Shadrack Scheirman
(503) 231 8585
Shadrack @ lclark.edu
box 5600

||| ||| ||||| ||| |||| |||||| ||| ||| |||||||| ||||
Y0-BZK-597

GELLHORN AND BYSE'S

Administrative Law

CASES AND COMMENTS

REVISED TENTH EDITION

by

Peter L. Strauss
Betts Professor of Law,
Columbia University

Todd D. Rakoff
Byrne Professor of Administrative Law,
Harvard University

Cynthia R. Farina
Professor of Law,
Cornell Law School

Foundation Press

NEW YORK, NEW YORK

2003

COPYRIGHT © 1940, 1947, 1954, 1960, 1970, 1974, 1979, 1987, 1995 FOUNDATION PRESS
COPYRIGHT © 2003 By FOUNDATION PRESS
     395 Hudson Street
     New York, NY 10014
     Phone Toll Free 1–877–888–1330
     Fax (212) 367–6799
     fdpress.com
Printed in the United States of America

ISBN 1–58778–594–3

TEXT IS PRINTED ON 10% POST CONSUMER RECYCLED PAPER

PREFACE

Preparing a preface for materials such as these, published in varying editions for more than sixty years, invites reflection on the continuing concerns and fluidity of Administrative Law. Enactment of the federal Administrative Procedure Act in 1946 shaped the basic structures of federal administrative law (and hence the course these materials imagine) in ways that have not changed much since. Yet if the basic statute has not been significantly amended, the mix of government activities with which it is concerned, the analytic tools scholars bring to bear on government, the technologies government employs, and the questions with which it attempts to deal have all changed dramatically. Written in an industrial age, informed by an optimistic perspective about the possibility and promise of expertise, and imagined for agencies whose major activities would best be classified as economic, the APA now faces the challenges of an information age, skepticism about the attainability of apolitical expertise, and a governmental apparatus whose more prominent regulatory concerns are hazards to health, safety and the environment. Political changes, fiscal pressures, and changes in management style that have already reshaped American industry combine to promise a significant downsizing of government. Those reductions, in turn, will inevitably influence the ways in which government seeks its ends.

The course in Administrative Law has long stood at the border between law and politics, and with the years that boundary has tended to shift. The Preface to the Eighth edition remarked on the surprising revival of separation of powers—the issue that dominated the first casebooks in our field. Today, changes in judicial styles of statutory interpretation, responding in part to changes in Congress, suggest a return to the formalism that also characterized earlier times. The Ninth edition highlighted the growth of political influence and political rationales in administrative process, and raised questions and suggestions about this trend. The intervening years, under Presidents Democrat and Republican, have witnessed a continuing tendency toward the rationalization of government around the President, seen as the one politically legitimate figure in executive government. Thus, this edition, the Tenth, brings some old cases to bear on new issues, and adds new materials to illuminate issues that have long been important to this course. It also seeks to initiate conversation about the predictable next set of issues facing administrative law: those of electronic government. Overall, we hope to empower you to understand the conventional framework of administrative law, to become acquainted with its institutions and the forces that influence them, and to face the changing future. In the intensely human and ultimately political business of striving for sound government, your editors do not suppose that movement will ever cease.

"Administrative Law" means different things to different people. In the setting of the law school course for which this book has been designed, the term refers to a body of largely procedural requirements resting upon administrative agencies which affect private interests through making rules, adjudicating cases, investigating, threatening, prosecuting, publicizing, disbursing benefits, and advising. These requirements have their source in Constitution, in statute and, to an extent the judges themselves have questioned, in judicial doctrine. Our stress is chiefly on requirements that are judicially enforceable, and that therefore are the special domain of lawyers. Attention is also directed, however, to aspects of control over administrators exercised by the legislative and executive branches of the government. The most pervasive control of all—that is, self-control, reinforced by professional attitudes within the public service—is difficult to depict; but assuredly it must not be overlooked, for without it the external controls would be of small moment. And, since most agencies have attorneys, this self-control is also often of special concern to lawyers.

More than its predecessors, this edition is organized around the principal procedural forms agencies use for regulation. Separate chapters now consolidate materials on agency adjudication and rulemaking that were previously developed more thematically. As few instructors will cover the entire book in a single course, we hope that this will ease the task of selection. We have tried to be conscious throughout of the likelihood that different instructors will find different sections of particular importance to the course they wish to offer.

Time is a major constraint in all law school courses, but the challenges are particularly severe in Administrative Law. Its students encounter a wide variety of procedure types, a tremendous range of agency actors (local and state as well as federal), and a broad spectrum of legal and political controls over their behavior. The resulting difficulties should be acknowledged.

When administrative lawyers work with a particular problem in practice, they will generally begin with a sense of the history and mission of the agency with which they are concerned, a history which often predetermines both procedure and substance. The agency's own statute will provide a sense of how to use it, of what procedures and what choices it opens; the attorney must consider as well what style of given regulation the agency has adopted (hard-line enforcement or softer); what its budget is and how it is treated by its appropriations committee; what the political atmosphere is and the attitude of important congressmen; what relationships exist between the agency and other federal agencies; what procedures it employs; who its personnel are and what their attitudes are; how competitors use or manipulate the statute for their own purposes; what the role of chance is in shaping the agency's agenda; what the general competence is of the staff being dealt with. One must know not only how to get meetings with agency officials but also what the publicity consequences are going to be of meeting with officials at varying levels; one must know what policy is likely to be driving the agency, for that will drive the procedures the agency chooses. And then there is the need to become thoroughly familiar with the mass of detail that bears on the particular issues to be presented for decision.

This sensitivity to circumstances, necessary as it is, should not be confused with the assertion sometimes made, that administrative law cannot be studied apart from a particular agency's program. Your editors firmly believe that common elements may be recognized in the affairs of administrative agencies. If general rules applicable to the behavior of the thousands of diverse instruments of government did not exist, surely judges and lawyers would be obliged to invent them, to assure the possibility of control and avoid unsustainable specialization. Our effort in this volume is to facilitate identification of resemblances as well as of differences, in the hope that your capacity to make critical and predictive judgments about administrative and judicial behavior will thus be enhanced.

We do so fully aware that procedures appropriate for allocation of a valuable radio license may poorly suit decisions on emission controls or welfare benefits. As important, in the limited number of classroom hours Administrative Law commands, and with the widely varying interests its students have, we cannot fully engage with the law the agencies themselves produce—labor law, utility law, corporation finance, land use (e.g., zoning and planning), trade recognition, health and safety, and so on. You must consider that substantive law in other appropriate courses, where it can be integrated with judicial and legislative contributions. Perhaps it will be helpful, however, to attend here to the elaborate statements about the context of agency action that you will often find in the opinions we have chosen. However unconscious this opinion-writing behavior may be, it serves to promote understanding of the particular agency and its circumstances, and so to suggest natural limits for what may appear a more general statement of law.

We have also thought it important to direct your attention to the other-than-judicial worlds in which agencies act and to which they respond. One of your editors once heard Peter Hutt, a distinguished Washington lawyer, tell a convention of administrative law professors that their courses overemphasized courts and litigation "... Over 90 percent of his practice ... is entirely informal, occurring outside hearings of any character. Litigation is avoided where it can be, and what the administrative law teacher must do is bring students to understand the variety of ways in which this can be done."[1] We intend these materials to expose those earlier stages and the issues that confront lawyers who participate in them; we have been conscious in editing to leave enough (and provide sufficient supplementation) to evoke their atmosphere and complexities.

Your editors can identify no single set of values against which to measure the success or failure of agencies or their procedures. In addition to the difficulties of reconciling "politics" and "law," consider the trio of not readily accommodated values that have been articulated in the Supreme Court's recent decisions about "due process" in administrative adjudication, the subject of Chapter VII. Fairness to interested persons, accuracy in decisionmaking, and reasonable social cost are all desirable— and none of them

1. Peter L. Strauss, Teaching Administrative Law: The Wonder of the Unknown,   33 J.Leg.Ed.1,8 (1983).

is achievable without consequence for the others. It is fair that the interested or aggrieved person participate in the process. It is fair that she be given appropriate procedural tools (including access to judicial review) with which to confront an often impersonal, sometimes blundering, bureaucracy. Yet the longer and more complex proceedings thus brought about may result in others being denied needed public services, significant additions to the cost of building a planned facility, or loss of the business required to keep a private concern economically viable. "Stopping the government in its tracks" would be a furtherance of fairness if the governmental tracks always went in the wrong direction; but few believe so unreservedly that that government is best which governs least. For the rest of us, fairness is not a likely product of governmental immobilization. Nor is it sound to view competition in values as occurring mostly between a public interest and a special interest. Identifiable Good Guys and Bad Guys may appear in tales of the West-that-never-was, but not (or certainly not clearly) in most modern affairs. In any interesting dispute, many public interests compete for consideration; rarely can an individual truly speak for *the* public interest rather than, far more modestly, for *a* public interest.

Difficult choices are inescapable—not soft choices between Definitely Good and Plainly Bad, but hard choices between one Good and another Good (or, more commonly, among a number of Goods that cannot be simultaneously achieved, so that some must be preferred over others). The desire to design procedures giving maximum assurance of fairness rubs against the desire to expedite governmental processes. The desire to give everybody a full chance to be heard rubs against recognition that adversary proceedings may not invariably be the best solvent of disagreements. The desire to bring administration into public view rubs against awareness that sometimes confidentiality facilitates resolution of difficult problems and may be as eagerly sought by members of the public as by members of the bureaucracy. The desire to encourage administrators to become fully informed before promulgating regulations having the force of law rubs against the fear of back door approaches to, and surreptitious pressure upon, the rulemakers.

Frictions like these generate considerable heat. Sometimes the heat produces litigation (which, regardless of outcome, can create further heat). Sometimes efforts to resolve matters in the legislature succumb to realities that produce gaps in statutory directions or cloudy language that thrusts upon administrators the responsibility—and the attendant heat – for value choices the lawmakers themselves could not agree upon. Criticizing what officials do may be far easier and more congenial than doing the job oneself. The techniques of law are unlikely to point to a single outcome or provide a settled resolution.

With all that said, it is still true that this is a law book about the administrative process, not a political-science text. Law's institutions and influences are omnipresent in American government. Partly this is so, because many administrators have been legally trained; partly, because bureaucratic organizations need the formal structures we associate with law; partly, because many agency actions are subject to judicial review and therefore come directly into the hands of the law in its most formal aspect. But the matter does not rest on institutional realities alone. Deep in the American spirit is the proposition that we ought to be governed by laws, not men; that the quest for law is part of the quest for freedom. From this point of view, administrative law is a normative enterprise that attempts to make the vast apparatus of the modern state conform to the standards which make the existence of that public power tolerable. Or, at least, the student of administrative law must always ask, to what extent does this subject rest on legal traditions rather than growing from the functional requisites of government alone. In what follows, we have avoided presenting as "settled doctrines" what are in fact still evolving patterns of interaction. We have sought instead to offer material that reveals the present state of evolution and that provides bases for realistic speculation concerning future growth of the law.

Finally, a note about usage. As in earlier editions, we have omitted without indication many citations and footnotes when we have reproduced opinions and other writings, renumbering the footnotes that we have retained. In quoted text, footnotes are also quotes unless preceded by "[Ed.]." And while we have indicated omissions of text by ellipses (...), we have ordinarily given only one such indication; omitted material may comprise phrases, sentences or paragraphs.

PETER STRAUSS
TODD RAKOFF
CYNTHIA R. FARINA

November 14, 2002

*

ACKNOWLEDGEMENTS

Bruce Ackerman, The New Separation of Powers, 113 Harv. L. Rev. 633, 706-09 (2000). Copyright © 1976 by the Harvard Law Review.

Bruce A. Ackerman, The Storrs Lectures: Discovering the Constitution, 93 Yale L.J. 1013 (1984). Reprinted by permission of The Yale Law Journal Company and William S. Hein Company.

Eugene Bardach and Robert A. Kagan, Going By the Book: The Problem of Regulatory Unreasonableness (New York: The Twentieth Century Fund, 1982). Reprinted with permission from the Twentieth Century Fund, New York.

David J. Barron & Elena Kagan, Chevron's Nondelegation Doctrine. The Supreme Court Review 201, 203-05 (2001). Copyright © 2001 by The University of Chicago Press.

William J. Brennan, Jr., Reason, Passion and "The Progress of the Law," 10 Cardozo L. Rev. 3, 19-22 (1988). Copyright ©1988 by Yeshiva University. This article was written as the Forty-Second Benjamin N. Cardozo Lecture of the Association of the Bar of the City of New York, Sept. 17, 1987. First published 42 The Record 948, copyright by The Association of the Bar of the City of New York. Reprinted by permission.

Lisa Schultz Bressman, Disciplining Delegation After Whitman v. American Trucking Ass'ns, 87 Cornell L. Rev. 452, 460, 461-62 (2002). Copyright ©2002 by The Cornell Law Review. Reprinted with permission of the author and the publication.

Rebecca L. Brown, Separated Powers and Ordered Liberty, 139 U. Pa. L. Rev. 1513 (1991). Copyright ©1991 by the University of Pennsylvania Law Review. Reprinted with permission of the author and the publication.

Robert A. Burt, The Constitution of the Family, 1979 Sup. Ct. Rev. 329, 341-42. Copyright ©1979 by the University of Chicago.

Steven G. Calabresi & Saikrishna B. Prakash, The President's Power to Execute The Laws, 104 Yale L.J. 541 (1994). Reprinted by permission of The Yale Law Journal Company and William S. Hein Company.

Stephen L. Carter, Constitutional Improprieties: Reflections on Mistretta, Morrison, and Administrative Government, 57 U. Chi. L. Rev. 357 (1990). Copyright ©1990 by the University of Chicago Law Review.

Erwin Chemerinsky, Federal Jurisdiction § 8.52 at 478-89 (3d ed. 1999). Copyright ©1999 by Aspen Press, Inc. Reprinted with permission of the author and the publisher.

Roger C. Cramton, A Comment on Trial-Type Hearings in Nuclear Power Plant Siting, 58 Virginia L.Rev. 585, 591-93 (1972). Copyright © 1972 by the Virginia Law Review Association. Reprinted by permission of the Virginia Law Review and Fred B. Rothman & Co.

Steven P. Croley, Theories of Regulation: Incorporating the Administrative Process. 98 Colum. L.Rev. 1 (1998). Reprinted by permission.

Steven R. Croley, White House Review of Agency Rulemaking: An Empirical Investigation (draft of Aug. 12, 2002). Reprinted by permission.

Cohn S. Diver, The Optimal Precision of Administrative Rules, 93 Yale L.J. 65, 89-91 (1983). Copyright © 1983 by the Yale Law Journal. Reprinted by permission of The Yale Law Journal Company and William S. Hein Company from The Yale Law Journal, Vol. 93, pages 65-109.

Christopher F. Edley, Jr., Administrative Law: Rethinking Judicial Control of Bureaucracy (1990) pp. 4-7 and 63-65, Yale University Press. Copyright © 1990 by the Yale University Press.

E. Donald Elliott, TQM-ing OMB: Or Why Regulatory Review Under Executive Order 12,291 Works Poorly And What President Clinton Should Do About It, 57 L. & Contemp.Probs. 167 (Spring 1994). Copyright © 1994 by Law and Contemporary Problems.

Harry T. Edwards, The Judicial Function and the Elusive Goal of Principled Decisionmaking. 1991 Wisconsin L.Rev. 837. Copyright © 1991 by The Board of Regents of the University of Wisconsin System. Reprinted by permission of the Wisconsin Law Review.

Jonathan L. Entin, Congress, The President, and The Separation of Powers: Rethinking the Value of Litigation, 43 Admin. L. Rev. 31 (1991). Copyright ©1991 by the Administrative Law Review.

Samuel Estreicher & Richard L. Revesz, Nonacquiescence by Federal Administrative Agencies, 98 Yale L.J. 679, 679-772 (1989). Copyright © 1989 by the Yale Law Journal. Reprinted by permission of The Yale Law Journal Company and Fred B. Rothman & Company.

Cynthia R. Farina, Conceiving Due Process, 3 Yale J. L. & Feminism, 189, 234-35 (1991). Reprinted by permission of the Yale Journal of Law & Feminism. Copyright ©1991 by the Yale Journal of Law & Feminism.

Cynthia R. Farina, Cognitive Psychology and Optimal Government Design, 87 Cornell L. Rev. 549, 562, 579, 597-98 (2002).

Cynthia R. Farina, Keeping Faith: Government Ethics and Government Ethics Regulation, 45 Admin.L. Rev. 287 (1993). Copyright © 1983 by the Administrative Law Review.

Cynthia R. Farina, Statutory Interpretation and the Balance of Power in the Administrative State, 89 Colum.L.Rev. 452, 487-88 (1989). Copyright © 1989 by the Directors of The Columbia Law Review Association, Inc.

Cynthia R. Farina, The Consent of the Governed: Against Simple Rules for a Complex World. 72 Chicago-Kent L.Rev. 987, 987-**989 (1997).** Copyright © 1997 by The Chicago-Kent Law Review.

Cynthia R. Farina, Undoing the New Deal Through the New Presidentialism, 22 Harv. J. L. & Pub. Policy 1(1998). Copyright ©1998 by Harvard Journal of Law and Public Policy. Reprinted by permission.

Louis Fisher, Congressional Abdication of War and Spending 180 (2000).
Copyright ©2000 by the Texas A & M University Press.

Owen M. Fiss, Reason in All Its Splendor, 56 Brooklyn L.Rev. 789, 801-03
(1990). Copyright ©1990 by the Brooklyn Law School.

Joan Flynn, The Costs and Benefits of "Hiding the Ball": NLRB Policymaking & The Failure of Judicial Review. 75 Boston U. L.Rev. 387-446
(1995). Reprinted with permission. Copyright © 1995 Trustees of
Boston University. Boston University bears no responsibility for any
errors which have occurred in reproducing this article.

William A. Fletcher, The Structure of Standing, 98 Yale L.J. 221, 227-28
(1988). Copyright 1988 by the Yale Law Journal. Reprinted by permission of The Yale Law Journal Company and William S. Hein Company.

Jody Freeman, Regulatory Negotiation and the Legitimacy Benefit, 9 N.Y.U.
Envtl. L.J. 60, 62-63, 138 (2000). Copyright © 2000 by the New York
University Environmental Law Review.

Jody Freeman, The Private Role in Public Governance, 75 N.Y.U. L. Rev.
543, 545-48 (2000). Copyright © 2000 by the New York University Law
Review.

James O. Freedman, Crisis and Legitimacy–The Administrative Process and
American Government, 9-11 (1978). Copyright © 1978 by Cambridge
University Press. Reprinted with the permission of Cambridge Univer-
sity Press.

James O. Freedman, Expertise And The Administrative Process, 28
Ad.L.Rev. 363 (1976). Copyright © 1976 by the Administrative Law
Review.

Monroe Freedman, "Corporate Bar Protects Its Own," Legal Times, June
15, 1992, p. 20. Reprinted by permission of the author and publisher.

William Funk, When Smoke Gets In Your Eyes: Regulatory Negotiation and
the Public Interest—EPA's Woodstove Standards, 18 Envtl.Law 55, 57.
Copyright © 1987 by Environmental Law. Reprinted with permission
of the author and the publication.

Merrick B. Garland, Deregulation and Judicial Review, 98 Harv.L.Rev. 505,
583 (1985). Copyright © 1985 by the Harvard Law Review Association.
Reprinted with permission of the author and the publication.

Ernest Gellhorn and Glen O. Robinson, Rulemaking "Due Process": An
Inconclusive Dialogue, 48 U.Chi.L.Rev. 201 (1981). Copyright ©1981 by
the University of Chicago Law Review.

Daniel J. Gifford, The Morgan Cases: A Retrospective View, 30 Ad.L.Rev.
Federal 237, 241-243, 256-57, 259 (1978). Copyright © 1978 by the
Administrative Law Review.

Mark H. Grunewald, The NLRB's First Rulemaking: An Exercise in Pragmatism, 41 Duke L.J. 274, 281-82 (1991). Copyright © 1991 by the

Duke Law Journal. Reprinted with permission of the author and the publication.

Phillip Harter, Assessing the Assessors: The Actual Performance of Negotiated Rulemaking, 9 N.Y.U. Envtl. L.J. 32, 33-35 (2001). Copyright © 2001 by the New York University Environmental Law Review.

Louis L. Jaffe, The Citizen As Litigant in Public Actions: The Non-Hohfeldian or Ideological Plaintiff, 116 U. Pa. L. Rev. 1033, 1037-38, 1044-45 (1968). Copyright ©1968 by the University of Pennsylvania Law Review. Reprinted with permission of the publication.

Louis L. Jaffe & Nathaniel Nathanson, Administrative Law: Cases and Materials 133-36 (1961). Copyright 1961.

Elena Kagan, Presidential Administration. 114 Harv.L.Rev. 2245, 2246-2249 (2001). Copyright © 2001 by The Harvard Law Review Association. Reprinted with permission of the author and the publication.

Bradley Karkkainen, Information as Environmental Regulation: TRI and Performance Benchmarking, Precursor to a New Paradigm: 89 Geo. L.J. 257, 286 ff. (2001). Copyright © 2001 Georgetown University Law Review.

Orin S. Kerr, Shedding Light on Chevron: An Empirical Study of the Doctrine in the U.S. Courts of Appeals. 15 Yale J. on Reg. 1 (1998). Copyright © 1998 by the Yale Law Journal. Reprinted by permission of The Yale Law Journal Company and Fred B. Rothman and Company.

Koch, Administrative Presiding Officials Today, 46 Ad. L. Rev. 271, 278-79 (1994). Copyright © 1994 by the Administrative Law Review.

Harold J. Krent, Executive Control Over Criminal Law Enforcement: Some Lessons From History, 38 Am. U. L. Rev. 275 (1989). Copyright ©1989 by the American University Law Review.

James M. Landis, The Administrative Process (1938) pp. 7, 30-38, 35-39, 46, Yale University Press. Copyright © 1938 by the Yale University Press.

Laura Langbein, Regulatory Negotiation and the Legitimacy Benefit, 9 N.Y.U Envtl. L.J. 60, 62-63, 138 (2000). Copyright © 2000 by the New York University Environmental Law Review.

Gary Lawson, The Rise and The Rise of the Administrative State, 107 Harv. L. Rev. 1231 (1994). Copyright ©1994 by the Harvard Law Review Association. Reprinted with permission of the author and the publication.

Richard J. Lazarus, The Neglected Question of Congressional Oversight of EPA, 54 Law & Contemp.Probs. 205 (1991). Copyright ©1991 by Law and Contemporary Problems.

Ronald M. Levin, Understanding Unreviewability in Administrative Law, 74 Minn. L. Rev. 689 (1990). Copyright ©1990 by the Minnesota Law Review. Reprinted with permission of the author and the publication.

Lawrence Lessig & Cass Sunstein, The President and the Administration, 94 Colum. L. Rev. 1, 2, 39-41 (1994). Copyright ©1994 by the Directors of the Columbia Law Review Association, Inc.

Peter L. Lindseth, Delegation is Dead, Long Live Delegation: Managing the Democratic Disconnect in the European Market-Polity; Good Governance in Europe's Integrated Market 144-150 (Joerges & Dehoouse, eds. 2002). Reprinted with permission.

Peter L. Lindseth, The Contradictions of Supranationalism: European Integration and the Constitutional Settlement of Administrative Governance, 1920s-1980s at 2-4 (PhD dissertation, Columbia University, 2002). Reprinted with permission.

Peter W. Low & John C. Jeffries, Jr., Federal Courts & The Law of Federal-State Relations 946-48 (4th ed. 1998). Copyright ©1998 by The Foundation Press, Inc. Reprinted with permission of the authors and the publisher.

Jonathan R. Macey, Transaction Costs and the Normative Elements of The Public Choice Model: An Application to Constitutional Theory, 74 Va. L. Rev. 471 (1988). Copyright ©1988 by the Virginia Law Review Association. Reprinted by permission from Fred B. Rothman & Company.

Jerry L. Mashaw, Bureaucratic Justice, 21-23 (1983). Copyright ©1983 by Yale University.

Jerry L. Mashaw, Due Process in the Administrative State 33-34 (1985).Copyright © 1985 by Yale University.

Jerry L. Mashaw, Greed, Chaos and Governance (1997) pp. 152-53, Yale University Press. Copyright © 1997 by the Yale University Press.

Jerry L. Mashaw, The Supreme Court's Due Process Calculus for Administrative Adjudication in Mathews v. Eldridge: Three Factors in Search of a Theory of Value, 44 U.Chi.L.Rev. 28, 48-49 (1976). Copyright ©1976-77 by the University of Chicago.

Jerry L. Mashaw & David L. Harfst, The Struggle for Auto Safety, 7-10, 6–11, 224–227 (1990). Copyright © 1990 by the President and Fellows of Harvard College. Reprinted by permission of the publishers, Harvard University Press, Cambridge, Mass.

Thomas O. McGarity, Presidential Control of Regulatory Agency Decisionmaking, 36 Am. U.L.Rev. 443, 450-51, 454-55, (1987). Copyright ©1987 by the American University Law Review.

Thomas O. McGarity, Substantive and Procedural Discretion in Administrative Resolution of Science Policy Questions: Regulating Carcinogens in EPA and OSHA, 67 Geo. L.J. 729, 732-736, 740-45, 750 (1979). Copyright © 1979 Georgetown Law Journal.

Thomas O. McGarity, The Internal Structure of EPA Rulemaking, 54 Law & Contemp. Probs., 57, 90-2 (Autumn 1991). Copyright © 1991 Law and Contemporary Problems.

Thomas W. Merrill, The Mead Doctrine: Rules and Standards, Meta-Rules and Meta-Standards. 54 Admin. L.Rev. 807, 833-834 (2002). Copyright © 2002 by American Bar Association. Reprinted by permission.

Thomas W. Merrill & Kristin E. Hickman, Chevron's Domain. 89 Georgetown L.J. 833, 916-17 (2001). Copyright © 2001 by the Georgetown

Law Journal. Reprinted by permission.

Geoffrey P. Miller, Rights and Structure in Constitutional Theory, 8 Social Philosophy & Policy 196 (1991). Copyright ©1991 by Cambridge University Press. Reprinted with permission of the author and the publisher.

Jonathan T. Molot, The Judicial Perspective in the Administrative State: Reconciling Modern Doctrines of Deference with the Judiciary's Structural Role. 53 Stanford L.Rev. 1, 76-79 (2000). Copyright © 2000 by the Board of Trustees of the Leland Stanford Junior University. Reprinted by permission of the Stanford Law Review.

Alan Morrison, The Administrative Procedure Act, 72 Va.L.Rev. 258, 256-258 (1986). Copyright © 1986 by the Virginia Law Review Association. Reprinted by permission from Fred B. Rothman & Company.

Gene R. Nichol, Jr., Rethinking Standing, 72 Calif. L. Rev. 68, 79-81 (1984). Copyright ©1984 by the Regents of the University of California. All Rights Reserved. Reprinted with permission of the author and the publisher.

Lars Noah, Scientific "Republicanism": Expert Peer Review and the Quest for Regulatory Deliberation, 49 Emory L.J. 1033, 1067, 1083 (2000). Copyright © 2000 by the Emory Law Journal.

Lars Noah, Sham Petitioning As a Threat To The Integrity Of the Regulatory Process, appearing in 74 N.C.L.Rev 1 (1995). Copyright © 1995 by the North Carolina Law Review Association. Reprinted with permission.

Craig N. Oren, Run Over by American Trucking, Part I: Can EPA Revive Its Air Quality Standards, 30 Environ. L. Reptr. 10653, 10660, 10662 (Nov. 1999). Copyright ©1999 by the Environmental Law Institute®, Washington D. C. Reprinted with permission from ELR®—The Environmental Law Reporter®. All rights reserved.

William F. Pedersen, Jr., Formal Records and Informal Rulemaking, 85 Yale L.J. 38, 64-65 (1975). Copyright © 1975-1976 by the Yale Law Journal Company, Inc. Reprinted by permission from Fred B. Rothman & Company.

Cesar Perales, The Fair Hearings Process: Guardian of the Social Service System, 56 Brooklyn L. Rev. 889, 889, 891-92 (1990). Copyright ©1990 by Brooklyn Law School.

Robert V. Percival, Presidential Management of the Administrative State: The Not-So-Unitary Executive, 51 Duke L.J. 963, 994, 968, 998-99 (2001). Copyright © 1979 Duke Law Journal

Richard J. Pierce, Jr., Seven Ways to Deossify Agency Rulemaking. 47 Admin.L.Rev. 59, 93-95 (1995). Copyright © 1995 by American Bar Association.

Richard Pierce, Jr., Use of the Federal Rules of Evidence in Federal Agency Adjudications, 39 Admin.L.Rev. 1, 17-19 (1987). Copyright © 1987 by American Bar Association.

Robert L. Rabin, Federal Regulation in Historical Perspective. 38 Stanford L.Rev. 1189, 1191-94, 1207, 1224, 1252-53, 1264-67, 1286-95, 1308-09, 1315-18, 1325-26 (1986). Copyright © 1986 by the author. Reprinted by permission.

Randy Rabinowitz, Punishment versus Cooperation in Regulatory Enforcement: A Case Study of OSHA, 49 Admin. L. Rev. 713, 720-24 (1997). Copyright © 1997 by the Administrative Law Review.

Jeffrey J. Rachlinski, Cognitive Psychology and Optimal Government Design, 87 Cornell L. Rev. 549, 562, 579, 597-98 (2002). Copyright © by the Cornell Law Review.

Todd D. Rakoff, Brock v. Roadway Express, Inc. and the New Law of Regulatory Due Process, 1987 Sup. Ct. Rev. 157, 18-85. Copyright ©1987 by the University of Chicago.

Todd D. Rakoff, The Shape of the Law in the American Administrative State, 11 Tel Aviv U. Studies in Law 9 (1992). Reprinted with permission.

Richard B. Saphire, Specifying Due Process Values: Toward a More Responsive Approach to Procedural Protection, 127 U. Pa. L. Rev. 111, (1978). Copyright ©1978 by the University of Pennsylvania Law Review. Reprinted with permission of the author and the publication.

Antonin Scalia, Vermont Yankee: The APA, the D.C. Circuit, and the Supreme Court, 1978 Sup. Ct. Rev. 345, 404-08. Copyright © 1978 by the University of Chicago Press.

Peter H. Schuck, Delegation and Democracy: Comments on David Schoenbrod, 20 Cardozo L. Rev. 775 (1999). Copyright ©1999 by the Cardozo Law Review. Reprinted with permission of the author and the publication.

Mark Seidenfeld, A Civil Republican Justification For the Bureaucratic State, 105 Harv. L. Rev. 1511, 1514, 1541-42 (1992). Copyright ©1992 by the Harvard Law Review Association. Reprinted with permission of the author and the publication.

Mark Seidenfeld, Demystifying Deossification: Rethinking Recent Proposals to Modify Judicial Review or Notice and Comment Rulemaking, published originally 75 Tex.L.Rev. 183 (1997). Copyright © 1997 by the Texas Law Review. Reprinted by permission.

Peter M. Shane, Political Accountability in a System of Checks and Balances: The Case of Presidential Review of Rulemaking. Published originally in 48 ARK. L. REV. 161 (1995). Copyright 1995 by the Arkansas Law Review and Bar Association Journal, Inc. Reprinted by permission. All rights reserved.

Sidney H. Shapiro, Agency Priority Setting and the Review of Existing Agency Rules, published in Volume 48 of the Administrative Law Review, at page 370. (1996) This article appears with permission of the Washington College of Law.

Sidney H. Shapiro, Punishment versus Cooperation in Regulatory Enforcement: A Case Study of OSHA, 49 Admin. L. Rev. 713, 720-24 (1997).

Copyright © 1997 by the Administrative Law Review.

Sidney A. Shapiro & Robert L. Glicksman, Congress, The Supreme Court, and The Quiet Revolution in Administrative Law, 1988 Duke L.J. 819. Copyright ©1988 by the Duke Law Journal. Reprinted with permission of the author and the publication.

William H. Simon, The Rule of Law and the Two Realms of Welfare Administration, 56 Brooklyn L. Rev. 777, 787 (1990). Copyright ©1990 by Brooklyn Law School.

Peter L. Strauss, Formal and Functional Approaches to Separation of Powers Questions–A Foolish Inconsistency?, 72 Cornell L. Rev. 488, 518-19 (1987). Copyright ©1987 by the Cornell Law Review.

Peter L. Strauss, Legislative Theory and The Rule of Law: Some Comments on Rubin, 89 Colum. L. Rev. 427, 442-43 (1989). Copyright ©1989 by the Directors of the Columbia Law Review Association, Inc.

Peter L. Strauss, Presidential Rulemaking, 72 Chicago-Kent L. Rev. 965 (1997). Copyright ©1997 by the Chicago Kent Law Review. All rights reserved.

Peter L. Strauss, Revisiting Overton Park: Political and Judicial Controls Over Administrative Actions Affecting the Community, 39U.C.L.A. LRev. 1251, 1253-54, 1256, 1318, 1323-1324 (1992). Copyright © 1992 by the Regents of the University of California. All Rights Reserved.

Peter L. Strauss, Was There a Baby in the Bathwater? A Comment on the Supreme Court's Legislative Veto Decision, 1983 Duke L.J. 789. Copyright ©1983 by the Duke Law Journal. Reprinted with permission of the author and the publication.

Peter L, Strauss, The Place of Agencies in Government: Separation of Powers and the Fourth Branch, 84 Colum.L.Rev. 573 (1984). Copyright ©1984 by the Directors of the Columbia Law Review Association, Inc.

Cass Sunstein, Constitutionalism After the New Deal, 101 Harv. L. Rev.421, 446-48 (1987). Copyright © 1987-88 by the Harvard Law Review Association.

Cass Sunstein, The Cost-Benefit State: The Future of Regulatory Protection 20-22 (2002). American Bar Association 2002. Reprinted by permission.

Cass Sunstein, Reviewing Agency Inaction After Heckler v. Chaney, 52 U.Chi.L.Rev. 653, 347, 1221(1985). Copyright © 1985 by the University of Chicago Law Review.

Cass Sunstein, Law and Administration After Chevron. 90 Colum.L.Rev. 2071, 2085-88 (1990). Copyright © 1990 by the Directors of The Columbia Law Review Association, Inc.

Cass R. Sunstein, What's Standing After Lujan? Of Citizen Suits, "Injuries," and Article III, 91 Mich. L. Rev. 163, 165 (1992). Copyright ©1992 by the Michigan Law Review. Reprinted with permission of the author and the publication.

Roberto Unger, Knowledge and Politics, 89-90 (1975). Copyright © 1975 by

Roberto Mangabeira linger. Reprinted with permission of The Free Press, A Division of Simon & Schuster, Inc.

Paul R. Verkuil, Comment: Rulemaking Ossification –A Modest Proposal. 47 Admin. L.Rev. 453, 457-458 (1995). Copyright © 1995 by American Bar Association. Reprinted by permission.

David C. Vladeck, Proceedings of the Second Annual Robert C. Byrd Conference on the Administrative Process, "Initiating Agency Action," 5 Admin. L.J. 1, 37-39 (1991). Copyright © 1991 by the Administrative Law Journal. Reprinted with permission.

Patricia M. Wald, The D. C. Circuit Here and Now, 55 Geo.Wash.L.Rev. 718, 720-21 (1987). Copyright ©1987 by the George Washington Law Review. Reprinted with permission of the author and the publication.

Lucie E. White, Subordination, Rhetorical Survival Skills, and Sunday Shoes: Notes on the Hearing of Mrs. G, 38 Buffalo L. Rev. 1, 2-4, 53-54 (1990). Copyright ©1990 Buffalo Law Review. Reprinted with permission of the author and the publication.

Stephen Williams, The Era of 'Risk-Risk' and the Problem of Keeping the APA Up to Date. 63 U. Chi. L. Rev. 1375 (1996). Copyright © 1996 by the University of Chicago.

*

SUMMARY OF CONTENTS

TABLE OF CONTENTS

**CHAPTER IX Obtaining Judicial Review: Access to Court
to Challenge Agency Action or Inaction** ------------------------ 1099

*

TABLE OF CASES

Principal cases are in bold type. Non-principal cases are in roman type.
Cases are listed by both the name of the plaintiff and of the defendant. The references are to Pages.

TABLE OF TEXT AND PERIODICAL CITATIONS

N

*

TABLE OF STATUTES

GELLHORN AND BYSE'S

ADMINISTRATIVE LAW

CASES AND COMMENTS

*

CHAPTER I

AN INTRODUCTION TO ADMINISTRATIVE LAW

SECTION 1.   AN INTRODUCTORY PROBLEM

(What follows is a real problem—the legal materials are genuine and the facts are true. It is a real problem in another sense, too—its pieces are hard to solve. Of course, if you are reading this at the beginning of your study of administrative law, you do not know much of what you would need to know to answer the questions posed in the way an experienced lawyer would. (Some of the questions are not so easy even if you do know what there is to know!) So the purpose of the problem is two-fold: first, to show you the kinds of questions administrative law tries to answer; and second, to invite you to use your imagination, along with the information given, to think about what some possible solutions might be.)

FIELD SANITATION

Each one of us, each day, needs to drink water and go to the bathroom. If we work full workdays, we probably need to do so during working hours. And we probably expect there to be clean water, a toilet, and a sink for us to use.

Of course, whether any workplace has reasonable sanitary facilities depends in part on what we mean by "reasonable." How far should employees have to walk in order to get to the fountain or the bathroom? What is an acceptable ratio of workers to toilets? How often, and to what standard, should bathrooms be cleaned?

These questions may sound mundane, but they have important public health consequences. Poor sanitation can cause intestinal and urinary tract infections, ranging from mild bouts to serious parasitic invasions. In many jobs, heat exposure is a serious risk, and the easy availability of pure water an important safeguard. Being able to wash hands and face can help reduce the danger of exposure to chemical residues. And, of course, there are also issues of personal comfort.

Question One: Assuming it were a totally open question, where in the legal universe should we put the law of workplace sanitation? Should it be a matter of tort, requiring an employer to take "reasonable care"? A matter of contract, so that employees get what they, individually or collectively, bargain for? Should we pass statutes, state or federal, specifying, say, the number of bathrooms that have to be provided, and stipulating civil and criminal penalties? Or should we give the matter over to a state or federal administrative agency to consider and regulate? Or, for that matter, should

1

we simply have no law on the subject, and leave the issue to the forces of reputation and social norms?

Whatever is hypothetically the best answer to the questions just put, the actual legal terrain was revolutionized when Congress enacted the Occupational Safety and Health Act of 1970. Its declared purpose was to "assure so far as possible every working man and woman in the Nation safe and healthful working conditions." 29 U.S.C. § 651(b). In addition to obligating employers to maintain workplaces "free from recognized hazards ... likely to cause death or serious physical harm," the Act said that employers had to comply with "occupational safety and health standards" promulgated according to the Act. 29 U.S.C. § 654(a). These standards were in turn defined to be regulations requiring conditions or practices "reasonably necessary or appropriate to provide safe or healthful employment and places of employment." 29 U.S.C. § 652(8).

Congress conferred the authority to pass these occupational safety and health standards on the Secretary of Labor. The Secretary of Labor is, of course, a member of the President's Cabinet. Insofar as high political judgment is involved in framing proper regulations, he or she may well be involved. But the Secretary can hardly do the work of, say, inquiring how many toilets there ought to be in a particular type of factory. Most of the work, then, is done by a division of the Department of Labor called, not surprisingly, the Occupational Safety and Health Administration (OSHA) headed by the Assistant Secretary for Occupational Safety and Health. In the year 2000, OSHA had 2176 employees.

As can be seen from its declared purpose, passage of the OSH Act put the federal government firmly into the business of workplace health and safety. This was also evident from the provisions of the Act which provided that agency employees could inspect "any factory, plant, establishment, construction site, or other area, workplace, or environment where work is performed" to see if the law was being obeyed. 29 U.S.C. § 657(a). But it takes time to promulgate sensible regulations. Accordingly the Act also directed the Secretary, as a starting point, to promulgate as binding standards, immediately and without normal procedures, what it called "national consensus standards": standards already in general use that had been promulgated by recognized professional organizations. 29 U.S.C. § 655(a). Beyond that, the Act said that "[I]n determining the priority for establishing standards ... the Secretary shall give due regard to the urgency of the need for ... standards for particular industries, trades, crafts, occupations, businesses, workplaces, or work environments." 29 U.S.C. § 655(g).

There were some "national consensus standards" for workplace sanitation, notably for permanent workplaces, and they were duly promulgated in April, 1971. 36 Fed. Reg. 10466. But there were no such standards for facilities for agricultural workers out in the field. In September, 1972, El Congreso, an organization speaking on behalf of Hispanic Americans, petitioned the agency to undertake public rulemaking to promulgate a field sanitation standard that would provide for drinking water, handwashing facilities and portable toilets.

Question Two: The agency has two issues it must address: first, does it make sense to spend time now on this regulation; and second, if it does go forward, what rule should it propose for the subsequent public proceedings. To this may be added a third matter: who should be making these decisions? Presumably there are staff in the agency who know something about workplace sanitation or farm conditions. Should they make the decision? Or should it be the Secretary or another top official? In addition, this particular statute provided two other choices. It established a federal research program relating to occupational safety and health, which is situated in the Department of Health and Human Services and known as the National Institute for Occupational Safety and Health. 29 U.S.C. § 669. Should NIOSH be consulted? And the Act also gave the Secretary the option of establishing an advisory committee to assist in setting standards. Such a committee has up to 15 people, including some federal government employees, a representative from state government, and "an equal number of persons qualified by experience and affiliation to present the viewpoint of the employers involved, and of persons similarly qualified to present the viewpoint of the workers involved." 29 U.S.C. § 656(b). How should the agency handle El Congreso's petition?

In the event, the petition was sent to a Standards Advisory Committee on Agriculture for factfinding and a recommendation; in December, 1974, that committee sent back a proposed field sanitation standard. The agency now had the following choices: First, because the committee was only advisory, the Secretary still had the option of deciding that there was no reason to have a rule—or he could publish the proposed standard to initiate a rulemaking proceeding in which the public would have a chance to comment on it. Second, if there were a rulemaking proceeding, at its end the agency could issue the proposed rule, could modify it in light of the comments it received, or could determine that a rule should not be issued. 29 U.S.C. § 655(b)(2–4).

OSHA did none of these things in any meaningful way. For a while it did nothing at all with the Advisory Committee's recommendation. Then, in April, 1976, it finally issued a Notice of Proposed Rulemaking, inviting public comment. But after the comment period closed, the agency again sat on its hands. It neither issued a rule nor said it wouldn't issue a rule.

As the agency dithered, El Congreso went to court. The Act, it pointed out, provided that final determinations in rulemakings were to be made within sixty days of the completion of the public proceedings. 29 U.S.C. § 655(b)(4). The court, El Congreso said, should order the Secretary to complete the standard.

Question Three: What should a court do? On the substantive side, the Act promises workers a healthful workplace, but leaves the enunciation of actual standards to the agency. On the process side, the Act tells the Secretary to complete the proceedings, but also gives him discretion as to the priorities of the agency. What is the role of the judiciary in a situation like this?

The actual course of this litigation was too complicated to reiterate here. (If you want to read the detail, see Farmworker Justice Fund, Inc. v. Brock, 811 F.2d 613, 614–19, vacated as moot, 817 F.2d 890 (D.C.Cir.

1987).) The upshot was that the courts told the Secretary to develop a timetable as to when the rule would be completed, which was ultimately done. In March, 1983, the agency issued an "Advance Notice" of rulemaking, saying it was reconsidering what standard it wanted to propose, and finally in March, 1984, it restarted the rulemaking proceeding.

The newly proposed rule differed from that suggested in 1976 primarily in being limited to farms with 11 or more field employees. This was a response to a stipulation Congress had enacted—not as part of the OSH Act itself, but rather as part of OSHA's funding. In successive years' appropriations bills, Congress prohibited the agency from spending any funds to "prescribe, issue, administer, or enforce any . . . regulation . . . applicable to any person . . . engaged in a farming operation which . . . employs ten or fewer employees."

An extensive rulemaking proceeding ensued. Hundreds of comments were submitted and 243 witnesses testified at five public hearings that were held. And this time the rulemaking actually produced a decision—a "final determination . . . that a federal field sanitation standard will not be issued at this time." 50 Fed. Reg. 15,086.

But, there is final and there is final. Eight days later, the newly appointed Secretary of Labor, William Brock, stated that he would reconsider the decision. This statement was made as part of his testimony during his Senate confirmation hearing.

Question Four: Congress of course passed the OSH Act. But consider now some of its subsequent actions. Congress limited the reach of the Act by adding language, year after year, to an appropriations bill. Why there rather than in the Act itself? And what about Brock's statement? Do you think it is purely coincidental that he promised to reconsider the regulation while he was facing the Senators? Note that these events seem to point in different political directions: one aids owners of small farms while the other helps farm workers. Are we witnessing a healthy involvement of politics, seeing the attention of the people's representatives at work to fine-tune regulatory policy? Or does Congress do a better job of representing the public interest when it formally legislates a major statute than it does when it sticks its nose into secondary matters?

Secretary Brock did get confirmed, and did reconsider. But he neither issued a rule nor didn't issue one. Instead, in October, 1985, he announced that promulgation of a national field sanitation standard would be delayed for two years so that the state governments could develop their own standards. If the states failed to provide adequate protection, then a federal standard would be promulgated.

The agency's justification for this decision had two prongs. First, it stated that the "clear evidence" adduced in the rulemaking proceeding showed that currently available facilities placed farmworkers' health at "unacceptable" risk. Regulation was indeed required. But, it went on, the Secretary "continues to believe that state action responsive to the need would be preferable to, and more effective than federal action. He therefore has decided to afford the states an opportunity to take adequate action . . ." 50 Fed. Reg. 42600.

Question Five: Politics again. Secretary Brock was appointed to his position by President Reagan and was part of his Cabinet. Reagan had campaigned, in part, on a platform that favored "returning" power to state government; he was a popular president and in 1985 had recently been reelected by a landslide. Brock (as the agency's statement shows) was willing to take personal responsibility for the "political" judgment to let the states have a last chance at regulating this matter. Do you think that is an adequate justification for what he did?

When the matter again went to court, the D.C. Circuit, rightly or wrongly, did not think the Secretary was justified (811 F.2d at 624–25):

> ... These remarks suggest that the October 21 decision was motivated, in part, by the Secretary's concept about the proper roles of the federal and state governments in our system. ...

> To the extent ... that the October decision rests on such a preference, the Secretary acted beyond the scope of his discretion. Although the Secretary might prefer that state governments regulate "public health issues" because they have "traditionally been a primary concern of state and local officials," Congress, in adopting the OSH Act, decided that the federal government would take the lead in regulating the field of occupational health. However much the Secretary might wish to "restore" what he considers to be "an appropriate balance of responsibility between state and federal governments," he is bound to enforce what Congress already determined to be the "appropriate balance ..." in the field of occupational safety and health.

The court ordered the Secretary to issue the regulation that he had admitted was necessary except for his hope for state action. This order was rendered moot, however, when the agency, very shortly thereafter, decided to move forward based on its own determination that the states had not done enough to warrant delaying federal action any further. And so, on May 1, 1987, a field sanitation standard was issued. It is still in force, 29 C.F.R. § 1928.110. Here are some of its provisions:

> (a) *Scope*. This Section shall apply to any agricultural establishment where eleven (11) or more employees are engaged on any given day in hand-labor operations in the field. ...

> (c) *Requirements*. Agricultural employers shall provide the following for employees engaged in hand-labor operations in the field, without cost to the employee:

> (1) *Potable drinking water*. ...

> (2) *Toilet and handwashing facilities*. (i) One toilet facility and one handwashing facility shall be provided for each twenty (20) employees or fraction thereof. ...

> (iii) Toilet and handwashing facilities shall be accessibly located and in close proximity to each other. The facilities shall be located within a one-quarter-mile walk of each hand laborer's place of work in the field. ...

(v) Toilet and handwashing facilities are not required for employees who perform field work for a period of three (3) hours or less ... during the day.

(3) *Maintenance.* Potable drinking water and toilet and handwashing facilities shall be maintained in accordance with appropriate public health sanitation practices. ...

The final rule was accompanied by a statement of its basis and purpose that extended over dozens of pages. 52 Fed. Reg. 16050. Among other things it said:

—That the rule covered an estimated 471,600 employees (25–30% of whom were women), of whom about half worked in California, Florida, or North Carolina.

—That according to a 1984 survey in the record, approximately 37% of farmworkers were not provided toilets; 55% had no handwashing facilities; and 21% had no drinking water.

—That there were many health risks associated with these conditions—for example, that farmworkers had parasitic infestations at rates 7 to 25 times higher than those prevailing in the population at large.

—That the cost of compliance with the rule for the typical agricultural employer would be about $1.09 per worker per day.

—And that there would be a substantial decrease in many health risks. While the data supporting this last point are hard to summarize, perhaps this paragraph from the statement gives the general picture:

> Where facilities are unavailable or inadequate, farmworkers are faced with alternatives that threaten their health because they cannot take care of their most basic physiological needs. Working in hot environments, if they minimize their fluid intake to try to limit their need to urinate, they risk dehydration and heat stress. If they drink water from irrigation pipes or ditches to quench their thirst, as some do, they risk being poisoned by agrichemicals or infected by pathogens from solid waste eliminated into the soil or ground water. They can try to retain their urine, but thereby, for women especially, risk getting urinary tract infections. Or they can simply urinate and defecate in the fields, subjecting their co-workers to exposure to communicable diseases.

Question Six: The Occupational Safety and Health Act and Administration are often mocked as an example of regulation gone haywire. Admittedly there is more in the record, but given what you know do you think that it is proper that the federal government has adopted this regulation? That it has imposed costs of this amount on private employers? That it has specified compliance to the degree of detail it has?

Of course, it is one thing to pass a regulation, and another to see that it is enforced. The OSH Act empowers the agency to inspect workplaces, and if the agency's inspector finds a violation of one of its standards, "he shall with reasonable promptness issue a citation to the employer." 29 U.S.C. § 658(a). The Act also provides for penalties that the agency may assess for serious or repeated violations of the standards. 29 U.S.C. § 666.

However, if the employer chooses to contest the citation or the proposed penalty, the case is heard, not by OSHA, but by a separate agency called the Occupational Safety and Health Review Commission. OSHRC is set up as what is sometimes called an "independent" agency. It is headed by a three-member Commission whose members serve for staggered six-year terms and can be removed only for "inefficiency, neglect of duty, or malfeasance in office." 29 U.S.C. § 661(b). (The Secretary of Labor, by contrast, serves at the President's pleasure.) Cases that go to OSHRC are heard in the first instance by internal hearing officers known as administrative law judges, and are then subject to review by the Commissioners themselves. From there, decisions are subject to judicial review in the Courts of Appeals.

Many contested cases will, of course, turn simply on establishing the facts. But we can imagine cases in which the interpretation of the field sanitation standard is at issue. For example, as we have seen, the rule applies to farms "where eleven or more employees are engaged on any given day ... in the field." How is this number to be reckoned? Do there have to be eleven hands working on the day the inspector comes? On more than half the days of the growing season? On an average day averaged over the whole year? On any one day during the whole year?

Questions like these arose shortly after the standard was adopted. In September, 1989, the Director of Compliance Programs for the agency sent a memorandum to the regional enforcement offices saying that the policy of the agency was that the standard would apply "to any agricultural establishment/employer that has employed, during the past twelve months, at any one time, eleven (11) or more employees ... in the field ... regardless of the number of employees engaged ... in the field on the day of inspection." (This letter, along with much else concerning OSHA, is available on the agency's website, www.osha.gov.) That appears to be the agency's latest word on the subject.

Question Seven (the last): Does this mean that "at any one time" is the law on how we reckon eleven? Presumably it does insofar as the field inspectors are concerned. But what if the employer contests it, arguing for some less stringent interpretation? Is OSHRC bound by the interpretation as it would be by a properly promulgated OSHA standard—or can it argue that it is not bound by interpretations issued by lower level agency personnel, and is instead entitled by its own grant of adjudicatory authority to interpret standards as it sees fit? And what about a Court of Appeals, if the matter should get there on review? Is it bound by OSHA's view? By OSHRC's view? Or should it be free to substitute its own judgment?

SECTION 2. THE BASICS

(If you were to log on to a hypothetical website—www.adlaw.gov—to find some fundamental background for understanding administrative law in general—or the preceding problem in particular—you might find something like the following. As with most sets of Frequently Asked Questions, the responses to these FAQs are only initial entry points for more sophisticated questions and answers which will arise throughout this book.)

FREQUENTLY ASKED QUESTIONS

- What is administrative law?
- What are administrative agencies?
- Is everything the government does considered agency action?
- Is administrative law important?
- Is administrative law just politics by another name?
- How are administrative agencies organized?
- How do administrative agencies do their work?
- How do administrative agencies make regulations?
- How do administrative agencies decide cases?
- How does administrative law contribute to social welfare?
- How does administrative law contribute to freedom?
- How does administrative law contribute to social justice?

What is administrative law?

Administrative law comprises the body of general rules and principles governing administrative agencies—governing both how they do their own work, and how the results of that work will be viewed, or reviewed, by the President, Congress, and the Courts. It exists at all levels of government—federal, state and local—and there are some just-forming principles of international administrative law, too. Federal administrative law, the subject of this website, can be found in many sources: the Constitution, executive orders, federal statutes, and decisions of the federal courts—as well as in the legal materials, decisions and rules of all sorts, developed by the agencies themselves.

Administrative law, as a body of general principles, needs to be distinguished from the particular substantive law implemented by each individual agency—distinguished, that is, from the tax law practiced by the IRS, the labor law of the National Labor Relations Board, or the occupational safety and health law of OSHA. Administrative law takes place on a more general, and more process-oriented, plane. The distinction is somewhat analogous to that between civil procedure and torts or contracts. Every torts or contracts case, because it came from a judicial proceeding, has a civil procedure matrix, even if the principal topic of dispute concerns a substantive torts or contracts doctrine. Similarly, administrative law treats of general questions like the process by which agency regulations must be made, or the authority agency regulations will have if reviewed in court, rather than of the more particular questions regarding labor or tax policy.

What are administrative agencies?

Administrative agencies are all the authorities and operating units of the government except for the constitutionally established entities: that is, except for the President, the Congress and the Courts. They are sometimes called "Agencies," but sometimes "Departments," sometimes "Boards," sometimes "Commissions"—they are all still agencies. Just as agents, in the ordinary sense of the term, carry out tasks for their principals, so, too, do agencies carry out the instructions of, and are responsible to, the three great constitutionally established, institutional "principals." Because administrative agencies are not established by the Constitution, they have to be created by statute.

Is everything the government does considered agency action?

Almost. When Congress passes a statute, that is not agency action, nor is a court's making a decision or the President's giving a speech. But when the Internal Revenue Service collects taxes, or the Bureau of Land Management leases public lands, or the National Labor Relations Board supervises a workplace election, or the Centers for Disease Control collect epidemiological data, or the Immigration and Naturalization Service deports an undocumented immigrant, or the Environmental Protection Agency sets a new air quality standard, or the Social Security Administration pays a pension—these all are indeed agency action.

However, some agency action is so given over to the discretion of the officials involved that it almost disappears from the ken of administrative law. The decisions of the Air Force as to what jets to order, or of a federal prosecutor whether to press charges, or for that matter of the State Department trying to set foreign policy in the Middle East, are all in some sense agency action, but unlikely to raise issues subject to administrative law control. And sometimes the length or breadth of agency discretion, in this large sense of the term "discretion," is uncertain, as, for example, in the degree to which Congress intended to give individual agencies the complete freedom to decide what priorities they should establish in carrying out their general mandates.

Is administrative law important?

Indeed! Given what has already been said, it is clear that it is almost impossible to be a lawyer for the government (except perhaps for those who prosecute ordinary crimes) without some knowledge of administrative law. But the same is really true for most practitioners with private clients. Most transactions these days have a regulatory aspect to them, and understanding any regulatory framework requires knowledge not merely of the substantive policies, but also of the types of processes and materials involved— the knowledge, in short, of administrative law. One might even go a bit further and say that it is hard even to read a newspaper knowledgeably without some understanding of administrative law. To speak only of matters growing out the events of 9/11/01: the implications of making airport security into a matter handled by a federal agency; the proper distribution of emergency funds to airlines in need of bailout and to the families of the departed; the powers and limits of a new Department of Homeland Security—these are all deeply affected by the doctrines of administrative law. Given the growth of federal government regulation over about the last century, administrative law is one of the best places to see how law works in the modern world. (Indeed, two members of the current Supreme Court—Justices Scalia and Breyer—used to be professors of administrative law, and at least three others were practitioners of it.)

Is administrative law just politics by another name?

Some say so. Because administrative agencies wield the government's power, they are of course intimately connected with many issues that are the subject of political debate. They are subject to constant oversight by the President and Congress. But because administrative law deals with the proper legal structure for that use of power and that process of oversight, it brings to bear the values of the law: values such as regularity, consistency, evenhandedness, participation. This tension—or if you like, this persistent problem of how to encapsulate political will in legal norms—bedevils administrative law. But this very closeness to, but separation from, politics also helps make the subject both interesting and important.

How are administrative agencies organized?

The Constitution says very little about the details of the structure of the federal government, so each agency is basically organized by the statute which puts it in business and tells it what its basic tasks are—indeed, this is often called the agency's "organic" statute. (Many times, but not always, the statute and the agency are eponyms: for example, the National Labor Relations Act establishing the National Labor Relations Board.) Nevertheless, and not surprisingly, there are many commonalities among most administrative agencies. There is a head of the agency, with a small cadre of advisers immediately responsible to that office; but the great bulk of agency personnel serve in "administrations," "services," "offices" or the like—subordinate units each with its own particular responsibilities and hierarchical organization. Thus, for example, the problem of controlling the gypsy moth is the immediate responsibility of a group of specialists in the Animal and Plant Health Inspection Service, headed by an Administrator and itself one of several bureaus under the authority of the Under Secretary for Marketing and Regulatory Programs, himself one of the several under secretaries under the authority of the Secretary of Agriculture. Legal staffs within agencies are typically segregated into special law offices. In any agency with substantial adjudicatory responsibilities, the administrative law judges and any appellate agency tribunal are wholly separated from both the staff of the agency and from the legal counsel of the agency. (Descriptions of the various federal departments and agencies, and organizational charts of their various units, can be found in the U.S. Government Manual, in paper or on-line at http://www.access.gpo.gov/nara/nara001.html.)

At the top of the agencies, there are, however, two different patterns. Some agencies are regulatory commissions, headed by multi-member bodies; these are usually free-standing bodies whose members can be removed from office by the President only for "cause," and accordingly are sometimes called "independent" agencies. The Federal Trade Commission is an example here. Other entities are headed by a single administrator who serves at the President's pleasure, and these are often nestled within larger entities headed by members of the President's Cabinet, whom the President can also discharge. The smaller units—for example, the Occupational Health and Safety Administration and the Mine Safety and Health Administration—and the larger unit that encompasses them—here, the Department of Labor—are all considered administrative agencies.

To determine who has what specific substantive responsibilities within an agency, one has to work with statutory law and with executive orders and agency rules that redelegate authority. Some of the procedural requirements of administrative law also vary by the form of organization of an agency—for example, the Government in the Sunshine Act applies to agencies headed by multi-member boards but not by single administrators. But the overwhelming majority of administrative law requirements do not turn on the particularities of each agency's organization. Rather, they are responsibilities placed on all agencies simply because they are agencies.

How do administrative agencies do their work?

Agencies act in a large variety of ways. The Chairman of the Federal Reserve Board may well influence the course of the economy—or at least of the financial markets—simply by giving a speech. The Department of Defense takes a more direct route to the same end—it spends a lot of money. Even these actions have a legal structure, depending as they do on delegated authority, not to mention appropriations! But agencies also do things that look more "law like," and it is those things that mostly come to mind when one speaks of administrative law. Agencies make regulations. A quick look at the Code of Federal Regulations (CFR) will show that agencies indeed make a great many regulations. Agencies decide particular disputes. The Social Security Administration alone adjudicates more disputes (over old-age pensions and disability claims) than all the federal courts put together. Agencies license activities or individuals. One cannot just decide to be a pilot and start carrying passengers for hire! And agencies enforce their statutes and regulations—by sending out inspectors, revoking licenses, levying penalties, or bringing criminal actions in court. Any particular agency can only do the things that its governing statutes authorize it to do, but the typical agency will indeed have all of these powers. Or in other words, individual agencies—say the Securities and Exchange Commission—can set priorities, administer budgets, make rules, decide cases, and pursue enforcement actions, and in doing so exercise legislative, executive, and judicial powers that would be split up at the Constitutional level among the Congress, the President, and the Courts.

How do administrative agencies make regulations?

Needless to say, this is in some respects a technical question that can only be answered after considerable study. In general, administrative rulemaking begins as you might expect—with a decision on the part of an agency to do something to carry out one of its statutory responsibilities. This is not necessarily an easy decision to make, because agencies usually have more they could do than they have time or money to do. Thus setting priorities, although usually thought of as a purely executive task, has important legal consequences. And along with the decision to do something is of course the issue of what to do. Here, most commonly, a team within the agency—some with technical expertise, some with legal expertise, and so forth—will develop a more-or-less worked out proposal. The archetypal procedure is then to conduct a "notice and comment" rulemaking—that is, to give notice that a rule is in the offing and to allow for those outside the agency to comment on the proposal. Staff then review that rulemaking record before making any rule final. Assuming that the proper procedures have been followed, and that the rule is substantively within the agency's statutory authority, final administrative rules have full legislative force, binding courts, agencies and citizens alike to their terms.

How do administrative agencies decide cases?

If you mean by "cases" the application of statutes or rules to individual circumstances, administrative agencies decide cases informally, and by the millions, all the time. (If, for example, you have been away from the United States and, on returning, turned in a customs form and passed through customs without paying duty, you have successfully "won" an administrative adjudication.) If you instead mean by "cases" the relatively formal proceedings that lead to final determinations of important matters and form precedents for future agency action, then you will not be mistaken if you think of them as trial-type proceedings—with some differences. Typically, agency cases are heard in the first instance before administrative law judges—officials who are not judges as understood in Article III of the Constitution, but yet have substantial civil service protection to help them maintain their independence. Often there is an intermediate level of review before a reasonably sheltered appeals panel. But if the case is important, or has significant contested issues, the ultimate decision may be made by an important agency official: the head of the agency, or the board or commission for agencies headed by multi-member groups. These officials also have political and policy responsibilities; they are not the same as appellate judges. But they are empowered to decide the issues in the adjudication. In short, there is often a closer connection between overt policy authority and case decision in administrative adjudication than in courtroom adjudication. This might be viewed as the genius of administrative adjudication, or as its fatal flaw. (Sometimes, indeed, Congress has shied away from this standard arrangement and separated adjudicatory matters from the rest of the agency's responsibilities. The Occupational Health and Safety Act, for example, created both a regulatory-and-enforcement agency, the well-known OSHA, and a separate case-hearing agency, the lesser-known OSHRC (Occupational Safety and Health Review Commission).)

How does administrative law contribute to social welfare?

The programs run by administrative agencies have tremendous impact on our economy and on other aspects of our welfare as a society. The Federal Reserve Board sets interest rates; the Securities and Exchange Commission tries to keep securities markets free of fraud; the Environmental Protection Agency sets and enforces pollution standards; the National Parks Service maintains our greatest natural treasures. Administrative law, as the law of the process by which these things happen, contributes to social welfare insofar as it improves the performance of these functions. Insofar, that is, as it contributes to agency decisions being better thought through, taking account of more varied interests, better communicated to those affected, paying greater attention to human dignity, and more rationally enforced—*and* does not create enormous burdens: making things more costly, more cumbersome, or too slow. Whether administrative law has this beneficial effect—or, perhaps better put, what should be the doctrines of administrative law so it will have this effect—is one of the persistent problems of the subject.

How does administrative law contribute to freedom?

Many administrative agencies regulate private activity. "Regulation" inherently reduces the freedom of some people compared to what they would have had if only common law rules applied. At the same time, regulation can increase the freedom of others. Whether any particular regulatory regime increases or decreases individual freedom overall, is thus a program-by-program question. But freedom is not just an individual matter; it also is a matter of the working of our governmental institutions. Administrative law serves to increase this social or political freedom when it makes the workings of the government more transparent to citizens and when it provides increased opportunities for them to participate in governmental affairs. Whether American administrative law adequately does this—or whether indeed it overdoes this—are persistent questions. But it is at least worth noting that many foreign legal scholars and law reformers consider some of the doctrines of American administrative law—for instance, the wide comment possibilities available during rulemaking, and the Freedom of Information Act—to be much better in this regard than their own existing arrangements.

How does administrative law contribute to social justice?

The programs run by administrative agencies also have tremendous impact on how benefits and burdens are distributed throughout the society—benefits as disparate as disability pensions, minimum wages, clean-ups of toxic wastes, and admission to the United States itself; burdens as disparate as filing forms, reengineering production processes, and, of course, paying taxes. The very disciplining of these activities to the regularity of the law—the reduction in arbitrariness of the distribution of either benefits or burdens—might be considered a considerable contribution to social justice. That administrative law doctrines make some real contribution of this sort is hard to deny. More difficult is the question whether administrative law conduces toward or away from social equality, or if not equality, then toward or away from the fair distribution of society's benefits. Seemingly technical doctrines can have distributive impacts. Indeed, those impacts have fueled some of the major disputes in the history of administrative law. What the final balance is—well, perhaps all that can be said with safety is that the issue is contentious.

SECTION 3.   THE DEVELOPMENT OF THE ADMINISTRATIVE STATE

Robert L. Rabin, Federal Regulation in Historical Perspective

38 Stan. L. Rev. 1189, 1191–94, 1207, 1224, 1252–53, 1264–67, 1286–95, 1308–09, 1315–18, 1325–26 (1986).

My account begins with the Populist era because of the formative influence of the Interstate Commerce Act on the development of the federal regulatory system. Beginning then, and in the ensuing years until the New Deal, a policing model of regulation [predominated]. . . .

The policing model closely corresponded to a widely shared philosophical and political perspective that stressed the limited responsibility of government for economic well-being . . . premised on an autonomous market-controlled economy. But adherents to this view were willing to concede that the market systematically generated certain "excessively competitive" practices such as the manufacture of products that seriously endangered health and safety or the setting of rates that were particularly discriminatory. When these practices occurred repetitively and constituted a nationwide problem, various factions—often including producer interests—regarded federal regulation as superior to the ad hoc approach of the pre-existing forms of government regulation, the judicially fashioned common law and state regulatory practices.

. . . The policing model was in tension with . . . a potentially stronger model of government intervention (more intrusive into market autonomy), anticipating government-encouraged business associational activities, [that] was consistently promoted in various forms—without much success—in the pre-New Deal years. . . . It was the New Deal that transformed the earlier "weak" associational impulses into a commitment to permanent market stabilization activity by the federal government. Along with this market-corrective model of economic regulation, the New Deal developed the framework for a transformed federal responsibility to assure individual economic security, and, more generally, triggered a substantial shift in traditional conceptions of the separate spheres of public and private activity.

. . . [T]he policing reforms of the Populist and Progressive eras . . . and the market-corrective programs of the New Deal and post-New Deal eras, represent points on a continuum of intervention strategies. They establish a distinctly American style of regulation, located between the opposing poles of public management and tort law. The style never entirely overcomes the competing visions offered by a planned economy, a welfare state, or an autonomous market, however. It is, in fact, a patchwork system that is resistant to any ideologically comprehensive rationale for regulation.

. . . In my view, the everyday politics of regulatory reform has been conducted without much concern for establishing a coherent theory of administrative government. This is hardly surprising. Reform groups as well as political actors have usually been driven either by narrow considerations of self-interest or spontaneous reactions to perceived crises rather than by comprehensive functional views on the role of regulation. As a result, regulatory legislation has been characterized by ambiguity of intention, leaving an open field for the judiciary to assume a substantial presence in defining the contours of administrative power. The courts, in turn, have failed to develop an enduring vision of the appropriate controls on agency power; instead, they have repeatedly provided an uncharitable reception to new regulatory reform movements, only to exercise greater sensitivity to the political process with the passage of time.

[Professor Rabin illustrates his thesis with detailed accounts of the political backgrounds of early federal agencies, the Interstate Commerce

Commission (1887) and the Federal Trade Commission (1915). The ICC, he argues, "did not reflect a coherent ideological approach to railroad regulation. And it was not one element in a more broadly conceived political agenda. Instead, the Commerce Act addressed a discrete set of immediately pressing problems in an equivocal fashion that reflected the difficult process of hammering out a legislative compromise." Similarly, "the substantive mandate given the newly formed FTC reflected a clear sense of irresolution reminiscent of the conflicting expectations that had characterized the Interstate Commerce Act. In the formation of both commissions, a long period of political debate and repeated efforts to articulate a set of principles precisely defining proscribed competitive behavior—or, in the alternative, creating a mechanism for rendering advisory opinions—resulted in a largely inconsequential directive to monitor and prohibit 'unreasonable' conduct. The failure of the Commerce Act to resolve ambivalent attitudes towards limiting competition in transportation by rail was extended to economic enterprise at large in the Trade Commission Act."]

In historical perspective, the New Deal appears as a distinct break from the past. The regulatory initiatives of the Populist and Progressive eras were largely discrete and limited measures—not dissimilar in kind from common law tort prohibitions against unfair trade practices. They were aimed largely at particularized fields of activity in which vigorous competition led to sharp market practices. Pre–New Deal regulatory initiatives rested on the common law assumption that minor government policing could ensure a smoothly functioning market.[1] But the Depression put to rest this constrained view of national power. Even the more traditional regulatory aspects of the New Deal conceived of government activity as a permanent bulwark against deep-rooted structural shortcomings in the market economy.

And the New Deal ventured considerably beyond the regulatory model developed in the Commerce Act. The [National Industrial Recovery Act] and [Agricultural Adjustment Act] represented countervailing strategies to the atomistic tendencies of the market—tendencies that appeared invariably to trigger downward price spirals. Along similar lines, the [National Labor Relations Act] served as a buffer against inequality of bargaining power in the labor market. It openly rejected free market assumptions about the mobility of labor. The [Tennessee Valley Administration] embraced comprehensive governmental planning as a tool for developing a social infrastructure in a regional economy suffering from perpetual depression. Once more, the legislation directly controverted assumptions of a self-correcting mechanism regulating the flow of market transactions.

The New Deal's distributional programs further demonstrated how far the new approach to government intervention departed from the old. The public works and social insurance programs undertaken by the New Dealers put the federal government squarely in the position of employer and insurer of last resort. Instead of indirectly creating incentives for changes in private market behavior, the new government programs established a

---

1. In the case of the railroads, some observers would have argued that more extensive regulation was required because the enterprise was "quasi-public" in nature. This view can be traced back at least as far as Munn v. Illinois, 94 U.S. 113 (1876).

reliance principle: The public came to look upon government as its guarantor against acute economic deprivation. As a result, the spheres of public and private activity were intermingled in ways that would have a pervasive effect on succeeding waves of administrative reform.

. . . Because the New Deal programs were largely uncoordinated ventures into areas in which no pre-existing regulatory framework existed, the procedural aspects of agency policymaking processes were often given short shrift. Thus, when questions of agency legitimacy were put to rest—and, correlatively, the permanence of a pervasive, discretionary system of government regulation became an accepted fact of life—it was only natural that political initiatives should focus on the decisionmaking procedures of the agencies.

The reaction against agency processes reached its peak in the late 1930s. In a widely publicized report published in 1938, Roscoe Pound, chairman of the special committee of the ABA on administrative law, excoriated the regulatory system for "administrative absolutism" and catalogued the suspect "tendencies" of administrative agencies, among them: (1) to decide without a hearing, (2) to decide on the basis of matters not before the tribunal, (3) to decide on the basis of preformed opinions, (4) to disregard jurisdictional limits, (5) to do what will get by, (6) to mix up rulemaking, investigation, and prosecution, as well as the functions of advocate, judge, and enforcement authority. [The ABA's efforts culminated in the 1940 Congressional passage (but subsequent Presidential veto) of the Walter–Logan bill, "an act which was both blatantly political (exempting 'favored' agencies) and quite restrictive (significantly enhancing the role of judicial and intra-agency review)."]

Roosevelt had not been deaf to the rising tide of procedural criticism, however. In 1939, he instructed his attorney general to appoint a committee to report on the "need for procedural reform in the field of administrative law."[2] After the war ended, this report served as the foundation for the drafting of the APA, which passed both houses unanimously in 1946.

The APA is, in essence, a highly conventional lawyer's view of how to tame potentially unruly administrators. It divides the universe of administrative action into two general decisionmaking categories, rulemaking and

2. See Attorney General's Committee on Administrative Procedure, Administrative Procedure in Government Agencies, S. Doc. No. 8, 77th Cong., 1st Sess. (1941). Kenneth Culp Davis has described the outcome of the committee's deliberations:

A committee of distinguished practitioners, judges, and professors was appointed, which set about its tasks in scholarly fashion. It went after the facts. Its staff interviewed administrative officers, subordinates in the agencies, and practitioners who had had cases before the agencies. A detailed monograph was written on each agency, and the committee and the agency then discussed the problems raised. Thereafter the committee held public hearings to receive opinions concerning the descriptions of procedures and the criticisms in the monographs. An elaborate report was finally prepared, which, with its appendices, fills 474 printed pages. This report, together with the monographs on which it is based, is still a primary source of information about the federal administrative process; even though it is out of date, no new comprehensive study has penetrated so far.

Kenneth C. Davis, Administrative Law Text 8–9 (3d ed. 1972).

adjudication. Drawing upon a legislative model, the Act provides notice-and-comment procedural safeguards for informal rulemaking and sets a limited "arbitrary and capricious" standard of judicial review. . . . By contrast, the APA contains provisions for adjudication which set out a fairly elaborate scheme of procedural requirements utilizing the judicial hearing as its decisionmaking model. . . .

Although the APA, as a generally applicable code of administrative procedure, was indisputably of great practical significance, it was nonetheless—in an important sense—a symbolic gesture. The Act was a formal articulation of agency due process in return for the newly recognized powers of wide-ranging administrative intervention in the economy. Symbolic benefits aside, the APA had considerable limitations. It did not purport to reshape the role of administrative government in the federal system; it established no new substantive areas of agency responsibility. Nor did the Act purport to alter common law judicial review principles establishing the allocation of authority between court and agency for deciding questions of law and fact. In addition, the Act failed to address the vast field of informal agency action—the entire range of interactions between agencies and regulated parties that take place outside the context of a formal hearing or a rulemaking proceeding. Finally, the Act spoke in the broad terms of a charter—"substantial evidence," "arbitrary and capricious," "statement of basis and purpose," and so forth—employing language sufficiently vague to allow the greatest leeway in the scope of administrative discretion to fashion regulatory policy in a particularized context.

On the judicial side, the [late 1930's] ushered in a period of unprecedented goodwill towards the regulatory system. With the final legitimation of the New Deal came the acceptance of a central precept of public administration: faith in the ability of experts to develop effective solutions to the economic disruptions created by the market system. Although this premise was not new—it had served as a foundation for early railroad regulation and as a basic tenet of Progressive thought—it came to political fruition with the New Deal agencies. And for the first time, the courts came to grips with the implications of expertise for the allocation of decisionmaking authority between court and agency.

. . . The enactment of the APA, however, created only a brief respite from criticism. By the early 1960s, a consensus existed that something was amiss.

Two groups of critics emerged. One group contended that the agencies were ignoring their mandate to establish clear and consistent policy guidelines—that economic regulation was adrift in a sea of irresolution. In the classic exposition, Henry Friendly challenged the agencies to abandon their practice of deciding major policy issues almost exclusively through case-by-case adjudication, and exhorted regulators to take advantage of their unique capacity to engage in long-term planning through administrative rulemaking.[3]

___

3. See Henry Friendly, The Federal Administrative Agencies: The Need for Better   Definition of Standards (1962).

Another school of critics expressed concern about the oppressive tendencies of the regulatory system. In a widely noted essay, Charles Reich stressed the dramatic fashion in which government largess had come to exercise a pervasive influence over the basic needs of the individual by setting the terms on which one might pursue an education, practice an occupation, or realize the expectation of economic security in later years.[4] While Friendly advocated greater reliance on rulemaking, Reich argued the need for more adequate procedural rights in adjudicatory settings.

The critical theses pursued by Friendly and Reich ... converged in their reliance on the traditional procedural mechanisms of rulemaking and adjudication for effecting regulatory reform. Just as the APA resorted to a simple dichotomous model—likening agency adjudication to the judicial process and agency rulemaking to the legislative process—so did the critics in the early 1960s pick up on the unfinished business of 1946.

Viewed in this context, [the National Environmental Policy Act of 1969 (NEPA)] represented a wholly different strategy for controlling administrative discretion. Most importantly, the Act had a powerful substantive impetus that was absent from earlier plenary regulatory reform proposals. In essence, APA-type reform took the agency's "mission" as given, and aimed at creating a formal decisionmaking methodology which would be more conducive to careful deliberation, and to achieving "correct" outcomes. By contrast, NEPA directly challenged the premise that mission-oriented agencies were discharging their responsibilities with a proper regard for "the public interest," as long as they failed to give focused consideration to the impact of their decisions on the environment. NEPA anticipated an altered process of decision rather than simply better procedures for decision; the environmental impact statement was to be "action-forcing" in that every federal regulatory agency was to reassess its mandate in view of the environmental consequences of any major decision it might reach.

In addition to this highly significant substantive requirement, NEPA brought a different procedural perspective to regulatory reform. ... NEPA was silent about hearings. ... [Its] primary thrust ... was its reliance upon an internal management technique that owed a greater debt to organization theory than to administrative law. Under the most optimistic scenario, the routinization of an impact statement requirement would necessitate specialized administrative personnel and the establishment of new channels of communication and information-flow within an agency. ... NEPA did, in fact, have a tremendous impact on the administrative system, although not necessarily that which might have been anticipated. Within months of the Act's passage, a federal court had enjoined the Trans–Alaska pipeline on grounds of failure to prepare an impact statement.[5] ... By 1975, the [Council on Environmental Quality] reported that in excess of a thousand impact statements had been filed annually over the preceding four years by federal agencies. ...

---

4. Charles A. Reich, The New Property, 73 Yale L.J. 733 (1964).

5. Wilderness Soc'y v. Morton, 479 F.2d 842 (D.C.Cir.1973), cert. denied, 411 U.S. 917 (1973).

The second pathbreaking piece of environmental regulatory legislation was the Clean Air Amendments of 1970 (CAA). In many ways, the design of this landmark pollution control scheme is at the polar extreme from NEPA. Where NEPA is a broadly stated charter of environmental rights consisting of barely a page of text, the CAA is an extraordinarily technical document as lengthy as a decent-sized novel (although hardly as readable). Where NEPA was designed to influence the mandate of every federal agency, the CAA is addressed to a single specialized agency headed by a sole administrator. Where NEPA is directed exclusively at the federal agencies, the CAA allocates major implementation responsibilities to the states. And finally, where NEPA is designed to effectuate internal management reforms within the federal bureaucracy, the CAA relies upon traditional rulemaking and adjudicative enforcement procedures—including private rights of action— and establishes various avenues for judicial review.

What unites the Clean Air Act with NEPA as a real innovation in regulatory design is congressional recourse to an action-forcing principle. The CAA, like NEPA, rejects the prevailing New Deal wisdom that agency experts could best bring their technical expertise to bear on problems of public policy if they were pointed in the right direction, whether allocation of air traffic routes, design of river rechannelization projects, or whatever, and told to regulate in "the public interest." ... NEPA was meant to widen the administrator's horizons. ... In setting stringent deadlines for administrative action, the CAA questioned the very will of the regulatory agencies to act. It warned that if air pollution controls were to be enforced by the New Deal strategy, 40 years of experience suggested that the regulators would delay, equivocate, and generally fail to establish in any precise way what "the public interest" required. Whereas NEPA's response was to rewrite the substantive mandate of the agencies, the CAA took the different tack of requiring that precise standards be established and explicit compliance timetables be met.

A new congressional mood was evident—a willingness to go beyond the blank-check delegation of the past. ... Whatever room for discretionary choice exists in defining "lowest achievable emissions" or "best available technology," the notion of unquestioning deference to administrative expertise was dealt a sharp blow by the establishment of firm deadlines for compliance with specified air quality standards. ...

Putting aside the singular implementation strategies associated with NEPA and the CAA, certain generalizations can be made about the salient characteristics of Public Interest era regulatory reform from a historical perspective. At the time of enactment both NEPA and the CAA stirred up almost no controversy, despite the arguably draconian implications of each regulatory scheme. ... Although there was an ineffectual eleventh-hour expression of industry protest, the CAA passed both houses of Congress with overwhelming majorities; in the case of NEPA, there was no discernible opposition.

Viewed in historical perspective, this phenomenon of virtual consensus support for landmark regulatory legislation turns out to be the norm rather than an aberration. From the enactment of the Interstate Commerce Act through the passage of New Deal legislation, major industrial groups were required to generate costly information, were circumscribed in access to markets, and were subjected to criminal enforcement schemes, with hardly a dissenting vote in Congress. Consequently, the smooth passage of the NEPA and the CAA should come as no surprise in itself.

In earlier times, however, the new regulatory scheme frequently produced apparent benefits to powerful regulated interests that helped to explain the relatively mild congressional opposition to proposals for substantial regulatory reform.[6] ... As James Q. Wilson has argued, much of the public interest regulation passed in the 1970s can be characterized politically as involving concentrated costs (on industry) and dispersed benefits (to "the public")[7]—not a scenario that traditionally augured well for the enactment of regulatory legislation. But in the 1970s, big business was truly on the defensive as the public seemed responsive to a wide variety of concerns about the quality of life. An entire series of initiatives resulted—on auto safety, product design, air and water pollution control, scenic conservation, and occupational health and safety, to mention only the most significant—which manifested a distinct bias against economic growth. The political climate made it virtually impossible to oppose such programs in principle—and focused objections can always be pursued in the process of agency implementation.

A second striking feature of the Public Interest era legislation is that it was not the product of a social movement for reform, nor even the outcome of pluralistic, interest group politics. As Wilson noted, the passage of NEPA and the CAA might well be characterized as instances of "entrepreneurial politics"—situations in which astute politicians adopted anticipatory strategies, setting the agenda for regulatory action prior to clearly articulated interest group demands for change.

A third aspect of the Public Interest era that warrants attention is the relatively limited ideological thrust of the reform measures that characterize the period. This assertion may seem at odds with the antigrowth theme evident throughout the era. Consider, however, that no substantial wealth redistribution impulse fueled the Public Interest reform efforts, and no discernible challenge was mounted against the autonomy of a market-based economy. Instead, the key legislation of the period suggested a return to the policing model of Progressivism. In the areas of pollution control, occupational safety, and consumer protection, the prevailing ideology anticipated the internalization of the previously unrecognized costs of industrial growth—a market-corrective strategy that posed no challenge to the premises of an exchange economy.

[In his essay, Professor Rabin examines judicial developments of the 1970's—cases that will attract sustained attention in this book—concluding that in them] the era of judicial deference that had spanned three decades

6. The strong version of this thesis is found in two historical studies, Gabriel Kolko, Railroads and Regulation 1877–1916 (1965) (dealing with the events leading to the enactment of the Interstate Commerce Act): Gabriel Kolko, Triumph of Conservatism (1963) (analyzing the origins of federal regulatory legislation in the Progressive era).

7. See James Q. Wilson, The Politics of Regulation 364–72 (1980).

was abruptly brought to an end. Regulation was once again viewed with a skeptical, if not jaundiced, eye. . . .

The legitimacy of the regulatory enterprise was not in question. Rather, the courts were centrally concerned with the question of how to control effectively the exercise of administrative discretion in the singularly perplexing cases of scientific and technological complexity. Deference to traditional processes of informal rulemaking and adjudication in such cases appeared to be tantamount to surrendering the function of judicial review.

Perhaps for the first time in a century of steady administrative expansion, the coordinate institutions—legislative and judicial—acted in tandem rather than moving in opposing directions. In the early 1970s, Congress recognized the need to address a variety of low-visibility collateral costs to health, safety, and the environment that were the legacy of relatively unimpeded long-term industrial growth. At the same time, the courts heralded the importance of these newly recognized values, and in doing so conducted a searching re-examination of fundamental principles of judicial review of administrative discretion. Confronting newly discovered problems in weighing scientific and technological uncertainty or in assessing the value of aesthetic and ecological concerns, the courts liberally construed the new social regulation. But correlatively, they imposed stringent standards of explanation and justification on the agencies responsible for implementing the new legislation. The courts thus fashioned a new judicial activism that first appeared as a dramatic reaction against the deferential judicial posture of the post-New Deal court. Then, as the decade wore on, the approach shifted back to a less intrusive (although still insistent) requirement that agencies demonstrate their competence rather than simply have it taken for granted.

By the late 1970s, . . . the expansionist period of the Public Interest era had . . . run its course. For the first time in a century, a discernible political movement sought to reassess the need for regulatory programs that administered markets as a means of promoting the health of particular industries. This movement was exceedingly widespread: The regulatory system came under close scrutiny by policy institutes and journals, academic disciplines, and politically influential public officials who all came to focus on a clear and dominant emerging theme—deregulation.

. . . The increased focus on deregulation was not principally a reaction to the latest wave of regulatory reform—the social regulation of the Public Interest era. No serious effort was mounted to revoke the recent congressional initiatives in the areas of health, safety, and environmental protection—let alone to reassess the need for earlier Progressive era efforts to establish policing controls on the market. Instead, the new criticism was leveled at administrative activity extending beyond the policing model; it constituted an attack—unparalleled in vigor—on price-and-entry regulation.

The economic regulatory agencies were chastised . . . on the grounds that widespread government intervention in support of price-and-entry regulation was suppressing competition and fostering economic waste. In unprecedented fashion, Congress responded with a series of deregulatory initiatives: the Airline Deregulation Act of 1978 (providing for total deregulation, in phases, of fare setting and entry restriction in air travel); the Motor Carrier Reform Act of 1980 and the Staggers Rail Act (relaxing rate and entry regulation of motor carriers and rail traffic, respectively); and the Depository Institutions Deregulation and Monetary Control Act of 1980 (eliminating interest ceilings on time and savings deposits).

The congressional embrace of deregulation marked a pause after a century of steady growth in the federal administrative system. Moreover, the rising storm of criticism over excessive regulation extended far beyond the field of legislative activity. Traditional administrative rulemaking—so-called command and control rulemaking—came under general attack for its economic inefficiency in failing to discriminate between low-cost and high-cost compliance activity. Critics excoriated administrative adjudication for its expense and delay. They further challenged agency priorities in establishing policy as failing to give precise consideration to the costs and benefits of various regulatory options—including the possibility of taking no action at all.

Lending a sympathetic ear, the Carter and Reagan administrations successively sought to sustain further the deregulatory mood through economic efficiency measures at the agency implementation stage—such as allowing the offsetting and trading of air pollution emissions credits under the Clean Air Act, and requiring cost-benefit justification from the agencies for 'major' regulatory initiatives prior to administrative action. Indeed, the Reagan administration appeared to pursue a broader-based de facto deregulation policy by appointing unsympathetic agency administrators and proposing drastic budget cuts in regulatory programs untainted by congressional disapproval.

. . . [A] half-century after the New Deal . . . [t]he system has grown by leaps and bounds, yet it remains devoid of any coherent ideological framework. In the political sphere, while a broadranging commitment to government intervention seems a continuing legacy of the New Deal, no consensus exists on the appropriate scope of federal regulatory activities. The long-standing tension between a regulatory system dedicated to effective policing of the market and one which would stimulate cooperation among private interests—a tension as venerable as the federal regulatory presence itself—has never been conclusively resolved. For the present, the minimalist policing model of regulation appears to be in the ascendancy, but only the most self-confident seer would predict the future. Indeed, even the welfare sector of the administrative system—an especially deep-rooted outgrowth of the New Deal—has not been immune from attack in the years since the demise of the War on Poverty.

In the courts, the legitimacy of regulation is no longer seriously questioned. But here, too, widespread recognition of the need for an expansive regulatory system has simply posed critical questions rather than resolved them. The courts have not developed a consistent approach to controlling agency discretion. Such an approach would have to draw on a theory of administrative expertise that dealt coherently with the technical and political dimensions of the regulatory process. Lacking an intelligible theoretical framework, the Supreme Court has oscillated between activism and restraint in reviewing agency decisions. Like Congress, the judicial system gets higher marks for pragmatism and flexibility in dealing with each successive wave of regulatory reform than it does for intellectual coherence and certainty of approach.

NOTES

(1) ELENA KAGAN, PRESIDENTIAL ADMINISTRATION, 114 Harv. L. Rev. 2245, 2246–2249 (2001):

"The history of the American administrative state is the history of competition among different entities for control of its policies. All three branches of government—the President, Congress, and Judiciary—have participated in this competition; so too have the external constituencies and internal staff of the agencies. Because of the stakes of the contest and the strength of the claims and weapons possessed by the contestants, no single entity has emerged finally triumphant, or is ever likely to do so. But at different times, one or another has come to the fore and asserted at least a comparative primacy in setting the direction and influencing the outcome of administrative process. In this time, that institution is the Presidency. We live today in an era of presidential administration. . . .

"For administrative law scholars, the claim of presidential administration may seem puzzling. . . . These scholars—concerned as they are with the actual practices of administrative control, as carried out in executive branch as well as independent agencies—may well have viewed the claim as arguable, though perhaps premature, if made ten or fifteen years ago, when President Reagan or Bush was in office. In the first month of his tenure, Reagan issued an executive order creating a mechanism by which the Office of Management and Budget (OMB), an entity within the Executive Office of the President (EOP), would review all major regulations of executive branch agencies. As Reagan's and then Bush's terms proceeded, and the antiregulatory effects of this system of review became increasingly evident, administrative law scholars took part in a sharp debate about its propriety. With the advent of the Clinton Administration, however, this debate receded. Although President Clinton issued his own executive order providing for OMB review of regulations, the terms of this order struck most observers as moderating the aggressive approach to oversight of administration taken in the Reagan and Bush Presidencies. Perhaps as important, the Clinton OMB chose to implement the order in a way generally sympathetic to regulatory efforts. Because objections to OMB review in the Reagan and Bush era arose in large part from its deregulatory tendencies, this reversal of substantive direction contributed to the waning of interest in, and even recognition of, the involvement of the President and his EOP staff in administration.

"In fact, as this Article will show, presidential control of administration, in critical respects, expanded dramatically during the Clinton years, making the regulatory activity of the executive branch agencies more and more an extension of the President's own policy and political agenda. Faced for most of his time in office with a hostile Congress but eager to show progress on domestic issues, Clinton and his White House staff turned to the bureaucracy to achieve, to the extent it could, the full panoply of his domestic policy goals. Whether the subject was health care, welfare reform, tobacco, or guns, a self-conscious and central object of the White House was to devise, direct, and/or finally announce administrative actions—regulations, guidance, enforcement strategies, and reports—to showcase and advance presidential policies. In executing this strategy, the White House in large measure set the administrative agenda for key agencies, heavily influencing what they would (or would not) spend time on and what they would (or would not) generate as regulatory product.

"The resulting policy orientation diverged substantially from that of the Reagan and Bush years, disproving the assumption some scholars have made, primarily on the basis of that earlier experience, that presidential supervision of administration inherently cuts in a deregulatory direction. Where once presidential supervision had worked to dilute or delay regulatory initiatives, it served in the Clinton years as part of a distinctly activist and pro-regulatory governing agenda. Where once presidential supervision had tended to favor politically conservative positions, it generally operated during the Clinton Presidency as a mechanism to achieve progressive goals. Or expressed in the terms most sympathetic to all these Presidents (and therefore most contestable), if Reagan and Bush showed that presidential supervision could thwart regulators intent on regulating no matter what the cost, Clinton showed that presidential supervision could jolt into action bureaucrats suffering from bureaucratic inertia in the face of unmet needs and challenges. . . ."

(2) The administrative state begins with a series of decisions to establish and empower administrative agencies. These decisions are probably best thought of not in absolute terms (administrative agencies are "good" or "bad") but in comparative terms (they are "better" or "worse"). Better or worse than what?

In political terms, the choice is usually phrased in terms of action, inaction, or reverse action: administrative agencies are equated with "regulation" and contrasted with the choices of "doing nothing" or "deregulation." From the standpoint of legal analysis, however, this is insufficient. The difficulty can be seen most clearly if we ask: what in the legal universe does "doing nothing" equate with? It doesn't equate with "no law," if only because there are very few things on which there is ever "no law." Indeed, "doing nothing" from the political point of view might well leave in place a highly articulated and demanding set of legal norms.

In the American legal system, there are two likely alternatives to the establishment of administrative agencies. First, there are common law regimes, created and implemented through the courts. Products liability law is, by and large, an example of a common-law legal regime. Second, there are statutory law regimes, in which legislatures establish rules that are directly enforceable in court. The law of sales under the Uniform Commercial Code is an example of this type of legal regime.

To decide whether to establish an administrative law regime to handle a particular topic, it is thus necessary to compare the advantages or disadvantages of it to each of these other possibilities. These pluses and minuses are of two general varieties. One is institutional: what are the advantages or disadvantages of creating special-purpose agencies staffed by appointed personnel rather than relying on the general-purpose legislatures and courts, each with a long tradition of legitimacy. The other is in terms of conferred powers: legislatures generally make rules, while courts usually decide cases; agencies can be given these powers within their jurisdictions, but also the powers to conduct inspections, grant licenses, broadcast information, undertake research, and other things as well. One might then ask overall, whether the probable use of this panoply of powers by a specialized organ of government resting on delegated powers is likely to be better or worse, in addressing the matter at hand, than having the legislature itself establish a set of directly-legally-effective rules, or than leaving the whole matter to the courts to work out as cases arise.

(3) STEVEN P. CROLEY, THEORIES OF REGULATION: INCORPORATING THE ADMINISTRATIVE PROCESS, 91 Colum. L. Rev. 1, 166–68 (1998): [This is an ambitious and thorough-going effort to test the realities of administrative procedure and action against four theories about regulation—public choice (treating regulators as economic actors in a 'market'), neopluralist (regulation as the outcome of competing group interests), public interest (regulation as ameliorative public response to market failures) and civic republicanism (regulation as the product of collective deliberation about goals and values). Prof. Croley argues that none of the theories fit the facts-on-the-ground very well, although on his assessment the second and third do best. He concludes:]

"That no theory of regulation is vindicated by a hands-on look at administrative process will not surprise some, and it should not. First of all, it is entirely possible that scholars like James Q. Wilson are correct when they argue that there can be no general political theory of regulation. Even the best generalizations that span different agencies, regulatory contexts, and particular regulatory problems may ultimately mislead more than they illuminate. But, Wilson's assertion notwithstanding, whether this is in fact the case cannot be known until scholars first try to reconcile their abstractions with observations from the trenches—with 'who,' 'when,' and 'where,' data about administrative decisionmaking.

"This article thus calls upon students of regulation to devote increased attention to the messy details of the administrative process, and, incidentally, upon students of administrative law to articulate more clearly how their arguments about what administrative law should look like fit into some broader conception of what agencies do. It thus challenges both the case-centric old school of administrative-law scholarship, which focuses on judicial doctrine with insufficient attention to how alternative doctrinal rules comport with one or more broader theoretical pictures of the regulatory regime, and the equation-centric new school of scholarship on the political economy of regulation, which either abstracts from administrative processes altogether or, at most, treats agencies as single players with insufficient attention to the legal context in which administrative decisionmakers operate. This is not to suggest that all students of administrative regulation fail to appreciate the benefits of close study of the administrative process. Much insightful work proves otherwise. Rather, while others have noted the connection, the administrative process has yet to be fully merged with theories of regulation (and vice versa). . . .

"Second, given that the American experiment with large scale administrative government is still (in the big picture) in its early stages, it would be surprising if students of regulation had already developed a complete and compelling understanding of administrative regulation. Students of the subject might more realistically seek to assimilate the partial and overlapping insights offered by the competing theories.

"This much, however, seems clear. Strong claims about the inevitability of regulatory failure due to regulated parties' privileged access to regulatory decisionmakers are untenable in the light of the decisionmaking procedures regulators employ, the broader legal environment in which regulatory decisions are made, and the available evidence about the types of parties that participate in regulatory decisionmaking. Moving down from the level of legislator incentives to the plane of agency implementation of very general legislative directives reveals a more complicated regulatory world than the public choice theory envisions. In it, rent-seekers' success requires much more than providing legislators with political resources, and thus the exploitation of the many by the few hardly appears a foregone conclusion. Instead, special interest domination seems more or less likely depending on the procedural opportunities available to other interests.

"The pressing question for scholars and policymakers thus becomes what procedural techniques for monitoring those delegated regulatory decisionmaking powers would better ensure that the exercise of that power does not create more problems than it solves. If ... regulatory outcomes really are a function of administrative process rules, then the right set of structural changes to those processes could have very beneficial results. Just what those changes might look like must be left for future analyses. But it is at least conceivable that a new, more unified theory of regulation could be developed that improved upon the basic conceptual frameworks of the neopluralist, public choice and public interest theories, but sought to supplement those with aspirations of the civic republican theory.

"Up to now, most regulatory scholars resisting the public choice theory's calls for deregulation have instead taken a very different track, turning to courts as the ultimate safeguard against the danger of rent-seeking. While that approach is sensible enough, especially given that judges are relatively insulated from the types of political pressures that produce undesirable regulations, there is no reason to place such a heavy burden on courts alone. Nor can it be clear just what oversight role is most appropriate for the courts, absent deeper understanding of exactly what they are overseeing. Between delegation and judicial review lies the black box of administrative process. Reformers who would preserve the regulatory regime should open it."

SECTION 4. PERSPECTIVES ON THE ENTERPRISE OF ADMINISTRATIVE LAW

Professor Rabin's article focuses on the reasons for, and modes of, regulation. Administrative law is closely connected to regulatory policy, but it is not the same thing. What is the purpose of the ways in which agency actions are clothed in legal forms and judicially reviewed? Here are some answers scholars have given, presented in chronological order:

(1) FELIX FRANKFURTER, THE TASK OF ADMINISTRATIVE LAW, 75 U. Penn. L. Rev., 614 (1927): "The widening area of what in effect is law-making authority, exercised by officials whose actions are not subject to ordinary court review, constitutes perhaps the most striking contemporary tendency of the Anglo–American legal order. The massive volumes of Statutory Rules and Orders, published annually since 1890, testify to the pervasive domain of delegated legislation in Great Britain. The formulation and publication of executive orders and rules and regulations are in this country still in a primitive stage, which only serves to render more portentous the operation of these forms of law. But the range of control conferred by Congress and the State legislatures upon subsidiary law-making bodies, variously denominated as heads of departments, commissions and boards, penetrates in the United States, as in Great Britain and the Dominions, the whole gamut of human affairs. Hardly a measure passes Congress the effective execution of which is not conditioned upon rules and regulations emanating from the enforcing authorities. These administrative complements are euphemistically called 'filling in the details' of a policy set forth in statutes. But the 'details' are of the essence; they give meaning and content to vague contours. The control of banking, insurance, public utilities, finance, industry, the professions, health and morals, in sum, the manifold response of government to the forces and needs of modern society, is building up a body of laws not written by legislatures, and of adjudications not made by courts and not subject to their revision. These powers are lodged in a vast congeries of agencies. We are in the midst of a process, largely unconscious and certainly unscientific, of adjusting the exercise of these powers to the traditional system of Anglo–American law and courts. A systematic scrutiny of these issues and a conscious effort towards their wise solution are the concerns of administrative law. The broad boundaries and far-reaching implications of these problems may be indicated by saying that administrative law deals with the field of legal control exercised by law-administering agencies other than courts, and the field of control exercised by courts over such agencies."

(2) JAMES M. LANDIS, THE ADMINISTRATIVE PROCESS, 7, 30–38, 46 (1938): "Two tendencies in the expanding civilization of the late nineteenth century seem to me to foreshadow the need for methods of government different in kind from those that had prevailed in the past. These are the rise of industrialism and the rise of democracy. Naturally, these two tendencies combined and interacted each upon the other, so that it becomes difficult to isolate cause and effect. For as a dynamic society does not move *in vacuo,* so an abstract classification of tendencies can have only a relative value. The rise of industrialism and the rise of democracy, however, brought new and difficult problems to government. A world that scarcely a hundred years ago could listen to Wordsworth's denunciation of railroads because their building despoiled the beauty of his northern landscapes is different, very different, from one that in 1938 has to determine lanes and flight levels for air traffic. While it was true that advances in transportation, communication, and mass production were in themselves disturbing elements, the profound problems were the social and economic questions

that flowed from the era of mechanical invention. To their solution some contribution derived from the rise of humanitarianism. But the driving force was the recognition by the governing classes of our civilization of their growing dependence upon the promotion of the welfare of the governed. Concessions to rectify social maladjustments thus had to be made, however grudgingly. And as the demands for positive solutions increased and, in the form of legislative measures, were precipitated upon the cathodes of governmental activity, *laissez faire*—the simple belief that only good could come by giving economic forces free play—came to an end.

"I have mentioned a broad distinction which underlies types of administrative agencies now in existence. That distinction relates to the difference between those administrative bodies whose essential concern is the economic functioning of the particular industry and those which have an extended police function of a particular nature. Although it is dangerous to deal in motives, yet the reasons which prompted a resort to the administrative process in the latter area would seem to be reasonably clear. In large measure these reasons sprang from a distrust of the ability of the judicial process to make the necessary adjustments in the development of both law and regulatory methods as they related to particular industrial problems.

"Admittedly, the judicial process suffers from several basic and more or less unchangeable characteristics. One of these is its inability to maintain a longtime, uninterrupted interest in a relatively narrow and carefully defined area of economic and social activity. ... A general jurisdiction leaves the resolution of an infinite variety of matters within the hands of courts. In the disposition of these claims judges are uninhibited in their discretion except for legislative rules of guidance or such other rules as they themselves may distill out of that vast reserve of materials that we call the common law. This breadth of jurisdiction and freedom of disposition tends somewhat to make judges jacks-of-all-trades and masters of none. ...

"To these considerations must be added two others. The first is the recognition that there are certain fields where the making of law springs less from generalizations and principles drawn from the majestic authority of textbooks and cases, than from a 'practical' judgment which is based upon all the available considerations and which has in mind the most desirable and pragmatic method of solving that particular problem. ...

"The second consideration is, perhaps, even more important. It is the fact that the common-law system left too much in the way of the enforcement of claims and interests to private initiative. Jhering's analysis of the 'struggle for law'—the famous essay in which he indicated that the process of carving out new rights had resulted from the willingness of individuals as litigants or as criminal defendants to become martyrs to their convictions—pointed only to a slow and costly method of making law. ...

"... The administrative process is, in essence, our generation's answer to the inadequacy of the judicial and the legislative processes. It represents our effort to find an answer to those inadequacies by some other method than merely increasing executive power. If the doctrine of the separation of power implies division, it also implies balance, and balance calls for equality. The creation of administrative power may be the means for the preservation of that balance, so that paradoxically enough, though it may seem in theoretic violation of the doctrine of the separation of power, it may in matter of fact be the means for the preservation of the content of that doctrine."

(3) JAMES O. FREEDMAN, CRISIS AND LEGITIMACY—THE ADMINISTRATIVE PROCESS AND AMERICAN GOVERNMENT, 9–11 (1978): "The criticism that historically has been directed toward the administrative agencies is significantly different in tone and quality from the criticism, robust though it often has been, that regularly has attended the manner in which Congress and the courts carry out their respective responsibilities. Those institutions have been challenged primarily with questions concerning the proper limits of their undoubted powers, the wisdom of particular decisions as a matter of policy or the national good, and the efficiency of the processes by which they reach their decisions. Most of these criticisms have been directed at actions and defects existing at the margins of institutional power, at temporary aberrations and malfunctions rather than at the legitimacy of the institutional power. On those few occasions when the criticism has been directed at the legitimacy of the institutional power itself, the power has survived wholly intact, its legitimacy undiminished.

"By contrast, the criticism of the administrative agencies has been animated by a strong and persisting challenge to the basic legitimacy of the administrative process itself. Criticisms of this character are stated in the reports commissioned by Presidents Roosevelt, Truman, Kennedy, and Nixon, as well as in an extensive body of literature analyzing the federal administrative process. That such criticism has so often been phrased in terms of crisis suggests that it is too serious, too fundamental, perhaps too deeply implicated in principle, to be met by theoretical constructs or by incremental adjustments of the kind that governments routinely rely upon when anomalies or inefficiencies of recent appearance or temporary duration seem to require a response.

"The subject of legitimacy is concerned with popular attitudes toward the exercise of governmental power. Such attitudes focus upon whether governmental power is being held and exercised in accordance with a nation's laws, values, traditions, and customs. That the legitimacy of the federal administrative process should still be in question at this late date may be surprising. But institutions of which so much is demanded, no matter how deep their historical roots, can hardly be expected to gain and sustain public acceptance when the very basis of their existence and their legitimacy is so consistently and forcefully challenged. Institutional legitimacy is an indispensable condition for institutional effectiveness. By endowing institutional decisions with an inherent capacity to attract obedience and respect, legitimacy permits an institution to achieve its goals without the regular necessity of threatening the use of force and creating renewed episodes of public resentment. Since the authority of any institution, as Max Weber so effectively argued, rests ultimately upon a popular belief in its legitimacy, substantial, persisting challenges to the legitimacy of governmental institutions must be regarded with concern, for such challenges threaten to impair the capacity of government to meet its administrative responsibilities effectively.

"But how do governmental institutions achieve a status of legitimacy in the American political setting? Why have the federal administrative agencies failed to achieve a status of legitimacy as complete as that of other governmental institutions? And what steps can Congress or the administrative agencies take to enhance the legitimacy of the administrative process?

"The recurrent sense of crisis attending the federal administrative process results from the failure of many Americans to appreciate the relevance of four principal sources of legitimacy to the role that administrative agencies play in American government. The legitimacy of the administrative process may be supported by public recognition that administrative agencies occupy an indispensable position in the constitutional scheme of government. The policies and performance of administrative agencies may further be accepted as legitimate to the extent that the public perceives the administrative process as embodying significant elements of political accountability. In addition, the effectiveness of administrative agencies in meeting their statutory responsibilities may enhance their legitimacy by strengthening public support in a nation that always has been impressed by effective performance. Finally, the legitimacy of the administrative process may be enhanced by the public's perception that its decision-making procedures are fair."

(4) CHRISTOPHER F. EDLEY, JR., ADMINISTRATIVE LAW: RETHINKING JUDICIAL CONTROL OF BUREAUCRACY, 4–7 (1990): "Historically, the separation of powers bulwarks were intended to minimize the risk of arbitrary government. Beginning in the late nineteenth century, however, and culminating with the Supreme Court's acquiescence in the New Deal's suggestion of administrative hegemony, courts and commentators increasingly recognized that a less rigid design was necessary to accommodate modern exigencies. In response, a variety of modern judicial doctrines and attitudes developed. The elements of this new approach to constraining bureaucratic discretion were the regularization of administrative processes, the presumptive availability of judicial review, and judicial deference to administrative expertise—expertise being itself a rational and professional constraint against arbitrariness. These elements were eventually reflected in the Administrative Procedure Act of 1946 (APA). It is too late in the day to protest the interment of separation of powers formalism, at least in the context of multifunction administrative agencies. But the underlying concern with arbitrary government remains with us, and the occasions for that concern multiply as unelected bureaucrats accumulate enormous policy and law-making discretion. The 'administrative' state is now inevitable because of the ever-lengthening agenda of complex public policy problems and the institutional limitations of legislatures. The broad delegations of power to those agencies—make the workplace 'reasonably' safe, assist the disabled who cannot engage in 'substantial gainful activity,' award licenses and allocate scarce resources in accordance with the 'public interest, convenience and necessity,' and similar formulas—create administrative discretion far more sweeping in scope and pervasiveness than the familiar and inherent ministerial discretion of the executive.

"As if to codify sweeping discretion, many statutes include a catchall delegation of substantive rule making authority to the agency, instructing the administrator to make any rules 'necessary' or 'appropriate' to accomplish the purposes of the statute. The sense that this discretion must be controlled continues to animate administrative law. As the bureaucracy's role has grown, so have the risks and benefits associated with official action. The stakes involved in judicial intervention to check malfeasance and misfeasance have also grown, so that familiar postures of judicial review now assume unfamiliar dimensions. In a way, discontent with judicial activism and the powerful social role of unelected judges is only a derivative problem, the principal one being awesome agency power.

"The Rule of Law approach to constraining discretion, which achieved maturity with the enactment of the APA, entails a strong role for subconstitutional judicial review. Such oversight by the unelected branch, however, is itself problematic in terms of those same values that cause us to fear official abuses in the first place. Thus, the continuing dilemma for administrative law has been that the effort to impose Rule of Law constraints on agencies must contend with the critique that judicial review simply replaces the *objectionable discretion of the administrator* with the *objectionable discretion of the judge*.

"There is a hopeful response to that critique. We have a continuing project of constructing and reforming a matrix of legal doctrines and attitudes intended to discipline the judges. That project reflects our powerful commitment to legal formality. If it is successful, the discipline judges themselves impose on administrators will not be simply another form of arbitrariness. But that is a rather large 'if.' "

(5) Jerry L. Mashaw and David L. Harfst, The Struggle for Auto Safety, 7–10 (1990): "The analysis of regulatory systems—why they emerge, how they operate, why they succeed or fail, who gains or loses from their operation—has been a thriving academic cottage industry for nearly two decades. This burgeoning interest is not difficult to explain. Not only is regulation a ubiquitous feature of late twentieth-century social, economic, and political life, but there has been enormous ferment in the regulatory arena. Regulation and deregulation both have been 'in' and 'out' as political ideas; regulatory and deregulatory statutes have emerged, sometimes in waves, sometimes in trickles, from Congress and from state legislatures. The individual and the social stakes in regulation are high.

"At the risk of oversimplification, we may assign prior analyses of regulation to two general categories. One is a policy analytic, or 'public welfare,' tradition with roots stretching back at least to the Progressive era. In that tradition the basic reference point is the 'public interest.' Inquiry concerns how best to design and operate regulatory agencies to serve that interest. This tradition is both normative and reformist in orientation. It seeks to distinguish good regulatory design from bad, explain why some systems succeed while others fail, and teach lessons about appropriate norms and techniques of regulatory administration.

"A second approach, with even older roots, is the tradition of political economy. In its more modern forms it is sometimes known as 'interest group theory' or 'capture theory.' This is a tradition more positive than normative in its focus. The central inquiry is why a particular regulatory regime takes the form that it takes or operates in a particular fashion.

Explanation is sought through attention not to the public welfare but to the underlying private interests that are affected by regulation. And although there are surely normative overtones to analyses that describe regulatory systems as, for example, designs to create government-sanctioned cartels for privileged interests, the explicit focus of most analyses is on explanation, not evaluation.

"These two traditions have much in common. Both assume that regulatory institutions, as well as the other political and legal institutions that make up the regulatory environment, are highly malleable. Both assume that contemporary political actors have a relatively free hand in designing and operating regulatory institutions to accommodate either public or private demands. Indeed, unless institutions are highly malleable, neither the design activities of the policy analysts nor the strategic maneuverings described by interest group aficionados have much point.

"To put the idea somewhat differently, both sets of analysts make easy transitions from motivations to behaviors. Policy analysts see institutional design and operation as an attempt by critical actors to realize some vision of the public interest. There may be mistakes, false starts, and failures, but this generally suggests only that the institutional designer should repair to the drawing board (or computer screen) to see in what respects the regulatory situation was misanalyzed. Political economists similarly view dominant coalitions as having the power, through selective political rewards and sanctions, to mold regulatory structures to suit their purposes. If regulatory institutions do not benefit their creators, it is usually because some other powerful political actor has made strategic moves that thwart the original coalition.

"In both traditions one finds complex analyses that try to take account of other factors. Some theorists give significant explanatory force to the power of new ideas and to external events or shocks that alter or redefine regulatory direction. Nor is personality, leadership, or entrepreneurship always absent from regulatory explanation.

"Yet both approaches tend to ignore a critical, often dominant, dimension of regulatory dynamics. Most accounts of regulatory behavior miss the inertial force of the general political and legal culture within which any regulatory regime must be constructed and operated. The dominant legal culture defines the repertoire of institutional techniques available to either policy-analytic planners or strategists concerned with political economy. Both must make their plans (or play their games) within the constraints that are established by broader institutions that elaborate and preserve the culture. Legal culture, as expressed through the operation of judicial review, the separation of powers, 'federalism,' and associated 'checks and balances,' provides a powerful, perhaps the most powerful, explanation for the particular form taken by regulatory regimes and for their ultimate success or failure.

"This is both a strong and a controversial claim. Do we really mean to argue that people, new ideas, external shocks, concentrations of economic power, and a host of other variables do not matter? Of course not. The legal culture is not the motive force for regulatory activity. It provides only broad models for and constraints on behavior. These models are subject both to situation-specific avoidance and long-term adaptation.

"Yet we do claim that viewed over the medium range—not a year or a century, but a few decades—legal convention exerts continuous and surprisingly sharp pressures on regulatory structures and regulatory behavior. Where regulatory policy goes and how it gets there can be traced in general, and sometimes in quite specific, terms to the way in which the regulatory regime reflects or challenges the conventional assumptions of the legal order."

(6) CYNTHIA R. FARINA, THE CONSENT OF THE GOVERNED: AGAINST SIMPLE RULES FOR A COMPLEX WORLD, 72 Chicago–Kent L. Rev. 987, 987–89 (1997): "The 1980s saw the emergence of a rich separation of powers jurisprudence that has been channeled, in this decade, into more focused attention on strengthening the hand of the President. The notion of strong presidential leadership of administrative government is not, of course, new. If the contemporary regulatory state could not have happened without the New Deal, the New Deal could not have happened without Franklin Roosevelt. Still, the current emphasis on presidential direction of domestic regulatory policy is different in kind, as well as intensity. Increasingly, scholars (and, at times, the judiciary) look to the President not only to improve the managerial competence and efficiency with which regulation occurs but also, and more deeply, to supply the elusive essence of democratic legitima tion. The ideological sources drawn upon are diverse—original intent, civic republicanism, public choice theory—but the central argument is consistent: The President, and the President alone, represents the entire citizenry. The President, uniquely, is situated to infuse into regulatory policymaking the will of the whole people.

"I argue here that this latest effort at making peace between regulatory government and representative democracy is fatally flawed. Despite the ingenuity and intensity with which strong presidentialism is advanced, it is premised upon a fundamentally untenable conception of the consent of the governed. The 'will of the people,' as invoked in that effort, is artificially bounded in time, homogenized, shorn of ambiguities—in short, fabricated. It obscures complex problems (recognized elsewhere in administrative law scholarship) of information, prediction, and risk perception. It slides over vexed questions (recognized elsewhere in scholarly literature about democracy) of when leaders should lead rather than follow and of how the act of governing becomes a process in which the collective will is formed, rather than merely implemented.

"My counter-proposition is a broad, and perhaps uncomfortably indeterminate one: No single mode of democratic legitimation can serve to mediate between the conflicted, protean, often inchoate will of the people and the modern regulatory enterprise. No single institution or practice is capable of performing the multiple tasks of registering, interpreting, educating, adapting, affording participation, facilitating deliberation, brokering accommodation, and umpiring conflict that are (or at least ought to be) entailed in shaping the public policy of a post-industrialized democracy with an activist regulatory government. There are no simple rules for this complex world. Rather, we must necessarily look to a plurality of institutions and practices as contributors to an ongoing process of legitimizing the regulatory state. Each of those institutions and practices will be partial and, of itself, insufficient. Each imposes its own kind of costs on the regulatory process. Each is capable, if overemphasized, of introducing its own kind of distortion.

"In sum, I am suggesting that the reconciliatory effort must abandon its yearning for a neat solution to the legitimacy problem and, instead, come to terms with 'the ugliness of democracy.' Whether actively exhilarated by the challenge, or merely resigned to the inescapable messiness, we scholars should understand the task of administrative law as an ongoing, and necessarily adaptive, inquiry into the optimal form and role for the variety of institutions and practices that hold legitimating potential."

* * *

A NOTE ON TEACHING AND STUDYING ADMINISTRATIVE LAW FROM THIS CASEBOOK

Administrative law is a big subject, and this is a big book. It would take a very big course of many semester hours to cover everything contained in the following chapters. None of your editors has ever given so large a course. We expect our users to be selective among the topics addressed, as we are. We have edited this book to facilitate this selectivity.

We have also edited this book to allow different users to take up its topics in varying sequences. Many administrative law topics are interrelated, to a degree you may not have encountered in other courses. Some have analogized the process of learning administrative law to watching a photographic negative develop in a darkroom. What you see at first are imprecise shapes whose details and relationships are unclear; only with time does a precise image emerge. "What are the standards to be applied on judicial review?" interacts with "When is judicial review available?" and with "What agency procedures are required in developing agency rules?" Cases presenting one of these issues explicitly or implicitly deal with the others. It is not reasonable to attempt to present the issues all at once, and different instructors will find one or another path through them to be appropriate. We have tried to edit the materials of this casebook to focus on the particular questions at hand, but also to, in various ways, signal or briefly anticipate the related issues you may not yet have dealt with in detail. By the end of the course, we trust, the interrelationships will emerge, and your review of the course will bring fresh understanding of your course's earliest topics.

In sum, we have tried to treat most topics in this book thoroughly and with intellectual rigor. We have done so in the belief that what is not directly covered in your course might still prove helpful to you in gaining fuller understanding of what *is* covered, and in the hope that after you have finished your course, our book will remain useful to you as a reference.

CHAPTER II

AGENCIES AND THE STRUCTURAL CONSTITUTION

Agencies are almost as old as the Constitution itself, yet controversy over their legal status has existed from the beginning of the Republic. The drafters of the Constitution chose not to specify the structure of the national government below the level of the three named constitutional actors: Congress, the President, and the Supreme Court. Instead, they empowered Congress to "make all Laws which shall be necessary and proper for carrying into Execution" not only "the foregoing [i.e., legislative] Powers" but also "all other Powers vested by this Constitution in the Government of the United States, or in any Department or Officer thereof." Art. 1, § 8, ¶ 18.

Pursuant to this provision—which Americans of the Founding era called the "Sweeping Clause"—the first Congress promptly created the Departments of Foreign Affairs, War, and the Treasury. The Post Office and the Department of the Navy followed within a few years. Intense debate preceded these acts. Although many of the first legislators had played key roles in the Philadelphia Convention and/or in the ratification process in their home states, they disagreed fundamentally about whether the Constitution gives the President sole and unqualified power to remove agency heads.[1] When even those so close to the Constitution's birth could not agree on this basic question, it seems unlikely that contemporary constitutional challenges to the administrative state will yield easy answers.

Such challenges have proliferated since 1980. Perhaps more accurately, in the last 25 years, *structural* constitutional challenges to agencies, their programs, and the methods of their oversight have emerged as major, and unprecedented, occasions to debate the legality of the administrative state. Throughout most of our history, constitutional litigation against regulation almost invariably involved *rights* provisions. In the early 20th century, substantive due process (epitomized by Lochner v. New York, 198 U.S. 45 (1905)) imposed significant, though transient, limits on government's regulatory ambitions. During the Cold War and Civil Rights Eras, procedural due process challenges began to work important changes in how agencies can allocate benefits and impose sanctions.[2] With the signal exception of

---

1. See Section 4.a, p. 140 below.

2. Because its commands apply to both the national government and the states, due process has the capacity significantly to affect the scope of regulation at both the federal and the local levels. The impact of *substantive* due process (and its modern relative, regulatory takings doctrine) is largely beyond the scope of this course; the important con-

the long line of nondelegation cases (considered in Section 1 below), few pre–1980 litigants ventured beyond the Bill of Rights and Fourteenth Amendment. John Marshall's expansive view of the Commerce Clause[3] had rendered that part of Article I an unpromising constitutional basis for challenging the growing federal regulatory presence. The Ninth and Tenth Amendments (and the principles of limited government and federalism they embody) might have seemed more congenial. But private attempts to mount such attacks were dismissed as non-justiciable.[4] And, when local governmental entities eventually began to assert Tenth Amendment claims for themselves, the Court (after equivocating) held that any federalism limits on national regulation were not judicially enforceable.[5]

By the end of the 20th century, however, the nature and outcome of constitutional litigation about regulation had undergone a sea change. To some extent, this change reflects a Supreme Court that has reversed, or at least substantially modified, existing constitutional doctrine. Decisions invigorating the Takings Clauses of the Fifth and (by incorporation) Fourteenth Amendments, and narrowing the Commerce Clause, invalidated some regulatory programs and limited the reach of others.[6] Similarly, decisions that enhanced state sovereign immunity and found Article III limits on private parties' ability to sue, curtailed some significant avenues of regulatory enforcement.[7] This recrafting of existing constitutional doctrine is redrawing the constitutional boundaries of the regulatory state—and the knowledgeable student of administrative law will keep these important developments in mind. Nonetheless, with the exception of standing and related justiciability doctrines explored in Chapter IX, they are largely beyond the scope of this course.

Very much at the heart of this course (and the subject of this Chapter) is the emergence of the structural Constitution as a force that may limit how agencies are organized, empowered, and overseen. In a series of cases as potentially far-reaching as they are jurisprudentially novel, litigants have insisted that a variety of administrative arrangements—some recent, others longstanding—violate particular provisions of Articles I, II, or III and, more generally, the constitutional principle of separation of powers.

Several factors contributed to this jurisprudential phenomenon. As a matter of intellectual history, the three presidential terms served by Ronald Reagan and George H. Bush were the renaissance of conservative constitutional theory—in particular, the vibrant resurgence of originalist and textualist forms of analysis. Although these methods of interpretation had been largely abandoned by constitutional rights theorists, they offered intriguing insights into questions of constitutional structure. As a matter of

straints imposed by *procedural* due process are the subject of Chapter VII.

3. See Gibbons v. Ogden, 9 Wheaton 1 (1824).

4. E.g., Frothingham v. Mellon, 262 U.S. 447 (1923) (challenge to federal Maternity Act of 1922).

5. See National League of Cities v. Usery, 426 U.S. 833 (1976) (invalidating, on 10th Amendment grounds, application of the Fair Labor Standards Act to the states) overruled by Garcia v. San Antonio Metro. Transit Auth., 469 U.S. 528 (1985).

6. See, e.g., United States v. Morrison, 529 U.S. 598 (2000); United States v. Lopez, 514 U.S. 549 (1995); First Eng. Evang. Luth. Church v. Los Angeles County, 482 U.S. 304 (1987).

7. See Chapter IX, Secs. 1, 2.

political reality, throughout the 1980s the Republican party appeared solidly in control of the White House. Since World War II, a pattern had emerged in which one of the major political parties dominated Congress while the other held the Presidency. Both history and electoral demographics predicted that the White House would tend to be Republican in such times of "divided government." As you consider the materials in this Chapter, note how often victory to those mounting separation-of-powers challenges would enhance Presidential control over agencies—either directly by recognizing new Presidential prerogatives, or indirectly by denying power to a Congress expectably held by the opposite political party. (The one exception, again, is the nondelegation cases. As you look at these cases in the next Section, consider how a vigorous nondelegation doctrine would affect Presidential power over domestic public policy. Note also that, in the end, nondelegation is the species of structural constitutional challenge that has had the least impact on the growth and operation of the regulatory state.)

It would be misleadingly simplistic, however, to explain the pro-Presidential tilt of modern separation-of-powers litigation solely by partisan politics. Undergirding much of this litigation is a value that is difficult to articulate as a legal claim, yet powerful as a constitutional norm: democratic legitimacy. As regulatory government has become more centralized, pervasive, and powerful, concern grows about how regulatory power will be rendered accountable to We, The People. As you consider the materials in this Chapter (and in other chapters as well), note the emerging theme of the President as providing a uniquely national focal point of democratic responsiveness. Consider also the argument that—in a world in which power is infinitely greater, physical distance far less limiting, and reaction time vastly more compressed than any world the Framers could have imagined—the Chief Executive is uniquely able to marshal and direct the social, economic, and military resources of the nation. In considering this, you might recall the history of the 1930s and 1940s. In the United States, the remarkably strong presidency of Franklin Roosevelt helped Americans recover from the Depression and presided over the emergence of the modern regulatory state. Other countries also looked to a charismatic Chief Executive as uniquely capable of leading the state in the 20th century. Eventually, however, the concentration of national hopes and powers in a single leader put the world in dire jeopardy. Do history and constitutional principles give us useful guidance in how to exploit the benefits of strong executive leadership while guarding against its perils?

SECTION 1.   THE CONSTITUTIONALITY OF EMPOWERING AGENCIES TO MAKE AND ENFORCE REGULATORY POLICY

"All legislative Powers herein granted shall be vested in a Congress of the United States, which shall consist of a Senate and House of Representatives."

U.S. Constitution, Art. I, § 1

"The Congress shall have Power . . . To make all Laws which shall be necessary and proper for carrying into Execution the foregoing Powers, and all other Powers vested by this Constitution in the Government of the United States, or in any Department or Officer thereof."

U.S. Constitution, Art. I, § 8, ¶ 18

"The Legislative cannot transfer the Power of Making Laws to any other hands. For it being but a delegated Power from the People, they, who have it, cannot pass it over to others. . . . And when the people have said, We will submit to rules, and be govern'd by Laws made by such Men, and in such Forms, no Body else can say other Men shall make Laws for them; nor can the people be bound by any Laws but such as are Enacted by those, whom they have Chosen, and Authorised to make Laws for them. The power of the Legislative being derived from the People by a positive voluntary Grant and Institution, can be no other, than what the positive Grant conveyed, which being only to make Laws, and not to make Legislators, the Legislative can have no power to transfer their Authority of making laws, and place it in other hands."

John Locke, Second Treatise of Civil Government (1690)

"That congress cannot delegate legislative power to the president is a principle universally recognized as vital to the integrity and maintenance of the system of government ordained by the constitution."

Field v. Clark, 143 U.S. 649 (1892)

American Trucking Associations, Inc. v. Environmental Protection Agency

United States Court of Appeals for the District of Columbia Circuit, 1999.
175 F.3d 1027.

■ Before WILLIAMS, GINSBURG, and TATEL, CIRCUIT JUDGES. PER CURIAM:

The Clean Air Act requires EPA to promulgate and periodically revise national ambient air quality standards ("NAAQS") for each air pollutant identified by the agency as meeting certain statutory criteria. See Clean Air Act §§ 108–09.[1] For each pollutant, EPA sets a "primary standard"—a concentration level "requisite to protect the public health" with an "ade-

---

1. [Ed.] The relevant statutory provisions are:

§ 108   (42 U.S.C. § 7408)

(a) *Air pollutant list; publication and revision by Administrator; issuance of air quality criteria for air pollutants.*

(1) For the purpose of establishing national primary and secondary ambient air quality standards, the Administrator shall within 30 days after December 31, 1970, publish, and shall from time to time thereafter revise, a list which in-

cludes each air pollutant—(A) emissions of which, in his judgment, cause or contribute to air pollution which may reasonably be anticipated to endanger public health or welfare; [and] (B) the presence of which in the ambient air results from numerous or diverse mobile or stationary sources; . . .

(2) The Administrator shall issue air quality criteria for an air pollutant within 12 months after he has included such pollutant in a list under paragraph (1).

quate margin of safety"—and a "secondary standard"—a level "requisite to protect the public welfare." § 109(b).

Air quality criteria for an air pollutant shall accurately reflect the latest scientific knowledge useful in indicating the kind and extent of all identifiable effects on public health or welfare which may be expected from the presence of such pollutant in the ambient air, in varying quantities. The criteria for an air pollutant, to the extent practicable, shall include information on—(A) those variable factors (including atmospheric conditions) which of themselves or in combination with other factors may alter the effects on public health or welfare of such air pollutant; (B) the types of air pollutants which, when present in the atmosphere, may interact with such pollutant to produce an adverse effect on public health or welfare; and (C) any known or anticipated adverse effects on welfare. . . .

(c) *Review, modification, and reissuance of criteria or information.*

The Administrator shall from time to time review, and, as appropriate, modify, and reissue any criteria or information on control techniques issued pursuant to this section. . . .

§ 109   (42 U.S.C. § 7409)

(a) *Promulgation.*

. . .

(2) With respect to any air pollutant for which air quality criteria are issued after December 31, 1970, the Administrator shall publish, simultaneously with the issuance of such criteria . . . proposed national primary and secondary ambient air quality standards for any such pollutant. The procedure provided for in paragraph (1)(B) of this subsection shall apply to the promulgation of such standards.

(b) *Protection of public health and welfare.*

(1) National primary ambient air quality standards prescribed under subsection (a) of this section shall be ambient air quality standards the attainment and maintenance of which in the judgment of the Administrator, based on such criteria and allowing an adequate margin of safety, are requisite to protect the public health. Such primary standards may be revised in the same manner as promulgated.

(2) Any national secondary ambient air quality standard prescribed under subsection (a) of this section shall specify a level of air quality the attainment and maintenance of which in the judgment of the Administrator, based on such criteria, is requisite to protect the public welfare from any known or anticipated adverse effects associated with the presence of such air pollutant in the ambient air. Such secondary standards may be revised in the same manner as promulgated. . . .

(d) *Review and revision of criteria and standards; independent scientific review committee; appointment; advisory functions.*

(1) Not later than December 31, 1980, and at five-year intervals thereafter, the Administrator shall complete a thorough review of the criteria published under [§ 108] and the national ambient air quality standards promulgated under this section and shall make such revisions in such criteria and standards and promulgate such new standards as may be appropriate in accordance with [§ 108] and subsection (b) of this section. . . .

(2)(A) The Administrator shall appoint an independent scientific review committee composed of seven members including at least one member of the National Academy of Sciences, one physician, and one person representing State air pollution control agencies.

(B) Not later than January 1, 1980, and at five-year intervals thereafter, the committee referred to in subparagraph (A) shall complete a review of the criteria published under [§ 108] and the national primary and secondary ambient air quality standards promulgated under this section and shall recommend to the Administrator any new national ambient air quality standards and revisions of existing criteria and standards as may be appropriate under [§ 108] and subsection (b) of this section.

(C) Such committee shall also (i) advise the Administrator of areas in which additional knowledge is required to appraise the adequacy and basis of existing, new, or revised national ambient air quality standards, (ii) describe the research efforts necessary to provide the required information, (iii) advise the Administrator on the relative contribution to air pollution concentrations of natural as well as anthropogenic activity, and (iv) advise the Administrator of any adverse public health, welfare, social, economic, or energy effects which may result from various strategies for attainment and maintenance of such national ambient air quality standards.

In July 1997 EPA issued final rules revising the primary and secondary NAAQS for particulate matter ("PM") and ozone. Numerous petitions for review have been filed for each rule. . . .

I. Delegation

Certain "Small Business Petitioners" argue in each case that EPA has construed §§ 108 & 109 of the Clean Air Act so loosely as to render them unconstitutional delegations of legislative power. We agree. Although the factors EPA uses in determining the degree of public health concern associated with different levels of ozone and PM are reasonable, EPA appears to have articulated no "intelligible principle" to channel its application of these factors; nor is one apparent from the statute. The nondelegation doctrine requires such a principle. See J.W. Hampton, Jr. & Co. v. United States, 276 U.S. 394, 409 (1928) [p. 68 below]. Here it is as though Congress commanded EPA to select "big guys," and EPA announced that it would evaluate candidates based on height and weight, but revealed no cutoff point. The announcement, though sensible in what it does say, is fatally incomplete. The reasonable person responds, "How tall? How heavy?"

EPA regards ozone definitely, and PM likely, as non-threshold pollutants, i.e., ones that have some possibility of some adverse health impact (however slight) at any exposure level above zero. . . . For convenience, we refer to both as non-threshold pollutants; the indeterminacy of PM's status does not affect EPA's analysis, or ours.

Thus the only concentration for ozone and PM that is utterly risk-free, in the sense of direct health impacts, is zero. Section 109(b)(1) says that EPA must set each standard at the level "requisite to protect the public health" with an "adequate margin of safety." These are also the criteria by which EPA must determine whether a revision to existing NAAQS is appropriate. For EPA to pick any non-zero level it must explain the degree of imperfection permitted. The factors that EPA has elected to examine for this purpose in themselves pose no inherent nondelegation problem. But what EPA lacks is any determinate criterion for drawing lines. It has failed to state intelligibly how much is too much.

We begin with the criteria EPA has announced for assessing health effects in setting the NAAQS for non-threshold pollutants. They are "the nature and severity of the health effects involved, the size of the sensitive population(s) at risk, the types of health information available, and the kind and degree of uncertainties that must be addressed." Although these criteria, so stated, are a bit vague, they do focus the inquiry on pollution's effects on public health. And most of the vagueness in the abstract formulation melts away as EPA applies the criteria: EPA basically considers severity of effect, certainty of effect, and size of population affected. These criteria . . . do not themselves speak to the issue of degree.

Read in light of these factors, EPA's explanations for its decisions amount to assertions that a less stringent standard would allow the relevant pollutant to inflict a greater quantum of harm on public health, and that a more stringent standard would result in less harm. Such arguments only support the intuitive proposition that more pollution will not benefit public health, not that keeping pollution at or below any particular level is "requisite" or not requisite to "protect the public health" with an "adequate margin of safety," the formula set out by § 109(b)(1).

Consider EPA's defense of the 0.08 ppm level of the ozone NAAQS. EPA explains that its choice is superior to retaining the existing level, 0.09 ppm, because more people are exposed to more serious effects at 0.09 than at 0.08. In defending the decision not to go down to 0.07, EPA never contradicts the intuitive proposition, confirmed by data in its Staff Paper, that reducing the standard to that level would bring about comparable changes. Instead, it gives three other reasons. The principal substantive one is based on the criteria just discussed:

> The most certain O_3-related effects, while judged to be adverse, are transient and reversible (particularly at O_3 exposures below 0.08 ppm), and the more serious effects with greater immediate and potential long-term impacts on health are less certain, both as to the percentage of individuals exposed to various concentrations who are likely to experience such effects and as to the long-term medical significance of these effects.

In other words, effects are less certain and less severe at lower levels of exposure. This seems to be nothing more than a statement that lower exposure levels are associated with lower risk to public health. . . .

In addition to the assertion quoted above, EPA cited the consensus of the Clean Air Scientific Advisory Committee ("CASAC") that the standard should not be set below 0.08. That body gave no specific reasons for its recommendations, so the appeal to its authority adds no enlightenment. The dissent stresses the undisputed eminence of CASAC's members, but the question whether EPA acted pursuant to lawfully delegated authority is not a scientific one. Nothing in what CASAC says helps us discern an intelligible principle derived by EPA from the Clean Air Act.

Finally, EPA argued that a 0.07 standard would be "closer to peak background levels that infrequently occur in some areas due to nonanthropogenic sources of O_3 precursors, and thus more likely to be inappropriately targeted in some areas on such sources." Ozone Final Rule. But a 0.08 level, of course, is also closer to these peak levels than 0.09. . . . EPA's language, coupled with the data on background ozone levels, may add up to a backhanded way of saying that, given the national character of the NAAQS, it is inappropriate to set a standard below a level that can be achieved throughout the country without action affirmatively extracting chemicals from nature. That may well be a sound reading of the statute, but EPA has not explicitly adopted it.

EPA frequently defends a decision not to set a standard at a lower level on the basis that there is greater uncertainty that health effects exist at lower levels than the level of the standard. And such an argument is likely implicit in its defense of the coarse PM standards. But the increasing-uncertainty argument is helpful only if some principle reveals how much uncertainty is too much. None does. . . .

EPA cites prior decisions of this Court holding that when there is uncertainty about the health effects of concentrations of a particular pollutant within a particular range, EPA may use its discretion to make the "policy judgment" to set the standards at one point within the relevant range rather than another. We agree. But none of those panels addressed the claim of undue delegation that we face here, and accordingly had no occasion to ask EPA for coherence (for a "principle," to use the classic term) in making its "policy judgment." The latter phrase is not, after all, a self-sufficient justification for every refusal to define limits. . . .

Where (as here) statutory language and an existing agency interpretation involve an unconstitutional delegation of power, but an interpretation without the constitutional weakness is or may be available, our response is not to strike down the statute but to give the agency an opportunity to extract a determinate standard on its own. Doing so serves at least two of three basic rationales for the nondelegation doctrine. If the agency develops determinate, binding standards for itself, it is less likely to exercise the delegated authority arbitrarily. See Amalgamated Meat Cutters v. Connally, 337 F.Supp. 737, 758–59 (D.D.C.1971) (Leventhal, J., for three-judge panel) [p. 73 below]. And such standards enhance the likelihood that meaningful judicial review will prove feasible. See id. at 759. A remand of this sort of course does not serve the third key function of non-delegation doctrine, to "ensure[ ] to the extent consistent with orderly governmental administration that important choices of social policy are made by Congress, the branch of our Government most responsive to the popular will," Industrial Union Dep't, AFL–CIO v. American Petroleum Inst., 448 U.S. 607, 685 (1980) ("Benzene") (Rehnquist, J., concurring) [p. 58 below]. The agency will make the fundamental policy choices. But the remand does ensure that the courts not hold unconstitutional a statute that an agency, with the application of its special expertise, could salvage. In any event, we do not read current Supreme Court cases as applying the strong form of the nondelegation doctrine voiced in Justice Rehnquist's concurrence. See Mistretta v. United States, 488 U.S. 361 (1989) [p. 74 below].

What sorts of "intelligible principles" might EPA adopt? . . . In theory, EPA could make its criterion the eradication of any hint of direct health risk. This approach is certainly determinate enough, but it appears that it would require the agency to set the permissible levels of both pollutants here at zero. No party here appears to advocate this solution, and EPA appears to show no inclination to adopt it.[2] EPA's past behavior suggests some readiness to adopt standards that leave non-zero residual risk. For example, it has employed commonly used clinical criteria to determine what qualifies as an adverse health effect. See Ozone Staff Paper at 59–60 (using

---

2. A zero-risk policy might seem to imply de-industrialization, but in fact even that seems inadequate to the task (and even if the calculus is confined to direct risks from pollutants, as opposed to risks from the concomitant poverty). First, PM (at least) results from almost all combustion, so only total prohibition of fire or universal application of some heretofore unknown control technology would reduce manmade emissions to zero. Second, the combustion associated with pas- toral life appears to be rather deadly. See World Bank, World Development Report 1992: Development and the Environment 52 (1992) (noting that "biomass" fuels (i.e., wood, straw, or dung) are often the only fuels that "poor households, mostly in rural areas" can obtain or afford, and that indoor smoke from biomass burning "contributes to acute respiratory infections that cause an estimated 4 million deaths annually among infants and children."

American Thoracic Society standards to determine threshold for "adverse health effect" from ozone). On the issue of likelihood, for some purposes it might be appropriate to use standards drawn from other areas of the law, such as the familiar "more probable than not" criterion.

Of course a one-size-fits-all criterion of probability would make little sense. There is no reason why the same probability should govern assessments of a risk of thousands of deaths as against risks of a handful of people suffering momentary shortness of breath. More generally, all the relevant variables seem to range continuously from high to low: the possible effects of pollutants vary from death to trivialities, and the size of the affected population, the probability of an effect, and the associated uncertainty range from "large" numbers of persons with point estimates of high probability, to small numbers and vague ranges of probability. This does not seem insurmountable. Everyday life compels us all to make decisions balancing remote but severe harms against a probability distribution of benefits; people decide whether to proceed with an operation that carries a 1/1000 possibility of death, and (simplifying) a 90% chance of cure and a 10% chance of no effect, and a certainty of some short-term pain and nuisance. To be sure, all that requires is a go/no-go decision, while a serious effort at coherence under § 109(b)(1) would need to be more comprehensive. For example, a range of ailments short of death might need to be assigned weights. Nonetheless, an agency wielding the power over American life possessed by EPA should be capable of developing the rough equivalent of a generic unit of harm that takes into account population affected, severity and probability. . . .

Alternatively, if EPA concludes that there is no principle available, it can so report to the Congress, along with such rationales as it has for the levels it chose, and seek legislation ratifying its choice. . . .

[Part II, which construes the statute as prohibiting consideration of costs, is omitted.]

We remand the cases to EPA for further consideration of all standards at issue. . . .

■ TATEL, CIRCUIT JUDGE, dissenting from Part I:

The Clean Air Act has been on the books for decades, has been amended by Congress numerous times, and has been the subject of regular congressional oversight hearings. The Act has been parsed by this circuit no fewer than ten times in published opinions delineating EPA authority in the NAAQS setting process. Yet this court now threatens to strike down section 109 of the Act as an unconstitutional delegation of congressional authority unless EPA can articulate an intelligible principle cabining its discretion. In doing so, the court ignores the last half-century of Supreme Court nondelegation jurisprudence, apparently viewing these permissive precedents as mere exceptions to the rule laid down sixty-four years ago in A.L.A. Schechter Poultry Corp. v. United States, 295 U.S. 495 (1935) [p. 69 below]. . . .

Section 109 requires EPA to publish air quality standards "the attainment and maintenance of which in the judgment of the Administrator, based on such criteria and allowing an adequate margin of safety, are requisite to protect the public health." Compare section 109 to the language of section 303 of the Communications Act of 1934, which gave the FCC authority to regulate broadcast licensing in the "public interest," and which the Supreme Court sustained in National Broadcasting Co. v. United States, 319 U.S. 190 (1943). The FCC's general authority to issue regulations "as public convenience, interest, or necessity requires" was sustained in United States v. Southwestern Cable Co., 392 U.S. 157 (1968). The Supreme Court has sustained equally broad delegations to other agencies, including the Price Administrator's authority to fix "fair and equitable" commodities prices, Yakus v. United States, 321 U.S. 414 (1944) [p. 71 below], the Federal Power Commission's authority to determine "just and reasonable" rates, FPC v. Hope Natural Gas Co., 320 U.S. 591 (1944), the War Department's authority to recover "excessive profits" earned on military contracts, Lichter v. United States, 334 U.S. 742 (1948), and the Attorney General's authority to regulate new drugs that pose an "imminent hazard to public safety," Touby v. United States, 500 U.S. 160 (1991) [p. 76 below]. . . .

[I]n setting standards "requisite to protect the public health," EPA discretion is not unlimited. The Clean Air Act directs EPA to base standards on "air quality criteria" that "accurately reflect the latest scientific knowledge useful in indicating the kind and extent of all identifiable effects on public health or welfare which may be expected from the presence of such pollutant in the ambient air, in varying quantities." § 109(b)(1); see also id. § 108(a)(2) [quoting this section]. . . . By directing EPA to set NAAQS at levels "requisite"—not reasonably requisite—to protect the public health with "an adequate margin of safety," the Clean Air Act tells EPA [to] ensure a high degree of protection.

. . . To identify which health effects were "significant enough" to warrant protection, EPA followed guidelines published by the American Thoracic Society. It then set the ozone and fine particle standards within ranges recommended by CASAC, the independent scientific advisory committee created pursuant to section 109 of the Act.

CASAC must consist of at least one member of the National Academy of Sciences, one physician, and one person representing state air pollution control agencies. In this case, CASAC also included medical doctors, epidemiologists, toxicologists and environmental scientists from leading research universities and institutions throughout the country. EPA must explain any departures from CASAC's recommendations. See 42 U.S.C. § 7607(d)(3). Bringing scientific methods to their evaluation of the Agency's Criteria Document and Staff Paper, CASAC provides an objective justification for the pollution standards the Agency selects. . . .

Beginning with CASAC's ozone recommendations—not one member recommended going below .08 ppm—EPA gave two perfectly rational explanations for the level it selected. First, it set the annual level based on the different types of health effects observed above and below .08 ppm. Particularly below .08, the Agency determined, "[t]he most certain [ozone-]related effects, while judged to be adverse, are *transient and reversible*." National Ambient Air Quality Standards for Ozone, 62 Fed. Reg. 38,856 (1997) (emphasis added). Characterizing this explanation as saying nothing more than that "lower exposure levels are associated with lower risk to public health," my colleagues find the Agency's reasoning unintelligible. But EPA did not find simply that public health risks decrease at lower levels. Instead, it found that public health effects *differ* below .08 ppm, i.e., that they are "transient and reversible."

Second, EPA explained that the level should not be set below naturally occurring background ozone concentrations. The Agency selected .08 ppm because it found that "a 0.07 ppm level would be closer to peak background levels that infrequently occur in some areas due to nonanthropogenic sources of [ozone] precursors, and thus more likely to be inappropriately targeted in some areas on such sources." 62 Fed.Reg. at 38,868/3. Of course, any level of ozone pollution above background concentrations is closer to background levels than one just above it. But as I read EPA's explanation, the Agency found that peak background levels sometimes occur at .07 ppm, not at .08 ppm. Indeed, the data EPA provided in its "Responses to Significant Comments" show a range of background concentrations from a low of .042 ppm in Olympic National Park in Washington to a high of .075 ppm in Quachita National Forest in Arizona. No region registered background levels above .075 ppm. In other words, by setting the annual standard at .08 rather than .07 ppm, EPA ensured that if a region surpasses the ozone standard, it will do so because of controllable human activity, not because of uncontrollable natural levels of ozone.

EPA offered an equally reasonable explanation for the fine particle pollution standard. Again limiting itself to the range approved by CASAC, EPA set the annual standard for PM sub2.5 pollution at the lowest level where it had confidence that the epidemiological evidence (filtered through peer-reviewed, published studies) displayed a statistically significant relationship between air pollution and adverse public health effects....

... Whether EPA arbitrarily selected the studies it relied upon or drew mistaken conclusions from those studies (as petitioners argue), or whether EPA failed to live up to the principles it established for itself (as my colleagues believe), has nothing to do with our inquiry under the nondelegation doctrine. Those issues relate to whether the NAAQS are arbitrary and capricious. The Constitution requires that Congress articulate intelligible principles; Congress has done so here.

A final point.... EPA regulates primarily by setting standards for states to develop their own plans. Indeed, because states have three years to submit implementation plans, which are themselves subject to notice, comment, public hearing, and frequent renegotiation, we will not know for years precisely how the ozone and particle NAAQS will actually affect individual businesses. Only if a state fails to produce an acceptable plan can EPA terminate federal highway funds or impose its own implementation plan. Because the Clean Air Act gives politically accountable state governments primary responsibility for determining how to distribute the burdens of pollution reduction and therefore how the NAAQS will affect specific industries and individual businesses, courts have less reason to second-guess the specificity of the congressional delegation. Moreover, if the states disagree with the standards EPA has set, they have 535 representatives in Congress to turn to for help....

American Trucking Associations, Inc. v. Environmental Protection Agency

United States Court of Appeals for the District of Columbia Circuit, 1999.
195 F.3d 4.

■ Opinion PER CURIAM on petitions for rehearing.

. . . In the EPA's petition for rehearing, counsel for the agency argue that § 109 of the Clean Air Act contains the following principle limiting the agency's discretion: "The levels [set in a NAAQS] must be necessary for public health protection: neither *more* nor *less* stringent than necessary, but 'requisite.' " Further, counsel claim that in setting the NAAQS at issue in this case the agency applied corollaries of this principle, one for particulate matter, one for ozone,[1] to derive determinate standards.

. . . [I]n the rulemakings that set the NAAQS, the EPA mentioned the corollary propositions its counsel now claim served as intelligible limiting principles, but the agency did not identify either as a limit upon its discretion; the EPA never suggested that it could not (or in a later rulemaking would not) base a NAAQS upon evidence that did not meet the 95 percent confidence level or that revealed adverse but transient effects. . . .

As we noted in our first opinion in this case, when "statutory language and an existing agency interpretation involve an unconstitutional delegation of power, but an interpretation without the constitutional weakness is or may be available, our response is not to strike down the statute but to give the agency an opportunity to extract a determinate standard on its own." Counsel for the EPA have now extracted from the statute what they contend is an intelligible principle limiting the EPA's discretion. We express no opinion upon the sufficiency of that principle; only after the EPA itself has applied it in setting a NAAQS can we say whether the principle, in practice, fulfills the purposes of the nondelegation doctrine. See Yakus v. United States; Amalgamated Meat Cutters v. Connally.

A final word about our nondelegation holding: The Supreme Court has long held that an ambiguous principle in a statute delegating power to an agency can gain "meaningful content from the purpose of the Act, its factual background and the statutory context in which [it] appear[s]." American Power & Light Co. v. SEC, 329 U.S. 90, 104 (1946); see also . . . Fahey v. Mallonee, 332 U.S. 245, 250 (1947) [p. 71 below]. . . . To choose among permissible interpretations of an ambiguous principle, of course, is to make a policy decision, and since Chevron it has been clear that "[t]he responsibilities for assessing the wisdom of such policy choices . . . are not judicial ones." Chevron U.S.A. Inc. v. NRDC, 467 U.S. 837, 866 (1984) [p. 61 below]. Accordingly, just as we must defer to an agency's reasonable interpretation of an ambiguous statutory term, we must defer to an agency's reasonable interpretation of a statute containing only an ambigu-

---

1. For particulate matter, counsel now state that the EPA's decision was determined by the norm of "the 95 percent confidence level to separate results that could be the product of chance from more convincing evi-dence of causation." For ozone, counsel now state that EPA inferred the existence of effects below 0.08 ppm, but nonetheless concluded that they were "less serious because they are 'transient and reversible.' "

ous principle by which to guide its exercise of delegated authority. . . . In sum, the approach of the Benzene case, in which the Supreme Court itself identified an intelligible principle in an ambiguous statute, has given way to the approach of Chevron. See Industrial Union Dep't v. American Petroleum Inst. (Benzene), 448 U.S. 607, 642, 646 (1980) (Stevens, J., plurality) (interpreting § 3(8) of the Occupational Health and Safety Act to require "a threshold finding . . . that significant risks are present," thereby finding in the statute an intelligible principle).[2]

■ [JUDGE TATEL dissented.]

ON RESPONDENT EPA'S SUGGESTION FOR REHEARING EN BANC
ORDER

PER CURIAM

Respondent EPA's Suggestion for Rehearing En Banc and the responses thereto have been circulated to the full court. The taking of a vote was requested. Thereafter, a majority of the judges of the court in regular active service did not vote in favor of the suggestion. Upon consideration of the foregoing, it is

ORDERED that the suggestion be denied.

■ SILBERMAN, CIRCUIT JUDGE, dissenting from the denial of rehearing en banc:

The panel's reliance on the nondelegation doctrine to reject EPA's interpretation of section 109 of the Clean Air Act is rather ingenious, but I regret that it seems to me to be fundamentally unsound. I do not think that doctrine can be employed to force an agency to narrow a broad legislative delegation from Congress. The doctrine, as Judge Tatel in dissent pointed out, is at this stage of constitutional "evolution" not in particularly robust health. Justice Rehnquist heroically attempted to inject vitality into the doctrine in his powerful concurrence in the Benzene case. But, sad to say, his view is not shared by a majority of the Court which has acknowledged only a theoretical limitation on the scope of congressional delegations to the executive branch. See Mistretta v. United States, 488 U.S. 361, 416 (1989) (Scalia, J., dissenting) ("What legislated standard, one must wonder, can possibly be too vague to survive judicial scrutiny, when we have repeatedly upheld, in various contexts, a 'public interest' standard?").

. . . I agree with Judge Tatel that the terminology of this section of the Clean Air Act does not come so close to those boundaries to raise a serious constitutional problem. If it did, and we were faced with two conflicting interpretations of the statute—both plausible—I have no doubt that a constitutionally dubious agency interpretation could be rejected even in a post-Chevron era.

. . . [T]he constitutional avoidance canon trumps Chevron deference. But that principle is not relevant to this case. Even assuming the statute

---

2. We note that Judge Silberman's dissent from the denial of rehearing en banc turns largely on his dim view of the Court's use of the non-delegation doctrine in Benzene, which he characterizes as "only a makeweight, tossed into the analysis . . . to help justify the result." Whatever the merits of Judge Silberman's critique of Benzene, we do not see how a lower court can properly rest its jurisprudence on the rejection of a Supreme Court decision.

was problematic, the panel was not faced with two competing constructions, one of which might be thought to avoid constitutional difficulty. Indeed, the panel concluded that there are no intelligible principles "apparent from the statute" that brought EPA's discretion within constitutionally acceptable limits. If the panel believed that was so, it should have held the statute unconstitutional. Instead the panel, purporting to rely on Chevron, remanded to EPA directing that agency to come up with an artificially narrow interpretation with various suggestions offered by the panel to accomplish that end.[1] By so doing, I believe the panel undermines the purpose of the nondelegation doctrine. That purpose is, of course, to ensure that Congress makes the crucial policy choices that are carried into law. The ability to make those policy choices (even if only at a broad level of generality) is what is meant by legislative power. See U.S. Const. art. I, § 1.

... That is not to say that EPA is totally free to exercise its authority at any point on the discretionary continuum that Congress delegated to it in the Clean Air Act. The Administrative Procedure Act's arbitrary and capricious standard also limits the agency's actions. [T]he broader the substantive statutory delegation the more likely that the agency's policy choices will be confined by the APA, rather than the substantive statute. In that regard, I am quite uncertain whether EPA's regulatory choice meets that test. Judge Tatel's emphasis on the agency's extensive procedures does not appear to me to answer the question. It would not matter whether the agency "actually adhered to a disciplined decisionmaking process," if its final product was unreasonable. If we were to rehear the case, I would focus on that issue. Doctrine aside, then, what is the practical difference between my approach and the panel's? The answer, I think, is that the panel engages—and by retaining jurisdiction promises to continue to engage—in a more searching review than the arbitrary and capricious standard would permit. By treating this case as a statutory interpretation question laden with constitutional implications the panel implicitly asserts a greater role for a reviewing court than is justified.

I respectfully dissent from our denial of rehearing en banc.

■ TATEL, CIRCUIT JUDGE, with whom HARRY T. EDWARDS, CHIEF JUDGE, and GARLAND, CIRCUIT JUDGE, join, dissenting from the denial of rehearing en banc:

... Not only did the panel depart from a half century of Supreme Court separation-of-powers jurisprudence, but in doing so, it stripped the Environmental Protection Agency of much of its ability to implement the Clean Air Act, this nation's primary means of protecting the safety of the air breathed by hundreds of millions of people.

Whitman v. American Trucking Associations, Inc.

Supreme Court of the United States, 2001.
531 U.S. 457.

■ JUSTICE SCALIA delivered the opinion of the Court.

These cases present the following questions: (1) Whether § 109(b)(1) of the Clean Air Act (CAA) delegates legislative power to the Administrator of

---

1. Like the plurality opinion in Benzene, these suggestions seem more directed to encouraging wiser policy choices than interpreting the statute at issue.

the Environmental Protection Agency (EPA). (2) Whether the Administrator may consider the costs of implementation in setting national ambient air quality standards (NAAQS) under § 109(b)(1). . . .

I

Section 109(a) of the CAA requires the Administrator of the EPA to promulgate NAAQS for each air pollutant for which "air quality criteria" have been issued under § 108. Once a NAAQS has been promulgated, the Administrator must review the standard (and the criteria on which it is based) "at five-year intervals" and make "such revisions . . . as may be appropriate." CAA § 109(d)(1). These cases arose when, on July 18, 1997, the Administrator revised the NAAQS for particulate matter and ozone. American Trucking Associations, Inc., and its co-respondents—which include, in addition to other private companies, the States of Michigan, Ohio, and West Virginia—challenged the new standards. . . .

II

[Respondents argue that the court of appeals erred in holding that] "economic considerations [may] play no part in the promulgation of ambient air quality standards under Section 109" of the CAA. . . . [S]ince the first step in assessing whether a statute delegates legislative power is to determine what authority the statute confers, we address that issue of interpretation first.

Section 109(b)(1) instructs the EPA to set primary ambient air quality standards "the attainment and maintenance of which . . . are requisite to protect the public health" with "an adequate margin of safety." Were it not for the hundreds of pages of briefing respondents have submitted on the issue, one would have thought it fairly clear that this text does not permit the EPA to consider costs in setting the standards. . . . The EPA, "based on" the information about health effects contained in the technical "criteria" documents compiled under § 108(a)(2) is to identify the maximum airborne concentration of a pollutant that the public health can tolerate, decrease the concentration to provide an "adequate" margin of safety, and set the standard at that level. Nowhere are the costs of achieving such a standard made part of that initial calculation.

Against this most natural of readings, respondents make a lengthy, spirited, but ultimately unsuccessful attack. They begin with the object of § 109(b)(1)'s focus, the "public health." When the term first appeared in federal clean air legislation—in the Act of July 14, 1955 which expressed "recognition of the dangers to the public health" from air pollution—its ordinary meaning was "[t]he health of the community." Webster's New International Dictionary 2005 (2d ed. 1950). Respondents argue, however, that § 109(b)(1), as added by the Clean Air Amendments of 1970, meant to use the term's secondary meaning: "[t]he ways and means of conserving the health of the members of a community, as by preventive medicine, organized care of the sick, etc." Ibid. Words that can have more than one meaning are given content, however, by their surroundings, and in the context of § 109(b)(1) this second definition makes no sense. Congress could not have meant to instruct the Administrator to set NAAQS at a level "requisite to protect" "the art and science dealing with the protection and improvement of community health." We therefore revert to the primary definition of the term: the health of the public.

Even so, respondents argue, many more factors than air pollution affect public health. In particular, the economic cost of implementing a very stringent standard might produce health losses sufficient to offset the health gains achieved in cleaning the air—for example, by closing down whole industries and thereby impoverishing the workers and consumers dependent upon those industries. That is unquestionably true, and Congress was unquestionably aware of it. Thus, Congress had commissioned in the Air Quality Act of 1967 "a detailed estimate of the cost of carrying out the provisions of this Act; a comprehensive study of the cost of program implementation by affected units of government; and a comprehensive study of the economic impact of air quality standards on the Nation's industries, communities, and other contributing sources of pollution." The 1970 Congress, armed with the results of this study, not only anticipated that compliance costs could injure the public health, but provided for that precise exigency. Section 110(f)(1) of the CAA permitted the Administrator to waive the compliance deadline for stationary sources if, inter alia, sufficient control measures were simply unavailable and "the continued operation of such sources is *essential . . . to the public health* or welfare." 84 Stat. 1683 (emphasis added). Other provisions explicitly permitted or required economic costs to be taken into account in implementing the air quality standards. [Justice Scalia cited half a dozen sections from other parts of the CAA that expressly direct the Administrator to consider cost in setting a standard.] Subsequent amendments to the CAA have added many more provisions directing, in explicit language, that the Administrator consider costs in performing various duties. We have therefore refused to find implicit in ambiguous sections of the CAA an authorization to consider costs that has elsewhere, and so often, been expressly granted.

Accordingly, to prevail in their present challenge, respondents must show a textual commitment of authority to the EPA to consider costs in setting NAAQS under § 109(b)(1). And because § 109(b)(1) and the NAAQS for which it provides are the engine that drives nearly all of Title I of the CAA, that textual commitment must be a clear one. Congress, we have held, does not alter the fundamental details of a regulatory scheme in vague terms or ancillary provisions—it does not, one might say, hide elephants in mouseholes. See MCI Telecommunications Corp. v. American Telephone & Telegraph Co., 512 U.S. 218, 231 (1994); FDA v. Brown & Williamson Tobacco Corp., [529 U.S. 120 (2000)]. Respondents' textual arguments ultimately founder upon this principle. . . .

It should be clear from what we have said that the canon requiring texts to be so construed as to avoid serious constitutional problems has no application here. No matter how severe the constitutional doubt, courts may choose only between reasonably available interpretations of a text. The text of § 109(b), interpreted in its statutory and historical context and with appreciation for its importance to the CAA as a whole, unambiguously bars cost considerations from the NAAQS-setting process, and thus ends the matter for us as well as the EPA.[2] We therefore affirm the judgment of the Court of Appeals on this point.

III

Section 109(b)(1) of the CAA instructs the EPA to set "ambient air quality standards the attainment and maintenance of which in the judgment of the Administrator, based on [the] criteria [documents of § 108] and allowing an adequate margin of safety, are requisite to protect the public health." The Court of Appeals held that this section as interpreted by the Administrator did not provide an "intelligible principle" to guide the EPA's exercise of authority in setting NAAQS. "[The] EPA," it said, "lack[ed] any determinate criteria for drawing lines. It has failed to state intelligibly how much is too much." The court hence found that the EPA's interpretation (but not the statute itself) violated the nondelegation doctrine. We disagree.

In a delegation challenge, the constitutional question is whether the statute has delegated legislative power to the agency. Article I, § 1, of the Constitution vests "[a]ll legislative Powers herein granted ... in a Congress of the United States." This text permits no delegation of those powers, and so we repeatedly have said that when Congress confers decisionmaking authority upon agencies Congress must "lay down by legislative act an intelligible principle to which the person or body authorized to [act] is directed to conform." J.W. Hampton, Jr., & Co. v. United States. We have never suggested that an agency can cure an unlawful delegation of legislative power by adopting in its discretion a limiting construction of the statute. Both Fahey v. Mallonee and Lichter v. United States, 334 U.S. 742, 783 (1948), mention agency regulations in the course of their nondelegation discussions, but Lichter did so because a subsequent Congress had incorporated the regulations into a revised version of the statute, and Fahey because the customary practices in the area, implicitly incorporated into the statute, were reflected in the regulations. The idea that an agency can cure an unconstitutionally standardless delegation of power by declining to exercise some of that power seems to us internally contradictory. The very choice of which portion of the power to exercise— that is to say, the prescription of the standard that Congress had omitted— would *itself* be an exercise of the forbidden legislative authority. Whether the statute delegates legislative power is a question for the courts, and an agency's voluntary self-denial has no bearing upon the answer.

We agree with the Solicitor General that the text of § 109(b)(1) of the CAA at a minimum requires that "[f]or a discrete set of pollutants and based on published air quality criteria that reflect the latest scientific knowledge, [the] EPA must establish uniform national standards at a level that is requisite to protect public health from the adverse effects of the

---

2. Respondents' speculation that the EPA is secretly considering the costs of attainment without telling anyone is irrelevant to our interpretive inquiry. If such an allegation could be proved, it would be grounds for vacating the NAAQS, because the Administrator had not followed the law. See, e.g., Chevron U.S.A. Inc. v. Natural Resources Defense Council, Inc. It would not, however, be grounds for this Court's changing the law.

pollutant in the ambient air." Tr. of Oral Arg., p. 5. Requisite, in turn, "mean[s] sufficient, but not more than necessary." Id., at 7. These limits on the EPA's discretion are strikingly similar to the ones we approved in Touby v. United States, which permitted the Attorney General to designate a drug as a controlled substance for purposes of criminal drug enforcement if doing so was "necessary to avoid an imminent hazard to the public safety." They also resemble the Occupational Safety and Health Act provision requiring the agency to "set the standard which most adequately assures, to the extent feasible, on the basis of the best available evidence, that no employee will suffer any impairment of health"—which the Court upheld in [the Benzene Case], and which even then-Justice Rehnquist, who alone in that case thought the statute violated the nondelegation doctrine, see id., at 671 (opinion concurring in judgment), would have upheld if, like the statute here, it did not permit economic costs to be considered.

The scope of discretion § 109(b)(1) allows is in fact well within the outer limits of our nondelegation precedents. In the history of the Court we have found the requisite "intelligible principle" lacking in only two statutes, one of which provided literally no guidance for the exercise of discretion, and the other of which conferred authority to regulate the entire economy on the basis of no more precise a standard than stimulating the economy by assuring "fair competition." See Panama Refining Co. v. Ryan, 293 U.S. 388 (1935) [p. 69 below]; A.L.A. Schechter Poultry Corp. v. United States. We have, on the other hand, upheld the validity of § 11(b)(2) of the Public Utility Holding Company Act of 1935, which gave the Securities and Exchange Commission authority to modify the structure of holding company systems so as to ensure that they are not "unduly or unnecessarily complicate[d]" and do not "unfairly or inequitably distribute voting power among security holders." American Power & Light Co. v. SEC, 329 U.S. 90, 104 (1946). We have approved the wartime conferral of agency power to fix the prices of commodities at a level that "will be generally fair and equitable and will effectuate the [in some respects conflicting] purposes of th[e] Act." Yakus v. United States. And we have found an "intelligible principle" in various statutes authorizing regulation in the "public interest." See, e.g., National Broadcasting Co. v. United States, 319 U.S. 190 (1943) (Federal Communications Commission's power to regulate airwaves); New York Central Securities Corp. v. United States, 287 U.S. 12 (1932) (Interstate Commerce Commission's power to approve railroad consolidations). In short, we have "almost never felt qualified to second-guess Congress regarding the permissible degree of policy judgment that can be left to those executing or applying the law." Mistretta v. United States, 488 U.S. 361, 416 (1989) (Scalia, J., dissenting).

It is true enough that the degree of agency discretion that is acceptable varies according to the scope of the power congressionally conferred. While Congress need not provide any direction to the EPA regarding the manner in which it is to define "country elevators," which are to be exempt from new-stationary-source regulations governing grain elevators, see 42 U.S.C. § 7411(i), it must provide substantial guidance on setting air standards that affect the entire national economy. But even in sweeping regulatory schemes we have never demanded, as the Court of Appeals did here, that statutes provide a "determinate criterion" for saying "how much [of the regulated harm] is too much." In Touby, for example, we did not require the statute to decree how "imminent" was too imminent, or how "necessary" was necessary enough, or even—most relevant here—how "hazardous" was too hazardous. Similarly, the statute at issue in Lichter authorized agencies to recoup "excess profits" paid under wartime Government contracts, yet we did not insist that Congress specify how much profit was too much. It is therefore not conclusive for delegation purposes that, as respondents argue, ozone and particulate matter are "nonthreshold" pollutants that inflict a continuum of adverse health effects at any airborne concentration greater than zero, and hence require the EPA to make judgments of degree. "[A] certain degree of discretion, and thus of lawmaking, inheres in most executive or judicial action." Mistretta v. United States, 488 U.S. at 417 (Scalia, J., dissenting) (emphasis deleted). Section 109(b)(1) of the CAA, which to repeat we interpret as requiring the EPA to set air quality standards at the level that is "requisite"—that is, not lower or higher than is necessary—to protect the public health with an adequate margin of safety, fits comfortably within the scope of discretion permitted by our precedent.

We therefore reverse the judgment of the Court of Appeals remanding for reinterpretation that would avoid a supposed delegation of legislative power. It will remain for the Court of Appeals—on the remand that we direct for other reasons—to dispose of any other preserved challenge to the NAAQS under the judicial-review provisions contained in 42 U.S.C. § 7607(d)(9). . . .

The judgment of the Court of Appeals is affirmed in part and reversed in part, and the cases are remanded for proceedings consistent with this opinion.

It is so ordered.

■ JUSTICE THOMAS, concurring.

I agree with the majority that § 109's directive to the agency is no less an "intelligible principle" than a host of other directives that we have approved. I also agree that the Court of Appeals' remand to the agency to make its own corrective interpretation does not accord with our understanding of the delegation issue. I write separately, however, to express my concern that there may nevertheless be a genuine constitutional problem with § 109, a problem which the parties did not address.

The parties to these cases who briefed the constitutional issue wrangled over constitutional doctrine with barely a nod to the text of the Constitution. Although this Court since 1928 has treated the "intelligible principle" requirement as the only constitutional limit on congressional grants of power to administrative agencies, the Constitution does not speak of "intelligible principles." Rather, it speaks in much simpler terms: "*All* legislative Powers herein granted shall be vested in a Congress." U.S. Const., Art. 1, § 1 (emphasis added). I am not convinced that the intelligible principle doctrine serves to prevent all cessions of legislative power. I believe that there are cases in which the principle is intelligible and yet the significance of the delegated decision is simply too great for the decision to be called anything other than "legislative."

As it is, none of the parties to these case has examined the text of the Constitution or asked us to reconsider our precedents on cessions of legislative power. On a future day, however, I would be willing to address the question whether our delegation jurisprudence has strayed too far from our Founders' understanding of separation of powers.

■ JUSTICE STEVENS, with whom JUSTICE SOUTER joins, concurring in part and concurring in the judgment.

. . . I wholeheartedly endorse the Court's result and endorse its explanation of its reasons, albeit with the following caveat.

The Court has two choices. We could choose to articulate our ultimate disposition of this issue by frankly acknowledging that the power delegated to the EPA is "legislative" but nevertheless conclude that the delegation is constitutional because adequately limited by the terms of the authorizing statute. Alternatively, we could pretend, as the Court does, that the authority delegated to the EPA is somehow not "legislative power." Despite the fact that there is language in our opinions that supports the Court's articulation of our holding, I am persuaded that it would be both wiser and more faithful to what we have actually done in delegation cases to admit that agency rulemaking authority is "legislative power."

The proper characterization of governmental power should generally depend on the nature of the power, not on the identity of the person exercising it. See Black's Law Dictionary 899 (6th ed. 1990) (defining "legislation" as, *inter alia,* "[f]ormulation of rule[s] for the future"). If the NAAQS that the EPA promulgated had been prescribed by Congress, everyone would agree that those rules would be the product of an exercise of "legislative power." The same characterization is appropriate when an agency exercises rulemaking authority pursuant to a permissible delegation from Congress.

My view is not only more faithful to normal English usage, but is also fully consistent with the text of the Constitution. In Article I, the Framers vested "All legislative Powers" in the Congress, Art. I, § 1, just as in Article II they vested the "executive Power" in the President, Art. II, § 1. Those provisions do not purport to limit the authority of either recipient of power to delegate authority to others. See 1 Davis & Pierce, Administrative Law Treatise § 2.6, 66 ("The Court was probably mistaken from the outset in interpreting Article I's grant of power to Congress as an implicit limit on Congress' authority to delegate legislative power"). Surely the authority granted to members of the Cabinet and federal law enforcement agents is properly characterized as "Executive" even though not exercised by the President.

It seems clear that an executive agency's exercise of rulemaking authority pursuant to a valid delegation from Congress is "legislative." As long as the delegation provides a sufficiently intelligible principle, there is nothing inherently unconstitutional about it. Accordingly, . . . I would hold that when Congress enacted § 109, it effected a constitutional delegation of legislative power to the EPA.

■ JUSTICE BREYER, concurring in part and concurring in the judgment.

... I ... agree with the Court's determination ... that the Clean Air Act does not permit the Environmental Protection Agency to consider the economic costs of implementation when setting national ambient air quality standards under § 109(b)(1) of the Act. But I would not rest this conclusion solely upon § 109's language or upon a presumption, such as the Court's presumption that any authority the Act grants the EPA to consider costs must flow from a "textual commitment" that is "clear." In order better to achieve regulatory goals—for example, to allocate resources so that they save more lives or produce a cleaner environment—regulators must often take account of all of a proposed regulation's adverse effects, at least where those adverse effects clearly threaten serious and disproportionate public harm. Hence, I believe that, other things being equal, we should read silences or ambiguities in the language of regulatory statutes as permitting, not forbidding, this type of rational regulation.

In this case, however, other things are not equal. Here, legislative history, along with the statute's structure, indicates that § 109's language reflects a congressional decision not to delegate to the agency the legal authority to consider economic costs of compliance. [Justice Breyer reviews these sources.]

Section 109(b)(1) directs the Administrator to set standards that are "requisite to protect the public health" with "an adequate margin of safety." But these words do not describe a world that is free of all risk—an impossible and undesirable objective. See [the Benzene Case] (the word "safe" does not mean "risk-free"). Nor are the words "requisite" and "public health" to be understood independent of context. We consider football equipment "safe" even if its use entails a level of risk that would make drinking water "unsafe" for consumption. And what counts as "requisite" to protecting the public health will similarly vary with background circumstances, such as the public's ordinary tolerance of the particular health risk in the particular context at issue.... The statute also permits the Administrator to take account of comparative health risks. That is to say, she may consider whether a proposed rule promotes safety overall. A rule likely to cause more harm to health than it prevents is not a rule that is "requisite to protect the public health." ...

... The statute's words, then, authorize the Administrator to consider the severity of a pollutant's potential adverse health effects, the number of those likely to be affected, the distribution of the adverse effects, and the uncertainties surrounding each estimate. They permit the Administrator to take account of comparative health consequences. They allow her to take account of context when determining the acceptability of small risks to health. And they give her considerable discretion when she does so.

This discretion would seem sufficient to avoid the extreme results that some of the industry parties fear. [T]he EPA ... retains discretionary authority to avoid regulating risks that it reasonably concludes are trivial in context. Nor need regulation lead to deindustrialization. Preindustrial society was not a very healthy society; hence a standard demanding the return of the Stone Age would not prove "requisite to protect the public health." ...

NOTES

(1) *Delegation and the Power/Duty to Engage in Cost–Benefit Analysis.* "Can/must EPA consider compliance costs in setting air quality standards?" is a question that placed the courts on the horns of a dilemma. If the answer is "no," the result might be profound regulatory irrationality. National resources are not unlimited; no goal—even public health—is sensibly pursued heedless of cost. Even within the area of public health itself, focusing on risks less costly to remediate may produce more beneficial results, sooner. Justice Breyer argued these points eloquently in Stephen Breyer, Breaking the Vicious Circle: Toward Effective Risk Regulation (1993), and we see, in his American Trucking concurrence, a valiant effort to find EPA some room for attending to such considerations. On the other hand, construing the CAA to prohibit consideration of cost would significantly narrow the statutory delegation, and limit executive adventurism. Particularly as regulatory mandates have become more complex and sweeping—e.g., to remediate air and water pollution across the nation as compared with, for example, to set reasonable rates for railroad carriage— would the power to balance costs against benefits become, in effect, carte blanche to engage in social engineering? Or is there a more subtle set of institutional incentives and constraints operating in this area?

CRAIG N. OREN, RUN OVER BY AMERICAN TRUCKING, PART I: CAN EPA REVIVE ITS AIR QUALITY STANDARDS?, 30 Environ. L. Rptr. 10653, 10660, 10662 (Nov. 1999): "Since the 1970s, a variety of scholars have argued that there is no way to obey the statute's command that ambient air quality standards be set without regard to cost. There are two reasons for this. One is scientific uncertainty about what effects are occurring and to whom. Given this uncertainty, any decision to set a standard trades off the cost of implementing the standard against the possibility that the standard may be efficacious. Second, and more fundamentally, available scientific data does not allow the identification of thresholds at which effects begin to occur. Instead, current knowledge suggests that, at any level of pollution, some effect may be happening to someone somewhere. The standard-setter must decide who should be protected and what effects should be protected against. Any such decision necessarily involves at least an implicit weighing of costs versus benefits. . . .

"EPA inevitably must therefore consider costs in standard-setting to help decide how stringent to make the standards. Indeed, EPA decisionmakers have admitted that they examine cost data when deciding on the levels of the standards. For this reason, it might seem obvious that EPA be required to justify its decisions in terms of cost. In that way a process of cost consideration that goes on behind the scenes would become visible for public comment and reaction. Yet, as American Trucking reiterates, the Act's text and legislative history make clear that EPA may not consider costs in standard-setting.

"Nonetheless, the exclusion of costs from the setting of air quality standards can be defended even if it is inevitable that costs be taken into account in setting the standards. The exclusion of costs [by the Act] can be explained as a means, albeit perhaps crude, of minimizing as much as possible the influence of cost calculations upon EPA's standard setting decisions and upon judicial review of those decisions. Consider, for example, EPA's previous revision of the ozone standard: Administrator Douglas Costle's decision in 1979 to promulgate an ambient standard for ozone of 0.12 ppm rather than the 0.10 standard urged by environmentalists or the 0.16 or 0.20 standard preferred by industry. Insofar as Costle chose to disregard the costs of implementation, the absence of cost language in the statute helped to protect him from public criticism and from judicial reversal for improperly ignoring costs. To put the point in administrative law terms, the Administrator's decision, to the extent it proceeds in the face of costs, is 'committed to agency discretion by law' [APA § 701(a)(2)] and hence unreviewable.[1] Considering the many difficulties of accurately determining the cost of attaining a given standard, much less intelligently weighing those costs against the benefits of attainment, Congress' decision to insulate the Administrator from cost-based arguments is an understandable way of assuring that standards be set.

"The exclusion of costs from the statute, while expanding Administrator Costle's discretion to be protective, also limited his ability to decide not to be protective. In rejecting the environmentalist 0.10 position, Costle had to frame his arguments in terms of the weakness of the scientific evidence for effects at very low level or the lack of public health significance of the effects that do exist. Consideration of cost may be implicit in considering whether a given effect is significant; but the Administrator who does not wish to safeguard health to the utmost is forced to address broader concerns than cost. Moreover, precisely because cost considerations cannot be invoked as a rationale for the decision, the Administrator is discouraged from putting much weight on cost. This acts to limit, though not eliminate, the Administrator's ability to decline to be protective.[2]"

Consider the many ways in which the estimation of compliance costs could play a role in air quality regulation: (1) It could guide EPA in its priority setting, causing the agency to focus first on controlling pollutants that promise the greatest health improvement per regulatory dollar spent. Regulatory target-setting is largely an internal agency process, with little external input and less procedural constraint.[3] Only in exceptional circumstances will such decisions be judicially reviewed.[4] (2) It could be data that the agency generates and reports to its principals in Congress and the

---

1. [Ed.] We explore this issue in Chapter IX, Sec. 3.b.

2. It can be countered that the device of excluding costs entirely from the statute is an overly simplistic means of minimizing the role of economic factors. There is some force to this objection. Telling the Administrator not to consider costs artificially distinguishes between the standard with no benefits, and the standard which has benefits that are offset by its costs; while both standards have an equal lack of utility, the Administrator will be able to justify promulgating the latter standard. On the other hand, consider the difficulties of drafting statutory language that would accomplish the same results with-

out explicitly barring cost consideration. Congress would be driven either to attempt to write a rigid formula for considering costs—probably impossible—or to provide the Administrator virtually untrammeled discretion.

3. Recent Presidents' efforts to exert more control over target-setting by forcing agencies to publish a regulatory agenda are considered in Chapter V, Sec. 3.b(ii).

4. Agency decisions not to take enforcement action in particular cases are presumptively unreviewable; decisions not to engage in rulemaking are reviewable, if at all, under a highly deferential standard. See p. 602 below; Chapter IX, Sec. 3.b.

White House. As Justice Scalia points out, even if the EPA isn't to consider the cost of cleaning up the nation's air, the political branches doubtless consider this information highly relevant to subsequent policymaking in the area. And once such data become public, they can generate regulatory (or deregulatory) momentum. (3) It could in fact influence EPA's decision about where to set the permissible standard, although the agency takes care to develop a public record that justifies the chosen standard on grounds apart from cost. This is the use complained of by industry in American Trucking, and accepted by Prof. Oren. (4) It could be a decisional factor overtly developed in the public record and explicitly used in the agency's justification of its regulatory choice. This, of course, is the use clearly impermissible after American Trucking.

Professor Jerry Mashaw has posited a "Law of Conservation of Administrative Discretion:" "[T]he amount of discretion in an administrative system is always constant. Elimination of discretion at one choice point merely causes the discretion that had been exercised there to migrate elsewhere in the system."[5] If the cost/benefit calculus is fundamental to rational regulation in general (as Justice Breyer argues) and to ambient air quality standards in particular (as Prof. Oren argues), might a comparable principle operate here?

(2) *The Ultimate Outcome.* On remand to review the reasonableness of the ozone and particulate rules, the D. C. Circuit found "the challenged air quality standards neither arbitrary nor capricious." American Trucking Ass'n v. EPA, 283 F.3d 355, 360–62 (D.C.Cir.2002).

(3) *Benzene and Chevron.* The disagreement between the majority and dissenters on the D.C. Circuit came, in part, from conflicting interpretations of two important Supreme Court cases.

INDUSTRIAL UNION DEPARTMENT, AFL-CIO v. AMERICAN PETROLEUM INSTITUTE, 448 U.S. 607 (1980) [THE BENZENE CASE]: In a regulatory effort in many ways similar to EPA's ozone and particulate matter rules, OSHA proposed to lower its existing standard for benzene in the workplace from 10 ppm to 1 ppm. The initial standard had been borrowed from the American National Standards Institute (ANSI), a private group that—pre-OSHA—promulgated voluntary "national consensus standards" for a number of workplace hazards. (In its early years, OSHA adopted several ANSI standards as a means of quickly establishing a relatively uncontroversial base of workplace safety regulation.) Subsequently, scientific studies confirmed a link between benzene and leukemia. The National Institute for Occupational Safety and Health (NIOSH)—a discrete, science-dominated agency located in the National Institutes of Health, with the mandate to advise OSHA about regulatory priorities—"strongly" recommended lowering the standard to 1 ppm as soon as possible. After the Fifth Circuit struck down OSHA's attempt to adopt a more stringent standard on an emergency basis, the agency began a full rulemaking that produced the regulation ultimately challenged in the Supreme Court.

Section 3(8) of the Occupational Safety and Health Act of 1970 states:

5. Jerry L. Mashaw, Greed, Chaos & Governance 154 (1997).

> The Secretary, in promulgating standards dealing with toxic materials or harmful physical agents ... shall set the standard which most adequately assures, to the extent feasible, on the basis of the best available evidence, that no employee will suffer material impairment of health or functional capacity even if such employee has regular exposure to the hazard dealt with by such standard for the period of his working life.

For a carcinogen like benzene, the ethical and practical limits of medical research make it difficult to establish the level below which lifelong exposure will not produce a material impairment of human health. Therefore, OSHA employed a "carcinogen policy" that assumed, in the absence of proof of a safe level, that any level above zero presents some cancer risk. Moreover, OSHA took the position that § 3(8) did not permit it to consider whether the costs of regulation outweighed the health benefits. Rather, it considered economic impact only to the extent of determining that compliance costs "will not be such as to threaten the financial welfare of the affected firms or the general economy." Taking into account the importance of benzene to various manufacturing processes, the omnipresence of small background amounts of benzene, and issues of technological workability (as well as the urging of NIOSH), OSHA settled on 1ppm as the minimum feasible exposure level. Estimated compliance costs varied across industry, ranging from a low of $1390 per employee to a high of $82,000 per employee.

The Court struck down the rule, producing five badly fractured opinions. For Justice Powell, who spoke only for himself, the problem was that OSHA incorrectly interpreted § 3(8) as precluding cost/benefit analysis; he was not willing to "assume that Congress intended OSHA to require reduction of health risks found to be significant *whenever* it also finds that the affected industry can bear the costs."[6] For the four-Justice plurality led by Justice Stevens and for Justice Rehnquist who wrote separately, the problem was delegation. Justice Stevens' opinion worried: "Expert testimony that a substance is probably a human carcinogen—either because it has caused cancer in animals or because individuals have contracted cancer following extremely high exposures—would justify the conclusion that the substance poses some risk of serious harm no matter how minute the exposure and no matter how many experts testified that they regarded the risk as insignificant. That conclusion would in turn justify pervasive regulation limited only by the constraint of feasibility. In light of the fact that there are literally thousands of substances used in the workplace that have been identified as carcinogens or suspect carcinogens, the Government's theory would give OSHA power to impose enormous costs that might produce little, if any, discernible benefit." Surprisingly, Justice Stevens paid no particular attention to the unusual Congressional command that OSHA be advised, in its choice of regulatory priorities, by

---

6. No one else addressed this issue. When, eventually, the Court did decide whether the Act contemplates cost-benefit analysis in setting workplace standards, it held—as with the Clean Air Act in American Trucking—that the agency could not consider costs in standard-setting. See American Textile Mfrs. Inst. Inc. v. Donovan, 452 U.S. 490 (1981).

NIOSH—an agency insulated in a "pure science" wing (the National Institutes of Health) of another department.

Therefore, he concluded, "In the absence of a clear mandate in the Act, it is unreasonable to assume that Congress intended to give the Secretary the unprecedented power over American industry that would result from the Government's view of [the Act] coupled with OSHA's cancer policy." The plurality limited this "unprecedented power" by using § 3(b), one of the basic definitional sections of the Act:

> The term "occupational safety and health standard" means a standard which requires conditions, or the adoption or use of one or more practices, means, methods, operations, or processes, reasonably necessary or appropriate to provide safe or healthful employment and places of employment.

Before OSHA can set (or reset) a standard, the plurality insisted, the agency must "determine that it is reasonably necessary and appropriate to remedy a significant risk of material health impairment"—i.e., the agency "must make a threshold finding that a place of employment is unsafe."[7] "If the Government was correct in arguing that neither § 3(8) nor § 6(b)(5) requires that the risk from a toxic substance be quantified sufficiently to enable the Secretary to characterize it as significant in an understandable way, the statute would make such a 'sweeping delegation of legislative power' that it might be unconstitutional under the Court's reasoning in A.L.A. Schechter Poultry Corp. v. United States and Panama Refining Co. v. Ryan. A construction of the statute that avoids this kind of open-ended grant should certainly be favored."

Justice Rehnquist agreed that the Act posed a nondelegation problem. However, he rejected the plurality's technique of "saving" the statute through a narrowing construction. His review of the legislative history persuaded him that Congress had recognized the thorny question of whether, and how, to balance lives saved against costs incurred—and had punted on it: "As formulated and enforced by this Court, the nondelegation doctrine serves three important functions. First, and most abstractly, it ensures to the extent consistent with orderly governmental administration that important choices of social policy are made by Congress, the branch of our Government most responsive to the popular will. Second, the doctrine guarantees that, to the extent Congress finds it necessary to delegate authority, it provides the recipient of that authority with an 'intelligible principle' to guide the exercise of the delegated discretion. See J.W. Hampton & Co. v. United States, 276 U.S. at 409; Panama Refining Co. v. Ryan, 293 U.S., at 430. Third, and derivative of the second, the doctrine ensures that courts charged with reviewing the exercise of delegated legislative discretion will be able to test that exercise against ascertainable standards.

"I believe the legislation at issue here fails on all three counts. The decision whether the law of diminishing returns should have any place in

---

7. Note that Justice Stevens substitutes "and" for "or" between "necessary" and "appropriate."

the regulation of toxic substances is quintessentially one of legislative policy. For Congress to pass that decision on to the Secretary in the manner it did violates, in my mind, John Locke's caveat ... that legislatures are to make laws, not legislators. Nor ... do the provisions at issue or their legislative history provide the Secretary with any guidance that might lead him to his somewhat tentative conclusion that he must eliminate exposure to benzene as far as technologically and economically possible. Finally, I would suggest that the standard of 'feasibility' renders meaningful judicial review impossible. ... It is difficult to imagine a more obvious example of Congress simply avoiding a choice which was both fundamental for purposes of the statute and yet politically so divisive that the necessary decision or compromise was difficult, if not impossible, to hammer out in the legislative forge...."

Justices Marshall, dissenting with three other Justices, would have sustained the rule: "While my Brother Rehnquist eloquently argues that there remains a place for [the nondelegation] doctrine in our jurisprudence, I am frankly puzzled as to why the issue is thought to be of any relevance here.... Congress has been sufficiently definite.... [I]t is clear that 'feasible' means technologically and economically achievable. Under the Act, the Secretary is afforded considerably more guidance than are other administrators acting under different regulatory statutes....

"The plurality's apparent suggestion that the nondelegation doctrine might be violated if the Secretary were permitted to regulate definite but nonquantifiable risks is plainly wrong. Such a statute would be quite definite and would thus raise no constitutional question under Schechter Poultry. Moreover, Congress could rationally decide that it would be better to require industry to bear 'feasible' costs than to subject American workers to an indeterminate risk of cancer and other fatal diseases."

CHEVRON, U.S.A. INC. V. NATURAL RESOURCES DEFENSE COUNCIL, 467 U.S. 837 (1984): Although not itself a nondelegation case, Chevron becomes relevant because (as argued by D.C. Circuit majority in American Trucking) one might conclude that "the approach of the Benzene case ... has given way to the approach of Chevron." Chevron, and the large body of caselaw and scholarship it has inspired, is considered fully in Chapter VIII. Here, we need only the basic outline of the decision.

At issue was a regulation in which the Reagan–Administration EPA proposed to reinterpret a crucial term in the Clean Air Act Amendments of 1977, to reach the opposite meaning used by the Carter–Administration EPA. Specifically, the question was whether "source" referred to each individual device (e.g., smokestack) that emitted pollutants or, instead, referred to the entire industrial unit (e.g., plant). The new regulation adopted the latter approach—which permits changes in individual emissions so long as net emissions of the industrial unit do not increase (the "bubble" approach). The D.C. Circuit invalidated the new interpretation. Finding that the issue was not definitively resolved by the statutory text or legislative history, that court examined the regulatory objectives of the relevant portion of the Clean Air Act. It concluded that the bubble approach was inconsistent with the statutory purpose of improving, not merely maintaining, air quality. The Supreme Court unanimously reversed, in an opinion by Justice Stevens (the author, four years earlier, of Benzene).

Once the D.C. Circuit concluded that Congress "had not spoken directly to the precise question at issue," Justice Stevens wrote, the question was "not whether in its view the [bubble] concept is 'inappropriate' in the general context of a program designed to improve air quality, but whether the Administrator's view that it is appropriate in the context of this particular program is a reasonable one." For present purposes, the opinion was most remarkable in recasting statutory interpretation, traditionally the domain of the judiciary, as a species of regulatory delegation—with the corresponding shift of primary responsibility to the agency: "Perhaps [Congress] consciously desired the Administrator to strike the balance [between various regulatory goals], thinking that those with great expertise and charged with responsibility for administering the provision would be in a better position to do so. Perhaps it simply did not consider the question at this level; and perhaps Congress was unable to forge a coalition on either side of the question, and those on each side decided to take their chances with the scheme devised by the agency. For judicial purposes, it matters not which of these things occurred.

"Judges are not experts in the field, and are not part of either political branch of the Government. Courts must, in some cases, reconcile competing political interests, but not on the basis of the judges' personal policy preferences. In contrast, an agency to which Congress has delegated policy-making responsibilities may, within the limits of that delegation, properly rely upon the incumbent administration's views of wise policy to inform its judgments. While agencies are not directly accountable to the people, the Chief Executive is, and it is entirely appropriate for this political branch of the Government to make such policy choices—resolving the competing interests which Congress itself either inadvertently did not resolve, or intentionally left to be resolved by the agency charged with the administration of the statute in light of everyday realities.

"When a challenge to an agency construction of a statutory provision, fairly conceptualized, really centers on the wisdom of the agency's policy, rather than whether it is a reasonable choice within a gap left open by Congress, the challenge must fail. In such a case, federal judges—who have no constituency—have a duty to respect legitimate policy choices made by those who do. The responsibilities for assessing the wisdom of such policy choices and resolving the struggle between competing views of the public interest are not judicial ones. . . . 'Our Constitution vests such responsibilities in the political branches.' TVA v. Hill, 437 U.S. 153, 195 (1978)."

You will be able better to assess what Chevron does, or doesn't, mean for judicial power to interpret regulatory statutes when you study the complete materials on the case in Chapter VIII. However, it is worth noting that even post-Chevron, a court nervous about regulatory authority may find a way to construe the statute against the possible delegation. This is what seems to have happened in MCI Telecommunications Corp. v. American Telephone and Telegraph Co., 512 U.S. 218 (1994), taken up as a principal case at p. 1052 below.

a.   NONDELEGATION AND THE PROBLEM OF TAXONOMY

The issues raised by the opinions in American Trucking can be grouped under two large questions. *First,* Is the delegation to EPA in §§ 108–09 of the Clean Air Act unconstitutional? This question in turn might be understood to comprise two related parts: Does the delegation fail under existing nondelegation precedent? If not, should that precedent be repudiated in favor of a more demanding standard? *Second,* If the statute is an unconstitutional delegation of power, how—and by whom—can that defect be remedied? The remaining materials in this Section explore these questions.

At the outset, though, we consider the threshold issue of taxonomy. Is it possible to classify the type of governmental power delegated by regulatory statutes? Is classification constitutionally necessary? If so, are the only choices "legislative," "executive,"and "judicial"?

THE FEDERALIST NO. 37 (JAMES MADISON): "Experience has instructed us that no skill in the science of Government has yet been able to discriminate and define, with sufficient certainty, its three great provinces—the Legislative, Executive, and Judiciary. . . . Questions daily occur in the course of practice which prove the obscurity which reigns in these subjects, and which puzzle the greatest adepts in political science."

FIELD V. CLARK, 143 U.S. 649, 693 (1892) (Harlan, J.): "The true distinction . . . is between the delegation of power to make the law, which necessarily involves a discretion as to what it shall be, and conferring authority or discretion as to its execution, to be exercised under and in pursuance of the law. The first cannot be done; to the latter no valid objection can be made." [internal quotes omitted]

PRINTZ V. UNITED STATES, 521 U.S. 898, 927 (1997): "The Government's distinction between 'making' law and merely 'enforcing' it, between 'policy-making' and mere 'implementation,' is an interesting one. . . . Executive action that has utterly no policymaking component is rare. . . ."

UNITED STATES V. GRIMAUD, 220 U.S. 506, 517 (1911): "It must be admitted that it is difficult to define the line which separates legislative power to make laws, from administrative authority to make regulations."

STEVEN G. CALABRESI, THE VESTING CLAUSES AS POWER GRANTS, 88 Nw. U. L. Rev. 1377, 1377, 1390 n. 45 (1994): "Anyone who sits down to read the U.S. Constitution from beginning to end must immediately be struck by . . . the stark division of the government of 'We the People' into three apparently coequal departments. That division leaps out at the reader because of the first three Articles of the Constitution each of which begins with a Vesting Clause that empowers a particular actor (or actors), and no one else, to act. . . .

". . . [The Vesting Clauses] appear clearly to divide the world of governmental powers into a finite set of three, each of which is assigned to *one and only one* governmental actor." (emphasis added)

MISTRETTA V. UNITED STATES, 488 U.S. 361, 417 (1989) (Scalia, J., dissenting): "[A] certain degree of discretion, and thus of lawmaking, inheres in most executive or judicial action."

WAYMAN V. SOUTHARD, 23 U.S. (10 Wheat) 1, 46 (1825) (Marshall, J.): "The difference between the departments undoubtedly is, that the legislature makes, the executive executes, and the judiciary construes the law; but the maker of the law may commit something to the discretion of the other departments, and the precise boundary of this power is a subject of delicate and difficult inquiry, into which a Court will not enter unnecessarily."

CLINTON V. CITY OF NEW YORK, 524 U.S. 417, 480 (1998) (Breyer, J., dissenting): "The power the Act conveys is the right kind of power. It is 'executive.' . . . [A]n exercise of that power 'executes' the Act. . . . The fact that one could also characterize this kind of power as 'legislative,' say, if Congress itself [through passage of a bill] prevented a provision from taking effect, is beside the point."

GARY LAWSON, THE RISE AND THE RISE OF THE ADMINISTRATIVE STATE, 107 Harv. L. Rev. 1231, 1239 (1994): "If the executive power 'means simply the power to carry out legislative commands regardless of their substance' . . . then there never was and never could be such a constitutional principle of nondelegation."

BOWSHER V. SYNAR, 478 U.S. 714, 749 (1986) (Stevens, J., concurring in the judgment): "One reason that the exercise of legislative, executive, and judicial powers cannot be categorically distributed among three mutually exclusive branches of Government is that governmental power cannot always be readily characterized with only one of those three labels. On the contrary, as our cases demonstrate, a particular function, like a chameleon, will often take on the aspect of the office to which it is assigned."

MARBURY V. MADISON, 5 U.S. (1 Cranch) 137, 177 (1803): "It is emphatically the province and duty of the judicial department to say what the law is. Those who apply the rule to particular cases, must of necessity expound and interpret that rule."

BOWSHER V. SYNAR, 478 U.S. 714, 733 (1986): "Interpreting a law enacted by Congress to implement the legislative mandate is the very essence of 'execution' of the law."

FREYTAG V. COMMISSIONER OF INTERNAL REVENUE, 501 U.S. 868, 912 (1991) (Scalia, J., concurring in part and concurring in the judgment): "It seems to me entirely obvious that the Tax Court, like the Internal Revenue Service, the FCC, and the NLRB, exercises executive power."

INS V. CHADHA, 462 U.S. 919, 952 (1983): "Examination of the action taken here . . . reveals that it was essentially legislative in purpose and effect. [It] had the purpose and effect of altering the legal rights, duties and relations of persons . . . outside the Legislative Branch."

INS V. CHADHA, 462 U.S. 919, 986 (1983) (White, J., dissenting). "There is no question but that agency rulemaking is lawmaking in any functional or realistic sense of the term. The Administrative Procedure Act, 5 U.S.C. § 551(4), provides that a 'rule' is an agency statement 'designed to implement, interpret, or prescribe law or policy.' When agencies are authorized to prescribe law through substantive rulemaking, the administrator's regulation is not only due deference, but is accorded 'legislative effect.' These regulations bind courts and officers of the Federal Government, may preempt state law, and grant rights to and impose obligations on the public. In sum, they have the force of law."

MISTRETTA V. UNITED STATES, 488 U.S. 361, 417 n. 2 (1989) (Scalia, J., dissenting): "An executive agency can ... be created with no power other than the making of rules, as long as that agency is subject to the control of the President and the President has executive authority related to the rulemaking. In such circumstances, the rulemaking is ultimately ancillary to the President's executive powers."

SECURITIES & EXCHANGE COMMISSION V. CHENERY CORP., 332 U.S. 194, 214 (1947) (Jackson, J., dissenting): "Now I realize fully what Mark Twain meant when he said, 'The more you explain it, the more I don't understand it.'"

One more, very different, possible answer to the classification question:

LAWRENCE LESSIG & CASS R. SUNSTEIN, THE PRESIDENT AND THE ADMINISTRATION, 94 Colum. L. Rev. 1, 39–41 (1994): "For most constitutionalists, resolving issues of what we call 'executive' power means deciding two different sets of questions. The first set relates to who performs the political functions of an executive—the power to conduct foreign affairs, for example, or the power to act as head of state. The second set of questions relates to who directs the *administrative* functions of an executive—in parliamentary systems, who controls the government.

"Consider three possibilities:

(1) a constitution could vest control over all political and administrative functions in the executive;

(2) a constitution could vest control over just the political functions in the executive, and control over the administrative functions in the legislature; and

(3) a constitution could vest control over all political and some administrative functions in the executive, but leave to the legislature the power to decide how much of the balance of administrative power should be afforded the President.

"Option two describes most existing constitutional systems; England is the most familiar example. Option one describes what most believe the framers created—a President with constitutional control over the administrative functions. But we believe that it is option three that describes best the original understanding of the framers' design. That is, we believe that the framers meant to constitutionalize just some of what we now think of as 'the executive power,' leaving the balance to Congress to structure as it thought proper....

"There are at least two ways to understand this claim that the framers did not intend to vest in the President control of all administrative functions.... One understanding would be that the framers had in their heads clear categories of 'executive power' (or in many cases equivalently 'political power') and 'administrative power,' and by constitutionally vesting in the President 'the executive power' they intended to vest constitutionally just 'executive power,' leaving the second category, 'administrative power,' for Congress to vest as it thought proper. This understanding relies on clear categories of governmental power.

"A second understanding does not turn on clear categorical understandings of these powers, but rather on a more ambiguous and undeveloped conception of what these powers could be. It understands the framers to believe that some powers fall clearly within the domain of 'the executive' (and these they constitutionalized), but the balance (what we would roughly call administrative) they believed would be assigned pragmatically, according to the values or functions of the particular power at issue. While the first understanding treats the framers as budding constitutional formalists, who simply chose not (or forgot, given the small number of administrative functions) to include a vesting clause for 'the administrative power,' the second treats them as speakers of a less categorical, more pragmatic, language...."

b.   Delegation in the Cases—The Long Road to American Trucking

Nearly two centuries of nondelegation caselaw reveals a Court that consistently talks a harsh line against the delegation of "legislative power," but rarely finds a statutory delegation it can't sustain.

Surveying this history, one of your editors has observed: "It is of course possible that the series of [nondelegation] cases ... ought to be dismissed as merely an elaborate charade, a ritual of approval that never had substance save for an interval in the 1930s when nondelegation allowed the Court a brief victory in a political war it ultimately lost. However, no one has convincingly explained why a Court that has repeatedly been willing, from Marbury v. Madison to Bowsher v. Synar [p. 176 below], to brave political controversy by telling Congress it has gone too far would choose to engage—for well over a century and through Justices as diverse as Marshall, Harlan, Taft, Cardozo and Stone—in whitewashing Congress's delegative propensities."[1] Hence, the suggestion that we "take[ ] seriously the idea that these cases chronicle the Court's purposeful struggle to construct, if possible, a constitutional model for the administrative state that would enable Congress to use means it deemed necessary to pursue ends it deemed appropriate, without sacrificing ideas and forms central to the Constitution." *Is* it possible to discern a principled and justifiable evolution of constitutional doctrine in the line of nondelegation cases? We invite you to decide:

Early Cases

Challenges to the constitutionality of statutory delegations date from the early years of the Republic. For almost 150 years, the Court sustained the challenged statutes by invoking one of two theories.

The first, the "contingency rationale," reasoned that an unconstitutional delegation had not occurred so long as the delegee was merely ascertaining the existence of certain conditions that triggered legal consequences specified in the statute. This rationale repeatedly worked to sustain delegations of authority to the President to set the terms of

---

1. Cynthia R. Farina, Statutory Interpretation and the Balance of Power in the   Administrative State, 89 Colum. L. Rev. 452, 480 (1989).

international trade. For example, the Non–Intercourse Act of 1809 barred trade with ports of Great Britain and France under pain of forfeiture of the vessel and its goods. In THE BRIG AURORA, 11 U.S. (7 Cranch) 382 (1813), the Court unanimously held that Congress could empower the President to "revive" a previous statute granting trading privileges with either country whenever he "declare[d] the fact" that it had "ceased to violate the neutral commerce" of the United States. Similarly, FIELD V. CLARK, 143 U.S. 649 (1892), (which contains the oft-cited quotation about delegation with which this Section begins, and which is much debated in the line-item veto case, Clinton v. City of New York, p. 224 below) upheld the Tariff Act of 1890. The Act set up a retaliatory tariff schedule on numerous imported agricultural products, to take effect, for whatever time the President "shall deem just," on any country that imposed on American products "duties or other exactions ... which ... [the President] may deem to be reciprocally unequal and unreasonable...." The majority concluded, "Legislative power was exercised when Congress declared that the suspension should take effect upon a named contingency. What the President was required to do was simply in execution of the act of Congress. ... He was the mere agent of the law-making department to ascertain and declare the event upon which its expressed will was to take effect." By this time, however, the contingency rationale was wearing thin. Two justices dissented, finding it impossible to see the delegation as one of mere factfinding.

The second rationale proved to have somewhat more staying power. WAYMAN V. SOUTHARD, 23 U.S. (10 Wheat.) 1 (1826), challenged a 1792 statute authorizing the Supreme Court to promulgate rules for the service of process and execution of judgments in the federal courts. Justice Marshall conceded that "the line has not been exactly drawn which separates those important subjects, which must be entirely regulated by the legislature itself, from those of less interest, in which a general provision may be made, and power given to those who are to act under such general provisions, to fill up the details." All the Court agreed, however, that the Process Act was on the constitutional side of that line. Almost ninety years later, the Court returned to the concept of "filling up the details" to sustain a regulation, promulgated by the Secretary of Agriculture, that required a permit to graze livestock in federal forest reserves.

A series of statutes from 1897–1905 authorized the creation of such reserves, directed the Secretary to "make provisions for the protection [of them] against destruction by fire and depredations," and set criminal penalties for violations of regulations made pursuant to the Act. In UNITED STATES V. GRIMAUD, 220 U.S. 506 (1911), two California ranchers, prosecuted for grazing their sheep without the requisite permit, argued that the Act unconstitutionally delegated the power to make criminal law. The contingency rationale was inapt—the statute said nothing about restricting the free-range grazing of livestock—but a unanimous Court reasoned that the Secretary was exercising only a "power to fill up the details:" "[The acts declare] that the privilege of using reserves for 'all proper and lawful purposes' is subject to the proviso that the person so using them shall comply 'with the rules and regulations covering said forest reservation.' ... The subjects as to which the Secretary can regulate are defined. The lands are set apart as a forest reserve. He is required to make provision to protect them from depredations and from harmful uses. He is authorized 'to regulate the occupancy and use and to preserve the forests from destruction.' A violation of reasonable rules regulating the use and occupancy of the property is made a crime, not by the Secretary, but by Congress. The statute, not the Secretary, fixes the penalty."

The New Deal Period—The Emergence, and the Test, of the Modern Doctrinal Approach

Eventually, though, regulatory statutes gave the delegee a bigger task than could be credibly described as "filling up the details." The case that set the modern doctrinal standard again involved a delegation of power to the President in the area of international trade.

J.W. HAMPTON, JR. & CO. v. UNITED STATES, 276 U.S. 394 (1928): The Tariff Act of 1922 directed the President to change the original statutory schedule of tariffs on various goods "[w]henever the President, upon investigation of the differences in costs of production of articles wholly or in part the growth or product of the United States and of like or similar articles wholly or in part the growth or product of competing foreign countries, shall find . . . that the duties fixed in this Act do not equalize the said differences in costs of production in the United States and the principal competing country." Moving tariff-setting more toward the bureaucratic mode of modern regulation, the Act authorized the President to act only after receiving the report of a new Tariff Commission. The Commission was to conduct "[i]nvestigations to assist the President in ascertaining differences in costs of production" and to "give reasonable public notice of its hearings and . . . reasonable opportunity to parties interested to be present, to produce evidence, and to be heard." Chief Justice Taft—himself a former President—reasoned for a unanimous Court that Congress could not practically undertake tariff adjustment itself. Therefore, as with the setting of transportation rates by the Interstate Commerce Commission, "common sense requires that . . . Congress may provide a Commission . . . to fix those rates, after hearing evidence and argument concerning them from interested parties, all in accord with a general rule that Congress first lays down. . . ." What is constitutionally required, he held, is "an intelligible principle to which the person or body authorized to fix such rates is directed to conform."

Although Hampton itself had resisted calling the delegated power "legislative," by 1933 the Court (speaking through Justice Cardozo) was quite frankly admitting that the Tariff Act of 1922 represented "in substance a delegation, though a permissible one, *of the legislative process*." Norwegian Nitrogen Prods. Co. v. U.S., 288 U.S. 294, 305 (1933). (italics added)

Within a few years, the new doctrinal formulation was put to severe test. "The depression which began in the Fall of 1929 had, by 1933, produced an economic crisis probably unequaled in the history of the United States. At least thirteen million persons were unemployed; wages received in mining, manufacturing, construction and transportation had declined from 17 to 6.8 billion dollars. Prices had fallen 37 per cent and industrial production had been cut almost in half." Robert L. Stern, The

Commerce Clause and the National Economy, 1933–1936, 59 Harv. L. Rev. 645, 653 (1946). Title I of the National Industrial Recovery Act of 1933 (NIRA) eschewed conventional regulatory techniques of market correction in favor of facilitating coordinated activities that might replace the market. "Business men, in combinations subject to Government approval, were to be allowed to eliminate wasteful competitive practices and cutthroat competition so as to enable them to halt the decline in prices, to pay the higher wage bills, and to restore business to a healthy condition." Id. The NIRA prompted the only occasions on which the Court has struck down a regulatory program on nondelegation grounds.

In addition to the ordinary effects of the depression, the petroleum industry faced "the ruinous consequences of uncontrolled overproduction from ... the opening of the vast East Texas field...." Stern, at 654. Section 9(c)[2] of the NIRA empowered the President to *federally* enforce conservation orders from *state* boards attempting to deal with this problem. PANAMA REFINING CO. V. RYAN, 293 U.S. 388 (1935), found no standard for the President to follow in deciding whether to close interstate commerce to "hot oil." The lengthy list of findings and purposes in § 1 did not help. "Among the numerous and diverse objectives broadly stated, the President was not required to choose. The President was not required to ascertain and proclaim the conditions prevailing in the industry which made the prohibition necessary. The Congress left the matter to the President without standard or rule, to be dealt with as he pleased." Only Justice Cardozo dissented.

Five months later, however, even Cardozo agreed that § 3 of the Act exceeded constitutional limits. This section authorized trade associations to draft "codes of fair competition" that could give a guild-like structure to trade. Once a code received Presidential approval, violations "shall be deemed an unfair method of competition in commerce within the meaning of the Federal Trade Commission Act"—carrying a criminal fine of up to $500 for each day of violation. Before approving the codes, the President was directed to "find (1) that such associations or groups impose no inequitable restrictions on admission to membership therein and are truly representative ... and (2) that such code or codes are not designed to promote monopolies or to eliminate or oppress small enterprises and will not operate to discriminate against them, and will tend to effectuate the policy of this title. ..." However, the approval process operated in secret without close supervision, and soon acquired a reputation for free-wheeling informality that could not have been reassuring. In A.L.A. SCHECHTER POULTRY CORP. V. UNITED STATES, 295 U.S. 495 (1935), the Court unanimously struck down the scheme.

---

2. "The President is authorized to prohibit the transportation in interstate and foreign commerce of petroleum and the products thereof produced or withdrawn from storage in excess of the amount permitted to be produced or withdrawn from storage by any state law or valid regulation or order prescribed thereunder, by any board, commission, officer, or other duly authorized agency of a State. Any violation of any order of the President issued under the provisions of this subsection shall be punishable by fine of not to exceed $1,000 or imprisonment for not to exceed six months, or both." 48 Stat. 200 (1933).

Chief Justice Hughes's opinion distinguished the procedures by which the FTC, ICC, and Federal Radio Commission (FRC) were to exercise their delegated power: "Provision was made for formal complaint, for notice and hearing, for appropriate findings of fact supported by adequate evidence, and for judicial review to give assurance that the action of the Commission is taken within its statutory authority." By contrast, the NIRA "dispenses with this administrative procedure and with any administrative procedure of an analogous character." Justice Cardozo, concurring, emphasized the sweep of § 3: "The delegated power of legislation which has found expression in this code is not canalized within banks that keep it from overflowing. It is unconfined and vagrant. . . . Here in effect is a roving commission to inquire into evils and upon discovery correct them." In particular, he carefully distinguished the arguably analogous mission of the FTC to eliminate "unfair methods of competition:" "If codes of fair competition are codes eliminating 'unfair' methods of competition ascertained upon inquiry to prevail in one industry or another, there is no unlawful delegation of legislative functions when the President is directed to inquire into such practices and denounce them when discovered. . . . But there is another conception of codes of fair competition. . . . By this other conception a code is not to be restricted to the elimination of business practices that would be characterized by general acceptance as oppressive or unfair. It is to include whatever ordinances may be desirable or helpful for the well-being or prosperity of the industry affected. . . . This is delegation running riot.[3]"

Mid-Century cases—Growing Emphasis on Effective External Checks

A new phase in nondelegation jurisprudence was prompted, once again, by turmoil in the economy. The domestic strain of a world at war produced The Emergency Price Control Act of 1942 (EPCA). The Price Administrator was to set maximum prices that "in his judgment will be generally fair and

---

3. See also Peter Irons, The New Deal Lawyers (1982) (providing insightful historical context, including how the NIRA Administrator's failure to construct a framework of legality contributed greatly to the outcome).

In Carter v. Carter Coal Co., 298 U.S. 238 (1936), another piece of New Deal legislation was invalidated on constitutional grounds. Not so obviously a "pure" nondelegation case, the Court's reasoning is heavily tinged with substantive due process. The Bituminous Coal Conservation Act of 1935 imposed a 15 percent tax on the coal of any producer who did not become a member of the Bituminous Coal Code. Moreover, once bargaining between companies who mined more than two thirds of the annual tonnage of coal and representatives of more than one-half of employed coal mine workers produced analogous wage and hours terms, all Code members had to accept those terms. Government officials had no voice in shaping or approving the arrangements thus made. The Court found this "legislative delegation in its

most obnoxious form; for it is not even delegation to an official or an official body, presumptively disinterested, but to private persons whose interests may be and often are adverse to the interests of others in the same business. . . . [I]n the very nature of things, one person may not be entrusted with the power to regulate the business of another, and especially of a competitor. And a statute which attempts to confer such power undertakes an intolerable and unconstitutional interference with personal liberty and private property."

The Schechter case has sometimes been explained on a similar basis. The classic discussion is Louis Jaffe, Law Making by Private Groups, 51 Harv. L.Rev. 201 (1937); thorough recent treatments may be found in David M. Lawrence, Private Exercise of Governmental Power, 61 Ind.L.J. 647 (1986), and Harold J. Krent, Legal Theory: Fragmenting the Unitary Executive, 85 Nw.U.L.Rev. 62 (1990).

equitable and will effectuate the purposes of this Act." These included: "to stabilize prices and to prevent speculative, unwarranted, and abnormal increases in prices and rents; to eliminate and prevent profiteering, hoarding, manipulation, speculation and other disruptive practices resulting from abnormal market conditions or scarcities caused by or contributing to the national emergency; [and] to assure that defense appropriations are not dissipated by excessive prices." "So far as practicable," he was to "ascertain and give due consideration to the prices prevailing between October 1 and October 15, 1941." After "consulting with representative members of the industry so far as practicable," he was to provide a "statement of the considerations involved" in prescribing prices. The EPCA originally contained a six–month sunset provision; it was extended for an additional year. YAKUS V. UNITED STATES, 321 U.S. 414 (1944), an appeal from a conviction for charging more than the regulated price of beef, sustained the Act against a nondelegation challenge. Important to the eight-member majority was the potential for institutions outside the agency to monitor the Administrator's use of power:

"... Acting within its constitutional power to fix prices, it is for Congress to say whether the data on the basis of which prices are to be fixed are to be confined within a narrow or a broad range. In either case the only concern of courts is to ascertain whether the will of Congress has been obeyed. This depends not upon the breadth of the definition of the facts or conditions which the administrative officer is to find but upon the determination whether the definition sufficiently marks the field within which the Administrator is to act so that it may be known whether he has kept within it in compliance with the legislative will.

"... Congress is not confined to that method of executing its policy which involves the least possible delegation of discretion to administrative officers. Only if we could say that there is an absence of standards for the guidance of the Administrator's action, so that it would be impossible in a proper proceeding to ascertain whether the will of Congress has been obeyed, would we be justified in overriding its choice of means for effecting its declared purpose of preventing inflation. The standards prescribed by the present Act, with the aid of the 'statement of the considerations' required to be made by the Administrator, are sufficiently definite and precise to enable Congress, the courts and the public to ascertain whether the Administrator, in fixing the designated prices, has conformed to those standards. Hence we are unable to find in them an unauthorized delegation of legislative power."

This emphasis on the possibility of external monitoring and control continued in FAHEY V. MALLONEE, 332 U.S. 245 (1947). The Home Owners' Loan Act delegated sweeping, and seemingly standardless, authority to bank regulators "to provide ... for the reorganization, consolidation, merger, or liquidation of [savings and loan associations.]" The Court reasoned: "Banking is one of the longest regulated and most closely supervised of public callings. It is one in which accumulated experience of supervisors, acting for many states under various statutes, has established well-defined practices for the appointment of conservators, receivers and liquidators. Corporate management is a field, too, in which courts have experience and many precedents have crystallized into well-known and generally acceptable standards. A discretion to make regulations to guide supervisory action in such matters may be constitutionally permissible while it might not be allowable . . . in uncharted fields." Other cases from this period that focus on the possibility of effective external checks, rather than the scope of the delegation as such, include American Power & Light Co. v. SEC, 329 U.S. 90 (1946), and Lichter v. United States, 334 U.S. 742 (1948).

In this period, the Court also developed the important technique of construing statutes to avoid nondelegation problems. The Passport Act of 1926 authorized the Secretary of State to "grant and issue passports . . . under such rules as the President shall designate and prescribe." A Cold–War era executive order permitted the Secretary "in his discretion to refuse to issue a passport." By regulation, the Secretary barred passports to members or supporters of the Communist Party, or persons believed to be going abroad in order to advance the Communist movement. A cognate regulation required passport applicants to execute an affidavit concerning past or present membership in the Communist Party. KENT V. DULLES, 357 U.S. 116 (1958), held that the Act did not authorize the Executive to refuse passports solely on the basis of the applicant's political commitments. Justice Douglas's opinion for a closely divided Court insisted that the "right to travel is a part of the 'liberty' of which the citizen cannot be deprived without due process of law. . . . We would be faced with important constitutional questions were we to hold that Congress . . . had given the Secretary authority to withhold passports to citizens because of their beliefs or associations. Congress has made no such provision in explicit terms; and absent one, the Secretary may not employ that standard to restrict the citizens' right of free movement."

This statutory interpretation technique—known as the "clear statement rule," because the court requires the legislature to speak with unambiguous clarity before assuming that a particular statutory meaning is contemplated—has since been used in a variety of areas where the Court perceives legislation to tread close to constitutional limits. In a case like Kent v. Dulles, Professor Cass Sunstein suggests, the clear statement technique provides a less drastic alternative to striking the statute down on nondelegation grounds: "The decision should be understood as an effort to ensure that the national legislature, not simply the executive branch, has deliberated on a question raising difficult constitutional questions relating to freedom of expression and the right to travel. This approach therefore responds to the delegation problem that would result from a decision to allow the executive branch to undertake constitutionally troublesome acts pursuant to an open-ended delegation of authority."[4]

Contemporary Cases

The impact of the Vietnam War on domestic wages and prices produced the Economic Stabilization Act of 1970. The Act delegated sweeping power to the President (and, via an implementing executive order, to the Cost of Living Council headed by the Secretary of the Treasury) not only to control

4.   Law and Administration After *Chevron,* 90 Colum.L.Rev. 2071, 2110–12 (1990).

wages, rents, and prices but also to decide when—if ever—a wage/price freeze would operate and how long it would endure. The Act was sustained in AMALGAMATED MEAT CUTTERS & BUTCHER WORKMEN V. CONNALLY, 337 F.Supp. 737 (D.D.C.1971). Writing for the special, three-judge court,[5] Judge Leventhal began "with the modest observation that the Constitution does not forbid every delegation of 'legislative' power." Yakus, he explained, emphasized that "[c]oncepts of control and accountability define the constitutional requirement. The principle permitting a delegation of legislative power, if there has been sufficient demarcation of the field to permit a judgment whether the agency has kept within the legislative will, establishes a principle of accountability under which compatibility with the legislative design may be ascertained not only by Congress but by the courts and the public."

In response to arguments that the Act delegated "a 'blank check' for internal affairs which is intolerable in our constitutional system," Judge Leventhal identified two significant limits on the delegation. First, a "background of wage and price controls in two wars," had generated an "administrative practice" that "was the subject of extensive judicial interpretation and review. This substantial background of prior law and practice ... provides more than adequate standards for the exercise of the authority granted by the Act." In particular that background, and the legislative history of the 1970 Act, implied that the delegated power to set wages and prices was to be guided by "a standard of broad fairness and avoiding gross inequity." Second, he discerned a "requirement that any action taken by the Executive under the law ... must be in accordance with further standards as developed by the Executive. This requirement, inherent in the Rule of Law and implicit in the Act, means that however broad the discretion of the Executive at the outset, the standards once developed limit the latitude of subsequent executive action. The importance in the present context of this self-limiting aspect of executive and agency discretion is brought out in Yakus v. United States.... The requirement of subsidiary administrative policy, enabling Congress, the courts and the public to assess the Executive's adherence to the ultimate legislative standard, is in furtherance of the purpose of the constitutional objective of accountability."

The first Supreme Court nondelegation opinion in this era was the Benzene case, excerpted at p. 58 above. You now can see that the plurality was using the Kent v. Dulles technique. The combination of the plurality's invocation of the clear statement rule (which suggested that the OSHA delegation was close to the constitutional line) and Justice Rehnquist's separate opinion (which thought the delegation was over the line) sent powerful signals to would-be challengers of regulatory statutes. Nondelega-

---

5. Judge Silberman's dismissive description of the case in American Trucking as "an old district court opinion" is misleading. Under a statutory process no longer in effect, challenges to the constitutionality of federal statutes had to be heard by a three-judge court comprised of two district and one circuit court judge, appeals from which could go immediately to the Supreme Court. Thus, the procedure combined the fact-finding capability of the trial court with the multi-judge deliberative process of the appeals court. Judge Leventhal was a distinguished member of the D.C. Circuit, whose opinions were almost uniformly held in high regard.

tion became the constitutional phoenix, powerfully resurgent after apparent oblivion. The result was three delegation opinions—all involving the criminal justice area—in the decade prior to American Trucking.

Prior to passage of the Sentencing Reform Act of 1984, criminal sentencing had been a matter of largely unchecked discretion in which all three branches participated. Congress typically specified a wide range of available penalties; trial judges were free to impose any sentence within this range (without explanation or judicial review); the Executive enjoyed essentially unsupervised discretion to parole prisoners before expiration of the stated terms. Unsurprisingly, so much unstructured discretion produced serious disparities. In 1984, Congress replaced this system by abolishing the parole system and by creating the United States Sentencing Commission. The Commission was directed to adopt, and then monitor and periodically revise, "mandatory sentencing guidelines." These guidelines set a much narrower range of sentencing possibilities, from which trial judges can deviate only on finding certain aggravating or mitigating factors. Judges must state their reasons, and limited appellate review is now available. The Commission is statutorily defined "as an independent commission in the judicial branch." Three of its seven members must be federal judges, whom the President selects from a list of six recommended by the Judicial Conference of the United States.

In MISTRETTA v. UNITED STATES, 488 U.S. 361 (1989), a convicted drug dealer attacked the Commission on a number of separation-of-powers grounds, including nondelegation. The Supreme Court, with only Justice Scalia dissenting, rejected all challenges. Justice Blackmun had an easy time with the delegation argument. "We cannot dispute petitioner's contention that the Commission enjoys significant discretion in formulating guidelines. . . . But our cases do not at all suggest that delegations of this type may not carry with them the need to exercise judgment on matters of policy."

With respect to Mistretta's more general separation-of-powers challenge, Justice Blackmun emphasized Justice Jackson's "pragmatic, flexible view of differentiated governmental power to which we are heir: 'While the Constitution diffuses power the better to secure liberty, it also contemplates that practice will integrate the dispersed powers into a workable government. It enjoins upon its branches separateness but interdependence, autonomy but reciprocity.' Youngstown Sheet & Tube Co. v. Sawyer, 343 U.S. 579, 635 (1952) (concurring opinion).

"In adopting this flexible understanding of separation of powers, we simply have recognized Madison's teaching that the greatest security against tyranny—the accumulation of excessive authority in a single branch—lies not in a hermetic division between the Branches, but in a carefully crafted system of checked and balanced power within each Branch. '[T]he greatest security,' wrote Madison, 'against a gradual concentration of the several powers in the same department, consists in giving to those who administer each department, the necessary constitutional means, and personal motives, to resist encroachments of the others.' The Federalist No. 51, p. 349 (J. Cooke ed. 1961). . . .

"It is this concern of encroachment and aggrandizement that has animated our separation-of-powers jurisprudence and aroused our vigilance against the 'hydraulic pressure inherent within each of the separate Branches to exceed the outer limits of its power.' Accordingly, we have not hesitated to strike down provisions of law that either accrete to a single branch powers more appropriately diffused among separate branches or that undermine the authority and independence of one or another coordinate branch. ... By the same token, we have upheld statutory provisions that to some degree commingle the functions of the Branches, but that pose no danger of either aggrandizement or encroachment."

The Sentencing Commission implicated none of these concerns. Although "an independent rulemaking body ... within the Judicial Branch" is "unquestionably a peculiar institution within the framework of our Government," the Constitution is not violated "by mere anomaly or innovation." To be sure, the Commission's decisions entail a "degree of political judgment about crime and criminality." However, "the Commission is not a court, does not exercise judicial power, and is not controlled by or accountable to members of the Judicial Branch." The judiciary's power is not unconstitutionally aggrandized because "[p]rior to the passage of the Act, the Judicial Branch, as an aggregate, decided precisely the questions assigned to the Commission: what sentence is appropriate to what criminal conduct under what circumstances." At the same time, the degree of Presidential control over Commission membership does not unconstitutionally encroach on judicial autonomy. "We simply cannot imagine that federal judges will comport their actions to the wishes of the President for the purpose of receiving an appointment to the Sentencing Commission." Moreover, the statutory "for cause" removal provision is "specifically crafted to prevent the President from exercising 'coercive influence' over independent agencies."

Justice Scalia's vigorous dissent advocated a provocative—and, from the Court's most vocal formalist, somewhat surprising—recasting of the nondelegation doctrine: "[W]hile the doctrine of unconstitutional delegation is unquestionably a fundamental element of our constitutional system, it is not an element readily enforceable by the courts. Once it is conceded, as it must be, that no statute can be entirely precise, and that some judgments, even some judgments involving policy considerations, must be left to the officers executing the law and to the judges applying it, the debate over unconstitutional delegation becomes a debate not over a point of principle but over a question of degree.

"Precisely because the scope of delegation is largely uncontrollable by the courts, we must be particularly rigorous in preserving the Constitution's structural restrictions that deter excessive delegation. The major one, it seems to me, is that the power to make law cannot be exercised by anyone other than Congress, except in conjunction with the lawful exercise of executive or judicial power. . . . In the present case, . . . a pure delegation of legislative power is precisely what we have before us. It is irrelevant whether the standards are adequate, because they are not standards related to the exercise of executive or judicial powers; they are, plainly and simply, standards for further legislation."

TOUBY V. UNITED STATES, 500 U.S. 160 (1991), attacked provisions of The Controlled Substance Act of 1970, which allows the Attorney General to designate illicit drugs on one of five schedules. Different schedules carry different penalties. The Act also provides an expedited temporary designation process, to allow the Drug Enforcement Agency rapidly to schedule emerging "designer drugs." The Act provides that a temporary designation, unlike permanent scheduling, "is not subject to judicial review."

Daniel and Lyrissa Touby were convicted for operating a home business that manufactured Euphoria, a drug temporarily listed on Schedule 1 (which merited the most severe penalties). Like sheep-rancher Grimaud 90 years earlier, they argued that the Act unconstitutionally delegated the power to define crimes. Conceding that the statute contained an "intelligible principle" with respect to temporary scheduling, they argued "that something more than an 'intelligible principle' is required when Congress authorizes another Branch to promulgate regulations that contemplate criminal sanctions." Justice O'Connor, for a unanimous Court, determined that the Act "passes muster even if greater congressional specificity is required in the criminal context." Her opinion went on to emphasize that the government conceded in its brief that the statutory bar on judicial review merely postpones a pre-enforcement challenge until the permanent scheduling is completed[6] and, in any event, "does not preclude an individual facing criminal charges from bringing a challenge to a temporary scheduling order as a defense to prosecution." The latter opportunity is "sufficient to permit a court to 'ascertain whether the will of Congress has been obeyed.'" (quoting Yakus).

Finally, in LOVING V. UNITED STATES, 517 U.S. 748 (1996), a soldier under sentence of death from a court martial challenged the delegation to the President of the power to set the conditions in which capital punishment would be imposed. Writing for the Court, Justice Kennedy rejected the challenge. He pointed out (citing Grimaud and Tobey) that "[t]here is no absolute rule ... against Congress' delegation of authority to define criminal punishments." Moreover, "the delegation here was to the President in his role as Commander in Chief." This role "require[s] him to take responsible and continuing action to superintend the military, including the courts-martial. The delegated duty, then, is interlinked with duties already assigned to the President by express terms of the Constitution, and the same limitations on delegation do not apply where the entity exercising the delegated authority itself possesses independent authority over the subject matter." [internal quote omitted] No one dissented.

TODD D. RAKOFF, THE SHAPE OF THE LAW IN THE AMERICAN ADMINISTRATIVE STATE, 11 Tel Aviv U. Studies in Law 9, 20, 21–23, 24, 39 (1992): "There is ... more than one way to divide up the power of government. The Constitution establishes three branches of government, legislative, executive and judicial; each has some power over a very large range of subject

---

6. "Pre-enforcement" review refers to an action—typically for declaratory and/or injunctive relief—challenging the legality of a rule after it is final but before it has been enforced against the plaintiff. See pp. 1182, 1252 below. When available, this option permits private parties to challenge the legality of agency action without running the risk of violating the rule and attempting to fend off sanctions by attacking it defensively.

matters, but is often unable to act effectively without the participation of one or both of the other branches. This is the 'separation of powers': branches of government that are 'omnicompetent' as regards subject-matter but 'unipowered' as regards the tools at their disposal. One could divide power the other way around. One could create organs of government that were 'omnipowered'—able to legislate, execute, adjudicate—but 'unicompetent'—entitled to exercise their many powers over only a small terrain. It is this second path that has been chosen in the fashioning of American regulatory agencies. . . .

"If the maxim that the only safe power is divided power is indeed a cultural norm, what would be taboo would be the creation of an organ of government at once omnipowered and omnicompetent. Congress would appear to operate on that maxim, as it has almost never tried to bring such an agency into being. The closest it has come was in the middle of the Great Depression, with the passage of the National Industrial Recovery Act. . . . But this example, far from disproving the force of the principle, in fact establishes it, for this Act is also the only one the Supreme Court has ever invalidated on the ground that it was, simply, an unlawful delegation of power. . . . Omnicompetence, or something near it, cannot, it seems, be delegated."

c.   THE FUTURE OF NONDELEGATION DOCTRINE

The Supreme Court's opinion in American Trucking may seem anticlimactic after the unabashed constitutional adventurism of the lower court opinions. Does it presage the end of the wave of delegation challenges inspired by the Benzene case? Certainly Justice Stevens (author of the Benzene plurality opinion) seems ready to renounce nondelegation analysis. On the other hand, Justice Thomas goes out of his way to invite a fundamental rethinking of the current doctrinal approach. And what are we to make of the fact that Justice Scalia's opinion for the Court returns to the pre-New Deal formalism of insisting that, whatever kind of power is delegated by regulatory statutes, it cannot be "legislative" power—especially in light of his position in Mistretta [pp. 63, 75 above] that "the scope of delegation is largely uncontrollable by the courts," *and* that "a certain degree of discretion, and thus of law-making, inheres in most executive or judicial action"?

The student (or lawyer, or judge) contemplating the optimal future of nondelegation jurisprudence might usefully focus on four questions posed by Professor Peter Schuck: "What is the nature of the delegation problem? What should be our goals in seeking to control delegation? In the absence of a nondelegation doctrine, is agency lawmaking effectively constrained? What would be the consequences of reviving the nondelegation doctrine?"[1] Here is a selection of views on various of these questions.

(1) JONATHAN R. MACEY, TRANSACTION COSTS AND THE NORMATIVE ELEMENTS OF THE PUBLIC CHOICE MODEL: AN APPLICATION TO CONSTITUTIONAL THEORY, 74 Va. L.

---

1.   Peter H. Schuck, Delegation and Democracy: Comments on David Schoenbrod, 20 Cardozo L.Rev. 775 (1999).

Rev. 471 (1988): "In any advanced society, persons in search of profit must decide whether to allocate their efforts to the private sector, where they pursue a strategy of wealth creation through trading, or to the public sector, where they (for good or ill) pursue a strategy of wealth transfer through rent-seeking. The latter strategy provides counter-incentives to wealth creation and eventually will sap a nation of its wealth. The core function of a well-ordered constitutional regime is to restrain such wealth transfers and guide transactions to the private sphere.

"... [T]he governmental structure created by the Constitution [can be] viewed as a means of raising transaction costs to interest groups intent on pursuing a policy of rent-seeking. These increased costs lower the incidence of redistributive wealth transfers to the politically powerful and, at the margin, guide profit seekers back to the private sector.

"The constitutional strategy of raising transaction costs manifests itself in two ways. The first is through language, textual admonitions to those in government not to shift costs to the politically weak. This strategy, however, is likely to prove ineffective over time. American constitutional history is a testament to the proposition that the language of constitutional directives, such as those contained in the contract clause, the commerce clause, and the takings clause, is almost infinitely malleable. As a result, constitutional directives do not hold much promise as effective constraints on rent-seeking behavior.

"Alternatively, constitutions can seek to constrain rent-seekers by creating institutional structures that effectively raise the transaction costs of organized interest group activity. It is this strategy that holds real promise for establishing a successful constitutional order. Structural features such as the executive veto, the independent judiciary, and the bicameral legislature (with differentiated house sizes) are best seen as structural devices that raise the costs of rent-seeking.

. . .

"... [Through delegation, however,] legislators who want to avoid controversial or indeterminate decisions as to which interest groups to favor can forfeit vast amounts of discretion (and thus responsibility and accountability) to administrative agencies, which function outside of the tripartite legislative process envisioned by our constitutional structure. The modern administrative agency lowers the cost to interest groups of influencing the political process; it conflicts in the most fundamental way imaginable with the core constitutional function of raising the transaction costs to interest groups of obtaining passage of favored legislation."

(2) MARK SEIDENFELD, A CIVIC REPUBLICAN JUSTIFICATION FOR THE BUREAUCRATIC STATE, 105 Harv. L. Rev. 1511, 1514, 1541–42 (1992): "Administrative agencies—the so-called fourth branch of government—may be the only institutions capable of fulfilling the civic republican ideal of deliberative decisionmaking. Congress adheres primarily to pluralistic norms and responds most directly to factional influence. ... Courts ... are too far removed from the voice of the citizenry, and judges' backgrounds are too homogenous and distinct from those of many Americans to ensure that judicially-defined policy will accord with the public values of the polity.

"Administrative agencies, however, fall between the extremes of the politically over-responsive Congress and the over-insulated courts. . . . The place of administrative agencies in government—subordinate and responsible to Congress, the courts, and the President—allows for the checks on agency decisionmaking that ensure politically informed discourse and prevent purely politically-driven outcomes. The bureaucratic structure of administrative agencies and the processes by which they frequently decide questions of policy also foster deliberative government. . . .

"At the core of almost every agency is a professional staff, chosen for its knowledge rather than for its political views or affiliations. The staff forms the base of a pyramid that has the ultimate decisionmakers, who are generally political appointees, at the apex. Although these appointees generate the agency's policy agenda, they depend on the bureaucrats below to evaluate the various alternatives for implementing broad policies. Career staff members derive their power primarily from their professional training and their relationships with interest group representatives who frequently control important information—in other words, from job-specific expertise. This expertise allows bureaucrats to exert significant influence on public policy even when their role is merely advisory. Although career staff rarely initiate consideration of general policies, the debate over policy alternatives often starts at lower levels and travels up the pyramid. This process has the potential to focus the debate on a professional understanding of the public interest rather than on accommodation of private interests. . . .

". . . In particular, the paradigmatic process for agency formulation of policy—informal rulemaking—is specifically geared to advance the requirements of civic republican theory. Informal rulemaking requires public notice sufficient to inform interest groups that the agency is considering a policy that might affect them. Any group that keeps abreast of developments at a particular agency or regularly reviews the Federal Register learns of the agency's commencement of an informal rulemaking proceeding. Comment procedures provide relatively easy access to the discourse among interest groups and the dialogue between those groups and decisionmakers. . . .

"With proper constraints on bureaucratic decisionmaking, the agencies' place in government, the professional nature of the agencies' staff, and the procedures agencies have traditionally used to set policy suggest that the administrative state holds the best promise for achieving the civic republican ideal of inclusive and deliberative lawmaking."

(3) JOHN HART ELY, DEMOCRACY AND DISTRUST, A THEORY OF JUDICIAL REVIEW, 131–33 (1980): "[T]he fact seems to be that on most hard issues our representatives quite shrewdly prefer not to have to stand up and be counted but rather to let some executive-branch bureaucrat, or perhaps some independent regulatory commission, 'take the inevitable political heat.' As Congressman Levitas put it, 'When hard decisions have to be made, we pass the buck to the agencies with vaguely worded statutes.' . . .

"Now this is wrong, not because it isn't 'the way it was meant to be' . . . but rather because it is undemocratic, in the quite obvious sense that by refusing to legislate, our legislators are escaping the sort of accountability that is crucial to the intelligible functioning of a democratic republic. . . .

There can be little point in worrying about the distribution of the franchise and other personal political rights unless the important policy choices are being made by elected officials. Courts thus should ensure not only that administrators follow those legislative policy directions that do exist . . . but also that such directions are given."

(4) JERRY L. MASHAW, GREED, CHAOS, AND GOVERNANCE, 152–53, 155 (1997): "Strangely enough it may make sense to imagine the delegation of political authority to administrators as a device for improving the responsiveness of government to the desires of the electorate. . . .

" . . . The high transaction costs of legislating specifically suggests that legislative activity directed to the modification of administration mandates will be infrequent. Agencies will thus persist with their statutory empowering provisions relatively intact over substantial periods of time.

"Voter preferences on the direction and intensity of governmental activities, however, are not likely to be so stable. Indeed, one can reasonably expect that a president will be able to affect policy in a four-year term only because being elected president entails acquiring the power to exercise, direct, or influence policy discretion. The group of executive officers we commonly call 'the administration' matters only because of the relative malleability of the directions that administrators have in their charge. . . . [I]t seems likely that the flexibility that is currently built into the processes of administrative governance by relatively broad delegations of statutory authority permits a more appropriate degree of administrative, or administration, responsiveness to the voter's [sic] will than would a strict nondelegation doctrine. . . ."

" . . . Responsiveness to the will of the people is not a unitary phenomenon that can be embodied in a single institution. Broad delegations recognize that tight accountability linkages at one point in the governmental system may reduce the responsiveness of the system as a whole."

(5) DAVID SCHOENBROD, POWER WITHOUT RESPONSIBILITY 183–84 (1993): "In making laws, Congress has to allocate both rights and duties in the very course of stating what conduct it prohibits, and so must make manifest the benefits and costs of regulation. When Congress delegates, it tends to do only half its job—to distribute rights without imposing the commensurate duties. So it promises clean air without restricting polluters and higher incomes for farmers without increasing the price of groceries. In striking poses popular to each and every constituency, Congress ducks the key conflicts. Those conflicts, however, will inevitably surface when the agency tries to translate the popular abstractions of the statutory goals—such as 'clean' air or 'orderly' agricultural markets—into rules of conduct. . . . [D]elegation allows legislators to claim credit for the benefits which a regulatory statute promises yet escape the blame for the burdens it will impose, because they do not issue the laws needed to achieve those benefits. The public inevitably must suffer regulatory burdens to realize regulatory benefits, but the laws will come from an agency that legislators can then criticize for imposing excessive burdens on their constituents. Just as deficit spending allows legislators to appear to deliver money to some people without taking it from others, delegation allows them to appear to deliver regulatory benefits without imposing regulatory costs."

(6) PETER H. SCHUCK, DELEGATION AND DEMOCRACY: COMMENTS ON DAVID SCHOEN-
BROD, 20 Cardozo L. Rev. 775 (1999): "[Professor Schoenbrod] fails to see
. . . that the particular attributes of the legislature's delegation—its
breadth, type, and level—are themselves fundamental policy choices. . . .
The optimal specificity and other delegation-related features of the legislation are among the questions on which almost all of the parties to these
legislative struggles—congressional committees, legislative staffs, the White
House, regulated firms, 'public interest' groups, state and local governments, and others—tend to stake out clear positions, for they know the
resolution of these questions may well determine the nature and effectiveness of the regulatory scheme being established. The issue of statutory
specificity is not resolved sub silentio or by default, as Professor Schoenbrod suggests. Rather, it is a focal point of the political maneuvering in the
legislature.

"Legislation is only part of the process of responsible lawmaking, and
it is becoming a less important part. In some important respects, this is for
the better. Today, the administrative agency is often the site where public
participation in lawmaking is most accessible, most meaningful, and most
effective.

"The administrative agency is often the most accessible site for public
participation because the costs of participating in the rulemaking and more
informal agency processes, where many of the most important policy
choices are in fact made, are likely to be lower than the costs of lobbying or
otherwise seeking to influence Congress. . . .

"The agency is often a more meaningful site for public participation
than Congress, because the policy stakes for individuals and interest groups
are most immediate, transparent, and well-defined at the agency level. One
can scarcely exaggerate the importance of this consideration to the legitimacy of democratic politics and to the substantive content of public policy.
After all, it is only at the agency level that the generalities of legislation are
broken down and concretized into discrete, specific issues with which
affected parties can hope to deal. . . . God and the devil are in the details of
policymaking, as they are in most other important things—and the details
are to be found at the agency level. . . .

"Finally, the agency is often the site in which public participation is
most effective. . . . [T]he agency is where the public can best educate the
government about the true nature of the problem that Congress has tried
to address. Only the interested parties, reacting to specific agency proposals
for rules or other actions, possess (or have the incentives to acquire) the
information necessary to identify, explicate, quantify, and evaluate the real-
world consequences of these and alternative proposals. . . . When policies
fail, it is usually. . . . because Congress did not fully appreciate how the
details of policy implementation would confound its purpose. Often, however, this knowledge can only be gained through active public participation in
the policymaking process at the agency level where these implementation
issues are most clearly focused and the stakes in their correct resolution
are highest."

(7) GARY LAWSON, THE RISE AND THE RISE OF THE ADMINISTRATIVE STATE, 107
Harv. L. Rev. 1231, 1239 (1994): "The task is . . . to determine when a

statute that vests discretionary authority in an executive (or judicial) officer has crossed the line. . . . [T]he core of the Constitution's nondelegation principle can be expressed as follows: Congress must make whatever policy decisions are sufficiently important to the statutory scheme at issue that Congress must make them. Although this circular formulation may seem farcical, it recognizes that a statute's required degree of specificity depends on context, takes seriously the well-recognized distinction between legislating and gap-filling, and corresponds reasonably well to judicial application of the nondelegation principle in the first 150 years of the nation's history."

(8) RICHARD B. STEWART, THE REFORMATION OF AMERICAN ADMINISTRATIVE LAW, 88 Harv. L.Rev. 1669, 1696–97 (1975): "How does the judge differentiate [cases in which the legislature has been as specific as is reasonably demanded] from those where the legislature is avoiding its 'proper' responsibilities? Such judgments are necessarily quite subjective, and a doctrine that made them determinative of an administrative program's legitimacy could cripple the program by exposing it to continuing threats of invalidation and encouraging the utmost recalcitrance by those opposed to its effectuation. Given such subjective standards, and the controversial character of decisions on whether to invalidate legislative delegations, such decisions will almost inevitably appear partisan, and might often be so."

(9) PETER L. STRAUSS, LEGISLATIVE THEORY AND THE RULE OF LAW: SOME COMMENTS ON RUBIN, 89 Colum. L. Rev. 427, 442–43 (1989): One "way to assess the failures or successes of the delegation doctrine might be to look at the behavior of government agencies in formulating and defending their work-product. Thousands of government attorneys spend much of their time demonstrating in internal memoranda, and when relevant in opinions, rulemakings, and judicial briefs, the bases on which proposed official action can be thought authorized (or not) by governing statutes. . . . Government attorneys do not think it relevant ('safe' is perhaps a better term) to argue that, since a statute was imprecise or broadly worded, the agency may do anything it pleases, or that a court or other outside observer cannot competently tell whether it is or is not acting within authority. They acknowledge the obligation to demonstrate authority—and with it, all the other issues about regularity that follow, such as consistency with (or an explanation of departure from) prior results, procedural correctness and the appropriate exercise of judgment.

"The delegation doctrine thus provides the impetus for agency concessions that the exercise of certain forms of discretion is subject to review for 'abuse.' Even if we must acknowledge at the outset that the agency will often succeed in justifying its conduct, precisely because the statutory formula is diffuse (very often deliberately) and agency discretion correspondingly large, the stance won—that the agency must be prepared to justify its behavior to outside assessors in accordance with principles of regularity and legality—is no trivial matter. The very fact of confidence in the possibility of supervision, and the winning of behavior from government that acknowledges its appropriateness and inevitability, lies at the heart of a commitment to the rule of law. This sense of delegation, . . . constitutional in character, remains vital."

(10) LISA SCHULTZ BRESSMAN, DISCIPLINING DELEGATION AFTER WHITMAN v. AMERICAN TRUCKING ASS'NS, 87 Cornell L. Rev. 452, 460, 461–62 (2002): "Administrative law is a more effective tool [than constitutional law] for addressing the delegation issue. . . . [C]ourts owe Congress a greater degree of leeway to formulate delegations under constitutional law than they owe agencies to exercise those delegations under administrative law. This conclusion proceeds directly from the practical recognition, acknowledged most fully by Justice Scalia in Mistretta v. United States, that Congress needs room to fix the limits of delegation 'according to common sense and the inherent necessities of [government].' [458 U.S. at 416 (dissenting op.)] Once courts permit Congress some latitude to write vague delegations, 'the debate over unconstitutional delegation becomes a debate not over a point of principle but over a question of degree.' [Id. at 415.] Courts should not 'second-guess' Congress on an issue that involves consideration of factors 'both multifarious and (in the nonpartisan sense) highly political.' [Id. at 416.] That is not to say that Congress always has good motives for delegating. But courts must give Congress the benefit of the doubt if we are to have modern government. Thus, they should respect Congress's determination and relinquishment of authority.

"At the same time, courts must insist that some governmental actor take responsibility for the hard choices of regulatory policy. Responsibility in this context means articulating the standards that direct and cabin administrative discretion. In a sense, Congress implicitly delegates that responsibility to agencies as part of their broader regulatory authority. *If courts allow Congress implicitly to delegate such responsibility, they must require agencies expressly to assume it. . . .*

"[Thus, precedent and policy support] a shift from constitutional law to administrative law for addressing the delegation issue. Using administrative law as a delegation doctrine obviously avoids revising constitutional doctrine or questioning the validity of a congressional statute. In addition, it provides theoretical grounding and practical guidance for requiring administrative standards. As a theoretical matter, administrative law already contains principles that fit comfortably with an administrative-standards requirement. These principles, together with an administrative-standards requirement, require agencies, in exchange for broad grants of policymaking authority, to demonstrate that they have used their authority in an open, regular, and rational fashion. They require agencies in general to articulate a basis for their policy determinations and, in particular, to articulate the standards for those determinations. In the absence of these principles, there is no protection (or recourse) against arbitrary lawmaking at any level of government. These principles also help to define administrative standards and suggest when they are missing."

d.   COMPARATIVE INSIGHTS: THE EXPERIENCE OF OTHER JURISDICTIONS

How do other democratic governments with regulatory ambitions deal with the issue of delegation?

(i) DELEGATION IN THE STATES

To begin close to home, we might look to the laboratories of the 50 states.[1] The separation-of-powers and checks-and-balances principles of the U.S. Constitution apply only to the national government. States are free to accept or reject these principles in whole or part and, while doubtless affected by U.S. Supreme Court views, can give them whatever interpretation seems appropriate.[2]

Indeed, state supreme courts have deployed the nondelegation doctrine with notable frequency to invalidate state regulatory schemes. Why do state judges appear to approach legislative delegations with a more aggressive skepticism than do their federal counterparts? Knowledgeable observers (who include a former Chief Justice of the Supreme Court of Oregon) have suggested several possibilities: "(i) The typical paucity of legislative history of state laws makes resort to it less promising, and more haphazard and unreliable when attempted. (ii) While federal law is recognized to be almost wholly statutory, counsel and judges in state courts tend to approach a public law case from a common law background of practice and with common law rather than statute law methods of briefing and argument. (iii) There may be a different degree of institutional respect and deference toward the legislative branch and its products; in any event, state courts are far less reluctant to hold that a legislature has misconstrued and exceeded its powers than federal courts are to hold that Congress has done so. (iv) Similarly state courts may have a different, and realistic, view of the professional capacity and impartiality of many agencies to whom power is delegated in the states as compared with federal agencies." Moreover, "[a] special class of problems more common in state law is the delegation of public decision-making authority to private groups, or to representatives of private groups appointed to part-time public positions."[3]

Boreali v. Axelrod

Court of Appeals of New York, 1987.[1]
71 N.Y.2d 1, 523 N.Y.S.2d 464, 517 N.E.2d 1350.

■ TITONE, J.

. . . [G]rowing concern about the deleterious effects of tobacco smoking led our State Legislature to enact a bill in 1975 restricting smoking in certain designated areas, specifically, libraries, museums, theaters and

---

1. "It is one of the happy incidents of the federal system that a single courageous state may, if its citizens choose, serve as a laboratory; and try novel social and economic experiments without risk to the rest of the country." New State Ice Co. v. Liebmann, 285 U.S. 262 (1932) (Brandeis, J., dissenting).

2. In theory, a state's choice of government structure might be so anomalous as to offend the federal constitution's guaranty to the states of a "republican form of government." U.S. Const. Art. IV, § 4. However,

since Luther v. Borden, 7 How. 1, 12 L.Ed. 581 (1849), claims under the Guaranty Clause (with the possible exception of voting rights claims, see New York v. United States, 505 U.S. 144, 183–86 (1992)) have been regarded as nonjusticiable political questions.

3. Hans Linde, George Bunn, Fredericka Paff, and W. Lawrence Church, Legislative and Administrative Processes 477–78 (2d ed. 1981).

1. [Ed.] The Court of Appeals is New York's highest court.

public transportation facilities. Efforts during the same year to adopt more expansive restrictions on smoking in public places were, however, unsuccessful. ... [W]hile some 40 bills on the subject have been introduced in the Legislature since 1975, none have passed both houses.

In late 1986 the Public Health Council (PHC) took action of its own. Purportedly acting pursuant to the broad grant of authority contained in its enabling statute, the PHC published proposed rules, held public hearings and, in February of 1987, promulgated the final set of regulations prohibiting smoking in a wide variety of indoor areas that are open to the public, including schools, hospitals, auditoriums, food markets, stores, banks, taxicabs and limousines. Under these rules, restaurants with seating capacities of more than 50 people are required to provide contiguous nonsmoking areas sufficient to meet customer demand. Further, employers are required to provide smoke-free work areas for nonsmoking employees and to keep common areas free of smoke, with certain limited exceptions for cafeterias and lounges. Affected businesses are permitted to prohibit all smoking on the premises if they so choose. Expressly excluded from the regulations' coverage are restaurants with seating capacities of less than 50, conventions, trade shows, bars, private homes, private automobiles, private social functions, hotel and motel rooms and retail tobacco stores. Additional "waivers" of the regulations' restrictions may be obtained from the Commissioner upon a showing of financial hardship. Implementation of these regulations, which were to become effective May 7, 1987, has been suspended during the pendency of this litigation. ...

Section 225(5)(a) of the Public Health Law authorizes the PHC to "deal with any matters affecting the ... public health." At the heart of the present case is the question whether this broad grant of authority contravened the oft-recited principle that the legislative branch of government cannot cede its fundamental policy-making responsibility to an administrative agency. As a related matter, we must also inquire whether, assuming the propriety of the Legislature's grant of authority, the agency exceeded the permissible scope of its mandate by using it as a basis for engaging in inherently legislative activities. While the separation of powers doctrine gives the Legislature considerable leeway in delegating its regulatory powers, enactments conferring authority on administrative agencies in broad or general terms must be interpreted in light of the limitations that the Constitution imposes (N.Y. Const., art. III, § 1). ...

Derived from the separation of powers doctrine, the principle that the legislative branch may not delegate all of its lawmaking powers to the executive branch has been applied with the utmost reluctance—even in the early case law. ... [M]any of this court's decisions uphold[] legislative delegations of authority that are circumscribed in only the most general of terms. Indeed, the precise provision that is at issue in this case—Public Health Law § 225(5)(a)—has been upheld against a constitutional challenge based upon the "nondelegation" doctrine (Chiropractic Assn. v. Hilleboe, 12 N.Y.2d 109, 119–120).[2]

---

2. [Ed.] The regulation at issue in Chiropractic Assn. restricted chiropractors' use of X–ray machinery, regardless of patient consent—a restriction not difficult to connect with the economic interests of medical radiologists as well as a concern for public safety.

This does not mean, however, that the regulations at issue here should be deemed valid without further analysis. To the contrary, the courts have previously struck down administrative actions undertaken under otherwise permissible enabling legislation where the challenged action could not have been deemed within that legislation without giving rise to a constitutional separation of powers problem (see, e.g., Industrial Union Dept. v. American Petroleum Inst., 448 U.S. 607, 645–646; National Cable Tel. Assn. v. United States, 415 U.S. 336, 341–342.)

A number of coalescing circumstances that are present in this case persuade us that the difficult-to-define line between administrative rule-making and legislative policy-making has been transgressed. While none of these circumstances, standing alone, is sufficient to warrant the conclusion that the PHC has usurped the Legislature's prerogative, all of these circumstances, when viewed in combination, paint a portrait of an agency that has improperly assumed for itself "[t]he open-ended discretion to choose ends" (Tribe, American Constitutional Law, p. 285), which characterizes the elected Legislature's role in our system of government.

First, while generally acting to further the laudable goal of protecting nonsmokers from the harmful effects of "passive smoking," the PHC has, in reality, constructed a regulatory scheme laden with exceptions based solely upon economic and social concerns. The exemptions the PHC has carved out for bars, convention centers, small restaurants, and the like, as well as the provision it has made for "waivers" based on financial hardship, have no foundation in considerations of public health. Rather, they demonstrate the agency's own effort to weigh the goal of promoting health against its social cost and to reach a suitable compromise. . . .

Striking the proper balance among health concerns, cost and privacy interests, however, is a uniquely legislative function. While it is true that many regulatory decisions involve weighing economic and social concerns against the specific values that the regulatory agency is mandated to promote, the agency in this case has not been authorized to structure its decision making in a "cost-benefit" model (cf., American Textile Mfrs. Inst. v. Donovan, 452 U.S. 490, 543–548 [Rehnquist, J., dissenting]) and, in fact, has not been given any legislative guidelines at all for determining how the competing concerns of public health and economic cost are to be weighed. Thus, to the extent that the agency has built a regulatory scheme on its own conclusions about the appropriate balance of trade-offs between health and cost to particular industries in the private sector, it was "acting solely on [its] own ideas of sound public policy" and was therefore operating outside of its proper sphere of authority (Matter of Picone v. Commissioner of Licenses, 241 N.Y. 157, 162). This conclusion is particularly compelling here, where the focus is on administratively created exemptions rather than on rules that promote the legislatively expressed goals, since exemptions ordinarily run counter to such goals and, consequently, cannot be justified as simple implementations of legislative values. . . .

The second, and related, consideration is that in adopting the anti-smoking regulations challenged here the PHC did not merely fill in the details of broad legislation describing the over-all policies to be implemented. Instead, the PHC wrote on a clean slate, creating its own comprehensive set of rules without benefit of legislative guidance. Viewed in that light, the agency's actions were a far cry from the "interstitial" rule making that typifies administrative regulatory activity.

A third indicator that the PHC exceeded the scope of the authority properly delegated to it by the Legislature is the fact that the agency acted in an area in which the Legislature had repeatedly tried—and failed—to reach agreement in the face of substantial public debate and vigorous lobbying by a variety of interested factions. While we have often been reluctant to ascribe persuasive significance to legislative inaction, our usual hesitancy in this area has no place here. Unlike the cases in which we have been asked to consider the Legislature's failure to act as some indirect proof of its actual intentions, in this case it is appropriate for us to consider the significance of legislative inaction as evidence that the Legislature has so far been unable to reach agreement on the goals and methods that should govern in resolving a society-wide health problem. Here, the repeated failures by the Legislature to arrive at such an agreement do not automatically entitle an administrative agency to take it upon itself to fill the vacuum and impose a solution of its own. Manifestly, it is the province of the people's elected representatives, rather than appointed administrators, to resolve difficult social problems by making choices among competing ends.

Finally, although indoor smoking is unquestionably a health issue, no special expertise or technical competence in the field of health was involved in the development of the antismoking regulations challenged here. Faced with mounting evidence about the hazards to bystanders of indoor smoking, the PHC drafted a simple code describing the locales in which smoking would be prohibited and providing exemptions for various special interest groups. The antismoking regulations at issue here are thus distinguishable from those at issue in Chiropractic Assn. v. Hilleboe, in which we stressed that the PHC's technical competence was necessary to flesh out details of the broadly stated legislative policies embodied in the Public Health Law.

Conclusion

Although Public Health Law § 225(5)(a) confers broad powers on the Public Health Council and there is no indication that the Legislature intended to circumscribe those powers when it enacted a limited antismoking measure of its own, the fundamental constitutional limitations on the respective powers of the legislative and executive branches foreclose a construction of the statute that would include the administrative activity challenged here. In promulgating its antismoking rules, the PHC transgressed the line that separates administrative rule making from legislating and thereby exceeded its statutory powers. Consequently, its actions cannot be upheld.

Accordingly, the order of the Appellate Division should be affirmed.

■ Bellacosa, J. (dissenting).

. . . The statutory authority for protecting the public health was delegated by the Legislature to the PHC 75 years ago in the broadest possible mandate and it has not been withdrawn or narrowed. Indeed, it has been exercised regularly with this court's express approbation. That power includes adoption and amendment to the Sanitary Code dealing with the root source of authority here—"matters affecting the security of life or health or the preservation and improvement of public health." . . . This antismoking regulation is a fortiori valid compared to the regulation in Chiropractic Assn. v. Hilleboe, which was a restriction on the freedom and access to chiropractic X-ray treatments, protecting patients from their own choices. Inasmuch as the Public Health Council could do that with our approbation, we search in vain for reasons in the majority's decision that the same statutory source of authority cannot protect the public health of innocent, involuntary *third-party victims* from others with this limited regulation. . . .

The Legislature declared its intent that there be a PHC in this State and empowered it to adopt a Sanitary Code for the preservation and improvement of the public health. The Legislature also wisely refrained from enacting a rigid formula for the exercise of the PHC's critical agenda of concerns because that calls for expert attention. That legislative forbearance represents both a sound administrative law principle and, at the threshold, a constitutional one as well. The Legislature could not have foreseen in 1913 the specific need for PHC regulations in areas of human blood collection, care and storage; X-ray film usage; pesticide labels; drinking water contamination; or a myriad of other public health topics. . . . While the court admits the difficulty under the high separation of powers standard of articulating the basis for drawing, and even finding, some line limiting the PHC's conceded exercise of authority, it nevertheless goes ahead and does so. Its line is no line, but rather an arbitrary judgment call of its own. It is this judicial branch intrusion which constitutes the truly egregious separation of powers breach into the exercise of prerogatives of the Legislature (Public Health Law § 225[4], [5][a] [enabling legislation]) and of the executive (10 NYCRR 25.2 [implementing regulation]).

NOTE

In the aftermath of Boreali, local boards of health across New York adopted regulations limiting smoking in public places. Many of these local agencies expressly framed their deliberations in an attempt to avoid the problems PHC had encountered in Boreali. (If you were counsel to a county board of health, how would you advise your client to proceed?) Somewhat peculiarly, litigation challenging these regulations has tended to occur in the federal courts. Restaurant owners have attacked the regulations as violating federal constitutional Equal Protection and First Amendment rights, and have added counts under the New York Constitution pursuant to supplemental jurisdiction. The result, in several cases, has been a decision rejecting the federal constitutional claims but enjoining the regulations on state constitutional grounds. Federal district judges have been uniformly unpersuaded that local health boards could successfully regulate "around" Boreali. The latest in the series is Dutchess/Putnam Restaurant

& Tavern Assoc., Inc. v. Putnam County Dep't of Health, 178 F.Supp.2d 396 (S.D.N.Y.2001). Thus far, both the Court of Appeals for the Second Circuit and the New York Court of Appeals have remained silent.

Texas Boll Weevil Eradication Foundation, Inc. v. Lewellen

Supreme Court of Texas, 1997.
952 S.W.2d 454.

■ PHILLIPS, CHIEF JUSTICE, delivered the Opinion of the Court as to Parts I, II, IV, and V, in which OWEN, JUSTICE, joins. GONZALEZ and BAKER, JUSTICES, join in Parts I, IV, and V of the Court's Opinion and in the judgment. HECHT, JUSTICE, joins in Parts IV and V of the Court's Opinion and in the judgment. CORNYN, ENOCH, SPECTOR and ABBOTT, JUSTICES, join in Parts I, II, and IV of the Court's Opinion.

Subchapter 74D of the Texas Agriculture Code (the Act) provides for the creation and operation of an "Official Cotton Growers' Boll Weevil Eradication Foundation." Subject to referendum approval from the affected cotton growers, this Foundation is authorized to operate boll weevil eradication programs and assess the growers for the cost. Appellees in these consolidated direct appeals, who are cotton growers subject to the Foundation's jurisdiction, filed declaratory judgment actions challenging the Foundation's assessments on a variety of constitutional and statutory grounds. The trial court in each case invalidated the assessments and enjoined their collection. . . .

We . . . conclude . . . that the Legislature made an unconstitutionally broad delegation of authority to the Foundation, a private entity, thereby violating Article II, Section 1 of the Texas Constitution. For this reason, without reaching all the other constitutional and statutory arguments raised by appellees, we affirm the judgments of the trial courts.

I

There is no dispute among the parties to these appeals or the numerous amici curiae that the Anthonomus grandis Boheman, an insect commonly known as the boll weevil, presents a major economic threat to the Texas cotton industry. This pest, which entered Texas from Mexico in 1892, causes an estimated $20 million in crop loss in Texas every year. To aid in the ongoing battle against the boll weevil, the Legislature in 1993 authorized the creation of the Official Cotton Growers' Boll Weevil Eradication Foundation. Instead of directly creating the Foundation, however, the Legislature merely authorized the Commissioner of Agriculture to certify some nonprofit organization representing cotton growers to create the Foundation and propose geographic eradication zones. The Act authorizes the creating organization or the Foundation to conduct referenda in each proposed eradication zone ("zone referenda") to determine whether those cotton growers desire to establish an official boll weevil eradication zone. Contemporaneous with the zone referendum, the growers are also to elect a member to represent them on the Foundation's board. If the growers vote not to establish a zone, their board selection is without effect.

Under the Act, once the initial zone has been created and the first board member elected, the growers of that zone must approve the assessment to fund the eradication at a subsequent referendum. Thereafter, the board is authorized to determine the assessment needed for each additional participating zone, which must be approved by the growers at a referendum. The Foundation may collect the assessment only if the assessment referendum passes. Approval of a zone and of the assessment each requires a vote of either two-thirds of the cotton growers in the zone or of those who farm more than one-half of the cotton acreage in the zone. The election of board members, on the other hand, requires only a plurality vote.

The Foundation exercises broad governmental powers. Besides being authorized to conduct elections in proposed eradication zones, the board may add an area to a zone under certain circumstances if approved by a referendum of cotton growers in the area. The board determines what eradication programs to conduct. The Foundation may impose penalties for late payment of assessments. A cotton grower who fails to pay an assessment within ten days of its due date must destroy his cotton crop. If the grower fails to do so, his crop is automatically declared a public nuisance. On the Foundation's recommendation, and after notice, the Department of Agriculture must destroy it, even if not infested with boll weevils, at the owner's cost. In addition, a cotton grower who violates the statute (including, presumably, by failing to pay an assessment or failing to destroy his own crop if payment is more than ten days late) is guilty of a Class C misdemeanor. Cotton which a delinquent grower has already produced and harvested is subject to a lien. Representatives of the Foundation may enter private property which is subject to eradication without the owner's permission for any purpose under the Act, including "the treatment, monitoring, and destruction of growing cotton or other host plants." Finally, the Commissioner and the Foundation may adopt rules necessary to carry out the purposes of the Act.

While growers in a zone must approve their assessments, they do not approve the type of eradication program or the amount of debt incurred by the Foundation to finance it. These matters are left to the Foundation's discretion. If the eradication program is discontinued for any reason, the Foundation may continue collecting assessments "as necessary to pay the financial obligations of the foundation."

Under the Act, some power is retained by the Commissioner of Agriculture. For example, the Foundation can change the number of board positions or the eradication zone representation on the board only with the Commissioner's approval. The Commissioner must also make rules to protect life and property from pesticides and other aspects of eradication programs. The Commissioner may prohibit planting cotton in zones when it would jeopardize the success of an eradication program. The Commissioner may exempt a cotton grower from payment of the Foundation's assessment penalties if payment would leave the grower with less than $15,000 taxable income. The Foundation may expend revenue only on "programs approved by the commissioner as consistent with this subchapter and applicable provisions of the constitution." Finally, the Commissioner must determine when elimination of boll weevils is no longer necessary to prevent economic loss to cotton growers.

After a referendum has passed, the cotton growers in the zone must be allowed to conduct referenda "periodically" under the terms prescribed in the initial referendum to determine whether to continue their assessments, although the Act says nothing about how often these referenda must occur. In addition, the Foundation must conduct a referendum on whether to discontinue the program on the petition of at least forty percent of the cotton growers in the zone. As noted, however, the Foundation may continue to collect assessments previously approved to pay its financial obligations.

[Part II concluded that the scheme did not violate Art. III, § 1(c) of the Texas Constitution, which provides that "[p]ersons engaged in mechanical and agricultural pursuits shall never be required to pay an occupation tax" because it involved a regulatory fee rather than a tax. Part III found it a close question whether limits on the ability to challenge the Foundation's assessments violated federal procedural due process and Texas "open courts" rights, but declined to resolve these issues in light of the conclusion on delegation. Part IV rejected equal protection and substantive due process claims.]

V

Finally, we turn to the growers' argument that the Legislature violated Article II, Section 1 of the Texas Constitution, requiring the separation of powers between the legislative, executive, and judicial branches, by improperly delegating governmental authority to the Foundation. In particular, the growers contend that the Foundation is a private entity whose directors are neither constrained before they act by meaningful standards nor made accountable after they act by administrative, judicial, or popular review. In response, the Foundation contends that both the Legislature's guidelines and the Commissioner of Agriculture's supervisory authority are constitutionally adequate.

A

. . . The prohibition on unwarranted delegation of lawmaking power is "rooted in the principle of separation of powers that underlies our tripartite system of Government." Mistretta v. United States, 488 U.S. 361, 371 (1989). The United States Constitution expressly vests legislative power in the Congress, see U.S. Const. art. I, § 1, and the Texas Constitution similarly vests legislative power in our Legislature. See Tex. Const. art. II, § 1; art. III, § 1. Thus, "Congress is not permitted to abdicate or to transfer to others the essential legislative functions with which it is vested." A.L.A. Schechter Poultry Corp. v. United States, 295 U.S. 495, 529 (1935). Likewise, in our State "[t]he power to pass laws rests with the Legislature, and that power cannot be delegated to some commission or other tribunal." Brown v. Humble Oil & Refining Co., 83 S.W.2d 935, 941 (1935).

Yet, like many truisms, these blanket pronouncements should not be read too literally. Even in a simple society, a legislative body would be hard put to contend with every detail involved in carrying out its laws; in a complex society it is absolutely impossible to do so. Hence, legislative delegation of power to enforce and apply law is both necessary and proper. E.g., Field v. Clark, 143 U.S. 649, 693–694 (1892). Such power must almost always be exercised with a certain amount of discretion, and at times the line between making laws and enforcing them may blur. [The court's long quotation from Justice Scalia's Mistretta dissent is omitted.] While warning against "allowing delegation of power to exercise unguided discretion in individual cases," Professor Davis points out that "the kind of government we have developed could not operate without" allowing legislatures to delegate rulemaking authority to administrative bodies. Kenneth Culp Davis, 1 Administrative Law Treatise § 3.1, at 150 (2d ed. 1978). . . . Even before the Depression, one state court noted: "It only leads to confusion and error to say that the power to fill up the details and promulgate rules and regulations is not legislative power." State ex rel. Wisconsin Inspection Bureau v. Whitman, 196 Wis. 472 (1928).

Even in its heyday, the nondelegation doctrine was sparingly applied, having been used by the United States Supreme Court to strike down a federal statute only three times. Since the Court retreated from its opposition to New Deal initiatives, it has consistently upheld congressional delegations.

Texas courts have also generally upheld legislative delegations to state or municipal agencies. We most recently did so in Edgewood Independent School District v. Meno, 917 S.W.2d 717, 740–741 (Tex.1995), where we said:

> The Texas Legislature may delegate its powers to agencies established to carry out legislative purposes, as long as it establishes "reasonable standards to guide the entity to which the powers are delegated." Railroad Comm'n v. Lone Star Gas Co., 844 S.W.2d 679, 689 (Tex. 1992) (quoting State v. Texas Mun. Power Agency, 565 S.W.2d 258, 273 (Tex.Civ.App.—Houston [1st Dist.] 1978, writ dism'd)). "Requiring the legislature to include every detail and anticipate unforeseen circumstances would ... defeat the purpose of delegating legislative authority." Id.

* * *

The separation of powers clause [Tex. Const. art. II, § 1] requires that the standards of delegation be "reasonably clear and hence acceptable as a standard of measurement." Jordan v. State Bd. of Ins., 160 Tex. 506, 334 S.W.2d [278,] 280 [(1960)].

But there are some indications that extreme judicial deference to legislative delegation may be declining. A number of Supreme Court justices have emphasized the need for adequate legislative standards. ... Moreover, "[m]any distinguished scholars and judges [have become] so concerned about the enormous discretionary power of agencies that they [have] urged reinvigoration of the doctrine." Kenneth Culp Davis & Richard J. Pierce, Jr., 1 Administrative Law Treatise § 2.6, at 74 (3d Ed. 1994).

State courts may have less need to reinvigorate the doctrine, since they have historically been more comfortable with striking down state laws on

this basis than their federal counterparts. Texas courts are no exception.
. . .

B

As difficult as the issue of proper legislative delegation may be, the considerations are even more complex when the delegation is made not to another department or agency of government, but to a private individual or group. While at first blush such delegations might seem manifestly unconstitutional, further reflection demonstrates that they also are frequently necessary and desirable. Presumably no one would argue that the state should not accord the full benefits and responsibilities of a marital union to a couple who was married by a minister, priest, or rabbi rather than a judge. Also, the delegation of authority to private associations to promulgate certain industrial and professional standards has been of immense benefit to the public. For example, a number of states have adopted existing or future versions of the National Electrical Code, promulgated by an industry association, turning a technical and complex task often quite beyond the competence of many city councils or even state legislatures over to a specialized private group. [internal quotation omitted]

Still, private delegations clearly raise even more troubling constitutional issues than their public counterparts. On a practical basis, the private delegate may have a personal or pecuniary interest which is inconsistent with or repugnant to the public interest to be served. More fundamentally, the basic concept of democratic rule under a republican form of government is compromised when public powers are abandoned to those who are neither elected by the people, appointed by a public official or entity, nor employed by the government. Thus, we believe it axiomatic that courts should subject private delegations to a more searching scrutiny than their public counterparts. . . .

C

[The court concluded that, although the Foundation had some attributes of a public agency, it was a private entity for purposes of applying the nondelegation doctrine.]

D

Now we must determine what standard to apply in determining whether the private delegation was appropriate. Because of the additional risks posed by such delegations to the proper separation of governmental powers, a number of factors should be considered by a reviewing court. . . .

. . . [W]e prefer to condense the various inquiries posed by scholars and courts to these eight factors:

1. Are the private delegate's actions subject to meaningful review by a state agency or other branch of state government?

2. Are the persons affected by the private delegate's actions adequately represented in the decisionmaking process?

3. Is the private delegate's power limited to making rules, or does the delegate also apply the law to particular individuals?

4. Does the private delegate have a pecuniary or other personal interest that may conflict with his or her public function?

5. Is the private delegate empowered to define criminal acts or impose criminal sanctions?

6. Is the delegation narrow in duration, extent, and subject matter?

7. Does the private delegate possess special qualifications or training for the task delegated to it?

8. Has the Legislature provided sufficient standards to guide the private delegate in its work? . . .

First, while the Foundation is subject to some oversight by the Commissioner of Agriculture, the review is uneven and incomplete. The Legislature did direct the Commissioner to promulgate rules regarding certain areas of the Foundation's operations. The Commissioner is required to adopt rules for the zone referenda and board elections, rules specifying hardship exemptions from assessment penalties, and rules "to protect individuals, livestock, wildlife, and honeybee colonies" in eradication areas. The Commissioner has complied with these directives. Indeed, the Commissioner's regulations relating to the protection of human life and the environment are fairly extensive. The Act also provides that the Commissioner may adopt rules regulating cotton planting in eradication zones and adopting a schedule of penalty fees, which he has also done.

The Commissioner could not, however, adopt any procedure for reviewing such critical decisions as the amount of assessments adopted by the growers, the total amount of funds expended on eradication, the amount of debt incurred by the Foundation, or the repayment terms for such debts.
. . .

Finally, contrary to the dissenting justices' conclusion, the Commissioner has no general authority to "revoke the Foundation's certification" if it fails to comply with the procedural provisions of the Act. The Act provides that "[t]he commissioner shall certify the petitioning organization selected under Section 74.103 of this code as the organization authorized to create an official boll weevil eradication foundation. . . . The commissioner may revoke the organization's certification on 60 days written notice if the organization fails to meet the requirements of this subchapter." It is clear that this section authorizes the Commissioner to revoke only the authority of the creating organization. Once the Foundation is created as an independent entity, the Commissioner has no authority to dissolve it, except when its eradication purpose has been fulfilled or it has become inoperative and abandoned. Thus, the first factor weighs against the delegation.

Judging the statute as it is written, rather than as it operated in practice, the second factor militates in favor of the private delegation. The growers in each zone are allowed to vote on whether to participate in the eradication program, and thereby subject themselves to the Foundation's jurisdiction, and are allowed to approve or reject any proposed assessment. Although the Foundation in actuality operated for nineteen months with a board controlled by Texas Cotton Producers' appointees, this process was inconsistent with the statutory contemplation that the Foundation should at all times by governed by the elected board. We thus do not consider that actual operation in reviewing the constitutionality of the Act.

The third factor weighs against the delegation. Far from merely devising eradication guidelines, the Foundation actually applied the programs it devised to all growers in zones where the program was approved. In accordance with its statutory authority, the Foundation collected assessments from individual growers and entered those growers' property to carry out its eradication programs.

The fourth factor also weighs against the delegation. The Foundation board members are cotton growers who have a direct pecuniary interest in the eradication programs implemented by the Foundation.

Under the circumstances of this case, the fifth factor does not weigh in our consideration of whether the statute as a whole is an unconstitutional delegation of authority to the Foundation. The Foundation is vested with authority to impose monetary penalties for late payment of the assessments and to direct the Department to destroy a delinquent growers' crops, and it is further empowered to adopt rules, a violation of which is a criminal offense. While this authority to impose penal sanctions strongly suggests an improper private delegation, principles of severability would allow us to strike down this power and still uphold the Act. ... Here, the assessment and expenditure provisions of the Act could be implemented without the penalty provisions. Thus, even though the penalty provisions seem to represent an unconstitutional delegation of authority to the Foundation, this should not weigh in judging the validity of the Foundation's core function under the Act, i.e., the levying and collecting of assessments and the expenditure of those assessments on eradication programs.

The sixth factor is inconclusive under the circumstances of this case. While the statute pertains to a specific, narrow purpose—eradication of the boll weevil and other cotton pests—it does not limit the program's cost and duration, other than to provide that the program is subject to the Sunset Act and that it should be discontinued once the boll weevil is eradicated.

The seventh factor, on its face, weighs against the delegation. While the Act is designed to allow those with firsthand experience in the cotton industry to lead the eradication effort, there is no assurance that those elected will actually have special qualifications or training regarding eradication of boll weevils, and there is absolutely no evidence that board actions were "taken for purposes which are independent of the statute," Professor Davis' salient test. DAVIS § 3.12, at 196 (2d ed.1978). The facts are thus quite distinct from a private delegation, say, for the promulgation of a municipal electrical code by an industry association consisting of electrical contractors, inspectors, and manufacturers. There is, of course, some tension between this factor and the second factor. It would ordinarily be difficult for a private delegation both to guarantee adequate representation of those affected by the delegation and to vest decisionmaking authority in a group of experts. There is no evidence in the record of a disinterested and yet eminent pre-existing entity to which the devising and implementing of a boll weevil eradication program could have been delegated. Thus, while the Act fails to meet the seventh factor, this failure is excused by the satisfaction of the second factor.

Finally, the eighth factor weighs against the delegation. The Legislature has provided very few statutory standards to guide the Foundation. While the Act provides the procedures for zone referenda and specifies the powers and duties of the board, it provides no guidance as to how assessments are to be set or the amount of debt that the Foundation may incur. Thus, in practice, the Foundation had free rein to incur over $9 million in debt in the Lower Rio Grande Valley Zone to be repaid by the growers there through several years of assessments, even though those growers voted within 21 months to discontinue their eradication program.

We recognize that the judicial branch should defer to the judgment of the people's elected representatives whenever possible, and we by no means suggest that a private delegation must satisfy all eight of these factors. We recognize also that courts should, when possible, read delegations narrowly to uphold their validity. ... Here, however, the invalidity of the delegation does not hinge on any one provision of the Act that might be narrowly interpreted; rather, the Act as a whole represents an overly broad delegation of legislative authority to a private entity, violating a majority of the eight factors we have set forth. Therefore, the Act cannot stand.

* * *

The nondelegation doctrine should be used sparingly, when there is, in Justice Cardozo's memorable phrase, "delegation running riot." A.L.A. Schechter Poultry Corp. v. United States, 295 U.S. 495, 553 (1935) (Cardozo, J., concurring). Because we believe this is an extraordinary case, we affirm the judgments of the trial courts.

[The five separate opinions, expressing various degrees of concurrence and dissent, are omitted.]

NOTE

Is the problem with delegating power to private groups one of fairness to particular persons who may be affected, or the expression of broader structural concerns? The fairness rationale was rejected by the United States Supreme Court in Friedman v. Rogers, 440 U.S. 1 (1979). Texas had placed the regulation of optometry in a board dominated by independent optometrists, one of two contending professional groups. The Supreme Court found no problem of federal due process raised by this arrangement, which was challenged by a member of the disfavored group. In any disciplinary hearing, the plaintiff could protect his "constitutional right to a fair and impartial hearing" by seeking disqualification of board members on conflict-of-interest grounds. See Gibson v. Berryhill, 411 U.S. 564 (1973). Plaintiff had "no constitutional right to be regulated by a Board ... sympathetic to the commercial practice of optometry." On the disqualification issue in these cases, see also pp. 421–22 below.

(ii) DELEGATION IN EUROPE

Although their constitutional traditions differ in important respects from those of the United States, Western European countries have also struggled with the basic democratic legitimacy concerns raised by legislative delegation of policymaking power to nonelected administrative bodies.

The first excerpt surveys post-World–War II experience in reconciling legislative supremacy with delegation of regulatory power to the executive (or, in usage more familiar in Europe than here, to "the government"). The growth of the European Community—and, in particular, its increasingly aggressive attempts to standardize economic and social regulatory policy across member countries—has further complicated those concerns. The second excerpt explores how nondelegation concerns might play out in a world of supranational delegation.

Peter Lindseth, Delegation is Dead, Long Live Delegation: Managing the Democratic Disconnect in the European Market–Polity

Good Governance in Europe's Integrated Market 144–150 (Joerges & Dehoouse, eds., 2002).

. . . Although legal and institutional approaches would differ in particulars, the process of reconciling delegation and parliamentary democracy [after World War II] would follow the same basic pattern in most western European states. The vast majority of rules of general application (i.e., legislative rules) would no longer be in the form of traditional legislation passed by parliament but would now take the form of regulations or other subordinate legislation produced in the executive and an increasingly complex and diffuse administrative sphere. The democratic legitimation of these rules would no longer be directly through a vote of individual legislators as such, but rather through the hierarchical control or supervision of the administrative sphere by government ministers (who were in turn responsible before parliament), supplemented by forms of direct legislative oversight and legal controls enforced by courts or other specialized administrative tribunals.

In countries like France and the Federal Republic of Germany, however, efforts were made in another direction as well, toward the protection of the "core" democratic functions of the legislature through the development of substantive constitutional constraints on the nature and scope of delegation. Article 80(1) of the West German Basic Law, for example, [required that the] "content, purpose and scope" of the delegation had to be specified in the enabling legislation itself, thus prohibiting indeterminate delegations. . . . The French constitution of 1946 seemed to take an even more restrictive line—providing in Article 13 that "[t]he National Assembly alone shall vote *la loi*. It cannot delegate this right." . . .

Defining the substantive consequences of these delegation constraints would occupy both German and French judges over the course of the 1950s. . . . What emerged in the postwar jurisprudence of the [German] Constitutional Court was not an inflexible, absolutist nondelegation doctrine—by its terms, Article 80(1) in fact *authorized* delegation—but rather a more subtle approach. The Court relied on a series of analytical formulas to constrain the executive's normative autonomy while nevertheless allowing the delegation to proceed.[1]

---

1. These included: the *Vorhersehbarkeitsformel*, which focused on whether the content of any future regulation was foreseeable from the statute itself; the *Selbstentcheid-*

Even though the [Court] sought to avoid applying Article 80(1) in an excessively strict sense, it also recognized the need to protect what it understood to be, in light of historical experience, the "essential" functions of the people's elected legislative representatives. This *Wesentlichkeitstheorie*, or "theory of essentialness," directly intersected with the Court's constitutional obligation to protect individual rights: Where a regulatory program implicated such rights or some other fundamental aspect of public policy, there was a heightened constitutional obligation on the part of the legislature to make the policy decisions itself on the face of the statute, rather than delegating that power to the executive. . . .

In France, a similar understanding of the democratic function of delegation constraints would also emerge in the postwar decades. . . . Consistent with established administrative jurisprudence, the Conseil d'Etat found that "certain matters are reserved to legislation," notably anything affecting the individual rights and liberties now incorporated by reference into the preamble of the 1946 constitution. In these sensitive domains, the legislature must formulate "the essential rules" itself, although it may also grant authority to the government to "complete" them. The constitution also prohibited a delegation that, "by its generality and its imprecision," constituted an abandonment by the National Assembly to the government of "the exercise of national sovereignty." In this sense, the Conseil viewed the need for constitutional constraint on delegation as a direct consequence of the democratic character of the constitution itself.

The constitutional environment in France obviously changed dramatically [with adoption of the constitution of 1958] both in terms of substance and institutional structure. Nevertheless, these changes, at least insofar as concepts of delegation are concerned, were less dramatic than originally supposed, despite the contrary implication of the new constitutional text . . . which now suggested that the executive possessed its own autonomous "regulatory" powers. . . . The Conseil constitutionnel and the Conseil d'Etat have interpreted the government's[2] powers as generally being limited to *mise en oeuvre*—or merely legislative implementation. . . .

If we shift our attention to postwar Britain, . . . we find of course that it never abandoned parliamentary supremacy as a fundamental constitutional doctrine. Thus, explicit recourse in that country to judicially-enforced constraints on delegation was out of the question. The focus of British efforts to constrain delegation would therefore be, at least initially, parliamentary and procedural, notably through the rationalization of parliamentary oversight mechanisms ("laying" procedures) under the Statutory

ungsformel, which focused on whether the legislature had itself decided the limits of the regulated area as well as the goals of the regulation; and the *Programmformel*, which focused on whether the statute had defined with sufficient clarity the regulatory program. The Court also relied on the presence in regulatory statutes of Bundestag veto powers over measures adopted by the executive—in effect, a kind of direct legislative over-

sight—viewing this veto power as compensation for the increased concentration of authority in the executive brought about by the delegation itself. Where Länder interests are implicated, the Bundesrat also possesses a right of veto that derives directly from the Basic Law itself.

    2. [Ed.] Keep in mind the European usage: "the government" meaning, to U.S. lawyers, "the Executive."

Instruments Act of 1946, as well as through a parallel effort a decade later to rationalize administrative adjudication and judicial review under the Tribunals and Inquiries Act of 1958. For much of the immediate postwar decade, however, the British courts deferred to the political imperatives of parliament and the government in the exercise of normative power outside the parliamentary realm.[3] Over the decade following the passage of the Tribunals and Inquiries Act, however, the courts would reverse this trend ... by becoming more active defenders of individual rights in the face of executive and administrative action, albeit within the confines imposed by British constitutional tradition.[4]

In some sense, British judges simply confronted through administrative case-law the same constitutional reality that their French and German counterparts also confronted through their written constitutional texts and jurisprudence. The diffusion and fragmentation of normative power both to, and within, the executive and administrative spheres directly challenged historically-grounded notions of "separation of powers"—in which the legislature would make the norms of general application, the executive would implement those norms as an agent of the legislature, and judges would adjudicate disputes as to the meaning and implementation of those norms. In the subsequent decades, few could deny that western European public law was now confronted by a much more complex reality. National legislatures, rather than specifying regulatory norms directly in the statute itself, now more often than not simply conferred power on executive bodies to make the rules via some form of subordinate legislation, subject to certain general statutory guidelines (*lois-cadres* in the French parlance). National executives thus came to enjoy not merely extensive legislative powers but also, concomitantly, broad adjudicative powers as well (at least in the first instance) over the vast array of disputes which arose in the implementation of the administrative programs under their charge. And as a consequence, national judicial power increasingly became concerned with the particulars of public (i.e., administrative and constitutional) law, taking on an important role in the supervision of the normative functions of the executive and the administration.

[E]ven as power shifted out of the parliamentary realm, [however,] the executive and administrative sphere never gained the ability to legitimize their normative activities in an autonomous manner. Rather, oversight by other branches—both judicial and legislative—continued to play important roles. Thus, even if the concentration of authority in the executive branch

---

3. This led to a series of disturbing precedents regarding the limited application of principles of natural justice (Nakkuda Ali v. Jayaratne, [1951] A.C. 66, and R. v. Commissioner of Police of the Metropolis ex parte Parker, [1953] 1 W.L.R. 1150); deference to the discretionary powers of the administration (see, e.g., Robinson v. Minister of Town and Country Planning, [1947] K.B. 702); and a broad reading of statutory provisions precluding judicial review (see, e.g., Woollett v. Minister of Agriculture and Fisheries, [1955] 1 Q.B. 103).

4. A now-famous series of major cases would reinvigorate the application of principles of natural justice (Ridge v. Baldwin, [1964] A.C. 40); impose much stricter judicial limits on ministerial discretion (Customs and Excise Commissioners v. Cure & Deeley Ltd., [1962] 1 Q.B. 340); give a much more narrow reading to preclusive clauses (Anisminic Ltd. v. Foreign Compensation Commission, [1969] 2 A.C. 147); and more generally use the doctrine of *ultra vires* to review a broad range of administrative illegalities.

seemed to signify a "fusion" rather than a "separation" of powers in the traditional sense ..., historically-grounded notions of democratic and constitutional government were, after a period of significant historical struggle, maintained through a separation of the *mechanisms of legitimation*—legislative, executive, and judicial.... In this way, administrative governance never attained—and has not attained—a kind of autonomous constitutional legitimacy, but rather its legitimacy has remained *mediated* through the traditional branches of government that are themselves historically endowed with constitutional authority.

* * *

The process of European integration has posed new constitutional questions and further complicated old ones. Professor Lindseth explains how nondelegation concepts operate in the supranational governmental order that is the contemporary European Community:

"... The Community system draws its authority not from a direct constitutional enactment of some definable European 'demos' but rather from lawful transfers of normative power from national parliaments as representatives of their respective national communities. Like administrative governance on the national level, the key sources of legitimacy in the Community are found in political and legal, and not directly democratic, control mechanisms. From this perspective, Community institutions operate as a multi-function agency—a category Americans know well—with executive, legislative, and adjudicative jurisdiction stretching across vast areas of economic and social regulation, unique in that it takes its mandate from multiple political principals, i.e., the Member State parliaments and their electorates.

"The transfer of regulatory authority to the Community system in the second half of the last century [can be seen as the supranational version of the] diffusion and fragmentation of normative power away from national parliaments which ... reached its full fruition in the postwar decades. ... European integration built directly on this reconciliation of administrative governance and parliamentary democracy, and thus it is no coincidence that supranationalism emerged as a viable political project in western Europe at precisely the moment in history when the basic constitutional foundations of administrative governance at the national level were also secured."

Professor Lindseth explains elsewhere,[5] "[d]elegation concerns were central to the 1993 decision of the German Federal Constitutional Court upholding the constitutionality of the Treaty on European of 1992 (the 'Maastricht Treaty')[:]

> The important factor is that the Federal Republic of Germany's membership and the rights and obligations which arise from it, in particular the legally binding direct activity of the European Communities in the domestic legal territory, have been defined foreseeably ... in Treaty.... If, for example, European institutions or governmental entities

---

5. Peter L. Lindseth, The Contradictions of Supranationalism: European Integration and the Constitutional Settlement of Administrative Governance, 1920s–1980s, at 2–4 (Ph.D. dissertation, Columbia University, 2002).

were to implement or to develop the Maastricht Treaty in a manner no longer covered by the Treaty in the form of it upon which the German Act of Accession is based, any legal instrument arising from such activity would not be binding in the German territory. German institutions would be prevented by reasons of constitutional law from applying such legal instruments in Germany. Accordingly, the German Federal Constitutional Court [in future cases involving EC regulatory mandates] must examine the question of whether or not legal instruments of European institutions or governmental entities may be considered to remain within the bounds of the sovereign rights accorded to them, or whether they may be considered to exceed those bounds.[6]

"Both national and supranational delegations, the Court implied, depended on parliament's adoption of enabling legislation containing sufficiently precise 'standards' which would allow the subsequent regulatory program to be 'foreseeable,' in some sense ensuring that the locus of legislative power ultimately remained with the national parliament, as the constitution demanded. Thereafter, it was the Court's job to police the exercise of the delegated normative power to ensure that it remained within the 'standardized' boundaries determined by the legislature. As in the domestic administrative state, moreover, the Court argued that, after the initial delegation, the democratic legitimacy of the Community's delegated legislative power flowed from oversight by the various national executives assembled in the Council of Ministers[7]—just as hierarchical oversight or control mechanisms by the national executive helped to legitimize delegated legislative power in the administrative sphere at the national level."

SECTION 2.   ASSESSING THE CONSTITUTIONALITY OF THE ADMINISTRATIVE STATE

"The Congress shall have Power ... To make all Laws which shall be necessary and proper for carrying into Execution the foregoing Powers, and all other Powers vested by this Constitution in the Government of the United States, or in any Department or Officer thereof."

U.S. Constitution, Art. I, § 8, ¶ 18

As you have probably realized, the delegation cases are one piece of a larger puzzle: How can we reconcile the modern regulatory state with a Constitution that is more than 200 years old, and yet still serves as our

---

6. This translation is drawn from 33 I.L.M. at 422–423.

7. See 33 I.L.M. at 421–422 ("the exercise of sovereign powers is largely determined by governments. If Community powers of this nature are based upon the democratic process of forming political will conveyed by each individual people, they must be exercised by an institution delegated by the governments of the Member States, which are themselves subject to democratic control."). The Court also relied on somewhat conventional notions of technocratic expertise, as well as the political incapacities of parliaments to rule on complex "technical" issues under electoral and interest group pressures, to justify the shift in normative power to an independent European Central Bank. Ibid., 439.

fundamental benchmark of political legitimacy? Your understanding of the Court's efforts to solve this puzzle—and your ability to reach your own solution—will be enhanced by learning something of the rich background of legal theory against which these issues are being litigated. The scholarship on separation of powers is broad and deep; here, we can only dip selectively into the vast body of work in the area. Perhaps most frustrating, this course cannot even begin to explore the primary historical materials so crucial to originalist arguments.

With these caveats, the materials that follow are designed to do two things. The first part presents a sampling of scholarly views about the ultimate question whether the administrative state can be squared with the Constitution. Here, the goal was diversity: to give you a sense of the range (rather than typicality) of possible answers to this most fundamental question. The second part offers some methodological guidance. The Constitution does not even contain the phrases "separation of powers," "checks and balances" or "administrative agency." How, then, might lawyers and judges go about constructing principled ways to assess the constitutionality of contemporary regulatory structures and practices? Here, you will be introduced to the dominant competing methodologies— formalism and functionalism—as well as to some alternative contenders.

a.   COMPETING VIEWS: IS THE REGULATORY STATE CONSTITUTIONAL?

Much of the commentary on this question identifies the New Deal as a constitutional watershed. Without doubt, this era brought an expansion in the regulatory ambitions of the national government that inaugurated the modern administrative state. The relationship between the states and the federal government—and, more fundamentally, between the government and the individual citizen—shifted profoundly. Keep in mind, however, that federal agencies existed and played a key role in national policymaking long before Franklin Roosevelt.

As noted in the introduction to this chapter, the First Congress quickly turned to the task—deliberately left to it by the framers of the Constitution[1]—of creating the internal structure of government. The Departments of Foreign Affairs (eventually, State), War and Treasury and the Post Office were solidly established and engaged in important (and often controversial) activities by the early 1800s. Federal regulation of the imports and exports of the growing nation, through tariff-setting and adjustment of trading privileges, significantly affected the domestic economy throughout the 19th century. The Departments of Agriculture and the Interior were in place by the time of the Civil War, poised to oversee the development and use of land in the westward expansion. After the War, the Populist and Progressive movements brought the first agencies in the "modern" form—

---

1. Early drafts of the Constitution specified a number of cabinet departments and vested them with particular responsibilities. This language was removed in the final days of drafting; one small vestige is the reference, in the Necessary and Proper Clause, to powers "*vested by this Constitution* in the Government of the United States, or *in any Department* or Officer thereof."

that is, existing outside a cabinet department. See Rabin, p. 13 above. The Interstate Commerce Commission was created in 1887 to regulate the practices of the crucially important network of interstate railroads. It was followed in 1914 by the Federal Trade Commission, with its much broader mandate to police unfair trade practices. In the intervening period, the Department of Commerce and Labor was created in 1903.

In sum, the New Deal is a significant constitutional moment, but the informed student of the modern administrative state will keep in mind that agencies—with diverse organizational structures and myriad substantive missions—were carrying out the important work of government from the earliest days of the Republic.

Gary Lawson, The Rise and the Rise of the Administrative State

107 Harv. L. Rev. 1231 (1994).

The post-New Deal administrative state is unconstitutional, and its validation by the legal system amounts to nothing less than a bloodless constitutional revolution. The original New Dealers were aware, at least to some degree, that their vision of the national government's proper role and structure could not be squared with the written Constitution: The Administrative Process, James Landis's classic exposition of the New Deal model of administration, fairly drips with contempt for the idea of a limited national government subject to a formal, tripartite separation of powers. Faced with a choice between the administrative state and the Constitution, the architects of our modern government chose the administrative state, and their choice has stuck. . . .

A. The Death of Limited Government

The advocates of the Constitution of 1789 were very clear about the kind of national government they sought to create. As James Madison put it: "The powers delegated by the proposed Constitution to the federal government are few and defined."[1] Those national powers, Madison suggested, would be "exercised principally on external objects, as war, peace, negotiation, and foreign commerce," and the states would be the principal units of government for most internal matters. . . .

Article I of the Constitution vests in the national Congress "[a]ll legislative powers herein granted," and thus clearly indicates that the national government can legislate only in accordance with enumerations of power. Article I then spells out seventeen specific subjects to which the federal legislative power extends: such matters as taxing and borrowing, interstate and foreign commerce, naturalization and bankruptcy, currency and counterfeiting, post offices and post roads, patents and copyrights, national courts, piracy and offenses against the law of nations, the military, and the governance of the nation's capital and certain federal enclaves. . . .

---

1. THE FEDERALIST No. 45, at 292 (James Madison) (Clinton Rossiter ed., 1961).

This is not the stuff of which Leviathan is made. None of these powers, alone or in combination, grants the federal government anything remotely resembling a general jurisdiction over citizens' affairs. . . .

B.   The Death of the Nondelegation Doctrine

The Constitution both confines the national government to certain enumerated powers and defines the institutions of the national government that can permissibly exercise those powers. Article I of the Constitution provides that "[a]ll legislative Powers herein granted shall be vested in a Congress of the United States, which shall consist of a Senate and House of Representatives." Article II provides that "[t]he executive Power shall be vested in a President of the United States of America." Article III specifies that "[t]he judicial Power of the United States, shall be vested in one supreme Court, and in such inferior Courts as the Congress may from time to time ordain and establish." The Constitution thus divides the powers of the national government into three categories—legislative, executive, and judicial—and vests such powers in three separate institutions. To be sure, the Constitution expressly prescribes some deviations from a pure tripartite scheme of separation, but this only underscores the role of the three Vesting Clauses in assigning responsibility for governmental functions that are not specifically allocated by the constitutional text. . . .

Although the Constitution does not tell us how to distinguish the legislative, executive, and judicial powers from each other, there is clearly some differentiation among the three governmental functions, which at least generates some easy cases. Consider, for example, a statute creating the Goodness and Niceness Commission and giving it power "to promulgate rules for the promotion of goodness and niceness in all areas within the power of Congress under the Constitution." If the "executive power" means simply the power to carry out legislative commands regardless of their substance, then the Goodness and Niceness Commission's rulemaking authority is executive rather than legislative power and is therefore valid. But if that is true, then there never was and never could be such a thing as a constitutional principle of nondelegation—a proposition that is belied by all available evidence about the meaning of the Constitution. . . . Certain powers simply cannot be given to executive (or judicial) officials, because those powers are *legislative* in character. . . .

. . . The United States Code is filled with statutes that create little Goodness and Niceness Commissions—each confined to a limited subject area such as securities, broadcast licenses, or (my personal favorite) import-ed tea.[2] These statutes are easy kills under any plausible interpretation of the Constitution's nondelegation principle. The Supreme Court, however, has rejected so many delegation challenges to so many utterly vacuous statutes that modern nondelegation decisions now simply recite these past

---

2.   [Ed.] The particular example invoked by Prof. Lawson illustrates the historical point made at the outset of this Section: The Board of Tea Experts, charged with preventing the importation of substandard tea, was a 19th century creation. See Tea Importation Act, Section 41, acts Mar. 2, 1897, ch. 358, Sec. 1, 29 Stat. 604. Its existence ended with Pub. L. 104–128, the Federal Tea Tasters Repeal Act of 1996.

holdings and wearily move on. Anything short of the Goodness and Niceness Commission, it seems, is permissible.

C. The Death of the Unitary Executive

Article II states that "[t]he executive Power shall be vested in a President of the United States of America." Although the precise contours of this "executive Power" are not entirely clear, at a minimum it includes the power to execute the laws of the United States. Other clauses of the Constitution, such as the requirement that the President "take Care that the Laws be faithfully executed," assume and constrain this power to execute the laws, but the Article II Vesting Clause is the constitutional source of this power—just as the Article III Vesting Clause is the constitutional source of the federal judiciary's power to decide cases.

Significantly, that power to execute the laws is vested, not in the executive department of the national government, but in "a President of the United States of America." The Constitution thus creates a unitary executive. Any plausible theory of the federal executive power must acknowledge and account for this vesting of the executive power in the person of the President.

Of course, the President cannot be expected personally to execute all laws. Congress, pursuant to its power to make all laws "necessary and proper for carrying into Execution" the national government's powers, can create administrative machinery to assist the President in carrying out legislatively prescribed tasks. But if a statute vests discretionary authority directly in an agency official (as do most regulatory statutes) rather than in the President, the Article II Vesting Clause seems to require that such discretionary authority be subject to the President's control. . . .

D. The Death of the Independent Judiciary

Article III provides that "[t]he judicial Power of the United States, shall be vested in one supreme Court, and in such inferior Courts as the Congress may from time to time ordain and establish." The judges of all such federal courts are constitutionally guaranteed tenure during good behavior as well as assurance that their salaries will not be diminished during their time in office. One of the principal functions of administrative agencies is to adjudicate disputes, yet administrative adjudicators plainly lack the essential attributes that Article III requires of any decisionmaker invested with "the judicial Power of the United States." Is adjudication by administrative agencies therefore another instance of abandonment of a fundamental constitutional principle?

Maybe. Administrative adjudication is problematic only if it must be considered an exercise of judicial power. But an activity is not exclusively judicial merely because it is adjudicative—that is, because it involves the application of legal standards to particular facts. Much adjudicative activity by executive officials—such as granting or denying benefits under entitlement statutes—is execution of the laws by any rational standard, though it also fits comfortably within the concept of the judicial power if conducted by judicial officers. This overlap between the executive and judicial functions is not surprising; under many pre-American conceptions of separation of powers, the judicial power was treated as an aspect of the executive power.

Agency adjudication is therefore constitutionally permissible under Article III as long as the activity in question can fairly fit the definition of executive power, even if it also fairly fits the definition of judicial power. Some forms of adjudication, however, are quintessentially judicial. The conviction of a defendant under the criminal laws, for example, is surely something that requires the exercise of judicial rather than executive power. . . . Wherever the line is drawn, however, at least some modern administrative adjudication undoubtedly falls squarely on the judicial side. Most notably, the imposition of a civil penalty or fine is very hard to distinguish from the imposition of a criminal sentence (especially when the criminal sentence is itself a fine). If the latter is judicial, it is difficult to see why the former is not as well. . . .

E.   The Death of Separation of Powers

The constitutional separation of powers is a means to safeguard the liberty of the people. In Madison's famous words, "[t]he accumulation of all powers, legislative, executive, and judiciary, in the same hands, whether of one, a few, or many, and whether hereditary, self-appointed, or elective, may justly be pronounced the very definition of tyranny."[3] The destruction of this principle of separation of powers is perhaps the crowning jewel of the modern administrative revolution. Administrative agencies routinely combine all three governmental functions in the same body, and even in the same people within that body.

Consider the typical enforcement activities of a typical federal agency—for example, of the Federal Trade Commission. The Commission promulgates substantive rules of conduct. The Commission then considers whether to authorize investigations into whether the Commission's rules have been violated. If the Commission authorizes an investigation, the investigation is conducted by the Commission, which reports its findings to the Commission. If the Commission thinks that the Commission's findings warrant an enforcement action, the Commission issues a complaint. The Commission's complaint that a Commission rule has been violated is then prosecuted by the Commission and adjudicated by the Commission. This Commission adjudication can either take place before the full Commission or before a semi-autonomous Commission administrative law judge. If the Commission chooses to adjudicate before an administrative law judge rather than before the Commission and the decision is adverse to the Commission, the Commission can appeal to the Commission. If the Commission ultimately finds a violation, then, and only then, the affected private party can appeal to an Article III court. But the agency decision, even before the bona fide Article III tribunal, possesses a very strong presumption of correctness on matters both of fact and of law.

This is probably the most jarring way in which the administrative state departs from the Constitution, and it typically does not even raise eyebrows. . . .

The actual structure and operation of the national government today has virtually nothing to do with the Constitution.

---

3.   THE FEDERALIST No. 47, at 301
(James Madison) (Clinton Rossiter ed., 1961).

Bruce A. Ackerman, The Storrs Lectures: Discovering the Constitution

93 Yale L.J. 1013 (1984).

[The Philadelphia Convention, by drafting a new constitution rather than suggesting amendments to the Articles of Confederation, exceeded the mandate it had received from the Continental Congress and the States. From the fact that the Convention "acted illegally in exceeding the authority" it was granted, Prof. Ackerman argues that the Framers came to recognize an extraordinary form of politics—constitutional politics—that is qualitatively different from normal politics. This kind of politics "under certain conditions, justifies a change in preexisting constitutional principles." In effect, it breaks the law in order to provide an opportunity in which The People can choose to amend their higher law. Prof. Ackerman points to Federalist 40, in which Madison justifies the acts of the Convention, as describing a moment of constitutional politics:]

> Let us view the ground on which the Convention stood.... They must have reflected that in all great changes of established governments, forms ought to give way to substance; that a rigid adherence [to forms] would render ... nugatory the transcendent and precious right of the people to "abolish or alter their governments ...," since it is impossible for the people spontaneously and universally to move in concert ...; and it is therefore essential that such changes be instituted by some informal and unauthorized propositions, made by some patriotic and respectable ... citizens.... [Indeed the Convention] must have recollected that it was by this irregular and assumed [method] that the States were first united against the danger with which they were threatened by their ancient government; ... nor could it have been forgotten that no little ill-timed scruples, no zeal for adhering to ordinary forms, were anywhere seen, except in those who wished to indulge, under these masks, their secret enmity to the substance contended for. They must have borne in mind that as the plan to be framed and proposed was to be submitted to *the people* themselves, the disapprobation of this supreme authority would destroy it forever; its approbation blot out antecedent errors and irregularities.

Hear the voice of the successful revolutionary. The highest form of political expression is to be found not in formal assemblies arising under preexisting law, but through an "irregular and assumed privilege" of proposing "informal and unauthorized propositions." If such proposals were accepted by irregular, but popularly elected, assemblies, we are to understand that the people themselves—the words are italicized in the original—had spoken; and if the People approved the revolutionary elite's considered proposals, this could "blot out ... errors and irregularities."

Strong stuff. At present, though, I am less interested in evaluating the Federalist theory of constitutional law than in presenting it to public view.... Although constitutional politics is the highest kind of politics, it should be permitted to dominate the nation's life only during rare periods of heightened political consciousness....

During the New Deal's first term, the President and Congress were no more entitled to pretend that they were speaking for We the People of the United States than any normal set of incumbents sitting in Washington, D.C. Moreover, the hard truth is that the New Deal did raise fundamental questions of constitutional legitimacy when viewed against the background of the individualistic principles enunciated after the American Revolution and the Civil War.

Thus, by resisting the initial New Deal experiments in the name of traditional principles, the Supreme Court [in the Lochner era] did not act in a constitutionally illegitimate fashion. Rather than permitting elected politicians to evade the fundamental questions of political principle raised by the New Deal, the Court's resistance in the name of the Old Constitution ... made it abundantly plain to the mass of private citizens that a fundamental constitutional initiative was being seriously entertained by their representatives in the nation's capital. If they did not approve of the new things that were being said in their name in Washington, D.C., the time had come to mobilize, as private citizens, on behalf of the Old Constitution....

... How, then, would the People respond to the competing visions of constitutional government offered by the Old Court and the New Deal as they proceeded to the polls in November of 1936? Would this election, like so many others in American history, yield an inconclusive outcome, permitting competing groups of normal politicians to continue battling indecisively from the competing centers of authority established by the separation of powers? Or would the People ... give a decisive victory to the party defending the vitality of the Old Constitution? Or, finally, would the People respond, as they had last done after the Civil War, by giving the party of constitutional re-vision a decisive electoral victory? [Roosevelt, of course, won decisively.]

In short, I propose to ... interpret the 1930's as a process of constitutional creation. Rather than acting under the explicit procedures established by Article V, however, We the People of the United States expressed its will through a higher lawmaking process that relied primarily upon the structural interaction of Articles I, II and III of the Constitution. Through their careful regulation of the terms of office held by representatives, senators, presidents, and Justices, these Articles process deep shifts in popular opinion very differently from a single-track constitution. Within our dualist structure, a single electoral victory by a new popular movement typically generates a highly charged dialogue among branches of government, rather than a straightforward victory for the new order. Those officials who gained office before the most recent election do not lightly accept the suggestion that their principles have been consigned by the People to the dustbin of history. So far as they are concerned, their rivals are transparent demagogues whose nostrums will only exacerbate the evils they profess to cure. Given the separation of powers, moreover, both sides are encouraged to appeal to the People in the hope that their own views will emerge victorious in succeeding elections. If this process is managed well, it will lead the adversaries to clarify the nature of the constitutional alternatives being proffered to the American People.

. . . The democratic struggle over constitutional principle will not end, moreover, until a series of decisive victories at the polls permits the newly triumphant spokesmen of the People to proclaim their new higher law from all three of the branches constituted by the first three Articles. It is only at this point that a structural amendment, as I shall call it, achieves its legitimate ratification under our dualist Constitution as it has evolved over the past two centuries. . . .

[O]nce we explicitly recognize that laissez-faire capitalism was legitimately repudiated by a process of structural amendment culminating in the 1930's, we are no longer obliged to save the welfare state at the cost of trivializing the process of [constitutional] interpretation. Instead, we can explain why it is right for modern lawyers to reject the particular conceptions of freedom of contract, private property, and states' rights dominant in the aftermath of the American Revolution and Civil War. We refuse to elaborate these themes for the same reason we refuse to listen to the Philadelphia Convention's opinions on race relations. On these matters, preexisting principles have been repealed, or at least profoundly revised, by successful constitutional solutions enacted into higher law by later generations of Americans.

Peter L. Strauss, The Place of Agencies in Government: Separation of Powers and the Fourth Branch

84 Colum. L. Rev. 573 (1984).

For the past few years the Supreme Court has been struggling with issues of government structure so fundamental that they might have been thought textbook simple, yet with results that seem to imperil the everyday exercise of law-administration. . . .

At the root of these problems lies a difficulty in understanding the relationships between the agencies that actually do the work of law-administration, whose existence is barely hinted at in the Constitution, and the three constitutionally named repositories of all governmental power— Congress, President, and Supreme Court. When, for example, a federal agency adopts a legislative "rule" following the procedures of the Administrative Procedure Act, how is this act to be understood constitutionally? In a colloquial sense, the agency is acting legislatively—that is, creating general statements of positive law whose application to an indefinite class awaits future acts and proceedings. Validly adopted legislative rules are identical to statutes in their impact on all relevant legal actors—those subject to their constraints, those responsible for their administration, and judges or others who may have occasion to consider them in the course of their activities. Does it follow that in the constitutional sense what the agency is doing should be regarded as an exercise of the "legislative Powers . . . granted" by article I, "all" of which are vested in Congress? Or, given statutory authorization, is it to be regarded as an exercise of the executive authority vested in the President by article II, the judicial power placed in the Supreme Court (and statutorily created inferior courts) by article III, or authority merely statutory in provenance? The Constitution names and ascribes functions only to the Congress, President and Supreme Court, sitting in uneasy relation at the apex of the governmental structure; it leaves undiscussed what might be the necessary and permissible relationships of each of these three constitutional bodies to the agency making the rule. Is it significant for any of these purposes whether the rulemaking authority has been assigned to a cabinet department or to an independent regulatory commission? Indeed, does it make sense to look to the Constitution, written so many years ago, for contemporary guidance or limits on the sorts of arrangements Congress can make?

Three differing approaches have been used in the effort to understand issues such as these. The first, "separation of powers," supposes that what government does can be characterized in terms of the kind of act performed—legislating, enforcing, and determining the particular application of law—and that for the safety of the citizenry from tyrannous government these three functions must be kept in distinct places. Congress legislates, and it only legislates; the President sees to the faithful execution of those laws and, in the domestic context at least, that is all he does; the courts decide specific cases of law-application, and that is their sole function. These three powers of government are kept radically separate, because if the same body exercised all three of them, or even two, it might no longer be possible to keep it within the constraints of law.

"Separation of functions" suggests a somewhat different idea, grounded more in considerations of individual fairness in particular proceedings than in the need for structural protection against tyrannical government generally. It admits that for agencies (as distinct from the constitutionally named heads of government) the same body often does exercise all three of the characteristic governmental powers, albeit in a web of other controls—judicial review and legislative and executive oversight. As these controls are thought to give reasonable assurance against systemic lawlessness, the separation-of-functions inquiry asks to what extent constitutional due process for the particular individual(s) who may be involved with an agency in a given proceeding requires special measures to assure the objectivity or impartiality of that proceeding. The powers are not kept separate, at least in general, but certain procedural protections—for example, the requirement of an on-the-record hearing before an "impartial" trier—may be afforded.

"Checks and balances" is the third idea, one that to a degree bridges the gap between these two domains. Like separation of powers, it seeks to protect the citizens from the emergence of tyrannical government by establishing multiple heads of authority in government, which are then pitted one against another in a continuous struggle; the intent of that struggle is to deny to any one (or two) of them the capacity ever to consolidate all governmental authority in itself, while permitting the whole effectively to carry forward the work of government. Unlike separation of powers, however, the checks-and-balances idea does not suppose a radical division of government into three parts, with particular functions neatly parceled out among them. Rather, the focus is on relationships and interconnections, on maintaining the conditions in which the intended struggle at the apex may continue. From this perspective, as from the perspective of separation of functions, it is not important how powers below the apex are treated; the important question is whether the relationship of each of the three named actors of the Constitution to the exercise of those powers is such as to promise a continuation of their effective independence and interdependence.

. . . I argue that, for any consideration of the structure given law-administration below the very apex of the governmental structure, the rigid separation-of-powers compartmentalization of governmental functions should be abandoned in favor of analysis in terms of separation of functions and checks and balances. . . . A shorthand way of putting the argument is that we should stop pretending that all our government (as distinct from its highest levels) can be allocated into three neat parts. The theory of separation-of-powers breaks down when attempting to locate administrative and regulatory agencies within one of the three branches; its vitality, rather, lies in the formulation and specification of the controls that Congress, the Supreme Court and the President may exercise over administration and regulation. . . .

[T]he important fact is that an agency is neither Congress nor President nor Court, but an inferior part of government. Each agency is subject to control relationships with some or all of the three constitutionally named branches, and those relationships give an assurance—functionally similar to that provided by the separation-of-powers notion for the constitutionally named bodies—that they will not pass out of control.[1] Powerful and potentially arbitrary as they may be, the Secretary of Agriculture and the Chairman of the SEC for this reason do not present the threat that led the framers to insist on a splitting of the authority of government at its very top. What we have, then, are three named repositories of authorizing power and control, and an infinity of institutions to which parts of the authority of each may be lent. The three must share the reins of control; means must be found of assuring that no one of them becomes dominant. But it is not terribly important to number or allocate the horses that pull the carriage of government. . . .

[G]iven the realities of contemporary government and the inescapable constraints of constitutional text and context, we can achieve the worthy ends of those who drafted our Constitution only if we give up the notion that it embodies a neat division of all government into three separate branches, each endowed with a unique portion of governmental power and employing no other. The apportionment was made, but it was made only as to those actors occupying the very apex of government—Congress, President, and Supreme Court. The remainder of government was left undefined, in the expectation that congressional judgments about appropriate structure would serve so long as they observed the two prescriptive judg-

---

1. For example, one may understand the delegation doctrine in this functional way, rather than as an indication "where" in government rulemaking occurs. That doc-trine requires both statutory authorization (a relationship with Congress) and a capacity on the part of the courts to assure legality (a relationship with the courts). . . .

ments embodied in the Constitution: that the work of law-administration be under the supervision of a unitary, politically accountable chief executive; and that the structures chosen permit, even encourage, the continuation of rivalries and tensions among the three named heads of government, in order that no one body become irreversibly dominant and thus threaten to deprive the people themselves of their voice and control.

b. CONTRASTING METHODOLOGIES

Formalism and Functionalism

REBECCA L. BROWN, SEPARATED POWERS AND ORDERED LIBERTY, 139 U. Pa. L. Rev. 1513 (1991): "Those who espouse the formalist view of separated powers seek judicial legitimacy by insisting upon a firm textual basis in the Constitution for any governmental act. They posit that the structural provisions of the Constitution should be understood solely by their literal language and the drafters' original intent regarding their application, giving little or no weight to the influence of changed circumstances or broad objectives such as good or efficient government. The formalist approach is committed to strong substantive separations between the branches of government, finding support in the traditional expositions of the theme of 'pure' separated powers, such as the maxim that 'the legislature makes, the executive executes, and the judiciary construes the law.' Thus the formalists attempt to ensure that exercise of governmental power comports strictly with the original blueprint laid down in articles I, II, and III of the Constitution. Under formalist thinking, the creation of independent administrative agencies, for example, is considered a violation of the Constitution because such agencies require the exercise of governmental power in ways that involve an overlap of expressly assigned functions, subject to the control of none of the three branches.

"The implications and consequences of formalism are significant. First, it depends upon a belief that legislative, executive, and judicial powers are inherently distinguishable as well as separable from one another. . . . Moreover, formalism, at least as promoted by Justice Scalia, appears to be concerned primarily with forcing the Court to adhere to bright-line rules to foster predictability and restraint in judging. . . . An additional consequence of formalism is that it tends to straitjacket the government's ability to respond to new needs in creative ways, even if those ways pose no threat to whatever might be posited as the basic purposes of the constitutional structure. And ironically, in light of the usual textualist support for judicial restraint, the Court is forced to engage in a relatively high degree of judicial activism. Formalism, although conceiving a narrow role for the Court, forces it to strike down any action for which it cannot find express textual justification in the Constitution, even when two branches of the federal government may have agreed or acquiesced in the use of certain powers.

"Finally, formalism supports majoritarianism. It is no accident that many of those who advocate the formalist view of constitutional interpretation for separation-of-powers issues also strongly favor greater strength for the Executive Branch—a majoritarian institution—through a 'unitary' theory of executive power. Formalism restricts innovation in sharing power and encourages independence of the branches; in the modern era it has most often been Congress, as the instigator of political change through legislation, that has initiated new modes of allocating or sharing power, at least in the domestic sphere. Thus, the formalist view as understood by the Burger and Rehnquist Courts has tended to work to restrict Congress to the advantage of the Executive. . . . [F]ormalism resists efforts to blend the areas of turf between Congress and the Executive; it promotes the passage of legislation and the execution of the laws strictly in the manner set forth in the Constitution. It thus ensures that the majoritarian political outcomes contemplated by the procedures outlined in articles I and II will not be compromised.

"In contrast, advocates of the 'functionalist' approach urge the Court to ask a different question: whether an action of one branch interferes with one of the core functions of another. The sharing of powers, in itself, is not repugnant to the functionalists, nor is the formation of alliances among the branches repugnant, as long as the basic principles of separated powers are not impaired. The functionalist view follows a different strand of separation-of-powers tradition from that of the formalists: the American variant that stresses not the independence, but the interdependence of the branches. 'While the Constitution diffuses power the better to secure liberty, it also contemplates that practice will integrate the dispersed powers into a workable government. It enjoins upon its branches separateness but interdependence, autonomy but reciprocity.'[1]

"Functionalism appears to bestow on judges a much greater discretion than does formalism. In order for the functionalist system to work, someone must determine what values or functions are central to the constitutional structure, and must define the extent to which changed circumstances should be permitted to influence that determination. Functionalist analysis is criticized, therefore, for its indeterminacy and the inevitability of ad hoc decisionmaking under its influence. In reality, however, the deference contemplated by functionalism has resulted in a less activist role for the Judiciary than has formalism—or at least it fosters activism of a different kind. While formalism nearly always results in striking down the challenged measure, functionalism nearly always upholds it. The activism of functionalism resides in the unguided discretion that it necessarily bestows on judges.

"The functionalist approach, like the formalist, is majoritarian in outcome. Because it encourages cooperation among branches, it would likely permit schemes to which Congress and the Executive, the two majoritarian branches, give their assent. Thus it is a theory that employs the principle of judicial restraint, and relies largely upon the departments of government themselves to work out what is best for them politically . . . ."

CYNTHIA R. FARINA, STATUTORY INTERPRETATION AND THE BALANCE OF POWER IN THE ADMINISTRATIVE STATE, 89 Colum. L.Rev. 452 (1989): "[O]ur tendency to

---

1. Youngstown Sheet & Tube Co. v. Sawyer, 343 U.S. 579, 635 (1952) (Jackson, J., concurring).

describe the constitutional scheme as one of 'separation of powers and checks and balances' can be misleading. This conventional, bifurcated phrasing obscures the fact that the latter represented, for those who drafted and defended the Constitution, a vital and indispensable aspect of the former. By the time of the ratification, the prevailing understanding of separation of powers was no longer a simplistic call for absolute segregation of conceptually distinct functions. The experience between independence and the Constitutional Convention had caused American political theorists to rethink the nature of governmental authority. They came to conclude that political power was, in Gordon Wood's words, 'essentially homogenous.'[2] Whether manifested as lawmaking, execution or adjudication, whether exercised by officials who were elected popularly, elected indirectly or appointed, all power in government shared the same fundamental quality: it was dangerous unless adequately offset and controlled. And so, notwithstanding their literal sense, the words 'separation of powers' came to connote something far more subtle and intricate than a mere, abstractly logical division. The phrase expressed the expectation that, through the carefully orchestrated disposition and sharing of authority, restraint would be found in power counterbalancing power.

"This complexity of American separation of powers theory is critical. . . . Those who forged the structural theory of the Constitution did not, of course, foresee the modern administrative agency—with its potent concentration of law making, law executing and adjudicating power—any more than they anticipated the federal commitment to social and economic intervention that created it. They were, however, acutely self-conscious that they were designing a plan for the future. Montesquieu had both reminded them of the inevitability of change and encouraged them to believe that a government designed on separation of powers principles could adapt: 'These three powers should naturally form a state of repose or inaction. But as there is a necessity for movement in the course of human affairs, they are forced to move, but still in concert.'[3] The peculiarly American conception of separation of powers that they developed sought balance, not stasis. The genius of a system in which authority was shared rather than rigidly divided was, Madison explained, that each part could respond to the movement of power over time. Change would simply prompt a readjustment, so long as each part retained 'the necessary constitutional means . . . to resist encroachments of the others.'[4]

"We can thus understand the structural model as one of dynamic equilibrium: As power flows among the power centers in government, new patterns of counterbalance emerge to provide restraint. The movement of power can be accepted so long as equilibrium can then be reestablished. The model is inherently flexible; new configurations of power may be formed. But its pliancy is not to be mistaken for unconditional license. Innovation in one area may call for a responsive shift in other areas. An

---

2. Gordon S. Wood, The Creation of the American Republic, 1776–87, at 604 (1969).

3. 1 Montesquieu, The Spirit of Laws, bk. XI, ch.6 at 172 (T. Nugent trans. 1878).

4. FEDERALIST No. 51, at 349 (J. Madison) (J. Cooke ed. 1961).

exercise of authority by one branch may become constitutionally necessary because of a realignment of power elsewhere in government."

STEPHEN L. CARTER, CONSTITUTIONAL IMPROPRIETIES: REFLECTIONS ON MISTRETTA, MORRISON, AND ADMINISTRATIVE GOVERNMENT, 57 U. Chi. L. Rev. 357 (1990): "Th[e] failure of the Court to produce a coherent theory [for dealing with separation of powers questions] is particularly ironic when placed alongside the reasonably consistent doctrines and workable tests that the Justices have developed to govern adjudication under such open-ended [constitutional] provisions as the First, Fifth, and Fourteenth Amendments. True, the doctrines have been challenged and their application to particular cases questioned, but for those who believe in judicial process, the simple fact of taking the Constitution seriously—which, in my view, the entire Court struggles to do when individual rights are at issue—is reassuring. When facing structural problems in general, however, and separation of powers questions in particular, the Justices sometimes seem to consider the possibility of constitutionalism almost as an afterthought.

"This approach might have matters exactly backward. Perhaps constitutionalism is more important in structural cases than in cases about rights. Perhaps it is important to have clear, determinate answers about the structure of government so that those who want to change the way the world works understand where the power lies. What might be needed is a constitutional 'safe harbor,' a part of constitutional governance that is shielded from the winds of change that blow constantly through society.... If all provisions of the Constitution are equally fluid, if relatively determinate results are no more possible in reading the Presentment Clause than in reading the Equal Protection Clause, then all of governance is essentially left up for grabs, and it becomes difficult to defend the claim that constitutionalism limits in any coherent sense the structure and operations of the government of the United States. In the words of Richard Epstein, 'The importance of a fixed constitutional framework and stable institutional arrangements is necessarily lost once the framework that was designed to place a limit upon politics becomes the central subject of the politics it was designed to limit.' If the structural provisions of the Constitution evolve freely as the felt political needs of the country change, then we might as well say that the federal government controls the Constitution rather than, as we teach school-children, the other way around.

"... The entire point of a constitution that governs structure is to enable government to function while restraining the ability of government to restructure itself."

Purposivism

REBECCA L. BROWN, SEPARATED POWERS AND ORDERED Liberty, 139 U. Pa. L. Rev. 1513 (1991) [internal quotations omitted]: "Missing from the analysis of both [functionalist and formalist] camps is an appropriate external value. By 'appropriate,' I mean a norm that is consistent with the reasons for separating powers in the first place. Few seem to be asking which (or what) approach to constitutional analysis—formalist, functionalist, or some other—will serve more reliably the underlying purposes of the constitutional provisions being interpreted. A counter-majoritarian approach better addresses the underlying purposes of separated powers. Unlike both the formalist and functionalist schools, an 'ordered-liberty' analysis would have the Court examine governmental acts in light of the degree to which they may tend to detract from fairness and accountability in the process of government. If process is impaired in this way, then the action poses a threat to individual liberty. The degree to which one branch may invade the institutional turf of another is irrelevant, as is the presence or absence of interbranch agreement to share turf. In either case, the Court should evaluate the potential effect of the action on the procedural rights of individuals. Interpreting the original body of the Constitution itself as containing such an inherent check on majority action effectuates a major tenet of the Framers.''

GEOFFREY P. MILLER, RIGHTS AND STRUCTURE IN CONSTITUTIONAL THEORY, 8 Social Philosophy & Policy 196 (1991): "There are a number of good reasons to suppose that concern for individual liberties should inform separation of powers analysis. Even an elementary analysis of the system of checks and balances reveals what appears to be a principle of liberty in operation. The overwhelmingly distinctive features of checks and balances is that almost all of them operate negatively. Each branch is given the power to negative—to veto—actions of the other branches.... The upshot is that a massive preference is built into the structure of the system of checks and balances for government inaction over government action. This principle of liberty is entirely consistent with the principles that inform the Bill fo Rights....

"[T]he appropriate type of 'liberty' to investigate in separation of powers cases is at an intermediate level of generality—not whether a particular plaintiff or defendant stands to lose her liberty in a particular case, nor whether the alleged erosion of checks and balances might lead to some breakdown of constitutional structure which in turn might impinge on individual liberty, but rather whether permitting the challenged governmental arrangement to exist across a range of similar cases would on average restrict individual liberty, as compared to the situation without such an arrangement....

"... Since the 1930s the Supreme Court has favored personal liberties and has relegated economic liberties to the back of the constitutional bus.... All the Framers were intensely concerned about preserving property rights. Their great intellectual mentor, Locke, viewed the preservation of private property as an essential part of the justification of government. It would be astonishing if the structure established in the original Constitution were not seen as protecting property rights.

"These considerations suggest that government arrangements should be examined in separation of powers cases not only to determine whether on balance they tend to restrict personal liberties but also whether or not over a broad range of cases the arrangement in question would threaten the sanctity and security of private property.''

Abstentionism

JONATHAN L. ENTIN, CONGRESS, THE PRESIDENT, AND THE SEPARATION OF POWERS: RETHINKING THE VALUE OF LITIGATION, 43 Admin. L. Rev. 31 (1991): "[T]he quest for ultimate judicial resolution of constitutional turf battles between Congress and the President has undesirable consequences for the nation as a whole. Separation of powers disputes implicate fundamental questions respecting the role of government, questions that rarely receive detailed attention in Supreme Court opinions. Excessive reliance upon the Court deceives us into thinking that these disputes are purely constitutional in nature and that only the Justices can resolve them. Demanding judicial resolution improperly diminishes the role of the political branches in interpreting the Constitution; emphasizing the constitutionality of a proposal diverts attention from its often dubious wisdom....

"Some commentators, mostly notably Dean Choper, have suggested that the judiciary refrain from deciding constitutional conflicts between Congress and the President. This approach would require substantial revision of the political question doctrine and would uphold interbranch accommodations that contravened express textual provisions of the Constitution. A less extreme analysis would defer to arrangements devised by Congress and the President provided that those arrangements were consistent with the constitutional text. The goal would be to discourage litigation by persuading the political branches that resort to the judicial process would rarely succeed. This in turn might create incentives for the legislature and the executive to assess the stakes of their disputes more realistically and to fashion workable solutions that would promote both free and responsible government.

"The recommendation against reliance upon judicial resolution of separation of powers disputes between Congress and the President does not necessarily apply to other constitutional issues. The rationale for the recommendation in this context is that the legislative and executive branches generally have ample resources with which to protect themselves. That is not true, for example, in individual rights cases, where the party asserting a constitutional violation frequently lacks meaningful access to the political process as a means of self-defense."

Public Choice Economics

Jonathan R. Macey, Transaction Costs and the Normative Elements of the Public Choice Model: an Application to Constitutional Theory, 74 Va. L. Rev. 471 (1988): "Perhaps the most fundamental precept of microeconomic theory is that people act as rational, utility-maximizing individuals. This model guided the framers of the United States Constitution as well.... Specifically, the drafters of the Constitution desired to create a system of government that would operate under the novel assumption that, in the ordinary course of human affairs, neither the governors nor the governed could be expected to be altruistic, other-regarding beings. Rather, ... consistent with basic economic principles, the framers of the Constitution assumed they were establishing a system of government that would guide the affairs of rational, highly self-interested economic actors who would be governed by other equally self-interested individuals....

. . .

"A basic presumption of the economic theory of legislation is that, all else equal, increasing levels of expenditures by an interest group on a particular issue increase that group's influence on that issue. The structure of government, however, greatly affects the marginal price that an interest group must pay to obtain the passage of a particular statute. Thus, constitutional drafters who are concerned about the welfare-reducing influence of special interest groups can design a governmental structure that makes it relatively costly to obtain passage of a statute.

"A venerable and straightforward application of the notion that altering the structure of government can affect the cost and thus the production function of legislation was offered by Montesquieu. Montesquieu argued that a separation of powers between the various functions of government would control governmental abuse by providing a check on the lawmaking ability of rival branches. The principle of separation of powers, advocated by Montesquieu and incorporated in many governmental organizational structures, is a way of increasing the costs to discrete special interest groups of achieving their legislative goals. Establishing a system of government with a separation of powers not only raises the equilibrium price for obtaining passage of a law, it also imposes varying costs on different interest groups, depending on the characteristics of each group and the nature of the legislation. . . .

"Establishing several independent branches of government that can block or impede the enactments of rival branches is a means of raising the cost of obtaining legislative enactments for all groups. If a two-thirds vote must be obtained in one elected body to override the veto of the executive, for example, the costs to an interest group of obtaining passage of a statute of which the executive disapproves must also go up. Similarly, if a third branch of government can invalidate or misconstrue (either intentionally or unintentionally) a legislative enactment, then the expected benefit of a statute is necessarily decreased.

"In sum, then, the classical justification for the separation of powers is that it raises the cost of special interest legislation by lowering the probability of its ultimately becoming law."

SECTION 3. THE CONSTITUTIONALITY OF EMPOWERING AGENCIES TO ADJUDICATE INDIVIDUAL DISPUTES

"The Judicial Power of the United States shall be vested in one supreme Court and in such inferior Courts as the Congress may from time to time ordain and establish. The Judges, both of the supreme and inferior Courts, shall hold their Offices during good Behavior, and shall, at stated Times, receive for their Services, a Compensation, which shall not be diminished during their Continuance in Office."

U.S. Constitution, Art. III, § 1

"In Suits at common law, where the value in controversy shall exceed twenty dollars, the right of trial by jury shall be preserved. . . ."

U.S. Constitution, Amend. VII

"The Congress shall have Power ... To make all Laws which shall be necessary and proper for carrying into Execution the foregoing Powers, and all other Powers vested by this Constitution in the Government of the United States, or in any Department or Officer thereof."

U.S. Constitution, Art. I, § 8, ¶ 18

The judicial power of the United States—the power to resolve specified categories of "Cases" and "Controversies" particularly important to the national government—is as clearly vested by the Constitution in the federal judiciary as the legislative power is in Congress. Hence, when Congress assigns adjudication of disputes to agencies, the problem is not that the legislative branch is giving away some of its own power. Rather, it is reallocating what seemingly ought to be judicial business—a possibly hostile interference with the work of a coordinate (perhaps especially vulnerable) branch.

The Constitution clearly envisions substantial Congressional power to structure the institutions that do the judicial work of the national government. Insofar as the text of Article III itself suggests, Congress need not create inferior federal courts at all. Apparently, it could rely on state courts for trial, and intermediate appellate, adjudication involving federal law. Relying on Congress' seemingly absolute power over whether the lower federal courts exist, the Supreme Court has long held that it may withhold parts of the Article III judicial power from whatever lower courts it does create. Even the Supreme Court's appellate jurisdiction is subject to "such Exceptions, and ... such Regulations as the Congress shall make." Art. III, § 2, ¶ 2. From your study of Constitutional Law or Federal Courts, you may already realize that defining the extent of Congress's authority in this area is one of the knottiest questions in American jurisprudence, and one the Court steadfastly avoids.[1] But what if Congress decides to create *federal* institutions to adjudicate claims within the federal judicial power—but *not* to give those adjudicators the Article III protections of life tenure and guarantee against reduction in compensation? These institutions may be designated "courts" (e.g., the Court of Federal Claims) and the adjudicators may be called "judges" (or "administrative law judges"), but they are not part of the judicial branch established by the Constitution.[2]

Why would Congress—or, for that matter, state legislatures operating under analogous state constitutional structures—take such a step? LOUIS JAFFE AND NATHANIEL NATHANSON, ADMINISTRATIVE LAW: CASES AND MATERIALS 133–36 (1961), describes the genesis of the workers' compensation board, one of the earliest forms of administrative agency. These boards implemented state legislative decisions to displace the common law of torts with

---

1. The classic treatment appears in Henry M. Hart, Jr., The Power of Congress to Limit the Jurisdiction of Federal Courts: An Exercise in Dialectic, 66 Harv. L.Rev. 1362 (1953). Those who want a brief introduction (or refresher) should read the Note on the Constitutionality of Precluding Review, p. 1224 below.

2. Acknowledging this, entities such as the Court of Federal Claims (whose judges are appointed for 15–year terms) are referred to as "Article I courts."

a substantively and procedurally simpler—and more employee-favoring—statutory scheme for compensating harms suffered from accidents in the workplace. (Eventually, Congress adopted this model at the federal level for workplace injuries suffered by railroad workers in interstate commerce and by longshoremen and harborworkers working on navigable waters). "... Stripped of minutiae, an industrial accident board adjudicates the claim of an industrial worker, sometimes against his employer, sometimes directly against a state insurance fund, that he has suffered an accidental injury growing out of and in the course of his employment. Our courts every day decide similar questions applying a superstructure of rules much more complicated and difficult. . . .

"The reasons why the business was not conferred on the courts are these. First, the [negligence-based] doctrines of the common law were inapposite [under statutes providing for no-fault regimes]. Second, the courts could not be trusted to apply statutory doctrines which departed so radically from the common law. The common law doctrines applicable to industrial accidents were a peculiar compound in part based on methods of production which were outmoded and in part based on the pervading business philosophy of laissez faire. The defendant employer was charged, if at all, only if negligent, and the plaintiff employee was disbarred if he too had been negligent. But in deciding the issue of negligence, the courts were unwilling to criticize too severely plant layouts and industrial operations. They were new, experimental. The investment in them seemed to the judges too precious and too rich in the potentiality of increased production to subject them to the uncertain effects of paying for the costs of industrial accident. It was held that if the employee could be thought to know of the risk he could be taken to have assumed it. Under the earlier conditions of hand-powered production, a worker could perhaps take care of himself. The philosophy of laissez faire added the emphasis of self-reliance regardless of risk. Yet it became clear that the machines inevitably consumed a constant number of arms and legs and eyes. The workers were without resources to absorb the cost to themselves and their families. . . .

"Nothing functionally intrinsic to the scheme, at least as at first conceived, required the creation of a new agency. Indeed, in some states, New Jersey was one, workmen's compensation was originally administered by the courts, but in most states, and finally in nearly all, specialized boards were set up. The courts were thought to be hostile to the purposes of the legislation and were incidentally too expensive and too much taken up with other business. What was needed was an agency which was sympathetic, which cost the worker little or nothing and had no other business. In what sense is such an agency administrative, as distinguished from a court? We see at once that the answer must run as much in terms of our constitutional system as in generic or functional terms. A court and a compensation board are fundamentally alike in that they determine controversies under the law upon the basis of evidence received in a hearing between the parties. (This is a shade more true of cases where the proceeding is against the employer than it is of proceedings against a state fund.) They are different in that a court as we know it today is a court of general jurisdiction, the board is restricted to one subject.[3] ... [T]hough expertness came to be an important aspect of its specialization, it came perhaps as a byproduct. It was the advocate rather than the expert who was sought. ..."

Doesn't the legislative attempt to vest adjudicatory authority in bodies that are not constitutional courts necessarily violate separation of powers?

Commodity Futures Trading Commission v. Schor

Supreme Court of the United States, 1986.
478 U.S. 833.

■ JUSTICE O'CONNOR delivered the opinion of the Court.

[Schor traded commodities futures through a broker at Conti Commodity Services, Inc., a firm regulated by the Commodity Futures Trading Commission. The CFTC is an independent regulatory commission, having roughly the same relationship to the commodities markets as the SEC has to the stock markets. Schor lost money in his trades, and so owed Conti a substantial sum. Alleging that this debit balance was the result of Conti's violations of the Commodity Exchange Act, 7 U.S.C. § 1 et seq., Schor sought "reparations" before the CFTC under § 14 of the Act. Section 14 provides that any person injured by violations of the CEA or CFTC regulations may apply to the Commission for an order directing the offender to pay reparations to the complainant and may enforce that order in federal district court. Congress created this procedure as an "inexpensive and expeditious" alternative to the courts or arbitration, S.Rep. No. 95–850, p. 11 (1978). The remedy is, however, non-exclusive; no rule prevents such a plaintiff from seeking arbitration or bringing a judicial action.

In the meantime, Conti had filed a diversity action in federal district court to recover Schor's debt. Schor counterclaimed in this action, reiterating his charges that the debit balance was due to Conti's violations of the CEA. Schor also twice suggested that the district court should dismiss or stay this federal action, to permit the CFTC to resolve it. (The CFTC had, by regulation, given defendants in reparations actions the right to raise, and have adjudicated, counterclaims "aris[ing] out of the ... transactions or occurrences set forth in the complaint." CFTC Rule 12.23(b)(2).) Although the District Court refused to *compel* Conti to try its contractual claim to the CFTC, Conti voluntarily dismissed its federal court action and counterclaimed in the reparations proceeding—apparently, to avoid the expense of litigating before two tribunals. Conti denied violating the CEA; it asserted that the debit balance resulted from Schor's trading, and was therefore a simple debt owed by Schor.

After discovery, briefing, and a hearing, the administrative law judge (ALJ) in Schor's reparations proceeding ruled in Conti's favor on both Schor's claims and Conti's counterclaims. Schor then for the first time challenged the CFTC's jurisdiction over Conti's counterclaim, asserting

3. [Ed.] The other salient difference, in the case of federal agencies, is the absence of the Article III touchstones: life tenure and protection against salary diminution.

that the CFTC lacked statutory authority for Rule 12.23(b)(2). The ALJ rejected this challenge, and the CFTC accepted his decision. When Schor sought judicial review, the D.C. Circuit, sua sponte, questioned whether CFTC could constitutionally adjudicate Conti's counterclaims. The Supreme Court had recently decided Northern Pipeline Construction Co. v. Marathon Pipe Line Co., 458 U.S. 50 (1982) ("Northern Pipeline"), which jolted the legal community by declaring the system of bankruptcy courts an unconstitutional assignment of adjudicatory power outside Article III. The D.C. Circuit found "[s]erious constitutional problems" with Rule 12.23(b)(2) under Northern Pipeline. To avoid these problems, it construed the CEA as not conferring on CFTC the power to adjudicate common-law counterclaims.

The Supreme Court responded that the strategy of construing statutes to avoid constitutional problems, while often sound, was confined to cases in which a limiting construction was reasonably available. Statutes could not to be rewritten to escape constitutional doubt. The Court read in the CEA an explicit congressional purpose to confer the jurisdiction Rule 12.23(b)(2) exercised. Thus, it was "squarely faced with the question of whether the CFTC's assumption of jurisdiction over common-law counterclaims violates Article III of the Constitution."]

III

Article III, § 1 directs that the "judicial Power of the United States shall be vested in one supreme Court and in such inferior Courts as the Congress may from time to time ordain and establish," and provides that these federal courts shall be staffed by judges who hold office during good behavior, and whose compensation shall not be diminished during tenure in office. Schor claims that these provisions prohibit Congress from authorizing the initial adjudication of common law counterclaims by the CFTC, an administrative agency whose adjudicatory officers do not enjoy the tenure and salary protections embodied in Article III.

Although our precedents in this area do not admit of easy synthesis, they do establish that the resolution of claims such as Schor's cannot turn on conclusory reference to the language of Article III. Rather, the constitutionality of a given congressional delegation of adjudicative functions to a non-Article III body must be assessed by reference to the purposes underlying the requirements of Article III. This inquiry, in turn, is guided by the principle that "practical attention to substance rather than doctrinaire reliance on formal categories should inform application of Article III." Thomas v. Union Carbide Agricultural Prod. Co., 473 U.S. 568 (1985). See also Crowell v. Benson, p. 127 below.

A

[The Court first considered whether, by bringing the reparations action and encouraging Conti to counterclaim there, Schor had waived any objections to the CFTC's jurisdiction. It reasoned that "Article III, § 1 serves both to protect the role of the independent judiciary within the constitutional scheme of tripartite government, and to safeguard litigants' right to have claims decided before judges who are free from potential domination by other branches of government." [internal quotes omitted.] The latter "personal" right was waivable and had "indisputably" been waived. The Court then turned to the former, "structural" claim.]

B

... [A]s "an inseparable element of the constitutional system of checks and balances[,]" Northern Pipeline, 458 U.S., at 58[,] Article III, § 1 safeguards the role of the Judicial Branch in our tripartite system by barring congressional attempts "to transfer jurisdiction [to non-Article III tribunals] for the purpose of emasculating" constitutional courts, National Insurance Co. v. Tidewater Co., 337 U.S. 582, 644 (1949) (Vinson, C.J., dissenting), and thereby preventing "the encroachment or aggrandizement of one branch at the expense of the other." Buckley v. Valeo, 424 U.S. 1, 122 (1976) (per curiam). To the extent that this structural principle is implicated in a given case, the parties cannot by consent cure the constitutional difficulty for the same reason that the parties by consent cannot confer on federal courts subject matter jurisdiction beyond the limitations imposed by Article III, § 2. ... [T]he limitations serve institutional interests that the parties cannot be expected to protect.

In determining the extent to which a given congressional decision to authorize the adjudication of Article III business in a non-Article III tribunal impermissibly threatens the institutional integrity of the Judicial Branch, the Court has declined to adopt formalistic and unbending rules. Thomas, supra. Although such rules might lend a greater degree of coherence to this area of the law, they might also unduly constrict Congress' ability to take needed and innovative action pursuant to its Article I powers. Thus, in reviewing Article III challenges, we have weighed a number of factors, none of which has been deemed determinative, with an eye to the practical effect that the congressional action will have on the constitutionally assigned role of the federal judiciary. Id. Among the factors upon which we have focused are the extent to which the "essential attributes of judicial power" are reserved to Article III courts, and, conversely, the extent to which the non-Article III forum exercises the range of jurisdiction and powers normally vested only in Article III courts, the origins and importance of the right to be adjudicated, and the concerns that drove Congress to depart from the requirements of Article III.

... [T]he congressional scheme [here] does not impermissibly intrude on the province of the judiciary. The CFTC's adjudicatory powers depart from the traditional agency model in just one respect: the CFTC's jurisdiction over common law counterclaims. While wholesale importation of concepts of pendent or ancillary jurisdiction into the agency context may create greater constitutional difficulties, we decline to endorse an absolute prohibition on such jurisdiction out of fear of where some hypothetical "slippery slope" may deposit us. Indeed, the CFTC's exercise of this type of jurisdiction is not without precedent. Thus, in ... Katchen v. Landy, 382 U.S. 323 (1966), this Court upheld a bankruptcy referee's power to hear and decide state law counterclaims against a creditor who filed a claim in bankruptcy when those counterclaims arose out of the same transaction. We reasoned that, as a practical matter, requiring the trustee to commence a plenary action to recover on its counterclaim would be a "meaningless gesture."

In the instant case, we are likewise persuaded that there is little practical reason to find that this single deviation from the agency model is fatal to the congressional scheme. ... The CFTC, like the agency in Crowell v. Benson deals only with a "particularized area of law," whereas the jurisdiction of the bankruptcy courts found unconstitutional in Northern Pipeline extended to broadly "all civil proceedings arising under title 11 or arising in or *related to* cases under title 11." CFTC orders, like those of the agency in Crowell, but unlike those of the bankruptcy courts are enforceable only by order of the District Court. CFTC orders are also reviewed under the same "weight of the evidence" standard sustained in Crowell, rather than the more deferential ["clearly erroneous"] standard found lacking in Northern Pipeline. The legal rulings of the CFTC, like the legal determinations of the agency in Crowell, are subject to de novo review. Finally, the CFTC, unlike the bankruptcy courts under the 1978 Act, does not exercise "all ordinary powers of district courts," and thus may not, for instance, preside over jury trials or issue writs of habeas corpus.

Of course, the nature of the claim has significance.... [It] is a "private" right for which state law provides the rule of decision. It is therefore a claim of the kind assumed to be at the "core" of matters normally reserved to Article III courts. Yet ... there is no reason inherent in separation of powers principles to accord the state law character of a claim talismanic power in Article III inquiries.

We have explained that "the public rights doctrine reflects simply a pragmatic understanding that when Congress selects a quasi-judicial method of resolving matters that 'could be conclusively determined by the Executive and Legislative Branches,' the danger of encroaching on the judicial powers" is less than when private rights, which are normally within the purview of the judiciary, are relegated as an initial matter to administrative adjudication. Thomas, supra, at 3337 (quoting Northern Pipeline, supra, 458 U.S., at 68). ... The risk that Congress may improperly have encroached on the federal judiciary is obviously magnified when Congress "withdraw[s] from judicial cognizance any matter which, from its nature, is the subject of a suit at the common law, or in equity, or admiralty" and which therefore has traditionally been tried in Article III courts, and allocates the decision of those matters to a non-Article III forum of its own creation. Murray's Lessee v. The Hoboken Land and Improvement Co., 59 U.S. 272, 18 How. 272, 284 (1855). Accordingly, where private, common law rights are at stake, our examination of the congressional attempt to control the manner in which those rights are adjudicated has been searching. In this case, however, "[l]ooking beyond form to the substance of what" Congress has done, we are persuaded that the congressional authorization of limited CFTC jurisdiction over a narrow class of common law claims as an incident to the CFTC's primary, and unchallenged, adjudicative function does not create a substantial threat to the separation of powers.

It is clear that Congress has not attempted to "withdraw from judicial cognizance" the determination of Conti's right to the sum represented by the debit balance in Schor's account. Congress gave the CFTC the authority to adjudicate such matters, but the decision to invoke this forum is left entirely to the parties and the power of the federal judiciary to take jurisdiction of these matters is unaffected. . . . This is not to say, of course, that if Congress created a phalanx of non-Article III tribunals equipped to handle the entire business of the Article III courts without any Article III supervision or control and without evidence of valid and specific legislative necessities, the fact that the parties had the election to proceed in their forum of choice would necessarily save the scheme from constitutional attack. But this case obviously bears no resemblance to such a scenario, given the degree of judicial control saved to the federal courts, as well as the congressional purpose behind the jurisdictional delegation, the demonstrated need for the delegation, and the limited nature of the delegation.

When Congress authorized the CFTC to adjudicate counterclaims, its primary focus was on making effective a specific and limited federal regulatory scheme, not on allocating jurisdiction among federal tribunals. . . . This reparations scheme itself is of unquestioned constitutional validity. It was only to ensure the effectiveness of this scheme that Congress authorized the CFTC to assert jurisdiction over common law counterclaims. Indeed, as was explained above, absent the CFTC's exercise of that authority, the purposes of the reparations procedure would have been confounded.

It also bears emphasis that . . . CFTC adjudication of common law counterclaims is incidental to, and completely dependent upon, adjudication of reparations claims created by federal law, and in actual fact is limited to claims arising out of the same transaction or occurrence as the reparations claim.

In such circumstances, the magnitude of any intrusion on the Judicial Branch can only be termed de minimus. Conversely, were we to hold that the Legislative Branch may not permit such limited cognizance of common law counterclaims at the election of the parties, it is clear that we would "defeat the obvious purpose of the legislation to furnish a prompt, continuous, expert and inexpensive method for dealing with a class of questions of fact which are peculiarly suited to examination and determination by an administrative agency specially assigned to that task." Crowell v. Benson, 285 U.S., at 46. We do not think Article III compels this degree of prophylaxis. . . .

The judgment of the Court of Appeals for the District of Columbia Circuit is reversed and the case remanded for further proceedings consistent with this opinion.

It is so ordered.

■ JUSTICE BRENNAN, with whom JUSTICE MARSHALL joins, dissenting.

[Justice Brennan (the author of Northern Pipeline) argued that Article III, § 1 generally "prohibit[s] the vesting of *any* judicial functions" outside the judiciary, subject to "three narrow exceptions" that had been recognized over time: for territorial courts, for military courts martial, and for "courts that adjudicate certain disputes concerning public rights." Only the latter was important here, and Justice Brennan saw no way to fit the CFTC's counterclaim authority within it. His opinion stressed both the formal theory of separation of powers and the particular function of the judiciary:]

The Framers understood that a principal benefit of the separation of judicial power from the legislative and executive powers would be the protection of individual litigants from decisionmakers susceptible to majoritarian pressures. Article III's salary and tenure provisions promote impartial adjudication by placing the judicial power of the United States "in a body of judges insulated from majoritarian pressures and thus able to enforce [federal law] without fear of reprisal or public rebuke." United States v. Raddatz, 447 U.S. 667, 704 (1980) (Marshall, J., dissenting). As Alexander Hamilton observed, "[t]hat inflexible and uniform adherence to the rights of the constitution and of individuals, which we perceive to be indispensable in the courts of justice can certainly not be expected from judges who hold their offices by a temporary commission." The Federalist No. 78, p. 546. This is so because:

"If the power of making [periodic appointments] was committed either to the Executive or Legislature, there would be danger of an improper complaisance to the branch which possessed it; if to both, there would be an unwillingness to hazard the displeasure of either; if to the People, or to persons chosen by them for the special purpose, there would be too great a disposition to consult popularity, to justify a reliance that nothing would be consulted but the Constitution and the laws." Ibid.

"Next to permanency in office," Hamilton added, "nothing can contribute more to the independence of the Judges than a fixed provision for their support" because "*a power over a man's subsistence amounts to a power over his will.*" Id. at 548 (emphasis in original). ...

These important functions of Article III are too central to our constitutional scheme to risk their incremental erosion. ... More than a century ago, we recognized that Congress may not "withdraw from [Article III] judicial cognizance any matter *which, from its nature, is the subject of a suit at the common law*, or in equity, or admiralty." Murray's Lessee v. Hoboken Land and Improvement Co., 59 U.S. 272, 18 How. 272, 284 (1856). ... The Court attempts to support the substantial alteration it works today in our Article III jurisprudence by pointing, inter alia, to legislative convenience; to the fact that Congress does not altogether eliminate federal court jurisdiction over ancillary state-law counterclaims; and to Schor's "consent" to CFTC adjudication of Conti Commodity's counterclaims.[1]

---

1. The Court also rests its holding on the fact that Congress has not assigned the same sweeping judicial powers to the CFTC that it had assigned to the bankruptcy courts under the Bankruptcy Act of 1978 and that we held violated Article III in Northern Pipeline Co. v. Marathon Pipe Line Co., 458 U.S. 50 (1982). While I agree with the Court that the grant of judicial authority to the CFTC is significantly narrower in scope than the grant to the bankruptcy courts under the 1978 Act, in my view, that difference does not suffice to cure the constitutional defects raised by the grant of authority over state-law counterclaims to the CFTC.

... Article III's prophylactic protections were intended to prevent ... abdication to claims of legislative convenience. The Court requires that the legislative interest in convenience and efficiency be weighed against the competing interest in judicial independence. In doing so, the Court pits an interest the benefits of which are immediate, concrete, and easily understood against one, the benefits of which are almost entirely prophylactic, and thus often seem remote and not worth the cost in any single case. Thus, while this balancing creates the illusion of objectivity and ineluctability, in fact the result was foreordained, because the balance is weighted against judicial independence. The danger of the Court's balancing approach is, of course, that as individual cases accumulate in which the Court finds that the short-term benefits of efficiency outweigh the long-term benefits of judicial independence, the protections of Article III will be eviscerated.

... The Framers established *three* coequal branches of government and intended to preserve *each* from encroachment by either of the others. The Constitution did not grant Congress the general authority to bypass the judiciary whenever Congress deems it advisable, any more than it granted Congress the authority to arrogate to itself executive functions.

[That the CFTC merely shares authority over the counterclaims with the federal judiciary was unpersuasive, Justice Brennan argued, because the principle established is without limit—it leaves Congress free to create alternative tribunals, competing with the Article III judiciary across an enormous range of subject matter.] [C]ontrary to the Court's intimations, dilution of judicial power operates to impair the protections of Article III regardless of whether Congress acted with the "good intention" of providing a more efficient dispute resolution system or with the "bad intention" of strengthening the Legislative Branch at the expense of the judiciary. ...

NOTES ON THE PRECEDENT UNDERLYING SCHOR

As a practical matter, Schor seems to have shut the constitutional Pandora's box opened, four years earlier, by Northern Pipeline. However, the theoretical issues raised by the assignment of adjudication to decision-makers who are not members of the Article III judicial branch are extremely, and persistently, difficult. In essence, the problem is the familiar slippery slope: If Congress can assign *some* adjudication of individual rights to Article I courts or administrative agencies, what principled limits prevent it from creating an entire system of adjudication outside of Article III? These Notes allow you to assess the Court's efforts, *prior* to Schor, to reconcile Congress's power (under the Necessary and Proper Clause) to specify the working systems of the federal government, with the important—if delphic—requirements of Article III. The next set of Notes considers *post*-Schor developments, as well as the effect of the Seventh Amendment.

(1) CROWELL v. BENSON, 285 U.S. 22 (1932): This case, on the threshold of the New Deal era, was the Court's first important engagement with the constitutional questions posed by using agencies rather than courts as primary adjudicators. The Longshoremen's and Harbor Workers' Act bor-

rowed the strategy of state workmen's compensation schemes (see p. 119 above) to provide a federal tort-substitute for injuries arising in certain maritime employments. Crowell, deputy commissioner of the United States Employees' Compensation Commission, ordered Benson to compensate injured Knudsen. Benson denied that Knudsen was acting as his employee at the time of injury.[1] Under the Act, Commission decisions were reviewable in the district courts—to whom the statute gave plenary authority to redecide any questions of law, but only limited authority to review conclusions of fact. Benson claimed, inter alia, that Congress could not constitutionally vest fact-finding authority in the agency rather than an Article III court. The Supreme Court accepted this argument only for a limited set of issues (which it called "jurisdictional"); this part of the decision is discussed at p. 973 below. In reasoning that is generally taken to validate administrative adjudication, the Court rejected the bulk of Benson's constitutional argument:

"The [constitutional] question ... can be deemed to relate only to determinations of fact. [The Court noted the Act's provision that the district court has plenary authority to decide legal questions.] ... The Congress did not attempt to define questions of law, and the generality of the description leaves no doubt of the intention to reserve to the Federal court full authority to pass upon all matters which this Court had held to fall within that category. There is thus no attempt to interfere with, but rather provision is made to facilitate, the exercise by the court of its jurisdiction to deny effect to any administrative finding which is without evidence or 'contrary to the indisputable character of the evidence,' or where the hearing is 'inadequate,' or 'unfair,' or arbitrary in any respect.

"As to determinations of fact, the distinction is at once apparent between cases of private right and those which arise between the Government and persons subject to its authority in connection with the performance of the constitutional functions of the executive or legislative departments. The Court referred to this distinction in Murray's Lessee v. Hoboken Land and Improvement Company [18 How. 272,] pointing out that 'there are matters, involving public rights, which may be presented in such form that the judicial power is capable of acting on them, and which are susceptible to judicial determination, but which Congress may or may not bring within the cognizance of the courts of the United States, as it may deem proper.' Thus the Congress, in exercising the powers confided to it, may establish 'legislative' courts (as distinguished from 'constitutional courts in which the judicial power conferred by the Constitution can be deposited') which are ... to serve as special tribunals 'to examine and determine various matters, arising between the government and others, which from their nature do not require judicial determination and yet are susceptible of it.' But 'the mode of determining matters of this class is completely within congressional control. Congress may reserve to itself the power to decide, may delegate that power to executive officers, or may

---

1. According to Benson, he had loaned Knudsen the barge on which the injury occurred, for some purpose of Knudsen's own. The injury happened while Knudsen was re- pairing a cable that he had, allegedly, improperly cut during this personal venture. Thus, said Benson, Knudsen was not acting "as an employee" at the time.

commit it to judicial tribunals.' Ex parte Bakelite Corporation, 279 U.S. 438, 451. Familiar illustrations of administrative agencies created for the determination of such matters are found in connection with the exercise of the congressional power as to interstate and foreign commerce taxation, immigration, the public lands, public health, the facilities of the post office, pensions and payments to veterans.

"The present case does not fall within the categories just described but is one of private right, that is, of the liability of one individual to another under the law as defined. But in cases of that sort, there is no requirement that, in order to maintain the essential attributes of the judicial power, all determinations of fact in constitutional courts shall be made by judges. On the common law side of the Federal courts, the aid of juries is not only deemed appropriate but is required by the Constitution itself. In cases of equity and admiralty, it is historic practice to call to the assistance of the courts, without the consent of the parties, masters and commissioners or assessors, to pass upon certain classes of questions, as, for example, to take and state an account or to find the amount of damages. While the reports of masters and commissioners in such cases are essentially of an advisory nature, it has not been the practice to disturb their findings when they are properly based upon evidence, in the absence of errors of law, and the parties have no right to demand that the court shall redetermine the facts thus found. . . .

"The statute has a limited application, being confined to the relation of master and servant, and the method of determining the questions of fact, which arise in the routine of making compensation awards to employees under the Act, is necessary to its effective enforcement. ... For the purposes stated, we are unable to find any constitutional obstacle to the action of the Congress in availing itself of a method shown by experience to be essential in order to apply its standards to the thousands of cases involved, thus relieving the courts of a most serious burden while preserving their complete authority to insure the proper application of the law."

Note that Crowell uses an analytical structure with two distinct categories. Cases involving "public rights" concern disputes between "the Government and persons subject to its authority in connection with the performance of the constitutional functions of the executive or legislative departments." Although Congress might choose to employ Article III courts to adjudicate these disputes (so long as the disputes otherwise satisfy the "case" and "controversy" criteria of Article III), it could also use its Necessary and Proper authority to set up administrative mechanisms for resolving them. The basic notion seems to be that these matters—the setting of rates and tariffs, the grant of immigration rights or veterans benefits, the payment of claims of government contractors, etc.—could have been resolved directly by Congress or by the President's delegees. Assigning their resolution to an agency thus does not impermissibly infringe on the judiciary's exclusive constitutional function.

Public Right

By contrast, cases involving "private rights"—"that is, of the liability of one individual to another under the law as defined"—have a different constitutional status. Here, an Article III court must be used. But, says Crowell, it need not itself perform every adjudicatory function. Analogizing

Private Right

the administrative agency to special masters, commissioners, or assessors—other traditionally-employed "adjuncts" to Article III courts—the Court permits Congress to transfer some tasks to the agency adjudicator. *Some*—not all. A statutory scheme in which (1) the agency action is reviewable by an Article III court; (2) the reviewing court can redetermine, de novo, all questions of law; and (3) the reviewing court can exercise some, more limited review over factual determinations, is constitutionally sufficient to permit the Employee Compensation Commission to determine Benson's liability to Knudsen. Are all three elements constitutionally necessary?

(2) For 50 years, the area was relatively quiescent. Then Northern Pipeline Construction Co. filed for bankruptcy and initiated a reorganization proceeding in Bankruptcy Court. As permitted by the Bankruptcy Act, it sued Marathon there on state-law contract claims. Marathon moved to dismiss, arguing that the Act unconstitutionally conferred Article III judicial power upon bankruptcy judges, who lacked lifetime tenure and salary protection. These judges were given substantially all the powers of Article III judges in civil cases: They could preside over a jury trial, issue declaratory judgments or writs of habeas corpus, etc. Their judgments would become final if unchallenged, but were subject to review by Article III courts. In NORTHERN PIPELINE CONSTRUCTION CO. v. MARATHON PIPE LINE CO., 458 U.S. 50 (1982), the Court agreed with Marathon that the Act was unconstitutional—although the Justices could not agree on a rationale.

The plurality opinion by Justice Brennan (joined by Justices Blackmun, Marshall, and Stevens) was highly formalistic. The bankruptcy courts could not be analyzed in the "public rights" category: "[A] matter of public rights must at a minimum arise 'between the government and others.'" (quoting Crowell). Within the private rights category, the bankruptcy courts could not be saved on the Crowell "adjunct" theory. So much authority had been vested in bankruptcy judges that it could not be said the district courts "retained 'the essential attributes of the judicial power'" (quoting Crowell) or that those courts "were subject to sufficient control by the Art. III district courts."

Justice Rehnquist joined by Justice O'Connor, wrote more narrowly. He stressed that Marathon was being forced to submit to the bankruptcy court a claim it could ordinarily prosecute in state court. "None of the cases has gone so far as to sanction the type of adjudication to which Marathon will be subjected against its will under the provisions of the ... Act. To whatever extent different powers granted under that Act might be sustained under the 'public rights' doctrine ..., I am satisfied that the adjudication of Northern's lawsuit cannot be so sustained."

Justice White wrote a classically functionalist dissent for himself, Chief Justice Burger, and Justice Powell. He conceded that the plurality's approach was accurate as an historical proposition.[2] But he found it untenable

---

2. "Any reader could easily take Article III to mean that although Congress was free to establish such lower courts as it saw fit, any court that it did establish would be an 'inferior' court exercising 'judicial Power of the United States' and so must be manned by judges possessing both life-tenure and a guaranteed minimal income. This would be an eminently sensible reading and one that, as the plurality shows, is well founded in both

as a contemporary answer to the question "what limits Art. III places on Congress' ability to create adjudicative institutions designed to carry out federal policy established pursuant to the substantive authority given Congress elsewhere in the Constitution. Whether fortunate or unfortunate, at this point in the history of constitutional law that question can no longer be answered by looking only to the constitutional text." Reviewing "one of the most confusing and controversial areas of constitutional law," Justice White found "no difference in principle between the work that Congress may assign to an Art. I court and that which the Constitution assigns to Art. III courts. Unless we want to overrule a large number of our precedents upholding a variety of Art. I courts—not to speak of those Art. I courts that go by the contemporary name of 'administrative agencies'—this conclusion is inevitable. It is too late to go back that far; too late to return to the simplicity of the principle pronounced in Art. III and defended so vigorously and persuasively by Hamilton in The Federalist Nos. 78–82.

". . . Article III is not to be read out of the Constitution; rather, it should be read as expressing one value that must be balanced against competing constitutional values and legislative responsibilities. This Court retains the final word on how that balance is to be struck." The presence of judicial review, and the absence of issues of high political interest, persuaded Justice White that the Bankruptcy Act did not unacceptably weaken the judicial branch or contribute to "a dangerous accumulation of power in one of the political branches of government."

Northern Pipeline provoked a sharply critical response. The implications for the bankruptcy system were serious enough—leading the Court to employ the extraordinary remedy of staying its judgment for more than three months "to afford Congress an opportunity to reconstitute the bankruptcy courts or to adopt other valid means of adjudication, without impairing the interim administration of the bankruptcy laws." More serious, in the view of many, were the implications for administrative adjudication in a range of regulatory programs.[3]

(3) Some of these concerns were allayed in THOMAS v. UNION CARBIDE AGRICULTURAL PRODUCTS CO., 473 U.S. 568 (1985): The 1978 amendments to the Federal Insecticide, Fungicide and Rodenticide Act (FIFRA) permitted EPA to use one manufacturer's research data about the health, safety and environmental effects of its product in considering another manufacturer's later application to register a similar product. The goal was to streamline the registration process and make it, overall, less costly. These data were, of course, quite expensive and time-consuming to generate, and firms argued that they represented highly valuable trade secrets. FIFRA required that the follow-on registrant offer to compensate the originating firm for use of the data; it provided for binding arbitration should the two parties

the documentary sources and the political doctrine of separation of powers that stands behind much of our constitutional structure."

3. See, e.g., Henry P. Monaghan, Marbury and the Administrative State, 83 Colum. L.Rev. 1, 18–20 (1983); Martin H. Redish,

Legislative Courts, Administrative Agencies, and the Northern Pipeline Decision, 1983 Duke L.J. 197; Peter L. Strauss, The Place of Agencies in Government: Separation of Powers and the Fourth Branch, 84 Colum. L.Rev. 573, 631–33 (1984).

be unable to agree on amount. The arbitrator's decision was subject to judicial review only for "fraud, misrepresentation or other misconduct." Pesticide manufacturers argued that the statutory scheme unconstitutionally substituted virtually final arbitral decision for judicial resolution of a "private rights" dispute. The eight justices who reached the merits agreed that the FIFRA scheme was constitutional.

Justice O'Connor's opinion (for five justices) echoed Justice White's Northern Pipeline dissent. Stating that "an absolute construction of Article III is not possible," she emphasized: "[T]he Court has long recognized that Congress is not barred from acting pursuant to its powers under Article I to vest decisionmaking authority in tribunals that lack the attributes of Article III courts." In a deliberate departure from the formalism of the Northern Pipeline plurality, she identified "the enduring lesson of Crowell" as "that practical attention to substance rather than doctrinaire reliance on formal categories should inform application of Article III." Even the definition of the categories seemed to be destabilized: "If the identity of the parties alone determined the requirements of Article III, under [the manufacturers'] theory the constitutionality of many quasi-adjudicative agencies involving claims between individuals would be thrown into doubt."

In any event, "the right created by FIFRA is not a purely 'private' right, but bears many of the characteristics of a 'public' right. Use of a registrant's data to support a follow-on registration serves a public purpose as an integral part of a program safeguarding the public health. Congress has the power, under Article I, to authorize an agency administering a complex regulatory scheme to allocate costs and benefits among voluntary participants in the program without providing an Article III adjudication. It also has the power to condition issuance of registrations or licenses on compliance with agency procedures. . . .

"We note as well that the FIFRA arbitration scheme incorporates its own system of internal sanctions and relies only tangentially, if at all, on the Judicial Branch for enforcement. The danger of Congress or the Executive encroaching on the Article III judicial powers is at a minimum when no unwilling defendant is subjected to judicial enforcement power as a result of the agency 'adjudication.' See, e.g., Hart, The Power of Congress to Limit the Jurisdiction of Federal Courts: An Exercise in Dialectic, 66 Harv. L.Rev. 1362 (1953). . . .

"Finally, . . . FIFRA at a minimum allows private parties to secure Article III review of the arbitrator's 'findings and determination' for fraud, misconduct, or misrepresentation. This provision protects against arbitrators who abuse or exceed their powers or willfully misconstrue their mandate under the governing law. Moreover, review of constitutional error is preserved, and FIFRA, therefore, does not obstruct whatever judicial review might be required by due process. . . .

"Our holding is limited to the proposition that Congress, acting for a valid legislative purpose pursuant to its constitutional powers under Article I, may create a seemingly 'private' right that is so closely integrated into a public regulatory scheme as to be a matter appropriate for agency resolution with limited involvement by the Article III judiciary."

The four Justices of the Northern Pipeline plurality wrote separately. Justices Brennan (joined by Justices Marshall and Blackmun) analyzed the FIFRA scheme as a "public rights" case. "In one sense the question of proper compensation ... is ... a dispute about 'the liability of one individual to another under the law as defined.' Crowell v. Benson (defining matters of private right). But the dispute arises in the context of a federal regulatory scheme that virtually occupies the field. ... Although a compensation dispute under FIFRA ultimately involves a determination of the duty owed one private party by another, at its heart the dispute involves the exercise of authority by a Federal Government arbitrator in the course of administration of FIFRA's comprehensive regulatory scheme." Justice Stevens concurred in dismissing the action because of perceived standing problems.

NOTES ON THE FUTURE OF THE PUBLIC/PRIVATE RIGHTS DISTINCTION, AND THE RELEVANCE OF THE SEVENTH AMENDMENT

> *"In Suits at common law, where the value in controversy shall exceed twenty dollars, the right of trial by jury shall be preserved...."*

U.S. Constitution, Amend. VII

(1) Just when the Court seemed comfortably to have interred the formalism of the Northern Pipeline plurality, "public rights" reemerged in a new constitutionally significant guise in GRANFINANCIERA, S.A. v. PAUL C. NORDBERG, CREDITOR TRUSTEE, 492 U.S. 33 (1989). Once again, the context was bankruptcy. The trustee in bankruptcy had sued in federal court to recover money allegedly fraudulenty transferred by the bankrupt to Grandfinanciera. The district court referred the action to the bankruptcy court, which refused Grandfinanciera's request for a jury trial on grounds that recovery of money transferred by fraud is an equitable, rather than a legal, cause of action. On appeal, the Supreme Court agreed that Grandfinanciera's Seventh Amendment rights were violated by this way of proceeding.

Justice Brennan, writing for five justices (including Chief Justice Rehnquist), held that the trustee's claim was legal, not equitable, in nature. He then turned to "whether the Seventh Amendment confers on petitioners a right to a jury trial in the face of Congress' decision to allow a non-Article III tribunal to adjudicate the claims against them." This question, he wrote, "requires the same answer as the question whether Article III allows Congress to assign adjudication of that action to a non-Article III tribunal." And surprisingly—in light of Thomas and Schor—both questions were said to turn on the public right/private right distinction: "Congress may only deny trials by jury in actions at law ... in cases where 'public rights' are litigated."

However, these crucial analytical categories were redrawn in a way particularly relevant to administrative adjudication: "In our most recent discussion of the 'public rights' doctrine ... we rejected the view that a matter of public right must at a minimum arise between the government and others. We held, instead, that the Federal Government need not be a party for a case to revolve around 'public rights.' The crucial question, in cases not involving the Federal Government, is whether 'Congress, acting for a valid legislative purpose pursuant to its constitutional powers under Article I, [has] create[d] a seemingly 'private' right that is so closely integrated into a public regulatory scheme as to be a matter appropriate for agency resolution with limited involvement by the Article III judiciary.'' (quoting his concurrence in Thomas; other internal quotes omitted) In this case, however, the trustee's claim was neither against the Federal Government nor ''closely intertwined with a federal regulatory program Congress has the power to enact.'' Thus it concerned a ''private right'' and the Seventh Amendment guarantee applied. (The Court was careful *not* to decide before whom—the bankruptcy judge or the district judge—the jury trial must be held.)

This reappearance of the ''public rights''/''private rights'' distinction produced three dissents and a strident concurrence. Justices White (joined by Justices Blackmun and O'Connor) viewed the bankruptcy system as an integrated body of law, particularly the province of Congress to design and administered by a ''specialized tribunal where juries have no place.'' Justice Scalia, writing only for himself, would have pushed the doctrine in the opposite direction. He advocated repudiating both Thomas and Schor and returning to the pure formalism of the originally stated distinction: ''In my view a matter of 'public rights,' whose adjudication Congress may assign to tribunals lacking the essential characteristics of Article III courts, 'must at a minimum arise between the government and others.' . . . It is clear that what we meant by public rights [in Murray's Lessee] were not rights important to the public, or rights created by the public, but rights *of the public*—that is, rights pertaining to claims brought by or against the United States. For central to our reasoning was the device of waiver of sovereign immunity . . . [which] can only be implicated . . . in suits where the Government is a party.''

The alternative test of whether a right was ''closely integrated into a public regulatory scheme,'' had been adopted ''as far as I can tell by sheer force of our office. . . . There was in my view no constitutional basis for that decision. . . . I do not think one can preserve a system of separation of powers on the basis of such intuitive judgments regarding 'practical effects' [as characterized Schor]. . . . This central feature of the Constitution must be anchored in rules, not set adrift in some multifactored 'balancing test'— and especially not in a test that contains as its last and most revealing factor 'the concerns that drove Congress to depart from the requirements of Article III.' ''

Might one respond to Justice Scalia that, even if the alternative test for a ''public right'' departs from the history of the concept, it does remain faithful to the rationale of the concept? If (to follow Justice Scalia), the presence of the government as a party is a *necessary* condition for a ''public right'' case, is it a *sufficient* condition? Consider one of the most important categories of cases in which the government is a party: criminal prosecutions. Under these precedents, could Congress choose agencies as the primary enforcement fora for the criminal law? See note 3 below.

(2) The Supreme Court's early analysis of the Seventh Amendment and administrative adjudication suggested that the jury trial right would rarely attach to "typical" regulatory programs. NLRB v. JONES & LAUGHLIN STEEL CORP., 301 U.S. 1 (1937), was a multi-pronged constitutional attack on the National Labor Relations Act and the NLRB. (You may have read the decision in Constitutional Law for its holding on the Commerce Clause power.) In rejecting the Jones & Laughlin's Seventh Amendment challenge, the Court reasoned tersely that the Amendment applied only to proceedings "in the nature of a suit at common law"—and NLRA proceedings were "unknown to the common law. Reinstatement of the employee and payment for time lost are requirements imposed for violation of the statute and are remedies appropriate for its enforcement."

Eventually, however, the Court cut back the breadth of this reasoning. In CURTIS v. LOETHER, 415 U.S. 189 (1974), a suit for damages for violation of the fair housing provisions of the Civil Rights Act of 1968, the Court insisted, "The Seventh Amendment does apply to actions enforcing statutory rights...." Its analysis seemed to turn on Congress's choice of primary enforcement forum: "[I]f the statute creates legal rights and remedies, enforceable in the ordinary courts of law," then an opportunity for jury trial must be provided. On the other hand, citing Jones & Laughlin, "the Seventh Amendment is generally inapplicable in administrative proceedings where jury trials would be incompatible with the whole concept of administrative adjudication and would substantially interfere with the NLRB's role in the statutory scheme."

Three years later, this distinction was further developed in ATLAS ROOFING CO., INC. v. OCCUPATIONAL SAFETY AND HEALTH REVIEW COMMISSION, 430 U.S. 442 (1977). On finding a violation of the OSH Act or OSHA rules, an OSHA inspector issues a citation setting a time for abatement of the violation and, possibly, proposing a "civil penalty" that can be quite substantial for willful or repeated violations. The employer can contest the abatement or penalty order in an evidentiary hearing before an administrative law judge of the Occupational Health and Safety Review Commission. (Appeal to the full Commission from the ALJ's decision is possible; as affirmed or modified, the initial decision becomes the final OSHRC order.) This order may be reviewed by the appropriate circuit court of appeals, at the instance of either the Secretary of Labor or the employer. In that review, the "findings of the Commission with respect to questions of fact, if supported by substantial evidence on the record considered as a whole, shall be conclusive." The Secretary may bring an action in federal district court to collect the assessed penalty; in such an action, neither the fact of the violation nor the propriety of the penalty assessed may be retried. Two employers—Atlas Roofing and Irey—had been cited for worksite violations that had resulted, in each case, in an employee's death. Irey was assessed a $7500 penalty; Atlas, a $600 penalty. They claimed that the statutory assessment scheme violated their right to trial by jury.

Justice White wrote for a unanimous Court (Justice Blackmun not participating): "... Petitioners claim that a suit in a federal court by the Government for civil penalties for violation of a statute is a suit for a money judgment which is classically a suit at common law, and that the defendant therefore has a Seventh Amendment right to a jury determination of all issues of fact in such a case. . . . We disagree. At least in cases in which 'public rights' are being litigated—e.g., cases in which the Government sues in its sovereign capacity to enforce public rights created by statutes within the power of Congress to enact—the Seventh Amendment does not prohibit Congress from assigning the factfinding function and initial adjudication to an administrative forum with which the jury would be incompatible.[1]

"Congress has often created new statutory obligations, provided for civil penalties for their violation, and committed exclusively to an administrative agency the function of deciding whether a violation has in fact occurred. . . . In sum, [NLRB v. Jones & Laughlan and Curtis v. Loether] stand clearly for the proposition that when Congress creates new statutory 'public rights,' it may assign their adjudication to an administrative agency with which a jury trial would be incompatible, without violating the Seventh Amendment's injunction that jury trial is to be 'preserved' in 'suits at common law.' Congress is not required by the Seventh Amendment to choke the already crowded federal courts with new types of litigation or prevented from committing some new types of litigation to administrative agencies with special competence in the relevant field. This is the case even if the Seventh Amendment would have required a jury where the adjudication of those rights is assigned to a federal court of law instead of an administrative agency. . . . "

"[Petitioners argue] that the right to jury trial was never intended to depend on the identity of the forum to which Congress has chosen to submit a dispute; otherwise, it is said, Congress could utterly destroy the right to a jury trial by always providing for administrative rather than judicial resolution of the vast range of cases that now arise in the courts. The argument is well put, but it overstates the holdings of our prior cases and is in any event unpersuasive. Our prior cases support administrative factfinding in only those situations involving 'public rights,' e.g., where the Government is involved in its sovereign capacity under an otherwise valid statute creating enforceable public rights. Wholly private tort, contract, and property cases, as well as a vast range of other cases as well, are not at all implicated.

"More to the point, it is apparent from the history of jury trial in civil matters that factfinding, which is the essential function of the jury in civil cases, was never the exclusive province of the jury under either the English or American legal systems at the time of the adoption of the Seventh Amendment; and the question whether a fact would be found by a jury turned to a considerable degree on the nature of the forum in which a litigant found himself. Critical factfinding was performed without juries in

---

1. These cases do not involve purely 'private rights.' In cases which do involve only 'private rights,' this Court has accepted factfinding by an administrative agency, without intervention by a jury, only as an adjunct to an Art. III court, analogizing the agency to a jury or a special master and permitting it in admiralty cases to perform the function of the special master. Crowell v. Benson, 285 U.S. 22, 51–65 (1932). The Court there said: 'On the common law side of the federal courts, the aid of juries is not only deemed appropriate but is required by the Constitution itself.' Id. at 51.

suits in equity, and there were no juries in admiralty, nor were there juries in the military justice system. The jury was the factfinding mode in most suits in the common-law courts, but it was not exclusively so: Condemnation was a suit at common-law but constitutionally could be tried without a jury. ... The question whether a particular case was to be tried in a court of equity without a jury or a court of law with a jury did not depend on whether the suit involved factfinding or on the nature of the facts to be found. Factfinding could be a critical matter either at law or in equity. Rather, as a general rule, the decision turned on whether courts of law supplied a cause of action and an adequate remedy to the litigant....

"Thus, history and our cases support the proposition that the right to a jury trial turns not solely on the nature of the issue to be resolved but also on the forum in which it is to be resolved. Congress found the common-law and other existing remedies for work injuries resulting from unsafe working conditions to be inadequate to protect the Nation's working men and women. It created a new cause of action, and remedies therefor, unknown to the common law, and placed their enforcement in a tribunal supplying speedy and expert resolutions of the issues involved. The Seventh Amendment is no bar to the creation of new rights or to their enforcement outside the regular courts of law."

(3) To repeat a question posed earlier, could Congress choose to enforce the criminal law outside the regular courts of law? (The relevant jury trial provision on the criminal side is the Sixth Amendment: "In all criminal prosecutions, the accused shall enjoy the right to a speedy and public trial, by an impartial jury of the State and district wherein the crime shall have been committed....") WONG WING v. UNITED STATES, 163 U.S. 228 (1896): In the blatantly racist series of Chinese Exclusion Acts, Congress followed up provisions that first excluded Chinese, then forbade the reentry of legally resident Chinese who had left the country temporarily, then required all Chinese to register with the Internal Revenue Service, with a requirement that noncomplying Chinese "shall be imprisoned at hard labor for a period not exceeding one year, and thereafter removed from the United States." This sanction was imposed by immigration officials without judicial trial or review. After having sustained all the previous measures as constitutional, the Court finally held that Congress exceeded its powers. "We regard it as settled by our previous decisions that the United States can, as a matter of public policy, by congressional enactment, forbid aliens or classes of aliens from coming within their borders, and expel aliens or classes of aliens from their territory, and can, in order to make effectual such decree of exclusion or expulsion, devolve the power and duty of identifying and arresting the persons included in such decree, and causing their deportation, upon executive or subordinate officials."

"But when congress sees fit to further promote such a policy by subjecting the persons of such aliens to infamous punishment at hard labor, or by confiscating their property, we think such legislation, to be valid, must provide for a judicial trial to establish the guilt of the accused.

"No limits can be put by the courts upon the power of congress to protect, by summary methods, the country from the advent of aliens whose race or habits render them undesirable as citizens, or to expel such if they have already found their way into our land, and unlawfully remain therein. But to declare unlawful residence within the country to be an infamous crime, punishable by deprivation of liberty and property, would be to pass out of the sphere of constitutional legislation, unless provision were made that the fact of guilt should first be established by a judicial trial. It is not consistent with the theory of our government that the legislature should, after having defined an offense as an infamous crime, find the fact of guilt, and adjudge the punishment by one of its own agents."

Obviously, the $7500 fine imposed against Irey and the $600 fine imposed against Atlas is significantly different from the hard labor imposed by an agency adjudicator upon Mr. Wong Wing. But, contemporary criminal statutes often provide for sanctions that include fines. How do the fines imposed by OSHA differ from such fines? Are they civil sanctions only because Congress has chosen to label them such?

(4) The premier academic commentators in this area conclude their consideration of the cases in this Section by asking, "[W]ould it be fair to say that the Supreme Court has brought little but confusion to this area since Crowell v. Benson?"[2] Nonetheless, administrative lawyers might read the line of cases as reducing to the following proposition: Whatever the Court might do around the edges, it is not about to disturb Congress's central judgment to entrust determination of individual rights and obligations under regulatory programs to administrative adjudicators. So read, the cases in this Section are consistent with the story told in other sections of this Chapter: Structural constitutional challenges produce analytic constructs that appear fundamentally to threaten established regulatory institutions. Some Congressional choices are indeed struck down. But, ultimately, core administrative structures and practices remain unscathed— although theoretical consistency and doctrinal integrity take some pretty severe hits in the process. If this seems a fair reading to you, consider what lessons, if any, the Justices should draw from a pattern of jurisprudence that seems to repeat itself with some frequency in the "new" structural constitutional litigation challenging the regulatory state.

SECTION 4.   CONTROLLING AGENCY POWER: CONSTITUTIONAL ISSUES IN CONGRESSIONAL AND PRESIDENTIAL OVERSIGHT EFFORTS

The constitutional issues posed by the administrative state are not exhausted by questions about the validity of the initial statutory assignment of power to agencies. Indeed, delegation simply opens the door to a whole different set of inquiries about how the assigned power can be influenced and controlled by the named constitutional actors.

---

2.   Richard H. Fallon, Daniel J. Meltzer, & David L. Shapiro, Hart & Wechsler's Federal Courts and the Federal System 401 (5th ed. 2003).

In the latter half of the 20th century, several trends converged to raise the stakes in the game of controlling delegated regulatory power. First, the quantum of power grew substantially. The ambitious national environmental, health and safety, and consumer-oriented programs created in the 1960s and 1970s cut across industries and beyond geographic region. See Rabin, p. 13 above. Agencies such as EPA and OSHA were directed to make highly technical and often largely predictive regulatory judgments that had enormous potential impact on the domestic economic and social order. With the strain put on the economy by the Vietnam War and by OPEC's success in capturing the monopoly profits of Mid-East oil, voices from all parts of the political spectrum increasingly demanded better "management" of regulation. Second, as noted earlier, the pattern of U.S. electoral politics since World War II has been a pattern of "divided government," in which one party has controlled the Presidency while its opponent has held one or both houses of Congress.[1] By the time Ronald Reagan was elected in 1980, Republican and Democratic policy preferences about regulation had become quite divergent. This divergence set up a dynamic of sharp competition between Congress and the President for influencing whether, and how, agencies deploy regulatory power. With the election of Bill Clinton in 1992, the political tables turned. The Clinton Administration combined moderately liberal policy objectives with a "good government" determination to increase centralized oversight and coordination; the result was even more aggressive Presidential control efforts.[2] As successive Congresses reacted to these various Presidential policy and managerial initiatives, old techniques for controlling agencies (such as appointment and removal of top officials) became more important, and new techniques (such as the legislative veto of substantive agency policy and centralized White House review of proposed rules) emerged.

You will not be surprised to discover that struggles for control of the administrative state tend to be framed as constitutional issues—and that the Constitution, when consulted, often addresses these very contemporary debates with delphic inscrutability. As you read the cases in this section, note the role played by the concepts of "aggrandizement" and "encroachment." The former focuses on whether one institution of government has

---

1. "In the century between Pierce and Truman, only two incoming presidents (Hayes and Cleveland) faced an opposition majority in at least one house of Congress; in that same period, midterm elections gave the opposing party control of at least one house fewer than a dozen times. By contrast, beginning with Eisenhower, six of the nine presidents have had to deal with a Congress at least one house of which was controlled by the opposition. Moreover, the trend towards divided government appears to be accelerating. Between 1946 and 1998, 32 of 52 years (62%) represent years of divided government; between 1980 and 1998, the comparable fig-

ure is 16 of 18 years (89%)." Cynthia R. Farina, The Consent of the Governed: Against Simple Rules for a Complex World, 72 Chi.-Kent L. Rev. 987, 999 n. 51 (1997). After the bizarre election of 2000, George W. Bush began his administration with an evenly divided Senate (tipped Republican by the tie-breaking power of the Vice–President) and a narrowly Republican House. The prompt defection by one Republican Senator to "independent" affiliation gave the Democrats razor-thin control of the Senate.

2. See Elena Kagan, Presidential Administration, 114 Harv. L. Rev. 2245 (2001).

inappropriately arrogated power to itself.[3] The latter asks whether a Branch has been significantly weakened by the incursion of another institution.

a. CONTROLLING POLICY BY CONTROLLING WHO MAKES IT— APPOINTMENT AND REMOVAL OF AGENCY OFFICIALS

"[The Congress shall have the power] To make all Laws which shall be necessary and proper for carrying into Execution the foregoing Powers, and all other Powers vested by this Constitution in the Government of the United States, or in any Department or Officer thereof."

U.S. Constitution, Art. I, § 8, ¶ 18

"[The House] shall have the sole Power of Impeachment. . . . The Senate shall have the sole Power to try all Impeachments."

U.S. Constitution, Art. I, §§ 2 ¶ 5, 3 ¶ 6

"The executive Power shall be vested in a President of the United States."

U.S. Constitution, Art. II, § 1

"[The President] shall . . . nominate, and by and with the Advice and Consent of the Senate, shall appoint Ambassadors, other public Ministers and Consuls, Judges of the supreme Court, and all other Officers of the United States, whose Appointments are not herein otherwise provided for, and which shall be established by Law; but the Congress may by Law vest the appointment of such inferior Officers, as they think proper, in the President alone, in the Courts of Law, or in the Heads of Departments."

U.S. Constitution, Art. II, § 2, ¶ 2

"He shall take Care that the Laws be faithfully executed. . . ."

U.S. Constitution, Art. II, § 3

Our discussion of controlling power through controlling personnel begins with the question of removal. Focusing first on the power to fire may seem as perverse as reading a novel from last chapter to first. And certainly if we look at the Framing, the preeminent question was who *appoints* the officers of government. The drafters found appointment a vexing structural problem, with the solution in Art. 2, § 2, ¶ 2 coming late in the drafting process as part of an intricate set of compromises. (This history is recounted in the majority opinion of the next principal case.) During the ratification process, the appointment power remained a much controverted issue, with the Anti–Federalists arguing that the Senate would conspire with the President to produce an Executive of distressingly monarchical cast. In the intensity of this debate, removal was a decidedly minor player.

---

3. Typically, Congress is the institution accused of aggrandizement. But recall Mistretta, p. 74 above, in which the Court considered whether the Sentencing Commission represented aggrandizement of the judiciary.

This changed, however, once the heady era of Constitution-making was over and the hard work of building a government had begun. When Congress in 1789 created the first Cabinet department—Foreign Affairs—everyone knew how the Secretary must be appointed, but the House could reach no consensus on what the Constitution meant for how he could be removed. The proposal under debate was whether the office of Secretary should be defined as terminable only "for cause"—that is, not at the President's pleasure. The perplexity surrounding the issue is epitomized by Representative James Madison. He asserted, in the initial debate, that "Congress may establish the office by law; therefore, most certainly, it is in the discretion of the Legislature to say upon what terms the office should be held, either during good behavior or during pleasure"—although he urged that Presidential removal at will was the best *policy*, for it concentrated responsibility for the Secretary's conduct solely in the President.[1] Within a month, however, Madison switched to the position that the Constitution makes removal an exclusive executive prerogative. He explained his changed position: "I have, since the subject was last before the House, examined the Constitution with attention, and I acknowledge that it does not perfectly correspond with the ideas I entertained of it from the first glance."[2] Ultimately, the House settled on Presidential removal at will—through the combined votes of those who believed it was the President's constitutional right and those who believed it was the course of soundest policy.[3] No reliable record exists of debate in the Senate, but we might reasonably infer comparable lack of consensus from the fact that the removal provision passed that chamber only on the Vice–President's tie-breaking vote. Indeed, the subsequent decision on structuring the Department of the Treasury underscores that the first Congress did not view the Constitution as demanding a single answer to the organizational issue: Unlike the Departments of Foreign Affairs and War (the second department created), Treasury was not denominated "an executive department," and one of its key officials—the Comptroller of the Treasury—was shielded

1. 1 Annals of Congress 389, 393–95 (1789).

2. Id. at 480. Madison was not the only prominent Framer to espouse multiple positions on the removal question. In Federalist 77, Alexander Hamilton as constitutional propagandist argues that "stability of administration" (a key Federalist theme in advocating ratification) will be enhanced by the fact that "[t]he consent of [the Senate] would be necessary to displace as well as to appoint." However by 1793, when Alexander Hamilton as Secretary of Treasury was writing as Pacificus in defense of strong Presidential powers, he cited the removal power as an important instance in which the Constitution vests a broad executive power. The 1810 edition of the Federalist Papers carries an amendatory note, apparently supplied by Hamilton, challenging the original contrary statement in Federalist No. 77.

3. Legal historians report that the House was divided into four major positions on the removal power: a very small group who believed impeachment to be the only constitutionally-authorized removal device, and three groups of virtually equal size who concluded that (1) removal was the constitutional prerogative of the President alone; (2) removal paralleled appointment, and therefore was vested jointly in President and Senate; and (3) removal was not constitutionally determined, and hence could be settled by Congress under its Necessary and Proper power. The classic account is Edward S. Corwin, Tenure of Office & The Removal Power Under the Constitution, 27 Colum. L. Rev. 353 (1927). See also Gerhard Caspar, Separating Power: Essays on the Founding Period 35–53 (1997); Louis Fisher, The Politics of Shared Power 49–53 (1987); Charles A. Miller, The Supreme Court and the Uses of History 61–64, 208–09 (1969).

from Presidential direction and removal.[4] The Post Office followed the Treasury model, thus establishing an early diversity of organizational form, one quite closely allied to the President, and the other with more independence and a greater orientation towards Congress.[5]

And so, the question of who is entitled to decide whether to remove an agency official became the oldest bone of constitutional contention in the regulatory state. The "Decision of 1789" (as the debate in the first Congress is now called) marked out the various competing positions, and satisfactorily reconciled none of them. Eighty years later, the removal question became part of the feud between an overwhelmingly Republican Congress and a Democratic President bent on thwarting any significant restructuring of race-relations through post-Civil War Reconstruction. The Tenure in Office Act of 1867 provided, inter alia, that members of the Cabinet would hold their office until the end of the Presidential term unless their earlier removal received Senate consent. It was enacted, in part, to secure the position of Secretary of War Edwin Stanton, who had served in that position under Lincoln and who supported Congress' position on Reconstruction. When President Andrew Johnson nonetheless removed Stanton, the House impeached him on this, and other, grounds. His defenses included the insistence that the Act was unconstitutional and ultimately the Senate failed, by one vote, to convict.

The removal issue reappeared on the eve of the New Deal—and, for the first time, the judiciary became involved in the debate. In the waning days of Woodrow Wilson's presidency, the Postmaster General fired Frank Myers, Postmaster of Portland, Oregon, before the end of his statutory four–year term. According to one version of the story, Myers was suspected of having committed fraud;[6] other versions paint the Postmaster General as something of a tin pot dictator with a personal grudge against Myers. In any event, a New York Times article written by Wilson's Solicitor General insisted that the President had "deliberately sought the issue:" "There was no conflict between him and Congress with reference to the Postmastership of Portland, Oregon . . . and President Wilson could easily have avoided the question."[7] The pertinent statute (the Act of July 12, 1876) provided: "Postmasters . . . shall be appointed and may be removed by the President *by and with the advice and consent of the Senate*, and shall hold their offices for four years unless sooner removed or suspended according to law." (emphasis added) Senate consent was never sought, and Myers sued for his lost salary. The case prompted the Supreme Court to the extraordinary

---

4. Other differences between Foreign Affairs and War on the one hand and Treasury on the other are detailed in Gerhardt Casper, An Essay in Separation of Powers: Some Early Versions and Practices, 30 Wm. & Mary L. Rev. 211, 239–40 (1989). Ironically, Representative James Madison was the strongest initial proponent of shielding the Comptroller from Presidential control. He argued that "there may be strong reasons why an officer of this kind should not hold his office at the pleasure of the executive branch." 1 Annals of Congress at 635–36.

When his allies in the Foreign Affairs debate bemoaned his switching sides yet again, he retreated. Id. at 638.

5. See Lawrence Lessig & Cass R. Sunstein, The President and the Administration, 94 Colum. L. Rev. 1, 71 (1994).

6. See Raines v. Byrd, 521 U.S. 811, 826 (1997).

7. New York Times, Nov. 7, 1926, § 9 p. 15.

step of requesting Senator George Pepper to present the position of Congress. (The position of "the United States" was that of the President, argued by the Solicitor General.) The case had to be argued twice, in successive terms. With a 70–page opinion for the Court written by former President and then-Chief Justice William Taft, and dissents written by Justices Holmes, Brandeis and McReynolds, it is one of the longest decisions in the Supreme Court Reports. And as you will see, notwithstanding President Wilson's determination to have the issue finally settled, even it could not lay the removal question to rest.

(i) THE REACH OF PRESIDENTIAL POWER

Myers v. United States

Supreme Court of the United States, 1926.
272 U.S. 52.

■ Mr. Chief Justice Taft delivered the opinion of the Court.

This case presents the question whether under the Constitution the President has the exclusive power of removing executive officers of the United States whom he has appointed by and with the advice and consent of the Senate.

. . . The government maintains that the [statutory requirement of Senate consent] is invalid, for the reason that under article 2 of the Constitution the President's power of removal of executive officers appointed by him with the advice and consent of the Senate is full and complete without consent of the Senate. . . .

Consideration of the executive power was initiated in the Constitutional Convention by the seventh resolution in the Virginia Plan introduced by Edmund Randolph. It gave to the executive "all the executive powers of the Congress under the Confederation," which would seem therefore to have intended to include the power of removal which had been exercised by that body as incident to the power of appointment. As modified by the committee of the whole this resolution declared for a national executive of one person to be elected by the Legislature, with power to carry into execution the national laws and to appoint to offices in cases not otherwise provided for. It was referred to the committee on detail, which recommended that the executive power should be vested in a single person to be styled the President of the United States, that he should take care that the laws of the United States be duly and faithfully executed, and that he should commission all the officers of the United States and appoint officers in all cases not otherwise provided by the Constitution. The committee further recommended that the Senate be given power to make treaties, and to appoint ambassadors and judges of the Supreme Court.

After the great compromises of the convention—the one giving the states equality of representation in the Senate, and the other placing the election of the President, not in Congress, as once voted, but in an electoral college, in which the influence of larger states in the selection would be more nearly in proportion to their population—the smaller states led by

Roger Sherman, fearing that under the second compromise the President would constantly be chosen from one of the larger states, secured a change by which the appointment of all officers, which theretofore had been left to the President without restriction, was made subject to the Senate's advice and consent, and the making of treaties and the appointments of ambassadors, public ministers, consuls, and judges of the Supreme Court were transferred to the President, but made subject to the advice and consent of the Senate. . . .

The vesting of the executive power in the President was essentially a grant of the power to execute the laws. But the President alone and unaided could not execute the laws. He must execute them by the assistance of subordinates. . . . As he is charged specifically to take care that they be faithfully executed, the reasonable implication, even in the absence of express words, was that as part of his executive power he should select those who were to act for him under his direction in the execution of the laws. The further implication must be, in the absence of any express limitation respecting removals, that as his selection of administrative officers is essential to the execution of the laws by him, so must be his power of removing those for whom he cannot continue to be responsible. It was urged that the natural meaning of the term "executive power" granted the President included the appointment and removal of executive subordinates. . . .

It is quite true that, in state and colonial governments at the time of the Constitutional Convention, power to make appointments and removals had sometimes been lodged in the Legislatures or in the courts, but such a disposition of it was really vesting part of the executive power in another branch of the government. . . .

The power to prevent the removal of an officer who has served under the President is different from the authority to consent to or reject his appointment. When a nomination is made, it may be presumed that the Senate is, or may become, as well advised as to the fitness of the nominee as the President, but in the nature of things the defects in ability or intelligence or loyalty in the administration of the laws of one who has served as an officer under the President are facts as to which the President, or his trusted subordinates, must be better informed than the Senate, and the power to remove him may therefor be regarded as confined for very sound and practical reasons, to the governmental authority which has administrative control. The power of removal is incident to the power of appointment, not to the power of advising and consenting to appointment, and when the grant of the executive power is enforced by the express mandate to take care that the laws be faithfully executed, it emphasizes the necessity for including within the executive power as conferred the exclusive power of removal. . . .

. . . The difference between the grant of legislative power under article 1 to Congress which is limited to powers therein enumerated, and the more general grant of the executive power to the President under article 2 is significant. The fact that the executive power is given in general terms strengthened by specific terms where emphasis is appropriate, and limited by direct expressions where limitation is needed, and that no express limit is placed on the power of removal by the executive is a convincing indication that none was intended. . . .

Made responsible under the Constitution for the effective enforcement of the law, the President needs as an indispensable aid to meet it the disciplinary influence upon those who act under him of a reserve power of removal. But it is contended that executive officers appointed by the President with the consent of the Senate are bound by the statutory law, and are not his servants to do his will, and that his obligation to care for the faithful execution of the laws does not authorize him to treat them as such. The degree of guidance in the discharge of their duties that the President may exercise over executive officers varies with the character of their service as prescribed in the law under which they act. The highest and most important duties which his subordinates perform are those in which they act for him. In such cases they are exercising not their own but his discretion. This field is a very large one. It is sometimes described as political. Kendall v. United States, 12 Pet 524, at page 610, 9 L. Ed. 1181. Each head of a department is and must be the President's alter ego in the matters of that department where the President is required by law to exercise authority. . . .

In all such cases, the discretion to be exercised is that of the President in determining the national public interest and in directing the action to be taken by his executive subordinates to protect it. In this field his cabinet officers must do his will. He must place in each member of his official family, and his chief executive subordinates, implicit faith. The moment that he loses confidence in the intelligence, ability, judgment, or loyalty of any one of them, he must have the power to remove him without delay. To require him to file charges and submit them to the consideration of the Senate might make impossible that unity and co-ordination in executive administration essential to effective action.

The duties of the heads of departments and bureaus in which the discretion of the President is exercised and which we have described are the most important in the whole field of executive action of the government. There is nothing in the Constitution which permits a distinction between the removal of the head of a department or a bureau, when he discharges a political duty of the President or exercises his discretion, and the removal of executive officers engaged in the discharge of their other normal duties. The imperative reasons requiring an unrestricted power to remove the most important of his subordinates in their most important duties must therefore control the interpretation of the Constitution as to all appointed by him. But this is not to say that there are not strong reasons why the President should have a like power to remove his appointees charged with other duties than those above described. The ordinary duties of officers prescribed by statute come under the general administrative control of the President by virtue of the general grant to him of the executive power, and he may properly supervise and guide their construction of the statutes under which they act in order to secure that unitary and uniform execution of the laws which article 2 of the Constitution evidently contemplated in vesting general executive power in the President alone. Laws are often passed with specific provision for adoption of regulations by a department or bureau head to make the law workable and effective. The ability and judgment manifested by the official thus empowered, as well as his energy and stimulation of his subordinates, are subjects which the President must consider and supervise in his administrative control. Finding such officers to be negligent and inefficient, the President should have the power to remove them. Of course there may be duties so peculiarly and specifically committed to the discretion of a particular officer as to raise a question whether the President may overrule or revise the officer's interpretation of his statutory duty in a particular instance. Then there may be duties of a quasi judicial character imposed on executive officers and members of executive tribunals whose decisions after hearing affect interests of individuals, the discharge of which the President cannot in a particular case properly influence or control. But even in such a case he may consider the decision after its rendition as a reason for removing the officer, on the ground that the discretion regularly entrusted to that officer by statute has not been on the whole intelligently or wisely exercised. Otherwise he does not discharge his own constitutional duty of seeing that the laws be faithfully executed.

[The Court then considered the argument that the removal provision could be sustained because postmasters were "inferior officers" within the meaning of the Appointments Clause:]

The power to remove inferior executive officers, like that to remove superior executive officers, is an incident of the power to appoint them, and is in its nature an executive power. The authority of Congress given by the excepting clause to vest the appointment of such inferior officers in the heads of departments carries with it authority incidentally to invest the heads of departments with power to remove. It has been the practice of Congress to do so and this court has recognized that power. The court also has recognized in the Perkins Case [116 U.S. 483 (1886)], that Congress, in committing the appointment of such inferior officers to the heads of departments, may prescribe incidental regulations controlling and restricting the latter in the exercise of the power of removal. But the court never has held, nor reasonably could hold, although it is argued to the contrary on behalf of the appellant, that the excepting clause enables Congress to draw to itself, or to either branch of it, the power to remove or the right to participate in the exercise of that power. To do this would be to go beyond the words and implications of that clause, and to infringe the constitutional principle of the separation of governmental powers.

Assuming, then, the power of Congress to regulate removals as incidental to the exercise of its constitutional power to vest appointments of inferior officers in the heads of departments, certainly so long as Congress does not exercise that power, the power of removal must remain where the Constitution places it, with the President, as part of the executive power. . . .

Our conclusion on the merits, sustained by the arguments before stated, is that article 2 grants to the President the executive power of the government—i.e., the general administrative control of those executing the laws, including the power of appointment and removal of executive officers—a conclusion confirmed by his obligation to take care that the laws be faithfully executed; that article 2 excludes the exercise of legislative power by Congress to provide for appointments and removals, except only as granted therein to Congress in the matter of inferior offices; that Congress is only given power to provide for appointments and removals of inferior officers after it has vested, and on condition that it does vest, their appointment in other authority than the President with the Senate's consent; that the provisions of the second section of article 2, which blend action by the legislative branch, or by part of it, in the work of the executive, are limitations to be strictly construed, and not to be extended by implication; that the President's power of removal is further established as an incident to his specifically enumerated function of appointment by and with the advice of the Senate, but that such incident does not by implication extend to removals the Senate's power of checking appointments; and, finally, that to hold otherwise would make it impossible for the President, in case of political or other difference with the Senate or Congress, to take care that the laws be faithfully executed. Judgment affirmed.

■ JUSTICE MCREYNOLDS, dissenting:

    . . . Nothing short of language clear beyond serious disputation should be held to clothe the President with authority wholly beyond congressional control arbitrarily to dismiss every officer whom he appoints except a few judges. There are no such words in the Constitution. . . .

    . . . The Legislature is charged with the duty of making laws for orderly administration obligatory upon all. It possesses supreme power over national affairs and may wreck as well as speed them. It holds the purse; every branch of the government functions under statutes which embody its will; it may impeach and expel all civil officers. The duty is upon it "to make all laws which shall be necessary and proper for carrying into execution" all powers of the federal government. We have no such thing as three totally distinct and independent departments; the others must look to the legislative for direction and support. "In republican government the legislative authority necessarily predominates." The Federalist, XLVI, XVII. Perhaps the chief duty of the President is to carry into effect the will of Congress through such instrumentalities as it has chosen to provide. . . .

    . . . The argument [that removal is inherently executive] assumes far too much. Generally, the actual ouster of an officer is executive action; but to prescribe the conditions under which this may be done is legislative. The act of hanging a criminal is executive; but to say when and where and how he shall be hanged is clearly legislative. . . .

    . . . Concerning the insistence that power to remove is a necessary incident of the President's duty to enforce the laws, it is enough now to say: The general duty to enforce all laws cannot justify infraction of some of them. Moreover, Congress, in the exercise of its unquestioned power, may deprive the President of the right either to appoint or to remove any inferior officer, by vesting the authority to appoint in another. Yet in that event his duty touching enforcement of the laws would remain. He must utilize the force which Congress gives. He cannot, without permission, appoint the humblest clerk or expend a dollar of the public funds.

. . .

Those who maintain that article 2, § 1, was intended as a grant of every power of executive nature not specifically qualified or denied, must show that the term "executive power" had some definite and commonly accepted meaning in 1787. This court has declared that it did not include all powers exercised by the King of England; and, considering the history of the period, none can say that it had then (or afterwards) any commonly accepted and practical definition. If any one of the descriptions of "executive power" known in 1787 had been substituted for it, the whole plan would have failed. . . .

■ JUSTICE BRANDEIS, dissenting.

. . . The ability to remove a subordinate executive officer, being an essential of effective government, will, in the absence of express constitutional provision to the contrary, be deemed to have been vested in some person or body. But it is not a power inherent in a chief executive. The President's power of removal from statutory civil inferior offices, like the power of appointment to them, comes immediately from Congress. It is true that the exercise of the power of removal is said to be an executive act, and that when the Senate grants or withholds consent to a removal by the President, it participates in an executive act. But the Constitution has confessedly granted to Congress the legislative power to create offices, and to prescribe the tenure thereof; and it has not in terms denied to Congress the power to control removals. . . .

The separation of the powers of government did not make each branch completely autonomous. It left each in some measure, dependent upon the others, as it left to each power to exercise, in some respects, functions in their nature executive, legislative and judicial. Obviously the President cannot secure full execution of the laws, if Congress denies to him adequate means of doing so. Full execution may be defeated because Congress declines to create offices indispensable for that purpose; or because Congress, having created the office, declines to make the indispensable appropriation; or because Congress, having both created the office and made the appropriation, prevents, by restrictions which it imposes, the appointment of officials who in quality and character are indispensable to the efficient execution of the law. If, in any such way, adequate means are denied to the President, the fault will lie with Congress. The President performs his full constitutional duty, if, with the means and instruments provided by Congress and within the limitations prescribed by it, he uses his best endeavors to secure the faithful execution of the laws enacted. Compare Kendall v. United States, 12 Pet. 524, 613, 626.

Checks and balances were established in order that this should be "a government of laws and not of men." As White said in the House in 1789, an uncontrollable power of removal in the Chief Executive "is a doctrine not to be learned in American governments." Such power had been denied in colonial charters, and even under proprietary grants and royal commissions. It had been denied in the thirteen states before the framing of the federal Constitution. The doctrine of the separation of powers was adopted by the convention of 1787 not to promote efficiency but to preclude the exercise of arbitrary power. The purpose was not to avoid friction, but, by means of the inevitable friction incident to the distribution of the governmental powers among three departments, to save the people from autocracy. In order to prevent arbitrary executive action, the Constitution provided in terms that presidential appointments be made with the consent of the Senate, unless Congress should otherwise provide; and this clause was construed by Alexander Hamilton in The Federalist, No. 77, as requiring like consent to removals. ... In America, as in England, the conviction prevailed then that the people must look to representative assemblies for the protection of their liberties. And protection of the individual, even if he be an official, from the arbitrary or capricious exercise of power was then believed to be an essential of free government.

■ JUSTICE HOLMES, dissenting:

... The arguments drawn from the executive power of the President, and from his duty to appoint officers of the United States (when Congress does not vest the appointment elsewhere), to take care that the laws be faithfully executed, and to commission all officers of the United States, seem to me spiders' webs inadequate to control the dominant facts. We have to deal with an office that owes its existence to Congress and that Congress may abolish to-morrow. Its duration and the pay attached to it while it lasts depend on Congress alone. Congress alone confers on the President the power to appoint to it and at any time may transfer the power to other hands. With such power over its own creation, I have no more trouble in believing that Congress has power to prescribe a term of life for it free from any interference than I have in accepting the undoubted power of Congress to decree its end. I have equally little trouble in accepting its power to prolong the tenure of an incumbent until Congress or the Senate shall have assented to his removal. The duty of the President to see that the laws be executed is a duty that does not go beyond the laws or require him to achieve more than Congress sees fit to leave within his power.

NOTES

(1) *Another Retelling of the Constitutional History.* FREYTAG V. COMMISSIONER OF INTERNAL REVENUE, 501 U.S. 868 (1991), posed the question whether special judges of the Tax Court were constitutionally appointed. See p. 174 below. In answering that question, Justice Blackmun had to decide whether the Tax Court was a "Department" within the meaning of the Appointments Clause: "The 'manipulation of official appointments' had long been one of the American revolutionary generation's greatest grievances against executive power, see G. Wood, The Creation of The American Republic 1776–1787, p. 79 (1969), because 'the power of appointment to offices' was deemed 'the most insidious and powerful weapon of eighteenth century despotism.' Id. at 143. Those who framed our Constitution addressed these concerns by carefully husbanding the appointment power to limit its diffusion. Although the debate on the Appointments Clause was brief, the

sparse record indicates the Framers' determination to limit the distribution of the power of appointment. The Constitutional Convention rejected Madison's complaint that the Appointments Clause did 'not go far enough if it be necessary at all': Madison argued that 'Superior Officers below Heads of Departments ought in some cases to have the appointment of the lesser offices.' 2 Records of the Federal Convention of 1787, pp. 627–628 (M. Farrand rev. 1966). The Framers understood, however, that by limiting the appointment power, they could ensure that those who wielded it were accountable to political force and the will of the people. Thus, the Clause bespeaks a principle of limitation by dividing the power to appoint the principal federal officers—ambassadors, ministers, heads of departments, and judges—between the Executive and Legislative Branches. Even with respect to 'inferior Officers,' the Clause allows Congress only limited authority to devolve appointment power on the President, his heads of departments, and the courts of law. . . ."

Having concluded that "[t]he Clause reflects our Framers' conclusion that widely distributed appointment power subverts democratic government," Justice Blackmun (for the five–member majority) held that "Department" refers to only Cabinet-level departments, which are "limited in number and easily identified. Their heads are subject to the exercise of political oversight and share the President's accountability to the people." "We cannot accept the Commissioner's assumption that every part of the Executive Branch is a department, the head of which is eligible to receive the appointment power. The Appointments Clause prevents Congress from distributing power too widely by limiting the actors in whom Congress may vest the power to appoint. Given the inexorable presence of the administrative state, a holding that every organ in the Executive Branch is a department would multiply indefinitely the number of actors eligible to appoint. The Framers recognized the dangers posed by an excessively diffuse appointment power and rejected efforts to expand that power. So do we. . . ."

This reading of the Appointments Clause history powerfully supports Justice Taft's reading of the removal authority, doesn't it?

(2) *Implications for the Civil Service.* The less attractive side of political accountability is political patronage—the giving out (and taking away) of public jobs based on partisan service or affiliation. Andrew Jackson is the President most associated with government employment by the spoils system, but some commentators say he was simply an exceptionally adept practitioner of a longstanding political art. During the Civil War, satirists attributed the Union loss at Bull Run to the opening of a federal job in New York—the entire Union army, the joke went, left the battlefield to apply. Eventually, momentum built for "good government" reform. Not only was the quadrennial turnover in the federal workforce inefficient, but the fact that government jobs could be acquired through political services or contributions devalued those positions in the eyes of the public and the holders themselves. The first wave of federal reform was the Pendleton Act of 1883. It created the Civil Service Commission that oversaw merit-based hiring via competitive examinations. Although it did not speak to removal in general, the Act specifically prohibited firing or demoting an employee for refusing

to contribute to a political fund, and instructed the Commission to issue regulations ensuring that no covered employee was fired or "prejudiced" for refusing to make a political contribution or render a political service. Eventually, the Lloyd–LaFollette Act of 1912 added a general "for cause" removal provision: "[N]o person in the classified Civil Service of the United States shall be removed therefrom except for such cause as will promote the efficiency of said service and for reasons given in writing...." (This legislation was born in Congressional outrage over Executive Orders by Presidents Teddy Roosevelt and Taft that prohibited federal employees from communicating directly with Congress without the permission of their supervisors—and enforced this gag order with dismissal.)

The legality of the civil-service system was confirmed by UNITED STATES v. PERKINS, 116 U.S. 483 (1886). Although Perkins concerned a particular statutory removal restriction in connection with the military, the Court's reasoning easily covered the Pendleton/Lloyd-LaFollette system: "We have no doubt that when congress, by law, vests the appointment of inferior officers in the heads of departments, it may limit and restrict the power of removal as it deems best for the public interest. The constitutional authority in congress to thus vest the appointment implies authority to limit, restrict, and regulate the removal by such laws as congress may enact in relation to the officers so appointed. The head of a department has no constitutional prerogative of appointment to offices independently of the legislation of congress, and by such legislation he must be governed, not only in making appointments, but in all that is incident thereto."

Note Chief Justice Taft's careful treatment of Perkins. Myers thus did not return the segment of federal employment covered by the Civil Service system to a patronage regime. How widespread was the system? When first created in 1883, the system comprised only about 10% of federal workers. By 1900, this ratio had risen to 40%, and the trend continued incrementally until the New Deal, when the size of the federal service increased dramatically. President Roosevelt was no fan of the Civil Service Commission and, at his instance, many of the new agencies were created outside its jurisdiction.[1] At all times, however, the layer of decisionmakers at the top of departments, bureaus, and commissions remained political appointees. And (as in the case of postmasters) many inferior officer appointments were left, by statute, to the constitutional default of Presidential nomination with Senate consent.

(3) *Contemporaneous Reaction.* Myers loosed a storm of commentary, surprisingly widespread and often positively incandescent in tone:

THE LITERARY DIGEST, Nov. 6, 1926 p.6 (reviewing newspapers from across the country): " 'New and autocratic powers' are given to the President by this decision which were 'not provided by the Constitution or contemplated by its framers,' declares the Milwaukee Journal [which also wrote,] 'powers have been given by Congress to commissions which no President has ever had, and which Congress almost certainly would not

---

1. Compare contemporary debates over the appropriate status of personnel in the Department of Homeland Security.

have given if it had been plain that a President might control the commission at will.' ... [Myers] 'nullifies to a large extent the check on the Executive that it was believed was vested in Congress,' agrees the Louisville Courier–Journal. In Portland, where Mr. Myers was postmaster ... The Oregon Journal similarly observes: 'A great power is placed in the hands of the President by the decision. It is a power scarcely in keeping with the system of checks and balances which the fathers incorporated in our system. It may be law, but is scarcely sound policy for the consent of the Senate to be required in an appointment, but not in a removal.'

"But these dailies, like the dissenting Justices seem to be in the minority. ... The layman, adds the [San Francisco Chronicle] will probably conclude that the Supreme Court in giving a freer hand to the Executive is acting 'in line with modern industrial practise.' The decision seems no less sensible and practical to papers like the Springfield Union, New York Sun, Times, and Evening Post; Newark News, Jersey City Journal, Atlanta Constitution, Memphis Commercial Appeal, and Chicago Daily News. 'Removal is and should remain an exclusive Executive function,' thinks the Chicago Evening Post. 'Common sense is on the side of the majority,' declares the Chicago Tribune:

> The President cannot maintain an effective control over the departments unless he has the right to appoint and remove, to hire and fire. Of the two the right to fire is probably the more important. It is the instrument with which he can bend men to his will. An executive can work with men not of his own choosing, provided he can remove those who do not accept his leadership. ...

"The decision is 'the severest blow the Senate has received in years,' says the Dallas News; it is a 'step toward stronger party government.' It concentrates the powers of government, and 'accordingly the country will expect results and exact accountability in proportion to the powers inherent in the office.' "

The Nation, Nov. 10, 1926, p. 468: "The decision is, as usual, political rather than legal. The settled habit of the court is so to interpret the Constitution as to prevent legislation which seems to disturb intrenched interests. The power of patronage in the President has been so long established and is such a powerful political weapon that to deny him the full benefits of it would cause a vast upheaval in political circles and make it possible seriously to hamper the Executive. The majority of the Supreme Court recoiled from such a decision."

The New Republic, Nov. 17, 1926, p. 371: "The wisdom of this decision, from the standpoint of administration may be as great as the Chief Justice affirms, or it may not. ... Even if the Constitution would have been wise had it done what six members of the Supreme Court have now done for it, it does not follow that the six members are justified in doing what they have done. They have swept off the statute books many provisions which many Congresses have put there. They have done so in the guise of interpreting the Constitution. To call this pseudo-interpretation a spider's web of reasoning is to flatter both its pattern and its power."

THE NEW YORK TIMES, Nov. 7, 1926, p. 5, § 1 (quoting Sen. Hiram Johnson): "As we have sometimes heard of late, there will be those who exclaim that what this country needs is another Mussolini and who rejoice in any extension of executive power. And, again, others who declare that the very liberty of the people is involved in the stability of official tenure. . . .

"The answer of those who upheld the arbitrary and illimitable power of the President is that the will of the Executive, made supreme now, will be exercised with the wisest discrimination and the highest purpose. But if the will of the Executive shall ever degenerate into mere caprice, or blind partisanship the agencies which have been established by Congress for the protection of the people will become the mere rewards of 'deserving' and active political henchmen."

Humphrey's Executor v. United States

Supreme Court of the United States, 1935.
295 U.S. 602.

■ MR. JUSTICE SUTHERLAND delivered the opinion of the Court.

. . . William E. Humphrey, the decedent, on December 10, 1931, was nominated by President Hoover to succeed himself as a member of the Federal Trade Commission, and was confirmed by the United States Senate. He was duly commissioned for a term of seven years, expiring September 25, 1938; and, after taking the required oath of office, entered upon his duties. On July 25, 1933, President Roosevelt addressed a letter to the commissioner asking for his resignation, on the ground "that the aims and purposes of the Administration with respect to the work of the Commission can be carried out most effectively with personnel of my own selection," but disclaiming any reflection upon the commissioner personally or upon his services. The commissioner replied, asking time to consult his friends. After some further correspondence upon the subject, the President on August 31, 1933, wrote the commissioner expressing the hope that the resignation would be forthcoming, and saying: "You will, I know, realize that I do not feel that your mind and my mind go along together on either the policies or the administering of the Federal Trade Commission, and, frankly, I think it is best for the people of this country that I should have a full confidence."

The commissioner declined to resign; and on October 7, 1933, the President wrote him: "Effective as of this date you are hereby removed from the office of Commissioner of the Federal Trade Commission."

Humphrey never acquiesced in this action, but continued thereafter to insist that he was still a member of the commission, entitled to perform its duties and receive the compensation provided by law at the rate of $10,000 per annum. . . .

The Federal Trade Commission Act creates a commission of five members to be appointed by the President by and with the advice and consent of the Senate, and section 1 provides: ". . . Any commissioner may be removed by the President for inefficiency, neglect of duty, or malfeasance in office. . . ." . . .

The commission is to be nonpartisan; and it must, from the very nature of its duties, act with entire impartiality. It is charged with the enforcement of no policy except the policy of the law. Its duties are neither political nor executive, but predominantly quasi judicial and quasi legislative. Like the Interstate Commerce Commission, its members are called upon to exercise the trained judgment of a body of experts "appointed by law and informed by experience."

The legislative reports in both houses of Congress clearly reflect the view that a fixed term was necessary to the effective and fair administration of the law. . . ."The work of this commission will be of a most exacting and difficult character, demanding persons who have experience in the problems to be met—that is, a proper knowledge of both the public requirements and the practical affairs of industry. It is manifestly desirable that the terms of the commissioners shall be long enough to give them an opportunity to acquire the expertness in dealing with these special questions concerning industry that comes from experience."

The report declares that one advantage which the commission possessed over the Bureau of Corporations (an executive subdivision in the Department of Commerce which was abolished by the act) lay in the fact of its independence, and that it was essential that the commission should not be open to the suspicion of partisan direction. The report quotes a statement to the committee by Senator Newlands, who reported the bill, that the tribunal should be of high character and "independent of any department of the government, . . . a board or commission of dignity, permanence, and ability, independent of executive authority, except in its selection, and independent in character."

The debates in both houses demonstrate that the prevailing view was that the Commission was not to be "subject to anybody in the government but . . . only to the people of the United States"; free from "political domination or control" or the "probability or possibility of such a thing"; to be "separate and apart from any existing department of the government—not subject to the orders of the President."

Thus, the language of the act, the legislative reports, and the general purposes of the legislation as reflected by the debates, all combine to demonstrate the congressional intent to create a body of experts who shall gain experience by length of service; a body which shall be independent of executive authority, except in its selection, and free to exercise its judgment without the leave or hindrance of any other official or any department of the government. To the accomplishment of these purposes, it is clear that Congress was of opinion that length and certainty of tenure would vitally contribute. And to hold that, nevertheless, the members of the commission continue in office at the mere will of the President, might be to thwart, in large measure, the very ends which Congress sought to realize by definitely fixing the term of office.

. . .

To support its contention that the removal provision of section 1, as we have just construed it, is an unconstitutional interference with the executive power of the President, the government's chief reliance is Myers v. United States. ... [T]he narrow point actually decided was only that the President had power to remove a postmaster of the first class, without the advice and consent of the Senate as required by act of Congress. In the course of the opinion of the court, expressions occur which tend to sustain the government's contention, but these are beyond the point involved and, therefore, do not come within the rule of stare decisis. In so far as they are out of harmony with the views here set forth, these expressions are disapproved....

The office of a postmaster is so essentially unlike the office now involved that the decision in the Myers Case cannot be accepted as controlling our decision here. A postmaster is an executive officer restricted to the performance of executive functions. He is charged with no duty at all related to either the legislative or judicial power. The actual decision in the Myers Case finds support in the theory that such an officer is merely one of the units in the executive department and, hence, inherently subject to the exclusive and illimitable power of removal by the Chief Executive, whose subordinate and aid he is. Putting aside dicta, which may be followed if sufficiently persuasive but which are not controlling, the necessary reach of the decision goes far enough to include all purely executive officers. It goes no farther; much less does it include an officer who occupies no place in the executive department and who exercises no part of the executive power vested by the Constitution in the President.

The Federal Trade Commission is an administrative body created by Congress to carry into effect legislative policies embodied in the statute in accordance with the legislative standard therein prescribed, and to perform other specified duties as a legislative or as a judicial aid. Such a body cannot in any proper sense be characterized as an arm or an eye of the executive. Its duties are performed without executive leave and, in the contemplation of the statute, must be free from executive control. In administering the provisions of the statute in respect of "unfair methods of competition," that is to say, in filling in and administering the details embodied by that general standard, the commission acts in part quasi legislatively and in part quasi judicially. In making investigations and reports thereon for the information of Congress under section 6, in aid of the legislative power, it acts as a legislative agency. Under section 7, which authorizes the commission to act as a master in chancery under rules prescribed by the court, it acts as an agency of the judiciary. To the extent that it exercises any executive function, as distinguished from executive power in the constitutional sense, it does so in the discharge and effectuation of its quasi legislative or quasi judicial powers, or as an agency of the legislative or judicial departments of the government.[1] ...

---

1. The provision of section 6(d) of the act which authorizes the President to direct an investigation and report by the commission in relation to alleged violations of the anti-trust acts, is so obviously collateral to the main design of the act as not to detract from the force of this general statement as to the character of that body.

The result of what we now have said is this: Whether the power of the President to remove an officer shall prevail over the authority of Congress to condition the power by fixing a definite term and precluding a removal except for cause will depend upon the character of the office; the Myers decision, affirming the power of the President alone to make the removal, is confined to purely executive officers; and as to officers of the kind here under consideration, we hold that no removal can be made during the prescribed term for which the officer is appointed, except for one or more of the causes named in the applicable statute.

To the extent that, between the decision in the Myers Case, which sustains the unrestrictable power of the President to remove purely executive officers, and our present decision that such power does not extend to an office such as that here involved, there shall remain a field of doubt, we leave such cases as may fall within it for future consideration and determination as they may arise.

NOTES

(1) *What Changed in Nine Years?* This defeat for President Roosevelt's ability to exert more control over the independent agencies—which then included the ICC, SEC, FCC, and FTC, among others—came on the same day as Schechter Poultry Corp. v. United States, p. 69 above, invalidated significant portions of the National Industrial Recovery Act on nondelegation grounds. In the nine years between Myers and Humphrey's Executor, Charles Hughes replaced William Taft as Chief Justice. With a record in public service matched only by Taft himself, Hughes came to the bench from a career in the executive: Two-term governor of New York, he lost narrowly to Woodrow Wilson in the presidential race of 1916; he served as Secretary of State to two Presidents and was initially appointed to the Court by President Taft. Justices Holmes and Sanford were replaced by Justices Cardozo (a supporter of the New Deal) and Roberts (who voted unevenly, but often in opposition). Thus, although two of the Myers majority (Taft and Sanford) had left by the time of Humphrey's Executor, two of the newcomers (Cardozo and Hughes) appeared generally sympathetic to Roosevelt or, at least, to the needs of a Chief Executive. Four Justices (Van Devanter, Sutherland, Butler and Stone) joined the majority in *both* cases. In contrast to the two years it took the Court to reach the split decision in Myers, the unanimous decision in Humphrey's Executor came down 26 days after the case was argued.

(2) WEINER V. UNITED STATES, 357 U.S. 349 (1958): The War Claims Act of 1948 established a three–person War Claims Commission (WCC) to adjudicate claims for compensation for injury or property damage at the hands of the enemy during World War II. The version initially passed by the House would have put limited categories of claims against Japan in the hands of the Federal Security Administrator, who was (in the Court's words) "indubitably an arm of the President." Other claims were merely to be investigated by a commission which would then report to Congress. The Senate completely rewrote the scheme, creating the more broadly empowered WCC. The Commission was "to be composed of three persons, at least two

of whom were to be members of the bar, to be appointed by the President, by and with the advice and consent of the Senate." No removal provision was specified, but the statute provided that the WCC was to complete its duties no later than three years after the deadline for filing claims.

In a reprise of Humphrey's Executor, President Eisenhower removed Commissioner Weiner (a Truman appointee), stating: "I regard it as in the national interest to complete the administration of the War Claims Act of 1948, as amended, with personnel of my own selection." Justice Frankfurter, for a unanimous Court, held that Weiner was entitled to back pay for wrongful removal. He began by noting the brief life of Chief Justice Taft's attempt in Myers to settle 150 years of controversy over removal: "The versatility of circumstances often mocks a natural desire for definitiveness."

"Humphrey's case was a cause celebre—and not least in the halls of Congress. And what is the essence of the decision in Humphrey's case? It drew a sharp line of cleavage between officials who were part of the Executive establishment and were thus removable by virtue of the President's constitutional powers, and those who are members of a body 'to exercise its judgment without the leave or hindrance of any other official or any department of the government,' as to whom a power of removal exists only if Congress may fairly be said to have conferred it. This sharp differentiation derives from the difference in functions between those who are part of the Executive establishment and those whose tasks require absolute freedom from Executive interference. . . .

"Thus, the most reliable factor for drawing an inference regarding the President's power of removal in our case is the nature of the function that Congress vested in the War Claims Commission. What were the duties that Congress confided to this Commission? And can the inference fairly be drawn from the failure of Congress to provide for removal that these Commissioners were to remain in office at the will of the President? . . . The terms of the War Claims Act of 1948 leave no doubt that such was not the conception of Congress regarding the War Claims Commission.

". . . Congress could, of course, have given jurisdiction over these claims to the District Courts or to the Court of Claims. The fact that it chose to establish a Commission to 'adjudicate according to law' the classes of claims defined in the statute did not alter the intrinsic judicial character of the task with which the Commission was charged. . . . If, as one must take for granted, the War Claims Act precluded the President from influencing the Commission in passing on a particular claim, a fortiori must it be inferred that Congress did not wish to have hang over the Commission the Damocles' sword of removal by the President for no reason other than that he preferred to have on that Commission men of his own choosing. . . ."

Two points to note about Weiner: First, the statute was silent about removal; in this case, the limitation on Presidential power was implied by the Court. Second, the author of the opinion—Felix Frankfurter—was a passionate New Dealer. A teacher of administrative law at Harvard, he mentored lawyers who held prominent places in presidential administrations from Woodrow Wilson to John Kennedy; before Franklin Roosevelt appointed him to the Court, he was one of the President's close advisers.

(3) *So, Where are the Independent Agencies "Located"?* FTC v. RUBEROID CO. 343 U.S. 470, 487 (1952) (Jackson, J., dissenting): "[The independent agencies] have become a veritable fourth branch of Government, which has deranged our three-branch legal theories. . . . Administrative agencies have been called quasi-legislative, quasi-executive, or quasi-judicial, as the occasion required in order to validate their functions within the separation-of-powers scheme of the Constitution. The mere retreat to the qualifying 'quasi' is implicit with confession that all recognized classifications have broken down, and 'quasi' is a smooth cover which we draw over our confusion as we might use a counterpane to cover a disordered bed."

FEDERAL MARITIME COMMISSION v. SOUTH CAROLINA STATE PORTS AUTHORITY, ___ U.S. ___, 122 S.Ct. 1864 (2002) (Breyer J., dissenting): "The legal body conducting the proceeding, the Federal Maritime Commission, is an 'independent' federal agency. Constitutionally speaking, an 'independent' agency belongs neither to the Legislative Branch nor to the Judicial Branch of Government.

"Although Members of this Court have referred to agencies as a 'fourth branch' of Government, FTC v. Ruberoid Co. (Jackson, J., dissenting), the agencies, even 'independent' agencies, are more appropriately considered to be part of the Executive Branch. See Freytag v. Commissioner, 501 U.S. 868, 910 (Scalia, J., concurring in part and concurring in judgment). The President appoints their chief administrators, typically a Chairman and Commissioners, subject to confirmation by the Senate. Cf. Bowsher v. Synar. The agencies derive their legal powers from congressionally enacted statutes. And the agencies enforce those statutes, i.e., they 'execute' them, in part by making rules or by adjudicating matters in dispute.

"The Court long ago laid to rest any constitutional doubts about whether the Constitution permitted Congress to delegate rulemaking and adjudicative powers to agencies. That, in part, is because the Court established certain safeguards surrounding the exercise of these powers. See, e.g., A.L.A. Schechter Poultry Corp. v. United States (nondelegation doctrine); Crowell [v. Benson] (requiring judicial review). And the Court denied that those activities as safeguarded, however much they might resemble the activities of a legislature or court, fell within the scope of Article I or Article III of the Constitution. Schechter Poultry, supra, at 529–530; Crowell, supra, at 50–53, 52; see also INS v. Chadha, 462 U.S. 919, 953, n. 16 (1983) (agency's use of rulemaking 'resemble[s],' but is not, lawmaking). Consequently, in exercising those powers, the agency is engaging in an Article II, Executive Branch activity. And the powers it is exercising are powers that the Executive Branch of Government must possess if it is to enforce modern law through administration.

"This constitutional understanding explains why both commentators and courts have often attached the prefix 'quasi' to descriptions of an agency's rulemaking or adjudicative functions. E.g., Humphrey's Executor v. United States. The terms 'quasi legislative' and 'quasi adjudicative' indicate that the agency uses legislative like or court like procedures but that it is not, constitutionally speaking, either a legislature or a court. See Whitman v. American Trucking Assns., Inc.; Freytag, supra, at 910, (Scalia, J., concurring in part and concurring in judgment)."

Justice Breyer's efforts to "locate" the independent agencies came in response to the majority's holding that the sovereign immunity which generally shields states from having to answer to private claims of constitutional or statutory violation before the courts, equally shields them from having to answer to private claims of regulatory violation before an agency adjudicator. The breadth of this holding is not nearly so great as you might think. It is well-established that a state's sovereign immunity cannot be asserted in litigation brought by the United States. Thus, regulatory enforcement actions prosecuted by the agency itself (the typical pattern) are unaffected by this holding. See Chapter IX, Sec. 1.

Justice Thomas, writing for the majority, was willing to assume, arguendo, that the FMC "does not exercise the judicial power of the United States" when adjudicating private regulatory claims. Why, then, are administrative proceedings subject to an immunity that has historically been attached to judicial proceedings? In an uncharacteristic resort to functionalist analysis, Justice Thomas accepted the view of the Fourth Circuit that the FMC proceeding "walks, talks, and squawks very much like a lawsuit." Extending the Wonderland-like topsy-turveyness of the opinion, he criticized Justice Breyer's textualism in a footnote that invites future trouble: "[I]t is ironic that Justice Breyer adopts such a textual approach in defending the conduct of an independent agency that itself lacks any textual basis in the Constitution." 102 S.Ct. at 1871 n. 8. Justices Scalia, O'Connor and Kennedy, and the Chief Justice, joined to make up the 5–4 majority.

(4) *Just What Difference Does "Independence" Make?* As Justice Breyer observes, independent agencies—like those in cabinet departments—have authority to engage in all the typical forms of governmental activity: to adopt rules, to make judgments about and carry out enforcement, and to decide contested cases within their "jurisdiction." So, just how different is the contemporary independent agency from its counterpart located in a cabinet department? PETER L. STRAUSS, THE PLACE OF AGENCIES IN GOVERNMENT: SEPARATION OF POWERS AND THE FOURTH BRANCH, 84 Colum.L.Rev. 573, 586–90 (1984): "As Presidents and political scientists are fond of remarking,[1] the White House does not control policymaking in the Executive Departments. The President and a few hundred political appointees are at the apex of an enormous bureaucracy whose members enjoy tenure in their jobs, are subject to the constraints of statutes whose history and provisions they know in detail, and often have strong views of the public good in the field in which they work. ... The bureaucracy constitutes an independent force ... and its cooperation must be won to achieve any desired outcome.

"Viewed from any perspective other than independence in policy formation, the legal regime within which [independent as well as executive] agencies function is highly unified under presidential direction. ... Thus, the property of independent as well as executive-branch agencies is managed by the General Services Administration, and their contracts are

---

1. President Truman is reported to have described his authority as the power "to bring people in and try to persuade them to do what they ought to do without persuasion. That's what I spend most of my time doing. That's what the powers of the President amount to." Clinton Rossiter, The American Presidency 149 (2d rev. ed. 1960).

entered in accordance with its procurement regulations. The Department of Justice, to varying degrees, represents their interests in court; the Office of Personnel Management and the Merit Systems Protection Board regulate their employment practices, pay scales and allocation of super-grade management posts. . . .

"Even in the arena of policy, one readily finds major respects in which agencies' work is centrally managed. The National Security Council and the Domestic Council coordinate interagency studies to develop national policy at the request of the President or a possibly affected agency, without necessary regard to the independence (or lack of it) of the agencies that may be affected. Similarly, the Office of Management and Budget coordinates agency comments on some proposed rules, promoting conferences and other collaborative efforts in order to produce a result maximally acceptable among all agencies concerned. OMB plays a coordinating role also when agencies find themselves in the jurisdictional disputes that are the inevitable consequence of the enormous number of regulatory measures Congress enacts and the many different agencies to which it assigns responsibility. . . . Overall, presidential coordination is an activity of importance, one in which the agencies generally cooperate and from which they receive benefit as well as occasional constraint.

"The independent agencies are often free, at least in a formal sense, of other relationships with the White House that characterize the executive branch agencies.[2] The President's influence reaches somewhat more deeply into the top layers of bureaucracy at an executive agency than at an independent commission. . . . Yet these differences are at best matters of degree. . . . Even in executive agencies, the layer over which the President enjoys direct control of personnel is very thin and political factors may make it difficult for him to exercise even those controls to the fullest. An administrator with a public constituency and mandate cannot be discharged—and understands that he cannot be discharged—without substantial political cost. Also for political reasons, one may be certain that independent commission consultation with the White House about appointments often occurs, even if subdued—as in so many other matters—by the lack of obligation so to consult."[3]

Morrison v. Olson

Supreme Court of the United States, 1988.
487 U.S. 654.

■ CHIEF JUSTICE REHNQUIST delivered the opinion of the Court.

[Title VI of the Ethics in Government Act was a response to the Watergate scandal that eventually forced President Nixon's resignation. It

---

2. [Ed.] For example, many of the independents are authorized to submit their budget proposals directly to Congress, without White House clearance. They are sometimes given freedom to litigate independent of Department of Justice control. Staff appointments, even at the highest level, are made by the Commission or its Chair; any clearance of them with the White House is informal. On the other hand, the Chair typically dominates the administrative side of the agency's business, selecting most staff, setting budgetary policy, and as a consequence commanding staff loyalties. And the power to select (and change) the Chair is given to the President.

3. [Ed.] Further discussion of whether the independent agencies differ significantly from executive branch agencies appears in the useful symposium, The Independence of Independent Agencies, 1988 Duke L.J. 215. Most of the authors share the assessment expressed in the text.

provided for politically independent investigation and, if appropriate, prosecution of high ranking executive-branch officials for violations of federal criminal laws. According to the Act—which has since expired without renewal—if the Attorney General received information "sufficient to constitute grounds to investigate whether any person [covered by the Act] may have violated any Federal criminal law," he was to conduct a preliminary investigation. Within 90 days, he had to notify the "Special Division" of the D.C. Circuit,[1] whether "reasonable grounds [exist] to believe that further investigation or prosecution is warranted." If not, "the division of the court shall have no power to appoint an independent counsel." But if the Attorney General did find such grounds, he was to ask the Special Division to appoint an independent counsel, providing "sufficient information to assist the [court] in selecting [her] and in defining [her] prosecutorial jurisdiction."

The Act gave the independent counsel "full power and independent authority to exercise all investigative and prosecutorial functions and powers of the Department of Justice, the Attorney General, and any other officer or employee of the Department of Justice." On appointment of an independent counsel, the Justice Department was required to suspend all investigations and proceedings regarding the matter. Counsel was instructed "except where not possible, [to] comply with the written or other established policies of the Department of Justice respecting enforcement of the criminal laws." The Special Division was empowered to determine if an investigation had reached a point justifying termination of the office. Beyond this, the power to remove was specified as "the personal action of the Attorney General and only for good cause, physical disability, mental incapacity, or any other condition that substantially impairs the performance of such independent counsel's duties." The Attorney General was required to report any such removal in detail to both the Special Division and the Judiciary Committees of the Senate and the House, and the independent counsel could obtain judicial review.

In 1986, Alexia Morrison was appointed independent counsel to investigate possible criminal violations by Theodore Olson while Assistant Attorney General in charge of the Department of Justice's Office of Legal Counsel. Olson had testified to a House Judiciary Committee investigating an earlier dispute between Congress and the Administrator of EPA. (In that earlier imbroglio, Administrator Ann Gorsuch had invoked presidential executive privilege to refuse documents sought by a committee investigating allegations of gross mismanagement at EPA. Eventually, Gorsuch was forced to resign.) The Judiciary Committee believed that Olson lied to it while testifying under oath, and it sought appointment of an independent counsel.

1. The Special Division consisted of three Circuit Court Judges appointed by the Chief Justice of the United States; one had to be a judge of the United States Court of Appeals for the District of Columbia, and no two could be from the same court. The judges were appointed for two–year terms.

In the course of her investigation, Morrison requested subpoenas against Olsen and two co-workers, Deputy Attorneys General Schmults and Dinkins. All three moved to quash the subpoenas, on grounds that the Act was unconstitutional. The District Court upheld the constitutionality of the Act, but a divided panel of the D. C. Circuit reversed.]

... The initial question is ... whether appellant is an "inferior" or a "principal" officer. ... We need not attempt here to decide exactly where the line falls between the two types of officers, because in our view appellant clearly falls on the "inferior officer" side of that line. Several factors lead to this conclusion.

First, appellant is subject to removal by a higher Executive Branch official. Although appellant ... possesses a degree of independent discretion to exercise the powers delegated to her under the Act, the fact that she can be removed by the Attorney General indicates that she is to some degree "inferior" in rank and authority. Second, appellant is empowered by the Act to perform only certain, limited duties. ... The Act specifically provides that in policy matters appellant is to comply to the extent possible with the policies of the Department.

Third, appellant's office is limited in jurisdiction. ... Finally, appellant's office is limited in tenure. ... In our view, these factors ... are sufficient to establish that appellant is an "inferior" officer in the constitutional sense.

... Appellees argue that even if appellant is an "inferior" officer, the Clause does not empower Congress to place the power to appoint such an officer outside the Executive Branch. ... On its face, the language of th[e Appointments Clause] admits of no limitation on interbranch appointments. Indeed, the inclusion of "as they think proper" seems clearly to give Congress significant discretion to determine whether it is "proper" to vest the appointment of, for example, executive officials in the "Courts of Law." ...

We also note that the history of the clause provides no support for appellees' position. Throughout most of the process of drafting the Constitution, the Convention concentrated on the problem of who should have the authority to appoint judges ... [T]here was little or no debate on the question of whether the Clause empowers Congress to provide for interbranch appointments, and there is nothing to suggest that the Framers intended to prevent Congress from having that power.

... Congress' decision to vest the appointment power in the courts [might] be improper if there was some "incongruity" between the functions normally performed by the courts and the performance of their duty to appoint. ... [But there is no] inherent incongruity about a court having the power to appoint prosecutorial officers. We have recognized that courts may appoint private attorneys to act as prosecutor for judicial contempt judgments.

[Noting that only appointments issues were actually before it, the Court nonetheless discussed arguments that the Special Division's functions were inconsistent with Article III. The Court's analysis warned against close judicial involvement with the independent counsel. "The Act simply does not give the Division the power to 'supervise' the independent counsel in the exercise of her investigative or prosecutorial authority." The Special Division's statutory power to terminate the office of the independent counsel "has not been tested in practice ... but it is the duty of federal courts to construe a statute in order to save it from constitutional infirmities. ... [T]he power to remove the counsel while an investigation or court proceeding is still underway ... is vested solely in the Attorney General. As we see it, 'termination' may occur only when the duties of the counsel are truly 'completed' or 'so substantially completed' that there remains no need for any continuing action by the independent counsel." So construed, the Special Division's powers would not threaten embroiling judges in "matters that are more properly within the Executive's authority."]

We emphasize, nevertheless, that the Special Division has *no* authority to take any action or undertake any duties that are not specifically authorized by the Act. The gradual expansion of the authority of the Special Division might in another context be a bureaucratic success story, but it would be one that would have serious constitutional ramifications. . . .

We now turn to consider whether the Act is invalid under the constitutional principle of separation of powers. ... Unlike both Bowsher v. Synar [p. 176 below] and Myers, this case does not involve an attempt by Congress itself to gain a role in the removal of executive officials other than its established powers of impeachment and conviction. The Act instead puts the removal power squarely in the hands of the Executive Branch; an independent counsel may be removed from office, "only by the personal action of the Attorney General, and only for good cause." There is no requirement of congressional approval of the Attorney General's removal decision, though the decision is subject to judicial review. In our view, the removal provisions of the Act make this case more analogous to Humphrey's Executor v. United States and Wiener v. United States than to Myers or Bowsher.

... We undoubtedly did rely on the terms "quasi-legislative" and "quasi-judicial" to distinguish the officials involved in Humphrey's Executor and Wiener from those in Myers, but our present considered view is that the determination of whether the Constitution allows Congress to impose a "good cause"-type restriction on the President's power to remove an official cannot be made to turn on whether or not that official is classified as "purely executive." The analysis contained in our removal cases is designed not to define rigid categories of those officials who may or may not be removed at will by the President,[2] but to ensure that Congress does not interfere with the President's exercise of the "executive power" and his constitutionally appointed duty to "take care that the laws be

---

2. The difficulty of defining such categories of "executive" or "quasi-legislative" officials is illustrated by a comparison of our decisions in cases such as Humphrey's Executor, Buckley v. Valeo, 424 U.S. 1, 140–141, (1976), and Bowsher.... As Justice White noted in his dissent in Bowsher, it is hard to dispute that the powers of the FTC at the time of Humphrey's Executor would at the present time be considered "executive," at least to some degree.

faithfully executed" under Article II. . . . We do not mean to suggest that an analysis of the functions served by the officials at issue is irrelevant. But the real question is whether the removal restrictions are of such a nature that they impede the President's ability to perform his constitutional duty, and the functions of the officials in question must be analyzed in that light.

Considering for the moment the "good cause" removal provision in isolation from the other parts of the Act at issue in this case, we cannot say that the imposition of a "good cause" standard for removal by itself unduly trammels on executive authority. . . . [Although the independent counsel performs] law enforcement functions that typically have been undertaken by officials within the Executive Branch . . . [and] the counsel exercises no small amount of discretion and judgment in deciding how to carry out her duties under the Act, we simply do not see how the President's need to control the exercise of that discretion is so central to the functioning of the Executive Branch as to require as a matter of constitutional law that the counsel be terminable at will by the President.

Nor do we think that the "good cause" removal provision at issue here impermissibly burdens the President's power to control or supervise the independent counsel, as an executive official, in the execution of her duties under the Act. . . . [B]ecause the independent counsel may be terminated for "good cause," the Executive, through the Attorney General, retains ample authority to assure that the counsel is competently performing her statutory responsibilities in a manner that comports with the provisions of the Act. . . . [T]he legislative history of the removal provision also makes clear that the Attorney General may remove an independent counsel for "misconduct." We do not think that this limitation as it presently stands sufficiently deprives the President of control over the independent counsel to interfere impermissibly with his constitutional obligation to ensure the faithful execution of the laws.[3]

The final question to be addressed is whether the Act, taken as a whole, violates the principle of separation of powers by unduly interfering with the role of the Executive Branch. . . . We observe first that this case does not involve an attempt by Congress to increase its own powers at the expense of the Executive Branch. Cf. Commodity Futures Trading Comm'n v. Schor, 478 U.S., at 856. Unlike some of our previous cases, most recently Bowsher v. Synar, this case simply does not pose a "dange[r] of congressional usurpation of Executive Branch functions." . . .

Similarly, we do not think that the Act works any *judicial* usurpation of properly executive functions. . . . As we pointed out in our discussion of the Special Division in relation to Article III, the various powers delegated by the statute to the Division are not supervisory or administrative, nor are they functions that the Constitution requires be performed by officials within the Executive Branch. . . .

3. We see no constitutional problem in the fact that the Act provides for judicial review of the removal decision. The purpose of such review is to ensure that an independent counsel is removed only in accordance with the will of Congress as expressed in the Act. The possibility of judicial review does not inject the Judicial Branch into the removal decision, nor does it, by itself, put any additional burden on the President's exercise of executive authority. . . .

Finally, we do not think that the Act "impermissibly undermine[s]" the powers of the Executive Branch, or "disrupts the proper balance between the coordinate branches [by] prevent[ing] the Executive Branch from accomplishing its constitutionally assigned functions," Nixon v. Administrator of General Services, 433 U.S., at 443. It is undeniable that the Act reduces the amount of control or supervision that the Attorney General and, through him, the President exercises over the investigation and prosecution of a certain class of alleged criminal activity. . . . Nonetheless, the Act does give the Attorney General several means of supervising or controlling the prosecutorial powers that may be wielded by an independent counsel. Most importantly, the Attorney General retains the power to remove the counsel for "good cause". . . . No independent counsel may be appointed without a specific request by the Attorney General, and the Attorney General's decision not to request appointment if he finds "no reasonable grounds to believe that further investigation is warranted" is committed to his unreviewable discretion. . . . In addition, the jurisdiction of the independent counsel is defined with reference to the facts submitted by the Attorney General, and once a counsel is appointed, the Act requires that the counsel abide by Justice Department policy unless it is not "possible" to do so. . . .

Reversed.

■ JUSTICE KENNEDY took no part in the consideration or decision of this case.

■ JUSTICE SCALIA, dissenting.

. . . "[T]he great security," wrote Madison, "against a gradual concentration of the several powers in the same department consists in giving to those who administer each department the necessary constitutional means and personal motives to resist encroachment of the others. The provision for defense must in this, as in all other cases, be made commensurate to the danger of attack." Federalist No. 51. Madison continued:

> But it is not possible to give to each department an equal power of self-defense. In republican government, the legislative authority necessarily predominates. The remedy for this inconveniency is to divide the legislature into different branches; and to render them, by different modes of election and different principles of action, as little connected with each other as the nature of their common functions and their common dependence on the society will admit. . . . As the weight of the legislative authority requires that it should be thus divided, the weakness of the executive may require, on the other hand, that it should be fortified.

The major "fortification" provided, of course, was the veto power. But in addition to providing fortification, the founders conspicuously and very consciously declined to sap the executive's strength in the same way they had weakened the legislature: by dividing the executive power. Proposals to have multiple executives, or a council of advisors with separate authority were rejected. Thus, while "[a]ll legislative Powers herein granted shall be vested in a Congress of the United States, which shall consist of a Senate *and* House of Representatives," U.S. Const., Art. I, § 1 (emphasis added), "[t]he executive Power shall be vested in *a President of the United States,*" Art. II, § 1, cl. 1. (emphasis added)

That is what this suit is about. Power. The allocation of power among Congress, the President and the courts in such fashion as to preserve the equilibrium the Constitution sought to establish—so that "a gradual concentration of the several powers in the same department," Federalist No. 51, can effectively be resisted. Frequently an issue of this sort will come before the Court clad, so to speak, in sheep's clothing: the potential of the asserted principle to effect important change in the equilibrium of power is not immediately evident, and must be discerned by a careful and perceptive analysis. But this wolf comes as a wolf.

[Justice Scalia argued that the Attorney General had no real choice about seeking appointment of an independent counsel in the face of the report of the Judiciary Committee. The public would ask how it could be that "a 3,000–page indictment drawn by our representatives over 2-1/2 years does not even establish ... that there were *'no reasonable grounds to believe'* ... merely that *'further investigation'* was warranted." Even if the courts are precluded from reviewing an Attorney General's decision not to seek appointment, "*Congress* is not prevented from reviewing it. The context of this statute is acrid with the smell of threatened impeachment." "Congress has effectively compelled a criminal investigation of a high-level appointee of the President in connection with his actions arising out of a bitter power dispute between the President and the Legislative Branch."]

... Art. II, § 1, cl. 1 of the Constitution provides: "The executive Power shall be vested in a President of the United States." ... [T]his does not mean *some* of the executive power, but *all of* the executive power. [Thus, decision here turns on two questions:] (1) Is the conduct of a criminal prosecution ... the exercise of purely executive power? (2) Does the statute deprive the President of the United States of exclusive control over the exercise of that power? ...

The Court concedes that "[t]here is no real dispute that the functions performed by the independent counsel are 'executive'" ... As for ... whether the statute before us deprives the President of exclusive control[:] ... That is indeed the whole object of the statute. Instead, the Court points out that the President, through his Attorney General, has at least *some* control. ... [T]he Court greatly exaggerates the extent of that "some" presidential control. ... As we recognized in Humphrey's Executor v. United States—indeed, what Humphrey's Executor was all about—limiting removal power to "good cause" is an impediment to, not an effective grant of, presidential control. ...

... [It] effects a revolution in our constitutional jurisprudence for the Court ... to sit in judgment of whether "the President's need to control the exercise of [the independent counsel's] discretion is *so central* to the functioning of the Executive Branch" as to require complete control. (emphasis added) ... It is not for us to determine, and we have never presumed to determine, how much of the purely executive powers of government must be within the full control of the President. The Constitution prescribes that they *all* are. ...

Is it unthinkable that the President should have such exclusive power, even when alleged crimes by him or his close associates are at issue? No more so than that Congress should have the exclusive power of legislation, even when what is at issue is its own exemption from the burdens of certain laws. No more so than that this Court should have the exclusive power to pronounce the final decision on justiciable cases and controversies, even those pertaining to the constitutionality of a statute reducing the salaries of the Justices. See United States v. Will, 449 U.S. 200, 211–217 (1980). A system of separate and coordinate powers necessarily involves an acceptance of exclusive power that can theoretically be abused. . . . Before this statute was passed, the President, in taking action disagreeable to the Congress, or an executive officer giving advice to the President or testifying before Congress concerning one of those many matters on which the two branches are from time to time at odds, could be assured that his acts and motives would be adjudged—insofar as the decision whether to conduct a criminal investigation and to prosecute is concerned—in the Executive Branch, that is, in a forum attuned to the interests and the policies of the Presidency. That was one of the natural advantages the Constitution gave to the Presidency, just as it gave Members of Congress (and their staffs) the advantage of not being prosecutable for anything said or done in their legislative capacities. See U.S. Const., Art. I, § 6, cl. 1. It is the very object of this legislation to eliminate that assurance of sympathetic forum. . . .

. . . [F]or the President's high-level assistants, who typically have no political base of support, it is as utterly unrealistic to think that they will not be intimidated by this prospect, and that their advice to him and their advocacy of his interests before a hostile Congress will not be affected, as it would be to think that the Members of Congress and their staffs would be unaffected by replacing the Speech or Debate Clause with a similar provision. It deeply wounds the President, by substantially reducing the President's ability to protect himself and his staff. That is the whole object of the law, of course, and I cannot imagine why the Court believes it does not succeed. . . .

Congress appropriates approximately $50 million annually for general legal activities, salaries and expenses of the Criminal Division of the Department of Justice. . . . By comparison, between May 1986 and August 1987, four independent counsel (not all of whom were operating for that entire period of time) spent almost $5 million (one-tenth of the amount annually appropriated to the entire Criminal Division), spending almost $1 million in the month of August 1987 alone. . . .

[Turning to the question whether prosecutor Morrison was an "inferior officer," Justice Scalia argued that only a "subordinate" could be so characterized.] . . . [I]t would be unpardonably careless to use the word ["inferior"] unless a relationship of subordination was intended. . . . To be sure, it is not a *sufficient* condition for "inferior" officer status that one be subordinate to a principal officer. Even an officer who is subordinate to a department head can be a principal officer. . . . But it is surely a *necessary* condition for inferior officer status that the officer be subordinate to another officer. . . . Because appellant is not subordinate to another officer, she is not an "inferior" officer and her appointment other than by the

President with the advice and consent of the Senate is unconstitutional....

The Court could have resolved the removal power issue in this case by
simply relying upon its erroneous conclusion that the independent counsel
was an inferior officer, and then extending our holding that the removal of
inferior officers appointed by the Executive can be restricted, to a new
holding that even the removal of inferior officers appointed by the courts
can be restricted. That would in my view be a considerable and unjustified
extension, giving the Executive full discretion in neither the selection nor
the removal of a purely executive officer. The course the Court has chosen,
however, is even worse....

Since our 1935 decision in Humphrey's Executor v. United States—
which was considered by many at the time the product of an activist, anti-
New Deal Court bent on reducing the power of President Franklin
Roosevelt—it has been established that the line of permissible restriction
upon removal of principal officers lies at the point at which the powers
exercised by those officers are no longer purely executive. Thus, removal
restrictions have been generally regarded as lawful for so-called "independent regulatory agencies," such as the Federal Trade Commission, the
Interstate Commerce Commission, and the Consumer Product Safety Commission, which engage substantially in what has been called the "quasi-
legislative activity" of rulemaking, and for members of Article I courts,
such as the Court of Military Appeals, who engage in the "quasi-judicial"
function of adjudication. It has often been observed, correctly in my view,
that the line between "purely executive" functions and "quasi-legislative"
or "quasi-judicial" functions is not a clear one or even a rational one. See
Bowsher v. Synar, 478 U.S. 714, 761, n. 3 (White, J., dissenting); FTC v.
Ruberoid Co., 343 U.S. 470, 487–488 (Jackson, J., dissenting). But at least
it permitted the identification of certain officers, and certain agencies,
whose functions were entirely within the control of the President. Congress
had to be aware of that restriction in its legislation. Today, however,
Humphrey's Executor is swept into the dustbin of repudiated constitutional
principles. ... What Humphrey's Executor (and presumably Myers) really
means, we are now told, is not that there are any "rigid categories of those
officials who may or may not be removed at will by the President," but
simply that Congress cannot "interefere with the President's exercise of
the 'executive power' and his constitutionally appointed duty to 'take care
that the laws be faithfully executed.' "

... Humphrey's Executor at least had the decency formally to observe
the constitutional principle that the President had to be the repository of
all executive power which, as Myers carefully explained, necessarily means
that he must be able to discharge those who do not perform executive
functions according to his liking....

By contrast, "our present considered view" is simply that *any* Executive officer's removal can be restricted, so long as the President remains
"able to accomplish his constitutional role." ... This is an open invitation
for Congress to experiment. What about a special Assistant Secretary of
State, with responsibility for one very narrow area of foreign policy, who
would not only have to be confirmed by the Senate but could also be

removed only pursuant to certain carefully designed restrictions? Could this possibly render the President "[un]able to accomplish his constitutional role"? . . . The possibilities are endless, and the Court does not understand what the separation of powers, what "[a]mbition . . . counteract[ing] ambition," Federalist No. 51 is all about, if it does not expect Congress to try them. . . .

Under our system of government, the primary check against prosecutorial abuse is a political one. . . . [W]hen crimes are not investigated and prosecuted fairly, nonselectively, with a reasonable sense of proportion, . . . the unfairness will come home to roost in the Oval Office. . . . That result, of course, was precisely what the Founders had in mind when they provided that all executive powers would be exercised by a *single* Chief Executive. . . . The people know whom to blame, whereas "one of the weightiest objections to a plurality in the executive . . . is that it tends to conceal faults and destroy responsibility." Federalist No. 70.

That is the system of justice the rest of us are entitled to, but what of that select class consisting of present or former high-level executive-branch officials? . . . An independent counsel is selected, and the scope of her authority prescribed, by a panel of judges. What if they are politically partisan, as judges have been known to be, and select a prosecutor antagonistic to the administration, or even to the particular individual who has been selected for this special treatment? There is no remedy for that, not even a political one. . . . The independent counsel thus selected proceeds to assemble a staff . . . [of] lawyers who are willing to lay aside their current careers for an indeterminate amount of time, to take on a job that has no prospect of permanence and little prospect for promotion. . . . What would be the reaction if, in an area not covered by this statute, the Justice Department posted a public notice inviting applicants to assist in an investigation and possible prosecution of a certain prominent person? . . .

. . . As described in the brief filed on behalf of three ex-Attorneys General from each of the last three administrations:

The . . . institutional environment of the Independent Counsel—specifically, her isolation from the Executive Branch and the internal checks and balances it supplies—is designed to heighten, not to check, all of the occupational hazards of the dedicated prosecutor; the danger of too narrow a focus, of the loss of perspective, of preoccupation with the pursuit of one alleged suspect to the exclusion of other interests. Brief for Edward H. Levi, Griffin B. Bell, and William French Smith as Amici Curiae 11.

. . . What would normally be regarded as a technical violation (there are no rules defining such things), may in her small world assume the proportions of an indictable offense. . . . How frightening it must be to have your own independent counsel and staff appointed, with nothing else to do but to investigate you until investigation is no longer worthwhile . . . with no basis for comparison, whether what you have done is bad enough, willful enough, and provable enough, to warrant an indictment. . . .

. . . A government of laws means a government of rules. Today's decision on the basic issue of fragmentation of executive power is ungoverned by rule, and hence ungoverned by law. ... Taking all things into account, we conclude that the power taken away from the President here is not really *too* much. The next time executive power is assigned to someone other than the President we may conclude, taking all things into account, that it *is* too much. That opinion, like this one, will not be confined by any rule. We will describe, as we have today (though I hope more accurately) the effects of the provision in question, and will authoritatively announce: "The President's need to control the exercise of the [subject officer's] discretion *is* so central to the functioning of the Executive Branch as to require complete control." This is not analysis; it is ad hoc judgment. ... It is guaranteed to produce a result, in every case, that will make a majority of the Court happy with the law. The law is, by definition, precisely what the majority thinks, taking all things into account, it *ought* to be. I prefer to rely upon the judgment of the wise men who constructed our system, and of the people who approved it, and of two centuries of history that have shown it to be sound. Like it or not, that judgment says, quite plainly, that "[t]he executive Power shall be vested in a President of the United States."

NOTES

(1) *Different Conclusions From a Common Perspective.* Mr. Olson, Chief Justice Rehnquist, and Justice Scalia all had past lives as the Assistant Attorney General heading the Office of Legal Counsel. A small, elite division of the Justice Department, OLC serves as counsel to the government and, particularly, to the White House. It is *the* place in the federal government with institutional responsibilities for constitutional issues, such as separation of powers. That these three shared this history as the President's lawyer in the Justice Department gave the case particular piquancy. Mr. Olson was appointed Solicitor General by President George W. Bush.

(2) *The Changing Political Fortunes of the Statute.* The independent counsel portion of the Ethics in Government Act had a sunset provision. Bitterly opposed by many Republicans, the statute was allowed to lapse during the George H. Bush administration. When Bill Clinton and associates were caught up in the Whitewater scandal, the Republican-controlled Congress passed the Independent Counsel Reauthorization Act of 1994. Prior to reauthorization, Attorney General Janet Reno had appointed Robert B. Fiske (a former U.S. Attorney and a moderate Republican) to investigate the scandal as a "special prosecutor" with administrative assurances of independence from the rest of the Department of Justice. The Reauthorization Act included language clearing the way for his designation as "independent counsel" in the matter, and Reno promptly moved the Special Division to make that appointment. In a move that was itself tainted with allegations of scandal, the Special Division instead appointed Kenneth Starr.[1] Starr's investigation grew to include incidents with no apparent link

---

1. Unlike Mr. Fiske, Mr. Starr lacked prosecutorial experience. He was also a more visibly partisan figure, who had been active in Republican election campaigns and had argued the Republican position on other Clinton "scandals." Prior to Starr's appointment, Judge David Sentelle, chief judge of the Special Division, lunched with North Carolina

to the original Whitewater allegations (most notoriously, the President's relationship with Monica Lewinsky) and extended through Clinton's second term. Plagued with allegations that it had become a partisan vendetta, the investigation finally concluded in March 2002, having cost a total of $64 million and produced 14 convictions or guilty pleas, none of which were in matters involving Bill or Hillary Clinton directly. See N. Y. Times Mar. 24, 2002, sec. 4, p. 1; http://icreport.access.gpo.gov. The Reauthorization Act itself expired in June 1999, with no significant support for renewal. Ironically, it was the Starr Whitewater investigation that most closely fulfilled Justice Scalia's prophesies.

(3) *Broader Implications for the Removal Question.* Morrison's importance, of course, transcends the particular statutory scheme it sanctioned. Has the Court, finally, settled an issue that resisted closure for over two centuries? At a minimum, isn't it now clear that Myers forbids only organizational arrangements that involve Congress *itself* in removal, and does not foreclose statutory regulation, within broad limits, of Presidential removal authority?

(a) *A better doctrinal approach?* First, consider the doctrinal formulation that Morrison substitutes for that of the Removal Trilogy. Does Morrison's functionalist question—"whether the removal restrictions are of such a nature that they impede[] the President's ability to perform his constitutional duty"—capture the various constitutional dimensions of allocating the removal power better than the Trilogy's formalist emphasis on power classification did? Is it likely to be more stable and predictable?

Justice Scalia (who, of course, objects in principle to any sort of balancing approach in this area) finds it especially wrongheaded to permit any interference with Presidential control over criminal prosecution. Is prosecution indeed a core executive function? HAROLD J. KRENT, EXECUTIVE CONTROL OVER CRIMINAL LAW ENFORCEMENT: SOME LESSONS FROM HISTORY, 38 Am. U. L. Rev. 275 (1989): "Most commentators agree that the Executive's power vis-a-vis the other branches rests on a continuum. At one end is the discharge of ministerial duties in civil matters, a function subject to considerable congressional and judicial intrusion. There is generally no dispute that Congress can direct an officer in the executive branch to make a report to Congress or to pay a specified amount to a claimant. At the other end of the spectrum are the discretionary conduct of foreign relations and authority to grant pardons, powers with which Congress and the judiciary can only minimally interfere. The Executive's more routine responsibility to exercise discretion in executing the broad mandates passed by Congress lies somewhere between the two poles. Because there is probably no presidential task completely immune from congressional regulation, some accommodation among the branches is required to determine whether a disputed congressional measure unduly intrudes into the prerogatives of the President. The accommodation, however, will differ substantially depending upon the nature and source of the executive power at a

Senators Jesse Helms and Lauch Faircloth. Sentelle, formerly a North Carolina lawyer, had been appointed to the D.C. Circuit with Helms's strong support. Faircloth had public-ly opposed Fiske's appointment. Press reports claimed that the men discussed whom the Special Division should appoint.

stake. Thus, the question avoided by the Morrison majority concerns where on the continuum the Executive's responsibility for criminal law enforcement should lie, towards the end with the foreign relations power, or towards the middle, closer to the Executive's duty to implement the many non-criminal laws enacted by Congress.

"There is no question but that the Executive historically has enjoyed substantial authority in overseeing and coordinating criminal law enforcement efforts.... Yet from the inception of the republic, the President has not exercised total dominion over criminal law enforcement matters.... First, Congress for almost a century directed that criminal law enforcement responsibility be decentralized, entrusting the bulk of such efforts to part-time district attorneys who had little contact with the President and his subordinates in the nation's capital. Second, private citizens, even after the Constitution was ratified, continued to play a prominent role in enforcing the criminal laws, just as they did at common law and continue to do today in England. Third, the initial and succeeding Congresses vested federal criminal law enforcement responsibilities in state officials, thereby removing a segment of overall enforcement from the Executive's direct control. Thus, Congress, by determining both who can enforce the criminal laws and how those laws should be enforced, has long helped shape and confine the Executive's discretion in criminal law enforcement matters....

"Viewed through a historical lens[, then], criminal law enforcement does not lie at the end of the continuum marking the Executive's greatest power in relation to the coordinate branches of government...."

(b) *A new meaning of removal only "for cause"?* Next, consider the apparent shift in meaning of "for cause" removal. In Humphrey's Executor and Weiner, statutory provisions permitting removal only for cause are seen as the touchstone of "independence." Yet Morrison describes the good-cause removal provision as "ample authority to assure that the counsel is competently performing her statutory responsibilities in a manner that comports with the provisions of the Act." And, as we will see in Bowsher v. Synar, p. 176 below, a majority of the Court concluded that the Comptroller General was under Congress's control because he could be removed by joint resolution for "permanent disability; inefficiency; neglect of duty; malfeasance; or a felony or conduct involving moral turpitude"—a list that appears merely to make specific the elements of good-cause removal. Does this shift suggest a new, more capacious understanding of what might constitute "cause" for removal?

Some indefiniteness about the boundaries of good cause for removal may be constitutionally beneficial, for uncertainty might induce all the relevant actors to be cautious. The outer limits appear clear: Insubordination is "cause," mere political preference is not. But the real question is, what are the bounds of the orders a President may properly give? Outside those bounds, refusal to obey is *not* insubordination. The set of Notes at p. 212 below explores the extent to which the President is entitled to order specific regulatory outcomes in policy disputes Congress has delegated to agencies for resolution. Here, you should recognize that the answer to this fundamental question has implications for the removal controversy. In particular, can the President remove an official citing, as "cause," that she has exercised her statutory discretion in a manner the President deems unwise or undesirable? If this question were to be answered "yes," wouldn't Justice Scalia and Chief Justice Taft have lost the doctrinal battle only to win the control war?

(4) *Political Realities Beyond Doctrinal Labels.* Legal doctrine is important, but politics plays at least as great a role in determining the relationship between the President and agency head(s). "Independent agencies, even if not required to do so, may nonetheless choose to align their policies with those of the President. It is hard to imagine that the Federal Trade Commission under James C. Miller III, for example, could have cooperated any more fully than it did with the Reagan administration's philosophy of economic regulation. Conversely, 'executive' agencies may not always be as cozy towards the White House as might be imagined. The Environmental Protection Agency under William Ruckelshaus [who took over as Administrator after the management debacle of Anne Gorsuch] tried to maintain at least something of an arm's-length relationship to the President. The 'independent' Civil Aeronautics Board was abolished in the late 1970s, and its functions folded into the 'purely executive' Department of Transportation. It is an open question whether this shift had any policy impact at all." Peter M. Shane, Independent Policymaking and Presidential Power: A Constitutional Analysis, 57 Geo. Wash. L. Rev. 596 (1989).

In other words, both the President and the "typical" independent agency understand that they exist within a complex political structure, in which the inevitability of long-term interaction with other powerful players makes it essential to cultivate relationships where possible—and to choose battles carefully. "The White House's treatment of cost-benefit analysis by independent regulatory commissions in conjunction with major rulemakings is a notable example. Both President Carter and President Reagan were advised [by their Office of Legal Counsel] that they had authority to include the independents in their executive orders promoting economic analysis of proposed rules as an element of regulatory reform.[2] Neither did include those agencies, reasoning that the political costs of arousing Congressional opposition, perhaps to the order as a whole, would be too great. In fact, the independents generally have complied with these executive orders: they have participated in the Regulatory Council, publish regular agendas of rulemaking, are attentive to White House inquiries about their progress, and otherwise behave as if they were in fact subject to the discipline from which they have been excused.

"The reasons for this acceptance of presidential input are clear. . . . It can be useful to be associated with national policy, to have a big and politically powerful 'friend,' when appearing before Congress. The [independent agencies] need goods the President can provide: budgetary and legislative support, assistance in dealing with other agencies, legal services, office space, and advice on national policy. They share a commitment to

---

2. See U.S. Dept. of Justice, Memorandum re Proposed Executive Order on Federal Regulation 7–13 (Feb. 12, 1981), reprinted in Role of The Office of Management and Budget in Regulation: Hearings Before the Subcomm. on Oversight and Investigations of the House Comm. on Energy and Commerce, 97th Cong., 1st Sess. 158–64 (1981).

achieving the public interest, and are likely to respect the President's motives and appreciate his political responsibility and support. They are flattered when their own advice is sought, and respectful of office when they are advised. In the circumstances, it is not surprising that the independent commissions can be susceptible to substantial presidential oversight." Peter L. Strauss, The Place of Agencies in Government: Separation of Powers and the Fourth Branch, 84 Colum. L. Rev. 573, 590–95 (1984).

(5) *The Meaning of "Inferior Officer."* Interpretation of the Appointments Clause with respect to "inferior" officers has continued in post-Morrison cases. EDMOND V. UNITED STATES, 520 U.S. 651 (1997), challenged the Secretary of Transportation's appointment of civilian members of the Coast Guard Court of Criminal Appeals, a military court. In sustaining their appointment as "inferior" officers, Justice Scalia echoed his own Morrison dissent, and wrote for all except Justice Souter: "Generally speaking, the term 'inferior officer' connotes a relationship with some higher ranking officer or officers below the President: whether one is an 'inferior' officer depends on whether he has a superior. It is not enough that other officers may be identified who formally maintain a higher rank, or possess responsibilities of a greater magnitude. If that were the intention, the Constitution might have used the phrase 'lesser officer.' Rather, in the context of a clause designed to preserve political accountability relative to important government assignments, we think it evident that 'inferior officers' are officers whose work is directed and supervised at some level by others who were appointed by presidential nomination with the advice and consent of the Senate." Justice Souter expressed unwillingness to decide the principal/inferior question based solely on whether the officer has a "relationship of [supervision and direction] with some higher ranking officer or officers below the President."

If it is now the law that an official must have a direct, hierarchical supervisor to be an "inferior" officer, it seems that a future Congress would encounter difficulty in reviving the independent counsel act. Conventional types of administrative arrangements, however, seem unaffected by Edmond. The same cannot be said about FREYTAG V. COMMISSIONER OF INTERNAL REVENUE, 501 U.S. 868 (1991), which potentially unsettles a broad range of existing agency appointments practices.

The Tax Court (itself a legislative, Article I court[3]) uses the services of "special trial judges" who hear cases and prepare proposed findings and opinions for the regular judges on the Court. These special judges are appointed by the chief judge of the Tax Court. If they are merely employees and not "officers of the United States," then no constitutional issue arises. All the Justices agreed, however, that their permanent status and significant discretion render them "officers." The question then became whether they are appointed by someone qualifying as "the Head of a Department" or by "the Courts of law." (There was no question that they are inferior,

---

3. For those who have not studied Section 3 of this Chapter, a legislative court is one whose judges do not have the requisite life tenure and protection against salary diminution required in those who exercise the Article III judicial power. Tax Court judges, for example, are appointed for a 15–year term.

rather than principal, officers.) The five–Justice majority held that the Chief Judge was not the "Head of a Department." As you may recall from the notes following Myers, see p. 149 above, Justice Blackmun reviewed the history of the Appointments Clause to conclude that "[t]he term 'Department' refers only to a part or divisions of the executive government, as the Department of State, or of the Treasury, expressly created and given the name of a department by Congress." (internal quotations omitted) This interpretation was necessary to avoid "excessively diffusing" the power of appointment, with a corresponding loss of accountability "to political force and the will of the people." "Confining the term 'Heads of Departments' in the Appointments Clause to executive divisions like the Cabinet-level departments constrains the distribution of the appointment power." The Tax Court did not meet this formal criterion. The majority went on to conclude, however, that the Tax Court *was* one of the "Courts of law" for appointments purposes. Justice Scalia, writing for himself and three other Justices, seemed to have the better of the argument in insisting that this phrase includes only courts having Article III status. He would have sustained the appointment system on grounds that the Tax Court was a "Department"—which he defined as "a free-standing, self-contained entity in the Executive Branch, whose [head] is removable by the President (and, save impeachment, no one else)." He added, in a footnote:

> I must confess that in the case of the Tax Court, as with some other independent establishments (notably, the so-called "independent regulatory agencies" such as the Federal Communications Commission and the Federal Trade Commission) permitting appointment of inferior officers by the agency head may not insure the high degree of insulation from congressional control that was the purpose of the appointments scheme elaborated in the Constitution. That is a consequence of our decision in Humphrey's Executor v. United States. . . . Depending upon how broadly one reads the President's power to dismiss "for cause," it may be that he has no control over the appointment of inferior officers in such agencies; and if those agencies are publicly regarded as beyond his control—a "headless Fourth Branch"—he may have less incentive to care about such appointments. . . . That is a reasonable position—though I tend to the view that adjusting the remainder of the Constitution to compensate for Humphrey's Executor is a fruitless endeavor. . . .

Considerable problems for common administrative structures are potentially created by the majority's broad definition of "inferior officer" (in contrast to mere employee) and narrow definition of "Department." Are any of the independent agencies "Departments," in the Freytag sense? They are not termed such by Congress. Neither is the EPA, the CIA, the Federal Reserve Banks, or a number of other agencies whose heads have long appointed personnel that surely qualify as "inferior officers," in the Freytag sense. In a footnote, the majority acknowledged these questions, but simply refused to address them.[4] Consequently, Freytag-inspired at-

---

4. "We do not address here any question involving an appointment of an inferior officer by the head of one of the principal agencies, such as the Federal Trade Commission, the Securities and Exchange Commission, the Federal Energy Regulatory Commis-

tacks on the appointment of various agency decisionmakers have since been made in divers administrative contexts. So far, the courts of appeals have resisted them. The opinions demonstrate more ingenuity in sidestepping the implications of Freytag, than fidelity to its language. E.g., Landry v. FDIC, 204 F.3d 1125 (D.C.Cir.2000) (ALJs who conduct administrative proceedings for the FDIC are not "inferior officers" because they render only proposed decisions and the FDIC makes its own factual findings); Silver v. Postal Service, 951 F.2d 1093 (9th Cir.1991) (Postal Service Board of Governors is a "department" capable of receiving authority to appoint the Postmaster General, as an inferior officer, because Freytag defines "department" as "executive divisions *like* the Cabinet-level departments" and the Postal Service was a cabinet level department prior to its reorganization). So far, the Supreme Court has refused to speak further on the issue.[5]

(ii) THE LIMITS OF CONGRESSIONAL PREROGATIVE

Bowsher v. Synar

Supreme Court of the United States, 1986.
478 U.S. 714.

■ CHIEF JUSTICE BURGER delivered the opinion of the Court.

[The Vietnam War, politically ambitious social programs, and politically popular tax cuts combined to quadruple the national debt between 1970 and the 1990s. Before the economic boom of the late 20th century produced unpredicted budget surpluses, conventional wisdom held that the federal budget could not be balanced through any "normal" political means. Congress had tried, for many years, to find reliable ways to tie itself to the mast of spending reduction. The challenge was finding some mechanism that kept all members securely in the cost-cutting boat, when each was eager to gain credit with his or her own constituencies by providing financial benefits to them. In 1985, with great political fanfare (and controversy), it enacted the Balanced Budget and Emergency Deficit Control Act—the Gramm–Rudman–Hollings Act. The Act contained a schedule of annual "maximum deficit amounts," that declined over five years to $0. Each year, the White House Office of Management and Budget and the Congressional Budget Office were independently to estimate the federal budget deficit for the coming year, and report their findings to the Comptroller General. As you might infer from the provision for separate estimates by agencies living at opposite ends of Pennsylvania Avenue, this process entailed highly debatable assumptions and predictions. The Comptroller was to review these reports and, if he concluded that the projected

sion, the Central Intelligence Agency, and the Federal Reserve Bank of St. Louis." Freytag, 501 U.S. at 887 n. 4.

5. Weiss v. United States, 510 U.S. 163 (1994), shed little additional light on the problem. The Court sustained the constitutionality of appointment, by the Judge Advocate General, of military trial and appeals judges by reasoning that the initial, Presidential appointment of these individuals to military service included, by implication, the possibility of assignment to perform judicial duties.

deficit would exceed statutory limits, he was to identify a set of "across the board" cuts, half of which (the Act specified) were to come from defense programs. On receiving the Comptroller's report, the President was to issue an order of "sequestration" requiring these reductions. If Congress did not legislate alternative reduction measures during a specified brief period, that order took effect.

The Comptroller General heads the General Accounting Office (GAO), an agency of more than 10,000 people who engage in audit and oversight activities on direction from Congress, its committees and, sometimes, individual members. The GAO was created as part of the Budget and Accounting Act of 1921. For the first time in American history, this Act had established an executive budget function centralized in the White House; the Act simultaneously created the Comptroller and the GAO to balance this newly created executive authority.

After resolving a threshold issue of standing, the Court turned to the merits:]

. . . The Constitution does not contemplate an active role for Congress in the supervision of officers charged with the execution of the laws it enacts. The President appoints "Officers of the United States" with the "Advice and Consent of the Senate." Once the appointment has been made and confirmed, however, the Constitution explicitly provides for removal of Officers of the United States by Congress only upon impeachment by the House of Representatives and conviction by the Senate. An impeachment by the House and trial by the Senate can rest only on "Treason, Bribery or other high Crimes and Misdemeanors." A direct congressional role in the removal of officers charged with the execution of the laws beyond this limited one is inconsistent with separation of powers. . . .

This Court first directly addressed this issue in Myers, . . . [holding] that for Congress to "draw to itself, or to either branch of it, the power to remove or the right to participate in the exercise of that power . . . would be . . . to infringe the constitutional principle of the separation of governmental powers." . . . Humphrey's Executor v. United States, relied upon heavily by appellants, . . . involved an issue not presented either in the Myers case or in this case—i.e., the power of Congress to limit the President's powers of removal of a Federal Trade Commissioner.[1] . . . The Court distinguished Myers, reaffirming its holding that congressional participation in the removal of executive officers is unconstitutional. . . . To permit the execution of the laws to be vested in an officer answerable only

---

1. Appellants therefore are wide of the mark in arguing that an affirmance in this case requires casting doubt on the status of "independent" agencies because no issues involving such agencies are presented here. The statutes establishing independent agencies typically specify either that the agency members are removable by the President for specified causes, see, e.g., 15 U.S.C. § 41 (members of the Federal Trade Commission may be removed by the President "for ineffi- ciency, neglect of duty, or malfeasance in office"), or else do not specify a removal procedure, see, e.g., 2 U.S.C. § 437c (Federal Election Commission). This case involves nothing like these statutes, but rather a statute that provides for direct Congressional involvement over the decision to remove the Comptroller General. Appellants have referred us to no independent agency whose members are removable by the Congress for certain causes short of impeachable offenses, as is the Comptroller General.

to Congress would, in practical terms, reserve in Congress control over the execution of the laws. ... The structure of the Constitution does not permit Congress to execute the laws; it follows that Congress cannot grant to an officer under its control what it does not possess. ... With these principles in mind, we turn to consideration of whether the Comptroller General is controlled by Congress.

... The critical factor lies in the provisions of the statute defining the Comptroller General's office relating to removability. Although the Comptroller General is nominated by the President from a list of three individuals recommended by the Speaker of the House of Representatives and the President pro tempore of the Senate, and confirmed by the Senate, he is removable only at the initiative of Congress. He may be removed not only by impeachment but also by Joint Resolution of Congress ["at any time" for "(i) permanent disability; (ii) inefficiency; (iii) neglect of duty; (iv) malfeasance; or (v) a felony or conduct involving moral turpitude."31 U.S.C. § 703(e)(1).][2] This provision was included, as one Congressman explained in urging passage of the Act, because Congress "felt that [the Comptroller General] should be brought under the sole control of Congress, so that Congress at the moment when it found he was inefficient and was not carrying on the duties of his office as he should and as the Congress expected, could remove him without the long, tedious process of a trial by impeachment." 61 Cong.Rec. 1081 (1921). ... The ultimate design was to "give the legislative branch of the Government control of the audit, not through the power of appointment, but through the power of removal." 58 Cong.Rec. 7211 (1919) (Rep. Taylor).

... [T]he dissent's assessment of the statute fails to recognize the breadth of the grounds for removal. The statute permits removal for "inefficiency," "neglect of duty," or "malfeasance." These terms are very broad and, as interpreted by Congress, could sustain removal of a Comptroller General for any number of actual or perceived transgressions of the legislative will. The Constitutional Convention chose to permit impeachment of executive officers only for "Treason, Bribery, or other high Crimes and Misdemeanors." It rejected language that would have permitted impeachment for "maladministration," with Madison arguing the "[s]o vague a term will be equivalent to a tenure during pleasure of the Senate." 2 Farrand 550. ...

This much said, we must also add that the dissent is simply in error to suggest that the political realities reveal that the Comptroller General is free from influence by Congress. ... It is clear the Congress has consistently viewed the Comptroller General as an officer of the Legislative Branch.

Against this background, we see no escape from the conclusion that, because Congress had retained removal authority over the Comptroller General, he may not be entrusted with executive powers. The remaining question is whether the Comptroller General has been assigned such powers in the Balanced Budget and Emergency Deficit Control Act of 1985.

2. Although the President could veto such a joint resolution, the veto could be overridden by a two-thirds vote of both Houses of Congress. Thus, the Comptroller General could be removed in the face of Presidential opposition. Like the District Court, we therefore read the removal provision as authorizing removal by Congress alone.

The primary responsibility of the Comptroller General under the instant Act is the preparation of a "report." This report must contain detailed estimates of projected federal revenues and expenditures. The report must also specify the reductions, if any, necessary to reduce the deficit to the target for the appropriate fiscal year. The reductions must be set forth on a program-by-program basis.

In preparing the report, the Comptroller General is to have "due regard" for the estimates and reductions set forth in a joint report submitted to him by the Director of CBO and the Director of OMB, the President's fiscal and budgetary adviser. However, the Act plainly contemplates that the Comptroller General will exercise his independent judgment and evaluation with respect to those estimates. The Act also provides that the Comptroller General's report "shall explain fully any differences between the contents of such report and the report of the Directors."

Appellants suggest that the duties assigned to the Comptroller General in the Act are essentially ministerial and mechanical so that their performance does not constitute "execution of the law" in a meaningful sense. On the contrary, we view these functions as plainly entailing execution of the law in constitutional terms. Interpreting a law enacted by Congress to implement the legislative mandate is the very essence of "execution" of the law. Under § 251, the Comptroller General must exercise judgment concerning facts that affect the application of the Act. He must also interpret the provisions of the Act to determine precisely what budgetary calculations are required. Decisions of that kind are typically made by officers charged with executing a statute. ... [And,] § 252(a)(3) ... gives the Comptroller General the ultimate authority to determine the budget cuts to be made. ...

Congress of course initially determined the content of the Balanced Budget and Emergency Deficit Control Act; and undoubtedly the content of the Act determines the nature of the executive duty. However, as *Chadha* makes clear, once Congress makes its choice in enacting legislation, its participation ends. Congress can thereafter control the execution of its enactment only indirectly—by passing new legislation. By placing the responsibility for execution of the Balanced Budget and Emergency Deficit Control Act in the hands of an officer who is subject to removal only by itself, Congress in effect has retained control over the execution of the Act and has intruded into the executive function. The Constitution does not permit such intrusion.

We now turn to the final issue of remedy. ... The language of the Balanced Budget and Emergency Deficit Control Act itself settles the issue. In § 274(f), Congress has explicitly provided "fallback" provisions in the Act that take effect "[i]n the event ... *any* of the reporting procedures described in section 251 are invalidated." § 274(f)(1) (emphasis added). ... Assuming that appellants are correct in urging that this matter must be resolved on the basis of congressional intent, the intent appears to have been for § 274(f) to be given effect in this situation. ...

Our judgment is stayed for a period not to exceed 60 days to permit Congress to implement the fallback provisions.

■ JUSTICE STEVENS, with whom JUSTICE MARSHALL joins, concurring in the judgment.

. . . [W]hen Congress, or a component or an agent of Congress, seeks to make policy that will bind the Nation, it must follow the procedures mandated by Article I of the Constitution—through passage by both Houses and presentment to the President. In short, Congress may not exercise its fundamental power to formulate national policy by delegating that power to one of its two Houses, to a legislative committee, or to an individual agent of the Congress such as the Speaker of the House of Representatives, the Sergeant at Arms of the Senate, or the Director of the Congressional Budget Office. INS v. Chadha, 462 U.S. 919 (1983). That principle, I believe, is applicable to the Comptroller General.

The fact that Congress retained for itself the power to remove the Comptroller General is important evidence supporting the conclusion that he is a member of the Legislative Branch of the Government. . . . [However,] Congress does not have the power to remove the Comptroller General at will, or because of disagreement with any policy determination that he may be required to make in the administration of this, or any other, Act. . . . Far from assuming that [the statutory] provision creates a " 'here-and-now subservience' " respecting all of the Comptroller General's actions, ante, at 3189, n. 5, we should presume that Congress will adhere to the law—that it would only exercise its removal powers if the Comptroller General were found to be permanently disabled, inefficient, neglectful, or culpable of malfeasance, a felony, or conduct involving moral turpitude.[3]

The notion that the removal power at issue here automatically creates some kind of "here-and-now subservience" of the Comptroller General to Congress is belied by history. There is no evidence that Congress has ever removed, or threatened to remove, the Comptroller General for reasons of policy. Moreover, the President has long possessed a comparable power to remove members of the Federal Trade Commission, yet it is universally accepted that they are independent of, rather than subservient to, the President in performing their official duties. . . . [T]he Humphrey's Executor analysis at least demonstrates that it is entirely proper for Congress to specify the qualifications for an office that it has created, and that the prescription of what might be termed "dereliction-of-duty" removal standards does not itself impair the independence of the official subject to such standards. . . .

Everyone agrees that the powers assigned to the Comptroller General by § 251(b) and § 251(c)(2) of the Gramm–Rudman–Hollings Act are extremely important. They require him to exercise sophisticated economic judgment concerning anticipated trends in the Nation's economy, projected levels of unemployment, interest rates, and the special problems that may

---

3. Just as it is "always appropriate to assume that our elected representatives, like other citizens, know the law," Cannon v. University of Chicago, 441 U.S. 677, 696–697 (1979), so too is it appropriate to assume that our elected representatives, like other citizens, will respect the law. As the proceedings in the United States Senate resulting from the impeachment of Justice Chase demonstrate, moreover, if that body were willing to give only lipservice to the governing standard, political considerations rather than "good behavior" would determine the tenure of federal judges. . . .

be confronted by the many components of a vast federal bureaucracy. His duties are anything but ministerial—he is not merely a clerk wearing a "green eye-shade" as he undertakes these tasks. Rather, he is vested with the kind of responsibilities that Congress has elected to discharge itself under the fallback provision that will become effective if and when § 251(b) and § 251(c)(2) are held invalid. Unless we make the naive assumption that the economic destiny of the Nation could be safely entrusted to a mindless bank of computers, the powers that this Act vests in the Comptroller General must be recognized as having transcendent importance.

The Court concludes that the Gramm–Rudman–Hollings Act impermissibly assigns the Comptroller General "executive powers." ... This conclusion is not only far from obvious but also rests on the unstated and unsound premise that there is a definite line that distinguishes executive power from legislative power. ...

One reason that the exercise of legislative, executive, and judicial powers cannot be categorically distributed among three mutually exclusive branches of Government is that governmental power cannot always be readily characterized with only one of those three labels. On the contrary, as our cases demonstrate, a particular function, like a chameleon, will often take on the aspect of the office to which it is assigned. For this reason, "[w]hen any Branch acts, it is presumptively exercising the power the Constitution has delegated to it." INS v. Chadha, 462 U.S., at 951.[4] ...

The powers delegated to the Comptroller General by § 251 of the Act before us today have [this] chameleon-like quality. ... [W]hen that delegation is held invalid, the "fallback provision" provides that the report that would otherwise be issued by the Comptroller General shall be issued by Congress itself. In the event that the resolution is enacted, the congressional report will have the same legal consequences as if it had been issued by the Comptroller General. In that event, ... surely no one would suggest that Congress had acted in any capacity other than "legislative." ... Under the District Court's analysis, and the analysis adopted by the majority today, it would therefore appear that the function at issue is "executive" if performed by the Comptroller General but "legislative" if performed by the Congress. In my view, however, the function may appropriately be labeled "legislative" even if performed by the Comptroller General or by an executive agency.

4. "Perhaps as a matter of political science we could say that Congress should only concern itself with broad principles of policy and leave their application in particular cases to the executive branch. But no such rule can be found in the Constitution itself or in legislative practice. It is fruitless, therefore, to try to draw any sharp and logical line between legislative and executive functions. Characteristically, the draftsmen of 1787 did not even attempt doctrinaire definitions, but placed their reliance in the mechanics of the Constitution. One of their principal devices was to vest the legislative powers in the two Houses of Congress and to make the President a part of the legislative process by requiring that all bills passed by the two Houses be submitted to him for his approval or disapproval, his disapproval or veto to be overridden only by a two-thirds vote of each House. It is in such checks upon powers, rather than in the classifications of powers, that our governmental system finds equilibrium." Ginnane, The Control of Federal Administration by Congressional Resolutions and Committees, 66 Harv.L.Rev. 569, 571 (1953) (footnote omitted).

Despite the statement in Article I of the Constitution that "All legislative Powers herein granted shall be vested in a Congress of the United States," it is far from novel to acknowledge that independent agencies do indeed exercise legislative powers. . . . Thus, I do not agree that the Comptroller General's responsibilities under the Gramm–Rudman–Hollings Act must be termed "executive powers," or even that our inquiry is much advanced by using that term. For, whatever the label given the functions to be performed by the Comptroller General under § 251—or by the Congress under § 274—the District Court had no difficulty in concluding that Congress could delegate the performance of those functions to another branch of the Government. If the delegation to a stranger is permissible, why may not Congress delegate the same responsibilities to one of its own agents? That is the central question before us today. . . .

The Gramm–Rudman–Hollings Act assigns to the Comptroller General the duty to make policy decisions that have the force of law. . . . Article I of the Constitution specifies the procedures that Congress must follow when it makes policy that binds the Nation: its legislation must be approved by both Houses of Congress and presented to the President. . . . If Congress were free to delegate its policymaking authority to one of its components, or to one of its agents, it would be able to evade "the carefully crafted restraints spelled out in the Constitution." Chadha, at 959. That danger—congressional action that evades constitutional restraints—is not present when Congress delegates lawmaking power to the executive or to an independent agency.

. . .

In my opinion, Congress itself could not exercise the Gramm–Rudman–Hollings functions through a concurrent resolution.[5] The fact that the fallback provision in § 274 requires a joint resolution rather than a concurrent resolution indicates that Congress endorsed this view. I think it equally clear that Congress may not simply delegate those functions to an agent such as the Congressional Budget Office. Since I am persuaded that the Comptroller General is also fairly deemed to be an agent of Congress, he too cannot exercise such functions. . . .

■ JUSTICE WHITE, dissenting.

. . . Before examining the merits of the Court's argument, I wish to emphasize what it is that the Court quite pointedly and correctly does *not* hold: namely, that "executive" powers of the sort granted the Comptroller by the Act may only be exercised by officers removable at will by the President. The Court's apparent unwillingness to accept this argument, which has been tendered in this Court by the Solicitor General,[6] is fully consistent with the Court's longstanding recognition that it is within the power of Congress under the "Necessary and Proper" Clause to vest authority that falls within the Court's definition of executive power in

5. [Ed.] A concurrent resolution requires only a majority of both houses; it is not presented to the President.

6. The Solicitor General appeared on behalf of the "United States," or, more properly, the Executive departments, which intervened to attack the constitutionality of the statute that the Chief Executive had earlier endorsed and signed into law.

officers who are not subject to removal at will by the President and are therefore not under the President's direct control. See, e.g., Humphrey's Executor v. United States; Wiener v. United States.[7] ... [W]ith the advent and triumph of the administrative state and the accompanying multiplication of the tasks undertaken by the Federal Government, the Court has been virtually compelled to recognize that Congress may reasonably deem it "necessary and proper" to vest some among the broad new array of governmental functions in officers who are free from the partisanship that may be expected of agents wholly dependent upon the President.

The Court's recognition of the legitimacy of legislation vesting "executive" authority in officers independent of the President does not imply derogation of the President's own constitutional authority—indeed, duty— to "take Care that the Laws be faithfully executed," for any such duty is necessarily limited to a great extent by the content of the laws enacted by the Congress. As Justice Holmes put it, "The duty of the President to see that the laws be executed is a duty that does not go beyond the laws or require him to achieve more than Congress sees fit to leave within his power." Myers v. United States, 272 U.S., at 177 (Holmes, J., dissenting). Justice Holmes perhaps overstated his case, for there are undoubtedly executive functions that, regardless of the enactments of Congress, must be performed by officers subject to removal at will by the President. Whether a particular function falls within this class or within the far larger class that may be relegated to independent officers "will depend upon the character of the office." Humphrey's Executor, 295 U.S., at 631. In determining whether a limitation on the President's power to remove an officer performing executive functions constitutes a violation of the constitutional scheme of separation of powers, a court must "focu[s] on the extent to which [such a limitation] prevents the Executive Branch from accomplishing its constitutionally assigned functions." Nixon v. Administrator of General Services, 433 U.S. 425, 443 (1977). "Only where the potential for disruption is present must we then determine whether that impact is satisfied by an overriding need to promote objectives within the constitutional authority of Congress." Ibid.

It is evident (and nothing in the Court's opinion is to the contrary) that the powers exercised by the Comptroller General under the Gramm– Rudman Act are not such that vesting them in an officer not subject to removal at will by the President would in itself improperly interfere with Presidential powers. ... Congress has created a precise and articulated set of criteria designed to minimize the degree of policy choice exercised by the officer executing the statute and to ensure that the relative spending priorities established by Congress in the appropriations it passes into law remain unaltered. .... [I]t is eminently reasonable and proper for Congress to vest the budget-cutting authority in an officer who is to the greatest

---

7. Although the Court in Humphrey's Executor characterized the powers of the Federal Trade Commissioner whose tenure was at issue as "quasi-legislative" and "quasi-judicial," it is clear that the FTC's power to enforce and give content to the Federal Trade Commission Act's proscription of "un-

fair" acts and practices and methods of competition is in fact "executive" in the same sense as is the Comptroller's authority under Gramm–Rudman—that is, it involves the implementation (or the interpretation and application) of an act of Congress. ...

degree possible nonpartisan and independent of the President and his political agenda and who therefore may be relied upon not to allow his calculations to be colored by political considerations. . . .

. . . [T]he question remains whether . . . the fact that the officer to whom Congress has delegated the authority to implement the Act is removable by a joint resolution of Congress should require invalidation of the Act. . . .

. . . Any removal under the statute would presumably be subject to post-termination judicial review to ensure that a hearing had in fact been held and that the finding of cause for removal was not arbitrary. These procedural and substantive limitations on the removal power militate strongly against the characterization of the Comptroller as a mere agent of Congress by virtue of the removal authority. . . . More importantly, the substantial role played by the President in the process of removal through joint resolution . . . obviates the possibility that the Comptroller will perceive himself as so completely at the mercy of Congress that he will function as its tool.[8] If the Comptroller's conduct in office is not so unsatisfactory to the President as to convince the latter that removal is required under the statutory standard, Congress will have no independent power to coerce the Comptroller unless it can muster a two-thirds majority in both Houses—a feat of bipartisanship more difficult than that required to impeach and convict. The incremental *in terrorem* effect of the possibility of congressional removal in the face of a presidential veto is therefore exceedingly unlikely to have any discernible impact on the extent of congressional influence over the Comptroller. . . .

■ [JUSTICE BLACKMUN, dissenting, argued that the only appropriate remedy in the case was to find unconstitutional the statutory removal provisions of the 1921 statute, *not* the Gramm–Rudman–Hollings Act. "I cannot see the sense of invalidating legislation of this magnitude in order to preserve a cumbersome, 65–year-old removal power that has never been exercised and appears to have been all but forgotten until this litigation."]

NOTES

(1) *Joint Resolutions vs. Ordinary Legislation.* Consider carefully the allocation of power in removal by joint resolution. If the President disagrees that removal is warranted, Congress can act only if two-thirds of both Representatives and Senators support removal. Because of the override possibility, Chief Justice Burger reasons, the Court should "read the removal provision as authorizing removal by Congress alone." This same reasoning would suggest—contrary to 200 years of political reality—that laws are enacted by Congress alone. How does this allocation of power in

---

8. The Court cites statements made by supporters of the Budget and Accounting Act indicating their belief that the Act's removal provisions would render the Comptroller subservient to Congress by giving Congress "absolute control of the man's destiny in office." The Court's scholarship, however, is faulty: at the time all of these statements were made—including Representative Sisson's statement of May 3, 1921—the proposed legislation provided for removal by concurrent resolution, with no Presidential role.

the Comptroller removal provision differ from the following hypothetical alternative?

Assume that the statutory removal provision vests "for cause" removal power in the President alone. Faced with an unsatisfactory (to it) Comptroller General, Congress presses the President to exercise his removal power, but he refuses to act. Congress then, by statute passed over the President's veto, abolishes the office. It promptly by statute (overriding a veto, if necessary) recreates it, and the Senate will confirm only a person named on the statutory list of three (a list, recall, prepared by the Speaker of the House and President pro tem of the Senate). Wouldn't this hypothetical course of events clearly be a constitutional way for Congress to control the Comptroller General? Does it differ in any constitutionally significant way from the actual removal provision?

(2) *Why the Choice of Formalism?* Bowsher was decided on the same day as CFTC v. Schor, p. 121 above, which sustained adjudication of securities-fraud claims and common-law counterclaims by the Commodities Futures Trading Commission in the face of an argument that such adjudication required an Article III court. A comparison of the two opinions reveals striking differences in tone and approach. Bowsher is a resolutely formalistic analysis; Schor takes a pragmatic, functionalist approach. Justice O'Connor, writing for the Court in Schor, tried to explain the difference: "Unlike Bowsher, this case raises no question of the aggrandizement of congressional power at the expense of a coordinate branch. Instead, the separation of powers question presented in this case is whether Congress impermissibly undermined, without appreciable expansion of its own power, the role of the Judicial Branch. In any case, we have, consistent with Bowsher, looked to a number of factors in evaluating the extent to which the congressional scheme endangers separation of powers principles under the circumstances presented, but have found no genuine threat to those principles to be present in this case."

PETER L. STRAUSS, FORMAL AND FUNCTIONAL APPROACHES TO SEPARATION OF POWERS QUESTIONS—A FOOLISH INCONSISTENCY? 72 Cornell L. Rev. 488, 518–19 (1987): "[T]here is no constitutional need to regard the functioning, day-to-day elements of government (that is, the agencies) as being 'in' any particular 'branch' (as distinct from having a relationship with the named constitutional actors). In such a case, the functional question would remain—namely, has so much been taken from the functioning of Actor X to impair its core function?—but the formal analysis would be irrelevant. The general question of control, of assuring the lawfulness and responsiveness of government, remains; yet so long as conventional lines of control running to each of the named heads of government are present—so long as Congress can revise the statute and must appropriate needed resources, the President may appoint and consult, the courts may review—the issue of aggrandizement simply disappears.

"... [The CFTC] enjoys a strong relationship with each of the constitutional actors it has thus, to some extent, displaced. It acts within the framework of congressional statutes, under the constraints of congressional appropriations, and subject to the ordinary routine of congressional oversight and political chaffering. The President appoints its members, who doubtless respond to his requests for advice or suggestions as to national policy, cooperate in his councils, depend upon him for logistic support, and suffer his discipline when they depart from their duty.

"Most important, given the particular dispute in Schor, the CFTC's decisions are subject to judicial controls in the usual fashion.... Given these arrangements, one can easily conclude that courts have been assured all the essentials of judicial power, in circumstances that do not threaten 'separation-of-powers' policy; one cannot see how either the President or Congress has been enlarged vis-a-vis the courts, or made more threatening in relation to them, or how the courts' capacity to maintain their relationship with the political heads of government has been diminished. Only formalism [could support] a negative judgment.

... [T]he problem underlying Bowsher cannot be understood in the same way. It is not simply that Congress chose a particular mechanism for protecting the 'independence' and 'objectivity' of the Comptroller General.... The Comptroller General's relationships with the President, from the proposing of his appointment onward, are strikingly weaker than those that characterize other agencies; the President and the courts both are utterly divorced from participating in the control of the particular functions under review; and the relationship between Congress and the Comptroller General is far more embracive and proprietary than the relationships that characterize the rest of government. Here one could fairly describe Congress as having appropriated to itself the President's characteristic functions (and made nugatory those of the courts). Functionalist and formalist could be equally concerned with these outcomes; that the Court chose a formalist analysis speaks to possible rhetorical advantages, but not to outcome."

NOTES ON CONGRESSIONAL ATTEMPTS TO CONTROL REGULATORY POLICY VIA APPOINTMENT AND CONFIRMATION

"[The President] shall ... nominate, and by and with the Advice and Consent of the Senate, shall appoint Ambassadors, other public Ministers and Consuls, Judges of the supreme Court, and all other Officers of the United States, whose Appointments are not herein otherwise provided for, and which shall be established by Law; but the Congress may by Law vest the appointment of such inferior Officers, as they think proper, in the President alone, in the Courts of Law, or in the Heads of Departments."

U.S. Constitution, Art. II, § 2, ¶ 2

"No Senator or Representative shall, during the Time for which he was elected, be appointed to any civil Office under the Authority of the United States, which shall have been created, or the Emoluments whereof shall have been encreased during such time; and no Person holding any Office under the United States, shall be a Member of either House during his Continuance in Office."

U.S. Constitution, Art. I, § 6, ¶ 2

Appointment

The Gramm–Rudman–Hollings Act's unprecedented solution to the problem of deficit spending posed several equally unprecedented constitutional questions. For example, can Congress delegate the "core" legislative power of setting spending levels?[1] Can any agency official be empowered to determine policy which the President is then *forced* to implement? To invalidate this innovative legislation by focusing on an arcane removal provision in another statute seemed to miss the "real" constitutional issues—especially since most knowledgeable observers agreed that the Comptroller General's independence from political control was exceeded only by that of the Chairman of the Federal Reserve Board.[2] *Whatever* was wrong with Gramm–Rudman–Hollings, it did not credibly seem to be that Congress was trying to control delegated power by controlling removal of the delegee.

By contrast, Congress has very definitely tried to use control over *appointment* for this purpose. And its "creative" appointments schemes have, as definitely, been rebuffed by the Court.

(1) *Background: Text and History.* The definitiveness with which the Court has scotched direct Congressional involvement in appointments reflects the explicitness of the Constitutional text: Whatever it might imply about the removal power, Art. II, § 2, ¶ 2 is quite explicit in allocating the appointment power. Moreover, the Ineligibility and Incompatibility Clauses of Article I, § 6, ¶ 2 hover in the background.

The policy reasons may seem obvious for preventing members of Congress from holding offices that they themselves have taken part in creating (or raising the salary of). However, practices during the revolutionary period provide additional insights into founding concerns. The filling of government offices and honorary positions was an historical prerogative of the King. These royal favors often brought significant wealth and power; indeed, this is the original Anglo–American meaning of political patronage. As the 18th century progressed, British political theorists and the early Americans alike came to regard the dispensation of honors and offices to members of Parliament as means by which the King could "corrupt" that body, and "render [it] the pliant tool of the Crown."[3] Similarly the royal colonial governors, importing this practice to their dealings with the colonial assemblies, "had sought to manipulate the representatives of the people by appointing them to executive or judicial posts, or by offering them opportunities for profits through the dispensing of government contracts and public money."[4] Hence, a provision that barred members of Congress from being appointed to any executive or

---

1. This argument was pressed before the three-judge lower court in the case. Synar v. U.S., 626 F.Supp. 1374 (D.D.C.1986). It was rejected in that court's per curiam opinion, reputed to have been written by then-judge Antonin Scalia.

2. As of the time Bowsher was decided, six Comptrollers had held the office since its creation in 1921. None had been threatened with, much less subjected to, removal. See F. Mosher, The GAO 242 (1979).

3. Jack N. Rakove, Original Meanings: Politics and Ideas in the Making of the Constitution, 209 (1996).

4. Gordon S. Wood, The Creation of the American Republic, 1776–1787 at 157 (1969).

judicial office during their legislative term—and, correspondingly, that prevented any person holding executive or judicial office from being simultaneously a member of Congress—erected a structural safeguard of legislative independence from executive blandishments. As you will see, the Court often cites the Incompatibility and Ineligibility Clauses as evidence of the Framers' determination to prevent Congressional involvement in execution of the laws. Of course, a wall by its very nature restrains *both* sides. But it is worth remembering that Art. 1, § 6, ¶ 2 was framed against a history in which the perceived problem was executive use of the appointment power to purchase the compliance of members of the legislature.

(2)   BUCKLEY V. VALEO, 424 U.S. 1 (1976), challenged Congress's first significant effort to control a modern regulatory program by directly participating in appointing the regulators. The Federal Election Act of 1971 attempted campaign finance reform by imposing various limitations on contributions and spending, to be overseen by a new eight-member agency, the Federal Election Commission. The FEC was given recordkeeping, disclosure, and investigatory functions as well as extensive rulemaking, adjudicatory, and enforcement powers. The extraordinary political sensitivity of this regulatory program was reflected in the equally extraordinary provisions for the Commission's selection: two members appointed by the President pro tempore of the Senate, two by the Speaker of the House, and two by the President (all subject to confirmation by *both* Houses of Congress), with the Secretary of the Senate and the Clerk of the House to be ex officio nonvoting members. All three appointing authorities were forbidden to choose both of their appointees from the same political party.

The case produced multiple conflicting opinions on the First Amendment implications of the contribution and spending limits, but no Justice thought that the Act's appointment innovation could be sustained. Were the FEC only empowered to conduct investigations, the Court reasoned, the appointment provisions would not have been objectionable; such powers are "in the same general category as . . . Congress might delegate to one of its own committees." But rulemaking, enforcement, and the Commission's other responsibilities represented "the performance of a significant governmental duty exercised pursuant to a public law," and were therefore to be exercised only by officers of the United States appointed according to one of the exclusive means specified in the Appointment Clause. Justice White's separate opinion concluded bluntly: "I . . . find singularly unpersuasive the proposition that because the FEC is implementing statutory policies with respect to the conduct of elections, which policies Congress has the power to propound, its members may be appointed by Congress. One might as well argue that the exclusive and plenary power of Congress over interstate commerce authorizes Congress to appoint the members of the Interstate Commerce Commission and of many other regulatory commissions; that its exclusive power to provide for patents and copyrights would permit the administration of the patent laws to be carried out by a congressional committee; or that the exclusive power of the Federal Government to establish post offices authorizes Congress itself or the Speaker of the House and the President pro tempore of the Senate to appoint postmasters and to enforce the postal laws. Congress clearly has the power to create federal offices and to define the powers and duties of those offices, Myers v. United

States, but no case in this Court even remotely supports the power of Congress to appoint an officer of the United States aside from those officers each House is authorized by Art. I to appoint to assist in the legislative processes."

(3) In METROPOLITAN WASHINGTON AIRPORTS AUTH. V. CITIZENS FOR THE ABATEMENT OF AIRCRAFT NOISE, 501 U.S. 252 (1991) and HECHINGER V. METROPOLITAN WASHINGTON AIRPORTS AUTH., 36 F.3d 97 (D.C.Cir.1994), cert. denied, 513 U.S. 1126 (1995), Congress tried a different tack. Again the regulatory issue was one in which Congress felt a particularly acute interest. Two of the three airports serving the Members (and other residents of the Washington, D.C. area) were federally owned and managed. A Congressionally approved interstate compact transferred their ownership to a Commission operated by Virginia, Maryland, and the District of Columbia. The Commission, in turn, acted under the watchful eye of a Review Board. In its first iteration, this Board consisted of nine members of Congress purportedly serving in their "individual capacities" as representatives of airport users. In 1991, the Supreme Court struck down that arrangement as effectively arrogating appointment and removal authority to Congress. Congress tried again, this time requiring that the Board consist of nine individuals who travel frequently, have experience in aviation, are registered as voters outside D.C., Maryland or Virginia, and are included in lists of candidates supplied to the Commission by House and Senate leaders. Not surprisingly, the D.C. Circuit thought this rearrangement did not cure the appointment problem, and the Supreme Court refused to address the matter again.

Confirmation

Congress (more accurately, one house of Congress) *can* constitutionally participate in deciding who will exercise delegated regulatory power through the Senate's authority to advise and consent in the appointment of principal officers. The confirmation process has generated an extraordinary amount of controversy in recent years. The challenges of divided government have become obvious when Presidents of one party have tried to get their nominees for administrative or judicial office through a Senate controlled by the other party. The most spectacular rejections (or near-rejections) have involved Supreme Court nominations, and the most blatant instances of Senate stonewalling have involved lower federal court vacancies. For our purposes, however, the most interesting cases—far less likely to achieve public notoriety—are the ones in which the Senate uses the confirmation process as a venue for obtaining assurances about how delegated regulatory authority will be exercised. Most confirmations are uneventful, but constituent pressure, interest-group lobbying and/or Senators' own policy concerns can transform a routine function into an occasion for demanding a regulatory course change, or seeking a concession from the Administration.

(4) *Oversight by Footdragging.* A now-classic example was the controversy, that came to a head in the George H. Bush Administration, over centralized White House review of major proposed rules. The Reagan Administration, building on the more modest efforts of earlier presidents, had issued a

series of executive orders requiring executive agencies to consider a number of factors in exercising their rulemaking authority. The most significant of these, Executive Order 12291, mandated cost-benefit analysis.[5] Compliance with these requirements was policed by the Office of Information and Regulatory Affairs (OIRA), to which agencies were required to submit proposed rules for clearance before publication.[6] OIRA is an office within the Office of Management and Budget (OMB). Originally created by Congress to alleviate the paperwork burden imposed on private parties by regulation,[7] it became the fulcrum of Reagan Administration regulatory review efforts. It was aggressive in blocking, or at least significantly delaying, rules that did not conform to Administration policies. Reputedly, it had frequent, nonpublic discussions with business and other regulated interests opposed to the rules it was reviewing.[8] By the time OIRA's initial statutory authorization expired, frustration in the Democratic Congress was high.

PETER M. SHANE, POLITICAL ACCOUNTABILITY IN A SYSTEM OF CHECKS AND BALANCES: THE CASE OF PRESIDENTIAL REVIEW OF RULEMAKING, 48 Ark. L. Rev. 161 (1994): "[The] regulatory review process got caught in a crossfire over the 1989 reauthorization of the Paperwork Reduction Act. That statute authorized [OIRA], which dominated the regulatory review effort under the Reagan Administrations and through the first half of the Bush Administration. With the statutory authorization for funding OIRA set to expire, critics sought to insert into the reauthorization bill a set of procedural constraints for OIRA regulatory review. These included comprehensive 'logging' requirements for all OMB activities and communications relating to review, the imposition of deadlines for the conduct of reviews, and a requirement for OMB to explain in writing its reasons for suggesting changes in any proposed regulation. When OMB threatened to recommend a veto of any such requirements, Richard Darman, the director of OMB, and Rep. John Conyers, Chair of the House Government Operations Committee, reached a 'sidebar' agreement to delete the statutory requirements in return for an OMB promise to implement the proposed changes administratively. Although the Darman–Conyers pact appeared to clear the path for House support of reauthorization, the Administration informed Rep. Conyers that it could not support the Darman deal because its provisions 'would seriously interfere with the president's constitutional duty to supervise the Executive Branch.'

"In retaliation, the Democratic Congress refused either to reauthorize OIRA or to confirm a presidential appointee to succeed Wendy Gramm, who had departed as OIRA Administrator in 1989. As a consequence, OIRA lacked an advice-and-consent appointee to wield its authority over executive agencies. Although OIRA continued to operate its regulatory review operation without an express statutory charter, the Council on Competi-

---

5. See Chapter V, Sec. 3.b(iv). Other executive orders required consideration of such substantive factors as federalism, interference with private property rights, and family values.

6. This process of centralized, White House review of major rules is examined in Chapter V.

7. See Chapter III, Sec. 2.b.

8. See p. 653 below.

tiveness stepped in to fill the political void and to set the tone of regulatory review in a way that OIRA could not."

The story illustrates the complex interactions possible in a system of checked and balanced power. The Senate constitutionally could—and did—refuse to allow an office to be filled until its views were heeded on the appropriate policy to be followed by that officer. But, the President could—and did—make a countermove. The task of jawboning executive agencies into line with Administration policies was transferred to a new internal White House entity, the Council on Competitiveness, headed by Vice President Quayle. Through the remainder of the Bush Administration, the Council took up the role of the effectively-neutralized OIRA.[9]

(5) *The Opportunity for Securing Specific Policy Commitments.* Although commentators continue to debate the propriety of Senators asking prospective federal judges about their views on substantive issues, the Senate routinely questions agency nominees about their policy positions—and may condition confirmation on assurances about what the nominee will do on a particular regulatory matter. Recall the case study of the OSHA field sanitation standard in Chapter 1. After the issue had bogged down for more than a dozen years in administrative back-and-forth and court-imposed deadlines, the agency issued a "final determination" that it would not propose a standard in the area. However, the Senate had before it the nomination of William E. Brock to become the new Secretary of Labor. Just over a week after the "final determination" was announced, Mr. Brock assured the Senators conducting his confirmation hearing that he would "reconsider" this decision. Confirmation proceeded and, in October 1985, the final determination was indeed revoked—although it took another 18 months, and a D. C. Circuit order, before the field sanitation standard actually emerged. For more on the history of the Senate's use of the confirmation power as an occasion to "speak" its views on regulatory policy—as well as discussion of the appropriate exercise of that power—see William G. Ross, The Senate's Constitutional Role in Confirming Cabinet Nominees and Other Executive Officers, 48 Syracuse L. Rev. 1123 (1998). See also G. Calvin MacKenzie, The Politics of Presidential Appointments (1981).

b.   CONTROLLING POLICY THROUGH VETO, DIRECTIVE, AND BUDGET

"All legislative Powers herein granted shall be vested in a Congress of the United States, which shall consist of a Senate and a House of Representatives."

U.S. Constitution, Art. I, § 1

"Every Bill which shall have passed the House of Representatives and the Senate, shall, before it becomes a Law, be presented to the President of the United States.... Every Order, Resolution, or Vote

---

9.   Don't think that additional moves in the game were impossible. Who provided the funds that allowed the Council on Competitiveness to operate? See the materials on use of the appropriations process to control policy at p. 233 below.

to which the Concurrence of the Senate and House of Representatives may be necessary (except on a question of Adjournment) shall be presented to the President of the United States; and before the Same shall take Effect, shall be approved by him, or being disapproved by him, shall be repassed by two thirds of the Senate and House of Representatives, according to the Rules and Limitations prescribed in the Case of a Bill."

U.S. Constitution, Art. I, § 7

"[The President] shall from time to time give to the Congress Information on the State of the Union, and recommend to their Consideration such Measures as he shall judge necessary and expedient."

U.S. Constitution, Art. II, § 3

"No money shall be drawn from the Treasury, but in Consequence of Appropriations made by Law . . . ."

U.S. Constitution, Art. I, § 9, ¶ 7

The modern regulatory state differs in fundamental ways from the form of governance imagined by the Framers. The common law is no longer the dominant system of legal regulation. "Policy formation has displaced the diffused and incremental operation of the common law as our primary means of social regulation, and agencies have displaced common-law courts as the primary means by which the regulation is effectuated. All these changes have been brought about by legislation. In the process, the nature of legislation itself has undergone a major change. It no longer consists of rules that displace or supplement the common law: contemporary legislatures allocate resources, create administrative agencies, issue vague guidelines or general grants of jurisdiction to those agencies, and enact a wide range of other provisions that bear little resemblance to our traditional concept of law."[1]

In this new order—in which statutes set in motion administrative processes for addressing economic and social problems—Congress often finds itself in the role of overseeing, rather than instigating, the making of public policy. "From their originally contemplated role as initiators of policy, the House and Senate now often occupy a reactive role, responding in formal and informal ways to policy generated by agencies. From his originally contemplated role as check upon hasty and imprudent legislation, the President as chief administrator now often forces Congress into the position of checking policy specified by the executive."[2] To be sure, regulatory statutes enacted late in the 20th century tended to be far more specific in their substantive and procedural directions than the majestically vague mandates received by agencies early in the century. (Reasons for this trend are considered at p. 235 below.) Still, this increased statutory specification—inappropriate "micromanagement" in the view of some—was often a

---

1. Edward L. Rubin, Law and Legislation in the Administrative State, 89 Colum. L. Rev. 369 (1989).

2. Cynthia R. Farina, The Consent of the Governed: Against Simple Rules for a Complex World, 72 Chi–Kent L. Rev. 987, 1018 (1997).

form of Congressional reaction to emergent patterns of agency action, or inaction, with which it was displeased.

What mechanisms may Congress use to supervise and correct the regulatory choices agencies make? To what extent may the President (who may well have different policy preferences than Congress) move beyond "merely" rationalizing and coordinating agency activities into substantively directing agency decisions? Both Capitol Hill and the White House have an array of powers and opportunities to influence agency policy choice. If you study the materials in Chapters IV and V on advocacy contacts to agency decisionmakers by members of Congress or presidential staff, you will encounter the ubiquitous oversight mechanism of "jawboning." Like such phone calls and private meetings, much political oversight is informal. And even more structured and public methods of oversight—such as committee hearings and spending restrictions—are often relatively unacknowledged by legal doctrine. However, the modern administrative law era has seen the creation of a handful of formal methods of oversight that have received legal, as well as political, attention. Although these methods have roots in constitutionally familiar practices, they are ultimately novel ways for Congress and the President to exert policy control. Two of them—the legislative veto and the so-called line-item veto—have faced (and fallen to) separation-of-powers challenge. Consider the methodology used by the Court in assessing the constitutionality of these innovations. Even if the Court reached the right result, are you satisfied with the reasoning through which it assessed these efforts to provide new instruments of governance for modern times? A third, increasingly significant method is the Presidential directive. This device may prove both the most important in its practical impact on regulatory policy, and the most elusive in its capacity to be legally analyzed and constrained.

(i) EFFORTS DIRECTLY TO OVERRIDE, OR TO COMMAND, REGULATORY DECISIONS

Immigration and Naturalization Service v. Chadha

Supreme Court of the United States, 1983.
462 U.S. 919.

■ CHIEF JUSTICE BURGER delivered the opinion of the Court.

[For most of our Nation's history, an alien found deportable under relevant immigration law could obtain permission to remain in the U.S. only by having someone in Congress orchestrate passage of a private bill. The Immigration and Nationality Act of 1952 changed this longstanding practice. Section 244 delegated to the Attorney General (who in turn delegated to the INS) the discretion to "suspend deportation" of any alien who has been physically present in the U.S. for at least seven years, is of good moral character, and "is a person whose deportation would, in the opinion of the Attorney General, result in extreme hardship to the alien, or to his spouse, parent, or child who is a citizen of the United States or an alien lawfully admitted for permanent residence." However, this power was conditioned upon neither House of Congress disagreeing.[1] Subsection (c) of § 244 provides:

> (1) Upon application by any alien who is found by the Attorney General to meet [these] requirements ... the Attorney General may in his discretion suspend deportation of such alien. If the deportation of any alien is suspended under the provisions of this subsection, a complete and detailed statement of the facts and pertinent provisions of law in the case shall be reported to the Congress with the reasons for such suspension. ...
>
> (2) [I]f during the session of the Congress at which a case is reported, or prior to the close of the session of the Congress next following the session at which a case is reported, either the Senate or the House of Representatives passes a resolution stating in substance that it does not favor the suspension of such deportation, the Attorney General shall thereupon deport such alien or authorize the alien's voluntary departure at his own expense under the order of deportation in the manner provided by law. If, within the time above specified, neither the Senate nor the House of Representatives shall pass such a resolution, the Attorney General shall cancel deportation proceedings.

Chadha, an East Indian born in Kenya who had been lawfully admitted on a nonimmigrant student visa, remained after the visa expired. After the INS ordered him to show cause why he should not be deported, he applied for—and received—a suspension of deportation. In conformity with § 244(c), Chadha's case was laid before Congress.]

On December 12, 1975, Representative Eilberg, Chairman of the Judiciary Subcommittee on Immigration, Citizenship, and International Law, introduced a resolution opposing "the granting of permanent residence in the United States to [six] aliens," including Chadha. The resolution was referred to the House Committee on the Judiciary. On December 16, 1975, the resolution was discharged from further consideration by the House Committee on the Judiciary and submitted to the House of Representatives for a vote. The resolution had not been printed and was not made available to other Members of the House prior to or at the time it was voted on. So far as the record before us shows, the House consideration of the resolution was based on Representative Eilberg's statement from the floor that

> [i]t was the feeling of the committee, after reviewing 340 cases, that the aliens contained in the resolution [Chadha and five others] did not meet these statutory requirements, particularly as it relates to hardship; and it is the opinion of the committee that their deportation should not be suspended.

The resolution was passed without debate or recorded vote. Since the House action was pursuant to § 244(c)(2), the resolution was not treated as an Article I legislative act; it was not submitted to the Senate or presented to the President for his action.

---

1. Prior to the 1952 Act, Congress experimented briefly with a system in which deportation could be suspended on the Attorney General's recommendation if Congress affirmatively approved by concurrent resolution. This proved not significantly less burdensome than the private bill system.

After the House veto of the Attorney General's decision to allow Chadha to remain in the United States, the immigration judge reopened the deportation proceedings to implement the House order deporting Chadha. [Chadha argued that § 244(c)(2) was unconstitutional but both the immigration judge and the Board of Immigration Appeals held that they had no power to rule on constitutionality.] On petition for review, the Ninth Circuit agreed with Chahda and directed the Attorney General "to cease and desist from taking any steps to deport this alien based upon the resolution enacted by the House of Representatives." . . . We granted certiorari . . . and we now affirm.

[The Court considered, and disposed of, several challenges to justiciability.]

III

We turn now to the question whether action of one House of Congress under § 244(c)(2) violates strictures of the Constitution. We begin, of course, with the presumption that the challenged statute is valid. Its wisdom is not the concern of the courts; if a challenged action does not violate the Constitution, it must be sustained. . . .

By the same token, the fact that a given law or procedure is efficient, convenient, and useful in facilitating functions of government, standing alone, will not save it if it is contrary to the Constitution. Convenience and efficiency are not the primary objectives—or the hallmarks—of democratic government and our inquiry is sharpened rather than blunted by the fact that Congressional veto provisions are appearing with increasing frequency in statutes which delegate authority to executive and independent agencies: "Since 1932, when the first veto provision was enacted into law, 295 congressional veto-type procedures have been inserted in 196 different statutes as follows: from 1932 to 1939, five statutes were affected; from 1940–49, nineteen statutes; between 1950–59, thirty-four statutes; and from 1960–69, forty-nine. From the year 1970 through 1975, at least one hundred sixty-three such provisions were included in eighty-nine laws." Abourezk, The Congressional Veto: A Contemporary Response to Executive Encroachment on Legislative Prerogatives, 52 Ind.L.Rev. 323, 324 (1977). . . .

The decision to provide the President with a limited and qualified power to nullify proposed legislation by veto was based on the profound conviction of the Framers that the powers conferred on Congress were the powers to be most carefully circumscribed. It is beyond doubt that lawmaking was a power to be shared by both Houses and the President. . . . The President's role in the lawmaking process also reflects the Framers' careful efforts to check whatever propensity a particular Congress might have to enact oppressive, improvident, or ill-considered measures. . . . The Court also has observed that the Presentment Clauses serve the important purpose of assuring that a "national" perspective is grafted on the legislative process: "The President is a representative of the people just as the members of the Senate and of the House are, and it may be, at some times, on some subjects, that the President elected by all the people is rather more representative of them all than are the members of either body of the

Legislature whose constituencies are local and not countrywide...." Myers v. United States, 272 U.S., at 123.

The bicameral requirement of Art. I, §§ 1, 7 was of scarcely less concern to the Framers than was the Presidential veto and indeed the two concepts are interdependent. By providing that no law could take effect without the concurrence of the prescribed majority of the Members of both Houses, the Framers reemphasized their belief, already remarked upon in connection with the Presentment Clauses, that legislation should not be enacted unless it has been carefully and fully considered by the Nation's elected officials. ... [I]n Federalist No. 51 Hamilton ... point[ed] up the need to divide and disperse power in order to protect liberty: "In republican government, the legislative authority necessarily predominates. The remedy for this inconveniency is to divide the legislature into different branches; and to render them, by different modes of election and different principles of action, as little connected with each other as the nature of their common functions and their common dependence on the society will admit." ...

We see therefore that the Framers were acutely conscious that the bicameral requirement and the Presentment Clauses would serve essential constitutional functions. The President's participation in the legislative process was to protect the Executive Branch from Congress and to protect the whole people from improvident laws. The division of the Congress into two distinctive bodies assures that the legislative power would be exercised only after opportunity for full study and debate in separate settings. The President's unilateral veto power, in turn, was limited by the power of two thirds of both Houses of Congress to overrule a veto thereby precluding final arbitrary action of one person. It emerges clearly that the prescription for legislative action in Art. I, §§ 1, 7 represents the Framers' decision that the legislative power of the Federal government be exercised in accord with a single, finely wrought and exhaustively considered, procedure.

IV

The Constitution sought to divide the delegated powers of the new federal government into three defined categories, legislative, executive and judicial, to assure, as nearly as possible, that each Branch of government would confine itself to its assigned responsibility. The hydraulic pressure inherent within each of the separate Branches to exceed the outer limits of its power, even to accomplish desirable objectives, must be resisted. Although not "hermetically" sealed from one another, Buckley v. Valeo, 424 U.S., at 121, the powers delegated to the three Branches are functionally identifiable. When any Branch acts, it is presumptively exercising the power the Constitution has delegated to it. When the Executive acts, it presumptively acts in an executive or administrative capacity as defined in Art. II. And when, as here, one House of Congress purports to act, it is presumptively acting within its assigned sphere.

Beginning with this presumption, we must nevertheless establish that the challenged action under § 244(c)(2) is of the kind to which the procedural requirements of Art. I, § 7 apply. Not every action taken by either House is subject to the bicameralism and presentment requirements of Art. I. Whether actions taken by either House are, in law and fact, an exercise of legislative power depends not on their form but upon "whether they contain matter which is properly to be regarded as legislative in its character and effect." S.Rep. No. 1335, 54th Cong., 2d Sess., 8 (1897).[2] Examination of the action taken here by one House pursuant to § 244(c)(2) reveals that it was essentially legislative in purpose and effect. [T]he House took action that had the purpose and effect of altering the legal rights, duties and relations of persons, including the Attorney General, Executive Branch officials and Chadha, all outside the legislative branch. Section 244(c)(2) purports to authorize one House of Congress to require the Attorney General to deport an individual alien whose deportation otherwise would be cancelled under § 244. The one-House veto operated in this case to overrule the Attorney General and mandate Chadha's deportation; absent the House action, Chadha would remain in the United States. Congress has acted and its action has altered Chadha's status.

The legislative character of the one-House veto in this case is confirmed by the character of the Congressional action it supplants. Neither the House of Representatives nor the Senate contends that, absent the veto provision in § 244(c)(2), either of them, or both of them acting together, could effectively require the Attorney General to deport an alien once the Attorney General, in the exercise of legislatively delegated authority,[3] had

2. [Ed.] This Judiciary Committee Report considered whether presentment was constitutionally required in connection with a "resolution" referred to in the River and Harbors Act of 1892. The Act limited surveys and preliminary estimates for building or repairing bridges to a list designated in the Act. It further provided that once a report was submitted on a listed project, no further report or estimate could be made in the fiscal year "unless ordered by a resolution of Congress." The Report concluded that this provision "partakes of the character of an ordinary request for information from a Department which has never been deemed to require the approval of the President."

3. [Ed. This controversial and oft-discussed note is Footnote 16 in the original opinion.] Congress protests that affirming the Court of Appeals in this case will sanction "lawmaking by the Attorney General.... Why is the Attorney General exempt from submitting his proposed changes in the law to the full bicameral process?" Brief of the United States House of Representatives 40. To be sure, some administrative agency action—rule making, for example—may resemble "lawmaking." See 5 U.S.C. § 551(4), which defines an agency's "rule" as "the whole or part of an agency statement of general or particular applicability and future effect designed to implement, interpret, or prescribe law or policy...." This Court has referred to agency activity as being "quasi-legislative" in character. Humphrey's Execu-

tor v. United States. Clearly, however, "[i]n the framework of our Constitution, the President's power to see that the laws are faithfully executed refutes the idea that he is to be a lawmaker." Youngstown Sheet & Tube Co. v. Sawyer, 343 U.S. 579, 587 (1952). When the Attorney General performs his duties pursuant to § 244, he does not exercise "legislative" power. The bicameral process is not necessary as a check on the Executive's administration of the laws because his administrative activity cannot reach beyond the limits of the statute that created it—a statute duly enacted pursuant to Art. I, §§ 1, 7. The constitutionality of the Attorney General's execution of the authority delegated to him by § 244 involves only a question of delegation doctrine. The courts, when a case or controversy arises, can always "ascertain whether the will of Congress has been obeyed," Yakus v. United States, 321 U.S. 414, 425 (1944), and can enforce adherence to statutory standards. See Ethyl Corp. v. EPA, 541 F.2d 1, 68 (C.A.D.C.) (en banc) (separate statement of Leventhal, J.), cert. denied, 426 U.S. 941 (1976). It is clear, therefore, that the Attorney General acts in his presumptively Art. II capacity when he administers the Immigration and Nationality Act. Executive action under legislatively delegated authority that might resemble "legislative" action in some respects is not subject to the approval of both Houses of Congress and the President for the reason that the Constitu-

determined the alien should remain in the United States. Without the challenged provision in § 244(c)(2), this could have been achieved, if at all, only by legislation requiring deportation.[4] Similarly, a veto by one House of Congress under § 244(c)(2) cannot be justified as an attempt at amending the standards set out in § 244(a)(1), or as a repeal of § 244 as applied to Chadha. Amendment and repeal of statutes, no less than enactment, must conform with Art. I.

The nature of the decision implemented by the one-House veto in this case further manifests its legislative character. After long experience with the clumsy, time consuming private bill procedure, Congress made a deliberate choice to delegate to the Executive Branch, and specifically to the Attorney General, the authority to allow deportable aliens to remain in this country in certain specified circumstances. It is not disputed that this choice to delegate authority is precisely the kind of decision that can be implemented only in accordance with the procedures set out in Art. I. Disagreement with the Attorney General's decision on Chadha's deportation—that is, Congress' decision to deport Chadha—no less than Congress' original choice to delegate to the Attorney General the authority to make that decision, involves determinations of policy that Congress can implement in only one way; bicameral passage followed by presentment to the President. Congress must abide by its delegation of authority until that delegation is legislatively altered or revoked.

Finally, we see that when the Framers intended to authorize either House of Congress to act alone and outside of its prescribed bicameral legislative role, they narrowly and precisely defined the procedure for such action. There are but four provisions in the Constitution, explicit and unambiguous, by which one House may act alone with the unreviewable force of law, not subject to the President's veto: (a) The House of Representatives alone was given the power to initiate impeachments; (b) The Senate alone was given the power to conduct trials following impeachment on charges initiated by the House and to convict following trial; (c) The Senate alone was given final unreviewable power to approve or to disapprove presidential appointments; (d) The Senate alone was given unreviewable power to ratify treaties negotiated by the President. Clearly, when the Draftsmen sought to confer special powers on one House, independent of the other House, or of the President, they did so in explicit, unambiguous terms. . . .

The veto authorized by § 244(c)(2) doubtless has been in many respects a convenient shortcut; the "sharing" with the Executive by Congress of its authority over aliens in this manner is, on its face, an appealing

---

tion does not so require. That kind of Executive action is always subject to check by the terms of the legislation that authorized it; and if that authority is exceeded it is open to judicial review as well as the power of Congress to modify or revoke the authority entirely. A one-House veto is clearly legislative in both character and effect and is not so checked; the need for the check provided by Art. I, §§ 1, 7 is therefore clear. Congress' authority to delegate portions of its power to administrative agencies provides no support for the argument that Congress can constitutionally control administration of the laws by way of a Congressional veto.

4. We express no opinion as to whether such legislation would violate any constitutional provision.

compromise.... The choices we discern as having been made in the Constitutional Convention impose burdens on governmental processes that often seem clumsy, inefficient, even unworkable, but those hard choices were consciously made by men who had lived under a form of government that permitted arbitrary governmental acts to go unchecked. There is no support in the Constitution or decisions of this Court for the proposition that the cumbersomeness and delays often encountered in complying with explicit Constitutional standards may be avoided, either by the Congress or by the President. With all the obvious flaws of delay, untidiness, and potential for abuse, we have not yet found a better way to preserve freedom than by making the exercise of power subject to the carefully crafted restraints spelled out in the Constitution.

We hold that the Congressional veto provision in § 244(c)(2) is severable from the Act and that it is unconstitutional. Accordingly, the judgment of the Court of Appeals is

Affirmed.

■ JUSTICE POWELL, concurring in the judgment.

The Court's decision ... apparently will invalidate every use of the legislative veto. The breadth of this holding gives one pause. Congress has included the veto in literally hundreds of statutes, dating back to the 1930s. Congress clearly views this procedure as essential to controlling the delegation of power to administrative agencies.[5] One reasonably may disagree with Congress' assessment of the veto's utility, but the respect due its judgment as a coordinate branch of Government cautions that our holding should be no more extensive than necessary to decide this case. In my view, the case may be decided on a narrower ground. When Congress finds that a particular person does not satisfy the statutory criteria for permanent residence in this country it has assumed a judicial function in violation of the principle of separation of powers. ...

. . .

... One abuse that was prevalent during the Confederation was the exercise of judicial power by the state legislatures. The Framers were well acquainted with the danger of subjecting the determination of the rights of one person to the "tyranny of shifting majorities." ... It was to prevent the recurrence of such abuses that the Framers vested the executive, legislative, and judicial powers in separate branches. Their concern that a legislature should not be able unilaterally to impose a substantial deprivation on one person was expressed not only in this general allocation of power, but also in more specific provisions, such as the Bill of Attainder Clause, Art. I, § 9, cl. 3. ... This Clause, and the separation of powers doctrine generally, reflect the Framers' concern that trial by a legislature lacks the safeguards necessary to prevent the abuse of power....

---

5. [T]he legislative veto has been included in a wide variety of statutes, ranging from bills for executive reorganization to the War Powers Resolution. Whether the veto complies with the Presentment Clauses may well turn on the particular context in which it is exercised, and I would be hesitant to conclude that every veto is unconstitutional on the basis of the unusual example presented by this litigation.

On its face, the House's action appears clearly adjudicatory.[6] The House did not enact a general rule; rather it made its own determination that six specific persons did not comply with certain statutory criteria. . . .

The impropriety of the House's assumption of this function is confirmed by the fact that its action raises the very danger the Framers sought to avoid—the exercise of unchecked power. In deciding whether Chadha deserves to be deported, Congress is not subject to any internal constraints that prevent it from arbitrarily depriving him of the right to remain in this country.[7] Unlike the judiciary or an administrative agency, Congress is not bound by established substantive rules. Nor is it subject to the procedural safeguards, such as the right to counsel and a hearing before an impartial tribunal, that are present when a court or an agency[8] adjudicates individual rights. The only effective constraint on Congress' power is political, but Congress is most accountable politically when it prescribes rules of general applicability. When it decides rights of specific persons, those rights are subject to "the tyranny of a shifting majority." . . .

■ JUSTICE WHITE, dissenting.

. . . The prominence of the legislative veto mechanism in our contemporary political system and its importance to Congress can hardly be overstated. It has become a central means by which Congress secures the accountability of executive and independent agencies. Without the legislative veto, Congress is faced with a Hobson's choice: either to refrain from delegating the necessary authority, leaving itself with a hopeless task of writing laws with the requisite specificity to cover endless special circumstances across the entire policy landscape, or in the alternative, to abdicate its law-making function to the executive branch and independent agencies. To choose the former leaves major national problems unresolved; to opt for the latter risks unaccountable policymaking by those not elected to fill that role. Accordingly, over the past five decades, the legislative veto has been placed in nearly 200 statutes. The device is known in every field of

---

6. The Court concludes that Congress' action was legislative in character because each branch "presumptively act[s] within its assigned sphere." The Court's presumption provides a useful starting point, but does not conclude the inquiry. Nor does the fact that the House's action alters an individual's legal status indicate, as the Court reasons, that the action is legislative rather than adjudicative in nature. In determining whether one branch unconstitutionally has assumed a power central to another branch, the traditional characterization of the assumed power as legislative, executive, or judicial may provide some guidance. But reasonable minds may disagree over the character of an act and the more helpful inquiry, in my view, is whether the act in question raises the dangers the Framers sought to avoid.

7. When Congress grants particular individuals relief or benefits under its spending power, the danger of oppressive action that the separation of powers was designed to avoid is not implicated. Similarly, Congress may authorize the admission of individual aliens by special acts, but it does not follow that Congress unilaterally may make a judgment that a particular alien has no legal right to remain in this country. . . .

8. We have recognized that independent regulatory agencies and departments of the Executive Branch often exercise authority that is "judicial in nature." Buckley v. Valeo, 424 U.S. 1, 140–141 (1976). This function, however, forms part of the agencies' execution of public law and is subject to the procedural safeguards, including judicial review, provided by the Administrative Procedure Act.

governmental concern: reorganization, budgets, foreign affairs, war powers, and regulation of trade, safety, energy, the environment and the economy.

The legislative veto developed initially in response to the problems of reorganizing the sprawling government structure created in response to the Depression. The Reorganization Acts established the chief model for the legislative veto. When President Hoover requested authority to reorganize the government in 1929, he coupled his request that the "Congress be willing to delegate its authority over the problem (subject to defined principles) to the Executive" with a proposal for legislative review. He proposed that the Executive "should act upon approval of a joint committee of Congress or with the reservation of power of revision by Congress within some limited period adequate for its consideration." Pub. Papers 432 (1929). . . .

Congress and the President applied the legislative veto procedure to resolve the delegation problem for national security and foreign affairs. World War II occasioned the need to transfer greater authority to the President in these areas. The legislative veto offered the means by which Congress could confer additional authority while preserving its own constitutional role. During World War II, Congress enacted over thirty statutes conferring powers on the Executive with legislative veto provisions. President Roosevelt accepted the veto as the necessary price for obtaining exceptional authority.

. . . The legislative veto balanced delegations of statutory authority in new areas of governmental involvement: the space program, international agreements on nuclear energy, tariff arrangements, and adjustment of federal pay rates.

During the 1970's the legislative veto was important in resolving a series of major constitutional disputes between the President and Congress over claims of the President to broad impoundment, war, and national emergency powers. The key provision of the War Powers Resolution, 50 U.S.C. § 1544(c), authorizes the termination by concurrent resolution of the use of armed forces in hostilities. A similar measure resolved the problem posed by Presidential claims of inherent power to impound appropriations. . . . These statutes were followed by others resolving similar problems: the National Emergencies Act, resolving the longstanding problems with unchecked Executive emergency power; the Arms Export Control Act, resolving the problem of foreign arms sales; and the Nuclear Non–Proliferation Act of 1978, resolving the problem of exports of nuclear technology.

In the energy field, the legislative veto served to balance broad delegations in legislation emerging from the energy crisis of the 1970's. In the educational field, it was found that fragmented and narrow grant programs "inevitably lead to Executive–Legislative confrontations" because they inaptly limited the Commissioner of Education's authority. The response was to grant the Commissioner of Education rulemaking authority, subject to a legislative veto. In the trade regulation area, the veto preserved Congressional authority over the Federal Trade Commission's broad mandate to make rules to prevent businesses from engaging in "unfair or deceptive acts or practices in commerce."

Even this brief review suffices to demonstrate that the legislative veto is more than "efficient, convenient, and useful." It is an important if not indispensable political invention that allows the President and Congress to resolve major constitutional and policy differences, assures the accountability of independent regulatory agencies, and preserves Congress' control over lawmaking. Perhaps there are other means of accommodation and accountability, but the increasing reliance of Congress upon the legislative veto suggests that the alternatives to which Congress must now turn are not entirely satisfactory.[9]

The history of the legislative veto also makes clear that it has not been a sword with which Congress has struck out to aggrandize itself at the expense of the other branches—the concerns of Madison and Hamilton. Rather, the veto has been a means of defense, a reservation of ultimate authority necessary if Congress is to fulfill its designated role under Article I as the nation's lawmaker. While the President has often objected to particular legislative vetoes, generally those left in the hands of congressional committees, the Executive has more often agreed to legislative review as the price for a broad delegation of authority. To be sure, the President may have preferred unrestricted power, but that could be precisely why Congress thought it essential to retain a check on the exercise of delegated authority....

... The power to exercise a legislative veto is not the power to write new law without bicameral approval or presidential consideration. The veto must be authorized by statute and may only negative what an Executive department or independent agency has proposed. On its face, the legislative veto no more allows one House of Congress to make law than does the presidential veto confer such power upon the President....

9. While Congress could write certain statutes with greater specificity, it is unlikely that this is a realistic or even desirable substitute for the legislative veto. ... For example, in the deportation context, the solution is not for Congress to create more refined categorizations of the deportable aliens whose status should be subject to change. In 1979, the Immigration and Naturalization Service proposed regulations setting forth factors to be considered in the exercise of discretion under numerous provisions of the Act, but not including § 244, to ensure "fair and uniform" adjudication "under appropriate discretionary criteria." 44 Fed.Reg. 36187 (1979). The proposed rule was canceled in 1981, because "[t]here is an inherent failure in any attempt to list those factors which should be considered in the exercise of discretion. It is impossible to list or foresee all of the adverse or favorable factors which may be present in a given set of circumstances."

Oversight hearings and congressional investigations have their purpose, but unless Congress is to be rendered a think tank or debating society, they are no substitute for the exercise of actual authority....

Finally, the passage of corrective legislation after agency regulations take effect or Executive Branch officials have acted entails the drawbacks endemic to a retroactive response.

Post hoc substantive revision of legislation, the only available corrective mechanism in the absence of post-enactment review could have serious prejudicial consequences; if Congress retroactively tampered with a price control system after prices have been set, the economy could be damaged and private interests seriously impaired; if Congress rescinded the sale of arms to a foreign country, our relations with that Country would be severely strained; and if Congress reshuffled the bureaucracy after a President's reorganization proposal had taken effect, the results could be chaotic.

Javits and Klein, Congressional Oversight and the Legislative Veto: A Constitutional Analysis, 52 N.Y.U.L.Rev. 455, 464 (1977).

If Congress may delegate lawmaking power to independent and executive agencies, it is most difficult to understand Article I as forbidding Congress from also reserving a check on legislative power for itself. Absent the veto, the agencies receiving delegations of legislative or quasi-legislative power may issue regulations having the force of law without bicameral approval and without the President's signature. It is thus not apparent why the reservation of a veto over the exercise of that legislative power must be subject to a more exacting test. In both cases, it is enough that the initial statutory authorizations comply with the Article I requirements. . . .

. . . Under the Court's analysis, the Executive Branch and the independent agencies may make rules with the effect of law while Congress, in whom the Framers confided the legislative power may not exercise a veto which precludes such rules from having operative force. . . .

The central concern of the presentation and bicameralism requirements of Article I is that when a departure from the legal status quo is undertaken, it is done with the approval of the President and both Houses of Congress—or, in the event of a presidential veto, a two-thirds majority in both Houses. This interest is fully satisfied by the operation of § 244(c)(2). The President's approval is found in the Attorney General's action in recommending to Congress that the deportation order for a given alien be suspended. The House and the Senate indicate their approval of the Executive's action by not passing a resolution of disapproval within the statutory period. Thus, a change in the legal status quo—the deportability of the alien—is consummated only with the approval of each of the three relevant actors. The disagreement of any one of the three maintains the alien's pre-existing status: the Executive may choose not to recommend suspension; the House and Senate may each veto the recommendation. The effect on the rights and obligations of the affected individuals and upon the legislative system is precisely the same as if a private bill were introduced but failed to receive the necessary approval. . . .

Thus understood, § 244(c)(2) fully effectuates the purposes of the bicameralism and presentation requirements. . . .

I regret that I am in disagreement with my colleagues on the fundamental questions that this case presents. But even more I regret the destructive scope of the Court's holding. It reflects a profoundly different conception of the Constitution than that held by the Courts which sanctioned the modern administrative state. Today's decision strikes down in one fell swoop provisions in more laws enacted by Congress than the Court has cumulatively invalidated in its history. I fear it will now be more difficult "to insure that the fundamental policy decisions in our society will be made not by an appointed official but by the body immediately responsible to the people," Arizona v. California, 373 U.S. 546, 626.

I must dissent.

NOTES

(1) *The Breadth of the Decision.* As Justice Powell says, Chadha was "an unusual example of the veto," fn. 5 above, in that it involved agency

adjudication. Far more typical—and important—was reservation of a veto power over agency exercise of delegated rulemaking authority. Two weeks after Chadha, the Court summarily affirmed two D.C. Circuit decisions, one invalidating a one-house veto in the context of rulemaking by an independent agency, and the other a two-house veto in a similar context. See Consumer Energy Council of America v. FERC, 673 F.2d 425 (D.C.Cir. 1982) and Consumers Union of United States v. FTC, 691 F.2d 575 (D.C.Cir.1982), both affirmed sub nom. Process Gas Consumers Group v. Consumer Energy Council of America, 463 U.S. 1216 (1983). Justice Powell did not participate in the decision; only Justice Rehnquist would have set the cases for argument.

Should it make a difference to the constitutional analysis whether the context is rulemaking (which is likely to set policy for a broad class of persons) rather than adjudication (which singles out an individual for regulatory consequences)? Should it make a further difference that the rulemaker is an "independent," rather than an executive, agency? Could the Court justifiably assume that a rule promulgated by an executive agency (or at least the kind of major rule that would attract veto attention in Congress) has the approval of the President? Could the Court justifiably assume that the President would have had no opportunity to weigh in decisively on a rule promulgated by an independent agency? Consider the following passages from the Court of Appeals opinion in Consumers Energy. The Natural Gas Policy Act of 1978 directed FERC to develop a system of "incremental pricing" that would ease the impact of deregulation on residential gas users by shifting costs to industrial users. FERC was statutorily directed to proceed in two phases. In Phase I, it was to adopt an incremental pricing rule that covered a limited class of industrial users. In Phase II, it was to adopt an expanded incremental pricing rule, by a specified date, applicable to all industrial users. Section 202(c) of the Act authorized either house to veto this rule within 30 days of promulgation. FERC adopted a Phase II rule in the allotted time, and the House passed a disapproval resolution. A consumers' group sued, to force FERC to put the rule into effect anyway:

"Clearly the President's . . . opportunity to veto [the Act initially] was not sufficient to cover the disapproval resolution; he had an opportunity to approve incremental pricing, to the extent adopted by FERC, but he did not have an opportunity to approve the abolition of extended incremental pricing, which is what the disapproval resolution effectively accomplished.[1] If, as Congressional amici contend, section 202(c) assigned to Congress 'a

---

1. Those who argue that an opportunity for presidential veto of the regulations is equivalent to an opportunity to veto the disapproval resolution, miss the crucial point that the presumption under a rulemaking statute is that the agency rule will take effect. The agency is authorized to formulate such a rule as it sees fit, in accordance with the statutory delegation. . . . A congressional attempt to stop the rule thus amends the original delegation. The President's opportu- nity to veto this disapproval—in effect to preserve the original delegation and prevent a change in the law—is quite different thing from an opportunity to veto the rule, and one which the Presentment Clause seeks to protect by requiring concurrence and presidential approval or concurrence of a supermajority. *Here, in any event, the rule was issued by an independent agency, so the President was not given a chance to "veto" it.* [emphasis added]

single, discrete, well-defined role' of 'deciding whether to expand a major experiment,' the President was entitled to participate in that decision. Otherwise, Congress has created a device which effectively expands the reach of its legislative power by permitting it to determine conclusively whether effective law is created or not.

"... [T]he effect of a congressional veto is to alter the scope of the agency's discretion. In this case, the practical effect probably was to withdraw the discretion altogether; Representative Brown seemed justified in saying, 'The overwhelming vote to disapprove phase II ... should be a clear message to the FERC not to send up another incremental pricing rule.' In other cases, exercise of the legislative veto may enable one house of Congress effectively to dictate that a specific type of rule be promulgated. In either case, one house of Congress is enabled to enact a policy to which the other house and the President did not agree originally, a result that violates the requirements of Article I, Section 7....

"... The fact that FERC is not subject to presidential control does not entitle Congress to direct FERC's administrative decisions. ... The Commission is an independent regulatory agency 'within the Department (of Energy)'.... Since the Supreme Court has upheld the constitutionality of such agency independence, Congressional amici argue that it is clear that the President can have no claim to participation in the making of FERC's rules. [While] it is true that the President, as representative of the Executive, does not have a claim to control the decisionmaking of independent agencies[,] ... it is an enormous, and unwarranted, jump from this to the conclusion that Congress may itself interfere with an independent agency's decisions without regard to separation of powers. Although FERC is substantially independent of the Executive, it nonetheless performs executive functions. The constitutionality of agency independence has not turned on a determination that certain agency functions are properly legislative rather than executive in nature. ... Indeed, it is ironic that Congressional amici attempt to place great significance on the Commission's independence and on the need for having a politically accountable check on the agency's decision. The fundamental justification for making agencies independent is that since they exercise adjudicatory powers requiring impartial expertise, political interference is undesirable. By then turning around and asserting that this independence is a justification for the one-house veto, Congress attempts simultaneously to decrease the power of the Executive and increase its own power."

(2) *Cleaning Up the Resulting Statutory Mess.* Chadha produced years of aftershocks as lower courts tried to determine whether the 200+ statutes containing a veto provision were entirely invalid or, alternatively, would remain fully effective except for the veto. This is the severability question. Traditionally, a court determines severability by asking whether the legislature would have wanted the balance of the statutory scheme to remain effective even without the invalid portion. As Justice White's account of the history emphasizes, the legislative veto was often the condition on which Congress agreed to the Executive's request for significant delegation of power. (Early uses involved reorganization, national security/foreign affairs, and discretion in spending appropriated funds; in the 1970s, Congress

began to attach the veto to "mainstream" delegations of substantive regulatory power.) Thus it was predictable that the effect of Chadha would be to topple the entire statutory delegation in some cases.

Generally speaking, the lower courts severed the veto provision from "conventional" regulatory statutes, leaving the substantive delegation intact. However, in contexts closer to the historical core of the veto's development, the courts sometimes recognized that the veto had been the quid pro quo for delegation, and accordingly invalidated the entire scheme. One such case—involving Presidential power to refuse to spend appropriated funds—is described at p. 224 below.

(3) *Congressional Reaction.* An aspect of U.S. constitutional history which we take for granted (but which lawyers from aspiring constitutional democracies recognize as remarkable) is the routine willingness of Congress and the President to acquiesce in even quite unpalatable judicial decisions. Official defiance of Supreme Court constitutional holdings is an extraordinary event for us. In the case of the legislative veto, the extraordinary occurred.

Louis Fisher, widely published analyst on the staff of the Congressional Research Service, reported in CONGRESSIONAL ABDICATION OF WAR AND SPENDING 180 (2000): "Following the Court's ruling, Congress amended a number of statutes by deleting legislative vetoes and replacing them with joint resolutions (which do go to the president.) Yet Congress continues to add committee vetoes to bills and presidents continue to signed them into law. In the years following Chadha, Congress enacted over four hundred of these statutory provisions." The vast majority of these placed veto conditions on agency use of appropriated funds. As Mr. Fisher explains, complex and inevitable inter-branch negotiations keep the veto alive in contexts such as appropriations. For example, NASA had established a pattern of cooperation with its appropriations committees: Statutory spending "caps" were placed on various programs (usually at the original executive budget request), but the statute authorized NASA to exceed those caps *if* it received committee approval. In 1984, President Reagan announced that he would implement statutes containing committee-veto provisions "in a manner consistent with the Chadha decision." The House Appropriations Committee responded that it would repeal both the committee veto provision and NASA's authority to exceed the caps. Thus, if NASA wanted to spend more, it would have to invoke the full Art. 1, § 7 process.

"NASA was aghast. It did not want to obtain a new public law every time it needed to exceed spending caps. To avoid that kind of administrative rigidity, NASA administrator James M. Beggs wrote to the Appropriations Committees and suggested a compromise. Instead of putting the caps in a public law, he recommended that they be placed in a conference report that explained how Congress expected a public law to be carried out. He then pledged that NASA would not exceed any ceiling identified in the conference report without first obtaining the prior approval of the Appropriations Committees." Id. at 181.

Are such side agreements legally enforceable? Probably not.[2] But particularly in the repeat-player world of appropriations, this does not

---

2. See, e.g., Burton v. Baker, 723 F.Supp. 1550 (D.D.C.1989) (dismissing, as nonjusticiable, an action by four members of the House to enforce a "Bipartisan Accord on

mean they can be ignored with impunity. "OMB Director James C. Miller III objected to a statutory provision that required the administration to obtain 'prior written approval' from the Appropriations Committees before transferring foreign assistance funds from one account to another. . . . The House Appropriations Committee gave a familiar reply: it would repeal the committee veto and, at the same time, repeal the administration's authority to transfer foreign assistance funds. . . . OMB beat a hasty retreat. The regular legislative language, including the committee veto, was enacted into law. When Miller repeated the challenge the next year, Congress followed through on its threat and deleted both the committee veto and the transfer authority. The two branches reached a compromise. . . . Congress removed the committee veto from the public law but required the administration to follow 'the regular notification procedures of the Committee on Appropriations' before transferring funds. . . . [T]hose procedures required the administration to notify the committees of each transfer. If no objection is raised during a fifteen-day review period, the administration may exercise the authority. If the committees object, the administration could proceed but only a great peril. By ignoring committee objections, the agency would most likely lose transfer authority the next year." Id. at 181–82.

(4) *Reprehensible Lawlessness, or Defensible Accommodation?* One might view these subsequent developments as unprincipled and unconstitutional collusion between Congress and the Executive. Certainly, it appears that the continued practice of using committee vetoes in appropriation survives judicial condemnation largely because doctrines such as standing render the veto nonjusticiable in this setting. See Chapter IX, Sec. 2.[3]

Or is there a different, and better, case to be made for the constitutional legitimacy of the legislative veto in the contexts—appropriations, reorganization, foreign affairs—in which it originally developed? PETER L. STRAUSS, WAS THERE A BABY IN THE BATHWATER? A COMMENT ON THE SUPREME COURT'S LEGISLATIVE VETO DECISION, 1983 Duke L.J. 789, 805–07, 816: "[Such] political uses of legislative vetoes warrant special analysis. . . . In these contexts it seems proper to characterize the veto, as [Justice White] does, as a means by which Congress could 'transfer greater authority to the President . . . while preserving its own constitutional role.' . . . [Such areas] concern chiefly public measures, primarily related to the internal organization of government and affecting the interests of private persons only indirectly; they reflect areas of direct presidential initiative and responsibil-

Central America" signed by the President, the Speaker of the House, and the House and Senate Majority and Minority Leaders).

3. Typically, no one can show cognizable individual injury traceable to appropriations or reorganization restrictions. A rare example to the contrary (and one which may not be reproducable given subsequent tightening of standing doctrine) is the pre-Chadha decision in American Fed. of Gov't Employees v. Pierce, 697 F.2d 303 (D.C.Cir.1982). The union of federal employees challenged a reorganization within the Department of Housing and Urban Development for failing to comply with a statutory provision requiring the agency to seek "prior approval of the Committee on Appropriations" before using funds to "plan, design, implement, or administer any reorganization" of the Department. (Why does Congress want to keep its hand in reorganization decisions?) The court, foreshadowing Chadha, held the requirement an unconstitutional aggrandizement of Congressional power.

ity. In these contexts, too, the veto represents an accommodation between the branches, often mutually desired as Justice White demonstrated, on matters of legitimate interest to each. Reorganization acts, measures concerned with budgetary adjustment (impoundment), foreign relations, and war (matters of the character Chief Justice Marshall long ago referred to as 'questions in their nature political,' [Marbury v. Madison, 5 U.S. (1 Cranch) 137 (1803)]), rarely appear in a form likely to attract or, more importantly, to justify judicial review. They may all be described fairly as a setting for horse-trading between the President and Congress: the authority subject to the veto will be that of the President himself; no alternative means of control is obvious; precise congressional standard-setting or structural arrangements are probably inadvisable; and a sharing of political authority is warranted by Congress' legitimate interests in the subject matter and the consequent desirability of committing Congress to support of the action to be taken. They evoke Justice Jackson's more enduring analysis in Youngstown Sheet & Tube Co. v. Sawyer that the power of government is at its peak when the President and Congress work supportively of each other's authority. To the extent Justice White speaks of the legislative veto in terms of Congressional accommodation directly with a powerful President requiring more power—as a means of preserving balance while accomplishing needed delegation to that other potential tyrant—his dissent is persuasive [in these contexts]. . . .

"... In ... a continuing relationship [such as the budget process], limiting one participant to episodic, formal, even clumsy acts is likely to produce rigidity and a covetousness about power that will hamper the effective conduct of government and may weaken the presidency far more than the alternative. The same is true for reorganization acts; in a government premised on the selection of a single executive as its head, it is internally sensible and externally non-threatening for the President to be the prime shaper of the internal structures of government, subject to congressional disapproval. . . ."

NOTES ON ALTERNATIVES TO THE LEGISLATIVE VETO: CONGRESSIONAL DIRECTION VIA LEGISLATION AND COMMITTEE OVERSIGHT

How effective are the alternative mechanisms available to Congress for overriding a particular regulatory policy choice?

(1) *Using the Full Article I, § 7 Process.* Two major barriers make it difficult for Congress to correct an agency's policy decision through the passage of legislation.

The first is institutional. WILLIAM N. ESKRIDGE, JR., PHILIP P. FRICKEY & ELIZABETH GARRETT, LEGISLATION AND STATUTORY INTERPRETATION 68 (2000): "The most salient aspect of the modern legislative process is that it is filled with a complex set of hurdles that proponents of a new policy must overcome before their bill becomes law. At each stage in the legislative process, a proposal can be changed or halted, new coalitions must be formed, and opportunities for logrolling, strategic behaviors, and deliberation are presented. Because those who control each of these choke points have the ability to kill a proposal, some political scientists have termed them *vetogates*. Vetogates emanate from a number of sources: some result from constitutional provisions, some from rules adopted formally by a legislative body, and some from norm or practices that are more informal." As commentators on the Constitution have been observing since The Federalist Papers, see, e.g., Federalist 73, the bicameralism and present-ment process is intentionally designed to make passage of legislation difficult. Put somewhat differently, the Art. 1, § 7 process privileges the legal status quo.[1] Ironically, then, once a broadly delegative statute is passed, the Constitution itself makes it hard for Congress to reign in or redirect the delegation.

The second barrier is political. In times of divided government—which, in the modern era, is most of the time—a Congress trying statutorily to override or preempt the agency's decision often has to muster a veto-proof supermajority in both houses. Put somewhat differently, the Art. 1, § 7 process, privileges the policy preferences of the Executive in a world of delegated regulatory power. For an excellent example of how the President can use his veto effectively to stymie a Congress trying to realign agency policy, see the aftermath of Rust v. Sullivan at p. 1046 below.

(2) *Experience Under the Congressional Review Act.* In 1995, Congress tried to overcome at least some of the institutional barriers to statutory revision of agency policy. It amended the Regulatory Flexibility Act to provide a process whereby "major" rules (defined essentially in terms of economic impact) must be laid before Congress for 60 legislative days before taking effect. See 5 U.S.C. § 801 et seq.; p. 701 below. This gives Congress an opportunity to pass a joint resolution of disapproval through a special, fast-track procedure that, inter alia, limits debate and amendments and curtails normal committee powers. If the joint resolution is passed (i.e., approved by a majority of both houses and signed by the President, or approved by a supermajority of both houses over his veto), the rule may not take effect.[2] Moreover, a rule that has been disapproved "may not be reissued in substantially the same form, and a new rule that is substantial-ly the same as such a rule may not be issued, unless the reissued or new rule is specifically authorized by a law enacted after the date of the joint resolution disapproving the original rule." 5 U.S.C. § 801(b)(2). Thus, the resolution of disapproval is intended to have the effect not only of invalidat-ing the particular rule but also of narrowing the agency's original statutory authority in the area.[3]

Since 1995, 409 rules have been laid before Congress; 17 joint resolu-tions of disapproval have been introduced; one has passed. Congressional

---

1. The classic modern explication is William N. Eskridge, Jr. & John Ferejohn, The Article I, Section 7 Game, 80 Geo. L.J. 523 (1992).

2. If a proposed resolution of disapprov-al is defeated in either chamber, the 60–day waiting period is terminated and the rule can become immediately effective. 5 U.S.C. § 801(a)(5).

3. For an argument that this aspect of the Act has significant nondelegation prob-lems—in that it delegates to courts the re-sponsibility to determine the new bounds of agency authority without any intelligible principle—see Daniel Cohen & Peter L. Strauss, Congressional Review of Agency Regulations, 49 Admin. L. Rev. 95 (1997).

Research Serv., Congressional Review of Agency Rulemaking 5–6 (Sept. 16, 2002). In the eleventh hour of the outgoing Clinton Administration, OSHA promulgated a regulation addressing ergonomic (repetitive motion) injuries. Incoming President George W. Bush signed the joint resolution of disapproval that had been quickly passed by the new, temporarily-Republican majority in both chambers. This history suggests that, even with a ticking clock and a streamlined legislative process, Congress can overcome the institutional and political barriers to legislative override only in extraordinary circumstances.

(3) *Committee Oversight.* Even though Congress as a whole may find it difficult to intervene and correct particular agency regulatory choices, subparts of Congress can be very actively engaged in review and response. In the 1960s–70s, Congress responded to growing federal regulatory ambitions by developing a complex system of committees that divided the labor of overseeing agencies.[4] One study found that between 1961 and 1983, the number of committee "oversight days" rose from about 150 per year to close to 600 per year.[5] Scholars have vigorously debated the desirability of the proliferation of committees—and the burgeoning of congressional staff that support their work. On one view, committees (and, particularly, their chairs) are opportunistic entrepreneurs of regional and special interest pandering whose preferences are likely to depart wildly from those of the median legislator. If this view is accurate, oversight by committee is probably a bad thing and certainly should not be equated with oversight by Congress as a whole. On the other hand, considerable empirical and theoretical work challenges this negative picture as overly simplistic. At least with respect to salient committees, some researchers argue that the data reveal committees acting as faithful agents of the chamber majority.[6] Wherever the truth lies, as the notes above on appropriations suggest, committees are often intimately engaged with monitoring, and attempting to influence the policy choices of, the agencies they oversee.

(4) *Committee Oversight in a Particular Regulatory Context.* Because of the breadth, importance, and contentiousness of its regulatory mission to improve air and water quality, EPA is a rich source of material on the virtues and vices of committee oversight. RICHARD J. LAZARUS, THE NEGLECTED QUESTION OF CONGRESSIONAL OVERSIGHT OF EPA, 54 Law & Contemp. Probs. 205 (1991): "[B]ecause EPA's jurisdiction has affected so many interest groups, the demand for the agency's oversight has grown exponentially among the committees and subcommittees in Congress, as has the number of oversight hearings regarding the agency's work. . . . At present, at least eleven standing House and nine standing Senate committees and up to 100 of their subcommittees share jurisdiction over EPA. . . .

"Congressional supervision of EPA each year includes lengthy and rigorous appropriations hearings on the agency's budget, numerous appearances by EPA officials at hearings, between 100 and 150 congressionally

---

4. See, e.g., Nelson W. Polsby, The Institutionalization of the House of Representatives, 62 Am. Pol. Sci. Rev. 144 (1968).

5. Joel Aberbach, Keeping a Watchful Eye 34–37 (1990).

6. The literature on both views is collected in Jeffrey J. Rachlinski & Cynthia R. Farina, Cognitive Psychology & Optimal Government Design, 87 Cornell L. Rev. 549, 573–74 n. 101 (2002).

commanded EPA reports to Congress, approximately 5,000 congressional inquiries to the agency, and doubtless even more frequent, less formal agency contacts. It also includes as many as forty GAO reports to Congress about EPA and its programs, and, when presidential appointments are made to the agency, confirmation hearings on those nominations. Finally, the Office of the Inspector General at the EPA (which was created in 1978) has played an active oversight function within the agency; EPA inspector generals' reports have frequently triggered, or otherwise been the subject of, formal congressional oversight. ... From 1971 to 1988, EPA officials appeared before each Congress between ninety-two and 214 times, testifying on 142 occasions in the first session of the 101st Congress alone. ... Even the Defense Department has appeared less often than EPA in some sessions of Congress....

"The significance of Congress's oversight of EPA is not confined to its intensity; it has also been remarkably and consistently negative.... After EPA was created, Senator Muskie's subcommittee quickly staked out its position as the agency's critical overseer. Muskie and others sharply criticized agency officials in widely publicized hearings in the early 1970s. The legislators strongly counseled the officials about the importance of consulting with the subcommittee prior to making important agency decisions. They also were sharply critical of any indication that either the White House or OMB was having undue influence on the agency's implementation and enforcement of the laws.

"When EPA failed to meet statutory deadlines, [various members of Congress] held hearings in which they chastised the agency for neglecting the public trust. Conversely, when EPA made politically unpopular decisions in an effort to comply with its statutory mandates, other members of Congress promptly joined in the public denunciation.

"Indeed, EPA's past twenty years have been marked by persistent allegations of corruption, scandal, and abuse of public trust. Early on there were congressional accusations of improper White House interference with pending litigation. There have been continuous congressional allegations that EPA has improperly allowed OMB to influence the substance of EPA rules.

"Congress has also frequently accused the agency of neglect and of overreaching. Congressional oversight of EPA's handling of the pesticides program in the mid–1970s illustrates both. Partly in response to congressional claims of excessive agency regulation, Administrator Russell Train reduced the role of lawyers in the general counsel's office, which had been a strong advocate of stringent pesticide regulation. Soon EPA was buffeted by allegations of agency neglect; agency lawyers, some of whom resigned in protest, were upset by the administrator's action and brought evidence to Congress' attention that EPA had relied on industry data in registering pesticides under the Federal Insecticide, Fungicide, and Rodenticide Act. To agency officials, their reliance on industry data was the necessary result of unrealistic statutory deadlines and reduced agency budgets. To Senate overseers, however, such reliance showed the agency's capture by industry and its subversion of congressional will at the expense of increased public health hazards....

"Without a doubt, EPA's most contentious time with Congress occurred during the tenure of Anne Gorsuch as EPA's administrator from 1981 to 1983. Intense congressional scrutiny of Gorsuch's management began soon after her confirmation. There were pervasive congressional concerns that Gorsuch and other political appointees at the agency were entering into 'sweetheart deals' with industry, manipulating programs for partisan political ends, and crippling the agency through requests for budget reductions. The confrontation with Congress, fueled by Congress' massive oversight efforts, was the decisive factor in causing Gorsuch, as well as most of the other political appointees at the agency, to resign."

NOTES ON PRESIDENTIAL POWER TO DIRECT AGENCY DECISIONS

"The executive Power shall be vested in a President of the United States."

U.S. Constitution, Art. II, § 1

"[H]e may require the Opinion, in writing, of the principal Officer in each of the executive Departments, upon any Subject relating to the Duties of their respective Offices...."

U.S. Constitution, Art. II, § 1

"[H]e shall take Care that the Laws be faithfully executed."

U.S. Constitution, Art. II, § 1

Modern Presidents since Richard Nixon have tried (with accelerating ambitiousness) to control agency policymaking at the *wholesale* level through requirements imposed by executive order. The most ubiquitous has been the mandate to supply a cost-benefit analysis of proposed major rules. This process, and its effects, are considered in Chapter V, Sec. 3.b(iv). Although centralized White House review has, in the view of many observers, had an appreciable affect on the content of proposed rules, here we are concerned with the somewhat different question of the extent of the President's power to direct *specific* regulatory outcomes.

Unlike early statutory delegations empowering the President himself to make decisions about tariffs and other international trade issues, see p. 66 above, modern regulatory statutes typically delegate decisional authority to some named officer of the United States—a Cabinet Secretary, an Administrator, or an independent Commission. Do these statutes vest the power of decision in the officer, such that while she can (should?) be guided by the President's views, the responsibility to decide is ultimately hers alone? May Congress constitutionally empower the officer to decide in a manner contrary to what the President would direct? May the President legitimately assert a directory authority in the absence of clear Congressional authorization?

The Emergence of Presidential Directory Authority

(1) *The Clinton Initiative.* The two Presidents usually identified as the most intent upon (and successful at) placing their personal stamp on federal regulatory policy are Franklin Roosevelt and Ronald Reagan. Clear-

ly, each of them offers a model for the President who is determined to direct the regulatory state. Yet, the greatest progress on this front may have been made by Bill Clinton. ELENA KAGAN, PRESIDENTIAL ADMINISTRATION, 114 Harv. L. Rev. 2245, 2281–82, 2290, 2298–99 (2001): "President Clinton treated the sphere of regulation as his own, and in doing so made it his own, in a way no other modern President had done. ... He accordingly developed a set of practices that enhanced his ability to influence or even dictate the content of administrative initiatives. He exercised this power with respect to a wide variety of agency action—rulemakings, more informal means of policymaking, and even certain enforcement activities....

"The claim of directive authority ... manifested itself most concretely and importantly in the frequent issuance of formal and published memoranda to executive branch agency heads instructing them to take specified action within the scope of the discretionary power delegated to them by Congress. These directives ... enabled Clinton and his White House staff to instigate, rather than merely check, administrative action. The memoranda became, ever increasingly over the course of eight years, Clinton's primary means, self-consciously undertaken, both of setting an administrative agenda that reflected and advanced his policy and political preferences and of ensuring the execution of this program....

"Even absent any assertion of directive authority, a President has many resources at hand to influence the scope and content of administrative action. Agency officials may accede to his preferences because they feel a sense of personal loyalty and commitment to him; because they desire his assistance in budgetary, legislative, and appointments matters; or in extreme cases because they respect and fear his removal power. President Reagan ... successfully relied on these points of leverage to induce reconsideration of some agency decisions; another President might be able to employ these devices to impel the initiation of administrative action. Conversely, even given the assertion of directive authority, a President may face considerable constraints in imposing his will on administrative actors. Their resistance to or mere criticism of a directive may inflict political costs on the President as heavy as any that would result from an exercise of the removal power. This fact of political life accounts in part for the consultations and compromises that prefaced many of the Clinton White House's uses of directive authority. In this context, to put the matter simply, persuasion may be more than persuasion and command may be less than command—making the line between the two sometimes hard to discover.

"All that said, a line remains, and by so often asserting legal authority to direct regulatory decisions, President Clinton crossed from one side of it to the other. Clinton's use of directives at the least signified a change in the form of presidential involvement in administrative decisionmaking. The unofficial became official, the subtle blatant, and the veiled transparent.... But more, the change in form likely led to a change in substance—a change in the practice itself—for two associated reasons. First, overt command sometimes, though not always, can accomplish what backdoor pressure cannot in impelling agency action and, perhaps even more important, locking in that action over time. Especially when agency resistance to presidential preferences need take only the form of inertia, publicity can serve as a useful weapon in the hands of a President—turning a spotlight on and creating a constituency for the action ordered, and thereby increasing the costs of noncompliance to agency officials. Second and more broadly, the explicit and repeated assertion of directive authority probably alters over time what Peter Strauss has called the 'psychology of government'—the understanding of agency and White House officials alike of their respective roles and powers. This change, in turn, makes presidential intervention in regulatory matters ever more routine and agency acceptance of this intervention ever more ready. The Clinton White House's use of presidential directives thus created the conditions for a significant enhancement of presidential power over regulatory matters.''

Assessing the Legality of Presidential Directory Claims

(2) MARBURY V. MADISON, 5 U.S. (1 Cranch) 137, 165–66 (1803) (Marshall, C.J.): "By the constitution of the United States, the president is invested with certain important political powers, in the exercise of which he is to use his own discretion, and is accountable only to his country in his political character, and to his own conscience. To aid him in the performance of these duties, he is authorized to appoint certain officers, who act by his authority and in conformity with his orders.

"In such cases, their acts are his acts; and whatever opinion may be entertained of the manner in which executive discretion may be used, still there exists, and can exist, no power to control that discretion. The subjects are political. They respect the nation, not individual rights, and being entrusted to the executive, the decision of the executive is conclusive. The application of this remark will be perceived by adverting to the act of congress for establishing the department of foreign affairs. This officer, as his duties were prescribed by that act, is to conform precisely to the will of the president. He is the mere organ by whom that will is communicated. . . .

"But when the legislature proceeds to impose on that officer other duties; when he is directed peremptorily to perform certain acts; when the rights of individuals are dependent on the performance of those acts; he is so far the officer of the law; is amenable to the laws for his conduct. . . .

"The conclusion from this reasoning is, that where the heads of departments are the political or confidential agents of the executive, merely to execute the will of the president, or rather to act in cases in which the executive possesses a constitutional or legal discretion, nothing can be more perfectly clear than that their acts are only politically examinable. But where a specific duty is assigned by law, and individual rights depend upon the performance of that duty, it seems equally clear that the individual who considers himself injured has a right to resort to the laws of his country for a remedy.''

(3) MYERS V. UNITED STATES, 272 U.S. 52 (1926) (Taft, C.J.): "The degree of guidance in the discharge of their duties that the President may exercise over executive officers varies with the character of their service as prescribed in the law under which they act. The highest and most important duties which his subordinates perform are those in which they act for him. In such cases they are exercising not their own but his discretion. This field

is a very large one. It is sometimes described as political. Kendall v. United States, 12 Pet. 524, at page 610, 9 L.Ed. 1181. Each head of a department is and must be the President's alter ego in the matters of that department where the President is required by law to exercise authority. . . .

"In all such cases, the discretion to be exercised is that of the President in determining the national public interest and in directing the action to be taken by his executive subordinates to protect it. In this field his cabinet officers must do his will. . . .

". . . The ordinary duties of officers prescribed by statute come under the general administrative control of the President by virtue of the general grant to him of the executive power, and he may properly supervise and guide their construction of the statutes under which they act in order to secure that unitary and uniform execution of the laws which article 2 of the Constitution evidently contemplated in vesting general executive power in the President alone. Laws are often passed with specific provision for adoption of regulations by a department or bureau head to make the law workable and effective. The ability and judgment manifested by the official thus empowered, as well as his energy and stimulation of his subordinates, are subjects which the President must consider and supervise in his administrative control. Finding such officers to be negligent and inefficient, the President should have the power to remove them. Of course there may be duties so peculiarly and specifically committed to the discretion of a particular officer as to raise a question whether the President may overrule or revise the officer's interpretation of his statutory duty in a particular instance. Then there may be duties of a quasi judicial character imposed on executive officers and members of executive tribunals whose decisions after hearing affect interests of individuals, the discharge of which the President cannot in a particular case properly influence or control. But even in such a case he may consider the decision after its rendition as a reason for removing the officer, on the ground that the discretion regularly entrusted to that officer by statute has not been on the whole intelligently or wisely exercised. Otherwise he does not discharge his own constitutional duty of seeing that the laws be faithfully executed."

(4) *The Constitutional Originalist Case.* STEVEN G. CALABRESI & SAIKRISHNA B. PRAKASH, THE PRESIDENT'S POWER TO EXECUTE THE LAWS, 104 Yale L.J. 541 (1994): "Because the President alone has the constitutional power to execute federal law, it would seem to follow that, notwithstanding the text of any given statute, the President must be able to execute that statute, interpreting it and applying it in concrete circumstances. It is a grave mistake to conceptualize the President's ability to execute federal law as a power to act in an executive officer's stead. Under the Constitution, executive officers can act only in the President's stead, since it is the President and the President alone who can delegate to them the constitutional power that they must have if they are to execute laws. For example, if Congress establishes by statute a Treasury Secretary with the power and responsibility to expend appropriations and also provides a degree of discretion in an appropriations act, it is a mistake to view that statute as creating any duty or authority that belongs to the Secretary, even if the statute is written that way. Rather, it is the President, under our Constitu-

tion, who must always be the ultimate empowered and responsible actor. This is because the Constitution establishes that the President *exclusively* controls the power to execute all federal laws, and therefore it must be the case that all inferior executive officers act in his stead. A statute stating that the Secretary of the Treasury and other Treasury personnel will execute appropriation and tax laws only establishes that these particular officers will assist the President in carrying those laws into execution. Congress lacks constitutional power to do anything more.

"If the President may make a decision that a statute purports to reserve for an inferior executive officer, by the same logic, the President must be able to nullify an action taken by an inferior executive officer. Once again, only the President has the constitutional power to execute federal law, and no governmental power may be exercised, including the law-execution power, without a basis in the Constitution for the exercise of the power. To give a nullification-power example, suppose the Secretary of the Treasury, in the exercise of her purportedly exclusive statutory discretion, decided to fine a bank for violation of certain banking laws. Because the Treasury Secretary would be ultimately exercising the President's 'executive power,' the President must be able, in effect, to reverse or nullify the Secretary's decision by withdrawing his delegation of the executive power, which the Constitution gives to him alone."

(5) *Getting to the Same Place by a Different Constitutional Route.* LAWRENCE LESSIG & CASS R. SUNSTEIN, THE PRESIDENT AND THE ADMINISTRATION, 94 Colum. L. Rev. 1, 2 (1994): "We think that the view that the framers constitutionalized anything like this vision of the executive is just plain myth. . . . We reach this conclusion with reluctance. A strongly unitary executive can promote important values of accountability, coordination, and uniformity in the execution of the laws, and to whatever extent these were the framers' values, they are certainly now ours. . . .

"We believe [however] that there is . . . a plausible structural argument on behalf of the hierarchical conception of the unitary executive. . . . [T]he national government has changed dramatically since the founding, and so too has the national presidency. In light of these changes, mechanical application of the founding understanding—to allow independent officials to engage in tasks that the framers never foresaw—may well disserve the very commitments that underlay the founding itself. Under current circumstances, a strongly unitary executive is the best way of keeping faith with the most fundamental goals of the original scheme. . . .

"Th[e] massive transformation in the institutional framework of American public law was entirely unanticipated by the framers, and it fundamentally altered the original constitutional design. We do not contend that administration was itself unanticipated, or that at the founding period it was trivial. On the contrary, the original period contained a precursor of the modern administrative state. But what we do now is not what was done then. . . .

"[I]n a period in which administrators exercise a wide range of discretionary authority, the very meaning of immunizing them from presidential control changes dramatically. When fundamental policy decisions are made by administrators, immunizing them from presidential control would have two significant consequences: first, it would segment fundamental policy decisions from direct political accountability and thus the capacity for coordination and democratic control; and second, it would subject these institutions to the perverse incentives of factions, by removing the insulating arm of the President, and increasing the opportunity for influence by powerful private groups. Neither of these consequences was favored by the framers. Indeed, both problems were specifically what the framers sought to avoid. For both these reasons—retaining accountability and avoiding factions—an interpreter could reasonably conclude either that it makes sense to understand the term 'executive' to include more of the administrative power than the framers would have (specifically) included, or alternatively, that a legislative effort to insulate what is misleadingly labeled 'administration' from the President is an improper exercise of legislative authority under the Necessary and Proper Clause....

"If all this is true, an argument for the strongly unitary executive under modern conditions takes the following form. From the actual administrative entities that the framers established, we can infer that the framers did not intend to allow administrative officials exercising broad policymaking authority to operate independently of the President. With respect to such officials, they made no explicit judgment, for their existence was not foreseen. The framers anticipated a much smaller national government, in which states would have the fundamental role and in which Congress would engage in basic policymaking, and they believed that the President would exercise a good deal of discretionary authority only in international relations. The execution of federal domestic law would often be mechanical, and crucially, nonpolitical. For this reason, the founding commitment to a unitary executive could coexist with a range of federal officials not directly subject to presidential control.

"A structural argument for a unitary executive, then, comes down to this: Where the framers allocated a power that they thought of as political, that power was allocated to people who were themselves politically accountable. This was part of the fundamental commitments to accountability and avoidance of factionalism. At the founding period, the existence of a degree of independence in administration could not realistically have been thought to compromise these commitments. Today, by contrast, a strong presumption of unitariness is necessary in order to promote the original constitutional commitments. The legislative creation of domestic officials operating independently of the President but exercising important discretionary policymaking power now stands inconsistent with founding commitments. ...

"[T]the basic conclusions of the argument are not obscure. To the extent that Congress has authorized executive officials to engage in adjudicative tasks, it may immunize those officials from presidential control by, for example, preventing presidential interference in ongoing cases and offering 'for cause' protection against discharge. ... But to the extent that an agency official makes discretionary decisions about the content of public policy, the best reading of the constitutional plan is that in general, the official may not be insulated from presidential supervision. ...

"If we are to translate [the Framers'] structural choices into current conditions, we may conclude that a largely hierarchical executive branch is the best way of keeping faith with the original plan. At least this is so if we are asking whether the President has a degree of removal and supervisory power over people who are authorized to make high-level discretionary decisions about the content of national policy."[1]

(6) *A Non-constitutional Alternative.* ELENA KAGAN, PRESIDENTIAL ADMINISTRATION, 114 Harv. L. Rev. 2245, 2319 (2001): "[A]lthough I am highly sympathetic to the view that the President should have broad control over administrative activity, I believe ... that the unitarians have failed to establish their claim for plenary control as a matter of constitutional mandate. The original meaning of Article II is insufficiently precise and, in this area of staggering change, also insufficiently relevant to support the unitarian position. And the constitutional values sometimes offered in defense of this claim are too diffuse, too diverse, and for these reasons, too easily manipulable to justify removing from the democratic process all decisions about the relationship between the President and administration—especially given that this result would reverse decades' worth of established law and invalidate the defining features of numerous and entrenched institutions of government. Second and equally important, the cases sustaining restrictions on the President's removal authority, whether or not justified, are almost certain to remain the law (at least in broad terms, if not in specifics); as a result, any serious attempt to engage the actual practice of presidential-agency relations must incorporate these holdings and their broader implications as part of its framework.

"But my acceptance of congressional authority in this area does not require the conclusion, assumed on the conventional view, that the President lacks all power to direct administrative officials as to the exercise of their delegated discretion. That Congress could bar the President from directing discretionary action does not mean that Congress has done so; whether it has is a matter of statutory construction. If Congress, in a particular statute, has stated its intent with respect to presidential involvement, then that is the end of the matter. But if Congress, as it usually does, simply has assigned discretionary authority to an agency official, without in any way commenting on the President's role in the delegation, then an interpretive question arises. One way to read a statute of this kind is to assume that the delegation runs to the agency official specified and to that official alone. But a second way to read such a statute is to assume that the delegation runs to the agency official specified, rather than to any other agency official, but still subject to the ultimate control of the President....

"When the delegation in question runs to the members of an independent agency, the choice between these two interpretive principles seems

---

1. Professors Lessig and Sunstein would, however, permit Congress to immunize specific regulatory policymaking from Presidential directory authority. In particular, they justify independence for the Federal Reserve Board because of the risk that "the money supply would be manipulated by the President for political reasons. Even a perception of this sort would have corrosive effects on democratic processes.... [I]t would likely have adverse effects on the economy as well." Id. at 108. *Can* the Fed be so easily distinguished from all other agencies?

fairly obvious. In establishing such an agency, Congress has acted self-consciously, by means of limiting the President's appointment and removal power, to insulate agency decisionmaking from the President's influence. In then delegating power to that agency (rather than to a counterpart in the executive branch), Congress must be thought to intend the exercise of that power to be independent. In such a case, the agency's heads are not subordinate to the President in other respects; making the heads subordinate in this single way would subvert the very structure and premises of the agency.

"When the delegation runs to an executive branch official, however, Congress's intent (to the extent it exists) may well cut in the opposite direction. Congress knows, after all, that executive officials stand in all other respects in a subordinate position to the President, given that the President nominates them without restriction, can remove them at will, and can subject them to potentially far-ranging procedural oversight. All these powers establish a general norm of deference among executive officials to presidential opinions, such that when Congress delegates to an executive official, it in some necessary and obvious sense also delegates to the President. It is true that these various powers do not give the President full ability to control an executive official's decisions, at least without incurring political costs; but then, for reasons discussed earlier, neither does directive power. I in no way mean here to conflate the two. But the very subtlety of the line between directive authority and other tools of presidential control—or stated more fully, between the 'command' expressed in the use of directive power and the 'influence' deriving from the use (or threatened use) of appointment, removal, and procedural oversight powers—provides reason to doubt any congressional intent to disaggregate them, in the absence of specific evidence of that desire. An interpretive principle presuming an undifferentiated presidential control of executive agency officials thus may reflect, more accurately than any other, the general intent and understanding of Congress."

The Implications of Recognizing Presidential Directory Authority—A More Skeptical View

(7) *In the Context of Rulemaking.* What if President Bush had directed EPA Administrator Christine Whitman to set the level of the revised standard for ozone at .085 parts per million? (Recall that the existing standard was .09 ppm; the agency's preference, recommended by its Science Advisory Council and settled after a lengthy notice-and-comment rulemaking, was .08 ppm). Could the EPA use such a presidential directive as an alternative to the time-consuming and doubtless aggravating process of reading and responding to hundreds of public comments?[2]

2. For those who have not yet studied the process that is modern APA rulemaking, here is the problem in a nutshell:

Let us suppose an agency has held a rulemaking proceeding that involved ... thousands of pages of written submissions. ... It has compiled a thousand-long-page rule-making record. It has then composed a statement showing that it has acted synoptically to consider every significant issue and arrive at the best possible decisions. Those who have been watching and participating in such a process are going to be ... outraged if,

How would the practice, and meaning, of notice-and-comment rule-making change if participants knew that the President could direct a different outcome after the fact? What place, if any, would judicial review have in such a world? PETER L. STRAUSS, PRESIDENTIAL RULEMAKING, 72 Chi.-Kent L. Rev. 965 (1997): "From the perspective simply of political responsi-bility, . . . the President appears to be a superior rulemaker to an agency, because he can be held directly accountable at the polls. Placing sweeping [quasi-]legislative authority in the hands of an actor himself at the apex of governmental authority, however, raises considerations quite distinct from those we face when an agency is empowered to act in a limited frame of government, and in relation with not only the President but also Congress and the courts. The President as lawmaker is more hazardous than the Environmental Protection Agency as lawmaker, precisely because he is omnicompetent, remote from effective check by courts or even Congress.[3] The embeddedness of the EPA, its focus and its relations with multiple, organizationally superior overseers, gives us the practical assurance that it will not run out of control. Dispersion of power . . . is the trumping consideration. The agency's rulemaking is preferred (indeed, tolerated) despite its diminished political responsibility just because it is not omni-competent, because it exists embedded in relationships with Congress and the courts as well as the White House. . . . That is the proposition that cannot easily be advanced about the President. That we cannot easily make it is what makes his participation as a rulemaker disturbing. . . .

"[A] President's public behavior suggesting that agency rules are *his* rules threatens to make us forget just this middle ground. It invites us to give up the constraints of law in favor of those of politics. While, from a political perspective, one can applaud a President who goes out of his way to take responsibility as well as credit for the policy judgments of his administration, this seems a high price to pay. To be sure, agency process, perhaps particularly rulemaking process, is increasingly seen as political rather than expert; that perception, in its way, has animated the recent apparent revival of interest in 'delegation,' and other respects in which political elements of the Constitution's structural arrangements have be-come prominent. . . . [Yet, even while] we accept that rulemaking is irreducibly political in some respects, we imagine components of expertise as well; otherwise we would not be fighting as hard as we do over proper elements of risk analysis—the best means for identifying and managing uncertainties about complex technical facts, and so forth. The issue is mediating between politics and law—recognizing the strengths and weak-nesses of each and finding ways of promoting their proper contribution—rather than pretending to locate the practice at either pole.

". . . For [the President] to make the bureaucrats believe that they are his is precisely to tear down the structures of law and regularity Congress has built up in relation to the presidency. It is Congress that gets to say

just before the agency publishes its final rule, the president calls to tell the agency what rule it should adopt.
Martin Shapiro, Who Guards the Guardians 112 (1988).

3. [Ed.] The concept of omnicompe-tence comes from Todd D. Rakoff, The Shape of the Law in the American Administrative State, 11 Tel Aviv U. Studies in Law 9, 39 (1992). See p. 76 above.

how many people work in the White House, how many in the Department of Labor; how many in political offices, how many in the Senior Executive Service. . . . This is of course a formal argument. It accepts the variety of political ways in which the President and those immediately around him chivvy in rulemaking, from the formal apparatus of Executive Order 12,866 to the informal checking and massaging that inevitably occur. The President in this respect is not too different from individual members of Congress and committees who may equally attempt to impress on administrative actors their views and the importance of respecting them in their discretionary activities. He is, to be sure, our chief executive, the one our Constitution has invested with executive power; but he wields that power, in these respects, within the constraints of law that Congress has established. No more could he assign to the Secretary of the Interior responsibilities Congress had placed in the hands of the Secretary of Agriculture, than can he depart from Congress's other assignments of responsibility. The bureaucrat or political appointee confronted by presidential chivvying can perhaps more easily see in this perspective the tension between duty and advice. . . . The stakes for the psychology of government, for the extent to which civil servants and political appointees imagine themselves acting within a culture of law, are rather high."

(8) *In the Context of Adjudication.* What if President Reagan—rather than the House of Representatives—had directed the Attorney General to delete Chadha's name from the group of 340 deportable aliens who, INS proceedings had determined, were eligible for compassionate suspension of deportation? EDWARD S. CORWIN, THE PRESIDENT: OFFICE AND POWERS 1787–1957, at 80–81 (4th rev. ed. 1957): "Suppose . . . that the law casts a duty upon a subordinate executive agency eo nomine, does the President thereupon become entitled, by virtue of his 'executive power' or of his duty to 'take care that the laws be faithfully executed,' to substitute his judgment for that of the agency regarding the discharge of such duty? . . . An affirmative answer would make all questions of law enforcement questions of discretion, the discretion moreover of an independent and legally uncontrollable branch of the government. By the same token, it would render it impossible for Congress, notwithstanding its broad powers under the 'necessary and proper' clause, to leave anything to the specially trained judgment of a subordinate executive official with any assurance that his discretion would not be perverted to political ends for the advantage of the administration in power."

At least as early as 1823, the President's chief legal adviser had opined that the President lacked the power to direct the outcome of an agency proceeding in an individual case. See The President and Accounting Officers, 1 Op. A.G. 1823 (Opinion of Attorney General William Wirt to President Monroe). In KENDALL V. U.S. EX REL STOKES, 37 U.S. 524 (1838), the Supreme Court held that mandamus was the proper remedy to force the postmaster general to remit a sum of money that Congress, via private bill, had directed him to pay as the appropriate resolution of a government contract dispute. The postmaster had argued that mandamus—the judicial direction to perform a nondiscretionary action—was inappropriate because he was "alone subject to the direction and control of the President." The Court responded: "To contend that the obligation imposed on the President to see the laws faithfully executed, implies a power to forbid their execution, is a novel construction of the constitution, and entirely inadmissible."

(9) *In the Context of Enforcement.* If adjudication is the hardest context in which to imagine Presidential power to direct administrators to reach particular outcomes, what about the seemingly easiest context—exercises of prosecutorial discretion? What if the investigation into whether Theodore Olson lied to a congressional committee had been conducted through normal Department of Justice procedures and, on learning that the Assistant U.S. Attorney in charge of the case had initiated a perjury prosecution, President Reagan had directed the AUSA to terminate the proceedings and abandon the case? What if a successor President, elected to office before the perjury statute of limitations ran, directed the AUSA to reinstitute the prosecution and, while she was at it, to add Olson's co-workers, Schmults and Dinkins, as co-defendants?

In 1831, the Attorney General advised President Andrew Jackson that he could direct the U.S. Attorney in New York to discontinue the prosecution of an action to condemn certain stolen jewels brought into the country in violation of the revenue laws. The context implicated the President's independent constitutional role in foreign affairs—the true owner of the jewels was the Princess of Orange, who had requested their return—but the Attorney General explicitly relied not on that ground, but rather on "the general supervisory powers which belong to his office, and which are necessary to enable him to perform the duty imposed upon him, of seeing that the law is faithfully executed." The Jewels of the Princess of Orange, 2 Op. A.G. 482 (1931). Still, even in the area of prosecution—where the President's claim to directory authority seems greatest—our politico-legal culture is not completely comfortable with direct Presidential disruption of the "standard operating procedure" for investigating and enforcing the law. Would the President's legitimate prerogatives be invaded if Congress enacted a statute directing the Internal Revenue Service to select tax returns for audit strictly upon objective criteria, and making it a felony for anyone (including any elected or appointed official) to coerce or induce the administrator to audit, or cease to audit, any particular person?

(ii) EFFORTS TO CONTROL POLICY BY CONTROLLING SPENDING

One of the most important determinates of regulatory behavior is virtually invisible to administrative *law*. Rarely do legislative decisions to appropriate, or executive decisions to spend, present themselves in a form that the judiciary will see as a "case" or "controversy." The other two branches, however, have long recognized the power of money to shape public policy. Conflicts over the President's power to refuse to spend appropriated monies—or to transfer them to other purposes—have been part of our history since at least the late 19th century.[1]

---

1. When President Grant set off a furor in Congress by refusing to spend appropriated river and harbor funds for what we would now term pork barrel projects. See Peter M. Shane & Harold H. Bruff, Separation of Powers Law 199 (1996) (quoting one House Member's Shakespearian ranting, "Upon what meat hath this our Ceasar fed?").

Necessarily, Congress cannot specify in detail the amounts and purposes of the monies needed to run the administrative state. Even if it had time enough to devote to thorough itemization, its specification would become obsolete almost immediately, as events varied needs and costs. Therefore, while the degree of appropriations specificity has varied with the times (and the level of trust between a particular legislature and Administration), executive discretion is an inevitable part of the appropriations process. Some exercises of this discretion are uncontroversial. If the government can accomplish a desired result for less than the projected expenditure, or if changed circumstances render the planned action unnecessary, it would be absurd to interpret the relevant appropriation as a mandate that all the money be spent, regardless. The Executive has long been permitted by Congress to make such "programmatic impoundments" with relatively little legislative involvement. (It is not hard to see such impoundments as simply effectuating Congressional intent—or, at least, what Congress would have intended had it known.) This discretion was codified in the Antideficiency Act of 1950, which authorized the President to establish reserves "to provide for contingencies, or to effect savings whenever savings are made possible by or through changes in requirements, greater efficiency of operations, or other developments subsequent to" the appropriation.

The real apple of discord is a very different sort of executive refusal to spend appropriated money, "policy impoundments." Largely a post-World War II phenomenon, policy impoundments reflect a President's disagreement with the purposes for which Congress appropriates money. In order to prevent, or at least minimize, a policy result Congress favors, the President simply refuses to spend the money needed (and appropriated) to accomplish it. Initially, Presidents used this strategy in the area of defense appropriations for weapons. Here, the constitutional Commander-in-Chief power provided an arguable basis for the President to assert and enforce a policy preference independent of Congress. By the presidency of Lyndon Johnson, however, policy impoundments were becoming a weapon in the domestic policymaking arena. Richard Nixon impounded nearly 20% of non-entitlement federal expenditures; in the process, several programs were terminated. The President's rationale was inflation control, but the particular programs chosen for economization reflected the regulatory policy disagreements between a Republican President and a Democratic Congress. This Presidential strategy did, finally, produce some litigation about the impoundment power, and several lower court opinions rejected the Executive's argument that policy impoundments were either authorized by statute or within the President's inherent constitutional authority. See, e.g., Missouri Highway Comm. v. Volpe, 479 F.2d 1099 (8th Cir.1973). The one case taken by the Supreme Court did not produce a definitive resolution.[2]

---

2. Train v. New York, 420 U.S. 35 (1975), was a challenge by New York City to President Nixon's instructions to EPA not to spend most of a sum of money appropriated, pursuant to the Federal Water Pollution Control Act, to provide federal financing for municipal sewage treatment facilities. By the time the case reached the Court, Nixon had resigned and the Executive had abandoned its claim to inherent Presidential impoundment authority. The only issues remaining were statutory ones of whether the Act intended to confer discretion as to the timing of spending the funds.

In the Congressional Budget and Impoundment Control Act of 1974, Congress responded to the Nixon controversy by changing the statutory scheme regulating impoundments. It deleted the phrase "other developments" from the Anti–Deficiency Act, and set up a procedure for policy impoundments. If the President were proposing to rescind an appropriation entirely, the proposal must be submitted to Congress and would be ineffective unless approved by a bill passed within a specified period. If the proposal were only to defer spending temporarily within the fiscal year, the proposal must be submitted to Congress and would become effective unless disapproved by a one-house veto. Of course, a decade later Chadha rendered this provision invalid. The D.C. Circuit then held that the veto was not severable. The legislative history, it concluded, "completely refutes the notion that Congress would have granted the President statutory authority to implement deferrals, thereby forcing itself to reenact an appropriations bill each time it disapproved of a deferral." City of New Haven v. United States, 809 F.2d 900 (D.C.Cir.1987). There the legal status of policy impoundments remained until the next amendment to the Anti–Deficiency Act: the perhaps fatally misnamed Line Item Veto Act of 1996.

Clinton v. City of New York

Supreme Court of the United States, 1998.
524 U.S. 417.

■ Justice Stevens delivered the opinion of the Court.

[Historically, the President's veto power has been exercised on a take-it-or-leave-it basis. He could sign a 700–page Omnibus Budget Reconciliation Act or veto it as a whole, but he could not single out and veto particularly objectionable provisions. The Line Item Veto Act permitted the President to sign a bill into law but then, in limited circumstances, to "cancel" portions of it. Specifically, he could "cancel in whole" "(1) any dollar amount of discretionary budget authority; (2) any item of new direct spending; or (3) any limited tax benefit." 2 U.S.C. § 691(a). The power had to be exercised within five days of signing and was conditioned on a number of substantive and procedural requirements, including prompt notification of Congress. Congress could then pass legislation disapproving the cancellation through an accelerated process.

Recognizing the legal novelty of this scheme, the Act attempted to confer standing on Members of Congress to raise constitutional challenges, and directed the Supreme Court to hear the case on an expedited basis. This attempt at rapid adjudication failed when the Court held that the plaintiffs lacked standing. Raines v. Byrd, 521 U.S. 811 (1997) See Chapter IX, Sec. 2. However, Presidential exercise of the cancellation power eventually provided two satisfactory plaintiffs. The Balanced Budget Act of 1997 contained a provision specifically relieving New York of an obligation to repay $2.6 billion in Medicaid overpayments that had resulted when the state failed to offset against its claims for federal reimbursement certain taxes it had collected from health-care providers. President Clinton disapproved of this provision, deeming it "preferential treatment that would have increased Medicaid costs, would have treated New York differently from all other States, and would have established a costly precedent for other States to request comparable treatment." As it qualified as an "item of new direct spending," he cancelled it. The Taxpayer Relief Act of 1997 included a provision that would have given advantageous tax treatment to certain farmers' cooperatives seeking to acquire refining or processing facilities. This "limited tax benefit" was cancelled by the President who stated that, while he endorsed the goal of "value-added farming" through cooperatives purchase of such facilities, the provision was inadequately tailored to benefit only small and medium sized cooperatives. The State of New York and Snake River Potato Growers, Inc. filed actions challenging the constitutionality of the Act. In the first sections of the opinion, the Court resolved a series of justiciability questions, including standing, in favor of the challengers.]

The Act requires the President to adhere to precise procedures whenever he exercises his cancellation authority. In identifying items for cancellation he must consider the legislative history, the purposes, and other relevant information about the items. He must determine, with respect to each cancellation, that it will "(i) reduce the Federal budget deficit; (ii) not impair any essential Government functions; and (iii) not harm the national interest." § 691(a)(3)(A). Moreover, he must transmit a special message to Congress notifying it of each cancellation within five calendar days (excluding Sundays) after the enactment of the canceled provision. It is undisputed that the President meticulously followed these procedures in these cases.

A cancellation takes effect upon receipt by Congress of the special message from the President. If, however, a "disapproval bill" pertaining to a special message is enacted into law, the cancellations set forth in that message become "null and void." The Act sets forth a detailed expedited procedure for the consideration of a "disapproval bill," but no such bill was passed for either of the cancellations involved in these cases.[1] A majority vote of both Houses is sufficient to enact a disapproval bill. The Act does not grant the President the authority to cancel a disapproval bill, but he does, of course, retain his constitutional authority to veto such a bill.

The effect of a cancellation is plainly stated.... [T]he cancellation prevents the item "from having legal force or effect." §§ 691e(4)(B)–(C). . . .

In both legal and practical effect, the President has amended two Acts of Congress by repealing a portion of each. "[R]epeal of statutes, no less than enactment, must conform with Art. I." INS v. Chadha, 462 U.S. 919, 954 (1983). . . . Although the Constitution expressly authorizes the President to play a role in the process of enacting statutes, it is silent on the subject of unilateral Presidential action that either repeals or amends parts of duly enacted statutes....

1. Congress failed to act upon proposed legislation to disapprove these cancellations. Indeed, despite the fact that the President has canceled at least 82 items since the Act was passed, Congress has enacted only one law, over a Presidential veto, disapproving any cancellation, see Pub.L. 105–159, 112 Stat. 19 (1998) (disapproving the cancellation of 38 military construction spending items).

The Government advances two related arguments to support its position that despite the unambiguous provisions of the Act, cancellations do not amend or repeal properly enacted statutes in violation of the Presentment Clause. First, relying primarily on Field v. Clark, 143 U.S. 649 (1892), the Government contends that the cancellations were merely exercises of discretionary authority granted to the President by [the Act]. Second, the Government submits that the substance of the authority to cancel tax and spending items "is, in practical effect, no more and no less than the power to 'decline to spend' specified sums of money, or to 'decline to implement' specified tax measures." Brief for Appellants 40. Neither argument is persuasive.

[After reviewing Field v. Clark, p. 67 above, Justice Stevens identified] three critical differences between the power to suspend the exemption from import duties and the power to cancel portions of a duly enacted statute. First, the exercise of the suspension power was contingent upon a condition that did not exist when the Tariff Act was passed: the imposition of "reciprocally unequal and unreasonable" import duties by other countries. In contrast, the exercise of the cancellation power within five days after the enactment of the Balanced Budget and Tax Reform Acts necessarily was based on the same conditions that Congress evaluated when it passed those statutes. Second, under the Tariff Act, when the President determined that the contingency had arisen, he had a duty to suspend; in contrast, while it is true that the President was required by the Act to make three determinations before he canceled a provision, those determinations did not qualify his discretion to cancel or not to cancel. Finally, whenever the President suspended an exemption under the Tariff Act, he was executing the policy that Congress had embodied in the statute. In contrast, whenever the President cancels an item of new direct spending or a limited tax benefit he is rejecting the policy judgment made by Congress and relying on his own policy judgment. . . .

Neither are we persuaded by the Government's contention that the President's authority to cancel new direct spending and tax benefit items is no greater than his traditional authority to decline to spend appropriated funds. The Government has reviewed in some detail the series of statutes in which Congress has given the Executive broad discretion over the expenditure of appropriated funds. For example, the First Congress appropriated "sum[s] not exceeding" specified amounts to be spent on various Government operations. In those statutes, as in later years, the President was given wide discretion with respect to both the amounts to be spent and how the money would be allocated among different functions. It is argued that the Line Item Veto Act merely confers comparable discretionary authority over the expenditure of appropriated funds. The critical difference between this statute and all of its predecessors, however, is that unlike any of them, this Act gives the President the unilateral power to change the text of duly enacted statutes. None of the Act's predecessors could even arguably have been construed to authorize such a change. . . .

. . . The Balanced Budget Act of 1997 is a 500-page document that became "Public Law 105–33" after three procedural steps were taken: (1) a bill containing its exact text was approved by a majority of the Members of the House of Representatives; (2) the Senate approved precisely the same text; and (3) that text was signed into law by the President. The Constitution explicitly requires that each of those three steps be taken before a bill may "become a law." Art. I, § 7. If one paragraph of that text had been omitted at any one of those three stages, Public Law 105–33 would not have been validly enacted. If the Line Item Veto Act were valid, it would authorize the President to create a different law—one whose text was not voted on by either House of Congress or presented to the President for signature. Something that might be known as "Public Law 105–33 as modified by the President" may or may not be desirable, but it is surely not a document that may "become a law" pursuant to the procedures designed by the Framers of Article I, § 7, of the Constitution.

If there is to be a new procedure in which the President will play a different role in determining the final text of what may "become a law," such change must come not by legislation but through the amendment procedures set forth in Article V of the Constitution.

The judgment of the District Court is affirmed.

It is so ordered.

■ JUSTICE KENNEDY, concurring.

A Nation cannot plunder its own treasury without putting its Constitution and its survival in peril. The statute before us, then, is of first importance, for it seems undeniable the Act will tend to restrain persistent excessive spending. Nevertheless, for the reasons given by Justice Stevens in the opinion for the Court, the statute must be found invalid. Failure of political will does not justify unconstitutional remedies.

. . . To say the political branches have a somewhat free hand to reallocate their own authority would seem to require acceptance of two premises: first, that the public good demands it, and second, that liberty is not at risk. The former premise is inadmissible. The Constitution's structure requires a stability which transcends the convenience of the moment. The latter premise, too, is flawed. Liberty is always at stake when one or more of the branches seek to transgress the separation of powers.

. . . In recent years, perhaps, we have come to think of liberty as defined by that word in the Fifth and Fourteenth Amendments and as illuminated by the other provisions of the Bill of Rights. The conception of liberty embraced by the Framers was not so confined. They used the principles of separation of powers and federalism to secure liberty in the fundamental political sense of the term, quite in addition to the idea of freedom from intrusive governmental acts. The idea and the promise were that when the people delegate some degree of control to a remote central authority, one branch of government ought not possess the power to shape their destiny without a sufficient check from the other two. In this vision, liberty demands limits on the ability of any one branch to influence basic political decisions. . . .

The principal object of the statute, it is true, was not to enhance the President's power to reward one group and punish another, to help one set of taxpayers and hurt another, to favor one State and ignore another. Yet these are its undeniable effects. The law establishes a new mechanism which gives the President the sole ability to hurt a group that is a visible target, in order to disfavor the group or to extract further concessions from Congress. . . .

■ Justice Scalia, with whom Justice O'Connor joins, and with whom Justice Breyer joins [in the section excerpted here], concurring in part and dissenting in part.

. . . Article I, § 7, of the Constitution obviously prevents the President from canceling a law that Congress has not authorized him to cancel. Such action cannot possibly be considered part of his execution of the law, and if it is legislative action, as the Court observes, " 'repeal of statutes, no less than enactment, must conform with Art. I.' " Ante, at 2103, quoting from INS v. Chadha. But that is not this case. . . . The Tariff Act of 1890 authorized the President to "suspend, by proclamation to that effect" certain of its provisions if he determined that other countries were imposing "reciprocally unequal and unreasonable" duties. This Court upheld the constitutionality of that Act in Field v. Clark. . . .

[Article 1, § 7] no more categorically prohibits the Executive reduction of congressional dispositions in the course of implementing statutes that authorize such reduction, than it categorically prohibits the Executive augmentation of congressional dispositions in the course of implementing statutes that authorize such augmentation—generally known as substantive rulemaking. There are, to be sure, limits upon the former just as there are limits upon the latter—and I am prepared to acknowledge that the limits upon the former may be much more severe. Those limits are established, however, not by some categorical prohibition of Art. I, § 7, which our cases conclusively disprove, but by what has come to be known as the doctrine of unconstitutional delegation of legislative authority: When authorized Executive reduction or augmentation is allowed to go too far, it usurps the nondelegable function of Congress and violates the separation of powers.

It is this doctrine . . . that is the issue presented by the statute before us here. . . .

Insofar as the degree of political, "lawmaking" power conferred upon the Executive is concerned, there is not a dime's worth of difference between Congress's authorizing the President to cancel a spending item, and Congress's authorizing money to be spent on a particular item at the President's discretion. And the latter has been done since the founding of the Nation. From 1789–1791, the First Congress made lump-sum appropriations for the entire Government—"sum[s] not exceeding" specified amounts for broad purposes. From a very early date Congress also made permissive individual appropriations, leaving the decision whether to spend the money to the President's unfettered discretion. . . . Examples of appropriations committed to the discretion of the President abound in our history. . . . The constitutionality of such appropriations has never seriously been questioned. . . .

The short of the matter is this: Had the Line Item Veto Act authorized the President to "decline to spend" any item of spending contained in the Balanced Budget Act of 1997, there is not the slightest doubt that authorization would have been constitutional. What the Line Item Veto Act does instead—authorizing the President to "cancel" an item of spending—is technically different. But the technical difference does not relate to the technicalities of the Presentment Clause, which have been fully complied with; and the doctrine of unconstitutional delegation, which is at issue here, is preeminently not a doctrine of technicalities. The title of the Line Item Veto Act, which was perhaps designed to simplify for public comprehension, or perhaps merely to comply with the terms of a campaign pledge, has succeeded in faking out the Supreme Court.

.   .   .

■ JUSTICE BREYER, with whom JUSTICE O'CONNOR and JUSTICE SCALIA join as to Part III, dissenting. . . .

II

. . . When our Nation was founded, . . . our population was less than 4 million, federal employees numbered fewer than 5,000, [and] the annual federal budget outlays totaled approximately $4 million. . . . At that time, a Congress, wishing to give a President the power to select among appropriations, could simply have embodied each appropriation in a separate bill, each bill subject to a separate Presidential veto.

Today, however, our population is about 250 million, the Federal Government employs more than 4 million people, the annual federal budget is $1.5 trillion, and a typical budget appropriations bill may have a dozen titles, hundreds of sections, and spread across more than 500 pages of the Statutes at Large. Congress cannot divide such a bill into thousands, or tens of thousands, of separate appropriations bills, each one of which the President would have to sign, or to veto, separately. Thus, the question is whether the Constitution permits Congress to choose a particular novel means to achieve this same, constitutionally legitimate, end. . . .

. . . [T]he fact that the Act may closely resemble a different, literally unconstitutional, arrangement is beside the point. To drive exactly 65 miles per hour on an interstate highway closely resembles an act that violates the speed limit. But it does not violate that limit, for small differences matter when the question is one of literal violation of law. No more does this Act literally violate the Constitution's words. . . .

III

The Court believes that the Act violates the literal text of the Constitution. A simple syllogism captures its basic reasoning:

Major Premise: The Constitution sets forth an exclusive method for enacting, repealing, or amending laws.

Minor Premise: The Act authorizes the President to "repea[l] or amen[d]" laws in a different way, namely by announcing a cancellation of a portion of a previously enacted law.

Conclusion: The Act is inconsistent with the Constitution.

I find this syllogism unconvincing, however, because its Minor Premise is faulty. When the President "canceled" the two appropriation measures now before us, he did not repeal any law nor did he amend any law. He simply followed the law, leaving the statutes, as they are literally written, intact.

. . . Imagine that the canceled New York health care tax provision at issue here had instead said the following:

> Section One. Taxes . . . that were collected by the State of New York from a health care provider before June 1, 1997 . . . are deemed to be permissible health care related taxes . . . *provided however that the President may prevent the just-mentioned provision from having legal force or effect if he determines x, y, and z.* (Assume x, y and z to be the same determinations required by the Line Item Veto Act.)

Whatever a person might say, or think, about the constitutionality of this imaginary law, there is one thing the English language would prevent one from saying. One could not say that a President who "prevent[s]" the deeming language from "having legal force or effect," has either repealed or amended this particular hypothetical statute. Rather, the President has followed that law to the letter. He has exercised the power it explicitly delegates to him. He has executed the law, not repealed it. . . .

. . . This is not the first time that Congress has delegated to the President or to others . . . a contingent power to deny effect to certain statutory language. See, e.g. 28 U.S.C. § 2072 (Supreme Court is authorized to promulgate rules of practice and procedure in federal courts, and "[a]ll laws in conflict with such rules shall be of *no further force and effect*") (emphasis added). . . .

IV

Because I disagree with the Court's holding of literal violation, I must consider whether the Act nonetheless violates separation-of-powers principles. There are three relevant separation-of-powers questions here: (1) Has Congress given the President the wrong kind of power, i.e., "non-Executive" power? (2) Has Congress given the President the power to "encroach" upon Congress' own constitutionally reserved territory? (3) Has Congress given the President too much power, violating the doctrine of "nondelegation?" These three limitations help assure "adequate control by the citizen's Representatives in Congress," upon which Justice Kennedy properly insists. And with respect to this Act, the answer to all these questions is "no."

Viewed conceptually, the power the Act conveys is the right kind of power. It is "executive." As explained above, an exercise of that power "executes" the Act. Conceptually speaking, it closely resembles the kind of delegated authority—to spend or not to spend appropriations, to change or not to change tariff rates—that Congress has frequently granted the President, any differences being differences in degree, not kind. . . . The fact that one could also characterize this kind of power as "legislative," say, if Congress itself (by amending the appropriations bill) prevented a provision from taking effect, is beside the point. This Court has frequently found that the exercise of a particular power, such as the power to make rules of broad applicability, or to adjudicate claims can fall within the constitutional purview of more than one branch of Government. . . .

The Court has upheld congressional delegation of rulemaking power and adjudicatory power to federal agencies. . . . It is far easier conceptually to reconcile the power at issue here with the relevant constitutional description ("executive") than in many of these cases. . . .

[O]ne cannot say that the Act "encroaches" upon Congress' power, when Congress retained the power to insert, by simple majority, into any future appropriations bill, into any section of any such bill, or into any phrase of any section, a provision that says the Act will not apply. Congress also retained the power to "disapprov[e]," and thereby reinstate, any of the President's cancellations. And it is Congress that drafts and enacts the appropriations statutes that are subject to the Act in the first place—and thereby defines the outer limits of the President's cancellation authority. . . .

Nor can one say the Act's grant of power "aggrandizes" the Presidential office. The grant is limited to the context of the budget. It is limited to the power to spend, or not to spend, particular appropriated items, and the power to permit, or not to permit, specific limited exemptions from generally applicable tax law from taking effect. These powers . . . resemble those the President has exercised in the past on other occasions. The delegation of those powers to the President may strengthen the Presidency, but any such change in Executive Branch authority seems minute when compared with the changes worked by delegations of other kinds of authority that the Court in the past has upheld.

The "nondelegation" doctrine represents an added constitutional check upon Congress' authority to delegate power to the Executive Branch. And it raises a more serious constitutional obstacle here. . . .

The Act before us seeks to create [an intelligible] principle in three ways. The first is procedural. The Act tells the President that, in "identifying dollar amounts [or] . . . items . . . for cancellation" (which I take to refer to his selection of the amounts or items he will "prevent from having legal force or effect"), he is to "consider," among other things, "the legislative history, construction, and purposes of the law which contains [those amounts or items, and] . . . any specific sources of information referenced in such law or . . . the best available information. . . ." The second is purposive. The clear purpose behind the Act, confirmed by its legislative history, is to promote "greater fiscal accountability" and to "eliminate wasteful federal spending and . . . special tax breaks." H.R. Conf. Rep. No. 104–491, p. 15 (1996). The third is substantive. The President must determine that, to "prevent" the item or amount "from having legal force or effect" will "reduce the Federal budget deficit; . . . not impair any essential Government functions; and . . . not harm the national interest."

The resulting standards are broad. But this Court has upheld standards that are equally broad, or broader. . . .

On the other hand, I must recognize that there are important differences between the delegation before us and other broad, constitutionally acceptable delegations to Executive Branch agencies—differences that argue against my conclusion. In particular, a broad delegation of authority to an administrative agency differs from the delegation at issue here in that agencies often develop subsidiary rules under the statute, rules that explain the general "public interest" language. Doing so diminishes the risk that the agency will use the breadth of a grant of authority as a cloak for unreasonable or unfair implementation. Moreover, agencies are typically subject to judicial review, which review provides an additional check against arbitrary implementation. The President has not so narrowed his discretionary power through rule, nor is his implementation subject to judicial review under the terms of the Administrative Procedure Act. See, e.g., Franklin v. Massachusetts, 505 U.S. 788, 801 (1992) (APA does not apply to President absent express statement by Congress).

While I believe that these last mentioned considerations are important, they are not determinative. The President, unlike most agency decision-makers, is an elected official. He is responsible to the voters, who, in principle, will judge the manner in which he exercises his delegated authority. Whether the President's expenditure decisions, for example, are arbitrary is a matter that in the past has been left primarily to those voters to consider. . . .

NOTES

(1) *What Was at Stake in the Decision.* The Line Item Veto Act culminated more than a decade of political debate about the wisdom of giving the President the power selectively to remove "pork" from omnibus appropriations statutes. See, e.g., Symposium, 16 St. Louis U. Pub. L. Rev. (1996). Numerous states give their governors such authority, and the data do not clearly establish that fiscal prudence has increased. See Matthew C. Bernstein, The Emperor Has No Clothes: The Line Item Veto Act of 1996 Exposed, 16 St. Louis U. Pub. L. Rev. 85 (1996). Some commentators argued that legislatures became adept at adjusting initial budget bills upward to neutralize eventual gubernatorial vetoes. Whether or not such strategic behavior could, or would, have resulted at the federal level, one thing was certain: The proportion of the federal budget that could have been affected by the cancellation authority was trivial. The bulk of the budget—and certainly the impelling force of deficits—has long been entitlement programs (e.g., Medicare/Medicaid) that do not constitute "discretionary" spending. So, in the end, the much ballyhooed line item veto was largely symbolic—at least in the budgetary realm.

Suppose, however, that the Court had sustained its constitutionality. Can you imagine a persuasive way to distinguish a statute that authorizes the President, *outside* the spending context, to cancel discrete provisions (or phrases, or words) in statutes? Wouldn't this clearly be the sort of unilateral Presidential rewriting of enacted law that the majority fears?

(2) *Agency Inaction: Refusing to "Spend" Resources on Policy-Making and Enforcing.* An Administration determined to terminate, or at least significantly curtail, a regulatory program can deploy strategies less blatant than impounding funds. Decisions about *when* to act—when to institute enforce-

ment proceedings; when to promulgate new rules—invariably fall largely within the Executive's discretion. No one expects 100% enforcement of all laws; indeed, Congress never allocates enough resources to accomplish this even if universal enforcement were good policy. Administrations set enforcement priorities, taking into account a variety of factors, only some of which are the enforcement equivalent of "programmatic impoundments." The Reagan Administration effectively pursued some of its deregulatory goals by an enforcement strategy more akin to "policy impoundments"—i.e., refusing to "spend" enforcement resources on programs of which the Administration did not approve.

HECKLER V. CHANEY, 470 U.S. 821 (1985), held that decisions not to take enforcement action are presumptively not judicially reviewable. Prisoners on death row had requested the Food and Drug Administration to regulate the use of drugs for human execution. They claimed that states were using drugs that had not been demonstrated to be safe and effective for the purpose. As the agency already regulated drugs used for animal euthanasia and drugs used on an experimental basis in prisons, the request was not as bizarre as it might at first sound. Although the APA expressly defines "agency action" to include "failure to act," 5 U.S.C § 551(13), the Court held that the normal APA presumption of reviewability is reversed when the agency has declined to act. Justice Rehnquist's opinion explained that refusal to enforce was likely to be based on factors "unsuitable" for judicial review. Also, "when an agency refuses to act it generally does not exercise its coercive power over an individual's liberty or property rights, and thus does not infringe upon areas that courts are often called upon to protect." The Court explicitly reserved the situation in which "it could justifiably be found that the agency has consciously and expressly adopted a general policy that is so extreme as to amount to an abdication of its statutory responsibilities." Of course, such a showing would be quite difficult. Justice Marshall alone argued against presumptive unreviewability. He would have sustained the FDA's decision after a review that gave considerable deference to the agency's explanation of its enforcement priorities. This latter approach has been used by some lower courts in the allied context of agency refusal to initiate a rulemaking. See, e.g., Brown v. Secretary of Health & Human Serv. 46 F.3d 102 (1st Cir.1995); American Horse Protection Assoc., Inc. v. Lyng, 812 F.2d 1 (D.C.Cir.1987).

NOTES ON APPROPRIATIONS: DIRECTING POLICY WITH THE PURSE STRINGS

> *"All Bills for raising Revenue shall originate in the House of Representatives; but the Senate may propose or concur with Amendments as on other Bills."*

U.S. Constitution, Art. 1, § 7, cl. 1

> *"No money shall be drawn from the Treasury, but in Consequence of Appropriations made by Law . . . ."*

U.S. Constitution, Art. 1, § 9, cl. 7

(1) *Money Talks*. Renowned constitutional historian Edward S. Corwin described the appropriations power as "the most important single curb in the Constitution on Presidential Power." The Constitution and What It Means Today 101 (13th ed. 1975). And indeed, Congress has become adept at using the appropriations power as a way to force course-corrections in administrative policy. Sometimes, members succeed in having a substantive rider included in an agency's appropriations bill, or in an omnibus funding bill. Other times, appropriations are explicitly conditioned on a change in agency policy. See Jaques B. LeBoeuf, Limitations on the Use of Appropriations Riders by Congress to Effectuate Substantive Policy Changes, 19 Hastings Const. L.Q. 457 (1992). Absent some sort of item veto, the President can reject the policy directive only at the usually-prohibitive cost of losing the entire funding package.

A particularly extensive illustration began during the first Reagan Administration. Through an executive order and an implementing "National Security Decision Directive" (NSDD), the Administration imposed significant new restrictions on what information federal employees could disclose. Three aspects became particularly controversial: (1) a redefinition of protected information to cover "classifi*able*" as well as "classified" matter; (2) a lifetime requirement that federal employees submit any publications for prior government clearance; and (3) more liberal agency use of polygraph examinations of employees. The Democratic Congress took a dim view of the new regime—in part because of civil liberties concerns but also, closer to home, because it had reason to believe that the restrictions were prompted by, and aimed at stopping, "whistleblower" communications from federal employees to Congress itself.

When a hostile oversight hearing by the Senate Committee on Governmental Affairs didn't faze Administration officials, Congress simply closed the purse. A provision was inserted in the State Department Authorization Act to delay, for six months, implementation of the pre-publication clearance requirement. A similar provision in the Defense Authorization Act blocked implementation by that Department of polygraph examinations. (One of the most explosive instances of employee whistleblowing to Congress had involved the way in which DOD was reporting weapons systems costs to Congress.) At that point, the Administration suspended the NSDD and began discussions with Congress. When President Reagan was reelected, however, the Administration became less conciliatory. It required employees to sign "Standard Form 189"—promising never to divulge in a "direct or indirect fashion" information that is classified or "classifiable"— as a condition of retaining their security clearances. Again a round of blistering oversight hearings produced no effect, and again Congress used appropriations. The Omnibus Continuing Resolution for 1988 contained this provision: "No funds appropriated in this or any other Act for fiscal year 1988 maybe used to implement or enforce the agreement[] in Standard Form 189"so long as it "contains the word classifiable." As the dispute continued into the Bush Administration, Congress rolled the ban over into other appropriations bills. Eventually the offending word was removed from the Form. More details can be found in Peter Shane & Harold Bruff, The Law of Presidential Power 154 (1988) and American Foreign Serv.

Ass'n v. Garfinkel, 732 F.Supp. 13 (D.D.C.1990), on remand from American Foreign Serv. Ass'n v. Garfinkel, 490 U.S. 153 (1989).

(2) *The Complex Politics of Appropriations Oversight.* As with oversight generally, see p. 210 above, EPA provides an especially rich case study. RICHARD J. LAZARUS, THE NEGLECTED QUESTION OF CONGRESSIONAL OVERSIGHT OF EPA, 54 Law & Contemp. Probs. 205 (1991): "The appropriations committees ... have been extremely effective in overseeing [EPA's] programs during the last twenty years. From the outset, these committees (particularly the House committees) have closely scrutinized EPA's programs through the budgetary process. Unlike members of the committees that drafted the environmental protection laws, many members of the appropriations committees were not advocates of the programs. They were instead often quite skeptical of the wisdom of those laws and sought to undermine their statutory mandates through the appropriation process.

"As a result of internal compromise, the leadership in Congress initially placed EPA's budget within the jurisdiction of the House appropriations subcommittee on the Department of Housing and Urban Development chaired by Representative Jamie Whitten, an outspoken critic of many of the environmental laws. Whitten used the appropriations process to conduct lengthy inquiries into the agency's implementation of those laws. He lobbied the administrator on pesticide matters of concern to agricultural interests, and he subsequently denounced EPA when it failed to heed his advice. He also openly stated his view that Congress may not have intended full implementation of the environmental laws that it had passed. According to Whitten, the appropriations process provided a way to 'limit use of money' in order to cut back on those laws."

(3) *The Challenge of Jumpstarting an Inactive Agency.* As these excerpts suggest, withholding funds can be very effective in bringing to heel an agency that wants to act. But what about an agency determined *not* to act? In the early 1980s, a Republican Administration strategy of de-regulation through non-action required a frustrated Democratic Congress to develop different tactical responses. Once again, EPA provides the best casestudy. SIDNEY A. SHAPIRO & ROBERT L. GLICKSMAN, CONGRESS, THE SUPREME COURT, AND THE QUIET REVOLUTION IN ADMINISTRATIVE LAW, 1988 Duke L.J. 819: "[L]egislators leveled two recurring charges at the EPA. First, Congress believed that the EPA was not acting when it should have been, or was acting too slowly. Second, legislators expressed a widespread concern that even when the EPA did act, it did so in a manner inconsistent with the objectives of its authorizing legislation. . . .

"As the EPA's regulatory responsibilities came up for reauthorization in the 1980s, a consensus developed in Congress to impose two kinds of more effective legislative controls on the EPA. In certain areas, to combat the agency's failure to act, or failure to act promptly, Congress removed some of the agency's regulatory discretion by mandating that regulation meet legislatively imposed deadlines or schedules. To combat the EPA's proclivity for implementing statutes in a manner contrary to congressional intent, Congress prescribed more detailed substantive criteria to guide the agency in implementing its regulatory responsibilities. In short, in recent statutory reauthorizations of environmental programs, Congress has rejected the traditional discretionary model for the EPA in favor of the coercive, prescriptive, and ministerial models of control.

"This model typically forces the agency to regulate by mandating some kind of agency action—such as listing chemicals as hazardous or issuing regulations applicable to industrial polluters—before a set deadline.[1] . . . Congress intends coercive statutes to accelerate the pace of regulation by making it easier for an agency to issue regulations and to facilitate legislative oversight. . . . Statutory deadlines also speed regulation because statutory beneficiaries can enforce deadlines in the courts. The Administrative Procedure Act (APA) authorizes courts to 'compel agency action . . . unreasonably delayed.' [S]tatutory deadlines increase the likelihood that a court will find an agency's delay unreasonable and will force the agency to remedy that delay."

Ultimately, however, the result was often bad regulatory policy. Coercive statutes set deadlines impossible to accomplish (at least, without considerably more resources), and they preempted informed regulatory priority-setting. As one particularly astute observer of the regulatory process concluded: "If political oversight is a good thing, then it is possible to have too much of a good thing. During the Reagan and Bush administrations, presidential and legislative oversight of regulatory policy reached its high-water mark, yet the effectiveness of regulatory policy deteriorated as a result." Sidney A. Shapiro, Political Oversight and the Deterioration of Regulatory Policy, 46 Admin. L. Rev. 1, 1 (1994).

This experience suggests the dark side of a system of checks and balances. What happens when each of two powerful Branches—with very different policy preferences and competing claims to represent the will of the people—attempts unilaterally to direct regulatory policy? A Branch's "claims of singular entitlement and ability to control the regulatory agenda establish a norm of confrontation, rather than collaboration. By raising the stakes for other actors in the system, such hegemonistic claims may trigger an oversight arms race. [T]his is exactly what happened in the 1980s, as Congress reacted to what it perceived as aggressive unilateral White House deregulatory initiatives with a variety of equally aggressive countermeasures—micro-management through hyper-detailed substantive statutory amendments; the imposition of rulemaking deadlines, regulatory hammers, and similar statutory action-forcing mandates; the increase in reports and other oversight data agencies are required to give Congress; the refusal to confirm nominees to key White House oversight positions; and the use of riders in appropriations bills to regain control over specific agency programs. If we encourage political actors to regard regulatory oversight as a battle for the soul of the administrative state, we may be unpleasantly surprised at the weapons each turns out to have available in its arsenal."[2]

---

1. "The 1984 amendments to the Resource Conservation and Recovery Act (RCRA) the 1986 amendments to the Comprehensive Environmental Response, Compensation, and Liability Act (CERCLA), the Safe Drinking Water Act (SDWA), and the Toxic Substances Control Act (TSCA), the 1987 amendments to the Clean Water Act (CWA) and the 1988 amendments to the Federal Insecticide, Fungicide, and Rodenticide Act (FIFRA) all include examples of coercive control devices that force the EPA to make decisions within a specified time." Id. at 829–30.

2. Cynthia R. Farina, Undoing the New Deal Through the New Presidentialism, 22 Harv. J.L. & Pub. Pol'y 227, 235 (1997).

CONCLUDING THOUGHTS

Section III (on the constitutionality of assigning adjudication to agencies rather than Article III courts) closed by suggesting a recurring story in the Court's separation-of-powers jurisprudence: Structural constitutional challenges produce analytic constructs that appear fundamentally to threaten established regulatory institutions. Some Congressional choices are indeed struck down. But, ultimately, core administrative structures and practices remain unscathed—although theoretical consistency and doctrinal integrity take some pretty severe hits in the process. If this story is indeed replayed in the various chapters of constitutional jurisprudence about the administrative state, is that jurisprudence the chronicle of failure? Or the testament of success?

After several decades of vigorous constitutional litigation, we find ourselves apparently where we started:

Agencies have the power to make rules with the force of law.

Agencies have the power to render binding adjudications of individual rights and duties under statutes.

Agencies have control relationships with Congress, the President, and the Judiciary. The precise boundaries of those relationships are legally indeterminate and politically contested.

So, has structural constitutional law made any progress? CHARLES L. BLACK, JR., THE PEOPLE & THE COURT: JUDICIAL REVIEW IN A DEMOCRACY 52 (1960): "The role of the Court has usually been conceived as that of *invalidating* . . ., of acting as a "check" on the other departments. It has played such a role on occasion, and may play it again in the future.

"But a case can be made for believing that the prime and most necessary function of the Court has been that of *validation*, not that of invalidation. What a government of limited powers needs, at the beginning and forever, is some means of satisfying the people that it has taken all steps humanly possible to stay within its power. That is the condition of its legitimacy, and its legitimacy, in the long run, is the condition of its life. And the Court, through its history has acted as the legitimator of the government."

CHAPTER III

PROCEDURAL FRAMEWORKS FOR ADMINISTRATIVE ACTION

SECTION 1. THE FUNDAMENTAL PROCEDURAL CATEGORIES OF ADMINISTRATIVE ACTION: ADJUDICATION AND RULEMAKING

a. THE CONSTITUTION

Londoner v. Denver

Supreme Court of the United States, 1908.
210 U.S. 373.

■ JUSTICE MOODY delivered the opinion of the court.

The plaintiffs in error began this proceeding in a state court of Colorado to relieve lands owned by them from an assessment of a tax for the cost of paving a street upon which the lands abutted. The relief sought was granted by the trial court, but its action was reversed by the Supreme Court of the State. ... The Supreme Court held that the tax was assessed in conformity with the constitution and laws of the State, and its decision on that question is conclusive. ...

The tax complained of was assessed under the provisions of the charter of the city of Denver, which confers upon the city the power to make local improvements and to assess the cost upon property specially benefited. ...

It appears from the charter that, in the execution of the power to make local improvements and assess the cost upon the property specially benefited, the main steps to be taken by the city authorities are plainly marked and separated: 1. The board of public works must transmit to the city council a resolution ordering the work to be done and the form of an ordinance authorizing it and creating an assessment district. This it can do only upon certain conditions, one of which is that there shall first be filed a petition asking the improvement, signed by the owners of the majority of the frontage to be assessed. 2. The passage of that ordinance by the city council, which is given authority to determine conclusively whether the action of the board was duly taken. 3. The assessment of the cost upon the landowners after due notice and opportunity for hearing.

In the case before us the board took the first step by transmitting to the council the resolution to do the work and the form of an ordinance authorizing it. It is contended, however, that there was wanting an essential condition of the jurisdiction of the board, namely, such a petition from the owners as the law requires. The trial court found this contention to be true. But, as has been seen, the charter gave the city council the authority

238

to determine conclusively that the improvements were duly ordered by the board after due notice and a proper petition. In the exercise of this authority the city council, in the ordinance directing the improvement to be made, adjudged, in effect, that a proper petition had been filed. ... The state Supreme Court held that the determination of the city council was conclusive that a proper petition was filed, and that decision must be accepted by us as the law of the State. The only question for this court is whether the charter provision authorizing such a finding, without notice to the landowners, denies to them due process of law. We think it does not. The proceedings, from the beginning up to and including the passage of the ordinance authorizing the work did not include any assessment or necessitate any assessment, although they laid the foundation for an assessment, which might or might not subsequently be made. Clearly all this might validly be done without hearing to the landowners, provided a hearing upon the assessment itself is afforded. The legislature might have authorized the making of improvements by the city council without any petition. If it chose to exact a petition as a security for wise and just action it could, so far as the Federal Constitution is concerned, accompany that condition with a provision that the council, with or without notice, should determine finally whether it had been performed. This disposes of the first assignment of error, which is overruled. ...

The fifth assignment, though general, vague and obscure, fairly raises, we think, the question whether the assessment was made without notice and opportunity for hearing to those affected by it, thereby denying to them due process of law. The trial court found as a fact that no opportunity for hearing was afforded, and the Supreme Court did not disturb this finding. The record discloses what was actually done, and there seems to be no dispute about it. After the improvement was completed the board of public works, in compliance with § 29 of the charter, certified to the city clerk a statement of the cost, and an apportionment of it to the lots of land to be assessed. Thereupon the city clerk, in compliance with § 30, published a notice stating, inter alia, that the written complaints or objections of the owners, if filed within thirty days, would be "heard and determined by the city council before the passage of any ordinance assessing the cost." Those interested, therefore, were informed that if they reduced their complaints and objections to writing, and filed them within thirty days, those complaints and objections would be heard, and would be heard before any assessment was made. ... Resting upon the assurance that they would be heard, the plaintiffs in error filed within the thirty days the following paper:

"Denver, Colorado, January 13, 1900.

"To the Honorable Board of Public Works and the Honorable Mayor and City Council of the City of Denver:

"The undersigned, by Joshua Grozier, their attorney, do hereby most earnestly and strenuously protest and object to the passage of the contemplated or any assessing ordinance against the property in Eighth Avenue Paving District No. 1, so called, for each of the following reasons, to wit:

Due Process

"1st. That said assessment and all and each of the proceedings leading up to the same were and are illegal, voidable and void, and the attempted assessment if made will be void and uncollectible.

"2nd. That said assessment and the cost of said pretended improvement should be collected, if at all, as a general tax against the city at large and not as a special assessment.

"3d. That property in said city not assessed is benefited by the said pretended improvement and certain property assessed is not benefited by said pretended improvement and other property assessed is not benefited by said pretended improvement to the extent of the assessment; that the individual pieces of property in said district are not benefited to the extent assessed against them and each of them respectively; that the assessment is arbitrary and property assessed in an equal amount is not benefited equally; that the boundaries of said pretended district were arbitrarily created without regard to the benefits or any other method of assessment known to law; that said assessment is outrageously large. . . .

"8th. Because the city had no jurisdiction in the premises. No petition subscribed by the owners of a majority of the frontage in the district to be assessed for said improvements was ever obtained or presented. . . .

"Wherefore, because of the foregoing and numerous other good and sufficient reasons, the undersigned object and protest against the passage of the said proposed assessing ordinance."

This certainly was a complaint against and objection to the proposed assessment. Instead of affording the plaintiffs in error an opportunity to be heard upon its allegations, the city council, without notice to them, met as a board of equalization, not in a stated but in a specially called session, and, without any hearing, adopted the following resolution:

"Whereas, complaints have been filed by the various persons and firms as the owners of real estate included within the Eighth Avenue Paving District No. 1, of the city of Denver against the proposed assessments on said property for the cost of said paving, . . . and Whereas, no complaint or objection has been filed or made against the apportionment of said assessment made by the board of public works of the city of Denver, but the complaints and objections filed deny wholly the right of the city to assess any district or portion of the assessable property of the city of Denver; therefore, be it

"Resolved, by the city council of the city of Denver, sitting as a board of equalization, that the apportionments of said assessment made by said board of public works be, and the same are hereby, confirmed and approved."

Subsequently, without further notice or hearing, the city council enacted the ordinance of assessment whose validity is to be determined in this case. The facts out of which the question on this assignment arises may be compressed into small compass. The first step in the assessment proceedings was by the certificate of the board of public works of the cost of the improvement and a preliminary apportionment of it. The last step was the enactment of the assessment ordinance. From beginning to end of the proceedings the landowners, although allowed to formulate and file complaints and objections, were not afforded an opportunity to be heard upon them. Upon these facts was there a denial by the State of the due process of law guaranteed by the Fourteenth Amendment to the Constitution of the United States?

In the assessment, apportionment and collection of taxes upon property within their jurisdiction the Constitution of the United States imposes few restrictions upon the States. In the enforcement of such restrictions as the Constitution does impose this court has regarded substance and not form. But where the legislature of a State, instead of fixing the tax itself, commits to some subordinate body the duty of determining whether, in what amount, and upon whom it shall be levied, and of making its assessment and apportionment, due process of law requires that at some stage of the proceedings before the tax becomes irrevocably fixed, the taxpayer shall have an opportunity to be heard, of which he must have notice, either personal, by publication, or by a law fixing the time and place of the hearing. It must be remembered that the law of Colorado denies the landowner the right to object in the courts to the assessment, upon the ground that the objections are cognizable only by the board of equalization.

Notice

If it is enough that, under such circumstances, an opportunity is given to submit in writing all objections to and complaints of the tax to the board, then there was a hearing afforded in the case at bar. But we think that something more than that, even in proceedings for taxation, is required by due process of law. Many requirements essential in strictly judicial proceedings may be dispensed with in proceedings of this nature. But even here a hearing in its very essence demands that he who is entitled to it shall have the right to support his allegations by argument however brief, and, if need be, by proof, however informal. Pittsburgh, & c. Railway Co. v. Backus, 154 U.S. 421, 426; Fallbrook Irrigation District v. Bradley, 164 U.S. 112, 171, et seq. It is apparent that such a hearing was denied to the plaintiffs in error. The denial was by the city council, which, while acting as a board of equalization, represents the State. The assessment was therefore void, and the plaintiffs in error were entitled to a decree discharging their lands from a lien on account of it. . . . Judgment reversed.

Opportunity to be heard

■ THE CHIEF JUSTICE and JUSTICE HOLMES dissent.

Bi–Metallic Investment Co. v. State Bd. of Equalization of Colorado

Supreme Court of the United States, 1915.
239 U.S. 441.

■ JUSTICE HOLMES delivered the opinion of the court.

This is a suit to enjoin the State Board of Equalization and the Colorado Tax Commission from putting in force, and the defendant Pitcher as assessor of Denver from obeying, an order of the boards increasing the valuation of all taxable property in Denver forty per cent. The order was sustained and the suit directed to be dismissed by the Supreme Court of the State. 56 Colo. 512, 138 P. 1010. See 56 Colo. 343, 138 P. 509. The plaintiff is the owner of real estate in Denver and brings the case here on the ground that it was given no opportunity to be heard and that therefore its property will be taken without due process of law, contrary to the Fourteenth Amendment of the Constitution of the United States. That is the only question with which we have to deal. ...

For the purposes of decision we assume that the constitutional question is presented in the baldest way—that neither the plaintiff nor the assessor of Denver, who presents a brief on the plaintiff's side, nor any representative of the city and county, was given an opportunity to be heard, other than such as they may have had by reason of the fact that the time of meeting of the boards is fixed by law. On this assumption it is obvious that injustice may be suffered if some property in the county already has been valued at its full worth. But if certain property has been valued at a rate different from that generally prevailing in the county the owner has had his opportunity to protest and appeal as usual in our system of taxation, Hagar v. Reclamation District, 111 U.S. 701, 709, 710, so that it must be assumed that the property owners in the county all stand alike. The question then is whether all individuals have a constitutional right to be heard before a matter can be decided in which all are equally concerned—here, for instance, before a superior board decides that the local taxing officers have adopted a system of undervaluation throughout a county, as notoriously often has been the case. The answer of this court in the State Railroad Tax Cases, 92 U.S. 575, at least as to any further notice, was that it was hard to believe that the proposition was seriously made.

Where a rule of conduct applies to more than a few people it is impracticable that every one should have a direct voice in its adoption. The Constitution does not require all public acts to be done in town meeting or an assembly of the whole. General statutes within the state power are passed that affect the person or property of individuals, sometimes to the point of ruin, without giving them a chance to be heard. Their rights are protected in the only way that they can be in a complex society, by their power, immediate or remote, over those who make the rule. If the result in this case had been reached as it might have been by the State's doubling the rate of taxation, no one would suggest that the Fourteenth Amendment was violated unless every person affected had been allowed an opportunity to raise his voice against it before the body entrusted by the state constitution with the power. In considering this case in this court we must assume that the proper state machinery has been used, and the question is whether, if the state constitution had declared that Denver had been undervalued as compared with the rest of the State and had decreed that for the current year the valuation should be forty per cent higher, the objection now urged could prevail. It appears to us that to put the question is to answer it. There must be a limit to individual argument in such matters if government is to go on. In Londoner v. Denver, 210 U.S. 373, 385, a local board had to determine "whether, in what amount, and upon whom" a tax for paving a street should be levied for special benefits. A relatively small number of persons was concerned, who were exceptionally affected, in each case upon individual grounds, and it was held that they had a right to a hearing. But that decision is far from reaching a general determination dealing only with the principle upon which all the assessments in a county had been laid.

Judgment affirmed.

NOTES ON LONDONER–BI–METALLIC

(1) *Just What is the Nature of the Londoner–Bi–Metallic Distinction?* Should the outcome in Londoner be any different if the street to be paved is many miles in length, and the affected plots and persons number in the tens of thousands? At what if any point would a Londoner right to a hearing emerge in the course of the following series of events? Respecting what issues or issues?:

1. In order to avoid rampant inflation in housing costs in areas heavily affected by World War II defense activities, Congress passes a statute which attempts to stabilize rents as of April 1, 1941. It authorizes an Administrator (1) to establish "defense-rental areas" and recommend rents for housing in those areas; and (2) if such recommendations fail to work, to set maximum rents that will be "generally fair and equitable" giving "due consideration" to rents prevailing on April 1, 1941.

2. The Administrator establishes a "defense-rental area" near a major army base and recommends that maximum rents should be those prevailing in the area on April 1, 1941.

3. Finding that his recommendation did not suffice, the Administrator establishes rent control in the area, fixing rents at those prevailing on April 1, 1941; for units rented for the first time after that date, the maximum rent is the rent initially charged, subject to being later reduced if that initial rent is higher than rents generally prevailing on April 1, 1941. Thousands of apartments are affected in this area, as they had been in others.

4. The Administrator orders a reduction in the maximum rents allowable in a particular apartment, which was first rented after April 1, 1941, on the ground that the rent initially charged exceeded the rate generally prevailing on April 1, 1941.

5. The Administrator denies the landlord's protest to the validity of the ordered reduction.

6. A court reviews the denial of the protest.[1]

If you conclude that "a relatively small number of persons was concerned" is not the key—that hearings might be required in the case of the longer road, or would be required for each of the thousands of particular apartments that might be made subject to rate reduction orders—three further questions suggest themselves:

First, in the large number situation, can you imagine procedural devices available within the framework of a right to hearing, that could work to control the number of hearings that had actually to be granted?

Second, can more explanatory power for the Londoner/Bi–Metallic distinction be found in Holmes's observation that, however many persons were concerned, they were persons "who were exceptionally affected, in

---

1. Bowles v. Willingham, 321 U.S. 503 (1944).

each case upon individual grounds"? Recall that Londoner confined the right to a hearing to those facts bearing on the appropriate assessment for each particular lot. Similarly, in considering stages 1 through 6 in the series set out above, you probably concluded that any hearing right would attach only to issues concerning what would be a "generally fair and equitable" rent for a particular apartment, having in mind the general condition of the area rental market on April 1, 1941. Yet individual circumstances are not the only kinds of facts agencies (or courts) must determine; they may be called upon to decide whether benzene is a human carcinogen; if so, how much cancer is likely to be caused at what concentrations of that chemical; and what would be the feasibility and/or cost of controlling benzene exposure to a given level in various industrial settings. Factual questions like these frequently arise both in agency adjudication and in agency rulemaking, and considering those procedures thus can entail the question whether relevant differences among types of fact would support a judgment that not all require a "hearing" of the nature Londoner appears to imagine. This question is conventionally framed in terms of a distinction between "adjudicative" and "legislative" facts.

Third, would it be helpful to see "in each case upon individual grounds" as implying a *political* explanation? It has been suggested that "the adjudicative/legislative distinction articulated in Bi–Metallic can arise from the singling out function of the adjudicative process. Professors [Kenneth C.] Davis and [Richard] Pierce view this as 'process-oriented protection' along the lines of that developed by Professor John Ely in Democracy and Distrust. 'When ... government singles out an individual for adverse action, the political process provides little protection. Individuals singled out for adverse action can be protected only by forcing the government to use a decisionmaking process that ensures fairness to the individual.' According to Davis and Pierce, '[t]hat is the purpose of the Due Process Clause.'" Michael Scaperlanda, Oklahoma Rejects Adjudicative Nature of Particularized Ratemaking, 9–SPG Nat. Resources & Env't 76, 79 (1995).

(2) PETER L. STRAUSS, REVISITING *OVERTON PARK*: POLITICAL AND JUDICIAL CONTROLS OVER ADMINISTRATIVE ACTIONS AFFECTING THE COMMUNITY, 39 UCLA L.Rev. 1251, 1256–57 (1992):

"A ... prominent distinction between the worlds of politics and law appears in Justice Holmes' opinion for the Court in the still influential *Bi-Metallic Investment Co. v. State Board of Equalization*. ... Although Holmes' conclusion was procedural—at issue was the application of the Due Process Clause of the Constitution to require quasi-adjudicatory process— the contrast he drew was grounded in conventional notions regarding the relative strengths and weaknesses of legal and political process. Politicians, not judges, should be responsible for setting the dimensions of social policy that may involve trades among the interests of broad groupings of citizens; judges' strengths lie in resolving discrete controversies between individuals, in which one wins, another loses, and broad social adjustments are secondary to the outcome of their concrete dispute. That contrast was given later, influential expression by Professor Lon Fuller, who noted the difference between the 'bi-polar' disputes characterizing typical judicial action and the 'polycentric' controversies that characterize legislatures and the policy-making side of administrative action. The give-and-take resolutions typical of the latter are more readily achieved by meliorative than winner-take-all procedures and are less easily justified in terms of a system structured as rational analysis than one grounded in accommodation."

(3) *How has the Distinction Fared in the Courts?*

(a) O'Connor, J., speaking for the Court in MINNESOTA STATE BOARD FOR COMMUNITY COLLEGES v. KNIGHT, 465 U.S. 271, 283–287 (1984):

"The Constitution does not grant to members of the public generally a right to be heard by public bodies making decisions of policy. . . .

"Policymaking organs in our system of government have never operated under a constitutional constraint requiring them to afford every interested member of the public an opportunity to present testimony before any policy is adopted. Legislatures throughout the nation, including Congress, frequently enact bills on which no hearings have been held or on which testimony has been received from only a select group. Executive agencies likewise make policy decisions of widespread application without permitting unrestricted public testimony. Public officials at all levels of government daily make policy decisions based only on the advice they decide they need and choose to hear. To recognize a constitutional right to participate directly in government policymaking would work a revolution in existing government practices.

"Not least among the reasons for refusing to recognize such a right is the impossibility of its judicial definition and enforcement. Both federalism and separation-of-powers concerns would be implicated in the massive intrusion into state and federal policymaking that recognition of the claimed right would entail. Moreover, the pragmatic considerations identified by Justice Holmes in Bi–Metallic Investment Co. v. State Board of Equalization are as weighty today as they were in 1915. Government makes so many policy decisions affecting so many people that it would likely grind to a halt were policymaking constrained by constitutional requirements on whose voices must be heard. 'There must be a limit to individual argument in such matters if government is to go on.' Absent statutory restrictions, the state must be free to consult or not to consult whomever it pleases.

"However wise or practicable various levels of public participation in various kinds of policy decisions may be, this Court has never held, and nothing in the Constitution suggests it should hold, that government must provide for such participation. In Bi–Metallic the Court rejected due process as a source of an obligation to listen. Nothing in the First Amendment or in this Court's case law interpreting it suggests that the rights to speak, associate, and petition require government policymakers to listen or respond to individuals' communications on public issues. . . . No other constitutional provision has been advanced as a source of such a requirement. Nor, finally, can the structure of government established and approved by the Constitution provide the source. It is inherent in a republican form of government that direct public participation in government policymaking is limited. See The Federalist No. 10 (Madison). Disagreement with public policy and disapproval of officials' responsiveness, as Justice Holmes suggested in Bi–Metallic, is to be registered principally at the polls."

(b) In CONISTON CORP. v. VILLAGE OF HOFFMAN ESTATES, 844 F.2d 461, 468 (7th Cir.1988), owners of land claimed that the village's "Board of Trustees" (the governing body of the village) violated due process in refusing to approve a site plan for land development; the Board, operating under no set criteria, reached its decision in executive session and gave no statement of reasons. *Held:* "These complaints might have considerable force if the zoning decision had been adjudicative in nature, but it was not." Posner, J., further explained: "It is not labels that determine whether action is legislative or adjudicative. A legislature is not allowed to circumvent the due process clause by the facile expedient of announcing that the state's courts and administrative agencies are henceforth to be deemed legislative bodies even though nothing in their powers and procedures has changed. But neither is the legislature required to judicialize zoning, and perhaps it would not be well advised to do so. The decision whether and what kind of land uses to permit does not have the form of a judicial decision. The potential criteria and considerations are too open-ended and ill-defined. Granted, much modern adjudication has this character, but the difference is that even modern courts hesitate to treat the decision-making process as a wide-open search for the result that is just in light of all possible considerations of distributive and corrective justice, while legislatures are free to range widely over ethical and political considerations in deciding what regulations to impose on society. The decision to make a judgment legislative is perforce a decision not to use judicial procedures, since they are geared to the making of more circumscribed, more 'reasoned' judgments."

As to the fact that "[t]he class here is small," the court thought that in zoning matters that contention had been foreclosed by City of Eastlake v. Forest City Enterprises, Inc., 426 U.S. 668 (1976), "upholding the decision to submit a single landowner's zoning application to a referendum." 844 F.2d at 469.

(c) Coniston was reinforced in PRO-ECO, INC. v. BOARD OF COMM'RS OF JAY COUNTY, IND. 57 F.3d 505, 513 (7th Cir.1995). Pro–Eco sought damages for the frustration of its wish to operate a land fill by a local moratorium ordinance. "The Board is an elected body that acted legislatively in enacting the moratorium. It did not deny Pro–Eco a permit or variance; rather, it enacted a generally applicable ordinance. Governing bodies may enact generally applicable laws, that is, they may legislate, without affording affected parties so much as notice and an opportunity to be heard. Bi–Metallic. 'The fact that a statute (or statute-like regulation) applies across the board provides a substitute safeguard.' Philly's v. Byrne, 732 F.2d 87, 92 (7th Cir.1984). It is likely, as Pro–Eco asserts, that the Board acted specifically because it saw Pro–Eco's landfill coming, and we have noted that 'more [process] may be required . . . where the legislation affects only a tiny class of people—maybe a class with only one member.' Philly's, 732 F.2d at 93. The Supreme Court, however, has held that even the functional equivalent of a petition for a variance may be put to a referendum. City of Eastlake v. Forest City Enters., Inc., 426 U.S. 668, 679 (1976). We do not believe that generally applicable prophylactic legislation provoked by the fear of one particular actor converts an elected body's legislative act into a quasi-judicial or administrative act that would require more process. . . . But we need not decide how little process the Board could have given here; Pro–Eco admits that it knew of the public hearing the Board held to discuss and adopt the moratorium and that a Pro–Eco representative attended that hearing. It does not allege, moreover, that its representative was denied an opportunity to speak. This is all 'that due process in zoning could possibly be thought to require. . . .' Coniston Corp. v. Village of Hoffman Estates, 844 F.2d 461, 469 (7th Cir.1988)."

NOTES ON PROCEDURES' ENDS AND MEANS

(1) *By What Standards Ought Procedures Be Assessed for Adequacy?* Precisely what procedures are required when the Constitution demands an individual hearing, is the question taken up in the Due Process chapter of these materials. Some instructors may choose to explore that chapter in tandem with this one. (Both, you will see, start off with Londoner—Bi-Metallic.) It nonetheless seems useful to continue here with an excerpt from ROGER C. CRAMTON, A COMMENT ON TRIAL-TYPE HEARINGS IN NUCLEAR POWER PLANT SITING, 58 Va.L.Rev. 585, 591–93 (1972), which asks more generally:

"What are the criteria for evaluating procedural systems?

"Procedures, for the most part, are a means to an end—the accomplishment of social purposes. But at the same time procedures in themselves may create or destroy important values. The usual statement of these values, in terms of 'fairness,' 'due process,' and the like suffers from undue generality, since the content of these value-laden words shifts from time to time and from person to person.

". . . We are reduced to a basic notion that in a society committed to a representative form of government, private persons should have a meaningful opportunity to participate in government decisions which directly affect them, especially when governmental action is based on individual rather than on general considerations.

"Beyond the fundamental principle of meaningful party participation, any evaluation of administrative procedures must rest on a judgment which balances the advantages and disadvantages of each procedural system. In striking this balance, I believe that the following formulation of competing considerations is more helpful than 'fairness' or 'due process': the extent to which the procedure furthers the accurate selection and determination of relevant facts and issues, the efficient disposition of business, and, when viewed in the light of the statutory objectives, its acceptability to the agency, the participants, and the general public.

"The first consideration, *accuracy,* serves as a short-hand reference to the rational aspects of a decision-making process. The ascertainment of truth, or, more realistically, as close an approximation of reality as human frailty permits, is a major goal of most decision-making. There are better and worse ways, in various contexts, of gathering relevant information, selecting or formulating controlling principles, and applying the correct principles to the probable facts. Accuracy, moreover, is not only a facet of each case but an aggregative or system characteristic of uniform and consistent results that give equal treatment to similarly situated persons. Accurate results in a particular instance ('justice in the individual case') may be less important in many areas than a high degree of consistency in the decision of a large number of cases.

"The second consideration, *efficiency,* emphasizes the time, effort, and expense of elaborate procedures. The work of the world must go on, and endless nit-picking, while it may produce a more nearly ideal solution, imposes huge costs and impairs other important values. In the polycentric administrative case, the efficiency of trial procedures meets the severest test. This criterion, unlike the others, is capable of quantitative statement since time and effort may usually be stated in dollar terms. Concern with public costs and expenditures must not be allowed to obscure the fact that the private costs of administrative delay are usually far higher than the total of governmental costs.

"The final consideration, *acceptability,* emphasizes the indispensable virtues of procedures that are considered fair by those whom they affect, as well as by the general public. Usually this translates into meaningful participation in the decisional process. The authority of decisions in a society resting on the consent of the governed is based on their general acceptability."

(2) *Are Such Standards Simply Lacking for "Legislative" Action?* PETER M. SHANE, BACK TO THE FUTURE OF THE AMERICAN STATE: OVERRULING BUCKLEY V. VALEO AND OTHER MADISONIAN STEPS, 57 U.Pitt.L.Rev. 443, 455 (1996): "Under the current state of due process law, the Due Process Clauses exercise no procedural leverage over legislative deliberations. Under the relevant precedents, it is black-letter judicial interpretation that procedural due process attaches only to the government's adjudicatory processes and not to legislative-style decision making, even when conducted by an administrative agency. . . . But such a reading of the Due Process Clauses seems facially wrong. A proper analysis should begin with the proposition that limiting the reach of procedural due process to adjudication does not accord with the Constitution's text. The point seems self-evident because the Due Process Clauses are routinely applied to the legislature in substantive due process cases. The question then ought to be posed whether legislative decisions that affect the rights and responsibilities of persons outside Congress deny liberty arbitrarily if such decisions are made under conditions in which no attention is given to the rudiments of sound decision-making procedure." See also Hans A. Linde, Due Process of Lawmaking, 55 Neb. L. Rev. 197 (1976).

(3) The distinction between making a rule and adjudicating a case is one of the most basic in all of jurisprudence. Here are some materials that bear on the question of how the distinction is, as a general matter, to be drawn, and on the difficulties in doing so:

(a) *The element of prospectivity:*

(i) Holmes, J., in Prentis v. Atlantic Coast Line Co., 211 U.S. 210, 226 (1908):

"A judicial inquiry investigates, declares and enforces liabilities as they stand on present or past facts and under laws supposed already to exist. That is its purpose and end. Legislation on the other hand looks to the future and changes existing conditions by making a new rule to be applied thereafter to all or some part of those subject to its power. The establishment of a rate is the making of a rule for the future, and therefore is an act legislative not judicial in kind."

(ii) Frederick Schauer, A Brief Note on the Logic Of Rules, with Special Reference to *Bowen v. Georgetown University Hospital*, 42 Admin.L.Rev. 447, 454 (1990):

"[N]othing ... in the necessity of drawing some ... distinction, suggests one answer or another to the question of when 'the future' starts. Some decisions will pertain to a certain narrow temporal time frame, and these will be the 'orders,' and others will pertain to an open-ended time frame, and these are the 'rules,' but *that* distinction has nothing to do with when that time frame is or starts and nothing to do with the relationship between the time frame and the time of the making of the decision.

"To put the same point differently (and perhaps slightly more clearly), we are now able to appreciate that the creation of an open-ended rule and the designation of the starting time for the open-ended period encompassed by that rule are two distinct issues."

(b) *The element of generality:*

(i) Ralph F. Fuchs, Procedure in Administrative Rule–Making, 52 Harv.L.Rev. 259, 263–64 (1938):

"The most obvious definition of rule-making and the one most often employed in the literature of administrative law asserts simply that it is the function of laying down general regulations as distinguished from orders that apply to named persons or to specific situations. Most acts of legislatures, although by no means all, establish rights and duties with respect either to people generally or to classes of people or situations that are defined but not enumerated. Conversely, the judgments of courts usually are addressed to particular individuals or to situations that are definitely specified. Similarly, administrative action can be classified into general regulations, including determinations whose effect is to bring general regulations into operation, and orders or acts of specific application.

" ... [I]t is feasible to distinguish a general regulation from an order of specific application on the basis of the manner in which the parties subject to it are designated. If they are named, or if they are in effect identified by their relation to a piece of property or transaction or institution which is specified, the order is one of specific application. If they are not named, but the order applies to a designated class of persons or situations, the order is a general regulation or a rule."

(ii) John Dickinson, Administrative Justice and the Supremacy of Law 17–20 (1927):

"Our constitutional distinction between 'legislative,' 'executive' and 'judicial' powers draws the courts frequently into discussions in which the 'legislative' or 'executive' aspect of an administrative act is generally emphasized at the expense of the 'judicial.' Thus, for example, the act of a public-utilities commission in fixing a rate has been held to be 'legislative' for constitutional purposes.

"From one aspect of juristic analysis, legislative it no doubt is—that is, from the aspect of its future operation and its applicability to a whole class of cases. But the writ of mandamus is future in its operation, and yet is not for that reason regarded as legislative; and if we examine rate-fixing from the standpoint of the general applicability of the resulting rate to an indefinite number of future cases as a class, we observe the significant peculiarity that, while the rate applies indifferently, indeed, as against all future shippers, it applies only to the particular carrier or carriers who were parties to the hearing and other proceedings before the commission, and for whom, as the outcome of those proceedings, the rate is prescribed. From the standpoint of shippers, therefore, the rate may no doubt be regarded as legislation, but from the standpoint of the carriers it seems quite as truly adjudication. Even with respect to the shippers, however, it may be likened to the procedure whereby an injunction is obtained against a group of persons designated by a class-description and not named personally in the bill. If the latter procedure is judicial, there is certainly an element of adjudication in administrative rate-fixing; and that is all I wish to insist on here. There is no intention to deny that rate-fixing involves as one of its elements the exercise of a function which may as well as not be called 'legislative.' The whole discussion should go to demonstrate the futility of trying to classify a particular exercise of administrative power as either wholly legislative or wholly judicial. The tendency of the administrative procedure is to foreshorten both functions into a continuous governmental act."

(c) *The element of "the rule of law":*

(i) Friedrich A. Hayek, The Constitution of Liberty 153–54 (1960):

"The conception of freedom under the law that is the chief concern of this book rests on the contention that when we obey laws, in the sense of general abstract rules laid down irrespective of their application to us, we are not subject to another man's will and are therefore free. It is because the lawgiver does not know the particular cases to which his rules will apply, and it is because the judge who applies them has no choice in drawing the conclusions that follow from the existing body of rules and the particular facts of the case, that it can be said that laws and not men rule. Because the rule is laid down in ignorance of the particular case and no man's will decides the coercion used to enforce it, the law is not arbitrary. This, however, is true only if by 'law' we mean the general rules that apply equally to everybody. This generality is probably the most important aspect of that attribute of law which we have called its 'abstractness.' As a true law should not name any particulars, so it should especially not single out any specific persons or group of persons."

(ii) Roberto M. Unger, Knowledge and Politics 89–90 (1975)[1]:

"To understand the nature of adjudication one must distinguish two different ways of ordering human relations. One way is to establish rules to govern general categories of acts and persons, and then to decide particular disputes among persons on the basis of the established rules. This is legal justice. The other way is to determine goals and then, quite independently of rules, to decide particular cases by a judgment of what decision is most likely to contribute to the predetermined goals, a judgment of instrumental rationality. This is substantive justice.

"In the situation of legal justice, the laws are made against the background of the ends they are designed to promote, even if the sole permissible end is liberty itself. Only after the rules have been formulated do decisions 'under the rules' become possible. Hence, the possibility of some sort of distinction between legislation and adjudication is precisely what defines legal justice. The main task of the theory of adjudication is to say when a decision can truly be said to stand 'under a rule,' if the rule we have in mind is the law of the state, applied by a judge. Only decisions 'under a rule' are consistent with freedom; others constitute arbitrary exercises of judicial power.

"Decisions made under rules must be capable of a kind of justification different from the justification for the rules themselves. The task of judging is distinct from that of lawmaking. Usually, the separation of functions will be accompanied and strengthened by a separation of powers: the person of the lawmaker will not be the same as the person of the law applier. . . .

"There are legal systems in which the line between legislation and adjudication is hazy from the start. This is especially true in a tradition of judge-made law like the Anglo–American common law. A system in which judges both make the law and apply it is not self-evidently inconsistent with a situation of legal justice as long as some screen can be interposed between reasons for having a rule and reasons for applying it to a particular case. . . .

"In substantive justice each decision is justified because it is the one best calculated to advance some accepted objective. The relation between a particular decision and the objective is that of a means to an end. For example, given the goal of increasing national production, a certain bargain should be enforced because its performance will increase output.

"The distinctive feature of substantive justice is the nonexistence of any line between legislation and adjudication. In the pure case of substantive justice, there is neither rulemaking nor rule applying, because rather than prescriptive rules there are only choices as to what should be accomplished and judgments of instrumental rationality about how to get it done."

b. THE FUNDAMENTAL STATUTE

ADMINISTRATIVE PROCEDURE ACT OF 1946[1]

§ 551 Definitions ...

(4) "rule" means the whole or a part of an agency statement of general or particular applicability and future effect designed to implement, interpret, or prescribe law or policy or describing the organization, procedure, or practice requirements of an agency and includes the approval or prescription for the future of rates, wages, corporate or financial structures or reorganization thereof, prices, facilities, appliances, services or allowances therefor or of valuations, costs, or accounting, or practices bearing on any of the foregoing;

(5) "rule making" means agency process for formulating, amending, or repealing a rule;

(6) "order" means the whole or a part of a final disposition, whether affirmative, negative, injunctive, or declaratory in form, of an agency in a matter other than rule making but including licensing;

(7) "adjudication" means agency process for the formulation of an order.

NOTES

(1) Provisions in the APA are sometimes referred to by the section numbers used in the Act itself (which appear in the right hand column in the Appendix, below) and sometimes by the sections numbers used in the codification of the Act in Title 5 of the United States Code (which appear as the regular section numbers in the Appendix). The latter form, generally used in this book, is more commonly used in judicial opinions.

(2) Note that the APA's definitions render *every* agency "final disposition, whether affirmative, negative, injunctive, or declaratory in form" *either* a rule *or* an order. The latter—i.e., the products of "adjudications"—is the residual category. The difficulties presented by the definition of "rule" are best explored in Chapter V, on rulemaking. Here, observe that the definition sections give two concrete examples of their application: The definition of an "order" includes "licensing"; and the definition of a "rule" includes "the approval or prescription for the future of rates, wages, corporate or financial structures or reorganization thereof, prices, facilities, appliances, services or allowances therefor or of valuations, costs, or accounting, or practices." Both of these activities are somewhat ambiguous in Londoner— Bi–Metallic terms; each typically involves particular applicants whose individual facts will be central to decision, on one side, and broadly diverse community interests and more social (polycentric) issues of fact on the other.

(3) The APA also distinguishes between formal and informal versions of both rulemaking and adjudication. This is done not by means of additional definitions, but rather by making those sections of the Act which define

---

1. The full text of the APA appears in the Appendix, at p. 1321 ff. below.

formal hearings (§§ 556 and 557) applicable only to certain proceedings: proceedings required to be "on the record." Thus, we find within § 553, "Rule making," that an informal procedure is defined in § 553(c), but that the subsection ends by saying: "When rules are required by statute to be made on the record after opportunity for an agency hearing, sections 556 and 557 of this title apply instead of this subsection." Rate-making proceedings, defined as rulemaking, are the most common form for which such requirements appear. As to adjudication, § 554, "Adjudications," starts right off by saying that it only applies "in every case of adjudication required by statute to be determined on the record after opportunity for an agency hearing"; later on, in § 554(c)(2), we find adjudications referred over for "hearing and decision on notice and in accordance with sections 556 and 557 of this title." For adjudications that are *not* "required by statute to be determined on the record after opportunity for an agency hearing," the only arguably applicable provision of the APA is § 555(e), requiring prompt notice of denials of requests, "accompanied by a brief statement of the grounds for denial" unless the denial is self-explanatory or in affirmation of a previous denial.

(4) When the statute was new, the Yale Law Journal published a chart of its basic structure. (The Federal Administrative Procedure Act: Codification or Reform, 56 Yale L.J. 670, 705 (1947).) With the thought that what was helpful to practitioners when the statute was first passed will also be helpful to students making their first pass at the statute, here (with slight modifications) is that chart:[1]

CHART OF ADMINISTRATIVE PROCEDURE ACT

	Rule Making	**Adjudication**
Informal	All: publication—sec. 552(a)(1); petitions to alter rules—sec. 553(e). Substantive only: notice, participation, statement of "basis and purpose," 30-day delay between publication and taking effect—sec. 553.	
Formal	Notice—section 553(b); hearing—sec. 556; intermediate and final decision—sec. 557; 30-day delay between publication and taking effect—sec. 553(d); publication—sec. 552(a)(1); petitions to alter rules—sec. 553(e).	Notice, informal settlement; separation of functions—sec. 554; hearing—sec. 556; intermediate and final decision—sec. 557; declaratory orders—section 554(e).

Needless to say, the statute in its entirety is more complex; this chart represents the beginning, not the end, of the matter. In particular, note

1. Provisions relating to administrative law judges have been omitted.

that even though licensing is explicitly mentioned in the general definition of adjudication, various portions of §§ 554(d), 556(d) and 557(b) make special provisions for initial licensing, the application process. So does § 558 of the Act. Similarly, ratemaking (explicitly made a part of the general definition of rulemaking) gets special treatment as a type of formal rulemaking—and is even mentioned in § 554(d), a provision about "adjudication." On working through these procedural variations, you would discover that they are roughly equivalent, and create for *both* that kind of "adjudication" that is action on an initial license application *and* that kind of "rulemaking" that is ratemaking a formal procedure of somewhat lesser intensity than ordinary on-the-record adjudication. In this concrete way, the Act's provisions accommodate the ambiguities of both the definitional sections and the constitutional test.

As remarked above, it is not so clear that the Act has nothing to say about informal adjudication; § 555 is discussed at p. 470 within.

Wong Yang Sung v. McGrath

Supreme Court of the United States, 1950.
339 U.S. 33.

■ MR. JUSTICE JACKSON delivered the opinion of the Court.

This habeas corpus proceeding involves a single ultimate question—whether administrative hearings in deportation cases must conform to requirements of the Administrative Procedure Act of June 11, 1946.

Wong Yang Sung, native and citizen of China, was arrested by immigration officials on a charge of being unlawfully in the United States through having overstayed shore leave as one of a shipping crew. A hearing was held before an immigrant inspector who recommended deportation. The Acting Commissioner approved; and the Board of Immigration Appeals affirmed.

Wong Yang Sung then sought release from custody by habeas corpus proceedings in District Court for the District of Columbia, upon the sole ground that the administrative hearing was not conducted in conformity with §§ 5 and 11 of the Administrative Procedure Act.[1] The Government

---

1. Particularly invoked are § 5(c), [now codified as 5 U.S.C. § 554(d)] which provides in part:

> The same officers who preside at the reception of evidence pursuant to section 7 shall make the recommended decision or initial decision required by section 8 except where such officers become unavailable to the agency. Save to the extent required for the disposition of ex parte matters as authorized by law, no such officer shall consult any person or party on any fact in issue unless upon notice and opportunity for all parties to participate; nor shall such officer be responsible to or subject to the supervision

or direction of any officer, employee, or agent engaged in the performance of investigative or prosecuting functions for any agency. No officer, employee, or agent engaged in the performance of investigative or prosecuting functions for any agency in any case shall, in that or a factually related case, participate or advise in the decision, recommended decision, or agency review pursuant to section 8 except as witness or counsel in public proceedings....;

and § 11, which provides in part:

> Subject to the civil-service and other laws to the extent not inconsistent with

admitted noncompliance, but asserted that the Act did not apply. The court, after hearing, discharged the writ and remanded the prisoner to custody, holding the Administrative Procedure Act inapplicable to deportation hearings. The Court of Appeals affirmed. 174 F.2d 158. Prisoner's petition for certiorari was not opposed by the Government and, because the question presented has obvious importance in the administration of the immigration laws, we granted review.

I

The Administrative Procedure Act of June 11, 1946, supra, is a new, basic and comprehensive regulation of procedures in many agencies, more than a few of which can advance arguments that its generalities should not or do not include them. Determination of questions of its coverage may well be approached through consideration of its purposes as disclosed by its background.

Multiplication of federal administrative agencies and expansion of their functions to include adjudications which have serious impact on private rights has been one of the dramatic legal developments of the past half-century. Partly from restriction by statute, partly from judicial self-restraint, and partly by necessity—from the nature of their multitudinous and semi-legislative or executive tasks—the decisions of administrative tribunals were accorded considerable finality, and especially with respect to fact finding. The conviction developed, particularly within the legal profession, that this power was not sufficiently safeguarded and sometimes was put to arbitrary and biased use.

Concern over administrative impartiality and response to growing discontent was reflected in Congress as early as 1929, when Senator Norris introduced a bill to create a separate administrative court. Fears and dissatisfactions increased as tribunals grew in number and jurisdiction, and a succession of bills offering various remedies appeared in Congress. Inquiries into the practices of state agencies, which tended to parallel or follow the federal pattern, were instituted in several states, and some studies noteworthy for thoroughness, impartiality and vision resulted.

The Executive Branch of the Federal Government also became concerned as to whether the structure and procedure of these bodies was conducive to fairness in the administrative process. President Roosevelt's

---

this Act, there shall be appointed by and for each agency as many qualified and competent examiners as may be necessary for proceedings pursuant to sections 7 and 8, who shall be assigned to cases in rotation so far as practicable and shall perform no duties inconsistent with their duties and responsibilities as examiners. Examiners shall be removable by the agency in which they are employed only for good cause established and determined by the Civil Service Commission (hereinafter called the Commission) after opportunity for hearing and upon the record thereof. Examiners shall receive compensation prescribed by the Commission independently of agency recommendations or ratings and in accordance with the Classification Act of 1923, as amended, except that the provisions of paragraphs (2) and (3) of subsection (b) of section 7 of said Act, as amended, and the provisions of section 9 of said Act amended, shall not be applicable.

[Ed.—These sentences of Section amended, are now codified §§ 3105 (first sentence), 7 tence), and 5372 (third s

Committee on Administrative Management in 1937 recommended complete separation of adjudicating functions and personnel from those having to do with investigation or prosecution. The President early in 1939 also directed the Attorney General to name "a committee of eminent lawyers, jurists, scholars, and administrators to review the entire administrative process in the various departments of the executive Government and to recommend improvements, including the suggestion of any needed legislation."

So strong was the demand for reform, however, that Congress did not await the Committee's report but passed what was known as the Walter–Logan bill, a comprehensive and rigid prescription of standardized procedures for administrative agencies. This bill was vetoed by President Roosevelt December 18, 1940, and the veto was sustained by the House. But the President's veto message made no denial of the need for reform. Rather it pointed out that the task of the Committee, whose objective was "to suggest improvements to make the process more workable and more just," had proved "unexpectedly complex." The President said, "I should desire to await their report and recommendations before approving any measure in this complicated field."

The committee divided in its views and both the majority and the minority submitted bills which were introduced in 1941. A subcommittee of the Senate Judiciary Committee held exhaustive hearings on three proposed measures, but, before the gathering storm of national emergency and war, consideration of the problem was put aside. Though bills on the subject reappeared in 1944, they did not attract much attention.

The McCarran–Sumners bill, which evolved into the present Act, was introduced in 1945. Its consideration and hearing, especially of agency interests, was painstaking. All administrative agencies were invited to submit their views in writing. A tentative revised bill was then prepared and interested parties again were invited to submit criticisms. The Attorney General named representatives of the Department of Justice to canvass the agencies and report their criticisms, and submitted a favorable report on the bill as finally revised. It passed both Houses without opposition and was signed by President Truman June 11, 1946.

The Act thus represents a long period of study and strife; it settles long-continued and hard-fought contentions, and enacts a formula upon which opposing social and political forces have come to rest. It contains many compromises and generalities and, no doubt, some ambiguities. Experience may reveal defects. But it would be a disservice to our form of government and to the administrative process itself if the courts should fail, so far as the terms of the Act warrant, to give effect to its remedial purposes where the evils it was aimed at appear.

II

Of the several administrative evils sought to be cured or minimized, only two are particularly relevant to issues before us today. One purpose was to introduce greater uniformity of procedure and standardization of administrative practice among the diverse agencies whose customs had ⁀arted widely from each other. We pursue this no further than to note that any exception we may find to its applicability would tend to defeat this purpose.

More fundamental, however, was the purpose to curtail and change the practice of embodying in one person or agency the duties of prosecutor and judge. The President's Committee on Administrative Management voiced in 1937 the theme which, with variations in language, was reiterated throughout the legislative history of the Act. The Committee's report, which President Roosevelt transmitted to Congress with his approval as "a great document of permanent importance," said:

> ... the independent commission is obliged to carry on judicial functions under conditions which threaten the impartial performance of that judicial work. The discretionary work of the administrator is merged with that of the judge. Pressures and influences properly enough directed toward officers responsible for formulating and administering policy constitute an unwholesome atmosphere in which to adjudicate private rights. But the mixed duties of the commissions render escape from these subversive influences impossible.
>
> Furthermore, the same men are obliged to serve both as prosecutors and as judges. This not only undermines judicial fairness; it weakens public confidence in that fairness. Commission decisions affecting private rights and conduct lie under the suspicion of being rationalizations of the preliminary findings which the commission, in the role of prosecutor, presented to itself. Administrative Management in the Government of the United States, Report of the President's Committee on Administrative Management, 36–37 (1937).

The Committee therefore recommended a redistribution of functions within the regulatory agencies. "It would be divided into an administrative section and a judicial section" and the administrative section "would formulate rules, initiate action, investigate complaints . . ." and the judicial section "would sit as an impartial, independent body to make decisions affecting the public interest and private rights upon the basis of the records and findings presented to it by the administrative section." Id. at 37.

Another study was made by a distinguished committee named by the Secretary of Labor, whose jurisdiction at the time included the Immigration and Naturalization Service. Some of the committee's observations have relevancy to the procedure under examination here. It said:

> The inspector who presides over the formal hearing is in many respects comparable to a trial judge. He has, at a minimum, the function of determining—subject to objection on the alien's behalf—what goes into the written record upon which decision ultimately is to be based. Under the existing practice he has also the function of counsel representing the moving party—he does not merely admit evidence against the alien; he has the responsibility of seeing that such evidence is put into the record. The precise scope of his appropriate functions is the first question to be considered. The Secretary of Labor's Committee on Administrative Procedure, The Immigration and Naturalization Service, 77 (Mimeo. 1940).

Further:

Merely to provide that in particular cases different inspectors shall investigate and hear is an insufficient guarantee of insulation and independence of the presiding official. The present organization of the field staff not only gives work of both kinds commonly to the same inspector but tends toward an identity of viewpoint as between inspectors who are chiefly doing only one or the other kind of work....

... We recommend that the presiding inspectors be relieved of their present duties of presenting the case against aliens and be confirmed [sic] entirely to the duties customary for a judge. This, of course, would require the assignment of another officer to perform the task of a prosecuting attorney. The appropriate officer for this purpose would seem to be the investigating inspector who, having prepared the case against the alien, is already thoroughly familiar with it....

A genuinely impartial hearing, conducted with critical detachment, is psychologically improbable if not impossible, when the presiding officer has at once the responsibility of appraising the strength of the case and of seeking to make it as strong as possible. Nor is complete divorce between investigation and hearing possible so long as the presiding inspector has the duty himself of assembling and presenting the results of the investigation.... Id. at 81–82.

And the Attorney General's Committee on Administrative Procedure, which divided as to the appropriate remedy, was unanimous that this evil existed. Its Final Report said:

These types of commingling of functions of investigation or advocacy with the function of deciding are thus plainly undesirable. But they are also avoidable and should be avoided by appropriate internal division of labor. For the disqualifications produced by investigation or advocacy are personal psychological ones which result from engaging in those types of activity; and the problem is simply one of isolating those who engage in the activity. Creation of independent hearing commissioners insulated from all phases of a case other than hearing and deciding will, the Committee believes, go far toward solving this problem at the level of the initial hearing provided the proper safeguards are established to assure the insulation.... Rep. Atty. Gen. Comm. Ad. Proc. 56 (1941), S. Doc. No. 8, 77th Cong., 1st Sess. 56 (1941).

The Act before us adopts in general this recommended form of remedial action. A minority of the Committee had, furthermore, urged an even more thoroughgoing separation and supported it with a cogent report. Id. at 203 et seq.

Such were the evils found by disinterested and competent students. Such were the facts before Congress which gave impetus to the demand for the reform which this Act was intended to accomplish. It is the plain duty of the courts, regardless of their views of the wisdom or policy of the Act, to construe this remedial legislation to eliminate, so far as its text permits, the practices it condemns.

III

Turning now to the case before us, we find the administrative hearing a perfect exemplification of the practices so unanimously condemned.

This hearing, which followed the uniform practice of the Immigration Service, was before an immigrant inspector, who, for purposes of the hearing, is called the "presiding inspector." Except with consent of the alien, the presiding inspector may not be the one who investigated the case. 8 C.F.R. 150.6(b). But the inspector's duties include investigation of like cases; and while he is today hearing cases investigated by a colleague, tomorrow his investigation of a case may be heard before the [examining] inspector whose case he passes on today. . . . The presiding inspector, when no examining inspector is present, is required to "conduct the interrogation of the alien and the witnesses in behalf of the Government and shall cross-examine the alien's witnesses and present such evidence as is necessary to support the charges in the warrant of arrest." 8 C.F.R. 150.6(b). It may even become his duty to lodge an additional charge against the alien and proceed to hear his own accusation in like manner. 8 C.F.R.150.6(l). Then, as soon as practicable, he is to prepare a summary of the evidence, proposed findings of fact, conclusions of law, and a proposed order. A copy is furnished the alien or his counsel, who may file exceptions and brief, 8 C.F.R. 150.7, whereupon the whole is forwarded to the Commissioner. 8 C.F.R. 150.9.

The Administrative Procedure Act did not go so far as to require a complete separation of investigating and prosecuting functions from adjudicating functions. But that the safeguards it did set up were intended to ameliorate the evils from the commingling of functions as exemplified here is beyond doubt. And this commingling, if objectionable anywhere, would seem to be particularly so in the deportation proceeding, where we frequently meet with a voteless class of litigants who not only lack the influence of citizens, but who are strangers to the laws and customs in which they find themselves involved and who often do not even understand the tongue in which they are accused. Nothing in the nature of the parties or proceedings suggests that we should strain to exempt deportation proceedings from reforms in administrative procedure applicable generally to federal agencies.

Nor can we accord any weight to the argument that to apply the Act to such hearings will cause inconvenience and added expense to the Immigration Service. Of course it will, as it will to nearly every agency to which it is applied. But the power of the purse belongs to Congress, and Congress has determined that the price for greater fairness is not too high. The agencies, unlike the aliens, have ready and persuasive access to the legislative ear and if error is made by including them, relief from Congress is a simple matter. . . .

We come, then, to examination of the text of the Act to determine whether the Government is right in its contentions: first, that the general scope of § 5 of the Act[, 5 U.S.C. § 554] does not cover deportation proceedings; and, second, that even if it does, the proceedings are excluded from the requirements of the Act by virtue of § 7[, 5 U.S.C. § 556].

IV.

The Administrative Procedure Act establishes a number of formal requirements to be applicable "In every case of adjudication required by statute to be determined on the record after opportunity for an agency hearing." The argument here depends upon the words "adjudication required by statute." The Government contends that there is no express requirement for any hearing or adjudication in the statute authorizing deportation, and that this omission shields these proceedings from the impact of § [554]. Petitioner, on the other hand, contends that deportation hearings, though not expressly required by statute, are required under the decisions of this Court, and the proceedings, therefore, are within the scope of § [554].

Both parties invoke many citations to legislative history as to the meaning given to these key words by the framers, advocates or opponents of the Administrative Procedure Act. Because § [554] in the original bill applied to hearings required "by law," because it was suggested by the Attorney General that it should be changed to "required by statute or Constitution," and because it finally emerged "required by statute," the Government argues that the section is intended to apply only when explicit statutory words granting a right to adjudication can be pointed out. Petitioner on the other hand cites references which would indicate that the limitation to statutory hearing was merely to avoid creating by inference a new right to hearings where no right existed otherwise. We do not know. The legislative history is more conflicting than the text is ambiguous.

But the difficulty with any argument premised on the proposition that the deportation statute does not require a hearing is that, without such hearing, there would be no constitutional authority for deportation. The constitutional requirement of procedural due process of law derives from the same source as Congress' power to legislate and, where applicable, permeates every valid enactment of that body. It was under compulsion of the Constitution that this Court long ago held that an antecedent deportation statute must provide a hearing at least for aliens who had not entered clandestinely and who had been here some time even if illegally. ...

We think that the limitation to hearings "required by statute" ... exempts from that section's application only those hearings which administrative agencies may hold by regulation, rule, custom, or special dispensation; not those held by compulsion.... They exempt hearings of less than statutory authority, not those of more than statutory authority. We would hardly attribute to Congress a purpose to be less scrupulous about the fairness of a hearing necessitated by the Constitution than one granted by it as a matter of expediency.

Indeed, to so construe the Immigration Act might again bring it into constitutional jeopardy. When the Constitution requires a hearing, it requires a fair one, one before a tribunal which meets at least currently prevailing standards of impartiality. A deportation hearing involves issues basic to human liberty and happiness and, in the present upheavals in lands to which aliens may be returned, perhaps to life itself. It might be difficult to justify as measuring up to constitutional standards of impartiality a hearing tribunal for deportation proceedings the like of which has been condemned by Congress as unfair even where less vital matters of property rights are at stake.

We hold that the Administrative Procedure Act, § [554], does cover deportation proceedings conducted by the Immigration Service.

V.

The remaining question is whether the exception of § [556(b)] of the Administrative Procedure Act [for specified classes of proceedings conducted "in whole or in part, by or before boards or other employees specially provided for by or designated under statute"] exempts deportation hearings held before immigrant inspectors. [The Court concluded that it did not.] Reversed.

■ MR. JUSTICE DOUGLAS and MR. JUSTICE CLARK took no part in the consideration or decision of this case.

■ MR. JUSTICE REED, dissenting, in an opinion here omitted, concluded that § 556(b) had exempted these proceedings from the Act.

NOTES

(1) The Court's confidence about Congress' purposes was apparently misplaced, for the specific holding of Wong Yang Sung was promptly reversed by legislation, and that reversal was subsequently upheld against constitutional challenge. See Marcello v. Bonds, 349 U.S. 302 (1955). Wong Yang Sung continues to be cited for the general proposition that aliens have due process rights in deportation hearings, but in federal due process cases today the APA is rarely cited. Giving concrete content to due process rights requires the Supreme Court and lower federal courts to say what procedures fairness requires for hearings necessitated by the Constitution, the analysis addressed in Chapter VII below. Today, these inquiries are made without relying on the APA as if it embodied Congress's assessment of the procedures required by the Constitution.

Wong Yang Sung's holding may survive in at least one respect. Under the Equal Access to Justice Act, "an agency that conducts an adversary adjudication" is to award counsel's fees to a prevailing private party unless the agency's position was "substantially justified" or the award would be "unjust." 5 U.S.C. § 504(a)(1). "An adversary adjudication" is relevantly defined as one occurring under APA § 554, so long as the government is represented by counsel or otherwise. In COLLORD V. DEPARTMENT OF THE INTERIOR, 154 F.3d 933, 936–37 (9th Cir.1998), mining claim holders prevailed in departmental adjudications of the validity of their mining claims under the General Mining Law of 1872. That statute does not itself require on-the-record hearings in such matters, but six years after the decision in Wong Yang Sung, the Department of the Interior had decided that due process required on-the-record hearings and that, therefore, under Wong Yang Sung, the APA governed. United States v. Keith O'Leary, 63 I.D. 341 (1956). This was enough for the Ninth Circuit. "Because the mining claim contest proceeding before us is governed by § 554, it is an 'adversary adjudication' under the natural reading of the words 'under section 554' in the EAJA. . . ." Reaching this result, however, required the court to distinguish a Supreme Court decision that had refused to apply the EAJA in an immigration context where due process required a hearing, the Marcello v.

Bonds situation. Ardestani v. Immigration and Naturalization Service, 502 U.S. 129 (1991).[1] For the Ninth Circuit, the distinction was that the statute overruling Wong Yang Sung had "'expressly superseded' the hearing provisions of the APA," citing 502 U.S. at 133; no alternative statutory procedures existed in this case. Should, then, the overruling be taken broadly, or limited to the immigration context, where Congress has supplied a fully articulated alternative procedure? The Ninth Circuit acknowledged that due process analysis now generally ignores the APA as a source of procedure, but refused to take this development as "undermin[ing]" its approach.

(2) A more contemporary account of the APA's genesis appears in Robert L. Rabin's "Federal Regulation in Historical Perspective," which you may have read at pp. 13–23 above. Here are two other brief excerpts, from articles written at about the time of its fortieth birthday:

(a) CASS SUNSTEIN, CONSTITUTIONALISM AFTER THE NEW DEAL, 101 Harv. L.Rev. 421, 446–48 (1987): "At least since the 1940's, many observers have invoked the traditional concerns underlying the distribution of national powers to challenge the role and performance of administrative agencies. . . .

"The first problem is that the New Deal agency combines executive, judicial, and legislative functions. To some degree, organic statutes and the APA attempt to separate these activities, but these measures have not produced a system that even remotely resembles the constitutional system of checks and balances. There is little competition among the different administrative functionaries within agencies, with 'ambition' operating to 'check ambition.' More often, the administrators are expected and believed to act in concert; indeed, that expectation was one of the reasons for the creation of the agency. What the New Deal administrators celebrated as a virtue—the combination of functions—is now often regarded as a vice, precisely because it causes some of the problems that gave rise to the original distribution of national powers.

"The second problem is that agency actors lack electoral accountability and often are not responsive to the public as a whole. Because of the absence of the usual electoral safeguards, agencies are peculiarly susceptible to factional pressure and often likely to act in their own interests. The New Deal conception of administration celebrated the rejection of these traditional concerns. Indeed, the repudiation of the system of separation and of checks and balances was a central feature of the New Deal reformation. By creating a new set of autonomous administrative actors, the New Deal critics sought to bypass the common law courts and, occasionally, the legislative process, both of which seemed to have fallen prey to factional control. But by evading the traditional safeguards, the New Deal reformers heightened the potential for abuses that the traditional system was designed to check.

"The initial reaction of the courts to these sorts of attack was predictable: they invalidated statutes creating agencies on constitutional grounds, invoking articles I, II, and III as well as the due process clause. The most

1. This case is briefly discussed at p. 333.

familiar example is Schechter Poultry Corp. v. United States [295 U.S. 495 (1935)] ... The constitutional assault eventually disintegrated in the face of prolonged and persistent popular support of regulatory administration. Taken as a whole, the process altered the constitutional system in ways so fundamental as to suggest that something akin to a constitutional amendment had taken place.

"After the constitutional challenge was rebuffed, the struggle between the advocates and the critics of New Deal administration resurfaced in the debate over the APA. During that debate, the Progressive critics of the common law sought administrative autonomy, while their opponents invoked pre-New Deal understandings of private liberty and of checks and balances in arguing for severe legal constraints on administrative agencies."

(b) MARTIN SHAPIRO, APA: PAST, PRESENT, FUTURE, 72 Va.L.Rev. 447, 452–454 (1986): "Turning to the APA itself, ... most ... contributors to this symposium rightly characterize it as a deal struck between opposing political forces. One should consider, however, who struck the deal and what its terms were. The battle of the thirties was between Republicans and conservative Democrats on the one hand and New Deal Democrats on the other, at a time when the New Deal consensus was not yet dominant in American politics. Consequently, the New Dealers were loath to compromise and loath to allow congressional initiatives against the president. ...

"By 1946, the New Deal consensus was absolutely and unassailably established, so the battle was by then really an internal one among New Dealers—between conservative and liberal Democrats, both of whom were firmly harnessed to the New Deal vision of the administrative state. At this point, the liberal New Dealers could afford to compromise in a statute that no longer appeared to threaten the strong presidency. . . .

"The APA as originally enacted divided all administrative law into three parts. For matters requiring adjudication, in which government action was directly detrimental to the specific legal interests of particular parties, the compromise was heavily weighted in favor of the conservatives. The ... demand for totally separate tribunals was ignored: the agencies themselves adjudicated these matters. But the agencies' processes were to be considered quasi-adjudication and were to be governed by adjudicative-style procedures, presided over by a relatively independent hearing officer, and freely subject to relatively strict judicial review.

"The second part, rulemaking, constituted an almost total victory for the liberal New Deal forces. Congress' delegation of vast lawmaking power to the agencies was acknowledged and legitimated. Rulemaking was to be quasi-legislative, not quasi-judicial. No adjudicatory-style hearings or hearing officers were required. Those not directly and immediately affected by the rule could not easily obtain judicial review. Under the APA, rulemaking generated no record to be reviewed, and the standard of review made an agency's decisions irreversible unless it had acted insanely. Although the agencies were acting in a quasi-legislative capacity, they were not required to jump through as many procedural hoops as Congress typically did in legislating. Congress normally held oral hearings on pending legislation, a full draft of which was already on the docket, and issued a rather elaborate committee report to explain a bill as it went to the floor of the House or Senate. In contrast, the APA simply required an agency to give notice only of its intention to make a rule. It did not have to submit a draft. It had to receive written comments, but no hearing was required. It merely had to provide a 'concise' and 'general' statement accompanying its rule.

"In the absence of a rulemaking record, reviewing courts were forced to presume that the agency had the facts to support its rule. Given the extremely broad and standardless delegations in most of the New Deal legislation of the thirties and forties, courts rarely found that a rule violated the terms of its parent statute. And it was rare indeed for a New Deal-appointed judge reviewing the work of a New Deal-staffed agency to find that the agency had acted like a lunatic, that is that it had been, in the words of the APA, 'arbitrary' and 'capricious.' Therefore, in the political bargain judicial review of rulemaking is about all the conservatives got, and they got very little of that.

"The third part of administrative law originally conceived by the APA included everything that government did that was neither adjudication nor rulemaking." Prof. Shapiro goes on to explain that this large mass of diverse activities fell into the default APA category of "adjudication." In the absence of some other statute requiring a hearing on the record, it was left without significant procedural requirements.

Justice Jackson, President Roosevelt's Attorney General from 1940 to 1941, participated in the development of the APA at an early stage. Thus, his opinion reflects the knowledge possessed by the generation of the framers. It also illustrates the then-prevailing approach towards statutory interpretation, which included relatively detailed attention to legislative materials.[2] As a statute of general application, and considerable importance to contemporary issues, how should the APA be interpreted today—as a statute of its times, or as an evolving text whose language takes meaning from ongoing circumstances? The case following raises this question, in the context of a discussion permitting preliminary attention to the differences between agencies and courts, and to the standards for judicial review of agency action. Both these themes attract considerable attention in these materials.

Dickinson, Acting Commissioner of Patents and Trademarks v. Mary E. Zurko et al.

Supreme Court of the United States, 1999.
527 U.S. 150..

■ JUSTICE BREYER delivered the opinion of the Court.

The Administrative Procedure Act (APA) sets forth standards governing judicial review of findings of fact made by federal administrative

---

2. In other opinions, Justice Jackson sometimes proved a coruscating critic of the Court's use of legislative history, even while acknowledging he had sometimes (as here) used it to considerable effect. United States v. Public Utilities Comm'n of California, 345 U.S. 295, 319 (1953); Schwegmann Bros. v. Calvert Distillers Corp., 341 U.S. 384, 395 (1951).

agencies. 5 U.S.C. § 706. We must decide whether § 706 applies when the Federal Circuit reviews findings of fact made by the Patent and Trademark Office (PTO). We conclude that it does apply, and the Federal Circuit must use the framework set forth in that section.

I

Section 706, originally enacted in 1946, sets forth standards that govern the "Scope" of court "review" of, *e.g.*, agency factfinding (what we shall call court/agency review). It says that a

reviewing court shall— . . .

(2) hold unlawful and set aside agency . . . findings . . . found to be—

(A) arbitrary, capricious, [or] an abuse of discretion, or . . .

(E) unsupported by substantial evidence in a case subject to sections 556 and 557 of this title or otherwise reviewed on the record of an agency hearing provided by statute; . . .

In making the foregoing determinations, the court shall review the whole record or those parts of it cited by a party. . . .

Federal Rule of Civil Procedure 52(a) sets forth standards that govern appellate court review of findings of fact made by a district court judge (what we shall call court/court review). It says that the appellate court shall set aside those findings only if they are "clearly erroneous." Traditionally, this court/court standard of review has been considered somewhat stricter (*i.e.*, allowing somewhat closer judicial review) than the APA's court/agency standards. . . .

II

The parties agree that the PTO is an "agency" subject to the APA's constraints, that the PTO's finding at issue in this case is one of fact, and that the finding constitutes "agency action." Hence a reviewing court must apply the APA's court/agency review standards in the absence of an exception.

The Federal Circuit rests its claim for an exception upon § 559. That section says that the APA does "not limit or repeal additional requirements . . . recognized by law." In the Circuit's view: (1) at the time of the APA's adoption, in 1946, the Court of Customs and Patent Appeals (CCPA), a Federal Circuit predecessor, applied a court/court "clearly erroneous" standard; (2) that standard was stricter than ordinary court/agency review standards; and (3) that special tradition of strict review consequently amounted to an "additional requirement" that under § 559 trumps the requirements imposed by § 706.

. . . Existence of the additional requirement must be clear. This is suggested both by the phrase "recognized by law" and by the congressional specification in the APA that "no subsequent legislation shall be held to supersede or modify the provisions of this Act except to the extent that such legislation shall do so expressly." 5 U.S.C. § 559. A statutory intent that legislative departure from the norm must be clear suggests a need for similar clarity in respect to grandfathered common-law variations. The

APA was meant to bring uniformity to a field full of variation and diversity. It would frustrate that purpose to permit divergence on the basis of a requirement "recognized" only as ambiguous. . . . [T]he 89 cases which, according to respondents and supporting *amici,* embody the pre-APA standard of review . . . do not reflect a well-established stricter court/court standard of judicial review for PTO factfinding. . . . [N]ot one of the 89 opinions actually uses the precise words "clear error" or "clearly errone-ous," which are terms of art signaling court/court review. Most of the 89 opinions use words like "manifest error," which is not now such a term of art.

. . . The Federal Circuit traced its standard of review back to *Morgan* v. *Daniels*, 153 U.S. 120, 38 L. Ed. 657, 14 S. Ct. 772 (1894), which it characterized as the foundation upon which the CCPA later built its review standards. . . . *Morgan* arose out of a Patent Office interference proceed-ing—a proceeding to determine which of two claimants was the first inventor. The Patent Office decided the factual question of "priority" in favor of one claimant; the Circuit Court, deciding the case "without any additional testimony," 153 U.S. at 122, reversed the Patent Office's factual finding and awarded the patent to the other claimant. This Court in turn reversed the Circuit Court, thereby restoring the Patent Office decision.

"What," asked Justice Brewer for the Court, "is the rule which should control the [reviewing] court in the determination of this case?" . . . [The Court] thought that the Circuit Court's standard sounded . . . like the rule used by "an appellate court in reviewing findings of fact made by the trial court." . . .

> *But this is something more than a mere appeal.* It is an application to the court to set aside the action of one of the executive departments of the government. . . . A new proceeding is instituted in the courts . . . to set aside the conclusions reached by the administrative depart-ment. . . . It is . . . not to be sustained by a mere preponderance of evidence. . . . It is a controversy between two individuals over a ques-tion of fact which has once been settled by a special tribunal, entrusted with full power in the premises. As such it might be well argued, were it not for the terms of this statute, that the decision of the patent office was a finality upon every matter of fact. Id. at 124 (emphasis added).

The Court, in other words, reasoned strongly that a court/court review standard is *not* proper; that standard is too strict; a somewhat weaker standard of review is appropriate. . . .

III

The Federal Circuit also advanced several policy reasons which in its view militate against use of APA standards of review. First, it says that both bench and bar have now become used to the Circuit's application of a "clearly erroneous" standard that implies somewhat stricter court/court review. It says that change may prove needlessly disruptive. . . . This Court, however, has not previously settled the matter. The Federal Cir-cuit's standard would require us to create § 559 precedent that itself could prove disruptive by too readily permitting other agencies to depart from uniform APA requirements. And in any event we believe the Circuit overstates the difference that a change of standard will mean in practice.

This Court has described the APA court/agency "substantial evidence" standard as requiring a court to ask whether a "reasonable mind might accept" a particular evidentiary record as "adequate to support a conclusion." Consolidated Edison Co. v. NLRB, 305 U.S. 197, 229 (1938). It has described the court/court "clearly erroneous" standard in terms of whether a reviewing judge has a "definite and firm conviction" that an error has been committed. United States v. United States Gypsum Co., 333 U.S. 364, 395 (1948). And it has suggested that the former is somewhat less strict than the latter. [citing Universal Camera Corp. v. NLRB, p. 940 below] At the same time the Court has stressed the importance of not simply rubber-stamping agency fact-finding. Id. at 490. The APA requires meaningful review; and its enactment meant stricter judicial review of agency factfinding than Congress believed some courts had previously conducted. Ibid. The upshot in terms of judicial review is some practical difference in outcome depending upon which standard is used. The court/agency standard, as we have said, is somewhat less strict that the court/court standard. But the difference is a subtle one—so fine that (apart from the present case) we have failed to uncover a single instance in which a reviewing court conceded that use of one standard rather than the other would in fact have produced a different outcome.

The difficulty of finding such a case may in part reflect the basic similarity of the reviewing task, which requires judges to apply logic and experience to an evidentiary record, whether that record was made in a court or by an agency. It may in part reflect the difficulty of attempting to capture in a form of words intangible factors such as judicial confidence in the fairness of the factfinding process. Jaffe, Judicial Review: "Substantial Evidence on the Whole Record," 64 Harv. L. Rev. 1233, 1245 (1951). It may in part reflect the comparatively greater importance of case-specific factors, such as a finding's dependence upon agency expertise or the presence of internal agency review, which factors will often prove more influential in respect to outcome than will the applicable standard of review.

These features of review underline the importance of the fact that, when a Federal Circuit judge reviews PTO factfinding, he or she often will examine that finding through the lens of patent-related experience—and properly so, for the Federal Circuit is a specialized court. That comparative expertise, by enabling the Circuit better to understand the basis for the PTO's finding of fact, may play a more important role in assuring proper review than would a theoretically somewhat stricter standard. . . .

For these reasons, the judgment of the Federal Circuit is reversed. We remand the case for further proceedings consistent with this opinion.

So ordered.

■ CHIEF JUSTICE REHNQUIST, with whom JUSTICE KENNEDY and JUSTICE GINSBURG join, dissenting.

The issue in this case is whether, at the time of the enactment of the Administrative Procedure Act (APA) over 50 years ago, judicial review of fact-finding by the Patent and Trademark Office (PTO) under the "clearly erroneous" standard was an "additional requirement ... recognized by law." 5 U.S.C. § 559. It is undisputed that, until today's decision, both the patent bench and the patent bar had concluded that the stricter "clearly erroneous" standard was indeed such a requirement placed upon the PTO.[1] Agency factfinding was thus reviewed under this stricter standard; in my view, properly so, since the APA by its plain text was intended to bring some uniformity to judicial review of agencies by *raising* the minimum standards of review and not by *lowering* those standards which existed at the time. Section 12 of the APA, which was ultimately codified as § 559, provided that "nothing in this Act shall be held to diminish the constitutional rights of any person or to limit or repeal additional requirements imposed by statute or otherwise recognized by law." Pub. L. 404, 79th Cong., 60 Stat. 237, 244 (1946). As a result, we must decide whether the "clearly erroneous" standard was indeed otherwise recognized by law in 1946.

This case therefore turns on whether the 89 or so cases identified by the Court can be read as establishing a requirement placed upon agencies that was more demanding than the uniform minimum standards created by the APA. In making this determination, I would defer, not to agencies in general as the Court does today, but to the Court of Appeals for the Federal Circuit, the specialized Article III court charged with review of patent appeals. In this case the unanimous en banc Federal Circuit and the patent bar both agree that these cases recognized the "clearly erroneous" standard as an "additional requirement" placed on the PTO beyond the APA's minimum procedures. I see no reason to reject their sensible and plausible resolution of the issue. . . .

I therefore dissent for the reasons given by the Court of Appeals.

NOTES

(1) On remand, now applying the "substantial evidence" test as directed, the Federal Circuit reinstated its previous result. In re Zurko, 258 F.3d 1379 (Fed.Cir.2001).

(2) Comparable issues about the appropriate standard of review arise in judicial proceedings. The majority says that, at least in theory, reviewing courts exercise more careful supervision over trial courts—and thus would be more likely to reverse them—than they exercise over administrative agencies. Why might it be appropriate for a reviewing court to leave undisturbed an administrative decision, that it imagines it would have reversed (as "clearly erroneous") if a trial court had made the identical decision on the identical record?

Varying standards of proof ("preponderance," "clear and convincing," "beyond a reasonable doubt") are commonplace at the trial level. They are thought to capture varying levels of confidence in the outcome, and are

---

1. It appears that even the PTO acquiesced in this interpretation for almost 50 years after the enactment of the APA.

justified in relation to the various interests involved. Can you imagine similar justifications for varying intensities of review?

Many instructors will choose to defer detailed exploration of the standards governing judicial review of agency action (Chapter VIII) until their students have become more familiar with proceedings at the agency level. Nonetheless, because these materials rely so extensively on judicial decisions (as most law school texts do), these students—you—will inevitably get some information about these standards through the pores. Zurko is useful for its introduction to these issues, as well as its focus on the role and interpretation of the APA generally.

(3) In DIRECTOR, OFFICE OF WORKERS' COMPENSATION PROGRAMS v. GREENWICH COLLIERIES, 512 U.S. 267 (1994), the dispute concerned the meaning of "burden of proof" under 5 U.S.C. § 556(d) [Section 7(c) of the APA]. Again, the issue is a familiar one for judges in judicial contexts. It concerns the standard that responsible officials must apply in deciding factual issues at trial. Section 556(d) provides that "[e]xcept as otherwise provided by statute, the proponent of a rule or order has the burden of proof." Does "burden of proof" refer to the "burden of going forward" (i.e., the burden of initially establishing a prima facie claim, shifting to the other side the obligation to rebut)? Or, rather, does it refer to the "burden of persuasion" (i.e., the burden of ultimately establishing a simple preponderance of evidence in one's own favor)? Both meanings are possible, and the choice could be significant.

In adjudicating benefits claims under the Black Lung Benefits Act (BLBA), 30 U.S.C. § 901 et seq., and the Longshore and Harbor Workers' Compensation Act (LHWCA), 33 U.S.C. § 901 et seq., the Department of Labor had long followed what it called a "true doubt" rule. Under this approach, a claimant had the burden of going forward; once she had carried that burden, however, the burden of persuasion shifted to the party opposing the benefits claim. As a result, the benefits claimant would win any case in which the factfinder found the evidence to be evenly balanced. The effect, which the Department grounded in statutory policy, was somewhat to favor benefit claimants.

After concluding that neither statute in question provided for an exception to § 556(d), Justice O'Connor's opinion for the Court turned to the meaning of "burden of proof": "Because the term 'burden of proof' is nowhere defined in the APA, our task is to construe it in accord with its ordinary or natural meaning. It is easier to state this task than to accomplish it, for the meaning of words may change over time, and many words have several meanings even at a fixed point in time. Here we must seek to ascertain the ordinary meaning of 'burden of proof' in 1946, the year the APA was enacted."

An extensive review of the cases and literature leading up to 1946— little of which had appeared in the briefs—persuaded the majority that "the emerging [1946] consensus on a definition of burden of proof" had fixed on the burden of persuasion, " 'the obligation which rests on one of the parties to an action to persuade the trier of the facts, generally the jury, of the truth of a proposition which he has affirmatively asserted by the pleadings.' W. Richardson, Evidence 143 (6th ed. 1944) [and other evidence treatises of the period].

"We ... presume Congress intended the phrase to have the meaning generally accepted in the legal community at the time of enactment. These principles lead us to conclude that the drafters of the APA used the term 'burden of proof' to mean the burden of persuasion.[2] ...

". . . [While] the Department relies on the Senate and House Judiciary Committee Reports on the APA to support its claim that burden of proof means only burden of production[,] ... [t]he legislative history the Department relies on is imprecise and only marginally relevant. Congress chose to use the term 'burden of proof' in the text of the statute, and given the substantial evidence that the ordinary meaning of burden of proof was burden of persuasion, this legislative history cannot carry the day."

The majority acknowledged Congress's recognition both of the merits of claims under the two statutes, and of the difficulty in proving them—and the consequent merit of departmental policies reflecting solicitude for benefits claimants. But the "true doubt" approach went a step too far. ". . . [I]t runs afoul of the APA, a statute designed 'to introduce greater uniformity of procedure and standardization of administrative practice among the diverse agencies whose customs had departed widely from each other.' Wong Yang Sung v. McGrath, 339 U.S. 33, 41 (1950). That concern is directly implicated here, for under the Department's reading each agency would be free to decide who shall bear the burden of persuasion. Accordingly, the Department cannot allocate the burden of persuasion in a manner that conflicts with the APA."

Justice Souter, with Justices Blackmun and Stevens joining him, strongly dissented, relying both on the agency's long practice under the statutes and on his own reading of the historical understandings leading up to the APA's enactment. That reading, like the majority's, was significantly grounded in chambers research rather than party briefs.

"Although the Court works hard to show that the phrase had acquired a settled meaning ... by the time the APA was passed in 1946, there is good evidence that the courts were still using the term either way. ... [and] commentators did not think the ambiguity of the phrase had disappeared ...

---

2. [Ed.] The Court's opinion then dealt with the question whether it was nonetheless bound by having previously decided in NLRB v. Transportation Management Corp., 462 U.S. 393, 404 n. 7 (1983), that § 556(d)'s "burden of proof" meant only the burden of going forward. It concluded that it was not bound by this holding, as only "one or two sentences" had been devoted, in a footnote, to a matter largely unbriefed there. The majority found that footnote to be in tension with an earlier opinion, Steadman v. SEC, 450 U.S. 91 (1981), which had not directly addressed the meaning of "burden of proof" but might be thought to have rested on some assumptions about that question. "We do not slight the importance of adhering to precedent, particularly in a case involving statutory interpretation. But here our precedents are in tension, and we think our approach in Steadman makes more sense than does the Transportation Management footnote. And although we reject Transportation Management's reading of § 7(c), the holding in that case remains intact."

"Although standard usage had not made a choice of meanings by 1946, Congress did make one, and the meaning it chose for the phrase as used in § 7(c) was 'burden of production.' . . .

". . . The commentators agree. 'The legislative history suggests that the term "burden of proof" was intended to denote the "burden of going forward."' 1 C. Koch, Administrative Law and Practice, § 6.42, p. 486 (1985); [and other modern commentators, relying inter alia on the legislative history the majority had dismissed]."[3]

NOTES ON CHANGING APPROACHES TO THE APA OVER THE YEARS

(1) In one of the many symposia provoked by the APA's fiftieth anniversary, editor Peter Strauss identified three broad approaches that had been used in interpreting it (PETER L. STRAUSS, CHANGING TIMES: THE APA AT FIFTY, 63 U.Chi.L.Rev. 1389, 1392–93 (1996)): "[T]his is a story of change, albeit one mostly led, rather than followed, by the Court. It falls roughly into three phases. This statute was produced against a backdrop of empirical study and political contention; it used broad strokes, in the language of those who had participated in the studies and struggles, to address practical problems. In its first years, the lawyers and judges who litigated and decided issues about its meaning had been, to a greater or lesser extent, witnesses to its creation, and they evidently expected their experiences to contribute to the statute's interpretation; . . . the habits of using legislative materials to illuminate statutory text were firmly in place.

"In the middle period, represented here by the procedural ferment and paradigm shifts of the seventies, lawyers' arguments were less likely to draw upon the debates of the forties, and the Court proved willing to reinterpret the text to fit contemporary developments. The apparent exception to that trend, Vermont Yankee Nuclear Power Corp. v. NRDC, might be thought to have involved a lower court's effort to give the statute meaning outside any reasonable possibility offered by the text, rather than a more general refusal to accommodate that text to contemporary understandings.

"Most recently, in the third phase, the Court has turned to formalism in matters of textual interpretation. Rejecting partnership assumptions about its relation with Congress that have characterized thinking about statutes since early in this century, it takes text as both time-bound and limiting. For the APA, that makes decisions turn on what its words would have been understood to mean as a matter of standard usage in 1946— usage independent of the political context and debates."

3. [Ed.] On the question developed in the next preceding footnote, Justice Souter also wrote at length, but in a different vein:

Today's abandonment of Transportation Management's holding is not only a mistake, but one that puts the Court at odds with that fundamental principle of precedent that "[c]onsiderations of stare decisis have special force in the area of statutory interpretation, for . . . Congress remains free to alter what we have done." . . .

(2) Much of the work of this course involves assessing the influence of important cases from the middle phase of APA development—cases you will come to know by name. One question you may often come to ask is whether their holdings are compromised by the more recent emphasis on 1946 understandings, as in the Zurko and Greenwich Collieries cases set out in the preceding pages. Or can these more recent approaches be readily distinguished? Because many of you will not yet have encountered in detail these important middle phase cases before you find them cited in your readings, here is a capsule introduction to the most important of them. Not incidentally, this introduction provides a foretaste of some of the more important questions about judicial review:

(a) ABBOTT LABORATORIES V. GARDNER, 387 U.S. 136 (1967), CB p. 1182 interpreted 5 U.S.C. § 704 in a manner that facilitated securing review of agency rulemaking as if in an action for declaratory judgment, immediately upon publication of a regulation and independent of any particular government effort to enforce it. For the previous twenty years, as Professor Shapiro suggests, rulemaking review had generally awaited enforcement. This pre-Abbott approach had three significant costs (or, depending on your perspective, benefits). First, regulated entities could challenge a regulation only if they were willing to violate it and gamble on being able to avoid sanctions by persuading the court that it was invalid. Second, regulatory beneficiaries who had hoped for more stringent regulation could rarely, if ever, get judicial review of the agency's decision. Third, agencies, through prosecutorial discretion about when to enforce, could substantially control the facts and circumstances of the cases that would receive judicial review.

(b) ASSOCIATION OF DATA PROCESSING SERVICE ORGANIZATIONS V. CAMP, 397 U.S. 150 (1970), ("ADAPSO"), CB p. 1129, interpreted 5 U.S.C. § 702's reference to "persons adversely affected or aggrieved within the meaning of a relevant statute" to confer standing on any one who could show an "injury in fact" to a concrete interest that was arguably within the set of interests protected or regulated by the statute in question. Before ADAPSO, most had understood § 702's language to refer to the relatively small number of particular statutes that explicitly authorized review by "persons affected or aggrieved." The ADAPSO formulation made it much easier for intended, and incidental, beneficiaries of regulation to challenge agency frustration of their hopes.

(c) For example, the ADAPSO approach to standing readily permitted opponents of a proposed federal highway grant, that would result in the bisection of a beloved urban park, to challenge the grant award. Recent statutes had directed the Secretary to take particular care to protect the values of urban parklands, and the opponents presented themselves as regular users of the park in question. They could bring their action although the statutes involved neither made any reference to judicial review of the Secretary of Transportation's decisions, nor included any provision for the opponents' participation in the informal adjudications that led to them. Section 706(2)(A) of the APA instructs a reviewing court to "set aside agency action, findings, and conclusions found to be ... arbitrary, capricious, [or] an abuse of discretion." CITIZENS TO PRESERVE OVERTON PARK V. VOLPE, 401 U.S. 402 (1971), CB p. 989, interpreted this language to require "searching" and "intense" review of the grant decision in light of a "full administrative record." In 1946, as Professor Shapiro's account above recalled, "arbitrary, capricious" review had been understood as a standard that "made an agency's decisions irreversible unless it had acted ... like a lunatic, that is that it had been, in the words of the APA, 'arbitrary' and 'capricious.'" Now the burden effectively shifted to the agency to demonstrate its sanity (reasonableness).

(d) In the wake of Overton Park, numerous court-of-appeals cases interpreted the simple requirements of § 553 rulemaking ("[g]eneral notice," an "opportunity to [comment]," and a "concise general statement of ... basis and purpose" accompanying a regulation when finally adopted) to comprise some rather elaborate procedural requirements: that agency data be exposed for comment; that significant changes in a proposal result in a second comment period; and that all significant comments be responded to in the statement of basis and purpose (which ought also fully to explain the agency's reasoning). These developments, although readily understandable as a reaction to the emergence of rulemaking as a major regulatory activity, would have been surprising to the legislators of 1946. In VERMONT YANKEE NUCLEAR POWER CORP. v. NATURAL RESOURCES DEFENSE COUNCIL, INC., 435 U.S. 519 (1978), CB p. 498, the Supreme Court emphatically rebuked the D.C. Circuit for having appeared to require *oral* procedures (testimony and cross-examination opportunities) in a rulemaking. This, the Court said, was inconsistent with the APA's "formula upon which opposing social and political forces have come to rest." But five years later, striking down a regulation that would have retrenched on important automobile safety requirements, MOTOR VEHICLE MANUFACTURERS ASSN. v. STATE FARM MUTUAL AUTOMOBILE INSURANCE CO., 463 U.S. 29 (1983), CB p. 1002, enunciated and applied review techniques that essentially confirmed the "paper hearing" aspects of the lower court cases. While orality could not be required, contemporary rulemaking requirements remain considerably more elaborate than a legislator would have imagined in 1946.

(e) CHEVRON, U.S.A., INC. v. NATURAL RESOURCES DEFENSE COUNCIL, INC., 467 U.S. 837 (1984), CB p. 1026, required the Court to decide how much deference (or even obedience) courts should give an agency's regulatory interpretation of its organic statute, when "traditional tools" of statutory interpretation were not sufficient precisely to resolve a question of statutory meaning or application. In these circumstances, the Supreme Court said, a reviewing court must accept the agency's "reasonable" choice among the possibilities statutory language permitted. Although a similar holding had been made in the years preceding the APA,[1] that holding turned on the particular statute involved; Chevron, like ADAPSO, generalized the proposition.

All of these summaries are extremely shorthand accounts of cases worth extensive class consideration; each has consumed volumes of attention in the literature. But these accounts will orient you to the importance and general meaning of cases that have become oft-cited classics. They also suggest the extent to which judicial improvisation during the APA's first

---

1. National Labor Relations Board v. Hearst, 322 U.S. 111 (1944), CB p. 979.

half century had changed the face from what a member of Congress, in 1946, might have had any reason to expect.

(3) As to the merits of the "third phase" approach, editor Strauss concluded in discussing the Greenwich Collieries opinion (63 U. Chi. L. Rev. at 1420) that:

"If the Court seriously intended to return the APA to its 1946 meanings, we will have been left with a far less flexible instrument of government than we had previously thought we possessed. Recall that in Wong Yang Sung, Justice Jackson characterized the Court's role as being 'so far as the terms of the Act warrant, to give effect to its remedial purposes where the evils it was aimed at appear.' Effecting 'remedial purposes' within a range that 'terms . . . warrant,' appropriately to the interpretive conventions of the time, reflects a far more fluid approach to meaning over the years than the effort to find 'ordinary meaning . . . in 1946.' And the intervening cases, as we have seen, unselfconsciously assumed an evolving statute—one whose evolution, to be sure, was limited by the possibilities of its text, but that nonetheless accommodated the shifting currents of administrative law development across the years. The APA's endurance for fifty years as a central reference point for the manifold activities of the federal government, like the Constitution's endurance for more than two hundred, can be understood only as a product of that flexibility. An interpretive theory that makes of statutes such static events undercuts the very project of having an APA."

Judge Stephen Williams had somewhat different thoughts. Stephen F. Williams, The Era of "Risk-Risk" and the Problem of Keeping the APA Up to Date, 63 U. Chi. L. Rev. 1375, 1385–87 (1996):

". . . I will step back a minute and ask more generally what the consuming public might reasonably expect from courts in their interpretation of a statute such as the APA—intended to guide the procedures of countless arms of the administrative state.

"Congress's decision to adopt the APA expressed, presumably, its belief that the courts—and perhaps the citizenry—needed some help. If Congress had fully embraced the judicial answers to the questions posed by administrative proliferation, a statute would not have been necessary. I apologize for mentioning the obvious, but anxiety over obsolescence tends to obscure the point. Absent constitutional imperatives, the congressional voice is decisive. Thus, to state the obvious, one criterion for sound interpretation of the APA must be fidelity to what Congress meant.

"A second criterion is that interpretations should lend themselves to reasonable application across the range of agencies and agency activities governed by the statute. . . . If one size must fit all, as in some sense it must under the APA, then those who define the permissible size must either build flexibility into the definition (for example, 'reasonable' availability) or find some other solution to the problem of variability. As applied to Greenwich Collieries, this principle might support reading 'burden of proof' as burden of production only. Because that reading leaves the more significant issue, burden of persuasion, untouched, it enables individual agencies to resolve it separately with a focus on context.

"Notice that each of these approaches to agency diversity has its costs. A pliable standard provides relatively little advance guidance. But a clear universal standard, deliberately set in lax terms (ones that leave agencies relatively unconstrained), may jeopardize private interests that Congress meant to protect.

"Third, there is surely an interest—the one that Strauss singles out for emphasis—in interpretations that fit current circumstances. . . .

"While Strauss focuses on keeping the APA current, I wonder if the central fault of Greenwich Collieries, by his lights, is really the Court's asserted failure to allow the meaning of the APA to flow with the times. . . . Strauss's real complaint—still a serious one—lies in regard to the second criterion that I hypothesized for APA interpretation, namely, the need to embrace disparate agencies and disparate activities. On that criterion, none of the options open to the Court was particularly appetizing . . . The Court could not adopt an elastic interpretation such as might be embodied in a concept of 'reasonableness.' It had to decide between two discrete possibilities, burden of production or burden of persuasion; Congress surely could not have meant the term to shift its meaning back and forth, from agency to agency, at the will of the courts. So long as the Court was forced to choose a one-size-fits-all meaning, the option with the advantage of being less intrusive upon agency choice (mere burden of production) came at the price of allowing agencies to deny some private parties the benefit of forcing their adversaries to carry the burden of persuasion—a benefit Congress intended them to have if the Court's reading of Congress's 1946 meaning was correct."

In TEXTUALISM AND CONTEXTUALISM IN ADMINISTRATIVE LAW, 78 B.U.L.Rev. 1023 (1998), Professor JONATHAN SIEGEL argues that "a dominant force in the construction of many administrative law statutes is neither the statutes' text nor the intentions of their authors, but background principles of administrative law." The Greenwich Collieries "opinion is inordinately focused on the abstract meaning of the three words, 'burden of proof,' to the exclusion of all other considerations. We hear a great deal in the Court's opinion about what these words meant to Lemuel Shaw in 1833 and how Justice Holmes credited that meaning on behalf of the Supreme Court ninety years later. Wholly absent from the Court's opinion, however, is any discussion of the background principles of administrative law that are usually so important in interpreting administrative law statutes. . . . The Court treated the phrase 'burden of proof' as a universal, indivisible atom that would necessarily have the same meaning wherever it might appear, so that its meaning in a federal statute about administrative law could be gleaned from its usage in a state supreme court opinion dealing with ordinary civil procedure."

c. ADDITIONAL SOURCES OF PROCEDURAL CONSTRAINT

These materials focus on the Administrative Procedure Act and a few other general procedural enactments folded into its structure, such as the Freedom of Information Act and Government in the Sunshine Act, Chapter VI below, and the Negotiated Rulemaking Act, pp. 627–38. Yet administrative lawyers need to be aware that a number of other statutes provide general structure for certain aspects of administrative procedure or judicial review. Title 28 of the U.S. Code and implementing rules of civil and appellate procedure contain enforcement procedures for subpoenas, provisions respecting jurisdiction and venue for judicial review, and the delegation of litigating responsibility to the Department of Justice and its officers. The Paperwork Reduction Act of 1980, briefly discussed at pp. 292–94 below, places generalized agency information-gathering under the supervision of the Office of Management and Budget (OMB), a White House agency we meet frequently in these pages. The Federal Advisory Committee Act p. 766, makes the White House also responsible to regulate agency use of private-public committees for consultation and policy development, and requires any such committees to work openly. Statutes and executive orders creating additional procedural obligations for rulemaking have become a major source of added complexity. See Chapter V.

More important, an awareness of general procedural requirements is just the beginning of solving any concrete problem of administrative procedure. The administrative lawyer must always consult the agency's own statutes, which often establish additional or differing procedural requirements. Thus, in reading the cases of the rulemaking chapter, you must be astute to see when the courts are responding to the general commands of APA § 553, and when to the particular requirements of a particular agency's organic statute. For adjudications not required to be decided "on the record," the agency's statute and regulations (and perhaps the Constitution) will provide the only external constraint on the procedures the agency will follow. Absent support from these sources, the courts are abjured from providing procedural specifications of their own.[1]

Within statutory and constitutional limits, agencies generally enjoy substantial freedom to shape the procedures they employ. Agencies often adopt detailed procedural regulations, which will usually be found in an early chapter of the agency's volume of the Code of Federal Regulations— the official annual compendium of regulations adopted by federal agencies, that is organized along the lines of the United States Code, and is several times as large. Any attorney involved with a particular agency or proceeding must pay careful attention to its procedural regulations and any internal interpretations they may have received.

SECTION 2.   PROCEEDINGS OUTSIDE THE FUNDAMENTAL PROCEDURAL CATEGORIES?—INFORMATION GATHERING

The great bulk of government activity affecting citizen interests occurs outside of and prior to the relatively structured interchanges that are the principal focus of these materials. Debates about constitutional due process and the application of the federal Administrative Procedure Act imagine proceedings analogous to trials or legislative deliberations; they take hold when a notice of proposed rulemaking is about to be published, a licence application filed, or a complaint seeking a sanction issued. Agencies gather information, make general policy, and enter contracts or make government

---

1. See Pension Benefit Guaranty Corp. v. LTV Corp., 496 U.S. 633 (1990), p. 472 below.

grants outside these frameworks. Just because the settings and agency actors are so diverse, courses in Administrative Law (like the APA) rarely grant them more than passing mention. Because citizens are most likely to come into contact with administrative agencies when the agencies are simply seeking information, the importance of information-gathering activities in particular makes a number of matters worthy of exploration here.

Information-gathering may occur by inspection, or through a general obligation to provide information in application forms or in reports, like tax returns or factory emission reports. Less important overall, yet more likely to involve a lawyer's services—are subpoenas that direct particular recipients to testify or to produce documents they possess, the familiar discovery instruments characteristic of adjudication. Moreover, the mere flow of information to government is only part of the significance of requiring information, and in many settings it is the lesser part. Primary conduct is often affected by the fact that an industry is subject to inspection of its facilities, or of records it is required to maintain; so, too, when people or businesses are required to report income or other data. But how much government's access to information affects primary conduct may depend on what people believe to be the actual likelihood of inspection or use—whether people believe that what they report is subject to some form of review or instead goes into a black hole.

Information is itself the raw material that fuels the implementation, even the shaping of policy. Information may be required in the course of adjudication or rulemaking, in advance of either of these activities, or in the service of other important, but less formal, agency functions: staff action on requests for governmental action, such as licensing or public grants; identifying industry problems or policy issues that may require agency response; monitoring circumstances in which enforcement activity may be required; preparing for dealings with the legislature or the executive on issues of policy or oversight involving matters within the agency's responsibility. As you proceed through the following pages, consider what goals are being enforced and where the information demands fit in furthering those goals.

A NOTE ON INFORMATION AS REGULATION—EPA'S TOXIC RESOURCES INVENTORY

In some situations, reporting or public disclosure may be effective and even sufficient to promote particular public policy goals. In this sense, information management can be understood as an alternative form of regulation. With the development of the Internet, government can expose data to any citizen with a computer in her home, and do so in ways that make it readily searchable and useful in ways that could hardly have been imagined a decade or so ago. In "Is the Toxics Release Inventory News to Investors," 16 Nat. Resources & Env't 292 (summer 2001), James T. Hamilton suggests that corporate awareness of "the reaction of stock prices to the release of . . . data" provides one credible explanation for the near halving of total releases of toxic substances manufacturing industries reported between 1988 and 1999. William F. Pedersen argues in Regulation and Information Disclosure: Parallel Universes and Beyond, 25 Harv. Envtl. L. Rev. 151 (2001), "the growth of social cost disclosure programs could lead to far-reaching changes in the status and function of federal regulatory agencies—but only if the agencies seize that opportunity themselves. The agencies must take affirmative responsibility for the accuracy, both in content and presentation, of the public message such programs convey. Without such an effort, social cost disclosure may duplicate most of the defects of our existing system of command-and-control regulation. Conversely, an agency that makes the effort will discover that social cost disclosure programs both require, and can help accomplish, a closer engagement of the agency in the dialogue that shapes goals for social cost control. That closer engagement could, in turn, encourage significant revisions to the command-and-control system itself."[1]

A prominent example is the Toxics Release Inventory maintained by the Environmental Protection Agency at its website, http://www.epa.gov/tri, under the authority of the 1986 Emergency Planning and Community Right-to-Know Act,[2] "the first regulatory statute of the contemporary 'information age,'" PROFESSOR BRADLEY C. KARKKAINEN in INFORMATION AS ENVIRONMENTAL REGULATION: TRI AND PERFORMANCE BENCHMARKING, PRECURSOR TO A NEW PARADIGM?, 89 GEO. L.J. 257, 286 ff. (2001):

"The Toxics Release Inventory (TRI) ... requires manufacturing and certain other industrial facilities to disclose releases and transfers of 654 specified toxic chemicals, subject to reporting thresholds and limited exemptions for trade secrets. The information must be provided on standardized forms and is entered into a publicly accessible computerized database, facilitating public access and enabling any interested party to aggregate the data in a variety of ways, and to generate inter-temporal, inter-facility, inter-firm, inter-sectoral, and inter-community comparisons.

"... TRI differs [from prior regulatory regimes relying on information] ... in that its primary purpose is not to police contractual arrangements by leveling the playing field between buyers and sellers or principals and agents. Instead, TRI aims squarely at measuring and disclosing the environmental performance of those parties most directly responsible for significant environmental impacts, with the aim of thereby improving performance outcomes.

"Mandatory production and disclosure of TRI information has prompted many firms to undertake ambitious voluntary emission reductions programs, often far beyond the levels required under current regulations. Both current EPA Administrator Carol Browner and her predecessor William Reilly have hailed TRI as one of the nation's most effective environmental laws—a view widely shared in the industry and among many environmentalists. Since TRI reporting began in 1988, reported releases of TRI-listed pollutants have dropped by nearly half, with the sharp downward trend continuing steadily year after year. ... [M]ost

---

1. Similar arguments about the potential effectiveness of disclosure programs, and the need for sophisticated care in constructing them, are made in William Sage, Regulat-ing Through Information: Disclosure Laws and American Health Care, 99 Colum. L. Rev. 1701 (1999).

2. 42 U.S.C. § 11023.

observers, including TRI-reporting firms, credit TRI with playing a central role in driving improvements in pollution performance. According to one EPA survey, some seventy percent of TRI reporting facilities indicate that they have intensified their waste reduction efforts under the influence of TRI....

"TRI achieves all this at a relatively low cost to the agency. EPA's direct administrative costs are approximately $25 million, a modest fraction if its $7 billion annual budget. ... Under TRI, the agency normally only needs to make the (relatively) low-threshold determination that a pollutant 'can reasonably be anticipated to cause' cancer or other chronic health effects at some level of exposure. ... Because its initial information threshold is so low, the agency can act more expeditiously and respond more readily to new information or changing circumstances, simply by adjusting the list of TRI-reported substances.[3] ...

"Direct compliance costs are also quite low. EPA estimates that the average facility requires about fifty person-hours of labor annually to produce each required report. The cumulative paperwork burden on regulated firms is not trivial, of course. But it is consistent with the level of reporting required of firms under conventional regulatory approaches simply as an incident of compliance monitoring. ... [I]f TRI does induce real reductions in pollutant releases, then some firms must be incurring the costs of investing in new technologies or processes, even if these are not properly labeled 'compliance costs.' But since firms have absolute flexibility under TRI to determine how, when, and to what extent they will reduce emissions, they are generally free to adopt the improvement targets, timetables, and strategies that best suit their individual circumstances. ...

"EPA's monitoring costs are also relatively low, although this may in part reflect under-enforcement. Failure to report or submission of grossly erroneous data can sometimes be detected without site investigations or complex measurement. There are, however, important caveats. Because reporting is required only beyond a threshold level of emissions, persistent non-reporters may go undetected because EPA has no reliable way to identify them. Consequently, some agency monitoring effort is required. ... As the agency has come to recognize TRI's role in driving performance gains, it has placed greater emphasis on TRI compliance and enforcement activities, and compliance has apparently increased. Monitoring the accuracy of required reports is a more daunting undertaking, however, and EPA has made only modest progress on that score."

As this last paragraph suggests, although agencies can often find needed information in existing governmental materials or in voluntary submissions, securing cooperation sometimes requires considerable agency effort. The means available to an agency for meeting its information requirements are varied. Agencies may seek to elicit cooperation by offering benefits conditioned upon the supply of information. This may seem more voluntary, when (for example) a firm is offered a choice between a cooperative regime, and one in which the agency assumes police responsibilities. Supplying information may seem less "optional" when (for example) an

---

3. [Ed.] See, e.g., Troy Corp. v. Browner, 120 F.3d 277 (D.C.Cir.1997).

agency's staff is unwilling to accept a license application until the firm has provided the information the staff says is necessary to complete the application. Sometimes compliance must be compelled rather than simply requested. Refusal to permit inspection or failure to make required reports may have negative consequences for an existing or hoped-for relationship with the agency; either may also provoke the agency to take the resistor to court—whether to secure access to the premises to be inspected, to require the supplying of information, or to collect a civil penalty.[4]

Different questions may be presented when the issue concerns information quality. Congress has not simply left it to the responsible agency to "take affirmative responsibility for the accuracy, both in content and presentation, of the public message [their] programs convey," as William Pedersen argued, p. 278, would be essential to their success. Section 515 of the Treasury and General Government Appropriations Act for Fiscal year 2001 (P.L. 106–554; H.R. 5658) requires the Director of the Office of Management and Budget to issue guidelines providing policy and procedural guidance to Federal agencies for ensuring and maximizing the quality, objectivity, utility, and integrity of information (including statistical information) shared and/or disseminated by Federal agencies under the Paperwork Reduction Act, briefly discussed at p. 292 below.[5] These guidelines are to require each agency not only to issue guidelines to these ends about information it disseminates, but also to "establish administrative mechanisms allowing affected persons to seek and obtain correction" of noncompliant information. The Director of OMB is also to monitor agency handling of complaints. If they provide the opportunity for diversion of agency effort and cost-infliction, not merely a spur to useful discipline, it is of course possible that the resulting administrative proceedings will make programs like TRI less timely and cost-effective.[6]

The next two subsections explore some useful programmatic issues affecting information acquisition, first by inspection and then by information demands. The Chapter then turns to problems of enforcing government information demands.[7] Once legal compulsion enters, our compound wish for a government that is effective, not excessively costly, and "safe" produces familiar tensions and conundrums. Indispensable as is the flow of facts to government, indispensable too is privacy—breathing room for

---

4. Unlike affirmatively supplying false information to the government, refusals to comply with information requests are rarely if ever criminal offenses. They often have no legal consequence until the agency brings an independent judicial proceeding seeking issuance of a warrant or of an order to produce, enforcement of a subpoena, or a civil sanction.

5. Initial stages in the carrying out of this responsibility may be found at 66 Fed-Reg 49718 (OMB Guidelines, Sept. 28, 2001) and http://www.whitehouse.gov/omb/inforeg/iqg_comments.pdf (OMB Memorandum for Presidential Management Council, June 10, 2002.)

6. An assessment of § 515's "fascinating remedial choices for the opponent of an agency press release or a new rule" appears in James T. O'Reilly, The 411 on 515: How OIRA's Expanded Information Roles in 2002 will Impact Rulemaking and Agency Publicity Actions, 54 Admin.L.Rev. 835 (2002). Concerns about the possibility that terrorists could use posted information, in the wake of the September 11, 2001 attack on the World Trade Towers, may also threaten the development of some programs.

7. One enforcement context, that for individual subpoenas, is briefly dealt with at p. 1067 below.

citizens—if we are to be safe from excessive government and free to pursue all those aspects of life that have little or nothing to do with government. Under the Fourth Amendment, one's person, house, papers and effects are not to be invaded without reason—generally, as demonstrated to a neutral magistrate. Under the Fifth Amendment, one may not be compelled to self-incrimination. Personal liberties confront programmatic needs, and you may find in these pages reason to wonder how well they have fared in that confrontation. Are there relevant differences between programmatic justifications for searches and those based on particularized suspicions—between generally imposed compulsions to maintain records or supply data, and compulsions arising out of *individual* circumstances already redolent with suspicion—that warrant different approaches to these liberties?

a. CHOICES OF GOVERNMENT REGULATORY STYLE IN INSPECTING

Industrial accidents and illnesses have long provided occasions for regulatory programs. In 2000, the AFL–CIO estimated, American workers suffered 16 work-related fatalities and almost 16,000 work-related injuries or illnesses each working day—touching one worker in sixteen each year.[1] Add the harder-to-estimate illnesses and the human consequences and economic losses are "staggering."[2] Some of the programs enacted in response operate retrospectively, seeking to compensate workers for injuries that have already occurred. As in the federal Occupational Safety and Health Act frequently encountered in these pages, however, the emphasis often is on safety measures to control hazards in advance of harm. These approaches require the government to become aware of workplace conditions in advance, and to cause employers to ameliorate them as appropriate. Failures here can produce calamity, as when "on September 3, 1991, 25 workers died and another 55 were injured when they were trapped behind locked doors as flames swept through the Imperial Food Products chicken processing plant in Hamlet, North Carolina."[3] The plant had never been inspected since it opened in 1980. It was the worst industrial accident in the state's history.[4]

Adequate standards for workplace safety, then, do not suffice; experience has shown the necessity of providing some means for encouraging or

---

1. AFL–CIO, Death on the Job: The Toll of Neglect 1 (11th ed. 2002); http://www.osha.gov/as/opa/oshafacts.html (last visited June 25, 2002).

2. Thomas O. McGarity and Sidney A. Shapiro, Workers at Risk: The Failed Promise of [OSHA], 4 (1993).

3. House Committee on Education and Labor, The Tragedy at Imperial Food Products, 102d Cong. 1st Sess., Comm. Print 102–N, 1 (1991).

4. Eighty years earlier, on March 25, 1911, 146 workers had died in New York City when they too were trapped by fire. This, too, was the worst industrial accident in the state's history. One of the two exits from the Triangle Shirtwaist Company's "loft" factory on the top three floors of a 10–story building was locked; the other was so narrow that only one person could pass at a time; the single fire escape became overloaded and collapsed. The building was adjacent to New York University Law School; a few months earlier, a professor who could see into the workrooms had urged officials to investigate the conditions. (The building had not been inspected since construction was completed.) Students and a professor who raced to the roof managed to rescue dozens. Eric G. Behrens, The Triangle Shirtwaist Company Fire of 1911: A Lesson in Legislative Manipulation, 62 Tex.L.Rev. 361 (1983).

assuring compliance. Physical inspection has been OSHA's principal enforcement tool; but just how that tool should best be deployed—a choice about government style—remains a significant matter of debate. Are inspectors best imagined as expert consultants, working with management and labor to achieve at lowest cost and with greatest net benefit ends that all are seeking? Or should they be imagined as street-level bureaucrats lacking the education necessary for trustworthy exercise of broad discretion, and possibly prone to graft (to supplement inferior wages)—persons who, for the protection of those whom they will inspect, had better be given a detailed manual specifying their activities? Or are they best seen as police officials entrusted with the responsibility for detecting violations and issuing citations? Can the agency properly differentiate in its approach between those firms who are disposed to be cooperative, and those who prefer to live at or beyond the edge of the permissible? How should any penalties be calculated in relation to the costs of compliance?[5]

NOTES ON THE CHOICES OF STYLE AND THEIR CONSTRAINTS

(1) *Cooperation With Management Understood to Share the Regulatory Incentive.* At the turn of the century, the ICC began inspecting the power railroad brakes and automatic couplers that federal law had just required railroads to use, in the hope of reducing the extraordinary incidence of death and serious injury among brakemen. It gave the following account in its Fourteenth Annual Report to Congress (1900):

"Recognizing that a law of this character can only be made effective by a system of supervision and inspection, Congress appropriated $15,000 at its last session to enable the Commission to keep informed regarding compliance with the safety-appliance act and to render its requirements effective. ... The inspections have served to give a general idea of the conditions existing, and this has been of great value. ... It has acquainted the railway presidents with conditions existing on their respective roads, of which they probably would not have been apprised in any other way. ... Railway equipment throughout the country is now interchangeable by reason of the general application of automatic couplers and brakes and standard-height drawbars required by the safety appliance act. It is reported, however, that probably 20 per cent of the couplers now used become nonautomatic through failure to keep them in proper repair. While in such condition it is agreed that they are far more dangerous to the men employed in handling the cars than the old link and pin coupler. ...

---

5. A study of "the direct impact of OSHA inspections on workplace injury rates," surveying experience at 6,842 manufacturing plants from 1979–85, found that "managerial attention does indeed respond to regulatory enforcement actions [although 'the expected penalty for violating almost any of OSHA's regulations is far below the cost of complying.'] Inspections imposing a penalty focus managerial attention on safety issues, thereby reducing injury rates in inspected firms to a greater extent than could be explained if firms simply abated the cited violations." Wayne B. Gray and John T. Scholz, Does Regulatory Enforcement Work? A Panel Analysis of OSHA Enforcement, 27 L. & Socy.Rev. 177, 179, 182–83 (1993). For a thoughtful contemporary analysis of the many factors involved, see Sidney A. Shapiro and Randy Rabinowitz, Voluntary Regulatory Compliance in Theory and Practice: The Case of OSHA, 52 Admin.L.Rev. 97 (2000).

"Under the instructions of the Commission inspections have been openly made, the inspector always introducing himself to the management and disclosing his identity. Railway officials generally are much interested in this inspection work, and the majority of them appear surprised to learn that so many automatic couplers are in the condition found by the inspectors. . . ."[6]

(2) *The relevance of underlying societal patterns:* In REGULATING AMERICA, REGULATING SWEDEN: A COMPARATIVE STUDY OF OCCUPATIONAL SAFETY AND HEALTH POLICY 196 (1981), STEVEN KELMAN speculated that the much greater Swedish reliance on persuasion may reflect fundamental differences in social attitude. "Out of the Swedish [political] tradition grows the notion that people ought to defer to the wishes of those in authority. Out of the American liberal tradition grows the notion that it is legitimate for people to define and pursue their own goals, independent of what the state thinks is best for them. ... The traditional problem of European states with established rulers has been to tame those rulers and let people breathe; that of America with its liberal tradition has been to tame the unruly so that other people can breathe."

"Perhaps the best single word to describe the American enforcement process," Kelman wrote, "is *formal* ... Inspections take the form of searches for violations. ... OSHA lays out the rules for its inspectors in ... a 122–page *Field Operations Manual* [compared to Sweden's] six pages ... The American enforcement system set up after 1970 was designed to be enforcement-minded, while the Swedish system was cooperation-minded."[7] To the enforcement-minded, inspection is a classic tool of command-and-control regulation—from the federal inspectors permanently resident in nuclear power plants or making surprise visits to mines and drug manufacturing plants, to the routine inspections of elevators, restaurants and buildings conducted by local governments. Despite the unarguable desirability of such goals as adequate housing, safe working conditions and pure food, the inspected may not see inspections as benevolent, and inspectors may see themselves as less concerned with the prevention or correction of undesired conditions than with the detection and punishment of wrongdoers.

(3) *The Costs and Benefits of Proceeding "by the Book".* EUGENE BARDACH and ROBERT A. KAGAN, GOING BY THE BOOK: THE PROBLEM OF REGULATORY UNREASONABLENESS, 4–5 (1982), composed a dialog between an official of OSHA and the pseudonymous Al Schaefer, director of workplace safety for a major aluminum manufacturer: "By all accounts, including those of a labor union safety officer, a regional OSHA official and a plant-level safety engineer with experience in other firms, Schaefer's company seems to have

---

6. Thomas K. McGraw's Prophets of Regulation (1984), gives a good account of this "cooperative" style of regulation in its account of Charles Adams, an early railroad regulator.

7. Steven Kelman, Enforcement of Occupational Safety and Health Regulations: A Comparison of Swedish and American Practices, in K. Hawkins and J. Thomas, eds., Enforcing Regulation 97, 99, 105, 108 (1984). See also David Vogel, National Styles of Regulation: Environmental Policy in Great Britain and the United States, 200 (1986) ("British [occupational health and safety] regulators rely more on conciliation than on coercion").

a positive attitude toward worker safety and an aggressive safety program. Still ... the 'major problem with OSHA,' he says, 'is that they mandate safety standards even where they are not the highest priority risk in a particular plant.' He gave an example involving an OSHA regulation that called for 'alternative means of egress' from public gathering places, such as restaurants. An OSHA inspector applied this rule to the lunchrooms in an aluminum smelting plant. The heart of the smelter is composed of long rows of furnaces (or 'pots') in which molten aluminum is transported along these rows by motorized vehicles. Small, airconditioned lunchrooms are adjacent to the 'potline' but separated from it by a cinder-block wall; the doors to the lunchroom do not open directly into the potline, but open off side corridors. The lunchrooms had no rear exits.

"OSHA said rear exits were required. The only justification OSHA could offer (other than the text of the regulation) was that if the molten aluminum spilled and went into the side corridors and a fire started, workers in the lunchrooms would be trapped.

" 'Now that citation does not represent a rational assessment of risk.' Schaefer says. 'Of course, it could happen. Almost anything could happen. Never mind that it's more likely that an earthquake could happen. Never mind that in the 15 years the plant has been operating nothing like that happened, or even any incidents that suggest it might happen.'

"Besides, he points out, because the lunchrooms are of cinder-block construction, the only thing that could burn is the wooden door. To cut through the other side and install a door, he says, would cost $6,000 per lunchroom, times 10 lunchrooms. 'This is a total misapplication of resources. I could use that money for real risk reduction in plenty of other places.'

"To Schaefer, OSHA appeared unreasonable. But was OSHA unreasonable? ... [A] rebuttal to Schaefer might have sounded like this: Either directly or through state agencies that enforce the OSHA regulations for us, we regulate worker safety and health in almost five million workplaces. They are extremely varied. If we had rules that were exactly suited to each hazard and each situation in every one of those workplaces, the inspector's manual would have to be transported in a truck. So we have to simplify and standardize, and obviously some cases of overinclusive rules and regulations are going to result. Remember, Al Schaefer or people like him can always file for a variance because the law does give us latitude to waive compliance in cases where equivalent protection is provided by other means. True, we don't let the inspector at the field level have the discretion to waive compliance. But that is because he would then be susceptible to manipulation, bribery, and perhaps intimidation. Besides, not all 3,000 occupational safety and health inspectors are sufficiently trained or clever or morally upright to be entrusted with discretionary power. It may be somewhat inconvenient for Al Schaefer and others in his position to seek waivers through the proper channels, and in some cases they just might choose to comply with regulatory rules rather than do it, but remember that workers' lives and well-being are at issue. If the system has to make errors, which of course it does, it is better to err on the side of safety. We at OSHA think that, our statutory mandate indicates that Congress thinks that, and public opinion polls suggest that the public overwhelmingly thinks so too."

Who, then, was unreasonable? Sharply at issue here are the problems of affordable training, discretion and official honesty. The "good cop" or the "good inspector" needs a high level of education and substantial freedom of action to be able to assess and bend to circumstances intelligently, to counsel as well as command. To the extent legal frameworks encourage legalism, they create a setting antithetical to the cooperative endeavor sought by well-motivated safety directors such as Schaefer. Yet an agency's "command and control" attitude *towards its own employees* may be a rational response to a less well-educated or less well-paid inspectorate, as well as to the need to control against the possibility of bad apples—and bad tendencies—among inspectors and among firms not as well-motivated as Schaefer's.

(4) SIDNEY A. SHAPIRO AND RANDY S. RABINOWITZ, PUNISHMENT VERSUS COOPERATION IN REGULATORY ENFORCEMENT: A CASE STUDY OF OSHA, 49 Admin.L.Rev. 713, 720–24 (1997): "There is little empirical evidence on the relative effectiveness of cooperative and legalistic enforcement policies. Most of the evidence is anecdotal and open to dispute. Bardach and Kagan, for example, suggest that eighty percent of regulated entities are strongly to weakly inclined to cooperate with regulatory agencies, but this estimate is based on one limited study and seat-of-pants estimates by regulators and others. . . . International studies also support the efficacy of cooperative approaches, but these studies are also impressionistic. . . .

"A mix of anecdotal and empirical evidence warns that cooperative approaches can decrease compliance if agencies permit law breakers to go unpunished. A Canadian study, for example, found that the same employers continued to violate health and safety regulations despite lenient treatment. Another empirical study which compared compliance in the pulp and paper industries in Canada and the United States found lower compliance rates in Canada, which the author attributed to the fact that Canadian enforcers were more lenient than their American counterparts when addressing noncompliance. An Australian analyst came to a similar conclusion based on his observations of efforts to enforce mine safety and health in Australia.

"OSHA's experience likewise suggests caution concerning cooperative approaches. The ineffective nature of the largely cooperative state enforcement programs was one reason why Congress created OSHA. Moreover, OSHA's effort at cooperation in the early 1980s was followed by a sharp increase in the number of workplace injuries. The Reagan administration, which believed that OSHA inspectors would be more effective as 'consultants' than as 'enforcers,' took a number of steps to reduce the level of enforcement in the early 1980s. By 1983, a previous downward trend in accident statistics reversed, and the accident rates continued to climb for the remainder of the decade.

"Two factors appear to explain these results. First, if a regulated entity lacks sufficient incentives to comply voluntarily with agency regulations, a cooperative enforcement approach is not likely to induce compliance. To the contrary, the agency's failure to punish the firm results in its continued noncompliance. Unless the firm's incentives are shifted by the imposition of penalties, its managers have no reason to change their behavior. Second, the failure to punish violators can lead to less voluntary compliance. If regulatory agencies fail to detect and punish violators, other firms will decline to comply because cooperation will put them at a competitive disadvantage with the noncompliers. In her examination of tax enforcement, for example, Margaret Levi stresses that active prosecution of violators is crucial because perceptions of 'exploitation' will encourage noncompliance.[8]"

(5) *The impacts of limited resources:* The importance of budgetary constraints is perhaps underscored by the situation that prevailed in the Labor Department and in North Carolina at the time of the Imperial fire. The 1970 federal OSH Act had established a "charter for federal-state cooperation,"[9] adopting the view that state enforcement of federal standards promotes efficiency and responsiveness.[10] The Act permits states to operate their own workplace safety and health programs if OSHA approves them. OSHA is then supposed to conduct "continuing evaluation" to ensure that each state program remains "at least as effective" as OSHA's own program. No approval had ever been revoked before the fire at Imperial Food Products, 281. One month after it, OSHA undertook limited federal concurrent enforcement, and that lasted for about three and a half years. OSHA formally redesignated the state plan "fully effective" on December 10, 1996. The state "has added no new workplace safety inspectors since 1993, despite a booming economy that added 40,000 new businesses during the past decade, a 25 percent jump. The number of workplace deaths is increasing, particularly among Hispanics. The poultry industry, which was a focus of enforcement after the fire in the Imperial Food Products plant, has seen a steady climb in the rate of workplace injuries over the past few years." Irwin Speizer, "Some Fear Safety Standards Have Leveled Off," The News & Observer, Raleigh, NC, Sept. 2, 2001, at A1.

AFL-CIO, DEATH ON THE JOB: THE TOLL OF NEGLECT 4 (11th ed. 2002): "There are only 2,238 federal and state OSHA inspectors responsible for enforcing the law at nearly eight million workplaces. In FY 2001, the 860 federal OSHA inspectors conducted 35,941 inspections (409 fewer than in FY 2000) and the state OSHA plans combined conducted 56,322 inspections (758 more than in FY 2000). ... At its current staffing levels and inspection levels, it would take federal OSHA 119 years to inspect each workplace under its jurisdiction just once. In six states (Florida, Louisiana, Mississippi, Georgia, New Hampshire and Nebraska), it would take more than 150 years for OSHA to pay a single visit to each workplace. In 21 states, it would take between 100 and 149 years to visit each workplace once. Inspection frequency is better in states with OSHA approved plans, yet still far from satisfactory. In these states, it would now take the state OSHAs a combined 62 years to inspect each worksite under state jurisdiction

---

8. Margaret Levi, Of Rule and Revenue 53 (1988).

9. Stephen A. Bokat (et al., eds.), Occupational Safety and Health Law, 62 (1988).

10. We cannot develop here the difficult questions of cooperative federalism, and associated problems of financial responsibilities for the implementation of federal mandates, that such a regime entails.

once...." (Based on OSHA data on inspection frequency for 1993, the 21 state programs then needed an average of 47 years to inspect each site for which they were responsible; in the other 29 states, OSHA needed an average of 98 years.) In North Carolina, the AFL–CIO study reports, it would take only 52 years to inspect each workplace once, and the reported rate of workplace injury and illness was also below the national average; North Carolina ranked 35th in its rate of workplace fatalities.

Obviously, priority-setting is crucial—e.g., industries are classified. The "high hazard" category includes poultry processing plants, which are "concentrated in the rural South [with almost half of the workers females.] ... 'Poultry is bigger than peanuts in Georgia, bigger than tobacco in North Carolina ...' [U]npleasant labor and low wages keep turnover high—exceeding 100% a year at many plants ..."[11] Even for high-hazard workplaces, however, for states where OSHA itself inspects, it "has resources to visit ... only once every thirteen years.... As a result, 'seventy-five percent of the sites where workers suffered serious accidents in 1994 and early 1995 had not had a federal safety inspection since 1990.' ... [Moreover,] OSHA enforcement creates fewer incentives for compliance than enforcement by other agencies for two reasons. First, OSHA is less likely than other agencies to detect rule violations because other agencies have more inspectors. The Mine Safety and Health Administration (MSHA), for example, has jurisdiction over far fewer employers, but it has about two hundred more inspectors than OSHA. ... In addition, unlike private rights of action that exist [in other regulatory contexts], no private right of action exists to enforce the OSH Act. ... [Worker compensation programs protect employers from tort law consequences of rule violations and,] after OSHA detects violations, it is more limited than other agencies in its ability to assess large fines." Sidney A. Shapiro and Randy Rabinowitz, Voluntary Regulatory Compliance in Theory and Practice: The Case of OSHA, 52 Admin.L.Rev. 97, 108–09 (2000).

One step North Carolina took after the Imperial Food Products fire was to have "food safety inspectors from the U.S. Department of Agriculture ... trained to identify workplace hazards." Ironically, the Imperial Foods plant had had federal inspectors on site every day—from the U.S. Department of Agriculture, monitoring the quality of the plant's product.[12] How shall we view the fact that they had ignored the visible padlocks on seven of the plant's nine exits, at least one of which was marked "Fire Exit Do Not Block"? A standard criticism of regulators is their undue narrowness or "tunnel vision." Yet, might a food safety inspector reasonably have feared that calling attention to even obvious workplace hazards would jeopardize her ability to carry out her own responsibility? Does limiting inspectors to single programs tend to limit their power in ways American political culture would generally applaud, even at the cost of resulting

---

11. Tony Horwitz, These Six Growth Jobs Are Dull, Dead–End, Sometimes Dangerous, Wall St.J., Dec. 1, 1994, 1, A8.

12. While these materials focus on workplace safety inspections, it may be apparent that similar accounts could be given of developments and problems with inspection of food for purity and healthfulness. Viz., Marian Burros, "Federal Audit Faults Department's Meat and Poultry Inspection System," The New York Times, July 10, 2002.

inefficiency? Should each agency be encouraged to explore what other agencies could help it, or what other programs it could help implement?

MAKING DO WITH LESS—NOTES ON A RETURN TO "COOPERATION" AND VOLUNTARISM

(1) NATIONAL PERFORMANCE REVIEW, CREATING A GOVERNMENT THAT WORKS BETTER AND COSTS LESS 62–63 (1993): "No army of federal auditors descends upon American businesses to audit their books; the government forces them to have the job done themselves. In the same way, no army of OSHA inspectors need descend upon corporate America. The health and safety of American workers could be vastly improved—without bankrupting the federal treasury.

"The Labor Secretary already is authorized to require employers to conduct certified self-inspections. OSHA should give employers two options with which to do so: They could hire third parties, such as private inspection companies; or they could authorize non-management employees, after training and certification, to conduct inspections. In either case, OSHA would set inspection and reporting standards and conduct random reviews, audits, and inspections to ensure quality.

"Within a year or two of issuing the new regulations, OSHA should establish a sliding scale of incentives designed to encourage workplaces to comply. Worksites with good health, safety, and compliance records would be allowed to report less frequently to the Labor Department, to undergo fewer audits, and to submit less paperwork. OSHA could also impose higher fines for employers whose health and safety records worsened or did not improve."

A June, 1994 recommendation of the Administrative Conference of the United States, "The Use of Audited Self–Regulation as a Regulatory Technique" encouraged reliance on this technique "in certain circumstances," while acknowledging that in others "audited self-regulation may present the significant risks of uneven enforcement, capture of the regulators by the regulated industry, and creating barriers to entry or competition." Positive signs, the Conference advised, include (1) an organized, expert and motivated industry; (2) clear rules that can be objectively applied to particular circumstances; and (3) an agency capable of effective supervision.[1]

---

1. 1 C.F.R. § 305.94–1. The Conference action was based on Douglas C. Michael, Federal Agency Use of Audited Self–Regulation as a Regulatory Technique, 47 Admin.L.Rev. 171 (1995).

Particularly in its emphasis on clear rules and objective application, this new direction stands in contrast with the efforts of some to return to fewer rules and broader discretion—as, for example, when Florida's Department of Transportation proposed a three-year test of replacing its rules "with loose guidelines that would set out goals but allow bureaucrats to make decisions on their own. 'Common sense and flexibility! That's a radical thought, but every once in a while we bureaucrats come up with something strange,' said Florida Transportation Secretary Ben G. Watts. ... 'We asked ourselves if we really believed government can be run differently. And we thought it could, and then we asked ourselves if we could run the agency without rules,' Watts said, recalling that nobody at the table had a heart attack." William Booth, "Florida Seeks to End Rule by the Book," The Washington Post, March 14, 1995, p. A:1.

(2) *A Program for Workplaces Initially Committed to Workplace Safety.* "Effective supervision" presents regulatory challenges that could be thought to re-present the issues of the preceding paragraphs. OSHA, for example, has been making increasing use of self-audited programs, as may be seen at a website devoted to "voluntary protection programs." See http://www.osha.gov/oshprogs/vpp. Charts there show strong growth in the number of sites in these programs, from 106 in 1992, the last year of the first Bush administration, to 819 in mid–2002, with a sharply increasing presence of state programs. The Voluntary Protection Program is limited to workplaces that have already established a demonstrable commitment to workplace safety. Each site must qualify through an application and initial inspection process that stresses the existence of effective on-site safety and health management, and then wins freedom from routine inspections. (Accidents, employee complaints, and chemical spills are handled through OSHA's established enforcement procedures.) The results, OSHA claims, are superior health and safety results at the enrolled sites, the generation of models of safety management that can be used elsewhere, and the development of resources for effective training in safety management. Accident rates at VPP sites are about half the industry average—which implies lower workers compensation costs and lost time costs, as well as increased morale. Of course, the need to qualify for enrolment may raise a question whether these outcomes are result from the program's success, or merely reflect its entrance standards.

While the program is perhaps better characterized as re-regulation than deregulation (as Prof. Charles Sabel remarked to one of your editors), the regulated entity gets more freedom to choose the means of compliance while OSHA, in turn, gets information that improves monitorability. It allows for better disposition of the monitors and improved performance measures—and, with these, greater ability to define acceptable paths to improvement from many different starting points. Still, administration of this program is not simple; it has called forth its own extensive "Policies and Procedures Manual" for responsible OSHA staff, posted to the program web page. For a general discussion of the advantages of such cooperative ventures, see Michael C. Dorf & Charles F. Sabel, A Constitution of Democratic Experimentalism, 98 Colum. L. Rev. 267 (1998).

(3) *Trading Enforcement for Cooperation in High-Hazard Worksites?* What of workplaces whose past experience suggests high levels of hazard rather than low ones? Here, OSHA developed another "partnership" approach, initially in the state of Maine. The 200 industries with the highest reported number of workers' compensation claims—1% of Maine's employers, but 30% of its workforce and 45% of its claims—were invited to participate in a cooperative program that would work to identify and correct safety problems. Those who accepted were promised a reduction in the incidence of "wall-to-wall inspections"; good faith efforts to stay with the program would also eliminate fines and sanctions. Of the "Maine Top 200," all but two joined the program, and their workers' compensation claim experience fell by 47.3%; the state as a whole saw a 27% drop in claims—a drop substantially explained by this performance in a group previously responsi-

ble for almost half the claims filed. For OSHA's Maine area director, the program also brought substantial rewards in the efficiency of his office's effort: a wall-to-wall inspection at a high hazard plant might involve six to nine officers on site for three months, then time to write findings, and months or years of litigation—with little sign, on later inspections, of permanent change. In three years, he thought, the new program had resulted in the identification and elimination of seven times as many safety hazards as OSHA could have found. See Charles Oliver, "Executive Update F," Investor's Business Daily 4, September 10, 1996.[2]

The success of this and other state programs prompted OSHA to issue a directive establishing a cooperative compliance program in high-hazard industries nationwide; over 12,000 were invited to join, under threat of immediate priority for comprehensive inspection if they did not. Given OSHA's constrained resources, of course, the reality of this threat depended on the degree of cooperation it would be able to secure. (There is also the possibility, as Shapiro and Rabinowitz suggest, 49 Admin.L.Rev. at 741, that "OSHA appears to be rewarding those employers with the worst safety records, which sends the wrong message.") On judicial review, this initiative was struck down, because OSHA had failed to comply with what the D.C. Circuit determined were the necessary procedures for adopting it, see Chamber of Commerce of the United States v. Department of Labor, 174 F.3d 206 (1999); the case is noted for other purposes at p. 728 below.

As may be apparent, the success of programs like these turns on the reality of the alternative—how real is the prospect of inspection. That, in turn, may be a function of OSHA's freedom to choose its targets. May it choose to concentrate its efforts on the most hazardous industries? The most hazardous workplaces within those industries, as shown by prior inspections? By reports of injuries filed? By worker compensation experience? The answers to such questions depend to some extent on OSHA's statutory authorization. But they may also depend on courts' responses to individuals who claim a constitutional right to be free of unreasonable searches and seizures when OSHA targets *their* premises under its inspection priorities.

(4) JODY FREEMAN, THE PRIVATE ROLE IN PUBLIC GOVERNANCE, 75 N.Y.U.L.Rev. 543, 545–48 (2000): "Administrative law, a field motivated by the need to legitimize the exercise of governmental authority, must now reckon with private power, or risk irrelevance as a discipline. Since the New Deal explosion of government agencies, administrative law has been defined by the crisis of legitimacy and the problem of agency discretion. ... Unsurprisingly, administrative law scholarship has organized itself largely around the need to defend the administrative state against accusations of illegitimacy, principally by emphasizing mechanisms that render agencies indirectly accountable to the electorate, such as legislative and executive oversight and judicial review. ... Only a handful of articles in the last sixty

---

2. Information about the Maine 200 program has been posted at various times on the OSHA website, that is now not accessible. At the time of this writing, URLs remaining active included http://www.osha.gov/oshin-fo/reinvent/prog1.html, http://www.osha.gov/html/Reinventing/app_1.html and http://www.osha.gov/media/oshnews/july95/osha95290.html.

years, by contrast, have ventured beyond the traditional preoccupation with agencies and the project of constraint. . . . [P]rivate power . . . has attracted significant attention only recently, in the wake of international trends toward privatization, deregulation, devolution, and the contracting out of services to private providers. . . .

"Private participation in governance is neither marginal nor restricted to the implementation of rules and regulations. A variety of nongovernmental actors, including corporations, public interest organizations, private standard setting bodies, professional associations, and nonprofit groups, engage in 'public' decision making in myriad ways. Nongovernmental actors perform 'legislative' and 'adjudicative' roles, along with many others, in a broad variety of regulatory contexts. They set standards, provide services, and deliver benefits. In addition, they help implement, monitor, and enforce compliance with regulations. Nongovernmental organizations exert, in the context of a larger network of relationships, coercive power. A careful inquiry into the private role in governance reveals not only its pervasiveness, but also the extent to which it operates symbiotically with public authority. That is, the relationship between public and private actors in administrative law cannot properly be understood . . . as if augmenting one necessarily depletes the other.

"Most administrative law theory now adheres to a hierarchical, agency-centered conception of administrative power in which the most pressing theoretical goal is to constrain agency discretion. Given the reality of public/private interdependence, I propose an alternative conception of administration as a set of negotiated relationships. Specifically, public and private actors negotiate over policy making, implementation, and enforcement. This evokes a decentralized image of decision making, one that depends on combinations of public and private actors linked by implicit or explicit agreements. . . . This alternative conception challenges the fundamental public/private distinction in administrative law. It invites a reconsideration of the agency as the primary unit of analysis in the field. . . . [T]he entity on which we ought to focus administrative law's scholarly attention is neither public nor private but something else: the set of negotiated relationships between the public and the private."

b.   REQUIRED FORMS AND REPORTS

How do EPA and OSHA collect the information they require to administer programs like TRI or to identify the "Maine 200"? Perhaps the most commonplace feature of regulatory regimes is an obligation to supply the government with information, either directly or by keeping it on hand for possible inspection. Experience with required forms and reports is as close at hand as the filing of an annual tax return or application for Social Security benefits, or a pharmacy's keeping its prescription records. To be valid, the requirement must be established by statute or an authorized regulation. Sanctions for non-compliance must be similarly defined; some, such as denial of a requested benefit, may be administered by the agency itself; others, such as criminal penalties, require judicial assistance. By contrast, the forms on which information is requested—paper or (increasingly) electronic—will likely be generated by purely internal bureaucratic routine.

For citizens and regulated entities alike, the burdens of such requirements are substantial. OMB's Office of Information and Regulatory Affairs (OIRA) is responsible for managing many different aspects of government information programs, as will shortly appear. On August 2, 2002 its website[1] reported 7,951 approved federal government information requirements of persons or organizations outside government, eliciting in excess of 66 billion responses, that consumed over 8 billion hours to produce, at a cost of $146 billion dollars. About two thirds of the time involved is imposed on business, one third on individuals. The great bulk of the time involved (but not of the number of requirements, responses or estimated cost) is attributed to the Department of the Treasury, home of the Internal Revenue Service. Despite the hopeful title of the legislation next described, these numbers have been steadily increasing in recent years. "[G]overnment information ... can be the means by which the dedicated public servant uncovers problems, reaches decisions, enforces laws, delivers services, and informs the public. But it also can be the means by which the faceless bureaucrat asks time-consuming or intrusive questions, forces seemingly arbitrary changes in business practices or personal behavior, and imposes significant costs on the economy."[2]

The next few paragraphs give a brief introduction to the PAPERWORK REDUCTION ACT, 44 U.S.C. §§ 3501–3520, which gives OIRA responsibility both for controlling and reducing the cumulating, expensive, sometimes even disturbing character of the paperwork burden, and for overseeing its gradual conversion into electronic form. "Paperwork reduction is what newspaper editors call a 'three-bowler.' (It has so little sex appeal that a reader's face will plop into his cereal bowl three times before he finishes the story in the morning paper.)"[3] Yet the struggles over it have large implications. Any effort at control quickly confronts the reality that much of the government's curiosity is firmly rooted in the programs it seeks to administer.[4] Information is required to assure that the rules of government programs are being respected; to permit intelligent decisions about the

---

1. http://www.whitehouse.gov/omb/library/OMBINV.html.

2. S. Rpt. 103–392, Paperwork Reduction Act of 1994, Committee on Governmental Affairs 18 (1994). The National Performance Review gave many examples of "industrial-era bureaucracies in an information age," such as the requirement of 14 different forms for every import transaction and as many as 40 for a single export transaction, at an estimated cost of at least $150–$200 per transaction. National Performance Review, Accompanying Report on Reengineering Through Information Technology, 38 (1993).

A very different example: employers of asbestos-exposed employees must retain medical records for the period of employment plus 30 years, because of the extended latency periods of the afflictions caused by asbestos. 29 C.F.R. § 1910.1001 (2001).

3. Richard Neustadt, Taming the Paperwork Tiger, Regulation p. 32 (Jan./Feb. 1981).

4. "Maybe we could suppress [red tape] if it were merely the nefarious work of a small group of villains or if it were a waste product easily separated from the things we want to government, but it is neither. ... What we need is a detached clinical approach rather than heated attacks, the delicate wielding of a scalpel rather than furious flailing about with a meat ax." Herbert Kaufman, Red Tape: Its Origins, Uses, and Abuses 97–98 (1977).

future course of policy; to understand the workings and needs of that part of the private sector being subject to regulation; and to inform the public about matters of common concern. Indeed, the lack of information critical to analyzing issues and controlling costs has led to "poor service quality, high costs, low productivity, unnecessary risks and burdens, and unexploited opportunities for improvement . . ."[5]

The Act requires any agency that seeks to collect information from outside government by identical questions or requirements posed to more than ten sources first to seek OIRA's approval. The governing standard is "whether the collection of information by the agency is necessary for the proper performance of the functions of the agency, including whether the information shall have practical utility." 44 U.S.C. § 3508. If the agency adopts its collection requirement by using the public procedures of rulemaking, see Chapter V, OIRA participates in that process;[6] if the agency proceeds only bureaucratically, OIRA itself makes the determination, and may itself conduct informal proceedings to that end. Anyone can track the requests made to OIRA (as well as find other information about the Act) at the information collection home on its website, http://www.whitehouse.gov/omb/inforeg/infocoll.html. OIRA can withhold permission to collect information, or make it subject to a condition that the information be obtained through a central collection agency able to coordinate this request with those of other agencies interested in similar data. Under even more hopefully titled amendments to the Act, the Government Paperwork Elimination Act, Ch. XVII of P.L. 105–277 (1998), OIRA is supervising agency efforts to comply by October, 2003 with a requirement to offer, "when practicable," the option of submitting, maintaining, or disclosing *all* information subject to the Act in electronic form.[7]

And OIRA's decisions are generally protected from judicial review of any kind. 44 U.S.C. § 3507(d)(6). Even the independent regulatory commissions are subject to this constraint, although a commission may override OIRA by a publicly explained majority vote. 44 U.S.C. § 3507(f). No one need comply with an information request required to be, but not, approved in this manner. You should notice that any federal government form you receive these days bears an OMB control number.[8] The implications of a

---

5. S.Rpt. 103–392, above n. 2 at 19, 30. Among specific losses attributed to information failures are overpayments of Medicare benefits and issuance of unauthorized student loans.

6. If it comments publicly in the rulemaking, § 3507(d)(4) permits the Director, "in the Director's discretion," to disapprove a collection (A) "not specifically required by an agency rule," (B) if the agency failed to comply with statutory requirements, (C) "if the Director finds within 60 days after the publication of the rule that the agency's response to the Director's comments . . . was unreasonable," or (D) if the Director finds the agency in its final rule has substantially modified what it initially proposed, without re-

submitting the modified collection requirement at least 60 days before issuing the final rule.

7. OMB, Implementation of the Government Paperwork Elimination Act, at http://www.whitehouse.gov/omb/fedreg/print/gpea.2.html, visited August 2 2002.

8. That the simple existence of a control number does not inevitably make this law self-enforcing is suggested by a June 10, 2002 memorandum from OIRA's Administrator, calling to agencies' attention that more than 400 violations of the Act had been documented for each of the two preceding fiscal years, of which more than 100 remained unresolved in each instance after several

failure to show that number can be quite dramatic.[9]

This centralization of control over information requirements in the presidency (through OIRA) is a presidential political control and coordination mechanism of surprising strength—and it is one that Congress, perhaps in frustration at the failure of information requirements to diminish—has steadily made stronger. While OIRA's function is focused on coordination and cost-reduction, and the statute explicitly disclaims any purpose to enlarge its authority over an agency's "substantive policies and programs," 44 U.S.C. § 3518(e), compliance with that limitation is itself in the hands of the White House and Executive Office Building. Is the statute a salutary recognition of the need for presidential coordination and of the benefits of sharing information across government (including the benefit of reducing duplicative information demands from agencies that may be unaware of each others' activities)? Or is it an invitation for influential regulated interests to undermine agency functioning by making covert use of White House friends? Similar questions about political controls are presented in some depth in other chapters; the degree of control statutorily authorized here is quite striking when compared to the level of statutory recognition generally given presidential direction of agency affairs.

c. RIGHTS TO REFUSE COOPERATION WITH INFORMATION DEMANDS

The Fourth Amendment to the United States Constitution, applicable as well to state and local governments through the Fourteenth Amendment, provides:

> The right of the people to be secure in their persons, houses, papers, and effects, against unreasonable searches and seizures, shall not be violated, and no Warrants shall issue, but upon probable cause, supported by Oath or affirmation, and particularly describing the place to be searched, and the persons or things to be seized.

Section 8(a) of the Occupational Safety and Health Act of 1970 (OSHA) provides that

> In order to carry out the purposes of this chapter, the Secretary, upon presenting appropriate credentials to the owner, operator, or agent in charge, is authorized—

---

months' notice. http://www.whitehouse.gov/omb/inforeg/violation_memo060602.pdf.

9. 44 U.S.C. § 3512 provides: "(a) Notwithstanding any other provision of law, no person shall be subject to any penalty for failing to comply with a collection of information that is subject to this chapter if—

> "(1) the collection of information does not display a valid control number assigned by the Director [of the OMB] in accordance with this chapter; . . . .

"(b) *The protection provided by this section may be raised in the form of a complete defense, bar, or otherwise at any time during the agency administrative process or judicial action applicable thereto.*" (emphasis added)

In Saco River Cellular, Inc. v. FCC, 133 F.3d 25 (D.C.Cir.1998), this provision required the unwinding of licensing proceedings ostensibly completed in 1986, but on the basis of information supplied on forms that did not bear a valid control number.

(1) to enter without delay and at reasonable times any factory, plant, establishment, construction site, or other area, workplace or environment where work is performed by an employee of an employer; and

(2) to inspect and investigate during regular working hours and at other reasonable times, and within reasonable limits and in a reasonable manner, any such place of employment and all pertinent conditions, structures, machines, apparatus, devices, equipment, and materials therein, and to question privately any such employer, owner, operator, agent, or employee.

84 Stat. 1590, 29 U.S.C. § 657(a) (1970). These two texts collided in

Marshall v. Barlow's, Inc.

Supreme Court of the United States, 1978.
436 U.S. 307.

[On Sept. 11, 1975, an OSHA inspector, after showing his credentials, requested permission from the owner of an electrical and plumbing installation business to inspect the working areas of that business, in Pocatello, Idaho. Mr. Barlow asked whether any complaint had been received about his company; the inspector answered no, the company had simply turned up in the agency's selection process. After ascertaining that the inspector had no search warrant, Mr. Barlow refused to allow entry, saying he was relying on his rights as guaranteed by the Fourth Amendment. On January 5, 1976, OSHA presented Mr. Barlow with a district court order directing him to allow entry. Mr. Barlow again refused, and sought injunctive relief against the warrantless search.]

■ MR. JUSTICE WHITE delivered the opinion of the Court.

Section 8(a) of the Occupational Safety and Health Act of 1970 (OSHA) empowers agents of the Secretary of Labor (the Secretary) to search the work area of any employment facility within the Act's jurisdiction. The purpose of the search is to inspect for safety hazards and violations of OSHA regulations. . . .

I

The Warrant Clause of the Fourth Amendment protects commercial buildings as well as private homes. To hold otherwise would belie the origin of that Amendment, and the American colonial experience. An important forerunner of the first 10 Amendments to the United States Constitution, the Virginia Bill of Rights, specifically opposed "general warrants, whereby an officer or messenger may be commanded to search suspected places without evidence of a fact committed." The general warrant was a recurring point of contention in the colonies immediately preceding the Revolution. The particular offensiveness it engendered was acutely felt by the merchants and businessmen whose premises and products were inspected for compliance with the several Parliamentary revenue measures that most irritated the colonists. . . .

This Court has already held that warrantless searches are generally unreasonable and that this rule applies to commercial premises as well as homes. In Camara v. Municipal Court, 387 U.S. 523, 528–29 (1967), we held: "[E]xcept in certain carefully defined classes of cases, a search of private property without proper consent is 'unreasonable' unless it has been authorized by a valid search warrant."

On the same day, we also ruled:

> ... The businessman, like the occupant of a residence, has a constitutional right to go about his business free from unreasonable official entries upon his private commercial property. The businessman, too, has that right placed in jeopardy if the decision to enter and inspect for violation of regulatory laws can be made and enforced by the inspector in the field without official authority evidenced by a warrant. See v. Seattle, 387 U.S. 541, 543 (1967).

... If the government intrudes on a person's property, the privacy interest suffers whether the government's motivation is to investigate violations of criminal laws or breaches of other statutory or regulatory standards. ... [A]n exception from the search warrant requirement has been recognized for "pervasively regulated business[es]," United States v. Biswell, 406 U.S. 311, 316 (1972), and for "closely regulated" industries "long subject to close supervision and inspection." Colonnade Catering Corp. v. United States, 397 U.S. 72, 74, 77 (1970). ... Certain industries have such a history of government oversight that no reasonable expectation of privacy could exist for a proprietor over the stock of such an enterprise. Liquor (Colonnade) and firearms (Biswell) are industries of this type; when an entrepreneur embarks upon such a business, he has voluntarily chosen to subject himself to a full arsenal of governmental regulation.[1] ...

The clear import of our cases is that the closely regulated industry of the type involved in Colonnade and Biswell is the exception. The Secretary would make it the rule. Invoking the Walsh–Healey Act of 1936 [see n. 1 above], the Secretary attempts to support a conclusion that all businesses involved in interstate commerce have long been subjected to close supervision of employee safety and health conditions. But ... [it] is quite unconvincing to argue that the imposition of minimum wages and maximum

---

1. [Ed.] The distinction between "closely regulated industries" and "ordinary enterprise," has recurred in various settings, with varying success, throughout our constitutional history. When "substantive due process" considerations called into question the permissible scope of state or federal regulation of enterprise, it served to segregate settings in which broad regulation was freely permitted from others subject to close constitutional scrutiny. Compare Munn v. Illinois, 94 U.S. 113 (1877) with Allgeyer v. Louisiana, 165 U.S. 578 (1897) and Lochner v. New York, 198 U.S. 45 (1905). Close scrutiny of *any* economic regulation was displaced as a test of regulatory authority by cases decided during the late 1930's and early 1940's, including one that upheld the Walsh–Healey Act imposing federal wage and hour standards, United States v. Darby, 312 U.S. 100 (1941). (See also Nebbia v. New York, 291 U.S. 502 (1934)).

In Shapiro v. United States, 335 U.S. 1 (1948) noted at p. 885 below, the Court rejected Justice Frankfurter's effort to rely on the distinction as a basis for recognizing the Fifth Amendment claims of a greengrocer legislatively required to keep what proved to be incriminatory records.

hours on employers who contracted with the government under the Walsh–Healey Act prepared the entirety of American interstate commerce for regulation of working conditions to the minutest detail. Nor can any but the most fictional sense of voluntary consent to later searches be found in the single fact that one conducts a business affecting interstate commerce; under current practice and law, few businesses can be conducted without having some effect on interstate commerce. . . .

The critical fact in this case is that entry over Mr. Barlow's objection is being sought by a Government agent. . . . What [employees] observe in their daily functions is undoubtedly beyond the employer's reasonable expectation of privacy. The government inspector, however, is not an employee. . . . Without a warrant he stands in no better position than a member of the public. . . . The owner of a business has not, by the necessary utilization of employees in his operation, thrown open the areas where employees alone are permitted to the warrantless scrutiny of Government agents. . . .

II

The Secretary . . . stoutly argues that the enforcement scheme of the Act requires warrantless searches, and that the restrictions on search discretion contained in the Act and its regulations already protect as much privacy as a warrant would. . . . Because "reasonableness is still the ultimate standard," Camara, at 539, the Secretary suggests that the Court decide whether a warrant is needed by arriving at a sensible balance between the administrative necessities of OSHA inspections and the incremental protection of privacy of business owners a warrant would afford. . . .

The Secretary submits that warrantless inspections are essential . . . because they afford the opportunity to inspect without prior notice and hence to preserve the advantages of surprise. . . . The risk is that during the interval between an inspector's initial request to search a plant and his procuring a warrant following the owner's refusal of permission, violations . . . could be corrected and thus escape the inspector's notice. To the suggestion that warrants may be issued ex parte and executed without delay and without prior notice, thereby preserving the element of surprise, the Secretary expresses concern for the administrative strain that would be experienced by the inspection system and by the courts, should ex parte warrants issued in advance become standard practice.

We are unconvinced, however, that requiring warrants to inspect will impose serious burdens on the inspection system or the courts, will prevent inspections necessary to enforce the statute, or will make them less effective. In the first place, the great majority of businessmen can be expected in normal course to consent to inspection without warrant; the Secretary has not brought to this Court's attention any widespread pattern of refusal.[2] In those cases where an owner does [refuse to permit an

---

2. We recognize that today's holding might itself have an impact on whether owners choose to resist requested searches; we can only await the development of evidence

inspector to enter the property or to complete his inspection] ... the Secretary has also promulgated a regulation providing that ... the inspector shall attempt to ascertain the reasons for the refusal and report to his superior, who shall "promptly take appropriate action, including compulsory process, if necessary." 29 C.F.R. § 1903.4.[3] ... Nor is it immediately apparent why the advantages of surprise would be lost if, after being refused entry, procedures were available for the Secretary to seek an ex parte warrant and to reappear at the premises without further notice to the establishment being inspected.

Whether the Secretary proceeds to secure a warrant or other process, with or without prior notice, his entitlement to inspect will not depend on his demonstrating probable cause to believe that conditions in violation of OSHA exist on the premises. Probable cause in the criminal law sense is not required. For purposes of an administrative search such as this, probable cause justifying the issuance of a warrant may be based not only on specific evidence of an existing violation but also on a showing that "reasonable legislative or administrative standards for conducting an ... inspection are satisfied with respect to a particular [establishment]." Camara, at 538. A warrant showing that a specific business has been chosen for an OSHA search on the basis of a general administrative plan for the enforcement of the Act derived from neutral sources such as, for example, dispersion of employees in various types of industries across a given area, and the desired frequency of searches in any of the lesser divisions of the area, would protect an employer's Fourth Amendment rights. ...

Nor do we agree that the incremental protections afforded the employer's privacy by a warrant are so marginal that they fail to justify the administrative burdens that may be entailed. The authority to make warrantless searches devolves almost unbridled discretion upon executive and administrative officers, particularly those in the field, as to when to search and whom to search. A warrant, by contrast, would provide assurances from a neutral officer that the inspection is reasonable under the Constitution, is authorized by statute, and is pursuant to an administrative plan containing specific neutral criteria. Also, a warrant would then and there advise the owner of the scope and objects of the search, beyond which limits the inspector is not expected to proceed. These are important functions for a warrant to perform, functions which underlie the Court's prior decisions that the Warrant Clause applies to inspections for compliance with regulatory statutes. ...

III

We hold that Barlow was entitled to a declaratory judgment that the Act is unconstitutional insofar as it purports to authorize inspections without warrant or its equivalent and to an injunction enjoining the Act's

not present on this record to determine how serious an impediment to effective enforcement this might be.

    3. ... [Section] 8(a) of the Act purports to authorize inspections without warrant; but

... it does not forbid the Secretary from proceeding to inspect only by warrant or other process. ...

enforcement to that extent.[4] The judgment of the District Court is therefore affirmed.

■ MR. JUSTICE STEVENS, with whom MR. JUSTICE BLACKMUN and MR. JUSTICE REHNQUIST join, dissenting.

. . . .

The Fourth Amendment contains two separate clauses, each flatly prohibiting a category of governmental conduct. The first clause states that the right to be free from unreasonable searches "shall not be violated"; the second unequivocally prohibits the issuance of warrants except "upon probable cause." In this case the ultimate question is whether the category of warrantless searches authorized by the statute is "unreasonable" within the meaning of the first clause.

. . . The routine OSHA inspections are, by definition, not based on cause to believe there is a violation on the premises to be inspected. Hence, if the inspections were measured against the requirements of the Warrant Clause, they would be automatically and unequivocally unreasonable. . . .

"[O]ur constitutional fathers were not concerned about warrantless searches, but about overreaching warrants. It is perhaps too much to say that they feared the warrant more than the search, but it is plain enough that the warrant was the prime object of their concern. Far from looking at the warrant as a protection against unreasonable searches, they saw it as an authority for unreasonable and oppressive searches. . . ."[5]

Since the general warrant, not the warrantless search, was the immediate evil at which the Fourth Amendment was directed, it is not surprising that the Framers placed precise limits on its issuance. The requirement that a warrant only issue on a showing of particularized probable cause was the means adopted to circumscribe the warrant power. . . .

Fidelity to the original understanding of the Fourth Amendment, therefore, leads to the conclusion that the Warrant Clause has no application to routine, regulatory inspections of commercial premises. If such inspections are valid, it is because they comport with the ultimate reasonableness standard of the Fourth Amendment. . . .

The Court's analysis does not persuade me that Congress' determination that the warrantless inspection power as a necessary adjunct of the exercise of the regulatory power is unreasonable. . . . [T]he Court's prediction of the effect a warrant requirement would have on the behavior of covered employers . . . is essentially empirical. On such an issue, I would defer to Congress' judgment regarding the importance of a warrantless search power to the OSHA enforcement scheme.

. . . .

4. The injunction entered by the District Court, however, should not be understood to forbid the Secretary from exercising the inspection authority conferred by § 8 pursuant to regulations and judicial process that satisfy the Fourth Amendment. . . .

5. Telford Taylor, Two Studies in Constitutional Interpretation, 41 (1969).

What purposes, then, are served by the administrative warrant procedure? The inspection warrant purports to serve three functions: to inform the employer that the inspection is authorized by the statute, to advise him of the lawful limits of the inspection, and to assure him that the person demanding entry is an authorized inspector. An examination of these functions in the OSHA context reveals that the inspection warrant adds little to the protections already afforded by the statute and pertinent regulations, and the slight additional benefit it might provide is insufficient to identify a constitutional violation or to justify overriding Congress' judgment that the power to conduct warrantless inspections is essential.

... Until today we have not rejected a congressional judgment concerning the reasonableness of a category of regulatory inspections of commercial premises. While businesses are unquestionably entitled to Fourth Amendment protection, we have "recognized that a business by its special nature and voluntary existence, may open itself to intrusions that would not be permissible in a purely private context." G.M. Leasing Corp. v. United States, 429 U.S. 338, 353 (1977). ...

The Court, however, concludes that the deference accorded Congress in Biswell and Colonnade should be limited to situations where the evils addressed by the regulatory statute are peculiar to a specific industry and that industry is one which has long been subject to Government regulation. ... I cannot agree that the respect due the congressional judgment should be so narrowly confined. ... The pertinent inquiry is not whether the inspection program is authorized by a regulatory statute directed at a single industry but whether Congress has limited the exercise of the inspection power to those commercial premises where the evils at which the statute is directed are to be found. Thus, in Biswell, if Congress had authorized inspections of all commercial premises as a means of restricting the illegal traffic in firearms, the Court would have found the inspection program unreasonable; the power to inspect was upheld because it was tailored to the subject matter of Congress' proper exercise of regulatory power. Similarly, OSHA is directed at health and safety hazards in the work place, and the inspection power granted the Secretary extends only to those areas where such hazards are likely to be found.

Finally, the Court would distinguish the respect accorded Congress' judgment in Colonnade and Biswell on the ground that businesses engaged in the liquor and firearms industry "accept the burdens as well as the benefits of their trade ..." In the Court's view, such businesses consent to the restrictions placed upon them, while it would be fiction to conclude that a businessman subject to OSHA consented to routine safety inspections. ... In both situations, the validity of the regulations depends not upon the consent of those regulated but on the existence of a federal statute embodying a congressional determination that the public interest in the health of the Nation's work force or the limitation of illegal firearms traffic outweighs the businessman's interest in preventing a government inspector from viewing those areas of his premises which relate to the subject matter of the regulation.[6]

6. Justice Brennan did not participate in the case.

NOTES ON THE CASES BEFORE BARLOW'S

(1) In FRANK V. MARYLAND, 359 U.S. 360 (1959), five Justices held that a city health officer's request to enter a Baltimore row-house to look for rats "touch[ed] at most upon the periphery" of Fourth Amendment protections. The inspector had seen indications of rat infestation outside the house; Frank had refused to allow entry and was fined. The Court stressed that such inspections were "an adjunct to a regulatory scheme for the general welfare and not as a means of enforcing the criminal law," noted that they were limited to "day time," that (unlike criminal searches) refusals were countered by fines not forced entry, and that there was "cause to suspect that a nuisance exists."

Frank dramatized the tension between "inspection[,] *the* indispensable law-enforcement device in the urban community," and the impulse to the dignity of privacy that underlies the Fourth Amendment. As Professor Bernard Schwartz recounted Baltimore's argument, "A man's house may still, in theory, be his castle, but that castle no longer sits on a hill isolated by a moat. The modern 'castle' is connected to a central water system, a sewage system, a garbage collection system, and, more often than not, to houses on either side. The paramount need in the metropolitan agglomerations ... is the enforcement of the plethora of health, sanitary, safety, and housing regulations which ensure that living conditions among the nation's urban masses remain tolerable. And over all hangs the problem of urban blight and decay—with the city engaged in an endless effort to maintain existing standards by preventive measures and slum clearance ..." Commentary on the Constitution of the United States—Rights of the Person, vol.I, 204–205 (1977). And, of course, corresponding issues arise in a wide variety of contexts—when customs agents want to disassemble a traveller's suitcase in search of smuggled contraband; when the Nuclear Regulatory Commission requires permittees to provide on-site office space and continuous, unimpeded access to its facilities for NRC inspectors as a condition of issuing a desired permit; and when a welfare agency conditions payment of benefits for children on agreement to occasional "home visits" to assess the quality of the children's environment.

(2) The Supreme Court overruled Frank eight years later, in the companion cases of CAMARA V. MUNICIPAL COURT, 387 U.S. 523, 530–32 (1967) and SEE V. SEATTLE, 387 U.S. 541 (1967). Camara was the lessee of an apartment that was not supposed to be used as a personal dwelling; he several times refused entry to a San Francisco public health inspector during daytime hours. See was the operator of a commercial warehouse who had refused a Fire Department inspector access to the warehouse during a routine, periodic canvass of premises subject to the city's Fire Code. Like Frank, both cases arose as prosecutions for violation of a statutory obligation to cooperate with an authorized inspection during business hours. In neither was forcible entry attempted. Rejecting possible distinctions between administrative and criminal searches, and between searches of a warehouse and an apartment, six Justices found that neither man could be penalized for insisting upon a warrant to permit a search. Justices Clark, Harlan and Stewart dissented, asserting that "reasonableness" was the proper constitutional inquiry, and that the searches at issue met that test. If the

question of reasonableness for routine inspections was transformed into an issue whether probable cause existed to issue a warrant, they worried, the inquiry would become a mere exercise; such a "pretense" would not only destroy the integrity of search warrants but "degrade the magistrate issuing them and soon bring disrepute not only upon the practice but upon the judicial process." They noted that a search warrant might be less desirable from the public's perspective, as well as expensive and wasteful. A warrant, obtainable ex parte, would permit a forced nighttime entry; the challenged ordinances restricted the hours when searches could occur, and they enforced searches only by imposing fines for refusals to admit, after an ordinary judicial hearing at which a defense could be offered. They also expressed concern that the holding would encourage resistance to essential community undertakings, threatening in this way public health and safety.

NOTES ON THE CLOSELY REGULATED INDUSTRY EXCEPTION

In discussing United States v. Biswell and Colonnade Catering v. United States, the Barlow's Court invokes an idea (akin to the right-privilege distinction discussed in Chapter VII) that some businesses really could not expect to exist absent state consent, and therefore their existence may be conditioned on waiver of what would otherwise be ordinary constitutional liberties. What would be an "unconstitutional condition" has never been an easy inquiry. Consider, for example, the pre-Barlow's case of WYMAN v. JAMES, 400 U.S. 309 (1971). Mrs. James, who received welfare on behalf of her son Maurice, was taken off the rolls when she refused to schedule a visit of her caseworker to her home, as participation in the program required. The Court found this a reasonable condition, despite the suggestion—supported by the state employees involved—that it was intended to search for evidence of child neglect. To be sure, the visit involved the home, and "the caseworker's posture in the home visit is ... both rehabilitative and investigative. But this latter aspect ... is given too broad a character and far more emphasis than it deserves if it is equated with a search in the traditional criminal law context. ... If consent to the visitation is withheld, no visitation takes place. The aid then never begins or merely ceases, as the case may be. ... The visit ... is made by a caseworker of some training[1] whose primary objective is, or should be, the welfare, not the prosecution, of the aid recipient. ... The caseworker is not a sleuth ... The home visit is not a criminal investigation ..."

In such a context, for the majority, a warrant procedure would be an insulting, counter-productive intrusion. For three dissenters, "Whatever the semantics, the central question is whether the government by force of

---

1. The amicus brief submitted on behalf of the Social Services Employees Union Local 371, AFSCME, AFL–CIO, the bargaining representative for the social service staff employed in the New York City Department of Social Services, recites that "caseworkers are either badly trained or untrained" and that "[g]enerally, a caseworker is not only poorly trained, but also young and inexperienced ..." Despite this astonishing description by the union of the lack of qualification of its own members for the work they are employed to do, we must assume that the caseworker possesses at least some qualifications and some dedication to duty.

its largesse has the power to 'buy up' rights guaranteed by the Constitution." "[T]he welfare visit is not some sort of purely benevolent inspection. ... Of course, caseworkers seek to be friends, but the point is that they are also required to be sleuths."

(1) In DONOVAN v. DEWEY, 452 U.S. 594 (1981), Justice Marshall, writing for most of the Barlow's majority, upheld warrantless inspection of a stone quarry. The Federal Mine Safety and Health Act requires the Secretary of Labor to develop health and safety standards to govern mines. Far more specific than the OSH Act on the subject of inspection, it directs that underground mines be inspected at least four times per year, surface mines at least twice per year. Moreover, followup inspections must be made to determine whether previously discovered violations had been corrected. Under § 103(a), "no advance notice of an inspection shall be provided to any person"; the Senate report explained that "[I]n [light] of the notorious ease with which many safety or health hazards may be concealed if advance warning of inspection is obtained, a warrant requirement would seriously undercut this Act's objectives."

In this case, an inspector had been following up after an inspection that had uncovered 25 violations, when the company's president refused to allow him to continue unless a warrant was obtained. The Court began by reasserting—perhaps recasting—a distinction it had drawn in Barlow's. It had reasoned there that "the 'reasonableness of a warrantless search ... will depend upon the specific enforcement needs and privacy guarantees of each statute' and that some statutes 'apply only to a single industry, where regulations might already be so pervasive that a Colonnade–Biswell exception ... could apply.'

"... [T]he only real issue before us is whether the [FMSHA] inspection program, in terms of the certainty and regularity of its application, provides a constitutionally adequate substitute for a warrant. We believe that it does. Unlike the statute at issue in Barlow's, the Mine Safety and Health Act applies to industrial activity with a notorious history of serious accidents and unhealthful working conditions. The Act is specifically tailored to address those concerns, and the regulation of mines it imposes is sufficiently pervasive and defined that the owner of such a facility cannot help but be aware that he 'will be subject to effective inspection.' Biswell, at 316. First, [unlike OSHA,] the Act requires inspection of *all* mines and specifically defines the frequency of inspection. ... Moreover, the Secretary must conduct followup inspections of mines where violations of the Act have previously been discovered, and must inspect a mine immediately if notified by a miner or a miner's representative that a violation of the Act or an imminently dangerous condition exists. Second, the standards with which a mine operator is required to comply are all specifically set forth in the Act or ... Regulations. ... Thus, rather than leaving the frequency and purpose of inspections to the unchecked discretion of Government officers, the Act establishes a predictable and guided federal regulatory presence. ...

"Finally, the Act provides a specific mechanism for accommodating any special privacy concerns that a specific mine operator might have. The Act prohibits forcible entries, and instead requires the Secretary, when refused entry onto a mining facility, to file a civil action in federal court to obtain an injunction against future refusals. . . . This proceeding provides an adequate forum for the mineowner to show that a specific search is outside the federal regulatory authority, or to seek from the district court an order accommodating any unusual privacy interests that the mineowner might have.

"Under these circumstances, it is difficult to see what additional protection a warrant requirement would provide. . . . Appellees contend, however, that even if § 103(a) is constitutional as applied to most segments of the mining industry, it nonetheless violates the Fourth Amendment as applied to authorize warrantless inspections of stone quarries . . . which came under federal regulation in 1966, [and] do not have a long tradition of government regulation. To be sure, in Colonnade this Court referred to 'the long history of the regulation of the liquor industry,' 397 U.S. at 75 . . . However, it is the pervasiveness and regularity of the federal regulation that ultimately determines whether a warrant is necessary to render an inspection program reasonable under the Fourth Amendment. . . . Of course, the duration of a particular regulatory scheme will often be an important factor . . . [but if it were the only criterion,] new or emerging industries, including ones such as the nuclear power industry that pose enormous potential safety and health problems, could never be subject to warrantless searches even under the most carefully structured inspection program . . .

"The Fourth Amendment's central concept of reasonableness will not tolerate such arbitrary results, and we therefore conclude that warrantless inspection of stone quarries, like similar inspections of other mines covered by the Act, are constitutionally permissible."

Justice Stevens concurred, agreeing that Dewey was distinguishable from Barlow's but finding the Dewey rationale "much closer to the reasoning in my dissent than to the reasoning" of the majority in Barlow's. "I need not confront the more difficult question whether Camara represented such a fundamental misreading of the Fourth Amendment that it should be overruled. I would merely observe that that option is more viable today."

Justice Rehnquist concurred in the judgment, because "the stone quarry here was largely visible to the naked eye without entrance onto the company's property. As this Court has held, the 'protection accorded by the Fourth Amendment to the people in their "persons, houses, papers, and effects,"' is not extended to the open fields."

Justice Stewart, who had joined in Frank and dissented in Camara, dissented here: "[A]s explained in Barlow's, the Colonnade–Biswell exception is a single and narrow one: the exception applies to businesses that are both pervasively regulated *and* have a long history of regulation. Today the Court conveniently discards the latter portion of the exception. Yet the very rationale for the exception—that the 'businessman . . . in effect consents to the restrictions placed upon him'—disappears without it. It can hardly be said that a businessman consents to restrictions on his business when those restrictions are not imposed until *after* he has entered the business. Yet, because it does not overrule Barlow's, that is precisely what the Court says today to many stone quarry operators.

"Under the peculiar logic of today's opinion, the scope of the Fourth Amendment diminishes as the power of governmental regulation increases. Yet I would have supposed that the mandates of the Fourth Amendment demand heightened, not lowered, respect, as the intrusive regulatory authority of government expands."

(2) In NEW YORK v. BURGER, 482 U.S. 691 (1987), Justice Blackmun (a dissenter in Marshall v. Barlow's) wrote for six Justices upholding the validity of a warrantless search of a New York City automobile junkyard. Owners of such junkyards were required by statute to register the business, to maintain a record book of the vehicles and parts in the junkyard, and to permit inspection of these records and related vehicles and/or parts "during ... regular and usual business hours." Failure either to register or to maintain the necessary records were substantial crimes under the statute. Here, the inspections were made despite the owner's admission that he had violated these provisions; and they were made by uniformed police officers. The officers found parts from a number of stolen vehicles. New York's highest court had unanimously concluded that the statutory scheme's sole justification was providing "the police an expedient means of enforcing penal sanctions for possession of stolen property. ... [The scheme did] little more than authorize general searches, including those conducted by the police, of certain commercial premises."

Rejecting the state court's characterization, the Court concluded that the junkyard was a pervasively regulated entity subject to warrantless inspections. That conclusion rested on three criteria, which had been met: a substantial government interest underlying the regulatory scheme; the necessity of warrantless inspections to further that scheme; and procedures giving adequate assurance of regularity—that the time, manner and scope of the searches would be reasonable. The Court noted that 37 other States had similar statutes, which a number of courts had upheld.

The Court also rejected the state court's conclusion that the administrative goal of the statute was mere pretext:

"[T]he Court of Appeals failed to recognize that a State can address a major social problem *both* by way of an administrative scheme *and* through penal sanctions. Administrative statutes and penal laws may have the same *ultimate* purpose of remedying the social problem, but they have different subsidiary purposes and prescribe different methods of addressing the problem. An administrative statute establishes how a particular business in a 'closely regulated' industry should be operated, setting forth rules to guide an operator's conduct of the business and allowing government officials to ensure that those rules are followed. Such a regulatory approach contrasts with that of the penal laws, a major emphasis of which is the punishment of individuals for specific acts of behavior.

"... New York, like many States, faces a serious social problem in automobile theft and has a substantial interest in regulating the vehicle-dismantling industry because of this problem. The New York penal laws address automobile theft by punishing it or the possession of stolen property, including possession by individuals in the business of buying and selling property. In accordance with its interest in regulating the automobile-junkyard industry, the State also has devised a regulatory manner of dealing with this problem. Section 415–a, as a whole, serves the regulatory goals of seeking to ensure that vehicle dismantlers are legitimate business-persons and that stolen vehicles and vehicle parts passing through automobile junkyards can be identified. ... Accordingly, to state that § 415–a5 is 'really' designed to gather evidence to enable convictions under the penal laws is to ignore the plain administrative purposes of § 415–a, in general, and § 415–a5, in particular.

"Finally, we fail to see any constitutional significance in the fact that police officers, rather than 'administrative' agents, are permitted to conduct the § 415–a5 inspection. ... [S]tate police officers, like those in New York, have numerous duties in addition to those associated with traditional police work. ... As a practical matter, many States do not have the resources to assign the enforcement of a particular administrative scheme to a specialized agency. So long as a regulatory scheme is properly administrative, it is not rendered illegal by the fact that the inspecting officer has the power to arrest individuals for violations other than those created by the scheme itself.[2] In sum, we decline to impose upon the States the burden of requiring the enforcement of their regulatory statutes to be carried out by specialized agents."

Justice Brennan's dissent, joined by Justices Marshall and (in most respects) O'Connor, stressed the extent of the retreat from Camara and See:

"Today ... the Court finds pervasive regulation in the barest of administrative schemes. Burger's vehicle-dismantling business is not closely regulated (unless most New York City businesses are). ... The Court also perceives careful guidance and control of police discretion in a statute that is patently insufficient to eliminate the need for a warrant. Finally, the Court characterizes as administrative a search for evidence of only criminal wrongdoing. As a result, the Court renders virtually meaningless the general rule that a warrant is required for administrative searches of commercial property.

"The provisions governing vehicle dismantling in New York simply are not extensive. ... Few substantive qualifications are required of an aspiring vehicle dismantler; no regulation governs the condition of the premises, the method of operation, the hours of operation, the equipment utilized, etc. This scheme stands in marked contrast to, e.g., the mine safety regulations relevant in Dewey....

"Here the State has used an administrative scheme as a pretext to search without probable cause for evidence of criminal violations. ... [I]t is factually impossible that the search was intended to discover wrongdoing subject to administrative sanction. Burger stated that he was not registered ... and that he did not have a police book, as required ... At that point he had violated every requirement of the administrative scheme. There is no administrative provision forbidding possession of stolen automobiles or

---

2. In [Biswell], the search in question was conducted by a city police officer and by a United States Treasury agent, 406 U.S. at 312, the latter being authorized to make arrests for federal crimes. See 27 C.F.R. § 70.28 (1986). The [IRS] agents involved in the search in [Colonnade, 397 U.S. at 73] had similar powers.

automobile parts. The inspection became a search for evidence of criminal acts when all possible administrative violations had been uncovered.

"... In no other administrative search case has this Court allowed the State to conduct an 'administrative search' which violated no administrative provision and had no possible administrative consequences."

(3) In PEOPLE v. KETA, 79 N.Y.2d 474, 496–98, 500–01, 583 N.Y.S.2d 920, 593 N.E.2d 1328, 1341–45 (1992), New York's Court of Appeals, now dividing 4–3, reaffirmed as a matter of state constitutional law its view that such junkyard searches violated the owner's rights,

"As Justice O'Connor has observed, statutes authorizing 'administrative searches' are 'the 20th century equivalent' of colonial writs of assistance (Illinois v. Krull, 480 U.S. 340, 364 [dissenting]), which were general warrants authorizing officials to search any and all residential and commercial premises, without particularized suspicion, to enforce various trade regulations and restrictions and, more specifically, to halt the rampant smuggling of untaxed goods. Such writs were an important component of colonial resentment against the Crown and, in fact, 'ignited the flame that led to American independence'. ... Given this history and the potential similarity between writs of assistance and statutorily authorized administrative searches, ... [and b]ecause the principles and standards set forth in [Burger] do not adequately serve those values, we decline to accept them as controlling in interpreting our own constitutional guarantees.

"... [T]he dissent's reliance on the 'staggering' statistics attesting to the growth of automobile theft in New York and the economic burdens such crime imposes are hardly a persuasive ground for relaxing [our constitutional] proscription against unreasonable searches and seizures. The alarming increase of unlicensed weapons on our urban streets and the catastrophic rise in the use of crack cocaine and heroin are also matters of pressing social concern, but few would seriously argue that those unfortunate facets of modern life justify routine searches of pedestrians on the street or any other suspension of the privacy guarantees that are there to protect all of our citizens. The fact is that, regrettably, there will always be serious crime in our society, and there will always be upsurges in the rate of particular crimes due to changes in the social landscape. Indeed, the writs of assistance were themselves a response of the colonial government to an unprecedented wave of criminal smuggling ..."

(4) In FERGUSON v. CITY OF CHARLESTON, 532 U.S. 67 (2001), the Medical University of South Carolina and Charleston city officials had agreed on a regime of urine testing for women showing characteristics thought consistent with their using cocaine while pregnant. Positive results could lead either to rehabilitative programs or to criminal prosecutions. City officials conceded that these undoubted searches were non-consensual. They asserted however, that the searches fit within a category of "special needs" cases that had upheld certain suspicionless searches performed for reasons unrelated to law enforcement. A majority of the Court, "consider[ing] all the available evidence in order to determine the relevant primary purpose," found that the focus was on criminal law enforcement against drug-abusing mothers. It therefore held the search unlawful. "[T]hroughout the development and application of the policy, the Charleston prosecutors and police

were extensively involved in [its] day-to-day administration. . . . While the ultimate goal of the program may well have been to get the women in question into substance abuse treatment and off of drugs, the immediate objective of the searches was to generate evidence *for law enforcement purposes* in order to reach that goal. . . . While state hospital employees, like other citizens, may have a duty to provide the police with evidence of criminal conduct they inadvertently acquire in the course of routine treatment, when they undertake to obtain such evidence from their patients *for the specific purpose of incriminating those patients*, they have a special obligation to make sure that the patients are fully informed about their constitutional rights, as standards of knowing waiver require." (Emphases in original). Justice Kennedy concurred specially, and the Chief Justice and Justices Scalia and Thomas strongly dissented.

NOTES ON PRACTICAL IMPACT AND OTHER ISSUES

(1) The immediate impact of Camara and Barlow's was suggested by data collected by an enterprising law student (data on continuing impact are unavailable): In the immediate wake of Camara, the San Francisco Department of Public Health had to obtain at most five warrants during an eight-month period in which it made more than 32,000 inspections. Note, Search Warrants and Administrative Area Searches, 3 Gonzaga L.Rev. 172, 189n (1968). After Barlow's (from October, 1978 to April, 1980), 2.6% of employers demanded warrants. See Mark Rothstein, OSHA After Ten Years: A Review and Some Proposed Reforms, 34 Vand. L. Rev. 71, 110 n. 234 (1981).

(2) OSHA has consistently been able to secure warrants for full inspections when a plant is chosen according to a neutral administrative plan. See, e.g., In re Establishment Inspection of Trinity Industries, 898 F.2d 1049 (5th Cir.1990). Discussion earlier in this Chapter, p. 289, outlined its initial successes in persuading the managers of hazardous worksites to work closely with it to effect risk reductions in exchange for promises to forego rigorous enforcement inspections during periods of good faith cooperation. A pilot program in Maine resulted in substantial workplace safety improvements *and* lowered enforcement costs for OSHA. Its effort to expand this program nationwide, was frustrated by litigation, however. OSHA has responded to this frustration by publishing directives setting "site specific targeting" priorities on an annual basis. The Directive for 2002 draws on data employers submit under statutory reporting obligations to calculate, for each of 80,000 establishments, a number reflecting the rate at which time is lost, per employee, from workplace accidents or injuries. The national average rate for all establishments is given as 3; the plan initially selects for "comprehensive" inspection *all* worksites with a rate of 14 or higher. It then adds 200 establishments randomly selected from among approximately 900 apparently successful worksites—worksites which themselves have rates lower than 8, although they belong to industrial groups with average rates higher than 8. This is done "to review the actual degree of compliance with OSHA requirements by establishments that report low . . . rates."[1] Should all these inspections be completed within a year, then

---

1. State programs may follow alternative high-hazard inspection targeting systems specified in their state plans.

OSHA will inspect as many worksites as it can with an experienced rate between 8 and 14.[2]

Would you expect a worksite chosen for inspection in accordance with this directive to satisfy the Fourth Amendment's requirements? Won't its owners have considerable incentive to challenge vigorously the legality of OSHA's policy, given their concern what a comprehensive inspection, with violations cited according to OSHA manuals, might reveal? Note the plan's implication that sites suffering lost time at rates as high as four times the national average probably will not be subject to comprehensive inspection.

(3) *Other Issues: Extent, Consent, Forcible Entry.* The preceding materials suggest the stresses administrative search has created for the Fourth Amendment. This is hardly the appropriate place to attempt a development of Fourth Amendment law generally.[3] Very briefly, then, some further pointers into the caselaw.

Extent: Conventional search warrants, in the Fourth Amendment's language, are to "particularly describ[e] the place to be searched, and the persons or things to be seized." Air Pollution Variance Bd. v. Western Alfalfa Corp., 416 U.S. 861 (1974) suggests that an inspector, lawfully on the premises, may react to any conditions that come effortlessly to view. Whether she may go further, and engage in a general inspection for workplace hazards, has been disputed; one side argues from administrative convenience, the other, from traditional understandings of the purpose of warrants and the possibility that employees may complain in order to harass. "Because administrative and legislative guidelines ensure that employers selected for inspection pursuant to neutral administrative plans have not been chosen simply for the purpose of harassment, courts have held that administrative plan searches may properly extend to the entire workplace. In the case of employee complaints, however, such safeguards are absent." Trinity Industries, Inc. v. OSH Review Commission, 16 F.3d 1455, 1460 (6th Cir.1994).

In PLATTEVILLE AREA APARTMENT ASS'N v. CITY OF PLATTEVILLE, 179 F.3d 574 (7th Cir.1999), a city ordinance authorized periodic inspections of rental housing to determine compliance with the city's housing code. That code included not only safety-related provisions, but also limitations on the number of adult occupants permissible in a single unit. In a college town, suspicions were rife that these limits were often violated in apartments rented out to students. Could the building inspector, in making inspections under search warrants obtained on the basis of administrative need and

---

2. OSHA Directive 02–02 (CPL 2), visited at http://www.osha.gov/pls/oshaweb/owad-isp.show_document?p_table=DIRECTIVES & p_id=2812 & p_text_version=FALSE

3. For example, to what extent data collection from a place external to inspected premises is to be regarded as a constitutional "search." Compare Dow Chemical Co. v. United States, 476 U.S. 227 (1986) (aerial surveillance of industrial complex using highly sophisticated photographic equipment from public navigable airspace is not a "search" of the factory) with Kyllo v. United States, 533 U.S. 27 (2001) (use of thermal imaging equipment from public street to reveal use of lamps suggestive of home marijuana factory—information not otherwise available to view without intrusion—is a "search" of the home).

regularity, open closets and drawers in an effort to find violations of these limitations? Posner, J: "All that the warrants at issue in the present case specify with regard to the object or scope of the search is ... violations of sections 23.13(b) and 23.16 of the housing code. The multiple occupancy restriction is in a different chapter ... and so is not encompassed by [this] reference. ... [T]here would be nothing to argue over if the building inspector could always discover the telltale signs of multiple occupancy without looking into places where no evidence of a violation of section 23.13(b) or 23.16 could be found. But apparently he cannot, for the City wants to preserve his right to rummage in closets and bureau drawers. ...

"... When the Supreme Court authorized administrative searches of residential housing, it didn't grant state and local governments carte blanche. The requirement of reasonableness that the Fourth Amendment imposes on all searches, whether or not pursuant to warrant, entails the striking of a balance.... Counting articles of underwear to determine how many people are living in an apartment may intrude on privacy further than the public interest in limiting apartment crowding justifies."

Consent: Courts are skeptical about claims of consent in criminal cases where searches have proved fruitful. "In a criminal search the inherent coercion of the badge and the presence of armed police make it likely that the consent to a criminal search is not voluntary. ... A criminal with something to hide is not likely to turn it over to the police on request unless he believes that he has no choice." UNITED STATES v. THRIFTIMART, INC., 429 F.2d 1006 (9th Cir.), cert. denied 400 U.S. 926 (1970). But not so for administrative searches. In this case, Food & Drug Administration inspectors routinely inspecting four company warehouses found insect-infested food. Upon arrival, the inspectors had requested permission to enter, and in each instance the local manager had said "Go ahead" or words of that nature. Although the managers had not been apprised of their right to refuse entry, nor had it been proven that they knew of this right, "[f]ood inspections occur with regularity. As here, the judgment as to consent to access is often a matter of company policy rather than of local managerial decision. FDA inspectors are unarmed and make their inspections during business hours. Also, the consent to an inspection is not only not suspect but is to be expected. The inspection itself is inevitable. Nothing is to be gained by demanding a warrant except that the inspectors have been put to trouble—an unlikely aim for the businessman anxious for administrative good will."

Forcible entry: In a criminal investigation, a search warrant may be executed by force; administrative searches typically require judicial enforcement rather than agency self-help. Thus, while Congress has ample power to authorize warrantless inspection of federally licensed dealers in alcoholic beverages, the Court in Colonnade Catering Corp. v. United States, 397 U.S. 72 (1970), excluded evidence seized as a result of a warrantless search, because Congress had not expressly provided for forcible entry. It had made refusal to admit the inspectors a criminal offense and that, the Court concluded, was the sole remedy available. The Federal Mine Safety and Health Act, considered in Dewey, above p. 303, provides for a civil action for injunctive or other relief if a warrantless search under its provisions is refused. An inspector holding an administrative warrant issued in support of an OSHA search, the Third Circuit has indicated, may be refused entry. The agency's remedy is to seek a civil contempt order in the issuing court— this will trigger a hearing in which the lawfulness of the search will be adversarially determined before it occurs.[4]

Results like these seem to move inspections from arguable equivalence to criminal searches, to an analogy to documentary production procedures. Procedures to compel production of information may begin with service of a subpoena on the possessor of the desired data. The subpoena typically has little bite until enforced by judicial decree. ZURCHER V. THE STANFORD DAILY, 436 U.S. 547 (1978), decided one week after Barlow's, involved a police search under warrant of a newspaper's offices for photographs thought likely to aid in identifying the perpetrators of a crime. A divided Court reversed a decision that would have compelled investigators to use subpoenas—thus giving warning—when seeking evidence from individuals not themselves suspects nor demonstrably likely to destroy or damage the evidence being sought: "The Fourth Amendment has itself struck the balance between privacy and public need, and there is no occasion or justification for a court to revise the Amendment and strike a new balance by denying the search warrant in the circumstances present here and by insisting that the investigation proceed by subpoena duces tecum, whether on the theory that the latter is a less intrusive alternative, or otherwise. . . . The seemingly blameless third party in possession of the fruits or evidence may not be innocent at all; and if he is, he may nevertheless be so related to or so sympathetic with the culpable that he cannot be relied upon to retain and preserve the articles that may implicate his friends, or at least not to notify those who would be damaged by the evidence that the authorities are aware of its location. In any event, . . . the delay involved in employing the subpoena duces tecum, offering as it does the opportunity to litigate its validity, could easily result in the disappearance of the evidence, whatever the good faith of the third party."

(4) *Summing Up.* ERIK G. LUNA, SOVEREIGNTY AND SUSPICION, 48 Duke L.J. 787, 790 (1999): "The current state of search and seizure law reflects an ongoing war of linguistic interpretation. The first clause of the Fourth Amendment (the Reasonableness Clause) generally prohibits 'unreasonable searches and seizures.' The second clause (the Warrant Clause) outlines the requirements for a valid warrant, expressly noting the necessary level of suspicion and the specific information that must be provided. The comma between the two Clauses, however, has become a virtual Mason–Dixon line. How the Clauses are to interact, if at all, is the central question that divides judges and scholars."

Has the time come to reconsider the soundness of the Camara–See– Barlow's approach? Our focus here is on what the Fourth Amendment means for administrative searches, but one cannot blink the fact that the Fourth Amendment's reach has been shrinking generally in recent years. To some, Camara has mattered enough to the Fourth Amendment generally to be blamed for "significantly undermin[ing] the role of probable cause

---

4. Babcock & Wilcox Co. v. Marshall, 610 F.2d 1128 (3d Cir.1979); Marshall v. Whittaker Corp., Berwick Forge & Fabricating Co., 610 F.2d 1141 (3d Cir.1979).

and set[ting] the stage for the long-term expansion of the reasonableness balancing test without proper justification of limits."[5] Do you agree that Camara was a "compromise between the government's argument that the Fourth Amendment did not apply at all and the petitioner's argument that a warrant based on traditional probable cause was required"?[6] "Is it not easier to read the words as written, and say that warrantless searches must simply be 'reasonable'? ... [T]he modern Court has explicitly upheld 'newfangled warrants' on less than probable cause in explicit violation of the core textual command of the Warrant Clause. History has been turned on its head, and loose, ex parte warrants—general warrants, really—now issue from central officialdom."[7]

(5) *And the Fifth Amendment Too.* One could without difficulty tell a similar story of stress and accommodation respecting the Fifth Amendment's assurance that "no person ... shall be compelled in any criminal case to be a witness against himself." Thus, when a "person" can point to a crime and believably assert that his response to some demand for information might serve as a link in a chain of evidence tending to convict him of that crime, he will be excused from responding. As a general matter, this privilege has been a strong one in American political history; fear of police coercion in criminal interrogations initially marked understanding of its scope. The widespread use of the Fifth Amendment by witnesses at congressional and administrative hearings during the anti-Communist hysteria of the early 1950s, and the political demagoguery that usually followed invocation of the privilege, have assured a broad reading of the amendment in other investigative contexts as well. The Supreme Court has strongly resisted efforts to punish invocation of the privilege, as by, for example, making use of the privilege a ground for removal from a public job.[8]

Nevertheless, recognizing the privilege's power to frustrate much regulatory activity, the courts have rarely found it available to resist information demands made in ordinary administrative contexts. In the first place, the privilege cannot be asserted by corporations or other artificial "persons,"[9] although such entities *are* protected by the Fifth Amendment's guarantees of due process and "just compensation" when property is taken

---

5. Scott E. Sundby, A Return to Fourth Amendment Basics: Undoing the Mischief of Camara and Terry, 72 Minn.L.Rev. 383, 385 (1988).

6. Scott E. Sundby, Everyman's Fourth Amendment: Privacy or Mutual Trust Between Government and Citizen?, 94 Colum.L.Rev. 1751, 1770, n. 62 (1994). Do you agree with Professor Sundby that "[d]espite its stated preference for the Warrant Clause, the Court has been quick to find a 'special need' justifying departure"? "With a little imagination, even the lowly Vehicle Identification Number can be made to sound as if it is crucial to civilized society." 94 Colum.L.Rev., at 1796–97. He argues that because searches impinge on citizens' trust in government, they should be limited either under the Reasonableness Clause by a specific serious public need justifying intrusion on the specific class subject to search—which could be satisfied in the Camara and See settings—or else by probable cause under the Warrant Clause.

7. Akhil R. Amar, Fourth Amendment First Principles, 107 Harv.L.Rev. 757, 784–85 (1994).

8. Gardner v. Broderick, 392 U.S. 273 (1968). A public employee could, however, be fired for refusing to answer questions directly and narrowly relating to the performance of her duties.

9. Such as partnerships, unions, or unincorporated associations. Hale v. Henkel, 201 U.S. 43 (1906); Bellis v. United States, 417 U.S. 85 (1974).

for public use. The Court reasons that the privilege seeks to protect the individual from having her will overborne by the state, an interest in personal integrity that artificial persons do not share.

Even real persons face numerous obstacles to using the privilege in the regulatory context. First, they may assert it only by affirmatively claiming it. For example, if a taxpayer's sources of income were unlawful, she could not use the privilege to excuse her failure to file an income tax return, but would have to file the return invoking the privilege on the line where earned income is to be reported. This is a more conspicuous gesture than most would wish to make. And any other response, if false, opens the citizen to prosecution for "false statement"—as in a recent decision sustaining a criminal conviction for having falsely responded "No" to government investigators' questions.[10] Second, the claim can be made only for "testimonial" communications. It is unavailable, for example, as a basis for resisting the taking of a fingerprint or other physical evidence. Third, it can be made only on the basis of potential criminal liability, not merely a tendency to bring about undesired regulatory consequences. Finally, the circumstances in which a claim can be made are highly limited: the papers must both belong to the claimant and be in her possession. Thus, if my papers are subpoenaed from my accountant or my bank, the privilege is not available, for it is not I being required to produce them; if my accountant's papers are sought from me, the fact that they incriminate me is irrelevant. Only if I can establish that the very fact of producing the papers in response to the subpoena is a testimonial act that might incriminate me, can a claim be made.[11] In a hearing process, where oral statements are sought, the application of the privilege is more obvious. Here the risk is that the claimant will be thought to have waived it by earlier answers indicating cooperation with the relevant line of the inquiry.

Here, one case may suffice to illustrate the pressures and arguable compromises:

Braswell v. United States

Supreme Court of The United States, 1988.
487 U.S. 99.

■ CHIEF JUSTICE REHNQUIST delivered the opinion of the Court.

This case presents the question whether the custodian of corporate records may resist a subpoena for such records on the ground that the act of production would incriminate him in violation of the Fifth Amendment. We conclude that he may not.

From 1965 to 1980, petitioner Randy Braswell operated his business—which comprises the sale and purchase of equipment, land, timber, and oil and gas interests—as a sole proprietorship. In 1980, he incorporated Worldwide Machinery Sales, Inc., a Mississippi corporation, and began conducting the business through that entity. In 1981, he formed a second

---

10. Brogan v. United States, 522 U.S. 398 (1998).

11. United States v. Doe, 465 U.S. 605 (1984); Baltimore City Dep't Social Services v. Bouknight, 493 U.S. 549 (1990).

Mississippi corporation, Worldwide Purchasing, Inc., and funded that corporation with the 100 percent interest he held in Worldwide Machinery. Petitioner was and is the sole shareholder of Worldwide Purchasing, Inc.

Both companies are active corporations, maintaining their current status with the State of Mississippi, filing corporate tax returns, and keeping current corporate books and records. In compliance with Mississippi law, both corporations have three directors, petitioner, his wife, and his mother. Although his wife and mother are secretary-treasurer and vice-president of the corporations, respectively, neither has any authority over the business affairs of either corporation.

In August 1986, a federal grand jury issued a subpoena to "Randy Braswell, President Worldwide Machinery Sales, Inc. [and] Worldwide Purchasing, Inc.," requiring petitioner to produce the books and records of the two corporations. The subpoena provided that petitioner could deliver the records to the agent serving the subpoena, and did not require petitioner to testify. Petitioner moved to quash the subpoena, arguing that the act of producing the records would incriminate him in violation of his Fifth Amendment privilege against self-incrimination. . . . There is no question but that the contents of the subpoenaed business records are not privileged. United States v. Doe, 465 U.S. 605 (1984); Fisher v. United States, 425 U.S. 391 (1976). Similarly, petitioner asserts no self-incrimination claim on behalf of the corporations; it is well established that such artificial entities are not protected by the Fifth Amendment. Petitioner instead relies solely upon the argument that his act of producing the documents has independent testimonial significance, which would incriminate him individually, and that the Fifth Amendment prohibits Government compulsion of that act. . . .

. . . [I]n United States v. Doe, the Court . . . [addressed] a claim by a sole proprietor that the compelled production of business records would run afoul of the Fifth Amendment . . . [because] respondent's act of producing the records would constitute protected testimonial incrimination. The Court concluded that respondent had established a valid Fifth Amendment claim. . . . By producing the records, respondent would admit that the records existed, were in his possession, and were authentic.

Had petitioner conducted his business as a sole proprietorship, Doe would require that he be provided the opportunity to show that his act of production would entail testimonial self-incrimination. But petitioner has operated his business through the corporate form, and we have long recognized that, for purposes of the Fifth Amendment, corporations and other collective entities are treated differently from individuals. This doctrine—known as the collective entity rule—has a lengthy and distinguished pedigree.

The rule was first articulated by the Court in the case of Hale v. Henkel, 201 U.S. 43 (1906). Hale, a corporate officer, had been served with a subpoena ordering him to produce corporate records and to testify concerning certain corporate transactions . . . [and] sought to resist the demand for the records by interposing a Fifth Amendment privilege on behalf of the corporation. The Court rejected that argument: "[W]e are of the opinion that there is a clear distinction . . . between an individual and a corporation, and ... the latter has no right to refuse to submit its books and papers for an examination at the suit of the State." Id., at 74. The Court explained that the corporation "is a creature of the State," ibid., with powers limited by the State. As such, the State may, in the exercise of its right to oversee the corporation, demand the production of corporate records. Id., at 75....

Although Hale settled that a corporation has no Fifth Amendment privilege, the Court did not address whether a corporate officer could resist a subpoena for corporate records by invoking his personal privilege—Hale had been protected by immunity. In Wilson v. United States, 221 U.S. 361 (1911), the Court answered that question in the negative [,] ... observing first that the records sought [from Wilson, the corporation's president,] were not private or personal, but rather belonged to the corporation. The Court continued:

"[Wilson] held the corporate books subject to the corporate duty. If the corporation were guilty of misconduct, he could not withhold its books to save it; and if he were implicated in the violations of law, he could not withhold the books to protect himself from the effect of their disclosures. The [State's] reserved power of visitation would seriously be embarrassed, if not wholly defeated in its effective exercise, if guilty officers could refuse inspection of the records and papers of the corporation. No personal privilege to which they are entitled requires such a conclusion. ..."

The next significant step in the development of the collective entity rule occurred in United States v. White, 322 U.S. 694 (1944), in which the Court held that a labor union is a collective entity unprotected by the Fifth Amendment. ...

The test ... is whether one can fairly say under all the circumstances that a particular type of organization has a character so impersonal in the scope of its membership and activities that it cannot be said to embody or represent the purely private or personal interests of its constituents, but rather to embody their common or group interests only. If so, the privilege cannot be invoked on behalf of the organization or its representatives in their official capacity. Labor unions—national or local, incorporated or unincorporated—clearly meet that test.

Id., at 701. In applying the collective entity rule to unincorporated associations such as unions, the Court jettisoned reliance on the visitatorial powers of the State over corporations owing their existence to the State— one of the bases for earlier decisions.

The frontiers of the collective entity rule were expanded even further in Bellis v. United States, 417 U.S. 85 (1974), in which the Court ruled that a partner in a [three-person law firm that had previously been dissolved] could not properly refuse to produce partnership records. ... After rehearsing prior precedent involving corporations and unincorporated associations, the Court examined the partnership form and observed that it had many of the incidents found relevant in prior collective entity decisions. ... The Court rejected the notion that the "formulation in White can be reduced to a simple proposition based solely upon the size of the organization. It is well settled that no privilege can be claimed by the custodian of corporate records, regardless of how small the corporation may be." Bellis held the partnership's financial records in "a representative capacity," and therefore, "his personal privilege against compulsory self-incrimination is inapplicable."

The plain mandate of these decisions is that without regard to whether the subpoena is addressed to the corporation, or as here, to the individual in his capacity as a custodian, a corporate custodian such as petitioner may not resist a subpoena for corporate records on Fifth Amendment grounds. Petitioner argues, however, that . . . [t]he collective entity decisions were concerned with the contents of the documents subpoenaed, . . . and not with the act of production. In Fisher and Doe, the Court moved away from the privacy-based collective entity rule, replacing it with a compelled-testimony standard under which the contents of business documents are never privileged but the act of producing the documents may be. Under this new regime, the act of production privilege is available without regard to the entity whose records are being sought. . . .

. . . We cannot agree, however, that [Doe] rendered the collective entity rule obsolete. The agency rationale undergirding the collective entity decisions, in which custodians asserted that production of entity records would incriminate them personally, survives. From Wilson forward, the Court has consistently recognized that the custodian of corporate or entity records holds those documents in a representative rather than a personal capacity. Artificial entities such as corporations may act only through their agents, Bellis, and a custodian's assumption of his representative capacity leads to certain obligations, including the duty to produce corporate records on proper demand by the Government. Under those circumstances, the custodian's act of production is not deemed a personal act, but rather an act of the corporation. Any claim of Fifth Amendment privilege asserted by the agent would be tantamount to a claim of privilege by the corporation—which of course possesses no such privilege. . . . A custodian may not resist a subpoena for corporate records on Fifth Amendment grounds.

Petitioner also attempts to extract support for his contention from Curcio v. United States, 354 U.S. 118 (1957). But rather than bolstering petitioner's argument, we think Curcio substantiates the Government's position. Curcio had been served with two subpoenas addressed to him in his capacity as secretary-treasurer of a local union, which was under investigation. One subpoena required that he produce union books, the other that he testify. Curcio appeared before the grand jury, stated that the books were not in his possession, and refused to answer any questions as to their whereabouts. Curcio was held in contempt for refusing to answer the questions propounded. We reversed the contempt citation, rejecting the Government's argument "that the representative duty which required the production of union records in the White case requires the giving of oral testimony by the custodian." . . .

The Curcio Court made clear that with respect to a custodian of a collective entity's records, the line drawn was between oral testimony and other forms of incrimination. "A custodian, by assuming the duties of his office, undertakes the obligation to produce the books of which he is custodian in response to a rightful exercise of the State's visitorial powers. But he cannot lawfully be compelled, in the absence of a grant of adequate immunity from prosecution, to condemn himself by his own *oral testimony*." 354 U.S., at 123–124 (emphasis added). . . . [T]he Court showed that it understood the testimonial nature of the act of production: "The custodian's act of producing books or records in response to a subpoena duces tecum is itself a representation that the documents produced are those demanded by the subpoena. Requiring the custodian to identify or authenticate the documents for admission in evidence merely makes explicit what is implicit in the production itself." In the face of this recognition, the Court nonetheless noted: "In this case petitioner might have been proceeded against for his failure to produce the records demanded by the subpoena duces tecum." . . .

We note further that recognizing a Fifth Amendment privilege on behalf of the records custodians of collective entities would have a detrimental impact on the Government's efforts to prosecute "white-collar crime," one of the most serious problems confronting law enforcement authorities. "The greater portion of evidence of wrongdoing by an organization or its representatives is usually found in the official records and documents of that organization. Were the cloak of the privilege to be thrown around these impersonal records and documents, effective enforcement of many federal and state laws would be impossible." White, 322 U.S., at 700. If custodians could assert a privilege, authorities would be stymied not only in their enforcement efforts against those individuals but also in their prosecutions of organizations. . . .

Although a corporate custodian is not entitled to resist a subpoena on the ground that his act of production will be personally incriminating, we do think certain consequences flow from the fact that the custodian's act of production is one in his representative rather than personal capacity. Because the custodian acts as a representative, the act is deemed one of the corporation and not the individual. Therefore, the Government concedes, as it must, that it may make no evidentiary use of the "individual act" against the individual. For example, in a criminal prosecution against the custodian, the Government may not introduce into evidence before the jury the fact that the subpoena was served upon and the corporation's documents were delivered by one particular individual, the custodian. The Government has the right, however, to use the corporation's act of production against the custodian. The Government may offer testimony—for example, from the process server who delivered the subpoena and from the individual who received the records—establishing that the corporation produced the records subpoenaed. The jury may draw from the corporation's act of production the conclusion that the records in question are authentic corporate records, which the corporation possessed, and which it produced in response to the subpoena. And if the defendant held a prominent position within the corporation that produced the records, the jury may, just as it would had someone else produced the documents, reasonably infer that he had possession of the documents or knowledge of their contents. Because the jury is not told that the defendant produced the records, any nexus between the defendant and the documents results solely from the corporation's act of production and other evidence in the case.[1]

Consistent with our precedent, the United States Court of Appeals for the Fifth Circuit ruled that petitioner could not resist the subpoena for corporate documents on the ground that the act of production might tend to incriminate him. The judgment is therefore

Affirmed.

■ JUSTICE KENNEDY, with whom JUSTICE BRENNAN, JUSTICE MARSHALL, and JUSTICE SCALIA join, dissenting.

Our long course of decisions concerning artificial entities and the Fifth Amendment served us well. It illuminated two of the critical foundations for the constitutional guarantee against self-incrimination: first, that it is an explicit right of a natural person, protecting the realm of human thought and expression; second, that it is confined to governmental compulsion.

It is regrettable that ... [a] case that might have served as the paradigmatic expression of the purposes served by the Fifth Amendment instead is used to obscure them ... [by denying] an individual his Fifth Amendment privilege against self-incrimination in order to vindicate the rule that a collective entity which employs him has no such privilege itself. To reach this ironic conclusion, the majority must blur an analytic clarity in Fifth Amendment doctrine that has taken almost a century to emerge. . . .

I

There is some common ground in this case. All accept the longstanding rule that labor unions, corporations, partnerships, and other collective entities have no Fifth Amendment self-incrimination privilege; that a natural person cannot assert such a privilege on their behalf; and that the contents of business records prepared without compulsion can be used to incriminate even a natural person without implicating Fifth Amendment concerns. Further, all appear to concede or at least submit the case to us on the assumption that the act of producing the subpoenaed documents will effect personal incrimination of Randy Braswell, the individual to whom the subpoena is directed....

In Boyd v. United States, 116 U.S. 616 (1886), we held that the compelled disclosure of the contents of "private papers" (which in Boyd was a business invoice), was prohibited not only by the Fifth Amendment

---

1. We reject the suggestion that the limitation on the evidentiary use of the custodian's act of production is the equivalent of constructive use immunity barred under our decision in Doe, 465 U.S., at 616–617. Rather, the limitation is a necessary concomitant of the notion that a corporate custodian acts as an agent and not an individual when he produces corporate records in response to a subpoena addressed to him in his representative capacity.

We leave open the question whether the agency rationale supports compelling a custodian to produce corporate records when the custodian is able to establish, by showing for example that he is the sole employee and officer of the corporation, that the jury would inevitably conclude that he produced the records.

but by the Fourth Amendment as well. The decision in Boyd generated nearly a century of doctrinal ambiguity as we explored its rationale and sought to define its protection for the contents of business records under the Fifth Amendment. . . . Its essential premise was rejected four years ago, when we held that the contents of business records produced by subpoena are not privileged under the Fifth Amendment, absent some showing that the documents were prepared under compulsion. United States v. Doe, 465 U.S. 605, 610–611, n. 8 (1984). . . . A subpoena does not, however, seek to compel creation of a document; it compels its production. . . . [T]he act of producing documents itself may communicate information separate from the documents' contents and that such communication, in some circumstances, is compelled testimony. An individual who produces documents may be asserting that they satisfy the general description in the subpoena, or that they were in his possession or under his control. Those assertions can convey information about that individual's knowledge and state of mind as effectively as spoken statements, and the Fifth Amendment protects individuals from having such assertions compelled by their own acts.

This is well-settled law, or so I had assumed. . . . In none of the collective entity cases cited by the majority, and in none that I have found, were we presented with a claim that the custodian would be incriminated by the act of production, in contrast to the contents of the documents.

The distinction is central. Our holding in Wilson was premised squarely on the fact that the custodian's claim rested on the potential for incrimination in the documents' contents, and we reasoned that the State's visitatorial powers over corporations included the authority to inspect corporate books. We compared the issue to that presented by cases involving public papers, explaining that "where, by virtue of their character and the rules of law applicable to them, the books and papers are held subject to examination by the demanding authority, the custodian has no privilege to refuse production although their contents tend to criminate him." . . . The act of producing documents stands on an altogether different footing. While a custodian has no necessary relation to the contents of documents within his control, the act of production is inescapably his own. Production is the precise act compelled by the subpoena, and obedience, in some cases, will require the custodian's own testimonial assertions. That was the basis of our recognition of the privilege in Doe. The entity possessing the documents in Doe was, as the majority points out, a sole proprietorship, not a corporation, partnership, or labor union. But the potential for self-incrimination inheres in the act demanded of the individual, and as a consequence the nature of the entity is irrelevant to determining whether there is ground for the privilege. . . . Once the Government concedes there are testimonial consequences implicit in the act of production, it cannot escape the conclusion that compliance with the subpoena is indisputably Braswell's own act. To suggest otherwise "is to confuse metaphor with reality." Pacific Gas & Electric Co. v. Public Utilities Comm'n of California, 475 U.S. 1, 33 (1986) (REHNQUIST, J., dissenting).

. . . In Curcio v. United States, 354 U.S. 118 (1957), we reviewed a judgment holding a union custodian in criminal contempt for failing to give oral testimony regarding the location and possession of books and records he had been ordered to produce. ... The majority is able to distinguish Curcio only by giving much apparent weight to the words "out of his own mouth," reading Curcio to stand for the proposition that the Constitution treats oral testimony differently than it does other forms of assertion. There is no basis in the text or history of the Fifth Amendment for such a distinction. The Self–Incrimination Clause speaks of compelled "testimony," and has always been understood to apply to testimony in all its forms. Physical acts will constitute testimony if they probe the state of mind, memory, perception, or cognition of the witness. The Court should not retreat from the plain implications of this rule and hold that such testimony may be compelled, even when self-incriminating, simply because it is not spoken.

The distinction established by Curcio, supra, is not, of course, between oral and other forms of testimony; rather it is between a subpoena which compels a person to "disclose the contents of his own mind," through words or actions, and one which does not. A custodian who is incriminated simply by the contents of the documents he has physically transmitted has not been compelled to disclose his memory or perception or cognition. A custodian who is incriminated by the personal knowledge he communicates in locating and selecting the document demanded in a Government subpoena has been compelled to testify in the most elemental, constitutional sense....

The heart of the matter, as everyone knows, is that the Government does not see Braswell as a mere agent at all; and the majority's theory is difficult to square with what will often be the Government's actual practice. The subpoena in this case was not directed to Worldwide Machinery Sales, Inc., or Worldwide Purchasing, Inc. It was directed to "Randy Braswell, President[,] Worldwide Machinery Sales, Inc.[,] Worldwide Purchasing, Inc." and informed him that "[y]ou are hereby commanded" to provide the specified documents. The Government explained at oral argument that it often chooses to designate an individual recipient, rather than the corporation generally, when it serves a subpoena because "[we] want the right to make that individual comply with the subpoena." This is not the language of agency. By issuing a subpoena which the Government insists is "directed to petitioner personally," it has forfeited any claim that it is simply making a demand on a corporation that, in turn, will have to find a physical agent to perform its duty. What the Government seeks instead is the right to choose any corporate agent as a target of its subpoena and compel that individual to disclose certain information by his own actions.

The majority gives the corporate agent fiction a weight it simply cannot bear. In a peculiar attempt to mitigate the force of its own holding, it impinges upon its own analysis by concluding that, while the Government may compel a named individual to produce records, in any later proceeding against the person it cannot divulge that he performed the act. But if that is so, it is because the Fifth Amendment protects the person without regard to his status as a corporate employee; and once this be admitted, the necessary support for the majority's case has collapsed.

. . .

II

The majority's abiding concern is that if a corporate officer who is the target of a subpoena is allowed to assert the privilege, it will impede the Government's power to investigate corporations, unions, and partnerships, to uncover and prosecute white-collar crimes, and otherwise to enforce its visitatorial powers. There are at least two answers to this. The first, and most fundamental, is that the text of the Fifth Amendment does not authorize exceptions premised on such rationales. Second, even if it were proper to invent such exceptions, the dangers prophesied by the majority are overstated.

Recognition of the right to assert a privilege does not mean it will exist in many cases. In many instances, the production of documents may implicate no testimonial assertions at all. ... Further, to the extent testimonial assertions are being compelled, use immunity can be granted without impeding the investigation. Where the privilege is applicable, immunity will be needed for only one individual, and solely with respect to evidence derived from the act of production itself. The Government would not be denied access to the records it seeks, it would be free to use the contents of the records against everyone, and it would be free to use any testimonial act implicit in production against all but the custodian it selects. In appropriate cases the Government will be able to establish authenticity, possession, and control by means other than compelling assertions about them from a suspect. . . .

The law is not captive to its own fictions. Yet, in the matter before us the Court employs the fiction that personal incrimination of the employee is neither sought by the Government nor cognizable by the law. That is a regrettable holding, for the conclusion is factually unsound, unnecessary for legitimate regulation, and a violation of the Self–Incrimination Clause of the Fifth Amendment of the Constitution. For these reasons, I dissent.

CHAPTER IV

THE PROCEDURAL CATEGORIES IN ACTION: ADJUDICATION

"Adjudication" should be a familiar concept for law students who have reached the point of taking a course in Administrative Law. Trials are the specific concern of courses in Civil and Criminal Procedure. Trials underlie most if not all first year courses, and numerous upperclass courses, such as Evidence, as well. Consequently, the materials of this chapter raise as their unifying question a comparative one: how do administrative adjudications deviate from the civil trials they often resemble, and why? The organization of these materials signal the principal comparisons to be made.

At the outset it may be useful to set out five analytic questions reflecting a variety of agency characteristics that will affect these comparisons:

1) *Is the adjudication one required by the Constitution's Due Process Clause, or is the adjudication one required by statute?* Despite the contrary indications in Wong Yang Sung v. McGrath, p. 254, procedural questions arising because a federal agency adjudication is required by the Due Process Clause are generally answered today by analysis of the body of precedents developed under that Clause, and not by reference to the APA's provisions. While you will find attention to the requirements of fairness (due process) as well as the specific demands of the APA throughout these materials, concerted attention to what due process requires, and how that is to be determined, is the work of Chapter VII.

2) *Is the adjudication one required to be decided "on the record" and hence subject to the APA's adjudicatory procedures?* How this determination is to be made is one subject of Seacoast Anti–Pollution League v. Costle, this Chapter's organizing case. If you answer this question in the negative—that is, if the adjudicatory procedures of APA §§ 554, 556 and 557 do *not* apply—you might find governing procedures in the agency's organic statute or in its regulations, but the APA itself provides virtually no procedural constraint.

3) *If required by statute to be decided "on the record," does the adjudication involve initial licensing, or some other matter?* The APA sections that govern agency procedures in on-the-record, or formal, adjudications—those adjudications that most resemble trials—are 5 U.S.C. §§ 554 and 556–58. A careful reading of these sections will reveal special accommodations made for initial licensing controversies. These accommodations may rest on judgments about (1) the routine character (or not) of the licensing;

(2) the need for unusually full engagement of an agency's expert staff in deciding license applications; (3) the (un)likelihood that license applications will involve the kinds of dispute for which we most emphatically demand trials, those entailing moral judgments about private behavior and/or factual controversies best resolved by hearing viva voce testimony; and/or (4) the likelihood that issues appearing to affect a license applicant's particular interests (Londoner) may also affect a wide range of community interests (Bi–Metallic), giving the dispute a polycentric character for which rigorous application of a "trial" model may be inappropriate.

4) *If required by statute to be decided "on the record," does the adjudication require adversarial procedures?* Americans are accustomed to an ideal of "trial" in which opposing parties contend before a neutral umpire who has no responsibility for presenting or assembling either the evidence or the arguments on the basis of which decision will be made. This ideal is not a necessary condition of justice. Well-regarded European and other legal systems have chosen what we call "inquisitorial" rather than "adversarial" models of procedure, in which the judge rather than the parties has the responsibility for developing the record for decision. Adversarial procedures dominate large, complex administrative adjudications in the United States, but nothing in the APA (or constitutional due process in the agency context) requires them. Indeed, the great bulk of federal administrative adjudicators conduct inquisitorial rather than adversarial proceedings. Wong Yang Sung was such a case in the immigration context; in federal disability insurance matters, the subject of a number of cases and studies in these pages, the trier is typically responsible for assembling and presenting the record, and questioning witnesses, as well as reaching decision. There is no government attorney "opposing" the claimant in these cases, whether or not the claimant appears (as she may) with the assistance of counsel.

5) *Does the case involve issues decided at trial, or on "appeal" within the agency?* Administrative adjudications have both trial and "appellate" stages. (The words signifying appeal are put in quotation marks because, as we will see and as § 557 of the APA makes explicit, an agency "reviewing" a decision of its hearing officers may decide the matter as if it were the trier of fact, and an appellate court reviewing its judgment must then treat it accordingly.) In at least one important agency, the Social Security Administration, decisions at the appellate stage do *not* create agency common law, in contra-distinction to judicial practice. This is a consequence of the large number of decisions having to be taken at that stage; the SSA gives its hearing officers any necessary *general* instructions by means of regulations and like policy instruments. Perhaps more important to understanding the special characteristics of administrative law, agency decisionmakers "at the top," unlike judges, have multiple responsibilities: agency heads adopt regulations, decide upon enforcement policies, deal with political overseers (Congress and President), manage a bureaucracy, are committed to achieving policy ends, give luncheon speeches in pursuit of them, serve for relatively brief terms, and in other ways take actions judges never do. The impact of these activities upon, and their interrelationship

with, agency adjudication present important questions that do not arise for courts.

SECTION 1. INITIAL HEARINGS IN FORMAL ADJUDICATION

We now turn to APA on-the-record adjudication, the form of administrative proceeding on which its drafters lavished the greatest attention and which was largely responsible for the political pressure leading to adoption of that Act. Bear in mind throughout (as the cases will themselves encourage seeing) that procedural requirements may be set by Constitution, authorizing statute, or agency regulation as well as the APA.

The process of formal adjudication before an administrative agency might be schematically represented as follows:

FLOW OF FORMAL ADJUDICATION IN AN AGENCY SETTING

ACTORS	STAGE	RELEVANT APA DIRECTIVES
Interested public License applicant Enforcement staff	INITIATING EVENT	
Agency staff Investigatory subject	INVESTIGATION	5 U.S.C. 555(c,d)
Agency staff or head Parties	DECISION TO GO FORWARD/NOTICE	5 U.S.C. 554, 558
Parties Agency staff ALJ	PRE-HEARING	5 U.S.C. 554, 555, 557(d)
Same	HEARING	5 U.S.C. 554(c, d), 556, 557(d)
ALJ or responsible official	DECISION	5 U.S.C. 554(d), 557, 558
Parties Agency staff Agency head or board	REVIEW	5 U.S.C. 557
Agency head or board	DECISION ON REVIEW	5 U.S.C. 557

[H198]

The materials that follow are organized with the thought of permitting consideration of the issues that may arise at these various stages of the hearing process.

Seacoast Anti–Pollution League v. Costle

United States Court of Appeals for the First Circuit, 1978.
572 F.2d 872, cert. denied, 439 U.S. 824 (1978).

■ Before COFFIN, CHIEF JUDGE, CAMPBELL and BOWNES, CIRCUIT JUDGES.

■ COFFIN, CHIEF JUDGE:

This case is before us on a petition by the Seacoast Anti–Pollution League and the Audubon Society of New Hampshire (petitioners) to review a decision by the Administrator of the Environmental Protection Agency (EPA). We have jurisdiction under 33 U.S.C. § 1369(b)(1). The petition presents several important issues relating to the applicability and effect of the Administrative Procedure Act (APA), 5 U.S.C. §§ 501 et seq., and the interpretation of the Federal Water Pollution Control Act of 1972 (FWPCA), 33 U.S.C. §§ 1251 et seq. In order to place those issues in context we set forth the procedural and factual background of the case.

The Public Service Company of New Hampshire (PSCO) filed an application with the EPA for permission to discharge heated water into the Hampton–Seabrook Estuary which runs into the Gulf of Maine. The water would be taken from the Gulf of Maine, be run through the condensor of PSCO's proposed nuclear steam electric generating station at Seabrook, and then be directly discharged back into the Gulf at a temperature 39° F higher than at intake. The water is needed to remove waste heat, some 16 billion BTU per hour, generated by the nuclear reactor but not converted into electrical energy by the turbine. Occasionally, in a process called backflushing, the water will be recirculated through the condensor, and discharged through the intake tunnel at a temperature of 120° F in order to kill whatever organisms may be living in the intake system.

Section 301(a) of the FWPCA prohibits the discharge of any pollutant unless the discharger, the point source operator, has obtained an EPA permit. Heat is a pollutant. Section 301(b) directs the EPA to promulgate effluent limitations. The parties agree that the cooling system PSCO has proposed does not meet the EPA standards because PSCO would utilize a once-through open cycle system—the water would not undergo any cooling process before being returned to the sea. Therefore, in August, 1974, PSCO applied not only for a discharge permit under § 402 of the FWPCA, but also an exemption from the EPA standards pursuant to § 316 of the FWPCA. Under § 316(a) a point source operator who "after opportunity for public hearing, can demonstrate to the satisfaction of the Administrator" that the EPA's standards are "more stringent than necessary to assure the projection [sic] and propagation of a balanced, indigenous population of shellfish, fish, and wildlife in and on the body of water" may be allowed to meet a lower standard. Moreover, under § 316(b) the cooling water intake structure must "reflect the best technology available for minimizing adverse environmental impact."

In January, 1975, the Regional Administrator of the EPA held a non-adjudicatory hearing at Seabrook. He then authorized the once-through system in June, 1975. Later, in October, 1975, he specified the location of the intake structure. The Regional Administrator granted a request by petitioners that public adjudicative hearings on PSCO's application be held. These hearings were held in March and April, 1976, pursuant to the EPA's regulations establishing procedures for deciding applications for permits under § 402 of the FWPCA. The hearings were before an administrative law judge who certified a record to the Regional Administrator for decision. The Regional Administrator decided in November, 1976, to reverse his original determinations and deny PSCO's application.

PSCO appealed the decision to the Administrator who agreed to review it. Thereafter, a new Administrator was appointed, and he assembled a panel of six in-house advisors to assist in his technical review. This panel met between February 28 and March 3, 1977, and submitted a report finding that with one exception PSCO had met its burden of proof. With respect to that exception, the effect of backflushing, the Administrator asked PSCO to submit further information, offered other parties the opportunity to comment upon PSCO's submission, and stated that he would hold a hearing on the new information if any party so requested and could satisfy certain threshold conditions. ... Petitioners did request a hearing, but the Administrator denied the request.

The Administrator's final decision followed the technical panel's recommendations and, with the additional information submitted, reversed the Regional Administrator's decision, finding that PSCO had met its burden under § 316. It is this decision that petitioners have brought before us for review.

Applicability of the Administrative Procedure Act

Petitioners assert that the proceedings by which the EPA decided this case contravened certain provisions of the APA governing adjudicatory hearings, 5 U.S.C. §§ 554, 556, and 557. Respondents answer that the APA does not apply to proceedings held pursuant to § 316 or § 402 of the FWPCA.

The dispute centers on the meaning of the introductory phrases of § 554(a) of the APA:[1]

> This section applies ... in every case of adjudication required by statute to be determined on the record after opportunity for an agency hearing. ...

---

1. The determination that the EPA must make under § 316 of the FWPCA is not a rule because it is not "designed to implement, interpret, or prescribe law or policy". 5 U.S.C. § 551(4). Rather the EPA must decide a specific factual question already prescribed by statute. Since the determination is not a rule, it is an order. 5 U.S.C. § 551(6). The agency process for formulating an order is an adjudication. 5 U.S.C. § 551(7). Therefore, § 554 rather than § 553 of the APA is the relevant section. The same result is dictated because § 316(a) of the FWPCA is a licensing, 5 U.S.C. § 551(9), since it results in the granting or denial of a form of permission. See 5 U.S.C. § 551(8). A license is an order. 5 U.S.C. § 551(6).

Both § 316(a) and § 402(a)(1) of the FWPCA provide for public hearings, but neither states that the hearing must be "on the record". We are now the third court of appeals to face this issue. The Ninth Circuit and the Seventh Circuit have each found that the APA does apply to proceedings pursuant to § 402. Marathon Oil Co. v. EPA, 564 F.2d 1253 (9th Cir.1977); United States Steel Corp. v. Train, 556 F.2d 822 (7th Cir.1977). We agree.

At the outset we reject the position of intervenor PSCO that the precise words "on the record" must be used to trigger the APA. The Supreme Court has clearly rejected such an extreme reading even in the context of rule making under § 553 of the APA. See United States v. Florida East Coast Ry. Co., 410 U.S. 224, 245. Rather, we think that the resolution of this issue turns on the substantive nature of the hearing Congress intended to provide.

We begin with the nature of the decision at issue. The EPA Administrator must make specific factual findings about the effects of discharges from a specific point source. On the basis of these findings the Administrator must determine whether to grant a discharge permit to a specific applicant. Though general policy considerations may influence the decision, the decision will not make general policy. Only the rights of the specific applicant will be affected. "As the instant proceeding well demonstrates, the factual questions involved in the issuance of section 402 permits will frequently be sharply disputed. Adversarial hearings will be helpful, therefore, in guaranteeing both reasoned decisionmaking and meaningful judicial review. In summary, the proceedings below were conducted in order 'to adjudicate disputed facts in particular cases,' not 'for the purposes of promulgating policy-type rules or standards.' " Marathon Oil Co., supra, at 1262.

This is exactly the kind of quasi-judicial proceeding for which the adjudicatory procedures of the APA were intended. As the Supreme Court has said, "Determination of questions of (the Administrative Procedure Act's) coverage may well be approached through consideration of its purposes as disclosed by its background." Wong Yang Sung v. McGrath, 339 U.S. 33, 36 (1950). One of the developments that prompted the APA was the "[m]ultiplication of federal administrative agencies and expansion of their functions to include adjudications which have serious impact on private rights." Id., 339 U.S. at 36–37. This is just such an adjudication. The panoply of procedural protections provided by the APA is necessary not only to protect the rights of an applicant for less stringent pollutant discharge limits, but is also needed to protect the public for whose benefit the very strict limitations have been enacted. If determinations such as the one at issue here are not made on the record, then the fate of the Hampton–Seabrook Estuary could be decided on the basis of evidence that a court would never see or, what is worse, that a court could not be sure existed. We cannot believe that Congress would intend such a result.

Our holding does not render the opening phrases of § 554 of the APA meaningless. We are persuaded that their purpose was to exclude "governmental functions, such as the administration of loan programs, which traditionally have never been regarded as adjudicative in nature and as a rule have never been exercised through other than business procedures."

Attorney General's Manual on the Administrative Procedure Act 40 (1947). Without some kind of limiting language, the broad sweep of the definition of "adjudication", defined principally as that which is not rule making, 5 U.S.C. § 551(6), (7), would include such ordinary procedures that do not require any kind of hearing at all. In short, we view the crucial part of the limiting language to be the requirement of a statutorily imposed hearing. We are willing to presume that, unless a statute otherwise specifies, an adjudicatory hearing subject to judicial review must be on the record. The legislative history of the APA and its treatment in the courts bear us out.

Adjusting default to Formal

For instance, one of the Senate documents explained the opening phrases of § 554 as follows:

> Limiting application of the sections to those cases in which statutes require a hearing is particularly significant, because thereby are excluded the great mass of administrative routine as well as pensions, claims, and a variety of similar matters in which Congress has usually intentionally or traditionally refrained from requiring an administrative hearing. Senate Comparative Print of June 1945, p. 7 (Sen. Doc. p. 22). Attorney General's Manual, supra, 41.

We note that this document looks to whether or not an adjudicative hearing is provided, not to whether the hearing must be on the record.

difference between Adjudicator y rule making*

This rationale and conclusion also are supported by our holding in South Terminal Corp. v. EPA, 504 F.2d 646, 660 (1st Cir.1974) ("public hearing" not tantamount to "on the record"), and the other rule making cases cited to us for similar propositions. The presumption in rule making cases is that formal, adjudicatory procedures are not necessary. A hearing serves a very different function in the rule making context. Witnesses may bring in new information or different points of view, but the agency's final decision need not reflect the public input. The witnesses are not the only source of the evidence on which the Administrator may base his factual findings. For these reasons, we place less importance on the absence of the words "on the record" in the adjudicatory context.

> It is believed that with respect to adjudication the specific statutory requirement of a hearing, without anything more, carries with it the further requirement of decision on the basis of the evidence adduced at the hearing. With respect to rule making, it was concluded, supra, that a statutory provision that rules be issued after a hearing, without more, should not be construed as requiring agency action "on the record", but rather as merely requiring an opportunity for the expression of views. That conclusion was based on the legislative nature of rule making, from which it was inferred, unless a statute requires otherwise, that an agency hearing on proposed rules would be similar to a hearing before a legislative committee, with neither the legislature nor the agency being limited to the material adduced at the hearing. No such rationale applies to administrative adjudication. In fact, it is assumed that where a statute specifically provides for administrative adjudication (such as the suspension or revocation of a license) after opportunity for an agency hearing, *such specific requirement for a hearing ordinarily implies the further requirement of decision in accordance with evidence adduced at the hearing.* Of course, the foregoing

discussion is inapplicable to any situation in which the legislative history or the context of the pertinent statute indicates a contrary congressional intent. Attorney General's Manual, supra, 42–43 (footnote and citation to statutory history omitted) (emphasis added).

Here the statute certainly does not indicate that the determination need not be on the record, and we find no indication of a contrary congressional intent. Therefore, we will judge the proceedings below according to the standards set forth in §§ 554, 556, and 557 of the APA.[2]

Compliance With the Administrative Procedure Act

Petitioners contend that two steps in the EPA's proceedings in this case violated the APA. We will look at each in turn.

1.   The Post–Hearing Submissions; The Request for Information

The Regional Administrator, in his initial decision, had determined that the record was insufficient to properly evaluate the environmental effects of backflushing. The Administrator's technical panel agreed. The Administrator asked PSCO to submit supplemental information on that subject. Other parties were given permission to comment on PSCO's submission. In addition, the Administrator provided that a hearing with respect to the submission would be held if four conditions designed to guarantee that the hearing could resolve a substantial issue of fact were met. PSCO submitted the requested information. Other parties, including petitioners, submitted comments, and petitioners requested a hearing. The Administrator denied the hearing because petitioners had failed to meet the threshold conditions.

Petitioners argue, first, that the Administrator could not rely on this information because it was not part of the exclusive record for decision. 5 U.S.C. § 556(e). Second, petitioners argue that even if the information was legitimately part of the record, the Administrator was obligated to provide an opportunity for cross-examination pursuant to 5 U.S.C. § 556(d).

. . . [W]e can find no fault with the Administrator's decision to seek further evidence. Indeed we think this procedure was a most appropriate way to gather the necessary information without the undue delay that would result from a remand.

The question remains, however, whether the procedures by which the Administrator gathered the information conformed to the governing law. The first point is whether the Administrator was empowered to require that the new evidence be submitted in written form. The Administrator may, under 5 U.S.C. § 556(d), so require in cases of initial licensing. This is

---

2. We agree with the Ninth Circuit that § 558(c) of the APA "does not independently provide that full adjudicatory hearings must be held" whenever an agency must pass on an application for a license. Marathon Oil Co., supra, at 1261, n.25. We think the language of § 558(c) applies to whatever kind of licensing proceeding the licensing statute has provided since it refers to "proceedings required to be conducted in accordance with sections 556 and 557 of (the APA) or other proceedings required by law." The most that can be said is that Congress assumed that most licensings would be governed by §§ 556 and 557.

an initial licensing. But ... [i]n this case § 316(a) of the FWPCA requires the EPA to afford an opportunity for a public hearing. We do not believe that an opportunity to submit documents constitutes a public hearing. ... The public hearing can be especially important in cases such as this one which turn not so much upon the actual baseline data (which presumably all parties will be happy to have submitted in written form) as upon experts' interpretation of the data. The experts' credibility is, therefore, very much at issue here.

While we believe that it was error for the Administrator not to hold a hearing to receive the responses to his request for information ... we cannot be sure that any purpose would be served by ordering a hearing on this issue at this stage in these proceedings. Petitioners' principal complaints are that either the Administrator could not take any evidence or that he was required to afford an opportunity for cross-examination. The latter complaint has no more basis than the former. A party to an administrative adjudicatory hearing does not have an absolute right to cross-examine witnesses. The plain language of 5 U.S.C. § 556(d) limits that right to instances where cross-examination is "required for a full and true disclosure of the facts."

We will order a remand for the limited purpose of allowing the Administrator to determine whether cross-examination would be useful. ... If the Administrator finds that cross-examination would help disclose the facts a hearing must be provided at which cross-examination would be available. If, however, the Administrator concludes that cross-examination would not serve any useful purpose then we will not require him to hold a hearing merely to have the already submitted statements read into the record.

2. Participation of the Technical Review Panel

Petitioners object to the Administrator's use of a panel of EPA scientists to assist him in reviewing the Regional Administrator's initial decision. The objection is two-fold: first, that the Administrator should not have sought such help at all; and, second, that the panel's report (the Report) to the Administrator included information not in the administrative record.

... The Administrator is charged with making highly technical decisions in fields far beyond his individual expertise. "The strength (of the administrative process) lies in staff work organized in such a way that the appropriate specialization is brought to bear upon each aspect of a single decision, the synthesis being provided by the men at the top." 2 K. Davis, Administrative Law Treatise 84 (1958). Therefore, "(e)vidence ... may be sifted and analyzed by competent subordinates." Morgan v. United States, 298 U.S. 468, 481 [(1936)]. The decision ultimately reached is no less the Administrator's simply because agency experts helped him to reach it.

A different question is presented, however, if the agency experts do not merely sift and analyze but also add to the evidence properly before the Administrator. ... To the extent the technical review panel's Report included information not in the record on which the Administrator relied,

§ 556(e) was violated. In effect the agency's staff would have made up for PSCO's failure to carry its burden of proof.

Our review of the Report indicates that such violations did occur. The most serious instance is on page 19 of the Report where the technical panel rebuts the Regional Administrator's finding that PSCO had failed to supply enough data on species' thermal tolerances by saying: "There is little information in the record on the thermal tolerances of marine organisms exposed to the specific temperature fluctuation associated with the Seabrook operation. However, the scientific literature does contain many references to the thermal sensitivity of members of the local biota." Whether or not these references do exist and whether or not they support the conclusions the panel goes on to draw does not concern us here. What is important is that the record did not support the conclusion until supplemented by the panel. The panel's work found its way directly into the Administrator's decision at page 27 where he discusses the Regional Administrator's concerns about insufficient data but then precipitously concludes, "On the recommendation of the panel, however, I find that ... local indigenous populations will not be significantly affected." This conclusion depends entirely on what the panel stated about the scientific literature.

Similar, though less egregious, examples occur in the Report at pages 13–14 ...; page 27 ...; and page 30 ... These find their way into the Administrator's decision at pages 25–26, 33–34, and 37, respectively.

... [T]hey supplied the information. They are free to do that as witnesses, but not as deciders.

The appropriate remedy under these circumstances is to remand the decision to the Administrator because he based his decision on material not part of the record. We are compelled to treat the use of the Report more severely than the use of the PSCO post-hearing submission because no party was given any opportunity to comment on the panel's Report. By contrast, all parties were given the opportunity to comment on PSCO's submission, and these comments were considered equally part of the record by the Administrator. ...

The Administrator will have the options of trying to reach a new decision not dependent on the panel's supplementation of the record; of holding a hearing at which all parties will have the opportunity to cross-examine the panel members and at which the panel will have an opportunity to amplify its position;[3] or of taking any other action within his power and consistent with this opinion.

Conclusion

Because of this resolution, we do not reach the question of whether the Administrator's opinion was supported by substantial evidence. 5 U.S.C.

---

3. We are prepared to say, on the basis of the record before us, that if the Administrator does choose to hold a hearing at which the technical panel members are witnesses, cross-examination will be "required for a full and true disclosure of the facts." 5 U.S.C. § 556(d). Consistent with our holding in respect to the PSCO submission, of course, the testimony of the panel members cannot become part of the record except at an adjudicatory hearing.

§ 706(2)(E). The Administrator must first set the record in order and reach his own conclusions on the state of the record as it will then stand.

So ordered.

NOTES

(1) Reading this opinion as a first encounter with APA adjudication points in several of the directions suggested by the questions at the chapter head. Proceedings before an administrative law judge are mentioned, but *this* opinion concerns a decision taken by the EPA's head. It arose on Public Service Co's application to EPA for a license ("permission to discharge"), but the active parties here represent broader community interests. Important questions are raised about the means by which the agency is to determine issues of "fact," and the issues of fact here call for expert judgment, not reconstruction of past events. These themes are taken up in the following subsections.

(2) The perhaps obvious first question for discussion is: how is an agency and/or reviewing court to tell whether an adjudication is "required by statute to be determined on the record after opportunity for agency hearing"? Do the attitudes toward APA interpretation embodied in Zurko, p. 264, and Greenwich Collieries, p. 269 above, tend to confirm the First Circuit's approach? Writing not long after, RICHARD J. PIERCE, JR., SIDNEY A. SHAPIRO, AND PAUL R. VERKUIL, ADMINISTRATIVE LAW AND PROCESS 300 (1985):

"The court's distinction [in Seacoast Anti–Pollution League] between rulemaking and adjudication makes good sense for two reasons. First, the general analogies reflected in the APA between rulemaking and legislating, on one side, and between adjudication and judicial trial, on the other, support the inference that Congress intended to require proceedings of a very different nature when it used an ambiguous term like hearing with reference to each.

"Second, the consequences of a holding that Congress did not intend to require trial-type procedures varies substantially, depending on whether that holding applies to a rulemaking or an adjudication."

(3) Four years after the excerpt just quoted, the D.C. Circuit decided in CHEMICAL WASTE MANAGEMENT, INC. v. EPA, 873 F.2d 1477 (1989) that it should accept EPA's judgment that the Resource and Conservation Recovery Act's (RCRA) use of "public hearing" required a formal APA adjudication *only* if the hearings in question could lead to a civil penalty or interference with the right to continue operations. "If the order calls upon the interim facility operator merely to undertake an investigation or to do so in combination with interim corrective measures," then the applicable procedures would be much less rigorous procedures specified in agency regulations. In such cases, EPA explained, factual issues "will relate almost entirely to technical (or policy) matters that create little need to establish witness veracity or credibility ... and can just as easily (perhaps more effectively) be resolved through analysis of the administrative record and written submissions and oral statements." The D.C. Circuit thought the Supreme Court's Chevron decision, briefly characterized at p. 273 above,

required it to accept the agency's reasonable judgment about the "ambiguous" term "public hearing" appearing in RCRA, a highly complex statute wholly committed to the EPA for administration. It found EPA's judgment, discriminating among various settings in which more or less formal hearing structures might seem appropriate, to be a reasonable one.

(a) Should EPA's interpretation be taken as one of RCRA, or of the APA? If the latter, the cases are clear that the Chevron proposition requiring acceptance of "reasonable" agency resolutions of statutory ambiguity does not properly apply. "The APA is not a statute that the Director is charged with administering." Metropolitan Stevedore Co. v. Rambo, 521 U.S. 121 n. 9. EPA argues, of course, that it is interpreting the words of RCRA—are they to be understood as necessarily embodying the APA's thrust? Again, does Zurko suggest an answer?

(b) If one applies the "Shepard's" test to both the Seacoast Anti–Pollution League case and the Chemical Waste Management case, one finds that neither opinion has been recanted by its own Circuit, and neither has been cited by the Supreme Court in the years since Chevron was decided. Nor, one might add, has the Supreme Court ever spoken directly to the issue at large. Professors Pierce, Shapiro and Verkuil, however, did bring a changed perspective to the second edition of their commentary:

"The language of the D.C. Circuit's opinion in Chemical Waste Management illustrates the extent to which judges' views concerning the desirability of formal adjudicatory process have changed over the decade of the 1980's. . . .

"The Supreme Court has not yet explicitly resolved the issue of when an agency is required to use formal adjudication. A sequence of four opinions issued between 1972 and 1990 suggests strongly, however, that the Court would adopt the D.C. Circuit's reasoning in Chemical Waste Management, rather than the First Circuit's reasoning in Seacoast." Administrative Law and Process 278–279 (2d ed., 1992).

The "four" opinions were, in addition to Chevron, United States v. Florida East Coast Railway, p. 487 below; Vermont Yankee Nuclear Power Corp. v. Natural Resources Defense Council, p. 498 below; and Pension Benefit Guaranty Corp. v. LTV Corp., p. 472. Encountering them may help you form your own view of this unresolved matter.

(4) Whether a proceeding is within § 554 has an important ancillary consequence as a result of the Supreme Court's interpretation of the Equal Access to Justice Act ("EAJA") in Ardestani v. INS, 502 U.S. 129 (1991). The EAJA provides, 5 U.S.C. § 504(a)(1), that "[a]n agency that conducts an adversary adjudication shall award, to a prevailing party other than the United States, fees and other expenses incurred by that party in connection with that proceeding, unless the adjudicative officer of the agency finds that the position of the agency was substantially justified or that special circumstances make an award unjust." "Adversary adjudication" is in turn defined as "an adjudication under section 554 of this title in which the position of the United States is represented by counsel or otherwise." 5 U.S.C. § 504(b)(1)(C)(i). Rafeh–Rafie Ardestani prevailed against INS efforts to deport her; the government did not argue that its position had been

"substantially justified"; the United States had been represented by counsel in the proceeding; so "the sole question presented in this case," wrote Justice O'Connor in her opinion for the Court, "is whether that proceeding was an adversary adjudication 'under section 554' within the meaning of the EAJA." 502 U.S. at 133. Held: it was not. Although making the EAJA applicable to deportation proceedings would "no doubt" serve the broad purposes of the Act, its terms of coverage were quite specific. The detailed provisions in the Immigration and Nationality Act governing adjudicatory hearings, including specific deviations from the APA pattern, meant that this adjudicatory hearing had been conducted solely and exclusively under the INA. It was therefore not "an adjudication under section 554" as the EAJA required. Justices Blackmun and Stevens dissented.

Where the Constitution requires a hearing, but the applicable statute contains no such detailed procedures, does Wong Yang Sung, p. 254, justify the conclusion that the adjudication is one "under section 554" and therefore the EAJA applies? The Ninth Circuit thought so, distinguishing Ardestani, in Collord v. U.S. Department of the Interior, 154 F.3d 933 (1998). Collord involved contested claims to federal land arising under the General Mining Law of 1872, matters for which APA-informed hearings had long been provided by the Department on the strength of an early reading of Wong Yang Sung. See 261 above.

a.   WHO IS ENTITLED TO PARTICIPATE?

The applicant in Seacoast, Public Service Company of New Hampshire, seems to have had no objection to the procedures EPA followed in the case. Who were Seacoast Anti–Pollution League, and what was the basis for their claim to procedural rigor greater than the license applicant in the case thought necessary to claim?

Office of Communication of the United Church of Christ v. Federal Communications Commission

United States Court of Appeals for the District of Columbia Circuit, 1966.
359 F.2d 994.

■ Before BURGER, McGOWAN and TAMM, CIRCUIT JUDGES.

■ BURGER, CIRCUIT JUDGE:

This is an appeal from a decision of the Federal Communications Commission granting to the Intervenor a one-year renewal of its license to operate television station WLBT in Jackson, Mississippi. Appellants filed with the Commission a timely petition to intervene to present evidence and arguments opposing the renewal application. The Commission dismissed Appellants' petition and, without a hearing, took the unusual step of granting a restricted and conditional renewal of the license. . . .

Because the question whether representatives of the listening public have standing to intervene in a license renewal proceeding is one of first impression, we have given particularly close attention to the background of these issues and to the Commission's reasons for denying standing to Appellants.

The complaints against Intervenor embrace charges of discrimination on racial and religious grounds and of excessive commercials. As the Commission's order indicates, the first complaints go back to 1955 when it was claimed that WLBT had deliberately cut off a network program about race relations problems on which the General Counsel of the NAACP was appearing and had flashed on the viewers' screens a "Sorry, Cable Trouble" sign. In 1957 another complaint was made to the Commission that WLBT had presented a program urging the maintenance of racial segregation and had refused requests for time to present the opposing viewpoint. Since then numerous other complaints have been made.

When WLBT sought a renewal of its license in 1958, the Commission at first deferred action because of complaints of this character but eventually granted the usual three-year renewal ...

Shortly after the outbreak of prolonged civil disturbances centering in large part around the University of Mississippi in September 1962, the Commission again received complaints that various Mississippi radio and television stations, including WLBT, had presented programs concerning racial integration in which only one viewpoint was aired. In 1963 the Commission investigated and requested the stations to submit detailed factual reports on their programs dealing with racial issues. On March 3, 1964, while the Commission was considering WLBT's responses, WLBT filed the license renewal application presently under review.

To block license renewal, Appellants filed a petition in the Commission urging denial of WLBT's application and asking to intervene in their own behalf and as representatives of "all other television viewers in the State of Mississippi." The petition stated that the Office of Communication of the United Church of Christ is an instrumentality of the United Church of Christ, a national denomination with substantial membership within WLBT's prime service area. It listed Appellants Henry and Smith as individual residents of Mississippi, and asserted that both owned television sets and that one lived within the prime service area of WLBT; both are described as leaders in Mississippi civic and civil rights groups. Dr. Henry is president of the Mississippi NAACP; both have been politically active. ...

The Commission's denial of standing[1] to Appellants was based on the theory that, absent a potential direct, substantial injury or adverse effect from the administrative action under consideration, a petitioner has no standing before the Commission and that the only types of effects sufficient to support standing are economic injury and electrical interference. It asserted its traditional position that members of the listening public do not suffer any injury peculiar to them ...

The Commission's rigid adherence to a requirement of direct economic injury in the commercial sense operates to give standing to an electronics manufacturer who competes with the owner of a radio-television station only in the sale of appliances, while it denies standing to spokesmen for the listeners, who are most directly concerned with and intimately affected by

---

1. [Ed.] Note that the use of "standing" here refers to rights of participation at   the agency level, not in the reviewing court.

the performance of a licensee. Since the concept of standing is a practical and functional one designed to insure that only those with a genuine and legitimate interest can participate in a proceeding, we can see no reason to exclude those with such an obvious and acute concern as the listening audience. . . .

Nor does the fact that the Commission itself is directed by Congress to protect the public interest constitute adequate reason to preclude the listening public from assisting in that task. The Commission of course represents and indeed is the prime arbiter of the public interest, but its duties and jurisdiction are vast, and it acknowledges that it cannot begin to monitor or oversee the performance of every one of thousands of licensees. . . .

The theory that the Commission can always effectively represent the listener interests in a renewal proceeding without the aid and participation of legitimate listener representatives fulfilling the role of private attorneys general is one of those assumptions we collectively try to work with so long as they are reasonably adequate. When it becomes clear, as it does to us now, that it is no longer a valid assumption which stands up under the realities of actual experience, neither we nor the Commission can continue to rely on it. . . .

The Commission's attitude in this case is ambivalent in the precise sense of that term. While attracted by the potential contribution of widespread public interest and participation in improving the quality of broadcasting, the Commission rejects effective public participation by invoking the oft-expressed fear that a "host of parties" will descend upon it and render its dockets "clogged" and "unworkable." The Commission resolves this ambivalence for itself by contending that in this renewal proceeding the viewpoint of the public was adequately represented since it fully considered the claims presented by Appellants even though denying them standing. It also points to the general procedures for public participation that are already available, such as the filing of complaints with the Commission, the practice of having local hearings, and the ability of people who are not parties in interest to appear at hearings as witnesses. . . .

We cannot believe that the Congressional mandate of public participation which the Commission says it seeks to fulfill was meant to be limited to writing letters to the Commission, to inspection of records, to the Commission's grace in considering listener claims, or to mere non-participating appearance at hearings. We cannot fail to note that the long history of complaints against WLBT beginning in 1955 had left the Commission virtually unmoved in the subsequent renewal proceedings, and it seems not unlikely that the 1964 renewal application might well have been routinely granted except for the determined and sustained efforts of Appellants at no small expense to themselves. Such beneficial contribution as these Appellants, or some of them, can make must not be left to the grace of the Commission. . . .

Unless the Commission is to be given staff and resources to perform the enormously complex and prohibitively expensive task of maintaining constant surveillance over every licensee, some mechanism must be developed so that the *legitimate* interests of listeners can be made a part of the record which the Commission evaluates. An initial applicant frequently floods the Commission with testimonials from a host of representative community groups as to the relative merit of their champion, and the Commission places considerable reliance on these vouchers; on a renewal application the "campaign pledges" of applicants must be open to comparison with "performance in office" aided by a limited number of responsible representatives of the listening public when such representatives seek participation.

We recognize the risk[ ] ... [that] regulatory agencies, the Federal Communications Commission in particular, would ill serve the public interest if the courts imposed such heavy burdens on them as to overtax their capacities. The competing consideration is that experience demonstrates consumers are generally among the best vindicators of the public interest. In order to safeguard the public interest in broadcasting, therefore, we hold that some "audience participation" must be allowed in license renewal proceedings. We recognize this will create problems for the Commission but it does not necessarily follow that "hosts" of protestors must be granted standing to challenge a renewal application or that the Commission need allow the administrative processes to be obstructed or overwhelmed by captious or purely obstructive protests. The Commission can avoid such results by developing appropriate regulations by statutory rulemaking. Although it denied Appellants standing, it employed ad hoc criteria in determining that these Appellants were responsible spokesmen for representative groups having significant roots in the listening community. These criteria can afford a basis for developing formalized standards to regulate and limit public intervention to spokesmen who can be helpful. ...

The responsible and representative groups eligible to intervene cannot here be enumerated or categorized specifically; such community organizations as civic associations, professional societies, unions, churches, and educational institutions or associations might well be helpful to the Commission. These groups are found in every community; they usually concern themselves with a wide range of community problems and tend to be representatives of broad as distinguished from narrow interests, public as distinguished from private or commercial interests.

The Commission should be accorded broad discretion in establishing and applying rules for such public participation, including rules for determining which community representatives are to be allowed to participate and how many are reasonably required to give the Commission the assistance it needs in vindicating the public interest. The usefulness of any particular petitioner for intervention must be judged in relation to other petitioners and the nature of the claims it asserts as basis for standing. Moreover it is no novelty in the administrative process to require consolidation of petitions and briefs to avoid multiplicity of parties and duplication of effort.

The fears of regulatory agencies that their processes will be inundated by expansion of standing criteria are rarely borne out. Always a restraining factor is the expense of participation in the administrative process, an economic reality which will operate to limit the number of those who will seek participation; legal and related expenses of administrative proceedings are such that even those with large economic interests find the costs burdensome. . . .

We are aware that there may be efforts to exploit the enlargement of intervention, including spurious petitions from private interests not concerned with the quality of broadcast programming, since such private interests may sometimes cloak themselves with a semblance of public interest advocates. But this problem, as we have noted, can be dealt with by the Commission under its inherent powers and by rulemaking.

In line with this analysis, we do not now hold that all of the Appellants have standing to challenge WLBT's renewal. We do not reach that question. As to these Appellants we limit ourselves to holding that the Commission must allow standing to one or more of them as responsible representatives to assert and prove the claims they have urged . . . The record is remanded to the Commission for further proceedings consistent with this opinion; jurisdiction is retained in this court.

NOTE

NATIONAL WELFARE RIGHTS ORG. V. FINCH, 429 F.2d 725 (D.C.Cir.1970): The Secretary of Health, Education and Welfare had initiated hearings to determine whether Nevada and Connecticut were conforming to requirements of the Aid to Families with Dependent Children program. If the states were found not in compliance, federal payments under the Act would stop. Hence, the initiation of hearings (itself an unusual administrative step) created substantial pressure to settle. NWRO and other welfare organizations responded to a public notice of these hearings by seeking to intervene. HEW decided that the groups could attend the hearing and submit views orally and in writing, but denied them full party status. The groups appealed. Although no statute expressly provided for intervention, Judge Wright, for the court, found "congressional silence" not controlling. Noting the broadening recognition of participatory rights, he readily concluded that NWRO would be able to secure judicial review of HEW's ultimate decision:

"The right of judicial review cannot be taken as fully realized, however, if appellants are excluded from participating in the proceeding to be reviewed. . . . [W]ithout participation . . ., issues which appellants here might wish to raise about the character of the states' plans may have been foreclosed as a topic for review. . . . As intervenors in conformity hearings appellants may serve the public interest in the maintenance of an efficient state-federal cooperative welfare system. . . .

"It is true that increased participation through intervention creates problems for both the tribunal and other parties; multiple and extended cross-examination may be deleterious to the administrative process. . . . Certainly keeping conformity hearings manageable may be a legitimate interest, but as this court set out in Virginia Petroleum Jobbers Ass'n v. FPC, 265 F.2d 364, 367 n. 1 (1959): 'Efficient and expeditious hearings should be achieved, not by excluding parties who have a right to participate, but by controlling the proceeding so that all participants are required to adhere to the issues and to refrain from introducing cumulative or irrelevant evidence.' The threat of hundreds of intervenors in conformity hearings is more apparent than real. The expense of participation, particularly for welfare beneficiaries, is a factor limiting participation; legal and related expenses can be burdensome. . . .

"In finding that appellants may intervene . . . we contemplate enlargement of the rights of participation already accorded them only to the extent of an additional right to present live witnesses and to cross-examine witnesses for other parties.[1] We do not hold that this intervenor status creates in appellants a right to participate in any way in the Secretary's informal efforts . . . to bring a state into conformity, nor do we limit his right to terminate a hearing, once called or begun, upon a determination by him that it is no longer necessary because he believes that conformity has been achieved. In such event, appellants are free to question that determination either indirectly by proceeding against the state, or directly against the Secretary by a suit asserting that he is acting beyond, or in conflict with, his statutory authority. In order to enhance orderly procedures regarding any such litigation as may ensue, the Secretary should provide the parties to a conformity hearing with a preliminary statement of his purpose to terminate the hearing, along with a statement of his reasons for termination and a copy of the proposed state plan on which the state and he have settled. The parties should then be afforded the opportunity to submit, for the Secretary's consideration and for the record, their views as to, or any information bearing upon, the merits of the proposed plan and the reasons for terminating the conformity hearing."

Envirocare of Utah, Inc. v. Nuclear Regulatory Commission

United States Court of Appeals for the District of Columbia Circuit, 1999.
194 F.3d 72.

■ BEFORE EDWARDS, CHIEF JUDGE, SENTELLE and RANDOLPH, CIRCUIT JUDGES.

■ RANDOLPH, CIRCUIT JUDGE:

Federal agencies may, and sometimes do, permit persons to intervene in administrative proceedings even though these persons would not have standing to challenge the agency's final action in federal court. Agencies, of course, are not constrained by Article III of the Constitution; nor are they governed by judicially-created standing doctrines restricting access to the federal courts. The criteria for establishing "administrative standing" therefore may permissibly be less demanding than the criteria for "judicial standing."

---

1. To the extent that appellees are apprehensive of chaos and confusion as an incident to this enlarged right, we remind that they have already recognized the right of appellants to be present at the hearings and to be heard through counsel. Reliance for proper control of the hearings and the orderly compilation of the hearing record must, of course, be on the hearing examiner. He is fully authorized to be the arbiter of the relevance of proffered testimony and of the proper scope of cross-examination, and to insist that all parties address themselves to the business at hand with dignity and dispatch.

Is the converse true? May an agency refuse to grant a hearing to persons who would satisfy the criteria for judicial standing and refuse to allow them to intervene in administrative proceedings? ...

I

Envirocare was the first commercial facility in the nation the Commission licensed to dispose of certain radioactive by-product material from offsite sources. The Commission had licensed other companies to dispose of such radioactive waste, but only if the waste was produced onsite. In the late 1990s, the Commission granted the applications of two such companies for amended licenses to allow them to dispose of radioactive waste received from other sites. International Uranium (USA) Corporation's facility in Utah became licensed to receive and dispose of approximately 25,000 dry tons of waste still remaining from the Manhattan Project and currently stored in New York State. Quivira Mining Company's facility in New Mexico, some 500 miles from Envirocare's operation, also became licensed to dispose of specified amounts of such material from offsite sources.

In both licensing proceedings before the Atomic Safety and Licensing Board, Envirocare requested a hearing and sought leave to intervene to oppose the amendment. Envirocare's basic complaint was "that the license amendment permits [the company] to become a general commercial facility like Envirocare, but that the NRC did not require [the company] to meet the same regulatory standards the agency imposed upon Envirocare when Envirocare sought its license to become a commercial disposal facility for" radioactive waste. Quivira Mining Co., 48 N.R.C. 1, 4, 1998 NRC LEXIS 30 (1998). The Licensing Board rejected Envirocare's requests for a hearing and for leave to intervene in both cases, and in separate opinions several months apart, the Commission affirmed.

... [T]he Commission ruled that Envirocare did not come within the following "standing" provision in the Atomic Energy Act: when the Commission institutes a proceeding for the granting or amending of a license, "the Commission shall grant a hearing upon the request of any person whose interest may be affected by the proceeding, and shall admit any such person as a party to such proceeding." 42 U.S.C. § 2239(a)(1)(A). ... Envirocare alleged economic injury, claiming that the less stringent application of regulations ... placed Envirocare at a competitive disadvantage ... [T]he Commission ... made explicit its view that judicial standing doctrines were not controlling in the administrative context and that its duty was to interpret the "interests" Congress intended to recognize in § 2239(a)(1)(A): "Our understanding of the AEA requires us to insist that a competitor's pecuniary aim of imposing additional regulatory restrictions or burdens on fellow market participants does not fall within those 'interests' that trigger a right to hearing and intervention under [§ 2239(a)(1)(A)]." International Uranium Corp., 48 N.R.C. at 264.

II

... The Commission ... is not an Article III court and thus is not bound to follow the law of standing derived from the "case or controversy" requirement. ... Whether the Commission erred in excluding Envirocare from participating in International Uranium's licensing proceeding therefore turns not on judicial decisions dealing with standing to sue, but on familiar principles of administrative law regarding an agency's interpretation of the statutes it alone administers. See Chevron U.S.A. Inc. v. Natural Resources Defense Council, Inc., 467 U.S. 837, 842 (1984). The governing provision—42 U.S.C. § 2239(a)(1)(A)—requires the Commission to hold a hearing "on the request of any person whose interest may be affected by the proceeding" and to allow such a person to intervene.[1] The term "interest" is not defined in the Act and it is scarcely self-defining.... But whatever the judicial mind thinks of today as an "interest" affected by a proceeding is not necessarily what Congress meant when it enacted this provision in 1954. At the time, judicial notions of standing were considerably more restrictive than they are now. The Supreme Court had put it this way: a private party could challenge federal government action in federal court only if the party had a legally protected interest, that is, "one of property, one arising out of contract, one protected against tortious invasion or one founded on a statute which confers a privilege." Tennessee Elec. Power Co. v. TVA, 306 U.S. 118, 137–38, (1939) ... It was not until the late 1950s that some decisions of this court began expanding the category of persons entitled to participate in agency proceedings on the theory that anyone who had standing to seek judicial review should have administrative standing. See, e.g., National Welfare Rights Org. v. Finch, 429 F.2d 725, 732–33 (D.C.Cir.1970); Office of Communication of United Church of Christ v. FCC, 359 F.2d 994, 1000–06 (D.C.Cir.1966); Virginia Petroleum Jobbers Ass'n v. FPC, 265 F.2d 364 (D.C.Cir.1959). (We will have more to say about these cases in a moment.)

Because we cannot be confident of what kinds of interests the 1954 Congress meant to recognize in § 2239(a)(1)(A)—because, in other words, the statute is ambiguous—the Commission's interpretation of this provision must be sustained if it is reasonable. See Chevron, 467 U.S. at 843. We think it is. For one thing, excluding competitors who allege only economic injury from the class of persons entitled to intervene in licensing proceedings is consistent with the Atomic Energy Act. The Act meant to increase private competition in the industry, not limit it. ...

In rendering its interpretation of § 2239(a)(1)(A), the Commission also properly took account of regulatory burdens on the agency. It wrote: "Competitors, though, whose only 'interest' is lost business opportunities,

---

1. Although it appears that the Administrative Procedure Act applies to the Nuclear Regulatory Commission, see 42 U.S.C. § 2231, Envirocare has not invoked the APA's administrative standing provision, which reads: "So far as the orderly conduct of public business permits, an interested person may appear before an agency or its responsible employees for the presentation, adjustment, or determination of an issue, request or controversy in a proceeding." 5 U.S.C. § 555(b).

Commentators have noted that the role of § 555(b) is unclear and very few courts have attempted to delineate its scope. See 3 K.C. Davis & Richard J. Pierce, Jr., Administrative Law Treatise § 16.10, at 63–65 (3d ed. 1994). One scholar, relying on the prefatory language of the provision, argues that § 555(b) does not create "an absolute, or even a conditional, right to be a party." David L. Shapiro, Some Thoughts on Intervention Before Courts, Agencies, and Arbitrators, 81 Harv. L. Rev. 721, 766 (1968). We express no view on whether § 555(b) would bring about a result different than the one reached by the Commission in its International Uranium opinion interpreting § 2239(a)(1)(A).

could readily burden our adjudicatory process with open-ended allegations designed not to advance public health and safety but as a dilatory tactic to interfere with and impose costs upon a competitor. Such an abuse of our hearing process would significantly divert limited agency resources, which ought to be squarely—genuinely—focused upon health and safety concerns." International Uranium, 48 N.R.C. at 265. . . .

We mentioned earlier several decisions of this court indicating that agencies should allow administrative standing to those who can meet judicial standing requirements. None of these cases interpreted the administrative standing provision of the Atomic Energy Act. All were decided before Chevron and for that reason alone cannot control our decision today. Furthermore, despite some broad language in Office of Communication about administrative standing, the agency there equated standing to appear before it with standing to obtain judicial review and so the court had no occasion to examine whether the two concepts might be distinct. In National Welfare Rights no statute gave individuals standing to intervene in agency proceedings to cut off federal grants-in-aid to states under the Social Security Act. Regardless of the agency's view that only states could participate in the administrative proceedings, which is what the statute said, the court ordered the agency to follow principles of judicial standing in order to "perfect[ ] the right to review." This mode of decisionmaking is contrary to the Supreme Court's later decision . . . prohibiting the judiciary from imposing procedures on an agency when a statute does not require them. See Vermont Yankee Nuclear Power Corp. v. Natural Resources Defense Council, Inc., 435 U.S. 519, 543–49 (1978). As to Virginia Petroleum Jobbers, the court there equated standing to intervene in agency proceedings with standing to seek judicial review on the basis that "the right to appeal from an order presupposes participation in the proceedings which led to it," 265 F.2d at 368, a proposition that has since been vigorously disputed. See Louis L. Jaffe, Judicial Control of Administrative Action 524–25 (1965). In any event, as we have said, all of these cases were pre-Chevron. Judged by current law, none gave sufficient weight to the agency's interpretation of the statute governing intervention in its administrative proceedings. . . .

The petitions for judicial review are denied.

NOTES ON INTERVENTION

(1) *Intervention as a Variable Concept?* When someone succeeds in intervening in a lawsuit in federal court, the traditional understanding (at least in the case of intervention as of right, and usually in the case of permissive intervention as well) is that they thereby attain full party status, with the entire bundle of participatory rights this status entails. Typically, these rights include engaging in discovery, making motions, presenting both written and oral argument, calling and cross-examining witnesses, undertaking appeals, and having a say in any proposed disposition of the case.

Judicial adjudication imagines only a limited set of principal roles: the decisionmaker, the party[ies] plaintiff, and the party[ies] defendant. Parties participate fully in the decisional process and, by virtue of that participation, are fairly held to be bound by the outcome of the process. With the time-honored exception of the amicus curiae, there is no room in the traditional paradigm for variable levels of participation. Even the amicus is understood to be only, as it were, a prompter: positioned offstage to provide whatever assistance might be requested, but having no formally acknowledged personal stake in the way the drama plays out. Although contemporary developments such as institutional public law litigation and mass tort class actions have strained the traditional paradigm, it remains essentially true that in (judicial) adjudication one is either a (full) party or merely a spectator.

"Intervention" at the agency level is apparently a far more variable procedural notion than "intervention" in the judicial setting. The cases you have read generally proceed on the assumption that intervention in agency proceedings does not *necessarily* entail a participatory role equivalent to that of the original parties; rather, the agency is envisioned as deciding (on a case-by-case basis?) which particular procedural "sticks" an intervenor will receive from the full participatory bundle. What might account for these very different assumptions about the meaning of "intervention," and empower judges to extend the range of interests to be given voice?

Particular organic statutes rarely speak decisively to the issue. Section 189(a) of the Atomic Energy Act of 1954, 42 U.S.C. § 2239(a), under which intervention was denied in Environcare, provides that in license application proceedings, the Commission shall "grant a hearing upon the request of any person whose interest may be affected by the proceeding, and shall admit any such person as a party to such proceeding." Other statutes that explicitly address party status or intervention typically contain only the loose directive that any person "upon good cause shown may be allowed" to intervene.[1] Often, the statute says nothing, thus apparently leaving the matter, at least in the first instance, to the agency's discretion. Just as crime victims have no formal participatory rights in criminal trials, one might ordinarily expect interventions to be much less readily granted in administrative proceedings for the imposition of a sanction than in proceedings like those here, for initial licensing; but party status for complainants and other private individuals is not unheard of in such proceedings, as in unfair labor practice proceedings before the NLRB, 29 C.F.R. § 102.8, and enforcement proceedings before the Occupational Safety and Health Review Commission, 29 C.F.R. § 2200.20–21.

In the APA, § 551(3) defines as a "party" anyone "named or admitted as a party, or properly seeking and entitled as of right to be admitted" or admitted "by an agency as a party for limited purposes." Then § 555(b) of the APA (mentioned by Judge Randolph in an Envirocare footnote, p. 341 above, as a possible alternative source of participatory rights) provides, "So far as the orderly conduct of public business permits, an interested person may appear before an agency or its responsible employees for the presenta-

---

1. Such language appears, for example, in the Federal Trade Commission Act.

tion, adjustment, or determination of an issue, request, or controversy ..."
Is an "interested person," then, someone other than a "party" (intervenor)? See Nichols v. Board of Trustees of the Asbestos Workers Local 24
Pension Plan, 835 F.2d 881, 898 (D.C.Cir.1987). As Judge Randolph remarks, Professor David Shapiro has argued that § 555(b) is a modest
mandate that may be satisfied through the grant of discrete participatory
rights—such as permission "to present written statements, to offer evidence, or in some instances to cross-examine"—that do not rise to the level
of full party status. David L. Shapiro, Some Thoughts on Intervention
Before Courts, Agencies, and Arbitrators, 81 Harv.L.Rev. 721, 766 (1968).

(2) Recall that the NWRO court found congressional silence no bar to
ordering that welfare recipients be included in proceedings to determine
states' conformity with federal benefit standards. Contrast this with the
1984 Supreme Court decision in BLOCK V. COMMUNITY NUTRITION INSTITUTE,
467 U.S. 340, 346–47. The case actually involved participation rights at the
level of judicial review: whether the statutory scheme precluded a consumer
group from obtaining judicial review of a milk marketing order issued by
the Secretary of Agriculture, outside the framework of administrative
challenges explicitly established by the governing legislation. (It is presented and discussed in this respect at p. 1188.) Intervention at the agency level
was not in issue. Nonetheless, Justice O'Connor's opinion (for a unanimous
court) contained the following dicta:

"The ... statutory scheme ... makes ... clear Congress' intention to
limit the classes entitled to participate in the development of market
orders. The Act contemplates a cooperative venture among the Secretary,
[milk] handlers, and [milk] producers the principal purposes of which are
to raise the price of agricultural products and to establish an orderly
system for marketing them. Handlers and producers—but not consumers—
are entitled to participate in the adoption and retention of market orders.
The Act provides for agreements among the Secretary, producers, and
handlers, for hearings among them, and for votes by producers and
handlers. Nowhere in the Act, however, is there an express provision for
participation by consumers in any proceeding. In a complex scheme of this
type, the omission of such a provision is sufficient reason to believe that
Congress intended to foreclose consumer participation in the regulatory
process."

(3) *Intervention and Standing.* Our present focus is on efforts by beneficiary groups and other private interests to influence regulatory policymaking
directly, by obtaining access to *agency* proceedings. The question of standing, as often discussed in the principal cases, concerns obtaining access to a
reviewing court, and has constitutional dimensions grounded in Article III
that are absent in the agency context. Standing is taken up in detail at p.
1117ff.

As a matter of legal doctrine, these two forms of voice are distinct. It is
black letter law that a party is not necessarily entitled to intervene at the
agency level merely because, under existing standing doctrine, she would be
entitled to seek judicial review of an unfavorable agency decision. "[I]t is
certainly possible that A's interests could be adequately represented before
the agency by B, a party to the proceedings; under these circumstances A

would have no right to intervene, but he might be entitled to appeal if he were adversely affected by a final order." Shapiro, 81 Harv.L.Rev. at 767. Conversely, intervention as of right at the agency level is not *limited* to parties who would later be entitled to judicial review. And finally, the fact that a party *was* admitted to the agency proceeding does not necessarily ensure standing to challenge the outcome.

As a matter of policy, there are good reasons for treating intervention at the agency level as distinct from standing to obtain judicial review. Intervention entails possible risks to hearing procedures—for example, permitting parties extended cross-examination. These risks are arguably controllable by the tribunal through limited participation rights. To the extent standing is grounded in Article III of the Constitution, that has no bearing on agency proceedings. Judicial review, on the other hand, is an all-or-nothing event, in which no compromise about the extent of participating rights is customary. Moreover, standing to obtain review is substantially affected by the constitutional requirement of case or controversy.

Even though the two forms of participation are sensibly regarded as distinct, judicial analysis of one often draws on the other for support. When standing doctrine was in a period of expansion, those seeking intervention benefitted from this linkage. But what happens to intervention when standing starts to contract? Envirocare, you may think, sends strong signals in this regard.

NOTES ON PUBLIC INTEREST REPRESENTATION

(1) *Public Interest Representation as a Model.* As the opinion in Envirocare accurately reflects, through the first half of this century American administrative law embodied a fairly narrow conception of which private interests were entitled to a voice in agency adjudication. The central legal problem posed by regulation was seen as one of defining and enforcing the permissible limits of government intrusion into private autonomy. Accordingly, rights of participation in agency proceedings (and, as is reflected at p. 1117 and following, rights of access to judicial review) were generally accorded only to private parties whose liberty or property interests—as traditionally defined by the common law—were being curtailed by agency action.

This restrictive view of the "relevant" private voices was changed as part of a legal, social and political transformation during the 1960s and early 1970s. Office of Communication—written, note, by one of the more conservative judges of the time—was a marker. The emergence of powerful, broadly-based movements in the areas of civil rights, health and safety, consumer protection, and the environment redefined the regulatory landscape. Government was called upon to take an affirmative role in ensuring social justice and enhancing physical and economic well-being. New regulatory initiatives were undertaken;[1] older regulatory programs faced demands that new considerations—such as environmental protection and equal

---

1. The Environmental Protection Agency, the Occupational Safety and Health Administration, the Consumer Product Safety Commission, and the Equal Employment Opportunity Commission all date from the 1960s–70s, a period of regulatory blossoming that rivaled the New Deal.

opportunity—be factored into the policymaking calculus. Yet, at the same time as government was taking on ambitious new regulatory agendas, questions were being raised about the ability of the administrative process, as traditionally structured, to in fact discern the "public interest." Political scientists and grassroots advocates alike charged that agencies had been "captured" by the interests they were supposed to regulate.[2] Legal scholars questioned the legitimacy and wisdom of standardless discretionary power exercised through informal, often closed, administrative processes.[3]

Skepticism about the quality of policy that emerged from agencies' "standard operating procedure," in conjunction with the rise of organized and vocal advocacy groups, produced a new emphasis on empowering otherwise underrepresented voices to participate meaningfully in the crafting of public policy. This emphasis eventually transformed administrative law in a variety of ways.[4] From simple models of "adjudication" and "legislation," the courts were moving toward an understanding of administrative action more consistent with its unique qualities as an analytic-policymaking enterprise. Most relevant for present purposes, these socio-legal developments led to a new assertion of the "rights" of beneficiaries of regulatory programs to participate in agency decisionmaking.

(2) An influential article published in the mid–1970s, RICHARD B. STEWART, THE REFORMATION OF AMERICAN ADMINISTRATIVE LAW, 88 Harv.L.Rev. 1667, 1759–62 (1975), reflected on this broader trend:

"The problem of administrative procedure is to provide representation for all affected interests; the problem of substantive policy is to reach equitable accommodations among these interests in varying circumstances; and the problem of judicial review is to ensure that agencies provide fair procedures for representation and reach fair accommodations."

"The expansion of the traditional model to afford participation rights in the process of agency decision and judicial review to a wide variety of affected interests must ultimately rest on the premise that such procedural changes will be an effective and workable means of assuring improved agency decisions. Advocates of extended access believe that an enlarged system of formal proceedings can, by securing adequate consideration of the interests of all affected persons, yield outcomes that better serve society as a whole. . . . [Moreover, such participation is said to be] valuable in itself because it gives citizens a sense of involvement in the process of government, and increases confidence in the fairness of government decisions. . . .

2. E.g., Theodore J. Lowi, The End of Liberalism (1969); Mark Green & Ralph Nader, Economic Regulation vs. Competition: Uncle Sam the Monopoly Man, 82 Yale L.J. 871 (1973).

3. E.g., Kenneth C. Davis, Discretionary Justice: A Preliminary Inquiry (1969); Charles A. Reich, The New Property, 73 Yale L.J. 733 (1964). For more extended discussion of the events sketched briefly in these paragraphs, see Richard B. Stewart, The Reformation of American Administrative Law, 88 Harv.L.Rev. 1669 (1975); Merrick B. Garland, Deregulation and Judicial Review, 98 Harv.L.Rev. 507 (1985).

4. See, e.g., Richard B. Stewart and Cass R. Sunstein, Public Programs and Private Rights, 95 Harv.L.Rev. 1193 (1982).

"The time has come for a critical assessment of this prescription for asserted biases and inadequacies in agency decisions. The judges' incipient transformation of administrative law into a scheme of interest representation is responding to powerful needs that have been neglected by other branches of government. There are serious perceived inadequacies in agency performance, and this perception must be addressed if attitudes towards government are not to degenerate into cynicism or despair. Moreover, the realities of agency performance may often indeed be far short of what is desirable or even tolerable. But whether a judicially implemented system of interest representation is an adequate or workable response to these needs is a question deserving the most careful consideration."

(3) *Balancing the Impact of Representation on the Agency?* The "interest representation" approach Professor Stewart identified was particularly concerned (as was the Office of Communication court) with agency failures to act on behalf of intended beneficiaries of regulatory regimes. Could an argument be constructed under which those beneficiaries would be stakeholders with claims equivalent to those of the regulated? Consider CASS R. SUNSTEIN, REVIEWING AGENCY INACTION AFTER HECKLER V. CHANEY, 52 U.Chi. L.Rev. 653, 666–69 (1985): "The original role of judicial review of administrative conduct was based on two related understandings. The first was that market ordering within the constraints of the common law was normal and natural. In light of this assumption, government intervention in the market appeared exceptional and was subject to special judicial control. For this reason, courts adopted what was in effect a one-way ratchet, consisting of legally enforceable constraints on regulation but no such constraints on inaction. The second understanding was that the purpose of judicial review was to safeguard traditional private rights as defined by the common law. The interests of those who were likely to benefit from administrative action were not traditional liberty or property interests and were thus not entitled to judicial protection. The political process was seen as the appropriate safeguard against unlawful inaction, especially since large numbers of people were often affected by failure to act. Together, these two understandings represent a Lochner-like view of the judicial role. The Lochner Court, too, saw the judicial role as the vindication of private rights, defined by reference to market ordering within the common law, against government 'intervention.'

"With the rise of the regulatory state, however, this Lochner-era approach to judicial review of administrative inaction is no longer tenable. And it should be unsurprising to find that this view arose and declined in constitutional and administrative law in parallel fashion. In the constitutional context, the Court recognized in West Coast Hotel v. Parrish, 300 U.S. 379 (1937), that common law ordering was in no sense 'natural,' but was the product of governmental choice: both action and inaction amount to decisions. It was pursuant to this view that a failure to act might be seen as, in the Court's words, a 'subsidy' to those who benefitted from the inaction. Similarly, in the administrative context, the notion that judicial review is limited in purpose to safeguarding traditional private rights and in scope to the promotion of traditional private autonomy has become unacceptable.

"... [T]he availability of political remedies does not, as a general rule, distinguish inaction from action. The possibility of political redress has not been thought sufficient to justify the elimination of judicial review of agency action. The same conclusion is properly reached in the context of inaction. Often political remedies are more readily used by well-organized members of regulated classes than by regulatory beneficiaries, who must overcome substantial barriers to the exercise of political power. At least in some contexts, differential access to the political process may well make judicial review of agency inaction a particularly necessary safeguard."

(4) Subsequent critics of the interest representation approach have come from opposing camps. MERRICK B. GARLAND, DEREGULATION AND JUDICIAL REVIEW, 98 Harv.L.Rev. 505, 583 (1985) is among those who have argued that "mere" participation rights do not go far enough:

> Doubts arose over whether the principal tool of the [interest representation approach], expanded public participation, was really capable of effectuating its purpose—enhancing protection for the intended beneficiaries of public programs. Procedural and quasi-procedural requirements could ensure an agency's awareness of the consequences of its actions and thereby eliminate truly irrational decisionmaking. But such requirements could do little to sway an agency that had decided on its course before undertaking the [regulatory action] and little to enforce an agency's fidelity to a legislative program for which it had no sympathy. ... [Moreover,] even an initially successful petitioner could find its victory rendered hollow when, on remand, the agency went through the required motions but reached the same results.

Others have condemned judicial enhancement of participation rights for increasing the time, expense and complexity of regulatory proceedings without reliably producing offsetting gains in the quality of regulatory decisionmaking. Thus, as suggested by Envirocare, rules facilitating party status may encourage manipulative use of process for economic advantage. LARS NOAH, SHAM PETITIONING AS A THREAT TO THE INTEGRITY OF THE REGULATORY PROCESS, 74 N. Car. L. Rev. 1 (1995): "The Federal Trade Commission recently announced plans to investigate the petitioning activities of companies in the pharmaceutical and medical device industries. Agency officials expressed concerns that firms were using frivolous patent litigation and petitions to the Food and Drug Administration to limit competition and market entry. The financial stakes in these industries are often enormous, and even relatively short delays in FDA approval of competing products could prove extremely valuable to a company with an approved product already on the market. ... It is difficult, of course, to gauge the prevalence of such behavior, and obvious differences exist among various agencies and regulated industries. Nonetheless, ... real opportunities exist for sham petitioning in administrative proceedings, especially when market entry requires some sort of agency licensing as in the pharmaceutical, transportation, communications, and energy industries.

"In light of the potential for abuse of the regulatory process, the next question is how best to minimize the risk of anticompetitive manipulation. By default rather than by design, application of the federal antitrust laws has become the preferred method of response by public and private litigants. Nevertheless, one might wonder whether the confidence expressed by the FTC in using the antitrust laws for these purposes is justified. Because the First Amendment protects persons' right to petition the government for redress of grievances, the Supreme Court has conferred broad immunity from antitrust scrutiny to businesses engaged in legislative lobbying, regulatory proceedings, and litigation. Although 'sham petitioning' is excluded from this immunity, serious limitations exist with a remedial approach dependent on the proscriptions of the Sherman Act. For example, . . . it is extremely difficult to establish that a regulatory petition is both objectively baseless and born of a subjective predatory intent, a two-part inquiry which raises some of the same difficulties that courts have faced in attempting to police the conduct of litigants. Objective baselessness may be particularly difficult to demonstrate in the administrative context because agencies enjoy greater policymaking discretion than do the courts. Indeed, where the standards for approval of licenses and applications make reference to undefined considerations of public interest, it may be impossible to show that a competitor's objections were objectively baseless. . . .

"Because the antitrust laws cannot adequately deter anticompetitive abuses of the regulatory process, agency procedures must be modified to address these concerns. . . . Just as courts have developed special standards of conduct, such as Rule 11 of the Federal Rules of Civil Procedure, to address real or perceived abuses in the context of litigation, agencies need to assume greater responsibility for controlling the behavior of participants in administrative proceedings. . . . In particular, agencies should impose greater restrictions on the rights of intervention by third parties. Although agencies permit and even encourage participation by persons with financial interests in licensing and other decisions, neither the constitutional right to petition nor guarantees of due process require that incumbent firms be given opportunities to block market entry by competitors. The decision-making activities of administrative agencies and courts differ, of course, in a variety of respects, and commentators properly have criticized the tendency to overlay the adversarial model on regulatory processes. In fact, legislators may intend that administrative agencies be more responsive to lobbying by interested persons even if that makes their procedures more vulnerable to anticompetitive manipulation. Nonetheless, legislators and agency officials must guard against sham petitioning when it threatens to undermine the integrity of the regulatory process. Opportunities for participation should not become invitations for fraudulent submissions or other misuses of administrative procedures."

The reference to F.R.Civ.P. 11 suggests a larger question of professional ethics: As a matter of good practice, what *should* a lawyer require as a "basis" for petitioning, before she advises or participates in invoking such administrative procedures on a client's behalf? Compare the related question about the ethics of scorched-earth comment practices in informal rulemaking, p. 548.

(5) *Adjudication as a Substitute for Politics?* Even when public beneficiary interests do underlie attempted litigation, the winner-take-all character of adjudicative approaches may give rise to doubts whether political or other consensual processes might not be more productive than empowering

persons with the capacity to litigate to command the course of administrative decisionmaking. PETER L. STRAUSS, REVISITING *OVERTON PARK*: POLITICAL AND JUDICIAL CONTROLS OVER ADMINISTRATIVE ACTIONS AFFECTING THE COMMUNITY, 39 UCLA L.Rev. 1251, 1323, 1328 (1992) reviews the political and legal history of one of the Supreme Court's major forays into interest representation, and concludes that the failures of citizen groups to achieve their goals prior to judicial involvement "were failures of persuasion, not the result of either institutional barriers to being heard or politicians insensitive to the importance of the values being promoted.

"In considering the claims and risks of 'public interest representation' ways of thinking about judicial review, it may be helpful to distinguish between judicial actions in the nature of 'representation reinforcement,' ... and actions that imagine the judicial role itself as a form of substitute politics. When judges act to strengthen political processes they find to be impaired ... the judicial intervention does not entail particular outcomes, and the overall impact may indeed be beneficial. ... Affirming the judicial role itself as a form of substitute politics respecting polycentric issues, in contrast, *does* entail particular outcomes, continuing politically inspired oversight, and continuing competition with other, explicitly political sources; and it can be expected to be more problematic. ... Thus, while in historic fact rights of participation at the agency level were built on the shoulders of decisions about standing to seek judicial review, consideration of the different ways politics works at the agency and judicial levels suggests stronger claims for agency participation than for judicial review."

On this theory, Office of Communication was probably rightly decided, for "Judge Burger could claim to have been strengthening agency process rather than injecting judicial politics; he was specifying participation rules for an administrative agency acting under political as well as judicial oversight, seeking political as well as legal ends."

The Overton Park case is considered at p. 989.

(6) *Litigation as a Strategy Within Continuing Administrative Relationships.* An intriguingly different perspective on the connection between voice in agency proceedings and voice in a reviewing court is offered in CARY COGLIANESE, LITIGATION WITHIN RELATIONSHIPS: DISPUTES & DISTURBANCES IN THE REGULATORY PROCESS, 30 Law & Soc'y Rev. 735 (1996). The conventional view of litigation sees the practice as a failure of social interaction: proof that the relationship between the parties has either irretrievably broken down, or was never successfully established in the first place. When Prof. Coglianese examined the pattern of regulatory litigation in the environmental area, however, he discovered that interest groups having the most extensive and long-standing relations with EPA tend to be the ones most likely to continue to press their policy positions in court if they do not succeed in obtaining their preferred resolution at the agency level. This observation leads him to posit an alternative, "disturbance theory" of litigation, which proposes that litigation's effect on relationships depends upon the nature of the litigation. In contrast to non-regulatory disputes, the type of litigating carried on in the EPA context—in which, for example, "groups communicate with agency staff to let them know that they are just suing over the policy decision, not attacking the character or competence of

the agency staff"—does not create significant disturbance within the ongoing relationship. Thus, he argues, the move from exercising voice in the agency to exercising voice in a reviewing court marks not a rupture of relationship or a "last-resort strategy reserved for outsiders," but rather is perceived by the regulatory players "as a legitimate institutional process for carrying on business as usual."

(7) *Whence Theory?* Other evidence of the interest representation approach—and further debates about its practical efficacy and normative justification—appear in the discussions of the hard look doctrine and related issues in standard of review (Chapter VIII), as well as in our consideration of the various threshold requirements for obtaining judicial review (Chapter IX). As the latter makes clear, much of the current argument over issues controlling access to judicial review, such as standing and ripeness, arises from fears for politicizing the courts should they come to be seen as the guardians of "a scheme of interest representation ... responding to powerful needs that have been neglected by other [advisedly political] branches of government." Stewart, above. What may become the next generation of metatheory about the administrative process reacts against the interest-representation model by drawing, variously, on the revived legal interest in republicanism, deliberative democracy, and collaborative processes. See, e.g., Mark Seidenfeld, A Civic Republican Justification for the Bureaucratic State, 105 Harv. L. Rev. 1511 (1992); Jim Rossi, Participation Run Amok: The Costs of Mass Participation for Deliberative Agency Decisionmaking, 92 Nw. U.L. Rev. 173 (1997); Jody Freeman, Collaborative Governance in the Administrative State, 45 U.C.L.A. L. Rev. 1 (1997). For a thoughtful and sympathetic, but ultimately challenging, response to those who would construct the next generation of metatheory, see Steven P. Croley, Theories of Regulation: Incorporating the Administrative Process, 91 Colum.L.Rev. 1 (1998).

b.   EVIDENTIARY ISSUES

While the student might expect that formal agency adjudications would be conducted under rules resembling the Federal Rules of Civil Procedure and/or of Evidence, a reading of §§ 554–57 will quickly reveal that no such provision is made. Pretrial practice, evidentiary practice, and other matters made the subject of uniform rules in federal trials are left to the statutes and regulations of particular agencies. A working group of the now defunct Administrative Conference of the United States,[1] convened to study the feasibility of model rules in the face of varying agency needs and practices, put the matter this way in 1988:

> At present, trial-type adjudications are held before scores of federal agencies, each having its own set of practice and procedure rules. To the extent that formal adjudications present similar practice and procedure considerations, substantial benefits can be anticipated if similarity also existed in federal agency practice and procedure rules. Such benefits might include: a reduction of adjudication costs both for the government and for private parties; expedition and simplification

---

1. See p. 479 below.

of administrative proceedings; and simplification of participation in the administrative process by administrative law judges or other agency adjudicators, federal agency attorneys, private practitioners, and other persons dealing with federal agencies. In order to encourage and facilitate the reduction of differences among practice and procedure rules applicable to federal agency formal adjudications, these Model Rules are offered for consideration.[2]

Your editors have chosen to represent the wide range of hearing issues possible to present by focusing on one question of evidentiary practice to which the APA does, at least partially, speak.

Central to decision in Seacoast Anti–Pollution League v. Costle, p. 325 above, was the court's concern about the manner in which the EPA administrator had resolved certain factual issues. One question, under § 556(d), was whether cross-examination was "required for a full and true disclosure of the facts." Note that this section further provides that in "applications for initial licenses an agency may, when a party will not be prejudiced thereby, adopt procedures for the submission of all or part of the evidence in written form." Is SAPL as much "a party" as Public Service Company of New Hampshire for these purposes? What would "prejudice" to it be, and how, if at all, should this test be understood to differ from that of the preceding sentence? Is "prejudice" the test that the SAPL court is proposing that the Administrator must meet, or has it concluded that the language of the constitutive EPA statute, § 316(a) of the FWPCA, operates to take this proceeding out of the special provision for initial licenses, so that the only question is whether cross-examination was "required for a full and true disclosure of the facts"? If you conclude that the court took the latter course, then you have found in this case a lesson important to learn in general—that procedures will be governed not only by the APA but also by the specific statutes underlying the particular proceeding.

The question about fact-finding that animates the materials of this section is this: Was the Administrator permitted to supplement the record developed at the hearing by relying on the "scientific literature" about, for example, the effect hot water discharges and/or thermal shock from their intermittent cessation would have on survival of marine organisms?[3] In part, this question has to do with the Administrator's use of a panel of agency scientists to help him understand the technological issues involved; we will take up this aspect below, at p. 394ff. Here, the question is one of evidentiary practice—whether, under *any* procedure, the Administrator could use information that had not been placed in the record at hearing. This issue is dealt with in § 556(e). It provides that "When an agency

2. Michael Cox, The Model Adjudication Rules (MARs), 11 T.M. Cooley L. Rev. 75, 76–77 (1994). Prof. Cox reports similar models having been proposed for state administrative law judges by a committee of the American Bar Association's National Conference of Administrative Law Judges, 76 at n. 5.

3. One of your editors, who had a limited professional association with the license application for this facility, recalls hearing that the organisms in question were softshell clam larvae, and that the projected kill was about the same as could be accounted for by the appetites of four of the great blue whales that once swam in these waters, before the American whaling industry depleted their stock.

decision rests on official notice of a material fact not appearing in the evidence in the record, a party is entitled, on timely request, to an opportunity to show the contrary." The SAPL court remarks that "To the extent the technical panel's Report included information not in the record on which the Administrator relied, § 556(e) was violated."

Castillo–Villagra v. Immigration and Naturalization Service

United States Court of Appeals for the Ninth Circuit, 1992.
972 F.2d 1017.

■ Before CHOY, NORRIS and KLEINFELD, CIRCUIT JUDGES.

■ KLEINFELD, CIRCUIT JUDGE:

This case turns on the breadth of the doctrine of administrative notice. We grant a petition for review of a decision of the Board of Immigration Appeals [Board or BIA] and reverse, because the Board improperly took notice of the effect of the change of government in Nicaragua on whether petitioners' fear of persecution was well-founded.

Teresa de Jesus Castillo–Villagra and her two adult daughters unsuccessfully sought asylum. They claimed that they had a well-founded fear of persecution by the Sandinistas because of their anti-Sandinista political opinions. While their case was pending, Violeta Chamorro, a democrat, was elected president of Nicaragua, and her democratic coalition, UNO, defeated the Sandinistas in an election. The Board of Immigration Appeals took administrative notice of the election and determined that because the Sandinistas had lost, the threat to petitioners from the Sandinistas had disappeared.

Petitioners were given no notice or opportunity to be heard regarding whether notice should be taken or whether the political changes in Nicaragua obviated their fear of returning. They claim that the Sandinistas retain enough power so that they still need asylum. Despite the election of the new president and parliamentary majority, the Sandinistas retained control of the army and the police, according to the State Department Country Report. The hearings were in December 1987 and February 1988, the Immigration Judge rendered his decision in February 1988, and the briefing on appeal before the BIA was completed in October 1989, all prior to the election, so no one had occasion to develop a record about the possibility that the Sandinistas might someday lose control. The election, with its surprise result in favor of UNO and Chamorro, was in April 1990. The BIA issued its decision in October 1990, without inviting supplementation of the record or briefs, yet based entirely on the election result subsequent to the record and briefs.

We determine that the Board should not have resolved the question of the effect of the change of government on petitioners without giving them notice of its intent to do so and an opportunity to show cause why notice should not be taken, or the record supplemented by further evidence. For these reasons, we reverse.

I. FACTS

The petitioners entered the United States without inspection, conceded deportability, and sought asylum under section 208 . . . [of the Immigration and Nationality Act], 8 U.S.C. § 1158(a).[1] They claim to have been members of a political group, the Movimiento Democratico Nicaraguense (MDN), which opposed the Sandinista regime in Nicaragua.

The State Department Country Report for Nicaragua for 1984 . . . explains how the then relatively new Sandinista regime sought to "intimidate the remaining opposition." The Sandinista methods of exercising power described by the State Department report and by the petitioners in their testimony give plausibility to petitioners' claims that the threat of Sandinista political persecution might have survived the election. . . .

At the hearing before the Immigration Judge, the older daughter, Maria Auxiliadora Aleman–Castillo, provided most of the testimony, because she spoke English. She said that in her small town, Jinotega, "everybody knows everybody's activities," and at the university, everybody knew who was anti-government. Maria testified that "we used to print out papers against the government" and "go to different schools and give them away to people." Both daughters and their mother were active in the MDN.

Maria testified, "if we come back we're gonna be incarcerated, we're gonna be persecuted, we're probably gonna disappear like our friend did. . . ." Because of the family's political opinions and activities, mobs of 20 to 50 people, who "used to live on the streets doing nothing" and had been given good government jobs and cars by the Sandinistas, stoned their house in Jinotega about 10 times, mostly in 1982. They also displayed an effigy in a context in which it was a death threat. She said: "We couldn't call the police because they were the police." All of their windows were knocked out. She was arrested once, together with her younger sister, Teresita, in an anti-government demonstration in Nandaime Carazo in 1982, held in jail about seven hours, and then released with a threat that the next time they would not get out for twenty years. . . . The family got out in September 1983. . . .

In his oral decision, the Immigration Judge found that the mother was lying and none of the three had a well-founded fear of persecution because of their political opinions. . . . The Immigration Judge believed that if they returned to Nicaragua and "simply went about their business without more," the government would not persecute them, although "[i]f they decided to get involved in demonstrations or distributing literature, perhaps they would be harassed." He therefore found that they were not entitled to asylum.

The Board of Immigration Appeals did not review the Immigration Judge's credibility determination, nor did it consider whether asylum could

---

1. [Ed.] 8 U.S.C. § 1158(a) provides for the granting of asylum "in the discretion of the Attorney General" after a determination that the alien is a refugee within the meaning of 8 U.S.C. § 1101(a)(42)(A); that section, in turn, defines "refugee" to mean, inter alia, a person outside the country of his or her nationality and unable or unwilling to return "because of persecution or a well-founded fear of persecution on account of race, religion, nationality, membership in a particular social group, or political opinion."

properly be denied if petitioners could avoid persecution by refraining from political activities. Instead, it resolved this case, along with a number of others involving anti-Sandinista Nicaraguans, by taking administrative notice that an anti-Sandinista coalition now controlled the government and Violeta Chamorro had been elected president, so anti-Sandinistas had nothing more to fear, whether they previously had a well-founded fear or not. Our review is limited to the BIA decision, and we may not base our decision upon the IJ's findings and decision independently of the BIA decision.

The Board issued its decision using language identical to that used in a large number of other cases before it involving anti-Sandinista Nicaraguans:

> After careful review of the record, we find no basis to support the respondents' contention that they have a well-founded fear of persecution. . . .

> In this regard, we take administrative notice that the Sandinista party no longer controls the Nicaraguan government. Effective April 25, 1990, a new coalition government, formed by parties in opposition to the Sandinistas ("UNO"), has succeeded the former government of the Sandinista party following national elections and the inauguration of Violeta Chamorro as the new president. Given that the Sandinista party no longer governs Nicaragua, under the present circumstances we do not find that the record now before us supports a finding that the respondents have a well-founded fear of persecution by the Sandinista government were they to return to Nicaragua.

It is plain from its use in the anti-Sandinista Nicaraguan cases that the phrase, "[a]fter careful review of the record," means review to determine whether this case fell into the category of anti-Sandinista Nicaraguan asylum cases, not to determine whether the claim of well-founded fear in the particular case should be accepted. The Board gave no reasons for its decision except for the facts of which it took administrative notice. The identical language was used in a large number of other cases, apparently as INS form language for Nicaraguan cases after Violeta Chamorro won the Nicaraguan presidential election.

II. JURISDICTION AND EXHAUSTION

[The court's discussion is omitted.]

III. ADMINISTRATIVE NOTICE

Petitioners' attorney explained that they had no quarrel with the BIA's taking notice that Violeta Chamorro had won election to the presidency, and that the UNO, a non-Sandinista coalition, had won a majority in parliament. Their claim is that the Sandinistas retain control of the police and the army, and still have sufficient sway to persecute their political adversaries, who include petitioners.

A. APA or INA?

To decide whether administrative notice was appropriate, first we must decide whether the question should be analyzed under the Administrative

Procedure Act or the Immigration and Naturalization Act. The petitioners argue that the Administrative Procedure Act ("the APA") bars administrative notice in the circumstances of this case. The APA provides that no subsequent statute shall be deemed to modify it "except to the extent that it does so expressly." 5 U.S.C. § 559. Section 242(b) of the Immigration and Nationality Act of 1952 ("the INA") (codified as amended at 8 U.S.C. § 1252(b)) sets out in some detail the procedural framework governing deportation proceedings, and provides that "[t]he procedure so prescribed shall be the sole and exclusive procedure for determining the deportability of an alien under this section." We conclude that the INA displaces the APA on this question. . . .

B.   Proper Scope of Notice.

Notice is a way to establish the existence of facts without evidence. In federal courts, notice may be taken of facts relating to the particular case, though no evidence is introduced, where the fact is "not subject to reasonable dispute," either because it is "generally known within the territorial jurisdiction," or is "capable of accurate and ready determination by resort to sources whose accuracy cannot reasonably be questioned." Fed.R.Evid. 201(b); see 9 John Henry Wigmore, Evidence § 2571, at 731–32 (J. Chadbourn rev. 1981).

The appropriate scope of notice is broader in administrative proceedings than in trials, especially jury trials. Partly this is because the rules of evidence are more liberal and the volume of cases is so much greater in administrative proceedings. Professor Kenneth Culp Davis distinguished between adjudicative facts, which are those concerning the immediate parties, and legislative facts, which help the tribunal determine law and policy and are ordinarily general facts not concerning the immediate parties. Kenneth Culp Davis, Judicial Notice, 55 Colum.L.Rev. 945, 952 (1955). Davis' argument that notice of legislative facts may properly be taken more liberally than notice of adjudicative facts generally has been accepted. See, e.g., Fed.R.Evid. 201 advisory committee's notes on 1972 proposed rules.

While in proceedings in court notice is quite restricted for adjudicative facts, it is broader in administrative proceedings. A case before an administrative agency, unlike one before a court, "is rarely an isolated phenomenon, but is rather merely one unit in a mass of related cases ... [which] often involve fact questions which have frequently been explored by the same tribunal." Walter Gellhorn, Official Notice in Administrative Adjudication, 20 Tex.L.Rev. 131, 136 (1941). The tribunal learns from its cases. Moreover, volume and repetition affect peoples' ability to pay attention. Because of the quantity of similar cases before an agency such as the INS, if notice is not taken more broadly in administrative hearings, litigants may have an uphill battle maintaining the attention of the administrative judges. Even if the law allows people to tell officials the exact same and obvious thing hundreds of times, the officials may find it very hard to listen attentively after the first dozen or two repetitions. Hearings may degenerate into an empty form if the adjudicators cannot focus attention upon what is noteworthy about the particular case. The broader notice available in administrative hearings may, if properly used, facilitate more genuine hearings, as opposed to "hearings" in which the finder of fact hears, but cannot, because of the repetition, listen.

But the administrative desirability of notice as a substitute for evidence cannot be allowed to outweigh fairness to individual litigants. . . . Notice of facts without warning may deny "the fair hearing essential to due process," and amount to "condemnation without trial." Ohio Bell Telephone Co. v. Public Utils. Comm'n, 301 U.S. 292, 300 (1937).

The facts of which the INS took notice in this case were in part legislative in nature. They included: (1) that Violeta Chamorro had been elected president, (2) that her non-Sandinista coalition had gained a majority in parliament, and (3) that the Sandinistas were ousted from power. The facts were also in part adjudicative, that the Castillo–Villagra family had nothing more to fear from the Sandinistas. The first two facts are plainly legislative and not debatable. It would be a waste of time to allow evidence regarding them. The third legislative fact, that the Sandinistas were ousted from power, was debatable, since the Sandinistas retained power over the police and the military. The adjudicative fact required both a debatable assumption about the amount of power retained by the Sandinistas, and an assumption about the particular salience of the Castillo–Villagra family as an irritant to Sandinistas who may retain enough power in Jinotega or the university to persecute them.

The question of proper scope and manner of administrative notice before the INS is one of first impression in the Circuit. We decided upon a somewhat analogous question in Banks v. Schweiker, 654 F.2d 637 (9th Cir.1981), although Banks is not controlling in this case because it arose in a social security context in which the APA and social security regulations applied. The reasoning in Banks, however, is applicable here, and we see no reason to choose a different path for INS cases.

In Banks we held that an adjudicator could properly take notice of how social security office personnel ordinarily dealt with inquiries such as Banks had made, as a basis for rejecting Banks' testimony as not credible. We rejected for administrative proceedings the applicability of the principle in Federal Rule of Evidence 201(b), that adjudicative facts may be noticed only if "not subject to reasonable dispute," and rejected in the administrative context the tradition of caution associated with taking notice under that rule. Instead, we adopted "a rule of convenience," that "the ALJ should take notice of adjudicative facts, whenever 'the ALJ at the hearing knows of information that will be useful in making the decision.'" Id. at 640–41 (quoting 3 Kenneth Culp Davis, Administrative Law Treatise § 15:18, at 200 (2d ed. 1980)).

The justifications for a rule of convenience apply equally in the INS context. The agency has a large volume of cases. Its officers work in a specialized area with many similar cases, so they grow familiar with conditions abroad from many witnesses and exhibits. The burden of producing evidence may be especially great when it involves changing political conditions in a foreign country. The repetitiveness of such evidence, as large numbers of petitioners from particular countries pass through the system, may interfere with its heuristic power. It is significant for the scope of notice that the asylum seeker has the burden of proof. Where the asylum seeker is given the opportunity to offer evidence rebutting the proposition of which notice is taken, notice does not substitute for evidence which the agency would otherwise have to produce. Instead, it directs the asylum seeker's presentation to the propositions likely to have a practical effect on the outcome.

The problem arises, in this case as in Banks, when the petitioner is denied a fair opportunity to rebut the proposition of which notice is taken. An essential concomitant of a rule of convenience is a fair opportunity to respond. . . .

There are three separable issues with regard to notice: (1) whether notice may be taken at all, (2) whether warning must be given before notice is taken, and (3) whether rebuttal evidence must be allowed against the proposition of which notice is taken. The distinctions between legislative and adjudicative facts, and between facts generally known and those known only to some, used in Federal Rule of Evidence 201, are but factors to be weighed in the administrative context.

Because of the multidimensional nature of administrative notice decisions, the only practical solution is to give the agency discretion, subject to review for abuse of discretion, not only for whether to take notice, but also for whether to allow rebuttal evidence and even for whether the parties must be notified that notice will be taken. . . . It is not necessary to warn that administrative notice will be taken of the fact that water runs downhill. Some propositions, however, may require that notice not be taken, or that warning be given, or that rebuttal evidence be allowed. The agency's discretion must be exercised in such a way as to be fair in the circumstances.[2]

The agency would not have to accord any opportunity to the applicants to offer evidence to rebut the propositions that Chamorro won the election and that UNO won a majority in parliament, since those facts are legislative, indisputable, and general. The agency should have warned that it would consider these facts even though they were not in existence at the time of the hearing and appellate briefs, so that the parties could have moved for leave to supplement their briefs, supplement the evidence, withdraw their applications for asylum, or seek other relief. The agency should also have warned, prior to final decision, that it intended to take notice that the Sandinistas were out of power, and that any well-founded fear of persecution the applicants might have had before the election could no longer be well-founded, and then given the parties an opportunity to show cause why notice should not be taken of these propositions. Depending on the showing made, fairness might or might not have required that the parties be allowed to present evidence on these propositions. . . .

---

2. In evaluating whether discretion was abused a court may find useful a number of factors formulated by Professor Davis. These include whether the facts at issue are: (1) narrow and specific or broad and general; (2) central or peripheral; (3) readily accepted or controversial; (4) purely factual or mixed with judgment, policy or political preference; (5) readily provable or provable only with difficulty or not at all; or, (6) facts about the parties or facts unrelated to them. . . .

To deny an opportunity to be heard in these circumstances was a denial of Due Process required by the Fifth Amendment. . . . The availability of a motion to reopen was not adequate, because the agency might have denied it, and deportation would not have been automatically stayed by the motion. The Board erred in taking notice of the change of government without providing the petitioners an opportunity to rebut the noticed facts.

We recognize that other circuits have resolved this question somewhat differently. . . .

The cases affirming the INS in these change of government cases, where administrative notice was taken, generally agree with the proposition that the asylum seeker is constitutionally entitled to present information which might rebut the proposition of which notice was taken, but assume that this could be done in the context of a motion to reopen, if it was not already done. We are not satisfied that we can make this presumption, in view of the "broad discretion" the agency has to deny motions for rehearing, which are "disfavored." INS v. Doherty, 502 U.S. 314 (1992).

In the case at bar, the applicants had a plausible claim that they might still have a well-founded fear of persecution despite the Chamorro election. The record they developed before the election allowed for the conclusion that Nicaragua had been dominated by the Sandinista party, and that Sandinista power flowed from the party, not just from the government. It may be that the party's permeation of society enables it to persecute opponents, even with the presidency and some departments of government in other hands. Perhaps the Nicaraguan government is not so strong and hierarchical as to render impotent any political movement which does not control the presidency. . . .

We take notice, for the limited purpose of determining whether the petitioners' claim is sufficiently plausible so that they should be allowed to present evidence, of the State Department country report on Nicaragua for 1990. This report says that the military and police remained under Sandinista control in 1990 despite the election, including the renamed General Directorate of State Security "which was responsible for numerous and significant human rights violations." The report notes continuing "politically motivated killings, some involving members of the security forces, police abuse of detainees," violence and killings by Sandinista supporters, and other political persecution similar to what Maria testified about before the election. . . .

. . . The point is, the propositions that the Sandinistas retain sufficient power to persecute petitioners, and that the petitioners have a well-founded fear of such persecution should they return to the town of Jinotega or the university in Managua, were seriously debatable, despite the election. Petitioners were never allowed to be heard on these propositions. Is their fear that they will be "disappeared" well-founded, despite the Chamorro election? Will the Sandinistas, because of their control of the police and military, still be in a position to carry out their threat of 20 years imprisonment if the sisters are caught demonstrating against them again? Will their house be stoned by party-orchestrated gangs because of their political opinions? Maybe petitioners' alleged fear of Sandinista persecution was ended by the election. Or maybe one swallow does not make a summer.

Neither we nor, without opportunity for a hearing, the BIA, can properly say whether applicants have a well-founded fear of persecution by the Sandinistas if they return to Nicaragua. . . .

We vacate the orders of deportation and remand for proceedings at which the asylum applicants may be heard on the appropriateness of notice and introduce evidence regarding the facts of which notice is taken.

NOTES

(1) *The Occasions for Notice.* One readily understands how, for a science-oriented agency such as the EPA in SAPL, the complexity and sweep of the technical issues with which it must deal may often tempt it to go into the library, as it were, to see what is to be found in the literature. For the INS, responding to the changing landscape of world politics presents similar pressures. The horrors of modern weaponry which created new refugees around the world; changes in substantive law which made it easier to apply for asylum; the existence of a backlog of cases before the INS which itself made applying for asylum attractive if only to delay deportation; new regimes which replaced old around the world—all these, and doubtless other, factors led to a flood of asylum claimants in the 1980's; then in 1996 the Illegal Immigration Reform and Immigration Response Act, by requiring relatively prompt application and other changes, somewhat constrained the flow. The number of asylum cases filed in the INS rose from 24,291 in fiscal 1984 to 101,679 in fiscal 1989;[1] asylum-seekers filed 66,356 applications in 2001.[2] As political regimes changed, as in Nicaragua, that general fact could influence the outcome of hundreds if not thousands of individual claims. The INS has continued to use official notice to determine questions of change in political regime and, consequently, threat: e.g., Fergiste v. INS, 138 F.3d 14 (1st Cir.1998) and Lucienne Yvette Civil v. INS, 140 F.3d 52 (1st Cir.1998), both concerning refugees from Haiti.

(2) OHIO BELL TELEPHONE CO. v. PUBLIC UTILITIES COMM. OF OHIO, 301 U.S. 292 (1937), cited in Castillo–Villagra, is still, despite its age, probably the leading Supreme Court decision concerning official notice in on-the-record proceedings. Consider to what extent its reasoning was grounded in claims of the utility to be heard on facts affecting its interests on individual grounds, and to what extent in considerations of sound procedure for the determination of contestable propositions of general fact.

At issue were the rates to be fixed for telephone service in Ohio, and, if overcharges there had been, the size of rebates to be ordered. To accomplish this under its governing law, the PUC was required to determine the value of the company's property as of a "date certain"; in a proceeding started in late 1924, the target date set was June 30, 1925. But the proceeding got away from the Commission, and a tentative valuation was

1. David A. Martin, Reforming Asylum Adjudication: On Navigating the Coast of Bohemia, 138 U.Pa.L.Rev. 1247, 1304 (1990)

2. See http://www.ins.usdoj.gov/graphics/ aboutins/statistics/workload.htm#monthly. According to the Department of Justice's Executive Office of Immigration Review, in fiscal 1984, the Board of Immigration Appeals received 3,000 cases; in FY 2000, nearly 30,000; the 60 immigration judges of 1990 have become more than 200.

not announced until January 10, 1931; then protests were filed, new hearings were held, and only on January 16, 1934, was the valuation as of June 30, 1925 determined. Eight-and-a-half years had passed and, just as importantly, the Great Crash had revolutionized the economy. The PUC then attempted a shortcut to determine the values for the intervening years, as well as the 1925 date, which the Supreme Court described as follows:

"The Commission did not confine itself . . . to a valuation of the property as of the date certain. It undertook also to fix a valuation for each of the years 1926 to 1933 inclusive. For this purpose it took judicial notice of price trends during those years, modifying the value which it had found as of the date certain by the percentage of decline or rise applicable to the years thereafter. The first warning that it would do this came in 1934 with the filing of its report. 'The trend of land valuation was ascertained', according to the findings, 'from examination of the tax value in communities where the company had its largest real estate holdings.' 'For building trends resort was had to price indices of the Engineering News Record, a recognized magazine in the field of engineering construction.' 'Labor trends were developed from the same sources.' Reference was made also to the findings of a federal court in Illinois as to the price levels upon sales of apparatus and equipment by Western Electric, an affiliated corporation. . . . The Commission consulted these findings as indicative of market trends and leaned upon them heavily. By resort to these and cognate sources, [the value of the company's property, and the amount of excess earnings that had to be refunded, were calculated down to the dollar]. . . . There being no excess revenue for the year 1933, the last year covered by the report, the Commission did not fix any percentage of reduction for the rates in future years. It did, however, prescribe a refund of the full amount of the excess for the years in which excess earnings were found to have been realized."

The Company protested, claiming the shelter of its federal right to due process. The Commission rejected the protests, as did the Ohio Supreme Court. In the Supreme Court of the United States, per Justice Cardozo: "Reversed and remanded."

"The fundamentals of a trial were denied to the appellant when rates previously collected were ordered to be refunded upon the strength of evidential facts not spread upon the record.

"The Commission had given notice that the value of the property would be fixed as of a date certain. Evidence directed to the value at that time had been laid before the triers of the facts in thousands of printed pages. To make the picture more complete, evidence had been given as to the value at cost of additions and retirements. Without warning or even the hint of warning that the case would be considered or determined upon any other basis than the evidence submitted, the Commission cut down the values for the years after the date certain upon the strength of information secretly collected and never yet disclosed. The company protested. It asked disclosure of the documents indicative of price trends, and an opportunity to examine them, to analyze them, to explain and to rebut them. The response was a curt refusal. Upon the strength of these unknown documents refunds have been ordered for sums mounting into millions, the

Commission reporting its conclusion, but not the underlying proofs. The putative debtor does not know the proofs today. This is not the fair hearing essential to due process. It is condemnation without trial. . . .

"What was done by the Commission is subject, however, to an objection even deeper. There has been more than an expansion of the concept of notoriety beyond reasonable limits. From the standpoint of due process—the protection of the individual against arbitrary action—a deeper vice is this, that even now we do not know the particular or evidential facts of which the Commission took judicial notice and on which it rested its conclusion. Not only are the facts unknown; there is no way to find them out. When price lists or trade journals or even government reports are put in evidence upon a trial, the party against whom they are offered may see the evidence or hear it and parry its effect. Even if they are copied in the findings without preliminary proof, there is at least an opportunity in connection with a judicial review of the decision to challenge the deductions made from them. The opportunity is excluded here. The Commission, withholding from the record the evidential facts that it has gathered here and there, contents itself with saying that in gathering them it went to journals and tax lists, as if a judge were to tell us, 'I looked at the statistics in the Library of Congress, and they teach me thus and so.' This will never do if hearings and appeals are to be more than empty forms."

(3) *Persuasiveness in the Face of Official Notice.* Beyond questions of opportunity to meet noticed facts and of admissibility, there remains, of course, the question of persuasion—a question that would be central on remand in Castillo–Villagra. Posner, C.J., in GRAMATIKOV V. INS, 128 F.3d 619, 619–20 (7th Cir.1997) faced an effort to overcome INS official notice of changes that had occurred in Bulgaria, where citizens had previously been prosecuted for opposition to communism and support for religion:

"Routinely in these cases the immigration service requests an evaluation by the State Department of the likelihood of persecution if asylum is denied. Routinely the State Department advises the service that the formerly communist nations, having abandoned communism, no longer persecute anticommunists; and having abandoned atheism along with the other tenets of communism, no longer persecute religious people either. The advice of the State Department is not binding, either on the service or on the courts; there is perennial concern that the Department soft pedals human rights violations by countries that the United States wants to have good relations with. So the alien is free to try to rebut the Department's advice, and since the rules of evidence are not applied in proceedings before the INS, he need not, in casting his net for helpful evidence, feel cabined by those rules.

"But when aliens try to rebut the State Department with self-serving, unsubstantiated, uncorroborated evidence about current political conditions in a country they left years ago, they will not convince the INS, and will certainly not furnish grounds upon which a reviewing court can reverse the agency given the deference that we are obliged to give decisions of the Board of Immigration Appeals. Rules of evidence or not, no responsible administrative or judicial body is going to give weight to unsubstantiated testimony that the alien believes that the bad guys are still running things. An alien who has lived in this country for years and is not an expert on the politics of his native country will ordinarily have no credible basis for testifying about the secret power structure of that country. He had better be able to point to a highly credible independent source of expert knowledge if he wants to contradict the State Department's evaluation of the likelihood of his being persecuted if he is forced to return home, an evaluation to which courts inevitably give considerable weight, despite the concern we noted earlier about the Department's tendency to downplay human-rights violations by governments with which the United States wants to have friendly relations."

NOTES ON JUDICIAL AND ADMINISTRATIVE APPROACHES TO EVIDENCE

(1) *The Implicit Comparison.* The court expresses its awareness that evidentiary matters are handled under different, more permissive rules before agencies than would be the case in court. In a federal trial in U.S. District Court, evidentiary questions would be governed by the Federal Rules of Evidence. By their terms, the Federal Rules of Evidence apply to federal courts, bankruptcy judges, and magistrates—not agencies. Rule 101. Congress can, of course, stipulate differently—e.g., 29 U.S.C. § 160(B), requiring the NLRB to rely on the rules of courtroom procedure "so far as practicable"—or agencies can similarly bind themselves through their own rules of procedure. But a study in the mid–80's reported that the rules of procedure in most agencies relied on the simple prescriptions of the APA. "There are 280 regulations that govern evidentiary decisionmaking by federal agencies. ... The majority—243 of 280—make no reference to the FRE and appear not to impose constraints on the discretion of ALJs to admit evidence. Often these provisions either parrot the APA or paraphrase it." Richard J. Pierce, Use of the Federal Rules of Evidence in Federal Agency Adjudications, 39 Admin.L.Rev. 1, 5–6 (1987).

In the particular case of the INS, the court remarks, the APA's Section 556(e) is also inapplicable. The INS procedural requirements referred to by the court have no directly comparable language, but do provide that "the alien shall have a reasonable opportunity to examine the evidence against him, to present evidence on his own behalf, and to cross-examine witnesses presented by the Government." 8 U.S.C. § 1252(b). One can understand why the Castillo–Villagras' attorney pressed for application of the APA; but would the case have been any different if the court had agreed with him?

(2) *Judicial Notice Under the Federal Rules of Evidence.* Section 201 of the Federal Rules of Evidence provides:

> (a) Scope of Rule. This rule governs only judicial notice of adjudicative facts.

> (b) Kinds of facts. A judicially noticed fact must be one not subject to reasonable dispute in that it is either (1) generally known within the territorial jurisdiction of the trial court or (2) capable of accurate and ready determination by resort to sources whose accuracy cannot reasonably be questioned.

(c) When discretionary. A court may take judicial notice, whether requested or not.

(d) When mandatory. A court shall take judicial notice if requested by a party and supplied with the necessary information.

(e) Opportunity to be heard. A party is entitled upon timely request to an opportunity to be heard as to the propriety of taking judicial notice and the tenor of the matter noticed. In the absence of prior notification, the request may be made after judicial notice has been taken.

(f) Time of taking notice. Judicial notice may be taken at any stage of the proceeding.

(g) Instructing jury. In a civil action or proceeding, the court shall instruct the jury to accept as conclusive any fact judicially noticed. . . .

(3) *The Limitation of Section 201 to "Adjudicative Facts".* Notice the limitation expressed in subsection (a). The Advisory Committee's Note to Section 201 explained this limitation in the following terms:

"(a). . . . The omission of any treatment of legislative facts results from fundamental differences between adjudicative facts and legislative facts. Adjudicative facts are simply the facts of the particular case. . . . The usual method of establishing adjudicative facts is through the introduction of evidence, ordinarily consisting of the testimony of witnesses. If particular facts are outside the area of reasonable controversy, this process is dispensed with as unnecessary. A high degree of indisputability is the essential prerequisite.

"Legislative facts are quite different. . . . Professor Morgan gave the following description of the methodology of determining domestic law:

In determining the content or applicability of a rule of domestic law, the judge is unrestricted in his investigation and conclusion. He may reject the propositions of either party or of both parties. He may consult the sources of pertinent data to which they refer, or he may refuse to do so. He may make an independent search for persuasive data or rest content with what he has or what the parties present. . . . [T]he parties do no more than to assist; they control no part of the process. Morgan, Judicial Notice, 57 Harv.L.Rev. 269, 270–271 (1944).

"This is the view which should govern judicial access to legislative facts. It renders inappropriate any limitation in the form of indisputability, any formal requirements of notice other than those already inherent in affording opportunity to hear and be heard and exchanging briefs, and any requirement of formal findings at any level. It should, however, leave open the possibility of introducing evidence through regular channels in appropriate situations."

Do the opinions in SAPL and/or Castillo–Villagra understand the distinction between adjudicative and legislative facts in the same way?

(4) *The Difficult Distinction Between Adjudicative and Legislative Facts.* In evoking the distinction between adjudicative and legislative facts, the opinion in Castillo–Villagra refers to KENNETH CULP DAVIS, JUDICIAL NOTICE,

55 Colum.L.Rev. 945, 952 (1955). Here is Davis's account, widely influential since it appeared:

"When a court or an agency finds facts concerning the immediate parties—who did what, where, when, how, and with what motive or intent—the court or agency is performing an adjudicative function, and the facts so determined are conveniently called adjudicative facts. When a court or an agency develops law or policy, it is acting legislatively; the courts have created the common law through judicial legislation, and the facts which inform the tribunal's legislative judgment are called legislative facts.

"Stated in other terms, the adjudicative facts are those to which the law is applied in the process of adjudication. They are the facts that normally go to the jury in a jury case. They relate to the parties, their activities, their properties, their businesses. Legislative facts are those which help the tribunal to determine the content of law and policy and to exercise its judgment or discretion in determining what course of action to take. Legislative facts are ordinarily general and do not concern the immediate parties. In the great mass of cases decided by courts and by agencies, the legislative element is either absent, unimportant, or interstitial, because in most cases the applicable law and policy have been previously established. But whenever a tribunal is engaged in the creation of law or of policy, it may need to resort to legislative facts, whether or not those facts have been developed on the record.

"The exceedingly practical difference between legislative and adjudicative facts is that, apart from facts properly noticed, the tribunal's findings of adjudicative facts must be supported by evidence, but findings or assumptions of legislative facts need not, frequently are not, and sometimes cannot be supported by evidence."

Clear distinctions like Professor Davis's are seductive, but often (as here) misleading—a proposition that perhaps informs the court's remark in Castillo–Villagra that the distinction is, "in the administrative context," merely a factor to be weighed. Consider the following two sentences from Davis's analysis:

> They are the facts that normally go to the jury in a jury case. They relate to the parties, their activities, their properties, their businesses.

The second of these sentences recalls Justice Holmes' observation in Bi–Metallic Investment Co. v. State Board of Equalization of Colorado, p. 241, explaining why due process had required an oral hearing in the earlier Londoner v. Denver, p. 238, but did not so require in Bi–Metallic. The Londoner claimants were "exceptionally affected, in each case upon individual grounds." But juries—and certainly agencies—do not only decide facts of this character, that relate uniquely "to the parties, their activities, their properties, their businesses." They might also be asked to consider such questions as the sensitivity of soft-shell clam larvae to thermal shock, a factual question on which the First Circuit reproached the EPA Administrator in SAPL. Administrative proceedings very often turn on factual propositions like these, that are not subject to variation "in each case upon individual grounds," but that nonetheless have qualities that might make one reluctant to credit their being decided by the vote of a legislature. What is the carcinogenicity of benzene? Over the years, what effect will intense nuclear radiation have on the tensile strength of steel used to build a nuclear reactor containment? Mr. Jones and Mrs. Smith don't differ in their relation to these questions. We might denominate them questions of general (often scientific) fact, to distinguish them both from the party-specific facts that are the core concern of due process analysis, and the very general propositions that are at the core of the "legislative fact" construct. Answering questions of general fact, often, will require considerable exercise of professional judgment as well as deep technical knowledge. They are not questions well adapted for resolution by lay fact-finders hearing viva voce testimony, and such procedures are not the ones generally chosen by others (the scientific community, for example) to whom their resolution is important. Yet neither would we consider them well suited to resolution by legislative vote, even though we can understand that legislative as well as judicial outcomes may turn on present beliefs about the best answers to them. For just those factual issues on which one is most likely to seek an expert's assistance, then, a neat allocation of facts into two categories, "adjudicative" and "legislative," is notably unhelpful.

(5) *Official Notice and Propositions of "General" Fact.* The previous note may suggest distinguishing between claims grounded in "due process" in the constitutional sense, and those grounded in ideas about sound process for the resolution of contestable factual issues. For those facts as to which parties have a claim grounded in their being "exceptionally affected, in each case upon individual grounds," one might say, sound process requires full party participation and indisputability is a sine qua non of official notice; for issues of general fact, indisputability is not required, but one might argue that sound process counsels a certain level of transparency in agency fact-finding, and an opportunity to show the contrary. Consider in this respect the Castillo–Villagra court's treatment of two issues: whether the Sandanistas had been ousted from power, and whether the Castillo–Villagra family, in particular, faced a continuing threat of persecution. Both were disputable. The second proposition fits easily within Holmes' Bi-Metallic formulation—the parties want an opportunity to show the particular hazards they face as individuals, uniquely a product of their personal situation; does the first?

In SAPL, the proposition about thermal shock has no individual variability—even for the utility that might be thought to have constitutionally protected interests at stake. Section 556(e) permits official notice, subject to a party's right, "on timely request, to an opportunity to show the contrary." Nothing in the opinion suggests that SAPL made such a request, that was refused, at the agency level. Did the court, then, err in finding EPA's treatment of the thermal shock issue inadequate? Or might it be argued that EPA's simple reference to "the scientific literature," without more, constituted deficient fact-finding, without regard to fairness concerns?

NOTES ON THE LIMITED APPLICATION OF THE HEARSAY RULE TO ADMINISTRATIVE PROCEEDINGS

(1) The inapplicability of courtroom rules of evidence has implications beyond the question of official notice, of course—and particularly with

regard to hearsay. On this topic, the APA says: "Any oral or documentary evidence may be received, but the agency as a matter of policy shall provide for the exclusion of irrelevant, immaterial, or unduly repetitious evidence." 5 U.S.C. § 556(d). For the overwhelming majority of agencies where there is no further restriction, this standard is understood—and rightly so, in light of its legislative history—to provide for the admission of hearsay evidence as a routine matter, although the weight of such evidence remains open to argument. RICHARD J. PIERCE, USE OF THE FEDERAL RULES OF EVIDENCE IN FEDERAL AGENCY ADJUDICATIONS, 39 ADMIN. L. REV. 1, 17–19 (1987):

"There are three reasons why it makes little sense to take the risk of erroneous exclusion of reliable evidence through application of highly technical exclusionary rules in the context of agency adjudications. First, the cost of such errors is as great in the agency adjudications context as it is in the trial context—if the ALJ erroneously excludes reliable evidence, the agency must either remand for further proceedings or decide the case on the basis of an incomplete record. Second, the risk of errors of exclusion is greater in the agency adjudication context than in the context of a jury trial. Third, there are good reasons to take this risk in the jury trial context that do not exist in the case of agency adjudications.

"Prompt resolution of difficult evidentiary issues ... presents even greater challenges and risks to agency ALJs than to federal trial judges. To resolve close evidentiary questions, a judge must focus specifically and with some care on the issues in the proceeding and on the relationship between a proffered item of evidence and those issues, for most such questions must be answered by reference to the purpose for which the evidence can be considered and its probative value when considered for that purpose. Yet, agency ALJs often have an incomplete understanding of the issues at the time they must rule on the admissibility of evidence. ALJs, unlike federal judges, do not resolve cases subject only to possible appeal. Rather, they issue initial decisions that are, for most purposes, functionally equivalent to recommendations to agency decisionmakers. Since the ALJ is not the final decisionmaker, she often has an imperfect understanding during the hearing of both the issues the agency ultimately will consider important and the probative value the agency will attach to various types of evidence with respect to those issues....

"The decision to take the risk of erroneous exclusion of evidence in jury trials is based in part on considerations of necessity that have no analogue in administrative adjudications. In a jury trial, there is little choice but to ask trial judges to resolve close evidentiary disputes through application of complicated and detailed exclusionary rules, and thereby to take the risk of a new trial or of a decision that is not based on all reliable evidence. In Dean Calabresi's words, juries are 'irresponsible' decisionmakers in the sense that they are not required to explain the bases for their decisions, including particularly the evidentiary bases for their findings of fact. Thus, if we want to preclude juries from basing findings on evidence considered unreliable by judges, we can do so only by precluding their exposure to that evidence in the first place.

"The considerations are entirely different in agency adjudications. Agencies and ALJs are required to state the bases for their findings of fact.

Their findings are then subject to judicial review under the substantial evidence standard. If an agency finding is based on unreliable evidence, the agency's action is reversed. Thus, there is a mechanism available in agency adjudications independent of rulings on the admissibility of evidence to insure that agency findings are based only on reliable evidence."

(2) *Can hearsay alone constitute "substantial evidence"?* Even if hearsay evidence is freely admitted, should it be treated as suspect? In 1938, Chief Justice Hughes stated that "[m]ere uncorroborated hearsay or rumor does not constitute substantial evidence." Consolidated Edison Co. v. NLRB, 305 U.S. 197, 230 (1938). The force of his comment was undercut—to a still undetermined extent—by RICHARDSON V. PERALES, 402 U.S. 389 (1971). This case was described by Justice Douglas, in his dissenting opinion, as follows: "This claimant for social security disability benefits had a serious back injury. The doctor who examined him testified that he was permanently disabled. His case is defeated, however, by hearsay evidence of doctors and their medical reports about this claimant. Only one doctor who examined him testified at the hearing. Five other doctors who had once examined the claimant did not testify and were not subject to cross-examination. But their reports were admitted in evidence. Still another doctor testified on the hearsay in the documents of the other doctors. All of this hearsay may be received, as the Administrative Procedure Act (5 U.S.C. § 556(d)) provides that '[a]ny oral or documentary evidence may be received.' But this hearsay evidence cannot by itself be the basis for an adverse ruling. The same section of the Act states that '[a] party is entitled . . . to conduct such cross-examination as may be required for a full and true disclosure of the facts.' " 402 U.S. at 411.

The majority, however, upheld, as a matter both of statute and of due process, the Social Security Administration's reliance on the written reports of the five doctors who were not cross-examined: "We conclude that a written report by a licensed physician who has examined the claimant and who sets forth in his report his medical findings in his area of competence may be received as evidence in a disability hearing and, despite its hearsay character and an absence of cross-examination, and despite the presence of opposing direct medical testimony and testimony by the claimant himself, may constitute substantial evidence supportive of a finding by the hearing examiner adverse to the claimant, when the claimant has not exercised his right to subpoena the reporting physician and thereby provide himself with the opportunity for cross-examination of the physician." 402 U.S. at 402.

At a minimum, Perales holds that hearsay evidence of substantial weight can be enough, by itself, to support a federal agency's decision even though the proponent of the statement does not produce the declarant; what remains unclear is whether the existence of the power of the other party to subpoena the declarant (here provided by Social Security regulations) is a necessary precondition of the holding, or merely a factor to be considered in assessing the overall situation.[1] States may apply a more

---

1. An observer might conclude that the difference between majority and dissent in Perales arose at least in part from factual propositions that were themselves the product of judicial notice, or at least experience. For Justice Blackmun, author of the majority

rigorous standard, as in Bean v. Montana Board of Labor Appeals, 290 Mont. 496, 965 P.2d 256 (1998) and People v. Ullrich, 328 Ill.App.3d 811, 767 N.E.2d 411 (2002). For discussion, see Richard J. Pierce, Jr., 2 Administrative Law Treatise § 10.4 (4th ed. 2002).

c.   THE REQUIREMENT OF FINDINGS

Armstrong v. Commodity Futures Trading Commission

United States Court of Appeals for the Third Circuit, 1993.
12 F.3d 401.

■ Before: GREENBERG, COWEN and SEITZ, CIRCUIT JUDGES.

■ SEITZ, CIRCUIT JUDGE.

Martin A. Armstrong petitions for review of a decision of the Commodity Futures Trading Commission (the "Commission") holding him individually responsible as a controlling person of corporations found to have violated Commission regulations. . . .

I.   Background

[Armstrong started working at a coin and stamp dealership at the age of 13; by 15, he was a millionaire. In his 20s he moved into commodities in general, and by his 30s (the time in question) he was publishing commodity forecasts and managing accounts. He did this through three different corporations. In 1985, and then again in 1987, the Commission charged Armstrong and the corporations with various violations, such as failing to register properly and failing to make proper disclosures to clients. The ALJ found all of them liable on all accounts. On appeal to the Commission, the first batch of charges were dismissed, but the findings of liability on the second complaint were affirmed. On a preliminary motion in the judicial review proceeding, another panel of the court of appeals dismissed these charges as against the corporations because they had ceased to do business. Only the question of Armstrong's individual liability on the second complaint remains.]

II.   Compliance With APA § 557(c)

A.   The Commission's Opinion

Armstrong complains that the Commission did not meet the requirements of the Administrative Procedure Act because it did not provide an

opinion and former General Counsel of the Mayo Clinic, "[w]e cannot, and do not, ascribe bias to the work of these independent physicians, or any interest on their part in the outcome of the administrative proceeding beyond the professional curiosity a dedicated medical man possesses. . . . One familiar with medical reports . . . will recognize their elements of detail and of value." For Justice Douglas, one HEW doctor was a simple bureaucrat: "The use of circuit-riding doctors who never see or examine claimants to defeat their claims should be beneath the dignity of a great nation. Three other doctors . . . were experts retained and paid by the Government. . . . The use by HEW of its stable of defense doctors without submitting them to cross-examination is the cutting of corners." One Justice sees a smoothly functioning, disinterested professional system; the other, adversarial combat.

adequate "statement of . . . findings and conclusions, and the reasons or basis therefor, on all the material issues of fact, law, or discretion presented on the record." 5 U.S.C. § 557(c). . . .

The purposes of the APA provision requiring specific findings and conclusions are to prevent arbitrary agency decisions, provide parties with a reasoned explanation for those decisions, settle the law for future cases, and furnish a basis for effective judicial review. Third Circuit Court of Appeals precedent emphasizes the need for adequate findings to ensure effective judicial review and eliminate appellate speculation.

An administrative agency need not provide an independent statement if it specifically adopts an ALJ's opinion that sets forth adequate findings and reasoning. Kenworth Trucks, Inc. v. NLRB, 580 F.2d 55, 62–63 (3d Cir.1978). In the wake of Vermont Yankee Nuclear Power Corp. v. Natural Resources Defense Council, Inc., 435 U.S. 519 (1978), our decision upon rehearing in Kenworth held that the NLRB was not required to separately elaborate reasons after specifically adopting the ALJ's findings and reasoning underlying a bargaining order.

No particular form of adoption is required if the agency's action permits meaningful appellate review. The Seventh Circuit has concluded that an agency order stating that "The initial decision is affirmed and the proceeding is terminated" is sufficient to indicate adoption of an ALJ's entire opinion. City of Frankfort, Ind. v. FERC, 678 F.2d 699, 708 & n. 18 (7th Cir.1982). The D.C. Circuit similarly accepted summary affirmance of enumerated issues by an agency in Cities of Bethany v. FERC, 727 F.2d 1131, 1144 (D.C.Cir.), cert. denied, 469 U.S. 917 (1984).

In the case before us, however, the Commission has not clearly adopted the ALJ's opinion. The Commission's entire opinion regarding the second complaint stated:

> Our review of the record and the briefs submitted by the parties establishes that the ALJ reached a substantially correct result on all the allegations raised in the Second Complaint. Because we also conclude that the parties have not raised important questions of law or policy concerning the ALJ's findings of fact and conclusions on these allegations, we affirm the Second Complaint without opinion.[2]
>
> 2.   The ALJ's decisions shall neither be cited as Commission precedent in any Commission proceeding, nor deemed an expression of the Commission's views on the issues raised in the Second Complaint.

In re Armstrong, [Current Transfer Binder] Comm.Fut.L.Rep.(CCH) ¶ 25657, at 40145 & n.2.

Summarily affirming the ALJ's opinion as "substantially correct" is insufficient because it does not permit intelligent appellate review. Kenworth, City of Frankfort, and Cities of Bethany approved summary affirmances when the agency adopted an entire opinion or specified parts of an opinion. However, the Commission's conclusion that the ALJ reached a "substantially correct" result leaves questions about which specific findings or conclusions by the ALJ were incorrect.

The footnote disclaiming the ALJ's decision as an expression of the Commission's views further undermines the Commission's assertion before us that it adopted the entire opinion. We assume that the Commission has the power to determine which of its decisions may be cited as precedent in future proceedings before it. However, the declaration that the opinion does not represent the Commission's views erodes our confidence that the Commission carefully considered and adopted each of the ALJ's findings and conclusions as contemplated by Kenworth.

We hold that a summary affirmance of all or part of an ALJ's opinion must leave no guesswork regarding what the agency has adopted. A decision by an ALJ that is only "substantially correct" should be fully correct by the time an agency imprints its seal of approval.

B.   The ALJ's Opinion

Although a remand is warranted based on the adoption issue alone, we proceed to review the Commission's and the ALJ's opinions in order to prevent an immediate return of the case to this court.

1.   The Single Enterprise Theory

[The ALJ concluded that Armstrong and the three corporations had acted as a single enterprise. But the complaint was not drafted on that theory, and the Commission disavowed it in its reversal of the finding of liability on the first complaint.]

2.   Controlling Person Liability

The only theory under which Armstrong was charged with individual liability in the second complaint was as a controlling person as defined in section 13(b) of the Commodity Exchange Act. This section provides:

> Any person who, directly or indirectly, controls any person who has violated ... any of the rules, regulations, or orders issued pursuant to this chapter may be held liable for such violation in any action brought by the Commission to the same extent as such controlled person. In such action, the Commission has the burden of proving that the controlling person did not act in good faith or knowingly induced, directly or indirectly, the act or acts constituting the violation. 7 U.S.C. § 13c(b).

Neither the ALJ's Initial Decision nor the Commission's opinion addressed Section 13(b). As discussed above, the Administrative Procedure Act requires an adequate "statement of ... findings and conclusions, and the reasons or basis therefor, on all the material issues of fact, law, or discretion presented on the record." 5 U.S.C. § 557(c). We do not understand how a statement of conclusion on a material issue of law can be adequate without mentioning the statutory provision or its language.

Section 13(b) requires at least two findings before concluding a respondent is liable as a controlling person: (1) that the respondent controlled a violator; and (2) that the controlling person did not act in good faith or knowingly induced the violation. First, the Commission contends that the ALJ's statement that Armstrong "had and exercised full domination and control over all operations of" [the corporations] is a sufficient finding that Armstrong controlled the corporations. However, this statement was made as part of the single enterprise discussion that the Commission vacated; its continuing validity is at least subject to question. Second, the Commission's appeal brief recites evidence in the record from which the ALJ could have found that Armstrong knowingly induced the violations. Nevertheless, there is still no finding by the ALJ or the Commission that Armstrong did knowingly induce the violations. Finally, and most importantly, there is no conclusion that Armstrong is liable as a controlling person under Section 13(b). Without a conclusion that Armstrong is liable for violations with which he was charged, Armstrong may not be individually penalized.

III.   Conclusion

We hold that the Commission's opinion does not comply with Section 557(c) of the Administrative Procedure Act because: (1) deeming an ALJ's opinion to be "substantially correct" does not rise to the level of adoption permitted by Kenworth; and (2) due to the ambiguous affirmance of the ALJ's opinion by the Commission and the vacation of the single enterprise theory resulting in the absence of findings supporting and a conclusion of "controlling person" status, there are insufficient findings to hold Armstrong liable as charged under Section 13(b) of the Commodity Exchange Act. Because it will be necessary for the Commission to reconsider Armstrong's liability as it considers more specific findings, reasons, and conclusions, we do not reach the weight of the evidence issues raised by Armstrong.

The decision of the Commission will be vacated and the matter remanded to the Commission for further appropriate proceedings.

NOTES

(1) *Why Require Findings and Conclusions?* HENRY J. FRIENDLY, "SOME KIND OF HEARING," 123 U.Pa.L.Rev. 1267, 1292 (1975): "A written statement of reasons, almost essential if there is to be judicial review, is desirable on many other grounds. The necessity for justification is a powerful preventive of wrong decisions. The requirement also tends to effectuate intra-agency uniformity. . . . A statement of reasons may even make a decision somewhat more acceptable to a losing claimant."

Thus, MATTER OF ISSUANCE OF PERMIT, 120 N.J. 164, 576 A.2d 784 (1990): The state Department of Environmental Protection (DEP), in issuing permits for discharges of chemically-treated effluents into the Atlantic Ocean, had to comply with the federal Clean Water Act's "ocean discharge criteria." "The impediment to judicial review is that there is nothing in the draft permit, the hearing examiner's report, the final permit, or elsewhere in the record that indicates how DEP concluded that [the permittee] complied with the [criteria]." While "interested parties and members of the public [a public hearing on renewal of the permit had been attended by 'hundreds of local residents'] appear to have been well informed about most significant aspects," the agency "did not fulfill its role as fact-finder." If DEP decided to allow degradation of water quality, its own regulations required it to find that degradation was "necessary to accommodate the important economic or social development in the area;" if the discharge was into waters whose quality was to be maintained, DEP had to indicate what it relied upon to decide water quality would be maintained. "By failing to make essential findings of fact on the record, DEP inhibited judicial review, requiring the reviewing court to speculate about the basis of its conclusions."

(2) *How Elaborate Must the Statement of Findings and Reasons Be?* Statutory requirements like APA § 557(c) might seem to demand of agency opinion writers a compulsive attention to detail. One hundred printed pages to show "findings and conclusions, and the reasons and basis therefore, on *all* the material issues of fact, law or discretion presented" is a not uncommon, if sometimes apparently unread, consequence.

When put to it, courts are frequently less demanding than such statutory phrases suggest, stressing simply the need to understand the administrative decision. That is to say, they require not some stylistic organization of the agency's utterance, but, rather, a communication (in whatever form) of precisely what has been decided, so that even if "the findings of the Commission ... leave much to be desired ... the path which it followed can be discerned." Colorado Interstate Gas Co. v. Federal Power Commission, 324 U.S. 581 (1945). Also not to be forgotten in this regard is the practical difference between the agency that renders relatively few decisions in a year, each of which may have substantial precedential significance, and the agency given the task of processing thousands upon thousands of particularistic cases. As Judge Easterbrook pointed out in Stephens v. Heckler, 766 F.2d 284 (7th Cir.1985), regarding the enormous job of processing claims for disability benefits, when agency decision-makers "slow down to write better opinions, that holds up the queue and prevents deserving people from receiving benefits."

At the same time, mere conclusory statements will not do. McElroy Electronics Corp. v. FCC, 990 F.2d 1351 (D.C.Cir.1993): The FCC rejected applications for a license as premature; but the mere act of denial was not enough. The order was remanded because "even a careful reader of the order ... could not have been expected to understand" what the Commission was requiring.

(3) *Is the Findings Requirement for Agencies Different From that for Courts?*

(a) *An agency superior reviewing a hearer's decision:* Would a court of appeals which affirmed a trial court summarily, saying merely that the trial judge "reached a substantially correct result," and that "the parties have not raised important questions of law or policy" be committing reversible error? If not, what is it about the administrative process that justifies requiring a more demanding practice of agencies reviewing ALJ decisions, as in Armstrong?

(b) *The findings requirement applicable to trials to the court, without a jury:* Federal Rule of Civil Procedure 52(a) requires that "in all actions tried upon the facts without a jury ... the court shall find the facts specially and state separately its conclusions of law thereon...." Is this arguably a more demanding standard than is appropriately applied to agency findings, because having agency findings serves the purpose of delegating authority to the agency, not the courts? Or is it arguably less demanding, because (as with evidentiary issues) the requirements for agency adjudication are appropriately less formal than those for judicial decisionmaking?

REICH v. NEWSPAPERS OF NEW ENGLAND, 44 F.3d 1060, 1079 (1st Cir.1995): "... [T]he purpose of [Rule 52(a)] is to apprise the appellate court of the grounds on which the trial court based its decision. Therefore, findings are sufficient so long as they 'indicate the factual basis for the ultimate conclusion.' Kelley v. Everglades Drainage District, 319 U.S. 415, 422 (1943). The 'judge need only make brief, definite, pertinent findings and conclusions upon the contested matters; there is no necessity for over-elaboration of detail or particularization of facts.' Applewood Landscaping & Nursery Co., Inc. v. Hollingsworth, 884 F.2d 1502, 1503 (1st Cir.1989) (quoting advisory committee note).' ... [A]nemic factual findings are not fatal to the decision so long as a complete understanding of the issues may be had from the record on appeal. ... Between the opinion and the record, we have garnered a thorough understanding of the proceedings below, and that is all that Rule 52(a) requires."

d.   THE PRESIDING OFFICER

The judicial opinions in the preceding cases directly concern themselves with the decision of the agency head—the Administrator of the EPA in SAPL, the Board of Immigration Appeals in Castillo–Villagra, the Commodities Futures Trading Commission in Armstrong. This is the usual character of judicial review, for—as the Armstrong court remarks—*if* the agency acts, then a reviewing court must regard the agency itself as having been the decisionmaker of first impression. Yet in each of these cases, initial hearings occurred before other officials—persons designated as "administrative law judges" in SAPL and Armstrong, and an immigration judge in Castillo–Villagra. (Recall from Wong Yang Sung and the notes following it, p. 254ff above, that immigration judges lack some of the protections of office of APA administrative law judges, although they serve a similar function.)

We will be focusing here chiefly on the "administrative law judges" (ALJs) described in the federal APA, rather than state administrative law judges or other federal administrative judges such as the immigration judges in Wong Yang Sung and Castillo–Villagra. Studies undertaken for the Administrative Conference of the United States in the early 1990s identified, in addition to the then almost 1200 federal ALJs, 2700 federal administrative adjudicators (AJs) hearing on-the-record administrative adjudications. Over 600 of these non-ALJ AJs have no other duties than hearing adjudications; in addition to the full-time immigration judges of the Immigration and Naturalization Service, they include the panel members of the Nuclear Regulatory Commission's Atomic Safety and Licensing Boards resolving licensing issues, the examiners of the Veterans' Administration adjudicating benefit claims, and the hearing officers of the Merit Systems Protection Board deciding issues of civil service discipline. The ALJ and AJ groups each resolve hundreds of thousands of on-the-record adjudications per year, performing work whose intrinsic difficulty or character would be difficult to tell apart. The fact that benefit applications for federal disability insurance are heard by administrative law judges, but deportation cases and civil service dismissals are tried before by hearing officers who are not ALJs, should be enough to suggest that no easy principle about the seriousness of the occasion for hearing rationalizes the diverse practice. See Charles Koch, Jr., Administrative Presiding Officials Today, 46 Ad.L.Rev. 271 (1994); John Frye, Survey of Non–ALJ Hearing Programs in the Federal Government, 44 Admin.L.Rev. 261 (1992); Paul Verkuil, Daniel Gifford, Charles Koch, Jr., Richard Pierce, Jr. and Jeffrey Lubbers, The Federal Administrative Judiciary (ACUS 1992).

Administrative law judges, a common feature of administrative adjudication at both federal and state levels, are an unusually well-insulated cadre of civil servants. For on-the-record proceedings, that closely resemble judicial trials in many respects, both the APA and the Model State Administrative Procedure Act describe both the procedures at hearing and the job protections of the hearer, but not the agency head, in ways that strongly invoke the judicial analogy. You may find it helpful to refer now to the APA provisions—pp. 1340–44 [§§ 556–7], and 1347–50 [§§ 3105, 7521, 5372, 3344, 1305]—keeping a particular eye on the prescribed character of the initial trier of fact. Federal administrative law judges are paid at the level of the senior executive service, but—although formally located within the particular agencies they serve—are virtually beyond agency control. Appointments must be made on a competitive basis, from the top few names on a list supplied by civil service authorities.[1] (On the constitutionality of this selection process, recall Freytag v. Commissioner, 501 U.S. 868, (1991), summarized above at p. 174; see also Michael Landry v. FDIC, 204 F.3d 1125 (D.C.Cir.2000)) Once made, appointments are permanent (without probationary period). Within the agency structure, administrative law judges must be free of supervision or direction from agency employees

---

1. This process is not without its difficulties. Under federal law, veterans and disabled veterans are entitled to a competitive preference, and as this edition goes to press litigation over the manner in which that preference is to be calculated and applied to the results of the merit selection process is consuming the Merit Systems Protection Board. See Azdell & Fishman v. Office of Personnel Management, 87 M.S.P.R. 133, 2000 WL 1617958 (2000) and subsequent orders on petitions for stay, 88 M.S.P.R. 319, 89 M.S.P.R. 23, 88 (2001). The preference is defended by few as a judicial qualification on the merits, but has proved to be politically unassailable.

Veterans, about one quarter of 799 candidates on the register, received about 40% of 213 initial ALJ appointments of ALJs made between October 1993 and July, 1994, according to data supplied to the ABA's Section of Administrative Law and Regulatory Practice by the Office of Personnel Management. Women constituted 2% of the veterans' group and minorities, 4%. The past use of veterans' preference had contributed to an overwhelming white and male ALJ cadre—a particular embarrassment, perhaps, for SSA, whose disability program disproportionately serves women and minority groups. Women and men score almost identically on the examination applicants are given. ACUS, The Federal Administrative Judiciary 109–113 (1992). See also Ninth Circuit Gender Bias Task Force, the Effects of Gender in the Federal Courts 98 ff. (1993); GAO, Racial Differences in Disability Decisions Warrants further Investigation (1992); Linda Mills, A Calculus for Bias: How Malingering Females and Dependent Housewives Fare in the Social Security Disability System, 16 Harv. W.L.J. 211 (1993).

responsible for the cases that may come before them; neither salary nor assignments nor any disciplinary measure can be controlled from within the agency, but (if adverse) must be the subject of formal proceedings before the federal Merit Systems Protection Board. Any conversations administrative law judges have with agency employees concerning the outcomes of formal proceedings they are hearing must be on the record— that is, there may be no private consultations.

Whether they serve in a cabinet department, an independent executive agency like the EPA, or an independent regulatory commission, an agency's administrative law judges will be found in a separate office, which may be located for bureaucratic purposes within the agency secretariat but which is independent of all other parts the agency. There will usually be a chief administrative law judge responsible for administrative matters in each agency. A proceeding is assigned at random, as it arises, and remains with the administrative law judge to whom it is assigned until the proceeding is completed, unless she is disqualified or leaves office, or (in rare cases) the agency directs that it be sent up without decision. In smaller agencies, her opinion may be reviewed directly by the agency head or commission itself. Frequently, however, provision is made for a judicial officer or review board to serve that function, and direct involvement of the agency head itself occurs only on a discretionary basis, analogous to the Supreme Court's certiorari practice. Whichever path is followed, conversations about the matters pending before the administrative law judges follow the common judicial protocols: they occur only in public, before all parties. If the head of an agency, reviewing an administrative law judge's decision, wishes help in understanding some aspect of the decision or of a complex record on which it is based, she must seek that assistance formally.

It might not seem a long step to creation of a system of administrative law courts located outside the agencies whose disputes they would consider, and such proposals have often been voiced. More than half the states use a central board of hearing examiners for some or all administrative adjudications.[2] At the federal level, resistance to such a court has been based on the varying tasks administrative law judges face in differing agencies, and the belief that the current legal regime protects their independence to a degree that would not be much improved by such a change. The overwhelming majority of American administrative law judges serve in the Social Security Administration, the National Labor Relations Board, or the Department of Labor; more than 1100 are in the SSA alone, resolving high-volume, small-scale questions such as eligibility for welfare or disability benefits;[3] only a handful, highly specialized and relatively few in number, serve in the major

---

2. See John W. Hardwicke, The Central Panel Movement: A Work in Progress, 53 Admin. L. Rev. 419 (2001); Christopher B. McNeil, The Model Act Creating a State Central Hearing Agency" Promises, Practical Problems, and a Proposal for Change, 53 Admin. L. Rev. 475 (2001).

3. In 1947, 125 (64%) of the federal government's 196 hearing officers worked in independent regulatory commissions deciding

regulatory matters; the remainder worked for cabinet agencies, including 13 who worked for the Social Security Administration. In 1999, following both extensive deregulation and an explosion in hearings in personal benefits programs, fewer than 200 of the more than 1300 federal administrative law judges worked in economic regulation or enforcement matters; the remainder decided personal benefits cases. Most federal ALJs, 1107,

federal regulatory agencies. A central agency might not be able to maintain the expertise in regulatory issues individual agencies can now encourage; in practice, its work would tend to be swamped by the demands of its mass-justice clientele. Locating hearing outside the agency, it is also feared, might tend to defuse agency responsibility for and control of policy even if (as is usually conceded) review of any decision by an administrative law judge serving on a central panel could be had within the agency itself.

Daniel J. Gifford, Federal Administrative Law Judges: The Relevance of Past Choices to Future Directions, 49 Admin.L.Rev. 1 (1997), provides a thorough and insightful account of the issues. Overall, he concludes, "The carefully structured decisionmaking model crafted into the APA was based upon experience in regulating, as opposed to administering, benefits. As a result, the premises upon which the adjudicatory structure were built have remained constant, while the work of adjudication has been transformed. The result is conducive to misunderstanding and conflict as ALJs assert their 'independence' from the agencies for which they work and as agencies assert control over policy. Many of these contemporary disputes over the allocation of decisional authority between ALJs and agencies could be resolved in light of the congressional concerns that engendered the APA and its distribution of decisionmaking authority between ALJs and the agencies."

As later materials in this chapter will develop, the variety of responsibilities and relationships those in agency leadership enjoy prevent enforcement for them of the standards of disengagement we insist upon for appellate judges. To the extent agencies are problem-solvers and policy-implementers, their leadership and their staff, as a whole, can be expected to have a point of view; and they can be expected to be pursuing that point of view through a variety of means—rulemakings, public addresses, congressional appearances, private meetings—rather than solely through the retrospective, highly structured, and somewhat leisurely activity of formal hearing on the record. Yet some circumstances may seem to require, at least at an initial stage, the detachment and objectivity of an impartial hearer, an individual or panel unacquainted with a controversy except as it may be revealed in the presence of the parties. That gives special importance to the position of an initial trier of fact, such as most agencies employ rather than hear matters directly at the agency level; the Supreme Court's characterization of the judicial function in reviewing agency fact-finding, set forth in Universal Camera Corp. v. NLRB, p. 940 below, was significantly shaped, many believe, by the relative isolation and single-function status of the Board's hearing examiner (today, an "administrative law judge") in relation to the NLRB itself.

were employed in the Social Security Administration, whose annual caseload, disposing of 597,000 cases, was about twice that of the federal district courts. For most ALJs today, then, daily work consists not of complex regulatory cases, but of reconciling the need for efficiency and dispatch in dealing with a sizable caseload, 38 hearings on average each month, with the wish for humanity in dealing with the most unfortunate. Social Security Bulletin Annual Statistical Supplement 2000.

(i) AN IMPARTIAL HEARER

The relative isolation and single-function status of the officer presiding at the initial hearing make her the most judge-like figure to encounter factual questions arising in agency adjudication. Yet in the agency context one must expect her also to have "expert acquaintance" with questions of general fact.[1] We start with a case arising in state courts, in which this problem (as well as, perhaps, others) is sharply presented. The Nebraska court treats Dr. Ann Bleed, the state hydrologist and also an important figure in the administrative proceedings, as if she were an administrative law judge in state administrative proceedings; can she use the expert knowledge of hydrology which she has acquired outside the four corners of this proceeding?

Central Platte Natural Resources Dist. v. Wyoming

Supreme Court of Nebraska, 1994.
245 Neb. 439, 513 N.W.2d 847.

■ JUDGES: HASTINGS, C.J., BOSLAUGH, WHITE, CAPORALE, FAHRNBRUCH, and LANPHIER, JJ., and GRANT, J., RETIRED.

■ WHITE, J.:

[Central Platte Natural Resources District filed six applications for permits to appropriate water for instream flows in the Central Platte River, a significant water source for Wyoming and Nebraska. That is, it sought to establish a legal right to have a certain volume of water flowing in the river—a right that would necessarily diminish the possibility of diverting water from the river for other uses at points upstream.] CPNRD essentially sought to reserve water rights in order to maintain food sources and habitats for five bird species. ... Wyoming objected to the applications. Wyoming owns land bordering the Platte River in Buffalo and Kearney Counties in Nebraska and intends to use that land as a whooping crane migrational habitat.

During July and September 1991, the Department of Water Resources held hearings on CPNRD's application. On July 2, 1992, the director granted three of the applications, granted in part and denied in part one of the applications, denied one application, and dismissed one application. Wyoming appealed from this decision. ...

[Much of the Nebraska Supreme Court's opinion concerned substantive issues of water law not important to develop here. The basic dispute was whether the Platte could reliably supply sufficient water to meet already established water rights and, in addition, those that the CPNRD was now seeking to establish. In this regard, the general desirability of instream flows, the models one would use to predict available water supplies, and economic models for estimating tradeoffs between economic and environmental benefits, were all hotly contested issues. For the Department to pass on these issues required that it develop and apply expertise in the hearing process. For these purposes, it took two routes. Departmental

---

1.   See pp. 364–66 above.

witnesses, among others, were called during the hearings to testify about available water resources and the various models that might be employed. After the hearing, the agency also turned to Dr. Ann Bleed for expert assistance in assessing the record and reaching judgment. Her participation was treated by the court as if she were a hearing officer,[1] and Wyoming asserted that that participation violated its rights to due process in on-the-record adjudication.]

Dr. Bleed is the state hydrologist. Dr. Bleed served as the State's "examining officer" at the hearing. The record reflects that, as examining officer, Dr. Bleed attended most of the hearing sessions and often cross-examined witnesses. . . .

Wyoming claims that Dr. Bleed was biased in two ways. First, Wyoming claims that Dr. Bleed favors the specific amount of instream flow requested in CPNRD's applications. Second, Wyoming claims that Dr. Bleed favors instream flows in general. Wyoming cites exhibit 113 as evidence of Dr. Bleed's bias. Exhibit 113 is a report prepared by Dr. Bleed, Dr. Suppalla, and two others . . . entitled "Economic, Environmental and Financing Optimization Analysis of Platte River Development Alternatives" and is published by the University of Nebraska. The study upon which the report is based had three general research objectives, one of which was to analyze the economic and environmental tradeoffs associated with alternative uses of the Platte River. To analyze these tradeoffs, the study correlated varying instream flow levels first with environmental consequences and then with economic consequences. The study concluded that instream flow constraints would not dramatically affect net economic returns. . . .

First, Wyoming accuses Dr. Bleed of having a specific bias in favor of the amount of flows requested in CPNRD's applications. Wyoming argues that the study sought to identify "optimum instream flows for the Central Platte River in relation to other water users" and that the study "adopted Alternative J . . . as the optimum flow levels." Wyoming then notes that the flows requested in CPNRD's applications are "strikingly similar" to Alternative J. Alternative J is one of 15 instream flow levels analyzed in the study.

Wyoming's claim that the study adopted Alternative J as the ideal is unfounded. . . . [After reviewing the few brief passages discussing Alternative J in the study, the court concluded that it may have been identified as a point at which economic and environmental tradeoffs began to become more significant, but was not presented as a normatively desirable choice.] Nothing in exhibit 113 indicated that the study authors designated or selected Alternative J as the ideal or optimum flow level.

---

1. In ruling on another issue, the court observed:

> Wyoming correctly notes that Dr. Bleed is not, technically, a judge. We would add that technically, the hearing officer is not a judge and the director is not a judge. . . . The hearing officer, the director, and Dr. Bleed are all performing adjudicative functions: the hearing officer is controlling the presentation of evidence, the director is deciding the ultimate outcome of the case, and Dr. Bleed, according to the explanations provided by the department, assists in the decisionmaking process by providing technical expertise.

To the extent that Dr. Bleed's participation in the study may have caused her to form an opinion as to the optimum flow level, such an opinion is not disqualifying. Although due process requires disqualification when the administrative adjudicator has actually prejudged the precise facts at issue, due process does not require the disqualification of one who has merely been exposed to or investigated the facts at issue. . . . Wyoming has not provided any evidence which would suggest that Dr. Bleed has prejudged the ideal level of instream flow for the Platte River. The evidence merely indicates that she has been exposed to and has investigated various instream flow levels.

Second, Wyoming fears that Dr. Bleed has a general bias in favor of instream flows. Wyoming does not cite us to any part of the record which would establish this bias. Exhibit 113 does not establish this bias—the tradeoff analysis reflects only an assumption that both instream and out-of-stream uses are positive and the two uses should somehow be brought into balance.

Even if Wyoming could establish that Dr. Bleed has a general bias in favor of instream flows, such a bias would not be disqualifying. An administrative adjudicator's prejudgment of a law or policy question is not disqualifying. See, Hortonville Dist. v. Hortonville Ed. Assn., 426 U.S. 482, 493 (1976) ("nor is a decisionmaker disqualified simply because he has taken a position, even in public, on a policy issue related to the dispute"). If such prejudgments were disqualifying, no judge could try the same issue of law twice. To put the case more strongly still: "If . . . 'bias' and 'partiality' be defined to mean the total absence of preconceptions . . . then no one has ever had a fair trial and no one ever will." In re J. P. Linahan, 138 F.2d 650, 651 (2d Cir.1943).

We therefore hold that the Department of Water Resources was not obligated to disqualify Dr. Bleed from assisting in the decisionmaking process. . . .

■ CAPORALE, J., concurring in part, and in part dissenting:

. . . I disagree with the majority's determination concerning Dr. Ann Bleed's participation in this matter.

She not only coauthored a report which involved the central issue the director was to decide and examined witnesses, she may . . . have been a part of the decisionmaking process. If she was, her participation as a coauthor of the article on the central issue before the director would entitle a reasonable disinterested observer to conclude that she had in some measure adjudged the facts in controversy. Such a circumstance, arising in an adjudicative setting, would provide a due process basis for disqualifying her as a decisionmaker. See, e.g., American General Ins. Co. v. F. T.C., 589 F.2d 462 (9th Cir.1979) (decision set aside because one commissioner had previously participated in case as counsel); Cinderella Career and Finishing Schools, Inc. v. F. T.C., 425 F.2d 583 (D.C.Cir.1970) (public statements of commission chairman indicating some measure of prejudgment, combined with other errors, required vacation of order).

In view of the department's contradictory characterizations of Bleed's role, the State of Wyoming should have been permitted to depose her in order to determine what that role in fact had been and was to be. I would therefore remand the entire matter for such to be done. If it were to develop that Bleed in fact served as a decisionmaker, I would vacate the entire order of the department and direct that proceedings begin anew.

NOTES

(1) In GROLIER, INC. V. FEDERAL TRADE COMMISSION, 615 F.2d 1215 (9th Cir.1980), the third ALJ assigned to a protracted deceptive practices case—the first had resigned, the second recused himself—revealed to the parties that years earlier, while Grolier had been under investigation, he had served as attorney-adviser to an FTC Commissioner. That Commissioner had attended at least one meeting concerning the investigation. Must the ALJ be disqualified? In remanding the case for further inquiry into the ALJ's former role, the court observed:

"In an effort to minimize any unfairness caused by ... consolidation of responsibilities, [in Section 554(d),] the APA mandates an internal separation of the investigatory-prosecutorial functions from adjudicative responsibilities. ... To violate section 554(d) ... an agency employee must, in the same or a factually related case, (1) engage in 'investigative or prosecuting functions,' and (2) 'participate or advise in the decision.' ...

"[The provisions reflect a recommendation contained in the Report of the Attorney General's Committee on Administrative Procedure 50 (1941), S.Doc. No. 8, 77th Cong., 1st Sess. 50 (1941), which gave at least] two reasons ... for this recommended separation: 'the investigators, if allowed to participate [in adjudication], would be likely to interpolate facts and information discovered by them ex parte and not adduced at the hearing, where the testimony is sworn and subject to cross-examination and rebuttal'; and '[a] man who has buried himself in one side of an issue is disabled from bringing to its decision that dispassionate judgment which Anglo–American tradition demands of officials who decide questions.'

" ... We conclude that ... Congress intended to preclude from decisionmaking in a particular case ... all persons who had, in that or a factually related case, been involved with ex parte information, or who had developed, by prior involvement with the case, a 'will to win.'[1] ...

"In resolving the question of ALJ von Brand's qualification to adjudicate the Grolier case, then, we must look to his activity during the time that he served as attorney-advisor to Commissioner MacIntyre. If he was sufficiently involved with the case to be apprised of ex parte information, 554(d) requires his disqualification. His current inability to recall that information is irrelevant. Once an attorney-advisor is shown to have been 'engaged in the performance of investigative or prosecuting functions' through prior acquaintance with ex parte information, 554(d) says he 'may not ... participate or advise in the decision ...' of the case. It does not condition this disqualification upon recollection of the ex parte facts.

---

1. In concluding that former attorney-advisors are not within the proscription of 554(d), the FTC focused solely upon the congressional desire to prevent adjudication by those who had developed a "will to win." In re Grolier, Inc., 87 F.T.C. 179, 180 (1976). With such a narrow focus, their conclusion was not unreasonable. It was erroneous, however, because it overlooked the equally important congressional desire to prevent adjudicative interpolation of ex parte facts.

"Grolier has the burden of showing ALJ von Brand's prior acquaintance with ex parte information. ... We do not say that the FTC must grant discovery [of all possibly relevant FTC documents]; but we do say that a flat refusal to disclose anything at all about ALJ von Brand's prior involvement in the Grolier case is error. The FTC must produce sufficient information to permit it and a reviewing court, to make an accurate 554(d) determination."

After a remand developed no facts suggesting that the ALJ had been personally involved in the earlier investigation, disqualification was denied. Grolier, Inc. v. FTC, 699 F.2d 983 (9th Cir.1983), cert. denied 464 U.S. 891 (1983). Are you satisfied that both the "will to win" and prior involvement with ex parte information in some official capacity warrant disqualification? See Michael Asimow, When the Curtain Falls: Separation of Functions in the Federal Administrative Agencies, 81 Colum.L.Rev. 759 (1981).

(2) *Judicial Disqualification.* Plainly enough, the right to an *impartial* trier of fact is not to be confused with a claim to one utterly indifferent to or unshaped by events such as may be put before him. All humans have attitudes of mind that, consciously or unconsciously, influence their judgments. Neither judges nor administrators approach their tasks with minds untouched by experience, reflection, and myth. Judges are shaped by "the predilections and the prejudices, the complex of instincts and emotions and habits and convictions, which make the man. ... The great tides and currents which engulf the rest of men do not turn aside in their course, and pass the judges by." B.N. Cardozo, The Nature of the Judicial Process 167–168 (1921). If a bias is to be regarded as so incapacitating as to prevent the tribunal's acting in a specific case, it must be much more focused upon particular parties, much more distorting in its results, much less amenable to modification by fuller information, by reason, or by competing social desiderata than are such generalized attitudes of mind.

For the federal judiciary, disqualification rules are set in some detail by 28 U.S.C. § 455. It requires, inter alia, disqualification "in any proceeding in which [the judge's] impartiality might reasonably be questioned," § 455(a). While some courts have thought this "heightened standard cannot apply to administrative law judges who, after all, are employed by the agency whose actions they review," Greenberg v. Board of Governors of the Federal Reserve System, 968 F.2d 164, 167 (2d Cir.1992), § 455 and the ABA Code of Judicial Conduct are regularly looked to for substantial guidance on what may serve to disqualify.[2] In a prosecution of (apparently) politically motivated vandals of government property, LITEKY v. UNITED STATES, 510 U.S. 540 (1994), the Court was unanimous that § 455(a)'s standard did not require disqualification of a judge who, at both this and an earlier hearing, was said to have shown some animus to their cause; but it was closely divided over the sweep of § 455(a). Justice Scalia, for five, reasoned from a subsequent subsection's limitation to essentially *personal* matters (§ 455(b)), that § 455(a) could rarely if ever reach attitudes formed in the performance of official function:

---

2. E.g., Reddy and Sorkvist v. CFTC, 191 F.3d 109, 119 (2d Cir.1999). See generally Peter L. Strauss, Disqualification of Decisional Officials in Rulemaking, 80 Colum.L.Rev. 990 (1980).

"The judge who presides at a trial may, upon completion of the evidence, be exceedingly ill disposed towards the defendant, who has been shown to be a thoroughly reprehensible person. But the judge is not thereby recusable for bias or prejudice, since his knowledge and the opinion it produced were properly and necessarily acquired in the course of the proceedings, and are indeed sometimes (as in a bench trial) necessary to completion of the judge's task. As Judge Jerome Frank pithily put it: 'Impartiality is not gullibility. Disinterestedness does not mean child-like innocence. If the judge did not form judgments of the actors in those courthouse dramas called trials, he could never render decisions.' In re J. P. Linahan, Inc., 138 F.2d 650, 654 (C.A.2 1943). Also not subject to deprecatory characterization as 'bias' or 'prejudice' are opinions held by judges as a result of what they learned in earlier proceedings. It has long been regarded as normal and proper for a judge to sit in the same case upon its remand, and to sit in successive trials involving the same defendant."

Agreeing as to result, Justice Kennedy wrote for four that "the Court's opinion announces a mistaken, unfortunate precedent in two respects. First, it accords nearly dispositive weight to the source of a judge's alleged partiality, to the point of stating that disqualification for intrajudicial partiality is not required unless it would make a fair hearing impossible. Second, the Court weakens the principal disqualification statute in the federal system, 28 U.S.C. § 455, by holding ... that the broad protections afforded by subsection (a) are qualified by limitations explicit in the specific prohibitions of subsection (b).

"... The relevant consideration under § 455(a) is the appearance of partiality, not where it originated or how it was disclosed. If, for instance, a judge presiding over a retrial should state, based upon facts adduced and opinions formed during the original cause, an intent to ensure that one side or the other shall prevail, there can be little doubt that he or she must recuse. Cf. Rugenstein v. Ottenheimer, 78 Ore. 371, 372, 152 P. 215, 216 (1915) (reversing for judge's failure to disqualify himself on retrial, where judge had stated: 'This case may be tried again, and it will be tried before me. I will see to that. And I will see that the woman gets another verdict and judgment that will stand.'). ... Still, we accept the notion that the 'conscientious judge will, as far as possible, make himself aware of his biases of this character, and, by that very self-knowledge, nullify their effect.' In re J. P. Linahan, Inc., 138 F.2d 650, 652 (C.A.2 1943). The acquired skill and capacity to disregard extraneous matters is one of the requisites of judicial office. As a matter of sound administration, moreover, it may be necessary and prudent to permit judges to preside over successive causes involving the same parties or issues. The public character of the prior and present proceedings tends to reinforce the resolve of the judge to weigh with care the propriety of his or her decision to hear the case.

"Out of this reconciliation of principle and practice comes the recognition that a judge's prior judicial experience and contacts need not, and often do not, give rise to reasonable questions concerning impartiality. ... [Yet a] judge may find it difficult to put aside views formed during some earlier proceeding. In that instance we would expect the judge to heed the judicial oath and step down, but that does not always occur. If through obduracy, honest mistake, or simple inability to attain self-knowledge the judge fails to acknowledge a disqualifying predisposition or circumstance, an appellate court must order recusal no matter what the source.''

(ii) MANAGERIAL CONTROLS

A somewhat different set of considerations are presented by an agency's responsibility for the effective carrying out of its policy responsibilities. To a considerable extent, of course, this may be carried out through the adoption of regulations setting agency policy, or through conventional agency review of ALJ judgments. Yet suppose the issue is not the correctness or not of a particular outcome, but the general industry with which an ALJ can be expected to pursue her work, or an ALJ's seeming general pattern of making decisions that are out of keeping with her fellows (or agency policy), or questions about the manner in which she conducts herself in hearings. Questions like these have particular importance for programs, notably those administered by the Social Security Administration, where caseloads are heavy, questions somewhat routine, and applicants appearing before the hearer are drawn, almost invariably, from among society's underprivileged.[1]

SSA's processes are enormously important—4.9 million disabled workers (6.5 million beneficiaries) received over $51billion in payments in 1999, at an administrative cost of $1.5 billion, or about 3% of system payout—a rather favorable ratio compared with, for example, the administrative cost component of the tort system.[2] Accuracy and uniformity are nonetheless difficult to achieve. This is in part a product of the difficulty of the inquiry, reflected in a number of cases studied elsewhere in these materials;[3] in part, it reflects the tremendous volume of matters to be decided. SSA's ALJs disposed of 597,000 cases in fiscal 1999. In the same year, the SSA Appeals Council, responsible for agency review of ALJ decisions, reported over 115,000 new matters added to its docket; and more than 13,000 new cases seeking review were filed in federal district court, in excess of 5% of its civil docket.[4]

SSA's ALJs consider only matters brought by applicants disappointed by the prior bureaucratic processing of their applications. These cases are not tried in conventional adversary fashion, with a government lawyer responsible for presenting the government's case. Rather, they are heard in an inquisitorial style. The presiding ALJ is responsible for seeing the government's information into the record, for the identification and direct examination of government witnesses, and for cross-examination of claim-

1. A number of similar programs are located in the Departments of Health and Human Services, and of Labor.

2. Although SSI and DI program benefits account for less than 20 percent of the total benefit payments made by SSA, they consume about well over half of its annual administrative resources. Social Security Administration: Agency Must Position Itself Now to Meet Profound Challenges (02–MAY–02, GAO–02–289t).

3. E.g., Stieberger v. Hechler, pp. 389 and 922 below; Heckler v. Campbell, p. 592 below; Mathews v. Eldridge, p. 839 below.

4. Social Security Administration, Annual Statistical Supplement 2000 117; see also Paul Verkuil and Jeffrey Lubbers, Alternative Approaches to Social Security Review of Disability Cases—A Report to the Social Security Advisory Board (March 1, 2002).

ant witnesses. On average, SSA ALJs rule in favor of applicants about 2/3 of the time, although this rate varies geographically, from 35 to 86 percent. Thus, of the roughly 600,000 matters that disappointed applicants brought to ALJs for hearing, about 200,000 were denied. Average ALJ processing time for a matter is 274 days.[5]

The 200,000 denials become about 115,000 proceedings before the Appeals Council. Since the government is unrepresented before the ALJ, over 95% of these proceedings result either directly or indirectly from applicant dissatisfaction; the small remainder are reviews the Appeals Council takes sua sponte for quality assurance or other special purposes.[6] The Appeals Council, like the SSA ALJs, proceeds nonadversarially; in about five of six cases, it ultimately affirms the ALJ's result. Thus, the 200,000 ALJ denials become about 180,000 final denials. The volume of Appeals Council decisions precludes the development of any "common law" of administrative review; rather, if the review process uncovers needs for new policy or clarification, that policy or clarification is supplied by regulation or similar directives to all decisionmakers in the system. The average time the Appeals Council takes to reach decision recently has been about eighteen months.[7]

Review in district court, again an eighteen month process, is more successful for the roughly 7% of denied applicants who seek it. About 6% of the cases brought result in outright reversal; about half, in remand—and about 60% of remanded cases result in a grant. Thus, about a third of the applicants who go to district court prevail, but they are a rather select group. In district court, of course, the government *is* represented, but through the office of the local US attorney (who has no programatic responsibilities, and whose experience is limited to this small proportion of cases.) Like ALJ grant statistics, the rates at which these results occur vary greatly from district to district; eight of the U.S.D.C. districts reported reversal rates less than 1%; three, on the other hand, reported reversal rates of more than 20%.[8] Among the more generous districts is the Southern District of New York, whence arose the following:

Nash v. Bowen

United States Court of Appeals for the Second Circuit, 1989.
869 F.2d 675.

■ Before FEINBERG, NEWMAN and ALTIMARI, CIRCUIT JUDGES.

■ ALTIMARI, CIRCUIT JUDGE:

[This appeal was the second in litigation generally challenging efforts by the Social Security Administration in the Department of Health and

---

5. Verkuil and Lubbers, above, at 35.

6. Verkuil and Lubbers report, at 36, that of 134,191 Appeals Council dispositions in FY 2000, 5,360 resulted from quality assurance and special reviews, 106,358 from applicant requests for review, and the remainder were associated with judicial review, which is always applicant initiated.

7. Ibid.

8. Id at 69–70. "A person whose claim for Social Security benefits is denied by an administrative law judge (ALJ) must in most

cases, before seeking judicial review of that denial, request that the Social Security Appeals Council review his claim," but need not necessarily specify in her request the particular issue on which she then seeks judicial review. Sims v. Apfel, 530 U.S. 103 (2000); see Dubin, Torquemada Meets Kafka: The Misapplication of the Issue Exhaustion Doctrine to Inquisitorial Administrative Proceedings, 97 Colum.L.Rev. 1289 (1997) and the discussion of exhaustion of administrative remedies, p. 1238 below.

Human Services to improve Administrative Law Judges' quality and efficiency. In 1975, faced with a backlog of over 100,000 cases, Robert L. Trachtenberg, then Director of SSA's Bureau of Hearings and Appeals, instituted a series of reforms. Simon Nash, an ALJ with three decades of experience in the Social Security Administration and the ALJ in charge of the Buffalo, New York field office of hearings and appeals, brought this action pro se, contending that these initiatives impaired ALJ's right to "decisional independence" under the Administrative Procedure Act. On the first appeal, which upheld Nash's standing, 613 F.2d 10 (1980), the court had described his allegations as follows:

"The first practice challenged in [Nash's] complaint is the Bureau's 'Regional Office Peer Review Program.' According to Nash, Trachtenberg [and other officials], as well as non-ALJ members of their staffs, known as 'Development Center Analysts' and 'Program Operation Officers,' review the work of ALJs outside the normal appellate process. In conjunction with this ongoing review, the appellees or their staffs give plaintiff and all other ALJs detailed, purportedly mandatory instructions concerning the proper length of hearings and opinions, the amount of evidence required in specific cases, and the proper use of expert witnesses. Through the Peer Review Program, the Bureau has allegedly arrogated to itself the power to control the conduct of hearings vested in ALJs by the Administrative Procedure Act, 5 U.S.C. § 556.

"Nash also avers that an arbitrary monthly production quota has been established for him and all his colleagues. Unless an ALJ renders a specified number of decisions per month, the agency, appellant claims, threatens to file incompetence charges against him with the Civil Service Commission. In his view, the agency's production quota constitutes a performance rating forbidden by the Administrative Procedure Act, 5 U.S.C. § 4301(2)(E) and 5 C.F.R. § 930.211.

"An additional threat to the ALJs statutory independence is allegedly posed by the so-called 'Quality Assurance Program,' which attempts to control the number of decisions denying Social Security Benefits. The agency has 'let it be known' that the average 50% 'reversal rate' for all ALJs is an 'acceptable' one. Appellant further claims in his amended complaint that the reversal rates of all ALJs are monitored, and those who deviate from the mean are counseled and admonished to bring their rates in line with the national average. This attempt to influence the ALJs' decisionmaking process, it is urged, violates 5 U.S.C. §§ 556 & 3105 and the Fifth Amendment to the Constitution."

The first Second Circuit opinion had also given a capsule account of the ALJ's place under the APA:

"As originally enacted in 1946, the Administrative Procedure Act (APA) vested hearing examiners (as ALJs were then called) with a limited independence from the agencies they served. The hearing examiners had previously been on a par with other agency employees, their compensation and promotion dependent upon agency ratings. The expanding scope of agency activity during the 1930s and early 1940s led to increasingly heavy criticism, however, because the hearing examiners came to be perceived as 'mere tools of the agency concerned.' Ramspeck v. Trial Examiners Conference, 345 U.S. 128, 131 (1953). In response, Congress enacted § 11 of the APA, removing control over the hearing examiners' tenure and compensation from the agencies and vesting it, to a large degree, in the Civil Service Commission.

"The APA provides that ALJs 'are entitled to pay prescribed by the Office of Personnel Management independently of agency recommendations or ratings.' 5 U.S.C. § 5372. In addition, section 4301 and its implementing regulation (5 C.F.R. § 930.211) exempts ALJs from the performance ratings prescribed for other civil service employees. ALJ tenure, moreover, is specially safeguarded by 5 U.S.C. § 554, which provides that ALJs, unlike other civil servants, may not be removed without a formal adjudication.

"These statutory provisions draw upon the more ancient wisdom grounded in history and contained in Article III, which safeguards federal judicial independence through still more stringent compensation and tenure provisions. . . . It is clear that these provisions confer a qualified right of decisional independence upon ALJs. First recognized by the Supreme Court in Ramspeck v. Trial Examiners Conference, 345 U.S. 128 (1953), this special status is a creation of statute, rather than the Constitution. And as their role has expanded, the ALJs functional comparability to judges has gained recognition."]

The district court explicitly determined that "[a]lthough the defendants may have engaged in some questionable practices which clearly caused great unrest among ALJs, . . . they did not infringe on the decisional independence of ALJs." The factual components of this conclusion, as with all findings of fact, cannot be set aside on appeal unless they are clearly erroneous.

. . . Policies designed to insure a reasonable degree of uniformity among ALJ decisions are not only within the bounds of legitimate agency supervision but are to be encouraged. . . . It is, after all, the Secretary who ultimately is authorized to make final decisions in benefit cases. An ALJ is a creature of statute and, as such, is subordinate to the Secretary in matters of policy and interpretation of law. Thus, the Secretary's efforts through peer review to ensure that ALJ decisions conformed with his interpretation of relevant law and policy were permissible so long as such efforts did not directly interfere with "live" decisions (unless in accordance with the usual administrative review performed by the Appeals Council). The efforts complained of in this case for promoting quality and efficiency do not infringe upon ALJs' decisional independence. . . .

Regarding the Secretary's policy of setting a minimum number of dispositions an ALJ must decide in a month, . . . [t]he setting of reasonable production goals, as opposed to fixed quotas, is not in itself a violation of the APA. The district court explicitly found that the numbers at issue constituted reasonable goals as opposed to unreasonable quotas. Judge Elfvin explained that

[a] minimum number of dispositions an ALJ must decide in a given period, provided this number is reasonable and not "etched in stone," is not a prescription of how, or how quickly, an ALJ should decide a particular case. It does not dictate the content of the decision.

Moreover, in view of the significant backlog of cases, it was not unreasonable to expect ALJs to perform at minimally acceptable levels of efficiency. Simple fairness to claimants awaiting benefits required no less. . . .

The Secretary's "reversal" rate policy embodied in the "Quality Assurance System," however, is cause for concern. To coerce ALJs into lowering reversal rates—that is, into deciding more cases against claimants—would, if shown, constitute . . . "a clear infringement of decisional independence." . . . [Nash] maintained that the reversal rate policy, in effect from approximately 1975 to 1985, was implemented under the guise of improving the quality and uniformity of ALJ decisions but was in fact a clear attempt by the Secretary to influence ALJs into deciding more cases in favor of the agency.

The Secretary concedes that he was very concerned about reversal rates, but only to the extent that they might indicate errors in the decisionmaking of ALJs. Testimony in the record revealed that reversal rates were used as a benchmark in deciding whether there *might* be problems in the adjudicatory methods of particularly high (or low) reversal rate ALJs. Statistical record evidence supported the agency's proffered correlation between actual errors of law or policy in ALJs decisions and extremes in their reversal rates. The agency maintained then, and maintains now, that reducing reversal rates was not the intent of the policy. Indeed, a handwritten notation by Associate Commissioner Hays on a 1982 internal agency memorandum placed the policy in perspective.

[T]here is *no* goal to reduce reversal rates—there is a goal to improve decisional quality [and] consistency, which is assumed to have as one effect a reduction of the reversal rate.

. . . Whatever legitimate concerns there may be about the soundness of the Secretary's practices regarding "reversal" rates, those concerns are more appropriately addressed by Congress or by courts through the usual channels of judicial review in Social Security cases. The bottom line in this case is that it was entirely within the Secretary's discretion to adopt reasonable administrative measures in order to improve the decisionmaking process. . . .

AFFIRMED.

NOTES

(1) Note again the unusual character of the SSA adjudicatory system, as compared with the model of adversarial trial we are accustomed to.

(2) *The Problem of Own-Motion Review.* The SSA concerns underlying Nash v. Bowen at one point found expression in a "Bellmon review program," adopted in response to a statutory requirement to "implement a program of reviewing, on [the Secretary's] own motion," ALJ decisions in

the disability insurance program.[1] Not surprisingly perhaps, the Secretary took this as a signal to check for excessive generosity in ALJ decisionmaking; the availability of Appeals Council review to disappointed applicants would already tend to check excessive denials. Under this program, "ALJs with individual allowance rates of 70 percent or higher and ALJs in hearing offices with aggregate allowance rates of 74 percent or higher were targeted for review. Half of the allowance decisions issued by targeted ALJs were evaluated by the Office of Hearings and Appeals for possible review, and 7 1/2 percent of the allowance decisions issued by these ALJs were formally reviewed by the Appeals Council. On April 1, 1982, the targeted ALJs were divided into four groups based on own-motion rates.[2] Each and every allowance decision by ALJs in the group with the highest own-motion rates was evaluated for possible review. In the group with the second-highest rates, 75 percent of the ALJs allowance decisions were thus evaluated; in the group with the third-highest rates, 50 percent; and in the group with the lowest rates, 25 percent. In addition, the program was expanded so that 15 percent of all allowance decisions by targeted ALJs were formally reviewed by the Appeals Council. Finally, the program was expanded to provide review of a national random sample of ALJ allowance decisions, ALJ decisions referred from the SSA Office of Disability Operations, and decisions of all new ALJs." W.C. v. Heckler, 629 F.Supp. 791, 793–94 (W.D.Wash.1985), affirmed 807 F.2d 1502 (9th Cir.1987). The spin this description suggestions, centering on excessive grants, is what produced the cautionary language in Nash, above. The program gradually changed, so that an ALJ's grant rate ceased to determine whether or at what intensity her decisions were reviewed.

Do you agree that it would be productive of bias, an interference with the necessary independence of the ALJs, to attempt to reduce or otherwise control "excessively high" ALJ grant rates? The government's argument was that Bellmon review was the equivalent of review that would be initiated by government prosecuting attorneys under a fully adversary scheme, and served to counterbalance the 50% rate at which review of *denials* of benefits was sought before the Appeals Council by disappointed applicants. Since no government attorney appears before the SSA ALJ, review of erroneous *grants* would not otherwise occur. The response, credited by Judge Sand in STIEBERGER V. HECKLER, 615 F.Supp. 1315, 1391 (S.D.N.Y.1985), vacated 801 F.2d 29 (2d Cir.1986) (a case seen for other purposes at p. 922 below) was that "[u]nder Bellmon Review, however, individual ALJs were singled out from the rest of their colleagues for appellate review based solely on the bottom-line results which these ALJs were reaching in disability determinations. This targeting process, regardless of the benevolence of the motives which may have prompted it, simply cannot be compared and equated with the everyday psychological burdens which all ALJs shared and continue to share with respect to claimant-

---

1. Social Security Disability Amendment of 1980, Pub.L. No. 96–265, § 304(g), 94 Stat. 441, 456.

2. An ALJ's own-motion rate during a given period is the number of his decisions corrected by the Appeals Council on own-motion review divided by the total number of his decisions evaluated for possible own-motion review.

initiated denial review." That the SSA's challenges in resolving disability claims remain a dominating issue is suggested by the continuing flow of GAO reports addressing its problems.[3] Currently, however, as noted above, quality control reviews—that is, reviews *not* initiated by a disappointed applicant—comprise less than 5% of the Appeals Council's caseload.

(3) *ALJ Discipline and the Chilling of "Judicial Independence."* Article III federal judges are protected from removal from office save by impeachment, as an important safeguard of their objectivity. The equivalent protection for ALJs is the requirement that any discipline be imposed outside the agency, through the Merit System Protection Board. In some cases, of course, disciplinary proceedings are brought against individual ALJs for the use of profane language, abusive behavior, and the like. Few find their way into reported cases, in part because of the costs to the agency of initiating such proceedings—the collective of social security administrative law judges is a frequent amicus opposing discipline even in the aggravated cases that do appear—and in part because the MSPB strongly favors settlement. See, e.g., Social Security Administration, Office of Hearing and Appeals v. Anyel, 58 M.S.P.R. 261 (1993) (frequent pressuring of often unsophisticated and language-handicapped applicants to proceed without counsel; failure to develop evidence on behalf of pro se applicants) and 66 M.S.R.P. 328 (1995) (settlement accepting 90 day suspension from duty as ALJ approved); Carr v. Social Security Administration, 185 F.3d 1318 (Fed.Cir.1999) ("On appeal, Ms. Carr does not challenge the findings of the Board that she persistently used vulgar and profane language, that she made demeaning comments and engaged in sexual harassment and ridicule, and that, by her conduct, she interfered with efficient and effective agency operations." Removal sustained despite claim of protection as "whistleblower").

CHARLES H. KOCH, JR., ADMINISTRATIVE PRESIDING OFFICIALS TODAY, 46 Ad.L.Rev. 271, 278–79 (1994) reported the results of surveys taken of large numbers of both ALJs and administrative judges in the early '90's. He learned, perhaps surprisingly, that the AJs perceived rather less threat to their independence for their relations with their agencies than did ALJs:

"... Fifteen percent of the non-SSA ALJs responded that threats to independence were a problem, with 8% saying this was frequently a problem. Nine percent responded that pressure to make different decisions was a problem and 4% found it to be a frequent problem. As with [an earlier study,] the SSA ALJs expressed more concern: 33% of the SSA ALJs found threats to independence to be a problem, with 21% saying this was a frequent problem. Twenty-six percent found pressure to make different decisions, with 10% finding it to be a frequent problem.

---

3. GAO Reports, accessible and searchable at http://www.gao.gov/reports.htm, often provide useful windows into the practical functioning of government agencies. An early summer 2002 search for recent studies including "Social Security Administration," "administrative law judge" and "disability" produced 14 responses. Social Security Administration: Agency Must Position Itself Now to Meet Profound Challenges (02–MAY–02, GAO–02–289T) and Social Security Disability: SSA Has Had Mixed Success in Efforts to Improve Caseload Management (21–OCT–99, GAO/T–HEHS–00–22) provide particularly helpful windows into the agency's continuing efforts and troubles.

"Because AJs have no formal protection, one might expect them to express a far higher level of anxiety. However, AJs reported less of a problem than ALJs. Ninety-one percent of the AJs described themselves as independent. About 70% reported that threats to independent judgment were not a problem, with 18% reporting that this was occasionally a problem and 10% reporting that it was frequently a problem. About 80% reported that pressure for different decisions was not a problem and most of the remainder reported that it was only occasionally a problem. Only 2% reported that it was frequently a problem.

"The contrast between the AJ and ALJ attitudes is significant because the AJs have none of the structural protections afforded ALJs. Thus, we asked the AJs to compare their position with that of ALJs. They divided nearly equally among greater, the same, or lesser, regarding independence from agency supervision and authority. These findings add support to the notion that structural protections are not important to a feeling of independence and perhaps to actual independence. In short, from the data, I must conclude that both a sense of independence and actual independence derive from other sources.

"The contrast between past and current attitudes and between ALJs and AJs held up when we asked whether they had experienced pressure to do things 'that are against their better judgment.' The 1992 ALJ Survey shows that 34% of the ALJs believed they were asked to do things that are against their better judgment, with 11% being frequently asked to do so. Thirteen percent of the SSA ALJs reported that they were frequently asked to do things against their better judgment and another 29% were occasionally asked to do so.[4] Only 6% of the non-SSA ALJs reported that they were frequently asked to do things against their better judgment, with another 13% saying they were asked to do so occasionally. Again these responses are more negative than the past responses.

"Responses from the AJs were more positive than those from the ALJs. About three-quarters reported that they were never or rarely asked do things in their work that were against their better judgment. Most of the rest said they were only sometimes asked to do so and only about 4% said they were often or usually asked to do so. Again, the group with less structural protection seemed less anxious."

Professor Koch' findings are, of course, the product of the atmosphere within which the AJs work. In early 2002, with the Department of Justice's Board of Immigration Appeals facing a backlog of more than 50,000 cases, Attorney General John Ashcroft proposed a variety of changes which, he asserted, would permit the backlog to be controlled—chiefly by making BIA review more routine, limited in relation to factual disputes and ordinarily to be handled by a single reviewing appellate administrative judge, not (as previously) a panel of three. This, he asserted, would permit the backlog to be eliminated within six months, and the number of BIA judges halved, from 23 to eleven. In the view of law professors T. Alexander Aleinikoff and David Martin, each a former general counsel of the Immigration and Nationalization Service, "This suggests that more might be at play here. A

---

4. 1992 ALJ Survey, SSA only, supra note 20, response 15e.

hint can be found in the reported comment of an unnamed top aide that the attorney general wants to make sure that the board and the department are 'on the same page.' The not-so-subtle threat is that the attorney general will use the next six months to monitor individual decisions and then purge those members whose substantive views don't conform to the attorney general's stated and unstated policy objectives, whatever their best professional judgment of the law.

"If the attorney general disagrees with a substantive decision of the board, current regulations permit him to have the final word, but in a way that is truer to the rule of law. Under established procedures, he may personally take BIA cases for review. But when that happens, the process is public and open, and the attorney general must write an opinion that carefully analyzes the legal questions and justifies his conclusions—without intruding on the independence of board members as they make their decisions resolving individual cases." T. Alexander Aleinikoff and David A. Martin, "Ashcroft's Immigration Threat," The Washington Post, Tuesday, February 26, 2002, Page A21.

As also happens occasionally to federal district judges, ALJs may be removed from further participation in a particular controversy, when the reviewing tribunal concludes that their behavior to that point suggests an inability to continue in an objective and fair manner. Roadway Express v. Reich, 34 F.3d 1068 (6th Cir.1994).

(4) *Should the Independence or Not of the Hearing Official Influence the Intensity of Judicial Review?* JONAL CORP. v. DISTRICT OF COLUMBIA, 533 F.2d 1192 (D.C.Cir.1976), cert. denied 429 U.S. 825 (1976), reviewed the District of Columbia's Contract Appeals Board's decision of a dispute arising out of Jonal's contract with the District to construct two buildings. Jonal challenged the fairness of the Board's action on the ground, inter alia, that it had been appointed by the Corporation Counsel of the District, who also appeared before the Board to argue the city's case. The majority, Judge Merhige writing, easily disposed of the case on the basis of Marcello v. Bonds, 349 U.S. 302 (1955), which in their view sustained similar arrangements in federal immigration cases.[5] Absent demonstrated personal bias, pecuniary interest, or prejudice apparent in the conduct of the proceedings, the majority concluded, Jonal had no complaint.

For Judge Harold Leventhal, in dissent, Marcello was not dispositive. In that case, rulings of inquiry officers were subject to "full administrative review" by a national board of immigration appeals *not* subject to INS supervision, and it was the judgment of this "insulated" review board that was found "entitled to substantial evidence deference by the courts." Here, on the other hand, the Corporation Counsel not only designated the members of the board from his staff, but also "considers itself free . . . to

---

5. "[T]he objection that the special inquiry officer was subject to the supervision and control of officials in the Immigration Service charged with investigative and prosecuting functions . . . is without substance when considered against the long-standing practice in deportation proceedings, judicially approved in numerous decisions in the federal courts, and against the special considerations applicable to deportation which Congress may take into account in exercising its particularly broad discretion in immigration matters." 349 U.S. at 311.

make such assignments, on a part-time duty basis, in such a way that on one day a lawyer may be a member of the board, ... although the day before and the day after he may be working alongside [the attorney who argued the city's case], or even under his supervision, in another matter." For Judge Leventhal, further inquiry was required to determine, in light of these working relationships, "whether, and to what extent, [the board's] decisions are entitled to the benefit of the 'substantial evidence' rule."[6]

SECTION 2.   FORMAL ADJUDICATION AT THE AGENCY LEVEL—ISSUES OF ROLE

When we turn from the initial hearer to the agency head ultimately responsible for decision, the landscape alters dramatically. This is the busy adjudicator first met in SAPL. With a few exceptions,[1] we are now dealing with an official or officials with myriad responsibilities, not all of them judicial or limited by "record" restraints. Any realistic account of an agency head's calendar would show little time for *personal* engagement with particular matters the agency must resolve; it would show many conversations, formal and informal, with agency staff who may have been associated with the case, about agency responsibilities that could bear on matters at issue; and it would show frequent contact on policy issues with other agencies, the White House, Congress and members of the public. Who can help the agency head reach decision, and in what ways? What conversations and interactions is she permitted to have, when on-the-record matters pend? Questions such as these return us to the committee of previously uninvolved scientific advisors the EPA Administrator assembled to assist his decision in SAPL.

The APA addresses particular proceedings, not the generality of agency business or the ways in which that business may bear on any one proceeding. For individual adjudications, it speaks to these issues in § 554 and § 557. Although these materials begin to consider decisionmaking at the top of the agency by examining a pair of decisions that predate the APA, it may be helpful at the outset to call attention to characteristics of these sections that bear on agency heads' multiple roles and the institutional nature of their decisionmaking. First, § 554(d), in addressing *internal* lines of communication, explicitly excludes from its coverage the "members of the body comprising the agency"—that is, its political head. Second, both § 554(d) and § 557(b) explicitly permit actively involved staff to work with agency decisionmakers in initial licensing or rate-making proceedings, in ways that would be forbidden in other on-the-record contexts. Separation of functions in an on-the-record proceeding within an agency is thus less

---

6. Compare Kalaris v. Donovan, 697 F.2d 376 (D.C.Cir.1983), cert. denied 462 U.S. 1119 (1983) (sitting member of Labor Department's Benefits Review Board may constitutionally be made subject to summary removal); NLRB v. Ohio New and Rebuilt Parts, Inc., 760 F.2d 1443 (6th Cir.1985) (performance ratings of NLRB regional directors as members of Federal Senior Executive Service did not create constitutionally unfair financial or other incentives).

1. Congress occasionally establishes agencies with chiefly quasi-judicial functions; the Occupational Safety and Health Review Commission is an example.

demanding in some contexts, and particularly at the agency's head, than judicial analogies might otherwise lead us to expect. Finally, while both sections 554 and 557(d) seek to restrain "ex parte" contacts, they use different language in doing so. The ex parte provisions of § 554(d)(1), which apply to all parties (i.e., including "adversarial" agency staff), only reach communications about "a fact in issue." In contrast, the ex parte provisions of § 557(d), which are addressed only to persons "outside the agency," apply more broadly—to all conversations "relevant to the merits of the proceeding." The pages following invite continued attention to the question whether the needs and realities of institutional decision, on the one hand, and the risks of unfairness, on the other, vary from proceeding to proceeding, or from level to level within the agency, in ways that explain these judgments.

a. THE OBLIGATIONS OF NOTICE AND HEARING

Morgan v. United States

Supreme Court of the United States, 1936.
298 U.S. 468.

■ MR. CHIEF JUSTICE HUGHES delivered the opinion of the Court. . . .

[Fifty suits, consolidated for the purpose of trial, were brought to restrain the enforcement of an order of the Secretary of Agriculture fixing the maximum rates to be charged by market agencies for buying and selling livestock at the Kansas City Stockyards. In 1930, acting under the authority of the Packers and Stockyards Act, the Secretary ordered an inquiry into the reasonableness of existing rates. The ultimate order fixing the rates was made in June, 1933. The plaintiffs in these suits attacked that order on the merits and also because (so they alleged) they had not been accorded the hearing required by Section 310 of the statute. This provided that the Secretary might fix rates "Whenever after full hearing . . . the Secretary is of the opinion that any rate . . . is or will be unjust, unreasonable or discriminatory. . . ." In substance, the plaintiffs complained that they had not had a "full hearing" because their respective cases had not been heard separately; because the trial examiner had prepared no tentative report, to be subject to oral argument and exceptions; because the Secretary had unlawfully delegated to the Acting Secretary the determination of issues with respect to the reasonableness of the rates involved; and because the Secretary, so they asserted on information and belief, "had not personally heard or read any of the evidence presented at any hearing in connection with this proceeding and had not heard or considered oral arguments relating thereto submitted on behalf of this petitioner and had not read or considered any briefs submitted by petitioner in this proceeding," but had obtained all his information about the proceeding by consulting "with employees in the Department of Agriculture, out of the presence of this petitioner or any representative of this petitioner." The Government successfully moved to strike these allegations, thus denying the plaintiffs any opportunity to require an answer or to prove the facts alleged. On the merits the District Court then sustained the order.

The record disclosed that the testimony in the case had been taken before an examiner; that there had been no formulation of an intermediate report; that oral argument upon the evidence was had before the Acting Secretary of Agriculture; that subsequently a brief was filed on plaintiffs' behalf; and that thereafter the Secretary had signed an order which prescribed rates upon the basis of findings of fact and of conclusions made, it was said, after "careful consideration of the entire record in this proceeding."]

All questions touching the regularity and validity of the proceeding before the Secretary are open to review. . . . When the Secretary acts within the authority conferred by the statute, his findings of fact are conclusive. . . . But, in determining whether in conducting an administrative proceeding of this sort the Secretary has complied with the statutory prerequisites, the recitals of his procedure cannot be regarded as conclusive. Otherwise the statutory conditions could be set at naught by mere assertion. If upon the facts alleged, the "full hearing" required by the statute was not given, plaintiffs were entitled to prove the facts and have the Secretary's order set aside. Nor is it necessary to go beyond the terms of the statute in order to consider the constitutional requirement of due process as to notice and hearing. For the statute itself demands a full hearing and the order is void if such a hearing was denied. . . .

Second. The outstanding allegation, which the District Court struck out, is that the Secretary made the rate order without having heard or read any of the evidence, and without having heard the oral arguments or having read or considered the briefs which the plaintiffs submitted. That the only information which the Secretary had as to the proceeding was what he derived from consultation with employees of the Department.

The other allegations of the stricken paragraph do not go to the root of the matter. Thus, it cannot be said that the failure to hear the respondents separately was an abuse of discretion. Again, while it would have been good practice to have the examiner prepare a report and submit it to the Secretary and the parties, and to permit exceptions and arguments addressed to the points thus presented—a practice found to be of great value in proceedings before the Interstate Commerce Commission—we cannot say that that particular type of procedure was essential to the validity of the hearing. The statute does not require it and what the statute does require relates to substance and not form.

Nor should the fundamental question be confused with one of mere delegation of authority. . . . If the Secretary had assigned to the [Acting] Secretary the duty of holding the hearing, and the [Acting] Secretary accordingly had received the evidence taken by the examiner, had heard argument thereon and had then found the essential facts and made the order upon his findings, we should have had simply the question of delegation. But while the [Acting] Secretary heard argument he . . . assumed no responsibility for the findings or order, and the Secretary, who had not heard, did assume that responsibility.

We may likewise put aside the contention as to the circumstances in which an Acting Secretary may take the place of his chief. . . . The Acting Secretary did not assume to make the order.

Third. What is the essential quality of the proceeding under review, and what is the nature of the hearing which the statute prescribes?

The proceeding is not one of ordinary administration, conformable to the standards governing duties of a purely executive character. It is a proceeding looking to legislative action in the fixing of rates of market agencies. And, while the order is legislative and gives to the proceeding its distinctive character (Louisville & Nashville R. Co. v. Garrett, 231 U.S. 298, 307), it is a proceeding which by virtue of the authority conferred has special attributes. The Secretary, as the agent of Congress in making the rates, must make them in accordance with the standards and under the limitations which Congress has prescribed. Congress has required the Secretary to determine, as a condition of his action, that the existing rates are or will be "unjust, unreasonable, or discriminatory." If and when he so finds, he may "determine and prescribe" what shall be the just and reasonable rate, or the maximum or minimum rate, thereafter to be charged. That duty is widely different from ordinary executive action. It is a duty which carries with it fundamental procedural requirements. There must be a full hearing. There must be evidence adequate to support pertinent and necessary findings of fact. Nothing can be treated as evidence which is not introduced as such. United States v. Abilene & Southern Ry. Co. [265 U.S. 274]. Facts and circumstances which ought to be considered must not be excluded. Facts and circumstances must not be considered which should not legally influence the conclusion. Findings based on the evidence must embrace the basic facts which are needed to sustain the order. . . .

A proceeding of this sort requiring the taking and weighing of evidence, determinations of fact based upon the consideration of the evidence, and the making of an order supported by such findings, has a quality resembling that of a judicial proceeding. Hence it is frequently described as a proceeding of a quasi-judicial character. The requirement of a "full hearing" has obvious reference to the tradition of judicial proceedings in which evidence is received and weighed by the trier of the facts. The "hearing" is designed to afford the safeguard that the one who decides shall be bound in good conscience to consider the evidence, to be guided by that alone, and to reach his conclusion uninfluenced by extraneous considerations which in other fields might have play in determining purely executive action. The "hearing" is the hearing of evidence and argument. If the one who determines the facts which underlie the order has not considered evidence or argument, it is manifest that the hearing has not been given.

There is thus no basis for the contention that the authority conferred by Section 310 of the Packers and Stockyards Act is given to the Department of Agriculture, as a department in the administrative sense, so that one official may examine evidence, and another official who has not considered the evidence may make the findings and order. In such a view, it would be possible, for example, for one official to hear the evidence and argument and arrive at certain conclusions of fact, and another official who had not heard or considered either evidence or argument to overrule those conclusions and for reasons of policy to announce entirely different ones. It is no answer to say that the question for the court is whether the evidence supports the findings and the findings support the order. For the weight ascribed by the law to the findings—their conclusiveness when made within the sphere of the authority conferred—rests upon the assumption that the officer who makes the findings has addressed himself to the evidence and upon that evidence has conscientiously reached the conclusions which he deems it to justify. That duty cannot be performed by one who has not considered evidence or argument. It is not an impersonal obligation. It is a duty akin to that of a judge. The one who decides must hear.

This necessary rule does not preclude practicable administrative procedure in obtaining the aid of assistants in the department. Assistants may prosecute inquiries. Evidence may be taken by an examiner. Evidence thus taken may be sifted and analyzed by competent subordinates. Argument may be oral or written. The requirements are not technical. But there must be a hearing in a substantial sense. And to give the substance of a hearing, which is for the purpose of making determinations upon evidence, the officer who makes the determinations must consider and appraise the evidence which justifies them. That duty undoubtedly may be an onerous one, but the performance of it in a substantial manner is inseparable from the exercise of the important authority conferred. . . .

Our conclusion is that the District Court erred in striking out the allegations of Paragraph IV of the bill of complaint with respect to the Secretary's action. The defendants should be required to answer these allegations and the question whether plaintiffs had a proper hearing should be determined.

The decree is reversed and the cause is remanded for further proceedings in conformity with this opinion.

Morgan v. United States

Supreme Court of the United States, 1938.
304 U.S. 1.

■ Mr. Chief Justice Hughes delivered the opinion for the Court:

[The trial held on remand permitted the Court to assess the procedures that had actually been followed by the Secretary:]

. . . The original administrative proceeding was begun on April 7, 1930, when the Secretary of Agriculture issued an order of inquiry and notice of hearing with respect to the reasonableness of the charges of appellants for stockyards services at Kansas City. The taking of evidence before an examiner of the Department was begun on December 3, 1930, and continued until February 10, 1931. The Government and appellants were represented by counsel and voluminous testimony and exhibits were introduced. In March, 1931, oral argument was had before the Acting Secretary of Agriculture and appellants submitted a brief. On May 18, 1932, the Secretary issued his findings and an order prescribing maximum rates. In view of changed economic conditions, the Secretary vacated that order and granted a rehearing. That was begun on October 6, 1932, and the taking of evidence was concluded on November 16, 1932. The evidence received at the first hearing was re-submitted and this was supplemented by additional testimony and exhibits. On March 24, 1933, oral argument was had before Rexford G. Tugwell as Acting Secretary.

It appears that there were about 10,000 pages of transcript of oral evidence and over 1,000 pages of statistical exhibits. The oral argument was general and sketchy. Appellants submitted the brief which they had presented after the first administrative hearing and a supplemental brief dealing with the evidence introduced upon the rehearing. No brief was at any time supplied by the Government. Apart from what was said on its behalf in the oral argument, the Government formulated no issues and furnished appellants no statement or summary of its contentions and no proposed findings. Appellants' request that the examiner prepare a tentative report, to be submitted as a basis for exceptions and argument, was refused.

Findings were prepared in the Bureau of Animal Industry, Department of Agriculture, whose representatives had conducted the proceedings for the Government, and were submitted to the Secretary, who signed them, with a few changes in the rates, when his order was made on June 14, 1933. These findings, 180 in number, were elaborate. ... No opportunity was afforded to appellants for the examination of the findings thus prepared in the Bureau of Animal Industry until they were served with the order. Appellants sought a rehearing by the Secretary but their application was denied on July 6, 1933, and these suits followed.

The part taken by the Secretary himself in the departmental proceedings is shown by his full and candid testimony. The evidence had been received before he took office. He did not hear the oral argument. The bulky record was placed upon his desk and he dipped into it from time to time to get its drift. He decided that probably the essence of the evidence was contained in appellants' briefs. These, together with the transcript of the oral argument, he took home with him and read. He had several conferences with the Solicitor of the Department and with the officials in the Bureau of Animal Industry and discussed the proposed findings. He testified that he considered the evidence before signing the order. The substance of his action is stated in his answer to the question whether the order represented his independent conclusion, as follows:

> My answer to the question would be that that very definitely was my independent conclusion as based on the findings of the men in the Bureau of Animal Industry. I would say, I will try to put it as accurately as possible, that it represented my own independent reactions to the findings of the men in the Bureau of Animal Industry.

Save for certain rate alterations, he "accepted the findings."

In the light of this testimony there is no occasion to discuss the extent to which the Secretary examined the evidence, and we agree with the Government's contention that it was not the function of the court to probe the mental processes of the Secretary in reaching his conclusions if he gave the hearing which the law required. The Secretary read the summary presented by appellants' briefs and he conferred with his subordinates who had sifted and analyzed the evidence. We assume that the Secretary sufficiently understood its purport. But a "full hearing"—a fair and open hearing—requires more than that. The right to a hearing embraces not only the right to present evidence but also a reasonable opportunity to know the claims of the opposing party and to meet them. The right to submit argument implies that opportunity; otherwise the right may be but a barren one. Those who are brought into contest with the Government in a quasi-judicial proceeding aimed at the control of their activities are entitled to be fairly advised of what the Government proposes and to be heard upon its proposals before it issues its final command.

No such reasonable opportunity was accorded appellants. The administrative proceeding was initiated by a notice of inquiry into the reasonableness of appellants' rates. No specific complaint was formulated. . . . In the absence of any report by the examiner or any findings proposed by the Government, and thus without any concrete statement of the Government's claims, the parties approached the oral argument.

Nor did the oral argument reveal these claims in any appropriate manner. The discussion by counsel for the Government was "very general," as he said, in order not to take up "too much time." It dealt with generalities both as to principles and procedure. . . .

Congress, in requiring a "full hearing," had regard to judicial standards—not in any technical sense but with respect to those fundamental requirements of fairness which are of the essence of due process in a proceeding of a judicial nature. If in an equity cause, a special master or the trial judge permitted the plaintiff's attorney to formulate the findings upon the evidence, conferred ex parte with the plaintiff's attorney regarding them, and then adopted his proposals without affording an opportunity to his opponent to know their contents and present objections, there would be no hesitation in setting aside the report or decree as having been made without a fair hearing. The requirements of fairness are not exhausted in the taking or consideration of evidence but extend to the concluding parts of the procedure as well as to the beginning and intermediate steps.

The answer that the proceeding before the Secretary was not of an adversary character, as it was not upon complaint but was initiated as a general inquiry, is futile. . . . In all substantial respects, the Government acting through the Bureau of Animal Industry of the Department was prosecuting the proceeding against the owners of the market agencies. The proceeding had all the essential elements of contested litigation, with the Government and its counsel on the one side and the appellants and their counsel on the other. It is idle to say that this was not a proceeding in reality against the appellants when the very existence of their agencies was put in jeopardy. Upon the rates for their services the owners depended for their livelihood, and the proceeding attacked them at a vital spot. . . .

The Government adverts to an observation in our former opinion that, while it was good practice—which we approved—to have the examiner, receiving the evidence in such a case, prepare a report as a basis for exceptions and argument, we could not say that that particular type of procedure was essential to the validity of the proceeding. That is true, for, as we said, what the statute requires "relates to substance and not form." . . . But what would not be essential to the adequacy of the hearing if the

Secretary himself makes the findings is not a criterion for a case in which the Secretary accepts and makes as his own the findings which have been prepared by the active prosecutors for the Government, after an ex parte discussion with them and without according any reasonable opportunity to the respondents in the proceeding to know the claims thus presented and to contest them. That is more than an irregularity in practice; it is a vital defect. . . .

As the hearing was fatally defective, the order of the Secretary was invalid. In this view, we express no opinion upon the merits. The decree of the District Court is

Reversed.

■ MR. JUSTICE BLACK dissents.

■ MR. JUSTICE CARDOZO and MR. JUSTICE REED took no part in the consideration and decision of this case.

NOTES

(1) *Morgan's Meaning.* The two Morgan cases just excerpted are the first and second Supreme Court efforts in a series of four decisions that, in each case, emphatically reversed the court of appeals. The fourth and last of these, 313 U.S. 409 (1941), resurfaced in the Overton Park case discussed at p. 989 below. Together with Morgan II's agreement "with the Government's contention that it was not the function of the court to probe the mental processes of the Secretary in reaching his conclusions if he gave the hearing which the law required," Morgan IV served to "place[ ] a veil of secrecy over the 'mental process' of the decision makers" in administrative proceedings. Daniel Gifford, The Morgan Cases: A Retrospective View, 30 Ad.L.Rev. 237 (1978). Note that Morgan I reviewed a judgment entered on the pleadings about a decision the Secretary of Agriculture made in 1933; Morgan II, reviewing the result of the ensuing trial, concerned the same 1933 decision. Together, the cases set a framework for analyzing high-level consideration of hearing records that remains influential to this day.

Does Morgan II fault the hearing officer for having failed to prepare an initial or recommended decision disclosing his own views about the case, to aid the Secretary? The Court's contemporaneous decision in NLRB v. MACKAY RADIO & TELEGRAPH CO., 304 U.S. 333 (1938) made clear that no such report was required; the issue was notice. In Mackay, the Labor Board had issued a formal complaint that the Company had discharged five men because of their union activities. After a trial examiner heard the evidence, and before either oral argument before the trial examiner or the making of an intermediate report by him, the Board transferred the case to Washington for its own decision. The Supreme Court found no problem in this procedure: "All parties to the proceeding knew from the outset that the thing complained of was discrimination against certain men by reason of their alleged union activities. . . . A review of the record shows that at no time during the hearings was there any misunderstanding as to what was the basis of the Board's complaint. . . . [Since] the issues and contentions of the parties were clearly defined and as no other detriment or disadvantage is claimed . . . the matter is not one calling for a reversal of the order. The Fifth Amendment guarantees no particular form of procedure; it protects substantial rights. . . ."

Section 557(b) of the Administrative Procedure Act subsequently provided that after a required trial-type hearing, the presiding employee (usually be an ALJ), "shall initially decide the case unless the agency requires, either in specific cases or by general rule, the entire record to be certified to it for decision." Even in those cases (with a few exceptions), either the person who presided over the hearing or another fully qualified person must "first recommend a decision"—a document clearly to be shared with the parties. Omission of an intermediate report of this character was sustained however, in an unusually protracted case that the Federal Communications Commission was pushing vigorously to conclusion. Communications Satellite Corp. v. FCC, 611 F.2d 883 (D.C.Cir.1977).

(2) *Institutional Decision.* Even putting aside the influence and demands of the Secretary's many other responsibilities, the size and complexity of his task in Morgan evidently moved the Court. He had a need for expert assistance and shared responsibilities, like that encountered in SAPL and in the Central Platte River case, 378. Used to the personally responsible judge, lawyers generally detest the anonymity of the "institutional decision." They believe that it encourages resort to information not embodied in the evidence of record; they fear that staff members with ideological axes to grind may exert an undetectable pressure upon the agency's announced judgment; they think that agency heads who are not themselves immersed in the facts of a case or who have not themselves weighed the arguments are especially easy prey for outside influences of various kinds.

On the other hand, institutional decisions are commonplaces of life outside the courtroom. Executives responsible for any large non-governmental organization, for example, would be surprised to learn that cutting themselves off from staff assistants would somehow make their decisions wiser or fairer. When various insights may enter into an important industrial judgment (such as whether a plant should be closed or whether a new manufacturing process should be initiated or whether funds for expansion should be raised by one device instead of another), business executives expect that economists, lawyers, engineers, public relations specialists, accountants, sales staff, and assorted underlings will cooperate in shaping the decision. The successful executive is usually more concerned about arriving at a sound decision than about her own virtuoso performance, more interested in results than in precedents. What is true of the business bureaucracy is equally true of other major non-governmental undertakings. In few universities, service clubs, trade associations, labor unions, or civic organizations, for example, do the chief officers individually form the conclusions they announce.

Writing at the time of Morgan, one analyst noted: "[Morgan I] seems so eminently reasonable on its face that some explanation is needed before its revolutionary character can be appreciated. The Secretary of Agriculture administers forty-two regulatory statutes. In addition, he administers a host of non-regulatory statutes, some of them, like the Soil Conservation and Domestic Allotment Act, of high national importance. Finally, he is a major political officer and takes part in the formulation of national policy as a member of the Cabinet. If he were to give to every order which he signs the consideration which the Morgan case requires, he would probably have to devote all his time to the conduct of matters which must be considered petty from a national viewpoint.

"What is to be done about this situation? Should the function of making orders be delegated to subordinate officials? There is considerable psychological value in having the signature of the Secretary himself on the order. It would carry less weight if signed by an unknown subordinate. There is also the danger of a relaxation of responsibility in case of a complete delegation. Even if the Secretary does not give full consideration to the evidence, he at least brings his attention to bear upon the problem and does review the order, however sketchily, before signing it." A. H. Feller, Prospectus for the Further Study of Federal Administrative Law, 47 Yale L.J. 647, 662–663 (1938).

(3) *Delegating the Judicial Function to Others.* Complete delegation of decisional power is exactly what did occur in the Agriculture Department as the end result of the Morgan series. Exercising power conferred on him to organize the department and to prescribe the duties of its officials, the Secretary of Agriculture in 1945 sloughed off even his nominal responsibility for decisions to be made on the record after a trial-type hearing. He vested final authority in such matters in the "Judicial Officer" of the Department of Agriculture, who issues final departmental decisions in his own name.

What are the hazards of such a delegation? In UTICA PACKING CO. V. BLOCK, 781 F.2d 71 (6th Cir.1986), a meat packer had initially been denied inspection facilities—debarred from the meat packing business—after a finding he had bribed inspectors. The Sixth Circuit had reversed that order because the Judicial Officer had failed to consider claimed mitigating circumstances. 705 F.2d 460. On remand, the Judicial Officer took the Sixth Circuit's action as in effect an instruction to let Utica Packing off the hook, and he did so. This outraged departmental officials, but they had no authority to seek judicial review of an order favorable to Utica Packing. They therefore arranged for the appointment of another Department of Agriculture official (one with no prior connection to the proceedings) as Judicial Officer pro tem, and moved this replacement official for reconsideration. So far as appeared, this proceeding was completely regular—without, for example, any ex parte communications to the new Judicial Officer what he should do. He reinstated the previous order, and Utica Packing again sought review. How should the case be argued for the Department? Utica Packing? Decided? Compare Kalaris v. Donovan, 697 F.2d 376, 397 (D.C.Cir.1983), cert. denied 462 U.S. 1119 (1983), finding that the members of the Department of Labor's Benefits Review Board "in the absence of a congressional statement to the contrary, ... serve indefinite terms at the discretion of their appointing officers"—so that they may be summarily removed from their posts.[1]

The Administrative Conference of the United States[2] commissioned two studies of agencies' delegations of adjudicative decisional authority to committed judicial officers or panels operating below the agency's political head. Both found and thoughtfully described a wide variety of institutional arrangements and experiences. Neither thought a single solution appropriate. Based on a 1983 study, Ronald A. Cass, Allocation of Authority in Bureaucracies: Empirical Evidence and Normative Analysis, 66 B.U.L.Rev. 1 (1986) found it hard to tell whether varying arrangements lead to

---

1. The court went on to find the arrangement "clearly constitutional" despite the spectre that the dismissal power would permit the Secretary to influence claims decisions outside the review process by replacing

the Board. "Congress has been creating quasi-judicial boards subject to Executive control for years, and the courts have not previously prevented them from doing so." At 401.

2. See p. 479 below.

concrete differences in result and thought "the frequent assertion of positive effects as the basis for a choice among alternative administrative processes ... misleading. The processes have relatively slight impact on empirical measures of agency decisionmaking, so far as can be ascertained from currently available data." Again surveying agency practices ten years later, Russell L. Weaver, Appellate Review in Executive Departments and Agencies, 48 Admin. L. Rev. 251 (1996) saw both advantages and disadvantages to "this trend toward depriving agency heads of their appellate review authority"—advantages in greater effective participatory rights for the parties in dealing with a committed judicial officer or review panel than a multi-function and political agency head, greater objectivity and continuity of decision, and greater incentive for the agency heads to do their policymaking by rulemaking; disadvantages in the possible conflicts or loss of control over important policy issues that could result, and the arguably deeper understanding available to the agency's head rather than a functionary. In the end, he thought the best arrangements were ones that committed routine matters to a committed appellate body, but permitted the agency head to claim major policy questions for her own decision on a discretionary basis.

(4) *The Split Enforcement Model.* As with OSHA and OSHRC, Congress has occasionally created a bureaucratic structure explicitly separating quasi-legislative and quasi-executive from quasi-judicial responsibilities. DANIEL J. GIFFORD, ADJUDICATION IN INDEPENDENT ADMINISTRATIVE TRIBUNALS: THE ROLE OF AN ALTERNATIVE AGENCY STRUCTURE, 66 Notre D.L.Rev. 965 (1991): "The structure of the highly visible regulatory agencies has largely shaped thinking about administrative law over the past half century. ... [T]raditional agency structure was designed to regulate by formulating policies in the adjudicatory process, and ... when policymaking through adjudication becomes impractical or inefficient, the structure of agency organization should, and generally does, change ... towards an organizational design in which the adjudicating tribunal is separate, practically if not always formally, from the policymakers. ...

"In the alternative administrative structure ... policy is developed through rulemaking, and the rulemaking organ does not participate in adjudication, except as a party. If the agency is administering a regulatory program, that same agency institutes enforcement proceedings against private parties who fail to comply with its policies. Or, if the program involves the distribution of benefits, the agency supervises the administration of the program, inter alia, by issuing rules when required. These agencies differ from the traditional regulatory agency because the agency head does not control the outcome of particular adjudications. ... Agency decisionmaking structures of this alternative type can be found both in state and federal regulatory and benefit systems. New York, for example, provides that the decision of the Industrial Commissioner administering the unemployment insurance laws is subject to review by an administrative law judge whose decision is, in turn, reviewed by an Unemployment Insurance Appeal Board with further review in the courts. ... On the federal level, the administration of OSHA, the Federal Mine Safety and Health Act, the Social Security disability program, the Veterans Administration, and the adjudicatory role of the National Transportation Safety

Board over the certificate suspension and revocation orders of the Secretary of Transportation are examples of similar nontraditional administrative structures.''

That policy is developed through rulemaking under a split enforcement model such as Professor Gifford has described leaves open the hard question how best to assure its intended implementation, highlighting the tradeoffs between coherence and individual fairness. If the rulemaking agency is empowered to seek judicial review of the adjudicating agency's decisions, it may be able to make its interpretations prevail, Martin v. OSHRC, 499 U.S. 144 (1991), but only by invoking yet another external body, the judiciary. Other treatments of the split-administration model include Richard H. Fallon, Jr., Enforcing Aviation Safety Regulations: The Case for A Split–Enforcement Model of Agency Adjudication, 4 Am.U.Admin.L.J. 389 (1991); George R. Johnson, Jr., The Split–Enforcement Model, Some Conclusions from the OSHA and MSHA Experiences, 39 Admin.L.Rev. 315 (1987).

(5) *Enhancing the ALJ's Fact-Finding Function.* Some part of these difficulties may seem to lie in the practice of treating the agency as the factfinder, rather than as a reviewer of facts found by a more objective other. Occasional statutory provisions like the Black Lung Benefits Act, 30 U.S.C. §§ 901–45, require agency reviewers to accept any ALJ factual finding supported by substantial evidence, converting the agency head into a review tribunal; in the view of Paul Verkuil, Daniel Gifford, Charles Koch, Jr., Richard Pierce, Jr. and Jeffrey Lubbers, The Federal Administrative Judiciary 168 (1992): "Conferring a high degree of finality on ALJ findings of fact is virtually certain to create interdecisional inconsistency, costly and time consuming battles for institutional hegemony, and policymaking cacophony. It will also raise serious questions concerning the constitutionality of any selection process that does not confer a broad power to appoint on the President, a cabinet officer, or a court of law."[3]

Proposals for dealing with the serious backlog of immigration cases in the Department of Justice's Executive Office of Immigration Review in 2002 included requiring the Board of Immigration Appeals to accept any immigration judge fact-finding that was not "clearly erroneous." Opposition to the proposal strikes these themes and also suggests, as a further impact, its implications for judicial review, and for BIA flexibility in asylum cases like Castillo–Villagra. Sometimes an ALJ's conclusions will have a practical finality, as may be suggested by a record like that in Morgan, or in the photograph opposite. The materials of Chapter VIII, § 3 treating substantial evidence review—notably Universal Camera Corp. v. NLRB, p. 940 below—illustrate the role that an administrative law judge's *report* plays in agency process. The weight assigned it on judicial review (of what are understood to be the *agency's* findings of fact) will permits us to see that report as one of the important instruments by which "separation of

---

3. [Ed.] The reference here is to Freytag v. Commissioner, 501 U.S. 868 (1991), 174 above. Even if we may describe as a mere "employee" an ALJ whose judgment will be wholly displaced by that of her agency in the event it is challenged, the authors implicitly argue, we may have to regard as an "inferior Officer" an ALJ whose judgment will not be so displaced.

functions" objectivity is enforced in the agency setting. The agency (which almost inevitably transcends those separations) must pay a "substantial evidence" price for any disagreement it may have with its hearing officer (who does not transcend those separations) as to the facts of the matter before it.

(6) DANIEL J. GIFFORD, THE MORGAN CASES: A RETROSPECTIVE VIEW, 30 Ad. L.Rev. 237, 256–57, 259 (1978): "That approximately 11,000 pages of transcript and exhibits had to be evaluated suggests that the major decisional problem in the Morgan cases was one of synthesizing vast amounts of material into an understandable form. But the Court never really addressed itself to the process of synthesis and evaluation, except negatively. It objected to the synthesizing function being performed off-the-record by officials from the Bureau of Animal Industry, but it did not suggest how that function ought to be performed. The Court said that the Secretary could use assistants to 'sift' and 'analyze' evidence, but that his decision nonetheless must be a 'personal' one based upon his own weighing of the evidence. It is unclear how the assistants may both sift and analyze on one hand, while the Secretary, on the other hand, makes a personal decision by weighing the evidence himself. The Court might have been thinking of the personal responsibility of a judge, who nevertheless receives assistance from his law clerk. Extrapolated to the functioning of a large agency, the Secretary might be said to decide 'personally' when he closely supervises his assistants and discusses their conclusions with them. Yet the line between the close supervision of assistants and a 'departmental' decision-making process which the Court condemned as impersonal is not easily drawn.

Photo by Robert Phillips—Courtesy of FORTUNE Magazine

"This paper mountain is only part of the testimony and documents pertaining to a single FPC gas case. The hearings to determine which new pipe line should be certified to serve midwestern markets ran for 143 days. Every one had his say *in extenso* and no doubt FPC hearing examiners like Edward B. Marsh, above, read each of the thousands of transcript pages. To the commissioners, however, they are mainly a monument to free speech. Said one: 'The industry spends so much time developing the records, they run from 10,000 to 20,000 pages, but we just haven't the time to read them' ", R.A. Smith, The Unnatural Problems of Natural Gas, 60 FORTUNE 120 (Sept. 1959).

"But there is more at stake than just the condensing of data. In a rate proceeding like that involved in the Morgan cases, there is likely to be little dispute as to what physical events did or did not transpire. Rather, it is the significance of those events which tends to be disputed, and it is the methods employed to evaluate the events which are crucial to the decision. While in a typical negligence trial the issues may be simple and the processes of evaluating the evidence require only the application of ordinary experience, in technical litigation the function of synthesizing the vast quantity of data into an understandable form and the process of evaluating it require both substantial time and special skills. Yet, the busy head of a large agency cannot normally devote a large amount of time to a single case, and he may not possess the necessary skills. Thus, it is both the mass of data and the complexities of the evaluation process which magnify the decision-making burden. . . .

"When the drafters of the APA incorporated the mechanism of a preliminary decision issued prior to final argument before the agency, they had been educated by the first two Morgan decisions and the Ohio Bell decision. Those decisions dramatized the decisional problems faced by a large, centralized agency in evaluating masses of data and complex exhibits. The drafters recognized that a means needed to be found for focusing the issues which did not command a large amount of the decision maker's time. They opted for a means involving a preliminary decision plus argument. As they saw it, that mechanism not only reduced the need for behind-the-scenes participation in the decisional process by the agency's employees (who have played an adversarial role in the formal proceedings), but it also permitted the parties to participate to a greater degree in the process of evaluating the evidence."

(7) Reconsider in the light of Morgan, the EPA Administrator's use of a panel of agency experts to permit him to master the record and issues in SAPL. How, if at all, does this differ from a judge's use of a law clerk? May such a clerk be instructed to search published works for judicially noticeable propositions about general fact—for example, what the psychological literature teaches about the capacity of persons acting in a official capacity to disregard information they may previously have encountered in that capacity, when their present responsibilities for decision limit them to a record subsequently made before them?

b.   THE IMPACT OF MULTIPLE ROLES

Most administrative agencies carry out multiple functions, as investigators, enforcers and rule-makers as well as adjudicators; at the top of the agency, its leadership may be performing all of these functions. This is the characteristic that most sharply distinguishes these agencies from courts—from Article I courts like the Tax Court, bankruptcy courts, or the Federal Claims Court as well as from Article III courts. Precisely because the agency head, unlike an ALJ, is not a committed, single-function adjudicator, she may have views that arise from prior activities in *other* functions, as investigator, rulemaker, congressional witness, or featured luncheon speaker, *before* she is asked to resolve the same issues in on-the-record adjudication; or she may be dealing with both simultaneously.

Where these views concern policy, it is perhaps easy to see that they are of limited concern. Although the wisdom or even the permissibility of a given policy or rule may be open to heated debate, persistent support of particular policies is what the public expects (and does not always receive) from its administrators, not an ill to be guarded against. Indeed, judges are not expected to "be neutral toward the purposes of the law" they enforce. Louis L. Jaffe, The Reform of Administrative Procedure, 2 Pub.Admin.Rev. 141, 149 (1942). No more are administrators supposed to lack enthusiasm for the policies they believe to be embodied in the statutes they administer. If the FTC is poorly disposed toward anti-competitive activity, or a workers' compensation board tends to resolve doubtful points in favor of allegedly disabled claimants, each can be accused only of carrying out the policy it was established to administer.

Does prior official exposure as Commissioners to particular *facts* controverted in on-the-record proceedings raise additional difficulties?

Federal Trade Commission v. Cement Institute

Supreme Court of the United States, 1948.
333 U.S. 683.

■ JUSTICE BLACK delivered the opinion of the Court.

We granted certiorari to review the decree of the Circuit Court of Appeals which, with one judge dissenting, vacated and set aside a cease and desist order issued by the Federal Trade Commission against the respondents. 7 Cir., 157 F.2d 533. Those respondents are: The Cement Institute, an unincorporated trade association composed of 74 corporations which manufacture, sell and distribute cement; the 74 corporate members of the Institute; and 21 individuals who are associated with the Institute. It took three years for a trial examiner to hear the evidence which consists of about 49,000 pages of oral testimony and 50,000 pages of exhibits. Even the findings and conclusions of the Commission cover 176 pages. The briefs with accompanying appendixes submitted by the parties contain more than 4,000 pages. The legal questions raised by the Commission and by the different respondents are many and varied. . . .

The proceedings were begun by a Commission complaint of two counts. The first charged that certain alleged conduct set out at length constituted an unfair method of competition in violation of § 5 of the Federal Trade Commission Act. 15 U.S.C. § 45. The core of the charge was that the respondents had restrained and hindered competition in the sale and distribution of cement by means of a combination among themselves made effective through mutual understanding or agreement to employ a multiple basing point system of pricing. It was alleged that this system resulted in the quotation of identical terms of sale and identical prices for cement by the respondents at any given point in the United States. This system had worked so successfully, it was further charged, that for many years prior to the filing of the complaint, all cement buyers throughout the nation, with rare exceptions, had been unable to purchase cement for delivery in any given locality from any one of the respondents at a lower price or on more favorable terms than from any of the other respondents.

The second count of the complaint, resting chiefly on the same allegations of fact set out in Count I, charged that the multiple basing point system of sales resulted in systematic price discriminations between the customers of each respondent. . . .

[The "multiple basing point delivered price system" worked as follows: The companies quoted prices of cement as delivered to the customer. They based these prices on the selling price at one of several fixed points, plus freight charges to the customer's location, regardless of whether the cement was actually shipped from that point. All sellers used the same system, and therefore quoted identical prices, regardless of their actual costs of production or of shipment.]

Resting upon its findings, the Commission ordered that respondents cease and desist from "carrying out any planned common course of action, understanding, agreement, combination, or conspiracy" to do a number of things, 37 F.T.C. 97, 258–262, all of which things, the Commission argues, had to be restrained in order effectively to restore individual freedom of action among the separate units in the cement industry. . . . [I]f the order stands, its terms are broad enough to bar respondents from acting in concert to sell cement on a basing point delivered price plan which so eliminates competition that respondents' prices are always identical at any given point in the United States.

Jurisdiction [omitted]

Alleged Bias of the Commission.—One year after the taking of testimony had been concluded and while these proceedings were still pending before the Commission, the respondent Marquette asked the Commission to disqualify itself from passing upon the issues involved. Marquette charged that the Commission had previously prejudged the issues, was "prejudiced and biased against the Portland cement industry generally," and that the industry and Marquette in particular could not receive a fair hearing from the Commission. After hearing oral argument the Commission refused to disqualify itself. . . .

Marquette introduced numerous exhibits intended to support its charges. In the main these exhibits were copies of the Commission's reports made to Congress or to the President, as required by § 6 of the Trade Commission Act. These reports, as well as the testimony given by members of the Commission before congressional committees, make it clear that long before the filing of this complaint the members of the Commission at that time, or at least some of them, were of the opinion that the operation of the multiple basing point system as they had studied it was the equivalent of a price fixing restraint of trade in violation of the Sherman Act. We therefore decide this contention, as did the Circuit Court of Appeals, on the assumption that such an opinion had been formed by the entire membership of the Commission as a result of its prior official investigations. But we also agree with that court's holding that this belief did not disqualify the Commission.

In the first place, the fact that the Commission had entertained such views as the result of its prior ex parte investigations did not necessarily mean that the minds of its members were irrevocably closed on the subject of the respondents' basing point practices. Here, in contrast to the Commission's investigations, members of the cement industry were legally authorized participants in the hearings. They produced evidence—volumes of it. They were free to point out to the Commission by testimony, by cross-examination of witnesses, and by arguments, conditions of the trade practices under attack which they thought kept these practices within the range of legally permissible business activities.

Moreover, Marquette's position, if sustained, would to a large extent defeat the congressional purposes which prompted passage of the Trade Commission Act. Had the entire membership of the Commission disqualified in the proceedings against these respondents, this complaint could not have been acted upon by the Commission or by any other government agency. Congress has provided for no such contingency. It has not directed that the Commission disqualify itself under any circumstances, has not provided for substitute commissioners should any of its members disqualify, and has not authorized any other government agency to hold hearings, make findings, and issue cease and desist orders in proceedings against unfair trade practices. Yet if Marquette is right, the Commission, by making studies and filing reports in obedience to congressional command, completely immunized the practices investigated, even though they are "unfair," from any cease and desist order by the Commission or any other governmental agency.

There is no warrant in the Act for reaching a conclusion which would thus frustrate its purposes. If the Commission's opinions expressed in congressionally required reports would bar its members from acting in unfair trade proceedings, it would appear that opinions expressed in the first basing point unfair trade proceeding would similarly disqualify them from ever passing on another. Thus experience acquired from their work as commissioners would be a handicap instead of an advantage. . . .

The Commission properly refused to disqualify itself. . . .

Findings and Evidence . . .

The Commission's findings of fact set out at great length and with painstaking detail numerous concerted activities carried on in order to make the multiple basing point system work in such way that competition in quality, price and terms of sale of cement would be nonexistent, and that uniform prices, job contracts, discounts, and terms of sale would be continuously maintained. The Commission found that many of these activities were carried on by the Cement Institute, the industry's unincorporated trade association, and that in other instances the activities were under the immediate control of groups of respondents. Among the collective methods used to accomplish these purposes, according to the findings, were boycotts; discharge of uncooperative employees; organized opposition to the erection of new cement plants; selling cement in a recalcitrant price cutter's sales territory at a price so low that the recalcitrant was forced to adhere to the established basing point prices; discouraging the shipment of cement by truck or barge; and preparing and distributing freight rate books which provided respondents with similar figures to use as actual or "phantom" freight factors, thus guaranteeing that their delivered prices (base prices plus freight factors) would be identical on all sales whether made to individual purchasers under open bids or to governmental agencies under sealed bids. These are but a few of the many activities of respondents which the Commission found to have been done in combination to reduce or destroy price competition in cement. . . .

Although there is much more evidence to which reference could be made, we think that the following facts shown by evidence in the record, some of which are in dispute, are sufficient to warrant the Commission's finding of concerted action.

When the Commission rendered its decision there were about 80 cement manufacturing companies in the United States operating about 150 mills. Ten companies controlled more than half of the mills and there were substantial corporate affiliations among many of the others. This concentration of productive capacity made concerted action far less difficult than it would otherwise have been. Out of those activities came the multiple basing point delivered price system. Evidence shows it to be a handy instrument to bring about elimination of any kind of price competition. . . . Thousands of secret sealed bids have been received by public agencies which corresponded in prices of cement down to a fractional part of a penny.[1]

. . . Respondents offered testimony that cement is a standardized product, that "cement is cement," that no differences existed in quality or usefulness, and that purchasers demanded delivered price quotations because of the high cost of transportation from mill to dealer. . . . Respondents introduced the testimony of economists to the effect that competition alone could lead to the evolution of a multiple basing point system of uniform delivered prices and terms of sale for an industry with a standardized product and with relatively high freight costs. These economists testified that for the above reasons no inferences of collusion, agreement, or understanding could be drawn from the admitted fact that cement prices of all United States producers had for many years almost invariably been the same in every given locality in the country. There was also considerable testimony by other economic experts that the multiple basing point system of delivered prices as employed by respondents contravened accepted economic principles and could only have been maintained through collusion. . . . [T]he Commission was not compelled to accept the views of respondents' economist-witnesses that active competition was bound to produce uniform cement prices. . . .

---

1. The following is one among many of the Commission's findings as to the identity of sealed bids: An abstract of the bids for 6,000 barrels of cement to the United States Engineer Office at Tucumcari, New Mexico, opened April 23, 1936, shows the following:

Name of Bidder	Price per Bbl.
Monarch	$3.286854
Ash Grove	3.286854
Lehigh	3.286854
Southwestern	3.286854
U.S. Portland Cement Co.	3.286854
Oklahoma	3.286854
Consolidated	3.286854
Trinity	3.286854
Lone Star	3.286854
Universal	3.286854
Colorado	3.286854

All bids subject to 10 cents per barrel discount for payment in 15 days. (Com.Ex. 175–A.) See 157 F.2d at 576.

Unfair Methods of Competition.—We sustain the Commission's holding that concerted maintenance of the basing point delivered price system is an unfair method of competition prohibited by the Federal Trade Commission Act. In so doing we give great weight to the Commission's conclusion, as this Court has done in other cases. Federal Trade Commission v. R. F. Keppel & Bro., 291 U.S. 304. In the Keppel case the Court called attention to the express intention of Congress to create an agency whose membership would at all times be experienced, so that its conclusions would be the result of an expertness coming from experience. We are persuaded that the Commission's long and close examination of the questions it here decided has provided it with precisely the experience that fits it for performance of its statutory duty. The kind of specialized knowledge Congress wanted its agency to have was an expertness that would fit it to stop at the threshold every unfair trade practice. . . .

[The Court's discussion of the price discrimination charge stated in count two is omitted.]

The Commission's order should not have been set aside by the Circuit Court of Appeals. Its judgment is reversed and the cause is remanded to that court with directions to enforce the order. It is so ordered.

Reversed and remanded.

■ JUSTICE DOUGLAS and JUSTICE JACKSON took no part in the consideration or decision of these cases.

■ [Dissent of JUSTICE BURTON omitted.]

NOTES

(1) JAMES M. LANDIS, THE ADMINISTRATIVE PROCESS 35–39 (1938):

"The demand for a power to initiate action was one of the primary purposes underlying the creation of the Federal Trade Commission. . . .

"The power to initiate action exists because it fulfills a long-felt need in our law. To restrict governmental intervention, in the determination of claims, to the position of an umpire deciding the merits upon the basis of the record as established by the parties, presumes the existence of an equality in the way of the respective power of the litigants to get at the facts. . . . In some spheres the absence of equal economic power generally is so prevalent that the umpire theory of administering law is almost certain to fail. Here government tends to offer its aid to a claimant, not so much because of the grave social import of the particular injury, but because the atmosphere and conditions created by an accumulation of such unredressed claims is of itself a serious social threat. . . .

"One other significant distinction between the administrative and the judicial processes is the power of 'independent' investigation possessed by the former. The test of the judicial process, traditionally, is not the fair disposition of the controversy; it is the fair disposition of the controversy *upon the record as made by the parties*. True, there are collateral sources of information which often affect judicial determinations. There is the more or less limited discretion under the doctrine of judicial notice; and there is the inarticulated but nonetheless substantial power to choose between competing premises based upon off-the-record considerations. But, in strictness, the judge must not know of the events of the controversy except as these may have been presented to him, in due form, by the parties. ...

"On the other hand, these characteristics, conspicuously absent from the judicial process, do attend the administrative process. For that process to be successful in a particular field, it is imperative that controversies be decided as 'rightly' as possible, independently of the formal record the parties themselves produce. The ultimate test of the administrative is the policy that it formulates; not the fairness as between the parties of the disposition of a controversy on a record of their own making."

(2) *Cement Institute Revisited.* Cement industry practices were again the subject of inquiry by the FTC's Bureau of Economics in the mid-'60's, leading to a 1966 Economic Report on Mergers and Vertical Integration in the Cement Industry. This staff report was the subject of public hearings, but the Commission in publishing it noted that it "has not approved, disapproved, or passed upon" it; no rule ever resulted from the analysis. In early 1967 the FTC did announce an enforcement policy; and in 1969, pursuing that policy, it issued a complaint challenging mid-'60's mergers of cement firms in the Kansas City Metropolitan Area—one of the twenty-two metropolitan areas that had been studied in the Economic Report. That complaint was sustained by an FTC ALJ after an extensive hearing, and then by the Commission. On appeal, the defendant, Ash Grove Cement Co., contended that the FTC's investigation of the cement industry and subsequent promulgation of the Economic Report and the Enforcement Policy caused it to prejudge the adjudicative proceeding below. ASH GROVE CEMENT Co. v. FTC, 577 F.2d 1368 (9th Cir.1978). The court had little difficulty rejecting this contention:

"Claims that an administrative agency is impermissibly biased because of its combination of investigative and adjudicative functions must overcome a presumption of honesty and integrity on the part of the decision-maker. ...

" ... That facts revealed by the staff investigation subsequently formed a part of the foundation for an enforcement proceeding is to be expected. Indeed, one of the purposes of industry investigations is to provide the agency with increased expertise in administering the law by exposing it to the factual background of relevant industries against which to judge individual mergers and acquisitions.

"Likewise, the fact that some of the Commissioners' conclusions expressed in the Enforcement Policy were mirrored in the complaint does not prove prejudgment.[1] The Enforcement Policy was openly cautious to phrase its conclusions tentatively. ...

" ... [I]t is incumbent on Ash Grove to make a showing that undue prejudice did occur. The facts suggest otherwise. In its proceeding against Ash Grove the FTC did not rely solely or even primarily on the Economic

---

1. Note that four of the five members of the Commission who decided the Ash Grove case (including three of the four-member majority) were not members of the Commission when the Enforcement Policy was developed.

Report or the Enforcement Policy to prove its case. Extensive independent evidence was introduced before the administrative law judge and was available upon review by the Commission. .... Ash Grove has not overcome the presumption of fairness by the FTC in its adjudicative enforcement procedures." The court then considered the sufficiency of the evidence, and the appropriateness of the remedy ordered, and upheld the Commission in all respects.

In Ash Grove Cement, however, the court was dealing with a large, busy agency—one structured below the very top to keep the work of investigating, prosecuting and judging in separate, if not watertight, compartments. It is unrealistic to regard most federal agencies as though all of their parts were moved by a single brain. On the whole, federal courts have been scantily impressed by lawyers' outcries against the combination of responsibilities to be found in large administrative bodies. Might a difference be perceived between such an agency and a smaller one, in which by hypothesis, the right hand may in fact know what the left hand is doing?

Withrow v. Larkin

Supreme Court of the United States, 1975.
421 U.S. 35.

■ MR. JUSTICE WHITE delivered the opinion of the Court.

[Appellee Larkin, a resident of Michigan, obtained a license to practice medicine in Wisconsin, and began performing abortions at a Milwaukee office, at a time when such operations were criminal acts. In June of 1973, he was informed that appellants, members of the state medical examining board, intended to conduct an investigation into certain aspects of his practice at a closed hearing which he and his attorney could attend. After unsuccessfully seeking to restrain the investigatory hearing, Larkin (through counsel) was present at the hearing; he was told that he could, if he wished, explain any of the evidence that had been presented, but was not otherwise invited to participate. In September, the board formally charged Larkin with practicing under an assumed name and other professional violations, and set a contested hearing for October. The possible outcomes of this hearing included temporary license suspension. Before the hearing could be held, Larkin persuaded a federal district court to restrain it pending trial of his claim that the statute was unconstitutional in its assignment of investigating and adjudicating roles to the same tribunal. Under distinct statutory authority, the Board then held a further investigatory hearing which resulted in a finding of "probable cause" to believe that Larkin had committed criminal violations of state law and a reference of the matter to the Milwaukee district attorney for prosecution in state court; possible outcomes in this proceeding included license revocation. A three-judge district court later found (after procedural complications not important to understanding here) that Larkin had shown a high likelihood of success in his constitutional claim not to be subjected to a contested hearing before the Board; accordingly, it enjoined preliminarily the conduct of the October hearing. The board then appealed to the Supreme Court.]

Concededly, a "fair trial in a fair tribunal is a basic requirement of due process." In re Murchison, 349 U.S. 133, 136 (1955). This applies to administrative agencies which adjudicate as well as to courts. Not only is a biased decisionmaker constitutionally unacceptable but "our system of law has always endeavored to prevent even the probability of unfairness." In pursuit of this end, various situations have been identified in which experience teaches that the probability of actual bias on the part of the judge or decisionmaker is too high to be constitutionally tolerable. Among these cases are those in which the adjudicator has a pecuniary interest in the outcome and in which he has been the target of personal abuse or criticism from the party before him.

The contention that the combination of investigative and adjudicative functions necessarily creates an unconstitutional risk of bias in administrative adjudication has a much more difficult burden of persuasion to carry. It must overcome a presumption of honesty and integrity in those serving as adjudicators; and it must convince that, under a realistic appraisal of psychological tendencies and human weakness, conferring investigative and adjudicative powers on the same individuals poses such a risk of actual bias or prejudgment that the practice must be forbidden if the guarantee of due process is to be adequately implemented. . . .

That is not to say that there is nothing to the argument that those who have investigated should not then adjudicate. The issue is substantial, it is not new, and legislators and others concerned with the operations of administrative agencies have given much attention to whether and to what extent distinctive administrative functions should be performed by the same persons. . . . Within the Federal Government itself, Congress has addressed the issue in several different ways, providing for varying degrees of separation from complete separation of functions to virtually none at all. For the generality of agencies, Congress has been content with § 5 of the Administrative Procedure Act, 5 U.S.C. § 554(d), which provides that no employee engaged in investigating or prosecuting may also participate or advise in the adjudicating function, but which also expressly exempts from this prohibition "the agency or a member or members of the body comprising the agency."

It is not surprising, therefore, to find that "[t]he case law, both federal and state, generally rejects the idea that the combination [of] judging [and] investigating functions is a denial of due process. . . ." 2 K. Davis, Administrative Law Treatise, § 13.02 (1958), at 175. Similarly, our cases, although they reflect the substance of the problem, offer no support for the bald proposition applied in this case by the District Court that agency members who participate in an investigation are disqualified from adjudicating. The incredible variety of administrative mechanisms in this country will not yield to any single organizing principle.

Appellee relies heavily on In re Murchison, supra, in which a state judge, empowered under state law to sit as a "one-man grand jury" and to compel witnesses to testify before him in secret about possible crimes, charged two such witnesses with criminal contempt, one for perjury and the other for refusing to answer certain questions, and then himself tried and convicted them. This Court found the procedure to be a denial of due process of law not only because the judge in effect became part of the prosecution and assumed an adversary position, but also because as a judge, passing on guilt or innocence, he very likely relied on "his own personal knowledge and impression of what had occurred in the grand jury room," an impression that "could not be tested by adequate cross-examination."

Plainly enough, Murchison has not been understood to stand for the broad rule that the members of an administrative agency may not investigate the facts, institute proceedings, and then make the necessary adjudications. The court did not . . . lay down any general principle that a judge before whom an alleged contempt is committed may not bring and preside over the ensuing contempt proceedings. The accepted rule is to the contrary.

Nor is there anything in this case that comes within the strictures of Murchison. When the Board instituted its investigative procedures, it stated only that it would investigate whether proscribed conduct had occurred. Later in noticing the adversary hearing, it asserted only that it would determine if violations had been committed which would warrant suspension of appellee's license. Without doubt, the Board then anticipated that the proceeding would eventuate in an adjudication of the issue; but there was no more evidence of bias or the risk of bias or prejudgment than inhered in the very fact that the Board had investigated and would now adjudicate.[1] Of course, we should be alert to the possibilities of bias that may lurk in the way particular procedures actually work in practice. The processes utilized by the Board, however, do not in themselves contain an unacceptable risk of bias. The investigative proceeding had been closed to the public, but appellee and his counsel were permitted to be present throughout; counsel actually attended the hearings and knew the facts presented to the Board. No specific foundation has been presented for suspecting that the Board had been prejudiced by its investigation or would be disabled from hearing and deciding on the basis of the evidence to be presented at the contested hearing. . . . Without a showing to the contrary, state administrators "are assumed to be men of conscience and intellectual discipline, capable of judging a particular controversy fairly on the basis of its own circumstances." United States v. Morgan, 313 U.S. 409, 421 (1941). . . .

Nor do we think the situation substantially different because the Board, when it was prevented from going forward with the contested hearing, proceeded to make and issue formal findings of fact and conclusions of law asserting that there was probable cause to believe that appellee had engaged in various acts prohibited by the Wisconsin statutes [, and transmitted them to the district attorney for his initiation of proceedings.]
. . .

Judges repeatedly issue arrest warrants on the basis that there is probable cause to believe that a crime has been committed and that the

---

1. Appellee does claim that state officials harassed him . . . because he performed abortions. . . . [T]he record does not provide a basis for finding . . . actual bias or prejudgment . . .

person named in the warrant has committed it. Judges also preside at preliminary hearings where they must decide whether the evidence is sufficient to hold a defendant for trial. Neither of these pretrial involvements has been thought to raise any constitutional barrier against the judge presiding over the criminal trial and, if the trial is without a jury, against making the necessary determination of guilt or innocence. Nor has it been thought that a judge is disqualified from presiding over injunction proceedings because he has initially assessed the facts in issuing or denying a temporary restraining order or a preliminary injunction. It is also very typical for the members of administrative agencies to receive the results of investigations, to approve the filing of charges or formal complaints instituting enforcement proceedings, and then to participate in the ensuing hearings. This mode of procedure does not violate the Administrative Procedure Act, and it does not violate due process of law. We should also remember that it is not contrary to due process to allow judges and administrators . . . reversed on appeal to confront the same questions a second time around. . . . [I]f the Board now proceeded after an adversary hearing to determine that appellee's license to practice should not be temporarily suspended, it would not implicitly be admitting error in its prior finding of probable cause. Its position most probably would merely reflect the benefit of a more complete view of the evidence afforded by an adversary hearing. . . .

That the combination of investigative and adjudicatory functions does not, without more, constitute a due process violation, does not, of course, preclude a court from determining from the special facts and circumstances present in the case before it that the risk of unfairness is intolerably high. Findings of that kind made by judges with special insights into local realities are entitled to respect, but injunctions resting on such factors should be accompanied by at least the minimum findings required by Rules 52(a) and 65(d).

The judgment of the District Court is reversed and the case is remanded to that court for further proceedings consistent with this opinion.

So ordered.

Judgment reversed and case remanded.

NOTES

(1) *A Question About Judicial Notice.* How does the Court know what it knows about the psychology of judges (or others acting in an official capacity) and their capacity to overcome prior conclusions? Do these propositions differ from those about the impact of thermal shock on soft-shell clam larvae that alarmed the First Circuit in Seacoast Anti–Pollution League v. Costle, the first case in this Chapter? Consider how one might go about focusing the attention of judges on the contestability of propositions such as these.

(2) *The Workability of the Test.* 2 RICHARD J. PIERCE, JR., ADMINISTRATIVE LAW TREATISE § 9.8 at 670 (4th ed. 2002) remarks that "[t]he Court in the Cement Institute opinion did not attempt to clarify the meaning of a 'closed

mind,' and no judicial opinion has been found that makes such an attempt. A typical good judge who has made a firm decision after a careful study that has led to what he considers to be full understanding may be properly unwilling to reexamine and in that respect may have a 'closed mind.' But the same judge may be willing to reconsider in the light of significant new facts or ideas. Does such a judge have a closed mind if no significant new facts or ideas are presented? If he does, then a closed mind is surely not a disqualification. If he does not, then a closed mind of a judge may be so rare as to be unworthy of discussion. The question about a judge or administrator who is unwilling to consider significant new facts or ideas about a position he has taken is not whether he should be disqualified for deciding a particular case; it is whether he is totally unfit to hold his position.

"The manner in which the Court ... avoided the question whether the Commissioners' minds were 'irrevocably closed' ... as a practical matter ... makes proof of closed minds virtually impossible. ... [T]he Court did not require the Commissioners to show that they had open minds, and the members of the industry had no means of proving that the minds were closed. ... [A]n allegation of closed minds is [usually] likely to bring the response the Court gave in the Cement Industry case."

(3) *The Nature of the Facts on Which Prior Judgments are Formed.* Does it make a difference whether the fact-finder's predisposition relates to a fact of the character we have called "general" (what is the impact of thermal shock on soft-shell clam larvae?) or one that can be expected to vary "in each case upon individual grounds" (what was the behavior of the Ash Grove company in the Kansas City cement market?)? Where the facts previously encountered while performing the functions of office are not general but individual to the parties before the tribunal—as clearly in Withrow and arguably, for the Kansas City area, in Ash Grove—how might counsel go about establishing the "special facts and circumstances" that, as Withrow recognized, might make "the risk of unfairness intolerably high"?

(4) *The Arguable Contribution of Agency Politics.* Many of the federal citations on disqualification of officials for bias involve the Federal Trade Commission. This may be partly a function of personality—one outspoken past chair of the agency, Paul Rand Dixon, figures in a great many of the cases. It may also be seen, however, as reflecting the agency's regulatory situation. As a consumer protection agency, the FTC represents diffuse interests against quite focused ones; consequently, it may feel more than most the need to publicize its good work on behalf of its constituency in order to rally political support in Congress, where its well-organized targets may otherwise be able to wield significant power. This factor may even encourage the appointment of crusaders like Dixon during activist periods. A pair of contrasting cases arising out of this explanatory function follow, the first involving Dixon, and the second not. Are both Commissioners' statements objectionable in your judgment? Neither? Or do you find valuable and workable distinctions between the two communications and their contexts?

TEXACO INC. v. FTC, 336 F.2d 754 (D.C.Cir.1964), vac. and remanded on other issues, 381 U.S. 739 (1965), involved Chairman Dixon. As did many large producers of petroleum products, Texaco strongly encouraged its franchised dealers to procure tires, batteries, and accessories (TBA) exclusively from a particular supplier, which then gave Texaco a commission on each sale made by Texaco dealers. The FTC had for years been seeking to establish that such links between TBA suppliers and gasoline producers were illegal, because they tended to restrict competition in TBA products. On-the-record proceedings against the various producers were in various states of completion when Chairman Dixon was invited to make a speech before the National Congress of Petroleum Retailers, Inc. The fact of the proceedings was well known, and the Commission had issued final cease-and-desist orders against some producers, finding the practices illegal; proceedings remained open against other producers, including Texaco. During his speech, Mr. Dixon said:

> Your problems are many, and many of them are the problems of the Federal Trade Commission, too; for the Commission is concerned with promoting fair competition ... We at the Commission are well aware of the practices which plague you and we have challenged their legality in many important cases. You know the practices—price fixing, price discrimination, and overriding commissions on TBA. You know the companies—Atlantic, Texas [i.e., Texaco], Pure, Shell, Sun, Standard of Indiana, American, Goodyear, Goodrich, and Firestone. ... Some of these cases are still pending before the Commission; some have been decided and are in the courts on appeal. You may be sure that the Commission will continue and, to the extent that increased funds and efficiency permit, will increase its efforts to promote fair competition in your industry.[1]

The FTC subsequently found that Texaco, too, had engaged in illegal conduct and issued a final order directing it to cease the promotion of Goodrich products. To the Court of Appeals, reversing, "a disinterested reader of Chairman Dixon's speech could hardly fail to conclude that he had in some measure decided that Texaco had violated the Act. ... We conclude that Chairman Dixon's participation in the hearing amounted in the circumstances to a denial of due process which invalidated the order under review. ... His Denver speech, made before the matter was submitted to the Commission, but while it was before the examiner, plainly reveals that he had already concluded that Texaco and Goodrich were violating the Act, and that he would protect the petroleum retailers from such abuses."[2]

---

1. As an exercise, try reading this paragraph aloud in a manner that clearly communicates prejudgment of Texaco-specific facts. Then see if you can read it with intonations that communicate commitments only on issues the Commission had already finally decided in other cases. If you can create two differing readings in this way, then consider whether the reviewing court knew the manner in which the speech had been given, and whether that should make any difference to the outcome.

2. Instead of remanding for reconsideration by the FTC without Chairman Dixon's participation, the court reviewed the FTC order on the merits, found it to be unsupported by substantial evidence, and directed that the complaint against Texaco and Goodrich be dismissed. It was on this issue that the Government petitioned for certiorari and obtained a remand. After fresh FTC action (without Chairman Dixon), an order against Texaco and Goodrich was finally sustained in FTC v. Texaco, Inc., 393 U.S. 223 (1968), rev'g 383 F.2d 942 (D.C.Cir.1967).

KENNECOTT COPPER CORP. v. FTC, 467 F.2d 67 (10th Cir.1972), cert. denied 416 U.S. 909, sought to compel Kennecott to divest itself of Peabody Coal, a large coal company it had recently acquired. The Commission had relied on a new theory in finding the merger unlawful; Kennecott was not a competitor in the coal industry, but the Commission concluded that *it would have become one* had it not bought Peabody outright. The Tenth Circuit sustained this theory, and turned to a news interview Commissioner Mary Jones had given while the case was pending:

> "Comm. Jones. When we look at the structure of a market, we must look at the barriers to entry. We have to determine whether the acquired company could have gone into the market on its own or whether its new presence might keep others out. Perhaps it's easier to see in a case like the Kennecott Copper–Peabody Coal *complaint*. We have here an instance of a copper company that was actually moving into the coal industry on its own. Kennecott was experimenting with a small, previously acquired coal property. The *complaint says* that Kennecott, in effect, eliminated itself as a probable new entrant into the coal industry when it went out and bought a major coal company. (Emphasis added.)

> "We have examined the cases and in each instance in which the courts considering the facts have ruled that the Commissioner had to be disqualified, action was entirely justified based on comments showing what appeared to be a prejudice or a viewpoint. No such commenting or editorializing is present here. From a reading of the statement in its entirety, it is clear that Commissioner Jones was discussing the *complaint* and was doing so in an effort to illustrate a point. . . . In other words, she is not shown to have prejudged the central issue of the case, namely, whether the effect of such acquisition may be substantially to lessen competition or to tend to create a monopoly. See Skelly Oil Company v. Federal Power Commission, 375 F.2d 6 at 17–18 (10th Cir.1967).

> "Effort was there being made to show that one of the Commissioners was disqualified based upon a public address. It was there said: ' . . . In our opinion no basis for disqualification arises from the fact or assumption that a member of an administrative agency enters a proceeding with advance views on important economic matters in issue. . . .' 375 F.2d at 18.

> "Public expressions with regard to pending cases cannot, of course, be approved because regardless of what is said such expressions tend not only to mar the image but to create embarrassment and to subject the proceedings to question. We do not, however, perceive any evidence of prejudging or the appearance of it."

(5) *Financial Incentives, and the Rule of Necessity.* Suppose circumstances in which there is no doubt that the agency's head is personally—not just officially—interested. One of the earliest definitions of due process denounced a hearing held before a decisionmaker financially interested in the outcome of the matter. Bonham's Case, 8 Coke 114a, 118a, 77 Eng.Rep. 646, 652 (1610). The Supreme Court has repeatedly enforced that principle in the strongest terms. E.g. Tumey v. Ohio, 273 U.S. 510 (1927); Ward v. Village of Monroeville, Ohio, 409 U.S. 57 (1972). The forcefulness of the position may be suggested by a court of appeals' willingness to say, in

advance of the Arkansas Motor Vehicle Commission's judgment in a pending matter, that it would be incompetent to act if the only one of its eight members who was financially interest in the outcome continued to sit. Yamaha Motor Corp. v. Riney, 21 F.3d 793 (8th Cir.1994).

Is it nonetheless permissible for the hearer to sit, if no alternative hearing body is authorized or available? Analysis of this issue conventionally begins with judges asked to pass on matters affecting their pay, which under the Constitution may not be reduced during their terms of office. UNITED STATES v. WILL, 449 U.S. 200 (1980), arose when Congress in several consecutive years passed legislation suspending cost-of-living increases that would otherwise have taken effect for all federal employees, including judges. Two of these suspensions became law before the beginning of the fiscal year to which they related, but two did not take effect until just after the fiscal year had begun. The Supreme Court concluded that the first two statutes did not, but the second two did, constitute forbidden reductions in judicial compensation. En route, it paused to consider the obvious and direct interest each of its members (and all other federal judges) had in the outcome:

"The Rule of Necessity had its genesis at least five and a half centuries ago and has been consistently applied in this country in both state and federal courts. In State ex rel. Mitchell v. Sage Stores Co., 157 Kan. 622, 143 P.2d 652 (1943), the Supreme Court of Kansas observed:

[I]t is well established that actual disqualification of a member of a court of last resort will not excuse such member from performing his official duty if failure to do so would result in a denial of a litigant's constitutional right to have a question, properly presented to such court, adjudicated."

At 213. The Court went on to find that Section 455 of the Judicial Code, discussed briefly above at p. 382, was not intended to alter this "time-honored" rule. The legislative reports "reflect a constant assumption that upon disqualification of a particular judge, another would be assigned to the case. And we would not casually infer that the Legislative and Executive Branches sought by the enactment of Para. 455 to foreclose federal courts from exercising 'the province and duty of the judicial department to say what the law is.' Marbury v. Madison, 5 U.S. (1 Cranch) 137, 177 (1803)." At 216–17. Similar litigation reached a similar end in the Court of Appeals for the Federal Circuit in 2001, but only after an unusual dissent from denial of certiorari by three Justices (Breyer, Scalia and Kennedy), Williams v. United States, 240 F.3d 1019, cert. den. ___ U.S. ___, 122 S.Ct. 1221 (2002).

In Gibson v. Berryhill, 411 U.S. 564 (1973), the Supreme Court found that members of the Alabama State Board of Optometry, all *independent* optometrists, could not consistently with due process adjudicate charges of "unprofessional conduct" brought against *employed* optometrists. "Independent" and "employed" optometrists enjoyed roughly equal shares of the Alabama market for eyeglasses, but the independents controlled the regulatory board and its policies. The protection they could thus provide for their trade gave them, the Court concluded, too substantial a pecuniary interest in the license revocation proceedings. The "doctrine of necessity" had been argued by the state in support of its board's competence; the Court did not mention the argument. Did it follow that state legislation might no longer create licensing boards composed in whole or in substantial part of professional members empowering them to define "unauthorized practice" by rule or adjudication in ways tending to enrich existing members of the profession, board members included? That proposition was emphatically rejected in Friedman v. Rogers, 440 U.S. 1 (1979), holding that impartiality was a matter to be assessed in the particular circumstances of individual disciplinary proceedings. In the view of a perceptive student analyst, " . . . If members of a profession are to be utilized, the possibility of bias based on personal economic interest will always be present. Given the advantages of professional expertise, courts are more likely to focus on the substantiality of the possible bias in each case, drawing the line only when the image of unfairness is quite distinct. Under this view, pecuniary interest based only on membership in the same profession seems unlikely to be considered disqualifying in many future cases. Yet Berryhill can be important if for no other reason than to indicate that courts should analyze the realities of the occupational licensing situation. If it is unworkable in this area to demand that all possibilities of bias be eliminated, then courts should recognize that bias might exist and adjust the procedural requirements and intensity of judicial review accordingly." Note, Due Process Limitations on Occupational Licensing, 59 U.Va.L.Rev. 1097, 1119 (1973).

(6) *Private Knowledge of Party-Specific Facts.* This section's cases thus far have largely involved administrators who had multiple exposure to matters (or expressed themselves incautiously) while serving in a single agency position. We know from the Grolier case, p. 381 above, that courts are much more sensitive to prior exposures to fact that occurred while serving in a different capacity. When one who was first a prosecutor becomes a judge, courts do *not* say that "the combination of investigative and adjudicatory functions does not, without more, constitute a" reason for disqualification, when the former prosecutor dealt with party-specific facts that are again before her as judge. See, e.g., Amos Treat & Co. v. SEC, 306 F.2d 260 (D.C.Cir.1962) (Commissioner had participated in investigation as a member of staff).

Is it ever permissible for the State to choose an adjudicatory body whose members are likely to have private knowledge of disputed facts? Imagine yourself a dentist and a part-time member of the State Dental Board, with responsibilities which include acting in disciplinary cases. In the course of your professional work you repeatedly encounter first-hand the prior efforts of your professional colleagues, and over time you have involuntarily acquired in this way a knowledge of their respective skills and practices. Wearing office whites, you know whether the cracked crown under your gaze is another sad example of Jones' general incompetence or, rather, an aberrational departure from Brown's customary skill. Does this inevitable but wholly private acquisition of extra-record information about the skills of fellow professionals who may one day be subjected to disciplinary proceedings argue for, or against, a State's choice to ask you for similar judgments in particular cases while wearing quasi-judicial black? If you are chosen, should you be expected to put that information wholly out of mind? Are public protection and/or individual fairness, on the whole, advanced or retarded by designating as judge of particular circumstances one who may find it easy to set those circumstances in a context of general performance? See Vakharia v. Swedish Covenant Hosp., 987 F.Supp. 633, 644 (N.D.Ill. 1997): "In a hospital setting it is inevitable that the members of the committee will have had prior involvement with the physician being reviewed and may even have general personal views about that physician's level of competence, but they can make the decision unless the record discloses actual bias."

In answering these questions, consider possible differences between the professional and the public view. The complaints about professional self-regulation reflected in litigation are most likely to come from fellow professionals. The loudest of these may concern he whom the current profession regards as a charlatan—an accolade, it should be remembered, once bestowed on Louis Pasteur. The complaints emerging from public policy debates may be quite different, and have a strikingly different source. From the public's perspective, it is more likely to be argued that assignment of fellow professionals to regulate professional conduct tends to produce too *much* understanding, a latitudinarianism that results for attorneys in disciplinary proceedings being brought only against the ambulance chaser, the misappropriator of funds, or the convicted felon—and not against the more subtly unethical or inept practitioner. The decisions of some authorities to confer disciplinary functions on a civil service "professional disciplinary board" with responsibility for all professions, or to include non-professionals in the tribunals, are in part the result of such suggestions. Putting aside their possible contribution to greater discipline, ought boards so constituted also to be favored as enhancing fairness? The competing argument is that their verdicts, whether destroying a career or failing to give the public full protection, are more likely to be irrational in relating the particular cases before them to general levels of professional skill and bearing than the conclusions of a panel of fellow professionals, some of whom may have had exposure to the individual's work ex cathedra.

c. OBSTACLES TO INTEGRITY ARISING FROM CONTACTS WITH OTHERS

Professional Air Traffic Controllers Organization v. FLRA

United States Court of Appeals for the District of Columbia Circuit, 1982.
685 F.2d 547.

■ Before ROBINSON, CHIEF JUDGE, MacKINNON and EDWARDS, CIRCUIT JUDGES.

■ HARRY T. EDWARDS, CIRCUIT JUDGE:

[The Professional Air Traffic Controllers Organization called its members out on strike August 3, 1981, in violation of a statute forbidding federal employees to strike their employer. Among the several proceedings resulting was an unfair labor practice hearing before the Federal Labor Relations Authority, threatening the revocation of PATCO's certification as the recognized union for the nation's air traffic controllers. That hearing was held before an FLRA ALJ August 10–11 and on August 14, after briefing, a recommended decision was announced stripping PATCO of its certification. Oral argument on review was held before the three members of the FLRA September 16, and the ALJ's decision was affirmed October 22. Members Frazier and Applewhaite voted unconditionally to revoke PATCO's certification; Chairman Haughton would have permitted PATCO a brief period to end the strike before that revocation, but joined the other two when that period elapsed without an appropriate PATCO response. The case was then brought to the D.C. Circuit for expedited judicial review.]

II.   Ex Parte Communications During the FLRA Proceedings

Unfortunately, allegations of improprieties during the FLRA's consideration of this case forced us to delay our review on the merits. Only a day before oral argument, the Department of Justice, which represents the FAA in this review, informed the court that the Department of Justice Criminal Division and the FBI had investigated allegations of an improper contact between a "well-known labor leader" and FLRA Member Applewhaite during the pendency of the PATCO case. . . . [W]e invoked a procedure that this court has occasionally employed in like situations in the past. Without assuming that anything improper had in fact occurred or had affected the FLRA Decision in this case, we ordered the FLRA "to hold, with the aid of a specially-appointed administrative law judge, an evidentiary hearing to determine the nature, extent, source and effect of any and all ex parte communications and other approaches that may have been made to any member or members of the FLRA while the PATCO case was pending before it."

Following our remand on the ex parte communications issue, John M. Vittone, an Administrative Law Judge with the Civil Aeronautics Board, was appointed to preside over an evidentiary proceeding. . . . ALJ Vittone's inquiry led to the disclosure of a number of communications with FLRA Members that were at least arguably related to the Authority's consideration of the PATCO case. We find the vast majority of these communications unobjectionable. Three occurrences, however, are somewhat more troubling and require our careful review and discussion. We first summarize ALJ Vittone's findings regarding them.

1.   The Meeting Between Member Applewhaite and FLRA General Counsel Gordon

On August 10, 1981 (one week after the unfair labor practice complaint against PATCO was filed), H. Stephan Gordon, the FLRA General Counsel, was in Member Applewhaite's office discussing administrative matters unrelated to the PATCO case. During Gordon's discussion with Member Applewhaite, Ms. Ellen Stern, an attorney with the FLRA Solicitor's office, entered Member Applewhaite's office to deliver a copy of a memorandum . . . Ms. Stern had prepared at the request of Member Frazier.[1] With

---

1. The Solicitor is the general legal advisor of the FLRA, including the Members. The Solicitor also represents the FLRA on appeals from FLRA orders and in other legal proceedings. [The General Counsel, by contrast, represents FLRA staff in appearances before the FLRA.]

General Counsel Gordon present, Ms. Stern proceeded to discuss her memorandum, which dealt with whether the Civil Service Reform Act makes revocation of a striking union's exclusive recognition status mandatory or discretionary and, assuming it is discretionary, what other disciplinary actions might be taken.

During Ms. Stern's discussion, both Member Applewhaite and General Counsel Gordon asked her general questions (e.g., regarding the availability of other remedies and whether she had researched the relevant legislative history). ... While the conversation at least implicitly focused on the PATCO case, the facts of the case and the appropriate disposition were not discussed. The discussion ended after ten or fifteen minutes.

ALJ Vittone concluded that "[t]he conversation had no effect or impact on Member Applewhaite's ultimate decision in the PATCO case."

2. Secretary Lewis' Telephone Calls to Members Frazier and Applewhaite

During the morning of August 13, 1981, Secretary of Transportation Andrew L. Lewis, Jr. telephoned Member Frazier. Secretary Lewis stated that he was not calling about the substance of the PATCO case, but wanted Member Frazier to know that, contrary to some news reports, no meaningful efforts to settle the strike were underway. Secretary Lewis also stated that the Department of Transportation would appreciate expeditious handling of the case. Not wanting to discuss the PATCO case with Secretary Lewis, Member Frazier replied, "I understand your position perfectly, Mr. Secretary." ...

Member Frazier also advised Member Applewhaite of Secretary Lewis' telephone call. In anticipation of a call, Member Applewhaite located the FLRA Rules regarding the time limits for processing an appeal from an ALJ decision in an unfair labor practice case. When Secretary Lewis telephoned and stated his concern that the case not be delayed, Member Applewhaite interrupted the Secretary to inform him that if he wished to obtain expedited handling of the case, he would have to comply with the FLRA Rules and file a written motion. Secretary Lewis stated that he was unaware that papers had to be filed and that he would contact his General Counsel immediately. The conversation ended without further discussion.

During the afternoon of August 13, the FAA filed a Motion to Modify Time Limits for Filing Exceptions, requesting that the time limit be reduced from the usual twenty-five days to seven days. On August 14, the FLRA General Counsel filed a similar motion. On August 17, PATCO filed an opposition to these motions and a motion to extend the time for filing exceptions to sixty days. On August 18, 1981, the FLRA Members considered the three pending motions, denied all three, and decided instead to reduce the usual twenty-five day period for filing exceptions to nineteen days.

Upon considering this evidence, Judge Vittone concluded that: (1) the FAA's filing of a motion to expedite may have been in response to Secretary Lewis' conversation with Member Applewhaite; (2) Chairman Haughton was unaware of Secretary Lewis' telephone calls when he considered the motions on August 18; (3) "Secretary Lewis' call had an undetermined effect on Member Applewhaite's and Member Frazier's decision to reduce the time period for filing exceptions,''; and (4) the telephone calls "had no effect on Member Applewhaite's or Member Frazier's ultimate decision on the merits of the PATCO case."

3.   Member Applewhaite's Dinner With Albert Shanker

Since 1974 Albert Shanker has been President of the American Federation of Teachers, a large public-sector labor union, and a member of the Executive Council of the AFL–CIO.[2] Since 1964 Mr. Shanker has been President of the AFT's New York City Local, the United Federation of Teachers. Before joining the FLRA, Member Applewhaite had been associated with the New York Public Employment Relations Board. Through their contacts in New York, Mr. Shanker and Member Applewhaite had become professional and social friends.

During the week of September 20, 1981, Mr. Shanker was in Washington, D.C. on business. On September 21, Mr. Shanker made arrangements to have dinner with Member Applewhaite that evening. Although he did not inform Member Applewhaite of his intentions when he made the arrangements, Mr. Shanker candidly admitted that he wanted to have dinner with Member Applewhaite because he felt strongly about the PATCO case and wanted to communicate directly to Member Applewhaite his sentiments, previously expressed in public statements, that PATCO should not be severely punished for its strike. ... After accepting the invitation, Member Applewhaite informed Member Frazier and Chairman Haughton that he was having dinner with Mr. Shanker.

Member Applewhaite and Mr. Shanker talked for about an hour and a half during their dinner on September 21. Most of the discussion concerned the preceding Saturday's Solidarity Day Rally, an upcoming tuition tax credit referendum in the District of Columbia, and mutual friends from New York. Near the end of the dinner, however, the conversation turned to labor law matters relevant to the PATCO case. The two men discussed various approaches to public employee strikes in New York, Pennsylvania and the federal government. Mr. Shanker expressed his view that the punishment of a striking union should fit the crime and that revocation of certification as a punishment for an illegal strike was tantamount to "killing a union." The record is clear that Mr. Shanker made no threats or promises to Member Applewhaite; likewise, the evidence also indicates that Member Applewhaite never revealed his position regarding the PATCO case.

Near the end of their conversation, Member Applewhaite commented that because the PATCO case was hotly contested, he would be viewed with disfavor by whichever side he voted against. Member Applewhaite also observed that he was concerned about his prospects for reappointment to the FLRA in July 1982. Mr. Shanker, in turn, responded that Member Applewhaite had no commitments from anyone and urged him to vote without regard to personal considerations. The dinner concluded and the two men departed.

2. The AFL–CIO presented oral argument to the FLRA in the PATCO case as amicus curiae. Mr. Shanker, however, was unaware of the amicus status of the AFL–CIO at all times relevant to our consideration.

The FLRA Decisional Process. On the afternoon of September 21, before the Applewhaite/Shanker dinner, the FLRA Members had had their first formal conference on the PATCO case, which had been argued to them five days earlier. Members Frazier and Applewhaite both favored revocation of PATCO's exclusive recognition status and took the position that PATCO would no longer be a labor organization within the meaning of the Civil Service Reform Act. Member Frazier favored an indefinite revocation; Member Applewhaite favored a revocation for a fixed period of one to three years. Chairman Haughton agreed that an illegal strike had occurred, but favored suspension, not revocation, of PATCO's collective bargaining status.

After September 21, Member Applewhaite considered other remedies, short of revocation, to deal with the PATCO strike. For over two weeks Member Applewhaite sought to find common ground with Chairman Haughton. Those efforts to agree on an alternative solution failed and, on October 9, Member Applewhaite finally decided to vote with Member Frazier for revocation. (Member Applewhaite apparently was concerned that the FLRA have a majority favoring one remedy, rather than render three opinions favoring three different dispositions.) . . . While these negotiations within the Authority were going on, Member Frazier became concerned that Mr. Shanker might have influenced Member Applewhaite's position in the case. On September 22, Member Frazier visited Member Applewhaite to inquire about his dinner with Mr. Shanker. Member Frazier understood Member Applewhaite to say that Shanker had said that if Member Applewhaite voted against PATCO, then Applewhaite would be unable to get work as an arbitrator when he left the FLRA. Member Frazier also understood Member Applewhaite to say that he was then leaning against voting for revocation. (ALJ Vittone found that Shanker had made no such threats during the dinner, and concluded that Member Frazier reached this conclusion based on some miscommunication or misunderstanding.)

On September 22 and again on September 28, Member Frazier advised Member Applewhaite to talk to Solicitor Freehling about his dinner with Mr. Shanker. . . . Member Frazier later asked Solicitor Freehling if Member Applewhaite had discussed his dinner with Mr. Shanker. Solicitor Freehling told Member Frazier that they had talked and that Member Applewhaite had concluded that there were no problems involved. Despite these assurances, Member Frazier contacted his personal attorney. Sometime in early October, Member Frazier's attorney contacted the FBI. The FBI interviewed Member Frazier on October 17 and then other FLRA Members and staff. FBI agents interviewed Member Applewhaite on October 22, the day the FLRA Decision issued. (Member Applewhaite was thus unaware of the FBI investigation until after he reached his final decision in the PATCO case.) . . .

C.   Applicable Legal Standards

1.   The Statutory Prohibition of Ex Parte Contacts and the FLRA Rules

The Civil Service Reform Act requires that FLRA unfair labor practice hearings, to the extent practicable, be conducted in accordance with the provisions of the Administrative Procedure Act. 5 U.S.C. § 7118(a)(6) (Supp. IV 1980). Since FLRA unfair labor practice hearings are formal adjudications within the meaning of the APA, section 557(d) governs ex parte communications. Id. § 557(d). . . .

Three features of the prohibition on ex parte communications in agency adjudications are particularly relevant to the contacts here at issue. First, by its terms, section 557(d) applies only to ex parte communications to or from an "interested person." . . . Second, the Government in the Sunshine Act defines an "ex parte communication" as "an oral or written communication not on the public record to which reasonable prior notice to all parties is not given, but . . . not includ[ing] requests for status reports on any matter or proceeding. . . ." 5 U.S.C. § 551(14) (1976). Requests for status reports are thus allowed under the statute, even when directed to an agency decisionmaker rather than to another agency employee. . . . Third, and in direct contrast to status reports, section 557(d) explicitly prohibits communications "relevant to the merits of the proceeding." The congressional reports state that the phrase should "be construed broadly and . . . include more than the phrase 'fact in issue' currently used in [section 554(d)(1) of] the Administrative Procedure Act." . . .

The disclosure of ex parte communications serves two distinct interests. Disclosure is important in its own right to prevent the appearance of impropriety from secret communications in a proceeding that is required to be decided on the record. Disclosure is also important as an instrument of fair decisionmaking; only if a party knows the arguments presented to a decisionmaker can the party respond effectively and ensure that its position is fairly considered. When these interests of openness and opportunity for response are threatened by an ex parte communication, the communication must be disclosed. . . .

2.   Remedies for Ex Parte Communications

Section 557(d) contains two possible administrative remedies for improper ex parte communications. The first is disclosure of the communication and its content. The second requires the violating party to "show cause why his claim or interest in the proceeding should not be dismissed, denied, disregarded, or otherwise adversely affected on account of [the] violation." . . . Under the case law in this Circuit, improper ex parte communications, even when undisclosed during agency proceedings, do not necessarily void an agency decision. . . . [A] court must consider whether, as a result of improper ex parte communications, the agency's decisionmaking process was irrevocably tainted so as to make the ultimate judgment of the agency unfair, either to an innocent party or to the public interest that the agency was obliged to protect.[3] In making this determination, a number of considerations may be relevant: the gravity of the ex parte communications;[4] whether the contacts may have influenced the agency's ultimate

---

3. We have also considered the effect of ex parte communications on the availability of meaningful judicial review. . . . If the off-the-record communications regard critical facts, the court will be particularly ill-equipped to resolve in the first instance any controversy between the parties. . . .

4. If the ex parte contacts are of such severity that an agency decision-maker should have disqualified himself, vacation of

decision; whether the party making the improper contacts benefited from the agency's ultimate decision; whether the contents of the communications were unknown to opposing parties, who therefore had no opportunity to respond; and whether vacation of the agency's decision and remand for new proceedings would serve a useful purpose. ... [A]ny such decision must of necessity be an exercise of equitable discretion.

D. Analysis of the Alleged Ex Parte Communications With FLRA Members ...

1. The Meeting Between Member Applewhaite and FLRA General Counsel Gordon

When General Counsel Gordon met with Member Applewhaite on August 10, the General Counsel's office was prosecuting the unfair labor practice complaint against PATCO before Chief ALJ Fenton. General Counsel Gordon was therefore a "person outside the agency" within the meaning of section 557(d) and the FLRA Rules. 5 C.F.R. § 2414.3(a) (1981). Still, the undisputed purpose of the meeting was to discuss budgetary and administrative matters. It was therefore entirely appropriate. The shared concerns of the Authority are not put on hold whenever the General Counsel prosecutes an unfair labor practice complaint.

The discussion relevant to the PATCO case arose only when Ms. Stern delivered a copy of her memorandum regarding decertification of striking unions to Member Applewhaite. ... Some occasional and inadvertent contacts between the prosecuting and adjudicating arms of a small agency like the FLRA may be inevitable. ... In hindsight, it may have been preferable if Member Applewhaite had postponed even this general conversation with Ms. Stern or if General Counsel Gordon had temporarily excused himself from Member Applewhaite's office. Nonetheless, we do not believe that this contact tainted the proceeding or unfairly advantaged the General Counsel in the prosecution of the case. Thus, we conclude that the conversation at issue here, even though possibly indiscreet and undesirable, does not void the FLRA Decision in this case.

2. Secretary Lewis' Telephone Calls to Members Frazier and Applewhaite

Transportation Secretary Lewis was undoubtedly an "interested person" within the meaning of section 557(d) and the FLRA Rules when he called Members Frazier and Applewhaite on August 13. Secretary Lewis' call clearly would have been an improper ex parte communication if he had sought to discuss the merits of the PATCO case. ... Although Secretary Lewis did not in fact discuss the merits of the case, even a procedural inquiry may be a subtle effort to influence an agency decision. ... We need not decide, however, whether Secretary Lewis' contacts were in fact improper. ... Member Applewhaite explicitly told Secretary Lewis that if he wanted the case handled more quickly than the normal course of FLRA business, then the FAA would have to file a written request. If ... Member

the agency decision and remand to an impartial tribunal is mandatory. Cf. Cinderella Career & Finishing Schools v. FTC, 425 F.2d 583, 591–92 (D.C.Cir.1970) (failure of single member of agency [Paul Rand Dixon] to disqualify himself for bias requires vacation of agency decision).

Applewhaite's comments led to the FAA's Motion to Modify Time Limits, *that was exactly the desired result.* . . . In these circumstances, and given ALJ Vittone's inability to find any effect of the calls on the Members' decision, we cannot find that the disposition of the motions was improperly influenced. . . .

3.   Member Applewhaite's Dinner With Albert Shanker

. . . At the outset, we are faced with the question whether Mr. Shanker was an "interested person" to the proceeding under section 557(d) and the FLRA Rules. . . . The House and Senate Reports agreed that the term covers "any individual or other person with an interest in the agency proceeding that is greater than the general interest the public as a whole may have." . . . Mr. Shanker was (and is) the President of a major public-sector labor union. As such, he has a special and well-known interest in the union movement and the developing law of labor relations in the public sector. . . . From August 3, 1981 to September 21, 1981, Mr. Shanker and his union made a series of widely publicized statements in support of PATCO. . . . Thus, Mr. Shanker's actions, as well as his union office, belie his implicit claim that he had no greater interest in the case than a member of the general public. . . .

Even if we were to adopt Mr. Shanker's position that he was not an interested person, we are astonished at his claim that he did nothing wrong.[5] Mr. Shanker frankly concedes that he "desired to have dinner with Member Applewhaite because he felt strongly about the PATCO case and he wished to communicate directly to Member Applewhaite sentiments he had previously expressed in public." . . . *It is simply unacceptable behavior for any person directly to attempt to influence the decision of a judicial officer in a pending case outside of the formal, public proceedings.* This is true for the general public, for "interested persons," and for the formal parties to the case. This rule applies to administrative adjudications as well as to cases in Article III courts. . . .

We do not hold, however, that Member Applewhaite committed an impropriety when he accepted Mr. Shanker's dinner invitation. Member Applewhaite and Mr. Shanker were professional and social friends. We recognize, of course, that a judge "must have neighbors, friends and acquaintances, business and social relations, and be a part of his day and generation." . . . Member Applewhaite was unaware of Mr. Shanker's purpose in arranging the dinner. He therefore had no reason to reject the invitation.

The majority of the dinner conversation was unrelated to the PATCO case. Only in the last fifteen minutes of the dinner did the discussion become relevant to the PATCO dispute . . . At this point, . . . Member Applewhaite should have promptly terminated the discussion. . . . We now

---

5. Mr. Shanker suggests that "[s]ince there is no sanction available against amici, it is reasonable to assume that the ex parte rules are not intended to apply in these circumstances." This argument is simply a non sequitur. The principal purpose of the ex parte rules is not to punish violators, but to preserve the integrity of the administrative process. Even when a nonparty is the source of an ex parte communication, a proceeding may be voided if the decision is irrevocably tainted. . . .

know that Mr. Shanker did *not* in any way threaten Member Applewhaite during their dinner. Mr. Shanker did *not* tell Member Applewhaite that if he voted to decertify PATCO he would be unable to get cases as an arbitrator if and when he left the FLRA. Mr. Shanker did *not* say that he was speaking "for top AFL–CIO officials" or that Member Applewhaite would need labor support to secure reappointment. Moreover, Mr. Shanker did *not* make any promises of any kind to Member Applewhaite, and Member Applewhaite did *not* reveal how he intended to vote in the PATCO case.

In these circumstances, we do not believe that it is necessary to vacate the FLRA Decision and remand the case. . . . Though plainly inappropriate, the ex parte communication was limited to a ten or fifteen minute discussion, often couched in general terms, of the appropriate discipline for a striking public employee union. This behavior falls short of the "corrupt tampering with the adjudicatory process" found by this court in WKAT, Inc. v. FCC, 296 F.2d 375, 383 (D.C.Cir.), cert. denied, 368 U.S. 841 (1961). . . . [T]he Applewhaite/Shanker dinner had no effect on the ultimate decision of Member Applewhaite or of the FLRA as a whole in the PATCO case. . . . Third, no party benefited from the improper contact. . . . Finally, we cannot say that the parties were unfairly deprived of an opportunity to refute the arguments propounded in the ex parte communication. . . .

E. Member Applewhaite's Alleged "Personal Interest" in the PATCO Case . . .

Based essentially on [member Applewhaite's brief conversation with Mr. Shanker about his reappointment prospects,] Member Frazier now proposes that Member Applewhaite had a personal interest in the outcome of the PATCO case . . . [and] argues that Member Applewhaite was disqualified from hearing the PATCO case.

We do not read as much into this conversation as does Member Frazier. It is not surprising that an agency member appointed by the President might be concerned about his prospects for reappointment. . . . The appropriate question here is not whether Member Applewhaite recognized that his decision might not be universally approved; rather, the correct inquiry is whether Member Applewhaite's concerns rendered him incapable of reaching a fair decision on the merits of the case before him.

The . . . conversation between Member Applewhaite and Mr. Shanker does not demonstrate an inability to fairly decide the case. Courts have long recognized "a presumption of honesty and integrity in those serving as adjudicators." Absent a strong showing to the contrary, an agency adjudicator is presumed to act in good faith and to be capable of ignoring considerations not on the record. . . . Member Applewhaite explained that this was no different from any arbitration case in which he had ruled—one party wins and the other loses. He testified: "I have always faced that problem[,] so I just have to call it like it is and . . . take my chances." Tr. 744. We have no reason to doubt this testimony. A remand on the basis of personal interest is therefore unnecessary.

[On the merits, the court upheld the FLRA order.]

■ SPOTTSWOOD W. ROBINSON, III, CHIEF JUDGE, concurring in part, and concurring in the judgment. . . .

From the special hearing emerges an appalling chronicle of attorneys, high government officials, and interested outsiders apparently without compunction about intervening in the course of FLRA's decisionmaking by means of private communications with those charged with resolving the case on the merits. We have an even more distressing picture of agency decisionmakers—whose role in this formal adjudication concededly approximated that of judges—seemingly ignorant of the substance of the ex parte rules, insensitive to the compromising potentialities of certain official and social contacts, and unwilling to silence peremptorily and firmly improper discussions that did transpire. . . . [T]he court's opinion administers a mild chiding where a ringing condemnation is in order.

I.   The Applewhaite–Gordon Incident

. . . [A]gencies such as FLRA fulfill, often simultaneously, the several roles of investigator, prosecutor, adjudicator, and policy formulator. Undoubtedly, this commingling of functions makes it more difficult to maintain a strict separation between those personnel who, on any given case, are cast in the role of advocate from those who occupy the position of judge in the matter. Once the agency is engaged in formal adjudication, however, such a separation is mandated by the APA, and is essential to the integrity of the administrative process. The perils of laxness on this point are well illustrated by the Applewhaite—Gordon incident. . . . The conversation was not merely indiscreet or undesirable; it was, purely and simply, a prohibited ex parte contact that should never have occurred. Gordon had no business remaining in the room once he realized that PATCO was the object of discussion. Applewhaite had no business permitting him to remain, and certainly was grossly at fault in soliciting Gordon's opinion. . . .

II.   Secretary Lewis' Calls to Members Frazier and Applewhaite

. . . Secretary Lewis' calls were highly unusual. Both [Frazier and Applewhaite] stated that they had never before been contacted by a Cabinet member on a pending case. Applewhaite also explained that persons seeking status information normally contact the staff in lieu of discussing such matters directly with the members. . . .

Agencies, like courts, promulgate rules of practice to assist outsiders in communicating in proper fashion with decisionmakers. These channels are quite adequate to accommodate any information that legitimately could be sought from or provided to those who will judge the case. For a high government officer to bypass established procedures and approach, directly and privately, members of an independent decisionmaking body about a case in which he has an official interest and on which they will be called to rule suggests, at the minimum, a deplorable indifference toward safeguarding the purity of the formal adjudicatory process. Regardless of the officer's actual intent, such a call could be felt by the recipient as political pressure; regardless of its actual effect, such a call could be perceived by the public as political pressure. . . .

IV.   The Applewhaite–Shanker Dinner

... Can the public really be expected to believe in the fairness and neutrality of the agency's formal adjudicatory processes when one of its decisionmakers permits an outspoken, highly visible official of a participating union to wine and dine him during deliberations on the case? ... [T]hose who take on this judicial role may no longer participate in the daily intercourse of life as freely as do others. They have a duty to the judicial system in which they have accepted membership fastidiously to safeguard their integrity—at the expense, if need be, of "neighbors, friends and acquaintances, business and social relations." This *is* their "part" in their "day and generation," and one who is unwilling to make the sacrifice is unsuited to the office....

■ MacKINNON, CIRCUIT JUDGE (concurring)....

The number of ex parte contacts that were disclosed at the remand hearing is appalling, as are the statements by counsel that such contacts were nothing more than what is normal and usual in administrative agencies and even in courts of law. ... In this connection 18 U.S.C. § 1505 should be noted. This section of the Criminal Code provides that it is an offense if one "corruptly ... *endeavors to influence,* obstruct or impede the due and proper administration of the law under which [a] proceeding is being had before [an] ... agency of the United States ..." (emphasis added). Private contacts with agency officials, with respect to pending adjudicatory matters, by interested parties or their agents, that endeavor to affect the decisional process, however subtle such contract may be, are *corrupt* endeavors to influence the "due and proper administration of the law" and those who so attempt may be indicted. The authorized punishment is imprisonment for not more than five years, or a $5,000 fine, or both. 18 U.S.C. § 1505.

ORGANIZATIONAL NOTE

Casebook editors sometimes suspect that opinions they encounter in the reporters were written with the classroom in mind, particularly when those opinion have been authored by former colleagues like Judge Edwards.[1] PATCO (like the Ticor case you may encounter in Chapter IX) is remarkable for capturing so many related questions in one place. Here, those questions concern the relationship of agency heads to the people around them—staff, other government officials, and private citizens who may be both personal friends and "interested persons." It catches, too, the influence of accidental crossings (unless you believe, as your editors do not, that the Gordon–Applewhaite–Stern meeting was advertent), headlines, internal politics (consider Member Frazier's decision to turn Member Applewhaite over to the FBI), and "the rotating door" through which agency leaders—and young lawyers—move in and out of government, with (we believe) both public benefits and public costs. It does so in the context of an unusual government agency; the FLRA, like the NLRB, is an almost wholly adjudicatory body; and, furthermore, it is one that *always* has a

---

1. Before his appointment to the bench, Judge Edwards was a Professor at the Uni- versity of Michigan Law School, specializing in Labor Law.

government agency on one side of the issues before it, with possibly oppressed or miscreant government employees on the other.

Most government agencies will not be so wholly committed to adjudication, and in adjudication will generally be dealing only with their own staff, not other government agencies, as a party. For them even more than for the FLRA, in your editors' experience, the PATCO issues are real ones. These issues cross the lives of agency officials daily and lurk behind every "chance" conversation. Sections 554(d) and 557(d), as well as independent conflict of interest legislation, speak to their resolution. The pages that follow, from which your instructor may make a limited selection, explore in some depth the three conversations that sparked this controversy: one within the agency, one with another government official, and the third with an interested "friend."

(i) GENERAL COUNSEL GORDON: INTERESTED AGENCY STAFF

General Counsel Gordon's participation in the conversation between Ms. Stern and Member Applewhaite suggests the difficulties that can arise, perhaps especially in a small agency, from the limited pool of expertise available to the agency, the variety of tasks agency staff are asked to perform, and the frequent informality with which work within an agency is done. As is common enough in even the most bureaucratic of institutions, people bring their whole selves to any conversation, not just what may happen to be identified with a single possible aspect of their work. Absent constraints of the kind normally to be found only in courtrooms, the conversation may correspondingly wander.

As we imagine will usually be the case, the PATCO conversation was unplanned, even unconscious. In an enforcement proceeding like the PATCO case, agency participants would and should have little doubt that separation of functions constraints have to be observed. The FLRA's own rules, as the court remarked, treated the General Counsel's office as if it were outside the agency for purposes of these proceedings; even if they had not thus brought § 557(d) into play, § 554(d) would have been understood to apply. Although § 554(d)(C) appears to exclude "the agency or a member or members of the body comprising the agency" from the ex parte ban, that exclusion serves only to permit those members themselves to serve multiple functions—not to authorize prosecuting counsel to have private conversations with them. Attorney General's Manual on the Administrative Procedure Act 58 (1947). All § 554(d) excludes for agency prosecutors, however, are off-the-record consultations about a "fact in issue" and participation or advice about "the decision, recommended decision, or agency review." To say that this language reaches general policy conversations in which the whole agency may be engaged, if they might also bear on particular matters in litigation, would introduce layers of formality into the day-to-day functioning of the agency, an arguably unwarranted cost. Many cases are pending all the time in traditional model regulatory agencies, raising issues implicating the full range of their responsibilities. Save where Congress has employed the alternative of an adjudicating agency distinct from the policymaker, the implication is fully institutional policy-making. If we think, then, that § 554(d) precludes conversations when it is evident that a pending case dominates them, but not when a general policy question is the driving force—then, how should we understand the Gordon/Stern/Apple-whaite conversation? Does the broader preclusion of § 557(d), applying to communications "relevant to the merits of the proceeding," further complicate matters, if the agency has defined General Counsel Gordon as being "outside the agency" for these purposes?

As previously noted, for formal rulemaking, and initial licensing proceedings, APA §§ 554, –6 and –7 enact a general solution to this problem of possible compartmentalization, one that permits the conversations to occur *even when it is clear that an on-the-record proceeding is at the center.* In these two classes of on-the-record proceedings, integrated staff assistance might be thought particularly important, and the risk of prejudice from participation of staff responsible for presentation might be thought particularly low. As in the Morgan cases, the use of staff advisers in such cases may be the product of deliberate decision about the use of the agency's resources. In the Seacoast Anti–Pollution League case that opens this chapter, the EPA Administrator took deliberate steps to reserve for himself experts *not* associated with the on-the-record matters he was required to decide. Yet an administrator's budget may not always be so richly endowed as to permit assembly of a second staff of experts, separate from those who may have testified or assisted in preparing the agency's staff for hearing. EPA Administrator Costle's own opinion in the administrative proceedings in SAPL included the following thought-provoking commentary:

"[T]he [Regional Administrator] apparently felt constrained to avoid discussion of the merits of the case with his technical staff after the hearing because they were 'parties' to the case and could not be consulted in the absence of the other parties. Consequently the RA was deprived of the opportunity to consult with experts experienced in the matter of thermal discharges, and reviewed the record with only the assistance of his legal staff and a biologist hired for the purpose. This unfortunate result appears to have occurred partly because the Agency took a position in favor of its determinations (i.e., in support of PSCo) at the hearings, thus becoming 'party' as well as judge. This seems to me to have been unnecessary and of dubious propriety.

"I am requesting my staff to review this aspect of the case with a view toward assuring that in future . . . cases RAs will have available to them adequate Agency resources to assist in the review of the record. In connection with the review of the regulations mentioned above, I am asking the Office of General Counsel to review the question of whether the Agency should act as a 'party' in 316(a) proceedings."

Now suppose, however, an agency with only one relevant expert in-house—the one who testified on the agency's behalf during the course of the hearings below—and the question is whether the agency head may consult with *that* person in getting to understand the record so that she can formulate her opinion.

American Telephone & Telegraph Co.

Federal Communications Commission, 1976.
60 FCC 1.

■ By the COMMISSION:

[The FCC had for a long time been considering revision of AT & T's rates for certain commercial telephone services—for so long, indeed, that it had now come under judicial order to resolve the issues presented within the next few months. Nader v. FCC, 520 F.2d 182, 205 (D.C.Cir.1975). Hearings before an ALJ were complete; the Chief of its Common Carrier Bureau, acting as a "responsible employee," 5 U.S.C. § 557(b)(1), had filed a recommended decision with the Commission. The Common Carrier Bureau had represented the FCC as one party before the ALJ, and AT & T and other parties now sought an order from the Commission prohibiting members of the Bureau from further participation in the decision.]

2. ... Pointing out that the Bureau staff adduced evidence through its own witnesses, cross-examined witnesses, and took positions on the highly controverted issues in the case, Bell argues that a fair and objective treatment of the evidence by the Bureau staff is precluded. As a result, Bell asserts, the Recommended Decision represents almost exclusively positions heretofore taken by the Bureau, crucial parts of the evidentiary record are disregarded, misstated or mischaracterized, and numerous statements are unsupported by the evidence. To permit the Bureau to advise the Commission ex parte as to the merits of the exceptions and briefs of the parties and to participate in the drafting of the Final Decision would, Bell urges, in effect permit the Bureau to review and evaluate the criticisms of its own decision; and that the procedure authorized herein is inconsistent with the principles of fairness and due process. Only by precluding the Bureau from further participation in the decision-making process, Bell maintains, can a fair and objective review of the Recommended Decision be obtained....

4. The Commission and the courts have consistently held that a tariff proceeding, such as the one under consideration, is rulemaking and separation of the Bureau from the decision-making process is not required by the Communications Act, the Administrative Procedure Act, or the due process clause of the Constitution.[1] American Telephone and Telegraph Co. v. FCC, 449 F.2d 439 (2d Cir.1971). While the court in American Telephone and Telegraph did indicate that the participation of a staff member of the Bureau in the preparation of a recommended decision was, as Bell asserts, "ill-advised," the fact remains that the court sustained the lawfulness of the Commission's procedure. The court therein expressly held that "despite our belief as to what might be desirable in such cases, we cannot see how, under present law, the commingling of functions practiced here is proscribed either by Section 409(c) of the Communications Act or by the due process clause of the Constitution" (449 F.2d at 454).

5. The Commission recently amended its rules to provide for a separated trial staff in restricted rulemaking proceedings involving common carrier matters.[2] However, it was specifically provided therein that the

---

1. [Ed.] A similar conclusion respecting the licensing exception to 5 U.S.C. § 554(d) is reached in Marathon Oil Co. v. Environmental Protection Agency, 564 F.2d 1253 (9th Cir.1977).

2. [Ed.] See Delay in the Regulatory Process, IV Study on Federal Regulation pre-

pared pursuant to S.Res. 71, Senate Committee on Governmental Affairs, 95th Cong., 1st Sess. 24 (Comm.Print 1977):

Since the passage of the APA, ... the distinction it makes between adjudicatory proceedings which are accusatory (in which separation of functions is re-

Commission would not "order separation of functions retroactively in proceedings wherein we had assigned the trial staff a decisional role, owing to the disruption this would entail." . . .

6. . . . In their exceptions to the Recommended Decision and in their briefs in support thereof the parties undoubtedly will advance all of their objections to the recommended findings and conclusions and will provide in detail the evidence of record and the arguments and contentions which, in their view, require contrary findings and conclusions. All such evidence, arguments and contentions will be given careful and thorough consideration. While we shall, of course, give like consideration to the views of the Common Carrier Bureau, the fact remains that the responsibility for making the final decision is ours and we shall discharge that responsibility in a fair and impartial manner upon the basis of what we determine will best serve the public interest after weighing and analyzing the evidence and the contentions of all parties. Moreover, as we stated in answer to a previous request by Bell in this proceeding for a separation of functions (A.T. & T., et al., 32 FCC2d at 90): "The final decision in 18128 will be made by the Commission. We will expect the participating staff to play its usual role of providing impartial expert advice and assistance to the Commission in its decisional process." We have no reason to believe that the staff of the Bureau will not continue to provide "impartial" as well as expert advice. . . .

Separate Statement of Chairman Richard E. Wiley, in which Commissioners Reid, Washburn and Quello join: . . .

If the question of separating the functions of the Bureau in this proceeding were being addressed for the first time, I believe that the better approach—from the standpoint of sound administrative procedure, but not necessarily as a matter of mandatory procedural due process—would be to grant the relief requested. And, certainly, this is my and the Commission's announced intention in future cases. Quite frankly, however, the time has passed when such an approach is feasible in the instant proceeding. The Court of Appeals has mandated that time is of the essence in this important and extremely complex docket and has established a deadline for its administrative conclusion. At this late date, the Commission realistically cannot turn to an entirely new staff which is unfamiliar with the complicated and interrelated issues raised in this rulemaking. Instead, I believe that the Commission must proceed, with appropriate caution, to consider the Bureau's Recommended Decision with the assistance of all available staff resources.

■ Dissenting Statement of Commissioner Glen O. Robinson in which Commissioner Benjamin L. Hooks joins: . . .

While separation of Common Carrier Bureau staff may not be required by the Administrative Procedure Act or by the due process clause of the

quired) and those which are not accusatory (in which separation of functions is not required), has largely been eroded. Instead, almost all agencies have voluntarily adopted approximately the same separation of functions rules that apply to other forms of adjudication for use in ratemaking and initial licensing as well. Similarly, agencies, for the most part, provide for decisions to be written by presiding ALJ's even where that is not legally required.

Fifth Amendment, American Telephone and Telegraph Co. v. FCC, 449 F.2d 439 (2d Cir.1971) (Telpak Sharing case), I think it is nevertheless injudicious to permit Bureau staff who participated in the investigation and prosecution of this case to advise us in its final disposition. More than injudicious, I consider it unfair.

The fact that the APA exempts cases such as this from the separations requirements imposed on other agency hearings (5 U.S.C. § 554(d)) does not persuade me to the contrary.[3] Whatever may be the strict legal requirements of the APA, where, as here, there is a clearly focused contest between specifically identified private interests and where the facts and arguments have been developed exclusively on the record in an evidentiary hearing, we should insulate ourselves from the investigative/prosecutorial staff of the Bureau as a matter of administrative discretion. The Commission does not dispute this in principle; in fact, it formally adopted new separation procedures in 1974 to deal with this very problem. Restricted Rulemaking Proceedings, 47 FCC 2d 1183 (1974). The only reason given by the majority for refusing to apply this concededly important element of fair procedure to this case is that to do so would cause disruption and delay while new, nonseparated staff made itself familiar with the case. But this explanation seems to me more an excuse than a reason. We are not required—we have not even been requested—to separate the entire Bureau or even all persons having familiarity with the general issues. All that is required is to separate those who have actively participated in the prosecution of the case through the time of the preparation of the recommended decision of the Bureau Chief. . . .

The fact that the majority is unwilling to separate itself from even part of the Bureau staff seems to me to underscore the very concern that AT & T and other parties have expressed: that the Commission will depend more on their advice than the arguments and facts on the official record which has been so elaborately and exhaustively constructed. Certainly one could forgive the parties, and the public, for so viewing it—and this appearance in itself should be a matter of concern to us.

---

3. I say this mindful of the court's suggestion in Telpak Sharing that rate-making cases such as this involve, in Professor Davis' terminology, "legislative" rather than "adjudicatory" facts—a distinction which Davis developed for determining the appropriateness of evidentiary procedures in deciding "factual" questions. I have elsewhere questioned the usefulness of that distinction as a general guideline in determining what form of agency proceeding is appropriate. See Robinson, The Making of Administrative Policy: Another Look at Rulemaking and Adjudication and Administrative Procedure Reform, 118 Pa. L.Rev. 485, 503–504 (1970). And I question its utility in this particular case in deciding what kinds of hearing procedures are fair. For one thing, I cannot say that all the issues here are "legislative" as opposed to "adjudi-

catory." Certainly the mere fact they involve "matters of statistics, economics and expert interpretation," American Tel. and Tel. Co., supra, at 455, does not make them such to my mind. Moreover, labels aside, I doubt that the court in Telpak Sharing intended to suggest that all "matters of statistics, economics and expert interpretation" are properly determinable outside the accepted processes of hearing procedures—particularly when the case is one for which an evidentiary hearing has been prescribed. [I]t is noteworthy that Professor Davis himself would not apply his legislative/adjudicative fact test in the manner suggested by the court in Telpak Sharing since he criticizes the FCC severely for its refusal to separate the Bureau staff in such cases. See Davis, supra, 1970 Supp. at pp. 445–57.

NOTES

(1) *The Intentionality of Permission to Consult.* DANIEL J. GIFFORD, THE MORGAN CASES: A RETROSPECTIVE VIEW, 30 Ad.L.Rev. 237, 241–243 (1978): "When the [Morgan] Court seemingly equated a 'judicial model' of decision-making with a 'full hearing' and perhaps with the fair procedure demanded by the due process clause, it made no distinction about the types of proceedings to which its strictures would apply. . . . [It] became apparent in the aftermath of the Morgan decisions that the pristine judicial model by which the Court seemed to be guided was inappropriate for ratemaking cases like the Morgan cases themselves, and perhaps was also inappropriate for other kinds of highly technical and complex cases. The studies and investigations of the Attorney General's Committee, which took place in 1940, had indicated that ex parte consultation, at least as to background matters, was common in rate proceedings, and that without such consultation the decisional process would be unduly hampered.

"These assessments profoundly affected the design of the Administrative Procedure Act. . . . These exemptions from [§ 554(d)] were justified on two grounds; first, that the hearing officer would be likely to need expert assistance in the decision of complex and technical issues and, second, that the isolation of the decision maker which a strict judicial decision-making model would impose would not be as necessary in non-accusatory proceedings where no stigma attached to an adverse determination."

(2) *Are Sharp Lines of Division Required for Fairness?* WILLIAM F. PEDERSEN, JR., THE DECLINE OF SEPARATION OF FUNCTIONS IN REGULATORY AGENCIES, 64 Va.L.Rev. 991 (1978): "The current debate over when and to what extent administrative agencies should use trial-type hearings to make decisions has focused primarily on the costs and the benefits of the hearings themselves. 'Separation-of-functions' requirements, however, are a more important but largely unperceived defect of these hearings. These provisions forbid agency employees who worked on a matter in its early stages from advising or consulting with those who handle succeeding stages. These barriers can hinder efficient agency operation and lower the quality of final administrative decisions.

"Admittedly, a separation-of-functions rule has its place in an 'accusatory' proceeding, in which one group of agency employees prosecutes a private party for a violation of the law and another group must sit in judgment. Most significant decisions by government agencies, however, simply do not fit this model. Instead, they involve the formulation or the application of policy, without any connotation of wrongdoing, regarding persons who are being regulated. Agencies and their staffs exist to make policy decisions, and there is no reason to suspect that staff members who work on the early stages of a nonaccusatory proceeding view the choices confronting them in a manner any less valid than do those who handle succeeding stages. . . .

"Five independent characteristics of formal adjudication may contribute to a fair disposition of a particular case: (1) a decision based on a publicly defined and publicly accessible record, (2) a mechanism for confrontation between opposing points of view, (3) a mechanism for probing and, where possible, resolving differences on factual and other matters, (4) separation-of-functions requirements, and (5) an independent, judge-like hearing officer. The framers of the APA concluded that all five of these elements must be present in accusatory cases but only the first three in policy decisions. They undermined their own work, however, by requiring the factual probing to take the form of a trial-type hearing even in policy-dominated cases.

"Whether a decision requires separation of functions depends not only upon its basic nature but also upon the procedures used to make it. Trial-type hearings cast the agency's trial staff in an adversarial role, which almost inevitably calls forth a partisan attitude, but the APA also expressly sanctions informal reliance on the advice of these same staff members in reaching a final decision. Naturally enough, private lawyers who have confronted this staff in the hearing object fiercely to its taking any part in the subsequent deliberations within the agency. Accordingly, in the years since passage of the APA, agencies gradually have adopted rules to bar those who take part in the hearing from playing any role in the preparation of the resulting decision, even when the APA would permit their involvement. . . .

"Clothing non-accusatory administrative hearings with more of the trappings of adjudicatory proceedings may make better theater, but it probably reduces their substantive importance. Agency trial staffs, because of the separation-of-functions rules, and hearing examiners, because of their misconceptions of their proper role, do not participate in the informal discussions that often generate the agency's governing policies. Unawareness of these policies or simple separation from their development may prevent the outcome of the initial hearing from reflecting what the agency as an institution would consider to be the proper result."

(3) *Obstacles to Needed Communication?* HARVEY J. SHULMAN, SEPARATION OF FUNCTIONS IN FORMAL LICENSING ADJUDICATIONS, 56 Notre D.L.Rev. 351 (1981): "In its report, the President's Commission on the Accident at Three Mile Island found that the NRC commissioners 'have adopted unnecessarily stringent ex parte rules to preserve their adjudicative impartiality. . . .'[1] Although the President's Commission declined to make any recommendations regarding these rules, the report of the Chief Counsel of the President's Commission blamed the ex parte rules, in part, for the 'strained communication system within NRC' which interferes with the agency's ability to protect public health and safety.[2] The Chief Counsel's Report noted that, although not required by the APA, the NRC's ex parte rules

---

1. [Ed.] U.S. President's Commission on the Accident at Three Mile Island, Report of the President's Commission on the Three Mile Island Accident 51 (1979). The accident in question was the most serious ever to occur at a U.S. nuclear power station. It destroyed the reactor in question, led to temporary evacuation in the Harrisburg, Pa. area, and generated penetrating questions whether the U.S. Nuclear Regulatory Commission had adequate lines of communication and other procedures for assessing and controlling the safety of nuclear power plants. Note that, like the FLRA, the NRC adopted rules treating its staff as if they were outside the agency; thus, "ex parte" as used here denotes internal separation-of-function barriers as well as constraints on communications with outsiders.

2. Report of the Office of Chief Counsel on the Nuclear Regulatory Commission 31 (1979).

apply to initial licensing cases and to all NRC staff. Thus, the report suggests that if the NRC were willing to relax its ex parte rules, many of the agency's problems could be better resolved. Similarly, [an NRC-commissioned report known as] the 'Rogovin Report' concluded that NRC members are isolated 'from detailed consideration of case-related safety issues by the so-called 'ex parte rule.'[3] The report stated that the NRC rule goes far beyond APA requirements in separating commissioners from 'those within their own agency who have the most knowledge and expertise about these questions.' The Rogovin Report called for the NRC ex parte rule to be 'very significantly limited and applied more rationally.' "

Shulman's discussion, like Pedersen's, is concerned more with the institutional impacts of separation of functions than the fairness issues that private participants experience and that inform the AT & T dissent. Professor John R. Allison explores the latter in detail in Ideology, Prejudgment, and Process Values, 28 N.Eng.L.Rev. 657 (1994) and Combinations of Decision–Making Functions, Ex Parte Communications, and Related Biasing Influences: A Process–Value Analysis, 1993 Utah L.Rev. 1135.

(4) *Do Agencies' Political Leadership Have Expert Regulatory Knowledge?*
(a) GENERAL ACCOUNTING OFFICE, POLITICAL APPOINTEES: TURNOVER RATES IN EXECUTIVE SCHEDULE POSITIONS REQUIRING SENATE CONFIRMATION (April 1994): The GAO studied turnover in high-level government positions during ten years (1981–91) spanning the Reagan and Bush administrations. It was principally concerned with turnover among senior political appointees serving in "at will" positions, such as characterize the executive departments, and independent executive agencies such as EPA. It found that these officials tend to serve "for periods that are significantly shorter than a presidential term"—a median length of service of 2.1 years in executive government as a whole, but 1.7 years in the Departments of Labor and Commerce and 1.8 years at EPA; among departments with significant regulatory responsibilities, Agriculture (2.9 years) and Health and Human Services (2.5 years) were toward the high end of the scale. Appointees to term-limited positions, such as commissioners of the independent regulatory commissions, tended to serve longer terms.[4] The data reported for regulatory commissions included the following:

Agency	Number of Positions	Total turnover	Statutory length of term	Median length of service
CFTC	5	9	5	4.4
EEOC	6	12	5	3.1
FCC	5	10	5	4.1
FERC	5	11	4	2.9
FLRA	4	11	5	2.9

3. NRC Special Inquiry Group, Three Mile Island: A Report to the Commissioners and to the Public 141 (1980).

4. The general trend is consistent with earlier studies, for example, The Regulatory Appointments Process, I Study on Federal Regulation pursuant to S.Res. 71, Senate Committee on Government Operations, 95th Cong. 1st Sess. 89 (Comm.Print 1977).

Agency	Number of Positions	Total turnover	Statutory length of term	Median length of service
FMC	5	10	5	3.1
FTC	5	11	7	3.5
NLRB	6	15	5	4.1
NRC	5	11	5	4.6
OSHRC	3	10	6	1.4
SEC	5	12	5	3.6

The data does not discriminate between forced and voluntary resignations. Even within the independent agencies, however, consider whether the short time commissioners serve suggests that they make a greater political than expert contribution.

(b) JAMES O. FREEDMAN, EXPERTISE AND THE ADMINISTRATIVE PROCESS, 28 Ad.L.Rev. 363 (1976): "To the extent that skepticism of administrative expertise is based on the premise that agency members have often lacked expertise in the substantive areas that they have been appointed to regulate, it misses the mark in a crucial respect. The continuing expertness of an administrative agency as to matters of technical substance can be more properly understood as deriving primarily from its staff, and not from the shifting membership of those who temporarily serve as commissioners. It is, indeed, the experience and specialization of a large and dedicated staff that has permitted agencies to channel the diverse expertise of many individuals into the process of institutional decisionmaking—one of the unique contributions of the modern administrative process. . . .

". . . Because so many agency members are themselves generalists rather than experts in any professional sense, they may be particularly well qualified to perform the necessary function of moderating the staff's assertions of expertise.

"This function requires agency members to use the staff's expertise wisely but not uncritically: to measure the staff's expertise against the counsels of common sense, to place the staff's expertise within the context of a wider experience with the world of affairs, to coordinate the staff's various kinds of expertise into a coherent program, and to estimate the extent to which the staff's technical expertise must share the direction of agency policy with values drawn from the world of political and social experience.

". . . [T]hose who point to the absence of a technical expertise in agency members may actually be directing attention to an expertise of a different kind—an expertise in the art of skepticism about expertise, a competence in the worldly art of the politically acceptable and socially wise.

". . . [T]he agency member who is not a technical expert becomes an essential guarantor of the common sense and political acceptability of proposals that originate from experts, whether they be agency staff members or private retainers. As Laski so well understood:

"In convincing the non-specialist Minister that a policy propounded is either right or wrong, the expert is already halfway to convincing the public of his plans; and if he fails in that effort to convince, the chances are that his plans are, for the environment he seeks to control, inadequate or mistaken.

"The agency member who is not an expert thus performs one of the defining acts of the statesman: he serves, in Laski's words, as 'the broker of ideas without whom no bridges can be built between the expert and the multitude.' "

(ii) SECRETARY LEWIS—PRESSURE FROM OTHER PARTS OF GOVERNMENT

Secretary Lewis's telephone calls in PATCO point to another common characteristic of agency life, whose recognition as a consideration by courts, particularly in connection with on-the-record proceedings, raises significant issues. Not only may agencies perform multiple functions in their own decision-making—the FTC conducting economic surveys *and* bringing antitrust proceedings, Wisconsin state officials initiating disciplinary charges *and* deciding their merit. As important, and again unlike courts, agencies frequently act in the context of policies or issues whose administration or resolution is shared with other official actors or spread over a variety of activities; and they act in the unruly world of politics, subject to a range of official and unofficial controls courts simply do not encounter. To what extent shall courts seek to control these external influences? We have already seen that judicial attitudes toward alleged bias may turn substantially on consideration whether the challenged distorting influence arose "extrajudicially," outside the hearing. Courts also are prone to distinguish impermissible "ex parte contacts" by interested outside participants in agency proceedings from permissible advice and support, as to policy issues, from the agency's own staff. Communications like the Secretary's call might be thought to fall on middle ground, and resolution of the questions to which they give rise is correspondingly uncertain.

Alternatively, suppose that a recent course of decision by a particular agency suggests to its oversight committee—responsible under the Legislative Reorganization Act of 1946, Sec. 136, 60 Stat. 832, to "exercise continuous watchfulness of the execution by the administrative agencies" of the laws within the committee's jurisdiction—that the agency is straying from the correct policy path. May oversight hearings be convened while aspects of the policy issues remain unresolved before the agency? Congressional conversations with bank examiners engaged in particular investigations have produced scandals. Direct, paid Congressional representation of clients in governmental proceedings is absolutely forbidden by law, though evasion is not unknown.[1] But how about legislators' expressions of opinion concerning the merits of an as yet unresolved and highly important policy question that may be brought to the fore by a pending application—such

---

1.   18 U.S.C. § 203(a) prohibits direct or indirect compensation to a Member of Congress in any proceeding in which the United States is a party or has a "substantial interest" before any department or agency. Other statutes explicitly prohibit Congressmen's practicing before named tribunals.

as, for example, whether a license should be granted for nuclear energy power plants or whether the effective date of a pollution control order should be postponed? Should legislators scrupulously abstain from indicating their judgment about an issue of public policy until the administrators have finally announced their own conclusion? A major change in contemporary mores would be effected if Congressmen were to be rigorously precluded from asking questions about or making remarks concerning current administrative cases. Where is the line to be drawn between legislative vigilance and legislative intermeddling?

Portland Audubon Society v. The Endangered Species Committee

United States Court of Appeals for the Ninth Circuit, 1993.
984 F.2d 1534.

■ BEFORE GOODWIN, D.W. NELSON, and REINHARDT, CIRCUIT JUDGES.

■ REINHARDT, CIRCUIT JUDGE:

[This case arose out of litigation concerning timber sales in the habitat of the northern spotted owl, an endangered species living in the old growth forests of Oregon. The Endangered Species Act stringently regulates federal (and other) activity affecting such habitats. Under the Act, *only* a high-level, seven-member committee[1] may authorize exemptions from the Act, after a process based on a record compiled in an on-the-record hearing before an ALJ, a report by the Secretary of the Interior, and any other hearings or written submissions the Committee may call for. 16 U.S.C. § 1536. An exemption requires five votes. The committee had authorized thirteen of forty-four proposed timber sales affecting northern spotted owl habitat after such proceedings, only the second exemption ever authorized under the Act. Environmental groups wished to show that this decision was the product of improper ex parte contacts. News stories had reported White House pressure to approve the sales, and the groups' lead counsel averred that his conversations "with several [knowledgeable] sources within the Administration . . . reveal that . . .

> a. The press reports of White House pressure on ESC decisionmakers to vote in favor of an exemption—particularly, on Administrator John Knauss . . . and Administrator William Reilly . . . —during the period preceding the ESC's vote on May 14 are accurate. Administrator Knauss met with Clayton Yeutter and other members of the White House staff on April 28, 1992, and several times thereafter. Administrator Knauss and his staff also had substantial on-going contacts with White House staff concerning the substance of his decision on the application for exemption by telephone and facsimile, as well as through staff intermediaries.

1. The committee is made up of the Secretaries of Agriculture, the Army and the Interior, the Administrators of EPA and the National Oceanic and Atmospheric Administration, the Chair of the Council of Economic Advisors, and presidential appointees from the affected state(s) with one collective vote.

b. Administrator Reilly also met with Clayton Yeutter and other White House staff, on May 5, 1992, and again on May 13, 1992.

c. ESC members were told by White House staff that the Bush Administration viewed an ESC decision to grant an exemption as extremely important politically. White House staff sought to persuade ESC members, including both Administrator Knauss and Administrator Reilly, to support an exemption.

d. Administrator Knauss ultimately voted to support granting the exemption for 13 timber sales. Administrator Reilly ultimately voted against the exemption.

The exemptions were granted by a 5–2 vote, so the change in Administrator Knauss's vote, if it occurred, was decisive. In this case, the environmental groups were seeking leave to conduct discovery into these matters, to supplement the record on review of the committee's exemption order.]

This case raises two important and closely related questions of statutory construction: 1) Are Committee proceedings subject to the ex parte communications ban of 5 U.S.C. § 557(d)(1)? and, 2) are communications from the President and his staff covered by that provision? For the reasons that follow, we answer both questions in the affirmative.

. . . Section 557(d)(1) is a broad provision that prohibits any ex parte communications relevant to the merits of an agency proceeding between "any member of the body comprising the agency" or any agency employee who "is or may reasonably be expected to be involved in the decisional process" and any "interested person outside the agency."[2] . . . [B]y virtue of the terms of APA § 554, sections 556 and 557 are applicable whenever that section applies. . . . Under the Endangered Species Act the Committee decides whether to grant or deny specific requests for exemptions based upon specific factual showings.[3] Thus, the Committee's determinations are quasi-judicial [and] constitute "adjudications" within the meaning of § 554(a).

. . . The Endangered Species Act as well as the applicable part of its regulations are intended to ensure that all Committee meetings, hearings, and records are open to the public. . . . If ex parte communications with Committee members were permissible, it would render futile the efforts contained in the remainder of the regulations to make the Committee's deliberative process open to the public. . . . [Finally,] the Committee is, in effect, an administrative court. Ex parte contacts are antithetical to the very concept of an administrative court reaching impartial decisions through formal adjudication. . . . Basic fairness requires that ex parte communications play no part in Committee adjudications, which involve high stakes for all the competing interests and concern issues of supreme

---

2. The government does not dispute that the Committee is an "agency" within the meaning of the APA. See 5 U.S.C. § 551(1).

3. . . . Section 1536(h)(1)(A) . . . provides, in relevant part, that Committee deter-minations shall be "on the record, based on the report of the Secretary, the record of the hearing [held before an ALJ] . . . and on such other testimony or evidence as it shall receive."

national importance. See [PATCO]. Behind-the-scenes contacts have no place in such a process.

... Although the APA's ban on ex parte communications is absolute and includes no special exemption for White House officials, the government advances three arguments in support of its position that section 557(d)(1) does not apply to the President and his staff.[4]

First, the government argues that because the President is the center of the Executive Branch and does not represent or act on behalf of a particular agency, he does not have an interest in Committee proceedings greater than the interest of the public as a whole. Therefore, the government contends, neither the President nor his staff is an "interested person." Next, the government maintains that the President and his staff do not fall within the terms of section 557(d)(1) because the President's interest as the Chief of the Executive Branch is no different from that of his subordinates on the Committee. Specifically, the government claims that by placing the Chairman of the President's Council of Economic Advisors on the Committee, Congress directly and expressly involved the Executive Office of the President in the decision-making process ... [and] communications between [committee members] and the White House staff cannot be considered to come from "outside the agency." Finally, the government argues that if the APA's ex parte communications ban encompasses the President and his aides, the provision violates the doctrine of separation of powers. We find all three of the government's arguments to be without merit.

... The government does not contest the validity of PATCO as it applies to Cabinet level officials and below. However, it argues that the President's broader policy role places him beyond the reach of the "interested person" language. ... We believe the President's position at the center of the Executive Branch renders him, ex officio, an "interested person" ... in every agency proceeding. No ex parte communication is more likely to influence an agency than one from the President or a member of his staff. No communication from any other person is more likely to deprive the parties and the public of their right to effective participation in a key governmental decision at a most crucial time. The essential purposes of the statutory provision compel the conclusion that the President and his staff are "interested persons" within the meaning of 5 U.S.C. § 557(d)(1).

The government's ... [argument that] the President is, for all intents and purposes, a "member" of the Committee and may attempt to influence its decisions ... amounts to a contention that the President is not "outside the agency" for the purposes of APA § 557(d)(1). The Supreme Court soundly rejected the basic logic of this argument in United States ex rel. Accardi v. Shaughnessy, 347 U.S. 260 (1954). The Court held that where legally binding regulations delegated a particular discretionary decision to

---

4. Neither the affidavit of the environmental groups' counsel nor the newspaper reports state that former President Bush personally met or lobbied Committee members. The government argues, however, that alleged ex parte communications with the Committee should be treated identically whether they are made by the President or by White House staff carrying out his policies.

the Board of Immigration Appeals, the Attorney General could not dictate a decision of the Board, even though the Board was appointed by the Attorney General, its members served at his pleasure, and its decision was subject to his ultimate review. Here, the Endangered Species Act explicitly vests discretion to make exemption decisions in the Committee and does not contemplate that the President or the White House will become involved in Committee deliberations. The President and his aides are not a part of the Committee decision-making process. They are ... covered by section 557's prohibition and are not free to attempt to influence the decision-making processes of the Committee through ex parte communications.[5] ...

The government next contends that any construction of APA § 557(d)(1) that includes presidential communications within the ban on ex parte contacts would constitute a violation of the separation of powers doctrine. It relies on language in Myers v. United States that states that the President has the constitutional authority to "supervise and guide" Executive Branch officials in "their construction of the statutes under which they act." 272 U.S. 52, 135 (1926). The government argues that including the President and his staff within the APA's ex parte communication ban would represent Congressional interference with the President's constitutional duty to provide such supervision and guidance to inferior officials. We reject this argument out of hand.

The Supreme Court established the test for evaluating whether an act of Congress improperly interferes with a presidential prerogative in Nixon v. Administrator of Gen. Services, 433 U.S. 425 (1977). First, a court must determine whether the act prevents the executive branch from accomplishing its constitutional functions. If the potential for such disruption exists, the next question is whether the impact is justified by an overriding need to promote objectives within the constitutional authority of Congress. We conclude that Congress in no way invaded any legitimate constitutional power of the President in providing that he may not attempt to influence the outcome of administrative adjudications through ex parte communications and that Congress' important objectives reflected in the enactment of the APA would, in any event, outweigh any de minimis impact on presidential power.

... [C]arried to its logical conclusion the government's position would effectively destroy the integrity of all federal agency adjudications. It is a fundamental precept of administrative law that an when an agency performs a quasi-judicial (or a quasi-legislative) function its independence must be protected. ... Myers itself clearly recognizes that "there may be duties of a quasi-judicial character imposed on executive officers and members of executive tribunals whose decisions after hearing affect inter-

---

5. The government's argument that the Chairman of the Council of Economic Advisors was put on the Committee to involve the Executive Office in Committee deliberations is spurious. The obvious reason for the inclusion of that official on the Committee is that the [Committee] must make difficult decisions with profound economic impact. Five of the six other members of the Committee are Executive Branch officials who also serve solely at the pleasure of the President. See Myers v. United States, 272 U.S. 52 (1926).

ests of individuals, the discharge of which the President can not in a particular case properly influence or control." 272 U.S. at 135. And in Humphrey's Executor v. United States the Court observed that "[t]he authority of Congress, in creating quasi-legislative or quasi-judicial agencies, to require them to act in discharge of their duties independently of executive control cannot well be doubted." 295 U.S. 602, 629 (1935). The government's position in this case is antithetical to and destructive of these elementary legal precepts, and we unequivocally reject it.

... Franklin v. Massachusetts, 112 S.Ct. 2767 (1992), considered the question of whether the President was an "agency" within the meaning of the APA. The Court determined he was not based on the textual silence of the statute and the Court's "respect for the separation of powers." Had the Court found the President to be an "agency" for the purposes of the APA, his performance of his statutory duties would have become reviewable by the judiciary under the abuse of discretion standard. Given ... [such] a significant innovation in inter-branch relations, the Court was unwilling to assume that Congress intended such a result in enacting the APA without an express statement to that effect.

By contrast, the question here is whether the President, like all other government officials and everyone else, is a "person" (specifically an "interested person") within the meaning of 5 U.S.C. § 557(d)(1) ... Our holding works no innovation comparable to that which would have occurred if the President had been found to be an "agency" within the meaning of the APA. As noted above, the general principle that the President may not interfere with quasi-adjudicatory agency actions is well settled. Therefore, our decision is fully consistent with Franklin ...

Congress might well have established a different procedure for granting exemptions from the Endangered Species Act. However, the language of the Act shows that it intended to create the Committee as a quasi-judicial adjudicatory body subject to the statutory restrictions that the APA imposes on such institutions. Congress clearly has the authority to do so, and thereby to ensure the independence of the agency from presidential control. We conclude that the members of the Committee, despite the Cabinet level status they otherwise enjoy, are, while serving in their Committee capacities, precisely the kinds of "members of executive tribunals" that Myers and Humphrey's Executor contemplate are to be free from presidential influence.

In view of the above, we hold that communications between the Committee and the President or his staff are subject to the APA's prohibition on ex parte contacts.

[Considering the question of remedy, the court found unpersuasive arguments that the requirement that the Committee's decision be supported by the record ensured that it would be appropriately reasoned and subject to full judicial review, and that discovery into the Committee's decisional processes would impermissibly inquire into the mental processes of Committee members.] If the record is not complete, then the requirement that the agency decision be supported by "the record" becomes almost meaningless. ... Unlike the documents requested in San Luis Obispo Mothers for Peace v. United States Nuclear Regulatory Comm'n,

751 F.2d 1287 (D.C.Cir.1984), vacated in part, 760 F.2d 1320, 1321 (D.C.Cir.1985)(en banc) [noted at p. 998 below], those sought here concern neither the internal deliberative processes of the agency nor the mental processes of individual agency members. Rather, the discovery requested here involves allegedly improper ex parte contacts between decisionmakers and outside parties. If such ex parte communications occurred, then the record must be supplemented to include those contacts so that proper judicial review may be conducted.

[The court directed a remand to the Committee, directing it]to hold, with the aid of a specially appointed administrative law judge, an evidentiary hearing to determine the nature, content, extent, source, and effect of any ex parte communications that may have transpired between any member of the Committee or its staff and the President or any member of his staff regarding the determination of the exemption application at issue. . . . [6]

■ GOODWIN, CIRCUIT JUDGE, concurring:

. . . I agree that all of the executive and cabinet level officials involved here are subject to APA's ban on ex parte communications. This holding, however, does not require us to answer the still open question whether the President himself also falls within the rule's purview. . . . [T]here is no evidence in the record that the then-incumbent President made any ex parte contacts with members of the [Committee]. Accordingly, we have no need to reach the issue whether the President is himself subject to the APA's ban on ex parte communications—a question which presents troubling separation of powers problems. . . .

NOTE

Crossing the Threshold of Inquiry. One of the higher hurdles for Portland Audubon's attorneys would have been getting the court to inquire into whether communications, appropriate or inappropriate, had been received. Notable judicial reluctance to make such inquiries was expressed in the Morgan cases, p. 397ff. and appears elsewhere in these materials.[1] What persuades the court to lift the presumption of regularity here? SOKAOGON CHIPPEWA COMMUNITY V. BABBITT, 929 F.Supp. 1165 (W.D.Wis.1996) and 961 F.Supp. 1276 (W.D.Wis.1997), settlement affirmed by 214 F.3d 941 (7th Cir.2000), involved the Chippewa tribes' effort to win departmental approval for acquisition of a greyhound racing facility; this would create a gambling facility in competition with facilities already being managed in the area by other tribes, and those tribes sought political help to persuade the Secretary of the Interior to deny the request. They apparently succeeded, and the Chippewas sued. The two district court opinions, by U.S.

6. [Ed.] An article appearing in BNA National Environment Daily April 22, 1993, suggested that the inquiry might never occur, because the government had withdrawn its exemption request. The Clinton Administration, a Department of the Interior press release asserted, "is not interested in looking backward or in resurfacing allegations about the previous Administration."

1. See Citizens to Preserve Overton Park v. Volpe, and discussion following, p. 989 ff; Sierra Club v. Costle, p. 684.

District Judge Barbara Crabb, explore at sophisticated length the problems of enquiring into political oversight in a system in which "congressional representatives are expected to represent the concerns of their constituents vigorously" and presidential oversight, too, "is permissible and desirable," but "at some point overzealous participation becomes detrimental to the agency's ability to act." The court at first denied discovery, concluding that plaintiffs had failed to cross the threshold "strong showing of bad faith or improper behavior"; on reconsideration, however, the court permitted discovery, concluding that it had not given "full consideration to the inferences to be drawn from the evidence presented by plaintiffs." Plaintiffs were entitled to have these inferences drawn in their rather than defendants' favor, she concluded; once this was done, there was "sufficient reason to suspect that an improper political influence affected plaintiff's application" to allow discovery to proceed. As reported by the Seventh Circuit in affirming the settlement order that eventually resulted, permitting the acquisition, the "allegations of impropriety [had] created a political firestorm that included Congressional hearings and the appointment of an Independent Counsel to investigate alleged misdeeds of White House and Department of the Interior officials."

Pillsbury Co. v. FTC

United States Court of Appeals for the Fifth Circuit, 1966.
354 F.2d 952.

■ Before TUTTLE, CHIEF JUDGE, and JONES and ANDERSON, CIRCUIT JUDGES.

■ TUTTLE, CHIEF JUDGE:

[In 1952 the FTC filed a complaint against Pillsbury, challenging its then-recent acquisition of competing flour millers as having had a substantial anti-competitive effect. This put in issue the meaning and application of Section 7 of the Clayton Act, as amended by the Cellar–Kefauver Anti–Merger Act of 1950. In 1953 its trial examiner dismissed the complaint; the FTC reinstated it on appeal and remanded for what proved to be a lengthy hearing. The complaint might have been reinstated on either of two bases—(1) that § 7 "per se" forbade a merger in which one company already having a substantial share of the business absorbed an active competitor; or (2) that the Commission's staff had shown prima facie that competition had actually been diminished, now requiring Pillsbury to come forward. In its 1953 order, the Commissioner adopted the latter, less dramatic approach to § 7. This conclusion of law could be expected to govern many cases then before the Commission, and to increase the difficulty it would encounter in blocking or discouraging corporate mergers.

The remanded hearings before the trial examiner were still in progress when, in 1955, the antitrust subcommittee of the Senate Judiciary Committee under Senator Kefauver's chairmanship summoned then FTC Chairman Howrey and members of his staff to appear. Chairman Howrey came before the Kefauver committee with the FTC's General Counsel Kintner, Commissioner Secrest, and Director of Litigation Sheehy (whose assistant Kern later became a commissioner). The Kefauver committee was volubly dissatisfied with the Commission's failure to adopt a "per se" rule. Especially critical were the questions and observations of Senator Kefauver, who commented at length on what he believed to be imperfections in the Commission's interpretation of the legislation he had sponsored. At one stage Chairman Howrey protested bitterly about the Senator's having "delved too deeply into the quasi-judicial mind in the Pillsbury matter"; he announced that he would have to disqualify himself from further participation in the Pillsbury case.[1] This case or the Pillsbury name was referred to more than 100 times during three hearings before this and other Congressional committees.

In 1960, adhering to its criticized interpretation of § 7, the FTC ordered Pillsbury to divest itself of the companies it had acquired. By this time, Howrey was no longer on the FTC. Kintner, who wrote the opinion, had become Chairman; Secrest was still a member; Kern, who had been Sheehy's assistant but was not personally at the hearings, had become a Commissioner; Commissioner Anderson, the fourth and last sitting member in the 1960 opinion, had had no contact with the hearings. Pillsbury sought review on the grounds that the Commission had misapplied the statute, had acted on improper evidence, and had not accorded Pillsbury due process because Congressional committees had interfered with the decisional process while the case was under consideration. The court focused on the last point alone. The alleged interference, as the reviewing court later remarked, was not an impropriety concealed from public view, but consisted, rather, of "questions and statements made by members of two Senate and House subcommittees having responsibility for legislation dealing with antitrust matters all clearly spread upon the record." After reviewing the details, including six pages devoted to reproducing questions and answers taken from Hearings Before the Subcommittee on Antitrust and Monopoly of the Committee on the Judiciary, United States Senate, Eighty–Fourth Congress (First Session) Part I, the court continued:]

... We conclude that the proceedings just outlined constituted an improper intrusion into the adjudicatory processes of the Commission and were of such a damaging character as to have required at least some of the members in addition to the chairman to disqualify themselves. We think it illuminating to quote Chairman Howrey's statement relative to his decision to disqualify himself, which he read into the record at the House subcommittee hearing. He said:

"... I wrote the opinion [in the Pillsbury case]. It is still a pending adjudication; and because of some of the penetrating questions over on the Senate side, I felt compelled to withdraw from the case because I did not think I could be judicial any more when I had been such an advocate of its views in answering questions."

1. At the time of this inquest, Chairman Howrey is said already to have informed the White House of his intention to resign; he had been a very forceful chairman for the FTC who had repeatedly "been summoned before committees in both houses to defend his sweeping staff reorganization and his FTC policies which—it was said—'were par-

tial to big business.'" Victor Kramer and J. Graham, Appointment to the Regulatory Agencies, 77, Senate Committee on Commerce, 94th Cong., 2d Sess. (Comm. Print 1976). In this context, his "withdrawal" from the case may have the guise of tactics more than injured judicial mien.

In view of the inordinate lapse of time in this proceeding, brought to undo what was done by mergers completed in 1951, we are naturally loathe to frustrate the proceedings at this late date. However, common justice to a litigant requires that we invalidate the order entered by a quasi-judicial tribunal that was importuned by members of the United States Senate, however innocent they intended their conduct to be, to arrive at the ultimate conclusion which they did reach. . . .

We are sensible of the fact that, pursuant to its quasi-legislative function, it frequently becomes necessary for a commission to set forth policy statements or interpretative rules (to be distinguished from strict "legislative" rules, see generally 1 Davis, Administrative Law §§ 5.03–04 (1958)) in order to inform interested parties of its official position on various matters. This is as it should be.

At times similar statements of official position are elicited in Congressional hearings. In this context, the agencies are sometimes called to task for failing to adhere to the "intent of Congress" in supplying meaning to the often broad statutory standards from which the agencies derive their authority, e.g., "substantially to lessen competition" or "to tend to create a monopoly." There are those who "take a rather dim view of [such] committee pronouncements as to what agency policy should be, save when this is incident to proposals for amendatory legislation." Friendly, The Federal Administrative Agencies 169 (Harvard University Press 1962). Although such investigatory methods raise serious policy questions as to the de facto "independence" of the federal regulatory agencies, it seems doubtful that they raise any constitutional issues. However, when such an investigation focuses directly and substantially upon the mental decisional processes of a Commission in a case which is pending before it, Congress is no longer intervening in the agency's legislative function, but rather, in its *judicial* function. . . .

To subject an administrator to a searching examination as to how and why he reached his decision in a case still pending before him, and to criticize him for reaching the "wrong" decision, as the Senate subcommittee did in this case, sacrifices the appearance of impartiality—the sine qua non of American judicial justice—in favor of some short-run notions regarding the Congressional intent underlying an amendment to a statute, unfettered administration of which was committed by Congress to the Federal Trade Commission (see 15 U.S.C. § 21).

It may be argued that such officials as members of the Federal Trade Commission are sufficiently aware of the realities of governmental, not to say "political," life as to be able to withstand such questioning as we have outlined here. However, this court is not so "sophisticated" that it can shrug off such a procedural due process claim merely because the officials involved should be able to discount what is said and to disregard the force of the intrusion into the adjudicatory process. We conclude that we can preserve the rights of the litigants in a case such as this without having any adverse effect upon the legitimate exercise of the investigative power of Congress. What we do is to preserve the integrity of the judicial aspect of the administrative process. See United States v. Morgan, 313 U.S. 409, 422 (1941).

We are fully aware of the reluctance expressed by the Supreme Court to disqualify the members of the Federal Trade Commission for bias or prejudice (a somewhat different basis than that urged here) in Federal Trade Commission v. Cement Institute, 333 U.S. 683. There the Court seems to have placed its decision largely on the grounds of necessity [which do not apply here]. . . .

Although we conclude that the course of the questioning before the Senate subcommittee in June 1955 deprived the petitioner of [a fair and impartial hearing], we are convinced that the Commission is not permanently disqualified to decide this case. We are convinced that the passage of time, coupled with the changes in personnel on the Commission, sufficiently insulate the present members from any untoward effect from what occurred in 1955.

It is extremely unfortunate that this complaint, seeking divestiture by Pillsbury of two other companies acquired by it, has taken this long to reach the present stage of the litigation. It commenced as a pioneer case under the new amendment to the law. However, in the meantime much law has been written as to the quantity and quality of proof needed under a Section 7 complaint while it has been pending. . . .

We conclude that the order appealed from must be vacated and the case remanded to the Commission. The Commission as now constituted can then determine what steps should then appropriately be taken in view of both the lapse of time and the present state of the case law applying Section 7.[2]

NOTES

(1) Had § 557(d)(1)(A) been in place at the time, would it have applied on the Pillsbury facts? If the General Counsel of the FTC had foreseen what the hearing before Senator Kefauver's committee would entail, would it have been appropriate for him to call committee counsel, to suggest that questioning be limited to the FTC's interpretation of Section 7, and that the Pillsbury case not be mentioned by name? (One of your editors witnessed many similar negotiations with oversight committees.) If the committee observed that constraint, but Senator Kefauver was just as forceful in conveying his sense how Section 7 ought to be interpreted, would that have avoided any § 557(d) problem? Would it make any real difference to the agency's perception of the political forces bearing on it? To the public's or Pillsbury's perception of the fairness of the hearing in which

---

2. [Ed.] On remand in 1966 the Commission (now with a membership wholly different from that of 1960) dismissed the complaint, noting sadly that the case was then fourteen years old, had elicited some 40,000 pages of testimony which pertained to market conditions more than a decade ago, and presented grave difficulties in fashioning effective relief after so long a passage of time. Bearing in mind that its funds and personnel resources were limited, the Commission concluded that the public interest would not be served by further proceedings. But the order which dismissed the complaint ended with a small growl: "Any future acquisitions by respondent will receive careful attention, and the Commission will take such action thereon as may be required in the public interest." Matter of Pillsbury Mills, Inc., 69 F.T.C. 482 (1966).

it was engaged? See Ronald M. Levin, Congressional Ethics and Constituent Advocacy in an Age of Mistrust, 95 Mich.L.Rev. 1, 39 (1996).

(2) The Fifth Circuit's understanding of decisionmaker psychology may be compared with that expressed by the Supreme Court in cases like FTC v. Cement Institute and Withrow v. Larkin, pp. 408 and 414. How does the Fifth Circuit know what it knows about the influence of Senator Kefauver's questioning, not on a witness before his committee, but on observers present in the committee hearing room? If you conclude that this question is unanswerable, you may agree with author Pierce, p. 417 above, that the law on this subject is rather malleable. In CALIFORNIA EX REL. STATE WATER RESOURCES BOARD V. FERC, 966 F.2d 1541 (9th Cir.1992), for example, FERC had been considering a license application for a small hydroelectric facility that would divert water from a stream that supported populations of brown and rainbow trout. Preserving fish habitat is one of its responsibilities, to be weighed alongside more obviously economic factors. After a quasi-judicial hearing, it fixed five cubic feet of water per second as the residual flow the applicant would have to leave in the stream; state and Department of the Interior officials then sought higher levels. FERC reopened the hearing, and raised the required flow level to 7 cfs—not nearly what the state or the Department wanted, but too much for the applicant—who thought this judgment had been influenced by FERC's "lengthy correspondence" on the matter with Chairman John Dingell of the House Energy and Commerce Committee. (Chairman Dingell acquired general notoriety among agency officials in the 1970's and 1980's for the forcefulness of his oversight tactics.) To the Ninth Circuit, "Chairman Dingell's three letters to FERC complaining about the 10(j) procedures FERC had initially followed in this case do not rise to the level of undue congressional influence described in Pillsbury, nor do they adversely affect the appearance of impartiality in this case. FERC's decision to correct a procedural problem was based on its own independent analysis of the record in this proceeding, and was an effort to establish fair procedures to allow the parties and the commission to investigate. The [relevant] amendments to the Federal Power Act were recent, and both Chairman Dingell and the Commission were understandably concerned about getting off to a good start with 10(j) dispute resolution efforts.

"Nor do we find the two letters from Chairman Dingell that urged FERC to weigh the view of the legislative history of [an act relating to the Department of the Interior's responsibilities] ... to constitute the type of undue congressional influence that would mandate reversal of the final FERC order on this issue based upon Pillsbury. FERC gave a reasoned explanation for the reversal of its original interpretation of [that act], and this provides substance for its claim that it addressed and resolved the ... issue under its own independent and detailed analysis.... While we hold the Commission erred in its ruling ..., the record does not disclose that its decision was the result of undue congressional influence. In short, Chairman Dingell's letters, expressing his views on [these two statutory] issues, do not constitute the type of intense and undue congressional influence that was present in Pillsbury."

In Pillsbury, the FTC had not backed away from the statutory interpretation Senator Kefauver had criticized. Here, following Congressman Dingell's intervention, FERC changed its mind on a factual (not a legal-policy) issue, and in just the direction he suggested. How can a court tell how much or what kind of pressure is "intense and undue"?

(3) ATX v. DEPARTMENT OF TRANSPORTATION, 41 F.3d 1522 (D.C.Cir.1994): Frank Lorenzo, who had earlier run several airlines suffering severe labor, safety and financial difficulties, was the major figure behind an application to DOT for permission to fly a new commercial airline, ATX. Spurred on by his former labor unions "among others", over sixty members of Congress (including the House Majority Whip and the chairs of aviation committees and subcommittees) registered strong opposition to ATX in letters to the Secretary. Two introduced legislation designed to prevent Lorenzo from reentering the airline industry. One member who had both written and sponsored legislation testified before the ALJ the Secretary assigned to hear the application, adding no new facts to the record; the ALJ permitted this testimony over ATX's objection because "I think that the Department and the decision maker in this case would be interested in the views of a Congressman." The Secretary responded to each letter with a form letter stating:

> I want to assure you that the Department will examine [the ATX] application thoroughly under the fitness requirements that we impose on all prospective airlines. Since [the ATX] application is currently under review, I hope that you will understand that it would be inappropriate for me to discuss the merits of the case with you.

and indicating that he planned to place the letters in the file for "contacts outside the record of the case." At the conclusion of a first hearing before the ALJ, an Assistant Secretary made responsible for reviewing that decision[3] required additional hearings, over ATX's objection, because "the public interest requires that our decision here should be based on a more completely developed record." First the ALJ, and then the Assistant Secretary in a 75–page opinion, concluded that the application should be denied.

What other steps might the Department have taken to protect the integrity of its quasi-judicial hearing process against the congressional barrage? Did it do enough?

(iii) ALBERT SHANKER—RELATIONS WITH THE REGULATED AND THE PUBLIC

The final element in PATCO concerned member Applewhaite's dinner with Albert Shanker, an old friend and also—as head of a major union of public employees—a person with obvious and strong interests in the outcome of the PATCO matter. That they discussed the pending case and, in close proximity, Applewhaite's employment concerns, understandably concerned the reviewing judges. Here, the more political and emphatically

---

3. Perhaps because, as the congressional letters pointed out, the Secretary had been Mayor of Denver, Colorado when the sudden bankruptcy of one of Mr. Lorenzo's earlier carriers stranded thousands of travellers there.

temporary character of an agency head's work brings the contrasts with a judicial model, and concomitant concerns about fairness, into the sharpest relief.

If we step back for a moment from the dinner and its rather pointed subjects of discussion, it may be easy to understand that the agency officials cannot stay as aloof from the worlds of politics and constituencies as can judges. For agencies, continuing contact with a regulated industry, the public, and the press can have central importance for effective regulation. Informal contacts, press interviews, convention addresses and the like may help the agency win needed support, reduce future enforcement requirements (by helping industry anticipate and plan for compliance), float a trial balloon, spur the provision of needed information, signal their staff about their preferences, or otherwise achieve wholly understandable and worthy ends, if it can discuss its program informally as it unfolds. For such reasons, speech-writing staffs burgeon, and Commissioner Jones may devote as much personal attention to his upcoming luncheon talk to the Environmental Alliance as to the draft opinion being prepared in the Gesellschaft case. Businessmen need to know how they might be planning for future requirements; the public, a basis on which to assess the agency's program and effectiveness; agency staff see such communications as a window into their bosses' thinking that—because addressed to other and important audiences—may be more reliable than what is said directly to them. Courts, having no direct policy responsibilities, are not faced with the need to motivate and inform a staff, to defend their policies or budget before a concerned legislature, to impress on the public the work being done on their behalf, or to enlist the understanding or reluctant support of industry at a convocation.

Idaho Historic Preservation Council, Inc. v. City Council of the City of Boise

Supreme Court of Idaho, 2000.
134 Idaho 651, 8 P.3d 646.

■ SILAK, JUSTICE

[S–Sixteen Limited Partnership (S–Sixteen) sought a certificate of appropriateness from the Boise City Historic Preservation Commission, to permit it to demolish a warehouse building within the city's South Eighth Street Historic District, an area established under state historic preservation laws. The Commission denied the application, and S–Sixteen appealed to the Boise city council. Sitting in a quasi-judicial capacity, which limited its decision to the record made before it, the city council granted the certificate. A number of council members remarked that they had received numerous telephone calls from concerned citizens while the matter was pending, but denied that their judgment had been influenced. An Idaho district court overturned the city council's decision on due process grounds, because its members had received but not recorded the telephone calls. The city council then appealed. The Idaho Supreme Court first determined that its task was to determine, de novo, whether a violation of the process due in a quasi-judicial proceeding had occurred. It then continued:]

This Court has held that when a governing body sits in a quasi-judicial capacity, it must confine its decision to the record produced at the public hearing, and that failing to do so violates procedural due process of law. This Court has also observed that when a governing body deviates from the public record, it essentially conducts a second fact-gathering session without proper notice, a clear violation of due process. Since the substance of the telephone calls received by the members of the City Council was not recorded or disclosed at the public hearing, the Commission had no opportunity to rebut any evidence or arguments the City Council may have received from the callers. The Court of Appeals has held that prior notice of fact-finding sessions, maintenance of a transcribable record, and the opportunity to present and rebut evidence are elements of "a common core" of procedural due process requirements. . . .

Under Idaho law, therefore, the City Council's receipt of phone calls violated due process of the law. The City Council argues that the quasi-judicial standard "requires some fine tuning" with respect to ex parte communications. In support of this assertion, the City Council cites two Oregon cases which further address the quasi-judicial standard established by the Oregon Supreme Court in Fasano v. Board of County Commissioners, 264 Ore. 574, 507 P.2d 23 (Or.1973). This Court quoted portions of the Fasano opinion when it adopted the quasi-judicial standard with respect to judicial review of planning and zoning decisions.

Since Fasano, the Oregon Supreme Court has addressed the issue of whether due process of law prohibits ex parte communications between third parties and local government officials considering a matter in a quasi-judicial capacity. In one case, Tierney v. Duris, 21 Ore. App. 613, 536 P.2d 435 (Or. 1975), the Oregon Supreme Court stated that not all ex parte contacts would constitute a violation of the due process standards set forth in Fasano:

> We hold there is no violation of Fasano when, as in this case: (1) the "ex parte contacts" were not with the proponents of change or their agents, but, rather, with relatively disinterested persons; (2) the contacts only amounted to an investigation of the merits or demerits of a proposed change; and, most importantly, (3) the occurrence and nature of the contacts were made a matter of record during a quasijudicial hearing so that the parties to the hearing then had an opportunity to respond. As we read Fasano its basic requirement is an impartial tribunal; ex parte contacts were just mentioned as one way in which impartiality could be compromised.

Tierney, 536 P.2d at 443

In Neuberger v. City of Portland, 288 Ore. 585, 607 P.2d 722 (Or. 1980), the Oregon Supreme Court further narrowed Fasano's application to ex parte contacts in quasi-judicial proceedings:

> Fasano should not be read as adopting a mechanical rule that any ex parte contact touching on a matter before a tribunal acting quasi-judicially renders the tribunal, or its affected members, unable to act in that matter. To the extent that the language in that opinion can be so understood we disapprove it. The issue is not whether there were any

ex parte contacts, but whether the evidence shows that the tribunal or its members were biased.

Neuberger, 607 P.2d at 725.

Even if this Court were persuaded that Tierney and Neuburger express the better rule, the requirements of procedural due process . . . were not met. The members of the City Council who accepted phone calls failed to disclose the name and other identifying information of the callers, and also failed to reveal the nature of the conversation, making it impossible for the Commission to effectively respond to the arguments that the callers may have advanced. While the district court found that it "[did] not appear that any of these telephone contacts improperly influenced any ultimate opinion given by the individual [City] Council members," there was no evidence to support this conclusion because of the City Council's failure to sufficiently identify the callers and provide a general description of what they said in favor of or in opposition to the destruction of the Foster Building. We hold, therefore, that the receipt of phone calls in this case, without more specific disclosure, violated procedural due process. . . .

This decision does not hold the City Council to a standard of judicial disinterestedness. As explained above, members of the City Council are free to take phone calls from concerned citizens and listen to their opinions and arguments prior to a quasi-judicial proceeding. In order to satisfy due process, however, the identity of the callers must be disclosed, as well as a general description of what each caller said. . . .

Affirmed.

■ JUSTICE KIDWELL, dissenting . . .

Local government officials who have been elected have a necessary obligation to be receptive to constituent concerns. I believe that the majority opinion, by imposing judicial burdens on quasi-judicial proceedings, could have a chilling effect on this process. Therefore, I respectfully dissent.

"Due process . . . is not a technical conception with a fixed content unrelated to time, place and circumstances" but "is flexible and calls for such procedural protections as the particular situation demands." Mathews v. Eldridge, 424 U.S. 319, 334, (1976) (internal quotations and citations omitted). The U.S. Supreme Court has noted that the "specific dictates of due process" in any given situation require considering "the risk of an erroneous deprivation of such interest through the procedures used, and the probable value, if any, of additional or substitute procedural safeguards" and "the fiscal and administrative burdens that the additional or substitute procedural requirement would entail." Id. at 335.

In any decision such as this, city council members will unavoidably receive unsolicited communications from their constituents—not only by telephone but even as they walk down the street. Requiring council members to record the name of each opinionated constituent and the substance of each conversation not only is "unduly burdensome," Gay v. County Comm'rs, 103 Idaho 626, 629, 651 P.2d 560, 563 (Ct.App.1982), but also does little to reduce the risk of erroneously depriving a party of its interest. . . . It should be sufficient for city council members to indicate or state at public hearings that they received unsolicited communications from the public at large, that they acquired no information that was not already in the record, and that they were not biased by the communications. . . .

In this case, all the council members who received constituent telephone calls disclosed the existence of the calls at the public hearing. Their statements on the record indicate that they considered the telephone calls cumulative and not of great import. Council member Terterling's statement seems to indicate that the parties were aware of the existence of a flyer encouraging telephone calls on one side of the issue. Council members Mapp and Baker specifically stated that they received telephone calls from both sides of the issue. Because the telephone calls were of little gravity, did not seem to influence the council's decision, did not come from parties, and were disclosed at the public hearing, vacating the decision would serve no useful purpose. Therefore, I would not reverse the city council's decision on the basis of the ex parte contacts.

■ JUSTICE SCHROEDER concurs.

NOTES ON INAPPROPRIATE RELATIONSHIPS

Commissioner Applewhaite's concern for his employment future was not simply inappropriate self-interest, but the natural product of our public policy choices. For an agency's top personnel, outside the Civil Service, tenure in office is anything but assured. Indeed we specifically choose to have government led by persons who are *not* part of a permanent bureaucracy; even at lower levels, for example in the general counsel's office, we encourage people to use a "revolving door" from and to the private sector. This choice risks that individuals will be tempted into acting today for future benefit while they are in government service, or that they later will put information or contacts acquired in government service to a use in for undesired private benefit in the outside world. But the choice also has benefits, in improving communication and understanding between government and the private sector in a mixed economy, and in maintaining citizen (and political) control of that part of the bureaucracy that *is* more-or-less permanent. Having made the choice, we render concerns like Applewhaite's inevitable.[1]

The "ex parte" and bias issues that can arise from commission speechmaking and other ordinary contacts with the private world have been suggested in preceding materials, see especially pp. 418–20 above, and

1. Christopher Camponovo, Indecent Proposal: Abraham Sofaer, Libya and the Appearance of Impropriety, 21 J.Leg.Prof. 23 (1996) reports an annual turnover rate of 14% at the Department of Justice, one lawyer in seven. Ross Eckert, The Life Cycle of Regulatory Commissioners, 24 J.Law & Ec. 113 (1981), drawing on publicly available data for commissioners at three major federal independent regulatory commissions through 1977, found that private use of government experience was the prevailing pattern. Although about half of the 174 persons *appointed* commissioners to the agencies came from related *public* sector jobs, and only one fifth from the regulated industry, the proportions were reversed on exit: fifty percent took jobs in or serving the regulated industries; only eleven percent, jobs in the related public sector. See also Bruce Ackerman, The New Separation of Powers, 113 Harv.L.Rev. 633, 706 (2000) asserting that "The median tenure of a political appointee . . . is now about two years. One third serve for less than one and a half years," and p. 467 below.

need not be readdressed here. The suggestion that Applewhaite's contact with Shanker was *in itself* irregular opens issues that may warrant further attention.

(1) *The Effect of Criminal Investigation.* Does the fact of an FBI investigation itself suggest that PATCO should be reversed? Should PATCO be heard to complain about a contact that, presumably, would have worked in its favor? In SOUTHWESTERN BELL TELEPHONE CO. V. OKLAHOMA CORPORATION COMMISSION, 873 P.2d 1001 (Okla.), cert. denied 513 U.S. 869 (1994), one of the three elected members of the Oklahoma Corporation Commission announced that for several years he had been cooperating with an FBI investigation of efforts by persons allegedly working on behalf of Southwestern Bell to bribe him and one or more of his fellow commissioners. He had, he said, received money from a utility attorney, lobbyist, and/or officer, and had advised senior corporate officers of "the conduct of persons associated with their firm." Southwestern Bell sought mandamus to force disqualification only of the member making the announcement, and not of the other commissioners, in advance of forthcoming commission rate hearings. The Oklahoma court evaded any question raised by this choice, by concluding that the doctrine of necessity would permit the commissioner to sit in a quasi-judicial proceeding and, very questionably, that the rate-making proceeding in which Bell sought this remedy was legislative in character and thus beyond the reach of due process concerns.

Framing an appropriate remedy for such improper conduct (short of criminal prosecution of responsible individuals, where warranted) can be daunting. The PATCO court was able to conclude that no remedy was required for the indiscretions that had occurred. What might an effective remedy have been? In some cases, disqualification has been administered, and plainly the threat that the agency will withhold whatever the communicator is seeking to gain can serve as a significant control. Thus, in WKAT, Inc. v. FCC, 296 F.2d 375 (D.C.Cir.1961), cert. denied 368 U.S. 841 (1961), cited by the PATCO court, the court disqualified a successful applicant for a television license worth millions, because of its improper ex parte efforts to influence the role of an FCC commissioner. This sanction cannot be applied invariably, however, without risking a hurt instead of an advantage to the public interest.

(2) *Lunches and Dinners with "Friends".* The problems of government ethics and government ethics regulation are far more subtle than criminal prohibitions against bribery; the implications of choosing an ethics regime for government employees' self-regard (and, hence, morale) as well as their futures outside government can be large. In general, such matters are the domain of the Office of Government Ethics, initially a part of the Office of Personnel Management but now a separate agency. Its nearly two hundred pages of regulations form Chapter XXVI of 5 C.F.R., binding on executive branch employees. Were a FLRA Commissioner to consult them today before going to dinner with an old friend who was also an official of a union interested in the outcome of a pending matter, or seek the counselling the OGE offers, he would find ample reason for caution. 5 C.F.R. § 2635.201 ff. In their detail—not only declaring a $20 maximum value for acceptable "gifts," for example, but also indicating that retail value must be observed, and stating principles on which the values of several trivial gifts must be

amalgamated—rules in such detail have been objectionable to some. "We see that meals pose a danger to morality, and that unfairness in the treatment of Citizen A versus Citizen B may spread alarmingly because of the allure which a good salad or a delicious piece of beef or a titillating highball may have for a servant of the public or his clerk. Rather than being a shield of good behavior, the enunciation of such rules seems to be an admission that the civil service is filled with weak characters whose will can be reduced to putty by a gift of spaghetti Bolognese. This is truly a libel upon the civil service." B. Boles, Correctives for Dishonest and Unfair Public Administrators, 363 The Annals 23 (1966).

The problems of government ethics regulation were the subject of study by a special ABA COMMITTEE ON GOVERNMENT STANDARDS, CYNTHIA R. FARINA, REPORTER, KEEPING FAITH: GOVERNMENT ETHICS AND GOVERNMENT ETHICS REGULATION, 45 Ad.L.Rev. 287 (1993): "The more zealous the effort to identify and legislate against wrongful conduct, the more elusive the goal of achieving ethical behavior has become. Each reform initiative has added another layer of regulation. The result is a complex and formidable rule structure, whose rationale is increasingly obscure and whose operation is increasingly arcane. Ethics is in danger of becoming an elaborate legalistic ritual, in which the application of multi-part tests substitutes for the internalization of values, and the establishment of multi-level clearance processes replaces the development of a supportive institutional culture. For government employees who must negotiate this ritual, the result is frustration and alienation. For citizens who hear all the ethics fanfare but nonetheless see government 'as usual,' the result is disillusionment and cynicism. . . .

"Of all areas of substantive ethics law, the rules defining and remedying conflicts of interest are the most central, and the most vexing. Here, the longstanding American commitment to citizen governance comes up against several fundamental ideals of ethical public service. The result is considerable tension and ambivalence.

"On the one hand, a continual stream of people entering government from the private sector is perceived as highly desirable. The current popularity of term-limitation laws reflects this perception. Movement between government and the private sector is valued as injecting energy, experience, practicality and perspective that would be lacking in government-by-professional-bureaucracy. On the other hand, there is an equally strong conviction that neither elected nor appointed officials should have financial interests or relationships outside government that compromise their exercise of power. . . . [T]he ethical obligations of Fidelity to the Public Interest and Scrupulous Integrity are central to our conception of public service as a public trust.

"For these reasons, public employees' connection with the world outside government is something simultaneously desired, and distrusted. Such links can bring invaluable knowledge and experience to public policymaking. At the same time, they can set the stage for distortion and corruption. Conflict-of-interest rules must balance the hope for the former against the fear of the latter.

"... [E]thics regulation will be both redundant and inadequate if it focuses merely on condemning the deliberate abuse of trust. It will be redundant because the criminal law (through the vehicles of bribery, illegal gratuities, embezzlement, etc.) already proscribes such behavior. It will be inadequate because the overwhelming majority of government employees, knowing themselves to be honorable persons who would never consciously misuse their position, can readily dismiss such proscriptions as irrelevant to their own professional lives—and so fail to reflect upon the insidious ways in which bias and self-interest can infect, almost unwittingly, the exercise of power. Hence, ethics regulation can make its most meaningful contribution by helping government employees to recognize, and take steps to defuse, situations that invite compromised behavior.

"In this sense, then, conflict-of-interest regulation should formally incorporate concerns about the *potential for* (i.e., the 'appearance'), as well as the *fact of*, impropriety. The basic rules in this area are appropriately delineated by asking, 'In what circumstances does it become difficult to believe that, even for a person of character and integrity, the capacity to act as a steward remains unimpaired?'[2] However, beyond this initial role in rule formulation, 'appearance of impropriety' is too vague and contestable a concept to function effectively as an independent benchmark in a system of ethics regulation."

NOTES ON THE REVOLVING DOOR

(1) *Permitted Employment Following Government Service.* Statutory regulation of the revolving door problem today occurs under the Ethics in

2. [Ed.] "Stewardship" was earlier identified as the defining characteristic of "public trust":

"The fiduciary, or steward. Although our society recognizes many kinds of fiduciaries, the essence of the role is always the same. The fiduciary, or steward, is one to whom power is given in order that his knowledge and skill can be brought to bear for the benefit of another. . . . [T]his transfer of power is neither a desperate confession of inability to rule ourselves, nor an unconditional submission to some outsider's superior claim to rule us. Those who receive the power to govern have no inherent right to it. Rather, the power that a free and willing citizenry gives to those who govern comes indelibly impressed with the duty to serve the interests of that citizenry. And, just as the power need not have been given, so it need not have been accepted. To take the power is to take on the responsibility of service with which it is invested."

The steward's obligations were identified as at least the following:

"*Fidelity to the Public Interest.* . . . In the cast of stock cultural characters, the 'faith- less steward,' who uses the power he has been given to serve the interests of someone other than his principal, epitomizes dishonor and betrayal. . . .

"*Scrupulous Integrity.* Daniel Webster once observed, 'In a government like ours, entirely popular, care should be taken in every part of the system, not only to do right, but to satisfy the community that right is done.' . . .

"*Competence and Diligence.* . . . While abuse of public power is clearly intolerable, the responsible use of public power is also compromised by mediocrity, complacency and neglect.

"*Discretion.* . . . Because the possession of [sensitive information about public and private persons and activities] is justified only to accomplish public purposes, those entrusted with it must treat it with utmost care. . . .

"*Responsiveness.* . . . The fundamental obligation to serve the public requires that government employees provide citizens with the assistance they need to comprehend their legal rights and duties, and to obtain meaningful access to official decisionmakers."

Government Act of 1978, 5 U.S.C. App., and implementing regulations of the Office of Government Ethics, 5 C.F.R. Part 2641. Federal criminal law had long provided that a former official may not appear for a private client after leaving government in a distinct matter (adjudication, grant, contract—but *not* rule) in which he had been "personally and substantially" involved while in government; and that he may not appear for a year respecting any like matter for which he had official "responsibility" during the year before he left government. A moment's reflection will show that these prohibitions are limited—there is no bar to advising a client so long as one does not appear; one's partner may appear; appearance is acceptable so long as it is not in connection with a "matter" within reach of one or the other rule; and, finally, waivers could on occasion be obtained. The Ethics in Government Act tightened post-employment constraints in some respects. As amended, 18 U.S.C. § 207 now extends the lifetime ban on participation in particular matters in which the former employee was "personally and substantially" involved to informal as well as formal appearances. In addition, for two years she is forbidden to counsel, aid, consult, advise, or assist others so appearing; the same extended two year ban applies to all matters formally under her official responsibility. For one year, high-level former employees are completely forbidden to make any approach to the agency, formal or informal, oral or written, seeking to influence outcomes—in this case, including rulemaking and whether or not the matter was pending during their tenure or within their responsibility.[1] In addition to the draconian (and consequently cumbersome and often reluctant) processes of criminal law, the agency concerned may impose a sanction as large as five years' disqualification to appear before it.

Is the former employee, then, wholly out in the cold? No, she may appear in whatever does not concern a "particular matter" she had the requisite connection with, unless she is subject to the one year ban on *all* business appearances before her former agency. And, so far as this statute is concerned, the disqualification is wholly personal. If she joins a law firm, her partners and associates can continue *their* appearances before her former agency; and once two years have expired, they can have her aid and counsel even in those matters respecting which she could not appear. To judge by newspaper accounts reasonably current at the time of this edition, and perhaps unsurprisingly, questionable behavior still occurs:

> CLINTON: "In his last months as a ranking official in the Clinton Administration, Michael J. Anderson made a pivotal decision in favor of the St. Regis Mohawk Indian tribe in a multibillion-dollar dispute over casino gambling, then left office for a job working on behalf of the tribe's gaming interests.
>
> "Anderson was the deputy chief of the Bureau of Indian Affairs when he was asked by the Mohawks last fall for help removing a major obstacle to the tribe's ambitious plans to open a casino in the Catskill Mountains of New York. . . .

---

1. Provision is made for the agency to seek its former employee's advice where the agency wants that advice, and the agency only is paying any compensation that may be received for it.

"Now, the Department of Interior's inspector general is investigating whether Anderson's decision in favor of the Mohawks was influenced by his job prospects, and whether he violated the federal revolving-door statute in his recent role as lobbyist for the tribe. . . ." Sean P. Murphy, "Official Took Job After Aid For Casino," Boston Globe, April 14, 2001, at A1.

BUSH: "Mr. Bush hasn't repeated Mr. Clinton's initial gestures. He has required lobbyists who assisted his transition to disclose their clients and financial interests. He also requires them to sign a 'code of ethics,' which prevents them from using nonpublic information they obtain to help current clients or attract new ones. But Mr. Bush didn't attempt to prevent them from immediately lobbying the individuals they worked with." Jim VandeHei, "Some Bush Aides Move From Interim Posts Back to Lobbyist Jobs," The Wall Street Journal, March 19, 2001, at A22.

The criminal provisions of the federal Ethics in Government Act received a strikingly narrow interpretation in United States v. Nofziger, 878 F.2d 442 (D.C.Cir.1989), cert. denied 493 U.S. 1003 (1989). While its specific holding, concerning scienter, appears to have been cut back somewhat by 1989 amendments to the statute, those amendments have also narrowed the scope of the statute—it now applies only to direct appearances or communications by the former employee; it is no longer a criminal offense for a former employee to counsel, aid, consult, advise or assist others who communicate or appear during the two years immediately following her government service. (A one-year ban on counseling, for members of the legislative branch as well as the executive branch, does apply in limited circumstances respecting trade and treaty negotiations.) See Eric Murdock, Finally, Government Ethics As If People Mattered: Some Thoughts on the Ethics Reform Act of 1989, 58 Geo.Wash.L.Rev. 502 (1990).

(2) ABA COMMITTEE ON GOVERNMENT STANDARDS, CYNTHIA R. FARINA, REPORTER, KEEPING FAITH: GOVERNMENT ETHICS AND GOVERNMENT ETHICS REGULATION, 45 Ad.L.Rev. 287 (1993): "Like conflict-of-interest regulation, regulation of the activities of individuals as they leave government service is simultaneously motivated and complicated by two contending forces. The public's interest lies *both* in making public service attractive to talented citizens who can contribute experience and perspective to government policymaking before returning to the private sector, *and* in ensuring that the power of government office is used for the public good rather than for private advantage. Historically, this latter interest has probably been undervalued by ethics regulation. Until the late 1980s, no comprehensive scheme existed for regulating the post-employment activities of Legislative and Executive Branch employees. And the statutory restrictions enacted at that time—while a commendable step—are, on the whole, quite modest. Hence, it is not surprising that more vigorous regulatory approaches, such as the lengthy lobbying bans contained in Executive Order 12,834, generate considerable enthusiasm.[2]

2. [Ed.] Immediately on taking office, President Clinton promulgated Executive Order 12834, 58 Fed.Reg. 5911 (1993), requiring all senior officials to promise as part of their

"... Nonetheless, we urge caution lest the zeal of regulatory reform produce an over-correction. For reasons of both political principle and pragmatic necessity, our country prizes the ability to draw on the skills of citizens who have been, and will return to be, private-sector managers, physical and social scientists, technical experts, and medical and legal professionals. Truly effective regulation in this area will forestall the exploitation of public office without so cabining post-employment activities that noncareer government service becomes undesirable to these people. Moreover, it will take into account the tacit but fundamental premise of citizen government: Most who serve are honorable persons who would disdain any intentional abuse of power or position.

"Of course, actually achieving this ideal of balanced regulation is not easy—particularly because it is not always clear precisely what ... is the answer to the question 'Which use of advantage in which situation is actually unethical?' Surely we are not prepared to say that *any* use at *any* time of *any* knowledge or influence acquired during government service on behalf of a party other than the federal government, is an abuse of the public trust. Taking such a position would mean that a lawyer who had clerked for the Supreme Court could never draft a certiorari petition for a private client, or that a scientist who had worked for the FDA could never take a job in commercial new drug development, or that an MBA who had worked for the SEC could never join an investment banking house. Neither sound ethics policy nor good government supports an approach in which individuals can enter government service only at the cost of radically reconfiguring their subsequent professional lives.

"We believe that the ethicality of using the advantages of former government employment tends to be a function of three factors:

"i) *The Nature of Former Official Responsibility*: Of greatest concern are situations in which the former employee had significant decisional responsibility, had access to sensitive information, or otherwise functioned in an influential role as draftsperson, strategizer or counselor.

"ii) *The Nature of the Matter*: Of greatest concern are situations that resemble adjudicatory 'cases'—i.e., that involve specific, identified parties and that are in some stage of contention, either between the government and other parties or among other parties with the government acting as referee.

"iii) *The Nature of the Aid Given the New Employer or Client*: Of greatest concern are situations in which the former employee functions directly or indirectly as advocate, and to a somewhat lesser degree as strategizer, draftsperson or counselor to help advance her new employer's position in an ongoing matter with the government.

"In addition, timeframe is likely to be relevant. Although the mere passage of time will not inevitably render the use of advantage ethically acceptable,

terms of employment with the federal government that after leaving government they would refrain from contact with their department, or parts of government that had been under their supervision, for five years.

the value of influence and sometimes knowledge does, as a practical matter, dissipate over time."

(3) MARK KELMAN, ON DEMOCRACY-BASHING: A SKEPTICAL LOOK AT THE THEORETICAL AND "EMPIRICAL" PRACTICE OF THE PUBLIC CHOICE MOVEMENT, 74 Va.L.Rev. 199 (1988): " . . . [S]ome empirical work, albeit of a fairly weak nature, suggest[s] that bureaucratic behavior is better explained by broad ideological beliefs than by simple self-interest. William Gormley, for instance, . . . found that the political party identification of FCC Commissioners better predicted voting on nonunanimous issues than did association with the industry prior to service.[3] Gormley's work, however, should hardly dissuade those who view Commissioner behavior as narrowly based in self-interest: the study does not account for employment opportunities after service, nor does it attempt to distinguish the significance of different issues facing the agency.[4] More interestingly, Jeffrey Cohen finds a (rather weak) tendency for past employment in the regulated broadcast industry to affect votes, but finds that people who will find employment in the regulated industry after their regulatory service are less than typically likely to side with the industry.[5] Because self-interested economic behavior is essentially forward-looking, and past ties to the industry might be expected to heavily influence Commissioners cognitively and ideologically, this finding should be especially disturbing for those who expect narrow self-interest to govern. Ross Eckert's hypothesis that regulated industries hire ex-regulators not as a bribe, but simply because such people are likely to have gained relevant technical expertise,[6] certainly seems consistent with Cohen's data. But . . . Cohen does nothing to weight the significance of distinct pro-and anti-industry votes, and he also does little to explain whether the (weak) tendency he notices of Commissioners to vote more frequently with the regulated industry in their last year on the job[7] is better explained by shifts in perception associated with experience in hearing industry claims, or is simply a jobseeking strategy.

"Public choice theorists may well spend so little time thinking about why people actually undertake public service careers because . . . motivational questions may be complicated. Survey evidence seems to support the commonsensical view that leaders quite frequently sacrifice financially

---

3. See William Gormley, A Test of the Revolving Door Hypothesis at the FCC, 23 Am.J.Pol.Sci. 665 (1979).

4. For instance, those Commissioners who had been employed before government service by the regulated broadcast industry were especially likely to side with the industry position on deregulation of cable industries. See id. at 676–78. It is surely plausible to me—and the author does nothing to allay my fears—that these votes alone were as materially consequential as were all the 53.2% of nonunanimous votes on which the ex-broadcast industry employees went against the expressed views of ex-employers. See id. at 674–75.

5. See Jeffrey Cohen, The Dynamics of the "Revolving Door" on the FCC, 30 Am. J.Pol.Sci. 689, 693–95 (1986) (those ultimately finding work in the industry supported it 44.9% of the time, compared to 55.4% for those who did not end up working in the industry).

6. See Ross Eckert, The Life Cycle of Regulatory Commissioners, 24 J.L. & Econ. 113, 120 (1981). This view is consistent with Paul Quirk's survey findings that regulators themselves (at least in some industries) believe that their activity has little impact on their ultimate employment prospects, Industry Influence in Federal Regulatory Agencies 148–74 (1981).

7. [A]t 704.

when entering public life[8] or care less about money than people who stay in the private sector,[9] but this evidence is largely ignored, accumulated without comment, by what amounts to ideological fiat. It is certainly much more difficult to 'test' the hypothesis that X acted out of exhibitionism or altruism than that he did so from desire for financial gain: there will rarely be externally verifiable correlates for nonfinancial motives. But there is no reason to adopt the economists' flattened motivational explanation, which has frequently been shown wanting, simply because it offers the most readily testable hypothesis.''

(4) BRUCE ACKERMAN, THE NEW SEPARATION OF POWERS, 113 Harv. L. Rev. 633, 706–09 (2000): "[T]he overwhelming majority of [political appointees] have substantial governmental experience, and many have worked previously in the agencies in which they receive their political appointments. Nonetheless, political appointees do not stay in office long enough to operate productively. The median tenure of a political appointee has been going down for some time and is now about two years. . . .

"These numbers introduce a very depressing, albeit prosaic, story. Most appointees must move to Washington, and they are inevitably distracted by the humdrum tasks of finding housing, caring for children and spouses, and the like—or commuting constantly to their hometowns. Because appointees to the same agency typically do not know one another beforehand, their first months on the job are inevitably spent learning each other's biases and idiosyncrasies. And the constant turnover makes this a never-ending enterprise. The result is a devastating lack of the teamwork that is essential for coherent policy development.

"Moreover, a series of short-term appointments yields a remorselessly short-term policy focus and a constantly shifting search for new panaceas. . . . Short-run, disjointed, ever-changing: this disheartening managerial pattern is confirmed by survey data suggesting that only twenty-eight percent of senior civil servants think of political appointees as possessing 'good management skills.' Many political appointees agree—only fifty-five percent think of themselves as good managers.

"Worse yet, there is no obvious way to induce political appointees to extend their stay in government. By definition, they cannot retain their jobs indefinitely—this would convert them into senior civil servants. It is only natural for them to view their positions as launching pads for acquiring more secure jobs. Moreover, it has become increasingly rare for political appointees to make a mini-career for themselves by linking jobs together into an extended stay in government—spending two years as an assistant secretary and then moving up for two more years as a deputy secretary. The revolving door now operates with relentless speed—two years in government, then out the door into the private sector.

"This constant churning brings new problems in its wake. Recurring vacancies take time to fill, averaging from six to twenty months at eight major agencies selected for study by the General Accounting Office. During all this time, necessary decisions pile up in administrative limbo as standins wait for the presidential appointee finally to arrive—perhaps only to

---

8. See Dean Mann & Jameson Doig, The Assistant Secretaries 162–64 (1965) (nonfinancial recruiting of Assistant Secretaries seems to be commonplace); U.S. Merit Sys. Protection Bd., The 1984 Report on the Senior Executive Service 15, chart 2.1 (1984)

(only 18% of senior executives gave pay levels as a reason to stay at their jobs).

9. See Edward Lawler, Pay and Organizational Effectiveness: A Psychological View 55–56 (1971).

learn that a crucial collaborator or superior has just announced her departure.

"What is more, the ongoing rush to the private sector generates an ongoing problem for the President: how is he to prevent his loyalists from selling out his programs in their effort to maximize their post-governmental income? The obvious solution: impose rules of ethics that prohibit departing appointees from cashing in too quickly and obviously on their preexisting connections. Putting aside the possibilities of evasion and the inevitable exploitation of loopholes, such initiatives can at best reduce, and not eliminate, the sellout incentive. Nevertheless, there is no reason to suppose that any President will try to change things anytime soon. Although his political loyalists may have bad incentives, at least they are his appointees—and that is a lot better than dealing with bureaucrats who look to his rivals in Congress for all their cues."

(5) ABA, MODEL RULES OF PROFESSIONAL CONDUCT (2002), RULE 1.11, "SUCCESSIVE GOVERNMENT AND PRIVATE EMPLOYMENT":

"(a) Except as law may otherwise expressly permit, a lawyer who has formerly served as a public officer or employee of the government:

"(1) is subject to Rule 1.9(c) [requiring the maintenance of confidentiality of information learned in representing a former client]; and

"(2) shall not otherwise represent a client in connection with a matter in which the lawyer participated personally and substantially as a public officer or employee, unless the appropriate government agency gives its informed consent, confirmed in writing, to the representation.

"(b) When a lawyer is disqualified from representation under paragraph (a), no lawyer in a firm with which that lawyer is associated may knowingly undertake or continue representation in such a matter unless:

"(1) the disqualified lawyer is timely screened from any participation in the matter and is apportioned no part of the fee therefrom; and

"(2) written notice is promptly given to the appropriate government agency to enable it to ascertain compliance with the provisions of this rule.

"(c) Except as law may otherwise expressly permit, a lawyer having information that the lawyer knows is confidential government information about a person acquired when the lawyer was a public officer or employee, may not represent a private client whose interests are adverse to that person in a matter in which the information could be used to the material disadvantage of that person. As used in this Rule, the term 'confidential government information' means information that has been obtained under governmental authority and which, at the time this Rule is applied, the government is prohibited by law from disclosing to the public or has a legal privilege not to disclose and which is not otherwise available to the public. A firm with which that lawyer is associated may undertake or continue representation in the matter only if the disqualified lawyer is timely screened from any participation in the matter and is apportioned no part of the fee therefrom.

"(d) Except as law may otherwise expressly permit, a lawyer currently serving as a public officer or employee:

"(1) is subject to Rules 1.7 ["Conflict of Interest: Current Clients"] and 1.9 ["Duties to Former Clients"]; and

"(2) shall not:

"(i) participate in a matter in which the lawyer participated personally and substantially while in private practice or nongovernmental employment, unless the appropriate government agency gives its informed consent, confirmed in writing; or

"(ii) negotiate for private employment with any person who is involved as a party or as attorney for a party in a matter in which the lawyer is participating personally and substantially, except that a lawyer serving as a law clerk to a judge, other adjudicative officer or arbitrator may negotiate for private employment as permitted by Rule 1.12(b) . . .

"(e) As used in this Rule, the term 'matter' includes:

"(1) any judicial or other proceeding, application, request for a ruling or other determination, contract, claim, controversy, investigation, charge, accusation, arrest or other particular matter involving a specific party or parties, and

"(2) any other matter covered by the conflict of interest rules of the appropriate government agency."

(6) *Questioning the Chinese Wall.* MONROE FREEDMAN, "CORPORATE BAR PROTECTS ITS OWN," Legal Times, June 15, 1992, p. 20: "The plain meaning of the American Bar Association's 1969 Model Code of Professional Responsibility (then in effect in virtually all jurisdictions) was not in dispute [in the late 1970's]. DR 9–101(B) of the ethical code said that a lawyer 'shall not accept private employment in a matter in which he had substantial responsibility while he was a public employee.' And DR 5–105(D) added that when the former government employee was disqualified, other lawyers in his firm were also disqualified.

"As explained in ABA Formal Opinion 342 (1975), these rules had 'long been recognized.' The one requiring imputed disqualification, the opinion said, 'is based upon the close, informational relationship among law partners and associates and upon the incentives, financial and otherwise, for partners to exchange information freely among themselves when the information relates to existing employment.'

"It is not surprising, therefore, that the Legal Ethics Committee of the D.C. Bar (which I then chaired) voted unanimously to give the rule its plain meaning, disqualifying the law firm as well as the lawyer. But before the committee's decision became official, the major corporate firms, for whom the revolving door was a way of life, mounted a wide-ranging campaign to defeat the opinion and to change the rules.[10]

---

10. [Ed.] In Armstrong v. McAlpin, 625 F.2d 433, 443 (2d Cir.1980) (en banc), vacated on other grounds 449 U.S. 1106 (1981), amicus briefs were filed by the United States, FTC, CAB, FERC, Federal Legal Council, SEC, ICC, FMC, CFTC and a number of distinguished former government lawyers, "all attesting to the importance of the issues raised on appeal. Thus, the United States asserts that a 'decision to reject screening procedures is certain to have a serious, adverse effect on the ability of Government legal offices to recruit and retain well-qualified attorneys'; this view is seconded by the other government amici. And the former government lawyers, including two former Attorneys General of the United States and two former Solicitors General of the United States, state that they are all 'affected at least indirectly, by the panel opinion's underlying assumption that government lawyers cannot be trusted to discharge their public responsibilities faithfully while in office, or to abide fully by screening procedures afterwards.' While the tone of these assertions may be overly apocalyptic, it is true that a

"For the first time, the corporate firms ran a slate of candidates for the D.C. Bar's governing board, which resulted in their capturing control of the board. The new board then replaced outgoing members of the Legal Ethics Committee with lawyers opposed to the opinion. As a result, the opinion was never issued.

"At the same time, the firms prevailed upon the ethics committees of the ABA and of the Association of the Bar of the City of New York to issue opinions designed to gut the imputed-disqualification rule. With no basis in the ethical rules, these opinions held that imputed disqualification could be overcome by 'screening' the former government lawyer with the consent of the government agency. In theory, the disqualified lawyer would be forbidden to talk about the case with his or her new partners. But how this screening could be effectively monitored by anyone outside the firm has never been answered.

"Corporate lawyers next succeeded in having Rule 1.11 of the ABA's 1983 Model Rules of Professional Conduct written to allow their firms to avoid imputed disqualification even without the consent of the government agency. And in a provision that no one had proposed in the earlier debates, MR 1.11 was written to permit the very lawyer who was personally and substantially involved in the matter on behalf of the government to switch sides as long as the government agency consents. This only compounds the conflict of interest, of course, because the government lawyer who gives consent will be setting a precedent favorable to herself when she goes through the revolving door."

SECTION 3.   INFORMAL ADJUDICATION

5 U.S.C. § 555

Ancillary matters

(a) This section applies, according to the provisions thereof, except as otherwise provided by this subchapter.

(b) A person compelled to appear in person before an agency or representative thereof is entitled to be accompanied, represented, and advised by counsel or, if permitted by the agency, by other qualified representative. A party is entitled to appear in person or by or with counsel or other duly qualified representative in an agency proceeding. So far as the orderly conduct of public business permits, an interested person may appear before an agency or its responsible employees for the presentation, adjustment, or determination of an issue, request, or controversy in a proceeding, whether interlocutory, summary, or otherwise, or in connection with an agency function. With due regard for the convenience and necessity of the parties or their representatives and within a reasonable time, each agency shall proceed to conclude a matter presented to it. This subsection

decision rejecting the efficacy of screening procedures in this context may have significant adverse consequences."

does not grant or deny a person who is not a lawyer the right to appear for or represent others before an agency or in an agency proceeding. ...

(e) Prompt notice shall be given of the denial in whole or in part of a written application, petition, or other request of an interested person made in connection with any agency proceeding. Except in affirming a prior denial or when the denial is self-explanatory, the notice shall be accompanied by a brief statement of the grounds for denial.

NOTE

As we have seen, p. 253 above, the structure of the APA suggests that it does not address "informal adjudication" per se. The framers found it too variable to be captured in a general statute. Indeed, the Eighth Edition of this casebook, published in 1987, opined (at page 247): "The APA contains provisions which prescribe procedures for formal rulemaking (§§ 553, 556 and 557) and formal adjudication (§§ 554, 556 and 557); and section 553 sets forth requirements for informal rulemaking. But there is no comparable APA section which establishes procedures for informal adjudication."

The text of § 555 is not happily drafted. What is the reader to make of the fact that subsection (a) seems to indicate that the section has its own, direct force, when the title of the section is "Ancillary matters"? What is one to glean from the contrast between the third sentence of part (b), which says it applies "in a proceeding ... or in connection with an agency function," and the first sentence of part (e), which says it applies to "any agency proceeding"?

As to the latter problem, some comfort can be found in the fact that "agency proceeding" is a statutorily defined term, § 551(12), that includes rulemaking, adjudication, and licensing. The Attorney General's Manual on the APA 63, 70 (1947) built on this definition and said that the right to appear in part (b) applies "not only in matters involving rule making, adjudication, and licensing, but also in connection with other agency functions," whereas the right to notice of denial of an application set out in part (e) "has no application to matters which do not relate to rule making, adjudication or licensing. Generally, it is not applicable to the mass of administrative routine unrelated to those proceedings."

Where does this leave informal adjudication? According to the APA, adjudication includes each agency action that leads to a final disposition and is not rulemaking, §§ 551(6) & (7), while informal adjudication includes all such adjudications not required to be determined on the record after a hearing, § 554(a). Thus, informal adjudication is an enormous category, encompassing numerous situations whose only common characteristics are residual. But if informal adjudication constitutes "adjudication" according to the definitions used in the statute, what is the "mass" of proceedings as to which the Attorney General believed interested persons are entitled to appear but not to be told the grounds for the denial of their petitions? If, however, informal adjudication is not within the meaning of "agency proceeding" as used in part (e), then does it not appear that the opinion in the following Supreme Court case was in error?

Pension Benefit Guaranty Corporation v. LTV Corporation

Supreme Court of The United States, 1990.
496 U.S. 633.

■ BLACKMUN, J. delivered the opinion of the Court:

[The Pension Benefit Guaranty Corporation (PGBC) is a wholly owned United States Government corporation protecting private workers' pension benefits, see 29 U.S.C. § 1302, modeled after the Federal Deposit Insurance Corporation. When it acts pursuant to the Employee Retirement Income Security Act of 1974 (ERISA), it is treated as an "agency" for APA purposes. In its assigned role, it had assumed substantial obligations of the LTV Steel employee pension plans when LTV filed for bankruptcy reorganization and it agreed to the "termination" of the LTV Steel plans. A principal reason for that filing was LTV's realization, in a poor market for steel, that its pension plans were underfunded by $2.1 billion.

In the reorganization, LTV negotiated new pension arrangements with its unions, free of the old liabilities. PBGC came to believe that these new arrangements would have the effect of putting LTV plan participants in the same financial position they would have occupied had the prior plans never been terminated. Now, however, a substantial part of their benefits would be paid by public sources (financed by premiums paid by all employers) through PGBC, rather than through LTV. PGCB's fixed policy was to object to follow-on plans designed to wrap around the insurance benefits it provided in this way. PGCB then acted to "restore" the plans it had previously terminated. This informal adjudication included meetings with LTV to "consider any additional information it might wish to supply." When LTV refused to comply with this decision, PGCB brought an action in District Court and, when it was refused enforcement there, in the Second Circuit, which found the restoration decision "arbitrary and capricious" under APA § 706.

In reversing, the Supreme Court considered a number of issues—for example, whether the PGCB was obliged to consider factors involved in bankruptcy law and labor law, as it had not done, as well as its responsibilities under ERISA.[1] Of particular importance here was the Court's consideration of the Second Circuit's ruling that the agency's procedures had been inadequate. In its prior decision in Vermont Yankee, briefly recounted at 273 above and taken up at 498 below, the Court had strongly stated that the APA established the maximum procedural requirements a reviewing court could require of rulemakings. Now the question was whether the same conclusion applied to informal adjudications, for which the APA itself supplies so few required procedures. While the Court split in some respects on other matters, it was unanimous on this issue:]

1. The Court held it was not. "Even if Congress' directive to the PBGC had not been so clear, we are not entirely sure that the Court of Appeals' holding makes good sense as a general principle of administrative law. ... [T]here are numerous federal statutes that could be said to embody countless policies. If agency action may be disturbed whenever a reviewing court is able to point to an arguably relevant statutory policy that was not explicitly considered, then a very large number of agency decisions might be open to judicial invalidation."

... Relying upon a passage in Bowman Transportation, Inc. v. Arkansas–Best Freight System, Inc., 419 U.S. 281, 288 n. 4 (1974), the court held that the PBGC's decision was arbitrary and capricious because the 'PBGC neither apprised LTV of the material on which it was to base its decision, gave LTV an adequate opportunity to offer contrary evidence, proceeded in accordance with ascertainable standards ..., nor provided [LTV] a statement showing its reasoning in applying those standards.' 875 F.2d, at 1021. The court suggested that on remand the agency was required to do each of these things.

The PBGC argues that this holding conflicts with Vermont Yankee Nuclear Power Corp. v. Natural Resources Defense Council, Inc., where, the PBGC contends, this Court made clear that when the Due Process Clause is not implicated and an agency's governing statute contains no specific procedural mandates, the Administrative Procedure Act establishes the maximum procedural requirements a reviewing court may impose on agencies. Although Vermont Yankee concerned additional procedures imposed by the Court of Appeals for the District of Columbia Circuit on the Atomic Energy Commission when the agency was engaging in informal rulemaking, the PBGC argues that the informal adjudication process by which the restoration decision was made should be governed by the same principles.

Respondents counter by arguing that courts, under some circumstances, do require agencies to undertake additional procedures. As support for this proposition, they rely on Citizens to Preserve Overton Park, Inc. v. Volpe, 401 U.S. 402 (1971). In Overton Park, the Court concluded that the Secretary of Transportation's "post hoc rationalizations" regarding a decision to authorize the construction of a highway did not provide "an [a]dequate basis for [judicial] review" for purposes of § 706 of the APA. Id., at 419. Accordingly, the Court directed the District Court on remand to consider evidence that shed light on the Secretary's reasoning at the time he made the decision. Of particular relevance for present purposes, the Court in Overton Park intimated that one recourse for the District Court might be a remand to the agency for a fuller explanation of the agency's reasoning at the time of the agency action. Subsequent cases have made clear that remanding to the agency in fact is the preferred course. ... Respondents contend that the instant case is controlled by Overton Park rather than Vermont Yankee, and that the Court of Appeals' ruling was thus correct.

We believe that respondents' argument is wide of the mark. We begin by noting that although one initially might feel that there is some tension between Vermont Yankee and Overton Park, the two cases are not necessarily inconsistent. Vermont Yankee stands for the general proposition that courts are not free to impose upon agencies specific procedural requirements that have no basis in the APA. At most, Overton Park suggests that § 706(2)(A) of the APA, which directs a court to ensure that an agency action is not arbitrary and capricious or otherwise contrary to law, imposes a general "procedural" requirement of sorts by mandating that an agency take whatever steps it needs to provide an explanation that will enable the court to evaluate the agency's rationale at the time of decision.

Here, unlike in Overton Park, the Court of Appeals did not suggest that the administrative record was inadequate to enable the court to fulfill its duties under § 706. Rather, to support its ruling, the court focused on "fundamental fairness" to LTV. With the possible exception of the absence of "ascertainable standards"—by which we are not exactly sure what the Court of Appeals meant—the procedural inadequacies cited by the court all relate to LTV's role in the PBGC's decisionmaking process. But the court did not point to any provision in ERISA or the APA which gives LTV the procedural rights the court identified. Thus, the court's holding runs afoul of Vermont Yankee and finds no support in Overton Park.

Nor is Arkansas–Best, the case on which the Court of Appeals relied, to the contrary. The statement relied upon (which was dictum) said: "A party is entitled, of course, to know the issues on which decision will turn and to be apprised of the factual material on which the agency relies for decision so that he may rebut it." That statement was entirely correct in the context of Arkansas–Best, which involved a formal adjudication by the Interstate Commerce Commission pursuant to the trial-type procedures set forth in §§ 5, 7 and 8 of the APA, 5 U.S.C. §§ 554, 556–557, which include requirements that parties be given notice of "the matters of fact and law asserted," § 554(b)(3), an opportunity for "the submission and consideration of facts [and] arguments," § 554(c)(1), and an opportunity to submit "proposed findings and conclusions" or "exceptions," § 557(c)(1), (2). The determination in this case, however, was lawfully made by informal adjudication, the minimal requirements for which are set forth in § 555 of the APA, and do not include such elements. A failure to provide them where the Due Process Clause itself does not require them (which has not been asserted here) is therefore not unlawful.

NOTES

(1) *A Timely and Adequate Response?* FRIENDS OF THE BOW v. THOMPSON, 124 F.3d 1210, 1220–21 (10th Cir.,1997). In the course of a dispute involving the sale of timber from Medicine Bow National Forest, an environmental group, Friends of the Bow, sent a letter to the Forest Supervisor, requesting that the Environmental Assessment (EA) on which the sale was based be updated because of changed circumstances. No direct response to this letter was given, but the Forest Service did prepare a 26 page "Supplemental Information Report" (SIR) explaining why no new environmental report was needed; this SIR was issued about a year after the letter in question, and a copy was given to the group. In subsequent litigation, one of the claims made by Friends was that this course of behavior violated section 555(b) of the APA, which requires an agency "within a reasonable time . . . to conclude a matter presented to it."

Ebel, J.: "The government maintains, and the district court agreed, that Friends' letter is not the sort of matter to which § 555(b) applies. There is little case law on this issue. However, we believe there is a substantial argument that § 555(b) does apply to Friends' letter, which is an explicit and colorably valid request for the Service to take action arguably required of it by law to prepare a supplemental EA. First, by its terms, § 555(b) applies to all 'matters' presented to the agency. Contrary to the government's position that the provision only applies to 'proceedings' in which a person is compelled to appear, the section specifically speaks to 'agency proceedings' in which a person is 'entitled to appear,' as well as 'agency functions' and 'matters,' terms which would appear to encompass all forms of agency action. Second, while the government points out that 'agency proceedings' only includes the rulemakings, adjudications, and licensings defined in § 551 of the APA, it fails to acknowledge that § 551 defines 'adjudication' as 'the formulation of an order,' and in turn defines 'order' expansively to include the 'whole or part of a final disposition . . . other than rule making but including licensing.' That section further defines 'agency action' broadly to include not only rule makings, licensings, and orders, but also the 'failure to act.' Id. § 551(13). Thus, we assume, for the purposes of this opinion, that § 555(b) applies to the letter.

"Nonetheless, even assuming § 555(b) applies to Friends' letter, the agency's response to the letter substantially complied with the requirements of the section, as well as with the 'brief statement' requirement of § 555(e). Friends does not dispute that the SIR is an adequate 'brief statement' of the agency's reasons for not conducting a supplemental EA. Thus, the only question is whether the SIR was issued within a 'reasonable time' as is required by § 555(b).

"Friends has not pointed to a single case in which a court has reversed an agency action under § 555(b) for failure to comply with the 'reasonable time' requirements. More typically, courts have occasionally granted mandamus to force agencies to act when there has been no response to a request for agency action. But, in this case, the agency did act, by issuing the SIR. In cases where agencies acted, courts have declined to overturn agency action on the basis of the delay in situations where the agency took much longer to respond than the approximately one year period at issue here, particularly where as here the party opposing the action benefited from the delay. Accordingly, we conclude the agency acted within a reasonable time in producing the SIR, particularly in light of the lengthy, detailed nature of Friends' request for action, and the thoroughness of the agency's eventual response."

(2) *A Brief Statement of the Grounds for Denial?* In ROELOFS v. SECRETARY OF THE AIR FORCE, 628 F.2d 594, 599–601 (D.C.Cir.1980), Roelofs petitioned the Air Force to have his General Discharge upgraded to an Honorable Discharge; his application was denied without a hearing and without any statement of the grounds for the decision. Held: he was entitled to a statement of reasons under § 555(e). Leventhal, J.:

"The APA embodies the notion that 'Rule of Administrative Law' places emphasis on 'a broad-gauged appraisal of the decision-making process, and assurance of its reliability.'[1] This entails the 'simple but fundamental' requirement that an agency or official set forth its reasons, a requirement that is essential to 'the integrity of the Administrative pro-

---

1. Childs v. United States Board of Parole, 511 F.2d 1270, 1287 (D.C.Cir.1974) (Leventhal, J., concurring in the result).

cess,' for it tends to require 'the agency to focus on the values served by its decision, ... hence releasing the clutch of unconscious preference and irrelevant prejudice.'[2]

"This notion achieves concrete expression in section 6(d) in the APA, now codified at 5 U.S.C. § 555(e). Section 555 is not limited to cases where a specific statutory prescription exists, but applies 'according to the provisions thereof.' Section 555(e) applies where 'a written application, petition, or other request ... made in connection with any proceedings' [sic] is denied. The requirement of 'a brief statement of the grounds for denial' obtains even though the request pertains to a matter of discretion or grace, not one of entitlement. ... In King v. United States, 492 F.2d 1337 (1974), the Seventh Circuit, in an opinion joined by Justice (then Judge) Stevens, held that an application for parole—like the case at hand, a matter of discretion rather than one of entitlement—was subject to the requirements of § 555(e). The fact that the proceeding for the disposition of appellant's individual application, filed in accordance with pertinent law and regulations, was informal, does not negate the applicability of § 555(e). ...

"The requirement of § 555(e) is modest. Indeed, it probably does not add to, and may even diminish, the burden put on an agency by the APA's provision for judicial review. Any aggrieved person can bring a lawsuit contending that the denial of the requested relief was arbitrary agency action. It would be a rare case indeed in which the plaintiff could not make a plausible enough contention to require the government to state the reasons for its action. When the reasons have not been asserted by the agency at the time the action is taken, there is a prospect of further proceedings to develop those reasons. The burden is lessened if the agency provides at least some statement of reasons at the time it takes its action. In this regard, we note that, in 1976, the government agreed to provide statements of reasons in cases like the appellants arising after January 31, 1977. While the consent judgment by which the government bound itself is not precedent and has not figured in our reasoning, it does suggest that the application of § 555(e) in this context does not impose an intolerable burden.

"It cannot be assumed that a remand to provide a statement of grounds would be a futile gesture."

(3) *The Necessities of Judicial Review?* Prior to the decision in PGBC, as Justice Blackmun's opinion suggests, lower courts had often rested their reasoning on what they had to know in order effectively to perform their functions under APA § 706, as explicated by the Court's 1971 decision in Citizens to Preserve Overton Park v. Volpe, 989. See, for example Independent U.S. Tanker Owners Committee v. Lewis, 690 F.2d 908 (D.C.Cir. 1982), another Maritime Administration decision. Exploration of this issue is best taken up in connection with Overton Park, but FLORIDA POWER & LIGHT CO. V. LORION, 470 U.S. 729, 743–45 (1985) may suggest a certain impatience with this approach. The question posed was whether, in the particular circumstances, jurisdiction to review the agency's decision belonged initially with the Court of Appeals:

---

2. Id. (citation omitted).

"If the record before the agency does not support the agency action, if the agency has not considered all relevant factors, or if the reviewing court simply cannot evaluate the challenged agency action on the basis of the record before it, the proper course, except in rare circumstances, is to remand to the agency for additional investigation or explanation. The reviewing court is not generally empowered to conduct a *de novo* inquiry into the matter being reviewed and to reach its own conclusions based on such an inquiry. . . . Moreover, a formal hearing before the agency is in no way necessary to the compilation of an agency record. As the actions of the [Nuclear Regulatory] Commission in compiling a 547–page record in this case demonstrate, agencies typically compile records in the course of informal agency action. The APA specifically contemplates judicial review on the basis of the agency record compiled in the course of informal agency action in which a hearing has not occurred. See 5 U.S.C. §§ 551(13), 704, 706.

"The factfinding capacity of the district court is thus typically unnecessary to judicial review of agency decisionmaking."

(4) *Fundamental Fairness?* The Due Process clauses of the Constitution, where applicable, generally accord considerably more procedural rights than those mentioned in § 555 even on the most generous interpretation. See Chapter VII, within. Counsel who can fit their clients' cases into the doctrines of due process are well advised to do so; which may, indeed, be one reason why the case law under § 555 is so sparse. But the claim of due process violation is not always easy to establish. In DISTRICT NO. 1, PACIFIC COAST DISTRICT, MARINE ENGINEERS' BENEFICIAL ASSN. V. MARITIME ADMINISTRATION, 215 F.3d 37 (D.C.Cir.2000), the D.C. Circuit confronted a contention that the Maritime Administration's (MarAd's) acceptance of and reliance upon ex parte communications denied it "fundamental fairness" in violation of both the APA and the Fifth Amendment:

"Although the APA prohibits ex parte contacts in an adjudication or rulemaking 'required by statute to be made on the record after opportunity for an agency hearing,' there is no such requirement applicable to the MarAd's review of an application. . . . In the absence of such a statutory command, of course, 'agencies are free to grant additional procedural rights in the exercise of their discretion, but reviewing courts are generally not free to impose them if the agencies have not chosen to grant them.' Vermont Yankee Nuclear Power Corp. v. NRDC, 435 U.S. 519, 524 (1978). Here the agency has not granted anyone the right to be free of ex parte communications. In the absence of any statutory or self-imposed limitation, we have no jurisdiction to review under the APA an agency's procedural decision regarding how best to make a substantive decision committed by law to the agency's discretion.

"The Union attempts to circumvent this analysis by arguing that once the MarAd requested comments from interested parties, it relinquished its discretion to 'accept and rely upon ex parte communications without giving the public an opportunity to respond to them.' The authorities the Union cites as support for that claim, however, do not stand for that broad proposition. In each case either the governing statute or a regulation or both required the agency to afford interested parties an opportunity to submit comments. As we have already noted, no statute or regulation requires the MarAd to afford interested parties the opportunity to submit comments on an application for a transfer of registry ... and, in the absence of such a requirement, whether the MarAd permits comments and how it deals with those comments are procedural decisions that, like the underlying substantive decision, are matters within the agency's discretion."

(5) STEPHEN P. CROLEY, THEORIES OF REGULATION: INCORPORATING THE ADMINISTRATIVE PROCESS, 98 Colum. L. Rev. 1, 117 (1998). "Because informal adjudication and the production of policy statements and similar guidelines are governed by no APA-prescribed procedures, it is difficult to generalize about how interested parties might participate in these types of agency decisions. Approaching agency personnel directly, however, is one such way. As Kay Schlozman and John Tierney explain:

> When the rules of administrative procedure do not prohibit it, organized interests commonly try to cultivate the favor of mid-level agency staff personnel.... Close contacts [with an agency] may ... furnish an organized interest with opportunities to comment informally on policy changes that may be incubating in the bureaucracy. In return, interest organizations are able to provide agency staff with policy ideas and useful technical information, including forecasts and policy analyses.... [T]hese informal contacts between groups and the agencies facilitate an easy two-way flow of information.[3]

In addition to interacting with agency staff, parties seeking to influence an informal agency decision might also contact political appointees at high levels of an agency, where some of the most important informal decisions are made. In any event, it is worth noting that for one important category of agency decisions, interested parties' participation is a matter of their own creativity, and that such participation often takes the form of ex parte communications, which are prohibited during formal rulemaking and formal adjudication processes."

SECTION 4.   ALTERNATIVE DISPUTE RESOLUTION

With the 1990 enactment of two statutes amending the APA, alternative dispute resolution formally took its place among the available modes of regulatory procedure. The Negotiated Rulemaking Act added a new Subchapter III (now, 5 U.S.C. §§ 561–70a, in the Appendix, at pp. 1355–61 "to establish a framework for the conduct of negotiated rulemaking, consistent with section 553 of this title, to encourage agencies to use the process when it enhances the informal rulemaking process." 5 U.S.C. § 561. It is discussed at pp. 627–38 below. On the adjudication side, the Administrative Dispute Resolution Act added a new Subchapter IV (now, 5 U.S.C. §§ 571–84, in the Appendix, at pp. 1361–69 explicitly to authorize, under certain circumstances, agency use of "settlement negotiations, conciliation, facilitation, mediation, factfinding, minitrials, and arbitration ..." 5 U.S.C. § 571(3). The Administrative Dispute Resolution Act of 1996, Pub.L.No. 104–320, 110 Stat. 3870, permanently reauthorized both Acts, adding the use of ombuds officers to the ADR approaches permitted, strengthening the confidentiality of proceedings by making explicit the FOIA exemption of

---

3. Kay Lehman Schlozman & John T. Tierney, Organized Interests and American Democracy 331 & n.21 (1986)

confidential communications, and enabling agencies to agree to binding arbitration.[1]

The former director of the Administrative Conference of the United States' Program on Dispute Resolution interprets the 1996 reauthorization as "[c]ollectively ... suggest[ing] that Congress, along with many federal agencies, have moved beyond an initial skepticism and concern over potential abuses to a point where they have begun to view ADR methods as safe and effective." See Charles Pou, Jr., Federal ADR & Negotiated Rulemaking Acts Receive Permanent Reauthorization, 22 ADMIN L. NEWS No. 2 (Winter 1997), which also summarizes the changes made by the 1996Act.

Mediation or arbitration of disputes can occur among government agencies,[2] as well as between agency and private citizen, but it is in the nature of such processes that they rarely produce materials suitable for casebooks like this one. Matters with substantial public policy components are unlikely to prove suitable; and when these procedures are used, their confidentiality will likely be important to all participants. See In re Grand Jury Proceedings, 148 F.3d 487 (5th Cir.1998); Department of Justice Federal Alternative Dispute Resolution Council, "Confidentiality in Federal Alternative Dispute Resolution Programs," 65 Fed.Reg. 83085 (Dec. 29, 2000). Nonetheless, the indications of broader use of ADR are evident: between fiscal year 1995 and 1999, the Justice Department's Office of Dispute Resolution reports—for its court-and-litigation-oriented divisions alone—the number of ADR processes completed grew from 509 to 2662.[3]

---

1. Another, far less positive accomplishment of the One–Hundred Fourth Congress was its abolition of the Administrative Conference of the United States (ACUS). Pub. L.No. 104–52, tit. IV, 109 Stat. 468 (1995). Between 1968 and 1995, this small agency had responsibilities for continuing analysis and development of federal administrative procedure. Headed by an Administrator appointed by the President, a small permanent staff, and a council of twelve appointed from public and private life, ACUS collected statistical data, produced occasional sourcebooks, and consulted on implementation of some administrative law statutes—notably the Government in the Sunshine Act, regulatory negotiation, and alternative dispute resolution. Its principal work, however, was done by a larger deliberative assembly drawn from government agencies and from the worlds of academia and private practice. This assembly periodically debated and adopted recommendations for the improvement of administrative procedures, based on empirical studies performed by academicians and (occasionally) individual attorneys. The recommendations often produced significant change at the administrative level and—as important—permitted professional views on such matters as hybrid rulemaking and presidential oversight of agency policymaking to coalesce in a relatively apolitical setting. You may encounter a number of them in this book. ACUS was

initally given an extensive mandate (in former 5 U.S.C. § 569 and 582) to provide training, advice, and other assistance to agencies conducting regulatory negotiations and to compile data on the use of ADR generally. These functions were replaced, in the 1996 reauthorization, by a direction to the President to designate an entity to "facilitate and encourage" alternative dispute resolution techniques. A web page for an Interagency Alternative Dispute Resolution Working Group created in 1998 can be found at http://www.adr.gov; its organization and that of the associated Federal ADR Council are described in the "Document" portion of the site. The attorney in charge of the Department of Justice's Office of Dispute Resolution maintains the web page.

2. See, e.g., "Referral of inter-agency dispute to CEQ under the National Environmental Policy Act," http://www.whitehous.gov/ceq/referrals.html. (visited June 17, 2002).

3. http://www.usdoj.gov/odr/statistics. htm; see also Jeffrey Senger, Turning the Ship of State, 2000 Journal of Dispute Resolution 79 (Mr. Senger was Deputy Senior Counsel for Dispute resolution in the Department of Justice when he wrote this during the Clinton administration, and in the Bush administration, as these materials are being compiled).

A contemporary indication of the factors bearing on ADR's use is given by the following extract:

Department of Transportation, "Statement of Policy on Alternative Dispute Resolution"

67 Fed. Reg. 40367 (June 12, 2002).

. . . ADR is a collaborative, consensual dispute resolution approach. It describes a variety of problem-solving processes that are used in lieu of litigation or other adversarial proceedings to resolve disagreements. ADR encompasses mediation, facilitation, conciliation, factfinding, mini-trials, negotiation, negotiated rulemaking, neutral evaluation, policy dialogues, use of ombuds, arbitration, and other processes that usually involve a neutral third party who assists the parties in preventing, minimizing the escalation of, and resolving disputes. The efficient and effective use of ADR will help us resolve disputes at an early stage, in an expeditious, cost-effective, and mutually acceptable manner.

The Department of Transportation is committed to advancing our national transportation goals though alternative dispute resolution. We will consider using ADR in all areas including workplace issues, formal and informal adjudication, issuance of regulations, enforcement and compliance, issuing and revoking licenses and permits, contract and grant award and administration, litigation brought by or against the Department, and other interactions with the public and the regulated community.

> We will ensure that neutrals disclose any actual or potential conflicts of interest.

> We will provide learning and development opportunities for our employees so that they will be able to use conflict resolution skills, understand the theory and practice of ADR, and apply ADR appropriately.

> We will use a variety of evaluation and assessment strategies to measure and improve our processes and our use of ADR.

> We will allocate resources to support the use of ADR.

> We will provide confidentiality consistent with the provisions of the Administrative Dispute Resolution Act and other applicable Federal laws.

. . . ADR is voluntary and the Department will not impose its use on parties. The decision-making on when to use ADR should reflect sound judgment that ADR offers the best opportunity to resolve the dispute. In appropriate disputes, the Department will use ADR in a good-faith effort to achieve consensual resolution. However, if necessary, we will litigate or participate in some other process to resolve a dispute.

. . .

Issued in Washington, DC on June 3, 2002.

Norman Y. Mineta,

Secretary of Transportation.

Appendix–ADR Considerations

A decision to use ADR may be made before or after a dispute arises. Several factors should be considered in making that decision. Some factors may favor the use of ADR while others may weigh against it. Although not intended as an exhaustive list of factors, the Department has determined that ADR may be helpful in resolving a particular dispute where one or more of the following factors are present:

1. *Identifiable Parties.* There is an identifiable group of constituents with interests (the parties) so that all reasonably foreseeable interests can be represented.

2. *Good Faith.* The parties are willing to participate in good faith.

3. *Communication.* The parties are interested in seeking agreement, but poor communication or personality conflicts between the parties adversely affect negotiations.

4. *Continuing Relationship.* A continuing relationship between the parties is important and desirable.

5. *Issues.* There are issues that are agreed to be ripe for a negotiated solution.

6. *Unrealistic View of the Issues.* The parties' demands or views of the issues are unrealistic. A discussion of the situation with a neutral may increase the parties' understanding and result in more realistic alternatives and options.

7. *Sufficient Areas of Compromise.* There are sufficient areas of compromise to make ADR worthwhile.

8. *Expectation of Agreement.* The parties expect to agree eventually, most likely before reaching the courtroom or engaging in other adversarial processes.

9. *Timing.* There is sufficient time to negotiate and ADR will not unreasonably delay the outcome of the matter in dispute. There is a likelihood that the parties will be able to reach agreement within a fixed time. There are no statutory or judicial deadlines that are adversely affected by the process. ADR may result in an earlier resolution of the dispute.

10. *Resources.* The parties have adequate resources (budget and people) and are willing to commit them to the process.

While many of these factors may apply to agency rulemaking, there may be some variation in the consideration. For example, with regard to "Expectation of Agreement," the consideration may be that all affected interests recognize that there is a problem that must be solved and that Federal regulation is the appropriate response. Furthermore, under the Negotiated Rulemaking Act, the head of the agency would determine whether negotiated rulemaking is in the public interest and would consider several factors concerning the parties, the timing, the costs, and the issues. See 5 U.S.C. § 561.

There are also factors that suggest that ADR should not be used. The Administrative Dispute Resolution Act of 1996 provides factors that suggest that ADR is inappropriate or may not be productive in a particular dispute resolution proceeding. See 5 U.S.C. § 572.

NOTE

With her customary perceptive pragmatism, Judge Patricia Wald provides a balanced assessment of the early course of administrative ADR in ADR & the Courts: An Update, 46 Duke L.J. 1445 (1997). One of the most thought-provoking contributions to the literature is Jody Freeman, Collaborative Governance in the Administrative State, 45 U.C.L.A. L. Rev. 1(1997). Prof. Freeman reviews several case studies of negotiated rulemaking and licensing, using them to demonstrate how these procedures are consistent with a movement from an adversarial, interest-representation model to a model of collaborative governance; she also emphasizes, however, the extent to which current administrative negotiation falls short of the ideal of true collaborative governance.

CHAPTER V

THE PROCEDURAL CATEGORIES IN ACTION: RULEMAKING

Imagine a visitor who seeks to catalog the variety of written texts American government uses to communicate its powers and its citizens' rights and obligations. She might organize those texts into the following pyramid:

One Constitution, ratified by "the people"

Hundreds of statutes, enacted by an elected Congress

Thousands of regulations, adopted by politically responsible agency heads

Tens of thousands of interpretations and other guidance documents, issued by agency bureaus

Countless advice letters, press releases, and other statements of understanding, generated by individual bureaucrats

The pyramid shape is descriptively accurate. The relative sizes of the Constitution and the United States Code are obvious. The Code of Federal Regulations, the annual compilation of the documents described by the third of the levels above, is considerably larger than the U.S.C. At any technologically sophisticated agency (e.g., the Federal Aviation Administration) the volume of its own interpretive and guidance documents, the fourth level, may equal that of the entire CFR.

While documents in any of the last three levels of the pyramid can fit APA § 551's definition of a "rule,"[1] this chapter is principally concerned with the procedures used to create regulations (level three). With limited exceptions, APA § 553 states two possible procedures for creating regulations: an on-the-record process verging on trial, rarely encountered these days; and a considerably less formal approach usually called "notice and comment rulemaking." This second procedure is the one commonly employed and conventionally described as "rulemaking" and, unless context requires otherwise, it is what the term "rulemaking" means in the following pages. Since "rule" (as defined by § 551(4)) can reach a much larger set of documents, the term "regulations" will generally be used to refer to texts that are the product of this rulemaking procedure. Be aware, howev-

---

1. 5 U.S.C. § 551(4): "Rule" means the whole or a part of an agency statement of general or particular applicability and future effect designed to implement, interpret, or prescribe law or policy or describing the organization, procedure, or practice requirements of an agency and includes the approval or prescription for the future of rates, wages, corporate or financial structures or reorganization thereof, prices, facilities, appliances, services or allowances therefor or of valuations, costs, or accounting, or practices bearing on any of the foregoing.

er, that judicial opinions and the literature often refer to these texts using the more inclusive term "rules." Our legal system treats regulations as binding text, subject only to the requirements that they be authorized by superior authority and appropriately adopted following the designated procedures. As we will see, courts are much more aggressive in testing the validity of regulations than statutes, and appropriately so. But if they are valid, regulations have legislative effect on government and citizen alike, until displaced by other text validly adopted at the same or a higher level.

This chapter's brief first section introduces the apparently straightforward text of § 553. Section 2 explores those statutory commands and their interpretation by the courts. Section 3 addresses rulemaking issues to which the APA does *not* speak. Here, the first question is what constraints govern the agency's use of rulemaking or adjudication to make new policy. Assuming it self-consciously chooses between these procedural forms, what factors may control its choices? The second set of issues involves congressional and presidential initiatives that have created a variety of procedural steps *preceding* notice of a proposed rulemaking. These issues include priority selection, required analysis of economic, environmental and other impacts, and the use of consensual processes to develop proposals. The third set of issues in Section 3 concerns the agency's decisional process *after* comments have been received. The cases here raise important questions about the relative importance of influence, politics, and expertise. Work in Section 3, then, should leave you with a picture of considerable encrustation of rulemaking procedures—"ossification" in the characterization of some. Finally, Section 4 addresses the fourth level of the pyramid suggested above—interpretive rules or statements of general policy, that seem to be the subject of § 552 as well as to be exempt from the notice-and-comment requirements of § 553. Here, you will encounter debate about whether these "publication rules" are legitimate instruments of agency policy, or a ruse to evade the higher procedural obligations associated with adopting regulations. The innumerable items at the base of the pyramid, while often in fact influential on private conduct, are denied any formal jural effect, and will not be examined here.

SECTION 1. THE STATUTORY FORMS OF RULEMAKING AND THE PROBLEM OF AUTHORITY

5 U.S.C. § 553

Rule making.

(a) This section applies, according to the provisions thereof, except to the extent that there is involved—

(1) a military or foreign affairs function of the United States; or

(2) a matter relating to agency management or personnel or to public property, loans, grants, benefits, or contracts.

(b) General notice of proposed rule making shall be published in the Federal Register, unless persons subject thereto are named and either personally served or otherwise have actual notice thereof in accordance with law. The notice shall include

(1) a statement of the time, place, and nature of public rule making proceedings;

(2) reference to the legal authority under which the rule is proposed; and

(3) either the terms or substance of the proposed rule or a description of the subjects and issues involved.

Except when notice or hearing is required by statute, this subsection does not apply—

(A) to interpretative rules, general statements of policy, or rules of agency organization, procedure, or practice; or

(B) when the agency for good cause finds (and incorporates the finding and a brief statement of reasons therefor in the rules issued) that notice and public procedure thereon are impracticable, unnecessary, or contrary to the public interest.

(c) After notice required by this section, the agency shall give interested persons an opportunity to participate in the rule making through submission of written data, views, or arguments with or without opportunity for oral presentation. After consideration of the relevant matter presented, the agency shall incorporate in the rules adopted a concise general statement of their basis and purpose. When rules are required by statute to be made on the record after opportunity for an agency hearing, sections 556 and 557 of this title apply instead of this subsection.

(d) The required publication or service of a substantive rule shall be made not less than 30 days before its effective date, except—

(1) a substantive rule which grants or recognizes an exemption or relieves a restriction;

(2) interpretative rules and statements of policy; or

(3) as otherwise provided by the agency for good cause found and published with the rule.

(e) Each agency shall give an interested person the right to petition for the issuance, amendment, or repeal of a rule.

NOTES

(1) *Formal or Informal Rulemaking?* Section 553 distinguishes between notice-and-comment procedures, for which it provides fully, and cases in which "rules are required by statute to be made on the record after opportunity for an agency hearing." The former procedures are often called "informal rulemaking." The latter, often called "formal rulemaking," involve compliance with §§ 556 and 557 instead of § 553(c).

In the early years of the APA, formal rulemaking was relatively common. Much agency rulemaking concerned economic matters, fitting § 551's definition of "rule" as including "the approval or prescription for the future of rates, wages, corporate or financial structures or reorganization thereof, prices, facilities, appliances, services or allowances therefor or of valuations, costs, or accounting, or practices bearing on any of the foregoing." It had long been settled that while legislatures might enact rates through the normal lawmaking process, the Due Process clause required individualized oral hearings if agencies were to be given the task of setting firm-specific rates. See, e.g., ICC v. Louisville & Nashville R. Co., 227 U.S. 88, 93 (1913). Under the APA, then, it was readily understood that such proceedings fit the "formal rulemaking" mode.

Save for this Note, we will not deal with formal rulemaking in this chapter. Formal rulemakings share a characteristic with initial licensing proceedings: From the applicant's perspective, the issue is its own particular, individual circumstances and this suggests the virtues of trial-type process; from the public's perspective, however, ratesetting and licensing raise a host of competing, "polycentric" policy issues whose resolution we would ordinarily expect to entrust to politics. See pp. 244 and 350 above. While the APA defines initial licensing as adjudication and ratesetting as rulemaking, the effect of the "formal rulemaking" provisions and the various special provisions that §§ 554–58 make for initial licensing is to set essentially equivalent procedural requirements for both. These special provisions are dealt with in various parts of the chapter on adjudication— for example, in relation to Seacoast Anti–Pollution League v. Costle, p. 325—and so they will not be explored further here.

Another reason for focusing on notice-and-comment rulemaking is that formal rulemakings have become quite rare. As a procedure, formal rulemaking was criticized for being a voracious consumer of agency resources, and giving excessive control over the development of the rule to the parties to the proceeding. For example, an FDA formal rulemaking to determine the percentage of peanuts a substance must contain in order to be labeled "peanut butter" took nine years and twenty weeks of hearings producing 8,000 pages of hearing record, to produce a six-page opinion to justify a decision to require at least 90% peanuts. Robert W. Hamilton, Procedures for the Adoption of Rules of General Applicability: The Need for Procedural Innovation in Administrative Rulemaking, 60 Calif.L.Rev. 1276, 1312–1313 (1972) reported more generally:

"It is surprising to discover that most agencies required to conduct formal hearings in connection with rulemaking in fact did not do so during the previous five years.... Thus, the primary impact of these procedural requirements is often not, as one might otherwise have expected, the testing of agency assumptions by cross-examination, or the testing of agency conclusions by courts on the basis of substantial evidence of record. Rather these procedures either cause the abandonment of the program (as in the Department of Labor), the development of techniques to reach the same regulatory goal but without a hearing (as FDA is now trying to do), or the promulgation of noncontroversial regulations by a process of negotiation and compromise (as FDA historically has done and Interior is encouraged to do). In practice, therefore, the principal effect of imposing rulemaking on a record has often been the dilution of the regulatory process rather than the protection of persons from arbitrary action."

In 1973, one year after publication of Hamilton's study, the Supreme Court assured the marginalization of formal rulemaking with its decision in UNITED STATES V. FLORIDA EAST COAST RAILWAY CO., 410 U.S. 224. The ICC had by regulation established "incentive" rates to encourage railroads to send empty freight cars back to their owners. Without such rates, railroads had no particular reason to return the cars, and cars that tended to go full in only one direction—refrigerator cars, say, carrying produce to urban markets—tended to pool there and create artificial and unnecessary shortages. Its statute directed it to act "after hearing" and the ICC had initially comtemplated oral trial-type procedures for its regulatory effort. However, after intense congressional pressure to move more quickly, the agency limited the railroads to written submissions.[1] The Supreme Court upheld the Commission. It held that the simple statutory reference to "hearing" was not enough to activate § 553(c)'s reference to cases in which "rules are required by statute to be made on the record after opportunity for an agency hearing." "The District Court[, in reaching the opposite conclusion,] observed that it was 'rather hard to believe that the last sentence of § 553(c) was directed only to the few legislative sports where the words "on the record" or their equivalent had found their way into the statute book.' 318 F.Supp., at 496. This is, however, the language which Congress used, and since there are statutes on the books that do use these very words, see, e.g., the Fulbright Amendment to the Walsh–Healey Act, 41 U.S.C. § 43a, and 21 U.S.C. § 371(e)(3), the regulations provision of the Food and Drug Act, adherence to that language cannot be said to render the provision nugatory or ineffectual. We recognized in United States v. Allegheny–Ludlum Steel Corp., 406 U.S. 742 (1972) that the actual words 'on the record' and 'after . . . hearing' used in § 553 were not words of art, and that other statutory language having the same meaning could trigger the provisions of §§ 556 and 557 in rulemaking proceedings. But we adhere to our conclusion, expressed in that case, that the phrase 'after hearing' in § 1(14)(a) of the Interstate Commerce Act does not have such an effect." Earlier cases like ICC v. Louisville & Nashville R. Co., above, were distinguished as involving the rates of a single railroad grounded in its individual financial circumstances, not uniform and nationwide incentive payments ordered to be made by all railroads subject to the regulation.

When a statute refers to "hearing" in the context of adjudication, rather than rulemaking, should the court similarly presume that informal procedures were intended? See Seacoast Anti–Pollution League v. Costle, p. 325.

(2) *The Statutory Text.* Here is a flowchart, shown on the following page, for the § 553 notice-and-comment rulemaking procedures. Considering, at this point, only the statutory text, how would you describe the requirements of this process?

---

1. The ICC actually proceeded as if under the special dispensation of § 556(d) permitting it to act just on the basis of written submissions, unless a party would be "preju- diced thereby"; as indicated in the text, the Supreme Court simply found that section inapplicable.

FLOW OF INFORMAL RULEMAKING

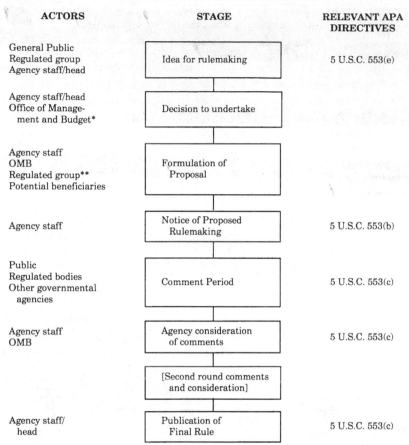

ACTORS	STAGE	RELEVANT APA DIRECTIVES
General Public Regulated group Agency staff/head	Idea for rulemaking	5 U.S.C. 553(e)
Agency staff/head Office of Management and Budget*	Decision to undertake	
Agency staff OMB Regulated group** Potential beneficiaries	Formulation of Proposal	
Agency staff	Notice of Proposed Rulemaking	5 U.S.C. 553(b)
Public Regulated bodies Other governmental agencies	Comment Period	5 U.S.C. 553(c)
Agency staff OMB	Agency consideration of comments	5 U.S.C. 553(c)
	[Second round comments and consideration]	
Agency staff/ head	Publication of Final Rule	5 U.S.C. 553(c)

* For treatment of the Executive Order that brings OMB into the rulemaking process, see p. 609 ff. below.

** For treatment of the possibility of negotiating the proposed rule, see p. 627 below.

[H199]

(3) *Some background to Section 553:* Here are some historical materials respecting § 553. Be warned that judicial understandings of § 553 have developed considerably since 1947.

(a) DEPARTMENT OF JUSTICE, ATTORNEY GENERAL'S MANUAL ON THE ADMINISTRATIVE PROCEDURE ACT 31–35 (1947): [In 1947, shortly after the APA was enacted, the Department of Justice prepared an extensive manual on the Act, primarily for the benefit of other government agencies. Although those agencies and their legal adviser were in important respects parties in interest, the Supreme Court has drawn upon this manual as "a contemporaneous interpretation" of the APA that is entitled to "some deference . . . because of the role played by the Department of Justice in drafting the legislation." Vermont Yankee Nuclear Power Corp. v. Natural Resources Defense Council, 435 U.S. 519 (1978), set forth below at p. 498]

"Informal rule making. In every case of proposed informal rule making subject to the notice requirements of section 4(a) [i.e., § 553(b)], section

4(b) [§ 553(c)] provides that 'the agency shall afford interested persons an opportunity to participate in the rule making through submission of written data, views, or arguments with or without opportunity to present the same orally in any manner.' The quoted language confers discretion upon the agency, except where statutes require 'formal' rule making subject to sections 7 and 8 [§§ 556 & 557], to designate in each case the procedure for public participation in rule making. Such informal rule making procedure may take a variety of forms: informal hearings (with or without a stenographic transcript), conferences, consultation with industry committees, submission of written views, or any combination of these. These informal procedures have already been extensively employed by Federal agencies. In each case, the selection of the procedure to be followed will depend largely upon the nature of the rules involved. The objective should be to assure informed administrative action and adequate protection to private interests.

"Each agency is affirmatively required to consider 'all relevant matter presented' in the proceeding; it is recommended that all rules issued after such informal proceedings be accompanied by an express recital that such material has been considered. It is entirely clear, however, that section 4(b) does not require the formulation of rules upon the exclusive basis of any 'record' made in informal rule making proceedings. Senate Hearings (1941) p. 444. Accordingly, except in formal rule making governed by sections 7 and 8, an agency is free to formulate rules upon the basis of materials in its files and the knowledge and experience of the agency, in addition to the materials adduced in public rule making proceedings.

"Section 4(b) provides that upon the completion of public rule making proceedings 'after consideration of all relevant matter presented, the agency shall incorporate in any rules adopted a concise general statement of their basis and purpose.' The required statement will be important in that the courts and the public may be expected to use such statements in the interpretation of the agency's rules. The statement is to be 'concise' and 'general.' Except as required by statutes providing for 'formal' rule making procedure, findings of fact and conclusions of law are not necessary. Nor is there required an elaborate analysis of the rules or of the considerations upon which the rules were issued. Rather, the statement is intended to advise the public of the general basis and purpose of the rules."

"*Formal rule making.* Section 4(b) [i.e., 5 U.S.C. § 553(c)] provides that 'Where rules are required by statute to be made on the record after opportunity for an agency hearing, the requirements of sections 7 [i.e., § 556] and 8 [i.e., § 557] shall apply in place of the provisions of this subsection.' Thus, where a rule is required by some other statute to be issued on the basis of a record after opportunity for an agency hearing, the public rule making proceedings must consist of hearing and decision in accordance with sections 7 and 8. . . .

"Statutes rarely require hearings prior to the issuance of rules of general applicability. Such requirements, where they exist, appear in radically different contexts. The Federal Food, Drug and Cosmetic Act (21 U.S.C. § 801) is almost unique in that it specifically provides that agency action issuing, amending or repealing specified classes of substantive rules may be taken only after notice and hearing, and that 'The Administrator shall base his order only on substantial evidence of record at the hearing and shall set forth as part of the order detailed findings of fact on which the order is based.' Upon review in a circuit court of appeals, a transcript of the record is filed, and 'the findings of the Administrator as to the facts, if supported by substantial evidence, shall be conclusive' (21 U.S.C. § 871). It is clear that such rules are 'required by statute to be made on the record after opportunity for an agency hearing.' . . .

"Statutes authorizing agencies to prescribe future rates (i.e., rules of either general or particular applicability) for public utilities and common carriers typically require that such rates be established only after an opportunity for a hearing before the agency. Such statutes rarely specify in terms that the agency action must be taken on the basis of the 'record' developed in the hearing. However, where rates or prices are established by an agency after a hearing required by statute, the agencies themselves and the courts have long assumed that the agency's action must be based upon the evidence adduced at the hearing. Sometimes the requirement of decision on the record is readily inferred from other statutory provisions defining judicial review. . . . It appears, therefore, that rules (as defined in section 2(c)) which are issued after a hearing required by statute . . . , and which are reviewable . . . on the basis of the evidence adduced at the agency hearing, must be regarded as 'required by statute to be made on the record after opportunity for an agency hearing.' . . .

"There are other statutes which require agencies to hold hearings before issuing rules, but contain no language from which the further requirement of decision 'on the record' can be inferred, nor any provision for judicial review on the record. . . . For example, the Federal Seed Act (7 U.S.C. § 1561) simply provides that 'prior to the promulgation of any rule or regulation under this chapter, due notice shall be given by publication in the Federal Register of intention to promulgate and the time and place of a public hearing to be held with reference thereto, and no rule or regulation may be promulgated until after such hearing.' . . . In this type of statute, there is no requirement, express or implied, that rules be formulated 'on the record.'

"There is persuasive legislative history to the effect that the Congress did not intend sections 7 and 8 to apply to rule making where the substantive statute merely required a hearing. In 1941, a subcommittee of the Senate Committee on the Judiciary held hearings on S. 674 (77th Cong., 1st sess.) and other administrative procedure bills. Section 209(d) of S. 674 provided with respect to rule making that 'where legislation specifically requires the holding of hearings prior to the making of rules, formal rulemaking hearings shall be held.' Mr. Ashley Sellers, testifying on behalf of the Department of Agriculture, called the subcommittee's attention to the fact that in various statutes, such as the Federal Seed Act, in which the Congress had required hearings to be held prior to the issuance of rules, the obvious purpose 'was simply to require that the persons interested in the proposed rule should be permitted to express their views.' Mr. Sellers drew a sharp distinction between such hearing requirements and the formal rule making requirements of the Federal Food, Drug and Cosmetic Act. Since this situation was thus specifically called to the subcommittee's attention, it is a legitimate inference that with respect to rule making the present dual requirement, i.e., 'after opportunity for an agency hearing' *and* 'on the record,' was intended to avoid the application of formal procedural requirements in cases where the Congress intended only to provide an opportunity for the expression of views.''

(b) MARTIN SHAPIRO, APA: PAST, PRESENT, FUTURE, 72 Va.L.Rev. 447, 452–454 (1986): See p. 263.

(c) ALAN MORRISON, THE ADMINISTRATIVE PROCEDURE ACT: A LIVING AND RESPONSIVE LAW, 72 Va.L.Rev. 253, 256–258 (1986): "While I have not undertaken any of these research projects, I have little doubt that anyone would disagree with the conclusion reached by then law professor and now Circuit Judge Antonin Scalia, who observed that 'perhaps the most notable development in federal government administration during the last two decades is the constant and accelerating flight away from individualized, adjudicatory proceedings to generalized disposition through rulemaking.'[2] This shift has occurred for a number of reasons.

"First, rulemaking is likely to produce a more rationally coherent rule for general application. Unlike adjudications, which are often focused on a single party, rulemaking allows an opportunity for all interested parties to comment. While results in adjudications are often determined by the particular facts before the agency, rulemaking allows, if not actually requires, the agency to take a broader look at an issue. Thus, instead of solving problems one at a time, the agency establishes an overall framework based on a coherent rationale and develops overarching principles that can be applied in future cases.

"Secondly, rulemaking is more efficient over the long term. Adjudications, centering as they do on the particulars of a given case, may require a substantial commitment of resources to establish the narrow set of facts necessary to reach a decision. This process must be repeated on many occasions before the final rule of law emerges. By contrast, a rulemaking, although it may require more effort than a single adjudication, will normally resolve a far larger range of issues. Thus, industry groups, consumers, labor unions, environmentalists, and other interested parties find it worthwhile to focus their efforts on a single rulemaking, although they might be unable to justify participating in any single adjudication, let alone an entire series of them. . . .

"Perhaps the single most important reason for the increase in rulemaking has been the advent of new substantive statutes designed to provide protection on an industrywide, or in some cases nationwide, basis for consumers, workers, or the environment.[3] Because many of these statutes leave the development of substantive standards to the relevant agencies, they specifically or effectively require rulemaking. Yet Congress,

---

2. Scalia, Vermont Yankee: the APA, the D.C. Circuit, and the Supreme Court, 1978 Sup.Ct.Rev. 345, 376.

3. See, e.g., National Traffic & Motor Vehicle Safety Act, 15 U.S.C. §§ 1381–1426; Consumer Product Safety Act, 15 U.S.C. §§ 2051–2083; Occupational Safety and Health Act, 29 U.S.C. §§ 651–678; Clean Air Act, 42 U.S.C. §§ 7401–7642.

aside from adding a few procedural modifications, has by and large been content to let the APA govern this rulemaking, as well as judicial review of its outcomes."

(4) *Notice-and-Comment Rulemaking Requires Statutory Authority.* Although courts tend to be permissive in finding rulemaking authority in generally worded statutory provisions, find such authority they must. Absent such a grant, agency views can not claim the force of legislation; although they may function as precedent within the agency, courts will treat them as persuasive rather than binding. While the non-delegation doctrine has relatively little bite, see Ch. II § 1 above, the requirement that Congress in fact have authorized agencies to adopt regulations permits courts the exercise of considerable control over agency authority, under the heading "ultra vires."

(5) *The Freedom of Information Act as Amendment.* Twenty years after adopting the APA, Congress amended it by the Freedom of Information Act (FOIA). This important legislation considerably expanded agency obligations to provide information to the public, enabling citizens to obtain particular agency records they wish to examine. Chapter VI considers FOIA in detail. Here we note two important collateral effects FOIA has had on rulemaking.

The first is a question. Consider the required contents of rulemaking notice in light of the FOIA obligation APA § 552(a)(3) has imposed since 1966: to make public, on request, any properly identified factual data in agency records, that does not fit one of seven narrowly defined exemptions. Must a Notice of Proposed Rulemaking issued under § 553(b) contain references to and make available any factual data (studies, etc.) known to the agency as arguably bearing upon its proposal? As you will learn if you study Chapter 6, "please disclose all factual studies and data in agency records that the agency has thus far considered in connection with the rulemaking on [subject] announced in the Federal Register on [date] at [page]" is a sufficiently definite (and otherwise proper) FOIA request. Persons interested in a rulemaking could (and certainly did) make such requests promptly on learning of a proposal. Although a requester couldn't count on getting the agency's response in time to inform her comments, the agency's obligation to disclose was evident, as was the likelihood that it would receive requests to do so. Can you convert this juxtaposition of statutory remedies into an argument that such data must be revealed *during* the notice-and-comment process?

Second, the FOIA considerably expanded the original versions of §§ 552(a)(1) and (2). These subsections provided respectively for Federal Register publication and for other forms of publication of operative agency documents—including a variety of documents that are not regulations adopted by § 553 procedures, and yet would be characterized as "rules" under § 551(4). Section 4 of this chapter considers these "publication" rules. For the moment, simply note the implication that *with appropriate publication (or actual notice),* agencies may rely upon these less formally generated rules when dealing with the public:

§ 552(a)(1) "Each agency shall separately state and currently publish in the Federal Register for the guidance of the public ... statements of general policy or interpretations of general applicability formulated and adopted by the agency ... Except to the extent that a person has actual and timely notice of the terms thereof, a person may not in any manner be required to resort to, or be adversely affected by, a matter required to be published in the Federal Register and not so published. ... ."

(2) [The subsection begins by describing other materials to be made "available for public inspection and copying" and also indexed. These include "final opinions" in adjudicated cases, "those statements of policy and interpretations which have been adopted by the agency and are not published in the Federal Register" and "administrative staff manuals and instructions to staff that affect a member of the public." Then the subsection continues:] "A final order, opinion, statement of policy, interpretation, or staff manual or instruction that affects a member of the public may be relied on, used, or cited as precedent by an agency against a party other than an agency only if [it has been appropriately indexed and made available, or actual and timely notice has been given]".

SECTION 2.   TIP OF THE ICEBERG—THE VISIBLE RULEMAKING PROCEDURES OF § 553

a.   PROCEDURES THAT MUST BE USED?

Sugar Cane Growers Cooperative of Florida v. Ann M. Veneman

United States Court of Appeals for the District of Columbia Circuit, 2002.
289 F.3d 89.

■ Before TATEL and GARLAND, CIRCUIT JUDGES, and SILBERMAN, SENIOR CIRCUIT JUDGE.

■ SILBERMAN, SENIOR CIRCUIT JUDGE: [In the summer of 2000, as a means of supporting the market price of domestically produced sugar and eliminating a costly-to-store government-owned surplus of sugar that was overhanging the market and depressing prices, the Department of Agriculture initiated a payment in kind program (PIK) authorized by the Food Security Act. Farmers bid for the right to receive sugar from the surplus to sell on the market (i.e., as if it were their crop), in return for plowing under a given acreage of already planted sugar-producing crops.[1] Because the stat-

---

1. A farmer's bid is his asking price for that amount of destruction, the price is expressed in terms of a percentage of the three-year average value of the crop yield for the acreage diverted. Thus, a farmer bidding 80 percent would receive eight dollars worth of sugar for every acre destroyed if his average acre produced ten dollars worth of sugar.

ute limited payments to $20,000 per producer, this program was attractive to northern growers of sugar beets but not to the typically larger southern growers of sugar cane. The sugar produced from these crops is indistinguishable. Typical winning bids were for about 85% of the sugar that could have been expected from the acreage to be plowed under. Important to the program's success was an assurance that participating farmers would not increase their future production over what they might have expected absent participation in the program. Thus, participants were told they could not participate in future PIK programs if they increased their future planted acreage. The Agency did not proceed by notice and comment in 2000, but no party challenged that decision or the program itself.

According to the sugar cane growers who brought this action, the sugar beet farmers participating in the program managed nonetheless to enrich themselves at the sugar cane growers' expense. They selected their lowest yield acreage as the acreage to be plowed under. Consequently, they experienced sugar yields from their remaining acreage (23.6 tons per acre) that were higher than the Department had calculated (22.8 tons per acre). Correspondingly, they received more government sugar as payment in kind than the Department had expected. Since this put more sugar on the market, the cane growers argued, prices were lower than they would otherwise have been.[2]

During the final weeks of the Clinton Administration, before data on the 2000 program was available, Department officials met with interested persons (including appellant representatives) to discuss a PIK program for the 2001 sugar crop. They indicated that the Department would not adapt a PIK program without notice and comment. Contacts continued until August 31, 2001, when the Department announced by press release that it had decided to implement a PIK program for the 2001 sugar crop without using APA rulemaking. It published a "Notice of Program Implementation" in the September 7, 2001 Federal Register, setting a 200,000 ton limit on total PIK volume in order to encourage more competitive bidding. The sugar cane growers were again effectively kept from participating by the payment/producer cap. Particularly troubling to them was that, although the program again provided that participation in *future* programs would be conditional upon not increasing the acreage planted in sugar, the Department waived the analogous eligibility restriction in the 2000 PIK program. Thus, farmers were free to participate in 2001 without regard to whether they had participated in 2000 and subsequently increased the acreage they planted in sugar.]

Appellants filed suit shortly after the press release appeared, seeking injunctive and declaratory relief. They argued that the Department violated the APA by promulgating a rule without notice-and-comment rulemaking.

[The court's discussion of appellants' standing is omitted.]

---

2. The government argued, in response, that the program had had a positive effect on the price of sugar. By reducing the government's sugar supply and storage fees, it argued, the program ameliorated the overhang effect and eased storage difficulties.

III.

Turning to the merits, we take up first appellants' APA claim. The APA sets forth several steps an agency must take when engaged in rulemaking: it must publish a general notice of proposed rulemaking in the Federal Register; give an opportunity for interested persons to participate in the rulemaking through submission of written data, views, or arguments; and issue publication of a concise general statement of the rule's basis and purpose. 5 U.S.C. § 553(b), (c). The government defends the Department's failure to engage in notice-and-comment rulemaking by asserting the PIK announcement was not really a rule and, even if it were, the failure to engage in rulemaking was a harmless error.[3]

The APA defines a rule very broadly as

the whole or a part of an agency statement of general or particular applicability and future effect designed to implement, interpret, or prescribe law or policy or describing the organization, procedure, or practice requirements of an agency and includes the approval or prescription for the future of rates, wages, corporate or financial structures or reorganizations thereof, prices, facilities, appliances, services or allowances therefor or of valuations, costs, or accounting, or practices bearing on any of the foregoing.

5 U.S.C. § 551(4). We have recognized that notwithstanding the breadth of the APA's definition an agency pronouncement that lacks the firmness of a proscribed standard . . . is not a rule. But the government . . . argues that because the announcement of the 2001 PIK program was an "isolated agency act" that did not propose to affect subsequent Department acts and had "no future effect on any other party before the agency" it was not a rule. The government would have us see its announcement of the PIK program as analogous to an agency's award of a contract pursuant to an invitation of bids or an agency's decision to approve an application or a proposal—in administrative law terms an informal adjudication (which is the technical term for an executive action).

Rule ?

We have little difficulty . . . in rejecting this argument. The August 31 press release, the September Questions and Answers and most notably the September 7 Notice of Program Implementation set forth the bid submission procedures which all applicants must follow, the payment limitations of the program, and the sanctions that will be imposed on participants if they plant more in future years than in 2001. It is simply absurd to call this anything but a rule "by any other name."

. . . [T]he government alternatively claims harmless error. We are told that appellants cannot identify any additional arguments they would have made in a notice-and-comment procedure that they did not make to the

---

3. Although the government also implies that it had good cause not to follow notice-and-comment rulemaking, it does not rely on that position, presumably because the Department did not assert it. Nor do we address amicus' argument that the 2001 PIK program was exempt from APA rulemaking requirements under 5 U.S.C. § 553(a)(2) because it constitutes agency action relating to "public property, loans, grants, benefits, or contracts." As the Department acknowledged, it has essentially waived that APA exemption. See 36 Fed. Reg. 13,804 (July 24, 1971); Rodway v. Dep't of Agriculture, 514 F.2d 809, 814 (D.C.Cir. 1975).

Department in the several informal sessions. And we are reminded that the Department did make certain changes to the 2001 PIK program in response to appellants' concerns. It is true that we have recognized certain technical APA errors as harmless. For example, in Sheppard v. Sullivan, 906 F.2d 756, 761–62 (D.C.Cir.1990), a challenge to an agency adjudication in a benefits case, we held that a failure to undertake formal notice and comment with respect to a program manual was harmless. But an utter failure to comply with notice and comment cannot be considered harmless if there is any uncertainty at all as to the effect of that failure. And in Sheppard, we initially observed that the agency did not even rely on that program manual in its challenged order; furthermore, we expressly concluded that the agency's substantive approach was "the only reasonable one."

Here the government would have us virtually repeal section 553's requirements: if the government could skip those procedures, engage in informal consultation, and then be protected from judicial review unless a petitioner could show a new argument—not presented informally—section 553 obviously would be eviscerated. The government could avoid the necessity of publishing a notice of a proposed rule and perhaps, most important, would not be obliged to set forth a statement of the basis and purpose of the rule, which needs to take account of the major comments—and often is a major focus of judicial review. . . .

There remains the question of remedy. Normally when an agency so clearly violates the APA we would vacate its action . . . and simply remand for the agency to start again. Unfortunately, because we denied preliminary relief in this case, the 2001 program was launched and crops were plowed under. The egg has been scrambled and there is no apparent way to restore the status quo ante. Appellants suggested that if we were to vacate, the Federal Court of Claims would have the responsibility of allocating damages. But that seems an invitation to chaos. Moreover, although the government did not—and could not have for the first time on appeal—assert a good cause for omitting notice and comment, it is at least possible that the Department could establish good cause because of timing exigencies.

Appellants insist that we have no discretion in the matter; if the Department violated the APA—which it did—its actions must be vacated. But that is simply not the law. Instead, "the decision whether to vacate depends on 'the seriousness of the order's deficiencies (and thus the extent of doubt whether the agency chose correctly) and the disruptive consequences of an interim change that may itself be changed.'" Allied–Signal, Inc. v. United States Nuclear Regulatory Commission, 988 F.2d 146, 150–51 (D.C.Cir.1993) (quoting International Union, UMW v. FMSHA, 920 F.2d 960, 966–67 (D.C.Cir.1990)). We have previously remanded without vacating when the agency failed to follow notice-and-comment procedures. See, e.g., Fertilizer Institute v. EPA, 935 F.2d 1303, 1312 (D.C.Cir.1991).

Accordingly, we reverse the district court's grant of summary judgment and remand to that court to in turn remand to the Department.

So ordered.

NOTE

The principal learning of this opinion seems straightforward. Section 4 below considers the more typical context in which the obligation to use notice and comment procedures is contested, when agencies purport to do by "interpretative rule" or "statement of general policy" what the parties argue must be accomplished by notice and comment procedures.

Here, it may be worth brief attention to the concluding paragraphs of the opinion. They assert that even after finding an agency violation of the APA, a court has remedial discretion merely to remand for further agency process, without vacating the action. The court treats this as routine—as indeed it has become. The approach recognizes both the extent of agency investment in the regulation, and the possibility of reliance on it by non-objecting parties. In light of judicially-created rules that sharply limit retrospective rulemaking, see p. 578 ff. below, vacating the regulation could defeat that reliance, and also tend to reward marginal appeals. These undesirable effects are diminished if the court can leave the regulation in effect while the agency reconsiders a particular issue or conducts further public proceedings. As the Allied–Signal quotation explains, it is in part a question of how far the agency's errors create doubt about the substantive validity of the regulation, and, in part, a question of how much disruption vacating the regulation will create.

Judicial authority for this course was sharply disputed in CHECKOSKY V. SEC, 23 F.3d 452 (D.C.Cir.1994). For Judge Silberman, cases like Allied–Signal stated good law, and justified merely remanding when the substantial issue was uncertainty as to what the agency had decided rather than doubt about its authority. 23 F.3d at 465. Judge Randolph dissented from the panel's decision to remand without vacating an SEC order that all judges agreed was arbitrary and capricious. Once that conclusion had been reached, he said, "the Administrative Procedure Act requires the court—in the absence of any contrary statute—to vacate the agency's action. ... Section 706(2)(A) provides that a 'reviewing court' faced with an arbitrary and capricious agency decision 'shall'—*not may*—'hold unlawful and set aside' the agency action. Setting aside means vacating; no other meaning is apparent." 23 F.3d at 491. No Supreme Court decision has directly considered the point and, as Sugar Cane Growers demonstrates, the practice continues unabated.

Don't assume that the agency will then inevitably "get it right." The Checkosky case came back to the Court of Appeals in 1998, Checkosky v. SEC, 139 F.3d 221 (D.C.Cir.1998). The Commission, in the court's view, did not do it right the second time, either. The court, exasperated, returned the case to the agency "with instructions to dismiss the proceedings." (Checkosky involved formal adjudication, rather than rulemaking. That makes an order to dismiss more comprehensible. Neither Judge Silberman for the panel nor Judge Randolph in dissent considered a distinction between rulemaking and adjudication in their initial debate.)

b. NO MORE THAN § 553 REQUIRES?

Vermont Yankee Nuclear Power Corp. v. Natural Resources Defense Council, Inc.[1]

Supreme Court of the United States, 1978.
435 U.S. 519.

[At the time of this litigation, the licensing of nuclear power plants occurred in two stages. The first authorized construction of the plant. These hearings were often quite extensive, and involved community voices and non-governmental groups like the NRDC, often in adamant opposition. The second stage was to license the plant's operation once built.[2] Both stages were adjudicatory hearings under the Atomic Energy Act of 1954, as amended, 42 U.S.C. § 2011 et seq., and under the APA. A wide range of factual issues might be contested at these hearings—from matters specific to the particular plant for which a construction or operating license was sought, to questions of a more general character that did not turn on facts about either the particular plant's location, or the people who would be operating it or exposed to its effects. This case arose because the agency responsible for regulating nuclear power plants—the Atomic Energy Commission when the matter started, the Nuclear Regulatory Commission by

1. [Ed.] If this was an administrative law case, how is it that no agency is named in the caption? The Nuclear Regulatory Commission was of course a party to the proceeding, and in the court of appeals it was a named party (Natural Resources Defense Council v. NRC and Aeschliman v. NRC are the names of the cases below). But Vermont Yankee Nuclear Power Corp.—whose license was going to be lost if the court of appeals' decision prevailed—was also a losing party below, and took the initiative in petitioning for certiorari. The Supreme Court retitles cases according to how the parties are aligned in the petition for review. Since there are commonly many parties in a complex review proceeding before a court of appeals, and since any losing party can petition for review, it is not uncommon for no agency to be named in what is surely, in fact, a review of an agency's work. (In Vermont Yankee itself, the agency had not been permitted to petition for certiorari by the Solicitor General, in light of the difficulty of determining "exactly what result [the court of appeals] did reach." It therefore was nominally a respondent before the Supreme Court, although arguing in support of the petitioner utilities.)

2. In order to obtain the construction permit, the utility must file a preliminary safety analysis report, an environmental report, and certain information regarding the antitrust implications of the proposed project. This application then undergoes exhaustive review by the Commission's staff and by the Advisory Committee on Reactor Safeguards (ACRS), a group of distinguished experts in the field of atomic energy. Both groups submit to the Commission their own evaluations, which then become part of the record of the utility's application. The Commission staff also undertakes the review required by the National Environmental Policy Act of 1969 (NEPA), 42 U.S.C. § 4321 et seq., and prepares a draft environmental impact statement, which, after being circulated for comment, is revised and becomes a final environmental impact statement. Thereupon a three-member Atomic Safety and Licensing Board conducts a public adjudicatory hearing, and reaches a decision which can be appealed to the Atomic Safety and Licensing Appeal Board, and currently, in the Commission's discretion, to the Commission itself. The final agency decision may be appealed to the courts of appeals. The same sort of process occurs when the utility applies for a license to operate the plant, except that a hearing need only be held in contested cases and may be limited to the matters in controversy.

the time it reached the Supreme Court[3] —attempted to use rulemaking to resolve some questions of the latter type.

These questions concerned the environmental impact the nuclear fuel cycle could be expected to have *outside* the plant grounds. For electricity to be generated at the plant, uranium would have to be mined, processed to enhance its potential as fuel, embodied in fuel elements, and then transported to the plant. After the fuel's potential to generate power had been exhausted, the resulting highly radioactive waste would somehow have to be transported, processed, and stored safely. Each of these operations could be expected to have environmental and safety impacts, but they would not be impacts specific to a particular plant. Workers would be injured, or the public threatened, in Utah where the mines were, or in the Ohio River valley where enrichment occurred, etc. The expectable impacts, moreover, could be expressed in relationship to units of power to be generated or, perhaps, to numbers of fuel rods made or used. Once one had determined these impacts in this way, the impact attributable to a particular plant could be straightforwardly calculated on the basis of its generating capacity.

For the agency, using rulemaking to fix these general impacts promised to take their factual questions out of individual licensing proceedings, where they would be repetitive and could perhaps be used simply for delay. The agency might also believe that a one-time process for determining these matters, open to any member of the public interested to participate, could be advantageous to accurate determination of the matters in issue. Still, for the parties opposing the licensing of a small nuclear reactor near Brattleboro, Vermont, this route would substitute the procedural rights of rulemaking for the procedural rights of adjudication. The procedures of rulemaking were arguably insufficiently rigorous and open to public control to be trustworthy in determining factual questions of large public moment. To what extent could the courts be persuaded to require processes for resolving such portentous factual issues in rulemaking, that would be like those otherwise available in agency adjudication?]

■ JUSTICE REHNQUIST delivered the opinion of the Court.

In 1946, Congress enacted the Administrative Procedure Act, which as we have noted elsewhere was not only "a new, basic and comprehensive regulation of procedures in many agencies," Wong Yang Sung v. McGrath, 339 U.S. 33 (1950), but was also a legislative enactment which settled "long-continued and hard-fought contentions, and enacts a formula upon which opposing social and political forces have come to rest." Id., at 40. Section 4 of the Act, 5 U.S.C. § 553 (1976 ed.), dealing with rulemaking, requires in subsection (b) that "notice of proposed rule making shall be published in the Federal Register ... ," describes the contents of that notice, and goes on to require in subsection (c) that after the notice the agency "shall give interested persons an opportunity to participate in the rule making through submission of written data, views, or arguments with

---

3. The licensing and regulatory functions of the Atomic Energy Commission (AEC) were transferred to the Nuclear Regulatory Commission (NRC) by the Energy Reorganization Act of 1974, 42 U.S.C. § 5801 et seq. (1970 ed., Supp. V). Hereinafter both the AEC and NRC will be referred to as the Commission.

or without opportunity for oral presentation. After consideration of the relevant matter presented, the agency shall incorporate in the rules adopted a concise general statement of their basis and purpose." Interpreting this provision of the Act in United States v. Allegheny–Ludlum Steel Corp., 406 U.S. 742 (1972), and United States v. Florida East Coast Ry. Co., 410 U.S. 224 (1973), we held that generally speaking this section of the Act established the maximum procedural requirements which Congress was willing to have the courts impose upon agencies in conducting rulemaking procedures. Agencies are free to grant additional procedural rights in the exercise of their discretion, but reviewing courts are generally not free to impose them if the agencies have not chosen to grant them. This is not to say necessarily that there are no circumstances which would ever justify a court in overturning agency action because of a failure to employ procedures beyond those required by the statute. But such circumstances, if they exist, are extremely rare.

Even apart from the Administrative Procedure Act this Court has for more than four decades emphasized that the formulation of procedures was basically to be left within the discretion of the agencies to which Congress had confided the responsibility for substantive judgments. In FCC v. Schreiber, 381 U.S. 279, 290 (1965), the Court explicated this principle, describing it as "an outgrowth of the congressional determination that administrative agencies and administrators will be familiar with the industries which they regulate and will be in a better position than federal courts or Congress itself to design procedural rules adapted to the peculiarities of the industry and the tasks of the agency involved." . . .

I

A

. . . These cases arise from two separate decisions of the Court of Appeals for the District of Columbia Circuit. In the first, the court remanded a decision of the Commission to grant a license to petitioner Vermont Yankee Nuclear Power Corp. to operate a nuclear power plant. Natural Resources Defense Council v. NRC, 547 F.2d 633 (1976). In the second, the court remanded a decision of that same agency to grant a permit to petitioner Consumers Power Co. to construct two pressurized water nuclear reactors to generate electricity and steam. Aeschliman v. NRC, 547 F.2d 622 (1976).[4]

B

In December 1967, after the mandatory adjudicatory hearing and necessary review, the Commission granted petitioner Vermont Yankee a permit to build a nuclear power plant in Vernon, Vt. Thereafter, Vermont Yankee applied for an operating license. Respondent Natural Resources Defense Council (NRDC) objected to the granting of a license, however, and therefore a hearing on the application commenced on August 10, 1971. Excluded from consideration at the hearings, over NRDC's objection, was

4. [Ed.] Both decisions were written by Chief Judge David Bazelon. Those parts of the Court's opinion principally concerning the Consumers Power reactor in Midland, Michigan are omitted.

the issue of the environmental effects of operations to reprocess fuel or dispose of wastes resulting from the reprocessing operations.[5] This ruling was affirmed by the Appeal Board in June 1972.

In November 1972, however, the Commission, making specific reference to the Appeal Board's decision with respect to the Vermont Yankee license, instituted rulemaking proceedings "that would specifically deal with the question of consideration of environmental effects associated with the uranium fuel cycle in the individual cost-benefit analyses for light water cooled nuclear power reactors." The notice of proposed rulemaking offered two alternatives, both predicated on a report prepared by the Commission's staff entitled Environmental Survey of the Nuclear Fuel Cycle. The first would have required no quantitative evaluation of the environmental hazards ... because the Environmental Survey had found them to be slight. The second would have specified numerical values for the environmental impact of ... the fuel cycle, which values would then be incorporated into a table ... to determine the overall cost-benefit balance for each operating license.

Much of the controversy in this case revolves around the procedures used in the rulemaking hearing which commenced in February 1973. In a supplemental notice of hearing the Commission indicated that while discovery or cross-examination would not be utilized, the Environmental Survey would be available to the public before the hearing along with the extensive background documents cited therein. All participants would be given a reasonable opportunity to present their position and could be represented by counsel if they so desired. Written and, time permitting, oral statements would be received and incorporated into the record. All persons giving oral statements would be subject to questioning by the Commission. At the conclusion of the hearing, a transcript would be made available to the public and the record would remain open for 30 days to allow the filing of supplemental written statements. More than 40 individuals and organizations representing a wide variety of interests submitted written comments. On January 17, 1973, the Licensing Board held a planning session to schedule the appearance of witnesses and to discuss methods for compiling a record. The hearing was held on February 1 and 2, with participation by a number of groups, including the Commission's staff, the United States Environmental Protection Agency, a manufacturer of reactor equipment, a trade association from the nuclear industry, a group of electric utility companies, and a group called Consolidated National Intervenors which represented 79 groups and individuals including respondent NRDC.

After the hearing, the Commission's staff filed a supplemental document for the purpose of clarifying and revising the Environmental Survey. Then the Licensing Board forwarded its report to the Commission without

---

5. The nuclear fission which takes place in light-water nuclear reactors apparently converts its principal fuel, uranium, into plutonium, which is itself highly radioactive but can be used as reactor fuel if separated from the remaining uranium and radioactive waste products. Fuel reprocessing refers to the process necessary to recapture usable plutonium. Waste disposal, at the present stage of technological development, refers to the storage of the very long lived and highly radioactive waste products until they detoxify sufficiently that they no longer present an environmental hazard. There are presently no physical or chemical steps which render this waste less toxic, other than simply the passage of time.

rendering any decision. The Licensing Board identified as the principal procedural question the propriety of declining to use full formal adjudicatory procedures. The major substantive issue was the technical adequacy of the Environmental Survey.

In April 1974, the Commission issued a rule which adopted the second of the two proposed alternatives described above. The Commission also approved the procedures used at the hearing,[6] and indicated that the record, including the Environmental Survey, provided an "adequate data base for the regulation adopted." Finally, the Commission ruled that to the extent the rule differed from the Appeal Board decisions in Vermont Yankee "those decisions have no further precedential significance," but that since "the environmental effects of the uranium fuel cycle have been shown to be relatively insignificant, . . . it is unnecessary to apply the amendment to applicant's environmental reports submitted prior to its effective date or to Final Environmental Statements for which Draft Environmental Statements have been circulated for comment prior to the effective date."

Respondents appealed from both the Commission's adoption of the rule and its decision to grant Vermont Yankee's license to the Court of Appeals for the District of Columbia Circuit.

C

[The description of the Consumers Power Co. case is omitted.]

D

With respect to the challenge of Vermont Yankee's license, the court first ruled that in the absence of effective rulemaking proceedings,[7] the Commission must deal with the environmental impact of fuel reprocessing and disposal in individual licensing proceedings. The court then examined the rulemaking proceedings and, despite the fact that it appeared that the agency employed all the procedures required by 5 U.S.C. § 553 and more, the court determined the proceedings to be inadequate and overturned the rule. Accordingly, the Commission's determination with respect to Vermont Yankee's license was also remanded for further proceedings.[8] . . .

---

6.   The Commission stated: . . .

"In our view, the procedures adopted provide a more than adequate basis for formulation of the rule we adopted. All parties were fully heard. Nothing offered was excluded. The record does not indicate that any evidentiary material would have been received under different procedures. Nor did the proponent of the strict 'adjudicatory' approach make an offer of proof—or even remotely suggest—what substantive matters it would develop under different procedures. In addition, we note that 11 documents including the Survey were available to the parties several weeks before the hearing, and the Regulatory staff, though not requested to do so, made available various drafts and handwritten notes. Under all of the circumstances, we conclude that adjudicatory type procedures were not warranted here."

7.   In the Court of Appeals no one questioned the Commission's authority to deal with fuel cycle issues by informal rulemaking as opposed to adjudication. Neither does anyone seriously question before this Court the Commission's authority in this respect.

8.   After the decision of the Court of Appeals the Commission promulgated a new interim rule pending issuance of a final rule. 42 Fed.Reg. 13803 (1977). . . .

As we read the opinion of the Court of Appeals, its view that reviewing courts may

II

A

[The Court first considered] whether the Commission may consider the environmental impact of the fuel processes when licensing nuclear reactors. In addition to the weight which normally attaches to the agency's determination of such a question, other reasons support the Commission's conclusion.

Vermont Yankee will produce annually well over 100 pounds of radioactive wastes, some of which will be highly toxic. The Commission itself . . . clearly recognizes that these wastes "pose the most severe potential health hazard. . . ." Many of these substances must be isolated for anywhere from 600 to hundreds of thousands of years. It is hard to argue that these wastes do not constitute "adverse environmental effects which cannot be avoided should the proposal be implemented," or that by operating nuclear power plants we are not making "irreversible and irretrievable commitments of resources." . . . For these reasons we hold that the Commission acted well within its statutory authority when it considered the back end of the fuel cycle in individual licensing proceedings.

B

We next turn to the invalidation of the fuel cycle rule. But before determining whether the Court of Appeals reached a permissible result, we must determine exactly what result it did reach, and in this case that is no mean feat. . . .

After a thorough examination of the opinion itself, we conclude that while the matter is not entirely free from doubt, the majority of the Court of Appeals struck down the rule because of the perceived inadequacies of the procedures employed in the rulemaking proceedings. The court first determined the intervenors' primary argument to be "that the decision to preclude 'discovery or cross-examination' denied them a meaningful opportunity to participate in the proceedings as guaranteed by due process." The court then went on to frame the issue for decision thus:

> Thus, we are called upon to decide whether the procedures provided by the agency were sufficient to ventilate the issues.

. . . [T]here is little doubt in our minds that the ineluctable mandate of the court's decision is that the procedures afforded during the hearings were inadequate. This conclusion is particularly buttressed by the fact that after the court examined the record, particularly the testimony of Dr. Pittman, and declared it insufficient, the court proceeded to discuss at some length the necessity for further procedural devices or a more "sensitive" applica-

in the absence of special circumstances justifying such a course of action impose additional procedural requirements on agency action raises questions of such significance in this area of the law as to warrant our granting certiorari and deciding the case. Since the vast majority of challenges to administrative agency action are brought to the Court of Appeals for the District of Columbia Circuit, the decision of that court in this case will serve as precedent for many more proceedings for judicial review of agency actions than would the decision of another Court of Appeals. Finally, this decision will continue to play a major role in the instant litigation regardless of the Commission's decision to press ahead with further rulemaking proceedings. . . .

tion of those devices employed during the proceedings. The exploration of the record and the statement regarding its insufficiency might initially lead one to conclude that the court was only examining the sufficiency of the evidence, but the remaining portions of the opinion dispel any doubt that this was certainly not the sole or even the principal basis of the decision. Accordingly, we feel compelled to address the opinion on its own terms, and we conclude that it was wrong.

In prior opinions we have intimated that even in a rulemaking proceeding when an agency is making a " 'quasi-judicial' " determination by which a very small number of persons are " 'exceptionally affected, in each case upon individual grounds,' " in some circumstances additional procedures may be required in order to afford the aggrieved individuals due process.[9] United States v. Florida East Coast Ry. Co., 410 U.S., at 242, 245, quoting from Bi–Metallic Investment Co. v. State Board of Equalization, 239 U.S. 441, 446 (1915). It might also be true, although we do not think the issue is presented in this case and accordingly do not decide it, that a totally unjustified departure from well-settled agency procedures of long standing might require judicial correction.

But this much is absolutely clear. Absent constitutional constraints or extremely compelling circumstances the "administrative agencies 'should be free to fashion their own rules of procedure and to pursue methods of inquiry capable of permitting them to discharge their multitudinous duties.' " FCC v. Schreiber, 381 U.S., at 290, quoting from FCC v. Pottsville Broadcasting Co., 309 U.S., at 143. . . .

Respondent NRDC argues that § 4 of the Administrative Procedure Act, 5 U.S.C. § 553, merely establishes lower procedural bounds and that a court may routinely require more than the minimum when an agency's proposed rule addresses complex or technical factual issues or "Issues of Great Public Import."

We have, however, previously shown that our decisions reject this view. We also think the legislative history, even the part which it cites, does not bear out its contention. The Senate Report explains what eventually became § 4 thus:

> This subsection states ... the minimum requirements of public rule making procedure short of statutory hearing. Under it agencies might in addition confer with industry advisory committees, consult organizations, hold informal "hearings," and the like. Considerations of practicality, necessity, and public interest ... will naturally govern the agency's determination of the extent to which public proceedings should go. Matters of great import, or those where the public submission of facts will be either useful to the agency or a protection to the public, should naturally be accorded more elaborate public procedures. S.Rep. No. 752, 79th Cong., 1st Sess., 14–15 (1945).

The House Report is in complete accord. ... And the Attorney General's Manual on the Administrative Procedure Act 31, 35 (1947), a contempora-

---

9. Respondent NRDC does not now argue that additional procedural devices were required under the Constitution. Since this was clearly a rulemaking proceeding in its purest form, we see nothing to support such a view.

neous interpretation previously given some deference by this Court because of the role played by the Department of Justice in drafting the legislation, further confirms that view. In short, all of this leaves little doubt that Congress intended that the discretion of the *agencies* and not that of the courts be exercised in determining when extra procedural devices should be employed.

There are compelling reasons for construing § 4 in this manner. In the first place, if courts continually review agency proceedings to determine whether the agency employed procedures which were, in the court's opinion, perfectly tailored to reach what the court perceives to be the "best" or "correct" result, judicial review would be totally unpredictable. And the agencies, operating under this vague injunction to employ the "best" procedures and facing the threat of reversal if they did not, would undoubtedly adopt full adjudicatory procedures in every instance. Not only would this totally disrupt the statutory scheme, through which Congress enacted "a formula upon which opposing social and political forces have come to rest," Wong Yang Sung v. McGrath, 339 U.S., at 40, but all the inherent advantages of informal rulemaking would be totally lost.

Secondly, it is obvious that the court in these cases reviewed the agency's choice of procedures on the basis of the record actually produced at the hearing, and not on the basis of the information available to the agency when it made the decision to structure the proceedings in a certain way. This sort of Monday morning quarterbacking not only encourages but almost compels the agency to conduct all rulemaking proceedings with the full panoply of procedural devices normally associated only with adjudicatory hearings.

Finally, and perhaps most importantly, this sort of review fundamentally misconceives the nature of the standard for judicial review of an agency rule. The court below uncritically assumed that additional procedures will automatically result in a more adequate record because it will give interested parties more of an opportunity to participate in and contribute to the proceedings. But informal rulemaking need not be based solely on the transcript of a hearing held before an agency. Indeed, the agency need not even hold a formal hearing. See 5 U.S.C. § 553(c). Thus, the adequacy of the "record" in this type of proceeding is not correlated directly to the type of procedural devices employed, but rather turns on whether the agency has followed the statutory mandate of the Administrative Procedure Act or other relevant statutes. If the agency is compelled to support the rule which it ultimately adopts with the type of record produced only after a full adjudicatory hearing, it simply will have no choice but to conduct a full adjudicatory hearing prior to promulgating every rule. In sum, this sort of unwarranted judicial examination of perceived procedural shortcomings of a rulemaking proceeding can do nothing but seriously interfere with that process prescribed by Congress. . . .

In short, nothing in the APA, . . . the circumstances of this case, the nature of the issues being considered, past agency practice, or the statutory mandate under which the Commission operates permitted the court to review and overturn the rulemaking proceeding on the basis of the procedural devices employed (or not employed) by the Commission so long as the Commission employed at least the statutory *minima*, a matter about which there is no doubt in this case.

There remains, of course, the question of whether the challenged rule finds sufficient justification in the administrative proceedings that it should be upheld by the reviewing court. Judge Tamm, concurring in the result reached by the majority of the Court of Appeals, thought that it did not. There are also intimations in the majority opinion which suggest that the judges who joined it likewise may have thought the administrative proceedings an insufficient basis upon which to predicate the rule in question. We accordingly remand so that the Court of Appeals may review the rule as the Administrative Procedure Act provides. We have made it abundantly clear before that when there is a contemporaneous explanation of the agency decision, the validity of that action must "stand or fall on the propriety of that finding, judged, of course, by the appropriate standard of review. If that finding is not sustainable on the administrative record made, then the Comptroller's decision must be vacated and the matter remanded to him for further consideration." Camp v. Pitts, 411 U.S. 138, 143 (1973). See also SEC v. Chenery Corp., 318 U.S. 80 (1943). The court should engage in this kind of review and not stray beyond the judicial province to explore the procedural format or to impose upon the agency its own notion of which procedures are "best" or most likely to further some vague, undefined public good.

III

[The Court's analysis of the companion case is omitted, except for the peroration, which follows:]

All this leads us to make one further observation of some relevance to this case. To say that the Court of Appeals' final reason for remanding is insubstantial at best is a gross understatement. Consumers Power first applied in 1969 for a construction permit—not even an operating license, just a construction permit. The proposed plant underwent an incredibly extensive review. The reports filed and reviewed literally fill books. The proceedings took years, and the actual hearings themselves over two weeks. To then nullify that effort seven years later because one report refers to other problems, which problems admittedly have been discussed at length in other reports available to the public, borders on the Kafkaesque. Nuclear energy may some day be a cheap, safe source of power or it may not. But Congress has made a choice to at least try nuclear energy, establishing a reasonable review process in which courts are to play only a limited role. The fundamental policy questions appropriately resolved in Congress and in the state legislatures are *not* subject to reexamination in the federal courts under the guise of judicial review of agency action. Time may prove wrong the decision to develop nuclear energy, but it is Congress or the States within their appropriate agencies which must eventually make that judgment. In the meantime courts should perform their appointed function. ... And a single alleged oversight on a peripheral issue, urged by parties who never fully cooperated or indeed raised the issue below, must not be made the basis for overturning a decision properly made after an otherwise exhaustive proceeding.

Reversed and remanded.[10]

■ JUSTICE BLACKMUN and JUSTICE POWELL took no part in the consideration or decision of these cases.

NOTES ON VERMONT YANKEE AND ITS IMPACT

(1) *Legislatively Required Hybrid Rulemaking.* Vermont Yankee is a screed against judicial improvisation with legislatively set procedures. Of course, Congress can add to § 553's procedural requirements, and to serve various ends it has often done so in agency-specific legislation. In the 1970s, both before and after Florida East Coast Railway, p. 487 above, Congress passed several important regulatory statutes which enlarged on the notice-and-comment process without moving fully to the trial-type process of formal rulemaking. These statutes created what is termed "hybrid" rulemaking processes. E.g., the Occupational Safety and Health Act of 1970, 29 U.S.C. § 651; the Consumer Product Safety Act of 1972, 15 U.S.C. § 2051; the Federal Trade Commission Improvement Act of 1975, 15 U.S.C. § 57a; the Toxic Substances Control Act of 1976, 15 U.S.C. § 2601; and the Clear Air Act Amendments of 1977, 42 U.S.C. § 7401. The FTC Improvement Act was among the most detailed of these statutes. Harry and Bryant Co. v. Federal Trade Commission, 726 F.2d 993, cert. denied, 469 U.S. 820 (1984), describes an FTC rulemaking on funeral industry practices that began in 1972 and finally produced a rulemaking in 1984, after fifty-two days of hearings at which 315 witnesses testified, 14,719 pages of transcripts were generated and approximately 4,000 additional pages of exhibits were introduced. More than 9000 documents were submitted in the comment period, comprising in excess of 20,000 pages.

In 1980, well before this particular FTC rulemaking had run its course, the Administrative Conference of the United States reported to Congress that even though oral procedures could offer certain advantages, nonetheless flexibility and resistance to procedural conservatism were required to avoid impairing the efficiency, acceptability, and quality of administrative decisions. Administrative Conference of the U.S., 1979 Report 42–3 (1980). Some confirmation of this observation might be found in CORROSION PROOF FITTINGS V. EPA, 947 F.2d 1201, 1211 (5th Cir.1991), a case involving EPA hybrid rulemaking under the authority of the Toxic Substances Control Act ("TSCA"), 15 U.S.C. § 2601. EPA had adopted a rule for products incorporating asbestos using TSCA procedures, and in the resulting hearings had permitted some, but not all, of the cross-examination desired by the appellants. Said the Fifth Circuit, "Section 19(c)(1)(B)(ii) of TSCA requires that we hold unlawful any rule promulgated where EPA restrictions on cross-examination 'precluded disclosure of disputed material facts which [were] necessary to a fair determination by the Administrator.' 15 U.S.C. § 2618(c)(1)(B)(ii). In promulgating this rule, the EPA allowed substantial

---

10. [Ed.] For further events in this effort to litigate the life cycle of nuclear wastes, see Baltimore Gas & Electric Co. v. Natural Resources Defense Council, Inc., 462 U.S. 87 (1983), discussed at p. 1016 below.

cross-examination of most, but not all, of its witnesses. Considering the importance TSCA accords to cross-examination, the EPA should have afforded interested parties full cross-examination on all of its major witnesses. We are mindful of the length of the asbestos regulatory process in this case, but Congress, in enacting the rules governing the informal hearing process under TSCA, specifically reserved a place for proper cross-examination on issues of disputed material fact. Precluding cross-examination of EPA witnesses—even a minority of them—is not the proper way to expedite the finish of a lengthy rulemaking procedure.''

One can find in these statutes, as in the cases that preceded Vermont Yankee, a sense that the stakes in some rulemakings are so high that additional procedural safeguards are called for. In one of the articles growing out of Vermont Yankee, then Professor (now ''The Honorable'') Antonin Scalia had this to say about the legislative fashioning of hybrid procedures (VERMONT YANKEE: THE APA, THE D.C. CIRCUIT, AND THE SUPREME COURT, 1978 Sup. Ct. Rev. 345, 404–08): ''What this discussion of the legislative process was meant to emphasize is the fundamental point that one of the functions of procedure is to limit power—not just the power to be unfair, but the power to act in a political mode, or the power to act at all. Such limitation is sometimes an incidental result of pursuing other functions, such as efficiency and fairness; but it may be an end in itself. . . .

''The procedural foundations of the judicial process were laid long ago, and the basic role of the courts seems firmly established by both tradition and constitutional prescription. There is little legislative inclination, therefore, to adjust upward and downward the power of the courts, and even less inclination to achieve this by fiddling with procedures. Not so with the agencies. Their powers are for the most part neither constitutionally prescribed nor well established, and their procedures are only recently formed. Thus, the tendency to alter procedures as a means of altering power is immeasurably stronger.

''Of course, once it is accepted that procedures are to be used as a means of expanding or restricting the power to act, the idea of any genuinely stable APA based on fairness and efficiency alone becomes visionary. It also becomes unrealistic to expect the framework of any such superstatute to contain only a few options of procedure among which later legislation must choose—such as the stark choice between formal and informal rulemaking offered under the current APA. . . . The degrees of activism and of political decision making which the Congress expects from (or, more precisely, which the legislative struggle finally induces its divergent factions to accord to) the FTC, the ICC, the INS, the FDA, and the CPSC may vary enormously—and so will the procedures which reflect those expectations.

''One can argue that things should be otherwise. That the Congress should be induced to forswear the use of procedures as a means of restricting power, and to pursue that goal, when desired, by some more sensible means (such as cutting budgets) or by some other equally senseless means (such as blindfolding every third bureaucrat). If such congressional self-denial were achieved, one might think a truly stable framework of administrative procedure could be established. There are two problems, however: one practical, one theoretical. As a practical matter, both the Congress and the lobbyists who appear before it would be foolhardy from a selfish standpoint—and perhaps even from the standpoint of the public interest—to abandon a compromise device which is so well insulated from effective criticism. . . . While 'hybrid rulemaking' may no longer be devised by the courts under the APA, it will continue to flourish in a multiplicity of special statutes that modify the APA's dispositions, at least so long as the APA itself provides so few variants (and those based on considerations of fairness and efficiency alone) from which to select.

"And there is a theoretical reason why this ought to be so. Congress can, indeed, refrain from making use of the connection between procedure and power, but it cannot make that connection itself disappear. Thus, to the extent that the choice of procedures is left to the agencies themselves, to that same extent the agencies are left to determine a substantial aspect of their own power. . . .

"It seems to me, therefore, that if the continuing fragmentation of mandated administrative procedure is to be abated, what is called for is a more modest expectation of what the APA can and should achieve, and a design that will accord with the realities. . . . I would settle for an APA that contains not merely three but ten or fifteen basic procedural formats—an inventory large enough to provide the basis for a whole spectrum of legislative compromises without the necessity for shopping elsewhere."

One theme that has perhaps already emerged in these pages is the risk of paralyzing rulemaking by imposing excessive procedural demands on it. This is often described in the literature as "ossification." Watch to see to what extent this tendency, when it appears, can be ascribed to the importance of the particular rulemaking involved. Should rulemaking procedures vary with the importance of the undertaking? As the materials of this chapter will reveal, considerable legislative and executive branch effort has been put into differentiating between "major" regulations—those likely to have a significant impact upon the national economy or sectors of it—and others of a more routine character. The APA has not been amended in this way, however. Should it be? Should courts draw from the unmistakable patterns of legislative and executive action a rationale for interpretation that was perhaps absent when Vermont Yankee was decided?

(2) Clark Byse, Vermont Yankee and the Evolution of Administrative Procedure: A Somewhat Different View, 91 Harv.L.Rev. 1823, 1828–29 (1978): "If the court is convinced that an adequate record for review can best be achieved by utilization of an additional procedural device, why should it not save everyone's time and energy by ordering the agency to utilize that device?

"There are at least three answers to such an argument. First, although the reviewing court may have convinced itself that an additional procedural device is indispensable, its conviction may well be erroneous. A particular procedural device is a means to an end, not the end itself. If the court has explained in what ways the record is inadequate, very likely there will be various means by which it can be made adequate. By prescribing a particular procedure the court prevents the agency, which has the firstline responsibility and experience in administering the statute, from utilizing that experience to provide the needed record in the most cost-effective fashion.

"Second, even if the judicially prescribed procedural device might, in some abstract sense, be thought to be the indispensable *modus operandi,* is it necessary or appropriate for the court to *order* the agency? I think not. If, as I believe and courts occasionally proclaim, courts and agencies constitute a 'partnership' in furtherance of the public interest and are 'collaborative instrumentalities of justice,' the judicial partner should be mindful of the sensitivities and responsibilities of the administrative partner; to the extent possible, the relationship should be one of collaboration, not command. This is not simply a matter of etiquette or abstract *noblesse oblige.* Rather it relates to an important aspect of our legal system that is sometimes overlooked, namely, that although the judiciary has a duty to uphold the law, it also has a duty to recognize and defer to the responsibilities of other components of government, including the administrative component. . . .

"Third, and most important, in enacting APA section 553 in 1946, Congress established a new general model of rulemaking procedure. There is no suggestion in the legislative history of the section that it was declaratory of the common law or that it was a delegation of power to the courts to develop desirable procedural models. On the contrary, the legislative history indicates that the question whether additional procedural devices are to be employed is an *agency* question, not a *judicial* question: '[c]onsiderations of practicality, necessity, and public interest . . . will naturally govern the *agency's* determination of the extent to which public proceedings should go.' "

(3) CHRISTOPHER F. EDLEY, JR., ADMINISTRATIVE LAW: RETHINKING JUDICIAL CONTROL OF BUREAUCRACY 228 (Yale Univ. Press 1990): "Because substance and procedure can be transmuted so readily, the effect of Vermont Yankee is simply to make a court that is inclined toward interventionism express its concerns and its remand instructions in quasi-procedural language that has a substantive resonance: explore more alternatives, give a more detailed explanation, disclose considerations and staff information, demonstrate adequate consideration of statutory factors, and so on. The risk is that the reviewing court may use modes of rhetoric and intervention that miscommunicate the course and nature of its dissatisfaction with the administrative action—all because in any particular circumstance, the court is concerned that its legitimate purview is somehow delimited by the substance-procedure categorization. This approach is misleading and self-defeating, in view of both the boundary problem in these two categories and the related and more fundamental point that proper evaluation of agency action requires an eye to both procedure and substance."

NOTES ON THE PROBLEMS OF FINDING CONTESTED "GENERAL" FACT

(1) *The State of the Record.* In an earlier passage in the essay just quoted, Professor Scalia suggested that the record supporting the values the

Commission's regulation had assigned to nuclear waste issues was indeed quite thin:

> The crucial factual issue in the case was the adequacy of existing high-level waste disposal techniques. The only supporting evidence on this point was a 20–page statement by the director of the Commission's Division of Waste Management and Transportation, which statement had been read during the oral hearings[1] and was subsequently incorporated into the Environmental Survey published after the comment period. On several important points it was strikingly devoid of detail and constituted little more than "conclusory reassurances." Although, in the [D.C. Circuit]'s view, "the vagueness of the presentation regarding waste disposal made detailed criticism of its specifics impossible," the petitioners had offered "a number of more general comments concerning the Commission's approach," including failure to distinguish between design objectives and performance objectives, failure to consider actual experience with waste disposal, and the unjustified assumption that organized human supervision necessary to continued maintenance of the proposed disposal techniques would be available "in perpetuity." The Commission's statement of basis and purpose for the rule did not respond specifically to any of these objections. 1978 Sup. Ct. Rev. 345, 352–54.

A quarter century after Vermont Yankee, questions about how to deal with the waste resulting from nuclear power generation are still unsettled. While this may be more the result of political struggles than technical uncertainties—and twenty-five years is very short in relation to how long the environment must be protected from contamination by this waste—our institutional failures to deal decisively with the questions emphasize the uncertainties of the Commission's approach. In this respect, is the opinion's peroration about the division between political and judicial responsibilities in the regulation of nuclear power an adequate response?

(2) *Regulations, Fact-Finding, and Procedures Familiar to Judges.* One inevitable risk for judges encountering open procedural questions is that they will tend to respond in terms of what they know as judges. You may already have seen one example of this in Withrow v. Larkin, p. 414. There, in assessing the constitutionality of an institutional arrangement in which an agency that had decided to seek criminal charges against an alleged abortionist was also responsible for deciding professional discipline matters,

---

1. [Ed.] This misstates matters a bit, but not much. The reference is to Dr. Pittman's testimony, discussed in the Court's opinion. One of your editors, then General Counsel of the NRC, had the opportunity to read the transcript of this testimony in the days immediately following decision by the D.C. Circuit. The transcript showed that Dr. Pittman first delivered his views viva voce and then stood down from the witness chair to permit testimony by another witness with a flight to catch. Dr. Pittman returned to the witness chair after this intermission and responded to questions from the board, including questions suggested by participants in the rulemaking. The original opinion issued by the D.C. Circuit, however, erroneously claimed that the board had asked Dr. Pittman no questions at all. These misstatements may have been the basis for then Professor, now Justice Scalia's characterization. The D.C Circuit opinion was amended to eliminate the misstatements, but not its conclusions, when the state of the transcript was called to its attention. No one could have characterized the record as thick, however.

Justice White asked whether "under a realistic appraisal of psychological tendencies and human weakness, conferring investigative and adjudicative powers on the same individuals poses such a risk of actual bias or prejudgment that the practice must be forbidden if the guarantee of due process is to be adequately implemented." To answer that question he drew on what he knew from experience as a judge.

One way to understand the Supreme Court's opinion in Vermont Yankee might be that the Court feared the D.C. Circuit had imported adjudicatory sensibilities and values into rulemaking. Legislatures do not typically proceed—and certainly need not proceed—by hearing live testimony about factual issues. When they hold hearings, the predominant talk is often about policy issues. Committee members or staff may ask questions, even belligerently at times; yet interested members of the public who are present in the hearing room (perhaps waiting to deliver their own views) never have the chance to ask questions themselves. At best they can send a note to a member or staffer suggesting them. Should a statute be enacted, any arguable failures of inquiry are of no concern to the courts. These adjudicatory sensibilities are simply out of place.

Another way to understand the D.C. Circuit opinion, however, might be that its motive power came not from a bias toward judicialized procedures, but rather from concern about the particular problems of finding "general" fact. In the adjudication chapter, at p. 364, you may already have found a brief discussion of Professor Kenneth C. Davis's influential distinction between legislative and adjudicative fact, and of how that distinction breaks down in high science-and-technology cases like Vermont Yankee. The Vermont Yankee regulation stated a series of values for health and other consequences to be expected from the fuel cycle processes occurring outside nuclear power plants. For example, what would be miners' exposure to radiation each time they handled the amount of uranium ore necessary to produce the nuclear fuel that could generate one Megawatt of electric power for a year? Or, an example that particularly concerned the D.C. Circuit, what might be the radiation exposure of members of the public living within X miles of storage facilities from the spent nuclear fuel resulting from the generation of 1 Megawatt of power? These are not questions concerning individuals "who were exceptionally affected, in each case upon individual grounds," as the Vermont Yankee Court remarks in invoking the Bi–Metallic decision. (Discussed at p. 504). At the same time however, *neither* are they the kinds of questions that we would likely think well resolved by legislative processes and votes. What processes might scientists use to resolve such questions of "general" fact? Is there room in § 553 for the courts to push rulemaking in *that* direction?

(3) *The D.C. Circuit Debate*. At the time of Vermont Yankee, the D.C. Circuit was deeply enmeshed in internal debate over how courts ought respond to challenges to regulations that turned on technical and scientific questions judges lacked the expertise to resolve—or perhaps, even, understand. This debate was captured best in an en banc decision, ETHYL CORP. v. EPA, 541 F.2d 1 (D.C.Cir.1976), cert. denied, 426 U.S. 941 (1976), reviewing an EPA regulation requiring annual reductions in the lead content of leaded gasoline. (This regulation is now often presented as a paradigm of a

regulation whose costs are strongly justified by its benefits.) In adopting the regulation, EPA had been required to decide a number of highly controverted factual propositions, make projections based on imperfect data, and in other ways reach technical or scientific judgments that the makers of lead additives strongly challenged. While this is not the place to consider the appropriate standard of judicial review (see Chapter VIII), the debate is well framed by these passages from the separate opinions of Chief Judge David Bazelon (who would shortly be the author of Vermont Yankee) and Judge Harold Leventhal (the author of several opinions urging considerably expanded notice, comment opportunity, and explanation—a concept that came to be called a "paper hearing"). Opinions of both judges are well represented in this chapter. Judge Leventhal frequently remarked to one of your editors that he understood Vermont Yankee to mean that he had won the debate.

Judge Bazelon: "I agree with the court's construction of the statute that the Administrator is called upon to make 'essentially legislative policy judgments' in assessing risks to public health. But I cannot agree that this automatically relieves the Administrator's decision from the 'procedural ... rigor proper for questions of fact.' Quite the contrary, this case strengthens my view that ' ... in cases of great technological complexity, the best way for courts to guard against unreasonable or erroneous administrative decisions is not for the judges themselves to scrutinize the technical merits of each decision. Rather, it is to establish a decision-making process that assures a reasoned decision that can be held up to the scrutiny of the scientific community and the public.' This record provides vivid demonstration of the dangers implicit in the contrary view, ably espoused by Judge Leventhal, which would have judges 'steeping' themselves 'in technical matters to determine whether the agency "has exercised a reasoned discretion."' It is one thing for judges to scrutinize FCC judgments concerning diversification of media ownership to determine if they are rational. But I doubt judges contribute much to improving the quality of the difficult decisions which must be made in highly technical areas when they take it upon themselves to decide, as did the panel in this case, that 'in assessing the scientific and medical data the Administrator made clear errors of judgment.' The process [of] making a de novo evaluation of the scientific evidence inevitably invites judges of opposing views to make plausible—sounding, but simplistic, judgments of the relative weight to be afforded various pieces of technical data. ...

"Because substantive review of mathematical and scientific evidence by technically illiterate judges is dangerously unreliable, I continue to believe we will do more to improve administrative decision–making by concentrating our efforts on strengthening administrative procedures:[2] 'When administrators provide a framework for principled decision–making, the result will be to diminish the importance of judicial review by enhancing the integrity of the administrative process, and to improve the quality of judicial review in those cases where judicial review is sought.' It does not

2. Environmental Defense Fund, Inc. v. Ruckelshaus, 439 F.2d 584, 598 (D.C.Cir. 1971) (Bazelon, C.J.).

follow that courts may never properly find that an administrative decision in a scientific area is irrational. But I do believe that in highly technical areas, where our understanding of the import of the evidence is attenuated, our readiness to review evidentiary support for decisions must be correspondingly restrained."

Judge Leventhal: "Taking [Chief Judge Bazelon's] opinion in its fair implication, as a signal to judges to abstain from any substantive review, it is my view that while giving up is the easier course, it is not legitimately open to us at present. In the case of legislative enactments, the sole responsibility of the courts is constitutional due process review. In the case of agency decision-making the courts have an additional responsibility set by Congress. Congress has been willing to delegate its legislative powers broadly—and courts have upheld such delegation—because there is court review to assure that the agency exercises the delegated power within statutory limits, and that it fleshes out objectives within those limits by an administration that is not irrational or discriminatory. . . .

"Our present system of review assumes judges will acquire whatever technical knowledge is necessary as background for decision of the legal questions. . . . The aim of the judges is not to exercise expertise or decide technical questions, but simply to gain sufficient background orientation. Our obligation is not to be jettisoned because our initial technical understanding may be meager when compared to our initial grasp of FCC or freedom of speech questions. When called upon to make de novo decisions, individual judges have had to acquire the learning pertinent to complex technical questions in such fields as economics, science, technology and psychology. Our role is not as demanding when we are engaged in review of agency decisions, where we exercise restraint, and affirm even if we would have decided otherwise so long as the agency's decisionmaking is not irrational or discriminatory.

"The substantive review of administrative action is modest, but it cannot be carried out in a vacuum of understanding. Better no judicial review at all than a charade that gives the imprimatur without the substance of judicial confirmation that the agency is not acting unreasonably. Once the presumption of regularity in agency action is challenged with a factual submission, and even to determine whether such a challenge has been made, the agency's record and reasoning has to be looked at. If there is some factual support for the challenge, there must be either evidence or judicial notice available explicating the agency's result, or a remand to supply the gap. . . ."

(4) *The Reach of Vermont Yankee.* Vermont Yankee is not the only case to have made strong arguments for procedural stasis, along the lines of the 1946 "formula upon which opposing social and political forces have come to rest."[3] Yet no one in 1946 was imagining the extent of health and safety regulation that would be called for a quarter century later, nor the intervention of the Freedom of Information Act and the transparency

---

3. Two more recent such Supreme Court opinions, Dickinson v. Zurko and Director, Office of Workers' Compensation Pro- grams v. Greenwich Collieries, are set out at pp. 264 and 269 above.

values that underlay it. Did the Court mean quite as much as it seemed to say in Vermont Yankee? Few today would attempt to use the courts to force the oral procedures of adjudication on a § 553 rulemaking. But what of other procedural issues—the extent of required notice? The meaning of an opportunity to comment? The level of detail necessary in a "concise general statement of basis and purpose?" In each of these areas, the better view (in your editors' judgment) is that the legislators of 1946 would not have thought they were providing for the procedures that the courts eventually required. Does it follow that the courts erred? Another way to put the question is to ask whether the procedures the Commission actually chose in the rulemaking that produced Vermont Yankee—considerably expanded notice, comment opportunity, and explanation—were simply voluntary measures that it imagined might improve the accuracy and public acceptability of its decision? Or, rather, were they steps that its general counsel *should* have advised might be required, even by courts taking what would ultimately prove to be the Vermont Yankee Court's view?

(5) THOMAS O. McGARITY, SUBSTANTIVE AND PROCEDURAL DISCRETION IN ADMINISTRATIVE RESOLUTION OF SCIENCE POLICY QUESTIONS: REGULATING CARCINOGENS IN EPA AND OSHA, 67 Geo.L.J. 729, 732–736, 740–45, 750 (1979): "In deciding whether to reduce human exposure to potentially carcinogenic chemicals, the agencies have been forced to resolve scientific questions that the scientific community itself has been unable to resolve. Due to these factual uncertainties, agencies and reviewing courts have recognized that they must resolve these questions partially on policy grounds. . . .

Trans–Scientific Issues

"Many highly technical questions that are cast in scientific terms cannot for various practical or moral reasons be answered by science. Alvin Weinberg, a prominent scientist, has coined the term 'trans-scientific' to describe this kind of issue. A perfect example of a trans-scientific issue is the extrapolation of carcinogenic effects at high-dose levels to low-dose levels. . . . [T]o demonstrate with ninety-five percent confidence that the carcinogenic response rate is less than one in a million, an experimenter need only feed three million animals at the human exposure rate and compare the response with three million control animals that have been raised under identical conditions but with no exposure to the chemical. As a practical matter, however, . . . this 'mega-mouse' experiment . . . would require feeding and caring for six million rodents for eighteen to twenty-four months. Scientists therefore test significantly fewer animals at much higher dosage rates. . . . The agency can never be certain whether a chemical that causes cancer at high doses will cause cancer at the lower doses to which humans are typically exposed.

"Regulators cannot, however, postpone decisions involving trans-scientific issues . . . Moreover, although most trans-scientific issues appear to be questions of fact, rather than questions of law or policy, a regulator clearly cannot reduce them to findings of fact in the traditional sense of that term. Correct answers to these questions may exist as a philosophical matter, but the 'truth' is ultimately unascertainable in either the scientific or the legal forum. Thus, a regulator who is given the responsibility for establishing a safe level for human exposure to a carcinogen has been given an impossible task if this entails establishing a threshold 'no-effect' level. The regulator cannot find as a factual matter whether a threshold 'no-effect' level exists. Nor can he establish an 'acceptable' exposure to a carcinogen, because he cannot determine the shape of the dose-response curve at low-dosage rates.[4] Therefore, a regulator must make a subjective, or policy-dominated decision. Moreover, the very nature of such trans-scientific issues deprives a regulator of any legitimate excuse for delaying a decision on these issues.

Decisionmaking Based on Insufficient Scientific Data

"Regulators frequently must decide scientific questions when data sufficient to reach a scientifically adequate decision do not exist. This situation differs from the trans-scientific problem because theoretically the scientific community could resolve the issue with whatever accuracy the regulator desires given sufficient time and resources. Thus, a regulator may be tempted to delay deciding a question until scientists develop more data, a solution that invariably receives the enthusiastic endorsement of the scientists who are performing experiments in the field. On the other hand, a regulator's delay in deciding whether to reduce human exposure to a potentially carcinogenic substance also prolongs public exposure to the chemical until a final decision is made. Therefore, as in the case of trans-scientific questions, regulators occasionally will have to decide questions on the basis of incomplete information even though these questions are, in theory, scientifically resolvable. . . .

Varying Scientific Interpretations

"Even though adequate information may be available concerning a particular scientific issue, scientists may differ in their interpretations of those data. For example, even when adequate bioassays for a chemical are available, pathologists often disagree in their diagnoses of the lesions they observe under their microscopes. . . .

"Differences in interpretation also arise over epidemiological studies. Because retrospective epidemiological data often lie on the borderline of statistical significance, how a scientist interprets particular findings often depends on subjective considerations. . . .

"Finally, disagreements over the adequacy of test methodologies can give rise to differences in interpretation of the results of a given experiment. . . .

"At stake in all of these disputes is a nebulous concept occasionally referred to as 'scientific judgment.' Scientists can objectively explain their

---

4. A dose-response curve shows the relationship between different exposure levels and the risk of cancer associated with those exposure levels. For the same reason that scientists cannot determine whether thresholds exist for certain chemicals, they cannot determine the shape of the dose-response curve for a chemical at low doses: The experiment to determine that question would require millions of animals. Several extrapolation models are currently vying for regulatory attention. All of the models fit the data well in the experimental dose range, but they diverge, often by several orders of magnitude, in the unexplored range that approximates human exposure. It is therefore impossible to choose among the models based solely on the experimental data available to the regulator.

interpretations of some kinds of data only to a point; past that point subjective considerations weigh heavily in their conclusions. These subjective considerations generally are not what lawyers label policy considerations. Although scientists are not immune from public policy preferences when they advise policymakers, scientific judgment has more to do with scientists' views, arising out of long years of study, on how things operate in the physical world with which they are familiar. As a result different scientists interpret the same data differently. The lay decisionmaker, having no scientific judgment of his own, is therefore unguided in determining which of the conflicting scientific judgments is the best. . . .

Disagreement Over Inferences

"Scientists often agree upon a single interpretation for existing data, but disagree over the proper inferences to draw from that interpretation. Scientists, like lawyers, draw inferences about unobserved events from observed data. For example, most scientists will infer that a substance will be carcinogenic in man if it is carcinogenic in laboratory animals. . . . The most compelling argument in favor of this use of animal tests is the lack of any better system for risk evaluation.[5] . . . Scientists still debate, however, whether a carcinogenic response in a single rodent species without duplication in another species is a sufficient basis to infer that a chemical poses a carcinogenic risk to man.

". . . [S]cience policy questions are by their very nature policy-dominated. . . . Further, the inherent uncertainties surrounding science policy questions dictate that the agency will never be able to reduce its solution of these questions to 'findings of fact' within the traditional legal meaning of that term. . . . Moreover, close judicial scrutiny of the administrative record, even if it results from formal procedures, will not reveal unequivocal support for the agency's decision. Scouring the record of an agency's resolution of science policy questions will only reveal unresolved conflicts between qualified scientists on highly technical questions, and strict judicial insistence upon formal 'findings of fact' will impose an impossible burden upon the agency. Finally, to the extent that a reviewing court is willing to defer to agency 'expertise' in choosing between the theories of equally respectable scientists, the court will simply force the agency to disguise policy decisions as factual determinations. Ultimately, this will result in less stringent judicial review of the legal and policy determinations upon which the agency in reality grounds its decisions."

(6) *Institutional Alternatives.* A number of institutional arrangements, both public and private, are possible for resolving the issues Professor McGarity raises. Thus, in the Benzene case about which you may have read, p. 58, Congress had established the National Institutes of Occupational Safety and Health as one of the National Institutes of Health, a group of scientific research-directing agencies in the Department of Health and

---

5. The most scientifically sound study of a chemical's carcinogenic properties would consist of feeding large quantities of the chemical to a cohort of humans over a period of 20 to 40 years and then sacrificing the humans to observe the presence or absence of neoplastic changes in particular organs. Obviously this experiment is morally unacceptable. . . .

Human Services. NIOSH is charged with advising the Department of Labor's Occupational Safety and Health Administration about particular workplace risks that warrant regulatory attention. Similarly, in Whitman v. American Trucking Associations, which appears at p. 38 ff., Congress had established a Clean Air Special Advisory Panel to assist in the assessment of air pollution risks. More generally, the Office of Information and Regulatory Affairs in the Office of Management and Budget—the White House bureaucracy chiefly responsible for the President's oversight of domestic regulation—has strongly encouraged the practice of peer review:

"We note that in 1996 the Congress, for health decisions under the Safe Drinking Water Act, adopted a basic standard of quality for the use of science in agency decisionmaking. Congress directed an agency, 'to the degree that an [a]gency action is based on science,' to use '(i) the best available, peer-reviewed science and supporting studies conducted in accordance with sound and objective scientific practices; and (ii) data collected by accepted methods or best available methods (if the reliability of the method and the nature of the decision justifies use of the data).'[6] We further note that, in 1996 the Congress adopted a basic quality standard for the dissemination of public information involving risk effects. Congress directed the agency, 'to ensure that the presentation of information [risk] effects is comprehensive, informative, and understandable.' Congress further directed the agency, 'in a document made available to the public in support of a regulation [to] specify, to the extent practicable—(i) each population addressed by any estimate [of applicable risk effects]; (ii) the expected risk or central estimate of risk for the specific populations [affected]; (iii) each appropriate upper-bound or lower-bound estimate of risk; (iv). each significant uncertainty identified in the process of the assessment of [risk] effects and the studies that would assist in resolving the uncertainty; and (v) peer-reviewed studies known to the [agency] that support, are directly relevant to, or fail to support any estimate of [risk] effects and the methodology used to reconcile inconsistencies in the scientific data.'[7] OMB recommends that each agency consider adopting or adapting these basic Congressional standards for judging the quality of scientific information about risk it uses and disseminates.

"*Peer Review.* For economically significant and major rulemakings, OMB recommends that agencies subject regulatory impact analyses [see p. 638 ff.] and supporting technical documents to independent, external peer review by qualified specialists. (Given the growing public interest in peer review at agencies, OMB recommends that (a) peer reviewers be selected primarily on the basis of necessary technical expertise, (b) peer reviewers be expected to disclose to agencies prior technical/policy positions they may have taken on the issues at hand, (c) peer reviewers be expected to disclose to agencies their sources of personal and institutional funding (private or public sector), and (d) peer reviews be conducted in an open and rigorous manner.) OIRA will be giving a measure of deference to agency analysis that has been developed in conjunction with such peer review procedures.''

6.   42 U.S.C. § 300g–1(b)(3)(A).   **7.**   42 U.S.C. § 300g–1(b)(3)(B).

"OMB Regulatory Review: Principles and Procedures," attached to John D. Graham, "Memorandum for the President's Management Council," Sept. 20, 2001, posted to http://www.whitehouse.gov/omb/inforeg/oira_review.html. The same memorandum describes OMB's responsibilities under an appropriations rider[8] to issue government-wide regulations providing policy and procedural guidance to agencies respecting the "quality, objectivity, utility and integrity of information" they disseminate—for example, in revealing studies in the course of rulemaking.

Do these legislative and executive measures adopt Judge Bazelon's side of the Bazelon–Leventhal debate? So long as they have been applied, is there less reason to adopt Judge Leventhal's attitude? As you work through the materials in this chapter, keep the Bazelon–Leventhal debate in mind. How does its resolution affect the advice agency counsel would give her client about the procedural course it should follow in rulemakings? How does its resolution affect the opportunities available to counsel for private parties seeking to influence the outcome of a rulemaking?

(i) "THE NOTICE SHALL INCLUDE ... (3) EITHER THE TERMS OR SUBSTANCE OF THE PROPOSED RULE OR A DESCRIPTION OF THE SUBJECTS AND ISSUES INVOLVED"

Natural Resources Defense Council v. United States Environmental Protection Agency

United States Court of Appeals for the Ninth Circuit, 2002.
279 F.3d 1180.

■ Before SIDNEY R. THOMAS, SUSAN P. GRABER, and RONALD M. GOULD, CIRCUIT JUDGES.

■ THOMAS, CIRCUIT JUDGE:

[Alaska's rugged terrain requires most trees cut from its forests to be bundled into log rafts at log transfer facilities ("LTFs") and then towed through marine waters to destinations such as sawmills and shipping ports. The rubbing that naturally occurs causes bark and woody debris to be rubbed or broken off and released into the water. In areas where the water lacks strong currents, this debris may remain undecayed for many years. Significant concentrations can accumulate, creating problems for marine life and degrading water quality. The United States Environmental Protection Agency ("EPA") recognized this as a pollutant discharge under the Clean Water Act of 1971 ("CWA"). Since the early 1980s, EPA has required the operators of LTFs to obtain National Pollutant Discharge Elimination System ("NPDES") permits for their activities.

Having a valid NPDES permit depends on a somewhat elaborate interaction between state and federal law. Alaska is responsible for setting water quality standards, subject to EPA's review and approval. Before the EPA can issue an NPDES permit for discharges into Alaskan waters, Alaska must certify (or waive its right to certify) that the proposed

---

8. Section 515 of the Treasury and General Government Appropriations Rider   for Fiscal Year 2001 (PL 106–554). See p. 280 above.

discharge will comply with its water quality standards. An NPDES permit may be either individual or general. General permits, the type relevant here, are issued when dischargers in the geographical area to be covered by the permit are relatively homogenous. General permits are authorized by administrative rulemaking procedures and are then available to any discharger who submits a "notice of intent" to discharge pursuant to them.

EPA identified bark and woody debris as a pollutant in the early 1980s. Although it initially grandfathered LTFs that had been in existence before October 22, 1985, in the mid–1990s it concluded that these operations did not comply with the CWA, because the terms under which they operated did not: (1) "include a zone of deposit for underwater accumulations of bark and woody debris at the LTF"; (2) "include uniform monitoring and reporting requirements"; or (3) "provide uniform application of best management practices and specific effluent limitations." EPA then issued for comment a draft general permit that would have modified nearly all LTFs in Alaska.

In part, EPA's proposal incorporated a feature of Alaskan law that, at that time, allowed LTFs a "zone of deposit" of up to one acre for bark and woody debris. This zone had to include all accumulations of 100 percent cover that exceeded four inches' depth at any point; only patchy distribution of bark was permitted beyond the one-acre zone. As part of its process, EPA advised the interested public that "persons wishing to comment on State Certification of the proposed general NPDES permit should submit written comments within this public notice period to the Alaska Department of Environmental Conservation" (ADEC), the state agency responsible for the necessary certification.

ADEC made public two drafts that continued the one-acre/four inch limit on continuous bark coverage, but added provisions for enforcement that suggested that in practice it would probably permit somewhat larger areas of deposit. It proposed to use 1.5 acres of continuous coverage to a depth of four inches at any point as the trigger for requiring LTFs to submit remediation plans showing "feasible" means of reducing their bark and woody debris deposits. Like the driver traveling 60 mph in a 55 mph speed zone, timber companies with continuous coverage LTF areas of 1.4 acres could be reasonably sure they would not be proceeded against. Subsequently, ADEC shared with EPA but did *not* circulate for public comment a final draft, in which it placed *no* specific size limit on zones of deposit but adopted more stringent enforcement criteria. This draft permitted each LTF's zone to be the entire area of water covered by its operations, but set as the trigger for requiring the submission of "feasible" remediation plans an accumulation of just an acre of continuous coverage four inches deep at any point. When EPA expressed concern that this change made the requirements less stringent than they previously had been, ADEC pointed out that it had thus reduced the trigger area for enforcement from one and a half acres to the one acre that had previously been the nominal limit on zones of deposit. EPA then accepted ADEC's certification for its general LTF permit. It then issued two general permits: one for pre–1985 LTFs, AK–G70–0000, and one for post–1985 LTFs, AK–

G70–1000. Both permits incorporated ADEC's project-area zone of deposit definition.]

III

A

Under the Administrative Procedures Act, the EPA must provide the public with notice and an opportunity to comment before it issues NPDES permits. 5 U.S.C. § 553(b)–(c); see also NRDC v. EPA, 863 F.2d 1420, 1428–29 (9th Cir.1988) (applying notice and comment requirement to general NPDES permit). Like other agencies, the EPA "must provide notice sufficient to fairly apprise interested persons of the subjects and issues before the Agency."

Of course, the final permit issued by the agency need not be identical to the draft permit. That would be antithetical to the whole concept of notice and comment. Indeed, it is "the expectation that the final rules will be somewhat different and improved from the rules originally proposed by the agency." Trans–Pac. Freight Conference v. Fed. Mar. Comm'n, 650 F.2d 1235, 1249 (D.C.Cir.1980). Thus, "the law does not require that every alteration in a proposed rule be reissued for notice and comment." First Am. Discount Corp. v. Commodity Futures Trading Comm'n, 222 F.3d 1008, 1015 (D.C.Cir.2000).

However, "a final rule which departs from a proposed rule must be a logical outgrowth of the proposed rule. . . . The essential inquiry focuses on whether interested parties reasonably could have anticipated the final rulemaking from the draft permit." NRDC v. EPA, 863 F.2d 1420, 1429 (9th Cir.1988). In determining this, one of the salient questions is "whether a new round of notice and comment would provide the first opportunity for interested parties to offer comments that could persuade the agency to modify its rule." Am. Water Works Ass'n v. EPA, 40 F.3d 1266, 1274 (D.C.Cir.1994)

B

In this instance, we conclude that the EPA's notice and comment procedure was inadequate because it did not afford interested parties the opportunity to comment on whether Alaska's proposed change in the zone of deposit definition conformed to the substantive requirements of Alaska law and, if not, whether the change required the issuance of a conditional permit or the denial of the permit altogether. . . .

In its draft permit, upon which public comment was solicited, the EPA noted:

> If issued, this general NPDES permit would authorize qualifying LTFs to discharge bark and woody debris into both near-shore and offshore marine waters in Alaska, except in areas excluded from coverage. The proposed general permit would not authorize new discharges into waters identified as critical or protected resources, waters which do not meet the ATTF siting guidelines, and waters already exceeding State Water Quality Standards for parameters relating to bark and woody debris. ADEC proposes to grant a one-acre zone of deposit for those LTFs authorized under this general permit.

... [While EPA was aware of Alaska's eventual decision to depart from this proposal, and wrote Alaska questioning it,] the public was never notified that Alaska was proposing to redefine the allowable zone of deposit, nor was the public afforded the opportunity to comment on the proposed change, either at the state or federal level.

... Given that the draft permit specifically referenced Alaska's proposed "one-acre zone of deposit" and conformance with the ATTF guidelines, interested parties could not have reasonably anticipated that the final permit would sanction the use of project-area zones of deposit that could exceed one acre. The fact that interested parties did not anticipate the paradigm shift from the draft to the final permit is underscored by the contents of the instant petition for review, which raises for the first time numerous issues about the proposed change in the conception of zones of deposit. These are precisely the type of comments that should have been directed in the first instance to the EPA, but which understandably were not because of the inadequate notice. Because the EPA's change of position from the draft permit was not "foreshadowed in proposals and comments advanced during the rulemaking," S. Terminal Corp. v. EPA, 504 F.2d 646, 658 (1st Cir.1974), the "decision clearly caught petitioners ... by surprise," Consumer Energy Council of Am. v. FERC, 673 F.2d 425, 446–47 n. 76 (D.C.Cir.1982)....

The EPA argues that the draft permit's references to the role of state law and the state certification process and the fact that the proposed zones of deposit might allow "patchy or discontinuous" bark coverage outside the one-acre zone of continuous coverage were sufficient to put interested parties on notice. However, nuance and subtlety are not virtues in agency notice practice. If the EPA were contemplating approving entirely new constructs for allowable zones of deposit and departing from the ATTF guidelines, it should have said so explicitly. More importantly, there is no question that the change was substantive. The EPA acknowledged as much in its letter to the State, noting that "the Department has changed its approach ... from the approach contained in the ATTF Guidelines, which has been used for authorizing ZODs since the guidelines were developed." Given the draft permit's stated "heavy reliance" on the ATTF Guidelines, there is no doubt that there was a fundamental policy shift, rather than a natural drafting evolution, between the draft permit and the final permit. ...

C

The fact that the certification process is vested with the state agency does not alter this conclusion. ...

Petition granted; remanded for further proceedings consistent with this opinion.

NOTES

(1) Focus on the general and disjunctive character of the text of § 553(b)(3) quoted from § 553 at the head of this subsection. Do you agree with the editors' judgment that the 1946 Congress would have found the

court's interpretation of the notice requirement surprising? Even if so, is the court then in error? Why or why not?

(2) Can you find in the text of § 553(b)(3) a basis for judgment by the Nuclear Regulatory Commission that its notice for the fuel cycle rulemaking should refer to and make available the staff documents and data on which the proposal was based? AIR TRANSPORT ASSOCIATION OF AMERICA V. FAA, 169 F.3d 1 (D.C.Cir.1999), faulted the Port Authority of New York for its failure to disclose certain data in an application that was then made the notice in a notice-and-comment proceeding. The Authority later sought to rely on this data without having provided an opportunity to comment. "[A]n agency engaged in informal rulemaking is not obliged to consider only record evidence. But . . . we have cautioned that the most critical factual material that is used to support the agency's position on review must have been made public *in the proceeding* and exposed to refutation. Still, the focus . . . is primarily on whether the final rule changes critically from the proposed rule rather than on whether the agency relies on supporting material not published for comment. The question is typically whether the agency's final rule so departs from its proposed rule as to constitute more surprise than notice. . . . [The court found that it did.]

"[T]he FAA argues that any procedural error stemming from its failure to provide adequate notice and an opportunity to comment was harmless. . . . It is true that to show prejudice, a 'petitioner objecting to the . . . late submission of documents must indicate with "reasonable specificity" what portions of the documents it objects to and how it might have responded if given the opportunity,' Air Transport Association v. CAB, 732 F.2d 219, 224 n. 11 (D.C.Cir.1984). But here petitioner had no knowledge of the new information until the final decision was made and had no subsequent opportunity to provide comments. Petitioner's reply brief does include the nature of its objection to the Port Authority's supplemental information, and it seems rather specific to us."

(3) Notices of Proposed Rulemaking ("NPRMs"—or sometimes "NOPRs" or "NPRs") appear in the Federal Register, which the federal government publishes every business day in paper and, today, online. Through their own websites and by mail and other means, agencies may also directly notify organizations and individuals of proposed rulemakings thought likely to be of interest to them. The Federal Register is scanned routinely by the legal staffs of corporations and unions, by trade associations and advocacy groups, and by independent lawyers with specialized practices or on behalf of particular clients.

Notice that § 553 says nothing whatever about the processes by which NPRMs are developed. As rulemaking has become more portentous, greater attention has been paid to the pre-NPRM period. Section 3 of this Chapter, below, explores this period, and the contemporary shape of rulemaking notice, in greater detail. Here, it may be useful to say that such notices occur very frequently. In 1999 and 2000, the last two years of the Clinton administration, 6140 documents appeared in the "Proposed Rules" section of the Federal Register. (A single document can, of course, make a proposal that appears as more than one numbered rule in the Code of Federal Regulations, if and when it is finally adopted.) 2558 NPRMs appeared in

2001, the first year of the Bush administration (perhaps held down somewhat by the frictions of transition).

(ii) "AFTER NOTICE REQUIRED BY THIS SECTION, THE AGENCY SHALL GIVE INTERESTED PERSONS AN OPPORTUNITY TO PARTICIPATE IN THE RULE MAKING THROUGH SUBMISSION OF WRITTEN DATA, VIEWS, OR ARGUMENTS WITH OR WITHOUT OPPORTUNITY FOR ORAL PRESENTATION"

United States v. Nova Scotia Food Products Corp.

United States Court of Appeals for the Second Circuit, 1977.
568 F.2d 240.

■ Before WATERMAN and GURFEIN, CIRCUIT JUDGES, and BLUMENFELD, DISTRICT JUDGE.

[In October 1969, after several incidents of the serious food poisoning botulism, the Food and Drug Administration issued a notice of proposed rulemaking concerning the processing of fish commonly sold as smoked and/or salted fish. The proposed rule reached all species of fish commercially handled this way—chub, eel, herring, salmon, sturgeon, trout, whitefish, etc. The FDA issued the rule in 1970, modifying its initial proposal in response to some comments it had received. However, the agency declined to make special provisions for particular species of fish until processors of a given species proposed a substitute they could prove adequate to protect the public from botulism. Whitefish processors apparently attempted no such demonstration. Six years later, the FDA successfully brought a district court action to enforce its rule against a whitefish processor, Nova Scotia Food Products Corp., that had not changed its processing methods to comply with the rule.]

■ GURFEIN, CIRCUIT JUDGE:

This appeal involving a regulation of the Food and Drug Administration is not here upon a direct review of agency action. It is an appeal from a judgment of the District Court for the Eastern District of New York (Hon. John J. Dooling, Judge) enjoining the appellants, after a hearing, from processing hot smoked whitefish except in accordance with time-temperature-salinity (T–T–S) regulations contained in 21 C.F.R. Part 122 (1977). The thorough analytical opinion of the District Court is reported at 417 F.Supp. 1364 (1976).

The injunction was sought and granted on the ground that smoked whitefish which has been processed in violation of the T–T–S regulation is "adulterated." Food, Drug and Cosmetics Act ("the Act"), 21 U.S.C. §§ 332(a), 331(k).

Appellant Nova Scotia receives frozen or iced whitefish in interstate commerce which it processes by brining, smoking and cooking. The fish are then sold as smoked whitefish.

The regulations cited above require that hot-process smoked fish be heated by a controlled heat process that provides a monitoring system positioned in as many strategic locations in the oven as necessary to assure a continuous temperature through each fish of not less than 180° F. for a minimum of 30 minutes for fish which have been brined to contain 3.5% Water phase salt or at 150° F. for a minimum of 30 minutes if the salinity was at 5% Water phase. Since each fish must meet these requirements, it is necessary to heat an entire batch of fish to even higher temperatures so that the lowest temperature for any fish will meet the minimum requirements.

Government inspection of appellants' plant established without question that the minimum T–T–S requirements were not being met. There is no substantial claim that the plant was processing whitefish under "insanitary conditions" in any other material respect. Appellants, on their part, do not defend on the ground that they were in compliance, but rather that the requirements could not be met if a marketable whitefish was to be produced. They defend upon the grounds that the regulation is invalid (1) because it is beyond the authority delegated by the statute; (2) because the FDA improperly relied upon undisclosed evidence in promulgating the regulation and because it is not supported by the administrative record; and (3) because there was no adequate statement setting forth the basis of the regulation. We reject the contention that the regulation is beyond the authority delegated by the statute, but we find serious inadequacies in the procedure followed in the promulgation of the regulation and hold it to be invalid as applied to the appellants herein.

The hazard which the FDA sought to minimize was the outgrowth and toxin formation of Clostridium botulinum Type E spores of the bacteria which sometimes inhabit fish. There had been an occurrence of several cases of botulism traced to consumption of fish from inland waters in 1960 and 1963 which stimulated considerable bacteriological research. These bacteria can be present in the soil and water of various regions. They can invade fish in their natural habitat and can be further disseminated in the course of evisceration and preparation of the fish for cooking. A failure to destroy such spores through an adequate brining, thermal, and refrigeration process was found to be dangerous to public health.

The Commissioner of Food and Drugs ("Commissioner"), employing informal "notice-and-comment" procedures under 21 U.S.C. § 371(a), issued a proposal for the control of C. botulinum bacteria Type E in fish. 34 F.R. 17,176 (Oct. 23, 1969). For his statutory authority to promulgate the regulations, the Commissioner specifically relied only upon § 342(a)(4) of the Act which provides:

"A food shall be deemed to be adulterated—

"(4) if it has been prepared, packed, or held under insanitary conditions whereby it may have become contaminated with filth, or whereby it may have been rendered injurious to health."

Similar guidelines for smoking fish had been suggested by the FDA several years earlier, and were generally made known to people in the industry. At that stage, however, they were merely guidelines without substantive effect as law. Responding to the Commissioner's invitation in the notice of proposed rulemaking, members of the industry, including appellants and the intervenor-appellant, submitted comments on the proposed regulation.

The Commissioner thereafter issued the final regulations in which he adopted certain suggestions made in the comments, including a suggestion by the National Fisheries Institute, Inc. ("the Institute"), the intervenor herein. 35 F.R. 17,401 (Nov. 13, 1970). The original proposal provided that the fish would have to be cooked to a temperature of 180° F. for at least 30 minutes, if the fish have been brined to contain 3.5% Water phase salt, with no alternative. In the final regulation, an alternative suggested by the intervenor "that the parameter of 150° F. for 30 minutes and 5% Salt in the water phase be established as an alternate procedure to that stated in the proposed regulation for an interim period until specific parameters can be established" was accepted, but as a permanent part of the regulation rather than for an interim period.

The intervenor suggested that "specific parameters" be established. This referred to particular processing parameters for different species of fish on a "species by species" basis. Such "species by species" determination was proposed not only by the intervenor but also by the Bureau of Commercial Fisheries of the Department of the Interior. That Bureau objected to the general application of the T–T–S requirement proposed by the FDA on the ground that application of the regulation to all species of fish being smoked was not commercially feasible, and that the regulation should therefore specify time-temperature-salinity requirements, as developed by research and study, on a species-by-species basis. The Bureau suggested that "wholesomeness considerations could be more practically and adequately realized by reducing processing temperature and using suitable concentrations of nitrite and salt." The Commissioner took cognizance of the suggestion, but decided, nevertheless, to impose the T–T–S requirement on all species of fish (except chub, which were regulated by 21 C.F.R. 172.177 (1977) (dealing with food additives)).

He did acknowledge, however, in his "basis and purpose" statement required by the Administrative Procedure Act ("APA"), 5 U.S.C. § 553(c), that "adequate times, temperatures and salt concentrations have not been demonstrated for each individual species of fish presently smoked." 35 F.R. 17,401 (Nov. 13, 1970). The Commissioner concluded, nevertheless, that "the processing requirements of the proposed regulations are the safest now known to prevent the outgrowth and toxin formation of C. botulinum Type E." He determined that "the conditions of current good manufacturing practice for this industry should be established without further delay." Id.

The Commissioner did not answer the suggestion by the Bureau of Fisheries that nitrite and salt as additives could safely lower the high temperature otherwise required, a solution which the FDA had accepted in the case of chub. Nor did the Commissioner respond to the claim of Nova Scotia through its trade association, the Association of Smoked Fish Processors, Inc., Technical Center that "(t)he proposed process requirements suggested by the FDA for hot processed smoked fish are neither commercially feasible nor based on sound scientific evidence obtained with the variety of smoked fish products to be included under this regulation." (Exhibit D, Tab A).

Nova Scotia, in its own comment, wrote to the Commissioner that "the heating of certain types of fish to high temperatures will completely destroy the product." It suggested, as an alternative, that "specific processing procedures could be established for each species after adequate work and experimention [sic] has been done—but not before." (Id.). We have noted above that the response given by the Commissioner was in general terms. He did not specifically aver that the T–T–S requirements as applied to whitefish were, in fact, commercially feasible.

When, after several inspections and warnings, Nova Scotia failed to comply with the regulation, an action by the United States Attorney for injunctive relief was filed on April 7, 1976, six years later, and resulted in the judgment here on appeal. The District Court denied a stay pending appeal, and no application for a stay was made to this court.

I

The argument that the regulation is not supported by statutory authority cannot be dismissed out of hand. ... [After 17 paragraphs of discussion, the court did dismiss it.]

II

Appellants contend that there is an inadequate administrative record upon which to predicate judicial review, and that the failure to disclose to interested persons the factual material upon which the agency was relying vitiates the element of fairness which is essential to any kind of administrative action. Moreover, they argue that the "concise general statement of ... basis and purpose" by the Commissioner was inadequate. 5 U.S.C. § 553.

The question of what is an adequate "record" in informal rulemaking has engaged the attention of commentators for several years. The extent of the administrative record required for judicial review of informal rulemaking is largely a function of the scope of judicial review. Even when the standard of review is whether the promulgation of the rule was "arbitrary, capricious, an abuse of discretion, or otherwise not in accordance with law," as specified in 5 U.S.C. § 706(2)(A), judicial review must nevertheless, be based on the "whole record" (id.). Adequate review of a determination requires an adequate record, if the review is to be meaningful. What will constitute an adequate record for meaningful review may vary with the nature of the administrative action to be reviewed. Review must be based on the whole record even when the judgment is one of policy, except that findings of fact such as would be required in an adjudicatory proceeding or in a formal "on the record" hearing for rulemaking need not be made. Citizens to Preserve Overton Park v. Volpe, 401 U.S. 402, 416–18 (1971). Though the action was informal, without an evidentiary record, the review must be "thorough, probing, [and] in depth." Id., 401 U.S. at 415.

This raises several questions regarding the informal rulemaking procedure followed here: (1) What record does a reviewing court look to? (2) How much of what the agency relied on should have been disclosed to interested persons? (3) To what extent must the agency respond to criticism that is material?

A

With respect to the content of the administrative "record," the Supreme Court has told us that in informal rulemaking, "the focal point for judicial review should be the administrative record already in existence, not some new record made initially in the reviewing court." See Camp v. Pitts, 411 U.S. 138, 142 (1973).

No contemporaneous record was made or certified.[1] When, during the enforcement action, the basis for the regulation was sought through pretrial discovery, the record was created by searching the files of the FDA and the memories of those who participated in the process of rulemaking. This resulted in what became Exhibit D at the trial of the injunction action. Exhibit D consists of (1) Tab A containing the comments received from outside parties during the administrative "notice-and-comment" proceeding and (2) Tabs B through L consisting of scientific data and the like upon which the Commissioner now says he relied but which were not made known to the interested parties.

Appellants object to the exclusion of evidence in the District Court "aimed directly at showing that the scientific evidence relied upon by the FDA was inaccurate and not based upon a realistic appraisal of the true facts. Appellants attempted to introduce scientific evidence to demonstrate that in fixing the processing parameters FDA relied upon tests in which ground fish were injected with many millions of botulism (sic) spores and then tested for outgrowth at various processing levels whereas the spore levels in nature are far less and outgrowth would have been prevented by far less stringent processing parameters." (Br. p. 33). The District Court properly excluded the evidence.

In an enforcement action, we must rely exclusively on the record made before the agency to determine the validity of the regulation. The exception to the exclusivity of that record is that "there may be independent judicial fact-finding when issues that were not before the agency are raised in a proceeding to *enforce* non-adjudicatory agency action." Overton Park, supra, 401 U.S. at 415 (1971). (Emphasis added.)

Though this is an enforcement proceeding and the question is close, we think that the "issues" were fairly before the agency and hence that de novo evidence was properly excluded by Judge Dooling. Our concern is, rather, with the manner in which the agency treated the issues tendered.

---

1. A practice developed in the early years of the APA of not making a formal contemporaneous record, but rather, when challenged, to put together a historical record of what had been available for agency consideration at the time the regulation was promulgated.... Professor Davis in a balanced review, has stated: "When the facts are of central importance and might be challenged, parties adversely affected by them should have a chance to respond to them. Clearly, whatever factual information the agency has considered should be a part of the record for judicial review." K. Davis, Administrative Law of the Seventies, § 29.01–6, pp. 672–73 (1976).

B

The key issues were (1) whether, in the light of the rather scant history of botulism in whitefish, that species should have been considered separately rather than included in a general regulation which failed to distinguish species from species; (2) whether the application of the proposed T–T–S requirements to smoked whitefish made the whitefish commercially unsaleable; and (3) whether the agency recognized that prospect, but nevertheless decided that the public health needs should prevail even if that meant commercial death for the whitefish industry. The procedural issues were whether, in the light of these key questions, the agency procedure was inadequate because (i) it failed to disclose to interested parties the scientific data and the methodology upon which it relied; and (ii) because it failed utterly to address itself to the pertinent question of commercial feasibility.

1.

The History of Botulism in Whitefish

The history of botulism occurrence in whitefish, as established in the trial record, which we must assume was available to the FDA in 1970, is as follows. Between 1899 and 1964 there were only eight cases of botulism reported as attributable to hot-smoked whitefish. In all eight instances, vacuum-packed whitefish was involved. All of the eight cases occurred in 1960 and 1963. The industry has abandoned vacuum-packing, and there has not been a single case of botulism associated with commercially prepared whitefish since 1963, though 2,750,000 pounds of whitefish are processed annually. Thus, in the seven-year period from 1964 through 1970, 17.25 million pounds of whitefish have been commercially processed in the United States without a single reported case of botulism. The evidence also disclosed that defendant Nova Scotia has been in business some 56 years, and that there has never been a case of botulism illness from the whitefish processed by it.

2.

The Scientific Data

Interested parties were not informed of the scientific data, or at least of a selection of such data deemed important by the agency, so that comments could be addressed to the data. Appellants argue that unless the scientific data relied upon by the agency are spread upon the public records, criticism of the methodology used or the meaning to be inferred from the data is rendered impossible.

We agree with appellants in this case, for although we recognize that an agency may resort to its own expertise outside the record in an informal rulemaking procedure, we do not believe that when the pertinent research material is readily available and the agency has no special expertise on the precise parameters involved, there is any reason to conceal the scientific data relied upon from the interested parties. As Judge Leventhal said in Portland Cement Ass'n v. Ruckelshaus, 486 F.2d 375, 393 (1973): "It is not consonant with the purpose of a rulemaking proceeding to promulgate rules

[handwritten margin note: Failure to Disclose Data. No meaningful Participation]

on the basis of inadequate data, or on data that [in] critical degree, *is known only to the agency.*" (Emphasis added.) This is not a case where the agency methodology was based on material supplied by the interested parties themselves. International Harvester Co. v. Ruckelshaus, 478 F.2d 615, 632 (1973). Here all the scientific research was collected by the agency, and none of it was disclosed to interested parties as the material upon which the proposed rule would be fashioned.[2] Nor was an articulate effort made to connect the scientific requirements to available technology that would make commercial survival possible, though the burden of proof was on the agency. This required it to "bear a burden of adducing a reasoned presentation supporting the reliability of its methodology." International Harvester, supra, 478 F.2d at 643 (1973).

Though a reviewing court will not match submission against counter-submission to decide whether the agency was correct in its conclusion on scientific matters (unless that conclusion is arbitrary), it will consider whether the agency has taken account of all "relevant factors and whether there has been a clear error of judgment." Overton Park, supra, 401 U.S. at 415–16. In this circuit we have said that "it is 'arbitrary or capricious' for an agency not to take into account all relevant factors in making its determination." Hanly v. Mitchell, 460 F.2d 640, 648 (2d Cir.), cert. denied, 409 U.S. 990 (1972).

If the failure to notify interested persons of the scientific research upon which the agency was relying actually prevented the presentation of relevant comment, the agency may be held not to have considered all "the relevant factors." We can think of no sound reasons for secrecy or reluctance to expose to public view (with an exception for trade secrets or national security) the ingredients of the deliberative process. Indeed, the FDA's own regulations now specifically require that every notice of proposed rulemaking contain "references to all data and information on which the Commissioner relies for the proposal (copies or a full list of which shall be a part of the administrative file on the matter ...)." 21 C.F.R. § 10.40(b)(1)(1977). And this is, undoubtedly, the trend.

We think that the scientific data should have been disclosed to focus on the proper interpretation of "insanitary conditions." When the basis for a proposed rule is a scientific decision, the scientific material which is believed to support the rule should be exposed to the view of interested parties for their comment. One cannot ask for comment on a scientific paper without allowing the participants to read the paper. Scientific research is sometimes rejected for diverse inadequacies of methodology; and statistical results are sometimes rebutted because of a lack of adequate gathering technique or of supportable extrapolation. Such is the stuff of scientific debate. To suppress meaningful comment by failure to disclose the basic data relied upon is akin to rejecting comment altogether. For unless there is common ground, the comments are unlikely to be of a quality that might impress a careful agency. The inadequacy of comment in

---

2. We recognize the problem posed by Judge Leventhal in International Harvester, supra, that a proceeding might never end if such submission required a reply ad infini- tum, ibid. Here the exposure of the scientific research relied on simply would have required a single round of comment addressed thereto.

turn leads in the direction of arbitrary decision-making. We do not speak of findings of fact, for such are not technically required in the informal rulemaking procedures. We speak rather of what the agency should make known so as to elicit comments that probe the fundamentals. Informal rulemaking does not lend itself to a rigid pattern. Especially, in the circumstance of our broad reading of statutory authority in support of the agency, we conclude that the failure to disclose to interested persons the scientific data upon which the FDA relied was procedurally erroneous. Moreover, the burden was upon the agency to articulate rationally why the rule should apply to a large and diverse class, with the same T–T–S parameters made applicable to all species.

C

Appellants additionally attack the "concise general statement" required by APA, 5 U.S.C. § 553, as inadequate. We think that, in the circumstances, it was less than adequate. It is not in keeping with the rational process to leave vital questions, raised by comments which are of cogent materiality, completely unanswered. The agencies certainly have a good deal of discretion in expressing the basis of a rule, but the agencies do not have quite the prerogative of obscurantism reserved to legislatures. . . .

The test of adequacy of the "concise general statement" was expressed by Judge McGowan in the following terms: "We do not expect the agency to discuss every item of fact or opinion included in the submissions made to it in informal rulemaking. We do expect that, if the judicial review which Congress has thought it important to provide is to be meaningful, the 'concise general statement of . . . basis and purpose' mandated by Section 4 will enable us to see what major issues of policy were ventilated by the informal proceedings and why the agency reacted to them as it did." Automotive Parts & Accessories Ass'n v. Boyd, 407 F.2d 330, 338 (1968). . . .

The Secretary was squarely faced with the question whether it was necessary to formulate a rule with specific parameters that applied to all species of fish, and particularly whether lower temperatures with the addition of nitrite and salt would not be sufficient. Though this alternative was suggested by an agency of the federal government, its suggestion, though acknowledged, was never answered.

Moreover, the comment that to apply the proposed T–T–S requirements to whitefish would destroy the commercial product was neither discussed nor answered. We think that to sanction silence in the face of such vital questions would be to make the statutory requirement of a "concise general statement" less than an adequate safeguard against arbitrary decision-making. . . .

One may recognize that even commercial infeasibility cannot stand in the way of an overwhelming public interest. Yet the administrative process should disclose, at least, whether the proposed regulation is considered to be commercially feasible, or whether other considerations prevail even if commercial infeasibility is acknowledged. This kind of forthright disclosure and basic statement was lacking in the formulation of the T–T–S standard made applicable to whitefish. It is easy enough for an administrator to ban everything. In the regulation of food processing, the worldwide need for food also must be taken into account in formulating measures taken for the protection of health. In the light of the history of smoked whitefish to which we have referred, we find no articulate balancing here sufficient to make the procedure followed less than arbitrary.

After seven years of relative inaction, the FDA has apparently not reviewed the T–T–S regulations in the light of present scientific knowledge and experience. In the absence of a new statutory directive by Congress regarding control of micro-organisms, which we hope will be worthy of its consideration, we think that the T–T–S standards should be reviewed again by the FDA.

We cannot, on this appeal, remand to the agency to allow further comments by interested parties, addressed to the scientific data now disclosed at the trial below. We hold in this enforcement proceeding, therefore, that the regulation, as it affects non-vacuum-packed hot-smoked whitefish, was promulgated in an arbitrary manner and is invalid.

When the District Court held the regulation to be valid, it properly exercised its discretion to grant the injunction. In view of our conclusion to the contrary, we must reverse the grant of the injunction and direct that the complaint be dismissed.

NOTES

(1) *The Timing of Judicial Review of Rulemaking.* Judge Gurfein's opinion begins by pointing out: "This appeal involving a regulation of the Food and Drug Administration is not here upon a direct review of agency action." As the need to make this statement suggests, the more common form of judicial review of rulemaking is a petition to review a new regulation, rather than an enforcement proceeding in which the invalidity of regulation is asserted as a defense. (This has been so since Abbott Laboratories v. Gardner, 387 U.S. 136 (1967), briefly described at p. 272 above, and set out at p. 1182 below.)

If you, as an attorney representing a regulated party, have the option of filing a petition for direct review of a regulation, or of waiting and defending against an enforcement action, what factors should you consider in making your choice?

(2) *Statutes and Regulations.* Imagine that Congress had debated and then enacted precisely the same text as the FDA adopted as its regulation—that is, statutorily preferring the administrative convenience of a provision reaching *all* forms of smoked and/or salted fish to species-by-species requirements. What would Nova Scotia's procedural rights have been in that process? How could Nova Scotia have challenged such a statute, and what would you expect to be the outcome of its challenge? To the extent you find differences, how can they be justified?

As Judge Gurfein's reasoning demonstrates, the question, how the factual basis of a regulation is to be established, is related to the question, what standards courts should use in reviewing the agency decision. This is the subject of Chapter VIII. For the reader who cannot wait, the chapter's case of greatest relevance here is Citizens to Preserve Overton Park, Inc. v. Volpe, summarized briefly at p. 272 above and set out at p. 989 below.

For the present, consider the matter without the complexities of judicial review. How should the facts that undergird agency rules be established? What are the implications of its being an *agency* that is making the decision? What are the implications of its being a *regulation* that is being adopted?

(3) *Participation in rulemaking.* Section 553(c) provides that the opportunity to participate in informal rulemaking shall be given to "interested persons." Section 551(2) defines "person" inclusively, barring only an agency itself. § 551(3) then defines "party" as a "person or agency" admitted or entitled to be admitted as a "party" "in an agency proceeding"; and § 551(12) defines "agency proceeding" to include rulemaking. Doesn't it seem clear that "party" is a subset of interested "persons"? Arguably, party status is relevant for *formal* rulemaking, where an oral hearing usually occurs and the procedures of §§ 556 and 557 generally apply. The reference to "interested persons" in § 553, however, suggests that any person or group who files timely comments is entitled to participate in an informal rulemaking. No agency has litigated the issue, and it is hard to imagine the situation in which it would be worth the agency's time to try to exclude a comment, rather than to accept it for whatever it is worth.

Whether filing of a comment, in and of itself, generates "standing" to seek judicial review of the final result is a different matter. See Chapter IX, Section 2 below. It is clear, however, that if a commenter does seek review, Federal Rule of Appellate Procedure 15(c)[3] does not require it to serve a copy of its petition for review on all other commenters, as party status would. "Because the rulemaking that is the subject of this petition for review was informal, the commenters were not 'parties ... admitted to participate in the proceedings' as envisioned under the rule. In informal rulemaking, any interested group or person may submit written comments to the agency or comment orally if the agency decides to hold a hearing. As such, no one is 'admitted to participate in the proceedings,' and no one becomes a party in a formal administrative adjudication." Sierra Club v. EPA, 118 F.3d 1324, 1326 (9th Cir.1997).

The level and extent of actual participation in the notice and comment process varies widely, as one would expect. Two turn-of-the-century rulemakings conducted on the Internet and involving small producer and consumer issues—organic farming and checking account privacy—drew hundreds of thousands of comments. Many were brief form submissions, but many others were extensive, unique comments. The 34 commenters in the rulemaking underlying the Nova Scotia Food Products case were probably a more typical number. Do we know enough to say whether, in the context of a rulemaking directed at all fish processing, the particular problems of whitefish processing bulked large? Whether those who sought

---

3. "At or before the time of filing a petition for review [of agency action], the petitioner shall serve a copy thereof on all parties who shall have been admitted to participate in the proceedings before the agency other than respondents [i.e., the agency itself] to be served by the clerk."

species-specific treatment filed comments attempting to demonstrate the adequacy of alternative measures for the species that concerned them? Might this be an element of the "Monday morning quarterbacking" problem that concerned the Court in Vermont Yankee?

(4) *"It is not consonant with the purpose of a rulemaking proceeding to promulgate rules on the basis of inadequate data, or on data that [in] critical degree, is known only to the agency."* This phrase is quoted by Judge Gurfein from Judge Harold Leventhal's influential opinion in Portland Cement Ass'n v. Ruckelshaus, 486 F.2d 375, 393 (D.C.Cir.1973).[4] Both Judge Leventhal's phrase and Judge Gurfein's approving quotation predate Vermont Yankee. Do they survive it? How would you argue that issue? One possibility might be to consider the implications of the Freedom of Information Act, p. 492, and the special difficulties associated with finding general fact, p. 510 ff. above.

Here are two post-Vermont Yankee efforts from the courts of appeals, addressing further issues:

(a) RYBACHEK v. EPA, 904 F.2d 1276, 1281, 1286 (9th Cir.1990), dealt with multiple challenges to EPA regulations issued under the Clean Water Act. The regulations addressed discharges into streams from placer mining operations; they had, in the judge's words, "particular impact on the gold-rich streambeds of Alaska." The first named challenger was "Rosalie A. Rybachek, North Pole, Alaska, pro se." "The Rybacheks allege that the EPA's addition of over 6,000 pages to the administrative record, after the public review-and-comment period had ended, violated their right to comment on the record.

"We disagree. The EPA has not violated the Rybacheks' right to meaningful public participation. The additional material was the EPA's response to comments made during a public-comment period. Nothing prohibits the Agency from adding supporting documentation for a final rule in response to public comments. In fact, adherence to the Rybacheks' view might result in the EPA's never being able to issue a final rule capable of standing up to review: every time the Agency responded to public comments, such as those in this rulemaking, it would trigger a new comment period. Thus, either the comment period would continue in a never-ending circle, or, if the EPA chose not to respond to the last set of public comments, any final rule could be struck down for lack of support in the record. The Rybacheks' unviolated right was to comment on the proposed regulations, not to comment in a never-ending way on the EPA's responses to their comments."

(b) OBER v. EPA, 84 F.3d 304, 314 (9th Cir.1996), concerned control of particulate matter in Phoenix, Arizona. The EPA proposed approval of the state's plan for implementing the Clean Air Act and set August 29 as the deadline for public comment. In December, at EPA's request, the state submitted an additional 300 pages of information responding to various comments which had suggested that additional control measures could be, and legally had to be, taken. The EPA accepted the state's justifications for not taking those measures, and approved the proposed plan. Held: Accep-

---

4. See the brief account of the Bazelon–Leventhal debate at pp. 513–14 above.

tance of this submission without offering others a chance to comment on it violated the APA.

But what about Rybachek's fear of a "never-ending circle"? Judge Trott wrote that "In Rybachek, the added materials were the EPA's own responses to comments received during the public comment period. Here, in contrast, the additional documentation was submitted by the State in response to the EPA's request for further information related to the rejection of control measures. Thus, the additional materials in Rybachek involved the EPA's internal assessment of comments from the public; whereas, here, the new information was solicited by the EPA from an interested party.

"Furthermore, in Rybachek, the EPA's responses related to the economic impact of the regulations on one group of miners. The additional information was not relied on or critical to the EPA's decision. Instead, the EPA decided not to alter the regulation based on the additional information it developed in response to the comments. Here, on the other hand, the added material related to the Implementation Plan's compliance with a critical statutory provision. . . ."

Do these distinctions make sense? Do they have a basis in § 553? If the EPA had made its request as part of its initial NPRM, and the state had submitted its documentation as part of its comment package on the final day of comments, what procedural rights would/should Ober have had to respond to it?

(c) Is there really *no* legitimate reason for an agency to conceal its data? Consider the following assessment of the dynamics generated by statutes requiring agencies to circulate Environmental Impact Statements before they act. Serge Taylor, Making Bureaucracies Think 270 (1984):

"In considering the role of science-like norms in politics we should look at what science can and cannot do, and the comparative advantage of science in helping us figure out what to do when knowledge is incomplete. . . . [T]he promise of an impact statement system is neither easily achieved nor free of unwanted side effects. In relying on competition among policy partisans to produce better knowledge, and through better knowledge, better decisions, impact statement systems are vulnerable to the ills associated with conflict of interest. Because the parties developing the information have policy stakes, they cannot be trusted to pursue or state the 'truth.' Because the participants cannot be trusted to value empirical objectivity more highly than political expediency, truth is pursued by an openly adversary process. In turn, for this adversary process to work effectively, analytical resources among the contending parties must not be extremely unbalanced. So 'analytical' resources are more widely distributed among the potential private and governmental critics of an agency. By having access to the development agency's data base, for example, these outsiders gain additional resources; . . . But solving the problem of merely pro forma adversariness exacerbates another problem: if policy partisans are used to enforce norms of analytical quality by way of competition, they will almost unavoidably be able to convert the procedures and analytical resources into political bargaining assets whose use does not necessarily serve a larger social purpose. Indeed, the mere anticipation that the other side will act to maximize its chances of prevailing on the policy issue, rather than to ascertain the evidence, may maintain a vicious circle in which both sides play fast and loose with the evidence. The convertibility of analytical into political assets puts a heavy burden on the oversight arrangements for formulating and adjudicating the rules of analysis."

NOTES ON THE NATURE OF A RULEMAKING RECORD

(1) Much of Judge Gurfein's opinion is concerned with the problems of judicial review (which are dealt with at other points in our casebook)[1] and, correspondingly, with the question what constitutes the "record" on which that review is to occur. He starts with the firm proposition that this record is to be the agency's record, not some new compilation made in court. We can understand this as one way of reinforcing the legislature's allocation of decisional authority. It is for the FDA, not the court, to consider the difficulties and proper responses concerning botulism in smoked and salted fish. Yet there are problems:

(a) *Temptation.* Judges may be tempted to add to the agency record despite the clear blackletter proposition Judge Gurfein correctly states, and they may find the temptation hard to resist. Consider this quotation from his own opinion, p. 529 above: "The history of botulism occurrence in whitefish, *as established in the trial record, which we must assume was available to the FDA in 1970*, is as follows." (Emphasis added.) What justified the district court in learning this history (which apparently included whitefish-induced botulism at about the time the FDA acted)? The court of appeals in reciting the continuation of this history beyond 1970?

(b) *Timing.* The timing of review here, and the focus specifically on whitefish, introduces some distortions. The court first entertaining a challenge in 1976 sees matters through the prism of whitefish in particular, rather than the whole range of species with which the rule deals; the agency is years removed from its focus on the general problem.

(c) *A variety of meanings for "record."* The word "record" has a variety of technical meanings in the law. Even if we assumed compilation of a rulemaking "record" during or immediately after the rulemaking, the informality of agency process introduces problems. We can imagine a mass of documents: statistical compilations and historical evidence, scientific analyses and economic studies made by concerned agency bureaus; analyses of the agency's legal authority, of its policy alternatives, and of the enforcement problems presented by these various alternatives; comments from those outside the agency; analyses of them by agency personnel; and, finally, the documents formally required by the APA (such as the notice of rulemaking) or by other statutes and/or executive orders. These are all documents that are in some sense identified to this particular rulemaking, and could be docketed if called for; it is not obvious that docketing is proper for all. Moreover, much that may influence the rulemaking does not have this readily identifiable character: expertise the agency and its employees have acquired over time; conversations within the agency never transcribed, that may more directly concern other issues; and conversations

---

1. This is yet another instance of the interrelatedness of administrative law issues, p. 34 above.

with outsiders—other government actors, and concerned members of the public—about issues important to the rulemaking. All of these build the context from which eventually a rule will emerge.

(2) *The Three "Records" of Agency Rulemaking.* We can, from this perspective, identify at least three quite different collections of material that might be thought of in "record" terms. The first would be the material that most directly concerned Judges Gurfein and Leventhal: the material available to be used by the public as the basis for commenting upon a proposed rule during the proceeding. We might call this the "record for participation." The second and most inclusive would be the world of materials that informs the agency's own decision-making processes generally and in the particular rulemaking. We might call this the "record for decision," although this mass of material is never finally gathered and identified. The third would be the documentary collection presented to a court as the basis for deciding whether the rule has sufficient basis to satisfy the applicable standard of judicial review. And we might call this the "record for review."

What are the relationships among the record for participation, the record for decision, and the record for review? Can the record for decision be larger than the record for participation, or must the agency disclose to the public everything which it considers? Can the record for decision be larger that the record for review, or must the agency produce in court all information it is aware of having considered, even if it was discarded as unreliable or outweighed? How, in this context, is the agency's acquired expertise (distributed among the many members of its staff) to be memorialized? Alternatively, can the record for decision be smaller than the record for review? Can the agency produce in court later-arising information which supports the rule it adopted but was not known at the time the rule was made? Under what circumstances will the answer be "yes," and when "no"? Questions such as these have provoked a considerable amount of litigation,—see, e.g., Idaho Farm Bureau Fed'n v. Babbitt, 58 F.3d 1392 (9th Cir.1995)—but no easy-to-state result. The difficulties which surround these questions might be put into three groups.

First, the ordinary workings of the legal system do not prepare us to think subtly about these issues. In ordinary courtroom litigation, we have a strong norm that the record for decision before the trial judge should be exactly the record of which the parties are aware, subject to the possibilities of judicial notice. We understand that the record for review by an appellate tribunal will be a direct outgrowth of this same record, limited perhaps by the scope of the questions open on appeal. As a general proposition for litigation, then, we think of the record for participation as enlarged upon only by what happens in open court; the resulting records for decision and for review are identical; we have little reason to work out their relationships in any finer sense. If we think now about the ordinary processes of legislation, the matter is at the other extreme. The "record" for public participation—the way in which non-official participants get to know that to which they must respond—is generated through a melange of hearings, reports, speeches, and gossip. There is no norm that connects this material the public "knows" to what legislators conscientiously determine to be an adequate basis (their "record") for decision. And in the ordinary processes of judicial review of legislation for constitutional validity, there is no need to produce either of these "records," (or non-records), in court. Legislation is not judged by comparison with them, but rather on the basis of assertions, and if need be, facts, developed in the judicial proceedings themselves. As a general proposition for legislation, then, the record for participation, the record for decision, and the record for review are radically disjunctive; again, we have little reason to work out their relationships in any finer sense.

Second, the drafters of the APA did not answer these questions when they created notice-and-comment rulemaking. As Judge Gurfein discusses in the principal case, the APA in § 706 calls for judicial review based on "the whole record." But in § 553, we find the record for participation described either skeletally—the notice has to include "the terms *or* substance of the proposed rule *or* a description of the subjects and issues involved" (emphasis added)—or very indirectly—"the agency shall give interested persons an opportunity to participate." And as to the record for decision, the statute says only that "[a]fter consideration of the relevant matter presented" the agency shall give "a concise general statement of [the rule's] basis and purpose." These phrases are intended to contrast with rulemaking "on the record," held only when another statute requires it. We can conclude that the text of the APA does not call for the close integration of the three types of record typical of adjudication. If it calls for some integration greater than what is typical of legislation, it does not define what this middle ground looks like.

Third, the opinions of the Supreme Court have not resolved the question, but have rather tended merely to restate the outer dimensions of the problem. Thus, we have opinions that say that even informal agency decisions are to be reviewed by judges based on the "whole record"—most notably the Overton Park case, relied on by Judge Gurfein and set out at p. 989. We have opinions that say that, as to the construction of the decisional record, the terms of § 553 describe all that, an agency need do—most notably the Vermont Yankee decision, set out at p. 498 above. But it has been left to the lower courts to work out the details of the relationships among the three types of records.

(3) *What the Agency Knows but Does Not Make Public.* As a concrete instance of the resulting difficulties, consider CENTER FOR AUTO SAFETY V. FEDERAL HIGHWAY ADMINISTRATION, 956 F.2d 309, 312–14 (D.C.Cir.1992): The Federal Highway Administration (FHWA) initially required states to inspect highway bridges every two years, but used rulemaking in 1988 to change the rule to allow states to apply for bridge-specific exemptions. Its statement of basis and purpose asserted that the "inspection interval can be increased for some categories of bridges with only a minimal or negligible increase in risk to the public." 52 Fed.Reg. at 11,094. When the agency was asked to reconsider this decision, it explained that it had considered two recent, draft studies of the rate at which various bridges deteriorate. Neither draft, however, had been put into what the agency formally denominated the "record" of the rulemaking proceeding. When the rule was challenged in court, the agency added a third such study it said it had relied on. Was this way of proceeding permissible? Per Clarence Thomas, finishing up a matter he had heard as a circuit court judge: no!

"The parties disputed the subsidiary question of what constitutes the administrative record subject to review. The FHWA filed with the district court the two drafts cited in its denial of reconsideration, together with a draft of a third bridge deterioration study. Attached to the studies was a declaration asserting that the agency had considered all of them during the rulemaking. The FHWA also filed a declaration explaining how it typically maintains its rulemaking records. According to that declaration, the 'formal Administrative Record' includes materials such as notices published and comments received, but it excludes less formal materials such as 'draft reports.' ...

"A 'record' is simply 'everything ... properly placed in evidence under defined rules of admissibility.' Pedersen, Formal Records and Informal Rulemaking, 85 Yale L.J. 38, 64 (1975). According to the FHWA's own testimony, the agency follows a defined, if informal, rule under which 'draft reports' are not admitted into the 'formal Administrative Record' maintained by the agency. Of course the agency could have maintained less strict evidentiary rules, consistent with the forgiving requirements of notice-and-comment rulemaking procedures, under which the draft studies would have been admitted. But having chosen, for whatever reason, to exclude the three draft bridge deterioration studies at the administrative stage, the FHWA cannot now rely on those same studies to provide the requisite evidentiary support during judicial review."

In referring to matters that are "admitted" into a record, is Judge Thomas applying the litigation idea of "record," in effect supposing that the "record" at the administrative stage was (must be?) the same for all? Or, as rulemaking has matured (with or without amendments to the APA), has it become incumbent on the agencies to define procedurally what will be the record for judicial review (as apparently the FHWA had done)—a definition the courts may then enforce as readily as any other procedural rule?

(4) *"Historical" and "Procedural" Records.* This problem resulted in an important recommendation by the now-defunct Administrative Conference of the United States,[2] that is well characterized and also criticized in the article Judge Thomas cited, WILLIAM F. PEDERSEN, JR., FORMAL RECORDS AND INFORMAL RULEMAKING, 85 Yale L.J. 38, 64–5 (1975): "The Administrative Conference of the United States has recommended that the record for judicial review of informal rulemaking should consist of (1) the notice of proposed rulemaking and any documents referred to in it; (2) the comments and documents submitted by interested persons; (3) transcripts of any hearings held in the course of the rulemaking; (4) reports of any advisory committees; (5) the agency's concise general statement or final order and any documents referred to in it; *and* (6) other factual information 'not included in the foregoing that was considered by the authority responsible for promulgation of the rule or that is proffered by the agency as pertinent to the rule.'

"The first five items cause no difficulty. Both under a historical approach to the record and under a procedural approach, they would certainly be included. But the first clause of the sixth recommendation comes down squarely on the side of the historical approach by explicitly recognizing the agency's right to include in the record whatever documents it 'considered'—even if they arose outside the APA notice and comment procedures. In addition, in defining the record as what was considered by

2. Recommendation 74–4: Preenforcement Judicial Review of Rules of General Applicability (1974); the Conference is discussed at p. 479 fn.1, above.

the 'authority responsible for promulgation of the rule,' the Administrative Conference misstates the nature of rulemaking. Only a very few, highly controversial issues can hope to receive detailed personal attention from the administrator of a busy agency, be he or she ever so competent. In all other cases, no single authority passes judgment on the rule. Different parts of the agency work on different parts of the rule, or on the same part from different angles—and the rule emerges. It follows from the lack of any meaningful central 'authority' that the phrase 'considered by the authority' also loses meaning, and sets no clear boundary to the size or content of the record. Given the diffuse nature of rulemaking, it will be a rare document that cannot claim to have been considered somewhere to some extent by someone in connection with the rulemaking, and a document almost as rare that will have received the personal attention of the administrator.

"The other test suggested by the Administrative Conference for including documents in the record—whether they are 'proffered by the agency as pertinent to the rule'—is even worse. It breaks free of the restriction implicit even in the historical approach that the record certified to the court should reflect what the agency *actually* weighed and evaluated in some manner at the time of the rulemaking. Indeed, it would apparently allow the agency to include whatever it thinks would help support its actions once litigation has begun.

"The relevant questions, which the Administrative Conference recommendation ignores, thus are the quality of the consideration given the documents involved and the manner in which they are determined to be relevant."

Apprised of the problem, Congress has hedged its bets, sometimes opting for the "procedural" and sometimes for the "historical" approach when enacting statutes actually containing definitions of the "rulemaking record" for judicial review purposes, as in § 307 of the Clean Air Act. American Bar Assoc. (J. Lubbers, Ed.), A Guide to Federal Agency Rulemaking 47 (3d. ed., 1998).[3]

Questions raised by various forms of administrative records also appear in Chapter VIII, and are elaborated upon in Section 3 of this chapter.

(iii) "AFTER CONSIDERATION OF THE RELEVANT MATTER PRESENTED, THE AGENCY SHALL INCORPORATE IN THE RULES ADOPTED A CONCISE GENERAL STATEMENT OF THEIR BASIS AND PURPOSE"

Independent U.S. Tanker Owners Committee v. Dole

United States Court of Appeals for the District of Columbia Circuit, 1987.
809 F.2d 847, cert. denied, 484 U.S. 819 (1987).

■ Before EDWARDS and BORK, CIRCUIT JUDGES, and SWYGERT, SENIOR CIRCUIT JUDGE.

■ BORK, CIRCUIT JUDGE:

These consolidated cases are before us on appeal from a decision of the district court, 620 F.Supp. 1289 (1985), which sustained the validity of a

---

3. The first two editions of this work were published by the Administrative Confer- ence, where Mr. Lubbers was long Research Director.

rule promulgated by the Secretary of Transportation. Appellants challenge the rule as exceeding the Secretary's statutory authority and as arbitrary and capricious agency action; they also raise a battery of specific procedural objections to the manner in which the rule was promulgated. We find that the Secretary was well within her statutory authority in promulgating the rule, but that she failed to provide an adequate account of how the rule serves the objectives set out in the governing statute, the Merchant Marine Act of 1936 (codified as amended at 46 U.S.C. §§ 1101–1295g (1982)).

I.

The rulemaking that gives rise to this case is the latest of numerous attempts by the Congress, the Maritime Administration, and the Department of Transportation to address the recurrent problems of the United States merchant marine fleet. The American fleet has had great difficulty competing in foreign commerce. American ships typically have higher construction and operating costs than their foreign competitors, not only because they typically must meet more stringent environmental and safety standards, but also because foreign ships often are subsidized and otherwise assisted by their own governments. Congress confronted these problems in 1936 and authorized the United States government to pay up to half the construction costs of American ships that will operate in foreign commerce. In addition, Congress authorized the government to subsidize the operating costs of these ships where necessary to meet foreign competition. Despite these provisions, American ships have continued to fare poorly against their competitors in foreign commerce.

Merchant ships that operate in the domestic shipping market do not receive these government subsidies. They are protected from the rigors of foreign competition, however, by the Jones Act, which requires all cargo transported between points in the United States to be carried on ships built in the United States, registered in the United States, and owned by American citizens. 46 U.S.C. § 883 (1982). They are also protected from having to compete against any of the ships that have received construction subsidies or operating subsidies from the government, except in a few specific and very limited instances. Since the Trans–Alaska Pipeline opened in 1977, however, the domestic fleet has been unable to satisfy the great new demand for large tankers to carry Alaskan oil to other points in the country. The Maritime Administration has responded to this situation by invoking its statutory authority to allow certain subsidized ships to operate in the domestic market for up to six months in a given year if the ships repay a proportional share of the construction subsidy that they have received. 46 C.F.R. Part 250 (1984). Yet this step has only partly solved the problem.

The rule at issue in this case permitted tanker vessels built with the assistance of a federal construction-differential subsidy, which had been barred from competing in domestic trade on account of that subsidy, to undertake domestic operations if they agreed to repay the unamortized portion of the subsidy plus interest during a period that began on June 6, 1985, and closed one year later. See Construction—Differential Subsidy Repayment; Total Payment Policy, 50 Fed.Reg. 19,170 (1985) (codified at 46 C.F.R. § 276.3 (1985)) (hereafter the "payback rule"). This rule addressed problems in both the foreign and domestic markets by providing an opportunity for ships that are not competitive in foreign commerce to enter the domestic market where the demand for their services has increased, but only by agreeing to relinquish their financial advantage over unsubsidized ships. The Maritime Administration has considered proposals for individual ships to repay their subsidies at least since 1964. In 1977, several owners of unsubsidized ships challenged the Administration's approval of repayment by one vessel in particular. The Supreme Court upheld the government's authority to approve subsidy repayment in exchange for permission to enter the domestic market. See Seatrain Shipbuilding Corp. v. Shell Oil Co., 444 U.S. 572, (1980). Shortly thereafter, the Administration established an interim rule that extended this authorization to undertake domestic shipping, upon repayment of the full subsidy plus interest, to a limited class of large tankers whose owners demonstrated "exceptional circumstances" of dismal prospects in foreign commerce to justify the application of the rule. See 45 Fed.Reg. 68,393 (1980). The interim rule was challenged, and this court invalidated it, finding that although the Administration had statutory authority to promulgate the rule, it had acted arbitrarily and capriciously by providing an inadequate discussion of the basis and purpose of the rule. See Independent U.S. Tanker Owners Comm. v. Lewis, 690 F.2d 908, 918–20 (D.C.Cir.1982). At that point, the Secretary of Transportation proposed the payback rule. This rule is similar to the earlier proposed interim rule except that it covers all tankers and does not require tankers to make any showing of "exceptional circumstances" to qualify for the benefits of subsidy repayment.

II.

Appellants initially question the Secretary's statutory authority to promulgate the payback rule. . . . [In our view she had that authority.]

III.

Appellants contend that even if the Secretary acted within her statutory authority in promulgating the payback rule, it should be invalidated because it is the product of agency action that was "arbitrary, capricious, an abuse of discretion, or not otherwise in accordance with law." 5 U.S.C. § 706(2)(A). In particular, appellants contend that the Secretary failed to provide a sufficiently reasoned discussion of why this rule was adopted and alternatives were rejected in light of the purposes of the Merchant Marine Act. . . .

It is unfortunate that, once more, we must agree with this contention. This court vacated the previous interim rule because the government "failed completely to fulfill its obligations" to set out an adequate statement of basis and purpose for the rule. Independent U.S. Tanker Owners Comm., 690 F.2d at 919. Now, four years later, we must vacate a similar rule on similar grounds.

Under the Administrative Procedure Act, when an agency initiates a rulemaking that the governing statute does not require to be undertaken "on the record," the agency is nonetheless bound to comply with the requirements for "notice and comment" rulemaking set out in 5 U.S.C. § 553. One requirement is that after the agency considers the comments presented by the participating parties, it "shall incorporate in the rules adopted a concise general statement of their basis and purpose." 5 U.S.C. § 553(c). This statement need not be an exhaustive, detailed account of every aspect of the rulemaking proceedings; it is not meant to be the more elaborate document, complete with findings of fact and conclusions of law, that is required in an on-the-record rulemaking. See id. § 557(c). On the other hand, this court has cautioned against "an overly literal reading of the statutory terms 'concise' and 'general' . . . [which] must be accommodated to the realities of judicial scrutiny." Automotive Parts & Accessories Ass'n v. Boyd, 407 F.2d 330, 338 (D.C.Cir.1968). At the least, such a statement should indicate the major issues of policy that were raised in the proceedings and explain why the agency decided to respond to these issues as it did, particularly in light of the statutory objectives that the rule must serve.

In Seatrain, the Supreme Court indicated that Congress gave the government broad power to implement the Merchant Marine Act so that the government could take steps that "directly further the general goals of the Act." 444 U.S. at 558. Those objectives are to foster the development and encourage the maintenance of an American merchant marine, in both foreign and domestic commerce, that is:

(a) sufficient to carry its domestic water-borne commerce and a substantial portion of the water-borne export and import foreign commerce of the United States and to provide shipping service essential for maintaining the flow of such domestic and foreign water-borne commerce at all times, (b) capable of serving as a naval and military auxiliary in time of war or national emergency, (c) owned and operated under the United States flag by citizens of the United States, insofar as may be practicable, (d) composed of the best-equipped, safest, and most suitable types of vessels, constructed in the United States and manned with a trained and efficient citizen personnel, and (e) supplemented by efficient facilities for shipbuilding and ship repair.

46 U.S.C. § 1101 (1982).

The Secretary's statement of basis and purpose fails to give an adequate account of how the payback rule serves these objectives and why alternative measures were rejected in light of them. The Secretary's treatment of these objectives, and of the concerns raised about them in the comment proceedings, is cursory at best. For example, concerns about whether this rule meets the statutory objective of maintaining an American merchant marine "sufficient to carry its domestic water-borne commerce and a substantial portion of the water-borne export and import foreign commerce" are met with the statement: "The Department believes that the [rule] will benefit the U.S. Merchant Marine." 50 Fed.Reg. 19,170, 19,173 (1985). Her discussion continues further, but it hardly improves:

Although it is true, as many commenters pointed out, that some tankers will be forced out of service by more efficient operators, the industry should be more competitive and efficient in the future, especially since some of the most efficient tankers in the U.S. flag fleet would be fully utilized. ... Overall, the industry should be left in a healthier, more viable condition.

Id. at 19,173–74. On the more dubious proposition that the fleet will remain able to carry "a substantial portion" of foreign commerce, the Secretary candidly acknowledges that "the final rule merely recognizes the existing condition of the U.S. tanker fleet. There currently exist few foreign trade employment opportunities for those vessels and the prospects for future employment in the foreign trade are far from bright." Id. at 19,174. Though this statement strongly suggests the view that this rule will hasten an American retreat from carriage of foreign commerce, the Secretary surprisingly asserts that the fleet will remain "more than adequate to carry an appropriate share of the U.S. foreign oil commerce if such opportunities should arise." Id. This remark is hard to fathom. If there is currently little hope for the employment of American vessels in foreign trade, then the payback rule will permit the total size of the American fleet to follow its natural tendency to decrease toward the level required by the domestic market. Under present conditions, therefore, the rule will make it impossible to retain a fleet that can carry all domestic traffic and "a substantial portion" of foreign traffic "at all times," which is explicitly set out as an objective in section (a) of the statute.

The Secretary's response to concerns about the rule's effects on the fleet as a naval auxiliary, to take another example, is similarly unsatisfying. The Navy warned that the projected loss under this rule of "handy-sized" tankers might have adverse implications for national security. The Secretary brushes aside this comment by stating her belief that "the outlook for these old, small product tankers is poor regardless of whether or not this rule is promulgated because of their age and the decline of the U.S. products trade." Id. She also claims that other non-fleet ships could fill in the gap, id., even though this observation may not help to satisfy the statutory objective that the fleet itself should constitute "a naval and military auxiliary in time of war or national emergency." 46 U.S.C. § 1101(b) (1982).

Rather than providing a more extensive discussion of the Merchant Marine Act's objectives, the Secretary chooses to rely on other policies in defending the rule. She identifies some of the "most important" reasons for the rule as being "economic efficiency," "use of underemployed resources," "increased competition," and "deregulation." 50 Fed.Reg. at 19,172. As she later elaborates: "It is the Department's position that the competitive forces of the market, rather than government regulation, should be relied upon, whenever feasible, to allocate transportation capacity and resources in the domestic trade. This rule reflects that position." Id. at 19,175. The central thrust of her approach, quite obviously, is to subject the merchant marine fleet to the discipline of the free market. Thus she finds it significant that the rule will leave the industry "in a healthier, more viable condition," id. at 19,174, and she finds it permissible that the condition of the fleet should depend on what economic opportunities become available in the world market. See id. This policy may well be defensible, yet it is not among the objectives specified in the Act, and if the Secretary has decided that it is implicit in or compatible with the statutory objectives, it would be useful for her to explain this decision somewhat more fully. She has failed to do so. The closest she comes is the conclusory statement that "it would not be appropriate to let the various program objectives reflected in the Act stand in the way of achieving the Act's broader policy mandates, including that of promoting a more competitive and efficient merchant fleet." Id. It may, however, be entirely appropriate for the Act's objectives to stand in the way of the payback rule, and perhaps to favor other alternatives, unless the Secretary can offer a fuller and more persuasive explanation for her view that the "broader policy mandates" of the Act include the promotion of a "more competitive and efficient merchant fleet."[1]

The Secretary's failure to link the policies served by this rule to the objectives set out in the Merchant Marine Act is particularly problematic because she does not explain in the statement of basis and purpose why she rejects proposed alternatives to the payback rule. One can find this explanation in the Regulatory Impact Analysis, Joint Appendix ("J.A.") at 1049, where the Secretary considers and rejects at least a half-dozen other suggested measures. Once again, however, her account focuses on non-statutory criteria that favor this rule, such as lower transportation costs, collateral fiscal benefits, and more "efficient" use of the fleet. J.A. at 1089, 1093. She admits that the rule "has a number of adverse impacts," including "the displacement of about 13 tankers ... most of which are militarily useful handy-sized tankers, loss of employment opportunities for about 800 seamen, and the possible default on several government loans," id. at 1093, problems that impinge on the statutory objectives and that might be avoided under some of the alternative measures. See, e.g., id. at 1091–92 (describing effects of "full-time permissions" option, "status quo" option, and "eliminate permissions" option).

In exercising her decisionmaking authority, the Secretary is certainly free to consider factors that are not mentioned explicitly in the governing statute, yet she is not free to substitute new goals in place of the statutory objectives without explaining how these actions are consistent with her authority under the statute. Her failure to link these non-statutory criteria with Congress' stated objectives in the Act thus makes it impossible for us to uphold the Secretary's decision to reject other measures and adopt this rule in response to the current problems of the merchant marine fleet. Her reliance on these non-statutory criteria is consistently a key point in her justifications for adopting this rule. In order to defend this action as "reasoned decisionmaking," the Secretary must spell out in more detail how her decision to adopt this rule and reject alternative measures by relying on policies of competition and deregulation can be squared with the statutory objectives that Congress specified as the primary guidelines for

---

1. It may be, of course, that present conditions in the world shipping market make it impossible for the Secretary to find a way to meet all of the statutory objectives. If this is the problem, she should discuss it frankly and directly when she considers which measures to adopt in light of the objectives explicitly set out in the Act.

administrative action in this area. We take no position on whether these policies can be squared with the Act. But in the absence of any such discussion, this court can only conclude that her action is "arbitrary, capricious, ... or not otherwise in accordance with law." 5 U.S.C. § 706(2)(A).

IV.

We therefore conclude that the Secretary violated section 553(c) of the Administrative Procedure Act by adopting this rule. In fashioning a remedy for an agency's failure to present an adequate statement of basis and purpose, this court may either remand for specific procedures to cure the deficiency without vacating the rule, see, e.g., National Nutritional Foods Ass'n v. Weinberger, 512 F.2d 688, 701, 703–04 (2d Cir.), cert. denied, 423 U.S. 827 (1975), or it may vacate the rule, thus requiring the agency to initiate another rulemaking proceeding if it would seek to confront the problem anew. See, e.g., Tabor v. Joint Bd. for Enrollment of Actuaries, 566 F.2d 705, 710–12 (D.C.Cir.1977). In this case, we vacate the rule because the Secretary's omissions are quite serious and raise considerable doubt about which of the proposed alternatives would best serve the objectives set out in the Merchant Marine Act. Yet we exercise our power to withhold issuance of our mandate until July 16, 1987 [six months from the date of decision], to avoid further disruptions in the domestic market and to allow the Secretary to undertake further proceedings to address the problems of the merchant marine trade. See Fed.R.App.P. 41(a). As of that date, the present rule will be vacated and conditions returned to the status quo ante, before the payback rule took effect, subject of course to any further action that may have been taken in the interim.

So ordered.

NOTES

(1) *"Concise General Statement of Basis and Purpose."* The Secretary—which is to say, the agency as a whole, and especially those responsible for crafting the statement of basis and purpose—seems to have provided considerably more by way of explanation than would accompany a statute, but in the eyes of the court the explanation is evidently too "concise" and too "general." Note that the panel is unanimous; Circuit Judges Harry Edwards and Robert Bork both had considerable academic and practical experience in administrative law before becoming judges, and both were well aware of Vermont Yankee and its teachings. What would it have taken for the Secretary adequately to have explained herself in light of her statutory authority? Consider STEPHEN BREYER, JUDICIAL REVIEW OF QUESTIONS OF LAW AND POLICY, 38 Admin.L.Rev. 363, 393 (1986):

"The reason agencies do not explore all arguments or consider all alternatives is one of practical limits of time and resources. Yet, to have to explain and to prove all this to a reviewing court risks imposing much of the very burden that not considering alternatives aims to escape. Of course, the reviewing courts may respond that only *important* alternatives and arguments must be considered. But, what counts as 'important'? District courts often find that parties, having barely mentioned a legal point at the trial level, suddenly make it the heart of their case on appeal, emphasizing its (sudden but) supreme importance. Appellate courts typically consider such arguments as long as they have been at least mentioned in the district court. But district courts, unlike agencies dealing with policy change, do not face, say, 10,000 comments challenging different aspects of complex policies. And, when appellate courts 'answer' an argument they write a few words or paragraphs, perhaps citing a case or two. A satisfactory answer in the agency context may mean factfinding, empirical research, detailed investigation. Accordingly, one result of strict judicial review of agency policy decisions is a strong conservative pressure in favor of the status quo."

(2) *Whose Statement?* As the opening to the previous note suggested, the Secretary is no more likely to have written the often extensive statement of basis and purpose accompanying an important rule, than to have written her Department's decision in an adjudicatory matter. The *internal* process-es agencies use to produce a proposed rule or rule are considered at some length in the next section. For the moment, by way of preparation for that material, consider THOMAS O. MCGARITY, THE INTERNAL STRUCTURE OF EPA RULEMAKING, 54 Law & Contemp.Probs. 57, 90–102 (Autumn, 1991). Profes-sor McGarity outlines four patterns of internal staff organization—all the product of bureaucratic management, not statutory requirement, and so subject to considerable variation. In the "Team Model," the basic decision-making unit is "the team composed of representatives from all of the institutional subunits within the agency that have an interest in the outcome of the rulemaking process." In the "Hierarchical Model," "a single office is responsible for all aspects of a rulemaking initiative except for the final determination of whether the rule is consistent with the particular statute involved." In the "Outside Advisor Model," a single office "retains primary responsibility," but "is free to call upon other offices in the agency for advice as needed." Finally, in the "Adversarial Model" offices within the agency having "different perspectives" are forced "to confront one another in an adversarial setting." Each model is in use somewhere in the federal government; the "team model" is the most common. As to it, Professor McGarity comments (at pp. 90–93):

"As we have seen, the team approach has several advantages over other models, the most significant of which is its capacity to bring multiple professional perspectives to bear on issues that arise in complex rulemak-ings. The team model allows the agency to base its decision on a wide range of information and analysis from multiple sources. It may also facilitate innovative, cross-disciplinary thinking about novel options for solving regu-latory problems. The very concept of a team connotes harmony and the pursuit of common goals that may take the adversarial edge off of interac-tions among persons with divergent professional perspectives and policy preferences. . . .

"Perhaps the most significant disadvantage of the team model is its potential to shift the locus of policymaking from upper-level political appointees to career staff. This shift can happen in several ways. First, a critical aspect of bureaucratic decisionmaking is the function of initially identifying the universe of possible options to solve the problem and the continuing process of narrowing those options to the one that the agency ultimately selects. The team model, especially as practiced at EPA, has a strong tendency to lodge this crucial aspect of rulemaking discretion at lower levels in the agency hierarchy. For example, one of the articulated goals of the EPA workgroup is to reach consensus on the proposed and final rules. Yet if the workgroup reaches consensus and that consensus is maintained (as is usually the case for important issues) throughout [higher level reviews] there is very little for the ultimate decisionmaker (the Administrator) to decide. If he or she asks for an options memorandum at this late stage in the rulemaking process, the result is likely to be a perfunctory effort in which the staff's preferred option is sandwiched between two impractical red herrings. The only real option for the decision-maker is to remand the entire matter to the staff with orders to start over. And even that is not a realistic option for rules that must be written by statutory or court-imposed deadlines. In reality, the important decisions (including significant policy determinations) are often made by the staff."

(3) *Gaming the System.* The agency's need to answer objections or suggested alternatives would seem to put a weapon in the hand of anyone interested in delaying or derailing a rulemaking proceeding. Are there ethical limits on how far a lawyer can go in exploiting the strategic possibilities of the situation? Can a lawyer lay down a barrage of comments and pursue a scorched earth policy just for its procedural effect? The relevant ABA Model Rules of Professional Conduct, Rules 3.1 and 3.2, appear to apply only to lawyers involved in adjudication. See Rule 3.9. But as a matter of ethics, should not their strictures against frivolous claims and positions taken merely for the purpose of frustrating opposing parties through delay, apply here too? Or is rulemaking so different from adjudication that no comparison can be drawn? The peroration to Vermont Yankee, p. 506 above, suggests some limits to judicial patience. Certainly one ought to address what one considers important; it is when another's comment leads the agency to alter its proposed rule that a previously minor matter may acquire greater urgency.

To the extent that an agency's obligation to consider various points, or to explain its resolution of them, is determined by the issues raised during the notice-and-comment proceeding, the nature of "reasoned decisionmaking" will be contingent on the history of the particular proceeding. Yet the agency ought to address *some* matters regardless whether anyone has commented on them—for example, its basic legal authority for promulgating the regulation at hand. The dividing line between these two sorts of issues is likely to be tested only when someone seeks judicial review on an issue not pressed before the agency itself. Here, the question is whether to treat the failure to comment on an issue as a procedural "default." Doing so gives commenters an incentive to raise matters initially before the agency. The cases addressing this question have done so in terms of the doctrine requiring "exhaustion" of administrative remedies, discussed at p. 1238 ff.

(4) Note that Independent Tankers, in delaying issuance of the mandate, improvises in an manner comparable to employs the practice of remanding without vacating, first encountered in the Sugar Cane Growers Cooperative case, at p. 493 above.

(5) *Rational Developments?* Looking back over the last three subsections, you should find considerable elaboration of § 553's requirements, well beyond what any 1946 legislator would have thought he was requiring. Can one say that these are *not* the unthinking product of adjudicatory analogies, but rather developments within the possibilities of § 553's language and purpose, and well adapted to what rulemaking has become? And, thus, that Vermont Yankee ought not to be read to foreclose them? They resonate with the words of Judge Leventhal, not Chief Judge Bazelon.

Writing a year before the Vermont Yankee decision, Professor Richard Stewart saw in a "requirement of reasoned elaboration" (including a requirement of responding to contrary arguments and evidence) and an expanded concept of agency records, the basis for a "paper hearing" that "combines many of the advantages of a trial-type adversary process (excepting oral testimony and cross-examination) while avoiding undue delay and cost." RICHARD STEWART, THE DEVELOPMENT OF ADMINISTRATIVE AND QUASI-CONSTITUTIONAL LAW IN JUDICIAL REVIEW OF ENVIRONMENTAL DECISIONMAKING: LESSONS FROM THE CLEAN AIR ACT, 62 Iowa L.Rev. 713, 731–33 (1977): "The development of a 'paper hearing' procedure and the related requirement that the Agency explain in detail the bases for its decision have contributed significantly to the improvement of EPA decisionmaking[1] because the Agency must be prepared to expose the factual and methodological bases for its decision and face judicial review on a record that encompasses the contentions and evidence of the Agency and its opponents, including responses by the Agency to criticism of its decision.

"Far more controversial are occasional court decisions that have gone beyond the requirements of detailed explanation and a 'paper hearing' to require, on a largely ad hoc basis, that EPA grant a limited trial-type hearing on specified issues. . . . A review of the actual procedures utilized by the parties upon remand in these and similar decisions indicated that the industries challenging EPA's position did not, in the end, insist upon the use of trial-type procedures; technical issues were instead thrashed out through exchange of documents and informal meetings between technical experts.

". . . Recognition of a 'paper hearing' procedure as a third standard model of administrative decision is likely to represent a better solution to the inadequacies of the two traditional paradigms (notice-and-comment

---

1. . . . Based on his own study of EPA decisions during his service over the past year as a member of the Committee on Environmental Decisionmaking, the author is firmly persuaded that the development of "paper hearing" procedures, combined with judicial willingness to scrutinize the grounds and evidence underlying EPA decisions, have contributed substantially to improve the quality of EPA decisionmaking. The reader is invited to make a personal assessment by comparing the adequacy of reasons and supporting evidence in early EPA decisions, such as those involved in Kennecott Copper Corp. v. EPA, 462 F.2d 846 (D.C.Cir.1972), or South Terminal Corp. v. EPA, 504 F.2d 646 (1st Cir.1974), with those in later decisions, such as Ethyl Corp. v. EPA, 541 F.2d 1 (D.C.Cir.), cert. denied, 426 U.S. 941 (1976).

procedures and adjudicatory procedures) than a series of ad hoc responses. The development of 'paper hearing' procedures at other agencies, and proposals by commentators, legislators, and the Administrative Conference, indicate that the 'paper hearing' model may well be widely imitated and eventually accepted as a procedural *tertium quid.*"

Today, both a collective "blackletter" of administrative law published by the Administrative Law and Regulatory Practice Section of the ABA,[2] and its published "Guide to Federal Agency Rulemaking," present these developments as uncontroversial, an established part of the law.

(iv) AND NOW, THE WORLDWIDEWEB

The question of providing contemporary meaning for § 553 has acquired particular impetus with the arrival of the information age. When § 553 was adopted, available technology helped to shape rulemaking realities. Invited comments were submitted to the agency—only. It could hardly be known who would submit. All commenters were subject to the same timetable for submission. One copy was enough, and reproduction technologies were limited (Xerox machines were still decades into the future). So if one wanted to see what another commenter had said, one would have to go to the place where the comments were kept—in the responsible Washington bureau—and hope for the opportunity to see them. The idea of responsive comment, in all these circumstances, was virtually inconceivable.

The 70's brought cheap photo-reproduction and the Freedom of Information Act, but comments were still physical, "located" documents one would need to go to (or ask for) to see. With the explosive development of the Internet and e-government, all this has changed. Increasingly, rulemaking is conducted on the World Wide Web, where comments can be submitted and made universally (and easily) available. As this casebook goes to press, the Bush administration has announced an ambitious program to make all rulemaking electronic. It will draw upon, inter alia, the experience accumulated in the Department of Transportation's Docket Management Service, http://dms.dot.gov. This site permits registration for automatic e-mail electronic notification of matters of interest—for example, new filings in a particular docket; it makes available for viewing all comments in all rulemakings in that busy Department (and thus readily permits you the student to gain an impression of rulemakings in action). Note that in distributing comments so quickly and widely, it gives reality to the possibility of responsive comments, for those with the resources and will to file them. Given the informality of rulemakings, late-filed comments will usually be received. Responsiveness to the comments of others that did not become available until shortly before a nominal filing deadline would be an understandable reason for lateness.

2. A Blackletter Statement of Federal Administrative Law, 54 Admin.L.Rev. 1, 30–35 (2002).

Might the result of conducting rulemakings on the Web be to make rulemaking more political (and correspondingly less "expert") by introducing elements of the referendum? Not all rulemakings will have wide popular appeal, but two early web-based rulemakings—one conducted by the Federal Deposit Insurance Corporation and one by the Department of Agriculture's Agricultural Marketing Service (AMS)—drew hundreds of thousands of comments, and resulted in substantial changes from the actions initially proposed. For example, the AMS published an NPRM in December, 1997, looking towards the adoption of certain standards for the growing, processing, and certification of organic foods. Five months later it announced that "as a result of the 200,000 comments USDA received on the initial proposal," it would be issuing a revised proposal embodying "national organic standards that organic farmers and consumers will embrace." Among the apparently unexpected controversies were initial proposals to include as "organic" the products of biotechnology, to permit the use of irradiation in food processing, and to allow the application of biosolids (municipal sludge) in organic food production. "If organic farmers and consumers reject our national standards, we have failed," the announcement reported the Secretary to have said. "Our task is to stimulate the growth of organic agriculture, ensure that consumers have confidence in the products that bear the organic label, and develop export markets for this growing industry." Vigorous development, visible and open to interaction, continued on the site for many months. The site offered a series of "issue papers" for which data was given and responses requested; a searchable database of over 100,000 individualized comments (along with a record of the signatures on many more form letters and postcards); and the transcripts of four hearings attended by organic farmers and consumers— "public listening sessions" evidently intended to make people feel they were being heard. The revised proposal did not issue until March, 2000, and the rule (7 C.F.R. Part 205) was published in the Federal Register December 21, 2000—one month before the Clinton administration ended. Over 300,000 comments had been filed. The agency website is still maintained, but the rulemaking material is no longer prominent there. http://www.ams.usda.gov/nop/.

The fact of web-based rulemaking has brought with it web sites dedicated to tracking it. "There's a lot out there for fast learners. And it's all free."[1] In addition to agency sites and the central repositories for the CFR (http://www.access.gpo.gov) and the Federal Register (http://www.nara.gov/fedreg), there are the two government monitors, OIRA (http://www.whitehouse.gov/omb/inforeg) and GAO (http://www.gao.gov), and a predictable variety of sites run by NGOs, liberal (http://www.ombwatch.org; http://www.citizen.org) and conservative (http://www.regradar.org; http://www.regulation.org; http://www.the-cre.com). The American Enterprise Institute and the Brookings Institution sponsor a joint project on regulation with a particularly useful set of links, http://www.aei.brookings.org/wnew/regulation.asp.

---

1. Cindy Skrzycki, "Web Sites Track Regulatory Changes," The Washington Post, April 24, 2001, E01.

(v) "THIS SUBSECTION DOES NOT APPLY . . . (B) WHEN THE AGENCY FOR GOOD CAUSE FINDS (AND INCORPORATES THE FINDING AND A BRIEF STATEMENT OF REASONS THEREFOR IN THE RULES ISSUED) THAT NOTICE AND PUBLIC PROCEDURE THEREON ARE IMPRACTICABLE, UNNECESSARY, OR CONTRARY TO THE PUBLIC INTEREST"

Utility Solid Waste Activities Group v. Environmental Protection Agency

United States Court of Appeals for the District of Columbia Circuit, 2000.
236 F.3d 749.

■ Before WILLIAMS, RANDOLPH, and TATEL, CIRCUIT JUDGES.

■ RANDOLPH, CIRCUIT JUDGE: [The Toxic Substances Control Act ("TSCA") forbids the "manufacture, processing, distribution in commerce or use" of any polychlorinated biphenyls (PCB) except in a "totally enclosed manner." 15 U.S.C. § 2605(e)(2)(A). While very useful for electrical equipment, PCBs are dangerous carcinogens; remarkably stable, they accumulate in fatty tissue and are readily absorbed through digestion and the skin. Nearly all manufacturing of PCBs has ceased, but cleanup and decontamination of former sites and spills remain major concerns.

EPA's cleanup and decontamination standards have long required corrective action for any spills involving solutions containing as little as 50 parts per million ("ppm") PCB. Successful cleanup would permit unrestricted subsequent use of solid surfaces; the test was a remaining surface concentration of at most 10 micrograms of PCBs per 100 square centimeters ("10 µg/100 cm^2"). The standards prohibited any use of contaminated porous surfaces (like concrete, or a wooden floor) where the residual surface contamination was more severe.

These standards came under fresh examination in a 1998 rulemaking. Many commenters raised questions whether complete prohibition of using these more severely contaminated surfaces was necessary. In response EPA promulgated 40 C.F.R. § 761.30(p)(1):

> Any person may use porous surfaces contaminated by spills of liquid PCBs at concentrations greater than or equal to 10 µg/100 cm^2 for the remainder of the useful life of the surfaces and subsurface material if the following conditions [setting parameters for cleaning, painting and marking the surfaces] are met: . . . .

Notice that this standard uses the 10 microgram *surface concentration* level EPA had sought as the end result of a clean-up, rather than the 50 microgram *spill concentration* level that had previously been the trigger for requiring a cleanup. The new regulation thus appears to express the judgment that surfaces contaminated at PCB concentrations of 10 micrograms per 100 square centimeters *and more* would not pose an unreasonable risk if appropriately cleaned, painted and marked. EPA's statement of basis and purpose explained the change in general terms, but did not mention this change of parameter:

EPA agrees with comments that the removal of porous materials contaminated by spills of liquid PCBs is economically burdensome and unnecessary where release of and exposure to the PCBs can be controlled. EPA believes that the [cleaning, painting and marking] conditions specified in § 761.30(p) will effectively prevent exposure to any residual PCBs in the contaminated porous material and therefore continued use of this material will not present an unreasonable risk.

63 Fed. Reg. at 35,398.

Apparently the change of parameter was an error. Without using § 553's notice and comment procedures, EPA soon amended § 761.30(p)(1) by substituting the 50 ppm spill concentration measure for the 10 microgram surface contamination measure. The result was to require the cleaning, painting and marking of *all* surfaces on which potentially contaminating spills had occurred, whether or not they already met the prior surface contamination standard, to permit their continued use. EPA characterized the amendment as a minor technical amendment to correct an obvious drafting error. It credibly asserted that the error resulted from careless use of a word processing find/replace command. Affected PCB makers and users sought review.]

I.

The Administrative Procedure Act's general rulemaking section, 5 U.S.C. § 553, sets down certain procedural requirements with which agencies must comply in promulgating legislative rules: there must be publication of a notice of proposed rulemaking; opportunity for public comment on the proposal; and publication of a final rule accompanied by a statement of the rule's basis and purpose. That EPA did not comply with the notice and comment requirements of APA § 553 in amending § 761.30(p) is certain. The question is whether EPA's justifications for not doing so will save the amended rule.

A.

... EPA thinks ... it possesses "inherent power" to correct "technical errors." It relies on a line of cases beginning with American Trucking Ass'ns v. Frisco Co., 358 U.S. 133 (1958), for the proposition that agencies may correct their mistakes without complying with the APA's procedural requirements. ... The Court noted that FED. R. CIV. P. 60(a) grants courts the power to correct clerical errors, and held that the Commission possessed the same power by analogy and pursuant to its broad enabling statute instructing the Commission to serve the "ends of justice." 358 U.S. at 145. "To hold otherwise would be to say that once an error has occurred the Commission is powerless to take remedial steps." Id. Later decisions, using the same analogy to judicial proceedings, have sustained an agency's inherent power to correct errors in an adjudication.

The judicial analogy does not work here. This was not an adjudication. EPA acted in a quasi-legislative fashion. The rule as initially promulgated was legislative in nature. Congress, with some regularity, particularly in the tax area, makes technical corrections to legislation, but it does so by enacting corrective legislation, not by issuing an order announcing the change. EPA is not quite so constrained. APA § 553(b)(B) permits it, and other agencies, to dispense with notice and comment "when the agency for good cause finds (and incorporates the finding and a brief statement of reasons therefor in the rules issued) that notice and public procedure thereon are impracticable, unnecessary, or contrary to the public interest." Unlike the Frisco Supreme Court case, the alternative here is not that EPA would be powerless to correct its mistakes. It has the power to do so, so long as it follows certain procedures. . . .

B.

In addition to its claim of inherent power to correct mistakes in rules, EPA contends that it brought itself within one or more of the APA's exceptions to notice and comment rulemaking.

APA § 553(b) requires notice of any proposed rule to be published in the Federal Register "unless persons subject thereto are named and either personally served or otherwise have actual notice thereof in accordance with law." 5 U.S.C. § 553(b). EPA's argument is that petitioners received "actual notice" when EPA published the change on its Internet site and when it held a meeting attended by counsel for Utility Solid Waste Activities Group. This court has never found that Internet notice is an acceptable substitute for publication in the Federal Register, and we refuse to do so now. In any event, EPA has not even alleged that the petitioners were "named" in the Internet publication, as APA § 553(b) would require if this sort of notice were sufficient. That counsel for one of the petitioners attended a meeting discussing the modification of § 761.30(p) is irrelevant. The other petitioner, General Electric, did not attend.

EPA also thinks it qualified for the exception to notice and comment rulemaking contained in APA § 553(b)(B). The claim is that its statement in the Federal Register accompanying the amendment—the amendments contained only "minor, routine clarifications that will not have a significant effect on industry or the public"—amounted to a finding of good cause and a statement of reasons. There are three grounds in APA § 553(b)(B) for finding good cause: notice and comment would be "impracticable, unnecessary, or contrary to the public interest." EPA does not tell us which of the three it meant to invoke, so we will discuss each. In doing so we are mindful of our precedents that the "good cause" exception is to be "narrowly construed and only reluctantly countenanced." Tennessee Gas Pipeline Co. v. FERC, 969 F.2d 1141, 1144 (D.C.Cir.1992). The exception is not an "escape clause"; its use "should be limited to emergency situations." American Fed'n of Gov't Employees v. Block, 655 F.2d 1153, 1156 (D.C.Cir.1981).

With respect to "impracticable" ground, the Attorney General's Manual explains "that a situation is 'impracticable' when an agency finds that due and timely execution of its functions would be impeded by the notice otherwise required in [§ 553]," as when a safety investigation shows that a new safety rule must be put in place immediately. United States Department of Justice, Attorney General's Manual on the Administrative Procedure Act 30–31 (1947). This ground for finding good cause cannot possibly apply here. There is no indication that 40 C.F.R. § 761.30(p), as it stood before the amendment, posed any threat to the environment or human health or that some sort of emergency had arisen. And EPA made no finding to this effect.

With respect to the "unnecessary" prong of the exception, one court has ruled that its use is "confined to those situations in which the administrative rule is a routine determination, insignificant in nature and impact, and inconsequential to the industry and to the public." South Carolina v. Block, 558 F. Supp. 1004, 1016 (D.S.C.1983). This formulation comports with the explanation in the Attorney General's Manual that " 'unnecessary' refers to the issuance of a minor rule in which the public is not particularly interested." Attorney General's Manual at 31. EPA's amendment of 40 C.F.R. § 761.30(p) does not fit that mold. ... In the original rule, porous surfaces contaminated by spills containing at least 50 ppm PCBs were not regulated by § 761.30(p) if the resulting PCB surface contamination was less than 10 μg/100 cm^2. As we understand the new regulations, these same surfaces now became subject to § 761.30(p) because the 10 μg/100 cm^2 surface contamination trigger has been repealed. ... EPA's amendment was, without doubt, something about which these members of the public were greatly interested.

As to the "public interest" ground for finding good cause, the Attorney General's Manual states that this "connotes a situation in which the interest of the public would be defeated by any requirement of advance notice," as when announcement of a proposed rule would enable the sort of financial manipulation the rule sought to prevent. Attorney General's Manual at 31. Nothing of the sort is present here . . . .

We therefore hold that EPA cannot take advantage of the exceptions contained in APA § 553(b)(B).

We hold as well that EPA cannot be excused from compliance with § 553 on the basis that its failure to engage in notice and comment rulemaking amounted to harmless error. This seems to us merely another way of saying that the change in the rule was unimportant, having no significant impact. We have already rejected that position. ...

The amendment to 40 C.F.R. § 761.30(p), as set forth in the June 1999 Federal Register, constituted agency action "without observance of [the] procedure required by law" and, as such, it is "unlawful and set aside." 5 U.S.C. § 706(2)(D).

Accordingly, the petitions for judicial review are granted.

NOTE

Behaviors like the EPA's in this case are commonly thought to be a product of the increasing rigor of § 553's rulemaking procedures. Agencies constrained in resources and convinced that action is required *now* are tempted to find other routes to accomplish their ends. Judges persuaded that this has occurred may prove emphatic that § 553's no-longer-so-simple procedures must be observed. An arguably similar agency technique that has emerged in recent years is the "interim-final" regulation. See, e.g., Michael Asimow, Interim–Final Rules: Making Haste Slowly, 51 Admin. L.

Rev. 703, 712–15 (1999). The agency publishes as immediately effective an "interim rule," which it may not expect to prove controversial; it states that the rule is also a proposal for final rulemaking, with comments possible in ordinary course. If it has correctly assessed the lack of controversy, the rule is in place and no harm is done. If the comments reveal a problem, it can be responded to—or in any event, a final rule published— before judicial review takes up the question of interim effectiveness.

The frequency with which the Internal Revenue Service issued "temporary regulations" and then never brought them to completion may have contributed to the enactment of 26 U.S.C. § 7805(e). The statute requires that any temporary regulation "shall also be issued as a proposed regulation" and provides that "Any temporary regulation [adopted after November 20, 1988] shall expire within 3 years" of its adoption. Should this solution be adopted for *all* interim-final regulations?

Section 4 of this Chapter will explore the most significant, and controversial, methods for agencies efforts to escape the rigors of informal rulemaking: the issuance of "interpretations," or "policy statements" that are (critics claim) masquerades for regulations requiring notice-and-comment procedures. First, however, we turn to a variety of issues and procedures that § 553 does not itself control. Beginning at the initiation of rulemaking and progressing to its conclusion, they reveal what lies beneath the iceberg's tip.

SECTION 3.   WHAT LIES BENEATH THE SURFACE—THE COURSE OF CONTEMPORARY RULEMAKING

a.   "CHOOSING" A MODE FOR POLICYMAKING

The principal procedural vehicles for major regulatory policymaking traditionally have been, and for the most part continue to be, informal rulemaking under § 553 and formal adjudication under §§ 554, 556 and 557. Here, we take up questions about the legal, institutional, and political factors that may encourage or constrain an agency with powers to use both, when it uses one of these vehicles rather than the other. What implications—for the agency, for the regulated and beneficiary communities, and for oversight institutions—follow from the type of policymaking mode employed? Must/should/may such an agency consider rulemaking the preferred policymaking option?

Securities & Exchange Commission v. Chenery Corp.

Supreme Court of the United States, 1947.
332 U.S. 194.

■ JUSTICE MURPHY delivered the opinion of the Court.

[The Public Utility Holding Company Act of 1935 aimed at dismantling the complex, highly leveraged pyramid structures common in the public utility industry; the collapse of many of these companies in the 1929 stock market crash had contributed to the Great Depression. Section 11(b) directed the SEC "as soon as practicable after January 1, 1938 ... [to] require by order, after notice and opportunity for hearing, that each registered holding company ... shall take such action as the Commission shall find necessary to limit the operations of the holding-company system of which such company is a part to a single integrated public-utility system ..." Section 11(e) permitted companies to forestall mandatory reorganization by proposing a "voluntary" plan. The SEC was to determine, after hearing, whether the proposal was "necessary to effectuate the provisions of [Section 11(b)] and fair and equitable to the persons affected by such plan." The Chenerys—officers, directors and controlling shareholders of Federal Water Service Corporation ("Federal")—had attempted voluntary reorganization under a plan in which they would retain a substantial role in the new enterprise; the SEC had refused to approve reorganization on these terms.]

This case is here for the second time. In SEC v. Chenery Corp., 318 U.S. 80 ["Chenery I"], we held that an order of the Securities and Exchange Commission could not be sustained on the grounds upon which that agency acted. We therefore directed that the case be remanded to the Commission for such further proceedings as might be appropriate. On remand, the Commission reexamined the problem, recast its rationale and reached the same result. The issue now is whether the Commission's action is proper in light of the principles established in our prior decision.

When the case was first here, we emphasized a simple but fundamental rule of administrative law. That rule is to the effect that a reviewing court, in dealing with a determination or judgment which an administrative agency alone is authorized to make, must judge the propriety of such action solely by the grounds invoked by the agency. If those grounds are inadequate or improper, the court is powerless to affirm the administrative action by substituting what it considers to be a more adequate or proper basis. To do so would propel the court into the domain which Congress has set aside exclusively for the administrative agency.

We also emphasized in our prior decision an important corollary of the foregoing rule. If the administrative action is to be tested by the basis upon which it purports to rest, that basis must be set forth with such clarity as to be understandable. It will not do for a court to be compelled to guess at the theory underlying the agency's action ...

Applying this rule and its corollary, the Court was unable to sustain the Commission's original action. ... During the period when successive reorganization plans proposed by the management were before the Commission, the officers, directors and controlling stockholders of Federal purchased a substantial amount [about 7 1/2%] of Federal's preferred stock on the over-the-counter market. Under the [proposed] plan, this preferred stock was to be converted into common stock of a new corporation; on the basis of the purchases of preferred stock, the management would have received more than 10% of this new common stock. It was frankly admitted that the management's purpose in buying the preferred stock was to protect its interest in the new company. It was also plain that there was no fraud or lack of disclosure in making these purchases.

But the Commission would not approve the [proposed] plan so long as the preferred stock purchased by the management was to be treated on a parity with the other preferred stock. It felt that the officers and directors of a holding company in process of reorganization under the Act were fiduciaries and were under a duty not to trade in the securities of that company during the reorganization period. And so the plan was amended to provide that the preferred stock acquired by the management, unlike that held by others, was not to be converted into the new common stock; instead, it was to be surrendered at cost plus [4 1/2% interest]. As amended, the plan was approved by the Commission over the management's objections.

The Court interpreted the Commission's order approving this amended plan as grounded solely upon judicial authority. The Commission appeared to have treated the preferred stock acquired by the management in accordance with what it thought were standards theretofore recognized by courts. If it intended to create new standards growing out of its experience in effectuating the legislative policy, it failed to express itself with sufficient clarity and precision to be so understood. Hence the order was judged by the only standards clearly invoked by the Commission. On that basis, the order could not stand. The opinion pointed out that courts do not impose upon officers and directors of a corporation any fiduciary duty to its stockholders which precludes them, merely because they are officers and directors, from buying and selling the corporation's stock. Nor was it felt that the cases upon which the Commission relied established any principles of law or equity which in themselves would be sufficient to justify this order.

The opinion further noted that neither Congress nor the Commission had promulgated any general rule proscribing such action as the purchase of preferred stock by Federal's management. And the only judge-made rule of equity which might have justified the Commission's order related to fraud or mismanagement of the reorganization by the officers and directors, matters which were admittedly absent in this situation.

[On remand from Chenery I, Federal's management again sought approval of a plan in which they would participate in the reorganized enterprise through conversion of the preferred stock they had acquired. The SEC again denied approval. The D.C. Circuit reversed, believing this to be inconsistent with Chenery I.]

The latest order of the Commission definitely avoids the fatal error of relying on judicial precedents which do not sustain it. This time, after a thorough reexamination of the problem in light of the purposes and standards of the Holding Company Act, the Commission has concluded that the proposed transaction is inconsistent with the . . . Act. It has drawn heavily upon its accumulated experience in dealing with utility reorganizations. And it has expressed its reasons with a clarity and thoroughness that admit of no doubt as to the underlying basis of its order.

The argument is pressed upon us, however, that the Commission was foreclosed from taking such a step following our prior decision. It is said that, in the absence of findings of conscious wrongdoing on the part of Federal's management, the Commission could not determine by an order in this particular case that it was inconsistent with the statutory standards to permit Federal's management to realize a profit through the reorganization purchases. All that it could do was to enter an order allowing an amendment to the plan so that the proposed transaction could be consummated. Under this view, the Commission would be free only to promulgate a general rule outlawing such profits in future utility reorganizations; but such a rule would have to be prospective in nature and have no retroactive effect upon the instant situation.

We reject this contention, for it grows out of a misapprehension of our prior decision and of the Commission's statutory duties. We held no more and no less than that the Commission's first order was unsupportable for the reasons supplied by that agency. But when the case left this Court, the problem whether Federal's management should be treated equally with other preferred stockholders still lacked a final and complete answer. It was clear that the Commission could not give a negative answer by resort to prior judicial declarations. And it was also clear that the Commission was not bound by settled judicial precedents in a situation of this nature. Still unsettled, however, was the answer the Commission might give were it to bring to bear on the facts the proper administrative and statutory considerations, a function which belongs exclusively to the Commission in the first instance. The administrative process had taken an erroneous rather than a final turn. Hence we carefully refrained from expressing any views as to the propriety of an order rooted in the proper and relevant considerations.

... The fact that the Commission had committed a legal error in its first disposition of the case certainly gave Federal's management no vested right to receive the benefits of such an order. After the remand was made, therefore, the Commission was bound to deal with the problem afresh, performing the function delegated to it by Congress. ...

The absence of a general rule or regulation governing management trading during reorganization did not affect the Commission's duties in relation to the particular proposal before it. The Commission was asked to grant or deny effectiveness to a proposed amendment to Federal's reorganization plan whereby the management would be accorded parity treatment on its holdings. It could do that only in the form of an order, entered after a due consideration of the particular facts in light of the relevant and proper standards. That was true regardless of whether those standards previously had been spelled out in a general rule or regulation. Indeed, if the Commission rightly felt that the proposed amendment was inconsistent with those standards, an order giving effect to the amendment merely because there was no general rule or regulation covering the matter would be unjustified.

It is true that our prior decision explicitly recognized the possibility that the Commission might have promulgated a general rule dealing with this problem under its statutory rule-making powers, in which case the issue for our consideration would have been entirely different from that which did confront us. But we did not mean to imply thereby that the failure of the Commission to anticipate this problem and to promulgate a general rule withdrew all power from that agency to perform its statutory duty in this case. To hold that the Commission had no alternative in this proceeding but to approve the proposed transaction, while formulating any general rules it might desire for use in future cases of this nature, would be to stultify the administrative process. That we refuse to do.

Since the Commission, unlike a court, does have the ability to make new law prospectively through the exercise of its rule-making powers, it has less reason to rely upon ad hoc adjudication to formulate new standards of conduct within the framework of the Holding Company Act. The function of filling in the interstices of the Act should be performed, as much as possible, through this quasi-legislative promulgation of rules to be applied in the future. But any rigid requirement to that effect would make the administrative process inflexible and incapable of dealing with many of the specialized problems which arise. Not every principle essential to the effective administration of a statute can or should be cast immediately into the mold of a general rule. Some principles must await their own development, while others must be adjusted to meet particular, unforeseeable situations. In performing its important functions in these respects, therefore, an administrative agency must be equipped to act either by general rule or by individual order. To insist upon one form of action to the exclusion of the other is to exalt form over necessity.

In other words, problems may arise in a case which the administrative agency could not reasonably foresee, problems which must be solved despite the absence of a relevant general rule. Or the agency may not have had sufficient experience with a particular problem to warrant rigidifying its tentative judgment into a hard and fast rule. Or the problem may be so specialized and varying in nature as to be impossible of capture within the boundaries of a general rule. In those situations, the agency must retain power to deal with the problems on a case-to-case basis if the administrative process is to be effective. There is thus a very definite place for the case-by-case evolution of statutory standards. And the choice made between proceeding by general rule or by individual, ad hoc litigation is one that lies primarily in the informed discretion of the administrative agency.

Hence we refuse to say that the Commission, which had not previously been confronted with the problem of management trading during reorganization, was forbidden from utilizing this particular proceeding for announcing and applying a new standard of conduct. That such action might have a retroactive effect was not necessarily fatal to its validity. Every case of first impression has a retroactive effect, whether the new principle is announced by a court or by an administrative agency. But such retroactivity must be balanced against the mischief of producing a result which is contrary to a statutory design or to legal and equitable principles. If that mischief is greater than the ill effect of the retroactive application of a new standard, it is not the type of retroactivity which is condemned by law.

. . . [The Commission's] view was that the amended plan would involve the issuance of securities on terms "detrimental to the public interest or the interest of investors" . . . and would result in an "unfair or inequitable distribution of voting power" among the Federal security holders . . . It was led to this result "not by proof that the [Chenerys] committed acts of conscious wrongdoing but by the character of the conflicting interests created by the interveners' program of stock purchases carried out while plans for reorganization were under consideration." [The Commission had emphasized both the "normal powers" possessed by management and the "special powers" management obtains during voluntary reorganization; it "felt that a management program of stock purchases would give rise to the temptation and the opportunity to shape the reorganization proceeding so as to encourage public selling on the market at low prices."]

The Commission further felt that its answer should be the same even where proof of intentional wrongdoing on the management's part is lacking. Assuming a conflict of interests, the Commission thought that the absence of actual misconduct is immaterial; injury to the public investors and to the corporation may result just as readily. "Questionable transactions may be explained away, and an abuse of investors and the administrative process may be perpetrated without evil intent, yet the injury will remain." Moreover, the Commission was of the view that the delays and the difficulties involved in probing the mental processes and personal integrity of corporate officials do not warrant any distinction on the basis of evil intent, the plain fact being "that an absence of unfairness or detriment in cases of this sort would be practically impossible to establish by proof."
. . .

The scope of our review of an administrative order wherein a new principle is announced and applied is no different from that which pertains to ordinary administrative action. The wisdom of the principle adopted is none of our concern. Our duty is at an end when it becomes evident that the Commission's action is based upon substantial evidence and is consistent with the authority granted by Congress. . . .

The Commission's conclusion here rests squarely in that area where administrative judgments are entitled to the greatest amount of weight by appellate courts. It is the product of administrative experience, appreciation of the complexities of the problem, realization of the statutory policies, and responsible treatment of the uncontested facts. It is the type of judgment which administrative agencies are best equipped to make and which justifies the use of the administrative process. Whether we agree or disagree with the result reached, it is an allowable judgment which we cannot disturb.

Reversed.

■ JUSTICE JACKSON, dissenting [joined by JUSTICE FRANKFURTER].

The Court by this present decision sustains the identical administrative order which only recently it held invalid. As the Court correctly notes, the Commission has only "recast its rationale and reached the same result." There being no change in the order, no additional evidence in the record and no amendment of relevant legislation, it is clear that there has been a shift in attitude between that of the controlling membership of the Court when the case was first here and that of those who have the power of decision on this second review.[1]

---

1. [Ed.] Chenery I had been a 4–3 decision, in which Justice Frankfurter wrote for himself, Chief Justice Stone, and Justices Roberts and Jackson. Justices Black, Reed and Murphy dissented. Justice Douglas had not participated, and there had been one

I feel constrained to disagree with the reasoning offered to rationalize this shift. It makes judicial review of administrative orders a hopeless formality for the litigant ... It reduces the judicial process in such cases to a mere feint. ...

... The basic assumption of the earlier opinion as therein stated was, *"But before transactions otherwise legal can be outlawed or denied their usual business consequences, they must fall under the ban of some standards of conduct prescribed by an agency of government authorized to prescribe such standards ..."* The basic assumption of the present opinion is stated thus: *"The absence of a general rule or regulation governing management trading during reorganization did not affect the Commission's duties in relation to the particular proposal before it."* This puts in juxtaposition the two conflicting philosophies which produce opposite results in the same case and on the same facts. The difference between the first and the latest decision of the Court is thus simply the difference between holding that administrative orders must have a basis in law and a holding that absence of a legal basis is no ground on which courts may annul them.

As there admittedly is no law or regulation to support this order, we peruse the Court's opinion diligently to find on what grounds it is now held that the Court of Appeals, on pain of being reversed for error, was required to stamp this order with its approval. We find but one. That is the principle of judicial deference to administrative experience. That argument is five times stressed in as many different contexts ...

What are we to make of this reiterated deference to "administrative experience" when in another context the Court says, "Hence, we refuse to say that the Commission, *which had not previously been confronted with the problem of management trading during reorganization,* was forbidden from utilizing this particular proceeding for announcing and applying *a new standard of conduct.'"*? (Emphasis supplied.)

The Court's reasoning adds up to this: The Commission must be sustained because of its accumulated experience in solving a problem with which it had never before been confronted!

Of course, thus to uphold the Commission by professing to find that it has enunciated a "new standard of conduct" brings the Court squarely against the invalidity of retroactive law-making. But the Court does not falter. "That such action might have a retroactive effect was not necessarily fatal to its validity." "But such retroactivity must be balanced against the mischief of producing a result which is contrary to a statutory design or to legal and equitable principles." Of course, if what these parties did really was condemned by "statutory design" or "legal and equitable principles," it could be stopped without resort to a new rule and there would be no retroactivity to condone. But if it had been the Court's view that some law already prohibited the purchases, it would hardly have been necessary

vacancy. By the time of Chenery II, Vinson had replaced Stone, Burton had replaced Roberts, and Rutledge had filled the vacancy. Justice Rutledge joined the three Chenery I dissenters to form the Chenery II majority, Justice Burton concurred in the judgment without opinion, and Chief Justice Vinson joined Justice Douglas in not participating. Of the original Chenery I majority, this left only Justices Frankfurter and Jackson to dissent.

three sentences earlier to hold that the Commission was not prohibited "from utilizing this particular proceeding for announcing and applying a *new standard of conduct.*" (Emphasis supplied.)

I give up. Now I realize fully what Mark Twain meant when he said, "The more you explain it, the more I don't understand it."

. . . [A]dministrative experience is of weight in judicial review only to this point—it is a persuasive reason for deference to the Commission in the exercise of its discretionary powers under and within the law. It cannot be invoked to support action outside of the law. . . .

The truth is that in this decision the Court approves the Commission's assertion of power to govern the matter *without* law, power to force surrender of stock so purchased whenever it will, and power also to overlook such acquisitions if it so chooses. The reasons which will lead it to take one course as against the other remain locked in its own breast, and it has not and apparently does not intend to commit them to any rule or regulation. This administrative authoritarianism, this power to decide without law, is what the Court seems to approve in so many words: "The absence of a general rule or regulation governing management trading during reorganization did not affect the Commission's duties . . ." This seems to me to undervalue and to belittle the place of law, even in the system of administrative justice. It calls to mind Mr. Justice Cardozo's statement that "Law as a guide to conduct is reduced to the level of mere futility if it is unknown and unknowable." . . .

NOTES ON CHENERY

(1) *Chenery I.* Before moving on to the principal case, it is worth emphasizing an enduring proposition from the *first* round of the Chenery litigation—a proposition that shaped the remaining episodes and much other administrative law:

> When the case was first here, we emphasized a simple but fundamental rule of administrative law. That rule is to the effect that a reviewing court, in dealing with a determination or judgment which an administrative agency alone is authorized to make, must judge the propriety of such action solely by the grounds invoked by the agency. If those grounds are inadequate or improper, the court is powerless to affirm the administrative action by substituting what it considers to be a more adequate or proper basis. To do so would propel the court into the domain which Congress has set aside exclusively for the administrative agency.
>
> We also emphasized in our prior decision an important corollary of the foregoing rule. If the administrative action is to be tested by the basis upon which it purports to rest, that basis must be set forth with such clarity as to be understandable. It will not do for a court to be compelled to guess at the theory underlying the agency's action . . .

The first paragraph describes a relationship between reviewing court and agency that differs markedly from that between reviewing court and trial court. Decisions from trial or intermediate appellate courts are regularly sustained for reasons other than the lower courts gave. The last sentence of the paragraph explains the difference: responsibility for setting policy has been allocated to the agency, not the courts. Doesn't the corollary "emphasized" in Chenery I (a decision predating passage of the APA) help explain how statements of basis and purpose have been encouraged into dimensions exceeding the "concise" and "general"? A second corollary formed the battleground for Chenery II—whether the agency, having been shown its reasoning error, may reach the same outcome using a different theory.

As remarked in editorial footnote 1, Chenery I was closely divided over the question whether existing *judicial* authority—in particular, equity cases defining the obligations of fiduciaries—was adequate to support the SEC's initial decision. If the legality of the Chenerys' conduct under equity precedents was indeed so close, is some of the sting removed from the "retroactivity" of the Commission's decision? That is, would the dissent's case be stronger if the SEC's action had come with no warning from existing legal sources that the Chenerys' course of conduct was, at the least, problematic? In considering the question of constraints on the agency's power to use adjudication vs. rulemaking as the vehicle for regulatory policymaking, pay careful attention to the possible difference between constraints based on reliance interests, and those grounded "merely" in beliefs about the peculiar strengths and weaknesses of these two procedural modes.

(2) *One or the Other?* Be careful to distinguish the question *how* an agency goes about making its law, from the question under what circumstances it may be under an obligation to do so, one way or another. Aspects of the latter question surface in these materials in the discussions of delegation, e.g., p. 83, due process, p. 832, and agency obligations of explanation, both in adjudications and in rulemaking. In PEARSON v. SHALALA, 164 F.3d 650 (D.C.Cir.1999), the court vacated and remanded for reconsideration the FDA's refusal to permit the marketers of dietary supplements to make certain health claims on the supplements' labels, on the ground that the available evidence to support the claim did not meet a statutory standard of "significant scientific agreement." The FDA had not explained just how it measured significance or otherwise defined the phrase: "[T]he APA requires the agency to explain why it rejects their proposed health claims—to do so adequately necessarily implies giving some definitional content to the phrase 'significant scientific agreement.' We think this proposition is squarely rooted in the prohibition under the APA that an agency not engage in arbitrary and capricious action. See 5 U.S.C. § 706(2)(A) (1994). It simply will not do for a government agency to declare—without explanation—that a proposed course of private action is not approved. To refuse to define the criteria it is applying is equivalent to simply saying no without explanation. . . .

"To be sure, Justice Stewart once said, in declining to define obscenity, 'I know it when I see it,' Jacobellis v. Ohio, 378 U.S. 184, 197 (1964) (Stewart, J., concurring), which is basically the approach the FDA takes to the term 'significant scientific agreement.' But the Supreme Court is not subject to the Administrative Procedure Act. Nor for that matter is the Congress. That is why we are quite unimpressed with the government's argument that the agency is justified in employing this standard without definition because Congress used the same standard in 21 U.S.C.A. § 343(r)(3)(B)(i). Presumably—we do not decide—the FDA in applying that statutory standard would similarly be obliged under the APA to give it content.

"That is not to say that the agency was necessarily required to define the term in its initial general regulation—or indeed that it is obliged to issue a comprehensive definition all at once. The agency is entitled to proceed case by case or ... sub-regulation by subregulation, but it must be possible for the regulated class to perceive the principles which are guiding agency action. Accordingly, on remand, the FDA must explain what it means by significant scientific agreement or, at minimum, what it does not mean."[1]

(3) *Rulemaking's Advantages?*

(a) RICHARD J. PIERCE, JR., TWO PROBLEMS IN ADMINISTRATIVE LAW: POLITICAL POLARITY ON THE DISTRICT OF COLUMBIA CIRCUIT AND JUDICIAL DETERRENCE OF AGENCY RULEMAKING, 1988 Duke L.J. 300, 308–09: "Judges and academics long ago reached rare consensus on the desirability of agency policymaking through the process of informal rulemaking. ... Rulemaking yields higher-quality policy decisions than adjudication because it invites broad participation in the policymaking process by all affected entities and groups, and because it encourages the agency to focus on the broad effects of its policy rather than the often idiosyncratic adjudicative facts of a specific dispute. Rulemaking enhances efficiency in three ways. It avoids the needless cost and delay of finding legislative facts through trial-type procedures[2]; it eliminates the need to relitigate policy issues in the context of disputes with no material differences in adjudicative facts; and, it yields much clearer 'rules' than can be extracted from a decision resolving a specific dispute. Rulemaking also provides greater fairness in three ways. It provides affected parties with clearer notice of what conduct is permissible and impermissible; it avoids the widely disparate temporal impact of agency policy decisions made and implemented through ad hoc adjudication; and, it allows all potentially affected segments of the public to participate in the process of determining the rules that will govern their conduct and affect their lives."

(b) E. DONALD ELLIOTT, RE-INVENTING RULEMAKING, 41 Duke L.J. 1490, 1492 (1992): "There can be no abstract answer to the question whether rulemaking or case–by–case evolution is the better way to make policy; in each case the answer depends on a variety of factors, including: how sure the agency is about what policy it wishes to adopt, how frequently the agency anticipates the question will come up, whether the issue is inherently entangled with other issues that can best be addressed comprehensively, and what other issues are currently pressing for the agency's attention." See also Glen O. Robinson, The Making of Administrative Policy: Another Look at Rulemaking and Adjudication and Administrative Procedure Reform, 118 U.Pa.L.Rev. 485, 535 (1970).

---

1. [Ed.] Compare Morton v. Ruiz, 415 U.S. 199 (1974), noted in Chapter 7, p. below.

2. [Ed.] See Heckler v. Campbell, p. 453 below.

AN ORGANIZATIONAL NOTE

A reader of Chenery II might wonder whether, in practice, agency "choice" between rulemaking and adjudication is ever likely to be forced—in one direction or the other—by judicial oversight. If an agency self-consciously acts as if it is principally making policy, rather than deciding a concrete case, is that a reason to require it to act by rulemaking rather than in the adjudicatory style of the common law? One frequent outcome of adjudication—as the Chenerys learned to their dismay—is that a rule new-minted in the decision is applied to prior behavior. In Chenery, one could respond to any fairness concerns about this by observing that the legality of their behavior was uncertain at the time the Chenerys acted. Competent counsel would have had to advise that rejection of their application on equitable grounds was possible. In what, if any, circumstances might fairness concerns require the use of prospective rulemaking to effect a change in agency policy? Suppose, on the other hand, there are no fairness concerns because the adoption of "new" agency policy had been clearly foreshadowed—for example by publication of a notice of proposed rulemaking, or by the agency's prior adoption of a rule that has been vacated and remanded for correction of errors that cast no doubt on the agency's authority properly to readopt the same rule? Then, may the agency act retrospectively *by rule*? Finally, do the procedural consequences for participants of the choice of rulemaking over adjudication—i.e., the substitution of a general right of comment for individual adjudicatory procedures—ever preclude the use of rulemaking? We have already seen this in Vermont Yankee, where the rulemaking substituted for adjudicatory determination of issues hard to cast in individualistic terms. But suppose a rule purports to settle matters having a more individual cast—whether, for example, airplane pilots are fit to fly after they reach age 60? Must an adjudicatory hearing be afforded each pilot on fitness to fly before his or her license is terminated? These are the questions of the following four subsections.

(i) THE SELF–CONSCIOUS USE OF ADJUDICATION FOR POLICY–MAKING

The National Labor Relations Board has been a focal point of concerns about the use of adjudication for setting policy. The NLRB operates in a setting—labor-management relations—of high political moment, characterized both by frequent legislative stalemates over enacting statutory revisions and by patterns of judicial review that vary considerably between pro- and anti-union areas of the country.[1] This setting at least partly explains a frequently noted characteristic of NLRB behavior over the decades: the

---

1. James J. Brudney, a Famous Victory: Collective Bargaining Protections and the Statutory Aging Process, 74 North Carolina Law Review 939, 987 (1996). The fact that circuits do not publish all opinions adds a further dimension to perceptions regarding the varying judicial sympathy accorded to agency judgments. From 1986 to 1993, the Fourth Circuit did not appear to be significantly pro or anti union when its published opinions were compared with those of other circuits, but that court became significantly anti-union when unpublished decisions were also included in the analysis. James J. Brudney, S. Schiavoni, and Deborah J. Merritt, Judicial Hostility Toward Labor Unions? Applying the Social Background Model to a Celebrated Concern, 60 Ohio State Law Journal 1675, 1725, 1732 (1999)

Board hardly ever engages in rulemaking about its regulatory concerns. Its first substantive rule was issued in the late 1980s, as you may shortly see. If you read the Supreme Court's recent decision in the Allentown Mack case, p. 953, you will see the Court highly suspicious that the NLRB had been manipulating its processes of case-by-case adjudication to achieve covert policy ends. As you have repeatedly learned elsewhere, the law that emerges from common-law style adjudication is often obscure.

In the late 60's, as enthusiasm for rulemaking was building, the NLRB experimented with adapting its adjudicatory processes towards rulemaking procedures. Having identified a policy issue in a pending matter, it would broadly invite interested parties—national unions, say—to participate as amicus curiae; and it would announce (as courts sometimes do when concerned about the unfairness of applying new common law to the parties before them) that a new policy would apply only prospectively. This practice first came to the Supreme Court's attention in NLRB v. WYMAN-GORDON CO., 394 U.S. 759 (1969). The Board had applied, as a precedent to the Wyman–Gordon Company, a standard adopted in an earlier adjudication involving another company, "Excelsior." In the Excelsior case, it had both invited wide "amicus" participation *and* decided to apply the new standard of employer conduct it announced there only prospectively. In a confusing and badly fractured set of opinions, differing majorities of Justices found (i) that the Excelsior standard was procedurally invalid (because its prospective application made it a "rule" which must be adopted through rulemaking, rather than adjudicative, procedures); and (ii) that the Board could nonetheless properly apply the standard as precedent to Wyman–Gordon in a subsequent adjudicatory proceeding. Four years later, the Second Circuit thought it had found a case in which the use of rulemaking *could* be required:

Bell Aerospace Co. v. National Labor Relations Board

United States Court of Appeals for the Second Circuit, 1973.
475 F.2d 485.

■ Before FRIENDLY, CHIEF JUDGE, and OAKES and TIMBERS, CIRCUIT JUDGES.

■ FRIENDLY, CHIEF JUDGE:

[Bell Aerospace Co. refused to bargain with the buyers at one of its facilities, claiming they were "managerial employees" outside the collective bargaining process established by the National Labor Relations Act. The Board concluded that the buyers were entitled to unionize. This conclusion was controversial in two respects. First, the Board apparently now interpreted the Act as excluding only those managerial personnel whose duties and alignment with the employer were such as to create a conflict of interest were they to unionize. A long line of earlier Board decisions (some of which predated an extensive round of congressional adjustments to the Act) had held *all* managerial employees to be excluded. Second, even if *some* managerial personnel were covered by the Act, a related line of Board decisions had treated buyers as allied with management—and therefore unable to unionize even under the new interpretation.

On the first point, the court concluded that congressional understanding of long–standing agency practice precluded the Board from reinterpreting the Act to exclude only managerial personnel whose unionization would create a conflict of interest.]

. . . On the other hand, despite the series of [Board decisions involving buyers], we do not think the Board would be precluded, on proper proceedings, from determining that buyers, or some types of buyers, are not true "managerial employees" and consequently come within the protection of [the Act]. It might seem that this conclusion would lead to the grant of enforcement here, since there was substantial evidence that Bell's buyers were not sufficiently high in the hierarchy to constitute "managerial employees," as that term has been defined [in earlier cases]. It does not
. . .

. . . [W]hile the Board was not precluded from reversing itself on the position that buyers, or some buyers, were not "managerial employees," we hold that, particularly in light of the justified contrary belief the Board had engendered, it could not do this in the manner that was done here. This is an appropriate case in which to give effect to the Supreme Court's observation in the second Chenery decision, largely disregarded by the Board for a quarter century:

> The function of filling in the interstices of the Act should be performed, as much as possible, through this quasi-legislative promulgation of rules to be applied in the future.

Such a holding is also in line with the considered dicta in NLRB v. Wyman–Gordon Co., 394 U.S. 759 (1969).

. . . [E]xpressions by a majority of the [Wyman–Gordon] Justices point against the procedure the Board followed here. The plurality opinion of Mr. Justice Fortas, joined by the Chief Justice, Mr. Justice Stewart and Mr. Justice White, emphasized:

> The rule-making provisions of that Act, which the Board would avoid, were designed to assure fairness and mature consideration of rules of general application. . . . They may not be avoided by the process of making rules in the course of adjudicatory proceedings.

Mr. Justice Douglas, [who had agreed with both of Wyman–Gordon's arguments], said this:

> A rule like the one in Excelsior is designed to fit all cases at all times. It is not particularized to special facts. It is a statement of far-reaching policy covering all future representation elections. It should therefore have been put down for the public hearing prescribed by the Act. The rule-making procedure performs important functions. It gives notice to an entire segment of society of those controls or regimentation that is forthcoming. It gives an opportunity for persons affected to be heard. . . . Agencies discover [through rule-making proceedings] that they are not always repositories of ultimate wisdom; they learn from the suggestions of outsiders and often benefit from that advice. . . . I would hold the agencies governed by the rule-making procedure strictly to its requirements and not allow them to play fast and loose as the National Labor Relations Board apparently likes to do.

Mr. Justice Harlan, likewise dissenting, after pointing to the Board's decision to apply the Excelsior rule only prospectively as implying that it was "such a departure from pre-existing understandings that it would be unfair to impose the rule upon the parties in pending matters," continued:

[I]t is precisely in these situations, in which established patterns of conduct are revolutionized, that rule-making procedures perform the vital functions that my Brother Douglas describes so well in a dissenting opinion with which I basically agree. . . . Either the rule-making provisions are to be enforced or they are not. Before the Board may be permitted to adopt a rule that so significantly alters pre-existing labor-management understandings, it must be required to conduct a satisfactory rule-making proceeding, so that it will have the benefit of wide-ranging argument before it enacts its proposed solution to an important problem.

. . . [I]f the statements quoted from the opinions of six Justices in Wyman–Gordon are to mean anything, they must be read as demanding rule-making here, and given the Board's long-standing negative attitude, as requiring a court to order it. The Board was prescribing a new policy, not just with respect to 25 buyers in Wheatfield, N.Y., but in substance, to use Mr. Justice Douglas' phrase, "to fit all cases at all times." There must be tens of thousands of manufacturing, wholesale and retail units which employ buyers, and hundreds of thousands of the latter. Yet the Board did not even attempt to inform industry and labor organizations . . . of its proposed new policy and to invite comment thereon, as it has sometimes done in the past, and did in Excelsior . . . Although policy-making by adjudication often cannot be avoided in unfair labor practice cases, since the parties have already acted and the Board must decide one way or the other, there is no such problem in a representation case.[1] Finally, the argument for rule-making is especially strong when the Board is proposing to reverse a long-standing and oft-repeated policy on which industry and labor have relied. To be sure, the change of policy here in question did not expose an employer to new and unexpected liability . . . The point rather is that when the Board has so long been committed to a position, it should be particularly sure that it has all available information before adopting another, in a setting where nothing stands in the way of a rule-making proceeding except the Board's congenital disinclination to follow [that] procedure . . .

The petition to review is granted and enforcement is denied . . .

National Labor Relations Board v. Bell Aerospace Co.

Supreme Court of the United States, 1974.
416 U.S. 267.

■ JUSTICE POWELL delivered the opinion of the Court.

[After canvassing administrative practice and legislative history, the Supreme Court agreed that the NLRB "is not now free" to reinterpret the

---

1. While nominally this comes before us as an unfair labor practice case, in substance the attack is on the Board's decision, unre- viewable at the time, in the representation proceeding.

Act to exclude only those managerial employees susceptible to conflicts of interest if unionized.]

In view of our conclusion, the case must be remanded to permit the Board to apply the proper legal standard in determining the status of these buyers. [citing Chenery I]. We express no opinion as to whether these buyers fall within the category of "managerial employees."

The Court of Appeals also held that, although the Board was not precluded from determining that buyers or some types of buyers were not "managerial employees," it could do so only by invoking its rulemaking procedures . . . We disagree.

At the outset, the precise nature of the present issue must be noted. The question is not whether the Board should have resorted to rulemaking, or in fact improperly promulgated a "rule," when in the context of the prior representation proceeding it held that the Act covers all "managerial employees" except those meeting the new "conflict of interest in labor relations" touchstone. Our conclusion that the Board applied the wrong legal standard makes consideration of that issue unnecessary. Rather, the present question is whether on remand the Board must invoke its rulemaking procedures if it determines, in light of our opinion, that these buyers are not "managerial employees" under the Act. The Court of Appeals thought that rulemaking was required because *any* Board finding that the company's buyers are not "managerial" would be contrary to its prior decisions and would presumably be in the nature of a general rule designed "to fit all cases at all times."

. . . Chenery II and Wyman–Gordon make plain that the Board is not precluded from announcing new principles in an adjudicative proceeding and that the choice between rulemaking and adjudication lies in the first instance within the Board's discretion. Although there may be situations where the Board's reliance on adjudication would amount to an abuse of discretion or a violation of the Act, nothing in the present case would justify such a conclusion. Indeed, there is ample indication that adjudication is especially appropriate in the instant context. As the Court of Appeals noted, "[t]here must be tens of thousands of manufacturing, wholesale and retail units which employ buyers, and hundreds of thousands of the latter." Moreover, duties of buyers vary widely depending on the company or industry. It is doubtful whether any generalized standard could be framed which would have more than marginal utility. The Board thus has reason to proceed with caution, developing its standards in a case-by-case manner with attention to the specific character of the buyers' authority and duties in each company. The Board's judgment that adjudication best serves this purpose is entitled to great weight.

The possible reliance of industry on the Board's past decisions with respect to buyers does not require a different result. It has not been shown that the adverse consequences ensuing from such reliance are so substantial that the Board should be precluded from reconsidering the issue in an adjudicative proceeding. Furthermore, this is not a case in which some new liability is sought to be imposed on individuals for past actions which were taken in good-faith reliance on Board pronouncements. Nor are fines or damages involved here. . . .

It is true, of course, that rulemaking would provide the Board with a forum for soliciting the informed views of those affected in industry and labor before embarking on a new course. But surely the Board has discretion to decide that the adjudicative procedures in this case may also produce the relevant information necessary to mature and fair consideration of the issues. Those most immediately affected, the buyers and the company in the particular case, are accorded a full opportunity to be heard before the Board makes its determination.

The judgment of the Court of Appeals is therefore affirmed in part and reversed in part, and the cause remanded to that court with directions to remand to the Board for further proceedings in conformity with this opinion.

[JUSTICES WHITE, BRENNAN, STEWART and MARSHALL concurred "that the Board was not required to resort to rulemaking in deciding this case." They dissented from the holding that the Act excludes all managerial employees.]

NOTES

(1) MARK H. GRUNEWALD, THE NLRB'S FIRST RULEMAKING: AN EXERCISE IN PRAGMATISM, 41 Duke L.J. 274, 281–82 (1991): "The policy product of Board adjudications generally takes one of two forms. First, there are cases in the common law mode that involve application of established policy to particular facts.[1] Cases of this kind, because of subtle changes over time, represent an evolutionary, incremental form of policymaking. Second, there are cases in which the Board, acting more in a legislative mode, uses the immediate controversy simply as a vehicle to announce more drastic policy changes without much regard for the particular facts.[2] When proceeding in the legislative mode, the essence of the policy product is indistinguishable from the product of a rulemaking. . . . [P]olicy formulated in this fashion [has] an important feature. It is formulated exclusively from *argument* and *evidence* that the *parties* to the proceeding offer (evaluated in light of the Board's expertise). Consequently, it formally lacks as a basis the breadth of data that rulemaking submissions can provide, and even the data upon which it is based is presented by a limited number of participants. The seriousness of these shortcomings is then a critical issue in evaluating the choice not to use notice and comment rulemaking in cases taking this form. Cases taking the traditional common law form raise no such questions and would arise even where true rules requiring more than mechanical application were in place.

"The breadth and sources of the data for policymaking are thus both obvious and fundamental concerns. Concern with policy clarity and stability is more subtle and perhaps peripheral. Because the line between the two

1. This class of cases is well illustrated by the fact–intensive unfair labor practice adjudications in which the Board determines whether particular bargaining meets the "good faith" standard of section 8(d) of the NLRA.

2. This class of cases is well illustrated by Excelsior Underwear, Inc. . . .

forms of adjudication described above is not always clear, important policy changes can be lost (or hidden) in the reasoning process of adjudication. Similarly, the opportunity exists for unanticipated policy shifts, unanticipated both in the sense of limited notice of the prospect of change and in the volatility of existing policy majorities in the face of changes in Board membership. Rulemaking thus provides clarity, not in the sense of the specificity of policy (which may vary from rule to rule), but in the identification of a decision as a policy choice. It also provides stability, not in the sense of unchangeable policy, but in policy that can not be changed without a process focused on the policy choice.

"Finally, the policymaking procedure can affect the efficiency of the enforcement process. To the extent that a single rulemaking can lay to rest important policy issues that would otherwise require a long series of adjudications, enforcement is advanced. Moreover, in rulemaking, the policymaking agenda can be set internally with a view toward enforcement needs, rather than externally in the form of cases that parties choose to press. Nevertheless, much of the value of rulemaking remains dependent upon time expended, resources consumed, and, most importantly, the form of the rulemaking product."

(2) *Differing Engagements by the Political Branches?* The quality of empirical data and the range of constituency viewpoints are not the only inputs affected when agencies make policy through rulemaking rather than adjudication. Suppose, as the prefatory notes suggested, that the Board's general avoidance of rulemaking is in part the product of its political situation. As a student law review editor perceptively noted, the NLRB's preference for adjudication allows it to "legislate in controversial areas without giving critics a clear and final rule to attack" and makes it "difficult for a congressional committee to justify spending valuable time on a matter for which the agency has announced no clear and final standard." NLRB Rulemaking: Political Reality Versus Procedural Fairness, 89 Yale L.J. 982, 995–96 (1980). Might the differing nature of political interactions as between rulemaking and adjudication influence other agencies as well? As you may already have learned in readings about the reach of presidential power, p. 143 ff. and p. 444 ff., White House "management" of rulemakings is considerably less constrained than its management of adjudications— even, one may suppose, for an "independent" agency like the NLRB. Might this encourage agencies to employ case-by-case policymaking?

Alan B. Morrison—for many years the lead attorney for Ralph Nader's NGO Public Citizen (and in that role responsible for many of the cases you read in these pages)—suggests that the much-touted capacity of rulemaking to produce clearer, more accessible articulation of policy may not be an unalloyed blessing from the agency's perspective: "... [A]s the Federal Trade Commission has discovered, proceeding by rulemaking also has its hazards, because it makes an agency's actions and policies more visible and hence more vulnerable to public and congressional criticism.[3] In the case of

---

3. The FTC's efforts to promulgate even a modest rule governing the sale of used cars provoked a legislative veto. ... Another area of FTC rulemaking that aroused public and congressional ire was regulation of children's advertising. See, e.g., 15 U.S.C. § 57a(i) (1982) (specifically prohibiting the FTC from promulgating rules to ban certain children's advertising as unfair).

the FTC, rulemaking has led to continued efforts to cut back the agency's powers, even though it largely avoids rulemaking today. In addition, because anyone can submit a comment in a rulemaking, without regard to the rules of evidence and without legal assistance, it is much easier for large segments of the public to become involved. This means rulemakings are often more controversial than adjudications, whose very processes are hidden from outsiders." 72 Va.L.Rev. at 255–56. Alan B. Morrison, The Administrative Procedure Act: A Living and Responsive Law, 72 Va. L. Rev. 253, 255–56 (1986). See also Antonin Scalia, "Back to Basics: Making Law Without Making Rules," Regulation 25, 27 (July/August 1981).

(3) *Judicial Differences.* Courts, too, may find rulemaking more conducive to intensive scrutiny of agency policymaking. In the view of some observers, rulemakings have fared relatively poorly in judicial review while courts have been "less demanding when they review agency policymaking under-taken through ad hoc adjudication of specific cases." Richard J. Pierce, Jr., Two Problems in Administrative Law: Political Polarity on the District of Columbia Circuit and Judicial Deterrence of Agency Rulemaking, 1988 Duke L.J. 300, 301. This phenomenon is blamed for compounding the "over–proceduralization" of notice-and-comment rulemaking, and hence further fueling the problem of "regulatory ossification"—with the result that agencies move away from rulemaking towards a regime in which policy is made through adjudication or, in some instances, is simply not made at all. See, e.g., Pierce, 1988 Duke L.J. at 301; Thomas McGarity & Sidney Shapiro, Report to the Administrative Conference on OSHA Rulemaking (1987); Jerry L. Mashaw & David L. Harfst, Regulation and Legal Culture: The Case of Motor Vehicle Safety, 4 Yale J. on Reg. 257, 299–302 (1987). We take up the judicial review dimension of the "regulatory ossification" controversy in Chapter VIII.

(4) *Is it a "Choice"?* In considering these various elements of the rulemak-ing vs. adjudication calculus, it is possible to overstate the deliberateness of the agency's behavior. Consider the findings made by of one of your editors after studying the Department of the Interior, PETER L. STRAUSS, RULES, ADJUDICATIONS, AND OTHER SOURCES OF LAW IN AN EXECUTIVE DEPARTMENT: REFLECTIONS ON THE INTERIOR DEPARTMENT'S ADMINISTRATION OF THE MINING LAW, 74 Colum.L.Rev. 1231, 1245–47, 1275 (1974): "The failure to use rulemak-ing is far less a product of conscious departmental choice than a result of impediments to the making of rules created by the Department's internal procedures. The channels which lead to rulemaking . . . are so clogged with obstacles, and the flow through them so sluggish, that staff members hesitate to use them. Several years may elapse between the initial move-ment towards a rule and its final promulgation. And like an adult game of 'Telephone,' Department personnel complain, what is suggested at the outset for possible rulemaking is often unrecognizable when and if a formal proposal ultimately emerges. Absent commitment at the highest levels, the process is one that is easily blocked at almost any stage by determined opposition. As a result, rulemaking may be consciously avoided by an

individual with an idea for policy change when other means for achieving the same policy ends appear to be available.

"... The procedures themselves do not reflect any policy determination as to when rulemaking is the preferred mode of policy articulation, unless general disfavor can be inferred from the obstacles imposed. ...

"... [T]he concept of 'allocation [of policymaking functions between rulemaking and adjudication]' suggests processes which do not occur. Coordination, unified control over the choice of policymaking technique, much less its outcome, is simply lacking. The principal determinants in the largely unconscious mechanisms by which issues find their way into one or another process are inertia and rulemaking procedures so choked as to be virtually impassable."

(ii) MIGHT THE RETROSPECTIVITY RESULTING FROM ADJUDICATION MAKE THIS CHOICE "UNFAIR"?

Epilepsy Foundation of Northeast Ohio v. National Labor Relations Board

United States Court of Appeals for the District of Columbia Circuit, 2001.
268 F.3d 1095.

■ Before: EDWARDS, ROGERS, and TATEL, CIRCUIT JUDGES.

■ EDWARDS, CIRCUIT JUDGE: [The Epilepsy Foundation challenged an NLRB decision finding that it had committed unfair labor practices when it discharged Ashraful Hasan and Arnis Borgs. Section 7 of the NLRA states that "employees shall have the right ... to engage in other concerted activities for the purpose of collective bargaining or other mutual aid or protection." 29 U.S.C. § 157. In NLRB v. J. Weingarten, Inc., 420 U.S. 251 (1975), the Supreme Court had interpreted § 7 as entitling a union employee to have a union representative present at an investigatory interview which she reasonably believes might result in disciplinary action. In subsequent years, the NLRB vacillated over whether the Weingarten rule gave non-union employees similar prerogatives. In 1982, it extended Weingarten, reasoning that employees in nonunion workplaces have a right to request the presence of a coworker in an investigatory interview which the employee reasonably believes could result in disciplinary action. It reversed itself in a 1985 case, holding that Weingarten principles do not apply in circumstances where there is no certified or recognized union. Three years later, in reaffirming this result, it acknowledged that "the statute might be amenable to other interpretations." Now, this issue reappeared in the Epilepsy Foundation's case. Borgs had unmistakably requested that Hasan be permitted to attend a meeting he and two supervisors, with whom he had certain issues, were scheduled to attend. One of the supervisors denied Borgs' request and, when Borgs refused to meet without Hasan, told him to go home for the day. When he returned the next morning, Borgs was fired for refusing to meet with his supervisors. The Board reinterpreted § 7 to extend the Weingarten rule to nonunion workplaces. It then applied the new rule retroactively and held the Foundation liable for Borgs' discharge.]

The Foundation claims that the holding in this case is unlawful because it cannot be squared with Weingarten. We disagree. The Court's decision in Weingarten did not deal with an employee's request for coworker representation in a nonunion setting, and the Board's decision in this case is a reasonable reading of § 7 of the NLRA. An otherwise reasonable interpretation of § 7 is not made legally infirm because the Board gives *renewed*, rather than new, meaning to a disputed statutory provision. It is a fact of life in NLRB lore that certain substantive provisions of the NLRA invariably fluctuate with the changing compositions of the Board. Because the Board's new interpretation is reasonable under the Act, it is entitled to deference.

[The court's extended discussion of Weingarten and the Board's interpretation of § 7 is omitted. It concluded:] ... The Board's conclusion obviously is debatable (because the Board has "changed its mind" several times in addressing this issue); but the rationale underlying the decision in this case is both clear and reasonable. That is all that is necessary to garner deference from the court. "When a challenge to an agency construction of a statutory provision, fairly conceptualized, really centers on the wisdom of the agency's policy, rather than whether it is a reasonable choice within a gap left open by Congress, the challenge must fail." Chevron U.S.A. Inc. v. Natural Res. Def. Council, Inc., 467 U.S. 837, 866 (1984). The Foundation's challenge here is merely an attack on the wisdom of the agency's policy, and, therefore, the challenge must fail.

B. Retroactivity

The Foundation argues that even if the NLRB's new interpretation of § 7 is upheld, the holding that Weingarten rights are applicable in non-union workplaces should not apply retroactively to impose damages for Borgs' discharge. We agree.

In considering whether to give retroactive application to a new rule, the governing principle is that when there is a "substitution of new law for old law that was reasonably clear," the new rule may justifiably be given prospectively-only effect in order to "protect the settled expectations of those who had relied on the preexisting rule." Williams Natural Gas Co. v. FERC, 3 F.3d 1544, 1554 (D.C.Cir.1993). By contrast, retroactive effect is appropriate for "new applications of [existing] law, clarifications, and additions." Pub. Serv. Co. of Colo. v. FERC, 91 F.3d 1478, 1488 (D.C.Cir. 1996).

In light of this governing principle, there is little doubt here that the Board erred in giving retroactive effect to its new interpretation of § 7. At the time when this case arose, the Board's policy on the application of Weingarten rights was absolutely clear—employees not represented by a union could not invoke Weingarten. Thus, Borgs unquestionably had no right to have a coworker present at an interview with his supervisors. And the employer obviously acted in conformity with the prevailing law in denying Borgs' request to have a coworker present during his scheduled interview. Neither Borgs nor the Foundation could have known for sure that the established law might change, so Borgs acted at his peril in defying his employer and the Foundation acted with no apparent risk in following the law.

In these circumstances, "notions of equity and fairness," see Cassell v. FCC, 154 F.3d 478, 486 (D.C.Cir.1998), militate strongly against retroactive application of the Board's "substitution of new law for old law that was reasonably clear." Indeed, it would be a "manifest injustice" to require the Foundation to pay damages to an employee who, without legal right, flagrantly defied his employer's *lawful* instructions. See Clark–Cowlitz Joint Operating Agency v. FERC, 826 F.2d 1074, 1081 (D.C.Cir.1987). We therefore decline to enforce the Board's decision on retroactivity.

[Discussion of Hasan's discharge, also upheld, is omitted.]

NOTES

(1) Judge Edwards wrote about this topic again in a complex telecommunications setting, in VERIZON TELEPHONE COMPANIES v. FCC, 269 F.3d 1098 (D.C.Cir.2001). Here, the FCC had adopted a different approach than it had established at an earlier stage in the same adjudication. Was the agency foreclosed from applying its new understanding—prompted in part by an intervening stage of judicial review—retroactively?

". . . [T]here is a robust doctrinal mechanism for alleviating the hardships that may befall regulated parties who rely on 'quasi-judicial' determinations that are altered by subsequent agency action. Over fifty years ago, in SEC v. Chenery Corp., 332 U.S. 194, 203 (1947), the Supreme Court cautioned that the ill effects of retroactivity 'must be balanced against the mischief of producing a result which is contrary to a statutory design or to legal and equitable principles.' . . .

"This court has not been entirely consistent in enunciating a standard to determine when to deny retroactive effect in cases involving 'new applications of existing law, clarifications, and additions' resulting from adjudicatory actions. In Clark–Cowlitz Joint Operating Agency v. FERC, 826 F.2d 1074, 1081–86 (D.C.Cir.1987), the en banc court adopted a non-exhaustive five-factor balancing test. In a subsequent case, however, we substituted a similar three-factor test. See Dist. Lodge 64 v. NLRB, 949 F.2d 441, 447–49 (D.C.Cir.1991). And in other cases, the court has jettisoned multi-pronged balancing approaches altogether. See Cassell v. FCC, 154 F.3d 478, 486 (D.C.Cir.1998) (declining to 'plow laboriously' through the Clark–Cowlitz factors, which 'boil down to a question of concerns grounded in notions of equity and fairness')."

In the case before it, the court found retroactive application permissible, relying "primarily on two factors. The first is the fact that the [challenged] FCC's policy . . . was never authoritatively articulated outside of the same complaint proceeding in which it was eventually reversed. Indeed, the two . . . decisions on which the . . . reliance argument primarily rests were part of a single chain of decisions triggered by [the] original complaint, a chain whose natural progression led to this court, where the Commission's holdings were vacated. Thus, the agency orders on which the [parties] claim to have relied not only had never been judicially confirmed, but were under unceasing challenge before progressively higher legal authorities. . . .

"The second factor pointing toward retroactive liability is that the agency pronouncements on which the [claimants] relied were subsequently held by this court to be mistaken as a matter of law. As such, the [FCC order challenged in this proceeding] was largely an exercise in error correction. We have previously held that administrative agencies have greater discretion to impose their rulings retroactively when they do so in response to judicial review, that is, when the purpose of retroactive application is to rectify legal mistakes identified by a federal court."

(2) *The Tentativeness and Contextuality of Adjudication.* Vacillation such as preceded the NLRB's decision in Epilepsy Foundation is perhaps extreme, yet we are accustomed to thinking of the law developed by adjudication, the common law, as more malleable than statutes. Any party to a common-law proceeding has the right to argue that a precedent ostensibly applicable to its situation should be distinguished or overruled. The record applicable to rulemaking review is the same, whatever court undertakes the review; but adjudicatory records differ from case to case. Might these factors lead an agency sure of its ground to prefer rulemaking to adjudication for developing policy? Consider SHELL OIL CO. v. FERC, 707 F.2d 230 (5th Cir.1983). In a prior agency adjudicatory proceeding ("Mullins & Prichard"), FERC had announced that gas from wells drilled through "sidetracking" would not qualify for higher, "new-gas" pricing. It reasoned that sidetracking—the process of drilling a new well at an angle from some point within an existing well—allows producers to utilize existing well footage "to a great degree;" therefore, gas from the new well should be priced like gas from the existing well. When Shell attempted to obtain new-gas pricing for gas from a sidetracked well, FERC applied the Mullins & Prichard "rule." Shell appealed to the Fifth Circuit, arguing that its factual circumstances differed from those of Mullins & Prichard. FERC responded that Shell's argument is "nothing more than an effort to reargue a matter that has been considered and settled by the Commission on general policy grounds." The court vacated the order denying Shell's new-gas pricing request:

"Agencies may establish rules of general application in a statutory rulemaking or an individual adjudication. The choice of methods is a matter within the agency's informed discretion. NLRB v. Bell Aerospace Co. But we must be mindful that these two methods of making rules differ fundamentally in the due process safeguards they provide. Rulemaking procedures require public notice and an opportunity for all interested parties to participate. ... By contrast, no due process guarantees are extended to non–parties in an individual adjudication, although non-parties may be greatly affected by a general rule an agency adopts in such a proceeding. Shell was afforded no meaningful opportunity in Mullins & Prichard to challenge the factual assumption that '[p]roducers undertaking sidetracking operations within the existing spacing or proration unit are able to utilize existing well footage to a great degree. ...' Due process requires that Shell be allowed to challenge that assumption here and now.

"Bell Aerospace makes clear that an agency may establish a general rule in an individual adjudication. But neither that decision nor any other precludes a later challenge to the validity of the rule by one who was not a party to the proceeding in which it was announced."

Did the facts on the basis of which FERC set its policy depend on the individual circumstances of each well-owner, persons who would be "exceptionally affected, in each case upon individual grounds" (as Holmes put it in Bi–Metallic, p. 241 above)? Or were they what we have been calling "general" facts, relatively independent of individual circumstances? Note that in concluding that "due process" entitles Shell to an individualized opportunity to be heard on the sidetracking policy, the court invokes a due process *of rulemaking* that the cases have yet to establish.[1]

Whether or not "due process" was actually at stake, the court's observation reflects general truths about the contrast between adjudication and rulemaking as instruments for policy development. In the former, other similarly situated regulated entities are at the mercy of the skills and circumstances of the particular litigants; they rarely receive notice that an issue of importance to them about to be decided; and their ability to participate is in any event constrained. The opportunity to argue for distinction or overruling—at least for the first few following cases—is a natural corollary. Normally, though, this is put in terms of an opportunity to argue, not a right to a hearing in the full sense; and lawyers know that adjudicators' tempers (and explanations) will grow short once the new doctrine has become firmly rooted. The final footnote of the court's opinion states: "Our decision of course does not preclude the Commission from establishing the identical rule on remand if it adduces sufficient evidence to support the underlying assumption."

(iii) FOREWARNED IS NOT ENOUGH—LIMITATIONS ON RETROSPECTIVE RULEMAKING

When the SEC initially received the Chenerys' proposed reorganization plan for Federal Water Service Corp., and first realized the potential problems posed by management's stock purchases, could it have (i) suspended action on all requests for approval of voluntary reorganizations (including Federal's) while it promulgated a "no insider dealing" rule, and then (ii) applied that rule to all the pending cases?

Bowen v. Georgetown University Hospital

Supreme Court of the United States, 1988.
488 U.S. 204.

■ JUSTICE KENNEDY delivered the opinion of the Court.

[The government reimburses health care providers for expenses incurred in treating Medicare beneficiaries. The Medicare Act authorizes the

---

1. We will encounter another side of this problem in the last part of this subsection. When the FAA fixed the retirement age of pilots at 60 by rule, because it feared older pilots would present undetectable safety haz- ards, it invited an unending parade of efforts by particular pilots to show that, whatever might generally be the case, they as individuals could safely continue to fly. See p. 587 below.

Secretary of Health and Human Services to promulgate cost-reimbursement regulations and states that "[s]uch regulations shall ... (ii) provide for the making of suitable retroactive corrective adjustments where, for a provider of services for any fiscal period, the aggregate reimbursement produced by the methods of determining costs proves to be either inadequate or excessive." 42 U.S.C. § 1395x(v)(1)(A). In June 1981, HHS issued a new schedule altering the method for calculating hospital costs. Various hospitals challenged the schedule, and in April 1983 the district court invalidated it on grounds that the agency should have employed notice–and–comment rulemaking. Rather than appealing, HHS paid the hospitals' pending reimbursement claims by applying the old method, and in February 1984 began the notice–and–comment process. In the meantime, Congress had amended the Act to provide a substantially different reimbursement process for years beginning in 1983. Hence, only the reimbursement calculation for 1981 and 1982 remained in dispute. The rulemaking aimed at reissuing the cost schedule invalidated by the district court and using that schedule to make "retroactive corrective adjustments" for those two years. The rulemaking concluded in November 1984 with reissuance of the "new" schedule. When HHS applied the rule to recoup the difference between the sums previously paid to the hospitals for 1981 and 1982, and the amount due under the revised formula, the hospitals again sued. The district court used a balancing approach to conclude that retroactive application was not justified in the circumstances; the court of appeals affirmed on grounds that the APA generally forbids retroactive rulemaking, and the Medicare Act specifically bars retroactive cost–limit rules.]

... It is axiomatic that an administrative agency's power to promulgate legislative regulations is limited to the authority delegated by Congress. In determining the validity of the Secretary's retroactive cost-limit rule, the threshold question is whether the Medicare Act authorizes retroactive rulemaking.

Retroactivity is not favored in the law. Greene v. United States, 376 U.S. 149, 160 (1964). Thus, congressional enactments and administrative rules will not be construed to have retroactive effect unless their language requires this result. By the same principle, a statutory grant of legislative rulemaking authority will not, as a general matter, be understood to encompass the power to promulgate retroactive rules unless that power is conveyed by Congress in express terms. Even where some substantial justification for retroactive rulemaking is presented, courts should be reluctant to find such authority absent an express statutory grant.

The Secretary contends that the Medicare Act provides the necessary authority to promulgate retroactive cost-limit rules in the unusual circumstances of this case. He rests on alternative grounds: first, the specific grant of authority to promulgate regulations to "provide for the making of suitable retroactive corrective adjustments," 42 U.S.C. § 1395x(v)(1)(A)(ii); and second, the general grant of authority to promulgate cost limit rules.
. . .

Retroactive only via express grant + Congress auth

[Section 1395x(v)(1)(A)] on its face permits some form of retroactive action. We cannot accept the Secretary's argument, however, that it provides authority for the retroactive promulgation of cost-limit rules. To the contrary, we agree with the Court of Appeals that [the section] directs the Secretary to establish a procedure for making case-by-case adjustments to reimbursement payments where the regulations prescribing computation methods do not reach the correct result in individual cases. The structure and language of the statute require the conclusion that the retroactivity provision applies only to case-by-case adjudication, not to rulemaking.

. . . [Moreover, t]he statutory provisions establishing the Secretary's general rulemaking power contain no express authorization of retroactive rulemaking. Any light that might be shed on this matter by suggestions of legislative intent also indicates that no such authority was contemplated. In the first place, where Congress intended to grant the Secretary the authority to act retroactively, it made that intent explicit. As discussed above, § 1395x(v)(1)(A)(ii) directs the Secretary to establish procedures for making retroactive corrective adjustments; in view of this indication that Congress considered the need for retroactive agency action, the absence of any express authorization for retroactive cost-limit rules weighs heavily against the Secretary's position.

The legislative history of the cost-limit provision directly addresses the issue of retroactivity. . . . [T]he House and Senate Committee Reports expressed a desire to forbid retroactive cost-limit rules: "The proposed new authority to set limits on costs . . . would be exercised on a prospective, rather than retrospective, basis so that the provider would know in advance the limits to Government recognition of incurred costs and have the opportunity to act to avoid having costs that are not reimbursable."

The Secretary's past administrative practice is consistent with this interpretation of the statute. . . .

The Secretary nonetheless suggests that, whatever the limits on his power to promulgate retroactive regulations in the normal course of events, judicial invalidation of a prospective rule is a unique occurrence that creates a heightened need, and thus a justification, for retroactive curative rulemaking. The Secretary warns that congressional intent and important administrative goals may be frustrated unless an invalidated rule can be cured of its defect and made applicable to past time periods. The argument is further advanced that the countervailing reliance interests are less compelling than in the usual case of retroactive rulemaking, because the original, invalidated rule provided at least some notice to the individuals and entities subject to its provisions.

Whatever weight the Secretary's contentions might have in other contexts, they need not be addressed here. The case before us is resolved by the particular statutory scheme in question. Our interpretation of the Medicare Act compels the conclusion that the Secretary has no authority to promulgate retroactive cost-limit rules.

The 1984 reinstatement of the 1981 cost-limit rule is invalid. The judgment of the Court of Appeals is affirmed.

■ JUSTICE SCALIA, concurring.

I agree with the Court that general principles of administrative law suggest that [§ 1395x(v)(1)(A)] does not permit retroactive application of the Secretary of Health and Human Service's 1984 cost-limit rule. I write separately because I find it incomplete to discuss general principles of administrative law without reference to the basic structural legislation which is the embodiment of those principles, the Administrative Procedure Act (APA). . . .

The first part of the APA's definition of "rule" states that a rule

means the whole or a part of an agency statement of general or particular applicability *and future effect* designed to implement, interpret, or prescribe law or policy or describing the organization, procedure, or practice requirements of an agency . . .

5 U.S.C. § 551(4) (emphasis added). The only plausible reading of the italicized phrase is that rules have legal consequences only for the future. It could not possibly mean that merely *some* of their legal consequences must be for the future, though they may also have legal consequences for the past, since that description would not enable rules to be distinguished from "orders," see 5 U.S.C. § 551(6), and would thus destroy the entire dichotomy upon which the most significant portions of the APA are based. (Adjudication—the process for formulating orders, see § 551(7)—has future as well as past legal consequences, since the principles announced in an adjudication cannot be departed from in future adjudications without reason.)

Nor could "future effect" in this definition mean merely "*taking effect in the future*," that is, having a future effective date even though, once effective, altering the law applied in the past. That reading, urged by the Secretary of Health and Human Services, produces a definition of "rule" that is meaningless, since obviously *all* agency statements have "future effect" in the sense that they do not take effect until after they are made.
. . .

In short, there is really no alternative except the obvious meaning, that a rule is a statement that has legal consequences only for the future. If the first part of the definition left any doubt of this, however, it is surely eliminated by the second part (which the Secretary's brief regrettably submerges in ellipsis). After the portion set forth above, the definition continues that a rule

includes the approval or prescription *for the future* of rates, wages, corporate or financial structures or reorganizations thereof, prices, facilities, appliances, services or allowances therefor or of valuations, costs, or accounting, or practices bearing on any of the foregoing.

5 U.S.C. § 551(4) (emphasis added). It seems to me clear that the phrase "for the future"—which even more obviously refers to future operation rather than a future effective date—is not meant to add a requirement to those contained in the earlier part of the definition, but rather to repeat, in a more particularized context, the prior requirement "of future effect." And even if one thought otherwise it would not matter for purposes of the

[margin note: Rules – Future]

[margin note: Adjudication]

present case, since the HHS "cost-limit" rules governing reimbursement are a "prescription" of "practices bearing on" "allowances" for "services."

... [The House] Report [accompanying the APA] states that "[t]he phrase 'future effect' does not preclude agencies from considering and, so far as legally authorized, dealing with past transactions in prescribing rules for the future." The Treasury Department might prescribe, for example, that for purposes of assessing future income tax liability, income from certain trusts that has previously been considered nontaxable will be taxable—whether those trusts were established before or after the effective date of the regulation. That is not retroactivity in the sense at issue here, *i.e.*, in the sense of altering the *past* legal consequences of past actions. Rather, it is what has been characterized as "secondary" retroactivity. A rule with exclusively future effect (taxation of future trust income) can unquestionably *affect* past transactions (rendering the previously established trusts less desirable in the future), but it does not for that reason cease to be a rule under the APA. Thus, with respect to the present matter, there is no question that the Secretary could have applied her new wage-index formulas to respondents in the future, even though respondents may have been operating under long-term labor and supply contracts negotiated in reliance upon the pre-existing rule. ...

A rule that has unreasonable secondary retroactivity—for example, altering future regulation in a manner that makes worthless substantial past investment incurred in reliance upon the prior rule—may for that reason be "arbitrary" or "capricious," see 5 U.S.C. § 706, and thus invalid. ... It is erroneous, however, to extend this "reasonableness" inquiry to purported rules that not merely affect past transactions but change what was the law in the past. Quite simply, a rule is an agency statement "of future effect," not "of future effect and/or reasonable past effect."

The profound confusion characterizing the Secretary's approach to this case is exemplified by its reliance upon our opinion in Chenery II. Even apart from the fact that that case was not decided under the APA, it has nothing to do with the issue before us here, since it involved adjudication rather than rulemaking. Thus, though it is true that our opinion permitted the Secretary, after his correction of the procedural error that caused an initial reversal to reach the same substantive result with retroactive effect, the utterly crucial distinction is that Chenery involved that form of administrative action where retroactivity is not only permissible but standard. Adjudication deals with what the law was; rulemaking deals with what the law will be. ... And just as Chenery suggested that rulemaking was prospective, the opinions in NLRB v. Wyman–Gordon Co., suggested the obverse: that adjudication could *not* be purely prospective, since otherwise it would constitute rulemaking. ... Side by side these two cases, Chenery and Wyman–Gordon, set forth quite nicely the "dichotomy between rulemaking and adjudication" upon which "the entire [APA] is based." 1947 Attorney General's Manual on the APA. ...

The dire consequences that the Secretary predicts will ensue from reading the APA as it is written ... are not credible. ... [W]here legal consequences hinge upon the interpretation of statutory requirements, and where no pre-existing interpretive rule construing those requirements is in effect, nothing prevents the agency from acting retroactively through adjudication. See NLRB v. Bell Aerospace Co.; Chenery II. . . .

NOTES

(1) *An impetus to remand erroneous agency actions without vacating them?* Earlier pages in this Chapter presented the D.C. Circuit's practice of remanding some rules infected by error *without* vacating them, debated by Judges Silberman and Randolph in the Checkosky case, p. 497 above. Bowen should help to understand at least one impulse behind that approach. Recall that HHS' unhappy odyssey in Bowen began when a reviewing court struck down the revised cost formula because of a procedural flaw. By the time the agency had again adopted the new formula, now through a legally unexceptionable process, three years had passed. This was the fact that generated the "need" for retroactive application of the rule in what might have been viewed as one continuous proceeding. Clearly the private parties had notice of possible regulatory consequences prior to the first round of the proceedings.

Consider the pressures that might be placed on a reviewing court by the prospect of a string of regulatory fiascos like Bowen. The D.C. Circuit finds some flaw requiring reversal in between 40% and 50% of all agency action it reviews.[1] By casting doubt on agencies' legal authority to cure defective rulemakings retrospectively, Bowen raises the stakes for a court trying to craft an appropriate remedy (and perhaps also for any agency deliberately choosing between adjudicatory and rulemaking approaches). The court's awareness of this link is illustrated by ICORE v. FCC, 985 F.2d 1075, 1081–82 (D.C.Cir.1993). In 1986, the FCC had adopted a rule that revised the formula by which local telephone companies were compensated for the interconnections they provide their customers with interstate long-distance carriers. The following year, the D.C. Circuit found that the Commission had failed to demonstrate a rational basis for the new formula. The court remanded the case to the agency without vacating the rule. The FCC reopened comment on the revised formula and, in 1991, readopted it with an augmented explanation. This time, the court found the explanation adequate. It then turned to petitioners' argument that use of the revised formula to govern compensation for the period 1986–91 constituted impermissible retroactive rulemaking:

"Here, of course, in contrast to [Bowen], the court considering the rule initially found it inappropriate to set the rule aside. The court's decision on that point represented a careful consideration of the risk of disruption and of the likelihood that the rule was altogether sound at the core. . . . Petitioners offer no reason why a rule so treated, and in fact applied during the entire interim period, should be treated the same as the rule initially 'struck down' in [Bowen]. Petitioners cite no case employing [Bowen] to

---

1. See Patricia M. Wald, Regulation at Risk: Are Courts Part of the Solution or Most of the Problem?, 67 S.Cal.L.Rev. 621, 636–38 (1994); Peter H. Schuck & E. Donald Elliott, To the *Chevron* Station: An Empirical Study of Federal Administrative Law, 1990 Duke L.J. 984, 1042. The D.C. Circuit's reversal rate tends to be somewhat higher than other circuits; it does, however, review more major rules than any other circuit.

cancel the effect of rules deliberately left standing by a court pending a remand. . . .

"Petitioners also claim that it would have been improper for this court not to vacate the rule once it found it arbitrary and capricious. . . . This and other federal circuit courts have repeatedly found it appropriate to remand an agency action without vacating it. [citing cases from 1975–1991]. To the extent that petitioners claim these decisions are invalidated by [Bowen], they confuse (1) the use of retroactive rulemaking to cure a gap created by judicial vacatur of a rule with (2) the judicial decision not to create such a gap. Nothing in [Bowen] speaks to the latter question. Nor do we share petitioners' apparent assumption that [Bowen]'s strictures *against filling* a gap through retroactive rulemaking yield an inference in favor of courts exercising their remedial discretion *in favor of creating* gaps that as a result will be impossible to fill."

ABA Recommended Remedy

Should this judicial discretion itself be constrained? In 1997, at the urging of the Section of Administrative Law & Regulatory Practice, the ABA adopted the following resolution:

[T]he American Bar Association recommends that:

1. When a reviewing court holds that a rule or order issued by a federal administrative agency must be remanded to the agency for further consideration, the court may exercise discretion in determining whether or not to refrain from vacating the agency's action pending the remand proceedings. The Administrative Procedure Act should be construed, or if necessary amended, to permit the exercise of such discretion.

2. In exercising this discretion, a reviewing court should normally strike the balance in favor of vacating the agency's action, unless special circumstances exist. Such special circumstances may be most often found to exist where, in the context of the proceeding as a whole:

(a) the agency's error did not preclude fair public consideration of a central issue in a rulemaking or a fair hearing on the necessary findings in an adjudication or other agency proceeding;

(b) the court finds a substantial likelihood that the agency, after further consideration, will be able to remedy its error and reach a similar overall result on a valid basis; and

(c) the challenging party's interest in obtaining relief from the agency's decision is clearly outweighed by the substantial and adverse impact that vacation of the agency's action would have on

(i) persons other than the Government who over time have reasonably relied on the agency action being remanded, or

(ii) persons other than the Government, during the interim period before agency action on remand to cure the error has become final, and such impact cannot be remedied after such interim period.

3. Where the court orders the remedy of remand without vacation, it should give serious consideration to specifying a time frame

within which the agency is to comply with the terms of the remand order. The importance of setting a time frame is heightened if the burden of a remand on the challenging party noticeably increases with its duration.

4.   Where the court orders the remedy of remand without vacation, it should also consider directing that, until agency action to cure the previous error has become final

(a) any statutory or administrative deadline for compliance with the remanded action should be extended; and

(b) any proceedings brought to enforce compliance with the remanded action should be stayed, or pursued only with permission of the court.

5.   In order to promote informed application of the above standards, courts should encourage parties to address remedial issues, such as the possibility of remand without vacation, in their briefs and at oral argument. In a given case, if further explanation is needed and undue delay will not result, the court should also consider inviting supplemental briefs directed to this issue.

If you read Sugar Cane Growers, p. 493 above, you might now consider whether and to what extent the court appears to have acted on these principles. Should it have? That is, do they appear to you to be a sound reconciliation of the competing issues?

(2) *The Problematics of "Retroactivity."* WILLIAM V. LUNEBURG, RETROACTIVITY AND ADMINISTRATIVE RULEMAKING, 1991 Duke L.J. 106, 109–10: "At the outset it should be noted that the formulation of a definition of retroactivity is no easy task, as the literature demonstrates. Take these relatively simple cases:

1.   The Environmental Protection Agency (EPA) for the first time adopts a standard for the release of sulfur dioxide from existing power plants. The regulation imposes civil penalties for pre-adoption releases of that pollutant in violation of the new standard.

2.   The EPA promulgates a new sulfur dioxide standard with a compliance date two years in the future. Most or all plants within the scope of the regulation will need to dismantle pollution-control technology installed in response to a prior, less stringent EPA regulation and invest in new stack gas cleaning equipment.

3.   A newly constructed power plant applies to the EPA for a permit to operate. The permit would have been granted under EPA regulations in effect during the construction phase of the facility, but it is denied based on new EPA regulations adopted between the time of application and final agency action on the permit.

"Under one common definition, a retroactive regulation gives pre-adoption conduct a different legal effect from the one it would have had without the adoption of the regulation. Under this view, only the first case posed above is clearly a case of formal retroactivity. The third case is somewhat problematic in that regard, and the second case would fall outside this account of retroactivity.[2] Yet all of these cases and variations provoke concern for the same reasons: They create 'surprise' and a potential for undermining 'reasonable' reliance by affected parties. When a certain activity occurred, apparently applicable legal principles either signaled approval or at least did not suggest disapproval. Retroactivity may threaten these expectations with 'disappointment' and unforeseen costs. The destabilizing effects of retroactive regulation suggest the need to come to terms with the permissible parameters of retroactivity."

(iv) LIMITS ON THE USE OF RULEMAKING TO ELIMINATE ISSUES OTHERWISE REQUIRING ADJUDICATORY HEARING?

One powerful attraction of rulemaking is that it may permit the agency to resolve recurring regulatory issues in a single proceeding—even if its governing statute grants qualified parties rights to adjudicatory hearings on particular matters, and the recurring issues involve contestable issues of general fact that could be the subject of trial type procedures in those adjudications. Thus, in the Vermont Yankee case, p. 498, the NRC used rulemaking to determine numerical values for a variety of safety and environmental issues concerning the nuclear fuel cycle. It could then simply plug these values into subsequent APA adjudications to license specific nuclear power plants. Rather than having to litigate these values in each individual case (with possible consequences for judicial review as well), the agency concentrated its efforts in one proceeding, which then became the focus of judicial review.[1] Are there any limits on this use of rulemaking to settle issues otherwise contestable in an adjudication to which a person is statutorily (or constitutionally) entitled? Must the agency provide at least the opportunity to be heard on why the generic resolution should not govern a specific case?

This issue has long troubled commercial airline pilots. If there are issues about their fitness to fly, their licenses ordinarily can be affected only by a full adjudicatory hearing. In 1959, after assessing the then state of medical knowledge and technology concerning the effects of aging, the Federal Aviation Administration concluded it could not reliably determine whether individual pilots remained medically fit after their 60th birthdays. Consequently, it provided by regulation that all commercial pilot licenses ceased to be valid on that day. There followed decades of generally unavailing effort to have the regulation reexamined, or to demonstrate the individual fitness of particular pilots for an exemption.

---

2.   [Ed.] Prof. Luneburg points out that the second hypothetical represents "secondary," as opposed to "primary," retroactivity.

1.   Some organic statutes enhance the efficiency of this procedure by requiring that judicial review be sought within a relatively short period after the rulemaking is completed. Even if there is no limitations period compelling prompt, pre–enforcement challenge, attacks on the rule made during a subsequent adjudication generally must be based on the "record" established during the rulemaking, not on a new record created at the time of the adjudication.

Bert M. Yetman et al. v. Jane Garvey, Administrator, FAA

United States Court of Appeals for the Seventh Circuit, 2001.
261 F.3d 664.

■ Before FLAUM, CHIEF JUDGE, AND RIPPLE AND DIANE P. WOOD, CIRCUIT JUDGES.

■ FLAUM, CHIEF JUDGE. Sixty-nine pilots, all either approaching or having reached the age of sixty, petitioned the Federal Aviation Administration ("FAA") for exemptions from the agency's "Age Sixty Rule." The FAA, which has never granted such an exemption, continued that trend by denying the pilots' requests. Petitioners now seek review of the FAA's decision in this court. For the reasons stated herein, we affirm the order of the FAA.

I. BACKGROUND

In Baker v. FAA, 917 F.2d 318 (7th Cir.1990), a group of airline captains sought review of an FAA order which had denied their petition for exemptions from an agency rule that prohibits those who have reached the age of sixty from serving as pilots. While we ultimately affirmed the decision of the FAA not to grant the requested exemptions, we cautioned the agency that its Age Sixty Rule was not sacrosanct and untouchable. Further, we counseled the FAA that serious consideration should be given to the petitioners' position that granting exemptions would not increase the risk of air travel accidents. Since that decision, over a decade has passed, but the FAA has held fast to its blanket policy of denying requests for exemptions. Thus, once again, a group of pilots, all either past the age of sixty or approaching that age, have come before this court in an effort to have us declare that the FAA's policy constitutes an abuse of discretion. [The court briefly recited the history of the regulation and pilot efforts to escape it or have it revised, stressing "advances in the medical field."]

Relevant to this review, ... 49 U.S.C. § 44701(f), [permits the FAA to] grant an exemption from its requirements if it finds that such an exemption is in the public interest. However, the FAA has established a rigorous benchmark for proving that an exemption is in the public interest.... [I]n 1995, the FAA further hardened its stance, announcing that future petitions for exemptions would be summarily denied unless the petitions contain a proposed technique, not previously discussed, to assess an individual pilot's abilities and risks of subtle and sudden incapacitation.

On April 11, 2000, a petition for exemptions was filed on behalf of Jerry L. Adams and sixty-eight other commercial airline pilots. In support of the petition, the pilots submitted their complete medical records and 286 additional exhibits. Besides evidence which tended to attack the basis of the Age Sixty Rule, the petitioners also included the recommendations of a panel of eight renowned physicians in the fields of cardiology, geriatric medicine, internal medicine, aerospace medicine, and neuropsychology ("Age Sixty Exemption Panel"). According to the petitioners, the Age Sixty Exemption Panel had developed a comprehensive and realistic protocol to evaluate the medical/neuropsychological status of pilots seeking to continue their services in airline operations after the age of sixty. Despite the panel's recommendation that the petitioners be granted exemptions, the FAA determined that the pilots' proffers did not meet the agency's promulgated standards, and thus summarily denied the petition. When the petitioners filed for review of that decision in this court, the FAA requested and received a remand in order to reconsider whether the petitioners had demonstrated that an exemption to the Age Sixty Rule was warranted. Following the remand, the FAA solicited comments from interested parties, receiving over eight hundred such statements. Nonetheless, in a fairly extensive opinion dated December 13, 2000, the FAA again denied the petitioners' requests, prompting this appeal.

II.   DISCUSSION

In reviewing the FAA's order, we are not to judge whether the petitioning pilots are fit to fly. Further, we are not to reexamine the validity of the Age Sixty Rule itself....[1] Rather, we focus solely on the petition for exemptions, reviewing the FAA's findings of fact for substantial evidence ... [and examining] the agency's decision to ensure that it was based on a consideration of the relevant factors and articulated a rational connection between the facts found and the choice made. ...

A.   Inconsistent Determinations

... [T]he deference accorded to agency action "should not be equated with a license to issue inconsistent determinations." ... Here, the pilots assert that ... the FAA has allowed certain pilots past the age of sixty to fly in United States airspace, and has granted exemptions to pilots with known medical conditions. Petitioners claim that the agency's failure to adequately explain why it has chosen to treat those pilots differently from the petitioners here renders the FAA's decision in this instance an abuse of discretion.

1.   Pilots Flying Past the Age of Sixty

In support of the assertion that the FAA has rendered inconsistent determinations, the pilots have advanced two circumstances in which the FAA has allowed pilots past the age of sixty to fly. First, the pilots note that while the FAA prohibits United States common carriers from employing healthy pilots who are over the age of sixty, at the same time, the agency allows foreign carriers operating in United States airspace to employ pilots who are beyond that age. Second, the petitioners point out that from 1995 through 1999, while the FAA sought to bring commuter planes under the safety rules that apply to major airline carriers, the agency allowed commuter airlines to employ pilots who were past the age of sixty. The petitioners further note that during that time period, National Transportation Safety Board ("NTSB") reports reveal that no accidents involving pilots over sixty occurred, though the regional airline pilots were operating

---

1. We recognize, however, that the distinction between the request for an exemption and the validity of the rule itself is a bit muddied. Were we to grant the petitioners' requests for exemptions, resolving that the evidence relied upon by the FAA could not support the age limitation, we would *ipso facto* be voiding the Age Sixty Rule itself, replacing it with a system of individualized testing for pilots who wish to fly beyond the age of sixty.

similar equipment and flying in and out of the same airports as the pilots for the larger commercial airlines.

[The court accepted the government's argument that foreign co-pilots over sixty were permitted to fly in United States airspace as a matter of treaty obligation, not belief about differing health issues.]

As for its decision to allow pilots over sixty to fly commuter planes between 1995 and 1999, the FAA seeks to explain the uniqueness of that situation. Responding to a series of high profile accidents involving commuter planes, the FAA, at the behest of the NTSB, sought to increase safety in scheduled passenger-carrying operations and to clarify, update, and consolidate the certification and operations requirements for persons who transport passengers or property by air for compensation or hire. 60 Fed. Reg. 65,832. Thus, in 1995, the agency determined that commuter airline pilots should be subject to the FAA regulations applicable to major airline carriers, including the Age Sixty Rule. Originally, when the FAA sought to bring Part 135 operations under the Part 121 requirements, it proposed that the Age Sixty Rule would take effect for commuter operations one year after publication of the final rule. However, in response to comments requesting a more delayed effective date, the FAA agreed to a four-year compliance period for pilots already employed by commuter airlines. The FAA asserts that by granting the extended compliance period, it provided pilots who had a reasonable expectation that they would be allowed to fly time to plan for retirement or for changing jobs, and allowed for regional airlines to recoup services for a longer period from pilots whom they had recently invested money in training. Thus, according to the FAA, these special circumstances provided a rational basis for the agency's decision to temporarily treat commuter pilots differently.

Statistics accumulated from the flights of foreign and commuter airline pilots, sixty and over, may provide the FAA with the data needed in order to determine whether continuation of the Age Sixty Rule is warranted. These pieces of evidence, and other comparable statistics, would certainly be relevant in a challenge to the Age Sixty Rule itself. But, under this exemption review, most are not. Here, we are limited to determining whether the FAA's decision to allow foreign and commuter pilots "virtual exemptions" while denying domestic pilots those opportunities constitutes an abuse of discretion. That being said, we find that the FAA has provided rational justifications for these supposed inconsistencies. . . .

2. Medical Exemptions For Disqualified Pilots Under Sixty

[The court concluded that the difference between over-sixty pilots whose *general* medical condition is in question, and younger pilots who have demonstrated recovery from specific, otherwise disqualifying medical conditions "is adequate to warrant the distinction that the FAA has drawn, and to preclude a finding that the FAA is acting arbitrarily and capriciously in this regard."]

3. Change In World Standards

Finally, the petitioners assert that the FAA's decision to deny their petition is inconsistent, given the fact that there has been a change in the world standard with regard to age limitations for pilots. Effective July 1, 1999, Europe's Joint Aviation Authority adopted age sixty-five as the standard retirement age for commercial pilots among its 29 member states. Furthermore, the petitioners note that the ICAO age sixty standard has been rejected by two-thirds of the ICAO member states. That the FAA has maintained its Age Sixty Rule in the face of viable alternatives, according to the pilots, goes to show that the agency has blindly adhered to an outdated rule.

Once again, we do not dispute that the practices of foreign carriers might provide guidance for the FAA in considering alternatives to its Age Sixty Rule. Perhaps statistics accumulated regarding foreign pilots over sixty will assist in showing that the age cutoff in this country should be raised, or dispensed with altogether. However, such evidence is of little significance in our review of the petition for exemptions. There is nothing inconsistent, arbitrary, or capricious in the FAA's decision to adopt a standard different from that of other countries. Caution, even excessive caution, will not constitute an abuse of discretion if the decision is made after considering the relevant medical advances. ... The pilots have not presented anything to suggest that the FAA has deliberately disregarded medical studies that other countries have not. Thus, we find the fact that other countries may have adopted an age sixty-five limitation (or even no limitation at all) not to warrant the granting of these exemptions.

B. Petitioner's Age Sixty Exemption Protocol

In addition to claiming that the FAA has a practice of rendering inconsistent determinations with regard to the Age Sixty Rule, the petitioners also present a more specific challenge to the FAA's decision in this case. Their contention is that the agency has disregarded the fact that these pilots have met the promulgated standard for granting exemptions—presenting (and passing) a protocol which can accurately gauge an individual pilot's abilities and risks of sudden incapacitation. The petitioners assert that they have been examined by the Age Sixty Exemption Panel, which was formed in 1999 specifically to evaluate the medical/neuropsychological status of airline pilots seeking to continue their employment after age sixty. According to the pilots, the panel has developed and approved medical and neuropsychological protocols for their use in evaluating the fitness of applicants for exemptions from 14 C.F.R. § 121.383(c). The testing which makes up the Age Sixty Exemption Protocol includes a complete medical history, physical examination, chem-screen profile, hemoccult, urinalysis, chest x-ray, audiometry, vision tests, tonometry, electrocardiogram, and exercise stress testing. The protocol also contains neuropsychological testing comprised of CogScreen Aeromedical Edition ("CogScreen–AE"), Wechsler Adult Intelligence Scale–Revised, Rey Auditory Verbal Learning Test, Trail Making Test, Controlled Oral Word Association Test, and the Paced Auditory Serial Addition Test. The Age Sixty Exemption Panel has determined that these tests, performed competently, together with other and further testing which may be medically and psychologically indicated, are sufficient to evaluate the fitness of pilots over sixty. Further, with regard to these sixty-nine pilots, the panel has utilized the protocol and concluded that subject to the satisfactory completion of the customary operational requirements of the FAA, the petitioners should be granted exemptions.

While the Age Sixty Exemption Protocol is certainly comprehensive, the vast majority of the protocol has been previously submitted to the FAA and rejected ... [Respecting new tests the petitioners had provided to substitute for some previously found insufficient,] the FAA maintains, and the petitioners do not truly dispute, that these substitutions have been made without improving the test battery's diagnostic or predictive value. Thus, we must focus on what is truly new and relevant in the Age Sixty Exemption Protocol—the Cogscreen–AE—and determine whether, when combined with the previously rejected protocol, it provides an adequate means of evaluating petitioners as they reach and pass the age of sixty.

[The court explored this test, and the FAA's negative reaction to it at some length.] ... We do not doubt that in the future, CogScreen–AE, and similar testing batteries may be sufficient gauges for assessing the abilities of pilots past the age of sixty. However, at this early stage, there is quite simply no evidence in the research literature that allows the FAA to establish a CogScreen–AE score or set of scores to identify when a pilot is incapable of safely operating an aircraft, nor is there evidence that Cog-Screen–AE provides an appropriate set of cognitive/psychomotor measures for making this prediction. ... Of course, in keeping in line with the requirement that the agency consider new advances, we expect that the FAA will continue to examine CogScreen–AE to determine whether it can be a sufficient tool for assessing pilots, and if so, what scores would be sufficient to allow for the granting of exemptions.

C. Accident Studies

[The court next explored at considerable length the propositions that "any undetected aging decrements or increased risks of incapacitation that accompanied pilots sixty and over were offset by the added experience that attends to pilots of that age" and that recent studies (and the experience with foreign and commuter pilots) "demonstrated that aviation accident rates do not go up with pilot age through the sixties." These propositions were to some extent settled by earlier litigation; respecting the newer studies, the FAA asserted flaws in them which the court was unable to disregard.]

But more generally, the FAA has proposed that all accident studies (including those relied upon by the petitioners) are inherently flawed. The agency notes that the major deficiency in all accident studies is that such analyses must rely upon surrogate data that does not reflect the reality and actual operating conditions and procedures of Part 121 operations, as there are no pilots over sixty that fly in Part 121 operations. While we, as a matter of first impression, might have concluded that the surrogate data was sufficiently comparable to Part 121 operations to allow for meaningful analysis, the FAA has determined otherwise, and we have accepted its determination. ... While it may seem unfair that by virtue of the Age Sixty Rule these pilots are being denied the opportunity to prove that they warrant exemptions, nevertheless, it is the petitioners' burden to present persuasive evidence that granting exemptions would not impair safety. If the FAA was justified in imposing the Age Sixty Rule in the first place, then we cannot say that simply because it is the rule itself which blocks the generation of data necessary to consider the propriety of granting exemptions to the rule, that it was unreasonable for the FAA to find that it lacks that data. . . . We find that the FAA, in accordance with our directive, has kept abreast of and considered new studies and advances in medical technology. Thus, we cannot conclude the FAA abused its discretion in not granting these exemptions on the basis of the aforementioned accident studies. . . .

. . . While our review of the evidence submitted by the petitioners might lead us to conclude that a strict age sixty cutoff, without exceptions, is a rule better suited to 1959 than to 2001, this court is not an expert in aerospace medicine, and Congress did not endow this court with the duty to make such a policy judgment. The FAA has the discretionary power to establish a rigid policy, whereby no exemptions are granted, until it is satisfied that medical standards can demonstrate an absence of risk factors in an individual sufficient to warrant a more liberal exemption policy from the Age Sixty Rule. Until the FAA determines that such standards exist, it may adhere inflexibly to a rule whose validity has been upheld by the courts and reevaluated by Congress, so long as it continues to consider, as we are satisfied it has done here, new advances in medical technology.

For the foregoing reasons, we affirm the order of the FAA.

NOTES

(1) *The Supreme Court's View.* A similar issue came to the Court in HECKLER V. CAMPBELL, 461 U.S. 458 (1983), five years after Vermont Yankee. Eligibility for Social Security disability benefits turns not only on the personal characteristics of the applicant, but also on the existence or not of jobs in the national economy that a person of the applicant's age, education, language skills, physical limitations, etc. could hold. Because the statute is not an unemployment statute, it does not matter whether those jobs are conveniently located to the applicant, or in fact unfilled, but the jobs do have to exist.[1] For many years, these issues were resolved through the testimony of vocational experts in each disability hearing. Then the Secretary of Health and Human Services adopted, by § 553 procedures, a set of medical-vocational guidelines to set these values for use in all disability hearings. Here's an example; as you can see, each line is, in legal effect, a separate rule.

---

1. The disability benefits scheme is a regulatory program we will encounter repeatedly in this course. A thoughtful observer might conclude that it is a program destined to fail; at the very least, the Social Security Act sets the responsible agencies a task that virtually guarantees charges of bureaucratic irrationality and inhumane administration. As a definitional matter, "disability" means *total* disability; unless the applicant is unable to engage in "*any* substantial gainful activity," 42 U.S.C. § 423(d)(1)(A) (emphasis added), she can receive no assistance whatsoever.

TABLE No. 2—RESIDUAL FUNCTIONAL CAPACITY: MAXIMUM SUSTAINED WORK CAPABILITY LIMITED TO LIGHT WORK AS A RESULT OF SEVERE MEDICALLY DETERMINABLE IMPAIRMENT(S)

Rule	Age	Education	Previous work experience	Decision
202.01	Advanced age	Limited or less	Unskilled or none	Disabled.
202.02	...do	...do	Skilled or semiskilled—skills not transferable.	Do.
202.03	...do	...do	Skilled or semiskilled—skills transferable [1].	Not disabled.
202.04	...do	High school graduate or more—does not provide for direct entry into skilled work [2].	Unskilled or none	Disabled.
202.05	...do	High school graduate or more—provides for direct entry into skilled work [2]	...do	Not disabled.
202.06	...do	High school graduate or more—does not provide for direct entry into skilled work [2].	Skilled or semiskilled—skills not transferable.	Disabled.
202.07	...do	...do	Skilled or semiskilled—skills transferable [2].	Not disabled.
202.08	...do	High school graduate or more—provides for direct entry into skilled work [2].	Skilled or semiskilled—skills not transferable.	Do.
202.09	Closely approaching advanced age.	Illiterate or unable to communicate in English.	Unskilled or none	Disabled.
202.10	...do	Limited or less—At least literate and able to communicate in English.	...do	Not disabled
202.11	...do	Limited or less	Skilled or semiskilled—skills not transferable.	Do.
202.12	...do	...do	Skilled or semiskilled—skills transferable.	Do.
202.13	...do	High school graduate or more.	Unskilled or none	Do.
202.14	...do	...do	Skilled or semiskilled—skills not transferable.	Do.
202.15	...do	...do	Skilled or semiskilled—skills transferable.	Do.
202.16	Younger individual	Illiterate or unable to communicate in English.	Unskilled or none	Do.
202.17	...do	Limited or less—At least literate and able to communicate in English.	...do	Do.
202.18	...do	Limited or less	Skilled or semiskilled—skills not transferable.	Do.
202.19	...do	...do	Skilled or semiskilled—skills transferable.	Do.
202.20	...do	High school graduate or more.	Unskilled or none	Do.
202.21	...do	...do	Skilled or semiskilled—skills not transferable.	Do.
202.22	...do	...do	Skilled or semiskilled—skills transferable.	Do.

[1] See 202.00(f)
[2] See 202.00(c).

The Court, Justice Powell writing, unanimously approved:

"... It is true that the statutory scheme contemplates that disability hearings will be individualized determinations based on evidence adduced at a hearing. See 42 U.S.C. § 423(d)(2)(A) (specifying consideration of each individual's condition); 42 U.S.C. § 405(b) (1976 ed., Supp. V) (disability determination to be based on evidence adduced at hearing). But this does not bar the Secretary from relying on rulemaking to resolve certain classes of issues. The Court has recognized that even where an agency's enabling statute expressly requires it to hold a hearing, the agency may rely on its rulemaking authority to determine issues that do not require case-by-case consideration. See FPC v. Texaco, Inc., 377 U.S. 33, 41–44 (1964); United States v. Storer Broadcasting Co., 351 U.S. 192, 205 (1956). A contrary holding would require the agency continually to relitigate issues that may be established fairly and efficiently in a single rulemaking proceeding.

"The Secretary's decision to rely on medical-vocational guidelines is consistent with Texaco and Storer. ... [I]n determining whether a claimant can perform less strenuous work, the Secretary must ... assess each claimant's individual abilities and then determine whether jobs exist that a person having the claimant's qualifications could perform. The first inquiry involves a determination of historic facts, and the regulations properly require the Secretary to make these findings on the basis of evidence adduced at a hearing. ... The second inquiry requires the Secretary to determine an issue that is not unique to each claimant—the types and numbers of jobs that exist in the national economy. This type of general factual issue may be resolved as fairly through rulemaking as by introducing the testimony of vocational experts at each disability hearing."

The Court took comfort from the use of rulemaking procedures to decide the factual issues underlying the grid, and from a regulatory provision making the grid inapplicable if it failed to capture the applicant's limitations. Concurrences by Justice Brennan and Marshall stressed the importance of sensitivity to the individual circumstances of the applicant.

(2) *The Efficiency of Rules.* COLIN S. DIVER, THE OPTIMAL PRECISION OF ADMINISTRATIVE RULES, 93 Yale L.J. 65, 89–91 (1983): "The grid rule is the latest stage in a relentless progression toward transparency and complexity in the disability standard. The factor most obviously responsible for this trend is transaction costs. The volume of determinations is immense and was, until recently, growing at a rapid rate. The number of hearings is still growing. Moreover, although the average cost of processing all DI [disability insurance] claims is modest ($171 in 1978), the cost per contested claim is a good deal higher. The total administrative cost of the disability insurance system in 1978 was $327 million.

"Raw numbers like these fail to do full justice to the importance of transaction costs. A 'hidden' transaction cost in any benefits system is the impact of delay on deserving applicants. The 551,500 applicants who received a favorable decision in 1976, for example, had to wait an average of 105 days for the award. The human costs of anxiety and deprivation from such delays are enormous.

"A second hidden transaction cost is the difficulty of controlling subordinate decisionmakers. A substantial degree of de facto decentralization is unavoidable in so enormous an operation. But the structure of the DI program promotes decentralization with a vengeance. Initial decisions (which become final determinations in the eighty-five percent of cases not appealed to SSA) are made by officers of fifty autonomous state agencies who are subject only to indirect supervision by SSA. These state agencies themselves are often administratively decentralized and rely heavily on consulting physicians and vocational experts. Within SSA, decisions are made by a cadre of about seven hundred fiercely independent Administrative Law Judges (ALJs) who preside at hearings where there are usually no representatives of SSA present. Any decisionmaking apparatus so fragmented—especially one which affects such large sums of money and so many people—cries out for tight, centralized control. Recent studies documenting inconsistencies among state agencies and ALJs have intensified pressures for reform.

"Demands for tighter supervision naturally focus attention on the clarity of substantive standards. The utility of conventional management control devices like reporting systems, performance appraisal, and quality review ultimately depends on the transparency of the underlying standards to be applied. It is one thing to document inconsistency in results by comparing two individuals' resolutions of a hypothetical case. But it is very difficult to remedy that inconsistency without having clear criteria. Without the dramatic increase in regulatory objectivity, SSA's massive quality control program and its impressive quantitative gains would be almost unthinkable."

(3) *Waiver.* Must a person whose claim to a hearing is apparently defeated by regulation-found facts always have the opportunity to show that those facts are inaccurate or otherwise inappropriate for her case? In Heckler, Storer, and Texaco, the Court prominently noted—and commented approvingly on—the presence of such safety valves in the challenged rules. But then there is FCC v. WNCN LISTENERS GUILD, 450 U.S. 582 (1981). The FCC promulgated a rule reversing its practice of taking into account, in a license renewal proceeding, the fact that a radio station had changed its programming format. The new rule rested on a deregulatory philosophy that the market would best promote diversity of entertainment formats. Only Justices Marshall and Brennan found the rule problematic. The issue, they argued, was not whether market forces would *in general* produce diversity, but rather whether the FCC must provide an opportunity to show in *particular* cases that the market would not work. For the other seven justices, however, the question was whether the deregulatory approach could be squared with the agency's statutory mandate. Having found that it could, the majority was apparently unconcerned with the safety valve issue. Justice White's opinion merely noted that previous cases had come to the Court with a waiver mechanism attached; the Court had not held that an agency may never adopt a rule which lacks one.

The approach of the court of appeals in Yetman is not atypical—assuring itself that the agency has taken a "hard look" at the question and, once so satisfied accepting the agency's judgment. Note that the issue could readily be put in terms falling on the adjudication side of the Bi–Metallic distinction (viz., what is the state of Mr. Yetman's health, and how likely is it to deteriorate over the next year(s) as he further ages?) as well as in more general ones (how capable is medical science of predicting the downward course of an aging person's health, as it may affect the safety of her 253 passengers in a commercial jet?) This framing suggests a possible due process link. Cf. Walters v. Nat'l Assoc. of Radiation Survivors, 473 U.S. 305, 337 (1985) (O'Connor, J., concurring), p. 851 below. In BELLSOUTH CORP. v. FCC, 162 F.3d 1215 (D.C.Cir.1999) the issue was the FCC's refusal to waive certain rules respecting cellular telephony:

"BellSouth focuses on the fact that granting its waiver would have involved a *de minimis* exception to the cap, ... that the Commission failed to give the requisite 'hard look' at its waiver request and that the Commission has effectively adopted a 'no waiver' policy for the spectrum cap. ... [W]e conclude that BellSouth has failed to show that the Commission's 'reasons for declining the waiver were 'so insubstantial as to render that denial an abuse of discretion.' '" Thomas Radio Co. v. FCC, 716 F.2d 921, 924 (D.C.Cir.1983) (quoting WAIT Radio v. FCC, 459 F.2d 1203, 1207 (D.C.Cir.1972) (WAIT II)).

"The 'hard look' requirement assures that a general rule serving the public interest for a broad range of situations will not be rigidly applied where its application would not be in the public interest.... Therefore, when an agency receives a request for waiver that is 'stated with clarity and accompanied by supporting data,' such requests 'are not subject to perfunctory treatment, but must be given a hard look.' While an agency must consider the relevant factors, in explaining the denial of a waiver request, 'the agency is not required to author an essay for the disposition of each application. It suffices, in the usual case, that we can discern the why and wherefore.' ICBC Corp. v. FCC, 716 F.2d 926, 929 (D.C.Cir.1983) (quotations omitted); see also P & R Temmer v. FCC, 743 F.2d 918, 932 (D.C.Cir.1984).

"At the same time, an agency that is required to give a 'hard look' at a waiver request is not necessarily required to have an existing waiver policy for all of its rules. The 'strict adherence to a general rule may be justified by the gain in certainty and administrative ease, even if it appears to result in some hardship in individual cases.' Turro v. FCC, 859 F.2d 1498, 1500 (D.C.Cir.1988); see also FCC v. WNCN Listeners Guild, 450 U.S. 582, 601 n. 44. Rigid and consistent adherence to a policy will be upheld if it is valid."

For recent thoughtful and thorough treatments of the waiver issue, see Harold Krent, Reviewing Agency Action for Inconsistency with Prior Rules and Regulations, 72 Chi–Kent L.Rev. 1187 (1997) and Jim Rossi, Waivers, Flexibility and Reviewability, 72 Chi–Kent L.Rev. 1359 (1997).

b. GETTING RULEMAKING STARTED

Whether or not agencies self-consciously choose *between* rulemaking and adjudication as the mode for developing policy, an agency that is going to engage in rulemaking commits to that effort well before the first event § 553 mentions, publication in the Federal Register of an NPRM. The public may play a part in initiating the process.

(i) PUBLIC INITIATION OF RULEMAKING

Section 553(e) requires "each agency [to] give an interested person the right to petition for the issuance, amendment, or repeal of a rule."

Professional Pilots Federation v. Federal Aviation Administration

United States Court of Appeals for the District of Columbia Circuit, 1997.
118 F.3d 758.

■ Before WALD, GINSBURG, and RANDOLPH, CIRCUIT JUDGES.

■ GINSBURG, CIRCUIT JUDGE: The Professional Pilots Federation and two individual pilots petition for review of two decisions of the Federal Aviation Administration: not to institute a rulemaking to relax the FAA Rule that requires commercial airline pilots to retire at age 60, and to extend application of the Rule to commuter airline operations. The Pilots contend, first, that the Rule unlawfully requires airlines to violate the Age Discrimination in Employment Act, see 29 U.S.C. § 621 et seq., and, second, that the FAA acted arbitrarily and capriciously, in violation of the Administrative Procedure Act, when it decided to retain and expand the scope of the Rule. Finding merit in neither contention, we deny the petitions for review.

I. Background

The FAA first promulgated the Age 60 Rule in 1959 pursuant to its mandate under the Federal Aviation Act of 1958 to ensure air safety. . . . The agency concluded that the Rule would promote air safety after finding "that available medical studies show that sudden incapacitation due to heart attacks or strokes becomes more frequent as men approach age sixty and present medical knowledge is such that it is impossible to predict with accuracy those individuals most likely to suffer attacks." The Second Circuit, reasoning that it was not for a court to substitute its own "untutored judgment for the expert knowledge" of the agency, accepted this conclusion and dismissed an early challenge to the Rule. Air Line Pilots Ass'n, Int'l v. Quesada, 276 F.2d 892 (2d Cir.1960)

The FAA has reconsidered the Rule on several occasions. . . . [details omitted] In 1979 the Congress directed the National Institutes of Health to determine whether the Rule was still medically warranted. See Pub. L. No. 96–171, 93 Stat. 1285. In its final report, the NIH concluded that there was "no special medical significance to age 60 as a mandatory age for retirement of airline pilots" but recommended that the age 60 limit be retained nonetheless because there was still no "medical or performance appraisal system that can single out those pilots who would pose the greatest hazard because of early, or impending, deterioration in health or performance." Report of the National Institute on Aging, Panel on the Experienced Pilots Study 1 (August 1981).

In 1982 the FAA considered relaxing the Rule in order to allow a small group of pilots to continue flying until age 62 in order to generate data on their performance under actual operating conditions. 47 Fed. Reg. 29,782 (July 8, 1982). The FAA ultimately determined, however, that "no medical or performance appraisal system can be identified that would single out pilots who would pose a hazard to safety." 49 Fed. Reg. 14,692, 14,695 (April 12, 1984). Unable "to distinguish those pilots who, as a consequence of aging, present a threat to air safety from those who do not," the agency decided not to experiment with changing the Rule.

The present litigation was stimulated, at least in part, by a 1993 study of the Age 60 Rule that was performed by Hilton Systems, Inc. for the FAA's Civil Aeromedical Institute. The Hilton Study correlated accident data for the period from 1976 to 1988 with pilot age and flying time. This analysis revealed "no support for the hypothesis that pilots of scheduled air carriers had increased accident rates as they neared the age of 60." On the contrary, the study found a "slight downward trend" in accident rates as pilots neared the age of 60. The authors cautioned, however, that this decrease might have resulted from "the FAA's rigorous medical and operational performance standards screening out, over time, pilots more likely to be in accidents."

Shortly after publication of the Hilton Study the FAA announced that it was again considering whether to institute a rulemaking concerning the Age 60 Rule and invited comments from the public on various aspects of the Hilton Study. 58 Fed. Reg. 21,336 (April 20, 1993). The agency held a public hearing in September 1993 at which 46 members of the public made presentations. The agency also received more than a thousand written comments.

In July 1993 the Professional Pilots Federation filed with the FAA a rulemaking petition to repeal the Rule. The Pilots maintained that "time and empirical evidence have shown that the blanket elimination of the country's most experienced pilots is not justified in the interests of safety and, therefore, is arbitrary and capricious, and violates this country's policy of prohibiting employment discrimination on the basis of age."

In early 1995 after a series of accidents involving commuter airlines, the FAA proposed in a separate rulemaking to bring certain commuter operations, previously conducted under Part 135, under ... the more stringent safety standards of Part 121, including the Age 60 Rule....

In December 1995 the FAA denied the Pilots' petitions to repeal the Age 60 Rule and decided not to institute a rulemaking in response to the Hilton Study. The agency determined that the "concerns regarding aging pilots and underlying the original rule have not been shown to be invalid or misplaced," and concluded that the Rule was still warranted as a safety measure. ... In addition the FAA adopted its proposed rule ... [making] certain commuter operations ... newly subject to the Age 60 Rule. The Pilots petitioned this court for review of both rulemaking decisions.

II.   Analysis

The Pilots challenge the FAA's decision not to institute a rulemaking to repeal the Age 60 Rule and its decision to apply the Rule to commuter airlines as violations of both the ADEA and the APA. First, the Pilots assert that by requiring the airlines to discriminate on the basis of age the Rule is in "direct conflict" with the ADEA. Second, they claim that the agency violated the APA by: (1) not affording adequate consideration to the reasonable alternatives proposed by various commenters; (2) reaching a decision that is against the weight of the evidence; and (3) failing to provide any reasoned basis for treating older pilots differently than other groups of pilots who create as great or greater a safety risk.

A.   The ADEA

[The court concluded that the ADEA did not prohibit the Age 60 Rule.]

B.   The APA Challenges

We will defer to the FAA's decisions to retain the Age 60 Rule and to bring commuter airlines under the Rule unless those decisions are "arbitrary, capricious, an abuse of discretion, or otherwise not in accordance with law." 5 U.S.C. § 706(2)(A). More particularly, the agency must have offered a reasoned explanation for its chosen course of action, responded to "relevant" and "significant" public comments, and demonstrated that it afforded adequate consideration to every reasonable alternative presented for its consideration.

With respect to its decision not to convene a rulemaking in order to repeal or modify the Age 60 Rule, the FAA argues that the appropriate standard of review is the even more deferential standard we apply to an agency's decision not to institute a rulemaking proceeding. Cellnet Communication, Inc. v. FCC, 965 F.2d 1106, 1111–12 (D.C.Cir.1992). That more deferential standard of review is indicated, however, only when the agency has clearly shown that "pragmatic considerations" would render the usual and somewhat more searching inquiry problematic because "the agency has chosen not to regulate for reasons ill-suited to judicial resolution, e.g., because of internal management considerations as to budget and personnel or for reasons made after a weighing of competing policies." In the case now before us the decision not to institute a rulemaking looking toward repeal of the Age 60 Rule was purportedly based upon the merits of the existing Rule. We see no need, therefore, to afford the agency more than the usual—and considerable—deference we show an agency when it adopts a rule implementing a statute it is charged with administering. We shall therefore apply the arbitrary and capricious standard of the APA.

1.   Consideration of alternatives

Various parties filing comments before the FAA proposed two alternatives to the present Rule. First, they suggested periodic performance checks designed to determine, on an individual basis, whether a pilot remains fit to fly. Second, they proposed allowing a group of pilots over the age of 60 to continue flying commercial passenger aircraft in order to gather the data that the FAA would need to make a reasoned decision about whether the current retirement age of 60 could safely be moved up to perhaps age 62 or 63. The Pilots now press both alternatives upon us.

[In an extended discussion, the panel accepted as rational the FAA's concern that "available tests: (1) evaluate only a pilot's present performance and cannot be used to predict the sudden onset of an age-related impairment, such as early or subclinical cognitive defects; (2) cannot measure the subtle degradation of skills that may prove serious in the cockpit; and (3) do not evaluate how a pilot responds to stress and fatigue." It rejected claims that the FAA was being inconsistent in permitting individualized testing of younger pilots with certain known medical conditions. "The risk of allowing the younger pilot to continue flying is negligible provided—and it is this critical proviso that our colleague in dissent seems to ignore—that 'the agency has been able to develop a means of assessment and surveillance specifically designed to demonstrate the individual's capabilities and to identify any adverse changes.' Doctors are not only unable to determine whether an older but apparently healthy pilot will be afflicted with a dangerous condition; they are also unable to predict with which of the myriad conditions that accompany advancing age an individual pilot is likely to be afflicted.[1]" It accepted the FAA's assertion that it could not study a select group of pilots over the age of 60 for testing of the

---

1. Contrary to the impression created by the dissent, the FAA did not suggest "that it is more difficult to monitor known medical conditions in an older pilot than in a younger pilot." Rather, the agency's concern was that it is more difficult to detect an unknown medical condition than to monitor a known medical condition.

regulation's hypothesis, because "it did not have confidence that it could identify a cohort of vintage pilots who would not be susceptible to subtle impairments or to sudden incapacitation. . . . [I]t would be unreasonable for the court to require that the FAA periodically suspend its safety regulations in order to determine anew, upon the basis of (potentially disastrous) experience, whether they are still needed." After considering, as well, a number of claims that the agency was acting inconsistently—as by permitting air taxi pilots over sixty, not under Part 121, to continue flying, or accepting under treaty obligations of the United States the qualifications of foreign co-pilots older than 60—the court concluded:]

The FAA may seem to have created something of a Catch–22 by announcing that it will not allow older pilots to fly until it has experiential data demonstrating the continued ability of such pilots to fly safely. On the other hand, it hardly seems reasonable to require that the Administrator periodically put his hand into the fire in order to ensure that he has precisely assessed the danger that it poses. If the FAA was justified in imposing the Rule in the first place then we cannot say that, simply because it is the Rule itself that blocks the generation of data necessary to reconsider the Rule, it was unreasonable for the FAA to find that it lacks those data. In sum, we hold that the FAA's decision not to convene a rulemaking to revise the Age 60 Rule was not arbitrary and capricious in violation of the APA.

■ WALD, CIRCUIT JUDGE, concurring in part and dissenting in part: The FAA has determined that the progressive anatomic, physiological, and cognitive decline generally associated with aging means that all pilots over the age of 60 represent too great a threat to aviation safety to be allowed to fly in part 121 operations, which constitute by far the bulk of commercial common carrier operations. The FAA based this determination not on evidence demonstrating that pilots over 60 perform less well than pilots under 60, but rather on the claim that there is no accurate means to identify which pilots are particularly at risk of suffering a sudden incapacitation or more subtle deterioration in their abilities and the age of 60 was within the age range where the incidence of diseases associated with aging sharply increases. This argument is essentially the same as that which the FAA offered when it first adopted the Age 60 Rule in 1959. The agency continued to adhere to the position that the Age 60 Rule is necessary to ensure the highest level of aviation safety despite the medical and technological developments over the ensuing nearly four decades, despite a growing trend among foreign aviation authorities to allow pilots over 60 to fly, and despite a recent report commissioned by the FAA which concluded there was no evidence of an increase in accidents associated with older pilots at least up to age 63.

. . . I believe that the FAA's justification for the rule simply does not pass muster under the APA.[2] It may be the case that our current medical

---

2. Although I disagree with the majority's analysis of the FAA's decision under the APA, I concur with the assessment that our usual standard of APA arbitrary and capricious review applies here, even though refus- als to initiate rulemaking ordinarily are accorded particular deference by a reviewing court, because the FAA based its refusal to initiate a rulemaking to rescind the Age 60

knowledge and testing protocols are unable to identify those older pilots who are at risk of sudden incapacitation or subtle deterioration in functioning, so that an arbitrary across-the-board age limit remains the only reliable means of achieving the highest possible level of aviation safety. However, the FAA has not yet provided an adequate justification on this go-round for its conclusion that this situation still exists, nor for its determination that aviation safety requires all common carrier pilots, even those carrying cargo only, to be subject to the age limit but not corporate or air-taxi pilots. The FAA's decision also suffers from a reliance on flawed and inapplicable studies of accident rates. Perhaps hardest to swallow is the FAA's continued refusal to try to obtain medical or performance data on older pilots at the same time as it claims that such evidence is required before any change in the rule can be countenanced. The agency's complacent acceptance of this Catch–22 situation, particularly given that the result is the continuation of a government-imposed regime of age discrimination, seems to me the epitome of arbitrary action. . . .

[Judge Wald explained these views at significant length, with detailed reference to the record and the various studies undertaken and reports made. She concluded:] Most importantly, the Age 60 Rule stands as an instance of government-mandated age discrimination for a particular group of employees. The ADEA manifests our country's rejection of measures that discriminate against individuals solely because of their age; its stated purpose was to "promote employment of older persons based on their ability rather than age . . . [and] to prohibit arbitrary age discrimination in employment." . . . [While the ADEA does not, in terms, require] the FAA in its role as a regulator of aviation . . . to demonstrate that the Age 60 Rule is a bona-fide occupational qualification and therefore acceptable under the Act . . . this does not mean that the FAA can ignore the ADEA altogether. The congressional condemnation of age discrimination embodied in the ADEA imposes a duty on the FAA to try to obtain data that might allow it to do away with its current reliance on an arbitrary across-the-board age cutoff as a method of ensuring aviation safety.[3] . . . Judges must be ever-vigilant to ensure that when enforcing the APA's requirement of reasoned decisionmaking they defer to agency expertise. The importance of such deference is most acute in regard to safety determinations, given the potential catastrophic effects of inadequate safety regulations. . . . However, deference to agency expertise cannot be allowed to become toleration of arbitrary agency action—or in this case inaction—even in an area as critical as aviation safety. Because I believe the FAA has failed to provide a reasoned explanation for its decision to retain the Age 60 Rule, I would remand to the agency for further proceedings.

Rule not on pragmatic resource concerns but on the merits of the rule.

3. A rider to the 1996 appropriations bill prohibited the National Transportation Safety Board from expending any funds to study the performance of pilots over 60. *See* Department of Transportation and Related Agencies Appropriations Act of 1997, Pub. L. No. 104–205, § 345, 110 Stat. 2951, 2976 (1996). But this rider was not in effect when the FAA rendered its decision, and thus is irrelevant to a determination of whether the FAA's failure to undertake measures to obtain data on older pilot functioning was reasonable.

NOTES

(1) *The Elusiveness of Judicial Controls.* If action on a petition under § 553(e) is a reviewable event, it is one in which the courts will almost invariably defer to the agency's refusal to initiate rulemaking when "the agency has chosen not to regulate for reasons ill-suited to judicial resolution, e.g., because of internal management considerations as to budget and personnel or for reasons made after a weighing of competing policies." As Judge Williams warned in Cellnet Communication, Inc. v. FCC, 965 F.2d 1106, 1111 (D.C.Cir.1992), refusals to initiate rulemaking are reviewed "with a deference so broad as to make the process akin to non-reviewability." Compare Heckler v. Chaney, 470 U.S. 821 (1985), which announced a presumption against reviewability of agency decisions not announced to take enforcement action, on analogy to the unreviewability of exercises of prosecutorial discretion; see p. 1218.

Even if a court is persuaded that rulemaking is required, it is after all the agency and not the court that must adopt the regulation, and the judicial tools for dealing with agency reluctance are limited. Consider the comments of David C. Vladeck, an attorney with the advocacy organization Public Citizens Litigation Group:

"What I would like to do is share with you [a] war stor[y] which I think illustrates many of the techniques that we have employed over the last ten years to get agencies off the dime and to actually regulate, and to reveal to you some of the pitfalls that we have encountered along the way.

"The ... story begins in August 1981, where the deregulatory pitch was at its zenith. ... At that time, OSHA was committed to doing as little as possible. And it was saying so as often and as loudly as it could in the press.

"At the same time, we had been approached by a number of unions that were concerned about a substance that was being used to sterilize hospital equipment—ethylene oxide—a very potent and carcinogenic gas. We filed a petition with the agencies, saying 'Look at the medical data regarding this substance. It shows that workers are under a very grave risk of harm. We urge that you regulate it promptly.'

"The response from OSHA: deafening silence. We wrote back and said, 'What about our petition? It has been sitting there for a while.' And again, the response from OSHA: deafening silence. ... We talked to everyone at OSHA who would listen. And they were very polite and listened to us. But the message that came across loud and clear was: 'We're not going to do anything.' And so we ran into court ... [A]fter a year of very intense litigation, Judge Parker issued a decision requiring the agency to go ahead and issue a rule. Judge Parker thought that twenty days would be plenty of time even though we never put in a request for a specific time period. But Judge Parker figured that if he could write an opinion in twenty days, the Agency should be able to put together a standard—generally 400 or 500 pages—in twenty days.

"Not surprisingly, the case went to the court of appeals which affirmed in part, and reversed in part. The court of appeals, told OSHA that it had thirty days to issue a standard, and one year to issue the rule.

"Well, that ought to have been the end of the story. But one of the first lessons that you have to learn about unreasonable delay litigation is that victories need to be preserved, because they can quickly escape unless you are vigilant. At the end of the first year, we got a call from OSHA's lawyers and they told us that they would not be able to meet the deadline. We went back before Judge Parker and the Agency was given until June 15 of that year.

"Finally, the Agency finalized a rule on June 15, 1984, the night before the standard was due, and sent it over for review to OMB. OMB then directed that a big chunk of the rule be deleted. And so the rule that went to the Federal Register had several hundred pages crossed out, with a little note that said, 'We had to take this out, because OMB didn't like it. We will reconsider this in an additional round of rulemaking.' We argued that this was not permitted. The Court did not agree with us.

"Finally, in December of that year, the Agency again acquiesced to OMB, finalizing the standard without this missing chunk. We sued again. We said, 'No, this part of the standard ought to be put back in.' A year and a half later, we got an opinion out of the D.C. Circuit saying, 'You're right, OSHA was wrong. Put it back in.' Of course, no time restraint was imposed.

"After another year and a half, we went back to the D.C. Circuit and said, 'They are engaging once again in unreasonable delay.' And, finally, again after prodding from the D.C. Circuit, OSHA completed its standard in January of 1989, almost eight years after our original rulemaking petition. And that is about as short as any of the cases I have had against OSHA."

Proceedings of the Robert C. Byrd Conf. on the Administrative Process, 5 Admin.L.J. 1, 37–39 (1991). See also An Introductory Problem, p. 1 above, and the case on which it is based, Farmworker Justice Fund, Inc. v. Brock, 811 F.2d 613, vacated as moot, 817 F.2d 890 (D.C.Cir.1987), in which OSHA sought to justify fourteen years of inaction on field sanitation standards for migrant farm workers, in part by the argument that it had other, higher priority rulemakings.

(2) *Who Petitions?* WILLIAM V. LUNEBURG, PETITIONING FEDERAL AGENCIES FOR RULEMAKING: AN OVERVIEW OF ADMINISTRATIVE AND JUDICIAL PRACTICE AND SOME RECOMMENDATIONS FOR IMPROVEMENT, 1988 Wisc.L.Rev. 1, 55–56 (1988): "Existing empirical data regarding the use and operation of the various petition processes are skimpy. The data compiled for the Administrative Conference of the United States indicate that often-regulated entities are the primary users. In the case of the National Highway Traffic Safety Administration, for example, vehicle and equipment manufacturers submit approximately one-half of the petitions, with trade associations, interest groups and private citizens accounting for the remainder. At the Nuclear Regulatory Commission, licensees have filed fifteen of the forty-one petitions presented since 1980; environmental and other public interest groups have filed nine; private citizens have filed seven; the federal government has filed one; trade associations have filed two; and a state government has filed one. Between 1981 and 1986, the Federal Trade Commission received

nine rulemaking petitions, four from industry and the rest from public interest organizations.''

(3) *Empowering the Powerless? Law vs. Discretion.* Other parts of these materials have explored the rise during the 1970's of a concern that the intended beneficiaries of regulation have opportunities, comparable to those of the regulated, to influence the course of agency action. [p. 334ff.] Petitioning for rulemaking (and enforcing agency attention to the petition) would be an obvious means to that end. If obtaining relief through the political process is often more difficult for regulatory beneficiaries than for well-organized members of regulated classes, see p. 345ff., might judicial review of agency inaction may be ''a particularly necessary safeguard'' if beneficiaries are in fact to secure some benefit from a regulatory scheme? Consider, in this respect, STATE OF IOWA EX REL. MILLER V. BLOCK, 771 F.2d 347, 350–55 (8th Cir.1985), cert. denied, 478 U.S. 1012 (1986): ''In 1983, a devastating drought parched the agricultural midwest, including southern Iowa. Farm output fell to a fraction of its ordinary level and many farmers skirted the brink of financial ruin. To mitigate this disaster, Iowa's governor requested that the Secretary [of Agriculture] implement several discretionary federal disaster relief programs, which the Secretary declined to do. [Suit to compel the Secretary to act was brought by six Iowa farm couples and the State of Iowa. The court held that the discretion granted by the Special Disaster Payments Program (SDPP) is not so broad as to preclude review of the Secretary's failure to promulgate *any* implementing regulations. The relevant statute provides that the Secretary ''*may* make disaster payments'' whenever he determines that farms within the federal crop insurance program have suffered substantial uncompensated disaster losses.[1] The court found ''illuminating'' the Senate Report on SDPP:]

''Although the statute 'does not specify the emergency situations' in which assistance under SDPP would be provided, Senator Heflin provided 'some idea of the situations in which the Secretary could reasonably be expected to implement the disaster payments program.' The list of examples, which was 'not meant to be inclusive,' included situations in which:

> (1) the Federal crop insurance policy excludes coverage for the disaster risk that caused the loss; (2) there was a lack of understanding of the crop insurance program among producers affected by the disaster; (3) the crop insurance program was not adequately sold in the area affected by the disaster, or the Federal Crop Insurance Corporation's educational efforts were inadequate; or (4) the Federal Crop Insurance Corporation used an inaccurate actuarial basis so that a producer affected by the disaster was unable to obtain coverage adequate to protect his crop sufficiently.

''The appellants also direct our attention to a General Accounting Office Report on USDA disaster aid payments under the Agriculture and Food Act of 1981. That report noted that the Act vests substantial discretionary authority in the Secretary to make these aid payments, yet it

---

1. By contrast, another part of the statute provides that the Secretary ''shall'' make disaster relief payments to farmers not covered by the federal crop insurance program at all.

concluded that 'USDA's use of this discretion should be based on objective criteria. However, USDA has not developed objective criteria to be used in awarding special disaster payments. This lack of criteria may result in subjective or inconsistent application of the Act.'

"Having reviewed the relevant legislative materials under the SDPP, we next review analogous case law to assist us in evaluating the statutes we have discussed. We find our recent decision in Allison v. Block, 723 F.2d 631 (8th Cir.1983), to be highly instructive. In that case, we considered the Secretary's failure to implement a program entirely, not simply his failure to grant aid in a particular case.[2] The Allisons, who had defaulted on Farmers Home Administration loans, sued the Secretary of Agriculture seeking a deferral of the foreclosure of their farm. [However, no administrative mechanism had been established by which deferrals, which had been authorized by statute, could be obtained.] The district court enjoined foreclosure on the Allisons' farm pending the Secretary's compliance with the deferral statute, 7 U.S.C. § 1981a (1982), and we affirmed.

". . . [W]e find that the Special Disaster Payments Program presents a straightforward case which compels judicial review of agency inaction. Despite the fact that the statute specifies three criteria for determining the inadequacy of federal crop insurance, the Secretary has deliberately taken no steps to implement proper procedures to protect applicants from potential abuses of discretion under the statute. Moreover, the criteria presuppose findings about the inadequacy of crop insurance; as in Allison, the criteria suggest a 'prima facie standard of eligibility for relief,' yet without substantive elaboration by the Secretary, the criteria and the relief program become no more than 'an empty procedural shell,' and the clear intent of Congress to establish a program is thwarted. We also observe that, as was the case in Allison, the legislative history of this measure relies on the word 'program,' which becomes nonsensical unless the Secretary promulgates procedural and substantive standards under which disaster assistance can be disbursed. Given the clear guidance of the statute, its supporting materials and case law, then, we find ample law to apply and we reject the district court's suggestion that judicial review was foreclosed by an absence of law.

"It is not the business of this Court to order the Secretary to make payments under the SDPP to specific farmers. But when Congress has created a program which contemplates that such payments will be made in appropriate circumstances, it is the clear duty of the Secretary to promulgate regulations which carry out the intent of Congress."

[Judge Fagg dissented on grounds that Heckler v. Chaney controlled and that "Congress has placed the determination of whether to implement

2. We regard this fact as the essential point distinguishing the Supreme Court's recent decision in Heckler v. Chaney from Allison and the case at bar. In Heckler, the Court extended the language of 5 U.S.C. § 701(a)(2) (which excludes from judicial review "agency action . . . committed to agency discretion by law") to insulate from review the FDA's decision not to enforce the law proscribing unapproved use and misbranding of a drug. We believe that Heckler's consideration of an agency's decision not to enforce the law in a single instance presents an issue distinguishable from the Secretary's decision not to promulgate general regulations embodying the intent of Congress.

the discretionary program encompassed in the SDPP entirely with the Secretary.''

(4) *The Problems of Remediating Inaction.* The opinion in Professional Pilots Federation reflects concerns about the appropriate relationship of courts and agencies—the scope of review problem taken up in Chapter 8. A full appreciation of the difficult problem of reviewing administrative discretion is best developed there, but the present readings illustrate remedial dilemmas judges may face. A court may be able to direct that rulemaking occur, but only the agency is capable of adopting a regulation and making the necessary discretionary judgments about content and enforcement. Consider, in this respect, MERRICK B. GARLAND, DEREGULATION AND JUDICIAL REVIEW, 98 Harv.L.Rev. 507, 563–65 (1985): "Even when an agency's inaction fails to survive review, the problem of remedy still looms. Historically, courts have resisted issuing orders directing agencies to take affirmative action. Instead, they have simply instructed agencies to explain or reconsider their decisions not to act. . . .

"There are several reasons for the general judicial reluctance to order affirmative relief. First, there are . . . prudential concerns . . . When there is no record evaluating the alternatives available to the agency, compelling the agency to act may well be ill-advised. Such an approach may also divert limited resources from an area of pressing need to one the agency has found not even worthy of consideration.

"Second, some commentators have argued that affirmative orders violate the separation of powers by encroaching upon the executive branch's function of executing the laws. . . . To be sure, because the essence of the executive function is the exercise of discretion, a court transgresses the separation of powers when it dictates that an agency take one particular action instead of others within its discretionary prerogative. Yet when a court merely orders an agency to act, leaving the choice of action to the agency's discretion, no trespass occurs. Nor does a court violate the separation of powers when its directs an agency to take a specific action that the agency has no discretion to refuse to take—either because it has a statutory duty to take such action, or because refusal would exceed (or abuse) the discretion the agency does possess.

"Nonetheless, affirmative orders do present a substantial question of institutional competence. When an agency resists a court order, effective enforcement may require the court itself to take evidence, weigh competing alternatives, and construct a satisfactory rule from whole cloth. In such circumstances, '[t]he ability of the courts to devise a fair and effective remedy' may often be in doubt.

"Finally, affirmative relief may also appear logically inappropriate in light of the limited scope of judicial review applied to inaction. Because such review requires only that the agency proffer a plausible explanation for its inaction, a court will ordinarily phrase an agency's failure to survive such review as a failure to provide a sufficient explanation. And when insufficient explanation is perceived as the defect, a remand for further explanation—rather than a direct order to take action—may appear to be the appropriate cure.''

Merrick Garland became Judge Garland of the D.C. Circuit, and followed his own advice, in the case of a rule delayed more than eight years behind "the express timetable set forth by Congress in the Mine Safety and Health Act of 1977." IN RE UNITED MINE WORKERS, 190 F.3d 545, 552–44, 556 (D.C.Cir.1999) was an action for mandamus seeking to force Mine Safety and Health Administration action on gaseous emissions from diesel engines used in underground coal mines. "As MSHA points out, the two gases of concern here represent only a small fraction of the over 600 contaminants of mine air at issue in the [NRPM for an omnibus air quality rulemaking, that the UMW was relying upon in its effort to force adoption of a final rule]. To single out diesel exhaust gases and designate them for expedited treatment might well delay rulemaking for other contaminants that are at least as dangerous to the health of the nation's miners." Yet, "[h]owever many priorities the agency may have, and however modest its personnel and budgetary resources may be, there is a limit to how long it may use these justifications to excuse inaction in the face of the congressional command to act within ninety days [of publishing an NPRM]." Rather than mandate adoption of a rule, as such, the court "retain[ed] jurisdiction over this case until there is a final agency disposition that discharges MSHA's obligations under the Mine Act. The agency is directed to advise the court on the date such disposition occurs, and of the status of this matter on each of the following dates unless final disposition has already occurred: December 31, 1999; June 30, 2000; December 31, 2000; and December 31, 2001. Prior to final agency action, the UMWA may petition this court to grant additional appropriate relief in the event MSHA fails to adhere substantially to a schedule that would ... constitute a good faith effort by MSHA to come into compliance with the Mine Act." In Cronin v. Browner, 90 F.Supp.2d 364 (S.D.N.Y.2000) one may find a district court wrestling with comparable problems at another overworked agency, EPA, and coming to a similar result.

(5) *Legislative Forcing.* As in the case just discussed, Congress has sometimes attempted to counteract administrative inaction by imposing mandatory statutory deadlines. Agency inaction has sometimes been attributable to the political differences characteristic of divided government—if there are conflicts in regulatory philosophy between Congress and the White House. More neutrally, delay may come from procedural elaborations on the notice-and-comment process introduced by hybrid rulemaking statutes. Action-forcing statutes have been particularly common in the environmental area. Typically they command particular agency action—such as determining whether certain chemicals are hazardous, or setting standards for certain classes of polluters—by a stated date.[3] Commentators have vigorously debated the regulatory wisdom, and the practical efficacy, of these action-forcing statutes.[4] SIDNEY A. SHAPIRO & ROBERT L. GLICKSMAN, CONGRESS,

---

3. Examples include the 1984 amendments to the Resource Conservation & Recovery Act, the 1986 amendments to the Comprehensive Environmental Response, Compensation, & Liability Act, the Safe Drinking Water Act, the Toxic Substance Control Act, the 1987 amendments to the Clean Water Act, and the 1988 amendments to the Federal Insecticide, Fungicide, & Rodenticide Act.

4. See, e.g., John S. Applegate, Worst Things First: Risk, Information, and Regulatory Structure in Toxic Substances Control, 9

THE SUPREME COURT, AND THE QUIET REVOLUTION IN ADMINISTRATIVE LAW, 1988 Duke L.J. 819, 834–36, provides a thorough survey, concluding that, although statutory deadlines "increase the likelihood" that a court will force the agency to act, courts "frequently seem uncomfortable enforcing such deadlines":

"Some courts believe that they must solicit a revised timetable from the agency and must accept it if the agency proceeds in good faith. While other courts deny any obligation to solicit the agency's views in drafting a timetable, most nevertheless do so. And judicial ire is greatest when an agency misses its own timetable. Thus, coercive statutes authorizing agencies to set initial deadlines are more likely to be strictly enforced than those imposing statutory deadlines on the agency.

"That the courts prefer agencies to set their own timetables for accelerated action illustrates one disadvantage of statutory deadlines—they place courts in the awkward position of second-guessing how an agency should use its resources. Moreover, since deadlines do not simplify the agency's substantive task, they can create unrealistic time pressures or more deadlines than an agency can realistically meet. In such circumstances, the agency is likely to take regulatory action that is hasty, without adequate evidentiary support, and thus unable to withstand judicial review, or to divert its resources to litigation in an effort to justify its failure to meet the deadlines. The agency's failure to meet its deadlines may also increase public pressure for more deadlines that the agency cannot meet. Even if the agency manages to comply with some deadlines, doing so may force it to misallocate its resources by shifting them from tasks it deems important to others it considers subsidiary."

Professors Shapiro and Glicksman go on to point out: "Perhaps the most important problem with using coercive delegations to reduce agency discretion is that even if an agency acts on time, a coercive statute requires only that the agency act, not that it act in a particular way. Thus, the coercive model's success in preventing an agency from subverting a congressional mandate may depend on a court's willingness to scrutinize the substance of the agency's decision." We take up this issue in Chapter VIII.

(6) *Delay in Completing Action vs. Refusal to Initiate Action.* What if the agency initiates a proceeding, receives comments (or takes testimony), and then retreats into years of silence? Attempts to persuade the court to jumpstart a stalled regulatory process often raise questions about both threshold issues such as jurisdiction and ripeness—considered in Chapter IX—and the appropriate standard of review on the merits. The germinal case in this area is TELECOMMUNICATIONS RESEARCH AND ACTION CENTER V. FCC,

Yale J. on Reg. 277 (1992); Michael Herz, Judicial Textualism Meets Congressional Micromanagement: A Potential Collision in Clean Air Act Interpretation, 16 Harv. Envtl.L.Rev. 175 (1992); Craig N. Oren, Detail and Delegation: A Study in Statutory Specificity, 15 Colum.J.Envtl.L. 143 (1990); Sidney A. Shapiro & Thomas O. McGarity, Reorienting OSHA: Regulatory Alternatives and Legislative Reform, 6 Yale J. on Reg. 1 (1989); Alden F. Abbott, The Case Against Federal Statutory and Judicial Deadlines: A Cost–Benefit Appraisal, 39 Admin.L.Rev. 171 (1987); John D. Graham, The Failure of Agency–Forcing: The Regulation of Airborne Carcinogens Under Section 112 of the Clean Air Act, 1985 Duke L.J. 100.

750 F.2d 70 (D.C.Cir.1984) ["TRAC"]. The court there defined "the hexagonal contours of a standard" for assessing claims of unreasonable delay:

> (1) the time agencies take to make decisions must be governed by a "rule of reason;" (2) where Congress has provided a timetable or other indication of the speed with which it expects the agency to proceed in the enabling statute, that statutory scheme may supply content for this rule of reason; (3) delays that might be reasonable in the sphere of economic regulation are less tolerable when human health and welfare are at stake; (4) the courts should consider the effect of expediting delayed action on agency activities of a higher or competing priority; (5) the court should also take into account the nature and extent of the interests prejudiced by delay; and (6) the court need not "find any impropriety lurking behind agency lassitude in order to hold that agency action is 'unreasonably delayed.'"

The D.C. Circuit periodically restates and reorders these factors,[5] but TRAC remains the pivotal case on judicial review of delay claims. For some circuits, specific congressional deadlines control these issues, e.g. Biodiversity Legal Fndn. v. Badgley, 284 F.3d 1046 (9th Cir.2002), but for the D.C. Circuit this is mainly a factor to be considered. Western Coal Traffic League v. Surface Transp. Bd., 216 F.3d 1168 (D.C.Cir.2000).

(ii) THE DECISION TO INITIATE RULEMAKING

Save for § 553(e)'s invitation to the public to petition for rulemaking, the APA is indifferent to what happens up to the point when an NPRM is published in the Federal Register. As might be expected, however, both agencies and their political overseers do a great deal of work in the pre-NPRM period. Increasingly, this work is the subject of statutory and executive order requirements.

First, the agency must decide what issues warrant rulemaking. This decision, in turn, requires both the setting of regulatory priorities—policy judgments that may transcend the agency's own substantive mandate—and the use of those priorities to identify appropriate subjects for regulations. Second, the agency must develop concrete proposals. Should those proposals be developed within the agency, or through negotiations with other concerned private and public actors? During the development phase, agencies must collect and analyze information, worry about enforcement possibilities and incentives, and develop a supportable view of their legal authority. Increasingly, they must also think about the costs the rule will impose, and consider how the rule will "play" with their immediate political constituencies (Congress and the White House) as well as with their more public environment. All this requires that they coordinate the various people in the agency who each know part, but not all, of what needs to be considered. Of course, as this happens, considerable institutional momentum builds.

Managing this process is one of the responsibilities that the heads, deputy heads, and assistants heads of departments, agencies, and adminis-

---

5. See, e.g., In re International Chemical Workers Union, 958 F.2d 1144, 1149 (D.C.Cir.1992), and the particularly compre-   hensive canvassing in Judge Robinson's opinion in Cutler v. Hayes, 818 F.2d 879, 896–98 (D.C.Cir.1987).

trations get paid to exercise. But the process is not entirely at their discretion. Quite apart from constraints imposed by each agency's specific regulatory authority, many legal requirements imposed since the APA's passage apply to the pre-NPRM period, and demand consideration of matters agencies might otherwise have ignored. Since 1969, the National Environmental Policy Act of 1969—the model from which other requirements have grown—has required the preparation of Environmental Impact Statements (or the less extensive Environmental Assessments) for actions likely to have an impact on environmental values. Drafts are to be made available for public comment before any such action (for example, the adoption of a regulation) is finally committed to. Not long after NEPA's passage, Richard Nixon began a practice, followed by all subsequent Presidents, of insisting that rulemakings likely to produce a significant effect on the economy be analyzed for their cost and benefit implications. Again, this analysis must be done in consultation with a White House office and it begins in advance of the NPRM. Subsequently, statutes and executive orders have required pre-NPRM impact analyses to analyze possible effects on small businesses, on states, localities and Indian tribes, on family values, etc. The result is a highly complex set of mandates for the would-be agency rulemaker. A grid prepared by Professor Mark Seidenfeld. "A Table of Requirements for Federal Administrative Rulemaking," 27 F.S.U.L. Rev. 533 (2000), arrays 18 different statutes or executive orders (other than the APA and the agency's own constitutive authority), against twenty-five different stages in the rulemaking process. Twelve of these stages precede the NPRM; twelve follow it.

Life has been made somewhat simpler than this sounds, although still complex, by permitting one "impact statement" generally to serve all applicable impact analysis requirements. And this is not the place, if any is, to examine each of the 450 intersections in Professor Seidenfeld's grid. Still the task is a daunting one and it is important for you to realize that the apparently straightforward requirements of § 553 have been encrusted in this way. The pages following will take up the aspects of the pre-NPRM process that strike your editors as the most important and/or representative. This subsection will address the problems of prioritization and initial commitment. The next will introduce you to negotiated rulemaking, a statutory process for developing consensual rulemaking proposals. A third subsection will explore the impact analysis process.

This sequence follows the timeline of a rulemaking as it would be experienced inside an agency or outside. All represent important recent developments. The impact analysis process became an established fixture of federal rulemaking with President Reagan's 1981 Executive Order 12,291. Negotiated Rulemaking first appeared in the statute books in 1990. Finally, elements of the priority-setting process were put in place by the Regulatory Flexibility Act of 1980, and elaborated on a few years later by Executive Order 12,498. Priority setting remains the most fluid (and also the least transparent) aspect of the contemporary pre-NPRM process.

It is perhaps worth noting at the outset a distortion that these developments have arguably introduced into both rulemaking and our perception of it. Their genesis lies in the explosion of health and safety regulations generated by statutes like the Occupational Safety and Health Act, the Clean Air Act, or the National Highway Traffic Safety Act—all enactments of the late 60's and early 70's. In consequence, one sees a great deal of attention to the choice among risks to address, at the point of initiation, and to cost-benefit analysis, at the point of rulemaking decision. Yet attempts to deal with the whole of administrative law as matters of risk regulation, or more broadly, cost-benefit analysis, greatly narrow the domain of administrative law. Much rulemaking is not about risk in any sensible sense, even giving allowance for the ways in which some analysts might see things like "deceptive practices" as matters of the risk of error. Much is not about maximizing welfare, but rather about providing minimum standards or redistributing power or income. Making new tax regulations is not a matter of risk or cost-benefit analysis; nor is deciding who merits disability benefits, nor how to allocate power between unions and management. Executive Order 12866, whose provisions on initiating rulemaking are about to be considered, arguably seeks to deal with this potential distortion by including in its initial statement of "Regulatory Philosophy" the following: "[I]n choosing among alternative regulatory approaches, agencies should select those approaches that maximize net benefits (including ... distributive impacts; and equity), unless a statute requires another regulatory approach." Is this more than a distraction from the general message conveyed by the Executive Order? Would it help you decide whether a rule on eligibility for farm mortgage foreclosure relief eligibility was net-beneficial? Watch out for any tendency of the writing in the field, including ours, to take the core examples where risk assessment or cost-benefit approaches do make sense—environmental regulation, safety regulation—and rewrite all of administrative law in that model.

Executive Order 12866[1]

Regulatory Planning and Review.

58 FR 51735 (Oct. 4, 1993), as amended by Executive Order 13258, 67 FR 9385 (Feb. 26, 2002).

Section 1.   Statement of Regulatory Philosophy and Principles.

(a) **The Regulatory Philosophy.** Federal agencies should promulgate only such regulations as are required by law, are necessary to interpret the law, or are made necessary by compelling public need, such as material failures of private markets to protect or improve the health and safety of the public, the environment, or the well-being of the American people. In deciding whether and how to regulate, agencies should assess all costs and benefits of available regulatory alternatives, including the alternative of not regulating. Costs and benefits shall be understood to include both quantifiable measures (to the fullest extent that these can be usefully estimated) and qualitative measures of costs and benefits that are difficult to quantify, but nevertheless essential to consider. Further, in choosing among alternative regulatory approaches, agencies should select those approaches that maximize net benefits (including potential economic, environmental, public health and safety, and other advantages; distributive

---

1. The whole text of Executive Order 12866 appears in the appendix.

impacts; and equity), unless a statute requires another regulatory approach.

(b) The Principles of Regulation. To ensure that the agencies' regulatory programs are consistent with the philosophy set forth above, agencies should adhere to the following principles, to the extent permitted by law and where applicable:

(1) Each agency shall identify the problem that it intends to address (including, where applicable, the failures of private markets or public institutions that warrant new agency action) as well as assess the significance of that problem.

(2) Each agency shall examine whether existing regulations (or other law) have created, or contributed to, the problem that a new regulation is intended to correct and whether those regulations (or other law) should be modified to achieve the intended goal of regulation more effectively.

(3) Each agency shall identify and assess available alternatives to direct regulation, including providing economic incentives to encourage the desired behavior, such as user fees or marketable permits, or providing information upon which choices can be made by the public.

(4) In setting regulatory priorities, each agency shall consider, to the extent reasonable, the degree and nature of the risks posed by various substances or activities within its jurisdiction.... [The remaining seven principles concern steps taken once a regulatory agenda has been set.]

Section 4.   Planning Mechanism

In order to have an effective regulatory program, to provide for coordination of regulations, to maximize consultation and the resolution of potential conflicts at an early stage, to involve the public and its State, local, and tribal officials in regulatory planning, and to ensure that new or revised regulations promote the President's priorities and the principles set forth in this Executive order, these procedures shall be followed, to the extent permitted by law:

(a) Agencies' Policy Meeting. Early in each year's planning cycle, the Director [of OMB] shall convene a meeting of the Advisors and the heads of agencies to seek a common understanding of priorities and to coordinate regulatory efforts to be accomplished in the upcoming year.

(b) Unified Regulatory Agenda. For purposes of this subsection, the term "agency" or "agencies" shall also include those considered to be independent regulatory agencies, as defined in 44 U.S.C. § 3502(10). Each agency shall prepare an agenda of all regulations under development or review, at a time and in a manner specified by the Administrator of [the Office of Management and Budget's Office of Information and Regulatory Affairs (OIRA)]. The description of each regulatory action shall contain, at a minimum, a regulation identifier number, a brief summary of the action, the legal authority for the action, any legal deadline for the action, and the name and telephone number of a knowledgeable agency official. Agencies may incorporate the information required under 5 U.S.C. § 602 [the Small

Business Regulatory Enforcement Fairness Act, originally the Regulatory Flexibility Act of 1980] . . . into these agendas.

(c) The Regulatory Plan. For purposes of this subsection, the term "agency" or "agencies" shall also include those considered to be independent regulatory agencies, as defined in 44 U.S.C. § 3502(10).

(1) As part of the Unified Regulatory Agenda, beginning in 1994, each agency shall prepare a Regulatory Plan (Plan) of the most important significant regulatory actions that the agency reasonably expects to issue in proposed or final form in that fiscal year or thereafter. The Plan shall be approved personally by the agency head and shall contain at a minimum:

(A) A statement of the agency's regulatory objectives and priorities and how they relate to the President's priorities;

(B) A summary of each planned significant regulatory action including, to the extent possible, alternatives to be considered and preliminary estimates of the anticipated costs and benefits;

(C) A summary of the legal basis for each such action, including whether any aspect of the action is required by statute or court order;

(D) A statement of the need for each such action and, if applicable, how the action will reduce risks to public health, safety, or the environment, as well as how the magnitude of the risk addressed by the action relates to other risks within the jurisdiction of the agency;

(E) The agency's schedule for action, including a statement of any applicable statutory or judicial deadlines; and

(F) The name, address, and telephone number of a person the public may contact for additional information about the planned regulatory action.

(2) Each agency shall forward its Plan to OIRA by June 1st of each year.

(3) Within 10 calendar days after OIRA has received an agency's Plan, OIRA shall circulate it to other affected agencies and the Advisors.

(4) An agency head who believes that a planned regulatory action of another agency may conflict with its own policy or action taken or planned shall promptly notify, in writing, the Administrator of OIRA, who shall forward that communication to the issuing agency and the Advisors.

(5) If the Administrator of OIRA believes that a planned regulatory action of an agency may be inconsistent with the President's priorities or the principles set forth in this Executive order or may be in conflict with any policy or action taken or planned by another agency, the Administrator of OIRA shall promptly notify, in writing, the affected agencies and the Advisors.

(6) The Director may consult with the heads of agencies with respect to their Plans and, in appropriate instances, request further consideration or inter-agency coordination.

(7) The Plans developed by the issuing agency shall be published annually in the October publication of the Unified Regulatory Agenda. This publication shall be made available to the Congress; State, local, and tribal governments; and the public. Any views on any aspect of any agency Plan, including whether any planned regulatory action might conflict with any other planned or existing regulation, impose any unintended consequences on the public, or confer any unclaimed benefits on the public, should be directed to the issuing agency, with a copy to OIRA.

Small Business Regulatory Enforcement Fairness Act[2]

5 U.S.C. § 602

Sec. 602.—Regulatory agenda

(a) During the months of October and April of each year, each agency shall publish in the Federal Register a regulatory flexibility agenda which shall contain—

(1) a brief description of the subject area of any rule which the agency expects to propose or promulgate which is likely to have a significant economic impact on a substantial number of small entities;

(2) a summary of the nature of any such rule under consideration for each subject area listed in the agenda pursuant to paragraph (1), the objectives and legal basis for the issuance of the rule, and an approximate schedule for completing action on any rule for which the agency has issued a general notice of proposed rulemaking, and

(3) the name and telephone number of an agency official knowledgeable concerning the items listed in paragraph (1).

(b) Each regulatory flexibility agenda shall be transmitted to the Chief Counsel for Advocacy of the Small Business Administration for comment, if any.

(c) Each agency shall endeavor to provide notice of each regulatory flexibility agenda to small entities or their representatives through direct notification or publication of the agenda in publications likely to be obtained by such small entities and shall invite comments upon each subject area on the agenda.

(d) Nothing in this section precludes an agency from considering or acting on any matter not included in a regulatory flexibility agenda, or requires an agency to consider or act on any matter listed in such agenda.

NOTES

(1) *Meet the Players*. E.O. 12866 refers to a number of White House actors of importance to contemporary rulemaking, and one agency official.

2. This section had its origin in the Regulatory Flexibility Act of 1980.

(a) The Office of Management and Budget (OMB) is the professional White House bureaucracy, with a permanent staff of about 500 that, save for its top leadership, continues through changing administrations. With limited exceptions for some (but not all) of the independent regulatory commissions, OMB controls agency submissions to Congress of draft legislation, testimony on proposed legislation, and budgetary requests. As the Executive Order suggests, OMB frequently serves as the tribunal before which inter-agency conflicts are resolved.[3] The President's equivalent of Congress's General Accounting Office, it develops management techniques generally for the Executive Branch. It is, thus, the office by which the President makes his priorities concrete.

(b) The Office of Information and Regulatory Affairs (OIRA) is the sub-division of OMB with the greatest responsibility for regulatory affairs. Operating with a professional staff of about 40, it is statutorily responsible for the coordination of government information policy, including the clearance of agency information demands under the Paperwork Reduction Act, p. 292. Under E.O. 12866 (and its predecessors), it assembles the government's regulatory agenda, and clears the regulatory impact statements that may subsequently be prepared for particular rulemakings. Presidents have generally appointed as its head accomplished professionals with significant experience in policy analysis and/or law. For example, Dr. John Graham, President Bush's Director as this casebook goes to press, is a widely published scholar who came to the office from a professorship focused on risk analysis at Harvard University's School of Public Health. The Director of OIRA has been subject to Senate confirmation since the administration of the first President Bush.

(c) The Regulatory Flexibility Act of 1980 and its successor, the Small Business Regulatory Enforcement Fairness Act (SBREFA), aim to protect small businesses from the impact of regulations that are manageable for larger corporations but likely to overwhelm smaller firms. Responsibility for policing compliance is given to the chief counsel of the Small Business Administration, an agency with particular responsibilities for the concerns of small businesses. In practice, however, OMB/OIRA controls predominate.[4]

(d) Until February 26, 2002, the Executive Order gave the Vice President responsibilities now assigned only to the Director and others in subsections (a) and (c)(3, 4, 5, and 6) of Section 4. This specific placement of the Vice President atop the administration's structure for setting its regulatory agenda brought clearly into public view a steady development of the previous quarter century. Beginning with the political negotiations that

---

3. For legal conflicts, the Office of Legal Counsel in the Department of Justice serves this bureaucratic function.

4. A "Memorandum of Understanding Between the Office of Advocacy, SBA and the Office of Information and Regulatory Affairs, OMB" Dated March 19, 2002 is posted to the

brought Nelson Rockefeller into the administration of Gerald Ford as Vice President, Vice Presidents had played an increasingly prominent role in coordinating domestic regulatory policy on the President's behalf. Any such role today is no longer a public one.

(2) *The Manhattan Telephone Book.* While the SBREFA obligation is limited to rulemaking initiatives "likely to have a significant economic impact on a substantial number of small entities," § 4 (b) of E.O. 12866 (like E.O. 12498 before it) applies to *all* rulemaking by *all* agencies, and the biannual Unified Agenda of Federal Regulations published by the Federal Register is correspondingly inclusive. Running two to four abstracts to a page, its print version is about three or four inches thick, the size of the Manhattan telephone book. Available and searchable in electronic form, the Unified Agenda lists agency actions in four stages of completion. The earliest, the "Pre-rule Stage," contains action to be undertaken within the next twelve months to determine whether to initiate rulemaking; it is thus substantially in advance even of the second stage, actions for which an NPRM is in the offing. The presence of "the name and telephone number of an agency official knowledgeable concerning the items listed" invites and permits immediate engagement in agency processes for those wishing it. A 1994 survey of organizations of all types that normally participate in notice-and-comment proceedings reported that about three-fourths of these organizations are in informal contact with agencies before the § 553 "notice" is issued, at least "regularly," and often "very frequently" or "always." Cornelius M. Kerwin, Rulemaking 202 (1994).

Presidential Management of the Regulatory State[1]

John D. Graham, Ph.D., Administrator, Office of Information and Regulatory Affairs.
Dec. 17, 2001.

I would like to introduce the session today with the following thought question: "Why would any clear thinking President ask a senior OMB official with a modest staff of 40 professionals to oversee the entire federal regulatory state?" Let me suggest, at the outset, that any such effort might justly be considered hopeless.

First, there are over 100 federal agencies and subagencies with regulatory mandates from Congress. They churn out 4,500 new rules each year. The 40 OMB professionals are obviously outnumbered by the thousands of regulatory specialists in the agencies.

Second, a wise regulatory system requires specialized expertise on a remarkable variety of subjects: agriculture, telecommunications, occupational safety and health, energy production and conservation, environmental protection, law enforcement, medicine and health care systems, and so forth. The responsible federal agencies have experienced professionals in each of these fields; the expertise at OMB is more limited.

Third, once a regulatory proposal is formally submitted to OMB, there is already powerful organizational momentum behind the proposal. Not only have agency staff devoted potentially years of work to data collection

OIRA website, http://www.white-house.gov/omb/inforeg/regpol.html.

1. Speech given to the Weidenbaum Center Forum, "Executive Regulatory Review: Surveying the Record, Making It Work," National Press Club, Washington, DC; in July, 2002 it could be found posted on the OIRA website, http://www.white-house.gov/omb/reginfo.

and analysis; policy officials at agencies may have managed delicate relationships among stakeholders. At this stage, OMB review is destined to make waves and bruise egos, which means that it will be resisted, sometimes fiercely and effectively.

Finally, it is sometimes argued that Congress, through legislative mandates and oversight, instructs or guides the efforts of agencies. From this perspective, any OMB "influence" in this bilateral relationship might be seen as extra-legal or even a perverse influence in democracy. And of course there is the cynical view that OMB is simply the place where nefarious deals are cut in the interests of lobbyists wearing alligator shoes and Rolex watches.

Not surprisingly, I do not share these views that Presidential management of the regulatory state is hopeless or perverse. I share the vision of Supreme Court Justice Stephen Breyer[2] who described an experienced cadre of civil servants in the Executive Office of the President who have broad expertise in the craft of regulatory policy. . . .

I think the following empirical fact is instructive: Every President since Richard Nixon, Democrat and Republican, has insisted on some type of centralized management of the regulatory state. . . . Given this history, it is instructive to consider why Presidents are so determined to manage the regulatory state.

First, the federal regulatory state is here to stay. Although economic regulation has seen much privatization over the last 20 years, the public and Congress have revealed a growing commitment to public health, safety and environmental regulation. . . .

Second, the economic costs of the regulatory state are substantial, exceeding $800 billion according to one recent estimate prepared for the Small Business Administration. Note that this figure is larger than the discretionary federal budget and . . . an average annual cost of almost $8,000 per household. Although many rules have enormous benefits for households, there is real concern that these dollars are not always invested wisely. . . .

Third, when two or more agencies disagree about a regulatory matter, the President needs an experienced unit to forge a consensus so that governance can proceed. OMB often plays that role in the regulatory arena. . . .

Finally, Presidents use the powers of OMB regarding agency action to advance Administration priorities and policy objectives. . . . We should remember that OMB is an office within the Executive Office of the President and its actions necessarily reflect Presidential priorities.

In this Administration, OMB's regulatory office is pursuing an agenda of smarter regulation. Despite what some of our critics charge, there is no grandiose plot to roll back safeguards or attempt an across-the-board sunset of existing regulations. What the President seeks is a smarter

---

2. [Ed.] The reference is to Justice   Effective Risk Regulation (1992).
Breyer's Breaking the Vicious Cycle: Toward

regulatory process based on sound science and economics: a smarter process adopts new rules when market and local choices fail, modifies existing rules to make them more effective or less costly, and rescinds outmoded rules whose benefits no longer justify their costs. We are pursuing this agenda under the terms of the Clinton–Gore executive order, which we believe ... is based on sound principles and procedures....

... [W]e have taken steps to enhance the openness of OMB's regulatory review process.... Through the Internet, it is now possible for the public to scrutinize how we use science and economics to stop bad rules and help agencies craft better ones. ... There may always be a need to hold some candid deliberations in the secluded quarters of the Old Executive Office Building. I certainly do not believe that the Executive Office of the President can operate in a fishbowl. However, I do believe that more openness at OMB about regulatory review will enhance public appreciation of the value and legitimacy of a centralized, analytical approach to regulatory policy.

Second, we are hiring the first scientists and engineers at OIRA to accompany a cadre of economists, statisticians, and information technology specialists. We believe this more diversified pool of expertise will enable us to ask better questions about agency proposals. We have reversed the 20–year decline in staffing at OIRA and have done so in a way that reflects the increasing importance of science-based regulation in the federal agencies.

Third, we have sent clear signals to agencies that we care about regulatory analysis, QUALITY regulatory analysis. We are using both the carrot and the stick. The carrot we have offered is more deferential OMB review of proposals that agencies have voluntarily subjected to independent peer review. ... The Bush Administration recognizes that we should consider and account for the consensus views of the leadership of the scientific community, regardless of whether it leads to a pro-or anti-regulation result. The stick has been a revival of the dreaded "return letter". ... Recently we have witnessed some agencies simply withdrawing rules rather than face a public return letter. Knowing that we care, agencies are beginning to invite OMB into the early stages of regulatory deliberations, where our analytical approach can have a much bigger impact.

Fourth, we have demonstrated that we are prepared to initiate new regulatory actions when they are sensible and based on sound science and economics. We have ... devised a modest tool called the "prompt letter" that enables OMB to publicly identify areas where agencies might improve regulatory policies. ... Unlike the more definitive Presidential directive, the prompt letter is a public request that is intended to stimulate agency and public deliberation. Final decisions about priorities remain with the agencies.

The prompt letter is not simply a pro-regulatory tool; we will be using it to encourage agency efforts to streamline the regulatory process. We do not believe that across-the-board reviews of all existing rules are a cost-effective use of agency resources; yet we have sought public comment and learned of 70 targeted suggestions to modify or rescind existing rules. We will be sharing these ideas with agencies through our forthcoming annual report on regulatory policy. We are also encouraging interested parties to prepare additional nominations for the public comment process on next year's annual report on the costs and benefits of regulation....

NOTES

(1) *An Open Process?* Administrator Graham had expanded on the thought that "the transparency of OIRA's regulatory review process is critical" in a memorandum to his staff dated October 18, 2001:[3]

> OIRA ... makes certain materials available after the publication of a rule that has been reviewed. Upon request by the public, OIRA will provide: the draft regulation as originally submitted; any agency analyses (e.g. RIA not published with rule) and other material submitted by the agency during the review; "change" pages, (i.e., pages of the draft where changes have occurred in the course of review); correspondence between OIRA and the agency exchanged during the review; and correspondence OIRA received from outside parties while the rule was under review....

> A. Definitions ...

>> 3. Rules under review:

>>> **Covered**: A rule is officially under review after an agency submits and OIRA records receipt of a clearance package. Consistent with the spirit of E.O. 12866 disclosure procedures and OIRA staff practice, OIRA also considers a rule to be under informal review after OIRA has started a substantive discussion with the agency concerning the provisions of a draft rule or OIRA has received the rule in draft.

>>> **Not covered**: Rules are not under review prior to the start of informal OIRA review ...

Would you expect the Regulatory Agenda process to be within OIRA's disclosure practices? Should it be? Or is this one of those settings in which "there may always be a need to hold some candid deliberations in the secluded quarters of the Old Executive Office Building"?

(3) *A Boon for Agency Leadership?* The "powerful organizational momentum" Dr. Graham addressed is not a problem for OIRA and the White House alone. The single person (or multi-member commission) in charge of a complex organization often might not learn of new policy initiatives under consideration in her agency until after they had taken definitive shape—a point at which it is considerably more difficult to get attention to issues or alternatives of interest to her.[4] Christopher DeMuth (the head of

---

3. Visited July 24, 2002, at http://www.whitehouse.gov/omb/inforeg/oira_disclosure_memo-b.html.

4. A poignant example surfaced in the spring of 2002. On a day Christie Whitman, the Administrator of EPA, was lunching with Secretary Gale Norton of the Department of the Interior, EPA filed official comments sharply critical on environmental grounds of a controversial Departmental initiative to facilitate the use of sno-mobiles in Yellowstone National Park. Whitman, unaware of the comments, had been unable to warn her colleague they were coming (or, indeed, to con-

OIRA when the predecessor of E.O. 12866 in this respect, E.O. 12498, was being considered) reportedly advised President Reagan that, in his judgment, the order would not only serve presidential authority, but also enhance the control of the agency's political head over her career bureaucrats. In putting together a draft regulatory agenda, as in developing an annual budget, the agency head would be required to confront at an early stage—and rationalize—competing views about priorities for her agency. More recently, discussing presidential directives to engage in rulemaking, PROF. JAMES F. BLUMSTEIN, REGULATORY REVIEW BY THE EXECUTIVE OFFICE OF THE PRESIDENT: AN OVERVIEW AND POLICY ANALYSIS OF CURRENT ISSUES, 51 Duke L.J. 851, 896–97 (2001), suggested a similar point: "... [T]he use of advance directives has much to commend it as compared to post hoc review. One way of viewing the after-the-fact OIRA reviews under Reagan and Bush is that they were developing, in a common law, case-by-case manner, a set of administration policies." ... [However, by the time the White House had] reached a decision, agency appointees were already locked into a particular stance, probably feeling duty-bound to represent forcefully the agency's viewpoint.

"[By contrast] the proactive, advance directive has the advantage of formulating an administration position at the front end. Responsible political appointees in the agency will have helped develop the directive, so the [Executive Office of the President] will have coopted them at an early stage. Once the administration takes a position, opposition becomes disloyalty. My sense is that that type of clearcut directive could help mobilize agency political appointees even when they face a hostile professional staff. The staff may be able to make changes at the margins, but the technique ensures the active involvement of the president's political agents (his appointees) within the agency. . . .

"If, as should be the case, agency staffs can accept EOP staff input as a legitimate part of an agency's decisionmaking process, that input should come as early in the process as possible. After-the-fact review inherently maximizes interagency conflict. . . . Broadening the horizon of agency staff is an important objective, and introducing staff to each other before decisions get too far along is an important way of allowing the staffs to see each other as professionals and to respect each other despite their differences in perspective. Staffs from agencies and OIRA should be encouraged to view each other as colleagues and as partners in the process. . . ."

These virtues of the unified regulatory agenda are only a potential. Both internal and external management skills are required to make it a credible opportunity for control from the top. A former General Counsel of EPA sympathetic to the exercise would report, ten years after the predecessor to E.O. 12866 in this respect (E.O. 12498) had been put in place, that the *centralizing* potential of the measure had not yet been realized and that OIRA review remained reactive. E. Donald Elliott, TQM-ing[5] OMB: Or Why

sider whether they ought to be filed). Katharine Q. Seelye, "Snowmobile Letter Surprises E.P.A. Leader and Interior Chief," N.Y. Times, May 3, 2002, at A14.

5. [Ed.] Total Quality Management, TQM, is the description given to contemporary management techniques for improving performance and doing away with excessive

Regulatory Review Under Executive Order 12,291 Works Poorly And What President Clinton Should Do About It, 57 L. & Contemp. Probs. 167 (1994). While EPA had developed principles similar to the executive order's for top-of-the-agency supervision of the allocation of agency effort, OIRA's contribution to this process was negligible. It spent "virtually no time reviewing the preliminary EPA submission" proposing to undertake a given rulemaking. During the Clinton administration, the President used the "presidential directives" Prof. Blumstein was directly addressing–memoranda to the heads of departments and agencies instructing them to undertake particular rulemakings. He sent 107 such directives, as compared to 9 in the Reagan and 4 in the first Bush administrations. Elena Kagan, Presidential Administration, 114 Harv.L.Rev. 2245, 2294 (2001). Yet these formal directives appear to have come from him (perhaps through his domestic advisors) and not through the OIRA bureaucratic process; so far as appears, they are not connected with the regulatory agenda process.

Not long after Dr. Graham assumed the leadership of OIRA in the second Bush administration, his office began issuing the occasional "prompt letters" his talk mentions,[6] inviting agencies to undertake rulemaking that seemed likely to prove beneficial.[7] "Prompt letters," OMB remarks in a recent draft report to Congress, "do not have the mandatory implication of a Presidential directive. . . . The prompt letter simply constitutes an OIRA request that an agency elevate a matter in priority, recognizing that agencies have limited resources and many conflicting demands for priority attention. The ultimate decision about priority setting remains in the hands of the regulatory agency."[8]

(4) *The President's Priorities*. Like directives, and as Prof. Blumstein's remarks make clear, the Regulatory Agenda directly serves the White House, and its interests in political controls over the acts of government. Suggesting considerable change from President Truman's famous laments,[9] E.O. 12866 in general, and Section 4 in particular, raise questions about presidential influence and control. SBREFA provides that "(d) Nothing in this section precludes an agency from considering or acting on any matter not included in a regulatory flexibility agenda, or requires an agency to consider or act on any matter listed in such agenda." Do you find such modesty attached to E.O. 12866? Or, rather, does it appear that agencies are *not* to engage in a rulemaking OIRA identifies as "a planned regulatory action [that] may be inconsistent with the President's priorities or the

---

bureaucraticization. TQM programs have brought sharp reductions in the administrative superstructures of many large private corporations.

6. http://www.whitehouse.gov/omb/inforeg/prompt_letter.html.

7. http://www.whitehouse.gov/omb/inforeg/return_letter.html.

8. OMB, Draft Report to Congress on the Costs and Benefits of Federal Regulations, 67 Fed.Reg. 15014, 15020 (March 28, 2002).

9. While acknowledging that "The buck stops here," he also complained "I thought I was the President, but when it comes to these bureaucrats I can't do a damned thing." For these and other complaints by Truman and others, see Elena Kagan, Presidential Administration, 114 Harv.L.Rev. 2245, 2272 (2001), citing for this one Richard P. Nathan, The Administrative Presidency 2 (1986).

principles set forth in this Executive order or [that] may be in conflict with any policy or action taken or planned by another agency"?[10]

The last of these issues, coordination with other agencies, is an important function OMB serves for the President. The practice of coordination, however, is often underappreciated by courts. The Benzene case, p. 58 above, provides two examples. First, Congress had specifically provided for the National Institutes of Occupational Safety and Health (a science agency constituted as part of the National Institutes of Health in the Department of Health and Human Services) to advise OSHA what, in its judgment, were important workplace health and safety issues to pursue. NIOSH had sent OSHA several urgent messages about the risks posed by benzene. The Court, worried that OSHA's discretion to choose regulatory targets was unconstrained, ignored this important structural arrangement and instead adopted a highly forced interpretation of OSHA's statutory mandate.[11] Second, OSHA had exempted retail gas stations from compliance with its regulation, saying it did so at the request of the Environmental Protection Agency. EPA had responsibility for setting benzene levels in air to which the public generally might be exposed. EPA, that is, was to regulate the benzene exposure of the driver sitting in her car, or perhaps pumping her own gas; while OSHA's job was the station attendant. However, the Court seemed to take the exemption as a signal of OSHA's irrationality, rather than as understandable temporizing to permit the working out of a genuine regulatory conflict.

The more important—and controversial—issue, however is Presidential control of agency policy preferences. Section 4 opens by requiring that "these procedures shall be followed, *to the extent permitted by law*," (emphasis added)—a phrase that suggests both command and possible limits. The back and forth between OIRA and agency about the Regulatory Agenda (unlike the processing of impact statements concerning particular proposed regulations, see p. 638ff. below) does *not* get memorialized on OIRA's website. Thus it is not possible to know much about how it happens, unless insiders, like Mr. Elliott, tell us how close the supervision is. Professor Elena Kagan observed President Clinton's practices under E.O. 12866 as Deputy Assistant to the President for Domestic Policy and Deputy Director of the Domestic Policy Council. She writes in remarkable and revealing detail about the increasing strength of "Presidential Administration"—and President Clinton's active engagement with (and efforts to seek political credit for) particular regulations.[12] Yet beyond remarking that Section 4 extends to the independent regulatory commissions as well as the conventional executive branch departments and agencies, she does not comment on its operation. We learn little about OIRA's or the Vice President's role in setting the regulatory agenda.

---

10. These formula are quite similar to ones familiar to agencies used to seeking OMB clearance for desired legislation, legislative testimony, or budgetary requests.

11. Similarly, the court of appeals in American Trucking Association v. Whitman, p. 41, gave little credit to the presence of a congressionally created Clean Air Scientific Advisory Council in expressing its concerns about the breadth of discretion conferred on the EPA administrator.

12. 114 Harv.L.Rev. 2245 (2001). Excerpts appear at pp. 213 and 218 above.

When Congress has directed an agency to develop regulations on a particular topic, two things seem clear: (1) "to the extent permitted by law" requires that these matters be permitted to appear in the Regulatory Agenda; (2) the fact that these regulations may be "inconsistent with the President's priorities or the principles set forth in [E.O. 12866]" is irrelevant to the agency's statutory responsibility to go forward. But suppose Congress has authorized an agency to *choose* regulatory targets within its field of responsibility, and it proposes its choice to OIRA. Does your conclusion differ? Consider two possibilities within this larger, very common situation.

First, suppose that, like the EPA in the American Trucking Association case, p. 38ff. above, the agency has a statute that does not permit it to consider costs in reaching its ultimate regulatory decisions. May the President or his delegate, having identified cost efficiency as one of his government-wide "priorities," direct the Administrator not to undertake particular rulemakings that she wishes to place on her agenda? Note that this is different from the question whether the President may require the Administrator to calculate and report cost data. The Constitution expressly provides that the President "may require the Opinion, in writing, of the principal Officer in each of the executive Departments, upon any subject relating to the Duties of their respective Offices."[13] If the President needs any further support for his informational demand, it comes from Congress's command that OMB report annually on the overall costs and benefits of federal regulation. That much is easy. The harder question is whether the President can go further and direct the Administrator not to pursue a particular regulatory target because of the likely cost of any forthcoming regulation. If you have studied the material in Chapter II, § 4(b), you know that this is a question that scholars heatedly debate,[14] and the Court has yet to clearly resolve as a constitutional matter. So what happens, in the real world, in the face of this legal uncertainty? Much doubtless is done in consensual fashion, among individuals who share a political administration and wish to keep their leader's trust. Even in the processes of consensus, however, background understandings of power and responsibility have considerable influence. Whether or not the matter ever comes to the courts, agency counsel and White House counsel need a clear view of their clients' legal rights and responsibilities.

Suppose, instead, that the agency's statute says nothing about considering cost (or, for that matter, any of the other factors that might show up on the list of presidential government-wide priorities implemented by OIRA in the regulatory review process). Absent an affirmative direction from Congress one way or the other, is an agency subject to presidential direction about its regulatory priorities? Professor Kagan argues that the answer—at least with respect to agencies in the executive branch—should be yes, as a matter of statutory construction.

(5) *Assessing Relative Risk*. In recent years, the concern about regulatory risk assessment has generated a significant volume of scholarship and

---

13. U.S. Const., Art. II, Sec. 2. cl. 1.

14. See, e.g., the excerpts from the works of Professors Oren and Kagan, quoted at pp. 56, 213 and 218 above.

political discussion. Two related themes have been prominent. One begins from the proposition that all regulation has an impact on the economy, and asserts that that overall impact should be determined and managed—that the United States should have a "regulatory budget" limiting and allocating the expenditures regulation requires of private firms, just as it has a fiscal budget limiting and allocating its own direct expenditures of funds. The second theme, underlying the thinking of many of the Justices in the Benzene case, understands regulation as a response to the risks that unregulated activity poses for the intended beneficiaries of regulation. It proposes that in allocating limited opportunities for regulatory action, government should favor targets with the highest ratio of benefits to costs. So put, both seem quite sensible propositions. Neither is currently well-developed in law, but it seems likely that during the useful life of this casebook both may become more so.

The regulatory budget idea is reflected in the Unfunded Mandate Reform Act of 1965, 2 U.S.C. § 1532 ff. and in certain sections of budgetary legislation,[15] which require OMB annually to report to Congress the costs and benefits of regulations and "unfunded mandates." These OMB reports, which can be found on the Internet,[16] reflect the difficulty of the enterprise. Thus, the draft report for 2002 lists as its first item a USDA rule on Roadless Area Conservation. It estimates $219,000 as the annual benefits, identified as savings of the maintenance costs that would be experienced if the areas were not roadless. It identifies over $200 million in costs—the jobs in road construction, mining and lumbering that presumably would exist if the roads were built, plus the value of phosphates, coal, gas and oil that will not be discovered and exploited in their absence. It will be apparent that all of these are estimates not of outlays, but of imagined opportunity costs. It isn't known that exploitable natural resources are there; that the areas remain roadless, after more than a century's thorough exploration of public lands generally, suggests at least the possibility that they are not. What about the benefit side of the calculus? The closest the document gets to acknowledging that there might be a variety of hard-to-quantify benefits to maintaining roadless wilderness areas is a concession that "A variety of other non-quantifiable benefits were mentioned in the preamble to the rule." OMB, DRAFT REPORT TO CONGRESS ON THE COSTS AND BENEFITS OF FEDERAL REGULATIONS, 67 Fed.Reg. 15014, 15025 (March 28, 2002).

Dr. Graham's scholarship before he joined OIRA centered on risk assessment, suggesting that this will be an important area for development during his tenure as its head. The Draft Report just cited strongly recommends a series of practices in risk assessment, including "formal, independent external peer review by qualified specialists." Such review, it urges, should occur openly, strictly on technical grounds, and with full disclosure by reviewers of their prior intellectual positions on the issues and possible

15. E.g., Treasury and General Government Appropriations Act, 2000, Pub. L. 106–58, § 628(a), 113 Stat. 430 (1999); Consolidated Appropriations Act of 2001, Pub. L. 106–554, § 624, 114 Stat. 2763 (2000).

16. http://www.whitehouse.gov/omb/inforeg/regpol-reports_congress.html.

financial or other conflicts of interest. The Draft Report promises "a measure of deference to agency analysis that has been developed in conjunction with such peer review procedures." At 15019. For particular high-consequence rulemakings already in progress, disciplined peer review of the originating agency's work may be more reliable than attempted oversight by OIRA's small and overworked staff, who are generally more expert in economic than technical analysis. Suppose, however, that the proposition is that *at the priority setting stage* the agency must submit its possible targets of opportunity to such an intensive, and external, review. What might the costs and benefits of this early public stage be? Might the reasons that contribute to OIRA's historical privacy about the Section 4 process be analogous to prosecutors' need for secrecy at the indictment stage?

Dr. Graham (at the time, still Director of Harvard University's Center for Risk Analysis) was one of twelve scholars and lawyers convened as a working group to assess S. 981 of the 105th Congress. This was a bipartisan and well-regarded legislative proposal for requiring agency risk assessment that Congress considered, but did not enact, during the second Clinton administration. Other participants included a former General Counsel of the EPA, a former Counsel to the President, and one of the editors of this volume. The proceedings are summarized in Regulatory Improvement Legislation: Risk Assessment, Cost Benefit Analysis and Judicial Review, 11 Duke Envtl L & Policy F 89 (2000). For a more skeptical view, see Celia Campbell–Mohn and John S. Applegate, Learning from NEPA: Guidelines for Responsible Risk Legislation, 23 Harv. Envtl L. Rev. 93 (1999).

(6) *The Dilemmas of Risk Selection.* The theme of failure in risk assessment underlies many contemporary writings about regulation. Three brief characterizations of important contributions:

(a) STEPHEN BREYER, BREAKING THE VICIOUS CIRCLE: TOWARD EFFECTIVE RISK REGULATION (1993) suggests that much of the seeming irrationality of governmental response to risk (at the legislative level as well as in rulemaking) is the product of innate human difficulties in assessing and choosing among relatively small risks. Designing effective governmental institutions that will, first, assess the level of risk in the face of usually incomplete information; second, clear-sightedly fix on effective means for dealing with the risks (the unintended consequences problem); and, finally, avoid responses driven by popular (mis)perceptions—these challenges are as difficult as any that legal institutions face, and easily fall victim to the fears of the moment.[17]

---

17. Jerry Mashaw and David Harfst's The Struggle for Auto Safety (1990) provides a concrete example. In the same legislative breath, amendments to the National Traffic and Motor Vehicle Safety Act helped stymie the development of air bags for a decade or more, and required a highly questionable commitment of regulatory resources to school bus safety. Risk assessment suggested that much greater gains were to be had from safety investments in cars than in school buses. Risk management techniques suggested that at least the immediate impact of making school buses more expensive would be to keep older buses on the road. Yet members of Congress and their constituents were unmoved. They preferred personal freedom in automobiles for themselves—despite quite substantial risks of death and serious injury, cheaply avoidable. They were horrified that anyone could propose to balance the possible saving of a child's life by making school buses

(b) RICHARD H. PILDES AND CASS R. SUNSTEIN, REINVENTING THE REGULATORY STATE, 62 U.Chi.L.Rev. 1 (1995): "It is hard to challenge the view that law and policy should be assessed on the basis of inquiries into the advantages and disadvantages of different courses of action. . . . Yet this process of seeking consistency can incorporate contentious assumptions about what it would mean for policy choices to be consistent and rational. In particular, this approach requires regulators to create a single metric along which diverse regulatory policies can be compared. . . . However, for laypeople, the most salient contextual features include: (1) the catastrophic nature of the risk; (2) whether the risk is uncontrollable; (3) whether the risk involves irretrievable or permanent losses; (4) the social conditions under which a particular risk is generated and managed, a point that connects to issues of consent, voluntariness, and democratic control; (5) how equitably distributed the danger is or how concentrated on identifiable, innocent, or traditionally disadvantaged victims, which ties to both notions of community and moral ideals; (6) how well understood the risk process in question is, a point that bears on the psychological disturbance produced by different risks; (7) whether the risk would be faced by future generations; and (8) how familiar the risk is. . . .

"The important point is that it can be fully rational to attend to contextual differences of this sort. . . . It is fully plausible to believe that expenditures per life saved ought to vary in accordance with (for example) the voluntariness of the risk or its catastrophic quality. Such beliefs appear widespread. Interviews with workers, for example, reveal that their valuations of workplace risks depend upon such contextual features as the overall structure of workplace relations, how much say workers have in how the risks are managed, and the nature of the particular jobs performed."

(c) LARS NOAH, SCIENTIFIC "REPUBLICANISM": EXPERT PEER REVIEW AND THE QUEST FOR REGULATORY DELIBERATION, 49 Emory L.J. 1033, 1067, 1083 (2000): "Concerns about the potential for added administrative burdens . . . deserve serious attention. If it does not help steer an agency early in the process, peer review of regulatory decisionmaking may become an ominous hurdle for agencies to surmount, both in terms of the difficulty of undergoing that scrutiny and because of the prospect of judicial invalidation triggered by the inevitable criticisms from expert peer reviewers. Moreover, if agencies sense that the blessing of outside scientists is necessary before proceeding with a rule, they may decide to settle for second-best regulatory options simply because these generate the least disagreement among the experts. . . .

"Few observers doubt that rulemaking has become 'ossified' during the past few decades, though disagreements persist about the precise causes and appropriate responses to this development. If the . . . criticisms of mandatory peer review have merit, agencies may face additional disincentives when they contemplate issuing or revising health and safety rules—

safer, against the relatively high regulatory costs of doing so. See also John Applegate, Worst Things First: Risk, Information, and Regulatory Structure in Toxic Substances Control, 9 Yale J. Reg. 277 (1992); Clayton Gillette and James Krier, Risk, Courts and Agencies, 138 U.Penn.L.R. 1027 (1990).

what some observers have christened 'paralysis by analysis.' Indeed, critics suggest that these sorts of reform proposals are designed for precisely that purpose, offering regulatory relief for industry in the guise of more rational procedures. Procedural reforms often do disguise legislative policy preferences about the substance of agency decisionmaking. Although they may appear to improve judgments, better procedures are rarely neutral in their effects. . . .

". . . Notwithstanding its centrality as a quality control mechanism for the scientific community, peer review does not provide a bromide for what some observers think ails our government—namely, overzealous bureaucrats issuing health and safety rules based on a misunderstanding or conscious disregard of the best available data. Involving outside scientists in the process undoubtedly will promote greater care and reflection, and these peer reviewers may help steer agencies clear of embarrassing and costly mistakes, but ultimately the independent experts cannot and should not displace the broader deliberative process about hard policy questions that science cannot answer. The New Deal faith in expertise continues to have strong appeal, especially as contrasted with the pluralist vision of agencies simply brokering compromises between competing interest groups. So long as independent peer review does not become a substitute for public participation or judicial review, it may provide a forum for genuine deliberation that can facilitate subsequent steps in the administrative process and help to better focus other forms of external scrutiny of agency decisionmaking."

(iii) REGULATORY NEGOTIATION

With the 1990 enactment of two statutes amending the APA, alternative dispute resolution formally took its place among the available modes of regulatory procedure.[1] The Negotiated Rulemaking Act added a new Subchapter III (now, 5 U.S.C. §§ 561–70a, in the Appendix at pp. 1355–61) "to establish a framework for the conduct of negotiated rulemaking, consistent with section 553 of this title, to encourage agencies to use the process when it enhances the informal rulemaking process." 5 U.S.C. § 561. On the adjudication side, the Administrative Dispute Resolution Act added a new Subchapter IV (now, 5 U.S.C. §§ 571–84, in the Appendix at pp. 1361–69) explicitly to authorize, under certain circumstances, agency use of "settlement negotiations, conciliation, facilitation, mediation, factfinding, minitrials, and arbitration . . ." 5 U.S.C. § 571(3). It is very briefly discussed at p. 478ff., but negotiated rulemaking is the principal ADR subject of administrative law interest, and warrants more extended treatment.

It is important to understand that negotiated rulemaking—"reg-neg" in the frequent shorthand—is a process for generating not final rules, but rulemaking *proposals*. That is, the product of a successful reg-neg must be published in the Federal Register and undergo the normal § 553 process.[2]

---

1. The original statutes had six year sunset provisions. Both have been reenacted in permanent form.

2. Different questions are presented when, as happens frequently, appellate challenges to agency rules are settled upon negotiated changes being made. See Jim Rossi,

ADR specialist Philip Harter, whose prominent advocacy of and involvement in this process have led some to call him the "father of negotiated rulemaking," described the negotiated rulemaking process in ASSESSING THE ASSESSORS: THE ACTUAL PERFORMANCE OF NEGOTIATED RULEMAKING, 9 N.Y.U. Envtl. L. J. 32, 33–35 (2001).[3]

"... [N]egotiated rulemaking is a process by which representatives of the interests that would be substantially affected by a rule, including the agency responsible for issuing the rule, negotiate in good faith to reach consensus on a proposed rule. ... The first step in a negotiated rulemaking is to conduct a 'convening,' in which the convenor:

> identifies the interests that will be substantially affected by the proposed rule and individuals or organizations that might represent those interests,

> identifies the issues of concern that need to be addressed in the negotiated rulemaking, and

> determines whether "the establishment of a negotiated rulemaking committee is feasible and appropriate in the particular rulemaking."

"If after the convening, the agency decides to go forward with a negotiated rulemaking, it publishes a Notice of Intent in the Federal Register and other publications likely to be read by those interested in the subject matter, announcing its intention ..., describing the subjects and scope of the rule to be developed, and listing the people or interests that will be on the committee. The notice also solicits comments on the decision to use reg-neg to develop the rule, and it invites those who believe they will be substantially affected by the rule, but who are not adequately represented on the committee, to apply for committee membership. The notice serves the important purposes of ensuring that no important interests are overlooked, and that everyone understands that the decision on the rule will, at least initially, be made in the committee, and informing interested parties that they need to come forward. Following the Notice of Intent, the committee is established and the actual negotiations begin.

"The members of the negotiated rulemaking committee determine what factual information or other data is necessary for them to make a reasoned decision, develop that information (which often comes from workgroups comprised of knowledgeable and interested individuals), analyze the information, examine the legal and policy issues involved in the regulation, and reach a consensus on the recommendation to make to the agency. As part of the consensus, each private interest agrees to support the recommendation and resulting rule to the extent that it reflects the agreement, and the agency agrees to use the recommendation as the basis of its action.

"Several implicit elements of this process merit emphasis: First, a senior representative of the agency is a full participant in the negotiations and deliberations of the negotiated rulemaking committee. Second, the committee makes its decision by consensus, which is defined by the

Bargaining in the Shadow of Administrative Procedure: The Public Interest in Rulemaking Settlement, 51 Duke L.J. 1015 (2001).

3. The quotations from Prof. Harter's article appear in a different order there.

Negotiated Rulemaking Act as the 'unanimous concurrence among the interests represented on a negotiated rulemaking committee.' Thus, each participating interest has veto power over the decision. Third, the agency agrees to use the consensus as the basis of a proposed rule, which necessarily means that the agency will follow the traditional process of publishing the proposal as a Notice of Proposed Rulemaking (NPRM) and receive comments on the proposal before issuing a final rule. As a matter of administrative law, the agency is also required to modify the proposed rule

NEGOTIATED RULEMAKING AT EPA

Source: ACUS Negotiated Rulemaking Sourcebook

EVALUATION

- Identify issues and deadlines
- Identify interested parties
- Compare to selection criteria
- Confirm management interest
- Select convenor

CONVENING—PHASE 1

- Identify additional parties
- Discuss RegNeg with parties
- Discuss issues with parties
- Determine willingness of parties to negotiate
- Report to agency
- Obtain agency management commitment
- Preliminary selection of 15–25 participants

CONVENING—PHASE 2

- Obtain parties' commitment to negotiate
- Publish "notice of intent to negotiate"
- Process FACA charter
- Select facilitator/mediator
- Respond to public comments on "notice"
- Adjust committee membership if necessary
- Arrange organizational meeting
- Arrange committee orientation/training

NEGOTIATIONS

- Establish groundrules/protocols
- Define "consensus"
- Set meeting schedule
- Publish notices of meetings
- Review available information and issues
- Review draft rule or proposals if available
- Establish work groups or subcommittees as necessary
- Negotiate text or outline of proposed rule

RULEMAKING

- Negotiations concluded
- If consensus is reached on language of rule:
  - Agency circulates draft for internal/external review
  - Agency publishes consensus as draft rule
- If consensus is reached only on issues or outline:
  - Agency drafts proposed rule
  - Agency circulates draft for internal/external review
  - Agency publishes NPRM
- If consensus is not reached:
  - Agency proceeds with rulemaking using discussions as a guide
  - Agency drafts and publishes NPRM
- Draft rule is subject to public comment
- Committee notified of public comments
- Agency revises rule if necessary
- Agency publishes final rule

[H200]

in response to significant, meritorious comments. Finally, the consensus of the committee becomes a recommendation to the agency; the agency alone retains the authority to issue the rule and may modify the proposal in response to comments or otherwise. That said, however, a negotiated rulemaking is a means by which the representatives of the affected interests actually share in making the regulatory decision, subject to the agency's constitutional responsibility to make the final decision. The resulting consensus is far more than a mere recommendation, especially since the agency itself endorses it during the deliberations."

Review the Act, in the Appendix at p. 1355ff. Does Harter's description appear apt? The preceding flowchart describing negotiated rulemaking at EPA may help in this exercise. Then consider the potential benefits and dangers of this method of writing rules in light of the comments and questions below.

NOTES

(1) *"The process ... embodies what many administrative law theorists viscerally fear: the last step from a system of arms-length interest representation—which preserves the agency's hierarchical authority—to one of direct interest group bargaining."*[1] WILLIAM FUNK, WHEN SMOKE GETS IN YOUR EYES: REGULATORY NEGOTIATION AND THE PUBLIC INTEREST—EPA'S WOODSTOVE STANDARDS, 18 Envtl.L. 55, 57 (1987), was an early and important critique of regulatory negotiation, that focused on possible threats to agency legality. Professor Funk considered an EPA negotiation (held before passage of the statute, but under comparable procedures) to develop emissions standards for residential wood stoves. The growing popularity of woodstoves, as a means of countering rising home heating costs, created new air pollution concerns when heavy stove usage produced detectable increases in airborne particulates and in a group of carcinogenic chemicals known as polycyclic organic matter (POMs). With Oregon leading the way, states and even municipalities began to impose emission limits on stoves sold within their borders. Manufacturers who might have preferred *no* regulation found state-to-state variation especially difficult: the permissible emission levels, and the testing procedures for establishing compliance with them, varied from jurisdiction to jurisdiction. Nationally, environmental groups and the state of New York had successfully sued EPA to compel it to regulate POMs from a variety of sources. Responding, EPA convened a negotiated rulemaking. The negotiating committee consisted of a representative of each of the following entities: EPA, National Resources Defense Council (a prominent national environmental organization), Oregon, Vermont, New York, Colorado, the Wood Heating Alliance (the trade organization of stove manufacturers), two specific stove manufacturers, two manufacturers of catalytic combustors (devices that potentially could reduce stove emissions), and the Consumer Federation of America.

Professor Funk describes the "stake" each member had in the outcome: "... [F]or each the proposed rule was a means to a particular end which was to the benefit of their particular organizations. For the Wood Heating Alliance and the manufacturers it represented, a national emissions limit on woodstoves would likely forestall the burgeoning movement

1. Jody Freeman and Laura Langbein, Regulatory Negotiation and the Legitimacy Benefit, 9 N.Y.U. Envtl. L.J. 60, 71 (2000).

by states and localities to create their own limitations. This would both reduce the likelihood of different standards and test methods as well as maximize the influence the Alliance could have on the substantive standards while minimizing the burden of obtaining that influence. For the states with their own woodstove regulations, the negotiation of a federal rule would perhaps enable them to achieve a substantive regulation under federal law that would allow federal funding of local enforcement, federal enforcement, or federally mandated local enforcement—in any case, reducing their internal funding difficulties. For states considering woodstove regulations, the regulatory negotiation would enable them to achieve the substantive regulation they sought without the financial or political cost within their state of developing the regulation. For the NRDC, a rule regulating woodstove emissions, whatever its basis or justification, would have the effect of reducing the emission of a pollutant NRDC believed to be harmful. For EPA, any new source performance standard rule to which the various states and NRDC would agree would eliminate the resource intensive litigation to which EPA would otherwise be subjected and would eliminate the demand for regulating POM as a hazardous pollutant. Even the Consumer Federation of America could further its 'consumer' goals by using the regulation to promote advertising and labeling requirements that would facilitate comparison shopping and consumer awareness."

With EPA supplying the structure, a multi-part compromise proposal emerged. In Professor Funk's eyes, many elements were at best problematic (and in some cases clearly invalid) under the Clean Air Act. For example, the Act is directed at "stationary sources" and their "owners or operators." Nonetheless, the standard ran primarily against manufacturers and retailers of the woodstoves—mass-produced consumer items hard to bring within the meaning of "stationary source." The proposed enforcement plan included no provision for pursuing the homeowners who bought and used them. The consensus standard provided for a phased-in compliance schedule, with a special delayed date for "small" manufacturers; the Act contains no authority to delay compliance for certain parties because of their economic situation. The negotiated standard would have required stoves to have labels giving information not only about emissions but also about fuel efficiency and heat output; the Act is concerned with pollution control, and confers no authority to act in order to improve consumer buying decisions. This last item is, in Professor Funk's view, a particularly good example of the way legality can be lost in the process of "getting to yes." The labeling requirement was opposed by the stove manufacturers' representatives on legality grounds, until some of the state participants indicated an inclination to impose (varying) consumer labeling requirements of their own. The manufacturers' representatives, after consulting their principals, withdrew their objections and negotiated a uniform national labeling standard as part of the package.

In Professor Funk's assessment, the woodstove emissions case study is an exemplar of how the negotiation process can produce "a proposed rule with which the parties are happy but which bears scant resemblance to what was contemplated by the statute":[2]

2. For more positive assessments of the woodstove emissions negotiations—albeit as-   sessments by participating parties—see EPA Office of Policy, Planning & Evaluation, An

"... [T]he theory and principles of regulatory negotiation are at war with the theory and principles of American administrative law applicable to rulemaking. . . .

"Of course, agencies are not to make their determinations in a vacuum. Procedural requirements assure input from interested parties, and recent executive orders institute a supervisory executive branch oversight of executive agencies' determinations. Moreover, this supervisory oversight can properly have a policy component; it need not be politically sterile. Nevertheless, the ultimate responsibility for the determination continues to rest with the agency. Not only is the final responsibility to be the agency's, but in the oft-quoted words of Scenic Hudson Preservation Conference v. FPC,[3] an agency's role as representative of the public interest 'does not permit it to act as an umpire blandly calling balls and strikes for adversaries appearing before it; the right of the public must receive active and affirmative protection at the hands of the [agency].'

"The concept of regulatory negotiation stands this role on its head, first, by reducing the agency to the level of a mere participant in the formulation of the rule, and second, by essentially denying that the agency has any responsibility beyond giving effect to the consensus achieved by the group. . . .

"This fundamental change in the role of the agency in the rulemaking process is mirrored by the fundamental change in the underlying theoretical justification for the eventual rule. As Harter admits: 'Under the traditional hybrid process, the legitimacy of the rule rests on a resolution of complex factual materials and rational extrapolation from those facts, guided by the criteria of the statute. Under regulatory negotiation, however, the regulation's legitimacy would lie in the overall agreement of the parties.' Stated another way, the parties to the rule are happy with it; therefore, it matters not whether the rule is rational or lawful. Discretion delegated to the agency by Congress is effectively exercised by the group of interested parties, constrained only by the need to obtain consensus. The law no longer directs or even necessarily constrains the outcome but has become merely a factor in the give-and-take necessary to achieve consensus.

"To say that regulatory negotiation turns the traditional concept of administrative rulemaking on its head does not, however, compel the conclusion that it is necessarily unlawful. . . . [S]upporters of regulatory negotiation may suggest that 'no harm, no foul.' . . .

"Reliance on the absence of disagreement as evidence of legitimacy for a regulation puts a premium on assuring that the negotiating group adequately represents all affected interests. There are, however, both practical and theoretical limitations on the number of interests that may be represented and the quality of representation each interest may obtain. Where the interest is strong enough to make itself known and felt, little

Assessment of EPA's Negotiated Rulemaking Activities (1987), reprinted in ACUS, Negotiated Rulemaking Sourcebook 23 (1990); Panel Discussion: Negotiated Rulemaking, 17 Envtl.L.Rep. 10245, 10251–53 (1987) (remarks of NRDC attorney).

3.   354 F.2d 608 (2d Cir.1965), cert. denied, 384 U.S. 941 (1966).

difficulty arises—either that interest will be represented in the negotiation or the negotiation in the end will not likely be successful. More problematic is where the interest is not well defined, organized, or strong. Reliance on the ... requirement for 'balanced membership' ... is not sufficient. ... For example, in the woodstove negotiation, the Consumer Federation of America (CFA) was supposed to represent the interests of the consumer, but consumers, as the CFA would be the first to admit, are hardly a homogenous entity. The CFA may have represented the interests associated with the mentality of a Consumers Reports reader, but it did not appear to lobby on behalf of poor, rural folk for whom the rule will provide little benefit and perhaps significant burden. Moreover, the fact that these people do not comment on the proposed rule or challenge a final rule in court hardly establishes that the rule is fair and wise as to them.

"The tendency of alternative dispute resolution to focus on the interests of the specific parties to the dispute without regard to broader values has been noted in the literature related to alternatives to litigation.[4] As Judge [Harry] Edwards [of the D.C. Circuit] has noted, there are important differences between alternative dispute resolution where only private interests and values are at stake and where public values and interests are involved.[5] '[I]f ADR is extended to resolve difficult issues of constitutional or public law—making use of nonlegal values to resolve important social issues or allowing those the law seeks to regulate to delimit public rights and duties—there is real reason for concern.' Regulatory negotiation, by reducing disputes over what is in the public interest to disputes between various private interests, and by substituting private agreement for public determinations made according to legal norms, transforms administrative rulemaking into an area of private law, and this is a fundamental alteration."

Is it realistic to expect—at least in the case of a significant issue of regulatory policy—that all affected interests *could* be represented at the negotiating table? Suppose Professor Funk is correct that the Consumer Federation of America probably did a better job of speaking for relatively affluent and well-educated woodstove purchasers than for the rural poor.[6] Is it plausible to think that such subgroups of the woodstove-buyer population would be meaningful players in a regulatory negotiation, even with § 568(c)'s authorization for agency funding of necessary but needy representatives? Of course, as Professor Funk also recognizes, such groups do not participate in the notice-and-comment process either—or, to follow Harter's analogy, in the legislative process.

4. See, e.g., Fiss, Owen, N., Against Settlement, 93 Yale L.J. 1073, 1085 (1984). See also Merry, Book Review: Disputing Without Culture, 100 Harv.L.Rev. 2057 (1987).

5. See Harry Edwards, Alternative Dispute Resolution: Panacea or Anathema?, 99 Harv.L.Rev. 668, 671–72, 676–77 (1986).

6. He is not the only one to suggest that regulatory negotiation imposes "dispro-

portionate costs ... on smaller groups with disproportionately fewer resources." Cornelius Kerwin & Laura Langbein, An Evaluation of Negotiated Rulemaking at the Environmental Protection Agency: Phase I (1993), unpublished manuscript cited in Jody Freeman and Laura Langbein, Regulatory Negotiation and the Legitimacy Benefit, 9 N.Y.U. Envtl. L.J. 60, 63 (2000).

One might therefore propose that (given a concededly imperfect world) negotiated rulemaking's explicit focus on interest representation provides the best procedural chance (though, concededly, it may not be a very large one) for identifying the politically powerless and enhancing their voice in regulatory policymaking. Or is there something in the conventional rulemaking process that works to protect the interests of poor, rural woodstove users despite their silence—something that is lost, or overridden, in regulatory negotiation? Professor Funk suggests that this "something" is the agency's independent judgment of where the public interest lies. Can one have faith in this "something" without embracing the New Deal credo of neutral policy science and objective bureaucratic expertise?

On the legality issue, Prof. Harter thinks the concerns overstated. "Everyone involved in negotiating a regulation must recognize on a fundamental level that the proposal must be within the agency's authority granted by statute if the agency is to use it as the basis for a rule. That is simply a recognition that neither the agency nor certainly the negotiating group is sovereign. Rather the agency must act within the bounds of discretion provided by Congress if its actions are to be a binding, official position. Thus, just as in the judicial review of a rule developed by another process, the court's first task must be to determine whether the rule is with the scope of the agency's authority. That process would be very much as it is customarily. Not only is this step required by the APA, it also serves several practical functions with respect to negotiating regulations." Philip J. Harter, The Role of Courts in Regulatory Negotiation—A Response to Judge Wald, 11 Colum. J. Env. L. 51, 61, (1986).

Perhaps, then, "expertise" is precisely the sacrifice negotiated rulemaking makes. Professor Susan Rose–Ackerman is highly critical of the use of negotiated rulemaking "for most environmental policy issues." It is not only that "[d]iffuse, unorganized interests—like consumers or those who breathe the air—will be hard to represent, and groups who claim to speak for such individuals will have difficulty proving their claims." Sound solutions in this area require "a knowledge base derived from scientific principles," and negotiation is not a methodology that helps the participants acquire technical expertise. Susan Rose–Ackerman, American Administrative Law Under Siege: Is Germany A Model?, 107 Harv.L.Rev. 1279, 1283 (1994).

(2) *External Politics.* Another player in the regulatory process that conceivably might be cast as the guardian of the public interest is the President— or, more mundanely, OIRA conducting rulemaking review pursuant to Executive Order 12,866, and statutes such as the Paperwork Reduction Act. In recent years, OIRA has emerged as the wildcard in the negotiated rulemaking process. With no formal place at the negotiating table, this agency can nonetheless cast a substantial shadow over the process, for rules that emerge from regulatory negotiation have no special dispensation from the various species of statutory and presidentially-ordered oversight. OIRA's role with respect to negotiated rules is the subject of considerable concern and debate. In the case of the woodstove emission standard, the agency disapproved the portion of the Proposed Rule mandating a consum-

er information label, on grounds that it exceeded EPA's legal authority.[7] This action, although obviously not "public-favoring" in the immediate sense, might be seen as an appropriate outside correction when the bargaining process caused the agency to veer away from the rule of law. Ultimately, however, the labelling requirement was included in the final rule, and no challenge was ever brought to it.

Integrating OIRA review into regulatory negotiation may present an even more fundamental problem than wildcard disruption of the work of the negotiating committee. Professor Rose–Ackerman points out a deep conflict between these two processes: "Regulatory negotiation is premised on the idea that the state is searching, not for the ideal answer, but for a solution to which everyone can agree. In contrast, cost-benefit analysis, the analytic technique behind market-like solutions, is predicated on a particular way of aggregating preferences that may not obtain unanimous consent. . . . Focused discussions with citizens to learn their preferences may be worthwhile, but that is a very different model of public involvement from the negotiated resolution of policy conflicts. Of course, [the two processes] need not be mutually exclusive alternatives; they could be complements. For example, the regulations that are needed under a market scheme could be produced by consensual methods. However, the commitment to least cost solutions . . . would rule out some of the political compromises that might arise under regulatory negotiation." Susan Rose Ackerman, Consensus Versus Incentives: A Skeptical Look at Regulatory Negotiation, 1994 Duke L.J. 1206, 1218–19.

(3) *Consensus.* "Consensus" is such a crucial concept to regulatory negotiation that it is worth considering exactly what it means. According to the statute, "consensus" means unanimity *unless* the committee decides it will mean something else. § 562(2). This power to define the standard for necessary agreement poses a real dilemma. As a practical matter, unanimity is hard to achieve and increases the chances of stalemate. At the same time, a less-than-unanimity standard increases the likelihood *both* of reaching "agreement" and of an unhappy member leaving the table and becoming a prospective challenger of any resulting rule. On a more theoretical level, negotiated rulemaking's claim to legitimacy as an interest-representative process becomes progressively weaker as the meaning of "consensus" moves away from unanimity. In sum, the definition of consensus is likely to affect both the dynamics of the negotiation and the credibility of the product. In view of this, Philip Harter has argued: ". . . [T]he most acceptable definition of consensus would be 'general agreement,' which means that no party dissents significantly from the shared position. General agreement, however, does not necessarily mean unanimity, because even if someone disagrees, the dissent may not be significant enough, either in weight or number, to destroy the agreement. Thus, the party may dissent on grounds that generally are viewed as irrational, or the party's interests may not be sufficiently affected to regard its dissent as significant. In group consensus a dissenting minor interest, one not directly and immediately

---

7. See Funk, 18 Envtl.L at 84. Professor Harter tells a similar story of concensus-disruptive presidential intervention in As-sessing the Assessors, p. 628 above, 9 N.Y.U. Envtl.L.J. at 47–48.

affected, can be disregarded even on a major issue.... The dissent of a major interest, however, could destroy a consensus even on a minor point. ... Ultimately, whether a consensus exists must be determined more by fingertip feel than by any sort of mathematical calculation. One negotiator has stated that if you have to count votes, you do not have a consensus. Rather, like pornography, consensus is hard to define, but you know it when you see it." Philip Harter, Negotiating Regulations: A Cure for Malaise? 71 Geo.L.J. 1, 93 (1982). Is this a workable concept of "consensus"? Does the answer to this question depend on whether the existence of consensus is being determined *contemporaneously*, in the course of the negotiation, as opposed to *after the fact* in the course of judicial review?

(4) *A cure for malaise?* Considerable controversy can be found in the literature about the promise and performance of negotiated rulemaking— whether, for example, it succeeds in shortening the time needed for rulemaking or in reducing the frequency or intensity of judicial review. For Professor Harter, "Reg-neg has proven to be an enormously powerful tool in addressing highly complex, politicized rules, the very kind that stall agencies when traditional or conventional procedures are used"; he takes as the measure of time saved not the ultimate appearance of a rule in the CFR, but the earlier point at which the achievement of consensus permits participants to plan confidently for the future.[8] For Professor Cary Coglianese of Harvard University's Kennedy School, "From 1983, when the Federal Aviation Administration (FAA) initiated the first federal negotiated rulemaking, to 1996, the year the Negotiated Rulemaking Act was permanently reauthorized, about a dozen federal agencies used the procedure to develop and issue at least one rule. All told, federal agencies had completed thirty-five rules using negotiated rulemaking, a number that amounted to less than 0.01% of all rules issued during the same period." and "Negotiated rulemaking demands a concentrated investment of time and resources by all involved, but without any clear corresponding return in terms of avoiding litigation or achieving other goals."[9] JODY FREEMAN AND LAURA I. LANGBEIN, REGULATORY NEGOTIATION AND THE LEGITIMACY BENEFIT, 9 N.Y.U. Envtl. L.J. 60, 62–63, 138 (2000) puts this controversy in perspective and offers these conclusions, based on the most extensive empirical research yet undertaken into negotiated rulemaking:

"Along virtually every important qualitative dimension, all participants in this study—whether business, environmental, or government— reacted more favorably to their experience with negotiated rules than do participants in conventional rulemaking. Contrary to the critics' expectations, Kerwin and Langbein[10] found that negotiation of rules reduced

---

8. Philip J. Harter, Assessing the Assessors: The Actual Performance of Negotiated Rulemaking, 9 N.Y.U. Envtl. L. J. 32, 56 (2000).

9. Cary Coglianese. Assessing the Advocacy of Negotiated Rulemaking: A Response to Philip Harter, 9 N.Y.U. Envtl. L.J. 386, 392, 447 (2001). Professor Harter's article cited in the previous footnote had been highly critical of Professor Coglianese's earlier Assessing Consensus: The Promise and Performance of Negotiated Rulemaking, 46 Duke L.J. 1255 (1997), which reported as the result of his empirical research that negotiated rulemaking as thus far experienced offered no advantages over conventional rulemaking in timesaving or litigation avoidance.

10. [Ed.] This is the unpublished study referenced in note 6 above; another analysis of its results appears as Laura I. Langbein

conflict between the regulator and regulated entities, and it was no less fair to regulated entities than conventional rulemaking. The data contradict claims that regulatory negotiation abrogates an agency's responsibility to implement laws written by Congress; indeed, the process may better enable the agency to fulfill that role. Regulatory negotiation clearly emerges, moreover, as a superior process for generating information, facilitating learning, and building trust. Most significantly, consensus-based negotiation increases legitimacy, defined as the acceptability of the regulation to those involved in its development. This legitimacy benefit, which was observed independently of the types of rules chosen for conventional versus negotiated rulemaking, and independently of differences among the participants, including their affiliation, is no small accomplishment and we argue that, in any event, it is more important than reducing transaction costs. . . .

"The empirical research on regulatory negotiation has just begun, and its relevance to larger questions of institutional design could not be greater. The data presented here paint a largely favorable picture of this particular decision-making innovation—it equals or outperforms conventional rulemaking on virtually every measure tested and produces greater satisfaction among participants—and there is no evidence that it exacerbates capture or leads the agency to abdicate responsibility. Perhaps most importantly, however, the data suggest that process matters. The legitimacy benefit produced by negotiated rulemaking is at least somewhat due to the process itself, not merely to satisfaction with outcomes. We imagine that other, similar, consensus-based processes might exert the same effect as well."

Even its most enthusiastic supporters agree that regulatory negotiation is not a panacea. Some types of regulatory problems appear to be more suited than others for this type of rulemaking. A "Negotiated Rulemaking Sourcebook" published by the former Administrative Conference of the United States,[11] which initially had bureaucratic responsibility for overseeing reg-neg, suggested the following "conditions . . . conducive to successful negotiation of rules":

- "A limited number of interests will be significantly affected, and they are such that individuals can be selected to represent them. A rule of thumb is that no more than 25 people would have to participate at any one time, although each interest may be represented by a caucus or 'team.' . . .

- The issues are known and ripe for decision. . . . [T]he matter must be sufficiently developed so the participants can focus on relatively well crystallized issues. . . .

- No party will have to compromise a fundamental value. . . . While the issues presented for agreement can be major and important, if they rise to the level of *faith*, agreement is unlikely. . . .

and Cornelius M. Kerwin, Regulatory Negotiation v. Conventional Rulemaking: Claims, Counterclaims and Empirical Evidence, 10 J. Pub. Admin. Res. & Theory 599 (2000).

11. See p. 479 above.

- The rule involves diverse issues. The parties will likely not agree if only one issue is presented. The advantage of negotiations is a type of 'Jack Sprat' rulemaking—what may be critical to one party may well not be so important to another. . . .

- The outcome is genuinely in doubt. If a party has the raw power— through political influence, a commanding position on the relevant facts, or bargaining strength—to dictate the results of the proceeding, it would likely be inappropriate to use a consensus process. Those without direct power would generally need the formal structure of the rulemaking process to protect their interests or to alter the relative power balance. . . .

- The parties view it as in their interest to use the process. . . . A party that feels forced to the table may go through the motions of participation, but it will likely not be a full, creative participant and may take actions subsequently to attempt to scuttle the product of any discussions.

- The agency is willing to use the process and participate in it. Experience shows rather dramatically that any agency can find creative ways to sabotage a process it does not like. . . .

- No one interest should be able to dominate the proceeding. All participants must feel that their concurrence in any agreement is essential.

- There should be a deadline for achieving consensus. A reasonably firm deadline for conclusion of negotiations will help the participants to keep moving toward a resolution at an efficient pace. The deadline may be externally imposed by statute or court order, or may be set by the agency."

(iv) IMPACT ANALYSIS

Executive Order 12866

Regulatory Planning and Review.

58 FR 51735 (October 4, 1993), as amended by Executive Order 13528, 67 FR 9385, Feb. 26, 2002.

[The Executive Order appears in the Appendix at p. 1370 and following. It is the principal text for this section of materials. In reading it, focus on Sections 1 and 6 through 10. Particularly note the several references to what is "authorized" or "required" "by law," and consider what those references imply for presidential authority over agency rulemaking. Note that, unlike Section 4, which is dealt with at p. 611ff., the operative commands here are directed only to executive branch officials holding office at the pleasure of the President, and not to the independent regulatory commissions. Is that a legal judgment, or a political one?]

Presidential Management of the Regulatory State[1]

John D. Graham, Ph.D., Administrator, Office of Information and Regulatory Affairs.
Dec. 17, 2001.

[The text of this speech is set out at p. 616 above].

AN HISTORICAL NOTE[2]

Since the administration of President Nixon, the White House has taken increasingly formal control of important ("major") rulemakings. It has asserted at least a supervisory if not a directory role in shaping the intellectual analysis of issues put on the rulemaking table, and even in assessing the justifications for particular conclusions. "[T]he history of the presidency in the twentieth century has been the history of Presidents' attempts to gain control of the sprawling federal bureaucracy."[3] "[P]residential oversight of the regulatory process, though relatively new, has become a permanent part of the institutional design of American government. This new institutional arrangement has occurred for reasons parallel to the development of a centralized budget in the 1920s. All Presidents are likely to seek assurance that an unwieldy federal bureaucracy conforms its actions to their basic principles. Any President is likely to be concerned about excessive public and private costs. And any President is likely to want to be able to coordinate agency activity so as to ensure consistency and coherence and to guard against the imposition of conflicting duties on people who must comply with the law. The result of these forces is that a centralizing and rationalizing body, housed within OMB and devoted to regulation, has emerged as an enduring, major, but insufficiently appreciated part of the national government."[4]

The device predominantly used, the "regulatory impact analysis," draws on the example legislatively set in the National Environmental Policy Act of 1969. NEPA had required agencies unaccustomed to considering the systemic consequences of their decisions to anticipate the adverse environmental changes their projects might bring about, and to consider means of reducing or avoiding them. Actively enforced by courts from the outset, the NEPA process often produced defensive measures or altered decisions.[5] Learning from this experience, and fearing adventitious use, Presidents have hesitated to permit private enforcement of the obligation to perform an impact analysis. Instead, enforcement comes from within the

---

1. Speech given to the Weidenbaum Center Forum, "Executive Regulatory Review: Surveying the Record, Marking It Work," National Press Club, Washington, DC; in July, 2002 it could be found posted on the OIRA website, http://www.whitehouse.gov/omb/reginfo.

2. A more extensive treatment, richly sourced and focusing particularly on the Clinton administration, may be found in Elena Kagan, Presidential Administration, 114 Harv.L.Rev. 2245, 2272–2319. Excerpts appear above at pp. 213 and 218.

3. Forrest McDonald, The American Presidency: An Intellectual History 329 (1994).

4. Richard H. Pildes and Cass R. Sunstein, Reinventing the Regulatory State, 62 U.Chi.L.Rev. 1 (1995).

5. 42 U.S.C. § 4331 et seq.; see Calvert Cliffs' Coordinating Comm., Inc. v. USAEC, 449 F.2d 1109 (D.C.Cir.1971); Serge Taylor, Making Bureaucracies Think (1984).

Executive Office of the President. During President Carter's administration, Executive Order 12044 required analysis of anticipated economic impacts and justifications for a limited number of important rulemakings. President Reagan built upon this development with Executive Orders 12291 and 12498, which placed a much wider range of rulemaking activities under the supervision of the Office of Information and Regulatory Analysis (OIRA) in the Office of Management and Budget. E.O. 12,291 specified analytic principles for rulemaking and provided richly for their enforcement from the White House. E.O. 12498 created an annual regulatory agenda under White House supervision, treated in Section 3(b)(ii) above.

Other impact requirements followed, some from the White House and others from Congress. For example, the Reagan administration contributed requirements to analyze regulatory impacts on federalism[6] and on family values.[7] A list appears in a table prepared by Professor Mark Seidenfeld. "A Table of Requirements for Federal Administrative Rulemaking," 27 F.S.U.L. Rev. 533 (2000). The proliferation of requirements, taken seriously, could significantly inhibit regulation; perhaps a "regulatory impact analysis" impact analysis was in order. However, an empirical survey, undertaken for the American Bar Association's Section of Administrative Law and Regulatory Practice, suggested that these subsidiary requirements—unlike the basic economic impact assessment requirement—had in fact not yet been seriously implemented. See Sidney Shapiro, Political Oversight and the Deterioration of Regulatory Policy, 46 Ad.L.Rev. 1 (1994). Congress's contributions began in 1980 with the Regulatory Flexibility Act, 5 U.S.C. §§ 601–612, encouraging the same sort of attention to regulatory impact on small businesses as NEPA had sought respecting impact on small fish. See Paul Verkuil, A Critical Guide to the Regulatory Flexibility Act, 1982 Duke L.J. 213. Like the executive orders, the 1980 Act was not subject to judicial enforcement.

In an era of divided government, with a Democrat Congress considerably more enthusiastic about regulation than a conservative Republican White House, OIRA became a lightning rod for concerns that the President was obstructing the "necessary" work of government agencies. Its director was made subject to Senate confirmation, and understandings about transparency in the process were negotiated. Even so, responding to concerns about the direction regulation was, or wasn't, taking, and feelings that the OIRA's processes were still insufficiently transparent and accountable, the Senate refused to confirm the first President Bush's nominee for the position. President Bush responded by creating a controversial "Council on Competitiveness" chaired by Vice President Quayle. The Council was responsible for political oversight of OIRA and the resolution of important disputes. It made little pretense of operating in public, preferring to "leave

6. Executive Order 12612, Federalism, defined a set of "Fundamental Federalism Principles" and required agencies to assess federalism impacts and to adhere to these principles "to the extent permitted by law." Preemption of state authority was to be minimized; state participation in federal proceedings, maximized.

7. Executive Order 12606 highlighted the importance of family values in American life, and instructed agencies to assess and (to the extent permitted by law) avoid any negative impact on those values.

no fingerprints."[8] "As a result," reports ELENA KAGAN, PRESIDENTIAL ADMINIS-TRATION, 114 Harv. L. Rev. 2281–82 (2001), "the Council provoked the same criticisms, except perhaps still more heated, formerly lodged against OIRA. . . .

"In light of this criticism, observers might have predicted that when a Democratic President assumed office in 1993, a radical curtailment of presidential supervision of administrative action would follow. Instead, the very opposite occurred. President Clinton, to be sure, replaced Reagan's executive orders on regulatory review [with Executive Order 12866] and eliminated Bush's Competitiveness Council. But . . . presidential control of administration . . . expanded significantly during the Clinton Presidency, moving in this eight-year period to the center of the regulatory landscape.

". . . Clinton came to view administration as perhaps the single most critical—in part because the single most available—vehicle to achieve his domestic policy goals. He accordingly developed a set of practices that enhanced his ability to influence or even dictate the content of administrative initiatives. He exercised this power with respect to a wide variety of agency action—rulemakings, more informal means of policymaking, and even certain enforcement activities. The new practices, to be sure, had significant limits, some internally and others externally imposed, and they left untouched a wide swath of regulatory activity. But to a considerable extent, Clinton built on the legacy Reagan had left him to devise a new and newly efficacious way of setting the policy direction of agencies—of converting administrative activity into an extension of his own policy and political agenda. In so doing, Clinton also showed that presidential supervision of administration could operate, contrary to much opinion, to trigger, not just react to, agency action and to drive this action in a regulatory, not deregulatory, direction."

Congress declined several chances to codify the Executive Order process into statutory form during the Clinton administration. However in 1996 it amended the Regulatory Flexibility Act to authorize judicial review to enforce its terms[9]—although litigants have had little success thus far. It also passed the Unfunded Mandates Reform Act of 1995, PL 104–4, which put legislative muscle behind the requirement, "unless otherwise prohibited by law," that agencies consider impacts on state, local and tribal governments *or the private sector* for rules that might "result in the expenditure . . . of $100,000,000 or more (adjusted annually for inflation) in any 1 year," 2 U.S.C. §§ 1531–32.[10] This analysis may be folded into any

8. See Peter M. Shane, Political Accountability in a System of Checks and Balances: The Case of Presidential Review of Rulemaking, 48 Ark.L.Rev. 161 (1995).

9. See Associated Fisheries of Maine, Inc. v. Daley, 127 F.3d 104 (1st Cir.1997); Symposium, 49 Admin.L.Rev. 111 (1997). However, an agency is under "no obligation to conduct a small entity impact analysis of effects on entities which it does not regulate." United Distribution Cos. v. FERC, 88 F.3d 1105, 1170 (D.C.Cir.1996).

10. Where the statutory threshold is crossed, § 1535 requires that "(a) . . . [T]he agency shall identify and consider a reasonable number of regulatory alternatives and from those alternatives select the least costly, most cost-effective or least burdensome alternative that achieves the objectives of the rule, . . .

(b) . . . unless—

(1) the head of the affected agency publishes with the final rule an explanation

other analysis the agency is required to perform. Judicial review is sharply limited, 2 U.S.C. § 1571, but OMB is required to make annual reports on OIRA's supervision. EPA's compliance with both RegFlex and UMRA was challenged in American Trucking Association v. Whitman, whose discussion of delegation questions is presented in Chapter II, § 1; both claims were summarily dismissed. 175 F.3d at 1043–44. This result is typical. Nonetheless, the fact of the statutes makes clear that Congress has accepted the validity of the executive order's approach. The obligations may not be judicially enforceable, but neither are they politically resistable.

The second President Bush has kept Executive Order 12866 in place, with OIRA under the direction of John Graham taking a publicly more disciplinarian stance than was evident under President Clinton's Director, Sally Katzen. (He has also considerably added to the transparency of OIRA's procedures; the OIRA website now reveals details of meetings and other matters previously inaccessible there.) The quoted talk fully reveals the public side of his early administration.

NOTES ON THE MECHANICS OF E.O. 12866

(1) *Insignificant, Significant, and Yet More Significant Regulations.* The Executive Order, generally mirrored in this respect by the supporting statutes, creates three different categories of regulations, determinable by the agency *or* the Administrator of OIRA. Under § 3(f),

> "Significant regulatory action" means any regulatory action that is likely to result in a rule that may:
>
> > (1) Have an annual effect on the economy of $100 million or more or adversely affect in a material way the economy, a sector of the economy, productivity, competition, jobs, the environment, public health or safety, or State, local, or tribal governments or communities;
> >
> > (2) Create a serious inconsistency or otherwise interfere with an action taken or planned by another agency;
> >
> > (3) Materially alter the budgetary impact of entitlements, grants, user fees, or loan programs or the rights and obligations of recipients thereof; or
> >
> > (4) Raise novel legal or policy issues arising out of legal mandates, the President's priorities, or the principles set forth in this Executive order.

Section 6(a)(3)(C), makes clear that actions meeting the economic impact standard of § 3(f)(1) are treated as more "significant" than the rest.

of why the least costly, most cost-effective or least burdensome method of achieving the objectives of the rule was not adopted; or

(2) the provisions are inconsistent with law."

Any invocation of the exceptions is a part of OMB's reporting obligation to Congress, but judicial enforcement is precluded.

Regulations that meet none of these tests of significance constitute the third level of White House engagement and procedure in rulemaking.

Contrast with this approach the Supreme Court's decision in Vermont Yankee Nuclear Power Corp. v. Natural Resources Defense Council, p. 498, which read APA § 553 as establishing a one-size-fits-all set of procedures. Then-Professor Antonin Scalia had criticized the Court's decision precisely for its failure to recognize that some rulemakings are more equal than others: "[O]nce it is accepted that procedures are to be used as a means of expanding or restricting the power to act, the idea of any genuinely stable APA based on fairness and efficiency alone becomes visionary. It also becomes unrealistic to expect the framework of any such superstatute to contain only a few options of procedure among which later legislation must choose—such as the stark choice between formal and informal rulemaking offered under the current APA." See p. 508. Indeed, one can see in the more demanding statutory "hybrid" rulemaking procedures Congress has provided for such important rulemakers as EPA and OSHA, a congressional recognition that some rulemakings have an impact that warrants deeper agency care, and more political and judicial oversight, than others. Not surprisingly, perhaps, when Justice Scalia wrote the majority opinion in Whitman v. American Trucking Assoc., the Court's most recent pronouncement on the delegation doctrine, p. 48, he made a similar point: "While Congress need not provide any direction to the EPA regarding the manner in which it is to define 'country elevators,' . . . exempt from new-stationary-source regulations governing grain elevators, see 42 U.S.C. § 7411(i), it must provide substantial guidance on setting air standards that affect the entire national economy." The three-tiered system of the E.O. 12866 reflects similar presidential judgments. Political favors aside, no one in the White House will care about the proper location of a marine buoy in Barnegat Sound, a matter on which the Coast Guard engages in notice and comment rulemaking. They will, however, have views about a rule regulating the risks of coastal oil pollution—and if that rule imposes massive economic costs on the maritime industry, their concerns will escalate.

One way to think about E.O. 12866, then, is as a reflection of variations in rulemaking procedure that—Vermont Yankee notwithstanding—could become part of the next "formula upon which opposing social and political forces have come to rest." Notice the various respects in which it embroiders on § 553's skeletal procedures, ratifying judicial and practice developments. For example, compare § 553(b)'s definition of required notice with § 6(a)(1)'s requirement that "*before issuing a notice of proposed rulemaking*, each agency should, where appropriate, seek the involvement of those who are intended to benefit from and those expected to be burdened by any regulation (including, specifically, State, local, and tribal officials)," (emphasis added) and § 6(a)(3)(B)'s requirements for agency submission to OIRA in connection with *any* "significant regulatory action" of

> (i) The text of the draft regulatory action, together with a reasonably detailed description of the need for the regulatory action and an explanation of how the regulatory action will meet that need; and

(ii) An assessment of the potential costs and benefits of the regulatory action, including an explanation of the manner in which the regulatory action is consistent with a statutory mandate and, to the extent permitted by law, promotes the President's priorities and avoids undue interference with State, local, and tribal governments in the exercise of their governmental functions.

If the proposed regulation meets the $100,000,000 or other impact tests of § 3(f)(1), still further preliminary analysis must be supplied. Will these items be available as part of the rulemaking record? Notice in this respect § 6(b)(4)(D):

After the regulatory action has been published in the Federal Register or otherwise issued to the public, or after the agency has announced its decision not to publish or issue the regulatory action, OIRA shall make available to the public all documents exchanged between OIRA and the agency during the review by OIRA under this section.

Just where to set the dividing lines among insignificant, significant, and more significant regulations is open to debate, but Professor Steven Croley's recent empirical study is suggestive.[1] During the Clinton administration—the most recent for which reliable figures are in hand—the federal government adopted roughly 5,000 regulations of all kinds annually. OIRA reviewed about 600 of these annually (the comparable figure was about four times as high in the Reagan and first Bush administrations). About 100 of these were regarded as economically major (this figure was less variable across administrations). OIRA review at any level, then, reached about fifteen percent of all regulations during the Clinton administration; "major" rule treatment, about two percent. Putting aside for the moment questions about White House control, does the 3–part division of rulemaking, with additional procedures provided for more important regulations, more aptly structure the rulemaking process?

If you wished to explore a concrete example of "significant" rulemaking under E.O. 12866, one candidate might be the Department of Transportation's rulemaking on Tire Pressure Monitoring Systems. This important rulemaking was statutorily directed under tight time deadlines in the wake of a dramatic series of accidents involving Ford Explorer motor vehicles and underinflated Firestone tires. In part responding to OIRA guidance, the National Highway Traffic Safety Administration has provided for continuing evaluation and development of its standards, after initially adopting a rule in June 2002. This process seems likely to keep the rulemaking active throughout the shelf-life of this edition. A search of the departmental docket at http://dms.dot.gov for Docket Number 8572 will reveal the current state of affairs. You will find (alongside the ordinary comments, and ample evidence of pre-NRPM public involvement) Dr. Graham's return letter of Feb. 12, 2002 (#202), a transcript of both the NHTSA Administrator's (#200) and Dr. Graham's (#201) subsequent congressional testimony before a House committee evidently concerned about the intervention, NGO letters reacting to Dr. Graham's letter

---

1. Steven P. Croley, White House Review of Agency Rulemaking: An Empirical   Investigation (draft of Aug. 12, 2002, cited with permission)

(##199, 204), NHTSA's memorandum indicating changes produced by the OIRA process (#237), and much else of possible interest.

(2) *The Practice of Cost-Benefit Analysis.* While disciplined exploration of cost-benefit analysis might consume a good deal of time, the following paragraphs from CASS R. SUNSTEIN, THE COST-BENEFIT STATE: THE FUTURE OF REGULATORY PROTECTION 20–22 (2002), should convey the principal ideas and issues: "First and foremost, a government committed to cost benefit analysis will attempt to analyze the consequences of regulations, on both the cost and benefit side. Such an analysis will include quantitative and qualitative accounts of expected effects, including, for example, a statement of the expected lives saved, curable cancers prevented, asthma attacks averted, and much more. . . .

". . . Many regulations do not impose substantial costs, and for routine or low-cost measures a formal analysis should not be required (and it has not been under the relevant executive orders). The central point is that the extent of the requisite analysis should depend on the magnitude of the regulation—and that a formal analysis should be required for all regulations imposing costs beyond some identified point. Quantification will be difficult or even impossible in some cases. For arsenic in drinking water, government cannot really come up with specific numbers to link exposure levels to deaths and illnesses. At this stage, science is able to produce only ranges of anticipated benefits, which are not precise but are nonetheless highly illuminating. For regulations protecting airport security in the face of terrorist threats, quantification of the benefits is at best a guess. We do not know the magnitude of the risks, and a full scale cost-benefit analysis would be silly. But even here, an effort to be as specific as possible about costs and anticipated efficacy is likely to help us to promote airport security in the most reasonable manner.

". . . [T]he cost-benefit state imposes a substantive requirement as well. In order to proceed, an agency should be required to conclude, in ordinary circumstances, that the benefits justify the costs, and to explain why. If, for example, a regulation is expected to save 80 lives, each valued at $6 million, and if it would cost $200 million, it is fully justified. But if a regulation is expected to save four lives and cost $400 million, an agency should ordinarily be barred from issuing it. If an agency seeks to proceed even though the benefits do not justify the costs, it should have to explain itself—by saying, for example, that those at risk are young children, and that because they cannot protect themselves, and because a number of years of life are involved, unusual steps should be taken.

"At this point, it might be possible to question whether a large amount of money (say, $400 million) would really be too much to spend to save a small number of lives (say, two). Who is to say that $400 million is too much? The best answer is heavily pragmatic. Each of us has limited resources, and we do not spend all of our budget on statistically low risks. We spent a certain amount, and not more, to protect against the risks associated with poor diet, motor vehicle accidents, fires, floods, and much more. In allocating our resources, we set priorities, partly to use resources to prevent the more serious safety problems and partly to use them on other things we care about, such as education, recreation, food, and entertainment. The same is true for governments, which cannot sensibly spend huge amounts on small hazards. If an agency requires a $400 million expenditure to save two lives, it will be expending resources that might well be spent on other matters, including the saving of more lives. Indeed, evidence suggests that high expenditures—of perhaps $15 million or more—will cause the loss of a statistical life, and hence that regulations with high costs and low benefits may cause more deaths than they prevent. . . .

"The point applies in every domain. If government refuses to regulate extremely low concentrations of arsenic in drinking water, it is probably because it believes that the health gains would be low and that the costs (in the form of higher water bills) would be significant. . . . It is not as if people are, with respect to some risk, either 'safe' or 'unsafe.' The real questions are whether and how to reduce the risks to which they are now subject. Cost-benefit analysis is tool for ensuring good answers to those questions.

"None of this suggests that the government should be rigidly bound to the 'bottom line.' Cost-benefit analysis ought not to place agencies in an arithmetic straightjacket. The benefits should ordinarily be required to exceed the costs, but regulators might reasonably decide that the numbers are not decisive if, for example, children are mostly at risk, or if the relevant hazard is faced mostly by poor people, or if the hazard at issue is involuntarily incurred or extremely difficult to control. . . . The basic ideas are simple: Agencies should be required to investigate both costs and benefits, to show that benefits justify costs most circumstances, and to offer a reasonable explanation for any decision to proceed when costs exceed benefits. [T]hese requirements should help to overcome problems that we all face in thinking about risk while at the same time reducing interest-group power and promoting accountability in government."

As you may already have seen, in some circumstances Congress appears to have forbidden costs to be taken into account in regulatory decisionmaking about health and safety issues (for example, the Clean Air Act, see Whitman v. ATA, p. 48), or to have allowed consideration of economic impact only a limited role in the regulatory equation (for example, the Occupational Safety and Health Act's regulation of hazardous substances in the workplace, see the Benzene case, p. 58). In these circumstances, what does E.O. 12866 require in the way of cost-benefit analysis? And what do these statutes permit?[2] In other regulatory settings, cost-benefit analysis may be statutorily required and, in consequence, the agency's calculations may be closely scrutinized on judicial review. Gas Appliance Manufacturers Assn. v. Department of Energy, 998 F.2d 1041 (D.C.Cir.1993).

(3) *Critiques of Cost–Benefit.*

(a) ERIC POSNER, CONTROLLING AGENCIES WITH COST-BENEFIT ANALYSIS: A POSITIVE POLITICAL THEORY PERSPECTIVE, 68 U.Chi.L.Rev. 1137, 1141, 1145 (2001): "Cost-benefit analysis is a puzzle for interest group theory because interest group theory assumes that the President and Congress seek to transfer resources to interest groups rather than to maximize efficiency.

---

2. See Craig Oren, Run Over by American Trucking, Part I, quoted at p. 56 above.

Cost-benefit analysis is a puzzle for welfare economists because it does not implement a plausible welfare standard such as the Pareto principle. And cost-benefit analysis is a puzzle for critics from the left, who point out that it undervalues environmental goods and the interests of the poor. . . . [T]hese puzzles are solved when cost-benefit analysis is put in the proper institutional context. The purpose of requiring agencies to perform cost-benefit analysis is not to ensure that regulations are efficient; it is to ensure that elected officials maintain power over agency regulation. Evaluation of cost-benefit analysis should be based on its usefulness for disciplining agencies and enhancing the control of elected officials, not on its instantiation of ethical principles that elected officials may or may not share. Many criticisms of cost-benefit analysis confuse the institutional justification of cost-benefit analysis and the normative goals of those who elect to use it. . . .

"Cost-benefit analysis is sometimes treated as a loose balancing of the advantages and disadvantages of a project. But this is not what is at stake in the policy dispute. The policy dispute concerns the process by which the welfare effects of projects are determined. When an agency conducts a cost-benefit analysis, it may spend thousands or millions of dollars collecting and analyzing data. The data usually come from studies of market behavior or surveys of consumer preferences, and the analysis often involves a great deal of extrapolation. Consider a proposed regulation to require the installation of scrubbers in the smokestacks of certain factories. The cost of the regulation will be calculated from market data on the price of the scrubbers, which must also take account of potential technological advances that may reduce that price. The benefit of the regulation will be determined using scientific studies on the effects of the pollutant on people's health and property. Health benefits will be calculated in terms of reduction of medical costs, and, if lives or life years are saved, in terms of the value of statistical lives—which themselves are calculated from studies that determine from market data how much money people are willing to pay to avoid small risks of death. If the pollutant causes damage to the environment, surveys will be used to determine how much people are willing to pay for clean air, or to preserve wildlife. The costs and benefits also must be discounted to reflect the passage of time. And alternative regulations must be considered; for example, shutting down the plants or installing another kind of scrubber may be more cost-effective. When the hard work of data collection and analysis is completed, the comparison of costs and benefits is straightforward."

(b) MARK SEIDENFELD, THE PSYCHOLOGY OF ACCOUNTABILITY AND POLITICAL REVIEW OF AGENCY RULES, 51 Duke L.J. 1059, 1091 (2001): "Of the three mechanisms [commonly discussed for oversight of agency rulemaking by elected officials—OMB (presidential) review, congressional review, and joint presidential-congressional review (fast-track enactment of approved rules as statutes)—] OMB review holds the greatest promise for improving the quality of staff decisionmaking. The agency knows that any rule with a significant economic impact will be subject to OMB review. This review is nominally process based, and when agency staff begins formulating the rule, it usually will not know the identity of the particular desk officer assigned to scrutinize the agency's cost-benefit analysis. For rules that attract significant political attention early on, however, the agency is apt to equate the preferences of the desk officer with the publicly announced views of the White House. This in turn will encourage the agency to formulate rules that are closer to the preferences of the president than the agency would if it were not subject to OMB review. An agency is also likely to presume that desk officers will be preoccupied with regulatory cost, which will induce the agency to adopt economically conservative rules rather than rules that promise uncertain but potentially large benefits at a certain and significant cost.''

Of course one need not assume that OMB review is optimal to, in Seidenfeld's words, ''satisfy the four criteria that psychologists have found necessary for accountability to improve the quality of decisionmaking.[3] OMB review might encourage the agency to take greater care in formulating rules, but not for every rule subject to review. Moreover, because the agency is apt to presume OIRA desk officers have a preoccupation with regulatory costs, OMB review generally will bias the outcome of agency rulemaking toward economically conservative rules.'' Id. At 1093–94.

(c) JAMES F. BLUMSTEIN, REGULATORY REVIEW BY THE EXECUTIVE OFFICE OF THE PRESIDENT: AN OVERVIEW AND POLICY ANALYSIS OF CURRENT ISSUES, 51 Duke L.J. 851, 879 (2001): ''The first two administrators of OIRA saw as perhaps the greatest benefit of OMB review improved agency ability to 'respond to the kinds of questions that OMB raises.' This was achieved when agencies either established or enhanced their inhouse capabilities to analyze their regulatory decisions. Thus, the very existence of external review can improve an agency's decisionmaking process by keeping the agency on its analytical toes. There is a value in keeping agency bureaucratic decisions intellectually honest and analytically rigorous, and external, centralized presidential regulatory review can bring this about by bringing to bear a new set of perspectives and analytical tools.''

Notice in this respect § 6(a)(2) of the Executive Order, requiring the ''agency head [to] designate a Regulatory Policy Officer who shall report to the agency head. The Regulatory Policy Officer shall be involved at each stage of the regulatory process to foster the development of effective, innovative, and least burdensome regulations and to further the principles set forth in this Executive order.'' What do you suppose the bureaucratic effect of this organizational requirement would be? What kinds of training would be appropriate for a ''Regulatory Policy Officer,'' and her supporting staff?

(d) JEFFREY J. RACHLINSKI & CYNTHIA R. FARINA, COGNITIVE PSYCHOLOGY AND OPTIMAL GOVERNMENT DESIGN, 87 Cornell L. Rev. 549, 562, 579, 597–98 (2002): ''The portrait psychologists paint of human judgment is one of constant effort to stretch limited cognitive resources. At an individual level,

---

3. [Ed.] These 4 criteria are: ''(1) [W]hether the decisionmaker is aware that he will be held accountable when he makes his decision, (2) whether he perceives the audience to which he is accountable as legitimate, (3) whether the audience demands a justification of the outcome of the decision rather than the processes by which the decisionmaker reached that outcome, and (4) whether he knows the outcome preferences of his audience, or even the identity of the audience well enough to surmise what its outcome preferences might be.'' Id at 1065.

people develop heuristics to enable them to manage the stimuli they encounter; these heuristics serve them well, but lead to systematic errors. Experts have knowledge, training, and experience that enable them to identify situations in which they cannot trust ordinary heuristics, and to approach problems from a different perspective. These advantages can indeed produce better decisions than laypeople make, but can also lead to overconfidence and a failure adequately to consider alternatives beyond the boundaries of their expertise.

"In light of this, a government that seeks to avoid bad decisions must be structured carefully to avoid predictable errors in judgment. . . .

"The problem with administrative agencies is the problem that all experts face: They are apt to be overconfident in their decisionmaking. Experts fail to look beyond the factors that their training and experience predispose them to consider; they tend not to test thoroughly their assumptions. Experts are right more often than laypersons, but not as often as they think. Furthermore, experts in administrative agencies are unlikely to mirror the range of values and priorities of the larger society they are supposed to serve. Most of the staff of the Army Corps of Engineers or the Environmental Protection Agency (EPA) will not have arrived at their employment at random. Those who join an agency with the principal mission of building dams probably do so because they like the prospect of building dams. Those who seek work at an agency charged with responsibility for the environment probably have strong views about the appropriate goals and means of environmental regulation. Consequently, agencies can become myopically focused on their missions. . . .

"In theory, OMB review . . . allows a technically sophisticated vetting of the agency's analysis before a group of examiners sufficiently adept to understand it but uninvested, either personally or professionally, in the particular proposal. . . .

"[The actual] practice has varied across administrations. . . . Assessments of OMB's performance over time are, not surprisingly, conflicting. Still, it appears reasonably safe to say that the agency's effectiveness in providing technically sophisticated external review was compromised whenever it was perceived as engaged in the very different function of reviewing policy proposals for conformity with the President's political or ideological agenda. This perception was highest in the first term of the Reagan Administration and abated somewhat in the Clinton Administration.[4] In any event, the pattern of staffing OIRA with ' "desk officers, who are typically young economists, lawyers, or policy analysts with little prior

---

4. *See* Thomas O. McGarity, Reinventing Rationality: The Role of Regulatory Analysis in the Federal Bureaucracy 286–87 (1991) (reporting "a strong sense among most agency analysts that a good analysis will not save a decision with which [Reagan-era] OMB disagrees and a poor analysis will not slow down a decision with which OMB agrees"); Tomkin, supra note 159, at 95, 102, 210, 216, 220–21, 256–57; Matthew Holden, Jr., Why Entourage Politics is Volatile, in The Managerial Presidency, supra note 104, at 61, 75 (reporting agency perceptions that Reagan OMB sided with and passed information along to industrial interests, and was " 'vindictive' " towards dissenting agencies); Terry M. Moe, The Politicized Presidency, in The Managerial Presidency, supra note 108, at 135, 151–52 (describing the role that "a new OMB unit, staffed by presidential partisans" played in the Reagan Administration's strategy for controlling regulatory policymaking).

experience in government or with the programs they oversee,"' seems ill-suited to providing technically adept expert review.

"Some commentors have argued vehemently that OMB pressure on agencies to conform to the President's policy agenda is a thoroughly appropriate—indeed, highly desirable—infusion of democratic control into regulatory decisionmaking. Others have as vigorously disputed the claim that presidential elections represent a regulatory policy mandate from the people that is carried out through White House review. We take no position, in this Article, on that debate. We simply observe that *whatever* the democratic value of review designed to achieve ideological or political influence over the regulatory policy process, such review is unlikely simultaneously to realize the potential of external review to catch and correct the cognitive illusions of agency experts."

In sum, although the White House is a thoroughly sensible location for evaluating proposed policy for consistency with the President's political and ideological agenda, it may not be the best locus for a technically sophisticated review process aimed at countering the cognitive errors of agency experts.

(4) *The OIRA Process.* A common observation about the OIRA process, reflected in the preceding Notes and in Dr. Graham's announcement that—two decades after formalization of the process in OIRA—he is adding some engineers and scientists to its 40–odd professionals, is that its contribution has been distorted by the economics and policy-analysis backgrounds of its professionals. Not only do they lack the depth of resources of the agencies they oversee, they bring a different set of professional skills to the analysis than may be dominant in the agency. The counter-argument, remarks Professor STEVEN P. CROLEY, WHITE HOUSE OVERSIGHT OF AGENCY RULEMAKING: AN EMPIRICAL INVESTIGATION 8–9 (forthcoming 2003) is that while "the OMB is not an expert in any substantive field, it has become an expert in the field of regulation itself. According to this view, OIRA has developed a special institutional capacity for distinguishing between regulation likely to advance sound regulatory policy, on the one hand, and regulation that however well intentioned may lead to unintended and undesirable consequences. In addition to mere coordination, in other words, White House review provides a 'quality check' on pending rules. On this view, OIRA 's small size and technocratic orientation are important virtues. Centralized expertise offers a needed antidote to the topsy-turvy world of congressional and bureaucratic politics."

Note that on this view, the politics of particular rulemakings—who will be hurt and who will be helped—are not central although general awareness of the President's policy preferences is. A review of the Executive Order may suggest that considerable care has been exercised to keep the desk professionals of OIRA away from politics in the first sense. Professor Croley briefly describes the bureaucratic structure at OIRA: "OIRA's Regulatory Review and Paperwork office is . . . divided into three branches, 'Natural Resources,' 'Commerce and Lands,' and 'Human Resources.' These branches allocate responsibility for rulemaking review by subject matter of submitted rules. . . . Each branch is headed by a 'Branch Chief' who together oversee some twenty-five to thirty 'desk officers' who perform the line-level rulemaking review. The Branch Chiefs answer to OIRA's Deputy Administrator, who in turn answers to the Administrator of OIRA, the agency's only political appointee.... The Administrator answers to the Director of OMB.

"Of the three current Branch Chiefs (as of late 2001), two are economists and one is a lawyer. The two and a half dozen desk officers, most of whom have advanced degrees, are trained in public policy, policy analysis, economics, or statistics. Following a critical report in the early 1980s by OMB Watch, a Washington, D.C. government watchdog group, ... OIRA became more particular in its hiring practices and currently requires new desk officers to have advanced training in quantitative methods. While much of the OIRA review process focuses on cost-benefit analysis, ... Executive Order 12866, like the Reagan orders before it, also contemplates that rules are to be reviewed for their compatibility with the President's principles and priorities more generally. On that subject, Executive Order 12866 provides that disagreements between OIRA staff and a rulemaking agency are to be resolved wherever possible by OIRA's Administrator, and in the event of an impasse ... by the Vice President or President directly. ... [D]irect presidential and vice presidential involvement ... may be instigated only by the Director of OMB or by the head of an agency.

"In the typical case, however, OIRA desk officers receive rule submissions from agencies and initiate the review process. ... The submission form, standardized by OMB, contains basic information about a submitted rule, including its stage of development and whether it is economically significant.... Agencies must also certify that a submitted rule complies with the substance of Executive Order 12866 with signatures of both the agency's designated regulatory contact person and the agency's relevant program official. The 12866 submission form must further contain contact information for a person at the agency 'who can best answer questions regarding the content' of the submitted rule. Through the course of the review process, desk officers often communicate with a rule's agency, focusing especially on the technical aspects of a given rule. ... Where questions arise concerning a rule's compatibility with the President's political objectives, on the other hand, the Administrator of OIRA assumes a lead role in the review process. ... [T]his entire review process took on average 25 days for rules reviewed under the Reagan orders, and 44 days for rules reviewed under the Clinton order." At 17–18.

(a) HAROLD BRUFF, PRESIDENTIAL MANAGEMENT OF AGENCY RULEMAKING, 57 Geo.Wash.L.Rev. 533 (1989) describes practice under the Reagan–Bush executive orders but in important respects little has changed: "It would not be sensible to [expect expertise or research from the desk officers,] in view of the vastly greater expertise and resources of the agencies. For example, EPA, with a staff of about 10,000, submits all its rules to four desk officers in OIRA, who receive some assistance from other OIRA and budget personnel. These officers have neither the time nor the expertise to evaluate conflicting interpretations of technical data in a rulemaking. ...

"... Negotiations usually produce tradeoffs at the margins of the agency proposal (as, indeed, they do in the budget process). An agency also has massive advantages in the size and expertise of its staff, and can respond in depth to any position taken by OIRA. An agency displeased by an OMB position, while appealing within the executive branch, can seek allies among the interest groups or in Congress. . . . Much depends on the bureaucratic level that a particular controversy reaches, and on the agency's power within the administration. No OIRA desk officer can realistically threaten to slash an agency's budget, but the OMB Director can. A Deputy Assistant Secretary in an agency cannot realistically threaten to appeal to the President, but the Secretary can. As with other issues in the bureaucracy, continuing controversy over a rule tends to rise up the chain of command in both the agency and OMB until resolution is reached. Final compromise on a relatively controversial rule will be reached among the senior political appointees in the administration. . . . [T]he ultimate steps of appealing to the presidential level or issuing a rule over OMB's objections are rare."

(b) E. Donald Elliott, TQM[5]-ing OMB: Or Why Regulatory Review Under Executive Order 12,291 Works Poorly And What President Clinton Should Do About It, 57 L. & Contemp. Probs. 167 (Spring 1994) was an account of experience under the first Bush administration that is believed significantly to have affected the content and administration of E.O. 12866 in the Clinton years.

"Between 1989 and 1991, I found myself, as General Counsel of the Environmental Protection Agency, on the front lines in perhaps the most contentious and troubled relationship between the OMB and the agencies. . . . [Its] excessive secrecy undermines public confidence in the policy process and is not truly necessary to assure full and frank discussion of options. . . . [Yet], in my experience, economic analysis by the OMB generally improves, as well as delays, the EPA rules. Indeed, many (perhaps as much as eighty percent) of the major issues raised by the OMB process had not previously received substantial consideration in internal EPA deliberations. On one hand, this is encouraging, in that it suggests that the OMB process is adding value. On the other hand, it is also deeply disturbing, because fundamental issues are raised very late in the process, when it is virtually impossible to do anything productive about them. . . . The essence of my complaint is not that the OMB is too powerful, but that because the regulatory review process is poorly designed, review does not effectively achieve its stated goals.

"Although the entity that conducts regulatory review is part of the Office of *Management* and Budget, the review process itself violates virtually every tenet of good management—probably because it was designed by lawyers. . . . [T]he basic modalities of review under Executive Order 12,291 were drawn, perhaps unconsciously, from appellate court review of agency rules. Episodic judicial review of agency decisions has not proved to be the most effective way of reshaping government policy. To be effective, a system of regulation must create compliance incentives for regulated parties, rather than rely on corrective action and oversight. . . .

---

5. [Ed.] Total Quality Management, TQM, is the description given to contemporary management techniques for improving performance and doing away with excessive bureaucraticization. TQM programs have brought sharp reductions in the administrative superstructures of many large private corporations.

"... Few career EPA employees believe in their heart of hearts that the temporary occupant of either the EPA Administrator's office or the White House is their ultimate 'customer.' Nor do they believe that giving either one whatever she or he wants necessarily translates into better quality. ... [T]he OMB will never be more effective at improving regulation until it recognizes the legitimacy of the statutory missions that Congress has given the agencies, missions that agency employees take seriously....

"Many of the conflicts in which political actors engage are unnecessary, because our present structure for identifying options is not well-suited to seeking out mutually beneficial ('win/win') options. The relationship between the EPA and the OMB is a good example of a 'game' that could be re-engineered to mutual benefit. Like rats in a maze, a husband and wife in a bad marriage, or the prisoners in the Prisoner's Dilemma, the EPA and the OMB continue to play out a struggle over options that neither of them would rationally choose if the game were restructured to maximize mutual achievement of goals. ... [T]he human systems in which we find ourselves are not given and immutable; rather than merely play the game, we can and must reflect on improving the system that creates our incentives."

(5) *Openness About the Process.* Much of the political battling about the early years of the regulatory review process concerned its lack of transparency and, correspondingly, fears that it was serving as a conduit for the views of the White House's political friends. It is in this respect that E.O. 12866 may differ most sharply from its predecessors.

(a) These differences were a focal concern of PETER M. SHANE, POLITICAL ACCOUNTABILITY IN A SYSTEM OF CHECKS AND BALANCES: THE CASE OF PRESIDENTIAL REVIEW OF RULEMAKING, 48 Ark. L.Rev. 161 (1995): "We are living through a period of intense debate—among both academics and politicians—regarding the appropriate presidential role in supervising our vast national bureaucracy. That debate has two distinct, if overlapping, dimensions. One is constitutional: does the Constitution, read historically or otherwise, command a particular model of presidential supervision? The second addresses questions of policy: does government function best when the President enjoys plenary authority over the entire policy output of the bureaucracy? Or is government more effective when policymaking influence is shared between the President and Congress, and among high-level bureaucratic administrators?

"The Reagan and Bush Administrations took explicit positions on both sets of issues. ... The RB position held that, as a matter of constitutional dictate, the President enjoys plenary authority over all policy making involved in the execution of the laws. ... [T]he Reagan and Bush Administrations' redesign of executive branch mechanisms ... reached an apotheosis with the activities of the now-defunct President's Council on Competitiveness, headed during the Bush Administration by Vice President Dan Quayle. The Council vigorously advocated a theory of the executive branch in which the President's policy roles, even in domestic affairs, are broadly discretionary, dischargeable in secret, relatively immune to congressional scrutiny (at least as to process), and subject to judicial review only in rare instances...."

"No executive order or other formal document 'chartered' the Council on Competitiveness. The sole public document marking its establishment and structure was a 'Fact Sheet' released in April 1989, by the Office of the Vice President. There is no indication that, while in operation, the Council followed regular procedures, published or otherwise. It had no formal or informal agreement with Congress over legislative access to the documentation of its deliberative contributions. It established no controls on the degree or nature of its substantive contacts with outside interests. The Council functioned chiefly not through its members—all presidential advisers, cabinet members, or designated representatives from particular agencies—but through the personal staff of the Vice President. By interagency memo, it asserted its jurisdiction over:

> not only regulations that are published for notice and comment, but also strategy statements, guidelines, policy manuals, grant and loan procedures, Advance Notices of Proposed Rulemaking, press releases and other documents announcing or implementing regulatory policy that affects the public.[6]

Given the Council's limited resources, the percentage of actual activities the Council could review was presumably quite small compared to the entire regulatory output of the federal executive. Nonetheless, according to the Vice President's self-expressed mandate, there was virtually no policy making activity that the Council regarded as categorically beyond its reach. . . .

" . . . As summarized by one recent commentator, the Council 'convinced agency heads to weaken, and in some cases eliminate, regulations relating to commercial aircraft noise, the protection of wetlands, mandatory recycling, and air pollution.'[7] . . . The Council [also] helped to derail an EPA effort to reduce sulphur dioxide emissions from the Navajo Generating Station, which, among other things, had obscured the view of Grand Canyon. The Council tried to press upon EPA a revised definition of protected 'wetlands,' which, by one estimate, would have lowered protections on one third of American wetlands, as earlier defined, including a majority of forested wetlands. The Council intervened to persuade the Federal Aviation Administration to relax its requirements for phasing out noisy aircraft under the Airport Noise and Capacity Act of 1990.

"Such was the regulatory oversight system dedicated most faithfully to a categorical separation of powers philosophy that, in turn, was touted as advancing the cause of accountability. . . . [I]t intervened in 'dozens of unpublicized controversies over important federal regulations, leaving what vice presidential aides call "no fingerprints" on the results of its interventions.'[8] The White House's efforts to avoid public disclosure of its oversight activity took multiple forms: resisting FOIA disclosure of documents be-

---

6. Memorandum for Heads of Executive Departments and Agencies From the Vice President re: Regulatory Review Process, at 1 (Mar. 22, 1991) (on file with author).

7. Caroline DeWitt, Comment, The President's Council on Competitiveness: Undermining the Administrative Procedure Act

with Regulatory Review, 6 Admin.L.J. 759, 762–63 (1993).

8. Bob Woodward & David S. Broder, "Quayle's Quest: Curb Rules, Leave 'No Fingerprints,' " Wash. Post , Jan. 9, 1992, at A1.

longing to President Reagan's Task Force on Regulatory Relief on the ground that the Task Force (and, by implication, the Council) was not a covered 'agency'; resisting access to information about the Council beyond published fact sheets and the testimony of individuals who did not participate in Council deliberations; keeping decisions at staff level to shield them from the greater publicity that would likely follow cabinet level involvement. Intriguingly, only one Council decision—pressuring EPA on pollution permit modifications—ever escalated to actual presidential involvement; the usual, albeit tacit, rule was to avoid appeals to the President wherever possible. It would not seem unrealistic that behind this approach lay a desire to buffer the President from criticism for Council policies, especially given a campaign promise to be the 'environmental president.' That would, of course, be the opposite of accountability.

"The covertness of the Council's approach is troubling not only because of its seeming inconsistency with customary norms of regulatory process, but also because evidence suggests extraordinary access to the Council for special business interests. The Council's recommended modifications to EPA's permit amendment regulations were essentially identical to suggestions earlier made to the EPA by Indiana-based pharmaceutical company Eli Lilly, the Pharmaceutical Manufacturers Association, and the Motor Vehicles Manufacturers Association. One of the Vice President's closest personal advisers, though not on the Council, was Mitch Daniels, former political director in the Reagan White House and an Eli Lilly vice president.

[Then, after an extended description and comparison of E.O. 12866 in relation to the Council's operation, Professor Shane's conclusion included the following:]

"... [W]hat accountability requires ... is a set of political conditions that is fairly complex. Perhaps the most important is widespread access to information about the nature of the decisions at issue. A second is policy dialogue, and a third, a multiplicity of opportunities for dialogue to be well-informed and salient to actual decision making. A fourth is flexibility in the value structure of bureaucratic decision making. The more procrustean the decision making environment, the less accountable it is to anyone but to the ultimate decisionmaker.

"By each of these measures, the model of regulatory oversight depicted in Executive Order No. 12,866 looks far more attractive than the model actually operationalized by President Bush's Council on Competitiveness. ..."

(b) Professor Croley's more recent study agrees (at 6–7, 29–44): "While important similarities outnumbered important differences, Executive Order 12866 did depart from the Reagan orders in several noteworthy respects. For example, intending to 'assure greater openness and accountability in the regulatory review process,' the Clinton order limited receipt of oral communications 'initiated by persons not employed by the executive branch of the Federal Government' regarding a rule under review to the Administrator of OIRA. The order furthermore required OIRA to disclose publicly information about communications between OIRA personnel and any person who is not employed by the executive branch, and to maintain a publicly available log containing the status of all regulatory actions, a notation of all written communications between OIRA personnel and outside parties, and the dates and names of individual participating in all substantive oral communications, including meetings and telephone conversations, between OIRA personnel and outside parties.''

Professor Croley's study devotes a great deal of attention to the meetings reflected in these logs. His review of 266 OIRA meeting logs for 1993–2000 (relating to 153 different rules—not a high number relative to the roughly 2000 rules reviewed in the same period) revealed that ''just over half (56%) of the rules that were the subject of OIRA meetings generated meetings attended solely by persons representing narrow interests [which he defined as corporate and trade association interests], while over a quarter (28%) generated meetings attended by persons representing both narrow and broad-based [NGO] interests, with solely broad-based interest meetings and inter-governmental meetings comprising the rest, ten percent and five percent respectively.'' Of the rules subject to meeting, about 6 in 7 were changed, a considerably higher proportion than the 1 in 2 he reported to have been changed overall.

His primary purpose in analyzing the meeting data was ''to facilitate inferential analysis concerning the relationship between the type of rule subject to a meeting or the types of interest present . . . and the likelihood that a rule subject to a meeting will be changed.'' His statistical analysis ''yield[ed] no statistically significant correlations. . . . That is to say, for the purposes of predicting a rule change, neither the rule's stage, nor its economic significance, nor outside parties' attempts to persuade OIRA staff . . . matter. . . . Nor are the types of interest present at an OIRA meeting associated with a greater or lesser likelihood that OIRA will require a change in the rule either. . . . [tables omitted] In fact, . . . the White House changed a disproportionately high number of rules that were the subject of meetings only with broad-based groups, though not quite to a statistically significant extent, a finding at odds with any simple picture of White House review according to which the White House delivers regulatory favors to economically powerful interest groups while ignoring broad-based interests. Nor does the fact that the White House heard only from state or local politicians or officials, or federal politicians acting on their behalf have any apparent effect on the White House's treatment of a rule under review. . . .

''Surprisingly, White House attendance at a meeting is not associated with a greater likelihood that a rule will be changed either. For just over a quarter of all OIRA meetings, the White House was represented variously by one or more persons from the Council of Economic Advisors, the Council on Environmental Quality, the Office of Scientific and Technology Policy, the Office of the Vice President, or some other White House agency. At such meetings, then, the White House is essentially represented twice—by OIRA itself, whose Administrator is almost always present (sometimes joined by one or more OIRA staffers), and by some other White House office. To the extent OIRA meetings provide the White House with an occasion for monitoring agencies to ensure that agency rules conform to the President's regulatory priorities, and for correcting instances when they do not, OIRA meetings attended by representatives from a White House agency besides OIRA should be especially useful for that purpose. Accordingly, one might expect that the White House' s presence at a meeting ... would increase the likelihood that the rule under review would be changed. It so happens, however, that there is no correlation between White House representation at a meeting and the likelihood that the rule in question will be changed...."

As Dr. Graham's talk reflects, his OIRA in the second Bush administration appears to be reinforcing the transparency commitments that permit such analyses. Dr. Graham has repeatedly told his staff and the public that he understands OIRA's credibility to depend upon them. See p. 619. Moreover, all the matters described in the sentence beginning "The order furthermore ...," at the bottom of p. 655 are now to be found, not in the relatively remote files where Professor Croley sought them out, but on OIRA's website. The Vice President, on the other hand, has engendered considerable political controversy by insisting that his consultations on energy policy—very substantially, it appears, with political friends—properly occurred out of the public's view.

(6) *Delay*. Especially for major rules, the required analyses can be time consuming, and the process of OMB review has threatened to be more so. On average, review time does not appear to be significant,[9] but one critical view of the process has been that "Because OMB was unable effectively to assess the wide range of regulations submitted to it, its principal function was to slow things down."[10] Consider in this respect the early decision in ENVIRONMENTAL DEFENSE FUND v. THOMAS, 627 F.Supp. 566 (D.D.C.1986): The Environmental Protection Agency's adoption of rules to regulate underground storage tanks for hazardous waste had been delayed well past a statutory deadline—in part, it transpired, because of the need to obtain OMB clearance under EO 12291. On the basis of internal documents released under seal, District Court Judge Thomas Flannery found this delay substantially attributable to policy disagreements between OMB and EPA over the approach to be taken. While accepting the timetable now proposed by the agency for completion of the rules, Judge Flannery addressed these words to the OMB:

"A certain degree of deference must be given to the authority of the President to control and supervise executive policymaking. Yet, the use of EO 12291 to create delays and to impose substantive changes raises some constitutional concerns. Congress enacts environmental legislation after years of study and deliberation, and then delegates to the expert judgment of the EPA Administrator the authority to issue regulations carrying out the aims of the law. Under EO 12291, if used improperly, OMB could withhold approval until the acceptance of certain content in the promulgation of any new EPA regulation, thereby encroaching upon the independence and expertise of EPA. Further, unsuccessful executive lobbying on Capitol Hill can still be pursued administratively by delaying the enactment

---

9. "This entire review process took on average 25 days for rules reviewed under the Reagan orders, and 44 days for rules reviewed under the Clinton order." P. 651 above.

10. Richard H. Pildes and Cass R. Sunstein, Reinventing the Regulatory State, 62 U.Chi.L.Rev. 1 (1995).

of regulations beyond the date of a statutory deadline. This is incompatible with the will of Congress and cannot be sustained as a valid exercise of the President's Article II powers. . . .

"This court declares that OMB has no authority to use its regulatory review under EO 12291 to delay promulgation of EPA regulations arising from the 1984 Amendments of the RCRA beyond the date of a statutory deadline. Thus, if a deadline already has expired, OMB has no authority to delay regulations subject to the deadline in order to review them under the executive order. If the deadline is about to expire, OMB may review the regulations only until the time at which OMB review will result in the deadline being missed. . . . While this may be an intrusion into the degree of flexibility the executive agencies have in taking their time about promulgating these regulations, this is simply a judicial recognition of law as passed by Congress and of the method for dealing with deadlines laid down by the President himself."

At the time, the issue was vigorously debated in Alan Morrison, OMB Interference With Agency Rulemaking: The Wrong Way To Write A Regulation, 99 Harv. L.Rev.1059 (1986), and Christopher DeMuth and Douglas Ginsburg, White House Review Of Agency Rulemaking, 99 Harv. L. Rev. 1075 (1986). Do §§ 6(a)(3)(D), 6(b)(2), and 7 of EO 12866 suggest acceptance of the holding in this case? Do they adequately address the timing problem? Note that statutes like the Unfunded Mandates Review Act suggest no particular congressional concern with this issue, where major rules are concerned. Accordingly, the timetable for such rules must allow considerable development time prior to the NPRM.

NOTES ON THE EXTENT OF PRESIDENTIAL AUTHORITY

If, in Judge Flannery's words just quoted, "a certain degree of deference must be given to the authority of the President to control and supervise executive policymaking," how much deference is that? Article II, Section 2 of the Constitution is explicit that "The President ... may require the Opinion, in writing, of the principal Officer in each of the executive Departments, upon any subject relating to the Duties of their respective Offices." Yet there is a certain distance between asking to consult, and dictating an outcome.

(1) CHAMBER OF COMMERCE v. REICH, 74 F.3d 1322 (D.C.Cir.1996), involved an executive order directing "It is the policy of the executive branch in procuring goods and services that, to ensure the economical and efficient administration and completion of Federal Government contracts, contracting agencies shall not contract with employers that permanently replace lawfully striking employees." Permanent replacement of lawfully striking employees is permitted by the National Labor Relations Act, so long as the strike is simply economic (i.e., not in protest of unfair employer labor practices). Legislative initiatives seeking a similar result had failed. The Secretary of Labor, Robert Reich, adopted a regulation implementing the President's executive order. Acknowledging the breadth of the President's ordinary discretion to direct government procurement policy under the Federal Procurement Act, the court stressed that that Act "was designed to

address broad concerns quite different from the more focused question of the appropriate balance of power between management and labor in collective bargaining." It struck down the implementing regulation—and so also condemned the executive order—as inconsistent with the NLRA.

"It does not seem to us possible to deny that the President's Executive Order seeks to set a broad policy governing the behavior of thousands of American companies and affecting millions of American workers. The President has, of course, acted to set procurement policy rather than labor policy. But the former is quite explicitly based—and would have to be based—on his views of the latter. For the premise of the Executive Order is the proposition that the permanent replacement of strikers unduly prolongs and widens strikes and disrupts the proper 'balance' between employers and employees. Whether that proposition is correct, or whether the prospect of permanent replacements deters strikes, and therefore an employer's right to permanently replace strikers is simply one element in the relative bargaining power of management and organized labor, is beside the point. Whatever one's views on the issue, it surely goes to the heart of United States labor relations policy. . . .

"That is not to say that the President, in implementing the Procurement Act, may not draw upon any secondary policy views that deal with government contractors' employment practices—policy views that are directed beyond the immediate quality and price of goods and services purchased. . . . But labor relations policy is different because of the NLRA and its broad field of pre-emption. No state or federal official or government entity can alter the delicate balance of bargaining and economic power that the NLRA establishes, whatever his or its purpose may be. . . . [T]he Executive Order is regulatory in nature and is pre-empted by the NLRA which guarantees the right to hire permanent replacements."

(2) ROBERT V. PERCIVAL, PRESIDENTIAL MANAGEMENT OF THE ADMINISTRATIVE STATE: THE NOT-SO-UNITARY EXECUTIVE, 51 Duke L.J. 963, 994, 968, 998–99 (2001): "President George H. W. Bush became directly involved in a few regulatory decisions, including a dispute over Food and Drug Administration (FDA) regulations to implement the Nutrition Labeling and Education Act of 1990. David Kessler, the commissioner of the FDA, has described how OMB (with the support of the Department of Agriculture) tried to require the FDA to modify its proposed food labeling regulations to mollify the meat industry, which wanted to obscure information about the fat content of foods. At a White House meeting, Health and Human Services Secretary Louis Sullivan showed the President a MacDonald's restaurant tray liner that contained nutritional information consistent with the FDA's approach. Sullivan argued that the FDA could not adopt the meat industry's proposal because it was not supported by the rulemaking record. This reportedly surprised President Bush, who stated:

> 'I'm a little puzzled. I'm being told that I can't just make a decision and have it promptly executed, that the Department can't just salute smartly and go execute whatever decision I make. Why is that?'

Kessler reports that he and Sullivan were prepared to resign if the White House ordered the FDA to issue the rules sought by the meat industry. Instead, to their surprise, the President directed that the regulations preferred by the FDA be promulgated, though he did not accept the FDA's proposal to apply them to restaurants. This appears to be an example of the President's dictating a decision to an agency head. However, because he chose the decision generally favored by the agency, the agency head accepted the decision and did not resign in protest."

Elsewhere in his essay, Professor Percival reasons that "The president's appointment and removal powers and the Framers' decision to vest executive authority in the president presumably give him considerable ability to influence decisions by executive officers. However, this does not provide a compelling case for concluding that the president may dictate decisions entrusted by Congress to the heads of executive agencies. Article II, Section 2's requirement that presidential appointments of executive officers be subject to the advice and consent of the Senate would have little meaning if the president simply could dictate the decisions such officers are required by law to make. By requiring Senate confirmation of the president's nominees to head cabinet agencies, the Constitution presumably envisions that these officers will have some degree of independence that makes it necessary for them to be acceptable not only to the president, but also to the Senate, one of the entities largely responsible for defining the powers, duties, and functions of their agencies. Moreover, if the president had authority to dictate the substance of agency decisions, why would the Framers have found it necessary to expressly grant him the authority to demand opinions in writing from executive officers? . . .

"The Clinton administration's assertion of presidential authority to resolve disputes between agencies is somewhat less troubling from a constitutional perspective than the notion of its resolving disputes between OMB and an agency. In circumstances where there is a dispute between two cabinet agencies that are pursuing incompatible approaches to a regulatory issue (as in the nutrition labeling example in which the Department of Health and Human Services and the Agriculture Department were fundamentally at odds), the case for having the president or vice president resolve the dispute is considerably stronger because the White House is uniquely situated to resolve conflicts between agencies. But if the dispute is between OMB and an agency head, a directive from the White House instructing the agency head how the dispute is to be resolved looks suspiciously like displacement of decisionmaking authority entrusted to agency heads by law. . . . The fact that the president may . . . redelegate decisions entrusted to him by law also does not imply that he has the authority to dictate decisions instead entrusted by law to other executive officials."

(3) ELENA KAGAN, PRESIDENTIAL ADMINISTRATION, 114 Harv.L.Rev. 2245 (2001), in 140 pages from which excerpts appear at pp. 213 and 218 above, elegantly makes the case for presidential directory authority, not as an ineluctable constitutional command but as the appropriate rule of interpretation when Congress has not been explicit about the matter.

"Presidential administration as most recently practiced—including, most controversially, the use of directive authority over executive branch agencies—comports with law not because, as some have claimed, the Constitution commands straight-line control of the administrative state, but because ... Congress generally has declined to preclude the President from controlling administration in this manner. Presidential administration in this form advances political accountability by subjecting the bureaucracy to the control mechanism most open to public examination and most responsive to public opinion. And presidential administration furthers regulatory effectiveness by providing not only the centralization necessary to achieve a range of technocratic goals but also the dynamic charge so largely missing today from both the administrative sphere and the surrounding political system."

As should be apparent, the transparency of presidential controls is a precondition to this argument.

(4) PETER L. STRAUSS, PRESIDENTIAL RULEMAKING, 72 Chicago–Kent L. Rev. 965 (1997), from which excerpts appear at p. 220 above, takes a view more like Professor Percival's.

(5) THOMAS O. MCGARITY, PRESIDENTIAL CONTROL OF REGULATORY AGENCY DECISIONMAKING, 36 Am. U.L.Rev. 443, 450–51, 454–55 (1987): "Good regulatory decisionmaking requires an appropriate balance between expertise and the generalist's perspective. That balance may be upset when expert agency decision makers must defer to political decision makers in the White House. We were rightly repelled to learn during the Watergate investigations of a plan to ensure a satisfactory outcome in an ongoing OSHA rulemaking concerning cotton dust in exchange for a large contribution from the textile industry to the Committee to Re-elect the President. Even when the exchange is not in coin, behind-the-scenes political tradeoffs severely undermine the integrity of the rulemaking process. We may not be shocked, but we are disturbed to hear that President Carter's need for Senator Byrd's support for the SALT II treaty was a major factor in the decision to adopt a sliding scale approach for the new source performance standard (NSPS) for coal-fired steam electric power plants.

"Congress, not the President alone, must provide the content of the policies that the agencies apply in individual rulemaking or adjudication proceedings. The policy component of regulatory decisionmaking is not the sort of overarching meta-policy that guides foreign policy and important budget decisions. It is, rather, a micro-policy that guides a decision maker in deciding which way to lean when the information and arguments on both sides of a regulatory issue appear about equally balanced. This kind of policy judgment is not likely to attain a very high position on the President's policy agenda even in an administration in which government regulation has a high political profile. Regulatory decision makers need the kind of policy guidance that Congress gives in individual statutes. In those not infrequent instances in which Congress has given vague policy guidance, a limited interpretational role for the President or his staff may be appropriate. But even here, it is not likely that the President or his aides in OMB will be more adept at divining congressional intent than the agency to which Congress has delegated decisionmaking power. ... To the extent that the President delegates his oversight function to personnel in agencies far removed from the Oval Office, accountability is attenuated, not enhanced. It is not readily apparent why, for example, an unelected appointee of OMB is any more accountable to the electorate than the Administrator of the Environmental Protection Agency, whose appointment has the Senate's advice and consent.

"Finally, secret interactions between the agencies and the White House or OMB staff in no way increase overall governmental accountability, because the electorate cannot distinguish those policies attributable to the agencies from those attributable to the President and his aides. Moreover, the President remains unaccountable for bad decisions that he or his staff may have influenced if the extent of that influence is not a matter of public record. The President can brush off the controversial results of his own secretly communicated policies, after-the-fact, as the regrettable outputs of an unaccountable bureaucracy.[1] . . .

"The related problem of staff abuse occurs when members of the President's staff attempt to implement their own policy agendas in the name of the President. As the . . . Iran–Contra scandal clearly demonstrates, the bureaucrats in the White House and OMB might not exercise the wisdom and restraint of the President himself. For example, a well-publicized instance of staff abuse occurred during the Carter administration when the Chairman of the Council of Economic Advisors (CEA) ordered the Assistant Secretary for Occupational Safety and Health to change a standard for protecting workers from exposure to cotton dust. When the Secretary of Labor demanded to meet with the President on the matter, the President overruled the CEA Chairman."

McGarity's complaints were registered before the increased transparency of E.O. 12866 made OIRA process more public, and before the order's commitments to limited as well as exposed political contacts with the outside world. Do these changes sufficiently answer his concerns? How are they enforced?

(6) CYNTHIA R. FARINA, THE CONSENT OF THE GOVERNED: AGAINST SIMPLE RULES FOR A COMPLEX WORLD, 72 Chi.-Kent. L. Rev. 987, 988–89 (1997): " . . . [T]he current emphasis on presidential direction of domestic regulatory policy . . . look[s] to the President not only to improve the managerial competence and efficiency with which regulation occurs but also, and more deeply, to supply the elusive essence of democratic legitimation. The ideological sources drawn upon are diverse—original intent, civic republicanism, public choice theory—but the central argument is consistent: The President, and the President alone, represents the entire citizenry. The President, uniquely, is situated to infuse into regulatory policymaking the will of the whole people.

"I argue here that this latest effort at making peace between regulatory government and representative democracy is fatally flawed. Despite the ingenuity and intensity with which strong presidentialism is advanced, it is premised upon a fundamentally untenable conception of the consent of the governed. The 'will of the people,' as invoked in that effort, is artificially

---

1. President Reagan attempted to explain the implementation of his rather clearly expressed budget policies as a bureaucratic blunder when he refused to take responsibility for the fact that the Department of Agriculture determined that catsup was a vegetable for purposes of the Department's school lunch program. See Wash. Post, Sept. 15, 1981, at A10, col. 2.

bounded in time, homogenized, shorn of ambiguities—in short, fabricated. It obscures complex problems (recognized elsewhere in administrative law scholarship) of information, prediction, and risk perception. It slides over vexed questions (recognized elsewhere in scholarly literature about democracy) of when leaders should lead rather than follow and of how the act of governing becomes a process in which the collective will is formed, rather than merely implemented.

"My counter-proposition is a broad, and perhaps uncomfortably indeterminate one: No single mode of democratic legitimation can serve to mediate between the conflicted, protean, often inchoate will of the people and the modern regulatory enterprise. No single institution or practice is capable of performing the multiple tasks of registering, interpreting, educating, adapting, affording participation, facilitating deliberation, brokering accommodation, and umpiring conflict that are (or at least ought to be) entailed in shaping the public policy of a post-industrialized democracy with an activist regulatory government. There are no simple rules for this complex world. Rather, we must necessarily look to a plurality of institutions and practices as contributors to an ongoing process of legitimizing the regulatory state. Each of those institutions and practices will be partial and, of itself, insufficient. Each imposes its own kind of costs on the regulatory process. Each is capable, if overemphasized, of introducing its own kind of distortion. In sum, . . . the reconciliatory effort must abandon its yearning for a neat solution to the legitimacy problem and, instead, come to terms with 'the ugliness of democracy.' "

c.   AFTER THE COMMENTS ARE IN—THE DECISION PROCESS IN RULEMAKING

In on-the-record proceedings, the very fact of limitation to "the record" controls the extent of institutional decisionmaking and other departures from the judicial model of decision. Reviewing courts are on familiar ground when "the record" is substantially the same for participants, decisionmaker, and reviewing court, and when the decision process is predictably hierarchical and subject more or less to judicial standards of objectivity. To be sure, as the materials in Chapter IV § 2 reflect, the unfamiliar can intrude into agency adjudication: agency decisionmakers have multiple obligations, consult with expert staff, experience political pressures, and often have some ongoing obligation to engage in public discourse about desirable regulatory outcomes. These thoroughly nonjudicial activities may be particularly prominent in initial licensing, the form of adjudication that most closely approaches the polycentric character of rulemaking. Nonetheless, in the adjudicatory context, we have a clear conception of the "ideal" into which these elements are intruding, and hence a better sense of the appropriate limits of any accommodation to be made.

In distinguishing rulemaking from adjudication for due process purposes, Justice Holmes' opinion in Bi–Metallic Investment Co. v. State Bd. of Equalization of Colorado, p. 241, insisted that the familiar judicial model is an inappropriate analogy when government is involved in making general policy. The APA-established institutions of rulemaking generally reflect that judgment, and subsequent Supreme Court analyses such as Vermont Yankee, p. 498, have reinforced it. Gone is any commitment to an initial decisionmaker of pointed objectivity and quasi-judicial mien, like the administrative law judge often used for the initial stages of adjudications. Ordinarily, rulemaking decision is thoroughly institutional from start to finish, involving whoever in the agency (and perhaps some outside the agency) has a relevant perspective to contribute. Decisions are taken not all at once, but over sometimes substantial lengths of time. They are highly dependent on institutional decisional processes.[1] Hence, the lawyers' instincts that may make us question institutional decisionmaking in the familiar setting of on-the-record adjudication have little proper bearing on informal rulemaking. If interested persons know even the formal public record of the rulemaking—the Notice of Proposed Rulemaking and the set of comments filed in response to it—that knowledge is a result of unusual industry and persistence. Federal Register publication (not service) suffices for notice; comments are filed only with the agency—and, often enough, at the last possible moment. Further, although the cases have required agencies to share their data in the interest of effective comment,[2] the institutional character of rulemaking means that the decisionmaker's record will vary widely from what even the most energetic participant (or reviewing judge) can know—both in content, and in the conversations that have shaped it. All this seems fairly to follow from the proposition that these are *not* proceedings required to be decided *on* the record. It follows as well from Holmes' Bi–Metallic conclusion that citizens' protection in such proceedings is to be found, not in the procedural apparatus of hearings, but in "their [political] power, immediate or remote, over those who make the rule." And as we see in, for example, Executive Order 12866, an elaborate political apparatus has grown up to channel such efforts in the most important rulemakings.

Yet when Holmes referred acceptingly in Bi–Metallic to "general statutes ... passed that affect the person or property of individuals, sometimes to the point of ruin," and to the political controls over their adoption, he was in fact addressing the work of an *elected* body. When EPA or OSHA adopt rules imposing costs across the American economy, one immediately recognizes that they are not the Congress. This difference sets up a continuing conflict between the importance of political control and the insistence on legal regularity. The tension is particularly striking when politics is at work in contexts in which the agency is unavoidably uncertain about levels of risk and/or the effectiveness of means to reduce it. Generalist reviewing courts might conclude that issues at the borders of the unknown merit particularly high deference to agency judgment, as a matter of expertise. Yet this instinct to defer may be sorely tested if it appears that politicians have not been equally restrained. And, to complicate matters further, any judicial inquiry into the actual decision process of rulemaking

---

1. If you have not already read Professor McGarity's brief description of models of agency decisionmaking, p. 547, it would be helpful to do so here.

2. See United States v. Nova Scotia Food Products Corp., p. 524, and Notes on the Nature of a Rulemaking Record, p. 536, for development of this point.

will be impeded by the rule that such inquiries are appropriate only if a high initial threshold of apparent irregularity has been crossed.[3]

Additional complications arise if the agency uses rulemaking to make decisions that seem equally appropriate (if not more so) for adjudication, leading courts to fear that it is attempting to escape the usual adjudicatory constraints on activities "off the record." SANGAMON VALLEY TELEVISION CORP. v. UNITED STATES, 269 F.2d 221 (D.C.Cir.1959) was such a case. In that early, pre-cable TV era, it was much more advantageous to have a franchise for one of the twelve "VHF" channels, 2–13, than one of the greater number of "UHF" channels. Not all TVs could receive UHF signals; those that could often did not receive them as well as VHF, for a VHF signal could be broadcast to a larger geographic area. The "rule" the FCC proposed would have had the effect of awarding a particular VHF franchise (Channel 2) to a particular St. Louis, Mo. television station in lieu of the UHF channel that station was currently assigned. It would also have reassigned the St. Louis station's UHF channel to Springfield, Illinois, to replace a franchise for Channel 2, currently in use. These assignments would have implemented an FCC policy to avoid intermixing of VHF and UHF transmission in the same television market. Congressional testimony disclosed that the St. Louis station's president had personally called on, and had written and telephoned FCC Commissioners to advocate shifting Channel 2 to St. Louis. Moreover, he had taken them to lunch, and had sent them turkeys as Christmas presents, while the matter was still under consideration. Apprised of the behavior, the D.C. Circuit concluded that "whatever the proceeding may be called, it involved not only allocation of TV channels among communities but also resolution of conflicting private claims to a valuable privilege, and that basic fairness requires such a proceeding to be carried on in the open. ... Accordingly the private approaches to the members of the Commission vitiated its action and the proceeding must be reopened."[4]

The next principal case threatened to generalize this understandable holding to virtually all rulemaking. Decided on the eve of Vermont Yankee, p. 498, it has been sharply criticized—particularly for its tendency to judicialize rulemaking and for its confusions about rulemaking procedures and records. So long as you approach it as a problematic case, it makes a good starting point for the materials of this section. In reading it, note both the standard rulemaking practices the FCC apparently invited and all participants apparently understood, and the depth of the court's apparent astonishment in learning about them. In particular, its reasoning about the "rulemaking record," is troubling, setting a framework against which the subsequent opinions of this section would have to contend; yet its doubts— once voiced—also served to alter the day-to-day conduct of rulemaking.

---

3. See p. 996ff.

4. Improper influence cases may be an artifact of the FCC's regulatory situation, in the same way that prejudgment cases seem to be for the FTC. VHF television channels in major urban markets have enormous economic value; but the government distributes them for the cost only of prevailing in FCC proceedings. Lunches and turkeys, in the circumstances, are very slight investments. Cf. WKAT, Inc. v. FCC, 296 F.2d 375 (D.C.Cir.), cert. denied 368 U.S. 841 (1961) (influence peddling in connection with award of Miami TV channel).

Here, then, is a case to be read less for its "law" than for insight into a set of enduring tensions and problems:

Home Box Office, Inc. v. Federal Communications Commission

United States Court of Appeals for the District of Columbia Circuit, 1977.
567 F.2d 9, cert. denied 434 U.S. 829 (1977).

■ Before WRIGHT, MacKINNON, CIRCUIT JUDGES, and WEIGEL, DISTRICT JUDGE:

Per Curiam.[1]

[In March 1975 the FCC ended a three-year notice-and-comment rulemaking proceeding by adopting four amendments to its rules governing the programs that could be shown by paid television services like HBO. If these services could show contemporary films and sports, commercial broadcasters feared, the quality of conventional television would inevitably be reduced. Viewers who could not be reached by (or afford to pay for) subscription television would be injured by this change. On the other hand, metropolitan viewers and paid service owners both denied that this harm would occur and asserted that restricting the material shown by subscription services would inhibit their commercial growth and deprive viewers of diversity. In this particular rulemaking, the FCC had held oral arguments in October, 1974. Ultimately, the committee decided to reduce somewhat the prior restrictions. The amendments satisfied neither the commercial nor the subscription broadcast interests (including associated viewer groups) and all promptly sought review in the D.C. Circuit. Henry Geller, General Counsel of the FCC until 1973 (by which time the rulemaking was well under way) and chairperson of a public interest group concentrating on broadcast matters, was one of those seeking review. He suggested to the court that participants in the rulemaking had frequently engaged in private contacts with Commissioners and others at the FCC.]

IV. Ex Parte Contacts

. . . In an attempt to clarify the facts this court sua sponte ordered the Commission to provide "a list of all of the ex parte presentations, together with the details of each, made to it, or to any of its members or representatives, during the rulemaking proceedings." In response to this order the Commission filed a document over 60 pages long which revealed, albeit imprecisely, widespread ex parte communications involving virtually every party before this court, including amicus Geller.[2]

. . . "Thus, in early 1974, then-Chairman Burch sought to complete action in this proceeding. Because the Commission was 'leaning' in its deliberations towards relaxing the existing rules . . . American Broadcast-

---

1. [Ed.] The court issued the opinion per curiam "because the complexity of the issues raised on appeal made it useful to share the effort required to draft this opinion among the members of the panel"; the part reproduced here was written by Judge J. Skelly Wright.

2. . . . There can be no waiver or estoppel raised here against our consideration of an issue vital to the public as a whole. Therefore, Mr. Geller's "dirty hands," if such they be, present no bar. . . .

ing Company's representatives contacted 'key members of Congress,' who in turn successfully pressured the Commission not to take such action.[3] . . ." [Quoting Geller's brief.] [I]n the crucial period between the close of oral argument on October 25, 1974 and the adoption of the First Report and Order on March 20, 1975, when the rulemaking record should have been closed while the Commission was deciding what rules to promulgate, . . . broadcast interests met some 18 times with Commission personnel, cable interests some nine times, motion picture and sports interests five times each, and "public interest" intervenors not at all. . . . [W]e are particularly concerned that the final shaping of the rules we are reviewing here may have been by compromise among the contending industry forces, rather than by exercise of the independent discretion in the public interest the Communications Act vests in individual commissioners. Our concern is heightened by the submission of the Commission's Broadcast Bureau to this court which states that in December 1974 broadcast representatives "described the kind of pay cable regulation that, in their view, broadcasters 'could live with.'" If actual positions were not revealed in public comments, . . . the elaborate public discussion in these dockets has been reduced to a sham.

Even the possibility that there is here one administrative record for the public and this court and another for the Commission and those "in the know" is intolerable. . . . [I]mplicit in the decision to treat the promulgation of rules as a "final" event in an ongoing process of administration is an assumption that an act of reasoned judgment has occurred, an assumption which further contemplates the existence of a body of material—documents, comments, transcripts, and statements in various forms declaring agency expertise or policy—with reference to which such judgment was exercised. Against this material, "the full administrative record that was before [an agency official] at the time he made his decision," Citizens to Preserve Overton Park v. Volpe, supra, . . . it is the obligation of this court to test the actions of the Commission for arbitrariness or inconsistency with delegated authority. . . . This course is obviously foreclosed if communications are made to the agency in secret and the agency itself does not disclose the information presented. . . . [A] reviewing court cannot presume that the agency has acted properly, but must treat the agency's justifications as a fictional account of the actual decisionmaking process and must perforce find its actions arbitrary.

. . . Even if the Commission had disclosed to this court . . . what was said to it ex parte, . . . we would not have the benefit of an adversarial

---

3. [S]ee remarks by Everett H. Erlich, Senior Vice President and General Counsel, ABC, before the ABC Television Network Affiliates, Los Angeles, May 10, 1974, at 1: "As most of you know, the FCC just prior to Chairman Burch's sudden departure was on the verge of modifying Pay–TV rules applicable to movies by loosening the 2 and 10–years limitations. They were also considering a so-called 'wild card' exception for 12 to 18 pictures a year which would have exempted entirely the most popular features from the application of any rule. We took the leadership in opposing these proposals with the result that key members of Congress made it known in no uncertain terms that they did not expect the Commission to act on such a far-reaching policy matter without guidance. The Commission got the message and has postponed for several months reconsideration of this particular issue . . ."

discussion among the parties. ... We have insisted, for example, that [relevant] information in agency files or consultants' reports ... be disclosed to the parties for adversarial comment. Similarly, we have required agencies to set out their thinking in notices of proposed rulemaking. This requirement not only allows adversarial critique of the agency but is perhaps one of the few ways that the public may be apprised of what the agency thinks it knows in its capacity as a repository of expert opinion. From a functional standpoint, we see no difference between assertions of fact and expert opinion tendered by the public, as here, and that generated internally in an agency: each may be biased, inaccurate, or incomplete—failings which adversary comment may illuminate. Indeed, the potential for bias in private presentations in rulemakings which resolve "conflicting private claims to a valuable privilege," seems to us greater than in cases where we have reversed agencies for failure to disclose internal studies. ...

Equally important is the inconsistency of secrecy with fundamental notions of fairness implicit in due process and with the ideal of reasoned decisionmaking on the merits which undergirds all of our administrative law. This inconsistency was recognized in Sangamon Valley Television Corp. v. United States, 269 F.2d 221 (D.C.Cir.1959), and ... [c]ertainly any ambiguity ... has been removed by recent congressional and presidential actions. In the Government in the Sunshine Act, for example, Congress has declared it to be "the policy of the United States that the public is entitled to the fullest practicable information regarding the decisionmaking processes of the Federal Government," and has taken steps to guard against ex parte contacts in formal agency proceedings.[4] Perhaps more closely on point is Executive Order 11920, 12 Weekly Comp. of Presidential Documents 1040 (1976), which prohibits ex parte contacts with members of the White House staff by those seeking to influence allocation of international air routes during the time route certifications are before the President for his approval. ... Thus this is a time when all branches of government have taken steps "designed to better assure fairness and to avoid suspicions of impropriety," White House Fact Sheet on Executive Order 11920 (June 10, 1976), and consequently we have no hesitation in concluding ... that due process requires us to set aside the Commission's rules here.

... [W]e recognize that informal contacts between agencies and the public are the "bread and butter" of the process of administration and are completely appropriate so long as they do not frustrate judicial review or raise serious questions of fairness. Reconciliation of these considerations in a manner which will reduce procedural uncertainty leads us to conclude that communications which are received prior to issuance of a formal notice of rulemaking do not, in general, have to be put in a public file. Of course, if the information contained in such a communication forms the basis for agency action, then, under well established principles, that information must be disclosed to the public in some form. Once a notice of proposed rulemaking has been issued, however, any agency official or employee who

---

4. Of course, the Sunshine Act by its terms does not apply here. Its ex parte contact provisions are couched as an amendment to 5 U.S.C. § 557, and as such the rules do not apply to rulemaking under § 4 of the Administrative Procedure Act, 5 U.S.C. § 553. Moreover, the Act was not in effect at the time of the events in question here.

is or may reasonably be expected to be involved in the decisional process of the rulemaking proceeding, should "refus[e] to discuss matters relating to the disposition of a [rulemaking proceeding] with any interested private party, or an attorney or agent for any such party, prior to the [agency's] decision . . .," Executive Order 11920, § 4, supra, at 1041. If ex parte contacts nonetheless occur, we think that any written document or a summary of any oral communication must be placed in the public file established for each rulemaking docket immediately after the communication is received so that interested parties may comment thereon. Compare Executive Order 11920, § 5.

. . . [W]e today remand the record to the Commission for supplementation . . . with the aid of a specially appointed hearing examiner . . .

■ [WEIGEL, DISTRICT JUDGE, concurred on other grounds.]

■ MacKINNON, CIRCUIT JUDGE, [belatedly filed a special concurrence]: . . .

To the extent that our Per Curiam opinion relies upon Overton Park to support its decision as to ex parte communications in this case, it is my view that it is exceeding the authority it cites because here there is no statutory requirement for specific findings nor are the regulations limited to the full administrative record. And our opinion follows up this excessive reliance on Overton Park by an overly broad statement of the rule. . . .

. . . [I]n this case . . . the rulemaking undeniably involved competitive interests of great monetary value and conferred preferential advantages on vast segments of the broadcast industry to the detriment of other competing business interests. The rule as issued was in effect an adjudication of the respective rights of the parties vis-a-vis each other. And since that is the nature of the case and controversy that we are deciding and to which our opinion is limited, I would make it clear that that is all we are deciding. I would not make an excessively broad statement to include dictum that could be interpreted to cover the entire universe of informal rulemaking. . . .

NOTES

(1) *Is this a Sound Result?* ERNEST GELLHORN AND GLEN O. ROBINSON, RULEMAKING "DUE PROCESS": AN INCONCLUSIVE DIALOGUE, 48 U.Chi.L.Rev. 201 (1981): "[*Publius:*] [E]x parte contacts . . . operate as an important check on the reliability of staff information and interpretation. Given the potential unreliability of staff-provided information, ex parte contacts with persons outside the agency are an important means of avoiding 'staff capture.' To be sure, one does not want an agency to rely entirely on outside informants, but neither does one want it to be the prisoner of agency staff. . . .

". . . Obtaining information is not the problem. Agencies seldom want for information or argument in a quantitative sense. If anything, they suffer from the opposite, what Alvin Toffler has described as 'information overload.' . . . What the agency rulemaker needs is both a means to get to the heart of the case, and an exchange of views with the advocates of competing positions in which he can test his, and their, understanding of the issues. It is somewhat ironic that one of the principal proponents of a ban on ex parte contacts, Judge Wright, should also interpret the APA as requiring rulemaking to provide 'a genuine dialogue between agency experts and concerned members of the public.' The formal submission of documents to an agency, in response to a formal public notice, seems unlikely to constitute a 'genuine' dialogue—but this would be the only permissible communication between the agency and the parties if the ban on ex parte contacts stands. . . . [T]o evaluate the true demand for different outcomes . . . is a vital component of rulemaking, just as it is of legislative lawmaking. . . . An agency is not simply an issuer of edicts; it is also an arbitrator of interests. Again Home Box Office is illustrative. Some of the ex parte contacts involved in that case apparently took place partly for the purpose of exploring possible compromises among the competing groups. It is difficult to envision how such compromise efforts, which are clearly desirable, could be made without some informal contacts. . . .

"*[Brutus:]* . . . [T]he rulemaker-as-arbitrator is not an appropriate model for agencies. No doubt rules often reflect compromises among competing interest groups. I do not deplore that. Even where rulemaking is a zero-sum game among different interests, agencies are properly sensitive to minimizing the losses to any particular group as a consequence of the rule being adopted. Bargaining is not objectionable except where it is done without rules, which would allow the decision to be unfairly skewed by irrelevant factors such as who was able to contact whom, when, and so forth. On the other hand, why do we have a structured rulemaking process with notice and comment and, in the Home Box Office case, even oral argument? Is this just a warmup for negotiations? I think not. It would seem to be an attempt to require rulemakers to do more than rubberstamp agreements by the affected parties. Instead, they must independently assure themselves, from the evidence produced by these procedures, that the rule is in fact in the public interest. That determination could be rendered illusory by unregulated ex parte contacts creating a predisposition in the rulemaker's mind.

"Moreover, I think it is somewhat naive to suppose that it is necessary for an agency rulemaker to have informal discussions with particular parties in order to gain an adequate understanding of their 'bottom line.' For example, I think your FCC commissioner in Home Box Office would, from the outset, have a pretty good sense of what was soft and what was firm in the positions of the parties as a result of his familiarity with the industry. If he did not, I doubt he would obtain it from ex parte discussions. The parties would be just as likely to seize such an opportunity to impress him with the fervor of their opinions and the rational basis thereof in hopes of securing a completely favorable decision, as they would be to reveal which of their claims they would be willing to concede without any quid pro quo."

(2) *The Judicial Retreat from Home Box Office.* The tensions between HBO's concern for the state of the rulemaking record on review and the institutional, legislative character of rulemaking decision led to a prompt retreat. In ACTION FOR CHILDREN'S TELEVISION [ACT] v. FCC, 564 F.2d 458 (D.C.Cir.1977), a different panel of the D.C.Circuit refused to apply HBO to

an FCC rulemaking involving television programming and advertising practices for children. Over 100,000 comments had been filed; six days of panel discussions and arguments had been held. Early on, the broadcast industry had undertaken "limited self-regulation"; after a private meeting with the FCC's Chairman following the Commission hearings, it adopted further measures to control advertising practice. When the Commission suspended its rulemaking, promising to monitor these self-regulatory measures, ACT sought review.

Holding only that HBO's "broad prescription is not to be applied retroactively," the panel's lengthy opinion left little doubt that it generally disapproved that presumption. "We do not propose to argue . . . that ex parte contacts always are permissible in informal rulemaking proceedings— they are of course not—but we do think . . . that ex parte contacts do not per se vitiate agency informal rulemaking action, but only do so if it appears from the administrative record under review that they may have materially influenced the action ultimately taken. . . .

"If we go as far as Home Box Office does in its ex parte ruling in ensuring a 'whole record' for our review, why not go further to require the decisionmaker to summarize and make available for public comment every status inquiry from a Congressman or any germane material—say a newspaper editorial—that he or she reads or their evening-hour ruminations? In the end, why not administer a lie-detector test to ascertain whether the required summary is an accurate and complete one? The problem is obviously a matter of degree, and the appropriate line must be drawn somewhere. In light of what must be presumed to be Congress' intent not to prohibit or require disclosure of all ex parte contacts during or after the public comment stage, we would draw that line at the point where the rulemaking proceedings involve 'competing claims to a valuable privilege.' It is at that point where the potential for unfair advantage outweighs the practical burdens, which we imagine would not be insubstantial, that such a judicially conceived rule would place upon administrators."

(3) *Agency Adoption Nonetheless.* As ACT suggests, the HBO court's attitude, and the line it drew at the point of the NPRM, might serve only to move private negotiations to an earlier point. (Indeed, the post-HBO development of requiring agencies to publish a regulatory agenda of planned rulemakings facilitates early, targeted private conversations with the agency.) This would tend to increase the formal rather than substantial qualities of the public comment process. Yet the general approach of HBO was substantially adopted, without legislative or judicial compulsion, by agency rulemakers.

The Administrative Conference of the United States,[1] drawing on a report by Professor Nathaniel L. Nathanson,[2] adopted a recommendation

---

1. See p. 479, n.1 above.

2. Professor Nathanson's report, published at 30 Ad.L.Rev. 377 (1978), concluded with an expression of "concern that [an absolute ban upon ex parte communications] might well prove self-defeating. It is obvi-ously impracticable to apply such a ban to communications occurring before the formal notice of proposed rulemaking is issued. Consequently, the effect of the ban might well be to encourage the agency and the more active or influential members of the

opposing any general prohibition on ex parte contacts in informal rulemakings, given the flexibility necessary for effective rulemaking. Nonetheless, the recommendation accepted that "certain restraints upon such communications may be desirable. Ex parte communications during the rulemaking process can give rise to three principal types of problems. First, decision makers may be influenced by communications made privately, thus creating a situation seemingly at odds with the widespread demand for open government; second, significant information may be unavailable to reviewing courts; and third, interested persons may be unable to reply effectively to information, proposals or arguments presented in an ex parte communication. In the context of Section 553 rulemaking, the first two problems can be alleviated by placing written communications addressed to a rule proposal in a public file, and by disclosure of significant oral communications by means of summaries or other appropriate techniques. The very nature of such rulemaking, however, precludes any simple solution to the third difficulty. The opportunity of interested persons to reply could be fully secured only by converting rulemaking proceedings into a species of adjudication in which such persons were identified as parties, and entitled to be, at least constructively, present when all information and arguments are assembled in a record. In general rulemaking, where there may be thousands of interested persons and where the issues tend to be broad questions of policy with respect to which illumination may come from a vast variety of sources not specifically identifiable, the constraints appropriate for adjudication are neither practicable nor desirable." 1 CFR § 305.77–3 (1993).[3] A few years later, nearly every agency with a substantial rulemaking docket reported to the conference that it was following the Conference's recommendations on written communications. Agency practice on handling oral ex parte communications was more varied. See Office of the Chairman of the Administrative Conference of the United States, A Guide to Federal Agency Rulemaking 166–68 (1983). As reflected in E.O. 12866 § 6(b)(4) and the National Highway Traffic Safety Administration's current electronic docket for its rule on monitoring tire pressures, p. 644, this trend appears not just to have continued, but to have been expanded into the pre-NPRM period. For a strong argument that "the legitimacy of rulemaking relies on public knowledge of private contacts with agency and White House officials even if an agency can successfully defend its rule against legal attacks on the basis of publicly available information," see Sidney A. Shapiro, Two Cheers for HBO: The Problem of the Nonpublic Record, 54 Admin L. Rev. 853 (2002).

(4) Should former General Counsel Geller have been participating in a private capacity in a rulemaking proceeding that had been well under way

---

industry involved to carry on their most significant discussions before the notice of proposed rulemaking is issued, thus reducing the statutory part of the proceeding to a relatively insignificant formality. If that should happen it would not be the first time that the complications of formal proceedings may have induced administrative agencies to accomplish their most important business by less formal means."

Compare the discussion of the Government in the Sunshine Act, at p. 762ff.

3. The demise of the Administrative Conference occurred before the CFR became available on the web through the GPO. The Administrative Conference recommendations were removed from the CFR in subsequent editions. See 58 FR 54271, Oct. 21, 1993.

while he was a high-level commission employee? The case arose before the Ethics in Government Act defined "rulemaking" as a "particular matter." 18 U.S.C. § 207(i)(3). Today, it seems unlikely that he could play any role on behalf of a client—whether he actually participated in the rulemaking (lifetime ban, § 207(a)(1)), had official responsibility for it (two year cooling off period, § 207(a)(2)), or was an officer of sufficiently high status (one-year general ban on contact with one's former agency, § 207(c)). But at that time, no established principle of ethical conduct forbade his appearance. See p. 462ff.

(i) AN OPEN–MINDED DECISIONMAKER?

C & W Fish Company, Inc. v. Fox

United States Court of Appeals for the District of Columbia Circuit, 1991.
931 F.2d 1556.

■ Before MIKVA, CHIEF JUDGE, SENTELLE AND HENDERSON, CIRCUIT JUDGES.

■ HENDERSON, CIRCUIT JUDGE:

On April 13, 1990, the Department of Commerce (Department), National Oceanic and Atmospheric Administration (NOAA), issued a final rule which, in part, bans the use of drift gillnets in the Atlantic King Mackerel Fishery. See 55 Fed.Reg. 14,833 (April 19, 1990). Various individuals involved in the fishing industry challenged the final rule on several grounds, including its allegedly ultra vires promulgation. The district court rejected all of the plaintiffs' challenges, granting summary judgment to the defendants. We affirm.

[The Magnuson Fishery Conservation and Management Act (Magnuson Act or Act), 16 U.S.C. §§ 1801–82, gives the Department authority to create national programs for fish conservation and management, while also preserving state roles. Eight Regional Fishery Management Councils representing state interests are granted authority over specific geographic regions. A Council can propose a Fishery Management Plan (FMP) subject to the Secretary's final approval, and must be given an opportunity to comment on any FMP the Secretary himself proposes. Within the Department, the Secretary's authority has been subdelegated in ways that may further promote state interests, as well as foster the development of departmental expertise. The Assistant Administrator for Fisheries (Assistant Administrator) of the National Oceans and Atmosphere Administration, who is also the Director of the National Marine Fisheries Service (NMFS), is an important intermediary recipient of this authority.

For years, the South Atlantic Regional Council and the Gulf Regional Council had been trying to ban gillnet fishing for various species,[1] including the Atlantic King Mackerel. In 1989, after a regional administrator had blocked several other efforts, they succeeded in getting a rule that imposed

---

1. As its name suggests, a gillnet is a net that traps fish who swim into it by catching their gills; although the size of openings in the nets offers some control, they inevitably catch unwanted fish (and other marine life); drift gillnets, a particular target of the Councils, are large nets permitted to drift through a fishing area, whose size may contribute to threats of overfishing.

limited constraints but permitted continued drift gillnet fishing for the Atlantic King Mackerel. In 1990, the Council submitted a renewed proposal to ban this practice, which the regional administrator rejected. He reasoned that "the evidence presented to support the new submission . . . had not changed since the first submission and did not warrant a change in agency policy."]

When the Regional Director's decision reached Dr. William Fox, the newly appointed NOAA Assistant Administrator, the rejected portions of the amendment gained new life. Fox—who before his appointment had been a strong advocate of the drift gillnet ban—inexplicably reported that the Regional Director had "approved" the new Amendment 3 and then, himself, approved the full plan, explaining the appropriateness of the ban. The Under Secretary and the Secretary subsequently approved the Councils' proposal, and NOAA implemented appropriate notice and comment rulemaking, 55 Fed.Reg. 5,242 (February 14, 1990) (proposed rule); 55 Fed.Reg. 14,833 (April 19, 1990) (final rule).

The issuance of the drift gillnet ban set the stage for this litigation. Immediately after the final rule was issued, two fish wholesalers and two individual fishermen filed suit against the Secretary of Commerce, Robert Mosbacher, and Assistant Administrator Fox in district court . . .

[After disposing of a number of other challenges, the court turned to appellants' contention], that Assistant Administrator Fox had an "unalterably closed mind" when he passed on the drift gillnet ban and, consequently, their due process right to an impartial decisionmaker was denied them. To support this claim, the appellants point to the fact that, immediately before his appointment, Fox was the chairman of the Florida Marine Fisheries Commission, an outspoken advocate of the drift gillnet ban. They also point to an article published after Fox was appointed, quoting Fox as stating " '[t]here's just no question that this kind of gear [i.e., drift gillnets] should be eliminated. . . . The drift nets run counter to everything we're trying to do for the fisheries.' " Wickstrom, "The Fox Goes to Washington," Florida Sportsman (Oct. 1989), JA 426. Last, the appellants claim that Fox's bias is demonstrated by his failure to conduct an adequate review of the issues or to consider the positions of his staff advisors.

First we reject the suggestion that we look to the adequacy of Fox's examination of the facts and issues in order to determine whether he was biased. In Association of National Advertisers, Inc. v. FTC, 627 F.2d 1151, 1170 (D.C.Cir.1979), cert. denied, 447 U.S. 921 (1980),[2] we held that an individual should be disqualified from rulemaking "only when there has been a clear and convincing showing that the Department member has an

---

2. [Ed.] This rulemaking regulated the advertising of sugared cereals on children's television programs. The movements for disqualification relied on a letter the FTC's Chairman, Michael Pertschuk, had sent to the head of the Food and Drug Administration, seeking to enlist his interest:

Setting legal theory aside, the truth is that we've been drawn into this issue because of the conviction which I know you share, that one of the evils flowing from the unfairness of children's advertising is the resulting distortion of children's perception of nutritional values. I see, at this point, our logical process as follows—Children's advertising is inherently unfair . . .

unalterably closed mind on matters critical to the disposition of the proceeding." See also Lead Industries Asso. v. EPA, 647 F.2d 1130, 1179–80 (D.C.Cir.), cert. denied, 449 U.S. 1042 (1980).[3] This showing should focus on the agency member's prejudgment, if any, rather than a failure to weigh the issues fairly. Whether Fox weighed the facts properly is to be examined only in determining if his decision was arbitrary or capricious. As we have often explained, this court will not second guess an agency decision or question whether the decision made was the best one.

The facts in this case do not even approach a "clear and convincing showing" that Fox had an "unalterably closed mind." As we reasoned in Association of National Advertisers, "[t]he mere discussion of policy or advocacy on a legal question . . . is not sufficient to disqualify an administrator." 627 F.2d at 1171 (footnote omitted). The harm that would result were courts to disqualify agency members whenever they express views in public, as Fox did here, is readily apparent: We would eviscerate the proper evolution of policymaking were we to disqualify every administrator who has opinions on the correct course of his agency's future actions. Administrators, and even judges, may hold policy views on questions of law prior to participating in a proceeding. The factual basis for a rulemaking is so closely intertwined with policy judgments that we would obliterate rulemaking were we to equate a statement on an issue of legislative fact with unconstitutional prejudgment.

* * *

An administrator's presence within an agency reflects the political judgment of the President and the Senate. . . . A Commission's view of what is best in the public interest may change from time to time. Commis-

---

3. [Ed.] Shortly before OSHA adopted a standard governing lead in the workplace, Assistant Secretary of Labor Eula Bingham, the official responsible for OSHA rulemaking, spoke at a labor union conference on the topic. On three controverted issues—whether exposed workers should be given alternative work at the same rate of pay; whether harmful effects were being experienced; and what would be the economic impact of the proposed standards—she told her "Brothers and Sisters" the following:

"As to the medical removal protection provision (MRP): I think that there may be some apprehension because Assistant Secretaries in the past have not always understood, or have not known how to spell the words medical removal protection, or rate retention . . . Well, I learned to spell those words a long time ago on the Coke Oven Advisory Committee, and if you want to know how I feel about it, you need only to look up my comments during those Committee hearings. As far

as I'm concerned, it is impossible to have a Lead Standard without it. . . .

"As to the dangers of lead: . . . I can tell you about a plant within 300 miles of the city where workers are told to go to the hospital from work and receive therapy that would drag out poison and precious metals. And then they're sent back to be poisoned again. I bet I could go down to the hospitals of this city and find a worker that is undergoing kidney dialysis, and I'll bet you a dinner that some of those workers have been in lead plants.

"As to economic feasibility: I have told some people that I have never aspired to be an economist, but I tell you I can smell a phony issue when I see one. And to say that safety and health regulations are inflationary is phony.

. . . "I don't understand a society such as ours who is not willing to pay a dollar more for a battery to insure that workers do not have to pay for that battery with their lives."

sions themselves change, underlying philosophies differ, and experience often dictates changes. We conclude that neither Fox's earlier advocacy nor his policy view as publicly expressed demonstrates an unalterably closed mind that would disqualify him as an impartial decisionmaker.

NOTES

(1) Given the court's action, what does it mean to have an "impartial decisionmaker" in rulemaking? How satisfactory do you find the political explanation for weak disqualification rules in rulemaking? Here, as in the two cited cases, the claims of disqualifying bias are made by those who are or might be the subject of the rule in question. Each rule reflects the action of an unusually outspoken, pro-regulation administrator, who may have been put in office for his or her views. Do the fairness claims of those subjected to regulation deserve more respect than these cases afford? See Peter L. Strauss, Disqualifications of Decisional Officials in Rulemaking, 80 Colum.L.Rev. 990 (1980); cf. ABA Committee on Government Standards, Cynthia Farina, Reporter, Keeping Faith: Government Ethics and Government Ethics Regulation, 45 Ad.L.Rev. 287 (1993).

(2) PLMRS NARROWBAND CORP. v. FCC, 182 F.3d 995, 1002 (D.C.Cir.1999): For years, the FCC had been committed to allocating certain potentially valuable franchises by lottery, under certain restrictions against commercial use. Long after the application process had begun, it opened for reconsideration the question whether the franchises should instead be allocated by auction, with the commercial use restrictions lifted. "In August 1995, before the Commission issued the *Third Notice of Proposed Rulemaking*, the Chairman unveiled in a speech the Commission's 'lineup of upcoming auctions,' including the auction in the third quarter of 1996 of the licenses at issue here. The Washington Legal Foundation then petitioned the Commission requesting that the Chairman recuse himself from voting upon the auction issue on the ground that he would be unable to give meaningful consideration to the public comments opposing an auction and favoring a lottery. Chairman Hundt did not recuse himself, and indeed voted to adopt the *Third Report and Order*, as did all the Commissioners.

"The day after the public release of that order Chairman Hundt responded to the WLF's petition. He explained that his 1995 statements indicated only his preliminary views, that his announcement of tentative auction dates 'included all *potential* services to be licensed' by auction in 1996, and that the Commission must begin to plan for an auction 'well in advance of any final Commission decision to authorize [one].' Letter from Chairman Hundt to Washington Legal Found. (March 13, 1997).

"Generally, we are unable to view the motivations of an agency official except as through a glass, darkly, and the glass may be tinted not by the official's unalterable prejudgment but by legitimate policy preconceptions; in a particular instance, the cause may be exceedingly difficult to discern. In order to avoid trenching upon the agency's policy prerogatives, therefore, we presume that policymakers approach their quasi-legislative task of rulemaking with an open mind—but not an empty one.

"[The protester's] burden is to make a 'clear and convincing showing that [Chairman Hundt had] an unalterably closed mind on matters critical to the disposition of the proceeding.' Association of Nat'l Adver. v. FTC, 627 F.2d 1151, 1170 (D.C.Cir.1979). That it has not done. Even if we assume Chairman Hundt was predisposed in favor of auctions as a matter of policy, that alone would not imply that he was unwilling to consider arguments to the contrary."

(3) As with the problem of bias in professional discipline hearings discussed at p. 420ff., the broader picture may suggest a different kind of problem. It may be that Commissioners tend to chat with those they are supposed to be regulating, and tend to softness rather than firmness of purpose. At the height of the public interest movement, a citizen-supported organization (Common Cause) surveyed personal appointments logs of several federal regulatory commissioners and found that even then almost half the record-ed contacts were with "industry representatives": less than 5% were with consumer or "public interest" representatives.[4] Compare the not-too-dis-similar results reported by Professor Steven Croley in analyzing meetings at OIRA, p. 656. Yet Professor Croley's results suggested no statistically significant correlation between meeting attendees and policy outcomes. Industry, of course, seeks understanding as urgently and as validly as the agency or any other participant before it. Absent an effort to influence a specific proceeding outside a procedurally—required exclusive record, its captains can hardly be criticized for trying to persuade bodies capable of inflicting substantial inconvenience and cost. After all, regulatory policy may be shaped by misapprehension as well as right-thinking attention to duty, and it is easier to correct error in early stages than after months of staff effort spent in building action plans. Common Cause conceded that "[i]ndustry has a constitutional right . . . to lobby government for favorable action. Consultation between regulatory officials and industry representa-

---

4. With Only One Ear 22 (1977). Press (13%), foreign visitors (11%), Congress (6%), Consultants (4%) and others (16%) supplied the balance. The "industry" group could not be broken down to reflect possibly competing interests. Id. at 9. Professor, formerly FCC Commissioner, Glen O. Robinson, remarks, "[I]ndustry capture is at best an awkward explanation for regulatory behavior in deal-ing with competing industry interests. For example, it is easy to find evidence of FCC bias towards the broadcast industry, but that very bias undermines any particular solici-tude towards the cable industry. It also would be difficult for the FCC to be captured simul-taneously by AT & T and interconnect equip-ment suppliers, nor could the agency at once be cozy with Motorola *and* radio common carriers. Because most important controver-sies involve conflicting industry constituents, the 'capture' explanation would appear to

have limited value as a guide to agency be-havior. . . .

"Because economic security is a charac-teristic of many, if not most, regulatory schemes, business interests tend to prefer regulation to the unsettling vicissitudes of competition. Herein lies the larger problem: not that *regulators* have been captured by industry but rather that *regulation* has been captured by industry. As I discovered during my term as a Commissioner, the FCC is entreated to promote many 'public interests,' but few are advanced with such heartfelt eloquence as the pleas of businessmen—most notably broadcasters and telephone company representatives—to protect their 'services' from the corrosive, unstabilizing effects of competition by imposing some new layer of anticompetitive regulations." The Federal Communications Commission: An Essay on Regulatory Watchdogs, 64 Va.L.Rev. 169, 191–192 (1978).

tives is an essential part of effective policy making in regulatory agencies."[5] It sought required logging of all contacts, as well as measures affirmatively to increase the level of public participation (such as government subsidization of that participation).

(ii) THE CONTRIBUTIONS OF AGENCY STAFF

The reasoning of the Fox court depends in good part on an argument from the legitimacy provided by "the political judgment of the President and the Senate" in making appointments. Should different considerations govern as one descends into the "expert" levels of the civil service, where institutional decisions will be strongly shaped?

United Steelworkers of America, AFL–CIO–CLC v. Marshall

United States Court of Appeals for the District of Columbia Circuit, 1980.
647 F.2d 1189, cert. denied 453 U.S. 913 (1981).

■ Before WRIGHT, CHIEF JUDGE, and ROBINSON and MACKINNON, JUDGES.

■ J. SKELLY WRIGHT, CHIEF JUDGE:[1]

[This case arose at an intermediate stage of a massive OSHA rulemaking to regulate worker exposure to airborne lead.[2] The agency proposed a permissible exposure limit (PEL) of 50 micrograms of lead per cubic meter of air (50 μg/m^3). Participants challenged the outcome from all sides, with industrial parties stressing procedural flaws. Regarding these, the court acknowledged that "OSHA was occasionally careless or inefficient in its procedures throughout this rulemaking," but felt itself constrained by Vermont Yankee, p. 498 above, and by the agency's practical problems in administering a proceeding with hundreds of participants and tens of thousands of pages of record. While] the OSH Act requires the agency to follow procedures more stringent than the minimal ones established in the Administrative Procedure Act, ... Congress' decision to impose the substantial evidence test on OSHA does not alter the essentially informal character of OSHA rulemaking. Industrial Union Dep't, AFL–CIO v. Hodgson, 499 F.2d 467, 472–473 (D.C.Cir.1974). ... Thus, as we examine the procedural claims in the lead proceeding, we must avoid imposing procedural constraints beyond those in APA § 553, the OSH Act, and the Due Process Clause, and we remain bound by judicial construction of the demands of APA § 553 as our source for the general principles of informal rulemaking. ...

B.   Improper Staff Role and Separation of Functions

[Lead Industries Assoc. (LIA), the main industrial challenger], aims its ... procedural attack at OSHA staff attorneys who, LIA argues, acted essentially as advocates for a stringent lead standard by consulting with and persuading the Assistant Secretary as she drew her conclusions from

---

5. With Only One Ear, at i.

1. [Ed.] Author of the ex parte portions of Home Box Office.

2. See, e.g., American Iron & Steel Inst. v. OSHA, 939 F.2d 975 (D.C.Cir.1991) (largely sustaining revised rule, but remanding in part for further development as to one industry).

the record. LIA would have us conclude that the agency decisionmaker engaged in ex parte, off-the-record contacts with one of the adverse sides in the rulemaking, thereby rendering the proceedings unfair. . . .

The key agency employee in question was Richard Gross, a lawyer in the Office of the Solicitor at OSHA, who served as a so-called "standard's attorney" throughout the rulemaking. . . . The standard's attorney was at the center of activity throughout the rulemaking. He worked with the regular OSHA staff in reviewing preliminary research and drafting the proposed standard, all the while offering informal legal advice. He helped organize the public hearings and, having immersed himself in the scientific literature and in the submitted public comments, he communicated regularly with the prospective expert witnesses. In these communications he briefed the witnesses on the issues they were to address in their testimony, explained the positions of the agency, the industry, and the unions on key questions, discussed the likely criticism of the experts' testimony, and asked the experts for any new information that supported or contradicted the OSHA proposal.[3] During the hearing itself he conducted all initial questioning of OSHA witnesses and cross-examined all other witnesses. After the hearings he assisted the Assistant Secretary by reviewing the evidence in the record, preparing summaries, analyses, and recommendations, and helping draft the Preamble to the final standard.

In a proceeding to create a general rule it makes little sense to speak of an agency employee advocating for one "side" over another. However contentious the proceeding, the concept of advocacy does not apply easily where the agency is not determining the specific rights of a specific party, and where the proposed rule undergoes detailed change in its journey toward a final rule. Indeed, as OSHA notes, the true adversaries here may well have been the industry and the unions, since the final standard, while in no sense a mathematical compromise, did fall between the old standard, to which the industry had resigned itself, and the extremely stringent one the unions urged. Thus, the standard's attorney may have been an advocate for *some* new lead standard, and probably even a stringent one, but not necessarily for one specific standard supported by one specific party.

Nevertheless, the adversary tone and format of the proceedings are obvious. . . . The Assistant Secretary might well have been able to assess the record more objectively—if less efficiently—had the standard's attorney

---

3. The letters of Gross' colleague, Donald Kuchenbecker, to two of the expert medical witnesses best reveal the work of the standard's attorney. ALD 66–82. The letters are exhaustively detailed and generally quite neutral in briefing the witnesses on the important medical issues and urging them to supply all new relevant evidence, including any at odds with a stringent lead standard. Nevertheless, Kuchenbecker did make some imprudent remarks. He told Dr. Piomelli that it "would not be helpful to OSHA" if the latter were to state that there was no correlation between air-lead and blood-lead measurements, and told both Dr. Piomelli and Dr. Seppalainen that OSHA wanted to avoid the "ticklish issue" of how to accommodate female workers of child-bearing age if feasibility limits required OSHA to set a standard that threatened such women but not other workers.

In context, these remarks do not overcome the generally objective import of the letters; moreover, Kuchenbecker himself did not advise the Assistant Secretary on the final standard, and we are loath to project his attitude onto Gross.

not been constantly at her side. Therefore, although we have some doubt about calling the standard's attorney an "advocate" in the context of such rulemaking,[4] we will *assume* he played that role so we can measure his conduct against the legal constraints on the agency.[5]

We note at the outset that nothing in the Administrative Procedure Act bars a staff advocate from advising the decisionmaker in setting a final rule. . . . Moreover, in establishing the special hybrid procedures in the OSH Act, Congress never intended to impose the separation-of-functions requirement it imposes in adjudications. The legislative history shows that Congress consistently turned back efforts to impose such formal procedures on OSHA standard-setting. . . .[U]nder the Supreme Court's decision in Vermont Yankee that is virtually the end of the inquiry. . . .

Rulemaking is essentially an institutional, not an individual, process, and it is not vulnerable to communication within an agency in the same sense as it is to communication from without. In an enormously complex proceeding like an OSHA standard setting, it may simply be unrealistic to expect an official facing a massive, almost inchoate, record to isolate herself from the people with whom she worked in generating the record. In any event, we rest our decision not on our own theory of agency management, but on the state of the law.

C.   Improper Use of Consultants

. . . OSHA relied heavily on David Burton Associates (DBA) and Nicholas Ashford and his Center for Policy Alternatives (CPA) in examining the data on feasibility and developing a "technology-forcing" rationale for the standard. The agency hired a number of other expert consultants, giving them fairly broad mandates to summarize and evaluate data in the record, prepare record data for computer processing, and help draft portions of the Preamble and the final standard. LIA argues that such reliance on outsiders invites abuse, even if one assumes the honesty of the ones in this case, since hired hands have a financial incentive to tell the agency what it wants to hear, and have no civil service protection against retaliation for telling uncomfortable truths. . . .

LIA's position . . . comes down to the challenge that OSHA has violated the principle of Morgan I: "The one who decides must hear," and an agency denies the parties a true hearing if the official who acts for the agency has not personally confronted the evidence and the arguments.

---

4. We also have some doubt as to the wisdom of singling out a staff *lawyer* in this case, when other, nonlegal, staff people probably participated with great vigor both in developing the agency position during the hearings and in advising the Assistant Secretary in drafting the final standard. . . .

5. We assume, however, only that the standard's attorney may have influenced the Assistant Secretary by reinforcing, according to his bias, certain information and arguments that they were put in the record of the public proceedings. Thus this is not a case where agency employees supplied the decisionmaker with actual new evidence which the agency has identified as part of the basis of its decision, but which it has refused to disclose except through a "blind reference." . . . [E]ven if he were predisposed on the lead standard, the standard's attorney's conduct remained within the general boundaries of the *deliberative* process and, however biased, his communications with the Assistant Secretary remained within the boundaries of *deliberative* material. . . .

Though Morgan I expressly allowed agency officials to rely on their subordinates in reviewing the record, it did not, of course, address the question of outside consultants. Nevertheless, applying the general principle of Morgan I, we see that LIA cannot buttress its general allegation of excessive reliance with any specific proof that the Assistant Secretary failed to confront personally the essential evidence and arguments in setting the final standard. Without at this point addressing the substantive validity of the lead standard, we note that in the lengthy Preamble and Attachments to the final standard the decisionmaker reviewed the evidence and explained the evidentiary bases for each part of the standard. Moreover, the Assistant Secretary demonstrated her independence from the consultants by strongly criticizing some of their conclusions on the key issue of feasibility.

To inquire further would be to probe impermissibly into the mental processes by which the Assistant Secretary made her decision. The unsupported allegation that hired consultants might have an incentive to act dishonestly cannot overcome the presumption that agency officials and those who assist them have acted properly. Thus we generally see no reason to force agencies to hire enormous regular staffs versed in all conceivable technological issues, rather than use their appropriations to hire specific consultants for specific problems.

LIA's second attack goes to *specific* uses of consultants, and alleges damage to the state of the rulemaking record, rather than to the Assistant Secretary's fulfillment of her personal responsibility. After closing the record, OSHA sought help from outside consultants in reviewing the record and preparing the Preamble. Two consultants were primary. The agency asked David Burton and DBA to help review the record to determine the feasibility of a permissible air-lead standard of 50 $\mu g/m^3$, as opposed to the 100 $\mu g/m^3$ standard the agency had proposed in the original notice of rulemaking, and on which most of the public commentary had focused. And OSHA asked Nicholas Ashford and CPA to analyze, in light of the record, the possibility of marking a correlation between air-lead levels and blood-lead levels. Both these consultants had previously aided OSHA by supplying on-the-record reports and testifying as expert witnesses at the public hearings. Both fulfilled the new requests by submitting written reports, of 117 and 192 pages respectively, neither of which the agency has released or placed in the rulemaking record. LIA contends that the reports are illegal ex parte communications which, like the communications with the staff advocates described earlier, constitute "secret briefs" and off-the-record evidence which LIA was deprived of a chance to rebut and the court a chance to review.

We note first that, as in the case of the staff-influence charge discussed earlier, LIA has not identified any hard data or new legal arguments which are contained only in the allegedly improper *ex parte* communications and on which OSHA demonstrably relied in setting the standard. Thus LIA has not shown that OSHA has materially prejudiced parties who were not privy to the communications. Rather, LIA asks us to infer that there must have been such *ex parte* evidence or legal argument ... The documents show that the communications between the agency and the consultants were simply part of the deliberative process of drawing conclusions from the public record. The consultants acted after the record was closed as the functional equivalent of agency staff, so the question of the legal propriety of OSHA's reliance on DBA and CPA is foreclosed by our earlier conclusion that neither the APA nor the Home Box Office doctrine imposes a separation-of-functions requirement on the agencies. Thus, even though we readily assume that OSHA used the consultants' reports—and even incorporated parts of them verbatim in the Preamble—LIA has suffered no legal prejudice from such use....

When performed by agency *staff*, [the] sort of sophisticated review of evidence [the consultants performed in this case] has always been recognized as legitimate participation in the deliberative process. And the circuit courts, in applying the intra-agency exemption to the Freedom of Information Act, 5 U.S.C. § 552(b)(5) (1976), have recognized that where outside consultants so engage in the deliberative process there is no *functional* difference between staff and consultants, and so there should be no *legal* difference. ...

In Lead Industries Ass'n, Inc. v. OSHA, 610 F.2d 70 (2d Cir.1979), Judge Friendly examined the same affidavits, agreements, and indices that we have examined, and concluded that both the DBA report and the CPA report contributed to the process by which the Assistant Secretary made her final decision. He conceded that the reports might contain some factual matter, but asserted that in a vast rulemaking like this one such information was necessarily incident to and not severable from the process of summary and analysis. He suggested, moreover, that to the extent the reports drew inferences from and weighed the evidence they were more truly "deliberative" and thus better candidates for [Freedom of Information Act] exemption than mere summaries of the record. ...

■ MacKinnon, Circuit Judge (dissenting): ...

Subsequent to the close of the record in this rulemaking, and prior to the promulgation of the final standard, OSHA contracted with outside consultants to perform an evaluation, presumably only of record evidence,[6] on two topics. First, the agency asked David Burton and David Burton Associates (DBA) to review the voluminous record and evaluate the feasibility of a permissible air-lead exposure standard of 50 $\mu g/m^3$. The rule as proposed in the notice, and virtually all of the record evidence, referred only to the feasibility of a permissible exposure limit of 100 $\mu g/m^3$. Burton and DBA had previously prepared reports for OSHA which had been introduced into the record, and *had testified as expert witnesses during the public hearings in support of the economic and technological feasibility of*

---

6. Without a review of the actual reports submitted by the consultants, which are not available, it cannot be determined whether or not they contain new, extra-record evidence. The majority reads vague statements from the contracts which designate the evaluating responsibilities of DBA and CPA, and concludes that only record evidence was to have been reviewed to formulate their analyses. However, far too little weight is given to the statement in the CPA contract to the effect that the consultant was permitted "to conduct additional research and prepare material supplementary to the above testimony. ..." This concern only magnifies the insuperable handicap with which the Court is afflicted by being forced to rule on the propriety of these reports, without ever seeing them. *This is a fatal defect in the record.*

the 100 µg/m³ proposed level. After the record was closed the agency also contracted with the Center for Policy Analysis and Nicholas Ashford to analyze the scientific and medical correlation between air-lead and blood-lead levels. Ashford had submitted a preliminary report on this correlation during the record period as an expert witness for OSHA. The lengthy analyses prepared by the consultants in fulfillment of their contractual responsibilities have *never* been released to the parties or the public, despite the fact that as far as the report on the economic and technological feasibility of 50 µg/m³ is concerned, it is the only in depth evidence on the topic in existence. The delegation of this task to these biased witnesses, and the failure to introduce the reports into evidence, constitute prejudicial error which requires the remand of the case to the agency on this point. As Chief Justice Hughes remarked in Morgan I, "[n]othing can be treated as evidence which is not introduced as such." In the absence of this report there is insufficient evidence to support the finding.

. . . No court should condone allowing paid consultants to legally change their hats from expert witnesses subject to cross-examination during the hearings, to "agency staff" hired after the close of hearings to evaluate the credibility of *their own testimony* and others. . . . Subjecting these consultants to cross-examination initially, and then giving them free rein to evaluate and weigh all contrary testimony, is in effect giving them free and unbridled rebuttal without the benefits that might flow from cross-examination. And OSHA cannot contend that the substance of these secret reports does not relate to "crucial issues" because they go to the very core of the standard. . . .

NOTES

(1) NATIONAL SMALL SHIPMENTS TRAFFIC CONFERENCE, INC. v. ICC, 725 F.2d 1442 (D.C.Cir.1984), reviewed a rulemaking that reexamined the way carriers allocate handling costs at freight truck terminals, among shippers of high and low bulk commodities. The final rule placed a higher proportion of the costs on smaller-size shippers. They complained that the bureaucratic decision process within the ICC had prevented staff analyses favorable to smaller-size shippers from reaching the Commission:

"Under existing law, an agency decisionmaking body such as the Commission may delegate detailed consideration of the administrative record to its subordinates while retaining the final power of decision for itself. Rather than wade through the entire record personally, then, members of the body are free to rely on summaries prepared by agency staff. Because of the strong presumption of regularity in administrative proceedings, reviewing courts will not normally entertain procedural challenges that members of the body inadequately considered the issues before reaching a final decision, or that staff reports on which the body relied imperfectly summarized the record under review, cf. Montrose Chemical Corp. v. Train, 491 F.2d 63, 71 (D.C.Cir.1974).

"At some point, however, staff-prepared synopses may so distort the record that an agency decisionmaking body can no longer rely on them in meeting its obligations under the law. . . . Certainly, if subordinates systematically eliminated from their reports all mention of record comments adverse to the agency's final action, the consideration requirement would not be satisfied unless the decisionmakers took independent steps to familiarize themselves with withheld portions of the record.

"This analysis suggests that petitioners do have a legal right that their comments reach Commission members in at least summary form, and that those comments be considered before final action is taken.[1] Neither the APA nor the due process clause, however, accords similar treatment to staff evaluations that move beyond a mere summary of record comments to express the independent judgments of subordinate agency personnel. An agency is free to structure its internal policy debate in any manner it deems appropriate. Mid-level managers may therefore filter out the evaluations of lower-level personnel if they so choose, so long as relevant record comments are not eliminated in the process as well. . . . [W]hat appears to have occurred is a lively debate in which other ICC offices seriously questioned the soundness of various aspects of the study methodology, and in which the Bureau responded with refined statistical analyses to support its conclusions. The Bureau of Accounts ultimately prevailed, not because it unfairly suppressed legitimate internal dissent, but because it convinced other division heads that its weight-only formula was not materially flawed by admitted shortcomings in the study's design and execution."

(2) LOUIS L. JAFFE, THE EFFECTIVE LIMITS OF THE ADMINISTRATIVE PROCESS: A RE-EVALUATION, 67 Harv.L.Rev. 1105, 1132–1133 (1954): "Where regulation is enacted there is conflict. Large forces find themselves in opposition, each seeking solutions which threaten social unity. In our society there is a broad basis of consent to the proposition that just at these points administration has a legitimate role in creating solutions. The agencies, specialized and experienced each in its way, are in a position to offer solutions that do not depart so far from the given technical base as to be unacceptable or unworkable. The permanent staff in particular is the repository of this experience. It is the matrix of thinking which can transcend the positions of the parties. Because it is anonymous it is more autonomous. It is politically less vulnerable, its opportunity for 'passing over' to the 'other side' is more restricted. For these reasons it has at times become the target for private interests who fear and resent its influence over the commissioners. To my mind this has much to do with the persistent efforts to devise procedures which isolate the commissions from their staffs."

(iii) PRESSURE FROM EXTERNAL GOVERNMENT ACTORS

Sierra Club v. Costle

United States Court of Appeals for the District of Columbia Circuit, 1981.
657 F.2d 298.

■ Before ROBB, WALD and GINSBURG, CIRCUIT JUDGES.

■ WALD, CIRCUIT JUDGE: [In June 1979, the Environmental Protection Agency (EPA) issued revised new source performance standards (NSPS) to

---

1. This right remains subject, however, to the long-standing rule that courts will not probe the mental processes of administrative decisionmakers absent strong evidence of bad faith or other misconduct. Overton Park, 401 U.S. at 420.

govern atmospheric emissions of sulfur dioxide and particulates by new coal-fired power stations. The standards resulted from long and contentious rulemaking under the special hybrid rulemaking procedures of the Clean Air Act.[1] They were promptly challenged from all sides.

One issue facing EPA was how to predict the impact of possible standards on utility planning. These were standards for *new* sources. To the extent they made construction of new plants expensive, they would encourage utilities to continue using older facilities having higher emission levels.[2] Moreover, if the sulfur dioxide emission standard was stated in terms of the total amount emitted by the plant, a utility might be able to choose among three strategies: (1) removing sulfur dioxide from emissions by the plant "scrubbing"; (2) burning coal with a low sulfur content; or (3) combining some scrubbing with purchase of lower sulfur coal. Choices about scrubbing were also possible; competing technologies differed in their effectiveness, reliability, and cost. Scrubbing 70% of the sulfur dioxide out of plant emissions would be less expensive and more reliable than attempting to scrub 90%; and removing 70% of the sulfur dioxide from low-sulfur coal emissions would produce much lower total emissions than removing 90% from high-sulfur coal emissions. (Indeed, very low sulfur coal would produce less sulfur dioxide if burned without *any* scrubbing than high-sulfur coal subject to 90% scrubbing.) While this seems a strong case for using low-sulfur coal, other considerations were important:

> Much low-sulfur coal is located in the West, where preventing any degradation of air quality is highly valued by many.

> Permitting utilities to scrub less if they use low-sulfur coal creates a reason not to buy high-sulfur coal, and that threatens the economy of regions with high sulfur coal deposits;

> Encouraging new plant demand for low-sulfur coal would raise coal prices for all plants, including old plants that might be able to reduce emissions economically only by switching to low sulfur coal.

> It will always be cheaper to install control equipment when building a new plant than to retrofit the plant later on.

1. For a thorough, spirited and highly critical account of this rulemaking see Bruce Ackerman and William Hassler, Clean Coal/Dirty Air (1981).

The dimensions of the controversy are suggested by the following footnote from the Court's opinion:

"The briefs submitted to this court on the merits total over 670 pages, the Joint Appendix contains 5,620 pages in twelve volumes, and the certified index to the record lists over 2,520 submissions. By the time of the publication of the final rule (EPA's statement accompanying the final rule took up 43 triple columns of single spaced type), EPA had performed or obtained from contractors approximately 120 studies, and collected over 400 items of reference literature, received almost 1,400 comments, written 650 letters and 200 interagency memos, held over 50 meetings and substantive telephone conversations with the public, and conducted four days of public hearings."

2. A contemporaneous discussion of the new source-old source problem appears in Peter Huber, The Old–New Division in Risk Regulation, 69 Va.L.Rev. 1025 (1983). With passage of the Clean Air Act Amendments of 1990, this problem was finally faced, and a mechanism for phasing out the old plants was established.

Thus, EPA had both a "new-old" problem and a fuel choice problem to consider in predicting the overall effect of a given emissions standard. To make its analysis, EPA developed a computer program to assess the impacts of various standards on a number of complex factors, including the following: total air emissions; new plant investment; consumer costs; energy production and consumption; fuel choice (coal, oil, gas, etc.); and the regional impacts on coal production and transportation. The program, and the assumptions on which it was based, were reviewed within government by a working group of representatives from several agencies (EPA, Energy, Council of Economic Advisors, Council on Wage and Price Stability). It had been subjected to public comments, and revised; the results were published and publicly discussed.

EPA ultimately adopted a variable standard. No new plant could emit more than 1.2 lbs of sulfur dioxide for each million British thermal units (MBtu) of heat energy produced by burning coal. If it would produce between 0.6 lbs and 1.2 lbs, it was required to use 90% scrubbing. If it would produce less sulfur than 0.6 lbs, it could employ 70% scrubbing. EPA's model indicated that this standard would "result in more coal capacity in newer and 'cleaner' utility plants, have a clear cost advantage, use less oil, and have an equivalent impact on coal production."

A lower ceiling on sulfur dioxide emissions would have been possible, but could have been adopted only at the cost of impairing the market for coal produced in the Eastern Midwest and Northern Appalachian coal regions. The Environmental Defense Fund (EDF) asserted that in fact EPA initially decided to adopt a ceiling of 0.55 lb/MBtu, and backed away from this under an "ex parte blitz" from the coal industry, the President, and Senator Robert Byrd. At the time, Byrd was Senate majority leader representing West Virginia; he was naturally and deeply interested in the economic health of the Northern Appalachian coal region. The "blitz" occurred partly through the submission of late comments and partly through high-level meetings with Executive branch officials (including one meeting with the President himself) and congressional officials, (including two with Senator Byrd).

The court considered multiple challenges to the rule, in an opinion of 125 pages. Here, we consider EDF's challenge to the "ex parte blitz." In discussion omitted here, the court held that the late-filed written submissions had been docketed in sufficient time to permit response and to satisfy the "procedural record" requirements of Section 307 of the Clean Air Act. It then turned to the meetings that had been held.]

The Clean Air Act does not explicitly treat the issue of post-comment period meetings with individuals outside EPA. Oral face-to-face discussions are not prohibited anywhere, anytime, in the Act. The absence of such prohibition may have arisen from the nature of the informal rulemaking procedures Congress had in mind. Where agency action resembles judicial action, where it involves formal rulemaking, adjudication, or quasi-adjudication among "conflicting private claims to a valuable privilege," [Sangamon Valley] the insulation of the decisionmaker from ex parte contacts is justified by basic notions of due process to the parties involved. But where agency action involves informal rulemaking of a policymaking sort, the concept of ex parte contacts is of more questionable utility.

Under our system of government, the very legitimacy of general policymaking performed by unelected administrators depends in no small part upon the openness, accessibility, and amenability of these officials to the needs and ideas of the public from whom their ultimate authority derives, and upon whom their commands must fall. As judges we are insulated from these pressures because of the nature of the judicial process in which we participate; but we must refrain from the easy temptation to look askance at all face-to-face lobbying efforts, regardless of the forum in which they occur, merely because we see them as inappropriate in the judicial context. Furthermore, the importance to effective regulation of continuing contact with a regulated industry, other affected groups, and the public cannot be underestimated. Informal contacts may enable the agency to win needed support for its program, reduce future enforcement requirements by helping those regulated to anticipate and shape their plans for the future, and spur the provision of information which the agency needs. The possibility of course exists that in permitting ex parte communications with rulemakers we create the danger of "one administrative record for the public and this court and another for the Commission."[3] Under the Clean Air Act procedures, however, "[t]he promulgated rule may not be based (in part or whole) on any information or data which has not been placed in the docket ..." Thus EPA must justify its rulemaking solely on the basis of the record it compiles and makes public. . . .

It still can be argued, however, that if oral communications are to be freely permitted after the close of the comment period, then at least some adequate summary of them must be made in order to preserve the integrity of the rulemaking docket, which under the statute must be the sole repository of material upon which EPA intends to rely. . . . [U]nless oral communications of central relevance to the rulemaking are also docketed in some fashion or other, information central to the justification of the rule could be obtained without ever appearing on the docket, simply by communicating it by voice rather than by pen, thereby frustrating the command of § 307 that the final rule not be "based (in part or whole) on any information or data which has not been placed in the docket ..."

EDF is understandably wary of a rule which permits the agency to decide for itself when oral communications are of such central relevance that a docket entry for them is required. Yet the statute itself[, which requires EPA to include in the rulemaking record "all data information and documents" on which it relies] vests EPA with discretion to decide whether "documents" are of central relevance and therefore must be placed in the docket; surely EPA can be given no less discretion in docketing oral communications, concerning which the statute has no explicit requirements whatsoever. . . .

Turning to the particular oral communications in this case, we find that only two of the nine contested meetings were undocketed by EPA.[4]

---

3. Home Box Office, Inc. v. FCC, p. 666 above.

4. [Ed.] The meetings were as follows:

March 14, 1979—one and one-half hours White House briefing for high level executive branch officials.

The agency has maintained that, as to the May 1 meeting where Senate staff people were briefed on EPA's analysis concerning the impact of alternative emissions ceilings upon coal reserves, its failure to place a summary of the briefing in the docket was an oversight. We find no evidence that this oversight was anything but an honest inadvertence; furthermore, a briefing of this sort by EPA which simply provides background information about an upcoming rule is not the type of oral communication which would require a docket entry under the statute.

The other undocketed meeting occurred at the White House and involved the President and his White House staff. . . .

(a) Intra–Executive Branch Meetings

We have already held that a blanket prohibition against meetings during the post-comment period with individuals outside EPA is unwarranted, and this perforce applies to meetings with White House officials. We have not yet addressed, however, the issue whether such oral communications with White House staff, or the President himself, must be docketed on the rulemaking record, and we now turn to that issue. . . .

We note initially that § 307 makes specific provision for including in the rulemaking docket the "written comments" of other executive agencies along with accompanying documents on any proposed draft rules circulated in advance of the rulemaking proceeding. Drafts of the final rule submitted to an executive review process prior to promulgation, as well as all "written comments," "documents," and "written responses" resulting from such interagency review process, are also to be put in the docket prior to promulgation.[5] This specific requirement does not mention informal meetings or conversations concerning the rule which are not part of the initial or final review processes, nor does it refer to oral comments of any sort. Yet it is hard to believe Congress was unaware that intra-executive meetings

April 5, 1979—Meeting of principal participants in the rulemaking called by EPA, with discussion among all of new data presented in connection with the meeting by EPA staff and the National Coal Association (NCA).

April 23, 1979—30–45 minute meeting in Senator Byrd's office with high level executive branch officials and NCA officials attending.

April 27, 1979—Briefing on technological issues for executive branch officials.

April 30, 1979—One hour briefing for the President and other executive branch officials.

April 30, 1979—Briefing on technological issues for White House staff.

May 1, 1979—Additional White House briefing on technological issues.

May 1, 1979—One hour briefing for Senate Committee staff members.

May 2, 1979—Meeting with Senator Byrd, executive branch and NCA officials.

The rule was promulgated in final form June 11, 1979.

5. These materials, although docketed, are excluded from the "record for judicial review." 42 U.S.C. § 7607(d)(7)(A). The logic of this exclusion of final draft comments from the agency's "record for judicial review" is not completely clear, but we believe it evinces a Congressional intent for the reviewing court to judge the rule solely upon the data, information, and comments provided in the public docket, as well as the explanations EPA provides when it promulgates the rule, and not to concern itself with who in the Executive Branch advised whom about which policies to pursue. . . .

and oral comments would occur throughout the rulemaking process. We assume, therefore, that unless expressly forbidden by Congress, such intra-executive contacts[6] may take place, both during and after the public comment period; the only real issue is whether they must be noted and summarized in the docket.

The court recognizes the basic need of the President and his White House staff to monitor the consistency of executive agency regulations with Administration policy. He and his White House advisers surely must be briefed fully and frequently about rules in the making, and their contributions to policymaking considered. The executive power under our Constitution, after all, is not shared—it rests exclusively with the President. The idea of a "plural executive," or a President with a council of state, was considered and rejected by the Constitutional Convention. Instead the Founders chose to risk the potential for tyranny inherent in placing power in one person, in order to gain the advantages of accountability fixed on a single source. . . .

The authority of the President to control and supervise executive policymaking is derived from the Constitution; the desirability of such control is demonstrable from the practical realities of administrative rulemaking. Regulations such as those involved here demand a careful weighing of cost, environmental, and energy considerations. They also have broad implications for national economic policy. Our form of government simply could not function effectively or rationally if key executive policymakers were isolated from each other and from the Chief Executive. Single mission agencies do not always have the answers to complex regulatory problems. An overworked administrator exposed on a 24–hour basis to a dedicated but zealous staff needs to know the arguments and ideas of policymakers in other agencies as well as in the White House.

We recognize, however, that there may be instances where the docketing of conversations between the President or his staff and other Executive Branch officers or rulemakers may be necessary to ensure due process. This may be true, for example, where such conversations directly concern the outcome of adjudications or quasi-adjudicatory proceedings; there is no inherent executive power to control the rights of individuals in such settings.[7] Docketing may also be necessary in some circumstances where a

---

6. In this case we need not decide the effect upon rulemaking proceedings of a failure to disclose so-called "conduit" communications, in which administration or interagency contacts serve as mere conduits for private parties in order to get the latter's off-the-record views into the proceeding. EDF alleges that many of the executive comments here fell into that category. We note that the Department of Justice Office of Legal Counsel has taken the position that it may be improper for White House advisers to act as conduits for outsiders. It has therefore recommended that Council of Economic Advisers officials summarize and place in rulemaking records a compilation of all written or oral comments they receive relevant to particular proceedings. EDF has given us no reason to believe that a policy similar to this was not followed here, or that unrecorded conduit communications exist in this case; we therefore decline to authorize further discovery simply on the unsubstantiated hypothesis that some such communications may be unearthed thereby. Cf. Citizens to Preserve Overton Park, Inc. v. Volpe, 401 U.S. 402, 420 (1971).

7. Myers v. United States, 272 U.S. 52, 135 (1926) ("there may be duties of a quasi-judicial character imposed on executive tribunals whose decisions after hearings affect the

statute like this one *specifically requires* that essential "information or data" upon which a rule is based be docketed. But in the absence of any further Congressional requirements, we hold that it was not unlawful in this case for EPA not to docket a face-to-face policy session involving the President and EPA officials during the post-comment period, since EPA makes no effort to base the rule on any "data or information" arising from that meeting. . . .

The purposes of full-record review which underlie the need for disclosing ex parte conversations in some settings do not require that courts know the details of every White House contact, including a Presidential one, in this informal rulemaking setting. After all, any rule issued here with or without White House assistance must have the requisite *factual support* in the rulemaking record, and under this particular statute the Administrator may not base the rule in whole or in part on any *"information or data"* which is not in the record, no matter what the source. The courts will monitor all this, but they need not be omniscient to perform their role effectively. Of course, it is always possible that undisclosed Presidential prodding may direct an outcome that *is* factually based on the record, but different from the outcome that would have obtained in the absence of Presidential involvement. In such a case, it would be true that the political process did affect the outcome in a way the courts could not police. But we do not believe that Congress intended that the courts convert informal rulemaking into a rarified technocratic process, unaffected by political considerations or the presence of Presidential power. In sum, we find that the existence of intra-Executive Branch meetings during the post-comment period, and the failure to docket one such meeting involving the President, violated neither the procedures mandated by the Clean Air Act nor due process.

(b) Meetings Involving Alleged Congressional Pressure

Finally, EDF challenges the rulemaking on the basis of alleged Congressional pressure, citing principally two meetings with Senator Byrd. EDF asserts that under the controlling case law the political interference demonstrated in this case represents a separate and independent ground for invalidating this rulemaking. But among the cases EDF cites in support of its position, only D.C. Federation of Civic Associations v. Volpe, 459 F.2d 1231 (D.C.Cir.1971), cert. denied 405 U.S. 1030 (1972), seems relevant to the facts here.

In D.C. Federation the Secretary of Transportation, pursuant to applicable federal statutes, made certain safety and environmental findings in designating a proposed bridge as part of the interstate highway system. Civic associations sought to have these determinations set aside for their failure to meet certain statutory standards, and because of possible tainting by reason of improper Congressional influence. Such influence chiefly included public statements by the Chairman of the House Appropriations Subcommittee on the District of Columbia, Representative Natcher, indi-

interest of individuals, the discharge of which the President cannot in a particular case properly influence or control").

cating in no uncertain terms that money earmarked for the construction of the District of Columbia's subway system would be withheld unless the Secretary approved the bridge. While a majority of this court could not decide whether Representative Natcher's extraneous pressure had in fact influenced the Secretary's decision, a majority did agree on the controlling principle of law: "that the decision [of the Secretary] would be invalid if based in whole or in part on the pressures emanating from Representative Natcher." In remanding to the Secretary for new determinations concerning the bridge, however, the court went out of its way to "emphasize that we have not found—nor, for that matter, have we sought—any suggestion of impropriety or illegality in the actions of Representative Natcher and others who strongly advocate the bridge." The court remanded simply so that the Secretary could make this decision strictly and solely on the basis of considerations made relevant by Congress in the applicable statute.

D.C. Federation thus requires that two conditions be met before an administrative rulemaking may be overturned simply on the grounds of Congressional pressure. First, the content of the pressure upon the Secretary is designed to force him to decide upon factors not made relevant by Congress in the applicable statute. Representative Natcher's threats were of precisely that character, since deciding to approve the bridge in order to free the "hostage" mass transit appropriation was not among the decision-making factors Congress had in mind when it enacted the highway approval provisions of Title 23 of the United States Code. Second, the Secretary's determination must be affected by those extraneous considerations.

In the case before us, there is no persuasive evidence that either criterion is satisfied. Senator Byrd requested a meeting in order to express "strongly" his already well-known views that the sulfur dioxide standards' impact on coal reserves was a matter of concern to him. EPA initiated a second responsive meeting to report its reaction to the reserve data submitted by the NCA.[8] In neither meeting is there any allegation that EPA made any commitments to Senator Byrd. The meetings did underscore Senator Byrd's deep concerns for EPA, but there is no evidence he attempted actively to use "extraneous" pressures to further his position. Americans rightly expect their elected representatives to voice their grievances and preferences concerning the administration of our laws. We believe it entirely proper for Congressional representatives vigorously to represent the interests of their constituents before administrative agencies engaged in informal, general policy rulemaking, so long as individual Congressmen do not frustrate the intent of Congress as a whole as expressed in statute, nor undermine applicable rules of procedure. Where Congressmen keep their comments focused on the substance of the proposed rule—and we have no substantial evidence to cause us to believe Senator Byrd did not do so here[9]—administrative agencies are expected to

8. [Ed.] See note 4 above.

9. The only hint we are provided that extraneous "threats" were made comes from a newspaper article which states, in part,

"The ceiling decision came after two weeks of what one Senate source called

'hard-ball arm-twisting' by Byrd and other coal state Senators. Byrd summoned Costle and White House adviser Stuart Eizenstat *strongly hinting* that the Administration needs his support on strategic arms limitation treaty (SALT) and the windfall profits

balance Congressional pressure with the pressures emanating from all other sources. To hold otherwise would deprive the agencies of legitimate sources of information and call into question the validity of nearly every controversial rulemaking.

In sum, we conclude that EPA's adoption of the 1.2 lbs./MBtu emissions ceiling was free from procedural error. The post-comment period contacts here violated neither the statute nor the integrity of the proceeding. . . .

Affirmed.

NOTES

(1) Judge Wald came to the bench from a career in public interest practice, and an important position in the Department of Justice. Perhaps her reaction to the rulemaking here owes something to that background. Note that most of the arguments concerning the inappropriateness of contacts are based § 307 of the Clean Air Act, which explicitly defines rulemaking records. See p. 540. The APA has no corresponding provision, suggesting that Judge Wald's reasoning from presidential responsibility would have even more force in the ordinary rulemaking case.

Instructive contrasts can be drawn between this case and a later decision involving presidential pressure on an adjudication, Portland Audubon Society v. The Endangered Species Committee, p. 444. One of the most evident was relied on by the Portland Audubon court to distinguish Sierra Club: "The decision in Costle that the contacts were not impermissible was based explicitly on the fact that the proceeding involved was informal rulemaking to which the APA restrictions on ex parte communications are not applicable. In fact, while the Costle court recognized that political pressure from the President may not be inappropriate in informal rulemaking proceedings, it acknowledged that the contrary is true in formal adjudications. Because Congress has decided that Committee determinations are formal adjudications, Costle supports, rather than contradicts, the conclusion that the President and his staff are subject to the APA's ex parte communication ban."

Perhaps less obvious is that the Portland Audubon petitioners met the burden of production necessary to justify judicial inquiry into possibly inappropriate political influence. By contrast, Judge Wald remarks that EDF simply asserted irregularities, without proof beyond a single newspaper article in the Washington Post, which did not suffice.[10] If Senator Byrd had, in fact, secured a concession from EPA in return for his support for

tax, according to Senate and Administration sources."

The Washington Post, May 5, 1979, at A–1 (emphasis supplied). We do not believe that a single newspaper account of strong "hint[s]" represents substantial evidence of extraneous pressure significant enough to warrant a finding of unlawful congressional interference.

10. What did not suffice for Judge Wald was nonetheless taken seriously by others. Compare Thomas O. McGarity, Presidential Control of Regulatory Agency Decisionmaking, 36 Am.U.L.Rev. 433 (1987), p. 223 above (believed) with Bruce A. Ackerman and William A. Hassler, Clean Coal/Dirty Air 179 n.24 (1981) (not proved).

the Panama Canal treaty, the D.C Federation principle would have been violated. The challenge lies in being able to invoke the sort of probing that cases like the Morgan series, p. 394ff. and Citizens to Preserve Overton Park v. Volpe, p. 989, strongly (and understandably?) discourage.

PLMRS Narrowband Corp. v. FCC, 182 F.3d 995, 1002 (D.C.Cir.1999), noted at p. 676, rejected a claim of disqualifying bias, remarking: "Generally, we are unable to view the motivations of an agency official except as through a glass, darkly, and the glass may be tinted not by the official's unalterable prejudgment but by legitimate policy preconceptions; in a particular instance, the cause may be exceedingly difficult to discern." In the same case, the court refused to give weight to a videotape of a Commission meeting (very early in the rulemaking process) in which the Commissioners could be heard referring approvingly to a factor a statute explicitly made irrelevant to their decision. "It is fundamental that 'agency opinions, like judicial opinions, speak for themselves.' Checkosky v. SEC, 23 F.3d 452, 489 (D.C.Cir.1994). Rendered at the conclusion of all the agency's processes and deliberations, they represent the agency's final considered judgment upon matters of policy the Congress has entrusted to it. ... We do not think the evidence that two Commissioners initially flirted with an impermissible rationale suffices to demonstrate that the permissible rationale given a year and one-half later in the Commission's published opinion was a mere pretext. Otherwise, it would seem, almost any slip of the tongue during an agency's decisionmaking process could be fatal, contrary to the settled principle that up to the point of announcement, agency decisions are freely changeable, as are the bases of those decisions."

What does it take, then, to meet the threshold burden? In Portland Audubon, petitioners produced two detailed news accounts, undergirded by counsel's sworn assertions of conversations with high officials in a position to corroborate those stories. When the White House itself provides this data for the rulemaking record, of course, these difficulties do not arise.

(2) HAZARDOUS WASTE TREATMENT COUNCIL V. EPA, 886 F.2d 355 (D.C.Cir. 1989), cert. denied 498 U.S. 849 (1990), was a rulemaking in which members of a congressional committee apparently succeeded in having their interpretation of earlier legislation adopted by the agency. Compare Pillsbury v. FTC, p. 450 above. EPA was acting under a statute that called upon it to specify methods "which substantially diminish the toxicity of [hazardous] waste or substantially reduce the likelihood of migration of hazardous constituents from the waste so that short-term and long-term threats to human health and the environment are minimized." EPA had initially proposed a rule that would pay some attention to the degree of risk the materials were thought to present, as well as to the technology available to deal with the hazards. Its final rule required adoption of the best demonstrated available technology (BDAT), even if the use of BDAT would produce more protection than would be required by relevant health screening standards. EPA's *complete* explanation of this choice, quoted by the court, was as follows:

> Although a number of comments on the proposed rule favored the first approach; that is, the use of screening levels to "cap" treatment that can be achieved under BDAT, several commenters, including eleven

members of Congress, argued strongly that this approach did not fulfill the intent of the law. They asserted that because of the scientific uncertainty inherent in risk-based decisions, Congress expressly directed the Agency to set treatment standards based on the capabilities of existing technology. The Agency believes that the technology-based approach adopted in today's final rule, although not the only approach allowable under the law, best responds to the above-stated comments. Accordingly, the final rule establishes treatment standards under RCRA section 3004(m) based exclusively on levels achievable by BDAT. The Agency believes that the treatment standards will generally be protective of human health and the environment. Levels less stringent than BDAT may also be protective. The plain language of the statute does not compel the Agency to set treatment standards based exclusively on the capabilities of existing technology. ... By calling for standards that minimize threats to human health and the environment, the statute clearly allows for the kind of risk-based standard originally proposed by the Agency. However, the plain language of the statute does not preclude a technology-based approach. This is made clear by the legislative history accompanying the introduction of the final section 3004(m) language. The legislative history provides that "[T]he requisite levels of [sic] methods of treatment established by the Agency should be the best that has been demonstrated to be achievable" and that "[T]he intent here is to require utilization of available technology in lieu of continued land disposal without prior treatment." (Vol. 130, Cong.Rec. 9178, (daily ed., July 25, 1984)). Thus, EPA is acting within the authority vested by the statute in selecting [sic] to promulgate a final regulation using its proposed alternative approach of setting treatment standards based on BDAT. The Agency believes that its major purpose in adopting the risk-based approach of the proposal (i.e., to allow different standards for relatively low-risk, low-hazard wastes) may be better addressed through changes in other aspects of its regulatory program. For example, EPA is considering the use of its risk-based methodologies to characterize wastes as hazardous pursuant to section 3001.

51 Fed.Reg. at 40,578.

The court might have held that the statute required the common-sense approach EPA had first proposed.[11] It agreed, however, that the meaning EPA chose was available. Nonetheless, "[t]his explanation is inadequate. It should go without saying that members of Congress have no power, once a statute has been passed, to alter its interpretation by post-hoc 'explanations' of what it means; there may be societies where 'history' belongs to those in power, but ours is not among them. In our scheme of things, we consider legislative history because it is just that: history. It forms the background against which Congress adopted the relevant statute. Post-enactment statements are a different matter, and they are not to be considered by an agency or by a court as legislative history. An agency has an obligation to consider the comments of legislators, of course, but on the

---

11. Cf. Stephen Breyer, Breaking the Vicious Circle: Toward Effective Risk Regula-tion (1993); Industrial Union Dept. AFL–CIO v. American Petroleum Inst., p. 58 above.

same footing as it would those of other commenters; such comments may have, as Justice Frankfurter [sic] said in a different context, 'power to persuade, if lacking power to control.' Skidmore v. Swift & Co., 323 U.S. 134, 140 (1944).

"It is unclear whether EPA recognized this fundamental point. On the one hand, it suggested that the adoption of a BDAT-only regime 'best respond[ed]' to the comments, suggesting that the statute required such a rule. On the other hand, EPA went on at some length to establish that the comments were in error, in that screening levels are permissible under the statute. EPA's 'rationale,' in other words, is that several members of Congress (among others) urged upon it the claim that Proposition X ('Congress mandated BDAT') requires Result A ('EPA adopts BDAT'), and that although Proposition X is inaccurate, the best response to the commenters is to adopt Result A."

A concurrence by Judge Silberman was even more pointed: "EPA's explanation ... is utterly devoid of any rationale whatsoever for the agency's statutory construction or its policy choice." Pressure, then, even if it may be acquiesced in, does not relieve the agency of its obligation of intelligible explanation.

(3) Oversight influence by the President and/or Congress occurs much more frequently than comes to light. Where the agency affirmatively embraces the guidance it receives, outsider may find it hard to establish that error occurred. In PUBLIC CITIZEN HEALTH RESEARCH GROUP v. TYSON, 796 F.2d 1479 (D.C.Cir.1986), OMB's objections under E.O. 12291, the predecessor to E.O. 12866, had contributed to OSHA's failure to adopt a short term exposure limit (STEL) for ethylene oxide in 1984. OMB's "contribution" came to light only because OSHA was acting under the time constraints of a previously set judicial deadline of June 15, 1984 for issuance of an ethylene oxide rule: "On June 13, 1984, OSHA sent the rule to OMB for review. The next day, OIRA Administrator DeMuth responded with a detailed letter objecting that the STEL was insufficiently supported by the health effects data and would not be cost effective. The speed and cogency of this response suggest strongly that OIRA had already negotiated with OSHA concerning the shape of the final rule, before its formal submission for review. The approach of the court's deadline would have compelled such a process if OIRA's review was to be meaningful. The next day, OSHA forwarded its final rule to the Federal Register. In its haste, OSHA simply deleted the STEL and all reference to it from the final standard, and blacked out the portions of the draft preamble referring to support for the STEL. Conceding that this decision was based 'largely in response to reservations expressed by the Office of Management and Budget,' OSHA then announced further rulemaking proceedings on the issue of a STEL. These proceedings also terminated without promulgation of a STEL."[12] Finding OSHA's refusal to adopt a STEL inadequately explained, the court did not have to decide "sharply contested" constitutional questions about the procedure. See p. 602 above.

---

12.   Harold Bruff, Presidential Management of Agency Rulemaking, 57 Geo. Wash. L.Rev. 533 (1989).

In NEW YORK V. REILLY, 969 F.2d 1147 (D.C.Cir.1992), EPA had proposed rules to govern new incinerators of municipal waste under provisions of the Clean Air Act (CAA). The proposals included a total ban on incinerating lead-acid vehicle batteries and a requirement that operators reduce the weight of incinerated waste by 25% through separating out recyclable or recoverable materials.

"On December 4, 1990, EPA submitted a package of final rules to the Office of Management and Budget (OMB) for review pursuant to Executive Order 12291. OMB did not approve the sections of the proposed rules covering materials separation and battery burning. EPA then appealed to the President's Council on Competitiveness.[13] In a 'Fact Sheet,' the Council rejected the proposed rules on materials separation as being inconsistent with 'several of the Administration's regulatory principles,' including their failure to 'meet the benefit/cost requirements for regulatory policy laid out in Executive Order 12291.'[14] The Fact Sheet also noted the Council's opinion that the materials separation requirement did not constitute a 'performance standard' and that it violated principles of federalism. EPA subsequently abandoned the materials separation and battery burning provisions when it promulgated its final rules. . . .

"Under the CAA, promulgated rules must be accompanied by 'an explanation of the reasons for any major changes in the promulgated rule from the proposed rule.' 42 U.S.C. § 7607(d)(6)(A). The Act also requires the court to sustain the Administrator's actions unless they are 'arbitrary, capricious, an abuse of discretion, or otherwise not in accordance with law.' 42 U.S.C. § 7607(d)(9)(A).[15] . . . [Applying this standard,] even if the evidence supports both sides of an issue, we will sustain the agency 'if a reasonable person could come to either conclusion on that evidence.' Public Citizen Health Research Group v. Tyson, 796 F.2d 1479, 1485 (D.C.Cir. 1986). We are particularly deferential when reviewing agency actions involving policy decisions based on uncertain technical information. Id. at 1505 ('As long as Congress delegates power to an agency to regulate on the borders of the unknown, courts cannot interfere with reasonable interpretations of equivocal evidence.')."

The court found adequate support for EPA's decision to omit the materials separation provision, and then turned to the Council's role. "After reviewing the record, we conclude that EPA did exercise its expertise in this case. The procedural history of the rules at issue demonstrates that the Council's views were important in formulating EPA's final policy decision regarding materials separation. The fact that EPA reevaluated its conclusions in light of the Council's advice, however, does not mean that

13. The Council was created in 1989 and served throughout the Bush administration. It was chaired by the Vice President and its members include other executive branch officials. Agencies whose regulations have not been approved by OMB may appeal OMB's decision to the Council.

14. The Fact Sheet did not mention the proposed rule prohibiting lead-acid battery combustion.

15. The Administrative Procedure Act contains no provision analogous to § 7607(d)(6)(A) and we express no opinion on the standard of review under the APA applicable to an agency decision not to adopt all or part of a proposed rule.

EPA failed to exercise its own expertise in promulgating the final rules.[16"] EPA's abandonment of the proposal prohibiting battery incineration, in the court's judgment, was not similarly supported by EPA's reasoning; it remanded that aspect to EPA for further explanation.

On July 31, 2002, neither Shepardizing nor a Lexis search for "(12,866 or 12866) and (president or OMB or OIRA)" returned any similar cases.

(4) *Pressure in the Realm of Uncertainty.* Note that both these cases involved not only presidential influence, but also Sierra Club's *other* characteristic: technical judgments of the greatest difficulty. Thus, the reviewing judges faced not only concerns about the impact of political oversight in the rulemaking, but also substantive complexities for which a generalist education had not prepared them. Both decisions note the "extreme deference" to agency judgments that courts must show when agencies act "on the borders of the unknown." Perhaps this gives particular point to Judge Wald's emphasis on accepting EPA decisions within the range of judgment the record may permit—even when the court knows that choice may have been swayed by presidential preferences.

Professor Elena Kagan argues that the fact of a presidential directive, signaling the intervention of a politically responsible official, should *increase* the extent to which courts defer to the "agency's" factual and policy judgments. Presidential Administration, 114 Harv. L. Rev. 2245 (2001), pp. 213 and 218 above. For Judge PATRICIA WALD AND JONATHAN SIEGEL, THE D.C. CIRCUIT AND THE STRUGGLE FOR CONTROL OF PRESIDENTIAL INFORMATION, 90 Geo.L.J. 737, 766 (2002), the President's participation is best protected by, instead, simply ignoring it on judicial review:

"The court's decision speaks volumes about the special solicitude the court shows for the activities of the President. The court rejected the old-fashioned, New Deal-era view of rulemaking as 'a rarified, technocratic process, unaffected by political considerations or the presence of Presidential power.' It recognized that the President has constitutionally derived power to control and supervise executive policymaking. The court found such power to be desirable, noting that the President's direction can give a valuable, national perspective to decisions made by single-mission agencies.

"Although the main significance of Sierra Club is its forthright recognition of the appropriate and inevitable role of politics in the administrative rulemaking process, the court's decision also has important implications for presidential information disputes. If an administrative rule could be overturned on the ground that pressure from the President caused an agency to act differently than it otherwise would have, then it would logically follow that petitioners challenging a rule would have a right to learn about the President's interactions with agency decisionmakers. The D.C. Circuit's

---

16. The petitioners also challenge some of the Council's comments. First, they challenge the Council's conclusion that the separation plan would violate principles of federalism because waste management is traditionally a state and local concern. Second, they challenge the Council's contention that the separation requirement is not a 'standard of performance' because it sets a strict standard rather than allowing flexibility in meeting a particular goal. We do not address the merits of either of these arguments as neither appears to have been a decisive factor in EPA's decision to omit the materials separation requirement.

opinion in Sierra Club protects this sensitive presidential information by making it legally irrelevant. Under Sierra Club, a presidential directive to an agency engaged in rulemaking will not add anything to the validity of the agency's final rule (which must be otherwise justified by the rulemaking record), but neither will it detract from the validity of that rule (assuming the rule is so justified). By decoupling the legal validity of the rule from any presidential action that may have led to it, the D.C. Circuit not only protected the President's flexibility to give direction to executive agencies, but also removed any reason why parties challenging the rule would have a valid need to know about the President's actions. The principle of Sierra Club therefore plays an important role in guarding the confidentiality of the President's activities."

If the agency can claim no review "credit" from the President's involvement, does that imply that, from a legal perspective, the decision is strictly the agency's to make and defend? Which of these two views, Professor Kagan's or Wald–Siegel's, should prevail, and why?

(iv) WHAT FUTURE SHAPE(S) FOR NOTICE-AND-COMMENT RULEMAKING?

It should now be evident that, at least for regulations of significance, rulemaking procedure has become far more complex than the authors of § 553 ever imagined—and principally in realms dominated by political rather than legal interactions. As the graphic opposite illustrates, the NPRM is no longer, (if it ever was) the point of first involvement for the public, or for political processes outside the agency. Rather, the Notice now caps an intensive series of political and analytic processes, generally open to the public, during which momentum inevitably builds for whatever proposal emerges as the compromise. In REINVENTING RULEMAKING, 41 Duke L.J. 1490, 1492–93 (1992), E. Donald Elliott, formerly Assistant Administrator and General Counsel of the EPA wrote: "What was once (perhaps) a means for securing public input into agency decisions has become today primarily a method for compiling a record for judicial review. No administrator in Washington turns to full-scale notice-and-comment rulemaking when she is genuinely interested in obtaining input from interested parties. Notice-and-comment rulemaking is to public participation as Japanese Kabuki theater is to human passions—a highly stylized process for displaying in a formal way the essence of something which in real life takes place in other venues. To secure the genuine reality, rather than a formal show, of public participation, a variety of techniques is available—from informal meetings with trade associations and other constituency groups, to roundtables, to floating 'trial balloons' in speeches or leaks to the trade press, to the more formal techniques of advisory committees and negotiated rulemaking."

To similar effect, Professor CORNELIUS M. KERWIN reported, in RULEMAKING 193 (2d ed. 1999), the results of his survey of 180 typical organizational participants: "Coalition formation and informal contacts before the notice of proposed rulemaking is issued are perceived to be the most effective. On reflection, these results should not be surprising. Contact with an agency before it has committed itself to a particular proposal allows the interest group to influence the earliest thinking about the content of the rule. Coalition formation increases the number of groups that will communicate a consistent message to an agency. Comments ... and grass-roots

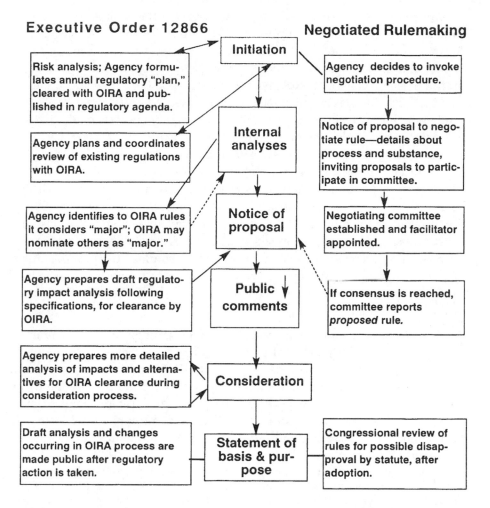

mobilization are also viewed as effective. However effective informal contacts may be, groups can ill-afford to fail to put their views on the public record by providing written comments ... Nearly half of the respondents rate informal contacts after the notice of proposed rulemaking as highly effective. This may point to situations in which agencies are surprised by the results of public comment and work informally with interest groups to fix the proposed rule."[1]

1. Professor Kerwin surveyed unions, trade associations, citizen groups, thinktanks, etc. His results are summarized in this table, appearing at p. 195 of his book:

Ratings by Interest Groups of the Effectiveness
of Techniques (percent)

Effectiveness	Written comments	Attendance at hearings	Formation of coalitions	Mobilization of grassroots support	Informal contact with agency before notice	Informal contact with agency after notice
Least effective	4.6	12.5	0.8	7.8	6.8	10.9
Somewhat effective	11.5	24.2	8.5	17.8	8.3	21.1
Effective	29.8	30.5	21.5	24.8	13.6	18.8
Very effective	38.2	21.1	38.5	34.1	37.9	32.8
Most effective	16.0	11.7	30.8	15.5	33.3	16.4

(1) *Return to Vermont Yankee.* As one of the Notes to Vermont Yankee's perhaps Quixotic call for strict adherence to the APA's terms as a "formula on which opposing social and political forces have come to rest," we quoted from ANTONIN SCALIA, VERMONT YANKEE: THE APA, THE D.C. CIRCUIT, AND THE SUPREME COURT, 1978 Sup. Ct. Rev. 345, 404–08: "It seems to me . . . that if the continuing fragmentation of mandated administrative procedure is to be abated, what is called for is a more modest expectation of what the APA can and should achieve, and a design that will accord with the realities. . . . I would settle for an APA that contains not merely three but ten or fifteen basic procedural formats—an inventory large enough to provide the basis for a whole spectrum of legislative compromises without the necessity for shopping elsewhere." If Congress wants to design new APA provisions on informal rulemaking, to what extent should it attempt to distinguish the routine, from the significant, from the more significant— and provide appropriately varying procedural formulas? In those formulas, what role should be played by the White House? The Congress? The courts? Members of the public who may be controlled, or benefitted, by the regulations adopted?

(2) *Monday Morning Quarterbacking.* The "Monday morning quarter-backing" that the Vermont Yankee court feared from free-wheeling judicial review is equally possible as a description of OIRA's participation—at least when it comes at the very end of the rule development process. And the agency subject to it may experience the very same temptations to slow down, to be conservative in choices and excessive in explanation. What is often called the "ossification"[2] of notice and comment rulemaking is

---

2. David Spence, "A Public Choice Progressivism, Continued" in Symposium: Getting Beyond Cynicism: New Theories of the Regulatory State, 87 Cornell L. Rev. 397, 413 n.64: "There is a very large literature on the ossification problem." See, e.g., Robert A. Anthony & David A. Codevilla, Pro–Ossification: A Harder Look at Agency Policy Statements, 31 Wake Forest L. Rev. 667, 676–80 (1996); Jody Freeman, Collaborative Governance in the Administrative State, 45 UCLA L. Rev. 1, 18 (1997) (arguing that 'adversarialism . . . has contributed to a rigid rulemaking and implementation process that fails to encourage creativity, adaptation, and cooperation in solving regulatory problems'); William Funk, Bargaining Toward the New Millennium: Regulatory Negotiation and the Subversion of the Public Interest, 46 Duke L.J. 1351 (1997) (defending formalism on democratic theory grounds); Thomas O. McGarity, A Cost–Benefit State, 50 Admin. L. Rev. 7, 26 (1998); Thomas O. McGarity, The Courts and the Ossification of Rulemaking: A Response to Professor Seidenfeld, 75 Tex. L. Rev. 525 (1997); Thomas O. McGarity, Some Thoughts on "Deossifying" the Rulemaking Process, 41 Duke. L.J. 1385 (1992); Richard J. Pierce, Jr., Seven Ways to Deossify Agency Rulemaking, 47 Admin. L. Rev. 59, 82–86 (1995); Mark Seidenfeld, Bending the Rules: Flexible Regulation and Constraints on Agency Discretion, 51 Admin. L. Rev. 429, 494–95 (1999) (arguing, among other points, that agencies' ability to evade procedural mandates helps ameliorate the ossification problem); Mark Seidenfeld, Demystifying Deossification: Rethinking Recent Proposals to Modify Judicial Review of Notice and Comment Rulemaking, 75 Tex. L. Rev. 483 (1997); Cass R. Sunstein, Congress, Constitutional Moments, and the Cost–Benefit

frequently ascribed to the influence of judicial review. You will be in a better position to assess that claim when you have studied the materials in Chapter VIII. Here we briefly consider two other possible culprits, rulemaking review and the Congressional Review Act—each of which imposes its own tax on agency resources.

(a) *Rulemaking review.* "Good government" recommendations frequently advocate periodic review of regulations for continuing utility and efficiency. While appealing in theory, such requirements can be a significant source of externally generated pressure on rulemaking activity.[3] From its inception, the Regulatory Flexibility Act required agencies to review all regulations affecting small business every ten years; the 1995 amendments put teeth into that obligation. Presidents have contributed their share of pressure. The first President Bush, in anticipation of the 1992 elections, announced a moratorium on new rulemaking while old regulations were reviewed. President Clinton, in Section 5 of E.O. 12866, required agencies to submit a "program" for periodic review of significant regulation. Current OIRA Director John Graham, recognizing the burden of universal review requirements, has asked the public for reasoned nominations of regulations needing review. THOMAS O. MCGARITY, JOGGING IN PLACE: THE BUSH ADMINISTRATION'S FRESHMAN YEAR ENVIRONMENTAL RECORD, 32 Envtl. L. Rep. 10709 (2002): "Another indication of the OIRA's desire to play a much more active role in day-to-day affairs is the invitation that it offered in May 2001, to the public to 'nominate specific regulations that we should propose for reform.' On the basis of the 71 submissions, the OIRA identified a list of 23 'high priority regulatory review issues' that warranted further attention and could potentially result in a 'prompt letter' to an agency demanding additional "deliberation and response." Thirteen of the 23 rules on the so-called hit list are environmental regulations. Included on the list are such recently completed actions as the Forest Service's roadless area conservation rule and EPA's arsenic in drinking water rule. All of the accepted recommendations came from either industry groups or the industry-supported Mercatus Center at George Mason University."

(b) *Congressional review of rules.* Congress created a potent rulemaking pressure point for itself in SBREFA, its 1995 revisions of the Regulatory Flexibility Act. Subtitle E establishes a formal mechanism for post-adoption congressional review of virtually *all* agency actions meeting the APA's definition of "rule"—that is, for interpretative rules and statements of general policy publication as well as regulations adopted following § 553's notice-and-comment procedure. See 5 U.S.C. § 801 et seq. "Major" rules (essentially, those meeting the test of E.O. 12866) may not take effect until the passage of 60 legislative days during which Congress can consider

---

State, 48 Stan. L. Rev. 247 (1996) (advocating more adaptive rules)." See also William S. Jordan, III, Ossification Revisited: Does Arbitrary and Capricious Review Significantly Interfere With Agency Ability to Achieve Regulatory Goals Through Informal Rulemaking? 94 Nw.U.L.Rev. 393, 443–44) (2000) (In a word, "No.")

3. Neil R. Eisner and Judith S. Kaleta, Federal Agency Review of Existing Regulations, 48 Admin.L.Rev. 139 (1996), report the results of a sixteen-agency survey of federal agency practice, suggesting both roadblocks and useful steps to secure effective agency program and minimize predictable resource constraints.

and pass resolutions of disapproval under "fast-track" procedures.[4] Other rules can be disapproved but are not stayed.

Significantly, the Act provides that if a resolution of disapproval is enacted, the resolution deprives the agency of authority to enact the same or a substantially similar rule, unless and until it receives a fresh legislative grant of authority to do so. 5 U.S.C. § 801(b)(2). One such resolution has thus far been adopted. It disapproved a regulation, adopted late in the Clinton administration, to protect workers from ergonomic injuries (the product of repetitive motion and, arguably, poorly designed work equipment). Although President Bush and his Secretary of Labor promised swift administrative action to produce a sound Republican solution to this workplace problem, the fact of the resolution's passage casts a shadow on the Department's legal authority to do so. "Under this procedure ... a simple and unelaborated 'No!' withdraws from agencies a range of substantive authority that cannot be determined without subsequent litigation. This uncertainty is in effect a delegation to the courts, without intelligible principle, of power to narrow agency authority. ... The text of the statute has not been changed; but Congress's particular and unexplained action raises the risk that a future court may find unauthorized a rule that otherwise would come within the language of the unamended enabling statute." Daniel Cohen & Peter L. Strauss, Congressional Review of Agency Regulations, 49 Admin. L. Rev. 95 (1997).

If, as President (or, for that matter, as the head of OIRA), you expected resolutions of disapproval to be rare at best, would/should that make you indifferent to the Congressional Review Act? In your editors' experience, few in Washington expect the Congressional Review Act to be used except during the weeks immediately following a change in presidential administrations—and only one of President Clinton's "midnight rules" suffered such a fate. Nonetheless, GAO and the agencies are assiduously engaged in the paperwork routines that Subtitle E creates, and this adds to the "expense" of rulemaking. See, e.g., Congressional Review Act: Implementation and Coordination, GAO/T–OGC–98–38, testimony by GAO's general counsel to a House oversight committee reporting that as of March 1998 115 major and 7,605 non-major rules had been received by his office. The same report found several hundred rules that had not been filed (and thus, under the statute, were ineffective), others whose effective date had not been postponed as required; and still more whose status as APA "rules" was not admitted. The report found several agencies that "told us they were unaware of CRA or of the CRA filing requirement," and repeatedly suggests that OIRA had not been cooperative in implementing the new statute. ·

(3) *An Example*. GAO reports on individual rules filed with it under the CRA reveal a good deal about the rigors of contemporary rulemaking. For example, OGC 98/45,[5] discussing an EPA rule, "National Emission

---

4. As these resolutions are presented to the President for signing or veto, no separation of powers problem is presented.

5. GAO's reports on major rules are accessible at http://www.gao.gov/deci-

sions/majrule/majrule.htm. As of July 31, 2002, 28 reports on major rules were indexed

Standards for Hazardous Air Pollutants for Source Category: Pulp and Paper Production; Effluent Limitations Guidelines, Pretreatment Standards, and New Source Performance Standards: Pulp, Paper, and Paperboard Category," 63 Fed. Reg.18504 (April 15, 1998), includes the following analysis:

"(i) Cost-benefit analysis

EPA performed an Economic Analysis of the final rule, including the Clean Air Act and Clean Water Act portions of the rule, and the analysis is summarized in the preamble to the final rule. ... The analysis shows that the combined costs of the air and water portions of the rule to be a capital cost of $1.393 billion, with operating and maintenance costs of $211 million and post-and pre-tax annualized costs of $229 million and $351 million, respectively.

While the analysis states that EPA is confident of the cost figures included in the analysis, an estimation of the benefits is more difficult because of EPA's inability to quantitatively evaluate all human and ecosystem benefits and to assign monetary values to these benefits for a comparison in a standard cost-benefit framework. For example, EPA was only able to monetize three of the seven air pollutants affected by the rule.

The analysis also discusses in qualitative terms the benefits of the rule regarding human health, including the health effects for Native American subsistence fishermen and reduction of projected non-cancer effects and improvements in fish and wildlife habitat.

"(ii) Agency actions relevant to the Regulatory Flexibility Act, 5 U.S.C. §§ 603–605, 607, and 609

EPA has certified that the final rule will not have a significant impact on a substantial number of small entities because, using the size standard of fewer than 750 employees, only four firms would be considered small entities. The cost of the Clean Water Act portion of the rule for these entities only exceeded 1 percent of revenues for one of the facilities and in no case did it exceed 3 percent. EPA estimates that the impact of the Clean Air Act maximum achievable control technology portion of the rule in combination with the Clean Water Act portion is that one facility owned by one of the four small entities may close as a result of the combined impact.

"(iii) Agency actions relevant to sections 202–205 of the Unfunded Mandates Reform Act of 1995, 2 U.S.C. §§ 1532–1535.

EPA has determined that the final rule, while not imposing a federal mandate that will result in the expenditure of $100 million or more in any one year, will impose such a mandate on the private sector. Therefore, in compliance with section 202 of the Unfunded Mandates Reform Act, EPA prepared a written statement, including a cost-benefit analysis, assessing the impact of the rule, which is summa-

there for 2002, 72 had been listed for 2001
(only one of those prior to President Bush's
inauguration); and 80 in 2000.

rized in the preamble to the final rule. . . . While EPA determined that the rule will not significantly or uniquely affect any state, local or tribal governments, EPA consulted with state and local air and water pollution control officials primarily regarding implementation issues.

Section 205 of the Act requires agencies to identify and consider a reasonable number of regulatory alternatives and to adopt the least costly, most cost-effective, or least burdensome alternative that achieves the objectives of the rule. The preamble discusses the alternatives considered and why EPA believes that the alternative selected is the least costly and least burdensome consistent with the requirements of the Clean Water Act and the Clean Air Act.

"(iv) Other relevant information or requirements under acts and executive orders Administrative Procedure Act, 5 U.S.C. §§ 551 et seq.

The final rule was issued pursuant to the notice and comment procedures contained in 5 U.S.C. § 553. On December 17, 1993, EPA published a notice of proposed rulemaking on the integrated air and water rules in the Federal Register. 58 Fed. Reg. 66078. On February 10, 1994, EPA held a public hearing so interested parties could present their views on the proposed rule. On March 8, 1996, a notice of proposed rulemaking was published concerning the air portions of the rule. All during this process, EPA issued many notices of data availability and held other meetings with numerous industry stakeholders, trade associations, environmental groups, states, and other interested parties.

In the preamble to the final rule, there is extensive discussion of the comments submitted and the actions and changes to the proposed rule that EPA made as a result of its consideration of the comments.

"Paperwork Reduction Act, 44 U.S.C. §§ 3501–3520

The final rule contains collections of information which are subject to approval by the Office of Management and Budget (OMB) under the Paperwork Reduction Act. The preamble to the final rule contains the required information regarding the collections, including the legal basis and reason for the collections, the number of respondents, and an estimate of the annual burden hours.

EPA estimates that there are approximately 490 respondents that are affected by the air emission rules and must submit an initial applicability notification. Of these 490 respondents, an estimated 155 respondents would be required to perform additional information collection. This results in an estimated burden of 320 hours over the first 3 years after promulgation at a 3–year cost of $29,600 per respondent. The collections have been sent to OMB for approval and the requirement is not effective until approved by OMB and a control number is issued.

"Statutory authorization for the rule

The final rule was issued pursuant to the authority of sections 301, 304, 306, 307, 308, 402, and 501 of the Clean Water Act, 33 U.S.C. §§ 1311, 1314, 1316, 1317, 1318, 1342, and 1361, and sections 112, 114, and 301 of the Clean Air Act, 42 U.S.C. §§ 7412, 7414, and 7601.

"Executive Order No. 12866

The final rule was determined to be an 'economically significant' regulatory action by the Office of Management and Budget. It was reviewed by OMB and approved as meeting the requirements of the Order."

* * * * * * *

Perhaps it is time for a thoughtful assessment of the costs and benefits of new procedural specifications. Additional procedures may make rulemaking more careful, politically responsive, expert and etc. They certainly make it more expensive, in both time and resource requirements. Agencies might then make fewer rules—a good in the eyes of some, but not all—or perhaps they will be tempted to find other means for accomplishing what to them appears to be their necessary business. This chapter began with a pyramid, depicting the relationships among constitutions, statutes, regulations, and lesser agency actions that might also fit the APA's definition of rules. Interpretive rules, statements of general policy, manuals for staff, and the like are ordinarily welcome to the regulated community, as indicators of agency direction and regularity. They offer some assurance that the discretion of the agency's street-level bureaucrats, who are the ones actually responsible for program administration, will be subject to constraint. Suppose, however, that ordinary rulemaking becomes so expensive or clogged that the agency seeks ways to accomplish *outside of § 553* results that properly call for its use?

SECTION 4.   THE PUBLICATION ALTERNATIVE TO NOTICE–AND–COMMENT RULEMAKING

5 U.S.C. § 552(a)(2): . . . A final order, opinion, statement of policy, interpretation, or staff manual or instruction that affects a member of the public may be relied on, used, or cited as precedent by an agency against a party other than an agency only if—

(i) it has been indexed and either made available or published as provided by this paragraph; or

(ii) the party has actual and timely notice of the terms thereof.

5 U.S.C. § 553(b): General notice of proposed rule making shall be published in the Federal Register . . . Except when notice or hearing is required by statute, this subsection does not apply—

(A) to interpretative rules, general statements of policy, or rules of agency organization, procedure, or practice . . .

Air Transport Association of America, Inc. v. Federal Aviation Administration

United States Court of Appeals for the District of Columbia Circuit, 2002.
291 F.3d 49.

■ Before EDWARDS, HENDERSON and GARLAND, CIRCUIT JUDGES.

■ KAREN LECRAFT HENDERSON, Circuit Judge: Air Transport Association of America, Inc. (ATA) and Regional Airline Association (RAA) seek review of the Federal Aviation Administration's November 20, 2000 interpretation (issued by letter) of Federal Aviation Regulation 121.471, 14 C.F.R. § 121.471 (FAR 121.471), and attendant Notice of Enforcement Policy (Notice) entitled "Flight Crewmember Flight Time Limitations and Rest Requirements," published in the Federal Register, 66 Fed. Reg. 27,548 (May 17, 2001). ATA contends the letter interpretation and Notice are inconsistent with the plain language of FAR 121.471. In addition, ATA maintains that the letter interpretation constitutes a substantive change to FAR 121.471 and, accordingly, requires notice-and-comment rulemaking under the Administrative Procedure Act (APA). We disagree.

I

[The regulation in question implemented FAA's statutory responsibility to "promote safe flight of civil aircraft in air commerce [by prescribing] regulations in the interest of safety for the maximum hours or periods of service of aircrew and other employees of air carriers." 49 U.S.C. § 44701(a)(4). The FAA had adopted, via notice and comment rulemaking, a number of "flight time limitations." In 1985, FAR 121.471 set flight time limits and rest requirements for "flight crew members engaged in air transportation." The NPRM for this rule noted that the "current Part 121 rule [governing large transport category airplanes] . . . provides no protection against acute short-term fatigue for crewmembers." As adopted, the regulation set maximum flight time limitations for crew members on yearly, monthly and weekly bases. Most important to the current controversy, it established a maximum of eight hours of flight time between "required rest periods." During the twenty-four consecutive hours preceding "the scheduled completion of any flight segment," a crewmember must be scheduled for a rest period of nine consecutive hours if "scheduled flight time" is for eight hours or fewer; ten consecutive hours if "scheduled flight time" is between eight and nine hours; and eleven consecutive hours if "scheduled flight time" is nine or more hours. The regulation did permit a pre-flight rest of only eight hours if a "compensatory rest period" of somewhat longer duration was provided immediately following the flight. "If a flight crewmember does not receive the required number of hours of rest, the operator and the flight crewmember are in violation of the regulation."

As fliers well know, scheduled and experienced flight times can differ—considerably—and this raised questions about the meaning of FAR 121.471.] On September 26, 2000 Captain Richard D. Rubin, Chairman of the Flight Time–Duty Time Committee of the Allied Pilots Association, submitted to the FAA several questions regarding FAR 121.741, which questions apparently arose as a result of changes in American Airlines's pilot reserve system. On November 20, 2000 FAA Deputy Counsel James Whitlow responded by letter (Whitlow Letter) to Rubin's questions. ... [After restating the rule's terms,] the Whitlow Letter provides that "look-back" rest[1] is computed by using "actual expected flight time and taxi-in time, based on the specific conditions that exist on the day, to determine the scheduled arrival time for purposes of determining whether a flight should be commenced." Whitlow Letter at 3. Irrespective of the carrier's published flight time, then, "scheduled flight time" under FAR 121.471 should be calculated (or recalculated) using the actual conditions on the day of departure regardless whether the length of the flight is longer or shorter than the originally scheduled flight time. Once this information is calculated, "if it is known, or reasonably should be known, that a flight segment will result in less than eight hours of look-back rest for a particular crew, the flight may not leave the gate."[2]

On January 18, 2001 ATA petitioned for review of the Whitlow Letter (No. 01–1027) and RAA intervened. Four months later, the FAA published in the Federal Register note of its intent to "rigorously enforce existing regulations governing flight crewmember rest requirements." Notice, 66 Fed. Reg. at 27,548 (May 17, 2001). The Notice incorporated the Whitlow Letter and advised that, within six months of the date of the Notice's publication, the FAA intended to begin a comprehensive review of flight scheduling practices and to "deal stringently with any violations." Id. ATA and RAA then filed separate petitions for review of the Notice (Nos. 01–1303 and 01–1306). We consolidated for review all three petitions. See July 25, 2001 Consolidation Order. On September 5, 2001 we granted ATA's motion to stay the Notice.

II.

A.   FAA's Interpretation of FAR 121.471

Because the Whitlow Letter constitutes the FAA's interpretation of its own regulation, that interpretation must be afforded substantial deference and upheld unless "plainly erroneous or inconsistent with the regulation." Thomas Jefferson Univ. v. Shalala, 512 U.S. 504, 512 (1994). Accordingly, we defer to the FAA's view unless "an alternative reading is compelled by the regulation's plain language or by other indications of the [agency's] intent at the time of the regulation's promulgation." 512 U.S. at 512. [The court determined that the FAA's interpretation met this test.]

---

1. The FAA defined "look-back rest" in an earlier rulemaking, noting that "the rest requirement is based on the number of flight hours looking back 24 hours from the completion of each flight segment. If a pilot is scheduled for 4 hours of flight time late on the first day and receives a reduced rest of 8 hours, he or she can only be scheduled for up to 5 hours of flight time the following morning, since the flight crewmember cannot be scheduled for 9 or more flight time hours in 24 consecutive hours, based on an 8 hour reduced rest period." Flight Time Limitations and Rest Requirements.

2. If the flight is away from the gate but not yet in the air, the flight may not take off. As a matter of enforcement policy, the FAA will not charge a violation of the rest requirements if a delay that first becomes known after the flight is in the air disrupts the scheduled flight time, provided the required minimum reduced rest and the compensatory rest occur at the completion of that flight segment.

Further, the Whitlow Letter is not inconsistent with the purpose of the 1985 amendment to FAR 121.471. Granted that simplified scheduling and added scheduling flexibility for carriers were two goals of the 1985 amendment, it does not necessarily follow that an interpretation cabining a carrier's flexibility is therefore unauthorized. The Whitlow Letter, while imposing a measure of rigidity, nonetheless maintains the system of flexible scheduling created by the amendment. Moreover, "protection against acute short-term fatigue" of crewmembers was also one of the FAA's goals. The rest requirement regulation was expressly promulgated under FAA's statutory authority to issue "reasonable rules and regulations governing, in the interest of safety, the maximum hours or periods of service of aircrew and other employees of air carriers." . . . Having concluded the FAA's interpretation via the Whitlow Letter represents a permissible construction of FAR 121.471, we do not believe the fact that it may lessen flexibility renders it invalid.

B. APA Issues

The FAA issued the Whitlow Letter without formal notice and comment procedures. In so doing, ATA claims, the FAA violated the APA because the Whitlow Letter (1) is a substantive, not an interpretative, rule and (2) materially changes the FAA's earlier interpretations of the required rest regulation. We disagree. The interpretation contained in the Whitlow Letter is "fairly encompassed" within the regulation it purports to construe and, therefore, under our circuit precedent is an interpretative rule exempt from notice-and-comment rulemaking. Moreover, none of the FAA's earlier interpretations of FAR 121.471 addresses precisely the issues addressed in the Whitlow Letter. Accordingly, the Whitlow Letter does not mark a departure from the past.

1. Substantive vs. Interpretative Rule

The APA requires federal agencies to publish "general notice of proposed rulemaking" in the Federal Register, 5 U.S.C. § 553(b), and "give interested persons an opportunity to participate in the rule making through submission of written data, views, or arguments," 5 U.S.C. § 553(c). Section 553, however, exempts "interpretative rules" and "general statements of policy" from notice and comment procedures. 5 U.S.C. § 553(b)(3)(A). Nonetheless, it is well established that an agency may not label a substantive change to a rule an interpretation simply to avoid the notice and comment requirements. See Appalachian Power Co. v. EPA, 208 F.3d 1015, 1024 (D.C.Cir.2000).

The distinction between a substantive rule and an interpretive rule can be less than clear-cut. One factor we consider in distinguishing between the two is "whether the interpretation itself carries the force and effect of law, . . . or rather whether it spells out a duty fairly encompassed within the regulation that the interpretation purports to construe." Paralyzed Veterans of America v. D.C. Arena, L.P., 117 F.3d 579, 588. The Whitlow Letter's interpretation of FAR 121.471, we believe, is "fairly encompassed" within the required rest regulation. . . . We cannot say that "in the absence of the [Whitlow Letter] there would not be an adequate legislative basis to . . . ensure the performance of duties." American Mining Congress v. Mine

Safety & Health Admin., 995 F.2d 1106, 1112 (D.C.Cir.1993). The provisions of FAR 121.471 incorporate ... the phrase "scheduled completion of any flight segment," which is reasonably understood to include a completion re-scheduled because of actual flight conditions. FAR 121.471 itself, then, provides the FAA with sufficient authority to impose the recalculation duty. The Whitlow Letter does not impose "new rights or duties," Orengo Caraballo v. Reich, 11 F.3d 186, 195 (D.C.Cir.1993), and therefore does not require notice-and-comment rulemaking.

2.   Relation to Prior Agency Interpretations

Even if the Whitlow Letter is an interpretative rule, ATA further contends, notice-and-comment rulemaking is nonetheless required because the Letter is inconsistent with earlier FAA interpretations of FAR 121.471. "Rulemaking," as defined in the APA, includes not only the agency's formulation, but also its modification, of a rule. See 5 U.S.C. § 551(5) ("rule making" includes "agency process for formulating, amending, or repealing a rule"); see also Paralyzed Veterans, 117 F.3d at 586 ("Under the APA, agencies are obligated to engage in notice and comment before formulating regulations, which applies as well to 'repeals' or 'amendments.'" (emphasis in original)). As the United States Supreme Court has noted, APA rulemaking is required if an interpretation "adopts a new position inconsistent with ... existing regulations." Shalala v. Guernsey Mem'l Hosp., 514 U.S. 87, 100 (1995). In Alaska Prof'l Hunters Ass'n v. FAA, 177 F.3d 1030 (D.C.Cir.1999), we held that "when an agency has given its regulation a definitive interpretation, and later significantly revises that interpretation, the agency has in effect amended its rule, which requires notice and comment." Id. at 1034 (citation omitted) (emphasis added); see also Paralyzed Veterans, 117 F.3d at 586 (agency violates APA if it makes a "fundamental change in its interpretation of a substantive regulation without notice and comment"). In Alaska Hunters, Alaskan guides who transport their customers to hunting and fishing sites by airplane challenged the FAA's requirement (imposed via a Notice to Operators) that they comply with FAA regulations applicable to commercial pilots. Id. at 1033. The Notice, promulgated without notice and comment, reversed the FAA's thirty-year interpretation that had exempted the guides. Id. The longstanding advice, we held, had become "an authoritative departmental interpretation, an administrative common law applicable to Alaskan guide pilots"; hence, the Notice changing that interpretation had to comply with notice-and-comment rulemaking. Id. at 1035.

ATA claims the Whitlow Letter changed "fifteen years of interpretations" because "recalculation of past rest periods has never [been] required, even though the opportunity to impose such a mandate was presented." [The court found this argument historically inaccurate. Although the agency had not previously taken the position expressed in the Whitlow letter, the matter had not been "definitively" spoken to. The Whitlow letter, "in clarifying a carrier's duty to recalculate previously computed rest periods based on actual flight schedules, addresses only a theretofore unresolved aspect of the rest requirement."]

For the foregoing reasons, the consolidated petitions for review are denied.

So ordered.

NOTES

(1) *The Utility of Advice.* Cases like Air Transport Association arise out of the tension of competing impulses. Return to the first page of this chapter and reflect again on the pyramid sketched there. Regulations can be more specific than statutes, which in turn are more specific than constitutions, but there remain nonetheless unsettled issues. This is particularly likely to prove the case when, responding to one frequent line of advice, agencies adopt "performance standards" telling the regulated what they must achieve, but not precisely how to do so.[1] Affected private persons can be expected to value both agency regularity in dealing with them, and the availability of agency advice on how it will approach these issues. When Mr. Rubin wrote Deputy Counsel Whitlow, his principal motivation was probably to seek an interpretation, not to lay the groundwork for a lawsuit. In National Automatic Laundry and Cleaning Council v. Shultz 443 F.2d 689 (D.C.Cir.1971), p. 1249 below, "Judge Harold Leventhal of the D.C. Circuit . . . learned that each year the U.S. Department of Labor's Wage and Hour Administration responded to 750,000 requests for advice about the interpretation and application of the Fair Labor Standards Act; 10,000 of these responses were signed by the Administrator herself and the rest, by staff. . . .

"When [one of your editors] was General Counsel of the Nuclear Regulatory Commission in 1975–77 . . . any regulation the Commission adopted was considered, often in detail, by the five Commissioners themselves. These Commission regulations generally set performance standards for nuclear safety . . . rather than specify the details of design—a difference often identified in the literature as that between having 'standards' and having 'rules.' The bulk of the work for one of the Commission's five bureaus was continually to generate guidance for license applicants and others about technical design issues raised by these regulatory standards. It issued this guidance in a volume dwarfing the regulations; and these guidance instruments, which the Commission expected to be the product of informal consultation by responsible staff with affected parties, were supervised by the Commission in only a general way. Another bureau, in charge of inspections and enforcement, produced copious guidance for the Commission's inspectors. Both sorts of guidance, understandably, were earnestly sought out by those the Commission regulated, and greatly influenced their conduct. From an internal perspective the guidance also contributed to the discipline of staff action, its predictability and regularity. Comparable practices and proportions, in response to similar levels of public demand for guidance and central agency interest in controlling a far-flung staff, can be found at many, if not all, regulatory agencies. The result is an enormous

---

1. See, e.g., E.O. 12866 § 1(b)(8): "Each agency . . . shall, to the extent feasible, specify performance objectives [in its reg- ulations], rather than specifying the behavior or manner of compliance that regulated entities must adopt."

output of publication rules, far greater than the pages of the Federal Register, and (in proportional terms) rarely challenged in litigation." PETER L. STRAUSS, PUBLICATION RULES IN THE RULEMAKING SPECTRUM: ASSURING PROPER RESPECT FOR AN ESSENTIAL ELEMENT, 53 Admin. L. Rev. 803 (2001).

Sections 552 and 553 plainly anticipate this outpouring, and provide a different procedural model for it: Unlike regulations, these documents do not have the force of a statute, but if published they may be relied upon in ways that could adversely affect members of the public—just as precedents can. Inspectors will follow the manual. This obedience is reassuring when it prevents a street-level bureaucrat from acting on whim or personal preference, but painful when it produces the assessment of a civil penalty. With the emergence of e-government, all these documents can be made readily available to search and perusal.[2]

The other side of the matter can be put in a variety of ways, largely reflected in the opinion's concerns. First, the knowledge that it will be able to interpret its regulations without notice-and-comment formality might tempt a lazy or devious agency to be less precise than it could and should be in drafting its notice-and-comment regulations—"to promulgate mush," as one court put it.[3] Courts rarely tell Congress that it has not drafted with adequate precision; absent special constitutional concerns, they interpret what the legislature has done as best they can. But as the agency both enacts *and* interprets, "regulatory vagueness" may appropriately be a more potent argument than "statutory vagueness" is. Second, an agency or its staff may sometimes use interpretation to reach a result that the language of a regulation cannot reasonably bear, or in other ways treat a publication rule as if it *did* have the force of a statute. By definition these rules cannot themselves be the source of legal obligation. Finally, if an agency has published one interpretation of its regulations, and then (perhaps in a new administration) changes its view, it may seem to be amending its regulation without using § 553 to do so. The increasing procedural costs of conventional rulemaking create a not inconsiderable temptation to cut corners in this way. Unsurprisingly, the cases judges see—chosen by litigants opposed to what the government has done—tend to highlight the dark side of publication rules, producing occasional expressions of annoyance or alarm.[4]

---

2. See, e.g., http://www.nhtsa.dot.gov/cars/rules/interps, which posts in searchable format all interpretation letters written by the counsel's office of the National Highway Traffic and Safety Administration, the agency responsible (inter alia) for automobile safety regulations. The site explicitly invites public reliance upon the opinions posted there (until they are withdrawn or changed). The web libraries all agencies are now required to maintain under the Electronic Freedom of Information Act, see p. 738 below, should contain electronic libraries of all such matters. The FAA collection is at http://www.faa.gov/avr/arm/index.cfm, including a link to an extensive "Regulatory and Guidance Library."

3. Paralyzed Veterans of America v. D.C. Arena L.P., 117 F.3d 579, 585 (D.C.Cir. 1997). The parallels to delegation concerns are obvious. For another analysis suggesting that delegation doctrine provides a useful framework for analyzing publication rule issues, see David Barron and Elena Kagan, Chevron's Nondelegation Doctrine, 2001 The Supreme Court Review 201.

4. E.g., Appalachian Power Co. v. EPA, 208 F.3d 1015 (D.C.Cir.2000): "The phenomenon we see in this case is familiar. Congress passes a broadly worded statute. The agency follows with regulations containing broad language, open-ended phrases, ambiguous standards and the like. Then as years pass, the agency issues circulars or guidance or

(2) *Procedural Concerns.* JAMES W. CONRAD, JR., DRAFT GUIDANCE ON THE APPROPRIATE USE OF RULES VERSUS GUIDANCE, 32 Env. L. Rep. 10721, 10722 (2002): "In thinking about regulation versus guidance questions, I have found it helpful to remember that people who care about these issues are basically concerned about three things:

"The opportunity to *have input before* a document is issued—the essence of notice-and-comment rulemaking;

"The opportunity to seek *judicial review* of the document afterwards; and

"The opportunity to act at variance with the document without becoming the subject of an enforcement action based on it, i.e., whether it is legally binding.

"These are three different things, addressed by different parts of the APA, and they do not always go together. Regulations normally require notice and comment, are generally reviewable, and are clearly enforceable; interpretive rules do not require notice and comment, are often reviewable, and in theory are not themselves enforceable (though the laws they interpret are); policy statements and the like do not require notice and comment, are often held non-reviewable, and also are not themselves enforceable. In thinking through a 'rulemaking by guidance' question, it is a good idea to start by considering which of these issues is the problem."

(a) *"The opportunity to have input before a document is issued."* Agencies often, but not invariably, provide opportunities for public discussion of guidance documents or interpretations before they are issued. When this has happened, should a reviewing court treat it as favorable to the agency, because the agency was honoring this value of notice-and-comment rulemaking? Or as a negative element, because the agency was apparently aware that § 553 procedures were required? Or as irrelevant? The cases often mention the fact, but appear to give it no significance.

(b) *"The opportunity to seek judicial review of the document afterwards."* The questions of finality and ripeness are taken up at 1246 ff. below. Although these are informal actions, the strong tendency (as in the principal cases opening and closing this section) is to treat them as eligible for pre-enforcement review in the same manner as a regulation would be.

(c) *"The opportunity to act at variance with the document without becoming the subject of an enforcement action based on it, i.e., whether it is*

memoranda, explaining, interpreting, defining and often expanding the commands in the regulations. One guidance document may yield another and then another and so on. Several words in a regulation may spawn hundreds of pages of text as the agency offers more and more detail regarding what its regulations demand of regulated entities. Law is made, without notice and comment, without public participation, and without publication in the Federal Register or the Code of Federal Regulations. With the advent of the Internet, the agency does not need these official publications to ensure widespread circulation; it can inform those affected simply by posting its new guidance or memoranda or policy statement on its web site. An agency operating in this way gains a large advantage.'It can issue or amend its real rules, i.e., its interpretative rules and policy statements, quickly and inexpensively without following any statutorily prescribed procedures.' Richard J. Pierce, Jr., Seven Ways to Deossify Agency Rulemaking, 47 Admin. L. Rev. 59, 85 (1995)."

legally binding." Here is where the problems lie. If Delta 432 pulls away from the gate despite a calculation showing that the rest parameters indicated in the Whitlow letter have not been and cannot be satisfied, Delta *will* become the subject of an enforcement action. But if the agency is well advised, that will be legally framed as an action to enforce FAR 121.471 itself, *not* the Whitlow letter. The interpretation conveyed by the letter will simply be a matter on which the agency can be expected to rely, precedent-like, in that action—and Delta will be as free to argue for another interpretation as any party ever is. If similar arguments have been heard ten times previously, its arguments may get no more respect than the arguments of southern attorneys contending against Brown v. Board of Education in the 1960's. But what is being enforced—what is binding—is FAR 121.471 (or the Fourteenth Amendment).

Thus, Williams, J., discussing interpretive (or as § 553 would have it, "interpretative") rules in AMERICAN MINING CONGRESS V. MINE SAFETY & HEALTH ADMIN., 995 F.2d 1106, 1111–12 (D.C.Cir.1993): "A non-legislative rule's capacity to have a binding effect is limited in practice by the fact that agency personnel at every level act under the shadow of judicial review. If they believe that courts may fault them for brushing aside the arguments of persons who contest the rule or statement, they are obviously far more likely to entertain those arguments. And, as failure to provide notice-and-comment rulemaking will usually mean that affected parties have had no prior formal opportunity to present their contentions, judicial review for want of reasoned decisionmaking is likely, in effect, to take place in review of specific agency actions implementing the rule. Similarly, where the agency must defend its view as an application of Chevron 'prong two' (i.e., where Congress has not 'clearly' decided for or against the agency interpretation), so that only reasonableness is at issue, agency disregard of significant policy arguments will clearly count against it. As Donald Elliott has said, agency attentiveness to parties' arguments must come sooner or later. 'As in the television commercial in which the automobile repairman intones ominously "pay me now, or pay me later," the agency has a choice. . . .' E. Donald Elliott, Reinventing Rulemaking, 41 Duke L.J. 1490, 1491 (1992). Because the threat of judicial review provides a spur to the agency to pay attention to facts and arguments submitted in derogation of any rule not supported by notice and comment, even as late as the enforcement stage, any agency statement not subjected to notice-and-comment rulemaking will be more vulnerable to attack not only in court but also within the agency itself.

"Not only does an agency have an incentive to entertain objections to an interpretive rule, but the ability to promulgate such rules, without notice and comment, does not appear more hazardous to affected parties than the likely alternative. Where a statute or legislative rule has created a legal basis for enforcement, an agency can simply let its interpretation evolve ad hoc in the process of enforcement or other applications (e.g., grants). The protection that Congress sought to secure by requiring notice and comment for legislative rules is not advanced by reading the exemption for 'interpretive rule' so narrowly as to drive agencies into pure ad hocery—an ad hocery, moreover, that affords less notice, or less convenient notice, to affected parties.

"Accordingly, insofar as our cases can be reconciled at all, we think it almost exclusively on the basis of whether the purported interpretive rule has 'legal effect', which in turn is best ascertained by asking (1) whether in the absence of the rule there would not be an adequate legislative basis for enforcement action or other agency action to confer benefits or ensure the performance of duties, (2) whether the agency has published the rule in the Code of Federal Regulations, (3) whether the agency has explicitly invoked its general legislative authority, or (4) whether the rule effectively amends a prior legislative rule. If the answer to any of these questions is affirmative, we have a legislative, not an interpretive rule."

(3) *An Interpretation "Fairly Encompassed" Within the Regulation it Purports to Construe.* "Fair warning" has often been a measure of whether § 553 procedures will be required. As suggested above, two concerns seem to animate this inquiry: First, whether, in general, the agency has been sufficiently assiduous in its regulatory effort, or instead has succumbed to the temptation "to promulgate mush." Second, whether the course it has taken is within the bounds of its established "law"—statutes, regulations, or established body of adjudicatory precedent. Both concerns seem to have figured in the closely divided Supreme Court opinions in SHALALA V. GUERN-SEY MEMORIAL HOSPITAL, 514 U.S. 87, 96, 99 (1995). Medicare regulations governed the reimbursement of hospitals for covered expenses; while detailed, they left some issues open. One such issue was resolved against the hospital in an adjudicatory proceeding in which the final agency adjudicator relied in part on a reimbursement guideline contained in the Provider Reimbursement Manual—despite that guideline's departure from "generally accepted accounting principles" (GAAP). The court of appeals reasoned that because this departure "effect[ed] a substantive change in the regulations," § 553 procedures were required to adopt it. The five member Supreme Court majority disagreed, finding the Secretary's interpretation "reasonable" and "consistent with the Medicare statute."

"To the extent the Medicare statute's broad delegation of authority imposes a rulemaking obligation, it is one the Secretary has without doubt discharged. The Secretary has issued regulations to address a wide range of reimbursement questions. The regulations are comprehensive and intricate in detail, addressing matters such as limits on cost reimbursement, apportioning costs to Medicare services, and the specific treatment of numerous particular costs. As of 1994, these regulations consumed some 640 pages of the Code of Federal Regulations. ... That her regulations do not resolve the specific timing question before us in a conclusive way, or "could use a more exact mode of calculating," does not, of course, render them invalid.... The APA does not require that all the specific applications of a rule evolve by further, more precise rules rather than by adjudication. ...

"... PRM § 233 is a prototypical example of an interpretive rule 'issued by an agency to advise the public of the agency's construction of the statutes and rules which it administers.' Chrysler Corp. v. Brown, 441 U.S. 281, 302, n. 31 (1979) (quoting Attorney General's Manual on the Administrative Procedure Act 30, n. 3 (1947)). Interpretive rules do not require notice and comment, although, as the Secretary recognizes, see Foreword to

PRM, they also do not have the force and effect of law and are not accorded that weight in the adjudicatory process.

"We can agree that APA rulemaking would still be required if PRM § 233 adopted a new position inconsistent with any of the Secretary's existing regulations. ... [H]owever, her regulations do not require reimbursement according to GAAP. PRM § 233 does not, as the Court of Appeals concluded it does, 'effect a substantive change in the regulations.'"

For four dissenters (Justice O'Connor writing for herself and Justices Scalia, Souter and Thomas), an independent reading of the Secretary's regulations established that the Department was generally committed to GAAP. Since PRM § 233 departs from those principles, it could be adopted only by § 553 procedures. For Professor John Manning, the majority's result is a predictable but unfortunate by-product of Supreme Court cases instructing courts to grant strong deference to agency interpretations. "[I]f an agency issues an imprecise or vague regulation, it does so secure in the knowledge that it can insist upon an unobvious interpretation, so long as its choice is not *'plainly* erroneous.' The Supreme Court's recent opinion in [Guernsey] illustrates the resulting latitude for both imprecision and vagueness."[5]

Regulatory vagueness appears to figure prominently in Chief Judge Edwards' opinion in UNITED STATES V. CHRYSLER CORP., 158 F.3d 1350 (D.C.Cir.1998). Chrysler had refused to recall 91,000 Chrysler and Dodge cars that the National Highway Traffic Safety Administration asserted were not in compliance with its standards respecting seat belts. The relevant standard specified a test the belt assemblies must pass, but did not specify the exact placement of the testing equipment. Chrysler passed the assemblies with the equipment in one position. NHTSA subsequently performed the test with the assemblies in another position which it interpreted its standard to require, and they failed that test. "[A] manufacturer cannot be found to be out of compliance with a standard if NHTSA has failed to give fair notice of what is required by the standard." That notice had not been given. The opinion implies that a clear interpretive rule would have sufficed. A perceptive student comment, United States v. Chrysler: The Conflict Between Fair Warning and Adjudicative Retroactivity in D.C. Circuit Administrative Law, 74 N.Y.U. L. Rev. 914, 918 (1999), finds the reach of "fair warning" broader than the retroactivity principles Judge Edwards applied in Epilepsy Foundation of Northeast Ohio v. NLRB, 268 F.3d 1095 (D.C.Cir.2001), set out at p. 574 above, although the two doctrines attempt to deal with the same underlying tension between fairness to the regulated party and the public's need for effective regulation. The note argues that the greater reach of "fair warning" compromises the public side of the equation, and "creates perverse incentives for regulated parties and administrative agencies, incentives which ultimately call into question the rule's efficacy at creating clear regulations."

(4) *If an agency has established one interpretation of its regulations, and then (perhaps in a new administration) changes its view, it may seem to be*

---

5. John F. Manning, Constitutional Structure and Judicial Deference to Agency Interpretations of Agency Rules, 96 Colum.L.Rev. 612, 657 (1996).

amending its regulation without using § 553 to do so. Judge Edwards'
Epilepsy Foundation opinion also stands in contrast to the D.C. Circuit's
second proposition, that once an agency has given a regulation a definitive
interpretation, a subsequent revision of that interpretation in effect
amends the regulation, requiring § 553 procedures. In Epilepsy Foundation, the NLRB had adopted a new, "reasonable" interpretation of Section
7 of the National Labor Relations Act. This was only the latest in a series of
vacillating interpretations. Although the Board was not permitted to apply
its new application to the complaining party in the face of reasonable
reliance on the prior one, Judge Edwards' opinion found the Board's
inconstant interpretational course in itself "understandable and unexceptionable. ... An otherwise reasonable interpretation of § 7 is not made
legally infirm because the Board gives *renewed*, rather than new, meaning
to a disputed statutory provision. It is a fact of life in NLRB lore that
certain substantive provisions of the NLRA invariably fluctuate with the
changing compositions of the Board. Because the Board's new interpretation is reasonable under the Act, it is entitled to deference. ... The Board's
conclusion obviously is debatable (because the Board has 'changed its mind'
several times in addressing this issue); but the rationale underlying the
decision in this case is both clear and reasonable. That is all that is
necessary to garner deference from the court."

In Interpreting Agency Enabling Acts: Misplaced Metaphors in Administrative Law, 41 Wm & Mary L. Rev. 1463, 1504–05 (2000), Professor Lars
Noah argues that this attitude, which imagines a common law role for
agencies that today's federal courts are prone to doubt for themselves,
"should arouse suspicion. ... [To be sure,] the failure [of courts] to defer
[to such agency revisions of view] where unforeseen circumstances render
an enabling statute's command anachronistic may lead to absurd results.
Thus, in order to combat obsolescence in antiquated enabling statutes that
Congress has failed to revisit, agencies may enjoy some updating function.

"This freedom is not, however, unconstrained. Courts must still determine whether a revised interpretation is reasonable...."

For revised interpretations of *regulations*, the fact that the agency both
adopts its regulations and interprets them may hold the key. It would take
Congress to alter NLRA Section 7, but an agency can amend its own
regulations. From this perspective, a "one bite at the interpretational
apple" standard may seem justified. Professor Manning's vagueness concerns, briefly quoted in discussing Guernsey in Note (3) above, may seem to
have particular force in this context; if the agency can freely change its
interpretations and expect strong judicial deference, it will readily be
satisfied with imprecise regulations, and may even experience some incentive to promulgate them.[6] Suppose, however, that the change is at a level of
detail unlikely to be dealt with by the agency's political leadership—if, for
example, NRC staff announces a slightly revised parameter for what they

---

6. See n. 5 above. Professor Manning
suggests a constitutional dimension for his
concern, arguing that the fact that agencies
both adopt and interpret regulations creates
"delegation" issues absent at the congressional level, that indeed make it inappropriate for courts to regard agency interpretations of unclear regulations with the same
respect as they do interpretations of unclear
statutes. Delegation issues figure importantly
in some other analyses of this issue, e.g.
Strauss, supra Note (1) and David Baron and
Elena Kagan, supra n. 3. Professor Manning's thesis, however, is best discussed in

will accept without further inquiry as suitable corrosion resistance in the reinforcing steel bars for a nuclear reactor's concrete containment, in light of recently published technical studies such as regularly underlie this kind of guidance?

Judge Henderson treats the Supreme Court's opinion in Guernsey as supporting the "one interpretational bite" proposition. However, Guernsey was given a somewhat different reading by the late Justice Byron White, sitting with the Ninth Circuit after his retirement in CHIEF PROBATION OFFICERS OF CALIFORNIA V. SHALALA, 118 F.3d 1327 (9th Cir.1997). Under the Emergency Assistance Program (EAP) administered by the Department of Health and Human Services, federal matching funds are available to states for emergency assistance to needy families with children. In 1993, HHS began approving state plans to provide benefits for children in the juvenile justice system. In 1995, HHS issued, without any public procedure, Action Transmittal No. ACF–AT–95–9. It advised that HHS would no longer fund such benefits because, on reconsideration of the statute and promulgated regulations, programs of this sort were not within the purpose of the EAP. State officials challenged the changed interpretation. Justice White construed Guernsey's reference to "adopt[ing] a new position inconsistent with any of the [agency's] existing regulations" to mean adopting a position inconsistent with existing regulatory *language*, not one inconsistent with existing regulatory *interpretations*. The agency did not claim to be changing properly promulgated regulations, but rather to be interpreting them more faithfully than it had before. Moreover, the Action Transmittal was in fact not contrary to any existing regulation having the force of law. The agency had simply changed its view of what constituted an appropriate emergency situation under the existing regulatory language. That the new interpretation would have significant effect on the operations of several states did not matter: impact was not the test. In order for notice and comment to be required, the new rule "would have to be inconsistent with another rule having the force of law, not just any agency interpretation regardless of whether it had been codified." 118 F.3d at 1337.

SCOTT H. AGSTREICH, SHORING UP CHEVRON: A DEFENSE OF SEMINOLE ROCK DEFERENCE TO AGENCY REGULATORY INTERPRETATIONS, 34 U.C. Davis L. Rev. 49, 79 (2000): "Although [the proposition that an agency is not free to reinterpret a regulation except by notice and comment rulemaking to amend the regulation] is settled law in the D.C. Circuit and was cited approvingly by the four dissenting Justices in [Geier v. American Honda Motor Co., 529 U.S. 861 (2000)], no other circuit currently follows this approach. The D.C. Circuit's rule has also come under attack from commentators, who claim that it does not comport with the APA. Although the D.C. Circuit is correct that Congress has spoken to the procedures that an agency must follow in amending or repealing a regulation, these commentators note that the APA's explicit exemption from those procedures for interpretive rules makes no distinction between initial and subsequent interpretations. ... The agency must explain its reasons for changing interpretations, and the new interpretation must itself be reasonable."

the context of judicial review issues, taken up
at p. 1086 in connection with United States v.
Mead Corp.

(5) *Does it Matter how an Initial Interpretation was Generated?* Judge Henderson's opinion relies on Alaska Prof'l Hunters Ass'n v. FAA, 177 F.3d 1030 (D.C.Cir.1999), for the proposition about changing interpretations. In that case, the "Notice to Operators" that brought professional guides within certain FAA flight regulations had been promulgated only after a considerable period of warning and informal discussion. By contrast the initial "thirty-year interpretation that had exempted the guides" was generated by the Alaska office of the FAA, with no indication it had come to prominent attention or been adopted in Washington. In Hoctor v. Department of Agriculture, 82 F.3d 165 (7th Cir.1996), a local departmental official had informally advised the owner of a game farm near Terre Haute, Indiana that fences six feet high would satisfy a DOA regulation requiring "structurally sound" fences around areas housing lions, tigers, and other big cats. A few years later, a centrally generated interpretive memorandum advised departmental officials that eight foot fences should be required for such animals.

When lower level officials acted in these ways, was the effect that the *agencies* had given their regulations definitive interpretations? One could perhaps separate the issue of justified reliance from the question whether, in general, the new interpretation is valid—although one would then run into the proposition that front-line bureaucrats are not ordinarily able to bind their agencies by their advice, see p. 1088 below. In both cases, the agencies had given the affected private parties substantial time to conform their behavior to the new understanding. Should *that* matter?

(6) *"Binding" Advice.* The Hoctor case just mentioned illustrates the difficulties inherent in the third of Mr. Conrad's questions. Imagine several stages in the Hoctor game farm proceedings. First an inspector visits the premises, measuring tape and manual in hand. He finds a six foot fence, and issues a citation. If the citation is for a "structurally unsound" fence, citing the relevant CFR section, does it matter that he has used the manual? Or that Hoctor knows what is in the manual? If the inspector errs, and issues a citation for "fence less than eight feet," has Hoctor been "bound" so long as the departmental adjudicator permits him to challenge what "structurally sound" means? Assume she concludes that "eight feet" is a sensible outcome for "structurally sound" in the context of fences having to contain big carnivorous cats, relying on the expertise of the responsible bureau and perhaps a number of similar results in prior adjudications. Now Hoctor is assuredly "bound," but has that been accomplished by the interpretation? Or by an adjudicatory process in which he had as much (or more) opportunity to affect the outcome as he would have had in a § 553 rulemaking?

(7) *Problematic Judicial Impact?* At the agency level, it has long been understood (and § 552 so suggests) that publication rules can be relied upon only in the manner of precedent. That is, those who might be adversely affected by them must be given the opportunity to argue their impropriety or inapplicability. "The critical distinction between a substantive rule and a general statement of policy is the different practical effect that these two types of pronouncements have in subsequent administrative proceedings. ... A properly adopted substantive rule establishes a standard

of conduct which has the force of law. In subsequent administrative proceedings involving a substantive rule, the issues are whether the adjudicated facts conform to the rule and whether the rule should be waived or applied in that particular instance. The underlying policy embodied in the rule is not generally subject to challenge before the agency.

"A general statement of policy, on the other hand, ... is not finally determinative of the issues or rights to which it is addressed. The agency cannot apply or rely upon a general statement of policy as law because a general statement of policy only announces what the agency seeks to establish as policy. A policy statement announces the agency's tentative intentions for the future. When the agency applies the policy in a particular situation, it must be prepared to support the policy just as if the policy statement had never been issued. An agency cannot escape its responsibility to present evidence and reasoning supporting its substantive rules by announcing binding precedent in the form of a general statement of policy." PACIFIC GAS & ELECTRIC CO. V. FEDERAL POWER COMMISSION, 506 F.2d 33 (D.C.Cir.1974).

Consider now the implications of the following passage in the ATA decision, p. 707, drawing on later precedent:

> Because the Whitlow Letter constitutes the FAA's interpretation of its own regulation, that interpretation must be afforded substantial deference and upheld unless "plainly erroneous or inconsistent with the regulation." Thomas Jefferson Univ. v. Shalala, 512 U.S. 504, 512 (1994) Accordingly, we defer to the FAA's view unless "an alternative reading is compelled by the regulation's plain language or by other indications of the [agency's] intent at the time of the regulation's promulgation." 512 U.S. at 512.

It would be inappropriate to anticipate here the discussion attending Chevron, U.S.A., Inc. v. Natural Resources Defense Council, Inc. and United States v. Mead Corp., pages 1026 and 1068 below, but note how much more potent these instructions seem to render the agency's "interpretation" for the court. Might a judge hearing agency counsel argue that she *must* accept an agency's not-plainly-erroneous interpretation of its regulations, citing these passages, feel that she as well as the appellant was being "bound," and react accordingly? Echoing Professor Manning's doubts, p. 716 above, consider Lars Noah, Divining Regulatory Intent: The Place for a "Legislative History" of Agency Rules, 51 Hastings L.J. 255, 289–90 (2000): "[Courts, in limiting themselves to asking] whether the agency's interpretation of [a regulation's] text is plainly erroneous ... seem largely unconcerned that this creates incentives for agencies to promulgate excessively vague legislative rules that leave the more difficult task of specification to the more flexible and unaccountable process of later 'interpreting' these open-ended regulations."

General Electric Company v. Environmental Protection Agency

United States Court of Appeals for the District of Columbia Circuit, 2002.
290 F.3d 377

■ Before GINSBURG, Chief Judge, and RANDOLPH and TATEL, Circuit Judges.

■ GINSBURG, Chief Judge: General Electric Co. petitions for review of the "PCB Risk Assessment Review Guidance Document" issued by the Environmental Protection Agency. The parties dispute (1) whether this case is ripe for review; (2) whether the Document is a "rule" within the meaning of § 19(a) of the Toxic Substances Control Act (TSCA), and hence whether the court has jurisdiction to review its promulgation; and (3) whether the Agency should have followed the procedures required for rulemaking in the TSCA and in the Administrative Procedure Act when it promulgated the Document. We conclude that the case is ripe for review, and that the Guidance Document is a legislative rule such that the court does have jurisdiction to entertain GE's petition and the Document should not have been issued without prior notice and an opportunity for public comment.

I. Background

The TSCA prohibits the manufacture, processing, distribution, and use (other than in a "totally enclosed manner") of polychlorinated biphenyls (PCBs) unless the EPA determines that the activity will not result in an "unreasonable risk of injury to health or the environment." 15 U.S.C. § 2605(e)(2) & (3). The Guidance Document governs the application of two regulations promulgated by the EPA under the TSCA to provide respectively for the cleanup and disposal of PCB remediation waste and for the disposal of PCB bulk product waste. See 40 C.F.R. §§ 761.61 ("cleanup and disposal options for PCB remediation waste"), 761.62 (how "PCB bulk product waste shall be disposed").

Under subsection (c) of each regulation a party may apply for permission to use a method other than one of the generic methods set out in the regulations for sampling, cleaning up, or disposing of PCB remediation waste, or for sampling or disposing of PCB bulk product waste. The EPA will approve applications under these subsections if the alternative method proposed does "not pose an unreasonable risk of injury to health or the environment." Id. The regulations do not, however, tell applicants how to conduct the necessary risk assessment.[1]

---

1. [Ed.] The "generic methods" mentioned consume 7 pages of the Federal Register, and describe in some detail techniques acceptable for use. The list necessarily reflects EPA's judgments about acceptable risks. It mentions that EPA designed these methods for smaller sites, and that "the procedure may be less practical for larger or more environmentally diverse sites." G.E. is responsible for PCB wastes at large and environmentally diverse sites. The generic procedures may be used there, but "an EPA Regional Administrator may authorize more practical procedures through paragraph (c) of this section." 40 C.F.R. § 761.61(a). Paragraph (c) provides for individual adjudication of applications, in the following terms:

c) *Risk-based disposal approval.* (1) Any person wishing to sample, cleanup, or dispose of PCB remediation waste in a manner other than prescribed in paragraphs (a) or (b) of this section, or store PCB remediation waste in a manner other than prescribed in § 761.65, must apply in writing to the EPA Regional Administrator in the Region where the sampling, cleanup, disposal or storage site is located, for sampling, cleanup, disposal or storage occurring in a single EPA Region; or to the Director of the National Program Chemicals Division, for sampling, cleanup, disposal or storage occurring in more than one EPA Region. Each application must contain information described in the notification required by § 761.61(a)(3). EPA may request other information that it believes necessary to evaluate the application. No person may conduct cleanup activities

That is where the Guidance Document comes in. It "provides an overview of risk assessment techniques, and guidance for reviewing risk assessment documents submitted under the final PCB disposal rule." Guidance Document at 10. Of particular relevance to this case, in the Guidance Document the EPA also explains that an applicant seeking to use an alternative method under § 761.61(c) may take either of two approaches to risk assessment. First, the applicant may calculate cancer and non-cancer risks separately. Id. To calculate cancer risks the applicant would have to use a cancer potency factor recognized by the EPA. Such cancer potency factors range, depending upon the exposure pathway and upon the composition of the PCB mixture, from .04 to 2.0 (mg/kg/day)–1. Id., Table 9, at 64. To calculate the non-cancer risks a different type of toxicity value—a reference dose, for example—would have to be used, and certain specified non-cancer risks would have to be taken into account. Id. at 21, 42.

The second approach endorsed in the Guidance Document is to use a "total toxicity factor" of 4.0 (mg/kg/day) 1 to account for cancer and non-cancer risks together. Id. In its brief the EPA explains that this approach "provides the applicant an opportunity to reduce the time and expense associated with the risk assessment" because the Agency is willing "to accept this 'default' toxicity value of 4.0 (mg/kg/ day)–1[ ] without requiring further justification."

II. Analysis

GE's primary argument is that the Guidance Document is a legislative rule and therefore should have been promulgated only after public notice and an opportunity for comment. In the alternative it contends that the Guidance Document is not supported by substantial evidence. Before considering these arguments about the merits, however, we must determine whether the case is ripe for review and whether we have jurisdiction to hear it.

A. Ripeness

[The court treated treat the question whether the Guidance Documents were eligible for pre-enforcement review in the same manner as it would have treated a regulation, and found them to be final agency actions ripe for review. In so doing, it rejected an EPA argument that the agency's flexibility in applying the documents could not be determined in advance of its decision on particular applications to use a technique other than the generic techniques specified in the text of the regulations.]

---

under this paragraph prior to obtaining written approval by EPA. (2) EPA will issue a written decision on each application for a risk-based method for PCB remediation wastes. EPA will approve such an application if it finds that the method will not pose an unreasonable risk of injury to health or the environment.

The Guidance Document at use here spells out approaches that EPA staff had determined would meet this burden of demonstrating the adequacy of alternative methods. Jump citations in the opinion reveal that it is at least 44 pages long.

B.   Jurisdiction under the TSCA

Before we can reach the merits, we must consider whether the Document is a "rule" subject to our review under § 19(a)(1)(A) of the TSCA, 15 U.S.C. § 2618(a)(1)(A). That section provides:

> Not later than 60 days after the date of the promulgation of a rule under section ... 2605(e) ... of this title, ... any person may file a petition for judicial review of such rule with the United States Court of Appeal for the District of Columbia Circuit.

GE contends that the term "rule" should be read broadly to track the definition in the APA. See 5 U.S.C. § 551(4). The EPA takes the narrower view that "direct appellate review is limited to legislative rules, i.e., rules which were (or should have been) promulgated through notice and comment rulemaking." We need not decide which interpretation of the term "rule" in § 19(a)(1)(A) is correct because we conclude that the Guidance Document is indeed a legislative rule.

GE argues that the Guidance Document is a legislative rule rather than a statement of policy or an interpretive rule because it gives substance to the vague language of 40 C.F.R. § 761.61(c) ("unreasonable risk of injury to health or the environment"), does so in an obligatory fashion, and is treated by the EPA as "controlling in the field." See Community Nutrition Inst. v. Young, 818 F.2d 943, 946 (D.C.Cir.1987); Appalachian Power, 208 F.3d at 1021. ... Although it is not entirely clear what in the EPA's view the Document is, the EPA comes closest to characterizing it as a statement of policy; thus:

> The portion of the guidance at issue here is simply an expression of EPA's policy judgment, based on the available scientific data and analysis, that when the "total toxicity" analysis is used, the 4.0 (mg/kg/day)–1 toxicity value is appropriate to avoid an unreasonable risk to health or the environment.

With the Agency's argument so understood, the question before us can be framed as whether the Guidance Document is a legislative rule or a statement of policy.

As GE argues, in cases where we have attempted to draw the line between legislative rules and statements of policy, we have considered whether the agency action (1) "imposes any rights and obligations" or (2) "genuinely leaves the agency and its decisionmakers free to exercise discretion." Community Nutrition Inst., 818 F.2d at 946; Chamber of Commerce v. Dep't of Labor, 174 F.3d 206, 212 (1999). In McLouth Steel Prods. Corp. v. Thomas, 838 F.2d 1317, 1320–21 (1988) we recognized that "in practice, there appears some overlap in the Community Nutrition criteria" because "if a statement denies the decisionmaker discretion in the area of its coverage, so that [the agency] will automatically decline to entertain challenges to the statement's position, then the statement is binding, and creates rights or obligations." We emphasized that an agency announcement has "present-day binding effect" if the agency is "simply unready to hear new argument" in proceedings governed by the announcement.

The EPA urges the court to consider three factors: "(1) the Agency's own characterization of its action; (2) whether the action was published in the Federal Register or the Code of Federal Regulations; and (3) whether the action has binding effects on private parties or on the agency." Molycorp, Inc. v. EPA, 197 F.3d 543, 545 (D.C.Cir.1999). As the EPA concedes, however, the third factor is the most important: "The ultimate focus of the inquiry is whether the agency action partakes of the fundamental characteristic of a regulation, i.e., that it has the force of law."

The two tests overlap at step three of the Molycorp formulation—in which the court determines whether the agency action binds private parties or the agency itself with the "force of law." This common standard has been well stated as follows:

> If a document expresses a change in substantive law or policy (that is not an interpretation) which the agency intends to make binding, or administers with binding effect, the agency may not rely upon the statutory exemption for policy statements, but must observe the APA's legislative rulemaking procedures.

Robert A. Anthony, Interpretive Rules, Policy Statements, Guidances, Manuals, and the Like—Should Federal Agencies Use Them to Bind the Public?, 41 Duke L.J. 1311, 1355 (1992).

Our cases likewise make clear that an agency pronouncement will be considered binding as a practical matter if it either appears on its face to be binding or is applied by the agency in a way that indicates it is binding. As Professor Robert A. Anthony cogently comments, the mandatory language of a document alone can be sufficient to render it binding:

> A document will have practical binding effect before it is actually applied if the affected private parties are reasonably led to believe that failure to conform will bring adverse consequences, such as ... denial of an application. If the document is couched in mandatory language, or in terms indicating that it will be regularly applied, a binding intent is strongly evidenced. In some circumstances, if the language of the document is such that private parties can rely on it as a norm or safe harbor by which to shape their actions, it can be binding as a practical matter.

Interpretive Rules, 41 Duke L.J. at 1328–29.

GE argues that the Guidance Document is binding both because it facially requires an applicant for a risk-based variance to calculate toxicity by one of two methods—either use a total toxicity factor of 4.0 (mg/kg/day)–1 or use a cancer potency factor and account for the specified non-cancer health risks—and because, considering the cost, delay, and uncertainty entailed in the latter course, "for all practical purposes, the Guidance is a rule that directs PCB toxicity to be measured by a 4.0 (mg/kg/day)–1 CPF."

The EPA counters that the Guidance Document lacks the force of law because it does not purport to be binding and because it has not been applied as though it were binding. First, we are told, the Document "allows great flexibility" because it not only "recognizes two broad approaches to risk assessment," but also acknowledges (at 44) that some risk assessments may have components that require the use of non-standard reference materials, unique exposure scenarios or assumptions, or require the use of unconventional methods for estimating risks. These risk assessments will need to be addressed on a case-by-case basis.

Second, the EPA says that it has not in practice "applied the guidance document inflexibly, as if it were a rule or regulation." By this, however, the EPA means only that it has received and approved applications based upon the use of the total toxicity factor and upon a separate analysis of cancer and non-cancer risks—and even this limited assertion is disputed by GE. Finally, the Agency contends that the Guidance Document is "an expression of EPA's judgment on values to be used in conducting risk assessments," much like the data in the Agency's Integrated Risk Information System (IRIS), which this court held are not subject to the requirements of notice and comment rulemaking. See Chemical Mfrs. Ass'n v. EPA, 307 U.S. App. D.C. 392, 28 F.3d 1259, 1263 (1994).

We think it clear that the Guidance Document does purport to bind applicants for approval of a risk-based cleanup plan under 40 C.F.R. § 761.61(c). Consider the principal directives: "When developing a risk-based cleanup application ... both the cancer and non-cancer endpoints must be addressed...." Guidance Document at 21. If an applicant chooses not to use the 4.0 total toxicity factor, then it "must, at a minimum account for the risk from non-cancer endpoints for neurotoxicity, reproductive and developmental toxicity, immune system suppression, liver damage, skin irritation, and endocrine disruption for each of the commercial mixtures found at the cleanup site." Id. Although the Guidance Document does, as noted, anticipate and acknowledge that "some risk assessments may have components that require the use of non-standard ... unique ... or unconventional methods for estimating risk," id. at 44, that does not undermine the binding force of the Guidance Document in standard cases. Furthermore, even though the Guidance Document gives applicants the option of calculating risk in either of two ways (assuming both are practical) it still requires them to conform to one or the other, that is, not to submit an application based upon a third way. And if an applicant does choose to calculate cancer and non-cancer risks separately, then it must consider the non-cancer risks specified in the Guidance Document. To the applicant reading the Guidance Document the message is clear: in reviewing applications the Agency will not be open to considering approaches other than those prescribed in the Document.

The Guidance Document also appears to bind the Agency to accept applications using a total toxicity factor of 4.0 (mg/kg/day)–1 to calculate the risk from both cancer and noncancer endpoints. Guidance Document at 21. The EPA recognized this in its principal brief: "By indicating that [a] total toxicity value [of 4.0 (mg/kg/day)–1] will be accepted without detailed justification, the guidance document offers an applicant an opportunity to reduce the time and expense associated with risk assessment." In its supplemental brief, however, the EPA backs away from this statement, asserting that the "EPA is not 'bound' to approve an application under Section 761.61(c) if the applicant uses a total toxicity factor of 4.0

(mg/kg/day)–1, even assuming that the application falls within the framework of the guidance document." How can this be? According to the Agency, its position with respect to the total toxicity factor "is a matter of policy" that "can be changed at any time to respond to, inter alia, advances in scientific knowledge." But the Guidance Document itself says nothing of the sort. Clearly the EPA's initial response more accurately describes the Agency's approach in the Document: Stating without qualification that an applicant may use a total toxicity factor of 4.0 (mg/kg/day)–1 strongly implies that use of that value will not be questioned; an applicant reasonably could rely upon that implication.

The EPA argues that the Guidance Document "neither adds to EPA's prior position nor imposes any further obligations on EPA or the regulated community" because the Agency had used the toxicity factor of 4.0 (mg/kg/day)–1 when it "established the generic cleanup standards in the 1998 regulations." In its supplemental brief, however, the Agency explicitly states that it does not think its use of 4.0 (kg/mg/day)–1 in the 1998 regulations requires it to approve use of that factor in an application under § 761.61(c). Because we conclude that the Guidance Document does bind the Agency to accept use of 4.0 (kg/mg/day)–1, it follows that the Document does indeed impose a "further obligation[ ] on the EPA." In this way the Guidance Document is not like the risk data at issue in Chemical Mfrs., which we held "constrain no one until ... applied in a particular rule."

Furthermore, the EPA does not contend that in practice it has not treated the Guidance Document as binding in the ways described above. The EPA does not claim, for example, that it has accepted any applications that (1) use neither of the two methods of risk assessment approved in the Guidance Document; or (2) calculate risk separately for cancer and non-cancer endpoints, but fail to calculate endpoints for all the non-cancer risks required by the Guidance Document to be addressed. Nor does the EPA contend that it has ever rejected an applicant's use of 4.0 (mg/kg/day)–1. Whether an applicant has successfully used the second method of risk assessment set out in the Guidance Document—as the EPA asserts and GE disputes—is immaterial because, even if both methods are practically available, the Document nonetheless binds applicants and the Agency in the ways described above.

In sum, the commands of the Guidance Document indicate that it has the force of law. On its face the Guidance Document imposes binding obligations upon applicants to submit applications that conform to the Document and upon the Agency not to question an applicant's use of the 4.0 (mg/kg/day)–1 total toxicity factor. This is sufficient to render it a legislative rule. Furthermore, the Agency's application of the Document does nothing to demonstrate that the Document has any lesser effect in practice. Consequently, we conclude that the Guidance Document is a legislative rule. The Guidance Document is therefore undisputedly a "rule" for purposes of § 19(a)(1)(A) of the TSCA, and the manner of its promulgation is subject to review.

C. The Merits

The EPA concedes that it did not comply with the procedural requirements of the TSCA and of the APA. More specifically, as GE points out, it failed to publish a notice of proposed rulemaking, give interested parties an opportunity to comment, and hold an informal hearing. Therefore, having held that the case is ripe for review and that the Guidance Document is a "rule" for purposes of the TSCA, it is clear that GE must prevail on the merits. The EPA agrees: "Either the petition must be dismissed for lack of jurisdiction or the PCB Guidance should be vacated." For this reason we need not consider GE's alternative argument on the merits, namely, that the Guidance Document is not supported by substantial evidence.

III.   Conclusion

GE's petition for review is granted because the EPA promulgated a legislative rule without following the procedures required by the TSCA and the APA. The Guidance Document is accordingly

Vacated.

NOTES

(1) *Regulatory Vagueness?* One might say of the EPA, paraphrasing the Supreme Court in Guernsey, p. 714, that "the [Adminstrator] has issued regulations to address a wide range of [PCB] questions. The Part 161 regulations are comprehensive and intricate in detail ... [consuming almost 200] pages of the Code of Federal Regulations." However, what these regulations did in detail was to deal with the typical PCB case, and not with the unusual situations presented by a large manufacturer like GE. The latter cases were left to what were, in effect, license application adjudications: The decisional standard was "unreasonable risk of injury to health or the environment," as illuminated by the detailed generic procedures. In providing in detail for the ordinary (and likely to be repeated) case, and establishing an adjudicatory mode for unusual settings, had EPA acted reasonably? Or was this a case in which it had "promulgated mush," or (as in Chrysler, page 715 above) left the regulated entity unacceptably uncertain what it must do?

(2) Professor Robert Anthony, repeatedly and approvingly quoted in the opinion, has been among the most vocal critics of agency use of guidance documents. His more recent writings include Robert A. Anthony, Three Settings in Which Nonlegislative Rules Should Not Bind, 53 Admin. L. Rev. (forthcoming Dec. 2001); Robert A. Anthony & David A. Codevilla, Pro-ossification: A Harder Look at Agency Policy Statements, 31 Wake Forest L. Rev. 667 (1996); and Robert A. Anthony, "Interpretive" Rules, "Legislative" Rules and "Spurious" Rules: Lifting the Smog, 8 Admin. L.J. Am. U. 1 (1994).

Responding to the article of Professor Anthony quoted by the majority, editor Strauss argued for a different perspective in thinking about publication rules: their salutary practical effect in binding *the agency*, on analogy to a precedent in adjudication. PETER L. STRAUSS, THE RULEMAKING CONTINUUM, 41 Duke L.J. 1463, 1465, 1482–83 (1992). When publication rules function in this way, he observed, individuals "are ordinarily unconcerned with procedural sufficiency; those who are subject to regulation would prefer to have the government declare its position on some controvertible issue of law or policy and then to be able to hold the government to it."

"Putting the matter this way also suggests the high stakes for the public, including the regulated public, in encouraging the adoption of publication rules. The usual interface between a member of the public and an agency does not involve the agency head, but a relatively low-level member of staff; earlier we used the example of the postal clerk, but the welfare worker, the District Forester, the IRS examiner, the Food and Drug Administration (FDA) inspector, or the application desk officer each suggest the same result—responsibility for initial processing of the public's business. Absent, again, some basis for a judgment that the agency's body of legislative rules are inadequate in themselves to permit the agency to function, the choice the public faces is between having the clerk apply his own interpretation of the agency's legislative rules, or having his decisions and actions further controlled by the agency's publication rules. As any reader who has faced an audit will likely attest, bureaucratic rationality is a major protection for the public having to deal with a bureaucracy, as well as an occasional annoyance. While recognizing the irritations, the affected public (especially the repeat players among them) will almost certainly prefer a state of affairs in which such instructions are publicly given and may be relied upon—that is, the lower-level bureaucrats are to follow them, and higher levels are to depart from them only with an explanation. Such instructions may not 'bind' a member of the public (although like agency caselaw they may affect or be cited against the public); binding agency staff is their very rationale." Perhaps if EPA has tied its hands to accept the 4.0 (mg/kg/day)–1 level, neighbors might have complained it was insufficiently protective. Still, according to EPA's arguments, the 4.0–1 level informed the detailed generic procedures of 761.61, which *had* resulted from notice-and-comment rulemaking. What is GE's complaint about being offered a safe harbor based on those values?

(3) *Enforcement Policies.*

(a) Some interpretations may produce comfort for the regulated, but an uneasy feeling among intended regulatory beneficiaries that their interests are not being sufficiently attended to. In COMMUNITY NUTRITION INSTITUTE V. YOUNG, 818 F.2d 943 (D.C.Cir.1987), the Food and Drug Administration had advised corn producers that it would not prosecute as "adulterated" (a statutory term) shipments of corn having 20 parts per billion or fewer of the unavoidable but harmful contaminant aflatoxin. Producers were told to apply for an exemption if they wished to exceed that limit. CNI objected to the unavoidable implication that FDA had committed itself not to prosecute the presence of aflatoxins below the stated limit. CNI argued that this effectively permitted their shipments up to the 20 ppm level–a level it thought much too high. Yet if the agency did bring suit to enjoin shipment of allegedly contaminated corn, it would have to prove that the corn was "adulterated" within the meaning of the governing statute, and not merely out-of-compliance with the action level. After failing to persuade the Supreme Court that FDA was required to establish a "tolerance level" for aflatoxin by regulation, Young v. CNI, 476 U.S. 974 (1986), CNI successfully persuaded the D.C.

Circuit on remand that setting the "action level" itself required the use of notice and comment rulemaking procedures. In the court's view, the agency had sufficiently bound itself for the action level to constitute a substantive, legislative rule. Judge Starr dissented, arguing that the single determinative test should be whether the agency's pronouncement has the force of law in subsequent proceedings against the regulated party. Would the public be better off without "action levels"? An article reviewing the case argued that "under those cases following the reasoning of [CNI v. Young], the more unstructured, variable and undisciplined the agency's prosecutorial approach, the more shielded an agency's prosecutorial discretion will be from public participation and, ultimately, judicial review. But, if regularity of agency enforcement action, centralized control of agency personnel, and imposition of public, agency-wide policy are desired—and they *are* desired by most critics of unchanneled agency discretion—then a rule that essentially penalizes an agency for restricting the discretion of its own personnel would appear to be counterproductive." Richard M. Thomas, Prosecutorial Discretion and Agency Self–Regulation: *CNI v. Young* and the Aflatoxin Dance, 44 Admin.L.Rev. 131, 155 (1992).

Here is the way the D.C. Circuit majority tried to handle the point: "Our holding today in no way indicates that agencies develop written guidelines to aid their exercise of discretion only at the peril of having a court transmogrify those guidelines into binding norms. We recognize that such guidelines have the not inconsiderable benefits of apprizing the regulated community of the agency's intentions as well as informing the exercise of discretion by agents and officers in the field. It is beyond question that many such statements are non-binding in nature and would thus be characterized by a court as interpretative rules or policy statements. We are persuaded that courts will appropriately reach an opposite conclusion only where, as here, the agency itself has given its rules substantive effect." 818 F.2d at 948. Are you convinced?

(b) CHAMBER OF COMMERCE OF THE UNITED STATES V. U.S. DEPARTMENT OF LABOR, 174 F.3d 206 (D.C.Cir.1999) ended OSHA's effort to expand, nationwide, its successful "Maine 200" program to encourage the operators of particularly hazardous worksites to enter into consultative relationships with it, p. 289 above. In a "policy statement" Directive, OSHA announced a plan to target the 12,500 most hazardous workplaces in the country for aggressive inspections—a plan certain to satisfy any Fourth Amendment constraints on its inspection routines, but well beyond its capacity to effect with the number of inspectors at its command. Essential to the plan was the "carrot" of a promise to reduce greatly the chance a workplace would be inspected if the employer agreed to participate in a "Cooperative Compliance Program" meeting declared OSHA guidelines. The Maine experience had been that 99% of employers chose the carrot—and that accident rates fell dramatically with the cooperative compliance regime in place. For the D.C. Circuit, this was not an offer OSHA was entitled to make without first undertaking notice-and-comment rulemaking.

"The Directive will affect employers' interests in the same way that a plainly substantive rule mandating a comprehensive safety program would affect their rights; that it so operates without having the force of law is therefore of little, if any, significance. In practical terms, the Directive places the burden of inspection upon those employers that fail to adopt a CSHP, and will have a substantial impact upon all employers within its purview—including those that acquiesce in the agency's use of "leverage" against them. Consequently, we conclude that the Directive is a substantive rather than a procedural rule.

". . . At first glance, one might think that a rule could not be considered a 'binding norm' unless it is backed by a threat of legal sanction. Beyond that first glance, however, its appeal is fleeting. . . . [T]he Directive provides that every employer that does not participate in the CCP will be searched. The effect of the rule is therefore not to "announce[ ] the agency's tentative intentions for the future," but to inform employers of a decision already made. Indeed, the OSHA admits in its brief that the inspection plan "leaves no room for discretionary choices by inspectors in the field." And the Directive itself suggests that the agency will not remove an employer from the CCP unless the employer fails to abide by the terms of the program. Therefore, although the Directive does not impose a binding norm in the sense that it gives rise to a legally enforceable duty, neither can it be shoehorned into the exception for policy statements."

(4) Can an agency make *any* use in subsequent proceedings of a statement of policy without running afoul of the APA? In PANHANDLE PRODUCERS & ROYALTY OWNERS ASS'N v. ECONOMIC REGULATORY ADMIN., 847 F.2d 1168 (5th Cir.1988), the organic statute permitted importation of natural gas unless it would "not be consistent with the public interest." Until 1984, importers had the burden of proof in demonstrating the need for, and reasonableness of, their proposals. In 1984, the agency announced in a policy statement that a proposed contract, if it contained flexible pricing and volume terms, would be presumed supported by need. "Parties opposing an import will bear the burden of demonstrating that the import arrangement is not consistent with the public interest." This statement, which might well be thought to have more than a merely "procedural" effect, was used to allocate the burden of proof in a proceeding and was cited in the ensuing order. The Fifth Circuit rejected a challenge by domestic gas producers. The agency did not treat the guidelines as binding precedent and responded to each argument made by opponents of the order. The agency was not bound to treat the situation as if the guidelines had never been written. "[T]he fact that a non-binding policy statement must be considered 'subject to complete attack' before being applied in particular cases does not mean that such a statement must be ignored *entirely* in those cases." 847 F.2d at 1175. Accord, Panhandle Producers and Royalty Owners Ass'n v. Economic Regulatory Admin., 822 F.2d 1105, 1110–11 (D.C.Cir.1987) ("Presumptions, so long as rebuttable, leave [the requisite degree of] freedom.").

(5) *The Legitimacy of Constrained Guidance.* TODD D. RAKOFF, THE CHOICE BETWEEN FORMAL AND INFORMAL MODES OF ADMINISTRATIVE REGULATION, 52 Admin.L.Rev. 159, 159–170 (2000): "On February 18, 1997, the United States Food and Drug Administration (FDA) issued a document entitled 'Good Guidance Practices' that set forth the agency's 'policies and proce-

dures for the development, issuance, and use of guidance documents."[1] [T]he document is important because it frankly recognizes and treats a category of administrative action called 'guidance.'

" 'Guidance' as a named, identified legal category is something new in American administrative law. The Administrative Procedure Acts of some countries, such as Japan and Korea, address concepts with this title, but ours does not. . . . This explicit recognition of 'guidance' is just one facet of the growing tendency of American administrative agencies to return to what we, in the United States, think of as informal administrative procedures. . . .

" . . . Americans are uneasy about governmental management of the economy; they favor administrative expertise and the furtherance of the public interest, but also want agencies to act in a law-like fashion.

"These two points of view could both be satisfied if it were possible to stipulate ahead of time, by broadly applicable rules of known application, the norms necessary to make private behavior consistent with the public interest. . . . [Yet the] experience of the twentieth century . . . is that this supposed program is, in fact, impossible to carry out in a modern society. The variety of situations to which any important rule must be applied is so vast that the process of application will inherently go beyond formal characterization, and instead will require judgments of policy. Moreover, the expertise required to choose the right path will often develop out of interaction between the administrative agency and the regulated party, and thus, in a rather strict sense, be unknowable ahead of time. Finally, the decisions to many modern problems require the reconciliation of multiple points of view, so that in many instances, the agency must be engaged more in balancing interests than in applying rules. In short, effective use of administrative power in modern circumstances necessitates substantial administrative discretion. . . .

"Since the 1960s, then, administrative law in the United States has exhausted the possibilities for developing an easily workable system of regulation within the procedural forms articulated in the APA. Agencies interested in pursuing their programs, rather than just slowing down, must search for ways to escape from [its] models of rulemaking and adjudication. We are in the midst of another round of discovering the virtues of informality. There is renewed interest in resolving particular disputes short of formal adjudication. Of greater general import, there is a trend toward setting regulatory policy in less formal ways. Techniques that previously were used as preliminaries to rulemaking or adjudication under the APA are now being used on the assumption that they will constitute the final disposition. Three such methods exemplify the trend: negotiated rulemaking, the use of interpretative rules, and organized 'guidance.' . . .

---

1. The Food and Drug Administration's Development, Issuance, and Use of Guidance Documents, 62 Fed. Reg. 8961 (1997). The approach taken by the FDA received congressional approval in the Food and Drug Administration Modernization Act of 1997, Pub. L. No. 105–115, § 405, 111 Stat. 2296, 2368–69 (codified as amended at 21 U.S.C. § 360bbb–1 (Supp. III 1997)).

"[The FDA's 'Good Guidance Practices' took the APA's lenient attitude toward interpretative rules and policy statements, and converted it into a wholly alternative system of regulation.] If we compare the mid–1990s with the late 1970s or early 1980s, we find that the number of FDA regulations adopted each year in accordance with the APA's rulemaking procedures declined by about fifty percent. By contrast, since the start of this decade there has been a striking increase in the number of FDA-issued documents intended to give guidance to the regulated industry but not adopted through public procedures. The rate per year for the 1990s is about four hundred percent greater than the rate for the 1980s. This decrease in the number of enacted rules, and this increase in the number of guidance documents led to cries that the required procedures were being subverted. Under pressure from industry, and to some extent from the courts as well, the FDA responded with a substantial, public proceeding—much like a rulemaking proceeding—in order to develop the very procedures by which this new process would be carried out.

"The ... definition of the term 'guidance documents' that the agency ultimately adopted ... cover[s] documents directed either to the agency's own staff or to the public that relate to: the evaluation or approval of proposed new drugs; the production and testing of regulated products; the agency's inspection and enforcement procedures; or documents that broadly describe 'the agency's policy and regulatory approach to an issue.' ... [Under the Good Guidance Practices,] guidance documents 'are not legally binding on the public or the agency. Rather, they explain how the agency believes the statutes and regulations apply to certain regulated activities.' Indeed, the FDA remains open to discussing 'alternative methods that comply with the [applicable] statute or regulations....' In short, guidance documents are meant to be statements of no legal consequence but immense practical consequence about virtually everything the agency regulates. ... [T]he FDA's program excludes from its scope 'communications directed to individual persons or firms,' ... [and does not claim the prerogative deliberately to go beyond its statutory authority], and thus in some sense still visualizes 'guidance' as rule-bound behavior. ...

"The 'Good Guidance Practices' statement divides guidance documents into two groups. The documents in the first, more important, group 'set forth first interpretations of statutory or regulatory requirements, changes in interpretation or policy that are of more than a minor nature, unusually complex scientific issues, or highly controversial issues.' The stipulated procedures for this group provide that the agency will publish a notice of the draft guidance in the Federal Register, accept written comments and perhaps hold public meetings regarding the draft, review the comments, and 'make changes to a guidance document in response to comments as appropriate.' It would not be far-fetched to rephrase these matters by saying that the FDA now proposes to issue its important regulations mostly in accordance with the notice-and-comment rulemaking procedure set forth in the APA, as it was understood before 1970.

"The only difference is that, at least in the agency's view, the entire matter will be beyond the purview of the courts. The promulgated policies will not legally bind the agency or regulated parties, and the stipulated procedures are not intended to confer procedural rights. But is that such a difference? The FDA appears to thinks it is not, as it proposes to set forth new interpretations of statutory requirements and other regulatory changes 'of more than a minor nature' in this fashion. It appears that the industry thinks it is not a great difference either, since it participated extensively in the proceeding to establish these 'good guidance practices.' In this highly regulated industry, in which all the players—including the agency, the drug companies, and even the representatives of consumers— are repeat players, it may well be that 'the force of law,' in the strict sense of enforceability in court, is of little value compared to 'the force of law' in the practical sense as dictated by existing relationships. . . .

". . . [T]he creation by the FDA of a whole organized system of rules contained in guidance documents can be seen either as an example of thoughtful and balanced institutional creativity, or as a brazen attempt to subvert the APA as construed by the courts."

See also Lars Noah, The FDA's New Policy on Guidelines: Having Your Cake and Eating it Too, 47 Cath. U.L. Rev. 113 (2001).

CHAPTER VI

OPEN GOVERNMENT AND THE FREEDOM OF INFORMATION ACT

SECTION 1. THE GENERAL SCOPE OF THE FREEDOM OF INFORMATION ACT

The Freedom of Information Act (or FOIA), codified at 5 U.S.C. § 552 as a sub-part of the Administrative Procedure Act (see pp. 1323–36 in the Appendix), departs further from the original APA than most of the other provisions studied in this book. When the APA was passed in 1946, it built on prior legislation by providing for what it called "Public Information" in three ways. (Ch. 324, § 3, 60 Stat. 238.) First, agencies were to publish their rules—their substantive rules, their general interpretations and statements of policy, and their rules of procedure—in the Federal Register. Second, they were to publish elsewhere (for example, in a series of their own reports) final opinions and orders in adjudicated cases, and rules of lesser generality—or in some other way act to make these materials available for public inspection. Finally, other types of agency records were to be made available "to persons properly and directly concerned" except where there was good cause for confidentiality.

One might say that these original provisions incorporated three general judgments. First, that agency law should be public. Second, that the core of agency law resided in substantive rules and decided cases, but that it extended somewhat more broadly to include at least the most significant policies and interpretations. And third, that other sorts of information that agencies had were properly made available only to a small group of outsiders, who had a demonstrably direct connection to the information at issue.

Starting in 1966, this part of the APA has been amended several times—much more so than the rest of the APA. Section 552(a)(1) still provides for rules of procedure, substantive rules, and "statements of general policy or interpretations of general applicability" to be published in the Federal Register. Section 552(a)(2) still provides for the opinions and orders in cases, and less general interpretations and statements of policy—supplemented now by "administrative staff manuals"—to be published in some other form, or made available (now including over the internet) for inspection and copying. (For further investigation of these two provisions, see the materials in this book on "Publication Rules," p. 705 above.) But section 552(a)(3) directs agencies to make available other records (a term which, by the way, is defined to include information stored in electronic formats) "to any person" based simply upon a request which "reasonably describes such records.'' Or, as the title of the enacting legislation would have it, there is now a presumption of freedom of information.

There are many details to consider regarding how this general presumption is carried out; but we should first pause to consider what might lie behind this departure from the original view that, beyond the legal materials generated by an agency, public access should be highly restricted. One possibility is that the APA now adopts a different view of what constitutes legally relevant materials: that it starts with the presumption that anything in an agency's files or data bases might influence agency action in pursuance of its statutory responsibilities, and thus from a purely operational viewpoint have legal importance. (One might see in this approach the way in which the freedom of information idea grew up with, and at times has historically substituted for, expanded disclosure by agencies in their own proceedings, such as was required in the Nova Scotia case, p. 524 above.) Another possibility is that, as the administrative state has grown larger, it has also grown potentially more fearsome; full disclosure is on this view a starting point for a process of policing agencies through public opinion and political pressure. And a third possibility is that governmental information is a resource which ought to be available to all for their own benefit, unless there is a reason to withhold it. On this view, disclosure of records in general is just a larger case of the many overt ways in which government collects information and provides it to private businesses and organizations, from Census data on down.

At one point, in specifying the fees to be charged for searching for, and duplicating, records, the statute distinguishes among these possible purposes, for it makes some difference as to the cost whether information is requested for a commercial use, is requested by a news reporter, is likely to contribute to public understanding of the government, and the like. See 5 U.S.C. § 552(4)(A). But the general design of the statute makes no such distinctions. The requester of records needs to describe the records wanted, but need not give any reason for wanting them. When the statute lists the grounds for the agency's refusing to surrender records (of which, more below), those grounds also do not depend on the reason for wanting the records produced. Whether in close cases it is possible to ignore suspicions as to the requester's probable purpose is, of course, a question that might reasonably be raised.

More broadly, the presumption in favor of disclosure—the idea that one need only describe the records wanted, and be willing to pay the fee, to be entitled to have the agency search for, and produce, anything corresponding to the request in its files—appears in many of the statute's subsidiary details. While the text of the statute *authorizes* agency nondisclosure in certain circumstances, it does not itself *require* non-disclosure. Further, it provides that if only parts of a document are exempt from disclosure, ''any reasonably segregable portion'' that does not share the infirmity must be produced. Both provisions seem to tell the agency that it will be easier to produce its records than not to produce them. And when the statute turns to judicial review, the same pressure to produce seems evident. Denials of requests can be taken to federal district court, and if the agency has not produced the documents relatively quickly, that delay can be deemed a denial. The complainant has a wide choice of venue. The court is authorized to assess attorney fees against the government if the complainant "substantially" prevails. Above all, not only is the district court told to "determine the matter de novo," it is also told that as to the applicability of any of the exemptions from disclosure "the burden is on the agency to sustain its action." 5 U.S.C. § 552(4)(B).

The statute lists nine general grounds for the agency's refusing to produce records that have been requested. They (like the rest of FOIA) are set out in the Appendix, 5 U.S.C. § 552(b)(1)(A) at p. 1332 below, and to understand the arguments in the cases one must of course consult the precise statutory language. For the purposes of grasping the general design of the statute, however, a truncated description of the nine will suffice:

(1) Classified records regarding national defense or foreign policy;

(2) Matters relating only to internal personnel rules and practices;

(3) Information specifically exempted from disclosure by some other statute;

(4) Trade secrets and confidential commercial information originating from a source outside the government;

(5) Intra- or inter-agency memoranda that fall within an ordinary litigation privilege, including executive privilege;

(6) Files on individuals, when disclosure would constitute an unwarranted invasion of personal privacy;

(7) Information compiled for law enforcement purposes, to the extent that disclosure would produce one of six specifically named harms;

(8) Certain records relating to the supervision of financial institutions; and

(9) Geological information regarding wells.

A couple of the listed items—the last two—are rather specific; but by and large the exemptions describe broad swaths of material to be exempted from the yet broader obligation to disclose records that have been requested. Moreover, the exemptions seem to assume a firmer set of background principles than perhaps exists—seem to assume, for example, that we already know, or can easily discover, what materials are ordinarily considered privileged, or represent trade secrets. Finally, although the exemptions include materials whose continued secrecy would be of interest to persons outside the agency—materials as varied as a corporation's process for making a miracle drug and an individual's tax return—the statute makes no explicit provision for these outsiders to be heard in the agency's (or court's) consideration of what should be disclosed. For all these reasons, the scope of the obligation of the agencies to disclose, or of their privilege not to disclose, or perhaps even of some obligation not to disclose, are much litigated topics. Indeed, those who read the advance sheets of the federal courts on matters involving administrative law cannot help but notice that FOIA is a leading contender for "the most litigated" of all administrative law matters.

NOTES

(1) Consistent with its information-providing theme, FOIA also requires each agency to prepare each year a report to the Attorney General detailing how it handled FOIA itself. 5 U.S.C. § 552(e)(1). The Attorney General is then instructed to make all the reports electronically available to the public at a single web site. 5 U.S.C. § 552(e)(3). Thus, you can find the reports at www.usdoj.gov/04foia, as well as in the electronic reading room each agency maintains at its own home page. A glance at some of these reports gives some indication of the scope and impact of the statute. For instance, the 2001 report for the entire Department of Health and Human Services (which consolidates the reports for operating divisions as varied as the Centers for Disease Control, the Food and Drug Administration, and the Indian Health Service) shows that the Department processed 62,599 FOIA requests, of which 48,226 were directly granted in full by the agency. Most of those not granted exhibited formal difficulties: the request was withdrawn, there was a problem about paying the fee, or the records did not in fact exist. 1,605 requests were denied on the merits and an additional 867 were granted only in part. For this agency, the most common exemption relied on was number six, the personal privacy exemption. 30 denials were reversed on internal appeal. And all of this action required the efforts of 169 full-time FOIA personnel, and some part-timers, for a total agency cost for FOIA processing (disregarding litigation) of $12,983,533. (The original Congressional estimates for implementing FOIA had been only in the hundreds of thousands of dollars for the whole government!) Of HHS's costs, only $964,711, or 7%, was recouped in fees.

The EPA in the same year spent $12,005,482 to process just 14,292 requests; perhaps they were more extensive. The pattern of response was similar: 9,319 requests were granted in full; only 62 were denied in full, 588 in part. Other requests fell by the wayside for miscellaneous reasons. At EPA, the most commonly used exemption was number 4, for confidential commercial information.

The Justice Department itself processed a whopping 194,612 requests, mostly through the Immigration and Naturalization Service and the Bureau of Prisons. Its denials, somewhat more frequent, were based mostly on exemption 6 or on exemption 7(c), which relates to personal privacy in records gathered for law enforcement purposes.

(2) Then-Acting Attorney General Robert Bork: FOIA presents problems akin to those "of the most difficult constitutional issues. . . . [A]djustment of [its] basic and conflicting values in individual cases, I find at least, a nerve-wracking task." Remarks quoted in Robert Saloschin, The FOIA–A Governmental Perspective, 35 Pub. Admin. Rev. 10, 13 (1975).

Then-professor Antonin Scalia: [The Freedom of Information Act is] "the Taj Mahal of the Doctrine of Unanticipated Consequences, the Sistine Chapel of Cost Benefit Analysis Ignored." "The defects of the . . . Act cannot be cured so long as we are dominated by the obsession that gave them birth—that the first line of defense against an arbitrary executive is do-it-yourself oversight by the public and its surrogate, the press." The Freedom of Information Act Has No Clothes, Regulation, March/April 1982 14, 15, 19.

Judge Patricia Wald: "If the debacles of the last few decades have taught us anything, they have taught us that too much secrecy breeds irresponsibility. ... [S]omething like [FOIA] had to be invented to prevent a 'curtain of fog and iron' from falling between the American public and its government. ... If the law fails, a piece of our freedom is chipped away. Times change—certain values, like open government, go in and out of favor. ... Watergate reinvigorated a feeble FOIA and produced FOIA amendments more important in many respects than the original bill. Yet, again, history and political fortunes changed, and the FOIA came to be viewed as a kind of flower child of the irresponsible seventies, constantly threatened with defoliation. Proofs of its actual harm to law enforcement or national security were relatively meager—the perceptions of potential informers and allies, not concrete evidence of positive harm, were invoked to discredit it. And in truth, the FOIA, like all basic freedoms, sometimes hurts the worthy and sometimes helps the unworthy.

"It takes constant vigilance, commitment, and common sense to make any law work. I hope we as citizens have all these qualities—in large measure to keep the FOIA around for a long time and to make it work." The Freedom of Information Act: A Short Case Study in the Perils and Paybacks of Legislating Democratic Values, 33 Emory L.J. 649, 654, 683 (1984).

(3) What are "agency records"? The Supreme Court focused on four factors: whether the documents were (1) in the agency's control; (2) generated within the agency; (3) placed into the agency's files; and (4) used by the agency "for any purpose." KISSINGER V. REPORTERS COMMITTEE FOR FREEDOM OF THE PRESS, 445 U.S. 136 (1980), involved three separate FOIA requests for the transcripts and summaries of Henry Kissinger's telephone conversations, which were maintained while he was Secretary of State and national security advisor to the President. Dr. Kissinger treated the notes as his own personal papers. While still in the State Department, he transferred them to a private location before two of the three FOIA requests were filed, and he entered an agreement deeding the notes to the Library of Congress. As to those two requests, the Court found that the State Department had not "withheld" anything because the documents had been removed from the State Department's possession prior to the filing of a FOIA request. "[T]he agency ha[d] neither the custody nor the control to enable it to withhold." The third FOIA request, filed before the telephone notes were removed from the State Department, sought notes of telephone conversations Dr. Kissinger had while he was in the Office of the President prior to becoming Secretary of State. Because FOIA does not include Presidential assistants in the definition of "agency," the records of those phone conversations were not *"agency"* records, and the mere physical transfer of those documents to the State Department did not by itself render them "agency records" because the "papers were not in the control of the State Department at any time. They were not generated in the State Department. They never entered the State Department's files, and they were not used by the Department for any purpose. If mere physical location of papers and materials could confer status as an 'agency record' Kissinger's personal books, speeches, and all other memorabilia stored in his office would have been agency records subject to disclosure under the FOIA."

(4) The most recent Congressional action regarding FOIA occurred in 1996, establishing what is commonly known as E–FOIA. The effects of those amendments are described in the Department of Justice's Freedom of Information Act Guide (2002) as follows:

"For the first thirty years of the FOIA's operation, three categories of records—'final opinions [and] . . . orders' rendered in the adjudication of administrative cases, specific agency policy statements, and certain administrative staff manuals 'that affect a member of the public'—were routinely made available in agency reading rooms. . . .

"The Electronic Freedom of Information Act Amendments of 1996 heavily modified the requirements of subsection [5 U.S.C. § 552](a)(2) by creating a fourth category of 'reading room' records, and by establishing a requirement for the electronic availability of 'reading room' records in what are referred to as 'electronic reading rooms.' The Electronic FOIA amendments greatly elevated the role of agency reading rooms—and, in turn, agency sites on the World Wide Web—in the processes of FOIA administration.

"First, in addition to the traditional three categories of 'reading room' records discussed above, agencies must also include any records processed and disclosed in response to a FOIA request that 'the agency determines have become or are likely to become the subject of subsequent requests for substantially the same records.' Under this provision, when records are disclosed in response to a FOIA request, an agency is required to determine whether they have been the subject of multiple FOIA requests (i.e., two or more additional ones) or, in the agency's best judgment based upon the nature of the records and the types of requests regularly received, are likely to be the subject of multiple requests in the future. . . .

"Second, the Electronic FOIA amendments require agencies to use electronic information technology to enhance the availability of their 'reading room' records: Agencies must make their newly created 'reading room' records (i.e., records created by agencies on or after November 1, 1996 in all four 'reading room' categories) available to the public by 'electronic means.' The Electronic FOIA amendments embody a strong statutory preference that this new electronic availability be provided by agencies in the form of online, Internet access—which is most efficient for both agencies and the public alike—and this expectation has been met by the development of agency FOIA sites on the World Wide Web.

"Under the Electronic FOIA amendments, all federal agencies now have FOIA sites on the World Wide Web to serve this 'electronic reading room' function, as well as for other FOIA-related purposes. This is a matter of great and growing importance to the processes of FOIA administration. . . ."

Whether or not compelled by the "likely to become the subject of subsequent requests" criterion, agencies are also increasingly putting on the web the whole docket in pending rulemaking proceedings, thus increasing both transparency and ease of participation.

If you want to try dipping into administrative materials on the web, to see what kinds of things these might be, you might look at the well-organized site that has been established for the September 11 Victim Compensation Fund, www.usdoj.gov/victimcompensation/.

(5) How should FOIA litigation proceed in court? The statute provides for agency claims of exemption to be tried de novo. But agencies don't want to have to disclose documents in order to litigate whether they ought to be disclosed. So the statute also provides for the judge to consider the disputed records in camera. But this in turn means first, that opposing counsel cannot easily argue the merits, and second, that the judge may have to review hundreds or thousands of pages by herself against a general claim that they fall into one exemption or another. Whether impressed by the first problem or not, the judges early on responded to the second one. Litigation under FOIA now usually proceeds on the basis of a "Vaughn index," named after the first case to require it, Vaughn v. Rosen, 484 F.2d 820 (D.C.Cir.1973), cert. denied 415 U.S. 977 (1974). In the Vaughn index, the agency itemizes and describes the records it does not want to produce, presents its justifications for not producing them, and cross-references the specific records with the specific justifications. These specified and indexed claims then become the basis for contest in court.

(6) Do you want to know what an agency knows about you? Now you know how to ask. One of the senior editors of this casebook used FOIA to inquire of the FBI whether it had any records about him—and found that his activities on behalf of the American Civil Liberties Union and the American Association of University Professors during the McCarthy era had in fact earned him that distinction. The report he received was, however, heavily redacted.

(7) Another avenue for getting personal information about oneself from the government is to pursue one's rights under the Privacy Act, codified at 5 U.S.C. § 552a. This long and detailed Act is especially addressed to government records of routine personal information—about education, medical history, financial transactions, criminal record, and so on. It specifies a mechanism, not only for seeing what the government knows, but also for having those records corrected if they are inaccurate. See 5 U.S.C. § 552a(d). With regard to records it governs, the Privacy Act starts from the opposite point of view from FOIA: it prohibits disclosure except to, or with the permission of, the person to whom each record pertains, or except as authorized under various specified (and restricted) conditions of disclosure. But a cross-reference to FOIA contained in the Privacy Act, 5 U.S.C. § 552a(b)(2), seems to have the consequence of telling agencies that they should release under FOIA that which FOIA requires to be released. Protection of privacy from the eyes of others thus depends on the scope of the FOIA exemptions.

SECTION 2.   FREEDOM OF INFORMATION AND THE OPERATIONAL NEEDS OF AGENCIES

a.   THE FLOW OF INFORMATION WITHIN AGENCIES

A moment's thought will show that if administrative agencies were allowed to work totally in secret, we would have no confidence that they were following the rule of law or allowing for adequate democratic participation. Another moment's thought will show that if administrative agencies were required to let everyone in the world know what they were doing and thinking at all times, their work would come to a halt. This tension reappears in numerous doctrines of administrative law—for example, in the question of what constitutes an adequate notice of proposed rulemaking. See Chapter 5, p. 519 above. The FOIA includes in its text both sides of the dilemma: a rule of disclosure and various exemptions based on the needs of government. Presumably it was meant to move the balance point further in the direction of disclosure than the operation of other rules of administrative law—but how far was it meant to go?

National Labor Relations Board v. Sears, Roebuck & Co.

Supreme Court of the United States, 1975.
421 U.S. 132.

■ MR. JUSTICE WHITE delivered the opinion of the Court.

[Sears urged a Regional Director of the Board to file an unfair labor practice complaint against a labor union with which it was engaged in collective bargaining. The Regional Director refused, guided in his judgment by internal advice received from the General Counsel of the Board; such refusals were appealable to an Office of Appeals in the General Counsel's Office. While preparing its appeal, Sears requested disclosure of various memoranda and related records generated by the Office of the General Counsel in deciding whether to issue other unfair labor practice complaints. The General Counsel resisted, principally on the ground of FOIA's fifth exemption, which excludes "inter-agency or intra-agency memorandums or letters which would not be available by law to a party other than an agency in litigation with the agency." Sears sued, claiming that the documents it sought were disclosable both as "final opinions" or "instructions to staff that affect a member of the public" (5 U.S.C. § 552(a)(2)) and as "identifiable records" not within any exemptive category (5 U.S.C. § 552(a)(3)). After the General Counsel failed in efforts to settle the dispute, the district court granted Sears sweeping relief. The court of appeals affirmed without opinion.]

A

The parties are in apparent agreement that Exemption 5 withholds from a member of the public documents which a private party could not discover in litigation with the agency. EPA v. Mink, 410 U.S. 73, 85–86 (1973). Since virtually any document not privileged may be discovered by the appropriate litigant, if it is relevant to his litigation; and since the Act clearly intended to give any member of the public as much right to disclosure as one with a special interest therein, it is reasonable to construe Exemption 5 to exempt those documents, and only those documents, normally privileged in the civil discovery context.[1] The privileges claimed

---

1. The ability of a private litigant to override a privilege claim set up by the Gov-   ernment, with respect to an otherwise disclosable document, may itself turn on the

by [the government] to be relevant to this case are (i) the "generally ... recognized" privilege for "confidential intra-agency advisory opinions ...," disclosure of which would be "injurious to the consultative functions of government ... ," EPA v. Mink, supra, at 86–87, (sometimes referred to as "executive privilege"), and (ii) the attorney-client and attorney work product privileges generally available to all litigants.

(i)

That Congress had the Government's executive privilege specifically in mind in adopting Exemption 5 is clear. ... The precise contours of the privilege in the context of this case are less clear, but may be gleaned from expressions of legislative purpose and the prior case law. The cases uniformly rest the privilege on the policy of protecting the "decision making processes of government agencies" ... and focus on documents "reflecting advisory opinions, recommendations and deliberations comprising part of a process by which governmental decisions and policies are formulated." Carl Zeiss Stiftung v. E.B. Carl Zeiss, Jena, 40 F.R.D., at 324 [D.D.C. 1966]. The point, plainly made in the Senate Report, is that the frank discussion of legal and policy matters in writing might be inhibited if the discussion were made public; and that the "decisions" and "policies formulated" would be the poorer as a result. ... As ... we have said in an analogous context, "[h]uman experience teaches that those who expect public dissemination of their remarks may well temper candor with a concern for appearances ... to the *detriment of the decisionmaking process*." United States v. Nixon, 418 U.S. 683, 705 (1974) (emphasis added).[2]

Manifestly, the ultimate purpose of this long-recognized privilege is to prevent injury to the quality of agency decisions. The quality of a particular agency decision will clearly be affected by the communications received by the decisionmaker on the subject of the decision prior to the time the decision is made. However, it is difficult to see how the quality of a decision will be affected by communications with respect to the decision occurring after the decision is finally reached; and therefore equally difficult to see how the quality of the decision will be affected by forced disclosure of such communications, as long as prior communications and the ingredients of the decisionmaking process are not disclosed. Accordingly, the lower courts have uniformly drawn a distinction between <u>predecisional communications</u>, which are <u>privileged</u>,[3] ... and communications made after the decision and

Predecisional Communications Privileged (exec priv)

---

extent of the litigant's need in the context of the facts of his particular case; or on the nature of the case. ... However, it is not sensible to construe the Act to require disclosure of any document which would be disclosed in the hypothetical litigation in which the private party's claim is the most compelling. Indeed, the House Report says that Exemption 5 was intended to permit disclosure of those intra-agency memoranda which would "routinely be disclosed" in private litigation, H.R.Rep. No. 1497, p. 10, and we accept this as the law.

2. Our remarks in United States v. Nixon were made in the context of a claim of "executive privilege" resting solely on the Constitution of the United States. No such claim is made here and we do not mean to intimate that any documents involved here are protected by whatever constitutional content the doctrine of executive privilege might have.

3. Our emphasis on the need to protect predecisional documents does not mean that

designed to explain it, which are not.[4] ... The public is only marginally concerned with reasons supporting a policy which an agency has rejected, or with reasons which might have supplied, but did not supply, the basis for a policy which was actually adopted on a different ground. In contrast, the public is vitally concerned with the reasons which did supply the basis for an agency policy actually adopted. These reasons, if expressed within the agency, constitute the "working law" of the agency and have been held by the lower courts to be outside the protection of Exemption 5. Exemption 5, properly construed, calls for "disclosure of all 'opinions and interpretations'—which embody the agency's effective law and policy, and the withholding of all papers which reflect the agency's group thinking in the process of working out its policy and determining what its law shall be." Davis, The Information Act: A Preliminary Analysis, 34 U.Chi.L.Rev. 761, 797 (1967).

This conclusion is powerfully supported by the other provisions of the Act. The affirmative portion of the Act, expressly requiring indexing of "final opinions," "statements of policy and interpretations which have been adopted by the agency," and "instructions to staff that affect a member of the public," 5 U.S.C. § 552(a)(2), represents a strong congressional aversion to "secret agency law," Davis, supra, at 797; and represents an affirmative congressional purpose to require disclosure of documents which have "the force and effect of law." We should be reluctant therefore to construe Exemption 5 to apply to the documents described in 5 U.S.C. § 552(a)(2); and with respect at least to "final opinions," which not only invariably explain agency action already taken or an agency decision already made, but also constitute "final dispositions" of matters by an agency, we hold that Exemption 5 can never apply.

(ii)

It is equally clear that Congress had the attorney work product privilege specifically in mind when it adopted Exemption 5 and that such a privilege had been recognized in the civil discovery context by the prior case law. ... Whatever the outer boundaries of the attorney work product rule are, the rule clearly applies to memoranda prepared by an attorney in contemplation of litigation which set forth the attorney's theory of the case and his litigation strategy.

the existence of the privilege turns on the ability of an agency to identify a specific decision in connection with which a memorandum is prepared. Agencies are, and properly should be, engaged in a continuing process of examining their policies; this process will generate memoranda containing recommendations which do not ripen into agency decisions; and the lower courts should be wary of interfering with this process.

4. We are aware that the line between predecisional documents and postdecisional documents may not always be a bright one. Indeed, even the prototype of the postdecisional document—the "final opinion"— serves the dual function of explaining the decision just made and providing guides for decisions of similar or analogous cases arising in the future. In its latter function, the opinion is predecisional; and the manner in which it is written may, therefore, affect decisions in later cases. For present purposes it is sufficient to note that final opinions are *primarily* postdecisional—looking back on and explaining, as they do, a decision already reached or a policy already adopted—and that their disclosure poses a negligible risk of denying to agency decisionmakers the uninhibited advice which is so important to agency decisions.

B

Applying these principles to the memoranda sought by Sears, it becomes clear that Exemption 5 does not apply to those Appeals and Advice Memoranda which conclude that no complaint should be filed and which have the effect of finally denying relief to the charging party; but that Exemption 5 does protect from disclosure those Appeals and Advice Memoranda which direct the filing of a complaint and the commencement of litigation before the Board.

(i)

Under the procedures employed by the General Counsel, Advice and Appeals Memoranda are communicated to the Regional Director *after* the General Counsel, through his Advice and Appeals Branches, has decided whether or not to issue a complaint; and represent an explanation to the Regional Director of a legal or policy decision already adopted by the General Counsel. In the case of decisions *not* to file a complaint, the Memoranda effect as "final" a "disposition" as an administrative decision can—representing, as it does, an unreviewable rejection of the charge filed by the private party. Disclosure of these Memoranda would not intrude on predecisional processes, and protecting them would not improve the quality of agency decisions, since when the Memoranda are communicated to the Regional Director, the General Counsel has already reached his decision and the Regional Director who receives them has no decision to make—he is bound to dismiss the charge. Moreover, the General Counsel's decisions not to file complaints together with the Advice and Appeals Memoranda explaining them, are precisely the kind of agency law in which the public is so vitally interested and which Congress sought to prevent the agency from keeping secret.[5] . . .

For essentially the same reasons, these Memoranda are "final opinions" made in the "adjudication of cases" which must be indexed pursuant to 5 U.S.C. § 552(a)(2)(A). . . .

(ii)

Advice and Appeals Memoranda which direct the filing of a complaint, on the other hand, fall within the coverage of Exemption 5. The filing of a complaint does not finally dispose even of the General Counsel's responsibility with respect to the case. The case will be litigated before and decided

---

5. The General Counsel argues that he makes no law, analogizing his authority to decide whether or not to file a complaint to a public prosecutor's authority to decide whether a criminal case should be brought, and claims that he does not adjudicate anything resembling a civil dispute. Without deciding whether a public prosecutor makes "law" when he decides not to prosecute or whether memoranda explaining such decisions are "final opinions," it is sufficient to note that the General Counsel's analogy is far from perfect. The General Counsel, unlike most prosecutors, may authorize the filing of a complaint with the Board only if a private citizen files a "charge." Unlike the victim of a crime, the charging party will, if a complaint is filed by the General Counsel, become a party to the unfair labor practice proceeding before the Board. And, if an unfair labor practice is found to exist, the ensuing cease and desist order will, unlike the punishment of the defendant in a criminal case, coerce conduct by the wrongdoer flowing particularly to the benefit of the charging party.

by the Board; and the General Counsel will have the responsibility of advocating the position of the charging party before the Board. The Memoranda will inexorably contain the General Counsel's theory of the case and may communicate to the Regional Director some litigation strategy or settlement advice. Since the Memoranda will also have been prepared in contemplation of the upcoming litigation, they fall squarely within Exemption 5's protection of an attorney's work product. At the same time, the public's interest in disclosure is substantially reduced by the fact ... that the basis for the General Counsel's legal decision will come out in the course of litigation before the Board; and that the "law" with respect to these cases will ultimately be made not by the General Counsel but by the Board or the courts.

We recognize that an Advice or Appeals Memorandum directing the filing of a complaint ... has many of the characteristics of the documents described in 5 U.S.C. § 552(a)(2). Although not a "final opinion" in the "adjudication" of a "case" because it does not effect a "final disposition," the Memorandum does explain a decision already reached by the General Counsel which has real operative effect—it permits litigation before the Board; and we have indicated a reluctance to construe Exemption 5 to protect such documents. We do so in this case only because the decision-maker—the General Counsel—must become a litigating party to the case with respect to which he has made his decision. The attorney work-product policies which Congress clearly incorporated into Exemption 5 thus come into play and lead us to hold that the ... Memoranda directing the filing of a complaint are exempt whether or not they are ... "instructions to staff that affect a member of the public."

C

Petitioner asserts that the District Court erred in holding that documents incorporated by reference in non-exempt Advice and Appeals Memoranda lose any exemption they might previously have held as "intra-agency" memoranda.[6] We disagree.

The probability that an agency employee will be inhibited from freely advising a decisionmaker for fear that his advice *if adopted,* will become public is slight. First, when adopted, the reasoning becomes that of the agency and becomes *its* responsibility to defend. Second, agency employees will generally be encouraged rather than discouraged by public knowledge that their policy suggestions have been adopted by the agency. Moreover, the public interest in knowing the reasons for policy actually adopted by an agency supports the District Court's decision below. Thus, we hold that, if an agency chooses *expressly* to adopt or incorporate by reference an intra-agency memorandum previously covered by Exemption 5 in what would otherwise be a final opinion, that memorandum may be withheld only on the ground that it falls within the coverage of some exemption other than Exemption 5.

6. It should be noted that the documents incorporated by reference are, in the main, factual documents which are probably not entitled to Exemption 5 treatment in the first place.

The Government also asserts that the District Court's order erroneously requires it to produce or create explanatory material in those instances in which an Appeals Memorandum refers to "the circumstances of the case." We agree. The Act does not compel agencies to write opinions in cases in which they would not otherwise be required to do so. It only requires disclosure of certain documents which the law requires the agency to prepare or which the agency has decided for its own reasons to create . . .

Judgment affirmed in part and reversed in part and case remanded.[7]

NOTES

(1) The documents at issue in the Sears case are more easily understood in light of the particular features of the National Labor Relations Act and NLRB practice. Unfair labor practice cases may begin with the filing of a charge by a private party, but they are adjudicated by the agency only if a complaint is filed, and a complaint can only be filed by agency personnel. In ordinary course, charges are considered by, and complaints are filed by, one of the Board's Regional Directors. No appeal lies from the filing of the complaint (although, of course, the underlying charge can be contested in the subsequent proceeding). If a complaint is not filed, however, application of the same rule would mean that the case would be over, since only the agency can file a complaint. Accordingly, the charging party is given the opportunity to contest the decision not to file a complaint by appealing to the Office of General Counsel of the Board, in Washington, D.C. There, a special Appeals Committee ultimately decides whether a complaint will issue. The decision is set out in an Appeals Memorandum either sustaining or overruling the Regional Director's judgment. Appeals Memoranda concerning prior cases on specified subjects were one class of documents requested by Sears.

In some cases concerning matters of special importance to the Board, Regional Directors are required to consult with Washington for "advice" before making their initial decision. The resulting Advice Memorandum will include the General Counsel's decision as to whether, on the stated facts, a complaint should issue. Advice Memoranda of this sort comprised the other class of documents that Sears sought.

(2) As the Court suggests, insofar as the various documents that were sought reflect rules or policies that constrain the enforcement authority of the agency, there is a question whether the APA may require them to be published quite apart from anyone's making an FOIA request. For discussion, see the treatment of "Publication Rules" in Chapter 5, Section 4, especially the discussion of CNI v. Young at p. 727 above.

(3) Does Exemption 5 cover "facts" as well as "opinion"? The Sears opinion's last footnote suggests that to qualify for Exemption 5, information must be not only predecisional but also deliberative, reflecting the

---

7. Chief Justice Burger concurred in the judgment; Justice Powell did not participate.

give-and-take of the consultative process. Then–Judge Ruth Ginsburg dealt with this issue in PETROLEUM INFORMATION CORP. V. DEPARTMENT OF INTERIOR, 976 F.2d 1429, 1434–35 (D.C.Cir.1992):

> Under [Exemption 5], factual information generally must be disclosed, but materials embodying officials' opinions are ordinarily exempt. ... Quarles v. Department of Navy, 893 F.2d 390 (D.C.Cir.1990) (observing that "the prospect of disclosure is less likely to make an adviser omit or fudge raw facts, while it is quite likely to have just such an effect" on materials reflecting agency deliberations). The fact/opinion distinction, however, is not always dispositive; in some instances, "the disclosure of even purely factual material may so expose the deliberative process within an agency" that the material is appropriately held privileged. [For example, Quarles] held exempt from FOIA disclosure Navy cost estimates prepared in the course of selecting a port for a battleship group. [We] explained that the estimates reflected a "complex set of judgments" that "partake of just that elasticity that has persuaded courts to provide shelter for opinions generally." [D]isclosure of the estimates could "chill" or distort eventual Navy deliberations concerning the award of a contract to construct the port ... [T]he "key question" in these cases [is] whether disclosure would tend to diminish candor within an agency.

(4) Exemption 5 requires not only that the records be privileged, but also that they be "inter-agency or intra-agency" records. What about records that come from outside the government? While they might be privileged as trade secrets—Exemption 4—in the ordinary case they would not represent part of the agency's own decisional process so as to be within Exemption 5. The difficult cases for the courts have been communications from those who are both without and within the agency, depending on how one views it.

Agencies often hire consultants—for example, as part of the rulemaking process. If they develop analytical factual studies, we would expect the resulting reports to be publicly available under FOIA—not to mention under modern notions of the publicly available record in a rulemaking proceeding. See p. 536 above. But sometimes their role is closer to the decisional process—for example, when they take the docket in a rulemaking proceeding after the comment period is closed, and do an analysis of it looking to a final result. What then? Several lower courts have held reports to agencies from paid consultants to be within Exemption 5. The Supreme Court, in its most recent decision under FOIA, refused to accept or reject those cases. In any event, said the Court, the cases did not operate to exempt materials filed by an Indian tribe attempting to persuade the government to exercise its fiduciary responsibilities towards Indians in one direction rather than another. DEPARTMENT OF THE INTERIOR AND BUREAU OF INDIAN AFFAIRS V. KLAMATH WATER USERS PROTECTIVE ASS'N, 532 U.S. 1 (2001).

(5) Courts have long recognized two general headings of executive privilege.[8] The first, corresponding roughly to Exemption 1, relates to what have

---

8. A noted legal scholar, once Attorney General of the United States, observed that

"[T]he term executive privilege ... fails to express the nature of the interests at issue;

been often described as state secrets—that is, matters relating to national security, either military or diplomatic. The second, reflected mainly in Exemptions 5 and 7, consists of "official information." The right to disclosure differs markedly with the two classifications. Because they pose patent dangers to the public interest, "disclosures that would impair national security or diplomatic relations are not required by the courts." Environmental Protection Agency v. Mink, 410 U.S. 73 (1973). On the other hand, the disclosure of "official information" involves a far lesser danger to the public interest. Accordingly, courts have long given greater scope to withholding under the Exemption 1. See FTC v. Warner Communications, Inc., 742 F.2d 1156 (9th Cir.1984); United States v. Nixon, 418 U.S. 683, 705–707, 710–711 (1974).

FOIA limits the reach of the stronger privilege to national defense or foreign policy matters that are "(A) specifically authorized under criteria established by an Executive order to be kept secret . . . and (B) are in fact properly classified pursuant to such Executive order." (The current order is E.O. No. 12,958.) Courts are to try these issues, like all others, de novo, with the burden on the agency to sustain its action. While this might appear to threaten the integrity of genuine state secrets—if, for example, the executive branch is now required to provide any classified document a person requests under FOIA to a district court, for its independent judgment whether the document has been properly classified—in operation Exemption 1 has remained a greater hurdle for FOIA requesters than any other exemption. Despite the statute's provisions, courts place substantial weight on agency affidavits asserting the grounds for classifying the particular documents sought, and will grant summary judgment based on them unless contrary evidence—inherently hard to produce against a claim of secrecy—is produced.

(6) IN RE SEALED CASE, 121 F.3d 729 (D.C.Cir.1997) concerns privileges before a criminal grand jury, not the Freedom of Information Act's exemptions. Nonetheless the similarities of the issues (the impact of denying confidentiality to predecisional matters on the receipt of advice within the executive branch) and procedures (district court in camera inspection of White House documents for which privilege was being asserted, and FOIA-like redaction of factual material) makes the extensive discussion of both substantive and procedural issues highly suggestive for FOIA litigation. The court found a "presidential communications privilege" for predecisional analyses intended to inform his judgment, whether or not these were written directly for the President's eyes. "Presidential advisers do not explore alternatives only in conversations with the President or pull their final advice to him out of thin air—if they do, their advice is not likely to be worth much. Rather, the most valuable advisers will investigate the factual context of a problem in detail, obtain input from all others with significant

its emotive value presently exceeds and consumes what cognitive value it might have possessed. The need for confidentiality is old, common to all governments, essential to ours since its formation." Edward Levi, Confidentiality and Democratic Government, 30 The Record 323 (1975). There seems little doubt that in its details, if not its core, this aspect of executive privilege is subject to statutory modification. Nixon v. Warner Communications, 435 U.S. 589 (1978); Nixon v. Administrator of General Services, 433 U.S. 425 (1977).

expertise in the area, and perform detailed analyses of several different policy options before coming to closure on a recommendation for the Chief Executive." The court nonetheless restricted this presidential communications privilege, which it characterized as broader and stronger than the general executive privilege for predecisional, infra-branch consultations ("deliberative process privilege"), to communications made or solicited by immediate presidential advisers, and intended specifically to aid them in "advising the President on official governmental matters."

b.   THE FLOW OF INFORMATION FROM THE OUTSIDE

The government is an insatiable consumer of information from the private sector. Banks cannot be regulated, nuclear power plants licensed, new drugs authorized, taxes collected, or censuses taken without detailed information that people do not readily share with others. Where the government must solicit cooperation rather than force disclosure, confidentiality may have to be guaranteed before cooperation is forthcoming. Even if disclosure could be forced or bargained for, as in rate regulation or technology licensing, sound public policy may support preserving confidentiality of some kinds of data (e.g., to foster innovation or to avoid creating circumstances conducive to unfair competition).

In considering the balance between disclosure and secrecy in this context, once again we must consider the basic structural features of the Act. In particular, we must remember that the Act does not allow the agency to distinguish among those *who* ask for information, nor (except with regard to fees) does it care *why* they are asking. Although many of the litigated cases (such as the one that follows) are brought by non-profit bodies, the most likely requester for commercial information in the Government's files is, not surprisingly, itself a commercial entity—which, even if not prepared to litigate, would certainly be happy to pick up some intelligence at not much cost. By statute made oblivious to the *who* and the *why*, agencies, and after them, the courts, must make their judgments based solely on *what* the Act's exemption from disclosure of proprietary information is read to protect.

Critical Mass Energy Project v. Nuclear Regulatory Commission

United States Court of Appeals for the District of Columbia Circuit, 1992.
975 F.2d 871 (1992), cert. denied 507 U.S. 984 (1993).

Before the court en banc.

■ BUCKLEY, CIRCUIT JUDGE:

Appellant seeks the release of certain reports that have been provided to the Nuclear Regulatory Commission by the Institute of Nuclear Power Operations on the understanding that they will be treated as confidential. In granting the petition to rehear the case *en banc*, we agreed to reconsider a seventeen-year-old decision, National Parks and Conservation Ass'n v. Morton, 498 F.2d 765 (D.C.Cir.1974), in which we established a two-part test for determining when financial or commercial information in the

Government's possession is to be treated as confidential under Exemption 4 of the Freedom on Information Act.[1] We reaffirm the test but confine it to information that persons are required to provide the Government. We hold that where, as here, the information sought is given to the Government voluntarily, it will be treated as confidential under Exemption 4 if it is of a kind that the provider would not customarily make available to the public.

. . .

This case involves a dispute between Critical Mass Energy Project ("CMEP") and the Nuclear Regulatory Commission ("NRC") over access to safety reports prepared by the Institute for Nuclear Power Operations ("INPO") and voluntarily transmitted to the NRC on the condition that the agency will not release the information to other parties without INPO's consent. INPO was formed after the 1979 Three Mile Island accident to promote safety and reliability in the operation of nuclear power plants. INPO is a nonprofit corporation whose membership includes all operators of nuclear power plants in the United States.

One of INPO's principal programs is the Significant Event Evaluation and Information Network ("SEE–IN"), a system for collecting, analyzing, and distributing information concerning the construction and operation of nuclear facilities. Compilation of these reports requires the solicitation of candid comments and evaluations from nuclear power plant employees. The reports are distributed on a voluntary basis to INPO members, certain other participants in the nuclear industry, and the NRC pursuant to the explicit understanding that they are not to be disclosed to additional persons without INPO's consent.

In 1984, CMEP asked the NRC, pursuant to FOIA, to provide it with copies of the INPO reports. The NRC denied the request, finding that they contained confidential commercial information and were therefore protected from disclosure by Exemption 4. CMEP then brought suit in district court challenging the NRC's determination.

[Description of prior proceedings, including two prior D.C. Circuit opinions, omitted.]

A. National Parks Reexamined

In challenging the definition of "confidential" presented in National Parks, the NRC and INPO ask us to set aside circuit precedent of almost twenty years' standing. In obedience to the principle of *stare decisis*, we reaffirm the definition but correct some misunderstandings as to its scope and application.

[The plaintiff in National Parks sought disclosure of audits and other financial materials concessioners submitted to the National Park Service.]

In summarizing [the] various purposes and justifications, we formulated the now familiar two-part test that defined as "confidential" any financial or commercial information whose disclosure would be likely either

---

1. [Ed.] Exemption 4 applies to "trade secrets and commercial or financial information obtained from a person and privileged or confidential"; "person" includes organizations and corporations.

"(1) to impair the Government's ability to obtain necessary information in the future; or (2) to cause substantial harm to the competitive position of the person from whom the information was obtained." 498 F.2d at 770 (footnote omitted). In applying this test to the facts of National Parks, we held that because

> the concessioners [were] *required* to provide this financial information ..., there is presumably no danger that public disclosure will impair the ability of the Government to obtain this information in the future.

Id. (emphasis in original). Then, because the record was incomplete as to the competitive harm that might be suffered by the concessioners on the release of the information, we remanded for further findings on that question. ...

While we indicated that the governmental interest is unlikely to be implicated where the production of information is compelled, we have since pointed out that there are circumstances in which disclosure could affect the reliability of such data. See Washington Post Co. v. HHS, 690 F.2d 252, 268–69 (D.C.Cir.1982). Thus, when dealing with a FOIA request for information the provider is required to supply, the governmental impact inquiry will focus on the possible effect of disclosure on its quality.

When a FOIA request is made for information that is furnished on a voluntary basis, however, we have identified a different aspect of the governmental interest in securing confidential information; the purpose served by the exemption in such instances is that of "encouraging cooperation with the Government by persons having information useful to officials." National Parks, 498 F.2d at 768. Moreover, we have taken note of the probable consequences of a breach of confidence by the Government:

> Unless persons having necessary information can be assured that it will remain confidential, they may decline to cooperate with officials, and the ability of the Government to make intelligent, well-informed decisions will be impaired.

Id. at 767. Thus, when information is obtained under duress, the Government's interest is in ensuring its continued reliability; when that information is volunteered, the Government's interest is in ensuring its continued availability.

A distinction between voluntary and compelled information must also be made when applying the "competitive injury" prong. In the latter case, there is a presumption that the Government's interest is not threatened by disclosure because it secures the information by mandate; and as the harm to the private interest (commercial disadvantage) is the only factor weighing against FOIA's presumption of disclosure, that interest must be significant. Where, however, the information is provided to the Government voluntarily, the presumption is that its interest will be threatened by disclosure as the persons whose confidences have been betrayed will, in all likelihood, refuse further cooperation. In those cases, the private interest served by Exemption 4 is the protection of information that, for whatever reason, "would customarily not be released to the public by the person from whom it was obtained" ... Sterling Drug, 450 F.2d at 709 (quoting Senate Report at 9).

B. Application of Exemption 4 to Information Provided on a Voluntary Basis

The Supreme Court has encouraged the development of categorical rules whenever a particular set of facts will lead to a generally predictable application of FOIA. See United States Dep't of Justice v. Reporters Comm. for Freedom of the Press, 489 U.S. 749 (1989). ... The circumstances of this case lend themselves to categorical treatment. It is a matter of common sense that the disclosure of information the Government has secured from voluntary sources on a confidential basis will both jeopardize its continuing ability to secure such data on a cooperative basis and injure the provider's interest in preventing its unauthorized release. Accordingly, while we reaffirm the National Parks test for determining the confidentiality of information submitted under compulsion, we conclude that financial or commercial information provided to the Government on a voluntary basis is "confidential" for the purpose of Exemption 4 if it is of a kind that would customarily not be released to the public by the person from whom it was obtained.

[T]his test ... is objective. As is the case with any claim under FOIA, the agency invoking Exemption 4 must meet the burden of proving the provider's custom. ...

Applying this rule to the INPO reports, we agree with the district court's conclusion that the information they contain is commercial in nature; that the reports are provided to the NRC on a voluntary basis; and that INPO does not customarily release such information to the public. On the basis of these findings, we hold that the INPO reports are confidential within the meaning of Exemption 4 and therefore protected from disclosure.

CMEP asserts that the test we announce today may lead government agencies and industry to conspire to keep information from the public by agreeing to the voluntary submission of information that the agency has the power to compel. CMEP alleges that the NRC had in fact planned to impose greatly expanded mandatory reporting requirements on its licensees until INPO undertook to manage the voluntary reporting system they would have replaced and to provide the NRC with access to the information generated by it.

We know of no provision in FOIA that obliges agencies to exercise their regulatory authority in a manner that will maximize the amount of information that will be made available to the public through that Act. Nor do we see any reason to interfere with the NRC's exercise of its own discretion in determining how it can best secure the information it needs. So long as that information is provided voluntarily, and so long as it is of a kind that INPO customarily withholds from the public, it must be treated as confidential.

... Accordingly, we affirm the district court's grant of summary judgment in favor of the NRC. To the extent that any of our other precedents may be read as inconsistent with our decision today, they are to that degree overruled.

[Judge Randolph's concurrence is omitted.]

■ RUTH B. GINSBURG, CIRCUIT JUDGE, joined by MIKVA, CHIEF JUDGE, WALD and EDWARDS, CIRCUIT JUDGES, dissenting:

... [T]he court ... removes from the governance of National Parks all cases in which commercial or financial information is given to the Government voluntarily. The cutback substantially revises the law of this circuit and diminishes as well sister circuit case law patterned on our National Parks decision. Stare decisis ... has not been appropriately observed in today's decision. Nor has the guiding purpose of the [FOIA]—to shed light on an agency's performance of its statutory duties—been well served by the en banc disposition. ...

The court today asserts that its revision of the National Parks test "is objective." That is true to the extent that my colleagues demand more than the stampmark "Confidential" to shield a document: the provider must have a confidentiality custom and the agency must prove that custom.[2] But the court's slackened test is not "objective" in the sense vital to ... National Parks. No longer is there to be an independent judicial check on the reasonableness of the provider's custom and the consonance of that custom with the purposes of Exemption 4 and of the Act of which the exemption is part. To the extent that the court allows providers to render categories of information confidential merely by withholding them from the public long enough to show a custom, the revised test is fairly typed "subjective" ...

... Henceforth, in this circuit, it will do for an agency official to agree with the submitter's ascription of confidential status to the information. There will be no objective check on, no judicial review alert to, "the temptation of government and business officials to follow the path of least resistance and say 'confidential' whenever they seek to satisfy the government's vast information needs." 9 to 5 Organization for Women Office Workers, 721 F.2d at 12 (Breyer, J. dissenting). Under the regime replacing National Parks, "the exemption [will] expand beyond what Congress intended." Id.

But the court sees virtue in a categorical rule, and such rules do have a place in FOIA's domain. ... A categorical approach, however, is not in order across the board under FOIA, without regard to the character of the information requested. Such an automatic approach is not suitable for judging the wide range of cases presenting contests under Exemption 4. ... This case is illustrative.

Critical Mass Energy Project seeks access to comprehensive reports, prepared by a consortium comprised of the entire nuclear utility industry, concerning the causes and potential hazards of "significant" safety-related

---

2. The court leaves unaddressed whether, as here, the custom must prevail in the industry or may be simply the provider's unique practice. Cf. H.R. Rep. No. 95–1382, 95th Cong., 2d Sess. 18 (1978) (rejecting as clearly inappropriate the withholding of "all information, no matter how innocuous, submitted by a corporation with a blanket policy of refusing all public requests for information").

events at nuclear power plants. See Critical Mass Energy Project v. NRC, 830 F.2d 278, 279–80 (D.C.Cir.1987). Disclosure of these reports, and the response of the Nuclear Regulatory Commission (NRC) to the information contained in them, would undoubtedly shed light on the character and adequacy of the Commission's pursuit of its mission to "encourage ... the development and utilization of [nuclear] energy for peaceful purposes to the maximum extent consistent ... with the health and safety of the public." 42 U.S.C. § 2013(d). The FOIA request we face seeks no "information about private citizens that happens to be in the warehouse of the Government"; disclosure is sought "not primarily in the commercial interest of the requester," but to advance public understanding of the nature and quality of the NRC's oversight operations or activities. See Reporters Committee for Freedom of the Press, 489 U.S. at 774, 775. "The public interest that the FOIA was enacted to serve," see id. at 775, is thus centrally at stake. ...

NOTES

(1) Obviously much of the court's analysis turns on its assessment of the consequences of what it is deciding, rather than on materials directly indicative of Congress' intent in enacting Exemption 4. What are the incentives created by alternative possible rules for the various parties involved? Considering not just the policies behind freedom of information, but also the desire to have well-working agencies, did the court pick the right set of rules?

(2) If determining the scope of protection of information furnished by private parties to the agency is a matter of balancing incentives, and if FOIA permits agencies to withhold the records named in the exemptions but does not require such withholding, does this mean that the agency is free, when it seems to it to be wise to do so, to release whatever proprietary information it wants? See the next principal case!

(3) Exemption 4's reference to "commercial or financial" information, unilluminated by the legislative history, led Professor Davis to characterize the exemption as "probably the most troublesome provision of the Act." Kenneth C. Davis, The Information Act: A Preliminary Analysis, 34 U. Chi. L. Rev. 761, 787 (1967). Critical Mass is criticized in Scott Raber, Reinventing a Less Vigorous [FOIA]: The Aftermath of [Critical Mass], 1994 Ann. Surv. Am. Law 79; but see Richard L. Rainey, Stare Decisis and Statutory Interpretation: An Argument for a Complete Overruling of the *National Parks Test,* 61 G.W. L. Rev. 1430 (1993).

SECTION 3.   PRIVATE PARTIES' DESIRES FOR SECRECY OF INFORMATION

A competitor seeking information about an adversary's business is no less a "person" entitled to demand information under FOIA than the most elevated public-interest claimant. Obviously, submitters of information often have a profound interest in assuring that agencies do not provide requested information if the agency could (under cases like Critical Mass Energy Project) deny it. Yet the busy agency functionary handling the request for information may not recognize its implications—he may have little sense of the supplier's business, or of the sophisticated analyses that might be made of what seem to be harmless data. Will there be a procedure for notifying submitters of the request, and an opportunity to justify the claim for confidentiality? Even if there is, FOIA requires disclosure unless an exemption applies, and the agency may disagree with the supplier of information about whether one does apply. And even if one applies, does the agency have discretion to disclose if it finds disclosure in the public interest, or if it chooses to avoid litigation? What if it simply errs? Don't the procedural provisions of FOIA in effect favor erring toward disclosure?

Chrysler Corp. v. Brown

Supreme Court of the United States, 1979.
441 U.S. 281.

■ MR. JUSTICE REHNQUIST delivered the opinion of the Court:

[As a major defense contractor, the Chrysler Corporation was required by Executive Orders 11246 and 11375 to observe non-discriminatory hiring practices and to furnish reports and other information about its programs to the Department of Defense Logistics Agency (DLA), pursuant to regulations of the Department of Labor's Office of Federal Contract Compliance Programs (OFCCP). Some of the information provided was commercially sensitive data—for example, "manning tables," listing job titles and the number of people performing each job—which might be useful to a competitor. OFCCP regulations stated that even though such information might be exempt from mandatory disclosure under the FOIA, "records obtained or generated pursuant to Executive Order 11246 (as amended) ... shall be made available for inspection and copying ... if it is determined that the requested inspection or copying furthers the public interest and does not impede any of the functions of the OFCC[P] or the Compliance Agencies except in the case of records disclosure of which is prohibited by law." Persons interested in monitoring Chrysler's employment practices filed FOIA requests for reports concerning two of its facilities. Pursuant to its regulations, DLA notified Chrysler of the requests and, later, of its intention to honor them. Chrysler then sought to enjoin the release of information that it asserted lay within the protection of Exemption 4. In district court it succeeded. The Third Circuit reversed, broadly sustaining the government's contentions: that FOIA created no right to withholding of information within its exemptions; that other confidentiality statutes created no private right of action; that the OFCCP regulations created any necessary authority to disclose, and were themselves within the Department of Labor's authority to adopt; and that, given authority to disclose, judicial review of the exercise of that authority would be limited to assuring procedural regularity and checking abuses of discretion. Since the administrative record was insufficient to perform such review, the Third Circuit directed the district court to remand the case to the agency for supplementation. At this point, the Supreme Court granted certiorari.]

In contending that the FOIA bars disclosure of the requested equal employment opportunity information, Chrysler relies ... specifically on Exemption 4. ... Chrysler contends that the nine exemptions in general, and Exemption 4 in particular, reflect a sensitivity to the privacy interests of private individuals and nongovernmental entities. That contention may be conceded without inexorably requiring the conclusion that the exemptions impose affirmative duties on an agency to withhold information sought. In fact, that conclusion is not supported by the language, logic or history of the Act.

... By its terms, subsection (b) [i.e., the list of exemptions] demarcates the limits of the agency's obligation to disclose; it does not foreclose disclosure.

That the FOIA is exclusively a disclosure statute is, perhaps, demonstrated most convincingly by examining its provision for judicial relief. Subsection (a)(4)(B) gives federal district courts "jurisdiction to enjoin the agency from withholding agency records and to order the production of any agency records improperly withheld from the complainant." 5 U.S.C. § 552(a)(4)(B). That provision does not give the authority to bar disclosure, and thus fortifies our belief that Chrysler, and courts which have shared its view, have incorrectly interpreted the exemption provisions of the FOIA. The Act is an attempt to meet the demand for open government while preserving workable confidentiality in governmental decision-making. Congress appreciated that with the expanding sphere of governmental regulation and enterprise, much of the information within Government files has been submitted by private entities seeking Government contracts or responding to unconditional reporting obligations imposed by law. There was sentiment that Government agencies should have the latitude, in certain circumstances, to afford the confidentiality desired by these submitters. But the congressional concern was with the *agency's* need or preference for confidentiality; the FOIA by itself protects the submitters' interest in confidentiality only to the extent that this interest is endorsed by the agency collecting the information.

Enlarged access to governmental information undoubtedly cuts against the privacy concerns of nongovernmental entities, and as a matter of policy some balancing and accommodation may well be desirable. We simply hold here that Congress did not design the FOIA exemptions to be mandatory bars to disclosure.[1] ...

---

1. It is informative in this regard to compare the FOIA with 49 U.S.C. § 1357, a section which authorizes the Administrator of the FAA to take antihijacking measures, including research and development into protection devices.

"Notwithstanding [FOIA], the Administrator shall prescribe such regulations as he may deem necessary to prohibit disclosure of any information obtained or developed in the conduct of research and development activities under this subsection if, in the opinion of the Administrator, the disclosure of such information- ...

"(B) would reveal trade secrets or privileged or confidential commercial or financial information obtained from any person ..." Id. § 1357(d)(2)(B).

Chrysler contends, however, that even if its suit for injunctive relief cannot be based on the FOIA, such an action can be premised on the Trade Secrets Act, 18 U.S.C. § 1905. The Act provides:

"Whoever, being an officer or employee of the United States or of any department or agency thereof, publishes, divulges, discloses, or makes known in any manner or to any extent not authorized by law any information coming to him in the course of his employment or official duties or by reason of any examination or investigation made by, or return, report or record made to or filed with, such department or agency or officer or employee thereof, which information concerns or relates to the trade secrets, processes, operations, style of work, or apparatus, or to the identity, confidential statistical data, amount or source of any income, profits, losses, or expenditures of any person, firm, partnership, corporation, or association; or permits any income return or copy thereof or any book containing any abstract or particulars thereof to be seen or examined by any person except as provided by law; shall be fined not more than $1,000 or imprisoned not more than one year, or both; and shall be removed from office or employment."

There are necessarily two parts to Chrysler's argument: that § 1905 is applicable to the type of disclosure threatened in this case, and that it affords Chrysler a private right of action to obtain injunctive relief.

A

The Court of Appeals held that § 1905 was not applicable to the agency disclosure at issue here because such disclosure was "authorized by law" within the meaning of the Act. The court found the source of that authorization to be the OFCCP regulations that DLA relied on in deciding to disclose information on the ... plants. Chrysler contends here that these agency regulations are not "law" within the meaning of § 1905.

It has been established in a variety of contexts that properly promulgated substantive regulations have the "force and effect of law." ... It would ... take a clear showing of contrary legislative intent before the phrase "authorized by law" in § 1905 could be held to have a narrower ambit than the traditional understanding. [After examining the relevant legislative history and finding no such clear showing, the Court rejected a Government argument that § 1905 was only an anti-leak statute applying to surreptitious, unofficial acts, and was therefore irrelevant to "official" agency actions, taken within channels. That reading, the Court thought, would "require an expansive and unprecedented holding that any agency action directed or approved by an agency head is 'authorized by law' "; such a holding would be contrary to repeated assurances to the Congress that § 1905 reached formal agency action as well as employee skullduggery. The Court then resumed discussion of whether the OFCCP regulations provided the required authorization.]

In order for a regulation to have the "force and effect of law," it must have certain substantive characteristics and be the product of certain procedural requisites. ... We [have] described a substantive rule—or a "legislative-type rule,"—as one "affecting individual rights and obligations." This characteristic is an important touchstone for distinguishing those rules that may be "binding" or have the "force of law."

Likewise the promulgation of these regulations must conform with any procedural requirements imposed by Congress. ... The pertinent procedural limitations in this case are those found in the APA.

The regulations relied on by the Government in this case as providing "authoriz[ation] by law" within the meaning of § 1905 certainly affect individual rights and obligations; they govern the public's right to information in records obtained under Executive Order 11246 and the confidentiality rights of those who submit information to OFCCP and its compliance agencies. It is a much closer question, however, whether they are the product of a congressional grant of legislative authority.

[The Court concluded that Congress had *not* authorized the OFCCP to adopt rules having the force and effect of law on information disclosure. (That holding, Justice Marshall emphasized in a concurrence, did not call into question the validity of OFCCP regulations as a whole.) The Court found also that the Secretary of Labor had not used notice and comment rulemaking procedures in adopting the regulations—thus confirming their character as merely interpretative regulations, "not the product of procedures which Congress prescribed as necessary prerequisites to giving a regulation the binding effect of law. An interpretative regulation or general statement of agency policy cannot be the 'authoriz[ation] by law' required by § 1905."]

B

[The Court rejected Chrysler's contention that § 1905 afforded a private right of action to enjoin disclosure in violation of the statute: We have] rarely implied a private right of action under a criminal statute and where [we did] so "there was at least a statutory basis for inferring that a civil cause of action of some sort lay in favor of someone." Nothing in § 1905 prompts such an inference. ... Most importantly, a private right of action under § 1905 is not "necessary to make effective the congressional purpose," J.I. Case Co. v. Borak, 377 U.S. 426, 433 (1964), for we find that review of DLA's decision to disclose Chrysler's employment data is available under the APA.

... Section 10(a) of the APA provides that "[a] person suffering legal wrong because of agency action, or adversely affected or aggrieved by agency action ..., is entitled to judicial review thereof." 5 U.S.C. § 702. [The Court held DLA's decision to disclose reviewable because] § 1905 and any "authoriz[ation] by law" contemplated by that section place substantive limits on agency action. Therefore, we conclude that DLA's decision ... is reviewable agency action and Chrysler is a person "adversely affected or aggrieved" within the meaning of § 10(a).

Both Chrysler and the Government agree that there is APA review of DLA's decision. They disagree on the proper scope of review. Chrysler argues that there should be de novo review, while the Government contends that such review is only available in extraordinary cases and this is not such a case.

The pertinent provisions of § 10(e) of the APA, 5 U.S.C. § 706 (1976), provide that a reviewing court shall

"(2) hold unlawful and set aside agency action, findings, and conclusions found to be—

"(A) arbitrary, capricious, an abuse of discretion, or otherwise not in accordance with law;

"(F) unwarranted by the facts to the extent that the facts are subject to trial de novo by the reviewing court."

For the reasons previously stated, we believe any disclosure that violates § 1905 is "not in accordance with law" within the meaning of 5 U.S.C. § 706(2)(A). De novo review by the District Court is ordinarily not necessary to decide whether a contemplated disclosure runs afoul of § 1905. The District Court in this case concluded that disclosure of some of Chrysler's documents was barred by § 1905, but the Court of Appeals did not reach the issue. We shall therefore vacate the Court of Appeals' judgment and remand for further proceedings consistent with this opinion in order that the Court of Appeals may consider whether the contemplated disclosures would violate the prohibition of § 1905.[2] Since the decision regarding this substantive issue—the scope of § 1905—will necessarily have some effect on the proper form of judicial review pursuant to § 706(2), we think it unnecessary, and therefore unwise, at the present stage of this case for us to express any additional views on that issue.

Vacated and remanded.[3]

NOTES

(1) Government-wide treatment of submitters' rights was established in 1987 by President Reagan's Executive Order No. 12,600, still in effect. It expanded submitters' ability to protect their submissions by providing for procedures for presubmission marking of documents as confidential and, if disclosure is later requested, for notification and an opportunity to explain why the request should be denied. 52 Fed.Reg. 23781 (June 25, 1987).

(2) The Chrysler case can make one's head spin with the number of sources of law it discusses and its variety of standards of judicial review. On comparison with earlier cases in this chapter, however, a fundamental contrast seems clear: On the one hand, a refusal to disclose information to a requester is to be reviewed by a court according to the procedures set out in FOIA itself: that is, de novo review with the agency bearing the burden

---

2. Since the Court of Appeals assumed for purposes of argument that the material in question was within an exemption to the FOIA, that court found it unnecessary expressly to decide that issue and it is open on remand. We, of course, do not here attempt to determine the relative ambits of Exemption 4 and § 1905, or to determine whether § 1905 is an exempting statute within the terms of the amended Exemption 3, 5 U.S.C. § 552(b)(3) (1976). Although there is a theoretical possibility that material might be outside Exemption 4 yet within the substantive provisions of § 1905, and that therefore the FOIA might provide the necessary "authoriz[ation] by law" for purposes of § 1905, that possibility is at most of limited practical significance in view of the similarity of language between Exemption 4 and the substantive provisions of § 1905.

3. Mr. Justice Marshall's concurrence is omitted.

of justifying non-disclosure. On the other hand, a complaint by a private supplier of information in an agency's files, that the agency is ready to disclose something it should hold secret, is to be reviewed by a court according to the standards set forth for ordinary judicial review in the Administrative Procedure Act. This process, as described more fully in the materials on judicial review in Chapter 8, normally is based on the record before the agency (rather than on material assembled de novo in court) and normally begins with a presumption in favor of the correctness of the agency's decision (although to varying degrees of intensity).

An example of how this APA review works in practice in a "reverse-FOIA" case is provided by BARTHOLDI CABLE CO. v. FCC, 114 F.3d 274 (D.C.Cir.1997). Bartholdi sold microwave video distribution services to apartment buildings in New York City, which had to be licensed by the FCC installation-by-installation. In the course of applying for some new licenses, the company discovered that it had already been providing some services without the needed license. The company conducted a comprehensive audit of its unauthorized operations, the report of which it transmitted to the FCC along with a request that the submission remain confidential. The agency refused to give the requested assurance, and Bartholdi went to court. Sentelle, J. (114 F.3d at 281–82):

"Exemption 4 of FOIA provides that an agency need not disclose information that is 'trade secrets and commercial or financial information obtained from a person and privileged or confidential.' 5 U.S.C. § 552(b)(4). The test for whether information is 'confidential' depends in part on whether the information was voluntarily or involuntarily disclosed to the government. If the information was voluntarily disclosed to the government, it will be considered confidential 'if it is of a kind that would customarily not be released to the public by the person from whom it was obtained.' Critical Mass Energy Project v. NRC. If the information was obtained under compulsion, it will be considered confidential only 'if disclosure ... is likely to have either of the following effects: (1) to impair the Government's ability to obtain necessary information in the future; or (2) to cause substantial harm to the competitive position of the person from whom the information was obtained.' National Parks and Conservation Ass'n v. Morton.

"Of course, the mere fact that information falls within a FOIA exemption does not of itself bar an agency from disclosing the information. Chrysler Corp. v. Brown. But we have held that information falling within Exemption 4 of FOIA also comes within the Trade Secrets Act, 18 U.S.C. § 1905, which prohibits the disclosure of, *inter alia*, 'trade secrets' and 'confidential statistical data.' CNA Fin. Corp. v. Donovan, 830 F.2d 1132, 1151 (D.C.Cir.1987) (holding that 'the scope of the [Trade Secrets] Act is at least co-extensive with that of Exemption 4 of FOIA'), cert. denied, 485 U.S. 977. Thus, generally when 'a party succeeds in demonstrating that its materials fall within Exemption 4, the government is precluded from releasing the information by virtue of the Trade Secrets Act.' McDonnell Douglas Corp. v. Widnall, 57 F.3d 1162, 1164 (D.C.Cir.1995). However, information otherwise protected by the Trade Secrets Act may be disclosed if 'authorized by law.' See 18 U.S.C. § 1905. The Supreme Court has held that the release of otherwise protected information to the public is 'authorized by law' if permitted by a regulation that is: (1) 'rooted in a grant of power by the Congress' to limit the scope of the Trade Secrets Act; (2) 'substantive,' rather than interpretive or procedural; and (3) consistent 'with any procedural requirements imposed by Congress' such as the APA. Chrysler.

"Section 0.457 of the Commission's regulations permits disclosure of exempt materials to the extent 'the policy considerations favoring nondisclosure' are outweighed by factors favoring disclosure. 47 C.F.R. § 0.457. The Commission has held that this regulation is 'authorized by law' as that phrase was defined by the Supreme Court in Chrysler. Pursuant to § 0.457, the [Commission's personnel] ruled that 'the public interest in disclosure of [Bartholdi's] materials would justify disclosure as a matter of our discretion even if the materials could be withheld under the FOIA.' The Commission affirmed this conclusion in its order, holding that 'public interest considerations favoring openness in our licensing proceedings outweigh any potential difficulty that the Government might experience in obtaining access to information in similar circumstances.' 11 F.C.C.R. at 2477.

"Bartholdi argues that § 0.457 of the Commission's regulations does not meet the definition of 'authorized by law' under Chrysler. But Bartholdi did not raise this challenge before the Commission. Bartholdi's application for review made no mention of Chrysler. Because Bartholdi failed to challenge the validity of § 0.457 before the Commission, we decline to consider the issue.

"Therefore, assuming the validity of § 0.457, we cannot conclude that the Commission acted arbitrarily in concluding that the public interest considerations in disclosure outweighed those in favor of confidentiality. As the Commission now explains, much of the information for which Bartholdi seeks confidential treatment is already publicly available. Moreover, the Commission concluded that the public has a compelling interest in the information at issue as it bears directly on Bartholdi's fitness as a license applicant. Bartholdi chastises the Commission for failing to articulate these rationales in its order. But a more explicit discussion in the Commission's order would have risked disclosure of the information Bartholdi was attempting to keep confidential. We cannot fault the Commission for attempting to maintain the confidentiality of Bartholdi's submissions pending judicial review."

(3) How much proprietary information has in fact been released under FOIA is a matter of dispute. The persistence of an active FOIA "industry" and the dominance of commercial sources as requesters suggest that valuable ore is in fact being mined.[4] A study for the Administrative

---

4. "The fact remains that the lion's share of information requested from those agencies that regulate businesses is made by corporations or corporate intermediaries. If these requesters are not interested in securing economic and valuable information, the release of which may be harmful to the information-submitting firms, *then what are they seeking?*" William Casey, Jr., John Marthin-sen, Lawrence Moss, The Economic Impact of the [FOIA], 12 AIPLA Q. Journ. 76, 80–81 (1984). The cited article is part of a symposium of four, all addressing "the evolution of FOIA into a significant avenue for distributing confidential technology among competitors." Arthur Whale, [Symposium] Introduction, 12 AIPLA Q. Journ. 2 (1984).

Conference of the United States found very little evidence of release of commercially valuable information, but Professor Stevenson, its author, acknowledged that submitters might not have wanted to call attention to what had been released, or that minor releases may not have come to attention. Russell Stevenson, Jr., Protecting Business Secrets Under the Freedom of Information Act: Managing Exemption 4, 34 Ad. L. Rev. 207, 218–222, 261 (1982).

Commercial data quite harmless standing alone may be very revealing when combined with other information publicly available or separately sought. An environmental lawyer counsels submitters that the interrelated nature of information makes "[a] submission ... like a crossword puzzle: knowing the answer to one clue helps in answering the next." For example, if a firm obtains publicly available data on a competing manufacturer's emissions, it may be able to estimate the facility's production. Submitters are advised to "draft the impossible crossword puzzle," test it for vulnerability, then take such steps as presubmission marking, negotiating with the agency and following-up with other agencies to which the information is forwarded. See David R. Andrews, Confidential Business Information Provided in Reports to the EPA May Ultimately be Disclosed Under [FOIA], Natl. L.J., Nov. 21, 1994, B4, B7.

(4) FOIA also asks agencies to consider the privacy needs of individuals. Exemption 6 applies to "personnel and medical files and similar files" when disclosure "would constitute a clearly unwarranted invasion of personal privacy" and Exemption 7 applies to law enforcement records when (among other things) disclosure "could reasonably be expected to constitute an unwarranted invasion of personal privacy." Here again, the structure of the Act has forced the courts to determine what is "unwarranted" without regard to the identity or particular purpose of the party requesting information (except when someone requests information about herself or himself). The result has been to encourage the formulation of rules organized by the type of information at issue. For example, in UNITED STATES DEPARTMENT OF JUSTICE V. REPORTERS COMMITTEE FOR FREEDOM OF THE PRESS, 489 U.S. 749, 774, 780 (1989), reporters requested the FBI "rap sheet" for a specific individual claimed to have organized crime connections. Stating that "the FOIA's central purpose is to ensure that the *Government's* activities be opened to the sharp eye of public scrutiny, not that information about *private citizens* that happens to be in the warehouse of the Government be so disclosed," Justice Stevens' opinion upheld the agency in refusing to produce the requested information. "We hold as a categorical matter that a third party's request for law-enforcement records or information about a private citizen can reasonably be expected to invade that citizen's privacy, and that when the request seeks no 'official information' about a Government agency, but merely records that the Government happens to be storing, the invasion of privacy is 'unwarranted.'"

(5) Can agencies legitimately refuse to disclose the names and addresses of those who submit comments in rulemaking proceedings? Commenters certainly might face bad publicity or other forms of harassment for taking

unpopular stands on controversial issues. At the same time, knowing who said what in the proceeding is one of the ways in which the public can monitor and evaluate the final outcome. Held: in the ordinary case, the interest in full disclosure must prevail. Alliance for Wild Rockies v. Dep't of the Interior, 53 F.Supp. 2d 32 (D.D.C.1999). The court, however, did not rule on the case of a commenter who had expressly requested anonymity.

SECTION 4.   GOVERNMENT IN THE SUNSHINE

Section of Administrative Law and Regulatory Practice, American Bar Association, A Blackletter Statement of Federal Administrative Law

54 Admin. L. Rev. 1, 75 (2002).

GOVERNMENT IN THE SUNSHINE ACT

The Government in the Sunshine Act, codified primarily at 5 U.S.C. § 552b, applies to any agency subject to FOIA and headed by a collegial body of two or more individual members, a majority of whom are appointed by the President with the advice and consent of the Senate, and to any subdivision of such an agency authorized to act on its behalf.

An agency subject to the Sunshine Act must give reasonable notice of its meetings and make every portion of its meetings open to public observation, unless the agency has properly decided to close the meeting, or a portion thereof, pursuant to one of the Act's ten exemptions. These exemptions generally mirror those in FOIA, with two notable exceptions: internal privileged communications that would not prematurely disclose proposed agency actions (FOIA Exemption 5) are not included, while discussions of most agency adjudicatory matters are. An agency may not close any portion of a meeting without a majority of the members voting to close that portion of the meeting. The agency has the burden of proving that the decision to close a meeting was lawful.

For purposes of the Act, the term "meeting" means the deliberations of at least the number of individuals required to take action on behalf of the agency where such deliberations determine or result in the joint conduct or disposition of official agency business, except that discussions of administrative matters such as scheduling a future meeting do not constitute meetings.

The Act provides district courts with subject matter jurisdiction to enforce the requirements of the Act relating to open meetings and records by declaratory judgment, injunctive relief, or other appropriate relief. Invalidation of the agency action is not a proper remedy under the Act, but requiring a meeting to be open or records to be disclosed is. A prevailing party is entitled to reasonable attorneys' fees and other litigation costs.

NOTES

(1) The Government in the Sunshine Act (or GITSA) was passed in 1976; it is reproduced as 5 U.S.C. § 552b in the Appendix, at pp. 1350–54. The

legislative history suggests that Congress decided that the Freedom of Information Act did not provide enough information to enable the public to "understand the reasons an agency has acted in a certain way, or even what exactly it has decided to do," because "[f]ormal statements in support of agency action are frequently too brief, or too general, to fully explain [a] Commission's reasoning, of the compromises that were made. By requiring important decisions to be made openly, [the new law] will create better public understanding of agency decisions." S.Rep. No. 94–354, 94th Cong., 1st Sess. 5.

(2) Consider three of the distinctions the Act makes, or fails to make:

(a) GITSA applies to agencies "headed by a collegial body." Thus the Nuclear Regulatory Commission is required to conduct its budget discussions in public. Common Cause v. NRC, 674 F.2d 921 (D.C.Cir. 1982). By contrast, discussions within the Department of Justice as to whether to seek the death penalty are beyond the reach of GITSA because DOJ is headed by the Attorney General. Nichols v. Reno, 931 F.Supp. 748 (D.Colo.1996), affirmed, 124 F.3d 1376 (10th Cir.1997).

(b) Predecisional deliberations among personnel in agencies headed by a single official will, as we have seen, be protected by Exemption 5 of FOIA. See NLRB v. Sears, Roebuck & Co., p. 740 above. Discussions of comparable issues by multi-member commissions will not be off-the-record, because GITSA does not have a comparable exclusion.[1]

(c) "Meeting" is defined by the Act to include not just formal occasions, but informal deliberations as long as enough of the agency's members to take action are present—e.g., 3 out of 5.

What do you think the combined incentive effect of these provisions will be?

(3) Whatever may have been the cause, following passage of GITSA the number of meetings at 59 executive and independent multi-member agencies declined 31% between 1979 and 1986. Just under 40% of those meetings were open, just over 40% closed, and the remainder were partly closed. Rogelio Garcia, Congressional Research Service, Public Access to Meetings Held under [GITSA] (1986).[2] According to an extensive survey undertaken for the Administrative Conference of the United States, DAVID WELBORN, W. LYON & L. THOMAS, IMPLEMENTATION AND EFFECTS OF THE FEDERAL [GITSA] (1984): (1) Members tended to behave somewhat differently in open than in closed meetings. They prepared more thoroughly for the open meetings, but used them more often to appeal to special interests; they refrained from asking important questions and engaged less frequently in candid exchange, sharp debate, or efforts at reconciling conflicts. (2) The authors believed there was "a shift in patterns of decision-making behavior, at least in some agencies, away from collegial processes toward seg-

---

1. Section 552b(c)(9)(B) does, however, provide protection against "premature disclosure" of information relating to some "proposed agency action[s]" when disclosure would "significantly frustrate implementation."

2. Reprinted in Senate Committee on Governmental Affairs, [GITSA]: History and Recent Issues, S.Prt. 101–54, 101st Cong. 1st Sess., 58 (1989).

mented, individualized processes in which, in the words of one commissioner, 'members are isolated from one another.'" Of 18 agencies surveyed, only officials at the Federal Election Commission thought "that the act had strengthened the collegium." The importance of meetings declined apparently "from an aversion to public discussion of certain topics." In addition, when open meetings with collegial interactions did occur, "meetings often ha[d] no bearing on results." Over 83% of survey respondents from agencies with full-time membership believed that "members now typically made up their minds on matters dealt with in open meetings *prior* to collective discussions." Further "the focus of decision-making activity has shifted toward the offices of individual members and to the staff level and involves three key sets of interactions. The first is between staff at the operating level who are handling a particular matter and the offices of the chairman and other members. The second is between members one-on-one, except presumably in three member agencies. The third is among staff assistants to members acting as surrogates for their principals. . . . All have distinct limitations as substitutes for collegial discussions."

Former Securities and Exchange Commissioner Bevis Longstreth found that:

> The Act tends to shift power in a multi-headed agency from the collegial body to its chairman. . . . As a result, the chairman typically meets with staff or outsiders alone, formulating policy without the benefit of timely and meaningful comment from other members of the collegial body. . . . [M]embers of the collegial body other than the chairman must rely upon information collected by their staff from the chairman's staff and on comments made when the issues have reached the final decisionmaking stage. In particular, the chairman's meetings with the staff have a powerful tendency to shape the staff's responses and recommendations, which might well be different if it were possible for the other members to be present.[3]

The Act's sponsor, Senator Lawton Chiles, replied:

> Longstreth finds fault in the fact that Cabinet agencies or single-headed agencies are not subject to the act. . . . The rationale for covering only multi-headed agencies was grounded in common sense and the nature of collegial agencies. Multi-headed agencies operate on the principle of give-and-take discussion between the members. There is a tradition of public dissent. While the agency takes a final action, it does not necessarily speak with one voice. Its deliberative process can and should be exposed to public scrutiny. The interior workings of a Cabinet secretary's decision-making process, on the other hand, may well be of great interest but are simply not accessible to public observation. . . . [A] critique that argues for a "modicum of darkness" aims at the heart of the law. To those who find open government inhibiting, I would remind them of President Truman's maxim about getting out of the kitchen.[4]

3. A Little Shade, Please—The Government-in-the-Sunshine Act Isn't Working, Washington Post, July 25, 1983, A13.

4. The Sunshine Act Does Too Work, Washington Post, Aug. 4, 1983, A21.

One of the final studies performed for the Administrative Conference of the United States, later presented to the American Bar Association's Section of Administrative Law and Regulatory Practice, reaffirmed the drift of most prior studies—that "true collective decisionmaking does not occur at agency public meetings" and that the Act "promotes inefficient practices within agencies which themselves contribute to the erosion of collegial decisionmaking and, correspondingly, to a decline in the quality of agency decisions that the public receives." Special Committee, Administrative Conference of the United States, Report and Recommendation by the Special Committee to Review the Government in the Sunshine Act, 49 Admin. L. Rev. 421, 423 (1997).

(4) The Sunshine Act exempts various forms of participation in agency adjudication, including specifically "disposition by the agency of a particular case of formal agency adjudication pursuant to the procedures in section 554 of this title or otherwise involving a determination on the record after opportunity for a hearing." 5 U.S.C. § 552b(c)(10). It thus appears that a Commission covered by the Act can discuss in closed session how to dispose of a case when it would have to discuss in public how to fashion a rule on a comparable topic. In light of the contrast between the Londoner and Bi-Metallic cases, p. 238 above, and the materials in the due process chapter—if you have already covered them—do you think this distinction is required by the Constitution? Regardless of its source, what do you think of the incentives the distinction establishes as regards the Chenery problem, p. 556 above?

(5) By 1976, when GITSA was enacted, every state had a statute requiring its agencies to hold their meetings in open, public session. That state governments led the federal government in adopting such laws may reflect more immediate practical impacts at the local level. Citizens are more likely to attend municipal meetings or go to the state capitol. The press, an acknowledged major beneficiary of the laws, finds at the federal level that the daily actions of the National Labor Relations Board compete with many significant "national news" items for attention. At the state or local level, reporters in Atlantic City may find meetings to revise the city charter well worth coverage. See Polillo v. Deane, 74 N.J. 562, 379 A.2d 211 (1977). The number of reported state cases reflects both the interest in open meetings and the potency of these laws. Violations in some states are grounds for invalidating action, even, as the Ohio statute provides, action taken in an open meeting but "result[ing] from deliberations in a meeting not open to the public." See State ex rel. Delph v. Barr, 44 Ohio St.3d 77, 541 N.E.2d 59 (1989). Some states provide for award of attorneys' fees and costs. For example, two University of Florida law students and an attorney were awarded $70,000 in fees for suing to open a law school dean selection process; one Florida newspaper was awarded over $100,000 in 1991; another won awards in six cases. University of Florida, Brechner Center for Freedom of Information, Brechner Report, Attorneys' Fee Awards under Florida's Sunshine Laws 1 (Feb. 26, 1994). Sanctions for violation can be severe. In Florida between 1977 and 1992, 86 officials were fined, many sentenced to community service and to studying the law, and one was removed. Brechner Center (release of Oct. 12, 1993). See generally Teresa D. Pupillo, The Changing Weather Forecast: Government in the Sunshine

in the 1990s—An Analysis of State Sunshine Laws, 71 Wash. U. L.Q. 1165 (1993).

(6) Another arena where sunlight has been tried as a disinfectant concerns advisory committees. These are bodies of citizens that agencies may appoint under the direction of statutes (or on their own initiative) to help them in the development and/or application of policy. (You may remember that such a committee was used to develop the initial draft of a Field Sanitation Standard under OSHA—see Chapter 1, p. 3.) From the observation that these committees were becoming numerous and that their membership was sometimes dominated by special interests, Congress developed in 1972 the FEDERAL ADVISORY COMMITTEE ACT, 5 U.S.C. App., which seeks to control their growth and operation through OMB clearance, public process, and requirements of balance in membership. Before an advisory committee can meet or take any action, it must file a detailed charter and give advance notice in the Federal Register; it must hold all meetings in public, keep detailed minutes, and make its records available to the public—along with any reports, records, or other documents it uses—unless they fall within GITSA or FOIA exemptions. Committees must be "fairly balanced in terms of the points of view represented," § 5(b)(2), and the Act requires precautions to ensure that their advice and recommendations "will not be inappropriately influenced by the appointing authority or by any special interest." § 5(b)(3).

As is evident throughout this book, especially in the materials on rulemaking, agency personnel must be in constant contact with those on the outside, many of whom have an interest or bias regarding the issue at hand. Does it make sense to require advisory committees to be "fairly balanced" and operate in the open? Or does this inhibit use of just those sources we should encourage agencies most to rely on?

An excellent analysis of the FACA is Steven B. Croley and William F. Funk, The Federal Advisory Committee Act and Good Government, 14 Yale J. Reg. 452 (1997).

CHAPTER VII

PROCEDURAL DUE PROCESS: CONSTITUTIONAL CONSTRAINTS ON ADMINISTRATIVE DECISIONMAKING

"No freeman shall be taken and imprisoned or disseized or exiled or in any way destroyed, nor will we go upon him nor send upon him, except by the lawful judgment of his peers and by the law of the land."

Magna Carta, Section XXXIX (1215)

"[N]o person shall ... be deprived of life, liberty, or property, without due process of law...."

U.S. Constitution, Amendment V (1791)

"... [N]or shall any State deprive any person of life, liberty, or property, without due process of law...."

U. S. Constitution, Amendment XIV (1868)

IMPORTANT NOTE ABOUT SCOPE

The lawyer may be forgiven for thinking that everywhere she turns, due process lies in wait. As Justice Stevens explained, this clause in the Fourteenth Amendment

is the source of three different kinds of constitutional protection. First, it incorporates specific protections defined in the Bill of Rights. Thus, the State, as well as the Federal Government, must comply with the commands in the First and Eighth Amendments; so too, the State must respect the guarantees in the Fourth, Fifth, and Sixth Amendments. Second, it contains a substantive component, sometimes referred to as "substantive due process," which bars certain arbitrary government actions "regardless of the fairness of the procedures used to implement them." Third, it is a guarantee of fair procedure, sometimes referred to as "procedural due process": the State may not execute, imprison, or fine a defendant without giving him a fair trial, nor may it take property without providing appropriate procedural safeguards.[1] ...

Administrative lawyers must make even a further division. As a "guarantee of fair procedure," due process speaks to both judicial and administrative proceedings. For courts it determines, for example, how far a state court's extra-territorial jurisdiction extends, e.g., International Shoe

---

1. Daniels v. Williams, 474 U.S. 327, 336–37 (1986) (concurring opinion).

Co. v. Washington, 326 U.S. 310 (1945); what procedures must accompany a writ of garnishment or other interlocutory property seizure, e.g., North Georgia Finishing, Inc. v. Di–Chem, Inc., 419 U.S. 601 (1975); or what notice is required before a binding adjudication of a party's rights, e.g., Richards v. Jefferson County, 517 U.S. 793 (1996). Here, however, we concentrate on how due process defines fair procedures when agencies are the decisionmakers.

These many facets of due process—substantive and procedural, civil and criminal, judicial and administrative—pose enormous challenges for the courts. Working from a single textual command to prevent an individual from being *deprived* of *life, liberty, or property* without *due process of law*, the judiciary is asked to evaluate the breathtakingly diverse acts of "disciplining prisoners and school children, suspending drivers' licenses and welfare benefits, terminating employment and parental rights, curtailing public programs, prosecuting public offenders, and compelling public access to beachfront property."[2] Are judges institutionally competent to implement "the guarantee of fair procedure" in these disparate settings? Yet, if courts defer to legislative or executive judgments on procedure, have they not betrayed the counter-majoritarian purposes of the Bill of Rights? And, if these constitutional waters were not treacherous enough already, there are the strong undercurrents of federalism whenever state and local government functions come under federal due process scrutiny.

In sum, the rise of the modern administrative state has put enormous strain on a constitutional concept born in 13th century England. Two aspects of due process doctrine have proven particularly vexatious for courts.

The first is the *trigger* question: What sorts of interests qualify as "life, liberty, or property"? We "know" that a protected interest is involved when government wants to put an individual to death, imprison him, or confiscate his money or land. What about when government wants to fire a police officer, discipline a child in public school, cut off disability benefits, revoke parole, or deny a license to sell alcoholic beverages or to practice law?

The second problematic question is: What process is *due* when government wants to harm a protected interest? Unless due process always means a full, trial-type hearing of the sort historically afforded by courts, how are we to determine which "sticks" in the possible "bundle" of process rights are required in a particular context? Moreover, when must they be afforded? Often, the agency wants to act swiftly—i.e., to suspend the benefit, the license, or the employee—and then offer a hearing as part of the ultimate decision to terminate. What process must be afforded prior to the "preliminary" decision and what can be reserved to the ultimate determination of cause to terminate? Finally, what is the venue for all this process? Must it

---

2. Cynthia R. Farina, Conceiving Due   (1991).
Process, 3 Yale J.L. & Feminism 189, 269

occur at the agency, or is it enough that the individual has a judicial cause of action, after the fact, to complain about the agency's decision?

The materials that follow explore these two large clusters of questions. Throughout, pay attention to methodology. What sources can (or should) be consulted in discovering the meaning of procedural due process in the modern administrative state: history and tradition? the practices of courts? natural law? What techniques can (or should) be employed: interest balancing? cost-benefit analysis? attempts to create several sets of rules each of which governs a certain category of administration action? Perhaps most fundamental, to what extent should the judiciary defer to the process judgments of the legislature that creates the program and the executive that implements it?

Finally, you should be aware of two other components of due process doctrine that will appear only briefly in this Chapter. One is the requirement, familiar from your study of Constitutional Law, of state action (federal action, for the Fifth Amendment due process clause). Historically, this has not been a significant issue in the administrative context, for it is usually obvious that the challenged action was undertaken by some level of government. Potential complications are introduced, however, by the trend towards "privatizing" regulatory functions. In addition to privatizing prisons, half-way houses and other aspects of the criminal detention system, government units are increasingly contracting out such diverse operations as running public schools and hospitals, performing motor vehicle licensing and street maintenance, and administering welfare programs and public housing.[3] In at least two cases, the Court has assumed that due process applies in prisons run by private contractors, but it has avoided squarely deciding the point.[4] And as courts are confronted with privatized operations in functions not so patently governmental as criminal detention, discerning the line between state and private actor will only become more difficult.

The other doctrinal component that has rarely been an issue in the administrative context is "deprivation." In the typical administrative due process case, the harmful conduct—withdrawing benefits, licenses or employment, or imposing some other sanction—is unequivocally intentional, even though the complaint may be that the official decision resulted from careless information gathering or processing. However, outside the "typical" regulatory context, the question has arisen about the mens rea required of the government actor causing the harm. At first, the Court held that negligently inflicted harm could count as a deprivation; within a short time, it repudiated that holding. See Daniels v. Williams, 474 U.S. 327 (1986), overruling in part Parratt v. Taylor, 451 U.S. 527 (1981). It appears that some intermediate mental states will suffice, but the doctrine is still very unsettled as to whether, and when, recklessness, deliberate indifference or gross negligence will be enough.

---

3. See, e.g., Jack M. Sabatino, Privatization and Punitives: Should Government Contractors Share the Sovereign's Immunities From Exemplary Damages? 58 Ohio St. L.J. 175, 179–85 (1997).

4. See Correctional Services Corp. v. Malesko, 534 U.S. 61 (2001) (federal); Richardson v. McKnight, 521 U.S. 399, 412 (1997) (state).

SECTION 1. GROWING PAINS: DUE PROCESS ENCOUNTERS THE AMBITIONS OF MODERN GOVERNMENT

"As to the words from Magna Charta, incorporated into the constitution ..., after volumes spoken and written with a view to their exposition, the good sense of mankind has at last settled down to this: that they were intended to secure the individual from the arbitrary exercise of the powers of government...."

Bank of Columbia v. Okely, 4 Wheat. 235, 244 (1819)

a. THE TRADITIONAL RIGHT/PRIVILEGE DISTINCTION AND ITS "DEMISE"

Bailey v. Richardson

United States Court of Appeals for the District of Columbia Circuit, 1950.
182 F.2d 46, aff'd by an equally divided Court, 341 U.S. 918 (1951).

■ PRETTYMAN, CIRCUIT JUDGE.

[After eight year's employment in the civil service, Dorothy Bailey was discharged "due to reduction in force;" a year later, she was reinstated. Civil Service Commission regulations made reinstatement subject to various conditions, including disqualification if "[o]n all the evidence, reasonable grounds exist for belief that the person involved is disloyal to the Government of the United States." Two months after her reinstatement, Ms. Bailey received a letter from the Commission's "Loyalty Board," saying in part: "[A]n investigation of you has been conducted under the provisions of Executive Order 9835, which established the Federal Employees Loyalty Program. This investigation disclosed information which, it is believed, you should have an opportunity to explain or refute." In particular, the Commission had received "information" that she was or had been a member of the Communist party and/or two other organizations "declared by the Attorney General to come within the purview" of the Loyalty Program.

She was asked to answer in writing a set of Interrogatories "based on the information received," and advised: "[Y]ou have the right, upon request, to an administrative hearing on the issues in the case before the Regional Loyalty Board. You may appear personally before the Board and be represented by counsel or representative of your own choice; and you may present evidence in your behalf."]

Miss Bailey answered the interrogatories directly and specifically, denying each item of information recited therein as having been received by the Commission, except that she admitted past membership for a short time in the American League for Peace and Democracy. She vigorously asserted her loyalty to the United States. She requested an administrative hearing. A hearing was held before the Regional Board. She appeared and testified and presented other witnesses and numerous affidavits. No person other than those presented by her testified.

On November 1, 1948, the Regional Board advised the Federal Security Agency, in which Miss Bailey was employed, that: "As a result of such investigation and after a hearing before this Board, it was found that, on all the evidence, reasonable grounds exist for belief that Miss Bailey is disloyal to the Government of the United States. Therefore, she has been rated ineligible for Federal employment; she has been barred from competing in civil service examinations for a period of three years, and your office is instructed to separate her from the service." . . .

Miss Bailey appealed to the Loyalty Review Board and requested a hearing. [N.B. The following details of that hearing come from Judge Edgerton's dissenting opinion:

"Appellant appeared and testified before a panel of the Loyalty Review Board. She submitted her own affidavit and the affidavits of some 70 persons who knew her, including bankers, corporate officials, federal and state officials, union members, and others. Again no one testified against her. She proved she had publicly and to the knowledge of a number of the affiants taken positions inconsistent with Communist sympathies. She showed not only by her own testimony but by that of other persons that she favored the Marshall Plan, which the Communist Party notoriously opposed, and that in 1940, during the Nazi–Soviet Pact, she favored Lend–Lease and was very critical of the Soviet position. In her union she urged its officers to execute noncommunist affidavits, opposed a foreign policy resolution widely publicized as pro-Russian, and favored what was then the official CIO resolution on foreign policy.

"Against all this, there were only the unsworn reports in the secret files to the effect that unsworn statements of a general sort, purporting to connect appellant with Communism, had been made by unnamed persons. Some if not all of these statements did not purport to be based on knowledge, but only on belief. Appellant sought to learn the names of the informants or, if their names were confidential, then at least whether they had been active in appellant's union, in which there were factional quarrels. The Board did not furnish or even have this information. Chairman Richardson said: "I haven't the slightest knowledge as to who they were or how active they have been in anything." All that the Board knew or we know about the informants is that unidentified members of the Federal Bureau of Investigation, who did not appear before the Board, believed them to be reliable. To quote again from the record: "Chairman Richardson: I can only say to you that five or six of the reports come from informants certified to us by the Federal Bureau of Investigation as experienced and entirely reliable."]

On February 9, 1949, the Chairman of the Loyalty Review Board advised the Federal Security Agency that the finding of the Regional Board was sustained. . . .

The case presented for Miss Bailey is undoubtedly appealing. She was denied reinstatement in her former employment because Government officials found reasonable ground to believe her disloyal. She was not given a trial in any sense of the word, and she does not know who informed upon her. Thus viewed, her situation appeals powerfully to our sense of the fair and the just. But the case must be placed in context and in perspective.

The Constitution placed upon the President and the Congress, and upon them alone, responsibility for the welfare of this country in the arena of world affairs. It so happens that we are presently in an adversary position to a government whose most successful recent method of contest is the infiltration of a government service by its sympathizers. This is the context of Miss Bailey's question.

The essence of her complaint is not that she was denied reinstatement; the complaint is that she was denied reinstatement without revelation by the Government of the names of those who informed against her and of the method by which her alleged activities were detected. So the question actually posed by the case is whether the President is faced with an inescapable dilemma, either to continue in Government employment a person whose loyalty he reasonably suspects or else to reveal publicly the methods by which he detects disloyalty and the names of any persons who may venture to assist him. . . .

The presentation of appellant's contentions is impressive. Each detail of the trial which she unquestionably did not get is depicted separately, in a mounting cumulation into analogies to the Dreyfus case and the Nazi judicial process. Thus, a picture of a simple black-and-white fact—that appellant did not get a trial in the judicial sense—is drawn in bold and appealing colors. But the question is not whether she had a trial. The question is whether she should have had one.

If the whole of this case were as appellant pictures it, if we had only to decide the question which she states and as she states it, our task would indeed be simple and attractively pleasant. But it is not so. We are dealing with a major clash between individual and public interests. We must ascertain with precision whether individual rights are involved, and we must then weigh the sum of those rights, if there be any, against the inexorable necessities of the Government. We must examine not only one side of the controversy but both sides.

[The court concluded that neither the statute nor the executive order entitled Ms. Bailey to more process than she received. However, it held that the three-year bar from federal service was a "punishment" which could be imposed only after compliance with the Sixth Amendment.]

It is next said on behalf of appellant that the due process clause of the Fifth Amendment requires that she be afforded a hearing of the quasi-judicial type before being dismissed. . . . It has been held repeatedly and consistently that Government employ is not "property" and that in this particular it is not a contract. We are unable to perceive how it could be held to be "liberty". Certainly it is not "life." So much that is clear would seem to dispose of the point. In terms the due process clause does not apply to the holding of a Government office.

Other considerations lead to the same conclusion. Never in our history has a Government administrative employee been entitled to a hearing of the quasi-judicial type upon his dismissal from Government service. That record of a hundred and sixty years of Government administration is the sort of history which speaks with great force. . . .

In the absence of statute or ancient custom to the contrary, executive offices are held at the will of the appointing authority, not for life or for fixed terms. If removal be at will, of what purpose would process be? To hold office at the will of a superior and to be removable therefrom only by constitutional due process of law are opposite and inherently conflicting ideas. Due process of law is not applicable unless one is being deprived of something to which he has a right.

Constitutionally, the criterion for retention or removal of subordinate employees is the confidence of superior executive officials. Confidence is not controllable by process . . . . .

We hold that the due process of law clause of the Fifth Amendment does not restrict the President's discretion or the prescriptive power of Congress in respect to executive personnel.

[The court next held that the First Amendment does not prevent dismissal of government employees because of political affiliations; absent statutory protection, Republican Presidents were entitled to dismiss Democrats, and so forth. Finally, it reached the contention that the allegation of disloyalty was, after all, different in kind.]

It is said . . . that disloyalty is akin to treason and that dismissal is akin to conviction. Forthwith it is asserted that Miss Bailey has been convicted of disloyalty. As we have seen, nothing resembling a conviction from the legal standpoint has been visited upon her. She was merely refused Government employment for reasons satisfactory to the appointing authorities.

But it is said that the public does not distinguish, that she has been stigmatized and her chance of making a living seriously impaired. The position implicit in that assertion . . . is that even if executive authorities had power to dismiss Miss Bailey without a judicial hearing, they had no power to hurt her while doing so; that is, they had no power to call her disloyal even if they had power to dismiss her for that reason. . . . But if no constitutional right of the individual is being impinged and officials are acting within the scope of official authority, the fact that the individual concerned is injured in the process neither invalidates the official act nor gives the individual a right to redress. . . . These harsh rules, which run counter to every known precept of fairness to the private individual, have always been held necessary as a matter of public policy, public interest, and the unimpeded performance of the public business. On behalf of the individual, our sense of justice rebels, but the counterbalancing essentials of effective government lead us to assent without equivocation to the rules of immunity.

. . . We cannot ignore the world situation in which not merely two ideologies but two potentially adverse forces presently exist, and certainly we cannot require that the President and the Congress ignore it. Infiltration of government service is now a recognized technique for the overthrow of government. We do not think that the individual rights guaranteed by the Constitution necessarily mean that a government dedicated to those rights cannot preserve itself in the world as it is. . . .

. . . Able pleas are made based upon the American passion for fair play and upon the sincere fears of patriotic men that unqueried and unrestricted power of removal in the President may lead to tyranny. Such pleas are to be neither ignored nor belittled, but their forum is the Congress and the President's office. . . .

Reversed in part, affirmed in part, and remanded with instructions.

■ [JUDGE EDGERTON's vigorous dissent argued that (1) the Executive Order establishing the Loyalty Program entitled plaintiff to more process than she got; (2) "dismissal for disloyalty is punishment and requires all the safeguards of a judicial trial"; and (3) her dismissal constituted an abridgement of the freedom of speech. He concluded: "The court thinks Miss Bailey's interest and the public interest conflict. I think they coincide. Since Miss Bailey's dismissal from a nonsensitive job has nothing to do with protecting the security of the United States, the government's right to preserve itself in the world as it is has nothing to do with this case. The ominous theory that the right of fair trial ends where defense of security begins is irrelevant."]

NOTES

(1) Bailey is an important chapter in the intellectual history of procedural due process doctrine because it epitomizes the traditional "right/privilege" distinction that the Court eventually claims to repudiate. Moreover, in its struggle to reconcile individual claims to fundamental fairness with Executive claims of national security, it has a sobering contemporary relevance.

(2) Another famous statement of the "right/privilege" approach came from Oliver Wendall Holmes while still a Justice of the Massachusetts Supreme Judicial Court. MCAULIFFE v. NEW BEDFORD, 155 Mass. 216, 220, 29 N.E. 517, 517–18 (1892), was a suit seeking reinstatement of a police officer who had been dismissed for engaging in political activities. The terse opinion dismissing the case did not even bother to describe the activities or indicate whether they had been conducted off-duty. "The petitioner may have a constitutional right to talk politics, but he has no constitutional right to be a policeman. There are few employments for hire in which the servant does not agree to suspend his constitutional right of free speech, as well as of idleness, by the implied terms of his contract. The servant cannot complain, as he takes the employment on the terms which are offered him."

EDGERTON, J., dissenting, in BAILEY v. RICHARDSON: "[Justice Holmes' statement] is greatly over-simplified. . . . [T]he premise that government employment is a privilege does not support the conclusion that it may be granted on condition that certain economic or political ideas not be entertained. Though members of minority parties have often been dismissed, in the past, to make room for members of a party in power, any comprehensive practice of that sort would today be unthinkable as well as illegal, and the Supreme Court has plainly indicated it would also be unconstitutional. The Court pointed out in [United Public Workers v. Mitchell, 330 U.S. 75 (1947)] that Congress could not 'enact a regulation providing that no Republican, Jew or Negro shall be appointed to federal office, or that no federal employee shall attend Mass or take any active part in missionary work.' ''

JACKSON, J., concurring in JOINT ANTI-FASCIST REFUGEE COMM. v. MCGRATH, 341 U.S. 123, 185 (1951): "The fact that one may not have a legal right to get or keep a government post does not mean that he can be adjudged ineligible illegally."

Can you have a right to fair procedures to retain something that the government did not have to give you in the first place? Try to articulate a theory of the objectives of the due process clause that would give Ms. Bailey some constitutional claim to procedural fairness without turning government jobs into something "owned" by the individual holding them.

(3) Note that Bailey was affirmed by an evenly divided Court. On the same day the Court held, 5–3, that three organizations designated as "Communist" by the Attorney General under the Loyalty Program stated a constitutional cause of action.[1] JOINT ANTI-FASCIST REFUGEE COMM. v. MCGRATH, 341 U.S. 123 (1951), produced a riot of opinions, some going off on procedural points not relevant here. Justice Black wrote that, in his view, the executive had no authority, with or without a hearing, to promulgate "officially prepared and proclaimed governmental blacklists."

Most important for our purposes is the opinion of Justice Frankfurter. In an eloquent argument that has been called "the finest exposition of the need for a 'hearing,' ''[2] Frankfurter offered an alternative to the right/privilege distinction:

"[The Attorney General's designation 'Communist'] imposes no legal sanction on these organizations other than that it serves as evidence in ridding the Government of persons reasonably suspected of disloyalty. It would be blindness, however, not to recognize that in the conditions of our time such designation drastically restricts the organizations, if it does not proscribe them. . . . Yet, designation has been made without notice, without disclosure of any reasons justifying it, without opportunity to meet the undisclosed evidence or suspicion on which designation may have been based, and without opportunity to establish affirmatively that the aims and acts of the organization are innocent. . . .

". . . '[D]ue process,' unlike some legal rules, is not a technical conception with a fixed content unrelated to time, place and circumstances. Expressing as it does in its ultimate analysis respect enforced by law for that feeling of just treatment which has been evolved through centuries of Anglo–American constitutional history and civilization, 'due process' cannot be imprisoned within the treacherous limits of any formula. Representing a profound attitude of fairness between man and man, and more particularly between the individual and government, 'due process' is compounded of history, reason, the past course of decisions, and stout confidence in the strength of the democratic faith which we profess. Due process is not a mechanical instrument. It is not a yardstick. It is a process. It is a delicate process of adjustment inescapably involving the exercise of judg-

1. The ninth justice, who did not participate in either case, was Justice Clark.

2. Henry J. Friendly, "Some Kind of Hearing," 123 U.Pa.L.Rev. 1267, 1277 (1975).

ment by those whom the Constitution entrusted with the unfolding of the process.

"... The precise nature of the interest that has been adversely affected, the manner in which this was done, the reasons for doing it, the available alternatives to the procedure that was followed, the protection implicit in the office of the functionary whose conduct is challenged, the balance of hurt complained of and good accomplished—these are some of the considerations that must enter into the judicial judgment. . . .

"This Court is not alone in recognizing that the right to be heard before being condemned to suffer grievous loss of any kind, even though it may not involve the stigma and hardships of a criminal conviction, is a principle basic to our society. . . .

"Man being what he is cannot safely be trusted with complete immunity from outward responsibility in depriving others of their rights. At least such is the conviction underlying our Bill of Rights. That a conclusion satisfies one's private conscience does not attest its reliability. The validity and moral authority of a conclusion largely depend on the mode by which it was reached. Secrecy is not congenial to truth-seeking and self-righteousness gives too slender an assurance of rightness. No better instrument has been devised for arriving at truth than to give a person in jeopardy of serious loss notice of the case against him and opportunity to meet it. Nor has a better way been found for generating the feeling, so important to a popular government, that justice has been done. . . .

"... The Attorney General is certainly not immune from the historic requirements of fairness merely because he acts, however conscientiously, in the name of security. ... Due process is perhaps the most majestic concept in our whole constitutional system. While it contains the garnered wisdom of the past in assuring fundamental justice, it is also a living principle not confined to past instances."

In anticipation of modern doctrinal developments, note two things in particular about this opinion. First, in Frankfurter's approach, what sort of event triggers the government's obligation to provide due process? Second, what methodology would Frankfurter have courts employ to determine the nature of the process that is due? The dissenters, in an opinion by Justice Reed, took a far more traditional doctrinal tack: "The contention [that process was constitutionally due] can be answered summarily by saying that there is no deprivation of any property or liberty of any listed organization by the Attorney General's designation."

(4) For the status of Bailey in contemporary procedural due process doctrine, see Board of Regents v. Roth, p. 803 below, at fn. 5.

Cafeteria & Restaurant Workers Union v. McElroy

Supreme Court of the United States, 1961.
367 U.S. 886.

■ JUSTICE STEWART delivered the opinion of the Court.

In 1956 the petitioner Rachel Brawner was a shortorder cook at a cafeteria operated by her employer, M & M Restaurants, Inc., on the premises of the Naval Gun Factory in the city of Washington. She had worked there for more than six years, and from her employer's point of view her record was entirely satisfactory.

The Gun Factory was engaged in designing, producing, and inspecting naval ordnance, including the development of weapons systems of a highly classified nature. ... [T]he installation was under the command of Rear Admiral D.M. Tyree, Superintendent. ... Identification badges were issued to persons authorized to enter the premises by the Security Officer, a naval officer subordinate to the Superintendent. ... Rachel Brawner had been issued such a badge.

[Section 5(b) of the contract between the U.S. and M & M prohibited M & M from using personnel who "(iii) fail to meet the security requirements or other requirements under applicable regulations of the Activity, as determined by the Security Officer of the Activity."]

On November 15, 1956, Mrs. Brawner was required to turn in her identification badge because of ... [a] determination that she had failed to meet the security requirements of the installation. The Security Officer's determination was subsequently approved by Admiral Tyree, who cited § 5(b)(iii) of the contract as the basis for his action. At the request of the petitioner Union, which represented the employees at the cafeteria, M & M sought to arrange a meeting with officials of the Gun Factory "for the purpose of a hearing regarding the denial of admittance to the Naval Gun Factory of Rachel Brawner." This request was denied by Admiral Tyree on the ground that such a meeting would "serve no useful purpose." ...

The petitioners brought this action ... seeking, among other things, to compel the return to Mrs. Brawner of her identification badge, so that she might be permitted to enter the Gun Factory and resume her former employment. [The court of appeals affirmed the district court's grant of summary judgment for the defendants.]

As the case comes here, two basic questions are presented. Was the commanding officer of the Gun Factory authorized to deny Rachel Brawner access to the installation in the way he did? If he was so authorized, did his action in excluding her operate to deprive her of any right secured to her by the Constitution?

[The Court concluded that commanding officer was so authorized, by regulations promulgated by the Secretary of the Navy and approved by the President.]

The question remains whether Admiral Tyree's action in summarily denying Rachel Brawner access to the site of her former employment violated the requirements of the Due Process Clause of the Fifth Amendment. This question cannot be answered by easy assertion that, because she had no constitutional right to be there in the first place, she was not deprived of liberty or property by the Superintendent's action. "One may not have a constitutional right to go to Baghdad, but the Government may not prohibit one from going there unless by means consonant with due process of law." Homer v. Richmond, 292 F.2d 719, 722. It is the petitioners' claim that due process in this case required that Rachel Brawner be advised of the specific grounds for her exclusion and be accorded a hearing at which she might refute them. We are satisfied, however, that under the circumstances of this case such a procedure was not constitutionally required.

The Fifth Amendment does not require a trial-type hearing in every conceivable case of government impairment of private interest. ... The very nature of due process negates any concept of inflexible procedures universally applicable to every imaginable situation. " '[D]ue process,' unlike some legal rules, is not a technical conception with a fixed content unrelated to time, place and circumstances." It is "compounded of history, reason, the past course of decisions. ..." Joint Anti–Fascist Comm. v. McGrath, 341 U.S. 123, 162–163 (concurring opinion).

[C]onsideration of what procedures due process may require under any given set of circumstances must begin with a determination of the precise nature of the government function involved as well as of the private interest that has been affected by governmental action. Where it has been possible to characterize that private interest (perhaps in oversimplification) as a mere privilege subject to the Executive's plenary power, it has traditionally been held that notice and hearing are not constitutionally required.

What, then, was the private interest affected by Admiral Tyree's action in the present case? It most assuredly was not the right to follow a chosen trade or profession. Rachel Brawner remained entirely free to obtain employment as a short-order cook or to get any other job, either with M & M or with any other employer. All that was denied her was the opportunity to work at one isolated and specific military installation.

Moreover, the governmental function operating here was not the power to regulate or license, as lawmaker, an entire trade or profession, or to control an entire branch of private business, but, rather, as proprietor, to manage the internal operation of an important federal military establishment. In that proprietary military capacity, the Federal Government, as has been pointed out, has traditionally exercised unfettered control.

... The Court has consistently recognized that an interest closely analogous to Rachel Brawner's, the interest of a government employee in retaining his job, can be summarily denied. It has become a settled principle that government employment, in the absence of legislation, can be revoked at the will of the appointing officer....

... [The Court distinguished United Public Workers v. Mitchell, relied on by Judge Edgerton in his Bailey dissent:] We may assume that Rachel Brawner could not constitutionally have been excluded from the Gun Factory if the announced grounds for her exclusion had been patently arbitrary or discriminatory—that she could not have been kept out because she was a Democrat or a Methodist. It does not follow, however, that she was entitled to notice and a hearing when the reason advanced for her exclusion was, as here, entirely rational and in accord with the contract with M & M.

Finally, it is to be noted that this is not a case where government action has operated to bestow a badge of disloyalty or infamy, with an attendant foreclosure from other employment opportunity. See Joint Anti–Fascist Comm. v. McGrath, 341 U.S. 123, 140–141; cf. Bailey v. Richardson, 182 F.2d 46, aff'd by an equally divided Court, 341 U.S. 918. All this record shows is that, in the opinion of the Security Officer of the Gun Factory, concurred in by the Superintendent, Rachel Brawner failed to meet the particular security requirements of that specific military installation. There is nothing to indicate that this determination would in any way impair Rachel Brawner's employment opportunities anywhere else[1].... For all that appears, the Security Officer and the Superintendent may have simply thought that Rachel Brawner was garrulous, or careless with her identification badge.

For these reasons, we conclude that the Due Process Clause of the Fifth Amendment was not violated in this case.

Affirmed.

■ JUSTICE BRENNAN, with whom THE CHIEF JUSTICE, JUSTICE BLACK and JUSTICE DOUGLAS join, dissenting.

... I read the Court's opinion to acknowledge that petitioner's status as an employee at the Gun Factory was an interest of sufficient definiteness to be protected by the Federal Constitution from some kinds of governmental injury.... In other words, if petitioner Brawner's badge had been lifted avowedly on grounds of her race, religion, or political opinions the Court would concede that some constitutionally protected interest— whether "liberty" or "property" it is unnecessary to state—had been injured. But, as the Court says, there has been no such open discrimination here. The expressed ground of exclusion was the obscuring formulation that petitioner failed to meet the "security requirements" of the naval installation where she worked. I assume for present purposes that separation as a "security risk," if the charge is properly established, is not unconstitutional. But the Court goes beyond that. It holds that the mere assertion by government that exclusion is for a valid reason forecloses further inquiry. That is, unless the government official is foolish enough to admit what he is doing—and few will be so foolish after today's decision— he may employ "security requirements" as a blind behind which to dismiss at will for the most discriminatory of causes.

Such a result in effect nullifies the substantive right—not to be arbitrarily injured by Government—which the Court purports to recognize. What sort of right is it which enjoys absolutely no procedural protection? I do not mean to imply that petitioner could not have been excluded from the installation without the full procedural panoply of first having been subjected to a trial, with cross-examination and confrontation of accusers, and proof of guilt beyond a reasonable doubt. I need not go so far in this case. For under today's holding petitioner is entitled to no process at all. She is

---

1. In oral argument government counsel emphatically represented that denial of access to the Gun Factory would not "by law or in fact" prevent Rachel Brawner from obtaining employment on any other federal property.

not told what she did wrong; she is not given a chance to defend herself. . . .

NOTES

(1) The right/privilege distinction was the way traditional due process doctrine analyzed the "trigger" question. That is, it was how courts decided whether the individual had been deprived of something that qualified as "life, liberty or property," so as to invoke the guarantee of "due" process. With astonishing lack of fanfare, Justice Stewart's opinion repudiates this traditional approach. What does the Court substitute? If you were the law clerk for a district judge the day after Cafeteria Workers comes down, would you explain the new due process analysis to your judge as the adoption of Justice Frankfurter's "grievous loss" approach? Justice Stewart balances the government's interest against the individual's interest. Does this come from Frankfurter? Does the balance determine whether due process is triggered? or what process is due? Does the Court perceive these as two separate inquiries?

(2) Note that Justice Holmes's McAuliffe formulation has also died a quiet death by the time of Cafeteria Workers. Even if Ms. Brawner has no constitutional right to a security clearance, the government cannot withdraw the clearance simply because she exercises her constitutional right to be a Democrat or a Methodist. Can you articulate a theory of constitutional rights that explains this result?

By contrast, government *can* constitutionally withdraw Rachel Brawner's security clearance because she is a security risk. This makes her case harder than Police Officer McAuliffe's. On what theory of the due process clause is Ms. Brawner entitled to process to prove that the government's apparently good faith belief in her riskiness is wrong? Recall Justice Brennan's assertion that the Court recognizes a constitutional right "not to be arbitrarily injured by Government?" This is an appealing theory of the due process clause, that resonates not only with Justice Frankfurters' eloquent exposition in Joint Anti–Fascist League but also with the much earlier statement in Bank of Columbia v. Okley, which begins this Section. But, how would this theory fare in the modern administrative state? Specifically, would it transform every challenge to administrative action as "arbitrary, capricious, or an abuse of discretion," APA § 706(2)(A), into a Fifth Amendment due process claim? And remember that the meaning of the Fourteenth Amendment—with its application to every state and local administrative decision—also hangs in the balance.

(3) Although the jettisoning of right/privilege in Cafeteria Workers may seem abrupt to contemporary students, it would not have been such a surprise to lawyers who lived through the 1950s and 1960s. CYNTHIA R. FARINA, ON MISUSING "REVOLUTION" AND "REFORM": PROCEDURAL DUE PROCESS AND THE NEW WELFARE ACT, 50 Admin. L. Rev. 591, 601–03 (1998): "In the 1950s—as Cold War hysteria about 'disloyalty' bred government intrusion into citizens' social and economic lives, unprecedented in its scope and heavy-handedness—it became increasingly hard for the judiciary to turn away victims of McCarthyism by merely parroting Justice Holmes' facile

distinction between 'rights' and 'privileges.' At the beginning of the decade, Dorothy Bailey unsuccessfully attacked her highly-publicized dismissal from government service on the basis of the unsworn testimony of un-named informants—but her argument that the Constitution protected her from thus losing the 'privilege' of government employment drew impassioned support from one dissenting judge on the D.C. Circuit, and so split the eight participating Justices that the case was affirmed by an equally divided Court. Four years later, the Court sustained New York's suspension of Edward Barsky's medical license after his conviction for contempt of Congress, emphasizing the state's 'substantially plenary power' over the 'privilege' of practicing medicine, but Justices Douglas, Black, and Frank-furter wrote strong dissents.[1] Within two years, a 5–4 Court overturned the summary discharge of state college professor Harry Slochower for invoking the Fifth Amendment in a congressional committee hearing—even as the majority disclaimed any intent to recognize 'a constitutional right to be an associate professor of German at Brooklyn College.'[2] And by the end of the decade a nearly unanimous Court, confronted again with an individually-devastating governmental job determination—revocation of William Greene's security clearance—based on unsworn, unnamed informants, found the procedure of such doubtful constitutionality that it invoked 'clear statement' principles to conclude that the Defense Department had not been authorized, by Congress or the President, to proceed in this fashion.[3]

"In the 1960s the Civil Rights movement, and the growth in the government's regulatory presence inaugurated by the Great Society programs, replaced McCarthyism as the impetus for movement in constitutional doctrine. The Fifth Circuit, in the face of established precedent that college students had no 'right' to an education at public expense, concluded that St. John Dixon could not be expelled from Alabama State College for participating in a lunch-counter sit-in, without the basic due process protections of notice and hearing.[4] The Supreme Court held that South Carolina could not deny Adell Sherbert unemployment benefits on grounds that, as a Seventh Day Adventist, she refused to work on Saturday; six Justices joined an opinion asserting that it was 'too late in the day' to suggest that First Amendment liberties could be infringed by the 'placing of conditions upon a benefit or privilege.'[5] Some lower federal courts extended the 'clear statement' strategy, used the previous decade by the Supreme Court in the Greene case, to invalidate summary government action in other regulatory settings. Some state courts questioned whether benefits such as welfare could be conditioned on consent to otherwise impermissible governmental behavior such as warrantless searches.

1. Barsky v. Board of Regents, 347 U.S. 442 (1954).

2. Slochower v. Board of Educ., 350 U.S. 551, 559 (1956).

3. Greene v. McElroy, 360 U.S. 474 (1959). [Ed.] Rachel Brawner's lawyers tried to use this strategy but, as the text notes, the Court held that Admiral Tyree's actions were authorized by the President and within the Secretary of the Navy's statutory delegation of power.

4. Dixon v. Alabama State Bd. of Educ., 294 F.2d 150 (5th Cir.), cert. denied, 368 U.S. 930 (1961).

5. Sherbert v. Verner, 374 U.S. 398 (1963).

"To be sure, several distinct jurisprudential strands become intertwined in these cases. Substantive due process claims (constitutional limits on *what* government can take from a citizen) weave round claims for procedural due process (constitutional limits on *how* government can take from a citizen). Interests that can insist upon the status of constitutional limitations on government action wholly apart from the Due Process Clause—e.g., First Amendment rights of religion, expression, and association; Fourth Amendment rights of privacy; Fifth Amendment rights against self-incrimination—become caught up in the tangled doctrine of 'unconstitutional conditions.' Strained statutory interpretation temporarily veils constitutional unease and determinedly (if disingenuously) creates some growing space for still-embryonic ways of reshaping constitutional understandings. Nonetheless, the common theme of these developments is clear: As modern society became more complex and interdependent, as Americans' collective political choices gave government a more pervasive role in regulating and supporting their individual social and economic lives, the right/privilege distinction became an increasingly inadequate touchstone for determining when the Constitution regulates interactions between government and the citizen."

(4) The other major development of the era having some relevance to the coming-of-age of procedural due process doctrine, is the jurisprudential debate over incorporation. Recall that prior to adoption of the Fourteenth Amendment in 1868, the Constitution imposed very different obligations, with respect to individual rights, on the national government than on the states. Specifically, the Bill of Rights applied only to the former. The Fourteenth Amendment—in particular, its due process clause—radically altered the constitutional landscape. For more than 100 years, the Court struggled to determine whether the Fourteenth Amendment due process clause encompasses rights and duties identical to those contained in the Bill of Rights. For our purposes, the relevant piece of this complicated story is the methodological debate between Justice Black on the one side and, on the other, a group of justices that included Cardozo, Frankfurter, and Harlan.

This latter group insisted that the Fourteenth Amendment was not intended to incorporate any of the first eight Amendments per se. Rather, these Justices interpreted the demands of Fourteenth Amendment due process by asking whether the claimed protection is "the very essence of a scheme of ordered liberty" or "a principle of justice so rooted in the traditions and conscience of our people as to be ranked as fundamental;" without it, would the state's action, looking at "the whole course of the proceedings ... offend those canons of decency and fairness which express the notions of justice of English-speaking peoples?"[6] Cf. Frankfurter's Joint Anti–Fascist Refugee Comm. opinion, p. 775 above. Sometimes this inquiry resulted in applying a particular constitutional protection found in the Bill of Rights (e.g., the right to counsel in capital cases) but for Justices taking

---

6. See Palko v. Connecticut, 302 U.S. 319 (1937) (Cardozo, J.); Adamson v. California, 332 U.S. 46 (Frankfurter, J., concurring).

this approach, "[t]he logically critical thing was not that the rights had been found in the Bill of Rights, but that they were deemed ... fundamental."[7]

By contrast, Justice Black read the Fourteenth Amendment as intended to incorporate the first eight Amendments *in toto*, with their accompanying judicial interpretations. Any other approach, he argued, was impossibly subjective and unpredictable. "I fear to see the consequences of the Court's practice of substituting its own concepts of decency and fundamental justice for the language of the Bill of Rights. ..." The natural law methodology, he argued, allows the Justices to "roam at will in the limitless area of their own beliefs as to reasonableness and actually select policies, a responsibility which the Constitution entrusts to the legislative representatives of the people."[8]

This debate most directly concerned criminal procedure. However, the deeper disagreement echoed the debates of the 1930s over judicial role. Would it be possible for the Court to give robust content to the counter-majoritarian guarantee of due process without engaging in constitutional interpretation by judicial fiat? These concerns were very much in the air when the Court confronted the question of what process is due when regulatory government harms the citizen—as you will recognize in the next case.

b.   THE MODERN WATERSHED

Goldberg v. Kelly

Supreme Court of the United States, 1970.
397 U.S. 254.

■ JUSTICE BRENNAN delivered the opinion of the Court.

The question for decision is whether a State that terminates public assistance payments to a particular recipient without affording him the opportunity for an evidentiary hearing prior to termination denies the recipient procedural due process in violation of the Due Process Clause of the Fourteenth Amendment.

---

7. Duncan v. Louisiana, 391 U.S. 145 (1968) (Harlan, J., dissenting). A different group of Justices believed that some, but not all, of the Bill of Rights were incorporated into the Fourteenth Amendment. This "selective incorporation" approach asks whether a particular Bill of Rights provision is "fundamental to the American scheme of justice" or "fundamental in the context of the criminal processes maintained by the American states." Justice Brennan falls in this group. Yet a fourth position was taken by some Justices (including Murphy and Rutledge), who interpreted the Fourteenth Amendment as selectively incorporating Bill of Rights pro-

visions *plus* any other protection necessary to fundamental fairness.

8. Justice Black continued to advocate total incorporation as the correct interpretation, but he voted with the selective incorporationists as the next best methodological choice: "I have been willing to support the selective incorporation doctrine ... as an alternative, although perhaps less historically supportable than complete incorporation [because it] keeps judges from roaming at will in their own notions of what policies outside the Bill of Rights are desirable and what are not." Duncan v. Louisiana, 391 U.S. at 171 (Black, J., concurring).

This action was brought in the District Court for the Southern District of New York by residents of New York City receiving financial aid under the federally assisted program of Aid to Families with Dependent Children (AFDC) or under New York State's general Home Relief program.[1] Their complaint alleged that the New York State and New York City officials administering these programs terminated, or were about to terminate, such aid without prior notice and hearing, thereby denying them due process of law.[2] At the time the suits were filed there was no requirement of prior notice or hearing of any kind before termination of financial aid. However, the State and city adopted procedures for notice and hearing after the suits were brought, and the plaintiffs, appellees here, then challenged the constitutional adequacy of those procedures.

[The revised procedures are as follows:] A caseworker who has doubts about the recipient's continued eligibility must first discuss them with the recipient. If the caseworker concludes that the recipient is no longer eligible, he recommends termination of aid to a unit supervisor. If the latter concurs, he sends the recipient a letter stating the reasons for proposing to terminate aid and notifying him that within seven days he may request that a higher official review the record, and may support the request with a written statement prepared personally or with the aid of an attorney or other person. If the reviewing official affirms the determination of ineligibility, aid is stopped immediately and the recipient is informed by letter of the reasons for the action. Appellees' challenge to this procedure emphasizes the absence of any provisions for the personal appearance of the recipient before the reviewing official, for oral presentation of evidence, and for confrontation and cross-examination of adverse witnesses. However, the letter does inform the recipient that he may request a post-termination "fair hearing."[3] This is a proceeding before an independent state hearing officer at which the recipient may appear personally, offer oral evidence, confront and cross-examine the witnesses against him, and have a record made of the hearing. If the recipient prevails at the "fair hearing" he is paid all funds erroneously withheld. A recipient whose aid is not restored by a "fair hearing" decision may have judicial review. The recipient is so notified.

I

The constitutional issue to be decided, therefore, is the narrow one whether the Due Process Clause requires that the recipient be afforded an

---

1. AFDC was established by the Social Security Act of 1935. It is a categorical assistance program supported by federal grants-in-aid but administered by the States according to regulations of the Secretary of Health, Education, and Welfare. ... Home Relief is a general assistance program financed and administered solely by New York state and local governments. ...

2. ... For example, Mrs. Altagracia Guzman alleged that she was in danger of losing AFDC payments for failure to cooperate with the City Department of Social Services in suing her estranged husband. She

contended that the departmental policy requiring such cooperation was inapplicable to the facts of her case.... Home Relief payments to Juan DeJesus were terminated because he refused to accept counseling and rehabilitation for drug addiction. Mr. DeJesus maintains that he does not use drugs. ...

3. ... In both AFDC and Home Relief the "fair hearing" must be held within 10 working days of the request, with decision within 12 working days thereafter. It was conceded in oral argument that these time limits are not in fact observed.

evidentiary hearing before the termination of benefits. The District Court held that only a pre-termination evidentiary hearing would satisfy the constitutional command, and rejected the argument of the state and city officials that the combination of the post-termination "fair hearing" with the informal pre-termination review disposed of all due process claims. The court said: "While post-termination review is relevant, there is one overpowering fact which controls here. By hypothesis, a welfare recipient is destitute, without funds or assets. . . . Suffice it to say that to cut off a welfare recipient in the face of . . . 'brutal need' without a prior hearing of some sort is unconscionable, unless overwhelming considerations justify it." The court rejected the argument that the need to protect the public's tax revenues supplied the requisite "overwhelming consideration." . . . We affirm.

Appellant does not contend that procedural due process is not applicable to the termination of welfare benefits. Such benefits are a matter of statutory entitlement for persons qualified to receive them.[4] Their termination involves state action that adjudicates important rights. The constitutional challenge cannot be answered by an argument that public assistance benefits are "a 'privilege' and not a 'right.'" Shapiro v. Thompson, 394 U.S. 618, 627 n. 6 (1969). Relevant constitutional restraints apply as much to the withdrawal of public assistance benefits as to disqualification for unemployment compensation, Sherbert v. Verner, 374 U.S. 398 (1963); or to denial of a tax exemption, Speiser v. Randall, 357 U.S. 513 (1958); or to discharge from public employment, Slochower v. Board of Higher Education, 350 U.S. 551 (1956). The extent to which procedural due process must be afforded the recipient is influenced by the extent to which he may be "condemned to suffer grievous loss," Joint Anti–Fascist Refugee Committee v. McGrath, 341 U.S. 123, 168 (1951) (Frankfurter, J., concurring), and depends upon whether the recipient's interest in avoiding that loss outweighs the governmental interest in summary adjudication. Accordingly, as we said in Cafeteria & Restaurant Workers Union v. McElroy, 367 U.S. 886, 895 (1961), "consideration of what procedures due process may require under any given set of circumstances must begin with a determina-

4. It may be realistic today to regard welfare entitlements as more like "property" than a "gratuity." Much of the existing wealth in this country takes the form of rights that do not fall within traditional common-law concepts of property. It has been aptly noted that

> [s]ociety today is built around entitlement. The automobile dealer has his franchise, the doctor and lawyer their professional licenses, the worker his union membership, contract, and pension rights, the executive his contract and stock options; all are devices to aid security and independence. Many of the most important of these entitlements now flow from government: subsidies to farmers and businessmen, routes for airlines and channels for television stations; long term contracts for defense, space, and education; social security pensions for individuals. Such sources of security, whether private or public, are no longer regarded as luxuries or gratuities; to the recipients they are essentials, fully deserved, and in no sense a form of charity. It is only the poor whose entitlements, although recognized by public policy, have not been effectively enforced.

Reich, Individual Rights and Social Welfare: The Emerging Legal Issues, 74 Yale L.J. 1245, 1255 (1965). See also Reich, The New Property, 73 Yale L.J. 733 (1964).

tion of the precise nature of the government function involved as well as of the private interest that has been affected by governmental action."

It is true, of course, that some governmental benefits may be administratively terminated without affording the recipient a pre-termination evidentiary hearing.[5] But we agree with the District Court that when welfare is discontinued, only a pre-termination evidentiary hearing provides the recipient with procedural due process. For qualified recipients, welfare provides the means to obtain essential food, clothing, housing, and medical care. Thus the crucial factor in this context—a factor not present in the case of the blacklisted government contractor, the discharged government employee, the taxpayer denied a tax exemption, or virtually anyone else whose governmental entitlements are ended—is that termination of aid pending resolution of a controversy over eligibility may deprive an eligible recipient of the very means by which to live while he waits. Since he lacks independent resources, his situation becomes immediately desperate. His need to concentrate upon finding the means for daily subsistence, in turn, adversely affects his ability to seek redress from the welfare bureaucracy.

Moreover, important governmental interests are promoted by affording recipients a pre-termination evidentiary hearing. From its founding the Nation's basic commitment has been to foster the dignity and well-being of all persons within its borders. We have come to recognize that forces not within the control of the poor contribute to their poverty. This perception, against the background of our traditions, has significantly influenced the development of the contemporary public assistance system. Welfare, by meeting the basic demands of subsistence, can help bring within the reach of the poor the same opportunities that are available to others to participate meaningfully in the life of the community. At the same time, welfare guards against the societal malaise that may flow from a widespread sense of unjustified frustration and insecurity. Public assistance, then, is not mere charity, but a means to "promote the general Welfare, and secure the Blessings of Liberty to ourselves and our Posterity." The same governmental interests that counsel the provision of welfare, counsel as well its uninterrupted provision to those eligible to receive it; pre-termination evidentiary hearings are indispensable to that end.

Appellant does not challenge the force of these considerations but argues that they are outweighed by countervailing governmental interests in conserving fiscal and administrative resources. These interests, the argument goes, justify the delay of any evidentiary hearing until after discontinuance of the grants. Summary adjudication protects the public fisc by stopping payments promptly upon discovery of reason to believe that a recipient is no longer eligible. Since most terminations are accepted with-

---

5. See ..., for example, Ewing v. Mytinger & Casselberry, Inc., 339 U.S. 594 (1950) (seizure of mislabeled vitamin product); North American Cold Storage Co. v. Chicago, 211 U.S. 306 (1908) (seizure of food not fit for human use).... In Cafeteria & Restaurant Workers Union v. McElroy, [367 U.S. 886, 896 (1961)] summary dismissal of a public employee was upheld because "[i]n [its] proprietary military capacity, the Federal Government ... has traditionally exercised unfettered control," and because the case involved the Government's "dispatch of its own internal affairs."

out challenge, summary adjudication also conserves both the fisc and administrative time and energy by reducing the number of evidentiary hearings actually held.

We agree with the District Court, however, that these governmental interests are not overriding in the welfare context. The requirement of a prior hearing doubtless involves some greater expense, and the benefits paid to ineligible recipients pending decision at the hearing probably cannot be recouped, since these recipients are likely to be judgment-proof. But the State is not without weapons to minimize these increased costs. Much of the drain on fiscal and administrative resources can be reduced by developing procedures for prompt pre-termination hearings and by skillful use of personnel and facilities. Indeed, the very provision for a post-termination evidentiary hearing in New York's Home Relief program is itself cogent evidence that the State recognizes the primacy of the public interest in correct eligibility determinations and therefore in the provision of procedural safeguards. Thus, the interest of the eligible recipient in uninterrupted receipt of public assistance, coupled with the State's interest that his payments not be erroneously terminated, clearly outweighs the State's competing concern to prevent any increase in its fiscal and administrative burdens. As the District Court correctly concluded, "[t]he stakes are simply too high for the welfare recipient, and the possibility for honest error or irritable misjudgment too great, to allow termination of aid without giving the recipient a chance, if he so desires, to be fully informed of the case against him so that he may contest its basis and produce evidence in rebuttal."

II

We also agree with the District Court, however, that the pre-termination hearing need not take the form of a judicial or quasi-judicial trial. We bear in mind that the statutory "fair hearing" will provide the recipient with a full administrative review.[6] Accordingly, the pre-termination hearing has one function only: to produce an initial determination of the validity of the welfare department's grounds for discontinuance of payments in order to protect a recipient against an erroneous termination of his benefits. Thus, a complete record and a comprehensive opinion, which would serve primarily to facilitate judicial review and to guide future decisions, need not be provided at the pre-termination stage. We recognize, too, that both welfare authorities and recipients have an interest in relatively speedy resolution of questions of eligibility, that they are used to dealing with one another informally, and that some welfare departments have very burdensome caseloads. These considerations justify the limitation of the pre-termination hearing to minimum procedural safeguards, adapted to the particular characteristics of welfare recipients, and to the limited nature of the controversies to be resolved. . . .

"The fundamental requisite of due process of law is the opportunity to be heard." Grannis v. Ordean, 234 U.S. 385, 394 (1914). The hearing must

---

6. Due process does not, of course, require two hearings. If, for example, a State simply wishes to continue benefits until after a "fair" hearing there will be no need for a preliminary hearing.

be "at a meaningful time and in a meaningful manner." Armstrong v. Manzo, 380 U.S. 545, 552 (1965). In the present context these principles require that a recipient have timely and adequate notice detailing the reasons for a proposed termination, and an effective opportunity to defend by confronting any adverse witnesses and by presenting his own arguments and evidence orally. These rights are important in cases such as those before us, where recipients have challenged proposed terminations as resting on incorrect or misleading factual premises or on misapplication of rules or policies to the facts of particular cases.[7] . . .

The city's procedures presently do not permit recipients to appear personally with or without counsel before the official who finally determines continued eligibility. Thus a recipient is not permitted to present evidence to that official orally, or to confront or cross-examine adverse witnesses. These omissions are fatal to the constitutional adequacy of the procedures.

The opportunity to be heard must be tailored to the capacities and circumstances of those who are to be heard. It is not enough that a welfare recipient may present his position to the decision maker in writing or secondhand through his caseworker. Written submissions are an unrealistic option for most recipients, who lack the educational attainment necessary to write effectively and who cannot obtain professional assistance. Moreover, written submissions do not afford the flexibility of oral presentations; they do not permit the recipient to mold his argument to the issues the decision maker appears to regard as important. Particularly where credibility and veracity are at issue, as they must be in many termination proceedings, written submissions are a wholly unsatisfactory basis for decision. The secondhand presentation to the decisionmaker by the caseworker has its own deficiencies; since the caseworker usually gathers the facts upon which the charge of ineligibility rests, the presentation of the recipient's side of the controversy cannot safely be left to him. Therefore a recipient must be allowed to state his position orally. Informal procedures will suffice; in this context due process does not require a particular order of proof or mode of offering evidence.

In almost every setting where important decisions turn on questions of fact, due process requires an opportunity to confront and cross-examine adverse witnesses. What we said in Greene v. McElroy, 360 U.S. 474, 496–497 (1959), is particularly pertinent here:

> Certain principles have remained relatively immutable in our jurisprudence. One of these is that where governmental action seriously injures an individual, and the reasonableness of the action depends on fact findings, the evidence used to prove the Government's case must be disclosed to the individual so that he has an opportunity to show that it is untrue. While this is important in the case of documentary evidence, it is even more important where the evidence consists of the testimony of individuals whose memory might be faulty or who, in fact, might be

---

7. This case presents no question requiring our determination whether due process requires only an opportunity for written submission, or an opportunity both for written submission and oral argument, where there are no factual issues in dispute or where the application of the rule of law is not intertwined with factual issues.

perjurers or persons motivated by malice, vindictiveness, intolerance, prejudice, or jealousy. . . .

Welfare recipients must therefore be given an opportunity to confront and cross-examine the witnesses relied on by the department.

"The right to be heard would be, in many cases, of little avail if it did not comprehend the right to be heard by counsel." Powell v. Alabama, 287 U.S. 45, 68–69 (1932). We do not say that counsel must be provided at the pre-termination hearing, but only that the recipient must be allowed to retain an attorney if he so desires. . . . We do not anticipate that this assistance will unduly prolong or otherwise encumber the hearing. . . .

Finally, the decisionmaker's conclusion as to a recipient's eligibility must rest solely on the legal rules and evidence adduced at the hearing. To demonstrate compliance with this elementary requirement, the decision maker should state the reasons for his determination and indicate the evidence he relied on, though his statement need not amount to a full opinion or even formal findings of fact and conclusions of law. And, of course, an impartial decision maker is essential. We agree with the District Court that prior involvement in some aspects of a case will not necessarily bar a welfare official from acting as a decision maker. He should not, however, have participated in making the determination under review.

Affirmed.

■ JUSTICE BLACK, dissenting.

The more than a million names on the relief rolls in New York, and the more than nine million names on the rolls of all the 50 States were not put there at random. The names are there because state welfare officials believed that those people were eligible for assistance. Probably in the officials' haste to make out the lists many names were put there erroneously in order to alleviate immediate suffering, and undoubtedly some people are drawing relief who are not entitled under the law to do so. Doubtless some draw relief checks from time to time who know they are not eligible, either because they are not actually in need or for some other reason. Many of those who thus draw undeserved gratuities are without sufficient property to enable the government to collect back from them any money they wrongfully receive. But the Court today holds that it would violate the Due Process Clause of the Fourteenth Amendment to stop paying those people weekly or monthly allowances unless the government first affords them a full "evidentiary hearing" even though welfare officials are persuaded that the recipients are not rightfully entitled to receive a penny under the law. In other words, although some recipients might be on the lists for payment wholly because of deliberate fraud on their part, the Court holds that the government is helpless and must continue, until after an evidentiary hearing, to pay money that it does not owe, never has owed, and never could owe. I do not believe there is any provision in our Constitution that should thus paralyze the government's efforts to protect itself against making payments to people who are not entitled to them.

. . . It somewhat strains credulity to say that the government's promise of charity to an individual is property belonging to that individual when the government denies that the individual is honestly entitled to receive such a payment.

... Although the majority attempts to bolster its decision with limited quotations from prior cases, it is obvious that today's result does not depend on the language of the Constitution itself or the principles of other decisions, but solely on the collective judgment of the majority as to what would be a fair and humane procedure in this case....

The Court apparently feels that this decision will benefit the poor and needy. In my judgment the eventual result will be just the opposite. While today's decision requires only an administrative, evidentiary hearing, the inevitable logic of the approach taken will lead to constitutionally imposed, time-consuming delays of a full adversary process of administrative and judicial review. In the next case the welfare recipients are bound to argue that cutting off benefits before judicial review of the agency's decision is also a denial of due process. Since, by hypothesis, termination of aid at that point may still "deprive an eligible recipient of the very means by which to live while he waits," I would be surprised if the weighing process did not compel the conclusion that termination without full judicial review would be unconscionable. After all, at each step, as the majority seems to feel, the issue is only one of weighing the government's pocketbook against the actual survival of the recipient, and surely that balance must always tip in favor of the individual. ... [T]he inevitable result of such a constitutionally imposed burden will be that the government will not put a claimant on the rolls initially until it has made an exhaustive investigation to determine his eligibility. While this Court will perhaps have insured that no needy person will be taken off the rolls without a full "due process" proceeding, it will also have insured that many will never get on the rolls, or at least that they will remain destitute during the lengthy proceedings followed to determine initial eligibility.

For the foregoing reasons I dissent from the Court's holding. The operation of a welfare state is a new experiment for our Nation. For this reason, among others, I feel that new experiments in carrying out a welfare program should not be frozen into our constitutional structure. They should be left, as are other legislative determinations, to the Congress and the legislatures that the people elect to make our laws.

[Wheeler v. Montgomery, 397 U.S. 280 (1970), a companion case involving the validity of California's welfare termination procedures, was decided on the basis of Goldberg. Chief Justice Burger, joined by Justice Black, wrote a dissenting opinion applicable to both Goldberg and Wheeler. Although agreeing "in large part with Mr. Justice Black's views," the Chief Justice added that since HEW had recently adopted new procedural regulations which "go far beyond the result reached today," the Court should "hold the heavy hand of constitutional adjudication and allow evolutionary" administrative experimentation.

Justice Stewart dissented in a brief opinion: "Although the question is for me a close one, I do not believe that the procedures that New York and California now follow in terminating welfare payments are violative of the United States Constitution. See Cafeteria & Restaurant Workers Union v. McElroy, 367 U.S. 886, 894–897."]

NOTES

(1) Goldberg is universally understood as making a sharp break with traditional analysis by extending constitutional protection to a consummate "privilege"—welfare. To some extent, this is the hindsight of history. Both the defendant and the United States appearing as amicus *conceded* that due process applied.[1] Thus, the litigants regarded the real issue as whether New York could treat benefit suspension as a preliminary decision accompanied by relatively informal process, with a final determination of ineligibility made through a post-suspension "fair hearing." However, because Justice Brennan goes beyond the parties' concession to explain why due process applies to welfare termination, the opinion is now read as setting the Court on the path of modern due process doctrine.

What exactly is this path? Is fair procedure constitutionally required because of the "brutal need" of recipients—in effect, accepting Justice Frankfurter's view that due process is triggered whenever the government imposes "grievous loss" on the individual? Or is the constitutionally crucial fact that "[s]uch benefits are a matter of statutory entitlement for persons qualified to receive them"? What turns on the distinction? Suppose that, after Goldberg is decided, the state of New York (with federal permission as necessary) revises its AFDC and Home Relief programs to provide: "Notwithstanding any other provision, benefits received under this Act may be terminated at the sole discretion of the unit supervisor, on recommendation of the caseworker." Would the John Kellys of the world still have a procedural due process claim?

In the Personal Responsibility and Work Opportunity Reconciliation Act of 1996, Congress abolished the AFDC program. As part of "welfare reform," it attempted to reverse the effect of Goldberg by preventing the new welfare regime from triggering due process. Can the legislature, by changing the terms of the statute, determine whether the individual is entitled to constitutional protection? We will return to this question after Board of Regents v. Roth. See p. 818 below.

(2) The "grievous loss" interpretation of Goldberg appeared to receive some support the following Term in WISCONSIN v. CONSTANTINEAU, 400 U.S. 433 (1971). The police chief of Hartford, Wisconsin, posted a notice in all liquor stores forbidding, for one year, the sale of liquor to Norma Constantineau. He acted under a statute that authorized such posting at the instance of various town officials or "the wife" of any person who "by excessive drinking" was harming himself, his family, or his neighbors. No notice or hearing was required. To sell or give intoxicating liquor to someone "posted" was a misdemeanor. Held: the statute was unconstitutional on its face. "We agree with the District Court that the private interest is such that those requirements of procedural due process must be

---

1. One of your editors was the lawyer in the Solicitor General's office who drafted the government's amicus brief for the Supreme Court. He recalls that federal lawyers regarded the applicability question as settled by the line of cases culminating in Cafeteria Workers. Similarly, Martha F. David, Brutal Need: Lawyers & The Welfare Rights Movement, 1960–1973 at 93 (1993) quotes the lead attorney for the City of New York that "nobody in our group had a taste for making conservative arguments that would be uncomfortable to defend."

met. It is significant that most of the provisions of the Bill of Rights are procedural, for it is procedure that marks much of the difference between rule by law and rule by fiat.

"We reviewed in Cafeteria and Restaurant Workers Union v. McElroy, the nature of the various 'private interest(s)' that have fallen on one side or the other of the line. Generalizations are hazardous as some state and federal administrative procedures are summary by reason of necessity or history. Yet certainly where the State attaches 'a badge of infamy' to the citizen, due process comes into play. '[T]he right to be heard before being condemned to suffer grievous loss of any kind, even though it may not involve the stigma and hardships of a criminal conviction, is a principle basic to our society.' Joint Anti–Fascist Refugee Committee v. McGrath, 341 U.S. 123, 168 (Frankfurter, J., concurring).

"Where a person's good name, reputation, honor, or integrity is at stake because of what the government is doing to him, notice and an opportunity to be heard are essential. 'Posting' under the Wisconsin Act may to some be merely the mark of illness, to others it is a stigma, an official branding of a person. The label is a degrading one. . . .' "

(3) Footnote 4 in the edited version of Goldberg quotes from an article by CHARLES REICH and cites his famous earlier work, THE NEW PROPERTY, 73 Yale L.J. 733 (1964). This is a remarkable and far-ranging essay. One of your editors has summarized its relevance to the issue at hand: "[The New Property's] central theme is a deeply liberal (if not libertarian) longing that the individual be able to retain a fundamental independence from the collective, an independence that is regarded as essential if the individual's unique identity is to exist and flourish. . . . Property, [Reich] argues, is the social construct that 'performs the function of maintaining independence, dignity and pluralism . . . by creating zones in which the majority has to yield to the owner. . . . Like the Bill of Rights, property represents a general, long range protection of individual and private interests, created by the majority for the ultimate good of all.'

"[For Reich], [p]roperty demarcates the essential boundary between the public and the private spheres. It insulates against the pressure to be, in contemporary jargon, politically correct. It forms the foundation of civil liberty. And the greatest danger to the traditional American way of life is, in Professor Reich's view, the emergence of the regulatory state. He points with concern to airlines, trucking companies, broadcasters, and taxicab owners whose survival depends upon regulatory permits and certificates; to doctors, lawyers, and pilots whose occupation turns on possessing an official license; to farmers whose livelihood is tied to government grazing permits and crop subsidies; to manufacturers and suppliers that rely upon government contracts; to universities that must have government grants for research and financial aid. Through this dependence, he worries, government obtains 'new rights to investigate, to regulate and to punish.' It gains the leverage to condition its favors on complying with [various] social welfare regulations; on being 'loyal' and eschewing activities thought to be subversive; on being of good 'moral character.'

"Up to this point, Charles Reich sounds more like a child of the '90s than of the '60s, preaching the text of radical deregulation rather than of socialist revolution. Where he makes a hard left turn is in his remarkable egalitarianism.... He is as concerned about regulating the 'moral character' of the longshoreman or the mother on welfare as of the businessman; about requiring some particular conception of 'loyalty' from the occupant of public housing or the recipient of unemployment compensation as from the lawyer or doctor; about conditioning the receipt of welfare upon giving up Fourth Amendment rights against unreasonable searches as conditioning the license to practice law upon giving up Fifth Amendment rights against self-incrimination. As he puts it, 'If the businessman, the teacher, and the professional man find themselves subject to the power of government largess, the man on public assistance is even more dependent.'

" . . . This concern about the autonomy of the individual citizen, caught up in the inexorable momentum of the regulatory state, led him to a radical—and radically egalitarian—prescription for reform:

> If individualism and pluralism are to be preserved, this must be done not by marching backwards, but by building these values into today's society. If public and private are now blurred, it will be necessary to draw a new zone of privacy. If private property can no longer perform its protective functions, it will be necessary to establish institutions to carry on the work that private property once did but can no longer do. . . . As we move toward a welfare state, largess will be an ever more important form of wealth. . . . It is necessary, then, that largess begin to do the work of property.

To 'do the work of property,' the licenses, permits, grants, and benefits that come from regulatory government must, he argued, be recast as 'rights' or 'Individual Stakes in the Commonwealth.' This reconceptualization entailed, first and foremost, substantive protection: from the imposition of unconstitutional conditions, from the temptation to use 'regulation of largess . . . [as] a handle for regulating everything else,' from the delegation of power to private organizations, from the retroactive accomplishment of 'takings' without just compensation. Procedural protection followed, largely derivatively: 'Because it is so hard to confine relevance and discretion, procedure offers a valuable means for restraining arbitrary action.' Viewing property, throughout its entire Anglo–American history, as a socio-political construct, Professor Reich saw no insuperable objections to our constructing a 'new property' to serve the needs of a new age."[2]

(4) The preceding notes have focused on Goldberg's significance for the question of what triggers due process. The case is also important for its assessment of what process is "due." We take up this issue in Section 3 below. At this point, though, you might consider the extent to which the procedures required by Goldberg prior to *suspension* of benefits were commonly regarded as part of a fundamentally fair administrative process. A survey of federal agency practice taken a few years after Goldberg reveals the following incidence of procedures that agencies chose to provide (i.e., were not under statutory or constitutional obligation to provide) in making

2. Cynthia R. Farina, On Misusing "Revolution" and "Reform": Procedural Due Process and the New Welfare Act, 50 Admin.L.Rev. 591, 605–09 (1998).

final decisions that "affect an individual's rights, obligations or opportunities"[3]:

Element of Hearing	Number of programs providing
Timely and adequate notice	40
Confronting adverse witnesses	10
Oral presentation of argument	21
Oral presentation of evidence	12
Cross-examination of adverse witnesses	9
Disclosure of opposing evidence	10
Right to retain and be represented by an attorney	16
Determination on the record	8
Statement of reasons and evidence relied on	37
Impartial decisionmaker	38

NOTES ON THE IDEAL OF PROCEDURAL FAIRNESS AND THE REALITY OF MASS ADMINISTRATIVE JUSTICE

Since Goldberg, the due process clause has been a force to be reckoned with by federal, state, and local governments embarking on programs of social regulation. The particular context—public assistance—presented both the most compelling case for protecting the individual against bureaucratic error or indifference, and the greatest political and organizational obstacles to realizing the "guarantee of fair procedure, sometimes referred to as procedural due process."[1] The 1990s' debates about welfare reform are only the latest in the long history of political ambivalence about the ends and means of public assistance programs. And, in any such program, the number of decisions that must be made (about initial eligibility, continued levels of benefits, and termination) is staggering. Any constitutionally-imposed procedure will have potentially massive implications for staffing, funding, and monitoring—and may have unforeseeable consequences for those served (or seeking to be served) by the program. After considering the following notes, ask yourself whether you would now decide Goldberg differently—and if so, how?

The focus: The individual or the system?

(1) WILLIAM J. BRENNAN, JR., REASON, PASSION, AND "THE PROGRESS OF THE LAW," 10 Cardozo L.Rev. 3, 19–22 (1988): "In many respects, the New York system for managing welfare terminations was a model of rationality. One who saw the due process clause as a mandate that the state govern according to reason could maintain that the welfare system was constitutionally adequate, for all were subject to rules that were impersonally applied. A significant issue in Goldberg therefore was whether progress in

---

3. Paul R. Verkuil, A Study of Informal Adjudication Procedures, 43 U.Chi.L.Rev. 739, 739 n.1 (1976).

1. Daniels v. Williams, 474 U.S. 327, 336–37 (1986) (Stevens, J., concurring) (internal quotes omitted).

the rationality of government always means progress in the law of due process.

"The Court said that it does not. The Court did so because it realized that the state's procedures lacked one vital element: appreciation of the drastic consequences of terminating a recipient's only means of subsistence. Provision of a hearing only *after* benefits were terminated was profoundly inappropriate for a person dependent upon the government for the very resources with which to live. . . . The brief for the recipient told the human stories that the state's administrative regime seemed unable to hear:

> After termination, Angela Velez and her four young children were evicted for non-payment of rent and all forced to live in one small room of a relative's already crowded apartment. The children had little to eat during the four months it took for the Department to correct its error. Esther Lett and her four children at once began to live on the handouts of impoverished neighbors; within two weeks all five required hospital treatment because of the inadequacy of their diet. Soon after, Esther Lett fainted in a welfare center while seeking an emergency food payment of $15 to feed herself and her children for three days. Pearl Frye and her 8 children 'had gone hungry,' living on peanut butter and jelly sandwiches and rice supplied by friends who were also dependent on public assistance. Juan DeJesus found himself homeless, living in temporary shelter provided by a friend.

"The Court also sought to leaven reason with experience in addressing the question of the procedures appropriate for the pretermination hearing. Written submissions, for instance, are a sufficient means of contesting government action in many contexts. Nonetheless, we said, '[w]ritten submissions are an unrealistic option for most recipients, who lack the educational attainment necessary to write effectively and who cannot obtain professional assistance.' The Court therefore deemed the opportunity for oral presentations to be an essential requirement of due process in welfare termination cases. . . .

"... Neither a judge nor an administrator who operates on the basis of reason alone can fully grasp that answer, for each is cut off from the wellspring from which concepts such as dignity, decency, and fairness flow. In Goldberg, the application of standard rules to all recipients was simply blind to the brute fact of dependence. A government insensitive to such a reality cannot be said to treat individuals with the respect that due process demands—not because its officials do not reason, but because they cannot understand."

(2) OWEN M. FISS, REASON IN ALL ITS SPLENDOR, 56 Brooklyn L.Rev. 789, 801–03 (1990): "The description in appellees' brief of the plight of Angela Velez, Esther Lett, Pearl Frye and Juan DeJesus and their families—in truth no more a story than a letter to Ann Landers is a work of literature—might have triggered an emotional response, but it would have been a mistake of the first order for the Court to have let these so-called 'human stories' stand for the social reality over which it governs.

"Because it lays down a rule for a nation and invokes the authority of the Constitution, the Court necessarily must concern itself with the fate of millions of people, all of whom touch the welfare system in a myriad of ways: some on welfare, some wanting welfare, some being denied welfare, some dispensing welfare, some creating and administering welfare, some paying for it. Accordingly, the Court's perspective must be systematic, not anecdotal: It should focus not on the plight of four or five or even twenty families, but consider the welfare system as a whole, which can only be understood as a complex interaction between millions of people and a host of bureaucratic and political institutions. The methods by which a court comes to know and understand a system as far-ranging and as complex as welfare are complicated and, as in the case of Goldberg v. Kelly itself, always in need of further refinement and improvement. But to describe these informational methods as storytelling, as has become fashionable these days on the left, trivializes what is at stake, unfairly disparages the enormous progress modern society has made in developing sophisticated techniques for assembling, presenting and evaluating empirical information, and throws into doubt the basic aspirations of all these informational processes, namely, finding the truth. A story is a story, sometimes a very good one, even if completely untrue."

Individualized attention or reasonable mass justice?

(3) *An Assessment at the Time:* DANIEL J. BAUM, THE WELFARE FAMILY AND MASS ADMINISTRATIVE JUSTICE 36–37 (1974): "Consider the enormity in sheer volume of [the] task in a city such as New York. There are approximately 1.5 million persons dependent on categorical aids in the state of New York. Most of these fall within AFDC, and most of the recipients, a total of 1.2 million, are resident in New York City. On a monthly average in the city, about 20,000 AFDC cases are terminated and another 20,000 are reduced. To handle this flow, the city Human Resources Administration employs an income maintenance staff of 2,500 and another 500 supervisors. And, said the unit head of that staff, 'there are always between 150 to 200 vacancies which we are now trying to fill as fast as we can.' . . .

"[W]ithout in any way imputing bad intent on the part of the city Human Resources Administration, there is no small question as to whether that agency can comply with the Court's order and the HEW regulations concerning advance notice . . ."

(4) *An Assessment 20 Years After Goldberg:* HON. CESAR A. PERALES, THE FAIR HEARINGS PROCESS: GUARDIAN OF THE SOCIAL SERVICE SYSTEM, 56 Brooklyn L.Rev. 889, 889, 891–92 (1990): "Twenty years ago, I was a young legal services lawyer representing public assistance recipients like John Kelly. For the last eight years, I have served as the Commissioner of the New York State Department of Social Services (the Department). . . .

"In 1969, the State Department of Social Services employed eleven hearing officers and a support staff of twenty. In 1989, the Department employed 105 hearing officers and a support staff numbering 141.

"In 1969, thirteen hundred appellants sought hearings and one thousand decisions resulted. In 1989, more than one hundred and fifty thousand hearings were requested and seventy-seven thousand decisions were issued.

"In 1969, hearing officers held an average of five hearings a week and drafted decisions in long hand which were then mailed or trucked to Albany for typing, review, and issuance. In 1989, hearing officers face calendars of twenty-eight to thirty-five scheduled hearings daily and draft decisions on a statewide computer system which can print and issue a decision in Albany the same day.[2]

"While the numbers are staggering, it is more than holding hearings that fulfills the promise of Goldberg. Not only must a hearing be impartial, but it must appear impartial to the appellant. The appellant should leave the hearing feeling that she had an opportunity to tell her story fully and to have an impartial person listen to that story. The appellant must know that the decision will be a fair one. Goldberg certainly does not stand for rubber stamp due process, and in that regard, the Department also fulfills the promise of Goldberg.

"Last year, eighty percent of the issues decided in hearings were decided in favor of appellants. By any measure, that is an impressive testament to the fairness of the hearing process. But, it is easy to overlook that the Goldberg promise is not only to those whose assistance has been wrongfully denied or discontinued. Even those whose assistance has been correctly denied or discontinued are afforded the opportunity to state their cases. They too are afforded the dignity of being listened to, of being taken seriously. . . ."

Equal treatment or bureaucratization?

(5) JERRY L. MASHAW, DUE PROCESS IN THE ADMINISTRATIVE STATE 33–34 (1985): "[Goldberg] presented welfare administrators with a significant problem. First, if a substantial percentage of the recipients noticed for termination exercised their appeal rights, the welfare departments would simply be unable to process the cases without a large infusion of funds for administration. Because of the complexity of welfare decision making, adequate preparation of cases to prove the correctness of termination decisions was likely to be quite costly. But the alternative would be even more expensive—leaving substantial numbers of ineligible persons on the rolls.

"These administrative difficulties reinforced a political difficulty. Welfare rolls were already increasing rapidly. State legislators were unwilling to provide more funds either for well-constructed hearings or for welfare benefits. A strategy was needed that would preserve fiscal integrity and produce defensible decisions.

"A number of tactical moves ultimately comprised the grand design. One was to tighten up and slow down the initial eligibility determination process. Another was to generalize and objectify the substantive eligibility criteria so that messy subjective judgments about individual cases would not have to be made and defended. This move led to the realization that professional social welfare workers were no longer needed. Costs could be reduced further by lowering the quality of the staff and by depersonalizing

---

2.   [Ed.] We invite you to calculate how long the average hearing lasts if the examiner works a standard 8–hour day.

staff-claimant encounters. If these reactions were not sufficient to restore fiscal balance, then payment levels could be reduced or allowed to remain stable in the face of rising prices. A tougher stance was also to be taken with respect to work requirements and prosecution of absent parents. Moreover, because hearings presumably protected the claimants' interests, internal audit procedures were skewed to ignore nonpayment and under-payment problems and concentrate on preventing over-payments and payments to ineligibles.''

(6) LUCIE E. WHITE, SUBORDINATION, RHETORICAL SURVIVAL SKILLS, AND SUNDAY SHOES: NOTES ON THE HEARING OF MRS. G, 38 Buffalo L. Rev. 1, 2–4, 53–54 (1990): ''[Goldberg] opened a far-reaching conversation among legal scholars over the meaning of procedural justice. . . . One group, seeing procedure as an *instrument* of just government, seeks devices that will most efficiently generate legitimate outcomes in a complex society. Other scholars, however, by taking the perspective of society's marginalized groups, give voice to a very different—I will call it a 'humanist'—vision. According to this vision, 'procedural justice' is a normative *horizon* rather than a technical problem. This horizon challenges us to realize the promise of formal procedural equality in the real world. . . .

"[T]he meaningful participation by all citizens in the governmental decisions that affect their lives . . . [is] a widely shared intuition about procedural justice in our political culture. [However,] there is a disjunction between this vision and the conditions in our society in which procedural rituals are actually played out. . . . Social subordination [by race, gender, or class] can lead disfavored groups to deploy verbal strategies that mark their speech as deviant when measured against dominant stylistic norms. These conditions . . . undermine the capacity of many persons in our society to use the procedural rituals that are formally available to them. . . .

". . . [R]emoving formal barriers to participation is not enough in our stratified society to achieve procedural justice, even in the modest sense of enabling all persons to participate in the rituals of their self-government on an equal basis. . . .

"Perhaps the greatest barrier to [a welfare recipient's] participation [in a termination hearing] is her well-founded fear of retaliation. . . . Without skilled advocates, poor people cannot invoke the laws that already forbid intentional retaliation. . . .

"In order to feel safe to speak out at a hearing, however, [the recipient] needs more than *post hoc* remedies against overt acts of retaliation. She also needs to feel economically secure, economically independent. . . . The social policies that might create such conditions are vigorously contested, and the political will that might enact them is not apparent. Without such economic security, however, *post hoc* measures to deter retaliation will never fully dismantle the barrier that intimidation imposes to her speech. . . .''

(7) NEW YORK TIMES, Oct. 10, 1990, section B, p. 3: ''The Human Resources Administration, which oversees welfare payments and benefits in New York City, takes almost 15,000 families off the welfare rolls each month for

administrative reasons like missed appointments with caseworkers and lack of proper documentation, a private report has found. . . .

"Welfare advocates say that despite recent improvements in the Human Resources Administration's method of notifying welfare clients to appear for interviews to determine if they are still eligible for benefits, a significant number of clients do not get notices in a timely manner because many live doubled up with friends and relatives. Others may not get notices because they live in homeless shelters or move from one overnight placement to another and do not receive mail.

"Notification is also very difficult for people who live in private substandard apartments in which mailboxes do not lock or are often vandalized. City welfare officials say they provide recipients with a written notice of upcoming interviews with their checks, but advocates caution that the notices say only that an interview is imminent but do not give a date or time."

Dignity or adversarial depersonalization?

(8) RICHARD B. SAPHIRE, SPECIFYING DUE PROCESS VALUES: TOWARD A MORE RESPONSIVE APPROACH TO PROCEDURAL PROTECTION, 127 U. Pa. L. Rev. 111, 118–24, 152 (1978): "The nexus between fairness and human dignity has been noted in much of our political and moral philosophy, and has occasionally been viewed as central to constitutional interpretation. . . .

" . . . In important respects, dignity can be said to relate to substantive outcomes of governmental action. . . . [B]asic notions of dignity might require that deprivatory action be premised upon the existence of facts or conditions that are generally believed to necessitate such action. In this situation, respect for human dignity would demand assurance that the facts upon which the action is based be determined by accurate and reliable means. . . .

" . . . However, there is another aspect of human dignity that seems essential to the ideal of fairness, and which has been viewed as central to western liberal political thought. This is the sense of dignity that springs, not from the outcomes of governmental decisions and conduct, but from the interaction between individuals and their government that occurs as part of the decisionmaking process. This aspect of dignity . . . will be referred to here as 'inherent dignity' (because it is inherent in the process by which decisions are reached and conduct is affected, yet it is independent of extrinsic, substantive outcomes). . . . Perhaps the most eloquent reference to it can be found in Justice Frankfurter's concurring opinion in Joint Anti–Fascist Refugee Committee v. McGrath. . . .

" . . . [This concept] is marked by at least two closely related characteristics. First, it reflects a view that fairness in government-individual relations can never be defined solely in terms of outcomes . . .; rather, the processes of interaction themselves are always important in their own right . . . . . Secondly, this concept of dignity reflects a view that individual perceptions and feelings about governmental processes are to be taken into account in assessing their legitimacy. . . .

"[T]he underlying concern of inherent dignity is that an individual subjected to deprivatory government action be given a meaningful opportunity to participate in the decisionmaking and/or decision-implementing process at a meaningful time. ... The opportunity for personal participation is the best assurance that the individual will understand what is about to happen to her and why, and is the essential prerequisite for satisfaction of the innate need to be treated as a responsible and independent human entity."

(9) WILLIAM H. SIMON, THE RULE OF LAW AND THE TWO REALMS OF WELFARE ADMINISTRATION, 56 Brooklyn L.Rev. 777, 787 (1990): "[I]f, as many have concluded, Goldberg is concerned not only with accurate decision making, but with the dignity of welfare beneficiaries, then the application of due process norms only through the hearing system has a further failing. This approach is unresponsive to the sense of oppression and degradation that the bureaucratized system engenders, as well as to the often gratuitous practical burdens of bureaucratic paper pushing and hoop jumping that the system imposes.

"This experience is in part a function of the design of the line worker's job, which focuses her attention on policing the claimant's satisfaction of a gauntlet of often meaningless bureaucratic tasks and leaves her powerless either to respond to contingencies of need that escape the rigid eligibility categories or to mitigate the irrationality of the procedural requirements. In places like New York City, where appeal rates are high, the hearing system seems to have the perverse effect of reducing pressure for general administrative reform and helping workers and administrators rationalize irresponsible behavior. Rather than correcting errors or trying to get their superiors to do so, the workers tell the beneficiaries to take their claims to hearing.

"At its best, the hearing system provides the beneficiary with the individualized, respectful attention contemplated by those who interpret Goldberg as an expression of 'dignitary' or 'process' values. But most beneficiaries never reach the hearing sphere and those who do reach it only rarely and briefly. The setting in which beneficiaries typically confront the welfare state is the line administrative one, and here their experience remains one of arbitrariness and indifference."

SECTION 2. CONTEMPORARY DOCTRINE: WHAT SORT OF INTERESTS TRIGGER DUE PROCESS PROTECTION?

Judge Henry Friendly, writing in 1975, noted that Goldberg sparked "a due process explosion in which the Court has carried the hearing requirement from one new area of government action to another. ... [I]ndeed, we have witnessed a greater expansion of procedural due process in the last five years than in the entire period since ratification of the Constitution."[1] Professor Jerry Mashaw quantified the explosion, finding that during the

---

1. Henry J. Friendly, "Some Kind of Hearing," 123 U. Pa. L. Rev. 1267, 1268 (1975).

1970s the number of complaints alleging procedural due process violations increased 350% from the 1960s. Federal civil litigation as a whole increased only 70% in the same period.[2] What effect would these developments have on evolution of the new due process doctrine?

Board of Regents of State Colleges v. Roth

Supreme Court of the United States, 1972.
408 U.S. 564.

■ JUSTICE STEWART delivered the opinion of the Court.

In 1968 the respondent, David Roth, was hired for his first teaching job as assistant professor of political science at Wisconsin State University–Oshkosh. He was hired for a fixed term of one academic year. The notice of his faculty appointment specified that his employment would begin on September 1, 1968, and would end on June 30, 1969.[1] The respondent completed that term. But he was informed that he would not be rehired for the next academic year.

The respondent had no tenure rights to continued employment. Under Wisconsin statutory law a state university teacher can acquire tenure as a "permanent" employee only after four years of year-to-year employment. Having acquired tenure, a teacher is entitled to continued employment "during efficiency and good behavior." A relatively new teacher without tenure, however, is under Wisconsin law entitled to nothing beyond his one-year appointment. There are no statutory or administrative standards defining eligibility for re-employment. State law thus clearly leaves the decision whether to rehire a nontenured teacher for another year to the unfettered discretion of university officials.

The procedural protection afforded a Wisconsin State University teacher before he is separated from the University corresponds to his job security. As a matter of statutory law, a tenured teacher cannot be "discharged except for cause upon written charges" and pursuant to certain procedures. A nontenured teacher, similarly, is protected to some extent *during* his one-year term. Rules promulgated by the Board of Regents provide that a nontenured teacher "dismissed" before the end of the year may have some opportunity for review of the "dismissal." But the Rules provide no real protection for a nontenured teacher who simply is not re-employed for the next year. He must be informed by February 1 "concerning retention or non-retention for the ensuing year." But "no

2. Jerry L. Mashaw, Due Process in the Administrative State 9–10 (1985).

1. The respondent had no contract of employment. Rather, his formal notice of appointment was the equivalent of an employment contract.

The notice of his appointment provided that: "*David F. Roth* is hereby appointed to the faculty of the Wisconsin State University Position number 0262. (Location:) *Oshkosh* as (Rank:) *Assistant Professor* of (Depart-

ment:) *Political Science* this (Date:) *first* day of (Month:) *September* (Year:) *1968.*" The notice went on to specify that the respondent's "appointment basis" was for the "academic year." And it provided that "[r]egulations governing tenure are in accord with Chapter 37.31, Wisconsin Statutes. The employment of any staff member for an academic year shall not be for a term beyond June 30th of the fiscal year in which the appointment is made."

reason for non-retention need be given. No review or appeal is provided in such case."

In conformance with these Rules, the President of Wisconsin State University–Oshkosh informed the respondent before February 1, 1969, that he would not be rehired for the 1969–1970 academic year. He gave the respondent no reason for the decision and no opportunity to challenge it at any sort of hearing.

The respondent then brought this action in Federal District Court alleging that the decision not to rehire him for the next year infringed his Fourteenth Amendment rights. He attacked the decision both in substance and procedure. First, he alleged that the true reason for the decision was to punish him for certain statements critical of the University administration, and that it therefore violated his right to freedom of speech.[2] Second, he alleged that the failure of University officials to give him notice of any reason for nonretention and an opportunity for a hearing violated his right to procedural due process of law.

The District Court granted summary judgment for the respondent on the procedural issue, ordering the University officials to provide him with reasons and a hearing. The Court of Appeals, with one judge dissenting, affirmed this partial summary judgment. We granted certiorari. The only question presented to us at this stage in the case is whether the respondent had a constitutional right to a statement of reasons and a hearing on the University's decision not to rehire him for another year. We hold that he did not.

I

The requirements of procedural due process apply only to the deprivation of interests encompassed by the Fourteenth Amendment's protection of liberty and property. When protected interests are implicated, the right to some kind of prior hearing is paramount.[3] But the range of interests protected by procedural due process is not infinite.

The District Court decided that procedural due process guarantees apply in this case by assessing and balancing the weights of the particular

---

2. While the respondent alleged that he was not rehired because of his exercise of free speech, the petitioners insisted that the nonretention decision was based on other, constitutionally valid grounds. The District Court came to no conclusion whatever regarding the true reason for the University President's decision. "In the present case," it stated, "it appears that a determination as to the actual bases of [the] decision must await amplification of the facts at trial. ... Summary judgment is inappropriate." 310 F.Supp. 972, 982.

3. Before a person is deprived of a protected interest, he must be afforded opportunity for some kind of a hearing, "except for extraordinary situations where some valid governmental interest is at stake that justi-

fies postponing the hearing until after the event." Boddie v. Connecticut, 401 U.S. 371, 379. "While '[m]any controversies have raged about ... the Due Process Clause,' ... it is fundamental that except in emergency situations (and this is not one) due process requires that when a State seeks to terminate [a protected] interest ..., it must afford 'notice and opportunity for hearing appropriate to the nature of the case' *before* the termination becomes effective." Bell v. Burson, 402 U.S. 535, 542. For the rare and extraordinary situations in which we have held that deprivation of a protected interest need not be preceded by opportunity for some kind of hearing, see, e.g., Phillips v. Commissioner of Internal Revenue, 283 U.S. 589, 597.

interests involved. It concluded that the respondent's interest in re-employment at Wisconsin State University–Oshkosh outweighed the University's interest in denying him re-employment summarily. Undeniably, the respondent's re-employment prospects were of major concern to him—concern that we surely cannot say was insignificant. And a weighing process has long been a part of any determination of the *form* of hearing required in particular situations by procedural due process.[4] But, to determine whether due process requirements apply in the first place, we must look not to the "weight" but to the *nature* of the interest at stake. We must look to see if the interest is within the Fourteenth Amendment's protection of liberty and property.

"Liberty" and "property" are broad and majestic terms. They are among the "[g]reat [constitutional] concepts . . . purposely left to gather meaning from experience. . . . [T]hey relate to the whole domain of social and economic fact, and the statesmen who founded this Nation knew too well that only a stagnant society remains unchanged." National Ins. Co. v. Tidewater Co., 337 U.S. 582, 646 (Frankfurter, J., dissenting). For that reason, the Court has fully and finally rejected the wooden distinction between "rights" and "privileges" that once seemed to govern the applicability of procedural due process rights.[5] The Court has also made clear that the property interests protected by procedural due process extend well beyond actual ownership of real estate, chattels, or money. By the same token, the Court has required due process protection for deprivations of liberty beyond the sort of formal constraints imposed by the criminal process.

Yet, while the Court has eschewed rigid or formalistic limitations on the protection of procedural due process, it has at the same time observed certain boundaries. For the words "liberty" and "property" in the Due Process Clause of the Fourteenth Amendment must be given some meaning.

II

"While this Court has not attempted to define with exactness the liberty . . . guaranteed [by the Fourteenth Amendment], the term has received much consideration and some of the included things have been definitely stated. Without doubt, it denotes not merely freedom from bodily restraint but also the right of the individual to contract, to engage in any of

Liberty

---

4. "The formality and procedural requisites for the hearing can vary, depending upon the importance of the interests involved and the nature of the subsequent proceedings." Boddie v. Connecticut, 401 U.S. 371, 378 (1971). See, e.g., Goldberg v. Kelly, 397 U.S. 254, 263. The constitutional requirement of opportunity for *some* form of hearing before deprivation of a protected interest, of course, does not depend upon such a narrow balancing process.

5. In a leading case decided many years ago, the Court of Appeals for the District of Columbia Circuit held that public employ-

ment in general was a "privilege," not a "right," and that procedural due process guarantees therefore were inapplicable. Bailey v. Richardson, 182 F.2d 46, aff'd by an equally divided Court, 341 U.S. 918. The basis of this holding has been thoroughly undermined in the ensuing years. For, as Mr. Justice Blackmun wrote for the Court only last year, "this Court now has rejected the concept that constitutional rights turn upon whether a governmental benefit is characterized as a 'right' or as a 'privilege.'" Graham v. Richardson, 403 U.S. 365, 374.

the common occupations of life, to acquire useful knowledge, to marry, establish a home and bring up children, to worship God according to the dictates of his own conscience, and generally to enjoy those privileges long recognized . . . as essential to the orderly pursuit of happiness by free men." Meyer v. Nebraska, 262 U.S. 390, 399. In a Constitution for a free people, there can be no doubt that the meaning of "liberty" must be broad indeed.

There might be cases in which a State refused to re-employ a person under such circumstances that interests in liberty would be implicated. But this is not such a case.

The State, in declining to rehire the respondent, did not make any charge against him that might seriously damage his standing and associations in his community. It did not base the nonrenewal of his contract on a charge, for example, that he had been guilty of dishonesty, or immorality. Had it done so, this would be a different case. For "[w]here a person's good name, reputation, honor, or integrity is at stake because of what the government is doing to him, notice and an opportunity to be heard are essential." Wisconsin v. Constantineau, 400 U.S. 433, 437 . . . See Cafeteria Workers v. McElroy, 367 U.S. 886, 898. In such a case, due process would accord an opportunity to refute the charge before University officials.[6] In the present case, however, there is no suggestion whatever that the respondent's "good name, reputation, honor, or integrity" is at stake.

Similarly, there is no suggestion that the State, in declining to re-employ the respondent, imposed on him a stigma or other disability that foreclosed his freedom to take advantage of other employment opportunities. The State, for example, did not invoke any regulations to bar the respondent from all other public employment in state universities. Had it done so, this, again, would be a different case. . . .[7]

To be sure, the respondent has alleged that the nonrenewal of his contract was based on his exercise of his right to freedom of speech. But this allegation is not now before us. The District Court stayed proceedings on this issue, and the respondent has yet to prove that the decision not to rehire him was, in fact, based on his free speech activities.

6. The purpose of such notice and hearing is to provide the person an opportunity to clear his name. Once a person has cleared his name at a hearing, his employer, of course, may remain free to deny him future employment for other reasons.

7. The District Court made an *assumption* "that non-retention by one university or college creates concrete and practical difficulties for a professor in his subsequent academic career." 310 F.Supp., at 979. And the Court of Appeals based its affirmance of the summary judgment largely on the premise that "the substantial adverse effect non-retention is likely to have upon the career interests of an individual professor" amounts to a limitation on future employment opportunities sufficient to invoke procedural due process guarantees. 446 F.2d, at 809. But even assuming, *arguendo*, that such a "substantial adverse effect" under these circumstances would constitute a state-imposed restriction on liberty, the record contains no support for these assumptions. There is no suggestion of how nonretention might affect the respondent's future employment prospects. Mere proof, for example, that his record of nonretention in one job, taken alone, might make him somewhat less attractive to some other employers would hardly establish the kind of foreclosure of opportunities amounting to a deprivation of "liberty."

Hence, on the record before us, all that clearly appears is that the respondent was not rehired for one year at one university. It stretches the concept too far to suggest that a person is deprived of "liberty" when he simply is not rehired in one job but remains as free as before to seek another. Cafeteria Workers v. McElroy, above, at 895–896.

III

The Fourteenth Amendment's procedural protection of property is a safeguard of the security of interests that a person has already acquired in specific benefits. These interests—property interests—may take many forms.

Thus, the Court has held that a person receiving welfare benefits under statutory and administrative standards defining eligibility for them has an interest in continued receipt of those benefits that is safeguarded by procedural due process. Goldberg v. Kelly, 397 U.S. 254. Similarly, in the area of public employment, the Court has held that a public college professor dismissed from an office held under tenure provisions, Slochower v. Board of Education, 350 U.S. 551, and college professors and staff members dismissed during the terms of their contracts, Wieman v. Updegraff, 344 U.S. 183, have interests in continued employment that are safeguarded by due process. Only last year, the Court held that this principle "proscribing summary dismissal from public employment without hearing or inquiry required by due process" also applied to a teacher recently hired without tenure or a formal contract, but nonetheless with a clearly implied promise of continued employment. Connell v. Higginbotham, 403 U.S. 207, 208.

Certain attributes of "property" interests protected by procedural due process emerge from these decisions. To have a property interest in a benefit, a person clearly must have more than an abstract need or desire for it. He must have more than a unilateral expectation of it. He must, instead, have a legitimate claim of entitlement to it. It is a purpose of the ancient institution of property to protect those claims upon which people rely in their daily lives, reliance that must not be arbitrarily undermined. It is a purpose of the constitutional right to a hearing to provide an opportunity for a person to vindicate those claims.

Property interests, of course, are not created by the Constitution. Rather, they are created and their dimensions are defined by existing rules or understandings that stem from an independent source such as state law—rules or understandings that secure certain benefits and that support claims of entitlement to those benefits. Thus, the welfare recipients in Goldberg v. Kelly, above, had a claim of entitlement to welfare payments that was grounded in the statute defining eligibility for them. The recipients had not yet shown that they were, in fact, within the statutory terms of eligibility. But we held that they had a right to a hearing at which they might attempt to do so.

Just as the welfare recipients' "property" interest in welfare payments was created and defined by statutory terms, so the respondent's "property" interest in employment at Wisconsin State University–Oshkosh was created and defined by the terms of his appointment. Those terms secured his interest in employment up to June 30, 1969. But the important fact in this case is that they specifically provided that the respondent's employment was to terminate on June 30. They did not provide for contract renewal absent "sufficient cause." Indeed, they made no provision for renewal whatsoever.

Thus, the terms of the respondent's appointment secured absolutely no interest in re-employment for the next year. They supported absolutely no possible claim of entitlement to re-employment. Nor, significantly, was there any state statute or University rule or policy that secured his interest in re-employment or that created any legitimate claim to it.[8] In these circumstances, the respondent surely had an abstract concern in being rehired, but he did not have a *property* interest sufficient to require the University authorities to give him a hearing when they declined to renew his contract of employment.

IV

Our analysis of the respondent's constitutional rights in this case in no way indicates a view that an opportunity for a hearing or a statement of reasons for nonretention would, or would not, be appropriate or wise in public colleges and universities. For it is a written Constitution that we apply. Our role is confined to interpretation of that Constitution.

We must conclude that the summary judgment for the respondent should not have been granted, since the respondent has not shown that he was deprived of liberty or property protected by the Fourteenth Amendment. The judgment of the Court of Appeals, accordingly, is reversed and the case is remanded for further proceedings consistent with this opinion.

It is so ordered.[9]

■ JUSTICE MARSHALL, dissenting.

... While I agree with Part I of the Court's opinion, setting forth the proper framework for consideration of the issue presented, and also with those portions of Parts II and III of the Court's opinion that assert that a public employee is entitled to procedural due process whenever a State stigmatizes him by denying employment, or injures his future employment prospects severely, or whenever the State deprives him of a property interest, I would go further than the Court does in defining the terms "liberty" and "property."

---

8. To be sure, the respondent does suggest that most teachers hired on a year-to-year basis by Wisconsin State University–Oshkosh are, in fact, rehired. But the District Court has not found that there is anything approaching a "common law" of re-employment, see Perry v. Sindermann, post, so strong as to require University officials to give the respondent a statement of reasons and a hearing on their decision not to rehire him.

9. [Ed.] See the Chronicle of Higher Education, Nov. 26, 1973, p. 3, col. 1: "David F. Roth ... has been awarded $6,746 in damages in federal district court. ... A six-person jury found that Mr. Roth's constitutional right to free speech was violated by [Wisconsin State University at Oshkosh]. ... Judge Doyle also has yet to rule on requests from Mr. Roth for reinstatement in his position at Oshkosh. ... Even if Judge Doyle orders his reinstatement, Mr. Roth is not likely to return to Oshkosh, since he now teaches at Purdue University."

... [W]hether or not a private employer is free to act capriciously or unreasonably with respect to employment practices, at least absent statutory or contractual controls, a government employer is different. The government may only act fairly and reasonably.

In my view, every citizen who applies for a government job is entitled to it unless the government can establish some reason for denying the employment. This is the "property" right that I believe is protected by the Fourteenth Amendment and that cannot be denied "without due process of law." And it is also liberty—liberty to work—which is the "very essence of the personal freedom and opportunity" secured by the Fourteenth Amendment. This Court has often had occasion to note that the denial of public employment is a serious blow to any citizen. See, e.g., Joint Anti–Fascist Refugee Committee v. McGrath, 341 U.S. 123, 185 (1951) (Jackson, J., concurring); United States v. Lovett, 328 U.S. 303, 316–317 (1946). Thus, when an application for public employment is denied or the contract of a government employee is not renewed, the government must say why, for it is only when the reasons underlying government action are known that citizens feel secure and protected against arbitrary government action.

Employment is one of the greatest, if not the greatest, benefits that governments offer in modern-day life. When something as valuable as the opportunity to work is at stake, the government may not reward some citizens and not others without demonstrating that its actions are fair and equitable. And it is procedural due process that is our fundamental guarantee of fairness, our protection against arbitrary, capricious, and unreasonable government action.

It may be argued that to provide procedural due process to all public employees or prospective employees would place an intolerable burden on the machinery of government. Cf. Goldberg v. Kelly, above. The short answer to that argument is that it is not burdensome to give reasons when reasons exist. Whenever an application for employment is denied, an employee is discharged, or a decision not to rehire an employee is made, there should be some reason for the decision. It can scarcely be argued that government would be crippled by a requirement that the reason be communicated to the person most directly affected by the government's action.

Where there are numerous applicants for jobs, it is likely that few will choose to demand reasons for not being hired. But, if the demand for reasons is exceptionally great, summary procedures can be devised that would provide fair and adequate information to all persons. As long as the government has a good reason for its actions it need not fear disclosure. It is only where the government acts improperly that procedural due process is truly burdensome. And that is precisely when it is most necessary. ...

■[CHIEF JUSTICE BURGER and JUSTICES WHITE, BLACKMUN, and REHNQUIST joined JUSTICE STEWART. JUSTICE POWELL took no part in the case. JUSTICES BRENNAN and DOUGLAS were, like JUSTICE MARSHALL, dissenters; their opinions have not been reproduced. Finally, CHIEF JUSTICE BURGER also filed a concurring opinion, reproduced following the next case.]

Perry v. Sindermann

Supreme Court of the United States, 1972.
408 U.S. 593.

■ JUSTICE STEWART delivered the opinion of the Court.

[In this case, considered with Board of Regents v. Roth, Robert Sindermann had worked for the state college system of Texas for ten years, the last four of which he was a full professor at Odessa Junior College. He had successive one-year contracts, as Odessa had no tenure system. In the 1968–69 academic year, he was elected president of the Texas Junior College Teachers Association and, as such, publicly opposed policies of the Board of Regents. In May 1969, his contract expired and the Regents voted not to offer him a new one. They issued a press release claiming he had been insubordinate, but gave him no official statement of reasons for nonrenewal and held no hearing in which he might challenge his discharge. Sindermann sued the Regents and the college's president, claiming a violation of his rights to free speech and procedural due process. The defendants denied that he had been fired in retaliation for his public criticism, and argued that they had no obligation to give him a hearing.

Based on a very slim record, the district court granted summary judgment for the college officials. The court of appeals reversed. As to free speech, it remanded for trial as to the actual reason for the Regents' decision. As to due process, it remanded to allow Sindermann to show that he had an "expectancy" of reemployment. The Court first considered the First Amendment claim, and held that this claim could be proved even if Sindermann lacked a contractual or tenure right to re-employment.]

For at least a quarter-century, this Court has made clear that even though a person has no "right" to a valuable governmental benefit and even though the government may deny him the benefit for any number of reasons, there are some reasons upon which the government may not rely. It may not deny a benefit to a person on a basis that infringes his constitutionally protected interests—especially, his interest in freedom of speech. ... [On remand, Sindermann must be given the opportunity to prove his allegations of retaliatory refusal to rehire.]

The respondent's lack of formal contractual or tenure security in continued employment at Odessa Junior College, though irrelevant to his free speech claim, is highly relevant to his procedural due process claim. But it may not be entirely dispositive.

We have held today in Board of Regents v. Roth that the Constitution does not require opportunity for a hearing before the nonrenewal of a nontenured teacher's contract, unless he can show that the decision not to rehire him somehow deprived him of an interest in "liberty" or that he had a "property" interest in continued employment, despite the lack of tenure or a formal contract. In Roth the teacher had not made a showing on either point to justify summary judgment in his favor.

Similarly, the respondent here has yet to show that he has been deprived of an interest that could invoke procedural due process protection. As in Roth, the mere showing that he was not rehired in one particular job, without more, did not amount to a showing of a loss of liberty. Nor did it amount to a showing of a loss of property.

But the respondent's allegations—which we must construe most favorably to the respondent at this stage of the litigation—do raise a genuine issue as to his interest in continued employment at Odessa Junior College. He alleged that this interest, though not secured by a formal contractual tenure provision, was secured by a no less binding understanding fostered by the college administration. In particular, the respondent alleged that the college had a *de facto* tenure program, and that he had tenure under that program. He claimed that he and others legitimately relied upon an unusual provision that had been in the college's official Faculty Guide for many years:

> *Teacher Tenure:* Odessa College has no tenure system. The Administration of the College wishes the faculty member to feel that he has permanent tenure as long as his teaching services are satisfactory and as long as he displays a cooperative attitude toward his co-workers and his superiors, and as long as he is happy in his work.

Moreover, the respondent claimed legitimate reliance upon guidelines promulgated by the Coordinating Board of the Texas College and University System that provided that a person, like himself, who had been employed as a teacher in the state college and university system for seven years or more has some form of job tenure. Thus, the respondent offered to prove that a teacher with his long period of service at this particular State College had no less a "property" interest in continued employment than a formally tenured teacher at other colleges, and had no less a procedural due process right to a statement of reasons and a hearing before college officials upon their decision not to retain him.

We have made clear in Roth that "property" interests subject to procedural due process protection are not limited by a few rigid, technical forms. Rather, "property" denotes a broad range of interests that are secured by "existing rules or understandings." A person's interest in a benefit is a "property" interest for due process purposes if there are such rules or mutually explicit understandings that support his claim of entitlement to the benefit and that he may invoke at a hearing.

A written contract with an explicit tenure provision clearly is evidence of a formal understanding that supports a teacher's claim of entitlement to continued employment unless sufficient "cause" is shown. Yet absence of such an explicit contractual provision may not always foreclose the possibility that a teacher has a "property" interest in re-employment. For example, the law of contracts in most, if not all, jurisdictions long has employed a process by which agreements, though not formalized in writing, may be "implied." 3 A. Corbin on Contracts §§ 561–572A (1960). Explicit contractual provisions may be supplemented by other agreements implied from "the promisor's words and conduct in the light of the surrounding circumstances." Id., at § 562. And, "[t]he meaning of [the promisor's] words and acts is found by relating them to the usage of the past." Ibid.

A teacher, like the respondent, who has held his position for a number of years, might be able to show from the circumstances of this service—and from other relevant facts—that he has a legitimate claim of entitlement to job tenure.... This is particularly likely in a college or university, like Odessa Junior College, that has no explicit tenure system even for senior members of its faculty, but that nonetheless may have created such a system in practice. See C. Byse & L. Joughin, Tenure in American Higher Education 17–28 (1959).[1]

In this case, the respondent has alleged the existence of rules and understandings, promulgated and fostered by state officials, that may justify his legitimate claim of entitlement to continued employment absent "sufficient cause." We disagree with the Court of Appeals insofar as it held that a mere subjective "expectancy" is protected by procedural due process, but we agree that the respondent must be given an opportunity to prove the legitimacy of his claim of such entitlement in light of "the policies and practices of the institution." 430 F.2d, at 943. Proof of such a property interest would not, of course, entitle him to reinstatement. But such proof would obligate college officials to grant a hearing at his request, where he could be informed of the grounds for his nonretention and challenge their sufficiency.

Therefore, while we do not wholly agree with the opinion of the Court of Appeals, its judgment remanding this case to the District Court is

Affirmed.[2]

■ CHIEF JUSTICE BURGER, concurring.

I concur in the Court's judgments and opinions in Sindermann and Roth, but there is one central point in both decisions that I would like to underscore. ... [T]he relationship between a state institution and one of its teachers is essentially a matter of state concern and state law. The Court holds today only that a state-employed teacher who has a right to re-employment under state law, arising from either an express or implied contract, has, in turn, a right guaranteed by the Fourteenth Amendment to some form of prior administrative or academic hearing on the cause for nonrenewal of his contract. Thus, whether a particular teacher in a particular context has any right to such administrative hearing hinges on a question of state law. ...

■ [CHIEF JUSTICE BURGER and JUSTICES WHITE, BLACKMUN and REHNQUIST joined JUSTICE STEWART. JUSTICE POWELL took no part in the case. JUSTICES BRENNAN, DOUGLAS, and MARSHALL agreed with the First Amendment portion of the

---

1. We do not now hold that the respondent has any such legitimate claim of entitlement to job tenure. For "[p]roperty interests ... are not created by the Constitution. Rather, they are created and their dimensions are defined by existing rules or understandings that stem from an independent source such as state law...." Board of Regents v. Roth, at 577. If it is the law of Texas that a teacher in the respondent's position has no contractual or other claim to job tenure, the respondent's claim would be defeated.

2. [Ed.] See the Odessa American, Nov. 12, 1972, p. 1, col. 1: "Robert P. Sindermann flew to Odessa Saturday and picked up the $48,000 check made out to him by Odessa College in settlement of his lawsuit stemming from the college's refusal to rehire him in 1969. ...

"The 43-year-old former Odessa College government teacher said one of the conditions of the settlement was that the college offered to reinstate him. 'I have politely declined the invitation,' Sindermann grinned."

Court's opinion, but also voted "to direct the District Court to enter summary judgment for respondent entitling him to a statement of reasons why his contract was not renewed and a hearing on disputed issues of fact."]

NOTES

(1) *Roth on "Property."* Goldberg made the break with traditional due process analysis, but Roth and Sindermann establish the modern doctrinal approach for determining whether a particular regulatory decision triggers the guarantee of due process. As you read the materials that follow, you should ask whether "entitlement analysis" has been any more successful than the right/privilege distinction in sorting out adverse government actions that merit constitutional procedural protection, from those in which the individual will receive only whatever procedure the political or administrative process has chosen to confer.

First, though, consider the implications of Roth's statement, "Property interests, of course, are not created by the Constitution. Rather, they are created *and their dimensions are defined* by existing rules or understandings that stem from an independent source such as state law. ... " (emphasis added). Does this description apply only to the "new property" of government benefits, licenses and jobs? Or does it affect the meaning of traditional property as well? Suppose that a state motor vehicle statute invested automobiles with all the conventional attributes of "property"— they could be bought, sold, leased, stolen at the risk of criminal sanctions, converted at the price of a tort judgment—but also provided that no person who bought a car manufactured *after* the statute was passed would be deemed to have a "right to continued ownership" as against the state. The statute leaves the decision whether to confiscate any particular automobile in the discretionary judgment of the governor.[1]

After Roth, would an order to confiscate a car that meets the statutory criterion trigger procedural due process protection? Would it trigger the constitutional requirement of just compensation? Can a statute define the dimensions of property interests so as to define them away—note, prospectively only? The answer is clearly yes for "new property." If you can come up with a theory that distinguishes cars from government jobs for purposes of constitutional protection, will that theory extend to the driver's license and the motor vehicle inspection and registration stickers that you need to use the car on the public highway? Compare Bell v. Burson, 402 U.S. 535 (1971) (holding, pre-Roth, that due process applies to suspension of a minister's driver's license because "[s]uspension ... involves state action that adjudicates important interests of the licensees") with Dixon v. Love, 431 U.S. 105 (1977) (post-Roth, citing Bell for the proposition that due process applies to the suspension of a trucker's driving license, but emphasizing that the Secretary of State "has limited his broad statutory discretion by an administrative regulation").

---

1.   The main elements of this hypothetical were originally posed by Henry P. Monaghan, Of "Liberty" and "Property", 62 Cornell L. Rev. 405, 440 (1977).

(2) *Roth on "Liberty."* Compare Part II of the majority's opinion, which deals with liberty. Note that, in contrast to property, the Court does not suggest that liberty depends on the content of ordinary, subconstitutional law. What is the source of the elements of liberty contained in the famous list Justice Stewart quotes from Meyer v. Nebraska? Are each of these liberties embodied in some part of the Constitutional text? If not, where do they reside in the Constitution—the due process clause itself, in its substantive dimension? Is the list exclusive? If not, how does a judge determine whether a claimed interest is constitutionally protected liberty? Is this the same sort of reasoning that gave us Lochner v. New York, 198 U.S. 45 (1905), and Roe v. Wade, 410 U.S. 113 (1973)?

NOTES ON THE THEORY OF ENTITLEMENT ANALYSIS

If the constitutional phrase *deprive any person of life, liberty, or property* "must be given some meaning" (Justice Stewart's phrase), is the meaning announced by Roth any stronger textually than the meaning asserted by the older cases? Isn't a distinction between "rights" (claims thought to exist prior to government action) and "privileges" (claims that depend on government grant) a perfectly good reading of the text? If the reason for rejecting this old distinction is that "only a stagnant society remains unchanged," as the Roth opinion suggests, why do we have to give an independent doctrinal significance to *each* element of the constitutional text?

(1) WILLIAM VAN ALSTYNE, CRACKS IN "THE NEW PROPERTY": ADJUDICATIVE DUE PROCESS IN THE ADMINISTRATIVE STATE, 62 Cornell L. Rev. 445, 484 (1977): "The concept of public sector status as property both overstates and understates the problem. It overstates the problem by carrying with it additional notions of personal entitlement and of sinecurism that no constitutional court since Lochner should desire to encourage. At the same time, it understates the problem by ignoring a vast number of situations in which it is impossible to describe the relationship as one giving rise to property, but in which the government's procedural grossness is nevertheless profoundly unfair and objectionable."

(2) JERRY L. MASHAW, DIGNITARY PROCESS: A POLITICAL PSYCHOLOGY OF LIBERAL DEMOCRATIC CITIZENSHIP, 39 U.Fla.L.Rev. 433, 437 (1987): "... Such an approach is functionally inadequate to address the problems of governmental or bureaucratic discretion that the due process clause was meant to address. The positive law trigger approach gives legal protection, or at least due process attention, where some legal protection already exists, while excluding due process concern where a legal regime seems to permit official arbitrariness. Although many have a taste for irony, few would choose Kafka or Ionesco as constitutional draftsmen."

(3) CYNTHIA R. FARINA, CONCEIVING DUE PROCESS, 3 Yale J. L. & Feminism 189, 200 (1991): "Precisely because we understand the essence of the Bill of Rights and 14th Amendment to be constraint on simple-majoritarian positive law, a doctrine that makes constitutional protection contingent upon the terms of such law is deeply disturbing if not actually, within our constitutional culture, incoherent."

(4) HENRY P. MONAGHAN, OF "LIBERTY" AND "PROPERTY", 62 Cornell L. Rev. 405, 409 (1977): "Prior to Roth, Supreme Court definitions of 'liberty' and 'property' had amounted to taking the words 'life, liberty, and property' as a unitary concept embracing all interests valued by sensible men. After Roth, however, each word of the clause must be examined separately; so examined, we find that they do not embrace the full range of state conduct having serious impact upon individual interests."

(5) RICHARD B. STEWART AND CASS R. SUNSTEIN, PUBLIC PROGRAMS AND PRIVATE RIGHTS, 95 Harv.L.Rev. 1195, 1257–58 (1982): "A formal definition of entitlements was not inevitable. The Court might have sought to identify those interests that are as central to individual well-being in contemporary society as were the interests protected at common law in a different era. The judicial discretion inherent in any such task has been a major factor in the Court's refusal to follow a functional approach. Moreover, if courts were to select certain 'important' interests as those deserving due process protection, they might be driven to give those interests substantive as well as procedural protection; procedural rights alone might be of little value if administrators were free to decide cases as they pleased as long as procedural formalities were observed. A functional approach could thus invite courts to rule the welfare state through a new form of substantive due process."

(6) STEPHEN F. WILLIAMS, LIBERTY AND PROPERTY: THE PROBLEM OF GOVERNMENT BENEFITS, 12 J. Legal Stud. 3, 13–14 (1983): "Besides drawing false analogies between [statutory] entitlements and property, entitlement theory has some adverse practical consequences. The first is that the entitlements theory is highly formalistic. By no intelligible criterion of value can it be said to sift out the more valuable from the less valuable interest in conditioned benefits. ... [S]ince it expressly rejects an evaluation of the weight of the interest, entitlements theory would only by coincidence protect the more weighty ones. ...

"Second, because of its formalistic character, the entitlements analysis imposes perverse incentives upon the legislative and executive branches. So long as the government keeps a 'beneficiary' on tenterhooks by making receipt of loss of a benefit discretionary, it can keep free of the trammels of due process. ... [T]he rule against unduly broad delegations will in some contexts prevent the use of totally discretionary criteria. Nonetheless, at the margin the entitlements approach sets up incentives against the evolution of clear substantive criteria for government allocation (or termination) of benefits—an odd way of protecting people from government."

(7) HENRY P. MONAGHAN, THE BURGER COURT AND "OUR FEDERALISM," 43 Law & Contemp. Probs. 39, 48–49 (Summer 1980): "[T]he general doctrine leaves the profession with a feeling that meaningful distinctions seldom exist between interests held to satisfy the threshold of liberty and property and those that do not."

(8) PATRICIA M. WALD, GOVERNMENT BENEFITS: A NEW LOOK AT AN OLD GIFTHORSE, 65 N.Y.U.L.Rev. 247, 260 (1990): "The Court's decision was hardly a renunciation of the right-privilege distinction. It simply redefined the boundary between the two."

NOTES ON THE PRACTICE OF ENTITLEMENT ANALYSIS

Despite criticism from most points on the ideological spectrum, entitlement analysis remains the doctrinal test for identifying "property." (More on identifying "liberty" in the next principal case.) Therefore, it becomes important to know exactly how one is to conduct this analysis. These notes highlight the most significant aspects of entitlement analysis.

What can give rise to an entitlement?

(1) *Institutional Practice.* Sindermann states that an entitlement can be found in the "unwritten common law" of the agency, as proved by "the existence of rules *and understandings*, promulgated *and fostered* by state officials . . ." (emphasis added) However, in subsequent cases the Court has given short shrift to institutional practice claims.[1] (The next principal case is a good example.) Plaintiffs relying on institutional practice seem to fail not because the court disbelieves in the reality of the practice, but rather because it is unwilling to give constitutional significance to a course of agency conduct not formally codified in positive law. Note the relationship of this point to the reliance issue explored in Note 6 below.

(2) *Government Contracts.* It may have occurred to you that, although Roth and Sindermann speak of entitlements as "property," the emphasis on "mutually explicit understandings that support [the] claim" sounds a great deal like contracts analysis. Indeed, the Court in Sindermann explicitly references contracts principles in explaining why Sindermann may have a provable claim to tenure. Does this mean that every federal, state, and local government procurement contract—from stealth bombers, to bus transportation for school children, to paperclips—can potentially support a due process claim if a dispute arises about payment? This question has vexed the courts of appeals but, in the 30+ years since Roth and Sindermann, the Supreme Court has made only tentative steps towards clarifying the issue.

AMERICAN MANUFACTURERS MUTUAL INS. CO. v. SULLIVAN, 526 U.S. 40 (1999), involved a Pennsylvania workers' compensation provision that authorizes insurers to withhold payments for medical treatment of injured employees until an independent "utilization review organization" examines the treatment and determines it to be "reasonable" and "necessary." Employees whose benefits were withheld under this provision sued, claiming that due process required notice and some sort of pre-withholding hearing. Seven Justices agreed that, on the particular statutory scheme, the withholding did not constitute state action. This, of course, was sufficient to dismiss the claim. The Court went on, however, to address the question whether the employees were deprived of a property interest. Pennsylvania law, like most workers' compensation schemes, requires employers to pay for reasonable and necessary medical treatment attributable to covered, work-related injuries. Chief Justice Rehnquist, for the five-member majority, reasoned that employees have an "entitlement" only *after* they establish

---

1. E.g., Leis v. Flynt, 439 U.S. 438, 442 (1979) (despite prevalence of practice, lawyer has no entitlement in being admitted pro hac vice where no statute or court rule limits judicial discretion). See also Connecticut Bd. of Pardons v. Dumschat, 452 U.S. 458, 465 (1981); Kentucky Dep't of Corrections v. Thompson, 490 U.S. 454, 475–76 (Marshall, J., dissenting).

that the treatment was indeed reasonable and necessary. He noted—in a footnote (#13) that has proved important to subsequent cases—that the employees "do not claim that they have a property interest in their claims for payment, as distinct from the payments themselves." Hence, withholding payment pending proof of reasonable necessity implicated no constitutionally protected interest. Justice Ginsburg provided the fifth vote on the understanding that the holding meant only that employees had no entitlement to "constant payment of each medical bill, within 30 days of receipt. . . . I do not doubt, however, that due process requires fair procedures for the adjudication of respondents' claims for workers' compensation benefits." Justices Breyer and Souter concurred in the judgment, adding "that there may be individual circumstances in which the receipt of earlier payments leads an injured person reasonably to expect their continuation, in which case that person may well possess a constitutionally protected 'property' interest." Compare Note (6) below. Justice Stevens insisted that the statutory right to payment of reasonably necessary medical treatment "whether described as a 'claim' for payment or a 'cause of action'[,] is unquestionably a species of property protected by the Due Process Clause. . . ." However, he concluded, "[i]t is not unfair in and of itself for a State to allow either a private or a publicly owned party to withhold payment of a state-created entitlement pending resolution of a dispute over its amount." Justice Scalia joined in the state action part of the holding, but said nothing about the entitlement part.

LUJAN V. G & G FIRE SPRINKLERS, INC., 532 U.S. 189 (2001), challenged a provision of the California Labor Code that permits governmental units to withhold payments from a contractor on a public works project if the contractor or any of its subcontractors fails to comply with Code requirements. Without conducting any sort of hearing before or after its determination, the Division of Labor Standards Enforcement (DSLE) concluded that G & G, a subcontractor on several projects, had failed to pay its workers the "prevailing wage" as the Code requires. It therefore directed that amounts equal to the underpayment, plus penalties, be withheld from contract payments to the prime contractors who used G & G. The prime contractors in turn (as required by the Code) withheld the disputed amount from payments to G & G on the subcontracts. The Court of Appeals held that G & G had a property interest in being paid in full for the work completed, and that due process required the DLSE to provide a hearing on the issue of Code violation, either before the withholding order or promptly thereafter. On remand to consider the impact of Sullivan, that court reaffirmed its decision. The Supreme Court unanimously reversed. Chief Justice Rehnquist's opinion "assume[d] without deciding that the withholding of money due [G & G] under its contracts occurred under color of state law, and that . . . [G & G] has a property interest . . . in its claim for payments under its contracts." However, because the (assumed) property interest was a *claim* for payment, rather than "any *present* entitlement . . . to exercise ownership dominion over real or personal property, or to pursue a gainful occupation," the Constitution would be satisfied by common law or statutory breach of contract remedies. (emphasis added) "If California makes ordinary judicial process available to respondent for resolving its contractual dispute, that process is due process." We will consider this holding further in Section 3.c (which explores the circumstances in which a post-deprivation judicial remedy can be all the process afforded, and due). For now, note that the question whether government contracts create property interests becomes far less significant, as a practical matter, if no process need be provided beyond ordinary contract remedies.

(3) *Keeping Entitlements vs. Getting them in the First Place.* Roth, Sindermann, and Goldberg involved individuals who were threatened with loss of a benefit they had been found qualified to obtain. What about the initial applicant for welfare, a license, or a governmental job? On the one hand, it is generally thought more grievous to take away something someone already has, than merely to fail to give it in the first place. Moreover, the burden on government might be far greater to provide individualized process at the application stage. On the other hand, Roth insists that "we must look not to the 'weight' but to the *nature* of the interest at stake." And in describing Goldberg, Justice Stewart's characterization is as accurate for initial applicants as it is for those attempting to forestall termination: "The recipients had not yet shown that they were, in fact, within the statutory terms of eligibility. But we held that they had a right to a hearing at which they might attempt to do so." Moreover, there are often factual issues that must be resolved if the agency is to make an accurate determination of eligibility.

In Griffeth v. Detrich, 603 F.2d 118 (9th Cir.1979), the plaintiffs challenged the constitutionality of the procedures used in San Diego County for reviewing applications for general relief. The district court held that applicants for such benefits had no protected interest. The court of appeals reversed. Its opinion emphasized that under state law the provision of general relief to qualified persons was mandatory: all who fit the statutory criteria would receive benefits.[2] A petition for certiorari was filed, and denied sub nom. Peer v. Griffeth, 445 U.S. 970 (1980). Justice Rehnquist dissented, arguing that the court of appeals "has taken a significant step in this case to expand the ruling of this Court in Goldberg v. Kelly, a step that I believe merits plenary consideration by the full Court."[3] Similarly in 1985, in Walters v. National Ass'n of Radiation Survivors, p. 851 below, Justice Rehnquist's opinion for the Court was careful to note that no Supreme Court case has squarely held that applicants for benefits

---

2. Accord Mallette v. Arlington County Employees' Supplemental Retirement System, 91 F.3d 630 (4th Cir.1996) (Virginia disability retirement benefits); Daniels v. Woodbury County, 742 F.2d 1128, 1132 (8th Cir.1984) (Iowa general relief statute). Compare Davis v. Ball Memorial Hosp. Ass'n, 640 F.2d 30, 38 (7th Cir.1980) (indigent patients had no property right because regulations contemplated that eligible applicants might exceed resources and did not mandate assistance when eligibility was found).

3. [Ed.] See also Gregory v. Pittsfield, 470 U.S. 1018, 1021 (1985), Justice O'Connor (joined by Justices Brennan and Marshall) dissenting from denial of certiorari: "The conclusion of the Supreme Judicial Court [of Maine] that an applicant for general assistance does not have an interest protected by the Due Process Clause is unsettling in its implication that less fortunate persons in our society may arbitrarily be denied benefits that a State has granted as a matter of right.... Although this Court has never addressed the issue whether applicants for general assistance have a protected property interest, see Peer v. Griffeth, 445 U.S. 970 (1980) (Rehnquist, J., dissenting from denial of certiorari), the weight of authority among lower courts is contrary to the conclusion of the Supreme Judicial Court."

have due process rights. 473 U.S. 305, 320 n. 8. The Sullivan case (Note 2 above) might have settled the issue, and one can see echoes of these earlier statements in Chief Justice Rehnquist's opinion for the 5–4 majority on the entitlement issue. However, given the failure of the employees in that case to press the issue (footnote 13) and Justice Ginsburg's careful qualification of her crucial fifth vote, it appears that the question remains open.

When we explore the second-level due process question (i.e., what process is due?), consider that the difference between *keeping* a benefit and *getting* one in the first place might be reflected in the amount of process due. Could the practical differences—to both the individual and the government—between termination and initial application be more sensitively dealt with at this stage, than at the trigger stage (where the only option is a binary choice)?

What law governs the question whether an entitlement is created?

(4) *"Fair Support."* Note the disposition of Sindermann's case: The case is remanded to the district court to allow Sindermann to prove his allegations that the Odessa College administration fostered the understanding that the school offered de facto tenure. However, the Court warns in a footnote, "If it is the law of Texas that a teacher in the respondent's position has no contractual or other claim to job tenure, the respondent's claim would be defeated." Thus, the district court is to place itself in the position of a Texas court and decide the question under Texas law. Initially, this might surprise you. Yet, the whole point of entitlement analysis is that the existence of a protected interest depends on how the legislature drafts the statute or the executive drafts the regulation. Is it not a logical extension to hold that *interpretation* of the statute or regulation (or, perhaps, institutional practice) is a task for the judiciary of the jurisdiction—and not for the federal courts acting as constitutional interpreters?

The answer to the question "what law governs whether an entitlement is created?" is actually somewhat more complicated. Although the Supreme Court has not decided this precise issue, we can look to analogous interactions of state law and federal constitutional command. The Contracts Clause is the best example. Article 1, § 10 prohibits states from enacting any "Law impairing the Obligation of Contracts." Contracts Clause jurisprudence is not so straightforward as this simple prohibition suggests, but two things are clear: The plaintiff must prove a contract to trigger the Clause, and the existence of a contract is a question of state law. At the same time, it is also clear that the Supreme Court will examine state law to assure itself that the state court's conclusion about the existence of a contract has "fair support" in the relevant precedents. As the Court explained in Indiana ex rel. Anderson v. Brand, "On such a question, one primarily of state law, we accord respectful consideration and great weight to the views of the state's highest court but, in order that the constitutional mandate may not become a dead letter, we are bound to decide for ourselves whether a contract was made.... This involves an appraisal of the statutes of the State and the decisions of its courts." 303 U.S. 95, 100 (1938). As you might imagine, the actual application of the fair support doctrine is a sensitive balance of federalism interests that has produced decisions sometimes hard to reconcile; you may explore these intricacies if you take a Federal Courts course.[4] For our purposes, the important point is that the courts of Texas probably would not have been free, for example, to repudiate in Sindermann's case a line of precedent that had recognized de facto tenure in circumstances like his.

(5) A variation on this question is presented by the Personal Responsibility & Work Opportunity Reconciliation Act of 1996, Pub.L.No. 104–103, 110 Stat. 2105—the federal statute that "reformed" the welfare system involved in Goldberg. In what initially appears to be a frontal attack on Goldberg, Section 401 of the Act reads "NO INDIVIDUAL ENTITLEMENT. This part shall not be interpreted to entitle any individual or family to assistance under any State program funded under this part." It turns out that, because of the particular history of welfare in this country, the term "entitlement" has several meanings unique to that regulatory context.

Because of this history, the purpose of § 401 is far more ambiguous than might at first appear.[5]

Consider, though, only the Roth meaning of entitlement—i.e., a statutory (or regulatory) set of decisional criteria that constrain the discretion of the agency and thereby create a "property" interest. On the one hand, Congress can indeed "overrule" Goldberg through the simple expedient of removing all mandatory eligibility criteria for welfare. On the other hand— at least so long as Marbury v. Madison is good law—Congress cannot simultaneously mandate eligibility criteria but direct the judiciary not to interpret them as constituting an entitlement for purposes of the due process clause. See also City of Boerne v. Flores, 521 U.S. 507 (1997) (invalidating Congress' attempt to overrule a Supreme Court decision interpreting the scope of the Fourteenth Amendment). Indeed, Section 402 of the Act directs that, in order to receive federal monies through the

---

4. A characteristically excellent discussion appears in R. Fallon, D. Meltzer, & D. Shapiro, Hart & Wechsler's The Federal Courts and the Federal System 527–41 (5th ed. 2003).

5. Cynthia R. Farina, On Misusing "Revolution" and "Reform": Procedural Due Process and the New Welfare Act, 50 Admin. L. Rev. 591, 618–23 (1998), argues that § 401 is best understood as directed not at Roth entitlement but rather at King v. Smith entitlement. This 1968 case, reported at 392 U.S. 309, held that the (old) federal statute created a cause of action for individual welfare recipients to enforce, against state programs, the beneficiary-favoring terms and conditions of the federal Aid to Families with Dependent Children (AFDC). As part of the political commitment to devolve control over program content from the national level to the states, the 1996 Act abandoned the long-standing AFDC eligibility criteria. Now, there are few provisions that could even arguably support a

recipient's claim that federal law entitles her to some more favorable benefits rule than the state has chosen to adopt. On this reading, § 401 emphasizes that individuals no longer have a federal statutory claim, enforceable in federal court, for benefits as against the state. Another possibly relevant meaning of "entitlement" in the welfare context is budgetary entitlement. Under AFDC, participating states were required (with the help of federal matching funds) to provide whatever level of funding proved necessary to pay the established level of benefits to all eligible recipients. (Many Social Security programs are "entitlement" programs in this budgetary sense.) The 1996 Act replaced this scheme with a lump sum payment, the Temporary Assistance for Needy Families block grants. As a result, federal law no longer requires states to fund up to the level of eligible need and, correspondingly, qualified applicants have no entitlement to aid once the allocated money runs out.

program, a state's implementing plan "shall set forth *objective criteria* for the delivery of benefits and *for the determination of eligibility.* ..." (emphasis added). Thus, by federal mandate, states must create through their implementing statutes or regulations precisely the sort of decisional standards that give rise to due process entitlements.

What about the individual's reasonable expectations?

(6) Justice Stewart, writing for the Court in Roth: "It is a purpose of the ancient institution of property to protect those claims upon which people rely in their daily lives, reliance that must not be arbitrarily undermined. It is a purpose of the constitutional right to a hearing to provide an opportunity for a person to vindicate those claims."

BISHOP V. WOOD, 426 U.S. 341 (1976): A personnel ordinance of the city of Marion, NC, provided: "A permanent employee whose work is not satisfactory over a period of time shall be notified in what way his work is deficient and what he must do if his work is to be satisfactory. If a permanent employee fails to perform work up to the standard of the classification held, or continues to be negligent, inefficient, or unfit to perform his duties, he may be dismissed by the City Manager." The employee is entitled, on request, to a "written notice" containing "the reasons for his discharge." Police officer Bishop successfully served a 6–month term as a "probationary" employee and became a "permanent" employee. Two years later, he was dismissed. He claimed a due process right to a pretermination hearing in which he could establish that he had not been negligent, inefficient, unfit to perform his duties, or otherwise deficient. Held: the ordinance did not create an property interest.

Justice Stevens for the Court admitted, "On its face, the ordinance on which petitioner relies may fairly be read as conferring such a guarantee. However, such a reading is not the only possible interpretation; the ordinance may also be construed as granting no right to continued employment but merely conditioning an employee's removal on compliance with certain specified procedures." The Court observed that there was no "authoritative interpretation of this ordinance by a North Carolina state court." However, the second possible interpretation was the one adopted by the federal district judge in the case. Noting that this judge "of course, sits in North Carolina and practiced law there for many years," the majority accepted his reading of the ordinance. Justice Brennan, joined by Justice Marshall, dissented: "[T]he strained reading of the local ordinance, which the Court deems to be 'tenable,' cannot be dispositive of the existence vel non of petitioner's 'property' interest.... [B]efore a state law is definitively construed as not securing a 'property' interest, the relevant inquiry is whether it was objectively reasonable for the employee to believe he could rely on continued employment.... At a minimum, this would require in this case an analysis of the common practices utilized and the expectations generated by respondents, and the manner in which the local ordinance would reasonably be read by respondent's employees."

How much discretion is too much?

(7) Rarely does a legislature intend to give an agency carte blanche in making regulatory decisions. At the same time, rarely are regulatory

decisions so heavily rule-bounded that the application of law to an individual case is purely ministerial. Within these two extremes, how much discretionary judgment is consistent with the concept of "entitlement"?[6] The Court has spoken to, and divided over, this question in the context of interests that might be considered more in the nature of "liberty" than "property." Nonetheless, the cases are included here because their discussion of discretion seems generally applicable.[7]

BOARD OF PARDONS V. ALLEN, 482 U.S. 369 (1987): Inmates of Montana State Prison claimed that their parole applications had been denied without due process. The relevant statute provided that the parole board "shall" release prisoners "when in its opinion there is reasonable probability that the prisoner can be released without detriment to the prisoner or to the community." Parole was to be ordered "only for the best interests of society and not as an award of clemency," and a prisoner shall be paroled "only when the board believes that he is able and willing to fulfill the obligations of a law-abiding citizen." Held: the statute creates an entitlement. Justice Brennan's majority opinion perceived "a distinction between two entirely distinct uses of the term discretion. In one sense of the word, an official has discretion when he or she 'is simply not bound by standards set by the authority in question.' R. Dworkin, Taking Rights Seriously 32 (1977). In this sense, officials who have been told to parole whomever they wish have discretion. . . . But the term discretion may instead signify that 'an official must use judgment in applying the standards set him [or her] by authority'; in other words, an official has discretion when the standards set by a statutory or regulatory scheme 'cannot be applied mechanically.' Dworkin, above; see also id., at 69 ('[W]e say that a man has discretion if his duty is defined by standards that reasonable [people] can interpret in different ways'). . . . [T]he presence of official discretion in this sense is not incompatible with the existence of a [constitutionally protected] interest in parole release when release is *required* after the Board determines (in its broad discretion) that the necessary prerequisites exist."

Justice O'Connor (for herself and Justices Rehnquist and Scalia) disagreed: "In my view, the distinction between an 'entitlement' and a mere 'expectancy' must necessarily depend on the degree to which the decisionmaker's discretion is constrained by law. An individual simply has nothing more than a mere hope of receiving a benefit unless the decision to confer that benefit is in a real sense channeled by law. Because the crucial inquiry in determining the creation of a protected interest is whether a statutory *entitlement* is created, it cannot be sufficient merely to point to the existence of some 'standard.' Instead, to give rise to a protected liberty interest, the statute must act to limit meaningfully the discretion of the decisionmaker. In the administrative law context we have long recognized that some purported standards 'are drawn in such broad terms that in a given case there is no law to apply.' Citizens to Preserve Overton Park v. Volpe, p. 989 below. Accordingly, we have held that some agency action is

---

6. A related question—Does due process itself require constraints on the amount of administrative discretion?—is explored in the set of notes at pp. 832 ff. below.

7. Meachum v. Fano, the next principal case, explores the movement of entitlement

analysis into liberty. On whether there is any difference between "liberty" and "property" entitlements, see Note 3 following that case.

committed to agency discretion within the meaning of the Administrative Procedure Act; as a result, agency action is not subject to judicial review if 'no judicially manageable standards are available for judging how and when an agency should exercise its discretion.' Heckler v. Chaney, p. 1218 below. It is no less critical in determining whether a statute creates a protected liberty interest to consider whether the statute includes standards that place real limits on decisionmaker discretion. Under our precedents, an entitlement is created by statute only if 'particularized standards or criteria' constrain the relevant decisionmakers."

Implicit in Justice Brennan's interpretation is the assumption that individualized process at the administrative level has value even when (especially when?) the agency decisionmaker is applying standards about which reasonable minds could disagree. Implicit in Justice O'Connor's interpretation is the assumption that there is no value (or, at least, no value relevant to the due process clauses) in requiring administrative process unless a court could ultimately, on judicial review, force the agency to decide in the individual's favor. Who has the better view?[8]

(8) Has Justice O'Connor ultimately prevailed? KENTUCKY DEP'T OF CORRECTIONS V. THOMPSON, 490 U.S. 454 (1989): Inmates in Kentucky claimed that state regulations governing prison visits were sufficient to entitle the inmates to some sort of procedure when prospective visitors were turned away. The six-justice majority ruled otherwise. The requirement that the statute or regulation contain " 'substantive predicates' to govern official decision-making" is only part of the test for finding an entitlement. "We have also articulated a requirement, implicit in our earlier decisions, that the regulations contain 'explicitly mandatory language,' i.e., specific directives to the decisionmaker that if the regulations' substantive predicates are present, a particular outcome must follow." Here, "[t]he regulations and procedures do provide certain 'substantive predicates' to guide the decisionmaker. The state procedures provide that a visitor 'may be excluded' when, inter alia, officials find reasonable grounds to believe that the 'visitor's presence in the institution would constitute a clear and probable danger to the institution's security or interfere with [its] orderly operation.' Among the more specific reasons listed for denying visitation are the visitor's connection to the inmate's criminal behavior, the visitor's past disruptive behavior or refusal to submit to a search or show proper identification, and the visitor's being under the influence of alcohol or drugs." And, Justice Blackmun conceded, these " 'substantive predicates'

---

8. Cf. Ohio Adult Parole Authority v. Woodard, 523 U.S. 272 (1998) (a prisoner on death row applying for clemency challenged Ohio's clemency process on a number of constitutional grounds; the Chief Justice, and Justices Scalia, Kennedy, and Thomas concluded that due process was not triggered: "[T]he heart of executive clemency ... is to grant clemency as a matter of grace, thus allowing the executive to consider a wide range of factors not comprehended by earlier judicial proceedings and sentencing determinations"; Justices O'Connor, Souter, Ginsberg and Breyer concluded that Woodward had a constitutionally protected "life" interest, but that Ohio procedures were constitutionally adequate; Justice Stevens agreed that a life interest was involved, but would have remanded for the district court to develop a full record on the adequacy of Ohio procedures.)

undoubtedly are intended to guide the duty officer's discretion in making the ultimate decision." However, they "lack the requisite relevant mandatory language. They stop short of requiring that a particular result is to be reached upon a finding that the substantive predicates are met." In sum, he concluded, "The overall effect of the regulations is not such that an inmate can reasonably form an objective expectation that a visit would necessarily be allowed absent the occurrence of one of the listed conditions. Or, to state it differently, the regulations are not worded in such a way that an inmate could reasonably expect to enforce them against the prison officials."

This time, Justice Stevens joined Justice Brennan in a dissent written by Justice Marshall: "I fail to see why mandatory language always is an essential element.... Once it is clear that a State has imposed substantive criteria in statutes or regulations to guide or limit official discretion, there is no reason to assume—as the majority does—that officials applying the statutes or regulations are likely to ignore the criteria if there is not some undefined quantity of the words 'shall' or 'must.' Drafters of statutes or regulations do not ordinarily view the criteria they establish as mere surplusage. Absent concrete evidence that state officials routinely ignore substantive criteria set forth in statutes or regulations (and there is no such evidence here), it is only proper to assume that the criteria are regularly employed *in practice,* thereby creating legitimate expectations worthy of protection by the Due Process Clause."

Viewed from an administrative law perspective, isn't Justice Stevens clearly correct about the intended impact of decisional criteria in statutes or regulations? How often do legislatures really mean for agencies to make decisions for any reason, or no reason at all? For that matter, how often to agency decisionmakers take official action for any reason, or no reason at all? Does all this suggest that something else is going on here?

*The dilemma of constitutionalizing procedural
rights in the regulatory state*

(9) To what extent should the structural constitutional principles of federalism (in the case of state agencies) and separation of powers (in the case of federal agencies) constrain the interpretation of constitutional rights principles such as due process? Recall the 1819 Supreme Court quotation that opened Section 1: "[T]he good sense of mankind has at last settled down to this: that [the words 'due process'] were intended to secure the individual from the arbitrary exercise of the powers of government...." Bank of Columbia v. Okely, 4 Wheat. 235, 244 (1819). Justice Brennan's more contemporary formulation (following in the footsteps of Justice Frankfurter) framed due process as the right "not to be arbitrarily injured by Government." Cafeteria & Restaurant Workers Union v. McElroy, above p. 776 (dissenting op.). Is it possible, in the modern regulatory state, to protect the individual from arbitrary injury by government without making the federal judiciary the "Constitution police" of federal, state, and local administrative practice?

The Court bluntly voiced its apprehensions about this in a set of three decisions rendered within three months:

PAUL v. DAVIS, 424 U.S. 693, 701 (1976), p. 896 below, holding that neither liberty nor property interests were involved when an individual's name and photo were unjustifiably circulated by local police officials to merchants as an "active shoplifter": "[Plaintiff's] reading would make of the Fourteenth Amendment a font of tort law to be superimposed upon whatever systems may already be administered by the States.... [T]he procedural guarantees of the Due Process Clause cannot be the source for such law." Cf. Wisconsin v. Constantineau, p. 791 above.

BISHOP v. WOOD, 426 U.S. 341 (1976), Note 6 above, refusing to find a property interest affected by the firing of a "permanent" employee: "The federal court is not the appropriate forum in which to review the multitude of personnel decisions that are made daily by public agencies. We must accept the harsh fact that numerous individual mistakes are inevitable in the day-to-day administration of our affairs.... The Due Process Clause of the Fourteenth Amendment is not a guarantee against incorrect or ill-advised personnel decisions."

MEACHUM v. FANO, 427 U.S. 215 (1976) below, holding that liberty was not involved when a prisoner was transferred to another, more stringent facility: "Holding that arrangements like this are within reach of the procedural protections of the Due Process Clause would place the Clause astride the day-to-day functioning of state prisons and involve the judiciary in issues and discretionary decisions that are not the business of federal judges. We decline to so interpret and apply the Due Process Clause. The federal courts do not sit to supervise state prisons, the administration of which is of acute interest to the States."

In each case, the Court reacted by refusing to recognize that government action implicated "liberty" or "property"—a conclusion that seemed, to put it mildly, strained. If legitimate federalism and separation-of-powers concerns existed in these cases, was there a better doctrinal solution? Consider this question again in Section 3, exploring "what process is due?"

Meachum v. Fano

Supreme Court of the United States, 1976.
427 U.S. 215.

■ JUSTICE WHITE delivered the opinion of the Court.

The question here is whether the Due Process Clause of the Fourteenth Amendment entitles a state prisoner to a hearing when he is transferred to a prison the conditions of which are substantially less favorable to the prisoner, absent a state law or practice conditioning such transfers on proof of serious misconduct or the occurrence of other events. We hold that it does not.

I

During a 2-1/2 month period in 1974, there were nine serious fires at the Massachusetts Correctional Institution at Norfolk a medium-security institution. Based primarily on reports from informants, the six respondent inmates were removed from the general prison population and placed in the

Receiving Building, an administrative detention area used to process new inmates. Proceedings were then had before the Norfolk prison Classification Board with respect to whether respondents were to be transferred to another institution ..., the living conditions at which are substantially less favorable than those at Norfolk. Each respondent was notified of the classification hearing and was informed that the authorities had information indicating that he had engaged in criminal conduct.

Individual classification hearings were held, each respondent being represented by counsel. Each hearing began by the reading of a prepared statement by the Classification Board. The Board then heard, in camera and out of the respondents' presence, the testimony of petitioner Meachum, the Norfolk prison superintendent, who repeated the information that had been received from informants. Each respondent was then told that the evidence supported the allegations contained in the notice but was not then—or ever—given transcripts or summaries of Meachum's testimony before the Board. Each respondent was allowed to present evidence in his own behalf; and each denied involvement in the particular infraction being investigated. ... Although respondents were aware of the general import of the informants' allegations and were told that the recommendations drew upon informant sources, the details of this information were not revealed to respondents and are not included in the Board's reports which are part of the record before us.

[The Board recommended that Fano, among others, be transferred to a maximum security facility. The Board's statement of reasons in Fano's case was: "1. The enclosed summary of informant information was considered. The sources are considered quite reliable in this case and tend to corroborate each other. In addition, the number of times the subject was named in conjunction with the unrest at Norfolk adds weight in the judgment of this board to the reliability of this information. 2. The seriousness of his involvements were considered extreme. The danger posed by weapons and materials used for violence weighs very heavily against remaining in this population. In addition, the type of involvement of this man as an organizer, leader and [e]nforcer was considered detrimental to the institution, and prohibitive to rehabilitative programming at MCI Norfolk at this time."]

... No respondent was subjected to disciplinary punishment upon arrival at the transfer prison. None of the transfers ordered entailed loss of good time or disciplinary confinement.

Meanwhile respondents had brought this action under 42 U.S.C. § 1983 ... alleging that respondents were being deprived of liberty without due process of law in that petitioners had ordered them transferred to a less favorable institution without an adequate factfinding hearing. They sought an injunction setting aside the ordered transfer, declaratory relief, and damages. [The District Court held in favor of the prisoners, and a divided panel of the Court of Appeals affirmed.]

II

... We reject at the outset the notion that *any* grievous loss visited upon a person by the State is sufficient to invoke the procedural protections of the Due Process Clause. In Board of Regents v. Roth, 408 U.S. 564

(1972), a university professor was deprived of his job, a loss which was surely a matter of great substance, but because the professor had no property interest in his position, due process procedures were not required in connection with his dismissal. We there held that the determining factor is the nature of the interest involved rather than its weight.

Similarly, we cannot agree that *any* change in the conditions of confinement having a substantial adverse impact on the prisoner involved is sufficient to invoke the protections of the Due Process Clause. The Due Process Clause by its own force forbids the State from convicting any person of crime and depriving him of his liberty without complying fully with the requirements of the Clause. But given a valid conviction, the criminal defendant has been constitutionally deprived of his liberty to the extent that the State may confine him and subject him to the rules of its prison system so long as the conditions of confinement do not otherwise violate the Constitution. . . .

Neither, in our view, does the Due Process Clause in and of itself protect a duly convicted prisoner against transfer from one institution to another within the state prison system. Confinement in any of the State's institutions is within the normal limits or range of custody which the conviction has authorized the State to impose. That life in one prison is much more disagreeable than in another does not in itself signify that a Fourteenth Amendment liberty interest is implicated when a prisoner is transferred. . . .

Wolff v. McDonnell, [418 U.S. 539 (1974)], on which the Court of Appeals heavily relied, is not to the contrary. Under that case, the Due Process Clause entitles a state prisoner to certain procedural protections when he is deprived of good-time credits because of serious misconduct. But the liberty interest there identified did not originate in the Constitution, which "itself does not guarantee good-time credit for satisfactory behavior while in prison." Id., at 557. The State itself, not the Constitution, had "not only provided a statutory right to good time but also specifies that it is to be forfeited only for serious misbehavior." Ibid. We concluded:

> [A] person's liberty is equally protected, even when the liberty itself is a statutory creation of the State. The touchstone of due process is protection of the individual against arbitrary action of government, Dent v. West Virginia, 129 U.S. 114, 123 (1889). Since prisoners in Nebraska can only lose good-time credits if they are guilty of serious misconduct, the determination of whether such behavior has occurred becomes critical, and the minimum requirements of procedural due process appropriate for the circumstances must be observed. Id., at 558.

The liberty interest protected in Wolff had its roots in state law, and the minimum procedures appropriate under the circumstances were held required by the Due Process Clause "to insure that the state-created right is not arbitrarily abrogated." Id., at 557. This is consistent with our approach in other due process cases such as . . . Board of Regents v. Roth; Perry v. Sindermann; Goldberg v. Kelly.

Here, Massachusetts law conferred no right on the prisoner to remain in the prison to which he was initially assigned, defeasible only upon proof of specific acts of misconduct. Insofar as we are advised, transfers between Massachusetts prisons are not conditioned upon the occurrence of specified events. On the contrary, transfer in a wide variety of circumstances is vested in prison officials. The predicate for invoking the protection of the Fourteenth Amendment as construed and applied in Wolff v. McDonnell is totally nonexistent in this case.

[I]t is argued that charges of serious misbehavior, as in this case, often initiate and heavily influence the transfer decision and that because allegations of misconduct may be erroneous, hearings should be held before transfer to a more confining institution is to be suffered by the prisoner. That an inmate's conduct, in general or in specific instances, may often be a major factor in the decision of prison officials to transfer him is to be expected unless it be assumed that transfers are mindless events.... But, as we have said, Massachusetts prison officials have the discretion to transfer prisoners for any number of reasons. Their discretion is not limited to instances of serious misconduct. As we understand it no legal interest or right of these respondents under Massachusetts law would have been violated by their transfer whether or not their misconduct had been proved in accordance with procedures that might be required by the Due Process Clause in other circumstances. Whatever expectation the prisoner may have in remaining at a particular prison so long as he behaves himself, it is too ephemeral and insubstantial to trigger procedural due process protections as long as prison officials have discretion to transfer him for whatever reason or for no reason at all.

Holding that arrangements like this are within reach of the procedural protections of the Due Process Clause would place the Clause astride the day-to-day functioning of state prisons and involve the judiciary in issues and discretionary decisions that are not the business of federal judges. We decline to so interpret and apply the Due Process Clause. The federal courts do not sit to supervise state prisons, the administration of which is of acute interest to the States. ...

The judgment of the Court of Appeals accordingly is

Reversed.

■ JUSTICE STEVENS, with whom JUSTICE BRENNAN and JUSTICE MARSHALL join, dissenting.

The Court's rationale is more disturbing than its narrow holding. If the Court had merely held that the transfer of a prisoner from one penal institution to another does not cause a sufficiently grievous loss to amount to a deprivation of liberty within the meaning of the Due Process Clause of the Fourteenth Amendment, I would disagree with the conclusion but not with the constitutional analysis. The Court's holding today, however, appears to rest on a conception of "liberty" which I consider fundamentally incorrect.

... According to the Court, a liberty interest may "originate in the Constitution," or it may have "its roots in state law." Apart from those two possible origins, the Court is unable to find that a person has a constitutionally protected interest in liberty.

If man were a creature of the State, the analysis would be correct. But neither the Bill of Rights nor the laws of sovereign States create the liberty which the Due Process Clause protects. . . . Of course, law is essential to the exercise and enjoyment of individual liberty in a complex society. But it is not the source of liberty, and surely not the exclusive source. . . .

. . . [I]f the inmate's protected liberty interests are no greater than the State chooses to allow, he is really little more than the slave described in the 19th century [prison] cases. I think it clear that even the inmate retains an unalienable interest in liberty at the very minimum the right to be treated with dignity which the Constitution may never ignore.

That does not mean, of course, that every adversity amounts to a deprivation within the meaning of the Fourteenth Amendment. There must be grievous loss, and that term itself is somewhat flexible. I would certainly not consider every transfer within a prison system, even to more onerous conditions of confinement, such a loss. On the other hand, I am unable to identify a principled basis for differentiating between a transfer from the general prison population to solitary confinement and a transfer involving equally disparate conditions between one physical facility and another. . . .

NOTES

Has entitlement analysis taken over "liberty" as well as "property"?

(1) Does Meachum signal the Court's determination to move liberty analysis away from the natural law/substantive due process realm of Meyer v. Nebraska (see Board of Regents v. Roth, p. 801 above) to the entitlement framework, in which the legislature and the executive have ultimate control?

In VITEK V. JONES, 445 U.S. 480 (1980), a Nebraska statute allowed transfer of a prisoner to a mental hospital if a physician or psychologist found him to be suffering a mental condition not treatable at the prison. Held: the transfer decision implicates a liberty interest. Why? The relevant statute created an "objective expectation, firmly fixed in state law and official penal complex practice, that a prisoner would not be transferred unless he suffered from a mental disease or defect that could not be adequately treated in the prison." (internal quote omitted) Justice White's opinion for the Court then went on to agree with the district court that "independently of [the Nebraska statute,] the transfer of a prisoner from a prison to a mental hospital must be accompanied by appropriate procedural protections. . . . None of our decisions holds that conviction for a crime entitles a State not only to confine the convicted person but also to determine that he has a mental illness and to subject him involuntarily to institutional care in a mental hospital. Such consequences visited on the prisoner are qualitatively different from the punishment characteristically suffered by a person convicted of crime. . . . [T]he stigmatizing consequences of a transfer to a mental hospital for involuntary psychiatric treatment, coupled with the subjection of the prisoner to mandatory behavior modification as a treatment for mental illness, constitute the kind of deprivations of liberty that requires procedural protections." WASHINGTON V. HARPER, 494 U.S. 210 (1990), followed a similar pattern of analysis. A prison Policy permitted administration of psychotropic drugs over a prisoner's objection if the prisoner suffers from "a mental disorder" and is "gravely disabled" or poses a "likelihood of serious harm" to himself or others. The Court first held that "[a]s a matter of state law, the Policy itself undoubtedly confers upon respondent a right to be free from the arbitrary administration of antipsychotic medication." It then professed "no doubt that, in addition to the liberty interest created by the State's Policy, respondent possesses a significant liberty interest in avoiding the unwanted administration of antipsychotic drugs under the Due Process Clause of the Fourteenth Amendment."

Is it more significant that, in each case, the Court found a liberty interest protected by due process itself? or that these statements came only after the Court had rooted the liberty entitlement firmly in local statute or regulation?

(2) Does it matter whether an entitlement is classified as "property" or "liberty"? In an opinion as peculiar in style as it is in substance, JAGO V. VAN CUREN, 454 U.S. 14 (1981), held that the Sindermann theory of an entitlement found in institutional practice was available to establish only a property interest, not a liberty interest. The brief 5–4 per curiam stated: "Principles of contract law naturally serve as useful guides in determining whether or not a constitutionally protected property interest exists. Such principles do not, however, so readily lend themselves to determining the existence of constitutionally protected liberty interests . . . ." This analysis is superficially appealing, but it blinks the more fundamental question: What makes something "liberty" rather than "property" in the world of entitlement analysis? For example, both employment and education have been labeled "property" interests by the Court, see Board of Regents v. Roth, p. 801 above; Goss v. Lopez, p. 862 below, even though Meyer v. Nebraska and other early substantive due process cases regarded both as aspects of liberty. See Henry P. Monaghan, Of "Liberty" and "Property", 62 Cornell L. Rev. 405, 434–45 (1977). More recently, the Court has described good time credits—reductions in sentence length that a prisoner can earn by good behavior—both as property (in Goss v. Lopez) and as liberty (in Meachum).

Is there a special due process doctrine for prison cases?

(3) One way to resolve some of the questions posed in the previous two notes is to conclude that liberty-as-entitlement is (or ought to be) a concept unique to the prison context. A central puzzle of modern procedural due process jurisprudence is whether, beneath the facade of a single analytical method invoked in all cases, the Court "really" has multiple due process doctrines that vary with the particular administrative context. Thus, for example, some observers insist that the cases make sense only if we distinguish the public employment decisions from the education decisions from the professional licensing decisions, etc. The strongest argument for this categorical approach is the prison context, particularly in light of the following case.

SANDIN v. CONNER, 515 U.S. 472 (1995), presented the Court with another in the seemingly interminable line of cases in which prison regulations were proffered as creating a constitutionally protected entitlement. Precisely because prisons are highly regimented institutions, many details of day-to-day life become the stuff of discretion-constraining rules. The lower courts had dealt with due process claims that involved receiving a tray rather than a bagged lunch, transfer to a cell without electrical outlets for a television, and being placed on a less desirable kind of diet—all grounded in highly specific substantive regulations. By contrast, DeMont Connor's due process claim arose in the serious context of imposition of 30 days disciplinary segregation for using "angry and foul" language to a guard conducting a rectal search. Nonetheless, Chief Justice Rehnquist's opinion for the 5–4 majority used the case to recast completely the practice of analyzing prisoners' liberty claims. Just as Meachum had reframed Wolff as "really" an entitlement case, so the Chief Justice reframed Meachum and its progeny:

"Because dictum in Meachum distinguished Wolff by focusing on whether state action was mandatory or discretionary, the Court in later cases laid ever greater emphasis on this somewhat mechanical dichotomy. [The Chief Justice reviewed a number of liberty entitlement cases.] As this methodology took hold, no longer did inmates need to rely on a showing that they had suffered a 'grievous loss' of liberty retained even after sentenced to terms of imprisonment. For the Court had ceased to examine the 'nature' of the interest with respect to interests allegedly created by the State. See Board of Regents of State Colleges v. Roth, 408 U.S. 564 (1972). In a series of cases ... the Court has wrestled with the language of intricate, often rather routine prison guidelines to determine whether mandatory language and substantive predicates created an enforceable expectation that the State would produce a particular outcome with respect to the prisoner's conditions of confinement. . . .

"By shifting the focus of the liberty interest inquiry to one based on the language of a particular regulation, and not the nature of the deprivation, the Court encouraged prisoners to comb regulations in search of mandatory language on which to base entitlements to various state-conferred privileges. Courts have, in response, and not altogether illogically, drawn negative inferences from mandatory language in the text of prison regulations. The Court of Appeals' approach in this case is typical: It inferred from the mandatory directive that a finding of guilt 'shall' be imposed under certain conditions the conclusion that the absence of such conditions prevents a finding of guilt.

"Such a conclusion may be entirely sensible in the ordinary task of construing a statute defining rights and remedies available to the general public. It is a good deal less sensible in the case of a prison regulation primarily designed to guide correctional officials in the administration of a prison. . . .

"[This approach] has produced at least two undesirable effects. First, it creates disincentives for States to codify prison management procedures in the interest of uniform treatment. Prison administrators need be concerned with the safety of the staff and inmate population. Ensuring that welfare often leads prison administrators to curb the discretion of staff on the front line who daily encounter prisoners hostile to the authoritarian structure of the prison environment. Such guidelines are not set forth solely to benefit the prisoner. They also aspire to instruct subordinate employees how to exercise discretion vested by the State in the warden, and to confine the authority of prison personnel in order to avoid widely different treatment of similar incidents. . . . States may avoid creation of 'liberty' interests by having scarcely any regulations, or by conferring standardless discretion on correctional personnel.

"Second, [this] approach has led to the involvement of federal courts in the day-to-day management of prisons, often squandering judicial resources with little offsetting benefit to anyone. In so doing, it has run counter to the view expressed in several of our cases that federal courts ought to afford appropriate deference and flexibility to state officials trying to manage a volatile environment. . . .

"In light of the above discussion, we believe that the search for a negative implication from mandatory language in prisoner regulations has strayed from the real concerns undergirding the liberty protected by the Due Process Clause. The time has come to return to the due process principles we believe were correctly established and applied in Wolff. . . .[1] States may under certain circumstances create liberty interests which are protected by the Due Process Clause. But these interests will be generally limited to freedom from restraint which, while not exceeding the sentence in such an unexpected manner as to give rise to protection by the Due Process Clause of its own force, see, e.g., Vitek, 445 U.S., at 493 (transfer to mental hospital), and Washington, 494 U.S., at 221–222 (involuntary administration of psychotropic drugs), nonetheless imposes atypical and significant hardship on the inmate in relation to the ordinary incidents of prison life."

Applying this new standard, the Court held that "Conner's discipline in segregated confinement did not present the type of atypical, significant deprivation in which a State might conceivably create a liberty interest." Justices Ginsburg's dissent (joined by Justice Stevens) returned to the more fundamental objections to liberty "entitlements": "I see the Due Process Clause itself, not Hawaii's prison code, as the wellspring of the protection due Conner. Deriving protected liberty interests from mandatory language in local prison codes would make of the fundamental right something more in certain States, something less in others. Liberty that may vary from Ossining, New York, to San Quentin, California, does not resemble the 'Liberty' enshrined among 'unalienable Rights' with which all persons are 'endowed by their Creator.' Declaration of Independence."

Justice Breyer's dissent, joined by Justice Souter, offered an alternative doctrinal solution: "There is no need . . . for [any] significant change in present law . . . to read the Constitution's Due Process Clause to protect inmates against deprivations of freedom that are important, not compara-

---

1. Such abandonment of [our previous] methodology does not technically require us to overrule any holding of this Court. . . .

tively insignificant. Rather, ... this concern simply requires elaborating, and explaining, the Court's present standards (without radical revision) in order to make clear that courts must apply them in light of the purposes they were meant to serve. As so read, the standards will not create procedurally protected 'liberty' interests where only minor matters are at stake.

"... [A]lthough this Court has said, and continues to say, that some deprivations of an inmate's freedom are so severe in kind or degree (or so far removed from the original terms of confinement) that they amount to deprivations of liberty, irrespective of whether state law (or prison rules) 'cabin discretion,' e.g., Vitek v. Jones; Washington v. Harper; cf. Joint Anti–Fascist Refugee Comm. v. McGrath, 341 U.S. 123 (1951) (Frankfurter, J., concurring), it is not easy to specify just when, or how much of, a loss triggers this protection. There is a broad middle category of imposed restraints or deprivations that, considered by themselves, are neither obviously so serious as to fall within, nor obviously so insignificant as to fall without, the Clause's protection.

"[T]he difficult line-drawing task that this middle category implies helps to explain why this Court developed its additional liberty-defining standard, which looks to local law (examining whether that local law creates a 'liberty' by significantly limiting the discretion of local authorities to impose a restraint). ...

"... The fact that a further deprivation of an inmate's freedom takes place under local rules that cabin the authorities' discretionary power to impose the restraint suggests, *other things being equal*, that the matter is more likely to have played an important role in the life of the inmate. It suggests, other things being equal, that the matter is more likely of a kind to which procedural protections historically have applied, and where they normally prove useful, for such rules often single out an inmate and condition a deprivation upon the existence, or nonexistence, of particular facts. It suggests, other things being equal, that the matter will not involve highly judgmental administrative matters that call for the wise exercise of discretion—matters where courts reasonably should hesitate to second-guess prison administrators. See Meachum, above. It suggests, other things being equal, that the inmate will have thought that he himself, through control of his own behavior, could have avoided the deprivation, and thereby have believed that (in the absence of his misbehavior) the restraint fell outside the 'sentence imposed' upon him. Finally, courts can identify the presence or absence of cabined discretion fairly easily and objectively, at least much of the time. These characteristics of 'cabined discretion' mean that courts can use it as a kind of touchstone that can help them, when they consider the broad middle category of prisoner restraints, to separate those kinds of restraints that, in general, are more likely to call for constitutionally guaranteed procedural protection, from those that more likely do not. ...

"[T]here is, therefore, no need to apply the 'discretion-cabining' approach—the basic purpose of which is to provide a somewhat more objective method for identifying deprivations of protected 'liberty' within a broad middle range of prisoner restraints—where a deprivation is unimportant enough (or so similar in nature to ordinary imprisonment) that it rather clearly falls outside that middle category. Prison, by design, restricts the inmates' freedom. And, one cannot properly view unimportant matters that happen to be the subject of prison regulations as substantially aggravating a loss that has already occurred. Indeed, a regulation about a minor matter, for example, a regulation that seems to cabin the discretionary power of a prison administrator to deprive an inmate of, say, a certain kind of lunch, may amount simply to an instruction to the administrator about how to do his job, rather than a guarantee to the inmate of a 'right' to the status quo. Thus, this Court has never held that comparatively unimportant prisoner 'deprivations' fall within the scope of the Due Process Clause even if local law limits the authority of prison administrators to impose such minor deprivations. And, in my view, it should now simply specify that they do not.

"I recognize that, as a consequence, courts must separate the unimportant from the potentially significant, without the help of the more objective 'discretion-cabining' test. Yet, making that judicial judgment seems no more difficult than many other judicial tasks. It seems to me possible to separate less significant matters such as television privileges, 'sack' versus 'tray' lunches, playing the state lottery, attending an ex-stepfather's funeral, or the limits of travel when on prison furlough, from more significant matters, such as the solitary confinement at issue here. Indeed, prison regulations themselves may help in this respect, such as the regulations here which separate (from more serious matters) 'low moderate' and 'minor' misconduct...."

Does Sandin rewrite entitlement analysis only in the prison context, or does it signal a broader revolution in modern procedural due process doctrine?[2] Thus far, the lower courts have read Sandin primarily as a prison case. Consider, however, the Chief Justice's two objections to Meachum's liberty-entitlement approach: It sets up perverse incentives for states to create standardless administrative regimes, and it involves the federal courts in day-to-day institutional management. As you have now seen, these objections can be (and have been) made to entitlement analysis in general, since it was first employed in Roth. The shortcomings of entitlement analysis are legion. The problem is finding an alternative methodology that would not be even worse. Can you imagine a way to generalize the Sandin majority's "atypical and significant hardship" standard, so that it could be applied outside the prison context?

NOTE ON WHETHER DUE PROCESS ITSELF REQUIRES STANDARDS TO LIMIT ADMINISTRATIVE DISCRETION

The premise of the Supreme Court's major entitlement cases seems to be that the Constitution does not itself demand substantive controls on the distribution of government-created property or liberty. If the legislative and

---

2. This question is debated in Richard J. Pierce, Jr., The Due Process Counterrevolution of the 1990s?, 96 Colum. L. Rev. 1973 (1996), and Cynthia R. Farina, On Misusing "Revolution" and "Reform": Procedural Due Process and the New Welfare Act, 50 Admin. L. Rev. 591 (1998).

executive branches are content to have officials exercise completely discretionary power, that is the end of the matter. There is, however, a contrary line of authority which suggests that due process itself has something to say about standardless administrative discretion.

(1) HOLMES V. NEW YORK CITY HOUSING AUTHORITY, 398 F.2d 262 (2d Cir.1968): Each year the Authority received approximately 90,000 applications for public housing, out of which it could select only 10,000 families for admission. In federally-aided projects, it was required to follow an objective scoring system to choose among applicants. For projects built with state and local money, however, there was no similar regulation. Plaintiffs alleged that they had applied for public housing, that they had never been advised of their eligibility or ineligibility, and that applications filed with the Authority were not processed according to any reasonable, or even ascertainable, system—not even by following a simple chronological waiting list. On interlocutory appeal, the court held that they stated a constitutional cause of action: "One charge made against the defendant, which has merit at least in connection with state-aided projects where the Authority has adopted no standards for selection among non-preference candidates, is that it thereby failed to establish the fair and orderly procedure for allocating its scarce supply of housing which due process requires. It hardly need be said that the existence of an absolute and uncontrolled discretion in an agency of government vested with the administration of a vast program, such as public housing, would be an intolerable invitation to abuse. See Hornsby v. Allen, 326 F.2d 605, 609–610 (5th Cir.1964). For this reason alone due process requires that selections among applicants be made in accordance with 'ascertainable standards,' id. at 612, and, in cases where many candidates are equally qualified under these standards, that further selections be made in some reasonable manner such as 'by lot or on the basis of the chronological order of application.' Hornsby v. Allen, 330 F.2d 55, 56 (5th Cir.1964) (on petition for rehearing). Due process is a flexible concept which would certainly also leave room for the employment of a scheme such as the 'objective scoring system' suggested in the resolution adopted by the Authority for federal-aided projects."

HORNSBY V. ALLEN, 326 F.2d 605 (5th Cir.1964), on which Holmes relied, involved similar issues regarding the procedures used by a liquor licensing board to distribute liquor licenses. Both cases precede Board of Regents v. Roth, yet both have been cited and discussed by lower courts in a number of post-Roth cases.[1] On the other hand, some cases have questioned their continued viability,[2] and a leading scholar in the area has described them as both "correctly decided" and "virtually moribund authorities." Jerry L. Mashaw, Dignitary Process: A Political Psychology of Liberal Democratic Citizenship, 39 U.Fla.L.Rev. 433, 437 (1987).

---

1. E.g., Madera v. Secretary of the Executive Office of Communities and Development, 418 Mass. 452, 636 N.E.2d 1326 (1994); Gates v. Chadwick, 812 F.Supp. 1233 (M.D.Ga.1993); Bowie v. Louisiana Public Service Comm., 627 So.2d 164 (La.1993); Johnson v. City of New York, 152 Misc.2d 576, 578 N.Y.S.2d 977 (N.Y.Sup.1991), af- firmed as modified, 192 A.D.2d 352, 596 N.Y.S.2d 33 (N.Y.App.Div.1993); Montgomery National Bank v. Clarke, 882 F.2d 87 (3d Cir.1989).

2. E.g., Wal–Mart Stores v. City of Cheyenne, 120 F.3d 271 (10th Cir.1997); South Gwinnett Venture v. Pruitt, 491 F.2d 5, 7 n. 1 (5th Cir.1974).

(2) Could the due process clause in its substantive dimension require the creation of the very discretion-constraining standards needed to trigger the clause in its procedural dimension? On the other hand, could due process really have *nothing* to say about government caprice in the allocation of at least very important benefits? Cf. Ohio Adult Parole Auth. v. Woodard, 523 U.S. 272, 288–89 (1998) (O'Connor, J., with whom Souter, Ginsburg, and Breyer join, concurring in part and concurring in the judgment): "I do not ... agree with the suggestion in the principal opinion that, because clemency [in capital cases] is committed to the discretion of the executive, the Due Process Clause provides no constitutional safeguards.... Judicial intervention might, for example, be warranted in the face of a scheme whereby a state official flipped a coin to determine whether to grant clemency, or in a case where the State arbitrarily denied a prisoner any access to its clemency process.")

(3) Fans of the Holmes–Hornsby approach, when looking for Supreme Court authority, usually cite MORTON v. RUIZ, 415 U.S. 199 (1974). Ruiz and his family, Papago Indians, moved 15 miles off the Papago reservation so that he could live and work at the Phelps–Dodge copper mines at Ajo, Arizona. They maintained close ties with the reservation and, said the Court, "have not been assimilated into the dominant culture." Twenty-seven years after the Ruizes moved, the miners went on strike, the state of Arizona refused general assistance to striking workers, and Ruiz applied for general assistance from the Bureau of Indian Affairs. The sole ground given for denying his application was that, although he lived *near* the reservation, the relevant portion of the BIA's internal Field Manual limited general assistance benefits to "Indians living *on* reservations." The statutory basis for the assistance program was phrased in very general language, and the annual appropriations acts were similarly vague. On appeal, the government argued that BIA's formal budget requests had always stated that "[g]eneral assistance will be provided to needy Indians on reservations." However, as confirmed by page after page of the agency's testimony before Congress, the BIA had always represented that "near" equaled "on."

In one sense, this was the end of the case. The BIA's central defense was that Congress had appropriated funds only for those living on reservations. This defense had failed. There was little doubt that if anyone "near" reservations would qualify, the Ruizes would. Instead of stopping there, however, Justice Blackmun's opinion for a unanimous Court went on to consider whether the agency's Field Manual might have some binding legal effect:

"Having found that the congressional appropriation was intended to cover welfare services at least to those Indians residing 'on or near' the reservation, it does not necessarily follow that the Secretary is without power to create reasonable classifications and eligibility requirements in order to allocate the limited funds available to him for this purpose. Thus, if there were only enough funds appropriated to provide meaningfully for 10,000 needy Indian beneficiaries and the entire class of eligible beneficiaries numbered 20,000, it would be incumbent upon the BIA to develop an eligibility standard to deal with this problem, and the standard, if rational and proper, might leave some of the class otherwise encompassed by the appropriation without benefits. But in such a case the agency must, at a minimum, let the standard be generally known so as to assure that it is being applied consistently and so as to avoid both the reality and the appearance of arbitrary denial of benefits to potential beneficiaries.

"Assuming, arguendo, that the Secretary rationally could limit the 'on or near' appropriation to include only the smaller class of Indians who lived directly 'on' the reservation . . ., the question that remains is whether this has been validly accomplished. The power of an administrative agency to administer a congressionally created and funded program necessarily requires the formulation of policy and the making of rules to fill any gap left, implicitly or explicitly, by Congress. In the area of Indian affairs, the Executive has long been empowered to promulgate rules and policies, and the power has been given explicitly to the Secretary and his delegates at the BIA. This agency power to make rules that affect substantial individual rights and obligations carries with it the responsibility not only to remain consistent with the governing legislation, but also to employ procedures that conform to the law. No matter how rational or consistent with congressional intent a particular decision might be, the determination of eligibility cannot be made on an ad hoc basis by the dispenser of the funds."

Commentators have been perplexed ever since about exactly what this condemnation of "ad hoc" agency behavior entails. It is hard to see how having field personnel operate under a rule in a departmental manual generates "ad hoc" behavior, since it should *increase* administrative consistency. Those who have already studied publication rules in Chapter V, Sec. 4 above, will recall the debate over how broadly to construe § 553(1)(A)'s exemption, from the notice-and-comment process, of interpretive rules and policy statements. One of the best arguments for liberal construction is that these documents can constrain the discretion of the agency's own personnel even though they cannot (because of the absence of notice and comment) bind the public. Alternatively, if the Court's concern was that the BIA had not in practice applied its own rule even-handedly—perhaps because case-by-case decisions were made by front-line employees without a mechanism for quality control—Justice Blackmun certainly did not say so.

Perhaps most important for our purposes, Justice Blackmun did not state the basis for his approach. Does the BIA have to develop a legal framework for distributing funds because this is what Congress intended? because this is a requirement of some federal common law of administrative procedure? because this forestalls a conclusion under the APA that the agency has acted arbitrarily and capriciously?[3] or because due process— applicable to state agencies as well—so requires?

(4) Occasional lower court cases follow Ruiz in requiring agencies to develop self-disciplining standards where the stakes for individuals are high—and in being less than clear on the legal basis of this requirement. The Eighth Circuit in two cases compelled the Secretary of Agriculture to promulgate standards implementing discretionary farm aid programs. See

---

3. This is the suggestion of the First Circuit in Trafalgar Capital Assocs. v. Cuomo, 159 F.3d 21, 35 n. 11 (1st Cir.1998).

Iowa ex rel. Miller v. Block, 771 F.2d 347 (8th Cir.1985) (suit to compel implementing regulations for statute providing that the Secretary "may make disaster payments" whenever he determines that farms within the federal crop insurance program have suffered "substantial uncompensated disaster losses."); Allison v. Block, 723 F.2d 631 (8th Cir.1983) (suit to compel implementing policies and procedures for exercising statutory discretion to defer foreclosure of farmers in default on federal loans).

In JEAN V. NELSON, 711 F.2d 1455 (11th Cir.1983), reh'g en banc, 727 F.2d 957 (11th Cir.1984), aff'd in part and rev'd in part, 472 U.S. 846 (1985), the Eleventh Circuit considered a number of statutory and constitutional challenges to federal detention of over 1000 Haitians being held in camps or prisons pending final determination of their right to remain in the country. By statute, the Attorney General "may in his discretion parole into the United States . . . any alien applying for admission." In 1954, the Commissioner of INS decided that mass detention pending processing was inhumane and unnecessary. Under the revised policy, only aliens "deemed likely to abscond or those whose freedom of movement could be adverse to national security or the public safety" would be detained. In 1981, as part of a crackdown on illegal immigration, the Reagan Administration returned to a policy of detaining undocumented aliens.

"Evidence concerning the substance of the Administration's 'new policy' reveals that the particulars of the new policy never were developed fully. Immigration inspectors were left to exercise discretion in an unguided fashion with the result that many individuals were deprived of their liberty in an arbitrary manner. [The court reviewed testimony of highly placed administration officials who 'contradicted one another several times, and did not agree on the substance of the policy.']

"The most significant and telling testimony was that dealing with the transfer of authority to those responsible for implementing the new policy. The testimony indicates that no one in the chain of command from the Attorney General to the immigration officers at Krome North, where the Haitians were detained, admitted to ever receiving or giving guidance as to who should be free and who should be incarcerated. . . . It is clear no one knew exactly what the policy was, and no one in authority attempted to supervise the exercise of discretion under the new policy. Not surprisingly, the discretion was exercised with harsh results. . . .

"As the district court recognized, this is a classic case of unguided and unfettered discretion. Cases are legion that discern the dangers of unguided discretion, preeminent among them the risk of selective and discriminatory enforcement. . . . The obvious solution, frequently recommended to avoid the dangers of discriminatory enforcement, would have been a specific policy adopted pursuant to notice and comment rulemaking. . . . The rulemaking requirements of the APA provide a minimum, not a maximum, to administrative procedure; they serve a crucial purpose in guiding administrative discretion. That is, and should be, the lesson of this case.

". . . We remand to the court below for such relief as is necessary to remedy the discrimination and effectuate the rationale of this decision. Such relief shall include, but is not limited to: (1) an injunction against discriminatory enforcement of the new policy, (2) the continued parole of class members, (3) record-keeping requirements so the district court may ensure the policy is effectuated in the future in a non-discriminatory manner, (4) [relief relating to claims of inadequate access to counsel], and (5) whatever further relief is necessary to ensure that all aliens, regardless of their nationality or origin, are accorded equal treatment."

All members of the plaintiff class were released on parole forthwith. However, the district court stayed the entry of its order enjoining future use of the incarceration-without-parole policy in order to permit INS to promulgate the policy in compliance with the APA. The INS promptly did so. Although the new rule expressly prohibited the use of racial or ethnic factors in the parole decision, the plaintiffs claimed that parole was still being discriminatorily denied by local INS officials. The 11th Circuit reheard the case en banc and held that the Fifth Amendment does not apply to unadmitted aliens. However, it remanded for further consideration of whether the current parole practice violated the new regulation. The Supreme Court granted certiorari, held that this nonconstitutional claim made it unnecessary to reach the Fifth Amendment issue, and affirmed the remand to the district court.

SECTION 3. CONTEMPORARY DOCTRINE: WHAT PROCESS IS DUE? AND WHEN?

"Many controversies have raged about the cryptic and abstract words of the Due Process Clause but there can be no doubt that at a minimum they require that deprivation of life, liberty or property by adjudication be preceded by notice and opportunity for hearing appropriate to the nature of the case."

Mullane v. Central Hanover Bank & Trust Co., 339 U.S. 306, 313 (1950)

Assuming that a protected liberty or property interest is at stake, what process does the Constitution require the agency to provide? Given the enormous range of federal, state, and local administrative contexts to which modern due process doctrine speaks, it should come as no surprise that the Court has resisted a "one size fits all" answer to this second step of due process analysis. As you read the materials in this section, keep in mind the synergy between two dimensions of "due" process: *what?* and *when?* By disaggregating the very large bundle of procedures comprised in a trial-type judicial hearing, and by accepting that some procedures could follow rather than precede deprivation, a court gains flexibility to respond to the range of administrative contexts. However, this flexibility comes at a cost. If each stick in the process bundle *plus* its timing is independently available, a very large number of process permutations is possible. Can the doctrine structure judicial choice in a manner both defensible in principle and predictable in practice?

Londoner v. Denver

Supreme Court of the United States, 1908.
210 U.S. 373.

(Reprinted p. 238 above).

Bi–Metallic Investment Co. v. State Bd. of Equalization of Colorado

Supreme Court of the United States, 1915.
239 U.S. 441.

(Reprinted p. 241 above).

NOTES

(1) The principle established by Londoner and Bi–Metallic is sometimes expressed by the shorthand, "Due process requires an individualized hearing in adjudication and not in rulemaking." But what about a regulatory decision which, although cast in the form of a universally applicable rule, will in fact deprive only one, or a very small number of, persons of property or liberty? That the APA may consider the decision a rulemaking—§ 551(4) defines a "rule" as "an agency statement of general *or particular* applicability and future effect"—cannot, of course, resolve the constitutional question. For example, if EPA promulgates a regulation limiting airborne emissions of a particular chemical, must it provide an oral hearing to the one and only manufacturer who produces this chemical in the area covered by the rule? The Tenth Circuit said no in Anaconda Co. v. Ruckelshaus, 482 F.2d 1301 (10th Cir.1973), reasoning that "there are many other interested parties and groups who are affected and are entitled to be heard." Other courts have been more wary: "[W]hen a rule adopted for general application applies only to a small number of persons, its characterization as legislation becomes suspect." Richardson v. Eastover, 922 F.2d 1152, 1158 (4th Cir.1991). Still, as the note cases at p. 245 illustrate, courts usually reject the claim that the regulation is really on the Londoner side of the line. They typically reason either that multiple interests have a stake in the issue, or that the type of factual and policy judgments grounding the regulation are identical whether one or many regulated entities are affected. These reasons address the practical cost and value of individualized hearings. Do they respond to the concern that an individual or small group is vulnerable to being singled out—and will be unable to protect their liberty or property through the political process? Doesn't the "right" constitutional answer to the case of the regulation that affects only a few persons depend on the objectives of procedural due process?

(2) Suppose, though, that agency action is clearly on the Londoner side of the line—for example, an agency comes to believe that the recipient of a statutory benefit no longer meets the statutory requirements and so proposes to terminate the benefit? What process must the agency afford? Recall Londoner's conclusion: "Many requirements essential in strictly judicial proceedings may be dispensed with *in proceedings of this nature.* But even here a hearing in its very essence demands that he who is entitled to it shall have the right to support his allegations by argument however brief and, if need be, by proof, however informal." (emphasis added) What characteristics define "proceedings of this nature," such that the agency can constitutionally dispense with many of the procedural "requirements essential in strictly judicial proceedings?" The process "due" under Londoner isn't, in the end, very much—although it must

include the opportunity for oral communication with the decisionmaker. Why is orality constitutionally essential? Will an opportunity for brief oral presentation of argument and proof always be enough to satisfy due process? If not, by what method is the agency (and the court) to gauge how much more is required?

Goldberg v. Kelly

Supreme Court of the United States, 1970.
397 U.S. 254.

(Reprinted p. 783 above).

NOTE

Goldberg is a prime example of the important synergy between "what"? and "when"? By the time the case reached the Court, New York by statute offered an initial informal hearing prior to suspension of benefits and a full evidentiary hearing after suspension. The controversy, therefore, was largely about timing. By what methodology does the Court decide which sticks in the process bundle must be provided prior to suspension of benefits? Note Justice Brennan's statement, "[T]he pre-termination hearing need not take the form of a judicial or quasi-judicial trial." What elements of a judicial trial are, in the end, missing from the Goldberg hearing?

New York's two-stage process might, instead, have been analogized to the criminal process. In that process, the individual charged with contravening the relevant legal standard may be given a preliminary hearing in which the government must show probable cause for its allegations. Alternatively, the government may seek an indictment before a grand jury, in which it must show a basis for filing the charge, but gets to do so ex parte. Any preliminary hearing is abbreviated in form and content—lacking, for example, any chance for cross-examination or affirmative proof of innocence. Unless the charges appear patently groundless and are dismissed, the individual must endure a significant level of interim deprivation until the opportunity for a trial in which the charges are fully adjudicated. At worst, he loses his liberty (if he is either refused bail or unable to post it); at best, he must bear the unrecoupable emotional and financial costs of being publicly accused of crime, putting up bail, and preparing for a full trial. We have long accepted this two-stage process as "due" despite the real interim deprivation it inflicts on the individual. Should the Goldberg Court have considered this analogy?

a.   THE EMERGENCE OF THE UTILITARIAN CALCULUS

Mathews v. Eldridge

Supreme Court of the United States, 1976.
424 U.S. 319.

■ JUSTICE POWELL delivered the opinion of the Court.

The issue in this case is whether the Due Process Clause of the Fifth Amendment requires that prior to the termination of Social Security disability benefit payments the recipient be afforded an opportunity for an evidentiary hearing.

I

Cash benefits are provided to workers during periods in which they are completely disabled under the disability insurance benefits program created by the 1956 amendments to Title II of the Social Security Act. 42 U.S.C. § 423.[1] Respondent Eldridge was first awarded benefits in June 1968. In March 1972, he received a questionnaire from the state agency charged with monitoring his medical condition. Eldridge completed the questionnaire, indicating that his condition had not improved and identifying the medical sources, including physicians, from whom he had received treatment recently. The state agency then obtained reports from his physician and a psychiatric consultant. After considering these reports and other information in his file the agency informed Eldridge by letter that it had made a tentative determination that his disability had ceased in May 1972. The letter included a statement of reasons for the proposed termination of benefits, and advised Eldridge that he might request reasonable time in which to obtain and submit additional information pertaining to his condition.

In his written response, Eldridge disputed one characterization of his medical condition and indicated that the agency already had enough evidence to establish his disability.[2] The state agency then made its final determination that he had ceased to be disabled in May 1972. This determination was accepted by the Social Security Administration (SSA), which notified Eldridge in July that his benefits would terminate after that month. The notification also advised him of his right to seek reconsideration by the state agency of this initial determination within six months.

Instead of requesting reconsideration Eldridge commenced this action.... [The district court agreed that the procedures violated due process, viewing the interest of disability recipients in uninterrupted benefits as indistinguishable from that of welfare recipients. The Court of Appeals

---

1. The program is financed by revenues derived from employee and employer payroll taxes. It provides monthly benefits to disabled persons who have worked sufficiently long to have an insured status, and who have had substantial work experience in a specified interval directly preceding the onset of disability. Benefits also are provided to the worker's dependents under specified circumstances. When the recipient reaches age 65 his disability benefits are automatically converted to retirement benefits. In fiscal 1974 approximately 3,700,000 persons received assistance under the program. Social Security Administration, The Year in Review 21 (1974).

2. Eldridge originally was disabled due to chronic anxiety and back strain. He subsequently was found to have diabetes. The tentative determination letter indicated that aid would be terminated because available medical evidence indicated that his diabetes was under control, that there existed no limitations on his back movements which would impose severe functional restrictions, and that he no longer suffered emotional problems that would preclude him from all work for which he was qualified. In his reply letter he claimed to have arthritis of the spine rather than a strained back.

affirmed. The Court discussed the relevant statutory review provisions, and determined that the courts had jurisdiction.]

III

A

. . . The Secretary does not contend that procedural due process is inapplicable to terminations of Social Security disability benefits. . . . Rather, the Secretary contends that the existing administrative procedures . . . provide all the process that is constitutionally due before a recipient can be deprived of that interest. . . . Eldridge agrees that the review procedures . . . would be adequate if disability benefits were not terminated until after the evidentiary hearing stage of the administrative process. The dispute centers upon what process is due prior to the initial termination of benefits, pending review.

In recent years this Court increasingly has had occasion to consider the extent to which due process requires an evidentiary hearing prior to the deprivation of some type of property interest even if such a hearing is provided thereafter. In only one case, Goldberg v. Kelly, has the Court held that a hearing closely approximating a judicial trial is necessary. . . .

. . . "Due process, unlike some legal rules, is not a technical conception with a fixed content unrelated to time, place and circumstances." Cafeteria Workers v. McElroy, 367 U.S. 886, 895 (1961). . . . Accordingly, resolution of the issue whether the administrative procedures provided here are constitutionally sufficient requires analysis of the governmental and private interests that are affected. Goldberg v. Kelly, above, at 263–266; Cafeteria Workers v. McElroy, above, at 895. More precisely, our prior decisions indicate that identification of the specific dictates of due process generally requires consideration of three distinct factors: First, the private interest that will be affected by the official action; second, the risk of an erroneous deprivation of such interest through the procedures used, and the probable value, if any, of additional or substitute procedural safeguards; and finally, the Government's interest, including the function involved and the fiscal and administrative burdens that the additional or substitute procedural requirement would entail. See, e.g., Goldberg v. Kelly, above, at 263–271.

We turn first to a description of the procedures for the termination of Social Security disability benefits, and thereafter consider the factors bearing upon the constitutional adequacy of these procedures.

B

The disability insurance program is administered jointly by state and federal agencies. State agencies make the initial determination whether a disability exists, when it began, and when it ceased. The standards applied and the procedures followed are prescribed by the Secretary, who has delegated his responsibilities and powers under the Act to the SSA.

In order to establish initial and continued entitlement to disability benefits a worker must demonstrate that he is unable to engage in any substantial gainful activity by reason of any medically determinable physical or mental impairment which can be expected to result in death or which has lasted or can be expected to last for a continuous period of not less than 12 months.... 42 U.S.C. § 423(d)(1)(A).

To satisfy this test the worker bears a continuing burden of showing, by means of "medically acceptable clinical and laboratory diagnostic techniques," § 423(d)(3), that he has a physical or mental impairment of such severity that

he is not only unable to do his previous work but cannot, considering his age, education, and work experience, engage in any other kind of substantial gainful work which exists in the national economy, regardless of whether such work exists in the immediate area in which he lives, or whether a specific job vacancy exists for him, or whether he would be hired if he applied for work. § 423(d)(2)(A)....

The continuing-eligibility investigation is made by a state agency acting through a "team" consisting of a physician and a nonmedical person trained in disability evaluation. The agency periodically communicates with the disabled worker, usually by mail—in which case he is sent a detailed questionnaire—or by telephone, and requests information concerning his present condition, including current medical restrictions and sources of treatment, and any additional information that he considers relevant to his continued entitlement to benefits.

Information regarding the recipient's current condition is also obtained from his sources of medical treatment. If there is a conflict between the information provided by the beneficiary and that obtained from medical sources such as his physician, or between two sources of treatment, the agency may arrange for an examination by an independent consulting physician. Whenever the agency's tentative assessment of the beneficiary's condition differs from his own assessment, the beneficiary is informed that benefits may be terminated, provided a summary of the evidence upon which the proposed determination to terminate is based, and afforded an opportunity to review the medical reports and other evidence in his case file. He also may respond in writing and submit additional evidence.

The state agency then makes its final determination, which is reviewed by an examiner in the SSA Bureau of Disability Insurance. If, as is usually the case, the SSA accepts the agency determination it notifies the recipient in writing, informing him of the reasons for the decision, and of his right to seek *de novo* reconsideration by the state agency.[3] Upon acceptance by the SSA, benefits are terminated effective two months after the month in which medical recovery is found to have occurred.

If the recipient seeks reconsideration by the state agency and the determination is adverse, the SSA reviews the reconsideration determination and notifies the recipient of the decision. He then has a right to an

---

3. The reconsideration assessment is initially made by the state agency, but usually not by the same persons who considered the case originally. R. Dixon, Social Security Disability and Mass Justice 32 (1973). Both the recipient and the agency may adduce new evidence.

evidentiary hearing before an SSA administrative law judge. The hearing is non-adversary, and the SSA is not represented by counsel. As at all prior and subsequent stages of the administrative process, however, the claimant may be represented by counsel or other spokesmen. If this hearing results in an adverse decision, the claimant is entitled to request discretionary review by the SSA Appeals Council, and finally may obtain judicial review.

Should it be determined at any point after termination of benefits, that the claimant's disability extended beyond the date of cessation initially established, the worker is entitled to retroactive payments. If, on the other hand, a beneficiary receives any payments to which he is later determined not to be entitled, the statute authorizes the Secretary to attempt to recoup these funds in specified circumstances.

C

Despite the elaborate character of the administrative procedures provided by the Secretary, the courts below held them to be constitutionally inadequate, concluding that due process requires an evidentiary hearing prior to termination. In light of the private and governmental interests at stake here and the nature of the existing procedures, we think this was error.

Since a recipient whose benefits are terminated is awarded full retroactive relief if he ultimately prevails, his sole interest is in the uninterrupted receipt of this source of income pending final administrative decision on his claim. His potential injury is thus similar in nature to that of the welfare recipient in Goldberg....

Only in Goldberg has the Court held that due process requires an evidentiary hearing prior to a temporary deprivation. It was emphasized there that welfare assistance is given to persons on the very margin of subsistence.... Eligibility for disability benefits, in contrast, is not based upon financial need.[4] Indeed, it is wholly unrelated to the worker's income or support from many other sources, such as earnings of other family members, workmen's compensation awards, tort claims awards, savings, private insurance, public or private pensions, veterans' benefits, food stamps, public assistance, or the "many other important programs, both public and private, which contain provisions for disability payments affecting a substantial portion of the work force. ..." Richardson v. Belcher, 404 U.S. 78, 85–87 (Douglas, J., dissenting).

As Goldberg illustrates, the degree of potential deprivation that may be created by a particular decision is a factor to be considered in assessing the validity of any administrative decisionmaking process. The potential deprivation here is generally likely to be less than in Goldberg, although the degree of difference can be overstated. As the District Court emphasized, to remain eligible for benefits a recipient must be "unable to engage in substantial gainful activity." Thus, ... there is little possibility that the

---

4. The level of benefits is determined by the worker's average monthly earnings during the period prior to disability, his age, and other factors not directly related to financial need. ...

terminated recipient will be able to find even temporary employment to ameliorate the interim loss.

As we recognized last Term in Fusari v. Steinberg, 419 U.S. 379, 389 (1975), "the possible length of wrongful deprivation of . . . benefits [also] is an important factor in assessing the impact of official action on the private interests." The Secretary concedes that the delay between a request for a hearing before an administrative law judge and a decision on the claim is currently between 10 and 11 months. Since a terminated recipient must first obtain a reconsideration decision as a prerequisite to invoking his right to an evidentiary hearing, the delay between the actual cutoff of benefits and final decision after a hearing exceeds one year.

In view of the torpidity of this administrative review process and the typically modest resources of the family unit of the physically disabled worker,[5] the hardship imposed upon the erroneously terminated disability recipient may be significant. Still, the disabled worker's need is likely to be less than that of a welfare recipient. In addition to the possibility of access to private resources, other forms of government assistance will become available where the termination of disability benefits places a worker or his family below the subsistence level. In view of these potential sources of temporary income, there is less reason here than in Goldberg to depart from the ordinary principle, established by our decisions, that something less than an evidentiary hearing is sufficient prior to adverse administrative action.

D

An additional factor to be considered here is the fairness and reliability of the existing pretermination procedures, and the probable value, if any, of additional procedural safeguards. Central to the evaluation of any administrative process is the nature of the relevant inquiry. See Friendly, "Some Kind of Hearing," 123 U.Pa.L.Rev. 1267, 1281 (1975). In order to remain eligible for benefits the disabled worker must demonstrate by means of "medically acceptable clinical and laboratory diagnostic techniques," 42 U.S.C. § 423(d)(3), that he is unable "to engage in any substantial gainful activity by reason of any *medically determinable* physical or mental impairment. . . ." § 423(d)(1)(A) (emphasis supplied). In short, a medical assessment of the worker's physical or mental condition is required. This is a more sharply focused and easily documented decision than the typical determination of welfare entitlement. In the latter case, a wide variety of information may be deemed relevant and issues of witness credibility and veracity often are critical to the decisionmaking process. Goldberg noted that in such circumstances "written submissions are a wholly unsatisfactory basis for decision."

---

5. *Amici* cite statistics compiled by the Secretary which indicate that in 1965 the mean income of the family unit of a disabled worker was $3,803, while the median income for the unit was $2,836. The mean liquid assets—i.e., cash, stocks, bonds—of these family units was $4,862; the median was $940. These statistics do not take into account the family unit's nonliquid assets—i.e., automobile, real estate, and the like. Brief for AFL–CIO et al. as *Amici Curiae* App. 4a.

By contrast, the decision whether to discontinue disability benefits will turn, in most cases, upon "routine, standard, and unbiased medical reports by physician specialists," Richardson v. Perales, 402 U.S. 389, 404 (1971) concerning a subject whom they have personally examined.[6] In Richardson the Court recognized the "reliability and probative worth of written medical reports," emphasizing that while there may be "professional disagreement with the medical conclusions" the "specter of questionable credibility and veracity is not present." To be sure, credibility and veracity may be a factor in the ultimate disability assessment in some cases. But procedural due process rules are shaped by the risk of error inherent in the truthfinding process as applied to the generality of cases, not the rare exceptions. The potential value of an evidentiary hearing, or even oral presentation to the decisionmaker, is substantially less in this context than in Goldberg.

[handwritten margin note: DP based on general case & not exception]

The decision in Goldberg also was based on the Court's conclusion that written submissions were an inadequate substitute for oral presentation because they did not provide an effective means for the recipient to communicate his case to the decisionmaker. Written submissions were viewed as an unrealistic option, for most recipients lacked the "educational attainment necessary to write effectively" and could not afford professional assistance. In addition, such submissions would not provide the "flexibility of oral presentations" or "permit the recipient to mold his argument to the issues the decision maker appears to regard as important." In the context of the disability-benefits-entitlement assessment the administrative procedures under review here fully answer these objections.

The detailed questionnaire which the state agency periodically sends the recipient identifies with particularity the information relevant to the entitlement decision, and the recipient is invited to obtain assistance from the local SSA office in completing the questionnaire. More important, the information critical to the entitlement decision usually is derived from medical sources, such as the treating physician. Such sources are likely to be able to communicate more effectively through written documents than are welfare recipients or the lay witnesses supporting their cause. The conclusions of physicians often are supported by X-rays and the results of clinical or laboratory tests, information typically more amenable to written than to oral presentation.

A further safeguard against mistake is the policy of allowing the disability recipient's representative full access to all information relied

---

6. The decision is not purely a question of the accuracy of a medical diagnosis since the ultimate issue which the state agency must resolve is whether in light of the particular worker's "age, education, and work experience" he cannot "engage in any ... substantial gainful work which exists in the national economy...." 42 U.S.C. § 423(d)(2)(A). Yet information concerning each of these worker characteristics is amenable to effective written presentation. The value of an evidentiary hearing, or even a limited oral presentation, to an accurate presentation of those factors to the decisionmaker does not appear substantial. Similarly, resolution of the inquiry as to the types of employment opportunities that exist in the national economy for a physically impaired worker with a particular set of skills would not necessarily be advanced by an evidentiary hearing. Cf. 1 K. Davis, Administrative Law Treatise § 7.06, p. 429 (1958). The statistical information relevant to this judgment is more amenable to written than to oral presentation.

upon by the state agency. In addition, prior to the cutoff of benefits the agency informs the recipient of its tentative assessment, the reasons therefor, and provides a summary of the evidence that it considers most relevant. Opportunity is then afforded the recipient to submit additional evidence or arguments, enabling him to challenge directly the accuracy of information in his file as well as the correctness of the agency's tentative conclusions. These procedures, again as contrasted with those before the Court in Goldberg, enable the recipient to "mold" his argument to respond to the precise issues which the decisionmaker regards as crucial.

Despite these carefully structured procedures, *amici* point to the significant reversal rate for appealed cases as clear evidence that the current process is inadequate. Depending upon the base selected and the line of analysis followed, the relevant reversal rates urged by the contending parties vary from a high of 58.6% for appealed reconsideration decisions to an overall reversal rate of only 3.3%.[7] Bare statistics rarely provide a satisfactory measure of the fairness of a decisionmaking process. Their adequacy is especially suspect here since the administrative review system is operated on an open-file basis. A recipient may always submit new evidence, and such submissions may result in additional medical examinations. Such fresh examinations were held in approximately 30% to 40% of the appealed cases in fiscal 1973, either at the reconsideration or evidentiary hearing stage of the administrative process. In this context, the value of reversal rate statistics as one means of evaluating the adequacy of the pretermination process is diminished. Thus, although we view such information as relevant, it is certainly not controlling in this case.

E

In striking the appropriate due process balance the final factor to be assessed is the public interest. This includes the administrative burden and other societal costs that would be associated with requiring, as a matter of constitutional right, an evidentiary hearing upon demand in all cases prior to the termination of disability benefits. The most visible burden would be the incremental cost resulting from the increased number of hearings and the expense of providing benefits to ineligible recipients pending decision. No one can predict the extent of the increase, but the fact that full benefits would continue until after such hearings would assure the exhaustion in most cases of this attractive option. Nor would the theoretical right of the Secretary to recover undeserved benefits result, as a practical matter, in any substantial offset to the added outlay of public funds. The parties submit widely varying estimates of the probable additional financial cost.

---

7. By focusing solely on the reversal rate for appealed reconsideration determinations amici overstate the relevant reversal rate. [I]n order fully to assess the reliability and fairness of a system of procedure, one must also consider the overall rate of error for all denials of benefits. Here that overall rate is 12.2%. Moreover, about 75% of these reversals occur at the reconsideration stage of the administrative process. Since the medi- an period between a request for reconsideration review and decision is only two months, Brief for AFL–CIO et al. as Amici Curiae App. 4a, the deprivation is significantly less than that concomitant to the lengthier delay before an evidentiary hearing. Netting out these reconsideration reversals, the overall reversal rate falls to 3.3%. See Supplemental and Reply Brief for Petitioner 14.

We only need say that experience with the constitutionalizing of government procedures suggests that the ultimate additional cost in terms of money and administrative burden would not be insubstantial.

Financial cost alone is not a controlling weight in determining whether due process requires a particular procedural safeguard prior to some administrative decision. But the Government's interest, and hence that of the public, in conserving scarce fiscal and administrative resources is a factor that must be weighed. At some point the benefit of an additional safeguard to the individual affected by the administrative action and to society in terms of increased assurance that the action is just, may be outweighed by the cost. Significantly, the cost of protecting those whom the preliminary administrative process has identified as likely to be found undeserving may in the end come out of the pockets of the deserving since resources available for any particular program of social welfare are not unlimited.

But more is implicated in cases of this type than ad hoc weighing of fiscal and administrative burdens against the interests of a particular category of claimants. The ultimate balance involves a determination as to when, under our constitutional system, judicial-type procedures must be imposed upon administrative action to assure fairness. . . . The judicial model of an evidentiary hearing is neither a required, nor even the most effective, method of decisionmaking in all circumstances. The essence of due process is the requirement that "a person in jeopardy of serious loss [be given] notice of the case against him and opportunity to meet it." Joint Anti–Fascist Comm. v. McGrath, 341 U.S., at 171–172 (Frankfurter, J., concurring). All that is necessary is that the procedures be tailored, in light of the decision to be made, to "the capacities and circumstances of those who are to be heard," Goldberg v. Kelly, 397 U.S., at 268–269 (footnote omitted), to insure that they are given a meaningful opportunity to present their case. In assessing what process is due in this case, substantial weight must be given to the good-faith judgments of the individuals charged by Congress with the administration of social welfare programs that the procedures they have provided assure fair consideration of the entitlement claims of individuals. This is especially so where, as here, the prescribed procedures not only provide the claimant with an effective process for asserting his claim prior to any administrative action, but also assure a right to an evidentiary hearing, as well as to subsequent judicial review, before the denial of his claim becomes final.

We conclude that an evidentiary hearing is not required prior to the termination of disability benefits and that the present administrative procedures fully comport with due process.

The judgment of the Court of Appeals is

Reversed.

■ JUSTICE STEVENS took no part in the consideration or decision of this case.

■ JUSTICE BRENNAN, with whom JUSTICE MARSHALL concurs, dissenting.

. . . [T]he Court's consideration that a discontinuance of disability benefits may cause the recipient to suffer only a limited deprivation is no argument. It is speculative. Moreover, the very legislative determination to provide disability benefits, without any prerequisite determination of need in fact, presumes a need by the recipient which is not this Court's function to denigrate. Indeed, in the present case, it is indicated that because disability benefits were terminated there was a foreclosure upon the Eldridge home and the family's furniture was repossessed, forcing Eldridge, his wife, and their children to sleep in one bed. Finally, it is also no argument that a worker, who has been placed in the untenable position of having been denied disability benefits, may still seek other forms of public assistance.

NOTES

(1) "[T]here is less reason here than in Goldberg to depart from *the ordinary principle*, . . . that something less than an evidentiary hearing is sufficient prior to adverse administrative action."(emphasis added) Does Matthews invert the traditional understanding of when process is due? If the "brutal need" of welfare recipients becomes the standard for departing from the "ordinary" rule, it is not surprising that Goldberg has remained unique in the amount of predeprivation process the Court has required.

Note that Justice Powell describes Goldberg as requiring an evidentiary hearing "prior to a *temporary* deprivation." (emphasis added) Does this language suggest that the Court is now inclined to view the suspension of benefits as more analogous to indictment than to conviction—such that some process is required to assure minimal support for the government's position but, once the government meets its burden in the preliminary hearing, the Constitution tolerates significant constraints on the individual pending full adjudication?

(2) This last question raises a fundamental question of methodology. To what sources should the Court look in determining what process is due? Should it specify agency procedure by choosing the best analogy from the range of civil and criminal judicial proceedings? Should it recognize administrative decisionmaking as unique, and therefore demanding a different conception of fair process? Consider Justice Frankfurter's view, concurring in Joint Anti–Fascist Comm. v. McGrath, 341 U.S. at 162–63:

"[D]ue process," unlike some legal rules, is not a technical conception with a fixed content unrelated to time, place and circumstances. Expressing as it does in its ultimate analysis respect enforced by law for that feeling of just treatment which has been evolved through centuries of Anglo–American constitutional history and civilization, "due process" cannot be imprisoned within the treacherous limits of any formula. Representing a profound attitude of fairness between man and man, and more particularly between the individual and government, "due process" is compounded of history, reason, the past course of decisions, and stout confidence in the strength of the democratic faith which we profess. Due process is not a mechanical instrument. It is not a yardstick. It is a process. It is a delicate process of adjustment inescapably involving the exercise of judgment by those whom the Constitution entrusted with the unfolding of the process.

... The precise nature of the interest that has been adversely affected, the manner in which this was done, the reasons for doing it, the available alternatives to the procedure that was followed, the protection implicit in the office of the functionary whose conduct is challenged, the balance of hurt complained of and good accomplished— these are some of the considerations that must enter into the judicial judgment. ...

Compare the views of Judge Henry J. Friendly in a now-famous article, published shortly before Mathews, that appears to have had significant impact on the majority's thinking in the case. In "SOME KIND OF HEARING," 123 U. Pa. L. Rev. 1267 (1975), Judge Friendly decried "the tendency to judicialize administrative procedures" that Goldberg produced. Instead, he suggested, "the required degree of procedural safeguards varies directly with the importance of the private interest affected and the need for and usefulness of the particular safeguard in the given circumstances and inversely with the burden and any other adverse consequences of affording it."

A balancing test, he admitted, might seem "uncertain and subjective," but he argued that "more elaborate specification of the relevant factors may help to produce more principled and predictable decisions." He offered the following list of "factors that have been considered to be elements of a fair hearing, roughly in order of priority":

1. An Unbiased Tribunal

2. Notice of the Proposed Action and the Grounds Asserted for It

3. An Opportunity to Present Reasons Why the Proposed Action Should Not be Taken

4. The Right to Call Witnesses

5. The Right To Know the Evidence Against One

6. The Right To Have Decision Based Only on the Evidence Presented

7. Counsel

8. The Making of a Record

9. A Statement of Reasons

10. Public Attendance

11. Judicial Review

He concluded: "In the mass justice area the Supreme Court has yielded too readily to the notions that the adversary system is the only appropriate model and that there is only one acceptable solution to any problem, and consequently has been too prone to indulge in constitutional codification. There is need for experimentation, particularly for the use of the investigative model, for empirical studies, and for avoiding absolutes."

(3) In the years following the decision in Mathews v. Eldridge, Professor Jerry Mashaw published a series of influential works about the problems of

administering the Social Security disability program.[1] JERRY L. MASHAW, BUREAUCRATIC JUSTICE, 21–23 (1983), observes that the program has been critiqued from multiple, conflicting perspectives; from these, he derives three larger competing models of administrative justice:

"There is a substantial critical literature on the administration of disability benefits under Titles II and XVI of the Social Security Act. One strand of the commentary is concerned that the disability program fails to provide adequate service to claimants and beneficiaries. This view at least implicitly characterizes the program's purposes as paternalistic and thera-peutic, purposes that would seem to require a major role for health care, vocational, social service, and other professionals in program administra-tion. The failure of the bureaucratic decision process to emphasize the role of professional judgment and to adopt a service orientation is seen as the program's major deficiency.

"A second, more 'legalistic' perspective is concerned primarily with the capacity of individual claimants to assert and defend their rights to disabili-ty benefits. This literature is concerned with such problems as the inade-quacy of the notices of denial sent to rejected applicants; the need for representation of claimants in disability hearings; the lack of adversarial testing of the evidence provided by participants in the adjudicatory process; the substantial reversal rate of those cases that are heard orally by independent administrative law judges and on review in federal courts. In sum, the concern is with the failure of the disability decision process to provide the essential ingredients of judicial trials.

"A third strand of the critical literature chides SSA for failing to manage the adjudication of claims in ways that produce predictable and consistent outcomes. The concern is that the system may be out of control, and the suggestions for reform are essentially managerial: SSA should provide more complete and objective criteria for the exercise of adjudicatory discretion; greater control should be gained over the internal routines of the disability decision services in the states; the system of management oversight and statistical quality assurance should be strengthened. In short, the system is viewed in bureaucratic terms and criticized for its inadequate management controls. . . .

"In reflecting on [this pattern of critique], I have come to some hypotheses that seem to have interesting implications, not just for the disability program but for the evaluation of administrative adjudication generally. First, these criticisms reflect distinct conceptual models of ad-ministrative justice. Second, each of the models is coherent and attractive. But, third, the models, while not mutually exclusive, are highly competi-tive: the internal logic of any one of them tends to drive the characteristics of the others from the field as it works itself out in concrete situations.

---

1. These include, in addition to the work quoted in the text, Jerry L. Mashaw, Charles J. Goetz, Frank I. Goodman, Warren F. Schwartz, Paul R. Verkuil and Milton M. Carrow, Social Security Hearings and Ap-peals: A Study of the Social Security Admin-istration Hearing System (1978), and Jerry L. Mashaw, Due Process in the Administrative State (1985).

"If these hypotheses are correct, then it may also follow that the best system of administrative adjudication may be the one most open to criticism. A compromise that seeks to preserve the values and to respond at once to the insights of all of these conceptions of justice will, from the perspective of each separate conception, appear incoherent and unjust. The best system of administrative adjudication that can be devised may fall tragically short of our inconsistent ideals."

Professor Mashaw denominates his models, respectively: "professional treatment," "moral judgment," and "bureaucratic rationality." Part of his argument is that traditional, individualized adjudication (although it sometimes takes place without formal adversarial process) is part of the moral judgment model, because in our culture individually adjudicated cases inevitably spill over beyond the mere application of existing rules to found facts (the bureaucratic rationality model) and begin to address broader, more diffuse questions of moral entitlement. Such cases lead, in Professor Mashaw's phrase, to a "contextual exploration of individual deservingness." As against this, he suggests we could have—and to some extent do have—programs which emphasize the application of professional judgment in a service relationship, or programs which emphasize cost-effective rational decisionmaking. Professor Mashaw makes a strong case for the third model; for a thoughtful review, see Lance Liebman and Richard B. Stewart, 96 Harv.L.Rev. 1952 (1983).

Walters v. National Association of Radiation Survivors

Supreme Court of the United States, 1985.
473 U.S. 305.

■ JUSTICE REHNQUIST delivered the opinion of the Court.

... Congress has by statute established an administrative system for granting service-connected death or disability benefits to veterans. See 38 U.S.C. § 301 et seq. The amount of the benefit award is not based upon need, but upon service connection—that is, whether the disability is causally related to an injury sustained in the service—and the degree of incapacity caused by the disability. A detailed system has been established by statute and Veterans' Administration (VA) regulation for determining a veteran's entitlement, with final authority resting with an administrative body known as the Board of Veterans' Appeals (BVA).... The controversy in this case centers on the opportunity for a benefit applicant or recipient to obtain legal counsel to aid in the presentation of his claim to the VA. Section 3404(c) of Title 38 provides [that the Administrator will award attorneys fees in successful cases in an amount not to exceed "$10 with respect to any one claim."] Section 3405 provides criminal penalties for any person who charges fees in excess of the limitation of § 3404.

... In 1978, ... approximately 800,000 claims ... were decided by the 58 regional offices of the VA. Slightly more than half of these were claims for service-connected disability or death, and the remainder were pension claims. Of the 800,000 total claims in 1978, more than 400,000 were allowed, and some 379,000 were denied. Sixty-six thousand of these denials were contested at the regional level; about a quarter of these contests were dropped, 15% prevailed on reconsideration at the local level, and the remaining 36,000 were appealed to the BVA. At that level some 4,500, or 12%, prevailed, and another 13% won a remand for further proceedings. Although these figures are from 1978, the statistics in evidence indicate that the figures remain fairly constant from year to year.

As might be expected in a system which processes such a large number of claims each year, the process prescribed by Congress for obtaining disability benefits does not contemplate the adversary mode of dispute resolution utilized by courts in this country. It is commenced by the submission of a claim form to the local veterans agency, which form is provided by the VA either upon request or upon receipt of notice of the death of a veteran. Upon application a claim generally is first reviewed by a three-person "rating board" of the VA regional office—consisting of a medical specialist, a legal specialist, and an "occupational specialist." A claimant is "entitled to a hearing at any time on any issue involved in a claim...." Proceedings in front of the rating board "are ex parte in nature"; no Government official appears in opposition. The principal issues are the extent of the claimant's disability and whether it is service-connected. The board is required by regulation "to assist a claimant in developing the facts pertinent to his claim," and to consider any evidence offered by the claimant. In deciding the claim the board generally will request the applicant's Armed Service and medical records, and will order a medical examination by a VA hospital. Moreover, the board is directed by regulation to resolve all reasonable doubts in favor of the claimant.

After reviewing the evidence the board renders a decision either denying the claim or assigning a disability "rating" pursuant to detailed regulations developed for assessing various disabilities. Money benefits are calculated based on the rating. The claimant is notified of the board's decision and its reasons, and the claimant may then initiate an appeal by filing a "notice of disagreement" with the local agency. If the local agency adheres to its original decision it must then provide the claimant with a "statement of the case"—a written description of the facts and applicable law upon which the panel based its determination—so that the claimant may adequately present his appeal to the BVA. Hearings in front of the BVA are subject to the same rules as local agency hearings—they are *ex parte*, there is no formal questioning or cross-examination, and no formal rules of evidence apply. The BVA's decision is not subject to judicial review. 38 U.S.C. § 211(a).[1]

The process is designed to function throughout with a high degree of informality and solicitude for the claimant. There is no statute of limitations, and a denial of benefits has no formal res judicata effect.... Perhaps more importantly for present purposes, however, various veterans' organizations across the country make available trained service agents, free of charge, to assist claimants in developing and presenting their claims. These service representatives are contemplated by the VA statute, and they are recognized as an important part of the administrative scheme. Appellees' counsel agreed at argument that a representative is available for any

---

1. [Ed.] § 211 is considered at p. 1204 below.

claimant who requests one, regardless of the claimant's affiliation with any particular veterans' group.[2]

[The district court held that plaintiffs had a strong likelihood of showing that the administrative scheme violated the due process clause, and entered a preliminary injunction enjoining the enforcement of §§ 3404–3405. The aid of the service representatives was unsatisfactory, said the trial court, because a heavy case load and lack of legal training led to inadequate research and failure to develop the facts. It was "standard practice . . . to submit merely a one to two page hand written brief." In reaching its conclusions the district court relied heavily on the problems presented by what it described as "complex cases," which apparently included those in which a disability was slow-developing and therefore difficult to find service-connected, as well as other cases involving difficult matters of medical judgment. There were no findings as to what proportion of the VA caseload comprised "complex cases". The evidence suggested, said Justice Rehnquist, "that the sum total of such claims is extremely small; in 1982, for example, roughly 2% of the BVA caseload consisted of 'agent orange' or 'radiation' claims, and what evidence there is suggests that the percentage of such claims in the regional offices was even less— perhaps as little as 3 in 1000."]

Appellees' first claim, accepted by the District Court, is that the statutory fee limitation, as it bears on the administrative scheme in operation, deprives a rejected claimant or recipient of "life, liberty or property, without due process of law," by depriving him of representation by expert legal counsel. . . .[3]

These general principles are reflected in the test set out in Mathews, which test the District Court purported to follow. . . .

The Government interest, which has been articulated in congressional debates since the fee limitation was first enacted in 1862 during the Civil War, has been this: that the system for administering benefits should be managed in a sufficiently informal way that there should be no need for the employment of an attorney to obtain benefits to which a claimant was entitled, so that the claimant would receive the entirety of the award without having to divide it with a lawyer. This purpose is reinforced by a similar absolute prohibition on compensation of any service organization representative. While Congress has recently considered proposals to modify the fee limitation in some respects, a Senate Committee Report in 1982 highlighted that body's concern "that any changes relating to attorneys' fees be made carefully so as not to induce unnecessary retention of

---

2. The VA statistics show that 86% of all claimants are represented by service representatives, 12% proceed pro se, and 2% are represented by lawyers. . . .

3. The District Court held that applicants for benefits, no less than persons already receiving them, had a "legitimate claim of entitlement" to benefits if they met the statutory qualifications. The court noted that this Court has never so held, although this Court has held that a person receiving such benefits has a "property" interest in their continued receipt. Since at least one of the claimants here alleged a diminution of benefits already being received, however, we must in any event decide whether "due process" under the circumstances includes the right to be represented by employed counsel. In light of our decision on that question, we need not presently define what class would be entitled to the process requested.

attorneys by VA claimants and not to disrupt unnecessarily the very effective network of nonattorney resources that has evolved in the absence of significant attorney involvement in VA claims matters." S.Rep. No. 97–466, p. 49 (1982). Although this same Report professed the Senate's belief that the original stated interest in protecting veterans from unscrupulous lawyers was "no longer tenable," the Senate nevertheless concluded that the fee limitation should with a limited exception remain in effect, in order to "protect claimants' benefits" from being unnecessarily diverted to lawyers.

In the face of this congressional commitment to the fee limitation for more than a century, the District Court had only this to say with respect to the governmental interest:

> The government has neither argued nor shown that lifting the fee limit would harm the government in any way, except as the paternalistic protector of claimants' supposed best interests. To the extent the paternalistic role is valid, there are less drastic means available to ensure that attorneys' fees do not deplete veterans' death or disability benefits.

It is not for the District Court or any other federal court to invalidate a federal statute by so cavalierly dismissing a long-asserted congressional purpose. If "paternalism" is an insignificant Government interest, then Congress first went astray in 1792, when by its Act of March 23 of that year it prohibited the "sale, transfer or mortgage . . . of the pension . . . [of a] soldier . . . before the same shall become due." Ch. 11, § 6, 1 Stat. 245. Acts of Congress long on the books, such as the Fair Labor Standards Act, might similarly be described as "paternalistic"; indeed, this Court once opined that "[s]tatutes of the nature of that under review, limiting the hours in which grown and intelligent men may labor to earn their living, are mere meddlesome interferences with the rights of the individual. . . ." Lochner v. New York, 198 U.S. 45, 61 (1905). That day is fortunately long gone, and with it the condemnation of rational paternalism as a legitimate legislative goal.

There can be little doubt that invalidation of the fee limitation would seriously frustrate the oft-repeated congressional purpose for enacting it. Attorneys would be freely employable by claimants to veterans benefits, and the claimant would as a result end up paying part of the award, or its equivalent, to an attorney. But this would not be the only consequence of striking down the fee limitation that would be deleterious to the congressional plan. . . .

. . . [T]he destruction of the fee limitation would bid fair to complicate a proceeding which Congress wished to keep as simple as possible. It is scarcely open to doubt that if claimants were permitted to retain compensated attorneys the day might come when it could be said that an attorney might indeed be necessary to present a claim properly in a system rendered more adversary and more complex by the very presence of lawyer representation. It is only a small step beyond that to the situation in which the claimant who has a factually simple and obviously deserving claim may nonetheless feel impelled to retain an attorney simply because so many other claimants retain attorneys. And this additional complexity will undoubtedly engender greater administrative costs, with the end result being that less Government money reaches its intended beneficiaries.

We accordingly conclude that under the Mathews v. Eldridge analysis great weight must be accorded to the Government interest at stake here. The flexibility of our approach in due process cases is intended in part to allow room for other forms of dispute resolution. ... It would take an extraordinarily strong showing of probability of error under the present system—and the probability that the presence of attorneys would sharply diminish that possibility—to warrant a holding that the fee limitation denies claimants due process of law. We have no hesitation in deciding that no such showing was made out on the record before the District Court....

... In this case we are fortunate to have statistics that bear directly on this question. ... These unchallenged statistics chronicle the success rates before the BVA depending on the type of representation of the claimant, and are summarized in the following figures taken from the record.

Ultimate Success Rates Before the Board of Veterans
Appeals by Mode of Representation

American Legion	16.2%
American Red Cross	16.8%
Disabled American Veterans	16.6%
Veterans of Foreign Wars	16.7%
Other nonattorney	15.8%
No representation	15.2%
Attorney/Agent	18.3%

The District Court opined that these statistics were not helpful, because in its view lawyers were retained so infrequently that no body of lawyers with an expertise in VA practice had developed, and lawyers who represented veterans regularly might do better than lawyers who represented them only *pro bono* on a sporadic basis. ...

We think the District Court's analysis of this issue totally unconvincing, and quite lacking in the deference which ought to be shown by any federal court in evaluating the constitutionality of an Act of Congress. We have the most serious doubt whether a competent lawyer taking a veteran's case on a *pro bono* basis would give less than his best effort, and we see no reason why experience in developing facts as to causation in the numerous other areas of the law where it is relevant would not be readily transferable to proceedings before the VA. ...

The District Court's treatment of the likely usefulness of attorneys is on the same plane with its efforts to quantify the likelihood of error under the present system. The court states several times in its opinion that lawyers could provide more services than claimants presently receive—a fact which may freely be conceded—but does not suggest how the availability of these services would reduce the likelihood of error in the run-of-the-mill case. Simple factual questions are capable of resolution in a nonadversarial context, and it is less than crystal clear why *lawyers* must be available to identify possible errors in *medical* judgment. The availability of particular lawyers' services in so-called "complex" cases might be more of a factor in preventing error in such cases, but on this record we simply do not know how those cases should be defined or what percentage of all of the cases before the VA they make up. Even if the showing in the District Court had been much more favorable, appellees still would confront the constitutional hurdle posed by the principle enunciated in cases such as Mathews to the effect that a process must be judged by the generality of cases to which it applies, and therefore process which is sufficient for the large majority of a group of claims is by constitutional definition sufficient for all of them. But here appellees have failed to make the very difficult factual showing necessary....

We have in previous cases, of course, not only held that the Constitution permits retention of an attorney, but that on occasion it requires the Government to provide the services of an attorney. [The Court then discussed a series of precedents concerning the provision of counsel in proceedings in which criminal, and other, sanctions were at issue.] But where, as here, the only interest protected by the Due Process Clause is a property interest in the continued receipt of Government benefits, which interest is conferred and terminated in a nonadversary proceeding, these precedents are of only tangential relevance. Appellees rely on Goldberg v. Kelly, 397 U.S. 254 (1970), in which the Court held that a welfare recipient subject to possible termination of benefits was entitled to be represented by an attorney....

We think that the benefits at stake in VA proceedings, which are not granted on the basis of need, are more akin to the Social Security benefits involved in Mathews than they are to the welfare payments upon which the recipients in Goldberg depended for their daily subsistence. Just as this factor was dispositive in Mathews in the Court's determination that no evidentiary hearing was required prior to a temporary deprivation of benefits, so we think it is here determinative of the right to employ counsel.
. . .

... Especially in light of the Government interests at stake, the evidence adduced before the District Court as to success rates in claims handled with or without lawyers shows no such great disparity as to warrant the inference that the congressional fee limitation under consideration here violates the Due Process Clause of the Fifth Amendment. What evidence we have been pointed to in the record regarding complex cases falls far short of the kind which would warrant upsetting Congress' judgment that this is the manner in which it wishes claims for veterans benefits adjudicated. The District Court abused its discretion in holding otherwise.

[In the final portion of its opinion, the Court rejected the argument that the fee limitation violated First Amendment rights.]

Reversed.

■ JUSTICE O'CONNOR, with whom JUSTICE BLACKMUN joins, concurring.

... [T]he record before us is insufficient to evaluate the claims of any individuals or identifiable groups. I write separately to note that such claims remain open on remand.

... In order to justify the sort of categorical relief the District Court afforded here, the fee limitation must pose a risk of erroneous deprivation of rights in the generality of cases reached by the injunctive relief. Cf. Mathews v. Eldridge. Given the nature of the typical claim and the simplified Veterans' Administration procedures, the record falls short of establishing any likelihood of such sweeping facial invalidity. . . .

Nevertheless, it is my understanding that the Court, in reversing the lower court's preliminary injunction, does not determine the merits of the appellees' individual "as applied" claims. The complaint indicates that appellees challenged the fee limitation both on its face and as applied to them, and sought a ruling that they were entitled to a rehearing of claims processed without assistance of an attorney. . . .

The merits of these claims are difficult to evaluate on the record of affidavits and depositions developed at the preliminary injunction stage. Though the Court concludes that denial of expert representation is not "*per se* unconstitutional," given the availability of service representatives to assist the veteran and the Veterans' Administration boards' emphasis on nonadversarial procedures, on remand, the District Court is free to and should consider any individual claims that the procedures did not meet the standards we have described in this opinion. [internal quotation omitted]

■ [JUSTICE BRENNAN's dissenting opinion is omitted]

■ JUSTICE STEVENS, with whom JUSTICE BRENNAN and JUSTICE MARSHALL join, dissenting.

The Court does not appreciate the value of individual liberty. It may well be true that in the vast majority of cases a veteran does not need to employ a lawyer, and that the system of processing veterans benefit claims, by and large, functions fairly and effectively without the participation of retained counsel. Everyone agrees, however, that there are at least some complicated cases in which the services of a lawyer would be useful to the veteran and, indeed, would simplify the work of the agency by helping to organize the relevant facts and to identify the controlling issues. What is the reason for denying the veteran the right to counsel of his choice in such cases? The Court gives us two answers: First, the paternalistic interest in protecting the veteran from the consequences of his own improvidence, and second, the bureaucratic interest in minimizing the cost of administering the benefit program. I agree that both interests are legitimate, but neither provides an adequate justification for the restraint on liberty imposed by the $10–fee limitation. . . .

At the time the $10–fee limitation was enacted [in 1862], Congress presumably considered that fee reasonable. The legal work involved in preparing a veteran's claim consisted of little more than filling out an appropriate form, and, in terms of the average serviceman's base pay, a $10 fee then was roughly the equivalent of a $580 fee today. At its inception, therefore, the fee limitation had neither the purpose nor the effect of precluding the employment of reputable counsel by veterans. . . . Thus, the law that was enacted in 1864 to protect veterans from unscrupulous lawyers—those who charge excessive fees—effectively denies today's veteran access to *all* lawyers who charge reasonable fees for their services.

In my opinion, the bureaucratic interest in minimizing the cost of administration is nothing but a red herring. Congress has not prohibited lawyers from participating in the processing of claims for benefits. . . . [T]here is no reason to believe that the *agency's* cost of administration will be increased because a claimant is represented by counsel instead of appearing pro se. The informality that the Court emphasizes is desirable because it no doubt enables many veterans, or their lay representatives, to handle their claims without the assistance of counsel. But there is no reason to assume that lawyers would add confusion rather than clarity to the proceedings. . . . Only if it is assumed that the average lawyer is incompetent or unscrupulous can one rationally conclude that the efficiency of the agency's work would be undermined by allowing counsel to partici-pate whenever a veteran is willing to pay for his services. I categorically reject any such assumption. . . .

The fundamental error in the Court's analysis is its assumption that the individual's right to employ counsel of his choice in a contest with his sovereign is a kind of second-class interest that can be assigned a material value and balanced on a utilitarian scale of costs and benefits. . . . [W]e are not considering a procedural right that would involve any cost to the Government. We are concerned with the individual's right to spend his own money to obtain the advice and assistance of independent counsel in advancing his claim against the Government.

. . . If the Government, in the guise of a paternalistic interest in protecting the citizen from his own improvidence, can deny him access to independent counsel of his choice, it can change the character of our free society. Even though a dispute with the sovereign may only involve property rights, or as in this case a statutory entitlement, the citizen's right of access to the independent, private bar is itself an aspect of liberty that is of critical importance in our democracy. . . .

. . . [T]he citizen's right to consult an independent lawyer and to retain that lawyer to speak on his or her behalf is an aspect of liberty that is priceless. It should not be bargained away on the notion that a totalitarian appraisal of the mass of claims processed by the Veterans' Administration does not identify an especially high probability of error. . . .

NOTES

(1) Pressure to introduce some elements of the adversary process into veterans' benefits determinations finally bore fruit in 1988 with the pas-sage of the Veterans' Judicial Review Act, P.L. 100–687, 102 Stat. 4105. Decisions of the Board of Veterans' Appeals are made reviewable, at the behest of a claimant, before a newly constituted United States Court of Veterans Appeals. Questions of law decided by this Article I tribunal are in turn reviewable by the Federal Circuit and, ultimately, the Supreme Court. The attorneys' fees provision (since renumbered 38 U.S.C. § 5904(c)) now states: "A fee may not be charged, allowed, or paid for services of agents and attorneys with respect to services provided before the date on which the Board of Veterans' Appeals first makes a final decision in the case." Representation for a fee is allowed thereafter, but is subject to review for

reasonableness, and in any case may not exceed 20% of the past-due benefits awarded. 38 U.S.C. § 5904(c), (d). Charging fees in excess of the stipulated limits remains a crime.

(2) One way to view Mathews is as a primer for litigators in how to build a due process case. From that perspective, how well did Radiation Survivors' counsel do? Consider, on this point, the concurrence of Justice O'Connor, whose vote helped form a majority. Reading between the lines, was she telling the attorneys what they ought to have done (and perhaps might still do on remand)? Are future litigators thus able to make their Mathews showing in terms of the "risk of error inherent in the truthfinding process as applied" not (as Mathews put it) "to the generality of cases," but rather to an important subset? How should counsel go about establishing the reasonableness of their proposed subset—or the risk of error within it?

On remand, the district court certified a class of plaintiffs whose claims involved exposure to ionizing radiation. It ultimately found that this class "made an extraordinarily strong showing of the probability of erroneous denial of ionizing radiation claims under the existing system, and an equally strong showing that assistance of counsel will sharply reduce that possibility." 782 F.Supp. 1392, 1409 (1992). The Ninth Circuit reversed, concluding that it was not enough to show that these cases were complex. Rather, what had to be shown (and wasn't) was that the agency's "process has produced or is substantially likely to produce a significant number of wrongful denials. ..." National Ass'n of Radiation Survivors v. Derwinski, 994 F.2d 583, 591 (9th Cir.1992), cert. denied, 510 U.S. 1023 (1993). Does the Ninth Circuit set plaintiffs' lawyers an impossible task? Does Mathews? See Note 4, p. 864 below.

(3) The veterans disability benefit program might be seen as exemplifying Mashaw's professional treatment model (p. 850 above). The discouragement of lawyers' involvement then becomes a means of protecting against the invasive pressure of the adversarial, moral judgment model. Does passage of the Veterans' Judicial Review Act suggest that the moral judgment model is too deeply ingrained in the American psyche for any other model to achieve stability? Consider, again, Justice Frankfurter, concurring in Joint Anti–Fascist Refugee Comm. v. McGrath, 341 U.S. 123, 171–72 (1951): "Man being what he is cannot safely be trusted with complete immunity from outward responsibility in depriving others of their rights. At least such is the conviction underlying our Bill of Rights. That a conclusion satisfies one's private conscience does not attest its reliability. The validity and moral authority of a conclusion largely depend on the mode by which it was reached. ... No better instrument has been devised for arriving at truth than to give a person in jeopardy of serious loss notice of the case against him and opportunity to meet it. Nor has a better way been found for generating the feeling, so important to a popular government, that justice has been done." If you believe that the Court got the constitutional answer wrong in Walters, are you assuming that the moral judgment model is too deeply ingrained in the American conception of due process for any other model to satisfy our constitutional instincts?

NOTES ON THE THEORY OF UTILITARIAN BALANCING

(1) TODD D. RAKOFF, BROCK V. ROADWAY EXPRESS, INC., AND THE NEW LAW OF REGULATORY DUE PROCESS, 1987 Sup. Ct. Rev. 157, 162, hypothesizing the reaction of the "typical American lawyer" to the Mathews balance: "No man's liberty or property are safe when the court simply asks case by case what procedures seem worthwhile and not too costly."

(2) JERRY L. MASHAW, THE SUPREME COURT'S DUE PROCESS CALCULUS FOR ADMINISTRATIVE ADJUDICATION IN MATHEWS v. ELDRIDGE: THREE FACTORS IN SEARCH OF A THEORY OF VALUE, 44 U.Chi.L.Rev. 28, 48–49 (1976): "The Eldridge Court conceives of the values of procedure too narrowly: it views the sole purpose of procedural protections as enhancing accuracy, and thus limits its calculus to the benefits or costs that flow from correct or incorrect decisions. No attention is paid to 'process values' that might inhere in oral proceedings or to the demoralization costs that may result from the grant-withdrawal-grant-withdrawal sequence to which claimants like Eldridge are subjected. Perhaps more important, as the Court seeks to make sense of a calculus in which accuracy is the sole goal of procedure, it tends erroneously to characterize disability hearings as concerned almost exclusively with medical impairment and thus concludes that such hearings involve only medical evidence, whose reliability would be little enhanced by oral procedure. As applied by the Eldridge Court the utilitarian calculus tends, as cost-benefit analyses typically do, to 'dwarf soft variables' and to ignore complexities and ambiguities.

"The problem with a utilitarian calculus is not merely that the Court may define the relevant costs and benefits too narrowly. However broadly conceived, the calculus asks unanswerable questions. For example, what is the social value, and the social cost, of continuing disability payments until after an oral hearing for persons initially determined to be ineligible? Answers to those questions require a technique for measuring the social value and social cost of government income transfers, but no such technique exists. Even if such formidable tasks of social accounting could be accomplished, the effectiveness of oral hearings in forestalling the losses that result from erroneous terminations would remain uncertain. In the face of these pervasive indeterminacies the Eldridge Court was forced to retreat to a presumption of constitutionality."

(3) RICHARD FALLON, JR., SOME CONFUSIONS ABOUT DUE PROCESS, JUDICIAL REVIEW, AND CONSTITUTIONAL REMEDIES, 93 Colum.L.Rev. 309, 336–37 (1993): "[D]ue process doctrine has acquired a managerial focus. While abjuring responsibility to guarantee individually correct decisions, the courts have generally acknowledged their obligation to identify and police, at wholesale if not at retail, the outer bounds of governmental lawfulness. The doctrine's macro-managerial concerns are reflected in cases that insist on minimally adequate availability of judicial review to ensure that the general structure of administrative schemes is fair ... and that apply the balancing test of Mathews v. Eldridge to ensure administrative procedures adequate to achieve a tolerable average level of accuracy in the application of law to fact."

(4) CYNTHIA R. FARINA, CONCEIVING DUE PROCESS, 3 Yale J. L. & Feminism 189, 234–35 (1991): "If due process is to mark out and defend a sphere in which the individual is reliably preserved from the demands of the collective, how can the extent of the protection the individual receives turn on some calculus explicitly designed to maximize aggregate welfare? When the claim of the individual is pitted against 'the sheer magnitude of the collective interests at stake,'[1] how often will the collective good not predominate? . . . The unnaturalness of using a social welfare balance to set the content of due process protection becomes apparent . . . if we imagine employing the Mathews approach to decide what process is due parties in traditional civil adjudication. And yet, the Court's tacit recognition that due process in the regulatory context must, somehow, be differently understood is ground in an inescapable reality: Providing mass justice is a staggering task. . . . If the Court is to avoid dictating a massive reordering of state and federal fiscal priorities, it must, it seems, weigh individual claims to process against the systematic costs of proceduralization.

"To venture into social welfare accounting is, however, to crack the lid of Pandora's box. . . . What is the judiciary doing second-guessing the political branches' judgment on how much should be spend to implement a given regulatory program? 'If the greatest good for the greatest number is the test for constitutionality under the due process clause, then it is hard to escape the notion that the best evidence of social welfare will always be the judgment of the legislature or its delegate.'[2] To engage, at this stage of the [due process] analysis, in an inevitably ad hoc and standardless assessment of the importance of the individual interest, and to use that assessment as the basis for restructuring administrative behavior, seems precisely the undisciplined judicial interference in local and national governance that the Court embraced entitlement analysis to avoid."

(5) LAURENCE H. TRIBE, AMERICAN CONSTITUTIONAL LAW 673–74 (2d ed. 1988): "[I]n centering its . . . mode of analysis around the instrumental importance of process, the Court has relaxed procedural protections in two important ways. First, by focusing on the reduction of error to the exclusion of more intrinsic concerns, the Court has eroded at least part of the traditional rationale for insisting that, with very few exceptions, the hearing required by due process *precede* rather than *follow* the deprivation at issue. A prior hearing had been required by the traditional conception of procedural due process under the precept that one should be able to continue living in quiet enjoyment of liberty or property unless and until there had been a fair determination that the state is entitled to intrude upon that situation of repose. But, as the more recent conception that the predominant value of process is accuracy has become ascendant, a *post*-deprivation remedy has more often sufficed to meet due process objections. . . . Second, the Court's [Matthews] holding that the degree and type of procedural protection that is due can be determined by weighing . . . not only overlooks the unquantifiable human interest in receiving decent

---

1. Richard Saphire, Specifying Due Process Values: Toward a More Responsive Approach to Procedural Protection, 127 U. Pa. L. Rev. 111, 155 (1978).

2. Jerry L. Mashaw, Due Process in the Administrative State 152 (1985).

treatment, but also provides the Court a facile means to justify the most cursory procedures by altering the relative weights to be accorded each of the three factors."

NOTES ON THE PRACTICE OF UTILITARIAN BALANCING

Is there a mandatory minimum of process?

(1) GOSS V. LOPEZ, 419 U.S. 565 (1975): Like other states, Ohio has a statutory scheme for compulsory education of children up to a certain age. One section authorized the suspension of a student for up to 10 days with no process beyond a letter from the principal to the student's parents explaining why the action had been taken. In a 5–4 opinion written by Justice White, the Court held that the lack of any pre-suspension process rendered the statute unconstitutional. Deprivation of the statutory entitlement to an education for up to 10 days is not de minimis. Moreover, suspension can tarnish a student's reputation, thus depriving him of a liberty interest. As to the process required, however, the Court departed strikingly from prior cases. All that is constitutionally required, in light of the interests implicated, the desire to avoid error, and the functional requisites of the institutional setting, is "an informal give-and-take between student and disciplinarian." The student must be given "notice of the charges against him and, if he denies them, an explanation of the evidence the authorities have and an opportunity to present his side of the story." (If the student's conduct creates an immediate threat of institutional disruption, the school can remove him first as long as it provides an opportunity for discussion immediately afterward.)

The opinion sparked speculation that "Goss process" represented the due process minimum: a four line dialogue containing reasons ("You started the food fight in the cafeteria."); opportunity for denial ("No way!"); explanation of evidence ("Five people saw you."); opportunity to respond ("No way!!! I was at my locker when it happened.").[1] This would seem the minimally defensible process that is "due" whenever government contemplates a deprivation of liberty or property. How burdensome could such skeletal process be?

In GRAY PANTHERS V. SCHWEIKER, 652 F.2d 146 (D.C.Cir.1980), an advocacy organization for elder people challenged the statutory provisions under which the only process provided to adjudicate denied Medicare claims of less than $100 was a written, internal review by the private insurance carrier. The court, Judge Patricia Wald writing, concluded that the Constitution required an oral hearing at some point. "To date, the Supreme Court has never expressly approved as meeting due process hearing requirements a procedure in which a claimant has been finally deprived of the right to government benefits without affording that individual an opportunity to appeal personally and orally to the decisionmaker.... Ambiguities which are not readily apparent on the face of a document can be disclosed and clarified with a few moments of oral exchange between the

---

1. An in-class experiment by one of your editors proved that Goss process can take as little as 12 seconds to accomplish.

individual and the decisionmaker.... An oral hearing requirement ... serves to ensure that decisionmakers recognize that their decisions affect the lives of human beings, a fact that is often obscured by a jumble of papers and depersonalized identification numbers.... [And] no other procedure so effectively fosters a belief that one has been dealt with fairly, even if there remains a disagreement with the result....

"We are convinced that simplified, streamlined, informal oral procedures are available which would be responsive to the concerns of Congress for efficiency and low cost yet which would provide claimants with the right to participate in decisions affecting their interests in cases where such participation is critical."

The case was remanded with directions to the parties to assist the district court in framing an order that would meet these criteria. When the case returned two years later, the court of appeals, Judge Mikva now writing, found the work not yet complete. GRAY PANTHERS V. SCHWEIKER, 716 F.2d 23 (D.C.Cir.1983). In part the problems were due to the government's failure fully to cooperate in the remanded proceedings. But in part they stemmed from the difficulty of constructing procedures that would be effective and yet reasonable in cost. "As a compromise, the Department has proposed a toll-free telephone system through which beneficiaries eventually would be able to speak with a carrier employee who is familiar with the particular facts of their disputed claim.... [W]e believe that the toll-free telephone system proposed by the Secretary—when combined with ... improved notice ... and the full written review procedures that currently exist—meets the dictates of due process for most of the claims at issue in this litigation.... [A] face-to-face meeting with the decisionmaker is not required for every claim. The telephone system will give many beneficiaries a chance to communicate orally with a carrier employee who is familiar with their particular claim, thereby improving the process somewhat for those beneficiaries who have trouble when they rely solely on written submissions or for whom a telephone is the most accessible means of communication....

"[T]he Gray Panthers argue that the proposed telephone system is overly burdensome on the elderly and infirm population with which we are concerned. Not only is it expected that 40% of the beneficiaries attempting to reach the toll-free number will receive a busy signal on their first try, but special problems exist for many beneficiaries trying to use a telephone because they have difficulty hearing or trouble comprehending a fast-paced telephone conversation. We do not mean to denigrate the concerns that the Gray Panthers raise—indeed, in response to these criticisms, we expect good faith efforts to be made by the Secretary to improve the telephone system in all ways that are feasible and practicable. But however much we might prefer, as a policy matter, to have face-to-face hearings mandated for all beneficiaries, we cannot say that the flexible requirements of due process are not satisfied by the complete procedural system that soon will be in place—including an improved written notice, the toll-free telephone system, and full written review procedures."

(2) The Supreme Court's second venture into procedural due process in the public school system involved corporal punishment. In that case, although

the Court agreed that paddling deprived the victim of a constitutional liberty interest, the majority held that *no* process (not even the Goss minimum) was due at the school level—either before or after paddling. The case is considered in full at p. 888 below.

The Use and Misuse of Data

(3) The Mathews "calculus" has been expressed by the following formula: The constitution demands more process (or, earlier process) only when

Interest of the claimant in avoiding interim harm	x	Increased accuracy of additional procedure	>	Government interest in avoiding more process

Did the Mathews Court really intend to adopt a cost-benefit methodology? Or did Justice Powell (and Judge Friendly in his influential article, "Some Kind of Hearing", see p. 849 above) mean instead something more akin to the various "balancing tests" encountered in other areas of constitutional law, such as the First Amendment? Would the latter have been more judicially manageable than the former? More predictable?

(4) Shouldn't the parties provide—and the courts insist on—some actual data? Look back at the section of Mathews in which the Court discusses error rates. Those percentages expressed as numbers of cases look approximately like the following: Of 1000 cases terminating benefits, 122 are eventually reversed (12.2%). Of these reversals, 91 come at the post-termination administrative reconsideration; the remaining 31 come at the post-termination evidentiary hearing. These 31 are from a group of 60 that go to hearing (58%). They represent 3% of the original set of 1000.

Which is the relevant error rate: 31 of 1000 total terminations? Or 31 of 60 cases that go to hearing? Or are these data like trying to compare apples and onions because we don't know how many termination appeals are abandoned at each step of the process (or are never appealed at all) and we don't know why. Do malingerers give up early, so that those going to evidentiary hearing are disproportionately the "good" cases? Or do many disabled persons give up because they lack the financial and emotional resources to pursue a multi-step bureaucratic process that takes a year to complete? How could we find the answers to these questions? Can a court responsibly conduct the Mathews balance without knowing the answers?

VAN HARKEN v. CITY OF CHICAGO, 103 F.3d 1346 (7th Cir.), cert. denied, 520 U.S. 1241 (1997): In 1987, Illinois joined a number of other states in authorizing municipalities to decriminalize parking violations. Chicago exercised this authority. So long as the violation was technically criminal, due process required safeguards consistent with conviction of other misdemeanors. Once the violation became merely civil, the city wanted to use truncated procedures. The parking ticket is deemed prima facie evidence of a violation. The owner can either pay the fine (which cannot exceed $100) or challenge the ticket in writing or in person. The police officer is not required to appear; the ticket is treated as an affidavit. Thus, the only witness will usually be the vehicle owner, whom the hearing officer is instructed to cross-examine searchingly. The hearing officer can (but is not required to) subpoena witnesses, including the police officer. If the owner's challenge is denied, he can seek review in the Circuit Court of Cook County by paying the normal filing fee: $200. Consistent with due process? Yes, according to the panel opinion written by Judge Posner. The supposed judicial review was illusory but unnecessary because the basic procedure complied with the Mathews test:

"The costs of procedural safeguards are fairly straightforward, which is not to say easy to quantify. For example, the cost of requiring the police officer who writes the ticket to appear in person at every hearing at which the ticket is challenged—one of the procedural safeguards that the plaintiffs in this case claim is required by the due process clause—depends on the number and length of hearings, the average time the police officer requires to get to and from the hearing, the reduction in his productivity from the interruption of his normal workday that attendance at such hearings requires, and the expense to the City of hiring additional policemen. We were told at argument without contradiction that the City issues 4 million parking tickets a year, of which 5 percent are challenged (200,000), a third of those in person rather than by mail and thus requiring an oral hearing (67,000). If the ticketing officer were required to attend, the number of hearings requested would undoubtedly be higher, because respondents would think it likely that the officer wouldn't show up—a frequent occurrence at hearings on moving violations. Suppose the number of hearings would be double what it is under the challenged procedures (that is, would be 134,000), but the police would show up at only half, putting us back to 67,000; and suppose that a hearing at which a police officer showed up cost him on average 2 hours away from his other work. Then this procedural safeguard for which the plaintiffs are contending would cost the City 134,000 police hours a year, the equivalent of 67 full-time police officers at 2,000 hours a year per officer. In addition, more hearing officers would be required, at some additional cost to the City, because each hearing would be longer as a result of the presence of another live witness. And all these are simply the monetary costs. Acquittals of violators due solely to the ticketing officer's failure to appear would undermine the deterrent efficacy of the parking laws and deprive the City of revenues to which it was entitled as a matter of substantive justice.

"The benefits of a procedural safeguard are even trickier to estimate than the costs. The benefits depend on the harm that the safeguard will avert in cases in which it prevents an erroneous result and the likelihood that it will prevent an erroneous result. We know the harm here to the innocent car owner found 'guilty' and forced to pay a fine: it is the fine, and it can be anywhere from $10 to $100, for an average of $55. We must ask how likely it is that error would be averted if the ticketing officer were present at the hearing and therefore subject to cross-examination. Suppose that in his absence the probability of an erroneous determination that the respondent really did commit a parking violation is 5 percent, and the officer's presence would cut that probability in half, to 2.5 percent. Then the average saving to the innocent respondent from this additional procedural safeguard would be only $1.38 ($55 x .025)—a trivial amount.

"These calculations are inexact, to say the least; but they help to show, what is pretty obvious without them, that the benefits of requiring the police officer to appear at every hearing are unlikely to exceed the costs."

Mass justice by hypothetical?

Does Mathews balancing apply outside the administrative context?

As the introduction to the Chapter observed, due process in its procedural dimension applies to an astonishing range of government decision-making. Is the Mathews calculus the methodology for determining what the Constitution requires in all of these contexts? What alternative sources can the Court look to in identifying what process is due?

(5) *The Process of Criminal Conviction.* MEDINA v. CALIFORNIA, 505 U.S. 437 (1992), rejected the use of Mathews to determine the constitutionality of procedures in the criminal context. Stating that "the Mathews balancing test was first conceived to address due process claims arising in the context of administrative law," the Court held that the appropriate inquiry, in criminal trial situations, is whether "some principle of justice so rooted in the traditions and conscience of our people as to be ranked as fundamental" has been offended. "[B]ecause the States have considerable expertise in matters of criminal procedure and the criminal process is grounded in centuries of common-law tradition, it is appropriate to exercise substantial deference to legislative judgments in this area." See, e.g., Coe v. Bell, 209 F.3d 815 (6th Cir.2000) (rejecting Mathews as the method for determining whether a state could constitutionally place on the defendant under sentence of death the burden of proving, by a preponderance, that he was not competent to be executed).

(6) *Civil Curtailment of Liberty.* PARHAM v. J.R., 442 U.S. 584 (1979), challenged the constitutionality of Georgia's procedures for allowing parents to commit their minor children to a mental health facility. Chief Justice Burger's opinion for the Court used Mathews to assess various aspects of the procedures, and found most (but not all) acceptable. Justice Stewart concurred in the judgment, using largely an historical analysis of parental control in this area. Justice Brennan, in a dissent joined by Justices Marshall and Stevens, would have found more aspects of Georgia's scheme unconstitutional, using an assessment of the interests of the child, the parents and the state that only vaguely resembled the Mathews calculus. Parham followed shortly on the heels of ADDINGTON v. TEXAS, 441 U.S. 418 (1979), in which the Chief Justice had invoked the Mathews calculus briefly to hold, for a unanimous Court, that due process requires use of an evidentiary standard at least as stringent as "clear and convincing evidence" in order to involuntarily commit a person to a mental health facility.

(7) *Process in Civil Adjudication.* It is somewhat less clear when Mathews is appropriate to analyze a challenge to aspects of civil adjudication. In UNITED STATES v. JAMES DANIEL GOOD REAL PROPERTY, 510 U.S. 43 (1993), the Court employed the Mathews calculus to confirm its view that the government could not constitutionally use an ex parte civil forfeiture proceeding to seize real property, absent exigent circumstances. Only Justices Rehnquist and Scalia, in dissent, argued against the use of a methodology conceived for "modern administrative law." Cf. Pacific Mutual Life Ins. Co. v. Haslip, 499 U.S. 1 (1991) (sustaining jury's punitive damages from due process challenge, using history and tradition; only Justice O'Connor's

dissent would have used Mathews.) Recently, however, DUSENBERY V. UNITED STATES, 534 U.S. 161 (2002), distinguished James Daniel Good. While Dusenbery was in prison on federal drug charges, the FBI instigated a statutory administrative procedure to forfeit cash seized during the search of his residence. To fulfill the statutory requirement of sending notice of the proceeding to each person who appeared to have an interest in the property, the FBI sent notice by certified mail to the prison, to the residence where he was arrested, and to an address in the town where his mother lived. Receiving no response within the allotted time, it turned the cash over to the U.S. Marshals Service. Dusenbery claimed he never received any of the notices, and argued that due process required the government to verify receipt of notice. Chief Justice Rehnquist, for the Court: "[W]e have never viewed Mathews as announcing an all-embracing test for deciding due process claims." Rather, when the issue is adequacy of notice, the appropriate test is from Mullane v. Central Hanover Bank & Trust Co., 339 U.S. 306 (1950), which determined the constitutional sufficiency of notice to beneficiaries on judicial settlement of accounts by the trustee of a common trust fund. That test—was the method of notice "reasonably calculated, under all the circumstances, to apprise interested parties of the pendency of the action and afford them an opportunity to present their objections?"—is satisfied here. The four dissenting justices agreed that Mullane was the appropriate precedent, but disagreed with its application on the facts.

(8) *Military Justice.* WEISS V. UNITED STATES, 510 U.S. 163 (1994), posed several constitutional challenges to the courts martial system. (For the Appointments Clause portion of the case, see p. 176 n.5 above.) In the portion relevant here, Weiss argued that the lack of a fixed term of office for military judges violated due process. Because "the Constitution contemplates that Congress has plenary control over rights, duties, and responsibilities in the framework of the Military Establishment, including regulations, procedures, and remedies related to military discipline," neither the Mathews calculus nor the Medina approach (note 5 above) applies. Rather, the question is whether the factors militating in favor of fixed terms for military judges "are so extraordinarily weighty as to overcome the balance struck by Congress." Chief Justice Rehnquist's opinion pointed out that a fixed term of office for a military judge "has never been a part of the military justice tradition." "Courts-martial . . . have been conducted in this country for over 200 years without the presence of a tenured judge." No one dissented from this conclusion.

(9) *Family Law.* LASSITER V. DEPARTMENT OF SOCIAL SERV., 452 U.S. 18 (1981), presented the question whether due process requires the state to provide counsel for an indigent parent in a proceeding to terminate her parental rights. Justice Stewart's opinion for the Court answered the question using the Mathews calculus—but the answer turned out to be "It depends." The parent's interest in the decision to terminate parental status is always extremely high; where criminal charges are also involved, it becomes even greater. The State shares with the parent an interest in a correct decision, and has a relatively weak pecuniary interest in avoiding the expense of appointed counsel and the cost of the lengthened proceedings his presence may cause; in some cases, though, it might have a stronger interest in

preserving informal procedures. Finally, the complexity of the proceeding and the incapacity of the uncounseled parent could be—but would not always be—great enough to make the risk of an erroneous deprivation of the parent's rights insupportably high. In the circumstances of *this* case, due process did not require appointment of counsel. The termination petition contained no allegations of neglect or abuse upon which criminal charges could be based; no expert witnesses testified; the case presented no specially troublesome points of law; and the presence of counsel could not have made a determinative difference for petitioner. However, in a case in which the parent's interests were at their strongest, the State's interests were at their weakest, and the risks of error were at their peak, the Mathews calculus would require that counsel be appointed. Justices Blackmun, Brennan and Marshall agreed with using Mathews, but dissented strenuously from the majority's case-by-case approach. They would have held that the state is always required to provide counsel to indigent parents threatened with termination proceedings.

Only Justice Stevens challenged the fundamental methodology: "The analysis employed in Mathews v. Eldridge, in which the Court balanced the costs and benefits of different procedural mechanisms for allocating a finite quantity of material resources among competing claimants, is an appropriate method of determining what process is due in property cases. Meeting the Court on its own terms, Justice Blackmun demonstrates that the Mathews v. Eldridge analysis requires the appointment of counsel in this type of case. I agree with his conclusion, but I would take one further step.

"In my opinion the reasons supporting the conclusion that the Due Process Clause of the Fourteenth Amendment entitles the defendant in a criminal case to representation by counsel apply with equal force to a case of this kind. The issue is one of fundamental fairness, not of weighing the pecuniary costs against the societal benefits. Accordingly, even if the costs to the State were not relatively insignificant but rather were just as great as the costs of providing prosecutors, judges, and defense counsel to ensure the fairness of criminal proceedings, I would reach the same result in this category of cases. For the value of protecting our liberty from deprivation by the State without due process of law is priceless."

SANTOSKY V. KRAMER, 455 U.S. 745 (1982), confirmed the relevance of Mathews in the family law area by using the calculus to strike down New York's use of the "fair preponderance of the evidence" standard of proof in proceedings to terminate parental rights for neglect. Justice Blackmun, for the 5–4 Court, concluded that the standard does not fairly allocate the risk of error between the state and the parent. Due process requires states to use at least the "clear and convincing evidence" standard. Justice Rehnquist's opinion for the four dissenters cited Mathews several times for general propositions, but did not use the calculus itself to conclude that the state's process was fundamentally fair and should be given deference.

What about regulatory deprivations of traditional property?

In an article written before he was appointed to the D.C. Circuit, Stephen Williams argued that a fatal flaw of the new due process jurisprudence was that, by spreading constitutional protection across the range of benefits and advantageous relationships with government offered by the regulatory state, the Court would dilute constitutional protection for traditional property. See Stephen F. Williams, Liberty and Property: The Problem of Government Benefits, 12 J. Legal. Stud. 3, 11–13 (1983). Are his fears confirmed by the following case?

(10) BROCK V. ROADWAY EXPRESS, INC., 481 U.S. 252 (1987): Section 405 of the Surface Transportation Assistance Act of 1982, 49 U.S.C.App. § 2305, protects trucking industry employees from being discharged for reporting safety violations, or for refusing to drive a vehicle that does not comply with federal or state safety regulations. On finding "reasonable cause to believe" that a discharge was retaliatory, the Secretary of Labor can issue an order requiring reinstatement. Roadway fired Hufstetler, alleging that he had disabled lights on his truck in order to obtain extra pay while waiting for repairs. Hufstetler grieved his discharge through the arbitration procedures of his union's collective bargaining agreement with Roadway, and lost. He then filed a complaint of retaliatory discharge under § 405. OSHA, the agency charged with investigating § 405 claims, notified Roadway of the complaint and interviewed Hufstetler and other Roadway employees. As provided in the Act, Roadway had an opportunity to meet with the field investigator and submit a written statement detailing the basis for its actions. It was not, however, given the names of the interviewed employees or the substance of their statements. Subsequently, the Regional Administrator issued a preliminary decision finding reasonable cause and ordering Hufstetler's immediate reinstatement with back pay. At that point, Roadway had a statutory right to request an evidentiary hearing, but this would not have stayed the reinstatement order. Instead, the Company went to court asserting that the procedures deprived it of its property (the contractual right to discharge for cause, as provided in the collective bargaining agreement) without due process. The government conceded that this was indeed a property interest.

Justice Marshall announced the judgment of the Court and wrote for himself and Justices Blackmun, Powell and O'Connor. He used the Mathews calculus—but with a twist: "We begin by accepting as substantial the Government's interests in promoting highway safety and protecting employees from retaliatory discharge. Roadway does not question the legislative determination that noncompliance with applicable state and federal safety regulations in the transportation industry is sufficiently widespread to warrant enactment of specific protective legislation encouraging employees to report violations. 'Random inspections by Federal and State law enforcement officials in various parts of the country [had] uniformly found widespread violation of safety regulations,' and § 405 was designed to assist in combating the 'increasing number of deaths, injuries, and property damage due to commercial motor vehicle accidents.' 128 Cong.Rec. 32509, 32510 (1982) (remarks of Sen. Danforth . . .).

"We also agree with the District Court that Roadway's interest in controlling the makeup of its workforce is substantial. In assessing the competing interests, however, the District Court failed to consider another private interest affected by the Secretary's decision: Hufstetler's interest in not being discharged for having complained about the allegedly unsafe condition of Roadway's trucks. This Court has previously acknowledged the 'severity of depriving a person of the means of livelihood.' Cleveland Board of Education v. Loudermill, 470 U.S. 532, 543 (1985) [p. 872 below] ... In light of the injurious effect a retaliatory discharge can have on an employee's financial status and prospects for alternative interim employment, the employee's substantial interest in retaining his job must be considered along with the employer's interest in determining the constitutional adequacy of the § 405 procedures. The statute reflects a careful balancing of 'the strong Congressional policy that persons reporting health and safety violations should not suffer because of this action' and the 'need to assure that employers are provided protection from unjustified refusal by their employees to perform legitimate assigned tasks.' 128 Cong.Rec. 32510 (1982).

"Reviewing this legislative balancing of interests, we conclude that the employer is sufficiently protected by procedures that do not include an evidentiary hearing before the discharged employee is temporarily reinstated. So long as the pre-reinstatement procedures establish a reliable 'initial check against mistaken decisions,' Loudermill, above, at 545, and complete and expeditious review is available, then the preliminary reinstatement provision of § 405 fairly balances the competing interests of the Government, the employer, and the employee, and a prior evidentiary hearing is not otherwise constitutionally required.

"We thus confront the crucial question whether the Secretary's procedures implementing § 405 reliably protect against the risk of erroneous deprivation, even if only temporary, of an employer's right to discharge an employee. We conclude that minimum due process for the employer in this context requires notice of the employee's allegations, notice of the substance of the relevant supporting evidence, an opportunity to submit a written response, and an opportunity to meet with the investigator and present statements from rebuttal witnesses. The presentation of the employer's witnesses need not be formal, and cross-examination of the employee's witnesses need not be afforded at this stage of the proceedings....

"Roadway contends that, absent an opportunity for the employer to confront and cross-examine the witnesses whose statements support the employee's complaint, the Secretary's preliminary procedures will produce unreliable decisions. We conclude, however, that as a general rule the employer's interest is adequately protected without the right of confrontation and cross-examination.... Providing the employer the relevant supporting evidence and a chance to meet informally with the investigator, to submit statements from witnesses and to argue its position orally, satisfies the constitutional requirement of due process for the temporary deprivation under § 405. Each of these procedures contributes significantly to the reliability of the Secretary's preliminary decision without extending inordinately the period in which the employee must suffer unemployment. To allow the employer and employee an opportunity to test the credibility of opposing witnesses during the investigation would not increase the reliability of the preliminary decision sufficiently to justify the additional delay. Moreover, the primary function of the investigator is not to make credibility determinations, but rather to determine simply whether reasonable cause exists to believe that the employee has been discharged for engaging in protected conduct. Ensuring the employer a meaningful opportunity to respond to the employee's complaint and supporting evidence maintains the principal focus on the employee's conduct and the employer's reason for his discharge. Final assessments of the credibility of supporting witnesses are appropriately reserved for the administrative law judge, before whom an opportunity for complete cross-examination of opposing witnesses is provided."

Justice Brennan concurred in part and dissented in part; he believed Roadway was entitled to "an opportunity to present contrary testimony and evidence and to cross-examine witnesses" before the reinstatement order issues. Also concurring and dissenting in part, Justice White, joined by the Chief Justice and Justice Scalia, would not have required the agency to disclose the witnesses' names and statements. "Given the purpose of § 405, I would not ignore the strong interest the Government may have in particular cases in not turning over the supporting information . . . prior to conducting the full administrative hearing."

Yet again, Justice Stevens, in dissent, was the sole voice against the Mathews methodology: "The plurality's willingness to sacrifice due process to the Secretary's obscure suggestion of necessity reveals the serious flaws in its due process analysis. It is wrong to approach the due process analysis in each case by asking anew what procedures seem worthwhile and not too costly. Unless a case falls within a recognized exception, we should adhere to the strongest presumption that the Government may not take away life, liberty, or property before making a meaningful hearing available. . . . Such a hearing necessarily includes the creation of a public record developed in a proceeding in which hostile witnesses are confronted and cross-examined.

"Traditions of fairness that have been long honored in American jurisprudence support the strongest possible presumption against *ex parte* proceedings. There is no support for the plurality's approval of the entry of a reinstatement order of indefinite duration based on uncross-examined and untested evidence."

(11) TODD D. RAKOFF, BROCK V. ROADWAY EXPRESS, INC. AND THE NEW LAW OF REGULATORY DUE PROCESS, 1987 Sup. Ct. Rev. 157, 184–85, explores "the fundamental reinterpretation of the Mathews test which occurs in Brock [when the Court states that] 'the employee's . . . interest . . . must be considered along with the employer's interest in determining the constitutional adequacy of the . . . procedures.' For there is no 'must' about this matter if the evil to which the constitutional provision is addressed implicates only one of these interests; if, that is, public deprivation of an interest is different from private deprivation. But Justice Marshall sees them as equal in kind and capable of being offset against each other. Because employees in the transportation industry 'may be threatened with discharge for cooperating with enforcement agencies, they need express protection against retaliation for reporting these violations.' Government coercion of employers will prevent employer coercion of employees. Thus, while government may have purely administrative interests of its own in the efficient conduct of its business, or may embrace diffuse public interests in, for example, highway safety, it may also be involved in reallocating

rights—including procedural rights—in order to achieve a fair balance between conflicting private interests.

"The Mathews test, as written, conceived of government as a provider of benefits or organizer of institutions, so that the government's interest, quasi-proprietary at least in part, stood on one side, while the private beneficiary stood on the other.... By contrast, the Mathews test as rephrased and then applied in Brock posits government as having a largely regulatory concern, and supposes that more than one private interest is affected by its decision. The details of Justice Marshall's argument are embraced by only four Justices, but this central point also appears in Justice White's opinion for a total of seven. On its face, the Court shows that it understands itself to be dealing with a different social situation. In this latter role, government is an umpire rather than an interested partici-pant. Despite the effort to use similar words, this is a far different model from the government-versus-private-beneficiary dynamics incorporated by implication in the original Mathews test."

(12) In UNITED STATES V. JAMES DANIEL GOOD REAL PROPERTY, 510 U.S. 43 (1993), the case determining the constitutionality of ex parte civil forfeiture of real property in Note 7 above, Chief Justice Rehnquist, in a dissent joined by Justice Scalia, argued that historical practice, rather than the Mathews calculus, was the appropriate methodology: "I reject the majori-ty's expansive application of Mathews.... [T]he Mathews balancing test was first conceived to address due process claims arising in the context of modern administrative law. No historical practices existed in this context for the Court to consider." Based on precedent in tax and other punitive and remedial areas, they would have upheld the constitutionality of ex parte forfeiture even absent exigent circumstances.

b.   THE RELEVANCE OF STATUTORY PROCESS TERMS

Cleveland Board of Education v. Loudermill

Supreme Court of the United States, 1985.
470 U.S. 532.

■ JUSTICE WHITE delivered the opinion of the Court.

In these cases we consider what pretermination process must be accorded a public employee who can be discharged only for cause.

I

In 1979 the Cleveland Board of Education ... hired respondent James Loudermill as a security guard. On his job application, Loudermill stated that he had never been convicted of a felony. Eleven months later, as part of a routine examination of his employment records, the Board discovered that in fact Loudermill had been convicted of grand larceny in 1968. By letter dated November 3, 1980, the Board's Business Manager informed Loudermill that he had been dismissed because of his dishonesty in filling out the employment application. Loudermill was not afforded an opportuni-ty to respond to the charge of dishonesty or to challenge his dismissal. On

November 13, the Board adopted a resolution officially approving the discharge.

[Under Ohio law, Loudermill was a "classified civil servant" who could be terminated only for cause. Loudermill appealed to the Cleveland Civil Service Commission, which held a hearing on January 29, 1981. Loudermill argued that he had thought that his larceny conviction was a misdemeanor rather than a felony, and the referee recommended reinstatement. However, in July, the full Commission upheld the dismissal. Loudermill's attorneys were advised of the result by mail on August 21. Loudermill sued, alleging that the relevant statute, Ohio Rev. Code Ann. § 124.34, was unconstitutional on its face for not providing an opportunity to respond to the charges prior to removal. He also alleged that the failure to give prompt postremoval hearings made the provision unconstitutional as applied. The District Court dismissed for failure to state a claim on which relief could be granted. A second case, involving Richard Donnelly, a bus mechanic for the Parma, Ohio, Board of Education, presented similar facts. Donnelly was reinstated after "a year of wrangling," but without backpay.]

... [T]he cases were consolidated for appeal. A divided panel of the Court of Appeals for the Sixth Circuit reversed in part and remanded.... [I]t concluded that the compelling private interest in retaining employment, combined with the value of presenting evidence prior to dismissal, outweighed the added administrative burden of a pretermination hearing. With regard to the alleged deprivation of liberty, and Loudermill's 9–month wait for an administrative decision, the court affirmed the District Court, finding no constitutional violation....

We ... now affirm in all respects.

II

Respondents' federal constitutional claim depends on their having had a property right in continued employment. If they did, the State could not deprive them of this property without due process.

Property interests are not created by the Constitution, "they are created and their dimensions are defined by existing rules or understandings that stem from an independent source such as state law...." Board of Regents v. Roth. The Ohio statute plainly creates such an interest. Respondents were "classified civil service employees," Ohio Rev.Code Ann. § 124.11 (1984), entitled to retain their positions "during good behavior and efficient service," who could not be dismissed "except ... for ... misfeasance, malfeasance, or nonfeasance in office," § 124.34. The statute plainly supports the conclusion, reached by both lower courts, that respondents possessed property rights in continued employment....[1]

---

1. The Cleveland Board of Education now asserts that Loudermill had no property right under state law because he obtained his employment by lying on the application. It argues that had Loudermill answered truthfully he would not have been hired. He therefore lacked a "legitimate claim of entitlement" to the position. Brief for Petitioner in No. 83–1362, pp. 14–15.

... [W]e must reject this submission.... The Board cannot escape its constitutional obligations by rephrasing the basis for termination as a reason why Loudermill should not have been hired in the first place.

The Parma Board argues, however, that the property right is defined by, and conditioned on, the legislature's choice of procedures for its deprivation. The Board stresses that in addition to specifying the grounds for termination, the statute sets out procedures by which termination may take place.[2] The procedures were adhered to in these cases. According to petitioner, "[t]o require additional procedures would in effect expand the scope of the property interest itself."

This argument, which was accepted by the District Court, has its genesis in the plurality opinion in Arnett v. Kennedy, 416 U.S. 134 (1974). Arnett involved a challenge by a former federal employee to the procedures by which he was dismissed. The plurality reasoned that where the legislation conferring the substantive right also sets out the procedural mechanism for enforcing that right, the two cannot be separated:

> The employee's statutorily defined right is not a guarantee against removal without cause in the abstract, but such a guarantee as enforced by the procedures which Congress has designated for the determination of cause.
>
> ... [W]here the grant of a substantive right is inextricably intertwined with the limitations on the procedures which are to be employed in determining that right, a litigant in the position of appellee must take the bitter with the sweet. Id., at 152–154.

This view garnered three votes in Arnett, but was specifically rejected by the other six Justices. See id., at 166–167 (Powell, J., joined by Blackmun, J.,); id., at 177–178, 185 (White, J.,); id., at 211 (Marshall, J., joined by Douglas and Brennan, JJ.)....

... [T]he "bitter with the sweet" approach misconceives the constitutional guarantee. If a clearer holding is needed, we provide it today. The point is straight-forward: the Due Process Clause provides that certain substantive rights—life, liberty, and property—cannot be deprived except pursuant to constitutionally adequate procedures. The categories of substance and procedure are distinct. Were the rule otherwise, the Clause would be reduced to a mere tautology. "Property" cannot be defined by the procedures provided for its deprivation any more than can life or liberty. The right to due process "is conferred, not by legislative grace, but by constitutional guarantee. While the legislature may elect not to confer a property interest in [public] employment, it may not constitutionally authorize the deprivation of such an interest, once conferred, without appropriate procedural safeguards." Arnett v. Kennedy, 416 U.S., at 167 (Powell, J., concurring in part and concurring in result in part).

---

2. After providing for dismissal only for cause, § 124.34 states that the dismissed employee is to be provided with a copy of the order of removal giving the reasons therefor. Within 10 days of the filing of the order with the Director of Administrative Services, the employee may file a written appeal with the State Personnel Board of Review or the Commission. "In the event such an appeal is filed, the board or commission shall forthwith notify the appointing authority and shall hear, or appoint a trial board to hear, such appeal within thirty days from and after its filing with the board or commission, and it may affirm, disaffirm, or modify the judgment of the appointing authority." Either side may obtain review of the Commission's decision in the State Court of Common Pleas.

In short, once it is determined that the Due Process Clause applies, "the question remains what process is due." Morrissey v. Brewer, 408 U.S. 471, 481 (1972). The answer to that question is not to be found in the Ohio statute.

III

An essential principle of due process is that a deprivation of life, liberty, or property "be preceded by notice and opportunity for hearing appropriate to the nature of the case." Mullane v. Central Hanover Bank & Trust Co., 339 U.S. 306, 313 (1950). We have described "the root requirement" of the Due Process Clause as being "that an individual be given an opportunity for a hearing *before* he is deprived of any significant property interest."[3] Boddie v. Connecticut, 401 U.S. 371, 379 (1971). This principle requires "some kind of a hearing" prior to the discharge of an employee who has a constitutionally protected property interest in his employment. . . .

The need for some form of pretermination hearing, recognized in these cases, is evident from a balancing of the competing interests at stake. These are the private interest in retaining employment, the governmental interest in the expeditious removal of unsatisfactory employees and the avoidance of administrative burdens, and the risk of an erroneous termination. See Mathews v. Eldridge.

First, the significance of the private interest in retaining employment cannot be gainsaid. We have frequently recognized the severity of depriving a person of the means of livelihood. While a fired worker may find employment elsewhere, doing so will take some time and is likely to be burdened by the questionable circumstances under which he left his previous job.

Second, some opportunity for the employee to present his side of the case is recurringly of obvious value in reaching an accurate decision. Dismissals for cause will often involve factual disputes. Even where the facts are clear, the appropriateness or necessity of the discharge may not be; in such cases, the only meaningful opportunity to invoke the discretion of the decisionmaker is likely to be before the termination takes effect. See Goss v. Lopez.[4]

The cases before us illustrate these considerations. Both respondents had plausible arguments to make that might have prevented their discharge. The fact that the Commission saw fit to reinstate Donnelly suggests that an error might have been avoided had he been provided an opportunity to make his case to the Board. As for Loudermill, given the Commis-

---

3. There are, of course, some situations in which a postdeprivation hearing will satisfy due process requirements. See North American Cold Storage Co. v. Chicago, 211 U.S. 306 (1908).

4. This is not to say that where state conduct is entirely discretionary the Due Process Clause is brought into play. See Meachum v. Fano, 427 U.S. 215, 228 (1976). Nor

is it to say that a person can insist on a hearing in order to argue that the decisionmaker should be lenient and depart from legal requirements. See Dixon v. Love, 431 U.S. 105, 114 (1977). The point is that where there is an entitlement, a prior hearing facilitates the consideration of whether a permissible course of action is also an appropriate one. . . .

sion's ruling we cannot say that the discharge was mistaken. Nonetheless, in light of the referee's recommendation, neither can we say that a fully informed decisionmaker might not have exercised its discretion and decided not to dismiss him, notwithstanding its authority to do so. In any event, the termination involved arguable issues,[5] and the right to a hearing does not depend on a demonstration of certain success.

The governmental interest in immediate termination does not outweigh these interests. As we shall explain, affording the employee an opportunity to respond prior to termination would impose neither a significant administrative burden nor intolerable delays. Furthermore, the employer shares the employee's interest in avoiding disruption and erroneous decisions; and until the matter is settled, the employer would continue to receive the benefit of the employee's labors. It is preferable to keep a qualified employee on than to train a new one. A governmental employer also has an interest in keeping citizens usefully employed rather than taking the possibly erroneous and counter-productive step of forcing its employees onto the welfare rolls. Finally, in those situations where the employer perceives a significant hazard in keeping the employee on the job,[6] it can avoid the problem by suspending with pay.

IV

The foregoing considerations indicate that the pretermination "hearing," though necessary, need not be elaborate. . . . Under state law, respondents were later entitled to a full administrative hearing and judicial review. The only question is what steps were required before the termination took effect.

In only one case, Goldberg v. Kelly, has the Court required a full adversarial evidentiary hearing prior to adverse governmental action. However, as the Goldberg Court itself pointed out, that case presented significantly different considerations than are present in the context of public employment. Here, the pretermination hearing need not definitively resolve the propriety of the discharge. It should be an initial check against mistaken decisions—essentially, a determination of whether there are reasonable grounds to believe that the charges against the employee are true and support the proposed action.

The essential requirements of due process, and all that respondents seek or the Court of Appeals required, are notice and an opportunity to respond. . . . The tenured public employee is entitled to oral or written

---

5. Loudermill's dismissal turned not on the objective fact that he was an ex-felon or the inaccuracy of his statement to the contrary, but on the subjective question whether he had lied on his application form. His explanation for the false statement is plausible in light of the fact that he received only a suspended 6–month sentence and a fine on the grand larceny conviction.

6. In the cases before us, no such danger seems to have existed. . . . As for Loudermill, petitioner states that "to find that we have a person who is an ex-felon as our

security guard is very distressful to us." Tr. of Oral Arg. 19. But the termination was based on the presumed misrepresentation on the employment form, not on the felony conviction. In fact, Ohio law provides that an employee "shall not be disciplined for acts," including criminal convictions, occurring more than two years previously. See Ohio Admin.Code § 124–3–04 (1979). Petitioner concedes that Loudermill's job performance was fully satisfactory.

notice of the charges against him, an explanation of the employer's evidence, and an opportunity to present his side of the story. To require more than this prior to termination would intrude to an unwarranted extent on the government's interest in quickly removing an unsatisfactory employee.

V

Our holding rests in part on the provisions in Ohio law for a full post-termination hearing. In his cross-petition Loudermill asserts, as a separate constitutional violation, that his administrative proceedings took too long[7] .... At some point, a delay in the post-termination hearing would become a constitutional violation.... A 9–month adjudication is not ... unconstitutionally lengthy *per se*. Yet Loudermill offers no indication that his wait was unreasonably prolonged other than the fact that it took nine months. The chronology of the proceedings set out in the complaint, coupled with the assertion that nine months is too long to wait, does not state a claim of a constitutional deprivation.[8]

... The judgment of the Court of Appeals is affirmed, and the case is remanded for further proceedings consistent with this opinion.

So ordered.

■ JUSTICE MARSHALL, concurring in Part II and concurring in the judgment.

... I write separately ... to reaffirm my belief that public employees who may be discharged only for cause are entitled, under the Due Process Clause of the Fourteenth Amendment, to more than respondents sought in this case. I continue to believe that *before the decision is made to terminate an employee's wages,* the employee is entitled to an opportunity to test the strength of the evidence "by confronting and cross-examining adverse witnesses and by presenting witnesses on [his] own behalf, whenever there are substantial disputes in testimonial evidence," Arnett v. Kennedy, 416 U.S. 134, 214 (1974) (Marshall, J., dissenting)....

To my mind, the disruption caused by a loss of wages may be so devastating to an employee that, whenever there are substantial disputes about the evidence, additional predeprivation procedures are necessary to minimize the risk of an erroneous termination. That is, I place significantly greater weight than does the Court on the public employee's substantial interest in the accuracy of the pretermination proceeding. After wage termination, the employee often must wait months before his case is finally resolved, during which time he is without wages from his public employment. By limiting the procedures due prior to termination of wages, the Court accepts an impermissibly high risk that a wrongfully discharged employee will be subjected to this often lengthy wait for vindication, and to

---

7. Loudermill's hearing before the referee occurred two and one-half months after he filed his appeal. The Commission issued its written decision six and one-half months after that....

8. The cross-petition also argues that Loudermill was unconstitutionally deprived of liberty because of the accusation of dishonesty that hung over his head during the administrative proceedings. As the Court of Appeals found, 721 F.2d, at 563, n. 18, the failure to allege that the reasons for the dismissal were published dooms this claim.

the attendant and often traumatic disruptions to his personal and economic life. . . .

■ [JUSTICE BRENNAN dissented from Part V of the Court's opinion; he claimed that Loudermill's complaint was sufficient to tender an issue concerning the constitutionality of the nine-month delay.]

■ JUSTICE REHNQUIST, dissenting.

In Arnett v. Kennedy, six Members of this Court agreed that a public employee could be dismissed for misconduct without a full hearing prior to termination. A plurality of Justices agreed that the employee was entitled to exactly what Congress gave him, and no more. The Chief Justice, Justice Stewart, and I said:

> Here appellee did have a statutory expectancy that he not be removed other than for "such cause as will promote the efficiency of [the] service." But the very section of the statute which granted him that right, a right which had previously existed only by virtue of administrative regulation, expressly provided also for the procedure by which "cause" was to be determined, and expressly omitted the procedural guarantees which appellee insists are mandated by the Constitution. Only by bifurcating the very sentence of the Act of Congress which conferred upon appellee the right not to be removed save for cause could it be said that he had an expectancy of that substantive right without the procedural limitations which Congress attached to it. . . . Where the focus of legislation was thus strongly on the procedural mechanism for enforcing the substantive right which was simultaneously conferred, we decline to conclude that the substantive right may be viewed wholly apart from the procedure provided for its enforcement. . . .

. . . [I]n one legislative breath Ohio has conferred upon civil service employees such as respondents in these cases a limited form of tenure during good behavior, and prescribed the procedures by which that tenure may be terminated. Here, as in Arnett, "[t]he employee's statutorily defined right is not a guarantee against removal without cause in the abstract, but such a guarantee as enforced by the procedures which [the Ohio legislature] has designated for the determination of cause." 416 U.S., at 152 (opinion of Rehnquist, J.). . . . We ought to recognize the totality of the State's definition of the property right in question, and not merely seize upon one of several paragraphs in a unitary statute to proclaim that in that paragraph the State has inexorably conferred upon a civil service employee something which it is powerless under the United States Constitution to qualify in the next paragraph of the statute. This practice ignores our duty under Roth to rely on state law as the source of property interests for purposes of applying the Due Process Clause of the Fourteenth Amendment. While it does not impose a federal definition of property, the Court departs from the full breadth of the holding in Roth by its selective choice from among the sentences the Ohio legislature chooses to use in establishing and qualifying a right.

Having concluded by this somewhat tortured reasoning that Ohio has created a property right in the respondents in these cases, the Court naturally proceeds to inquire what process is "due" before the respondents may be divested of that right. This customary "balancing" inquiry conducted by the Court in these cases reaches a result that is quite unobjectionable, but it seems to me that it is devoid of any principles which will either instruct or endure. The balance is simply an ad hoc weighing which depends to a great extent upon how the Court subjectively views the underlying interests at stake. The results in previous cases and in these cases have been quite unpredictable. To paraphrase Justice Black, today's balancing act requires a "pretermination opportunity to respond" but there is nothing that indicates what tomorrow's will be. Goldberg v. Kelly, 397 U.S. 254, 276 (1970) (Black, J., dissenting). The results from today's balance certainly do not jibe with the result in Goldberg or Mathews v. Eldridge, 424 U.S. 319 (1976).[9] The lack of any principled standards in this area means that these procedural due process cases will recur time and again. Every different set of facts will present a new issue on what process was due and when. One way to avoid this subjective and varying interpretation of the Due Process Clause in cases such as these is to hold that one who avails himself of government entitlements accepts the grant of tenure along with its inherent limitations.

Because I believe that the Fourteenth Amendment of the United States Constitution does not support the conclusion that Ohio's effort to confer a limited form of tenure upon respondents resulted in the creation of a "property right" in their employment, I dissent.

NOTE

As Loudermill explains, the plurality opinion in ARNETT v. KENNEDY, 416 U.S. 134 (1974), written by Justice Rehnquist for himself and Chief Justice Burger and Justice Stewart, rejected a similar due process challenge on the ground "that where the grant of a substantive right is inextricably

---

9. Today the balancing test requires a pretermination opportunity to respond. In Goldberg we required a full-fledged trial-type hearing, and in Mathews we declined to require any pretermination process other than those required by the statute. At times this balancing process may look as if it were undertaken with a thumb on the scale, depending upon the result the Court desired. For example, in Mathews we minimized the importance of the benefit to the recipient, stating that after termination he could always go on welfare to survive. Today, however, the Court exalts the recipient's interest in retaining employment; not a word is said about going on welfare. Conversely, in Mathews we stressed the interests of the State, while today, in a footnote, the Court goes so far as to denigrate the State's interest in firing a school security guard who had lied about a prior felony conviction.

Today the Court purports to describe the State's interest but does so in a way that is contrary to what petitioner Boards of Education have asserted in their briefs. The description of the State's interests looks more like a make-weight to support the Court's result. The decision whom to train and employ is strictly a decision for the State. The Court attempts to ameliorate its ruling by stating that a State may always suspend an employee with pay, in lieu of a predischarge hearing, if it determines that he poses a threat. This does less than justice to the State's interest in its financial integrity and its interest in promptly terminating an employee who has violated the conditions of his tenure, and ignores Ohio's current practice of paying back wages to wrongfully discharged employees.

intertwined with the limitations on the procedures which are to be employed in determining that right, a litigant ... must take the bitter with the sweet."

Arnett differed from Loudermill in three respects. First, Kennedy was a federal employee, and the statute in question was a federal statute. This difference appears to be irrelevant to all the Justices. Second, although the federal statute did not provide for an evidentiary hearing until after dismissal, it did give the employee 30 days notice of the reasons for his proposed discharge, a chance to respond (including a chance to submit affidavits), and an opportunity to appear personally before the official who had the authority to make the final decision. The votes of Justices Powell and Blackmun—who were necessary to make a majority—turned on this fact. The case predates Mathews, but these Justices performed an independent assessment to conclude that the procedures provided by the statute were "a reasonable accommodation of the competing interests" and hence satisfied due process. Third, the most important ground for Kennedy's dismissal was that he had slandered the very person authorized to conduct the pretermination proceeding. Justice White (the author of Loudermill) agreed with Justices Powell and Blackmun that the statutory process was generally adequate, but thought that, in the particular case, the employee was entitled to decision by an unbiased decisionmaker.

Justice Marshall, with whom Justices Douglas and Brennan joined, dissented on grounds very similar to those stated in his Loudermill opinion.

NOTES ON THE THEORY OF "THE BITTER WITH THE SWEET"

(1) HENRY P. MONAGHAN, OF "LIBERTY" AND "PROPERTY," 62 Cornell L. Rev. 405, 438–39 (1977): "The thrust of [Justice Rehnquist's approach] is to break down any distinction between substance and procedure and to assert that, in some contexts at least, procedural safeguards are themselves indispensable aspects of the 'property' itself. There is probably nothing inherently illogical in this approach. 'Property' may be viewed as merely a series of discrete rights and powers, the property teacher's 'bundle of sticks.' And there is no a priori reason to exclude 'procedural sticks' from the bundle. But our legal traditions strongly oppose this mode of analysis. In countless contexts we distinguish between substance and procedure, and subject the procedural aspects of 'property' rights to independent constitutional scrutiny."

(2) RODNEY A. SMOLLA, THE REEMERGENCE OF THE RIGHT-PRIVILEGE DISTINCTION IN CONSTITUTIONAL LAW: THE PRICE OF PROTESTING TOO MUCH, 35 Stan.L.Rev. 69, 75 (1982): "Clearly the strongest motive force behind entitlement theory ... is deference to majoritarian sovereignty. In its most extreme form entitlement doctrine rejects the existence of a dichotomy between 'substantive' and 'procedural' aspects of an interest in largess. It is possible to treat the creation of a welfare program or a parole system as purely political affairs, as matters of legislative choice beyond the pale of judicial review, while nonetheless arguing that minimum procedural integrity in the administration of those programs is a matter of constitutional right. Entitlement theory in its purest form repudiates that division, and proceeds instead on the assumption that the procedural accoutrements that accompany an interest in largess are among the defining characteristics of the interest itself. Under this theory the level of procedural protection that

surrounds a government job, for example, is a political expression of the importance of the job to the body politic; as such it is as much a matter of legislative prerogative as the level of salary assigned to that class of job holder.''

(3) FRANK H. EASTERBROOK, SUBSTANCE AND DUE PROCESS, 1982 Sup. Ct. Rev. 85, 112–13: "Substance and process are intimately related. The procedures one uses determine how much substance is achieved, and by whom. Procedural rules usually are just a measure of how much the substantive entitlements are worth, of what we are willing to sacrifice to see a given goal attained. The body that creates a substantive rule is the logical judge of how much should be spent to avoid errors in the process of disposing of claims to that right. The substantive rule itself is best seen as a promised benefit coupled with a promised rate of mistake: the legislature sets up an $X\%$ probability that a person will receive a certain boon. The Court cannot logically be reticent about revising the substantive rules but unabashed about rewriting the procedures to be followed in administering those rules.''

(4) CYNTHIA R. FARINA, CONCEIVING DUE PROCESS, 3 Yale J. L. & Feminism 189, 230 (1991): "We might object that the average person—the person not trained in economics—does not understand a law that promises a benefit of $X allocated according to a procedure that has an error rate of Y% as 'really' only promising a benefit of X discounted by Y. Still, so long as the process terms of the law are as clear and accessible as the substantive terms, we are hard pressed to explain why the individual's expectations would be shaped by only the 'sweet' substance without reference to the 'bitter' procedures. . . . Thomas Grey suggests that people may not read 'the fine print' of procedural terms, assuming instead a 'normal' or 'reasonable' level of accuracy in implementation.[1] Even if this is so, the law traditionally has little sympathy for the expectations of people who don't read what's right in front of them.''

(5) To sum up: Can you (like the Loudermill majority) distinguish a property right from the procedures that provide a remedy for its violation? If you can, can you assess the right's importance to its holder (in order to conduct the Mathews balance) without referring to the importance which it is accorded by state or federal sub-constitutional law? If you can do both of these things, why do you care whether sub-constitutional law has recognized the property right in the first place? On the other hand, if you do care, why do you not also care about the procedures sub-constitutional law has provided for protecting the right? But if you did care about the procedural as well as the substantive provisions of sub-constitutional law, what would be left for the due process clause to do?

NOTES ON THE PRACTICE OF "THE BITTER WITH THE SWEET"

Is it substance? Or procedure?

(1) GOSS v. LOPEZ, 419 U.S. 565 (1975): In this case, you will recall, see p. 862 above, the Court held that a public school student is constitutionally

---

1. Thomas Grey, Procedural Fairness and Substantive Rights, in Nomos: Due Process, at 195 (J. Roland Pennock & John Chapman eds. 1977).

entitled to some, albeit brief, process before being suspended for 10 days. Ohio law, the majority reasoned, creates an entitlement to a free education for children between the ages of 6 and 21. Deprivation of this entitlement, via suspension, triggers at least minimal due process protection. The dissent fundamentally disagreed: "In identifying property interests subject to due process protections, the Court's past opinions make clear that these interests 'are created *and their dimensions are defined* by existing rules or understandings that stem from an independent source such as state law,' Board of Regents v. Roth, 408 U.S., at 577. The Ohio statute that creates the right to a 'free' education also explicitly authorizes a principal to suspend a student for as much as 10 days. Thus the very legislation which 'defines' the 'dimension' of the student's entitlement, while providing a right to education generally, does not establish this right free of discipline imposed in accord with Ohio law. Rather, the right is encompassed in the entire package of statutory provisions governing education in Ohio—of which the power to suspend is one. The Court thus disregards the basic structure of Ohio law in posturing this case as if Ohio had conferred an unqualified right to education...." You might think you recognize, in this quotation, the voice of Justice Rehnquist advocating "the bitter with the sweet." The surprise is that the author is Justice Powell, who nine months earlier had emphatically rejected Rehnquist's position in Arnett. Justice Blackmun, who joined in Powell's Arnett opinion, also joined him here. Justice Rehnquist and Chief Justice Burger, quite predictably, also dissented. However, Justice Stewart, who had been persuaded by Justice Rehnquist in Arnett, was with the Goss majority.

Is the moral of Goss that in due process—just as in choice-of-laws analysis and applications of Erie v. Thompson—the line between substance and procedure can be elusive? Or is the moral that (as many of the commentators in the previous note cluster pointed out) a doctrine that gives sub-constitutional law *complete* control over whether a protected interest arises and *no* control over the process by which it will be granted or taken away, is deeply conflicted?

(2) A variation on the problem of separating substantive terms from procedural terms was present in O'BANNON v. TOWN COURT NURSING CENTER, 447 U.S. 773 (1980). Medicare and Medicaid programs entitle aged, disabled, and poor persons to receive certain nursing home care. In turn, a nursing home is entitled to receive reimbursement for furnishing that care if it is certified as a "skilled nursing facility." These two entitlements intersect in 42 U.S.C. § 1396a(a)(23), which provides that a patient may get nursing home care "from any institution ... qualified to perform the ... services ... who undertakes to provide him such services...." Is the patient entitled to a hearing before the government "decertifies" the nursing home because once the *home* is no longer "qualified," the *patient* must uproot and go elsewhere? For an aged or infirm person, such a move may be very traumatic—but has there been a deprivation of protected interest? Held: No. First, the substantive entitlement of the patients was not the "right to remain in the home of one's choice absent specific cause for transfer" (as the court of appeals thought) but rather a "right to continued benefits to pay for care in the qualified institution of his choice," with "no enforceable expectation of continued benefits to pay for care in an

institution that has been determined to be unqualified." Second, the decision to decertify is not a direct withdrawal of benefits, and indeed may well be in the patients' interests; the possible "indirect and incidental" impact of the government's enforcement action does not amount to a deprivation of a protected interest. Justice Brennan dissented; Justice Marshall did not participate.

Can process terms create an entitlement?

(3) LOGAN v. ZIMMERMAN BRUSH CO., 455 U.S. 422 (1982): The Illinois Fair Employment Practices Act (FEPA) prohibited employment discrimination against the handicapped, and required the implementing state agency to hold a factfinding hearing on discrimination complaints within 120 days of filing. If the agency found "substantial evidence" of prohibited discrimination, it was required to either eliminate the problem via negotiation or institute formal enforcement proceedings. Apparently through inadvertence, Logan's complaint was not scheduled for hearing within 120 days. The Illinois Supreme Court held that the 120–day limit was jurisdictional; having failed to meet it, the agency lost jurisdiction over Logan's claim. Held: Due process requires the agency to hear the claim. "The hallmark of property, the Court has emphasized, is an individual entitlement grounded in state law, which cannot be removed except 'for cause.' ... The right to use the FEPA's adjudicatory procedures shares these characteristics. A claimant has more than an abstract desire or interest in redressing his grievance: his right to redress is guaranteed by the State, with the adequacy of his claim assessed under what is, in essence, a 'for cause' standard, based upon the substantiality of the evidence. And an FEPA claim, which presumably can be surrendered for value, is at least as substantial as the right to an education labeled as property in Goss v. Lopez." Having chosen to provide this entitlement to an administrative hearing and remedy, Illinois had to provide an opportunity to vindicate it. "To put it as plainly as possible, the State may not finally destroy a property interest without first giving the putative owner an opportunity to present his claim of entitlement.... A system or procedure that deprives persons of their claims in a random manner, as is apparently true of [the 120 day limit], necessarily presents an unjustifiably high risk that meritorious claims will be terminated. And the State's interest in refusing Logan's procedural request is, on this record, insubstantial." Although some of the other Justices found an equal protection rationale more apt, no one dissented from reversing the Illinois Supreme Court's judgment.

(4) In OLIM v. WAKINEKONA, 461 U.S. 238 (1983), an inmate of a Hawaii prison was transferred to a mainland facility and claimed a due process violation. He could not establish that the relevant state statutes or prison regulations contained substantive standards constraining the discretion of prison authorities to make such transfers. However, the Court of Appeals found significant the fact that "[t]he Hawaii regulations clearly guarantee prisoners specified procedural protections before any transfer involving a 'grievous loss,' and they define an interstate transfer as a 'grievous loss.' [These included a hearing before an "impartial committee," in which the prisoner has the right to see all non-confidential material, present witnesses, and cross examine other witnesses, as well as a requirement that

the committee base its decision "only upon evidence presented at the hearing to which the individual had an opportunity to respond or any evidence which may subsequently come to light after the formal hearing"]. These regulations are not without substantive content. Their clear import is that a transfer will not be carried out absent a hearing directed to proof of the facts alleged in the notice received beforehand by the prisoner. In our view, these regulations create a justifiable expectation that a prisoner will not be transferred absent the specified procedures. They consequently give rise to a constitutionally protected liberty interest." 664 F.2d 708 (9th Cir.1981). The Supreme Court disagreed. Justice Blackmun, for the 6–member majority: "The Court of Appeals ... erred in attributing significance to the fact that the prison regulations require a particular kind of hearing before the administrator can exercise his unfettered discretion.... Process is not an end in itself. Its constitutional purpose is to protect a substantive interest to which the individual has a legitimate claim of entitlement. If officials may transfer a prisoner 'for whatever reason or for no reason at all,' Meachum, 427 U.S., at 228, there is no such interest for process to protect. The State may choose to require procedures for reasons other than protection against deprivation of substantive rights, of course, but in making that choice the State does not create an independent substantive right." (The state gave the following explanation of the procedural requirements: "The hearings required by Rule IV not only enable the officials to gather information and thereby to exercise their discretion intelligently, but also have a therapeutic purpose: inmate participation in the decisionmaking process, it is hoped, reduces tension in the prison.")

c. THE RELEVANCE OF POST-DEPRIVATION JUDICIAL REMEDIES

Sub-constitutional law may provide a variety of causes of action to complain of harm inflicted by government officials. These range from common law remedies in tort or contract, to criminal prosecutions, to statutory provisions (such as the APA at the federal level) for judicial review of administrative action. Sometimes, waivers of sovereign immunity will allow for judicial remedies against the governmental entity itself for the wrong done by its employees. See Chapter IX below. Can these remedies—typically available only after the deprivation, and sited in the courts rather than at the agency—constitute all the process that is constitutionally "due" in connection with an administrative deprivation of liberty or property?

North American Cold Storage Co. v. Chicago
Supreme Court of the United States, 1908.
211 U.S. 306.

[Section 1161 of the Revised Municipal Code of the City of Chicago required owners of facilities for cold storage of perishable food items to "put, preserve and keep such article of food supply in a clean and wholesome condition, and ... not allow the same, nor any part thereof, to become putrid, decayed, poisoned, infected, or in any other manner rendered or made unsafe or unwholesome for human food." Further, health department inspectors were authorized "to enter any and all such premises ... at any time of any day and to forthwith seize, condemn and destroy any such putrid, decayed, poisoned and infected food, which any such inspector may find in and upon said premises." Pursuant to this ordinance, city officials ordered North American Cold Storage to deliver to them, for purposes of destruction, forty-seven barrels of poultry which allegedly had become putrid. The Company refused. The City then threatened to destroy summarily anything in the warehouse deemed unfit for human consumption; it banned further deliveries to or from the warehouse and promised to imprison anyone attempting to avoid the ban. Business was completely halted, and the Company sought an injunction.]

■ JUSTICE PECKHAM ... delivered the opinion of the court.

... The general power of the State to legislate upon the subject embraced in the above ordinance of the city of Chicago, counsel does not deny. Nor does he deny the right to seize and destroy unwholesome or putrid food, provided that notice and opportunity to be heard be given the owner or custodian of the property before it is destroyed. We are of opinion, however, that provision for a hearing before seizure and condemnation and destruction of food which is unwholesome and unfit for use, is not necessary. ... The right to so seize and destroy is, of course, based upon the fact that the food is not fit to be eaten. Food that is in such a condition, if kept for sale or in danger of being sold, is in itself a nuisance, and a nuisance of the most dangerous kind, involving, as it does, the health, if not the lives, of persons who may eat it. A determination on the part of the seizing officers that food is in an unfit condition to be eaten is not a decision which concludes the owner. The ex parte finding of the health officers as to the fact is not in any way binding upon those who own or claim the right to sell the food. If a party cannot get his hearing in advance of the seizure and destruction he has the right to have it afterward, which right may be claimed upon the trial in an action brought for the destruction of his property, and in that action those who destroyed it can only successfully defend if the jury shall find the fact of unwholesomeness as claimed by them. ...

Miller v. Horton, 152 Mass. 540, 26 N.E. 100, is in principle like the case before us. It was an action brought for killing the plaintiff's horse. The defendants admitted the killing but justified the act under an order of the board of health, which declared that the horse had the glanders, and directed it to be killed. The court held that the decision of the board of health was not conclusive as to whether or not the horse was diseased, and said that: "Of course there cannot be a trial by jury before killing an animal supposed to have a contagious disease, and we assume that the legislature may authorize its destruction in such emergencies without a hearing beforehand. But it does not follow that it can throw the loss upon the owner without a hearing. If he cannot be heard beforehand he may be heard afterward. The statute may provide for paying him in case it should appear that his property was not what the legislature had declared to be a nuisance and may give him his hearing in that way. If it does not do so, the statute may leave those who act under it to proceed at their peril, and the owner gets his hearing in an action against them." ...

Complainant, however, contends that there was no emergency requiring speedy action for the destruction of the poultry in order to protect the public health from danger resulting from consumption of such poultry. It is said that the food was in cold storage, and that it would continue in the same condition it then was for three months, if properly stored, and that therefore the defendants had ample time in which to give notice to complainant or the owner and have a hearing of the question as to the condition of the poultry, and as the ordinance provided for no hearing, it was void. But we think this is not required. The power of the legislature to enact laws in relation to the public health being conceded, as it must be, it is to a great extent within legislative discretion as to whether any hearing need be given before the destruction of unwholesome food which is unfit for human consumption. If a hearing were to be always necessary, even under the circumstances of this case, the question at once arises as to what is to be done with the food in the meantime. Is it to remain with the cold storage company, and if so under what security that it will not be removed? To be sure that it will not be removed during the time necessary for the hearing, which might frequently be indefinitely prolonged, some guard would probably have to be placed over the subject-matter of investigation, which would involve expense, and might not even then prove effectual. What is the emergency which would render a hearing unnecessary? We think when the question is one regarding the destruction of food which is not fit for human use the emergency must be one which would fairly appeal to the reasonable discretion of the legislature as to the necessity for a prior hearing, and in that case its decision would not be a subject for review by the courts. As the owner of the food or its custodian is amply protected against the party seizing the food, who must in a subsequent action against him show as a fact that it was within the statute, we think that due process of law is not denied the owner or custodian by the destruction of the food alleged to be unwholesome and unfit for human food without a preliminary hearing. . . .

Affirmed.

■ JUSTICE BREWER dissents.

NOTES

(1) Even after nearly a century of doctrinal evolution, the North American Cold Storage principle remains a vital aspect of procedural due process. FEDERAL DEPOSIT INS. CORP. V. MALLEN, 486 U.S. 230 (1988): As part of its regulatory charge to guard against losses from bank failures, the Federal Deposit Insurance Corporation is authorized to suspend summarily an officer of an insured bank who has been indicted for a felony involving dishonesty or breach of trust and whose continued service could pose a threat to the depositors or to public confidence in the bank. The statute provides that an administrative hearing need not be given until 30 days after the suspension, and might not be concluded for an additional 60 days. Held, by a unanimous Court: no violation of due process. "An important government interest, accompanied by a substantial assurance that the deprivation is not baseless or unwarranted, may in limited cases demanding prompt action justify postponing the opportunity to be heard until after the

initial deprivation. See North American Cold Storage Co. v. Chicago." As to the possible 90 day delay, the length of time was a proper item of concern, but in this case the Court was not convinced that Congress had overstepped its limits. GILBERT V. HOMAR, 520 U.S. 924 (1997), relied on North American Cold Storage and Mallen in holding that a state university could constitutionally summarily suspend, without pay, a police officer arrested for and charged with a drug felony. Justice Scalia wrote for a unanimous Court. The purpose of a pre-suspension hearing—to assure that there are reasonable grounds to support the suspension—has already been assured by the arrest and charge. The State has a significant interest in immediately suspending employees charged with felonies who occupy positions of public trust and visibility, such as police officers. So long as the lost income is relatively insubstantial and the post-suspension hearing is prompt, due process "does not require the government to give an employee charged with a felony a paid leave at taxpayer expense."

(2) So long as prompt post-deprivation process is available in which the owner can contest the government's action and, if successful, recover the property or its value, need the government show exigent circumstances in order to, in effect, take now and pay later? A long line of cases affirms the power of state and federal governments to require taxpayers to pay a contested assessment and then bring an action for refund. Justice Brandeis for a unanimous Court in PHILLIPS v. COMMISSIONER, 283 U.S. 589 (1931): "Where only property rights are involved, mere postponement of the judicial enquiry is not a denial of due process, if the opportunity given for the ultimate judicial determination of the liability is adequate. Delay in the judicial determination of property rights is not uncommon where it is essential that governmental needs be immediately satisfied. For the protection of public health, a State may order the summary destruction of property by administrative authorities without antecedent notice or hearing. North American Cold Storage Co. v. Chicago.... Because of the public necessity, the property of citizens may be summarily seized in war-time. And at any time, the United States may acquire property by eminent domain, without paying, or determining the amount of the compensation before the taking."

On the other hand, in UNITED STATES V. JAMES DANIEL GOOD REAL PROPERTY, 510 U.S. 43 (1993), the Court split 5–4 on whether a civil forfeiture of real property could be done summarily in the absence of exigent circumstances. Four and one-half years after James Good pleaded guilty to drug offenses (and 3–1/2 years after he had completed his jail sentence), the government convinced a magistrate, in an ex parte proceeding, that it had probable cause to seize the house and land on which the drugs had been found. The government then seized the property without prior notice to Good or the tenants then occupying it. The Court (Justice Kennedy writing) held that where property is seized, not to preserve evidence of criminal wrongdoing but to assert ownership and control, "[w]e tolerate some exceptions to the general rule requiring predeprivation notice and hearing, ... only in extraordinary situations where some valid governmental interest is at stake that justifies postponing the hearing until after the event." (internal quotes omitted) "It is true that, in cases decided over a century ago, we permitted the ex parte seizure of real property when the

Government was collecting debts or revenue. Without revisiting these cases, it suffices to say that their apparent rationale—like that for allowing summary seizures during wartime, . . . and seizures of contaminated food, see North American Cold Storage Co. v. Chicago,—was one of executive urgency. 'The prompt payment of taxes,' we noted, 'may be vital to the existence of a government.' Springer v. United States, 102 U.S. 586, 594 (1880). See also G.M. Leasing Corp. v. United States, 429 U.S. 338, 352, n. 18 (1977) ('The rationale underlying [the revenue] decisions, of course, is that the very existence of government depends upon the prompt collection of the revenues')." Here, no such executive urgency existed. Unlike such personal property as the boats and automobiles that had been involved in other cases, real property cannot leave the jurisdiction. For dissenting Justices Rehnquist and Scalia, the majority opinion both disregarded the long history of ex parte seizures of real and personal property through civil forfeiture, and failed convincingly to distinguish the tax cases. For Justices O'Connor and Thomas, it was also relevant that Good had been convicted at the time the forfeiture began; the majority's concern that the property rights of an "innocent owner" might be forfeited before hearing was thus completely misplaced.

(3) Does the legality of summary deprivation depend on the secure existence of a post-seizure remedy that will make the property owner whole? The proposition in the Massachusetts horse-with-glanders case discussed in North American Cold Storage—that the responsible officials would be personally liable in tort to the owner if the horse were not, in fact, diseased—was overruled by Gildea v. Ellershaw, 363 Mass. 800, 298 N.E.2d 847 (1973). The Supreme Judicial Court held that a public official who acts in good faith within the scope of his official duty is not liable for "negligence or other error . . . at the suit of a private individual claiming to have been damaged thereby." Federal law similarly recognizes a variety of official immunities which wholly or partially shield state and federal actors from damages liability for acts that turn out to have been unjustified by law. See Chapter IX, Sec. 5.a below. And, when the property owner attempts to recover her loss from the government entity itself, she may well encounter the barrier of sovereign immunity. Supreme Court cases in the tax area have stated that adequate post-payment remedies must be provided if the government denies pre-deprivation process, see, e.g., Reich v. Collins, 513 U.S. 106 (1994); Mc Kesson Corp. v. Division of Alcoholic Beverages & Tobacco, 496 U.S. 18, 36–37 (1990). However, recent Court decisions in the areas of Eleventh Amendment and sovereign immunity have created considerable doubt about the extent to which the state and federal governments must consent to be liable in damages for even constitutional violations by their officials. See Chapter IX, Sec. 1.c below.

(4) So far we have been considering property. What, if anything, do these cases mean for summary deprivation of liberty?

Ingraham v. Wright
Supreme Court of the United States, 1977.
430 U.S. 651.

■ JUSTICE POWELL delivered the opinion of the Court.

. . . Petitioners' evidence may be summarized briefly. In the 1970–1971 school year many of the 237 schools in Dade County used corporal punishment as a means of maintaining discipline pursuant to Florida legislation and a local School Board regulation.... The authorized punishment consisted of paddling the recalcitrant student on the buttocks with a flat wooden paddle measuring less than two feet long, three to four inches wide, and about one-half inch thick. The normal punishment was limited to one to five "licks" or blows with the paddle and resulted in no apparent physical injury to the student. School authorities viewed corporal punishment as a less drastic means of discipline than suspension or expulsion....

... The evidence, consisting mainly of the testimony of 16 students, suggests that the regime at Drew [Junior High] was exceptionally harsh. The testimony of [plaintiffs James] Ingraham and [Roosevelt] Andrews, in support of their individual claims for damages, is illustrative. Because he was slow to respond to his teacher's instructions, Ingraham was subjected to more than 20 licks with a paddle while being held over a table in the principal's office. The paddling was so severe that he suffered a hematoma requiring medical attention and keeping him out of school for several days. Andrews was paddled several times for minor infractions. On two occasions he was struck on his arms, once depriving him of the full use of his arm for a week.

The District Court made no findings on the credibility of the students' testimony. Rather, assuming their testimony to be credible, the court found no constitutional basis for relief. [A panel of the Fifth Circuit voted to reverse but, upon rehearing en banc, the judgment of the district court was affirmed.]

We granted certiorari, limited to the questions of cruel and unusual punishment and procedural due process.

II

[Corporal punishment dates back to colonial times, as does the common law principle (now incorporated in the Restatement (Second) of Torts) that teachers are privileged to use reasonable but not excessive force to discipline children.]

III

... An examination of the history of the [Eighth] Amendment and the decisions of this Court construing the proscription against cruel and unusual punishment confirms that it was designed to protect those convicted of crimes. We adhere to this longstanding limitation and hold that the Eighth Amendment does not apply to the paddling of children as a means of maintaining discipline in public schools....

IV

The Fourteenth Amendment prohibits any state deprivation of life, liberty, or property without due process of law. Application of this prohibition requires the familiar two-stage analysis: We must first ask whether the asserted individual interests are encompassed within the Fourteenth Amendment's protection of "life, liberty or property"; if protected interests are implicated, we then must decide what procedures constitute "due process of law." Following that analysis here, we find that corporal punishment in public schools implicates a constitutionally protected liberty interest, but we hold that the traditional common-law remedies are fully adequate to afford due process.

A

"[T]he range of interests protected by procedural due process is not infinite." Board of Regents v. Roth, [408 U.S.] at 570. We have repeatedly rejected "the notion that *any* grievous loss visited upon a person by the State is sufficient to invoke the procedural protections of the Due Process Clause." Meachum v. Fano, 427 U.S., at 224. Due process is required only when a decision of the State implicates an interest within the protection of the Fourteenth Amendment. And "to determine whether due process requirements apply in the first place, we must look not to the 'weight' but to the *nature* of the interest at stake." Roth, at 570–571.

The Due Process Clause of the Fifth Amendment, later incorporated into the Fourteenth, was intended to give Americans at least the protection against governmental power that they had enjoyed as Englishmen against the power of the Crown. The liberty preserved from deprivation without due process included the right "generally to enjoy those privileges long recognized at common law as essential to the orderly pursuit of happiness by free men." Meyer v. Nebraska, 262 U.S. 390, 399 (1923). Among the historic liberties so protected was a right to be free from, and to obtain judicial relief for, unjustified intrusions on personal security.

While the contours of this historic liberty interest in the context of our federal system of government have not been defined precisely, they always have been thought to encompass freedom from bodily restraint and punishment. It is fundamental that the state cannot hold and physically punish an individual except in accordance with due process of law.

This constitutionally protected liberty interest is at stake in this case. There is, of course, a *de minimis* level of imposition with which the Constitution is not concerned. But at least where school authorities, acting under color of state law, deliberately decide to punish a child for misconduct by restraining the child and inflicting appreciable physical pain, we hold that Fourteenth Amendment liberty interests are implicated.[1]

B

The question remains what process is due. [quotation omitted] Were it not for the common-law privilege permitting teachers to inflict reasonable corporal punishment on children in their care, and the availability of the traditional remedies for abuse, the case for requiring advance procedural safeguards would be strong indeed. But here we deal with a punishment—

---

1. Unlike Goss v. Lopez, this case does not involve the state-created property interest in public education. The purpose of corporal punishment is to correct a child's behavior without interrupting his education. That corporal punishment may, in a rare case, have the unintended effect of temporarily removing a child from school affords no basis for concluding that the practice itself deprives students of property protected by the Fourteenth Amendment. . . .

paddling—within that tradition, and the question is whether the common-law remedies are adequate to afford due process.

... Whether in this case the common-law remedies for excessive corporal punishment constitute due process of law must turn on an analysis of the competing interests at stake, viewed against the background of "history, reason, [and] the past course of decisions." The analysis requires consideration of three distinct factors: "First, the private interest that will be affected ...; second, the risk of an erroneous deprivation of such interest ... and the probable value, if any, of additional or substitute procedural safeguards; and finally, the [state] interest, including the function involved and the fiscal and administrative burdens that the additional or substitute procedural requirement would entail." Mathews v. Eldridge, 424 U.S. 319, 335 (1976).

1

Because it is rooted in history, the child's liberty interest in avoiding corporal punishment while in the care of public school authorities is subject to historical limitations....

The concept that reasonable corporal punishment in school is justifiable continues to be recognized in the laws of most States....

This is not to say that the child's interest in procedural safeguards is insubstantial....

We turn now to a consideration of the safeguards that are available under applicable Florida law.

2

Florida has continued to recognize, and indeed has strengthened by statute, the common-law right of a child not to be subjected to excessive corporal punishment in school. Under Florida law the teacher and principal of the school decide in the first instance whether corporal punishment is reasonably necessary under the circumstances in order to discipline a child who has misbehaved. But they must exercise prudence and restraint. For Florida has preserved the traditional judicial proceedings for determining whether the punishment was justified. If the punishment inflicted is later found to have been excessive—not reasonably believed at the time to be necessary for the child's discipline or training—the school authorities inflicting it may be held liable in damages to the child and, if malice is shown, they may be subject to criminal penalties.[2]

Although students have testified in this case to specific instances of abuse, there is every reason to believe that such mistreatment is an aberration. The uncontradicted evidence suggests that corporal punishment in the Dade County schools was, "[w]ith the exception of a few cases, ... unremarkable in physical severity." Moreover, because paddlings are usually inflicted in response to conduct directly observed by teachers in their

---

2. ... Both the District Court and the Court of Appeals expressed the view that the common-law tort remedy was available to the petitioners in this case. And petitioners con- ceded in this Court that a teacher who inflicts excessive punishment on a child may be held both civilly and criminally liable under Florida law. ...

presence, the risk that a child will be paddled without cause is typically insignificant. In the ordinary case, a disciplinary paddling neither threatens seriously to violate any substantive rights nor condemns the child "to suffer grievous loss of any kind." Anti–Fascist Comm. v. McGrath, 341 U.S., at 168 (Frankfurter, J., concurring).

In those cases where severe punishment is contemplated, the available civil and criminal sanctions for abuse—considered in light of the openness of the school environment—afford significant protection against unjustified corporal punishment. Teachers and school authorities are unlikely to inflict corporal punishment unnecessarily or excessively when a possible consequence of doing so is the institution of civil or criminal proceedings against them.[3]

It still may be argued, of course, that the child's liberty interest would be better protected if the common-law remedies were supplemented by the administrative safeguards of prior notice and a hearing.... But where the State has preserved what "has always been the law of the land," United States v. Barnett, 376 U.S. 681 (1964), the case for administrative safeguards is significantly less compelling.[4] ...

3

But even if the need for advance procedural safeguards were clear, the question would remain whether the incremental benefit could justify the cost. Acceptance of petitioners' claims would work a transformation in the law governing corporal punishment in Florida and most other States. Given the impracticability of formulating a rule of procedural due process that varies with the severity of the particular imposition, the prior hearing petitioners seek would have to precede *any* paddling, however moderate or trivial.

Such a universal constitutional requirement would significantly burden the use of corporal punishment as a disciplinary measure.... Teachers, properly concerned with maintaining authority in the classroom, may well prefer to rely on other disciplinary measures—which they may view as less

---

3. The low incidence of abuse, and the availability of established judicial remedies in the event of abuse, distinguish this case from Goss v. Lopez, 419 U.S. 565 (1975). The Ohio law struck down in Goss provided for suspensions from public school of up to 10 days without "any written procedure applicable to suspensions." Id., at 567. Although Ohio law provided generally for administrative review, the Court assumed that the short suspensions would not be stayed pending review, with the result that the review proceeding could serve neither a deterrent nor a remedial function. 419 U.S., at 581 n. 10. In these circumstances, the Court held the law authorizing suspensions unconstitutional for failure to require "that there be at least an informal give-and-take between student and disciplinarian, preferably prior to the suspen-

sion...." Id., at 584. The subsequent civil and criminal proceedings available in this case may be viewed as affording substantially greater protection to the child than the informal conference mandated by Goss.

4. "[P]rior hearings might well be dispensed with in many circumstances in which the state's conduct, if not adequately justified, would constitute a common-law tort. This would leave the injured plaintiff in precisely the same posture as a common-law plaintiff, and this procedural consequence would be quite harmonious with the substantive view that the fourteenth amendment encompasses the same liberties as those protected by the common law." Monaghan, Of "Liberty" and "Property," 62 Cornell L.Rev. 405, 431 (1977) (footnote omitted)....

effective—rather than confront the possible disruption that prior notice and a hearing may entail.[5] Paradoxically, such an alteration of disciplinary policy is most likely to occur in the ordinary case where the contemplated punishment is well within the common-law privilege.[6] . . .

"At some point the benefit of an additional safeguard to the individual affected . . . and to society in terms of increased assurance that the action is just, may be outweighed by the cost." Mathews v. Eldridge, 424 U.S., at 348. We think that point has been reached in this case. In view of the low incidence of abuse, the openness of our schools, and the common-law safeguards that already exist, the risk of error that may result in violation of a schoolchild's substantive rights can only be regarded as minimal. Imposing additional administrative safeguards as a constitutional requirement might reduce that risk marginally, but would also entail a significant intrusion into an area of primary educational responsibility. We conclude that the Due Process Clause does not require notice and a hearing prior to the imposition of corporal punishment in the public schools, as that practice is authorized and limited by the common law. . . .

Affirmed.

■ JUSTICE WHITE, with whom JUSTICE BRENNAN, JUSTICE MARSHALL, and JUSTICE STEVENS join, dissenting.

Today the Court holds that corporal punishment in public schools, no matter how severe, can never be the subject of the protections afforded by the Eighth Amendment. It also holds that students in the public school systems are not constitutionally entitled to a hearing of any sort before beatings can be inflicted on them. . . .

The reason that the Constitution requires a State to provide "due process of law" when it punishes an individual for misconduct is to protect the individual from erroneous or mistaken punishment that the State would not have inflicted had it found the facts in a more reliable way. In Goss v. Lopez, 419 U.S. 565 (1975), the Court applied this principle to the school disciplinary process, holding that a student must be given an informal opportunity to be heard before he is finally suspended from public school.

> Disciplinarians, although proceeding in utmost good faith, frequently act on the reports and advice of others; and the controlling facts and the nature of the conduct under challenge are often disputed. *The risk of error is not at all trivial,* and it should be guarded against if that may be done without prohibitive cost or interference with the educational process. Id., at 580. (Emphasis added.)

To guard against this risk of punishing an innocent child, the Due Process Clause requires, not an "elaborate hearing" before a neutral party, but

---

5. If a prior hearing, with the inevitable attendant publicity within the school, resulted in rejection of the teacher's recommendation, the consequent impairment of the teacher's ability to maintain discipline in the classroom would not be insubstantial.

6. The effect of interposing prior procedural safeguards may well be to make the

punishment more severe by increasing the anxiety of the child. For this reason, the school authorities in Dade County found it desirable that the punishment be inflicted as soon as possible after the infraction.

simply "an informal give-and-take between student and disciplinarian" which gives the student "an opportunity to explain his version of the facts."

The Court now holds that these "rudimentary precautions against unfair or mistaken findings of misconduct," id., at 581, are not required if the student is punished with "appreciable physical pain" rather than with a suspension, even though both punishments deprive the student of a constitutionally protected interest. . . .

[The Florida] tort action is utterly inadequate to protect against erroneous infliction of punishment for two reasons. First, under Florida law, a student . . . has no remedy at all for punishment imposed on the basis of mistaken facts . . .[7] The "traditional common-law remedies" on which the majority relies thus do nothing to protect the student from the danger that concerned the Court in Goss—the risk of reasonable, good-faith mistake in the school disciplinary process.

Second, and more important, even if the student could sue for good-faith error in the infliction of punishment, the lawsuit occurs after the punishment has been finally imposed. The infliction of physical pain is final and irreparable; it cannot be undone in a subsequent proceeding. There is every reason to require, as the Court did in Goss, a few minutes of "informal give-and-take between student and disciplinarian" as a "meaningful hedge" against the erroneous infliction of irreparable injury. 419 U.S., at 583–584.

The majority's conclusion that a damages remedy for excessive corporal punishment affords adequate process rests on the novel theory that the State may punish an individual without giving him any opportunity to present his side of the story, as long as he can later recover damages from a state official if he is innocent. . . . There is no authority for this theory, nor does the majority purport to find any, in the procedural due process decisions of this Court. . . .

I would reverse the judgment below.

■ JUSTICE STEVENS, dissenting.

. . . Notwithstanding my disagreement with the Court's holding . . . my respect for Mr. Justice Powell's reasoning in Part IV–B of his opinion for the Court prompts these comments.

The constitutional prohibition of state deprivations of life, liberty, or property without due process of law does not, by its express language, require that a hearing be provided *before* any deprivation may occur. To be sure, the timing of the process may be a critical element in determining its adequacy—that is, in deciding what process is due in a particular context. Generally, adequate notice and a fair opportunity to be heard in advance of any deprivation of a constitutionally protected interest are essential. The

---

7. The majority's assurances to the contrary, it is unclear to me whether and to what extent Florida law provides a damages action against school officials for excessive corporal punishment. Giving the majority the benefit of every doubt, I think it is fair to say that the most a student punished on the basis of mistaken allegations of misconduct can hope for in Florida is a recovery for unreasonable or bad-faith error. But I strongly suspect that even this remedy is not available. . . .

Court has recognized, however, that the wording of the command that there shall be no deprivation "without" due process of law is consistent with the conclusion that a postdeprivation remedy is sometimes constitutionally sufficient.

When only an invasion of a property interest is involved, there is a greater likelihood that a damages award will make a person completely whole than when an invasion of the individual's interest in freedom from bodily restraint and punishment has occurred. . . .

NOTE

ROBERT A. BURT, THE CONSTITUTION OF THE FAMILY, 1979 Sup. Ct. Rev. 329, 341–42: "[I]n Ingraham v. Wright, Mr. Justice Powell identified a problem of central concern to him . . . : 'If a prior hearing, with the inevitable attendant publicity within the school, resulted in rejection of the teacher's recommendation, the consequent impairment of the teacher's ability to maintain discipline in the classroom would not be insubstantial.'
. . .

"It would be unfair, however, to portray the Court in Ingraham or its conservative nucleus as intending to condone or encourage brutality by teachers, parents, or judges. This nucleus intends to encourage an unquestioning attitude toward, and a reciprocally firm and self-confident attitude by, constituted authority. An idealized image of conflict-free interpersonal relations appears to lie beneath this intention. Mr. Justice Powell reveals this in his Goss v. Lopez dissent: 'The role of the teacher in our society historically has been an honored and respected one, rooted in the experience of decades that has left for most of us warm memories of our teachers, especially those of the formative years of primary and secondary education.' It might thus appear an insult to these honored memories if the Supreme Court were now to abandon '[our reliance] for generations upon the experience, good faith and dedication of those who staff our public schools.' "

JANE RUTHERFORD, THE MYTH OF DUE PROCESS, 72 B.U.L.Rev. 1, 41 (1992): "[T]he 'law of the land' is merely a myth in both senses of the word. It is a cultural story because its content depends on which time period the law is drawn from, how elastically we read that law, and whether we define that law specifically or generally. By characterizing law as historical fact, however, the Court has managed to define the law in favor of more powerful parties. As a result, due process has been transformed from a shield for the powerless to a weapon for the powerful. Accordingly, historical due process is also a myth that carries false promises of protection. One way to balance the power more fairly is to ensure that relatively powerless parties can participate on an equal footing."

Is it legitimate, in considering the reach of constitutional due process, to take into account the degree to which an extension of procedural rights will alter institutional power relationships? Is it responsible not to consider these possible consequences?

NOTES ON THE QUESTION WHETHER COMMON LAW OR STATUTORY REMEDIES ARE ALL THE PROCESS THAT IS "DUE"

(1) PAUL V. DAVIS, 424 U.S. 693 (1976), was a famous—perhaps infamous—and certainly remarkable case decided the term before Ingraham. The name and photograph of Davis, a newspaper photographer, were included in a flier of "Active Shoplifters" circulated to area merchants by Paul, a police chief. In fact, Davis had been arrested a year-and-a-half before, had pleaded not guilty at his arraignment, and had not been further prosecuted. Alleging that he had been branded without having ever been tried, and that his future employment opportunities would be impaired, Davis filed suit under 42 U.S.C. § 1983 seeking damages for violation of his due process rights. In an opinion by Justice Rehnquist, for the same five justices who constituted the Ingraham majority, held: No deprivation of a constitutionally protected interest.

Most of Justice Rehnquist's opinion was devoted to showing that the interest in reputation asserted by Davis was not "liberty" or "property." Given statements decrying the official stigmatization of a person's good name that stretched back at least as far as Joint Anti–Fascist Refugee Comm. v. McGrath (1951) (p. 775 above), this required some fancy footwork. For example, Wisconsin v. Constantineau, the 1971 case which held that "posting" of persons for excessive drinking was unconstitutional without notice and hearing (p. 791 above), was distinguished as turning not on the stigma of being called a drunkard, but rather on loss of "the right to purchase liquor." (To see how this claim was reconciled with the Constantineau Court's statement that "[w]here a person's good name, reputation, honor, or integrity is at stake because of what the government is doing to him, notice and an opportunity to be heard are essential," consult 424 U.S. at 708.) What Davis alleged, Justice Rehnquist reasoned, was simply a common law defamation. "[Accepting Davis's argument] would seem almost necessarily to result in every legally cognizable injury which may have been inflicted by a state official acting under 'color of law' establishing a violation of the Fourteenth Amendment."

Paul was one of a trilogy of cases, decided in a 3–month span, in which the Court openly worried about the capacity of the new due process doctrine to involve federal courts in the day-to-day operation of state and local governments. (The other two cases were Bishop v. Wood, involving firing of a police officer, and Meachum v. Fano, involving prison discipline. In all three cases, plaintiffs with due process claims that seemed strong under existing precedent, lost. See p. 823 above.) Paul may have been understandable from the federalism perspective, but as an exposition of due process doctrine, it was lambasted in the academic press. See, e.g., David L. Shapiro, Mr. Justice Rehnquist: A Preliminary View, 90 Harv.L.Rev. 293, 324–28 (1976). Of particular importance was the extended discussion in HENRY P. MONAGHAN, OF "LIBERTY" AND "PROPERTY," 62 Cornell L.Rev. 405 (1977). The Paul opinion's treatment of precedent, said Professor Monaghan, was "wholly startling." Moreover, even if the constitutional status of the interest in reputation were an open question, Justice Rehnquist's discussion was wide of the mark. "[I]t is an unsettling conception of 'liberty' that protects an individual against state interference with his access to liquor but not with his reputation in the community." Id. at 426.

Professor Monaghan then went further, and attempted to reconstruct Paul v. Davis by focusing on the process due rather than the interest protected. The Court's problem, he said, grew out of its insistence in Goldberg on prior hearings. Common-law plaintiffs sue in court after being injured and, in many cases, common-law-like "property" or "liberty" interests could be treated procedurally the same way. That is, a subsequent cause of action for damages could satisfy government's obligation to afford due process. "This view, if accepted, would have disposed of the procedural due process objection in Paul." Id. at 431. This part of Professor Monaghan's article turns up in the majority opinion in Ingraham (footnote 4 in the above-edited version). Justice Stevens (who had not participated in Paul v. Davis) made the point more explicitly in his Ingraham dissent: "In the property context, therefore, frequently a postdeprivation state remedy may be all the process that the Fourteenth Amendment requires. It may also be true—although I do not express an opinion on the point—that an adequate state remedy for defamation may satisfy the due process requirement when a State has impaired an individual's interest in his reputation. On that hypothesis, the Court's analysis today gives rise to the thought that Paul v. Davis may have been correctly decided on an incorrect rationale. Perhaps the Court will one day agree with Mr. Justice Brennan's appraisal of the importance of the constitutional interest at stake in [Paul] and nevertheless conclude that an adequate state remedy may prevent every state-inflicted injury to a person's reputation from violating 42 U.S.C. § 1983."

(2) The next significant line of cases involved prisoners who lost something that was indubitably "property" at the hands of prison personnel. In PARRATT V. TAYLOR, 451 U.S. 527 (1981), a mail order hobby kit worth $23.50 disappeared between its arrival at the prison and its delivery to Taylor. The loss, Taylor alleged, was due to the negligence of prison officials. Justice Rehnquist, writing for the Court: "Although [Taylor] has been deprived of property under color of state law, the deprivation did not occur as a result of some established state procedure. Indeed, the deprivation occurred as a result of the unauthorized failure of agents of the State to follow established state procedure. There is no contention that the procedures themselves are inadequate nor is there any contention that it was practicable for the State to provide a predeprivation hearing. Moreover, the State of Nebraska has provided respondent with the means by which he can receive redress for the deprivation. The State provides a remedy to persons who believe they have suffered a tortious loss at the hands of the State. See Neb.Rev.Stat. § 81–8,209 et seq. (1976). Through this tort claims procedure the State hears and pays claims of prisoners housed in its penal institutions. This procedure was in existence at the time of the loss here in question but respondent did not use it. It is argued that the State does not adequately protect the respondent's interests because it provides only for an action against the State as opposed to its individual employees, it contains no provisions for punitive damages, and there is no right to a trial by jury. Although the state remedies may not provide the respondent with all the relief which may have been available if he could have proceeded

under § 1983, that does not mean that the state remedies are not adequate to satisfy the requirements of due process. The remedies provided could have fully compensated the respondent for the property loss he suffered, and we hold that they are sufficient to satisfy the requirements of due process." This conclusion, the Justice pointed out, "is also quite consistent with the approach taken by the Court in Ingraham v. Wright."[1]

The rationale of Parratt was extended in HUDSON v. PALMER, 468 U.S. 517 (1984). Prisoner Palmer alleged that Hudson, a guard, had intentionally destroyed some of his noncontraband property during a "shakedown" search of his cell. The lower courts concluded that, even though the action here was (allegedly) intentional, the logic of Parratt applied. The Supreme Court, per Chief Justice Burger, agreed. "While Parratt is necessarily limited by its facts to negligent deprivations of property, it is evident, as the Court of Appeals recognized, that its reasoning applies as well to intentional deprivations of property. The underlying rationale of Parratt is that when deprivations of property are effected through random and unauthorized conduct of a state employee, predeprivation procedures are simply 'impracticable' since the state cannot know when such deprivations will occur. We can discern no logical distinction between negligent and intentional deprivations of property insofar as the 'practicability' of affording predeprivation process is concerned. The state can no more anticipate and control in advance the random and unauthorized intentional conduct of its employees than it can anticipate similar negligent conduct. Arguably, intentional acts are even more difficult to anticipate because one bent on intentionally depriving a person of his property might well take affirmative steps to avoid signalling his intent." Palmer went on to argue that "relief under applicable state law 'is far from certain and complete' because a state court might hold that petitioner, as a state employee, is entitled to sovereign immunity." The Court disposed of this argument by observing that the district court explicitly, and the court of appeals implicitly, had consulted Virginia law and determined that immunity was not available for intentional torts.[2]

(3) The boundaries of the Parratt–Hudson doctrine were clarified in ZINERMON v. BURCH, 494 U.S. 113 (1990). Burch was admitted to a state mental hospital, and kept there for 5 months, based on his "voluntary" signature, which was given while he was known to be heavily medicated and disoriented. He claimed that defendants (physicians and other staff at the hospital) should have admitted him pursuant to Florida's "involuntary placement procedure," under which he would have been afforded a hearing and representation. Relying on Parratt–Hudson, the defendants argued that Burch had, at most, a claim for damages under the state law of unlawful confinement. Florida had perfectly good statutory procedures governing involuntary commitment, as Burch admitted, and therefore the

---

1. Insofar as it held that a *negligent* action by government officials could constitute a "deprivation," Parratt was overruled by Daniels v. Williams, 474 U.S. 327 (1986), and Davidson v. Cannon, 474 U.S. 344 (1986).

2. Cf. Daniels v. Williams, 474 U.S. 327, 342 (1986) (Stevens, J., concurring in the judgment) ("[T]he mere fact that a State elects to provide some of its agents with a sovereign immunity defense in certain cases does not justify the conclusion that its remedial system is constitutionally inadequate.")

gravamen of the complaint was that there was a random, unauthorized departure from the normal procedures. But held, 5–4, per Justice Blackmun: Failure adequately to inquire into whether Burch was capable of voluntary consent, if proven, would constitute a denial of due process: "Parratt is not an exception to the Mathews balancing test, but rather an application of that test to the unusual case in which one of the variables in the Mathews equation—the value of predeprivation safeguards—is negligible in preventing the kind of deprivation at issue." Therefore, Parratt could be applied to deprivations of liberty as well as property. But "[t]his case . . . is not controlled by Parratt and Hudson, for three basic reasons:

"First, petitioners cannot claim that the deprivation of Burch's liberty was unpredictable. Under Florida's statutory scheme, only a person competent to give informed consent may be admitted as a voluntary patient. There is, however, no specified way of determining, before a patient is asked to sign admission forms, whether he is competent. It is hardly unforeseeable that a person requesting treatment for mental illness might be incapable of informed consent. . . . Any erroneous deprivation will occur, if at all, at a specific, predictable point in the admission process—when a patient is given admission forms to sign. . . .

"Second, we cannot say that predeprivation process was impossible here. Florida already has an established procedure for involuntary placement. The problem is only to ensure that this procedure is afforded to all patients who cannot be admitted voluntarily, both those who are unwilling and those who are unable to give consent. . . . [T]here is nothing absurd in suggesting that, had the State limited and guided petitioners' power to admit patients, the deprivation might have been averted. . . .

"Third, petitioners cannot characterize their conduct as 'unauthorized' in the sense the term is used in Parratt and Hudson. The State delegated to them the power and authority to effect the very deprivation complained of here, Burch's confinement in a mental hospital, and also delegated to them the concomitant duty to initiate the procedural safeguards set up by state law to guard against unlawful confinement. In Parratt and Hudson, the state employees had no similar broad authority to deprive prisoners of their personal property, and no similar duty to initiate (for persons unable to protect their own interests) the procedural safeguards required before deprivations occur. The deprivation here is 'unauthorized' only in the sense that it was not an act sanctioned by state law. . . ."

If Zinermon, as thus distinguished, marks the bounds of the Parratt–Hudson doctrine that government may provide all the process "due" by offering post-deprivation tort or statutory judicial remedies, where does this leave Ingraham? Does Zinermon constitute a rejection of Prof. Monaghan's effort to reframe Paul v. Davis?

(4) The latest word in this area appears to further muddy the waters. Those of you who studied the collection of Notes on the Practice of Entitlement Analysis, p. 814 above, will recall that one of the most vexing questions raised by entitlement reasoning is whether government contracts (conceptualized as a set of mutually explicit understandings that constrain the discretion of the government procurement officer) now become "property" for due process purposes. In LUJAN V. G & G FIRE SPRINKLERS, INC., 532

U.S. 189 (2001), p. 815 above, the Court pretermitted this question in favor of speaking to the question of what process is due. Chief Justice Rehnquist, writing for a unanimous Court: "In [prior cases], the claimant was denied a right by virtue of which he was presently entitled either to exercise ownership dominion over real or personal property, or to pursue a gainful occupation. Unlike those claimants, respondent has not been denied any present entitlement. G & G has been deprived of payment that it contends it is owed under a contract, based on the State's determination that G & G failed to comply with the contract's terms. G & G has only a claim that it did comply with those terms and therefore that it is entitled to be paid in full. Though we assume for purposes of decision here that G & G has a property interest in its claim for payment, it is an interest, unlike the interests discussed above, that can be fully protected by an ordinary breach-of-contract suit. In Cafeteria & Restaurant Workers v. McElroy, we said: 'The very nature of due process negates any concept of inflexible procedures universally applicable to every imaginable situation. "[D]ue process, unlike some legal rules, is not a technical conception with a fixed content unrelated to time, place and circumstances. It is compounded of history, reason, the past course of decisions" [Joint Anti–Fascist Refugee Comm. v. McGrath, 341 U.S. 123, 171–72 (1951) (Frankfurter, J., concurring)]. We hold that if California makes ordinary judicial process available to respondent for resolving its contractual dispute, that process is due process."

The Chief Justice then turned to whether such process was indeed available to G & G. After surveying California statutes and cases, he concluded: "It thus appears that subcontractors like respondent may pursue their claims for payment by bringing a standard breach-of-contract suit against the contractor under California law. Our view is necessarily tentative, since the final determination of the question rests in the hands of the California courts, but respondent has not convinced us that this avenue of relief is closed to it."

Does G & G Fire Sprinklers constitute a vindication of Prof. Monaghan's effort to reframe Paul v. Davis?

CODA

One of your editors, surveying the Court's handiwork since Goldberg v. Kelly, concluded:

"In essence, a federal court enforcing current due process doctrine says to the national political branches and to the states:

We will prevent you from depriving an individual, without due process, of those interests which you have chosen to define in a certain fashion—that is, through use of specific, mandatory, substantive standards that meaningfully constrain the discretion of the official decisionmaker. Rest assured, you really are in control here. We have nothing to say about how, or even whether, you define interests in the first instance; we have nothing to say about interests you choose to define in some other fashion. Indeed, we are primarily concerned about what you *really meant* to do, not what the individual might reasonably have *thought* you did. And our standard for standards, if you will, has gotten pretty high, just as we've become very hesitant to hold you to anything that you haven't expressly and formally undertaken. But keep this also in mind. As to interests which you *have* defined in the critical fashion, your views about the process appropriate to implement those interests are not controlling on us.

"This is doctrine so patently absurd that criticizing it seems about as challenging as shooting fish in a barrel. Only by disassembling it, and understanding how each piece came to be present, can we appreciate that the alternatives threatened to make of due process either the warrant for boundless judicial intervention in administrative government, or the meaningless rubber stamp of whatever process the legislature decides is due."[3]

If you want to pursue the question of how procedural due process might be reconstructed, here is a sampling of very diverse proposals: Henry P. Monaghan, Of "Liberty" and "Property," 62 Cornell L.Rev. 405 (1977); Richard B. Saphire, Specifying Due Process Values: Toward a More Responsive Approach to Procedural Protection, 127 U. Pa. L. Rev. 111 (1978); Rodney A. Smolla, The Reemergence of the Right–Privilege Distinction in Constitutional Law: The Price of Protesting Too Much, 35 Stan.L.Rev. 69 (1982); Frank H. Easterbrook, Substance and Due Process, 1982 Sup. Ct. Rev. 85; Stephen Williams, Liberty and Property: The Problem of Government Benefits, 12 J. Legal. Stud. 3, 11–13 (1983); Edward L. Rubin, Due Process and the Administrative State, 72 Cal.L.Rev. 1044 (1984); Jerry L. Mashaw, Due Process in the Administrative State (1985); Lawrence Alexander, The Relationship Between Procedural Due Process and Substantive Constitutional Rights, 39 U. Fla.L.Rev. 323 (1987); Cynthia R. Farina, Conceiving Due Process, 3 Yale J.L. & Feminism 189 (1991); Jane Rutherford, The Myth of Due Process, 72 B.U. L. Rev. 1 (1992); Richard J. Pierce, Jr., The Due Process Counterrevolution of the 1990s?, 96 Colum. L. Rev. 1973 (1996); Rebecca E. Zeitlow, Giving Substance to Process: Countering the Due Process Counterrevolution, 75 Denv. U. L. Rev. 9 (1997).

3. Cynthia R. Farina, Conceiving Due Process, 3 Yale J.L. & Feminism 189, 221 (1991).

CHAPTER VIII

SCOPE OF REVIEW OF ADMINISTRATIVE ACTION

We turn now to the questions raised when courts are asked to review directly the substance of an agency's action. The fact that courts are in this business has an impact on many of the doctrines addressed elsewhere in this book—for instance, in the question raised several times in the chapters on rulemaking and adjudication, of what procedures agencies must follow in order to build an adequate record for this review process. And if you have already studied those chapters, you will already have met some of the doctrines you will also meet here—doctrines signaled by terms such as "arbitrary and capricious," "reasonable interpretation," "substantial evidence" and the like. But now we will look at the relationship of court and agency, concerning matters of substance, in a systematic way. Traditionally this is known as the question of "scope of review," but it might as well be called an inquiry into "intensity of review."

When judicial review occurs, on what subjects and how closely is the court to inquire? To what degree are the various elements of decision—facts, judgment, policy, law—left to the agency? To what extent are they to be decided by the reviewing court? One might imagine two polar positions: that the administrative determination in issue is conclusive, or that the court should make the determination by itself "de novo." Neither of these is readily described as "review" at all; they represent conclusions that the matter at issue is the unique business of the agency or of the courts, rather than a shared concern to be allocated between them. But we should expect most matters to be of shared concern, if only because Congress routinely provides both for agency determination of matters in the first instance, and for judicial review of those determinations. Most matters fall at neither pole, and thus a more nuanced determination of the proper allocation must be made.

Congress has usually, but not always, placed review of important administrative decisions in the keeping of the courts of appeals. These courts are, of course, already in the business of reviewing the non-administrative-law determinations of the federal trial courts, and so one is tempted to draw an analogy between the appellate court/trial court relationship and the appellate court/administrative agency one. But while there are some similarities—for instance, in the fact that both trial courts and agencies are equipped to hold evidentiary hearings, while appellate courts are not—there are also some important differences. For example, agencies, unlike district courts, have political responsibilities. And the President and the Congress have oversight relationships with agencies that tend to control the exercise of those political responsibilities. Probably the courts should not assume control of those responsibilities, too. Thus, this particular factor suggests the appropriateness of a relationship more remote and less embracing than that between appellate and trial courts for the kinds of issues that it embraces.

Considerations like these—considerations based on the systematic structural features of courts, agencies, and the other branches of government—form the groundwork on which the law of "scope of review" is built. Your editors would, however, be dissemblers, were they not also to point out that there is a strong counter-tradition on this subject, to be met both among scholars and among practitioners. This counter-tradition stakes out what can perhaps best be called a strong "realist" position. On this view, what judicial review comes down to, whatever words the judges mouth, is whether the judges do, or do not, agree with the agency on the underlying merits (or politics) of the substantive decision—and nothing more. There is no "deference," but only agreement or disagreement. Even on this view, of course, it would behoove the student to learn the lingo used to describe judicial review, in order, as a lawyer, to play her or his assigned part in the supposed charade. But your editors do not agree. They think that the subject is not mere window dressing; they think there are substantial structural issues that do imply that judges ought to interfere more here, and less there, and that these considerations ought to be reflected in the doctrinal formulations of scope of review. (Whether the particular doctrines presently articulated by the courts properly reflect these considerations is, of course, another question.)

It being a free country, you are of course entitled to decide for yourself.

SECTION 1. PERSPECTIVES ON THE PRACTICE OF JUDICIAL REVIEW

a. SOME GENERAL CLAIMS

(1) "The availability of judicial review is the necessary condition, psychologically if not logically, of a system of administrative power which purports to be legitimate, or legally valid." Louis L. Jaffe, Judicial Control of Administrative Action 320 (1965).

(2) "Congress has been willing to delegate its legislative powers broadly—and courts have upheld such delegation—because there is court review to assure that the agency exercises the delegated power within statutory limits...." Ethyl Corp. v. EPA, 541 F.2d 1, 68 (D.C.Cir.1976) (Leventhal, J., concurring), cert. denied, 426 U.S. 941 (1976).

(3) "Why should anyone believe that particular issues raised in episodic litigation between parties having peculiar litigating interests should provide the judiciary with sufficient information for it to understand the administrative, political, social, economic, or scientific reality of a congressional-administrative program, much less provide an opportunity to take effective action to mold that reality in desirable forms? That the courts generally do not hold such a belief is a testament to their wisdom. That they sometimes act as if they did is perhaps a result of our general

tendency to exert unreasonable pressure on all public institutions. If we demand persistently enough that the judges pull our chestnuts out of the fire, they will sometimes try." Jerry L. Mashaw, Bureaucratic Justice: Managing Social Security Disability Claims 7–9 (1983).

(4) *"Courts usually substitute judgment on the kind of questions of law that are within their special competence, but on other questions they limit themselves to deciding reasonableness; they do not clarify the meaning of reasonableness but retain full discretion in each case to stretch it in either direction.* The italicized statement is in general an adequate summary of the main idea of the law of scope of review and may be more reliable than the many complexities and refinements that are constantly repeated in judicial opinions." Kenneth C. Davis, Administrative Law Treatise 332 (2d ed. 1984).

(5) "[The intensity of review is affected by] the character of the administrative agency, the nature of the problems with which it deals, the nature and consequences of the administrative action, the confidence which the agency has won, the degree to which the review would interfere with the agency's functions or burden the courts, the nature of the proceedings before the administrative agency, and similar factors." Report of the Attorney General's Committee on Administrative Procedure 91 (1941).

(6) "The rules governing judicial review have no more substance at the core than a seedless grape." Ernest Gellhorn & Glen O. Robinson, Perspectives in Administrative Law, 75 Colum.L.Rev. 771, 780–81 (1975).

(7) "We should not assume that our judges are dissemblers." Clark Byse, Scope of Judicial Review in Informal Rulemaking, 33 Admin.L.Rev. 183, 193 (1981).

(8) "[A] standard of review ... generally cannot eliminate the risk [that the court will substitute its preferences. Yet] the only kind of review that does not entail that risk is no review, and that is the one 'standard' clearly incompatible with the will of Congress." Merrick B. Garland, Deregulation and Judicial Review, 98 Harv.L.Rev. 505, 558 (1985).

b. A JUDGE'S POINT OF VIEW

Harry T. Edwards, The Judicial Function and the Elusive Goal of Principled Decisionmaking
1991 Wis.L.Rev. 837.

Today, more than eleven years after becoming a judge, ... I still believe in and subscribe to principled decisionmaking, but it is no longer entirely clear to me that partisan politics and ideological maneuvering have no meaningful influence on judicial decisionmaking. ... [I]n my view, most judges still share a belief that principled decisionmaking is the essence of the judicial function. What has changed, I think, is the nature of certain external pressures felt by judges; these pressures are both created and exacerbated by the continuing distortion of public perceptions, in which the judicial function is increasingly viewed as just one more "political" enterprise. ...

The more that judges are assessed in terms of "political" (result-oriented) decisionmaking, the more likely it is that this will become a self-fulfilling prophecy. Even if judges are able to resist the temptation to conform to the false perception, continued assessments of judicial performance in political terms will promote a "new reality," for most people will come to believe that the judicial function is nothing more than a political enterprise. No matter how good the intentions of its servants, the judiciary will be sharply devalued and incompetent to fulfill its role as mediator in a society with lofty but sometimes conflicting ambitions. This would be a horror to behold. ... I have felt damned by an increasingly common image of the judiciary, and particularly of the D.C. Circuit, as a fundamentally political body.

Fortunately, the present reality of decisionmaking on the D.C. Circuit does not match the public perception. There is no doubt that there are ideological differences among the judges and that these differences may have an impact in the disposition of certain "very hard" (and even "hard") cases. ... Perhaps the most fundamental reality of D.C. Circuit decisionmaking is that, contrary to popular belief, circuit judges rarely disagree with one another over the disposition of particular cases. The vast majority of case dispositions involve unanimous decisions. In the court's 1983–84 year, for instance, dissents were filed in only 5.8% of the total cases decided; of those cases decided by full opinion, only 13% generated a dissent. A statistical analysis of 1989–90 reveals that dissents were filed in only 2.6% of the total cases decided; of those cases decided by full opinion, only roughly 10% included a dissent. Thus, the rate of dissents in 1989–90 actually dropped below the rate for 1983–84. Most notably, the dissent rate on what I call "mixed panels"—panels with judges appointed by Presidents of different political affiliations—did not exceed the general dissent rate in either year. Clearly, the image of an ideologically divided circuit court on which judges heed some political call to action is far from the truth.

In my view, most cases are "easy," in that the pertinent legal rules are readily identified and applied to the facts at hand, revealing a single "right answer." ... [R]oughly one-half of the cases I hear each year are "easy" and virtually all of these are disposed of without dissent. ... In a second category of ["hard"[1] cases] ... each party is able to advance at least one plausible legal argument in its favor. ... [But after] ... research and review ... the arguments of one party to a "hard" case seem to me demonstrably stronger than those of the other, and the case is decided accordingly. ... [A]pproximately 35 to 45% of the cases before the court are "hard" in this sense. In my experience, judges hearing these cases generally feel themselves bound by their view of the law, and identify the sounder arguments without recourse to their own political opinions. Not surprisingly, therefore, there is substantial agreement among judges as to the proper disposition of "hard" cases.

---

1. [Ed.] The judge's examples of "hard" and "very hard" cases included civil rights actions and two First Amendment cases, one involving a Ku Klux Klan march, the other a 6–5 decision dismissing a defamation suit by a Marxist political science professor against two syndicated columnists.

That leaves from 5 to 15% of our cases in the "very hard" category, making it by far the smallest of the three. In this narrow set of cases, careful research and reflection fail to yield conclusive answers. The relevant legal materials, thoroughly studied, show only that the competing arguments advanced by the parties are equally strong, and the judges who must decide are left in a state of equipoise. Disposition of this small number of cases, then, requires judges to exercise a measure of discretion, drawing to some degree on their own social and moral beliefs. That judges may find themselves in disagreement as to the outcome of these "very hard" cases is thus to be expected, and represents something quite different from stark political decisionmaking.

The important point, I think, is that so-called "very hard" cases are viewed as such not because they raise situations in which judges are inclined to engage in result-oriented decisionmaking, but, rather, because these cases admit of no clear answer. And when there is no discernible "right" answer to a case, it is more likely (although not inevitable) that decisionmaking may be influenced by political or ideological considerations.

NOTE

Harry Edwards is, of course, a well-known member of the United States Court of Appeals for the District of Columbia Circuit, a court that, because of its location and some specific statutory assignments, does a disproportionate amount of administrative review work. In recent years, there have been a spate of academic studies of the question whether reviewing judges are acting out of "principle" or out of "politics." While the methodologies of the studies have varied, and have become increasingly sophisticated, the core elements have been to assign judges an "ideology" based on the party of the President who appointed them, and then to look more at how they voted than at what they said. In one such study, based on environmental law decisions coming from the D.C. Circuit and written in part in direct response to Judge Edward's claims, Professor Richard Revesz drew the following conclusions:

> First, ideology significantly influences judicial decisionmaking on the D.C. Circuit. Second, ideological voting is more prevalent in cases ... that are less likely to be reviewed by the United States Supreme Court. Third, a judge's vote ... is greatly affected by the identity of the other judges sitting on the panel.

Richard L. Revesz, Environmental Regulation, Ideology, and the D.C. Circuit, 83 Va. L. Rev. 1717, 1719 (1997). Revesz explained his third claim more graphically a few pages later: "The findings show, quite strongly, that Democratic judges 'vote as Democrats' only when there are at least two Democrats on the panel; and that similarly, Republican judges 'vote as Republicans' only when there are at least two Republicans on the panel." (Id. at 1765–66.)

Judge Edwards was not convinced. In a reply, Collegiality and Decision Making on the D.C. Circuit, 84 Va. L. Rev. 1335 (1998), he claimed that Revesz's study—and another in the same vein—was gravely flawed. Much of the criticism was methodological and detailed, and must be read in full to be evaluated. Judge Edwards concluded that at most Revesz had shown that composition of the three-judge panels influenced judicial discussion in a way fully consistent with the view that the judges were supposed to discuss cases with each other and try to reach a collegial result. One general point Judge Edwards made, however, went to the heart of studies like these, id. at 1365:

> Ignoring the self-description of judges would be one thing if judging were a mechanical process, or one performed by people incapable of self-consciousness. But judging is a human activity, performed by human beings trained to think critically about their endeavor. To understand it fully requires considering the way those who perform the activity understand it.

Do you agree?

(To see Professor Revesz's response to Judge Edwards' response, see Ideology, Collegiality, and the D.C. Circuit: A Reply to Chief Judge Harry T. Edwards, 85 Va.L.Rev. 805 (1999).)

c.   WHAT THE APA PROVIDES

5 U.S.C. § 706   Scope of Review

To the extent necessary to decision and when presented, the reviewing court shall decide all relevant questions of law, interpret constitutional and statutory provisions, and determine the meaning or applicability of the terms of an agency action. The reviewing court shall:

(1) compel agency action unlawfully withheld or unreasonably delayed; and

(2) hold unlawful and set aside agency action, findings, and conclusions found to be—

(A) arbitrary, capricious, an abuse of discretion, or otherwise not in accordance with law;

(B) contrary to constitutional right, power, privilege, or immunity;

(C) in excess of statutory jurisdiction, authority, or limitations, or short of statutory right;

(D) without observance of procedure required by law;

(E) unsupported by substantial evidence in a case subject to sections 556 and 557 of this title or otherwise reviewed on the record of an agency hearing provided by statute; or

(F) unwarranted by the facts to the extent that the facts are subject to trial de novo by the reviewing court.

In making the foregoing determinations, the court shall review the whole record or those parts of it cited by a party, and due account shall be taken of the rule of prejudicial error.

NOTES

(1) It may seem surprising to find the judicial review provisions of the APA included under a section of this chapter called "Perspectives on the Practice of Judicial Review." The APA is, after all, governing law. But there is no doubt that the courts handle § 706 of the APA differently from

many of the other provisions of the statute. Sometimes the judges cite it, and sometimes not. Sometimes the judges seem to rely on its particular wording, and sometimes not. It is too early in the chapter, of course, to formulate a view of what the underlying pattern is. But in what follows, it is certainly worth asking what the source of judicial authority—and judicial limit—in judicial review is, or ought to be. Is substantive review a common law process, thrust upon the courts by the existence of jurisdictional statutes sending cases their way? Is it a statutory process, defined and limited by the provisions of the APA or of various organic statutes? Or is it based on the Constitution, on the theory that broad delegations of authority to agencies would not be constitutionally valid without some substantial judicial oversight?

(2) Whatever the answers to the preceding questions, it certainly does not hurt to be familiar with the mechanics of the provisions. As an initial exercise, see if you can refer each of the blocks in the following table to the appropriate language and subsection in § 706:

	On-the-record proceeding	Notice-and-comment rulemaking	Informal adjudication
Findings of fact			
Judgment (application of law to facts)			
Discretion (policy formulation)			
Conclusions of law			

[H17]

SECTION 2.   THE BASELINE NORM OF LEGAL REGULARITY

a.   CONSISTENCY OF APPLICATION

Shaw's Supermarkets, Inc. v. National Labor Relations Board

United States Court of Appeals for the First Circuit, 1989.
884 F.2d 34.

■ Before BREYER and SELYA, CIRCUIT JUDGES, and CAFFREY, SENIOR DISTRICT JUDGE.

■ BREYER, CIRCUIT JUDGE.

The National Labor Relations Board (the "Board") found that Shaw's Supermarkets ("Shaw") violated National Labor Relations Act ("NLRA") § 8(a)(1) during a representation election held at Shaw's Wells, Maine distribution facility in January 1987. In the election, 71 votes were cast for no union, 46 votes for a Teamsters local, and one vote for an independent union. The finding of violation rested primarily upon the fact that five days before the election, a Shaw vice president [made statements to employees that in the Board's view] taken in context, constituted a "threat of reprisal" against collective organizing ... The Board ordered a new election. The Board now asks us to enforce its order.

... Under NLRA § 7, employees have the right to "self-organization, to form, join, or assist labor organizations, to bargain collectively through representatives of their own choosing ..." Employers may not "interfere with, restrain, or coerce employees in the exercise of" those rights. NLRA § 8(a)(1). Moreover, the NLRA expressly states that a "threat of reprisal or force or promise of benefit" does not constitute otherwise protected "express[ion]." NLRA § 8(c). Thus the NLRA prohibits employer speech during an election campaign which contains a "threat of reprisal" and thereby "interfere[s] with, restrain[s] or coerce[s]" employees in the exercise of their rights to "form, join or assist" labor unions. See NLRB v. Gissel Packing Co., Inc., 395 U.S. 575, 618 (1969). Whether any particular employer speech amounts to such a "threat of reprisal" depends upon the context in which the speech is uttered. And, as a general rule, the law gives the Board, not the courts, the authority to examine the circumstances, to find the facts, and to decide whether the remarks, in context, amounted to an unlawful threat. ...

In January 1987, in the midst of a union representation campaign, and five days before the election, Charles Wyatt, Shaw's vice president for distribution, held three meetings with three different groups of employees. In response to questions at the first meeting, Wyatt said that if a union won "the employees would be guaranteed minimum wages and workmen's comp and that's where our collective bargaining process would begin." He made the same statement to the other two groups of employees. Wyatt also told all the employees that "typically the art of collective bargaining is a give and take process and that ... we would start with minimum wages and workmen's comp and build from that point." Wyatt referred to a union as a "third party." He also said that "the first contract is generally the toughest or hardest to negotiate ... and that generally it could take up to a year." Wyatt's audience contained both full-time employees, then earning up to $11.70 an hour, and part-time employees, then earning about $5.00 an hour; the federal minimum wage at that time was $3.55 an hour.

The Board found no other unfair labor practices committed by Shaw during this election campaign. We can find nothing else in the record that might sharpen the details or color the background of the "context" of the bargaining campaign, either in the Board's or the company's favor. And as Board counsel told us at oral argument, neither can the Board.

Were the Board writing on a blank slate, were there no set of Board cases on the subject, we should likely find sufficient basis in the record to sustain the Board's conclusion. Statements like those at issue here—that the company will "begin" its bargaining at "minimum wages and workmen's comp," that it will "build from that point"—might, depending on the context, innocently represent a legal truth about how the collective bargaining process works, legitimately remind employees that a union might trade certain payments or benefits that many workers now enjoy in order to obtain other payments or benefits, or improperly constitute a threat that, if the union wins, the employer will strip benefits back to the minimum, forcing the union to struggle even to keep the status quo. In deciding how to react to these statements, a court must recognize that the Board is expert, not simply about the factual context of the individual case, but also about how employees are likely to understand certain forms of words in the mine-run of cases. Thus, if the Board were to conclude that it should always assume that employees would reasonably take words of the sort at issue here as threats of regressive bargaining in the absence of added employer explanation to the contrary, we believe (though we need not, and do not decide) that a court could not easily say the Board was acting outside the authority that the law grants it.

The problem in this case for the Board, however, is that (a) it is not writing on a blank slate, but has written on the subject often in the past; (b) the Board has not said that it wishes to depart from its several prior cases on the subject; yet (c) as we shall discuss below, the prior cases dictate a result in Shaw's favor.

The law that governs an agency's significant departure from its own prior precedent is clear. ... The agency has a

> duty to explain its departure from prior norms. The agency may flatly repudiate those norms, deciding, for example, that changed circumstances mean that they are no longer required in order to effectuate congressional policy. Or it may narrow the zone in which some rule will be applied, because it appears that a more discriminating invocation of the rule will best serve congressional policy. Or it may find that, although the rule in general serves useful purposes, peculiarities of the case before it suggest that the rule not be applied in that case. *Whatever the ground for departure from prior norms, however, it must be clearly set forth so that the reviewing court may understand the basis of the agency's action and so may judge the consistency of that action with the agency's mandate.* ...
>
> [If] the agency distinguishes earlier cases[, it must] assert ... distinctions that, when fairly and sympathetically read in the context of the entire opinion of the agency, reveal the policies it is pursuing.

Atchison, Topeka & Santa Fe Railway Co. v. Wichita Board of Trade, 412 U.S. 800, 808–09 (1973) (plurality opinion) (emphasis added).

> It is, of course, true that the Board is free to adopt new rules of decision and that the new rules of law can be given retroactive application. Nevertheless the Board may not depart sub silentio from its usual rules of decision to reach a different, unexplained result in a single case. ... "[T]here may not be a rule for Monday, another for Tuesday, a rule for general application, but denied outright in a specific case." Mary Carter Paint Co. v. FTC, 333 F.2d 654, 660 (5th Cir.1964) (Brown, J., concurring), rev'd on other grounds, 382 U.S. 46 (1965). "[A]n inadequately explained departure solely for purposes of a

particular case, or the creation of conflicting lines of precedent governing the identical situation, is not to be tolerated."

NLRB v. International Union of Operating Engineers, Local 925, 460 F.2d
589, 604 (5th Cir.1972) (citations omitted).

The Board says that Wyatt's statements fell within a category it calls
"bargaining from scratch." It has held the making of such statements
unlawful when, in context, a reasonable employee would take them as a
coercive threat that an employer will engage in "regressive bargaining," by
removing wages and benefits if the union wins. The Board has distinguished lawful from unlawful "bargaining from scratch" statements by
ascribing importance to the varying elements of the factual contexts
embodied in its past precedent.

[The court reviewed eight NLRB cases, from 1968–1986, in which the
Board had concluded that an employer's "bargaining from scratch" statement did *not*, in context, amount to a threat of "regressive bargaining."] In
many of these cases ... the statements in context seem to us just as
threatening (if not more so) than those in the present case. We do not see
how, after reading the record in this case and the opinions in the cases we
have just mentioned, one could reasonably find no violation in those earlier
cases yet find a violation in this case. Wyatt used language virtually
identical to that used in the cases just listed. ... The record does not reveal
any other elements suggesting regressive bargaining. Indeed, Board counsel
at oral argument simply stated that he "did not know" just what it was in
the context of the prior cases finding no violation that "made these same
statements" benign there, yet harmful here. Counsel's statement, in our
view, honestly reflects the circumstances, for we do not see how one can
distinguish prior cases in which the Board found "no violation."

Of course, there are other cases in which the Board found that a
"bargaining from scratch" statement violated the law. [The court reviewed
four NLRB decisions from the 1977–86 period.] ... In almost all these
cases, the "bargaining from scratch" speech was accompanied by other
serious unfair labor practices, such as the discriminatory treatment of labor
organizers. ... [Moreover,] the language and context suggested, far more
strongly than here, a threat to eliminate benefits before bargaining. ...

In finding the Board's decision in this case inconsistent with its
precedents, we do not intend to impose upon the Board the time consuming
obligation of microscopically examining prior cases; nor to encourage counsel to examine past precedent with an eye towards raising hosts of legalistic
arguments and distinctions. Here, however, the past cases trace a relatively
clear line. Nor do we believe that past cases are a straitjacket, inhibiting
experimentation or change. ... [T]he Board remains free to modify or
change its rule; to depart from, or to keep within, prior precedent, as long
as it focuses upon the issue and explains why change is reasonable. Unless
an agency either follows or consciously changes the rules developed in its
precedent, those subject to the agency's authority cannot use its precedent
as a guide for their conduct; nor will that precedent check arbitrary agency
action.

For these reasons we decline to enforce the Board's order, and we remand the case to the Board.

NOTES

(1) The most clearly troubling species of inconsistent administrative behavior occurs when someone is penalized for conduct that all available official signals at the time led him to believe was lawful. As Justice Cardozo put it, "Law as a guide to conduct is reduced to the level of mere futility if it is unknown and unknowable." Benjamin N. Cardozo, The Growth of the Law 3 (1924). Do you think Shaw's vice-president was briefed by counsel about the intricacies of the Board's "bargaining from scratch" doctrine before meeting with Shaw's employees? If so, what did counsel say?

But demands for administrative consistency might be justified even in the absence of concerns about upsetting actual reliance. Writing for the plurality in Atchison, Topeka & Santa Fe, Justice Marshall reasoned:

> This is essentially a corollary of the general rule requiring that the agency explain the policies underlying its action. A settled course of behavior embodies the agency's informed judgment that, by pursuing that course, it will carry out the policies committed to it by Congress. There is, then, at least a presumption that those policies will be carried out best if the settled rule is adhered to.

412 U.S. at 807–08.

The difference between reliance-upsetting inconsistency and "mere" inconsistency can also be seen in the range of administrative options on remand. Then-Judge Breyer's opinion in Shaw is careful to emphasize that the agency is not forever locked into its original regulatory policy; it *can* change its mind, so long as it acknowledges that change is occurring and justifies the new position. At that point, the court will have to determine, just as in any other administrative review situation, whether the agency's action is procedurally and substantively lawful. In the "mere inconsistency" situation, that is the end of the matter. However, with inconsistency of the reliance-upsetting sort, yet another hurdle looms before the agency: Can it apply the "new" policy to the particular party before it, or is the disruption of reliance so severe (as balanced against the government's interest in immediate application of the new policy) as to constitute unlawful retroactivity? This latter question, which at some point implicates due process, is explored more thoroughly at p. 574 above.

(2) BUSH–QUAYLE '92 PRIMARY COMM., INC. v. FEC, 104 F.3d 448(D.C.Cir.1997): The Primary Committee challenged an order of the FEC that it repay federal matching funds, received under the Presidential Primary Matching Payment Account Act, because the Committee had claimed reimbursement for costs that were not "qualified campaign expenses" within the Act. The court sustained the agency's reading as reasonable. The Committee insisted, however, that the FEC had disbursed matching funds for analogous expenditures during President Reagan's 1984 primary campaign. Judge Sentelle observed that the FEC's method of distinguishing this prior decision was "essentially a bare assertion that the two cases are different":

"The Commission's cursory treatment of seemingly relevant precedent is inadequate. We have stated previously, 'While here the agency's vice was not complete inattention to its prior policies, its discussion is so perplexing as to sow doubt whether this is a process of reasoned policy making, with a change in direction put in effect for a navigational objective, or the confusion of an agency that is rudderless and adrift.' ... Remand will permit the Commission to justify its approach or to reconsider its repayment determination. If the Commission chooses to provide a more detailed explanation, we can then ascertain whether some principled reason exists for distinguishing between the cases or whether the decision of whether an expenditure is qualified has been so subjective as to be arbitrary and capricious. Until we have a more adequate discussion from the Commission of the departure from the approach used in Reagan–Bush, it would be imprudent to address petitioners' claim that they suffered a due process violation from lack of notice. We therefore decline to address this claim at this time." (Id. at 454–55.)

(3) Distinct from, though surely related to, consistency with prior adjudicatory decisions, is the principle that an agency must follow its own regulations until they are validly amended or rescinded. The agency has this obligation *even if* it had no duty to adopt the particular rules in the first place. This principle is often called the "Accardi doctrine" from the case in which it first played a prominent role[1]; its most dramatic applications come from the Watergate scandal. When Attorney General Robert Bork, on Richard Nixon's order, fired Archibald Cox as Watergate Special Prosecutor, Judge Gerhardt Gesell held the action unlawful. Although the Attorney General generally had the power to fire a federal prosecutor at will, he had limited his own authority by promulgating a regulation that the Watergate Special Prosecutor would be fired only "for extraordinary improprieties." As Cox had not engaged in such behavior, the Attorney General had no power to fire him. Nader v. Bork, 366 F.Supp. 104 (D.D.C.1973). When Cox's successor, Leon Jaworski, obtained a subpoena ordering President Nixon to produce certain tape recordings, and Nixon refused to comply on grounds of executive privilege, the President argued that the judiciary could not intervene in an "intra-executive dispute." The Supreme Court unanimously held that, because the Attorney General had explicitly delegated to the Special Prosecutor the power to contest any invocation of executive privilege in connection with his investigations, "the Executive Branch is bound by" that regulation. United States v. Nixon, 418 U.S. 683 (1974).

A more recent Supreme Court use of the principle appears in INS v. Yang, 519 U.S. 26 (1996). By statute, the Immigration & Naturalization Service has authority to waive deportation in certain circumstances. This case began when the INS refused to waive the deportation of Yang, on grounds that he had engaged in a pattern of fraud and deceit in obtaining admission to the United States. Yang argued, and the Ninth Circuit agreed, that the statute did not authorize the agency to consider fraud relating to original admission in making the judgment whether to waive deportation. The Supreme Court unanimously disagreed with this construction of the

---

1. Accardi v. Shaughnessy, 347 U.S. 260 (1954).

statute. But, Yang wasn't out of court yet. The INS had voluntarily established a policy of not considering such evidence in its waiver decisions. The Court explained, "Though the agency's discretion is unfettered at the outset, if it announces and follows—by rule or settled course of adjudication—a general policy by which its exercise of discretion will be governed, an irrational departure from that policy (as opposed to an avowed alteration of it) could constitute action that must be overturned as 'arbitrary, capricious, [or] an abuse of discretion' within the meaning of the Administrative Procedure Act." Ultimately, however, Yang lost. The Court concluded that the INS had not capriciously ignored its policy. Rather, it had "interpreted" its policy narrowly to apply only to aliens who committed a single, isolated act of fraud to gain entry, and not to those who engaged in a pattern of fraudulent acts. As the policy was the INS' voluntary act of self-restraint, the agency could "within reason" refine it, and the Court found this refinement reasonable.

(4) Yet another aspect of the consistency norm is the concern for evenhandedness. "Government is at its most arbitrary when it treats similarly situated people differently"[2]—an axiom that Judge Friendly called "the most basic principle of jurisprudence." Henry J. Friendly, Indiscretion About Discretion, 31 Emory L.J. 747, 758 (1982). Although generally (if not universally) acknowledged as an essential condition of a just legal system, the principle of "like treatment of like cases" can be surprisingly difficult to realize: recall the difficulties first-year law students have in deciding if fact patterns are, or are not, distinguishable.

In the Shaw's case, Judge (now Justice) Breyer could at least work from formal, published N.L.R.B. opinions. What of less formal agency determinations? In Davis v. Commissioner, 69 T.C. 716 (1978), the Internal Revenue Service had disallowed part of a small charitable deduction claimed by Professor K.C. Davis for books received from West Publishing Co., used, and then donated to the University of Chicago Law Library. Contesting this position in the Tax Court, Davis (a famous professor of administrative law) obtained through discovery IRS "letter rulings" issued to Members of Congress who received free copies of the Congressional Record, gave them to charitable organizations, and deducted the value of the gifts.[3] After receiving four such rulings, Davis—insisting that the agency must act evenhandedly—sought additional discovery of all pertinent letter rulings (at that time, not generally available to the public) in the IRS's "reference file." Discovery was denied. As another Tax Court judge had said two years earlier in a similar effort by Professor Davis over a different deduction,

> It has long been the position of this Court that our responsibility is to apply the law to the facts of the case before us . . . ; how the Commissioner may have treated other taxpayers has generally been considered irrelevant in making that determination. Any change in that position

---

2. Etelson v. OPM, 684 F.2d 918, 926 (D.C.Cir.1982).

3. "Letter rulings" are issued with less structured intra-agency review than "revenue rulings," which are officially published and on which all taxpayers are encouraged to rely. The IRS considers itself bound by revenue rulings until revoked, but bound by letter rulings only as to the addressee taxpayer.

would have widespread ramifications in the administration and application of the Federal tax laws and in the conduct of our work. ... Over 11,000 new cases were commenced in this Court in the past year, and although many of those cases are settled, the Court still has a herculean task to keep abreast of its caseload. Were we to embrace the principles urged by Mr. Davis, the task would be magnified. Every trial would be extended, for it would then become necessary to allow the petitioner to inquire into the Commissioner's treatment of other similarly situated taxpayers. ... [T]he notion of equal justice has strong appeal in our society and might lead to the conclusion that his position should ultimately be adopted. Yet, a full appreciation of the ramifications of this matter makes abundantly clear that it should be approached cautiously.

Davis v. Commissioner, 65 T.C. 1014, 1022–23 (1976).

We might further consider the prospects of achieving evenhandedness in a massive benefits regime like the Social Security disability program. Professor Jerry Mashaw's several writings on Social Security disability administration illuminate these issues. His first study, completed in 1978, produced a damning indictment from a perspective much like Professor Davis': individual cases were being decided without discernible pattern. "The inconsistency of the disability process is patent. Indeed, it is widely believed that the outcome of cases depends more on who decides the case than on what the facts are."[4] But, as Mashaw explored in his later work, Bureaucratic Justice[5], intolerance of *any* degree of inconsistency is premised on a "model of individual justice." Alternatively, a "model of bureaucratic rationality" would frame the issues as whether *gross* errors have been avoided and marginal errors *evenly distributed* (that is, about as many wrongful grants as wrongful denials) at reasonable cost. These conditions will maximize the extent to which programmatic purposes are achieved and, thus, overall fairness is accomplished. For the "similarly situated" people at the margin of eligibility, inconsistent treatment is a necessary cost of a workable scheme; all that can realistically be asked—that the judgment on eligibility not be "too wrong"—will have been achieved.

Butz v. Glover Livestock Commission Co., Inc.

Supreme Court of the United States, 1973.
411 U.S. 182.

■ JUSTICE BRENNAN delivered the opinion of the Court.

The Judicial Officer of the Department of Agriculture, acting for the Secretary of Agriculture, found that respondent, a registrant under the Packers and Stockyards Act, 7 U.S.C. § 181 et seq., willfully violated ... the Act by incorrect weighing of livestock, and ... by entries of false

---

4. Jerry L. Mashaw, Charles J. Goetz, Frank I. Goodman, Warren F. Schwartz, Paul R. Verkuil & Milton M. Carrow, Social Security Hearings and Appeals: A Study of the Social Security Administration Hearing System xxi (1978).

5. Jerry L. Mashaw, Bureaucratic Justice: Managing Social Security Disability Claims (1983).

weights. An order was entered directing that respondent cease and desist from the violations and keep correct accounts, and also suspending respondent as a registrant under the Act for 20 days. Upon review of the decision and order, the Court of Appeals for the Eighth Circuit upheld, as supported by substantial evidence, the findings that respondent violated the Act by short-weighting cattle, and also sustained the cease-and-desist order and the order to keep correct accounts. The Court of Appeals, however, set aside the 20-day suspension. We granted certiorari to consider whether, in doing so, the Court of Appeals exceeded the scope of proper judicial review of administrative sanctions. . . .

Respondent operates a stockyard in Pine Bluff, Arkansas. As a registered "market agency" . . . respondent is authorized to sell consigned livestock on commission, subject to the regulatory provisions of the Act and the Secretary's implementing regulations. Investigations of respondent's operations in 1964, 1966, and 1967 uncovered instances of underweighing of consigned livestock. Respondent was informally warned to correct the situation, but when a 1969 investigation revealed more underweighing, the present proceeding was instituted by the Administrator of the Packers and Stockyards Administration.

Following a hearing and the submission of briefs, the Department of Agriculture hearing examiner found that respondent had "intentionally weighed the livestock at less than their true weights, issued scale tickets and accountings to the consignors on the basis of the false weights, and paid the consignors on the basis of the false weights." The hearing examiner recommended, in addition to a cease-and-desist order and an order to keep correct records, a 30-day suspension of respondent's registration under the Act.

The matter was then referred to the Judicial Officer. After hearing oral argument, the Judicial Officer filed a decision and order accepting the hearing examiner's findings and adopting his recommendations of a cease-and-desist order and an order to keep correct records. The recommended suspension was also imposed but was reduced to 20 days. The Judicial Officer stated:

> It is not a pleasant task to impose sanctions but in view of the previous warnings given respondent we conclude that we should not only issue a cease and desist order but also a suspension of respondent as a registrant under the act but for a lesser period than recommended by complainant and the hearing examiner.

The Court of Appeals agreed that 7 U.S.C. § 204 authorized the Secretary to suspend "any registrant found in violation of the Act," that the suspension procedure here satisfied the relevant requirements of the Administrative Procedure Act, 5 U.S.C. § 558, and that "the evidence indicates that [respondent] acted with careless disregard of the statutory requirements and thus meets the test of 'willfulness.' " The court nevertheless concluded that the suspension order was "unconscionable" under the circumstances of this case. The court gave two reasons. The first, relying on four previous suspension decisions, was that the Secretary's practice was not to impose suspensions for negligent or careless violations but only for violations found to be "intentional and flagrant," and therefore that the suspension in respondent's case was contrary to a policy of "achiev[ing] . . . uniformity of sanctions for similar violations." The second reason given was that "[t]he cease and desist order coupled with the damaging publicity surrounding these proceedings would certainly seem appropriate and reasonable with respect to the practice the Department seeks to eliminate."

The applicable standard of judicial review in such cases required review of the Secretary's order according to the "fundamental principle . . . that where Congress has entrusted an administrative agency with the responsibility of selecting the means of achieving the statutory policy 'the relation of remedy to policy is peculiarly a matter for administrative competence.' " American Power Co. v. SEC, 329 U.S. 90, 112 (1946). Thus, the Secretary's choice of sanction was not to be overturned unless the Court of Appeals might find it "unwarranted in law or . . . without justification in fact . . ." Id. at 112–13; FTC v. Universal–Rundle Corp., 387 U.S. 244, 250 (1967). The Court of Appeals acknowledged this definition of the permissible scope of judicial review but apparently regarded respondent's suspension as "unwarranted in law" or "without justification in fact." We cannot agree that the Secretary's action can be faulted in either respect on this record.

We read the Court of Appeals' opinion to suggest that the sanction was "unwarranted in law" because "uniformity of sanctions for similar violations" is somehow mandated by the Act. We search in vain for that requirement in the statute. The Secretary may suspend "for a reasonable specified period" any registrant who has violated any provision of the Act. 7 U.S.C. § 204. Nothing whatever in that provision confines its application to cases of "intentional and flagrant conduct" or denies its application in cases of negligent or careless violations. Rather, the breadth of the grant of authority to impose the sanction strongly implies a congressional purpose to permit the Secretary to impose it to deter repeated violations of the Act, whether intentional or negligent. The employment of a sanction within the authority of an administrative agency is thus not rendered invalid in a particular case because it is more severe than sanctions imposed in other cases. FTC v. Universal–Rundle Corp., 387 U.S., at 250, 251.

Moreover, the Court of Appeals may have been in error in acting on the premise that the Secretary's practice was to impose suspensions only in cases of "intentional and flagrant conduct." The Secretary's practice, rather, apparently is to employ that sanction as in his judgment best serves to deter violations and achieve the objectives of that statute. Congress plainly intended in its broad grant to give the Secretary that breadth of discretion. Therefore, mere unevenness in the application of the sanction does not render its application in a particular case "unwarranted in law."

Nor can we perceive any basis on this record for a conclusion that the suspension of respondent was so "without justification in fact" "as to constitute an abuse of [the Secretary's] discretion." American Power Co. v. SEC, 329 U.S., at 115. The Judicial Officer rested the suspension on his view of its necessity in light of respondent's disregard of previous warnings. The facts found concerning the previous warnings and respondent's disregard of these warnings were sustained by the Court of Appeals as based on ample evidence. In that circumstance, the overturning of the suspension authorized by the statute was an impermissible intrusion into the administrative domain.

Similarly, insofar as the Court of Appeals rested its action on its view that, in light of damaging publicity about the charges, the cease-and-desist order sufficiently redressed respondent's violations, the court clearly exceeded its function of judicial review. The fashioning of an appropriate and reasonable remedy is for the Secretary, not the court. The court may decide only whether, under the pertinent statute and relevant facts, the Secretary made "an allowable judgment in [his] choice of the remedy."

Reversed.

■ JUSTICE STEWART, with whom JUSTICE DOUGLAS joins, dissenting.

The only remarkable thing about this case is its presence in this Court. For the case involves no more than the application of well-settled principles to a familiar situation ... The Court of Appeals did nothing more than review a penalty imposed by the Secretary of Agriculture that was alleged by the respondent to be discriminatory and arbitrary. ... Had [it] used the talismanic language of the Administrative Procedure Act, and found the penalty to be either "arbitrary, capricious, an abuse of discretion, or otherwise not in accordance with law," 5 U.S.C. § 706(2)(A), I have no doubt that certiorari would have been denied. But the Court of Appeals made the mistake of using the wrong words, saying that the penalty was "unconscionable," because it was "unwarranted and without justification in fact."[1]

Today the Court holds that the penalty was not "unwarranted in law," because it was within permissible statutory limits. But this ignores the valid principle of law that motivated the Court of Appeals—the principle that like cases are to be treated alike. As Professor Jaffe has put the matter:

> The scope of judicial review is ultimately conditioned and determined by the major proposition that the constitutional courts of this country are the acknowledged architects and guarantors of the integrity of the legal system. ... An agency is not an island entire of itself. It is one of the many rooms in the magnificent mansion of the law. The very subordination of the agency to judicial jurisdiction is intended to proclaim the premise that each agency is to be brought into harmony with the totality of the law; the law as it is found in the statute at hand, the statute book at large, the principles and conceptions of the "common law," and the ultimate guarantees associated with the Constitution.

[Louis L. Jaffe, Judicial Control of Administrative Action 589–90 (1965).] The reversal today of a wholly defensible Court of Appeals judgment accomplishes two unfortunate results. First, the Court moves administrative decisionmaking one step closer to unreviewability, an odd result at a time when serious concern is being expressed about the fairness of agency

---

1. The Court of Appeals borrowed this phrasing of the test from this Court's opinion in American Power Co. v. SEC, 329 U.S. 90, 112–113.

justice.[2] Second, the Court serves notice upon the federal judiciary to be wary indeed of venturing to correct administrative arbitrariness. . . .

NOTES

(1) Distinguish the Agency's decision to bring a particular enforcement proceeding from the sanction it decides to give once the proceeding is successful. The former, akin to a D.A.'s decision to prosecute, has been held to be presumptively unreviewable unless the particular organic statute contains standards constraining the agency's enforcement discretion; it is discussed along with Heckler v. Chaney, p. 1218 below. Does it follow that the principle of "uniformity of sanctions for similar violations" should apply only if mandated by the particular organic statute? Or are the situations distinguishable?

(2) Traditionally, trial judges had considerable, and virtually unreviewable, discretion in setting criminal sentences. Cumulating criticism of the resulting disparities in punishment finally led to the Comprehensive Crime Control Act's provision of (i) a process for formulating federal sentencing guidelines, see Mistretta v. United States, p. 74 above, and (ii) appellate review of application of those guidelines. Should a court confronting the Butz issue today—conscious of the fact that Congress has been moved to curb discretion in the criminal sentencing context—develop standards of consistency in the administrative sentencing context? If so, would the standards be a matter of federal common law or a construction of § 706(2)(A)'s direction to set aside arbitrary or capricious agency action?

(3) CORDER v. UNITED STATES, 107 F.3d 595 (8th Cir.1997): Mary Corder owned a small 7–Eleven food store in St. Louis. An employee working alone at the store exchanged a total of $305 in cash for $610 in food stamp coupons offered by an undercover Department of Agriculture investigator. The Department's Food & Consumer Service (FCS) then charged Corder with illegal trafficking in violation of the Food Stamp Program. Corder, who proved that she neither knew about, nor had benefited from, the violations, and that she had in place a comprehensive compliance policy and employee training program, requested FCS to assess a civil monetary penalty in lieu of permanently disqualifying her from the Program. The agency granted this request; however, it not only required that she repay the $610 actual loss but also imposed the maximum penalty authorized by statute, $40,000. Corder sought judicial review of the sanction, and the Eighth Circuit held that the formula used to determine this monetary penalty was arbitrary and capricious, at least as applied to Corder:

"From the standpoint of its economic impact on Corder and her enterprise, the penalty is indistinguishable from a criminal fine. Congress has specified the factors that are relevant in imposing criminal fines, including defendant's ability to pay, the burden a fine will impose on defendant and any dependents, the loss defendant inflicted upon others, and so forth. See 18 U.S.C. § 3572. In reviewing criminal fines, this court

---

2. See generally K. Davis, Discretionary Justice: A Preliminary Inquiry (1969), reviewed by Wright, Beyond Discretionary Justice, 81 Yale L.J. 575.

ensures that the sentencing court has properly considered those factors. Similarly, many statutes authorizing civil fines carefully prescribe the factors an agency must consider in imposing such penalties, and reviewing courts ensure that agencies obey those statutory mandates.

"In the 1988 amendment, Congress did not specify the factors FCS must consider in imposing a civil monetary penalty in lieu of permanent disqualification. Instead, Congress generally directed FCS to exercise discretion so that 'the punishment will more closely fit the crime.' We do not construe this as a grant of standardless discretion to impose whatever fine the agency pleases. Rather, we believe it is a clear signal that FCS should follow principles of fairness that Congress has more clearly delineated in other laws administered by the Department of Agriculture, such as the Packers and Stockyards Act, 7 U.S.C. § 213(b): 'In determining the amount of the civil penalty to be assessed under this section, the Secretary shall consider the gravity of the offense, the size of the business involved, and the effect of the penalty on the person's ability to continue in business.'

"Following the 1988 amendment, FCS adopted a formula in § 278.6(j) of the regulations that considers none of these factors. The formula starts with one violator-specific fact—the violator's average monthly food stamp redemptions in the year prior to the violation. It then applies a series of arithmetic multipliers designed, as best we can determine, to guarantee that nearly every unknowing first offender will incur the statutory maximum $40,000 penalty. This is not the exercise of informed agency discretion. It is another example of implementing regulations that reflect a hostile attitude toward the alternative monetary sanction Congress enacted in 1988. We conclude that a fine based entirely on this formula, as Corder's fine admittedly was, must be overturned as arbitrary, capricious, and contrary to the statute."

(For a more favorable view of the agency's application of its guidelines, see Vasudeva v. U.S., 214 F.3d 1155 (9th Cir.2000).)

(4) FTC v. UNIVERSAL–RUNDLE CORP., 387 U.S. 244 (1967)—cited prominently in Glover Livestock—involved FTC sanctions against a plumbing-fixture manufacturer for engaging in the anticompetitive practice of giving some of its customers discounts that were unavailable to their competitors. Universal–Rundle had asked the Commission to stay its cease and desist order and "investigate and institute whatever proceedings are deemed appropriate . . . to correct the industry-wide practice by plumbing fixture manufacturers of granting discounts in prices on truckload shipments." Universal–Rundle submitted affidavits that (i) competitors offered even larger discounts than it had done, (ii) it was the sixth largest of seven main plumbing manufacturers, and (iii) during each of the past three years, it had lost money while its five larger competitors had made money. The FTC denied the stay, saying that a general allegation of wrongdoing by competitors was insufficient to trigger an industry-wide proceeding or to withhold enforcement of the order against Universal–Rundle's demonstrated wrongdoing. The court of appeals concluded that the agency had abused its discretion in denying the stay in light of Universal–Rundle's evidentiary offering; the FTC was instructed on remand to conduct an inquiry. The Supreme Court

(quoting from Moog Industries v. FTC, 355 U.S. 411 (1958)) unanimously reversed the court of appeals, 387 U.S. at 249–50:

> The decision as to whether to postpone enforcement of a cease-and-desist order "depends on a variety of factors peculiarly within the expert understanding of the Commission." Thus, "although an allegedly illegal practice may appear to be operative throughout an industry, whether such appearances reflect fact" is a question "that call[s] for discretionary determination by the administrative agency." Because these determinations require the specialized experienced judgment of the Commission, they cannot be overturned by the courts "in the absence of a patent abuse of discretion."

The Court distinguished precedent that "indicates [the FTC] does not have unbridled power to institute proceedings which will arbitrarily destroy one of many law violators in an industry" on grounds that "this is not such a case."

(5) Should beneficiaries of a regulatory scheme be able to complain that a decision as to sanctions was arbitrary and capricious because it was too *lenient*?

(6) Finally, we should remember that a significant amount of agency behavior in the area of enforcement and sanctions—as in all aspects of regulation—occurs beyond the ken of a reviewing court. A good reminder comes from Lars Noah, Administrative Arm–Twisting in the Shadow of Congressional Delegations of Authority, 1997 Wis. L. Rev. 873. Professor Noah explores the phenomenon of "arm-twisting," in which an agency uses informal coercion—threats to deny a license, refuse to enter into a procurement agreement, disseminate adverse publicity, or impose some sanction—indirectly to achieve "voluntary" compliance with objectives the agency (at least sometimes) could not achieve directly. After comparing this behavior with such analogues as plea bargaining and negotiated land-use conditions, Prof. Noah points out that the practice is not amenable to judicial control, so that the only realistic curbs for inappropriate use of arm-twisting are congressional oversight and agency self-restraint.

If the parties ultimately reach agreement, should we take this behavior as evidence of a win-win solution? Or as evidence of official duress? Compare the discussion of negotiated rulemaking, at p. 627 above.

b.   CONSISTENCY OF RULE DECLARATION

When the Shaw's Supermarket case (p. 908 above) was sent back to the NLRB, the agency was submissive but not repentant (Shaw's Supermarkets, Inc., 303 N.L.R.B. 382 (1991)):

> We respectfully decline the court's invitation to change extant Board law. For, with due respect to the court, we continue to believe that, under that law, conduct like that involved herein is unlawful. However, given the law of this case, we shall dismiss the complaint.

That an agency act within the bounds the court sets in the very case it has remanded—which, of course, sometimes allows the agency to do what it did before, if it has a new but proper basis for doing so—is probably the least that judicial review could mean. When agencies fail to live by this "law of the case"—or when courts' believe that agencies have failed to do this—the courts are quick to react. See, e.g., NLRB v. Goodless Brothers Electric Co., 285 F.3d 102 (1st Cir.2002). But what about next time? Is "the law of the *next* case" that announced by the court in a prior case, or that adhered to by the unrepentant agency? This is a surprisingly hard question to answer.

Stieberger v. Heckler

United States District Court for the Southern District of New York, 1985.
615 F.Supp. 1315, vacated and remanded, 801 F.2d 29 (2d Cir.1986).

■ SAND, DISTRICT JUDGE.

Plaintiffs, Theresa Stieberger and the City of New York, have instituted this action [against] the United States Department of Health and Human Services ("HHS") and the Social Security Administration ("SSA") [to challenge] the "non-acquiescence" policy, under which Administrative Law Judges ("ALJs") have been instructed to disregard the decisions of federal courts within the circuit in which they sit when those decisions conflict with the Secretary's own policies ... Plaintiffs contend that the non-acquiescence policy has ... unlawfully discriminated between those claimants who are able to secure judicial review and those who do not have access to judicial review in violation of the Administrative Procedure Act ("APA"), the Social Security Act, the Due Process Clause of the Fifth Amendment to the United States Constitution, and the principle of separation of powers. ... Plaintiffs have moved ... for a preliminary injunction.
...

It is important at the outset to set forth the precise nature of the "non-acquiescence" with which we are concerned in this case. Defendants acknowledge that they are bound by the judgments or orders of federal courts in the specific cases in which they are issued. Thus, this case does not involve the "law of the case" doctrine or principles of res judicata. At the other end of the legal spectrum, plaintiffs do not contend that the Secretary is legally obligated to follow a circuit court decision in a circuit other than the circuit in which the decision was rendered. Thus, plaintiffs do not argue that the decision of the first circuit court to decide an issue should have controlling, nationwide effect. What is at issue in this case is the Secretary's refusal to follow a circuit court ruling in subsequent cases within the same circuit.

[The particular legal issue involved was the "treating physician rule." The Second Circuit had a well-established standard concerning the weight to be given the medical opinion of the claimant's own physician in establishing the existence of a disability: "absent substantial evidence to the contrary, such opinions are binding on the Secretary; these opinions need not be supported by objective clinical or laboratory findings in order to be accorded such weight." The Secretary's standard was that "other things being equal, the fact that a physician treated a claimant will increase the weight which his or her opinion is accorded"; this standard was derived from a Fifth Circuit decision. The court concluded that the Secretary's standard was significantly different than the Second Circuit's in the weight it accorded the treating physician's opinion.]

... [SSA's original nonacquiescence] policy has been expressed in a variety of different forms. Section 1–161 of the [Agency's] Handbook, containing instructions for ALJs to follow in deciding Social Security cases, provided that

> While the ALJs are bound by decisions of the United States Supreme Court, they should also make every reasonable effort to follow the district or circuit court[']s views regarding procedural or evidentiary matters when handling similar cases in that particular district or circuit.

> However, where a district or circuit court[']s decision contains interpretations of the law, regulations, or rulings [that] are inconsistent with the Secretary's interpretations, the ALJs should not consider such decisions binding on future cases simply because the case is not appealed. In certain cases SSA will not appeal a court decision it disagrees with, in view of the special circumstances of the particular case (e.g., the limited effect of the decision).

> When SSA decides to acquiesce in a district court decision, or a circuit court decision [that] is inconsistent with our previous interpretation of the law, regulations, or rulings, SSA will take appropriate action to implement changes by means of regulations, rulings, etc. ALJs will be promptly advised of such action.

... In a January 7, 1982 memo to agency ALJs, defendant Louis B. Hays, former ... Associate Commissioner, stated unequivocally that

> [T]he federal courts do not run SSA's programs ... ALJs are responsible for applying the Secretary's policies and guidelines regardless of court decisions below the level of the Supreme Court. Court decisions can result in the changing of policies, but it is not the role of ALJs to independently institute those changes.

... The SSA has implemented its non-acquiescence policy in two ways. First, the SSA may simply ignore a circuit court decision by leaving unaltered and continuing to adhere to an agency regulation or other interpretive guideline which conflicts with the decision. Second, the Secretary has from time to time promulgated Social Security Rulings which specifically direct agency personnel, including ALJs, not to abide by a particular circuit court decision. Ten SSRs have been issued since 1966, seven of which are still in effect. ...

Defendants advance a number of interrelated legal arguments in support of an overall theory of why its policy of intracircuit non-acquiescence is lawful. Briefly stated, defendants first contend that the SSA, as part of a co-equal branch of the federal Government, is not bound by the doctrine of *stare decisis* ... [The agency asserts] the right, generally held by other litigants (e.g., private parties), to continue to adhere to and advocate its own view of what the law should be, free of any duty to continually conform its conduct to what the law has been said to be by a federal circuit court. Defendants note that the SSA, as a governmental agency with a duty to administer nationwide legal standards in Social

Security matters, is also different from the ordinary civil litigant and accordingly must be permitted to follow a policy of non-acquiescence in unfavorable circuit court decisions in order to preserve what it believes are the correct uniform legal standards under the Social Security Act. Defendants assert that the right to relitigate adverse circuit court rulings through a non-acquiescence policy is supported by the Supreme Court's decision in United States v. Mendoza, 464 U.S. 154 (1984), in which the Court held that the doctrine of non-mutual collateral estoppel does not apply against the United States.[1]

While the Supreme Court has apparently not directly confronted the issue of whether intra-circuit non-acquiescence is a lawful exercise of administrative agency authority, ... the SSA's non-acquiescence policy has been the subject of almost universal condemnation by those courts which have considered its legality [citing circuit and/or district court opinions from the Second, Fourth, Sixth, Eighth, Ninth and Tenth Circuits]. ... Courts are not alone in their condemnation of the Secretary's non-acquiescence policy. Members of Congress have also expressed considerable concern with respect to the legality and wisdom of the Secretary's non-acquiescence policy. See, e.g., H.R.No. 1039, 98th Cong., 2d Sess. 37–38 ("1984 Conference Report") (noting undesirability and questionable legality of non-acquiescence policy). Members of the executive branch itself have noted their disagreement with the policy by refusing to defend or adhere to the policy in judicial proceedings. See June 25, 1984 letter from United States Attorney for the Southern District of New York to Chief Judge Motley stating that

> It is our view that this policy, whatever it does permit, surely does not allow the United States Attorney's Office, HHS or any other federal agency to refuse to follow clear rules of law decided by the United States Court of Appeals ... [T]here has never been any support to my knowledge for the notion that federal agencies within a particular Circuit could disagree with and refuse to follow clear rulings of that Circuit. We have not defended cases in the past by disregarding the law of this Circuit and will not do so in the future.[2]

Even ALJs have objected to the policy, not only on constitutional grounds but also because Appeals Council reversal of ALJ decisions which are consistent with federal court precedent makes ALJ decisionmaking appear unduly erroneous ...

These authorities have stated the legal basis for their disapproval of the non-acquiescence policy by invoking several well-established legal doc-

---

1. Defendants also argue that ALJs are subordinates of the Secretary and thus are obligated to adhere to and apply the Secretary's policy as embodied in her rules and regulations, even if contrary to the decision of a federal circuit court. We fail to see how this argument is responsive to plaintiffs' contention that the Secretary's instruction to ALJs—that they need not consider a circuit court decision as binding if it conflicts with the Secretary's own policy—is unlawful, and that ALJ decisions rendered pursuant to such instructions are therefore invalid. ...

2. As a consequence of this position, the memoranda submitted with respect to the validity of the SSA's non-acquiescence policy have been prepared by the Department of Justice's Washington, D.C. Civil Division and HHS' General Counsel's Office.

trines: separation of powers; the rule of law; *stare decisis*; due process; equal protection. The policy has been challenged on statutory grounds as well. Although legal theories have varied, these authorities have spoken with virtual unanimity in their condemnation of the practice of intra-circuit non-acquiescence and in their determination that such a policy is unlawful.

Nor is the SSA the first executive agency to assert the right to disregard, or continue to challenge, circuit court decisions in subsequent cases within the same circuit, only to have this assertion rejected by the courts [citing cases involving the NLRB, the Railroad Retirement Board, the FCC, OSHA and the Postal Service].

We find the reasoning of these decisions fully applicable here. Our system of constitutional government is undoubtedly a unique and complex one, with three distinct branches of government with independently derived legal authority and substantially separate functions . . . Undoubtedly, too, the lines of separation between these functions are not always clear-cut. The judiciary necessarily exercises enforcement-related functions as an incident of its interpretive and adjudicative activities, while the executive, particularly in the modern era of elaborate administrative agency regulation of a multitude of commercial, social, economic, scientific and employment-related affairs, is permitted to exercise a degree of interpretive authority in its enforcement of the law. However, only a fundamental reordering of this constitutional balance would permit the SSA to exercise the power to which it claims an entitlement in this case. The fundamental principles of our constitutional scheme, as articulated in decisions such as Marbury v. Madison, 5 U.S. (1 Cranch) 137 (1803) (judicial determination of constitutionality of congressional legislation), Cooper v. Aaron, 358 U.S. 1, 17–19 (1958) (state executive and legislative officials' duty to obey federal court decisions), and United States v. Nixon, 418 U.S. 683 (1974) (judicial determination of scope of presidential power), establish the authority of federal courts to render decisions which bind all other participants in our constitutional system of government. Thus, the SSA's status as an agency of a co-equal branch of the federal government clearly is not an impediment to the imposition of a requirement that it adhere to decisions of federal courts in accordance with the doctrine of separation of powers. The judiciary's duty and authority, as first established in Marbury, "to say what the law is" would be rendered a virtual nullity if coordinate branches of government could effectively and unilaterally strip its pronouncements of any precedential force. . . .

. . . None of the [policy] considerations relied upon in Mendoza is in any significant way threatened by a rule of mandatory intra-circuit acquiescence in circuit court decisions[3] . . . [T]he SSA is free, when confronted with an unfavorable Second Circuit decision, . . . to apply and advocate its legal position in the eleven other federal judicial circuits in the country. . . .

---

3. The government's conduct in Mendoza, a case instituted in the Central District of California, essentially constituted nonacquiescence in the decision of a federal district judge from the Northern District of California. It has been recognized that the decision of a federal district judge is generally regarded as persuasive, but not binding, authority by other judges within the same district. We do not understand plaintiffs to challenge any failure of the Secretary to acquiesce in the decisions of federal district courts.

If successful, the SSA will reaffirm its right to adhere in other forums to what it believes is the preferred view of the law, will create the conditions which maximize the likelihood of Supreme Court review of the issue (i.e., the creation of inter-circuit conflicts) and possible nationwide resolution of the issue in the SSA's favor, and may even create the conditions for possible re-examination of the adverse decision by the very circuit which rendered it.

Defendants suggest that this alternative leaves them at the mercy of claimants, whose decision to appeal becomes a precondition to Supreme Court review, absent a decision by the Solicitor General to seek review of the unfavorable decision in the first instance. Certainly, defendants cannot seriously contest the fact that claimants will create the opportunity for Supreme Court review by appealing unfavorable decisions (i.e., decisions favorable to the Secretary) of other circuit courts. Indeed, the Supreme Court, in United States v. Stauffer Chemical Co., the companion case to Mendoza, rejected an argument by the Environmental Protection Agency to the contrary. As for the appropriateness of the Supreme Court review sought by a claimant in a particular case, the Solicitor General not only takes into account prudential considerations which make it undesirable for the *government* to seek appellate review, but also has the unique opportunity, as the executive branch's principal spokesperson before the Court, to explain to the *Supreme Court* why *it* should not grant review in a particular case. Thus, the fact that Supreme Court review of an unfavorable circuit court decision will often be claimant-initiated should not interfere with the SSA's ability to insure that such review occur only in cases which it considers appropriate vehicles for Supreme Court review.

The Secretary also retains the full ability to seek more immediate review of an unfavorable decision if the conditions for doing so are in fact appropriate. The Secretary can petition for review of a circuit court decision either by the panel that rendered the decision or by the circuit court en banc. If unsuccessful, the Secretary can seek Supreme Court review if the circuit court's decision either conflicts with those of other circuits, thus making the issue ripe for Supreme Court resolution, or is *consistent* with those of several other circuits, thus making a Supreme Court decision on the issue the only realistic judicial alternative to further, potentially fruitless inter-circuit consideration of the issue. While the decision to seek Supreme Court review of an unfavorable circuit court ruling is a complicated one to which both legal and policy considerations apply, we perceive a certain illogic in permitting the Secretary to so heavily rely on this circumstance in support of a non-acquiescence policy which essentially renders Supreme Court review of an unfavorable decision either unnecessary (because the agency can simply refuse to follow the circuit court decision in subsequent cases) or undesirable (because the Supreme Court may affirm the unfavorable decision, thus giving it nationwide effect). ... The Secretary is also free to pursue a legislative remedy for an unfavorable circuit court decision by seeking congressional amendment of the relevant provision of the Social Security Act. ...

Defendants also assert that it is the duty of the SSA to administer the Social Security Act in a way which promotes nationwide uniformity, and that its intra-circuit non-acquiescence policy is necessary to achieve this goal. In support of this argument, defendants point to § 10 of the 1984 amendments to the Social Security Act, which requires the Secretary to "establish by regulation uniform standards which shall be applied at all levels of determination, review, and adjudication in determining whether individuals are under disabilities ..."

The defendants' argument not only fails to dispel the serious doubts concerning the legal validity of its policy, but in fact highlights some of the most troubling consequences of that policy. At the outset, we note that the desire for uniform national standards in disability cases as expressed by Congress does not necessarily lead to the conclusion that intra-circuit non-acquiescence is a necessary or appropriate means of achieving this goal. ... [W]hile Congress considered legislation to eliminate (the House version) or regulate (the Senate version) the SSA's non-acquiescence policy, its decision not to legislate on the issue was hardly an endorsement either of the policy or its legality. The Conference Report states as follows:

> The conference agreement deletes both the House and Senate language. The conferees do not intend that the agreement to drop both provisions be interpreted as approval of "non-acquiescence" by a federal agency to an interpretation of a U.S. Circuit Court of Appeals as a general practice. On the contrary, ... the conferees urge that a policy of non-acquiescence be followed only in situations where the Administration has initiated or has the reasonable expectation and intention of initiating the steps necessary to receive a review of the issue in the Supreme Court.

> *The conferees reaffirm the congressional intent that the Secretary resolve policy conflicts promptly in order to achieve consistent uniform administration of the program. This objective may be achieved in at least two ways other than non-acquiescence when the agency is faced with conflicting interpretations of the meaning and intent of the Social Security Act: either to appeal the issue to the Supreme Court, or to seek a legislative remedy from the Congress.* ... The conferees recognize that the realities of litigation do not make it appropriate or feasible to appeal every adverse decision with which the Secretary continues to disagree. In such instances, however, the conferees strongly insist that Congress' judgment as to the appropriate policy should prevail. The conferees expect the Secretary to propose what she believes to be appropriate remedial legislation for congressional consideration. ... (emphasis added)

... [In addition, the Conference Committee Report recognized] the inherent unfairness of the Secretary's policy to the very persons whom the Social Security Act was designed to protect. ... The consequence of the SSA's non-acquiescence policy is simply this: one set of rules applies to those claimants fortunate enough to procure legal representation, persistent enough to appeal an adverse determination of the various non-acquiescing levels of the agency to a federal court bound to follow the Court of Appeals ruling, and healthy enough to endure this belabored process; a different and adverse rule will govern the rights of those claimants who are unrepresented, insufficiently persistent in their efforts to invoke the benefits of favorable judicial rulings, or incapable of doing so. The arbitrariness of such a system is evident simply from its description.

The Secretary emphasizes the disuniformity of a rule which would require the SSA to apply one legal standard in Connecticut but another in California. We have just as much, if not more, difficulty with a policy whereby one claimant is governed by one legal standard but his neighbor, lacking in either financial resources, litigational persistence, or physical or mental stamina, is governed by another. . . .

A comparison of the SSA with other agencies which adhere to a non-acquiescence policy further reveals the dubious legality of the SSA's particular non-acquiescence policy. . . . [T]he IRS and NLRB can at least offer a practical explanation for such behavior. Under the venue provisions governing the situs of litigation with these two agencies, private parties are often able to bring suit in any one of a number of circuits. . . . [S]ince it is often difficult for the agency to predict in which circuit the litigation may ultimately be brought, and thus to know which circuit's law to apply, the existence of intra-circuit non-acquiescence often will be apparent only when the situs of the appeal has been determined. In this situation, non-acquiescence at the agency level is a more readily understandable phenomenon.

In SSA cases, such venue uncertainty is largely absent. . . . Given the physical, fiscal and employment-related disabilities of many such claimants, it is usually the case that judicial review will occur in the circuit where the claimant resides. Thus, the SSA usually knows well in advance of the judicial review process in which circuit the controversy is likely to arise.

We also believe that the SSA's role in the federal statutory scheme is unique with respect to the impact of its decision-making authority on the statute's intended beneficiaries. Were we dealing with administrative policy concerning the labor laws or tax regulations, there would be the solace of knowing that most litigants will be relatively affluent and sophisticated so that their legal rights will be pressed by privately retained counsel. Here, we deal with a quite different group of claimants. According to statistics provided by defendants, almost half (49.2%) of all claimants are without legal representation in their pursuit of disability benefits, and approximately three out of every eight claimants (37.6%) are without any representation whatsoever, legal or otherwise. The consequences of this phenomenon are obvious. If every claimant denied benefits as a result of the application of the non-acquiescence policy were properly represented, the case would automatically be appealed to the federal courts, which would reverse the decision and perhaps also award costs and counsel fees under 28 U.S.C. § 2412(d)(1)(A) [the Equal Access to Justice Act, which provides for fee awards against the government "unless the court finds that the position of the United States was substantially justified or that special circumstances make an award unjust."] This practice would soon prove to be too expensive, and the Secretary either would abandon the non-acquiescence policy or would seek a revision of the Court of Appeals' determination from either the Supreme Court or Congress. To the extent, therefore, that the non-acquiescence policy has a budgetary motivation, it must be premised on the assumption that a significant number of HHS claimants will be unrepresented and unaware of their rights. . . .

In its persistent refusal to abide by authoritative interpretations of the very statute which it is charged with administering, the SSA has created a litigation burden of unprecedented proportions on the courts,[4] litigants and administrative agency personnel, resulting in the needless expenditure of resources on the determination, judicial review of, and frequent redetermination (after remand) of disability claims. It has caused needless delays in compensating claimants who are forced to endure the multi-layered administrative process before obtaining the benefits which courts have said are their entitlement and, undoubtedly, the outright denial of benefits for other claimants who are unable or otherwise fail to pursue their claims to the courts. It has frustrated congressional intent, by virtue of the agency's persistent failure to apply the law in accordance with this intent as interpreted by the federal appellate courts in accordance with Marbury. It even has placed its own ALJs in the untenable position of "trying to serve two masters": the courts, who interpret the Constitution and laws which ALJs have sworn to uphold; and the Secretary, who has essentially instructed ALJs that they may disregard such interpretations in favor of her own. That these consequences reflect a serious departure from any reasonable conception of an orderly system of justice simply cannot be gainsaid.

In conclusion, we believe that plaintiffs are likely to succeed in showing that the Secretary's non-acquiescence policy as practiced up until approximately two months ago was inconsistent with the constitutionally required separation of powers and effected an arbitrary and unlawful discrimination among disability claimants. [The court then examined the SSA's revised version of non-acquiescence, concluded that it did not "alleviate the concerns we have previously expressed," and issued a preliminary injunction.]

NOTES

(1) *The Ultimate Outcome of the Litigation.* On appeal, the Second Circuit vacated Judge Sand's order because, in an intervening case, it had entered an injunction obligating the Secretary "to formulate and issue instructions to all adjudicators, state and federal, concerning the content of the treating physician rule and the requirement of its use." This injunction, in its view, "substantially reduces the need for" the preliminary relief Judge Sand had awarded. Stieberger was finally settled in 1992, with SSA agreeing to: (i) send letters offering to reexamine over 200,000 otherwise-closed disability cases; (ii) instruct all employees to follow Second Circuit holdings involving New York residents, and provide them with a manual containing stipulated quotations from Second Circuit disability decisions; and (iii) follow a specified set of procedures for subsequent Second Circuit precedent. For criticism of the settlement, see Robert J. Axelrod, Comment, The Politics of

---

4. Statistics from early 1984 regarding the Secretary's termination of disability benefits reveal that of the approximately 470,000 individuals who had their disability benefits terminated since March 1981, benefits were reinstated on appeal to 160,000 claimants and an additional 120,000 cases were still pending.

Nonacquiescence: The Legacy of *Stieberger v. Sullivan,* 60 Brook.L.Rev. 765 (1994).

The last chapter of the Stieberger saga brought ultimate defeat from the perspective of plaintiff disability recipients, but victory (or at least acceptable closure) from the perspective of the legal system. SSA promulgated a new rule incorporating its preferred view of the treating physician rule. The rule was challenged and, deferring to the agency, the Second Circuit sustained it as a reasonable interpretation. Schisler v. Sullivan, 3 F.3d 563 (2d Cir.1993). One might take issue with the correctness of the Second Circuit's decision on the merits, but at least SSA's post-Steiberger strategy saw the agency employing an unexceptionable means for pursuing its view of preferred regulatory policy.

(2) *The Precedents on Collateral Estoppel.* In UNITED STATES V. STAUFFER CHEMICAL CO., 464 U.S. 165 (1984), the Supreme Court held that "the doctrine of mutual defensive collateral estoppel is available against the government to preclude relitigation of the same issue already litigated against the same party in another case involving virtually identical facts." 464 U.S. at 169. That, of course, still left the government free to litigate the same issue with other parties. Might those other parties be able to preclude litigation of an issue under the doctrine of non-mutual (and perhaps even "offensive") collateral estoppel, as is increasingly recognized in ordinary civil litigation? If so, the civil procedure doctrine of issue preclusion might well settle the administrative law question of nonacquiescence. But in Stauffer's companion case, UNITED STATES V. MENDOZA, 464 U.S. 154 (1984), the Court said that no such result was contemplated. Per Justice Rehnquist (464 U.S. at 159–61):

"We have long recognized that 'the Government is not in a position identical to that of a private litigant,' both because of the geographic breadth of Government litigation and also, most importantly, because of the nature of the issues the Government litigates. It is not open to serious dispute that the Government is a party to a far greater number of cases on a nationwide basis than even the most litigious private entity; in 1982, the United States was a party to more than 75,000 of the 206,193 filings in the United States District Courts. In the same year the United States was a party to just under 30% of the civil cases appealed from the District Courts to the Court of Appeals. Government litigation frequently involves legal questions of substantial public importance; indeed, because the proscriptions of the United States Constitution are so generally directed at governmental action, many constitutional questions can arise only in the context of litigation to which the Government is a party. Because of those facts the Government is more likely than any private party to be involved in lawsuits against different parties which nonetheless involve the same legal issues.

"A rule allowing nonmutual collateral estoppel against the Government in such cases would substantially thwart the development of important questions of law by freezing the first final decision rendered on a particular legal issue. Allowing only one final adjudication would deprive this Court of the benefit it receives from permitting several courts of appeals to explore a difficult question before this Court grants certiorari. Indeed, if nonmutual estoppel were routinely applied against the Government, this Court would have to revise its practice of waiting for a conflict to develop before granting the Government's petitions for certiorari.

". . . The Court of Appeals faulted the Government in this case for failing to appeal a decision that it now contends is erroneous. But the Government's litigation conduct in a case is apt to differ from that of a private litigant. Unlike a private litigant who generally does not forego an appeal if he believes that he can prevail, the Solicitor General considers a variety of factors, such as the limited resources of the Government and the crowded dockets of the courts, before authorizing an appeal. The application of nonmutual estoppel against the Government would force the Solicitor General to abandon those prudential concerns and to appeal every adverse decision in order to avoid foreclosing further review.

"In addition to those institutional concerns traditionally considered by the Solicitor General, the panoply of important public issues raised in governmental litigation may quite properly lead successive administrations of the Executive Branch to take differing positions with respect to the resolution of a particular issue. While the Executive Branch must of course defer to the Judicial Branch for final resolution of questions of constitutional law, the former nonetheless controls the progress of Government litigation through the federal courts. It would be idle to pretend that the conduct of Government litigation in all its myriad features, from the decision to file a complaint in the United States district court to the decision to petition for certiorari to review a judgment of the court of appeals, is a wholly mechanical procedure which involves no policy choices whatever. . . ."

The government, of course, relied heavily on Mendoza in arguing the principal case. But does it follow from the government's right to nonacquiesce in the individual rulings of over 1000 federal district judges (which is what Mendoza effectively means) that it also can ignore the collegial decisions of the 13 federal circuit courts of appeals?

(3) *SSA's New Nonacquiescence Policy.* As Judge Sand's opinion recognizes, the SSA did not invent the practice of nonacquiescence. Other agencies had sporadically asserted the power to ignore judicial decisions with which they did not agree (at least, outside the particular case and so long as the rendering court was not the Supreme Court), and the IRS and the NLRB had a long and open history of nonacquiescing.

What made the SSA's venture into nonacquiescence so explosive? In part, it was the massiveness of the regulatory program. The judiciary confronted the real possibility of being overwhelmed by thousands of claimants, each needing an individualized order to the agency to obey "the law." In part, it was concern for an especially vulnerable beneficiary group. And, in part, it was the political visibility of the issue. SSA's actions took place within the larger context of the Reagan Administration's unapologetic agenda to cut social welfare programs—an agenda which sparked alarm and resistance among many public interest groups, but which was not broadly unpopular. Perhaps it was not surprising, then, that Congress jawboned the agency for its nonacquiescence posture but settled, in the end, for tinkering with the substantive law of the disability program (statutorily endorsing the courts of appeals' interpretations) and punting on the larger questions about what the Executive was up to.

In 1990, SSA adopted regulations that provided for intracircuit nonacquiescence only when (i) the occurrence of "an activating event" such as subsequent decisions or legislative action "raises the question of whether the circuit court would reach the same decision if the issue(s) previously decided were presented to it again"; or (ii) the General Counsel, after consulting with the Justice Department, concurs and SSA publishes in the Federal Register a notice that it will continue to apply its own interpretation on the disputed issue.[1] Why did SSA finally curtail its nonacquiescence policy—at least as a public stance? Martha Derthick, Agency Under Stress: The Social Security Administration in American Government 152 (1990), observes:

> The courts are overwhelmingly important in their own right, and no agency can afford to be consistently at odds with them, liable to constant reversal. . . . In the disability review, the costs of nonacquiescence were not confined to the courtroom. They extended to the SSA's relations with the state governments, on which the agency depended for execution of its administrative routine. And . . . these costs extended as well to the agency's portrayal on the front pages of the nation's newspapers.

(4) *The Broader Debate.* Few contemporary administrative law issues have generated the heat—and the literature—occasioned by nonacquiescence.[2] Federal judges reacted to nonacquiescence with outrage. Judge Pregerson likened SSA's policy to the pre-Civil War southern states' doctrine of nullification of federal authority;[3] Judge Posner berated the NLRB for "dealing with judicial precedent in a disingenuous, evasive, and in short dishonest manner."[4] Government attorneys required to advance SSA's nonacquiescence position often reported great ethical and moral discomfort with it.[5] Is the practice unmitigated agency lawlessness, or is it more complicated than that?

In a report prepared for the Administrative Conference of the U.S., Professors Estreicher and Revesz advocated "a middle course" between defenders and critics of nonacquiescence, a course that "recognizes a role for the courts in policing agency practices in this area, but also acknowledges the legitimacy of an agency's desire to maintain a uniform administration of its governing statute while it reasonably seeks the national validation of its preferred position." SAMUEL ESTREICHER & RICHARD L. REVESZ,

---

1. This did not moot the litigation in Stieberger because, in Judge Sand's view, the regulations "improperly shift the responsibility for guaranteeing SSA's acquiescence away from the agency itself." 738 F.Supp. 716, 758 (S.D.N.Y.1990).

2. For a collection of the literature—citations to which occupy more than a page—see Dan T. Coenen, The Constitutional Case Against Intracircuit Nonacquiescence, 75 Minn.L.Rev. 1339, 1340–42 n.4 (1991).

3. Lopez v. Heckler, 713 F.2d 1432, 1441 (9th Cir.1983).

4. Nielsen Lithographing Co. v. NLRB, 854 F.2d 1063, 1067 (7th Cir.1988).

5. In addition to the discussion of this in Stieberger, see Susan G. Mezey, No Longer Disabled: The Federal Courts and the Politics of Social Security Disability xi-xii, 133–34, 178 (1988), who also reports discomfort among ALJs directed to ignore circuit precedent. For discussion of the ethical dimension, see Jack B. Weinstein & Gay A. Crosthwait, Some Reflections on Conflicts Between Government Attorneys and Clients, 1 Touro L.Rev. 1, 8 (1985).

NONACQUIESCENCE BY FEDERAL ADMINISTRATIVE AGENCIES, 98 Yale L.J. 679 (1989). Their analysis, which implicates the issues posed by Stauffer and Mendoza as well, begins by examining the case for *inter*circuit nonacquiescence[6]—which is widely, and relatively uncontroversially, practiced by agencies:

"Consider, for example, the question whether EPA can use independent contractors in enforcement proceedings under the Clean Air Act—the question at stake in United States v. Stauffer Chemical Co. If the first court of appeals to face this question determined that EPA could not use independent contractors, a bar against intercircuit nonacquiescence would prevent the agency from using such contractors anywhere in the country. In addition, it is unlikely that any private party would have standing to argue that the agency should be given the option of using such contractors. Thus, no subsequent court would have the opportunity to decide whether independent contractors are part of the permissible arsenal of enforcement options. . . . It is true that even in this scenario, the Supreme Court could grant certiorari, or Congress could amend the governing statute to explicitly authorize the use of independent contractors. But . . . from a managerial perspective, there are important costs attached to involving either of these institutions, which have limited decisional resources, in problems that could be resolved by the circuits themselves. More fundamentally, although our legal system generally assumes that Congress will be able to correct judicial errors, the combined influence of inertial forces and unwillingness to open up what may have been a controversial legislative compromise to reexamination may severely limit the occasions for congressional intervention of this type. . . .

Turning, then, to *intra*circuit nonacquiescence, Professors Estreicher & Revesz identify the following considerations in favor of the practice:

First, "A bar against intracircuit nonacquiescence . . . delays the harmonization of federal law. Were such a bar in place, conflicts could be harmonized without intervention by the Supreme Court only if the courts of appeals that ruled *for* the agency reconsidered their position. The courts that ruled against it would ordinarily not have an occasion to reexamine their prior rulings, even where they might have found persuasive the views of the other circuits."

Second, "[A bar against intracircuit nonacquiescence] undermines important goals of uniformity that underlie the administrative law system. The problems of disuniformity can be divided into three major categories: externalities, interstate competition, and fairness.

"Externalities—in the sense of cross-circuit effects—are present when economic activity that takes place in one region produces adverse effects in another region. . . .

"Another central goal of federal regulation is to prevent regions from competing for industry by offering a more favorable economic climate at the expense of other societal goals. For example, federal regulation in the labor field can be justified, in part, as an attempt to prevent interstate

---

6. That is, refusing to follow the precedent of a court of appeals *other than* the one that will review the agency's decision in the case at hand.

competition for industry at the expense of worker protection. If one circuit takes a more restrictive view than does the NLRB of what constitutes a mandatory subject for collective bargaining, employers in that circuit have more entrepreneurial flexibility, and perhaps lower labor costs, than their counterparts in other circuits, creating incentives for new industry to establish itself in that circuit and for existing industry to move there from other circuits. As long as the conflict among the circuits persists, there will be undesirable regional competition.

"Finally, uniformity promotes some fairness values. Whether the agency acts as regulator of private sector activity or administers a benefit program, Congress intended by enacting federal law to promote horizontal uniformity—equal treatment of regulatees or claimants regardless of where in this country the dispute or claim arose. To the extent the agency is required to alter its policy to conform to adverse circuit rulings, the federal interest in horizontal uniformity is undermined."

Third, "If an agency cannot engage in intracircuit nonacquiescence, it will have to administer its statute differently in various parts of the country ... Differential administration can impose significant costs on an agency. ... For example, enforcement staff, often non-lawyers who are normally responsible for large caseloads, may find it difficult to become familiar not only with the agency's own policy but also with adverse court of appeals decisions. Such personnel are typically informed of their agency's policies by means of instruction manuals prepared by the agency's General Counsel. If such officials are to follow a policy of acquiescence, they will have to be separately instructed on the case law of the relevant circuits. And whenever the agency loses a case in a court of appeals, these documents will have to be updated. More importantly, if officials in different parts of the country must operate under different legal regimes, it will be difficult for the agency to use a single training system for all such officials or to evaluate them pursuant to uniform standards. A portion of the economies of scale that attach to centralized administration will thereby be lost."

On the other hand, they observe the following countervailing costs of intracircuit nonacquiescence:

First, the "central cost" is "distributional unfairness." "A litigant's ability to obtain the benefit of the case law of the reviewing court of appeals will depend on whether he has sufficient resources to pursue an appeal to the federal courts. The result is analogous to one in which a litigant before a court is told that he can purchase the rule of law which will govern the disposition of his case and that more favorable rules of law are progressively more expensive. ... A by-product of these distributional effects is the lack of uniformity in the output of the administrative lawmaking system. When lack of resources prevents a litigant's challenge to the agency's nonacquiescence in court, the result will be vertical disuniformity—disuniformity in outcome between those who pursue their case into the courts and those who do not. Like horizontal disuniformity, which is present when different circuits adjudicate under different legal standards, vertical disuniformity also undermines the goals of uniform administration of federal law. Vertical disuniformity is especially troublesome because the negative impact of the differential policy will probably fall disproportionately on those parties least able to bear it."

Second, "Nonacquiescence is likely to increase the volume of cases reaching the federal courts. ... Because a litigant will probably prevail simply through the application of stare decisis, there will be a strong incentive to seek review, since, in balancing the costs and benefits of challenging the agency action, the discount for the risk of not prevailing before the court will be very small...."

Professors Estreicher & Revesz conclude, on balance, that "either a per se prohibition or an unqualified endorsement of intracircuit nonacquiescence would be undesirable ... [I]ntracircuit nonacquiescence is justified only where it is an adjunct to litigation designed to yield a uniform rule in favor of the agency's preferred policy. ... [W]e translate this general principle into [the following] judicially manageable standards. ... [A]gencies should not engage in intracircuit nonacquiescence unless (1) the agency has responsibility for securing a nationally uniform policy with respect to the question that was the subject of the adverse judicial decision; (2) there is a justifiable basis for belief that the agency's position falls within the scope of its delegated discretion; and (3) the agency is reasonably seeking the vindication of its position both in the courts of appeals and before the Supreme Court."

These recommendations proved highly controversial, and ACUS tabled them. The report drew a critical response from two of the Stieberger plaintiffs' counsel, Matthew Diller & Nancy Morawetz, Intracircuit Nonacquiescence and the Breakdown of the Rule of Law: A Response to Estreicher & Revesz, 99 Yale L.J. 801 (1990), which in turn prompted Samuel Estreicher & Richard L. Revesz, The Uneasy Case Against Intracircuit Nonacquiescence: A Reply, 99 Yale L.J. 831 (1990).

(5) *And the Obligations of the Judge.* DEPARTMENT OF ENERGY V. FEDERAL LABOR RELATIONS AUTHORITY, 106 F.3d 1158 (4th Cir.1997): In a case involving labor relations within the federal government, the FLRA and the Department of Justice narrowly avoided a confrontation with the Fourth Circuit over nonacquiescence. In the administrative decision appealed from, FLRA had written that it "respectfully declined to follow" Fourth Circuit precedent on a certain point, in favor of contrary D.C. Circuit precedent. At oral argument, counsel was asked to file post-argument briefs on this position. FLRA counsel submitted a letter asserting that: (i) decision in the case did not in fact turn on the disputed precedent; and (ii) even if it did, because applicable venue provisions permitted a review petition to be brought in either circuit that had already ruled contrarily on the point, the agency would inevitably be placed in the apparent position of nonacquiescing. The Department of Justice also filed a letter, which went further than FLRA to insist that "[e]ven where there is no multiple-venue provision, we do not believe that there is any constitutional requirement or any other inflexible rule that a federal agency must apply the legal principles announced in a court of appeals decision to the administration of a statutory program, either generally or in matters arising in the particular circuit." The letter went on to assure the court, "Of course, in many instances an agency will, as a matter of policy and comity, follow circuit precedent." The

majority of the panel, apparently agreeing with FLRA's first point that the case did not turn directly on the disputed precedent, ignored the Executive's assertion of its right not to acquiesce. Judge Luttig, however, was not so restrained, 106 F.3d at 1165–66:

"I appreciate the precarious position in which the FLRA finds itself by virtue of the multiple-venue provision ... when it first adjudicates a dispute. Indeed, recognizing the awkwardness, I cannot fault the agency for taking the position that, at the adjudicatory stage of its proceedings, it may follow that case law which it prefers. However, I cannot, and do not, accept the Department of Justice's and the agency's quite different, and, in my view, extraordinary, position that, even absent a multiple-venue provision and even outside the context of a particular litigation, the agency is not bound by the principles of law set forth in the opinions of this Court 'in matters arising in [this] particular circuit.' ...

"In any event, regardless of the precariousness of the FLRA's position (because of the multiple-venue provision ...) when it originally adjudicates a dispute, and regardless of whether the agency is bound to apply the law of this Circuit in matters arising within this Circuit following an adverse decision or is bound by one of our prior decisions when before this Court, I, as a judge of this Court, am bound by the prior decisions of this Court. I am not free, as the agency believes it is, to conduct myself unconstrained by law. Nor am I, as the Authority is, subject to any kind of multiple-venue provision; I am bound by the law of but one circuit. Therefore, when faced with an agency decision in which the agency expressly refuses to follow the law of this Circuit, I can conclude only that that decision is arbitrary, capricious and inconsistent with law, ... just as I am bound to hold that a district court abuses its discretion when it applies the incorrect law. In other words, although it may arguably be defensible, at least in the first instance, that the agency chooses not to apply the law of this Court, that understandable choice does not affect my obligation to judge the agency's action under the laws of this Circuit. And, given that the agency did not apply the law of this Circuit, its decision is, ipso facto, 'not in accordance with law.' For this reason alone, I concur in the judgment of the court denying enforcement of the FLRA's decision."

(By the way, and not irrelevantly, when the underlying issue in this case got to the Supreme Court in a later case, that Court decided that *both* the Fourth Circuit *and* the D.C. Circuit had it wrong—and that the particular question was best left to (substantive) agency discretion! See National Federation of Fed. Employees, Local 1309 v. Department of Interior, 526 U.S. 86 (1999). In so deciding, the Supreme Court relied on the Chevron case, set forth at p. 1026 below. When you get to that case, you might consider how much it is driven by the policies that undergird the nonacquiescence debate.)

SECTION 3.   JUDICIAL REVIEW OF AGENCY FACTUAL DETERMINATIONS

The Federal Rules of Civil Procedure instruct district judges, who do not have explicit policymaking functions, to frame their results in terms of "findings of fact" and "conclusions of law." F.R.C.P. 52(a). In describing the way in which administrative law judges should prepare their reports in on-the-record proceedings, the APA encourages a similar bifurcation. 5 U.S.C. § 557(c). Yet, as we have already seen in a variety of contexts, the world of actual decision is a good deal more complicated than this comfortable duality. Even for trial judges, the process of bringing "fact" and "law" together is a complex one. While appellate courts conventionally build on the distinction, and assert that they exercise independent ("de novo") judgment on all legal questions, the inevitable truth is that they do—as they must—recognize a wide range of trial court "discretion" on questions that could be called legal, relating to issues of trial management, remedy, and the like.[1] Exercise of discretion on such issues is reviewed neither for clear error (a finding-of-fact standard) nor for correctness (the conclusion-of-law standard), but for unreasonableness (arbitrariness, capriciousness, or abuse of discretion). For agencies—who have assigned policy-making responsibilities, and whose staffing and institutional structure permit them to make complex "factual" and law-applying judgments of a character foreign to the courts—the fact/law distinction is even less helpful *if* it is thought to embrace the universe of possibilities. It is, on the other hand, a familiar framework that can serve (or at least historically has served) as a useful starting point in thinking about standards of review.

The conceptual problems of the fact/law distinction are well known:

No two terms of legal science have rendered better service than "law" and "fact." They are basic assumptions; irreducible minimums and the most comprehensive maximums at the same instant. They readily accommodate themselves to any meaning we desire to give them. In them and their kind a science of law finds its strength and durability. They are the creations of centuries. What judge has not found refuge in them? The man who could succeed in defining them would be a public enemy.

L. Green, Judge and Jury 270–71 (1930). Consider in this respect the following brief account of the distinction, given by Louis L. Jaffe, perhaps the leading scholar of the relationship of judge to agency in the APA's first quarter-century:

How then do we distinguish fact from law? *It will be more meaningful, I think, to put the question: how do we distinguish a finding of fact from a conclusion of law?* In this way we emphasize that we are concerned with the function and the functioning of the decisional process: what is the officer doing, we ask, when he "finds" a fact and how does this action differ from his making a conclusion of law? Thus we may perhaps avoid the unanchored abstractness of distinguishing between fact and law *simpliciter. A finding of fact is the assertion that a phenomenon has happened or is or will be happening independent of or anterior to any assertion as to its legal effect.* It can, for example, be made by a person who is ignorant of the applicable law. Thus a statute

---

1. Maurice Rosenberg, Judicial Discretion of the Trial Court, Viewed From Above, 22 Syracuse L.Rev. 635 (1971).

may provide compensation for injuries arising out of and during the course of employment. It has been found that an employee while at work has been intentionally hit on the head by a fellow employee. This is a finding of fact. It owes nothing to the compensation statute. If, however, it is asserted that the injury arose out of the employment and is therefore compensable, the assertion is something more than a finding of fact; it is, in our view, a conclusion of law. The assertion cannot be derived by one who is ignorant of the applicable statutes. It is, unless it is a purely arbitrary exercise of power, an assertion that the purpose of the statute will be served by awarding compensation.[2]

Do you agree that Jaffe's first example is independent of law? Of the compensation statute? Note the presence of such ideas as "at work," "employee," "intentionally" and "fellow employee"—all of which you will recognize as being the subject of law classes. How about the second example—are you happy to characterize the conclusion that the injury is compensable as necessarily raising a question of statutory meaning as such? Where, then, do "mixed" questions belong: in the limited review class of "questions of fact," or the independent review class of "questions of law"? Judge Friendly said that under Jaffe's view "the making of a contract would be a question of law, not of fact." NLRB v. Marcus Trucking Co., 286 F.2d 583, 590 (2d Cir.1961). Professor Jaffe responded: "I would demur to his conclusion that under my view 'the making of a contract' is necessarily a question of law. That depends on whether what is at issue are the events, the intentions, etc., which are asserted to constitute a contract. If so, the questions are questions of fact. ... I do, however, agree with him that if the conclusion to be drawn from the facts involves no more than applying the statute with no further and explicit questions raised as to its 'meaning,' the reviewing court should accept it, but not because it is a finding of fact. Rather, in my view, ... a law-applying judgment is *presumptively* within the area of the agency's discretion."[3]

In reviewing fact-finding from the trial courts, appellate courts apply two standards, depending on whether the facts were found by the trial judge (sitting without a jury), or by the jury. Factual findings in non-jury decisions are reviewed under the "clearly erroneous" standard—a measure that falls short of appellate redetermination, although it leaves some room for appellate court oversight. Judge John Gibbons of the Third Circuit explained the basis for deference to the trial judge as fact-finder in dissenting from his colleagues' reversal of a district judge's opinion based on documentary evidence: "The concurrence of several [appellate] judges in a factual inference possibly increases the likelihood of achieving truth in the cosmic sense. ... [But] the primary function of appellate courts is the correction of errors of law. The primary function of the trial court is to make a record and from it to determine the relevant facts.

"Even in instances where an appellate court is in as good a position to decide as the trial court, it should not disregard the trial court's finding, for to do so impairs confidence in the trial courts and multiplies appeals with

---

2. Judicial Control of Administrative Action 547–48 (1965).

3. Id. at 549–50.

attendant expense and delay. In addition to encouraging the filing of appeals, the majority's rule has the disadvantage of increasing the already considerable burden on this court with respect to those that are filed. ... The 'we are in as good a position as the trial court' rationale is, of course, a possible model for an appellate court system. But it is a model which imposes enormous costs without commensurate social benefits. The judicial process is at best a less than scientific method of determining the facts. The process is at its least scientific in determining such facts as subjective motivation. All that can be expected is the opportunity to present to a neutral factfinder the parties' respective versions, under rules designed to assure a measure of fairness, and to let that fact finder draw inferences. Since certainty is impossible no matter how often the process is repeated, society's interest emphasizes finality at that point. The clearly erroneous standard accepts the strong interest in finality, while the majority's 'we are in as good a position as the trial court' rule ignores it. The late Judge Charles E. Clark, who drafted Rule 52(a), recognized that society's interest in finality outweighed any competing interest in allowing even those philosopher kings with whom he sat on the Second Circuit to perform anew the task of drawing inferences." Davis v. United States Steel Supply, 32 Fed.R.Serv.2d (Callaghan) 727, 739–40 (3d Cir.1981) (Gibbons, J., dissenting), vacated 688 F.2d 166, 178 (3d Cir.1982). Judge Gibbons' view has substantially prevailed. See Anderson v. Bessemer City, 470 U.S. 564 (1985).

In cases tried to a jury, the fact-review function of the appellate court is yet more constrained. "[E]vidence sufficient to support a jury verdict may not suffice to support a trial judge's finding. ... We must sustain a general or a special jury verdict when there is some evidence which the jury might have believed, and when a reasonable inference from that evidence will support the verdict, regardless of whether that evidence is oral or by deposition." Orvis v. Higgins, 180 F.2d 537, 539, 540 n. 7 (2d Cir.1950) (Frank, J.). Which of these standards, if either, provides the best reference point for a judge considering her function in reviewing *administrative* fact-finding?

We begin this inquiry with judicial review of agency fact-finding that most resembles the product of a trial, that is, of fact-finding in an on-the-record hearing. In 1912, reviewing an ICC rate reduction order issued under a statute that contained no specific scope-of-review provision, the Supreme Court stated that a court would "not consider the expediency or wisdom of the order, or whether, on like testimony, it would have made a similar ruling. ... [The Commission's] conclusion, of course, is subject to review, but when supported by evidence is accepted as final; not that its decision, involving as it does so many and such vast public interests, can be supported by a mere scintilla of proof—but the courts will not examine the facts further than to determine whether there was substantial evidence to sustain the order." ICC v. Union Pacific Ry. Co., 222 U.S. 541, 547–48 (1912). "Substantial evidence" quickly became the conventional test, although courts may have found "greater difficulty in applying the [substantial evidence] test than in formulating it." Stork Restaurant, Inc. v. Boland, 282 N.Y. 256, 26 N.E.2d 247, 255 (N.Y.1940). Congress has often used the phrase, as it did as early as the Federal Trade Commission Act of 1914, where it provided that "Findings of fact, if supported by substantial evidence, shall be conclusive."[4] Even when Congress omitted the word "substantial," courts often supplied it, as when the Supreme Court said: "[T]he statute, in providing that 'the findings of the [National Labor Relations] Board as to the facts, if supported by evidence, shall be conclusive' means supported by substantial evidence." Consolidated Edison Co. v. NLRB, 305 U.S. 197, 229 (1938).

Just what "substantial evidence" was, was variously described. Judge Learned Hand called it "the kind of evidence on which responsible persons are accustomed to rely in serious affairs." NLRB v. Remington Rand, Inc., 94 F.2d 862, 873 (2d Cir.1938). Judge Jerome Frank of the Second Circuit, in the Orvis case quoted just above, thought the test "the same as in the case of a jury, the findings being treated like a special verdict." When the APA was adopted in 1946, Congress codified the "substantial evidence" test as the general standard of review for on-the-record fact-finding. Lively debate began about what, if any, change the Act made in the scope of judicial review of such findings of fact. The major, perhaps definitive, answer came five years later:

Universal Camera Corp. v. National Labor Relations Board

Supreme Court of the United States, 1951.
340 U.S. 474.

■ JUSTICE FRANKFURTER delivered the opinion of the Court.

[The question before the Board was whether an employee had been fired because he had testified supporting the union's position in an NLRB representation proceeding, or solely because subsequently he had accused the personnel manager of drunkenness. The trial examiner, crediting the employer's testimony and finding that antiunion animus had not entered into the discharge, recommended dismissing the complaint. A divided Board made the opposite finding and held the discharge to be an unfair labor practice. The Second Circuit also divided, granting enforcement per Judge Learned Hand but with express misgivings about the Board's assessment of the evidence; Judge Hand's opinion voiced views that conflicted with those of the Sixth Circuit, whose decision was reviewed in a companion case.]

The essential issue raised by this case and its companion . . . is the effect of the Administrative Procedure Act and the legislation colloquially known as the Taft–Hartley Act, 5 U.S.C. § 1001 et seq.; 29 U.S.C. § 141 et seq., on the duty of Courts of Appeals when called upon to review orders of the National Labor Relations Board. . . .

I.

Want of certainty in judicial review of Labor Board decisions partly reflects the intractability of any formula to furnish definiteness of content for all the impalpable factors involved in judicial review. But in part doubts as to the nature of the reviewing power and uncertainties in its application

---

4. 15 U.S.C. § 41.

derive from history, and to that extent an elucidation of this history may clear them away.

The Wagner Act [the original National Labor Relations Act] provided: "The findings of the Board as to the facts, if supported by evidence, shall be conclusive." Act of July 5, 1935, § 10(e), 29 U.S.C. § 160(e). This Court read "evidence" to mean "substantial evidence," and we said that "(s)ubstantial evidence is more than a mere scintilla. It means such relevant evidence as a reasonable mind might accept as adequate to support a conclusion." Consolidated Edison Co. v. National Labor Relations Board, 305 U.S. 197, 229. Accordingly, it "must do more than create a suspicion of the existence of the fact to be established. . . . it must be enough to justify, if the trial were to a jury, a refusal to direct a verdict when the conclusion sought to be drawn from it is one of fact for the jury." National Labor Relations Board v. Columbian Enameling & Stamping Co., 306 U.S. 292, 300.

The very smoothness of the "substantial evidence" formula as the standard for reviewing the evidentiary validity of the Board's findings established its currency. But the inevitably variant applications of the standard to conflicting evidence soon brought contrariety of views and in due course bred criticism. Even though the whole record may have been canvassed in order to determine whether the evidentiary foundation of a determination by the Board was "substantial," the phrasing of this Court's process of review readily lent itself to the notion that it was enough that the evidence supporting the Board's result was "substantial" when considered by itself. It is fair to say that by imperceptible steps regard for the fact-finding function of the Board led to the assumption that the requirements of the Wagner Act were met when the reviewing court could find in the record evidence which, when viewed in isolation, substantiated the Board's findings. . . .

Criticism of so contracted a reviewing power reinforced dissatisfaction felt in various quarters with the Board's administration of the Wagner Act in the years preceding the war. The scheme of the Act was attacked as an inherently unfair fusion of the functions of prosecutor and judge. Accusations of partisan bias were not wanting. The "irresponsible admission and weighing of hearsay, opinion, and emotional speculation in place of factual evidence" was said to be a "serious menace." No doubt some, perhaps even much, of the criticism was baseless and some surely was reckless.[1] What is here relevant, however, is the climate of opinion thereby generated and its effect on Congress. Protests against "shocking injustices" and intimations of judicial "abdication" with which some courts granted enforcement of the Board's order stimulated pressures for legislative relief from alleged administrative excesses.

The strength of these pressures was reflected in the passage in 1940 of the Walter–Logan Bill. It was vetoed by President Roosevelt, partly because it imposed unduly rigid limitations on the administrative process, and

---

1. Professor Gellhorn and Mr. Linfield reached the conclusion in 1939 after an extended investigation that "the denunciations find no support in fact." Gellhorn and Linfield, Politics and Labor Relations, 39 Col. L.Rev. 339, 394.

partly because of the investigation into the actual operation of the administrative process then being conducted by an experienced committee appointed by the Attorney General. It is worth noting that despite its aim to tighten control over administrative determinations of fact, the Walter–Logan Bill contented itself with the conventional formula that an agency's decision could be set aside if "the findings of fact are not supported by substantial evidence."

The final report of the Attorney General's Committee was submitted in January, 1941. The majority concluded that "(d)issatisfaction with the existing standards as to the scope of judicial review derives largely from dissatisfaction with the fact-finding procedures now employed by the administrative bodies." Departure from the "substantial evidence" test, it thought, would either create unnecessary uncertainty or transfer to courts the responsibility for ascertaining and assaying matters the significance of which lies outside judicial competence. Accordingly, it recommended against Legislation embodying a general scheme of judicial review.[2]

Three members of the Committee registered a dissent. Their view was that the "present system or lack of system of judicial review" led to inconsistency and uncertainty. They reported that under a "prevalent" interpretation of the "substantial evidence" rule "if what is called 'substantial evidence' is found anywhere in the record to support conclusions of fact, the courts are said to be obliged to sustain the decision without reference to how heavily the countervailing evidence may preponderate—unless indeed the stage of arbitrary decision is reached. Under this interpretation, the courts need to read only one side of the case and, if they find any evidence there, the administrative action is to be sustained and the record to the contrary is to be ignored." Their view led them to recommend that Congress enact principles of review applicable to all agencies not excepted by unique characteristics. One of these principles was expressed by the formula that judicial review could extend to "findings, inferences, or conclusions of fact unsupported, upon the whole record, by substantial evidence." So far as the history of this movement for enlarged review reveals, the phrase "upon the whole record" makes its first appearance in this recommendation of the minority of the Attorney General's Committee. This evidence of the close relationship between the phrase and the criticism out of which it arose is important, for the substance of this formula for judicial review found its way into the statute books when Congress with unquestioning—we might even say uncritical—unanimity enacted the Administrative Procedure Act.

One is tempted to say "uncritical" because the legislative history of that Act hardly speaks with that clarity of purpose which Congress supposedly furnishes courts in order to enable them to enforce its true will. On

---

2. Referring to proposals to enlarge the scope of review to permit inquiry whether the findings are supported by the weight of the evidence, the majority said: "[T]he wisdom of a general change to review of the 'weight of evidence' is questionable. If the change would require the courts to determine independently which way the evidence preponderates, administrative tribunals would be turned into little more than media for transmission of the evidence to the courts. It would destroy the values of adjudication of fact by experts or specialists in the field involved. It would divide the responsibility for administrative adjudications." Final Report, 91–92.

the one hand, the sponsors of the legislation indicated that they were reaffirming the prevailing "substantial evidence" test. But with equal clarity they expressed disapproval of the manner in which the courts were applying their own standard. The committee reports of both houses refer to the practice of agencies to rely upon "suspicion, surmise, implications, or plainly incredible evidence," and indicate that courts are to exact higher standards "in the exercise of their independent judgment" and on consideration of "the whole record."[3]

Similar dissatisfaction with too restricted application of the "substantial evidence" test is reflected in the legislative history of the Taft–Hartley Act [amending the National Labor Relations Act in 1947]. ... Early committee prints in the Senate provided for review by "weight of the evidence" or "clearly erroneous" standards. But, as the Senate Committee Report relates, "it was finally decided to conform the statute to the corresponding section of the Administrative Procedure Act where the substantial evidence test prevails. In order to clarify any ambiguity in that statute, however, the committee inserted the words 'questions of fact, if supported by substantial evidence on the record considered as a whole....' "[4]

This phraseology was adopted by the Senate. The House conferees agreed. ...

It is fair to say that in all this Congress expressed a mood. And it expressed its mood not merely by oratory but by legislation. As legislation that mood must be respected, even though it can only serve as a standard for judgment and not as a body of rigid rules assuring sameness of applications. Enforcement of such broad standards implies subtlety of mind

---

3. The following quotation from the report of the Senate Judiciary Committee indicates the position of the sponsors. "The 'substantial evidence' rule set forth in section 10(e) is exceedingly important. As a matter of language, substantial evidence would seem to be an adequate expression of law. The difficulty comes about in the practice of agencies to rely upon (and of courts to tacitly approve) something less—to rely upon suspicion, surmise, implications, or plainly incredible evidence. It will be the duty of the courts to determine in the final analysis and in the exercise of their independent judgment, whether on the whole record the evidence in a given instance is sufficiently substantial to support a finding, conclusion, or other agency action as a matter of law. In the first instance, however, it will be the function of the agency to determine the sufficiency of the evidence upon which it acts—and the proper performance of its public duties will require it to undertake this inquiry in a careful an dispassionate manner. Should these objectives of the bill as worded fail, supplemental legislation will be required." S.Rep. No. 752, 79th Cong., 1st Sess. 30–31. The House Committee Report is to substantially the same effect. H.R.Rep. No. 1980, 79th Cong., 2d Sess. 45.

4. S.Rep. No. 105, 80th Cong., 1st Sess. 26–27. The Committee did not explain what the ambiguity might be.... Senator Taft gave this explanation to the Senate of the meaning of the section: "In the first place, the evidence must be substantial; in the second place, it must still look substantial when viewed in the light of the entire record. That does not go so far as saying that a decision can be reversed on the weight of the evidence. It does not go quite so far as the power given to a circuit court of appeals to review a district-court decision, but it goes a great deal further than the present law, and gives the court greater opportunity to reverse an obviously unjust decision on the part of the National Labor Relations Board." 93 Cong.Rec. 3839.

and solidity of judgment. But it is not for us to question that Congress may assume such qualities in the federal judiciary.

From the legislative story we have summarized, two concrete conclusions do emerge. One is the identity of aim of the Administrative Procedure Act and the Taft–Hartley Act regarding the proof with which the Labor Board must support a decision. The other is that now Congress has left no room for doubt as to the kind of scrutiny which a court of appeals must give the record before the Board to satisfy itself that the Board's order rests on adequate proof. . . .

Whether or not it was ever permissible for courts to determine the substantiality of evidence supporting a Labor Board decision merely on the basis of evidence which in and of itself justified it, without taking into account contradictory evidence or evidence from which conflicting inferences could be drawn, the new legislation definitively precludes such a theory of review and bars its practice. The substantiality of evidence must take into account whatever in the record fairly detracts from its weight. This is clearly the significance of the requirement in both statutes that courts consider the whole record. Committee reports and the adoption in the Administrative Procedure Act of the minority views of the Attorney General's Committee demonstrate that to enjoin such a duty on the reviewing court was one of the important purposes of the movement which eventuated in that enactment.

To be sure, the requirement for canvassing "the whole record" in order to ascertain substantiality does not furnish a calculus of value by which a reviewing court can assess the evidence. Nor was it intended to negative the function of the Labor Board as one of those agencies presumably equipped or informed by experience to deal with a specialized field of knowledge, whose findings within that field carry the authority of an expertness which courts do not possess and therefore must respect. Nor does it mean that even as to matters not requiring expertise a court may displace the Board's choice between two fairly conflicting views, even though the court would justifiably have made a different choice had the matter been before it de novo. Congress has merely made it clear that a reviewing court is not barred from setting aside a Board decision when it cannot conscientiously find that the evidence supporting that decision is substantial, when viewed in the light that the record in its entirety furnishes, including the body of evidence opposed to the Board's view.

There remains, then, the question whether enactment of these two statutes has altered the scope of review other than to require that substantiality be determined in the light of all that the record relevantly presents. A formula for judicial review of administrative action may afford grounds for certitude but cannot assure certainty of application. Some scope for judicial discretion in applying the formula can be avoided only by falsifying the actual process of judging or by using the formula as an instrument of futile casuistry. It cannot be too often repeated that judges are not automata. The ultimate reliance for the fair operation of any standard is a judiciary of high competence and character and the constant play of an informed professional critique upon its work.

Since the precise way in which courts interfere with agency findings cannot be imprisoned within any form of words, new formulas attempting to rephrase the old are not likely to be more helpful than the old. There are no talismanic words that can avoid the process of judgment. The difficulty is that we cannot escape, in relation to this problem, the use of undefined defining terms.

Whatever changes were made by the Administrative Procedure and Taft–Hartley Acts are clearly within this area where precise definition is impossible. Retention of the familiar "substantial evidence" terminology indicates that no drastic reversal of attitude was intended.

But a standard leaving an unavoidable margin for individual judgment does not leave the judicial judgment at large even though the phrasing of the standard does not wholly fence it in. The legislative history of these Acts demonstrates a purpose to impose on courts a responsibility which has not always been recognized. Of course it is a statute and not a committee report which we are interpreting. But the fair interpretation of a statute is often "the art of proliferating a purpose," revealed more by the demonstrable forces that produced it than by its precise phrasing. The adoption in these statutes of the judicially-constructed "substantial evidence" test was a response to pressures for stricter and more uniform practice, not a reflection of approval of all existing practices. To find the change so elusive that it cannot be precisely defined does not mean it may be ignored. . . .

We conclude, therefore, that the Administrative Procedure Act and the Taft–Hartley Act direct that courts must now assume more responsibility for the reasonableness and fairness of Labor Board decisions than some courts have shown in the past. Reviewing courts must be influenced by a feeling that they are not to abdicate the conventional judicial function. Congress has imposed on them responsibility for assuring that the Board keeps within reasonable grounds. That responsibility is not less real because it is limited to enforcing the requirement that evidence appear substantial when viewed, on the record as a whole, by courts invested with the authority and enjoying the prestige of the Courts of Appeals. The Board's findings are entitled to respect; but they must nonetheless be set aside when the record before a Court of Appeals clearly precludes the Board's decision from being justified by a fair estimate of the worth of the testimony of witnesses or its informed judgment on matters within its special competence or both.

From this it follows that enactment of these statutes does not require every Court of Appeals to alter its practice. Some—perhaps a majority—have always applied the attitude reflected in this legislation. To explore whether a particular court should or should not alter its practice would only divert attention from the application of the standard now prescribed to a futile inquiry into the nature of the test formerly used by a particular court.

Our power to review the correctness of application of the present standard ought seldom to be called into action. Whether on the record as a whole there is substantial evidence to support agency findings is a question which Congress has placed in the keeping of the Courts of Appeals. This Court will intervene only in what ought to be the rare instance when the standard appears to have been misapprehended or grossly misapplied.

II.

. . .

The decision of the Court of Appeals is assailed on two grounds. It is said (1) that the court erred in holding that it was barred from taking into account the report of the examiner on questions of fact insofar as that report was rejected by the Board, and (2) that the Board's order was not supported by substantial evidence on the record considered as a whole, even apart from the validity of the court's refusal to consider the rejected portions of the examiner's report.

The latter contention is easily met. . . . [I]t is clear from the court's opinion in this case that it in fact did consider the "record as a whole," and did not deem itself merely the judicial echo of the Board's conclusion. The testimony of the company's witnesses was inconsistent, and there was clear evidence that the complaining employee had been discharged by an officer who was at one time influenced against him because of his appearance at the Board hearing. On such a record we could not say that it would be error to grant enforcement.

The first contention, however, raises serious questions to which we now turn.

III.

The Court of Appeals deemed itself bound by the Board's rejection of the examiner's findings because the court considered these findings not "as unassailable as a master's."[5] They are not. . . . The responsibility for decision . . . placed on the Board is wholly inconsistent with the notion that it has power to reverse an examiner's findings only when they are "clearly erroneous." Such a limitation would make so drastic a departure from prior administrative practice that explicitness would be required.

The Court of Appeals concluded from this premise "that, although the Board would be wrong in totally disregarding his findings, it is practically impossible for a court, upon review of those findings which the Board itself substitutes, to consider the Board's reversal as a factor in the court's own decision. This we say, because we cannot find any middle ground between doing that and treating such a reversal as error, whenever it would be such, if done by a judge to a master in equity." Much as we respect the logical acumen of the Chief Judge of the Court of Appeals, we do not find ourselves pinioned between the horns of his dilemma.

We are aware that to give the examiner's findings less finality than a master's and yet entitle them to consideration in striking the account, is to introduce another and an unruly factor into the judgmatical process of

---

5. Rule 53(e)(2), Fed.Rules Civ.Proc., gives finality to the findings of a master unless they are clearly erroneous.

review. But we ought not to fashion an exclusionary rule merely to reduce the number of imponderables to be considered by reviewing courts.

The Taft–Hartley Act provides that "The findings of the Board with respect to questions of fact if supported by substantial evidence on the record considered as a whole shall be conclusive." Surely an examiner's report is as much a part of the record as the complaint or the testimony. According to the Administrative Procedure Act, "All decisions (including initial, recommended, or tentative decisions) shall become a part of the record ..." § 557(c). We found that this Act's provision for judicial review has the same meaning as that in the Taft–Hartley Act. The similarity of the two statutes in language and purpose also requires that the definition of "record" found in the Administrative Procedure Act be construed to be applicable as well to the term "record" as used in the Taft–Hartley Act.

It is therefore difficult to escape the conclusion that the plain language of the statutes directs a reviewing court to determine the substantiality of evidence on the record including the examiner's report. The conclusion is confirmed by the indications in the legislative history that enhancement of the status and function of the trial examiner was one of the important purposes of the movement for administrative reform.

This aim was set forth by the Attorney General's Committee on Administrative Procedure: "In general, the relationship upon appeal between the hearing commissioner and the agency ought to a considerable extent to be that of trial court to appellate court. Conclusions, interpretations, law, and policy should, of course, be open to full review. On the other hand, on matters which the hearing commissioner, having heard the evidence and seen the witnesses, is best qualified to decide, the agency should be reluctant to disturb his findings unless error is clearly shown."

Apparently it was the Committee's opinion that these recommendations should not be obligatory. For the bill which accompanied the Final Report required only that hearing officers make an initial decision which would become final in the absence of further agency action, and that agencies which differed on the facts from their examiners give reasons and record citations supporting their conclusion. This proposal was further moderated by the Administrative Procedure Act. It permits agencies to use examiners to record testimony but not to evaluate it, and contains the rather obscure provision that an agency which reviews an examiner's report has "all the powers which it would have in making the initial decision."

But this refusal to make mandatory the recommendations of the Attorney General's Committee should not be construed as a repudiation of them. Nothing in the statutes suggests that the Labor Board should not be influenced by the examiner's opportunity to observe the witnesses he hears and sees and the Board does not. Nothing suggests that reviewing courts should not give to the examiner's report such probative force as it intrinsically commands. . . .

We do not require that the examiner's findings be given more weight than in reason and in the light of judicial experience they deserve. The "substantial evidence" standard is not modified in any way when the Board and its examiner disagree. We intend only to recognize that evidence supporting a conclusion may be less substantial when an impartial, experienced examiner who has observed the witnesses and lived with the case has drawn conclusions different from the Board's than when he has reached the same conclusion. The findings of the examiner are to be considered along with the consistency and inherent probability of testimony. The significance of his report, of course, depends largely on the importance of credibility in the particular case. To give it this significance does not seem to us materially more difficult than to heed the other factors which in sum determine whether evidence is "substantial." . . .

We therefore remand the cause to the Court of Appeals. On reconsideration of the record it should accord the findings of the trial examiner the relevance that they reasonably command in answering the comprehensive question whether the evidence supporting the Board's order is substantial. But the court need not limit its reexamination of the case to the effect of that report on its decision. We leave it free to grant or deny enforcement as it thinks the principles expressed in this opinion dictate.

Judgment vacated and cause remanded.

■ MR. JUSTICE BLACK AND MR. JUSTICE DOUGLAS concur with parts I and II of this opinion but as to part III agree with the opinion of the court below, 2 Cir., 179 F.2d 749, 753.

NOTES

(1) "Weight of the evidence," "clearly erroneous," "substantial evidence"—can you tell the labels apart? If so, *how* do you tell them apart—by comparing them with one another, by relating them to a known institutional process (such as the deference given to a jury verdict), or by reformulating them? Justice Frankfurter has a serious jurisprudential problem: he believes that Congress has indeed said *something* in enacting the APA (and the Taft–Hartley Act) but he also believes that "the precise way in which courts interfere with agency findings cannot be imprisoned within any form of words." If you were a Court of Appeals judge (or her clerk), would you be confident you now understand your role?

(2) DICKINSON V. ZURKO, 527 U.S. 150 (1999) has already appeared in these pages p. 264 above, with regard to its holding that the APA controls the Federal Circuit's review of findings of fact made by the Patent and Trademark office. In the course of that opinion, Justice Breyer distinguishes between what he labels "court/court" review of findings of fact (by which he means appellate review of findings of fact made by a trial judge, not the jury), and "court/agency" review. He then writes (527 U.S. at 162–163): "This Court has described the APA court/agency 'substantial evidence' standard as requiring a court to ask whether a 'reasonable mind might accept' a particular evidentiary record as 'adequate to support a conclusion.' Consolidated Edison, 305 U.S., at 229. It has described the court/court 'clearly erroneous' standard in terms of whether a reviewing judge has a 'definite and firm conviction' that an error has been committed.

United States v. United States Gypsum Co., 333 U.S. 364 (1948). And it has suggested that the former is somewhat less strict than the latter. Universal Camera, 340 U.S., at 477, 488 (analogizing 'substantial evidence' test to review of jury findings and stating that appellate courts must respect agency expertise). At the same time the Court has stressed the importance of not simply rubber-stamping agency factfinding. *Id.*, at 490. The APA requires meaningful review; and its enactment meant stricter judicial review of agency factfinding than Congress believed some courts had previously conducted. *Ibid.*

"The upshot in terms of judicial review is some practical difference in outcome depending upon which standard is used. The court/agency standard, as we have said, is somewhat less strict than the court/court standard. But the difference is a subtle one—so fine that (apart from the present case) we have failed to uncover a single instance in which a reviewing court conceded that use of one standard rather than the other would in fact have produced a different outcome. Cf. International Brotherhood of Electrical Workers v. NLRB, 448 F.2d 1127, 1142 (C.A.D.C.1971) (Leventhal, J., dissenting) (wrongly believing—and correcting himself—that he had found the 'case dreamed of by law school professors' where the agency's findings, though 'clearly erroneous,' were 'nevertheless' supported by 'substantial evidence').

"The difficulty of finding such a case may in part reflect the basic similarity of the reviewing task, which requires judges to apply logic and experience to an evidentiary record, whether that record was made in a court or by an agency. It may in part reflect the difficulty of attempting to capture in a form of words intangible factors such as judicial confidence in the fairness of the factfinding process. Universal Camera, supra, at 489. It may in part reflect the comparatively greater importance of case-specific factors, such as a finding's dependence upon agency expertise or the presence of internal agency review, which factors will often prove more influential in respect to outcome than will the applicable standard of review."

Relying on the fact that the Federal Circuit has a much narrower, more specialized scope of jurisdiction—focused on trademark and patent decisions—than the other Circuit Courts of Appeals, Justice Breyer then continues with the following remark (527 U.S. at 163): "These features of review underline the importance of the fact that, when a Federal Circuit judge reviews PTO factfinding, he or she often will examine that finding through the lens of patent-related experience—and properly so, for the Federal Circuit is a specialized court. That comparative expertise, by enabling the Circuit better to understand the basis for the PTO's finding of fact, may play a more important role in assuring proper review than would a theoretically somewhat stricter standard."

(3) While we are on the matter, is it a good idea that judicial review of administrative action usually is done by courts with a large, general jurisdiction? Harold Bruff, Specialized Courts in Administrative Law, 443 Admin.L.Rev. 329, 331 (1991):

> A premise of our nation's usual resort to courts of general jurisdiction
> is that sound decisionmaking results from exposure to a wide range of

problems, rather than from initiation into an arcane set of mysteries. Generalization has two related benefits. Some loosely related legal issues may produce direct cross-fertilization of insights. More often, a wider perspective aids judgment by forestalling the exaggerated importance that long immersion may lend to some social problem. A broadened perspective may be especially important in those who review the action of bureaucracies that are themselves narrowly focused.

Are you convinced? European countries typically rely on specialized courts to review regulatory decisions—and even we have our Federal Circuit and our Tax Court.

(4) In its treatment of the examiner's (now ALJ's) report, the Universal Camera Court suggests a principle of allocation of responsibility as between examiner and agency. It places significant weight on the apoliticality of the examiner's place and function in the agency, a characteristic that lends "impartiality" to her judgments—impartiality is, if you like, what her participation contributes. The agency, on the other hand, has responsibility for the development and implementation of policy in light of its experience and statutory powers. This agency responsibility may lead the agency to develop policy-laden principles or presumptions for interpreting fact patterns that commonly arise in the course of its work. A simple issue of witness credibility, on the one hand, evokes the examiner's objectivity as well as her presence when the testimony was given. On the other hand, the idea that sudden and drastic employment actions are associated with anti-union animus is not based only in objective fact; policy-based commitments to the protection of union organizing activity contribute to it—and if such commitments are statutorily appropriate, one may see that such an inference is grounded in the agency's responsibilities, not the examiner's. Judge Frank explained the distinction on remand in Universal Camera in the following terms:

> An examiner's finding binds the Board only to the extent that it is a "testimonial inference," or "primary inference," i.e., an inference that a fact to which a witness orally testified is an actual fact because the witness so testified and because observation of the witness induces a belief in that testimony. The Board, however, is not bound by the examiner's "secondary inferences," or "derivative inferences," i.e., facts to which no witness orally testified but which the examiner inferred from facts orally testified by witnesses whom the examiner believed. The Board may reach its own "secondary inferences" and we must abide by them unless they are irrational; in that way, the Board differs from a trial judge (in a jury-less case) who hears and sees the witnesses, for although we are usually bound by his "testimonial inferences" we need not accept his "secondary inferences" even if rational, but where other rational "secondary inferences" are possible, we may substitute our own.

190 F.2d 429, 432 (2d Cir.1951).

PENASQUITOS VILLAGE, INC. v. NLRB, 565 F.2d 1074 (9th Cir.1977) exemplifies both the distinction and its frequent difficulty. Once again the question for the Board was whether a challenged discharge reflected employee misbehavior, or employer anti-union animus. A supervisor testified that he had observed two discharged employees loafing on the job; one had a few months earlier been suspended for similar misconduct; after verifying that he had the authority to fire them, he did so. The employees presented evidence of their status as union organizers and of alleged coercive interrogation. At least one of the employees was shown to have testified untruthfully in important respects, and the ALJ resolved "clear-cut questions of credibility" in favor of the employer. The case was also marked, however, by circumstances (abrupt employment discipline, occurring very shortly after union organizing activity had come to light) that past Board decisions had identified as signs of anti-union animus. Disagreeing with its ALJ's assessment, the Board concluded that the discharges had been improper. Were its derivative inferences, based on general experience and labor policy, enough to constitute "substantial evidence" on the record as a whole, when opposed to the ALJ's testimonial inferences that the employer's witnesses had been truthtellers, and the employees not, in describing the circumstances that led up to the discharges?

Judge Wallace, for the majority, 565 F.2d at 1078 et seq.: "even when the record contains independent, credited evidence supportive of the Board's decision, a reviewing court will review more critically the Board's findings of fact if they are contrary to the administrative law judge's factual conclusions. ... All aspects of the witness's demeanor—including the expression of his countenance, how he sits or stands, whether he is inordinately nervous, his coloration during critical examination, the modulation or pace of his speech and other non-verbal communication—may convince the observing trial judge that the witness is testifying truthfully or falsely. These same very important factors, however, are entirely unavailable to a reader of the transcript, such as the Board or the Court of Appeals. But it should be noted that the administrative law judge's opportunity to observe the witnesses' demeanor does not, by itself, require deference with regard to his or her derivative inferences. Observation of demeanor makes weighty only the observer's testimonial inferences.

"Deference is accorded the Board's factual conclusions for a different reason—Board members are presumed to have broad experience and expertise in labor-management relations. ... Further, it is the Board to which Congress has delegated administration of the Act. The Board, therefore, is viewed as particularly capable of drawing inferences from the facts of a labor dispute. Accordingly, it has been said that a Court of Appeals must abide by the Board's derivative inferences, if drawn from not discredited testimony, unless those inferences are 'irrational' ...

"... [I]n this case, credibility played a dominant role. The administrative law judge's testimonial inferences reduce significantly the substantiality of the Board's contrary derivative inferences. Particularly, removing the Board's finding of anti-union animus based upon alleged unlawful threats and interrogations, leaves poorly substantiated the Board's other conclusion that the discharges were improperly motivated. Considering the record as a whole, we conclude that the Board's conclusion that Penasquitos committed unlawful labor practices is not supported by substantial evidence and must, therefore, be set aside."

Judge Duniway's partial dissent expressed doubt, 565 F.2d at 1084–85: "The notion that special deference is owed to the determination of a trier of fact, . . . is deeply imbedded in the law. . . . As a generalization, it is unassailable. . . . [Yet] I venture to suggest that, as to every one of the factors that Judge Wallace lists, one trier of fact may take it to indicate that the witness is truthful and another may think that it shows that the witness is lying. . . . Every trial lawyer knows, and most trial judges will admit, that it is not unusual for an accomplished liar to fool a jury (or, even, heaven forbid, a trial judge) into believing him because his demeanor is so convincing. The expression of his countenance may be open and frank; he may sit squarely in the chair, with no squirming; he may show no nervousness; his answers to questions may be clear, concise and audible, and given without hesitation; his coloration may be normal—neither pale nor flushed. In short, he may appear to be the trial lawyer's ideal witness. He may also be a consummate liar."

(5) Distinct from the court's function in reviewing facts is the *standard of proof* by which the agency is to find facts initially. " 'The function of a standard of proof . . . is to "instruct the factfinder concerning the degree of confidence our society thinks he should have in the correctness of factual conclusions for a particular type of adjudication." ' " Cruzan v. Director, Missouri Dept. of Health, 497 U.S. 261, 282 (1990) (quoting precedents).

What standard of proof is called for in formal proceedings by APA § 556(d)? "Except as otherwise provided by statute, the proponent of a rule or order has the burden of proof. . . . A sanction may not be imposed or rule or order issued except on consideration of the whole record or those parts thereof cited by a party *and supported and in accordance with the reliable, probative, and substantial evidence.*" In Steadman v. SEC, 450 U.S. 91 (1981), the SEC used the preponderance-of-the-evidence standard to establish violations of the antifraud and related securities law provisions. It then ordered the long-time head of several investment companies permanently barred from any association with any such companies. Steadman argued that such severe sanctions required a clear-and-convincing standard. The courts of appeals had been divided. Seven Justices held that the "somewhat opaque" language of § 556(d), in light of legislative history, adopted the traditional standard the SEC used. Two dissenters argued that at common law, fraud had to be proved by clear and convincing evidence and there was no indication that Congress intended to change that practice.

(6) A second issue distinct from, but often discussed in conjunction with, scope of review of factual determinations, is who bears the *burden* of meeting the standard of proof when the agency is finding facts and drawing conclusions. Section 556(d) says that "[e]xcept as otherwise provided by the statute, the proponent of a rule or order has the burden of proof." The Court has interpreted this to mean that the "proponent" has the burden of persuasion, and not merely the burden of producing evidence initially. See Director, Office of Workers' Compensation Programs v. Greenwich Collieries, 512 U.S. 267 (1994), also discussed at page 269 above.

(7) Finally, quite apart from evidence or "substantial evidence," Justice Frankfurter's opinion is an excellent example of what can be done to construe a statute using legislative history in both senses of the term: the

documents that Congress produced, and the problems and controversies that produced the Act. The opinion also seems to many readers to be verbose. It is one of the most famous decisions in this casebook. Did you like it?

Allentown Mack Sales and Service, Inc. v. National Labor Relations Board

Supreme Court of the United States, 1998.
522 U.S. 359.

■ JUSTICE SCALIA delivered the opinion of the Court.

Under longstanding precedent of the National Labor Relations Board, an employer who believes that an incumbent union no longer enjoys the support of a majority of its employees has three options: to request a formal, Board-supervised election, to withdraw recognition from the union and refuse to bargain, or to conduct an internal poll of employee support for the union. The Board has held that the latter two are unfair labor practices unless the employer can show that it had a "good faith reasonable doubt" about the union's majority support. We must decide whether the Board's standard for employer polling is rational and consistent with the National Labor Relations Act, and whether the Board's factual determinations in this case are supported by substantial evidence in the record.

I

Mack Trucks, Inc., had a factory branch in Allentown, Pennsylvania, whose service and parts employees were represented by Local Lodge 724 of the International Association of Machinists and Aerospace Workers, AFL–CIO. Mack notified its Allentown managers in May of 1990 that it intended to sell the branch, and several of those managers formed Allentown Mack Sales, Inc., the petitioner here, which purchased the assets of the business on December 20, 1990, and began to operate it as an independent dealership. From December 21, 1990, to January 1, 1991, Allentown hired 32 of the original 45 Mack employees.

During the period before and immediately after the sale, a number of Mack employees made statements to the prospective owners of Allentown Mack Sales suggesting that the incumbent union had lost support among employees in the bargaining unit. In job interviews, eight employees made statements indicating, or at least arguably indicating, that they personally no longer supported the union. In addition, Ron Mohr, a member of the union's bargaining committee and shop steward for the Mack Trucks service department, told an Allentown manager that it was his feeling that the employees did not want a union, and that "with a new company, if a vote was taken, the Union would lose." And Kermit Bloch, who worked for Mack Trucks as a mechanic on the night shift, told a manager that the entire night shift (then 5 or 6 employees) did not want the union.

On January 2, 1991, Local Lodge 724 asked Allentown Mack Sales to recognize it as the employees' collective-bargaining representative, and to begin negotiations for a contract. The new employer rejected that request by letter dated January 25, claiming a "good faith doubt as to support of the Union among the employees." The letter also announced that Allentown had "arranged for an independent poll by secret ballot of its hourly employees to be conducted under guidelines prescribed by the National Labor Relations Board." The poll, supervised by a Roman Catholic priest, was conducted on February 8, 1991; the union lost 19 to 13. Shortly thereafter, the union filed an unfair-labor-practice charge with the Board.

The Administrative Law Judge (ALJ) concluded that Allentown was a "successor" employer to Mack Trucks, Inc., and therefore inherited Mack's bargaining obligation and a presumption of continuing majority support for the union. The ALJ held that Allentown's poll was conducted in compliance with the procedural standards enunciated by the Board ... but that it violated §§ 8(a)(1) and 8(a)(5) of the National Labor Relations Act (Act), because Allentown did not have an "objective reasonable doubt" about the majority status of the union. The Board adopted the ALJ's findings and agreed with his conclusion that Allentown "had not demonstrated that it harbored a reasonable doubt, based on objective considerations, as to the incumbent Union's continued majority status after the transition." The Board ordered Allentown to recognize and bargain with Local 724.

On review in the Court of Appeals for the District of Columbia Circuit, Allentown challenged both the facial rationality of the Board's test for employer polling and the Board's application of that standard to the facts of this case. The court enforced the Board's bargaining order, over a vigorous dissent. 83 F.3d 1483 (1996). We granted certiorari.

II

Allentown challenges the Board's decision in this case on several grounds. First, it contends that because the Board's "reasonable doubt" standard for employer polls is the same as its standard for unilateral withdrawal of recognition and for employer initiation of a Board-supervised election (a so-called "Representation Management," or "RM" election), the Board irrationally permits employers to poll only when it would be unnecessary and legally pointless to do so. Second, Allentown argues that the record evidence clearly demonstrates that it had a good-faith reasonable doubt about the union's claim to majority support. Finally, it asserts that the Board has, *sub silentio* (and presumably in violation of law), abandoned the "reasonable doubt" prong of its polling standard, and recognizes an employer's "reasonable doubt" only if a majority of the unit employees renounce the union. In this Part of our opinion we address the first of these challenges; the other two, which are conceptually intertwined, will be addressed in Parts III and IV.

Courts must defer to the requirements imposed by the Board if they are "rational and consistent with the Act," Fall River Dyeing & Finishing Corp. v. NLRB, 482 U.S. 27, 42 (1987), and if the Board's "explication is not inadequate, irrational or arbitrary," NLRB v. Erie Resistor Corp., 373 U.S. 221, 236 (1963). Allentown argues that it is irrational to require the same factual showing to justify a poll as to justify an outright withdrawal of recognition, because that leaves the employer with no legal incentive to poll. Under the Board's framework, the results of a poll can never supply an otherwise lacking "good faith reasonable doubt" necessary to justify a withdrawal of recognition, since the employer must already have that same reasonable doubt before he is permitted to conduct a poll. Three Courts of Appeals have found that argument persuasive.

While the Board's adoption of a unitary standard for polling, RM elections, and withdrawals of recognition is in some respects a puzzling policy, we do not find it so irrational as to be "arbitrary [or] capricious" within the meaning of the Administrative Procedure Act, 5 U.S.C. § 706. . . .

III

The Board held Allentown guilty of an unfair labor practice in its conduct of the polling because it "ha[d] not demonstrated that it held a reasonable doubt, based on objective considerations, that the Union continued to enjoy the support of a majority of the bargaining unit employees." We must decide whether that conclusion is supported by substantial evidence on the record as a whole. Universal Camera Corp. v. NLRB, 340 U.S. 474 (1951). Put differently, we must decide whether on this record it would have been possible for a reasonable jury to reach the Board's conclusion.

Before turning to that issue, we must clear up some semantic confusion. The Board asserted at argument that the word "doubt" may mean either "uncertainty" or "disbelief," and that its polling standard uses the word only in the latter sense. We cannot accept that linguistic revisionism. "Doubt" is precisely that sort of "disbelief" (failure to believe) which consists of an uncertainty rather than a belief in the opposite. If the subject at issue were the existence of God, for example, "doubt" would be the disbelief of the agnostic, not of the atheist. A doubt is an uncertain, tentative, or provisional disbelief. See, e.g., Webster's New International Dictionary 776 (2d ed. 1949) (def. 1: "A fluctuation of mind arising from defect of knowledge or evidence; uncertainty of judgment or mind; unsettled state of opinion concerning the reality of an event, or the truth of an assertion, etc."); 1 The New Shorter Oxford English Dictionary 734 (1993) (def. 1: "Uncertainty as to the truth or reality of something or as to the wisdom of a course of action; occasion or room for uncertainty"); American Heritage Dictionary 555 (3d ed. 1992) (def. 1: "A lack of certainty that often leads to irresolution").

The question presented for review, therefore, is whether, on the evidence presented to the Board, a reasonable jury could have found that Allentown lacked a genuine, reasonable uncertainty about whether Local 724 enjoyed the continuing support of a majority of unit employees. In our view, the answer is no. The Board's finding to the contrary rests on a refusal to credit probative circumstantial evidence, and on evidentiary demands that go beyond the substantive standard the Board purports to apply.

The Board adopted the ALJ's finding that 6 of Allentown's 32 employees had made "statements which could be used as objective considerations supporting a good-faith reasonable doubt as to continued majority status by the Union." (These included, for example, the statement of Rusty Hoffman that "he did not want to work in a union shop," and "would try to find another job if he had to work with the Union.") The Board seemingly also accepted (though this is not essential to our analysis) the ALJ's willingness to assume that the statement of a seventh employee (to the effect that he "did not feel comfortable with the Union and thought it was a waste of $35 a month,") supported good-faith reasonable doubt of his support for the union—as in our view it unquestionably does. And it presumably accepted the ALJ's assessment that "7 of 32, or roughly 20 percent of the involved employees" was not alone sufficient to create "an objective reasonable doubt of union majority support." . . . But there was much more.

For one thing, the ALJ and the Board totally disregarded the effect upon Allentown of the statement of an eighth employee, Dennis Marsh, who said that "he was not being represented for the $35 he was paying." The ALJ, whose findings were adopted by the Board, said that this statement "seems more an expression of a desire for better representation than one for no representation at all." It seems to us that it is, more accurately, simply an expression of dissatisfaction with the union's performance—which could reflect the speaker's desire that the union represent him more effectively, but could also reflect the speaker's desire to save his $35 and get rid of the union. The statement would assuredly engender an uncertainty whether the speaker supported the union, and so could not be entirely ignored.

But the most significant evidence excluded from consideration by the Board consisted of statements of two employees regarding not merely their own support of the union, but support among the work force in general. Kermit Bloch, who worked on the night shift, told an Allentown manager "that the entire night shift did not want the Union." The ALJ refused to credit this, because "Bloch did not testify and thus could not explain how he formed his opinion about the views of his fellow employees." Unsubstantiated assertions that other employees do not support the union certainly do not establish the fact of that disfavor with the degree of reliability ordinarily demanded in legal proceedings. But under the Board's enunciated test for polling, it is not the fact of disfavor that is at issue (the poll itself is meant to establish that), but rather the existence of a reasonable uncertainty on the part of the employer regarding that fact. On that issue, absent some reason for the employer to know that Bloch had no basis for his information, or that Bloch was lying, reason demands that the statement be given considerable weight.

Another employee who gave information concerning overall support for the union was Ron Mohr, who told Allentown managers that "if a vote was taken, the Union would lose" and that "it was his feeling that the employees did not want a union." The ALJ again objected irrelevantly that "there is no evidence with respect to how he gained this knowledge." In addition, the Board held that Allentown "could not legitimately rely on [the statement] as a basis for doubting the Union's majority status," because Mohr was "referring to Mack's existing employee complement, not to the individuals who were later hired by [Allentown]." This basis for disregarding Mohr's statements is wholly irrational. Local 724 had never won an election, or even an informal poll, within the actual unit of 32 Allentown employees. Its claim to represent them rested entirely on the Board's presumption that the workforce of a successor company has the same disposition regarding the union as did the work force of the predecessor company, if the majority of the new workforce came from the old one. The Board cannot rationally adopt that presumption for purposes of imposing the duty to bargain, and adopt precisely the opposite presumption (i.e., contend that there is no relationship between the sentiments of the two work forces) for purposes of determining what evidence tends to establish a reasonable doubt regarding union support. Such irrationality is impermissible even if, as Justice Breyer's dissent suggests, it would further the Board's political objectives.

It must be borne in mind that the issue here is not whether Mohr's statement clearly establishes a majority in opposition to the union, but whether it contributes to a reasonable uncertainty whether a majority in favor of the union existed. We think it surely does. Allentown would reasonably have given great credence to Mohr's assertion of lack of union support, since he was not hostile to the union, and was in a good position to assess antiunion sentiment. Mohr was a union shop steward for the service department, and a member of the union's bargaining committee; according to the ALJ, he "did not indicate personal dissatisfaction with the Union." It seems to us that Mohr's statement has undeniable and substantial probative value on the issue of "reasonable doubt."

Accepting the Board's apparent (and in our view inescapable) concession that Allentown received reliable information that 7 of the bargaining-unit employees did not support the union, the remaining 25 would have had to support the union by a margin of 17 to 8—a ratio of more than 2 to 1—if the union commanded majority support. The statements of Bloch and Mohr would cause anyone to doubt that degree of support, and neither the Board nor the ALJ discussed any evidence that Allentown should have weighed on the other side. The most pro-union statement cited in the ALJ's opinion was Ron Mohr's comment that he personally "could work with or without the Union," and "was there to do his job." ... Giving fair weight to Allentown's circumstantial evidence, we think it quite impossible for a rational factfinder to avoid the conclusion that Allentown had reasonable, good-faith grounds to doubt—to be *uncertain about*—the union's retention of majority support.

IV

That conclusion would make this a fairly straightforward administrative-law case, except for the contention that the Board's factfinding here was not an aberration. ... The Board ... does defend its factfinding in this case by saying that it has regularly rejected similarly persuasive demonstrations of reasonable good-faith doubt in prior decisions. The Court of Appeals in fact accepted that defense, relying on those earlier, similar decisions to conclude that the Board's findings were supported by substantial evidence here. That the current decision may conform to a long pattern is also suggested by academic commentary. ...

It is certainly conceivable that an adjudicating agency might consistently require a particular substantive standard to be established by a quantity or character of evidence so far beyond what reason and logic would require as to make it apparent that the *announced* standard is not *really* the effective one. And it is conceivable that in certain categories of cases an adjudicating agency which purports to be applying a preponderance standard of proof might so consistently demand in fact more than a preponderance, that all should be on notice from its case law that the genuine burden of proof is more than a preponderance. The question arises, then, whether, if that should be the situation that obtains here, we ought to measure the evidentiary support for the Board's decision against the standards consistently applied rather than the standards recited. As a theoretical matter (and leaving aside the question of legal authority), the Board could certainly have raised the bar for employer polling or withdrawal of recognition by imposing a more stringent requirement than the reasonable-doubt test, or by adopting a formal requirement that employers establish their reasonable doubt by more than a preponderance of the evidence. Would it make any difference if the Board achieved precisely the same result by formally leaving in place the reasonable-doubt and preponderance standards, but consistently applying them as though they meant something other than what they say? We think it would.

The Administrative Procedure Act, which governs the proceedings of administrative agencies and related judicial review, establishes a scheme of "reasoned decisionmaking." Motor Vehicle Mfrs. Assn. of United States, Inc. v. State Farm Mut. Automobile Ins. Co., 463 U.S. 29, 52 (1983). Not only must an agency's decreed result be within the scope of its lawful authority, but the process by which it reaches that result must be logical and rational. Courts enforce this principle with regularity when they set aside agency regulations which, though well within the agencies' scope of authority, are not supported by the reasons that the agencies adduce. See SEC v. Chenery Corp., 318 U.S. 80 (1943); SEC v. Chenery Corp., 332 U.S. 194 (1947). The National Labor Relations Board, uniquely among major federal administrative agencies, has chosen to promulgate virtually all the legal rules in its field through adjudication rather than rulemaking. See, e.g., NLRB v. Bell Aerospace Co., 416 U.S. 267, 294–295 (1974). . . . But adjudication is subject to the requirement of reasoned decisionmaking as well. It is hard to imagine a more violent breach of that requirement than applying a rule of primary conduct or a standard of proof which is in fact different from the rule or standard formally announced. And the consistent repetition of that breach can hardly mend it.

Reasoned decisionmaking, in which the rule announced is the rule applied, promotes sound results, and unreasoned decisionmaking the opposite. The evil of a decision that applies a standard other than the one it enunciates spreads in both directions, preventing both consistent application of the law by subordinate agency personnel (notably administrative law judges), and effective review of the law by the courts. . . .

Because reasoned decisionmaking demands it, and because the systemic consequences of any other approach are unacceptable, the Board must be required to apply in fact the clearly understood legal standards that it enunciates in principle, such as good-faith reasonable doubt and preponderance of the evidence. Reviewing courts are entitled to take those standards to mean what they say, and to conduct substantial-evidence review on that basis. Even the most consistent and hence predictable Board departure from proper application of those standards will not alter the legal rule by which the agency's factfinding is to be judged.

... In the regime envisioned by the dissent—a regime in which inadequate factual findings become simply a revision of the standard that the Board's (adjudicatorily adopted) rules set forth, thereby converting those findings into rule-interpretations to which judges must defer—the "substantial evidence" factual review provision of the APA becomes a nullity. ...

For the foregoing reasons, we need not determine whether the Board has consistently rejected or discounted probative evidence so as to cause "good faith reasonable doubt" or "preponderance of the evidence" to mean something more than what the terms connote. The line of precedents relied on by the ALJ and the Court of Appeals could not render irrelevant to the Board's decision, and hence to our review, any evidence that tends to establish the existence of a good-faith reasonable doubt. It was therefore error, for example, for the ALJ to discount Ron Mohr's opinion about lack of union support because of "the Board's historical treatment of unverified assertions by an employee about another employee's sentiments." And it was error for the Court of Appeals to rely upon the fact that "[t]he Board has consistently questioned the reliability of reports by one employee of the antipathy of other employees toward their union." Assuming that those assessments of the Board's prior behavior are true, they nonetheless provide no justification for the Board's factual inferences here. Of course the Board is entitled to be skeptical about the employer's claimed reliance on second-hand reports when the reporter has little basis for knowledge, or has some incentive to mislead. But that is a matter of logic and sound inference from all the circumstances, not an arbitrary rule of disregard to be extracted from prior Board decisions. ...

We conclude that the Board's "reasonable doubt" test for employer polls is facially rational and consistent with the Act. But the Board's factual finding that Allentown Mack Sales lacked such a doubt is not supported by substantial evidence on the record as a whole. The judgment of the Court of Appeals for the D.C. Circuit is therefore reversed, and the case is remanded with instructions to deny enforcement.

It is so ordered.

■ CHIEF JUSTICE REHNQUIST, with whom JUSTICE O'CONNOR, JUSTICE KENNEDY, and JUSTICE THOMAS join, concurring in part and dissenting in part.

I concur in the judgment of the Court and in Parts I, III, and IV. However, I disagree that the Board's standard is rational and consistent with the National Labor Relations Act, and I therefore dissent as to Part II. ...

■ JUSTICE BREYER, with whom JUSTICE STEVENS, JUSTICE SOUTER, and JUSTICE GINSBURG join, concurring in part and dissenting in part.

I concur in Parts I and II and dissent from Parts III and IV of the Court's opinion. In Parts III and IV, the Court holds unlawful an agency conclusion on the ground that it is "not supported by substantial evidence." That question was not presented to us in the petition for certiorari. In deciding it, the Court has departed from the half-century old legal standard governing this type of review. See Universal Camera Corp. v. NLRB, 340 U.S. 474, 490–491 (1951). It has rewritten a Board rule without adequate justification. It has ignored certain evidentiary presumptions developed by the National Labor Relations Board (Board) to provide guidance in the application of this rule. And it has failed to give the kind of leeway to the Board's factfinding authority that the Court's precedents mandate.

To decide whether an agency's conclusion is supported by substantial evidence, a reviewing court must identify the conclusion and then examine and weigh the evidence. As this Court said in 1951, "[w]hether on the record as a whole there is substantial evidence to support agency findings is a question which Congress has placed in the keeping of the Courts of Appeals." Universal Camera, supra, at 491. The Court held that it would "intervene only in what ought to be the rare instance when the standard appears to have been misapprehended or grossly misapplied." Ibid. Consequently, if the majority is to overturn a Court of Appeals' "substantial evidence" decision, it must identify the agency's conclusion, examine the evidence, and then determine whether the evidence is so obviously inadequate to support the conclusion that the reviewing court must have seriously misunderstood the nature of its legal duty.

The majority opinion begins by properly stating the Board's conclusion, namely that the employer, Allentown, did not demonstrate that it "held a reasonable doubt, *based on objective considerations*, that the Union continued to enjoy the support of a majority of the bargaining unit employees."

The opinion, however, then omits the words I have italicized and transforms this conclusion, rephrasing it as: "Allentown lacked a genuine, reasonable uncertainty about whether Local 724 enjoyed the continuing support of a majority of unit employees."

Key words of a technical sort that the Board has used in hundreds of opinions written over several decades to express what the Administrative Law Judge (ALJ) here called "objective reasonable doubt" have suddenly disappeared, leaving in their place what looks like an ordinary jury standard that might reflect, not an agency's specialized knowledge of the workplace, but a court's common understanding of human psychology. The only authority cited for the transformation, the dictionary, in fact offers no support, for the majority has looked up the wrong word, namely "doubt," instead of the right word, "objective." . . .

To illustrate the problem with the majority's analysis, I must describe the factual background, the evidence, and the ALJ's findings, in some detail. . . .

Consider Marsh's statement. Marsh said, as the majority opinion notes, that " 'he was not being represented for the $35 he was paying.' " The majority says that the ALJ was wrong not to count this statement in the employer's favor. But the majority fails to mention that Marsh made this statement to an Allentown manager while the manager was interviewing Marsh to determine whether he would, or would not, be one of the 32 employees whom Allentown would re-employ. The ALJ, when evaluating all the employee statements, wrote that statements made to the Allentown managers during the job interviews were "somewhat tainted as it is likely that a job applicant will say whatever he believes the prospective employer wants to hear." In so stating, the ALJ was reiterating the Board's own normative general finding that employers should not "rely in asserting a good-faith doubt" upon "[s]tatements made by employees during the course of an interview with a prospective employer." Middleboro Fire Apparatus, Inc., 234 N.L.R.B. 888, 894 enf'd, 590 F.2d 4 (1st Cir.1978). The Board also has found that " '[e]mployee statements of dissatisfaction with a union are not deemed the equivalent of withdrawal of support for the union.' " Either of these general Board findings (presumably known to employers advised by the labor bar), applied by the ALJ in this particular case, provides more than adequate support for the ALJ's conclusion that the employer could not properly rely upon Marsh's statement as help in creating an "objective" employer doubt.

I do not see how, on the record before us, one could plausibly argue that these relevant general findings of the Board fall outside the Board's lawfully delegated authority. The Board in effect has said that an employee statement *made during a job interview with an employer who has expressed an interest in a nonunionized work force* will often tell us precisely nothing about that employee's true feelings. That Board conclusion represents an exercise of the kind of discretionary authority that Congress placed squarely within the Board's administrative and fact-finding powers and responsibilities. Nor is it procedurally improper for an agency, rather like a common law court, (and drawing upon its accumulated expertise and exercising its administrative responsibilities) to use adjudicatory proceedings to develop rules of thumb about the likely weight assigned to different kinds of evidence. Consider next Bloch's statement, made during his job interview with Worth, that those on the night shift (five or six employees) "did not want the Union." The ALJ thought this statement failed to provide support, both for reasons that the majority mentions (" 'Bloch did not testify and thus could not explain how he formed his opinion about the views of his fellow employees' "), and for reasons that the majority does not mention ("no showing that [the other employees] made independent representations about their union sympathies to [Allentown] and they did not testify in this proceeding").

The majority says that "reason demands" that Bloch's statement "be given considerable weight." But why? The Board, drawing upon both reason and experience, has said it will "view with suspicion and caution" one employee's statements "purporting to represent the views of other employees." [Citing cases.] Indeed, the Board specifically has stated that this type of evidence does not qualify as "objective" within the meaning of the "objective reasonable doubt" standard. Wallkill Valley General Hospital, 288 N.L.R.B. at 109–110 (finding that statement by one employee that other employees opposed the union "cannot be found to provide *objective* considerations" because statement was a "bare assertion," was "subjective," and "lacking in demonstrable foundation"; statement by another employee about the views of others was similarly "insufficiently reliable and definite to contribute to a finding of *objective* considerations") (emphases added).

. . . Why is it unreasonable for an ALJ to disregard a highly general conclusory statement such as Bloch's, a statement that names no names, is unsupported by any other concrete testimony, and was made during a job interview by an interviewer who foresees a nonunionized workforce? To put the matter more directly, how can the majority substitute its own judgment for that of the Board and the ALJ in respect to such detailed workplace-related matters . . .?

Finally, consider the Allentown manager's statement that Mohr told him that "if a vote was taken, the Union would lose." . . .

One can find reflected in the majority opinion some of the reasons the ALJ gave for discounting the significance of Mohr's statement. The majority says of the ALJ's first reason (namely that "there is no evidence with respect to how" Mohr "gained this knowledge") that this reason is "irrelevan[t]." But why so? The lack of any specifics provides some support for the possibility that Mohr was overstating a conclusion, say, in a job-preserving effort to curry favor with Mack's new managers. More importantly, since the absence of detail or support brings Mohr's statement well within the Board's pre-existing cautionary evidentiary principle (about employee statements regarding the views of other employees), it diminishes the reasonableness of any employer reliance.

The majority discusses a further reason, namely that Mohr was referring to a group of 32 employees of whom Allentown hired only 23, and "the composition of the complement of employees hired would bear on whether this group did or did not support the Union." The majority considers this reason "wholly irrational," because, in its view, the Board cannot "rationally" assume that "the work force of a successor company has the same disposition regarding the union as did the work force of the predecessor company, if the majority of the new work force came from the old one," while adopting an opposite assumption "for purposes of determining what evidence tends to establish a reasonable doubt regarding union support."

The irrationality of these assumptions, however, is not obvious. The primary objective of the National Labor Relations Act is to secure labor peace. To preserve the status quo ante may help to preserve labor peace; the first presumption may help to do so by assuming (in the absence of contrary evidence) that workers wish to preserve that status quo; the second, by requiring detailed evidence before dislodging the status quo, may help to do the same. . . .

The majority fails to mention the ALJ's third reason for discounting Mohr's statement, namely, that Mohr did not indicate "whether he was speaking about a large majority of the service employees being dissatisfied with the Union or a small majority." It fails to mention the ALJ's belief that the statement was "almost off-the-cuff." It fails to mention the ALJ's reference to the "Board's historical treatment of unverified assertions by an employee about other employees' sentiments" (which, by itself, would justify a considerable discount). And, most importantly, it leaves out the

ALJ's conclusion. The ALJ did not conclude that Mohr's statement lacked evidentiary significance. Rather, the ALJ concluded that the statement did not provide "*sufficient* basis, even when considered with other employee statements relied upon, to meet the Board's objective reasonable doubt standard."

Given this evidence, and the ALJ's reasoning, the Court of Appeals found the Board's conclusion adequately supported. That conclusion is well within the Board's authority to make findings and to reach conclusions on the basis of record evidence, which authority Congress has granted, and this Court's many precedents have confirmed.

In sum, the majority has failed to focus upon the ALJ's actual conclusions, it has failed to consider all the evidence before the ALJ, it has transformed the actual legal standard that the Board has long administered without regard to the Board's own interpretive precedents, and it has ignored the guidance that the Board's own administrative interpretations have sought to provide to the bar, to employers, to unions, and to its own administrative staff. The majority's opinion will, I fear, weaken the system for judicial review of administrative action that this Court's precedents have carefully constructed over several decades.

For these reasons, I dissent.

NOTES

(1) The NLRB attorney argued that "doubt," as regards the "good faith reasonable doubt" rule, meant "disbelief," not "uncertainty." Justice Scalia's contrary ruling played an important part in his subsequent evaluation of the evidence.

(a) Should the Supreme Court have deferred to counsel's interpretation as a reasonable choice made by an agency? The usual rule is that the power of interpretation lies with the officials of the agency, to be exercised at the time they make their decisions, not with the agency's lawyers in court, after the fact. This principle seems to be a straightforward derivation from ideas of political legitimacy (i.e., responsibility lies with those to whom authority has been delegated) and of deliberation (i.e., "post hoc" rationalizations are no substitute for careful consideration at the time of decision-making). Nonetheless, there has been some erosion of the principle in recent years, perhaps because a little clarification in court can save a lot of time on remand. See p. 1000 within.

(b) Assuming that we discount what the NLRB's attorney says, it surely does matter what the NLRB itself thought the word meant. It might have thought that "doubt" meant "disbelief"; or "uncertainty"; or there may have been no single meaning shared by members of the Board. Justice Scalia does not pursue this question, presumably because he is willing to rule that "doubt" must mean "uncertainty" based on its dictionary meaning. (Regarding the use of dictionaries to construe legal language, see within at page 1060ff.) Once he has so ruled, shouldn't he just remand the case on the authority of the Chenery cases (page 556 above)? Shouldn't the agency be given the opportunity, or the responsibility, of applying the now clarified standard to the facts of the case?

(2) If we turn now to the Supreme Court's relationship to the Court of Appeals, Justice Breyer starts his opinion by saying that Justice Scalia's approach is contrary to Universal Camera's placing substantial evidence "in the keeping of the Court of Appeals." Whether or not this is technically right, most observers would probably agree that Scalia's opinion goes further into the facts of a "substantial evidence" case than any recent Supreme Court opinion they can easily call to mind. Does this indicate a new approach for the future? It is too soon to tell.

(3) Perhaps what motivates Justice Scalia's inquiry is his view that the "substantial evidence" rule not only polices arbitrary fact-finding, but also prevents there being a gap between "the standards consistently applied" and "the standards recited"—or in other words, that the "substantial evidence" rules serves a "rule of law" function as well as an "adjudicatory fairness" one. In the first year of law school, students learn that there is often a gap between the rule a common-law court claims to follow and the rule it actually applies. Indeed, it is often said that it is through the development of such gaps that progress is made. Does Justice Scalia, in his insistence that law consists of enunciated rules, adopt a jurisprudence that does not fit the American legal system? Or are there reasons why such behavior is simultaneously acceptable from common-law judges and reprehensible from agencies?

(4) JOAN FLYNN, THE COSTS & BENEFITS OF "HIDING THE BALL": NLRB POLICYMAKING & THE FAILURE OF JUDICIAL REVIEW, 75 B.U. L. REV. 387 (1995) provides the "academic commentary" to which Justice Scalia refers for the proposition that "the current decision may conform to a long pattern." Prof. Flynn argues that the NLRB consistently and deliberately engages in "policymaking in the guise of factfinding." In one species of this covert policymaking, "there is often a significant disparity between the Board's articulated adjudicative standard and its application of that standard. This dichotomy . . . is typified by a test that sounds flexible, but that the Board applies in a rigid, near-absolute fashion." Prof. Flynn identifies the "good faith doubt" standard as "[p]erhaps the best example of this phenomenon." Ironically, the article concludes that, despite the normative and practical costs of the Board's practice of "hiding the ball," this is on balance the best strategy for implementing the objectives of the labor statutes:

"In my judgment, the Board's roundabout ways result in a greater effectuation of the Act's purposes than would be achieved were the Board to abandon its present methods and open the door to closer judicial supervision. In advancing this conclusion, I do not mean to downplay my earlier criticisms of the Board's general performance or to discount the seriousness of the inefficiencies that flow from the Board's subterranean methodology; one could hardly mistake the status quo for perfection.

"The costs of the Board's methodology, however, may actually be less than would appear at first glance. Despite the invitation to litigation and delay that the Board's current practices seem to provide, the vast majority of cases are in fact resolved without litigation and fairly expeditiously. The Board's use of veiled policymaking, moreover, appears in many instances to be directed not simply toward protecting the Board's turf and maximizing the agency's power at the expense of the courts, but also toward protecting important statutory goals from the substantial possibility of judicial obstruction.

"Were the Board, in contrast, to come clean with the courts, the probable result would not be the oft-called-for agency-court partnership, but rather increased judicial infringement upon the Board's policymaking role. Although the Board could in theory make policy in a straightforward and aboveboard manner without ceding its rightful authority over federal labor policy, reality points in the other direction.

"As the rulemaking agencies have learned the hard way, the federal courts simply cannot be trusted to keep their fingers out of the policymaking pie. 'Procedural' review of agency decision making, it seems, is all too readily converted into an instrument of encroachment on agencies' substantive policymaking powers. Given the courts' apparent antipathy toward collective values, this lesson is particularly likely to hold true for a candid and forthright NLRB. Administrative law principles aside, the judicial usurpation that I foresee is liable to do more to impede the goals underlying the National Labor Relations Act than to advance them. In its emphasis on collective values in a highly individualistic society and its recognition of the strike as the ultimate means of dispute resolution in a nation that has seemingly never been comfortable with 'disruptive' exercises of employee power, the Act remains, a full sixty years after its passage, the object of substantial judicial misunderstanding and even opposition. When this consideration is added to the courts' sorry record of largely counterproductive attempts to improve on other federal agencies' policymaking, it appears that the benefits of the NLRB's hide-the-ball methodology to our national labor policy may well, in the end, exceed the costs."

(5) Even if you are not ready to adopt Prof. Flynn's arguments for subterfuge, isn't there something to be said for the fact that the Board has been acting (in the opinion of the Court of Appeals) in full daylight? Justice Scalia says that "[t]he question arises, then, whether ... we ought to measure the evidentiary support for the Board's decision against the standards consistently applied rather than the standards recited." His answer is *no*—but doesn't the interest in consistency counsel that the answer should be *yes*? See the Shaw's Supermarket case, p. 908 above.

Association of Data Processing Service Organizations, Inc. v. Board of Governors of the Federal Reserve System

United States Court of Appeals for the District of Columbia Circuit, 1984.
745 F.2d 677.

■ Before GINSBURG and SCALIA, CIRCUIT JUDGES, and VAN PELT, sitting by designation.

■ SCALIA, CIRCUIT JUDGE:

The Association of Data Processing Service Organizations, Inc. ("ADAPSO"), a national trade association representing the data processing industry, and two of its members petition this court for review of two orders of the Board of Governors of the Federal Reserve System, pursuant to 12 U.S.C. § 1848 (1982). In No. 82–1910, they seek review of the Board's July 9, 1982 order approving Citicorp's application to establish a subsidiary, Citishare, to engage in certain data processing and transmission services. In No. 82–2108, they seek review of the Board's August 23, 1982 order, entered after notice and comment rulemaking, amending those portions of Regulation Y which dealt with the performance of data processing activities by bank holding companies. We consolidated the two appeals.

The Bank Holding Company Act of 1956 requires all bank holding companies to seek prior regulatory approval before engaging in nonbanking activities. The restrictions do not apply to:

> activities . . . which the Board after due notice and opportunity for hearing has determined (by order or regulation) to be so closely related to banking or managing or controlling banks as to be a proper incident thereto. . . . In determining whether a particular activity is a proper incident to banking or managing or controlling banks the Board shall consider whether its performance by an affiliate of a holding company can reasonably be expected to produce benefits to the public, such as greater convenience, increased competition, or gains in efficiency, that outweigh possible adverse effects, such as undue concentration of resources, decreased or unfair competition, conflicts of interests, or unsound banking practices.

12 U.S.C. § 1843(c)(8). Section 1848, the source of our review authority, provides that "[t]he findings of the Board as to the facts, if supported by substantial evidence, shall be conclusive."

On February 23, 1979, Citicorp applied for authority to engage . . . in the processing and transmission of banking, financial, and economic related data through timesharing, electronic funds transfer, home banking and other techniques. . . . The Board published notice of Citicorp's application, which was protested by ADAPSO, and set it for formal hearing. Before the hearing was held, Citicorp amended its application to add certain activities and to request amendment of Regulation Y to permit the activities it had specified. The Board published an Amended Order for Hearing and invited public comments and participation. A formal hearing was held before an Administrative Law Judge in which the merits of both the application and the proposed rule were considered. . . . [M]ore than sixty companies and individuals submitted written comments on the proposed rule. . . . [T]he ALJ decided that the activities proposed by Citicorp were closely related to banking and would produce benefits to the public which would outweigh their costs [and] also recommended amendments to Regulation Y that would permit those activities contained in the Citicorp application. On July 9, 1982, the Board adopted the ALJ's recommendation to approve the Citicorp application, with certain restrictions. On August 23, 1982, the Board adopted the ALJ's recommended amendments to Regulation Y, again with certain restrictions. ADAPSO, and two of its members, participants in the actions below, filed these petitions for review.

I. Standard of Review

We are faced at the outset with a dispute regarding the proper standard of review. These consolidated appeals call for us to review both an on-the-record adjudication and an informal notice and comment rulemaking. Petitioners contend that the substantial evidence standard, which presumably authorizes more rigorous judicial review, should govern our review of both orders. The Board agrees, noting that § 1848 applies a substantial evidence standard to factual determinations. . . . Intervenor Citicorp contends that while the substantial evidence standard should govern review of the Citicorp order, Regulation Y should be upset only if arbitrary or capricious. . . . The parties' submissions on this point reflect considerable confusion, which is understandable when one examines decisions defining the standard of review under this statute. . . . The courts of appeals, however, have applied the substantial evidence standard of § 1848 to Board adjudications such as the authorization in the first order here under review, while applying the arbitrary or capricious standard, despite § 1848, to Board rules, including specifically amendments of Regulation Y. In fact one appellate opinion has, like this one, addressed precisely the situation in which *both* an adjudicatory authorization *and* an amendment of Regulation Y were at issue in the same case—and applied the § 1848 substantial evidence standard to the former but the arbitrary or capricious to the latter. This would make a lot of sense if, as the Board has argued in some cases, § 1848 in its totality applies only to adjudication rather than rulemaking, since it is limited to "orders" of the Board, a word which the [APA] defines to mean the product of an adjudication. [APA] § 551(4), (6). Such a technical interpretation of the provision, however, has been uniformly and quite correctly rejected. That leaves the courts with the difficult task of explaining why the last sentence of § 1848, unlike all the rest of it, should be deemed to apply only to adjudication and not to rulemaking. Difficult, because there is nothing in either the text[1] or the legislative history of the section to suggest such a result. The courts applying the arbitrary or capricious standard to Board rulemaking . . . dispose of this problem either by totally ignoring it, or by noting that the parties "do not appear to contest" the point, or by the *ipse dixit* that "[w]e interpret [the last sentence of § 1848] to apply to findings of fact 'on the record' in an adjudicatory hearing as contrasted with a rulemaking proceeding."

We think that there is no basis for giving the last sentence of § 1848 anything less than the general application given to the rest of the section.

---

1. 12 U.S.C. § 1848 reads as follows:

Any party aggrieved by an order of the Board under this chapter may obtain a review of such order in the United States Court of Appeals within any circuit wherein such party has its principal place of business or in the Court of Appeals in the District of Columbia by filing in the court, within thirty days after the entry of the Board's order, a petition praying that the order of the Board be set aside. A copy of such petition shall be forthwith transmitted to the Board by the clerk of the court, and thereupon the Board shall file in the court the record made before the Board. . . . Upon the filing of such petition the court shall have the jurisdiction to affirm, set aside, or modify the order of the Board and to require the Board to take such action with regard to the matter under review as the court deems proper. The finding of the Board as to the facts, if supported by substantial evidence, shall be conclusive.

... [I]n their application to the requirement of factual support the substantial evidence test and arbitrary or capricious test are one and the same. The former is only a specific application of the latter. ... The "scope of review" provisions of the APA, § 706(2), are cumulative. Thus, an agency action which is supported by the required substantial evidence may in another regard be "arbitrary, capricious, an abuse of discretion, or otherwise not in accordance with law"—for example, because it is an abrupt and unexplained departure from agency precedent. Paragraph (A) of subsection 706(2)—the "arbitrary or capricious" provision—is a catch-all, picking up administrative misconduct not covered by the other more specific paragraphs. Thus, in those situations where paragraph (E) has no application (informal rulemaking, for example, which is not governed by §§ 556 and 557 to which paragraph (E) refers), paragraph (A) takes up the slack, so to speak, enabling the courts to strike down, as arbitrary, agency action that is devoid of needed factual support. When the arbitrary or capricious standard is performing that function of assuring factual support, there is no *substantive* difference between what it requires and what would be required by the substantial evidence test, since it is impossible to conceive of a "nonarbitrary" factual judgment supported only by evidence that is not substantial in the APA sense—i.e., not " 'enough to justify, if the trial were to a jury, a refusal to direct a verdict when the conclusion sought to be drawn ... is one of fact for the jury.' " Illinois Central R.R. v. Norfolk & Western Ry., 385 U.S. 57, 66 (1966) (quoting NLRB v. Columbian Enameling & Stamping Co., 306 U.S. 292, 300 (1939)).

We have noted on several occasions that the distinction between the substantial evidence test and the arbitrary or capricious test is "largely semantic," and have indeed described that view as "the emerging consensus of the Court of Appeals" ... The distinctive function of paragraph (E)—what it achieves that paragraph (A) does not—is to require substantial evidence to be found *within the record of closed-record proceedings* to which it exclusively applies. The importance of that requirement should not be underestimated. It is true that, as the Supreme Court said in Camp v. Pitts, 411 U.S. 138, 142, even informal agency action (not governed by paragraph (E)) must be reviewed only on the basis of "the administrative record already in existence." But that is quite a different and less onerous requirement, meaning only that whether the administrator was arbitrary must be determined on the basis of what he had before him when he acted, and not on the basis of "some new record made initially in the reviewing court," id. That "administrative record" might well include crucial material that was neither shown to nor known by the private parties in the proceeding—as indeed appears to have been the situation in Camp v. Pitts itself. It is true that, in informal rulemaking, at least the most critical factual material that is used to support the agency's position on review must have been made public in the proceeding and exposed to refutation. That requirement, however, does not extend to all data, and it only applies in rulemaking and not in other informal agency action, since it derives not from the arbitrary or capricious test but from the command of 5 U.S.C. § 553(c) that "the agency ... give interested persons an opportunity to participate in the rule making." See Portland Cement Association v. Ruckelshaus, 486 F.2d 375, 393 n. 67 (D.C.Cir.1973).

Consolidated cases such as those before us here—involving simultaneous review of a rule (whose factual basis is governed only by paragraph (A)'s catch-all control against "arbitrary or capricious" action) and of a formal adjudication dealing with the same subject (whose factual basis is governed by paragraph (E)'s requirement of substantial evidence)—demonstrate why the foregoing interpretation of the two standards is the only interpretation that makes sense. If the standards were substantively different ... the Citicorp order, authorizing one bank holding company's data processing services, would be subject to more rigorous judicial review of factual support than the Regulation Y order which, due to its general applicability, would affect the operations of every bank holding company in the nation. Or, to put the point another way: If the Board had never issued any Regulation Y, and simply determined in the context of a particular application that the provision of timesharing services is "closely related" to banking, that determination, which could be reconsidered and revised in the context of the next adjudication, would require more factual support than the same determination in a rulemaking, which would have immediate nationwide application and, until amended by further rulemaking, would have to be applied to all subsequent applications.

This seemingly upside-down application of varying standards is not an issue in the present case since, as we have observed, § 1848 makes it clear that only *one* standard—the substantial evidence test—applies to review of all Board actions. The relevance of the foregoing discussion here is to determine what that standard *means*. What we have said suggests that the normal (APA) meaning of the "substantial evidence" terminology connotes a substantive standard no different from the arbitrary or capricious test. One cannot dismiss out of hand, however, the possibility that, in this particular statute, a different meaning was intended—in which case that different standard would govern review of both rulemaking and adjudication. A number of "substantial evidence" review provisions have been attached to rulemaking authority, particular in recent years. See, e.g., 29 U.S.C. § 655(f) (1982) (Occupational Safety and Health Act); 30 U.S.C. § 816(a) (1982) (Federal Coal Mine Health and Safety Act); 15 U.S.C. § 1193(e)(3) (1982) (Flammable Fabrics Act); 15 U.S.C. § 57a(e)(3)(A) (1982) (FTC Improvement of Act of 1975). It is conceivable that some of these were intended, as the Fifth Circuit found with regard to such a provision in the Consumer Product Safety Act, 15 U.S.C. § 2060 (1982), to require the courts "to scrutinize [agency] actions more closely than an 'arbitrary or capricious' standard would allow." Aqua Slide 'N' Dive Corp. v. CPSC, 569 F.2d 831, 837 (5th Cir.1978). Congress's unpropitious use of the "substantial evidence" APA language for such a purpose is plausible, since the standard has acquired a reputation for being more stringent.[2] One should not be too quick, however, to impute such a congressional intent. There is surely little appeal to an ineffable review standard that lies somewhere in-between the quantum of factual support required to go to a

---

2. The reason for this reputation, one may surmise, is that under the APA the substantial evidence test applies almost exclusively to formal adjudication (formal rulemaking is rare), which is, by contrast to rulemaking, characteristically long on facts and short on policy—so that the inadequacy of factual support is typically the central issue in the judicial appeal and is the most common reason for reversal.

jury (the traditional "substantial evidence" test) and the "preponderance of the evidence" standard that would apply in de novo review. . . . The Supreme Court has evidently rejected the notion that [§ 1848] alters normal APA review requirements, since the Court's opinions reviewing Board action deem the provision unworthy of mention, and specifically accord the Board "the greatest deference." We hold, therefore, that the § 1848 "substantial evidence" requirement applicable to our review here demands a quantum of factual support no different from that demanded by the substantial evidence provision of the APA, which is in turn no different from that demanded by the arbitrary or capricious standard. . . .

NOTES

(1) To understand the problem of this case, it is useful to spend a few moments looking at the structure of § 706(2) of the APA, page 907 above. Six distinct standards of review are there articulated. For purposes of considering review of factual propositions, we can put to one side standards (B), relating to consistency with the constitution, (C), relating to consistency with statutes, and (D), relating to procedure. Subsection (E) states the substantial evidence standard but by its reference to sections 556 and 557 limits that standard to formal proceedings. Where, then, are the standards for reviewing the factual predicates for informal agency action, and especially for notice-and-comment rulemaking? The only other specific reference to "facts" is in standard (F), and that refers to a trial de novo. Could it be that the factual propositions underlying rules are to be tried de novo in court? Whether or not that is what the drafters had in mind, it is too awful to contemplate. Apart from the consummate inefficiency involved, review of rulemaking is typically assigned by statute to the courts of appeals, which of course lack the means for de novo factfinding. And so we turn to the catchall standard (A), and even though its terms seem to refer to action "not in accordance with law," we say that the words "arbitrary" and "capricious" also refer to action not sufficiently in accordance with the facts. But since we have had to manhandle a statute which seems not to have addressed this issue very well, it is no surprise that we end up with some terms, but not much guidance as to what they mean. Hence the court's problem.

(2) If one looks for it, one can find Supreme Court statements that seem to suggest that the "arbitrary and capricious" standard is less demanding than the "substantial evidence" test; that the two standards are the same; and even perhaps that the "arbitrary and capricious" standard is more demanding. In the most recent case to discuss substantial evidence, Dickinson v. Zurko (above at pages 264 and 948), the Court decided that findings of fact of the Patent and Trademark Office were to be reviewed by the Federal Circuit under the standards set by § 706 of the APA. Which standard? 527 U.S. at 158:

> Indeed, it apparently remains disputed to this day (a dispute we need not settle today) precisely which APA standard—"substantial evidence" or "arbitrary, capricious, abuse of discretion"—would apply to court review of PTO factfinding. See 5 U.S.C. § 706(2)(E) (applying the

term "substantial evidence" where agency factfinding takes place "on the record"); see also Association of Data Processing Service Organizations, Inc. v. Board of Governors of Federal Reserve System, 745 F.2d 677, 683–84 (C.A.D.C.1984) (Scalia, J.) (finding no difference between the APA's "arbitrary, capricious" standard and its "substantial evidence" standard as applied to court review of agency factfinding.)

What authority would you find in a "see also" cite in a statement by six Justices (including Justice Scalia) that is clearly dictum?[1]

(3) Do the two previous notes appear to you to be mere quibbling? If so, do you think the bigger issues in reviewing the factual basis for rules made after notice and comment are likely to be the kind of record, the kind of factual issues, and the kind of result that typify informal rulemaking and distinguish it from formal adjudication? Or even in light of these functional differences, does there remain the inescapable question of (to use Justice Frankfurter's term from the Universal Camera case, p. 940 above) the "mood" Congress intended the courts to adopt?

(4) As then-Judge Scalia remarks, Congress has on a number of occasions seemed to signal that it wishes more intensive review than it understands "arbitrary or capricious" to provide; it has done so by specifying "substantial evidence" review of particular agency actions, such as OSHA's notice-and-comment rulemaking, that would ordinarily be examined under § 706(2)(A). INDUSTRIAL UNION DEPARTMENT, AFL–CIO v. HODGSON, 499 F.2d 467 (D.C.Cir.1974) was an early D.C. Circuit encounter with such a statutory requirement. The court found the challenge daunting (499 F.2d at 469–470): "Congress—with no apparent awareness of anomaly—has explicitly combined an informal agency procedure with a standard of review traditionally conceived of as suited to formal adjudication or rulemaking. The federal courts, hard pressed as they are by the flood of new tasks imposed upon them by Congress, surely have some claim to be spared additional burdens deriving from the illogic of legislative compromise. At the least, it would have been helpful if there had been some recognition by Congress that the quick answer it gave to a legislative stalemate posed serious problems for a reviewing court, and that there would inevitably have to be some latitude accorded it to surmount those problems consistently with the legislative purposes. The duty remains, in any event, to decide the case before us in accordance with our statutory mandate, however dimly the rationale, if any, underlying it can be perceived. ...."

In the course of responding to this challenge, the court voiced thoughts that have had a broader influence (499 F.2d at 474–76): "[I]n some degree the record approaches the form of one customarily conceived of as appropriate for substantial evidence review. In other respects, it does not. ... From extensive and often conflicting evidence, the Secretary in this case made numerous factual determinations. With respect to some of those questions,

---

1. In In re Gartside, 203 F.3d 1305 (Fed.Cir.2000), the Federal Circuit subsequently decided that PTO findings of fact should be reviewed under the substantial evidence test, because although not developed through an APA formal hearing, they were reviewed on the record developed in a statutorily required hearing as also mentioned in § 706(2)(E). In the Circuit's view, it was choosing the more demanding standard of review.

the evidence was such that the task consisted primarily of evaluating the data and drawing conclusions from it. The court can review that data in the record and determine whether it reflects substantial support for the Secretary's findings. But some of the questions involved in the promulgation of these standards are on the frontiers of scientific knowledge, and consequently as to them insufficient data is presently available to make a fully informed factual determination. Decisionmaking must in that circumstance depend to a greater extent upon policy judgments and less upon purely factual analysis. Thus, in addition to currently unresolved factual issues, the formulation of standards involves choices that by their nature require basic policy determinations rather than resolution of factual controversies. . . . Regardless of the manner in which the task of judicial review is articulated, policy choices of this sort are not susceptible to the same type of verification or refutation by reference to the record as are some factual questions. Consequently, the court's approach must necessarily be different no matter how the standards of review are labeled. That does not mean that such decisions escape exacting scrutiny, for, as this court has stated in a similar context: 'This exercise need be no less searching and strict in its weighing of whether the agency has performed in accordance with the Congressional purposes, but, because it is addressed to different materials, it inevitably varies from the adjudicatory model. The paramount objective is to see whether the agency, given an essentially legislative task to perform, has carried it out in a manner calculated to negate the dangers of arbitrariness and irrationality in the formulation of rules for general application in the future.' Automotive Parts and Accessories Ass'n v. Boyd, 407 F.2d 330, 338 (D.C.Cir.1968). . . .

"What we are entitled to at all events is a careful identification by the Secretary, when his proposed standards are challenged, of the reasons why he chooses to follow one course rather than another. Where that choice purports to be based on the existence of certain determinable facts, the Secretary must, in form as well as substance, find those facts from evidence in the record. By the same token, when the Secretary is obliged to make policy judgments where no factual certainties exist or where facts alone do not provide the answer, he should so state and go on to identify the considerations he found persuasive."

(5) When EPA argued that for informal rulemaking under the Toxic Substances Control Act, the substantial evidence standard "tend[s] to converge" with the arbitrary and capricious standard, it lost. CORROSION PROOF FITTINGS v. EPA, 947 F.2d 1201, 1213 n. 13 (5th Cir.1991): "Considering that Congress specifically rejected the arbitrary and capricious standard in the TSCA context, we will not act now to read that same standard back in by holding that the two standards are in fact one and the same." The 1976 House Conference Report had included this: "The conferees recognize that in rulemaking proceedings such as those . . . in this bill . . . the traditional standard of review is that of 'arbitrary and capricious.' However, the conferees have adopted the 'substantial evidence' test because they intend that the reviewing court focus on the rulemaking record to see if the . . . action is supported by that record." (1976 U.S.C.C.A.N. (90 Stat.) 4539, 4581).

Similarly, in 1992 the Eleventh Circuit reversed a major OSHA rule-making after holding that the court "must take a 'harder look' at OSHA's action than we would if we were reviewing the action under the more deferential arbitrary and capricious standard," AFL–CIO v. OSHA, 965 F.2d 962 (11th Cir.1992).

Are these courts of appeals to be faulted for unduly aggressive review? Or are they to be defended for carrying out statutes that, being 25–30 years old, reflect an early and perhaps naïve conception of the challenges that rulemakers confront?

(6) WILLIAM F. PEDERSEN, JR., FORMAL RECORDS AND INFORMAL RULEMAKING, 85 Yale L.J. 38, 59 (1975): ". . . [D]etailed factual review of [EPA] regulations by those with the power to change them takes place in two forums only—at the level of the office of primary interest and working group inside EPA, and in court. The working group generally will understand the technical complexities of a regulation. So to a great extent will members of the industry being regulated. But the review process within the agency and the executive branch does not spur a working group to make sure that the final regulation adequately reflects these complexities. To the extent that internal review is the only review worried about, comments by the affected industry or (to pick a less frequent case) by environmental groups may not be given the kind of detailed consideration they deserve. Since the higher levels of review are unwilling or unable to consider the more complex issues, the best hope for detailed, effective review of complex regulations is the judiciary."

NOTE ON THE SPECIAL PROBLEM OF REVIEWING "CONSTITUTIONAL" OR "JURISDICTIONAL" FACTS

Should otherwise applicable standards of fact review be superseded by more intense judicial scrutiny when the issue has constitutional implications? For example, § 8(c) of the National Labor Relations Act, 29 U.S.C. § 158(c), provides that an employer's right to attempt to dissuade its employees from unionizing does not include expressions constituting a "threat of reprisal or force or promise of benefit." How closely should the court review the NLRB's conclusions that certain statements were an "unfair labor practice" rather than protected free speech? Surely, any question of the First Amendment's legal content (e.g., is § 8(c) itself consistent with the Constitution?) is wholly up to the court; it is hard to imagine any serious theoretical or pragmatic argument for deference to the agency on such a question.[1] But how should responsibility be allocated for *applying* First Amendment law to the particular facts or, indeed, for *finding* what those facts were? ". . . [M]any lawyers would insist that who finds the facts is far more important than who applies the law . . ." Henry P. Monaghan, Constitutional Fact Review, 85 Colum.L.Rev. 229, 255 n.141 (1985).

---

1. See Henry P. Monaghan, *Marbury* and the Administrative State, 83 Colum.L.Rev. 1 (1983).

In constitutional litigation unrelated to the administrative process, the Supreme Court has sometimes required that appellate review include an independent appraisal of the factual foundation of the decision below. For example, in defamation suits by "public figures," the First Amendment permits liability only if the defendant acted with "actual malice." In Bose Corp. v. Consumers Union of U.S., Inc., 466 U.S. 485, 501 n. 17 (1984), a 6–member majority held that this finding must be independently re-examined on appeal:

> Regarding certain largely factual questions in some areas of the law, the stakes—in terms of impact on future cases and future conduct—are too great to entrust them finally to the judgment of the trier of fact.[2]

Would similar treatment apply to the NLRB's finding that an employer's speech during a representation battle was unprotected threats or promises?

A more straightforwardly regulatory question raising this problem is whether rates set through administrative ratemaking are so low as to constitute an uncompensated taking. Early in the last century, the Court described the takings question as "depend[ing] upon the valuation of the property, the income to be derived from the proposed rate and the proportion between the two—pure matters of fact."[3] It had held that due process requires judicial review of allegedly confiscatory rates,[4] but had not clarified the scope of that review. This uncertainty was resolved in Ohio Valley Water Co. v. Ben Avon, 253 U.S. 287 (1920). An Ohio trial court determined that the Public Service Commission set unconstitutionally low water rates. The Ohio Supreme Court, conducting what we would now consider substantial evidence review of the administrative ratemaking record, found the Commission's decision adequately supported and chided the trial judge for substituting his judgment for that of the agency. The Supreme Court, in turn, reversed the Ohio Supreme Court:

> . . . [I]f the owner claims confiscation of his property will result, the State must provide a fair opportunity for submitting that issue to a judicial tribunal for determination *upon its own independent judgment as to both law and facts*; otherwise the [rate] order is void because in conflict with the due process clause . . . (emphasis added).

Although Ben Avon immediately sparked voluminous criticism, the Court extended constitutional fact review beyond ratemaking two years later. In Ng Fung Ho v. White, 259 U.S. 276 (1922), individuals being detained as illegal aliens under an administrative deportation warrant petitioned for habeas corpus, arguing that they were in fact U.S. citizens. Justice Brandeis' opinion for the Court agreed that a citizen could not lawfully be deported, and held that due process requires independent

---

2.   Another area in which de novo appellate reconsideration has occurred—at least historically—involves constitutional challenges to state criminal convictions. See, e.g., Ashcraft v. Tennessee, 322 U.S. 143 (1944) (allegation of coerced confession); Norris v. Alabama, 294 U.S. 587 (1935) (allegation of systematic racial discrimination in jury selec-

tion). This issue has been subsumed in the complicated law of federal habeas corpus, and review of such claims is now addressed by statute. See 28 U.S.C. § 2254 (d)(8).

3.   Prentis v. Atlantic Coast Line, 211 U.S. 210, 228 (1908).

4.   Chicago, Milwaukee & St. Paul Ry. v. Minnesota, 134 U.S. 418 (1890).

judicial determination of what he labelled the "essential jurisdictional fact" of citizenship.

A decade later, the "jurisdictional fact" idea played a crucial role in CROWELL V. BENSON, 285 U.S. 22 (1932). You may already have considered Crowell at page 127 above, in connection with the separation-of-powers question of what adjudicative functions may be assigned to decisionmakers other than Article III courts. You will recall that the case involved the Longshoremen's and Harbor Workers' Act, a federal workers' compensation scheme covering certain maritime employment. The Court upheld the use of a compensation commissioner to determine claims under the Act— thus sanctioning the general practice of administrative adjudication. However, in another portion of the opinion, the Court held that de novo review was required on certain issues (285 U.S. at 54–57):

"What has been said thus far relates to the determination of claims of employees within the purview of the Act. A different question is presented where the determinations of fact are fundamental or 'jurisdictional,' in the sense that their existence is a condition precedent to the operation of the statutory scheme. These fundamental requirements are that the injury occur upon navigable waters of the United States and that the relation of master and servant exist. These conditions are indispensable to the application of the statute, not only because the Congress has so provided explicitly ... but also because the power of the Congress to enact the legislation turns upon the existence of these conditions.[5]

"... [As to these two facts], the question is not the ordinary one as to the propriety of provision for administrative determinations. ... It is rather a question of the appropriate maintenance of the Federal judicial power in requiring the observance of constitutional restrictions. It is the question whether the Congress may substitute for constitutional courts ... an administrative agency—in this instance a single deputy commissioner— for the final determination of the existence of the facts upon which the enforcement of the constitutional rights of the citizen [i.e., the employer being held strictly liable] depend. The recognition of the utility and convenience of administrative agencies for the investigation and finding of facts within their proper province, and the support of their authorized action, does not require the conclusion that there is no limitation of their use, and that the Congress could completely oust the courts of all determinations of fact by vesting the authority to make them with finality in its own instrumentalities or in the Executive Department. That would be to sap the judicial power as it exists under the Federal Constitution, and to establish a government of a bureaucratic character alien to our system, wherever fundamental rights depend, as not infrequently they do depend,

---

5. [Ed.] The constitutional significance of the injury's occurring on the navigable waters of the U.S. is that it brings the Act under the admiralty power of Art. I § 8. The significance of the master-servant issue may be harder to appreciate today; at the time of Crowell, efforts on the part of some states and the federal government to move from the common-law negligence regime to the strict- liability scheme of workers' compensation statutes had been challenged on substantive due process grounds. They had been sustained, but not without difficulty, as legitimate police power regulation of the employment relationship. An attempt to extend no- fault liability beyond that relationship could have failed the then-applicable "substantive due process" test.

upon the facts, and finality as to facts becomes in effect finality in law." Thus, the Court held, the federal district court reviewing the Deputy Commissioner must make this determination "upon its own record and the facts elicited before it."

The alarm and indignation Crowell elicited in the commentary surpassed the response to Ben Avon. If "jurisdictional facts" were triable de novo, what would be the point of having an administrative process? Would other criteria for recovery under the statute also be deemed "jurisdictional"? And how could the jurisdictional fact reasoning be confined to this particular regulatory scheme? Apparently recognizing the potential voraciousness of the creature he had unleashed in Ng Fung Ho, Justice Brandeis dissented in Crowell, beginning a determined (if not terribly convincing) attempt to confine the jurisdictional fact doctrine to the immigration context. More persuasive, as an intellectual matter, was the perceptive analysis of scholar John Dickinson:

> There can be little doubt that the rule of the Ben Avon case rests at bottom on unconscious acceptance of the particular brand of philosophy designated as "naive realism." It rests on the assumption that the existence of a fact is something absolute and fixed, and capable of being apprehended rightly or wrongly, correctly or incorrectly. The legal authority of the administrative body is consequently regarded as depending on the *real* or *actual* presence of a fact, independently of anyone's correct or incorrect apprehension of it, or conclusion about it. From this point of view, the reasonableness or lack of reasonableness of the administrative body's conclusion makes obviously no difference. [The trouble with this attitude is that the court has no better access to the fact itself than does the administrative body; its "finding" is, after all, only its conclusion and no more identical with the fact itself than is the administrative finding.] If it is thus understood that conclusion is merely being checked against conclusion, it should be enough for the reviewing tribunal to pass on whether the conclusion below was reasonable.

John Dickinson, Crowell v. Benson: Judicial Review of Administrative Questions of "Constitutional Fact," 80 U.Pa.L.Rev. 1055, 1074 (1932).

The criticism largely prevailed and, in retrospect, Crowell was the highwater mark of jurisdictional/constitutional fact reasoning in regulatory cases. One of Crowell's requirements, an independent record made in court, was apparently abandoned only four years later by the justice who had first announced it. In ST. JOSEPH STOCK YARDS CO. V. UNITED STATES, 298 U.S. 38, 53–54 (1936), Chief Justice Hughes blandly asserted:

> ... [The] judicial duty to exercise an independent judgment does not require or justify disregard of the weight which may properly attach to findings upon hearing and evidence. On the contrary, the judicial duty is performed in the light of the proceedings already had and may be greatly facilitated by the assembling and analysis of the facts in the course of the [administrative] determination. Judicial judgment may be nonetheless appropriately independent because informed and aided by the sifting procedure of an expert ... agency.

On its face, St. Joseph (yet another confiscatory rate challenge) reaffirmed both Crowell and Ben Avon[6]; however, the Court's description of how the required "independent" judicial judgment would operate had begun to sound suspiciously like substantial evidence review:

> ... [A]s the question is whether the [administrative] action has passed beyond the lowest limit of the permitted zone of reasonableness into the forbidden reaches of confiscation, judicial scrutiny must of necessity take into account the entire [administrative] process, including the reasoning and findings upon which the [administrative] action rests. We have said that "in a question of ratemaking there is a strong presumption in favor of the conclusions reached by an experienced administrative body after a full hearing." The established principle which guides the court in the exercise of its judgment on the entire case is that the complaining party carries the burden of making a convincing showing and that the court will not interfere with the exercise of the ratemaking power unless confiscation is clearly established. ... [A]s the ultimate determination whether or not rates are confiscatory ordinarily rests upon a variety of subordinate or primary findings of fact as to particular elements, such findings made by a[n] ... agency after hearing will not be disturbed save as in particular instances they are plainly shown to be overborne.

Although the Court did closely review the evidence before upholding the rate order, the district court judgment it affirmed had explicitly employed a substantial evidence standard.

These opinions all occurred during the early years of the New Deal, before the Court had accepted the major expansion in federal regulatory power that era brought. Within five years of St. Joseph, "substantive due process" and the other forms of judicial resistance to the regulatory state had been abandoned. The Court, in a pair of related opinions, reversed findings of confiscatory regulatory action where the lower courts had exercised independent judgment—with not so much as a mention (by majority or dissenting justices) of Ben Avon or St. Joseph.[7] And in 1944, FPC v. Hope Natural Gas Co., 320 U.S. 591, sufficiently relaxed the due process standard for a lawful rate that confiscation challenges virtually disappeared from the constitutional landscape.[8] The jurisdictional fact portion of Crowell itself—although never explicitly overruled—was never extended beyond the two particular "facts" of navigable waters and employment, nor has it affected regulatory schemes other than the Longshoremen's & Harbor Workers' Compensation Act. The doctrine of independent determination of constitutional or jurisdictional facts never became the significant factor in judicial review of administrative action that might have been predicted from its forceful articulation by the pre-New Deal Court.

---

6. Justice Brandeis concurred in the result only.

7. See Railroad Comm'n v. Rowan & Nichols Oil Co., 310 U.S. 573 (1940) and 311 U.S. 570 (1941).

8. Hope held that the method of valuation used in the ratemaking is not a reviewable issue; the only constitutional inquiry is whether the rate that resulted falls within a "zone of reasonableness."

Nonetheless, the concerns underlying the doctrine have not disappeared. Where the facts implicate constitutional values beyond an agency's limited responsibilities, we can expect reviewing courts to be alert to claims that administrative determinations have trenched on core constitutional values. Thus, when the National Park Service denied permits for demonstrations (i) in Lafayette Park to groups of more than 500 and (ii) on the White House sidewalk to groups of more than 100, the reviewing court responded:

> The expertise of those entrusted with the protection of the President does not qualify them to resolve First Amendment issues, the traditional province of the judiciary. A balancing of First Amendment freedoms against the requirements of Presidential safety may be left to other agencies in the first instance. But absent a compelling showing—which has not been begun here—that courts cannot evaluate the questions of fact involved in estimating danger to the President, the final judgment must rest with the courts.[9]

As seen in Chapter 7, the vast litigation over whether administrative procedures satisfy the commands of due process reveals few instances of deference to agency judgments about adequate process. The same is true of the Fourth Amendment and agencies' power to investigate or to require information, considered in Chapter 3. Beyond these sorts of cases, however, little constitutional basis exists for requiring special review of an agency's determination of the facts that establish its jurisdiction—i.e., the jurisdiction it does have, rather than the constitutional limits on its actions. Nonetheless, as the next section will reveal, debate continues, on policy grounds, on whether an agency's determination of its own jurisdiction should receive less judicial deference than other sorts of determinations within the agency's responsibilities.

SECTION 4. JUDICIAL REVIEW OF AGENCY DETERMINATIONS BEYOND THE FACTS

a. HISTORICAL BUILDING-BLOCK CASES

Whatever the problems of reviewing findings of fact, the proper standard of review is far more controversial when other kinds of "questions" are under review. (Even what these "questions" should be called is controversial.) We start our inquiry with a pair of cases that, as much as any, defined for an earlier generation an appropriate framework. Both predate—by a couple of years—passage of the APA; but here, unlike with substantial evidence on the record as a whole, the APA was, at least initially, treated as merely restating prior practice.[1]

9. A Quaker Action Group v. Hickel, 421 F.2d 1111, 1118 (D.C.Cir.1969).

1. When the APA was passed in 1946, the House conferees said it's provisions on review would "preclude" various decisions, specifically including the first of our cases,

Hearst. Justice Frankfurter noted this in the Universal Camera opinion (see footnote 22 of the original) but seemed to think that as to this particular case, the conferees were confused. In any case, the Court treated Hearst, at least for a while, as unimpaired by passage

National Labor Relations Board v. Hearst Publications, Inc.

Supreme Court of the United States, 1944.
322 U.S. 111.

■ Justice Rutledge delivered the opinion of the Court.

These cases arise from the refusal of respondents, publishers of four Los Angeles daily newspapers, to bargain collectively with a union representing newsboys who distribute their papers on the streets of that city. Respondents' contention that they were not required to bargain because the newsboys are not their "employees" within the meaning of that term in the National Labor Relations Act, 29 U.S.C. § 152,[1] presents the important question which we granted certiorari to resolve ... [T]he Board made findings of fact and concluded that the regular full-time newsboys selling each paper were employees within the Act and that questions affecting commerce concerning the representation of employees had arisen. It designated appropriate units and ordered elections. 28 N.L.R.B. at 1006. At these the union was selected as their representative by majorities of the eligible newsboys. [Respondents then refused to bargain with that union, and the Board found this refusal was an unfair labor practice; the court of appeals refused enforcement, deciding that "employee" was to be interpreted consistently with the tests of the common law, and that under those tests the newsboys were not employees.]

The papers are distributed to the ultimate consumer through a variety of channels, including ... newsboys who sell on the streets of the city and its suburbs. ...

The newsboys work under varying terms and conditions. They may be "bootjackers," selling to the general public at places other than established corners, or they may sell at fixed "spots." They may sell only casually or part-time, or full-time; and they may be employed regularly and continuously or only temporarily. The units which the Board determined to be appropriate are composed of those who sell full-time at established spots. Those vendors, misnamed boys, are generally mature men, dependent upon the proceeds of their sales for their sustenance, and frequently supporters of families. Working thus as news vendors on a regular basis, often for a number of years, they form a stable group with relatively little turnover, in contrast to schoolboys and others who sell as bootjackers, temporary and casual distributors.

[The Court then set forth several paragraphs of detail about the newsboys' supervision, compensation and conditions of work.]

In this pattern of employment the Board found that the newsboys are an integral part of the publishers' distribution system and circulation organization. And the record discloses that the newsboys and checkmen feel

---

of the APA. Of course, if the case had come up after 1946, some of its phrasing would have differed.

1. Section 2(3) of the Act provides that "The term 'employee' shall include any em-
ployee, and shall not be limited to the employees of a particular employer, unless the Act explicitly states otherwise. ..."

they are employees of the papers and respondents' supervisory employees, if not respondents themselves, regard them as such.

I

The principal question is whether the newsboys are "employees." Because Congress did not explicitly define the term, respondents say its meaning must be determined by reference to common-law standards. In their view "common-law standards" are those the courts have applied in distinguishing between "employees" and "independent contractors" when working out various problems unrelated to the Wagner Act's purposes and provisions.

The argument assumes that there is some simple, uniform and easily applicable test which the courts have used, in dealing with such problems, to determine whether persons doing work for others fall in one class or the other. Unfortunately this is not true. Only by a long and tortuous history was the simple formulation worked out which has been stated most frequently as "the test" for deciding whether one who hires another is responsible in tort for his wrongdoing. But this formula has been by no means exclusively controlling in the solution of other problems. And its simplicity has been illusory because it is more largely simplicity of formulation than of application. ... [T]hey have arisen principally, first, in the struggle of the courts to work out common-law liabilities where the legislature has given no guides for judgment, more recently also under statutes which have posed the same problem for solution in the light of the enactment's particular terms and purposes. ... [W]ithin a single jurisdiction a person who, for instance, is held to be an "independent contractor" for the purpose of imposing vicarious liability in tort may be an "employee" for the purposes of particular legislation, such as unemployment compensation. ...

Two possible consequences could follow. One would be to refer the decision of who are employees to local state law. The alternative would be to make it turn on a sort of pervading general essence distilled from state law. Congress obviously did not intend the former result. It would introduce variations into the statute's operation as wide as the differences the forty-eight states and other local jurisdictions make in applying the distinction for wholly different purposes. Persons who might be "employees" in one state would be "independent contractors" in another. ... Persons working across state lines might fall in one class or the other, possibly both, depending on whether the Board and the courts would be required to give effect to the law of one state or of the adjoining one, or to that of each in relation to the portion of the work done within its borders.

Both the terms and the purposes of the statute, as well as the legislative history, show that Congress had in mind no such patchwork plan for securing freedom of employees' organization and of collective bargaining. The Wagner Act is federal legislation, administered by a national agency, intended to solve a national problem on a national scale. ...

II

Whether, given the intended national uniformity, the term "employee" includes such workers as these newsboys must be answered primarily from the history, terms and purposes of the legislation. The word "is not treated by Congress as a word of art having a definite meaning ..." Rather "it ... must be read in the light of the mischief to be corrected and the end to be attained." South Chicago Coal & Dock Co. v. Bassett, 309 U.S. 251.

Congress, on the one hand, was not thinking solely of the immediate technical relation of employer and employee. It had in mind at least some other persons than those standing in the proximate legal relation of employee to the particular employer involved in the labor dispute. It cannot be taken, however, that the purpose was to include all other persons who may perform service for another or was to ignore entirely legal classifications made for other purposes. Congress had in mind a wider field than the narrow technical legal relation of "master and servant," as the common law had worked this out in all its variations, and at the same time a narrower one than the entire area of rendering service to others. The question comes down therefore to how much was included of the intermediate region between what is clearly and unequivocally "employment," by any appropriate test, and what is as clearly entrepreneurial enterprise and not employment. ...

Congress ... sought to find a broad solution, one that would bring industrial peace by substituting, so far as its power could reach, the rights of workers to self-organization and collective bargaining for the industrial strife which prevails where these rights are not effectively established. Yet only partial solutions would be provided if large segments of workers about whose technical legal position such local differences exist should be wholly excluded from coverage by reason of such differences. Yet that result could not be avoided, if choice must be made among them and controlled by them in deciding who are "employees" within the Act's meaning. Enmeshed in such distinctions, the administration of the statute soon might become encumbered by the same sort of technical legal refinement as has characterized the long evolution of the employee-independent contractor dichotomy in the courts for other purposes. The consequences would be ultimately to defeat, in part at least, the achievement of the statute's objectives. Congress no more intended to import this mass of technicality as a controlling "standard" for uniform national application than to refer decision of the question outright to the local law.

The Act, as its first section states, was designed to avert the "substantial obstructions to the free flow of commerce" which result from "strikes and other forms of industrial strife or unrest" by eliminating the causes of that unrest. It is premised on explicit findings that strikes and industrial strife themselves result in large measure from the refusal of employers to bargain collectively and the inability of individual workers to bargain successfully for improvements in their "wages, hours, or other working conditions" with employers who are "organized in the corporate or other forms of ownership association." Hence the avowed and the interrelated purposes of the Act are to encourage collective bargaining and to remedy the individual worker's inequality of bargaining power by "protecting the exercise ... of full freedom of association, self-organization, and designation of representatives of their own choosing, for the purpose of negotiating the terms and conditions of their employment or other mutual aid or protection." 49 Stat. 449, 450.

The mischief at which the Act is aimed and the remedies it offers are not confined exclusively to "employees" within the traditional legal distinctions separating them from "independent contractors." Myriad forms of service relationship, with infinite and subtle variations in the terms of employment, blanket the nation's economy. Some are within this Act, others beyond its coverage. Large numbers will fall clearly on one side or on the other, by whatever test may be applied. But intermediate there will be many, the incidents of whose employment partake in part of the one group, in part of the other, in varying proportions of weight. And consequently the legal pendulum, for purposes of applying the statute, may swing one way or the other, depending upon the weight of this balance and its relation to the special purpose at hand.

. . . Interruption of commerce through strikes and unrest may stem as well from labor disputes between some who, for other purposes, are technically "independent contractors" and their employers as from disputes between persons who, for those purposes, are "employees" and their employers. . . . Inequality of bargaining power in controversies over wages, hours and working conditions may as well characterize the status of the one group as of the other. The former, when acting alone, may be as "helpless in dealing with an employer," as "dependent . . . on his daily wage" and as "unable to leave the employ and to resist arbitrary and unfair treatment" as the latter. For each, "union . . . [may be] essential to give . . . opportunity to deal on equality with their employer." And for each, collective bargaining may be appropriate and effective for the "friendly adjustment of industrial disputes arising out of differences as to wages, hours, or other working conditions." 49 Stat. 449. In short, when the particular situation of employment combines these characteristics, so that the economic facts of the relation make it more nearly one of employment than of independent business enterprise with respect to the ends sought to be accomplished by the legislation, those characteristics may outweigh technical legal classification for purposes unrelated to the statute's objectives and bring the relation within its protections. . . .

It is not necessary in this case to make a completely definitive limitation around the term "employee." That task has been assigned primarily to the agency created by Congress to administer the Act. Determination of "where all the conditions of the relation require protection" involves inquiries for the Board charged with this duty. Everyday experience in the administration of the statute gives it familiarity with the circumstances and backgrounds of employment relationships in various industries, with the abilities and needs of the workers for self organization and collective action, and with the adaptability of collective bargaining for the peaceful settlement of their disputes with their employers. The experience thus acquired must be brought frequently to bear on the question who is an employee under the Act. Resolving that question, like determining whether unfair labor practices have been committed, "belongs to the usual administrative routine" of the Board. Gray v. Powell, 314 U.S. 402, 411. . . .

In making that body's determinations as to the facts in these matters conclusive, if supported by evidence, Congress entrusted to it primarily the decision whether the evidence establishes the material facts. Hence in reviewing the Board's ultimate conclusions, it is not the court's function to substitute its own inferences of fact for the Board's, when the latter have support in the record. . . . Undoubtedly questions of statutory interpretation, especially when arising in the first instance in judicial proceedings, are for the courts to resolve, giving appropriate weight to the judgment of those whose special duty is to administer the questioned statute. Norwegian Nitrogen Products Co. v. United States, 288 U.S. 294. But where the question is one of specific application of a broad statutory term in a proceeding in which the agency administering the statute must determine it initially, the reviewing court's function is limited. Like the commissioner's determination under the Longshoremen's & Harbor Workers' Act, that a man is not a "member of a crew" or that he was injured "in the course of his employment" and the Federal Communications Commission's determination that one company is under the "control" of another, the Board's determination that specified persons are "employees" under this Act is to be accepted if it has "warrant in the record" and a reasonable basis in law.

In this case the Board found that the designated newsboys work continuously and regularly, rely upon their earnings for the support of themselves and their families, and have their total wages influenced in large measure by the publishers who dictate their buying and selling prices, fix their markets and control their supply of papers. Their hours of work and their efforts on the job are supervised and to some extent prescribed by the publishers or their agents. Much of their sales equipment and advertising materials is furnished by the publishers with the intention that it be used for the publisher's benefit. Stating that "the primary consideration in the determination of the applicability of the statutory definition is whether effectuation of the declared policy and purposes of the Act comprehend securing to the individual the rights guaranteed and protection afforded by the Act," the Board concluded that the newsboys are employees. The record sustains the Board's findings and there is ample basis in the law for its conclusion. . . .

The judgments are reversed and the causes are remanded . . .

■ [JUSTICE REED concurred in the result. JUSTICE ROBERTS dissented:]

. . . I think it plain that newsboys are not "employees" of the respondents within the meaning and intent of the National Labor Relations Act. When Congress, in § 2(3) said: "The term 'employee' shall include any employee, . . ." it stated as clearly as language could do it that the provisions of the Act were to extend to those who, as a result of decades of tradition which had become part of the common understanding of our people, bear the named relationship. Clearly also Congress did not delegate to the National Labor Relations Board the function of defining the relationship of employment so as to promote what the Board understood to be the underlying purpose of the statute. The question who is an employee, so as to make the statute applicable to him, is a question of the meaning of the Act and, therefore, is a judicial and not an administrative question. . . .

NOTES

(1) This is a carefully written opinion. Justice Rutledge treats some of the questions he considers as matters for the Court to decide for itself, and some as matters for which "the reviewing court's function is limited." Can you pinpoint the place in the opinion where he shifts from one stance to the other? Can you say why?

(2) Compare the nearly contemporaneous Packard Motor Car Co. v. NLRB, 330 U.S. 485 (1947). "The question presented by this case," said Justice Jackson, "is whether foremen are entitled as a class to these rights of self-organization [and] collective bargaining . . . assured to employees generally by the National Labor Relations Act."

Packard's 1100 foremen wanted to organize as a unit of the Foremen's Assn. of America, representing supervisory employees exclusively. The foremen supervised Packard's 32,000 rank-and-file workers, represented by the United Auto Workers; foremen were relatively highly paid and responsible for maintaining quantity and quality of production under overall control by management; foremen could not hire or fire but could discipline and recommend promotion, demotion, etc. The NLRB decided the foremen were "employees," and then decided that they constituted an appropriate bargaining unit. Packard refused to bargain, claiming foremen were not "employees."

The Act, as we have seen, provided that " 'employee' shall include any employee" but also said that " 'employer' includes any person acting in the interest of an employer, directly or indirectly. . . ." How to put these two provisions together, in relation to foremen, was, said the Court, a "naked question of law" as to which "administrative interpretation" (which had waivered over time on the question) was irrelevant. Nevertheless, the Court affirmed the Board, none of the Justices deferring to the Board on this "tremendously important" policy affecting industry nation-wide, but a majority agreeing with the Board about how the Act treated foremen. (Hearst was cited only once, by the dissent, and only for the proposition that "the term 'employee' must be considered in the context of the Act.")[1]

(3) Roy A. Schotland, Scope of Review of Administrative Action—Remarks Before the D.C. Circuit Judicial Conference, 34 Fed.B.J. 54, 58 (1975): "the phrases 'questions of fact' and 'questions of law' are not only misleading, but also tend to invite focus on the wrong factors. The inquiry, when deciding what is the appropriate scope of review, of course should be not into the nature of the issue to be decided, e.g., fact or law, but rather should focus upon how much of the resolution of the issue is to be by the judge, how much by the agency. Thus, we should speak of factfinding, which obviously is mainly for the administrator; law-declaring, which has to do with general construction of a statute wholly independently of the particular controversy at bar, which will be mainly, and very often entirely, for our best experts at such matters as statutory construction, you judges; and the last function, spoken of in the familiar but muddling way as 'mixed

---

1. Congress promptly amended the definition of "employee" to exclude "supervisory employees." The next generation of questions about which employees can unionize is exemplified by the Bell Aerospace case, p. 569 above.

question,' is what I call law-applying, or applying a statute or other item of law to the particular facts at bar, a function which in the normal course is mainly for the agency because in the normal course, the decisions will have little bearing on any other decision. That is, it's part of the normal particularized administration of the statute and its resolution belongs mainly to the body with the first-line responsibility for that administration."

Skidmore v. Swift & Co.

Supreme Court of the United States, 1944.
323 U.S. 134.

■ JUSTICE JACKSON delivered the opinion of the Court.

Seven employees of the Swift and Company packing plant at Fort Worth, Texas, brought an action under the Fair Labor Standards Act, to recover overtime, liquidated damages, and attorneys' fees, totaling approximately $77,000. . . .

It is not denied that the daytime employment of these persons was working time within the Act. . . .

Under their oral agreement of employment, however, petitioners undertook to stay in the fire hall on the Company premises, or within hailing distance, three and a half to four nights a week. This involved no task except to answer alarms, either because of fire or because the sprinkler was set off for some other reason. No fires occurred during the period in issue, the alarms were rare, and the time required for their answer rarely exceeded an hour. For each alarm answered the employees were paid in addition to their fixed compensation an agreed amount, fifty cents at first, and later sixty-four cents. The Company provided a brick fire hall equipped with steam heat and air-conditioned rooms. It provided sleeping quarters, a pool table, a domino table, and a radio. The men used their time in sleep or amusement as they saw fit, except that they were required to stay in or close by the fire hall and be ready to respond to alarms. It is stipulated that "they agreed to remain in the fire hall and stay in it or within hailing distance, subject to call, in event of fire or other casualty, but were not required to perform any specific tasks during these periods of time, except in answering alarms." The trial court found the evidentiary facts as stipulated; it made no findings of fact as such as to whether under the arrangement of the parties and the circumstances of this case, which in some respects differ from those of [a companion case], the fire hall duty or any part thereof constituted working time. It said, however, as a "conclusion of law" that "the time plaintiffs spent in the fire hall subject to call to answer fire alarms does not constitute hours worked, for which overtime compensation is due them under the Fair Labor Standards Act, as interpreted by the Administrator and the Courts," and in its opinion observed, "of course we know pursuing such pleasurable occupations or performing such personal chores does not constitute work." The Circuit Court of Appeals affirmed.

For reasons set forth in [that companion case], we hold that no principle of law found either in the statute or in Court decisions precludes waiting time from also being working time. We have not attempted to, and we cannot, lay down a legal formula to resolve cases so varied in their facts as are the many situations in which employment involves waiting time. Whether in a concrete case such time falls within or without the Act is a question of fact to be resolved by appropriate findings of the trial court. . . . This involves scrutiny and construction of the agreements between the particular parties, appraisal of their practical construction of the working agreement by conduct, consideration of the nature of the service, and its relation to the waiting time, and all of the surrounding circumstances. Facts may show that the employee was engaged to wait, or they may show that he waited to be engaged. His compensation may cover both waiting and task, or only performance of the task itself. Living quarters may in some situations be furnished as a facility of the task and in another as a part of its compensation. The law does not impose an arrangement upon the parties. It imposes upon the courts the task of finding what the arrangement was. . . .

Congress did not utilize the services of an administrative agency to find facts and to determine in the first instance whether particular cases fall within or without the Act. Instead, it put this responsibility on the courts. . . . But it did create the office of Administrator, impose upon him a variety of duties, endow him with powers to inform himself of conditions in industries and employments subject to the Act, and put on him the duties of bringing injunction actions to restrain violations. Pursuit of his duties has accumulated a considerable experience in the problems of ascertaining working time in employments involving periods of inactivity and a knowledge of the customs prevailing in reference to their solution. From these he is obliged to reach conclusions as to conduct without the law, so that he should seek injunctions to stop it, and that within the law, so that he has no call to interfere. He has set forth his views of the application of the Act under different circumstances in an interpretative bulletin and in informal rulings. They provide a practical guide to employers and employees as to how the office representing the public interest in its enforcement will seek to apply it. Wage and Hour Division, Interpretative Bulletin No. 13. . . .

There is no statutory provision as to what, if any, deference courts should pay to the Administrator's conclusions. And, while we have given them notice, we have had no occasion to try to prescribe their influence. The rulings of this Administrator are not reached as a result of hearing adversary proceedings in which he finds facts from evidence and reaches conclusions of law from findings of fact. They are not, of course, conclusive, even in the cases with which they directly deal, much less in those to which they apply only by analogy. They do not constitute an interpretation of the Act or a standard for judging factual situations which binds a district court's processes, as an authoritative pronouncement of a higher court might do. But the Administrator's policies are made in pursuance of official duty, based upon more specialized experience and broader investigations and information than is likely to come to a judge in a particular case. They do determine the policy which will guide applications for enforcement by injunction on behalf of the Government. Good administration of the Act and good judicial administration alike require that the standards of public enforcement and those for determining private rights shall be at variance only where justified by very good reasons. The fact that the Administrator's policies and standards are not reached by trial in adversary form does not mean that they are not entitled to respect. This Court has long given considerable and in some cases decisive weight to Treasury Decisions and to interpretative regulations of the Treasury and of other bodies that were not of adversary origin.

We consider that the rulings, interpretations and opinions of the Administrator under this Act, while not controlling upon the courts by reason of their authority, do constitute a body of experience and informed judgment to which courts and litigants may properly resort for guidance. The weight of such a judgment in a particular case will depend upon the thoroughness evident in its consideration, the validity of its reasoning, its consistency with earlier and later pronouncements, and all those factors which give it <u>power to persuade</u>, if lacking power to control.

Deference to extent has persuasive power

The court in the [companion] case weighed the evidence . . . in the light of the Administrator's rulings and reached a result consistent therewith. The evidence in this case in some respects, such as the understanding as to separate compensation for answering alarms, is different. Each case must stand on its own facts. But in this case, although the District Court referred to the Administrator's Bulletin, its evaluation and inquiry were apparently restricted by its notion that waiting time may not be work, an understanding of the law which we hold to be erroneous. Accordingly, the judgment is reversed and the cause remanded for further proceedings consistent herewith.

Reversed.

NOTES

(1) SAMUEL HERMAN, THE ADMINISTRATION AND ENFORCEMENT OF THE FAIR LABOR STANDARDS ACT, 6 Law & Contemp.Probs. 368, 378–80 (1939). "A rule-making power had been contained in the Act as originally introduced. The issuance of 'interpretative bulletins' by the Wage and Hour Division stemmed from the failure of Congress to include a rule-making provision in the Act. The bulletins were the creature of necessity . . . [and] self-denying as witnessed by the following typical statement:

> . . . [I]nterpretations announced by the Administrator, except in certain specific instances where the statute directs the Administrator to make various regulations and definitions, serve only to indicate the construction of the law which will guide the Administrator in the performance of his administrative duties, unless he is directed otherwise by the authoritative rulings of the courts, or unless he shall subsequently decide that a prior interpretation is incorrect.

" . . . The interpretative bulletins are not binding on industry; they are merely legal advice—good, perhaps the best. While industry is advised to comply, if in doubt, the employer is not immune if, in reliance upon an interpretative bulletin, he concludes that the Act is not applicable to him.

He may be subsequently prosecuted under Section 16(a), sued by an employee under Section 16(b), or enjoined under Section 17."

(2) Justice Jackson's penultimate paragraph is—as we shall see—much quoted. It is certainly well written, but what exactly does it mean? The weight to be given the Administrator's interpretation by the court on remand, we are told, depends on "those factors which give it power to persuade." Does this mean that if the court is persuaded that the Administrator is right, it should follow his interpretation (which is now, since it has been persuaded, also the court's interpretation)—and if not, it should not? This is not news. It is also not deference. The court will simply be doing in its own voice what it now thinks it is right to do. We would not say that a court persuaded by the excellent brief of a private litigant to decide in its favor is deferring to the litigant's lawyers.

(3) If you responded to the previous note by saying to yourself that, whatever the words, Jackson did mean for the court to give some extra weight to the agency's judgments, to defer to them to some extent, then how do you get by the point, also in the paragraph, that these interpretations are "not controlling upon the courts by reason of their authority." Is the crucial word here "controlling"—so that a court can still *choose* to defer to the opinion of the agency much as a trial court might defer to the opinion of an expert witness once convinced the witness was really an expert?

(4) Does it bother you that Congress did not give the Administrator the power to make rules? Does it bother you that no law gave Swift & Co. an opportunity to be heard before the agency on the interpretive question presented? (Recall, if you have studied them, the materials on publication rules, Chapter V, Section 4 above.)

(5) If you think that Skidmore stands for a principle of deference which is legitimate, what is that principle? How does it fit with your interpretation of the Hearst case? How far does it extend?

TRANSITIONAL NOTE

Our gravitation to models based on judicial proceedings—not to mention our natural yearning for generalization[1]—might lead us to categorize the preceding cases in terms of questions of fact and questions of law, or perhaps more subtly in terms of fact-finding, law-declaring, and law-

---

1. "Confronted with disturbing variety, we often feel a tension from which a generalization, an abstraction, relieves us. It serves as a de-problemizer, aiding us to pass from an unstable, problematical, situation to a more stable one. It satisfies a craving, meets what Emerson called 'the insatiable demand of harmony in man,' a demand which translates itself into the so-called 'law' of 'the least effort.' But the solution of a problem through the invention of a new generalization is no final solution: The new generalization breeds new problems. Stressing a newly perceived likeness between many particular happenings, which had theretofore seemed unlike, it may blind us to continuing unlikenesses. Hypnotized by a label, which emphasizes identities, we may be led to ignore differences. In all fields of thought that evil is encountered. Nowhere can it do more harm than in democratic government—and in democratic courthouse government in particular." Guiseppi v. Walling, 144 F.2d 608, 618–19 (2d Cir.1944) (Frank, J.), aff'd sub nom. Gemsco, Inc. v. Walling, 324 U.S. 244 (1945).

applying. But note that most of these cases involved on-the-record adjudication. The traditional frame of reference may be less helpful in classifying the array of issues that agencies decide in informal adjudication, notice-and-comment rulemaking, discretionary treatment of waivers or sanctions, agencies' prescription of their own procedures, etc. Yet courts—and legislatures—have tended to retain the familiar analytical categories, and to deemphasize the relevance of the procedural form in which the issues come before the agency.

However, over the last thirty years, a series of Supreme Court decisions has, to the eyes of many observers at least, considerably changed the rules governing substantive judicial review. What is less obvious is how the new rules should be stated, or even what the operative categories are. Some might organize these cases by the traditional categories, seeing in them the same subjects as appear in the older cases, but with different predicates. Others might emphasize the shift from the paradigm of on-the-record adjudication to the paradigm of informal adjudication and rulemaking, and see in the different procedural frame at the agency level forces leading to new reviewing postures as well. Still others might emphasize the intrusion of an increased awareness of "politics" and "policy" as determinants of agency action, and the consequent complexification of the simpler world of "law" and "fact." What follows, then, requires the student of the law—either the neophyte student or the "student" who has been studying the matter for many years—to analyze on two (or more) levels at once (i) how are the principles, as stated within the traditional frame of reference still used by statutes and opinions, changing? and (ii) how are the frames of reference themselves being, if not superseded, at least refashioned?

How complex the modern world is! How interesting, too!

b.   THE PRESENT-DAY FRAMEWORK

We turn now to a series of cases which, taken together, define the modern law of judicial review of matters beyond determination-of-the-facts. Because they react off one another, they are presented in historical order. What analytical pattern they exhibit is, of course, one of the questions to be asked.

Citizens to Preserve Overton Park, Inc. v. Volpe

Supreme Court of the United States, 1971.
401 U.S. 402.

■ Opinion of the Court by JUSTICE MARSHALL, announced by JUSTICE STEWART.

The growing public concern about the quality of our natural environment has prompted Congress in recent years to enact legislation designed to curb the accelerating destruction of our country's natural beauty. We are concerned in this case with 4(f) of the Department of Transportation Act of 1966, as amended, and § 18(a) of the Federal–Aid Highway Act of 1968, 82 Stat. 823, 23 U.S.C. § 138.[1] . . .

---

1. [Each section says:] "It is hereby declared to be the national policy that special effort should be made to preserve the natural beauty of the countryside and public park

Petitioners, private citizens as well as local and national conservation organizations, contend that the Secretary [of Transportation] has violated these statutes by authorizing the expenditure of federal funds for the construction of a six-lane interstate highway through a public park in Memphis, Tennessee. Their claim was rejected by the District Court, which granted the Secretary's motion for summary judgment, and the Court of Appeals for the Sixth Circuit affirmed. After oral argument, this Court granted a stay that halted construction and, treating the application for the stay as a petition for certiorari, granted review. We now reverse the judgment below and remand for further proceedings in the District Court.

Overton Park is a 342–acre city park located near the center of Memphis. The park contains a zoo, a nine-hole municipal golf course, an outdoor theater, nature trails, a bridle path, an art academy, picnic areas, and 170 acres of forest. The proposed highway, which is to be a six-lane, high-speed, expressway, will sever the zoo from the rest of the park. Although the roadway will be depressed below ground level except where it crosses a small creek, 26 acres of the park will be destroyed. ...

Although the route through the park was approved by the Bureau of Public Roads in 1956 and by the Federal Highway Administrator in 1966, the enactment of § 4(f) ... prevented distribution of federal funds for the section of the highway designated to go through Overton Park until the Secretary of Transportation determined whether the requirements of § 4(f) had been met. ... In April 1968, the Secretary announced that he concurred in the judgment of local officials that I–40 should be built through the park. ... Final approval for the project—the route as well as the design—was not announced until November 1969, after Congress had reiterated in § 138 of the Federal–Aid Highway Act that highway construction through public parks was to be restricted. [The Secretary's approval of federal funds for the highway was not] accompanied by a statement of the Secretary's factual findings. He did not indicate why he believed there were no feasible and prudent alternative routes or why design changes could not be made to reduce the harm to the park.

Petitioners contend that the Secretary's action is invalid without such formal findings and that the Secretary did not make an independent determination but merely relied on the judgment of the Memphis City Council. ...[2]

and recreation lands, wildlife and waterfowl refuges, and historic sites. ... After [August 23, 1968], the Secretary shall not approve any program or project which requires the use of any publicly owned land from a public park, recreation area, or wildlife and waterfowl refuge of national, State, or local significance as determined by the Federal, State, or local officials having jurisdiction thereof, or any land from an historic site of national, State or local significance as so determined by such officials unless (1) there is no feasible and prudent alternative to the use of such land, and (2) such program includes all possible planning to minimize harm to such park, recreational area, wildlife and waterfowl refuge, or historic site resulting from such use."

2. [Ed.] The judgment of the Memphis City Council had been obtained pursuant to a statutory provision requiring consultation with local officials. In conducting these consultations, the Secretary had insisted that the Council consider only issues of community values and not costs—as the federal government would pay most of the expenses—and he regarded this instruction as an important

Respondents argue that it was unnecessary for the Secretary to make formal findings, and that he did, in fact, exercise his own independent judgment which was supported by the facts. In the District Court, respondents introduced affidavits, prepared specifically for this litigation, which indicated that the Secretary had made the decision and that the decision was supportable. These affidavits were contradicted by affidavits introduced by petitioners. . . .

The District Court and the Court of Appeals found that formal findings by the Secretary were not necessary and refused to order the deposition of the former Federal Highway Administrator because those courts believed that probing of the mental processes of an administrative decisionmaker was prohibited. And, believing that the Secretary's authority was wide and reviewing courts' authority narrow in the approval of highway routes, the lower courts held that the affidavits contained no basis for a determination that the Secretary had exceeded his authority.

We agree that formal findings were not required. But we do not believe that in this case judicial review based solely on litigation affidavits was adequate.

A threshold question—whether petitioners are entitled to any judicial review—is easily answered. Section 701 of the Administrative Procedure Act . . . provides that the action of "each authority of the Government of the United States," which includes the Department of Transportation, is subject to judicial review except where there is a statutory prohibition on review or where "agency action is committed to agency discretion by law." In this case, there is no indication that Congress sought to prohibit judicial review and there is most certainly no "showing of 'clear and convincing evidence' of a . . . legislative intent" to restrict access to judicial review. Abbott Laboratories v. Gardner, 387 U.S. 136, 141 (1967). . . .

Similarly, the Secretary's decision here does not fall within the exception for action "committed to agency discretion." This is a very narrow exception. Berger, Administrative Arbitrariness and Judicial Review, 65 Colum.L.Rev. 55 (1965). The legislative history of the Administrative Procedure Act indicates that it is applicable in those rare instances where "statutes are drawn in such broad terms that in a given case there is no law to apply." S.Rep. No. 752, 79th Cong., 1st Sess., 26 (1945).

Section 4(f) of the Department of Transportation Act and § 138 of the Federal–Aid Highway Act are clear and specific directives. . . . [The statutory] language is a plain and explicit bar to the use of federal funds for construction of highways through parks—only the most unusual situations are exempted.

Despite the clarity of the statutory language, respondents argue that the Secretary has wide discretion. They recognize that the requirement that there be no "feasible" alternative route admits of little administrative

means of implementing § 4(f). Those local hearings were widely reported in the Memphis press, and the issues were hotly debated. One outcome of that process was that the city used the money it received for the 26 acres of Overton Park needed for the highway to buy several hundred acres of land for parks scattered throughout the city. Creation of the new parks was complete at the time of the lawsuit.

discretion. For this exemption to apply the Secretary must find that as a matter of sound engineering it would not be feasible to build the highway along any other route. Respondents argue, however, that the requirement that there be no other "prudent" route requires the Secretary to engage in a wide-ranging balancing of competing interests. They contend that the Secretary should weigh the detriment resulting from the destruction of parkland against the cost of other routes, safety considerations, and other factors, and determine on the basis of the importance that he attaches to these other factors whether, on balance, alternative feasible routes would be "prudent."

But no such wide-ranging endeavor was intended. It is obvious that in most cases considerations of cost, directness of route, and community disruption will indicate that parkland should be used for highway construction whenever possible. Although it may be necessary to transfer funds from one jurisdiction to another, there will always be a smaller outlay required from the public purse when parkland is used since the public already owns the land and there will be no need to pay for right-of-way. And since people do not live or work in parks, if a highway is built on parkland no one will have to leave his home or give up his business. Such factors are common to substantially all highway construction. Thus, if Congress intended these factors to be on an equal footing with preservation of parkland there would have been no need for the statutes.

Congress clearly did not intend that cost and disruption of the community were to be ignored by the Secretary. But the very existence of the statutes[3] indicates that protection of parkland was to be given paramount importance. The few green havens that are public parks were not to be lost unless there were truly unusual factors present in a particular case or the cost or community disruption resulting from alternative routes reached extraordinary magnitudes. If the statutes are to have any meaning, the Secretary cannot approve the destruction of parkland unless he finds that alternative routes present unique problems.

Plainly, there is "law to apply" and thus the exemption for action "committed to agency discretion" is inapplicable. But the existence of judicial review is only the start: the standard for review must also be determined. For that we must look to § 706 of the Administrative Procedure Act ... [A] "reviewing court shall ... hold unlawful and set aside agency action, findings, and conclusions found" not to meet six separate standards. In all cases agency action must be set aside if the action was "arbitrary, capricious, an abuse of discretion, or otherwise not in accordance with law" or if the action failed to meet statutory, procedural, or constitutional requirements. 5 U.S.C. § 706(2)(A), (B), (C), (D). In certain narrow, specifically limited situations, the agency action is to be set aside if

---

3. The legislative history of both § 4(f) of the Department of Transportation Act ... and § 138 of the Federal–Aid Highway Act ... is ambiguous. The legislative committee reports tend to support respondents' view that the statutes are merely general directives to the Secretary requiring him to consider the importance of parkland as well as cost, community disruption, and other factors. Statements by proponents of the statutes as well as the Senate committee report on § 4(f) indicate, however, that the Secretary was to have limited authority. Because of this ambiguity it is clear that we must look primarily to the statutes themselves to find the legislative intent.

the action was not supported by "substantial evidence." And in other equally narrow circumstances the reviewing court is to engage in a de novo review of the action and set it aside if it was "unwarranted by the facts."

Petitioners argue that the Secretary's approval of the construction of [the highway] through Overton Park is subject to one or the other of these latter two standards of limited applicability. First, they contend that the "substantial evidence" standard of § 706(2)(E) must be applied. In the alternative, they claim that § 706(2)(F) applies and that there must be a de novo review to determine if the Secretary's action was "unwarranted by the facts." Neither of these standards is, however, applicable.

Review under the substantial-evidence test is authorized only when the agency action is taken pursuant to a rulemaking provision of the Administrative Procedure Act itself, 5 U.S.C. § 553, or when the agency action is based on a public adjudicatory hearing. See 5 U.S.C. §§ 556, 557. The Secretary's decision to allow the expenditure of federal funds to build [the highway] through Overton Park was plainly not an exercise of a rulemaking function. And the only hearing that is required by either the Administrative Procedure Act or the statutes regulating the distribution of federal funds for highway construction is a public hearing conducted by local officials for the purpose of informing the community about the proposed project and eliciting community views on the design and route. 23 U.S.C. § 128. The hearing is nonadjudicatory, quasi-legislative in nature. It is not designed to produce a record that is to be the basis of agency action—the basic requirement for substantial-evidence review.

Petitioners' alternative argument also fails. De novo review of whether the Secretary's decision was "unwarranted by the facts" is authorized by § 706(2)(F) in only two circumstances. First, such de novo review is authorized when the action is adjudicatory in nature and the agency factfinding procedures are inadequate. And, there may be independent judicial factfinding when issues that were not before the agency are raised in a proceeding to enforce nonadjudicatory agency action. Neither situation exists here.

Even though there is no de novo review in this case and the Secretary's approval of the route ... does not have ultimately to meet the substantial-evidence test, the generally applicable standards of § 706 require the reviewing court to engage in a substantial inquiry. Certainly, the Secretary's decision is entitled to a presumption of regularity. See, e.g., Pacific States Box & Basket Co. v. White, 296 U.S. 176, 185 (1935). But that presumption is not to shield his action from a thorough, probing, in-depth review.

The court is first required to decide whether the Secretary acted within the scope of his authority. This determination naturally begins with a delineation of the scope of the Secretary's authority and discretion. L. Jaffe, Judicial Control of Administrative Action 359 (1965). As has been shown, Congress has specified only a small range of choices that the Secretary can make. Also involved in this initial inquiry is a determination of whether on the facts the Secretary's decision can reasonably be said to be within that range. The reviewing court must consider whether the Secretary properly construed his authority to approve the use of parkland as limited to situations where there are no feasible alternative routes or where feasible alternative routes involve uniquely difficult problems. And the reviewing court must be able to find that the Secretary could have reasonably believed that in this case there are no feasible alternatives or that alternatives do involve unique problems.

Scrutiny of the facts does not end, however, with the determination that the Secretary has acted within the scope of his statutory authority. Section 706(2)(A) requires a finding that the actual choice made was not "arbitrary, capricious, an abuse of discretion, or otherwise not in accordance with law." To make this finding the court must consider whether the decision was based on a consideration of the relevant factors and whether there has been a clear error of judgment. . . . Although this inquiry into the facts is to be searching and careful, the ultimate standard of review is a narrow one. The court is not empowered to substitute its judgment for that of the agency.

Hard Look Doctrine

The final inquiry is whether the Secretary's action followed the necessary procedural requirements. Here the only procedural error alleged is the failure of the Secretary to make formal findings and state his reason for allowing the highway to be built through the park.

Undoubtedly, review of the Secretary's action is hampered by his failure to make such findings, but the absence of formal findings does not necessarily require that the case be remanded to the Secretary. Neither the Department of Transportation Act nor the Federal–Aid Highway Act requires such formal findings. Moreover, the Administrative Procedure Act requirements that there be formal findings in certain rulemaking and adjudicatory proceedings do not apply to the Secretary's action here. See 5 U.S.C. §§ 553(a)(2), 554(a). And, although formal findings may be required in some cases in the absence of statutory directives when the nature of the agency action is ambiguous, those situations are rare. Plainly, there is no ambiguity here; the Secretary has approved the construction of [the highway] through Overton Park and has approved a specific design for the project. . . .

. . . Moreover, there is an administrative record that allows the full, prompt review of the Secretary's action that is sought without additional delay which would result from having a remand to the Secretary.

That administrative record is not, however, before us. The lower courts based their review on the litigation affidavits that were presented. These affidavits were merely "post hoc" rationalizations, Burlington Truck Lines v. United States, 371 U.S. 156, 168–169 (1962), which have traditionally been found to be an inadequate basis for review. Burlington Truck Lines v. United States, supra; SEC v. Chenery Corp., 318 U.S. 80, 87 (1943). And they clearly do not constitute the "whole record" compiled by the agency: the basis for review required by § 706 of the Administrative Procedure Act.

Thus it is necessary to remand this case to the District Court for plenary review of the Secretary's decision. That review is to be based on the full administrative record that was before the Secretary at the time he made his decision. But since the bare record may not disclose the factors that were considered or the Secretary's construction of the evidence it may be necessary for the District Court to require some explanation in order to determine if the Secretary acted within the scope of his authority and if the Secretary's action was justifiable under the applicable standard.

The court may require the administrative officials who participated in the decision to give testimony explaining their action. Of course, such inquiry into the mental processes of administrative decisionmakers is usually to be avoided. United States v. Morgan, 313 U.S. 409, 422 (1941). And where there are administrative findings that were made at the same time as the decision, as was the case in Morgan, there must be a strong showing of bad faith or improper behavior before such inquiry may be made. But here there are no such formal findings and it may be that the only way there can be effective judicial review is by examining the decisionmakers themselves. See Shaughnessy v. Accardi, 349 U.S. 280 (1955).

The District Court is not, however, required to make such an inquiry. It may be that the Secretary can prepare formal findings including the information required by DOT Order 5610.1 that will provide an adequate explanation for his action. Such an explanation will, to some extent, be a "post hoc rationalization" and thus must be viewed critically. If the District Court decides that additional explanation is necessary, that court should consider which method will prove the most expeditious so that full review may be had as soon as possible.

Reversed and remanded.

[JUSTICE BLACK, joined by JUSTICE BRENNAN, dissented on the ground that "it is our duty" to remand this case to the Secretary so he can "give this whole matter the hearing it deserves in full good-faith obedience to the Act of Congress." JUSTICE BLACKMUN, although joining in the Court's opinion and judgment, filed a brief concurring opinion. JUSTICE DOUGLAS did not participate.]

NOTES ON THE PARTICULAR PROCEEDINGS

(1) Overton Park came before the Court in a rush: a motion for a stay was treated by the Court as a petition for certiorari and granted December 7, 1970; petitioner's brief was due on December 21, 1970; the government's, January 4, 1971; and oral argument was heard January 11. The opinion was handed down in early March. The central question briefed and argued was the meaning of the park-use provisions of the highway acts. For all that, the case has had tremendous influence as an interpretation of the APA and the process of judicial review. (The case also makes some errors in its statements about the APA—did you spot them?)

(2) On remand, the district court conducted a 27–day trial that included affidavits of the Secretary and testimony of subordinates. It held: (1) Secretary Volpe had never actually made the route or corridor determination which was required by section 4 of the Department of Transportation Act; and (2) even if the Secretary had made such a determination, it was based on an incorrect view of the law. Accordingly, in January 1972, the district court remanded the case to the Secretary to make a route determi-

nation in accordance with the applicable law. 335 F.Supp. 873. The Secretary rendered his decision in January 1973. He stated in part: "On the basis of the record before me and in light of guidance provided by the Supreme Court, I find that an Interstate highway as proposed by the State through Overton Park cannot be approved. . . . I cannot find . . . that there are no prudent and feasible alternatives to the use of parkland nor that the broader environmental protection objectives of the NEPA and the Federal–Aid Highway Act have been met, nor that the existing proposal would comply with FHWA standards on noise." The State of Tennessee then sought review in the district court, contending that the Secretary was required either to approve the Overton Park route or to specify an alternate route. The district court agreed with the State but its decision was reversed by the Sixth Circuit. Citizens to Preserve Overton Park, Inc. v. Brinegar, 494 F.2d 1212 (6th Cir.1974), cert. denied, 421 U.S. 991 (1975).

(3) The Supreme Court's opinion in Overton Park is as important for its description of the process to be followed in judicial review as for its stipulation of the standard to which agency action is to be held. These process points echo throughout this book, and indeed the opinion could have been printed in at least two other places.

First, Justice Marshall's treatment of § 701 of the APA, and its "presumption" of judicial review, has been very influential. For treatment of the matter, see Chapter 9, § 3 below.

Second, Justice Marshall's treatment of the last sentence of § 706 of the APA—as ordinarily requiring the review even of informal agency action to focus on the "whole record" before the agency, despite the fact that the action was informal precisely because no statute required the proceeding to be "on the record"—has reverberated throughout administrative law ever since. See, for example, United States v. Nova Scotia Food Products Corp., page 524 above. See also Association of Data Processing Service Organizations, earlier in this chapter, page 965.

NOTES ON DECISION–MAKERS' MENTAL PROCESSES

(1) As Justice Marshall's discussion shows, Overton Park's treatment of the connection between administrative findings and the investigation of decision-makers' mental processes has its origin in United States v. Morgan, 313 U.S. 409 (1941). (On the Morgan cases more generally, see p. 394 above.) There, the Secretary of Agriculture—the decider—had been required to appear in trial court and testify as to how he reached his conclusions, including his attention to the record and his consultation with subordinates. This, said the Supreme Court, should never have been done: "Just as a judge cannot be subjected to such a scrutiny, . . . so the integrity of the administrative process must be equally respected." When Overton Park distinguished Morgan, and when a substantial judicial inquiry followed, there was some fear that this curtain of privacy had been rent.

However, this one of Justice Marshall's shots proved to be important largely because of the way it ricocheted. In CAMP v. PITTS, 411 U.S. 138 (1973), an application to organize a new national bank was denied by the Comptroller of the Currency; no hearing or findings were required, but a brief explanation was given by letter.[1] Upon the applicants' suit for review, the district court went over the administrative record of information from bank examiners and other interested parties, and granted summary judgment for the Comptroller. The court of appeals reversed and remanded for trial de novo because the Comptroller had "inadequately and inarticulately resolved the [respondents'] presentation." The court directed that respondents "will open the trial with proof of their application and compliance with the statutory inquiries, and proffer of any other relevant evidence." Then, "[t]estimony may . . . be adduced by the Comptroller or intervenors manifesting opposition, if any, to the new bank." On the basis of the record thus made, the district court was instructed to make its own findings of fact and conclusions of law in order to determine "whether the [respondents] have shown by a preponderance of evidence that the Comptroller's ruling is capricious or an abuse of discretion." 463 F.2d 632, 634 (4th Cir.1972).

The Supreme Court reversed per curiam, closing as follows (411 U.S. at 141–43):

". . . It is quite plain from our decision in Citizens to Preserve Overton Park v. Volpe that de novo review is appropriate only where there are inadequate factfinding procedures in an adjudicatory proceeding, or where judicial proceedings are brought to enforce certain administrative actions. Neither situation applies here. The proceeding in the District Court was obviously not brought to enforce the Comptroller's decision, and the only deficiency suggested in agency action or proceedings is that the Comptroller inadequately explained his decision. As Overton Park demonstrates, however, that failure, if it occurred in this case, is not a deficiency in fact-finding procedures such as to warrant the de novo hearing ordered in this case.

"The appropriate standard for review was, accordingly, whether the Comptroller's adjudication was arbitrary, capricious, an abuse of discretion, or otherwise not in accordance with law, as specified in 5 U.S.C. § 706(2)(A). In applying that standard, the focal point for judicial review should be the administrative record already in existence, not some new record made initially in the reviewing court.

"If, as the Court of Appeals held and as the Comptroller does not now contest, there was such failure to explain administrative action as to frustrate effective judicial review, the remedy was not to hold a de novo hearing but, as contemplated by Overton Park, to obtain from the agency, either through affidavits or testimony, such additional explanation of the reasons for the agency decision as may prove necessary. We add a caveat, however. Unlike Overton Park, in the present case there was contemporaneous explanation of the agency decision. The explanation may have been

---

1. The letter read in part: "On each application we endeavor to develop the need and convenience factors in conjunction with all other banking factors and in this case we were unable to reach a favorable conclusion as to the need factor. The record reflects that this market area is now served by the Peoples Bank with deposits of $7.2MM, The Bank of Hartsville with deposits of $12.8MM, The First Federal Savings and Loan Association with deposits of $5.4MM, The Mutual Savings and Loan Association with deposits of $8.2MM and the Sonoco Employees Credit Union with deposits of $6.5MM. The aforementioned are as of December 31, 1968."

curt, but it surely indicated the determinative reason for the final action taken: the finding that a new bank was an uneconomic venture in light of the banking needs and the banking services already available in the surrounding community. The validity of the Comptroller's action must, therefore, stand or fall on the propriety of that finding, judged, of course, by the appropriate standard of review. If that finding is not sustainable on the administrative record made, then the Comptroller's decision must be vacated and the matter remanded to him for further consideration. See SEC v. Chenery Corp., 318 U.S. 80 (1943)."

Few agencies will have difficulty choosing between the 27 day trial-on-remand in Overton Park itself, and the alternative of making some findings as suggested in the preceding paragraph!

(2) Of course, Overton Park does say that, even where there are findings, there can be "inquiry into the mental processes" when there is "a strong showing of bad faith or improper behavior" on the part of administrative decisionmakers. One of the more dramatic recent invocations of this principle occurred in SAN LUIS OBISPO MOTHERS FOR PEACE v. NRC, 751 F.2d 1287 (D.C.Cir.1984), vacated in part pending rehearing en banc, 760 F.2d 1320 (D.C.Cir.1985), aff'd, 789 F.2d 26 (D.C.Cir.1986) (en banc). After on-the-record hearings, the NRC had published an opinion approving operation of a controversial nuclear reactor in Southern California; on review, supported by statements from a dissenting Commissioner and the chair of a Congressional oversight committee, petitioners attempted to show irregularities in the Commission's decision-making process. They adduced a transcript that had been made of Commission discussions that were otherwise properly closed to the public under the federal Government in the Sunshine Act, see p. 762 above. A majority of the panel first hearing the case, Judges Wilkey (writing) and Bork, refused even to examine the materials in camera:

"Precedent aside, judicial reliance on an agency's stated rationale and findings is central to a harmonious relationship between agency and court, one which recognizes that the agency and not the court is the principal decisionmaker. . . . Inclusion in the record of documents recounting deliberations of agency members is especially worrisome because of its potential for dampening candid and collegial exchange between members of multi-head agencies. . . .

"The Supreme Court has declared that 'where there are administrative findings that were made at the same time as the decision . . . there must be a *strong showing* of bad faith or improper behavior before such inquiry [into the mental processes of administrative decisionmakers] may be made.' [Citing Overton Park.] . . . Petitioners' allegations, while serious, have not been documented with the requisite degree of specificity to warrant either supplementing the record or reviewing the transcripts in camera. The ease with which charges of 'bad faith' could be leveled, combined with the inordinate burden resolution of such claims would entail for courts, persuade us to decline petitioners' invitation to review the transcripts and to supplement the record.

". . . A great many parties could make similar accusations of impropriety in future litigation. On their view of the law, petitioners, and other parties to future proceedings of this sort, could successfully move for supplementation as long as one sympathetic Commissioner, Congressman, or investigative reporter was willing to attest that, based on his reading of the transcript, the agency's decision was rendered in 'bad faith.' Allegations of an 'unbalanced presentation,' 'insufficient attention to arguments of the agency's staff'—indeed, virtually any accusation of irregularity in the agency's decisionmaking process—would require discovery and supplementation of the record.

"The ease with which accusations of impropriety can be made must be compared to the difficulty judges would face investigating such charges—difficulties the dissent ignores. Courts do not have a limitless capacity to review documents in camera on the off-chance that something might turn up. . . . In addition . . . over-eagerness by courts to review documents in camera and to supplement the administrative-created record fails to respect the autonomy of administrative agencies."

For Judge Wald, in dissent, "the unprecedented nature of the *specific* allegations of misconduct lodged by the chairman of one of the NRC oversight committees and one of the commissioners of the NRC, viewed against the disturbing background of the plant's troubled safety history, seem to me clearly sufficient to meet the special exceptions criteria allowing further inquiry by this court. Courts have recognized that supplementation of an administrative record may be justified, in the interest of effective judicial review, where there are *credible* accusations that an agency has relied on material outside the record or has acted improperly or in bad faith. . . . I see no reason not to take the middle course, i.e., an *in camera* examination by the court of the transcripts and related documents before making the ultimate determination to deny Petitioners' Motion to Supplement the Record. I simply believe the stakes are so high and the nature and source of the accusations sufficiently credible as to make a 'business as usual'—'see no evil, hear no evil, confront no evil'—attitude on our part untenable, if we are to provide meaningful judicial review."

When en banc consideration was ordered, petitioners were permitted to file the transcripts with the court. The en banc majority, Judge Bork now writing, reiterated the panel majority's conclusion that the transcripts alone could not be sufficient to establish "the requisite bad faith and improper conduct" to warrant an inquiry into the deliberative processes of the Commission. Judge Bork stressed "the analogy to the deliberative processes of a court . . . Without the assurance of secrecy, the court could not fully perform its functions." Judge Mikva, who indicated that he had reviewed the transcripts, concurred only in the result on this issue. He thought supplementation of the record to include the transcripts would have been justified had petitioners made an allegation "strongly supported by the record, affidavits, and specific references to the transcripts, that the agency has acted in bad faith or with improper purpose. . . . [A]n absolute judicial refusal to inspect transcripts at the threshold of judicial inquiry sweeps too broadly . . . [and] creates incentives for concealment from the public and reviewing courts." On the facts, petitioners had not met Judge Mikva's standard. Four dissenting judges did not reach this issue.

(3) If the courts will accept an explicated administrative decision that addresses all the relevant factors and justifies the choices made, and, except in extreme circumstances, will not go behind that decision to look at actual motives, why, as Justice Marshall says, will they reject a " 'post hoc' rationalization" filed in court that offers the same justification? Notice that what he rejects are affidavits from properly authorized agency personnel, and not just an explanation offered in the agency's brief. Is his worry that the affidavits will be meaningless unless a "record" accompanies them? Or is it that a contemporaneous decision will have certain role-specific assurances of care that a later statement prepared for court use will not? (By the way, there has been some relaxation of the "no-post-hoc-rationalization" rule in recent years. See, e.g., National Wildlife Federation v. Browner, 127 F.3d 1126 (D.C.Cir.1997).

NOTES ON OVERTON PARK'S STANDARD OF REVIEW

(1) If we turn now to Overton Park's substantive standard of review, we see that Justice Marshall says that the first question is "whether the Secretary acted within the scope of his authority." To determine this, the court must ascertain whether the Secretary properly construed the limits of his authority and whether the choice he made could reasonably be said to be within those limits. The Justice then goes on to say that judicial review under the "arbitrary or capricious" standard "does not end" at this point. Why not? What is the basis for saying that judicial review goes beyond the determination that an agency has decided to do something properly within its statutory authority?

(2) How many factors are comprised in the "relevant factors" the agency has to consider? Is the set of "relevant factors" determined by some notion of what makes for good policy, or is it determined by the framework of the legal regime? And if the latter, by which framework? Consider PENSION BENEFIT GUARANTY CORP. v. LTV CORP., 496 U.S. 633 (1990), a case presented at page 472 above. PBGC is a federal agency established by the Employee Retirement Income Security Act of 1974 (ERISA) to "insure" certain pension benefits—somewhat like the FDIC's insuring of bank deposits. The lower court found that the agency, which often acts in situations in which bankruptcy and labor law are relevant, in this case had "focused inordinately on ERISA" and given too little consideration to those other areas of law. Justice Blackmun wrote for the Court that the requirement imposed on PBGC by the lower court was irreconcilable with the statute's "plain language." He continued (496 U.S. at 646):

"Even if Congress' directive to the PBGC had not been so clear, we are not entirely sure that the Court of Appeals' holding makes good sense as a general principle of administrative law. The PBGC points up problems that would arise if federal courts routinely were to require each agency to take explicit account of public policies that derive from federal statutes other than the agency's enabling act. To begin with, there are numerous federal statutes that could be said to embody countless policies. If agency action may be disturbed whenever a reviewing court is able to point to an arguably relevant statutory policy that was not explicitly considered, then a very large number of agency decisions might be open to judicial invalidation.

"The Court of Appeals' directive ... is questionable for another reason as well. Because the PBGC can claim no expertise in the labor and bankruptcy areas, it may be ill-equipped to undertake the difficult task of discerning and applying the 'policies and goals' of those fields."

In your view, does this narrowing of agency focus make for good or bad policy? Is it a result required by the nondelegation doctrine?

(3) Lastly, it is worth considering whether the Court's treatment of the federal highway statutes was itself based on a particular view of the administrative process. PETER L. STRAUSS, REVISITING *OVERTON PARK*: POLITICAL AND JUDICIAL CONTROLS OVER ADMINISTRATIVE ACTIONS AFFECTING THE COMMUNITY, 39 U.C.L.A. L.Rev. 1251, 1253–54, 1269, 1276, 1318–24 (1992): "The statute the Overton Park Court had to interpret was open to readings both of text and of legislative history that would either credit or discredit the workability of political controls. The Court chose a reading that maximized the possibilities of judicial control of agency decision through litigation, reasoning in part that only this reading could vindicate the policies that underlay the statute in question. The alternative reading would have credited the possibility of effective political controls, and the Court concluded that in the context before it these controls would inevitably fail. Overton Park thus presents us not only with the use of the courts as a surrogate for political action, but also with a declaration by the Court that only the surrogate can work. ...

" ... [I]t has been thought the courts may have a special role to play in correcting disfunctions (such as malapportionment) that impeded generally the functioning of the political system. Translating that thought to the arena of administrative law underlay the development of public interest representation arguments from the '60's forward, and also appears to explain the questioned proposition in Overton Park. ...

" ... [I]f the inquiry whether politics *could* work to control the decisions in question was an appropriate one, the negative answer the Court gave—that politics could not have worked to control those decisions—was in error. Political controls, so far as one can tell, were the only controls Congress had considered; and in the instance, they were working well. A fuller appreciation for the Overton Park controversy, whether viewed from Washington, D.C. or Memphis, Tennessee shows wide and effective engagement of a variety of political actors in the controversy. The effect of the Court's action in surrogate politics was to empower one of those actors to an extent that had not been contemplated, and that is not sustainable on any general political view. ...

" ... [T]he steady course of development in highway planning processes had been towards increasing involvement of local authorities and increasing opportunities for generating political pressure on issues of location. ... While the statutory provisions specifically at issue in Overton Park concerned park and environmental values, these provisions were only a part of a larger development. ... Where the Secretary naturally (and one could say appropriately) understood this statute in the context of the variety of new arrangements that had been made in the highway statutes and bureaucracies, the Court saw isolated diktat. The Court's opinion, strikingly, admits that the legislative history does not resolve the choice between these two approaches, and justifies its choice on its own understanding of the policy considerations involved. . . .

". . . [E]ven if we could imagine judges successfully resolving polycentric disputes, we might not often choose to have them do so; much as we may accept redistribution as a proper end of legislation, we seem unlikely to accept either that end or legislation's concomitant arbitrariness in outcome as a proper output of adjudication. . . . [J]udicial doctrine created to serve the imagined political interests of the pauper needs to be equally available in litigation brought by the prince. One need remember only that the prince is likely to have more in the way of litigating resources and, over time, more control over who becomes a judge. Inviting judges to interfere with particular outcomes in the absence of constitutional or like instructions, simply on the grounds that political processes may have been inadequate, is inviting the whirlwind.

"Both the temptations and the justifications for judges to imagine their role in political terms may seem greater when they are overseeing administrative action. Electoral controls over administrators are at best indirect. Although those controls exist in forms judges emphatically do not experience—viz., the legislative oversight hearing, or the possibility of policy-based dismissal—their very inappropriateness for judges may in itself contribute to judicial underestimation of their legitimacy and/or effectiveness and may make judges think judicial control all the more important."

Motor Vehicle Manufacturers Association of the United States, Inc. v. State Farm Mutual Automobile Insurance Co.

Supreme Court of the United States, 1983.
463 U.S. 29.

■ Justice White delivered the opinion of the Court.

The development of the automobile gave Americans unprecedented freedom to travel, but exacted a high price for enhanced mobility. Since 1929, motor vehicles have been the leading cause of accidental deaths and injuries in the United States. In 1982, 46,300 Americans died in motor vehicle accidents and hundreds of thousands more were maimed and injured. While a consensus exists that the current loss of life on our highways is unacceptably high, improving safety does not admit to easy solution. In 1966, Congress decided that at least part of the answer lies in improving the design and safety features of the vehicle itself. But much of the technology for building safer cars was undeveloped or untested. Before changes in automobile design could be mandated, the effectiveness of these changes had to be studied, their costs examined, and public acceptance considered. This task called for considerable expertise and Congress responded by enacting the National Traffic and Motor Vehicle Safety Act of 1966, 15 U.S.C. § 1381. The Act, created for the purpose of "reduc[ing] traffic accidents and deaths and injuries to persons resulting from traffic accidents," § 1381, directs the Secretary of Transportation or his delegate to issue motor vehicle safety standards that "shall be practicable, shall meet the need for motor vehicle safety, and shall be stated in objective terms." § 1392(a). In issuing these standards, the Secretary is directed to consider "relevant available motor vehicle safety data," whether the proposed standard "is reasonable, practicable and appropriate" for the particular type of motor vehicle, and the "extent to which such standards will contribute to carrying out the purposes" of the Act. § 1392(f)(1), (3), (4).[1]

The Act also authorizes judicial review under [APA § 706] of all "orders establishing, amending, or revoking a Federal motor vehicle safety standard," § 1392(b). Under this authority, we review today whether NHTSA acted arbitrarily and capriciously in revoking the requirement in Motor Vehicle Safety Standard 208 that new motor vehicles produced after September 1982 be equipped with passive restraints to protect the safety of the occupants of the vehicle in the event of a collision. . . .

I

The regulation whose rescission is at issue bears a complex and convoluted history. Over the course of approximately 60 rulemaking notices, the requirement has been imposed, amended, rescinded, reimposed, and now rescinded again.

As originally issued by the Department of Transportation in 1967, Standard 208 simply required the installation of seatbelts in all automobiles. It soon became apparent that the level of seatbelt use was too low to reduce traffic injuries to an acceptable level. The Department therefore began consideration of "passive occupant restraint systems"—devices that do not depend for their effectiveness upon any action taken by the occupant except that necessary to operate the vehicle. Two types of automatic crash protection emerged: automatic seatbelts and airbags. The automatic seatbelt is a traditional safety belt, which when fastened to the interior of the door remains attached without impeding entry or exit from the vehicle, and deploys automatically without any action on the part of the passenger. The airbag is an inflatable device concealed in the dashboard and steering column. It automatically inflates when a sensor indicates that deceleration forces from an accident have exceeded a preset minimum, then rapidly deflates to dissipate those forces. The life-saving potential of these devices was immediately recognized, and in 1977, after substantial on-the-road experience with both devices, it was estimated by NHTSA that passive restraints could prevent approximately 12,000 deaths and over 100,000 serious injuries annually.

In 1969, the Department formally proposed a standard requiring the installation of passive restraints . . . and in 1972, the agency amended the Standard to require full passive protection for all front seat occupants of vehicles manufactured after August 15, 1975. In the interim, vehicles built between August 1973 and August 1975 were to carry either passive

---

1. The Secretary's general authority to promulgate safety standards under the Act has been delegated to the Administrator of the National Highway Traffic Safety Administration (NHTSA). 49 C.F.R. § 1.50(a). . . .

restraints or lap and shoulder belts coupled with an "ignition interlock" that would prevent starting the vehicle if the belts were not connected. On review, the agency's decision to require passive restraints was found to be supported by "substantial evidence" and upheld. Chrysler Corp. v. Department of Transportation, 472 F.2d 659 (C.A.6 1972).[2]

In preparing for the upcoming model year, most car makers chose the "ignition interlock" option, a decision which was highly unpopular, and led Congress to amend the Act to prohibit a motor vehicle safety standard from requiring or permitting compliance by means of an ignition interlock or a continuous buzzer designed to indicate that safety belts were not in use. Motor Vehicle and Schoolbus Safety Amendments of 1974. The 1974 Amendments also provided that any safety standard that could be satisfied by a system other than seatbelts would have to be submitted to Congress where it could be vetoed by concurrent resolution of both Houses.

The effective date for mandatory passive restraint systems was extended for a year until August 31, 1976. But in June 1976, Secretary of Transportation William Coleman, Jr., initiated a new rulemaking on the issue. After hearing testimony and reviewing written comments, Coleman extended the optional alternatives indefinitely and suspended the passive restraint requirement.[3] Although he found passive restraints technologically and economically feasible, the Secretary based his decision on the expectation that there would be widespread public resistance to the new systems. He instead proposed a demonstration project involving up to 500,000 cars installed with passive restraints, in order to smooth the way for public acceptance of mandatory passive restraints at a later date.

Coleman's successor as Secretary of Transportation disagreed. Within months of assuming office, Secretary Brock Adams decided that the demonstration project was unnecessary. He issued a new mandatory passive restraint regulation [that] mandated the phasing in of passive restraints beginning with large cars in model year 1982 and extending to all cars by model year 1984. The two principal systems that would satisfy the Standard were airbags and passive belts; the choice of which system to install was left to the manufacturers. In Pacific Legal Foundation v. Department of Transportation, 593 F.2d 1338, cert. denied, 444 U.S. 830 (1979), the Court of Appeals upheld Modified Standard 208 as a rational, nonarbitrary regulation consistent with the agency's mandate under the Act. The Standard also survived scrutiny by Congress, which did not exercise its authority under the legislative veto provision of the 1974 Amendments.

Over the next several years, the automobile industry geared up to comply with Modified Standard 208. ... In February 1981, however,

---

2. The court did hold that the testing procedures required of passive belts did not satisfy the Safety Act's requirement that standards be "objective."

3. [Ed.] In a step unprecedented except by his own similar actions on other matters (e.g., landing rights in the United States for supersonic airliners), Secretary Coleman personally presided over these hearings. Persons familiar with the hearings were impressed by his complete preparation and command of all material. The final decision was directly his own to a degree that is becoming rare even among leading judges. When one of your editors asked ex-Secretary Coleman how other high officials could possibly find the time to perform as he had, the response was: "Fewer cocktail parties."

Secretary of Transportation Andrew Lewis reopened the rulemaking due to changed economic circumstances and, in particular, the difficulties of the automobile industry. Two months later, the agency ordered a one-year delay in the application of the Standard to large cars, extending the deadline to September 1982 and at the same time, proposed the possible rescission of the entire Standard. After receiving written comments and holding public hearings, NHTSA issued a final rule (Notice 25) that rescinded the passive restraint requirement contained in Modified Standard 208.

II

In a statement explaining the rescission, NHTSA maintained that it was no longer able to find, as it had in 1977, that the automatic restraint requirement would produce significant safety benefits. ... In 1977, the agency had assumed that airbags would be installed in 60% of all new cars and automatic seatbelts in 40%. By 1981 it became apparent that automobile manufacturers planned to install the automatic seatbelts in approximately 99% of the new cars. For this reason, the lifesaving potential of airbags would not be realized. Moreover, it now appeared that the overwhelming majority of passive belts planned to be installed by manufacturers could be detached easily and left that way permanently. Passive belts, once detached, then required "the same type of affirmative action that is the stumbling block to obtaining high usage levels of manual belts." For this reason, the agency concluded that there was no longer a basis for reliably predicting that the Standard would lead to any significant increased usage of restraints at all.

In view of the possibly minimal safety benefits, the automatic restraint requirement no longer was reasonable or practicable in the agency's view. The requirement would require approximately $1 billion to implement and the agency did not believe it would be reasonable to impose such substantial costs on manufacturers and consumers without more adequate assurance that sufficient safety benefits would accrue. In addition, NHTSA concluded that automatic restraints might have an adverse effect on the public's attitude toward safety. Given the high expense and limited benefits of detachable belts, NHTSA feared that many consumers would regard the Standard as an instance of ineffective regulation, adversely affecting the public's view of safety regulation and, in particular, "poisoning ... popular sentiment toward efforts to improve occupant restraint systems in the future." ... [The court of appeals reversed.]

III

Unlike the Court of Appeals, we do not find the appropriate scope of judicial review to be the "most troublesome question" in [this case]. Both the [1966] Act and the 1974 Amendments concerning occupant crash protection standards indicate that motor vehicle safety standards are to be promulgated under the informal rulemaking procedures of § 553 of the Administrative Procedure Act. The agency's action in promulgating such standards therefore may be set aside if found to be "arbitrary, capricious, an abuse of discretion, or otherwise not in accordance with law." 5 U.S.C. § 706(2)(A). Citizens to Preserve Overton Park v. Volpe, 401 U.S. 402, 414

(1971). We believe that the rescission or modification of an occupant-protection standard is subject to the same test. Section 103(b) of the Act states that the procedural and judicial review provisions of the Administrative Procedure Act "shall apply to all orders establishing, amending, or revoking a Federal motor vehicle safety standard," and suggests no difference in the scope of judicial review depending upon the nature of the agency's action.

Petitioner Motor Vehicle Manufacturers Association (MVMA) disagrees, contending that the rescission of an agency rule should be judged by the same standard a court would use to judge an agency's refusal to promulgate a rule in the first place—a standard petitioner believes considerably narrower than the traditional arbitrary-and-capricious test. . . . We reject this view. The Motor Vehicle Safety Act expressly equates orders "revoking" and establishing safety standards; neither that Act nor the APA suggests that revocations are to be treated as refusals to promulgate standards. . . . Moreover, the revocation of an extant regulation is substantially different than a failure to act. Revocation constitutes a reversal of the agency's former views as to the proper course. A "settled course of behavior embodies the agency's informed judgment that, by pursuing that course, it will carry out the policies committed to it by Congress. There is, then, at least a presumption that those policies will be carried out best if the settled rule is adhered to." Atchison, T. & S.F.R. Co. v. Wichita Bd. of Trade, 412 U.S. 800, 807–808 (1973). Accordingly, an agency changing its course by rescinding a rule is obligated to supply a reasoned analysis for the change beyond that which may be required when an agency does not act in the first instance.

In so holding, we fully recognize that "[r]egulatory agencies do not establish rules of conduct to last forever," American Trucking Ass'ns., Inc. v. Atchison, T. & S.F.R. Co., 387 U.S. 397, 416 (1967), and that an agency must be given ample latitude to "adapt their rules and policies to the demands of changing circumstances." Permian Basin Area Rate Cases, 390 U.S. 747, 784 (1968). But the forces of change do not always or necessarily point in the direction of deregulation. In the abstract, there is no more reason to presume that changing circumstances require the rescission of prior action, instead of a revision in or even the extension of current regulation. If Congress established a presumption from which judicial review should start, that presumption—contrary to petitioners' views—is not *against* safety regulation, but *against* changes in current policy that are not justified by the rulemaking record. While the removal of a regulation may not entail the monetary expenditures and other costs of enacting a new standard, and, accordingly, it may be easier for an agency to justify a deregulatory action, the direction in which an agency chooses to move does not alter the standard of judicial review established by law.

The Department of Transportation . . . argues that under [the "arbitrary and capricious" standard], a reviewing court may not set aside an agency rule that is rational, based on consideration of the relevant factors, and within the scope of the authority delegated to the agency by the statute. We do not disagree with this formulation.[4] The scope of review under the "arbitrary and capricious" standard is narrow and a court is not to substitute its judgment for that of the agency. Nevertheless, the agency must examine the relevant data and articulate a satisfactory explanation for its action including a "rational connection between the facts found and the choice made." Burlington Truck Lines, Inc. v. United States, 371 U.S. 156, 168. . . . Normally, an agency rule would be arbitrary and capricious if the agency has relied on factors which Congress has not intended it to consider, entirely failed to consider an important aspect of the problem, offered an explanation for its decision that runs counter to the evidence before the agency, or is so implausible that it could not be ascribed to a difference in view or the product of agency expertise. The reviewing court should not attempt itself to make up for such deficiencies; we may not supply a reasoned basis for the agency's action that the agency itself has not given. SEC v. Chenery Corp., 332 U.S. 194, 196 (1947) . . . For purposes of this case, it is also relevant that Congress required a record of the rulemaking proceedings to be compiled and submitted to a reviewing court, § 1394, and intended that agency findings under the Act would be supported by "substantial evidence on the record considered as a whole. . . ."

IV

[The course of Congressional consideration of this matter does not suggest application of any special standard of review.]

V

The ultimate question before us is whether NHTSA's rescission of the passive restraint requirement of Standard 208 was arbitrary and capricious. . . .

A

The first and most obvious reason for finding the rescission arbitrary and capricious is that NHTSA apparently gave no consideration whatever to modifying the Standard to require that airbag technology be utilized. Standard 208 sought to achieve automatic crash protection by requiring automobile manufacturers to install either of two passive restraint devices: airbags or automatic seatbelts. There was no suggestion in the long rulemaking process that led to Standard 208 that if only one of these options were feasible, no passive restraint standard should be promulgated. Indeed, the agency's original proposed standard contemplated the installation of inflatable restraints in all cars. Automatic belts were added [in 1971] as a means of complying with the Standard because they were believed to be as effective as airbags in achieving the goal of occupant crash protection. . . . At that time, the passive belt approved by the agency could not be detached. Only later, at a manufacturer's behest, did the agency approve of the detachability feature—and only after assurances that the

---

4. The Department of Transportation suggests that the arbitrary-and-capricious standard requires no more than the minimum rationality a statute must bear in order to withstand analysis under the Due Process Clause. We do not view as equivalent the presumption of constitutionality afforded legislation drafted by Congress and the presumption of regularity afforded an agency in fulfilling its statutory mandate.

feature would not compromise the safety benefits of the restraint. Although it was then foreseen that 60% of the new cars would contain airbags and 40% would have automatic seatbelts, the ratio between the two was not significant as long as the passive belt would also assure greater passenger safety.

The agency has now determined that the detachable automatic belts will not attain anticipated safety benefits because so many individuals will detach the mechanism. Even if this conclusion were acceptable in its entirety, . . . standing alone it would not justify any more than an amendment of Standard 208 to disallow compliance by means of the one technology which will not provide effective passenger protection. . . . Given the effectiveness ascribed to airbag technology by the agency, the mandate of the Act to achieve traffic safety would suggest that the logical response to the faults of detachable seatbelts would be to require the installation of airbags. At the very least this alternative way of achieving the objectives of the Act should have been addressed and adequate reasons given for its abandonment. But the agency not only did not require compliance through airbags, it also did not even consider the possibility in its 1981 rulemaking. Not one sentence of its rulemaking statement discusses the airbags-only option. . . . [W]hat we said in Burlington Truck Lines, Inc. v. United States, 371 U.S., at 167, is apropos here: "There are no findings and no analysis here to justify the choice made, no indication of the basis on which the [agency] exercised its expert discretion. We are not prepared to and the Administrative Procedure Act will not permit us to accept such . . . practice. . . . Expert discretion is the lifeblood of the administrative process, but 'unless we make the requirements for administrative action strict and demanding, *expertise*, the strength of modern government, can become a monster which rules with no practical limits on its discretion.' " We have frequently reiterated that an agency must cogently explain why it has exercised its discretion in a given manner, and we reaffirm this principle again today.

Agency must cogently explain

The automobile industry has opted for the passive belt over the airbag, but surely it is not enough that the regulated industry has eschewed a given safety device. For nearly a decade, the automobile industry waged the regulatory equivalent of war against the airbag and lost—the inflatable restraint was proven sufficiently effective. Now the automobile industry has decided to employ a seatbelt system which will not meet the safety objectives of Standard 208. This hardly constitutes cause to revoke the Standard itself. Indeed, the Act was necessary because the industry was not sufficiently responsive to safety concerns. . . .

. . . [P]etitioners recite a number of difficulties that they believe would be posed by a mandatory airbag standard. These range from questions concerning the installation of airbags in small cars to that of adverse public reaction. But these are not the agency's reasons for rejecting a mandatory airbag standard. Not having discussed the possibility, the agency submitted no reasons at all. . . .

Petitioners also invoke our decision in Vermont Yankee Nuclear Power Corp. v. NRDC, 435 U.S. 519 (1978) as though it were a talisman under which any agency decision is by definition unimpeachable. Specifically, it is submitted that to require an agency to consider an airbags-only alternative is, in essence, to dictate to the agency the procedures it is to follow. Petitioners both misread Vermont Yankee and misconstrue the nature of the remand that is in order. In Vermont Yankee, we held that a court may not impose additional procedural requirements upon an agency. We do not require today any specific procedures which NHTSA must follow. Nor do we broadly require an agency to consider all policy alternatives in reaching decision. It is true that a rulemaking "cannot be found wanting simply because the agency failed to include every alternative device and thought conceivable by the mind of man . . . regardless of how uncommon or unknown that alternative may have been. . . ." 435 U.S., at 551. But the airbag is more than a policy alternative to the passive restraint Standard; it is a technological alternative within the ambit of the existing Standard. We hold only that given the judgment made in 1977 that airbags are an effective and cost-beneficial life-saving technology, the mandatory passive restraint rule may not be abandoned without any consideration whatsoever of an airbags-only requirement.

B

Although the issue is closer, we also find that the agency was too quick to dismiss the safety benefits of automatic seatbelts. NHTSA's critical finding was that, in light of the industry's plans to install readily detachable passive belts, it could not reliably predict "even a 5 percentage point increase as the minimum level of expected usage increase." The Court of Appeals rejected this finding because there is "not one iota" of evidence that Modified Standard 208 will fail to increase nationwide seatbelt use by at least 13 percentage points, the level of increased usage necessary for the Standard to justify its cost. Given the lack of probative evidence, the court held that "only a well-justified refusal to seek more evidence could render rescission non-arbitrary." 680 F.2d, at 232.

Petitioners object to this conclusion. In their view, "substantial uncertainty" that a regulation will accomplish its intended purpose is sufficient reason, without more, to rescind a regulation. We agree with petitioners that just as an agency reasonably may decline to issue a safety standard if it is uncertain about its efficacy, an agency may also revoke a standard on the basis of serious uncertainties if supported by the record and reasonably explained. Rescission of the passive restraint requirement would not be arbitrary and capricious simply because there was no evidence in direct support of the agency's conclusion. It is not infrequent that the available data does not settle a regulatory issue and the agency must then exercise its judgment in moving from the facts and probabilities on the record to a policy conclusion. Recognizing that policymaking in a complex society must account for uncertainty, however, does not imply that it is sufficient for an agency to merely recite the terms "substantial uncertainty" as a justification for its actions. . . . [T]he agency must explain the evidence which is available, and must offer a "rational connection between the facts found and the choice made." Burlington Truck Lines, Inc. v. United States, supra, 371 U.S. at 168. Generally, one aspect of that explanation would be a justification for rescinding the regulation before engaging in a search for further evidence. . . .

We start with the accepted ground that if used, seatbelts unquestionably would save many thousands of lives and would prevent tens of thousands of crippling injuries. Unlike recent regulatory decisions we have reviewed, the safety benefits of wearing seatbelts are not in doubt, and it is not challenged that were those benefits to accrue, the monetary costs of implementing the standard would be easily justified. We move next to the fact that there is no direct evidence in support of the agency's finding that detachable automatic belts cannot be predicted to yield a substantial increase in usage. The empirical evidence on the record, consisting of surveys of drivers of automobiles equipped with passive belts, reveals more than a doubling of the usage rate experienced with manual belts.[5] Much of the agency's rulemaking statement—and much of the controversy in this case—centers on the conclusions that should be drawn from these studies. The agency maintained that the doubling of seatbelt usage in these studies could not be extrapolated to an across-the-board mandatory standard because the passive seatbelts were guarded by ignition interlocks and purchasers of the tested cars are somewhat atypical.[6] Respondents insist these studies demonstrate that Modified Standard 208 will substantially increase seatbelt usage. We believe that it is within the agency's discretion to pass upon the generalizability of these field studies. This is precisely the type of issue which rests within the expertise of NHTSA, and upon which a reviewing court must be most hesitant to intrude.

But accepting the agency's view of the field tests on passive restraints indicates only that there is no reliable real-world experience that usage rates will substantially increase. To be sure, NHTSA opines that "it cannot reliably predict even a 5 percentage point increase as the minimum level of expected increased usage." But this and other statements that passive belts will not yield substantial increases in seatbelt usage apparently take no account of the critical difference between detachable automatic belts and current manual belts. A detached passive belt does require an affirmative act to reconnect it, but—unlike a manual seatbelt—the passive belt, once reattached, will continue to function automatically unless again disconnected. Thus, inertia—a factor which the agency's own studies have found significant in explaining the current low usage rates for seatbelts[7]—works

---

5. Between 1975 and 1980, Volkswagen sold approximately 350,000 Rabbits equipped with detachable passive seatbelts that were guarded by an ignition interlock. General Motors sold 8,000 1978 and 1979 Chevettes with a similar system, but eliminated the ignition interlock on the 13,000 Chevettes sold in 1980. NHTSA found that belt usage in the Rabbits averaged 34% for manual belts and 84% for passive belts. Regulatory Impact Analysis (RIA) at IV–52, App 108. For the 1978–1979 Chevettes, NHTSA calculated 34% usages for manual belts and 72% for passive belts. On 1980 Chevettes, the agency found these figures to be 31% for manual belts and 70% for passive belts.

6. "NHTSA believes that the usage of automatic belts in Rabbits and Chevettes would have been substantially lower if the automatic belts in those cars were not equipped with a use-inducing device inhibiting detachment." Notice 25, 46 Fed.Reg. at 53422 (1981). [The "atypicality" was also that small car owners used seatbelts more than others did, and that most owners with passive belts in these cars had voluntarily paid extra for them.]

7. NHTSA commissioned a number of surveys of public attitudes in an effort to better understand why people were not using manual belts and to determine how they would react to passive restraints. The surveys reveal that while 20% to 40% of the public is

in *favor* of, not *against*, use of the protective device. Since 20% to 50% of motorists currently wear seatbelts on some occasions, there would seem to be grounds to believe that seatbelt use by occasional users will be substantially increased by the detachable passive belts. Whether this is in fact the case is a matter for the agency to decide, but it must bring its expertise to bear on the question. . . .

The agency also failed to articulate a basis for not requiring nondetachable belts under Standard 208. It is argued that the concern of the agency with the easy detachability of the currently favored design would be readily solved by a continuous passive belt, which allows the occupant to "spool out" the belt and create the necessary slack for easy extrication from the vehicle. The agency did not separately consider the continuous belt option, but treated it together with the ignition interlock device in a category it titled "Option of Adoption of Use–Compelling Features." The agency was concerned that use-compelling devices would "complicate extrication of [an] occupant from his or her car." "[T]o require that passive belts contain use-compelling features," the agency observed, "could be counterproductive [given] . . . widespread, latent and irrational fear in many members of the public that they could be trapped by the seatbelt after a crash." In addition, based on the experience with the ignition interlock, the agency feared that use-compelling features might trigger adverse public reaction.

By failing to analyze the continuous seatbelts in its own right, the agency has failed to offer the rational connection between facts and judgment required to pass muster under the arbitrary-and-capricious standard. . . . NHTSA did not suggest that the emergency release mechanisms used in nondetachable belts are any less effective for emergency egress than the buckle release system used in detachable belts. In 1978, when General Motors obtained the agency's approval to install a continuous passive belt, it assured the agency that nondetachable belts with spool releases were as safe as detachable belts with buckle releases. NHTSA was satisfied that this belt design assured easy extricability: "[t]he agency does not believe that the use of [such] release mechanisms will cause serious occupant egress problems. . . ." While the agency is entitled to change its view on the acceptability of continuous passive belts, it is obligated to explain its reasons for doing so.

The agency also failed to offer any explanation why a continuous passive belt would engender the same adverse public reaction as the ignition interlock, and, as the Court of Appeals concluded, "every indication in the record points the other way." We see no basis for equating the two devices: the continuous belt, unlike the ignition interlock, does not interfere with the operation of the vehicle. More importantly, it is the agency's responsibility, not this Court's, to explain its decision.

opposed to wearing manual belts, the larger proportion of the population does not wear belts because they forgot or found manual belts inconvenient or bothersome. In another survey, 38% of the surveyed group responded that they would welcome automatic belts, and 25% would "tolerate" them. NHTSA did not comment upon these attitude surveys in its explanation accompanying the rescission of the passive restraint requirement.

VI

"An agency's view of what is in the public interest may change, either with or without a change in circumstances. But an agency changing its course must supply a reasoned analysis. ..." Greater Boston Television Corp. v. FCC, 444 F.2d 841, 852 (1970), cert. denied, 403 U.S. 923 (1971). We do not accept all of the reasoning of the Court of Appeals but we do conclude that the agency has failed to supply the requisite "reasoned analysis" in this case. Accordingly, we vacate the judgment of the Court of Appeals and remand the case to that court with directions to remand the matter to the NHTSA for further consideration consistent with this opinion.

So ordered.

■ JUSTICE REHNQUIST, with whom the CHIEF JUSTICE, JUSTICE POWELL, and JUSTICE O'CONNOR join, concurring in part and dissenting in part.

I join parts, I, II, III, IV, and V–A of the Court's opinion. In particular, I agree that, since the airbag and continuous spool automatic seatbelt were explicitly approved in the Standard the agency was rescinding, the agency should explain why it declined to leave those requirements intact. In this case, the agency gave no explanation at all. ...

I do not believe, however, that NHTSA's view of detachable automatic seatbelts was arbitrary and capricious. ... [T]he agency's explanation, while by no means a model, is adequate. The agency acknowledged that there would probably be some increase in belt usage, but concluded that the increase would be small and not worth the cost of mandatory detachable automatic belts. ...

The agency's changed view of the standard seems to be related to the election of a new President of a different political party. It is readily apparent that the responsible members of one administration may consider public resistance and uncertainties to be more important than do their counterparts in a previous administration. A change in administration brought about by the people casting their votes is a perfectly reasonable basis for an executive agency's reappraisal of the costs and benefits of its programs and regulations. As long as the agency remains within the bounds established by Congress,[8] it is entitled to assess administrative records and evaluate priorities in light of the philosophy of the administration.

NOTES ON THE SCOPE AND SIGNIFICANCE OF STATE FARM

(1) One year after State Farm, NHTSA issued a rule requiring passive restraints unless by April 1989, two-thirds of the nation's population were covered by state laws that both required seatbelts and met other criteria

---

8. Of course, a new administration may not refuse to enforce laws of which it does not approve, or to ignore statutory standards in carrying out its regulatory functions. But in this case, as the Court correctly concludes, ... Congress has not required the agency to require passive restraints.

including educational efforts and enforcement. Most states enacted seat belt laws—but most of these laws did not satisfy the other criteria. Thus, a federal passive restraint requirement finally became effective in 1989. Most automakers chose to meet the requirement with airbags, and in 1991 Congress made the airbags requirement permanent, effective in 1996. Pub.L.No. 102–240, § 2508.

(2) Petitioners reliance on the Vermont Yankee case, (which is set out at page 498 above,) can be more easily understood in light of the flow of judicial review decisions in the decade or so before the principal case. In the oft-cited case (indeed, cited in the very decision we just read) of GREATER BOSTON TELEVISION CORP. v. FCC, 444 F.2d 841 (D.C.Cir.1970), cert. denied, 403 U.S. 923 (1971), Judge Leventhal said in 1970 that "[t]he function of the court is to assure that the agency has given reasoned consideration to all the material facts and issues." In spelling out this idea, he explained, 444 F.2d at 851:

> Its supervisory function calls on the court to intervene not merely in case of procedural inadequacies, or bypassing of the mandate in the legislative charter, but more broadly if the court becomes aware, especially from a combination of danger signals, that the agency has not really taken a "hard look" at the salient problems, and has not genuinely engaged in reasoned decision-making. If the agency has not shirked this fundamental task, however, the court exercises restraint and affirms the agency's action even though the court would on its own account have made different findings or adopted different standards.

In the succeeding years, this set of ideas was taken up by other judges, in the D.C. Circuit and elsewhere, to frame their process of review, especially of informal rulemaking. "As originally articulated," Judge Wald wrote in 1980, "the words 'hard look' described the agency's responsibility and not the court's. However, the phrase subsequently evolved to connote the rigorous standard of judicial review applied to increasingly utilized informal rulemaking proceedings or to other decisions made upon less than a full trial-type record." National Lime Assoc. v. EPA, 627 F.2d 416, 451 n. 126 (D.C.Cir.1980).

As can be seen from Judge Leventhal's statement, the "hard look" approach did not necessarily distinguish possible procedural requirements from possible substantive ones, and indeed terms like "quasi-procedural, quasi-substantive" were sometimes used to describe various items. Different judges gave different emphases, some more to the procedural side, some to the substantive. The structure of the problem can be seen in the Nova Scotia Food Products case, decided in 1977 and already set out at page 524 above. There, one of Judge Gurfein's objections was that the agency should have explained why it rejected a salient alternative urged on it in the comment process. Was this requirement to address alternatives based on § 553(c), requiring the agency to "incorporate in the rules adopted a concise general statement of their basis and purpose"? Was it based on § 706(2)(A), telling the court to "set aside agency action ... found to be ... arbitrary, capricious ... or otherwise not in accordance with law"? Or was it based on neither of these, and justified only if the reviewing courts had the power to create a common law of judicial review?

This last is what the State Farm petitioners hoped the Supreme Court would conclude. Then Vermont Yankee—which emphatically denied the existence of such a power—would be the death of "hard look." (Insofar as the Overton Park case also had "hard look" elements, petitioners also hoped the Court would narrow Overton Park in light of Vermont Yankee.)

(3) MERRICK B. GARLAND, DEREGULATION AND JUDICIAL REVIEW, 98 Harv. L. Rev. 505, 545 (1985): "The Court could hardly have been more explicit in approving the judicial imposition of quasi-procedural requirements. Reciting a veritable litany of such requirements, Justice White held that an agency must 'articulate a satisfactory explanation for its action,' rely on its own and not appellate counsel's '*post hoc* rationalizations,' 'supply a reasoned analysis' justifying any reversal of course, 'examine the relevant data,' 'consider[ ] . . . the relevant factors,' and consider 'alternative way[s] of achieving . . . objectives.' In response to the Solicitor General's claim that such requirements violate the spirit of Vermont Yankee, the Court replied with words as strong as those used in Vermont Yankee itself: 'Vermont Yankee,' said the Court, is not 'a talisman under which any agency decision is by definition unimpeachable.' The requirements of explanation and consideration of alternatives do not 'impose additional procedural requirements upon an agency.'

". . . Despite the Court's quasi-procedural rhetoric, it would be a mistake to interpret State Farm as applicable to that dimension of the hard look doctrine alone. Indeed, the Court rejected the Solicitor General's view of the scope of substantive review as firmly as it rejected his attack on quasi-procedural requirements. To his argument that the arbitrary and capricious standard mandates only that an agency exercise the minimum rationality required of a legislature by the due process clause, the Court replied, 'We do not view as equivalent the presumption of constitutionality afforded legislation drafted by Congress and the presumption of regularity afforded an agency in fulfilling its statutory mandate.' Rather, the Court held, an agency must articulate a 'satisfactory' explanation for its actions that does not 'run[ ] counter to the evidence before the agency' and that demonstrates a '"rational connection between the facts found and the choice made." ' "

(4) The Government's attempt to equate "arbitrary and capricious" review of agency action with "rationality" review of legislation (to which the previous note refers) can be traced back to PACIFIC STATES BOX & BASKET CO. V. WHITE, 296 U.S. 176 (1935). This case concerned a rule of the Oregon Division of Plant Industry fixing official standards for containers used to package raspberries and strawberries—standards which could not be met by the fruit baskets petitioner made. The circumstances suggested, but no finding stated, that the Oregon board might have found that use of a single container type (among the 34 available) would enhance consumer protection against short measures. Acknowledging that no such finding would be required of a legislature, petitioner urged that findings were constitutionally requisite for the actions of administrators wielding delegated powers. A unanimous court, speaking through Justice Brandeis, found that that contention was "without support in authority or reason, and rests upon misconception. Every exertion of the police power, either by the legislature

or by an administrative body, is an exercise of delegated power. . . . Where the regulation is within the scope of authority legally delegated, the presumption of the existence of facts justifying its specific exercise attaches alike to statutes . . . and to orders of administrative bodies. . . . [T]he statute did not require special findings; doubtless because the regulation authorized was general legislation, not an administrative order in the nature of a judgment directed against an individual concern." 296 U.S. at 185–86.

(5) CHRISTOPHER F. EDLEY, JR., ADMINISTRATIVE LAW: RETHINKING JUDICIAL CONTROL OF BUREAUCRACY 63–65 (1990): "The Supreme Court analyzed NHTSA's action strictly in terms of the paradigm of expertise, applying a fairly rigorous, 'adequate consideration' brand of arbitrary and capricious review. The majority concluded that NHTSA erred by failing to analyze obvious and important alternatives to total rescission of the rule, including a requirement that manufacturers use nondetachable automatic seatbelts rather than detachable ones, or that they use airbags. Thus, science and implicit norms about good science were the Court's touchstones for evaluating the adequacy of the agency's decision making process as described in NHTSA's statement of basis and purpose in the rule making record.

"In contrast, Justice Rehnquist, joined by three others in partial dissent, noted the undeniable role of politics in the decision: NHTSA's action was most easily understandable as the result of the 1980 election and a consequent change in regulatory philosophy, and such shifts are entitled to deference. . . .

"By contrast, nowhere does the majority refer to an election, to regulatory philosophy, or to the possibility that politics might have played any role, positive or negative, in NHTSA's decision.

"If politics means anything short of crass interest group giveaways, then politics was plainly involved in the rescission of the passive restraints regulation. Not only had candidate Reagan spoken out about deregulation generally, he had specifically discussed the auto industry and even the passive restraints regulation. Presidential appointees throughout the government were thoroughly committed to wholesale deregulation. It is totally implausible to suggest that NHTSA's evaluation of the scientific evidence and consideration of the regulatory alternatives were pursued within the . . . paradigm of neutral, objective expertise. The regulatory result was all but ordained by the election results. The misidentification of the paradigm as science rather than politics gives the Court's decision an odd quality. If the strong role I posit for politics *was* permissible and indeed cause for deference (emphasizing the positive attributes of that paradigm), as Rehnquist suggested in State Farm, then failure of the agency and the Court to identify the political element in the agency's action may have resulted in too little judicial deference. If instead the strong role of politics was *not* permissible (emphasizing the negative), then perhaps an even more interventionist posture would have been appropriate, whether through the doctrinal content of the Court's reasoning or through the specificity of the remand order."

In a review of Professor Edley's book, Judge Stephen Williams responded:

In State Farm ... the agency had at the outset of the rulemaking process revealed a political judgment in the least appetizing form imaginable. Far from stressing the financial burden that passive restraints would impose on auto buyers, it explained that it was reopening the issue because of "the difficulties of the automobile industry." This gaffe might well have undercut any effort to find in the statute a power to reject a safety device on the grounds of standard cost-benefit analysis, and, for whatever reason, the agency never made such an effort (at least so far as the public record shows). Rather, it appeared to adopt a substantive standard tilting strongly toward regulation, under which it would require a proposed safety device if it offered any significant benefits (at least if they were not overwhelmed by costs). It then found that passive restraints did not measure up even to this criterion. Given those agency choices, the vulnerable point of the decision was its science, and there the challengers attacked. Thus, the Court did not "identify" a paradigm; the agency and litigants did.

The Roots of Deference, 100 Yale L.J. 1103, 1107–08 (1991).

(6) Particularly in scientific and technological matters, "uncertainty" is a major element in administrative judgment. Events conspire to demand action before knowledge is complete. How ought uncertainty be managed by agencies, and how ought their acknowledgement of it be treated by courts on review? An exemplary case is BALTIMORE GAS & ELECTRIC CO. v. NRC, 462 U.S. 87 (1983), the second appearance of the Vermont Yankee dispute in the Supreme Court. Here, the Court unanimously upheld the NRC's decision that licensing of nuclear power plants could proceed in the face of high uncertainty, fully acknowledged, about the environmental effects of nuclear waste disposal.

The NRC had responded to Vermont Yankee I as follows: Licensing boards dealing with particular applications could take evidence about the health and other effects of nuclear plant operation, but were to assume that waste fuel could be adequately disposed of without harm to the environment. The Commission acknowledged the remote possibility that water might enter a waste depository, resulting in release of radioactive materials; but it predicted that bedded-salt repositories would be satisfactory and it found the evidence "tentative but favorable" that such sites would be found. Further, the NRC found any undue optimism in those assumptions offset by related assumptions that were probably conservative in nature. It concluded: "On the individual reactor licensing level, where the proceedings deal with fuel cycle issues only peripherally, the Commission sees no advantage in having licensing boards repeatedly weigh for themselves the effect of uncertainties on the selection of fuel cycle impacts for use in cost-benefit balancing. This is a generic question properly dealt with in the rulemaking. ... The Commission concludes, having noted that uncertainties exist, that for the limited purpose of the fuel cycle rule it is reasonable to base impacts on the assumption which the Commission believes the probabilities favor, i.e., that bedded-salt repository sites can be found which will provide effective isolation of radioactive waste from the biosphere." 44 Fed.Reg. 45362, 45369 (1979).

A divided court of appeals, per Judge Bazelon, found the NRC's treatment both arbitrary and violative of NEPA. NRDC v. NRC, 685 F.2d 459 (D.C.Cir.1982). If the NRC's "zero-release assumption" was viewed as a finding of fact, it was arbitrary because admittedly surrounded with uncertainty. If, instead, the assumption was viewed as a "decisionmaking device" permitting the Commission to use generic rulemaking to evaluate environmental impacts common to all licensing decisions, the Commission was arbitrarily failing to take account of environmentally relevant factors. Dissenting, Judge Wilkey said that "the effect of the majority's analysis is to state that it is error for the Commission to proceed in the face of admitted uncertainties."

A unanimous Supreme Court, speaking through Justice O'Connor, reversed (462 U.S. at 98–105): "[N]o one suggests that the uncertainties are trivial or the potential effects insignificant if time proves the zero-release assumption to have been seriously wrong. After confronting the issue, though, the Commission has determined that the uncertainties concerning the development of nuclear waste storage facilities are not sufficient to affect the outcome of any individual licensing board.

"It is clear that the Commission, in making this determination, has made the careful consideration and disclosure required by NEPA. The sheer volume of proceedings before the Commission is impressive. Of far greater importance, the Commission's Statement of Consideration announcing the final ... rule shows that it has digested this mass of material and disclosed all substantial risks. ... Our only task is to determine whether the Commission has considered the relevant factors and articulated a rational connection between the facts found and the choice made."

NOTES ON THE WISDOM (OR NOT) OF THE STATE FARM APPROACH

(1) "It is a great tonic," wrote William Pedersen, former Deputy General Counsel of the EPA, "to discover that even if a regulation can be slipped or wrestled through various layers of internal or external review [inside the bureaucracy] without significant change, the final and most prestigious reviewing forum of all—a circuit court of appeals—will inquire into the minute details of methodology, data sufficiency and test procedure and will send the regulations back if these are lacking. The effect of such judicial opinions within the agency reaches beyond those who were concerned with the specific regulations reviewed. They serve as a precedent for future rulewriters and give those who care about well-documented and well-reasoned decisionmaking a lever with which to move those who do not." Formal Records and Informal Rulemaking, 85 Yale L.J. 38, 60 (1975).

(2) R. Shep Melnick, Regulation and the Courts: The Case of the Clean Air Act 294–98 (1983):

"Most writers who have evaluated the courts' performance in reviewing national air quality standards have praised the judiciary for improving the EPA's technical analysis and expanding public participation. ... [But] many jurists and scholars have warned that the adjudicatory process is not capable of explaining complex scientific issues to generalist judges. However, the number of occasions on which judges have misread scientific evidence is extremely small. By overturning only those decisions based on glaring error, the courts have managed to avoid becoming enmeshed in disputes between experts. Judges appear to recognize their own limitations when reviewing clinical, epidemiological, and toxicological studies.

"What the adjudicatory process has not seemed to convey to key federal judges, though, is the fact that health effects thresholds[1] do not exist for most pollutants. While most scientists agree on this and congressional committees have conceded that the health effects threshold is little more than a myth, the courts continue to insist upon a 'health only' approach that rests on the threshold assumption. . . . [B]y insisting upon a 'health only' approach, the courts have helped reduce national standards to the status of long-term targets. . . . If the courts have had an unfortunate effect on standard setting, it is not because they have misinterpreted scientific evidence, but rather because they have been guided by an idea—a judicially protected, quasi-constitutional 'right' to health—that is incompatible with the medical evidence on the effects of pollution. No amount of documentation, no number of 'hard looks,' no corps of science clerks will solve the courts' problem until judges reexamine the views on public health and the regulatory process that guide their laborious review of air quality standards."

(3) JERRY L. MASHAW AND DAVID L. HARFST, THE STRUGGLE FOR AUTO SAFETY (1990): This vivid exploration of NHTSA's shift from enacting rules to overseeing vehicle recalls chronicles what the authors deem to be "the virtual abandonment of its safety mission":

"From today's vantage point, the optimism of 1966 seems rather quaint. . . . Of some fifty general safety regulations adopted under the [Act], forty-five (90 percent) were issued prior to 1974. Not one of the fifty was first issued after 1976. By contrast, motor vehicle recalls have increased from about fifteen million motor vehicles between 1966 and 1970 . . . to over thirty-nine million vehicles between 1976 and 1980. Indeed, during the period 1972–1977, the agency supervised the recall of more American automobiles than were sold new. . . . These changes began long before the Reagan Administration. . . . Something happened at NHTSA. . . .

"The most authoritative studies of the causes of automobile accidents indicate that, at most, 13 percent involve some mechanical failure [and most of those] result from inadequate maintenance, not from defective design or construction. . . . [Moreover, only about] 50 percent of owners respond to recall notices. . . . By contrast the best, though very imperfect, studies of the effects of NHTSA's modest vehicle standards suggest an overall improvement in vehicle safety of around 30 percent. If true, that is on the order of fifteen thousand lives saved and one hundred thousand serious injuries prevented per year."

The most persuasive explanation of the shift from rules to recalls, Mashaw and Harfst argue, is the impact of the "legal culture," of which judicial review is a large, but not the only, part:

---

1. [Ed.] That is, levels above 0% beneath which it can confidently be expected that human health will not be affected.

"The primary demands of the legal culture of regulation—that regulatory policy be subject to the rule of law through judicial review and procedurally open to affected interests—have been much in evidence throughout the history of federal motor vehicle safety regulation. Indeed, as we have seen, these demands have been mutually reinforcing. Judicial review has been 'proceduralized' in order to accord with our post-New Deal ideology of judicial policy restraint. And by focusing on 'process rationality,' the judiciary has leveraged both the strategic and the legal positions of regulatory participants. Not only must the agency listen with care, but participants may use their access to provide multiple grounds for later legal reversal of the agency's choices.

"[First NHTSA Administrator Dr.] William Haddon's reluctance to proceed without bulletproof, scientific evidence may have been born of scientific fussiness, but it was prescient nevertheless. [Chief Counsel] Frank Berndt's desire to shape policy as an adjunct to litigation strategy may have proceeded from the myopia of a traditionalist lawyer, but the legal environment ratified his instincts. Not only did his litigation successes exalt his bureaucratic position, but legal failures cast out his enemies as well. Both the agency's product—recalls in place of rules—and its internal organization came to reflect the rewards and sanctions that that legal culture, via judicial review, bestowed.

"Ironically, given their explicit posture of limited intervention, the courts become crucial actors in shaping the regulatory environment. The legal culture thereby scripts the roles of the other actors in the drama of regulation. In their own decisions, moreover, the courts tend to 'act out,' or at least be guided by, the premises of the general legal culture rather than the more specific purposes or commitments of a particular regulatory regime. Judicial review is by 'generalist' judges, not by special administrative courts. Viewing particular statutory systems through generalist legal lenses constructs the image of legitimate regulation.

" 'Rationality' understood from the perspective of the systems analytic premises of the 1966 Motor Vehicle Safety Act, for example, surely does not counsel the judicial acceptance of NHTSA's recall activity. Recalls make sense, if at all, only against the backdrop of the general remedial assumptions of products liability law. Nor can a technology-forcing, rulemaking enterprise possibly withstand a rationality review that evaluates technological reasonableness by reference to the legal culture's conventional standard of reasonable conduct. Where the adequacy of product design is at issue, the law generally gauges reasonableness in terms of current practice. It is just such a standard that generalist judges have imported into the review of regulatory action at NHTSA. But as we have also seen, the 'state of the art' justifies the status quo, not technology forcing.

"The result of judicial requirements for comprehensive rationality has been a general suppression of the use of rules. In this regard, the experience at the Consumer Product Safety Commission and the Occupational Safety and Health Administration is similar to NHTSA's. Even an agency like the Environmental Protection Agency, which can hardly act at all except by rule, has found its activities both halted and skewed by judicial review. NHTSA's experience is not aberrational.

"This is not all there is to the story. Politics, personality, external events, and many other factors also shaped regulatory output and agency structure. What may not have been so obvious, however, is the way that some of the most important of these influences also reflect basic assumptions of the legal culture and interact with judicial review to shape regulatory policymaking. The legal culture has subtle and complicated as well as direct and dramatic impact.

"Notice, for example, the submerged yet powerful message in the Supreme Court's decision in State Farm, that the political directions of a particular administration are inadequate to justify regulatory policy. The agency must carry out the statute that Congress enacted. That, again, is one of the legal culture's firmest commitments. But looking at the act's language and legislative history ... what was Congress saying? ... Given the legislative processes of 1966 and 1974, and the differences between the Congress as a whole and the Congress in committees, and the conflicts and ambiguities in congressional positions in all forms, whose or what will was the agency meant to follow?

"The fundamental separation of powers that prevents the courts from insisting on congressional clarity and specificity and that keeps the President from meddling in congressional lawmaking ... leaves the regulators legally and politically exposed. They have a political job without a political mandate, and they are subject to judicial review for 'legality.' The basic assumptions of the rule of law and the separation of powers in our legal culture virtually make 'administrative policymaking' an oxymoron. Regulation must proceed legally, therefore, under the cover of a fiction—that regulation is only the application of law to fact, the carrying out of statutory instructions. ...

"It is true that although the President ordinarily may not dictate domestic law, the Chief Executive has policy influence, often verging on control, through appointments, removals, and coordination to 'see that the laws are faithfully executed.' Yet, sensitive to constitutional convention, this last power (or, perhaps responsibility) tends to be exercised through structural and procedural devices designed to nudge administrators in the direction of an administration's overall views, not through attempts to mandate policy. The most conspicuous executive monitoring device in the late 1980s, for example, is OMB review of major proposed regulations through the medium of 'comments' on required regulatory-impact analyses.

"Peculiar notions about the separation of powers thus produce not only a proceduralized rationality review of rules in the courts, but also 'proceduralized' executive oversight. The resulting multiple tiers of process can have dramatic effects on regulatory output. Put in terms of NHTSA's shift from rules to recalls, for example, even if courts gave the factual predicate for a recall the same extensive examination that they gave NHTSA's rules, the recall process would be substantially more expeditious than rulemaking. Recall activity does not have to pass through the gauntlet of a regulatory flexibility analysis or OMB review."

(4) AFL-CIO v. OSHA, 965 F.2d 962 (11th Cir.1992), is a striking example of the intersection (or should one say "collision"?) between an agency's efforts to get its job done and judicial review. In one rulemaking, set out in

a statement of 652 pages, OSHA set permissible exposure limits (or PELs: the maximum amounts of contaminants in air to which workers may be exposed over a given time period) for 428 toxic substances. Although the court found the substances had little in common, it upheld use of a single rulemaking. But it remanded because "with rare exceptions, the individual substance discussions ... are virtually devoid of reasons for setting those individual standards. In most cases, OSHA cited a few studies and then established a PEL without explaining why the studies mandated the particular PEL chosen.

" 'While our deference to the agency is at a peak for its choices among scientific predictions, we must still look for *some* articulation of reasons for those choices.' [citing a 1989 D.C. Circuit decision.] ... The only explanation given by OSHA in the final rule for setting its standard where a significant risk of material health impairment remains was that the time and resource constraints of attempting to promulgate an air contaminants standard of this magnitude prevented detailed analysis of these substances. [OSHA, noting that since its creation it had issued only 24 substance-specific and three generic health standards, argued that 'using past approaches ... it would take decades to review currently used chemicals' let alone keep up with new ones.]

"The agency further claims that no quantification was required because OSHA's final standards 'fall [ ] within a zone of reasonableness.' However, without any quantification or any explanation, this court cannot determine what that 'zone of reasonableness' is or if these standards fall within it. ... OSHA's overall approach to this rulemaking is so flawed that we must vacate the whole revised [standard].

"We have no doubt that the agency acted with the best of intentions. It may well be, as OSHA claims, that this was the only practical way of accomplishing a much needed revision of the existing standards and of making major strides towards improving worker health and safety. ... Unfortunately, OSHA's approach to this rulemaking is not consistent with the requirements of the OSH Act."

Earlier in the opinion, the court had noted that the OSH Act, Section 6(f), provides that "the determinations of the Secretary shall be conclusive if supported by substantial evidence in the record considered as a whole." Therefore, said the court, "we must take a 'harder look' at OSHA's action than we would if we were reviewing the action under the more deferential arbitrary and capricious standard ..." See the notes following the ADAP-SO Case, p. 971 above.

Compare TROY CORP. v. BROWNER, 120 F.3d 277 (D.C.Cir.1997). There the EPA, in a single proceeding, added 286 chemicals to the list of toxic chemicals whose release into the environment must be reported in some detail to the EPA and subsequently to the public in what is known as the Toxic Release Inventory. The Court of Appeals upheld the EPA for all but two of the chemicals involved. 120 F.3d at 284: "The AFL–CIO v. OSHA decision upon which appellants rely does not suggest a contrary result. As always, of course, the questions of sufficiency of an agency's stated reasons under the arbitrary and capricious review of the APA is fact-specific and record-specific. That OSHA had not given sufficient reasons under a different statute applying a different (substantial evidence) standard of review on a different factual record would not compel a similar result on our part even if that case were a binding precedential decision from our own circuit, which, of course, it is not. More specifically, from the Eleventh Circuit's decision it appears that OSHA's failure to give reasons in that case was systemic and purposeful. Here ... the EPA undertook an on-the-record review of the data as to each candidate chemical. While we might describe the record of some of the chemical-by-chemical reviews as 'brief' or 'sketchy,' that would not necessarily be pejorative. That a standard, such as the statutory standard in this case, is strict, does not require that the evidence to meet it be voluminous, and especially does not required that it be voluminously recorded." Even at that, the court reviewed each of the chemical-by-chemical listings petitioners complained of, and remanded two to the agency. One fell afoul of the consistency norm, because differently treated from an apparently similar situation in which EPA in 1994 had decided not to list the chemical. In the other, EPA appeared in its published documents to rely on two studies of the chemical conducted in the Soviet Union in the 1960s; they were, by the EPA's own standards, poorly documented. EPA's claim to have looked at a third, better study did not appear in the rulemaking record. "We hold that the EPA's reliance on tests that were largely undocumented violates the agency's Guidelines and evidences arbitrary and capricious agency action."

(5) The switch from rulemaking to recalls at NHTSA chronicled by Mashaw and Harfst, the inability of OSHA to accomplish the rulemaking it needs to do which is suggested by AFL v. OSHA, and perhaps even the effort the EPA had to expend to successfully justify listing chemicals for an informational purpose, are illustrations of what some scholars have suggested is a general trend toward "ossification" of the federal rulemaking process. RICHARD J. PIERCE, JR., SEVEN WAYS TO DEOSSIFY AGENCY RULEMAKING, 47 Admin.L.Rev. 59, 93–95 (1995), which evaluates several possible solutions, had this to say about substantive judicial review: "Judicially induced rulemaking ossification is a serious problem that courts can and should reduce. The problem can be addressed effectively through many doctrinal routes, however, and it is neither necessary nor desirable to sacrifice other important goals of the legal system in the process of deossifying rulemaking. ...

"[The proposal to give] interpretative rules and policy statements the same binding effect as legislative rules presents a close[] case. This potential doctrinal solution would be more effective because it would eliminate the primary source of judicially induced ossification of rulemaking. It is hard to imagine how a reviewing court could enforce the duty to engage in reasoned decisionmaking against an agency in the absence of the kind of record produced by the notice and comment procedure. Agencies that act by rule still would be affected by the risk of judicial rejection of a rule based on disingenuous judicial attribution to Congress of an intent Congress never had, but consistent application of Chevron[2] would render that risk manageable. The cost of this doctrinal solution is loss of the advantages of the notice and comment procedure to institutions other than reviewing

---

2.   [Ed.] Chevron is the next principal case in this book.

courts. I find that cost intolerably high, partly because I believe the notice and comment procedure provides significant benefits to agencies, to the agencies' politically accountable superiors in both branches, and to the public, and partly because I believe that rulemaking can be deossified without paying such a high price.

"Reducing the scope of the duty to engage in reasoned decisionmaking also presents a close question, but one of a different type. This doctrinal solution would be only partially effective. It might reduce the deterrent effect by 50 percent, for instance, because agencies would still be affected by the need to comply with the now narrower duty to engage in reasoned decisionmaking and by the still significant risk of judicial rejection of a rule based on a conclusion that the agency failed to comply with that duty in some respect. Reducing the scope of the duty leaves unaffected the unpredictable intensity of judicial review of the adequacy of an agency's reasoning with respect to an issue that is within the scope of the duty. The potential cost of the partial solution would appear in the form of an increased tendency for agencies to use narrow decisional frameworks, e.g., to ignore or to discount the potential unintended adverse effects of a rule that lie outside the agency's primary focus of attention in the rulemaking or outside the agency's statutory responsibilities. I cannot quantify these costs with confidence, but I fear they could be large.

"Of course, we need not confine our research for potential solutions to those suggested in recent judicial decisions. Tom McGarity has urged adoption of a conceptually appealing solution.[3] He argues that judges should apply the duty to engage in reasoned decisionmaking the way a professor grades a pass-fail paper that treats a complicated subject the professor knows little about. His analogy is compelling, but I lack confidence that circuit courts actually would apply such a standard if the Supreme Court announced it, and I doubt that the Supreme Court would be able to enforce such a standard against reluctant circuit court judges. It is simply too easy for judges to say they are applying such a standard while they continue instead to evidence the seemingly unlimited hubris that has long been apparent in many judicial decisions reviewing complicated regulatory rules that raise issues beyond the understanding of most judges.

"McGarity's proposed solution could be restated in a functionally equivalent form that the Court could enforce more effectively. The Court could reverse State Farm and abolish the judicially enforceable duty to engage in reasoned decisionmaking. The Court could instruct circuit courts to return to the prior method of applying the arbitrary and capricious test to agency rules that was replaced by the duty to engage in reasoned decisionmaking. That method is illustrated by the Court's opinion in Pacific States Box & Basket Co. v. White. The Court rejected petitioner's claim that a rule was arbitrary and capricious because the agency's lawyer was able to identify some plausible public purpose that the rule might further. This solution would impose some costs in the form of loss of the benefits attributable to the judicially enforced duty to engage in reasoned

---

3. Thomas   O.   McGarity,   Some Thoughts on "Deossifying" the Rulemaking Process, 1992 Duke L.J. 1385, 1453.

decisionmaking. As a skeptic with respect to the magnitude of the benefits often attributed to that duty, I would be willing to pay that price to deossify rulemaking. In such a reconstituted legal environment, reviewing courts would retain the power and the duty to review agency rules to determine whether they violate clear statutory or constitutional constraints on agency discretion at the behest of anyone adversely affected by the rule."

(6) Professor Pierce's article prompted an alternative solution in PAUL R. VERKUIL, COMMENT: RULEMAKING OSSIFICATION—A MODEST PROPOSAL, 47 Admin. L. Rev. 453, 457–58 (1995): ". . . Pierce correctly identifies the social costs of rulemaking ossification and argues for restrained judicial review of the reasoning process as a means of reviving informal rulemaking. . . . The problem is trust in the undemocratic decider, the agency. The lack of trust by the Congress and the public in the bureaucracy makes it difficult to see how restrained review would be accepted. Is there then a solution to the problem? I believe there is. . . . The idea is to have major rules—those that are subject to ossification—come back to Congress on a fast-track basis to be enacted into statutes.

"This process should create not more than 100–200 such statutory actions per year. These rules can be sent back to Congress after they have been promulgated by the agencies. This means that informal rulemaking procedures (involving the public) and OMB oversight (involving the President) already will have occurred. The fast-track process would require both houses of Congress to introduce bills automatically; not refer them to committees; nor table or filibuster; and to vote up or down within a specified time. Although the process is unusually constraining, it has been utilized most recently with success in approving decisions of the Base Closing Commission.

"The benefits of this approach are several. It utilizes the openness, inclusiveness, and rationality of the rulemaking process to ensure high-quality results; it takes the courts out of the substantive review process for the problematic category of rules; it forces Congress to be accountable and confront difficult risk assessment choices; it involves the President in the process through presentment (and earlier through OMB review); and it restores Pacific States Box rationality review to the resulting legislative enactments. Voila, Pierce wins, and so do we.

"What are the costs? It asks a lot of an institution mired in politics and inefficiency to do its legislative duty under the Constitution. Presumably some rules will succeed and some will not, but that is true with judicial review as well. . . . Yet Congress can reform itself. The base closing format has worked. If politics derails a rule, then that is the democratic process at work. . . .

(7) Another view: MARK SEIDENFELD, DEMYSTIFYING DEOSSIFICATION: RETHINKING RECENT PROPOSALS TO MODIFY JUDICIAL REVIEW OR NOTICE AND COMMENT RULEMAKING, 75 Tex. L. Rev. 483, 499–502 (1997):

"I am skeptical . . . whether a more deferential attitude toward agency decisionmaking will relieve the problems created by hard look review without forfeiting the benefits that flow from such review.

"First, calls for a new metaphor, such as 'pass/fail' review, do not take into account judges' motivations in establishing administrative law doctrine. According to a leading model, judges tend to balance their ability to dictate outcomes consistent with their own values against the impact that deviating from existing doctrine will have on their judicial reputations and pride in their judicial abilities. Increasing the indeterminacy of administrative law doctrine allows judges to pursue their preferred outcomes without paying a reputational price. If that is so, then the replacement of one fuzzy metaphor with another that sounds more deferential is unlikely to have any significant impact on the outcome of challenges to particular rules. In the end, calls for pass/fail review, without any operational guidelines constraining how courts should decide what passes and what fails are unlikely to alter the actual operation of judicial review.

"Second, raising the level of deference to agency rulemaking may not reduce an agency's incentives to engage in excessive data collection and analysis. Simply making review more 'agency friendly' will not tell the agency how to perform its analyses in a manner sufficient to pass judicial review. Moreover, without delving into the details of a rulemaking record and questioning the agency's rationale in light of data and arguments submitted by challengers of the rule, most judges lack the expertise with the substantive areas of agency regulation to know whether the agency, in adopting the rule, has reached a reasonable decision. Hence, even under a more deferential standard of review, courts will have to consult the record and ensure that it is consistent with the agency's reasoning. This in turn sends a message to the agency that its chances of success on review increase if it collects additional data and performs more analysis. Thus, significant incentives remain for an agency to overtax its scarce regulatory resources.

"Third, easing of judicial review may have a detrimental impact on the agency deliberative process. For example, courts could dramatically reduce the uncertainty created by judicial review simply by eliminating meaningful review; they could affirm any rule that was not wholly irrational. That would still leave congressional and presidential review to ensure against unwise agency rulemaking. But both congressional and presidential review increase the propensity for agency rules to benefit groups with narrow interests. By demanding that agencies publicly justify their rules, however, judicial review can discourage the adoption and interpretation of rules preferred by special interest groups. Increasing the likelihood that a rule will be upheld by relaxing the requirements that an agency explain its decision to a court might, by the same token, increase the proportion of rules driven by pressure from special interest groups or an agency agenda that is at odds with the general public's desire for regulation."

(Professor Seidenfeld's own proposals are set out at 75 Tex. L. Rev. 503–24.)

(8) In an effort to test some of the empirical assumptions of the ossification debate, Prof. William Jordan looked at all of the rulemaking proceedings remanded by the D. C. Circuit in the decade from 1985 to 1995, 61 cases in all, and tried to determine what happened to the agency's regulatory effort after the Circuit had spoken. WILLIAM S. JORDAN, OSSIFICATION REVISITED: DOES

ARBITRARY AND CAPRICIOUS REVIEW SIGNIFICANTLY INTERFERE WITH AGENCY ABILITY TO ACHIEVE REGULATORY GOALS THROUGH INFORMAL RULEMAKING, 94 Northwestern L. Rev. 393 (2000). He found that in a very high percentage of the cases (about 80%) agencies were able to keep their programs going: because the court itself had used the option of remanding for further proceedings without vacating the rule in the meantime; because what was called for was better explanation, and once that was offered the rule survived any further judicial proceedings; because what was wrong with the rule was sufficiently minor that a work-around was possible without disrupting the agency's overall program; or, in the rare case, because Congress intervened. Moreover, the delays involved in carrying on were not that great—on average, within two years.

"If the prospect of judicial review deters agencies from informal rulemaking because they fear they will not succeed, the results of this research suggest that there is little basis for this concern. In light of these figures, the image of agency failure is inaccurate. For example, Professor Mashaw and Harfst's study of NHTSA's early experience, which apparently deterred the agency from relying upon informal rulemaking, appears to be an isolated oddity in this consistent history of agency success and prompt recovery. Indeed, perhaps NHTSA's experience is not just an oddity, but an anachronism. NHTSA's major defeats came in the early days of hard look review. It is hardly surprising that agencies might have suffered significant setbacks as courts were beginning to demand more than they had before. There was undoubtedly a learning curve before agencies generally became used to the new demands and able to provide the necessary support for their rulemaking initiatives. The results of this research suggest that agencies have moved well along on the curve from the 1970s." Id. at 441.

Of course, there are costs associated both with the greater efforts needed to meet expected judicial demands and with having to revise plans to accommodate judicial objections after litigation. Thus, Professor Jordan suggests, the real question in the "ossification" debate is not whether the administrative state will grind to a halt, but more simply whether the benefits of hard look review are worth the opportunity costs it imposes in a world in which agency resources are both inherently and politically limited.

Chevron, U.S.A., Inc. v. Natural Resources Defense Council, Inc.

Supreme Court of the United States, 1984.
467 U.S. 837.

■ JUSTICE STEVENS delivered the opinion of the Court.

In the Clean Air Act Amendments of 1977, Pub.L. 95–95, 91 Stat. 685, Congress enacted certain requirements applicable to States that had not achieved the national air quality standards established by the Environmental Protection Agency (EPA) pursuant to earlier legislation. The amended Clean Air Act required these "nonattainment" States to establish a permit program regulating "new or modified major stationary sources" of air pollution. Generally, a permit may not be issued for a new or modified major stationary source unless several stringent conditions are met. The

EPA regulation promulgated to implement this permit requirement allows a State to adopt a plantwide definition of the term "stationary source." Under this definition, an existing plant that contains several pollution-emitting devices may install or modify one piece of equipment without meeting the permit conditions if the alteration will not increase the total emissions from the plant. The question presented by this case is whether EPA's decision to allow States to treat all of the pollution-emitting devices within the same industrial grouping as though they were encased within a single "bubble" is based on a reasonable construction of the statutory term "stationary source."

I

The EPA regulations containing the plantwide definition of the term stationary source were promulgated on October 14, 1981. 46 Fed.Reg. 50766. Respondents filed a timely petition for review in the United States Court of Appeals for the District of Columbia Circuit pursuant to 42 U.S.C. § 7607(b)(1). The Court of Appeals set aside the regulations. Natural Resources Defense Council, Inc. v. Gorsuch, 685 F.2d 718 (1982).

The court observed that the relevant part of the amended Clean Air Act "does not explicitly define what Congress envisioned as a 'stationary source,' to which the permit program . . . should apply," and further stated that the precise issue was not "squarely addressed in the legislative history." In light of its conclusion that the legislative history bearing on the question was "at best contradictory," it reasoned that "the purposes of the nonattainment program should guide our decision here."[1] Based on two of its precedents concerning the applicability of the bubble concept to certain Clean Air Act programs, the court stated that the bubble concept was "mandatory" in programs designed merely to maintain existing air quality, but held that it was "inappropriate" in programs enacted to improve air quality. Since the purpose of the permit program—its "raison d'etre," in the court's view—was to improve air quality, the court held that the bubble concept was inapplicable in this case under its prior precedents. It therefore set aside the regulations embodying the bubble concept as contrary to law. We . . . now reverse.

The basic legal error of the Court of Appeals was to adopt a static judicial definition of the term stationary source when it had decided that Congress itself had not commanded that definition. . . .

II

When a court reviews an agency's construction of the statute which it administers, it is confronted with two questions. First, always, is the question whether Congress has directly spoken to the precise question at issue. If the intent of Congress is clear, that is the end of the matter; for the court, as well as the agency, must give effect to the unambiguously

---

1. The court remarked in this regard: "We regret, of course, that Congress did not advert specifically to the bubble concept's application to various Clean Air Act programs, and note that a further clarifying statutory directive would facilitate the work of the agency and of the court in their endeavors to serve the legislators' will."

expressed intent of Congress.[2] If, however, the court determines Congress has not directly addressed the precise question at issue, the court does not simply impose its own construction on the statute, as would be necessary in the absence of an administrative interpretation. Rather, if the statute is silent or ambiguous with respect to the specific issue, the question for the court is whether the agency's answer is based on a permissible construction of the statute.[3]

Permissible Standard

"The power of an administrative agency to administer a congressionally created ... program necessarily requires the formulation of policy and the making of rules to fill any gap left, implicitly or explicitly, by Congress." Morton v. Ruiz, 415 U.S. 199, 231 (1974). If Congress has explicitly left a gap for the agency to fill, there is an express delegation of authority to the agency to elucidate a specific provision of the statute by regulation. Such legislative regulations are given controlling weight unless they are arbitrary, capricious, or manifestly contrary to the statute. Sometimes the legislative delegation to an agency on a particular question is implicit rather than explicit. In such a case, a court may not substitute its own construction of a statutory provision for a reasonable interpretation made by the administrator of an agency.

We have long recognized that considerable weight should be accorded to an executive department's construction of a statutory scheme it is entrusted to administer, and the principle of deference to administrative interpretations

> has been consistently followed by this Court whenever decision as to the meaning or reach of a statute has involved reconciling conflicting policies, and a full understanding of the force of the statutory policy in the given situation has depended upon more than ordinary knowledge respecting the matters subjected to agency regulations. See e.g., Labor Board v. Hearst Publications, Inc., 322 U.S. 111; Securities & Exchange Comm'n v. Chenery Corp., 332 U.S. 194. ... If this choice represents a reasonable accommodation of conflicting policies that were committed to the agency's care by the statute, we should not disturb it unless it appears from the statute or its legislative history that the accommodation is not one that Congress would have sanctioned.

United States v. Shimer, 367 U.S. 374, 382, 383 (1961).

In light of these well-settled principles it is clear that the Court of Appeals misconceived the nature of its role in reviewing the regulations at issue. Once it determined, after its own examination of the legislation, that Congress did not actually have an intent regarding the applicability of the

---

2. The judiciary is the final authority on issues of statutory construction and must reject administrative constructions which are contrary to clear congressional intent. If a court, employing traditional tools of statutory construction, ascertains that Congress had an intention on the precise question at issue, that intention is the law and must be given effect.

3. The court need not conclude that the agency construction was the only one it permissibly could have adopted to uphold the construction, or even the reading the court would have reached if the question initially had arisen in a judicial proceeding.

bubble concept to the permit program, the question before it was not whether in its view the concept is "inappropriate" in the general context of a program designed to improve air quality, but whether the Administrator's view that it is appropriate in the context of this particular program is a reasonable one. Based on the examination of the legislation and its history which follows, we agree with the Court of Appeals that Congress did not have a specific intention on the applicability of the bubble concept in these cases, and conclude that the EPA's use of that concept here is a reasonable policy choice for the agency to make.

[The Court reviewed the legislative history at length, remarking that the issue before it concerned "one phrase" from a "small portion" of "a lengthy, detailed, technical, complex, and comprehensive response to a major social issue," the Clean Air Act Amendments of 1977, that in turn was only part of a much larger statutory scheme under EPA's administration. "The legislative history of the portion of the 1977 Amendments dealing with nonattainment areas," it remarked, "does not contain any specific comment on the 'bubble concept' or the question whether a plantwide definition of a stationary source is permissible under the permit program. It does, however, plainly disclose that in the permit program Congress sought to accommodate the conflict between the economic interest in permitting capital improvements to continue and the environmental interest in improving air quality."]

VI

[Turning to the administrative history of implementation, the Court noted that EPA had at first proposed interpretations like that under challenge.]

In August 1980, however, the EPA adopted a regulation that, in essence, applied the basic reasoning of the Court of Appeals in this case. The EPA took particular note of the two then-recent Court of Appeals decisions, which had created the bright-line rule that the bubble concept should be employed in a program designed to maintain air quality but not in one designed to enhance air quality. Relying heavily on those cases, EPA adopted a dual definition of "source" for nonattainment areas that required a permit whenever a change in either the entire plant, or one of its components, would result in a significant increase in emissions even if the increase was completely offset by reductions elsewhere in the plant. ...

In 1981 a new administration took office and initiated a "Government-wide reexamination of regulatory burdens and complexities." 46 Fed.Reg. 16281. In the context of that review, the EPA reevaluated the various arguments that had been advanced in connection with the proper definition of the term "source" and concluded that the term should be given the same definition in both nonattainment areas and PSD [preventing significant deterioration] areas.

In explaining its conclusion, the EPA first noted that the definitional issue was not squarely addressed in either the statute or its legislative history and therefore that the issue involved an agency "judgment as how to best carry out the Act." It then set forth several reasons for concluding that the plantwide definition was more appropriate. ... These conclusions were expressed in a proposed rulemaking in August 1981 that was formally promulgated in October.

VII

[The Court turned to arguments offered by the respondents to show that the statute had a clear meaning.]

Statutory Language

We are not persuaded that parsing of general terms in the text of the statute will reveal an actual intent of Congress. We know full well that this language is not dispositive; the terms are overlapping and the language is not precisely directed to the question of the applicability of a given term in the context of a larger operation. To the extent any congressional "intent" can be discerned from this language, it would appear that the listing of overlapping, illustrative terms was intended to enlarge, rather than to confine, the scope of the agency's power to regulate particular sources in order to effectuate the policies of the Act.

Legislative History

Based on our examination of the legislative history, we agree with the Court of Appeals that it is unilluminating. The general remarks pointed to by respondents "were obviously not made with this narrow issue in mind and they cannot be said to demonstrate a Congressional desire ..." Jewell Ridge Coal Corp. v. Mine Workers, 325 U.S. 161, 168–169 (1945).... We find that the legislative history as a whole is silent on the precise issue before us. It is, however, consistent with the view that the EPA should have broad discretion in implementing the policies of the 1977 Amendments.

More importantly, that history plainly identifies the policy concerns that motivated the enactment; the plantwide definition is fully consistent with one of those concerns—the allowance of reasonable economic growth—and, whether or not we believe it most effectively implements the other, we must recognize that the EPA has advanced a reasonable explanation for its conclusion that the regulations serve the environmental objectives as well. Indeed, its reasoning is supported by the public record developed in the rulemaking process, as well as by certain private studies.[4]

Our review of the EPA's varying interpretations of the word "source"—both before and after the 1977 Amendments—convince us that the agency primarily responsible for administering this important legislation has consistently interpreted it flexibly—not in a sterile textual vacuum, but in the context of implementing policy decisions in a technical and complex arena. The fact that the agency has from time to time changed its

---

4. "Economists have proposed that economic incentives be substituted for the cumbersome administrative-legal framework. The objective is to make the profit and cost incentives that work so well in the marketplace work for pollution control. ... [The 'bubble' or 'netting' concept] is a first attempt in this direction. By giving a plant manager flexibility to find the places and processes within a plant that control emissions most cheaply, pollution control can be achieved more quickly and cheaply." L. Lave & G. Omenn, Cleaning the Air: Reforming the Clean Air Act 28 (1981) (footnote omitted).

interpretation of the term source does not, as respondents argue, lead us to conclude that no deference should be accorded the agency's interpretation of the statute. An initial agency interpretation is not instantly carved in stone. On the contrary, the agency, to engage in informed rulemaking, must consider varying interpretations and the wisdom of its policy on a continuing basis. Moreover, the fact that the agency has adopted different definitions in different contexts adds force to the argument that the definition itself is flexible, particularly since Congress has never indicated any disapproval of a flexible reading of the statute.

Significantly, it was not the agency in 1980, but rather the Court of Appeals that read the statute inflexibly to command a plantwide definition for programs designed to maintain clean air and to forbid such a definition for programs designed to improve air quality. The distinction the court drew may well be a sensible one, but our labored review of the problem has surely disclosed that it is not a distinction that Congress ever articulated itself, or one that the EPA found in the statute before the courts began to review the legislative work product. We conclude that it was the Court of Appeals, rather than Congress or any of the decisionmakers who are authorized by Congress to administer this legislation, that was primarily responsible for the 1980 position taken by the agency.

Policy

The arguments over policy that are advanced in the parties' briefs create the impression that respondents are now waging in a judicial forum a specific policy battle which they ultimately lost in the agency and in the 32 jurisdictions opting for the bubble concept, but one which was never waged in the Congress. Such policy arguments are more properly addressed to legislators or administrators, not to judges.

In this case, the Administrator's interpretation represents a reasonable accommodation of manifestly competing interests and is entitled to deference: the regulatory scheme is technical and complex, the agency considered the matter in a detailed and reasoned fashion, and the decision involves reconciling conflicting policies. Congress intended to accommodate both interests, but did not do so itself on the level of specificity presented by this case. Perhaps that body consciously desired the Administrator to strike the balance at this level, thinking that those with great expertise and charged with responsibility for administering the provision would be in a better position to do so; perhaps it simply did not consider the question at this level; and perhaps Congress was unable to forge a coalition on either side of the question, and those on each side decided to take their chances with the scheme devised by the agency. For judicial purposes, it matters not which of these things occurred.

Judges are not experts in the field, and are not part of either political branch of the Government. Courts must, in some cases, reconcile competing political interests, but not on the basis of the judges' personal policy preferences. In contrast, an agency to which Congress has delegated policy-making responsibilities may, within the limits of that delegation, properly rely upon the incumbent administration's views of wise policy to inform its judgments. While agencies are not directly accountable to the people, the

Chief Executive is, and it is entirely appropriate for this political branch of the Government to make such policy choices—resolving the competing interests which Congress itself either inadvertently did not resolve, or intentionally left to be resolved by the agency charged with the administration of the statute in light of everyday realities.

When a challenge to an agency construction of a statutory provision, fairly conceptualized, really centers on the wisdom of the agency's policy, rather than whether it is a reasonable choice within a gap left open by Congress, the challenge must fail. In such a case, federal judges—who have no constituency—have a duty to respect legitimate policy choices made by those who do. The responsibilities for assessing the wisdom of such policy choices and resolving the struggle between competing views of the public interest are not judicial ones: "Our Constitution vests such responsibilities in the political branches." TVA v. Hill, 437 U.S. 153, 195 (1978).

We hold that the EPA's definition of the term "source" is a permissible construction of the statute which seeks to accommodate progress in reducing air pollution with economic growth. "The Regulations which the Administrator has adopted provide what the agency could allowably view as . . . [an] effective reconciliation of these twofold ends. . . ." United States v. Shimer, 367 U.S., at 383.

The judgment of the Court of Appeals is reversed.

■ JUSTICE MARSHALL and JUSTICE REHNQUIST did not participate in the consideration or decision of these cases.

■ JUSTICE O'CONNOR did not participate in the decision of these cases.

NOTES ON THE NOTORIETY OF CHEVRON

(1) Soundbites on Chevron's importance:

(a) "[T]he decision has established itself as one of the very few defining cases in the last twenty years of American public law." Cass R. Sunstein, Law and Administration After *Chevron*, 90 Colum. L. Rev. 2071, 2075 (1990).

(b) "Now for you agency case lawyers. Chevron is the password. In every case involving statutory interpretation, think Chevron." Judge Patricia Wald, speaking on "Advocacy from the Viewpoint of an Appellate Judge," Fourth Annual Appellate Advocacy Program, Washington D.C., Oct. 28, 1994, at 9.

(c) "The loss of forests necessary to make the paper to print all of the articles written on the proper standard of review in interpreting statutes following [Chevron] might well have justified requiring the Supreme Court to issue an environmental impact statement along with the opinion." Jerry L. Mashaw, Improving the Environment of Agency Rulemaking: An Essay on Management, Games, and Accountability, 57 Law & Contemp. Probs. 185, 229 n.116 (1994).

(2) Searches of Westlaw, Federal Database CTA (i.e., U.S. Circuit Courts of Appeals decisions), conducted on September 22, 2002, revealed the following:

"401 U.S. 402" (i.e., Overton Park, decided in 1971): 1458 citing cases;

"463 U.S. 29" (i.e., State Farm, decided in 1983): 819 citing cases;

"467 U.S. 837" (i.e., Chevron, decided in 1984): 3287 citing cases.

(A rather closer competitor to Chevron is Universal Camera, the leading "substantial evidence" case (see p. 940 above). It had 3204 citing cases—but it was decided in 1951!)

(3) Compare Robert V. Percival, Environmental Law in the Supreme Court: Highlights from the Marshall Papers, 23 Envtl.L.Rep. 10606, 10613 (1993): "One surprise is the absence of any evidence in the written record indicating that the Justices realized the full implications of their landmark administrative law decision in ... Chevron. There is no comment in the written exchanges among the Justices that reflects any appreciation of the major change in administrative law the decision effected. ... [T]he Marshall papers indicate that the decision was reached without any significant debate over Justice Stevens' draft opinion, which was initially circulated among the Justices on June 11, 1984. On June 12, Justices Rehnquist and Marshall circulated notes indicating without explanation that they were recusing themselves from the case. [Justice O'Connor also recused herself because a family estate owned stock in one of the parties. By June 18, all others had joined the opinion.] The only comment in the memos concerning the substance of [the] opinion is the statement by Chief Justice Burger that 'I am now persuaded you have the correct answer to this case.' "

NOTES ON THE MEANING OF CHEVRON

(1) How does the Chevron test work? Perhaps its most important feature, considered strictly as a matter of doctrinal analysis, is that the test has two steps. This provokes two important questions: First, how do we know whether we are in step one or step two? Second, what is the difference in approach between the two steps? Let us begin with the first of these.

To use Justice Stevens' formulations, we are in step one "if the intent of Congress is clear," while we are in step two "if the statute is silent or ambiguous." Clarity or ambiguity is the test. Of course, all language is ambiguous with regard to something, but Stevens definitely states that the test is ambiguity (or not) with regard to "the precise question at issue." And in a footnote he indicates that the way to determine whether Congress had, or didn't have, a clear intent, is by using "traditional tools of statutory construction."

This formulation makes it rather plain that Chevron deference is not based on there being an inextricable mixture of fact and law that the agency especially "knows" about. As one commentator has said: "The distinction is not between issues of law and fact, which does not seem to have much to do with Chevron. The distinction is between issues of law and policy, which is at the core of Chevron." Michael Herz, Deference Running Riot: Separating Interpretation and Lawmaking under Chevron, 6 Admin. L. J. 187, 223 (1992). Even if this claim is a bit overstated, its basic implication—that under Chevron, agencies get to make decisions that from a traditional law/fact/mixed question analysis are only about questions of law—obviously raises questions of legitimacy. (Of these questions, more later; for the moment we are looking simply at the question of how to employ the doctrine.)

If ambiguity means ambiguity as to the meaning of the statute itself (which seems to be the case), much turns on how one thinks judges should ascribe meaning to statutory language. Thus, many of the subsequent controversies regarding Chevron-in-practice have been, in effect, contests between different theories of statutory construction—between, for example, those who think that "legislative history" is useful and those who do not.

Turning now to the question of the differences in operation between the two steps of the test, Stevens' formulation of the question under the second step is "whether the agency's answer is based on a permissible construction of the statute." Is this just a broader statement of the outer limits of what the statute will permit, requiring thinking similar to that done in determining Congress' intent for step one? Some have read it that way—so that the whole Chevron test, in effect, is whether the agency's interpretation of the statute is "reasonable." Or, at the other extreme, does this language signal the kind of thinking that lies behind application of the "arbitrary and capricious" standard? Some have read it that way, too—so that in effect Chevron and State Farm merge at step two.

It would doubtless be a mistake to think that all these issues were in Justice Stevens' mind when he wrote Chevron, or that we would find definite answers to them if only we read his opinion with exquisite care. The questions have been, and remain, much alive. In the notes that follow, some possible analyses will be suggested. But each of the three later principal cases in this Chapter were written in Chevron's shadow, and so they, too, are authorities on how the Chevron test is understood at the present time.

(2) NATIONAL CREDIT UNION ADMIN. V. FIRST NAT. BANK, 522 U.S. 479 (1998), is a good recent example of Chevron "step one" in action. Section 109 of the Federal Credit Union Act stipulates that "Federal credit union membership shall be limited to groups having a common bond or association, or to groups within a well-defined neighborhood, community, or rural district." Beginning in 1982, the National Credit Union Administration allowed credit unions to be composed of more than one employer group, each having its own "common bond." In the instant case, NCUA approved amendments to the charter of AT & T Family Federal Credit Union, which had expanded to include not only employees of AT & T, but also employees of Duke Power, American Tobacco, Lee Apparel, and so forth; five commercial banks and the American Bankers Association brought suit. (Regarding the standing issues in the case, see page 1163 within.)

THOMAS, J., for the Court, 522 U.S. at 499–503:

"Turning to the merits, we must judge the permissibility of the NCUA's current interpretation of § 109 by employing the analysis set forth in Chevron U.S.A. Inc. v. Natural Resources Defense Council, Inc., 467 U.S.

837 (1984). Under that analysis, we first ask whether Congress has 'directly spoken to the precise question at issue.' ... Because we conclude that Congress has made it clear that the same common bond of occupation must unite each member of an occupationally defined federal credit union, we hold that the NCUA's contrary interpretation is impermissible under the first step of Chevron.

"As noted, § 109 requires that '[f]ederal credit union membership shall be limited to groups having a common bond of occupation or association, or to groups within a well-defined neighborhood, community, or rural district.' Respondents [i.e., the banks] contend that because § 109 uses the article 'a'— i.e., 'one'—in conjunction with the noun 'common bond,' the 'natural reading' of § 109 is that all members in an occupationally defined federal union must be united by one common bond. Petitioners [i.e., the NCUA and the credit union] reply that because § 109 uses the plural noun 'groups,' it permits multiple groups, each with its own common bond, to constitute a federal credit union.

"Like the Court of Appeals, we do not think that either of these contentions, standing alone, is conclusive. The article 'a' could be thought to convey merely that one bond must unite only the members of each group in a multiple-group credit union, and not all of the members in the credit union taken together. Similarly, the plural word 'groups' could be thought to refer not merely to multiple groups in a particular credit union, but rather to every single 'group' that forms a distinct credit union under the NCUA. Nonetheless, as the Court of Appeals correctly recognized, additional considerations compel the conclusion that the same common bond of occupation must unite all of the members of an occupationally defined federal credit union.

"First, the NCUA's current interpretation makes the phrase 'common bond' surplusage when applied to a federal credit union made up of multiple unrelated employer groups, because each 'group' in such a credit union already has its own 'common bond.' To use the facts of this case, the employees of AT & T and the employees of the American Tobacco Company each already had a 'common bond' before being joined together as members of ATTF. ... If the phrase 'common bond' is to be given any meaning when these employees are joined together, a different 'common bond'—one extending to each and every employee considered together—must be found to unite them. Such a 'common bond' exists when employees of different subsidiaries of the same company are joined together in a federal credit union; it does not exist, however, when employees of unrelated companies are so joined. ...

"Second, the NCUA's interpretation violates the established canon of construction that similar language contained within the same section of a statute must be accorded a consistent meaning. Section 109 consists of two parallel clauses: Federal credit union membership is limited 'to groups having a common bond of occupation or association, *or* to groups within a well-defined neighborhood, community, or rural district' (emphasis added). The NCUA concedes that even though the second limitation permits geographically defined credit unions to have as members more than one 'group,' all of the groups must come from the same 'neighborhood, community, or rural district.' The reason that the NCUA has never interpreted, and does not contend that it could interpret, the geographical limitation to allow a credit union to be composed of members from an unlimited number of unrelated geographic units, is that to do so would render the geographical limitation meaningless. Under established principles of statutory interpretation, we must interpret the occupational limitation in the same way.

"... Reading the two parallel clauses in the same way, we must conclude that, just as all members of a geographically defined federal credit union must be drawn from the same 'neighborhood, community or rural district,' members of an occupationally defined federal credit union must be united by the same 'common bond of occupation.'

"Finally, by its terms, § 109 requires that membership in federal credit unions 'shall be limited.' The NCUA's interpretation—under which a common bond of occupation must unite only the members of each unrelated employer group—has the potential to read these words out of the statute entirely. The NCUA has not contested that, under its current interpretation, it would be permissible to grant a charter to a conglomerate credit union whose members would include the employees of every company in the United States. Nor can it: Each company's employees would be a 'group,' and each such 'group' would have its own 'common bond of occupation.' Section 109, however, cannot be considered a *limitation* on credit union membership if at the same time it permits such a *limitless* result.

"For the foregoing reasons, we conclude that the NCUA's current interpretation of § 109 is contrary to the unambiguously expressed intent of Congress and is thus impermissible under the first step of Chevron."[1]

(3) Are the two parts of the Chevron test different in kind or only degree? Judge Williams, 30 F.3d at 193, on the denial of rehearing in SWEET HOME CHAPTER v. BABBITT, 17 F.3d 1463 (D.C.Cir.1994), reversed 515 U.S. 687 (1995):

> The government faults the panel for failing to specify whether the regulation's excess of statutory authority failed under the first or second "step" of the analysis set forth in Chevron and in a more general way for failing to give the agency the deference that is its due under Chevron. Because the court in determining whether Congress "unambiguously expressed" its intent on the issue is to employ all the "traditional tools of statutory construction," INS v. Cardoza–Fonseca, the factors involved in the first "step" are also pertinent to whether an agency's interpretation is "reasonable." Thus the exact point where an agency interpretation falls down may be unclear. (Indeed, the Chevron Court itself never specified which step it was applying at any point in its analysis.)

Compare Judge Silberman in the same case (30 F.3d at 194–95):

> I quite agree with the panel that "the factors involved in the first 'step' are also pertinent to whether an agency's interpretation is

---

1. We have no need to consider § 109's legislative history, which, as both courts below found, is extremely "murky" and a "slender reed on which to place reliance."

'reasonable' "; but when thinking of the statute at that second step, one must assume that the statute has more than one plausible construction as it applies to the case before you. If the agency offers one— it prevails.

And Thomas W. Merrill, Judicial Deference to Executive Precedent, 101 Yale L.J. 969, 977 (1992):

> ... [I]n contrast to the previous approach, the two-step structure makes deference an all-or-nothing matter. If the court resolves the question at step one, then it exercises purely independent judgment and gives no consideration to the executive view. If it resolves the question at step two, then it applies a standard of maximum deference. In effect, Chevron transformed a regime that allowed courts to give agencies deference along a sliding scale into a regime with an on/off switch.

(4) Can you put Chevron together with State Farm and Overton Park? ARENT V. SHALALA, 70 F.3d 610 (D.C.Cir.1995): The Nutrition Labeling and Education Act of 1990, enforced by the FDA, required manufacturers of food to provide various items of nutritional information on the foods' labels. For raw produce and fish—not manufactured items—it established voluntary guidelines under which the retail stores provide nutritional information to the customer. The Act then required the FDA to convert this voluntary scheme into a mandatory set of labeling requirements if it found that food stores were not in "substantial compliance" with the guidelines.

The Act required the agency to issue a regulation defining what constituted "substantial compliance," with the following stipulations:

> The regulation shall provide that there is not substantial compliance if a significant number of retailers have failed to comply with the guidelines. The size of the retailers and the portion of the market served by retailers in compliance with the guidelines shall be considered in determining whether the substantial-compliance standard has been met.

In the event, the regulation provided that individual stores would be considered in compliance if they provided information for at least 90% of their fish and vegetables, and the industry as a whole would be in compliance if at least 60% of the surveyed stores were in compliance; the size of the stores and the markets they served were taken into account in determining the protocol for the stipulated survey.

This suit challenged both the validity of the regulation and of the subsequent determination by the FDA, based on its survey, that the industry was in substantial compliance.

Edwards, C.J., for the majority (70 F.3d at 614–17):

"Although the parties argue this case in terms of both Chevron analysis and arbitrary and capricious review, they interpret the case as one involving review of an agency's construction of a statute and look primarily to Chevron for the appropriate analytical framework. We, however, do not find Chevron controlling. In challenging the FDA's regulation defining 'substantial compliance,' appellants seek traditional arbitrary and capricious review governed by Motor Vehicle Manufacturers Ass'n v. State Farm Mutual Automobile Insurance Co., 463 U.S. 29 (1983). We recognize that, in some respects, Chevron review and arbitrary and capricious review overlap at the margins. But it would be a mistake to view this case as one involving typical Chevron review.

"Chevron is principally concerned with whether an agency has authority to act under a statute. Thus, a reviewing court's inquiry under Chevron is rooted in statutory analysis and is focused on discerning the boundaries of Congress' delegation of authority to the agency; and as long as the agency stays within that delegation, it is free to make policy choices in interpreting the statute, and such interpretations are entitled to deference. . . . In such a case, the question for the reviewing court is whether the agency's construction of the statute is faithful to its plain meaning, or, if the statute has no plain meaning, whether the agency's interpretation 'is based on a permissible construction of the statute.'

"In the present case, however, there is no question that the FDA had authority to define the circumstances constituting food retailers' substantial compliance with the NLEA's voluntary labeling guidelines. The only issue here is whether the FDA's discharge of that authority was reasonable. Such a question falls within the province of traditional arbitrary and capricious review under 5 U.S.C. § 706(2)(A) (1988). Thus, in the present case, State Farm is controlling regarding the standard of review.

"In State Farm, the Court held: [long quotation omitted]. Under this standard of review, it is clear that the FDA's regulations must be upheld.

"The FDA certainly took account of the relevant factors in devising its sixty-percent, industry-wide standard for food retailers' 'substantial compliance' under the NLEA. . . .

"The FDA also has articulated an explanation for its decision that demonstrates its reliance on a variety of relevant factors and represents a reasonable accommodation in light of the facts before the agency. . . .

"Given the record before the agency, the FDA's sixty-percent figure is not unreasonable and it certainly does not reveal 'a clear error of judgment.' Overton Park, 401 U.S. at 416. Moreover, the statutory intent was not to assure one-hundred-percent compliance, but rather 'substantial' compliance, and the FDA's sixty-percent standard does ensure that a major portion of the retail food market will receive nutritional information. . . .

Wald, J., concurring (70 F.3d at 619–620):

"While I agree with the panel's conclusion that the Food and Drug Administration's ('FDA') rule is justifiable, I would resolve the case under the Chevron step two challenge which was presented by the parties and addressed by the trial court, rather than grounding our decision on a different facet of Administrative Procedure Act ('APA') review." . . .

"Chevron allocates power to interpret statutes among the branches of government by creating a presumption that agencies, rather than the courts, are the preferred institution for filling in statutory gaps. The first step of Chevron is straightforward; if the statutory language is clear, it controls. The second step, where in my view the majority goes astray, entrusts agencies with authority to interpret statutory ambiguities, provided they do so in a manner that is reasonable and consistent with the language and purposes of the statute. By contrast, garden-variety APA review under § 706 focuses more heavily on the agency's decisionmaking process; to survive arbitrary and capricious review, 'the agency must examine the relevant data and articulate a satisfactory explanation for its action, including a rational connection between the facts found and the choice made.' Motor Vehicle Mfrs. Ass'n v. State Farm Mut. Auto. Ins. Co., 463 U.S. 29, 43 (1983).

"Given these differences in the central concerns behind the two analytic frameworks, there are certainly situations where a challenge to an agency's regulation will fall squarely within one rubric, rather than the other. For example, we might invalidate an agency's decision under Chevron as inconsistent with its statutory mandate, even though we do not believe the decision reflects an arbitrary policy choice. Such a result might occur when we believe the agency's course of action to be the most appropriate and effective means of achieving a goal, but determine that Congress has selected a different—albeit, in our eyes, less propitious—path. Conversely, we might determine that although not barred by statute, an agency's action is arbitrary and capricious because the agency has not considered certain relevant factors or articulated any rationale for its choice. . . .

"But I agree with the panel that despite these distinctions, the Chevron and State Farm frameworks often do overlap. . . .

"The case before us arguably falls within this area of overlap. In reviewing the FDA's regulations, our task was to determine whether the agency rationally considered the factors set forth in the NLEA when it defined 'substantial compliance.' Accordingly, I would not argue that State Farm is altogether irrelevant to our analysis, but given the scope and function of Chevron step two analysis, neither would I find State Farm applicable to the exclusion of Chevron, as the majority does. Petitioners' appeal ultimately does stand or fall on whether the FDA heeded Congress' admonitions that it may not find 'substantial compliance' if 'a significant number of retailers' have failed to comply, and that it must consider '[t]he size of the retailers and the portion of the market served by retailers in compliance with the guidelines' when making this determination. This language is sufficiently concrete to permit review of whether the agency's interpretation is reasonable and consistent with Congress' purpose in enacting the NLEA. In fact, I believe it well within the bounds of typical Chevron step two analysis, which is why the majority's opinion troubles me somewhat. If this case falls totally outside Chevron, many other cases marching under its banner must be similarly exiled. The majority's unequivocal rejection of the Chevron analytic framework utilized by the parties and the trial court in this case provides no clues as to the boundary lines for Chevron and APA review."

And one professor's commentary (RONALD M. LEVIN, THE ANATOMY OF CHEVRON: STEP TWO RECONSIDERED, 72 Chi.-Kent L. Rev. 1253, 1276 (1997)):

My view is that both Chief Justice Edwards and Judge Wald were right—except in arguing that the other was wrong. For they were debating an artificial question. In the remainder of this article I will suggest that the D.C. Circuit's strenuous efforts to divide up the terrain between arbitrariness review and *Chevron* step two should be abandoned; the court, as well as other courts, would do better simply to treat these two modes of analysis as equivalent. I will maintain that step one review and arbitrariness review, properly defined, can cover all the types of inquiries that courts actually use step two to address. The effort to find some middle step that falls within neither of the former two types of review is not only unnecessary, but actually undesirable because it defines the scope of those two inquiries in an unjustifiably narrow fashion.

(5) By the way, in case you had any doubt, Chevron also applies to agency construction of statutes which takes place, not in rulemaking, but in the course of case-by-case adjudication. E.g., I.N.S. v. Aguirre–Aguirre, 526 U.S. 415 (1999).

NOTES ON THE WISDOM OF CHEVRON

(1) CYNTHIA R. FARINA, STATUTORY INTERPRETATION AND THE BALANCE OF POWER IN THE ADMINISTRATIVE STATE, 89 Colum. L. Rev. 452, 487–88 (1989): "The great success with which nondelegation analysis evolved to accommodate a regulation-favoring political consensus has, unfortunately, produced an insidious 'bottom-line' myopia—a tendency to focus only on the consequence that Congress may broadly delegate regulatory power, while ignoring the doctrinal construct that developed to make this outcome possible. A belief in legislative primacy obviously occupied an important place in that construct. Congress was accorded great deference to transfer power and thereby radically restructure American government. But the Court's long struggle to reconcile the growth of agencies with the Constitution yielded a solution far more complex than carte blanche for Congress to give agencies whatever power it wishes them to have. The administrative state became constitutionally tenable because the Court's vision of separation of powers evolved from the simple (but constraining) proposition that divided powers must not be commingled, to the more flexible (but far more complicated) proposition, that power may be transferred *so long as* it will be adequately controlled.

"A crucial aspect of the capacity for external control upon which the permissibility of delegating regulatory power hinged was judicial policing of the terms of the statute. ... Judge Leventhal expressed the point most succinctly: 'Congress has been willing to delegate its legislative powers broadly—and the courts have upheld such delegation—because there is court review to assure that the agency exercises the delegated power within statutory limits.' Whether or not Judge Leventhal correctly interpreted the legislature's motives, he aptly characterized the course of nondelegation theory in the courts. The constitutional accommodation ultimately reached in the nondelegation cases implied that principal power to say what the statute means must rest *outside* the agency in the courts.

"Hence, a key assumption of Chevron's 'judicial usurpation' argument—that Congress may give agencies primary responsibility not only for making policy within the limits of their organic statutes, but also for defining those limits whenever the text and surrounding legislative materials are ambiguous—is fundamentally incongruous with the constitutional course by which the Court came to reconcile agencies and separation of powers. Of course, to demonstrate that one of Chevron's central premises cannot be squared with the doctrinal structure built in the nondelegation cases is not necessarily to establish that this structure was worth preserving. Was it merely a delusion that separation of powers could be honored through a theory of nondelegation that permitted the concentration of great policy-making and executing authority in administrative agencies, but which insisted that agencies could not then also hold the power to say what their organic statutes mean? An examination of the origins and content of that constitutional principle suggests not. The vision of separation of powers embodied in mature nondelegation analysis—a vision that came to ask whether power was being adequately checked, rather than whether powers were remaining divided—was in essence true to the constitutional vision."

(2) JERRY L. MASHAW, GREED, CHAOS AND GOVERNANCE, 152–53 (1997): "Strangely enough, it may make sense to imagine the delegation of political authority to administrators as a device for improving the responsiveness of government to the desires of the general electorate. This argument can be made even if we accept many of the insights of the political and economic literature that premises its predictions of congressional and voter behavior on a direct linkage between benefits transferred to constituents and the election or reelection of representatives. All we need do is not forget there are also presidential elections and that, as the Supreme Court reminds us in *Chevron*, presidents are heads of administrations.

"Assume then that voters view the election of representatives to Congress through the lens of the most cynical interpretation of the modern public choice literature on congressional behavior. In short, the voter chooses a representative for that representative's effectiveness in supplying governmental goods and services to the local district, including the voter. The representative is a good representative or a bad representative depending upon his or her ability to provide the district with at least its fair share of governmental largesse. In this view, the congressperson's position on various issues of national interest is of modest, if any, importance. The only question is, Does he or she 'bring home the bacon.'

"The voter's vision of presidential electoral politics is arguably quite different. The president has no particular constituency to which he or she has special responsibility to deliver benefits. Presidents are hardly cut off from pork-barrel politics. Yet issues of national scope and the candidates' positions on those issues are the essence of presidential politics. Citizens vote for a president based almost wholly on a perception of the difference that one or another candidate might make to general governmental policies.

"If this description of voting in national elections is reasonably plausible, then the utilization of vague delegations to administrative agencies takes on significance as a device for facilitating responsiveness to voter preferences expressed in presidential elections. The high transactions costs of legislating specifically suggests that legislative activity directed to the modification of administration mandates will be infrequent. Agencies will thus persist with their statutory empowering provisions relatively intact over substantial periods of time.

"Voter preferences on the direction and intensity of governmental activities, however, are not likely to be so stable. Indeed, one can reasonably expect that a president will be able to affect policy in a four-year term only because being elected president entails acquiring the power to exercise, direct, or influence policy discretion. The group of executive officers we commonly call 'the administration' matters only because of the relative malleability of the directives that administrators have in their charge. If congressional statutes were truly specific with respect to the actions that administrators were to take, presidential politics would be a mere beauty contest."

(3) Justice Stevens' opinion does not discuss the APA. Do you think Chevron is consistent with the text of § 706?

(4) Cass R. Sunstein, Law and Administration After *Chevron*, 90 Colum. L.Rev. 2071, 2085–88 (1990): "When Congress has expressly said that deference is or is not appropriate, the matter is relatively simple. As stated above, the text and background of the APA suggest a firm belief in the need for judicial checks on administration, particularly with respect to the interpretation of law. The view that courts should always defer to agency interpretation is, therefore, a poor reconstruction of the instructions of the APA. It remains possible, however, that particular substantive statutes displace the APA and accord law-interpreting power to the agency. If so, the courts should defer in such cases on the ground that the relevant law *is* what the agency says that it is. The APA's provision for independent judicial interpretation of law is not inconsistent, then, with Chevron's deference to the agency's interpretation if Congress has, under particular statutes, granted the relevant authority to administrative agencies.

"Frequently, however, Congress does not speak in explicit terms on the question of deference. When this is so, the court's task is to make the best reconstruction that it can of congressional instructions. And if Congress has not made a clear decision one way or the other, the choice among the alternatives will call for an assessment of which strategy is the most sensible one to attribute to Congress under the circumstances. This assessment is not a mechanical exercise of uncovering an actual legislative decision. It calls for a frankly value-laden judgment about comparative competence, undertaken in light of the regulatory structure and applicable constitutional considerations.

"If all this is so, the Chevron approach might well be defended on the ground that the resolution of ambiguities in statutes is sometimes a question of policy as much as it is one of law, narrowly understood, and that agencies are uniquely well situated to make the relevant policy decisions. In some cases, there is simply no answer to the interpretive question if it is posed as an inquiry into some real or unitary instruction of the legislature. Sometimes congressional views cannot plausibly be aggregated in a way that reflects a clear resolution of regulatory problems, many of them barely foreseen or indeed unforeseeable. In these circumstances, legal competence, as narrowly understood, is insufficient for decision. The resolution of the ambiguity calls for an inquiry into something other than the instructions of the enacting legislature. And in examining those other considerations, the institution entrusted with the decision must make reference to considerations of both fact and policy.

"Chevron nicely illustrates the point. The decision about whether to adopt a plantwide definition of 'source' required distinctly administrative competence because it called for a complex inquiry, not foreseen by Congress, into the environmental and economic consequences of the various possibilities. If regulatory decisions in the face of ambiguities amount in large part to choices of policy, and if Congress has delegated basic implementing authority to the agency, the Chevron approach might reflect a belief, attributable to Congress in the absence of a clear contrary legislative statement, in the comparative advantages of the agency in making those choices.

"At least as a general rule, these suggestions argue powerfully in favor of administrative rather than judicial resolution of hard statutory questions. The factfinding capacity and electoral accountability of the administrators are far greater than those of courts. Chevron is best understood and defended as a frank recognition that sometimes interpretation is not simply a matter of uncovering legislative will, but also involves extratextual considerations of various kinds, including judgments about how a statute is best or most sensibly implemented. Chevron reflects a salutary understanding that these judgments of policy and principle should be made by administrators rather than judges."

[The idea that Chevron only provides a default rule is, by the way, not merely theoretical. Occasionally since the decision Congress has provided for a different standard of review. See, e.g., 15 U.S.C. § 6714(e) (2000), regarding differences between state and federal insurance regulation.]

(5) JONATHAN T. MOLOT, THE JUDICIAL PERSPECTIVE IN THE ADMINISTRATIVE STATE: RECONCILING MODERN DOCTRINES OF DEFERENCE WITH THE JUDICIARY'S STRUCTURAL ROLE, 53 Stanford L. Rev. 1, 76–79 (2000): "The error in Chevron's logic lies in its equating any statutory ambiguity at all with a failure on the part of Congress to legislate. Chevron posits that whenever Congress' statutory instructions do not resolve an interpretive question conclusively, this must mean Congress either failed to 'consider the question,' 'was unable to forge a coalition on either side of the question,' or else consciously decided to delegate the question to the relevant agency. Chevron thus ignores the reality that the Founders highlighted over two centuries ago: Even when a majority of legislators *do* contemplate a legislative issue broadly conceived and *do* agree to address it with substantive instructions, statutory ambiguity may nonetheless remain over the particular questions that will arise under that statute. Recall Madison's observation that '[a]ll new laws, though penned with the greatest technical skill and passed on the fullest and most mature deliberation, are considered as more or less obscure and

equivocal, until their meaning be liquidated and ascertained by a series of particular . . . adjudications.'[1] . . .

"It is beyond controversy that statutes often are ambiguous and that outside the administrative context judges are responsible for resolving those ambiguities. Whether Congress may be said to have 'delegated' legislative authority to the judiciary each time it leaves an ambiguity is unimportant: Courts must make decisions using traditional tools of statutory interpretation regardless of the label attached. Thus the very same statutory instructions, yielding the very same level of ambiguity that Chevron treats as a delegation in the administrative context, will be treated outside the administrative context as ordinary legislation subject to ordinary judicial interpretation.

"There is a substantial cost to treating as a 'delegation' the sort of ordinary statutory instructions that would be subject to ordinary judicial interpretation outside the administrative context. . . . [S]ince virtually '[a]ll new laws' start out ambiguous as applied to various circumstances and do not become clear until interpreted in 'particular . . . adjudications,' legislators historically have had incentives to engage in careful deliberation and drafting to guide judicial resolution of statutory ambiguities. This careful deliberation and drafting not only appropriately ensures some legislative control over law application, but also may have the corollary benefit of improving the laws that legislators enact.

"But the sort of careful deliberation and drafting that legislators might use to guide judicial interpretation will be wasted on an administrative agency. The agency will tend to choose among reasonable interpretive options based on political considerations and policy concerns rather than anything in Congress' statute. As a result, legislators wishing to guide administrative decisions under Chevron must resort to . . . tactics that differ significantly from the careful deliberation and drafting they might use to guide judges.

"[As one such tactic,] legislators may decide to engage in what scholars have dubbed 'micromanagement' of administrative regulation. If conventional drafting tools generally cannot eliminate ambiguity (and the administrative leeway that goes with it under Chevron), legislators nonetheless have tried in some instances to go beyond conventional drafting. They have drafted statutory provisions with such 'striking specificity' as to preclude deference at Chevron Step I and compel administrative outcomes in keeping with their legislative bargains. . . .

"But if highly specific drafting of detailed statutory provisions succeeds in securing legislative control over administrative outcomes, such drafting by no means ensures the fair, sensible laws that our constitutional structure was designed to promote. . . ."

(6) Peter L. Strauss, One Hundred Fifty Cases Per Year: Some Implications of the Supreme Court's Limited Resources for Judicial Review of Agency Action, 87 Colum. L. Rev. 1093, 1121 (1987): " . . . [I]t is helpful to view Chevron through the lens of the Supreme Court's severely restricted

---

1. The Federalist No. 37 (James Madison).

capacity directly to enforce uniformity upon the courts of appeals in those courts' review of agency decisionmaking. When national uniformity in the administration of national statutes is called for, the national agencies responsible for that administration can be expected to reach single readings of the statutes for which they are responsible and to enforce those readings within their own framework. ... If, however, one accepts not only that language is imprecise, but also that congressional language (in particular) is frequently indeterminate, it follows that that reading could never be demonstrably correct, but merely reasonable if within the range of indeterminacy, or incorrect if beyond it. Any reviewing panel of judges from one of the twelve circuits, if made responsible for precise renditions of statutory meaning, could vary in its judgment from the agency's, and from the judgments of other panels in other circuits, without being wrong. The variance might even occur in predictable ways, if simple diversity were overlaid by geographical bias. The Supreme Court's practical inability in most cases to give its own precise renditions of statutory meaning virtually assures that circuit readings will be diverse. By removing the responsibility for precision from the courts of appeals, the Chevron rule subdues this diversity, and thus enhances the probability of uniform national administration of the laws.

"Rather than see Chevron just as a rule about agency discretion ... it can be seen as a device for managing the courts of appeals that can reduce (although not eliminate) the Supreme Court's need to police their decisions for accuracy."

(One might reconsider, in light of this excerpt, the material on interjudicial nonuniformity and agency "nonacquiescence" near the beginning of this chapter, p. 922 above.)

NOTES ON THE IMPACT OF CHEVRON

(1) Does it matter if the Supreme Court announces a new doctrinal formulation regarding the standard for judicial review? Professors Peter H. Schuck and E. Donald Elliott examined almost 2,000 courts of appeals decisions from 1984–85 and 1988. In To The *Chevron* Station: An Empirical Study of Federal Administrative Law, 1990 Duke L.J. 984, they reported "strong evidence" that outcomes changed from a pre-Chevron affirmance rate of 71% to a post-Chevron rate of 81%, between the six months before Chevron came down in 1984 and a six-month period in 1985. By 1988, the affirmance rate was 76% (with remands twice as frequent as reversals, whereas in 1984–85 they had been about equal).

A more recent study of all the courts of appeals decisions from 1995 and 1996 that cited Chevron reported that agency interpretations were upheld 73% of the time. Of those that were rejected, 59% failed step one; in 18%, the statute was declared ambiguous but the agency's interpretation was ruled unreasonable, failing step two; and in 23%, the agency's interpretation failed a general test of "reasonability" which conflated steps one and two. Orin S. Kerr, Shedding Light on *Chevron*: An Empirical Study of the *Chevron* Doctrine in the U.S. Courts of Appeals, 15 Yale J. on Reg. 1 (1998).

Of course, rates of affirmance and reversal do not tell the whole story. They are affected not only by what the courts do, but by which cases lawyers choose to bring to court. If Chevron made it easier for agencies to win, it correspondingly made it more risky to bring an action challenging an agency decision (or, in the case of an agency enforcement action, to choose to oppose). Or, in other words, the value of winning against the agency now had to be discounted by a larger percentage representing the likelihood of losing. Accordingly, one would expect over time for counsel representing parties opposed to agency action to bring fewer marginal cases. Assuming the costs of bringing an action against an agency (litigation costs plus the more practical costs of opposing an agency one deals with) remain constant, and assuming that the amounts at stake in proceedings on average also remain constant, over the long run the rates of affirmance and reversal might be expected to return to their prior state— even if the courts were using a different standard of review—since those rates would represent the discounted value of bringing actions.

(2) Recall the long history of policy vacillation in the State Farm case, and Justice Rehnquist's partial dissent stressing that "[t]he agency's changed view of the standard seems to be related to the election of a new President of a different political party. ... A change in administration brought about by the people casting their votes is a perfectly reasonable basis for an executive agency's reappraisal of the costs and benefits of its programs and regulations ... within the bounds established by Congress."

In Chevron, a case where, once again, the agency's position had shifted over time, all six voting Justices signed Justice Steven's observation endorsing agency reliance, within the limits established by delegation, "upon the incumbent administration's views of wise policy," and two of the nonparticipating Justices had been among the State Farm partial dissenters. This judicial proposition has substantial implications for relationships between the executive and legislative branches. For if each administration's present choice can survive judicial review, Congress will be unable to change it unless it can secure either presidential agreement or the votes necessary to override a veto. Thus a change of administration may bring in its wake new "interpretations" that, however unwelcome to Congress, cannot easily be overcome.

RUST V. SULLIVAN, 500 U.S. 173 (1991), presents a particularly dramatic example of this effect of Chevron. Title X of the Public Health Service Act, 42 U.S.C. §§ 300–300a–6, had provided, since enactment in 1970, for federal grant support of family planning clinics. While grantees were supposed to "offer a broad range of acceptable and effective family planning methods and services," the Act also stipulated that none of the grant money "shall be used in programs where abortion is a method of family planning." How far did this prohibition go? The initial regulations under the statute, issued in 1971, simply required that a Title X project "not provide abortions." Further guidelines issued in the mid–1970's expressly permitted non-directive counseling of pregnant women as to their options, including abortion. Guidelines issued in 1981 mandated such counseling upon a patient's request. But in 1988, after a notice-and-comment proceeding, the Department of Health and Human Services promulgated new regulations that at every turn required grant recipients to avoid giving advice or making referrals concerning abortion. If a patient asked for information, the grantee was allowed to say that "the project does not consider abortion an appropriate method of family planning."

The Court sustained the regulations, 5 to 4. Much of Justice Rehnquist's opinion for the majority was devoted to answering the challengers' claim that the regulations violated constitutional guarantees of free speech and substantive due process. But, as even this brief history shows, he had to address substantial questions of statutory interpretation and administrative discretion, too. As to the statute, the reach of its reference to "programs where abortion is a method of family planning" was uncertain, and not clarified by the legislative history. "The broad language of Title X" Justice Rehnquist said, "plainly allows the Secretary's construction of the statute." He continued (500 U.S. at 186–87):

"Petitioners argue, however, that the regulations are entitled to little or no deference because they 'reverse a longstanding agency policy that permitted nondirective counseling and referral for abortion,' and thus represent a sharp break from the Secretary's prior construction of the statute. . . .

"This Court has rejected the argument that an agency's interpretation 'is not entitled to deference because it represents a sharp break with prior interpretations' of the statute in question. Chevron, 467 U.S. at 862. In Chevron, we held that a revised interpretation deserves deference because '[a]n initial agency interpretation is not instantly carved in stone' and 'the agency, to engage in informed rulemaking, must consider varying interpretations and the wisdom of its policy on a continuing basis.' An agency is not required to 'establish rules of conduct to last forever,' Motor Vehicle Mfrs. Assn. of United States v. State Farm Mutual Automobile Ins. Co., but rather 'must be given ample latitude to "adapt [its] rules and policies to the demands of changing circumstances." '

"We find that the Secretary amply justified his change of interpretation with a 'reasoned analysis.' Motor Vehicle Mfrs. The Secretary explained that the regulations are a result of his determination, in the wake of the critical reports of the General Accounting Office (GAO) and the Office of the Inspector General (OIG), that prior policy failed to implement properly the statute and that it was necessary to provide 'clear and operational guidance to grantees to preserve the distinction between Title X programs and abortion as a method of family planning.' 53 Fed.Reg. 2923–2924 (1988). He also determined that the new regulations are more in keeping with the original intent of the statute, are justified by client experience under the prior policy, and are supported by a shift in attitude against the 'elimination of unborn children by abortion.' We believe that these justifications are sufficient to support the Secretary's revised approach. Having concluded that the plain language and legislative history are ambiguous as to Congress' intent in enacting Title X, we must defer to the Secretary's permissible construction of the statute."

The dissenting Justices wrote three opinions. Much of Justice Blackmun's opinion was devoted to arguing that the regulations violated the first and fifth amendments. Justice Stevens' rested on the first step of the

Chevron test: "I am convinced that the 1970 Act did not authorize the Secretary to censor the speech of grant recipients or their employees." Justice O'Connor, making a point Justice Blackmun had also made, relied on a "long-standing canon of statutory construction" (500 U.S. at 223–25):

> "[W]here an otherwise acceptable construction of a statute would raise serious constitutional problems, the Court will construe the statute to avoid such problems unless such construction is plainly contrary to the intent of Congress." Edward J. DeBartolo Corp. v. Florida Gulf Coast Building & Construction Trades Council, 485 U.S. 568, 575 (1988). . . . In these cases, we need only tell the Secretary that his regulations are not a reasonable interpretation of the statute; we need not tell Congress that it cannot pass such legislation. If we rule solely on statutory grounds, Congress retains the power to force the constitutional question by legislating more explicitly. It may instead choose to do nothing. That decision should be left to Congress; we should not tell Congress what it cannot do before it has chosen to do it. It is enough in this case to conclude that neither the language nor the history of § 1008 compels the Secretary's interpretation, and that the interpretation raises serious First Amendment concerns. On this basis alone, I would . . . invalidate the challenged regulations.

If we view this debate in terms of its allocations of power to various institutions, Justice O'Connor's opinion would have required action on the part of both Congress and the President (or an extraordinary majority in Congress) to reinstate the prohibitions contained in the regulations. By contrast, Justice Rehnquist's deference to the agency put a similar burden of action on those who would have removed the prohibitions. This, as it turned out, was not merely a theoretical point. In 1992, Congress passed a bill requiring Title X projects to provide their clients with non-directive counseling on various matters, including termination of pregnancy. But it was vetoed by President Bush on September 25, 1992, 28 Weekly Comp. Pres. Doc. 1759, with the consequence that even though both Houses of Congress opposed the regulations, they remained in force.

On February 5, 1993—very shortly after President Clinton took office—the new Secretary of HHS published an "Interim Rule," effective immediately for "good cause" pending a new notice and comment proceeding, which said in part:

> " . . . [T]he Secretary suspends the 1988 rules and announces that, on an interim basis, the agency's nonregulatory compliance standards that existed prior to February 2, 1988 . . . will be used to administer the Family Planning Program.

> "Under these compliance standards, Title X projects would be required, in the event of an unplanned pregnancy and where the patient requests such action, to provide nondirective counseling to the patient on options relating to her pregnancy, including abortion, and to refer her for abortion, if that is the option she selects."

(3) "Construction to avoid a constitutional question" and "deference to long-standing administrative constructions"—two "canons" of statutory construction at stake in Rust v. Sullivan—are but examples of a much

longer list of maxims which have been used, now and again, either to construe Congress' work or to determine whether to defer to the work of construction already done by an agency. In the past few years, the Supreme Court—and the lower courts—have had occasion to consider the interaction (or collision) of Chevron with many such canons. (For a good long list, see Russell Weaver, Some Realism About *Chevron*, 58 Mo. L. Rev. 129, 162 & n.223 (1993).)

In some cases, Chevron conflicted with a canon having substantive overtones. For example, in EEOC v. Arabian American Oil Co., 499 U.S. 244 (1991), the Court held that the "[l]ong-standing principle of American law 'that legislation of Congress, unless a contrary intent appears, is meant to apply only within the territorial jurisdiction of the United States'" overrode any deference due under Chevron to the EEOC's interpretation of Title VII as applying extraterritorially. In the same vein, compare Muscogee (Creek) Nation v. Hodel, 851 F.2d 1439 (D.C.Cir.1988), cert. denied, 488 U.S. 1010 (1989) (applying the canon that ambiguous statutes should be construed in favor of American Indians, and noting that but for the canon, deference to the agency's interpretation would have been appropriate) with Haynes v. United States, 891 F.2d 235 (9th Cir.1989) (declining to apply the same canon when Chevron deference was appropriate, on the grounds that the canon is a guideline, not substantive law, and that extended administrative practice deserves deference).

In other cases, more directly relevant to the doctrines of administrative law, the question was the relationship between Chevron and one of the maxims regarding deference to agency work that had been developed under the pre-*Chevron* regime—for example, the long-standing construction rule. Some of these rules represented the older, multi-factored approach to deference and their invocation could thus undermine the "rule-ness" of the Chevron decision. Not surprisingly, they have caused trouble.

For example, in INS v. Cardoza–Fonseca, 480 U.S. 421 (1987), the Court held that use of the "traditional tools of statutory construction" showed that the agency's reading of the statute was flawed. As it announced this holding, the Court dropped this footnote, 480 U.S. at 446, n.30:

An additional reason for rejecting the Government's request for heightened deference to its position is the inconsistency of the positions the BIA has taken through the years. An agency interpretation of a relevant provision which conflicts with the agency's earlier interpretation is "entitled to considerably less deference" than a consistently held agency view. [Citation of pre-Chevron cases.]

This canon, needless to say, does not do much work in Justice Rehnquist's opinion in Rust v. Sullivan; indeed, as we have just seen, he spends a paragraph developing the opposite proposition that agencies must be given "ample latitude" to adapt their interpretations of the law to changing conditions.

Rust, however, was not the last word on the point. In the yet more recent Good Samaritan Hospital v. Shalala, 508 U.S. 402 (1993), the Court stated that "the consistency of an agency's position is a factor in assessing the weight that position is due," followed by a quotation from the above-quoted footnote from Cardoza–Fonseca. This was also the position taken in Thomas Jefferson Univ. v. Shalala, 512 U.S. 504 (1994). And so it goes.

Whether canons of interpretation are very useful—or just give judges something to say—is debatable. Sometimes, it seems, there are just canons firing in all directions. E.g., WILLIAMS V. BABBITT, 115 F.3d 657 (9th Cir. 1997), cert. denied, 523 U.S. 1117 (1998): The Reindeer Act of 1937 provides that "Live reindeer in Alaska . . . acquired by the Secretary of the Interior . . . and live reindeer in Alaska . . . owned by the said natives . . . shall not be sold or transferred . . . to anyone other than . . . natives of Alaska." Williams, non-native, intended to import reindeer to Alaska from Canada for commercial purposes. The Department of the Interior ruled that he could not; based on the Act's policy, structure, and legislative history, Interior said, it "must be construed to prohibit non-Native entry into the reindeer industry in Alaska, regardless of the source of the reindeer involved." *Held*, per Judge Kozinski: Williams wins. Under 9th Circuit precedent, construing statutes in favor of natives is a less powerful rule than is Chevron. Under Chevron, the issue is close, since the Act simply does not say that non-natives cannot herd reindeer. But for 60 years natives were assumed to have a monopoly, and thus this interpretation is "entitled the added force of a long-standing construction." But that brings us face-to-face with the maxim counseling avoidance of constitutional questions. Rust v. Sullivan can be made consistent with that canon by saying that "[o]nly if the agency's proferred interpretation raises *serious* constitutional concerns may a court refuse to defer under Chevron." Here, that was the case. The reindeer preference does not relate to native land, tribal status or culture; indeed, reindeer were not imported to Alaska until the turn of the century. As a more general racial preference, the agency's rule raises a serious question of equal protection doctrine. "We therefore interpret the Reindeer Act as not precluding non-natives in Alaska from owning and importing reindeer."

(4) There are also several cases which have had to choose between Chevron deference and the Court's own pre-Chevron precedents construing a particular statute. Some of these precedents might have been written differently, had Chevron been the law; but in any case, they still hold sway. See, for example, Lechmere v. NLRB, 502 U.S. 527 (1992), which held an NLRB interpretation invalid as contrary to a Supreme Court precedent construing the National Labor Relations Act, despite the dissent's complaint that the precedent itself was fundamentally at odds with Chevron.

THOMAS W. MERRILL AND KRISTIN E. HICKMAN, CHEVRON'S DOMAIN, 89 Geo. L.J. 833, 916–17 (2001): "Most accurately considered, however, the question of what to do about judicial precedent does not present an exception to Chevron, but illustrates the need for a transitional rule—a special rule of adjustment that mediates between the pre-Chevron and the post-Chevron worlds. This can be seen by considering, first, what role judicial precedent should play in a world in which all relevant decisions have been made in full awareness of Chevron and its two-step procedure. In such a world, all judicial precedent should be self-consciously rendered as either a 'step-one precedent' or a 'step-two precedent.' If step one, then the previous court will have determined that the statute had an unambiguous meaning that forecloses the exercise of any interpretational discretion on the part of the agency; the statute either compelled or forbade the previous agency view. Such a precedent would obviously be entitled to full stare decisis effect in a later case presenting the same interpretational issue. Such a decision, in effect, tells us that the statute has only one possible meaning, which precludes any exercise of agency discretion.

"In contrast, if the previous judicial decision was a step-two precedent, then the court found that the statute admits of the exercise of agency discretion in its interpretation. If the court upheld the agency interpretation at step two, then we know that the previous agency interpretation was reasonable. This does not, however, foreclose the possibility that a different agency interpretation would also be reasonable. If the court struck down the previous agency interpretation at step two, then we know the previous interpretation was unreasonable. But this too does not mean that a different agency interpretation would not be reasonable. In either event, the previous judicial decision should not be given full stare decisis effect in fixing the meaning of the statute. Instead, it should be given stare decisis effect only for the proposition that the statute admits of multiple interpretations—in other words, for the proposition that the case should be resolved at step two—and that at least one interpretation (the agency's previous interpretation) was either reasonable or unreasonable. The fact that the court upheld (or invalidated) the agency's prior construction of the statute would not, however, be determinative in deciding whether the current interpretation is permissible. Thus, in a post-Chevron world in which all relevant decisions are taken in full awareness of Chevron's two-step procedure, judicial precedent should be categorized as being either step-one precedent or step-two precedent, and should be given the stare decisis effect appropriate to its status.

"The analysis becomes more complicated, however, when we introduce the possibility that one or more of the relevant judicial decisions were *not* rendered in full awareness of the Chevron framework. The most obvious circumstance is where the judicial precedent predates 1984. . . .

"There are really only two options for such decisions. One is to examine each pre-Chevron precedent on a case-by-case basis, in an attempt to determine as best as is possible whether the precedent would have been a step-one precedent or a step-two precedent if, counterfactually, the court had applied the Chevron doctrine. The other is to adopt a blanket presumption that all pre-Chevron precedent is step-one precedent. . . . The Supreme Court's treatment of its own precedent is best understood as adopting the second option."

A FINAL THOUGHT ON CHEVRON

After reviewing the tasks State Farm assigned to courts and to agencies, and the tasks Chevron assigned to courts and to agencies, then-First–Circuit–Judge Stephen Breyer asked of the combination: "Is this not the exact opposite of a rational system?" Judicial Review of Questions of Law and Policy, 38 Admin. L. Rev. 363, 397 (1986).

MCI Telecommunications Corp. v. American Telephone and Telegraph Co.

Supreme Court of the United States, 1994.
512 U.S. 218.

5 - 3

■ JUSTICE SCALIA delivered the opinion of the Court.

Section 203(a) of Title 47 of the United States Code requires communications common carriers to file tariffs with the Federal Communications Commission, and § 203(b) authorizes the Commission to "modify" any requirement of § 203. These cases present the question whether the Commission's decision to make tariff filing optional for all nondominant long distance carriers is a valid exercise of its modification authority.

I

[The Communications Act of 1934 requires long distance carriers to file their tariffs with the FCC and to charge only the filed rates. When the Act was passed, AT & T monopolized long distance service, but in the 1970's technological advances made it possible for others, like MCI, to compete. In a series of orders from 1980 on, the FCC responded to the increased competition by relaxing the filing requirements for nondominant carriers—that is, for everyone but AT & T. The policy ran into some difficulty with the D.C. Circuit Court of Appeals, but the agency persisted. In 1992, the Commission concluded a rulemaking proceeding by declaring that filing of tariffs was optional for all nondominant carriers, and that the Communications Act authorized this deregulation. The D.C. Circuit reversed per curiam; MCI and the United States petitioned for certiorari, and the Court granted the petitions.]

II

Section 203 of the Communications Act contains both the filed rate provisions of the Act and the Commission's disputed modification authority. It provides in relevant part:

(a) Filing; public display.

Every common carrier, except connecting carriers, shall, within such reasonable time as the Commission shall designate, file with the Commission and print and keep open for public inspection schedules showing all charges ..., whether such charges are joint or separate, and showing the classifications, practices, and regulations affecting such charges. ...

(b) Changes in schedule; discretion of Commission to modify requirements.

(1) No change shall be made in the charges, classifications, regulations, or practices which have been so filed and published except after one hundred and twenty days notice to the Commission and to the public, which shall be published in such form and contain such information as the Commission may by regulations prescribe.

(2) The Commission may, in its discretion and for good cause shown, modify any requirement made by or under the authority of this

section either in particular instances or by general order applicable to special circumstances or conditions except that the Commission may not require the notice period specified in paragraph (1) to be more than one hundred and twenty days.

(c) Overcharges and rebates.

No carrier, unless otherwise provided by or under authority of this chapter, shall engage or participate in such communication unless schedules have been filed and published in accordance with the provisions of this chapter and with the regulations made thereunder; and no carrier shall (1) charge, demand, collect, or receive a greater or less or different compensation for such communication ... than the charges specified in the schedule then in effect, or (2) refund or remit by any means or device any portion of the charges so specified, or (3) extend to any person any privileges or facilities in such communication, or employ or enforce any classifications, regulations, or practices affecting such charges, except as specified in such schedule.

47 U.S.C. § 203 (1988 ed. and Supp. IV).

The dispute between the parties turns on the meaning of the phrase "modify any requirement" in § 203(b)(2). Petitioners argue that it gives the Commission authority to make even basic and fundamental changes in the scheme created by that section. We disagree. The word "modify"—like a number of other English words employing the root "mod-" (deriving from the Latin word for "measure"), such as "moderate," "modulate," "modest," and "modicum"—has a connotation of increment or limitation. Virtually every dictionary we are aware of says that "to modify" means to change moderately or in minor fashion. See, e.g., Random House Dictionary of the English Language 1236 (2d ed. 1987) ("to change somewhat the form or qualities of; alter partially; amend"); Webster's Third New International Dictionary 1452 (1976) ("to make minor changes in the form or structure of; alter without transforming"); 9 Oxford English Dictionary 952 (2d ed. 1989) ("[t]o make partial changes in; to change (an object) in respect of some of its qualities; to alter or vary without radical transformation"); Black's Law Dictionary 1004 (6th ed. 1990) ("[t]o alter; to change in incidental or subordinate features; enlarge; extend; amend; limit; reduce").

In support of their position, petitioners cite dictionary definitions contained in or derived from a single source, Webster's Third New International Dictionary 1452 (1976) ("Webster's Third"), which includes among the meanings of "modify," "to make a basic or important change in." Petitioners contend that this establishes sufficient ambiguity to entitle the Commission to deference in its acceptance of the broader meaning, which in turn requires approval of its permissive detariffing policy. See Chevron U.S.A. Inc. v. Natural Resources Defense Council, Inc., 467 U.S. 837, 843 (1984). In short, they contend that the courts must defer to the agency's choice among available dictionary definitions, citing National Railroad Passenger Corp. v. Boston and Maine Corp., 503 U.S. 407 (1992).

Most cases of verbal ambiguity in statutes involve, as Boston and Maine did, a selection between accepted alternative meanings shown as such by many dictionaries. One can envision (though a court case does not immediately come to mind) having to choose between accepted alternative meanings, one of which is so newly accepted that it has only been recorded by a single lexicographer. (Some dictionary must have been the very first to record the widespread use of "projection," for example, to mean "forecast.") But what petitioners demand that we accept as creating an ambiguity here is a rarity even rarer than that: a meaning set forth in a single dictionary (and, as we say, its progeny) which not only supplements the meaning contained in all other dictionaries, but contradicts one of the meanings contained in virtually all other dictionaries. Indeed, contradicts one of the alternative meanings contained in the out-of-step dictionary itself—for as we have observed, Webster's Third itself defines "modify" to connote both (specifically) major change and (specifically) minor change. It is hard to see how that can be. When the word "modify" has come to mean both "to change in some respects" and "to change fundamentally" it will in fact mean neither of those things. It will simply mean "to change," and some adverb will have to be called into service to indicate the great or small degree of the change.

If that is what the peculiar Webster's Third definition means to suggest has happened—and what petitioners suggest by appealing to Webster's Third—we simply disagree. "Modify," in our view, connotes moderate change. It might be good English to say that the French Revolution "modified" the status of the French nobility—but only because there is a figure of speech called understatement and a literary device known as sarcasm. And it might be unsurprising to discover a 1972 White House press release saying that "the Administration is modifying its position with regard to prosecution of the war in Vietnam"—but only because press agents tend to impart what is nowadays called "spin." Such intentional distortions, or simply careless or ignorant misuse, must have formed the basis for the usage that Webster's Third, and Webster's Third alone, reported.[1] It is perhaps gilding the lily to add this: In 1934, when the Communications Act became law—the most relevant time for determining a statutory term's meaning—Webster's Third was not yet even contemplated. To our knowledge all English dictionaries provided the narrow definition of "modify," including those published by G. & C. Merriam Company. See Webster's New International Dictionary 1577 (2d ed. 1934); Webster's Collegiate Dictionary 628 (4th ed. 1934). We have not the slightest doubt that is the meaning the statute intended.

Beyond the word itself, a further indication that the § 203 authority to "modify" does not contemplate fundamental changes is the sole exception to that authority which the section provides. One of the requirements of § 203 is that changes to filed tariffs can be made only after 120 days' notice to the Commission and the public. § 203(b)(1). The only exception to the Commission's § 203(b)(2) modification authority is as follows: "except that the Commission may not require the notice period specified in paragraph (1) to be more than one hundred and twenty days." Is it conceivable that the statute is indifferent to the Commission's power to eliminate the tariff-

---

1. That is not an unlikely hypothesis. Upon its long-awaited appearance in 1961, Webster's Third was widely criticized for its portrayal of common error as proper usage. . . .

filing requirement entirely for all except one firm in the long-distance sector, and yet strains out the gnat of extending the waiting period for tariff revision beyond 120 days? We think not. The exception is not as ridiculous as a Lilliputian in London only because it is to be found in Lilliput: in the small-scale world of "modifications," it is a big deal.

Since an agency's interpretation of a statute is not entitled to deference when it goes beyond the meaning that the statute can bear, see, e.g., Pittston Coal Group v. Sebben, 488 U.S. 105, 113, (1988); Chevron, 467 U.S., at 842–843, the Commission's permissive detariffing policy can be justified only if it makes a less than radical or fundamental change in the Act's tariff-filing requirement. The Commission's attempt to establish that no more than that is involved greatly understates the extent to which its policy deviates from the filing requirement, and greatly undervalues the importance of the filing requirement itself.

To consider the latter point first: For the body of a law, as for the body of a person, whether a change is minor or major depends to some extent upon the importance of the item changed to the whole. Loss of an entire toenail is insignificant; loss of an entire arm tragic. The tariff-filing requirement is, to pursue this analogy, the heart of the common-carrier section of the Communications Act. In the context of the Interstate Commerce Act, which served as its model, this Court has repeatedly stressed that rate filing was Congress's chosen means of preventing unreasonableness and discrimination in charges: "[T]here is not only a relation, but an indissoluble unity between the provision for the establishment and maintenance of rates until corrected in accordance with the statute and the prohibitions against preferences and discrimination." Texas and Pacific R. Co. v. Abilene Cotton Oil Co., 204 U.S. 426, 440 (1907). . . .

. . . Rate filings are, in fact, the essential characteristic of a rate-regulated industry. It is highly unlikely that Congress would leave the determination of whether an industry will be entirely, or even substantially, rate-regulated to agency discretion—and even more unlikely that it would achieve that through such a subtle device as permission to "modify" rate-filing requirements.

Bearing in mind, then, the enormous importance to the statutory scheme of the tariff-filing provision, we turn to whether what has occurred here can be considered a mere "modification." The Commission stresses that its detariffing policy applies only to nondominant carriers, so that the rates charged to over half of all consumers in the long-distance market are on file with the Commission. It is not clear to us that the proportion of customers affected, rather than the proportion of carriers affected, is the proper measure of the extent of the exemption (of course all carriers in the long-distance market are exempted, except AT & T). But even assuming it is, we think an elimination of the crucial provision of the statute for 40% of a major sector of the industry is much too extensive to be considered a "modification." What we have here, in reality, is a fundamental revision of the statute, changing it from a scheme of rate regulation in long-distance common-carrier communications to a scheme of rate regulation only where effective competition does not exist. That may be a good idea, but it was not the idea Congress enacted into law in 1934.

Finally, petitioners earnestly urge that their interpretation of § 203(b) furthers the Communications Act's broad purpose of promoting efficient telephone service. They claim that although the filing requirement prevented price discrimination and unfair practices while AT & T maintained a monopoly over long-distance service, it frustrates those same goals now that there is greater competition in that market. Specifically, they contend that filing costs raise artificial barriers to entry and that the publication of rates facilitates parallel pricing and stifles price competition. We have considerable sympathy with these arguments (though we doubt it makes sense, if one is concerned about the use of filed tariffs to communicate pricing information, to require filing by the dominant carrier, the firm most likely to be a price leader). ... But our estimations, and the Commission's estimations, of desirable policy cannot alter the meaning of the Federal Communications Act of 1934. For better or worse, the Act establishes a rate-regulation, filed-tariff system for common-carrier communications, and the Commission's desire "to 'increase competition' cannot provide [it] authority to alter the well-established statutory filed rate requirements," Maislin Industries, U.S., Inc. v. Primary Steel, Inc., 497 U.S. 116, 135 (1990). As we observed in the context of a dispute over the filed-rate doctrine more than 80 years ago, "such considerations address themselves to Congress, not to the courts," Armour Packing Co. v. United States, 209 U.S. 56, 82 (1908).

We do not mean to suggest that the tariff-filing requirement is so inviolate that the Commission's existing modification authority does not reach it at all. Certainly the Commission can modify the form, contents, and location of required filings, and can defer filing or perhaps even waive it altogether in limited circumstances. But what we have here goes well beyond that. It is effectively the introduction of a whole new regime of regulation (or of free-market competition), which may well be a better regime but is not the one that Congress established.

The judgment of the Court of Appeals is affirmed.

■ JUSTICE O'CONNOR took no part in the consideration or decision of these cases.

■ JUSTICE STEVENS, with whom JUSTICE BLACKMUN and JUSTICE SOUTER join, dissenting.

The communications industry has an unusually dynamic character. In 1934, Congress authorized the Federal Communications Commission (FCC) to regulate "a field of enterprise the dominant characteristic of which was the rapid pace of its unfolding." National Broadcasting Co. v. United States, 319 U.S. 190, 219, (1943). The Communications Act (the Act) gives the FCC unusually broad discretion to meet new and unanticipated problems in order to fulfill its sweeping mandate "to make available, as far as possible, to all the people of the United States, a rapid, efficient, Nation-wide and world-wide wire and radio communication service with adequate facilities at reasonable charges." 47 U.S.C. § 151. This Court's consistent interpretation of the Act has afforded the Commission ample leeway to interpret and apply its statutory powers and responsibilities. The Court today abandons that approach in favor of a rigid literalism that deprives the FCC of the flexibility Congress meant it to have in order to implement the core policies of the Act in rapidly changing conditions.

I

At the time the Communications Act was passed, the telephone industry was dominated by the American Telephone & Telegraph Company and its affiliates. Title II of the Act, which establishes the framework for FCC regulation of common carriers by wire, was clearly a response to that dominance. As the Senate Report explained, "[u]nder existing provisions of the Interstate Commerce Act the regulation of the telephone monopoly has been practically nil. This vast monopoly which so immediately serves the needs of the people in their daily and social life must be effectively regulated." S.Rep. No. 781, 73d Cong., 2d Sess., 2 (1934).

. . . Congress doubtless viewed the filed rate provisions as an important mechanism to guard against abusive practices by wire communications monopolies. But it is quite wrong to suggest that the mere process of filing rate schedules—rather than the substantive duty of reasonably priced and nondiscriminatory service—is "the heart of the common-carrier section of the federal Communications Act."

II

In response to new conditions in the communications industry, including stirrings of competition in the long-distance telephone market, the FCC in 1979 began reexamining its regulatory scheme. . . .

III

. . . The Commission plausibly concluded that any slight enforcement benefits a tariff-filing requirement might offer were outweighed by the burdens it would put on new entrants and consumers. Thus, the sole question for us is whether the FCC's policy, however sensible, is nonetheless inconsistent with the Act.

In my view, each of the Commission's detariffing orders was squarely within its power to "modify any requirement" of § 203. Subsection 203(b)(2) plainly confers at least some discretion to modify the general rule that carriers file tariffs, for it speaks of "any requirement." Subsection 203(c) of the Act, ignored by the Court, squarely supports the FCC's position; it prohibits carriers from providing service without a tariff "unless otherwise provided by or under authority of this Act." Subsection 203(b)(2) is plainly one provision that "otherwise provides" and thereby authorizes service without a filed schedule. The FCC's authority to modify § 203's requirements in "particular instances" or by "general order applicable to special circumstances or conditions" emphasizes the expansive character of the Commission's authority: modifications may be narrow or broad, depending upon the Commission's appraisal of current conditions. From the vantage of a Congress seeking to regulate an almost completely monopolized industry, the advent of competition is surely a "special circumstance or condition" that might legitimately call for different regulatory treatment.

The only statutory exception to the Commission's modification authority provides that it may not extend the 120–day notice period set out in § 203(b)(1). See § 203(b)(2). The Act thus imposes a specific limit on the Commission's authority to stiffen that regulatory imposition on carriers, but does not confine the Commission's authority to relax it. It was no stretch for the FCC to draw from this single, unidirectional statutory limitation on its modification authority the inference that its authority is otherwise unlimited.

According to the Court, the term "modify," as explicated in all but the most unreliable dictionaries, rules out the Commission's claimed authority to relieve nondominant carriers of the basic obligation to file tariffs. Dictionaries can be useful aids in statutory interpretation, but they are no substitute for close analysis of what words mean as used in a particular statutory context. Even if the sole possible meaning of "modify" were to make "minor" changes, further elaboration is needed to show why the detariffing policy should fail. The Commission came to its present policy through a series of rulings that gradually relaxed the filing requirements for nondominant carriers. Whether the current policy should count as a cataclysmic or merely an incremental departure from the § 203(a) baseline depends on whether one focuses on particular carriers' obligations to file (in which case the Commission's policy arguably works a major shift) or on the statutory policies behind the tariff-filing requirement (which remain satisfied because market constraints on nondominant carriers obviate the need for rate-filing). When § 203 is viewed as part of a statute whose aim is to constrain monopoly power, the Commission's decision to exempt nondominant carriers is a rational and "measured" adjustment to novel circumstances—one that remains faithful to the core purpose of the tariff-filing section. See Black's Law Dictionary 1198 (3d ed. 1933) (defining "modification" as "A change; an alteration which introduces new elements into the details, or cancels some of them, but leaves the general purpose and effect of the subject-matter intact").

The Court seizes upon a particular sense of the word "modify" at the expense of another, long-established meaning that fully supports the Commission's position. That word is first defined in Webster's Collegiate Dictionary 628 (4th ed. 1934) as meaning "to limit or reduce in extent or degree."[2] The Commission's permissive detariffing policy fits comfortably within this common understanding of the term. The FCC has in effect adopted a general rule stating that "if you are dominant you must file, but if you are nondominant you need not." The Commission's partial detariff-

---

2. See also 9 Oxford English Dictionary 952 (2d ed. 1989) ("2. To alter in the direction of moderation or lenity; to make less severe, rigorous, or decided; to qualify, tone down. ...); Random House Dictionary of the English Language 1236 (2d ed. 1987) ("5. to reduce or lessen in degree or extent; moderate; soften; to modify one's demands"); Webster's Third New International Dictionary 1452 (1981) ("1: to make more temperate and less extreme: lessen the severity of; ... 'traffic rules were modified to let him pass' ");

Webster's New Collegiate Dictionary 739 (1973) ("1. to make less extreme; MODERATE"); Webster's Seventh New Collegiate Dictionary 544 (1963) (same); Webster's Seventh New International Dictionary 1577 (2d ed. 1934) ("2. To reduce in extent or degree; to moderate; qualify; lower; as, to modify heat, pain, punishment"); N. Webster, American Dictionary of the English Language (1828) ("To moderate; to qualify; to reduce in extent or degree. Of his grace He modifies his first severe decree. Dryden").

ing policy—which excuses nondominant carriers from filing on condition that they remain nondominant—is simply a relaxation of a costly regulatory requirement that recent developments had rendered pointless and counterproductive in a certain class of cases.

A modification pursuant to § 203(b)(1), like any other order issued under the Act, must of course be consistent with the purposes of the statute. On this point, the Court asserts that the Act's prohibition against unreasonable and discriminatory rates "would not be susceptible of effective enforcement if rates were not publicly filed." That determination, of course, is for the Commission to make in the first instance. But the Commission has repeatedly explained that (i) a carrier that lacks market power is entirely unlikely to charge unreasonable or discriminatory rates, (ii) the statutory bans on unreasonable charges and price discrimination apply with full force regardless of whether carriers have to file tariffs, (iii) any suspected violations by nondominant carriers can be addressed on the Commission's own motion or on a damages complaint filed pursuant to § 206, and (iv) the FCC can reimpose a tariff requirement should violations occur. The Court does not adequately respond to the FCC's explanations, and gives no reason whatsoever to doubt the Commission's considered judgment that tariff-filing is altogether unnecessary in the case of competitive carriers; the majority's ineffective enforcement argument lacks any evidentiary or historical support.

The filed tariff provisions of the Communications Act are not ends in themselves, but are merely one of several procedural means for the Commission to ensure that carriers do not charge unreasonable or discriminatory rates. The Commission has reasonably concluded that this particular means of enforcing the statute's substantive mandates will prove counterproductive in the case of nondominant long distance carriers. Even if the 1934 Congress did not define the scope of the Commission's modification authority with perfect scholarly precision, this is surely a paradigm case for judicial deference to the agency's interpretation, particularly in a statutory regime so obviously meant to maximize administrative flexibility. Whatever the best reading of § 203(b)(2), the Commission's reading cannot in my view be termed unreasonable. It is informed (as ours is not) by a practical understanding of the role (or lack thereof) that filed tariffs play in the modern regulatory climate and in the telecommunications industry. Since 1979, the FCC has sought to adapt measures originally designed to control monopoly power to new market conditions. It has carefully and consistently explained that mandatory tariff-filing rules frustrate the core statutory interest in rate reasonableness. The Commission's use of the "discretion" expressly conferred by § 203(b)(2) reflects "a reasonable accommodation of manifestly competing interests and is entitled to deference: the regulatory scheme is technical and complex, the agency considered the matter in a detailed and reasoned fashion, and the decision involves reconciling conflicting policies." Chevron U.S.A. Inc. v. Natural Resources Defense Council, Inc., 467 U.S. 837, 865, (1984). The FCC has permissibly interpreted its § 203(b)(2) authority in service of the goals Congress set forth in the Communications Act. We should sustain its eminently sound, experience-tested, and uncommonly well explained judgment.

I respectfully dissent.

NOTES ON MCI'S APPROACH TO STATUTORY INTERPRETATION

(1) NOTE, LOOKING IT UP: DICTIONARIES AND STATUTORY INTERPRETATION, 107 Harv. L. Rev. 1437, 1454 (1994): A LEXIS search of Supreme Court precedents revealed the following:

NUMBER OF REFERENCES[c] TO DICTIONARIES, 1842 TERM–1992 TERM

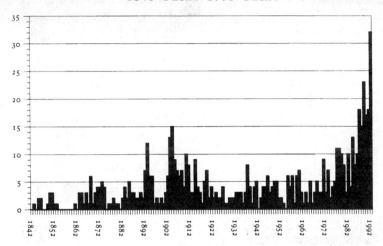

[c] Includes all cases that use the words "dictionary" or "dictionaries." Search of LEXIS, Genfed library, US file (Jan. 4, 1994).

(2) Side-by-side with the rise of dictionaries has been an increased wariness on the part of some Justices in relying on Committee Reports, floor debates, and other sources of "legislative history." For a good exposition of Justice Scalia's opposition to the use of legislative history, and of Justice Stevens' endorsement of its use, see their respective opinions in Bank One Chicago, N.A. v. Midwest Bank & Trust Co., 516 U.S. 264 (1996). For an example of Justice Scalia's willingness to consider other sources of meaning for a text, such as trade usage, see his opinion for a unanimous Court in Atlantic Mutual Ins. Co. v. Commissioner of Internal Revenue, 523 U.S. 382 (1998).

(3) JOHN F. MANNING, TEXTUALISM AND THE EQUITY OF THE STATUTE, 101 Colum. L. Rev. 1, 108–109 (2001): "If textualists were literalists, it would be easy to understand the attraction to equitable interpretation. Modern textualists, however, are not literalists. In contrast to their early-twentieth-century predecessors in the 'plain meaning' school, they do not claim that interpretation can occur 'within the four corners' of a statute, or that 'the duty of interpretation does not arise' when a text is 'plain.' Rather, modern textualists acknowledge that language has meaning only in context. As discussed, they believe that statutory language, like all language, conveys

meaning only because a linguistic community attaches common understandings to words and phrases, and relies on shared conventions for deciphering those words and phrases in particular contexts. Hence, textualists ask how 'a skilled, objectively reasonable user of words' would have understood the statutory text, as applied to the problem before the court.

"The 'reasonable user' approach gives textualists significant room to account for the nuances of language, a factor that is especially significant in a mature legal system with a rich set of background legal understandings and conventions. Textualists, of course, often consult dictionaries as an important historical record of the ways in which speakers have used words in the past. But they do not stop there. ... Like any reasonable language user, textualists pay attention to the glosses often put on language (even in ordinary usage), the specialized connotations of established terms of art, and the background conventions that sometimes tell readers how to fill in the gaps inevitably left in statutory directions. Each of these considerations focuses on faithfully decoding the text, while sharply reducing the basic justification for the equity of the statute."

(4) THOMAS W. MERRILL, TEXTUALISM AND THE FUTURE OF THE CHEVRON DOCTRINE, 72 Wash. U. L.Q. 351, 354, 371–73 (1994): "Textualism is clearly ascendant [in recent Supreme Court opinions]. The use of legislative history (a disfavored tool among textualists) is dropping precipitously, while the use of dictionaries (a favored tool) is moving up.

" ... [T]extualism triumphant would lead to a permanent subordination of the Chevron doctrine.

"This has to do with the style of judging associated with textualism. Intentionalism mandates an 'archeological' excavation of the past, producing opinions written in the style of the dry archivist sifting through countless documents in search of the tell-tale smoking gun of congressional intent. Textualism, in contrast, seems to transform statutory interpretation into a kind of exercise in judicial ingenuity. The textualist judge treats questions of interpretation like a puzzle to which it is assumed there is one right answer. The task is to assemble the various pieces of linguistic data, dictionary definitions, and canons into the best (most coherent, most explanatory) account of the meaning of the statute. This exercise places a great premium on cleverness. In one case the outcome turns on the placement of a comma, in another on the inconsistency between a comma and rules of grammar, in a third on the conflict between quotation marks and the language of the text. One day arguments must be advanced in support of broad dictionary definitions; the next day in support of narrow dictionary definitions. New canons of construction and clear statement rules must be invented and old ones reinterpreted.

"This active, creative approach to interpretation is subtly incompatible with an attitude of deference toward other institutions—whether the other institution is Congress or an administrative agency. In effect, the textualist interpreter does not *find* the meaning of the statute so much as *construct* the meaning. Such a person will very likely experience some difficulty in deferring to the meanings that other institutions have developed.

"... By changing the focus from what Congress intended to what the ordinary reader would understand, textualism adopts, at least implicitly, a model of the court as an autonomous interpreter, applying its own judicially-prescribed conventions and canons for understanding the code that Congress has built up over the years. Once the Court grows comfortable with the autonomous interpreter model, its creativity in matters of statutory interpretation begins to expand apace, exemplified perhaps most clearly by the proliferating use of canons.

"Whatever the explanation for the active, creative style associated with textualism, it is fair to say that this attitude is out of sync with the Chevron doctrine, based as it is on a generalized model of the courts as faithful agents of the politically accountable branches of government. To the extent this change in style explains what appears to be an inverse relationship between the rise of textualism and the waning of Chevron, it suggests that the eclipse of the deference doctrine is likely to last as long as textualism remains dominant."

(4) A study of the Courts of Appeals cases that relied on Chevron in 1995 and 1996 tried to test the prediction that judges from different interpretive schools would apply Chevron differently—to test, that is, whether "textualist" judges would be less likely to find ambiguity under the first part of the Chevron test. Judges appointed by Presidents Reagan and Bush, who presumably were more likely to be textualist than those appointed by Presidents Carter and Clinton, in fact found ambiguity at very nearly the same rate as the other group; no statistically significant differences were found. ORIN S. KERR, SHEDDING LIGHT ON *CHEVRON*: AN EMPIRICAL STUDY OF THE *CHEVRON* DOCTRINE IN THE U.S. COURTS OF APPEALS, 15 Yale J. on Reg. 1, 42 (1998). The author comments, 15 Yale J. on Reg. at 57–59:

"In light of the substantial body of scholarship that accepts the claims of the interpretive paradigm, it is surprising that its claims are unsupported by the data. The question arises: Where did proponents of the interpretive model go wrong? I propose that the model errs by understating the degree to which theories of statutory interpretation are normative, rather than descriptive. I submit that jurists internalize interpretative norms based on their largely intuitive understandings of the proper role of the judiciary in a constitutional democracy, not on their personal answer to the hermeneutic question of how much meaning can be extracted from text. Roughly speaking, those judges who follow text more closely tend to profess a belief in a more limited, rule-following judiciary, while those who endorse a more dynamic interpretative method tend to appreciate judicial rule-making power. Whether a judge advocates or rejects textualism does not reflect the judge's capacity to find more or less meaning in text. Instead, it means that the judge believes that the body politic is better served by judges who try more or less hard to find what meaning may be there.

"The reason that the interpretive model fails in the Chevron context, then, is that Chevron asks judges an interpretive question in a context that disrupts the usual relationship between the outcomes served and the political theories that typically inform judges' interpretive methods. Chevron upsets the usual relationship between interpretation and the judicial role in two ways. First, statutory ambiguity no longer expands judicial power; it constricts it, limiting the judicial role to deferential review for unreasonableness. Conversely, finding meaning in the text no longer limits judicial power; it expands it by granting to the courts plenary review of administrative action. Second, Chevron transforms a judge's degree of commitment to the text from a means of allocating power between the legislature and the judiciary (its usual function) into a means of allocating power between the judiciary and the executive. Finding meaning in the text no longer enhances the power of the legislature over the judiciary; instead, it emphasizes the power of the judiciary over the executive. I propose that these disruptions of the typical association between interpretative method and the judicial role explains why judges do not approach Chevron's first step with their usual interpretive associations intact. Chevron's atypical interpretive context in effect suspends judges' normative associations between their approaches to text and political theory.

"Consider the case of a judge who adopts an expansive view of the judicial function and believes that the proper judicial role is to ensure that the broad policy concerns of Congress are carried out in a fair and just way. Because textualism requires a judge to adhere to text instead of purpose and justice, the judge would likely eschew textualism and instead find that most texts were ambiguous enough to allow the judge to fashion a just remedy. In the Chevron context, however, the ambiguity that would normally allow the judge to fashion a just remedy backfires. A finding of ambiguity instead binds the judge to accept a wide range of agency action, even if the judge perceives that action as unjust. Ambiguity ceases to be an engine of judicial authority and becomes an engine of uncabined executive power.

"In the absence of the usual forces pulling and pushing judges toward different interpretive approaches, judges who typically are influenced by very different normative interpretive traditions adopt roughly equivalent understandings of how ambiguous is ambiguous enough at step one. This does not mean that all judges will agree in every case, of course (although most cases are unanimous), but it does mean that no one set of judges will be led to adopt a particularly different vision of Chevron."

(5) Is a book called a dictionary the only form of dictionary? Another possible source for ascertaining the meaning of legal terms is, of course, prior legal materials. In Director, Office of Workers' Compensation Programs v. Greenwich Collieries, 512 U.S. 267 (1994), see page 269 above, the Supreme Court referred to legal treatises to determine the meaning of "burden of proof" at the time the APA was passed. A yet broader reference to legal materials as, in effect, providing a dictionary, occurred in NATIONWIDE MUTUAL INS. CO. V. DARDEN, 503 U.S. 318 (1992). Darden, who sold insurance for Nationwide, claimed to be an "employee" and so entitled to retirement benefits protected by ERISA (Employee Retirement Income Security Act of 1974); Nationwide viewed him as an independent contractor who by violating an agreement not to compete had forfeited his contractual rights. Justice Souter for a unanimous Court (503 U.S. at 322–23):

"We have often been asked to construe the meaning of 'employee' where the statute containing the term does not helpfully define it. Most recently we confronted this problem in Community for Creative Non–

Violence v. Reid, 490 U.S. 730 (1989), a case in which a sculptor and a non-profit group each claimed copyright ownership in a statute the group had commissioned from the artist. ... Because the Copyright Act nowhere defined the term 'employee,' we unanimously applied the 'well established' principle that

> [w]here Congress uses terms that have accumulated settled meaning under ... the common law, a court must infer, unless the statute otherwise dictates, that Congress means to incorporate the established meaning of these terms. ... In the past, when Congress has used the term "employee" without defining it, we have concluded that Congress intended to describe the conventional master-servant relationship as understood by common-law agency doctrine. ...

"While we supported this reading of the Copyright Act with other observations, the general rule stood as independent authority for the decision.

"So too should it stand here." ...[1]

Compare NATIONSBANK OF NORTH CAROLINA V. VARIABLE ANNUITY LIFE INS. CO., 513 U.S. 251 (1995): The National Bank Act authorizes national banks to "carry on the business of banking" but prohibits them from selling "insurance." The question in this case was raised by the Comptroller of the Currency's characterization of annuities as incidental to the banking business and not insurance. *Held*: both of the determinations were "reasonable," and therefore to be sustained under Chevron.

Justice Ginsburg, also for a unanimous court (513 U.S. at 262):

> As our decisions underscore, a characterization fitting in certain contexts may be unsuitable in others. See, e.g., Atlantic Cleaners & Dyers, Inc. v. United States, 286 U.S. 427, 433 (1932) ("meaning [of words] well may vary to meet the purposes of the law"; courts properly give words "the meaning which the legislature intended [they] should have in each instance"); cf. Cook, "Substance" and "Procedure" in the Conflict of Laws, 42 Yale L.J. 333, 337 (1933) ("The tendency to assume that a word which appears in two or more legal rules, and so in connection with more than one purpose, has and should have precisely the same scope in all of them, runs all through legal discussions. It has all the tenacity of original sin and must constantly be guarded against."). ... The Comptroller has concluded that the federal regime is best served by classifying annuities according to their functional characteristics. Congress has not ruled out that course, see Chevron, 467 U.S., at 842; courts, therefore, have no cause to dictate to the Comptroller ... the constraint [the challenger] espouses.

NOTES ON BROADER VIEWS OF MCI

(1) PETER STRAUSS, ON RESEGREGATING THE WORLDS OF STATUTE AND COMMON LAW, 1994 Sup. Ct. Rev. pp. 429, 495–97: "Perhaps the root issue for Justice Scalia [in the MCI case] is one of delegation—a factor that has been

---

1. Are you worried about the contrary approach to "employee" taken in the Hearst case, p. 979 above? See 503 U.S. at 324–25.

important to him in other contexts. It is not merely the largeness of the change being effected, but also that accepting it will entail accepting that an agency can be empowered to change its mandate. For Justice Stevens, author of striking passages in Chevron strongly endorsing delegation, the FCC has 'unusually broad discretion to meet new and unanticipated problems in order to fulfill its sweeping mandate'; this power to 'modify' is no different in kind from the Commission's responsibility to allocate licenses and otherwise act in accordance with 'public convenience, interest, or necessity.' Justice Scalia accepts broad delegations only because he cannot imagine a judicially manageable standard for telling the good from the bad, a handicap he does not face if he can plausibly construe an agency's authority in a narrow way. It is revealing in this respect that he never explains how he concludes that the New Deal Congress that so broadly empowered all the agencies it created, not just the FCC, intended here only a narrow grant of authority.

"The result, in any event, is essentially formal and text-bound. Whether the FCC has rightly caught the implications of new market conditions and adapted its regulatory regime to them are not issues for the Court. '[O]ur estimations, and the Commission's estimations, of desirable policy cannot alter the meaning of the Federal Communications Act of 1934. ... [A] whole new regime of regulation (or of free-market competition) ... may well be a better regime but is not the one that Congress established.' Of course, the validity of the 'but is not' clause depends on one's conclusions about the meaning of 'modify,' one's general estimation of the breadth of authority Congress bestowed on the Commission, and also on one's acceptance or not of agency and/or judicial authority to follow Congress's lead by using existing text to adapt law to changing circumstances. ... Looking to the general climate of change, in regulation and in technology, it is hard to imagine that the FCC erred. The general trend of legislation, the absence of any legislative effort to correct the Commission, indeed the Commission's dogged persistence in its deregulatory course despite prior discouragement from the courts—all suggest that this was the right reading. It was one that both ancient and contemporary understandings of 'modify' would permit. The insistence that Congress unmistakably act tends, again, to deny the coherence-building judicial function."

(2) "In 1996, the Food and Drug Administration (FDA), after having expressly disavowed any such authority since its inception, asserted jurisdiction to regulate tobacco products." So began FDA v. BROWN & WILLIAMSON TOBACCO CORP., 529 U.S. 120 (2000). In an opinion by Justice O'Connor for five members of the court, *held*: the FDA's assertion of jurisdiction was unwarranted. First, the Food, Drug and Cosmetic Act (FDCA) was premised on ensuring that drugs were either safe or taken off the market. The FDA's own approach to cigarettes—involving regulation of advertising, labeling, and promotion, but not banning sale to adults—would do neither. "The inescapable conclusion is that there is no room for tobacco products within the FDCA's regulatory scheme." Second, since 1965 Congress had enacted six statutes regarding tobacco, each time acting on the premise, supported by the the FDA at the time, that the FDA lacked jurisdiction. "Under these circumstances, it is clear that Congress' tobacco-specific

legislation has effectively ratified the FDA's previous position that it lacks jurisdiction to regulate tobacco." She continued (529 U.S. at 159–161):

"Finally, our inquiry into whether Congress has directly spoken to the precise question at issue is shaped, at least in some measure, by the nature of the question presented. Deference under Chevron to an agency's construction of a statute that it administers is premised on the theory that a statute's ambiguity constitutes an implicit delegation from Congress to the agency to fill in the statutory gaps. In extraordinary cases, however, there may be reason to hesitate before concluding that Congress has intended such an implicit delegation.

"This is hardly an ordinary case. Contrary to its representations to Congress since 1914, the FDA has now asserted jurisdiction to regulate an industry constituting a significant portion of the American economy. . . . Owing to its unique place in American history and society, tobacco has its own unique political history. Congress, for better or for worse, has created a distinct regulatory scheme for tobacco products, squarely rejected proposals to give the FDA jurisdiction over tobacco, and repeatedly acted to preclude any agency from exercising significant policymaking authority in the area. Given this history and the breadth of the authority that the FDA has asserted, we are obliged to defer not to the agency's expansive construction of the statute, but to Congress' consistent judgment to deny the FDA this power.

"Our decision in MCI Telecommunications Corp. v. American Telephone & Telegraph Co., 512 U.S. 218 (1994), is instructive. That case involved the proper construction of the term 'modify' in § 203(b) of the Communications Act of 1934. The FCC contended that, because the Act gave it the discretion to 'modify any requirement' imposed under the statute, it therefore possessed the authority to render voluntary the otherwise mandatory requirement that long distance carriers file their rates. We rejected the FCC's construction, finding 'not the slightest doubt' that Congress had directly spoken to the question. In reasoning even more apt here, we concluded that '[i]t is highly unlikely that Congress would leave the determination of whether an industry will be entirely, or even substantially, rate-regulated to agency discretion—and even more unlikely that it would achieve that through such a subtle device as permission to "modify" rate-filing requirements.'

"As in MCI, we are confident that Congress could not have intended to delegate a decision of such economic and political significance to an agency in so cryptic a fashion. To find that the FDA has the authority to regulate tobacco products, one must not only adopt an extremely strained understanding of 'safety' as it is used throughout the Act—a concept central to the FDCA's regulatory scheme—but also ignore the plain implication of Congress' subsequent tobacco-specific legislation. It is therefore clear, based on the FDCA's overall regulatory scheme and the subsequent tobacco legislation that Congress has directly spoken to the question at issue and precluded the FDA from regulating tobacco products."

Compare Justice Breyer's dissent for four (529 U.S. at 190–91):

"[O]ne might claim that courts, when interpreting statutes, should assume in close cases that a decision with 'enormous social consequences' should be made by democratically elected Members of Congress rather than by unelected agency administrators. Cf. Kent v. Dulles, 357 U.S. 116, 129 (1958) (assuming Congress did not want to delegate the power to make rules interfering with exercise of basic human liberties). If there is such a background canon of interpretation, however, I do not believe it controls the outcome here.

"Insofar as the decision to regulate tobacco reflects the policy of an administration, it is a decision for which that administration, and those politically elected officials who support it, must (and will) take responsibility. And the very importance of the decision taken here, as well as its attendant publicity, means that the public is likely to be aware of it and to hold those officials politically accountable. Presidents, just like Members of Congress, are elected by the public. Indeed, the President and Vice President are the only public officials whom the entire Nation elects. I do not believe that an administrative agency decision of this magnitude—one that is important, conspicuous, and controversial—can escape the kind of public scrutiny that is essential in any democracy. And such a review will take place whether it is the Congress or the Executive Branch that makes the relevant decision."

Whichever view you favor, is MCI now to be understood as precedent only for a certain type of situation? If so, does it represent purposive reasoning in a textualist disguise?

(3) The possibility that a court will intensify its review when dealing with the outer limits of an agency's power can act as a siren song to lawyers for regulated parties, tempting them to frame even the "ordinary" case in terms of the agency's supposed overreaching of its jurisdiction. This temptation is even stronger if there is also the chance of judicial intervention early enough to completely derail the administrative proceeding. Doctrines governing the availability of judicial review, such as those requiring the exhaustion of administrative proceedings, control this problem to some extent. See Chapter 9, section 4 below.

Especially in investigatory and enforcement proceedings, however, another avenue to judicial process often open to regulated parties is to resist an administrative subpoena, forcing the agency to go to court to have it enforced. The APA directs courts to enforce a subpoena "to the extent that it is found to be in accordance with law," § 555(d). By and large the courts have interpreted this directive so as not to hinder the fundamentals of the administrative process. The agency must, of course, show that it has the power to issue subpoenas, but grants of the power are liberally construed. Some traditional legal grounds do operate to narrow some subpoenas—to exclude information within the scope of the attorney-client privilege or to require specification and perhaps narrowing of vague or unreasonably burdensome requests. The Fourth and Fifth Amendments at one time powerfully constrained the breadth of agency subpoenas, but as construed by the Supreme Court since the 1940s they impose few limits. See Richard J. Pierce, Jr., Administrative Law Treatise § 4.1 (4th ed., 2002). As to questions of statutory authority, the subpoena must be issued in pursuit of an authorized objective and germane to a lawful subject of inquiry. But, perhaps to avoid throwing up the very roadblocks litigants hope for, courts generally give the agency very wide latitude on these matters. "We have repeatedly admonished," said the First Circuit, "that questions concerning the scope of an agency's substantive authority to regulate are not to be resolved in subpoena enforcement proceedings. . . . As long as the agency's assertion of authority is not apocryphal, a procedurally sound subpoena must be enforced." United States v. Sturm, Ruger & Co., 84 F.3d 1, 5–6 (1st Cir.1996). Which is not to say that resisters never prevail. Thus, when a tribal fish and wildlife commission claimed to be within the Fair Labor Standards Act exemption for law enforcement officials and no factual information was needed to resolve the question of coverage, Judge Posner found that the Secretary of Labor's argument that the subpoena be enforced without addressing the issue of statutory coverage "need not detain us long. . . . The Commission should not be burdened with having to comply with a subpoena. . . ." Reich v. Great Lakes Indian Fish and Wildlife Commission, 4 F.3d 490, 491–92 (7th Cir.1993).

United States v. Mead Corporation

Supreme Court of the United States, 2001.
533 U.S. 218.

■ SOUTER, J., delivered the opinion of the Court, in which REHNQUIST, C.J., AND STEVENS, O'CONNOR, KENNEDY, THOMAS, GINSBURG, AND BREYER, JJ., joined. SCALIA, J., filed a dissenting opinion.

■ JUSTICE SOUTER delivered the opinion of the Court.

The question is whether a tariff classification ruling by the United States Customs Service deserves judicial deference. The Federal Circuit rejected Customs's invocation of Chevron U.S.A. Inc. v. Natural Resources Defense Council, Inc., 467 U.S. 837 (1984), in support of such a ruling, to which it gave no deference. We agree that a tariff classification has no claim to judicial deference under Chevron, there being no indication that Congress intended such a ruling to carry the force of law, but we hold that under Skidmore v. Swift & Co., 323 U.S. 134 (1944), the ruling is eligible to claim respect according to its persuasiveness.

I

A

Imports are taxed under the Harmonized Tariff Schedule of the United States (HTSUS), 19 U.S.C. § 1202. Title 19 U.S.C. § 1500(b) provides that Customs "shall, under rules and regulations prescribed by the Secretary [of the Treasury] . . . fix the final classification and rate of duty applicable to . . . merchandise" under the HTSUS. Section 1502(a) provides that

> [t]he Secretary of the Treasury shall establish and promulgate such rules and regulations not inconsistent with the law (including regulations establishing procedures for the issuance of binding rulings prior to the entry of the merchandise concerned), and may disseminate such information as may be necessary to secure a just, impartial, and

uniform appraisement of imported merchandise and the classification and assessment of duties thereon at the various ports of entry.[1]

The Secretary provides for tariff rulings before the entry of goods by regulations authorizing "ruling letters" setting tariff classifications for particular imports. 19 CFR § 177.8 (2000). A ruling letter

> represents the official position of the Customs Service with respect to the particular transaction or issue described therein and is binding on all Customs Service personnel in accordance with the provisions of this section until modified or revoked. In the absence of a change of practice or other modification or revocation which affects the principle of the ruling set forth in the ruling letter, that principle may be cited as authority in the disposition of transactions involving the same circumstances. § 177.9(a).

After the transaction that gives it birth, a ruling letter is to "be applied only with respect to transactions involving articles identical to the sample submitted with the ruling request or to articles whose description is identical to the description set forth in the ruling letter." § 177.9(b)(2). As a general matter, such a letter is "subject to modification or revocation without notice to any person, except the person to whom the letter was addressed," § 177.9(c), and the regulations consequently provide that "no other person should rely on the ruling letter or assume that the principles of that ruling will be applied in connection with any transaction other than the one described in the letter," *ibid.* Since ruling letters respond to transactions of the moment, they are not subject to notice and comment before being issued, may be published but need only be made "available for public inspection," 19 U.S.C. § 1625(a), and, at the time this action arose, could be modified without notice and comment under most circumstances, 19 CFR § 177.10(c) (2000).

Any of the 46 port-of-entry Customs offices may issue ruling letters, and so may the Customs Headquarters Office. ... Most ruling letters contain little or no reasoning, but simply describe goods and state the appropriate category and tariff. A few letters, like the Headquarters ruling at issue here, set out a rationale in some detail.

B

Respondent, the Mead Corporation, imports "day planners," three-ring binders with pages having room for notes of daily schedules and phone numbers and addresses, together with a calendar and suchlike. The tariff schedule on point falls under the HTSUS heading for "[r]egisters, account books, notebooks, order books, receipt books, letter pads, memorandum pads, diaries and similar articles," HTSUS subheading 4820.10, which comprises two subcategories. Items in the first, "[d]iaries, notebooks and address books, bound; memorandum pads, letter pads and similar articles," were subject to a tariff of 4.0% at the time in controversy. Objects in the second, covering "[o]ther" items, were free of duty.

---

1. The statutory term "ruling" is defined by regulation as "a written statement ... that interprets and applies the provisions of the Customs and related laws to a specific set of facts." 19 CFR § 177.1(d)(1) (2000).

Between 1989 and 1993, Customs repeatedly treated day planners under the "other" HTSUS subheading. In January 1993, however, Customs changed its position, and issued a Headquarters ruling letter classifying Mead's day planners as "Diaries ..., bound" subject to tariff under subheading 4820.10.20. That letter was short on explanation, but after Mead's protest, Customs Headquarters issued a new letter, carefully reasoned but never published, reaching the same conclusion. This letter considered two definitions of "diary" from the Oxford English Dictionary, the first covering a daily journal of the past day's events, the second a book including "printed dates for daily memoranda and jottings; also ... calendars. ..." Customs concluded that "diary" was not confined to the first, in part because the broader definition reflects commercial usage and hence the "commercial identity of these items in the marketplace." As for the definition of "bound," Customs concluded that HTSUS was not referring to "bookbinding," but to a less exact sort of fastening described in the Harmonized Commodity Description and Coding System Explanatory Notes to Heading 4820, which spoke of binding by "reinforcements or fittings of metal, plastics, etc."

Customs rejected Mead's further protest of the second Headquarters ruling letter, and Mead filed suit in the Court of International Trade (CIT). The CIT granted the Government's motion for summary judgment, adopting Customs's reasoning without saying anything about deference. 17 F.Supp.2d 1004 (1998).

Mead then went to the United States Court of Appeals for the Federal Circuit. ...

The Federal Circuit ... reversed the CIT and held that Customs classification rulings should not get Chevron deference, ... Rulings are not preceded by notice and comment as under the Administrative Procedure Act (APA), 5 U.S.C. § 553, they "do not carry the force of law and are not, like regulations, intended to clarify the rights and obligations of importers beyond the specific case under review." 185 F.3d, at 1307. The appeals court thought classification rulings had a weaker Chevron claim even than Internal Revenue Service interpretive rulings, to which that court gives no deference; unlike rulings by the IRS, Customs rulings issue from many locations and need not be published. 185 F.3d, at 1307–1308.

The Court of Appeals accordingly gave no deference at all to the ruling classifying the Mead day planners and rejected the agency's reasoning as to both "diary" and "bound." It thought that planners were not diaries because they had no space for "relatively extensive notations about events, observations, feelings, or thoughts" in the past. Id., at 1310. And it concluded that diaries "bound" in subheading 4810.10.20 presupposed "unbound" diaries, such that treating ring-fastened diaries as "bound" would leave the "unbound diary" an empty category. Id., at 1311.

We granted certiorari, in order to consider the limits of Chevron deference owed to administrative practice in applying a statute. We hold that administrative implementation of a particular statutory provision qualifies for Chevron deference when it appears that Congress delegated authority to the agency generally to make rules carrying the force of law, and that the agency interpretation claiming deference was promulgated in the exercise of that authority. Delegation of such authority may be shown in a variety of ways, as by an agency's power to engage in adjudication or notice-and-comment rulemaking, or by some other indication of a comparable congressional intent. The Customs ruling at issue here fails to qualify, although the possibility that it deserves some deference under Skidmore leads us to vacate and remand.

II

A

When Congress has "explicitly left a gap for an agency to fill, there is an express delegation of authority to the agency to elucidate a specific provision of the statute by regulation," Chevron, 467 U.S., at 843–844, and any ensuing regulation is binding in the courts unless procedurally defective, arbitrary or capricious in substance, or manifestly contrary to the statute. APA, 5 U.S.C. §§ 706(2)(A), (D). But whether or not they enjoy any express delegation of authority on a particular question, agencies charged with applying a statute necessarily make all sorts of interpretive choices, and while not all of those choices bind judges to follow them, they certainly may influence courts facing questions the agencies have already answered. "[T]he well-reasoned views of the agencies implementing a statute 'constitute a body of experience and informed judgment to which courts and litigants may properly resort for guidance,' " Bragdon v. Abbott, 524 U.S. 624, 642 (1998) (quoting Skidmore, 323 U.S., at 139–140), and "[w]e have long recognized that considerable weight should be accorded to an executive department's construction of a statutory scheme it is entrusted to administer . . . ." Chevron, *supra,* at 844. The fair measure of deference to an agency administering its own statute has been understood to vary with circumstances, and courts have looked to the degree of the agency's care, its consistency, formality, and relative expertness, and to the persuasiveness of the agency's position. The approach has produced a spectrum of judicial responses, from great respect at one end, to near indifference at the other. Justice Jackson summed things up in Skidmore v. Swift & Co.:

> The weight [accorded to an administrative] judgment in a particular case will depend upon the thoroughness evident in its consideration, the validity of its reasoning, its consistency with earlier and later pronouncements, and all those factors which give it power to persuade, if lacking power to control. 323 U.S., at 140.

Since 1984, we have identified a category of interpretive choices distinguished by an additional reason for judicial deference. This Court in Chevron recognized that Congress not only engages in express delegation of specific interpretive authority, but that "[s]ometimes the legislative delegation to an agency on a particular question is implicit." 467 U.S., at 844. Congress, that is, may not have expressly delegated authority or responsibility to implement a particular provision or fill a particular gap. Yet it can still be apparent from the agency's generally conferred authority and other statutory circumstances that Congress would expect the agency to be able to speak with the force of law when it addresses ambiguity in the statute or fills a space in the enacted law, even one about which "Congress did not actually have an intent" as to a particular result. *Id.,* at 845. When circumstances implying such an expectation exist, a reviewing court has no business rejecting an agency's exercise of its generally conferred authority to resolve a particular statutory ambiguity simply because the agency's chosen resolution seems unwise, but is obliged to accept the agency's position if Congress has not previously spoken to the point at issue and the agency's interpretation is reasonable; cf. 5 U.S.C. § 706(2) (a reviewing court shall set aside agency action, findings, and conclusions found to be "arbitrary, capricious, an abuse of discretion, or otherwise not in accordance with law").

We have recognized a very good indicator of delegation meriting Chevron treatment in express congressional authorizations to engage in the process of rulemaking or adjudication that produces regulations or rulings for which deference is claimed. It is fair to assume generally that Congress contemplates administrative action with the effect of law when it provides for a relatively formal administrative procedure tending to foster the fairness and deliberation that should underlie a pronouncement of such force.[2] Thus, the overwhelming number of our cases applying Chevron deference have reviewed the fruits of notice-and-comment rulemaking or formal adjudication.[3] That said, and as significant as notice-and-comment is in pointing to Chevron authority, the want of that procedure here does not decide the case, for we have sometimes found reasons for Chevron deference even when no such administrative formality was required and none was afforded, see, *e.g.*, NationsBank of N.C., N.A. v. Variable Annuity Life Ins. Co., 513 U.S. 251, 256–257, 263 (1995).[4] The fact that the tariff classification here was not a product of such formal process does not alone, therefore, bar the application of Chevron.

There are, nonetheless, ample reasons to deny Chevron deference here. The authorization for classification rulings, and Customs's practice in making them, present a case far removed not only from notice-and-comment process, but from any other circumstances reasonably suggesting that Congress ever thought of classification rulings as deserving the deference claimed for them here.

B

No matter which angle we choose for viewing the Customs ruling letter in this case, it fails to qualify under Chevron. On the face of the statute, to begin with, the terms of the congressional delegation give no

2. See Merrill & Hickman, Chevron's Domain, 89 Geo. L.J. 833, 872 (2001) ("[I]f Chevron rests on a presumption about congressional intent, then Chevron should apply only where Congress would want Chevron to apply. In delineating the types of delegations of agency authority that trigger Chevron deference, it is therefore important to determine whether a plausible case can be made that Congress would want such a delegation to mean that agencies enjoy primary interpretational authority").

3. For rulemaking cases, see, e.g., [19 cases cited]. For adjudication cases, see e.g., [8 cases cited].

4. In NationsBank of N.C., N.A. v. Variable Annuity Life Ins. Co., 513 U.S. 251, 256–257 (1995), we quoted longstanding precedent concluding that "[t]he Comptroller of the Currency is charged with the enforcement of banking laws to an extent that warrants the invocation of [the rule of deference] with respect to his deliberative conclusions as to the meaning of these laws" (internal quotation marks omitted).

indication that Congress meant to delegate authority to Customs to issue classification rulings with the force of law. We are not, of course, here making any global statement about Customs's authority, for it is true that the general rulemaking power conferred on Customs, see 19 U.S.C. § 1624, authorizes some regulation with the force of law, or "legal norms." It is true as well that Congress had classification rulings in mind when it explicitly authorized, in a parenthetical, the issuance of "regulations establishing procedures for the issuance of binding rulings prior to the entry of the merchandise concerned," 19 U.S.C. § 1502(a). The reference to binding classifications does not, however, bespeak the legislative type of activity that would naturally bind more than the parties to the ruling, once the goods classified are admitted into this country. And though the statute's direction to disseminate "information" necessary to "secure" uniformity, 19 U.S.C. § 1502(a), seems to assume that a ruling may be precedent in later transactions, precedential value alone does not add up to Chevron entitlement; interpretive rules may sometimes function as precedents, see Strauss, The Rulemaking Continuum, 41 Duke L.J. 1463, 1472–1473 (1992), and they enjoy no Chevron status as a class. In any event, any precedential claim of a classification ruling is counterbalanced by the provision for independent review of Customs classifications by the CIT, see 28 U.S.C. §§ 2638–2640; . . .

It is difficult, in fact, to see in the agency practice itself any indication that Customs ever set out with a lawmaking pretense in mind when it undertook to make classifications like these. Customs does not generally engage in notice-and-comment practice when issuing them, and their treatment by the agency makes it clear that a letter's binding character as a ruling stops short of third parties; Customs has regarded a classification as conclusive only as between itself and the importer to whom it was issued, 19 CFR § 177.9(c) (2000), and even then only until Customs has given advance notice of intended change, §§ 177.9(a), (c). Other importers are in fact warned against assuming any right of detrimental reliance. § 177.9(c).

Indeed, to claim that classifications have legal force is to ignore the reality that 46 different Customs offices issue 10,000 to 15,000 of them each year. Any suggestion that rulings intended to have the force of law are being churned out at a rate of 10,000 a year at an agency's 46 scattered offices is simply self-refuting. Although the circumstances are less startling here, with a Headquarters letter in issue, none of the relevant statutes recognizes this category of rulings as separate or different from others; there is thus no indication that a more potent delegation might have been understood as going to Headquarters even when Headquarters provides developed reasoning, as it did in this instance.

In sum, classification rulings are best treated like "interpretations contained in policy statements, agency manuals, and enforcement guidelines." Christensen v. Harris County, 529 U.S., 576, 587 (2000). They are beyond the Chevron pale.

C

To agree with the Court of Appeals that Customs ruling letters do not fall within Chevron is not, however, to place them outside the pale of any

Chevron did not overrule Skidmore

deference whatever. Chevron did nothing to eliminate Skidmore's holding that an agency's interpretation may merit some deference whatever its form, given the "specialized experience and broader investigations and information" available to the agency, 323 U.S., at 139, and given the value of uniformity in its administrative and judicial understandings of what a national law requires, *id.*, at 140.

There is room at least to raise a Skidmore claim here, where the regulatory scheme is highly detailed, and Customs can bring the benefit of specialized experience to bear on the subtle questions in this case: whether the daily planner with room for brief daily entries falls under "diaries," when diaries are grouped with "notebooks and address books, bound; memorandum pads, letter pads and similar articles," HTSUS subheading 4820.10.20; and whether a planner with a ring binding should qualify as "bound," when a binding may be typified by a book, but also may have "reinforcements or fittings of metal, plastics, etc.," Harmonized Commodity Description and Coding System Explanatory Notes to Heading 4820, p. 687. A classification ruling in this situation may therefore at least seek a respect proportional to its "power to persuade." Such a ruling may surely claim the merit of its writer's thoroughness, logic and expertness, its fit with prior interpretations, and any other sources of weight.

D

Underlying the position we take here, like the position expressed by Justice Scalia in dissent, is a choice about the best way to deal with an inescapable feature of the body of congressional legislation authorizing administrative action. That feature is the great variety of ways in which the laws invest the Government's administrative arms with discretion, and with procedures for exercising it, in giving meaning to Acts of Congress. Implementation of a statute may occur in formal adjudication or the choice to defend against judicial challenge; it may occur in a central board or office or in dozens of enforcement agencies dotted across the country; its institutional lawmaking may be confined to the resolution of minute detail or extend to legislative rulemaking on matters intentionally left by Congress to be worked out at the agency level.

Although we all accept the position that the Judiciary should defer to at least some of this multifarious administrative action, we have to decide how to take account of the great range of its variety. If the primary objective is to simplify the judicial process of giving or withholding deference, then the diversity of statutes authorizing discretionary administrative action must be declared irrelevant or minimized. If, on the other hand, it is simply implausible that Congress intended such a broad range of statutory authority to produce only two varieties of administrative action, demanding either Chevron deference or none at all, then the breadth of the spectrum of possible agency action must be taken into account. Justice Scalia's first priority over the years has been to limit and simplify. The Court's choice has been to tailor deference to variety. This acceptance of the range of statutory variation has led the Court to recognize more than one variety of judicial deference, just as the Court has recognized a variety of indicators that Congress would expect Chevron deference.[5]

---

5. It is, of course, true that the limit of Chevron deference is not marked by a hard-edged rule. But Chevron itself is a good example showing when Chevron deference is

Our respective choices are repeated today. Justice Scalia would pose the question of deference as an either-or choice. On his view that Chevron rendered Skidmore anachronistic, when courts owe any deference it is Chevron deference that they owe. Whether courts do owe deference in a given case turns, for him, on whether the agency action (if reasonable) is "authoritative." The character of the authoritative derives, in turn, not from breadth of delegation or the agency's procedure in implementing it, but is defined as the "official" position of an agency, and may ultimately be a function of administrative persistence alone.

The Court, on the other hand, said nothing in Chevron to eliminate Skidmore's recognition of various justifications for deference depending on statutory circumstances and agency action; Chevron was simply a case recognizing that even without express authority to fill a specific statutory gap, circumstances pointing to implicit congressional delegation present a particularly insistent call for deference. Indeed, in holding here that Chevron left Skidmore intact and applicable where statutory circumstances indicate no intent to delegate general authority to make rules with force of law, or where such authority was not invoked, we hold nothing more than we said last Term in response to the particular statutory circumstances in Christensen, to which Justice Scalia then took exception, just as he does again today.

We think, in sum, that Justice Scalia's efforts to simplify ultimately run afoul of Congress's indications that different statutes present different reasons for considering respect for the exercise of administrative authority or deference to it. Without being at odds with congressional intent much of the time, we believe that judicial responses to administrative action must continue to differentiate between Chevron and Skidmore, and that continued recognition of Skidmore is necessary for just the reasons Justice Jackson gave when that case was decided.[6]

. . .

Since the Skidmore assessment called for here ought to be made in the first instance by the Court of Appeals for the Federal Circuit or the Court of International Trade, we go no further than to vacate the judgment and remand the case for further proceedings consistent with this opinion.

It is so ordered.

■ JUSTICE SCALIA, dissenting.

Today's opinion makes an avulsive change in judicial review of federal administrative action. Whereas previously a reasonable agency application

warranted, while this is a good case showing when it is not. Judges in other, perhaps harder, cases will make reasoned choices between the two examples, the way courts have always done.

6. Surely Justice Jackson's practical criteria, along with Chevron's concern with congressional understanding, provide more reliable guideposts than conclusory references to the "authoritative" or "official." Even if those terms provided a true criterion, there would have to be something wrong with a standard that accorded the status of substantive law to every one of 10,000 "official" customs classifications rulings turned out each year from over 46 offices placed around the country at the Nation's entryways.

of an ambiguous statutory provision had to be sustained so long as it represented the agency's authoritative interpretation, henceforth such an application can be set aside unless "it appears that Congress delegated authority to the agency generally to make rules carrying the force of law," as by giving an agency "power to engage in adjudication or notice-and-comment rulemaking, or ... some other [procedure] indicati[ng] comparable congressional intent," and "the agency interpretation claiming deference was promulgated in the exercise of that authority." What was previously a general presumption of authority in agencies to resolve ambiguity in the statutes they have been authorized to enforce has been changed to a presumption of no such authority, which must be overcome by affirmative legislative intent to the contrary. And whereas previously, when agency authority to resolve ambiguity did not exist the court was free to give the statute what it considered the best interpretation, henceforth the court must supposedly give the agency view some indeterminate amount of so-called Skidmore deference. We will be sorting out the consequences of the Mead doctrine, which has today replaced the Chevron doctrine, for years to come. I would adhere to our established jurisprudence, defer to the reasonable interpretation the Customs Service has given to the statute it is charged with enforcing, and reverse the judgment of the Court of Appeals.

I

Only five years ago, the Court described the Chevron doctrine as follows: "We accord deference to agencies under Chevron ... because of a presumption that Congress, when it left ambiguity in a statute meant for implementation by an agency, understood that the ambiguity would be resolved, first and foremost, by the agency, and desired the agency (rather than the courts) to possess whatever degree of discretion the ambiguity allows," Smiley v. Citibank (South Dakota), N. A., 517 U.S. 735, 740–741 (1996). Today the Court collapses this doctrine, announcing instead a presumption that agency discretion does not exist unless the statute, expressly or impliedly, says so. While the Court disclaims any hard-and-fast rule for determining the existence of discretion-conferring intent, it asserts that "a very good indicator [is] express congressional authorizations to engage in the process of rulemaking or adjudication that produces regulations or rulings for which deference is claimed." Only when agencies act through "adjudication[,] notice-and-comment rulemaking, or ... some other [procedure] indicati[ng] comparable congressional intent [whatever that means]" is Chevron deference applicable—because these "relatively formal administrative procedure[s] [designed] to foster ... fairness and deliberation" bespeak (according to the Court) congressional willingness to have the agency, rather than the courts, resolve statutory ambiguities. Once it is determined that Chevron deference is not in order, the uncertainty is not at an end—and indeed is just beginning. Litigants cannot then assume that the statutory question is one for the courts to determine, according to traditional interpretive principles and by their own judicial lights. No, the Court now resurrects, in full force, the pre-Chevron doctrine of Skidmore deference.... The Court has largely replaced Chevron, in other words, with that test most beloved by a court unwilling to be held to rules (and most feared by litigants who want to know what to expect): th'ol' "totality of the circumstances" test.

The Court's new doctrine is neither sound in principle nor sustainable in practice.

A

As to principle: The doctrine of Chevron—that all *authoritative* agency interpretations of statutes they are charged with administering deserve deference—was rooted in a legal presumption of congressional intent, important to the division of powers between the Second and Third Branches. When, Chevron said, Congress leaves an ambiguity in a statute that is to be administered by an executive agency, it is presumed that Congress meant to give the agency discretion, within the limits of reasonable interpretation, as to how the ambiguity is to be resolved. By committing enforcement of the statute to an agency rather than the courts, Congress committed its initial and primary interpretation to that branch as well. . . .

The basis in principle for today's new doctrine can be described as follows: The background rule is that ambiguity in legislative instructions to agencies is to be resolved not by the agencies but by the judges. Specific congressional intent to depart from this rule must be found—and while there is no single touchstone for such intent it can generally be found when Congress has authorized the agency to act through (what the Court says is) relatively formal procedures such as informal rulemaking and formal (and informal?) adjudication, and when the agency in fact employs such procedures. . . . [T]he Court's principal criterion of congressional intent to supplant its background rule seems to me quite implausible. There is no necessary connection between the formality of procedure and the power of the entity administering the procedure to resolve authoritatively questions of law. The most formal of the procedures the Court refers to—formal adjudication—is modeled after the process used in trial courts, which of course are not generally accorded deference on questions of law. The purpose of such a procedure is to produce a closed record for determination and review of the facts—which implies nothing about the power of the agency subjected to the procedure to resolve authoritatively questions of law. . . .

B

As for the practical effects of the new rule:

(1)

The principal effect will be protracted confusion. As noted above, the one test for Chevron deference that the Court enunciates is wonderfully imprecise: whether "Congress delegated authority to the agency generally to make rules carrying the force of law, . . . as by . . . adjudication[,] notice-and-comment rulemaking, or . . . some other [procedure] indicati[ng] comparable congressional intent." But even this description does not do justice to the utter flabbiness of the Court's criterion, since, in order to maintain the fiction that the new test is really just the old one, applied consistently throughout our case law, the Court must make a virtually open-ended exception to its already imprecise guidance: In the present case, it tells us, the absence of notice-and-comment rulemaking . . . is not enough to decide the question of Chevron deference, "for we have sometimes found reasons for Chevron deference even when no such administrative formality was required and none was afforded." The opinion then goes on to consider a grab bag of other factors—including the factor that used to be the sole criterion for Chevron deference: whether the interpretation represented the *authoritative* position of the agency. It is hard to know what the lower courts are to make of today's guidance.

(2)

Another practical effect of today's opinion will be an artificially induced increase in informal rulemaking. Buy stock in the GPO. Since informal rulemaking and formal adjudication are the only more-or-less safe harbors from the storm that the Court has unleashed; and since formal adjudication is [often] not an option . . . informal rulemaking . . . will now become a virtual necessity. As I have described, the Court's safe harbor requires not merely that the agency have been given rulemaking authority, but also that the agency have *employed* rulemaking as the means of resolving the statutory ambiguity. (It is hard to understand why that should be so. Surely the mere *conferral* of rulemaking authority demonstrates—if one accepts the Court's logic—a congressional intent to allow the agency to resolve ambiguities. And given that intent, what difference does it make that the agency chooses instead to use another perfectly permissible means for that purpose?) Moreover, the majority's approach will have a perverse effect on the rules that do emerge, given the principle (which the Court leaves untouched today) that judges must defer to reasonable agency interpretations of their own regulations. Agencies will now have high incentive to rush out barebones, ambiguous rules construing statutory ambiguities, which they can then in turn further clarify through informal rulings entitled to judicial respect.

(3)

Worst of all, the majority's approach will lead to the ossification of large portions of our statutory law. Where Chevron applies, statutory ambiguities remain ambiguities subject to the agency's ongoing clarification. They create a space, so to speak, for the exercise of continuing agency discretion. As Chevron itself held, the Environmental Protection Agency can interpret "stationary source" to mean a single smokestack, can later replace that interpretation with the "bubble concept" embracing an entire plant, and if that proves undesirable can return again to the original interpretation. For the indeterminately large number of statutes taken out of Chevron by today's decision, however, ambiguity (and hence flexibility) will cease with the first judicial resolution. Skidmore deference gives the agency's current position some vague and uncertain amount of respect, but it does not, like Chevron, *leave* the matter within the control of the Executive Branch for the future. Once the court has spoken, it becomes *unlawful* for the agency to take a contradictory position; the statute now *says* what the court has prescribed. . . .

One might respond that such ossification would not result if the agency were simply to readopt its interpretation, after a court reviewing it under Skidmore had rejected it, by repromulgating it through one of the Chevron-eligible procedural formats approved by the Court today. Approving this procedure would be a landmark abdication of judicial power. It is worlds apart from Chevron proper, where the court does not *purport* to give the statute a judicial interpretation—except in identifying the scope of the statutory ambiguity, as to which the court's judgment is final and irreversible. (Under Chevron proper, when the agency's authoritative interpretation comes within the scope of that ambiguity—and the court therefore approves it—the agency will not be "overruling" the court's decision when it later decides that a different interpretation (still within the scope of the ambiguity) is preferable.) By contrast, under this view, the reviewing court will not be holding the agency's authoritative interpretation within the scope of the ambiguity; but will be holding that the agency has not used the "delegation-conferring" procedures, and that the court must therefore *interpret the statute on its own*—but subject to reversal if and when the agency uses the proper procedures. . . .

There is, in short, no way to avoid the ossification of federal law that today's opinion sets in motion. What a court says is the law after according Skidmore deference will be the law forever, beyond the power of the agency to change even through rulemaking.

(4)

And finally, the majority's approach compounds the confusion it creates by breathing new life into the anachronism of Skidmore, which sets forth a sliding scale of deference owed an agency's interpretation of a statute that is dependent "upon the thoroughness evident in [the agency's] consideration, the validity of its reasoning, its consistency with earlier and later pronouncements, and all those factors which give it power to persuade, if lacking power to control"; in this way, the appropriate measure of deference will be accorded the "body of experience and informed judgment" that such interpretations often embody, 323 U.S., at 140. Justice Jackson's eloquence notwithstanding, the rule of Skidmore deference is an empty truism and a trifling statement of the obvious: A judge should take into account the well-considered views of expert observers.

It was possible to live with the indeterminacy of Skidmore deference in earlier times. But in an era when federal statutory law administered by federal agencies is pervasive, and when the ambiguities (intended or unintended) that those statutes contain are innumerable, totality-of-the-circumstances Skidmore deference is a recipe for uncertainty, unpredictability, and endless litigation. To condemn a vast body of agency action to that regime (all except rulemaking, formal (and informal?) adjudication, and whatever else might now and then be included within today's intentionally vague formulation of affirmative congressional intent to "delegate") is irresponsible.

II

The Court's pretense that today's opinion is nothing more than application of our prior case law does not withstand analysis. . . .

III

To decide the present case, I would adhere to the original formulation of Chevron. " 'The power of an administrative agency to administer a congressionally created . . . program necessarily requires the formulation of policy and the making of rules to fill any gap left, implicitly or explicitly, by Congress,' " 467 U.S., at 843, (quoting *Morton v. Ruiz,* 415 U.S. 199, 231, (1974)). We accordingly presume—and our precedents have made clear to Congress that we presume—that, absent some clear textual indication to the contrary, "Congress, when it left ambiguity in a statute meant for implementation by an agency, understood that the ambiguity would be resolved, first and foremost, by the agency, and desired the agency (rather than the courts) to possess whatever degree of discretion the ambiguity allows," Smiley, 517 U.S., at 740–741. Chevron sets forth an across-the-board presumption, which operates as a background rule of law against which Congress legislates: Ambiguity means Congress intended agency discretion. Any resolution of the ambiguity by the administering agency that is authoritative—that represents the official position of the agency—must be accepted by the courts if it is reasonable.

Nothing in the statute at issue here displays an intent to modify the background presumption on which Chevron deference is based. . . .

There is no doubt that the Customs Service's interpretation represents the authoritative view of the agency. Although the actual ruling letter was signed by only the Director of the Commercial Rulings Branch of Customs Headquarters' Office of Regulations and Rulings, the Solicitor General of the United States has filed a brief, cosigned by the General Counsel of the Department of the Treasury, that represents the position set forth in the ruling letter to be the official position of the Customs Service. No one contends that it is merely a "post hoc rationalizatio[n]" or an "agency litigating positio[n] wholly unsupported by regulations, rulings, or administrative practice."[7]

There is also no doubt that the Customs Service's interpretation is a reasonable one, whether or not judges would consider it the best. I will not belabor this point, since the Court evidently agrees: An interpretation that was unreasonable would not merit the remand that the Court decrees for consideration of Skidmore deference.

---

7. The Court's parting shot, that "there would have to be something wrong with a standard that accorded the status of substantive law to every one of 10,000 'official' customs classifications rulings turned out each year from over 46 offices placed around the country at the Nation's entryways" misses the mark. I do not disagree. The "authoritativeness" of an agency interpretation does not turn upon whether it has been enunciated by someone who is actually employed by the agency. It must represent the judgment of central agency management, approved at the highest levels. I would find that condition to have been satisfied when, a ruling having been attacked in court, the general counsel of the agency has determined that it should be defended. If one thinks that that does not impart sufficient authoritativeness, then surely the line has been crossed when, as here, the General Counsel of the agency and the Solicitor General of the United States have assured this Court that the position represents the agency's authoritative view. . . .

IV

... For the reasons stated, I respectfully dissent from the Court's judgment. I would uphold the Customs Service's construction of Subheading 4820.10.20 of the Harmonized Tariff Schedule of the United States, 19 U.S.C. § 1202, and would reverse the contrary decision of the Court of Appeals. I dissent even more vigorously from the reasoning that produces the Court's judgment, and that makes today's decision one of the most significant opinions ever rendered by the Court dealing with the judicial review of administrative action. Its consequences will be enormous, and almost uniformly bad.

NOTES ON WHAT MEADS MEANS

(1) Just one year before Mead, in CHRISTENSEN V. HARRIS COUNTY, 529 U.S. 576 (2000), the Court considered the status of an opinion letter issued by the Department of Labor's Wage and Hour Division applying the Fair Labor Standards Act to a particular set of circumstance. Holding against the agency's interpretation, the Court, in an opinion by Justice Thomas, refused to give it Chevron deference. 529 U.S. at 587:

> Here ... we confront an interpretation contained in an opinion letter, not one arrived at after, for example, a formal adjudication or notice-and-comment rulemaking. Interpretations such as those in opinion letters—like interpretations contained in policy statements, agency manuals, and enforcement guidelines, all of which have the force of law—do not warrant Chevron-style deference.

Instead, the interpretation was entitled to Skidmore deference, but in applying that standard Justice Thomas found the agency's interpretation "unpersuasive."

Justice Thomas spoke for five members of the Court. Justice Scalia agreed with the result reached, not because he would refuse Chevron deference, but because even granting that deference he considered the agency's statutory interpretation unreasonable. In terms not unlike those used in Mead, he specifically abjured Skidmore deference. Justices Stevens, Breyer and Ginsburg dissented in two opinions, the gist of which was that the Department got it right, whether viewed as a matter of Skidmore or Chevron.

Christensen was, thus, in some sense a dress-rehearsal for Mead. But in Mead, Justice Souter speaks with the authority of eight Justices, and delivers an opinion in which Skidmore deference is clearly part of the holding, since it forms the basis for the instructions to the court below upon remand.

(2) PETER L. STRAUSS, PUBLICATION RULES IN THE RULEMAKING SPECTRUM: ASSURING PROPER RESPECT FOR AN ESSENTIAL ELEMENT, 53 Admin. L. Rev. 803, 822–23 (2001): "The Supreme Court's recent decision in Christensen v. Harris County and its very recent decision in United States v. Mead Corp.,

have focused attention on how one might articulate the way in which agency judgments on matters of law or policy should influence reviewing courts. Putting aside the possibility of treating agency views as simply irrelevant, two models live in the cases. The first might be described as 'obedience'—courts encountering agency decisions they conclude the agencies were authorized to take must accept the conclusions they embody rather than displace them with their own independent judgment on the matter. The second, as 'weight'—the court is responsible for decision of a matter; but, in so deciding it will treat the agency views as constituent elements of its own decision, as persuasive if not controlling material whose force derives from the agency's office and the dignity of its action. The 'obedience' model is firmly associated in the Court's canon with its decision in Chevron U.S.A., Inc. v. Natural Resources Defense Council that, within the possibilities of meaning a statute's language could be given, a matter for the courts to decide, a reviewing court must accept any reasonable interpretation given that language by the agency Congress has empowered to implement the statute. The 'weight' model was best articulated by Justice Jackson in Skidmore v. Swift & Co. . . .

"Christensen, which arose in precisely the same context as Skidmore, held that Skidmore weight rather than Chevron obedience remained the correct measure of the force of an agency upon judicial interpretation of text where the agency interpretation was expressed in a publication rule. Mead Corp., which concerned a Customs Service tariff classification ruling, reiterated the point, with rather more (and more satisfactory) attention to the nature of that weight and its influence on judicial judgment."

(3) Regarding the interpretation of the Skidmore standard, see the notes following that case, p. 985 above.

(4) What do you make of Justice Souter's way of presenting the landscape of deference in Section II of his opinion? Is Skidmore's multifactored analysis of deference now the core principle, with Chevron representing merely the limiting case of "most" deference because "an additional reason for judicial deference applies"? Or is Skidmore merely a clean-up principle, kept alive so as to give judges more choices than Chevron or nothing? And to the same effect, what do you make of his footnote 5?

In this regard, consider the Court's account (in 1999) of its reasons for deferring to the Federal Labor Relations Authority on a matter concerning the rules governing bargaining between the Department of the Interior and its employees. NATIONAL FEDERATION OF FEDERAL EMPLOYEES, LOCAL 1309 v. DEPARTMENT OF THE INTERIOR, 526 U.S. 86, 99–100. Per JUSTICE BREYER:

> The statutory ambiguity is perfectly consistent, however, with the conclusion that Congress delegated to the Authority the power to determine—within appropriate legal bounds, see, *e.g.,* 5 U.S.C. § 706; Chevron—whether, when, where, and what sort of midterm bargaining is required. The Statute's delegation of rulemaking, adjudicatory, and policymaking powers to the Authority supports this conclusion. This conclusion is also supported by precedent recognizing the similarity of the Authority's public-sector and the National Labor Relations Board's private-sector roles. As we have recognized, the Authority's function is "to develop specialized expertise in its field of labor relations and to

use that expertise to give content to the principles and goals set forth in the Act," and it "is entitled to considerable deference when it exercises its 'special function of applying the general provisions of the Act to the complexities' of federal labor relations." Bureau of Alcohol, Tobacco and Firearms v. FLRA, 464 U.S. 89, 97, (1983) (quoting NLRB v. Erie Resistor Corp., 373 U.S. 221, 236, (1963)).

We conclude that Congress "left" the matters of whether, when, and where midterm bargaining is required "to be resolved by the agency charged with the administration of the statute in light of everyday realities." Chevron, at 865–866.

(5) What happens if an agency has the authority to fill in the statute but the case lacks some of the Skidmore factors? Consider the debate in the pre-Mead case of DiCENSO v. CISNEROS, 96 F.3d 1004 (7th Cir.1996). The question was whether a particular incident of sexual harassment was sufficient to create a hostile housing environment, and thus entitle a tenant to damages against her landlord, under the Fair Housing Act, 42 U.S.C. § 3601 et seq. After an adjudicatory preceeding, the ALJ said no; on review within the Department of Housing and Urban Development, the Secretary's designee said yes; and then there was review in the Seventh Circuit. Defer to the agency? *Held*: No.

BAUER, J., for the majority:

Chevron requires us to defer to the decisions of executive agencies where the agency has a particular expertise in the conflicting policy considerations that underlie a statute, or where the agency previously has considered the matter at issue in a detailed and reasoned fashion. Neither of these situations exist here. ... HUD has not even enacted guidelines regarding hostile housing environment sex discrimination. Rather, as the HUD Secretary's designee acknowledged, a determination of what constitutes a hostile environment in the housing context requires the same analysis courts have undertaken in the Title VII context. Such a determination does not require deference to an administrative agency.

FLAUM, J., dissenting:

It is well-established that considerable weight should be given to an agency's construction of a statutory scheme that it has been entrusted to administer. The Supreme Court has held that HUD's interpretation of the FHA "ordinarily commands considerable deference" since "HUD [is] the federal agency primarily assigned to implement and administer [it]" ... Thus an agency's interpretation of the statute that it administers commands deference, irrespective of whether that interpretation emerges as a result of an adjudicative proceeding or a rulemaking process. ... We "may not substitute [our] own construction of a statutory provision for a reasonable interpretation made by the administrator of an agency." Chevron.

Which of these views is more consistent with Mead?

(6) Does the majority opinion (as Justice Scalia says) create a "safe-harbor" for agency interpretations incorporated in notice-and-comment-made rules or formal adjudications? Or does the opinion leave open the

possibility that even for such interpretations Chevron deference depends on what a court can glean about Congressional intent in the particular statutory scheme?

Assuming the Court did mean to create a safe harbor, do you agree with Justice Scalia that Mead will create an unfortunate "artificially induced increase in informal rulemaking"? Or do you think the Court, without saying so, intended to create a counterbalancing incentive to the "ossification" and anti-rulemaking pressures some have found in the regime of State Farm review (see p. 1017 above)?

NOTES ON WHAT MEAD APPLIES TO, AND HOW

(1) The "ruling letter," says the Court, is "best treated like interpretations contained in policy statements, agency manuals, and enforcement guidelines." This is the closest we get to an answer of how the "ruling letter" would be classified under the APA. Probably it is an interpretative rule, but possibly it could be labeled an informal adjudication. In either case, it would seem, to put the matter a bit loosely, to be a lesser version of something else: of a formal adjudication or of a notice-and-comment-made "legislative" rule. And it seems this contrast plays an important part in the Court's reasoning.

How, then, should we analyze other types of things agencies produce which do not quite so easily fit this "less impressive/more impressive" framework? For example, what of agency rules of procedure—which are exempted from § 553 processes yet have no more formal APA analog (although agencies can, of course, consistent with Vermont Yankee, choose to hold a notice-and-comment proceeding to adopt them)?

In EDELMAN v. LYNCHBURG COLLEGE, 535 U.S. 106 (2002), a majority of the Supreme Court decided to duck this question. Under Title VII of the Civil Rights Act of 1964, complainants have to file a "verified charge" with the EEOC within a limited time after the event complained of; the issue in Edelman was the validity of an EEOC rule of procedure which allowed a verification filed after the charge, and after the passing of the limited time, to relate back to the original filing. Per JUSTICE SOUTER (122 S.Ct. at 1150):

"The other issue insignificant in this case, however prominent it is in much of the litigation that goes on over agency rulemaking, is the degree of deference owed to the regulation by reviewing courts. We agree with the Government as *amicus* that deference under Chevron does not necessarily require an agency's exercise of express notice-and-comment rulemaking power; we so observed in United States v. Mead, ([W]e have sometimes found reasons for Chevron deference even when no such administrative formality was required and none was afforded). But there is no need to resolve any question of deference here. We find the EEOC rule not only a reasonable one, but the position we would adopt even if there were no formal rule and we were interpreting the statute from scratch. Because we so clearly agree with the EEOC, there is no occasion to defer and no point in asking what kind of deference, or how much."

JUSTICE O'CONNOR, joined by JUSTICE SCALIA, concurred in an opinion that did reach the deference issue, albeit perhaps on unusual facts (122 S.Ct. at 1154–55):

"I think the EEOC's regulation is entitled to Chevron deference. We have, of course, previously held that because the EEOC was not given rulemaking authority to interpret the *substantive* provisions of Title VII, its substantive regulations do not receive Chevron deference, but instead only receive consideration according to the standards established in Skidmore v. Swift & Co. The EEOC has, however, been given "authority from time to time to issue . . . suitable *procedural* regulations to carry out the provisions of" Title VII, 42 U.S.C. § 2000e–12(a) (emphasis added). The regulation at issue here, which permits relation back of amendments to charges filed with the EEOC, is clearly such a procedural regulation. See, *e.g.,* Fed. Rule Civ. Proc. 15 (establishing rules for amendments to pleadings and relation back as part of the Federal Rules of Civil Procedure). Thus, as the Court recognizes, the EEOC was exercising authority explicitly delegated to it by Congress when it promulgated this rule.

"The regulation was also promulgated pursuant to sufficiently formal procedures. Although the EEOC originally issued the regulation without undergoing formal notice-and-comment procedures, it was repromulgated pursuant to those procedures in 1977. We recognized in United States v. Mead Corp., that although notice-and-comment procedures are not required for Chevron deference, notice-and-comment is 'significant . . . in pointing to Chevron authority,' and that an 'overwhelming number of our cases applying Chevron deference have reviewed the fruits of notice-and-comment rulemaking or formal adjudication.' I see no reason why a repromulgation pursuant to notice-and-comment procedures should be less entitled to deference than an original promulgation pursuant to those procedures.

"Moreover, the regulation is codified in the Code of Federal Regulations, 29 CFR § 1601.12(b) (1977), and so is binding on all the parties coming before the EEOC, as well as on the EEOC itself. In this regard, it is distinguishable from the Customs Service ruling letters at issue in Mead Corp., which we found not to be binding on third parties and to be changeable by the Customs Service merely upon notice, and to which we therefore denied Chevron deference.

"Because I believe the regulation is entitled to review under Chevron, and because the regulation is reasonable, I concur in the judgment."

(2) And while we are at it, what is the appropriate deference to give to statutory interpretations embodied in regulations issued pursuant to the "good cause" exemption from § 553? Does their lack of procedural formality translate to less deference even though (assuming the exemption was properly used) there was good reason to issue them in the way the agency did?

(3) The Court appears to have meant what it said, when it said that even for ordinary substantive regulatory interpretations, notice-and-comment rulemaking was not the only road to Chevron's heaven. In BARNHART V. WALTON, 535 U.S. 212 (2002), in an opinion written by Justice Breyer and joined by all but Justice Scalia, the Court sustained an interpretation of the

Social Security Administration which had appeared in many documents—rulings and official manuals—over many years. This interpretation, said the Court, was entitled to Chevron deference even though not the product of a notice-and-comment proceeding:

> In this case, the interstitial nature of the legal question, the related expertise of the Agency, the importance of the question to administration of the statute, the complexity of that administration, and the careful consideration the Agency has given the question over a long period of time all indicate that Chevron provides the appropriate legal lens through which to view the legality of the Agency interpretation here at issue. See Mead.

(4) A separable, and rather common, issue is: assuming the legal validity of an existing regulation, how much deference is owed to an agency's interpretation of ambiguities in its own rule?

In Udall v. Tallman, 380 U.S. 1, 16, (1965), the Court had said: "When the construction of an administrative regulation rather than a statute is in issue, deference is even more clearly in order." In THOMAS JEFFERSON UNIV. V. SHALALA, 512 U.S. 504, 512 (1994), the Court, per JUSTICE KENNEDY, followed this lead, and, quoting several cases, wrote:

> . . . [T]he agency's interpretation must be given "controlling weight unless it is plainly erroneous or inconsistent with the regulation." In other words, we must defer to the Secretary's interpretation unless an "alternative reading is compelled by the regulation's plain language or by other indications of the Secretary's intent at the time of the regulation's promulgation." This broad deference is all the more warranted when, as here, the regulation concerns "a complex and highly technical regulatory program," in which the identification and classification of relevant "criteria necessarily require significant expertise and entail the exercise of judgment grounded in policy concerns."

Dissenting, JUSTICE THOMAS, joined by JUSTICES STEVENS, O'CONNOR AND GINSBURG, found that the regulation was "hopelessly vague" and unworthy of deference (512 U.S. at 525):

> . . . [T]he Secretary has merely replaced statutory ambiguity with regulatory ambiguity. It is perfectly understandable, of course, for an agency to issue vague regulations, because to do so maximizes agency power and allows the agency greater latitude to make law through adjudication than through the more cumbersome rulemaking process.

The dissenters in Thomas Jefferson University received support in JOHN F. MANNING, CONSTITUTIONAL STRUCTURE AND JUDICIAL DEFERENCE TO AGENCY INTERPRETATIONS OF AGENCY RULES, 96 Colum. L. Rev. 612, 617 (1996):

> If an agency's rules mean whatever it says they mean (unless the reading is plainly erroneous), the agency effectively has the power of self-interpretation. This authority permits an agency to supply the meaning of regulatory gaps or ambiguities of its own making and relieves the agency of the cost of imprecision that it has produced. This state of affairs makes it that much less likely that an agency will give clear notice of its policies either to those who participate in the

rulemaking process prescribed by the Administrative Procedure Act (APA) or to the regulated public. The present arrangement also contradicts a major premise of our constitutional scheme and of contemporary separation of powers case law that a fusion of lawmaking and law-exposition is especially dangerous to our liberties.

Professor Manning further explicated the difference he saw between Chevron and a case like Thomas Jefferson University in this fashion, 96 Colum. L. Rev. at 639:

> In a Chevron case, the reviewing court asks whether agency action—usually the promulgation of a rule, an agency enforcement action, or an adjudication—is consistent with an authorizing statute. If the reviewing court is effectively bound by the agency's interpretation of the statute, separation remains between the relevant lawmaker (Congress) and at least one entity (the agency) with independent authority to interpret the applicable legal text. In contrast, [in a case like Thomas Jefferson University] the reviewing court asks whether the agency action—typically an enforcement action or adjudication—is consistent with an agency regulation. In those circumstances, if the court is bound by the agency's interpretation of the meaning of its own regulation, there is no independent interpreter; the agency lawmaker has effective control of the exposition of the legal text that it has created. In short, whereas Chevron retains *one* independent interpretive check on lawmaking by Congress, [this other line of cases] leaves in place *no* independent interpretive check on lawmaking by an administrative agency.

In his dissent in Mead, Justice Scalia charges that "the majority's approach will have a perverse effect on the rules that do emerge, given the principle (which the Court leaves untouched today) that judges must defer to reasonable agency interpretations of their own regulations. . . . Agencies will now have high incentive to rush out barebones, ambiguous rules construing statutory ambiguities, which they can then in turn further clarify through informal ruling entitled to judicial respect." Can it be that informal agency interpretations of their organic statutes will, under Mead, get only Skidmore (or perhaps no) deference, while informal agency interpretations of their own regulations will do much better? Is this simply carrying out the Mead calculus and deferring in a situation characterized by high expertise and at most interstitial effect? Or does Professor Manning's argument convince you that this is upside down?

So far, the Court does not seem to have changed its approach. For example, in Barnhart v. Walton, 535 U.S. 212 (2002) the Court again cited Udall v. Tallman for the proposition that "Courts grant an agency's interpretation of its own regulations considerable legal leeway." See also p. 707, above.

(5) Side by side with the deference-to-own-interpretation-of-regulations approach is a line of lower-court cases that protect regulated parties from being penalized for agency enforcement of standards of which they had no fair notice. If a regulation is sufficiently ambiguous, it may not give adequate notice of what it requires, although of course the agency's enforcement personnel may have given actual notice of the agency's inter-

pretation in interactions with the regulated party. Absent such actual notice, it is thus possible to have (a) a properly adopted regulation, to which the court will defer as a reasonable interpretation of an ambiguous statute; (b) a less formal agency interpretation of that regulation, to which the court will defer as an interpretation of an ambiguous regulation; (c) conditions which violate the agency's interpretation of the law; but (d) no liability because the combined ambiguity in (a) and (b)—overcome by the combined deference in (a) and (b)—prevent the regulated party from having had fair notice of what it was required to do. For an example, see Beaver Plant Operations, Inc. v. Herman, 223 F.3d 25 (1st Cir.2000), and United States v. Chrysler Corp., p. 715 above.

NOTES ON ESTOPPEL

(1) The Mead Court points out that the agency was careful to make clear in its ruling letter that the ruling could be modified without notice, and that no one should rely on it except the person to whom it was issued for the transaction particularly described. Can the agency avoid its obligation to be consistent (see p. 908ff. above) that easily?

(2) Suppose we take a yet more extreme case: Someone in an agency advises a private party as to the law governing her situation, and the agency later determines that the advice was improvident or wrong? Suppose, for example, that a taxpayer was advised by an IRS agent over the phone that she will not have to pay taxes if she does thus-and-so, and an IRS auditor later determines that that advice was incorrect. If the private party has relied on the agency's advice in the interim, can she estop the agency? (You will notice that this, in effect, is the Mead situation in reverse: The agency wants to disavow the effect of an informal interpretation of the law made by a subordinate employee while the outside party wants to assert its binding effect.)

The short answer to the question, ninety-some-percent reliable, is that the government cannot be estopped. The longer answer is that the Supreme Court has made a practice of always stopping short of saying "never" while at the same time refusing actually to find an estoppel in any particular set of facts before it; and that the lower courts have occasionally found a set of facts extreme enough to convince them. Some of the fact patterns that the Supreme Court has found insufficient seem at first glance (or maybe even later) to be rather compelling. In one leading case, an agent for a federal crop insurance plan told a farmer that a particular kind of crop was insurable; the farmer insured it with the government; after the drought hit, the government determined that a regulation not known to the agent or the farmer prevented coverage, and refused payment; *held*: no estoppel. Federal Crop Ins. Corp. v. Merrill, 332 U.S. 380 (1947). In another, a retired Navy employee consulted with the Navy's personnel department before taking another job which might threaten his disability annuity, and was told it would not; took the job; and then lost payments under his annuity because, although not reflected in the Navy's own manuals, a few years earlier Congress had amended the statute to tighten eligibility requirements; *held*: no estoppel. Office of Personnel Management v. Richmond, 496 U.S. 414 (1990).

The Court's attitude can be better understood if the consequences of allowing lower level employees to estop the government are considered. In effect such a ruling would allow bad advice plus private reliance to take the place of the otherwise applicable law—to override the terms of a statute or the limitations of an appropriation. Moreover, liability for bad advice might well create an incentive for agencies to give no advice—in which case the cure might be worse than the disease.

In an appropriate case, of course, the facts that might establish an estoppel might also be recharacterized in the terms of some other doctrine that seems to threaten less far-reaching consequences—perhaps in terms of the government's having "waived" a right, or in terms of the government's abusing its discretion in not taking its own course of advice into account when deciding what to do, or in terms, as discussed in a note above, of the government's having failed to give "fair notice" of what its regulations require.

NOTES ON THE EARLY ACADEMIC RETURNS ON MEAD

The Mead case threatens to become as much a cottage industry for academics as Chevron was. Here are some of the early assessments:

(1) THOMAS W. MERRILL, THE MEAD DOCTRINE: RULES AND STANDARDS, META-RULES AND META-STANDARDS, 54 Admin. L. Rev. 807, 833–34 (2002): "On the whole, 'the Mead doctrine' is a sound development. Mead clarifies that Chevron rests on congressional intent, and correctly concludes from this that Chevron applies only when Congress has given some signal that the agency, rather than the court, is to be the primary interpreter of statutory ambiguity. The decision also correctly concludes that the relevant signal of Congress's intent in this regard is a delegation of power to act with the force of law. By linking Chevron and congressional intent, Mead helps achieve a reconciliation between Chevron and the judicial review provisions of the APA. Indeed, by insisting that the agency gets strong deference only when it acts within the scope of delegated power to act with the force of law, and not otherwise, Mead goes part way toward restoring an important aspect of the nondelegation doctrine. . . .

"To be sure, the decision comes up short in terms of articulating a meta-rule to guide lower courts in future controversies. Mead says Chevron applies only when Congress has delegated authority to an agency to act with the force of law, but it treats 'force of law' as (at most) a standard to be applied by looking to a variety of factors. The Court's decision to treat 'force of law' as a standard rather than a rule is regrettable. But nothing the Court did or said precludes future decisions that brush away the fuzziness in the majority's exposition, leaving us with a clear and defensible meta-rule.

"Finally, notwithstanding Justice Scalia's fulminations, Mead secures a bright future for the Chevron doctrine. It is now clear that Chevron deference is significantly more powerful than ordinary deference. It is also clear that Chevron applies whenever agencies exercise delegated lawmaking authority from Congress. With these propositions established, judges are more likely to take Chevron seriously. This includes the Justices of the Supreme Court. In the past, a number of Justices have ignored Chevron or applied a watered down version of Chevron. In Mead, eight Justices trimmed back on the scope of Chevron, but gave it a sounder jurisprudential foundation and signaled that it enjoys the full support of the Court in its new, slimmed-down form. In the long run the compact, but powerful, Chevron doctrine should enhance, rather than retard, the transfer of interpretational power from courts to agencies."

(2) WILLIAM S. JORDAN, III, JUDICIAL REVIEW OF INFORMAL STATUTORY INTERPRETATIONS: THE ANSWER IS CHEVRON STEP TWO, NOT CHRISTENSEN OR MEAD, 54 Admin. L. Rev. 719, 719–20 (2002): "The U.S. Supreme Court has taken the wrong approach to review of informal statutory interpretations issued by administrative agencies. First, in Christensen v. Harris County, then in United States v. Mead Corp., the Court created a cumbersome, unworkable regime under which courts must draw increasingly fine distinctions using impossibly vague standards. If courts are able to draw such fine distinctions, they will then, presumably with some frequency, issue binding statutory interpretations that usurp clearly delegated agency lawmaking authority. The net result is chaos—encouragement of extensive argument on the fine distinctions necessary to determine the applicable standard of review, inadequate attention to the substantive questions of statutory meaning, and direct conflict between judicial and executive authority."

(3) DAVID J. BARRON AND ELENA KAGAN, CHEVRON'S NONDELEGATION DOCTRINE, 2001 The Supreme Court Review 201, 203–05: "We ... argue in this article that an inquiry into actual congressional intent, of the kind the Mead Court advocated, cannot realistically solve this question of the proper scope of Chevron. Although Congress has broad power to decide what kind of judicial review should apply to what kind of administrative action, Congress so rarely discloses (or, perhaps, even has) a view on this subject as to make a search for legislative intent chimerical and a conclusion regarding that intent fraudulent in the mine run of cases. ... Given the difficulty of determining actual congressional intent, some version of constructive—or perhaps more frankly said, fictional—intent must operate in judicial efforts to delineate the scope of Chevron. After considering other alternatives, we aver that this construction should arise from and reflect candid policy judgments, of the kind evident in Chevron itself, about the allocation of interpretive authority between administrators and judges with respect to various kinds of agency action.

"Underneath the rhetoric of legislative intent, an approach of this kind in fact animates the Mead decision, but the Court's reliance on the two stock dichotomies of administrative process failed to generate the most appropriate distribution of interpretive power. The Court emphasized most heavily the divide between formal and informal procedures, suggesting that, except in unusual circumstances, only decisions taken in formal procedural contexts merit Chevron deference. But this preference for formality in administration, even in cases when not statutorily required, fails to acknowledge the costs associated with the procedures specified in the APA, which only have increased in significance since that statute's enactment. The Court similarly noted at times the divide between generality and particularity in administrative decision making, suggesting that actions exhibiting the former trait should receive greater judicial deference.

But administrative law doctrine long has resisted, for good reason, the temptation to pressure the choice between general and particular decision making, in light of the many and fluctuating considerations, usually best known to an agency itself, relevant to this choice. None of this is to say that interpretive authority in areas of statutory ambiguity or silence always should rest with agency officials; it is only to say that in allocating this power in a way consistent with important administrative values, courts can do better than to rely on the two usual (indeed, hoary) 'either-ors' of agency process.

"We contend that the deference question should turn on a different feature of agency process, traditionally ignored in administrative law doctrine and scholarship—that is, the position in the agency hierarchy of the person assuming responsibility for the administrative decision. More briefly said, the Court should refocus its inquiry from the 'how' to the 'who' of administrative decision making. If the congressional delegatee of the relevant statutory grant of authority takes personal responsibility for the decision, then the agency should command obeisance, within the broad bounds of reasonableness, in resolving statutory ambiguity; if she does not, then the judiciary should render the ultimate interpretive decision. This agency nondelegation principle serves values familiar from the congressional brand of the doctrine, as well as from Chevron itself: by offering an incentive to certain actors to take responsibility for interpretive choice, the principle advances both accountability and discipline in decision making.
. . .

"The aspect of institutional design we emphasize here—call it the high level/low level distinction—justifies the result the Court reached in Mead, but only by fortuity. In other cases our approach would diverge significantly from the Court's—in granting deference even in the absence of formality or generality and, conversely, in refusing deference even in the face of these attributes. This approach also would diverge from Justice Scalia's, given the nearly unlimited deference he favors. But oddly enough, we see our approach as in some sense, even if in a sense unrecognized by the Justices themselves, present in all of their different views on the issue: because this is so, we see some potential for the Court to move toward, and even converge on, the . . . doctrine we advocate. . . ."

Department of Housing and Urban Development v. Rucker

Supreme Court of the United States, 2002.
535 U.S. 125.

■ CHIEF JUSTICE REHNQUIST delivered the opinion of the Court.

With drug dealers "increasingly imposing a reign of terror on public and other federally assisted low-income housing tenants," Congress passed the Anti–Drug Abuse Act of 1988. 42 U.S.C. § 11901(3) (1994 ed.). The Act, as later amended, provides that each "public housing agency shall utilize leases which . . . provide that any criminal activity that threatens the health, safety, or right to peaceful enjoyment of the premises by other tenants or any drug-related criminal activity on or off such premises, engaged in by a public housing tenant, any member of the tenant's household, or any guest or other person under the tenant's control, shall be cause for termination of tenancy." 42 U.S.C. § 1437d(*l*)(6) (1994 ed., Supp. V). Petitioners say that this statute requires lease terms that allow a local public housing authority to evict a tenant when a member of the tenant's household or a guest engages in drug-related criminal activity, regardless of whether the tenant knew, or had reason to know, of that activity. Respondents say it does not. We agree with petitioners.

Respondents are four public housing tenants of the Oakland Housing Authority (OHA). Paragraph 9(m) of respondents' leases, tracking the language of § 1437d(*l*)(6), obligates the tenants to "assure that the tenant, any member of the household, a guest, or another person under the tenant's control, shall not engage in . . . [a]ny drug-related criminal activity on or near the premise[s]." Respondents also signed an agreement stating that the tenant "understand[s] that if I or any member of my household or guests should violate this lease provision, my tenancy may be terminated and I may be evicted."

In late 1997 and early 1998, OHA instituted eviction proceedings in state court against respondents, alleging violations of this lease provision. The complaint alleged: (1) that the respective grandsons of respondents William Lee and Barbara Hill, both of whom were listed as residents on the leases, were caught in the apartment complex parking lot smoking marijuana; (2) that the daughter of respondent Pearlie Rucker, who resides with her and is listed on the lease as a resident, was found with cocaine and a crack cocaine pipe three blocks from Rucker's apartment;[1] and (3) that on three instances within a 2–month period, respondent Herman Walker's caregiver and two others were found with cocaine in Walker's apartment. OHA had issued Walker notices of a lease violation on the first two occasions, before initiating the eviction action after the third violation.

United States Department of Housing and Urban Development (HUD) regulations administering § 1437d(*l*)(6) require lease terms authorizing evictions in these circumstances. The HUD regulations closely track the statutory language, and provide that "[i]n deciding to evict for criminal activity, the [public housing authority] shall have discretion to consider all of the circumstances of the case. . . ." 24 CFR § 966.4(*l*)(5)(i) (2001). The agency made clear that local public housing authorities' discretion to evict for drug-related activity includes those situations in which "[the] tenant did not know, could not foresee, or could not control behavior by other occupants of the unit." 56 Fed.Reg. 51560, 51567 (1991).

After OHA initiated the eviction proceedings in state court, respondents commenced actions against HUD, OHA, and OHA's director in United States District Court. They challenged HUD's interpretation of the statute under the Administrative Procedure Act, 5 U.S.C. § 706(2)(A), arguing that 42 U.S.C. § 1437d(*l*)(6) does not require lease terms authorizing the eviction of so-called "innocent" tenants, and, in the alternative,

---

1. In February 1998, OHA dismissed the unlawful detainer action against Rucker, after her daughter was incarcerated, and thus no longer posed a threat to other tenants.

that if it does, then the statute is unconstitutional. The District Court issued a preliminary injunction, enjoining OHA from "terminating the leases of tenants pursuant to paragraph 9(m) of the 'Tenant Lease' for drug-related criminal activity that does not occur within the tenant's apartment unit when the tenant did not know of and had no reason to know of, the drug-related criminal activity."

A panel of the Court of Appeals reversed, holding that § 1437d(*l*)(6) unambiguously permits the eviction of tenants who violate the lease provision, regardless of whether the tenant was personally aware of the drug activity, and that the statute is constitutional. See Rucker v. Davis, 203 F.3d 627 (C.A.9 2000). An en banc panel of the Court of Appeals reversed and affirmed the District Court's grant of the preliminary injunction. See Rucker v. Davis, 237 F.3d 1113 (2001). That court held that HUD's interpretation permitting the eviction of so-called "innocent" tenants "is inconsistent with Congressional intent and must be rejected" under the first step of Chevron U.S.A. Inc. v. Natural Resources Defense Council, Inc., 467 U.S. 837, 842–843 (1984).

We granted certiorari, and now reverse, holding that 42 U.S.C. § 1437d(*l*)(6) unambiguously requires lease terms that vest local public housing authorities with the discretion to evict tenants for the drug-related activity of household members and guests whether or not the tenant knew, or should have known, about the activity.

That this is so seems evident from the plain language of the statute. It provides that "each public housing authority shall utilize leases which . . . provide that . . . any drug-related criminal activity on or off such premises, engaged in by a public housing tenant, any member of the tenant's household, or any guest or other person under the tenant's control, shall be cause for termination of tenancy." 42 U.S.C. § 1437d(*l*)(6) (1994 ed., Supp. V). The en banc Court of Appeals thought the statute did not address "the level of personal knowledge or fault that is required for eviction." 237 F.3d, at 1120. Yet Congress' decision not to impose any qualification in the statute, combined with its use of the term "any" to modify "drug-related criminal activity," precludes any knowledge requirement. As we have explained, "the word 'any' has an expansive meaning, that is, 'one or some indiscriminately of whatever kind.' " United States v. Gonzales, 520 U.S. 1, 5, (1997). Thus, *any* drug-related activity engaged in by the specified persons is grounds for termination, not just drug-related activity that the tenant knew, or should have known, about.

The en banc Court of Appeals also thought it possible that "under the tenant's control" modifies not just "other person," but also "member of the tenant's household" and "guest." 237 F.3d, at 1120. The court ultimately adopted this reading, concluding that the statute prohibits eviction where the tenant "for a lack of knowledge or other reason, could not realistically exercise control over the conduct of a household member or guest." *Id.*, at 1126. But this interpretation runs counter to basic rules of grammar. The disjunctive "or" means that the qualification applies only to "other person." Indeed, the view that "under the tenant's control" modifies everything coming before it in the sentence would result in the nonsensical reading that the statute applies to "a public housing tenant . . .

under the tenant's control." HUD offers a convincing explanation for the grammatical imperative that "under the tenant's control" modifies only "other person": "by 'control,' the statute means control in the sense that the tenant has permitted access to the premises." 66 Fed.Reg. 28781 (2001). Implicit in the terms "household member" or "guest" is that access to the premises has been granted by the tenant. Thus, the plain language of § 1437d(*l*)(6) requires leases that grant public housing authorities the discretion to terminate tenancy without regard to the tenant's knowledge of the drug-related criminal activity.

Comparing § 1437d(*l*)(6) to a related statutory provision reinforces the unambiguous text. . . .

The en banc Court of Appeals next resorted to legislative history. The Court of Appeals correctly recognized that reference to legislative history is inappropriate when the text of the statute is unambiguous. 237 F.3d, at 1123. Given that the en banc Court of Appeals' finding of textual ambiguity is wrong, there is no need to consult legislative history.[2]

Nor was the en banc Court of Appeals correct in concluding that this plain reading of the statute leads to absurd results. The statute does not *require* the eviction of any tenant who violated the lease provision. Instead, it entrusts that decision to the local public housing authorities, who are in the best position to take account of, among other things, the degree to which the housing project suffers from "rampant drug-related or violent crime," 42 U.S.C. § 11901(2) (1994 ed. and Supp. V), "the seriousness of the offending action," 66 Fed.Reg., at 28803, and "the extent to which the leaseholder has . . . taken all reasonable steps to prevent or mitigate the offending action," *ibid.* It is not "absurd" that a local housing authority may sometimes evict a tenant who had no knowledge of the drug-related activity. Such "no-fault" eviction is a common "incident of tenant responsibility under normal landlord-tenant law and practice." 56 Fed.Reg., at 51567. Strict liability maximizes deterrence and eases enforcement difficulties.

And, of course, there is an obvious reason why Congress would have permitted local public housing authorities to conduct no-fault evictions: Regardless of knowledge, a tenant who "cannot control drug crime, or other criminal activities by a household member which threaten health or safety of other residents, is a threat to other residents and the project." 56 Fed.Reg., at 51567. With drugs leading to "murders, muggings, and other forms of violence against tenants," and to the "deterioration of the physical environment that requires substantial governmental expenditures," 42 U.S.C. § 11901(4) (1994 ed., Supp. V), it was reasonable for Congress to permit no-fault evictions in order to "provide public and other federally assisted low-income housing that is decent, safe, and free from illegal drugs," § 11901(1) (1994 ed.).

---

2. Even if it were appropriate to look at legislative history, it would not help respondents. . . .

In another effort to avoid the plain meaning of the statute, the en banc Court of Appeals invoked the canon of constitutional avoidance. But that canon "has no application in the absence of statutory ambiguity." United States v. Oakland Cannabis Buyers' Cooperative, 532 U.S. 483, 494 (2001). "Any other conclusion, while purporting to be an exercise in judicial restraint, would trench upon the legislative powers vested in Congress by Art. I, § 1, of the Constitution." United States v. Albertini, 472 U.S. 675, 680 (1985). There are, moreover, no "serious constitutional doubts" about Congress' affording local public housing authorities the discretion to conduct no-fault evictions for drug-related crime. Reno v. Flores, 507 U.S. 292, 314, n. 9 (1993) (emphasis deleted).

The en banc Court of Appeals held that HUD's interpretation "raise[s] serious questions under the Due Process Clause of the Fourteenth Amendment," because it permits "tenants to be deprived of their property interest without any relationship to individual wrongdoing." 237 F.3d, at 1124–1125 (citing Scales v. United States, 367 U.S. 203, 224–225, (1961); Southwestern Telegraph & Telephone Co. v. Danaher, 238 U.S. 482 (1915)). But both of these cases deal with the acts of government as sovereign. In Scales, the United States criminally charged the defendant with knowing membership in an organization that advocated the overthrow of the United States Government. In Danaher, an Arkansas statute forbade discrimination among customers of a telephone company. The situation in the present cases is entirely different. The government is not attempting to criminally punish or civilly regulate respondents as members of the general populace. It is instead acting as a landlord of property that it owns, invoking a clause in a lease to which respondents have agreed and which Congress has expressly required. Scales and Danaher cast no constitutional doubt on such actions.

The Court of Appeals sought to bolster its discussion of constitutional doubt by pointing to the fact that respondents have a property interest in their leasehold interest, citing Greene v. Lindsey, 456 U.S. 444 (1982). This is undoubtedly true, and Greene held that an effort to deprive a tenant of such a right without proper notice violated the Due Process Clause of the Fourteenth Amendment. But, in the present cases, such deprivation will occur in the state court where OHA brought the unlawful detainer action against respondents. There is no indication that notice has not been given by OHA in the past, or that it will not be given in the future. Any individual factual disputes about whether the lease provision was actually violated can, of course, be resolved in these proceedings.

We hold that "Congress has directly spoken to the precise question at issue." Chevron U.S.A. Inc. v. Natural Resources Defense Council, Inc., 467 U.S., at 842. Section 1437d(l)(6) requires lease terms that give local public housing authorities the discretion to terminate the lease of a tenant when a member of the household or a guest engages in drug-related activity, regardless of whether the tenant knew, or should have known, of the drug-related activity.

Accordingly, the judgment of the Court of Appeals is reversed, and the cases are remanded for further proceedings consistent with this opinion.

It is so ordered.

■ JUSTICE BREYER took no part in the consideration or decision of these cases.

NOTES

(1) According to the opinion below, 237 F.3d 1113, Pearlie Rucker (the named plaintiff) "is a sixty-three-year-old woman who has lived in public housing since 1985. She lives with her mentally disabled daughter, her two grandchildren, and one great-granddaughter. OHA sought to evict Rucker because her daughter was found in possession of cocaine three blocks from the apartment. Rucker asserts that she regularly searches her daughter's room for evidence of alcohol and drug use and has never found any evidence or observed any sign of drug use by her daughter." Later in the opinion the court reports that "HUD conceded at oral argument that there was nothing more Pearlie Rucker could have done to protect herself from eviction, but argued that the statute authorized her eviction nonetheless."

(2) The crucial statutory language is "any drug-related criminal activity on or off such premises, engaged in by a public housing tenant, any member of the tenant's household, or any guest or other person under the tenant's control, shall be cause for termination of tenancy." The court below began by saying that this text was ambiguous (237 F.3d at 1119–20):

> The parties debate the significance that should be attributed to the use of the phrase "under the tenant's control." HUD argues that this phrase modifies only the term "other person" and that "control" means only that this other person has the tenant's consent to be in the tenant's unit. The tenants contend that "control" involves the "exercise of a restraining or directing influence" over another, and that this applies to all of the words in the group, i.e., household members, guests *and* other persons. The tenants further argue that it is implicit from the use of this wording that Congress intended tenants to be held accountable for the actions of those persons who are subject to their control, but that the statute does not impose sanctions on tenants who have taken reasonable steps to prevent criminal drug activity from occurring, but, for a lack of knowledge or other reason, could not realistically be expected to exercise control over the conduct of another. The text of subsection (6), viewed in isolation, does not compel either party's interpretation. We therefore turn to the specific context in which the language is used and the broader context of the statute as a whole.

The Ninth Circuit then (as Chief Justice Rehnquist reports) resolved the ambiguity by looking to other sources of interpretation.

(3) The Ninth Circuit, en banc, split: 7 saying that the statute was unambiguously against the agency, 4 saying that the statute was clear and in favor of the agency's interpretation; if we add in the district judge, we get 8 to 4 against, before we reach the big nine. The Supreme Court votes 8 to 0 (one recusing) to hold that the statute unambiguously favors the agency. So now we have a total of 12 to 8 in favor of the agency. Both sides say the statute is unambiguous. How can that be?

(4) Do you think the words "any" and "or" have as fixed a meaning as Chief Justice Rehnquist does? (And by the way, do you think the just-preceding sentence would mean something different if it said: "Do you think the words "any" *or* "or" have as fixed a meaning as Chief Justice Rehnquist does?)

(5) Let us assume that *if* the statute was ambiguous, *then* the agency had selected one of the reasonable possible interpretations. On that assumption, under Chevron the Ninth Circuit ultimately had to say the statute was unambiguous in order to hold against the agency. But the Supreme Court would have reached the same result it did, upholding the agency, if it had said that the statute was ambiguous, and then deferred to the agency's interpretation. Yet the Court speaks entirely in its own voice in construing the statute, refers to agency explanations only when it agrees with them, and mentions Chevron only in the penultimate paragraph after all the work has been done. Is the holding of the case different because of the approach the Court took? Or is the seeming constraint on future agency action—should the agency ever want to change its mind—mere dictum?

(6) More to present purposes, why did the Court approach the case as it did? Is there something about it (in light of the three principal cases we have just read) that makes it unsuited for judicial deference? Compare Arthur Conan Doyle, Silver Blaze, 2 The Annotated Sherlock Holmes 261, 277 (1967):

> " 'Is there any other point to which you would wish to draw my attention?'
>
> 'To the curious incident of the dog in the night-time.'
>
> 'The dog did nothing in the night-time.'
>
> 'That was the curious incident,' remarked Sherlock Holmes.' "

(7) Or is the Supreme Court circa 2002 just a little less enthusiastic about Chevron (or for that matter any flavor of deference) than it has been in the past? In another recent case, National Cable & Telecommunications Assoc. v. Gulf Power Co., 534 U.S. 327 (2002), Justice Kennedy appeared to go a bit out of his way to assert the Court's own position, even while upholding the agency: "This is our own, best reading of the statute, which we find unambiguous. If the statute were thought ambiguous, however, the FCC's reading must be accepted nonetheless, provided it is a reasonable interpretation. See Chevron." And in S.E.C. v. Zandford, 535 U.S. 813 (2002), which turned on the scope of the very important anti-fraud section 10(b) of the Securities Exchange Act, and rule 10–b(5) thereunder, Justice Stevens began his analysis by citing some S.E.C. decisions and saying that the S.E.C.'s interpretation, developed "in the context of formal adjudication, is entitled to deference if it is reasonable," (citing Mead). By the end of his opinion, however, the Court, although upholding the agency, speaks in its own voice: citing judicial precedents this time, "the SEC complaint describes a fraudulent scheme in which the securities transactions and breaches of fiduciary duty coincide. Those breaches were therefore ... within the meaning of § 10(b)." Is something afoot? Should something be afoot?

SECTION 5.   THE BEST THERE IS ON JUDICIAL REVIEW

Louis L. Jaffe, Judicial Control of Administrative Action

589–90 (1965).

The scope of judicial review is ultimately conditioned and determined by the major proposition that the constitutional courts of this country are the acknowledged architects and guarantors of the integrity of the legal system. I use integrity here in its specific sense of unity and coherence and in its more general sense of the effectuation of the values upon which this unity and coherence are built. In a society so complex, so pragmatic as our, unity is never realized, nor is it necessary that it should be. Indeed, there is no possibility of agreement on criteria for absolute unity; what is contradiction to one man is higher synthesis to another. But within a determined context there may be a sense of contradiction sufficient to create social distress; and it is one of the grand roles of our constitutional courts to detect such contradictions and to affirm the capacity of our society to integrate its purposes. I have said much of statutory purpose as the guiding consideration in evaluating the validity of administrative action. It must be admitted, however, that the statute often has little or nothing to say concerning whatever matter is at hand. It may do no more than establish the general framework of power—"jurisdiction"—within which the agency must establish a system of rules and principles. I have suggested that normally the courts should tolerate agency law making which does not in the courts' opinion seem clearly contrary to the statutory purposes as the courts understand them. But the statute under which an agency operates is not the whole law applicable to its operation. An agency is not an island entire of itself. It is one of the many rooms in the magnificent mansion of the law. The very subordination of the agency to judicial jurisdiction is intended to proclaim the premise that each agency is to be brought into harmony with the totality of the law; the law as it is found in the statute at hand, the statute book at large, the principles and conceptions of the "common law," and the ultimate guarantees associated with the Constitution.

OBTAINING JUDICIAL REVIEW: ACCESS TO COURT TO CHALLENGE AGENCY ACTION OR INACTION

With a few exceptions such as the Federal Circuit in trademark and patent cases, judicial review of agency action takes place in courts of general jurisdiction. Unlike many other countries with a developed, centralized regulatory process, the United States has not opted to channel regulatory oversight either to substantively specialized courts or to public-law courts that are deliberately structured as part of the administrative enterprise. This choice has substantive implications that you may have discussed when you studied the materials on scope of review; here, we are concerned with the procedural implications: Cases challenging agency action will be expected to conform to the forms and practices of ordinary civil litigation— at least absent some justification for deviating. What this means, as a practical matter, is that the lawyer considering a lawsuit to challenge agency action must resolve many of the same questions that occur in planning any litigation:

Which courts are available? (jurisdiction and venue)

What causes of action are possible? What claims, defenses and remedies are available with each?

Can the proposed plaintiff raise the claims sought to be adjudicated? If not, what claims can this plaintiff raise—and who might be able to raise the others? (standing)

When can the action be brought? When is too early? (hypotheticality and ripeness) When is too late? (statute of limitations and mootness)

To be sure, there are some questions unique to administrative litigation. For example, the timing issue has additional dimensions when an agency is involved: specifically, whether there are administrative remedies that must be exhausted before coming to court and, occasionally, whether the agency will be deemed to have "primary jurisdiction" over the area. Perhaps most fundamental, any litigation against the government, its agencies, or its officers for tasks within the scope of their employment encounters the significant hurdle of immunity: *sovereign* immunity for the government and its agencies; *official* immunity in suits against the officers personally. Clearing, or sidestepping, this hurdle is easy in some cases and difficult in others—but it must be accomplished if the suit is to go forward.

Because a lawsuit challenging agency action has so much in common, procedurally, with other civil litigation, the topics considered in this Chapter will resonate with issues you may have studied in Civil Procedure, Federal Courts, perhaps even Constitutional Law. (Remember that Article III empowers the federal courts to resolve only disputes that can be considered "cases" or "controversies;" therefore, many of the doctrines governing access to judicial review have constitutional dimensions.)

In an important sense, however, even familiar aspects of justiciability can have distinctive implications in the context of regulatory litigation. If you have already studied Chapter VIII on scope of review, you know that judicial review gives courts significant power to affect the course of regulation—to facilitate it, to redirect it, to stultify it, even to stymie it altogether. Who can invoke this power against the agency? When? For what sorts of claims? With what kinds of remedies? Such questions are answered by the various doctrines of justiciability. These technical, "procedural" rules define the moves and countermoves available in the judicial review stage of the regulatory game. And because judicial review could upset what has already occurred in the game, the behavior of players in the earlier stages is likely to be shaped with this end game in mind.

In sum, as you work to understand the intricacies of the various justiciability doctrines, try also to understand their larger importance to the administrative process. This process involves several types of actors: At a minimum, these include (1) the agency, (2) the regulated community, (3) those who are intended beneficiaries of the administrative program, and (4) those who benefit incidentally from regulation. (Two other, highly important actors are Congress and the President, but they rarely appear overtly in the end game of judicial review.) The rules of justiciability allocate access to, and protection from, judicial review among these various actors. Does success for one—with "success" defined as standing, or review now, or recognition of an immunity defense—necessarily mean a correlative loss for others? Or are there instances in which alterations in the extent, or allocation, of the power of judicial review help, or hurt, all (or most) of the actors? More fundamentally, can we reliably predict the ultimate magnitude and distribution of benefits and burdens? And, given all this, which institution is in the best position—as a matter of principle or pragmatism—to decide what configuration of judicial review is optimal for the contemporary administrative state?

SECTION 1.   METHODS OF OBTAINING JUDICIAL REVIEW

In general, it is easy to institute an action in federal court to litigate a question of federal law. The intricacies of common law pleading have been abandoned,[1] and the basic federal question jurisdictional statute no longer has an amount-in-controversy requirement.[2] However, the lawyer seeking

---

1. "There shall be one form of action to be known as a 'civil action.'" Fed.R.Civ.Proc. 2.

2. 28 U.S.C. § 1331. From 1875, when Congress first conferred general federal question jurisdiction, until 1976 there was a juris-

dictional amount requirement identical to that in diversity cases. In 1976, Congress deleted this requirement in actions against federal officers and agencies; in 1980, the requirement was deleted for all § 1331 cases.

review of administrative action inevitably faces an obstacle not present in federal-question suits between private parties: sovereign immunity. The federal government and its agencies are immune from suit unless Congress has given consent.[3] Fortunately, this consent exists for most claims seeking prospective relief, and for many claims seeking damages. Moreover, it is sometimes possible to maneuver around sovereign immunity where consent has not been given, typically through the fiction of suing the official rather than the agency. Nevertheless, the administrative lawyer must always be alert to the background problems of suing the sovereign. And even within the broad areas in which immunity has been waived, she should be aware that she may have a choice among alternative sources of jurisdiction, and several possible causes of action. Some may be more desirable than others, in the procedural advantages they offer and the substantive claims and defenses they permit. Thus, it is important to recognize the various, potentially available methods of obtaining review. The best route in a particular case will often be easy to discern, but you should be making an informed and deliberate choice for your client.

The methods of obtaining review of agency action are conventionally grouped into three categories:

"Special Statutory Review"—review authorized by the particular organic statute(s) under which the agency is acting

"General Statutory Review"—review authorized by the APA

"Nonstatutory Review"—a somewhat misleading term, in that this category now includes not only common-law and equity forms of action, but also actions authorized by statutes *other* than the agency's organic statute or the APA. The core of nonstatutory review are actions for declaratory and injunctive relief, and for remedies that historically are termed the "prerogative" (or "extraordinary") writs. These actions have in common the strategy of subverting sovereign immunity by suing the official, rather than the agency, for prospective relief. Also included, historically, were common-law actions against officials to recover damages in tort or contract for wrongful administrative actions. Today, these have been largely supplanted by statutory remedies against the United States itself: the Federal Tort Claims Act and the Tucker Act.

Each of these categories is discussed in turn.

a. SPECIAL STATUTORY REVIEW

"The form of proceeding for judicial review is the special statutory review proceeding relevant to the subject matter in a court specified by statute *or, in the absence or inadequacy thereof, any applicable form of legal action . . ."*

Administrative Procedure Act, 5 U.S.C. § 703 (emphasis added)

---

3. At the risk of stating the obvious, the general federal-question jurisdictional grant, 28 U.S.C. § 1331, is *not* also a general consent by the United States to be sued on claims of federal law.

Not surprisingly, regulatory statutes often contain provisions specifically authorizing judicial review of at least some of the actions in which the agency engages. Searching the relevant organic statute(s) for such provisions—which define what § 703 terms a "special statutory review proceeding"—is the lawyer's first step. Why? Such provisions often designate the level of the court system (i.e., district or appellate) at which review is to be initiated. Moreover, they are usually interpreted as

> (i) granting subject matter jurisdiction,
> (ii) providing a cause of action, *and*
> (iii) waiving sovereign immunity, for claims within their scope.

In addition, they might

> (iv) specify venue,
> (v) set a statute of limitations,
> (vi) determine whether certain intra-agency remedies must be exhausted,
> (vii) confer standing, *and/or*
> (viii) provide supplementary or alternative standards of review.

Lawyers accustomed to the ordinary civil litigation process may be surprised to learn that the typical special statutory review proceeding begins directly in the court of appeals, by filing a petition for review.[1] If you have already studied the materials on rulemaking and adjudication in Chapters III–V, you will appreciate why Congress so often chooses to site review in the circuit courts from the outset: The record on which agency action is reviewed is almost always the record created *at the agency*. Hence, there is no need for the district court's capacity to hold evidentiary hearings—indeed, it would usually be inappropriate to attempt to build a new record outside the agency.[2] Siting review in the court of appeals offers the immediate benefit of deliberation by a panel of three appellate judges, and very often (because the Supreme Court grants so few petitions for certiorari) results in the review petition being resolved relatively quickly through a single round of litigation.

Still, there are important instances of special statutory review sited in the trial court. For example, the Social Security Act provides for review of benefit denials or terminations "in the district court of the United States

---

1. Some statutes, especially in the environmental area, consolidate review in the D.C. Circuit. Alternatively, the petition can usually be filed in any circuit in which the petitioner resides or the cause of action arose. If more than two parties seek review in different circuits within ten days of the agency's decision, the cases will be consolidated in a circuit selected by lot, although forum non conveniens may be employed to adjust the lottery selection. See 28 U.S.C. § 2112(a). Through a combination of statutory direction and litigant choice, the D.C. Circuit hears the lion's share of petitions for review of rules. In many years, the Ninth Circuit has the largest number of administrative review filings, but this reflects a disproportionately high number of immigration appeals. See generally http://www.uscourts.gov/caseload2001/tables/b01mar01.pdf.

2. See Camp v. Pitts, p. 996 above; see also U.S. v. Nova Scotia Food Prod. Corp., p. 524 above. Occasionally, the court of appeals is authorized to transfer the case to the district court if further evidentiary development proves necessary. See, e.g., 8 U.S.C. § 1105a(a)(5); 28 U.S.C. § 2347(b)(3).

for the judicial district in which the plaintiff resides, or has his principal place of business...." 42 U.S.C. §§ 405(g), 421(d). When a statute directs for review to begin in the district court, the reason is often a concern for reducing the travel burden on private litigants, as well as a greater likelihood that the court has been statutorily authorized to take additional evidence as part of its review.

When special statutory review provisions apply, they typically preempt other potential avenues of judicial review.[3] "This sort of jurisdiction is favored because it represents Congress's particular estimate of an optimal allocation of business between a specific agency and the courts. This special jurisdiction, and the accompanying form of review, may provide a space in which agencies for a time may act unimpeded by the courts." Alfred C. Aman, Jr. & William T. Mayton, Administrative Law 353 (1993).

Note, though, that APA § 703 expressly acknowledges the possibility that a special statutory review proceeding might be "absent[t] or inade-qua[te]." When might this occur? First, and most obviously, the relevant organic statute may not mention judicial review at all. As we will see in Section 3 below, such silence is usually *not* construed to mean no review. Rather, the litigant will be permitted to use a species of general statutory or nonstatutory review. Second, the organic statute might provide for review of agency actions *other than* the particular type of which the litigant wishes to complain. For example, one of the most significant Supreme Court justiciability decisions in the modern era was prompted by attempts to obtain review of a *rule* when the organic statute spoke only of review of "*orders*." See Abbott Laboratories v. Gardner, p. 1182 below. A more contemporary example occurs when regulatory beneficiaries seek judicial remedies for agency failure to act or unreasonable delay. See Heckler v. Chaney, p. 1218 below; p. 602 above. Finally, the special review proceeding may be arguably inadequate because the litigant is unable or unwilling to comply with one of the statutory conditions, or because she seeks a type of remedy not provided by the statute. Whether the litigant is permitted to use other forms of review will depend on the court's assessment, in light of the legislative evidence and regulatory objectives of the particular adminis-trative scheme, whether Congress intended the special review proceeding to be exclusive—even with its alleged shortcomings.

One other important species of special statutory review proceeding is the "enforcement action." Even agencies that are broadly authorized to investigate and adjudicate alleged wrongdoing and impose sanctions are usually not empowered to enforce those sanctions. If the regulated entity does not voluntarily accept the penalty imposed, the agency typically has to petition the court for a judicial order of enforcement. In deciding whether to issue this order, the court reviews the agency's decision just as if an aggrieved person had filed a petition for review.[4] Indeed, the court often

---

3. See Thunder Basin Coal Co. v. Reich, 510 U.S. 200 (1994); Whitney Nat'l Bank v. Bank of New Orleans, 379 U.S. 411 (1965).

4. "Except to the extent that prior, ade-quate, and exclusive opportunity for judicial review is provided by law, agency action is subject to judicial review in civil or criminal proceedings for judicial enforcement." 5 U.S.C. § 703.

receives cross-petitions, as the agency seeks to have its sanction decision enforced while the regulated entity seeks to have it vacated.

b.   GENERAL STATUTORY REVIEW

"Agency action made reviewable by statute and final agency action for which there is no other adequate remedy in a court are subject to judicial review."

Administrative Procedure Act, 5 U.S.C. § 704

If a special statutory review proceeding is absent, inadequate, or deemed non-exclusive, the cause of action most commonly used is the one created by the APA itself. The APA cause of action is highly versatile and has many advantages, although the informed lawyer will recognize its distinctive characteristics.

"The 'right of action' in such cases is expressly created by the [APA], which states that 'final agency action for which there is no other adequate remedy in a court [is] subject to judicial review,' § 704, at the behest of '[a] person ... adversely affected or aggrieved by agency action.' § 702." Japan Whaling Ass'n v. American Cetacean Soc., 478 U.S. 221, 231 n. 4 (1986). In this action, the court is empowered to "compel agency action unlawfully withheld or unreasonably delayed," § 706(1), as well as to "hold unlawful and set aside agency action, findings, and conclusions found to" fall within any of the six conditions listed in § 706(2). The APA does not itself confer subject matter jurisdiction on the federal courts. Califano v. Sanders, 430 U.S. 99 (1977). Typically, this is easily remedied by pleading 28 U.S.C. § 1331, the general federal-question statute.

Section 1331 confers jurisdiction on the *district* courts and so (in contrast to the typical special statutory review proceeding) a review proceeding under the APA typically begins in the trial court.[1] This forum difference almost invariably implies a longer course of litigation, and may become significant if there is ambiguity about whether a special statutory proceeding applies, or is intended to be exclusive. The Supreme Court tends to resolve such questions in favor of the special statutory process, on the theory that direct appellate review is more efficient—at least for the sorts of agency actions that raise major issues of law or policy and are reviewed solely on the agency record.[2]

There is one significant exception to the rule that general statutory review begins in the district court. In the important and widely-followed decision Telecommunications Research & Action Center v. FCC, 750 F.2d 70 (D.C.Cir.1984) ["TRAC"], the D.C. Circuit held that where an organic

---

1. Absent a subject-specific venue provision, venue is proper in the district where the defendant resides, where "a substantial part of the events or omissions giving rise to the claim occurred," or where the plaintiff resides so long as no real property is involved. 28 U.S.C. § 1391(e).

2. See, e.g., Florida Power & Light Co. v. Lorion, 470 U.S. 729 (1985); Harrison v. PPG Indus., Inc., 446 U.S. 578 (1980). For thoughtful discussion of the several factors, in addition to judicial economy, that should be considered in defining the optimal forum for review, see III Richard J. Pierce, Jr., Administrative Law Treatise § 18.2 (4th ed. 2002).

statute commits review of *final* agency action to the court of appeals, that court has exclusive jurisdiction over *all* suits seeking relief that "might affect" its future statutory review power.[3] If you studied the materials in Chapter V on dealing with agency inaction and unreasonable delay, p. 602 above, you have already seen a context in which the TRAC principle can operate to locate APA-based review immediately in the appeals court.

Because the APA addresses several other justiciability issues—in particular, standing and exhaustion—those directions will be applied when a litigant relies on the APA cause of action. With respect to standing, APA § 702[4] may afford standing that is broader, or narrower, than that afforded by the special statutory review proceeding. For example, a litigant seeking review in a special statutory proceeding having a citizen-suit provision will generally not have to satisfy the zone-of-interest test that is required in APA standing. E.g., Bennett v. Spear, p. 1172 below. With respect to exhaustion, APA § 704 specifies precise criteria for when administrative remedies must be employed before seeking review; this direction supplants the multi-factor interest balance that will determine exhaustion requirements in non-APA causes of action. See Darby v. Cisneros, p. 1238 below.

Perhaps most significant, the APA contains an important, though not absolute, waiver of sovereign immunity. As originally enacted, the statute did not explicitly address the problem of sovereign immunity. The consequences were confusion about what could be accomplished within the APA itself, considerable reliance on nonstatutory forms of action outside the APA, and emphatic scholarly criticism.[5] Finally, in 1976 Congress responded with a set of four related provisions to facilitate judicial review of agency action—at least when the remedy sought is specific relief rather than damages. The first amended 28 U.S.C. § 1331 to delete the jurisdictional amount requirement in actions against the United States, any federal agency, or any federal employee or officer in his official capacity.[6] The second amended 28 U.S.C. § 1391(e) to permit joinder of third parties in civil litigation in which the government is defendant. The third, codified in APA § 702, waived sovereign immunity for non-damages claims:

3. Although one hopes not to need it, 28 U.S.C. § 1651 provides some protection for the lawyer who files in the wrong forum. It directs that the action be transferred to the appropriate court "if [transfer] is in the interest of justice," and provides that the action shall then "proceed as if it had been filed in the court to which it is transferred on the date upon which it was actually filed" in the transferor court.

4. "A person suffering legal wrong because of agency action, or adversely affected or aggrieved by agency action within the meaning of a relevant statute, is entitled to judicial review thereof."

5. See, e.g., Kenneth Culp Davis, Suing the Government by Falsely Pretending to Sue an Officer, 29 U. Chi. L. Rev. 435 (1962);

Louis L. Jaffe, Judicial Control of Administrative Action 197–256 (1965); Clark Byse, Proposed Reforms in Federal "Nonstatutory" Judicial Review: Sovereign Immunity, Indispensable Parties, Mandamus, 75 Harv. L. Rev. 1479 (1962); Roger C. Cramton, Nonstatutory Review of Federal Administrative Action: The Need for Statutory Reform of Sovereign Immunity, Subject Matter Jurisdiction, and Parties Defendant, 68 Mich. L. Rev. 387 (1970); Kenneth Culp Davis, Sovereign Immunity Must Go, 22 Admin. L. Rev. 383 (1970) ; David E. Engdahl, Immunity and Accountability for Positive Governmental Wrongs, 44 U. Colo. L. Rev. 1 (1972).

6. Four years later, the amount in controversy requirement was deleted entirely from § 1331.

> An action in a court of the United States seeking relief other than money damages and stating a claim that an agency or an officer or employee thereof acted or failed to act in an official capacity or under color of legal authority shall not be dismissed nor relief therein be denied on the ground that it is against the United States or that the United States is an indispensable party. The United States may be named as a defendant in any such action, and a judgment or decree may be entered against the United States: Provided, that any mandatory or injunctive decree shall specify the Federal officer or officers (by name or by title) and their successors in office, personally responsible for compliance. Nothing herein (1) affects other limitations on judicial review or the power or duty of the court to dismiss any action or deny relief on any other appropriate legal or equitable ground; or (2) confers authority to grant relief if any other statute that grants consent to suit expressly or impliedly forbids the relief which is sought.

The fourth, codified in APA § 703, provided, "If no special statutory proceeding is applicable, the action for judicial review may be brought against the United States, the agency by its official title, or the appropriate officer." The accompanying House Report explained the purpose of these changes as "remov[ing] technical barriers to the consideration on the merits of citizens' complaints against the Federal Government, its agencies or employees." H. Rep. No. 94–1656, 94th Cong., 2d Sess. 3 (1976).

Because of the 1976 legislation, most garden-variety administrative review claims seeking to challenge the procedural or substantive validity of agency rules or orders proceed against the agency, by name, without any sovereign immunity concerns. The exception to this comes when the challenged administrative decision itself involves the payment of money, for the statutory consent to suit expressly excludes "money damages." In BOWEN V. MASSACHUSETTS, 487 U.S. 879 (1988), the Court construed § 702 to permit Massachusetts to contest an HHS decision denying the state $6,000,000 in Medicaid reimbursements. Five Justices concluded that the reimbursement Massachusetts would receive if it prevailed on the merits would constitute not "money damages" but rather an equitable remedy for money owed. A sixth Justice agreed with the alternative reasoning that the State did not request an order actually compelling the government to pay money—even though everyone expected it would do so if a court overturned the agency decision. However, the courts of appeals, particularly the D.C. Circuit, have tended to read Bowen narrowly and to resist litigants' attempts to use § 702 for making equitable claims to the payment of money.[7] A monetary claim against the United States that is not within the scope of the waiver must generally be brought under the Tucker Act (for contracts, takings and other non-tort claims), p. 1289 below, or the Federal Tort Claims Act, p. 1278 below.

---

7. See, e.g., Hubbard v. Administrator, 982 F.2d 531 (D.C.Cir.1992) (en banc) (back pay claim not within § 702 consent to suit); Slaughter v. FBI, 991 F.2d 799 (7th Cir. 1993); Ward v. Brown, 22 F.3d 516 (2d Cir. 1994) (following Hubbard, although finding adequate waiver of sovereign immunity in the Back Pay Act, 5 U.S.C. § 5596). Cf. Department of the Army v. Blue Fox, 525 U.S. 255 (1999) (subcontractor cannot use § 702 to seek equitable lien on funds held by the Army for work on prime contract).

c. "NONSTATUTORY" REVIEW

When the 1976 amendments established unambiguously that APA-based review could proceed against agencies by name without sovereign immunity concerns, the need for nonstatutory forms of review disappeared in the typical case seeking review of rulemaking or administrative adjudication. However, APA-based review does not serve every need. The government official or entity whose action is challenged may not be within the purview of the APA.[1] Or, the action complained of may not be reachable under that statute.[2] Finally, the injured party may find the APA cause of action insufficient because she principally desires compensation rather than prospective relief. In such circumstances, and lacking any usable special statutory review proceeding, the lawyer looks for an appropriate form of "nonstatutory review."[3]

Nonstatutory review has produced some of our most important opinions defining the legitimate scope of government action: Marbury v. Madison,[4] Osborn v. Bank of the United States,[5] and Youngstown Sheet and Tube Co. v. Sawyer[6] all proceeded through nonstatutory forms of action. Originating in the need to provide some avenue for judicial review of the conduct of government employees whose sovereign principal refused to waive its immunity from suit, nonstatutory review proceeded against the official *individually*. The proceedings tended to be of two general types: actions to obtain retrospective relief in the form of damages, and actions to obtain specific, or prospective, relief in the form of injunctions or other judicial orders. Today, statutes operate in both areas to codify, supplement, or sometimes even supplant the original nonstatutory forms. (This is why "nonstatutory review" as a term of art includes certain obviously statutory proceedings.) Nonetheless, important elements remain uncodified.

(i) DAMAGES ACTIONS

Historically, if an administrative action invaded liberty or property interests protected by the common law, the injured citizen sued the responsible official in tort or contract. When the official defended by citing his statutory authority, the court could inquire into the scope of that authority, and resolve allegations of its abuse. If the administrative action were found not justified under the legal authority claimed, the official would be liable personally to the complainant for the damages caused. See, e.g., North American Cold Storage Co. v. Chicago, p. 884 above.

---

1. For example, the President is not an "agency" within the meaning of the APA, Dalton v. Specter, 511 U.S. 462 (1994). Similarly, claims that state agencies have violated federal statutes or the Constitution cannot be brought under the APA.

2. E.g., Webster v. Doe, p. 1209 below (finding CIA employment decision not reviewable under the APA because "committed to agency discretion by law," but reviewable for claimed due process and equal protection violations).

3. For a lucid and illuminating examination of the history and forms of nonstatutory review, see Jonathan R. Siegel, Suing the President: Nonstatutory Review Revisited, 97 Colum. L. Rev. 1612 (1997)[hereinafter "Nonstatutory Review Revisited"].

4. 5 U.S. (1 Cranch) 137 (1803).

5. 22 U.S. (9 Wheat.) 738 (1824).

6. 343 U.S. 579 (1952).

Of course, such a regime tends to be hard on government officials whose personal assets are at risk in the event of a mistaken administrative decision. Consequently, courts developed "official immunity" defenses that protected official judgment in varying degrees. See, e.g., Butz v. Economou, p. 1258 below.[1] Eventually, legislatures intervened to provide alternative or supplanting causes of action against the government itself. At the federal level, officials now have complete statutory immunity for torts committed "while acting within the scope of [their] office or employment." 28 U.S.C. § 2679(b)(1). The exclusive remedy is against the United States, on a respondeat superior theory, under the Federal Tort Claims Act (FTCA)— even though this statutory consent to liability has significant procedural restrictions and substantive gaps. See Section 5(b) below.[2] For claims "not sounding in tort"—most importantly, contract and takings claims—a remedy directly against the United States can be sought under the Tucker Act. See id.

Damages actions against government officials personally remain important in two areas:

First, damages can be sought against both federal and state officials for constitutional violations committed in the course of their duties. In the case of federal officials, the cause of action comes directly from the Constitution. See Bivens v. Six Unknown Federal Narcotics Agents, 403 U.S. 388 (1971). The FTCA immunity from personal liability does *not* extend to constitutional wrongs,[3] although the official will have the benefit of official immunity defenses. See Section 5(a) below. Such "Bivens actions" can be brought only against the individual official, not against the agency,[4] and there are circumstances in which the Court will refuse to imply the cause of action even where only the official himself is being sued.[5] In the case of state and

---

1. Such remedies are not ideal from the perspective of the injured citizen either. The law of when a government employee can be held personally liable for harm from official action can be quite complex, and has significant gaps. See Hart & Wechsler at 938–960; Revisiting Nonstatutory Review at 1644–62.

2. For example, most intentional torts are excluded, 28 U.S.C. § 2680(h), and there is a significant categorical exception for "the exercise or performance or the failure to exercise or perform a discretionary function ... whether or not the discretion involved be abused." § 2680(a). Nevertheless, the statutory bar on employees' personal liability applies even when one of the statutory exclusions precludes recovery from the government. United States v. Smith, 499 U.S. 160 (1991). In such circumstances, victims are remitted to whatever relief they can obtain through administrative settlement, see 28 U.S.C. §§ 2672, 2675; George A. Bermann, Federal Tort Claims at the Agency Level: The FTCA Administrative Process, 35 Case

W.Res.L.Rev. 509, 512 (1985), or from Congress via a private bill. See generally M. Jones & F. Davis, Profile of a Congressional Reference Case, 28 Mo.B.J. 69 (1972); Jeffrey M. Glosser, Congressional Reference Cases in the U.S. Court of Claims: A Historical and Current Perspective, 25 Am.U.L.Rev. 595 (1976).

3. See 28 U.S.C. § 2679(b)(2)(A).

4. Federal Deposit Ins. Corp. v. Meyer, 510 U.S. 471 (1994); Correctional Services Corp. v. Malesko, 534 U.S. 61 (2001) (private corporation acting as government contractor).

5. A constitutional cause of action will not be implied when either (1) Congress has provided an alternative remedy deemed equally effective; or (2) the court perceives "special factors counseling hesitation." These criteria have proved controversial in application. See generally Hart & Wechsler at 804–25. The tenor of the Court's recent opinions in the area has been decidedly negative, see, e.g., Correctional Services Corp. v. Malesko,

local officials, the cause of action for damages from constitutional violations is statutory. 42 U.S.C. § 1983[6] has spawned a massive body of law that is very selectively considered in Section 5(b) below. For present purposes, the basic contours of the § 1983 cause of action are: (i) Damages claims against state and local officials, in their individual capacity, are subject to the same official immunity defenses available to federal officials in Bivens actions; (ii) The statute can be used to seek damages against government entities below the level of the state itself; these entities (counties, municipalities, etc.) can assert no immunity defenses, but their liability for their employees' actions is limited in a number of ways;[7] (iii) States (and state agencies) cannot be sued under this statute.[8]

Second, as the result of a 1980 Supreme Court decision,[9] § 1983 may be available to obtain damages for violations of federal statutes, as well as the Constitution. Not all federal statutes can be enforced through § 1983. The nature of the statutory duty involved, and the existence and nature of other available enforcement mechanisms must be considered.[10] Particularly on the first of these requirements (which is now framed as requiring Congressional intent to create an "individually enforceable" right), recent Supreme Court decisions appear to apply a more demanding standard.[11] Still, the potential significance of this development is considerable.

(ii) SPECIFIC RELIEF: INJUNCTIONS, DECLARATIONS AND THE PREROGATIVE WRITS

For at least a century, federal courts have used injunctive relief to correct administrative violations of federal rights.[1] For even longer, the prerogative writs—a "highly creative development of the English law" borrowed by early American courts[2]—have been available to test the legality of official action.[3] In both instances, a proceeding against the

534 U.S. 61 (2001), and it seems clear that, at a minimum, expansion of the Bivens remedy is unlikely.

6. "Every person who, under color of any statute, ordinance, regulation, custom, or usage, of any State or Territory ..., subjects, or causes to be subjected, any citizen of the United States or other person within the jurisdiction thereof to the deprivation of any rights, privileges, or immunities secured by the Constitution and laws, shall be liable to the party injured in an action at law, suit in equity, or other proper proceeding for redress."

7. Most significantly, there is no respondeat superior liability; the wrongdoing must be pursuant to official policy or custom. Monell v. Department of Social Serv., 436 U.S. 658, 691 (1978). Also, punitive damages may not be recovered. City of Newport v. Fact Concerts, 453 U.S. 247 (1981).

8. Will v. Michigan Dept. of State Police, 491 U.S. 58 (1989); Quern v. Jordan, 440 U.S. 332 (1979).

9. Maine v. Thiboutot, 448 U.S. 1 (1980).

10. See Golden State Transit Corp. v. Los Angeles, 493 U.S. 103, 106–07 (1989).

11. See Gonzaga University v. Doe, 536 U.S. 273 (2002); Blessing v. Freestone, 520 U.S. 329 (1997).

1. E.g., American School of Magnetic Healing v. McAnnulty, 187 U.S. 94 (1902). A few years later, the germinal case of Ex parte Young, 209 U.S. 123 (1908), afforded injunctive relief in a claim of constitutional wrongdoing by a state administrative official.

2. Hart & Wechsler at 940.

3. E.g., Marbury v. Madison, 5 U.S. (1 Cranch) 137 (1803). See Louis L. Jaffe & Edith G. Henderson, Judicial Review and the Rule of Law: Historical Origins, 72 Law Q.Rev. 345 (1956).

official served to circumvent the immunity of the sovereign. Unlike damages actions—which ostensibly affect only the personal pocketbook of the official (even if he would be indemnified by his government employer)—these remedies directly affect official behavior and policy. In this sense, they rest upon a fiction: Ordering an official to conform his (official) behavior to law is not a suit against the sovereign because the sovereign does not authorize its agents to violate the law. Thus, in Marbury v. Madison, the writ of mandamus was an appropriate vehicle for judicial inquiry into the legality of the Secretary of State's failure to do an act "in the performance of which he is not placed under the particular direction of the President, and the performance of which the President cannot lawfully forbid, and therefore is never presumed to have forbidden." 5 U.S. (1 Cranch) 137, 171 (1803).[4] In Ex parte Young, Minnesota's Attorney General could be enjoined from enforcing a confiscatory rate order against the plaintiffs without "affect[ing] the State in its sovereign or governmental capacity. It is simply an illegal act upon the part of a state official in attempting by the use of the name of the State to enforce a legislative enactment which is void because unconstitutional. ... [H]e is in that case stripped of his official or representative character...." 209 U.S. 123, 160 (1908).[5]

Even today, injunctive relief requires no specific statutory authorization; declaratory relief has been authorized by 28 U.S.C. § 2201. Judicially crafted defenses of official immunity are generally not available in suits for prospective relief. See p. 1275 below. Of the five original prerogative writs, only habeas corpus and mandamus remain significant in federal administrative practice.[6] Habeas corpus, used to challenge the legality of physical custody, has recently become prominent for its capacity to obtain review of the detention of aliens and persons in the military. A number of statutory provisions determine the conditions of its availability in a variety of contexts.[7] Mandamus relief is now codified in 28 U.S.C. § 1361, entitled

---

4. At least, it would have been an appropriate vehicle if the relevant jurisdictional statute had been constitutional.

5. Although Ex parte Young itself involved a state official and a claim of constitutional illegality, its principle has been extended both to federal officials and to claims of statutory violation. See Hart & Wechsler at 959.

6. The others are quo warranto (usually limited to challenging an official's right to office), prohibition (used to prevent a judicial or quasi-judicial body from exceeding its jurisdiction when no other remedy is available), and certiorari (used to require a lower tribunal to certify the record of its proceedings to a higher tribunal for purposes of review). The writ of certiorari is, of course, alive and well as a review mechanism *within* the court system; however, fairly early in the life of the administrative state, the Supreme Court held that it could not be used to bring the record of an administrative agency before the federal courts. See Degge v. Hitchcock, 229 U.S. 162 (1913). By contrast, this writ remains an important, if "baffling," part of state administrative law practice. See 2 Frank E. Cooper, State Administrative Law 644 (1965). 28 U.S.C. § 1651, the All Writs Act, authorizes the Supreme Court and the lower federal courts to "issue all writs necessary or appropriate in aid of their respective jurisdictions and agreeable to the usages and principles of law."

7. E.g., 28 U.S.C. §§ 2241, 2254. See also 28 U.S.C. § 2255 (providing an alternative to habeas for federal prisoners). The Supreme Court's power to issue habeas corpus (and the other prerogative writs) as part of its original jurisdiction exists apart from statute, although the extent and conditions of this power are unsettled. See Hart & Wechsler at 312–16.

"Action to compel an officer of the United States to perform his duty": "The district courts shall have original jurisdiction of any action in the nature of mandamus to compel an officer or employee of the United States or any agency thereof to perform a duty owed to the plaintiff."

Section 703 of the APA expressly acknowledges the important tradition of nonstatutory review when it provides: "The form of proceeding for judicial review is ... in the absence or inadequacy of [a special statutory review proceeding], any applicable form of legal action, including actions for declaratory judgments or writs of prohibitory or mandatory injunction or habeas corpus, in a court of competent jurisdiction." Prior to the 1976 legislation authorizing suits against the United States itself for non-damages relief, it would have been apparent that this language was intended to preserve the various avenues of relief that ran individually against agency officials in order to avoid sovereign immunity problems. Now that § 702 expressly authorizes specific relief against the agency itself, the nonstatutory forms retain little practical independent significance for cases that can be brought under the APA.[8]

Where the APA is unavailable, however, the traditional nonstatutory avenues for declaratory and injunctive relief, and for mandamus, continue to function.[9] These remedies are not always straightforward. In some circumstances, complex questions may arise about whether an order running against the official is appropriate or whether, instead, the requested relief is "really" against the government (and so barred by immunity).[10] With respect to mandamus, there is a fundamental split in view about the scope of available review. The traditional approach distinguishes between "ministerial" and "discretionary" duties, insisting that mandamus is appropriate only to compel performance of a "clear, nondiscretionary duty." Humane Society v. Clinton, 236 F.3d 1320, 1328 (Fed.Cir.2001).[11] The alternative approach, which tends to have the support of scholars, is that mandamus lies whenever an official acts beyond the scope of her lawful authority. On this view, mandamus functions very much like abuse-of-discretion review under APA § 706(2).[12] Some courts seem determined to

8. For example, although some circuits take the position that the availability of the APA § 706 remedy of compelling "agency action unlawfully withheld or unreasonably delayed" precludes mandamus relief under § 1361, e.g., Smilde v. Herman, 201 F.3d 449 (10th Cir.1999), others allow the two forms of relief to go forward in parallel as "essentially the same." E.g., Independence Min. Co., Inc. v. Babbitt, 105 F.3d 502, 507 & n. 6 (9th Cir.1997). See also Idaho Watersheds Project v. Hahn, 2002 WL 31109002 (9th Cir.2002); R.T. Vanderbilt Co. v. Babbitt, 113 F.3d 1061, 1065 (9th Cir.1997).

9. See, e.g., Rhode Island Dept. of Environmental Management v. U.S., 304 F.3d 31 (1st Cir., 2002); Chamber of Commerce of U.S. v. Reich 74 F.3d 1322 (D.C.Cir.1996).

10. See generally Hart & Wechsler at 938–60; 14 Charles A. Wright, Arthur R. Miller & Edward H. Cooper, Federal Practice and Procedure § 3655 at. 358–83; Nonstatutory Review Revisited at pp. 1622–62. At least with respect to entities that meet the APA definition of "agency," the 1976 waiver of sovereign immunity codified in APA § 702 "applies to any suit, whether under the APA, § 1331, § 1361, or any other statute." Hart & Wechsler at 968–69. See, e.g., Chamber of Commerce of U.S. v. Reich 74 F.3d at 1328.

11. See, e.g., Heckler v. Ringer, 466 U.S. 602, 612 (1984); 14 Wright, Miller & Cooper § 3655 at 406 & n. 58. See generally Hart & Wechsler at 941–42.

12. Chief Justice Taft, himself a former Chief Executive, articulated this approach in

straddle the debate by quoting the traditional approach but then concluding that the court can determine the *extent* of discretion the applicable statute confers and, if necessary, direct the administrative actor to redecide the matter under a proper understanding of the scope of her authority.[13]

(iii) SPECIAL PROBLEMS OF SUING STATES TO ENFORCE REGULATORY OBLIGATIONS: STATE SOVEREIGN IMMUNITY AND THE ELEVENTH AMENDMENT

Although we often do not think of states as included in the class of regulated entities, in many administrative programs Congress has chosen to require state agencies to conform to the same regulatory obligations imposed on private parties. Initially, the Supreme Court perceived Tenth Amendment problems with such statutes, but it soon abandoned that approach.[1] Now, so long as Congress (i) avoids strategies of regulating that amount to "commandeering" the processes of state government,[2] and (ii) makes sufficiently clear its intention that states be included in the class of those regulated,[3] it can require state agencies to comply with federal standards governing emission of pollution and treatment of hazardous waste, worker health and safety, discrimination, intellectual property rights, etc.

It would seem logical that if Congress has the constitutional authority to impose such substantive obligations on states, it also has the authority

Work v. Rives, 267 U.S. 175 (1925). See also Wright, Miller & Cooper, § 3655 at 412 nn. 60, 62.

The traditional view of mandamus is often traced to the section of Marbury v. Madison in which Chief Justice Marshall distinguished between "ministerial" obligations of government officials, whose fulfillment mandamus could compel, and "discretionary" powers, with which the writ could not interfere. 5 U.S. (1 Cranch) at 168–73. Significantly, however, the example Marshall gives of a "discretionary" function is the Secretary of State's performance of his foreign affairs responsibilities. Hence, he seems to have had in mind a type of discretion unconstrained by judicially manageable legal standards (discretion as to which there is now said to be "no law to apply," see p. 1209 below), and not the far more common type of official judgment that we understand to be discretion bounded by enforceable legal standards (such as the Secretary of Transportation's decision to route a highway through Overton Park, p. 989 above). Thus, cases that use mandamus to determine whether an official is acting without proper authority or in abuse of statutory discretion are in fact reconcilable with Marbury.

13. E.g., Buchanan v. Apfel, 249 F.3d 485 (6th Cir.2001) (mandamus will lie to challenge agency's use of a cap for permissible attorneys' fees; the "Commissioner has neglected his clear, nondiscretionary duty to follow both case law and his own administrative regulations"); Barron v. Reich 13 F.3d 1370 (9th Cir.1994) ("While mandamus may not be used to impinge upon an official's legitimate use of discretion, even in an area generally left to agency discretion, there may well exist statutory or regulatory standards delimiting the scope or manner in which such discretion can be exercised. In these situations, mandamus will lie when the standards have been ignored or violated.") (internal quotes omitted).

1. See Garcia v. San Antonio Metro. Transit Auth., 469 U.S. 528 (1985), overruling National League of Cities v. Usery, 426 U.S. 833 (1976).

2. See New York v. United States, 505 U.S. 144 (1992); Printz v. United States, 521 U.S. 898 (1997).

3. E.g., Vermont Agency of Natural Resources v. United States ex rel. Stevens, 529 U.S. 765 (2000); Gregory v. Ashcroft, 501 U.S. 452 (1991); cf. Atascadero State Hosp. v. Scanlon, 473 U.S. 234 (1985).

to provide for normal methods of legal enforcement against them. This, however, is not the law.

In a complex and highly contested series of decisions, the Court has held that states' sovereign immunity from suit without their consent is embodied in the Constitution, and that nothing in Article I or the Bill of Rights gives Congress the power to abrogate that immunity. See Seminole Tribe of Florida v. Florida, 517 U.S. 44 (1996); Florida Prepaid Postsecondary Educ. Expense Bd. v. College Sav. Bank, 527 U.S. 627 (1999) ["Florida Prepaid"].[4] Because most regulatory programs are enacted under the Commerce Clause, the Spending Clause, or other more specific Article I provisions, this holding has enormous implications for attempts by regulatory beneficiaries to enforce statutory obligations against states. For example, Florida Prepaid held that patent holders could not sue a state agency in federal court to recover damages for infringement *even though* Congress had recently amended the patent laws explicitly to reach states, because Florida had not waived its immunity. Subsequently, the Court extended this holding to suits brought by private parties in *state* court to enforce federal law. Alden v. Maine, 527 U.S. 706 (1999), permitted the courts of Maine to dismiss, on sovereign immunity grounds, an action by state probation officers to recover overtime payments required by the Fair Labor Standards Act *even though* states are expressly subject to the FLSA; the employees had gone to state court after their FLSA claim in federal court was dismissed under Seminole Tribe. Finally, the Court extended the principle to administrative adjudication, holding that private parties cannot force states to appear before federal agencies to answer for federal regulatory violations.[5]

How can regulatory obligations be enforced against states and their agencies? The most doctrinally straightforward answer is enforcement action undertaken by the federal government itself. States cannot assert sovereign immunity in actions by the United States (or its agencies).[6] Thus, immunity will not be a problem in the very common enforcement paradigm in which the federal agency itself, or the U.S. Attorney, brings the complaint.[7] But this solution, while indubitably possible, is not a panacea. What if the federal agency refuses a request to institute enforcement action?

---

4. See generally Hart & Wechsler, at 1004–39.

5. Federal Maritime Com'n v. South Carolina State Ports Auth., 535 U.S. 743 (2002) (sovereign immunity prevented cruise ship company from using Federal Maritime Commission proceeding to obtain injunctive relief and reparations from South Carolina agency for violation of Shipping Act).

6. E.g., United States v. Texas, 143 U.S. 621, 644–45 (1892); United States v. Mississippi, 380 U.S. 128, 140–41 (1965). Similarly, the immunity cannot be asserted in a suit brought by another state. E.g., Kansas v. Colorado, 206 U.S. 46, 83 (1907).

7. See, e.g., Rhode Island Dep't of Environmental Management v. U.S., 304 F.3d 31 (1st Cir., 2002), in which former state employees attempted to use a statutory procedure before the Secretary of Labor to complain that the state agency had fired them in retaliation for reporting violations of federal waste disposal laws. The court recognized that, after South Carolina State Ports Authority, Rhode Island could not be forced to participate in the administrative proceeding as it was then structured. However, the opinion pointed out, if the Secretary of Labor intervened to become a party—as applicable regulations permitted—the immunity problem would be resolved. Id. at 53–54.

Such a refusal is almost certainly unreviewable.[8] Even if the agency is sympathetic, it is unlikely to have the resources to undertake all the enforcement it would prefer.[9] Thus, regulatory beneficiaries injured by state noncompliance will often be left to their own devices. Fortunately, those devices do include one significant, though remedially limited, option.

As described above, for nearly a century the federal courts have employed a legal fiction to allow enforcement of federal obligations against state actors despite sovereign immunity: a suit brought against *the responsible state official by name* seeking an injunction that the official conform his conduct to federal law. These "Ex parte Young" actions—so called after the original case[10]—can achieve future compliance with regulatory obligations through the device of an injunction (or, sometimes, simply a declaration) that specifies the official defendant's duties under federal law.[11] What cannot be accomplished in such actions is retrospective, compensatory relief that requires the payment of money from the state treasury.[12] Thus, for example, the probation officers in Alden could have obtained an injunction against the responsible state official, by name, directing the future payment of overtime as required by the FLSA.[13] However, there now appears to be no remedial mechanism through which they can themselves obtain recovery of the unpaid overtime to which the FLSA entitled them.[14]

8. See Heckler v. Chaney, p. 602 above and p. 1218 below.

9. Demonstrating a remarkable indifference to the practical demands of administering a system of nationwide law enforcement, the Alden majority tartly remarked that, although the Solicitor General appeared in the case to assert the interest of the United States in having the suit go forward, "the United States apparently found the same interests insufficient to justify sending even a single attorney to Maine to prosecute this litigation." 527 U.S. at 759. The majority did not explain why the interests of the United States in having the suit go forward were not adequately demonstrated by the actions of Congress in passing legislation expressly authorizing such lawsuits, and of the Executive in appearing to argue for its constitutionality.

10. 209 U.S. 123 (1908).

11. See, e.g., Verizon Md., Inc. v. Public Serv. Comm'n, 535 U.S. 635 (2002).

12. Edelman v. Jordan, 415 U.S. 651 (1974). A convoluted line of cases defines the border between permissible prospective relief that incidentally involves the payment of money and impermissible retrospective relief. See Hart & Weschler, at 995–99.

13. In Alden, the state had changed its overtime policies to comply with the FLSA,

so future compliance was not an issue. The possibility of using Ex parte Young to accomplish reinstatement of the alleged whistle-blowers in Rhode Island Dep't of Environmental Management was noted by the First Circuit, although the court concluded that the state of the record was insufficient to determine whether in fact such a claim had been properly pleaded. 304 F.3d at 52.

14. Cf. Alden, 527 U.S. at 810 (noting that the statute authorizes the Secretary of Labor to bring suit to recover unpaid overtime for the benefit of particular employees).

It is, of course, possible that a state would waive its immunity from suit. Like the federal government, many states have consented, by statute, to be sued under specified circumstances. Such statutes are highly unlikely to include consent to suit in federal court, and may not include consent to suit on federal claims (although see Howlett v. Rose, 496 U.S. 356 (1990), which suggests some limits on the state's ability to discriminate against federal claims.) However, it may be possible to recast the regulatory wrongdoing as, for example, a tort for which damages are recoverable under a state tort claims scheme. It is also possible in some circumstances to argue that the state has consented to suit by its conduct in the specific litigation. What if,

The law of Eleventh Amendment sovereign immunity is so contentious, and so much in flux, that Congress' options for enhancing enforcement of regulatory obligations against states are very unclear. In theory, it *can* abrogate state's immunity when it legislates pursuant to the remedial authority of section 5 of the Fourteenth Amendment.[15] In fact, recent Supreme Court decisions have set such stringent standards for invoking this authority that few regulatory programs are likely to qualify.[16] In theory, it is possible for Congress to condition a state's participation in certain regulatory programs on its waiving its sovereign immunity. After initially accepting the notion that a state could be deemed to have consented to suit merely by undertaking activity in a regulated area in which Congress had provided for judicial enforcement, the Court has rejected this idea of "constructive consent."[17] However, it still appears possible for Congress to enact an express requirement that states consent to suit in order to obtain some benefit the federal government is not otherwise required to confer upon them.[18] This strategy would seem most promising in programs that disburse federal funds under the Spending Clause. Finally, a strong argument has been made that Congress could expand the device of qui tam actions to authorize their use to enforce regulatory commands against states.[19] A form of statutorily authorized remedy that has existed since the Founding, qui tam actions are, in effect, bounty actions brought by private individuals for the benefit of the United States— typically, to uncover fraud on the government or similar forms of wrongdoing. See p. 1153 below. The Court recently gave a qualified constitutional endorsement to such actions when brought against private defendants, but refused to construe the relevant statute as intended to authorize qui tam proceedings against states.[20] Thus the question of Congress' power to do so is still open. Although the argument in favor of the qui tam solution is conceptually strong—and although the need seems great for some approach that realigns the scope of Congress' power to impose substantive duties on states with the scope of its power to provide for judicial enforcement of those duties—the tenor of recent Supreme Court decisions is not favorable.

for example, the beneficiary initially files suit in state court (e.g., taking advantage of a statutory immunity waiver), and the state defendant removes to federal court? In Lapides v. Board of Regents, 535 U.S. 613 (2002), a unanimous Court held that such litigation conduct constitutes a waiver of any 11th Amendment immunity. On the question of whether Congress can force state consent to suit as a condition of participating in a regulatory program, see the next paragraph in the text.

15. Fitzpatrick v. Bitzer, 427 U.S. 445 (1976).

16. E.g., Florida Prepaid, supra (patent act amendments do not qualify); United States v. Morrison, 529 U.S. 598 (2000) (Violence Against Women Act does not qualify); Kimel v. Florida Bd. of Regents, 528 U.S. 62 (2000) (Age Discrimination in Employment Act does not qualify).

17. College Sav. Bank v. Florida Prepaid Postsecondary Educ. Expense Bd., 527 U.S. 666 (1999), overruling Parden v. Terminal Ry., 377 U.S. 184 (1964).

18. See, e.g., Petty v. Tennessee–Missouri Bridge Comm'n, 359 U.S. 275 (1959) (condition of approving interstate compact); South Dakota v. Dole, 483 U.S. 203 (1987) (condition of fund disbursement under Spending Clause).

19. See Evan H. Caminker, State Immunity Waivers for Suits by the United States, 98 Mich. L. Rev. 92 (1999).

20. Vermont Agency of Natural Resources v. United States ex rel. Stevens, 529 U.S. 765 (2000).

d. INTERIM RELIEF

"On such conditions as may be required and to the extent necessary to prevent irreparable injury, the reviewing court, including the court to which a case may be taken on appeal from or on application for certiorari or other writ to a reviewing court, may issue all necessary and appropriate process to postpone the effective date of an agency action or to preserve status or rights pending conclusion of the review proceedings."

Administrative Procedure Act, 5 U.S.C. § 705

Once you have determined which of these various methods is most appropriate for challenging the particular agency action involved, an important practical question may arise: Can the agency action be suspended while judicial review takes its course? Section 705 of the APA speaks explicitly to this question. Alternatively, the relevant organic statute might specifically authorize a stay. If all else fails, the Supreme Court has suggested that the power to issue a stay does not depend upon specific authorization but is "part of [the court's] traditional equipment for the administration of justice." Scripps–Howard Radio, Inc. v. FCC, 316 U.S. 4, 9–10 (1942).

VIRGINIA PETROLEUM JOBBERS ASS'N v. FPC, 259 F.2d 921, 925 (D.C.Cir. 1958), sets forth a widely followed outline of the factors typically considered on application for a stay:

"(1) Has the petitioner made a strong showing that it is likely to prevail on the merits of its appeal? Without such a substantial indication of probable success, there would be no justification for the court's intrusion into the ordinary processes of administration and judicial review.

"(2) Has the petitioner shown that without such relief, it will be irreparably injured? The key word in this consideration is *irreparable*. Mere injuries, however substantial, in terms of money, time and energy necessarily expended in the absence of a stay, are not enough. The possibility that adequate compensatory or other corrective relief will be available at a later date, in the ordinary course of litigation, weighs heavily against a claim of irreparable harm. But injury held insufficient to justify a stay in one case may well be sufficient to justify it in another, where the applicant has demonstrated a higher probability of success on the merits.

"(3) Would the issuance of a stay substantially harm other parties interested in the proceedings? On this side of the coin, we must determine whether, despite showings of probable success and irreparable injury on the part of petitioner, the issuance of a stay would have a serious adverse effect on other interested persons. Relief saving one claimant from irreparable injury, at the expense of similar harm caused another, might not qualify as the equitable judgment that a stay represents.

"(4) Where lies the public interest? In litigation involving the administration of regulatory statutes designed to promote the public interest, this factor necessarily becomes crucial. The interests of private litigants must give way to the realization of public purposes. The public interest may, of course, have many faces, . . . both fostering competition and preserving the economic viability of existing [enterprises]; both expediting administrative or judicial action and preserving orderly procedure."

SECTION 2. STANDING TO INVOKE JUDICIAL REVIEW

Over thirty years ago, in an opinion that transformed the law on who can invoke judicial review of agency action, Justice Douglas opined, "Generalizations about standing to sue are largely worthless as such." Association of Data Processing Serv. Orgs. v. Camp, p. 1129 below. Of course, this is not what the lawyer (or law student) wants to hear, but the convoluted course of standing doctrine in the last three decades bears out Justice Douglas' warning.

Of all the components of justiciability, standing doctrine most clearly shows the strain of changing—and conflicting—views about the appropriate role of the judiciary in the regulatory process. Standing is the key to the courthouse door; those who possess the key, possess power. To be sure, being permitted to complain about agency behavior is a long way from having that complaint legally validated and judicially remedied. Still, from the agency's perspective, the very act of being haled into court and required to defend its action involves considerable costs. Hence, parties who are capable of imposing such costs at the *end* of the regulatory process become parties whose interests must be reckoned with *during* the regulatory process. In this sense, standing represents judicially-enhanced voice. As you consider the evolution of the various strands of standing doctrine, consider which voices gain, and lose, in the process—and what impact this modulation is likely to have on the course of regulatory policymaking.

Moreover, because standing is quintessentially judge-made law, consider also the responsibility the judiciary bears as it decides who, if anyone, shall be entitled to trigger judicial scrutiny of agency conduct. These decisions can have significant implications for the Executive Branch that administers regulatory programs and for the Legislative Branch that creates them. To what extent *should* the contours of standing doctrine reflect the wishes of the political branches? In the late 1960s and into the 1970s, social and political movements to enhance public participation in regulatory processes encouraged (and were, in turn, encouraged by) changes in administrative law that opened agency proceedings to a range of interested parties. Although some of those legal changes were statutory, many—particularly in the areas of rights to participate at the agency level[1] and access to judicial review—came about through administrative common-lawmaking by federal judges. By the 1980s, however, the "interest representation" model of the administrative process had come under attack on both practical and philosophical grounds. In an era when regulatory ossification has become a byword and separation of powers has experienced a renaissance, the Supreme Court has become increasingly self-conscious about its role as gatekeeper of the federal courthouse.

---

1. See p. 334 above.

a. OVERVIEW: THE CONTEMPORARY DOCTRINAL FRAMEWORK

Allen v. Wright

Supreme Court of the United States, 1984.
468 U.S. 737.

■ JUSTICE O'CONNOR delivered the opinion of the Court.

[Under the Internal Revenue Code, racially discriminatory schools may not receive charitable tax-exempt status.[1] Parents of African–American children attending public schools in school districts undergoing desegregation in seven states, brought a nationwide class action challenging the adequacy of IRS efforts to enforce this prohibition. They claimed that IRS standards and procedures fail to identify schools that in fact discriminate, with the result that such schools are obtaining, and keeping, tax-exempt status. They asserted that this failure violates both the Code and the Constitution, and sought an injunction requiring denial of tax-exempt status to all private schools

> which have insubstantial or nonexistent minority enrollments, which are located in or serve desegregating public school districts, and which either
>
> (1) were established or expanded at or about the time the public school districts in which they are located or which they serve were desegregating;
>
> (2) have been determined in adversary judicial or administrative proceedings to be racially segregated; or
>
> (3) cannot demonstrate that they do not provide racially segregated educational opportunities for white children avoiding attendance in desegregating public school systems.[2]

The district court dismissed the complaint for lack of standing. The court of appeals reversed.]

Respondents allege in their complaint that many racially segregated private schools were created or expanded in their communities at the time the public schools were undergoing desegregation. According to the complaint, many such private schools, including 17 schools or school systems identified by name in the complaint (perhaps some 30 schools in all), receive tax exemptions.... Respondents allege that ... some of the tax-exempt racially segregated private schools created or expanded in desegregating districts in fact have racially discriminatory policies.[3] ...

---

1. The IRS has had a formal policy to this effect since 1971; the Supreme Court confirmed this interpretation in Bob Jones Univ. v. United States, 461 U.S. 574 (1983).

2. The requested relief was substantially similar to enforcement guidelines that were promulgated by IRS in 1978 and 1979. The agency withdrew the guidelines after Congressional action described at footnote 4 below.

3. The complaint generally uses the phrase "racially segregated school" to mean simply that no or few minority students attend the school, irrespective of the school's maintenance of racially discriminatory policies or practices. Although the complaint, on its face, alleges that granting tax-exempt status to any "racially segregated" school in a desegregating public school district is unlaw-

Respondents allege that the challenged Government conduct harms them in two ways. The challenged conduct

> (a) constitutes tangible federal financial aid and other support for racially segregated educational institutions, and

> (b) fosters and encourages the organization, operation and expansion of institutions providing racially segregated educational opportunities for white children avoiding attendance in desegregating public school districts and thereby interferes with the efforts of federal courts, HEW and local school authorities to desegregate public school districts which have been operating racially dual school systems.

Thus, respondents do not allege that their children have been the victims of discriminatory exclusion from the schools whose tax exemptions they challenge as unlawful. Indeed, they have not alleged at any stage of this litigation that their children have ever applied or would ever apply to any private school. Rather, respondents claim a direct injury from the mere fact of the challenged Government conduct and, as indicated by the restriction of the plaintiff class to parents of children in desegregating school districts, injury to their children's opportunity to receive a desegregated education. The latter injury is traceable to the IRS grant of tax exemptions to racially discriminatory schools, respondents allege, chiefly because contributions to such schools are deductible from income taxes ... and the "deductions facilitate the raising of funds to organize new schools and expand existing schools in order to accommodate white students avoiding attendance in desegregating public school districts."

... [T]he District Court permitted intervention as a defendant by petitioner Allen, the head of one of the private school systems identified in the complaint. Thereafter, progress in the lawsuit was stalled for several years. During this period, the Internal Revenue Service reviewed its challenged policies and proposed new Revenue Procedures to tighten requirements for eligibility for tax-exempt status for private schools. In 1979, however, Congress blocked any strengthening of the IRS guidelines....[4] The District Court thereupon considered and granted the defendants' motion to dismiss the complaint, concluding that respondents lack standing, that the judicial task proposed by respondents is inappropriately

ful, it is clear that respondents premise their allegation of illegality on discrimination, not on segregation alone. ...

4. Treasury, Postal Service, and General Government Appropriations Act of 1980, §§ 103 and 615, 93 Stat. 562, 577. Section 615 of the Act, known as the Dornan Amendment, specifically forbade the use of funds to carry out the IRS's proposed Revenue Procedures. Section 103 of the Act, known as the Ashbrook Amendment, more generally forbade the use of funds to make the requirements for tax-exempt status of private schools more stringent than those in effect

prior to the IRS's proposal of its new Revenue Procedures. These provisions expired on October 1, 1980, but Congress maintained its interest in IRS policies regarding tax exemptions for racially discriminatory private schools. The Dornan and Ashbrook Amendments were reinstated for the period December 16, 1980, through September 30, 1981. For fiscal year 1982, Congress specifically denied funding for carrying out not only administrative actions but also court orders entered after the date of the IRS's proposal of its first revised Revenue Procedure. No such spending restrictions are currently in force.

intrusive for a federal court, and that awarding the requested relief would be contrary to the will of Congress. . . .

Article III of the Constitution confines the federal courts to adjudicating actual "cases" and "controversies." As the Court explained in Valley Forge Christian College v. Americans United for Separation of Church and State, Inc., 454 U.S. 464, 471–476 (1982), the "case or controversy" requirement defines with respect to the Judicial Branch the idea of separation of powers on which the Federal Government is founded. The several doctrines that have grown up to elaborate that requirement are "founded in concern about the proper—and properly limited—role of the courts in a democratic society." Warth v. Seldin, 422 U.S. 490, 498 (1975). . . . The case-or-controversy doctrines state fundamental limits on federal judicial power in our system of government.

The Art. III doctrine that requires a litigant to have "standing" to invoke the power of a federal court is perhaps the most important of these doctrines. "In essence the question of standing is whether the litigant is entitled to have the court decide the merits of the dispute or of particular issues." Warth v. Seldin. Standing doctrine embraces several judicially self-imposed limits on the exercise of federal jurisdiction, such as the general prohibition on a litigant's raising another person's legal rights, the rule barring adjudication of generalized grievances more appropriately addressed in the representative branches, and the requirement that a plaintiff's complaint fall within the zone of interests protected by the law invoked. The requirement of standing, however, has a core component derived directly from the Constitution. A plaintiff must allege personal injury fairly traceable to the defendant's allegedly unlawful conduct and likely to be redressed by the requested relief.

Like the prudential component, the constitutional component of standing doctrine incorporates concepts concededly not susceptible of precise definition. The injury alleged must be, for example, "distinct and palpable," and not "abstract" or "conjectural" or "hypothetical." The injury must be "fairly" traceable to the challenged action, and relief from the injury must be "likely" to follow from a favorable decision. These terms cannot be defined so as to make application of the constitutional standing requirement a mechanical exercise.

The absence of precise definitions, however, . . . hardly leaves courts at sea in applying the law of standing. . . . Determining standing in a particular case may be facilitated by clarifying principles or even clear rules developed in prior cases. Typically, however, the standing inquiry requires careful judicial examination of a complaint's allegations to ascertain whether the particular plaintiff is entitled to an adjudication of the particular claims asserted. Is the injury too abstract, or otherwise not appropriate, to be considered judicially cognizable? Is the line of causation between the illegal conduct and injury too attenuated? Is the prospect of obtaining relief from the injury as a result of a favorable ruling too speculative? These questions and any others relevant to the standing inquiry must be answered by reference to the Art. III notion that federal courts may exercise power only "in the last resort, and as a necessity," and only when adjudication is "consistent with a system of separated powers and [the dispute is one] traditionally thought to be capable of resolution through the judicial process," Flast v. Cohen, 392 U.S. 83, 97 (1968).

Respondents allege two injuries in their complaint to support their standing to bring this lawsuit. First, they say that they are harmed directly by the mere fact of Government financial aid to discriminatory private schools. Second, they say that the federal tax exemptions to racially discriminatory private schools in their communities impair their ability to have their public schools desegregated. ... We conclude that neither suffices to support respondents' standing. The first fails ... because it does not constitute judicially cognizable injury. The second fails because the alleged injury is not fairly traceable to the assertedly unlawful conduct of the IRS.[5]

1

Respondents' first claim of injury can be interpreted in two ways. It might be a claim simply to have the Government avoid the violation of law alleged in respondents' complaint. Alternatively, it might be a claim of stigmatic injury, or denigration, suffered by all members of a racial group when the Government discriminates on the basis of race. Under neither interpretation is this claim of injury judicially cognizable.

This Court has repeatedly held that an asserted right to have the Government act in accordance with law is not sufficient, standing alone, to confer jurisdiction on a federal court. In Schlesinger v. Reservists Committee to Stop the War, 418 U.S. 208 (1974), for example, the Court rejected a claim of citizen standing to challenge Armed Forces Reserve commissions held by Members of Congress as violating the Incompatibility Clause....[6] As citizens, the Court held, plaintiffs alleged nothing but "the abstract injury in nonobservance of the Constitution...." More recently, in Valley Forge we rejected a claim of standing to challenge a Government conveyance of property to a religious institution. Insofar as the plaintiffs relied simply on " 'their shared individuated right' " to a Government that made no law respecting an establishment of religion, we held that plaintiffs had not alleged a judicially cognizable injury. "[A]ssertion of a right to a particular kind of Government conduct, which the Government has violated by acting differently, cannot alone satisfy the requirements of Art. III without draining those requirements of meaning." See also United States

---

5. The "fairly traceable" and "redressability" components of the constitutional standing inquiry were initially articulated by this Court as "two facets of a single causation requirement." C. Wright, Law of Federal Courts § 13, p. 68 n.43 (4th ed. 1983). To the extent there is a difference, it is that the former examines the causal connection between the assertedly unlawful conduct and the alleged injury, whereas the latter examines the causal connection between the alleged injury and the judicial relief requested. Cases such as this, in which the relief requested goes well beyond the violation of law alleged, illustrate why it is important to keep the inquiries separate if the "redressability" component is to focus on the requested relief. Even if the relief respondents request might have a substantial effect on the desegregation of public schools, whatever deficiencies exist in the opportunities for desegregated education for respondents' children might not be traceable to IRS violations of law—grants of tax exemptions to racially discriminatory schools in respondents' communities.

6. [Ed.] "No person holding any Office under the United States, shall be a Member of either House during his Continuance in Office." Art. I, § 6.

v. Richardson, 418 U.S. 166 (1974).[7] Respondents here have no standing to complain simply that their Government is violating the law.

Neither do they have standing to litigate their claims based on the stigmatizing injury often caused by racial discrimination. There can be no doubt that this sort of noneconomic injury is one of the most serious consequences of discriminatory government action and is sufficient in some circumstances to support standing. Our cases make clear, however, that such injury accords a basis for standing only to "those persons who are personally denied equal treatment" by the challenged discriminatory conduct.

. . . If the abstract stigmatic injury were cognizable, standing would extend nationwide to all members of the particular racial groups against which the Government was alleged to be discriminating by its grant of a tax exemption to a racially discriminatory school, regardless of the location of that school. . . . A black person in Hawaii could challenge the grant of a tax exemption to a racially discriminatory school in Maine. Recognition of standing in such circumstances would transform the federal courts into "no more than a vehicle for the vindication of the value interests of concerned bystanders." United States v. SCRAP, 412 U.S. 669, 687 (1973). Constitutional limits on the role of the federal courts preclude such a transformation.

2

It is in their complaint's second claim of injury that respondents allege harm to a concrete, personal interest that can support standing in some circumstances. The injury they identify—their children's diminished ability to receive an education in a racially integrated school—is, beyond any doubt, not only judicially cognizable but, as shown by cases from Brown v. Board of Educ., 347 U.S. 483 (1954), to Bob Jones Univ. v. United States, 461 U.S. 574 (1983), one of the most serious injuries recognized in our legal system. Despite the constitutional importance of curing the injury alleged by respondents, however, the federal judiciary may not redress it unless standing requirements are met. In this case, respondents' second claim of injury cannot support standing because the injury alleged is not fairly traceable to the Government conduct respondents challenge as unlawful.

The illegal conduct challenged by respondents is the IRS's grant of tax exemptions to some racially discriminatory schools. The line of causation between that conduct and desegregation of respondents' schools is attenuated at best. From the perspective of the IRS, the injury to respondents is highly indirect and "results from the independent action of some third party not before the court," Simon v. Eastern Ky. Welfare Rts. Org., p. 1172 below.

The diminished ability of respondents' children to receive a desegregated education would be fairly traceable to unlawful IRS grants of tax

---

7. [Ed.] Richardson refused standing to a federal taxpayer who sued to force disclosure of CIA expenditures. He claimed that the statute exempting the CIA from generally-applicable budget disclosure requirements violated the Accounts Clause of the Constitution, Art. 1, § 9, which states: "[A] regular Statement and Account of the Receipts and Expenditures of all public Money shall be published from time to time."

exemptions only if there were enough racially discriminatory private schools receiving tax exemptions in respondents' communities for withdrawal of those exemptions to make an appreciable difference in public-school integration. Respondents have made no such allegation. It is, first, uncertain how many racially discriminatory private schools are in fact receiving tax exemptions. Moreover, it is entirely speculative, as respondents themselves conceded in the Court of Appeals, whether withdrawal of a tax exemption from any particular school would lead the school to change its policies. It is just as speculative whether any given parent of a child attending such a private school would decide to transfer the child to public school as a result of any changes in educational or financial policy made by the private school once it was threatened with loss of tax-exempt status. It is also pure speculation whether, in a particular community, a large enough number of the numerous relevant school officials and parents would reach decisions that collectively would have a significant impact on the racial composition of the public schools.

The links in the chain of causation between the challenged Government conduct and the asserted injury are far too weak for the chain as a whole to sustain respondents' standing. . . .

The idea of separation of powers that underlies standing doctrine explains why our cases preclude the conclusion that respondents' alleged injury "fairly can be traced to the challenged action" of the IRS. Simon v. Eastern Kentucky Welfare Rights Org. That conclusion would pave the way generally for suits challenging, not specifically identifiable Government violations of law, but the particular programs agencies establish to carry out their legal obligations. Such suits, even when premised on allegations of several instances of violations of law, are rarely if ever appropriate for federal-court adjudication.

> Carried to its logical end, [respondents'] approach would have the federal courts as virtually continuing monitors of the wisdom and soundness of Executive action; such a role is appropriate for the Congress acting through its committees and the "power of the purse;" it is not the role of the judiciary, absent actual present or immediately threatened injury resulting from unlawful governmental action.

Laird v. Tatum, 408 U.S. 1, 15 (1972).

. . . "When a plaintiff seeks to enjoin the activity of a government agency, even within a unitary court system, his case must contend with 'the well-established rule that the Government has traditionally been granted the widest latitude in the 'dispatch of its own internal affairs.' "
. . . [T]hat principle, grounded as it is in the idea of separation of powers, counsels against recognizing standing in a case brought, not to enforce specific legal obligations whose violation works a direct harm, but to seek a restructuring of the apparatus established by the Executive Branch to fulfill its legal duties. The Constitution, after all, assigns to the Executive Branch, and not to the Judicial Branch, the duty to "take Care that the Laws be faithfully executed." We could not recognize respondents' standing in this case without running afoul of that structural principle. . . .

"The necessity that the plaintiff who seeks to invoke judicial power stand to profit in some personal interest remains an Art. III requirement." Simon v. Eastern Ky. Welfare Rts. Org. Respondents have not met this fundamental requirement. The judgment of the Court of Appeals is accordingly reversed, and the injunction issued by that court is vacated.

■ [JUSTICE MARSHALL did not participate; JUSTICE BRENNAN's dissenting opinion is omitted.]

■ JUSTICE STEVENS, with whom JUSTICE BLACKMUN joins, dissenting.

Three propositions are clear to me: (1) respondents have adequately alleged "injury in fact;" (2) their injury is fairly traceable to the conduct that they claim to be unlawful; and (3) the "separation of powers" principle does not create a jurisdictional obstacle to the consideration of the merits of their claim.

Respondents, the parents of black school children, have alleged that their children are unable to attend fully desegregated schools because large numbers of white children in the areas in which respondents reside attend private schools which do not admit minority children. The Court, Justice Brennan, and I all agree that this is an adequate allegation of "injury in fact." . . . This kind of injury may be actionable whether it is caused by the exclusion of black children from public schools or by an official policy of encouraging white children to attend nonpublic schools. A subsidy for the withdrawal of a white child can have the same effect as a penalty for admitting a black child. . . . The critical question in these cases, therefore, is whether respondents have alleged that the Government has created that kind of subsidy. . . .

An organization that qualifies for preferential treatment under § 501(c)(3) of the Internal Revenue Code, because it is "operated exclusively for . . . charitable . . . purposes," is exempt from paying federal income taxes, and [under § 170] persons who contribute to such organizations may deduct the amount of their contributions when calculating their taxable income. Only last Term we explained the effect of this preferential treatment:

> Both tax exemptions and tax-deductibility are a form of subsidy that is administered through the tax system. A tax exemption has much the same effect as a cash grant to the organization of the amount of tax it would have to pay on its income. Deductible contributions are similar to cash grants of the amount of a portion of the individual's contributions.

The purpose of this scheme, like the purpose of any subsidy, is to promote the activity subsidized; the statutes "seek to achieve the same basic goal of encouraging the development of certain organizations through the grant of tax benefits." Bob Jones University v. United States. If the granting of preferential tax treatment would "encourage" private segregated schools to conduct their "charitable" activities, it must follow that the withdrawal of the treatment would "discourage" them. . . .

This causation analysis is nothing more than a restatement of elementary economics: when something becomes more expensive, less of it will be purchased. . . . If racially discriminatory private schools lose the "cash grants" that flow from the operation of the statutes, the education they provide will become more expensive and hence less of their services will be purchased. Conversely, maintenance of these tax benefits makes an education in segregated private schools relatively more attractive, by decreasing its cost. Accordingly, without tax exempt status, private schools will either not be competitive in terms of cost, or have to change their admissions policies, hence reducing their competitiveness for parents seeking "a racially segregated alternative" to public schools, which is what respondents have alleged many white parents in desegregating school districts seek. In either event the process of desegregation will be advanced.... Thus, the laws of economics, not to mention the laws of Congress embodied in §§ 170 and 501(c)(3), compel the conclusion that the injury respondents have alleged—the increased segregation of their children's schools because of the ready availability of private schools that admit whites only—will be redressed if these schools' operations are inhibited through the denial of preferential tax treatment.

Considerations of tax policy, economics, and pure logic all confirm the conclusion that respondents' injury in fact is fairly traceable to the Government's allegedly wrongful conduct. The Court therefore is forced to introduce the concept of "separation of powers" into its analysis. . . .

The Court could mean one of three things by its invocation of the separation of powers. First, it could simply be expressing the idea that if the plaintiff lacks Article III standing to bring a lawsuit, then there is no "case or controversy" within the meaning of Article III and hence the matter is not within the area of responsibility assigned to the Judiciary by the Constitution. . . . While there can be no quarrel with this proposition, in itself it provides no guidance for determining if the injury respondents have alleged is fairly traceable to the conduct they have challenged.

Second, the Court could be saying that it will require a more direct causal connection when it is troubled by the separation of powers implications of the case before it. That approach confuses the standing doctrine with the justiciability of the issues that respondents seek to raise. The purpose of the standing inquiry is to measure the plaintiff's stake in the outcome, not whether a court has the authority to provide it with the outcome it seeks. . . . If a plaintiff presents a nonjusticiable issue, or seeks relief that a court may not award, then its complaint should be dismissed for those reasons, and not because the plaintiff lacks a stake in obtaining that relief and hence has no standing. . . .

Third, the Court could be saying that it will not treat as legally cognizable injuries that stem from an administrative decision concerning how enforcement resources will be allocated. This surely is an important point. Respondents do seek to restructure the IRS's mechanisms for enforcing the legal requirement that discriminatory institutions not receive tax-exempt status. Such restructuring would dramatically affect the way in which the IRS exercises its prosecutorial discretion. The Executive requires latitude to decide how best to enforce the law, and in general the Court may well be correct that the exercise of that discretion, especially in the tax context, is unchallengeable.[8]

However, as the Court also recognizes, this principle does not apply when suit is brought "to enforce specific legal obligations whose violation works a direct harm." ... Here, respondents contend that the IRS is violating a specific constitutional limitation on its enforcement discretion. There is a solid basis for that contention. ... Similarly, respondents claim that the Internal Revenue Code itself, as construed in Bob Jones, constrains enforcement discretion. It has been clear since Marbury v. Madison that "[i]t is emphatically the province and duty of the judicial department to say what the law is." Deciding whether the Treasury has violated a specific legal limitation on its enforcement discretion does not intrude upon the prerogatives of the Executive, for in so deciding we are merely saying "what the law is." Surely the question whether the Constitution or the Code limits enforcement discretion is one within the Judiciary's competence. . . .

NOTE

Standing as a distinct legal concept is largely a phenomenon of the last half of the 20th century.[1] Before that time, litigation occurred principally within the private-rights pattern in which the question of *who* could seek relief was elided with the question whether the complaint *stated a cause of action.*[2] Two socio-legal developments altered this: a new conception of the nature and function of constitutional rights, fueled by the civil rights movement; and the emergence of the administrative state, with its complex of broadly applicable statutory rights and duties. Allen v. Wright—an administrative law challenge to whether the agency is fulfilling its statutory mandate that echoes the great constitutional struggles for desegregated

---

8. [Ed.] The following Term in Heckler v. Chaney, the Court held that agency decision not to take enforcement action is presumptively nonreviewable. See p. 1218 below. Moreover, in other contexts, the Court had shown considerable resistance to judicial redirection of institutional enforcement practices. See, e.g., Rizzo v. Goode, 423 U.S. 362 (1976) (setting aside on justiciability grounds a court order requiring a city police force to institute a comprehensive procedure for dealing with citizen complaints about brutality and racism). See also O'Shea v. Littleton, 414 U.S. 488 (1974); Laird v. Tatum, 408 U.S. 1 (1972).

1. See Joseph Vining, Legal Identity: The Coming of Age of Public Law 55 (1978). To pursue in more depth the ideas sketched in this Note, see Abram Chayes, The Role of the Judge in Public Law Litigation, 89 Harv. L.Rev. 1281 (1976); Henry P. Monaghan, Constitutional Adjudication: The Who and When, 82 Yale L.J. 1363 (1973); Louis L.

Jaffe, Standing to Secure Judicial Review: Public Actions, 74 Harv.L.Rev. 1265 (1961); Richard B. Stewart, The Reformation of American Administrative Law, 88 Harv. L.Rev. 1669 (1975); Cass R. Sunstein, Standing and the Privatization of Public Law, 88 Colum.L.Rev. 1432 (1988). For a revisionist account arguing that standing was an important aspect of 19th and early 20th century equity practice and that a vigorous "public rights" model coexisted throughout with the common law model, see Steven L. Winter, The Metaphor of Standing and the Problem of Self–Governance, 40 Stan.L.Rev. 1371 (1988).

2. For example, if *A* makes a contract with *B* for the benefit of *C*, and *B* fails to perform, *C*'s ability to sue *B* was conceptualized not as a question of whether *C* has "standing," but rather as a question of whether a third party beneficiary has a legally enforceable interest in the contract.

education—is born of both these developments. And the split on the Court reflects deep judicial ambivalence about the role the judiciary has come to play.

(a) *Transforming the Constitution from "shield" to "sword."* Traditionally, suits raising constitutional issues began with the pleading of a common law wrong. (E.g., the defendant police officer committed trespass and assault by breaking into the plaintiff's home to make an arrest.) The government official would answer by asserting official authority and privilege. The plaintiff would then raise the Constitution to counter that assertion. (E.g., the Fourth Amendment required a warrant before entry.) The constitutional argument, if accepted, stripped the government defendant of his official authority and he stood liable as any other tortfeasor. Although this approach provided some relief for unconstitutional government action that could be framed as a common law injury,[3] official behavior creating harm that could not be expressed as a tort or contract cause of action could be remedied, if at all, only through the constricted channels of the prerogative writs.[4] As the Twentieth Century progressed, concern about constitutional injuries that defied expression through the common law framework—such as school segregation—led to new litigation patterns. Aggrieved individuals insisted, and courts came to agree, that the Constitution itself creates interests which, *irrespective* of any common law injury, can support affirmative claims for judicial relief from government action.[5]

Cut loose from common-law definitions of judicially-cognizable claims, courts then confronted the prospect of "a potential nation of plaintiffs"[6]: Who are appropriate parties to instigate a judicial inquiry into the constitutionality of government action? Sometimes, the answer is easy. African–American children barred from attending a public school because of their race are clearly proper parties to raise an equal protection challenge to segregation. In other cases, the answer is more complex. As WILLIAM A. FLETCHER, THE STRUCTURE OF STANDING, 98 Yale L.J. 221, 227–28 (1988), explains, "[F]ederal litigation in the 1960's and 1970's increasingly involved attempts to establish and enforce public, often constitutional, values by litigants who were not individually affected by the conduct of which they complained in any way markedly different from most of the population. The most prominent example is probably Flast v. Cohen, [392 U.S. 83 (1968)], in which the Court granted standing to a federal taxpayer to challenge federal expenditures of funds for parochial schools allegedly in violation of the establishment clause. Mrs. Flast's interest in the dispute was not markedly different from that of most of the rest of the population,

3. Even in such cases, the damages or other relief were determined by the principles of the applicable common law cause of action—principles which might or might not make whole the victim of unconstitutional government behavior.

4. See p. 1109 above.

5. This development culminates in cases in which the federal courts imply a

cause of action directly from a constitutional provision. See, e.g., Bivens v. Six Unknown Named Agents of the Fed. Bureau of Narcotics, 403 U.S. 388 (1971) (judicially-created cause of action for damages for violation of the Fourth Amendment).

6. Peter W. Low & John C. Jeffries, Jr., Federal Courts and the Law of Federal–State Relations 333 (4th ed. 1998).

and the impact of the expenditures on her federal tax bill was ... 'minute and indeterminable.' ... Yet the Court granted standing because it sensed, without being able to articulate it fully, that a broad grant of standing was an appropriate mechanism to implement the establishment clause interest at stake."

By the 1980s, the Court had become far more articulate about the implications of standing, but its sense of the appropriateness of broadly granting access to litigate constitutional issues had changed. Although Flast has never been formally overruled, it has become the exceptional case. More illustrative of the contemporary approach is Valley Forge Christian College v. Americans United for Separation of Church & State (relied upon in Allen), which held that neither taxpayers, citizens, nor an organization self-identified as concerned with establishment clause issues had standing to challenge an agency's gift of land and buildings valued at more than half a million dollars to a Christian seminary.

(b) *The emergence of the administrative state.* The other major factor in the evolution of modern standing law was the creation of regulatory programs, in which numerous individuals and entities had a stake. Again, Prof. (now Judge) Fletcher explains: "As private entities increasingly came to be controlled by statutory and regulatory duties, as government increasingly came to be controlled by statutory and constitutional commands, and as individuals sought to control the greatly augmented power of the government through the judicial process, many kinds of plaintiffs and would-be plaintiffs sought the articulation and enforcement of new and existing rights in the federal courts. ... Among the difficult questions posed by the enormous growth of administrative agencies in the 1930's, one of the most prominent was how to determine who could sue to enforce the legal duties of an agency. It was not feasible to infer simply from the existence of an agency's duty that any plaintiff who might benefit from the performance of the duty should have the right to enforce it. In some circumstances, the most desirable scheme might be to permit standing broadly, conferring the right to sue on 'private attorneys general' who, for reasons of public policy, should be permitted to sue as appropriate guardians of the public interest. In other circumstances, the most desirable scheme might be to grant standing narrowly, refusing to give it even to some of those directly affected by the actions of the agency." 98 Yale L.J. at 225–26.

The materials that follow explore the judiciary's continuing struggle to derive appropriate principles for determining who can "sue to enforce the legal duties of an agency."

b. WHAT SORT OF INTERESTS COUNT?

"A person suffering legal wrong because of agency action, or adversely affected or aggrieved by agency action within the meaning of a relevant statute, is entitled to judicial review thereof."

Administrative Procedure Act, 5 U.S.C. § 702

Association of Data Processing Service Organizations, Inc. v. Camp

Supreme Court of the United States, 1970.
397 U.S. 150.

■ JUSTICE DOUGLAS delivered the opinion of the Court.

[A trade organization of providers of data processing services challenged a ruling by the Comptroller of the Currency that national banks could enter the data processing business. The lower courts dismissed for lack of standing.]

... Generalizations about standing to sue are largely worthless as such. One generalization is, however, necessary and that is that the question of standing in the federal courts is to be considered in the framework of Article III which restricts judicial power to "cases" and "controversies." As we recently stated in Flast v. Cohen, "[I]n terms of Article III limitations on federal court jurisdiction, the question of standing is related only to whether the dispute sought to be adjudicated will be presented in an adversary context and in a form historically viewed as capable of judicial resolution." ...

The first question is whether the plaintiff alleges that the challenged action has caused him injury in fact, economic or otherwise. There can be no doubt but that petitioners have satisfied this test. The petitioners not only allege that competition by national banks in the business of providing data processing services might entail some future loss of profits for the petitioners, they also allege that [one] respondent was performing or preparing to perform such services for two customers for whom [one] petitioner had previously agreed or negotiated to perform such services. ...

The Court of Appeals viewed the matter differently, stating:

[A] plaintiff may challenge alleged illegal competition when as complainant it pursues (1) a legal interest by reason of public charter or contract, ... (2) a legal interest by reason of statutory protection, ... or (3) a "public interest" in which Congress has recognized the need for review of administrative action and plaintiff is significantly involved to have standing to represent the public....[1]

Those tests were based on prior decisions of this Court, such as Tennessee Electric Power Co. v. TVA, p. 1132 below, where private power companies sought to enjoin TVA from operating, claiming that the statutory plan under which it was created was unconstitutional. The Court denied the competitors' standing, holding that they did not have that status "unless the right invaded is a legal right—one of property, one arising out of contract, one protected against tortious invasion, or one founded on a statute which confers a privilege."

---

1. The first two tests applied by the Court of Appeals required a showing of a "legal interest." But the existence or non-existence of a "legal interest" is a matter quite distinct from the problem of standing. The third test mentioned by the Court of Appeals, which rests on an explicit provision in a regulatory statute conferring standing and is commonly referred to in terms of allowing suits by "private attorneys general," is inapplicable to the present case. See FCC v. Sanders Bros. Radio Station, p. 1132 below.

The "legal interest" test goes to the merits. The question of standing is different. It concerns, apart from the "case" or "controversy" test, the question whether the interest sought to be protected by the complainant is arguably within the zone of interests to be protected or regulated by the statute or constitutional guarantee in question. Thus the Administrative Procedure Act grants standing to a person "aggrieved by agency action within the meaning of a relevant statute." 5 U.S.C. § 702. That interest, at times, may reflect "aesthetic, conservational, and recreational" as well as economic values. . . . We mention these noneconomic values to emphasize that standing may stem from them as well as from the economic injury on which petitioners rely here. Certainly he who is "likely to be financially" injured, FCC v. Sanders Bros. Radio Station, may be a reliable private attorney general to litigate the issues of the public interest in the present case. . . . Where statutes are concerned, the trend is toward enlargement of the class of people who may protest administrative action. The whole drive for enlarging the category of aggrieved "persons" is symptomatic of that trend. . . .

The Court of Appeals for the First Circuit held in Arnold Tours, Inc. v. Camp, 408 F.2d 1147, 1153, that by reason of § 4 [of the Bank Service Corporation Act][2] a data processing company has standing to contest the legality of a national bank performing data processing services for other banks and bank customers:

> Section 4 had a broader purpose than regulating only the service corporations. It was also a response to the fears expressed by a few senators, that without such a prohibition, the bill would have enabled "banks to engage in a nonbanking activity," and thus constitute "a serious exception to the accepted public policy which strictly limits banks to banking." We think Congress has provided the sufficient statutory aid to standing even though the competition may not be the precise kind Congress legislated against.

We do not put the issue in those words, for they implicate the merits. We do think, however, that § 4 arguably brings a competitor within the zone of interests protected by it. . . .

Whether anything in the Bank Service Corporation Act or the National Bank Act gives petitioners a "legal interest" that protects them against violations of those Acts, and whether the actions of respondents did in fact violate either of those Acts, are questions which go to the merits and remain to be decided below.

We hold that petitioners have standing to sue and that the case should be remanded for a hearing on the merits.

[A companion case, BARLOW v. COLLINS, 397 U.S. 159, employed the "zone of interests" standard to grant standing to tenant farmers seeking to challenge a regulation of the Secretary of Agriculture that revised the terms on which farmers could assign federal crop payments. The following opinion was written in that case:]

---

2. [Ed.] "No bank service corporation may engage in any activity other than the   performance of bank services for banks."

■ JUSTICE BRENNAN, with whom JUSTICE WHITE joins, concurring in the result and dissenting.

. . . The Court's approach to standing, set out in Data Processing, has two steps: (1) . . . the first step is to determine "whether the plaintiff alleges that the challenged action has caused him injury in fact;" (2) if injury in fact is alleged, the relevant statute or constitutional provision is then examined to determine "whether the interest sought to be protected by the complainant is arguably within the zone of interests to be protected or regulated by the statute or constitutional guarantee in question."

My view is that the inquiry in the Court's first step is the only one that need be made to determine standing. . . . By requiring a second, nonconstitutional step, the Court comes very close to perpetuating the discredited requirement that conditioned standing on a showing by the plaintiff that the challenged governmental action invaded one of his legally protected interests.[3]

NOTES

(1) *The Background of Data Processing: Pre–APA Doctrine and the Debate About the Intent of § 702.* Data Processing's interpretation of § 702 created the liberal standing regime that has characterized modern U.S. administrative law. It was also a surprising resolution to a legal controversy that had raged among commentators and lower courts for decades.

(a) *The "legal right"/"legal interest" standard.* Traditionally, a plaintiff complaining of government action had to show that the official had invaded an interest either protected by the common law, see p. 1127 above, or created as an individual right by statute. Absent such an interest, the plaintiff could plead no legally-cognizable harm—she had suffered, at most, damnum absque injuria.[1] As the Second Circuit explained in 1943, "[U]nless the citizen first shows that, if the defendant were a private person having no official status, the particular defendant's conduct or threatened conduct would give rise to a cause of action against him by that particular citizen, the court cannot consider whether the defendant officer's conduct is or is not authorized by statute; for the statute comes into the case, if at all, only by way of a defense or of justification for acts of the defendant." Associated Indus. of N.Y. State v. Ickes, 134 F.2d 694, 700, vacated as moot, 320 U.S. 707 (1943).

Because we are now accustomed to a broad definition of litigable injury, it can be difficult to appreciate the significance of a doctrine that refused review of government action unless that action had invaded an interest "of a recognized character at common law, or a substantive private legally protected interest created by statute." Id. Two Supreme Court cases early in the modern regulatory era illustrate this traditional approach. The

---

3. [Ed.] Justice Brennan went on to argue that "a canvass of relevant statutory materials must be made . . . not to determine standing, but to determine an aspect of reviewability, that is, whether Congress meant to deny or to allow judicial review of the agency action at the instance of the plaintiff."

1. That is, "damage without wrongful act" or loss for which there is no legal remedy.

Interstate Commerce Act requires the Interstate Commerce Commission to set "just and reasonable" rates for railroad carriage. In Alexander Sprunt & Son v. United States, 281 U.S. 249 (1930), one group of shippers challenged a Commission order that reduced the freight rates charged to another group. The Supreme Court acknowledged that the order caused the complaining shippers real economic harm, but denied them standing because neither the common law nor the Interstate Commerce Act gave them a "right" to be protected from competition. Their only statutory right—to be *themselves* charged reasonable rates—was not implicated by an order setting the rates of others. In Tennessee Elec. Power Co. v. Tennessee Valley Auth., 306 U.S. 118 (1939), the Court applied similar reasoning to deny private utilities standing to challenge the constitutionality of a statute that created a new federal corporation to generate power. Whether or not the TVA exceeded Congress' powers under Article I, the Constitution created no private interest in being free from competition from a government corporation.

(b) *The "aggrieved person" alternative, and the emergence of the "private attorney general."* In the Communications Act of 1934, Congress departed from this traditional conception of who could seek judicial review of the legality of agency action. Section 402(b) authorized judicial review of an FCC order granting or denying a broadcast license by (1) a license applicant, and (2) *"any other person aggrieved* or whose interests are adversely affected by any decision of the Commission granting or refusing any such application." (emphasis added). In FCC v. SANDERS BROS., 309 U.S. 470 (1940), an existing radio station challenged an order licensing a proposed new station. Once again, the relevant statute was interpreted not to create a legal right to be free of competition. Nevertheless, the Supreme Court allowed the action to proceed because of § 402(b)(2): "The [agency] insists that as economic injury to the respondent was not a proper issue before the Commission it is impossible that § 402(b) was intended to give the respondent standing to appeal, since absence of right implies absence of remedy. This view would deprive subsection (2) of any substantial effect. Congress had some purpose in enacting section 402(b)(2). It may have been of the opinion that one likely to be financially injured by the issuance of a license would be the only person having a sufficient interest to bring to the attention of the appellate court errors of law in the action of the Commission in granting the license. It is within the power of Congress to confer such standing to prosecute an appeal." Two years later, the Court elaborated: "The Communications Act of 1934 did not create new private rights [i.e., in competitors to be protected from market entrants]. The purpose of the Act was to protect the public interest in communications. ... [T]hese private litigants have standing only *as representatives of the public interest."* SCRIPPS-HOWARD RADIO INC. v. FCC, 316 U.S. 4, 14 (1942) (emphasis added).

Together, Sanders Bros. and Scripps-Howard established a concept that would become centrally important to regulatory standing. The would-be plaintiff must have suffered an actual injury traceable to the agency's action; as the Second Circuit explained in Ickes, "not every person is a 'person aggrieved'." 134 F.2d at 705. Even Congress cannot authorize judicial review of agency action "in the absence of an actual justiciable controversy." Id. at 704. However, that injury need not be to an interest that is itself legally protected. Rather, a regulatory statute can authorize anyone who is actually harmed by the agency's action to challenge the agency's compliance with its statutory responsibility to serve the public interest—to act, "so to speak, as *private Attorney Generals.*" Id. at 704 (emphasis added).[2] (For a more contemporary restatement of this concept by the Supreme Court, see Sierra Club v. Morton, note 4 below.)

(c) *What was APA § 702 intended to do?* Sanders Bros. and Scripps–Howard represented a significant theoretical shift, but their immediate impact on regulatory standing was limited because they rested on the relatively atypical phrasing of the Communications Act. Then Congress enacted the APA, providing in § 702: "A person suffering legal wrong because of agency action, or adversely affected or aggrieved by agency action within the meaning of a relevant statute, is entitled to judicial review thereof." A major controversy ensued. Lower courts and some scholars took the position that § 702 merely codified existing standing law—that is, a "legal interest" is required unless the particular organic statute empowers "aggrieved" persons to sue.[3] On the other hand, influential commentator Professor K.C. Davis pointed to legislative history that described § 702 as "confer[ring] a right of review upon any person adversely affected *in fact* by agency action or aggrieved within the meaning of any statute," and argued that Congress intended to broaden regulatory standing by adopting generally the Sanders Bros./Scripps–Howard approach.[4] Nearly 25 years after the APA was enacted, Data Processing settled the question.

(2) *The Meaning of § 702 Resolved: Compromise.* On the one hand, Data Processing interprets the APA as intended to depart from the traditional conception of standing. Under § 702, the injury that gives access to judicial review need not be the same as the legal claim that will justify judicial relief. As Dean Nichol points out, even the new standing terminology underscored this departure: "Consider the appellation itself—injury *in fact*—as distinguished, one supposes, from injury protected by law." Gene R. Nichol, Jr., Rethinking Standing, 72 Cal.L.Rev. 68, 74 (1984). In this

---

2. Ickes itself would be an easy standing case today. The plaintiffs were industrial consumers of coal who challenged an administrative order increasing the minimum prices for bituminous coal. They claimed that the agency had acted outside its statutory authority, and that the order was unsupported by substantial evidence on the facts. Although the Bituminous Coal Act was designed to provide price supports for coal producers, it explicitly acknowledged consumer interests and charged the agency with giving "due regard to the interests of the consuming public," and protecting "the consumer of coal against unreasonably high prices therefor." 134 F.2d at 706 (quoting the statute). Thus, not only did § 6(b) of the Act contain the broad "any person aggrieved" standing authorization, but also the

plaintiffs were among the intended beneficiaries of the regulatory scheme. It underscores how far our understanding of legally cognizable injury has changed that the Second Circuit was faced with, and had to work hard to resolve, a serious argument that these plaintiffs were merely attempting to assert "public rights" rather than presenting a justiciable "case or controversy."

3. See, e.g., Louis L. Jaffe, Judicial Control of Administrative Action 528–30 (1965).

4. See, e.g., 3 Kenneth C. Davis, Administrative Law § 22.02 at 211–12 (1958). See also Kenneth C. Davis, "Judicial Control of Administrative Action:" A Review, 66 Colum.L.Rev. 635, 668–69 (1966).

new regime, the data processors (like the rival radio stations in Sanders Bros. and Scripps–Howard before them) have standing because of competitive harm, even though competitive harm is not a factor that the relevant organic statutes require the agency to take into account—and, hence, not a basis on which its action can be attacked as arbitrary, capricious or otherwise outside its statutory authority.

On the other hand, injury in fact (or, in the Sanders Bros./Scripps–Howard terminology, being a "person aggrieved") is not sufficient under § 702. The would-be plaintiff must also show that her interest is "arguably within the zone of interests protected or regulated" by the relevant statute. Professor William Fletcher suggests that this requirement represented "a gesture toward Jaffe's position" about the meaning of APA § 702 by a Court that was adopting K.C. Davis' position about injury in fact. 98 Yale L.J. at 258. Note Justice Brennan's concern that the zone-of-interest gloss on § 702 will recreate the traditional regime. Prof. Fletcher agrees that the Data Processing formulation is "a very unsatisfactory resolution to the Davis–Jaffe debate." You will be in a better position to assess these criticisms when we consider the line of zone-of-interests precedent at p. 1162 below.

(3) *Finding Surrogates to Speak for the Intended Beneficiaries of Regulation*. Recall the principal players in the regulatory game who may be involved in judicial review: (1) the agency; (2) the regulated community; (3) intended beneficiaries of the regulatory program; and (4) incidental beneficiaries of the program. The data processors are incidental beneficiaries of statutes like the Bank Service Corp. Act: Their market position is enhanced if banks are prevented from offering non-banking services. At the same time, protecting their interests is *not* the Comptroller General's statutory mandate. To put it somewhat differently, proving that the agency caused this harm will not advance their case on the merits because the statute does not make competitive injury one of the legally relevant criteria in the administrative decision. As the First Circuit explained in the Arnold Tours case quoted in Data Processing, "The plaintiffs have not pointed to, nor have we in our research discovered, any evidence that Congress in delimiting the scope of banking activity . . . was concerned . . . with competitors in the businesses impliedly prohibited. . . . Rather, the limitations were for the purpose of insuring the stability, liquidity, and safety of the banks." 408 F.2d at 1151. Thus, just as Clark Kent enters the phone booth and Superman emerges, so the data processors get in the courthouse door on the basis of their own competitive injury but (because causing such harm is not a basis for reversing the agency) they must then take up the mantle of "private attorney general to litigate the issues of the public interest."

In general, courts are extremely reluctant to allow a party to litigate anyone's rights but her own. Recall that Allen identifies the "jus tertii" principle—no raising the rights of third parties—as one of the prudential restrictions on standing. Why shouldn't the intended beneficiaries of regulation speak for themselves? Who are the intended beneficiaries of regulatory restrictions on banking? Presumably, the general banking public. Do you think that anyone in this group could establish standing to complain that the Comptroller has allowed banks to offer limited data processing services?

Recall that, under Allen, Article III requires a real, individualized, nonspeculative injury traceable to the Comptroller's decision and redressible by a court order overturning that decision. (The zone-of-interests test would not, of course, be a problem for intended beneficiaries.)

If it appears unlikely that an intended beneficiary could get (or would be motivated to seek) standing—perhaps because the collective nature of the regulatory goods produced makes it difficult to establish a credible threat of individualized injury—then a surrogate must be found. More accurately, a surrogate must be found if we do not want judicial review to be one-sided: that is, correcting only errors of *over*-regulation because only regulated entities can invoke it. Justice Douglas reasons that parties with a competitive economic interest in the regulatory outcome are likely to be good advocates in a reviewing court for whether the agency's action serves the "public interest." Put more bluntly, those with money at stake will be motivated to make whatever sorts of arguments it takes to get the agency reversed. Are you as confident that the motives of incidental beneficiaries will align with the interests of the general public, or the particular subgroup meant to benefit from regulation? If regulatory standing law is going to relax "the general prohibition on a litigant's raising another person's legal rights," Allen, 468 U.S. at 751, are there other potential plaintiffs who would be a better voice for the public interest?

(4) SIERRA CLUB V. MORTON, 405 U.S. 727 (1972), rejected one possible solution to the question posed at the end of the previous note. The Forest Service had invited bids from private developers to construct a year-round recreational facility in the theretofore pristine wilderness area of Mineral King Valley in the Sierra Nevada Mountains. Walt Disney Enterprises won the competition, with a plan to build a complex of motels, restaurants, swimming pools, ski lifts and lodges on the valley floor and the adjoining mountain slopes. An access highway would be constructed, in part through Sequoia National Park, to bring in the then-estimated 14,000 daily visitors. The Sierra Club, one of the nation's oldest environmental organizations, sued. The Club pleaded that it had standing based on its "special interest in the conservation and the sound maintenance of the national parks, game refuges and forests of the country." It deliberately avoided pleading facts—such as its founder, John Muir's, having a cabin in the affected area—that would have placed individual members personally in the pathway of environmental impact.

In a 4–3 decision (two Justices not participating), Justice Stewart rejected the concept of an ideological plaintiff: "[T]he complaint alleged that the development 'would destroy or otherwise adversely affect the scenery, natural and historic objects and wildlife of the park and would impair the enjoyment of the park for future generations.' We do not question that this type of harm may amount to an 'injury in fact' sufficient to lay the basis for standing under § [702] of the APA. Aesthetic and environmental well-being, like economic well-being, are important ingredients of the quality of life in our society, and the fact that particular environmental interests are shared by the many rather than the few does not make them less deserving of legal protection through the judicial process. But the 'injury in fact' test requires more than an injury to a cognizable interest. It requires that the party seeking review be himself among the injured.

"... The Sierra Club failed to allege that it or its members would be affected in any of their activities or pastimes by the Disney development. Nowhere in the pleadings or affidavits did the Club state that its members use Mineral King for any purpose, much less that they use it in any way that would be significantly affected by the proposed actions of the respondents.

"The Club apparently regarded any allegations of individualized injury as superfluous, on the theory that this was a 'public' action involving questions as to the use of natural resources, and that the Club's longstanding concern with and expertise in such matters were sufficient to give it standing as a 'representative of the public.' This theory reflects a misunderstanding of our cases involving so-called 'public actions' in the area of administrative law....

"Taken together, Sanders and Scripps–Howard ... established a dual proposition: the fact of economic injury is what gives a person standing to seek judicial review under the statute, but once review is properly invoked, that person may argue the public interest in support of his claim that the agency has failed to comply with its statutory mandate. It was in the latter sense that the 'standing' of the appellant in Scripps–Howard, existed only as a 'representative of the public interest.' It is in a similar sense that we have used the phrase 'private attorney general' to describe the function performed by persons upon whom Congress has conferred the right to seek judicial review of agency action. See Data Processing....

"... It is clear that an organization whose members are injured may represent those members in a proceeding for judicial review.[5] But a mere 'interest in a problem,' no matter how longstanding the interest and no matter how qualified the organization is in evaluating the problem, is not sufficient by itself to render the organization 'adversely affected' or 'aggrieved' within the meaning of the APA. The Sierra Club is a large and long-established organization, with a historic commitment to the cause of protecting our Nation's natural heritage from man's depredations. But if a 'special interest' in this subject were enough to entitle the Sierra Club to commence this litigation, there would appear to be no objective basis upon which to disallow a suit by any other bona fide 'special interest' organization however small or short-lived. And if any group with a bona fide 'special interest' could initiate such litigation, it is difficult to perceive why any individual citizen with the same bona fide special interest would not also be entitled to do so.

"The requirement that a party seeking review must allege facts showing that he is himself adversely affected does not insulate executive action from judicial review, nor does it prevent any public interests from being

5. [Ed.] An organization can serve as plaintiff on behalf of its individual members when "(a) its members would otherwise have standing to sue in their own right; (b) the interests it seeks to protect are germane to the organization's purpose; and (c) neither the claim asserted nor the relief requested requires the participation of individual members in the lawsuit." Hunt v. Washington State Apple Adver. Comm., 432 U.S. 333, 343 (1977).

protected through the judicial process. It does serve as at least a rough attempt to put the decision as to whether review will be sought in the hands of those who have a direct stake in the outcome. That goal would be undermined were we to construe the APA to authorize judicial review at the behest of organizations or individuals who seek to do no more than vindicate their own value preferences through the judicial process.[6] ...'' Justices Douglas, Blackmun, and Brennan dissented.

Six bids were submitted to the Forest Service. Would a disappointed competitor of Walt Disney Enterprises, who had submitted a more modest development proposal, have standing to complain that the Forest Service decision inadequately protected the wilderness environment? How about a company who offered guided wilderness hiking tours through the area? Are any of these better plaintiffs than Sierra Club reliably to litigate the environmental issues raised by development of Mineral King? Is that the wrong question? In fact, standing was easily established in the case. On remand, the Sierra Club was permitted to, and did, amend its complaint to add individual members who used the Mineral King area. However, as the next principal case suggests, finding an individual plaintiff will not always be so easy.

(5) *In Favor of the Ideological Plaintiff.* LOUIS L. JAFFE, THE CITIZEN AS LITIGANT IN PUBLIC ACTIONS: THE NON-HOHFELDIAN OR IDEOLOGICAL PLAINTIFF, 116 U.Pa.L.Rev. 1033, 1037–38, 1044–45 (1968): "The usual justification for [the rejection of 'ideological' plaintiffs] runs in terms of the necessary conditions for the rational exercise of the judicial power. The court, not being a representative institution, not having initiating powers and not having a staff for the gathering of information, must rely on the parties and their advocates to frame the problem and to present the opposing considerations relevant to its solution. It is argued that unless the plaintiff is a person whose legal position will be affected by the court's judgment, he cannot be relied on to present a serious, thorough, and complete argument. I do not know whether there is any way of finding out whether non-Hohfeldian plaintiffs are less zealous than Hohfeldian ones.[7] My own recourse is to my understanding of human nature, which tells me that there is no predictable difference between the two. If it were thought that

6. Every school boy may be familiar with Alexis de Tocqueville's famous observation, written in the 1830's, that "scarcely any political question arises in the United States that is not resolved, sooner or later, into a judicial question." 1 Democracy in America 280 (1945). Less familiar, however, is De Tocqueville's further observation that judicial review is effective largely because it is not available simply at the behest of a partisan faction, but is exercised only to remedy a particular, concrete injury. "It will be seen, also, that by leaving it to private interest to censure the law, and by intimately uniting the trial of the law with the trial of an individual, legislation is protected from wanton assaults and from the daily aggressions of

party spirit. The errors of the legislator are exposed only to meet a real want; and it is always a positive and appreciable fact that must serve as the basis of a prosecution."

7. [Ed.] An Hohfeldian plaintiff is one who, in accord with the traditional common law approach, "proffers for judicial determination a question concerning *his own* legal status"—i.e., who is "seeking a determination that he [himself] has a right, a privilege, an immunity or a power." 116 U.Pa.L.Rev. at 1033 (emphasis added). The source is Wesley N. Hohfeld, Some Fundamental Legal Conceptions as Applied in Judicial Reasoning, 23 Yale L.J. 16 (1913), which develops an elaborate scheme for analyzing claims in the common-law context of property rights.

self-aggrandizement is a more dependable motive than ideological interest, I would point out that it usually requires a financial outlay to undertake a lawsuit.... But the very fact of investing money in a lawsuit from which one is to acquire no further monetary profit argues, to my mind, a quite exceptional kind of interest, and one peculiarly indicative of a desire to say all that can be said in support of one's contention. From this I would conclude that, insofar as the argument for a traditional plaintiff runs in terms of the need for effective advocacy, the argument is not persuasive.

"The second argument for a restrictive definition of case and controversy is that the judicial power ... is inconsistent with the fundamental premises of a democratic system and has proved to be a block to effective government. ...

"It has now become a commonplace that the individual citizen in our vast, multitudinous complexes feels excluded from government. Thus, while governmental power expands, individual participation in the exercise of power contracts. This is unfortunate because the feeling of helplessness and exclusion is itself an evil, and because the individuals and organized groups are a source of information, experience, and wisdom. It has been remarked that administrative agencies are sometimes captured by particular interests. This assertion has been, in my opinion, somewhat overdone, but there can be no question that there is danger that officials and their staffs will become attached to certain positions and to certain accommodations which narrow their visions. For these reasons procedural devices, which enable citizen groups to participate in the decision-making process and to invoke judicial controls, are very valuable. ...

" ... From the very beginning, both our Constitution and our practice has sought to protect the individual qua individual and qua member of a minority from the abuse of power by the majority or by government in the name of the majority, despite the fact that majority rule through representation is the central institution of our democracy. Furthermore, democracy in our tradition emphasizes citizen participation as much as it does majority rule. Citizen participation is not simply a vehicle for minority protection, but a creative element in government and lawmaking. The usual ... citizen suit is thoroughly consistent with the primacy of majority rule. The issue will be the statutory authority of the official action, and the lawsuit itself will be prescribed by statute. The conservation and broadcasting cases emerge, then, as excellent examples of the lawsuit as a form of citizen participation within a framework established by majority rule."

(6) *A More Skeptical Assessment.* PETER L. STRAUSS, REVISITING OVERTON PARK: POLITICAL AND JUDICIAL CONTROLS OVER ADMINISTRATIVE ACTIONS AFFECTING THE COMMUNITY, 39 UCLA L.Rev. 1251, 1327 (1992): "If we consider participation in the judicial review process as a surrogate for an impaired political-democratic process, we must immediately be struck that the pricing of judicial review makes it an extremely inaccurate marker for the competing interests that may be involved in the proceeding. The investment of $100,000 in a review proceeding may inflict investment costs in the millions on the builder of an opposed project, making it less likely the project will be built even if the permission to construct it is eventually upheld. Ostensible concern with the survival of a striped bass fishery may

mask wealthy landowners' interest in preserving an unspoiled mountain view or 'any-way-we-can' opposition to the construction of a nuclear power plant. In a political process, we might expect those interests to be tested against others with, often, some form of accommodation in the outcome. But we would not expect a settlement reflecting a balance of strength of interests to be the result of a judicial proceeding, and the way the costs of judicial review are experienced makes it unlikely that accommodation will occur in its shadow.[8]"

(i) "INJURY IN FACT"

Lujan v. Defenders of Wildlife

Supreme Court of the United States, 1992.
504 U.S. 555.

■ JUSTICE SCALIA delivered the opinion of the Court with respect to Parts I, II, III–A, and IV, and an opinion with respect to Part III–B in which CHIEF JUSTICE REHNQUIST, JUSTICE WHITE, and JUSTICE THOMAS join.

[Section 7(a)(2) of the Endangered Species Act of 1973 divides responsibility for the protection of endangered species between the Secretary of the Interior and the Secretary of Commerce. Each federal agency is required to consult with the appropriate Secretary to ensure that any action funded by the agency is not likely to jeopardize the continued existence or habitat of any endangered or threatened species. Both Secretaries initially promulgated a joint regulation interpreting § 7(a)(2) to apply to actions taken in foreign nations; then, they jointly revised the rule to limit the section's geographic scope to the United States and the high seas. Wildlife conservation and other environmental organizations sued, claiming that the revised rule misinterpreted the statute. The court of appeals reversed the district court's dismissal of the suit for lack of standing. On remand, the district court denied the government's motion for summary judgment on standing, and granted the plaintiffs' cross motion on the merits. It ordered publication of a new rule returning to the original interpretation of § 7(a)(2). The court of appeals affirmed.]

II

. . . When the suit is one challenging the legality of government action or inaction, the nature and extent of facts that must be averred (at the summary judgment stage) or proved (at the trial stage) in order to establish

---

8. Political resolutions are commonly said to be rendered inaccurate by the difficulties large groups with relatively diffuse interests face in organizing and acting collectively, as compared with smaller, more focused "special interests." While the prospect of using judicial remedies may help overcome these difficulties in some absolute sense, if they can be obtained more cheaply than political relief and hence with the cooperation of fewer members of the collectivity, one should not overlook that the special interest groups enjoy the same cost advantages in using judicial rather than political remedies as the more diffuse consumerist groups. Unless the judicial forum is for some reason biased toward consumerist outcomes—a proposition that must be the less likely the more that use of the courts is seen to be an alternative form of politics—little reason exists to think, then, that the difficulties suggested by the collective action problems of large, diffuse groups of citizens will be solved in this way.

standing depends considerably upon whether the plaintiff is himself an object of the action (or forgone action) at issue. If he is, there is ordinarily little question that the action or inaction has caused him injury, and that a judgment preventing or requiring the action will redress it. When, however, as in this case, a plaintiff's asserted injury arises from the government's allegedly unlawful regulation (or lack of regulation) of someone else, much more is needed. In that circumstance, causation and redressability ordinarily hinge on the response of the regulated (or regulable) third party to the government action or inaction—and perhaps on the response of others as well. The existence of one or more of the essential elements of standing "depends on the unfettered choices made by independent actors not before the courts and whose exercise of broad and legitimate discretion the courts cannot presume either to control or to predict," and it becomes the burden of the plaintiff to adduce facts showing that those choices have been or will be made in such manner as to produce causation and permit redressability of injury. Thus, when the plaintiff is not himself the object of the government action or inaction he challenges, standing is not precluded, but it is ordinarily "substantially more difficult" to establish. Allen v. Wright.

III

We think the Court of Appeals failed to apply the foregoing principles in denying the Secretary's motion for summary judgment. . . .

A

Respondents' claim to injury is that the lack of consultation with respect to certain funded activities abroad "increas[es] the rate of extinction of endangered and threatened species." Of course, the desire to use or observe an animal species, even for purely aesthetic purposes, is undeniably a cognizable interest for purpose of standing. See, e.g., Sierra Club v. Morton. "But the 'injury in fact' test requires more than an injury to a cognizable interest. It requires that the party seeking review be himself among the injured." Id. . . .

. . . [T]he Court of Appeals focused on the affidavits of two Defenders' members—Joyce Kelly and Amy Skilbred. Ms. Kelly stated that she traveled to Egypt in 1986 and "observed the traditional habitat of the endangered nile crocodile there and intend[s] to do so again, and hope[s] to observe the crocodile directly," and that she "will suffer harm in fact as a result of [the] American . . . role . . . in overseeing the rehabilitation of the Aswan High Dam on the Nile . . . and [in] develop[ing] . . . Egypt's . . . Master Water Plan." Ms. Skilbred averred that she traveled to Sri Lanka in 1981 and "observed th[e] habitat" of "endangered species such as the Asian elephant and the leopard" at what is now the site of the Mahaweli Project funded by the Agency for International Development (AID), although she "was unable to see any of the endangered species;" "this development project," she continued, "will seriously reduce endangered, threatened, and endemic species habitat including areas that I visited . . . [, which] may severely shorten the future of these species;" that threat, she concluded, harmed her because she "intend[s] to return to Sri Lanka in the future and hope[s] to be more fortunate in spotting at least the endangered elephant and leopard." When Ms. Skilbred was asked at a subsequent deposition if and when she had any plans to return to Sri Lanka, she reiterated that "I intend to go back to Sri Lanka," but confessed that she had no current plans: "I don't know [when]. There is a civil war going on right now. I don't know. Not next year, I will say. In the future."

We shall assume for the sake of argument that these affidavits contain facts showing that certain agency-funded projects threaten listed species— though that is questionable. They plainly contain no facts, however, showing how damage to the species will produce "imminent" injury to Ms. Kelly and Skilbred. That the women "had visited" the areas of the projects before the projects commenced proves nothing. As we have said in a related context, " '[p]ast exposure to illegal conduct does not in itself show a present case or controversy regarding injunctive relief . . . if unaccompanied by any continuing, present adverse effects.' " And the affiants' profession of an "inten[t]" to return to the places they had visited before—where they will presumably, this time, be deprived of the opportunity to observe animals of the endangered species—is simply not enough. Such "some day" intentions—without any description of concrete plans, or indeed even any specification of when the some day will be—do not support a finding of the "actual or imminent" injury that our cases require.

Besides relying upon the Kelly and Skilbred affidavits, respondents propose a series of novel standing theories. The first, inelegantly styled "ecosystem nexus," proposes that any person who uses any part of a "contiguous ecosystem" adversely affected by a funded activity has standing even if the activity is located a great distance away. This approach, as the Court of Appeals correctly observed, is inconsistent with our opinion in Lujan v. National Wildlife Federation, 497 U.S. 871 (1990), which held that a plaintiff claiming injury from environmental damage must use the area affected by the challenged activity and not an area roughly "in the vicinity" of it. It makes no difference that the general-purpose section of the ESA states that the Act was intended in part "to provide a means whereby the ecosystems upon which endangered species and threatened species depend may be conserved." To say that the Act protects ecosystems is not to say that the Act creates (if it were possible) rights of action in persons who have not been injured in fact, that is, persons who use portions of an ecosystem not perceptibly affected by the unlawful action in question.

Respondents' other theories are called, alas, the "animal nexus" approach, whereby anyone who has an interest in studying or seeing the endangered animals anywhere on the globe has standing; and the "vocational nexus" approach, under which anyone with a professional interest in such animals can sue. Under these theories, anyone who goes to see Asian elephants in the Bronx Zoo, and anyone who is a keeper of Asian elephants in the Bronx Zoo, has standing to sue because the Director of AID did not consult with the Secretary regarding the AID-funded project in Sri Lanka. This is beyond all reason. . . .

[In Part IIIB of the opinion, which represented the views of only four Justices, Justice Scalia argued that Defenders failed the redressability, as well as injury, requirements. The agencies involved in the particular projects were not named defendants, and Justice Scalia saw no reason to expect that they would in fact consult simply because a court ordered the

Secretaries to return to the extraterritorial interpretation. Justice Stevens protested that no agency would ignore an authoritative construction of the ESA by the Supreme Court; Justice Scalia responded that, as standing must be determined at the outset of the lawsuit, "it could certainly not be known [at that point] that the suit would reach this Court."]

IV

The Court of Appeals found that respondents had standing for an additional reason: because they had suffered a "procedural injury." The so-called "citizen-suit" provision of the ESA provides, in pertinent part, that "any person may commence a civil suit on his own behalf (A) to enjoin any person, including the United States and any other governmental instrumentality or agency . . . who is alleged to be in violation of any provision of this chapter." 16 U.S.C. § 1540(g). The court held that, because § 7(a)(2) requires interagency consultation, the citizen-suit provision creates a "procedural righ[t]" to consultation in all "persons"—so that anyone can file suit in federal court to challenge the Secretary's (or presumably any other official's) failure to follow the assertedly correct consultative procedure, notwithstanding their inability to allege any discrete injury flowing from that failure. To understand the remarkable nature of this holding one must be clear about what it does *not* rest upon: This is not a case where plaintiffs are seeking to enforce a procedural requirement the disregard of which could impair a separate concrete interest of theirs (e.g., the procedural requirement for a hearing prior to denial of their license application, or the procedural requirement for an environmental impact statement before a federal facility is constructed next door to them).[1] Nor is it simply a case where concrete injury has been suffered by many persons, as in mass fraud or mass tort situations. Nor, finally, is it the unusual case in which Congress has created a concrete private interest in the outcome of a suit against a private party for the government's benefit, by providing a cash bounty for the victorious plaintiff. Rather, the court held that the injury-in-fact requirement had been satisfied by congressional conferral upon all persons of an abstract, self-contained, noninstrumental "right" to have the Executive observe the procedures required by law. We reject this view.[2]

1. There is this much truth to the assertion that "procedural rights" are special: The person who has been accorded a procedural right to protect his concrete interests can assert that right without meeting all the normal standards for redressability and immediacy. Thus, under our case-law, one living adjacent to the site for proposed construction of a federally licensed dam has standing to challenge the licensing agency's failure to prepare an Environmental Impact Statement, even though he cannot establish with any certainty that the Statement will cause the license to be withheld or altered, and even though the dam will not be completed for many years. (That is why we do not rely, in the present case, upon the Government's argument that, even if the other agencies were obliged to consult with the Secretary, they might not have followed his advice.) What respondents' "procedural rights" argument seeks, however, is quite different from this: standing for persons who have no concrete interests affected—persons who live (and propose to live) at the other end of the country from the dam.

2. The dissent's discussion of this aspect of the case distorts our opinion. We do not hold that an individual cannot enforce procedural rights; he assuredly can, so long as the procedures in question are designed to protect some threatened concrete interest of his that is the ultimate basis of his standing. The dissent, however, asserts that there exist "classes of procedural duties . . . so enmeshed

We have consistently held that a plaintiff raising only a generally available grievance about government—claiming only harm to his and every citizen's interest in proper application of the Constitution and laws, and seeking relief that no more directly and tangibly benefits him than it does the public at large—does not state an Article III case or controversy [citing, inter alia, Richardson, Schlesinger, and Valley Forge]. . . .

To be sure, our generalized-grievance cases have typically involved Government violation of procedures assertedly ordained by the Constitution rather than the Congress. But there is absolutely no basis for making the Article III inquiry turn on the source of the asserted right. Whether the courts were to act on their own, or at the invitation of Congress, in ignoring the concrete injury requirement described in our cases, they would be discarding a principle fundamental to the separate and distinct constitutional role of the Third Branch—one of the essential elements that identifies those "Cases" and "Controversies" that are the business of the courts rather than of the political branches. "The province of the court," as Chief Justice Marshall said in Marbury v. Madison, "is, solely, to decide on the rights of individuals." Vindicating the public interest (including the public interest in government observance of the Constitution and laws) is the function of Congress and the Chief Executive. The question presented here is whether the public interest in proper administration of the laws (specifically, in agencies' observance of a particular, statutorily prescribed procedure) can be converted into an individual right by a statute that denominates it as such, and that permits all citizens (or, for that matter, a subclass of citizens who suffer no distinctive concrete harm) to sue. If the concrete injury requirement has the separation-of-powers significance we have always said, the answer must be obvious: To permit Congress to convert the undifferentiated public interest in executive officers' compliance with the law into an "individual right" vindicable in the courts is to permit Congress to transfer from the President to the courts the Chief Executive's most important constitutional duty, to "take Care that the Laws be faithfully executed," Art. II, § 3. It would enable the courts, with the permission of Congress, "to assume a position of authority over the governmental acts of another and co-equal department," and to become " 'virtually continuing monitors of the wisdom and soundness of Executive action.' " Allen v. Wright. We have always rejected that vision of our role:

with the prevention of a substantive, concrete harm that an individual plaintiff may be able to demonstrate a sufficient likelihood of injury just through the breach of that procedural duty." If we understand this correctly, it means that the government's violation of a certain (undescribed) class of procedural duty satisfies the concrete-injury requirement by itself, without any showing that the procedural violation endangers a concrete interest of the plaintiff (apart from his interest in having the procedure observed). We cannot agree. The dissent is unable to cite a single case in which we actually found standing solely on the basis of a "procedural right" unconnected to the plaintiff's own concrete harm. Its suggestion that we did so in Japan Whaling Association v. American Cetacean Society, 478 U.S. 221 (1986), and Robertson v. Methow Valley Citizens Council, 490 U.S. 332 (1989), is not supported by the facts. In the former case, we found that the environmental organizations had standing because the "whale watching and studying of their members w[ould] be adversely affected by continued whale harvesting;" and in the latter we did not so much as mention standing, for the very good reason that the plaintiff was a citizens' council for the area in which the challenged construction was to occur, so that its members would obviously be concretely affected.

When Congress passes an Act empowering administrative agencies to carry on governmental activities, the power of those agencies is circumscribed by the authority granted. This permits the courts to participate in law enforcement entrusted to administrative bodies only to the extent necessary to protect justiciable individual rights against administrative action fairly beyond the granted powers. ... This is very far from assuming that the courts are charged more than administrators or legislators with the protection of the rights of the people. Congress and the Executive supervise the acts of administrative agents. ... But under Article III, Congress established courts to adjudicate cases and controversies as to claims of infringement of individual rights whether by unlawful action of private persons or by the exertion of unauthorized administrative power.

Stark v. Wickard, 321 U.S. 288 (1944). "Individual rights," within the meaning of this passage, do not mean public rights that have been legislatively pronounced to belong to each individual who forms part of the public.

Nothing in this contradicts the principle that "[t]he ... injury required by Art. III may exist solely by virtue of 'statutes creating legal rights, the invasion of which creates standing.'" [These other cases] involved Congress's elevating to the status of legally cognizable injuries concrete, de facto injuries that were previously inadequate in law.... As we said in Sierra Club, "[Statutory] broadening [of] the categories of injury that may be alleged in support of standing is a different matter from abandoning the requirement that the party seeking review must himself have suffered an injury." ...

We hold that respondents lack standing to bring this action and that the Court of Appeals erred in denying the summary judgment motion filed by the United States. The opinion of the Court of Appeals is hereby reversed, and the cause remanded for proceedings consistent with this opinion.

■ JUSTICE KENNEDY, with whom JUSTICE SOUTER joins, concurring in part and concurring in the judgment.

Although I agree with the essential parts of the Court's analysis, I write separately to make several observations.

I agree with the Court's conclusion in Part III–A that, on the record before us, respondents have failed to demonstrate that they themselves are "among the injured." ... While it may seem trivial to require that Ms. Kelly and Skilbred acquire airline tickets to the project sites or announce a date certain upon which they will return, this is not a case where it is reasonable to assume that the affiants will be using the sites on a regular basis, see Sierra Club v. Morton, nor do the affiants claim to have visited the sites since the projects commenced. ...

I also join Part IV of the Court's opinion with the following observations. As government programs and policies become more complex and far-reaching, we must be sensitive to the articulation of new rights of action that do not have clear analogs in our common-law tradition. Modern litigation has progressed far from the paradigm of Marbury suing Madison to get his commission.... In my view, Congress has the power to define injuries and articulate chains of causation that will give rise to a case or controversy where none existed before, and I do not read the Court's opinion to suggest a contrary view. In exercising this power, however, Congress must at the very least identify the injury it seeks to vindicate and relate the injury to the class of persons entitled to bring suit. The citizen-suit provision of the Endangered Species Act does not meet these minimal requirements, because while the statute purports to confer a right on "any person ... to enjoin ... the United States and any other governmental instrumentality or agency ... who is alleged to be in violation of any provision of this chapter," it does not of its own force establish that there is an injury in "any person" by virtue of any "violation."

The Court's holding that there is an outer limit to the power of Congress to confer rights of action is a direct and necessary consequence of the case and controversy limitations found in Article III. I agree that it would exceed those limitations if, at the behest of Congress and in the absence of any showing of concrete injury, we were to entertain citizen-suits to vindicate the public's nonconcrete interest in the proper administration of the laws. While it does not matter how many persons have been injured by the challenged action, the party bringing suit must show that the action injures him in a concrete and personal way....

■ [JUSTICE STEVENS concurred in the judgment on grounds that the new rule correctly interpreted the intended geographical scope of the ESA. He concluded respondents did have standing.]

■ JUSTICE BLACKMUN, with whom JUSTICE O'CONNOR joins, dissenting.

I part company with the Court in this case in two respects. First, I believe that respondents have raised genuine issues of fact—sufficient to survive summary judgment—both as to injury and as to redressability. Second, I question the Court's breadth of language in rejecting standing for "procedural" injuries. I fear the Court seeks to impose fresh limitations on the constitutional authority of Congress to allow citizen-suits in the federal courts for injuries deemed "procedural" in nature. ...

I think a reasonable finder of fact could conclude from the information in the affidavits and deposition testimony that either Kelly or Skilbred will soon return to the project sites, thereby satisfying the "actual or imminent" injury standard. ... By requiring a "description of concrete plans" or "specification of when the some day [for a return visit] will be," the Court, in my view, demands what is likely an empty formality. No substantial barriers prevent Kelly or Skilbred from simply purchasing plane tickets to return to the Aswan and Mahaweli projects. ...

I fear the Court's demand for detailed descriptions of future conduct will do little to weed out those who are genuinely harmed from those who are not. More likely, it will resurrect a code-pleading formalism in federal court summary judgment practice, as federal courts, newly doubting their jurisdiction, will demand more and more particularized showings of future harm. ...

The Court concludes that any "procedural injury" suffered by respondents is insufficient to confer standing. It rejects the view that the "injury-in-fact requirement ... [is] satisfied by congressional conferral upon all person of an abstract, self-contained, noninstrumental 'right' to have the

Executive observe the procedures required by law." Whatever the Court might mean with that very broad language, it cannot be saying that "procedural injuries" as a class are necessarily insufficient for purposes of Article III standing.

Most governmental conduct can be classified as "procedural." Many injuries caused by governmental conduct, therefore, are categorizable at some level of generality as "procedural" injuries. Yet, these injuries are not categorically beyond the pale of redress by the federal courts. . . .

The Court expresses concern that allowing judicial enforcement of "agencies' observance of a particular, statutorily prescribed procedure" would "transfer from the President to the courts the Chief Executive's most important constitutional duty, to 'take Care that the Laws be faithfully executed.'" In fact, the principal effect of foreclosing judicial enforcement of such procedures is to transfer power into the hands of the Executive at the expense—not of the courts—but of Congress, from which that power originates and emanates.

Under the Court's anachronistically formal view of the separation of powers, Congress legislates pure, substantive mandates and has no business structuring the procedural manner in which the Executive implements these mandates. To be sure, in the ordinary course, Congress does legislate in black-and-white terms of affirmative commands or negative prohibitions on the conduct of officers of the Executive Branch. In complex regulatory areas, however, Congress often legislates, as it were, in procedural shades of gray. That is, it sets forth substantive policy goals and provides for their attainment by requiring Executive Branch officials to follow certain procedures, for example, in the form of reporting, consultation, and certification. . . .

The consultation requirement of § 7 of the Endangered Species Act is [such an] action-forcing statute. Consultation is designed as an integral check on federal agency action, ensuring that such action does not go forward without full consideration of its effects on listed species. . . .

. . . Congress could simply impose a substantive prohibition on executive conduct; it could say that no agency action shall result in the loss of more than 5% of any listed species. Instead, Congress sets forth substantive guidelines and allows the Executive, within certain procedural constraints, to decide how best to effectuate the ultimate goal. The Court never has questioned Congress' authority to impose such procedural constraints on executive power. Just as Congress does not violate separation of powers by structuring the procedural manner in which the Executive shall carry out the laws, surely the federal courts do not violate separation of powers when, at the very instruction and command of Congress, they enforce these procedures.

. . . Here Congress seeks not to delegate "executive" power but only to strengthen the procedures it has legislatively mandated. . . . Ironically, this Court has previously justified a relaxed review of congressional delegation to the Executive on grounds that Congress, in turn, has subjected the exercise of that power to judicial review. The Court's intimation today that procedural injuries are not constitutionally cognizable threatens this under-standing upon which Congress has undoubtedly relied. . . .

It is to be hoped that over time the Court will acknowledge that some classes of procedural duties are so enmeshed with the prevention of a substantive, concrete harm that an individual plaintiff may be able to demonstrate a sufficient likelihood of injury just through the breach of that procedural duty. For example, in the context of the NEPA requirement of environmental-impact statements, this Court has acknowledged "it is now well settled that NEPA itself does not mandate particular results [and] simply prescribes the necessary process," but "these procedures are almost certain to affect the agency's substantive decision." . . .

. . . There may be factual circumstances in which a congressionally imposed procedural requirement is so insubstantially connected to the prevention of a substantive harm that it cannot be said to work any conceivable injury to an individual litigant. But, as a general matter, the courts owe substantial deference to Congress' substantive purpose in im-posing a certain procedural requirement. . . . There is no room for a per se rule or presumption excluding injuries labeled "procedural" in nature.

In conclusion, I cannot join the Court on what amounts to a slash-and-burn expedition through the law of environmental standing. . . .

NOTES

Lujan has been termed "one of the most important standing cases since World War II,"[1] a decision that "will mark a transformation in the law of standing."[2] Your understanding of this controversial case may benefit from considering the decision in two parts: (1) the Court's reaction to Defenders' first standing claim, which was a fairly conventional (if somewhat stretched) claim of particularized injury from harm to identified elements of the environment; (2) the Court's analysis of Defenders' second standing claim, which relied on the citizen-suit provision of the statute to obviate the need for individualized substantive environmental injury in favor of what the Court terms "procedural injury."

The conventional standing claim—closing the court house door to beneficiaries of regulation?

(1) PATRICIA M. WALD,[3] THE D.C. CIRCUIT: HERE AND NOW, 55 Geo.Wash. L.Rev. 718, 720–21 (1987): "More is undoubtedly demanded of plaintiffs now to make the necessary showing of a particularized injury. This is not difficult when the injury has already occurred. But the more common and harder case in our court is that of an organization claiming among its members persons who will suffer in the future from some national regula-

1. Cass R. Sunstein, What's Standing After Lujan? Of Citizen Suits, "Injuries," and Article III, 91 Mich.L.Rev. 163, 165 (1992).

2. Gene R. Nichol, Jr., Justice Scalia, Standing, and Public Law Litigation, 42 Duke L.J. 1141, 1142 (1993).

3. [Ed.] Judge Wald had a long and distinguished tenure on the D.C. Circuit—including serving as its chief judge for many years—before she took senior status and was appointed by the Secretary General of the United Nations to the International Criminal Tribunal for the former Yugoslavia.

tory policy not yet in effect. Sometimes the government itself does not know precisely the locations or the identities of the people to whom its policies will apply. Yet, in some cases, the [organic] statute itself requires that challenges be made to the regulations within sixty days of issuance. Even if judicial gloss can ease the sixty-day restraint, there is often an understandable desire on the part of both the government and possible victims to have a quick, coherent, unified challenge to the regulations at issue. Yet particularized injuries may be impossible to prove at this stage.

"There are, as the court realizes, profound public policy dimensions to standing decisions in such cases. When complex national regulatory policies are challenged, litigation can last several years and only a limited number of private citizens can afford the course. Congress, in setting stringent time limits for challenge in major regulatory statutes, likely assumed that organizations with resources would be the principal challengers. Yet if the criteria for showing the necessary injury for standing and especially for associational standing are too strict, a court creates a one-way street for challenge, open to regulated industries only and closed to consumers, environmentalists, or other public interest groups. While this concern does not, of course, resolve the primary question of whether Article III case or controversy standing is present in each case, it is my experience that there is usually no real dispute that a genuine case or controversy exists about the effects of a regulatory policy on certain segments of the citizenry, i.e., that certain types of persons will arguably be hurt by the policy, and even that the national organizational plaintiff has among its members some such citizens. The court must decide how much specificity to require in identifying these citizens in advance of the policy going into effect. Making everyone play the waiting game until the regulation has actually been applied to particular persons and caused particular results has practical consequences for all the players: industry and the government cannot be sure of the validity of a new policy in which they invest money and efforts, and members of the public must stand by and wait until lightning strikes a specific victim before doing anything."

(2) *The Implications of an Asymmetrical Standing Doctrine.* Review carefully Part II of the opinion, in which Justice Scalia sets out a general theory of how regulatory standing should operate. Note that, in this conception, "there is ordinarily little question" that the regulated entity will have standing to challenge agency action or inaction. By contrast, when the would-be plaintiff is a beneficiary of regulation, "standing is not precluded, but it is ordinarily 'substantially more difficult to establish.' "[4] How is regulatory decisionmaking likely to be affected if the rules governing access to judicial review are skewed in favor of some regulatory players and against others? In such a system, judicial review becomes a one-way rachet: It systematically corrects over-regulation but rarely addresses (because it rarely hears about) under-regulation.

In an article published before he joined the Court, Justice Scalia acknowledged that a standing doctrine that systematically disfavors beneficiary claims would tend to result in regulatory statutes being under-

---

4. You might consult Allen v. Wright to see the context from which the internal quote is taken. Note that Justice O'Connor, the author of Allen, dissented in Lujan.

enforced. He argued that this is "a good thing" because the Executive's "ability to lose or misdirect laws can be said to be one of the prime engines of social change." Executive branch under-enforcement reflects changing political will about the regulatory program; as the Justice put it, "Yesterday's herald is today's bore." ANTONIN SCALIA, THE DOCTRINE OF STANDING AS AN ESSENTIAL ELEMENT OF THE SEPARATION OF POWERS, 17 Suffolk U.L.Rev. 881, 897 (1983). CASS R. SUNSTEIN, WHAT'S STANDING AFTER *LUJAN*? OF CITIZEN SUITS, "INJURIES," AND ARTICLE III, 91 Mich.L.Rev. 163, 165 (1992), responded: "... In a case of beneficiary or citizen standing, courts are not enforcing 'executive branch adherence to legislative policies that the political process itself would not enforce.' [quoting Scalia] Instead, they are requiring the executive branch to adhere to the law, that is, to outcomes that the political process has endorsed. In Lujan, for example, the plaintiffs would have won [on the merits of their statutory argument] only if they could have shown an unambiguous legislative judgment in their favor.[5] Standing would produce 'legislative policies that the political process itself would not enforce' only if courts systematically misinterpreted statutes. But this seems to be an unsupportable assumption.

"In addition, it is hardly a good thing if agency implementation defeats legislative judgments. ... [S]uppose that an agency decides that the ESA should not be applied to American activities in foreign nations, when in fact Congress plainly intended that the ESA should apply abroad. Is this a good thing? On the contrary, it is a violation of democratic aspirations and (more relevant still) of the system for national lawmaking set up by Articles I and II of the Constitution. If agency enforcement beyond that intended by Congress is not 'a good thing,' even where the agency responds to political pressures, it is not 'a good thing' where an agency undertakes a pattern of enforcement that violates congressional will through abdication or failure to act. Asymmetry on this point would simply translate judicial antipathy to regulation into administrative law. The foreclosure of standing cannot plausibly be defended as a means of allowing the bureaucracy to implement the law in a manner that conflicts with the governing statute."

Professor Richard Pierce put the concern in somewhat different terms. Although "sympathetic to ... reducing the role of the judiciary in making government policy," Prof. Pierce worried that Lujan would be the "source of widespread harm to the process of agency policymaking, reducing dramatically the range of interests effectively represented in most agency proceedings," thereby "increas[ing] significantly the tendency for agency policies to be distorted by factionalism." RICHARD J. PIERCE, JR., LUJAN V. DEFENDERS OF WILDLIFE: STANDING AS A JUDICIALLY IMPOSED LIMIT ON LEGISLATIVE POWER, 42 Duke L.J. 1170, 1170–71 (1993).

(3) *The "Problem" of No Plaintiff.* Should the majority have recognized conventional regulatory standing, based on the Kelly and Skilbred affida-

---

5. [Ed.] For those who have not yet studied Chevron, p. 1026 above, an agency empowered to issue rules with the force of law receives considerable judicial deference for a rule interpreting ambiguous statutory language. Unless the reviewing court con-cluded that Congress had a clearly discernible intent with respect to extraterritorial application of the consultation requirement, Defenders would have lost to any reasonable interpretation the Secretaries proffered.

vits? The requirement of "actual or imminent" injury is understood to come from Article III itself. Does it trivialize the Constitution to suggest that the injury assessment would have come out differently if either Ms. Kelly or Ms. Skilbred had purchased an airline ticket before filing suit? *Would* purchasing a ticket have been enough, in the majority's view? If not, is there any plaintiff who could litigate the question whether the Secretaries had properly interpreted the scope of the ESA consultation requirement?

In a series of constitutional cases that predate Lujan, the Court held that a claim to standing is not helped by the argument that no one will have standing if this plaintiff does not.[6] Indeed, some of these cases go so far as to say that the apparent absence of any other viable plaintiff is good evidence that the matter does not belong in the courts.[7] Is the "no plaintiff" answer less acceptable in cases seeking review of agency action for conformity with the organic statute? Should Congress be given more latitude to "create" plaintiffs in such circumstances? Nearly a decade before Lujan, DAVID A. LOGAN, STANDING TO SUE: A PROPOSED SEPARATION OF POWERS ANALYSIS, 1984 Wisc.L.Rev. 37, 69–70, argued that the constitutional cases represent an appropriate prudential avoidance of friction between the judiciary and the political branches, but that the issue is different with respect to statutory claims:

> As a general proposition, the Court should defer to Congress and grant standing to 'any person' who is injured in a way colorably contemplated by the remedial legislation unless express legislative history or a clear failure to meet the minimum content of article III compels a contrary judgment. By deferring in this way to Congress' broad power to act to cure social ills, the Court serves the principle of separation of powers.

In light of Lujan, Prof. Pierce, 42 Duke L.J. at 1200, elaborates: "The reasoning in [Lujan] reallocates power among the institutions of government in three related ways. First, in authorizing, indeed requiring, judges to choose whether to characterize a particular form of injury or causal relationship in a manner that permits the judge to enforce or not to enforce a particular statutory command, it gives courts discretion to decide which congressional policy decisions bind agencies. Judges are more likely to choose characterizations that result in judicial enforcement of a congressional policy decision when they agree with the policy reflected in the statute than when they disagree with that policy. Second, it confers on agencies discretion to ignore many congressional policy decisions. Indeed, extended to its logical limit, the reasoning of the opinion could confer on agencies discretion to ignore *all* statutory commands or prohibitions that regulated firms prefer they ignore. Third, it takes from Congress the power to make many judicially enforceable policy decisions. Again, carried to its logical limit, the reasoning ... could preclude Congress from making any

---

6. See United States v. Richardson, 418 U.S. 166, 179 (1974); Schlesinger v. Reservists Comm. to Stop the War, 418 U.S. 208, 227 (1974); Valley Forge Christian College v. Americans United for Separation of Church & State, Inc., 454 U.S. 464, 489 (1982).

7. Richardson, 418 U.S. at 179; Valley Forge, 454 U.S. at 489.

enforceable policy decisions that have the effect of benefiting only groups rather than identifiable individuals."

Standing based on a citizen–suit provision—Article
II and the conundrum of "procedural rights"

(4) *Who Should Determine the Breadth of Regulatory Standing?* Although older regulatory statutes rarely contain a "citizen suit" provision like that in the ESA, such provisions became common in newer environmental legislation.[8] Why might Congress choose to include this device in these regulatory contexts? PETER L. STRAUSS, REVISITING OVERTON PARK: POLITICAL AND JUDICIAL CONTROLS OVER ADMINISTRATIVE ACTIONS AFFECTING THE COMMUNITY, 39 UCLA L.Rev. 1251, 1324–25 (1992): "The very possibility of bringing an action places in the hands of the initiator the capacity to inflict transaction costs on others that may themselves bend the outcomes of polycentric issues toward its interests. . . . Wide distribution of the capacity to inflict the costs that judicial review entails can protect agencies from the effective co-option that may result when this punishment can be inflicted only from one direction—and the agency therefore bends its actions to avoiding those costs. Indeed, Congress may choose widely to distribute the right to challenge agency behavior in court both as a means of assuring agency fidelity to its aims and as a reliable device for signaling to it when administration is going astray—as a substitute, as it were, for its own political oversight."

Because rules governing access to judicial review can significantly impact both agency functioning and substantive regulatory policy, Congress has a significant stake in defining the level and distribution of regulatory standing. Adjusting the *level* of rights to judicial review can increase policing of agency compliance with statutory directives and enhance substantive and procedural rationality, but carries the risk of obstruction and ossification. Adjusting the *distribution* of rights to judicial review can create differential agency incentives to attend to various interests in the regulatory process—incentives that will either support, or undermine, the substantive objectives of the statute. Thus, in setting up a new regulatory program, Congress may consider the allocation of standing to be an important part of the program's implementing architecture.

At the same time, however, the relationship of standing to the Article III judicial power implies a core set of justiciability requirements that transcend ordinary legislation. It is clear, at least in principle, that the

---

8. See, e.g., Clean Air Act, 42 U.S.C. § 7604(a) ("any person may commence a civil action on his own behalf" against a private or governmental polluter or against the EPA Administrator for failing to perform a nondiscretionary duty); Resource Conservation & Recovery Act, 42 U.S.C. § 6972(a) ("any person may commence a civil action on his own behalf ... against the Administrator where there is alleged a failure of the Administrator to perform any act or duty under this chapter which is not discretionary").

In some statutes, nominally "citizen suit" provisions in fact explicitly contemplate more conventional standing analysis. See, e.g., Clean Water Act, which states that "any citizen may commence a civil action on his own behalf" against an alleged polluter, 33 U.S.C. § 1365(a), but which defines a "citizen" as "a person ... having an interest which is or may be adversely affected" by the alleged violation. § 1365(g).

prudential elements of standing may be altered by statute. For example, the zone-of-interests requirement may be dispensed with by a particular organic statute. E.g., Bennett v. Spear, p. 1172 below. The extent to which statutes can affect the constitutional elements of standing is a more complex matter. By defining new legally protected interests, a statute may create an injury for standing purposes where none previously existed.[9] If this were not so, standing doctrine would operate to freeze the set of injuries capable of receiving legal redress at those recognized by the common law. Similarly, legislative determinations can guide the court's assessment of causation.[10] Deference in this area acknowledges that the decision to accept a particular causal chain as sufficient to justify relief depends both on factual findings about real world behavior, and on policy judgments about acceptable degrees of contingency in linking the plaintiff's harm to the defendant's behavior. Nonetheless, most of us have the constitutional intuition that there must be limits to Congress' power to affect the constitutional components of standing.

(5) *Bringing Article II into Standing Doctrine*. Lujan was the first case in which the Court invalidated an explicit grant of standing in a regulatory statute.[11] Prior to Lujan, most commentators would have acknowledged that true citizen-suit provisions present a tricky constitutional question, and the lower courts were divided about the need for conventional particularized injury in the presence of an applicable citizen-suit provision.[12] The constitutional conundrum, however, was generally thought to be reconciling Congress' Article I power to create new legally cognizable claims with the Article III "case" or "controversy" requirement. In an extraordinary stroke, Lujan reframed the terms of the constitutional debate by insisting that the *real* problem with citizen-suit provisions was Article II.

In determining the extent of Congress' power to confer standing to enforce agency compliance with regulatory statutes, how helpful is it to invoke the "Take Care" Clause? Professor Sunstein, who generally favors

---

9. "The actual or threatened injury required by Article III may exist solely by virtue of statutes creating legal rights, the invasion of which creates standing." Warth v. Seldin, 422 U.S. 490, 500 (1975) (internal quotations omitted). For example, in Traffi-cante v. Metropolitan Life Ins. Co., 409 U.S. 205 (1972), existing tenants were permitted to sue their landlord for discriminating in rental decisions against persons of color. The relevant statute gave standing to one "who claims to have been injured by a discriminatory housing practice." The plaintiffs claimed damages for lost social benefits of living in an integrated community, lost business and professional advantages, and stigma as residents of a "white ghetto." Justices White, Powell and Blackmun concurred but wrote separately to explain that, absent the statute, they would have "great difficulty in concluding that petitioners' complaint in this case pre-sented a case or controversy." See also Havens Realty v. Coleman, 455 U.S. 363, 373 (1982).

10. See, e.g., Friends of the Earth, Inc. v. Laidlaw Envtl. Serv., p. 1180 below; Lujan, 504 U.S. at 580 (Kennedy, J., concurring in part and in the judgment).

11. Earlier cases, such as Allen v. Wright, did not involve provisions in the organic statute that attempted to grant standing to a class of which the plaintiff was a member.

12. Compare Metropolitan Wash. Coalition for Clean Air v. District of Columbia, 511 F.2d 809, 814 n. 26 (D.C.Cir.1975) (plaintiff suing under Clean Air Act citizen-suit provision need not allege injury) with NRDC, Inc. v. EPA, 507 F.2d 905, 908–11 (9th Cir.1974) (contra).

strong presidential oversight of agencies and management of regulation,[13] argues that Article II is a red herring: "If a plaintiff with a plane ticket can sue under the ESA without offense to Article II, then it makes no sense to say that Article II is violated if a plaintiff lacking such a ticket initiates a proceeding. Beneficiary standing poses no Article II issue." 91 Mich. L. Rev. at 213. As an historical matter, the Take Care Clause was apparently designed to emphasize that the President does not have the power (used against Parliament by some of the Kings), to suspend laws with which he disagrees.[14] This explanation accounts for the phraseology, which appears to impose a duty on the President ("he *shall* Take Care . . .") rather than to grant a prerogative assertable against Congress. As a conceptual matter, can Lujan's interpretation of the Clause be squared with *any* private suit to have the judiciary review agency action for compliance with law?

(6) *The Relevance of "Bounty" Statutes.* "Statutes providing for actions by a common informer, who himself had no interest whatever in the controversy other than that given by statute, have been in existence for hundreds of years in England, and in this country ever since the foundation of our Government." Marvin v. Trout, 199 U.S. 212, 225 (1905). Suits under these bounty statutes, which typically establish a penalty for official wrongdoing and provide that anyone who brings such wrongdoing to the attention of the court will receive a share of the penalty, are called "popular" (because given to "the people" in general) or *qui tam* (because the plaintiff is one *who* sues *as well* for the state as for himself) actions. "These statutes provided a common mechanism to regulate, by judicial sanction, governmental officials where there was likely to be no aggrieved party with a private cause of action."[15] Suppose that Congress amended the citizen-suit provision of ESA to provide that a successful plaintiff would receive a reward of $1,000. Why are professional bounty hunters better plaintiffs ("better" from either a constitutional or a prudential perspective) than professional environmentalists such as Defenders of Wildlife?[16]

STEEL CO. V. CITIZENS FOR A BETTER ENVIRONMENT, 523 U.S. 83 (1998), held that the Emergency Planning & Community Right-to-Know Act could not constitutionally authorize private suits to complain of *past* violations of the Act's requirement that companies file annual reports about the nature and quantity of hazardous chemical use. Justice Scalia's opinion reasoned that a

---

13. See p. 216 above.

14. See George Van Cleve, Congressional Power to Confer Broad Citizen Standing in Environmental Cases, 29 Envtl. L. Rep. (Envtl. L. Inst.) 10,028, 10,036 (1999); Martin S. Flaherty, The Most Dangerous Branch, 105 Yale L.J. 1725, 1792–95 (1996); Christopher N. May, Presidential Defiance of "Unconstitutional" Laws: Reviving the Royal Prerogative, 21 Hastings Con. L. Q. 865, 873 (1994).

15. Stephen L. Winter, The Metaphor of Standing and the Problem of Self–Governance, 40 Stan.L.Rev. 1371, 1407 (1988). See also Evan Caminker, The Constitutionality of *Qui Tam* Actions, 99 Yale L.J. 341 (1989).

16. Vermont Ag. of Natural Res. v. U.S. ex rel. Stevens, 529 U.S. 765 (2000), held that a qui tam suit under the False Claims Act satisfied Article III standing requirements. Justice Scalia, for the Court, focused on the long history of such actions in Anglo–American jurisprudence, and reasoned that injury-in-fact arose from the status of the "qui tam relator [as], in effect, suing as a partial assignee of the United States." However, footnote 8 warns: "In so concluding, we express no view on the question whether qui tam suits violate Article II, in particular the Appointments Clause of § 2 and the Take Care Clause of § 3," citing Lujan.

statutory citizen-suit scheme in which the only available remedies for noncompliance were penalties payable to the United States (rather than to the private plainiffs) ran afoul of Lujan. Justice Stevens, concurring only in the judgment, responded:

> It is hard to see ... how EPCRA's citizen-suit provision impinges on the power of the Executive. ... [U]nder the Court's own reasoning, respondent would have had standing if Congress had authorized some payment to respondent. ... Yet it is unclear why the separation of powers question should turn on whether the plaintiff receives monetary compensation. In either instance, a private citizen is enforcing the law. If separation of powers does not preclude standing when Congress creates a legal right that authorizes compensation to the plaintiff, it is unclear why separation of powers should dictate a contrary result when Congress has created a legal right but has directed that payment be made to the federal Treasury. Indeed, in this case (assuming for present purposes that respondent correctly reads the statute) not only has Congress authorized standing, but the Executive Branch has also endorsed its interpretation of Article III. [The United States had appeared as amicus curiae arguing in favor of standing.] It is this Court's decision, not anything that Congress or the Executive has done, that encroaches on the domain of other branches of the Federal Government.

(7) *The Meaning and Significance of "Procedural Injury."* Why is the Take Care Clause more offended by claims of procedural agency illegality than substantive agency illegality?

As you are well aware if you've studied Chapters III–V, administrative law in general—and the APA in particular—uses procedural requirements to improve the quality of agency decisionmaking, control the exercise of regulatory power, and enhance the perceived legitimacy of administrative action. Moreover, Congress sometimes imposes procedures to enhance regulatory policymakers' sensitivity to certain interests. The environmental impact statement required by NEPA is a good example. Not surprisingly, then, much judicial review of agency action involves claims that a particular action must be set aside not because it is substantively indefensible (although this claim may also be made), but rather because it was reached "without observance of procedure required by law." APA § 706(2)(D). When Lujan states that "an abstract, self-contained, noninstrumental 'right' to have the Executive observe the procedures required by law" cannot constitutionally support standing, does it mean that the only cognizable procedural injuries are those which the plaintiff can prove resulted in a substantively harmful decisional outcome?

The stakes riding on the answer are high. Several statutes that we now regard as a fundamental part of modern regulatory government afford procedural rights to all citizens without regard to substantive interest. The right to attend meetings under the Government in the Sunshine Act (GITSA) is a good example. An individual whose property will be impacted by a particular regulatory decision has no more right to attend a meeting within the scope of GITSA than does an administrative law professor who simply wants to be able to say that she has sat in on one meeting of every existing federal agency. The Federal Advisory Committee Act (FACA) establishes similar rights with respect to federal advisory committee meetings. A related example is FOIA—under which the law is clear that any person is entitled to receive information within the scope of the statute, without regard to why the information is sought. See Chapter VII. A final example is § 553 of the APA, which appears to create a general right to comment on a properly noticed proposed rule uncontingent on having any particular substantive connection to the issues at stake. After Lujan, are these rights judicially enforceable only by someone who can demonstrate that "the procedures in question are designed to protect some threatened concrete interest of his that is the ultimate basis of his standing"? The next principal case begins to provide some answers.

Federal Election Commission v. Akins

Supreme Court of the United States, 1998.
524 U.S. 11.

■ JUSTICE BREYER delivered the opinion of the Court.

The Federal Election Commission (FEC) has determined that the American Israel Public Affairs Committee (AIPAC) is not a "political committee" as defined by the Federal Election Campaign Act of 1971 (FECA or Act), 2 U.S.C. § 431(4), and, for that reason, the FEC has refused to require AIPAC to make disclosures regarding its membership, contributions, and expenditures that FECA would otherwise require. We hold that respondents, a group of voters, have standing to challenge the Commission's determination in court, and we remand this case for further proceedings.

[FECA attempts to remedy actual or perceived corruption of the electoral process by imposing limits on the amounts that individuals, corporations, "political committees" (including political action committees), and political parties can contribute to a candidate for federal political office. It also requires that groups which fall within the definition of a "political committee" must register with the FEC, appoint a treasurer, keep names and addresses of contributors, track the amount and purpose of disbursements, and file complex FEC reports that include lists of donors giving in excess of $200 per year, contributions, expenditures, and other disbursements.

Akins, et al. described themselves as a group of voters with views opposed to those of AIPAC. They filed a complaint with the FEC, alleging that AIPAC met the statutory definition of "political committee" and had unlawfully failed to register and to make public the statutorily listed information about members, contributions, and expenditures. They asked the FEC to find that AIPAC had violated the Act and to order AIPAC to make public the information that FECA demands of a "political committee." AIPAC moved to dismiss the complaint on grounds that it was not a "political committee" within the meaning of the Act. The FEC interpreted the Act's definition of "political committee" to include only organizations that have as a "major purpose" the nomination or election of candidates.

AIPAC, it concluded, was fundamentally an issue-oriented lobbying organization, not a campaign-related organization, and hence fell outside the Act.

As permitted by FECA, respondents filed a petition in district court seeking review of the FEC's determination dismissing their complaint. That court granted summary judgment for the FEC, and a panel of the D.C. Circuit affirmed. The court took the case en banc and reversed, concluding that the FEC misinterpreted the Act's definition of a "political committee." The Court took certiorari on both the questions of standing, and the merits; it decided only the former.]

The Solicitor General argues that respondents lack [both prudential and Article III] standing....

We do not agree with the FEC's "prudential standing" claim. Congress has specifically provided in FECA that "[a]ny person who believes a violation of this Act ... has occurred, may file a complaint with the Commission." § 437g(a)(1). It has added that "[a]ny party aggrieved by an order of the Commission dismissing a complaint filed by such party ... may file a petition" in district court seeking review of that dismissal. § 437g(a)(8)(A). History associates the word "aggrieved" with a congressional intent to cast the standing net broadly—beyond the common-law interests and substantive statutory rights upon which "prudential" standing traditionally rested. Scripps-Howard Radio, Inc. v. FCC; FCC v. Sanders Bros. Radio Station; Associated Indus. of N.Y. v. Ickes.

Moreover, prudential standing is satisfied when the injury asserted by a plaintiff " 'arguably [falls] within the zone of interests to be protected or regulated by the statute ... in question.' " NCUA (quoting Data Processing). The injury of which respondents complain—their failure to obtain relevant information—is injury of a kind that FECA seeks to address. Buckley v. Valeo, [424 U.S. 1] 66–67 [1976]("political committees" must disclose contributors and disbursements to help voters understand who provides which candidates with financial support). We have found nothing in the Act that suggests Congress intended to exclude voters from the benefits of these provisions, or otherwise to restrict standing, say, to political parties, candidates, or their committees.

Given the language of the statute and the nature of the injury, we conclude that Congress, intending to protect voters such as respondents from suffering the kind of injury here at issue, intended to authorize this kind of suit. Consequently, respondents satisfy "prudential" standing requirements. Cf. Raines v. Byrd, 521 U.S. 811, 820, n. 3 (1997) (explicit grant of authority to bring suit "eliminates any prudential standing limitations and significantly lessens the risk of unwanted conflict with the Legislative Branch").

Nor do we agree with the FEC or the dissent that Congress lacks the constitutional power to authorize federal courts to adjudicate this lawsuit. Article III, of course, limits Congress' grant of judicial power to "cases" or "controversies." That limitation means that respondents must show, among other things, an "injury in fact"....

The "injury in fact" that respondents have suffered consists of their inability to obtain information—lists of AIPAC donors (who are, according to AIPAC, its members), and campaign-related contributions and expenditures—that, on respondents' view of the law, the statute requires that AIPAC make public. There is no reason to doubt their claim that the information would help them (and others to whom they would communicate it) to evaluate candidates for public office, especially candidates who received assistance from AIPAC, and to evaluate the role that AIPAC's financial assistance might play in a specific election. Respondents' injury consequently seems concrete and particular. Indeed, this Court has previously held that a plaintiff suffers an "injury in fact" when the plaintiff fails to obtain information which must be publicly disclosed pursuant to a statute. Public Citizen v. Department of Justice, 491 U.S. 440, 449 (1989) (failure to obtain information subject to disclosure under Federal Advisory Committee Act "constitutes a sufficiently distinct injury to provide standing to sue"). See also Havens Realty Corp. v. Coleman, 455 U.S. 363, 373–374(1982) (deprivation of information about housing availability constitutes "specific injury" permitting standing). . . .

The FEC's strongest argument is its contention that this lawsuit involves only a "generalized grievance." . . . The FEC points out that respondents' asserted harm (their failure to obtain information) is one which is " 'shared in substantially equal measure by all or a large class of citizens.' " (quoting Warth v. Seldin, 422 U.S. 490, 499 (1975)). This Court, the FEC adds, has often said that "generalized grievance[s]" are not the kinds of harms that confer standing. Whether styled as a constitutional or prudential limit on standing, the Court has sometimes determined that where large numbers of Americans suffer alike, the political process, rather than the judicial process, may provide the more appropriate remedy for a widely shared grievance.

The kind of judicial language to which the FEC points, however, invariably appears in cases where the harm at issue is not only widely shared, but is also of an abstract and indefinite nature—for example, harm to the "common concern for obedience to law." L. Singer & Sons v. Union Pacific R. Co., 311 U.S. 295, 303 (1940); see also Allen v. Wright. Cf. Lujan (injury to interest in seeing that certain procedures are followed not normally sufficient by itself to confer standing); Perkins v. Lukens Steel Co., 310 U.S. 113, 125 (1940) (plaintiffs lack standing because they have failed to show injury to "a particular right of their own, as distinguished from the public's interest in the administration of the law"). The abstract nature of the harm—for example, injury to the interest in seeing that the law is obeyed—deprives the case of the concrete specificity that characterized those controversies which were "the traditional concern of the courts at Westminster," Coleman, 307 U.S. at 460 (Frankfurter, J., dissenting); and which today prevents a plaintiff from obtaining what would, in effect, amount to an advisory opinion.

Often the fact that an interest is abstract and the fact that it is widely shared go hand in hand. But their association is not invariable, and where a harm is concrete, though widely shared, the Court has found "injury in fact." See Public Citizen, 491 U.S., at 449–450 ("The fact that other citizens or groups of citizens might make the same complaint after unsuccessfully demanding disclosure . . . does not lessen [their] asserted injury").

Thus the fact that a political forum may be more readily available where an injury is widely shared (while counseling against, say, interpreting a statute as conferring standing) does not, by itself, automatically disqualify an interest for Article III purposes. Such an interest, where sufficiently concrete, may count as an "injury in fact." This conclusion seems particularly obvious where (to use a hypothetical example) large numbers of individuals suffer the same common-law injury (say, a widespread mass tort), or where large numbers of voters suffer interference with voting rights conferred by law. We conclude that, similarly, the informational injury at issue here, directly related to voting, the most basic of political rights, is sufficiently concrete and specific such that the fact that it is widely shared does not deprive Congress of constitutional power to authorize its vindication in the federal courts.

Respondents have also satisfied the remaining two constitutional standing requirements. The harm asserted is "fairly traceable" to the FEC's decision about which respondents complain. Of course, as the FEC points out it is possible that even had the FEC agreed with respondents' view of the law, it would still have decided in the exercise of its discretion not to require AIPAC to produce the information. Cf. Heckler v. Chaney, p. 1218 below. But that fact does not destroy Article III "causation," for we cannot know that the FEC would have exercised its prosecutorial discretion in this way. Agencies often have discretion about whether or not to take a particular action. Yet those adversely affected by a discretionary agency decision generally have standing to complain that the agency based its decision upon an improper legal ground. See, e.g., Abbott Laboratories v. Gardner, p. 1182 below (discussing presumption of reviewability of agency action); Citizens to Preserve Overton Park, Inc. v. Volpe, p. 989 above. If a reviewing court agrees that the agency misinterpreted the law, it will set aside the agency's action and remand the case—even though the agency (like a new jury after a mistrial) might later, in the exercise of its lawful discretion, reach the same result for a different reason. SEC v. Chenery Corp., p. 556 above. Thus respondents' "injury in fact" is "fairly traceable" to the FEC's decision not to issue its complaint, even though the FEC might reach the same result exercising its discretionary powers lawfully. For similar reasons, the courts in this case can "redress" respondents' "injury in fact."

Finally, the FEC argues that we should deny respondents standing because this case involves an agency's decision not to undertake an enforcement action—an area generally not subject to judicial review. In Heckler, this Court noted that agency enforcement decisions "ha[ve] traditionally been 'committed to agency discretion,'" and concluded that Congress did not intend to alter that tradition in enacting the APA. We deal here with a statute that explicitly indicates the contrary.

In sum, respondents, as voters, have satisfied both prudential and constitutional standing requirements. They may bring this petition for a declaration that the FEC's dismissal of their complaint was unlawful. . . .

■ JUSTICE SCALIA, with whom JUSTICE O'CONNOR and JUSTICE THOMAS join, dissenting.

The provision of law at issue in this case is an extraordinary one, conferring upon a private person the ability to bring an Executive agency into court to compel its enforcement of the law against a third party. Despite its liberality, the Administrative Procedure Act does not allow such suits, since enforcement action is traditionally deemed "committed to agency discretion by law." 5 U.S.C. § 701(a)(2); Heckler v. Chaney. If provisions such as the present one were commonplace, the role of the Executive Branch in our system of separated and equilibrated powers would be greatly reduced, and that of the Judiciary greatly expanded. ...

[Justice Scalia began by arguing that FECA did not intend to give every person who can file complaints the right also to obtain judicial review if that complaint is rejected. He then turned to the majority's standing analysis.]

What is noticeably lacking in the Court's discussion of our generalized-grievance jurisprudence is all reference to two words that have figured in it prominently: "particularized" and "undifferentiated." "Particularized" means that "the injury must affect the plaintiff in a personal and individual way." Lujan. If the effect is undifferentiated and common to all members of the public, ... the plaintiff has a "generalized grievance" that must be pursued by political, rather than judicial, means. These terms explain why it is a gross oversimplification to reduce the concept of a generalized grievance to nothing more than "the fact that [the grievance] is widely shared," thereby enabling the concept to be dismissed as a standing principle by such examples as "large numbers of individuals suffer[ing] the same common-law injury (say, a widespread mass tort), or ... large numbers of voters suffer[ing] interference with voting rights conferred by law." The exemplified injuries are widely shared, to be sure, but each individual suffers a particularized and differentiated harm. One tort victim suffers a burnt leg, another a burnt arm—or even if both suffer burnt arms they are different arms. One voter suffers the deprivation of his franchise, another the deprivation of hers. With the generalized grievance, on the other hand, the injury or deprivation is not only widely shared but it is undifferentiated. The harm caused to ... Mr. Akins by the allegedly unlawful failure to enforce FECA is precisely the same as the harm caused to everyone else: unavailability of a description of AIPAC's activities.

... A system in which the citizenry at large could sue to compel Executive compliance with the law would be a system in which the courts, rather than the President, are given the primary responsibility to "take Care that the Laws be faithfully executed." We do not have such a system because the common understanding of the interest necessary to sustain suit has included the requirement ... that the complained-of injury be particularized and differentiated, rather than common to all the electorate. When the Executive can be directed by the courts, at the instance of any voter, to remedy a deprivation that affects the entire electorate in precisely the same way—and particularly when that deprivation (here, the unavailability of information) is one inseverable part of a larger enforcement scheme—there has occurred a shift of political responsibility to a branch designed not to protect the public at large but to protect individual rights. ... If today's decision is correct, it is within the power of Congress to authorize any interested person to manage (through the courts) the Executive's enforcement of any law that includes a requirement for the filing and public availability of a piece of paper. This is not the system we have had, and is not the system we should desire.

Because this statute should not be interpreted to confer upon the entire electorate the power to invoke judicial direction of prosecutions, and because if it is so interpreted the statute unconstitutionally transfers from the Executive to the courts the responsibility to "take Care that the Laws be faithfully executed," I respectfully dissent.

NOTES

(1) *Domesticating Lujan?* Recall that Allen v. Wright characterized the "rule barring adjudication of generalized grievances" as a prudential restriction on standing. (This characterization was consistent with earlier cases.) Congress clearly can obviate prudential standing limitations. Faced with explicit statutory intent to create broad standing to ensure compliance with the ESA, Lujan recast the generalized grievance restriction as a dimension of the constitutional injury requirement. How does Akins characterize the "rule barring adjudication of generalized grievances"? In light of Akins, could Congress ensure judicial review of the ESA consultation requirement by amending the Act to add the following: "The results of the consultation required by this Act shall be incorporated into a report, and this report shall be available to any person upon request"?

(2) *Information Requirements as a Type of Regulation.* If you studied the materials in Chapter III on government information gathering, you will already appreciate that the choice to require the production and disclosure of information is not only "regulation," but also a specific *strategy* of regulation. FECA's required public disclosure of designated categories of campaign finance information is one of Congress' earliest uses of this strategy; government ethics requirements that high-level officials periodically disclose information about their financial holdings is another. Both may be seen as part of the larger movement (epitomized in the Government in the Sunshine Act and FOIA) to open government processes to citizen oversight. In recent years, Congress has chosen to employ this strategy more frequently in private-sector regulation as well. Statutes such as the Worker Adjustment & Retraining Notification Act and the Emergency Planning & Community Right to Know Act require periodic public reporting of information regarding private entities' behavior. Such requirements allow citizens to monitor activities that will predictably have significant spillover effects, and to bring community and political pressures to bear to affect whether and how those activities are conducted. As such, public reporting requirements represent a milder, and more localized, remedial strategy for regulating potentially harmful private behavior than, for example, imposing a regime of centralized administrative oversight and standard-setting. If Akins had come out the other way, to what extent would this strategy have been effectively removed from Congress's array of possible regulatory techniques?

(3) *Making Peace Between Lujan and Akins?* The Administrative Law Section of the ABA undertook a project to collate and restate the law that had emerged under the APA since its enactment in 1946. Here is the Section's attempt to provide a theory for explaining and reconciling Lujan and Akins, while preserving existing law on private enforcement of statutes such as GITSA, FACTA, and FOIA and offering a method of analyzing new claims.[1] Is the effort a success?

"Injury from Violation of Procedural Requirements"

"When a challenged agency action harms an underlying substantive interest of the plaintiff, she has standing to challenge the agency's failure to follow proper procedures even though she cannot prove that the procedural error actually changed the substantive outcome. For example, a taxpayer whose tax liability is increased by a new regulation can challenge the adequacy of the notice of proposed rulemaking, even though it cannot be shown that but for the error, a more favorable regulation would have ensued.

"Cognizable injury may also arise from procedural violation without a showing that the violation endangers a concrete substantive interest of the plaintiff, but there is some uncertainty about the situations in which this can occur. The uncertainty stems from the holding in Lujan v. Defenders of Wildlife that, in at least some situations, a violation of procedural duties alone fails to satisfy the Article III injury requirement.

"It is clear, notwithstanding Lujan, that Congress can confer upon individuals a right personally to obtain notice of, observe, or get information about an agency activity without regard to their having a particular substantive interest, and that this right can be judicially enforced without reference to any additional, underlying substantive injury. Examples of such rights include the right to attend meetings and otherwise have access to government proceedings under the Government In The Sunshine Act and the Federal Advisory Committee Act. Freedom of Information Act rights and voter rights to certain information under the Federal Election Campaign Act are analogous sorts of rights, denial of which will support standing without regard to proof of harm to a particular, underlying substantive interest.

"It is also clear, from Lujan itself, that Congress does not have the power to confer standing upon individuals to enforce a procedural requirement without regard to their underlying substantive interests *if* the procedural requirement entails a purely internal agency activity as to which persons like the plaintiff have no legal claim to involvement or information. The Endangered Species Act consultation provision challenged in Lujan was such a purely internal executive-branch activity, in which outsiders were given no statutory right of participation or access.

"The area of uncertainty comes when a procedural requirement:

---

1. Administrative Law Section of the ABA, The Administrative Procedure Act Project, 54 Admin. L. Rev. 1, 54–55 (2002).

(1) *does* entail a right on the part of a person like the plaintiff *individually* to obtain notice of, observe, participate in, or get information about an agency activity, but

(2) Congress has not been explicit as to whether the requirement was intended to be enforceable without regard to the plaintiff's having a particular underlying substantive interest, and the Supreme Court has not yet provided a definitive construction of the statute.

Examples include APA § 553 notice-and-comment requirements and the public-hearing requirements in numerous organic statutes.

"Although some lower courts have construed Lujan as automatically requiring an underlying substantive interest in all such cases, this interpretation is not inevitable. The procedural requirement sought to be enforced in Lujan was not such a right of individual participation or access, a distinction that seems important in light of the continued enforceability of individual (though widely shared) rights of notice, participation, and information such as those created by GITSA, FACA, FOIA and FECA. It may be that the availability of standing in such cases properly depends, in the first instance, on construing the particular statute or regulation that creates the procedural requirement. Specifically, the question would be whether this particular statute or regulation intended to confer a right of individual participation, access, etc., enforceable without regard to whether the agency action on the merits threatens a discrete substantive interest of the plaintiff."

(ii) "ARGUABLY WITHIN THE ZONE OF INTERESTS PROTECTED OR REGULATED BY THE LAW INVOKED"

As Data Processing redefined the law of regulatory standing, the would-be challenger of agency action must show not only personalized injury of a cognizable nature, but also that this injury is "arguably within the zone of interests protected or regulated" by the relevant organic statutes. Hence, the zone-of-interests test was apparently conceived as an additional hurdle for regulatory standing. However, the test was announced in a part of Justice Douglas' opinion that speaks approvingly of "the trend ... toward enlargement of the class of people who may protest administrative action," and for nearly a decade thereafter, the zone test played so insignificant a role in Supreme Court standing discussions that Professor K.C. Davis' influential Treatise took the position that it had been abandoned as a separate prerequisite.[1]

In 1981, the D.C. Circuit in CONTROL DATA CORP. v. BALDRIGE, 655 F.2d 283, 293 (D.C.Cir.), cert. denied, 454 U.S. 881, surveyed appellate cases and found "more variety than uniformity among the approaches to the zone test. Some courts, reacting strongly to the Supreme Court's vague formulation of the test, have expressed disagreement with the standard, clearly misapplied it, or virtually ignored it. Other courts, taking a more active approach, have attempted to refine the test into a workable standard." The

---

1. Kenneth C. Davis, Administrative Law of the Seventies § 22.02–11 at 509 (Supp. 1976).

panel then proceeded to issue an opinion that placed the D.C. Circuit prominently within the group of "more active" courts. It interpreted the zone test to require an affirmative showing, based on the language or legislative history of the relevant organic statute, that "the interest asserted by a party in the particular instance is one *intended by Congress* to be protected or regulated by the state under which suit is brought." (emphasis added)

The following year, a different panel followed Control Data to deny standing to a trade association of the copper industry seeking to challenge a Treasury Department decision reducing the amount of copper in pennies from 95% to 2.4%. COPPER & BRASS FABRICATORS COUNCIL, INC. V. DEP'T OF TREASURY, 679 F.2d 951 (D.C.Cir.1982). More noteworthy than the particular outcome was the separate opinion of then-Judge Ruth Bader Ginsburg: "I write separately (1) to emphasize the need for further enlightenment from Higher Authority as to the vitality and proper application of the 'zone' test, and (2) because I am uncertain whether the Control Data standard ... is fully consistent with the leading Supreme Court decisions announcing and applying the 'zone' test. ... [T]he Control Data standard 'requires some indicia ... that the litigant before the court *was intended* to be protected, benefitted or regulated by the statute under which suit is brought.' (Emphasis added). However, the 'zone' test announced by the Supreme Court requires only that the litigant be '*arguably* within the zone of interests to be protected or regulated by the statute or constitutional guarantee in question.' Data Processing (emphasis added). ...

"... Were redressable 'injury in fact' the sole test for standing, the copper fabricators would clear the first threshold to adjudication of their claim. How much more the 'zone' test demands and even the situations in which the test applies present questions left murky by the Supreme Court. Clarification from the Court would facilitate the expeditious, even-handed disposition of standing controversies by lower courts."

The Supreme Court took up the challenge, issuing four "zone" opinions in a decade. The following is the most recent; the earlier three are described in the case and in the Note material. Has the Court succeeded in clarifying the zone test?

National Credit Union Administration v. First National Bank & Trust Co.

Supreme Court of the United States, 1998.
522 U.S. 479.

■ JUSTICE THOMAS delivered the opinion of the Court, except as to footnote 6 in which JUSTICE SCALIA does not concur.

[Section 109 of the Federal Credit Union Act (FCUA), 12 U.S.C. § 1759, provides that "[f]ederal credit union membership shall be limited to groups having a common bond of occupation or association, or to groups within a well-defined neighborhood, community, or rural district." Until 1982, the National Credit Union Administration (NCUA) and its predecessors interpreted § 109 to require that the same common bond of occupation unite every member of an occupationally defined federal credit union. In 1982, however, NCUA reinterpreted § 109 to permit federal credit unions to be composed of multiple unrelated employer groups, each having its own common bond of occupation. As a result, AT & T Family Federal Credit Union (ATTF) requested (and received) NCUA permission to amend its charter to add as members employees of Lee Apparel Co., Coca–Cola Bottling Co., Ciba–Geigy Corp., Duke Power Co., and the American Tobacco Co. Five banks and the American Bankers Association (the Banks) challenged the charter approval, arguing that the revised interpretation of § 109 was impermissible. The district court dismissed the complaint, holding that the Banks were not within the zone of interests of § 109. The D.C. Circuit reversed. It agreed that "Congress did not, in 1934, intend to shield banks from competition from credit unions;" hence the Banks could not be said to be "intended beneficiaries" of § 109. However, the panel considered the Banks' interests sufficiently congruent with those of § 109's intended beneficiaries that they were "suitable challengers" to the chartering decision. Turning to the merits, it then held that NCUA's interpretation was impermissible. Other circuits had reached the opposite conclusion on both questions.]

Although our prior cases have not stated a clear rule for determining when a plaintiff's interest is "arguably within the zone of interests" to be protected by a statute, they nonetheless establish that we should not inquire whether there has been a congressional intent to benefit the would-be plaintiff. In Data Processing, the Office of the Comptroller of the Currency had interpreted the National Bank Act[ ] . . . to permit national banks to perform data processing services for other banks and bank customers. . . . In holding that the plaintiffs[, a data processing corporation and its trade association,] had standing, we stated that [§ 702] required only that "the interest sought to be protected by the complainant [be] arguably within the zone of interests to be protected or regulated by the statute . . . in question." In determining that the plaintiffs' interest met this requirement, we noted that although the relevant federal statutes . . . did not "in terms protect a specified group[,] . . . their general policy is apparent; and those whose interests are directly affected by a broad or narrow interpretation of the Acts are easily identifiable." "[A]s competitors of national banks which are engaging in data processing services," the plaintiffs were within that class of "aggrieved persons" entitled to judicial review of the Comptroller's interpretation. . . .

[In Clarke v. Securities Industry Ass'n, 479 U.S. 388 (1987),] a securities dealers trade association sued the Comptroller, this time for authorizing two national banks to offer discount brokerage services both at their branch offices and at other locations inside and outside their home States. The plaintiff contended that the Comptroller's action violated the McFadden Act, which permits national banks to carry on the business of banking only at authorized branches, and to open new branches only in their home States and only to the extent that state-chartered banks in that State can do so under state law.

We again held that the plaintiff had standing under the APA. Summarizing our prior holdings, we stated that although the "zone of interests" test "denies a right of review if the plaintiff's interests are ... marginally related to or inconsistent with the purposes implicit in the statute," id., "there need be no indication of congressional purpose to benefit the would-be plaintiff," id. We then determined that by limiting the ability of national banks to do business outside their home States, "Congress ha[d] shown a concern to keep national banks from gaining a monopoly control over credit and money." The interest of the securities dealers in preventing national banks from expanding into the securities markets directly implicated this concern because offering discount brokerage services would allow national banks "access to more money, in the form of credit balances, and enhanced opportunities to lend money, viz., for margin purchases." The case was thus analogous to Data Processing ... : "[There,] the question was what activities banks could engage in at all; here, the question is what activities banks can engage in without regard to the limitations imposed by state branching law."

Our prior cases, therefore, have consistently held that for a plaintiff's interests to be arguably within the "zone of interests" to be protected by a statute, there does not have to be an "indication of congressional purpose to benefit the would-be plaintiff." Clark, 479 U.S. at 399–400. The proper inquiry is simply "whether the interest sought to be protected by the complainant is *arguably* within the zone of interests to be protected ... by the statute." Data Processing, 397 U.S. at 153 (emphasis added). Hence in applying the "zone of interests" test, we do not ask whether, in enacting the statutory provision at issue, Congress specifically intended to benefit the plaintiff. Instead, we first discern the interests "arguably ... to be protected" by the statutory provision at issue; we then inquire whether the plaintiff's interests affected by the agency action in question are among them.

Section 109 provides that "[f]ederal credit union membership shall be limited to groups having a common bond of occupation or association, or to groups within a well-defined neighborhood, community, or rural district." By its express terms, § 109 limits membership in every federal credit union to members of definable "groups." Because federal credit unions may, as a general matter, offer banking services only to members, § 109 also restricts the markets that every federal credit union can serve. Although these markets need not be small, they unquestionably are limited. The link between § 109's regulation of federal credit union membership and its limitation on the markets that federal credit unions can serve is unmistakable. Thus, even if it cannot be said that Congress had the specific purpose of benefitting commercial banks, one of the interests "arguably ... to be protected" by § 109 is an interest in limiting the markets that federal credit unions can serve.[1] This interest is precisely the interest of respon-

---

1. [Ed. This is footnote 6 in the original opinion, which Justice Scalia refused to join.] The legislative history of § 109, upon which petitioners so heavily rely, supports this conclusion. Credit unions originated in mid–19th-century Europe as cooperative associations that were intended to provide credit to persons of small means; they were usually organized around some common theme, either geographic or associational. Following the European example, in the 1920's many States passed statutes authorizing the chartering of credit unions, and a number of

dents affected by the NCUA's interpretation of § 109. As competitors of federal credit unions, respondents certainly have an interest in limiting the markets that federal credit unions can serve, and the NCUA's interpretation has affected that interest by allowing federal credit unions to increase their customer base. . . .

Petitioners attempt to distinguish this action principally on the ground that there is no evidence that Congress, when it enacted the FCUA, was at all concerned with the competitive interests of commercial banks, or indeed at all concerned with competition. Indeed, petitioners contend that the very reason Congress passed the FCUA was that "[b]anks were simply not in the picture" as far as small borrowers were concerned, and thus Congress believed it necessary to create a new source of credit for people of modest means.

The difficulty with this argument is that similar arguments were made unsuccessfully in. . . . Data Processing . . . and Clarke. . . . In Data Processing, we considered it irrelevant that the statutes in question "d[id] not in terms protect a specified group," because "their general policy [was] apparent[,] and those whose interests [were] directly affected by a broad or narrow interpretation of [the statutes] [were] easily identifiable." . . . And in Clarke, we did not debate whether the Congress that enacted the McFadden Act was concerned about the competitive position of securities dealers. The provisions at issue in each of these cases, moreover, could be said merely to be safety-and-soundness provisions, enacted only to protect national banks and their depositors and without a concern for competitive effects. We nonetheless did not hesitate to find standing.

We therefore cannot accept petitioners' argument that respondents do not have standing because there is no evidence that the Congress that enacted § 109 was concerned with the competitive interests of commercial banks. To accept that argument, we would have to reformulate the "zone of interests" test to require that Congress have specifically intended to benefit a particular class of plaintiffs before a plaintiff from that class could have standing under the APA to sue. We have refused to do this in our prior cases, and we refuse to do so today.

those statutes contained provisions similar to § 109's common bond requirement.

During the Great Depression, in contrast to widespread bank failures at both the state and national level, there were no involuntary liquidations of state-chartered credit unions. See S.Rep. No. 555, 73d Cong., 2d Sess., 2 (1934). The cooperative nature of the institutions, which state-law common bond provisions reinforced, was believed to have contributed to this result. See Credit Unions: Hearing before a Subcommittee of the Senate Committee on Banking and Currency, 73d Cong., 1st Sess., 19–20, 26 (1933). A common bond provision was thus included in the District of Columbia Credit Union Act, which Congress passed in 1932; it was identical to the FCUA's common bond provision enacted

two years later. When Congress enacted the FCUA, sponsors of the legislation emphasized that the cooperative nature of credit unions allowed them to make credit available to persons who otherwise would not qualify for loans. See S.Rep. No. 555, supra, at 1, 3.

The legislative history thus confirms that § 109 was thought to reinforce the cooperative nature of credit unions, which in turn was believed to promote their safety and soundness and allow access to credit to persons otherwise unable to borrow. Because, by its very nature, a cooperative institution must serve a limited market, the legislative history of § 109 demonstrates that one of the interests "arguably . . . to be protected" by § 109 is an interest in limiting the markets that federal credit unions can serve.

Petitioners also mistakenly rely on our decision in Air Courier Conf. v. Postal Workers, 498 U.S. 517 (1991). In Air Courier, we held that the interest of Postal Service employees in maximizing employment opportunities was not within the "zone of interests" to be protected by the postal monopoly statutes, and hence those employees did not have standing under the APA to challenge a Postal Service regulation suspending its monopoly over certain international operations. We stated that the purposes of the statute were solely to increase the revenues of the Post Office and to ensure that postal services were provided in a manner consistent with the public interest. Only those interests, therefore, and not the interests of Postal Service employees in their employment, were "arguably within the zone of interests to be protected" by the statute. Cf. Lujan v. National Wildlife Federation (stating that an agency reporting company would not have prudential standing to challenge the agency's failure to comply with a statutory mandate to conduct hearings on the record). We further noted that although the statute in question regulated competition, the interests of the plaintiff employees had nothing to do with competition. See Air Courier, 498 U.S. at 528, n.5 (stating that "[e]mployees have generally been denied standing to enforce competition laws because they lack competitive and direct injury"). In this action, not only do respondents have "competitive and direct injury," but, as the foregoing discussion makes clear, they possess an interest that is "arguably ... to be protected" by § 109.

Respondents' interest in limiting the markets that credit unions can serve is "arguably within the zone of interests to be protected" by § 109. Under our precedents, it is irrelevant that in enacting the FCUA, Congress did not specifically intend to protect commercial banks. Although it is clear that respondents' objectives in this action are not eleemosynary in nature,[2] under our prior cases that, too, is beside the point.

[If you have already studied the materials on scope of review, you may recall that the balance of the Court's opinion holds that NCUA's current interpretation of § 109 is impermissible under the Chevron Step 1—i.e., "Congress has made it clear that the same common bond of occupation must unite each member of an occupationally defined federal credit union." P. 1034 above.]

The judgment of the Court of Appeals is therefore affirmed.

■ JUSTICE O'CONNOR, with whom Justice STEVENS, JUSTICE SOUTER, and JUSTICE BREYER join, dissenting.

In determining that respondents have standing under the zone-of-interests test ... the Court applies the test in a manner that is contrary to our decisions and, more importantly, that all but eviscerates the zone-of-interests requirement....

Under the Court's approach, every litigant who establishes injury in fact under Article III will automatically satisfy the zone-of-interests re-

---

2. The data processing companies ... and securities dealers that challenged the Comptroller's rulings in our prior cases certainly did not bring suit to advance the noble goal of maintaining the safety and soundness of national banks, or to promote the interests of national bank depositors.

quirement, rendering the zone-of-interests test ineffectual. See Air Courier, at 524, ("mistak[e]" to "conflat[e] the zone-of-interests test with injury in fact"). . . .

[T]he Court's conclusion that respondents "have" an interest in "limiting the [customer] markets that federal credit unions can serve" means little more than that respondents "have" an interest in enforcing the statute. The common bond requirement limits a credit union's membership, and hence its customer base, to certain groups, and in the Court's view, it is enough to establish standing that respondents "have" an interest in limiting the customers a credit union can serve. The Court's additional observation that respondents' interest has been "affected" by the NCUA's interpretation adds little to the analysis. . . . A party . . . will invariably have an interest in enforcing a statute when he can establish injury in fact caused by an alleged violation of that statute. . . .

Our decision in Air Courier . . . cannot be squared with the Court's analysis in this action. Air Courier involved a challenge by postal employees to a decision of the Postal Service suspending its statutory monopoly over certain international mailing services. The postal employees alleged a violation of the Private Express Statutes (PES)—the provisions that codify the Service's postal monopoly—citing as their injury in fact that competition from private mailing companies adversely affected their employment opportunities. We concluded that the postal employees did not have standing under the zone-of-interests test, because "the PES were not designed to protect postal employment or further postal job opportunities." [However,] the postal employees would have established standing under the Court's analysis in this action: The employees surely "had" an interest in enforcing the statutory monopoly, given that suspension of the monopoly caused injury to their employment opportunities.

In short, requiring simply that a litigant "have" an interest in enforcing the relevant statute amounts to hardly any test at all. That is why our decisions have required instead that a party "establish that *the injury he complains of* . . . falls within the 'zone of interests' sought to be protected by the statutory provision" in question. [Lujan] at 883 (emphasis added). In Air Courier, for instance, after noting that the asserted injury in fact was "an adverse effect on employment opportunities of postal workers," we characterized "[t]he question before us" as "whether the adverse effect on the employment opportunities of postal workers . . . is within the zone of interests encompassed by the PES."

Our decision last Term in Bennett v. Spear is in the same vein. There, the Fish and Wildlife Service, in an effort to preserve a particular species of fish, issued a biological opinion that had the effect of requiring the maintenance of minimum water levels in certain reservoirs. A group of ranchers and irrigation districts brought suit asserting a "competing interest in the water," alleging, in part, injury to their commercial interest in using the reservoirs for irrigation water. 520 U.S. at 160. The plaintiffs charged that the Service had violated a provision of the Endangered Species Act requiring "use [of] the best scientific and commercial data available." [W]e assessed whether the injury asserted by the plaintiffs fell within the zone of interests protected by the "best data" provision, and concluded that the economic interests of parties adversely affected by erroneous biological opinions are within the zone of interests protected by that statute. Id. at 176–177 (observing that one purpose of the "best data" provision "is to avoid needless economic dislocation produced by agency officials zealously but unintelligently pursuing their environmental objectives"). . . .

. . . Clarke v. Securities Industry Ass'n . . . involved provisions of the McFadden Act allowing a national bank to establish branch offices only in its home State, and then only to the extent that banks of the home State were permitted to have branches under state law. The statute defined a "branch" office essentially as one that offered core banking services. The Comptroller allowed two banks to establish discount brokerage offices at locations outside the allowable branching area, on the rationale that brokerage services did not constitute core banking services and that the offices therefore were not "branch" offices. Representatives of the securities industry challenged the Comptroller's action, alleging a violation of the statutory branching limitations. . . . [W]e found that . . . Congress had "arguably legislated against . . . competition" through those provisions. Specifically, Congress demonstrated "a concern to keep national banks from gaining a monopoly control over credit and money through unlimited branching." Id.; see also id. at 402 (Stevens, J., concurring in part and concurring in judgment) ("The general policy against branching was based in part on a concern about the national banks' potential for becoming massive financial institutions that would establish monopolies on financial services"). The Court makes no analogous finding in this action that Congress, through the common bond provision, sought to prevent credit unions from gaining "monopoly control" over the customers of banking services.

It is true, as the Court emphasizes repeatedly, that we did not require in this line of decisions that the statute at issue was designed to benefit the particular party bringing suit. . . . Respondents thus need not establish that the common bond provision was enacted specifically to benefit commercial banks, any more than they must show that the provision was intended to benefit Lexington State Bank, Piedmont State Bank, or any of the particular banks that filed this suit.

In each of the competitor standing cases, though, we found that Congress had enacted an "anti-competition limitation," see Bennett, 520 U.S. at 176 (discussing Data Processing), or, alternatively, that Congress had "legislated against . . . competition," see Clarke, and accordingly, that the plaintiff-competitor's "commercial interest was sought to be protected by the anti-competition limitation" at issue, Bennett. . . . The Court fails to undertake that analysis here.

Applying the proper zone-of-interests inquiry to this action, I would find that competitive injury to respondents' commercial interests does not arguably fall within the zone of interests sought to be protected by the common bond provision. . . . The [statutory] language suggests that the common bond requirement is an internal organizational principle concerned primarily with defining membership in a way that secures a financially sound organization. There is no indication in the text of the provision or in the surrounding language that the membership limitation was even arguably designed to protect the commercial interests of competitors. . . .

The operation of the common bond provision does not likewise denote a congressional desire to legislate against competition. First, the common bond requirement does not purport to restrict credit unions from becoming large, nationwide organizations, as might be expected if the provision embodied a congressional concern with the competitive consequences of credit union growth.

More tellingly, although the common bond provision applies to all credit unions, the restriction operates against credit unions individually: The common bond requirement speaks only to whether a particular credit union's membership can include a given group of customers, not to whether credit unions in general can serve that group. . . . In this sense, the common bond requirement does not limit credit unions collectively from serving any customers, nor does it bar any customers from being served by credit unions.

In Data Processing . . . and Clarke, by contrast, the statutes operated against national banks generally, prohibiting all banks from competing in a particular market: Banks in general were barred from providing a specific type of service (Data Processing . . .), or from providing services at a particular location (Clarke). . . .

The circumstances surrounding the enactment of the FCUA also indicate that Congress did not intend to legislate against competition through the common bond provision. . . . The requirement of a common bond was . . . meant to ensure that each credit union remains a cooperative institution that is economically stable and responsive to its members' needs. As a principle of internal governance designed to secure the viability of individual credit unions in the interests of the membership, the common bond provision was in no way designed to impose a restriction on all credit unions in the interests of institutions that might one day become competitors. Indeed, the very notion seems anomalous, because Congress' general purpose was to encourage the proliferation of credit unions, which were expected to provide service to those would-be customers that banks disdained. [internal quotes omitted]

That the common bond requirement would later come to be viewed by competitors as a useful tool for curbing a credit union's membership should not affect the zone-of-interests inquiry. The pertinent question under the zone-of-interests test is whether Congress intended to protect certain interests through a particular provision, not whether, irrespective of congressional intent, a provision may have the effect of protecting those interests. See Clarke, 479 U.S. at 394 (the "matter [is] basically one of interpreting congressional intent"). . . .

. . . The zone-of-interests test "seeks to exclude those plaintiffs whose suits are more likely to frustrate than to further statutory objectives," Clarke, 479 U.S. at 397, n.12, and one can readily envision circumstances in which the interests of competitors, who have the incentive to suppress credit union expansion in all circumstances, would be at odds with the statute's general aim of supporting the growth of credit unions that are cohesive and hence financially stable.

... [T]he plaintiff's injury is at best "marginally related" to the interests sought to be protected by the statute, Clarke, 479 U.S. at 399, and the most that can be said is that the provision has the incidental effect of benefitting the plaintiffs. That was not enough to establish standing in Air Courier, and it should not suffice here....

NOTES

(1) *Further Enlightenment?* Based on the four opinions from Clarke through NCUA, if you were the law clerk for a court of appeals judge, what would you tell your judge the zone-of-interests test means? Here is some information not found in the various NCUA opinions:

Clarke explicitly cites the D.C. Circuit's Control Data decision with disapproval; Justices Stevens and O'Connor and Chief Justice Rehnquist refused to join what they characterized as a "wholly unnecessary exegesis" on the zone test, while Justice Scalia did not participate in the case at all. Chief Justice Rehnquist wrote the Court's opinion in Air Courier Conference, which is the first case in which the Court used the zone test to *deny* standing. The opinion reasons, in part, that in passing the relevant postal statutes, Congress had not intended to benefit employees of the Postal Service. Justices Stevens, Marshall and Brennan refused to join this opinion. Justice Scalia wrote the Court's opinion in Bennett. He agreed that the interests of the plaintiff—an agricultural firm landowner—were clearly not aligned with the "species preservation" purpose of the Endangered Species Act as a whole. However, no one dissented from the conclusion that the landowner was within the zone of interests of the particular statutory provision the agency was said to have violated: a requirement to assess species damage using "the best scientific and commercial data available." This provision was interpreted as intended "to avoid needless economic dislocation produced by agency officials zealously but unintelligently pursuing their environmental objectives." Can you reconcile Justice Scalia, Justice Kennedy and Chief Justice Rehnquist joining the narrow majorities in both Air Couriers and NCUA?

(2) *Relationship Between the "Zone" Test and Beneficiary Standing Generally.* Historically, standing by disappointed competitors of regulatory entities was granted on the theory of private attorney general: Such parties, whose economic harm gave them both the requisite Article III injury and an incentive to litigate vigorously, would then (according to the theory) "litigate the issues of the public interest." See p. 1132 above. If contemporary justiciability rules provide access for the intended beneficiaries of regulation to speak for themselves, do actions by incidental beneficiaries do more than increase costs and impose delay? On the other hand, if justiciability rules are shifting to disfavor beneficiary suits vis-a-vis suits by regulated entities, see p. 1148 above, should the zone test be relaxed?

(3) *The Prudential Nature of the Zone Test.* Whatever the zone test ultimately means, Congress can dispense with it. Two sorts of statutory

standing provisions are typically understood as expressing Congressional intent to confer standing to the full extent Article III permits.

The first type are statutes authorizing suit by any "person aggrieved." Those familiar with the history of standing recognize the provenance of such language as the pathbreaking expansion of standing in the Federal Communications Act, p. 1132 above.[1] The second type are statutes that attempt to confer true citizen-suit standing. Bennett v. Spear, 520 U.S. 154 (1997), involved two causes of action: one under the APA; the other under the Endangered Species Act. The language about the zone test quoted in NCUA referred to standing for the first cause of action. The standing provision of the ESA, however, was the citizen-suit provision at issue in Lujan. Justice Scalia concluded that the intent to grant broad standing manifested in this provision, even if insufficient under Lujan to accomplish everything Congress desired, was nonetheless enough to obviate the zone test. After Lujan, shouldn't this construction be given to any other true citizen-suit provision?[2]

c.   TRACEABILITY AND REDRESSABILITY

Allen v. Wright

Supreme Court of the United States, 1984.
468 U.S. 737.

(Reprinted p. 1118 above)

NOTES

(1) The causation portion of Allen was prefigured in SIMON V. EASTERN KENTUCKY WELFARE RIGHTS ORGANIZATION, 426 U.S. 26 (1976) ("EKWRO"). The IRS issued a revenue ruling deleting an existing requirement that a hospital must provide free services to indigent persons in order to qualify for charitable, tax-exempt status. Low-income persons and organizations representing them sued, arguing that the new interpretation violated the Internal Revenue Code. Justice Powell, for the five-member majority, held that the suit must be dismissed for lack of standing: "The obvious interest of all respondents, to which they claim actual injury, is that of access to hospital services. In one sense, of course, they have suffered injury to that interest. The complaint alleges specific occasions on which each of the

---

1. See FEC v. Akins, 524 U.S. 11, 19 (1998); see also Department of Comm. v. House of Representatives, 525 U.S. 316, 328 (1999) (phrase means "Congress has eliminated any prudential concerns").

2. An occasional lower court has suggested that jus tertii principles might limit standing even when the zone test has been dispensed with. This is a problematic approach, at least if the third parties whose "rights" the plaintiff seeks to litigate are those of intended beneficiaries of the regulatory program. The zone test serves much the same function as jus tertii doctrine. If the statutory language appears designed to confer broad standing—by using citizen-suit language or the historical "aggrieved person" form—then it is reasonable to assume an intent to permit any plaintiff satisfying the Article III minima to litigate an administrative failure to protect the interests of the regulatory beneficiaries.

individual respondents sought but was denied hospital services solely due to his indigency, and in at least some of the cases it is clear that the needed treatment was unavailable, as a practical matter, anywhere else. ... But injury at the hands of a hospital is insufficient by itself to establish a case or controversy in the context of this suit, for no hospital is a defendant. The only defendants are officials of the Department of the Treasury, and the only claims of illegal action respondents desire the courts to adjudicate are charged to those officials. Although the law of standing has been greatly changed in recent years, ... the 'case or controversy' limitation of Art. III still requires that a federal court act only to redress injury that fairly can be traced to the challenged action of the defendant, and not injury that results from the independent action of some third party not before the court.

"The complaint here alleged only that petitioners, by the adoption of Revenue Ruling 69–545, had 'encouraged' hospitals to deny services to indigents.[1] The implicit corollary of this allegation is that a grant of respondents' requested relief, resulting in a requirement that all hospitals serve indigents as a condition to favorable tax treatment, would 'discourage' hospitals from denying their services to respondents. But it ... is purely speculative whether the denials of service specified in the complaint fairly can be traced to petitioners' 'encouragement' or instead result from decisions made by the hospitals without regard to the tax implications.

"It is equally speculative whether the desired exercise of the court's remedial powers in this suit would result in the availability to respondents of such services. So far as the complaint sheds light, it is just as plausible that the hospitals to which respondents may apply for service would elect to forgo favorable tax treatment to avoid the undetermined financial drain of an increase in the level of uncompensated services. It is true that the individual respondents have alleged, upon information and belief, that the hospitals that denied them service receive substantial donations deductible by the donors. This allegation could support an inference that these hospitals, or some of them, are so financially dependent upon the favorable tax treatment afforded charitable organizations that they would admit respondents if a court required such admission as a condition to receipt of that treatment. But this inference is speculative at best. ...

"Prior decisions of this Court establish that unadorned speculation will not suffice to invoke the federal judicial power. In Linda R. S. v. Richard D., the mother of an illegitimate child averred that state-court interpretation of a criminal child support statute as applying only to fathers of legitimate children violated the Equal Protection Clause of the Fourteenth Amendment. She sought an injunction requiring the district attorney to enforce the statute against the father of her child. We held that the mother

---

1. ... [We note] that it is entirely speculative whether even the earlier Ruling would have assured the medical care they desire. It required a hospital to provide care for the indigent only "to the extent of its financial ability." ... Thus a hospital could not maintain ... a general policy of refusing care to all patients unable to pay. But the number of such patients accepted, and whether any particular applicant would be admitted, would depend upon the financial ability of the hospital to which admittance was sought.

lacked standing, because she had 'made no showing that her failure to secure support payments results from the nonenforcement, as to her child's father, of [the statute].' 410 U.S. 614, 618 (1973). The prospect that the requested prosecution in fact would result in the payment of child support instead of jailing the father was 'only speculative.' Similarly, last Term in Warth v. Seldin, we held that low-income persons seeking the invalidation of a town's restrictive zoning ordinance lacked standing because they had failed to show that the alleged injury, inability to obtain adequate housing within their means, was fairly attributable to the challenged ordinance instead of to other factors. In language directly applicable to this litigation, we there noted that plaintiffs relied 'on little more than the remote possibility, unsubstantiated by allegations of fact, that their situation might have been better had [defendants] acted otherwise, and might improve were the court to afford relief.' 422 U.S. 490, 507 (1975).

"The principle of Linda R. S. and Warth controls this case. As stated in Warth, that principle is that indirectness of injury, while not necessarily fatal to standing, 'may make it substantially more difficult to meet the minimum requirement of Art. III: to establish that, in fact, the asserted injury was the consequence of the defendants' actions, or that prospective relief will remove the harm.' Respondents have failed to carry this burden. Speculative inferences are necessary to connect their injury to the challenged actions of petitioners. Moreover, the complaint suggests no substantial likelihood that victory in this suit would result in respondents' receiving the hospital treatment they desire. A federal court, properly cognizant of the Art. III limitation upon its jurisdiction, must require more than respondents have shown before proceeding to the merits."

Justice Stevens did not participate. Justice Stewart concurred, adding that he "cannot now imagine a case, at least outside the First Amendment area, where a person whose own tax liability was not affected ever could have standing to litigate the federal tax liability of someone else." Justice Brennan, joined by Justice Marshall (who had authored the opinion in Linda R.S.), concurred in the judgment on grounds that ambiguities in the scope of the new Revenue Ruling made premature the issue whether the IRS had illegally encouraged *all* nonprofit hospitals to withdraw indigent services. Assuming the majority's interpretation of the Ruling, however, he disputed the Court's standing analysis: "First, the Court's treatment of the injury-in-fact standing requirement is simply unsupportable in the context of this case. The wrong of which respondents complain is that the disputed Ruling gives erroneous economic signals to nonprofit hospitals whose subsequent responses affect respondents; they claim the IRS is offering the economic inducement of tax-exempt status to such hospitals under terms illegal under the Internal Revenue Code. Respondents' claim is not, and by its very nature could not be, that they have been and will be illegally denied the provision of indigent medical services by the hospitals. Rather, if respondents have a claim cognizable under the law, it is that the Internal Revenue Code requires the Government to offer economic inducements to the relevant hospitals only under conditions which are likely to benefit respondents. The relevant injury in light of this claim is, then, injury to this beneficial interest as respondents alleged, injury to their 'opportunity and ability' to receive medical services. . . .

"... [T]he most disturbing aspect of today's opinion is the Court's insistence on resting its decision regarding standing squarely on the irreducible Art. III minimum of injury in fact, thereby effectively placing its holding beyond congressional power to rectify. Thus, any time Congress chooses to legislate in favor of certain interests by setting up a scheme of incentives for third parties, judicial review of administrative action that allegedly frustrates the congressionally intended objective will be denied, because any complainant will be required to make an almost impossible showing. ...

"In modern-day society, dominated by complex legislative programs and large-scale governmental involvement in the everyday lives of all of us, judicial review of administrative action is essential both for protection of individuals illegally harmed by that action and to ensure that the attainment of congressionally mandated goals is not frustrated by illegal action. ..."

(2) *The Difference Between "Traceability" and "Redressability."* Traceability and redressability are conceptually distinct—but, as a practical matter, are they resolved in tandem? Most of the time, yes. There is, however, an important kind of case in which they operate separately. If the relevant statutes or other law limit the court's remedial options, then even though the injury is traceable to the defendant's actions, it may be incapable of redress through any of the available remedies.

In STEEL CO. v. CITIZENS FOR A BETTER ENVIRONMENT, 523 U.S. 83 (1998), a plaintiff who was injured by the defendant's seven-year failure to file reports required by the Emergency Planning & Community Right-to-Know Act[2] was denied standing because the wrongdoing had ceased before suit was filed, the plaintiff had failed to demonstrate likelihood of recurrence, and the only available statutory remedies were prospective injunctive relief and civil penalties payable to the government. Scalia, J., for the Court: "If respondent had alleged a continuing violation or the imminence of a future violation, the injunctive relief requested would remedy that alleged harm. But there is no such allegation here—and on the facts of the case, there seems no basis for it. Nothing supports the requested injunctive relief except respondent's generalized interest in deterrence, which is insufficient for purposes of Article III.

"Justice Stevens thinks it is enough that respondent will be gratified by seeing petitioner punished for its infractions and that the punishment will deter the risk of future harm. If that were so, our holdings in Linda R.S. v. Richard D. and [EKWRO] are inexplicable. Obviously, such a principle would make the redressability requirement vanish. By the mere bringing of his suit, every plaintiff demonstrates his belief that a favorable judgment will make him happier. But although a suitor may derive great comfort and joy from the fact that the United States Treasury is not cheated, that a wrongdoer gets his just deserts, or that the nation's laws

---

2. EPCRA is designed "to inform the public about the presence of hazardous and toxic chemicals, and to provide for emergency response in the event of health-threatening release," and requires users of specified hazardous chemicals to make annual public reports about the nature and quantity of the chemicals they use, as well as to provide information on their disposal methods.

are faithfully enforced, that psychic satisfaction is not an acceptable Article III remedy because it does not redress a cognizable Article III injury. See, e.g., Allen v. Wright."

Justice Stevens (joined on this point by Justices Ginsburg and Souter) concurred in the judgment after concluding that the EPCRA was not intended to authorize citizen suits for wholly past violations. More broadly, he took issue with the majority's redressability analysis: " 'Redressability,' of course, does not appear anywhere in the text of the Constitution. Instead, it is a judicial creation of the past 25 years, see [EKWRO]; Linda R.S. v. Richard D.—a judicial interpretation of the 'Case' requirement of Article III. . . .

"When one private party is injured by another, the injury can be redressed in at least two ways: by awarding compensatory damages or by imposing a sanction on the wrongdoer that will minimize the risk that the harm-causing conduct will be repeated. Thus, in some cases a tort is redressed by an award of punitive damages; even when such damages are payable to the sovereign, they provide a form of redress for the individual as well.

"History supports the proposition that punishment or deterrence can redress an injury. In past centuries in England, in the American colonies, and in the United States, private persons regularly prosecuted criminal cases. The interest in punishing the defendant and deterring violations of law by the defendant and others was sufficient to support the 'standing' of the private prosecutor even if the only remedy was the sentencing of the defendant to jail or to the gallows. Given this history, the Framers of Article III surely would have considered such proceedings to be 'Cases' that would 'redress' an injury even though the party bringing suit did not receive any monetary compensation. . . ."

NOTES ON THE RELATIONSHIP BETWEEN DEFINING THE INJURY AND FINDING CAUSATION

(1) *What's in a Name? A Rose by Any Other Name* . . . GENE R. NICHOL, JR., RETHINKING STANDING, 72 Calif.L.Rev. 68, 79–81 (1984): "For more than a decade, standing doctrine has required that the injury asserted by the plaintiff be likely to be redressed by a favorable decision. The nature of the interplay between redressability and injury, however, has apparently escaped the Burger Court.

"[Linda R.S., Warth v. Seldin, and EKWRO] demonstrate the ease with which the Court, by toying with the scope of the injury at issue, can raise or lower the redressability hurdle. In Linda R.S., Warth, and [EKWRO], the Court overstated the injuries that the plaintiffs sought to have redressed. In Linda R.S., the Court refused jurisdiction because even a decree requiring nondiscriminatory enforcement would not ensure support. But why was obtaining the payment of child support considered the relevant injury? The mother in Linda R.S. sought to be treated on an equal basis with married mothers. Her injury—denial of equal treatment—would undoubtedly have been redressed by an affirmative decree requiring enforcement of child support obligations against unmarried fathers. Similarly, the Warth plaintiffs sought not only to obtain housing in Penfield. They also asserted their interest in equal participation in a housing market not distorted by unconstitutional zoning practices. The denial of a meaningful opportunity to persuade others to construct low cost housing in Penfield, for example, would have been redressed by a determination that the ordinance was unconstitutional. The indigents in [EKWRO] had no objection to receiving hospital access, but the interest they asserted would more appropriately be described as having hospital decisions concerning the services offered to indigents accurately reflect an earlier incentive structure implicitly approved by the Congress. Again, that injury would have been redressed by the claim presented.

"... Equal protection cases provide the clearest examples of the Court's inability to maintain a principled line. In Regents of the University of California v. Bakke, [438 U.S. 265 (1978),] a substantial question arose concerning Alan Bakke's ability to prove that he would have been admitted to medical school absent the contested affirmative action program. The Court skirted the standing issue, however, by declaring that the university's 'decision not to permit Bakke to compete for all 100 places' was the relevant injury. That harm would, of course, be redressed by a favorable ruling. If, however, the Warth plaintiffs could redress their injuries only by showing that they would actually obtain housing, and if the mother in Linda R.S. was required to show that she would actually receive support payments, Bakke should have been made to prove that he would have gotten into medical school. The interest in equal opportunity was insufficient to provide standing in Linda R.S. and Warth, but it eventually got Alan Bakke into medical school."

See also NORTHEASTERN FLA. CHAPTER OF ASSOC. GEN. CONTRACTORS V. JACKSONVILLE, 508 U.S. 656 (1993), which permitted an association of contractors to challenge the city's minority set-aside program. The city challenged the organization's standing because it could not prove that its members would have won the contracts in the absence of the set-aside provision. The Court responded: "When the government erects a barrier that makes it more difficult for members of one group to obtain a benefit than it is for members of another group, a member of the former group seeking to challenge the barrier need not allege that he would have obtained the benefit but for the barrier in order to establish standing." The redressable injury, the Court continued, was the imposition of the barrier, not the inability to obtain the benefit. The Court conceded that there was "undoubtedly some tension" between this approach and earlier cases, including Warth v. Seldin.

(2) *The High Stakes of the Injury–Causation Connection for Regulatory Standing.* PATRICIA M. WALD, THE D.C. CIRCUIT: HERE AND NOW, 55 Geo.Wash. L.Rev. 718, 721–24 (1987): "[T]he part of standing in greatest turmoil in the circuit today is the requirement of causation between the action complained of and the purported injury to the plaintiff. Regulation typically involves a complex relationship between administrative agencies and affected industries; an injury to a third party is often caused by—and can be remedied only by—the cooperation of both the agency and the industry. Increasingly, we see the agency argue that what it does or does not do is

irrelevant, because even if the agency had acted correctly, the third party would still have done what it did, causing the plaintiff's injury. This sounds a great deal like the old proximate cause argument in tort law: a defendant seeks to be excused from its negligence because another party intervened in the chain of events and became the actor most immediately responsible for the plaintiff's injury. The crucial difference between this argument in standard tort law and modern standing doctrine is that in the first case proximate cause is used to allocate ultimate financial responsibility among the various blameworthy parties. In standing law, however, it is used at the opening gun of the litigation to prevent the merits of the controversy from ever being heard.

"Government regulation in modern life is a very complex matrix—it is hard to pin down the cause and effect relationship of a myriad of relevant interacting factors on the regulated entities' behavior. One can make reasonable predictions but hardly ever offer precise proof of how one actor will react to the other. Standing inquiries about causation can deteriorate into very refined judgments about what real world actors will or will not do under varied circumstances, judgments that often must be made on the basis of judges' intuitive reactions, economic dogma, or logical tautology without benefit of legislative, administrative, or even evidentiary inquiry.

"Sometimes the plaintiff can produce the required 'but for' evidence in these tripartite standing cases. . . . But in other cases the court was not willing to assume that if the government had done its job differently, the third party would have responded so as to obviate the plaintiff's injury. In Center for Auto Safety v. NHTSA (CAFE I), 793 F.2d 1322 (D.C.Cir.1986), the membership association complained that the agency's failure to promulgate stringent fuel efficiency regulations deprived members of the opportunity to purchase fuel efficient cars. Standing was upheld by a divided panel. Later, in the same year, another panel relied upon CAFE I to justify standing in a related challenge by the same association to EPA's fuel efficiency testing procedures. In Center for Auto Safety v. Thomas (CAFE II), 806 F.2d 1071 (D.C.Cir.1986), Judge Bork, while agreeing that the CAFE I precedent applied, indicated that he, like Justice Scalia, who had dissented in the earlier case, thought the causation and redressability prongs of the standing test had not been met, i.e., the plaintiff had failed 'to identify any particular types of fuel-efficient light truck or any particular fuel-saving model options that their members desire but are or will be unable to purchase,' and, in any case, the industry could choose to pay fines instead of complying with any new regulations. The crucial rationale supporting the panel's majority finding of causation in CAFE I was that *Congress itself* had legislated the requisite causation and redressability by determining that the automobile industry would comply with more stringent fuel efficiency requirements instead of paying fines and so produce more fuel efficient cars.

"The court voted to en banc CAFE II; we will settle, at least temporarily, the interesting separation of powers question of whether a *congressional* determination that certain regulations will affect the behavior of an industry in a certain way is enough to satisfy the causation and redressability aspects of standing or whether the court may insist on conducting its own independent causation inquiry in each case.[1]

"There is no sidestepping the enormous amount of judgment involved when courts make cause-and-effect predictions for standing purposes about future actions of national industries faced with government regulations. The verbal formulas are there but few would try to reconcile their application by different courts to different sets of circumstances. Inevitably, the judgment that in particular cases, causation is too remote or is direct enough to allow standing reflects the court's feelings about the appropriate domain of the executive, the legislature, and the courts. Judges inclined to be highly deferential to the executive branch in its regulatory activities and cautious about judicial intervention will more likely take a hard line on standing issues. Judges who believe that Congress has the right to legislate on such issues as what is a reasonable nexus between regulation and statutory goals, and to require that challenges to legislation be rendered promptly, may more readily vote to confer standing on organizational plaintiffs. In the D.C. Circuit, the standing doctrine has indeed become a surrogate for profound differences about larger separation of powers questions. At the same time our skirmishes have immense and immediate practical implications for access to the courts to challenge major administrative actions."

(3) *The Theory Behind Defining the Injury as Decreased Probability of an Outcome Favorable to the Plaintiff.* FRANK H. EASTERBROOK, FOREWORD: THE COURT AND THE ECONOMIC SYSTEM, 98 Harv.L.Rev. 4, 40–41 (1984): "The [Allen] Court concludes that the plaintiffs, black parents and children in public schools who disclaimed interest in attending the bigoted private schools, were unaffected by the IRS's policies. Some earlier cases can be read to say that private parties are not injured in fact by prosecutorial policies. [citing Linda R.S.] But it is hard to take seriously the claim that enforcement of legal rules does not affect bystanders. The rule against murder is designed to prevent other people from slaying me, as well as others, and I suffer an injury if the police announce that they will no longer enforce that rule in my neighborhood. I will keep off the streets, hire guards, pay for locks, and still face an increased chance of being killed. Only a judge who secretly believes that the law does not influence behavior would find no injury in fact. Someone who feeds me a poison that increases my chances of dying next year has injured me, even if I am neither dead nor sure to die, and I may recover damages from him. The reduction in my expected life span is a real injury. This is the basis of recovery in many mass tort cases. The same reasoning establishes injury in fact when the government declines to enforce a law that was designed in part for my benefit. The court cannot know that any identified plaintiff will be better off if the law is enforced, but the law is about probabilities, not certainties.

---

1. [Ed.] Judge Wald's expectation that the issue would be resolved by the en banc court proved incorrect. See Center for Auto Safety v. Thomas, 847 F.2d 843, order vacated on limited rehearing, 856 F.2d 1557 (D.C.Cir.1988). Five judges (including Ruth Bader Ginsburg) who had been appointed by presidents before Ronald Reagan held that petitioners had standing; five judges, all Reagan or Bush appointees, held that they did not.

A plaintiff need not show a sure gain from winning in order to prove that some probability of gain is better than none."

For an effort to apply this theory to causation in administrative standing generally, see The Administrative Procedure Act Project, 54 Admin. L. Rev. 1, 58–59 (2002).

(4) *Congressional Power to Affect Conclusions of Traceability and Redressability.* Just as statutes can define new cognizable injuries, so they can "articulate chains of causation that will give rise to a case or controversy where none existed before." Lujan, 504 U.S. at 580 (Kennedy, J., concurring in part and in the judgment). Some early lower court cases had refused to defer to legislative determinations about causation, but the Supreme Court recently resolved a difficult redressability question by looking in part to Congressional findings that, the Court said, "warrant[] judicial attention and respect." FRIENDS OF THE EARTH V. LAIDLAW ENVTL. SERV., INC., 528 U.S. 167, 185 (2000), continued the inquiry (begun in Steel Company v. Citizens for A Better Environment, p. 1175 above) into private plaintiffs' standing to seek regulatory penalties payable to the government. At the time suit was filed, Laidlaw was (allegedly) repeatedly discharging more mercury into the water than allowed by its discharge permit. The plaintiffs sought declaratory and injunctive relief against future excessive discharges, as well as civil penalties (payable to the United States) for past violations. The district court assessed civil penalties, but denied injunctive relief on grounds that Laidlaw had achieved substantial compliance during the lawsuit. The plaintiffs appealed only the adequacy of the penalty order. The court of appeals reasoned that their failure to appeal the denial of injunctive relief removed their personal stake in the outcome. The Supreme Court disagreed.

Ginsburg, J., for the seven-member majority: "Laidlaw is right to insist that a plaintiff must demonstrate standing separately for each form of relief sought. See, e.g., Los Angeles v. Lyons, 461 U.S. [95, 109 (1983)](notwithstanding the fact that plaintiff had standing to pursue damages, he lacked standing to pursue injunctive relief). But it is wrong to maintain that citizen plaintiffs facing ongoing violations never have standing to seek civil penalties.

"We have recognized on numerous occasions that all civil penalties have some deterrent effect. [internal quotes omitted.] More specifically, Congress has found that civil penalties in Clean Water Act cases do more than promote immediate compliance by limiting the defendant's economic incentive to delay its attainment of permit limits; they also deter future violations. This congressional determination warrants judicial attention and respect. 'The legislative history of the Act reveals that Congress wanted the district court to consider the need for retribution and deterrence, in addition to restitution, when it imposed civil penalties. ... [The district court may] seek to deter future violations by basing the penalty on its economic impact.' Tull v. United States, 481 U.S. 412, 422–423 (1987).

"It can scarcely be doubted that, for a plaintiff who is injured or faces the threat of future injury due to illegal conduct ongoing at the time of suit, a sanction that effectively abates that conduct and prevents its recurrence provides a form of redress. Civil penalties can fit that description. To the extent that they encourage defendants to discontinue current violations and deter them from committing future ones, they afford redress to citizen plaintiffs who are injured or threatened with injury as a consequence of ongoing unlawful conduct.

"... [I]t is reasonable for Congress to conclude that an actual award of civil penalties does in fact bring with it a significant quantum of deterrence over and above what is achieved by the mere prospect of such penalties. A would-be polluter may or may not be dissuaded by the existence of a remedy on the books, but a defendant once hit in its pocketbook will surely think twice before polluting again.

"We recognize that there may be a point at which the deterrent effect of a claim for civil penalties becomes so insubstantial or so remote that it cannot support citizen standing. The fact that this vanishing point is not easy to ascertain does not detract from the deterrent power of such penalties in the ordinary case. Justice Frankfurter's observations for the Court, made in a different context nearly 60 years ago, hold true here as well:

> How to effectuate policy—the adaptation of means to legitimately sought ends—is one of the most intractable of legislative problems. Whether proscribed conduct is to be deterred by qui tam action or triple damages or injunction, or by criminal prosecution, or merely by defense to actions in contract, or by some, or all, of these remedies in combination, is a matter within the legislature's range of choice. Judgment on the deterrent effect of the various weapons in the armory of the law can lay little claim to scientific basis.

Tigner v. Texas, 310 U.S. 141, 148 (1940). What of Steel Company? "We specifically noted in that case that there was no allegation in the complaint of any continuing or imminent violation, and that no basis for such an allegation appeared to exist. ... Steel Co. held that private plaintiffs, unlike the Federal Government, may not sue to assess penalties for wholly past violations, but our decision in that case did not reach the issue of standing to seek penalties for violations that are ongoing at the time of the complaint and that could continue into the future if undeterred." The case was remanded for the court of appeals to consider, inter alia, the effect of the intervening closing of Laidlaw's plant. Justice Kennedy concurred but noted his reservations about the "[d]ifficult and fundamental questions ... raised when we ask whether exactions of public fines by private litigants, and the delegation of Executive power which might be inferable from the authorization, are permissible in view of the responsibilities committed to the Executive by Article II of the Constitution of the United States." However, he considered these issues insufficiently raised and briefed in the case. Justice Scalia, joined by Justice Thomas, dissented.

SECTION 3. REVIEWABILITY: AGENCY ACTIONS SUBJECT TO JUDICIAL SCRUTINY

When the organic statute does not expressly authorize judicial review—either being completely silent on the subject or speaking of review with respect to some, but not all, types of administrative action—the question arises whether the court is nonetheless empowered to scrutinize the agency's behavior. Answering this question almost invariably begins with the framework established by the following case, which (like the Data Processing opinion on standing three years later, p. 1129 above) substantially altered existing concepts of justiciability and laid the groundwork for the contemporary era of judicial review.

Abbott Laboratories v. Gardner

Supreme Court of the United States, 1967.
387 U.S. 136.

■ JUSTICE HARLAN delivered the opinion of the Court.

In 1962 Congress amended the Federal Food, Drug, and Cosmetic Act to require manufacturers of prescription drugs to print the "established name" of the drug "prominently and in type at least half as large as that used thereon for any proprietary name or designation for such drug," on labels and other printed material. The "established name" is one designated by the Secretary of Health, Education, and Welfare[1] ...; the "proprietary name" is usually a trade name under which a particular drug is marketed. The underlying purpose of the 1962 amendment was to bring to the attention of doctors and patients the fact that many of the drugs sold under familiar trade names are actually identical to drugs sold under their "established" or less familiar trade names at significantly lower prices. The Commissioner of Food and Drugs, exercising authority delegated to him by the Secretary, published proposed regulations designed to implement the statute. After inviting and considering comments submitted by interested parties the Commissioner promulgated the following regulation for the "efficient enforcement" of the Act:

> If the label or labeling of a prescription drug bears a proprietary name or designation for the drug or any ingredient thereof, the established name, if such there be, corresponding to such proprietary name or designation, shall accompany each appearance of such proprietary name or designation.

A similar rule was made applicable to advertisements for prescription drugs.

The present action was brought by a group of 37 individual drug manufacturers and by the Pharmaceutical Manufacturers Association, ... which includes manufacturers of more than 90% of the Nation's supply of prescription drugs. They challenged the regulations on the ground that the Commissioner exceeded his authority under the statute.... The District Court ... granted the declaratory and injunctive relief sought, finding that the statute did not sweep so broadly as to permit the Commissioner's "every time" interpretation. The Court of Appeals for the Third Circuit reversed without reaching the merits of the case. It held first that under

---

1. [Ed.] The "established" name has become, in common parlance, the drug's "generic" name.

the statutory scheme provided by the Federal Food, Drug, and Cosmetic Act pre-enforcement[2] review of these regulations was unauthorized and therefore beyond the jurisdiction of the District Court. Second, the Court of Appeals held that no "actual case or controversy" existed and, for that reason, that no relief under the Administrative Procedure Act or under the Declaratory Judgment Act was in any event available. . . .

I

The first question we consider is whether Congress by the Federal Food, Drug, and Cosmetic Act intended to forbid pre-enforcement review of this sort of regulation promulgated by the Commissioner. The question is phrased in terms of "prohibition" rather than "authorization" because a survey of our cases shows that judicial review of a final agency action by an aggrieved person will not be cut off unless there is persuasive reason to believe that such was the purpose of Congress. Early cases in which this type of judicial review was entertained have been reinforced by the enactment of the Administrative Procedure Act, which embodies the basic presumption of judicial review to one "suffering legal wrong because of agency action, or adversely affected or aggrieved by agency action within the meaning of a relevant statute," 5 U.S.C. § 702, so long as no statute precludes such relief or the action is not one committed by law to agency discretion, 5 U.S.C. § 701(a). The Administrative Procedure Act provides specifically not only for review of "[a]gency action made reviewable by statute" but also for review of "final agency action for which there is no other adequate remedy in a court," 5 U.S.C. § 704. The legislative material elucidating that seminal act manifests a congressional intention that it cover a broad spectrum of administrative actions,[3] and this Court has echoed that theme by noting that the Administrative Procedure Act's "generous review provisions" must be given a "hospitable" interpretation. Shaughnessy v. Pedreiro, 349 U.S. 48, 51. Again in Rusk v. Cort, 369 U.S. 367, 379–380, the Court held that only upon a showing of "clear and convincing evidence" of a contrary legislative intent should the courts restrict access to judicial review.

Given this standard, we are wholly unpersuaded that the statutory scheme in the food and drug area excludes this type of action. The Government relies on no explicit statutory authority for its argument that pre-enforcement review is unavailable, but insists instead that because the statute includes a specific procedure for such review of certain enumerated kinds of regulations, not encompassing those of the kind involved here, other types were necessarily meant to be excluded from any pre-enforcement review. The issue, however, is not so readily resolved; we must go further and inquire whether in the context of the entire legislative scheme

Access to Judicial Review under APA presumed unless Cong intent otherwise

---

2. That is, a suit brought by one before any attempted enforcement of the statute or regulation against him.

3. See H.R. Rep. No. 1980, 79th Cong., 2d Sess., 41 (1946):

To preclude judicial review under this bill a statute, if not specific in withhold-

ing such review, must upon its face give clear and convincing evidence of an intent to withhold it. The mere failure to provide specially by statute for judicial review is certainly no evidence of intent to withhold review.

the existence of that circumscribed remedy evinces a congressional purpose to bar agency action not within its purview from judicial review. As a leading authority in this field has noted, "The mere fact that some acts are made reviewable should not suffice to support an implication of exclusion as to others. The right to review is too important to be excluded on such slender and indeterminate evidence of legislative intent." Louis Jaffe, Judicial Control of Administrative Action 357 (1965)....

II

A further inquiry must, however, be made. The injunctive and declaratory judgment remedies are discretionary, and courts traditionally have been reluctant to apply them to administrative determinations unless these arise in the context of a controversy "ripe" for judicial resolution. Without undertaking to survey the intricacies of the ripeness doctrine it is fair to say that its basic rationale is to prevent the courts, through avoidance of premature adjudication, from entangling themselves in abstract disagreements over administrative policies, and also to protect the agencies from judicial interference until an administrative decision has been formalized and its effects felt in a concrete way by the challenging parties. The problem is best seen in a twofold aspect, requiring us to evaluate both the fitness of the issues for judicial decision and the hardship to the parties of withholding court consideration.

As to the former factor, we believe the issues presented are appropriate for judicial resolution at this time. First, all parties agree that the issue tendered is a purely legal one: whether the statute was properly construed by the Commissioner to require the established name of the drug to be used *every time* the proprietary name is employed. Both sides moved for summary judgment in the District Court, and no claim is made here that further administrative proceedings are contemplated. It is suggested that the justification for this rule might vary with different circumstances, and that the expertise of the Commissioner is relevant to passing upon the validity of the regulation. This of course is true, but the suggestion overlooks the fact that both sides have approached this case as one purely of congressional intent, and that the Government made no effort to justify the regulation in factual terms.

Second, the regulations in issue we find to be "final agency action" within the meaning of [APA] § 704, as construed in judicial decisions. ... The regulation challenged here, promulgated in a formal manner after announcement in the Federal Register and consideration of comments by interested parties is quite clearly definitive. There is no hint that this regulation is informal, or only the ruling of a subordinate official, or tentative. It was made effective upon publication, and the Assistant General Counsel for Food and Drugs stated in the District Court that compliance was expected.

The Government argues, however, that the present case can be distinguished from [earlier cases allowing preenforcement review] on the ground that in those instances the agency involved could implement its policy directly, while here the Attorney General must authorize criminal and seizure actions for violations of the statute. In the context of this case, we do not find this argument persuasive. These regulations are not meant to advise the Attorney General, but purport to be directly authorized by the statute. Thus, if within the Commissioner's authority, they have the status of law and violations of them carry heavy criminal and civil sanctions. Also, there is no representation that the Attorney General and the Commissioner disagree in this area; the Justice Department is defending this very suit. . . .

This is also a case in which the impact of the regulations upon the petitioners is sufficiently direct and immediate as to render the issue appropriate for judicial review at this stage. These regulations purport to give an authoritative interpretation of a statutory provision that has a direct effect on the day-to-day business of all prescription drug companies; its promulgation puts petitioners in a dilemma that it was the very purpose of the Declaratory Judgment Act to ameliorate. As the District Court found on the basis of uncontested allegations, "Either they must comply with the every time requirement and incur the costs of changing over their promotional material and labeling or they must follow their present course and risk prosecution." The regulations are clear-cut, and were made effective immediately upon publication; as noted earlier the agency's counsel represented to the District Court that immediate compliance with their terms was expected. If petitioners wish to comply they must change all their labels, advertisements, and promotional materials; they must destroy stocks of printed matter; and they must invest heavily in new printing type and new supplies. The alternative to compliance—continued use of material which they believe in good faith meets the statutory requirements, but which clearly does not meet the regulation of the Commissioner—may be even more costly. That course would risk serious criminal and civil penalties for the unlawful distribution of "misbranded" drugs.

It is relevant at this juncture to recognize that petitioners deal in a sensitive industry, in which public confidence in their drug products is especially important. To require them to challenge these regulations only as a defense to an action brought by the Government might harm them severely and unnecessarily. Where the legal issue presented is fit for judicial resolution, and where a regulation requires an immediate and significant change in the plaintiffs' conduct of their affairs with serious penalties attached to noncompliance, access to the courts under the Administrative Procedure Act and the Declaratory Judgment Act must be permitted, absent a statutory bar or some other unusual circumstance. . . .

Finally, the Government urges that to permit resort to the courts in this type of case may delay or impede effective enforcement of the Act. We fully recognize the important public interest served by assuring prompt and unimpeded administration of the Pure Food, Drug, and Cosmetic Act, but we do not find the Government's argument convincing. First, in this particular case, a preenforcement challenge by nearly all prescription drug manufacturers is calculated to speed enforcement. If the Government prevails, a large part of the industry is bound by the decree; if the Government loses, it can more quickly revise its regulation.

The Government contends, however, that if the Court allows this consolidated suit, then nothing will prevent a multiplicity of suits in various jurisdictions challenging other regulations. The short answer to this contention is that the courts are well equipped to deal with such eventualities. The venue transfer provision, 28 U.S.C. § 1404(a), may be invoked by the Government to consolidate separate actions. Or, actions in all but one jurisdiction might be stayed pending the conclusion of one proceeding. A court may even in its discretion dismiss a declaratory judgment or injunctive suit if the same issue is pending in litigation elsewhere. . . . Further, the declaratory judgment and injunctive remedies are equitable in nature, and other equitable defenses may be interposed. If a multiplicity of suits are undertaken in order to harass the Government or to delay enforcement, relief can be denied on this ground alone. . . .

In addition to all these safeguards against what the Government fears, it is important to note that the institution of this type of action does not by itself stay the effectiveness of the challenged regulation. There is nothing in the record to indicate that petitioners have sought to stay enforcement of the "every time" regulation pending judicial review. See 5 U.S.C. § 705. If the agency believes that a suit of this type will significantly impede enforcement or will harm the public interest, it need not postpone enforcement of the regulation and may oppose any motion for a judicial stay on the part of those challenging the regulation. It is scarcely to be doubted that a court would refuse to postpone the effective date of an agency action if the Government could show, as it made no effort to do here, that delay would be detrimental to the public health or safety.

Lastly, although the Government presses us to reach the merits of the challenge to the regulation in the event we find the District Court properly entertained this action, we believe the better practice is to remand the case to the Court of Appeals for the Third Circuit to review the District Court's decision that the regulation was beyond the power of the Commissioner.

■ [On the same day as Abbott Laboratories, the Court decided two companion cases. In TOILET GOODS ASS'N, INC. v. GARDNER, 387 U.S. 158—hereinafter referred to as "Toilet Goods (access rule)"—cosmetic manufacturers brought a pre-enforcement challenge to regulations requiring them to afford FDA employees access to the manufacturing processes and formulae involved in making color additives. The regulations provided that, if such access were denied, the FDA Commissioner "may immediately suspend" the manufacturer's certificate to sell additives and "may continue such suspension until adequate corrective action has been taken." The Court, with only Justice Douglas dissenting, held that this challenge was not ripe:]

. . . [T]here can be no question that this regulation . . . is "final agency action" . . . Also, we recognize the force of petitioners' contention that the issue as they have framed it presents a purely legal question: whether the regulation is totally beyond the agency's power under the statute. . . . These points which support the appropriateness of judicial resolution are, however, outweighed by other considerations. The regulation serves notice only that the Commissioner *may* under certain circumstances order inspection of certain facilities and data, and that further certification of additives *may* be refused to those who decline to permit a duly authorized inspection until they have complied in that regard. At this juncture we have no idea whether or when such an inspection will be ordered and what reasons the

Commissioner will give to justify his order. The statutory authority assert- ed for the regulation is the power to promulgate regulations "for the efficient enforcement" of the Act. Whether the regulation is justified thus depends ... on whether the statutory scheme as a whole justified promul- gation of the regulation. This will depend not merely on an inquiry into statutory purpose, but concurrently on an understanding of what types of enforcement problems are encountered by the FDA, the need for various sorts of supervision in order to effectuate the goals of the Act, and the safeguards devised to protect legitimate trade secrets. We believe that judicial appraisal of these factors is likely to stand on a much surer footing in the context of a specific application of this regulation than could be the case in the framework of the generalized challenge made here.

We are also led to this result by considerations of the effect on the petitioners of the regulation.... This is not a situation in which primary conduct is affected—when contracts must be negotiated, ingredients tested or substituted, or special records compiled. This regulation merely states that the Commissioner may authorize inspectors to examine certain pro- cesses or formulae; no advance action is required of cosmetics manufactur- ers.... Moreover, no irremediable adverse consequences flow from requir- ing a later challenge to this regulation by a manufacturer who refuses to allow this type of inspection. Unlike the other regulations challenged in this action, in which seizure of goods, heavy fines, adverse publicity for distributing "adulterated" goods, and possible criminal liability might penalize failure to comply, a refusal to admit an inspector here would at most lead only to a suspension of certification services to the particular party, a determination that can then be promptly challenged through an administrative procedure, which in turn is reviewable by a court.

■ [In the other case, GARDNER v. TOILET GOODS ASS'N, INC., 387 U.S. 167— hereinafter referred to as "Toilet Goods (additives rule)"—the manufactur- ers challenged a rule that broadly interpreted the statutory phrase "color additives" and narrowly interpreted a statutory exemption for "hair dyes," for purposes of pre-marketing clearance requirements. The majority found this pre-enforcement challenge ripe under Abbott. JUSTICE FORTAS dissented, in the following opinion that applied to Abbott as well:]

... The Court, by today's decisions ..., has opened Pandora's box. Federal injunctions will now threaten programs of vast importance to the public welfare. ... It is cold comfort—it is little more than delusion—to read in the Court's opinion that "It is scarcely to be doubted that a court would refuse to postpone the effective date of an agency action if the Government could show ... that delay would be detrimental to the public health or safety." Experience dictates, on the contrary, that it can hardly be hoped that some federal judge somewhere will not be moved as the Court is here, by the cries of anguish and distress of those regulated, to grant a disruptive injunction.

... [T]he Court has concluded that the damage to petitioners if they have to engage in the required redesign and reprint of their labels and printed materials without threshold review outweighs the damage to the public of deferring during the tedious months and years of litigation a cure for the possible danger and asserted deceit of peddling plain medicine under fancy trademarks and for fancy prices which, rightly or wrongly, impelled the Congress to enact this legislation. I submit that a much stronger showing is necessary than the expense and trouble of compliance and the risk of defiance. Actually, if the Court refused to permit this shotgun assault, experience and reasonably sophisticated common sense show that there would be orderly compliance without the disaster so dramatically predicted by the industry, reasonable adjustments by the agency in real hardship cases, and where extreme intransigence involving substantial violations occurred, enforcement actions in which legality of the regulation would be tested in specific, concrete situations. I respectfully submit that this would be the correct and appropriate result. Our refusal to respond to the vastly overdrawn cries of distress would reflect not only healthy skepticism, but our regard for a proper relationship between the courts on the one hand and Congress and the administrative agencies on the other. It would represent a reasonable solicitude for the purposes and programs of the Congress. And it would reflect appropriate modesty as to the competence of the courts.

■ [JUSTICE BRENNAN did not participate in decision of any of the three cases.]

NOTE

Abbott is a watershed case on both the questions *whether* review is available and *when* it can occur. The second of these, the issue of "ripeness," is taken up in Section 4 below. Here, we focus on the issue of reviewability per se. As Abbott explains, the APA strongly favors review but does not universally guarantee it. Section 701 establishes two sets of circumstances in which, notwithstanding the "presumption" of review, the APA will not assist a party seeking judicial scrutiny of agency behavior. These circumstances are explored in the materials that follow.

a.   § 701(a)(1): STATUTORY PRECLUSION OF REVIEW

"(a) This chapter [i.e., §§ 701–706] applies, according to the provisions thereof, except to the extent that—

(1) statutes preclude judicial review;"

Administrative Procedure Act, § 701(a)(1)

Block v. Community Nutrition Institute

Supreme Court of the United States, 1984.
467 U.S. 340.

■ JUSTICE O'CONNOR delivered the opinion of the Court.

[Pursuant to his power under the Agricultural Marketing Agreement Act, the Secretary of Agriculture sets minimum prices that milk handlers (those who process dairy products) must pay to milk producers (i.e., dairy farmers). The Act—which long predates the APA—directs that these "milk marketing orders" be formulated through a rulemaking process that includes public hearing and comment. However, it also stipulates that marketing orders can become effective only after a vote of approval by a majority of handlers and a supermajority of producers. The Secretary can, in limited circumstances, implement an order even if the requisite percentage of handlers fail to approve it; by contrast, approval by a supermajority of producers is always required.

Milk marketing orders issued several years before this lawsuit assigned reconstituted milk (milk made by adding water to milk powder) to one of the higher price classes. The plaintiffs—who included consumers, a non-profit organization promoting good nutrition for lower income families, and a milk handler—petitioned the Secretary to begin a rulemaking to change this classification. They argued that it made reconstituted milk uneconomical for handlers to process, thus depriving consumers of a source of less expensive milk. The Secretary invited comments on the proposed change, but there the process stalled. Eventually, the plaintiffs filed suit both challenging inaction on their rulemaking petition, and attacking the existing orders. This prompted the Secretary to announce that he would not proceed further with the proposed rulemaking, and the inaction claim was dismissed as moot. The district court then dismissed the substantive challenge as well. As to the consumers and nonprofit organization, it found both a lack of standing and a legislative intent to preclude review at the instance of such parties; it found that the milk handler had failed to exhaust its administrative remedies. The court of appeals reversed as to the consumers. It concluded that standing existed, and that the structure and purposes of the Act did not reveal "the type of clear and convincing evidence of congressional intent needed to overcome the presumption in favor of judicial review."]

. . . Whether and to what extent a particular statute precludes judicial review is determined not only from its express language, but also from the structure of the statutory scheme, its objectives, its legislative history, and the nature of the administrative action involved. . . .

It is clear that Congress did not intend to strip the judiciary of all authority to review the Secretary's milk market orders. The Act's predecessor, the Agricultural Adjustment Act of 1933, contained no provision relating to administrative or judicial review. In 1935, however, Congress added a mechanism by which dairy handlers could obtain review of the Secretary's market orders. . . . Section 608c(15) requires handlers first to exhaust the administrative remedies made available by the Secretary.[1] . . . These provisions for handler-initiated review make evident Congress' de-

---

1. [Ed.] "(A) Any handler subject to an order may file a written petition with the Secretary of Agriculture, stating that any such order or any provision of any such order or any obligation imposed in connection therewith is not in accordance with law and praying for a modification thereof or to be exempted therefrom. He shall thereupon be given an opportunity for a hearing upon such petition, in accordance with regulations made by the Secretary of Agriculture, with the approval of the President. After such hearing, the Secretary shall make a ruling upon the prayer of such petition which shall be final, if in accordance with law.

(B) The District Courts of the United States in any district in which such handler is an inhabitant, or has his principal place of business, are vested with jurisdiction in equity to review such ruling, provided a bill in equity for that purpose is filed within twenty days from the date of the entry of such ruling." 7 U.S.C. § 608c(15).

sire that *some* persons be able to obtain judicial review of the Secretary's market orders.

The remainder of the statutory scheme, however, makes equally clear Congress' intention to limit the classes entitled to participate in the development of market orders. The Act contemplates a cooperative venture among the Secretary, handlers, and producers the principal purposes of which are to raise the price of agricultural products and to establish an orderly system for marketing them. Handlers and producers—but not consumers—are entitled to participate in the adoption and retention of market orders. The Act provides for agreements among the Secretary, producers, and handlers[;] for hearings among them[;] and for votes by producers and handlers. Nowhere in the Act, however, is there an express provision for participation by consumers in any proceeding. In a complex scheme of this type, the omission of such a provision is sufficient reason to believe that Congress intended to foreclose consumer participation in the regulatory process. See Switchmen v. National Mediation Board, p. 1197 below.

To be sure, the general purpose sections of the Act allude to general consumer interests. But the preclusion issue does not only turn on whether the interests of a particular class like consumers are implicated. Rather, the preclusion issue turns ultimately on whether Congress intended for that class to be relied upon to challenge agency disregard of the law. The structure of this Act indicates that Congress intended only producers and handlers, and not consumers, to ensure that the statutory objectives would be realized.

Respondents would have us believe that, while Congress unequivocally directed handlers first to complain to the Secretary that the prices set by milk market orders are too high, it was nevertheless the legislative judgment that the same challenge, if advanced by consumers, does not require initial administrative scrutiny. There is no basis for attributing to Congress the intent to draw such a distinction. The regulation of agricultural products is a complex, technical undertaking. Congress channelled disputes concerning marketing orders to the Secretary in the first instance because it believed that only he has the expertise necessary to illuminate and resolve questions about them. Had Congress intended to allow consumers to attack provisions of marketing orders, it surely would have required them to pursue the administrative remedies provided in § 608c(15)(A) as well. The restriction of the administrative remedy to handlers strongly suggests that Congress intended a similar restriction of judicial review of market orders.

Allowing consumers to sue the Secretary would severely disrupt this complex and delicate administrative scheme. It would provide handlers with a convenient device for evading the statutory requirement that they first exhaust their administrative remedies. A handler may also be a consumer and, as such, could sue in that capacity. Alternatively, a handler would need only to find a consumer who is willing to join in or initiate an action in the district court. The consumer or consumer-handler could then raise precisely the same exceptions that the handler must raise administratively. ... For these reasons, we think it clear that Congress intended that judicial review of market orders issued under the Act ordinarily be confined to suits brought by handlers in accordance with 7 U.S.C. § 608c(15).

The Court of Appeals viewed the preclusion issue from a somewhat different perspective. First, it recited the presumption in favor of judicial review of administrative action that this Court usually employs. It then noted that ... no legislative history or statutory language directly and specifically supported the preclusion of consumer suits. In these circumstances, the Court of Appeals reasoned that the Act could not fairly be interpreted to overcome the presumption favoring judicial review and to leave consumers without a judicial remedy. We disagree. . . .

The presumption favoring judicial review of administrative action is just that—a presumption. This presumption, like all presumptions used in interpreting statutes, may be overcome by specific language or specific legislative history ... [, by] contemporaneous judicial construction barring review and the congressional acquiescence in it, or [by] the collective import of legislative and judicial history behind a particular statute. More important for purposes of this case, the presumption favoring judicial review of administrative action may be overcome by inferences of intent drawn from the statutory scheme as a whole. See, e.g., Switchmen v. National Mediation Board. . . .

In this case, the Court of Appeals did not take [a] balanced approach to statutory construction. . . . Rather, it recited this Court's oft-quoted statement that "only upon a showing of 'clear and convincing evidence' of a contrary legislative intent should the courts restrict access to judicial review." Abbott Laboratories v. Gardner. See also Dunlop v. Bachowski. According to the Court of Appeals, the "clear and convincing evidence" standard required it to find unambiguous proof, in the traditional evidentiary sense, of a congressional intent to preclude judicial review at the consumers' behest. Since direct statutory language or legislative history on this issue could not be found, the Court of Appeals found the presumption favoring judicial review to be controlling.

This Court has, however, never applied the "clear and convincing evidence" standard in the strict evidentiary sense the Court of Appeals thought necessary in this case. Rather, the Court has found the standard met, and the presumption favoring judicial review overcome, whenever the congressional intent to preclude judicial review is "fairly discernible in the statutory scheme." In the context of preclusion analysis, the "clear and convincing evidence" standard is not a rigid evidentiary test but a useful reminder to courts that, where substantial doubt about the congressional intent exists, the general presumption favoring judicial review of administrative action is controlling. That presumption does not control in cases such as this one, however, since the congressional intent to preclude judicial review is "fairly discernible" in the detail of the legislative scheme. . . .

... [P]reclusion of consumer suits will not threaten realization of the fundamental objectives of the statute. Handlers have interests similar to those of consumers. Handlers, like consumers, are interested in obtaining reliable supplies of milk at the cheapest possible prices. Handlers can therefore be expected to challenge unlawful agency action and to ensure that the statute's objectives will not be frustrated.[2] ... Accordingly, the judgment of the Court of Appeals is reversed.

■ JUSTICE STEVENS took no part in the decision of this case.

Bowen v. Michigan Academy of Family Physicians

Supreme Court of the United States, 1986.
476 U.S. 667.

■ JUSTICE STEVENS delivered the opinion of the Court.

[Michigan Academy, an association of family physicians, and several individual family physicians challenged a regulation of the Secretary of Health and Human Services that set higher Medicare reimbursement levels for "board certified" family physicians than for identical services performed by non-board certified family physicians. They claimed this distinction violated both the Medicare Act and the Fifth Amendment. The lower courts agreed with their statutory argument and hence did not reach the constitutional claim. In seeking certiorari, the Secretary did not challenge the decision on the merits but contended only that the Act precluded review.]

I

We begin with the strong presumption that Congress intends judicial review of administrative action. From the beginning "our cases [have established] that judicial review of a final agency action by an aggrieved person will not be cut off unless there is persuasive reason to believe that such was the purpose of Congress." Abbott Laboratories v. Gardner. In Marbury v. Madison, a case itself involving review of executive action, Chief Justice Marshall insisted that "[t]he very essence of civil liberty certainly consists in the right of every individual to claim the protection of the laws." Later, in the lesser known but nonetheless important case of United States v. Nourse, 34 U.S. 8, 9 Pet. 8, 28–29 (1835), the Chief Justice noted the traditional observance of this right and laid the foundation for the modern presumption of judicial review:

> It would excite some surprise if, in a government of laws and of principle, furnished with a department whose appropriate duty it is to decide questions of right, not only between individuals, but between the government and individuals, a ministerial officer might, at his discretion, issue this powerful process ... leaving to the debtor no remedy, no appeal to the laws of his country, if he should believe the claim to be unjust. But this anomaly does not exist; this imputation cannot be cast on the legislature of the United States.

Committees of both Houses of Congress have endorsed this view. In undertaking the comprehensive rethinking of the place of administrative agencies in a regime of separate and divided powers that culminated in the

---

2. Whether handlers would pass on to consumers any savings they might secure through a successful challenge to the market order provisions is irrelevant. Consumers' interest in market orders is limited to lowering the prices charged to handlers in the hope that consumers will then reap some benefit at the retail level.

passage of the Administrative Procedure Act, the Senate Committee on the Judiciary remarked:

> Very rarely do statutes withhold judicial review. It has never been the policy of Congress to prevent the administration of its own statutes from being judicially confined to the scope of authority granted or to the objectives specified. Its policy could not be otherwise, for in such a case statutes would in effect be blank checks drawn to the credit of some administrative officer or board.

The Committee on the Judiciary of the House of Representatives agreed that Congress ordinarily intends that there be judicial review, and emphasized the clarity with which a contrary intent must be expressed:

> The statutes of Congress are not merely advisory when they relate to administrative agencies, any more than in other cases. To preclude judicial review under this bill a statute, if not specific in withholding such review, must upon its face give clear and convincing evidence of an intent to withhold it. The mere failure to provide specially by statute for judicial review is certainly no evidence of intent to withhold review.

Taking up the language in the House Committee Report, [Abbott] reaffirmed ... that "only upon a showing of 'clear and convincing evidence' of a contrary legislative intent should the courts restrict access to judicial review." This standard has been invoked time and again when considering whether the Secretary has discharged "the heavy burden of overcoming the strong presumption that Congress did not mean to prohibit all judicial review of his decision," Dunlop v. Bachowski.[1]

Subject to constitutional constraints, Congress can, of course, make exceptions to the historic practice whereby courts review agency action. The presumption of judicial review is, after all, a presumption, and "like all presumptions used in interpreting statutes, may be overcome...." Block v. Community Nutrition Institute. [Here, the Secretary contended that review was both implicitly and explicitly precluded. The former contention rested on a distinction between Part A of the program (a government administered insurance plan, mandatory for everyone eligible for Medicare, that covers a portion of costs such as hospitalization) and Part B (an optional coverage, provided by private insurance carriers under contract with the agency, that individuals can purchase to supplement Part A benefits). The regulation at issue was promulgated under Part B. The Government argued that § 1395ff implicitly forecloses review of any Part B determination because it explicitly provides for review of comparable Part A determinations.[2]]

---

1. Of course, this Court has "never applied the 'clear and convincing evidence' standard in the strict evidentiary sense;" nevertheless, the standard serves as "a useful reminder to courts that, where substantial doubt about the congressional intent exists, the general presumption favoring judicial review of administrative action is controlling." Block v. Community Nutrition Institute. ...

2. The pertinent text of § 1395ff provides:

(a) *Entitlement to and amount of benefits.* The determination of whether an individual is entitled to benefits under part A or part B, and the determination of the amount of benefits under part A, shall be made by the

II

Section 1395ff on its face is an explicit authorization of judicial review, not a bar. As a general matter, " '[t]he mere fact that some acts are made reviewable should not suffice to support an implication of exclusion as to others. The right to review is too important to be excluded on such slender and indeterminate evidence of legislative intent.' " Abbott Laboratories v. Gardner (quoting L. Jaffe, Judicial Control of Administrative Action 357 (1965)).

In the Medicare program, however, the situation is somewhat more complex. . . . Subject to an amount-in-controversy requirement, individuals aggrieved by delayed or insufficient payment with respect to benefits payable under Part B are afforded an "opportunity for a fair hearing by the *carrier*," § 1395u (emphasis added); in comparison, and subject to a like amount-in-controversy requirement, a similarly aggrieved individual under Part A is entitled "to a hearing thereon by the *Secretary* . . . and to judicial review," § 1395ff(b). "In the context of the statute's precisely drawn provisions," we held in United States v. Erika, Inc., 456 U.S. 201, 208 (1982), that the failure "to authorize further review for determinations of the amount of Part B awards . . . provides persuasive evidence that Congress deliberately intended to foreclose further review of such claims." Not limiting our consideration to the statutory text, we investigated the legislative history which "confirm[ed] this view," and disclosed a purpose to " 'avoid overloading the courts' " with " 'trivial matters,' " a consequence which would " 'unduly ta[x]' " the federal court system with " 'little real value' " to be derived by participants in the program (quoting 118 Cong. Rec. 33992 (1972) (remarks of Sen. Bennett)).

Respondents' federal-court challenge to the validity of the Secretary's regulation is not foreclosed by § 1395ff as we construed that provision in Erika. The reticulated statutory scheme, which carefully details the forum and limits of review of "any determination . . . of . . . the amount of benefits under part A," § 1395ff(b), and of the "amount of . . . payment" of benefits under Part B, § 1395u, simply does not speak to challenges mounted against the *method* by which such amounts are to be determined rather than the *determinations* themselves. As the Secretary has made clear, "the legality, constitutional or otherwise, of any provision of the Act or regulations relevant to the Medicare Program" is not considered in a "fair hearing" held by a carrier to resolve a grievance related to a determination of the amount of a Part B award. As a result, an attack on the validity of a regulation is not the kind of administrative action that we

Secretary in accordance with regulations prescribed by him.

(b) *Appeal by individuals.* Any individual dissatisfied with any determination under subsection (a) of this section as to

(A) whether he meets the [eligibility requirements for part A], or

(B) whether he is eligible to enroll and has enrolled pursuant to the provisions of part B . . . , or,

(C) the amount of the benefits under part A (including a determination where such amount is determined to be zero)

shall be entitled to a hearing thereon by the Secretary . . . and to judicial review of the Secretary's final decision after such hearing. . . .

described in Erika as an "amount determination" which decides "the amount of the Medicare payment to be made on a particular claim" and with respect to which the Act impliedly denies judicial review.

That Congress did not preclude review of the method by which Part B awards are computed (as opposed to the computation) is borne out by the very legislative history we found persuasive in Erika. [Justice Stevens quotes the House and Senate Reports on the original legislation and the Conference Committee Report on pertinent 1972 amendments, all referring to complaints regarding "the amount of benefits."] Senator Bennett's introductory explanation to the amendment confirms that preclusion of judicial review of Part B awards—designed "to avoid overloading the courts with quite minor matters"—embraced only "decisions on a claim for payment for a given service." The Senator feared that "[i]f judicial review is made available where any claim is denied, as some court decisions have held, the resources of the Federal court system would be unduly taxed and little real value would be derived by the enrollees. The proposed amendment would merely clarify the original intent of the law and prevent the overloading of the courts with trivial matters because the intent is considered unclear." . . .

Careful analysis of the governing statutory provisions and their legislative history thus reveals that Congress intended to bar judicial review only of determinations of the amount of benefits to be awarded under Part B. Congress delegated this task to carriers who would finally determine such matters in conformity with the regulations and instructions of the Secretary. We conclude, therefore, that those matters which Congress did *not* leave to be determined in a "fair hearing" conducted by the carrier—including challenges to the validity of the Secretary's instructions and regulations—are not impliedly insulated from judicial review by [§ 1395ff].

III

In light of Congress' express provision for carrier review of millions of what it characterized as "trivial" claims, it is implausible to think it intended that there be *no* forum to adjudicate statutory and constitutional challenges to regulations promulgated by the Secretary. The Government nevertheless maintains that this is precisely what Congress intended to accomplish [when § 1395ii of the Medicare Act incorporates by reference § 405(h) of the Social Security Act. Section 405(h) provides:]

Finality of Secretary's decision

The findings and decision of the Secretary after a hearing shall be binding upon all individuals who were parties to such hearing. No findings of fact or decision of the Secretary shall be reviewed by any person, tribunal, or governmental agency except as herein provided. No action against the United States, the Secretary, or any officer or employee thereof shall be brought under section 1331 or 1346 of title 28 to recover on any claim arising under this subchapter.

The Government contends that the third sentence of § 405(h) by its terms prevents any resort to the grant of general federal-question jurisdiction contained in 28 U.S.C. § 1331.[3] . . . Respondents counter that . . .

---

3. The Government also argues that the challenged regulation is a "decision of the Secretary" which the second sentence of § 405(h) excepts from "revie[w] by any . . .

Congress' purpose was to make clear that whatever specific procedures it provided for judicial review of final action by the Secretary were exclusive, and could not be circumvented by resort to the general jurisdiction of the federal courts.

. . . [W]e need not pass on the meaning of § 405(h) in the abstract to resolve this case. Section 405(h) does not apply on its own terms to Part B of the Medicare program, but is instead incorporated *mutatis mutandis* by § 1395ii. The legislative history of both the statute establishing the Medicare program and the 1972 amendments thereto provides specific evidence of Congress' intent to foreclose review only of "amount determinations"—i.e., those "quite minor matters," (remarks of Sen. Bennett), remitted finally and exclusively to adjudication by private insurance carriers in a "fair hearing."[4] By the same token, matters which Congress did *not* delegate to private carriers, such as challenges to the validity of the Secretary's instructions and regulations, are cognizable in courts of law. In the face of this persuasive evidence of legislative intent, we will not indulge the Government's assumption that Congress contemplated review by carriers of "trivial" monetary claims, but intended no review at all of substantial statutory and constitutional challenges to the Secretary's administration of Part B of the Medicare program. This is an extreme position, and one we would be most reluctant to adopt without "a showing of 'clear and convincing evidence,' " Abbott Laboratories v. Gardner, to overcome the "strong presumption that Congress did not mean to prohibit all judicial review" of executive action, Dunlop v. Bachowski. We ordinarily presume that Congress intends the executive to obey its statutory commands and, accordingly, that it expects the courts to grant relief when an executive agency violates such a command. That presumption has not been surmounted here.[5]

The judgment of the Court of Appeals is affirmed.

■ JUSTICE REHNQUIST took no part in the consideration or decision of this case.

NOTES ON IMPLIED PRECLUSION OF REVIEW

(1) *A Wrong Turn in APA Interpretation at the Outset?* Look again at the language of § 701(a)(1). Should this provision *ever* be satisfied by anything

---

tribunal." The Government's assumption that the regulation is such a decision, however, ignores the contextual definition of "decision" in the first sentence as those determinations made by "the Secretary after a hearing." The purpose of the first two sentences of § 405(h) . . . is to assure that administrative exhaustion will be required. Respondents' attack on the regulation here is not subject to such a requirement because there is no hearing, and thus no administrative remedy, to exhaust.

4. In this connection it bears mention that the legislative history summarized in the preceding section speaks to provisions for appeal generically, and is thus as probative of congressional intent in enacting § 1395ii as it is of § 1395ff.

5. Our disposition avoids the "serious constitutional question" that would arise if we construed § 1395ii to deny a judicial forum for constitutional claims arising under part B of the Medicare program. . . .

short of an explicit statutory direction that review not occur?[1] Recall that Abbott Labs admits the possibility that a statute could implicitly foreclose review. However, both the reasoning and the outcome of that case set so formidable a standard for preclusion that, until recent years, courts and commentators looking for a case in which the Supreme Court actually found implied preclusion had to fall back on the pre-APA opinion in SWITCHMEN'S UNION v. NATIONAL MEDIATION BD., 320 U.S. 297 (1943). The Switchmen's Union, engaged in a representation battle with a rival union, had argued that yardmen in certain parts of the New York Central system should be permitted to vote for separate representatives. The Board decided it had no authority to permit representation of a unit composed of fewer than all the employees of a given craft. Accordingly, it ordered a system-wide election, which Switchmen's lost. The Union went to court, arguing that the Board had misinterpreted its statutory power. The Supreme Court held the Board's decision unreviewable.

Writing for four of the seven Justices who participated, Justice Douglas reviewed the legislative history of the disputed portion of the statute: "Commissioner Eastman, draftsman of the 1934 amendments, ... stated that whether one organization or another was the proper representative of a particular group of employees was 'one of the most controversial questions in connection with labor organization matters.' He stated that it was very important 'to provide a neutral tribunal which can make the decision and get the matter settled.' But the problem was deemed to be so 'highly controversial' that it was thought that the prestige of the Mediation Board might be adversely affected by the rulings which it would have to make in these jurisdictional disputes. Accordingly [the provision] was drafted so as to give to the Mediation Board the power to 'appoint a committee of three neutral persons who after hearing shall within ten days designate the employees who may participate in the election.' That was added so that the Board's 'own usefulness of settling disputes that might arise thereafter might not be impaired.' Where Congress took such great pains to protect the Mediation Board in its handling of an explosive problem, we cannot help but believe that if Congress had desired to implicate the federal judiciary and to place on the federal courts the burden of having the final say on any aspect of the problem, it would have made its desire plain. ... [T]he intent seems plain—the dispute was to reach its last terminal point when the administrative finding was made. There was to be no dragging out of the controversy into other tribunals of law."

Although much cited, Switchmen's Union was more often distinguished than followed.[2] Even in the labor area, where its precedential

---

1.   For an historical argument that the answer to this question should be "no," see Daniel B. Rodriguez, The Presumption of Reviewability: A Study in Canonical Construction and Its Consequences, 45 Vand.L.Rev. 743, 754–57 (1992).

2.   Professor (now Dean) Rodriguez suggests that Switchmen's Union "was very much a product of its times, that is, a part of a genre of post-New Deal, pre-APA adminis-

trative law decisions in which the New Deal's defenders on the Court fashioned rules that would ensure the survival and vitality of this grand regulatory experiment. Since the battle was essentially between a Democratic majority in Congress and President Roosevelt on one side and conservative judges appoint by Roosevelt's predecessors on the other, the Court's New Dealers characteristically would

impact was greatest, Switchmen's could be (and often was) contrasted with LEEDOM V. KYNE, 358 U.S. 184 (1958). There, a group of professional employees sought review of an NLRB order certifying a bargaining unit that included both professional and nonprofessional workers. Although the relevant statute prohibited the certification of mixed units "unless a majority of such professional employees vote for inclusion," the Board had refused to take such a vote. The agency argued that Board orders in certification proceedings are not reviewable final orders. The Court disagreed:

> This case, in its posture before us, involves unlawful action of the Board [which] has inflicted an injury on the [respondent]. Does the law, apart from the review provisions of the ... Act, afford a remedy? We think the answer surely must be yes. This suit is not one to "review," in the sense of that term as used in the Act, a decision of the Board made within its jurisdiction. Rather it is one to strike down an order of the Board made in excess of its delegated powers and contrary to a specific prohibition in the Act. ... Where, as here, Congress has given a "right" to the professional employees it must be held that it intended that right to be enforced, and the courts ... encounter no difficulty in fulfilling its purpose. (internal quotes omitted)[3]

(2) *Retreat from the Presumption of Reviewability?* Abbott Lab's insistence on "clear and convincing evidence" of Congressional intent to preclude review was not universally applauded. Professor K.C. Davis repeatedly attacked the Abbott formulation as insupportable and unwise.[4] Was CNI (which you may previously have considered in studying intervention in agency adjudication, p. 344 above) an appropriate regulatory context for revisiting the Abbott formulation?

Agricultural price supports date from the 1930s. As Justice O'Connor's opinion recounts, the milk marketing agreement program originally contained no provision for judicial review; a provision allowing handlers to

---

take positions that restricted the role of the courts." 45 Vand.L.Rev. at 755.

3. Dean Rodriguez explains Leedom as an example of how shifting political tides were reflected in reviewability decisions: "Some twenty years or so after the APA was passed, liberals and conservatives changed teams. Where the spectre of judicial review had seemed so threatening to New Dealers, liberals in the public interest era understood that federal administrative agencies and a Republican President presented their own set of dangers. Moreover, the Supreme Court now was the Warren Court, or more importantly from the standpoint of administrative law, the D.C. Court of Appeals was the Wright–Bazelon court." Rodriguez, 45 Vand. L.Rev. at 758.

Like Switchmen's Union, Leedom itself tends to be cited more often than followed. As Prof. William Funk explains, "To litigants seeking review under a variety of circum-

stances where review was precluded either explicitly or implicitly, the rule of Leedom v. Kyne was attractive; it suggested an exception to preclusion whenever the agency allegedly had acted ultra vires. Courts over the years, however, have interpreted the exception narrowly, finding the exception to exist only where the agency action was plainly beyond its authority or, as one court put it, when the agency decision is 'infused with an error which is of a summa or magna quality as contraposed to decisions which are simply cum error.' " William Funk, Supreme Court News, 17 Admin.L.News 5 (Spring 1992). See also the limited interpretation of Leedom in Board of Governors of the Fed. Reserve Sys. v. MCorp Fin., Inc., 502 U.S. 32 (1991).

4. See, e.g., Administrative Law of the Seventies § 28.08 at 631 (1976); Administrative Law Treatise § 28.09 at 495 (1982 Supp.).

obtain review of the Secretary's orders *after* they had exhausted administrative remedies was added in 1935. To be sure, the statute does not mention suits by consumers, but is the explanation a deliberate legislative choice to deny them review? Or is the more likely explanation that the possibility of suits by consumers was not within legal contemplation at that time? See p. 1126 above. Given the statutory provision for public hearings during the rulemaking portion of the marketing order process, how can the Court state that "[h]andlers and producers—but not consumers—are entitled to participate" in adoption of the orders, and assert that "Congress intended to foreclose consumer participation in the regulatory process"? If we recognize this as gratuitous, inaccurate, and potentially mischievous dicta, can you nonetheless articulate a reason why immediate consumer access to court to challenge marketing orders might be inconsistent with the statutory scheme?

(3) *Abbott Redux*? Note that the consequence of accepting the agency's § 701(a)(1) argument in CNI was not to exempt its action from *all* judicial scrutiny. Rather, the effect was merely to circumscribe the kinds of parties who can trigger review. (Is CNI a standing case in disguise?) To be sure, restricting *who* may be heard can substantially change *what* will be said. But if Justice O'Connor is correct that handlers' interests in challenging milk market orders are likely to be aligned with those of consumers (Is she?), no significant voice will be lost as a result of the decision. This might suggest that the Court was looking for an opportunity for conspicuously "reinterpreting" Abbott.

But then can we explain Michigan Academy's equally conspicuous rehabilitation of the "clear and convincing evidence" formulation? Or the fact that neither CNI nor Michigan Academy contain any separate concurrences or dissents (although Justice Stevens, author of the latter opinion, did not participate in the former case)? Not surprisingly, courts of appeals have responded to the uncomfortable pair of cases by either (i) citing both as if they embody a single, integrated approach to preclusion;[5] or (ii) emphasizing CNI when finding preclusion and Michigan Academy when finding reviewability.[6]

In GUTIERREZ DE MARTINEZ V. LAMAGNO, 515 U.S. 417 (1995), a 5–4 majority rejected the argument that the Federal Tort Claims Act implicitly precluded review of the Attorney General's certification that the defendant

---

5. E.g., Center for Auto Safety v. Dole, 846 F.2d 1532, 1535 (D.C.Cir.1988) (opinion on rehearing) ("Compelling legislative history or a law's own structure may manifest a Congressional intent to deny review when the statute itself is silent on the matter. See Community Nutrition Institute v. Block. But appellees have pointed to no 'clear and convincing' evidence, see Bowen v. Michigan Academy of Family Physicians, that Congress meant to take this unusual step with this Act.").

6. Compare Southern Pines Associates v. United States, 912 F.2d 713 (4th Cir.1990)

(review of EPA "compliance orders" implicitly precluded by Clean Water Act, citing Community Nutrition) with Farmers Union Milk Marketing Cooperative v. Yeutter, 930 F.2d 466 (6th Cir.1991) (allowing review of milk marketing order at instance of producers, despite equal absence of any statutory provision for review by such parties; extending Community Nutrition to producers as well as consumers would "effectively undermine the presumption in favor of judicial review that the Supreme Court has consistently reaffirmed. See, e.g., Bowen v. Michigan Academy of Family Physicians").

employee was acting within the scope of his employment at the time of the alleged tort. The FTCA provides: "Upon certification by the Attorney General that the defendant employee was acting within the scope of his office or employment at the time of the incident out of which the claim arose, any civil action or proceeding commenced upon such claim in a United States district court shall be deemed an action against the United States under the provisions of this title and all references thereto, and the United States shall be substituted as the party defendant."[7] Typically, then, certification is against the government's interest, for it makes the United States liable for any tortious damage caused by its employee. The Act explicitly provides for review of the Attorney General's decision at the behest *of the employee* when the A.G. *refuses* to certify. Here, however, the tort had occurred in a foreign country, and clearly fell within an exception as to which the Act had not waived the sovereign immunity of the United States. See p. 1279 below. Thus, certification was the death of this lawsuit.

Justice Ginsburg's opinion identifies as a consideration "weigh[ing] heavily in our analysis" that "federal judges traditionally proceed from the 'strong presumption that Congress intends judicial review,'" quoting Bowen and citing Abbott. She also quoted the "lesser known but nonetheless important" case of United States v. Nourse. Pointing out that a case like Guitierrez de Martinez' provides the Attorney General with a strong incentive to "do a favor" for both the government and the employee by certifying, she concluded that "the argument for unreviewability in such an instance runs up against a mainstay of our system of government . . . [:]'No man is allowed to be a judge in his own case.'" (quoting Federalist No. 10) Justice O'Connor concurred in most of this opinion and in the judgment.

Justice Souter, joined by Justices Scalia and Thomas and Chief Justice Rehnquist, dissented. Citing CNI, he argued that consideration of the text and the entire statutory scheme revealed a legislative intent that certification be unreviewable; hence, there was no room for the Abbott presumption to operate. The strong dissent was the more remarkable because the United States had sided with Guitierrez de Martinez in favor of reviewability; to provide the needed adversary presentation, the Court had to request the employee to appear and argue that review was precluded.[8]

NOTES ON EXPRESS PRECLUSION OF REVIEW

Whatever interpretive difficulties occur in discerning an *implied* legislative intent that agency action be unreviewable, it should be fairly simple to determine whether a statute *explicitly* precludes review. Yet the cases

---

7. The dissenting Justices considered this language as, at least arguably, an instance of express statutory preclusion.

8. Eighteen months before Gutierrez de Martinez, no Justice had dissented from the conclusion that the Federal Mine Safety and Health Act's comprehensive scheme of enforcement and administrative review implicitly precludes a mine owner's pre-enforcement challenge to an order designating two Union organizers as employee representatives for safety inspections. See Thunder Basin Coal Co. v. Reich, 510 U.S. 200 (1994). The mine owner could obtain review by refusing to comply with the order and forcing the agency to begin enforcement proceedings. Thus all Justices agreed that the issue was *when*, rather than *whether*, review would occur.

tend to show courts engaged in very narrow, even tortured, reading of statutory language that apparently bars review. What explains judicial reluctance to conclude that Congress really did intend to preclude review of administrative action? constitutional command? the APA's background presumption of reviewability? judicial officiousness? Are some claims of agency illegality more compelling than others?

(1) LINDAHL V. OFFICE OF PERSONNEL MGMT., 470 U.S. 768 (1985): Under the Civil Service Retirement Act, OPM "shall determine questions of disability and dependency" under the federal government's disability retirement program. "The decisions of the Office concerning these matters are final and conclusive and are not subject to review." 5 U.S.C. § 8347(c). The Navy told Lindahl, a security guard at a naval shipyard, that he was being retired on disability because acute and chronic bronchitis rendered him "unable to perform the full range of duties required of your position as a Police Officer." He did not contest this decision. After he had been retired, OPM denied him a retirement annuity on grounds that he had failed to establish that his disability prevented him from doing his job. He sought review, arguing that the burden of proof was improperly placed on him, and that the Navy improperly dismissed him before OPM had resolved his disability status.

Justice Brennan, for the Court, held that § 8347(c) precludes review of only OPM's *factual* determinations regarding disability. Review is available to determine whether "there has been a substantial departure from important procedural rights, a misconstruction of the governing legislation, or some like error 'going to the heart of the administrative determination.'" Justices White, Rehnquist and O'Connor and Chief Justice Burger dissented.

(2) MCNARY V. HAITIAN REFUGEE CTR., 498 U.S. 479 (1991), challenged INS practice in implementing an amnesty program for certain alien farmworkers created by the The Immigration Reform and Control Act of 1986. Eligibility was determined by a personal interview with each applicant; the plaintiffs claimed that the interview process was conducted in an arbitrary manner in violation of due process. The agency claimed unreviewability, relying on § 210(e) of the Act, which begins: "There shall be no administrative or judicial review of a determination respecting an application for adjustment of status ... except in accordance with this subsection," and goes on to provide for review of status denials "only" in the context of review (to be conducted by the court of appeals) of an exclusion or deportation order.

Justice Stevens, writing for the Court, rejected the agency's argument. Section 210(e)'s language prohibiting review "of *a determination* respecting *an application*" refers to direct review of individual denials of amnesty status, not to "general collateral challenges to unconstitutional practices and policies used by the agency in processing applications." Therefore, the district court could hear challenges to the procedures used by INS. "[A]s a practical matter," the plaintiffs would be unable to obtain meaningful judicial review of their constitutional claims if they were remitted to the § 210(e) procedure. Aliens would have to surrender themselves for deportation in order to receive any judicial review, a "price ... tantamount to a complete denial of judicial review for most undocumented aliens." More-over, a court of appeals reviewing an individual determination would most likely not have a sufficient record to assess whether a pattern of unconsti-tutional practices existed, and would lack the district court's factfinding capacity to develop such a record. "It is presumable that Congress legislates with knowledge of our basic rules of statutory construction, and given our well-settled presumption favoring interpretations of statutes that allow judicial review of administrative action, see Michigan Academy of Family Physicians, coupled with the limited review provisions of § 210(e), it is most unlikely that Congress intended to foreclose all forms of meaningful judicial review."

Chief Justice Rehnquist and Justice Scalia dissented, arguing that the presumption favoring review "comes into play only where there is a genuine ambiguity as to whether Congress intended" to preclude review, and that there was no such ambiguity here.[1]

(3) *The Medicare & Social Security Acts.* As Michigan Academy suggests, the complex reviewability provisions of the Medicare Act, and its incorpo-ration by reference of the Social Security Act's preclusion language, have prompted considerable litigation about reviewability. The most recent in the series is SHALALA V. ILLINOIS COUNCIL ON LONG–TERM CARE, INC., 529 U.S. 1 (2000). Medicare Part A provides payment to nursing homes that care for Medicare beneficiaries after hospitalization. To receive payment, a home must meet various standards enforced through periodic inspection. Inspec-tors report "deficiencies," which lead to imposition of sanctions or "reme-dies." The Illinois Council on Long Term Care, Inc., an association of about 200 nursing homes, attacked HHS regulations promulgated pursuant to statutory amendments that both tightened nursing home standards and broadened the Secretary's remedial authority. The challenged regulations (and a related manual) specify how remedies will be assessed. They divide deficiencies into three categories of seriousness, depending upon severity, prevalence, relation to other deficiencies, and the home's compliance histo-ry. Each category corresponds to a set of remedies. These range from terminating the home's provider agreement (where, e.g., deficiencies "im-mediately jeopardize the health or safety of . . . residents,") through civil penalties, transfer of residents, denial of some or all reimbursement, and state monitoring, to no sanction (where, e.g., the home is in "[s]ubstantial compliance," with deficiencies representing no more than a "potential for [causing] minimal harm"). The statute and regulations also create various review procedures when sanctions are imposed.

The Council brought suit under 28 U.S.C. § 1331, claiming the regula-tions were unconstitutionally vague; in excess of the agency's statutory authority; inconsistent with procedural due process; and not properly

---

1. The practical value of McNary for those seeking review of INS policies and prac-tices was substantially curtailed by Reno v. Catholic Soc. Serv., 509 U.S. 43 (1993), which construed "virtually identical" review provi-sions in a different section of the Immigra-tion Reform and Control Act. Although reaf-firming that the preclusion provision covers only *individual* determinations of adjustment of status, and not challenges to INS policies and practices, CSS held that the latter sorts of challenges will rarely be *ripe* for review until the policy or practice is applied in the individual's case (at which point, of course, the statutory preclusion *would* be triggered). CSS is considered further at p. 1255 below.

promulgated under the APA. For a 5–4 majority, Justice Breyer held that the suit was precluded by the combination of (i) provisions of the Medicare Act that set up a review process for homes "dissatisfied … with a determination [that the provider fails to comply with the provisions of the Act]", 42 U.S.C. § 1395cc(h)(1); and (ii) § 405(h) of the Social Security Act which, as you learned in Michigan Academy, the Medicare Act incorporates by reference.[2]

These provisions, Justice Breyer concluded, "reach beyond ordinary administrative law principles of 'ripeness' and 'exhaustion of administrative remedies' … [which contain exceptions that] permit early review when, for example, the legal question is 'fit' for resolution and delay means hardship, or when exhaustion would prove 'futile.' … [By demanding] the 'channelling' of virtually all legal attacks through the agency, [this interplay of statutory provisions] assures the agency greater opportunity to apply, interpret, or revise policies, regulations, or statutes without possibly premature interference by different individual courts applying 'ripeness' and 'exhaustion' exceptions case by case. But this assurance comes at a price, namely, occasional individual, delay-related hardship. In the context of a massive, complex health and safety program such as Medicare, embodied in hundreds of pages of statutes and thousands of pages of often interrelated regulations, any of which may become the subject of a legal challenge in any of several different courts, paying this price may seem justified. In any event, such was the judgment of Congress. …"

Michigan Academy was explained as refusing to find preclusion "where application of § 405(h) would not simply channel review through the agency, but would mean no review at all," thus illustrating "the distinction that this Court has often drawn between a total preclusion of review and postponement of review." Justice Breyer rejected the Council's argument that various limitations on use of "the special review channel that the Medicare statutes create" amounted to "the practical equivalent of a total denial of judicial review."

The four dissenters emphatically took issue with most of the majority's analysis. Justice Stevens argued that Michigan Academy, properly understood, limited the scope of § 405(h) preclusion to Medicare recipients' claims for benefits. Health care providers' "challenges to the Secretary's regulations simply do not fall within the 'to recover' language of § 405(h) that was obviously drafted to describe pecuniary claims." Justice Scalia agreed that the case should go forward under Michigan Academy—although he expressed himself "doubtful whether [that case] was correctly decided." Justice Thomas (writing for himself and Justices Scalia, Kennedy and Stevens on this point), argued at length that § 405(h) is triggered only "when a particular fact-bound determination is in dispute, but not in the case, as here, of a 'challeng[e] to the validity of the Secretary's instructions and regulations'." He went further (in reasoning not joined by Justice Scalia) to argue that "the [Abbott] presumption favors not merely judicial review 'at some point,' but *preenforcement* judicial review." He explained:

---

2. The pertinent language of § 405(h) is: "No action against the United States, the [Secretary], or any officer or employee thereof shall be brought under section 1331 … of title 28 to recover on any claim arising under this subchapter."

"There is a practical reason why we employ the presumption not only to questions of whether judicial review is available, but also to questions of when judicial review is available. Delayed review—that is, a requirement that a regulated entity disobey the regulation, suffer an enforcement proceeding by the agency, and only then seek judicial review—may mean no review at all. For when the costs of 'presenting' a claim via the delayed review route exceed the costs of simply complying with the regulation, the regulated entity will buckle under and comply, even when the regulation is plainly invalid. And we can expect that this consequence will often flow from an interpretation of an ambiguous statute to bar preenforcement review." Justice Thomas found compelling the nursing homes' arguments that forcing them to challenge the regulations only in defense to a sanctions order was the practical equivalent of foreclosing review entirely.

(4) *The Veterans' Benefit Cases.* Like the Medicare/Social Security context, the veterans' benefit area has provided fertile ground for preclusion controversies. Prior to 1970, the statutory language read:

> [T]he decisions of the Administrator [of Veterans Affairs] on any question of law or fact concerning a claim for benefits or payments under any law administered by the Veterans' Administration shall be final and conclusive and no other official or any court of the United States shall have power or jurisdiction to review any such decision.

72 Stat. 1115 (1958). Although this preclusion of review was generally respected, the D.C. Circuit had repeatedly held that, because the statute used the phrase "concerning a *claim* for benefits," it did not preclude review of agency action *terminating* benefits.[3] Growing numbers of suits seeking review of benefit terminations led Congress in 1970 to amend the statute to read:

> [T]he decisions of the Administrator on any question of law or fact under any law administered by the Veterans' Administration providing benefits for veterans and their dependents or survivors shall be final and conclusive and no other official or any court of the United States shall have power or jurisdiction to review any such decision by an action in the nature of mandamus or otherwise.

38 U.S.C. § 211(a)(1970). The accompanying House Report explained that Congress had acted to "make it perfectly clear that the Congress intends to exclude from judicial review all determinations with respect to noncontractual benefits provided for veterans and their dependents and survivors."

Four years later, JOHNSON v. ROBISON, 415 U.S. 361, 366–67 (1974), interpreted the new § 211(a). Conscientious objector William Robison claimed that the First and Fifth Amendments were violated by a statutory provision denying generally available veterans' educational benefits to conscientious objectors who had completed alternative service. Writing for a unanimous Court on this point,[4] Justice Brennan rejected the agency's argument that § 211(a) barred the action: "Such a construction would, of

---

3. E.g., Wellman v. Whittier, 259 F.2d 163 (D.C.Cir.1958); Thompson v. Gleason, 317 F.2d 901 (D.C.Cir.1962); Tracy v. Gleason, 379 F.2d 469 (D.C.Cir.1967).

4. Justice Douglas dissented from the majority's resolution of the merits of the constitutional claims.

course, raise serious questions concerning the constitutionality of § 211(a), and in such case it is a cardinal principle that this Court will first ascertain whether a construction of the statute is fairly possible by which the [constitutional] question[s] may be avoided." (Internal quotes omitted.)

"Plainly, no explicit provision of § 211(a) bars judicial consideration of appellee's constitutional claims. That section provides that 'the *decisions* of the Administrator on any question of law or fact *under* any law administered by the Veterans' Administration providing benefits for veterans ... shall be final and conclusive and no ... court of the United States shall have power or jurisdiction to review any such decision....'" (emphasis added) The prohibitions would appear to be aimed at review only of those decisions of law or fact that arise in the *administration* by the Veterans' Administration of a *statute* providing benefits for veterans. A decision of law or fact 'under' a statute is made by the Administrator in the interpretation or application of a particular provision of the statute to a particular set of facts. Appellee's constitutional challenge is not to any such decision of the *Administrator*, but rather to a decision of *Congress* to create a statutory class entitled to benefits that does not include ... conscientious objectors who performed alternate civilian service. Thus, as the District Court stated: 'The questions of law presented in these proceedings arise under the Constitution, not under the statute whose validity is challenged.' "

After Johnson, lower federal courts held that § 211(a) did not preclude review of claims that VA procedures violated due process[5] or that VA regulations exceeded its statutory authority.[6] The Supreme Court reentered the field in TRAYNOR V. TURNAGE, 485 U.S. 535 (1988).[7] Honorably discharged veterans were entitled to educational benefits under the G.I. Bill. However, benefits had to be used within ten years of their discharge unless the time was extended because of a "physical or mental disability which was not the result of ... [their] own willful misconduct." The VA promulgated a rule that defined "primary" alcoholism (i.e., alcoholism unrelated to an underlying psychiatric disorder) as "willful misconduct." Veterans denied extensions challenged the rule as violating § 504 of the Rehabilitation Act of 1973, which prohibits discrimination on the basis of handicap in federal programs. The Second Circuit had held such claims precluded by § 211(a); the D.C. Circuit (with then-Judge Scalia dissenting) had held them reviewable. In the portion of the majority opinion dealing with reviewability,

---

5. E.g., Arnolds v. Veterans' Admin., 507 F.Supp. 128, 130–31 (N.D.Ill.1981); Plato v. Roudebush, 397 F.Supp. 1295, 1301–04 (D.Md.1975).

6. E.g., American Fed'n of Gov't Employees v. Nimmo, 711 F.2d 28, 31 (4th Cir. 1983); Evergreen State College v. Cleland, 621 F.2d 1002, 1007–08 (9th Cir.1980); University of Maryland v. Cleland, 621 F.2d 98, 100–01 (4th Cir.1980); Merged Area X (Educ.) v. Cleland, 604 F.2d 1075, 1078 (8th Cir.1979); Wayne State Univ. v. Cleland, 590 F.2d 627, 631–32 (6th Cir.1978).

7. In an intervening decision, the Court had held that § 211(a) did not preclude *state* courts from determining that veterans' benefits are income that can be reached in awarding child support. Rose v. Rose, 481 U.S. 619 (1987). Although the preclusion argument was tendered principally by the appellant veteran (who had been held in contempt for defying state-court orders to pay support), the Solicitor General appeared as amicus curiae urging the Court to adopt the veteran's interpretation of § 211(a).

Justice White wrote for all participating Justices:[8] "We have repeatedly acknowledged 'the strong presumption that Congress intends judicial review of administrative action.' Michigan Academy of Family Physicians. The presumption in favor of judicial review may be overcome 'only upon a showing of "clear and convincing evidence" of a contrary legislative intent.' Abbott Laboratories v. Gardner. We look to such evidence as 'specific language or specific legislative history that is a reliable indicator of congressional intent,' or a specific congressional intent to preclude judicial review that is 'fairly discernible in the detail of the legislative scheme.' Michigan Academy of Family Physicians, quoting Block v. CNI.

"The text and legislative history of § 211(a) . . . provide no clear and convincing evidence of any congressional intent to preclude a suit claiming that § 504 of the Rehabilitation Act, a statute applicable to all federal agencies, has invalidated an otherwise valid regulation issued by the Veterans' Administration and purporting to have the force of law. Section 211(a) insulates from review decisions of law and fact 'under any law administered by the Veterans' Administration,' that is, decisions made in interpreting or applying a particular provision of that statute to a particular set of facts. But the cases now before us involve the issue whether the law sought to be administered is valid in light of a subsequent statute whose enforcement is not the exclusive domain of the Veterans' Administration. There is no claim that the regulation at issue is inconsistent with the statute under which it was issued; and there is no challenge to the Veterans' Administration's construction of any statute dealing with veterans' benefits, except to the extent that its construction may be affected by the Rehabilitation Act. Nor is there any reason to believe that the Veterans' Administration has any special expertise in assessing the validity of its regulations construing veterans' benefits statutes under a later passed statute of general application. Permitting these cases to go forward will not undermine the purposes of § 211(a) any more than did the result in Johnson."[9]

(5) *The Habeas Cases.* ZADVYDAS V. DAVIS, 533 U.S. 678 (2001): "[T]he primary federal habeas corpus statute, 28 U.S.C. § 2241, confers jurisdiction upon the federal courts to hear [cases involving aliens in custody pending deportation]." See § 2241(c)(3) (authorizing any person to claim in federal court that he or she is being held 'in custody in violation of the

---

8. Justices Kennedy and Scalia did not participate. Justices Blackmun, Brennan and Marshall dissented from the parts of the opinion sustaining the VA's position on the merits.

9. In 1988, the saga of § 211(a) took a very different turn when the Veterans' Judicial Review Act, Pub.L.No. 100–687, 102 Stat. 4105, created a new Article I court, the Court of Veterans Appeals, to review VA benefit decisions. The scope of review is similar to that provided by § 706 of the APA, except that findings of fact are to be set aside only if "clearly erroneous" (rather than "unsupport-

ed by substantial evidence"). The judgments of this court are in turn reviewable by the Court of Appeals for the Federal Circuit. The Federal Circuit may not, however, review "a challenge to a factual determination" or "a challenge to a law or regulation as applied to the facts of a particular case" unless the case "presents a constitutional issue." The Act also provides for review of VA rulemaking in the Federal Circuit. For changes in attorneys' fees limits to accommodate this new review structure, see Note 1 following Walters v. National Assoc. of Radiation Survivors, at p. 858 above.

Constitution or laws ... of the United States'). Before 1952, the federal courts considered challenges to the lawfulness of immigration-related detention, including challenges to the validity of a deportation order, in habeas proceedings. Beginning in 1952, an alternative method for review of deportation orders, namely actions brought in federal district court under the Administrative Procedure Act (APA), became available. And in 1961 Congress replaced district court APA review with initial deportation order review in courts of appeals. The 1961 Act specified that federal habeas courts were also available to hear statutory and constitutional challenges to deportation (and exclusion) orders. These statutory changes left habeas untouched as the basic method for obtaining review of continued custody after a deportation order had become final. See Cheng Fan Kwok v. INS, 392 U.S. 206, 212, 215–216 (1968) (holding that [the new procedure] applied only to challenges to determinations made during deportation proceedings and motions to reopen those proceedings).

"More recently, Congress has enacted several statutory provisions that limit the circumstances in which judicial review of deportation decisions is available." Specifically, the Antiterrorism and Effective Death Penalty Act of 1996 (AEDPA) and the Illegal Immigration Reform and Immigrant Responsibility Act of 1996 (IIRIRA) contained, between them, four separate provisions precluding judicial review. In Zadvydas, two deportable aliens whose country of origin refused to accept them were being held indefinitely by U.S. authorities. (The statute provided for a period of detention while deportation was being attempted, but the period had expired without success in repatriation.) They claimed that such indefinite suspension was unconstitutional. Justice Breyer began by explaining that "none [of the statutory limits on review] applies here. One provision, 8 U.S.C. § 1231(h), simply forbids courts to construe that section 'to create any ... procedural right or benefit that is legally enforceable'; it does not deprive an alien of the right to rely on 28 U.S.C. § 2241 to challenge detention that is without statutory authority. Another provision, 8 U.S.C. § 1252(a)(2)(B)(ii), says that 'no court shall have jurisdiction to review' decisions 'specified ... to be in the discretion of the Attorney General.' The aliens here, however, do not seek review of the Attorney General's exercise of discretion; rather, they challenge the extent of the Attorney General's authority under the post-removal period detention statute. And the extent of that authority is not a matter of discretion. We conclude that § 2241 habeas corpus proceedings remain available as a forum for statutory and constitutional challenges to post-removal-period detention." On the merits, the Court construed the Act to contain an implicit "reasonable time" limitation on detention—and concluded that this reasonable time is presumptively six months. Four justices dissented on the merits, but did not contest the majority's conclusion on reviewability.

A few days earlier in INS v. St. Cyr, 533 U.S. 289 (2001), the Court held that habeas review was available despite 8 U.S.C. § 1252(a)(2)(C): "Notwithstanding any other provision of law, no court shall have jurisdiction to review any final order of removal against an alien who is removable by reason of having committed [one or more enumerated] criminal offense[s]." St. Cyr had pleaded guilty to a listed offense; at the time of the plea, the Attorney General had broad statutory authority to waive deportation.

However, AEDPA and IIRIRA took effect before the INS began deportation proceedings, and the Attorney General took the position that they had withdrawn her discretion to waive deportation. St. Cyr challenged this interpretation as unlawfully "retroactive." Justice Stevens (joined by Justices Kennedy, Souter, Ginsburg and Breyer) relied heavily on "the strong presumption in favor of judicial review of administrative action, *Michigan Academy of Family Physicians*, and the longstanding rule requiring a clear statement of congressional intent to repeal habeas jurisdiction." Moreover, preclusion of review "of a pure question of law by any court would give rise to substantial constitutional questions" under the Suspension Clause, Art. 1, § 9, ¶ 2. Therefore, § 1252(a)(2)(C)'s reference to "jurisdiction to review" would not be interpreted to include habeas corpus jurisdiction. "In the immigration context, 'judicial review' and 'habeas corpus' have historically distinct meanings." On the merits, the majority held that repeal of the Attorney General's waiver power did not apply retroactively.

Justice Scalia, joined by Chief Justice Rehnquist and Justices Thomas and O'Connor (on this issue[10]), dissented vehemently on both reviewability and the merits. He asserted that "ambiguity in the utterly clear language" of IIRIRA and AEDPA could be found only by "fabricat[ing] a superclear statement, 'magic words' requirement ... unjustified in law and unparalleled in any other area of our jurisprudence."[11]

(6) RONALD M. LEVIN, UNDERSTANDING UNREVIEWABILITY IN ADMINISTRATIVE LAW, 74 Minn. L.Rev. 689, 739–40 (1990): "[T]he Court tends to allow some issues to be precluded more readily than other issues. At the top of the scale, ... the presumption against preclusion of constitutional grievances against an agency is practically irrebuttable. The Court also has proved less willing to find preclusion in cases involving administrative rules than in cases involving agency adjudication, and less willing to foreclose legal challenges than factual ones, especially where the legal issues are not within the administering agency's expertise. At the bottom of the hierarchy are issues of fact and application of law to fact, which the Court allows to be precluded more readily than any others.

"In most of these cases, the Court also found technical grounds for reading the statutes to support these results; thus the Court's lawmaking was peripheral and somewhat covert. Yet these holdings clearly have been informed by practical judgments about the relative importance of judicial

---

10. Justice O'Connor did not join the part of the dissent where Justice Scalia disputed the majority's reading of the Suspension Clause.

11. Similar questions had been raised, in the criminal rather than administrative context, by a provision of AEDPA stating that second (or "successive") petitions for habeas corpus must be dismissed unless authorized, under stringent statutory criteria, by a court of appeals—and then providing that such court-of-appeals "gatekeeping" decisions "shall not be appealable and shall not be the subject of a petition for rehearing or for a writ of certiorari." After the Eleventh

Circuit denied him permission to file a successive petition, a death row inmate sought a writ of habeas corpus directly from the Supreme Court. In *Felker v. Turpin*, 518 U.S. 651 (1996), Chief Justice Rehnquist for a unanimous Court held that the gatekeeping provision was constitutional—but that AEDPA did not withdraw the Court's authority to hear an original habeas petition under § 2241. Justice Stevens, in a concurrence joined by Justices Souter and Breyer, added the view that the AEDPA also did not affect the Court's jurisdiction under the All Writs Act, 28 U.S.C. § 1651.

review of various kinds of issues. One would have been astonished if the Court had adopted any of the opposite distinctions—for example, if it had made factual contentions reviewable in a situation in which legal issues were unreviewable."

b. § 701(a)(2): "Committed to Agency Discretion by Law"

"(a) This chapter [i.e., §§ 701–706] applies, according to the provisions thereof, except to the extent that—

. . .

(2) agency action is committed to agency discretion by law."

Administrative Procedure Act, § 701(a)(2)

Webster v. Doe

Supreme Court of the United States, 1988.
486 U.S. 592.

■ Chief Justice Rehnquist delivered the opinion of the Court.

Section 102(c) of the National Security Act of 1947 provides that:

[T]he Director of Central Intelligence may, in his discretion, terminate the employment of any officer or employee of the Agency whenever he shall deem such termination necessary or advisable in the interests of the United States. . . .

50 U.S.C. § 403(c). In this case we decide whether, and to what extent, the termination decisions of the Director under § 102(c) are judicially reviewable.

[John Doe had been employed by the CIA for nine years. During that time, his evaluations consistently rated him an excellent or outstanding employee and he was promoted from clerk-typist to covert electronics technician. In January 1982, Doe voluntarily informed the CIA that he was a homosexual. Almost immediately, he was placed on paid administrative leave; he was extensively questioned by a polygraph officer concerning his homosexuality and possible security violations. He denied having sexual relations with any foreign nationals and maintained that he had not disclosed classified information to any of his sexual partners—statements which the polygraph indicated were truthful. In April 1982, the CIA's Office of Security told Doe that his homosexuality posed a threat to security, although it declined to explain the nature of the danger. Doe was then asked to resign. When he refused, the Office recommended to the CIA Director that Doe be dismissed. After reviewing Doe's records and evaluations, the Director did so, invoking § 102(c). Doe filed suit in the District Court, alleging that the decision (i) was arbitrary, capricious and an abuse of discretion in violation of the APA, and (ii) deprived him of his constitutional rights. He sought declaratory and injunctive relief in the form of reinstatement or, at least, of an order that the Director reevaluate the termination and provide a statement of reasons. The government moved to dismiss on grounds that the Director's decision was unreviewable.]

In Citizens to Preserve Overton Park, Inc. v. Volpe, p. 989 above, this Court explained the distinction between §§ 701(a)(1) and (a)(2). Subsection (a)(1) is concerned with whether Congress expressed an intent to prohibit judicial review; subsection (a)(2) applies "in those rare instances where 'statutes are drawn in such broad terms that in a given case there is no law to apply.' " (citing S.Rep. No. 752, 79th Cong., 1st Sess., 26 (1945)).

We further explained what it means for an action to be "committed to agency discretion by law" in Heckler v. Chaney, 470 U.S. 821 (1985). Heckler required the Court to determine whether the Food and Drug Administration's decision not to undertake an enforcement proceeding against the use of certain drugs in administering the death penalty was subject to judicial review. We noted that, under § 701(a)(2), even when Congress has not affirmatively precluded judicial oversight, "review is not to be had if the statute is drawn so that a court would have no meaningful standard against which to judge the agency's exercise of discretion." . . .

Both Overton Park and Heckler emphasized that § 701(a)(2) requires careful examination of the statute on which the claim of agency illegality is based. In the present case, respondent's claims against the CIA arise from the Director's asserted violation of § 102(c) of the NSA. As an initial matter, it should be noted that § 102(c) allows termination of an Agency employee whenever the Director "shall *deem* such termination necessary or advisable in the interests of the United States" (emphasis added), not simply when the dismissal *is* necessary or advisable to those interests. This standard fairly exudes deference to the Director, and appears to us to foreclose the application of any meaningful judicial standard of review. . . .

So too does the overall structure of the NSA. Passed shortly after the close of the Second World War, the NSA created the CIA and gave its Director the responsibility "for protecting intelligence sources and methods from unauthorized disclosure." Section 102(c) is an integral part of that statute, because the Agency's efficacy, and the Nation's security, depend in large measure on the reliability and trustworthiness of the Agency's employees. . . . Section 102(c) . . . exhibits the Act's extraordinary deference to the Director in his decision to terminate individual employees.

We thus find that the language and structure of § 102(c) indicate that Congress meant to commit individual employee discharges to the Director's discretion, and that § 701(a)(2) accordingly precludes judicial review of these decisions under the APA. . . .

In addition to his claim that the Director failed to abide by the statutory dictates of § 102(c), . . . [r]espondent charged that petitioner's termination of his employment deprived him of property and liberty interests under the Due Process Clause of the Fifth Amendment, denied him equal protection of the laws, and unjustifiably burdened his right to privacy. Respondent asserts that he is entitled, under the APA, to judicial consideration of these claimed violations.

We share the confusion of the Court of Appeals as to the precise nature of respondent's constitutional claims. It is difficult, if not impossible, to ascertain from the amended complaint whether respondent contends that his termination, based on *his* homosexuality, is constitutionally impermissible, or whether he asserts that a more pervasive discrimination policy exists in the CIA's employment practices regarding *all* homosexuals. This ambiguity in the amended complaint is no doubt attributable in part to the inconsistent explanations respondent received from the Agency itself regarding his termination. Prior to his discharge, respondent had been told by two CIA security officers that his homosexual activities themselves violated CIA regulations. In contrast, the Deputy General Counsel of the CIA later informed respondent that homosexuality was merely a security concern that did not inevitably result in termination, but instead was evaluated on a case-by-case basis.

Petitioner maintains that, no matter what the nature of respondent's constitutional claims, judicial review is precluded by the language and intent of § 102(c). In petitioner's view, all Agency employment termination decisions, even those based on policies normally repugnant to the Constitution, are given over to the absolute discretion of the Director, and are hence unreviewable under the APA. We do not think § 102(c) may be read to exclude review of constitutional claims. We emphasized in Johnson v. Robison, p. 1204 above, that where Congress intends to preclude judicial review of constitutional claims its intent to do so must be clear. ... We require this heightened showing in part to avoid the "serious constitutional question" that would arise if a federal statute were construed to deny any judicial forum for a colorable constitutional claim. See Michigan Academy of Family Physicians, p. 1192 above.

Our review of § 102(c) convinces us that it cannot bear the preclusive weight petitioner would have it support. As detailed above, the section does commit employment termination decisions to the Director's discretion, and precludes challenges to these decisions based upon the statutory language of § 102(c). A discharged employee thus cannot complain that his termination was not "necessary or advisable in the interests of the United States," since that assessment is the Director's alone. Subsections (a)(1) and (a)(2) of § 701, however, remove from judicial review only those determinations specifically identified by Congress or "committed to agency discretion by law." Nothing in § 102(c) persuades us that Congress meant to preclude consideration of colorable constitutional claims arising out of the actions of the Director pursuant to that section; we believe that a constitutional claim based on an individual discharge may be reviewed by the District Court.[1] We agree with the Court of Appeals that there must be further proceedings in the District Court on this issue.

Petitioner complains that judicial review even of constitutional claims will entail extensive "rummaging around" in the Agency's affairs to the detriment of national security. But petitioner acknowledges that Title VII claims attacking the hiring and promotion policies of the Agency are

---

1. Petitioner asserts that respondent fails to present a colorable constitutional claim when he asserts that there is a general CIA policy against employing homosexuals. Petitioner relies on our decision in Bowers v. Hardwick, 478 U.S. 186 (1986), to support this view. This question was not presented in the petition for certiorari, and we decline to consider it at this stage of the litigation.

routinely entertained in federal court, and the inquiry and discovery associated with those proceedings would seem to involve some of the same sort of rummaging. Furthermore, the District Court has the latitude to control any discovery process which may be instituted so as to balance respondent's need for access to proof which would support a colorable constitutional claim against the extraordinary needs of the CIA for confidentiality and the protection of its methods, sources, and mission.

Petitioner also contends that even if respondent has raised a colorable constitutional claim arising out of his discharge, Congress in the interest of national security may deny the courts the authority to decide the claim and to order respondent's reinstatement if the claim is upheld. For the reasons previously stated, we do not think Congress meant to impose such restrictions when it enacted § 102(c) of the NSA. Even without such prohibitory legislation from Congress, of course, traditional equitable principles requiring the balancing of public and private interests control the grant of declaratory or injunctive relief in the federal courts. On remand, the District Court should thus address respondent's constitutional claims and the propriety of the equitable remedies sought. . . .

■ JUSTICE KENNEDY took no part in the consideration or decision of this case.

■ JUSTICE O'CONNOR, concurring in part and dissenting in part.

I agree that the APA does not authorize judicial review [here]. . . . I do not understand the Court to say that the exception in § 701(a)(2) is necessarily or fully defined by reference to statutes "drawn in such broad terms that in a given case there is no law to apply." See Citizens to Preserve Overton Park, Inc. v. Volpe. . . . I disagree, however, with the Court's conclusion that a constitutional claim challenging the validity of an employment decision covered by § 102(c) may nonetheless be brought in a federal district court. Whatever may be the exact scope of Congress' power to close the lower federal courts to constitutional claims in other contexts, I have no doubt about its authority to do so here. . . .

■ JUSTICE SCALIA, dissenting.

I agree with the Court's apparent holding, that the Director's decision to terminate a CIA employee is "committed to agency discretion by law". . . . But because I do not see how a decision can, either practically or legally, be both unreviewable and yet reviewable for constitutional defect, I regard [the last part] of the opinion as essentially undoing [the first part]. . . .

Before proceeding to address [the last part] of the Court's opinion, which I think to be in error, I must discuss one significant element of the analysis in [the first part]. Though I subscribe to most of that analysis, I disagree with the Court's description of what is required to come within subsection (a)(2) of § 701. . . . Our precedents amply show that "commit[ment] to agency discretion by law" includes, but is not limited to, situations in which there is "no law to apply."

. . . [This] test can account for the nonreviewability of certain issues, but falls far short of explaining the full scope of the areas from which the courts are excluded. For the fact is that there is no governmental decision that is not subject to a fair number of legal constraints precise enough to be susceptible of judicial application—beginning with the fundamental constraint that the decision must be taken in order to further a public purpose rather than a purely private interest; yet there are many governmental decisions that are not at all subject to judicial review. A United States Attorney's decision to prosecute, for example, will not be reviewed on the claim that it was prompted by personal animosity. Thus, "no law to apply" provides much less than the full answer to whether § 701(a)(2) applies.

The key to understanding the "committed to agency discretion *by law* "provision of § 701(a)(2) lies in contrasting it with the "*statutes* preclude judicial review" provision of § 701(a)(1). Why "statutes" for preclusion, but the much more general term "law" for commission to agency discretion? The answer is, as we implied in Chaney, that the latter was intended to refer to "the 'common law' of judicial review of agency action"—a body of jurisprudence that had marked out, with more or less precision, certain issues and certain areas that were beyond the range of judicial review. That jurisprudence included principles ranging from the "political question" doctrine, to sovereign immunity (including doctrines determining when a suit against an officer would be deemed to be a suit against the sovereign), to official immunity, to prudential limitations upon the courts' equitable powers, to what can be described no more precisely than a traditional respect for the functions of the other branches reflected in the statement in Marbury v. Madison that "[w]here the head of a department acts in a case, in which executive discretion is to be exercised; in which he is the mere organ of executive will; it is again repeated, that any application to a court to control, in any respect, his conduct, would be rejected without hesitation." See, e.g., Switchmen v. National Mediation Board, p. 1197 above. Only if all that "common law" were embraced within § 701(a)(2) could it have been true that, as was generally understood, "[t]he intended result of [§ 701(a)] is to restate the existing law as to the area of reviewable agency action." Attorney General's Manual on the APA 94 (1947). Because that is the meaning of the provision, we have continued to take into account for purposes of determining reviewability, post-APA as before, not only the text and structure of the statute under which the agency acts, but such factors as whether the decision involves "a sensitive and inherently discretionary judgment call," Department of Navy v. Egan, 484 U.S. 518, 527 (1988), whether it is the sort of decision that has traditionally been nonreviewable, Heckler v. Chaney, and whether review would have "disruptive practical consequences," see Southern R. Co. v. Seaboard Allied Milling Corp., 442 U.S. 444, 457 (1979). . . .

All this law, shaped over the course of centuries and still developing in its application to new contexts, cannot possibly be contained within the phrase "no law to apply." It is not surprising, then, that although the Court recites the test it does not really apply it. Like other opinions relying upon it, this one essentially announces the test, declares victory and moves on. It is not really true " 'that a court would have no meaningful standard against which to judge the agency's exercise of discretion,' " supra, quoting Chaney. The standard set forth in § 102(c) . . . at least excludes dismissal out of personal vindictiveness, or because the Director wants to give the job to his cousin. Why, on the Court's theory, is respondent not entitled to assert the presence of such excesses, under the "abuse of discretion" standard of § 706? ...

Before taking the reader through the terrain of the Court's holding that respondent may assert constitutional claims in this suit, I would like to try to clear some of the underbrush, consisting primarily of the Court's ominous warning that "[a] 'serious constitutional question' ... would arise if a federal statute were construed to deny any judicial forum for a colorable constitutional claim."

The first response to the Court's grave doubt about the constitutionality of denying all judicial review to a "colorable constitutional claim" is that the denial of all judicial review is not at issue here, but merely the denial of review in United States district courts. As to that, the law is, and has long been, clear. Article III, § 2, of the Constitution extends the judicial power to "all Cases ... arising under this Constitution." But Article III, § 1, provides that the judicial power shall be vested "in one supreme Court, *and in such inferior Courts as the Congress may from time to time ordain and establish*" (emphasis added). We long ago held that the power not to create any lower federal courts at all includes the power to invest them with less than all of the judicial power. ... [See] Sheldon v. Sill, 49 U.S. (8 How.) 441, 449 (1850). Thus, if there is any truth to the proposition that judicial cognizance of constitutional claims cannot be eliminated, it is, at most, that they cannot be eliminated from state courts, and from this Court's appellate jurisdiction over cases from state courts (or cases from federal courts, should there be any) involving such claims. Narrowly viewed, therefore, there is no shadow of a constitutional doubt that we are free to hold that the present suit, whether based on constitutional grounds or not, will not lie.

It can fairly be argued, however, that our interpretation of § 701(a)(2) indirectly implicates the constitutional question whether state courts can be deprived of jurisdiction, because if they cannot, then interpreting § 701(a)(2) to exclude relief here would impute to Congress the peculiar intent to let state courts review Federal Government action that it is unwilling to let federal district courts review. ... I turn, then, to the substance of the Court's warning that judicial review of all "colorable constitutional claims" arising out of the respondent's dismissal may well be constitutionally required. What could possibly be the basis for this fear? Surely not some general principle that *all* constitutional violations must be remediable in the courts. The very text of the Constitution refutes that principle, since it provides that "[e]ach House shall be the Judge of the Elections, Returns and Qualifications of its own Members," Art. I, § 5, and that "for any Speech or Debate in either House, [the Senators and Representatives] shall not be questioned in any other Place," Art. I, § 6. Claims concerning constitutional violations committed in these contexts—for example, the rather grave constitutional claim that an election has been stolen—cannot be addressed to the courts. Even apart from the strict text of the Constitution, we have found some constitutional claims to be beyond judicial review because they involve "political questions." The doctrine of sovereign immunity—not repealed by the Constitution, but to the contrary at least partly reaffirmed as to the States by the Eleventh Amendment—is a monument to the principle that some constitutional claims can go unheard. No one would suggest that, if Congress had not passed the Tucker Act, the courts would be able to order disbursements from the Treasury to pay for property taken under lawful authority (and subsequently destroyed) without just compensation. . . . In sum, it is simply untenable that there must be a judicial remedy for every constitutional violation. Members of Congress and the supervising officers of the Executive Branch take the same oath to uphold the Constitution that we do, and sometimes they are left to perform that oath unreviewed, as we always are.

. . . It seems to me clear that courts would not entertain, for example, an action for backpay by a dismissed Secretary of State claiming that the reason he lost his Government job was that the President did not like his religious views—surely a colorable violation of the First Amendment. I am confident we would hold that the President's choice of his Secretary of State is a "political question." But what about a similar suit by the Deputy Secretary of State? Or one of the Under Secretaries? Or an Assistant Secretary? Or the head of the European Desk? Is there really a constitutional line that falls at some immutable point between one and another of these offices at which the principle of unreviewability cuts in, and which cannot be altered by congressional prescription? I think not. . . .

. . . It seems to me the Court is attempting the impossible feat of having its cake and eating it too. . . . If the § 102(c) assessment is really "the Director's alone," the only conceivable basis for review of respondent's dismissal (which is what this case is about) would be that the dismissal was not *really* the result of a § 102(c) assessment by the Director. But respondent has never contended that, nor could he. . . . Even if the basis for the Director's assessment was the respondent's homosexuality, and even if the connection between that and the interests of the United States is an irrational and hence an unconstitutional one, if that assessment is really "the Director's alone" there is nothing more to litigate about. . . .

Since the Court's disposition contradicts its fair assurances, I must assume that the § 102(c) judgment is no longer "the Director's alone," but rather only "the Director's alone except to the extent it is colorably claimed that his judgment is unconstitutional." I turn, then, to the question of where this exception comes from. As discussed at length earlier, the Constitution assuredly does not require it. Nor does the text of the statute. . . .

Perhaps, then, a constitutional right is by its nature so much more important to the claimant than a statutory right that a statute which plainly excludes the latter should not be read to exclude the former unless it says so. That principle has never been announced—and with good reason, because its premise is not true. An individual's contention that the Government has reneged upon a $100,000 debt owing under a contract is much more important to him—both financially and, I suspect, in the sense of injustice that he feels—than the same individual's claim that a particular federal licensing provision requiring a $100 license denies him equal protection of the laws, or that a particular state tax violates the Commerce Clause. A citizen would much rather have his statutory entitlement correctly acknowledged after a constitutionally inadequate hearing, than have it incorrectly denied after a proceeding that fulfills all the requirements of the Due Process Clause. The *only* respect in which a constitutional claim is necessarily more significant than any other kind of claim is that, regardless of how trivial its real-life importance may be in the case at hand, it can be asserted against the action of the legislature itself, whereas a nonconstitutional claim (no matter how significant) cannot. That is an important distinction, and one relevant to the constitutional analysis that I conducted above. But it has no relevance to the question whether, as between executive violations of statute and executive violations of the Constitution—both of which are equally unlawful, and neither of which can be said, *a priori*, to be more harmful or more unfair to the plaintiff—one or the other category should be favored by a presumption against exclusion of judicial review. . . .

NOTES

(1) *Historical Approaches to the Conundrum of § 701(a)(2) and § 706(2)(A).* Section 701(a)(2) withdraws otherwise available judicial review from "agency actions committed to agency discretion by law." Section 706(2)(A) directs courts to set aside agency action found to "arbitrary, capricious or *an abuse of discretion.*" If a court is not to review discretionary action, when would it have occasion to find discretion abused? Could an agency "abuse" its discretion in § 706 terms, and yet be immune under § 701(a)(2) from judicial correction? Early in the modern administrative law era, three prominent scholars advocated three very different solutions to the puzzle:

Kenneth Culp Davis argued that § 701(a)(2) must be taken literally, to mean that some exercises of agency discretion are unreviewable even in the event of abuse. He thought courts should distinguish "unreviewable discretion" from "reviewable discretion" based on "(a) intent of Congress to cut off review, (b) inappropriateness of the subject matter for judicial consideration, *or* (c) some other reason that a court deems sufficient for unreviewability."[1]

At the other extreme, Raoul Berger insisted that *abuses* of discretion are always judicially correctable (unless, under § 701(a)(1), a statute has precluded review). In Prof. Berger's view, § 701(a)(2) functions primarily as a reminder to judges that agencies have been delegated substantial discretion, with the *lawful* exercise of which courts should not interfere.[2]

In the middle (though inclining more toward the Berger end of the spectrum), Louis Jaffe proposed that § 701(a)(2) comes into play only in those rare instances when an agency is given unfettered discretion:

---

1. Administrative Law of the Seventies § 28.16–1 at 641, § 28.08 at 634–35 (1976).

2. See Administrative Arbitrariness and Judicial Review, 65 Colum.L.Rev. 55 (1965). The interchange that ensued between Professors Davis and Berger on this point has been characterized as "probably the longest—and possibly the most vitriolic—debate in the history of law reviews." Ronald M. Levin, Understanding Unreviewability in Administrative Law, 74 Minn. L.Rev. 689, 694–95 (1990).

A power may appear to be granted in absolute terms and the character of the power or the statutory history of the grant may support the apparent implication. ... But such an interpretation of a statute should be tolerated only on a very strong showing. ... The upshot is that *there are very few discretions, however broad, substantially affecting the person or property of an individual which cannot at some point come under judicial surveillance.*[3]

Whose theory prevailed in the Supreme Court? Whose theory is closest to the position of the Webster dissenters?

(2) *Contemporary Scholarly Assessment.* RONALD M. LEVIN, UNDERSTANDING UNREVIEWABILITY IN ADMINISTRATIVE LAW, 74 Minn.L.Rev. 689, 740–41 (1990): "[W]hatever one thinks of the results that Justice Scalia favored ..., the manner in which he analyzed section 701(a)(2) was essentially correct. The Supreme Court should acknowledge the common law role ... by replacing the formalistic Overton Park analysis with a pragmatic approach to section 701(a)(2).

"Under such an analysis, a court could legitimately consider a wide variety of historical, utilitarian, and prudential arguments in deciding whether to refrain from judicial review in a given case. Of course, individual judges should not have unfettered discretion to accept or reject any administrative case presented to the courts. The Supreme Court, and to a lesser extent lower courts, could establish case law rules declaring a broad class of agency actions unreviewable. Or, at times, the courts might prefer to resort, as the Supreme Court did in Chaney, to the weaker device of a 'presumption,' which implies that courts in subsequent cases may sometimes make reasoned departures from the general rule. At still other times, a court might find the accepted rules and presumptions unhelpful and, therefore, embark on a fresh examination of competing policy issues. Over time, various aspects of the law of unreviewability probably would fluctuate between rule and ad hoc decisions, as often occurs in subject areas governed by the common law."

Are you persuaded?

(3) *Regulations as "Law to Apply."* What if the agency adopts a regulation indicating how it will go about exercising its statutorily-unconstrained discretion? It is likely then to lose its § 701(a)(2) defense to judicial review. See, e.g., McAlpine v. United States, 112 F.3d 1429 (10th Cir.), cert. denied 522 U.S. 984 (1997); Stehney v. Perry, 101 F.3d 925 (3d Cir.1996). Isn't this the logical justiciability corollary of the substantive proposition that agencies must follow their own regulations? See p. 913 above. Consider, however, the resulting disincentives for agencies to exercise self-discipline through discretion-constraining regulations. Cf. Harold J. Krent, Reviewing Agency Action for Inconsistency with Prior Rules and Regulations, 72 Chi–Kent L. Rev. 1187 (1997). Recognizing this, might a reviewing court hesitate before interpreting an agency statement as a binding commitment to limit its own power?

---

3. Judicial Control of Administrative Action 375 (1965).

NOTES ON REVIEWABILITY OF AGENCY REFUSALS TO ACT

(1) *Agency Nonenforcement Decisions.* HECKLER v. CHANEY, 470 U.S. 821 (1985), involved an attempt by prisoners on death row to persuade the Food and Drug Administration to regulate the use of drugs for human execution. The petitioners argued that the drugs had not been tested to verify their capacity to produce quick and painless death, and that their use in human execution constituted both the "unapproved use of an approved drug" and misbranding within the meaning of the Food, Drug and Cosmetic Act. The FDA refused on grounds that (1) the agency's jurisdiction in the area was unclear, but should not in any event be exercised to interfere with state criminal justice practices; and (2) agency enforcement in the area of unapproved use of approved drugs was generally initiated "only when there is a serious danger to the public health or a blatant scheme to defraud," neither of which was present here.

The D.C. Circuit found the refusal reviewable, focusing both on the Abbott presumption of reviewability and on an FDA Policy Statement that the agency was "obligated" to investigate unapproved uses of approved drugs when such uses became "widespread" or "endanger[ed] the public health." Because the agency currently regulated both drugs used for animal euthanasia and clinical trials on prisoners of unapproved uses of approved drugs, the panel majority found the agency's response irrational. The Supreme Court, then-Justice Rehnquist writing, reversed in an opinion joined by all but Justice Marshall. Although affirming Overton Park's statement that § 701(a)(2) is a "very narrow exception" to the presumption of reviewability, Justice Rehnquist concluded that "tradition, case law, and sound reasoning" established that the presumption does not apply to non-enforcement decisions.

"Overton Park did not involve an agency's refusal to take requested enforcement action. It involved an affirmative act of approval under a statute that set clear guidelines for determining when such approval should be given. Refusals to take enforcement steps generally involve precisely the opposite situation, and in that situation we think the presumption is that judicial review is not available. This Court has recognized on several occasions over many years that an agency's decision not to prosecute or enforce, whether through civil or criminal process, is a decision generally committed to an agency's absolute discretion. This recognition of the existence of discretion is attributable in no small part to the general unsuitability for judicial review of agency decisions to refuse enforcement.

"The reasons for this general unsuitability are many. First, an agency decision not to enforce often involves a complicated balancing of a number of factors which are peculiarly within its expertise. Thus, the agency must not only assess whether a violation has occurred, but whether agency resources are best spent on this violation or another, whether the agency is likely to succeed if it acts, whether the particular enforcement action requested best fits the agency's overall policies, and, indeed, whether the agency has enough resources to undertake the action at all. An agency generally cannot act against each technical violation of the statute it is charged with enforcing. The agency is far better equipped than the courts to deal with the many variables involved in the proper ordering of its priorities. ...

"In addition to these administrative concerns, we note that when an agency refuses to act it generally does not exercise its *coercive* power over an individual's liberty or property rights, and thus does not infringe upon areas that courts often are called upon to protect. Similarly, when an agency *does* act to enforce, that action itself provides a focus for judicial review, inasmuch as the agency must have exercised its power in some manner. The action at least can be reviewed to determine whether the agency exceeded its statutory powers. Finally, we recognize that an agency's refusal to institute proceedings shares to some extent the characteristics of the decision of a prosecutor in the Executive Branch not to indict—a decision which has long been regarded as the special province of the Executive Branch, inasmuch as it is the Executive who is charged by the Constitution to 'take Care that the Laws be faithfully executed.' U.S. Const., Art. II, § 3.

"We of course only list the above concerns to facilitate understanding of our conclusion that an agency's decision not to take enforcement action should be presumed immune from judicial review under § 701(a)(2). For good reasons, such a decision has traditionally been 'committed to agency discretion,' and we believe that the Congress enacting the APA did not intend to alter that tradition. In so stating, we emphasize that the decision is only presumptively unreviewable; the presumption may be rebutted where the substantive statute has provided guidelines for the agency to follow in exercising its enforcement powers.[1] Thus, in establishing this presumption in the APA, Congress did not set agencies free to disregard legislative direction in the statutory scheme that the agency administers. Congress may limit an agency's exercise of enforcement power if it wishes, either by setting substantive priorities, or by otherwise circumscribing an agency's power to discriminate among issues or cases it will pursue. ..."

Neither of these occurred in the FDCA. The Act's general enforcement provision, § 372, provides only that "[t]he Secretary is *authorized* to conduct examinations and investigations...." (emphasis added) The section on criminal sanctions does state that violators "shall be imprisoned ... or fined" but such language, the Court pointed out, "is commonly found" in criminal statutes and is not understood to mandate prosecution of *every* violator. As to the argument that the Act's substantive prohibition of "misbranding" provided law to apply, "[t]hese provisions are simply irrelevant to the agency's discretion to refuse to initiate proceedings." The Court dismissed the Policy Statement on which the appeals court had relied as "vague" and "in any event ..., attached to a rule that was never adopted."

---

1. We do not have in this case a refusal by the agency to institute proceedings based solely on the belief that it lacks jurisdiction. Nor do we have a situation where it could justifiably be found that the agency has 'consciously and expressly adopted a general policy' that is so extreme as to amount to an abdication of its statutory responsibilities. Although we express no opinion on whether such decisions would be unreviewable under § 701(a)(2), we note that in those situations the statute conferring authority on the agency might indicate that such decisions were not "committed to agency discretion."

Justice Brennan concurred to point out that "the Court properly does not decide today that nonenforcement decisions are unreviewable in cases where (1) an agency flatly claims that it has no statutory jurisdiction to reach certain conduct; (2) an agency engages in a pattern of nonenforcement of clear statutory language, as in Adams v. Richardson, 480 F.2d 1159 (1973) (en banc);[2] (3) an agency has refused to enforce a regulation lawfully promulgated and still in effect;[3] or (4) a nonenforcement decision violates constitutional rights.[4] It is possible to imagine other nonenforcement decisions made for entirely illegitimate reasons, for example, nonenforcement in return for a bribe, judicial review of which would not be foreclosed by the nonreviewability presumption. . . ." What justifies this set of "exceptions" to the nonreviewability presumption—presumed Congressional intent? judicial manageability? the APA itself?

Justice Marshall concurred only in the judgment, "to argue for a different basis of decision: that refusals to enforce, like other agency actions, are reviewable in the absence of a 'clear and convincing' congressional intent to the contrary, but that such refusals warrant deference when, as in this case, there is nothing to suggest that an agency with enforcement discretion has abused that discretion." Justice Marshall noted that the prisoners had offered no evidence that the reasons FDA gave were pretextual, and agreed with the majority that the Act does not require prosecution of all violations. Given the presence of enforcement discretion, "the basis on which the agency chose to exercise this discretion—that other problems were viewed as more pressing—generally will be enough to pass muster." Hence, he concluded, FDA's decision was sustainable *on the merits*.

". . . [A]rguments about prosecutorial discretion do not necessarily translate into the context of agency refusals to act. . . . Criminal prosecutorial decisions vindicate only intangible interests, common to society as a whole, in the enforcement of the criminal law. The conduct at issue has already occurred; all that remains is society's general interest in assuring that the guilty are punished. In contrast, requests for administrative enforcement typically seek to prevent concrete and future injuries that Congress has made cognizable—injuries that result, for example, from misbranded drugs, such as alleged in this case, or unsafe nuclear power plants—or to obtain palpable benefits that Congress has intended to bestow. . . . Entitlements to receive these benefits or to be free of these

---

2. [Ed.] In Adams, African–American students sued HEW alleging failure to enforce Title VI of the Civil Rights Act of 1964, which prohibits racial discrimination in public educational institutions receiving federal funds. The court ordered HEW to undertake a variety of enforcement measures, including (i) commencing enforcement proceedings against more than 100 school districts already determined to have engaged in past segregation and (ii) requiring 85 others to explain their racially disproportionate enrollments.

3. Cf. Motor Vehicle Manufacturers Assn. v. State Farm Mutual Ins. Co., p. 1002 above.

4. [Ed.] The majority opinion had cited, on this point, Johnson v. Robison, p. 1204 above (claim that refusal to award veterans' educational benefits to conscientious objectors who performed alternative service violates First Amendment) and Yick Wo v. Hopkins, 118 U.S. 356, 372–74 (1886) (claim of racially discriminatory enforcement of laundry license law).

injuries often run to specific classes of individuals whom Congress has singled out as statutory beneficiaries. The interests at stake in review of administrative enforcement decisions are thus more focused and in many circumstances more pressing than those at stake in criminal prosecutorial decisions. A request that a nuclear plant be operated safely or that protection be provided against unsafe drugs is quite different from a request that an individual be put in jail or his property confiscated as punishment for past violations of the criminal law. Unlike traditional exercises of prosecutorial discretion, 'the decision to enforce—or not to enforce—may itself result in significant burdens on a ... statutory beneficiary.' ... To the extent arguments about traditional notions of prosecutorial discretion have any force at all in this context, they ought to apply only to an agency's decision to decline to seek penalties against an individual for past conduct, not to a decision to refuse to investigate or take action on a public health, safety, or welfare problem.

"... [A]ttempting to draw a line for purposes of judicial review between affirmative exercises of coercive agency power and negative agency refusals to act is simply untenable; one of the very purposes fueling the birth of administrative agencies was the reality that governmental refusal to act could have just as devastating an effect upon life, liberty, and the pursuit of happiness as coercive governmental action. ... The lower courts, facing the problem of agency inaction and its concrete effects more regularly than do we, have responded with a variety of solutions to assure administrative fidelity to congressional objectives: a demand that an agency explain its refusal to act, a demand that explanations given be further elaborated, and injunctions that action 'unlawfully withheld or unreasonably delayed,' 5 U.S.C. § 706, be taken. Whatever the merits of any particular solution, one would have hoped the Court would have acted with greater respect for these efforts by responding with a scalpel rather than a blunderbuss. ..."

Is a (rebuttable) presumption against reviewability of agency enforcement decisions correct as an interpretation of the APA? Is it significant that § 551(13) expressly defines "agency action" as including "failure to act"? Or that the first direction of § 706 is that the "reviewing court shall—compel agency action unlawfully withheld or unreasonably delayed"? Does the majority's reasoning reduce to the view that regulatory beneficiaries have less claim to judicial review of government behavior than regulated entities? For an argument that Heckler v. Chaney represents "a Lochner-like view of the judicial role," see Cass R. Sunstein, Reviewing Agency Inaction After Heckler v. Chaney, 52 U. Chi. L. Rev. 653 (1985).

(2) *Refusal to Initiate Rulemaking.* Should the presumption of nonreviewability apply as well to decisions not to undertake rulemaking? FARMWORKER JUSTICE FUND, INC. V. BROCK, 811 F.2d 613, vacated as moot, 817 F.2d 890 (D.C.Cir.1987), WILLIAMS, J., concurring in part and dissenting in part:[5] "... Chaney relied on three features of nonenforcement decisions. First, such

---

5. [Ed]. The rest of the panel agreed with Judge Williams that Chaney did not preclude review of refusals to initiate rulemaking. The panel majority, however, found the agency's refusal unjustified, while Judge Williams would have sustained it. If you did the case study in Chapter I, you are familiar with the facts of this case.

decisions usually require agency expertise and coordination in setting priorities for the use of scarce resources. Second, they usually involve the agency's decision *not* to 'exercise its *coercive* power over an individual's liberty or property rights.' (emphasis in original) Third, they are akin to prosecutorial decisions not to indict." [Judge Williams concluded that the first two of these—which he summarized as the "resource allocation" and "non-use of the state's coercive power against a citizen's liberty or property" elements of nonenforcement decisions—were equally present in refusals to make rules.]

"[However, the] third element, the analogy to prosecutorial discretion, appears to distinguish this case from Chaney. The Chaney Court does not identify the characteristics shared by prosecutorial discretion and agency nonenforcement (other than the two elements previously mentioned), but two such characteristics leap to mind. First, prosecutors and agencies typically have to make innumerable decisions not to enforce or to seek indictment. Second, each such decision typically is very fact-rich, requiring deep involvement in the details of the individual case at issue and little legal analysis. By contrast, decisions not to initiate rulemaking are less likely to be frequent and more likely to turn on the scope of the agency's authority. Almost by definition, *rule* making, or its negative, entails consideration of broad issues that are likely to become, or to turn upon, issues of law.

"Supporting this analysis is the Court's distinction of cases where an agency 'has "consciously and expressly adopted a general policy" that is so extreme as to amount to an abdication of its statutory responsibilities.' Such abdications would presumably be infrequent and, when they occurred, would present issues of legal interpretation rarely seen in the typical fact-intensive decision against enforcement. Thus it appears that the prosecutorial discretion analogy (apart from its recapitulation of Chaney's first two factors) does not forcefully apply to a decision not to initiate a rulemaking (or act as the Secretary has here).

"Moreover, under the [APA,] refusal of a petition to initiate rulemaking provides a focus for judicial review not present in conventional nonenforcement cases. In distinguishing enforcement action from nonenforcement, the Court in Chaney noted that 'when an agency *does* act to enforce, that action itself provides a focus for judicial review,' allowing a court 'at least ... to determine whether the agency exceeded its statutory powers.'

"Here the APA provides a similar focal point. It requires every agency to provide opportunities to 'petition for the issuance, amendment, or repeal of a rule,' 5 U.S.C. § 553(e), and to give notice of denial of applications or petitions and 'a brief statement of the grounds for denial,' § 555(e). The combination of these requirements suggests a legislative expectation that agencies either declining to initiate rulemaking, or delaying final promulgation on the sort of theory alleged here, must reveal their thought processes. That expectation in turn suggests that courts may review such determinations for errors of law.

"In sum, I find noninstitution of a rulemaking distinguishable from nonenforcement decisions in that the former tend to be (1) less frequent, (2) more typically fraught with legal analysis (and therefore potential legal error), and (3) characteristically accompanied by public justification under the APA. Thus I believe that Chaney does not overturn prior decisions allowing review of agency decisions not to initiate rulemakings and, by inference, decisions of the sort the Secretary has made here.

"Our cases, however, have rightly emphasized the high degree of deference to which a decision not to initiate rulemaking is entitled, and that such a refusal is to be overturned 'only in the rarest and most compelling of circumstances,' WWHT, Inc. v. FCC, 656 F.2d 807, 818 (D.C.Cir.1981). Such judicial interventions, we have observed, 'primarily involve plain errors of law, suggesting that the agency has been blind to the source of its delegated power.' "

A few weeks later, the panel in another case unanimously adopted Judge Williams' rationale for not extending Chaney to the context of rulemaking. AMERICAN HORSE PROTECTION ASS'N, INC. V. LYNG, 812 F.2d 1 (D.C.Cir.1987), reviewed denial of a petition to amend allegedly inadequate regulations on the use of devices that deliberately injure show horses to improve their performance. Although agreeing with petitioners about the inadequacy of the agency's reasons for not acting, the court's opinion cautions: "Review under the 'arbitrary and capricious' tag line . . . encompasses a range of levels of deference to the agency, and Chaney surely reinforces our frequent statements that an agency's refusal to institute rulemaking proceedings is at the high end of the range." Subsequent D.C. Circuit cases speak of the "extremely limited, highly deferential scope" of review used in this context. National Customs Brokers & Forwarders Ass'n of Am., Inc. v. United States, 883 F.2d 93, 96 (D.C.Cir.1989). Indeed, Judge Williams himself subsequently warned that refusals to initiate rulemaking are reviewed "with a deference so broad as to make the process akin to non–reviewability." Cellnet Comm., Inc. v. FCC, 965 F.2d 1106, 1111 (D.C.Cir.1992). But compare Professional Pilots Fed'n, p. 596 above, applying "ordinary" arbitrary and capricious review because the refusal to engage in rulemaking was deemed a judgment on the merits of the proposal.

(3) *Refusal to Spend Money.* In LINCOLN V. VIGIL, 508 U.S. 182 (1993), Justice Souter for a unanimous Court described § 701(a)(2) jurisprudence as recognizing "certain categories of administrative decisions that courts traditionally have regarded as 'committed to agency discretion.' " Citing Justice Scalia's Webster dissent, he listed: (i) decisions not to take enforcement action; (ii) refusals to grant reconsideration of an action because of material error; and (iii) decisions to terminate an employee in the interests of national security. He then added another category: decisions about allocating funds from a lump-sum appropriation.

At issue was the Indian Health Service's decision to terminate a program that directly provided evaluative and clinical services to handicapped Native American children in the Southwest. The Service phased out this program in favor of what it described as a "nationwide" program. Children who had been receiving services sued, arguing that the decision violated various organic statutes, the APA, and the Fifth Amendment. They also argued that the Service had represented the Program's continuation to Congress, and that Congress had appropriated funds on that representation. The district court held that the Service's decision was reviewable, and that it was a "legislative rule" requiring § 553 notice-and-comment procedures. The court of appeals affirmed. In reversing on the threshold issue of reviewability, Justice Souter's opinion pointed out that no program-specific appropriation had been made, and reasoned: "The allocation of funds from a lump-sum appropriation is [an] administrative decision traditionally regarded as committed to agency discretion. After all, the very point of a lump-sum appropriation is to give an agency the capacity to adapt to changing circumstances and meet its statutory responsibilities in what it sees as the most effective or desirable way. . . .

"Like the decision against instituting enforcement proceedings, then, an agency's allocation of funds from a lump-sum appropriation requires 'a complicated balancing of a number of factors which are peculiarly within its expertise:' whether its 'resources are best spent' on one program or another; whether it 'is likely to succeed in fulfilling its statutory mandate'; whether a particular program 'best fits the agency's overall policies;' and, 'indeed, whether the agency has enough resources' to fund a program 'at all.' Heckler, 470 U.S. at 831. As in Heckler, so here, the 'agency is far better equipped than the courts to deal with the many variables involved in the proper ordering of its priorities.' Of course, an agency is not free simply to disregard statutory responsibilities: Congress may always circumscribe agency discretion to allocate resources by putting restrictions in the operative statutes (though not . . . just in the legislative history). And, of course, we hardly need to note that an agency's decision to ignore congressional expectations may expose it to grave political consequences. But as long as the agency allocates funds from a lump-sum appropriation to meet permissible statutory objectives, § 701(a)(2) gives the courts no leave to intrude. '[T]o [that] extent,' the decision to allocate funds 'is committed to agency discretion by law.' § 701(a)(2)."

Compare the complicated issue of Presidential power to make programmatic impoundments of appropriated funds. See p. 223 above.

NOTE ON THE CONSTITUTIONALITY OF PRECLUDING REVIEW

Justice Scalia's Webster dissent is perhaps most remarkable for its confident rejection of the proposition that "serious constitutional questions" are posed by denying judicial review of constitutional claims. As the reviewability cases testify, the judicial impulse to construe statutes to avoid these questions is strong—and has transcended political lines. Judges as diverse as Robert Bork and John Minor Wisdom have described the issue as "complex," "profound," "ancient and difficult;"[1] the topic is one of the most deeply and widely debated in contemporary constitutional law scholarship.[2] We have to leave exhaustive exploration of this area to the course

1. Bartlett v. Bowen, 816 F.2d 695, 711 (D.C.Cir.1987) (Bork, J., dissenting); American Ass'n of Councils of Med. Staffs of Private Hosp. v. Califano, 575 F.2d 1367, 1372 (5th Cir.1978), cert. denied, 439 U.S. 1114 (1979).

2. Accessing the vast literature can be a formidable task; excellent help is provided in

Paul M. Bator, Paul J. Mishkin, Daniel J. Meltzer & David L. Shapiro, Hart & Wechsler's The Federal Courts & the Federal System 319–465 (5th 2003) and Peter W. Low & John C. Jeffries, Jr., Federal Courts & The Law of Federal–State Relations 213–38 (4th ed. 1998) & most current Supplement. Com-in Federal Courts; what follows merely sketches the contours of a rich and convoluted intellectual landscape.

The problem begins, as Justice Scalia suggests, in the language of Article III. Although contemporary lawyers take the extensive federal court system for granted, very little of that system is explicitly mandated by the Constitution. Article III, § 1 provides: "The judicial Power of the United States shall be vested in one Supreme court, and in such inferior Courts as the Congress *may from time to time ordain and establish.*" Inasmuch as the very existence of the lower federal courts is apparently left to Congress' judgment (the argument goes), access to such courts for relief from allegedly illegal government action is necessarily a matter of legislative grace rather than constitutional right. Moreover, even with respect to the Supreme Court, Article III confers "appellate Jurisdiction, both as to Law and Fact, *with such Exceptions, and under such Regulations as the Congress shall make.*" Hence (it can be argued), access to the Supreme Court is also contingent on congressional authorization.[3] The view that Congress has plenary power over the jurisdiction of both Supreme and lower federal courts draws some support from history and precedent. Early on, the Court took the position that Article III is not self-executing—i.e., the federal courts, even the Supreme Court, require an affirmative *statutory* grant of jurisdiction. In the 200+ years since the Constitution was adopted, the full range of federal judicial power defined in Article III has never been statutorily vested in either the Supreme Court or the lower federal courts.[4] And there is language in Supreme Court cases that accords with the plenary power view, both as to original jurisdiction of the lower courts[5] and appellate jurisdiction of the Supreme Court.[6]

The plenary power interpretation of Article III has been espoused by enough distinguished scholars that it has been labelled the "traditional view."[7] Those holding this view typically urge that Congress *should* not use its power to withdraw jurisdiction, but insist that the power does exist as part of the constitutional system of checks and balances. Some have even argued that the very fact of the courts' dependence upon continued legislative acquiescence legitimates judicial review in a democracy.[8] At least in its

plete citations to the works of the scholars mentioned in this Note can be found in either of these sources.

3. Even a strongly literalist interpretation acknowledges that the Supreme Court's *original* jurisdiction could not be withdrawn by Congress, but Article III defines that jurisdiction as the very limited group of "all Cases affecting Ambassadors, other public Ministers and consuls, and those in which a State shall be Party."

4. For example, the statutory grant of diversity jurisdiction has always included an amount in controversy limitation. See, e.g., The First Judiciary Act, 1 Stat. 73 (1789) ($500 minimum required). Hence, although clearly within the "judicial Power of the United States" as defined by Article III, di-

versity cases involving less than $500 have never been heard, as an original or appellate matter, by federal courts. Moreover, the Supreme Court has never been authorized to review diversity cases of any dollar value coming from state courts.

5. See Sheldon v. Sill, 49 U.S. (8 How.) 441 (1850).

6. See Ex parte McCardle, 74 U.S. (7 Wall.) 506 (1868).

7. Adherents of this view have included Henry Hart, Herbert Wechsler, Gerald Gunther, Paul Bator, Martin Redish and William Van Alstyne.

8. Charles Black and Herbert Wechsler have made this argument.

mainstream form, however, the traditional view does not concede that there could be *no* judicial forum for asserting constitutional claims. Rather, as Henry Hart put it, the concern that Congress might leave constitutional rights without a remedy is answered by: "The state courts. In the scheme of the Constitution, they are the primary guarantors of constitutional rights, and in many cases they may be the ultimate ones."[9] Because the state courts do not derive their jurisdiction from Congress in the first instance (it is argued), they will always be open for the raising of constitutional claims, and the Supremacy Clause requires that such claims be heard and honored.

The traditional view has been seriously challenged. Its opponents point out that even a confirmed textualist might discern alternative meaning in the language of Article III.[10] Moreover, the Supreme Court opinions cited to support the plenary power view can all be read more narrowly, and (as implied by contemporary interpretive gymnastics to avoid "the serious constitutional questions") the Court has never squarely held that Congress may foreclose *all* judicial review of a constitutional claim. With respect to the traditionalist reliance on the state courts as ultimate remediators of constitutional rights, opponents point to a line of Supreme Court cases that call into question the power of state courts to give many forms of relief against federal officials and agencies.[11] The critics also emphasize that many state court judges do not enjoy the protection from political reprisal afforded by Article III's life tenure and salary provisions.[12]

Two principal types of theories have emerged as alternatives to the traditional, plenary power view. One type, the "essential function" arguments, uses constitutional history, structure and purpose to insist that Congress cannot withdraw jurisdiction when the result would be to vitiate

9. This is the concluding section of Hart's famous dialogue, The Power of Congress to Limit the Jurisdiction of Federal Courts: An Exercise in Dialectic, 66 Harv. L.Rev. 1362 (1953). The Dialogue remains a primary, if somewhat cryptic, source in this area.

10. For example, with respect to the Supreme Court's appellate jurisdiction, Raoul Berger and others have contended (and still others have disputed) that historical evidence supports reading the "Exceptions" clause as modifying only the word "Fact," such that Congress may control Supreme Court review of factual findings but not conclusions of law. Leonard Ratner (expanding upon a brief remark in Henry Hart's famous Dialogue) has argued that, in the legal mileau of the Framers, an "exception" could not destroy the "essential characteristics" of the subject to which it applies, while authority to adopt a "regulation" did not confer the power of complete prohibition.

With respect to the lower federal courts, Akhil Amar has posited a difference between Article III's subject-matter defined heads of jurisdiction (e.g., federal question, admiralty) and party-defined heads of jurisdiction (e.g., diversity, U.S. as party). Noting that the former are described using the language "*all* Cases" while the latter are described with only the unmodified word "Controversies," Amar argues that Congress *must* vest jurisdiction of the former category in some federal court, original or appellate. Amar's thesis, a revival in part of a position attributed to Justice Story, has generated a small whirlwind of debate within the larger controversy.

11. These cases seem to establish that state courts cannot employ habeas corpus or mandamus to remedy the illegal acts of federal officials. On the other hand, damage awards and, apparently, orders for possession of specific property are possible. Injunctive relief is an open question. See generally Richard S. Arnold, The Power of State Courts to Enjoin Federal Officers, 73 Yale L.J. 1385 (1964).

12. Lawrence Sager, in particular, has argued this point.

the essential functions of the federal judiciary. Initially propounded with respect to the Supreme Court's appellate jurisdiction, variations of the original "essential functions" theory have gone further to contend that the vast expansion of modern litigation—beyond anything the Framers might have imagined—now requires a lower federal court system as well.[13] The central debate sparked by these arguments is, of course, how to define the "essential functions" of the federal judiciary—with traditionalists insisting that their critics are engaged in "constitutional wishful thinking" and "question-begging."[14]

The second category of alternative theories, the "independent unconstitutionality" arguments, finds limits on Congress' jurisdiction-withdrawing power in constitutional provisions outside Article III. On the most basic level, virtually all commentators (including traditionalists) agree that Congress cannot limit judicial review through a restriction that itself violates some specific constitutional right—for example, closing the courthouse doors to African Americans or Jews. "Independent unconstitutionality" theorists argue for an even broader effect. Some contend that the equal protection clause, and perhaps substantive due process, prevent Congress from withdrawing jurisdiction over particular kinds of cases (e.g., school prayer challenges) because of hostility to the Court's holdings in the area.[15] Others have emphasized procedural due process, arguing that the process "due" in many contexts is judicial process.[16] Some support for the latter position can be found in the line of "constitutional" or "jurisdictional fact" cases, although the continuing precedential value of those cases is debatable.[17] More solid (though narrower) support is found in UNITED STATES v. MENDOZA-LOPEZ, 481 U.S. 828 (1987). An alien being prosecuted for illegal entry following deportation attempted to defend on grounds that the underlying deportation order was invalid; the Court agreed with the government that Congress had intended to foreclose such a defense. It held,

---

13. Leonard Ratner, a leading proponent of the original "essential functions" theory, would identify the essential functions of the Supreme Court as (i) providing the ultimate resolution of disputed questions of federal law, especially the Constitution, and (ii) maintaining the supremacy of federal law, especially the Constitution, when state law conflicts. Theodore Eisenberg is the principal proponent of the variation that insists that the existence of the lower federal courts has become constitutionally required; Eisenberg's theory would allow Congress to limit jurisdiction (using, for example, amount-in-controversy requirements) for "neutral" policy reasons such as efficiency. Lawrence Sager, another prominent essential-functions theorist, identifies the "essential function" as "supervision of state conduct to assure general compliance with the Constitution," a function which (he argues) Congress must permit the lower federal courts to perform if it wishes to withdraw jurisdiction from the Supreme Court.

14. These characterizations come from Martin Redish and Gerald Gunther, respectively.

15. Laurence Tribe has most clearly articulated this theory. In an interesting variation on the argument, Lea Brilmeyer and Stefan Underhill have pointed to a series of conflicts-of-laws cases which, they contend, supports the proposition that jurisdictional statutes cannot validly discriminate against constitutional claims.

16. Traditionalists are likely to agree with this point, at least in principle. The debate comes over how broadly one defines the cases in which judicial process is required, as well as over whether that process could constitutionally be satisfied by a hearing in state, rather than federal, court.

17. See "Note on the Special Problem of Reviewing 'Constitutional' or 'Jurisdictional' Facts," p. 973 above.

however, that this intent could not be honored in circumstances where judicial review of the original deportation proceeding had been effectively precluded: "[W]here a determination made in an administrative proceeding is to play a critical role in the subsequent imposition of a criminal sanction, there must be *some* meaningful review of the administrative proceeding."[18] Cf. Zadvydas v. Davis, 533 U.S. 678, 692 (2001) ("This Court has suggested ... that the Constitution may well preclude granting 'an administrative body the unreviewable authority to make determinations implicating fundamental rights.' Superintendent v. Hill, 472 U.S. 445 (1985), see also Crowell v. Benson, 285 U.S. at 87 (Brandeis, J., dissenting) ('Under certain circumstances, the constitutional requirement of due process is a requirement of judicial process.')").

Mendoza–Lopez presented the most compelling paradigm for recognizing a constitutional right to judicial review of agency action: the government was seeking to deprive an individual of his physical liberty on the basis of an administrative order that the defendant claimed was itself entered in violation of due process. (Mendoza–Lopez had argued, and the majority agreed, that the procedures used in his original deportation hearing were fundamentally unfair in a variety of ways.) But what if the challenged agency action has harmed an individual "only" by denying her something that does not (under current procedural due process entitlement analysis) constitute a "liberty" or "property" interest? And what if the claim is not that the agency action was *unconstitutional* but rather "merely" *unlawful*—either because it exceeded the agency's statutory authority or because it was an arbitrary and capricious exercise of discretion? In a highly respected book on judicial review, Louis Jaffe wrote: "The availability of judicial review is the necessary condition, psychologically if not logically, of a system of administrative power which purports to be legitimate, or legally valid."[19] As the previous discussion suggests, it is difficult enough to determine whether the Constitution mandates judicial review of claims that agencies have acted *unconstitutionally*. Is there any plausible argument that judicial review to ensure agencies' fidelity to *sub*-constitutional law is constitutionally, as well as psychologically, required? For arguments that judicial review is part of the constitutional quid pro quo for broad delegations of power, see pp. 70–77 above, and Cynthia R. Farina, Statutory Interpretation and the Balance of Power in the Administrative State, 89 Colum.L.Rev. 452, 487, 497–98 (1989).[20]

18. Chief Justice Rehnquist, with Justices O'Connor and White, dissented on grounds that the alien had not demonstrated the kind of "exceptional circumstances" that would justify permitting collateral attack on the underlying deportation order. Only Justice Scalia (writing a year before his Webster opinion) perceived no constitutional problem with "mak[ing] it a felony for deportees—irrespective of the legality of their deportations—to reenter the United States illegally."

19. Judicial Control of Administrative Action 320 (1965).

20. Other thoughtful arguments for a separation-of-powers based theory of required judicial review include Richard H. Fallon, Jr., Of Legislative Courts, Administrative Agencies, and Article III, 101 Harv.L.Rev. 915, 937–43 (1988); Todd D. Rakoff, The Shape of the Law in the American Administrative State, 11 Tel Aviv U. Studies in Law 9 (1992); Peter L. Strauss, The Place of Agencies in Government: Separation of Powers and the Fourth Branch, 84 Colum. L. Rev. 573, 579–80 (1984); Cass R. Sunstein, Constitutionalism After the New Deal, 101 Harv. L.Rev. 421, 463–74 (1987).

SECTION 4. THE TIMING OF JUDICIAL INTERVENTION

Ticor Title Insurance Co. v. Federal Trade Commission

United States Court of Appeals for the District of Columbia Circuit, 1987.
814 F.2d 731.

■ Before EDWARDS and WILLIAMS, CIRCUIT JUDGES, and JOYCE HENS GREEN, DISTRICT JUDGE. Separate opinions filed by CIRCUIT JUDGE EDWARDS, CIRCUIT JUDGE WILLIAMS and DISTRICT JUDGE JOYCE HENS GREEN.

■ HARRY T. EDWARDS, CIRCUIT JUDGE:

In this case we are asked to rule on a facial constitutional challenge to section 5(b) of the Federal Trade Commission Act, [15 U.S.C. § 45(b) (1982),] which authorizes the Federal Trade Commission to initiate and prosecute complaints against persons suspected of engaging in unfair methods of competition, or unfair or deceptive trade practices. Pursuant to this statutory authority, the FTC issued a complaint against the appellants, six title insurance companies, charging that they illegally restrained competition by fixing prices for title search and examination services. ... [T]hey have ... brought this action seeking a declaration that section 5(b) of the Act is unconstitutional and an injunction against the ongoing prosecution and all future FTC prosecutions.

The appellants' constitutional challenge centers on Article II of the Constitution.... According to the appellants, Article II prohibits the FTC, an independent federal agency outside the direct control and supervision of the President, from exercising the law enforcement powers conferred upon it by section 5(b) of the Act. Without passing on the merits of this argument, the District Court dismissed the appellants' claim, holding that it was not yet ripe for adjudication. ... Judge Green would affirm the District Court's determination ... Judge Williams, on the other hand, would hold that the filing of a complaint against the appellants was not final agency action.... I would affirm the judgment of the District Court on the prudential ground of exhaustion.

The issue presented by this complaint is relatively straightforward. The appellants have brought a facial constitutional challenge under the general federal question statute, 28 U.S.C. § 1331.... The appellants, however, also purport to have nonconstitutional (or statutory) defenses to the FTC complaint, which they are currently asserting before an ALJ in an ongoing administrative proceeding. The question posed by this appeal, then, is whether the appellants must exhaust their *nonconstitutional* defenses in the ongoing administrative proceeding before bringing their *constitutional* challenge to the agency's authority in federal court. ...

On two recent occasions, this circuit has considered whether to require litigants to pursue available remedies on nonconstitutional claims where the litigant has brought a constitutional challenge to the very authority of the government to take action against him. Most recently, in Hastings v. Judicial Conf. of the United States, 770 F.2d 1093 (D.C.Cir.1985), cert.

denied, 477 U.S. 904 (1986), we considered whether a United States District Court judge should be allowed to challenge the facial constitutionality of the Judicial Councils Reform and Judicial Conduct and Disability Act of 1980, which establishes an elaborate mechanism by which federal judges may be investigated and disciplined by their fellow judges for "conduct prejudicial to the effective and expeditious administration of the business of the courts." In Hastings, we held that we should postpone review of the constitutional question until the procedures outlined in the statute had actually been applied to Judge Hastings. . . .

In a separate portion of the opinion, however, we considered whether to pass on the constitutionality of certain informal fact-gathering powers that *had* been exercised under the statute. Again, we declined to reach the constitutional issue, reasoning that to do so "would contravene another aspect of avoidance—the policy [against] rendering judgment on the constitutionality of proceedings *while* the proceedings themselves are going on." (emphasis in opinion). We found that disruption of the ongoing proceedings would be justified only if the plaintiff could demonstrate that he would suffer "serious and irremediable injury" in the absence of immediate judicial review. We concluded that Judge Hastings had not made a showing of irreparable injury because the proceedings to which he was subject might terminate at any number of points before sanctions were imposed against him. The effect of our holding was to require Judge Hastings to defend himself in the statutory proceedings before bringing his constitutional challenge to the facial validity of the statute in federal court.

Two years before the decision in Hastings, a different panel of the court issued an opinion in Andrade v. Lauer, 729 F.2d 1475 (D.C.Cir.1984). Andrade is significant because it is not easily reconciled with the judgment in Hastings. In Andrade, employees of the Office of Juvenile Justice and Delinquency Prevention—an agency within the Department of Justice—challenged the implementation of a reduction in force ("RIF"), pursuant to which they were removed or demoted from their positions at the agency. The employees challenged the RIF on [two statutory grounds and on a constitutional, Appointments Clause, ground].

The first issue addressed in Andrade was whether the employees were required to pursue their nonconstitutional and constitutional claims through the "statutory and contractual" grievance procedure contained in their union's contract with the Department of Justice. Congress had mandated that public sector collective bargaining agreements contain a procedure for resolving grievances in cases involving RIFs. . . . Because Congress had defined a "grievance" to include any complaint regarding a "claimed violation, misinterpretation, or misapplication of any law, rule, or regulation affecting conditions of employment," we held that the employees were required to pursue their *personnel* and *statutory* claims through the available steps of the grievance procedure. . . . We held, however, that the employees were not required to pursue their *constitutional* claim through the grievance procedure before raising that claim in federal court, because the grievance procedure was not the appropriate forum in which to adjudicate a constitutional challenge. The decisionmakers in that forum, we reasoned, had neither the qualifications nor the expertise to articulate or develop the separation of powers principles implicated by the Appointments Clause.

Having found that the constitutional question was to be decided by the court rather than by the decisionmakers in the grievance procedure, we turned our attention to whether we should nevertheless postpone judicial review until the employees had submitted their *nonconstitutional* claims through the grievance procedure. We held that exhaustion of remedies on the nonconstitutional claims was unnecessary, despite the fact that a favorable decision on the employees' nonconstitutional claims would moot their constitutional claims. . . .

Apart from the obvious differences in the results reached in Hastings and Andrade, it is important to recognize that the cases rely on distinct legal theories. The principal holding in Hastings is that the plaintiff's claim was not "ripe" for judicial review; whereas in Andrade the court held that the plaintiffs need not "exhaust" their administrative remedies before pursuing their constitutional claims in court. . . .

. . . [A]lthough the case law is sometimes confusing on this point, the purposes and tests associated with the application of each doctrine are distinct:

> Ripeness and exhaustion are complementary doctrines which are designed to prevent unnecessary or untimely judicial interference in the administrative process.
>
> If the agency proceeding is still at an early stage and the party seeking review has the right to an administrative hearing or review, the court will decline to hear his appeal on the ground that he has failed to exhaust his administrative remedies. Judicial intervention may not be necessary because the agency can correct any initial errors at subsequent stages of the process; moreover, the agency's position on important issues of fact and law may not be fully crystallized or adopted in final form. . . .
>
> The ripeness doctrine looks to similar factors in determining the availability of review—that is, the fitness of the issues for judicial determination and the hardship to the parties that would result from granting or denying review—but it has a different focus and a different basis from exhaustion. The exhaustion doctrine emphasizes the position of the party seeking review; in essence, it asks whether he may be attempting to short circuit the administrative process or whether he has been reasonably diligent in protecting his own interests. Ripeness, by contrast, is concerned primarily with the institutional relationships between courts and agencies, and the competence of the courts to resolve disputes without further administrative refinement of the issues. In extreme cases, the ripeness doctrine serves to implement the policy behind Article III of the Constitution. Since the judicial power is limited to cases and controversies, federal courts cannot decide purely abstract or theoretical claims, or render advisory opinions.

E. Gellhorn & B. Boyer, Administrative Law and Process 316–19 (1981). . . .

I begin my analysis with the general rule—recognized even in An- drade—that exhaustion of available administrative remedies is a prerequi- site to obtaining judicial relief.... The appellants contend that this general rule should not be applied where the constitutional challenge goes to the very authority of the administrative body to conduct the relevant proceed- ings. In such circumstances, they argue, imposition of an exhaustion requirement would force litigants to submit to the very procedures they challenge as unconstitutional. In addition, ... [e]xhaustion, they argue, is typically required in order to give the agency an opportunity to apply its expertise and to develop facts that will aid the court in reviewing the final agency action. Here, however, ... the agency is not equipped to pass on the constitutionality of its enabling statute. Likewise, there is no need for factual development by the agency, because the exact nature of the law enforcement powers exercised by the Commission are well-known....[2]

Although the appellants' arguments have some real force,[3] they are insufficient under the facts of this case to warrant a departure from the general rule of exhaustion. ... [T]he courts have identified two exceptions to the general rule of exhaustion. The first exception, derived from the Supreme Court's decision in Leedom v. Kyne, p. 1198 above, permits immediate judicial review of a challenge to agency authority where the agency's assertion of jurisdiction "would violate a *clear right* of a petitioner by disregarding a *specific* and *unambiguous* statutory, regulatory, or consti- tutional directive." The second exception permits immediate judicial review where postponement of review would cause the plaintiff irreparable injury. However, relying on the Supreme Court's pronouncement in Renegotiation Board v. Bannercraft Clothing Co., 415 U.S. 1, 24 (1974), courts have uniformly recognized that "[m]ere litigation expense, even substantial and unrecoupable cost, does not constitute irreparable injury."

In the instant case, the appellants are plainly unable to invoke either of the above exceptions. First, the appellants cannot possibly maintain that the Commission's exercise of law enforcement powers is *clearly* unconstitu- tional. The status of independent agencies such as the FTC was upheld by the Supreme Court in Humphrey's Executor v. United States, p. 153 above.... Although it is at least arguable that the Supreme Court might be

---

2. In this respect, the appellants con- tend that this case differs markedly from Hastings. In Hastings, they observe, this court dealt with a recently enacted statute that had never been fully applied. It was therefore imperative that the court have be- fore it an actual application of the statute before passing on its facial constitutionality. Here, they argue, the FTC has exercised stat- utory law enforcement powers for decades, and there is no need for the court to educate itself on the workings of the challenged stat- ute.

3. I agree with the appellants that the constitutionality of section 5(b) of the Act is for this court, and not the agency, to decide. See, e.g., Weinberger v. Salfi, 422 U.S. 749,

764–67 (1975) (where all possible nonconsti- tutional objections to denial of social security benefits have been eliminated, and the *sole* issue for decision is the constitutionality of a statutory requirement, exhaustion is unnec- essary, because the agency is without juris- diction or competence to decide the constitu- tional question). I also agree that this case is somewhat unlike Hastings, where we dealt with a more complicated and untested statu- tory scheme. However, I would not foreclose the possibility that we might learn something from the application of the statute to these particular appellants that might aid us in deciding which, if any, of the powers con- ferred upon the Commission may be exer- cised consistent with the Constitution.

persuaded to alter its current position, that possibility falls far short of establishing that the Commission has acted in such direct conflict with the Constitution as to warrant immediate judicial intervention. Second, the only injury alleged by the appellants is the cost of defending themselves in the pending Commission proceedings. . . .

Given that neither of these two exceptions apply, I find no basis for departing from the general rule. . . . [First, the] interest in avoiding premature judicial involvement is heightened where the plaintiffs raise a *constitutional* challenge to agency action. In several different contexts, the Supreme Court has admonished courts not to decide important constitutional questions, and possibly invalidate congressional legislation, where a controversy may be resolved on some independent, nonconstitutional ground. . . . Second, I think it unwise to embrace an exception to the exhaustion doctrine that would permit interruption of ongoing agency proceedings whenever a litigant raises a non-frivolous challenge to the legitimacy of those proceedings. Such an exception would encourage litigants to bypass the orderly processes of administrative agencies and would intolerably interfere with the ability of those agencies to perform the tasks assigned to them by Congress. . . . For these reasons, I would adhere to the salutary rule of exhaustion, and affirm the District Court's dismissal of the appellants' complaint on that ground. . . .

■ WILLIAMS, CIRCUIT JUDGE:

. . . Since the challenged agency action was not "final" . . ., I would hold this suit barred on that jurisdictional ground, and would not address the related prudential issues of exhaustion and ripeness.[4]

Perhaps the most telling commentary on the chaotic state of the law governing our threshold inquiry is Professor Davis's observation that

> "[p]roblems of finality are in the area where the law of exhaustion joins or overlaps with the law of ripeness. . . . Finality may be a part of exhaustion, a part of ripeness, or a third subject; courts do not clarify the classification, for they need not."

4 K. Davis, Administrative Law Treatise § 26:10, at 458 (2d ed. 1983) (citation omitted) But while courts often mingle the three doctrines, they are analytically distinct. The mingling is natural enough. All three serve the interests in agency autonomy and judicial economy. All depend, in varying degrees, on the view that further administrative activity (or inactivity) may give effective victory to the complaining party, thus obviating the need for judicial intervention. All to a degree balance those interests against a concern that a rogue agency must not unduly burden private parties.

But the distinctions remain important. First, there is a difference in focus. While exhaustion is directed to the steps a litigant must take, finality looks to the conclusion of activity by the agency. And while ripeness depends on the fitness of issues for judicial review, see Abbott Laboratories v. Gardner, p. 1182 above, finality in administrative law plays a role closely

---

4. The ripeness doctrine, in extreme cases, is responsive to constitutional concerns and is jurisdictional, but the constitutional component of ripeness is not at issue here.

akin to the doctrine of the same name restricting interlocutory review of trial courts in the federal system, see 28 U.S.C. § 1291. For our immediate purposes, the more critical distinction is that while exhaustion and ripeness are judge-made *prudential* doctrines, finality is, where applicable, a *jurisdictional* requirement.

Thus, a finding of finality (or of an applicable exception) is essential when the court's reviewing authority depends on one of the many statutes permitting appeal only of "final" agency action. . . .

Administrative orders are final when "they impose an obligation, deny a right or fix some legal relationship as a consummation of the administrative process." Chicago & Southern Air Lines, Inc. v. Waterman Steamship Corp., 333 U.S. 103, 113 (1948) (citations omitted) Though that language itself leaves critical issues open, the precedents resolve them clearly enough for this case.

First, a long line of decisions establishes that the expense of an administrative proceeding—the sole burden that appellants allege here—does not qualify as the imposition of a burden or denial of a right. As we said in Alcoa v. United States:

> [T]hese are not the sorts of rights and obligations to which the quoted test refers. It is firmly established that agency action is not final merely because it has the effect of requiring a party to participate in an agency proceeding.

790 F.2d 938, 941 (D.C.Cir.1986) (citing FTC v. Standard Oil of California ("SOCAL"), 449 U.S. 232, 241–43 (1980)). . . .

Second, an administrative act is not "final" merely because it constitutes the agency's last word on a discrete legal issue in the course of a proceeding. In SOCAL, for example, the Commission had initiated enforcement proceedings, predicated on an assertion that it had "reason to believe" that SOCAL was violating the FTC Act. The Court, acknowledging that the issuance of the complaint was "definitive on the question whether the Commission avers" such a threshold finding, held that the averment was nonetheless not "definitive" in the relevant sense. Similarly, the fact that the Commission is most unlikely to change its position on the constitutionality of a § 5 proceeding . . . does not convert the Commission's assertion of jurisdiction into final agency action.

. . .

Third, an agency's decision to initiate proceedings does not become final merely because the challenger attacks the agency's jurisdiction, even where the attack raises a pure question of law. . . . To be sure, since the Commission in all likelihood cannot pass on the constitutionality of its own enabling statute, denial of immediate review does not serve the purpose of enabling the Commission "to correct its own mistakes and . . . apply its expertise." SOCAL, 449 U.S. at 242. In addition, petitioners claim that subjection to an unconstitutional proceeding constitutes a peculiarly offensive burden from which they should be relieved as promptly as possible. However, as noted above, the SOCAL Court assumed that the Commission would not alter its position on the challenged determination, yet it saw no reason to relax the customary finality rule. And, even if we accept the dubious proposition that unconstitutional burdens are *ipso facto* "heavier" than those of statutory illegality, the constitutional dimension of appellants' burden entails a concern that militates powerfully against immediate review: the "fundamental rule of judicial restraint," forbidding resolution of constitutional questions before it is necessary....

Review of nonfinal agency action is available in "the most exceptional circumstances." The classic and oft-quoted formulation is that of Judge Leventhal:

> [A] federal court ... [may] take jurisdiction before final agency action ... only ... in a case of "clear right" such as outright violation of a clear statutory provision [citing Leedom v. Kyne] or violation of basic rights established by a structural flaw, and not requiring in any way a consideration of interrelated aspects of the merits....

Association of National Advertisers, Inc. v. FTC, 627 F.2d 1151, 1180 (D.C.Cir.1979) (Leventhal, J., concurring) (emphasis omitted), cert. denied, 447 U.S. 921 (1980). In this case, it is quite plain that neither exception applies.[5]

That the clear-right exception is unavailable is self-evident. ... Little in the law is clearer than the proposition that petitioners' right, if any, is not clear. See Bowsher v. Synar, p. 176 above; Humphrey's Executor v. United States, p. 153 above.

The structural-flaw exception is even less promising. ... [S]imple initiation of enforcement proceedings in the face of a jurisdictional attack could not, alone, qualify as a "structural flaw;" mere subjection to the proceeding itself is not an injury incurable by review at the completion of the agency's work.

I would therefore affirm for want of final agency action....

■ JOYCE HENS GREEN, DISTRICT JUDGE:

... I write separately ... to explain why I believe that the constitutional question posed by this case is not yet ripe for review, and why, in my view, the ripeness doctrine provides the soundest basis for the result we reach today.

... "[A] court should be loath to interfere, by means of injunction, with ongoing [agency] proceedings." Hastings v. Judicial Conference. Administrative agencies are "entitled to a measure of comity sufficient to preclude disruptive injunctive relief by federal courts absent a showing that serious and irremediable harm will otherwise result." Ripeness is one of the judicial doctrines, along with exhaustion and finality, designed, in part, to prevent such disruption. In Abbott Laboratories v. Gardner, p. 1182

---

5. ... [I]nitiation of a complaint might in some circumstances impose a burden— beyond that of mere litigation—severe enough to meet the finality requirement. Judge Green's treatment of the "hardship" aspect of ripeness seems congruent with the traditional analysis of burdens for finality purposes. It is this very congruence that has led courts to discuss finality solely as an *aspect* of ripeness. Despite the overlap, finality is a separate requirement which, because of its jurisdictional character, must be addressed first. ...

above, the Supreme Court announced the now familiar two-part test for determining whether a challenge to administrative action is ripe for review. The Abbott Laboratories formulation requires courts "to evaluate both the fitness of the issues for judicial decision and the hardship to the parties of withholding court consideration." Like the District Court, I conclude that appellants' constitutional challenge satisfies the first of these two prongs, but founders on the second and is therefore unripe. Unlike my colleagues on this panel, however, I believe that the ripeness doctrine presents the only bar to immediate judicial consideration of appellants' claims, as the policies and purposes underlying the finality and exhaustion requirements do not dictate further postponement of judicial review.

There are, as Judge Edwards notes, areas of overlap between the exhaustion and ripeness doctrines. Both incorporate what might be termed "administrative refinement" concerns that spring in equal measure from the desire, on the one hand, to preserve agency autonomy, and the recognition, on the other hand, that there are limits to judicial competence. Thus, the exhaustion doctrine is designed in part to permit an agency to formalize or crystallize its policies, detect and correct its errors, develop a factual record where necessary, and apply its expertise where appropriate. Similarly, under the ripeness doctrine's "fitness of the issues" prong, courts must determine first whether the challenge to the agency's action or proceedings raises purely legal questions (which are presumptively suitable for judicial review) or questions requiring further factual development, and second whether either "the court or the agency would benefit from the postponement of review until the agency action or policy in question has assumed either a final or more concrete form."

These concerns, whether cast in exhaustion or ripeness terms, have been satisfied in the present case. Here, as in Abbott Laboratories, appellants have raised a purely legal question—namely, whether an independent agency, in this case the FTC, can exercise prosecutorial or executive powers. There is not even a suggestion . . . that the constitutional validity of the agency's exercise of such authority might vary according to the circumstances of each prosecution, or that the validity of the exercise of such authority may be more readily assessed in the context of a concrete factual setting. . . . Additionally, no purpose would be served by allowing the Commission an opportunity to correct its own mistakes or apply its expertise here, since the agency enjoys no expertise in matters of constitutional law, and in any event may not declare its own enabling statute unconstitutional. . . .

Turning then to the ripeness doctrine's "hardship to the parties" inquiry, appellants have identified the cost of defending themselves in allegedly unconstitutional administrative proceedings as the principal harm they will suffer if this court withholds review. . . . In SOCAL, the Court observed that litigation and its accompanying expense and annoyance is one of the costs of living under government, and held that such expense, even if substantial and unrecoupable, does not constitute irreparable injury. . . . Indeed, if the expense of such a defense were sufficient to satisfy the second prong of the ripeness test, that half of the test would be rendered superfluous in all cases involving challenges to ongoing administrative proceedings. . . .

Appellants attempt to distinguish SOCAL on the ground that the challenge raised in that case implicated the underlying merits of the FTC proceedings, while here the constitutional challenge is entirely unrelated to the merits of the administrative complaint currently pending against them. . . . [This distinction] highlights an essential difference . . . between the ripeness doctrine on the one hand, and exhaustion and finality on the other. The nature of appellants' challenge is such that further exhaustion is essentially futile, since the agency will not and cannot alter its determination that it possesses the prosecutorial authority it seeks to exercise here. The fact that appellants suffer no hardship other than the expense and bother of litigating before the agency in no way renders further exhaustion any less futile, or the agency's assertion of its authority any less final, thus neither the exhaustion nor finality doctrines should bar judicial review of that challenge. Because the nature of appellants' challenge does not increase the expense of participating in those proceedings, however, and because the ripeness test always requires some showing of harm greater than mere litigation expense, the distinction appellants draw between this case and SOCAL does not buttress their claim that the constitutional challenge they seek to litigate is ripe.

Appellants also argue that this court's failure to reach the merits of their claims will deprive them of their right to be free from unconstitutional, coercive prosecutions, and that unless their constitutional challenge is adjudicated before that prosecution concludes, this right will be irretrievably lost. This court's decision in Hastings, however, effectively disposes of this contention. . . . Judge Hastings, like appellants here, presumably lost his right to be free from an allegedly unconstitutional investigation into his conduct, yet this court found that he had not demonstrated a sufficiently serious and irreparable injury to justify interruption of the ongoing proceedings. . . .

Finally, appellants rely on Andrade v. Lauer, a decision which, at first blush, is not easily reconciled with the Hastings opinion. . . . I agree with appellants that if this case is analyzed only in terms of exhaustion, Andrade dictates that we find their claims reviewable. Here, as there, appellants' constitutional claims cannot be raised in the administrative proceedings; the agency lacks the necessary expertise to resolve such claims; judicial resolution of the claims would not do violence to Congress' administrative scheme because that scheme does not envision administrative resolution of such issues; the claims themselves do not require further factual development as they raise purely legal questions; and there is considerable public interest in resolving those claims as the constitutional violation, if there be one, is continuous. As in Andrade, therefore, the underlying purposes of the exhaustion requirement are so little served by postponement of review that the requirement should not bar judicial consideration of the claims presented. It is for this reason that I cannot join the opinion of Judge Edwards, for as I see it, the inherent flexibility of the exhaustion doctrine militates in *favor* of judicial review in a case such as this. . . .

Ripeness, by contrast, is a two-part test that always requires some showing of hardship. ... Since administrative agencies, as autonomous bodies, always have an interest in avoiding judicial interruption of their proceedings, courts require some showing of hardship to warrant judicial intrusion into the agency's domain, even where the issues are otherwise generally fit for review. ... [W]hile the absence of any significant harm does not bar judicial review under the exhaustion doctrine where that doctrine's purposes are otherwise not served by postponement, a lack of such harm does stand as a barrier under the Abbott Laboratories formulation of the ripeness test, as that test established hardship as an independent requirement. Nor is this surprising, given the ripeness doctrine's concern for preventing judicial encroachment on administrative autonomy: without the requirement of some showing of hardship, courts could interrupt agency proceedings whenever judges felt competent to decide the question under agency consideration. Such a rule would make agencies but a poor relation of the courts, reducing their function in many instances to the mere collection of data and refinement of issues for judicial resolution. Without establishing what minimum showing of hardship is required when the issues are otherwise fit for review, it is enough for present purposes to note that the cost of participating in agency proceedings is inadequate. ... Accordingly, I would hold that the District Court properly dismissed this case as unripe. ...

* * *

As the three opinions in Ticor illustrate, the seemingly simple question of *when* judicial review is timely may implicate three distinct but overlapping doctrines: exhaustion of administrative remedies, finality, and ripeness. (You might find it helpful to think of the first as focusing on party behavior, the second on agency behavior, and the third on judicial behavior.) Each doctrine is explored, in turn, in a set of Notes below.

NOTES ON EXHAUSTION OF ADMINISTRATIVE REMEDIES

Exhaustion in cases brought under the APA

"Actions reviewable

... Except as otherwise expressly required by statute, agency action otherwise final is final for the purposes of this section whether or not there has been presented or determined an application for a declaratory order, for any form of reconsideration, or, unless the agency otherwise requires by rule and provides that the action meanwhile is inoperative, for an appeal to superior agency authority."

Administrative Procedure Act, § 704

(1) *Preemption of Common-Law Interest Balancing.* In Darby v. Cisneros, 509 U.S. 137 (1993), a real estate developer sought review of an ALJ decision that he had engaged in improper financial practices and should be barred from participating in HUD programs for 18 months. Under HUD regulations, an ALJ's decision "shall be final unless ... the Secretary or the Secretary's designee, within 30 days of receipt of a request decides as a matter of discretion to review the [ALJ's] finding. ... Any party may request such a review in writing within 15 days of receipt of the [ALJ's]

determination." The agency argued that Darby's failure to request review under this regulation foreclosed judicial review.

For a unanimous Court,[1] Blackmun, J.: "This case presents the question whether federal courts have the authority to require that a plaintiff exhaust available administrative remedies before seeking judicial review under the Administrative Procedure Act, where neither the statute nor agency rules specifically mandate exhaustion as a prerequisite to judicial review. At issue is the relationship between the judicially created doctrine of exhaustion of administrative remedies and the statutory requirements of § [704] of the APA. . . .

"Petitioners argue that this provision means that a litigant seeking judicial review of a final agency action under the APA need not exhaust available administrative remedies unless such exhaustion is expressly required by statute or agency rule. . . . Respondents contend that [the section] is concerned solely with timing, that is, when agency actions become 'final,' and that Congress had no intention to interfere with the courts' ability to impose conditions on the timing of their exercise of jurisdiction to review final agency actions. . . . It perhaps is surprising that it has taken over 45 years since the passage of the APA for this Court definitively to address this question. . . .

". . . [T]he text of the APA leaves little doubt that petitioners are correct. Under [§ 702], '[a] person suffering legal wrong because of agency action, or adversely affected or aggrieved by agency action within the meaning of a relevant statute, *is entitled to judicial review thereof.*' (emphasis added) Although [§ 702] provides the general right to judicial review of agency actions under the APA, [§ 704] establishes when such review is available. When an aggrieved party has exhausted all administrative remedies expressly prescribed by statute or agency rule, the agency action is 'final for the purposes of this section' and therefore 'subject to judicial review' under the first sentence. While federal courts may be free to apply, where appropriate, other prudential doctrines of judicial administration to limit the scope and timing of judicial review, [§ 704], by its very terms, has limited the availability of the doctrine of exhaustion of administrative remedies to that which the statute or rule clearly mandates.

". . . Congress clearly was concerned with making the exhaustion requirement unambiguous so that aggrieved parties would know precisely what administrative steps were required before judicial review would be available. If courts were able to impose additional exhaustion requirements beyond those provided by Congress or the agency, the last sentence of [§ 704] would make no sense. . . . Of course, the exhaustion doctrine continues to apply as a matter of judicial discretion in cases not governed by the APA. But where the APA applies, an appeal to 'superior agency authority' is a prerequisite to judicial review *only* when expressly required by statute or when an agency rule requires appeal before review and the administrative action is made inoperative pending that review." Because

---

1. Chief Justice Rehnquist and Justices Scalia and Thomas did not join in a section of the opinion, not reproduced here, in which Justice Blackmun considered the legislative history of the APA.

neither the governing statute nor HUD regulations *mandated* an appeal to the Secretary, the Court held that Darby's action must be permitted to go forward.[2]

(2) *The Continued Importance of Finality and Ripeness.* Air España v. Brien, 165 F.3d 148 (2d Cir.1999), underscores that participating in an agency's internal review processes might make judicial review premature *even if* those processes do not meet the stringent exhaustion standards of § 704. Airlines who transport improperly documented foreign nationals to the United States are liable to sanctions, including monetary penalties. The INS had imposed fines on Air España, which the airline appealed to the Board of Immigration Appeals. Simultaneously, the airline sought judicial review. Held: Even though neither the statute nor INS rules required exhaustion of the BIA appeal route, while the appeal was pending the fine order was not final. Ripeness required either exhaustion of the BIA appeal process, or waiver of those appeal rights.

Exhaustion in cases with no applicable statutory exhaustion requirement

(3) *The Classic Exhaustion Requirement.* On the day that the NLRB began an unfair labor practice hearing against Bethlehem Shipbuilding Corp., the company sought (and obtained from the district court) an injunction against further administrative proceedings. When the court of appeals affirmed, the Supreme Court granted certiorari. In Myers v. Bethlehem Shipbuilding Corp., 303 U.S. 41 (1938), Justice Brandeis, for a unanimous Court, explained why the case must be dismissed: "There is no claim by the Corporation that the statutory provisions and the rules of procedure prescribed for such hearings are illegal; or that the Corporation was not accorded ample opportunity to answer the complaint of the Board; or that opportunity to introduce evidence on the allegations made will be denied. The claim is that the provisions of the Act are not applicable to the Corporation's business at the Fore River Plant, because the operations conducted there are not carried on, and the products manufactured are not sold, in interstate or foreign commerce; that, therefore, the Corporation's relations with its employees at the plant cannot burden or interfere with such commerce; that hearings would, at best, be futile; and that the holding of them would result in irreparable damage to the Corporation, not only by reason of their direct cost and the loss of time of its officials and employees, but also because the hearings would cause serious impairment of the good will and harmonious relations existing between the Corporation and its employees, and thus seriously impair the efficiency of its operations.

"... The District Court is without jurisdiction to enjoin the hearing.... It is true that the Board has jurisdiction only if the complaint concerns interstate or foreign commerce. Unless the Board finds that it does, the complaint must be dismissed. And if it finds that interstate or

---

2. Note that both § 704 itself and the Darby case require the lawyer to consult any exhaustion requirements in the relevant organic statute(s). Is there a reverse-Darby effect as well: i.e., no judicial discretion to excuse a litigant's failure to exhaust administrative remedies that satisfy § 704? The Fourth Circuit thought so in Volvo GM Heavy Truck Corp. v. Department of Labor, 118 F.3d 205 (4th Cir.1997).

foreign commerce is involved, but the Circuit Court of Appeals concludes that such finding was without adequate evidence to support it, or otherwise contrary to law, the Board's petition to enforce it will be dismissed, or the employer's petition to have it set aside will be granted. Since the procedure before the Board is appropriate and the judicial review so provided is adequate, Congress had power to vest exclusive jurisdiction in the Board. . . .

"Obviously, the rule requiring exhaustion of the administrative remedy cannot be circumvented by asserting that the charge on which the complaint rests is groundless and that the mere holding of the prescribed administrative hearing would result in irreparable damage. Lawsuits also often prove to have been groundless; but no way has been discovered of relieving a defendant from the necessity of a trial to establish the fact."

Note that in finding the NRLB procedure appropriate, and judicial review of its outcomes adequate, the Court gave Bethlehem Shipbuilding half a loaf. The administrative scheme, the Court held, was not facially invalid; the obligation to submit to the administrative process was not, in itself, unfair. Consider how often justiciability doctrines, while ostensibly denying review, in fact afford partial review in this way.

(4) *Waiver*. McKart v. United States, 395 U.S. 185 (1969), was a criminal prosecution for wilful failure to report for induction into the army. McKart had been protected from the draft by a statutory exemption for a sole surviving son whose father had been killed in action. When his mother died as well, he was reclassified and ordered to report. He neither reported nor attempted to use Selective Service processes for challenging the reclassification. When he tried to defend the prosecution on grounds that he remained entitled to the statutory exemption, the lower court refused to allow the defense because he had failed to exhaust his administrative remedies.

Note that this case presents a different kind of exhaustion problem than that involved in Myers. As Justice Brandeis takes pains to point out, if the administrative proceeding in Myers is allowed to take its course, the agency will decide whether Bethlehem is an employer in interstate commerce and, if Bethlehem loses on the merits, this question will be preserved for eventual judicial review. Hence, insisting on exhaustion "simply" delays judicial consideration of this claim. By contrast, the effect of requiring exhaustion in McKart would be to foreclose the statutory exemption claim entirely, for the opportunity to invoke the relevant administrative processes had passed. McKart unanimously held that the statutory claim could be raised. Justice Marshall, writing for the Court, reasoned that (i) invoking exhaustion in criminal cases can have "exceedingly harsh" results; (ii) the issue was a purely legal question of statutory interpretation; and (iii) the high stakes of a criminal prosecution made it unlikely that failure to require exhaustion in this case would encourage draftees to bypass available administrative remedies.

Compare the result, two years later, in another draft prosecution, McGee v. United States, 402 U.S. 479 (1971). McGee also failed to resort to administrative remedies to dispute his classification status; here, though, Justice Marshall (writing for all but Justice Douglas) invoked the exhaustion requirement. Even though the Government conceded that the local draft board had had no basis, on the materials before it, for denying McGee's claimed exemption as a ministerial student or conscientious objector, the Court concluded: "Unlike the dispute about statutory interpretation involved in McKart, McGee's claims to exempt status . . . depended on the application of expertise by administrative bodies in resolving underlying issues of fact. Factfinding for purposes of Selective Service classification is committed primarily to the administrative process, with very limited judicial review. . . . McKart expressly noted that as to classification claims turning on the resolution of particularistic fact questions, 'the Selective Service System and the courts may have a stronger interest in having the question decided in the first instance by the local board. . . .' "

(5) *The Relevant Considerations.* In MCCARTHY V. MADIGAN, 503 U.S. 140 (1992), a prisoner sought damages for allegedly unconstitutional denial of medical care. The prison argued that he must first exhaust internal prison grievance procedures. Blackmun, J: "[In general,] [e]xhaustion is required because it serves the twin purposes of protecting administrative agency authority and promoting judicial efficiency.

"As to the first of these purposes, the exhaustion doctrine recognizes the notion, grounded in deference to Congress' delegation of authority to coordinate branches of government, that agencies, not the courts, ought to have primary responsibility for the programs that Congress has charged them to administer. . . . The exhaustion doctrine also acknowledges the commonsense notion of dispute resolution that an agency ought to have an opportunity to correct its own mistakes with respect to the programs it administers before it is haled into federal court. Correlatively, exhaustion principles apply with special force when 'frequent and deliberate flouting of administrative processes' could weaken an agency's effectiveness by encouraging disregard of its procedures. McKart v. United States.

"As to the second of the purposes, exhaustion promotes judicial efficiency in at least two ways. When an agency has the opportunity to correct its own errors, a judicial controversy may well be mooted, or at least piecemeal appeals may be avoided. And even where a controversy survives administrative review, exhaustion of the administrative procedure may produce a useful record for subsequent judicial consideration, especially in a complex or technical factual context.

"Notwithstanding these substantial institutional interests, federal courts are vested with a 'virtually unflagging obligation' to exercise the jurisdiction given them. 'We have no more right to decline the exercise of jurisdiction which is given, than to usurp that which is not given.' Cohens v. Virginia, 19 U.S. 264, 6 Wheat. 264, 404 (1821). Accordingly, this Court has declined to require exhaustion in some circumstances even where administrative and judicial interests would counsel otherwise. . . . [Our] precedents have recognized at least three broad sets of circumstances in which the interests of the individual weigh heavily against requiring administrative exhaustion. First, requiring resort to the administrative remedy may occasion undue prejudice to subsequent assertion of a court action. Such prejudice may result, for example, from an unreasonable or indefinite timeframe for administrative action. Even where the administrative decisionmaking schedule is otherwise reasonable and definite, a particular plaintiff may suffer irreparable harm if unable to secure immediate judicial consideration of his claim. By the same token, exhaustion principles apply with less force when an individual's failure to exhaust may preclude a defense to criminal liability. McKart v. United States.

"Second, an administrative remedy may be inadequate 'because of some doubt as to whether the agency was empowered to grant effective relief.' For example, an agency, as a preliminary matter, may be unable to consider whether to grant relief because it lacks institutional competence to resolve the particular type of issue presented, such as the constitutionality of a statute. . . . Alternatively, an agency may be competent to adjudicate the issue presented, but still lack authority to grant the type of relief requested. Montana Bank v. Yellowstone County, 276 U.S. 499, 505 (1928) (taxpayer seeking refund not required to exhaust where 'any such application [would have been] utterly futile since the county board of equalization was powerless to grant any appropriate relief' in face of prior controlling court decision).

"Third, an administrative remedy may be inadequate where the administrative body is shown to be biased or has otherwise predetermined the issue before it. . . ."

Exhaustion was not required here because damages—the only remedy McCarthy sought—were not available through the prison grievance procedure, and because his Eighth Amendment claim of "deliberate indifference" to medical needs neither implicated the Bureau of Prison's general interest in prison control and management, nor represented the sort of issue on which the agency possessed special expertise that would be useful to a court. Compare SIMS V. APFEL, 530 U.S. 103 (2000), permitting judicial review at the behest of a claimant for Social Security disability benefits who had exhausted her administrative remedies as to her claim per se, but who had not raised every *issue* in her agency appeal to the Social Security Appeals Counsel. Neither the statute nor SSA regulations required issue exhaustion. Justice Thomas, for a plurality that included Justices Stevens, Souter and Ginsburg, reasoned that a judicially imposed requirement of issue exhaustion would be inappropriate given the nature of Social Security proceedings. The ALJ (and the Council on review) are not like trial courts that merely decide on the basis of adversarial presentations; rather, they have an inquisitorial duty to develop the facts pro and con awarding benefits. In such a context, requiring issue exhaustion makes little sense. Justice O'Connor concurred, to make a majority, on grounds that SSA had failed to notify claimants of any issue exhaustion requirement. Justice Breyer, for the four dissenters, argued that the differences between the agency and a court actually *favored* an issue exhaustion requirement.

(5) *Primary Jurisdiction*. Related to, though distinct from, exhaustion of administrative remedies is the doctrine of primary jurisdiction. "At times, both an agency and a court may have original jurisdiction over the same case or issue. In this context of concurrent jurisdiction, the question addressed by the doctrine of primary jurisdiction is whether, when a party chooses to initiate an action in the court, that court may decline . . . to hear

the action in favor of an initial agency decision in the matter." Alfred C. Aman, Jr., & William T. Mayton, Administrative Law 422 (1993). The Supreme Court's 1907 decision in TEXAS & PACIFIC RY. V. ABILENE COTTON OIL Co., 204 U.S. 426, established that the federal courts *do* have this discretionary power. In that case, a shipper sued in federal court to recover from the railroad an allegedly excessive rate. Even though the Interstate Commerce Act expressly preserved this common-law remedy, the Court held that the shipper must "primarily invoke redress through the Interstate Commerce Commission." If, as in Abilene Cotton Oil, a court concludes that the agency has primary jurisdiction over the entire *dispute*, it will dismiss the case outright. Alternatively, a court might conclude that primary jurisdiction exists over only an *issue*, in which case it will retain jurisdiction over the dispute while the agency's resolution of the issue is obtained.

Like exhaustion, the doctrine of primary jurisdiction is more accurately described as a set of policy considerations, applied in a fact-specific manner, than as a collection of formulaic rules. Factors that are commonly considered include: the need for uniform resolution of the particular regulatory issue,[3] the degree to which proper resolution is likely to require the agency's specialized expertise,[4] and the risk that judicial resolution would impede the agency's ability to accomplish its regulatory mission.[5] The doctrine has sometimes proved controversial in its application. In a classic primary jurisdiction case, FAR EAST CONF. V. UNITED STATES, 342 U.S. 570 (1952), the Supreme Court ordered that an anti-trust action brought by the Department of Justice against a group of steamship operators be dismissed on grounds that the Federal Maritime Board had primary jurisdiction to determine whether the rate practices at issue were permissible under the Shipping Act. Subsequently, the FMB approved the practices. The Supreme Court then held that the practices violated both the Shipping Act and the Sherman Act. FMB v. Isbrandtsen Co., 356 U.S. 481 (1958).

As this series illustrates, invocation of primary jurisdiction can result in considerable delay and extra litigation expense, for the dispute as to which the agency's opinion is sought can usually find its way back into court on petition for review of that opinion. Nonetheless, it is argued, the benefits are worth the costs.[6] Indeed, courts have discerned new impetus for invocation of primary jurisdiction in Chevron v. NRDC, p. 1026 above. AYUDA V. THORNBURGH, 880 F.2d 1325, 1344 (D.C.Cir.1989), vacated on other grounds, 498 U.S. 1117 (1991): "Although the doctrine of primary jurisdiction was originally rooted in the notion that agencies have greater expertise, experience, and flexibility than courts in dealing with regulatory matters, see Far East Conference, as well as in a desire for uniform application of the law, see id., ... abstention in favor of agencies charged with resolving conflicting statutory policies also promotes the proper rela-

3. See, e.g., Texas & Pacific Ry. Co. v. Abilene Cotton Oil Co., 204 U.S. 426 (1907).

4. See, e.g., United States v. Western Pac. Ry. Co., 352 U.S. 59 (1956).

5. See, e.g., Allnet Comm. Serv. v. National Exchange Carrier Ass'n, 965 F.2d 1118 (D.C.Cir.1992).

6. See, e.g., II Richard J. Pierce, Jr., Administrative Law Treatise 937 (4th ed. 2002).

tionships between courts and administrative agencies. This follows natural-ly from Chevron, which explained that deference to agencies was appropri-ate not only because of agency expertise but also because Congress is presumed to delegate the policy choices inherent in resolving statutory ambiguities to the agency charged with implementation of the statute." Compare NORTHWEST AIRLINES, INC. V. COUNTY OF KENT, 510 U.S. 355 (1994), in which several airlines sued in district court claiming that airport user fees imposed by Kent County contravened federal statutes that authorized "reasonable" user fees. The district court and court of appeals concluded that the fees were not unreasonable. On the airlines' petition for certiorari, the Supreme Court affirmed on this ground, but suggested in dicta that it would have invoked primary jurisdiction had the County filed a cross-petition raising the issue: "The Secretary of Transportation . . . is equipped, as courts are not, to survey the field nationwide, and to regulate based on a full view of the relevant facts and circumstances. If we had the benefit of the Secretary's reasoned decisions concerning the [Act's] permis-sion for the charges in question, we would accord that decision substantial deference. See Chevron v. NRDC."

(6) *Exhaustion in Rulemaking?* All the preceding discussion has involved administrative adjudication. What if a rule is challenged on grounds never raised in the notice-and-comment process? Does exhaustion have any role to play in review of rules?

Two initial observations: There is nothing like "party" status in rulemaking; moreover, in the typical regulatory context, neither statute nor regulation requires that persons seeking to challenge the rule in court must have participated in the notice-and-comment process.[7]

In addition, consider the several types of challenges that might be made to a rule: (1) facial constitutional and statutory authority for the rule (which usually can be determined without any need for an administrative record); (2) procedural compliance in the rulemaking; (3) factual support for and judgment reasonability of the rulemaking; (4) as-applied constitu-tional and statutory authority for the rulemaking; (5) other issues unique to the particular enforcement context. Of these, Type 1 seems most unlikely to implicate "exhaustion" concerns. If, for example, Joe's Furni-ture didn't participate in a Consumer Product Safety Commission rulemak-ing that resulted in enforcement against it when it sold furniture that wasn't fire-safe, can't Joe *always* argue a Type 1 issue: "Congress provided in a recent rider that you have no authority to enforce your rule on this subject" or "Your statutes say you can't adopt rules about furniture"? (Or, at least, can't Joe's always do so absent some extraordinary statutory limitation on when or how such arguments must be made?) At the other extreme, Types 4 & 5 will virtually *never* be ripe for challenge until the enforcement stage, at which point the usual exhaustion analysis will tell us whether they need to be raised first during the agency adjudication apply-

---

7. For an exceptional counter-example, see the Federal Communications Act, 47 U.S.C. § 405, which permits judicial review only at the request of someone who has ei-ther participated in the agency proceeding or petitioned the agency for reconsideration.

ing the rule. This leaves Types 2 & 3, which are probably the most common kinds of challenges in pre-enforcement review. Could one argue that these challenges are most sensibly made only by people who participated in the rulemaking and raised the issues there? (At a minimum, isn't it sensible to insist that *someone* in the rulemaking must prominently have raised them?)

A small but potentially significant number of recent decisions appear to be taking this position. In National Ass'n of Manufacturers v. Department of the Interior, 134 F.3d 1095 (D.C.Cir.1998), a trade association which participated in a CERCLA rulemaking was told that a few references to the issue "buried in hundreds of pages of technical comments" it had submitted were inadequate to preserve the issue for review—despite arguments that the agency knew about the issue because it had addressed it in prior related rulemakings. See also 1001 Friends of Maryland v. Browner, 265 F.3d 216 (4th Cir.2001); cf. Vermont Yankee, p. 498 above. In Southwestern Pa. Growth Alliance v. Browner, 121 F.3d 106 (3d Cir.1997), the court refused to consider a statutory point that might have been, but apparently was not, raised before the agency, once it had concluded that it (the court) would have benefitted from the agency's "special expertise regarding the workings of the Clean Air Act." Yet in American Forest & Paper Ass'n v. EPA, 137 F.3d 291 (5th Cir.1998), where the issue appeared to concern an agency's legal authority per se (a Type 1 issue), the court refused to impose any requirement that the party (or someone else) have flagged the issue in the rulemaking. Compare NRDC v. EPA, 824 F.2d 1146 (D.C.Cir.1987), a unanimous en banc opinion considering NRDC's arguments even though the group had not participated in the rulemaking, where other parties had made the arguments and EPA had in fact responded to them.

These cases conspicuously lack discussion of whether, when, why, or how exhaustion doctrine developed in the context of agency adjudication should be applied to rulemaking. Perhaps they signal a kind of responsiveness to ossification concerns, see p. 1022 above. That is, they display a judicial conviction that—for at least some types of issues—parties should not be able to hold the agency to consideration of factors, criticisms, and alternatives not actually and prominently raised in the comment process. Note, though, that even if the underlying judicial impulse is sensible, using the exhaustion rubric opens the courts to criticism if (as in these cases) they fail to recognize the relevance of Darby's interpretation of APA § 704. For an ambitious argument that exhaustion and ripeness doctrines (among other things) are inappropriate vestiges of judicial common-lawmaking that should be recognized as completely supplanted by the APA, see John F. Duffy, Administrative Common Law in Judicial Review, 77 Tex. L. Rev. 113 (1998).

NOTES ON FINALITY

Finality is the most amorphous of the several doctrines through which courts regulate the timing of judicial review. A legal grab bag, the finality rubric is applied to an assortment of questions about the appropriateness of intervention at a particular moment in the administrative process.

(1) *Analogy to Interlocutory Appeals.* One sort of finality problem arises when the contested agency determination, though complete in itself, is embedded in a larger, ongoing administrative proceeding. In FTC v. STANDARD OIL CO. OF CAL., 449 U.S. 232 (1980) ["SOCAL"], eight major oil companies, charged by the FTC with unfair and monopolistic practices in connection with the late–1970s gasoline shortage, argued that the administrative complaint had unlawfully been filed in response to political pressure, rather than on the statutorily required basis of "reason to believe" that an unfair method of competition had been used. The FTC had explicitly considered, and rejected, this claim—not just once in denying a motion to dismiss the complaint, but again on SOCAL's petition for reconsideration. No one suggested that the agency's resolution of the "reason to believe" issue was tentative or likely to be modified, yet the Supreme Court unanimously rejected the attempted resort to the courts.

Judicial refusal to intervene on finality grounds in such circumstances can be analogized to the presumption against interlocutory appeals within the court system. As Judge Friendly has explained, "Many of the considerations supporting the final judgment rule with respect to appeals from decisions of lower courts are equally present in the case of agency action: The agency may find in favor of respondent; the case may be settled; the reviewing court, in any event, will be in a better position to assess the matter when all the cards have been played." PEPSI CO., INC. v. FTC, 472 F.2d 179, 185 (2d Cir.1972), cert. denied, 414 U.S. 876 (1973). Nonetheless, just as in the case of interlocutory decisions within the court system, immediate review of interlocutory agency action may be available in unusual circumstances. For example, in Pepsico itself, the court allowed an appeal of FTC's refusal to join 513 Pepsi bottlers in a complaint that charged Pepsico with anticompetitive practices for restricting its bottlers from selling outside designated geographical areas. "While Pepsico and its bottlers cannot be heard to complain of the Commission's attempt to [restructure the industry], arguably they should not be placed under that threat in a proceeding that must prove to be a nullity" if the bottlers were indeed indispensable parties.[1] Review is most likely to occur in circumstances where the petitioner can make a credible claim that failure to grant immediate review will result in irrevocable loss of the very right asserted. See, e.g., Alabama Power Co. v. FERC, 993 F.2d 1557, 1566–67 (D.C.Cir. 1993) (allowing review of decision to initiate a rate investigation, despite general rule that such decisions are unreviewable nonfinal orders, where petitioner alleged an earlier settlement in which FERC had agreed that such investigations would occur no more often than every three years; "deprivation [of the alleged contractual right to be free from the burden of

---

1. The Second Circuit affirmed the agency action on the merits. Other soft-drink manufacturers against whom the FTC had filed parallel complaints were not successful in persuading other courts of appeals interlo-cutorily to review the agency's joinder rulings. See Coca–Cola Co. v. FTC, 475 F.2d 299 (5th Cir.), cert. denied, 414 U.S. 877 (1973); Seven–Up Co. v. FTC, 478 F.2d 755 (8th Cir.), cert. denied, 414 U.S. 1013 (1973).

investigation] cannot be cured by a subsequent Commission decision that petitioners' formula rates are not excessive").

(2) *Multiple Regulatory Actors.* Another sort of finality problem may occur when a regulatory scheme requires several officials each to play a part in the regulatory decision. *Whose* actions constitute "final agency action"? The Supreme Court has encountered several such schemes in which the President is the ultimate official actor. In these cases, the Court has generally invoked lack of finality as a reason for refusing to review the actions of other officials involved in the process. In Franklin v. Massachusetts, 505 U.S. 788 (1992), Massachusetts' attempt to regain a seat lost in the House because of the decennial reapportionment failed at the threshold when five Justices concluded that the Secretary of Commerce's Census Report was not final action: "In this case, the action that creates an entitlement to a particular number of Representatives and has a direct effect on the reapportionment is the President's statement to Congress, not the Secretary's report to the President." Having also held that the President is not an "agency" within the meaning of the APA, the majority therefore concluded that "there is no final agency action that may be reviewed under the APA standards."[2] Similarly, Dalton v. Specter, 511 U.S. 462 (1994), held that the actions of the Secretary of Defense and the Base Closing Commission are not "final agency action" since their reports identifying military bases for closure have "no direct consequences."[3] Cf. Public Citizen v. U.S. Trade Representative, 5 F.3d 549 (D.C.Cir.1993), cert. denied, 510 U.S. 1041 (1994) (relying on Franklin to dismiss NEPA challenge to final, signed draft of North American Free Trade Agreement since "the agreement will have no effect . . . unless and until the President submits it to Congress").

Are these cases explained by judicial solicitude for preserving the President's constitutionally unique freedom to act? Cf. Japan Whaling Ass'n v. American Cetacean Soc., 478 U.S. 221 (1986) (holding final and reviewable the Secretary of Commerce's certification to the President that another country was endangering fisheries; the certification automatically triggered sanctions, regardless of any discretionary action the President might choose to take). Absent direct involvement of the President, would (should?) other officials be able to avoid review on finality grounds by pointing out that their decision was a necessary, but not sufficient, component of a complex regulatory action?

(3) *Guidance Documents.* Yet another dimension of finality appears when a party insists that the agency has definitively committed itself to a position, but this position has not been expressed in a form conventionally understood as having the force of law. If you studied the materials in Chapter V on interpretive rules, statements of policy and similar "publication rules," see p. 705 above, you are already familiar with the growing agency trend to supply "guidance" to the public without undertaking the full process of notice-and-comment rulemaking. The best treatment of the justiciability

2. Justices Stevens, Blackmun, Kennedy and Souter found the Census Report final but rejected Massachusetts' challenge on the merits.

3. Justices Stevens, Blackmun, Souter and Ginsburg would have dismissed on grounds of reviewability, without reaching the finality question.

issues posed by such cases (which some courts consider problems of ripeness, rather than finality) remains an early opinion by Judge Leventhal.

In NATIONAL AUTOMATIC LAUNDRY & CLEANING COUNCIL v. SHULTZ, 443 F.2d 689 (D.C.Cir.1971), the petitioners had requested a letter ruling from the Administrator of the Wage & Hour Division of the Department of Labor to "confirm" that laundromat employees were not affected by recent amendments to the Fair Labor Standards Act. When the ruling did not comport with their hopes, they sought a declaratory judgment that the Administrator had misinterpreted the statute. At the time, the Division issued about 750,000 letter rulings annually; fewer than 1.5% of these were signed by the Administrator himself (the rest came from a regional or field official). None of the rulings possessed independent binding force, but they did signal when the agency might seek judicial enforcement of the Act against an employer. Moreover, they might have supported a private cause of action by affected employees. In either of these events, the courts were likely to pay considerable deference to the Administrator's views, and the possible consequences of being found a violator included liability for double damages to the injured employees and, in extreme cases, criminal sanctions.

Judge Leventhal provided a framework for assessing when administrative "guidance" should be deemed reviewable final agency action: "A businessman unable to obtain a final, authoritative ruling on the matter at hand is nevertheless interested in an 'advisory' indication, perhaps from a subordinate official, which can serve the purpose of providing an informed though not binding prediction. There are sound reasons why such advisory letters and opinions should not be subject to judicial review. This technique of apprising persons informally as to their rights and liabilities has been termed an 'excellent practice in administrative procedure.' There is surely a need for such informality in the administration of the Fair Labor Standards Act, a law deemed 'full of baffling questions of application.' ... Advisory opinions should, to the greatest extent possible, be available to the public as a matter of routine; it would be unfortunate if the prospect of judicial review were to make an agency reluctant to give them.

"It is because of a disinclination to intervene in case of a ruling that is only an 'advisory,' that the early cases under the Act denied declaratory judgments, notwithstanding the risk of employee double damage actions, to employers contesting bulletins or more specific notifications of coverage from the Wage and Hour Administration. As the court put it in F.W. Maurer & Sons Co. v. Andrews, 30 F.Supp. 637, 638 (E.D.Pa.1939), the courts cannot give relief merely because the 'petitioner has a real problem' and 'a genuine need for legal advice.'

"There are two separate matters involved. One of these is the need for authoritative determination within the office or agency before its ruling can be termed final. ... But there seems little room for the application of that doctrine when the interpretative ruling is signed by the head of the agency. In this situation we are not troubled by the questions that might arise as to the nature or extent of delegation to a subordinate official. ...

"[Second, e]ven the head of an agency, it may be contended, operates on more than one level of deliberativeness. And it may be urged that a ruling made without that kind of assurance of deliberativeness that is presented by a hearing, or a structured controversy, may be the kind of ruling that is more truly subject to reconsideration. Certainly we know that the head of an agency may make tentative rulings and may reconsider rulings previously made. . . . We think the sound course is to accept the ruling of a board or commission, or the head of an agency, as presumptively final. If it does not indicate on its face that it is only tentative, it would be likely to be accepted as authoritative, and given [judicial] deference. . . . This presumption could be negatived, of course, if the agency adopted a rule prescribing its procedure in such a way as to identify certain actions as tentative and subject to reconsideration, prescribing the means of obtaining such reconsideration. Indeed, even in the absence of such structuring in regulations prescribing agency procedures, a court might decline to entertain a litigation if it was presented not with legal defenses interposed by counsel, but with an affidavit of the agency head advising the court that the ruling in question was tentative, and outlining the method of seeking reconsideration. . . . [S]uch a submission would [likely] undercut plaintiff's need for judicial review since it would support the conclusion that the interpretation of the employer, not being contrary to any administrative ruling, had enough merit to qualify as a view held on a reasonable basis and in good faith, which suffices as a defense to a double damage action.[4]
. . .

"Plainly there is a need for advisory interpretations by agency officials. The overwhelming bulk of these are not given by the agency head, and are not within the scope of our ruling announced today. When a general, interpretative ruling signed by the head of an agency has been crystallized following reflective examination in the course of the agency's interpretative process, and is accordingly entitled to deference not only as a matter of fact from staff and citizenry expected to conform but also as a matter of law from a court reviewing the question, there coexist both multiple signposts of authoritative determination, finality and ripeness, and a concomitant indication that the resultant pointing toward prompt judicial review will benefit the total administrative process by resolving uncertainties without intolerable burden or disruption."

Compare the assessment contemplated by Judge Leventhal with the analysis required by United States v. Mead, p. 1068 above, as a predicate for giving Chevron deference to an agency's interpretation. Note that Judge Leventhal's resolution allows the agency considerable power over whether the challenged statement will constitute a final, "authoritative determination" for purposes of review. For a more recent case giving the agency far less control, see APPALACHIAN POWER v. EPA, 208 F.3d 1015 (D.C.Cir.2000), in which electric power companies and a petrochemical industry trade associa-

---

4. [Ed.] Later in the opinion, Judge Leventhal added: "Even if the interpretation is not being reconsidered, the agency may invoke the sound discretion of the court on the ground that an [enforcement] action was in preparation or imminent. If filing of such an action close in time permits an equally convenient determination, the court's sound discretion permits the deferral . . . of the action for declaratory relief."

tion sought review of an EPA "guidance" document that allegedly imposed unauthorized requirements on states administering operating permit programs under the Clean Air Act. Judge Randolph first determined that the challenged document was "binding" because it set forth "a position [EPA] plans to follow in reviewing State-issued permits, a position it will insist State and local authorities comply with in setting the terms and conditions of permits issued to petitioners, a position EPA officials in the field are bound to apply."

He then turned to whether it was "final:" "Of course, an agency's action is not necessarily final merely because it is binding. Judicial orders can be binding; a temporary restraining order, for instance, compels compliance but it does not finally decide the case. In the administrative setting, 'two conditions must be satisfied for agency action to be "final"': First, the action must mark the consummation of the agency's decision-making process—it must not be of a merely tentative or interlocutory nature. And second, the action must be one by which rights or obligations have been determined, or from which legal consequences will flow.' Bennett v. Spear, 520 U.S. 154, 178 (1997). [internal quotes omitted] The first condition is satisfied here. The 'Guidance,' as issued in September 1998, followed a draft circulated four years earlier and another, more extensive draft circulated in May 1998. This latter document bore the title 'EPA Draft Final Periodic Monitoring Guidance.'[5] On the question whether States *must* review their emission standards ... to determine if the standards provide enough monitoring, the Guidance is unequivocal—the State agencies must do so. ...

"EPA may think that because the Guidance, in all its particulars, is subject to change, it is not binding and therefore not final action. There are suggestions in its brief to this effect. But all laws are subject to change. ... The fact that a law may be altered in the future has nothing to do with whether it is subject to judicial review at the moment. On the issue whether the challenged portion of the Guidance has legal consequences, EPA points to the concluding paragraph of the document, which contains a disclaimer: 'The policies set forth in this paper are intended solely as guidance, do not represent final Agency action, and cannot be relied upon to create any rights enforceable by any party.' This language is boilerplate; since 1991 EPA has been placing it at the end of all its guidance documents. See Peter L. Strauss, The Rulemaking Continuum, 41 Duke L.J. 1463, 1485 (1992) (referring to EPA's notice as 'a charade, intended to keep the proceduralizing courts at bay'). Insofar as the 'policies' mentioned in the disclaimer consist of requiring State permitting authorities to search for deficiencies in existing monitoring regulations and replace them through terms and conditions of a permit, 'rights' may not be created but 'obligations' certainly are—obligations on the part of the State regulators and those they regulate. At any rate, the entire Guidance, from beginning to end—except the last paragraph—reads like a ukase.[6] It commands, it

---

5. In the title to the Guidance we have before us, EPA dropped the word 'final.'

6. [Ed.] For those who (like some of the editors of this casebook) are unacquainted

with the word "ukase," it comes from czarist Russia and means fiat, an order by absolute and—by connotation, arbitrary—authority.

requires, it orders, it dictates. Through the Guidance, EPA has given the States their 'marching orders' and EPA expects the States to fall in line, as all have done. . . . Petitioners tell us, and EPA does not dispute, that many of them are negotiating their [discharge] permits[, and] that State authorities, with EPA's Guidance in hand, are insisting on [monitoring procedures that comply with the Guidance]. The short of the matter is that the Guidance, insofar as relevant here, is final agency action, reflecting a settled agency position which has legal consequences both for State agencies administering their permit programs and for companies like those represented by petitioners who must obtain . . . permits in order to continue operating."

NOTES ON RIPENESS

(1) *The Modern Watershed for Pre-enforcement Review of Rules.* Please review Part II of Abbott Lab. v. Gardner and the opinion of Justice Fortas in the companion Toilet Goods Ass'n cases, pp. 1184, 1187 above.

(2) *The Benefits and Costs of Pre-enforcement Review.* Abbott Laboratories inaugurated an era in which pre-enforcement review is the common pattern of rulemaking review. To be sure, strategic considerations might sometimes lead a regulated entity to wait until the point of enforcement to attack the rule. Consider, for example, United States v. Nova Scotia Food Prod. Corp., p. 524 above, in which FDA's attempt to enforce its fish-processing regulations against a smoked whitefish manufacturer provided a specific factual context for attacks on the rule that might well have received short shrift (if they were raised at all) in the more abstract setting of a broad-based, pre-enforcement challenge. In general, though, pre-enforcement review offers several attractive features. Jerry L. Mashaw & David L. Harfst, The Struggle for Auto Safety 246–47 (1990): "Costs of compliance with invalid rules are saved, uncertainty about the legality of regulation is more quickly removed, all affected parties receive similar treatment (no one need comply while a challenge is pending, and weak or disfavored organizations cannot be singled out by the agency for enforcement action), and regulators are held strictly accountable because they cannot suppress legal contests through enforcement compromises."

Notwithstanding these "good arguments for immediate judicial review," Mashaw & Harfst urge Congress to reform the auto safety program overseen by the National Highway Transportation Safety Administration by abolishing pre-enforcement review of NHTSA rules: "[First, a]ltering the timing of review shifts the incentives of manufacturers strongly in the direction of serious attempts at compliance. Second, because delaying review shifts incentives, it promotes the development of more credible information on both compliance costs and engineering feasibility. Judicial review will be better informed on the critical issues that are now routinely presented but seldom substantiated by more than industry and agency conjecture. Third, in such a regime, if real problems of implementation develop, NHTSA will have every reason to delay enforcement and modify the rule. If problems are relatively tractable, manufacturers will have incentives to comply. Negotiation between the two parties who are best informed should thus resolve most conflicts, and the need to present them to a decidedly second-best form of institutional decision making—litigation—should occur much less frequently. Fourth, in those cases that are presented to the judiciary, the questions would tend to be focused, limited, and practical rather than diffuse, multiple, and abstract. This not only limits the prospects for agency exhaustion and judicial error but transforms the remedial situation as well."

Mashaw & Harfst's proposal is a carefully targeted conclusion to their analysis of almost 25 years of "information and experience" from a particular regulatory scheme. Sweeping much more broadly, some commentators have argued that Abbott's holding on pre-enforcement review ought to be generally overruled (either judicially or legislatively) as one important step in curing regulatory ossification. RICHARD J. PIERCE, JR., SEVEN WAYS TO DEOSSIFY AGENCY RULEMAKING, 47 Admin.L.Rev. 59, 89–91 (1995): "[M]any scholars believe that the Court's 1967 opinion in Abbott was one of the major causes of the ensuing significant increase in the stringency of judicial review of legislative rules. Before Abbott, . . . [c]ourts typically relied on the record of the enforcement proceeding as the primary basis for review of the rule, and most rules were upheld. . . . Proponents of reversal of Abbott believe that the unavailability of pre-enforcement review . . . will deossify rulemaking by restoring the legal environment that existed prior to Abbott. . . . [In addition, they anticipate that the] lack of availability of pre-enforcement review of rules will deter parties from seeking review. . . . Violation of a rule that is held to be valid often exposes the regulatee to the risk of large civil and criminal penalties, as well as other adverse regulatory and public relations consequences. Those risks are likely to induce regulatees to comply with a rule, even if they believe the rule to be invalid. . . . [Finally, r]eversal of Abbott also could deossify rulemaking in a third way. Beneficiaries of regulatory statutes can obtain judicial review of agency rules only in the pre-enforcement context. Thus, reversal of Abbott would have effects identical to those created by elimination of beneficiaries' standing to obtain judicial review of rules.[1]"

Consider carefully the set of assumptions about the regulatory process on which these arguments rest. Professor Pierce, although a vigorous critic of many aspects of contemporary judicial review of rulemaking, concludes that this particular proposal would deossify rulemaking "at a social cost [that is] intolerably high." Given the adverse consequences to regulated entities of losing an enforcement action, "agencies often could predict with confidence that a rule will never be subject to judicial review;" hence, "reversal of Abbott could produce a legal environment in which agencies frequently issue rules that conflict with statutes or with the Constitution." The virtual elimination of beneficiary challenges would create an additional problem: "Asymmetric access to judicial review . . . would introduce a powerful systemic anti-regulation bias in the implementation of all regulatory systems. . . ."

(3) *Pre-enforcement Review and Beneficiary Challenges: The Other Lujan Case.* Do you understand why the option of pre-enforcement review is

---

1. [Ed.] See Lujan v. Defenders of Wildlife and accompanying notes, p. 1139 above.

essential to beneficiary challenges? What if the agency simply doesn't bring enforcement actions? See Heckler v. Chaney, p. 1218 above. Even if an enforcement action is brought, would a beneficiary group be permitted to intervene and argue that because the rule isn't stringent enough, even greater sanctions should be imposed against the defendant than the agency proposes? Obviously, then, regulatory beneficiaries have a significant stake in the preservation of pre-enforcement review. Just as Justice Scalia's general theory of regulatory standing would disfavor beneficiary challenges, see Lujan v. Defenders of Wildlife, p. 1139 above, so does his general theory of ripeness.

LUJAN V. NATIONAL WILDLIFE FED., 497 U.S. 871, 890–94 (1990), involved a challenge to what environmentalists claimed was an unlawful Bureau of Land Management "program" of opening previously protected public lands to private development. Justice Scalia's opinion for the five-member majority concluded that the environmentalists did not have standing and that, in any event, their complaint did not identify a final agency action ripe for review: "The term 'land withdrawal review program' (which as far as we know is not derived from any authoritative text) does not refer to a single BLM order or regulation, or even to a completed universe of particular BLM orders and regulations. It is simply the name by which petitioners have occasionally referred to the continuing (and thus constantly changing) operations of the BLM in reviewing withdrawal revocation applications and the classifications of public lands and developing land use plans as required by the FLPMA. It is no more an identifiable 'agency action'—much less a 'final agency action'—than a 'weapons procurement program' of the Department of Defense or a 'drug interdiction program' of the Drug Enforcement Administration. As the District Court explained, the 'land withdrawal review program' extends to, currently at least, '1250 or so individual classification terminations and withdrawal revocations.'

"Respondent alleges that violation of the law is rampant within this program—failure to revise land use plans in proper fashion, failure to submit certain recommendations to Congress, failure to consider multiple use, inordinate focus upon mineral exploitation, failure to provide required public notice, failure to provide adequate environmental impact statements. Perhaps so. But respondent cannot seek *wholesale* improvement of this program by court decree, rather than in the offices of the Department or the halls of Congress, where programmatic improvements are normally made."

Then the Justice lays out a general theory of ripeness: "Under the terms of the APA, respondent must direct its attack against some particular 'agency action' that causes it harm. Some statutes permit broad regulations to serve as the 'agency action,' and thus to be the object of judicial review directly, even before the concrete effects normally required for APA review are felt. Absent such a provision, however, a regulation is not ordinarily considered the type of agency action 'ripe' for judicial review under the APA until the scope of the controversy has been reduced to more manageable proportions, and its factual components fleshed out, by some concrete action applying the regulation to the claimant's situation in a fashion that harms or threatens to harm him. (The major exception, of course, is a substantive rule which as a practical matter *requires the plaintiff to adjust his conduct immediately*. Such agency action is 'ripe' for review at once, whether or not explicit statutory review apart from the APA is provided. See Abbott Lab. v. Gardner; Toilet Goods (additives rule). Cf. Toilet Goods (access rule).)'' (emphasis added)[2] Note that the italicized description applies principally—if not exclusively—to members of the regulated community. Where, in this description, do challenges by beneficiaries fit?[3]

How the Court ought conceptualize ripeness standards for beneficiary suits was specifically discussed by Justice O'Connor, concurring in the judgment in RENO V. CATHOLIC SOC. SERV., INC., 509 U.S. 43, 68–71,78 (1993). The Immigration Reform and Control Act of 1986 established a special amnesty process whereby certain aliens illegally in this country could apply for regularization of their status and permanent residency. INS issued regulations narrowly interpreting two of the four statutory criteria for eligibility. Immigrants' rights groups, in class actions on behalf of aliens who would be rendered ineligible for legalization under INS' interpretation, challenged the rules as inconsistent with the Act and violative of equal protection. The majority held that most of the challenges were not ripe until an immigrant had applied for benefits and been denied.[4]

In this case, of course, the challenged regulation spoke directly to beneficiary behavior, in a way that environmental, health, and safety regulations typically do not. However, Justice O'Connor addressed the issue more broadly, and seemed concerned to limit the potential sweep of Lujan v. NWF: "An anticipatory suit by a would-be beneficiary, who has not yet applied for the benefit that the rule denies him, poses different ripeness problems than a pre-enforcement suit against a duty-creating rule, see Abbott Laboratories v. Gardner. Even if he succeeds in his anticipatory action, the would-be beneficiary will not receive the benefit until he actually applies for it; and the agency might then deny him the benefit on grounds other than his ineligibility under the rule. By contrast, a successful

2. See also Thunder Basin Coal Co. v. Reich, 510 U.S. 200, 220 (1994) (Scalia, J., concurring in part and concurring in the judgment) (characterizing pre-enforcement review as "the exception" rather than "the rule.")

3. Cf. Ohio Forestry Ass'n v. Sierra Club, 523 U.S. 726 (1998), in which the Sierra Club challenged the Forest Service management plan for Wayne National Forest as permitting too much clear-cut logging. Justice Breyer, for a unanimous Court, deemed the challenge unripe because no logging could occur without preparation of a site-specific proposal that would be subject to public comment and judicial review. Judicial intervention now would interfere with the agency's ability to refine the plan, in light of specific site proposals. On the other hand, the opinion does contain some good news for environmentalists seeking review of land manage-

ment plans. Two types of challenges to such plans would be presently ripe, Justice Breyer explained: an attack under NEPA for failure to develop an adequate environmental impact statement, and an attack on an element of the plan having immediate effect (such as opening trails to motorized vehicles).

4. The Court remanded for exploration of allegations that the INS engaged in a practice of "front-desking," in which employees refused even to accept applications from immigrants whom the agency considered ineligible under the challenged interpretation. "[A] class member whose application was 'front-desked' would have felt the effects of the [challenged regulations] in a particularly concrete manner, for his application for legalization would have been blocked then and there; his challenge to the regulation should not fail for lack of ripeness."

suit against the duty-creating rule will relieve the plaintiff immediately of a burden that he otherwise would bear.

"Yet I would not go so far as to state that a suit challenging a benefit-conferring rule is necessarily unripe simply because the plaintiff has not yet applied for the benefit. ... If it is 'inevitable' that the challenged rule will 'operat[e]' to the plaintiff's disadvantage—if the court can make a firm prediction that the plaintiff will apply for the benefit, and that the agency will deny the application by virtue of the rule—then there may well be a justiciable controversy that the court may find prudent to resolve.

"... As for Lujan v. National Wildlife Federation, the Court['s] ... language does not suggest that an anticipatory challenge to a benefit-conferring rule will of necessity be constitutionally unripe, for otherwise an 'explicit statutory review' provision would not help cure the ripeness problem. Rather, Lujan points to the prudential considerations that weigh in the ripeness calculus: the need to 'fles[h] out' the controversy and the burden on the plaintiff who must 'adjust his conduct immediately.' These are just the kinds of factors identified in the two-part, prudential test for ripeness that Abbott Laboratories articulated. ..." Justice Stevens, in a dissenting opinion joined by Justices White and Blackmun, "agree[d] with Justice O'Connor that the Court's [ripeness] rationale is seriously flawed."

(5) *Ripeness Doctrine and Asymmetrical Access to Judicial Review.* CASS R. SUNSTEIN, STANDING AND THE PRIVATIZATION OF PUBLIC LAW, 88 Colum.L.Rev. 1432, 1447 (1988), offers an explanation for the doctrinal movement, in cases such as Data Processing and Abbott Laboratories, from restrictive justiciability concepts of the common-law model to a more expansive conception of who has a judicially-cognizable stake in the regulatory process: "[The] very distinction [between regulated entities and regulatory beneficiaries] depended on a conceptual foundation that had become anachronistic precisely because it was dependent on common-law baselines. Whether someone is the object of regulation or its beneficiary cannot be decided without an independent theory outlining what it is that government ordinarily or properly does. Regulated entities are themselves the beneficiaries of statutory limits on agency power—and of the common law—insofar as those sources of law protect them from public or private incursions into their legally created spheres. The beneficiaries are the objects of regulation insofar as positive law authorizes such intrusions and affords them less protection from private conduct than they would like. Indeed, the very term 'statutory beneficiary,' as conventionally used, assumes that the common law is the ordinary backdrop or the usual state of affairs, and that departures from that state should be understood as providing special benefits and special burdens. It is not surprising that assumptions of this sort became impossible to sustain in the wake of the New Deal attack on the common law."

Do Lujan v. NWF and Reno signal a reversal of the doctrinal trend? What theory of "what it is that government ordinarily or properly does" could justify a contemporary return to a set of ripeness principles that provide—to borrow Professor Pierce's phrase in note 2 above—"asymmetric access to judicial review"?

(7) *Statutes that Require Pre-enforcement Review?* The converse issue arises under statutes that try to ensure prompt determination of the validity of regulations by imposing strict time limits (typically, 30–90 days from promulgation) for seeking judicial review. Unexcused failure to obtain pre-enforcement review precludes later attacks on the rule—even as a defense to civil or criminal enforcement proceedings.[5] "Excusable" failure includes situations in which the challenge would not have been ripe within the statutory period; hence, a shift in ripeness doctrine away from entertaining pre-enforcement challenges could significantly affect the operation of these statutory limitations.

How should a court, faced with an apparently untimely challenge, determine whether the challenge would have been ripe within the statutory period? EAGLE-PICHER INDUS. V. EPA, 759 F.2d 905, 914 (D.C.Cir.1985), considered the difficulties of conducting a retrospective ripeness calculation and concluded: "As a general proposition ..., if there is *any* doubt about the ripeness of a claim, petitioners must bring their challenge in a timely fashion or risk being barred. Courts simply are not well-suited to answering hypothetical questions which involve guessing what the court might have done in the past. Furthermore, if we were routinely to conduct retrospective ripeness analyses where a late petitioner offers no compelling justification for not having filed his claim in a timely manner, we would wreak havoc with the congressional intention that repose be brought to final agency action. Consequently, except where events occur or information becomes available after the statutory review period expires that essentially create a challenge that did not previously exist, or where a petitioner's claim is, under our precedents, *indisputably* not ripe until the agency takes further action, we will be very reluctant, in order to save a late petitioner from the strictures of a timeliness requirement, to engage in a retrospective determination of whether we would have held the claim ripe had it been brought on time."

SECTION 5. ACTIONS FOR DAMAGES AS A FORM OF REVIEW

Today, when we think about judicial review of administrative action, we typically envision a proceeding instigated under the organic statute or the APA, often in the court of appeals, that seeks *specific* relief: that is, a declaration that the agency has acted unlawfully and an order that the agency remedy this illegality by acting or ceasing to act in a particular way. See Section I above. Historically, however, the "typical" judicial review proceeding would have taken the form of a claim for money damages. As the Attorney General's Committee on Administrative Procedure put it in 1946, on the eve of enactment of the APA: "[T]he basic judicial remedy for the protection of the individual against illegal official action is a private action for damages against the official in which the court determines, in the

---

5. If you studied the challenge to EPA's revised ozone and particulate matter standards in American Trucking, p. 38 above, you have seen such a statute in action: Section 307(b) of the Clean Air Act sets a 60–day limit for challenges to final EPA action; had the trucking association not sought pre-enforcement review, it would almost certainly have been barred from raising its arguments in an enforcement proceeding.

usual common law manner and with the aid of a jury, whether or not the officer was legally authorized to do what he did in the particular case." Although damages actions no longer serve as the principal procedural vehicle for obtaining judicial review of regulatory action, they remain an important mechanism for calling on government officials to demonstrate that their conduct conforms with applicable constitutional, statutory and common-law standards.

Damages actions against agency officials *personally* raise hard questions about balancing the interest of the individual in being compensated for injury caused by unlawful government action, against the interest of the community in having government employees go about the business of making and implementing public policy without constant fear of personal liability for a wrong (or arguably wrong) decision. Subsection (a) introduces the various immunity defenses that have evolved to accommodate these competing interests.

Subsection (b) considers the increased availability of damages actions against the government *entity* for harm caused by the unlawful acts of its officials. The United States has now statutorily waived its sovereign immunity to suit for some torts of its employees and for most non-tort claims. With respect to states and state agencies, there is still no blanket waiver or abrogation of sovereign immunity that permits damages actions for violations of federal law. However, in 1978 the Supreme Court revised its interpretation of 42 U.S.C. § 1983 to permit such actions against governmental entities below the level of the state, e.g., municipalities.

a.   DAMAGES ACTIONS AGAINST GOVERNMENT OFFICIALS

North American Cold Storage Co. v. Chicago

Supreme Court of the United States, 1908.
211 U.S. 306.

(Reprinted p. 884 above).

Butz v. Economou

Supreme Court of the United States, 1978.
438 U.S. 478.

■ JUSTICE WHITE delivered the opinion of the Court.

This case concerns the personal immunity of federal officials in the Executive Branch from claims for damages arising from their violations of citizens' constitutional rights. . . .

Respondent controls Arthur N. Economou and Co., Inc., which was at one time registered with the Department of Agriculture as a commodity futures commission merchant. . . . On February 19, 1970, following an audit, the Department of Agriculture issued an administrative complaint alleging that respondent, while a registered merchant, had willfully failed to maintain the minimum financial requirements prescribed by the Department. . . . A hearing was held before the Chief Hearing Examiner of the

Department, who filed a recommendation sustaining the administrative complaint. The Judicial Officer of the Department, to whom the Secretary had delegated his decisional authority in enforcement proceedings, affirmed the Chief Hearing Examiner's decision. On respondent's petition for review, the Court of Appeals for the Second Circuit vacated the order of the Judicial Officer. It reasoned that "the essential finding of willfulness ... was made in a proceeding instituted without the customary warning letter, which the Judicial Officer conceded might well have resulted in prompt correction of the claimed insufficiencies."

While the administrative complaint was pending before the Judicial Officer, respondent filed this lawsuit in Federal District Court. Respondent sought initially to enjoin the progress of the administrative proceeding, but he was unsuccessful in that regard. On March 31, 1975, respondent filed a second amended complaint seeking damages. Named as defendants were the individuals who had served as Secretary and Assistant Secretary of Agriculture during the relevant events; the Judicial Officer and Chief Hearing Examiner; several officials in the Commodity Exchange Authority; the Agriculture Department attorney who had prosecuted the enforcement proceeding; and several of the auditors who had investigated respondent or were witnesses against respondent.

The complaint stated that prior to the issuance of the administrative complaints respondent had been "sharply critical of the staff and operations of Defendants and carried on a vociferous campaign for the reform of Defendant Commodity Exchange Authority to obtain more effective regulation of commodity trading." ... The complaint charged that each of the administrative complaints had been issued without the notice or warning required by law; ... and that following the issuance of the amended complaint, the defendants had issued a "deceptive" press release that "falsely indicated to the public that [respondent's] financial resources had deteriorated, when Defendants knew that their statement was untrue and so acknowledge[d] previously that said assertion was untrue."

[The complaint presented ten "causes of action," including claims under the due process clause and the First Amendment. The district court granted defendants' motion to dismiss, holding that they were entitled to absolute immunity on their showing that "their alleged unconstitutional acts were within the outer perimeter of their authority and discretionary." The court of appeals reversed, holding that only qualified, "good faith" immunity was available.]

The single submission by the United States on behalf of petitioners is that all of the federal officials sued in this case are absolutely immune from any liability for damages even if in the course of enforcing the relevant statutes they infringed respondent's constitutional rights and even if the violation was knowing and deliberate. Although the position is earnestly and ably presented by the United States, we are quite sure that it is unsound and consequently reject it.

In Bivens v. Six Unknown Fed. Narcotics Agents, 403 U.S. 388 (1971), the victim of an arrest and search claimed to be violative of the Fourth Amendment brought suit for damages against the responsible federal agents. ... [W]e rejected the claim that the plaintiff's remedy lay only in the state court under state law, with the Fourth Amendment operating merely to nullify a defense of federal authorization. We held that a violation of the Fourth Amendment by federal agents gives rise to a cause of action for damages consequent upon the unconstitutional conduct. ... [W]e reserved the question whether the agents involved were "immune from liability by virtue of their official position," and remanded the case for that determination. On remand, the Court of Appeals for the Second Circuit, as has every other Court of Appeals that has faced the question, held that the agents were not absolutely immune and that the public interest would be sufficiently protected by according the agents and their superiors a qualified immunity.

In our view, the Courts of Appeals have reached sound results. ...

The Government places principal reliance on Barr v. Matteo, 360 U.S. 564 (1959). In that case, the acting director of an agency had been sued for malicious defamation by two employees whose suspension for misconduct he had announced in a press release. The defendant claimed an absolute or qualified privilege, but the trial court rejected both and the jury returned a verdict for plaintiff. [The court of appeals held that the defendant was entitled to a qualified privilege that would protect him from liability if he had acted without malice and with reasonable grounds for believing that his statements were true. It remanded for a new trial.] ... [This] Court was divided in reversing the judgment of the Court of Appeals, and there was no opinion for the Court.[1] The plurality opinion inquired whether the conduct complained of was among those "matters committed by law to [the official's] control" and concluded, after an analysis of the specific circumstances, that the press release was within the "outer perimeter of [his] line of duty" and was "an appropriate exercise of the discretion which an officer of that rank must possess if the public service is to function effectively." ... Barr clearly held that a false and damaging publication, the issuance of which was otherwise within the official's authority, was not itself actionable and would not become so by being issued maliciously. ...

Barr does not control this case. It did not address the liability of the acting director had his conduct not been within the outer limits of his duties, but from the care with which the Court inquired into the scope of his authority, it may be inferred that had the release been unauthorized, and surely if the issuance of press releases had been expressly forbidden by statute, the claim of absolute immunity would not have been upheld. ... It is apparent also that a quite different question would have been presented had the officer ignored an express statutory or constitutional limitation on his authority.

Barr did not, therefore, purport to depart from the general rule, which long prevailed, that a federal official may not with impunity ignore the limitations which the controlling law has placed on his powers. The immunity of federal executive officials began as a means of protecting them in the execution of their federal statutory duties from criminal or civil

---

1. Justice Harlan's opinion in Barr was joined by three other Justices. The majority was formed through the concurrence in the judgment of Justice Black, who emphasized in a separate opinion the strong public interest in encouraging federal employees to ventilate their ideas about how the Government should be run.

actions based on state law. A federal official who acted outside of his federal statutory authority would be held strictly liable for his trespassory acts. For example, Little v. Barreme, 6 U.S. 170, 2 Cranch 170 (1804), held the commander of an American warship liable in damages for the seizure of a Danish cargo ship on the high seas. Congress had directed the President to intercept any vessels reasonably suspected of being en route *to* a French port, but the President had authorized the seizure of suspected vessels whether going *to* or *from* French ports, and the Danish vessel seized was en route *from* a forbidden destination. The Court, speaking through Mr. Chief Justice Marshall, held that the President's instructions could not "change the nature of the transaction, or legalize an act which, without those instructions, would have been a plain trespass." . . .

. . . [The official in Barreme] did not merely mistakenly conclude that the circumstances warranted a particular seizure, but failed to observe the limitations on [his] authority by making seizures not within the category or type of seizures [he was] authorized to make. Kendall v. Stokes, 3 How. 87 (1845), addressed a different situation. The case involved a suit against the Postmaster General for erroneously suspending payments to a creditor of the Post Office. Examining and, if necessary, suspending payments to creditors were among the Postmaster's normal duties, and it appeared that he had simply made a mistake in the exercise of the discretion conferred upon him. He was held not liable in damages since "a public officer, acting to the best of his judgment and from a sense of duty, in a matter of account with an individual [is not] liable in an action for an error of judgment." Having "the right to examine into this account" and the right to suspend it in the proper circumstances, the officer was not liable in damages if he fell into error. . . .

In Spalding v. Vilas, 161 U.S. 483 (1896), on which the Government relies, the principal issue was whether the malicious motive of an officer would render him liable in damages for injury inflicted by his official act that otherwise was within the scope of his authority. The Postmaster General was sued for circulating among the postmasters a notice that assertedly injured the reputation of the plaintiff and interfered with his contractual relationships. . . . Spalding made clear that a malicious intent will not subject a public officer to liability for performing his authorized duties as to which he would otherwise not be subject to damages liability. But Spalding did not involve conduct manifestly or otherwise beyond the authority of the official, nor did it involve a mistake of either law or fact in construing or applying the statute. It did not purport to immunize officials who ignore limitations on their authority imposed by law. . . .

Insofar as cases in this Court dealing with the immunity or privilege of federal officers are concerned, this is where the matter stood until Barr v. Matteo. There, as we have set out above, immunity was granted even though the publication contained a factual error, which was not the case in Spalding. The plurality opinion and judgment in Barr also appear—although without any discussion of the matter—to have extended absolute immunity to an officer who was authorized to issue press releases, who was assumed to know that the press release he issued was false and who therefore was deliberately misusing his authority. Accepting this extension of immunity with respect to state tort claims, however, we are confident that Barr did not purport to protect an official who has not only committed a wrong under local law, but also violated those fundamental principles of fairness embodied in the Constitution.[2] Whatever level of protection from state interference is appropriate for federal officials executing their duties under federal law, it cannot be doubted that these officials, even when acting pursuant to congressional authorization, are subject to the restraints imposed by the Federal Constitution. ... [I]f they are accountable when they stray beyond the plain limits of their statutory authority, it would be incongruous to hold that they may nevertheless willfully or knowingly violate constitutional rights without fear of liability.

Although it is true that the Court has not dealt with this issue with respect to federal officers, we have several times addressed the immunity of state officers when sued under 42 U.S.C. § 1983 for alleged violations of constitutional rights. ... In Scheuer v. Rhodes, 416 U.S. 232 (1974), ... the Governor of a State, the senior and subordinate officers of the state National Guard, and a state university president had been sued on the allegation that they had suppressed a civil disturbance in an unconstitutional manner. We explained that the doctrine of official immunity from § 1983 liability, although not constitutionally grounded and essentially a matter of statutory construction, was based on two mutually dependent rationales:

> (1) the injustice, particularly in the absence of bad faith, of subjecting to liability an officer who is required, by the legal obligations of his position, to exercise discretion; (2) the danger that the threat of such liability would deter his willingness to execute his office with the decisiveness and the judgment required by the public good.

The opinion also recognized that executive branch officers must often act swiftly and on the basis of factual information supplied by others, constraints which become even more acute in the "atmosphere of confusion, ambiguity, and swiftly moving events" created by a civil disturbance. Although quoting at length from Barr v. Matteo, we did not believe that there was a need for absolute immunity from § 1983 liability for these high-ranking state officials. Rather the considerations discussed above indicated:

> ... It is the existence of reasonable grounds for the belief formed at the time and in light of all the circumstances, coupled with good-faith belief, that affords a basis for qualified immunity of executive officers for acts performed in the course of official conduct.

... [W]ith impressive unanimity, the Federal Courts of Appeals have concluded that federal officials should receive no greater degree of protection from *constitutional* claims than their counterparts in state government.[3] ... We agree with the perception of these courts that, in the

---

2. We view this case, in its present posture, as concerned only with constitutional issues. ... The Second Circuit has subsequently read [its opinion in the case] as limited to that context. The argument before us as well has focused on respondent's constitutional claims, and our holding is so limited.

3. As early as 1971, Judge, now Attorney General, Bell, concurring specially in a judgment of the Court of Appeals for the

absence of congressional direction to the contrary, there is no basis for according to federal officials a higher degree of immunity from liability when sued for a constitutional infringement as authorized by Bivens than is accorded state officials when sued for the identical violation under § 1983.[4] . . .

As we have said, the decision in Bivens established that a citizen suffering a compensable injury to a constitutionally protected interest could invoke the general federal-question jurisdiction of the district courts to obtain an award of monetary damages against the responsible federal official. As Mr. Justice Harlan, concurring in the judgment, pointed out, the action for damages recognized in Bivens could be a vital means of providing redress for persons whose constitutional rights have been violated. The barrier of sovereign immunity is frequently impenetrable.[5] Injunctive or declaratory relief is useless to a person who has already been injured. "For people in Bivens' shoes, it is damages or nothing." . . . If, as the Government argues, all officials exercising discretion were exempt from personal liability, a suit under the Constitution could provide no redress to the injured citizen, nor would it in any degree deter federal officials from committing constitutional wrongs. Moreover, no compensation would be available from the Government, for the Tort Claims Act prohibits recovery for injuries stemming from discretionary acts, even when that discretion has been abused.[6]

This is not to say that considerations of public policy fail to support a limited immunity for federal executive officials. We consider here, as we did in Scheuer, the need to protect officials who are required to exercise their discretion and the related public interest in encouraging the vigorous exercise of official authority. . . . We therefore hold that, in a suit for damages arising from unconstitutional action, federal executive officials exercising discretion are entitled only to the qualified immunity specified in Scheuer, subject to those exceptional situations where it is demonstrated that absolute immunity is essential for the conduct of the public business.

Fifth Circuit, recorded his "continuing belief that all police and ancillary personnel in this nation, whether state or federal, should be subject to the same accountability under law for their conduct." Anderson v. Nosser, 438 F.2d 183, 205 (1971). He objected to the notion that there should be "one law for Athens and another for Rome." . . .

4. In Apton v. Wilson, 506 F.2d 83, 93 (1974), Judge Leventhal compared the Governor of a State with the highest officers of a federal executive department:

. . . Having a wider territorial responsibility than the head of a state government, a Federal cabinet officer may be entitled to consult fewer sources and expend less effort inquiring into the circumstances of a localized problem. But

these considerations go to the showing an officer vested with a qualified immunity must make in support of "good faith belief;" they do not make the qualified immunity itself inappropriate. The head of an executive department, no less than the chief executive of a state, is adequately protected by a qualified immunity.

5. At the time of the Bivens decision, the Federal Tort Claims Act prohibited recovery against the Government for [assault, battery, false imprisonment or false arrest]. The statute was subsequently amended in light of Bivens to lift the bar against . . . these claims when arising from the act of federal law enforcement officers.

6. [Ed.] See p. 1280 below.

. . . Federal officials will not be liable for mere mistakes in judgment, whether the mistake is one of fact or one of law. But we see no substantial basis for holding, as the United States would have us do, that executive officers generally may with impunity discharge their duties in a way that is known to them to violate the United States Constitution or in a manner that they should know transgresses a clearly established constitutional rule. . . . Insubstantial lawsuits can be quickly terminated by federal courts alert to the possibilities of artful pleading. . . .

Although a qualified immunity from damages liability should be the general rule for executive officials charged with constitutional violations, our decisions recognize that there are some officials whose special functions require a full exemption from liability. In each case, we have undertaken "a considered inquiry into the immunity historically accorded the relevant official at common law and the interests behind it."

In Bradley v. Fisher, 80 U.S. 335, 13 Wall. 335 (1871), the Court analyzed the need for absolute immunity to protect judges from lawsuits claiming that their decisions had been tainted by improper motives. . . . Judges were often called to decide "[c]ontroversies involving not merely great pecuniary interests, but the liberty and character of the parties, and consequently exciting the deepest feelings." Such adjudications invariably produced at least one losing party, who would "accep[t] anything but the soundness of the decision in explanation of the action of the judge." "Just in proportion to the strength of his convictions of the correctness of his own view of the case is he apt to complain of the judgment against him, and from complaints of the judgment to pass to the ascription of improper motives to the judge." If a civil action could be maintained against a judge by virtue of an allegation of malice, judges would lose "that independence without which no judiciary can either be respectable or useful." Thus, judges were held to be immune from civil suit "for malice or corruption in their action whilst exercising their judicial functions within the general scope of their jurisdiction."[7]

The principle of Bradley was extended to federal prosecutors through the summary affirmance in Yaselli v. Goff, 275 U.S. 503 (1927). . . . We recently reaffirmed the holding of Yaselli in Imbler v. Pachtman, 424 U.S. 409 (1976), a suit against a state prosecutor under § 1983. The Court's examination of the leading precedents led to the conclusion that "[t]he common-law immunity of a prosecutor is based upon the same considerations that underlie the common-law immunit[y] of judges." . . . A qualified immunity might have an adverse effect on the functioning of the criminal justice system, not only by discouraging the initiation of prosecutions, but also by affecting the prosecutor's conduct of the trial. . . .

Despite these precedents, the Court of Appeals concluded that all of the defendants in this case—including the Chief Hearing Examiner, Judicial Officer, and prosecuting attorney—were entitled to only a qualified immunity. The Court of Appeals reasoned that officials within the Executive Branch generally have more circumscribed discretion and pointed out that,

7. In Pierson v. Ray, 386 U.S. 547 (1967), we recognized that state judges sued on constitutional claims pursuant to § 1983 could claim a similar absolute immunity. . . .

unlike a judge, officials of the Executive Branch would face no conflict of interest if their legal representation was provided by the Executive Branch. The Court of Appeals recognized that "some of the Agriculture Department officials may be analogized to criminal prosecutors, in that they initiated the proceedings against [respondent], and presented evidence therein," but found that attorneys in administrative proceedings did not face the same "serious constraints of time and even information" which this Court has found to be present frequently in criminal cases.

We think that the Court of Appeals placed undue emphasis on the fact that the officials sued here are—from an administrative perspective—employees of the Executive Branch. Judges have absolute immunity not because of their particular location within the Government but because of the special nature of their responsibilities. This point is underlined by the fact that prosecutors—themselves members of the Executive Branch—are also absolutely immune. ... The cluster of immunities protecting the various participants in judge-supervised trials stems from the characteristics of the judicial process rather than its location. As the Bradley Court suggested, controversies sufficiently intense to erupt in litigation are not easily capped by a judicial decree. The loser in one forum will frequently seek another, charging the participants in the first with unconstitutional animus. Absolute immunity is thus necessary to assure that judges, advocates, and witnesses can perform their respective functions without harassment or intimidation.

At the same time, the safeguards built into the judicial process tend to reduce the need for private damages actions as a means of controlling unconstitutional conduct. The insulation of the judge from political influence, the importance of precedent in resolving controversies, the adversary nature of the process, and the correctability of error on appeal are just a few of the many checks on malicious action by judges. Advocates are restrained not only by their professional obligations, but by the knowledge that their assertions will be contested by their adversaries in open court. Jurors are carefully screened to remove all possibility of bias. Witnesses are, of course, subject to the rigors of cross-examination and the penalty of perjury. Because these features of the judicial process tend to enhance the reliability of information and the impartiality of the decisionmaking process, there is a less pressing need for individual suits to correct constitutional error.

We think that adjudication within a federal administrative agency shares enough of the characteristics of the judicial process that those who participate in such adjudication should also be immune from suits for damages. The conflicts which federal hearing examiners seek to resolve are every bit as fractious as those which come to court. ... Moreover, federal administrative law requires that agency adjudication contain many of the same safeguards as are available in the judicial process. The proceedings are adversary in nature. See 5 U.S.C. § 555(b). They are conducted before a trier of fact insulated from political influence. See § 554(d). A party is entitled to present his case by oral or documentary evidence, § 556(d), and the transcript of testimony and exhibits together with the pleadings constitute the exclusive record for decision. § 556(e). The parties are entitled to know the findings and conclusions on all of the issues of fact, law, or discretion presented on the record. § 557(c).

. . . [W]e think that the risk of an unconstitutional act by one presiding at an agency hearing is clearly outweighed by the importance of preserving the independent judgment of these men and women. We therefore hold that persons subject to these restraints and performing adjudicatory functions within a federal agency are entitled to absolute immunity from damages liability for their judicial acts. Those who complain of error in such proceedings must seek agency or judicial review.

We also believe that agency officials performing certain functions analogous to those of a prosecutor should be able to claim absolute immunity with respect to such acts. The decision to initiate administrative proceedings against an individual or corporation is very much like the prosecutor's decision to initiate or move forward with a criminal prosecution. . . . We turn finally to the role of an agency attorney in conducting a trial and presenting evidence on the record to the trier of fact. We can see no substantial difference between the function of the agency attorney in presenting evidence in an agency hearing and the function of the prosecutor who brings evidence before a court. . . .

There remains the task of applying the foregoing principles to the claims against the particular petitioner-defendants involved in this case. Rather than attempt this here in the first instance, we vacate the judgment of the Court of Appeals and remand the case to that court with instructions to remand the case to the District Court for further proceedings consistent with this opinion.

■ Justice Rehnquist, with whom Chief Justice [Burger], Justice Stewart, and Justice Stevens join, concurring in part and dissenting in part.

I concur in that part of the Court's judgment which affords absolute immunity. . . . I cannot agree, however, with the Court's conclusion that in a suit for damages arising from allegedly unconstitutional action federal executive officials, regardless of their rank or the scope of their responsibilities, are entitled to only qualified immunity even when acting within the outer limits of their authority. . . .

. . . No one seriously contends that the Secretary of Agriculture or the Assistant Secretary . . . had wandered completely off the official reservation in authorizing prosecution of respondent for violation of regulations promulgated by the Secretary. . . . This is precisely what the Secretary and his assistants were empowered and required to do. That they would on occasion be mistaken in their judgment that a particular merchant had in fact violated the regulations is a necessary concomitant of any known system of administrative adjudication. . . .

. . . At one point the Court observes that . . . "an executive officer would be vulnerable if he took action 'manifestly or palpably' beyond his authority or ignored a clear limitation on his enforcement powers." From that proposition, which is undeniably accurate, the Court appears to conclude that anytime a plaintiff can paint his grievance in constitutional colors, the official is subject to damages unless he can prove he acted in good faith. . . . Putting to one side the illogic and impracticability of distinguishing between constitutional and common-law claims for purposes of immunity, which will be discussed shortly, this sort of immunity analysis badly misses the mark. It amounts to saying that an official has immunity until someone alleges he has acted unconstitutionally. But that is no immunity at all: The "immunity" disappears at the very moment when it is needed. The critical inquiry in determining whether an official is entitled to claim immunity is not whether someone has in fact been injured by his action; that is part of the plaintiff's case in chief. The immunity defense turns on ... whether the official was acting within the outer bounds of his authority. Only if the immunity inquiry is approached in this manner does it have any meaning. That such a rule may occasionally result in individual injustices has never been doubted, but at least until today, immunity has been accorded nevertheless. As Judge Learned Hand said in Gregoire v. Biddle, 177 F.2d 579, 581 (2d Cir.1949):

> The justification for doing so is that it is impossible to know whether the claim is well founded until the case has been tried, and that to submit all officials, the innocent as well as the guilty, to the burden of a trial and to the inevitable danger of its outcome, would dampen the ardor of all but the most resolute, or the most irresponsible, in the unflinching discharge of their duties. Again and again the public interest calls for action which may turn out to be founded on a mistake, in the face of which an official may later find himself hard put to it to satisfy a jury of his good faith. There must indeed be means of punishing public officers who have been truant to their duties; but that is quite another matter from exposing such as have been honestly mistaken to suit by anyone who has suffered from their errors. As is so often the case, the answer must be found in a balance between the evils inevitable in either alternative. In this instance it has been thought in the end better to leave unredressed the wrongs done by dishonest officers than to subject those who try to do their duty to the constant dread of retaliation. . . .

... [I]f we allow a mere allegation of unconstitutionality, obviously unproved at the time made, to require a Cabinet-level official ... to lay aside his duties and defend such an action on the merits, the defense of official immunity will have been abolished in fact if not in form. The ease with which a constitutional claim may be pleaded in a case such as this, where a violation of statutory or judicial limits on agency action may be readily converted by any legal neophyte into a claim of denial of procedural due process under the Fifth Amendment, will assure that. . . .

It likewise cannot seriously be argued that an official will be less deterred by the threat of liability for unconstitutional conduct than for activities which might constitute a common-law tort. The fear that inhibits is that of a long, involved lawsuit and a significant money judgment, not the fear of liability for a certain type of claim. . . .

... Marbury v. Madison leaves no doubt that the high position of a Government official does not insulate his actions from judicial review. But that case, like numerous others which have followed, involved equitable-type relief by way of mandamus or injunction. In the present case, respondent sought damages in the amount of $32 million. . . .

My biggest concern, however, is not with the illogic or impracticality of today's decision, but rather with the potential for disruption of Government that it invites. The steady increase in litigation, much of it directed against governmental officials and virtually all of which could be framed in constitutional terms, cannot escape the notice of even the most casual observer. From 1961 to 1977, the number of cases brought in the federal courts under civil rights statutes increased from 296 to 13,113. It simply defies logic and common experience to suggest that officials will not have this in the back of their minds when considering what official course to pursue. It likewise strains credulity to suggest that this threat will only inhibit officials from taking action which they should not take in any event. . . .

NOTES

(1) *The Cause of Action for Constitutional Injuries.* As Butz explains, damages actions against government officials for violation of constitutional rights comprise two principal groups. In the case of non-federal officials, the cause of action is statutory, 42 U.S.C. § 1983:

> Any person who, under color of any statute, ordinance, regulation, custom, or usage, of any State or Territory or the District of Columbia, subjects, or causes to be subjected, any citizen of the United States or any other person within the jurisdiction thereof to the deprivation of any rights, privileges, or immunities secured by the Constitution and laws, shall be liable to the party injured in an action at law, a suit in equity, or other proper proceeding for redress, except that in any action brought against a judicial officer for an act or omission taken in such officer's judicial capacity, injunctive relief shall not be granted unless a declaratory decree was violated or declaratory relief was unavailable. . . .

Congress has not provided a comparable statutory remedy against those acting under color of federal law. For federal officials, the Supreme Court has been willing in some circumstances to imply a cause of action directly from the Constitution. Bivens, the first case in this area, involved the Fourth Amendment. Subsequently, the Supreme Court allowed such actions under the First, Fifth and Eighth Amendments, and lower courts have expanded the list even further. See Erwin Chemerinsky, Federal Jurisdiction § 9.1 (3d ed. 1999). "Bivens actions"—as they have come to be called—are unavailable when Congress provides an alternative remedy viewed as equally effective or when, even absent legislative remedial action, there are "special factors counselling hesitation." Carlson v. Green, 446 U.S. 14, 18–19 (1980). Under these exceptions, the Court has refused to imply a cause of action under the Fifth Amendment for military personnel who were the victims of alleged racial discrimination by superior officers, Chappell v. Wallace, 462 U.S. 296 (1983); for soldiers who were severely injured when deceptively subjected by the Army to LSD experimentation, United States v. Stanley, 483 U.S. 669 (1987); and for disability recipients whose procedural due process rights were violated in benefit termination decisions, Schweiker v. Chilicky, 487 U.S. 412 (1988)—all situations in which an alternative remedy was completely unavailable, or significantly limited.

(2) *The Evolving Meaning of Qualified Immunity.* HARLOW V. FITZGERALD, 457 U.S. 800, 813–19 (1982): Earnest Fitzgerald, a Defense Department employee and well-known "whistle-blower," found himself unemployed after an Air Force reorganization abolished his job. Claiming he was the victim of retaliation for testifying before Congress about defense program cost overruns, Fitzgerald brought a First Amendment Bivens action against a number of people including Bryce Harlow, a presidential aide. Harlow denied involvement in the matter and, even after considerable discovery, evidence of his role remained at most "inferential." The district court denied his motion for summary judgment, and an immediate appeal was taken on the immunity issue.

Justice Powell wrote for the Court: "The resolution of immunity questions inherently requires a balance between the evils inevitable in any available alternative. In situations of abuse of office, an action for damages may offer the only realistic avenue for vindication of constitutional guarantees. It is this recognition that has required the denial of absolute immunity to most public officers. At the same time, however, it cannot be disputed seriously that claims frequently run against the innocent as well as the guilty—at a cost not only to the defendant officials, but to society as a whole. . . .

"In identifying qualified immunity as the best attainable accommodation of competing values, . . . we relied on the assumption that this standard would permit '[i]nsubstantial lawsuits [to] be quickly terminated.' Butz v. Economou. Yet petitioners advance persuasive arguments that the dismissal of insubstantial lawsuits without trial—a factor presupposed in the balance of competing interests struck by our prior cases—requires an adjustment of the 'good faith' standard established by our decisions.

"Qualified or 'good faith' immunity is an affirmative defense that must be pleaded by a defendant official. Decisions of this Court have established that the 'good faith' defense has both an 'objective' and a 'subjective' aspect. The objective element involves a presumptive knowledge of and respect for 'basic, unquestioned constitutional rights.' Wood v. Strickland, 420 U.S. 308, 322 (1975). The subjective component refers to 'permissible intentions.' Characteristically the Court has defined these elements by identifying the circumstances in which qualified immunity would *not* be available. Referring both to the objective and subjective elements, we have held that qualified immunity would be defeated if an official *'knew or reasonably should have known* that the action he took within his sphere of official responsibility would violate the constitutional rights of the [plaintiff], *or* if he took the action *with the malicious intention* to cause a deprivation of constitutional rights or other injury. . . .' (emphasis added)

"The subjective element of the good-faith defense frequently has proved incompatible with our admonition in Butz that insubstantial claims should not proceed to trial. Rule 56 of the Federal Rules of Civil Procedure provides that disputed questions of fact ordinarily may not be decided on motions for summary judgment. And an official's subjective good faith has been considered to be a question of fact that some courts have regarded as inherently requiring resolution by a jury.

"In the context of Butz' attempted balancing of competing values, it now is clear that substantial costs attend the litigation of the subjective good faith of government officials. Not only are there the general costs of subjecting officials to the risks of trial—distraction of officials from their governmental duties, inhibition of discretionary action, and deterrence of able people from public service. There are special costs to 'subjective' inquiries of this kind. Immunity generally is available only to officials performing discretionary functions. In contrast with the thought processes accompanying 'ministerial' tasks, the judgments surrounding discretionary action almost inevitably are influenced by the decisionmaker's experiences, values, and emotions. These variables explain in part why questions of subjective intent so rarely can be decided by summary judgment. Yet they also frame a background in which there often is no clear end to the relevant evidence. Judicial inquiry into subjective motivation therefore may entail broad-ranging discovery and the deposing of numerous persons, including an official's professional colleagues. Inquiries of this kind can be peculiarly disruptive of effective government.

"Consistently with the balance at which we aimed in Butz, we conclude today that bare allegations of malice should not suffice to subject government officials either to the costs of trial or to the burdens of broad-reaching discovery. We therefore hold that government officials performing discretionary functions generally are shielded from liability for civil damages insofar as their conduct does not violate clearly established statutory or constitutional rights of which a reasonable person would have known.[1]

"Reliance on the objective reasonableness of an official's conduct, as measured by reference to clearly established law, should avoid excessive disruption of government and permit the resolution of many insubstantial claims on summary judgment. On summary judgment, the judge appropriately may determine, not only the currently applicable law, but whether that law was clearly established at the time an action occurred.[2] If the law at that time was not clearly established, an official could not reasonably be expected to anticipate subsequent legal developments, nor could he fairly be said to 'know' that the law forbade conduct not previously identified as unlawful. Until this threshold immunity question is resolved, discovery should not be allowed. If the law was clearly established, the immunity defense ordinarily should fail, since a reasonably competent public official should know the law governing his conduct. Nevertheless, if the official pleading the defense claims extraordinary circumstances and can prove that he neither knew nor should have known of the relevant legal standard,

---

1. This case involves no issue concerning the elements of the immunity available to state officials sued for constitutional violations under 42 U.S.C. § 1983. We have found previously, however, that it would be "untenable to draw a distinction for purposes of immunity law between suits brought against state officials under § 1983 and suits brought

directly under the Constitution against federal officials."

2. ... [W]e need not define here the circumstances under which 'the state of the law' should be evaluated by reference to the opinions of this Court, of the Courts of Appeals, or of the local District Court.

the defense should be sustained. But again, the defense would turn primarily on objective factors.

"By defining the limits of qualified immunity essentially in objective terms, we provide no license to lawless conduct. The public interest in deterrence of unlawful conduct and in compensation of victims remains protected by a test that focuses on the objective legal reasonableness of an official's acts. Where an official could be expected to know that certain conduct would violate statutory or constitutional rights, he should be made to hesitate; and a person who suffers injury caused by such conduct may have a cause of action. But where an official's duties legitimately require action in which clearly established rights are not implicated, the public interest may be better served by action taken 'with independence and without fear of consequences.' Pierson v. Ray, 386 U.S. 547, 554 (1967).[3]"

When Harlow states that "bare allegations of malice should not suffice to subject government officials either to the costs of trial or to the burdens of broad-reaching discovery," does it mean that plaintiffs alleging malicious government action have a higher-than-normal burden of producing evidence in order to avoid dismissal—or does it mean that even *proof* of bad motive cannot defeat the assertion of immunity? Crawford–El v. Britton, 523 U.S. 574 (1998): "Under [the Harlow] standard, a defense of qualified immunity may not be rebutted by evidence that the defendant's conduct was malicious or otherwise improperly motivated. Evidence concerning the defendant's subjective intent is simply irrelevant to that defense." Official immunity defenses are judge-made law. Under Harlow as clarified in Crawford–El, an unscrupulous official can engage in a malicious misuse of her official authority whenever the relevant legal standards are objectively unclear. (Keep in mind that, if the official's conduct either is not unlawful or does not cause harm, she wins on the merits without regard to any immunity.) In setting the qualified immunity standard, has the Court properly calibrated the risk that damages actions will deter legitimate government activities?

(3) *The Case for Fearing Over-Deterrence.* PETER W. LOW & JOHN C. JEFFRIES, JR., FEDERAL COURTS & THE LAW OF FEDERAL–STATE RELATIONS 946–48 (4th ed. 1998): "In most situations, society relies on private decision-makers to evaluate the expected costs and benefits of certain actions, including the possibility of civil liability, and to make decisions roughly congruent with the social interest. In the context of damage actions against government officials, however, many factors combine to make it likely that the prospect of personal liability will induce government officials to engage in excessive defensive activity and thus to sacrifice the public good in favor of individual protection. These factors are detailed in an analysis of the working environment of the street-level official by Peter H. Schuck in Suing Government: Citizen Remedies for Official Wrongs 60–77 (1983).

"The person most likely to be sued . . . is, in Schuck's parlance, the 'street-level official.' Examples include police officers, prison authorities,

---

3. We emphasize that our decision applies only to suits for civil *damages* arising from actions within the scope of an official's duties and in 'objective' good faith. We express no view as to the conditions in which injunctive or declaratory relief might be available.

public school officials, and welfare administrators. Because these officials personally and directly deliver basic government services, they constantly interact with individual citizens on matters of intense concern. Many of these interactions are non-consensual and thus likely to be characterized by conflict and mutual suspicion. The goals that these officials are directed to pursue—maintaining order, educating students, and the like—are often complex and ambiguous, and the choice of means to attain them is irreducibly judgmental.

"Moreover, the official often has a duty to act. While the private citizen is usually free to do nothing, if that seems the best course, the public official may be commanded by law to intervene on behalf of the public interest. Since government action is likely to be coercive, it is especially productive of conflict and harm. Indeed, virtually any choice of action or inaction risks harm to someone. . . .

"Not only are such decisions potentially harmful to others; they are also likely to be attended by significant risk of error. Many officials must act more or less instantly, in situations that border on emergency, and on the basis of inadequate information. Under such circumstances, it is difficult to capture appropriate decision-making in dependable rules. Not that the effort is lacking. As Schuck points out, the street-level official is typically required to administer and abide by a host of rules, but rules 'so voluminous, ambiguous, contradictory, and in flux that officials can only comply with or enforce them selectively.' In short, says Schuck, the officials 'are actually awash in discretion.'

"Most important of all, public officials are typically unable to appropriate to themselves the benefits that flow from their decisions. The costs of malfeasance or mistake can be visited upon the official by a suit for damages, but the benefits of good performance tend to run to the public at large. The resulting incentive structure may conduce to defensive, cost-minimizing behavior, even if it entails a net loss in social benefits. . . . 'Officials tend to orient their decisions about whether, when, and how to act less toward maximizing . . . net benefits, which they cannot appropriate, than toward minimizing . . . those costs that they would incur personally.'

"Among these costs is the risk of being sued. The magnitude of this risk depends not only on the expected cost of adverse judgments, but also on the expected cost of having to defend such actions and on the demoralization or other nonpecuniary cost of being sued. As Schuck points out, an important element of nonpecuniary cost is uncertainty—uncertainty concerning 'the outcome of the case; its duration; its effect upon the official's creditworthiness; the circumstances under which the official may receive (or lose) free counsel and indemnification of any settlement or adverse judgment; the quality of legal representation that the defending agency will provide; and potential conflicts of interest on the part of the defending agency or assigned counsel.' . . .

"Finally, it is worth noting that the expected costs and benefits to officials of their own decisions are typically not symmetrical. To put the point very crudely, action is likely to be more costly than inaction. This imbalance is due in part to what Jerry Mashaw has termed a 'cause of action' problem. See Jerry L. Mashaw, Civil Liability of Government Officers: Property Rights and Official Accountability, 42 Law & Contemp. Probs. 8 (1978). The individual who is injured by affirmative misconduct is likely to be able to state a cause of action against the responsible official. The harm to the citizen and its connection to the official's conduct are likely to be clear. By contrast, persons injured by an official's failure to act may find it more difficult to state a claim for relief. The connection between harm to the citizen and official inaction may be indirect and obscure, and causation therefore difficult to establish. Furthermore, enforcement authority is typically discretionary in nature. As a result, the official may be protected from liability for an omission by the absence of any duty to act. For these reasons, the likelihood of being sued for erroneous action exceeds the risk for erroneous inaction, and the incentives of government officials ... may therefore be skewed toward defensive behavior.

"For these reasons, the prospect of unintended deterrence of legitimate government activity has loomed very large in debates over official immunities."

(4) *Are There Any Actual Data?* THEODORE EISENBERG & STEWART J. SCHWAB, THE REALITY OF CONSTITUTIONAL TORT LITIGATION, 72 Cornell L.Rev. 641, 685–86 (1987): "A further issue in constitutional tort litigation is who pays for these recoveries. Many are concerned that the threat of personal fiscal loss adversely affects individual official behavior. This study[4] does not directly assess such effects because doing so requires knowing individuals' perceptions of the threat of personal liability and their behavioral responses to it, information beyond the scope of this project. We can, however, offer some guidance about the magnitude of this threat. In cases in which court records showed payments to plaintiffs, we recorded the defendant's status as an institution or individual. We found no case in which court records showed that an individual official had borne the cost of an adverse constitutional tort judgment.

"This does not mean that there were no such cases, nor does it reflect the legal costs incurred by a defendant in the unusual case in which a government employer does not furnish its officials with an attorney. Nevertheless, it does suggest that rampant official fear of personal liability may be an overreaction."

(5) *Applying the Qualified Immunity Standard: Identifying "clearly established statutory or constitutional rights of which a reasonable person would have known."* Cases after Harlow have emphasized that the presence of qualified immunity is a question of law for the court (rather than fact, for the jury) that must be resolved in the plaintiff's favor before discovery is permitted. See Hunter v. Bryant, 502 U.S. 224 (1991); Siegert v. Gilley, 500 U.S. 226, 231 (1991). Far less clear is precisely how the trial judge ought to

---

4. [Ed.] Professors Eisenberg & Schwab have conducted virtually the only empirical studies of constitutional tort litigation. Their results called into question many of the intuitions in this area, including the belief that this category of litigation is overwhelming the federal courts and fiscally overburdening government entities. Their results are summarized in Theodore Eisenberg, Civil Rights Legislation 151–62 (4th ed. 1996).

determine the existence of "clearly established rights" that a reasonable official "could be expected to know."

In Elder v. Holloway, 510 U.S. 510 (1994), the district court had dismissed, on immunity grounds, a § 1983 action against police officers based on an unconstitutional search—even though, *before* the search occurred, the Ninth Circuit had issued an opinion holding such searches violative of the Fourth Amendment. The Supreme Court had not ruled on the issue; apparently, the appellate opinion was not known to either the lawyers who tried the case or the district judge (not to mention the police officers who conducted the search). The Supreme Court unanimously reversed dismissal of the action. In United States v. Lanier, 520 U.S. 259 (1997), the Court unanimously reversed a Sixth Circuit en banc ruling that the defendant state-court judge, who had sexually assaulted five women in his chambers, could not be convicted of criminally violating their constitutional rights[5] absent a prior decision establishing that such conduct was unconstitutional as well as criminal. Justice Souter's opinion explained that Harlow's "clearly established right" requirement "is simply the adaptation of the fair warning standard to give officials ... the same protection from civil liability and its consequences that individuals have traditionally possessed in the face of vague criminal statutes." Most recently, Hope v. Pelzer, 536 U.S. 730 (2002), reemphasized the "fair warning" purpose of the qualified immunity inquiry. Hope, a state prisoner, alleged violation of his Eighth Amendment rights when he was punished for disruptive conduct on a chain gang by being twice handcuffed with raised hands to a hitching post for extended periods without adequate water. The Eleventh Circuit agreed that the conduct was cruel and unusual punishment but dismissed on qualified immunity grounds because the facts of Hope's situation were not "materially similar" to those of any previously decided case. Justice Stevens, writing for the 6–3 majority, reversed. If, "in the light of pre-existing law, the unlawfulness is apparent," then it need not be shown "that the very action in question has previously been held unlawful." Here, a prior decision of the Supreme Court had held that "unnecessary and wanton infliction of pain" violated the Eighth Amendment, two Eleventh Circuit cases had condemned punishment that included handcuffing inmates to a fence for extended periods, an Alabama regulation that restricted the use of hitching posts had not been followed, and a U.S. Department of Justice report had advised the state department of corrections to stop using the practice because of constitutional concerns. Justice Thomas, dissenting for himself, the Chief Justice and Justice Scalia, argued inter alia that several recent district court cases in the Circuit had upheld very similar practices, and that the guards in question had never seen the DOJ report.

The "clearly established law" standard has given the lower courts a great deal of difficulty, and even the recent decision in Hope v. Pelzer is unlikely to calm the area significantly. What is the right interpretation? As is often the case, the answer depends on what we are trying to accomplish. RICHARD H. FALLON, DANIEL J. MELTZER, & DAVID L. SHAPIRO, HART & WECHSLER'S

---

5. Under 18 U.S.C. § 242, the criminal analogue of § 1983.

THE FEDERAL COURTS AND THE FEDERAL SYSTEM 1134 (5th ed. 2003)[6]: "The threshold issue with respect to official immunity is whether to frame the problem as one about the appropriate scope of remedies against individual officials or about government's liability for the costs of government. Under the first of these approaches, if excessive caution by enforcement officers is a substantial worry, formulation of an immunity standard in terms of new law (i.e., precluding liability for conduct that was not a violation of clearly established law) seems a sensible response. And if officials are easily deterred from conscientious action by the threat of personal liability, an unusually broad conception of new law may be appropriate. But if the second approach is followed and doctrines of official liability are seen as evolving because they were functionally necessary surrogates for governmental liability [see p. 1107 above], then there would be greater concern for the cost to the victims of unlawful conduct. The second approach would therefore suggest a narrowing of the scope of official immunity, perhaps preserving immunity only for 'exceptional circumstances' in which, for example, later case law established the unconstitutionality of previously accepted and widespread [official] practices. Such a course would pressure government to provide indemnification and thereby internalize the costs of government, which in turn would permit victims to obtain relief even if the official[s] themselves were judgment-proof."

(6) *Other Levels of Official Immunity, and the Effect of the Kind of Relief Requested.* As Butz explains, the level of immunity varies with the nature and level of the particular official's function. It also varies with the type of relief requested. As you review the various possibilities, ask yourself whether they reflect a coherent theory of the appropriate balance between compensating individual harm and protecting the legitimate activities of government:

Judicial Officials. In suits for money damages, judges have absolute immunity for judicial functions, "however erroneous the act may have been, and however injurious in its consequences it may have proved to the plaintiff,"[7] and even if the act was malicious. E.g., Stump v. Sparkman, 435 U.S. 349 (1978) (immunity for state court judge who, without statutory authority, ordered a "somewhat retarded" 15–year old young woman sterilized on her mother's request, without hearing or appointment of a guardian; the woman was told she was having an appendectomy and discovered the truth only after she married and tried to have children). By contrast, judges receive only qualified immunity for administrative or executive actions. See, e.g., Forrester v. White, 484 U.S. 219 (1988) (allegedly gender-based firing of probation officer). As Butz indicates, these immunity rules apply as well to ALJs and other agency officials performing adjudicative tasks, but linedrawing has proven difficult. See, e.g., Cleavinger v. Saxner, 474 U.S. 193 (1985) (prison disciplinary committee given only qualified immunity). In any event, absolute judicial immunity does *not*

---

6. [Ed.] This excerpt in turns quotes portions of Richard H. Fallon, Jr., & Daniel J. Meltzer, New Law, Non–Retroactivity, and Constitutional Remedies, 104 Harv. L. Rev. 1731 (1991). All punctuation indicating internal quotes has been omitted.

7. Bradley v. Fisher, 80 U.S. 335, 347 (1871).

extend to suits for prospective relief, or to attorneys' fee awards. Pulliam v. Allen, 466 U.S. 522 (1984).

Actors Who Are an Integral Part of the Judicial Process. A variety of actors intimately connected with the adjudicative process share the judge's absolute immunity. These include witnesses[8] and court officers such as clerks (lower court precedent only).[9] Also included are prosecutors to the extent they are engaged in in-court, prosecutorial tasks. See Imbler v. Pachtman, 424 U.S. 409 (1976) (knowing use of perjured testimony that resulted in conviction, and 9–year incarceration, of innocent person). Absolute immunity does not extend, however, to prosecutors' investigative or other activities outside the courtroom. See, e.g., Mitchell v. Forsyth, 472 U.S. 511 (1985) (decision to wiretap); Burns v. Reed, 500 U.S. 478 (1991) (approval of interrogation of suspect under hypnosis); Buckley v. Fitzsimmons, 509 U.S. 259 (1993) (fabrication of evidence and false statements at a press conference). As with judges, even absolute immunity does not apply in suits for prospective relief.

Legislative Officials. Members of Congress and their aides have absolute immunity in suits for *both* money damages *and* prospective relief because of the Speech & Debate Clause, Article I, § 6.[10] State and local legislators have been accorded analogous immunity.[11] This immunity exists only for legislative tasks. E.g., Hutchinson v. Proxmire, 443 U.S. 111 (1979) (qualified immunity applies to press release).

The Chief Executive. Although, under Scheuer v. Rhodes, state governors receive only qualified immunity, the President of the United States has absolute immunity for money damages for acts done while President[12] —although not for acts prior to taking office.[13] The President's amenability to prospective relief is uncertain; the Court has expressed separation-of-powers reservations about such relief.[14]

(7) *Personal Liability of the Employee vs. Entity Liability of the Government.* In 1988 Congress, at the urging of the Department of Justice, amended the Federal Tort Claims Act to provide that the *only* available remedy for torts committed by federal employees during the course of their employment is against the United States pursuant to the FTCA.[15] The

---

8. Briscoe v. LaHue, 460 U.S. 325 (1983) (police officer witness who committed perjury). There is some question whether this holding is limited to witnesses who are police officers.

9. E.g., Rodriguez v. Weprin, 116 F.3d 62 (2d Cir.1997). But cf. Antoine v. Byers & Anderson, Inc., 508 U.S. 429 (1993) (no absolute immunity for court reporter).

10. Eastland v. U.S. Servicemen's Fund, 421 U.S. 491 (1975); Gravel v. U.S., 408 U.S. 606 (1972).

11. See Supreme Court of Virginia v. Consumers Union, 446 U.S. 719 (1980); Lake Country Estates v. Tahoe Regional Planning Agency, 440 U.S. 391 (1979); Tenney v. Brandhove, 341 U.S. 367 (1951).

12. Nixon v. Fitzgerald, 457 U.S. 731 (1982).

13. Clinton v. Jones, 520 U.S. 681 (1997).

14. See Franklin v. Massachusetts, 505 U.S. 788 (1992).

15. Federal Employees Liability Reform & Tort Compensation Act of 1988 [often called the "Westfall Act"], Pub.L.No. 100– 694, 102 Stat. 4564 (codified at 28 U.S.C. § 2679(b)(1) (1988)).

"Upon certification by the Attorney General that the defendant employee was acting within the scope of his office or employment at the time of the incident out of which the claim arose, [the action] shall be deemed an

Supreme Court has broadly interpreted this statutory immunity: Even when the FTCA withholds consent to recovery from the United States, see p. 1278 below, the employee may not be sued personally. See United States v. Smith, 499 U.S. 160 (1991) (military doctor not subject to individual malpractice suit even though case fell within FTCA exception for injuries sustained in a foreign country). The 1988 amendments expressly exclude *constitutional* torts from the Act's reach. See 28 U.S.C. § 2679(b)(2)(a).[16] Hence, Bivens actions remain alive and well, and litigants now have an added incentive to frame injurious official conduct as a constitutional wrong if at all possible.[17]

3 RICHARD J. PIERCE, JR., ADMINISTRATIVE LAW TREATISE § 19.2 at 1391–92 (2002): "Allowing tort actions against government employees, rather than government, has three . . . adverse effects. First, sympathy for the plight of the public employee defendant often induces courts to adopt unduly narrow interpretations of constitutional and statutory rights. Some of the most insupportably narrow interpretations of the Due Process Clause, for instance, have been adopted in § 1983 actions, where the Court knew that a broader interpretation would have the effect of exposing a public employee to potential catastrophic tort liability. See, e.g., Ingraham v. Wright, p. 888 above (public school can inflict corporal punishment without any prior proceeding). . . . Second, sympathy for the plight of the public servant defendant often induces juries to resolve close factual disputes in favor of the defendant and to award lower damages than would otherwise be warranted. Third, plaintiffs who are seriously injured by unlawful government conduct rarely can recover their full damages from a government employee defendant because government employees rarely have unencumbered assets sufficient to satisfy a large judgment. . . .

"Tort law would provide a more appropriate constraint on government action and a more secure source of compensation for victims of torts committed by government if all potential exposure to tort liability were transferred from public employees to government. . . . "

action against the United States under the provisions of [the FTCA], and the United States shall be substituted as the party defendant." 28 U.S.C. § 2679(d)(1). If the case was filed in state court, the Attorney General's certification also triggers removal to the federal district court. § 2679(d)(2).

16. Commentators have been critical of the Act's distinction between common law and constitutional torts. Professor Pierce argues: "From a public policy perspective, negligent violation of a constitutionally based rule of conduct is indistinguishable from negligent violation of a common law rule of conduct. In many contexts, rules of conduct that have their source in the Constitution are more difficult to predict, understand, and apply than common law tort rules. It is much easier, for instance, for a government truck driver to know and apply the rules of the road than for a government benefit administrator to know and apply the rules of procedural due process. . . . " III Richard J. Pierce, Jr., Administrative Law Treatise § 19.4 at 1434 (2002).

17. A given injurious occurrence may, of course, support both common law and constitutional tort theories. The possibility of an FTCA claim against the United States is not sufficient, per se, to prevent implication of a Bivens action against the individual officer. See Carlson v. Green, 446 U.S. 14 (1980) (mother of prisoner who died from allegedly improper medical care could maintain Eighth Amendment action against prison officials even though an FTCA claim might lie against the federal government).

b. DAMAGES ACTIONS AGAINST GOVERNMENT ENTITIES

(i) THE FEDERAL TORT CLAIMS ACT

Not until the passage of the Federal Tort Claims Act in 1946 did the United States consent to accept, in any significant degree, liability for the tortious conduct of its employees.[1] The scope of this consent has been broadened in subsequent years, and today the FTCA represents a substantial remedy for official wrongdoing. The core provision is 28 U.S.C. § 2674: "The United States shall be liable . . . in the same manner and to the same extent as a private individual under like circumstances. . . ."

This consent is subject to several procedural restrictions. The government "shall not be liable for interest prior to judgment or for punitive damages." Id.[2] Jury trial is not available. 28 U.S.C. § 2402. Attorneys' fees are limited.[3] Finally, there is a stringent exhaustion requirement: Before suit can be filed, a claim must be presented to the responsible agency and denied. 28 U.S.C. § 2675(a).[4] Absent newly discovered evidence or intervening facts, the amount of the claim presented to the agency limits the amount recoverable by suit. § 2675(b). This process must be completed before the lawsuit is initiated; a complaint filed while a claim is pending will be dismissed even if the agency then denies the claim. McNeil v. United States, 508 U.S. 106 (1993).

More significant than these procedural restrictions are the several substantive qualifications and exceptions contained in the Act. These provisions preserve the federal government's sovereign immunity in many important areas. Since 1988, the Act has also provided that federal employees may not be sued personally for torts committed during the scope of their employment. See p. 1276 above. The practical consequence is that victims of tortious government action falling within one of the substantive exceptions or qualifications can obtain compensation for their injuries, if at all, only through the extraordinary processes of direct administrative settlement or passage of a private bill by Congress.[5]

Actionable Conduct in General. 28 U.S.C. § 1346, conferring jurisdiction on the district court to hear FTCA actions, elaborates on the basic liability defined in § 2674 by speaking of a "negligent or wrongful act or omission" as to which "a private person[ ]would be liable to the claimant in accordance with the law of the place where the act or omission occurred." Several conclusions have been held to flow from this language. First,

---

1. A large number of highly specific waivers of sovereign immunity also exist, but they represent a small portion of the federal government's total possible liability for the wrongful acts of its employees.

2. On the classification of damages as "punitive," see Molzof v. United States, 502 U.S. 301 (1992).

3. To 25% of a judgment, or 20% of an administrative settlement, 28 U.S.C. § 2678—low by comparison with typical contingent fees in personal injury cases.

4. The agency's failure to make "final disposition" of the claim within six months can be deemed a denial. § 2675(a).

5. See generally George A. Bermann, Federal Tort Claims at the Agency Level: The FTCA Administrative Process, 35 Case W.Res.L.Rev. 509, 516 (1985); Note, Denial of Atomic Veterans' Claims: The Enduring Fallout from Feres v. United States, 24 Wm. & Mary L.Rev. 259 (1983).

recovery cannot be had on a strict liability theory; at least negligence must be proved.[6] Second, except to the extent that it is specifically displaced by FTCA provisions, state law ("the law of the place where the act or omission occurred") provides the rule of decision.[7] Third, recovery against the United States (or its agencies) cannot be had for *constitutional* torts, inasmuch as such torts sound in federal, not state, law.[8]

Because the Act uses "a private person" as the reference for liability, the government has repeatedly argued that the United States cannot be held liable for torts arising out of "core governmental functions"—i.e., activities for which there are no private analogues. The Supreme Court has disapproved this interpretation at least three times[9] but, perhaps because the argument is closely related to the scope of the "discretionary function" exception (below), it persists.

Activities Outside the United States. Any claim arising in a foreign country is excluded. 28 U.S.C. § 2680(k).

Exception for Unconstitutional Statutes or Unlawful Regulations. An FTCA claim will not lie for "an act or omission of an employee of the Government, exercising due care, in the execution of a statute or regulation, whether or not such statute or regulation be valid." 28 U.S.C. § 2680(a). "It was not 'intended that the constitutionality of legislation [or] the legality of regulations . . . should be tested through the medium of a damage suit for tort.'" Dalehite v. United States, 346 U.S. 15, 27 (1953) (quoting legislative hearings on FTCA).

The Miscellany of Subject–Specific Exceptions. The Act excludes liability for a number of specific activities: carriage of the mail; admiralty suits for which other remedies are provided; administration of the Trading with the Enemy Act of 1917; quarantines; monetary system regulation; combatant activities during time of war[10]; activities of the TVA, the Panama Canal Co., and federal land and credit banks. 28 U.S.C. § 2680.

Exception for Most Intentional Torts. In one of the two most significant gaps in FTCA recovery, consent to liability is explicitly withheld for "[a]ny claim arising out of assault, battery, false imprisonment, false arrest, malicious prosecution, abuse of process, libel, slander, misrepresentation, deceit, or interference with contract rights"—except that an action for any

---

6. Laird v. Nelms, 406 U.S. 797, 799 (1972); Dalehite v. United States, 346 U.S. 15, 45 (1953).

7. E.g., FDIC v. Meyer, 510 U.S. 471, 478 (1994).

8. Id. at 477–78.

9. See Berkovitz v. United States, p. 1280 below.

10. The Supreme Court has substantially broadened this exception beyond its terms, such that the government is now effectively immune from liability for all injuries to military personnel while they are in the service. This immunity—referred to as the "Feres doctrine" from the original case, Feres v. United States, 340 U.S. 135 (1950)—extends even to willful and egregious wrongdoing. See, e.g., United States v. Stanley, 483 U.S. 669 (1987) (deceptive administration of LSD to soldiers who thought they had volunteered to test protective gear for chemical warfare). It has drawn sharp criticism from commentators. E.g., Jonathan P. Tomes, *Feres* to *Chappell* to *Stanley*: Three Strikes and Servicemembers Are Out, 25 U.Rich. L.Rev. 93 (1990); Barry Kellman, Judicial Abdication of Military Tort Accountability: But Who Is to Guard the Guards Themselves?, 1989 Duke L.J. 1597.

of the first six torts can be maintained if the employee involved was a federal "investigative or law enforcement officer[ ]."[11] 28 U.S.C. § 2680(h).

Discretionary Function Exception. The other significant gap in the government's consent to liability for its employees' torts is § 2680(a), which excludes:

> Any claim based upon an act or omission of an employee of the Government ... based upon the exercise or performance or the failure to exercise or perform a discretionary function or duty on the part of a federal agency or an employee of the Government, whether or not the discretion involved be abused.

As in other settings in which legal consequences turn on the discretionary/ministerial distinction, reaching a sound and predictable definition of "discretionary function" has proved vexing:

Berkovitz v. United States

Supreme Court of the United States, 1988.
486 U.S. 531.

■ JUSTICE MARSHALL delivered the opinion of the Court.

The question in this case is whether the discretionary function exception of the Federal Tort Claims Act bars a suit based on the Government's licensing of an oral polio vaccine and on its subsequent approval of the release of a specific lot of that vaccine to the public.

On May 10, 1979, Kevan Berkovitz, then a 2–month-old infant, ingested a dose of Orimune, an oral polio vaccine manufactured by Lederle Laboratories. Within one month, he contracted a severe case of polio. The disease left Berkovitz almost completely paralyzed and unable to breathe without the assistance of a respirator. The Communicable Disease Center, an agency of the Federal Government, determined that Berkovitz had contracted polio from the vaccine.

Berkovitz, joined by his parents as guardians, subsequently filed suit against the United States in Federal District Court.[1] The complaint alleged that the United States was liable for his injuries under the FTCA.... The Government moved to dismiss the suit for lack of subject-matter jurisdiction on the ground that the agency actions fell within the discretionary function exception of the FTCA. The District Court denied this motion. [The Court of Appeals reversed.]

... [The discretionary function] exception, as we stated in our most recent opinion on the subject, "marks the boundary between Congress'

---

11.   As Butz explains, see p. 1258 above, this "exception to the exception" was added in 1974, after outcry over some especially shocking behavior on the part of federal narcotics officers. See Jack Boger, Mark Gitenstein & Paul R. Verkuil, The Federal Tort Claims Act Intentional Torts Amendment: An Interpretive Analysis, 54 N.C.L.Rev. 497

(1976). The exception cannot be circumvented by suing on a theory that the tortfeasor's superior negligently provided inadequate supervision. United States v. Shearer, 473 U.S. 52, 55 (1985).

1.   Petitioners also sued Lederle Laboratories in a separate civil action. That suit was settled before the instant case was filed.

willingness to impose tort liability upon the United States and its desire to protect certain governmental activities from exposure to suit by private individuals." United States v. Varig Airlines, 467 U.S. 797, 808 (1984).

The determination of whether the discretionary function exception bars a suit against the Government is guided by several established principles. This Court stated in Varig that "it is the nature of the conduct, rather than the status of the actor, that governs whether the discretionary function exception applies in a given case." In examining the nature of the challenged conduct, a court must first consider whether the action is a matter of choice for the acting employee. This inquiry is mandated by the language of the exception; conduct cannot be discretionary unless it involves an element of judgment or choice. See Dalehite v. United States, 346 U.S. 15, 34 (1953) (stating that the exception protects "the discretion of the executive or the administrator to act according to one's judgment of the best course"). Thus, the discretionary function exception will not apply when a federal statute, regulation, or policy specifically prescribes a course of action for an employee to follow. In this event, the employee has no rightful option but to adhere to the directive. . . .

Moreover, assuming the challenged conduct involves an element of judgment, a court must determine whether that judgment is of the kind that the discretionary function exception was designed to shield. The basis for the discretionary function exception was Congress' desire to "prevent judicial 'second-guessing' of legislative and administrative decisions grounded in social, economic, and political policy through the medium of an action in tort." United States v. Varig Airlines. The exception, properly construed, therefore protects only governmental actions and decisions based on considerations of public policy. . . .

This Court's decision in Varig Airlines illustrates these propositions. The two cases resolved in that decision were tort suits by the victims of airplane accidents who alleged that the Federal Aviation Administration had acted negligently in certifying certain airplanes for operation. The Court characterized the suits as challenging the FAA's decision to certify the airplanes without first inspecting them and held that this decision was a discretionary act for which the Government was immune from liability. . . . Congress had given the Secretary of Transportation broad authority to establish and implement a program for enforcing compliance with airplane safety standards. In the exercise of that authority, the FAA, as the Secretary's designee, had devised a system of "spot-checking" airplanes for compliance. This Court first held that the establishment of that system was a discretionary function within the meaning of the FTCA because it represented a policy determination as to how best to "accommodat[e] the goal of air transportation safety and the reality of finite agency resources." The Court then stated that the discretionary function exception also protected "the acts of FAA employees in executing the 'spot-check' program" because under this program the employees "were specifically empowered to make policy judgments regarding the degree of confidence that might reasonably be placed in a given manufacturer, the need to maximize compliance with FAA regulations, and the efficient allocation of agency resources.'' . . .[2]

In restating and clarifying the scope of the discretionary function exception, we intend specifically to reject the Government's argument, pressed both in this Court and the Court of Appeals, that the exception precludes liability for any and all acts arising out of the regulatory programs of federal agencies. That argument is rebutted first by the language of the exception, which protects ''discretionary'' functions, rather than ''regulatory'' functions. The significance of Congress' choice of language is supported by the legislative history. . . .[3] This coverage accords with Congress' purpose in enacting the exception: to prevent ''[j]udicial intervention in . . . the political, social, and economic judgments'' of governmental—including regulatory—agencies. United States v. Varig Airlines. Moreover, this Court twice before has rejected a variant of the Government's position. See Indian Towing Co. v. United States, 350 U.S. 61, 64–65 (1955) (disapproving argument that FTCA precludes liability for the performance of ''uniquely governmental functions''); Rayonier, Inc. v. United States, 352 U.S. 315, 318–319 (1957) (same). . . . To the extent we have not already put the Government's argument to rest, we do so now. The discretionary function exception applies only to conduct that involves the permissible exercise of policy judgment. . . .

Petitioners' suit raises two broad claims. First, petitioners assert that the [Division of Biologic Sciences of the National Institutes of Health] violated a federal statute and accompanying regulations in issuing a license to Lederle Laboratories to produce Orimune. Second, petitioners argue that the Bureau of Biologics of the [Food & Drug Administration] violated federal regulations and policy in approving the release of the particular lot of Orimune that contained Kevan Berkovitz's dose. . . .

---

2. The decision in Indian Towing Co. v. United States, 350 U.S. 61 (1955), also illuminates the appropriate scope of the discretionary function exception. The plaintiff in that case sued the Government for failing to maintain a lighthouse in good working order. The Court stated that the initial decision to undertake and maintain lighthouse service was a discretionary judgment. The Court held, however, that the failure to maintain the lighthouse in good condition subjected the Government to suit under the FTCA. The latter course of conduct did not involve any permissible exercise of policy judgment.

3. The House of Representatives Report on the final version of the FTCA discussed the application of the discretionary function exception to the activities of regulatory agencies by stating that it would preclude application of the Act to

a claim against a regulatory agency, such as the Federal Trade Commission or the Securities and Exchange Commission, based upon an alleged abuse of discretionary authority by an officer or employee, whether or not negligence is alleged to have been involved. . . . The bill is not intended to authorize a suit for damages to test the validity of or provide a remedy on account of such discretionary acts even though negligently performed and involving an abuse of discretion. Nor is it desirable or intended that the constitutionality of legislation, or the legality of a rule or regulation should be tested through the medium of a damage suit for tort. However, the common-law torts of employees of regulatory agencies would be included within the scope of the bill to the same extent as torts of nonregulatory agencies.

This passage illustrates that Congress intended the discretionary function exception to apply to the *discretionary* acts of regulators, rather than to all regulatory acts.

Under federal law, a manufacturer must receive a product license prior to marketing a brand of live oral polio vaccine. . . . In deciding whether to issue a license, the DBS is required to comply with certain statutory and regulatory provisions. The Public Health Service Act provides:

> Licenses for the maintenance of establishments for the propagation or manufacture and preparation of products [including polio vaccines] may be issued only upon a showing that the establishment and the products for which a license is desired meet standards, designed to insure the continued safety, purity, and potency of such products, prescribed in regulations. . . .

A regulation similarly provides that "[a] product license shall be issued only upon examination of the product and upon a determination that the product complies with the standards prescribed in the regulations. . . ." In addition, a regulation states that "[a]n application for license shall not be considered as filed" until the DBS receives the information and data regarding the product that the manufacturer is required to submit. These statutory and regulatory provisions require the DBS, prior to issuing a product license, to receive all data the manufacturer is required to submit, to examine the product, and to make a determination that the product complies with safety standards.

Petitioners' first allegation with regard to the licensing of Orimune is that the DBS issued a product license without first receiving data that the manufacturer must submit showing how the product, at the various stages of the manufacturing process, matched up against regulatory safety standards. The discretionary function exception does not bar a cause of action based on this allegation. . . . The DBS has no discretion to issue a license without first receiving the required test data; to do so would violate a specific statutory and regulatory directive. . . .

Petitioners' other allegation regarding the licensing of Orimune is difficult to describe with precision. Petitioners contend that the DBS licensed Orimune even though the vaccine did not comply with certain regulatory safety standards. This charge may be understood in any of three ways. . . . If petitioners aver that the DBS licensed Orimune either without determining whether the vaccine complied with regulatory standards or after determining that the vaccine failed to comply, the discretionary function exception does not bar the claim. Under the scheme governing the DBS's regulation of polio vaccines, the DBS may not issue a license except upon an examination of the product and a determination that the product complies with all regulatory standards. . . . If petitioners' claim is that the DBS made a determination that Orimune complied with regulatory standards, but that the determination was incorrect, the question of the applicability of the discretionary function exception requires a somewhat different analysis. In that event, the question turns on whether the manner and method of determining compliance with the safety standards at issue involve agency judgment of the kind protected by the discretionary function exception. Petitioners contend that the determination involves the application of objective scientific standards, whereas the Government asserts that the determination incorporates considerable "policy judgment." In making these assertions, the parties have framed the issue appropriately. . . . The parties, however, have not addressed this question in detail, and they have given us no indication of the way in which the DBS interprets and applies the regulations setting forth the criteria for compliance. ... We therefore leave it to the District Court to decide, if petitioners choose to press this claim, whether agency officials appropriately exercise policy judgment in determining that a vaccine product complies with the relevant safety standards.

The regulatory scheme governing release of vaccine lots is distinct from that governing the issuance of licenses. The former set of regulations places an obligation on manufacturers to examine all vaccine lots prior to distribution to ensure that they comply with regulatory standards. These regulations, however, do not impose a corresponding duty on the Bureau of Biologics. Although the regulations empower the Bureau to examine any vaccine lot and prevent the distribution of a noncomplying lot, they do not require the Bureau to take such action in all cases. The regulations generally allow the Bureau to determine the appropriate manner in which to regulate the release of vaccine lots, rather than mandating certain kinds of agency action. ... Given this regulatory context, the discretionary function exception bars any claims that challenge the Bureau's formulation of policy as to the appropriate way in which to regulate the release of vaccine lots. In addition, if the policies and programs formulated by the Bureau allow room for implementing officials to make independent policy judgments, the discretionary function exception protects the acts taken by those officials in the exercise of this discretion. ...

Viewed in light of these principles, petitioners' claim regarding the release of the vaccine lot from which Kevan Berkovitz received his dose survives the Government's motion to dismiss. Petitioners allege that, under the authority granted by the regulations, the Bureau of Biologics has adopted a policy of testing all vaccine lots for compliance with safety standards and preventing the distribution to the public of any lots that fail to comply. Petitioners further allege that notwithstanding this policy, which allegedly leaves no room for implementing officials to exercise independent policy judgment, employees of the Bureau knowingly approved the release of a lot that did not comply with safety standards. ... If those allegations are correct—that is, if the Bureau's policy did not allow the official who took the challenged action to release a noncomplying lot on the basis of policy considerations—the discretionary function exception does not bar the claim. Because petitioners may yet show, on the basis of materials obtained in discovery or otherwise, that the conduct challenged here did not involve the permissible exercise of policy discretion, the invocation of the discretionary function exception to dismiss petitioners' lot release claim was improper. ... The judgment of the Court of Appeals is accordingly reversed, and the case is remanded for further proceedings consistent with this opinion.

United States v. Gaubert

Supreme Court of the United States, 1991.
499 U.S. 315.

■ JUSTICE WHITE delivered the opinion of the Court.

... This FTCA suit arises from the supervision by federal regulators of the activities of Independent American Savings Association (IASA), a

Texas-chartered and federally insured savings and loan. Respondent Thomas A. Gaubert was IASA's chairman of the board and largest shareholder. In 1984, officials at the [Federal Home Loan Bank Board] sought to have IASA merge with Investex Savings, a failing Texas thrift. Because [the Board] and [the Dallas Federal Home Loan Bank] were concerned about Gaubert's other financial dealings, they requested that he sign a "neutralization agreement" which effectively removed him from IASA's management. They also asked him to post a $25 million interest in real property as security for his personal guarantee that IASA's net worth would exceed regulatory minimums. Gaubert agreed to both conditions. Federal officials then provided regulatory and financial advice to enable IASA to consummate the merger with Investex. Throughout this period, the regulators instituted no formal action against IASA. Instead, they relied on the likelihood that IASA and Gaubert would follow their suggestions and advice.

In the spring of 1986, the regulators threatened to close IASA unless its management and board of directors were replaced; all of the directors agreed to resign. The new officers and directors, including the chief executive officer who was a former [Dallas FHLB] employee, were recommended by [Dallas FHLB]. After the new management took over, [Dallas FHLB] officials became more involved in IASA's day-to-day business. They recommended the hiring of a certain consultant to advise IASA on operational and financial matters; they advised IASA concerning whether, when, and how its subsidiaries should be placed into bankruptcy; they mediated salary disputes; they reviewed the draft of a complaint to be used in litigation; they urged IASA to convert from state to federal charter; and they actively intervened when the Texas Savings and Loan Department attempted to install a supervisory agent at IASA. In each instance, [Dallas FHLB]'s advice was followed.

Although IASA was thought to be financially sound while Gaubert managed the thrift, the new directors soon announced that IASA had a substantial negative net worth. On May 20, 1987, Gaubert filed an administrative tort claim with the [Board], [Dallas FHLB], and FSLIC, seeking $75 million in damages for the lost value of his shares and $25 million for the property he had forfeited under his personal guarantee. That same day, the FSLIC assumed the receivership of IASA. After Gaubert's administrative claim was denied six months later, he filed the instant FTCA suit in the United States District Court for the Northern District of Texas, seeking $100 million in damages for the alleged negligence of federal officials in selecting the new officers and directors and in participating in the day-to-day management of IASA. The District Court granted the motion to dismiss filed by the United States, finding that all of the challenged actions of the regulators fell within the discretionary function exception to the FTCA. [The Court of Appeals affirmed as to claims concerning the merger, neutralization agreement, personal guarantee, and replacement of Independent's management, but reversed as to claims which concerned the regulators' activities after they assumed a supervisory role in IASA's day-to-day affairs.]

Where Congress has delegated the authority to an agency or to the executive branch to implement the general provisions of a regulatory statute and to issue regulations to that end, there is no doubt that planning-level decisions establishing programs are protected by the discretionary function exception, as is the promulgation of regulations by which the agencies are to carry out the programs. In addition, the actions of Government agents involving the necessary element of choice and grounded in the social, economic, or political goals of the statute and regulations are protected.

Thus, in Dalehite [v. United States, 346 U.S. 15 (1953)], the exception barred recovery for claims arising from a massive fertilizer explosion. The fertilizer had been manufactured, packaged, and prepared for export pursuant to detailed regulations as part of a comprehensive federal program aimed at increasing the food supply in occupied areas after World War II. Not only was the cabinet-level decision to institute the fertilizer program discretionary, but so were the decisions concerning the specific requirements for manufacturing the fertilizer. . . .

Under the applicable precedents, therefore, if a regulation mandates particular conduct, and the employee obeys the direction, the Government will be protected because the action will be deemed in furtherance of the policies which led to the promulgation of the regulation. If the employee violates the mandatory regulation, there will be no shelter from liability because there is no room for choice and the action will be contrary to policy. On the other hand, if a regulation allows the employee discretion, the very existence of the regulation creates a strong presumption that a discretionary act authorized by the regulation involves consideration of the same policies which led to the promulgation of the regulation.

Not all agencies issue comprehensive regulations, however. Some establish policy on a case-by-case basis, whether through adjudicatory proceedings or through administration of agency programs. Others promulgate regulations on some topics, but not on others. In addition, an agency may rely on internal guidelines rather than on published regulations. In any event, it will most often be true that the general aims and policies of the controlling statute will be evident from its text.

When established governmental policy, as expressed or implied by statute, regulation, or agency guidelines, allows a Government agent to exercise discretion, it must be presumed that the agent's acts are grounded in policy when exercising that discretion. For a complaint to survive a motion to dismiss, it must allege facts which would support a finding that the challenged actions are not the kind of conduct that can be said to be grounded in the policy of the regulatory regime. The focus of the inquiry is not on the agent's subjective intent in exercising the discretion conferred by statute or regulation, but on the nature of the actions taken and on whether they are susceptible to policy analysis.[1]

---

1. There are obviously discretionary acts performed by a Government agent that are within the scope of his employment but not within the discretionary function exception because these acts cannot be said to be based on the purposes that the regulatory regime seeks to accomplish. If one of the officials involved in this case drove an auto-

In light of our cases and their interpretation of § 2680(a), it is clear that the Court of Appeals erred in holding that the exception does not reach decisions made at the operational or management level of the bank involved in this case. A discretionary act is one that involves choice or judgment; there is nothing in that description that refers exclusively to policymaking or planning functions. Day-to-day management of banking affairs, like the management of other businesses, regularly requires judgment as to which of a range of permissible courses is the wisest. Discretionary conduct is not confined to the policy or planning level. . . .

We now inquire whether the Court of Appeals was correct in holding that some of the acts alleged in Gaubert's Amended Complaint were not discretionary acts within the meaning of § 2680(a). . . .

We first inquire whether the challenged actions were discretionary, or whether they were instead controlled by mandatory statutes or regulations. Berkovitz v. United States. . . . [N]either party has identified formal regulations governing the conduct in question. . . . 12 U.S.C. § 1464(a) authorizes the [Board] to examine and regulate [federal savings and loan associations], "giving primary consideration to the best practices of thrift institutions in the United States." Both the District Court and the Court of Appeals recognized that the agencies possessed broad statutory authority to supervise financial institutions. The relevant statutory provisions were not mandatory, but left to the judgment of the agency the decision of when to institute proceedings against a financial institution and which mechanism to use. . . . We are unconvinced by Gaubert's assertion that because the agencies did not institute formal proceedings against IASA, they had no discretion to take informal actions as they did. Although the statutes provided only for formal proceedings, there is nothing in the language or structure of the statutes that prevented the regulators from invoking less formal means of supervision of financial institutions. . . .

Gaubert also argues that the challenged actions fall outside the discretionary function exception because they involved the mere application of technical skills and business expertise. But this is just another way of saying that the considerations involving the day-to-day management of a business concern such as IASA are so precisely formulated that decisions at the operational level never involve the exercise of discretion within the meaning of § 2680(a), a notion that we have already rejected in disapproving the rationale of the Court of Appeals' decision. It may be that certain decisions resting on mathematical calculations, for example, involve no choice or judgment in carrying out the calculations, but the regulatory acts alleged here are not of that genre. Rather, it is plain to us that each of the challenged actions involved the exercise of choice and judgment.

. . . Although Gaubert contends that day-to-day decisions concerning IASA's affairs did not implicate social, economic, or political policies, even the Court of Appeals recognized that these day-to-day "operational" deci-

---

mobile on a mission connected with his official duties and negligently collided with another car, the exception would not apply. Although driving requires the constant exer-

cise of discretion, the official's decisions in exercising that discretion can hardly be said to be grounded in regulatory policy.

sions were undertaken for policy reasons of primary concern to the regulatory agencies:

> [T]he federal regulators here had two discrete purposes in mind as they commenced day-to-day operations at IASA. First, they sought to protect the solvency of the savings and loan industry at large, and maintain the public's confidence in that industry. Second, they sought to preserve the assets of IASA for the benefit of depositors and shareholders, of which Gaubert was one.

... By Gaubert's own admission, the regulators replaced IASA's management in order to protect the FSLIC's insurance fund; thus it cannot be disputed that this action was based on public policy considerations. The regulators' actions in urging IASA to convert to federal charter and in intervening with the state agency were directly related to public policy considerations regarding federal oversight of the thrift industry. So were advising the hiring of a financial consultant, advising when to place IASA subsidiaries into bankruptcy, intervening on IASA's behalf with Texas officials, advising on litigation policy, and mediating salary disputes. ...

Because from the face of the Amended Complaint, it is apparent that all of the challenged actions of the federal regulators involved the exercise of discretion in furtherance of public policy goals, the Court of Appeals erred in failing to find those claims barred by the discretionary function exception.... We therefore reverse the decision ... and remand for further proceedings consistent with this opinion.

■ JUSTICE SCALIA, concurring in part and concurring in the judgment.

... The Court of Appeals in this case concluded that a choice involves policy judgment (in the relevant sense) if it is made at a planning rather than an operational level within the agency. I agree with the Court that this is wrong. I think, however, that the level at which the decision is made is often *relevant* to the discretionary function inquiry, since the answer to that inquiry turns on *both* the subject matter *and* the office of the decisionmaker. In my view a choice is shielded from liability by the discretionary function exception if the choice is, under the particular circumstances, one that ought to be informed by considerations of social, economic, or political policy and is made by an officer whose official responsibilities include assessment of those considerations.

This test, by looking not only to the decision but also to the officer who made it, recognizes that there is something to the planning vs. operational dichotomy—though the "something" is not precisely what the Court of Appeals believed. Ordinarily, an employee working at the operational level is not responsible for policy decisions, even though policy considerations may be highly relevant to his actions. The dock foreman's decision to store bags of fertilizer in a highly compact fashion is not protected by this exception because, even if he carefully calculated considerations of cost to the government versus safety, it was not his responsibility to ponder such things; the Secretary of Agriculture's decision to the same effect *is* protected, because weighing those considerations is his task. ...

Moreover, not only is it necessary for application of the discretionary function exception that the decisionmaker be an official who possesses the relevant policy responsibility, but also the decisionmaker's close identification with policymaking can be strong evidence that the other half of the test is met—i.e., that the subject-matter of the decision is one that ought to be informed by policy considerations. I am much more inclined to believe, for example, that the manner of storing fertilizer raises economic policy concerns if the decision on that subject has been reserved to the Secretary of Agriculture himself. That it is proper to take the level of the decision-maker into account is supported by the phrase of the FTCA immediately preceding the discretionary function exception, which excludes governmental liability for acts taken, " 'exercising due care, in the execution of a . . . regulation, whether or not such . . . regulation be valid.' " Dalehite. We have taken this to mean that regulations "[can] not be attacked by claimants under the Act." Id. This immunity represents an absolute statutory presumption, so to speak, that all regulations involve policy judgments that must not be interfered with. I think there is a similar presumption, though not an absolute one, that decisions reserved to policy-making levels involve such judgments—and the higher the policy-making level, the stronger the presumption. . . .

NOTE

KENNETH C. DAVIS, ADMINISTRATIVE LAW OF THE EIGHTIES § 27.12 at 451 (1989):

"With the hindsight of nearly half a century, one can now easily see that the original [FTCA] should have said that the government is not liable for making law or governmental policy, instead of saying that the government is not liable for exercising a discretionary function. The word 'discretionary' was unfortunate. The right word was 'policy.' "

5 KENNETH C. DAVIS, ADMINISTRATIVE LAW TREATISE § 27.13 at 73–74 (2d ed. 1984):

"The proposition that negligence or other fault in making law is not a tort is generally a sound proposition, even if it might be less than an absolute. If Congress itself is negligent in enacting swine-flu legislation, what is enacted is still law, and it is therefore binding on a tort court; even if the legislation is invalid, the government is not liable in tort because of the [FTCA exception for implementation of statutes and regulations]. If the negligence is not that of Congress but is that of a delegate of Congress, the enactment is still law. . . . Governmental policy made by those who are authorized to make it is as binding on courts as law made by those who are authorized to make it."

(ii) THE TUCKER ACT

The United States' consent to suit for *non-tort* claims considerably predates the FTCA. The Tucker Act, passed in 1887, waives immunity for claims "founded either upon the Constitution, or any Act of Congress or any regulation of an executive department, or upon any express or implied contract with the United States, or for liquidated or unliquidated damages in cases not sounding in tort." 28 U.S.C. § 1491. With certain exceptions, suit on claims up to $10,000 may be brought in either the district court or the Court of Federal Claims; jurisdiction over larger claims is exclusive in the Claims Court. 28 U.S.C. §§ 1491(a)(1), 1346(a)(2).[1] The Claims Court (so called to distinguish it from its predecessor, the Court of Claims, which had heard Tucker Act cases for nearly a century) is an Article I court whose decisions are reviewed by the Court of Appeals for the Federal Circuit. Consistent with this status, its ability to grant declaratory and injunctive relief is circumscribed. See 28 U.S.C. § 1491(a)(2), (3).

The vast majority of actions under the Act involve express or implied contracts. This might seem surprising, given the statute's expansive language. However, the restriction to cases "not sounding in tort" has long been interpreted as excluding claims for personal injuries. The non-contractual claims permitted by the Act have been interpreted as comprising two classes:

> (1) the plaintiff has paid money over to the Government, directly or in effect, and seeks return of all or part of that sum; and

> (2) . . . money has not been paid but the plaintiff asserts that he is nevertheless entitled to payment from the treasury.

Alfred C. Aman, Jr. & William T. Mayton, Administrative Law 545 (2d ed. 2001). Tax refund suits are a classic example of the first category. The second has been construed to require that the particular law relied upon "be interpreted as mandating compensation." United States v. Mitchell, 463 U.S. 206, 217 (1983). Claims for just compensation under the Takings Clause of the Fifth Amendment illustrate this category. See generally David M. Cohen, Claims for Money in the Claims Court, 40 Cath.U.L.Rev. 533 (1991).

The relationship between the waiver of immunity in the Tucker Act (with its concomitant requirement of using the Claims Court for major claims) and the waiver of immunity in § 702 of the APA (which applies generally to suits in Article III courts) has been much debated since Bowen v. Massachusetts, p. 1106 above. Bowen held that § 702's exclusion of actions seeking "money damages" did not apply to Massachusetts' attempt to recover $6 million in Medicaid reimbursements from the Secretary of Health and Human Services. Reasoning that the claim sounded in equity for restitution, rather than at law for damages, the Court upheld the power of the district court to order the payment. For an illuminating analysis of the genesis and implications of Bowen, see Richard H. Fallon, Jr., Claims Court at the Crossroads, 40 Cath.U.L.Rev. 517 (1991). For lower court cases struggling to preserve the traditional understanding of the Claims Court's role, through narrow interpretation of the Bowen opinion, see, e.g., Transohio Savings Bank v. Director, Office of Thrift Supervision, 967 F.2d 598 (D.C.Cir.1992); Hubbard v. Administrator of EPA, 982 F.2d 531 (D.C.Cir.1992) (en banc); City of Houston v. Department of Housing & Urban Development, 24 F.3d 1421 (D.C.Cir.1994).

(iii) SECTION 1983

The law surrounding the cause of action created by 42 U.S.C. § 1983 is so complex and voluminous that it can virtually sustain a course by itself.

---

1. Claims for recovery of taxes can be brought in the district courts, regardless of amount; on the other hand, any claim falling under the Contract Disputes Act of 1978 must be brought in the Claims Court. 28 U.S.C. § 1346(a).

The materials here sketch the portion of that law concerned with obtaining a remedy against certain governmental entities for violations of federal rights. Before reading these materials, you should review the basic contours of the § 1983 cause of action set out at p. 1109 above.

Owen v. City of Independence

Supreme Court of the United States, 1980.
445 U.S. 622.

■ JUSTICE BRENNAN delivered the opinion of the Court.

[Owen, police commissioner of Independence, was fired after an acrimonious dispute over administration of the police department. Alleging that the dismissal violated due process and seeking damages, he sued the City and, in their official capacities, the City Manager and the City Council.[1]]

Monell v. New York City Dept. of Social Services, 436 U.S. 658 (1978), overruled Monroe v. Pape, 365 U.S. 167 (1961), insofar as Monroe held that local governments were not among the "persons" to whom 42 U.S.C. § 1983 applies and were therefore wholly immune from suit under the statute. Monell reserved decision, however, on the question whether local governments, although not entitled to an absolute immunity, should be afforded some form of official immunity in § 1983 suits. In this action ..., the Court of Appeals for the Eighth Circuit held that respondent city of Independence, Mo., "is entitled to qualified immunity from liability" based on the good faith of its officials.... We granted certiorari. We reverse.

... By its terms, § 1983 "creates a species of tort liability that on its face admits of no immunities." Imbler v. Pachtman, 424 U.S. 409, 417 (1976). Its language is absolute and unqualified; no mention is made of any privileges, immunities, or defenses that may be asserted. Rather, the Act imposes liability upon *"every person"* who, under color of state law or custom, "subjects, or causes to be subjected, any citizen of the United States ... to the deprivation of any rights, privileges, or immunities secured by the Constitution and laws." And Monell held that these words were intended to encompass municipal corporations as well as natural "persons."

Moreover, the congressional debates surrounding the passage of § 1 of the Civil Rights Act of 1871, 17 Stat. 13—the forerunner of § 1983— confirm the expansive sweep of the statutory language. ...

However, notwithstanding § 1983's expansive language and the absence of any express incorporation of common-law immunities, we have, on several occasions, found that a tradition of immunity was so firmly rooted

---

1. This is in contrast to suing the officials "in their *individual* capacity," in which case any liability decision would take into account the official immunity rules considered in the previous section, and any judgment rendered would run against the officials personally and be satisfied from their own assets (to the extent that the government chose not to indemnify them). In "official capacity" suits, the official is not at personal risk; any monetary judgment runs against, and is satisfied directly from, governmental funds.

in the common law and was supported by such strong policy reasons that "Congress would have specifically so provided had it wished to abolish the doctrine." Pierson v. Ray, 386 U.S. 547, 555 (1967). ... Where the immunity claimed by the defendant was well established at common law at the time § 1983 was enacted, and where its rationale was compatible with the purposes of the Civil Rights Act, we have construed the statute to incorporate that immunity. But there is no tradition of immunity for municipal corporations, and neither history nor policy supports a construction of § 1983 that would justify the qualified immunity accorded the city of Independence by the Court of Appeals. ...

... [I]n the hundreds of cases from [the era preceding enactment of § 1983] awarding damages against municipal governments for wrongs committed by them, one searches in vain for much mention of a qualified immunity based on the good faith of municipal officers. Indeed, where the issue was discussed at all, the courts had rejected the proposition that a municipality should be privileged where it reasonably believed its actions to be lawful. In the leading case of Thayer v. Boston, 36 Mass. 511, 515–516 (1837), for example, Chief Justice Shaw explained:

> There is a large class of cases, in which the rights of both the public and of individuals may be deeply involved, in which it cannot be known at the time the act is done, whether it is lawful or not. The event of a legal inquiry, in a court of justice, may show that it was unlawful. Still, if it was not known and understood to be unlawful at the time, if it was an act done by the officers having competent authority, either by express vote of the city government, or by the nature of the duties and functions with which they are charged, by their offices, to act upon the general subject matter, and especially if the act was done with an honest view to obtain for the public some lawful benefit or advantage, reason and justice obviously require that the city, in its corporate capacity, should be liable to make good the damage sustained by an individual, in consequence of the acts thus done.

To be sure, there were two doctrines that afforded municipal corporations some measure of protection from tort liability. The first sought to distinguish between a municipality's "governmental" and "proprietary" functions; as to the former, the city was held immune, whereas in its exercise of the latter, the city was held to the same standards of liability as any private corporation. ... The governmental-proprietary distinction owed its existence to the dual nature of the municipal corporation. On the one hand, the municipality was a corporate body, capable of performing the same "proprietary" functions as any private corporation, and liable for its torts in the same manner and to the same extent, as well. On the other hand, the municipality was an arm of the State, and when acting in that "governmental" or "public" capacity, it shared the immunity traditionally accorded the sovereign. ...

That the municipality's common-law immunity for "governmental" functions derives from the principle of sovereign immunity ... explains why that doctrine could not have served as the basis for the qualified privilege respondent city claims under § 1983. First, because sovereign immunity insulates the municipality from unconsented suits altogether, the presence or absence of good faith is simply irrelevant. The critical issue is whether injury occurred while the city was exercising governmental, as opposed to proprietary, powers or obligations—not whether its agents reasonably believed they were acting lawfully in so conducting themselves.[2] More fundamentally, however, the municipality's "governmental" immunity is obviously abrogated by the sovereign's enactment of a statute making it amenable to suit. Section 1983 was just such a statute. . . .

The second common-law distinction between municipal functions—that protecting the city from suits challenging "discretionary" decisions—was grounded not on the principle of sovereign immunity, but on a concern for separation of powers. A large part of the municipality's responsibilities involved broad discretionary decisions on issues of public policy—decisions that affected large numbers of persons and called for a delicate balancing of competing considerations. For a court or jury, in the guise of a tort suit, to review the reasonableness of the city's judgment on these matters would be an infringement upon the powers properly vested in a coordinate and coequal branch of government. . . . But a municipality has no "discretion" to violate the Federal Constitution; its dictates are absolute and imperative. And when a court passes judgment on the municipality's conduct in a § 1983 action, it does not seek to second-guess the "reasonableness" of the city's decision nor to interfere with the local government's resolution of competing policy considerations. Rather, it looks only to whether the municipality has conformed to the requirements of the Federal Constitution and statutes. . . .

In sum, we can discern no "tradition so well grounded in history and reason" that would warrant the conclusion that in enacting § 1 of the Civil Rights Act, the 42d Congress *sub silentio* extended to municipalities a qualified immunity based on the good faith of their officers. . . .

Our rejection of a construction of § 1983 that would accord municipalities a qualified immunity for their good-faith constitutional violations is compelled both by the legislative purpose in enacting the statute and by considerations of public policy. The central aim of the Civil Rights Act was to provide protection to those persons wronged by the " '[m]isuse of power, possessed by virtue of state law and made possible only because the wrongdoer is clothed with the authority of state law.' " Monroe v. Pape. . . . How "uniquely amiss" it would be, therefore, if the government itself— "the social organ to which all in our society look for the promotion of liberty, justice, fair and equal treatment, and the setting of worthy norms and goals for social conduct"—were permitted to disavow liability for the injury it has begotten. A damages remedy against the offending party is a vital component of any scheme for vindicating cherished constitutional guarantees, and the importance of assuring its efficacy is only accentuated when the wrongdoer is the institution that has been established to protect the very rights it has transgressed. Yet owing to the qualified immunity

---

2. The common-law immunity for governmental functions is thus more comparable to an absolute immunity from liability for conduct of a certain character, which defeats a suit at the outset, than to a qualified immunity, which "depends upon the circumstances and motivations of [the official's] actions, as established by the evidence at trial." Imbler v. Pachtman, 424 U.S. at 419, n.13.

enjoyed by most government officials, see Scheuer v. Rhodes, many victims of municipal malfeasance would be left remediless if the city were also allowed to assert a good-faith defense. Unless countervailing considerations counsel otherwise, the injustice of such a result should not be tolerated.[3]

Moreover, § 1983 was intended not only to provide compensation to the victims of past abuses, but to serve as a deterrent against future constitutional deprivations, as well. The knowledge that a municipality will be liable for all of its injurious conduct, whether committed in good faith or not, should create an incentive for officials who may harbor doubts about the lawfulness of their intended actions to err on the side of protecting citizens' constitutional rights. Furthermore, the threat that damages might be levied against the city may encourage those in a policymaking position to institute internal rules and programs designed to minimize the likelihood of unintentional infringements on constitutional rights. Such procedures are particularly beneficial in preventing those "systemic" injuries that result not so much from the conduct of any single individual, but from the interactive behavior of several government officials, each of whom may be acting in good faith.[4]

Our previous decisions conferring qualified immunities on various government officials are not to be read as derogating the significance of the societal interest in compensating the innocent victims of governmental misconduct. Rather, in each case we concluded that overriding considerations of public policy nonetheless demanded that the official be given a measure of protection from personal liability. The concerns that justified those decisions, however, are less compelling, if not wholly inapplicable, when the liability of the municipal entity is at issue.

In Scheuer v. Rhodes, the Chief Justice identified the two "mutually dependent rationales" on which the doctrine of official immunity rested:

> (1) the injustice, particularly in the absence of bad faith, of subjecting to liability an officer who is required, by the legal obligations of his position, to exercise discretion; (2) the danger that the threat of such liability would deter his willingness to execute his office with the decisiveness and the judgment required by the public good.[5]

The first consideration is simply not implicated when the damages award comes not from the official's pocket, but from the public treasury. It

3. The absence of any damages remedy for violations of all but the most "clearly established" constitutional rights, see Wood v. Strickland, could also have the deleterious effect of freezing constitutional law in its current state of development, for without a meaningful remedy aggrieved individuals will have little incentive to seek vindication of those constitutional deprivations that have not previously been clearly defined.

4. In addition, the threat of liability against the city ought to increase the attentiveness with which officials at the higher levels of government supervise the conduct of their subordinates. The need to institute sys-

tem-wide measures in order to increase the vigilance with which otherwise indifferent municipal officials protect citizens' constitutional rights is, of course, particularly acute where the frontline officers are judgment-proof in their individual capacities.

5. Wood v. Strickland mentioned a third justification for extending a qualified immunity to public officials: the fear that the threat of personal liability might deter citizens from holding public office. Such fears are totally unwarranted, of course, once the threat of personal liability is eliminated.

hardly seems unjust to require a municipal defendant which has violated a citizen's constitutional rights to compensate him for the injury suffered thereby. ... Elemental notions of fairness dictate that one who causes a loss should bear the loss.

It has been argued, however, that revenue raised by taxation for public use should not be diverted to the benefit of a single or discrete group of taxpayers, particularly where the municipality has at all times acted in good faith. On the contrary, the accepted view is that stated in Thayer v. Boston—"that the city, in its corporate capacity, should be liable to make good the damage sustained by an [unlucky] individual, in consequence of the acts thus done." After all, it is the public at large which enjoys the benefits of the government's activities, and it is the public at large which is ultimately responsible for its administration. Thus, even where some constitutional development could not have been foreseen by municipal officials, it is fairer to allocate any resulting financial loss to the inevitable costs of government borne by all the taxpayers, than to allow its impact to be felt solely by those whose rights, albeit newly recognized, have been violated.[6]

The second rationale mentioned in Scheuer also loses its force when it is the municipality, in contrast to the official, whose liability is at issue. At the heart of this justification for a qualified immunity for the individual official is the concern that the threat of *personal* monetary liability will introduce an unwarranted and unconscionable consideration into the decisionmaking process, thus paralyzing the governing official's decisiveness and distorting his judgment on matters of public policy. The inhibiting effect is significantly reduced, if not eliminated, however, when the threat of personal liability is removed. First, as an empirical matter, it is questionable whether the hazard of municipal loss will deter a public officer from the conscientious exercise of his duties; city officials routinely make decisions that either require a large expenditure of municipal funds or involve a substantial risk of depleting the public fisc. More important, though, is the realization that consideration of the *municipality's* liability for constitutional violations is quite properly the concern of its elected or appointed officials. Indeed, a decisionmaker would be derelict in his duties if, at some point, he did not consider whether his decision comports with constitutional mandates and did not weigh the risk that a violation might result in an award of damages from the public treasury. ...

... Doctrines of tort law have changed significantly over the past century, and our notions of governmental responsibility should properly reflect that evolution. No longer is individual "blameworthiness" the acid

6. Monell v. New York City Dept. of Social Services, indicated that the principle of loss-spreading was an insufficient justification for holding the municipality liable under § 1983 on a *respondeat superior* theory. Here, of course, quite a different situation is presented. Petitioner does not seek to hold the city responsible for the unconstitutional actions of an individual official "*solely* because it employs a tortfeasor." Rather, liability is predicated on a determination that "the action that is alleged to be unconstitutional implements or executes a policy statement, ordinance, regulation, or decision officially adopted and promulgated by that body's officers." In this circumstance—when it is the local government itself that is responsible for the constitutional deprivation—it is perfectly reasonable to distribute the loss to the public as a cost of the administration of government, rather than to let the entire burden fall on the injured individual.

test of liability; the principle of equitable loss-spreading has joined fault as a factor in distributing the costs of official misconduct.

We believe that today's decision, together with prior precedents in this area, properly allocates these costs among the three principals in the scenario of the § 1983 cause of action: the victim of the constitutional deprivation; the officer whose conduct caused the injury; and the public, as represented by the municipal entity. The innocent individual who is harmed by an abuse of governmental authority is assured that he will be compensated for his injury. The offending official, so long as he conducts himself in good faith, may go about his business secure in the knowledge that a qualified immunity will protect him from personal liability for damages that are more appropriately chargeable to the populace as a whole. And the public will be forced to bear only the costs of injury inflicted by the "execution of a government's policy or custom, whether made by its lawmakers or by those whose edicts or acts may fairly be said to represent official policy." Monell v. New York City Dept. of Social Services.

■ JUSTICE POWELL, with whom CHIEF JUSTICE [BURGER], JUSTICE STEWART, and JUSTICE REHNQUIST join, dissenting.

... The allocation of public resources and the operational policies of the government itself are activities that lie peculiarly within the competence of executive and legislative bodies. When charting those policies, a local official should not have to gauge his employer's possible liability under § 1983 if he incorrectly—though reasonably and in good faith—forecasts the course of constitutional law. ... Because today's decision will inject constant consideration of § 1983 liability into local decisionmaking, it may restrict the independence of local governments and their ability to respond to the needs of their communities. ...

The Court now argues that local officials might modify their actions unduly if they face personal liability under § 1983, but that they are unlikely to do so when the locality itself will be held liable. This contention denigrates the sense of responsibility of municipal officers, and misunderstands the political process. Responsible local officials will be concerned about potential judgments against their municipalities for alleged constitutional torts. Moreover, they will be accountable within the political system for subjecting the municipality to adverse judgments. If officials must look over their shoulders at a strict municipal liability for unknowable constitutional deprivations, the resulting degree of governmental paralysis will be little different from that caused by fear of personal liability.

In addition, basic fairness requires a qualified immunity for municipalities. The good-faith defense ... incorporates the idea that liability should not attach unless there was notice that a constitutional right was at risk. ... The Court nevertheless suggests that, as a matter of social justice, municipal corporations should be strictly liable even if they could not have known that a particular action would violate the Constitution. After all, the Court urges, local governments can "spread" the costs of any judgment across the local population. The Court neglects, however, the fact that many local governments lack the resources to withstand substantial unanticipated liability under § 1983. ... By simplistically applying the theorems of welfare economics and ignoring the reality of municipal finance, the

Court imposes strict liability on the level of government least able to bear it.[7] . . .

[Justice Powell argued at length that the majority had misinterpreted both the legislative history of § 1983 and the state of 19th century law regarding municipal immunity. He also estimated that "[t]oday's decision also conflicts with the current [municipal immunity] law in 44 States and the District of Columbia."] The Court turns a blind eye to this overwhelming evidence that municipalities have enjoyed a qualified immunity and to the policy considerations that for the life of this Republic have justified its retention. This disregard of precedent and policy is especially unfortunate because suits under § 1983 typically implicate evolving constitutional standards. A good-faith defense is much more important for those actions than in those involving ordinary tort liability. The duty not to run over a pedestrian with a municipal bus is far less likely to change than is the rule as to what process, if any, is due the busdriver if he claims the right to a hearing after discharge.

The right of a discharged government employee to a "name clearing" hearing was not recognized until our decision in Board of Regents v. Roth, page 801 above. That ruling was handed down 10 weeks after Owen was discharged and 8 weeks after the city denied his request for a hearing. By stripping the city of any immunity, the Court punishes it for failing to predict our decision in Roth. As a result, local governments and their officials will face the unnerving prospect of crushing damages judgments whenever a policy valid under current law is later found to be unconstitutional. I can see no justice or wisdom in that outcome.

NOTES

(1) *Personal Liability of the Employee vs. Entity Liability of the Government.* PETER W. LOW & JOHN C. JEFFRIES, JR., FEDERAL COURTS AND THE LAW OF FEDERAL–STATE RELATIONS 965–66 (4th ed. 1998): "Before Monell, damages could be obtained from a police officer who violated constitutional rights but not from the city that ordered the officer to do so. Justice Powell commented on the 'oddness' of that result. There is something odd, is there not, in holding an agent exclusively liable for acts specifically authorized by the principal? And yet, exactly this situation prevails with respect to state officials. They can be sued for damages under § 1983, but the state itself is immune from suit.[1] Does this make sense? Is there any justification in policy for treating states and municipalities differently?[2]

7. Ironically, the State and Federal Governments cannot be held liable for constitutional deprivations. The Federal Government has not waived its sovereign immunity against such claims, and the States are protected by the Eleventh Amendment.

1. [Ed.] Will v. Michigan Dep't of State Police, 491 U.S. 58 (1989), held that "person" in § 1983 does not include states.

2. Note the argument of William P. Murphy, who suggests in Reinterpreting

"Person" in Section 1983: The Hidden Influence of Brown v. Board of Education, 9 Black L.J. 97 (1985), that Monell was necessary to remove the 'very serious danger' of derailing desegregation suits against school boards. By contrast, Murphy suggests, the exclusion of states from the concept of 'person' in § 1983 has no large impact on desegregation litigation.

"As a practical matter, the issue of state or municipal liability for the *authorized* acts of its employees matters only when the official cannot be held personally liable. Where liability can be imposed on the official as an individual, the government will have a strong incentive to indemnify its employees against loss incurred in implementing official policy. Not only may the government feel a moral obligation to hold its employee harmless for following orders; but it will also find that indemnification is necessary to recruit and retain qualified employees. Few would be so bold as to accept government office without some protection against personal liability for government error. Perhaps for that reason, the states follow the policy of defending state officers in actions under § 1983 and reimbursing them for any damages assessed, despite the formal immunity of the 11th amendment."

(2) *Punitive Damages.* In CITY OF NEWPORT V. FACT CONCERTS, INC., 453 U.S. 247 (1981), the City reneged on an entertainment license when City Council learned that Blood, Sweat and Tears had been booked to replace an originally-scheduled jazz performer. Concerned that the rock group "would attract a rowdy and undesirable audience," the City told the promoter that it could either allow the band to perform subject to a condition that they not play rock music, or cancel the event. In the promoter's § 1983 action for violation of its first amendment and due process rights, the jury returned a verdict of $72,910 in compensatory damages and $200,000 in punitive damages against the City. Although the City had not objected to the jury instruction authorizing such damages, the Supreme Court reversed the judgment, holding that municipalities (in contrast to municipal officials individually) may not held liable under § 1983 for punitive damages.[3] After conducting the familiar historical survey of tort law and concluding that "courts that had considered the issue prior to 1871 were virtually unanimous in denying such damages against a municipal corporation," Justice Blackmun's opinion turned to "whether considerations of public policy dictate a contrary result":

"Punitive damages by definition are not intended to compensate the injured party, but rather to punish the tortfeasor whose wrongful action was intentional or malicious, and to deter him and others from similar extreme conduct. Regarding retribution, it remains true that an award of punitive damages against a municipality 'punishes' only the taxpayers, who took no part in the commission of the tort. These damages are assessed over and above the amount necessary to compensate the injured party. Thus, there is no question here of equitably distributing the losses resulting from official misconduct. Cf. Owen v. City of Independence. Indeed, punitive damages imposed on a municipality are in effect a windfall to a fully compensated plaintiff, and are likely accompanied by an increase in taxes or a reduction of public services for citizens footing the bill. Neither reason nor justice suggests that such retribution should be visited upon the shoulders of blameless or unknowing taxpayers."

Addressing "[t]he other major objective of punitive damages"—deterrence—the Court reasoned: (i) "[I]t is far from clear that municipal

---

3. The dissenters, Justices Brennan, Marshall and Stevens, would have held the City to its failure to object at the time of jury instruction.

officials, including those at the policymaking level, would be deterred from wrongdoing by the knowledge that large punitive awards could be based on the wealth of their municipality"; (ii) "There is also no reason to suppose that corrective action, such as the discharge of offending officials who were appointed and the public excoriation of those who were elected, will not occur unless punitive damages are awarded"; (iii) "[T]here is available a more effective means of deterrence"—punitive damages awards against the responsible official *individually*; and (iv) "[A]lthough the benefits associated with awarding punitive damages against municipalities ... are of doubtful character, the costs may be very real"—particularly in light of emerging law allowing § 1983 to be used for statutory, as well as constitutional, violations.

The case on the other side was made by Judge Goldberg in Webster v. City of Houston, 689 F.2d 1220 (5th Cir.1982). Seventeen year old Randy Webster stole a van; when police stopped it, Webster was thrown to the ground and shot in the head—even though he was unarmed and, according to witnesses, made no resistance. One of the officers placed a "throw down" weapon in Webster's hand and reported that Webster had brandished the gun as he emerged from the van. An internal investigation did not acknowledge the deception, despite eyewitness testimony and discrepancies in the physical evidence. Webster's parents sued the officers and the city, and received a verdict of compensatory damages sufficient only to cover his funeral expenses and punitive damages of $1.2 million against the officers and $200,000 against the city. The Fifth Circuit agreed that the evidence supported a finding that the Police Department covertly approved the "throw down gun" tactic and acquiesced in a cover up; however, it set aside the punitive damages award against Houston in light of Fact Concerts. Judge Goldberg's concurrence, although accepting this disposition, argued that the Supreme Court had been wrong to adopt an *absolute* bar against punitive damages:

"First, while the Court in Newport argued that punitive damages against the municipality would not deter *individual* misconduct, here we have *municipal* or *group* misconduct. Second, whereas in Newport the Court relied on sanctions from superiors as a sufficient deterrent, in this case the bad policy actually exists due to the collective inaction of the superiors. ... Third, in Newport the Court suggested that damages assessed directly against the offending official were a better deterrent. But while damages assessed directly against an individual might deter individual misconduct, at whom do we point the finger of guilt in the case of tragic collective apathy? ... Finally, the Court in Newport argued that punitive damages for lost ticket sales might deprive the citizens of other services because of financial burdens from increased liability. But in this *core* section 1983 case, that is exactly what Congress wanted. It is necessary that the threatened damages cause some deprivation for the populace so that they will be nudged out of their blissful ignorance, 'and the effect will be most wholesome.' ... The function of damages is to force the decisionmaker to consider the costs of his or her actions as well as the benefits and promote socially correct decisionmaking. The point of damages, then, is to 'internalize' costs to the decisionmaker.

"The choice between compensatory and punitive damages should be made based on whether one or the other will properly internalize the social costs and produce socially correct decisions. If all the parties bearing all the costs and enjoying all the benefits are before the court, then compensatory damages will properly account for all costs and benefits. ... If, however, the situation is such that not all of the costs will come before the court, then compensatory damages will be inadequate to internalize the costs and punitive damages are needed. This is much more likely to happen when the relevant decision is one promulgating a policy, as in the present case, rather than one regarding a discrete event, as in Newport. ...

"The full costs of a policy might not be before a court because not all instances of the policy's application are known. For example, if a policy results in ten citizens suffering a cost of $10, but only one of those instances is discovered, compensatory damages would not internalize all the costs. If a court can tell that nine instances of application are likely to remain undiscovered, when one *does* come before it, the court should assess $90 punitive damages to internalize the costs of the undiscovered applications. ... [Here,] it is hard to avoid the inference that some cases are not coming before the courts.

"Another instance in which punitive damages are needed to internalize social costs is if some social costs are known but are diffused widely through society. This point highlights the key difference between Newport and this case, the reason it would be an injustice to award punitive damages in Newport and a greater injustice not to award them here. In Newport the total social damages from the incident are summed up in the lost profits of the promoters.... This case, however, produces social costs of the gravest nature. Without trivializing the most grievous injury done to the Webster family, it makes a travesty of the most fundamental values of our society to ignore the damages done to *them* by Houston's policy. The most primal reason for banding together in social groups is protection from violence. When members of the very institution created to protect us from violence instead inflict it, the social fabric is torn. This is but a tear, however, because we can all understand the possibility of uncontrollable renegades. But when the crime is concealed in accordance with the tacit policy of that institution, the social fabric is ripped into tattered rags.

"It is only by threat of punitive damages that we can be sure policy-makers will be cognizant of this grave social cost. It is only by threat of punitive damages that we can arouse policymakers from their dozing to eradicate policies such as this."

(3) *"Pursuant to an Official Policy or Custom."* ERWIN CHEMERINSKY, FEDERAL JURISDICTION § 8.5.2 at 478–89 (3d ed. 1999), offers an insightful synthesis of the law on one of the most difficult aspects of local government § 1983 liability—Monell's requirement that the challenged acts be done "pursuant to an official policy or custom":

"After Monell, there are at least five possible ways to establish the existence of a policy or custom sufficient to impose § 1983 liability on a municipal government. First, and most obviously, actions by the municipal legislative body constitute official policies. As the Supreme Court observed in Pembaur v. City of Cincinnati, [475 U.S. 469, 480 (1986)], 'No one has ever doubted ... that a municipality may be liable under § 1983 for a single decision by its properly constituted legislative body—whether or not that body had taken similar action in the past or intended to do so in the future—because even a single decision by such a body unquestionably constitutes an act of official government policy.' ...

"Second, official policy exists when there are actions by municipal agencies or boards that exercise authority delegated by the municipal legislative body. In Monell, for example, the plaintiffs challenged regulations adopted by the Department of Social Services and the Board of Education requiring pregnant employees to take unpaid leaves of absence. The Court found that actions of these agencies 'unquestionably involves official policy.'

"Third, actions by those with final authority for making a decision in the municipality constitute official policy.... In Pembaur, police officers who were frustrated in trying to serve subpoenas called an assistant prosecutor for further instructions. The assistant prosecutor conferred with the county prosecutor, who issued instructions 'to go in and get [the witnesses].' The police then obtained an axe and chopped down the door.... The Supreme Court held that 'municipal liability under § 1983 attaches where—and only where—a deliberate choice to follow a course of action is made from among various alternatives by the official or officials responsible for establishing final policy with respect to the subject matter in question.' In other words, the Court reasoned that municipal liability could not be imposed merely because an employee had discretion in the discharge of his or her duties. An official must 'be responsible for establishing final government policy' in order for municipal liability to attach to his or her decision. Such authority could be granted legislatively or be delegated from higher officials. Its existence is a question of state [rather than federal] law.[4] Based on the relevant Ohio law, the Court concluded that the prosecutor had authority for making the final decision and, hence, his decision constituted the City's official policy....

"A fourth way of demonstrating an official policy is by establishing a government policy of inadequate training or supervision. When, if at all, is the failure to train officers adequately, or the lack of supervision, or the failure to respond to complaints a municipal policy? ... In City of Canton v. Harris, [489 U.S. 378 (1989)], the Supreme Court ... held that demonstrating a policy of inadequate training requires proof of deliberate indifference by the local government. The plaintiff, Geraldine Harris, claimed to have been injured by the failure of the city to instruct police officers to recognize medical ailments and to summon treatment. She was ill at the police station following her arrest, but the officers did not provide or summon any medical assistance. ... The Court indicated at least two types of situations that would justify a conclusion of deliberate indifference.... One is failure to provide adequate training in light of foreseeable serious consequences that could result from the lack of instruction. For example, the court indicated that lack of instruction in the use of firearms or in the

---

4. [Ed.] The relevant law includes state and local laws and "customs or usage having the force of law;" the meaning of that law is a question for the judge, not for the jury. Jett v. Dallas Independent School District, 491 U.S. 701, 737 (1989).

use of deadly force could constitute 'deliberate indifference.' A second type of situation ... is where the city fails to act in response to repeated complaints of constitutional violations by its officers. ...

"A fifth and final way to establish municipal liability under § 1983 would be to demonstrate the existence of a 'custom.' The Supreme Court, however, has provided little guidance as to what constitutes a 'custom'. ... In Pembaur and [City of St. Louis v. Praprotnik, 485 U.S. 112 (1988)], the Court explicitly reaffirmed that municipal governments could be sued for their customs ... even though such a custom has not received formal approval from the official legislative body. But because the plaintiffs did not allege a municipal custom, the Court did not reach the issue. Some lower courts have found customs to exist based on well-settled practices within the city. ... Other courts have ... concluded that customs exist only where 'actual or constructive knowledge of such custom was attributable to the governing body or an official to whom that body had delegated policymaking authority.' ..."

THE CONSTITUTION OF THE UNITED STATES OF AMERICA

We the People of the United States in Order to form a more perfect Union, to establish Justice, insure domestic Tranquility, provide for the common defense, promote the general Welfare, and secure the Blessings of Liberty to ourselves and our Posterity, do ordain and establish this Constitution for the United States of America.

ARTICLE I

Section 1.

All legislative Powers herein granted shall be vested in a Congress of the United States which shall consist of a Senate and House of Representatives.

Section 2.

[1] The House of Representatives shall be composed of Members chosen every second Year by the People of the several States, and the Electors in each State shall have the Qualifications requisite for Electors of the most numerous Branch of the State Legislature.

[2] No Person shall be a Representative who shall not have attained to the Age of twenty-five Years, and been seven Years a Citizen of the United States, and who shall not, when elected, be an Inhabitant of that State in which he shall be chosen.

[3] Representatives and direct Taxes shall be apportioned among the several States which may be included within this Union, according to their respective Numbers, which shall be determined by adding to the whole Number of free Persons, including those bound to Service for a Term of Years, and excluding Indians not taxed, three fifths of all other Persons. The actual Enumeration shall be made within three Years after the first Meeting of the Congress of the United States, and within every subsequent Term of ten Years, in such Manner as they shall by Law direct. The Number of Representatives shall not exceed one for every thirty Thousand, but each State shall have at Least One Representative; and until such enumerations shall be made, the State of New Hampshire shall be entitled to chuse three, Massachusetts eight, Rhode Island and Providence Plantations one, Connecticut five, New York six, New Jersey four, Pennsylvania eight, Delaware one, Maryland six, Virginia ten, North Carolina five, South Carolina five, and Georgia three.

[4]   When vacancies happen in the Representation from any State, the Executive Authority thereof shall issue Writs of Election to fill such Vacancies.

[5]   The House of Representatives shall chuse their Speaker and other Officers, and shall have the sole Power of Impeachment.

Section 3.

[1]   The Senate of the United States shall be composed of two Senators from each State, chosen by the Legislature thereof, for six Years; and each Senator shall have one Vote.

[2]   Immediately after they shall be assembled in Consequence of the first Election, they shall be divided as equally as may be into three Classes. The Seats of the Senators of the first Class shall be vacated at the Expiration of the second Year, of the second Class at the Expiration of the fourth Year, and of the third class at the Expiration of the sixth Year, so that one third may be chosen every second Year; and if Vacancies happen by Resignation, or otherwise, during the Recess of the Legislature of any State, the Executive thereof may make temporary Appointments until the next Meeting of the Legislature, which shall then fill such Vacancies.

[3]   No Person shall be a Senator who shall not have attained to the Age of thirty Years, and been nine Years a Citizen of the United States, and who shall not, when elected, be an Inhabitant of that State for which he shall be chosen.

[4]   The Vice President of the United States shall be President of the Senate, but shall have no Vote, unless they be equally divided.

[5]   The Senate shall chuse their other Officers, and also a President pro tempore, in the Absence of the Vice President, or when he shall exercise the Office of President of the United States.

[6]   The Senate shall have the sole Power to try all Impeachments. When sitting for that Purpose, they shall be on Oath or Affirmation. When the President of the United States is tried, the Chief Justice shall preside: And no Person shall be convicted without the Concurrence of two thirds of the Members present.

[7]   Judgment in Cases of Impeachment shall not extend further than to removal from Office, and disqualification to hold and enjoy any Office of honor, Trust or Profit under the United States: but the Party convicted shall nevertheless be liable and subject to Indictment, Trial, Judgment and Punishment, according to Law.

Section 4.

[1]   The Times, Places and Manner of holding Elections for Senators and Representatives, shall be prescribed in each State by the Legislature thereof; but the Congress may at any time by Law make or alter such Regulations, except as to the Places of chusing Senators.

[2]   The Congress shall assemble at least once in every Year, and such Meeting shall be on the first Monday in December, unless they shall by Law appoint a different Day.

Section 5.

[1] Each House shall be the Judge of the Elections, Returns and Qualifications for its own Members, and a Majority of each shall constitute a Quorum to do Business; but a smaller Number may adjourn from day to day, and may be authorized to compel the Attendance of absent Members, in such Manner, and under such Penalties as each House may provide.

[2] Each House may determine the Rules of its Proceedings, punish its Members for disorderly Behaviour, and, with the Concurrence of two thirds, expel a Member.

[3] Each House shall keep a Journal of its Proceedings, and from time to time publish the same, excepting such Parts as may in their Judgment require Secrecy; and the Yeas and Nays of the Members of either House on any questions shall, at the Desire of one fifth of those Present, be entered on the Journal.

[4] Neither House, during the Session of Congress, shall, without the Consent of the other, adjourn for more than three days, nor to any other Place than that in which the two Houses shall be sitting.

Section 6.

[1] The Senators and Representatives shall receive a Compensation for their Services, to be ascertained by Law, and paid out of the Treasury of the United States. They shall in all Cases, except Treason, Felony and Breach of the Peace, be privileged from Arrest during their Attendance at the Session of their respective Houses, and in going to and returning from the same; and for any Speech or Debate in either House, they shall not be questioned in any other Place.

[2] No Senator or Representative shall, during the Time for which he was elected, be appointed to any civil Office under the Authority of the United States, which shall have been created, or the Emoluments whereof shall have been encreased during such time; and no Person holding any Office under the United States, shall be a Member of either House during his Continuance in Office.

Section 7.

[1] All Bills for raising Revenue shall originate in the House of Representatives, but the Senate may propose or concur with Amendments as on other Bills.

[2] Every Bill which shall have passed the House of Representatives and the Senate, shall, before it become a Law, be presented to the President of the United States; If he approve he shall sign it, but if not he shall return it with his Objections to that House in which it shall have originated, who shall enter the Objections at large on their Journal, and proceed to reconsider it. If after such Reconsideration two thirds of the House shall agree to pass the Bill, it shall be sent, together with the Objections, to the other House, by which it shall likewise be reconsidered, and if approved by two thirds of that House, it shall become a Law. But in all such Cases the Votes of both Houses shall be determined by Yeas and Nays, and the Names of the Persons voting for and against the Bill shall be

entered on the Journal of each House respectively. If any Bill shall not be returned by the President within ten Days (Sundays excepted) after it shall have been presented to him, the Same shall be a Law, in like Manner as if he had signed it, unless the Congress by their Adjournment prevent its Return, in which Case it shall not be a Law.

[3]   Every Order, Resolution, or Vote to Which the Concurrence of the Senate and House of Representatives may be necessary (except on a question of Adjournment) shall be presented to the President of the United States; and before the Same shall take Effect, shall be approved by him, or being disapproved by him, shall be repassed by two thirds of the Senate and House of Representatives, according to the Rules and Limitations prescribed in the Case of a Bill.

Section 8.

[1]   The Congress shall have Power To lay and collect Taxes, Duties, Imports and Excises, to pay the Debts and provide for the common Defence and general Welfare of the United States; but all Duties, Imports and Excises shall be uniform throughout the United States;

[2]   To borrow money on the credit of the United States;

[3]   To regulate Commerce with foreign Nations, and among the several States, and with the Indian Tribes;

[4]   To establish a uniform Rule of Naturalization, and uniform Laws on the subject of Bankruptcies throughout the United States;

[5]   To coin Money, regulate the value thereof, and of foreign Coin, and fix the Standard of Weights and Measures;

[6]   To provide for the Punishment of counterfeiting the Securities and current Coin of the United States;

[7]   To establish Post Offices and post Roads;

[8]   To promote the Progress of Science and useful Arts, by securing for limited Times to Authors and Inventors exclusive Right to their respective Writings and Discoveries;

[9]   To constitute Tribunals inferior to the supreme Court;

[10]   To define and punish Piracies and Felonies committed on the high Seas, and Offences against the Law of Nations;

[11]   To declare War, grant Letters of Marque and Reprisal, and make Rules concerning Captures on Land and Water;

[12]   To raise and support Armies, but no Appropriation of Money to that Use shall be for a longer Term than two Years;

[13]   To provide and maintain a Navy;

[14]   To make Rules for the Government and Regulation of the land and naval Forces;

[15]   To provide for calling forth the Militia to execute the Laws of the Union, suppress Insurrections and repel Invasions;

[16]   To provide for organizing, arming, and disciplining, the Militia and for governing such Part of them as may be employed in the Service of

the United States, reserving to the States respectively, the Appointment of the Officers, and the Authority of training the Militia according to the discipline prescribed by Congress;

[17]   To exercise exclusive Legislation in all Cases whatsoever, over such District (not exceeding ten Miles square) as may, by Cession of particular States, and the Acceptance of Congress, become the Seat of the Government of the United States, and to exercise like Authority over all Places purchased by the Consent of the Legislature of the State in which the Same shall be, for the Erection of Forts, Magazines, Arsenals, dock-Yards, and other needful buildings;—And

[18]   To make all Laws which shall be necessary and proper for carrying into Execution the foregoing Powers, and all other Powers vested by this Constitution in the Government of the United States, or in any Department or Officer thereof.

Section 9.

[1]   The Migration or Importation of such Persons as any of the States now existing shall think proper to admit, shall not be prohibited by the Congress prior to the Year one thousand eight hundred and eight, but a Tax or duty may be imposed on such Importation, not exceeding ten dollars for each Person.

[2]   The privilege of the Writ of Habeas Corpus shall not be suspended, unless when in Cases of Rebellion or Invasion the public Safety may require it.

[3]   No Bill of Attainder or ex post facto Law shall be past.

[4]   No Capitation, or other direct, Tax shall be laid, unless in Proportion to the Census on Enumeration herein before directed to be taken.

[5]   No Tax or Duty shall be laid on Articles exported from any State.

[6]   No Preference shall be given by any Regulation of Commerce or Revenue to the Ports of one State over those of another: nor shall Vessels bound to, or from, one State, be obliged to enter, clear or pay Duties in another.

[7]   No money shall be drawn from the Treasury, but in Consequence of Appropriations made by Law, and a regular Statement and Account of the Receipts and Expenditures of all public Money shall be published from time to time.

[8]   No Title of Nobility shall be granted by the United States: And no Person holding any Office of Profit or Trust under them, shall, without the Consent of the Congress, accept of any present, Emolument, Office, or Title, of any kind whatever, from any King, Prince, or foreign State.

Section 10.

[1]   No State shall enter into any Treaty, Alliance, or Confederation; grant Letters of Marque and Reprisal; coin Money; emit Bills of credit; make any Thing but gold and silver Coin a Tender in Payment of Debts; pass any Bill of Attainder, ex post facto Law, or Law impairing the Obligation of Contracts, or grant any Title of Nobility.

[2]   No State shall, without the Consent of Congress, lay any Imposts or Duties on Imports or Exports, except what may be absolutely necessary for executing its inspection Laws: and the net Produce of all Duties and Imposts, laid by any State on Imports and Exports, shall be for the Use of the Treasury of the United States; and all such Laws shall be subject to the Revision and Controul of the Congress.

[3]   No State shall, without the Consent of Congress, lay any Duty of Tonnage, keep Troops, or Ships of War in time of Peace, enter into any Agreement or Compact with another State, or with a foreign Power, or engage in War, unless actually invaded, or in such imminent Danger as will not admit of delay.

ARTICLE II

Section 1.

[1]   The executive Power shall be vested in a President of the United States of America. He shall hold his Office during the Term of four Years, and, together with the Vice President, chosen for the same Term, be elected, as follows:

[2]   Each State shall appoint, in such Manner as the Legislature thereof may direct, a Number of Electors, equal to the whole Number of Senators and Representatives to which the State may be entitled in the Congress: but no Senator or Representative, or Person holding an Office of Trust or Profit under the United States, shall be appointed an Elector.

[3]   The Electors shall meet in their respective States, and vote by Ballot for two Persons, of whom one at least shall not be an Inhabitant of the same State with themselves. And they shall make a List of all the Persons voted for, and of the Number of Votes for each; which List they shall sign and certify, and transmit sealed to the Seat of the Government of the United States, directed to the President of the Senate. The President of the Senate shall, in the Presence of the Senate and House of Representatives, open all the Certificates, and the Votes shall then be counted. The Person having the greatest Number of Votes shall be the President, if such Number be a Majority of the whole Number of Electors appointed; and if there be more than one who have such Majority, and have an equal Number of Votes, then the House of Representatives shall immediately chuse by Ballot one of them for President; and if no Person have a Majority, then from the five highest on the List the said House shall in like Manner chuse the President. But in chusing the President, the Votes shall be taken by States, the Representation from each State having one Vote; a quorum for this Purpose shall consist of a Member or Members from two thirds of the States, and a Majority of all the States shall be necessary to a Choice. In every Case, after the Choice of the President, the Person having the greatest Number of Votes of the Electors shall be the Vice President. But if there should remain two or more who have equal Votes, the Senate shall chuse from them by Ballot the Vice President.

[4]   The Congress may determine the Time of chusing the Electors, and the Day on which they shall give their Votes; which Day shall be the same throughout the United States.

[5]   No Person except a natural born Citizen, or a Citizen of the United States, at the time of the Adoption of this Constitution, shall be eligible to the Office of President; neither shall any Person be eligible to that Office who shall not have attained to the Age of thirty five Years, and been fourteen Years a Resident within the United States.

[6]   In case of the removal of the President from Office, or of his Death, Resignation or Inability to discharge the Powers and Duties of the said Office, the Same shall devolve on the Vice President, and the Congress may by Law provide for the Case of Removal, Death, Resignation or Inability, both of the President and Vice President, declaring what Officer shall then act as President, and such Officer shall act accordingly, until the Disability be removed, or a President shall be elected.

[7]   The President shall, at stated Times, receive for his Services, a Compensation, which shall neither be increased nor diminished during the Period for which he shall have been elected, and he shall not receive within that Period any other Emolument from the United States, or any of them.

[8]   Before he enter on the Execution of his Office, he shall take the following Oath or Affirmation: "I do solemnly swear (or affirm) that I will faithfully execute the Office of President of the United States, and will to the best of my Ability, preserve, protect and defend the Constitution of the United States."

Section 2.

[1]   The President shall be Commander in Chief of the Army and Navy of the United States, and of the Militia of the several States, when called into the actual Service of the United States; he may require the Opinion, in writing, of the principal Officer in each of the executive Departments, upon any subject relating to the Duties of their respective Offices, and he shall have Power to grant Reprieves and Pardons for Offences against the United States, except in Cases of Impeachment.

[2]   He shall have Power, by and with the Advice and Consent of the Senate, to make Treaties, provided two thirds of the Senators present concur; and he shall nominate, and by and with the Advice and Consent of the Senate, shall appoint Ambassadors, other public Ministers and Consuls, Judges of the supreme Court, and all other Officers of the United States, whose Appointments are not herein otherwise provided for, and which shall be established by Law: but the Congress may by Law vest the Appointment of such inferior Officers, as they think proper, in the President alone, in the Courts of Law, or in the Heads of Departments.

[3]   The President shall have Power to fill up all Vacancies that may happen during the Recess of the Senate, by granting Commissions which shall expire at the End of their next Session.

Section 3.

He shall from time to time give to the Congress Information of the State of the Union, and recommend to their Consideration such Measures as he shall judge necessary and expedient; he may, on extraordinary occasions, convene both Houses, or either of them, and in Case of Disagreement between them, with Respect to the time of Adjournment, he may adjourn them to such Time as he shall think proper; he shall receive Ambassadors and other public Ministers, he shall take Care that the Laws be faithfully executed, and shall Commission all the Officers of the United States.

Section 4.

The President, Vice President and all civil Officers of the United States, shall be removed from Office on Impeachment for, and Conviction of Treason, Bribery, or other high Crimes and Misdemeanors.

ARTICLE III

Section 1.

The judicial Power of the United States, shall be vested in one supreme Court, and in such inferior Courts as the Congress may from time to time ordain and establish. The Judges, both of the supreme and inferior Courts, shall hold their Offices during good Behaviour, and shall, at stated Times, receive for their Services, a Compensation, which shall not be diminished during their Continuance in Office.

Section 2.

[1]   The judicial Power shall extend to all Cases, in Law and Equity, arising under the Constitution, the Laws of the United States, and Treaties made, or which shall be made, under their Authority;—to all Cases affecting Ambassadors, other public Ministers and Consuls;—to all Cases of admiralty and maritime Jurisdiction;—to Controversies to which the United States shall be a Party;—to Controversies between two or more States;—between a State and Citizens of Another State;—between Citizens of different States;—between Citizens of the same State claiming Lands under Grants of different States, and between a State, or the Citizens thereof, and foreign States, Citizens or Subjects.

[2]   In all Cases affecting Ambassadors, other public Ministers and Consuls, and those in which a State shall be Party, the supreme Court shall have original Jurisdiction. In all the other Cases before mentioned, the supreme Court shall have appellate Jurisdiction, both as to Law and Fact, with such Exceptions, and under such Regulations as the Congress shall make.

[3]   The trial of all Crimes, except in Cases of Impeachment, shall be by Jury; and such Trial shall be held in the State where the said Crimes shall have been committed; but when not committed within any State, the Trial shall be at such Place or Places as the Congress may by Law have directed.

Section 3.

[1]   Treason against the United States, shall consist only in levying War against them, or in adhering to their Enemies, giving them Aid and Comfort. No Person shall be convicted of Treason unless on the Testimony of two Witnesses to the same overt Act, or on Confession in open Court.

[2]   The Congress shall have Power to declare the Punishment of Treason, but no Attainder of Treason shall work Corruption of Blood, or Forfeiture except during the Life of the Person attained.

ARTICLE IV

Section 1.

Full Faith and Credit shall be given in each State to the public Acts, Records, and judicial Proceedings of every other State. And the Congress may by general Laws prescribe the Manner in which such Acts, Records and Proceedings shall be proved, and the Effect thereof.

Section 2.

[1]   The Citizens of each State shall be entitled to all Privileges and Immunities of Citizens in the several States.

[2]   A Person charged in any State with Treason, Felony, or other Crime, who shall flee from Justice, and be found in another State, shall on demand of the executive Authority of the State from which he fled, be delivered up, to be removed to the State having Jurisdiction of the Crime.

[3]   No Person held to Service or Labour in one State, under the Laws thereof, escaping into another, shall, in Consequence of any Law or Regulation therein, be discharged from such Service or Labour, but shall be delivered up on Claim of the Party to whom such Service or Labour may be due.

Section 3.

[1]   New States may be admitted by the Congress into this Union, but no new State shall be formed or erected within the Jurisdiction of any other State; nor any State be formed by the Junction of two or more States, or Parts of States, without the Consent of the Legislatures of the States concerned as well as of the Congress.

[2]   The Congress shall have Power to dispose of and make all needful Rules and Regulations respecting the Territory or other Property belonging to the United States; and nothing in this Constitution shall be so constructed as to Prejudice any claims of the United States, or of any particular State.

Section 4.

The United States shall guarantee to every State in this Union a Republican Form of Government, and shall protect each of them against Invasion; and on Application of the Legislature, or of the Executive (when the Legislature cannot be convened) against domestic Violence.

ARTICLE V

The Congress, whenever two thirds of both Houses shall deem it necessary, shall propose Amendments to this Constitution, or, on the Application of the Legislature of two thirds of the several States, shall call a Convention for proposing Amendments, which, in either Case, shall be valid to all Intents and Purposes, as part of this Constitution, when ratified by the Legislatures of three fourths of the several States, or by Conventions in three fourths thereof, as the one or the other Mode of Ratification may be proposed by the Congress; Provided that no Amendment which may be made prior to the Year One thousand eight hundred and eight shall in any Manner affect the first and fourth Clauses in the Ninth Section of the first Article; and that no State, without its Consent, shall be deprived of its equal Suffrage in the Senate.

ARTICLE VI

[1]   All Debts contracted and Engagements entered into, before the Adoption of this Constitution, shall be as valid against the United States under this Constitution, as under the Confederation.

[2]   This Constitution, and the Laws of the United States which shall be made in Pursuance thereof; and all Treaties made, or which shall be made, under the Authority of the United States, shall be the supreme Law of the Land; and the Judges in every State shall be bound thereby, any Thing in the Constitution or Laws of any State to the Contrary notwithstanding.

[3]   The Senators and Representatives before mentioned, and the Members of the several State Legislatures, and all executive and judicial Officers, both of the United States and of the several States, shall be bound by Oath or Affirmation, to support this Constitution; but no religious Test shall ever be required as a Qualification to any Office or public Trust under the United States.

ARTICLE VII

The Ratification of the Conventions of nine States, shall be sufficient for the Establishment of this Constitution between the States so ratifying the Same.

Done in Convention by the Unanimous Consent of the States present the Seventeenth Day of September in the Year of our Lord one thousand seven hundred and Eighty seven and of the Independence of the United States of America the Twelfth.

AMENDMENT 1 [1791]

Congress shall make no law respecting an establishment of religion, or prohibiting the free exercise thereof; or abridging the freedom of speech, or of the press; or the right of the people peaceably to assemble, and to petition the Government for a redress of grievances.

AMENDMENT 2 [1791]

A well regulated Militia, being necessary to the security of a free State, the right of the people to keep and bear Arms, shall not be infringed.

AMENDMENT 3 [1791]

No Soldier shall, in time of peace be quartered in any house, without the consent of the Owner, nor in time of war, but in a manner to be prescribed by law.

AMENDMENT 4 [1791]

The right of the people to be secure in their persons, houses, papers, and effects, against unreasonable searches and seizures, shall not be violated, and no Warrants shall issue, but upon probable cause, supported by Oath or affirmation, and particularly describing the place to be searched, and the persons or things to be seized.

AMENDMENT 5 [1791]

No person shall be held to answer for a capital, or otherwise infamous crime, unless on a presentment or indictment of a Grand Jury, except in cases arising in the land or naval forces, or in the Militia, when in actual service in time of War or public danger; nor shall any person be subject for the same offence to be twice put in jeopardy of life or limb; nor shall be compelled in any criminal case to be a witness against himself, nor be deprived of life, liberty, or property, without due process of law; nor shall private property be taken for public use, without just compensation.

AMENDMENT 6 [1791]

In all criminal prosecutions, the accused shall enjoy the right to a speedy and public trial, by an impartial jury of the State and district wherein the crime shall have been committed, which district shall have been previously ascertained by law, and to be informed of the nature and cause of the accusation; to be confronted with the witnesses against him; to have compulsory process for obtaining witnesses in his favor, and to have the Assistance of Counsel for his defence.

AMENDMENT 7 [1791]

In Suits at common law, where the value in controversy shall exceed twenty dollars, the right of trial by jury shall be preserved, and no fact tried by a jury, shall be otherwise re-examined in any Court of the United States, than according to the rules of the common law.

AMENDMENT 8 [1791]

Excessive bail shall not be required, nor excessive fines imposed, nor cruel and unusual punishments inflicted.

AMENDMENT 9 [1791]

The enumeration in the Constitution, of certain rights, shall not be construed to deny or disparage others retained by the people.

AMENDMENT 10 [1791]

The powers not delegated to the United States by the Constitution, nor prohibited by it to the States, are reserved to the States respectively, or to the people.

AMENDMENT 11 [1798]

The Judicial power of the United States shall not be construed to extend to any suit in law or equity, commenced or prosecuted against one of the United States by Citizens of another State, or by Citizens or Subjects of any Foreign State.

AMENDMENT 12 [1804]

The Electors shall meet in their respective states and vote by ballot for President and Vice–President, one of whom, at least, shall not be an inhabitant of the same state with themselves; they shall name in their ballots the person voted for as President, and in distinct ballots the person voted for as Vice–President, and they shall make distinct lists of all persons voted for as President, and of all persons voted for as Vice–President, and of the number of votes for each, which lists they shall sign and certify, and transmit sealed to the seat of the government of the United States, directed to the President of the Senate;—The President of the Senate shall, in the presence of the Senate and House of Representatives, open all the certificates and the votes shall then be counted;—The person having the greatest number of votes for President, shall be the President, if such number be a majority of the whole number of Electors appointed; and if no person have such majority, then from the persons having the highest numbers not exceeding three on the list of those voted for as President, the House of Representatives shall choose immediately, by ballot, the President. But in choosing the President, the votes shall be taken by states, the representation from each state having one vote; a quorum for this purpose shall consist of a member or members from two-thirds of the states, and a majority of all the states shall be necessary to a choice. And if the House of Representatives shall not choose a President whenever the right of choice shall devolve upon them, before the fourth day of March next following, then the Vice–President shall act as President, as in the case of the death or other constitutional disability of the President.—The person having the greatest number of votes as Vice–President, shall be the Vice–President, if such number be a majority of the whole number of Electors appointed, and if no person have a majority, then from the two highest numbers on the list, the Senate shall choose the Vice–President; a quorum for the purpose shall consist of two-thirds of the whole number of Senators, and a majority of the whole number shall be necessary to a choice. But no person constitutionally ineligible to the office of President shall be eligible to that of Vice–President of the United States.

AMENDMENT 13 [1865]

Section 1.

Neither slavery nor involuntary servitude, except as a punishment for crime whereof the party shall have been duly convicted, shall exist within the United States, or any place subject to their jurisdiction.

Section 2.

Congress shall have power to enforce this article by appropriate legislation.

AMENDMENT 14 [1868]

Section 1.

All persons born or naturalized in the United States, and subject to the jurisdiction thereof, are citizens of the United States and of the State wherein they reside. No State shall make or enforce any law which shall abridge the privileges or immunities of citizens of the United States; nor shall any State deprive any person of life, liberty, or property, without due process of law; nor deny to any person within its jurisdiction the equal protection of the laws.

Section 2.

Representatives shall be apportioned among the several States according to their respective numbers, counting the whole number of persons in each State, excluding Indians not taxed. But when the right to vote at any election for the choice of electors for President and Vice President of the United States, Representatives in Congress, the Executive and Judicial officers of a State, or the members of the Legislature thereof, is denied to any of the male inhabitants of such State, being twenty-one years of age, and citizens of the United States, or in any way abridged, except for participation in rebellion, or other crime, the basis of representation therein shall be reduced in the proportion which the number of such male citizens shall bear to the whole number of male citizens twenty-one years of age in such State.

Section 3.

No person shall be a Senator or Representative in Congress, or elector of President and Vice President, or hold any office, civil or military, under the United States, or under any State, who, having previously taken an oath, as a member of Congress, or as an officer of the United States, or as a member of any State legislature, or as an executive or judicial officer of any State, to support the Constitution of the United States, shall have engaged in insurrection or rebellion against the same, or given aid or comfort to the enemies thereof. But Congress may by a vote of two-thirds of each House, remove such disability.

Section 4.

The validity of the public debt of the United States, authorized by law, including debts incurred for payment of pensions and bounties for services in suppressing insurrection or rebellion, shall not be questioned. But neither the United States nor any State shall assume or pay any debt or obligation incurred in aid of insurrection or rebellion against the United States, or any claim for the loss of emancipation of any slave; but all such debts, obligations and claims shall be held illegal and void.

Section 5.

The Congress shall have the power to enforce, by appropriate legislation, the provisions of this article.

AMENDMENT 15 [1870]

Section 1.

The right of citizens of the United States to vote shall not be denied or abridged by the United States or by any State on account of race, color, or previous condition of servitude.

Section 2.

The Congress shall have power to enforce this article by appropriate legislation.

AMENDMENT 16 [1913]

The Congress shall have power to lay and collect taxes on incomes, from whatever source derived, without apportionment among the several States, and without regard to any census or enumeration.

AMENDMENT 17 [1913]

[1] The Senate of the United States shall be composed of two Senators from each State, elected by the people thereof for six years, and each Senator shall have one vote. The electors in each State shall have the qualifications requisite for electors of the most numerous branch of the State legislatures.

[2] When vacancies happen in the representation of any State in the Senate, the executive authority of such State shall issue writs of election to fill such vacancies: Provided, That the legislature of any State may empower the executive thereof to make temporary appointments until the people fill the vacancies by election as the legislature may direct.

[3] This amendment shall not be so construed as to affect the election or term of any Senator chosen before it becomes valid as part of the Constitution.

AMENDMENT 18 [1919]

Section 1.

After one year from the ratification of this article the manufacture, sale, or transportation of intoxicating liquors within, the importation thereof into, or the exportation thereof from the United States and all territory subject to the jurisdiction thereof for beverage purposes is hereby prohibited.

Section 2.

The Congress and the several States shall have concurrent power to enforce this article by appropriate legislation.

Section 3.

This article shall be inoperative unless it shall have been ratified as an amendment to the Constitution by the legislatures of the several States as provided in the Constitution, within seven years from the date of the submission hereof to the States by the Congress.

AMENDMENT 19 [1920]

[1] The right of citizens of the United States to vote shall not be denied or abridged by the United States or by any State on account of sex.

[2] Congress shall have power to enforce this article by appropriate legislation.

AMENDMENT 20 [1933]

Section 1.

The terms of the President and Vice President shall end at noon on the 20th day of January, and the terms of Senators and Representatives at noon on the 3d day of January, of the years in which such terms would have ended if this article had not been ratified; and the terms of their successors shall then begin.

Section 2.

The Congress shall assemble at least once in every year, and such meeting shall begin at noon on the 3d day of January, unless they shall by law appoint a different day.

Section 3.

If, at the time fixed for the beginning of the term of the President, the President elect shall have died, the Vice President elect shall become President. If a President shall not have been chosen before the time fixed for the beginning of his term, or if the President elect shall have failed to qualify, then the Vice President elect shall act as President until a President shall have qualified; and the Congress may by law provide for the case wherein neither a President elect nor a Vice President elect shall have qualified, declaring who shall then act as President, or the manner in which one who is to act shall be selected, and such person shall act accordingly until a President or Vice President shall have qualified.

Section 4.

The Congress may by law provide for the case of the death of any of the persons from whom the House of Representatives may choose a President whenever the right of choice shall have devolved upon them, and for the case of the death of any of the persons from whom the Senate may choose a Vice President whenever the right of choice shall have devolved upon them.

Section 5.

Sections 1 and 2 shall take effect on the 15th day of October following the ratification of this article.

Section 6.

This article shall be inoperative unless it shall have been ratified as an amendment to the Constitution by the legislatures of three-fourths of the several States within seven years from the date of its submission.

AMENDMENT 21 [1933]

Section 1.

The eighteenth article of amendment to the Constitution of the United States is hereby repealed.

Section 2.

The transportation or importation into any State, Territory, or possession of the United States for delivery or use therein of intoxicating liquors, in violation of the laws thereof, is hereby prohibited.

Section 3.

This article shall be inoperative unless it shall have been ratified as an amendment to the Constitution by conventions in the several States, as provided in the Constitution, within seven years from the date of the submission hereof to the States by the Congress.

AMENDMENT 22 [1951]

Section 1.

No person shall be elected to the office of the President more than twice, and no person who has held the office of President, or acted as President, for more than two years of a term to which some other person was elected President shall be elected to the office of President more than once. But this Article shall not apply to any person holding the office of President when this Article was proposed by the Congress, and shall not prevent any person who may be holding the office of President, or acting as President, during the term within which this Article becomes operative from holding the office of President or acting as President during the remainder of such term.

Section 2.

This article shall be inoperative unless it shall have been ratified as an amendment to the Constitution by the legislatures of three-fourths of the several States within seven years from the date of its submission to the States by the Congress.

AMENDMENT 23 [1961]

Section 1.

The District constituting the seat of Government of the United States shall appoint in such manner as the Congress may direct:

A number of electors of President and Vice President equal to the whole number of Senators and Representatives in Congress to which the District would be entitled if it were a State, but in no event more than the least populous State; they shall be in addition to those appointed by the States, but they shall be considered, for the purposes of the election of President and Vice President, to be electors appointed by a State; and they shall meet in the District and perform such duties as provided by the twelfth article of amendment.

Section 2.

The Congress shall have power to enforce this article by appropriate legislation.

AMENDMENT 24 [1964]

Section 1.

The right of citizens of the United States to vote in any primary or other election for President or Vice President, for electors for President or Vice President, or for Senator or Representative in Congress, shall not be denied or abridged by the United States or any State by reason of failure to pay any poll tax or other tax.

Section 2.

The Congress shall have power to enforce this article by appropriate legislation.

AMENDMENT 25 [1967]

Section 1.

In case of the removal of the President from office or of his death or resignation, the Vice President shall become President.

Section 2.

Whenever there is a vacancy in the office of the Vice President, the President shall nominate a Vice President who shall take office upon confirmation by a majority vote of both Houses of Congress.

Section 3.

Whenever the President transmits to the President pro tempore of the Senate and the Speaker of the House of Representatives his written declaration that he is unable to discharge the powers and duties of his office, and until he transmits to them a written declaration to the contrary, such powers and duties shall be discharged by the Vice President as Acting President.

Section 4.

Whenever the Vice President and a Majority of either the principal officers of the executive departments or of such other body as Congress may by law provide, transmit to the President pro tempore of the Senate and the Speaker of the House of Representatives their written declaration that the President is unable to discharge the powers and duties of his office, the Vice President shall immediately assume the powers and duties of the office as Acting President.

Thereafter, when the President transmits to the President pro tempore of the Senate and the Speaker of the House of Representatives his written declaration that no inability exists, he shall resume the powers and duties of his office unless the Vice President and a majority of either the principal officers of the executive department or of such other body as Congress may by law provide, transmit within four days to the President pro tempore of the Senate and the Speaker of the House of Representatives their written declaration that the President is unable to discharge the powers and duties of his office. Thereupon Congress shall decide the issue, assembling within forty-eight hours for that purpose if not in session. If the Congress, within twenty-one days after receipt of the latter written declaration, or, if Congress is not in session, within twenty-one days after Congress is required to assemble, determines by two-thirds vote of both Houses that the President is unable to discharge the powers and duties of his office, the Vice President shall continue to discharge the same as Acting President; otherwise, the President shall resume the powers and duties of his office.

AMENDMENT 26 [1971]

Section 1.

The right of citizens of the United States, who are eighteen years of age or older, to vote shall not be denied or abridged by the United States or by any State on account of age.

Section 2.

The Congress shall have the power to enforce this article by appropriate legislation.

AMENDMENT 27 [1992]

No law, varying the compensation for the services of the Senators and Representatives, shall take effect, until an election of Representatives shall have intervened.

ADMINISTRATIVE PROCEDURE ACT

[Public Law 404–79th Congress, approved June 11, 1946, 60 Stat. 237; as codified by An Act to enact title 5, United States Code, September 6, 1966, Public Law 89–554, 80 Stat. 378; and as amended through P.L. 107–245 (2002).]

TITLE 5.   GOVERNMENT ORGANIZATION AND EMPLOYEES

CHAPTER 5.   ADMINISTRATIVE PROCEDURE

* * *

Subchapter II—Administrative Procedure

Parallel sections of 1946 Act

§ 551. Definitions

SEC. 2

For the purpose of this subchapter—

(1) "agency" means each authority of the Government of the United States, whether or not it is within or subject to review by another agency, but does not include—   SEC. 2(a).

    (A) the Congress;

    (B) the courts of the United States;

    (C) the governments of the territories or possessions of the United States;

    (D) the government of the District of Columbia;

or except as to the requirements of section 552 of this title—

    (E) agencies composed of representatives of the parties or of representatives of organizations of the parties to the disputes determined by them;

    (F) courts martial and military commissions;

(G) military authority exercised in the field in time of war or in occupied territory; or

(H) functions conferred by sections 1738, 1739, 1743, and 1744 of title 12; chapter 2 of title 41; subchapter II of chapter 471 of title 49; or sections 1884, 1891–1902, and former section 1641(b)(2), of title 50, appendix;

(2) "person" includes an individual, partnership, corporation, association, or public or private organization other than an agency;   SEC. 2(b).

(3) "party" includes a person or agency named or admitted as a party, or properly seeking and entitled as of right to be admitted as a party, in an agency proceeding, and a person or agency admitted by an agency as a party for limited purposes;

(4) "rule" means the whole or a part of an agency statement of general or particular applicability and future effect designed to implement, interpret, or prescribe law or policy or describing the organization, procedure, or practice requirements of an agency and includes the approval or prescription for the future of rates, wages, corporate or financial structures or reorganization thereof, prices, facilities, appliances, services or allowances therefor or of valuations, costs, or accounting, or practices bearing on any of the foregoing;   SEC. 2(c).

(5) "rule making" means agency process for formulating, amending, or repealing a rule;

(6) "order" means the whole or a part of a final disposition, whether affirmative, negative, injunctive, or declaratory in form, of an agency in a matter other than rule making but including licensing;   SEC. 2(d).

(7) "adjudication" means agency process for the formulation of an order;

(8) "license" includes the whole or a part of an agency permit, certificate, approval, registration, charter, membership, statutory exemption or other form of permission;   SEC. 2(e).

(9) "licensing" includes agency process respecting the grant, renewal, denial, revocation, suspension, annulment, withdrawal, limitation, amendment, modification, or conditioning of a license;

(10) "sanction" includes the whole or a part of an agency—   SEC. 2(f).

(A) prohibition, requirement, limitation, or other condition affecting the freedom of a person;

(B) withholding of relief;

(C) imposition of penalty or fine;

(D) destruction, taking, seizure, or withholding of property;

(E) assessment of damages, reimbursement, restitution, compensation, costs, charges, or fees;

(F) requirement, revocation, or suspension of a license; or

(G) taking other compulsory or restrictive action;

(11) "relief" includes the whole or a part of an agency—

(A) grant of money, assistance, license, authority, exemption, exception, privilege, or remedy;

(B) recognition of a claim, right, immunity, privilege, exemption, or exception; or

(C) taking of other action on the application or petition of, and beneficial to, a person;

(12) "agency proceeding" means an agency process as defined by paragraphs (5), (7), and (9) of this section; and

Sec. 2(g).

(13) "agency action" includes the whole or a part of an agency rule, order, license, sanction, relief, or the equivalent or denial thereof, or failure to act.

(14)[1] "Ex parte communication" means an oral or written communication not on the public record with respect to which reasonable prior notice to all parties is not given, but it shall not include requests for status reports on any matter or proceeding covered by this subchapter.

§ 552. Public information; agency rules, opinions, orders, records, and proceedings (The Freedom of Information Act)[2];

Sec. 3. (as amended)

(a) Each agency shall make available to the public information as follows:

(1) Each agency shall separately state and currently publish in the Federal Register for the guidance of the public—

(A) descriptions of its central and field organization and the established places at which, the employees (and in the case of a uniformed service, the members) from whom, and the methods whereby, the public may

---

1. Added by P.L. 94–409, 90 Stat. 1247 (1976).

2. While Section 3 of the original APA contained a limited provision respecting public records, the bulk of this section is the result of subsequent legislation. See P.L. 89–554, 80 Stat. 383 (1966); P.L. 90–23, 81 Stat. 54 (1967); P.L. 93–502, 88 Stat. 1561 (1974);

P.L. 94–409, 90 Stat. 1247 (1976); P.L. 95–454, 92 Stat. 1225 (1978); P.L. 98–620, 98 Stat. 3357 (1984); P.L. 99–570, 100 Stat. 3207 (1986), and P.L. 104–231, 110 Stat. 3049 (1996). The last of these is known as the "Electronic Freedom of Information Act Amendments of 1996," and provided the various provisions for web-based access.

obtain information, make submittals or requests, or obtain decisions;

(B) statements of the general course and method by which its functions are channeled and determined, including the nature and requirements of all formal and informal procedures available;

(C) rules of procedure, descriptions of forms available or the places at which forms may be obtained, and instructions as to the scope and contents of all papers, reports, or examinations;

(D) substantive rules of general applicability adopted as authorized by law, and statements of general policy or interpretations of general applicability formulated and adopted by the agency; and

(E) each amendment, revision, or repeal of the foregoing.

Except to the extent that a person has actual and timely notice of the terms thereof, a person may not in any manner be required to resort to, or be adversely affected by, a matter required to be published in the Federal Register and not so published. For the purpose of this paragraph, matter reasonably available to the class of persons affected thereby is deemed published in the Federal Register when incorporated by reference therein with the approval of the Director of the Federal Register.

(2) Each agency, in accordance with published rules, shall make available for public inspection and copying—

(A) final opinions, including concurring and dissenting opinions, as well as orders, made in the adjudication of cases;

(B) those statements of policy and interpretations which have been adopted by the agency and are not published in the Federal Register;

(C) administrative staff manuals and instructions to staff that affect a member of the public;

(D) copies of all records, regardless of form or format, which have been released to any person under paragraph (3) and which, because of the nature of their subject matter, the agency determines have become or are likely to become the subject of subsequent requests for substantially the same records; and

(E) a general index of the records referred to under subparagraph (D);

unless the materials are promptly published and copies offered for sale. For records created on or after November 1, 1996, within one year after such date, each agency shall make such records available, including by computer telecommunications or, if computer telecommunications means have not been established by the agency, by other electronic means. To the extent required to prevent a clearly unwarranted invasion of personal privacy, an agency may delete identifying details when it makes available or publishes an opinion, statement of policy, interpretation, staff manual, instruction, or copies of records referred to in subparagraph (D). However, in each case the justification for the deletion shall be explained fully in writing, and the extent of such deletion shall be indicated on the portion of the record which is made available or published, unless including that indication would harm an interest protected by the exemption in subsection (b) under which the deletion is made. If technically feasible, the extent of the deletion shall be indicated at the place in the record where the deletion was made. Each agency shall also maintain and make available for public inspection and copying current indexes providing identifying information for the public as to any matter issued, adopted, or promulgated after July 4, 1967, and required by this paragraph to be made available or published. Each agency shall promptly publish, quarterly or more frequently, and distribute (by sale or otherwise) copies of each index or supplements thereto unless it determines by order published in the Federal Register that the publication would be unnecessary and impracticable, in which case the agency shall nonetheless provide copies of such index on request at a cost not to exceed the direct cost of duplication. Each agency shall make the index referred to in subparagraph (E) available by computer telecommunications by December 31, 1999. A final order, opinion, statement of policy, interpretation, or staff manual or instruction that affects a member of the public may be relied on, used, or cited as precedent by an agency against a party other than an agency only if—

> (i) it has been indexed and either made available or published as provided by this paragraph; or

> (ii) the party has actual and timely notice of the terms thereof.

(3)(A) Except with respect to the records made available under paragraphs (1) and (2) of this subsection, each agency, upon any request for records which (i) reasonably describes such records and (ii) is made in accordance with published rules stating the time, place, fees (if any), and procedures to be followed, shall make the records promptly available to any person.

> (B) In making any record available to a person under this paragraph, an agency shall provide the record in any form or format requested by the person if the record is readily reproducible by the agency in that form or format. Each agency shall make reasonable

efforts to maintain its records in forms or formats that are reproducible for purposes of this section.

(C) In responding under this paragraph to a request for records, an agency shall make reasonable efforts to search for the records in electronic form or format, except when such efforts would significantly interfere with the operation of the agency's automated information system.

(D) For purposes of this paragraph, the term "search" means to review, manually or by automated means, agency records for the purpose of locating those records which are responsive to a request.

(4)(A)(i) In order to carry out the provisions of this section, each agency shall promulgate regulations, pursuant to notice and receipt of public comment, specifying the schedule of fees applicable to the processing of requests under this section and establishing procedures and guidelines for determining when such fees should be waived or reduced. Such schedule shall conform to the guidelines which shall be promulgated, pursuant to notice and receipt of public comment, by the Director of the Office of Management and Budget and which shall provide for a uniform schedule of fees for all agencies.

(ii) Such agency regulations shall provide that—

(I) fees shall be limited to reasonable standard charges for document search, duplication, and review, when records are requested for commercial use;

(II) fees shall be limited to reasonable standard charges for document duplication when records are not sought for commercial use and the request is made by an educational or noncommercial scientific institution, whose purpose is scholarly or scientific research; or a representative of the news media; and

(III) for any request not described in (I) or (II), fees shall be limited to reasonable standard charges for document search and duplication.

(iii) Documents shall be furnished without any charge or at a charge reduced below the fees established under clause (ii) if disclosure of the information is in the public interest because it is likely to contribute significantly to public understanding of the operations or activities of the government and is not primarily in the commercial interest of the requester.

(iv) Fee schedules shall provide for the recovery of only the direct costs of search, duplication, or review. Review costs shall include only the direct costs incurred during the initial examination of a document for the purposes of determining whether the documents must be disclosed under this section and for the purposes of withholding any portions exempt from disclosure under this section. Review costs may not include any costs incurred in resolving issues of law or policy that may be raised in the course of processing a request under this section. No fee may be charged by any agency under this section—

(I) if the costs of routine collection and processing of the fee are likely to equal or exceed the amount of the fee; or

(II) for any request described in clause (ii)(II) or (III) of this subparagraph for the first two hours of search time or for the first one hundred pages of duplication.

(v) No agency may require advance payment of any fee unless the requester has previously failed to pay fees in a timely fashion, or the agency has determined that the fee will exceed $250.

(vi) Nothing in this subparagraph shall supersede fees chargeable under a statute specifically providing for setting the level of fees for particular types of records.

(vii) In any action by a requester regarding the waiver of fees under this section, the court shall determine the matter de novo: *Provided*, That the court's review of the matter shall be limited to the record before the agency.

(B) On complaint, the district court of the United States in the district in which the complainant resides, or has his principal place of business, or in which the agency records are situated, or in the District of Columbia, has jurisdiction to enjoin the agency from withholding agency records and to order the production of any agency records improperly withheld from the complainant. In such a case the court shall determine the matter de novo, and may examine the contents of such agency records in camera to determine whether such records or any part thereof shall be withheld under any of the exemptions set forth in subsection (b) of this section, and the burden is on the agency to sustain its action. In addition to any other matters to which a court accords substantial weight, a court shall accord substantial weight to an affidavit of an agency concerning the agency's determination as to technical feasibility under paragraph (2)(C) and subsection (b) and reproducibility under paragraph (3)(B).

(C) Notwithstanding any other provision of law, the defendant shall serve an answer or otherwise plead to any complaint made under this subsection within thirty days after service upon the defendant of the pleading in which such complaint is made, unless the court otherwise directs for good cause shown.

[(D) Repealed. Pub.L. 98–620, Title IV, § 402(2), Nov. 8, 1984, 98 Stat. 3357.]

(E) The court may assess against the United States reasonable attorney fees and other litigation costs reasonably incurred in any case under this section in which the complainant has substantially prevailed.

(F) Whenever the court orders the production of any agency records improperly withheld from the complainant and assesses against the United States reasonable attorney fees and other litigation costs, and the court additionally issues a written finding that the circumstances surrounding the withholding raise questions whether agency personnel acted arbitrarily or capriciously with respect to the withholding, the Special Counsel shall promptly initiate a proceeding to determine whether disciplinary action is warranted against the officer or employee who was primarily responsible for the withholding. The Special Counsel, after investigation and consideration of the evidence submitted, shall submit his findings and recommendations to the administrative authority of the agency concerned and shall send copies of the findings and recommendations to the officer or employee or his representative. The administrative authority shall take the corrective action that the Special Counsel recommends.

(G) In the event of noncompliance with the order of the court, the district court may punish for contempt the responsible employee, and in the case of a uniformed service, the responsible member.

(5) Each agency having more than one member shall maintain and make available for public inspection a record of the final votes of each member in every agency proceeding.

(6)(A) Each agency, upon any request for records made under paragraph (1), (2), or (3) of this subsection, shall—

> (i) determine within 20 days (excepting Saturdays, Sundays, and legal public holidays) after the receipt of any such request whether to comply with such request and shall immediately notify the person making such request of such determination and the reasons therefor, and of the right of such

person to appeal to the head of the agency any adverse determination; and

(ii) make a determination with respect to any appeal within twenty days (excepting Saturdays, Sundays, and legal public holidays) after the receipt of such appeal. If on appeal the denial of the request for records is in whole or in part upheld, the agency shall notify the person making such request of the provisions for judicial review of that determination under paragraph (4) of this subsection.

(B)(i) In unusual circumstances as specified in this subparagraph, the time limits prescribed in either clause (i) or clause (ii) of subparagraph (A) may be extended by written notice to the person making such request setting forth the unusual circumstances for such extension and the date on which a determination is expected to be dispatched. No such notice shall specify a date that would result in an extension for more than ten working days, except as provided in clause (ii) of this subparagraph.

(ii) With respect to a request for which a written notice under clause (i) extends the time limits prescribed under clause (i) of subparagraph (A), the agency shall notify the person making the request if the request cannot be processed within the time limit specified in that clause and shall provide the person an opportunity to limit the scope of the request so that it may be processed within that time limit or an opportunity to arrange with the agency an alternative time frame for processing the request or a modified request. Refusal by the person to reasonably modify the request or arrange such an alternative time frame shall be considered as a factor in determining whether exceptional circumstances exist for purposes of subparagraph (C).

(iii) As used in this subparagraph, "unusual circumstances" means, but only to the extent reasonably necessary to the proper processing of the particular requests—

(I) the need to search for and collect the requested records from field facilities or other establishments that are separate from the office processing the request;

(II) the need to search for, collect, and appropriately examine a voluminous amount of separate and distinct records which are demanded in a single request; or

(III) the need for consultation, which shall be conducted with all practicable speed, with another agency having a substantial interest in the determination of the request or among two or more components of the agency having substantial subject-matter interest therein.

(iv) Each agency may promulgate regulations, pursuant to notice and receipt of public comment, providing for the aggregation of certain requests by the same requestor, or by a group of requestors acting in concert, if the agency reasonably believes that such requests actually constitute a single request, which would otherwise satisfy the unusual circumstances specified in this subparagraph, and the requests involve clearly related matters. Multiple requests involving unrelated matters shall not be aggregated.

(C)(i) Any person making a request to any agency for records under paragraph (1), (2), or (3) of this subsection shall be deemed to have exhausted his administrative remedies with respect to such request if the agency fails to comply with the applicable time limit provisions of this paragraph. If the Government can show exceptional circumstances exist and that the agency is exercising due diligence in responding to the request, the court may retain jurisdiction and allow the agency additional time to complete its review of the records. Upon any determination by an agency to comply with a request for records, the records shall be made promptly available to such person making such request. Any notification of denial of any request for records under this subsection shall set forth the names and titles or positions of each person responsible for the denial of such request.

(ii) For purposes of this subparagraph, the term "exceptional circumstances" does not include a delay that results from a predictable agency workload of requests under this section, unless the agency demonstrates reasonable progress in reducing its backlog of pending requests.

(iii) Refusal by a person to reasonably modify the scope of a request or arrange an alternative time frame for processing a request (or a modified request) under clause (ii) after being given an opportunity to do so by the agency to whom the person made the request shall be considered as a factor in determining whether exceptional circumstances exist for purposes of this subparagraph.

(D)(i) Each agency may promulgate regulations, pursuant to notice and receipt of public comment, providing for multitrack processing of requests for records based on the amount of work or time (or both) involved in processing requests.

(ii) Regulations under this subparagraph may provide a person making a request that does not qualify for the fastest multitrack processing an opportunity to limit the scope of the request in order to qualify for faster processing.

(iii) This subparagraph shall not be considered to affect the requirement under subparagraph (C) to exercise due diligence.

(E)(i) Each agency shall promulgate regulations, pursuant to notice and receipt of public comment, providing for expedited processing of requests for records—

(I) in cases in which the person requesting the records demonstrates a compelling need; and

(II) in other cases determined by the agency.

(ii) Notwithstanding clause (i), regulations under this subparagraph must ensure—

(I) that a determination of whether to provide expedited processing shall be made, and notice of the determination shall be provided to the person making the request, within 10 days after the date of the request; and

(II) expeditious consideration of administrative appeals of such determinations of whether to provide expedited processing.

(iii) An agency shall process as soon as practicable any request for records to which the agency has granted expedited processing under this subparagraph. Agency action to deny or affirm denial of a request for expedited processing pursuant to this subparagraph, and failure by an agency to respond in a timely manner to such a request shall be subject to judicial review under paragraph (4), except that the judicial review shall be based on the record before the agency at the time of the determination.

(iv) A district court of the United States shall not have jurisdiction to review an agency denial of expedited processing of a request for records after the agency has provided a complete response to the request.

(v) For purposes of this subparagraph, the term "compelling need" means—

(I) that a failure to obtain requested records on an expedited basis under this paragraph could reasonably be expected to pose an imminent threat to the life or physical safety of an individual; or

(II) with respect to a request made by a person primarily engaged in disseminating information, urgency to inform the public concerning actual or alleged Federal Government activity.

(vi) A demonstration of a compelling need by a person making a request for expedited processing shall be made by a statement certified by such person to be true and correct to the best of such person's knowledge and belief.

(F) In denying a request for records, in whole or in part, an agency shall make a reasonable effort to estimate the volume of any requested matter the provision of which is denied, and shall provide any such estimate to the person making the request, unless providing such estimate would harm an interest protected by the exemption in subsection (b) pursuant to which the denial is made.

(b) This section does not apply to matters that are—

(1)(A) specifically authorized under criteria established by an Executive order to be kept secret in the interest of national defense or foreign policy and (B) are in fact properly classified pursuant to such Executive order;

(2) related solely to the internal personnel rules and practices of an agency;

(3) specifically exempted from disclosure by statute (other than section 552b of this title), provided that such statute (A) requires that the matters be withheld from the public in such a manner as to leave no discretion on the issue, or (B) establishes particular criteria for withholding or refers to particular types of matters to be withheld;

(4) trade secrets and commercial or financial information obtained from a person and privileged or confidential;

(5) inter-agency or intra-agency memorandums or letters which would not be available by law to a party other than an agency in litigation with the agency;

(6) personnel and medical files and similar files the disclosure of which would constitute a clearly unwarranted invasion of personal privacy;

(7) records or information compiled for law enforcement purposes, but only to the extent that the production of such law enforcement records or information (A) could reason-

ably be expected to interfere with enforcement proceedings, (B) would deprive a person of a right to a fair trial or an impartial adjudication, (C) could reasonably be expected to constitute an unwarranted invasion of personal privacy, (D) could reasonably be expected to disclose the identity of a confidential source, including a State, local, or foreign agency or authority or any private institution which furnished information on a confidential basis, and, in the case of a record or information compiled by criminal law enforcement authority in the course of a criminal investigation or by an agency conducting a lawful national security intelligence investigation, information furnished by a confidential source, (E) would disclose techniques and procedures for law enforcement investigations or prosecutions, or would disclose guidelines for law enforcement investigations or prosecutions if such disclosure could reasonably be expected to risk circumvention of the law, or (F) could reasonably be expected to endanger the life or physical safety of any individual;

(8) contained in or related to examination, operating, or condition reports prepared by, on behalf of, or for the use of an agency responsible for the regulation or supervision of financial institutions; or

(9) geological and geophysical information and data, including maps, concerning wells.

Any reasonably segregable portion of a record shall be provided to any person requesting such record after deletion of the portions which are exempt under this subsection. The amount of information deleted shall be indicated on the released portion of the record, unless including that indication would harm an interest protected by the exemption in this subsection under which the deletion is made. If technically feasible, the amount of the information deleted shall be indicated at the place in the record where such deletion is made.

(c)(1) Whenever a request is made which involves access to records described in subsection (b)(7)(A) and—

(A) the investigation or proceeding involves a possible violation of criminal law; and

(B) there is reason to believe that (i) the subject of the investigation or proceeding is not aware of its pendency, and (ii) disclosure of the existence of the records could reasonably be expected to interfere with enforcement proceedings,

the agency may, during only such time as that circumstance continues, treat the records as not subject to the requirements of this section.

(2) Whenever informant records maintained by a criminal law enforcement agency under an informant's name or

personal identifier are requested by a third party according to the informant's name or personal identifier, the agency may treat the records as not subject to the requirements of this section unless the informant's status as an informant has been officially confirmed.

(3) Whenever a request is made which involves access to records maintained by the Federal Bureau of Investigation pertaining to foreign intelligence or counterintelligence, or international terrorism, and the existence of the records is classified information as provided in subsection (b)(1), the Bureau may, as long as the existence of the records remains classified information, treat the records as not subject to the requirements of this section.

(d) This section does not authorize withholding of information or limit the availability of records to the public, except as specifically stated in this section. This section is not authority to withhold information from Congress.

(e)(1) On or before February 1 of each year, each agency shall submit to the Attorney General of the United States a report which shall cover the preceding fiscal year and which shall include—

(A) the number of determinations made by the agency not to comply with requests for records made to such agency under subsection (a) and the reasons for each such determination;

(B)(i) the number of appeals made by persons under subsection (a)(6), the result of such appeals, and the reason for the action upon each appeal that results in a denial of information; and

(ii) a complete list of all statutes that the agency relies upon to authorize the agency to withhold information under subsection (b)(3), a description of whether a court has upheld the decision of the agency to withhold information under each such statute, and a concise description of the scope of any information withheld;

(C) the number of requests for records pending before the agency as of September 30 of the preceding year, and the median number of days that such requests had been pending before the agency as of that date;

(D) the number of requests for records received by the agency and the number of requests which the agency processed;

(E) the median number of days taken by the agency to process different types of requests;

(F) the total amount of fees collected by the agency for processing requests; and

(G) the number of full-time staff of the agency devoted to processing requests for records under this section, and the total amount expended by the agency for processing such requests.

(2) Each agency shall make each such report available to the public including by computer telecommunications, or if computer telecommunications means have not been established by the agency, by other electronic means.

(3) The Attorney General of the United States shall make each report which has been made available by electronic means available at a single electronic access point. The Attorney General of the United States shall notify the Chairman and ranking minority member of the Committee on Government Reform and Oversight of the House of Representatives and the Chairman and ranking minority member of the Committees on Governmental Affairs and the Judiciary of the Senate, no later than April 1 of the year in which each such report is issued, that such reports are available by electronic means.

(4) The Attorney General of the United States, in consultation with the Director of the Office of Management and Budget, shall develop reporting and performance guidelines in connection with reports required by this subsection by October 1, 1997, and may establish additional requirements for such reports as the Attorney General determines may be useful.

(5) The Attorney General of the United States shall submit an annual report on or before April 1 of each calendar year which shall include for the prior calendar year a listing of the number of cases arising under this section, the exemption involved in each case, the disposition of such case, and the cost, fees, and penalties assessed under subparagraphs (E), (F), and (G) of subsection (a)(4). Such report shall also include a description of the efforts undertaken by the Department of Justice to encourage agency compliance with this section.

(f) For purposes of this section, the term—

(1) "agency" as defined in section 551(1) of this title includes any executive department, military department, Government corporation, Government controlled corporation, or other establishment in the executive branch of the Government (including the Executive Office of the President), or any independent regulatory agency; and

(2) "record" and any other term used in this section in reference to information includes any information that would be an agency record subject to the requirements of this section when maintained by an agency in any format, including an electronic format.

(g) The head of each agency shall prepare and make publicly available upon request, reference material or a guide for requesting records or information from the agency, subject to the exemptions in subsection (b), including—

(1) an index of all major information systems of the agency;

(2) a description of major information and record locator systems maintained by the agency; and

(3) a handbook for obtaining various types and categories of public information from the agency pursuant to chapter 35 of title 44, and under this section.

§ 552a.   Records maintained on individuals

[This section, also known as the Privacy Act, is omitted.]

§ 552b.   Open meetings

[See p. 1350 within].

§ 553.   Rule making

Sec. 4.

(a) This section applies, according to the provisions thereof, except to the extent that there is involved—

(1) a military or foreign affairs function of the United States; or

(2) a matter relating to agency management or personnel or to public property, loans, grants, benefits, or contracts.

(b) General notice of proposed rule making shall be published in the Federal Register, unless persons subject thereto are named and either personally served or otherwise have actual notice thereof in accordance with law. The notice shall include—

Sec. 4(a).

notice

(1) a statement of the time, place, and nature of public rule making proceedings;

(2) reference to the legal authority under which the rule is proposed; and

(3) either the terms or substance of the proposed rule or a description of the subjects and issues involved.

Except when notice or hearing is required by statute, this subsection does not apply—

(A) to interpretative rules, general statements of policy, or rules of agency organization, procedure, or practice; or

(B) when the agency for good cause finds (and incorporates the finding and a brief statement of reasons therefor in the rules issued) that notice and public procedure thereon are impracticable, unnecessary, or contrary to the public interest.

(c) After notice required by this section, the agency shall give interested persons an opportunity to participate in the rule making through submission of written data, views, or arguments with or without opportunity for oral presentation. After consideration of the relevant matter presented, the agency shall incorporate in the rules adopted a concise general statement of their basis and purpose. When rules are required by statute to be made on the record after opportunity for an agency hearing, sections 556 and 557 of this title apply instead of this subsection.

Sec. 4(b).

Comment

(d) The required publication or service of a substantive rule shall be made not less than 30 days before its effective date, except—

Sec. 4(c).

30 days

(1) a substantive rule which grants or recognizes an exemption or relieves a restriction;

(2) interpretative rules and statements of policy; or

(3) as otherwise provided by the agency for good cause found and published with the rule.

(e) Each agency shall give an interested person the right to petition for the issuance, amendment, or repeal of a rule.

Sec. 4(d).

§ 554. Adjudications

Sec. 5.

(a) This section applies, according to the provisions thereof, in every case of adjudication required by statute to be determined on the record after opportunity for an agency hearing, except to the extent that there is involved—

(1) a matter subject to a subsequent trial of the law and the facts de novo in a court;

(2) the selection or tenure of an employee, except an administrative law judge appointed under section 3105 of this title;

(3) proceedings in which decisions rest solely on inspections, tests, or elections;

(4) the conduct of military or foreign affairs functions;

(5) cases in which an agency is acting as an agent for a court; or

(6) the certification of worker representatives.

(b) Persons entitled to notice of an agency hearing shall be timely informed of—

Sec. 5(a).

(1) the time, place, and nature of the hearing;

(2) the legal authority and jurisdiction under which the hearing is to be held; and

(3) the matters of fact and law asserted.

When private persons are the moving parties, other parties to the proceeding shall give prompt notice of issues controverted in fact or law; and in other instances agencies may by rule require responsive pleading. In fixing the time and place for hearings, due regard shall be had for the convenience and necessity of the parties or their representatives.

(c) The agency shall give all interested parties opportunity for—   SEC. 5(b).

(1) the submission and consideration of facts, arguments, offers of settlement, or proposals of adjustment when time, the nature of the proceeding, and the public interest permit; and

(2) to the extent that the parties are unable so to determine a controversy by consent, hearing and decision on notice and in accordance with sections 556 and 557 of this title.

(d) The employee who presides at the reception of evidence pursuant to section 556 of this title shall make the recommended decision or initial decision required by section 557 of this title, unless he becomes unavailable to the agency. Except to the extent required for the disposition of ex parte matters as authorized by law, such an employee may not—   SEC. 5(c).

(1) consult a person or party on a fact in issue, unless on notice and opportunity for all parties to participate; or

(2) be responsible to or subject to the supervision or direction of an employee or agent engaged in the performance of investigative or prosecuting functions for an agency.

An employee or agent engaged in the performance of investigative or prosecuting functions for an agency in a case may not, in that or a factually related case, participate or advise in the decision, recommended decision or agency review pursuant to section 557 of this title, except as witness or counsel in public proceedings. This subsection does not apply—

(A) in determining applications for initial licenses;

(B) to proceedings involving the validity or application of rates, facilities, or practices of public utilities or carriers; or

(C) to the agency or a member or members of the body comprising the agency.

(e) The agency, with like effect as in the case of other orders, and in its sound discretion, may issue a declaratory order to terminate a controversy or remove uncertainty.

SEC. 5(d).

§ 555. Ancillary matters

SEC. 6.

(a) This section applies, according to the provisions thereof, except as otherwise provided by this subchapter.

(b) A person compelled to appear in person before an agency or representative thereof is entitled to be accompanied, represented, and advised by counsel or, if permitted by the agency, by other qualified representative. A party is entitled to appear in person or by or with counsel or other duly qualified representative in an agency proceeding. So far as the orderly conduct of public business permits, an interested person may appear before an agency or its responsible employees for the presentation, adjustment, or determination of an issue, request, or controversy in a proceeding, whether interlocutory, summary, or otherwise, or in connection with an agency function. With due regard for the convenience and necessity of the parties or their representatives and within a reasonable time, each agency shall proceed to conclude a matter presented to it. This subsection does not grant or deny a person who is not a lawyer the right to appear for or represent others before an agency or in an agency proceeding.

SEC. 6(a).

(c) Process, requirement of a report, inspection, or other investigative act or demand may not be issued, made, or enforced except as authorized by law. A person compelled to submit data or evidence is entitled to retain or, on payment of lawfully prescribed costs, procure a copy or transcript thereof, except that in a nonpublic investigatory proceeding the witness may for good cause be limited to inspection of the official transcript of his testimony.

SEC. 6(b).

(d) Agency subpenas authorized by law shall be issued to a party on request and, when required by rules of procedure, on a statement or showing of general relevance and reasonable scope of the evidence sought. On contest, the court shall sustain the subpena or similar process or demand to the extent that it is found to be in accordance with law. In a proceeding for enforcement, the court shall issue an order requiring the appearance of the witness or the production of the evidence or data within a reasonable time under penalty of punishment for contempt in case of contumacious failure to comply.

SEC. 6(c).

(e) Prompt notice shall be given of the denial in whole or in part of a written application, petition, or other request of an interested person made in connection with any agency proceeding. Except in affirming a prior denial or when the denial is self-explanatory, the notice shall be accompanied by a brief statement of the grounds for denial.

SEC. 6(d).

§ 556. Hearings; presiding employees; powers and duties; burden of proof; evidence; record as basis of decision

SEC. 7.

(a) This section applies, according to the provisions thereof, to hearings required by section 553 or 554 of this title to be conducted in accordance with this section.

(b) There shall preside at the taking of evidence—

SEC. 7(a).

(1) the agency;

(2) one or more members of the body which comprises the agency; or

(3) one or more administrative law judges appointed under section 3105 of this title.

This subchapter does not supersede the conduct of specified classes of proceedings, in whole or in part, by or before boards or other employees specially provided for by or designated under statute. The functions of presiding employees and of employees participating in decisions in accordance with section 557 of this title shall be conducted in an impartial manner. A presiding or participating employee may at any time disqualify himself. On the filing in good faith of a timely and sufficient affidavit of personal bias or other disqualification of a presiding or participating employee, the agency shall determine the matter as a part of the record and decision in the case.

(c) Subject to published rules of the agency and within its powers, employees presiding at hearings may—

SEC. 7(b).

(1) administer oaths and affirmations;

(2) issue subpenas authorized by law;

(3) rule on offers of proof and receive relevant evidence;

(4) take depositions or have depositions taken when the ends of justice would be served;

(5) regulate the course of the hearing;

(6) hold conferences for the settlement or simplification of the issues by consent of the parties or by the use of alternative means of dispute resolution as provided in subchapter IV of this chapter [5 U.S.C. §§ 571 et seq.];

(7) inform the parties as to the availability of one or more alternative means of dispute resolution, and encourage use of such methods;

(8) require the attendance at any conference held pursuant to paragraph (6) of at least one representa-

tive of each party who has authority to negotiate concerning resolution of issues in controversy;

(9) dispose of procedural requests or similar matters;

(10) make or recommend decisions in accordance with section 557 of this title; and

(11) take other action authorized by agency rule consistent with this subchapter.

(d) Except as otherwise provided by statute, the propo-   Sec. 7(c).
nent of a rule or order has the burden of proof. Any oral or documentary evidence may be received, but the agency as a matter of policy shall provide for the exclusion of irrelevant, immaterial, or unduly repetitious evidence. A sanction may not be imposed or rule or order issued except on consideration of the whole record or those parts thereof cited by a party and supported by and in accordance with the reliable, probative, and substantial evidence. The agency may, to the extent consistent with the interests of justice and the policy of the underlying statutes administered by the agency, consider a violation of section 557(d) of this title sufficient grounds for a decision adverse to a party who has knowingly committed such violation or knowingly caused such violation to occur.[3] A party is entitled to present his case or defense by oral or documentary evidence, to submit rebuttal evidence, and to conduct such cross-examination as may be required for a full and true disclosure of the facts. In rule making or determining claims for money or benefits or applications for initial licenses an agency may, when a party will not be prejudiced thereby, adopt procedures for the submission of all or part of the evidence in written form.

(e) The transcript of testimony and exhibits, together   Sec. 7(d).
with all papers and requests filed in the proceeding, constitutes the exclusive record for decision in accordance with section 557 of this title and, on payment of lawfully prescribed costs, shall be made available to the parties. When an agency decision rests on official notice of a material fact not appearing in the evidence in the record, a party is entitled, on timely request, to an opportunity to show the contrary.

§ 557. Initial decisions; conclusiveness; review by   Sec. 8.
agency; submissions by parties; contents of decisions; record

(a) This section applies, according to the provisions thereof, when a hearing is required to be conducted in accordance with section 556 of this title.

---

3. This sentence added by P.L. 94–409, 90 Stat. 1247 (1976).

(b) When the agency did not preside at the reception of the evidence, the presiding employee or, in cases not subject to section 554(d) of this title, an employee qualified to preside at hearings pursuant to section 556 of this title, shall initially decide the case unless the agency requires, either in specific cases or by general rule, the entire record to be certified to it for decision. When the presiding employee makes an initial decision, that decision then becomes the decision of the agency without further proceedings unless there is an appeal to, or review on motion of, the agency within time provided by rule. On appeal from or review of the initial decision, the agency has all the powers which it would have in making the initial decision except as it may limit the issues on notice or by rule. When the agency makes the decision without having presided at the reception of the evidence, the presiding employee or an employee qualified to preside at hearings pursuant to section 556 of this title shall first recommend a decision, except that in rule making or determining application for initial licenses—

SEC. 8(a).

(1) instead thereof the agency may issue a tentative decision or one of its responsible employees may recommend a decision; or

(2) this procedure may be omitted in a case in which the agency finds on the record that due and timely execution of its functions imperatively and unavoidably so requires.

(c) Before a recommended, initial, or tentative decision, or a decision on agency review of the decision of subordinate employees, the parties are entitled to a reasonable opportunity to submit for the consideration of the employees participating in the decisions—

SEC. 8(b).

(1) proposed findings and conclusions; or

(2) exceptions to the decisions or recommended decisions of subordinate employees or to tentative agency decisions; and

(3) supporting reasons for the exceptions or proposed findings or conclusions.

The record shall show the ruling on each finding, conclusion, or exception presented. All decisions, including initial, recommended, and tentative decisions, are a part of the record and shall include a statement of—

(A) findings and conclusions, and the reasons or basis therefor, on all the material issues of fact, law, or discretion presented on the record; and

(B) the appropriate rule, order, sanction, relief, or denial thereof.

(d)(1)[4] In any agency proceeding which is subject to subsection (a) of this section, except to the extent required for the disposition of ex parte matters as authorized by law—

(A) no interested person outside the agency shall make or knowingly cause to be made to any member of the body comprising the agency, administrative law judge, or other employee who is or may reasonably be expected to be involved in the decisional process of the proceeding, an ex parte communication relevant to the merits of the proceeding;

(B) no member of the body comprising the agency, administrative law judge, or other employee who is or may reasonably be expected to be involved in the decisional process of the proceeding, shall make or knowingly cause to be made to any interested person outside the agency an ex parte communication relevant to the merits of the proceeding;

(C) a member of the body comprising the agency, administrative law judge, or other employee who is or may reasonably be expected to be involved in the decisional process of such proceeding who receives, or who makes or knowingly causes to be made, a communication prohibited by this subsection shall place on the public record of the proceeding:

(i) all such written communications;

(ii) memoranda stating the substance of all such oral communications; and

(iii) all written responses, and memoranda stating the substance of all oral responses, to the materials described in clauses (i) and (ii) of this subparagraph;

(D) upon receipt of a communication knowingly made or knowingly caused to be made by a party in violation of this subsection, the agency, administrative law judge, or other employee presiding at the hearing may, to the extent consistent with the interests of justice and the policy of the underlying statutes, require the party to show cause why his claim or interest in the proceeding should not be dismissed, denied, disregarded, or otherwise adversely affected on account of such violation; and

(E) the prohibitions of this subsection shall apply beginning at such time as the agency may designate, but in no case shall they begin to apply later than the time at which a proceeding is noticed for hearing unless the person responsible for the communication

4. Subsection (d) was added by P.L. 94–409, 90 Stat. 1247 (1976).

has knowledge that it will be noticed, in which case the prohibitions shall apply beginning at the time of his acquisition of such knowledge.

(2) This subsection does not constitute authority to withhold information from Congress.

§ 558. Imposition of sanctions; determination of applications for licenses; suspension, revocation, and expiration of licenses

SEC. 9.

(a) This section applies, according to the provisions thereof, to the exercise of a power or authority.

(b) A sanction may not be imposed or a substantive rule or order issued except within jurisdiction delegated to the agency and as authorized by law.

SEC. 9(a).

(c) When application is made for a license required by law, the agency, with due regard for the rights and privileges of all the interested parties or adversely affected persons and within a reasonable time, shall set and complete proceedings required to be conducted in accordance with sections 556 and 557 of this title or other proceedings required by law and shall make its decision. Except in cases of willfulness or those in which public health, interest, or safety requires otherwise, the withdrawal, suspension, revocation, or annulment of a license is lawful only if, before the institution of agency proceedings therefor, the licensee has been given—

SEC. 9(b).

(1) notice by the agency in writing of the facts or conduct which may warrant the action; and

(2) opportunity to demonstrate or achieve compliance with all lawful requirements.

When the licensee has made timely and sufficient application for a renewal or a new license in accordance with agency rules, a license with reference to an activity of a continuing nature does not expire until the application has been finally determined by the agency.

§ 559. Effect on other laws; effect of subsequent statute

SEC. 12.

This subchapter, chapter 7, and sections 1305, 3105, 3344, 4301(2)(E), 5372, and 7521, and the provisions of section 5335(a)(B) of this title that relate to administrative law judges, do not limit or repeal additional requirements imposed by statute or otherwise recognized by law. Except as otherwise required by law, requirements or privileges relating to evidence or procedure apply equally to agencies and persons. Each agency is granted the authority necessary to comply with the requirements of this subchapter through the issuance of rules or otherwise. Subsequent statute may not be held to supersede or modify this subchapter, chapter 7, sections 1305, 3105, 3344, 4301(2)(E), 5372, or 7521, or the provisions of section 5335(a)(B) of this title that relate to administrative law judges, except to the extent that it does so expressly.

[For Regulatory Negotiation and Alternative Dispute Resolution, see p. 1354 below.]

* * *

CHAPTER 7.   JUDICIAL REVIEW

§ 701.   Application; definitions

(a) This chapter applies, according to the provisions thereof, except to the extent that—   SEC. 10.

  (1) statutes preclude judicial review; or

  (2) agency action is committed to agency discretion by law.

(b)(1) ["agency" is defined precisely as in § 551(1)(A) through (H), above];

  (2) "person", "rule", "order", "license", "sanction", "relief", and "agency action" have the meanings given them by section 551 of this title.

§ 702.   Right of review

A person suffering legal wrong because of agency action,   SEC. 10(a).
or adversely affected or aggrieved by agency action within the meaning of a relevant statute, is entitled to judicial review thereof.[5] An action in a court of the United States seeking relief other than money damages and stating a claim that an agency or an officer or employee thereof acted or failed to act in an official capacity or under color of legal

---

5. Material after first sentence added by P.L. 94–574, 90 Stat. 2721 (1976).

authority shall not be dismissed nor relief therein be denied on the ground that it is against the United States or that the United States is an indispensable party. The United States may be named as a defendant in any such action, and a judgment or decree may be entered against the United States: Provided, That any mandatory or injunctive decree shall specify the Federal officer or officers (by name or by title), and their successors in office, personally responsible for compliance. Nothing herein (1) affects other limitations on judicial review or the power or duty of the court to dismiss any action or deny relief on any other appropriate legal or equitable ground; or (2) confers authority to grant relief if any other statute that grants consent to suit expressly or impliedly forbids the relief which is sought.

§ 703.   Form and venue of proceeding

The form of proceeding for judicial review is the special statutory review proceeding relevant to the subject matter in a court specified by statute or, in the absence or inadequacy thereof, any applicable form of legal action, including actions for declaratory judgments or writs of prohibitory or mandatory injunction or habeas corpus, in a court of competent jurisdiction. If no special statutory review proceeding is applicable, the action for judicial review may be brought against the United States, the agency by its official title, or the appropriate officer.[6] Except to the extent that prior, adequate, and exclusive opportunity for judicial review is provided by law, agency action is subject to judicial review in civil or criminal proceedings for judicial enforcement.

SEC. 10(b).

§ 704.   Actions reviewable

Agency action made reviewable by statute and final agency action for which there is no other adequate remedy in a court are subject to judicial review. A preliminary, procedural, or intermediate agency action or ruling not directly reviewable is subject to review on the review of the final agency action. Except as otherwise expressly required by statute, agency action otherwise final is final for the purposes of this section whether or not there has been presented or determined an application for a declaratory order, for any form of reconsideration, or, unless the agency otherwise requires by rule and provides that the action meanwhile is inoperative, for an appeal to superior agency authority.

SEC. 10(c).

6. Preceding sentence added by P.L. 94–574, 90 Stat. 2721 (1976).

§ 705. Relief pending review

When an agency finds that justice so requires, it may   SEC. 10(d).
postpone the effective date of action taken by it, pending
judicial review. On such conditions as may be required and
to the extent necessary to prevent irreparable injury, the
reviewing court, including the court to which a case may be
taken on appeal from or on application for certiorari or
other writ to a reviewing court, may issue all necessary and
appropriate process to postpone the effective date of an
agency action or to preserve status or rights pending conclusion of the review proceedings.

§ 706. Scope of review

To the extent necessary to decision and when presented,   SEC. 10(e).
the reviewing court shall decide all relevant questions of
law, interpret constitutional and statutory provisions, and
determine the meaning or applicability of the terms of an
agency action. The reviewing court shall—

(1) compel agency action unlawfully withheld or unreasonably delayed; and

(2) hold unlawful and set aside agency action, findings,
and conclusions found to be—

   (A) arbitrary, capricious, an abuse of discretion, or
   otherwise not in accordance with law;

   (B) contrary to constitutional right, power, privilege,
   or immunity;

   (C) in excess of statutory jurisdiction, authority, or   *ultra vir*
   limitations, or short of statutory right;

   (D) without observance of procedure required by
   law;

   (E) unsupported by substantial evidence in a case
   subject to sections 556 and 557 of this title or otherwise reviewed on the record of an agency hearing
   provided by statute; or

   (F) unwarranted by the facts to the extent that the
   facts are subject to trial de novo by the reviewing
   court.

In making the foregoing determinations, the court shall
review the whole record or those parts of it cited by a party,
and due account shall be taken of the rule of prejudicial
error.

§ 3105. Appointment of administrative law judges[7]

Each agency shall appoint as many administrative law   SEC. 11 (1st
judges as are necessary for proceedings required to be   sentence).

---

7. Substitution of "administrative law   elsewhere in the APA, was effected by P.L.
judge" for "hearing examiner," here and   95–251, 92 Stat. 183 (1978).

conducted in accordance with sections 556 and 557 of this title. Administrative law judges shall be assigned to cases in rotation so far as practicable, and may not perform duties inconsistent with their duties and responsibilities as administrative law judges.

§ 7521. Actions against administrative law judges[8]

(a) An action may be taken against an administrative law judge appointed under section 3105 of this title by the agency in which the administrative law judge is employed only for good cause established and determined by the Merit Systems Protection Board on the record after opportunity for hearing before the Board.

SEC. 11 (2d sentence).

(b) The actions covered by this section are—

(1) a removal;

(2) a suspension;

(3) a reduction in grade;

(4) a reduction in pay; and

(5) a furlough of 30 days or less;

but do not include—

(A) a suspension or removal [in the interest of national security];

(B) a reduction-in-force action . . .; or

(C) any action initiated [by the Special Counsel of the Board].

§ 5372. Administrative law judges[9]

(a) For the purposes of this section, the term "administrative law judge" means an administrative law judge appointed under section 3105.

SEC. 11 (3d sentence).

(b)(1)(A) There shall be 3 levels of basic pay for administrative law judges (designated as AL–1, 2, and 3, respectively), and each such judge shall be paid at 1 of those levels, in accordance with the provisions of this section.

(B) Within level AL–3, there shall be 6 rates of basic pay, designated as AL–3, rates A through F, respectively. Level AL–2 and level AL–1 shall each have 1 rate of basic pay.

(C) The rate of basic pay for AL–3, rate A, may not be less than 65 percent of the rate of basic pay for level

---

8. As amended by the Civil Service Reform Act of 1978, P.L. 95–454, 92 Stat. 1137. The following sections were also amended in minor respects.

9. Added by P.L. 101–509, Title V, § 529, 104 Stat. 1445 (1990) with succeeding amendments through P.L. 106–97, § 1 (1999); the section it replaced authorized OPM to set pay levels "independently of agency recommendations or ratings" and in accordance with general civil service practice.

IV of the Executive Schedule, and the rate of basic pay for AL–1 may not exceed the rate for level IV of the Executive Schedule.

(2) The Office of Personnel Management shall determine, in accordance with procedures which the Office shall by regulation prescribe, the level in which each administrative-law-judge position shall be placed and the qualifications to be required for appointment to each level.

(3)(A) Upon appointment to a position in AL–3, an administrative law judge shall be paid at rate A of AL–3, and shall be advanced successively to rates B, C, and D of that level at the beginning of the next pay period following completion of 52 weeks of service in the next lower rate, and to rates E and F of that level at the beginning of the next pay period following completion of 104 weeks of service in the next lower rate.

(B) The Office of Personnel Management may provide for appointment of an administrative law judge in AL–3 at an advanced rate under such circumstances as the Office may determine appropriate.

(4) Subject to paragraph (1), effective at the beginning of the first applicable pay period commencing on or after the first day of the month in which an adjustment takes effect under section 5303 in the rates of basic pay under the General Schedule, each rate of basic pay for administrative law judges shall be adjusted by an amount determined by the President to be appropriate.

(c) The Office of Personnel Management shall prescribe regulations necessary to administer this section.

§ 3344. Details; administrative law judges

An agency as defined by section 551 of this title which occasionally or temporarily is insufficiently staffed with administrative law judges appointed under section 3105 of this title may use administrative law judges selected by the Office of Personnel Management from and with the consent of other agencies.

SEC. 11 (4th sentence).

§ 1305. Administrative law judges

For the purpose of sections 3105, 3344, 4301(2)(D), and 5372 of this title and the provisions of section 5335(a)(B) of this title that relate to administrative law judges, the Office of Personnel Management may, and for the purpose of section 7521 of this title, the Merit Systems Protection Board may investigate, prescribe regulations, appoint advisory committees as necessary, recommend legislation, sub-

SEC. 11 (5th sentence).

pena witnesses and records, and pay witness fees as established for the courts of the United States.

§ 552b.   Open meetings[10] (The Government in the Sunshine Act)

(a) For purposes of this section—

(1) the term "agency" means any agency, as defined in section 552(e) of this title, headed by a collegial body composed of two or more individual members, a majority of whom are appointed to such position by the President with the advice and consent of the Senate, and any subdivision thereof authorized to act on behalf of the agency;

(2) the term "meeting" means the deliberations of at least the number of individual agency members required to take action on behalf of the agency where such deliberations determine or result in the joint conduct or disposition of official agency business, but does not include deliberations required or permitted by subsection (d) or (e); and

(3) the term "member" means an individual who belongs to a collegial body heading an agency.

(b) Members shall not jointly conduct or dispose of agency business other than in accordance with this section. Except as provided in subsection (c), every portion of every meeting of an agency shall be open to public observation.

(c) Except in a case where the agency finds that the public interest requires otherwise, the second sentence of subsection (b) shall not apply to any portion of an agency meeting, and the requirements of subsections (d) and (e) shall not apply to any information pertaining to such meeting otherwise required by this section to be disclosed to the public, where the agency properly determines that such portion or portions of its meeting or the disclosure of such information is likely to—

(1) disclose matters that are (A) specifically authorized under criteria established by an Executive order to be kept secret in the interests of national defense or foreign policy and (B) in fact properly classified pursuant to such Executive order;

(2) relate solely to the internal personnel rules and practices of an agency;

(3) disclose matters specifically exempted from disclosure by statute (other than section 552 of this title), provided that such statute (A) requires that the matters be withheld from the public in such a manner as to leave no discretion on the issue, or (B) establishes particular criteria for withholding or refers to particular types of matters to be withheld;

(4) disclose trade secrets and commercial or financial information obtained from a person and privileged or confidential;

10. Added by P.L. 94–409, 90 Stat. 1241 (1976).

(5) involve accusing any person of a crime, or formally censuring any person;

(6) disclose information of a personal nature where disclosure would constitute a clearly unwarranted invasion of personal privacy;

(7) disclose investigatory records compiled for law enforcement purposes, or information which if written would be contained in such records, but only to the extent that the production of such records or information would (A) interfere with enforcement proceedings, (B) deprive a person of a right to a fair trial or an impartial adjudication, (C) constitute an unwarranted invasion of personal privacy, (D) disclose the identity of a confidential source and, in the case of a record compiled by a criminal law enforcement authority in the course of a criminal investigation, or by an agency conducting a lawful national security intelligence investigation, confidential information furnished only by the confidential source, (E) disclose investigative techniques and procedures, or (F) endanger the life or physical safety of law enforcement personnel;

(8) disclose information contained in or related to examination, operating, or condition reports prepared by, on behalf of, or for the use of an agency responsible for the regulation or supervision of financial institutions;

(9) disclose information the premature disclosure of which would—

(A) in the case of an agency which regulates currencies, securities, commodities, or financial institutions, be likely to (i) lead to significant financial speculation in currencies, securities, or commodities, or (ii) significantly endanger the stability of any financial institution; or

(B) in the case of any agency, be likely to significantly frustrate implementation of a proposed agency action,

except that subparagraph (B) shall not apply in any instance where the agency has already disclosed to the public the content or nature of its proposed action, or where the agency is required by law to make such disclosure on its own initiative prior to taking final agency action on such proposal; or

(10) specifically concern the agency's issuance of a subpena, or the agency's participation in a civil action or proceeding, an action in a foreign court or international tribunal, or an arbitration, or the initiation, conduct, or disposition by the agency of a particular case of formal agency adjudication pursuant to the procedures in section 554 of this title or otherwise involving a determination on the record after opportunity for a hearing.

(d)(1) Action under subsection (c) shall be taken only when a majority of the entire membership of the agency (as defined in subsection (a)(1)) votes to take such action. A separate vote of the agency members shall be taken with respect to each agency meeting a portion or portions of which are proposed to be closed to the public pursuant to subsection (c), or with respect to any information which is proposed to be withheld under subsection (c). A single vote may be taken with respect to a series of meetings, a portion or portions of which are proposed to be closed to the public, or with respect to any information concerning such series of meetings, so long as each meeting in such series involves the same particular matters and is scheduled to be held no more than thirty days after the initial meeting in such series. The vote of each agency member participating in such vote shall be recorded and no proxies shall be allowed.

(2) Whenever any person whose interests may be directly affected by a portion of a meeting requests that the agency close such portion to the public for any of the reasons referred to in paragraph (5), (6), or (7) of subsection (c), the agency, upon request of any one of its members, shall vote by recorded vote whether to close such meeting.

(3) Within one day of any vote taken pursuant to paragraph (1) or (2), the agency shall make publicly available a written copy of such vote reflecting the vote of each member on the question. If a portion of a meeting is to be closed to the public, the agency shall, within one day of the vote taken pursuant to paragraph (1) or (2) of this subsection, make publicly available a full written explanation of its action closing the portion together with a list of all persons expected to attend the meeting and their affiliation.

. . .

(e)(1) In the case of each meeting, the agency shall make public announcement, at least one week before the meeting, of the time, place, and subject matter of the meeting, whether it is to be open or closed to the public, and the name and phone number of the official designated by the agency to respond to requests for information about the meeting. Such announcement shall be made unless a majority of the members of the agency determines by a recorded vote that agency business requires that such meeting be called at an earlier date, in which case the agency shall make public announcement of the time, place, and subject matter of such meeting, and whether open or closed to the public, at the earliest practicable time.

(2) The time or place of a meeting may be changed following the public announcement required by paragraph (1) only if the agency publicly announces such change at the earliest practicable time. The subject matter of a meeting, or the determination of the agency to open or close a meeting, or portion of a meeting, to the public, may be changed following the public announcement required by this subsection only if (A) a majority of the entire membership of the agency determines by a recorded vote that agency business so requires and that no earlier announcement of the change was possible, and (B) the agency publicly announces such change and the vote of each member upon such change at the earliest practicable time.

. . .

(f)(1) For every meeting closed pursuant to paragraphs (1) through (10) of subsection (c), the General Counsel or chief legal officer of the agency shall publicly certify that, in his or her opinion, the meeting may be closed to the public and shall state each relevant exemptive provision. A copy of such certification, together with a statement from the presiding officer of the meeting setting forth the time and place of the meeting, and the persons present, shall be retained by the agency. The agency shall maintain a complete transcript or electronic recording adequate to record fully the proceedings of each meeting, or portion of a meeting, closed to the public, except that in the case of a meeting, or portion of a meeting, closed to the public pursuant to paragraph (8), (9)(A), or (10) of subsection (c), the agency shall maintain either such a transcript or recording, or a set of minutes. Such minutes shall fully and clearly describe all matters discussed and shall provide a full and accurate summary of any actions taken, and the reasons therefor, including a description of each of the views expressed on any item and the record of any rollcall vote (reflecting the vote of each member on the question). All documents considered in connection with any action shall be identified in such minutes.

(2) The agency shall make promptly available to the public, in a place easily accessible to the public, the transcript, electronic recording, or minutes (as required by paragraph (1)) of the discussion of any item on the agenda, or of any item of the testimony of any witness received at the meeting, except for such item or items of such discussion or testimony as the agency determines to contain information which may be withheld under subsection (c)....

. . .

(h)(1) The district courts of the United States shall have jurisdiction to enforce the requirements of subsections (b) through (f) of this section by declaratory judgment, injunctive relief, or other relief as may be appropriate. Such actions may be brought by any person against an agency prior to, or within sixty days after, the meeting out of which the violation of this section arises, except that if public announcement of such meeting is not initially provided by the agency in accordance with the requirements of this section, such action may be instituted pursuant to this section at any time prior to sixty days after any public announcement of such meeting. Such actions may be brought in the district court of the United States for the district in which the agency meeting is held or in which the agency in question has its headquarters, or in the District Court for the District of Columbia. In such actions a defendant shall serve his answer within thirty days after the service of the complaint. The burden is on the defendant to sustain his action. In deciding such cases the court may examine in camera any portion of the transcript, electronic recording, or minutes of a meeting closed to the public, and may take such additional evidence as it deems necessary. The court, having due regard for orderly administration and the public interest, as well as the interests of the parties, may grant such equitable relief as it deems appropriate, including granting an injunction against future violations of this section or ordering the agency to make available to the public such portion of the transcript, recording, or minutes of a meeting as is not authorized to be withheld under subsection (c) of this section.

(2) Any Federal court otherwise authorized by law to review agency action may, at the application of any person properly participat-

ing in the proceeding pursuant to other applicable law, inquire into violations by the agency of the requirements of this section and afford such relief as it deems appropriate. Nothing in this section authorizes any Federal court having jurisdiction solely on the basis of paragraph (1) to set aside, enjoin, or invalidate any agency action (other than an action to close a meeting or to withhold information under this section) taken or discussed at any agency meeting out of which the violation of this section arose.

(i) The court may assess against any party reasonable attorney fees and other litigation costs reasonably incurred by any other party who substantially prevails in any action brought in accordance with the provisions of subsection (g) or (h) of this section, except that costs may be assessed against the plaintiff only where the court finds that the suit was initiated by the plaintiff primarily for frivolous or dilatory purposes. In the case of assessment of costs against an agency, the costs may be assessed by the court against the United States.

. . .

(k) Nothing herein expands or limits the present rights of any person under section 552 of this title, except that the exemptions set forth in subsection (c) of this section shall govern in the case of any request made pursuant to section 552 to copy or inspect the transcripts, recordings, or minutes described in subsection (f) of this section. . . .

(*l*) This section does not constitute authority to withhold any information from Congress, and does not authorize the closing of any agency meeting or portion thereof required by any other provision of law to be open.

. . .

PROCEDURES OF CONSENSUS— REGULATORY NEGOTIATION AND ALTERNATIVE DISPUTE RESOLUTION

(The sections set out below were added to the Administrative Procedure Chapter of 5 U.S.C. in 1990. Both were enacted as experimental regimes. The Negotiated Rulemaking Act originally provided that no new negotiated rulemakings were to be initiated after November 29, 1996; this provision was itself repealed on October 19, 1996. The Administrative Dispute Resolution Act, originally set to terminate on October 1, 1995, was, with some amendment, similarly extended. Both are now apparently permanent parts of federal administrative law.)

Further provisions of these Acts, directed to the agencies, sought to assure the needed bureaucratic commitments. P.L. 101–552, § 3, 104 Stat. 2736 (1990), as amended by P.L. 104–320, § 4(a), 110 Stat. 3871 (1996), provided, inter alia, for the development of agency policies for the use of alternative means of dispute resolution and case management that embraced "(A) formal and informal adjudications; (B) rulemakings; (C) enforcement actions; (D) issuing and revoking licenses or permits; (E) contract administration; (F) litigation brought by or against the agency; and (G) other agency actions." To accomplish this, "The head of each agency shall designate a senior official to be the dispute resolution specialist of the agency," and provide regular training for her and other employees in the "theory and practice of negotiation, mediation, arbitration, or related techniques." Procedures for grants and contracts are to be modified to authorize and encourage the use of ADR techniques in their administration. Section 9 of the 1990 statute required agencies to develop "a policy with regard to the representation by persons other than attorneys of parties in alternative dispute resolution proceedings" and appears to create a presumption for allowing non-lawyer representation unless it finds generically that "the subject areas of the applicable proceedings or the procedures are so complex or specialized that only attorneys may adequately provide such representation or assistance."

NEGOTIATED RULEMAKING PROCEDURE

§ 561. Purpose

The purpose of this subchapter [5 U.S.C. §§ 561 et seq.] is to establish a framework for the conduct of negotiated rulemaking, consistent with section 553 of this title, to encourage agencies to use the process when it enhances the informal rulemaking process. Nothing in this subchapter should be construed as an attempt to limit innovation and experimentation with the negotiated rulemaking process or with other innovative rulemaking procedures otherwise authorized by law.

§ 562. Definitions

For the purposes of this subchapter, the term—

(1) "agency" has the same meaning as in section 551(1) of this title;

(2) "consensus" means unanimous concurrence among the interests represented on a negotiated rulemaking committee established under this subchapter, unless such committee—

    (A) agrees to define such term to mean a general but not unanimous concurrence; or

    (B) agrees upon another specified definition;

(3) "convener" means a person who impartially assists an agency in determining whether establishment of a negotiated rulemaking committee is feasible and appropriate in a particular rulemaking;

(4) "facilitator" means a person who impartially aids in the discussions and negotiations among the members of a negotiated rulemaking committee to develop a proposed rule;

(5) "interest" means, with respect to an issue or matter, multiple parties which have a similar point of view or which are likely to be affected in a similar manner;

(6) "negotiated rulemaking" means rulemaking through the use of a negotiated rulemaking committee;

(7) "negotiated rulemaking committee" or "committee" means an advisory committee established by an agency in accordance with this Subchapter and the Federal Advisory Committee Act [5 U.S.C. Appx.] to consider and discuss issues for the purpose of reaching a consensus in the development of a proposed rule;

(8) "party" has the same meaning as in section 551(3) of this title;

(9) "person" has the same meaning as in section 551(2) of this title;

(10) "rule" has the same meaning as in section 551(4) of this title; and

(11) "rulemaking" means "rule making" as that term is defined in section 551(5) of this title.

§ 563. Determination of need for negotiated rulemaking committee

(a) Determination of need by the agency. An agency may establish a negotiated rulemaking committee to negotiate and develop a proposed rule, if the head of the agency determines that the use of the negotiated rulemaking procedure is in the public interest. In making such a determination, the head of the agency shall consider whether—

(1) there is a need for a rule;

(2) there are a limited number of identifiable interests that will be significantly affected by the rule;

(3) there is a reasonable likelihood that a committee can be convened with a balanced representation of persons who—

(A) can adequately represent the interests identified under paragraph (2); and

(B) are willing to negotiate in good faith to reach a consensus on the proposed rule;

(4) there is a reasonable likelihood that a committee will reach a consensus on the proposed rule within a fixed period of time;

(5) the negotiated rulemaking procedure will not unreasonably delay the notice of proposed rulemaking and the issuance of the final rule;

(6) the agency has adequate resources and is willing to commit such resources, including technical assistance, to the committee; and

(7) the agency, to the maximum extent possible consistent with the legal obligations of the agency, will use the consensus of the committee with respect to the proposed rule as the basis for the rule proposed by the agency for notice and comment.

(b) Use of conveners.

(1) Purposes of conveners. An agency may use the services of a convener to assist the agency in—

(A) identifying persons who will be significantly affected by a proposed rule, including residents of rural areas; and

(B) conducting discussions with such persons to identify the issues of concern to such persons, and to ascertain whether the establishment of a negotiated rulemaking committee is feasible and appropriate in the particular rulemaking.

(2) Duties of conveners. The convener shall report findings and may make recommendations to the agency. Upon request of the agency, the convener shall ascertain the names of persons who are willing and qualified to represent interests that will be significantly affected by the proposed rule, including residents of rural areas. The report and any recommendations of the convener shall be made available to the public upon request.

§ 564. Publication of notice; applications for membership on committees

(a) Publication of notice. If, after considering the report of a convener or conducting its own assessment, an agency decides to establish a negotiated rulemaking committee, the agency shall publish in the Federal Register and, as appropriate, in trade or other specialized publications, a notice which shall include—

(1) an announcement that the agency intends to establish a negotiated rulemaking committee to negotiate and develop a proposed rule;

(2) a description of the subject and scope of the rule to be developed, and the issues to be considered;

(3) a list of the interests which are likely to be significantly affected by the rule;

(4) a list of the persons proposed to represent such interests and the person or persons proposed to represent the agency;

(5) a proposed agenda and schedule for completing the work of the committee, including a target date for publication by the agency of a proposed rule for notice and comment;

(6) a description of administrative support for the committee to be provided by the agency, including technical assistance;

(7) a solicitation for comments on the proposal to establish the committee, and the proposed membership of the negotiated rulemaking committee; and

(8) an explanation of how a person may apply or nominate another person for membership on the committee, as provided under subsection (b).

(b) Applications for membership o[n] committee. Persons who will be significantly affected by a proposed rule and who believe that their interests will not be adequately represented by any person specified in a notice under subsection (a)(4) may apply for, or nominate another person for, membership on the negotiated rulemaking committee to represent such interests with respect to the proposed rule. Each application or nomination shall include—

(1) the name of the applicant or nominee and a description of the interests such person shall represent;

(2) evidence that the applicant or nominee is authorized to represent parties related to the interests the person proposes to represent;

(3) a written commitment that the applicant or nominee shall actively participate in good faith in the development of the rule under consideration; and

(4) the reasons that the persons specified in the notice under subsection (a)(4) do not adequately represent the interests of the person submitting the application or nomination.

(c) Period for submission of comments and applications. The agency shall provide for a period of at least 30 calendar days for the submission of comments and applications under this section.

§ 565.   Establishment of committee

(a) Establishment.

(1) Determination to establish committee. If after considering comments and applications submitted under section 564, the agency determines that a negotiated rulemaking committee can adequately represent the interests that will be significantly affected by a proposed rule and that it is feasible and appropriate in the particular rulemaking, the agency may establish a negotiated rulemaking committee. In establishing and administering such a committee, the agency shall comply with the Federal Advisory Committee Act [5 U.S.C. Appx.] with respect to such committee, except as otherwise provided in this subchapter.

(2) Determination not to establish committee. If after considering such comments and applications, the agency decides not to establish a negotiated rulemaking committee, the agency shall promptly publish notice of such decision and the reasons therefor in the Federal Register and, as appropriate, in trade or other specialized publications, a copy of which shall be sent to any person who applied for, or nominated another person for membership on the negotiating rulemaking committee to represent such interests with respect to the proposed rule.

(b) Membership. The agency shall limit membership on a negotiated rulemaking committee to 25 members, unless the agency head determines that a greater number of members is necessary for the functioning of the committee or to achieve balanced membership. Each committee shall include at least one person representing the agency.

(c) Administrative support. The agency shall provide appropriate administrative support to the negotiated rulemaking committee, including technical assistance.

§ 566.   Conduct of committee activity

(a) Duties of committee. Each negotiated rulemaking committee established under this subchapter shall consider the matter proposed by the agency for consideration and shall attempt to reach a consensus concerning a proposed rule with respect to such matter and any other matter the committee determines is relevant to the proposed rule.

(b) Representatives of agency on committee. The person or persons representing the agency on a negotiated rulemaking committee shall participate in the deliberations and activities of the committee with the same rights and responsibilities as other members of the committee, and shall be authorized to fully represent the agency in the discussions and negotiations of the committee.

(c) Selecting facilitator. Notwithstanding section 10(e) of the Federal Advisory Committee Act [5 U.S.C. Appx. § 10(e)], an agency may nominate either a person from the Federal Government or a person from outside the Federal Government to serve as a facilitator for the negotiations of the committee, subject to the approval of the committee by consensus. If the committee does not approve the nominee of the agency for facilitator, the agency shall submit a substitute nomination. If a committee does not approve any nominee of the agency for facilitator, the committee shall select by consensus a person to serve as facilitator. A person designated to represent the agency in substantive issues may not serve as facilitator or otherwise chair the committee.

(d) Duties of facilitator. A facilitator approved or selected by a negotiated rulemaking committee shall—

(1) chair the meetings of the committee in an impartial manner;

(2) impartially assist the members of the committee in conducting discussions and negotiations; and

(3) manage the keeping of minutes and records as required under section 10(b) and (c) of the Federal Advisory Committee Act [5 U.S.C. Appx. § 10(b), (c)], except that any personal notes and materials of the facilitator or of the members of a committee shall not be subject to section 552 of this title.

(e) Committee procedures. A negotiated rulemaking committee established under this subchapter may adopt procedures for the operation of the committee. No provision of section 553 of this title shall apply to the procedures of a negotiated rulemaking committee.

(f) Report of committee. If a committee reaches a consensus on a proposed rule, at the conclusion of negotiations the committee shall transmit to the agency that established the committee a report containing the proposed rule. If the committee does not reach a consensus on a proposed rule, the committee may transmit to the agency a report specifying any areas in which the committee reached a consensus. The committee may include in a report any other information, recommendations, or materials that the committee considers appropriate. Any committee member may include as an addendum to the report additional information, recommendations, or materials.

(g) Records of committee. In addition to the report required by subsection (f), a committee shall submit to the agency the records required under section 10(b) and (c) of the Federal Advisory Committee Act [5 U.S.C. Appx. § 10(b), (c)].

§ 567. Termination of committee

A negotiated rulemaking committee shall terminate upon promulgation of the final rule under consideration, unless the committee's charter contains an earlier termination date or the agency, after consulting the committee, or the committee itself specifies an earlier termination date.

§ 568. Services, facilities, and payment of committee member expenses

(a) Services of conveners and facilitators.

(1) In general. An agency may employ or enter into contracts for the services of an individual or organization to serve as a convener or facilitator for a negotiated rulemaking committee under this subchapter, or may use the services of a Government employee to act as a convener or a facilitator for such a committee.

(2) Determination of conflicting interests. An agency shall determine whether a person under consideration to serve as convener or facilitator of a committee under paragraph (1) has any financial or other interest that would preclude such person from serving in an impartial and independent manner.

(b) Services and facilities of other entities. For purposes of this subchapter, an agency may use the services and facilities of other Federal agencies and public and private agencies and instrumentalities with the consent of such agencies and instrumentalities, and with or without reimbursement to such agencies and instrumentalities, and may accept voluntary and uncompensated services without regard to the provisions of section 1342 of title 31. The Federal Mediation and Conciliation Service may provide services and facilities, with or without reimbursement, to assist agencies under this subchapter, including furnishing conveners, facilitators, and training in negotiated rulemaking.

(c) Expenses of committee members. Members of a negotiated rulemaking committee shall be responsible for their own expenses of participation in such committee, except that an agency may, in accordance with section 7(d) of the Federal Advisory Committee Act [5 U.S.C. Appx. § 7(d)], pay for a member's reasonable travel and per diem expenses, expenses to obtain technical assistance, and a reasonable rate of compensation, if—

(1) such member certifies a lack of adequate financial resources to participate in the committee; and

(2) the agency determines that such member's participation in the committee is necessary to assure an adequate representation of the member's interest.

(d) Status of member as Federal employee. A member's receipt of funds under this section or section 569 shall not conclusively determine for purposes of sections 202 through 209 of title 18 whether that member is an employee of the United States Government.

§ 569. Encouraging negotiated rulemaking[11]

(a) The President shall designate an agency or designate or establish an interagency committee to facilitate and encourage agency use of negotiated rulemaking. An agency that is considering, planning, or conducting a negotiated rulemaking may consult with such agency or committee for information and assistance.

(b) To carry out the purposes of this subchapter, an agency planning or conducting a negotiated rulemaking may accept, hold, administer, and utilize gifts, devises, and bequests of property, both real and personal, if that agency's acceptance and use of such gifts, devises or bequests do not create a conflict of interest. Gifts and bequests of money and proceeds from sales of other property received as gifts, devises or bequests shall be deposited in the Treasury and shall be disbursed upon the order of the head of such agency. Property accepted pursuant to this section, and the proceeds thereof, shall be used as nearly as possible in accordance with the terms of the gifts, devises or bequests.

§ 570. Judicial review

Any agency action relating to establishing, assisting, or terminating a negotiated rulemaking committee under this subchapter shall not be subject to judicial review. Nothing in this section shall bar judicial review of a rule if such judicial review is otherwise provided by law. A rule which is the product of negotiated rulemaking and is subject to judicial review shall not be accorded any greater deference by a court than a rule which is the product of other rulemaking procedures.

§ 570a. Authorization of appropriations.

There are authorized to be appropriated such sums as may be necessary to carry out the purposes of this subchapter.

ALTERNATIVE MEANS OF DISPUTE RESOLUTION IN THE ADMINISTRATIVE PROCESS

§ 571. Definitions

For the purposes of this subchapter [5 U.S.C. §§ 571 et seq.], the term—

(1) "agency" has the same meaning as in section 551(1) of this title;

(2) "administrative program" includes a Federal function which involves protection of the public interest and the determination of rights, privileges, and obligations of private persons through rule making, adjudication, licensing, or investigation, as those terms are used in subchapter II of this chapter;

(3) "alternative means of dispute resolution" means any procedure that is used to resolve issues in controversy, including, but not limited to, conciliation, facilitation, mediation, factfinding, minitrials, arbitration, and use of ombuds, or any combination thereof;

---

11. Added by P.L. 104–320, 110 Stat. 3873 (1996).

(4) "award" means any decision by an arbitrator resolving the issues in controversy;

(5) "dispute resolution communication" means any oral or written communication prepared for the purposes of a dispute resolution proceeding, including any memoranda, notes or work product of the neutral, parties or nonparty participant; except that a written agreement to enter into a dispute resolution proceeding, or final written agreement or arbitral award reached as a result of a dispute resolution proceeding, is not a dispute resolution communication;

(6) "dispute resolution proceeding" means any process in which an alternative means of dispute resolution is used to resolve an issue in controversy in which a neutral is appointed and specified parties participate;

(7) "in confidence" means, with respect to information, that the information is provided—

(A) with the expressed intent of the source that it not be disclosed; or

(B) under circumstances that would create the reasonable expectation on behalf of the source that the information will not be disclosed;

(8) "issue in controversy" means an issue which is material to a decision concerning an administrative program of an agency, and with which there is disagreement—

(A) between an agency and persons who would be substantially affected by the decision; or

(B) between persons who would be substantially affected by the decision;

(9) "neutral" means an individual who, with respect to an issue in controversy, functions specifically to aid the parties in resolving the controversy;

(10) "party" means—

(A) for a proceeding with named parties, the same as in section 551(3) of this title; and

(B) for a proceeding without named parties, a person who will be significantly affected by the decision in the proceeding and who participates in the proceeding;

(11) "person" has the same meaning as in section 551(2) of this title; and

(12) "roster" means a list of persons qualified to provide services as neutrals.

§ 572. General authority

(a) An agency may use a dispute resolution proceeding for the resolution of an issue in controversy that relates to an administrative program, if the parties agree to such proceeding.

(b) An agency shall consider not using a dispute resolution proceeding if—

(1) a definitive or authoritative resolution of the matter is required for precedential value, and such a proceeding is not likely to be accepted generally as an authoritative precedent;

(2) the matter involves or may bear upon significant questions of Government policy that require additional procedures before a final resolution may be made, and such a proceeding would not likely serve to develop a recommended policy for the agency;

(3) maintaining established policies is of special importance, so that variations among individual decisions are not increased and such a proceeding would not likely reach consistent results among individual decisions;

(4) the matter significantly affects persons or organizations who are not parties to the proceeding;

(5) a full public record of the proceeding is important, and a dispute resolution proceeding cannot provide such a record; and

(6) the agency must maintain continuing jurisdiction over the matter with authority to alter the disposition of the matter in the light of changed circumstances, and a dispute resolution proceeding would interfere with the agency's fulfilling that requirement.

(c) Alternative means of dispute resolution authorized under this subchapter are voluntary procedures which supplement rather than limit other available agency dispute resolution techniques.

§ 573. Neutrals

(a) A neutral may be a permanent or temporary officer or employee of the Federal Government or any other individual who is acceptable to the parties to a dispute resolution proceeding. A neutral shall have no official, financial, or personal conflict of interest with respect to the issues in controversy, unless such interest is fully disclosed in writing to all parties and all parties agree that the neutral may serve.

(b) A neutral who serves as a conciliator, facilitator, or mediator serves at the will of the parties.

(c) The President shall designate an agency or designate or establish an interagency committee to facilitate and encourage agency use of dispute resolution under this subchapter. Such agency or interagency committee, in consultation with other appropriate federal agencies and professional organizations experienced in matters concerning dispute resolution, shall—

(1) encourage and facilitate agency use of alternative means of dispute resolution, and

(2) develop procedures that permit agencies to obtain the services of neutrals on an expedited basis.

(d) An agency may use the services of one or more employees of other agencies to serve as neutrals in dispute resolution proceedings. The agencies may enter into an interagency agreement that provides for the reimbursement by the user agency or the parties of the full or partial cost of the services of such an employee.

(e) Any agency may enter into a contract with any person for services as a neutral, or for training in connection with alternative means of dispute resolution. The parties in a dispute resolution proceeding shall agree on compensation for the neutral that is fair and reasonable to the Government.

§ 574. Confidentiality

(a) Except as provided in subsections (d) and (e), a neutral in a dispute resolution proceeding shall not voluntarily disclose or through discovery or compulsory process be required to disclose any dispute resolution communication or any communication provided in confidence to the neutral, unless—

(1) all parties to the dispute resolution proceeding and the neutral consent in writing, and, if the dispute resolution communication was provided by a nonparty participant, that participant also consents in writing;

(2) the dispute resolution communication has already been made public;

(3) the dispute resolution communication is required by statute to be made public, but a neutral should make such communication public only if no other person is reasonably available to disclose the communication; or

(4) a court determines that such testimony or disclosure is necessary to—

(A) prevent a manifest injustice;

(B) help establish a violation of law; or

(C) prevent harm to the public health or safety,

of sufficient magnitude in the particular case to outweigh the integrity of dispute resolution proceedings in general by reducing the confidence of parties in future cases that their communications will remain confidential.

(b) A party to a dispute resolution proceeding shall not voluntarily disclose or through discovery or compulsory process be required to disclose any information concerning any dispute resolution communication, unless—

(1) the communication was prepared by the party seeking disclosure;

(2) all parties to the dispute resolution proceeding consent in writing;

(3) the dispute resolution communication has already been made public;

(4) the dispute resolution communication is required by statute to be made public;

(5) a court determines that such testimony or disclosure is necessary to—

    (A) prevent a manifest injustice;

    (B) help establish a violation of law; or

    (C) prevent harm to the public health and safety,

of sufficient magnitude in the particular case to outweigh the integrity of dispute resolution proceedings in general by reducing the confidence of parties in future cases that their communications will remain confidential;

(6) the dispute resolution communication is relevant to determining the existence or meaning of an agreement or award that resulted from the dispute resolution proceeding or to the enforcement of such an agreement or award; or

(7) except for dispute resolution communications generated by the neutral, the dispute resolution communication was provided to or was available to all parties to the dispute resolution proceeding.

(c) Any dispute resolution communication that is disclosed in violation of subsection (a) or (b), shall not be admissible in any proceeding relating to the issues in controversy with respect to which the communication was made.

(d)(1) The parties may agree to alternative confidential procedures for disclosures by a neutral. Upon such agreement the parties shall inform the neutral before the commencement of the dispute resolution proceeding of any modifications to the provisions of subsection (a) that will govern the confidentiality of the dispute resolution proceeding. If the parties do not so inform the neutral, subsection (a) shall apply.

    (2) To qualify for the exemptions established under subsection (j), an alternative confidential procedure under this subsection may not provide for less disclosure than the confidential procedures otherwise provided under this section.

(e) If a demand for disclosure, by way of discovery request or other legal process, is made upon a neutral regarding a dispute resolution communication, the neutral shall make reasonable efforts to notify the parties and any affected nonparty participants of the demand. Any party or affected nonparty participant who receives such notice and within 15 calendar days does not offer to defend a refusal of the neutral to disclose the requested information shall have waived any objection to such disclosure.

(f) Nothing in this section shall prevent the discovery or admissibility of any evidence that is otherwise discoverable, merely because the evidence was presented in the course of a dispute resolution proceeding.

(g) Subsections (a) and (b) shall have no effect on the information and data that are necessary to document an agreement reached or order issued pursuant to a dispute resolution proceeding.

(h) Subsections (a) and (b) shall not prevent the gathering of information for research or educational purposes, in cooperation with other agencies, governmental entities, or dispute resolution programs, so long as the parties and the specific issues in controversy are not identifiable.

(i) Subsections (a) and (b) shall not prevent use of a dispute resolution communication to resolve a dispute between the neutral in a dispute resolution proceeding and a party to or participant in such proceeding, so long as such dispute resolution communication is disclosed only to the extent necessary to resolve such dispute.

(j) A dispute resolution communication which is between a neutral and a party and which may not be disclosed under this section shall also be exempt from disclosure under section 552(b)(3).

§ 575. Authorization of arbitration

(a)(1) Arbitration may be used as an alternative means of dispute resolution whenever all parties consent. Consent may be obtained either before or after an issue in controversy has arisen. A party may agree to—

(A) submit only certain issues in controversy to arbitration; or

(B) arbitration on the condition that the award must be within a range of possible outcomes.

(2) The arbitration agreement that sets forth the subject matter submitted to the arbitrator shall be in writing. Each such arbitration agreement shall specify a maximum award that may be issued by the arbitrator and may specify other conditions limiting the range of possible outcomes.

(3) An agency may not require any person to consent to arbitration as a condition of entering into a contract or obtaining a benefit.

(b) An officer or employee of an agency may offer to use arbitration for the resolution of issues in controversy unless such officer or employee—

(1) would otherwise have authority to enter into a settlement concerning the matter; or

(2) is otherwise specifically authorized by the agency to consent to the use of arbitration.

(c) Prior to using binding arbitration under this subchapter, the head of an agency, in consultation with the Attorney General and after taking into account the factors in section 572(b), shall issue guidance on the appropriate use of binding arbitration and when an officer or employee of the agency has authority to settle an issue in controversy through binding arbitration.

§ 576. Enforcement of arbitration agreements

An agreement to arbitrate a matter to which this subchapter applies is enforceable pursuant to section 4 of title 9, and no action brought to enforce such an agreement shall be dismissed nor shall relief therein be denied on the grounds that it is against the United States or that the United States is an indispensable party.

§ 577. Arbitrators

(a) The parties to an arbitration proceeding shall be entitled to participate in the selection of the arbitrator.

(b) The arbitrator shall be a neutral who meets the criteria of section 573 of this title.

§ 578. Authority of the arbitrator

An arbitrator to whom a dispute is referred under this subchapter may—

(1) regulate the course of and conduct arbitral hearings;

(2) administer oaths and affirmations;

(3) compel the attendance of witnesses and production of evidence at the hearing under the provisions of section 7 of title 9 only to the extent the agency involved is otherwise authorized by law to do so; and

(4) make awards.

§ 579. Arbitration proceedings

(a) The arbitrator shall set a time and place for the hearing on the dispute and shall notify the parties not less than 5 days before the hearing.

(b) Any party wishing a record of the hearing shall—

(1) be responsible for the preparation of such record;

(2) notify the other parties and the arbitrator of the preparation of such record;

(3) furnish copies to all identified parties and the arbitrator; and

(4) pay all costs for such record, unless the parties agree otherwise or the arbitrator determines that the costs should be apportioned.

(c)(1) The parties to the arbitration are entitled to be heard, to present evidence material to the controversy, and to cross-examine witnesses appearing at the hearing.

(2) The arbitrator may, with the consent of the parties, conduct all or part of the hearing by telephone, television, computer, or other electronic means, if each party has an opportunity to participate.

(3) The hearing shall be conducted expeditiously and in an informal manner.

(4) The arbitrator may receive any oral or documentary evidence, except that irrelevant, immaterial, unduly repetitious, or privileged evidence may be excluded by the arbitrator.

(5) The arbitrator shall interpret and apply relevant statutory and regulatory requirements, legal precedents, and policy directives.

(d) No interested person shall make or knowingly cause to be made to the arbitrator an unauthorized ex parte communication relevant to the merits of the proceeding, unless the parties agree otherwise. If a communication is made in violation of this subsection, the arbitrator shall ensure that a memorandum of the communication is prepared and made a part of the record, and that an opportunity for rebuttal is allowed. Upon receipt of a communication made in violation of this subsection, the arbitrator may, to the extent consistent with the interests of justice and the policies underlying this subchapter, require the offending party to show cause why the claim of such party should not be resolved against such party as a result of the improper conduct.

(e) The arbitrator shall make the award within 30 days after the close of the hearing, or the date of the filing of any briefs authorized by the arbitrator, whichever date is later, unless—

(1) the parties agree to some other time limit; or

(2) the agency provides by rule for some other time limit.

§ 580. Arbitration awards

(a)(1) Unless the agency provides otherwise by rule, the award in an arbitration proceeding under this subchapter shall include a brief, informal discussion of the factual and legal basis for the award, but formal findings of fact or conclusions of law shall not be required.

(2) The prevailing parties shall file the award with all relevant agencies, along with proof of service on all parties.

(b) The award in an arbitration proceeding shall become final 30 days after it is served on all parties. Any agency that is a party to the proceeding may extend this 30–day period for an additional 30–day period by serving a notice of such extension on all other parties before the end of the first 30–day period.

(c) A final award is binding on the parties to the arbitration proceeding, and may be enforced pursuant to sections 9 through 13 of title 9. No action brought to enforce such an award shall be dismissed nor shall relief therein be denied on the grounds that it is against the United States or that the United States is an indispensable party.

(d) An award entered under this subchapter in an arbitration proceeding may not serve as an estoppel in any other proceeding for any issue that was resolved in the proceeding. Such an award also may not be used as precedent or otherwise be considered in any factually unrelated proceeding, whether conducted under this subchapter, by an agency, or in a court, or in any other arbitration proceeding.

§ 581. Judicial review

(a) Notwithstanding any other provision of law, any person adversely affected or aggrieved by an award made in an arbitration proceeding conducted under this subchapter may bring an action for review of such award only pursuant to the provisions of sections 9 through 13 of title 9.

(b) A decision by an agency to use or not to use a dispute resolution proceeding under this subchapter shall be committed to the discretion of the agency and shall not be subject to judicial review, except that arbitration shall be subject to judicial review under section 10(b) of title 9.

§ 582. Repealed.

§ 583. Support services

For the purposes of this subchapter, an agency may use (with or without reimbursement) the services and facilities of other Federal agencies, state, local, and tribal governments, public and private organizations and agencies, and individuals, with the consent of such agencies, organizations, and individuals. An agency may accept voluntary and uncompensated services for purposes of this subchapter without regard to the provisions of section 1342 of title 31.

§ 584. Authorization of Appropriations.

There are authorized to be appropriated such sums as may be necessary to carry out the purposes of this chapter.

REGULATORY PLANNING AND REVIEW

Executive Order 12866, 58 FR 51735 (9/30/93) as amended
by Executive Order 13258, 67 FR 9385 (2/26/02)

The American people deserve a regulatory system that works for them, not against them: a regulatory system that protects and improves their health, safety, environment, and well-being and improves the performance of the economy without imposing unacceptable or unreasonable costs on society; regulatory policies that recognize that the private sector and private markets are the best engine for economic growth; regulatory approaches that respect the role of State, local, and tribal governments; and regulations that are effective, consistent, sensible, and understandable. We do not have such a regulatory system today.

With this Executive order, the Federal Government begins a program to reform and make more efficient the regulatory process. The objectives of this Executive order are to enhance planning and coordination with respect to both new and existing regulations; to reaffirm the primacy of Federal agencies in the regulatory decisionmaking process; to restore the integrity and legitimacy of regulatory review and oversight; and to make the process more accessible and open to the public. In pursuing these objectives, the regulatory process shall be conducted so as to meet applicable statutory requirements and with due regard to the discretion that has been entrusted to the Federal agencies.

Accordingly, by the authority vested in me as President by the Constitution and the laws of the United States of America, it is hereby ordered as follows:

Sec. 1.   Statement of Regulatory Philosophy and Principles.

(a) The Regulatory Philosophy. Federal agencies should promulgate only such regulations as are required by law, are necessary to interpret the law, or are made necessary by compelling public need, such as material failures of private markets to protect or improve the health and safety of the public, the environment, or the well-being of the American people. In deciding whether and how to regulate, agencies should assess all costs and benefits of available regulatory alternatives, including the alternative of not regulating. Costs and benefits shall be understood to include both quantifiable measures (to the fullest extent that these can be usefully estimated) and qualitative measures of costs and benefits that are difficult to quantify, but nevertheless essential to consider. Further, in choosing among alternative regulatory approaches, agencies should select those approaches that maximize net benefits (including potential economic, environmental, public health and safety, and other advantages; distributive impacts; and equity), unless a statute requires another regulatory approach.

(b) The Principles of Regulation. To ensure that the agencies' regulatory programs are consistent with the philosophy set forth above, agencies should adhere to the following principles, to the extent permitted by law and where applicable:

(1) Each agency shall identify the problem that it intends to address (including, where applicable, the failures of private markets or public institutions that warrant new agency action) as well as assess the significance of that problem.

(2) Each agency shall examine whether existing regulations (or other law) have created, or contributed to, the problem that a new regulation is intended to correct and whether those regulations (or other law) should be modified to achieve the intended goal of regulation more effectively.

(3) Each agency shall identify and assess available alternatives to direct regulation, including providing economic incentives to encourage the desired behavior, such as user fees or marketable permits, or providing information upon which choices can be made by the public.

(4) In setting regulatory priorities, each agency shall consider, to the extent reasonable, the degree and nature of the risks posed by various substances or activities within its jurisdiction.

(5) When an agency determines that a regulation is the best available method of achieving the regulatory objective, it shall design its regulations in the most cost-effective manner to achieve the regulatory objective. In doing so, each agency shall consider incentives for innovation, consistency, predictability, the costs of enforcement and compliance (to the government, regulated entities, and the public), flexibility, distributive impacts, and equity.

(6) Each agency shall assess both the costs and the benefits of the intended regulation and, recognizing that some costs and benefits are difficult to quantify, propose or adopt a regulation only upon a reasoned determination that the benefits of the intended regulation justify its costs.

(7) Each agency shall base its decisions on the best reasonably obtainable scientific, technical, economic, and other information concerning the need for, and consequences of, the intended regulation.

(8) Each agency shall identify and assess alternative forms of regulation and shall, to the extent feasible, specify performance objectives, rather than specifying the behavior or manner of compliance that regulated entities must adopt.

(9) Wherever feasible, agencies shall seek views of appropriate State, local, and tribal officials before imposing regulatory requirements that might significantly or uniquely affect those governmental entities. Each agency shall assess the effects of Federal regulations on State, local, and tribal governments, including specifically the availability of resources to carry out those mandates, and seek to minimize those burdens that uniquely or significantly affect such governmental entities, consistent with achieving regulatory objectives. In addition, as appropriate, agencies shall seek to harmonize Federal regulatory actions with related State, local, and tribal regulatory and other governmental functions.

(10) Each agency shall avoid regulations that are inconsistent, incompatible, or duplicative with its other regulations or those of other Federal agencies.

(11) Each agency shall tailor its regulations to impose the least burden on society, including individuals, businesses of differing sizes, and other entities (including small communities and governmental entities), consistent with obtaining the regulatory objectives, taking into account, among other things, and to the extent practicable, the costs of cumulative regulations.

(12) Each agency shall draft its regulations to be simple and easy to understand, with the goal of minimizing the potential for uncertainty and litigation arising from such uncertainty.

Sec. 2.   Organization. An efficient regulatory planning and review process is vital to ensure that the Federal Government's regulatory system best serves the American people.

(a) The Agencies. Because Federal agencies are the repositories of significant substantive expertise and experience, they are responsible for developing regulations and assuring that the regulations are consistent with applicable law, the President's priorities, and the principles set forth in this Executive order.

(b) The Office of Management and Budget. Coordinated review of agency rulemaking is necessary to ensure that regulations are consistent with applicable law, the President's priorities, and the principles set forth in this Executive order, and that decisions made by one agency do not conflict with the policies or actions taken or planned by another agency. The Office of Management and Budget (OMB) shall carry out that review function. Within OMB, the Office of Information and Regulatory Affairs (OIRA) is the repository of expertise concerning regulatory issues, including methodologies and procedures that affect more than one agency, this Executive order, and the President's regulatory policies. To the extent permitted by law, OMB shall provide guidance to agencies and assist the President and regulatory policy advisors to the President in regulatory planning and shall be the entity that reviews individual regulations, as provided by this Executive order.

(c) Assistance. In fulfilling his responsibilities under this Executive order, the President shall be assisted by the regulatory policy advisors within the Executive Office of the President and by such agency officials and personnel as the President may, from time to time, consult.

Sec. 3.   Definitions. For purposes of this Executive order:

(a) "Advisors" refers to such regulatory policy advisors to the President as the President may from time to time consult, including, among others: (1) the Director of OMB; (2) the Chair (or another member) of the Council of Economic Advisers; (3) the Assistant to the President for Economic Policy; (4) the Assistant to the President for Domestic Policy; (5) the Assistant to the President for National Security Affairs; (6) the Director of the Office of Science and Technology

Policy; (7) the Deputy Assistant to the President and Director for Intergovernmental Affairs; (8) the Assistant to the President and Staff Secretary; (9) the Assistant to the President and Chief of Staff to the Vice President; (10) the Assistant to the President and Counsel to the President; (11) the Chairman of the Council on Environmental Quality and Director of the Office of Environmental Policy; (12) the Assistant to the President for Homeland Security; and (13) the Administrator of OIRA, who also shall coordinate communications relating to this Executive order among the agencies, OMB, the other Advisors, and the Office of the Vice President.

(b) "Agency," unless otherwise indicated, means any authority of the United States that is an "agency" under 44 U.S.C. 3502(1), other than those considered to be independent regulatory agencies, as defined in 44 U.S.C. 3502(10).

(c) "Director" means the Director of OMB.

(d) "Regulation" or "rule" means an agency statement of general applicability and future effect, which the agency intends to have the force and effect of law, that is designed to implement, interpret, or prescribe law or policy or to describe the procedure or practice requirements of an agency. It does not, however, include:

(1) Regulations or rules issued in accordance with the formal rulemaking provisions of 5 U.S.C. 556, 557;

(2) Regulations or rules that pertain to a military or foreign affairs function of the United States, other than procurement regulations and regulations involving the import or export of non-defense articles and services;

(3) Regulations or rules that are limited to agency organization, management, or personnel matters; or

(4) Any other category of regulations exempted by the Administrator of OIRA.

(e) "Regulatory action" means any substantive action by an agency (normally published in the Federal Register) that promulgates or is expected to lead to the promulgation of a final rule or regulation, including notices of inquiry, advance notices of proposed rulemaking, and notices of proposed rulemaking.

(f) "Significant regulatory action" means any regulatory action that is likely to result in a rule that may:

(1) Have an annual effect on the economy of $100 million or more or adversely affect in a material way the economy, a sector of the economy, productivity, competition, jobs, the environment, public health or safety, or State, local, or tribal governments or communities;

(2) Create a serious inconsistency or otherwise interfere with an action taken or planned by another agency;

(3) Materially alter the budgetary impact of entitlements, grants, user fees, or loan programs or the rights and obligations of recipients thereof; or

(4) Raise novel legal or policy issues arising out of legal mandates, the President's priorities, or the principles set forth in this Executive order.

Sec. 4. Planning Mechanism. In order to have an effective regulatory program, to provide for coordination of regulations, to maximize consultation and the resolution of potential conflicts at an early stage, to involve the public and its State, local, and tribal officials in regulatory planning, and to ensure that new or revised regulations promote the President's priorities and the principles set forth in this Executive order, these procedures shall be followed, to the extent permitted by law:

(a) Agencies' Policy Meeting. Early in each year's planning cycle, the Director shall convene a meeting of the Advisors and the heads of agencies to seek a common understanding of priorities and to coordinate regulatory efforts to be accomplished in the upcoming year.

(b) Unified Regulatory Agenda. For purposes of this subsection, the term "agency" or "agencies" shall also include those considered to be independent regulatory agencies, as defined in 44 U.S.C. 3502(10). Each agency shall prepare an agenda of all regulations under development or review, at a time and in a manner specified by the Administrator of OIRA. The description of each regulatory action shall contain, at a minimum, a regulation identifier number, a brief summary of the action, the legal authority for the action, any legal deadline for the action, and the name and telephone number of a knowledgeable agency official. Agencies may incorporate the information required under 5 U.S.C. 602 and 41 U.S.C. 402 into these agendas.

(c) The Regulatory Plan. For purposes of this subsection, the term "agency" or "agencies" shall also include those considered to be independent regulatory agencies, as defined in 44 U.S.C. 3502(10).

(1) As part of the Unified Regulatory Agenda, beginning in 1994, each agency shall prepare a Regulatory Plan (Plan) of the most important significant regulatory actions that the agency reasonably expects to issue in proposed or final form in that fiscal year or thereafter. The Plan shall be approved personally by the agency head and shall contain at a minimum:

(A) A statement of the agency's regulatory objectives and priorities and how they relate to the President's priorities;

(B) A summary of each planned significant regulatory action including, to the extent possible, alternatives to be considered and preliminary estimates of the anticipated costs and benefits;

(C) A summary of the legal basis for each such action, including whether any aspect of the action is required by statute or court order;

(D) A statement of the need for each such action and, if applicable, how the action will reduce risks to public health, safety, or the environment, as well as how the magnitude of the risk addressed by the action relates to other risks within the jurisdiction of the agency;

(E) The agency's schedule for action, including a statement of any applicable statutory or judicial deadlines; and

(F) The name, address, and telephone number of a person the public may contact for additional information about the planned regulatory action.

(2) Each agency shall forward its Plan to OIRA by June 1st of each year.

(3) Within 10 calendar days after OIRA has received an agency's Plan, OIRA shall circulate it to other affected agencies and the Advisors.

(4) An agency head who believes that a planned regulatory action of another agency may conflict with its own policy or action taken or planned shall promptly notify, in writing, the Administrator of OIRA, who shall forward that communication to the issuing agency and the Advisors.

(5) If the Administrator of OIRA believes that a planned regulatory action of an agency may be inconsistent with the President's priorities or the principles set forth in this Executive order or may be in conflict with any policy or action taken or planned by another agency, the Administrator of OIRA shall promptly notify, in writing, the affected agencies and the Advisors.

(6) The Director may consult with the heads of agencies with respect to their Plans and, in appropriate instances, request further consideration or inter-agency coordination.

(7) The Plans developed by the issuing agency shall be published annually in the October publication of the Unified Regulatory Agenda. This publication shall be made available to the Congress; State, local, and tribal governments; and the public. Any views on any aspect of any agency Plan, including whether any planned regulatory action might conflict with any other planned or existing regulation, impose any unintended consequences on the public, or confer any unclaimed benefits on the public, should be directed to the issuing agency, with a copy to OIRA.

(d) **Regulatory Working Group.** Within 30 days of the date of this Executive order, the Administrator of OIRA shall convene a Regulatory Working Group ("Working Group"), which shall consist of representatives of the heads of each agency that the Administrator determines to have significant domestic regulatory responsibility and the Advisors. The Administrator of OIRA shall chair the Working Group and shall periodically advise the Director on the activities of the Working Group. The Working Group shall serve as a forum to assist agencies in identifying and analyzing important regulatory issues (including, among others (1) the development of innovative regulatory techniques, (2) the methods, efficacy, and utility of comparative risk assessment in regulatory decisionmaking, and (3) the development of short forms and other streamlined regulatory approaches for small businesses and other entities). The Working Group shall meet at least quarterly and may meet as a whole or in subgroups of agencies with an interest in particular issues or subject areas. To inform its discussions, the Working Group may commission analytical studies and reports by OIRA, the Administrative Conference of the United States, or any other agency.

(e) Conferences. The Administrator of OIRA shall meet quarterly with representatives of State, local, and tribal governments to identify both existing and proposed regulations that may uniquely or significantly affect those governmental entities. The Administrator of OIRA shall also convene, from time to time, conferences with representatives of businesses, nongovernmental organizations, and the public to discuss regulatory issues of common concern.

Sec. 5. Existing Regulations. In order to reduce the regulatory burden on the American people, their families, their communities, their State, local, and tribal governments, and their industries; to determine whether regulations promulgated by the executive branch of the Federal Government have become unjustified or unnecessary as a result of changed circumstances; to confirm that regulations are both compatible with each other and not duplicative or inappropriately burdensome in the aggregate; to ensure that all regulations are consistent with the President's priorities and the principles set forth in this Executive order, within applicable law; and to otherwise improve the effectiveness of existing regulations:

(a) Within 90 days of the date of this Executive order, each agency shall submit to OIRA a program, consistent with its resources and regulatory priorities, under which the agency will periodically review its existing significant regulations to determine whether any such regulations should be modified or eliminated so as to make the agency's regulatory program more effective in achieving the regulatory objectives, less burdensome, or in greater alignment with the President's priorities and the principles set forth in this Executive order. Any significant regulations selected for review shall be included in the agency's annual Plan. The agency shall also identify any legislative mandates that require the agency to promulgate or continue to impose regulations that the agency believes are unnecessary or outdated by reason of changed circumstances.

(b) The Administrator of OIRA shall work with the Regulatory Working Group and other interested entities to pursue the objectives of this section. State, local, and tribal governments are specifically encouraged to assist in the identification of regulations that impose significant or unique burdens on those governmental entities and that appear to have outlived their justification or be otherwise inconsistent with the public interest.

(c) The Director, in consultation with the Advisors, may identify for review by the appropriate agency or agencies other existing regulations of an agency or groups of regulations of more than one agency that affect a particular group, industry, or sector of the economy, or may identify legislative mandates that may be appropriate for reconsideration by the Congress.

Sec. 6. Centralized Review of Regulations. The guidelines set forth below shall apply to all regulatory actions, for both new and existing regulations, by agencies other than those agencies specifically exempted by the Administrator of OIRA:

(a) Agency Responsibilities.

(1) Each agency shall (consistent with its own rules, regulations, or procedures) provide the public with meaningful participation in the regulatory process. In particular, before issuing a notice of proposed rulemaking, each agency should, where appropriate, seek the involvement of those who are intended to benefit from and those expected to be burdened by any regulation (including, specifically, State, local, and tribal officials). In addition, each agency should afford the public a meaningful opportunity to comment on any proposed regulation, which in most cases should include a comment period of not less than 60 days. Each agency also is directed to explore and, where appropriate, use consensual mechanisms for developing regulations, including negotiated rulemaking.

(2) Within 60 days of the date of this Executive order, each agency head shall designate a Regulatory Policy Officer who shall report to the agency head. The Regulatory Policy Officer shall be involved at each stage of the regulatory process to foster the development of effective, innovative, and least burdensome regulations and to further the principles set forth in this Executive order.

(3) In addition to adhering to its own rules and procedures and to the requirements of the Administrative Procedure Act, the Regulatory Flexibility Act, the Paperwork Reduction Act, and other applicable law, each agency shall develop its regulatory actions in a timely fashion and adhere to the following procedures with respect to a regulatory action:

(A) Each agency shall provide OIRA, at such times and in the manner specified by the Administrator of OIRA, with a list of its planned regulatory actions, indicating those which the agency believes are significant regulatory actions within the meaning of this Executive order. Absent a material change in the development of the planned regulatory action, those not designated as significant will not be subject to review under this section unless, within 10 working days of receipt of the list, the Administrator of OIRA notifies the agency that OIRA has determined that a planned regulation is a significant regulatory action within the meaning of this Executive order. The Administrator of OIRA may waive review of any planned regulatory action designated by the agency as significant, in which case the agency need not further comply with subsection (a)(3)(B) or subsection (a)(3)(C) of this section.

(B) For each matter identified as, or determined by the Administrator of OIRA to be, a significant regulatory action, the issuing agency shall provide to OIRA:

(i) The text of the draft regulatory action, together with a reasonably detailed description of the need for the regulatory action and an explanation of how the regulatory action will meet that need; and

(ii) An assessment of the potential costs and benefits of the regulatory action, including an explanation of the manner in which the regulatory action is consistent with a statutory mandate and, to the extent permitted by law, promotes the President's priorities and avoids undue interference with State, local, and tribal governments in the exercise of their governmental functions.

(C) For those matters identified as, or determined by the Administrator of OIRA to be, a significant regulatory action within the scope of section 3(f)(1), the agency shall also provide to OIRA the following additional information developed as part of the agency's decisionmaking process (unless prohibited by law):

(i) An assessment, including the underlying analysis, of benefits anticipated from the regulatory action (such as, but not limited to, the promotion of the efficient functioning of the economy and private markets, the enhancement of health and safety, the protection of the natural environment, and the elimination or reduction of discrimination or bias) together with, to the extent feasible, a quantification of those benefits;

(ii) An assessment, including the underlying analysis, of costs anticipated from the regulatory action (such as, but not limited to, the direct cost both to the government in administering the regulation and to businesses and others in complying with the regulation, and any adverse effects on the efficient functioning of the economy, private markets (including productivity, employment, and competitiveness), health, safety, and the natural environment), together with, to the extent feasible, a quantification of those costs; and

(iii) An assessment, including the underlying analysis, of costs and benefits of potentially effective and reasonably feasible alternatives to the planned regulation, identified by the agencies or the public (including improving the current regulation and reasonably viable nonregulatory actions), and an explanation why the planned regulatory action is preferable to the identified potential alternatives.

(D) In emergency situations or when an agency is obligated by law to act more quickly than normal review procedures allow, the agency shall notify OIRA as soon as possible and, to the extent practicable, comply with subsections (a)(3)(B) and (C) of this section. For those regulatory actions that are governed by a statutory or court-imposed deadline, the agency shall, to the extent practicable, schedule rulemaking proceedings so as to permit sufficient time for OIRA to conduct its review, as set forth below in subsection (b)(2) through (4) of this section.

(E) After the regulatory action has been published in the Federal Register or otherwise issued to the public, the agency shall:

(i) Make available to the public the information set forth in subsections (a)(3)(B) and (C);

(ii) Identify for the public, in a complete, clear, and simple manner, the substantive changes between the draft submitted to OIRA for review and the action subsequently announced; and

(iii) Identify for the public those changes in the regulatory action that were made at the suggestion or recommendation of OIRA.

(F) All information provided to the public by the agency shall be in plain, understandable language.

(b) OIRA Responsibilities. The Administrator of OIRA shall provide meaningful guidance and oversight so that each agency's regulatory actions are consistent with applicable law, the President's priorities, and the principles set forth in this Executive order and do not conflict with the policies or actions of another agency. OIRA shall, to the extent permitted by law, adhere to the following guidelines:

(1) OIRA may review only actions identified by the agency or by OIRA as significant regulatory actions under subsection (a)(3)(A) of this section.

(2) OIRA shall waive review or notify the agency in writing of the results of its review within the following time periods:

(A) For any notices of inquiry, advance notices of proposed rulemaking, or other preliminary regulatory actions prior to a Notice of Proposed Rulemaking, within 10 working days after the date of submission of the draft action to OIRA;

(B) For all other regulatory actions, within 90 calendar days after the date of submission of the information set forth in subsections (a)(3)(B) and (C) of this section, unless OIRA has previously reviewed this information and, since that review, there has been no material change in the facts and circumstances upon which the regulatory action is based, in which case, OIRA shall complete its review within 45 days; and

(C) The review process may be extended (1) once by no more than 30 calendar days upon the written approval of the Director and (2) at the request of the agency head.

(3) For each regulatory action that the Administrator of OIRA returns to an agency for further consideration of some or all of its provisions, the Administrator of OIRA shall provide the issuing agency a written explanation for such return, setting forth the pertinent provision of this Executive order on which OIRA is relying. If the agency head disagrees with some or all of the bases for the return, the agency head shall so inform the Administrator of OIRA in writing.

(4) Except as otherwise provided by law or required by a Court, in order to ensure greater openness, accessibility, and accountability in the regulatory review process, OIRA shall be governed by the following disclosure requirements:

(A) Only the Administrator of OIRA (or a particular designee) shall receive oral communications initiated by persons not employed by the executive branch of the Federal Government regarding the substance of a regulatory action under OIRA review;

(B) All substantive communications between OIRA personnel and persons not employed by the executive branch of the Federal Government regarding a regulatory action under review shall be governed by the following guidelines:

(i) A representative from the issuing agency shall be invited to any meeting between OIRA personnel and such person(s);

(ii) OIRA shall forward to the issuing agency, within 10 working days of receipt of the communication(s), all written communications, regardless of format, between OIRA personnel and any person who is not employed by the executive branch of the Federal Government, and the dates and names of individuals involved in all substantive oral communications (including meetings to which an agency representative was invited, but did not attend, and telephone conversations between OIRA personnel and any such persons); and

(iii) OIRA shall publicly disclose relevant information about such communication(s), as set forth below in subsection (b)(4)(C) of this section.

(C) OIRA shall maintain a publicly available log that shall contain, at a minimum, the following information pertinent to regulatory actions under review:

(i) The status of all regulatory actions, including if (and if so, when and by whom) Presidential consideration was requested;

(ii) A notation of all written communications forwarded to an issuing agency under subsection (b)(4)(B)(ii) of this section; and

(iii) The dates and names of individuals involved in all substantive oral communications, including meetings and telephone conversations, between OIRA personnel and any person not employed by the executive branch of the Federal Government, and the subject matter discussed during such communications.

(D) After the regulatory action has been published in the Federal Register or otherwise issued to the public, or after the agency has announced its decision not to publish or issue the regulatory action, OIRA shall make available to the public all documents exchanged between OIRA and the agency during the review by OIRA under this section.

(5) All information provided to the public by OIRA shall be in plain, understandable language.

Sec. 7. Resolution of Conflicts.

(a) To the extent permitted by law, disagreements or conflicts between or among agency heads or between OMB and any agency that cannot be resolved by the Administrator of OIRA shall be resolved by the President with the assistance of the Chief of Staff to the President ("Chief of Staff"), with the relevant agency head (and, as appropriate, other interested government officials). Presidential consideration of such disagreements may be initiated only by the Director, by the head of the issuing agency, or by the head of an agency that has a significant interest in the regulatory action at issue. Such review will not be undertaken at the request of other persons, entities, or their agents.

(b) Resolution of such conflicts shall be informed by recommendations developed by the Chief of Staff, after consultation with the Advisors (and other executive branch officials or personnel whose responsibilities to the President include the subject matter at issue). The development of these recommendations shall be concluded within 60 days after review has been requested.

(c) During the Presidential review period, communications with any person not employed by the Federal Government relating to the substance of the regulatory action under review and directed to the Advisors or their staffs or to the staff of the Chief of Staff shall be in writing and shall be forwarded by the recipient to the affected agency(ies) for inclusion in the public docket(s). When the communication is not in writing, such Advisors or staff members shall inform the outside party that the matter is under review and that any comments should be submitted in writing.

(d) At the end of this review process, the President, or the Chief of Staff acting at the request of the President, shall notify the affected agency and the Administrator of OIRA of the President's decision with respect to the matter.

Sec. 8. Publication. Except to the extent required by law, an agency shall not publish in the Federal Register or otherwise issue to the public any regulatory action that is subject to review under section 6 of this Executive order until (1) the Administrator of OIRA notifies the agency that OIRA has waived its review of the action or has completed its review without any requests for further consideration, or (2) the applicable time period in section 6(b)(2) expires without OIRA having notified the agency that it is returning the regulatory action for further consideration under section 6(b)(3), whichever occurs first. If the terms of the preceding sentence have not been satisfied and an agency wants to publish or otherwise issue a regulatory action, the head of that agency may request Presidential consideration through the Director, as provided under section 7 of this order. Upon receipt of this request, the Director shall notify OIRA and the Advisors. The guidelines and time period set forth in section 7 shall apply to the publication of regulatory actions for which Presidential consideration has been sought.

Sec. 9. Agency Authority. Nothing in this order shall be construed as displacing the agencies' authority or responsibilities, as authorized by law.

Sec. 10. Judicial Review. Nothing in this Executive order shall affect any otherwise available judicial review of agency action. This Executive order is intended only to improve the internal management of the Federal Government and does not create any right or benefit, substantive or procedural, enforceable at law or equity by a party against the United States, its agencies or instrumentalities, its officers or employees, or any other person.

Sec. 11. Revocations. Executive Orders Nos. 12291 and 12498; all amendments to those Executive orders; all guidelines issued under those orders; and any exemptions from those orders heretofore granted for any category of rule are revoked.

William J. Clinton

The White House

September 30, 1993.

INDEX

References are to Pages

†